February 24–28, 2014
New York, New York, USA



Association for Computing Machinery

*Advancing Computing as a Science & Profession*

wsdm
New York City

# WSDM'14

## Proceedings of the 7th ACM International Conference on
# Web Search and Data Mining

*Sponsored by:*
***ACM SIGIR, ACM SIGKDD, ACM SIGMOD, & ACM SIGWEB***

*Supported by:*
***Google, Microsoft Research, Abode, American Express, Etsy, Facebook, Yahoo!, and Johnson Research Labs***

Association for
Computing Machinery

*Advancing Computing as a Science & Profession*

**The Association for Computing Machinery**
**2 Penn Plaza, Suite 701**
**New York, New York 10121-0701**



**ISBN:** 978-1-4503-2351-2 (Digital)

**ISBN:** 978-1-4503-3097-8 (Print)

Additional copies may be ordered prepaid from:

**ACM Order Department**
PO Box 30777
New York, NY 10087-0777, USA

Phone: 1-800-342-6626 (USA and Canada)
+1-212-626-0500 (Global)
Fax: +1-212-944-1318
E-mail: acmhelp@acm.org
Hours of Operation: 8:30 am – 4:30 pm ET

Printed in the USA

# Welcome from the General Chairs

Welcome to New York, NY for the Seventh Annual ACM International Conference on Web Search and Data Mining (WSDM).

Though under ten years old, WSDM has quickly become the premier venue for presentation of cutting edge research in web search and data mining. In the four years since it was last hosted in New York City, the conference has kept pace with the rapid development of web technologies and products.

Successfully organizing a conference would not be possible without the dedicated work of many people. Principal among these are the Program Committee Chairs, Carlos Castillo and Donald Metzler who worked with a Senior Program Committee of twenty-five people to select the research that will be presented during the main conference. As for the rest of the conference agenda, Practice and Experience Talks Chair Jimmy Lin took the initiative in organizing speakers for industrial research talks that weave together cutting-edge academic research with real-world practice from top industry experts. Tutorial Chairs Vanessa Murdock and Jie Tang organized a superb slate of tutorials; Workshop Chair Brian Davison did the same for workshops. Doctoral Consortium Chairs Susan Dumais and Oren Kurland arranged a full day for PhD students to discuss their research and get feedback. We thank them all, as well as the authors and presenters who contributed their work.

We are also grateful to those who organized conference logistics. Treasurer Hema Raghavan worked with the General Chairs and ACM to keep the conference on budget. Sponsorship Chairs Jake Hofman and Sergei Vassilvitskii pulled together an excellent group of sponsors. Proceedings Chair Claudia Hauff put together all the materials for the proceedings and program booklets, and Publicity Chair Michael Bendersky maintained the conference web site and social media feeds. Local Chair Oksana Yakhnenko organized volunteers and worked with the Crowne Plaza staff to ensure smooth operations. Last but not least, we would like to thank the staff of the Crowne Plaza Times Square and the conference organization team at ACM for all their help.

WSDM is co-sponsored by ACM SIGIR, SIGKDD, SIGMOD, and SIGWEB, and receives generous support from a number of companies and organizations. Google and Microsoft generously supported the conference at the Platinum level; Adobe, American Express, Etsy, Facebook, and Yahoo! contributed at the Silver level; Johnson Research Labs contributed at the Bronze level.

We hope that you find this program exciting and that you take the opportunity to explore our little city with your colleagues.

**Ben Carterette**
*University of Delaware*

**Fernando Diaz**
*Microsoft*

# Welcome from the Program Chairs

It is our great pleasure to welcome you to the Seventh ACM International Conference on Web Search and Data Mining (WSDM 2014) held on February 24—28, 2014 in New York City, New York, USA. As with previous installments, WSDM attracted many high quality submissions covering a broad spectrum of Web search and data mining topics. WSDM continues be a leading forum for reporting the latest research developments in the field. We are delighted to present here the proceedings of the conference.

We received a total of 355 submissions from a diverse group of 44 countries and regions, of which 64 were accepted for full paper publication in the proceedings, thus achieving an acceptance rate of 18%. The accepted papers are from 20 different countries and represent a nice mix of academic and industrial research, making this a truly international and diverse forum. Some of the most popular research topics this year include Web search, computational advertising, recommender systems, and social networks.

As in the past, WSDM 2014 continues to be a single track conference. To accommodate this, 19 papers were chosen to be presented as long presentations, while the remaining 45 will be presented as short presentations. As in the past, all authors of accepted papers were afforded the opportunity to present a poster during the poster session. There were many remarkable papers submitted to the conference. We chose 10 of the most exceptional papers as Best Paper Award candidates.

Putting together a high quality program was a huge team effort. None of it would have been possible without the spectacular hard work of the 125 Program Committee members (representing 28 countries) and the 25 Senior Program Committee members. To encourage diversity within these committees, members spanning a wide spectrum of backgrounds (e.g., level of experience, academia vs. industry, geographic region, and gender) were chosen.

In addition to the reviewers and meta-reviewers, we would also like to thank the WSDM Steering Committee and the Organizers, Ben Carterette and Fernando Diaz, who provided amazing guidance and support at every step along the way. Last, but certainly not least, we would like to thank the authors and attendees, as they make the conference possible in the first place.

We hope that you will find this program interesting and thought-provoking. Our goal was not only to give you the opportunity to share ideas with other researchers and practitioners from around the world, but also to foster new research and innovation in this dynamically changing field.

**Carlos Castillo**
*Qatar Computing Research Institute*

**Donald Metzler**
*Google*

# Table of Contents

## Session: Advertising



## Session: Log Analysis



## Session: Recommender Systems

## Session: Recommender Systems and Networks



## Session: Networks: Communities and Labeling



## Session: Networks: Centrality and Influence

## Session: Natural Language Processing; Topic Models



## Session: Topic Models; Linked Data



## Session: Peer Production: Data Analysis

## Session: Doctoral Consortium



## Session: Tutorials



## Session: Workshop Summaries

# WSDM 2014 Conference Organization

**General Chairs:** Ben Carterette (*University of Delaware, USA)*
Fernando Diaz *(Microsoft Research, USA)*

**Program Chairs:** Carlos Castillo (*Qatar Computing Research Institute, Qatar)*
Donald Metzler *(Google, USA)*

**Tutorial Chairs:** Vanessa Murdock (*Microsoft Research*)
Jie Tang (*Tsinghua University, China*)

**Proceedings Chair:** Claudia Hauff *(Delft University of Technology, The Netherlands)*

**Local Chair:** Oksana Yakhnenko (*Google, USA*)

**Workshop Chair:** Brian Davison (*Lehigh University, USA)*

**Doctoral Consortium Chairs:** Susan Dumais (*Microsoft Research, USA*)
Oren Kurland (*Technion – Israel Institute of Technology*)

**Treasurer and Registration Chair:** Hema Raghavan (*IBM Research, USA)*

**Sponsorship Chairs:** Jake Hofman (*Microsoft Research, USA*)
Sergei Vassilvitskii (*Google, USA*)

**Practice & Experience Talks Chair:** Jimmy Lin (*University of Maryland*)

**Web Presence & Publicity Chair:** Michael Bendersky (*Google, USA*)

**Steering Committee:** Rakesh Agrawal (*Microsoft Research, USA*)
Ricardo Baeza-Yates (*Yahoo! Labs, Spain and University of Chile, Chile*)
Ziv Bar-Yossef (*Technion and Google, Israel*)
Soumen Chakrabarti (*IIT Bombay, India*)
Monika Henzinger (*University of Vienna, Austria*)
Jon Kleinberg (*Cornell University, USA*)
Marc Najork (*Microsoft Research, USA*)

# WSDM 2014 Program Committee

Lise Getoor *(University of Maryland, USA)*
Fosca Giannotti *(ISTI-CNR, Italy)*
David Gleich *(Purdue University, USA)*
Nazli Goharian *(Georgetown University, USA)*
Manuel Gomez Rodriguez *(Stanford University / MPI for Biological Cybernetics)*
Gregory Grefenstette *(Exalead)*
Antonio Gulli *(Microsoft)*
Francesco Gullo *(Yahoo! Research Barcelona, Spain)*
Dimitrios Gunopulos *(University of Athens, Greece)*
Jiafeng Guo *(Institute of Computing Technology, Chinese Academy of Sciences, China)*
Maxim Gurevich *(Google)*
Jiawei Han *(University of Illinois at Urbana-Champaign, USA)*
Monika Henzinger *(University of Vienna, Austria)*
Katja Hofmann *(University of Amsterdam, The Netherlands)*
Liangjie Hong *(Yahoo! Labs, USA)*
Vagelis Hristidis *(UC Riverside, USA)*
Estevam Hruschka Junior *(Federal University of Sao Carlos, Brazil)*
Grace Hui Yang *(Georgetown University, USA)*
Samuel Ieong *(Microsoft Research, USA)*
Alejandro Jaimes *(Yahoo! Research Barcelona, Spain)*
Shen Jialie *(Singapore Management University)*
Jing Jiang *(Singapore Management University)*
Vanja Josifovski *(Google)*
Jaap Kamps *(University of Amsterdam, The Netherlands)*
Makoto P. Kato *(Kyoto University, Japan)*
Henry Kautz *(University of Rochester, USA)*
Irwin King *(The Chinese University of Hong Kong)*
George Kollios *(Boston University, USA)*
Yehuda Koren *(Google)*
Alexander Kotov *(Emory University, USA)*
Nick Koudas *(University of Toronto, Canada)*
Georgia Koutrika *(HP Labs)*
Ravi Kumar
Oren Kurland *(Technion, Israel Institute of Technology)*
Mayank Lahiri
Mounia Lalmas *(Yahoo! Research Barcelona, Spain)*
Theodoros Lappas *(Boston University, USA)*
Silvio Lattanzi *(Google)*
Kristen Lefevre *(University of Michigan, USA)*
Daniel Lemire *(Université du Québec à Montréal, Canada)*
Ronny Lempel *(Yahoo! Labs Israel)*
Kristina Lerman *(University of Southern California, USA)*
Jure Leskovec *(Stanford University, USA)*
Cane Leung *(Huawei)*
Hang Li *(Huawei)*
Edo Liberty *(Yahoo! Research, USA)*
Ee-Peng Lim *(Singapore Management University)*
Yu-Ru Lin *(Harvard/Northeastern Universities, USA)*
Yan Liu *(University of Southern California, USA)*
Bing Liu *(University of Illinois at Chicago, USA)*
Huan Liu *(Arizona State University, USA)*
Chao Liu *(Tencent Inc)*
Hao Ma *(Microsoft Research)*
Yoelle Maarek *(Yahoo! Labs)*
Michael Mahoney *(Stanford University, USA)*
Mark Manasse *(Microsoft Research, USA)*
Winter Mason *(Stevens Institute of Technology, USA)*
Yutaka Matsuo *(University of Tokyo, Japan)*
Edgar Meij *(Yahoo! Research Barcelona, Spain)*
Massimo Melucci *(University of Padua, Italy)*
Donald Metzler *(Google)*
Peter Mika *(Yahoo! Research Barcelona, Spain)*
Vahab Mirrokni *(Google Research)*
Alan Mislove *(Northeastern University, USA)*
Michael Mitzenmacher *(Harvard University, USA)*
Alistair Moffat *(University of Melbourne, Australia)*
Kamesh Munagala *(Duke University, USA)*
Vanessa Murdock *(Microsoft, USA)*
Hamid Nazerzadeh *(USC Marshall School of Business, USA)*
Jennifer Neville *(Purdue University, USA)*
Iadh Ounis *(University of Glasgow, UK)*
Rasmus Pagh *(IT University of Copenhagen, Denmark)*
Themis Palpanas *(University of Trento, Italy)*

Weike Pan *(Hong Kong Baptist University)*
Spiros Papadimitriou *(Rutgers University, USA)*
Stelios Paparizos *(Microsoft Research)*
Srini Parthasarathy
Jian Pei *(Simon Fraser University, Canada)*
Dan Pelleg *(Yahoo!)*
Evaggelia Pitoura *(University of Ioannina, Greece)*
Benjamin Piwowarski *(UPMC, France)*
Kira Radinsky *(Technion - Israel Insitute of Technology)*
Filip Radlinski *(Microsoft Research, UK)*
Justin Rao *(Microsoft Research, USA)*
Chandan K. Reddy *(Wayne State University, USA)*
Matthew Richardson *(Microsoft Research, USA)*
Lars Schmidt-Thieme *(University of Hildesheim, Germany)*
Giovanni Semeraro *(University of Bari, Italy)*
Pavel Serdyukov *(Yandex, Russia)*
Hua-Wei Shen *(Institute of Computing Technology, Chinese Academy of Sciences, China)*
Milad Shokouhi *(Microsoft Research, UK)*
Luo Si *(Purdue University, USA)*
Fabrizio Silvestri *(ISTI - CNR, Italy)*
Vikas Sindhwani *(IBM Research, USA)*
Yangqiu Song *(Hong Kong University of Science & Technology)*
Mauro Sozio *(Télécom ParisTech, France)*
Fabian M. Suchanek *(Max Planck Institute for Informatics, Germany)*
Torsten Suel *(Yahoo! Research)*
Yizhou Sun *(UIUC, USA)*
Idan Szpektor *(Yahoo! Research)*
Domenico Talia *(University of Calabria, Italy)*
Katsumi Tanaka *(Kyoto University, Japan)*
Jie Tang *(Tsinghua University, China)*
Jaime Teevan *(Microsoft Research, USA)*
Evimaria Terzi *(Boston University, USA)*
Martin Theobald *(Max Planck Institute for Informatics, Germany)*
Paul Thomas *(CSIRO, Australia)*
Panayiotis Tsaparas *(University of Ioannina, Greece)*
Antti Ukkonen *(Helsinki Institute for Information Technology, Finland)*
Eli Upfal *(Brown University, USA)*
Sergei Vassilvitskii *(Google)*
Andrea Vattani *(University of California, San Diego, USA)*
Petros Venetis *(Stanford University, USA)*
Rossano Venturini *(University of Pisa, Italy)*
Sebastiano Vigna *(University of Milan, Italy)*
Vishwa Vinay *(Microsoft Research, UK)*
Jun Wang *(University College London, UK)*
Haifeng Wang *(Baidu)*
Haixun Wang *(Microsoft Research Asia)*
Quan Wang *(Peking University, China)*
Ingmar Weber *(Qatar Computing Research Institute, Qatar)*
Gerhard Weikum *(Max-Planck Institute for Informatics, Germany)*
Evan Xiang *(Hong Kong University of Science & Technology)*
Lexing Xie *(Australian National University, Australia)*
Hui Xiong *(Rutgers University, USA)*
Qiang Yang *(Hong Kong University of Science & Technology)*
Emine Yilmaz *(University College London, UK)*
Dawei Yin
Philip Yu *(University of Illinois at Chicago, USA)*
Cong Yu *(Google Research)*
Nicholas Jing Yuan *(Microsoft Research Asia)*
Yisong Yue *(Carnegie Mellon University, USA)*
Georgios Zervas *(Yale University, USA)*
Kun Zhang *(Max-Planck-Institute for Intelligent Systems, Germany)*
Nan Zhang
Elena Zheleva *(LivingSocial)*
Vincent Wenchen Zheng *(Advanced Digital Sciences Center)*
Yu Zheng *(Microsoft Research Asia)*
Xingquan Zhu *(University of Technology, Sydney, Australia)*

# WSDM 2014 Additional Reviewers

Mohammad Ali Abbasi
Avishek Anand
Ashton Anderson
Cigdem Aslay
Florian Baeurle
Andrew Bagdanov
Saeideh Bakhshi
Lamberto Ballan
Nicola Barbieri
Daniel Bengs
Anand Bhalgat
Christina Brandt
Björn Brodén
Bjoern Buchhold
Florian Burle
André Carvalho
Aitao Chen
Bowei Chen
Chuang Chen
Tony Chen
Chen Cheng
Shiwen Cheng
Luca Chiarandini
Freddy Chong Tat Chua
Lorenzo Coviello
Paolo Cremonesi
Wanyun Cui
Bhavana Dalvi
Engin Demir
Cong Dinh
Yuxiao Dong
Alessandro Epasto
Dora Erdos
Andrea Esuli
Mohammadamin Fazli
Yang Feng
Sela Ferdman
Dario Di Fina
Yanjie Fu
Huiji Gao
Marco de Gemmis
Shima Gerani
Behzad Golshan
Ming Gong
Mingming Gong
Josif Grabocka
Huan Gui
Morgan Harvey
Elmar Haussmann
Tao Hoang
Juhua Hu
Xia Hu
Yuheng Hu
Giacomo Inches
Suradej Intagorn
Adam Jatowt
Xin Jin
Svebor Karaman
Ioannis Katakis
Mostafa Keikha
Umer Khan
Yubin Kim
Abhishek Kumar
Shamanth Kumar
Shankar Kumar
Monica Landoni
Baichuan Li
Wei Li
Tom Minka
Joyce Miranda
Tanushree Mitra
Anna Monreale
Fred Morstatter
Davide Mottin
Defu Lian
Qiao Lian
Guang Ling
Bin Liu
Daniel Liu
Jialu Liu
Yandong Liu
Pasquale Lops
Ahmad Mahmoody
Tong Man
Alex Mathews
Michael Mathioudakis
Charalampos Mavroforakis
Julian McAuley
Yelena Mejova
Xiao Meng
Shahin Rahmatollahi Namin
Franco Maria Nardini
Fedelucio Narducci
Afshin Nikzad
Hiroaki Ohshima
Rifat Ozcan
Umberto Panniello
Luca Pappalardo
Diego Pennacchioli
Yinian Qi
Meng Qu
Rajiur Rahman
Vineeth Rakesh
Suhas Ranganath
Theodoros Rekatsinas
Xiang Ren
Andrei Rikitiansky
Salvatore Rinzivillo
Matteo Riondato
Giulio Rossetti
Eduardo Ruiz
Antonia Saravanou
Nicolas Schilling
Lorenzo Seidenari
Dafna Shahaf
Marc Sloan
Yuxin Su
Umar Syed
Kartik Talamadupula
Maryam Tavakol
Huihsin Tseng
Mikalai Tsytsarau
Emmanouil Tzouridis
Ozgur Ulusoy
Tiberio Uricchio
George Valkanas
Bhanukiran Vinzamuri
Yana Volkovich
Pengyuan Wang
Robert West
Matthew Wiley
Martin Wistuba
Fangzhao Wu
Le Wu
Chenyan Xiong
Li Xiong
Takehiro Yamamoto
Haiqin Yang
Jaewon Yang
Yu Yang
Honglin Yu
Kui Yu
Reza Zafarani
Fuzheng Zhang
Hongyi Zhang
Weinan Zhang
Shenglin Zhao
Xiaoxue Zhao
Xin Zhao
Guoqing Zheng
Hao Zhong
Yuan Zhong
Zhuojie Zhou
Honglei Zhuang

# WSDM 2014 Sponsors & Supporters

Sponsors:

SIGIR
Special Interest Group
on Information Retrieval

Supporters:

# Data that Matter: Opportunities in Crisis Informatics Research

Leysia Palen
Project EPIC
Computer Science
University of Colorado Boulder
palen@colorado.edu

## ABSTRACT

In an increasingly global society and on a planet experiencing effects of climate change, large-scale emergencies both instigated by humans and arising from nature can devastate human life and our tightly- woven social fabric. With a promise of improved warning and coordination, a prevailing hope is that information and communication technology (ICT) can help reduce the impacts of large-scale disruptions, including political crises, natural disasters, pandemics, and terrorist threats. Much of the focus of development has been on the formal emergency response effort.

However, social computing is changing the way we understand information distribution. By viewing the citizenry as a powerful, self-organizing, and collectively intelligent force, ICT is now playing a remarkable and transformational role in the way society responds to mass emergencies and disasters. Furthermore, this view of a civil society that can be augmented by ICT is based on social and behavioral knowledge about how people truly respond in disaster, rather than on simplified and mythical portrayals of people unable to help themselves [2]. Indeed, long before the advent of widely available social computing platforms, research has shown that disaster victims themselves are the true —first responders, frequently acting on the basis of knowledge not available to officials [1, 3, 6].

We argue that this transformative view is critical to our global future: When large-scale emergencies happen, there is often no way to survive it in practical terms unless we rely on each other for help. The urgency and scale of many disaster events are such that no one— not even the most experienced and best technology-equipped responders—can rescue all victims or direct all people over the span of the event as to what the best course of action might be. Climate change and population migration to geographically vulnerable areas mean that naturally occurring hazards will exert increasingly extensive damage. Man-made and terrorist threats can also have greater potential to cause lasting damage to the social and built environment. It is instead necessary, through innovative ICT, to leverage the power of the collective intelligence of the citizenry to support natural instincts, which are to search for reliable information using any means possible to optimize for local conditions [5].

This view challenges fundamental assumptions about how information should be controlled and disseminated to ensure public safety. That officials can and should provide the best information during emergencies, and that the public can and should primarily rely on official information appears to be a difficult-to-resist, near- universal human hope. However, it is critical that we adopt a view of broad public participation in emergency response—and make such a view viable.

*Crisis informatics* addresses socio- technical concerns in large-scale emergency response. Additionally it expands consideration to include not only official responders (who tend to be the focus in policy and technology-focused matters), but also members of the public. It therefore views emergency response as a much broader socio-technical system where information is disseminated within and between official and public channels and entities. Crisis informatics wrestles with methodological concerns as it strives to develop new theory and support informed development of ICT and policy [4].

In this talk, I will review the state of the art in research, and where future opportunities in computing research lie.

## Categories and Subject Descriptors

H.5.3 Groups & Organization Interfaces—collaborative computing; computer-supported cooperative work

## Keywords

Crisis informatics, disaster, emergency, social computing, social media, Human-Computer Interaction

## 1. BIOGRAPHY

Leysia Palen is an Associate Professor of Computer Science at the University of Colorado Boulder, USA. She is a faculty fellow with the ATLAS Institute and the Institute of Cognitive Science. She is also a Full Adjunct Professor at the University of Agder in Norway.

Prof. Palen is a leader in the area of crisis informatics, an area she forged with her graduate students and colleagues at Colorado. She brings her training in human-computer interaction (HCI), computer-supported cooperative work and social computing to bear on understanding and advancing socio-technical issues of societal import. She conducts empirical research in the interpretivist tradition. However, in the advancing arena of large-scale on-line interaction (the "big data" of crisis response), she adapts quantitative techniques that then allow the application of qualitative methods and the "ethnographic eye" to closely observe


*WSDM'14*, February 24–28, 2014, New York, New York, USA.
ACM 978-1-4503-2351-2/14/02.
http://dx.doi.org/10.1145/2556195.2559898

and describe social structures in such technology-mediated situations.

Prof. Palen is the author of over 70 articles and a co-edited book in the areas of human computer interaction, computer supported cooperative work, mobility, and crisis informatics. She has been awarded $3.4M as Principal Investigator and $1.1M as co-Principal Investigator in grants from the US National Science Foundation, including an NSF CAREER award in 2006. She is an Associate Editor for the Human Computer Interaction Journal (Taylor and Francis) and for the Computer-Supported Cooperative Work Journal (Springer).

At the University of Colorado Boulder, Prof. Palen directs the Project EPIC (Empowering the Public with Information during Crisis) research effort, and co-directs the Center for Software & Society.

Leysia Palen is a graduate of the University of California, San Diego with a BS in Cognitive Science, and of the University of California, Irvine with an MS and PhD in Information and Computer Science. As an undergraduate, she spent time at the University of Stirling, Scotland, and as faculty member at the University of Aarhus, Denmark and the University of Agder, Norway. She has worked at Boeing Commercial, USWEST Advanced Technologies, Microsoft and Xerox PARC.

## 2. REFERENCES


[1] Aguirre, B., Wenger, D., Glass, T., Diaz-Murillo, M. & Vigo, G. (1995). The Social Organization of Search and Rescue: Evidence from the Guadalajara Gasoline Explosion. *International Journal of Mass Emergencies and Disasters,* 13:93–106.

[2] Fischer III, H. (1998). *Response to Disaster: Fact Versus Fiction & Perpetuation, 2nd ed.*, University Press of America.

[3] Kendra, J. & Wachtendorf, T. (2006). Community Innovation and Disasters. In Rodríguez, H., Quarantelli, E. & Dynes, R. (Eds.), *Handbook of Disaster Research*: 316–334. Springer.

[4] Palen, L., KM Anderson, G. Mark, J. Martin, D. Sicker, M. Palmer, D. Grunwald (2010). A Vision for Technology-Mediated Support for Public Participation & Assistance in Mass Emergencies & Disasters. *Association of Computing Machinery and British Computing Society's 2010 Conference on Visions of Computer Science.*

[5] Sorenson, J. & Sorenson, B. (2006). Community Processes: Warning and Evacuation. In Rodríguez, H., Quarantelli, E. & Dynes, R. (Eds.) *Handbook of Disaster Research*, Springer, New York, pp. 183-199.

[6] Stallings, R. A. & Quarantelli, E. L. (1985). Emergent Citizen Groups and Emergency Management. *Public Administration Review* 45: 93–100.

# Improving the Efficiency of Multi-site Web Search Engines

Guillem Francès*
Universitat Pompeu Fabra
Barcelona, Spain
guillem.frances@upf.edu

Xiao Bai
Yahoo Labs
Barcelona, Spain
xbai@yahoo-inc.com

B. Barla Cambazoglu
Yahoo Labs
Barcelona, Spain
barla@yahoo-inc.com

Ricardo Baeza-Yates
Yahoo Labs
Barcelona, Spain
rbaeza@acm.org

## ABSTRACT

A multi-site web search engine is composed of a number of search sites geographically distributed around the world. Each search site is typically responsible for crawling and indexing the web pages that are in its geographical neighborhood. A query is selectively processed on a subset of search sites that are predicted to return the best-matching results. The scalability and efficiency of multi-site web search engines have attracted a lot of research attention in recent years. In particular, research has focused on replicating important web pages across sites, forwarding queries to relevant sites, and caching results of previous queries. Yet, these problems have only been studied in isolation, but no prior work has properly investigated the interplay between them.

In this paper, we take this challenge up and conduct what we believe is the first comprehensive analysis of a full stack of techniques for efficient multi-site web search. Specifically, we propose a document replication technique that improves the query locality of the state-of-the-art approaches with various replication budget distribution strategies. We devise a machine learning approach to decide the query forwarding patterns, achieving a significantly lower false positive ratio than a state-of-the-art thresholding approach with little negative impact on search result quality. We propose three result caching strategies that reduce the number of forwarded queries and analyze the trade-off they introduce in terms of storage and network overheads. Finally, we show that the combination of the best-of-the-class techniques yields very promising search efficiency, rendering multi-site, geographically distributed web search engines an attractive alternative to centralized web search engines.

*This research was carried out during the author's internship at Yahoo Labs Barcelona.


*WSDM'14*, February 24–28, 2014, New York, New York, USA.

http://dx.doi.org/10.1145/2556195.2556249.

## Categories and Subject Descriptors

H.3.3 [**Information Storage Systems**]: Information Retrieval Systems

## Keywords

Distributed web search; query processing; document replication; query forwarding; result caching; efficiency

## 1. INTRODUCTION

As the vast amount of data available in the Web and the number of users accessing it keep their steady growth, an emerging line of research has focused on the scalability problems faced by single-site, centralized web search engines [3, 10, 13, 21]. An interesting alternative, multi-site distributed web search engines were shown to reduce the resource consumption in query processing and thus the financial costs of search engines, while also decreasing query response times experienced by users [3]. In multi-site web search engines, the document collection is partitioned into a number of distributed indexes, usually based on the geographical proximity between web servers and users. The objective is to exploit the so-called query locality, i.e., the fact that a large fraction of queries can find their top $k$ best-matching documents in the index of the local site to which they are issued, saving the need to process them on non-local sites and thus reducing query response latencies and query processing workloads.

Multi-site web search engines raise three major research problems regarding query processing, which forms the focus of our work. First, since each search site indexes only a subset of the documents, for some queries, some of the best-matching documents may not be present in the local index. Therefore, a query forwarding strategy is necessary to determine, every time a query is received at a local site, which non-local search sites may have indexed the missing best-matching documents for the query, so that the query can be forwarded to those sites. In order to avoid unnecessary increases in query response time, it is important to forward queries only to those sites that indexed the best-matching documents. Second, forwarding queries increases the query response time due to the network latency among sites. If we replicate and locally index those documents that are frequently fetched from remote sites, more queries can benefit from query locality, thus decreasing query response times.

The challenge here is to determine the right documents to replicate on the sites in order to achieve high query locality with low replication overhead. Third, as commonly used in centralized search engines, a result cache is useful for reducing query response times and query processing workload. In addition to the problems faced by result caches in centralized search engines (e.g., admission, eviction, invalidation), for a multi-site search engine, it is also important to determine in which sites the results of a query should be cached.

**Contributions.** We propose and evaluate new strategies for each of the outlined problems (document replication, query forwarding, and multi-site result caching) and conduct what we believe is the first realistic simulation of the full stack of strategies in a multi-site search engine:

- We propose a document replication technique that relies on per-document utility to select the documents to be replicated on each site, improving the query locality of state-of-the-art approaches up to 5.88% with various replication budget distribution strategies.
- For the query forwarding problem, we propose a machine learning approach that exploits the trade-off between result quality and query response time. Without using any document replication or result caching techniques, our approach is able to increase the fraction of locally processed queries up to 61% with respect to a state-of-the-art approach.
- We describe three new multi-site result caching strategies, improving the query locality up to 3.4% with respect to that of the local caching approach.
- We conduct extensive experiments with real-life data and study the interplay among the proposed techniques. We show that the combination of the best-of-the-class techniques improves the average query response time of a state-of-the-art approach up to 24% with little sacrifice from the result quality.

**Paper outline.** In Section 2, we provide some background on multi-site web search engines. Section 3 describes the data and setup used in our simulations. Sections 4, 5, and 6 present the strategies we propose for document replication, query forwarding, and multi-site result caching, respectively. Section 7 evaluates the combination of the best-of-the-class techniques. Section 8 surveys the related work. The paper is concluded in Section 9.

# 2. MULTI-SITE WEB SEARCH

## 2.1 Preliminaries

**Notation.** We assume a distributed web search engine composed of a set $\mathcal{S}=\{s_1, s_2, \ldots, s_m\}$ of $m$ geographically distributed sites. A set $\mathcal{D}=\{d_1, d_2, \ldots, d_n\}$ of $n$ documents is partitioned among these $m$ sites. Each site $s_i$ maintains a local index built on a disjoint subset $\mathcal{D}_i$ of documents such that $\mathcal{D}=\bigcup_{1\leq i\leq m}\mathcal{D}_i$ and $\mathcal{D}_i \cap \mathcal{D}_j = \emptyset$, for $1 \leq j \leq m$ and $i \neq j$.[1] We denote by $size(d)$ the number of postings contributed to the inverted index by document $d$.[2] Also, for document set $\mathcal{D}$, we define $size(\mathcal{D}) = \sum_{d\in\mathcal{D}} size(d)$. Each site $s_i$ serves a set $Q_i$ of queries that are issued to the site. We denote by $f_i(q)$ the number of times a query $q$ was issued to $s_i$ (in a given query set). Finally, we denote by $R(q) \subseteq \mathcal{D}$ the global top-$k$ result set for query $q$ (i.e., the result set that would be returned by a centralized search engine).[3]

**Query forwarding.** Upon the reception of a query at some search site $s_i$, a query forwarder decides in which search sites the best-matching documents of the query might have been indexed. Based on this decision, the query is forwarded to a number of sites and processed on their indexes. The top-$k$ result sets retrieved from the contacted sites are then merged at the local site $s_i$ and returned to the user.[4]

**Replication.** The occurrence of documents in query result sets is highly skewed. Therefore, replicating a certain subset of documents (typically, the most popular documents) on search sites considerably reduces the number of forwarded queries [3, 21]. We assume that each site $s_i$ maintains a replicated index built on a subset $\mathcal{R}_i \subseteq \mathcal{D}\setminus\mathcal{D}_i$ of documents that are not present in the local index of the site.

**Caching.** Finally, some form of result caching might be used in order to reduce query response times as well as the overall system workload.

## 2.2 Performance Metrics

**Query locality.** For a given combination of document replication, query forwarding, and result caching strategies, we define query locality as the fraction of queries that are answered by the local site they are submitted to without necessitating any forwarding. Increasing the query locality allows lower query response times and also helps decreasing the overall system workload.

**Query forwarding accuracy.** Given a query $q$ received at site $s_i$, the query forwarder on that site needs to decide whether to process $q$ on the index of each site $s_j$ ($1 \leq j \leq m$). Each of these $m$ binary decisions might turn out to be a true positive (TP), a true negative (TN), a false positive (FP), or a false negative (FN). If the decision is not to forward the query to $s_j$, we have an FN if $s_j$ has indexed some best-matching document in $R(q)$ (and that document is not locally replicated), or a TN otherwise. If the decision is to forward the query to $s_j$, we have an FP if $s_j$ has indexed no best-matching documents, or a TP otherwise. An FN degrades the quality of search results since the final result set will be missing some best-matching documents. On the other hand, it might reduce the average response time and system workload. An FP might increase the average response time (because the user might have to wait for unnecessary query processing and round-trip time due to forwarding) as well as increasing the system workload. However, it does not affect the quality of results. We report the FP and FN rates as well as the overall accuracy for different query forwarding strategies.

**Result quality.** We aim at generating the same result set that a centralized search engine can provide. In order to measure the degradation in the result quality (caused by the FN rate of the query forwarder), we use a number of standard metrics. These metrics compare the result sets returned by the distributed architecture against those that would be returned by a centralized architecture, using the latter as a ground truth. We measure the quality at different result ranks, considering only the first $p$ results (for practical reasons, we restrict ourselves to $p \in \{1, 5, 10\}$). The three metrics we used are summarized below:

[1] We assume that the partitioning of documents on sites is determined according to some external design factor.

[2] This is equal to the number of unique terms in the document.

[3] In the rest of the paper, we assume a standard value of $k=10$.

[4] In contrast to previous approaches, we allow the query forwarder not to process $q$ on the local site $s_i$, as described later.

(i) *Exact match rate at rank p (EMR@p).* We define the exact match rate as the fraction of queries for which the top-$k$ results returned by the distributed architecture are identical to the top-$k$ results returned by the centralized architecture.
(ii) *Average overlap at rank p (overlap@p).* For a given query $q$, let $D_p(q)$ and $R_p(q)$ be the sets containing the first $p$ results returned by the distributed and centralized architectures, respectively. We define the overlap at rank $p$ for query $q$ as the fraction of results in $R_p(q)$ that are also present in $D_p(q)$, i.e., $|D_p(q) \cap R_p(q)|/|R_p(q)|$.[5] The obtained overlap values are averaged over all queries in a test query set.
(iii) *Average normalized discounted cumulative gain at rank p (NDCG@p).* Finally, we measure the average NDCG metric. Here, we assume that a document is relevant if and only if it belongs to the top-$k$ result set of the centralized architecture. We normalize the DCG computed for a query by the ideal DCG attained by the centralized architecture.[6]

**Query response time.** We estimate query response times by simulating the processing of queries in a distributed web search engine and report the distribution of response times.
**System workload.** We estimate the workload incurred by a query as the sum of the lengths of the inverted lists that need to be traversed when processing the query. We average the workload estimates over all queries in a query set.

# 3. EXPERIMENTAL SETUP

**Datasets.** We simulate a distributed search engine composed of five sites, located in five different major continents. For each site, we sample consecutive queries from the corresponding search frontend of a commercial web search engine. Queries are normalized by case-folding, stop-word removal, term uniquing, and alphabetical ordering of query terms. The full query set is split roughly 75%–25% between a training set (5.25 million queries), which we use to compute the replication utility of the documents and to train our query forwarding models, and a test set (1.72 million queries), which we use to compute the performance metrics. The document collection contains about 200 million web pages obtained after various cleansing and filtering steps such as spam filtering. A proprietary classifier is used to assign the documents to a home country (some documents are not assigned to any of the five sites). This classifier uses features such as document language, IP address, and domain name, among others.
**Simulation parameters.** For each search site, we build a separate index using the documents assigned to it. Each site is assumed to have computational resources proportional to its index size. The simulated response times include query processing times and network latencies. For the former, we assume a processing cost of 200 ns per posting and a fixed preprocessing overhead of 20 ms per query, as in [13]. The top $k$ query results are retrieved using the open-source search engine Terrier. For the latter, we considered the user-to-site and site-to-site network latencies, estimated based on the geodesic distances between the users and sites.

[5]We note that this metric becomes identical to the recall metric if the results in $R_p(q)$ are the only results considered as relevant.
[6]Because the ideal DCG is computed based on the ranking generated by the centralized architecture, our metric is slightly different than the standard NDCG definition in [19].

**Baselines.** We compare the performance of the proposed query forwarding approach against the state-of-the-art linear-programming-based forwarding model (`LP`) proposed in [13]. To facilitate the interpretation of our results, we often show the performance of an oracle query forwarder (`ORACLE`) that always knows, for any given query, in which search sites the top $k$ best-matching documents are indexed.

# 4. DOCUMENT REPLICATION

As mentioned before, document replication helps increasing the query locality in a distributed search engine. Replicating too many documents, however, defeats the purpose of a distributed search engine. Moreover, query processing times may increase when the replicated indexes are too large. Typically, the storage overhead of replicated documents are constrained by an upper-bound on the replication amount. Herein, we aim to devise a replication strategy that selects a set $\mathcal{R}_i \subset D \setminus D_i$ of documents and builds a replicated index on those documents for each site $s_i$ such that
(i) the total size of the replicated documents remains below a given fraction $b$ of the global document collection's size (i.e., $\sum_{1 \le i \le m} size(\mathcal{R}_i) \le b \times size(\mathcal{D})$), and
(ii) the query locality, i.e., the fraction of queries that can be processed locally without any quality loss (on both local and replicated indexes), is maximized.

In the rest of the section, we first categorize different document replication strategies (Section 4.1). We then propose a new document selection heuristic (Section 4.2). Finally, we show that this heuristic outperforms existing heuristics in terms of query locality (Section 4.3), assuming the presence of the `ORACLE` query forwarder.

## 4.1 Document Replication Strategies

Figure 1 illustrates the way different strategies replicate documents across the search sites. Figure 1(a) illustrates the case without any document replication, with each site indexing its own disjoint subset of documents.
**Identical replication.** A simple strategy is to replicate the same set $\mathcal{R}$ of documents on all sites (Figure 1(b)). Since part of the replicated documents may already exist in the local collection $\mathcal{D}_i$ of site $s_i$ (the dotted regions within the replicated indexes in Figure 1(b)), only those documents in $\mathcal{R}_i = \mathcal{R} \setminus \mathcal{D}_i$ are used to build the replicated index. At query processing time, this avoids the potential redundancy due to duplicate scoring of documents that appear in both indexes. To bound the total size of replicated documents, we just need to ensure that $size(\mathcal{R}) \le \frac{b}{m} \times size(\mathcal{D})$.
**Individual replication.** Identical replication possesses an obvious drawback: the documents best-suited for replication on site $s_i$ might not be the best documents for site $s_j$ since the users of each search site might have different information needs. A possible improvement is to replicate a distinct subset of documents on each site such that the replicated documents are selected depending on the query stream of the site. We study the following two alternatives for this kind of replication.
(i) *Global replication budget.* In this alternative, the total size of the replicated indexes is constrained, i.e., $\sum_{1 \le i \le m} size(\mathcal{R}_i) \le b \times size(\mathcal{D})$. As shown in Figure 1(c), a site with a small local index may have a large replicated index (e.g., site 3) and a site with a large local index may have a small replicated index (e.g., site 1).

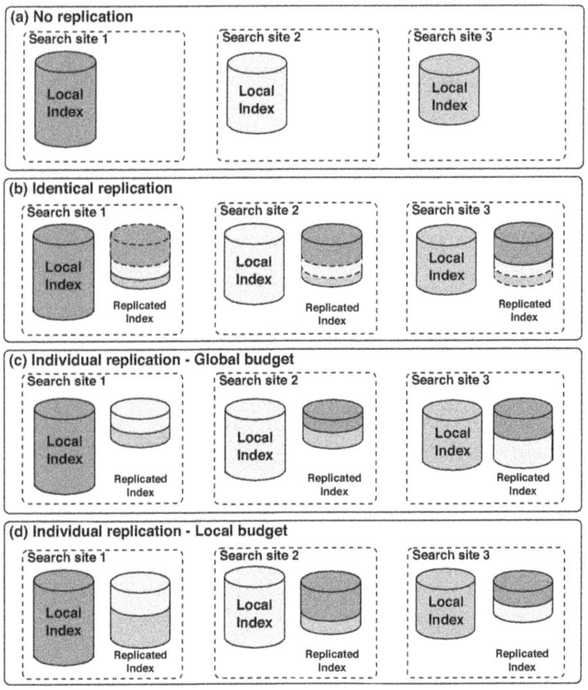


Figure 1: Different document replication strategies.

(ii) *Local replication budget.* In a distributed search engine, the amount of storage and computational resources available in search sites may show high variation. Under a global replication budget, replicating a large number of documents on a small search site with limited resources may require redistribution of resources among the sites or an investment in new resources. A potential solution is to use a local replication budget and limit the size of the replicated index on each site $s_i$ to a certain fraction $b$ of the local index size, i.e., $size(\mathcal{R}_i) \leq b \times size(\mathcal{D}_i)$ (Figure 1(d)).

## 4.2 Document Selection Heuristics

Herein, we present a generic heuristic that selects the documents to be replicated at each site, for any given replication strategy. For a given query set $Q$, it has been shown that the computation of the replicated subsets $\mathcal{R}_i$ that maximize the fraction of top-$k$ relevant documents that are indexed locally can be reduced to the 0-1 knapsack problem [14, 21],[7] which is known to be NP-hard. In our work, we rely on a greedy heuristic where the documents are sorted in descending order of their replication utility and progressively selected in this order until the replication budget is exhausted. We next define how the replication utility of a document is estimated.

For a given site $s_i$, let $\overline{R}_i(q) = R(q) \setminus \mathcal{D}_i$ be the set of documents that appear in the top-$k$ result set of $q$ and are not indexed in the local index of $s_i$. We define the utility of replicating a document $d \in \mathcal{D} \setminus \mathcal{D}_i$ on site $s_i$ with respect to query $q$ as

$$u_{i,q}(d) = \begin{cases} \frac{1}{|\overline{R}_i(q)| \times size(d)}, & \text{if } d \in R(q); \\ 0, & \text{otherwise.} \end{cases}$$

[7]The basic idea is to assign each document a weight equal to its size and a utility proportional to the number of top-$k$ result sets where it appears.

Given this, we define the global utility of replicating a document $d \in \mathcal{D} \setminus \mathcal{D}_i$ on site $s_i$ as the sum of the individual utility of each query $q$ weighted by its frequency $f_i(q)$, i.e.,

$$u_i(d) = \sum_{q \in Q_i} f_i(q) \times u_{i,q}(d).$$

The choice of $u_i(d)$ stems from the following observations: (i) replicating a non-local document in $R(q)$ is more likely to increase the query locality of site $s_i$ if query $q$ is frequently issued to site $s_i$ (i.e., larger $f_i(q)$), (ii) as there are fewer non-local documents in $R(q)$, it becomes more likely that replicating one of these non-local documents will let $q$ be processed locally, and (iii) the utility should be computed per unit document size, not per document. With this utility definition, we build the replicated document sets $\mathcal{R}_i$ for each replication strategy discussed in Section 4.1 as follows:

**Identical replication.** We compute the utility $u(d)$ of replicating a document as the sum of the utilities of replicating it on each site, i.e., $u(d) = \sum_{1 \leq i \leq m} u_i(d)$ and select documents in descending order of $u(d)$ values until the replication budget $\frac{b}{m} \times size(\mathcal{D})$ is exhausted.

**Individual replication with global budget.** Since a site can replicate any number of documents as long as the global replication budget is not exhausted, we rank the $\langle u_i(d), s_i \rangle$ pairs in descending order of $u_i(d)$ values and select the document with the highest $u_i(d)$ value for replication on site $s_i$ until the global replication budget $b \times size(\mathcal{D})$ is exhausted.

**Individual replication with local budget.** The size of replicated documents in a site should not exceed the local budget of the site. For each site $s_i$, we rank the documents in descending order of their $u_i(d)$ values and select them in this order until the local budget $b \times size(\mathcal{D}_i)$ is exhausted.

## 4.3 Experiments on Performance

In this section, we compare the performance of the proposed heuristic against the frequency-based heuristic used for identical replication in [13], where the utility of replicating a document is computed as the total frequency of the queries having the document in their top-$k$ results divided by the size of the document. We refer to this heuristic as `Identical-OF`, where `OF` stands for optimizing frequency. Moreover, we compare our heuristic against the `ORT` (optimizing response time) heuristic used in [21] for individual replication both with global (`Individual-ORT-G`) and local (`Individual-ORT-L`) replication budgets. In [21], the utility of replicating a document, is computed as in [13], but only non-local documents are considered for replication. We refer to the three replication strategies using our heuristics as `Identical-OU`, `Individual-OU-G`, and `Individual-OU-L`, where `OU` stands for optimizing utility.

**Query locality.** If no documents are replicated, 44.40% of queries can be processed entirely locally (44.80% in case of unique queries). Figure 2 compares our heuristic against the three baseline heuristics under different replication strategies for varying replication budgets. We observe that (i) replicating documents significantly improves the number of locally processed queries (e.g., replicating only 1% of documents improves the query locality by 36% assuming all queries are used), (ii) individual replication outperforms identical replication, (iii) for individual replication, using global budgets outperforms using local budgets, and (iv) our heuristic (`*-OU-*`) improves the query locality metric by 0.34% to 1.32% in case of all queries and by 0.73% to

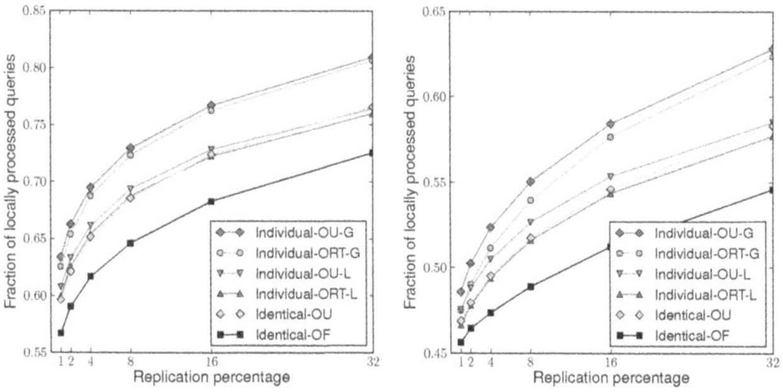


(a) All queries. (b) Unique queries.

Figure 2: Effectiveness of document replication.

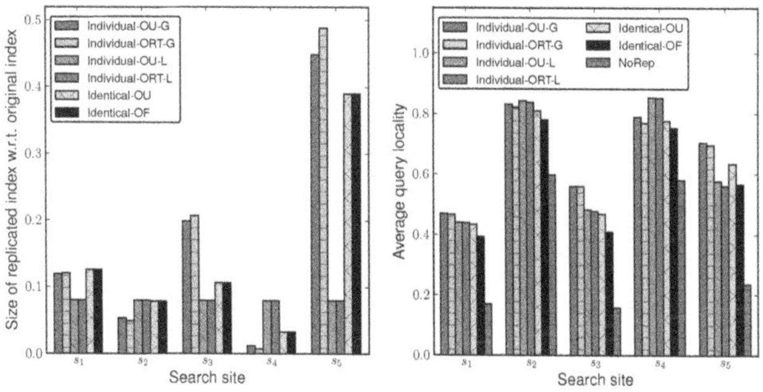


(a) Storage overhead. (b) Locally processed queries.

Figure 3: Load distribution among sites ($b = 8\%$).

2.22% in case of unique queries relative to the two individual replication strategies. The improvement with respect to identical replication is up to 5.88%. Interestingly, the improvement is higher in case of unique queries. This will be important once we add a cache layer (Section 6).

**Load distribution.** We study the load distribution among different sites by measuring the per-site storage overhead due to replication. This overhead is measured in terms of the ratio between the replicated and local index sizes. According to Figure 3(a), individual replication with a global budget replicates more documents in sites having smaller local indexes (e.g., $s_5$) while individual replication with local budgets results in a more balanced replication pattern.[8] In Figure 3(b), we observe that sites with larger local indexes have higher query locality. This explains why individual replication with a global budget results in larger query locality than individual replication with local budgets.

# 5. QUERY FORWARDING

In this section, we describe the solution we propose for the query forwarding problem. Given $m$ distributed search sites, we cast the problem as $m^2$ independent binary decision problems arising from every possible site pair. Thus, each local site $s_i$ has $m$ available binary classifiers $c_{i,1}, c_{i,2}, \ldots, c_{i,m}$, where $c_{i,j}$ is in charge of deciding, for any query received at site $s_i$, whether it is worth processing the query on the index residing at site $s_j$. We present the type of machine learning features we consider in Section 5.1, and we evaluate them in Section 5.2. We detail the query forwarding architecture in Section 5.3 and report on its performance in Section 5.4.

**Interplay with document replication.** Query forwarding in multi-site search engines typically determines where to forward a query according to the likelihood of a remote site to index some of the best-matching documents of the query [3]. In Section 4.3, we saw that individual replication outperforms identical replication. However, in the individual replication strategy, documents are usually replicated on a subset of the sites. Because of this, determining the optimal subset of sites to which the query should be forwarded becomes much more involved. Since this issue is beyond the classical query forwarding problem we aim to solve, in the rest of the paper, we assume that query forwarding is coupled with the identical replication strategy.[9]

[8]For easier visualization, Figure 3 assumes a fixed replication budget $b = 8\%$. Other values of $b$ exhibit a similar behavior.

[9]The above-mentioned problem does not exist in case of identical replication, where a replicated document becomes locally accessible in all sites, eliminating the need for query forwarding.

Table 1: Feature categories

| Type | Category | # |
|---|---|---|
| Pre-retrieval | Term lengths | 8 |
| | Term IDFs | 20 |
| | Term scores | 32 |
| | Query language | 1 |
| | Query popularity | 15 |
| | Query performance | 12 |
| Post-retrieval | Local query score | 8 |
| | LP forwarder decision | 4 |

## 5.1 Feature Extraction

Given the model described above, each query $q$ submitted to a site $s_i$ can be seen as the source of $m$ different machine learning instances $q_{i,1}, \ldots, q_{i,m}$, where the data instance $q_{i,j}$ will solely be used to train the binary classifier $c_{i,j}$ and contains features about (i) the local site $s_i$, (ii) the remote site $s_j$, (iii) some third sites $s_k$, where $k \notin \{i, j\}$,[10] and (iv) any meaningful combination of the previous options. Finally, the label (i.e., our ground truth) of every query instantiation $q_{i,j}$ is a binary variable indicating whether site $s_j$ contains at least one document from $\mathcal{R}(q) \setminus (\mathcal{D}_i \cup \mathcal{R}_i)$, i.e., a document that should be in the top-$k$ result set returned to the user and not available in neither index in site $s_i$.

Table 1 shows a summary of the different feature categories that we have considered. It is important to note that pre-retrieval features can be extracted prior to the local processing of the query, whereas post-retrieval features can be computed afterwards. We next give a brief description of these different categories.

**Term lengths, IDFs and scores.** We extract some basic features about the query and the terms in it. We also use some per-term and per-site frequency statistics as well as information on the maximum contribution of any term appearing in the site index to the score of a query containing the term.[11] As previously mentioned, we extract a number of features from that information, including features that try to capture the possible contribution of third sites to the result set.

[10] For instance, by encoding the maximum score that the lowest-scoring term is able to achieve at a third site, we expect our query forwarder to be more informed than the previous thresholding models [3, 13], which by nature only take into account the information from the local-remote site pair.

[11]As pointed out in [12], the storage overhead of keeping this *site* × *term* score matrix is negligible.

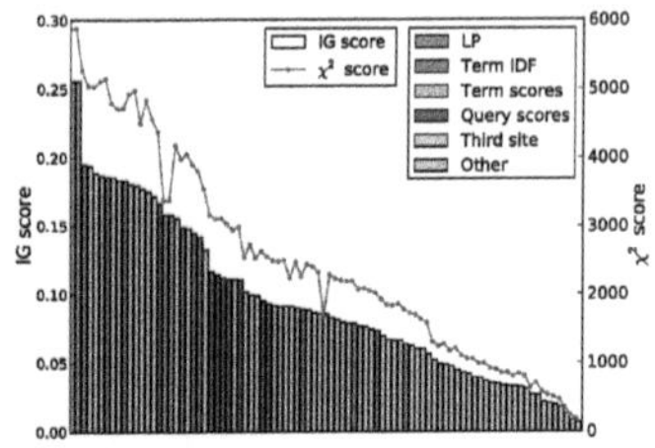


Figure 4: Individual feature scores.

**Query language.** Another feature which can be intuitively expected to capture the relevance of the indexes in different sites is the language of the query, especially given that documents are assigned to sites using language as a feature. We try to predict the language of the query by using a character-level, n-gram-based predictor.

**Per-site query popularity.** This is a simple set of features encoding information about whether the query belongs to the most frequent queries issued to the local site, for different percentile-based definitions of most frequent queries.

**Query performance.** We also extract some features related to the query performance predictors: $\gamma_1$ and $\gamma_2$, which predict how good the results of a query will be on a given index [18]. These predictors are based on the distribution of IDF values over different terms of a query and can be easily computed in the pre-retrieval stage.

**Local query score.** This set contains a number of features related to the scores obtained after processing the query on the local index.

**LP forwarder decision.** We compute some features using the LP-based query forwarding model described in [13].

## 5.2 Feature Evaluation

We investigate the importance of individual query features by computing both the information gain (IG) and chi-squared ($\chi^2$) scores of each feature. IG measures the reduction in entropy when the feature value is known, and $\chi^2$ measures the lack of independence between a feature and class values. Both metrics have been previously reported to perform well as feature selection methods [24].

Figure 4 shows IG and $\chi^2$ scores averaged over the query instances arising from different site pairs and are ordered by decreasing IG score types. The first thing to note is that the relative performance of individual features is roughly the same for both scores. As expected, the most informative features are those extracted from the LP formulation. A bit surprisingly, the post-retrieval query score features based on the local processing of the query are less informative than pre-retrieval features based on term scores and term IDFs. However, we note that we are only measuring the performance of features when they are considered in isolation. Therefore, the informativeness of some feature combinations might not be properly captured. It is also worth noting that features capturing information of term scores in sites other than the local-remote pair (labeled as the third site features) carry a certain amount of information. Finally, let us note that the features showing the worst performance are those related to query popularity, on the one hand, and to query language, on the other hand. This is probably due to the difficulty of accurately predicting the language of queries, given their very short length.

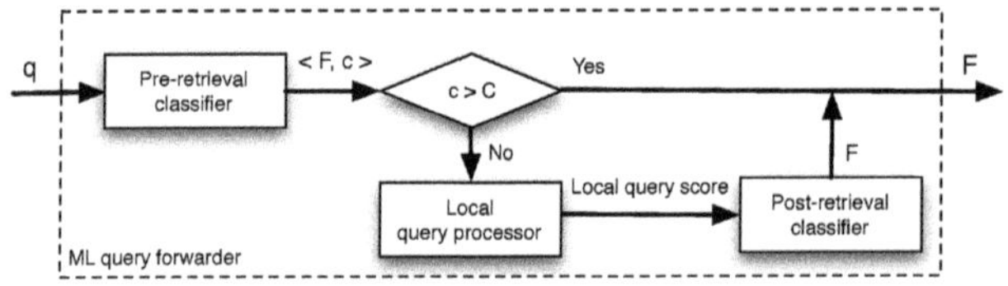


Figure 5: Architecture of the ML query forwarder.

## 5.3 Machine-Learned Query Forwarder

Figure 5 illustrates the proposed machine-learned query forwarder. The forwarder is composed of two different classifiers. On one hand, we have a pre-retrieval classifier which only uses pre-retrieval features and thus can be run right upon the reception of the query. Since this classifier dismisses post-retrieval features, however, it will predictably be less accurate than the full post-retrieval classifier, which employs all available features. In order to exploit the trade-off between the result quality and efficiency, we choose to trust the set $F$ of forwarding decisions made by the pre-retrieval classifier only if the confidence score $c \in [0.5, 1]$ of the classifier is high enough, i.e., higher than a given threshold $C$.[12] The ML architecture is thus parametrized by the confidence threshold $C$, and different values of $C$ will result in query forwarders with different properties: lower thresholds will be able to trigger the forwarding process earlier, but at the cost of being less precise and thus producing both inferior results and a higher chance of unnecessarily overloading remote sites. Also, we note that this architecture gives us the option not to process the query locally, as opposed to previous approaches.

As the classification model, we choose to combine a set of 100 base decision trees through the bagging ensemble method [9]. We use an off-the-shelf implementation of both the bagging method and the fast REP classification tree provided by the WEKA package [17]. In our preliminary experiments, other machine learning approaches such as random forest classifiers showed slightly better accuracy rates, but their training time was significantly larger. Given the large number of classifiers and the size of the datasets, we chose to use the bagging classifier.

In order to assess the value of using large training sets, we analyze the accuracy of our pre-retrieval classifiers as the amount of training queries increases, in the no-replication scenario. We hold out a fraction of our training dataset for testing purposes and train the forwarders with subsets of varying size from the remaining fraction. The resulting accuracies (averaged over all different site pairs) do not attain any saturation point before reaching the maximum training set size. Increasing the number of training queries from 10K to 100K, for instance, raises the accuracy from 88.72% to 90.86%. Using all the available queries results in a further boost up to 92.75% accuracy. We thus only report henceforth on query forwarders trained with the full training set.

## 5.4 Experiments on Performance

We now report the accuracy and the query locality metric attained by our classification strategy and defer the discus-

[12]We note that this confidence score is actually the estimated probability of the decision to be correct. Hence, since we are dealing with a binary decision problem, the score always lies in the range [0.5, 1].

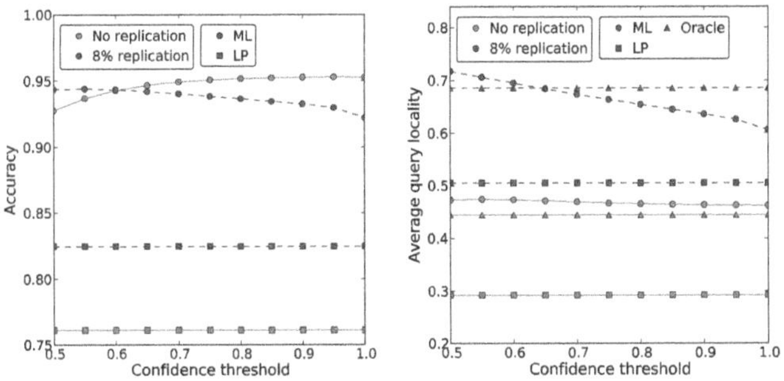


(a) Accuracy. (b) Query locality.

Figure 6: Performance of different query forwarders.

Table 2: Confusion matrix values (%)

| | Replication budget ($b$) | | | | | | | |
|---|---|---|---|---|---|---|---|---|
| | 0% | | | | 8% | | | |
| | TP | TN | FP | FN | TP | TN | FP | FN |
| ORACLE | 42.97 | 57.03 | 0.00 | 0.00 | 32.22 | 67.78 | 0.00 | 0.00 |
| LP | 42.97 | 33.14 | 23.89 | 0.00 | 32.21 | 50.26 | 17.53 | 0.00 |
| $ML_{0.5}$ | 38.61 | 54.14 | 2.89 | 4.36 | 28.56 | 65.79 | 1.99 | 3.66 |
| $ML_{0.75}$ | 40.41 | 54.67 | 2.36 | 2.57 | 30.41 | 63.43 | 4.35 | 1.81 |
| $ML_{1.0}$ | 40.64 | 54.64 | 2.39 | 2.33 | 30.72 | 61.49 | 6.29 | 1.50 |

sion of other metrics to Section 7. Figure 6(a) compares the accuracy of our ML forwarder against that of the LP baseline, varying the confidence threshold and assuming two different replication scenarios (no replication and 8% identical replication). Table 2 further presents the true positive (TP), true negative (TN), false positive (FP), and false negative (FN) rates ($ML_C$ stands for our ML forwarder with confidence threshold $C$). We note that due to the false positives, in some cases the ML forwarder has higher query locality than ORACLE. In both replication scenarios, the accuracy of the ML forwarder significantly exceeds that of the LP forwarder (for any confidence threshold), due to the high FP rate of the LP model. Unexpectedly, in the replicated scenario, the accuracy decreases as the confidence threshold increases, i.e., as more queries are forwarded according to the post-retrieval query forwarder. To investigate this issue, in Figure 7, we show a graphical breakdown of the evolution of the confusion matrix values for increasing confidence threshold values. The accuracy decrease in the replicated scenario turns out to be caused by an increase in the FP rate, although the FN rate actually decreases. This might be due to the higher imbalance caused by document replication. A potential solution is to weight false positives and false negatives non-uniformly, e.g., penalizing false positives more than false negatives when training the classifiers. We explore this possibility and its outcome in Section 7.

Figure 6(b), on the other hand, compares the query locality achieved by different forwarding strategies. As expected, both LP and ML forwarders are able to exploit the higher query locality allowed by the document replication. Compared to the LP forwarder, however, the lower FP rates of our approach ensure significant increase in query locality (10%–20% more queries are locally processed). Again, we note that in the replicated scenario, the increase in the FP rate that we just mentioned has a negative impact on the query locality for high confidence thresholds.

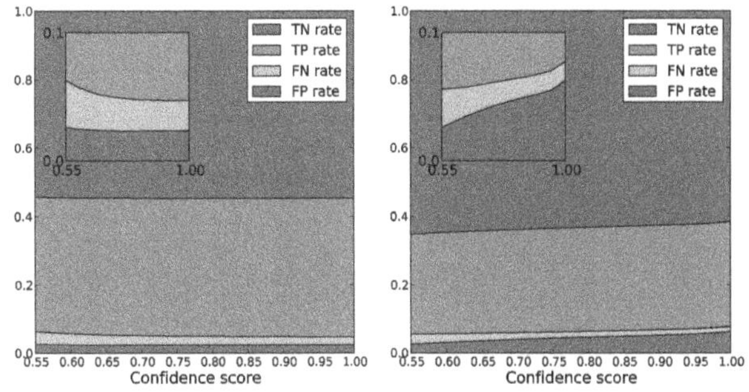


(a) No replication. (b) 8% replication.

Figure 7: Confusion matrix values. The inset details the lower section of the graph for easier visualization.

# 6. RESULT CACHING

Result caching is an important technique for improving the performance of search engines. The results of recurrent queries can be served by the cache, eliminating the need to process the query on the index. In previously proposed multi-site search architectures, each site typically maintains its own result cache, which contains the results of queries issued to itself. In this section, we are interested in designing cache architectures for multi-site search engines, where the search sites coordinate among each other to decide when and where query results should be cached. The proposed architectures further reduce the need for query forwarding. We limit ourselves to infinite-capacity caches, as assumed in [1]. To maintain the freshness of results served by the cache, we expire cached entries with a simple time-to-live (TTL) mechanism.

## 6.1 Result Caching Strategies

**Local cache.** A straightforward, yet common result caching approach in multi-site search architectures is to assume a local, independent cache in each search site [13]. When a site receives a query whose results are already cached, the results are served immediately by the local cache if the age of the cached results is less than a predefined TTL value. Otherwise, the query could be processed locally and also forwarded to non-local sites depending on the decision of the query forwarder. The lack of coordination between the caches cause certain queries to be processed redundantly although their results are already cached in one or more search sites.

**Global cache.** An effective way to reduce the number of queries that require processing is to replicate cached query results on all sites. Once a query is added to the local cache of a site, it is sent to the rest of the sites and cached also remotely.[13] This approach ensures that any site can serve the query results from its cache (until the TTL expires).

**Partial cache.** In the global caching approach, certain cache entries are replicated on sites where they will never be requested again. Moreover, the storage and communication overheads are high. To alleviate these problems, the results of a query may be replicated only on the sites to which the query is forwarded during the query processing.

[13]This can be achieved either on a per-query basis or in batch mode, according to the desired trade-off between the hit rate and the communication cost.

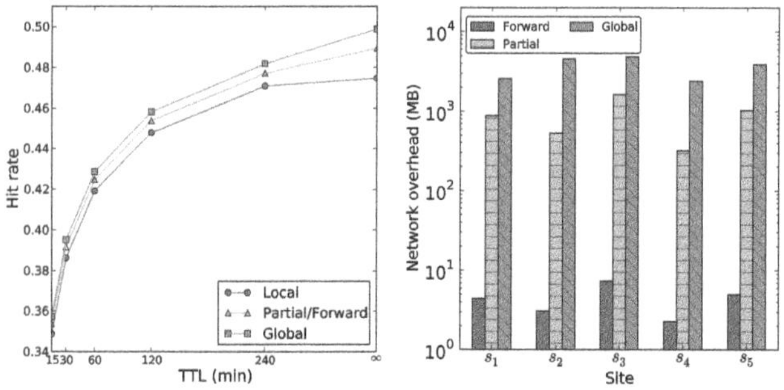


(a) Hit rate w.r.t. TTL. (b) Network overhead.

Figure 8: Performance of different caching strategies.

This partial caching approach is motivated by the fact that the contacted sites are more likely to index documents that are relevant to the query and hence the query will be issued those sites with higher probability.

**Forward cache.** A variation of the partial caching approach for reducing the communication overhead is to cache, in site $s_j$, a pointer to site $s_i$, whenever a query is forwarded from $s_i$ to $s_j$. If $s_j$ receives the same query in the future, it simply requests the results from the cache on $s_i$ instead of processing the query. The validity of the cached pointer entries are expired by the same TTL mechanism used before. Queries that are processed locally are maintained in the cache as in the local caching approach.

## 6.2 Experiments on Performance

In this section, we evaluate the performance of different result caching strategies. Figure 8(a) shows the hit rate as the value of TTL increases. As expected, the global caching approach consistently achieves the highest hit rate compared to other strategies, as the results of queries are replicated across all caches. Taking a TTL of two hours as an example, the average hit rate in case of a global cache is 3.4% higher than that in case of a local cache, and 1.1% higher than those in case of partial cache and forward cache.[14] In Figure 8(b), we observe that the global cache incurs higher network and storage overheads. Nevertheless, since our caches are assumed to have unlimited capacity and the communication of cached results between the sites can be performed offline, in the rest of the paper, we choose to focus only on the performance of the global caching approach.

In Figure 9, we observe that the query locality increases along with the TTL value, for both replication budgets (0% and 8%) and query forwarding strategies that we take into consideration. More importantly, we observe that the proposed ML query forwarder outperforms the baselines for all TTL values. Besides, even if the difference between not using a cache (i.e., zero TTL) and using a cache (e.g., a TTL of minutes) decreases when documents are replicated, using a cache still improves the query locality by at least 9.3% for different query forwarding strategies.

# 7. GLOBAL RESULTS

In this section, we report the performance in terms of result quality and query response time. We first report on these metrics independently and then study the combined effect of different strategies.[15] Table 3 shows some result quality metrics for our ML forwarder assuming three different confidence thresholds $C \in \{0.5, 0.75, 1.0\}$ at different rank positions $p \in \{1, 5, 10\}$. *O@p*, *N@p* and *E@p* stand for overlap@p, NDCG@p and EMR@p, respectively. The results are consistent with what we saw in the previous sections: as the confidence threshold increases, the quality improves (according to all metrics). This is because the post-retrieval forwarder, which has a smaller FN rate, is used more often.

In Figure 10, we analyze the variation of query response time across different queries. The figure shows the cumulative percentage of queries that are answered below a certain time threshold. In the scenario with replication, for instance, 53.51% of the test queries are answered in less than 300ms when using the LP forwarder, whereas by using our ML strategy, this percentage is increased to a value in the 62.09%–71.43% range, depending on the confidence threshold.

We now turn our attention to the trade-off between both metrics, this time taking into account the impact of caching strategies (Figure 11(a)). In the figure, the solid markers denote a simulation without caching while the hollow markers include the effect of a global cache with a two-hour TTL. The markers from left to right correspond to ML forwarders with increasing confidence threshold $C \in [0.5, 1]$. As expected, the average response time increases as the result quality increases. Without caching and taking the LP forwarder as a baseline, the proposed ML forwarder achieves a significant reduction in average response time: in the 20%–22% range (no replication) or 15%–25% (8% replication), depending on the confidence threshold, in exchange for a small loss in re-

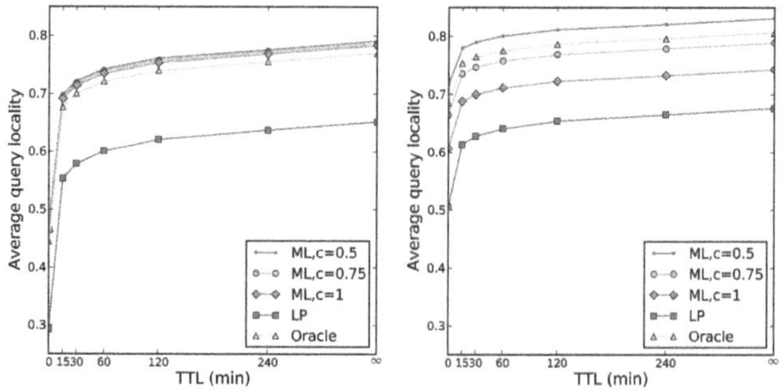


(a) No replication. (b) 8% replication.

Figure 9: Impact of global cache on query locality.

Table 3: Quality metrics at different result positions ($p$)

| | | Replication budget ($b$) | | | | | |
|---|---|---|---|---|---|---|---|
| | | 0% | | | 8% | | |
| C | p | O@p | N@p | E@p | O@p | N@p | E@p |
| 0.5 | 1 | 0.965 | 0.965 | 96.52 | 0.970 | 0.971 | 97.04 |
| | 5 | 0.957 | 0.959 | 94.41 | 0.964 | 0.965 | 95.33 |
| | 10 | 0.934 | 0.945 | 82.73 | 0.944 | 0.953 | 85.54 |
| 0.75 | 1 | 0.983 | 0.983 | 98.32 | 0.991 | 0.991 | 99.07 |
| | 5 | 0.978 | 0.979 | 97.07 | 0.987 | 0.988 | 98.21 |
| | 10 | 0.964 | 0.971 | 89.22 | 0.977 | 0.982 | 92.34 |
| 1.0 | 1 | 0.988 | 0.988 | 98.84 | 0.997 | 0.997 | 99.69 |
| | 5 | 0.983 | 0.984 | 97.61 | 0.994 | 0.994 | 98.92 |
| | 10 | 0.970 | 0.976 | 90.23 | 0.984 | 0.989 | 93.66 |

[14] We assume that the queries are forwarded by the ORACLE query forwarder.

[15] Note that caching has no impact on the result quality.

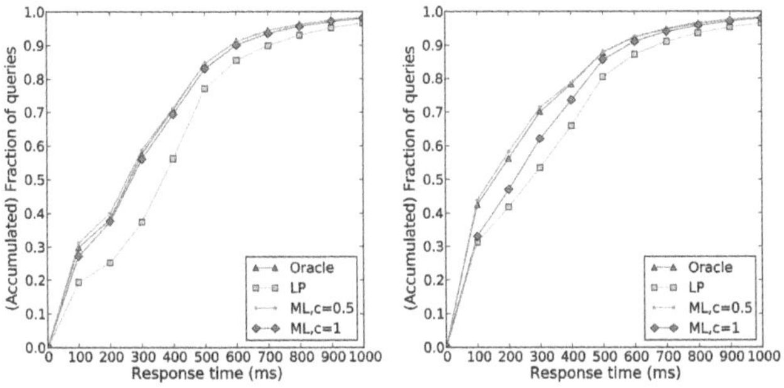


(a) No replication. (b) 8% replication.

Figure 10: Distribution of the query response time.

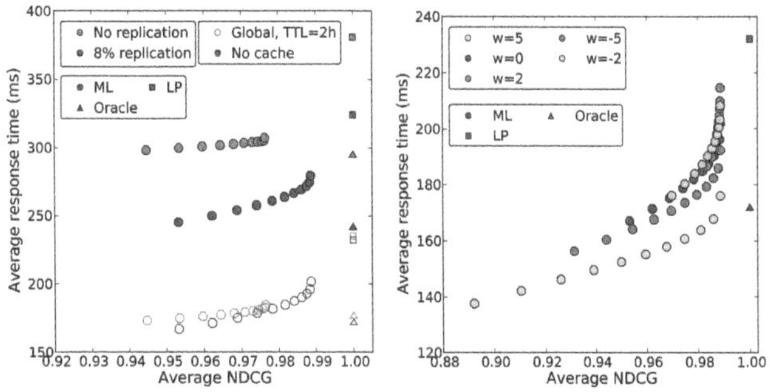


(a) No training weights. (b) Varying training weights.

Figure 11: Trade-off between result quality and time.

sult quality. If we focus on the scenario with replication and pick a confidence threshold of 0.7, our approach offers an improvement of 19.5% in the average response time while the average NDCG remains as high as 0.978, and 91.65% of queries obtain a result set identical to that of a centralized architecture. We omit the relative improvements in query processing workload since they follow a similar pattern.

Regarding the impact of the cache layer, we observe that caching neutralizes the advantages of replication as far as the response time is concerned, up to the point where larger index sizes due to replication and the induced larger query processing time outweighs the benefits achieved by the replication itself. This might be partly due to the fact that the replication strategy is specifically tailored to query frequencies in the original query stream, which is largely modified by the presence of a cache layer. To circumvent this problem, one should simulate a fixed caching strategy paired with a fixed TTL value and tailor the replication decisions to the resulting, post-cache query stream.

**Varying training weights.** In Section 5.4, we hinted at an alternative, orthogonal way of exploring the quality-time trade-off that consisted of modifying the balance between false positives and false negatives by weighting them non-uniformly while training the query forwarder. We show the results of applying this strategy in Figure 11(b), where for easier visualization only a scenario with 8% replication coupled with a global cache with a two-hour TTL, is depicted. $w=x$ stands for an `ML` forwarder such that during the training phase an FP is considered $x$ times as negative as an FN (e.g., the $w=-2$ stands for those forwarders where an FN is considered twice as harmful as an FP). It can be seen that this strategy further widens the flexibility that the `ML` forwarder offers to the system designer. In exchange for a larger quality loss, the average query response time can now be decreased to as little as 137ms (a 40% reduction with respect to the `LP` forwarder). More interestingly, on the other extreme, we can reach a 0.99 NDCG quality and decrease the average response time to 176ms, which is almost as good as the `ORACLE` forwarder. This means a significant reduction of 24% with respect to the state-of-the-art `LP` forwarder.[16]

# 8. RELATED WORK

There is a rich literature on query forwarding, document replication, and result caching. Herein, we provide a brief survey of related work on these topics, limiting the context to multi-site web search. A broader survey on scalability and efficiency of web search engines can be found in [10].

**Query forwarding.** In the multi-site web search framework, the query forwarding problem is first investigated by Baeza-Yates et al. [3]. The authors propose a simple technique for estimating the maximum score a query can achieve on each search site. The forwarding decisions are made based on the outcome of a comparison between the estimated maximum scores and the lowest score in the top $k$ result set computed by the local search site. The authors show that, with the proposed technique, many queries can be processed solely in local search sites without sacrificing the result quality. The work of Cambazoglu et al. [10] further increases the rate of locally processed queries by using a linear-programming technique. The technique exploits the co-occurrence of query terms in documents and yields tighter upper bound score estimations. In our work, we use a machine-learned query forwarding technique, which achieves further performance improvements over the linear programming model used in [13]. Finally, Baeza-Yates et al. [4] also investigate the use of machine learning techniques in a distributed search engine, although the scope of their simulation is much more limited and their focus is on two-tiered systems with high index size imbalance.

**Document replication.** There are two prior studies on document replication in multi-site web search engines [8, 21]. Brefeld et al. [8] employ machine learning techniques to select the data center(s) where a newly discovered document should be replicated. Since no past popularity information (i.e., the number of views in web search results) is available for new documents, the features used by the learning model are mainly extracted from the document content (e.g., the language feature). Kayaaslan et al. [21] consider a scenario where past popularity information is available for every document. They propose three algorithmic optimizations that aim to reduce the response latency, query processing workload, and the loss in result quality. The replication heuristic proposed in our work achieves further improvements over the heuristic described in [21] in terms of the query locality metric. Besides [8] and [21], Cambazoglu et al. [13] also evaluate a simple replication heuristic, where a small fraction of frequently viewed documents are replicated on all search sites. However, document replication does not form the main focus of their work. Finally, Blanco et al. [7] investigate the problem of assigning documents to search sites with the most similar content, obtaining a one-to-one mapping between the newly crawled documents and search sites.

[16]These response time gains (not shown in the figure) are virtually the same even without the cache layer.

**Result caching.** Result caching is long recognized as an important technique for improving search engine performance [22]. So far, various caching policies are proposed to increase the hit rates [2, 15] or to reduce the query workload of search backends [16, 23]. Recent studies mainly focus on refreshing result caches [11, 20] and cache invalidation [1, 5, 6]. To the best of our knowledge, our work is the first to investigate result caching strategies in the context of multi-site web search.

## 9. CONCLUSIONS

In this paper, we studied the interplay between three important mechanisms in a multi-site web search engine: document replication, query forwarding, and result caching. For each of these mechanisms, we proposed new strategies that outperform the existing state-of-the-art approaches. Most notably, we explored the fundamental trade-off between result quality, on the one hand, and query response time and system workload, on the other hand. The use of a machine-learned query forwarding strategy can allow system designers to exploit this trade-off and obtain significant improvements in query response time and overall system workload, in exchange for a little quality loss. We note that our machine learning technique can be improved through active learning on forwarding mistakes, i.e., adding false positives and false negatives to the training data.

## 10. ACKNOWLEDGEMENTS

This work was supported by the LEADS project (ICT-318809), funded by the European Community, and the Torres Quevedo Program from the Spanish Ministry of Science and Innovation, co-funded by the European Social Fund.

## 11. REFERENCES

[1] S. Alici, I. S. Altingovde, R. Ozcan, B. B. Cambazoglu, and O. Ulusoy. Timestamp-based result cache invalidation for web search engines. In *Proc. 34th Int'l ACM SIGIR Conf. Research and Development in Information Retrieval*, pages 973–982, 2011.

[2] R. Baeza-Yates, A. Gionis, F. Junqueira, V. Murdock, V. Plachouras, and F. Silvestri. The impact of caching on search engines. In *Proc. 30th Int'l ACM Conf. Research and Development in Information Retrieval*, pages 183–190, 2007.

[3] R. Baeza-Yates, A. Gionis, F. Junqueira, V. Plachouras, and L. Telloli. On the feasibility of multi-site web search engines. In *Proc. 18th ACM Int'l Conf. Information and Knowledge Management*, pages 425–434, 2009.

[4] R. Baeza-Yates, V. Murdock, and C. Hauff. Efficiency trade-offs in two-tier web search systems. In *Proc. 32nd Int'l ACM Conf. Research and Development in Information Retrieval*, pages 163–170, 2009.

[5] X. Bai and F. P. Junqueira. Online result cache invalidation for real-time web search. In *Proc. 35th Int'l ACM SIGIR Conf. Research and Development in Information Retrieval*, pages 641–650, 2012.

[6] R. Blanco, E. Bortnikov, F. Junqueira, R. Lempel, L. Telloli, and H. Zaragoza. Caching search engine results over incremental indices. In *Proc. 33rd Int'l ACM SIGIR Conf. Research and Development in Information Retrieval*, pages 82–89, 2010.

[7] R. Blanco, B. B. Cambazoglu, F. P. Junqueira, I. Kelly, and V. Leroy. Assigning documents to master sites in distributed search. In *Proc. 20th ACM Int'l Conf. Information and Knowledge Management*, pages 67–76, 2011.

[8] U. Brefeld, B. B. Cambazoglu, and F. P. Junqueira. Document assignment in multi-site search engines. In *Proc. 4th ACM Int'l Conf. Web Search and Data Mining*, pages 575–584, 2011.

[9] L. Breiman. Bagging predictors. *Machine learning*, 24(2):123–140, 1996.

[10] B. B. Cambazoglu and R. Baeza-Yates. Scalability challenges in web search engines. In M. Melucci, R. Baeza-Yates, and W. B. Croft, editors, *Advanced Topics in Information Retrieval*, volume 33 of *The Information Retrieval Series*, pages 27–50. Springer Berlin Heidelberg, 2011.

[11] B. B. Cambazoglu, F. P. Junqueira, V. Plachouras, S. Banachowski, B. Cui, S. Lim, and B. Bridge. A refreshing perspective of search engine caching. In *Proc. 19th Int'l Conf. World Wide Web*, pages 181–190, 2010.

[12] B. B. Cambazoglu, V. Plachouras, F. Junqueira, and L. Telloli. On the feasibility of geographically distributed web crawling. In *Proc. 3rd Int'l Conf. Scalable Information Systems*, pages 31:1–31:10, 2008.

[13] B. B. Cambazoglu, E. Varol, E. Kayaaslan, C. Aykanat, and R. Baeza-Yates. Query forwarding in geographically distributed search engines. In *Proc. 33rd Int'l ACM Conf. Research and Development in Information Retrieval*, pages 90–97, 2010.

[14] T. H. Cormen, C. Stein, R. L. Rivest, and C. E. Leiserson. *Introduction to Algorithms*. McGraw-Hill Higher Education, 2nd edition, 2001.

[15] T. Fagni, R. Perego, F. Silvestri, and S. Orlando. Boosting the performance of web search engines: caching and prefetching query results by exploiting historical usage data. *ACM Trans. Inf. Syst.*, 24(1):51–76, 2006.

[16] Q. Gan and T. Suel. Improved techniques for result caching in web search engines. In *Proc. 18th Int'l Conf. World Wide Web*, pages 431–440, 2009.

[17] M. Hall, E. Frank, G. Holmes, B. Pfahringer, P. Reutemann, and I. H. Witten. The WEKA data mining software: an update. *ACM SIGKDD Explorations Newsletter*, 11(1):10–18, 2009.

[18] B. He and I. Ounis. Inferring query performance using pre-retrieval predictors. In *String Processing and Information Retrieval*, pages 43–54. Springer, 2004.

[19] K. Järvelin and J. Kekäläinen. Cumulated gain-based evaluation of IR techniques. *ACM Trans. Inf. Syst.*, 20(4):422–446, 2002.

[20] S. Jonassen, B. B. Cambazoglu, and F. Silvestri. Prefetching query results and its impact on search engines. In *Proc. 35th Int'l ACM SIGIR Conf. Research and Development in Information Retrieval*, pages 631–640, 2012.

[21] E. Kayaaslan, B. B. Cambazoglu, and C. Aykanat. Document replication strategies for geographically distributed web search engines. *Inf. Process. Manage.*, 49(1):51–66, 2013.

[22] E. P. Markatos. On caching search engine query results. *Computer Comm.*, 24(2):137–143, 2001.

[23] R. Ozcan, I. S. Altingovde, and O. Ulusoy. Cost-aware strategies for query result caching in web search engines. *ACM Trans. Web*, 5(2):9:1–9:25, 2011.

[24] Y. Yang and J. O. Pedersen. A comparative study on feature selection in text categorization. In *Proc. 14th Int'l Conf. Machine Learning*, pages 412–420, 1997.

# A Self-Adapting Latency/Power Tradeoff Model for Replicated Search Engines

Ana Freire[1], Craig Macdonald[2], Nicola Tonellotto[3], Iadh Ounis[2], Fidel Cacheda[1]

[1] University of A Coruña, Campus de Elviña s/n, 15017 A Coruña, Spain
[2] University of Glasgow, G12 8QQ Glasgow, UK
[3] National Research Council of Italy, Via G. Moruzzi 1, 56124 Pisa, Italy

{ana.freire, fidel.cacheda}@udc.es[1], {craig.macdonald, iadh.ounis}@glasgow.ac.uk[2], {nicola.tonellotto}@isti.cnr.it[3]

## ABSTRACT

For many search settings, distributed/replicated search engines deploy a large number of machines to ensure efficient retrieval. This paper investigates how the power consumption of a replicated search engine can be automatically reduced when the system has low contention, without compromising its efficiency. We propose a novel self-adapting model to analyse the trade-off between latency and power consumption for distributed search engines. When query volumes are high and there is contention for the resources, the model automatically increases the necessary number of active machines in the system to maintain acceptable query response times. On the other hand, when the load of the system is low and the queries can be served easily, the model is able to reduce the number of active machines, leading to power savings. The model bases its decisions on examining the current and historical query loads of the search engine. Our proposal is formulated as a general dynamic decision problem, which can be quickly solved by dynamic programming in response to changing query loads. Thorough experiments are conducted to validate the usefulness of the proposed adaptive model using historical Web search traffic submitted to a commercial search engine. Our results show that our proposed self-adapting model can achieve an energy saving of 33% while only degrading mean query completion time by 10 ms compared to a baseline that provisions replicas based on a previous day's traffic.

**Categories & Subject Descriptors:** H.3.3 [Information Storage & Retrieval]: Information Search & Retrieval

**Keywords:** Search Engines; Power Consumption.

## 1. INTRODUCTION

Commercial web search engines are expected to process queries under tight response time constraints and be able to operate under heavy query traffic loads. Operating under these conditions requires building a very large infrastructure involving thousands of computers, with corresponding continuous operating costs. In particular, electricity costs (including power and cooling) form an important part of the operational costs of search engine companies [14]. Indeed, in 2011, Google's overall power consumption was reported[1] to be 2.68 million MWh.

The user query volume typically received by a Web search engine varies through the course of the day [27]. In order to guarantee that each query is processed with sub-second response times, the computing/communication infrastructure has to support worst-case query volume, which typically reaches its maximum during the day time. Hence, the typical approach taken by Web search engines is to deploy a distributed search architecture relying on a very large data centre to deal with the worst-case query volumes [13]. The main goal of this high-level approach is to maximise the query throughput of a search engine, providing users with effective query results in a timely manner. Supporting worst-case query volumes in large data centres has the obvious drawback that the power consumption/electricity costs are not taken into account, resulting in a potential waste of power and money when the query volume is low. Instead, it is possible to *dynamically adapt* the behaviour of the search engine – according to the variations of the query load – while providing acceptable query latencies and minimising the number of machines used to process the queries.

We argue that a tradeoff can be enforced between the machines devoted to processing queries and query processing deadlines, and that this tradeoff can be adapted during the operational cycle of a Web search engine, in order to minimise the number of machines processing the queries while ensuring acceptable latencies. Moreover, we contend that this tradeoff can be adapted dynamically to changing query volumes in very short times. To attain this, we propose a mathematical model of a replicated search engine with a query broker and many independent query processors, each managing a replica of the index. This model permits the number of query processors to be dynamically changed according to the query arrivals and proposed latency and power consumption cost functions. By estimating the arrival times and processing requirements of future queries, we derive self-adapting mechanisms for the search engine model that can reduce power consumption without negatively impacting efficiency, by means of dynamic optimisation schemes [2]. Moreover, we provide thorough ex-

[1]Google Green: `http://www.google.com/green/`.


*WSDM'14,* February 24–28, 2014, New York, New York, USA.
Copyright 2014 ACM 978-1-4503-2351-2/14/02 ...$15.00.
http://dx.doi.org/10.1145/2556195.2556246.

periments using 1 million queries submitted to a real Web search engine over the course of 2 days, to demonstrate the power savings that can be obtained without marked impact on the efficiency of the search engine.

The main contributions of this paper are the following:

- We propose a self-adapting model for replicated search systems that establishes a trade-off between latency and power consumption in terms of the number of replicated query servers required as query load varies throughout the day.
- We show how this model can be instantiated for different methods of forecasting the query traffic at a given time – based on current and historical query loads – as well as with a variety of latency functions.
- We thoroughly demonstrate experimentally how the proposed model can reduce the power consumption of a search engine by 33% with little decrease in the overall efficiency of the search engine.

This paper is structured as follows: Section 2 discusses the existing literature on distributed search and green efforts in information technology. In Section 3, we introduce our model, by describing the dynamic system and the general cost function, while Section 4 presents the deterministic approach that considers the previous and also the current state of the system for predicting query traffic. Section 5 proposes power and latency cost functions. In Section 6, we concretely state the research questions that we investigate, as well as detailing the baselines and experimental setup. Section 7 reports our experimental results, with concluding remarks following in Section 8.

# 2. BACKGROUND

As well as effectively answering the users' information needs, a search engine must be efficient, as users are not willing to wait long for queries to be answered [26]. For large settings, the efficient answering of queries typically encompasses the distribution of the search engine index across multiple machines. As our work is concerned with the analysis of distributed search engines, and their power consumption, in the remainder of this section we provide the necessary background on distributed search engine architectures (Section 2.1) and on previous work on reducing power consumption within information technology (IT) (Section 2.2).

## 2.1 Distributed/Replicated Search

Increasing the parallelism of a search engine through distributed architectures offers a route to increased per-request efficiency without loss of effectiveness. In such *document-partitioned* architectures, a query server stores the index shard for a subset of the documents in the corpus. When a query arrives at a *query broker*, it broadcasts the query to all shards, in order to later collect and merge the results and produce the final top K retrieved set for presentation to the user [1]. To ensure high throughput rates, shards are often replicated, so that one of multiple *query servers* can provide the results for a single shard [4]. Indeed, with multiple *replicas* of the same shard, more queries can be processed in parallel on identical shard copies, thus reducing the waiting time of incoming queries, as well as providing fault tolerance properties. Without loss, we focus on a single broker, single-shard environment with multiple replicas on different query

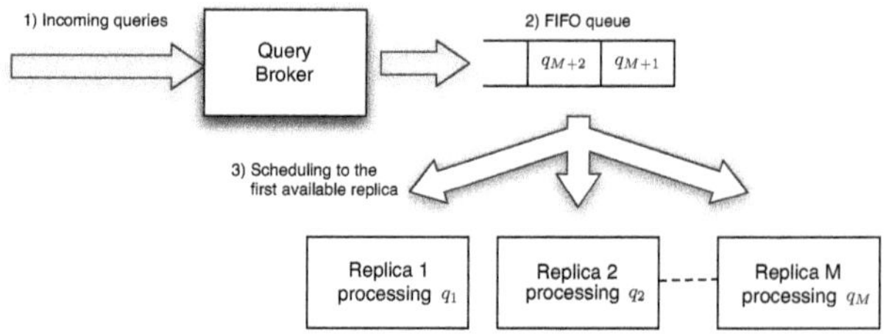


Figure 1: Our reference architecture.

server machines. Indeed, as the replicated query servers allocated to a single shard represent independent partitions of the search engine's index, the techniques proposed in this paper could easily be applied for multiple shard environments, by independent application on each shard individually.

Our reference architecture assumes a single-shard search engine implemented by a query broker and $M$ independent replicas that manage a copy of the index (Fig. 1). Queries are received by the broker and are queued up in a buffer. While complex queue re-ordering strategies can benefit overall response times [9, 20], in our architecture, the query processing nodes serve from the front of the queue: at any given time if the search engine has less than $M$ queries, some processing nodes are idle, while if the search engine has more than $M$ queries, some queries are queued in the buffer.

## 2.2 Green IT

In recent years, the consciousness of environmental problems tied to Green-House Gases has increased. In 2007, analyst Gartner estimated that Information and Communication Technology is responsible for 2% of the total emissions [11]. Much research effort has been dedicated to achieve power savings for data centres or Internet servers [8, 17, 19, 21, 30] taking into account different factors such as the devices' power consumption and/or cooling systems. Moreover, large IT companies such as Microsoft[2] and Google[3] are making efforts in reducing their carbon emissions, while also publishing their carbon footprints and goals.

Some directions on how to proceed in order to save power consumption in data centres are given in [19], where Lin et al. showed that the most effective and aggressive power saving comes from turning off components that are not used, such as CPU, disk, and memory, which consume substantial power when they are turned on, even with no active workload. Nevertheless, they remark on several challenges regarding this technique: the workload scheduling of the remaining active systems to preserve performance and the cost of waking up a sleeping component.

Many of the afore-mentioned works are focused on achieving power savings in data centres for general Internet services (e.g. [19, 21]). However, few works have addressed this problem within search engines, where user queries equate to (short-lived) jobs. Chowdhury [5] recently introduced the term *Green IR*, that maps this concern into the information retrieval field. His roadmap for improving environmental impact of information retrieval systems addresses the power efficiency of end-user devices as well as within the search engine itself. Within his roadmap, our work is clearly focused on the intra-data centre efficiency of the search engine.

[2]`http://www.microsoft.com/environment/`
[3]`http://www.google.com/green/`

In contrast, the work of [16] addressed power efficiency at the inter-data centre level, by distributing query volume between geographically distant data centres based on workload and electricity prices. Recently, Sazoglu et al. [25] propose a novel metric for result caching that considers the financial cost of a cache miss. Nevertheless, to the best of our knowledge, no previous work has presented an intra-data centre model that turns the servers on or off depending on the incoming query traffic needs. Indeed, our model, proposed in the next section, can examine the historical and current query traffic patterns to predict the number of query server replicas now needed, and obtain power savings within a single data centre by eliminating query servers that are not currently needed.

# 3. DYNAMIC OPTIMISATION MODEL

We consider a replicated search engine processing user queries, as explained above with reference to Figure 1. Each query submitted to the search engine experiences a completion time defined as the sum of its waiting time (the time that the query has spent enqueued), its processing time (the time spent processing the query by a query processor) and any network delays between the broker and the corresponding replica. Assuming identical query processors, the processing time of a query is independent from the node actually processing the query: the same query will be processed in the same amount of time on each node.

We consider a daily-based operational cycle of the search engine, in that we analyse the behaviour of the search engine during a single day. Periodically during the day, we *observe* the state of the search engine and thus *decide* how to change it, with the objective of minimising a certain cost, i.e., an undesirable behaviour. In our scenario, this behaviour is represented by the unnecessary usage of machines that are not required to service the query load with acceptable timeliness. In doing so, we must take into account that the outcome of each decision cannot be fully predicted, due to some random unknown parameters – such as the number of queries that will be received. Moreover, each decision cannot be taken in isolation, since we want to balance lowering the present cost with potentially higher future costs – for instance, turning off currently unused machines that might be needed shortly. To achieve these aims, we model the search engine as an optimal decision problem of a discrete dynamic system over a finite number of stages [2]. Computing systems have been previously modelled as dynamic systems in order to leverage automatic control theory to address the dynamics of resource management [12], such as email server [23] and web servers [6]. However, this work represents the first instantiation of a dynamic decision problem within search engine power/latency modelling.

In the remainder of this section, we provide a short introduction to the general dynamic decision problem [2] (Section 3.1), a dynamic model of a replicated search engine with multiple query processors (Section 3.2), a discussion on the cost function for our dynamic model (Section 3.3), and a summary of the resulting decision problem (Section 3.4).

## 3.1 General Dynamic Decision Problem

A dynamic decision problem model must be composed by: (1) an underlying *discrete-time dynamic system* and (2) a *cost function that is additive over time* [2]. In the following, we introduce the notation necessary to describe a general decision problem model, which we later instantiate for our proposed search engine model. All notation used in our instantiation for a search engine problem model is summarised in Table 1. Firstly, we assume that time is slotted and indexed by $k = 0, 1, 2, \ldots, N$. Time slots are sampled every $T_s$ seconds. The dynamic system has the form:

Table 1: Notation used within our model.

| Symbol | Explanation |
|---|---|
| $N$ | number of time slots (per day) |
| $T_s$ | length of a time slot (in secs) |
| $M$ | number of available machines |
| $x_k$ | queued queries at the beginning of time slot $k$ |
| $u_k$ | processing nodes during time slot $k$ |
| $w_k$ | incoming queries during time slot $k$ |
| $y_k$ | processed queries at the end of time slot $k$ |
| $\bar{w}_k$ | estimated incoming queries during time slot $k$ |
| $v_k$ | mean query processing time during time slot $k$ |
| $\bar{v}_k$ | estimated mean average query processing time during time slot $k$ |
| $f_k(\cdot)$ | generic state update function |
| $g_k(\cdot)$ | generic cost function |
| $P_k(\cdot)$ | power cost function |
| $L_k(\cdot)$ | latency cost function |
| $h_k(\cdot)$ | query processing function |

$$x_{k+1} = f_k(x_k, u_k, w_k) \qquad k = 0, 1, \ldots, N-1 \tag{1}$$

where $k$ indexes discrete time, $x_k$ represents the state of the system that is relevant for its future operation, $u_k$ is the decision variable to be selected at time $k$ and $w_k$ is a random parameter. In general, we deal with a *finite time horizon*, i.e., we observe and optimise the system during a fixed number of time slots, indexed from 0 to $N$ – for instance, over a 24 hour period. The random parameter (or noise, or disturbance, or exogenous input) $w_k$ is characterised by a probability distribution that may depend explicitly on $x_k$ and $u_k$ but not on the values of prior disturbances $w_0, \ldots, w_{k-1}$. Given an initial state $x_0$ and a sequence of decisions $u_0, \ldots, u_{N-1}$, the states $x_k$ and the disturbances $w_k$ are random variables with distributions defined through Equation (1).

The cost function defines the expected cost of the decision at time $k$, and is additive in the sense that the cost incurred at $k$, denoted by $g_k(x_k, u_k, w_k)$, accumulates over time. Note that $g_k$ is a random variable, since it depends on $x_k$ and $w_k$. Hence the expected total cost $J(x_0)$ is:

$$J(x_0) = E\left[g_N(x_N) + \sum_{k=0}^{N-1} g_k(x_k, u_k, w_k)\right] \tag{2}$$

where the expectation is taken over the random variables $x_k$ and $w_k$ and $g_N(x_N)$ is a terminal cost incurred at the end of the process, depending on the final state. Hence, an *optimal decision sequence* $u_0^*, \ldots, u_{N-1}^*$ is the decision sequence that minimises the cost $J(x_0)$.

## 3.2 Search Engine Dynamic Model

Following the above formulation of a general dynamic decision problem, we now instantiate a dynamic decision model for a search engine. In each time slot $k$, depending on the number of pending queries in the buffer, the search engine allocates a number of processing nodes among the $M$ available. Increasing the number of processing nodes decreases the overall waiting time for the queries in the buffer but increases the service cost and power consumption associated with the system.

At the beginning of each time slot, a decision must be taken regarding the number of processing nodes to be used in that slot. Decisions cannot be viewed in isolation since we want to balance two conflicting goals: minimising the power consumption of the search engine, and maximising the search engine's efficiency. We denote by:

- $x_k$: the number of queries waiting to be processed (i.e., currently enqueued) at the start of the $k$th time slot.
- $u_k$: the number of *active* processing nodes at the start of the $k$th time slot.
- $y_k$: the number of queries processed by the search engine during the $k$th time slot (with a given probability distribution).
- $w_k$: the number of queries arriving to the search engine during the $k$th time slot (with a given probability distribution).

We assume that any incoming query is queued, and that if there are waiting queries, any processing node that finishes to process a query will immediately start to process another query. Thus, the number of queries waiting to be processed evolves according to the following discrete-time equation:

$$x_{k+1} = x_k - y_k + w_k \tag{3}$$

The dynamic equation (3) does not explicitly depend on the number of active processing nodes $u_k$. However, the number of queries processed by the search engine during the $k$th time slot $y_k$ depends explicitly on $u_k$, according to the following general equation:

$$y_k = h_k(x_k, u_k, v_k) \tag{4}$$

This models the fact that, in a given time slot, the number of processed queries depends on three quantities: the number of queries waiting to be processed $x_k$, the number of processing nodes $u_k$, and a random component $v_k$ modelling the mean service time of the queries. To summarise, the complete model for the search engine under examination is:

$$x_{k+1} = x_k - h_k(x_k, u_k, v_k) + w_k \tag{5}$$

where we leave to later in Section 4 the specification of the query processing function $h_k(x_k, u_k, v_k)$, which defines how many queries of $x_k$ can be processed by $u_k$ machines with a given service time pattern of $v_k$.

## 3.3 Search Engine Cost Function

A public software service such as a search engine has two main stakeholders: the service provider and the service user. In general, the service provider aims to maximise the revenue from the service, increasing the income and reducing its operating expenditure. One of the main costs of a running service is the expenditure on power required to run the machines hosting the service. From the point of view of the user, a search service is desired to be efficient (timely), i.e., the latency between the submission of a query and the display of the first search results should be minimised.

Clearly, the operating cost of a search infrastructure depends on the number of machines operating the service, and the final revenue depends on the number of satisfied users, i.e., how many users receive their search results with acceptable latency. Indeed, search engines users have less tolerance for slower search engines [26], and may abandon their search request [18] if the search engine takes too long to respond. Such abandonment can lead to the loss of users to other search services, leading to a loss of potential revenue from these users.

Given that the number of queries submitted to a search engine varies during the day [27], the number of processing nodes can be varied according to the demand. At the start of each time slot, a decision regarding the number of processing nodes to be used must be taken. Decisions need to balance two conflicting goals: minimise the search engine power consumption and maximise the search engine efficiency (by reducing latency). Hence, we have two types of costs that should both be considered:

1. Power cost $P_k(x_k, u_k, v_k, w_k)$, increasing in the number of processing nodes used;
2. Latency cost $L_k(x_k, u_k, v_k, w_k)$, increasing in the number of queries waiting to be processed and decreasing in the number of processing nodes used.

As the latency costs increase, the model aims to minimise the overall cost by emptying the query queue faster. On the other hand, as the power costs increase, the system will attempt to trade higher latencies for lower power. In order to model this power-latency tradeoff, we propose cost combinations of the following type:

$$g_k(\cdot) = \lambda P_k(\cdot) + (1 - \lambda) L_k(\cdot) \tag{6}$$

for various values of $\lambda \in [0, 1)$. For $\lambda = 0$, the cost function represented by Equation (6) ignores any power cost, and leads to the maximum number of available processing nodes being used in every time slot, as this achieves the minimum possible queueing delay. If $\lambda = 1$ is allowed, the cost function would ignore any latency cost, leading to the limit case of no processing nodes being used for processing, thereby maximising power savings but leading to infinite waiting times. Varying $\lambda$ in $[0, 1)$, we can achieve any average query latency from infinite to the minimum possible traded off against the corresponding power consumption of the search system. We note that both cost functions assume values in the same range. Without loss of generality, later in Section 5, we devise particular cost functions ranging in the [0,1] interval, where 0 means no cost and 1 means maximum cost.

## 3.4 Latency/Power Decision Problem

We now formulate the general dynamic decision problem by adapting Equations (1) & (2) to our search engine and cost models:

$$\begin{aligned} \underset{u_k}{\text{minimise}} \quad & E\left[\sum_{k=0}^{N-1} \lambda P_k(x_k, u_k, v_k, w_k) + \right. \\ & \left. (1-\lambda) L_k(x_k, u_k, v_k, w_k)\right] \\ \text{subject to} \quad & x_{k+1} = x_k - h_k(x_k, u_k, v_k) + w_k, \\ & k = 0, 1, \ldots, N-1 \end{aligned} \tag{7}$$

As described above, $\lambda$ is an exploratory parameter that must be fixed at the beginning, while $w_k$ and $v_k$ are random variables describing the number of incoming and processed queries at the $k$th time slot respectively. The state variables $x_k$ are computed through $N$ instances of Equation (5), depending on these two random variables and the query processing functions $h_k(\cdot)$. Given these dependencies, the state variables are random variables as well, hence the expectation in the cost function must be computed over these three sets of random variables, in a stochastic manner. The query processing functions $h_k(\cdot)$ will be defined in the next section, where we describe some approximations that allow the stochastic decision problem (7) to be sub-optimally solved in a deterministic manner.

# 4. DETERMINISTIC APPROXIMATION

Problems like (7) cannot typically be solved analytically, and their solution algorithms are computationally very intensive [2]. For these reasons, these problems, where the exact value of all variables are unknown deterministically, are solved sub-optimally in practice. In order to deal with the stochastic decision problem (7), we propose to solve a suboptimal scheme that consists of computing, at each stage, a decision that would be optimal if the uncertain quantities were fixed at some typical values. In doing so, we replace the stochastic nature of the decision problem with a simpler *deterministic* version at each stage and then we solve the deterministic problem. Within this section we discuss:

1. how to estimate the 'typical' value of the random variables, which we denote by $\bar{w}_k$ and $\bar{v}_k$, representing the estimated number of queries arriving during the $k$th time slot and the estimated mean service time during the $k$th time slot (Section 4.1);
2. how to derive a deterministic approximation for problem (7) with query processing functions $h_k(\cdot)$ depending on our estimations (Section 4.2);
3. how to solve the deterministic problem using dynamic programming, if we know all the estimates of the random variables for the whole day, and how to solve the deterministic problem with simple subsequent steps, if we know the estimates of the random variables for the next time slot only (Section 4.3).

## 4.1 Random variables estimation

In order to compute the estimated values of the random variables $w_k$ and $v_k$, we adopt the following estimation schemes, based on historical data.

For the service times of queries, the typical assumption is that these are independent and identically distributed random variables [3]. However, we assume that the service times exhibit a *seasonal* trend among days, hence the mean service time of the queries in the $k$-th time slot is equal to the mean service time of queries in the same time slot of a previous day, i.e., $\bar{v}_k = v_{k-SN}$, where $S$ defines the step, i.e., the number of previous days, and $N$ is the total number of time slots in a day. For instance, $S = 1$ means that $\bar{v}_k$ is estimated using data from the previous day, while $S = 7$ means that $\bar{v}_k$ is estimated using data from the same day in the previous week.

For the number of queries arriving during the $k$th time slot, we will assume two different estimation schemes:

- In the *seasonal estimator*, we estimate the number of incoming queries with the actual number of incoming queries in the same time slot of a previous day, i.e.:

$$\bar{w}_k = w_{k-SN}$$

- In the *seasonal estimator with drift*, the previous day value is adjusted with the current trend of arrivals [24] experienced in the last two time slots, such that:

$$\bar{w}_k = w_{k-SN} + (w_{k-1} - w_{k-2})$$

While the seasonal estimator is a viable solution for days exhibiting the same query submission and execution patterns (e.g., two subsequent weekdays or the same day in two subsequent weeks), the seasonal estimator with drift takes into account potential and unpredictable changes in query volume patterns, such as reduced query volumes during holidays or increased query volumes during major events (e.g., disasters, breaking news, or sport events). However, for this estimator, the value of $\bar{w}_k$ is known for only the next time slot ahead.

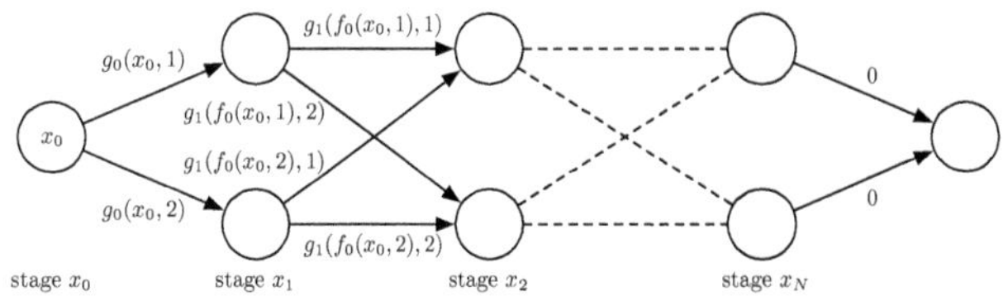


Figure 2: Transition graph for a deterministic problem with 2 machines.

## 4.2 Deterministic Problem Formulation

Given the mean query service time $v_k$, it is straightforward to model the processing of queries in our search engine model. If a single node can process $T_s/v_k$ queries in the $T_s$ seconds duration of the $k$th time slot, then $u_k$ identical processing nodes can serve $u_k \cdot T_s/v_k$ queries during the same slot, resulting in the following expression for $h_k$:

$$h_k(\cdot) = u_k \cdot T_s/v_k \tag{8}$$

Since we use the estimated mean service time $\bar{v}_k$ instead of the actual mean service time $v_k$, the approximation of the stochastic decision problem (7) with the random variables' estimated values leads to the following deterministic problem formulation:

$$\begin{aligned} \underset{u_k}{\text{minimise}} \quad & \sum_{k=0}^{N-1} \lambda P_k(x_k, u_k, \bar{v}_k, \bar{w}_k) + \\ & (1-\lambda) L_k(x_k, u_k, \bar{v}_k, \bar{w}_k) \\ \text{subject to} \quad & x_{k+1} = \max\{0, x_k - u_k \cdot T_s/\bar{v}_k + \bar{w}_k\} \\ & k = 0, 1, \ldots, N-1 \end{aligned} \tag{9}$$

where the $\max\{\cdot\}$ function avoids to process more queries than the number of queries available to process. In contrast to problem (7), problem (9) is deterministic as there is no longer any probability distributions associated to $v_k$ and $w_k$ (and hence $x_k$). Such deterministic formulation can be tractably solved [2], as described next.

## 4.3 Deterministic Problem Solutions

Consider the deterministic problem formulation defined in Equation (9) where each state $x_k$ can assume a finite set of values. Then, at any state $x_k$, a decision $u_k$ can be associated with a transition from state $x_k$ to state $f_k(x_k, u_k) = x_k - u_k \cdot T_s/\bar{v}_k + \bar{w}_k$ at a cost $g_k(x_k, u_k) = \lambda P_k(x_k, u_k, \bar{v}_k, \bar{w}_k) + (1-\lambda) L_k(x_k, u_k, \bar{v}_k, \bar{w}_k)$. As illustrated in Figure 2, the deterministic problem can be equivalently represented by a graph, where the arcs correspond to transitions between states at successive stages and each arc has an associated cost corresponding to $g_k(\cdot)$. Decision sequences correspond to paths across the graph, originating at the initial state (node at stage 0, where $x_0 = 0$), and terminating at a final node linked to all terminal states (nodes at stage $N-1$) with no associated transition cost or, alternatively, with a cost proportional to the number of remaining unprocessed queries. If we view the cost of an arc as its length, we see that the deterministic problem of Equation (9) is equivalent to finding a minimum length path from the initial node (at stage $x_0$) to the artificial terminal node with no transition costs of the graph.

If the service times and the number of arriving queries are estimated using only historical data (e.g. based on a previous day, the seasonal estimator), then the transition costs of the whole graph for the current day can be computed a priori. Hence, it is possible to use dynamic programming to solve the general shortest path problem [2], but also algorithms specifically designed for the shortest path problem solution, such as the Dijkstra algorithm [7]. We denote this solution algorithm as LONGTERM.

On the other hand, if we estimate the number of arriving queries with the seasonal drift approach, the estimates of the number of queries $w_k$ depend not just on the historical data, but also on the current load being experienced by the search engine. Hence, it is not possible to compute all the transition costs in the graph at the start of the day [2]. Instead, at each step we truncate the *estimation horizon* (i.e. how ahead the costs are calculated) to the next step only and resort to a *one step limited lookahead* strategy, where, at each stage, we select the next stage reachable with minimum cost from current stage[4]. We will denote this solution algorithm with SHORTTERM. Moreover, as discussed in Section 4.1, we expect SHORTTERM to improve LONGTERM, as it considers the query volume being currently experienced by the search engine in addition to the volume experienced on a previous day.

# 5. COST FUNCTIONS

The previous two sections define our model for balancing power/latency tradeoff, as well as a deterministic approximation. In this section, we study two cost functions to analytically express the power/latency tradeoff as the linear combination expressed in Equation (6). These cost functions allow us to model the benefits/drawback of using a variable number of machines.

## 5.1 Power Cost Function

The power cost function $P_k(x_k, u_k, \bar{v}_k, \bar{w}_k)$ represents the electric power consumption of the whole search engine and it is directly proportional to the energy costs of operating the search engine. Firstly, we discuss the power usage of a single processing node. We distinguish between three states that a node can be in:

1. ON. The node is fully operational and busy processing a query. The node consumes power at a rate of $P_{\text{on}}$.
2. STANDBY. The node is available, but is currently sleeping. The node consumes power at a rate of $P_{\text{standby}}$.
3. OFF. The node is off, and it consumes no power.

Switching a node between two states is associated to a *switching cost*. The switching cost typically consists of two components: a time component and a power component. The time component depends on node characteristics and the search engine implementation, while the power component depends on the power consumed by the node during setup time (typically coinciding with $P_{\text{on}}$). While the switching time ON $\leftrightarrow$ STANDBY is almost instantaneous, the time required to switch between ON and OFF and vice-versa is not negligible: for most data centres [10], this switching time can reach 200 seconds. This setup time can negatively impact on the latency of the queries to be processed by the node, and must be avoided. As the modelling of switching times is not considered in our cost functions, we limit our machine operational states to ON and STANDBY.

[4]We leave an examination of strategies with larger lookaheads to future work.

Given these costs, we assume that a fully operational node is consuming $P_{\text{on}}$ Watts per $T_s$ seconds, while a STANDBY node is not turned off but consuming $P_{\text{standby}}$ Watts per $T_s$ seconds. So, at a given time slot $k$, the total energy consumed by a search engine with $u_k$ active processing nodes out of a possible $M$ is:

$$P_{\text{on}} T_s u_k + P_{\text{standby}} T_s (M - u_k)$$

Please note that this energy consumption is an upper bound approximation of the actual power costs, because we are implicitly assuming that all active node will always be processing queries. By normalising this quantity by the maximum consumable energy for $M$ machines, we obtain the following expression for the power cost function $P_k(\cdot)$:

$$P_k(\cdot) = P(u_k) = \frac{1}{M P_{\text{on}}} \left[ P_{\text{on}} u_k + P_{\text{standby}} (M - u_k) \right] \quad (10)$$

Note that the power cost function does not depend on $k$, $x_k$, $\bar{v}_k$ or $\bar{w}_k$, and that it varies between $P_{\text{standby}}/P_{\text{on}}$ and 1.

## 5.2 Latency Cost Function

The latency cost function $L_k(x_k, u_k, \bar{v}_k, \bar{w}_k)$ represents the cost incurred when the time required to process queries increases. In order to provide a simple analytic expression for this cost, consider the following situation. At the beginning of time slot $k$, we have $x_k$ queued queries, waiting to be processed by $u_k$ nodes with an average service time per node of $\bar{v}_k$ seconds. During the $k$-th time slot, we receive $\bar{w}_k$ new queries to process. We want to compute the average latency of $x_k + \bar{w}_k$ queries. The first batch of $u_k$ queries can be processed by a single replica after $\bar{v}_k$ seconds, the second batch of $u_k$ queries is processed after $2\bar{v}_k$ seconds, and so on. We have a total of $B = (x_k + \bar{w}_k)/u_k$ batches of queries, so the last batch of at most $u_k$ queries is processed after $B\bar{v}_k$ seconds. Hence, at a given time slot $k$, the query completion time $T_k$ of $x_k + \bar{w}_k$ queries by $u_k$ replicas can be computed by:

$$T_k = \frac{x_k + \bar{w}_k}{u_k} \bar{v}_k \quad (11)$$

While this definition of completion time assumes that queries arrive such that the query processors are always busy during the time slot, it behaves as expected: $T_k$ decreases when the number of processing nodes increases, and increases when the number of queued queries, the number of arriving queries or the average query processing time increases.

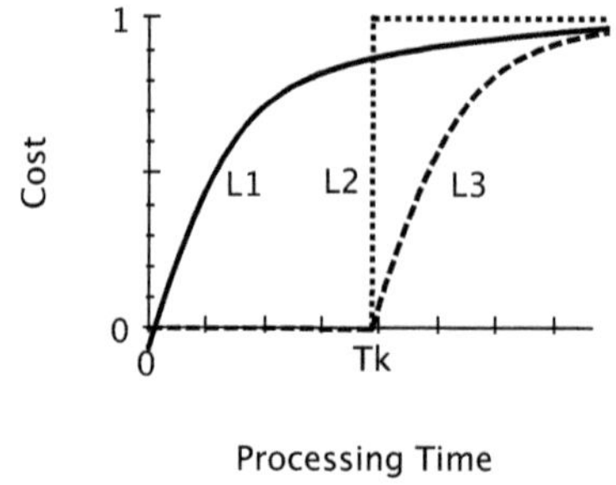


Figure 3: Illustration of latency cost function shapes.

To normalise this completion time in the [0,1] interval, we adapt the latency metrics in [29]:

$$L_k^1(\cdot) = 1 - \exp(\alpha T_k) \tag{12}$$

$$L_k^2(\cdot) = \begin{cases} 0 & \text{if } T_k \leq T_s \\ 1 & \text{otherwise} \end{cases} \tag{13}$$

$$L_k^3(\cdot) = \begin{cases} 0 & \text{if } T_k \leq T_s \\ 1 - \exp(\alpha(T_k - T_s)) & \text{otherwise} \end{cases} \tag{14}$$

While all metrics consider processing of all queries in the time slot, in contrast to $L_k^1$, $L_k^2$ and $L_k^3$ model a certain tolerance level for query execution time, based on the processing of all queries in the time slot ($T_s$). Figure 3 illustrates each of the latency cost functions. The exponential parameter $\alpha > 0$ controls how rapidly the latency cost increases as a function of query completion time.

# 6. EXPERIMENTAL SETUP

In the next section, we experimentally investigate to determine the potential of our proposed model for reducing the power consumption of a search engine without negatively impacting on its efficiency. In particular, three research questions are addressed, as follows:

1. Do our proposed self-adaptive models using seasonal data and current query traffic achieve comparable latency values compared to reasonable baselines while achieving savings in power consumption?

2. How do power and efficiency properties of LONGTERM and SHORTTERM differ?

3. How should the latency cost function be modelled within our self-adaptive models?

In the remainder of this section, we define the experimental setup to address these research questions, covering the search engine (Section 6.1), evaluation measures (Section 6.2), baselines (Section 6.3), and parameter settings (Section 6.4).

## 6.1 Search Engine, Documents & Queries

To evaluate the proposed model, we determine the processing times for real user queries submitted to a search engine platform. In particular, we index 50M Web documents from the TREC ClueWeb09 corpus (category B) using the Terrier IR platform[5] [22] – ClueWeb09 cat. B is intended to reflect the first tier of a commercial Web search engine index. While indexing the corpus, standard stopwords are removed and Porter stemming applied.

For queries, we use two days of queries (approx one million queries) from the MSN 2006 query log[6]. In particular, we use queries from 19th May 2006 as testing and - by setting $S = 11$ - use the historical queries from 8th May 2006 as training data for estimating the random variables. Figure 4 presents the number of queries over the course of each day. During retrieval, we use the WAND dynamic pruning technique applying BM25 to rank 1000 documents for each query, recording the processing time of the query by a single replica. All efficiency experiments are made with a quad-core Intel Xeon 2.4GHz, with 8GB RAM, with inverted indexes are stored on a 160GB SATA drive.

[5]http://terrier.org/

[6]http://research.microsoft.com/en-us/um/people/nickcr/wscd09/

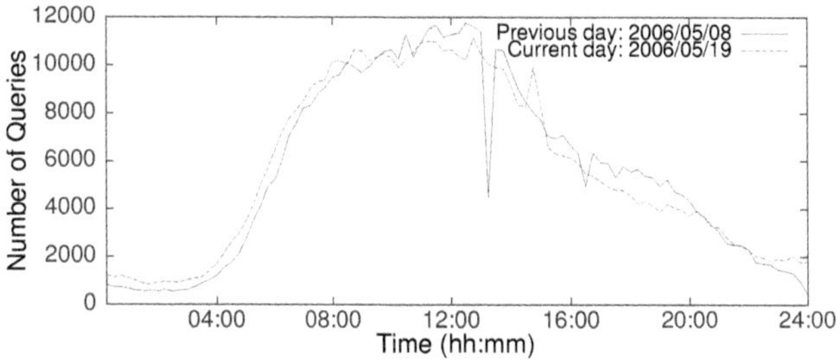


Figure 4: Number of queries arriving per 15 minute slot for both days.

## 6.2 Evaluation Measures

As our work concerns balancing the tradeoff between search engine efficiency and power consumption, we measure both aspects within our work. In particular, we measure the mean and 90th percentile response time for queries as the configuration of the search engine is varied across the evaluation period (denoted ACT and 90%CT, respectively). Response times are measured in milliseconds (ms).

Concurrently, we measure the power usage of the search engine for the same period based on the number of machines active at any point (denoted E and measured in KWh), as well as the maximum number of machines that were active (denoted Max Mch). We note that with some configurations of the search engine when there are insufficient replicas available, the search engine will become backlogged with excessive number of queued queries. To prevent any skew in the results, we drop queries that are not answered within 5 seconds, thereby returning an error page to the user of that query. Clearly this is an undesirable scenario, and hence, we count the number of unanswered queries (denoted %UQ).

To summarise, we consider as a success when, compared to a baseline approach (described in the next section), the maximum number of active query server replicas and resulting power consumption of the search engine can be reduced, without marked negative impact upon the experience of the search engine users, as portrayed by increased response times and higher rates of unanswered queries.

## 6.3 Baselines

To evaluate our proposed model, we define two reasonable baselines for determining $u_k$ for $i = 0, \ldots, N-1$, in other words for defining how many machines are active at any slot.

The first baseline – which we call **Naïve** – is motivated by the provisioning of search engines to cope with worst-case query volume [13], and consists in choosing the maximum number $M$ of machines in each time slot, ignoring completely any power consumption. In this case, we assume maximum power cost, to reflect the fact that the $M$ machines are will continue to be allocated queries, e.g. by round-robin.

The second baseline, that we call **Threshold**, consists in fixing a time threshold for the query completion times, and using the previous day average arrival times, the average processing times and the number of queued queries in the same time slot in Equation (11). In doing this, we can derive the decisions $u_k$ for $i = 0, \ldots, N-1$ that will be applied to the current day. In this case, we assume that each of the selected $u_k$ processing nodes for a specific time slot consume maximum power, as they may be allocated queries in a round robin basis, even if the current query load is lower than the previous day query load. On the other hand, the other $M - u_k$ nodes in a STANDBY state consume $P_{standby}$ power each. Then, if we consider the definition of latency as per Equation (11), and fix the time threshold to $T^*$, we can compute $u_k$ as:

$$u_k = \frac{\bar{w}_k}{T^*}\bar{v}_k$$

where we assume that in each time slot the choice of $u_k$ was able to process all the incoming queries, so that $x_k = 0$. The value of $T^*$ is determined by the length of the time slot, as we want all the queries of a slot to be processed before proceeding to the next slot.

Of these two baselines, it is clear that the power consumption of Threshold will be less than Naïve, as Threshold affords the opportunity to save power for nodes that are not expected to be required. However, compared to LongTerm, Threshold may disable nodes that would soon be required, as it cannot examine the impact of a power decision across the remainder of the day.

## 6.4 Parameter Settings

To instantiate our model, we invoke various parameter settings as follows. Firstly, to calculate the power consumption of a replicated processing node, we use the energy ratings from the EU Energy Star programme [28] for a small server as follows: $P_{on} = 62W$, $P_{standby} = 2W$, following the reported use of commodity-sized servers within commercial search engines [13]. Within latency cost functions (Equations (12)-(14)), we follow Wang et al. [29] and use $\alpha = -0.01$ for the ClueWeb09 cat. B corpus. For slot duration, we set $T_s = 15$ minutes, reflecting an interval that identifies general changing trends in query volumes that the model can quickly respond to, rather than random fluctuations that might be detected by shorter slot durations. Finally, as queries arrive on average at 15 per second, we use $M = 15, 20$ as the number of replica query processors. The remaining parameter of our model, namely the power/latency tradeoff $\lambda$ are experimental variables that we vary within the next section.

# 7. RESULTS

In this section, we aim to determine if our proposed self-adapting model allows the system to markedly reduce power consumption with latency comparable to that achieved by the baselines. In particular, Section 7.1 firstly determines the efficiency and power properties of our two baselines. Section 7.2 addresses our first and second research questions, by comparing the LongTerm and ShortTerm approaches with the baselines and with each other. Finally, in Section 7.3, we address our final research question concerning the choice of latency cost function within the model.

## 7.1 Baselines

The top part of Table 2 reports, for $M = 15, 20$ replicas, the various evaluation measures achieved by the two baselines in this paper, namely Naïve, which keeps the maximal number of replicas active, and Threshold, which actives the number of replicas that would have sustained the traffic of the previous day. Within the table, we report efficiency measures (average and 90th percentile response times, measured in milliseconds), the number of unanswered queries, the peak number of machines used, and the total energy consumption over the course of the day (KWh). The time slot size is maintained at $Ts = 15$ minutes.

Analysing the response times for the baselines within Table 2, we note that mean response times around 850ms are achievable by both approaches. Moreover, while the Threshold approach can reduce the energy consumption compared to Naïve by putting machines into standby mode (by 47% for $M = 15$ and 57% for $M = 20$), this comes at the expense of marginally increased response times (approx. 6ms). To summarise, we find that, as expected the Threshold approach results in markedly decreased energy consumption compared to Naïve, with little marked impact on response times.

## 7.2 Self-adaptive Power/Latency Models

The bottom two parts of Table 2 report the evaluation measures for the LongTerm and ShortTerm approaches. For both approaches and both $M = 15, 20$ replicas, we vary the power/ latency tradeoff parameter $\lambda$, to determine its impact on both efficiency and energy consumption. In this section, the $L_1$ latency cost function (Equation (12)) is applied.

Firstly, we discuss the LongTerm approach, which estimates the expected number of queries solely based on the query volume in the same time slot of the previous day. Overall, for some values of $\lambda$, this approach provides completion times generally comparable with the baselines, i.e. less than 900ms. However, such values can be obtained with marked reductions in energy use. For instance, compared to Threshold, the setting of $M = 20, \lambda = 0.5$ produces a 5% increase in mean completion times and 4% in 90th percentile completion time; this is achieved with a 42% reduction in consumed energy, and a peak usage of 7 replicas – down from 19. For $M = 15$, $\lambda = 0.5$, the query load can be serviced with only 6.3KWh of energy use and only 6 replicas, at the cost of 14% increase in mean completion time compared to Threshold, and a small increase in the number of unanswered queries.

Such results demonstrate the promise of the proposed LongTerm approach: given enough replicas to service peak demands ($M = 20$), it can achieve marked energy savings compared to the Threshold baseline. Indeed, LongTerm has the advantage that by being able to derive the cost of a decision until the end of the day, compared to Threshold it has less tendency to overfit to any fluctuations in query volume experienced by the search engine on the previous day.

Next, we examine the results for the ShortTerm approach in the bottom part of Table 2. Recall, as explained in Section 4, that compared to LongTerm, ShortTerm also takes into account the actual number of arrived queries during the previous slot, while LongTerm only considers the query traffic from the previous day. In general, we find that for $\lambda = 0.25$, ShortTerm exhibits an improved power/latency trade over the results exhibited by the LongTerm approach. In particular, with mean response times that are only a few milliseconds different from the results of the Threshold and Naïve baselines, ShortTerm achieves marked energy savings (33% and 64% respectively for $M = 15$; 26% and 68% for $M = 20$).

This further marked reduction in energy consumption shows that the ShortTerm method can more accurately predict the query load in the next slot by considering the query load in the previous slot. As LongTerm makes the estimation based on previous query volume alone, it selects a higher number of machines, while ShortTerm can reduce the necessary number of replicas, with corresponding energy

Table 2: Performance comparison among LongTerm, ShortTerm and the Baselines for different $M$ and $\lambda$ values.

| $\lambda$ | ACT(ms) | 90%CT | % UQ | Max Mch | E(KWh) | ACT(ms) | 90%CT | % UQ | Max Mch | E(KWh) |
|---|---|---|---|---|---|---|---|---|---|---|
| | $M = 15$ | | | | | $M = 20$ | | | | |
| Baselines | | | | | | | | | | |
| Naïve | 847 | 1,349 | 0 | 15 | 22.3 | 846 | 1,349 | 0 | 20 | 29.8 |
| Threshold | 853 | 1,354 | 0.03 | 15 | 12.0 | 853 | 1,354 | 0.03 | 19 | 12.9 |
| LongTerm | | | | | | | | | | |
| 0.25 | 848 | 1,350 | 0 | 15 | 12.0 | 848 | 1,349 | 0 | 17 | 12.1 |
| 0.5 | 969 | 1,394 | 1.35 | 6 | 6.3 | 896 | 1,409 | 0.08 | 7 | 7.4 |
| 0.75 | 3,194 | 3,886 | 19.19 | 2 | 2.7 | 2,299 | 3,049 | 4.68 | 3 | 4.2 |
| ShortTerm | | | | | | | | | | |
| 0.25 | 857 | 1,356 | 0.03 | 8 | 8.0 | 854 | 1,354 | 0.02 | 10 | 9.5 |
| 0.5 | 1,536 | 2,260 | 1.36 | 4 | 4.8 | 1,007 | 1,567 | 0.31 | 5 | 5.7 |
| 0.75 | 3,225 | 3,724 | 11.84 | 2 | 2.9 | 2,956 | 3,700 | 10.69 | 2 | 3.4 |

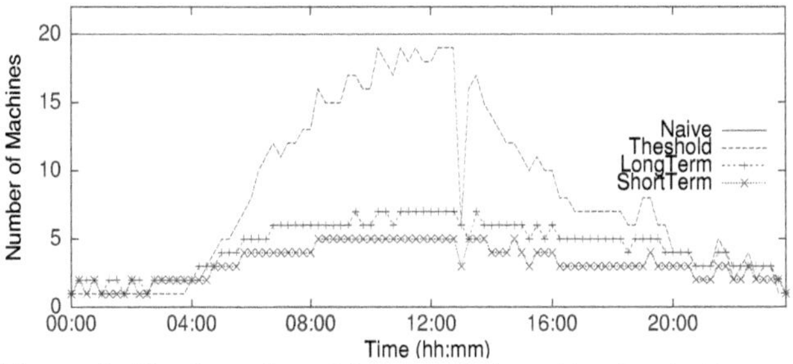


Figure 5: Number of machines used along the day by LongTerm and ShortTerm ($\lambda = 0.5$, $M = 20$) and the two baselines, namely Naïve and Threshold.

savings. This is clearly illustrated in Figure 5, which shows the number of machines used by each approach for $M = 20$ and $\lambda = 0.5$, as well as the two baselines. LongTerm and ShortTerm clearly reduce the number of active machines, but are less sensitive than Threshold to the sudden decrease in query traffic at approx. 13:00 on the training day. Moreover, ShortTerm uses less query processors than LongTerm over the day, confirming the power results shown in Table 2.

In summary, in answer to our first research question, we find that our proposed self-adapting models can markedly reduce power consumption, without marked impact on efficiency. With respect to the second research question, of the proposed LongTerm and ShortTerm instantiations, ShortTerm demonstrates the highest promise, as by considering recent query traffic conditions, it is able to reduce the number of required query processors along the day, without marked degradations in query response time. Indeed, with $\lambda = 0.25$ and $M = 15$ ShortTerm achieves a 33% of power improvement by producing only a 1% increasing in latency; with $\lambda = 0.5$ and $M = 20$ ShortTerm achieves around mean completion times of 1 second but attains a 24% power saving and maintains the percentage of unanswered queries under 0.05%.

## 7.3 Modelling Latency Costs

In this section, we address our final research question, examining how the latency of the search engine should be modelled within our proposed approach. Firstly, recall that Wang et al. [29] proposed three different efficiency metrics, which we used as inspiration for efficiency cost functions in Section 5.2. In particular, the latency of the search engine can be modelled with an exponential decay function (Equation (12), denoted $L^1$), a step function with a fixed penalty after a time threshold has expired (Equation (13), $L^2$) or a step function followed by an exponential decay (Equations (14), $L^3$). As we consider the processing of queries within a time slot, we set the time threshold as the slot length $T_s = 15$ minutes.

Table 3: Comparison of latency functions, while varying $\lambda$.

| | ACT(ms) | 90%CT | % UQ | Max Mch | E(KWh) |
|---|---|---|---|---|---|
| $\lambda = 0.25$ | | | | | |
| $L^1$ | 848 | 1,349 | 0 | 17 | 12.1 |
| $L^2$ | 869 | 1,380 | 0.04 | 20 | 14.2 |
| $L^3$ | 880 | 1,401 | 0.07 | 19 | 12.0 |
| $\lambda = 0.5$ | | | | | |
| $L^1$ | 896 | 1,409 | 0.07 | 7 | 7.4 |
| $L^2$ | 849 | 1,350 | 0.01 | 20 | 14.2 |
| $L^3$ | 860 | 1,357 | 0.03 | 7 | 7.6 |
| $\lambda = 0.75$ | | | | | |
| $L^1$ | 2,299 | 3,049 | 4.68 | 3 | 4.2 |
| $L^2$ | 3,544 | 4,113 | 22.77 | 9 | 3.9 |
| $L^3$ | 2,235 | 3,030 | 4.5 | 3 | 4.3 |

Table 3 shows the comparison between the chosen latency functions for the LongTerm approach for $M = 20$. We also vary $\lambda$, in case the choice of $\lambda$ can impact upon the choice of the latency function. On a first inspection of Table 3, we observe that latency function $L^1$ achieves the lowest response times and energy consumptions. This can be explained with reference to Figure 3: For $L^2$, the cost function becomes 1 as soon as queries cannot be completed on time. Hence, if the latency exceeds the time threshold even by a small amount, the latency cost is 1, and the model resorts to the power function to decide between options. As it is power conservative in nature, a smaller number of machines will be chosen. In contrast, by using the exponential decay, $L^1$ and $L^3$ represent 'softer' latency cost function, and hence can permit small inefficiencies for power savings. Of these, the simpler $L^1$ is more appropriate than $L^3$, for the same reasoning as for $L^2$. In summary, in addressing our final research question concerning how the latency cost should be modelled, we find that the exponential increase of cost as latency increases represents the most promising function, as per Equation (12).

# 8. CONCLUSIONS

While various have been dedicated to reduce power consumption regarding IT systems, few works apply this concept to the information retrieval field. In this work we propose a mathematical model for a replicated search engine that allows the establishment of a trade-off between latency and power consumption. Based on the query traffic from a previous day, the system predicts the incoming query flow and increases, decreases or maintains the number of available replicated query processors to answer the queries under acceptable latencies. Experiments are conducted in comparison to two baselines: Naïve (always uses the maximum number of machines) and Threshold (calculates the number of necessary machines to ensure latency values under a threshold), using 1 million queries submitted to a real commercial search engine. Our results show that our self-adapting model can achieve an energy savings of 33% while only degrading mean query completion time by 10ms compared to a baseline that provisions replicas based on a previous day's traffic, while more substantial energy savings can be attained while accepting marginally larger efficiency degradations.

In this paper, we focused on the power savings achievable when switching replicated query servers between standby and actively processing search queries. There are advantages to such a scenario, because during off-peak times standby query servers may be re-purposed to other offline tasks, such as indexing, ads/recommendations generation, and pre-caching of result lists [15]. For future work, we will consider a more complex scenario where servers are fully powered down when not required, but incur delay on startup.

# 9. ACKNOWLEDGEMENTS

Ana Freire and Fidel Cacheda acknowledge the support from the Spanish Government (TIN2009-14203), Xunta de Galicia (CN2012/211) and FEDER funds. Craig Macdonald and Iadh Ounis acknowledge the support of EC-funded project SMART (FP7-287583). Nicola Tonellotto acknowledges the support of EC-funded projects InGeoClouds (FP7-297300) and MIDAS (FP7-318786).

# 10. REFERENCES

[1] R. Baeza-Yates and B. Ribeiro-Neto. *Modern Information Retrieval.* Addison Wesley, 1999.

[2] D. P. Bertsekas. *Dynamic programming and optimal control.* Athena Scientific, 2nd ed, 2000.

[3] S. Buettcher, C. L. A. Clarke, and G. V. Cormack. *Information Retrieval: Implementing and Evaluating Search Engines.* The MIT Press, 1st ed, 2010.

[4] F. Cacheda, V. Carneiro, V. Plachouras, and I. Ounis. Performance analysis of distributed information retrieval architectures using an improved network simulation model. *Inf. Process. Manage.*, 43(1):204–224, 2007.

[5] G. Chowdhury. An agenda for green information retrieval research. *Inf. Process. Manage.*, 48(6):1067–1077, 2012.

[6] Y. Diao, N. Gandhi, J. Hellerstein, S. Parekh, and D. Tilbury. Using MIMO feedback control to enforce policies for interrelated metrics with application to the Apache web server. In *Proc. of the Network Operations and Management Symposium 2002*, pages 219–234.

[7] E. Dijkstra. A note on two problems in connexion with graphs. *Numerische Mathematik*, 1(1):269–271, 1959.

[8] D. Economou, S. Rivoire, and C. Kozyrakis. Full-system power analysis and modeling for server environments. In *Proc. of the Workshop on Modeling Benchmarking and Simulation*, 2006.

[9] A. Freire, C. Macdonald, N. Tonellotto, I. Ounis, and F. Cacheda. Hybrid query scheduling for a replicated search engine. In *Proc. of ECIR 2013*, pages 435–446.

[10] A. Gandhi and M. Harchol-Balter. How data center size impacts the effectiveness of dynamic power management. In *Proc. of 49th Allerton conference on Communication, Control, and Computing*, pages 1164–1169, 2011.

[11] Gartner. Green IT: The new industry shockwave. *Presentation at Symposium/ITXPO conference*, 2007.

[12] J. L. Hellerstein, Y. Diao, S. Parekh, and D. M. Tilbury. *Feedback Control of Computing Systems.* John Wiley & Sons, 2004.

[13] L. A. Barroso, J. Dean, and U. Hölzle. Web search for a planet: The Google cluster architecture. *IEEE Micro*, 23(2):22–28, 2003.

[14] U. Hoelzle and L. A. Barroso. *The Datacenter as a Computer: An Introduction to the Design of Warehouse-Scale Machines.* Morgan and Claypool Publishers, 1st ed, 2009.

[15] S. Jonassen, B. B. Cambazoglu, and F. Silvestri. Prefetching query results and its impact on search engines. In *Proc. of SIGIR 2012*, pages 631–640.

[16] E. Kayaaslan, B. B. Cambazoglu, R. Blanco, F. P. Junqueira, and C. Aykanat. Energy-price-driven query processing in multi-center web search engines. In *Proc. of SIGIR 2011*, pages 983–992.

[17] B. Khargharia, S. Hariri, and M. S. Yousif. Autonomic power and performance management for computing systems. *Cluster Computing*, 11(2):167–181, 2008.

[18] E. Kharitonov, C. Macdonald, P. Serdyukov, and I. Ounis. Incorporating efficiency in evaluation. In *Proc. of the Modeling User Behavior for Information Retrieval Evaluation Workshop at SIGIR 2013.*

[19] J. Liu, F. Zhao, X. Liu, and W. He. Challenges towards elastic power management in Internet data centers. *Proc. of Cyber-Physical Systems Workshop at ICDCS 2009.*

[20] C. Macdonald, N. Tonellotto, and I. Ounis. Learning to predict response times for online query scheduling. In *Proc. of SIGIR 2012*, pages 621–630.

[21] L. Mastroleon, N. Bambos, C. Kozyrakis, and D. Economou. Automatic power management schemes for internet servers and data centers. In *Proc. of GLOBECOM 2005*, page 5.

[22] I. Ounis, G. Amati, V. Plachouras, B. He, C. Macdonald, and C. Lioma. Terrier: A high performance and scalable information retrieval platform. In *Proc. of the Open Source IR Workshop at SIGIR 2006*, pages 18–25.

[23] S. Parekh, N. Gandhi, J. Hellerstein, D. Tilbury, T. Jayram, and J. Bigus. Using control theory to achieve service level objectives in performance management. *Real-Time Syst.*, 23(1/2):127–141, 2002.

[24] K. Radinsky, K. Svore, S. Dumais, J. Teevan, A. Bocharov, and E. Horvitz. Modeling and predicting behavioral dynamics on the web. In *Proc. WWW 2012*, pages 599–608.

[25] F. B. Sazoglu, B. B. Cambazoglu, R. Ozcan, I. S. Altingovde, and O. Ulusoy A financial cost metric for result caching. In *Proc. of SIGIR 2013*, pages 873–876.

[26] E. Shurman and J. Brutlag. Performance related changes and their user impacts. In *Velocity: Web Performance and Operations Conference*, 2009.

[27] F. Silvestri. Mining query logs: Turning search usage data into knowledge. *Foundations and Trends in Information Retrieval*, 4(1-2):1–174, 2010.

[28] EU Energy Star: http://eu-energystar.org.

[29] L. Wang, J. Lin, and D. Metzler. Learning to efficiently rank. In *Proc. of SIGIR 2010*, pages 138–145.

[30] Z. Wang, N. Tolia, and C. Bash. Opportunities and challenges to unify workload, power, and cooling management in data centers. *SIGOPS Oper. Syst. Rev.*, 44(3):41–46, 2010.

# Heterogeneous Graph-Based Intent Learning with Queries, Web Pages and Wikipedia Concepts

Xiang Ren[†]* Yujing Wang[‡] Xiao Yu[†] Jun Yan[‡] Zheng Chen[‡] Jiawei Han[†]
[†] University of Illinois at Urbana-Champaign, Urbana, IL, USA
[‡] Microsoft Research, Beijing, China
[†]{xren7, xiaoyu, hanj}@illinois.edu [‡]{yujwang, junyan, zhengc}@microsoft.com

## ABSTRACT

The problem of learning user search intents has attracted intensive attention from both industry and academia. However, state-of-the-art intent learning algorithms suffer from different drawbacks when only using a single type of data source. For example, query text has difficulty in distinguishing ambiguous queries; search log is bias to the order of search results and users' noisy click behaviors. In this work, we for the first time leverage three types of objects, namely queries, web pages and Wikipedia concepts collaboratively for learning generic search intents and construct a heterogeneous graph to represent multiple types of relationships between them. A novel unsupervised method called *heterogeneous graph-based soft-clustering* is developed to derive an intent indicator for each object based on the constructed heterogeneous graph. With the proposed co-clustering method, one can enhance the quality of intent understanding by taking advantage of different types of data, which complement each other, and make the implicit intents easier to interpret with explicit knowledge from Wikipedia concepts. Experiments on two real-world datasets demonstrate the power of the proposed method where it achieves a 9.25% improvement in terms of NDCG on search ranking task and a 4.67% enhancement in terms of Rand index on object co-clustering task compared to the best state-of-the-art method.

## Categories and Subject Descriptors

H.3.3 [**Information Storage and Retrieval**]: Information Search and Retrieval—*clustering, search process*

## General Terms

Algorithms; Experimentation

## Keywords

Search Intent; Wikipedia; Heterogeneous Graph Clustering

*This work was partially done when the first author was visiting Microsoft Research, Beijing, China.


*WSDM'14,* February 24–28, 2014, New York, New York, USA.
Copyright 2014 ACM 978-1-4503-2351-2/14/02 ...$15.00.
http://dx.doi.org/10.1145/2556195.2556222.

## 1. INTRODUCTION

Understanding user search intent is one of the most fundamental and critical problems faced by modern search engines. Research studies have been conducted extensively on identifying search intents in order to better satisfy users' information needs. Identifying the intents behind a query helps distinguish ambiguous or multi-faceted queries [16], suggest related queries [30], and guide users to corresponding vertical search engines [15]. Additionally, matching web pages and search intents together can benefit search result presentation through search result diversification.

There are mainly two categories of intent definitions, based on whether or not the intent is pre-defined. Intents such as search tasks [17] require intent labels defined in advance while others such as topics [1] do not rely on any existing ontology. In this work we focus on learning generic search intents which can fit into all domains without any kind of pre-defined intent category.

Traditional intent learning methods utilize only text information from queries or web pages [29]. Such methods cannot handle ambiguous or multi-faceted queries properly. Later studies leverage web search log to facilitate user interest interpretation when learning search intents [7]. One general assumption is that multiple web pages tend to share the same search intent if they are clicked under similar queries. Unfortunately, this assumption has some intrinsic limitation due to the nature of web search. User clicks might be biased by the order of search results, and are typically observed for only a small fraction of web pages. Users may click web pages which are irrelevant to their real search intents by mistake, bringing noise to the search log.

Recent studies attempt to tackle the aforementioned issues by either using search session data [24] and sponsored search data [27], or combining search log with different data sources such as query text [20, 16] and search session data [22]. In particular, semantic information such as named entities [15] and Wikipedia concepts [28, 4] have proven to be effective in terms of learning and interpreting search intents. However, existing methods can only learn intents within a specific domain such as cars or movies, and often can only handle concept-related queries. To our best knowledge, no previous works leverage query, web page and Wikipedia concepts collaboratively to learn generic search intents.

In this paper we propose a novel search intent definition by utilizing three types of objects, namely query, web page and semantic concept from Wikipedia. A heterogeneous graph-based framework is proposed to derive intents from query text data, web page content, click-through log and

Wikipedia concepts simultaneously. The unified optimization approach takes advantages of different types of data, which complement each other, and ameliorate the aforementioned drawbacks when using a single data source. For example, given the query "office", the proposed method is able to identify several search intents including software intent for Microsoft Office, entertainment intent for the NBC TV show "The Office" and daily supplies intent for office supplies as needed. However, using only query text, entity mentions in query or the search log we are not able to find all possible intents as stated above because (1) search queries are often short and ambiguous; and (2) user click is biased to more popular web pages related to Microsoft Office.

In our solution, we construct a heterogeneous graph using many types of data to encode query-page, page-page and page-concept relations where the relation strength indicates how similar two objects are, in terms of their search intents (see Figure 1). To learn search intents through the heterogeneous graph structure, we face three challenges: (1) how to model the relationships between objects to preserve the semantic information in the constructed heterogeneous graph; (2) how to incorporate different types of relations in a unified intent learning framework; (3) how to predict intents for newly emerged objects. We develop a graph-based soft-clustering method to learn how likely an object belongs to each search intent from the heterogeneous graph, yielding an intent indicator for each object. An approximate algorithm is further designed to first embed all types of objects into a unified feature space and then apply soft-clustering methods on the embedded intent features to obtain intent indicators. With the proposed method, we can simultaneously (1) identify information needs behind queries; (2) understand what intents a web page can satisfy; and (3) recognize Wikipedia concepts that can best interpret different intents.

Experiments on both search ranking, which evaluates the effectiveness of intent features, and object co-clustering of queries, web pages and concepts demonstrate the power of our method. For search ranking, the proposed method achieves a 9.35% improvement in terms of NDCG on the commercial data set and a 23.99% growth in terms of MRR on AOL data set. For object co-clustering, our method gets a 4.67% enhancement in terms of Rand index on the commercial data set compared to the best state-of-the-art method. Our case study on object co-clustering results shows that the learned intents can be well interpreted by the Wikipedia concepts within each intent cluster.

The rest of paper is organized as follows. Section 3 introduces the construction of heterogeneous graphs and provides a formal problem definition. Section 4 proposes the heterogeneous graph-based soft-clustering method, along with the computational complexity analysis. We provide experimental results and analysis in Section 5, and conclude our work together with ideas on future work in Section 6.

## 2. RELATED WORK

### 2.1 Query Intent Learning

The problem of learning query intent has been studied intensively and characterized along different dimensions, such as search subgoals [27], search tasks [17], search missions [1], topics [1], subtopics [16], patterns [6] and taxonomy [28]. Nevertheless, we categorize existing methods into query classification and query clustering.

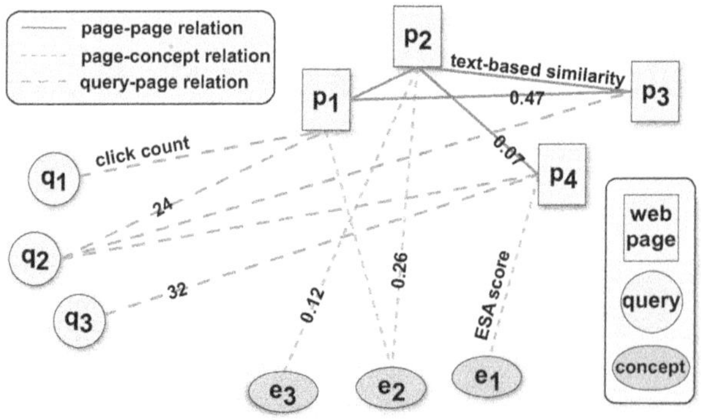


**Figure 1: An illustration of the constructed heterogeneous graph which consists of three types of objects: queries, web pages and Wikipedia concepts, and three types of relations: query-page relation, page-page relation and page-concept relation.**

Query classification aims to classify queries into pre-defined intents such as search goals or search tasks [17]. Instead of using only query keywords, quite a few studies turn to different resources, including search log [18], Wikipedia concepts [15] and search session data [5].

As an alternative, grouping queries into intents by means of query clustering has also been popularly studied [24, 28, 20, 1, 16, 27, 6]. Traditional document clustering methods cannot work well on queries due to their limited number of keywords. Search log which contains user interests is one kind of data widely used for query clustering [7], and is further combined with query content to achieve better performance [20]. Search session data [30] and sponsored search data [27] are also widely utilized for finding query relations and intents.

Our work is similar to [6] in terms of the motivation of seeking a better interpretation for learned intents. However, we achieve the interpretation by leveraging semantic concepts in Wikipedia. Compared to building taxonomy from entity-related queries [28], we collect external semantic concepts from Wikipedia, which is able to handle broader kinds of queries. Although there are studies such as [25], which learn user intents for queries and web pages simultaneously, and work such as [4], which explores heterogeneous relationships between queries and Wikipedia concepts, to our best knowledge, our work is the first for learning generic search intents behind queries, web pages and Wikipedia concepts in an unified graph-based framework.

### 2.2 Clustering on Graphs

Another group of related work is graph-based clustering which groups single or multiple types of objects with respect to their graph structure. Typical methods include spectral clustering on homogeneous graph and co-clustering on bipartite graph [8, 26].

In particular, Guan *et al.* [12] exploit affinity and bipartite relationships between users, documents and social tags by graph embedding in recommendation. Recently, several studies exploit heterogeneous graphs which consist of heterogeneous types of objects and/or relationships by clustering [19]. For example, affinity relationships can be incorporated into co-clustering of bipartite graph [11]. Clustering of multiple types of objects in a heterogeneous graph which consists of multiple relationships are also studied [23].

The differences between our method and the above studies are (1) we study both affinity relationships and bipartite relationships in a co-clustering framework, and (2) we consider features of multiple types of objects simultaneously.

# 3. BACKGROUND

In this section, we provide the background of the problem which includes the details on construction of heterogeneous graph and the formal problem definition.

## 3.1 Heterogeneous Graph Construction

We use a heterogeneous graph, which consists of multiple types of objects and/or multiple types of relationships, to preserve different kinds of information from different data sources. The basic idea to construct the graph is that two objects are linked with larger relation strength if they are more likely to share similar search intent.

Specifically, we have three types of objects: queries $\mathcal{Q} = \{q_1, ..., q_{|\mathcal{Q}|}\}$ issued by different users in search log, web pages $\mathcal{P} = \{p_1, ..., p_{|\mathcal{P}|}\}$ clicked by different users in search log, and Wikipedia concepts $\mathcal{E} = \{e_1, ..., e_{|\mathcal{E}|}\}$ related to web pages[1]. There are three types of relations between these objects including query-page relation extracted from click-through log, page-page relation based on web page text, and page-concept relation provided by explicit semantic analysis (ESA) [9], leading to three subgraphs $H_{\mathcal{Q},\mathcal{P}}$, $G_{\mathcal{P}}$ and $J_{\mathcal{P},\mathcal{E}}$, respectively. In this way, information from these data sources can be learned to preserve the heterogeneous graph structure. We denote the constructed heterogeneous graph as $G$ and show an illustration in Figure 1.

### *3.1.1 Query-page Subgraph*

Click-through relations between queries and web pages form a bipartite query-page subgraph. We assume that a query and a web page are more likely to share the same intent if the number of users who click the web page after issuing the query is larger. For example, if most of users end at clicking web pages of Microsoft Office after they issue the query "office", "office" is more likely to carry software intent rather than intents relevant to entertainment.

The query-web page bipartite subgraph is also called *click graph* in the literature [7], where a query $q \in \mathcal{Q}$ is linked to a web page $p \in \mathcal{P}$ if and only if $p$ has been clicked by at least one user after issuing query $q$ in the search log. The edge weight is defined as click-through counts between $q$ and $p$, reflecting the relation strength. We use $\mathbf{C} \in \mathbb{R}^{|\mathcal{Q}|\times|\mathcal{P}|}$ to denote adjacency matrix of the click graph, where $C_{ij}$ is equal to click counts from $i$-th query to $j$-th web page.

### *3.1.2 Web Page Subgraph*

Text in a web page is a good source for identifying what search intents a web page can satisfy. For instance, if we find a web page containing keywords (*e.g.*, words with highest TF-IDF scores) such as "Microsoft" , "install" and "download", we are more confident to say this web page can accomplish software intent rather than entertainment intent. Therefore, we assume that two web pages might satisfy similar search intents if their textual content are similar.

Specifically, we extract keywords from title and body of all web pages based on TF-IDF scores which form an $m$-dimensional term space, and generate TF-IDF vectors for all the web pages as their textual features, denoted by $\mathbf{P} \in \mathbb{R}^{|\mathcal{P}|\times m}$. We further follow the construction of K-nearest neighbor (KNN) graph [2] to build a web page affinity subgraph whose adjacency matrix is denoted by $\mathbf{Y} \in \mathbb{R}^{|\mathcal{P}|\times|\mathcal{P}|}$. Specifically, each web page is linked to its K most similar web pages in terms of their textual features $\mathbf{P}$ as follows:

$$Y_{ij} = \begin{cases} \text{sim}(\mathbf{P}_i, \mathbf{P}_j), & \text{if } \mathbf{P}_i \in N_K(\mathbf{P}_j) \text{ or } \mathbf{P}_j \in N_K(\mathbf{P}_i); \\ 0, & \text{otherwise.} \end{cases} \tag{1}$$

where $\text{sim}(\mathbf{P}_i, \mathbf{P}_j)$ is Cosine similarity score between $\mathbf{P}_i$ and $\mathbf{P}_j$, *i.e.*, $\text{sim}(\mathbf{P}_i, \mathbf{P}_j) = (\mathbf{P}_i \cdot \mathbf{P}_j^T)/(\|\mathbf{P}_i\|\|\mathbf{P}_j\|)$, and $N_K(\mathbf{a})$ denotes K nearest neighbors of $\mathbf{a}$.

### *3.1.3 Page-concept Subgraph*

We extract web page-concept relations using explicit semantic analysis (ESA) [9], which can measure the semantic relevance between a Wikipedia concept and a given web page. For instance, given the web page about Microsoft Office, Wikipedia concept "microsoft_word" receives ESA score as 0.24 while "room_(architecture)" gets approximately 0 score, showing that "microsoft_word" is more likely to share the same intent with the web page. Similarly, two web pages are assumed more likely to share the same search intent if their related concepts are similar.

For simplicity, we only consider the top-300 most relevant concepts for each web page, and represent all web pages in the resulting $|\mathcal{E}|$-dimension concept space as ESA score vectors, denoted as $\mathbf{P}_{\mathcal{E}} \in \mathbb{R}^{(|\mathcal{P}|\times|\mathcal{E}|)}$. We further define the page-concept bipartite subgraph $J_{\mathcal{P},\mathcal{E}}$ by an adjacency matrix $\mathbf{P}_{\mathcal{E}} \in \mathbb{R}^{|\mathcal{P}|\times|\mathcal{E}|}$ as follows:

$$P_{\mathcal{E},ij} = \begin{cases} \text{sim}(p_i, e_j), & \text{if } p_i \in N_K(e_j) \text{ or } e_j \in N_K(p_i); \\ 0, & \text{otherwise.} \end{cases} \tag{2}$$

where $\text{sim}(p_i, e_j)$ denotes the ESA scores between web page $p_i$ and concept $e_j$; and $\sum_{j=1}^{|\mathcal{E}|} P_{\mathcal{E},ij} = 1$.

## 3.2 Problem Definition

In this work, we cast the search intent learning problem into heterogeneous graph-based soft-clustering of queries, web pages and concepts simultaneously where each cluster can be explained as one search intent.

Suppose there are $k$ different search intents behind all three types of objects, we first define three indicator matrices $\mathbf{F}_{\mathcal{Q}} \in [0,1]^{|\mathcal{Q}|\times k}$, $\mathbf{F}_{\mathcal{P}} \in [0,1]^{|\mathcal{P}|\times k}$, and $\mathbf{F}_{\mathcal{E}} \in [0,1]^{|\mathcal{E}|\times k}$ which describe the confidence of queries, web pages and concepts belonging to different search intents, respectively. The definition of search intent learning problem is as follows:

DEFINITION 1 (PROBLEM DEFINITION). *Suppose there are $k$ distinct search intents for queries, web pages and concepts. Given a constructed heterogeneous graph $G$, its adjacency matrices $\mathbf{C}$, $\mathbf{Y}$ and $\mathbf{P}_{\mathcal{E}}$, and web pages' textual features $\mathbf{P}$, learn $\mathbf{F}_{\mathcal{Q}}$, $\mathbf{F}_{\mathcal{P}}$ and $\mathbf{F}_{\mathcal{E}}$ as soft-clustering indicators for all three types of objects simultaneously.*

# 4. LEARNING INTENTS ON GRAPHS

In this section, we explain our method for learning unified search intents in details. An approximate method for efficient learning of concept intent is first developed. We then derive an optimization problem which preserve the heterogeneous graph structure and developed an efficient algorithm

[1]In the rest of the paper, we use the term "concept" to represent Wikipedia concept for simplicity.

based on graph embedding and fuzzy clustering for solving the optimization. Finally, we extend our method to predict intent for unseen queries and web pages.

## 4.1 Efficient Learning of Concept Intents

In practice, the concept number in knowledge base is huge (*e.g.*, Wikipedia contains 4,308,113 English concepts[2]), resulting in an even larger parameter space when learning concept intent indicator $\mathbf{F}_{\mathcal{E}}$, *i.e.*, $\mathcal{O}(|\mathcal{E}|d)$. Therefore, we propose to approximately compute concept intent features by first aggregating information from web page-concept subgraph into an concept-based web page affinity subgraph, and then deriving concept intent indicator based on learned web page intent indicator $\mathbf{F}_{\mathcal{P}}$ and web page-concept subgraph $\mathbf{P}_{\mathcal{E}}$. Through this way, the computational burden is largely reduced by getting rid of the parameter space of $\mathbf{F}_{\mathcal{E}}$ during the learning process.

Specifically, web page-concept relationships in the bipartite subgraphs $J_{\mathcal{P},\mathcal{E}}$ are encoded into concept-based web page relationships by measuring web page-web page similarity in terms of their related concepts $\mathbf{P}_{\mathcal{E}i}$ and $\mathbf{P}_{\mathcal{E}j}$, respectively. We represent $J_{\mathcal{P}}$ by an adjacency matrix $\mathbf{E} \in \mathbb{R}^{|\mathcal{P}|\times|\mathcal{P}|}$ whose element is dot product of $\mathbf{P}_{\mathcal{E}i}$ and $\mathbf{P}_{\mathcal{E}j}$, *i.e.*, $E_{ij} = \mathbf{P}_{\mathcal{E}i}\mathbf{P}_{\mathcal{E}j}^T$. With this modification, the heterogenous graph $G$ is now transformed into a simplified formation, consisting of a click graph, a text-based affinity graph of web pages, and an concept-based affinity graph for web pages. After learning the web page intent features, we can further derive the intent feature for $j$-th concept as follows:

$$\mathbf{F}_{\mathcal{E}j} = \mathbf{P}_{\mathcal{E}\cdot j}^T \cdot \mathbf{F}_{\mathcal{P}}, \quad \text{for } j = 1, 2, \ldots, |\mathcal{E}|, \tag{3}$$

where $\mathbf{P}_{\mathcal{E}\cdot j}$ is the $j$-th column of matrix $\mathbf{P}_{\mathcal{E}}$.

In the following sections, we will introduce the detailed algorithm for learning intent features of queries and web pages based on the simplified heterogeneous graph $G$.

## 4.2 Problem Formulation

In this section, a heterogeneous graph-based soft-clustering optimization problem is derived for unified search intent learning and an approximate algorithm is developed to efficiently solve the optimization problem.

Mathematically, we model each type of relationship into a cost function based on locality preserving idea [2], which requires two nearby objects in $G$ to have similar intent indicators, and further derive the optimization problem by using weighted summation of these cost functions as the objective function and imposing soft-clustering constraints on the intent indicators:

$$\begin{aligned}\min_{\mathbf{F}_{\mathcal{Q}},\mathbf{F}_{\mathcal{P}}} \mathcal{L}(\mathbf{F}_{\mathcal{Q}},\mathbf{F}_{\mathcal{P}}) &= \lambda_{\mathcal{QP}} \cdot \sum_{i=1}^{|\mathcal{Q}|}\sum_{j=1}^{|\mathcal{P}|} C_{ij}\|\mathbf{F}_{\mathcal{Q}i} - \mathbf{F}_{\mathcal{P}j}\|_2^2 \\ &+\lambda_T \cdot \sum_{i,j=1}^{|\mathcal{P}|} Y_{ij}\|\mathbf{F}_{\mathcal{P}i} - \mathbf{F}_{\mathcal{P}j}\|_2^2 + \lambda_{\mathcal{E}} \cdot \sum_{i,j=1}^{|\mathcal{P}|} E_{ij}\|\mathbf{F}_{\mathcal{P}i} - \mathbf{F}_{\mathcal{P}j}\|_2^2 \\ \text{s.t.}\ & \mathbf{F}_{\mathcal{Q}} \in [0,1]^{|\mathcal{Q}|\times k}, \quad \mathbf{F}_{\mathcal{P}} \in [0,1]^{|\mathcal{P}|\times k},\end{aligned} \tag{4}$$

where $\|\cdot\|_2$ denotes the $L_2$ norm, *i.e.*, $\|\mathbf{a}\|_2^2 = \sum_i a_i^2$. $\lambda_{\mathcal{QP}}$, $\lambda_T$ and $\lambda_{\mathcal{E}}$ are tuning parameters which control the trade-off between three types of relationships. Note that $0 \leq \lambda_{\mathcal{QP}}, \lambda_T, \lambda_{\mathcal{E}} \leq 1$.

[2]http://en.wikipedia.org/wiki/Wikipedia:Statistics

Query-web page relationship is modeled by the first term in Equation (4). Minimizing the term forces linked queries and web pages in click graph $\mathbf{C}$ to have similar intent indicator if click count between them is large. With the definition of two diagonal degree matrices $\mathbf{D}^{(\mathcal{P})}$ and $\mathbf{D}^{(\mathcal{Q})}$, where $D_{ii}^{(\mathcal{Q})} = \sum_{j=1}^{|\mathcal{P}|} C_{ij}$ and $D_{jj}^{(\mathcal{P})} = \sum_{i=1}^{|\mathcal{Q}|} C_{ij}$, we can rewrite $L_2$ norm of the first term into trace form and transform summation into matrix multiplication as follows:

$$\begin{aligned}&\sum_{i=1}^{|\mathcal{Q}|}\sum_{j=1}^{|\mathcal{P}|} C_{ij} \cdot \|\mathbf{F}_{\mathcal{Q}i} - \mathbf{F}_{\mathcal{P}j}\|_2^2 \\ =\ & \mathrm{Tr}\Big(\sum_{i=1}^{|\mathcal{Q}|} D_{ii}^{(\mathcal{Q})} \cdot \mathbf{F}_{\mathcal{Q}i}\mathbf{F}_{\mathcal{Q}i}^T + \sum_{j=1}^{|\mathcal{P}|} D_{jj}^{(\mathcal{P})} \cdot \mathbf{F}_{\mathcal{P}j}\mathbf{F}_{\mathcal{P}j}^T \\ & -2 \cdot \sum_{i=1}^{|\mathcal{Q}|}\sum_{j=1}^{|\mathcal{P}|} C_{ij} \cdot \mathbf{F}_{\mathcal{Q}i}\mathbf{F}_{\mathcal{P}j}^T\Big) \\ =\ & \mathrm{Tr}\left(\mathbf{F}_{\mathcal{Q}}^T\mathbf{D}^{(\mathcal{Q})}\mathbf{F}_{\mathcal{Q}} + \mathbf{F}_{\mathcal{P}}^T\mathbf{D}^{(\mathcal{P})}\mathbf{F}_{\mathcal{P}} - 2\cdot\mathbf{F}_{\mathcal{Q}}^T\mathbf{C}\mathbf{F}_{\mathcal{P}}\right).\end{aligned} \tag{5}$$

Here we utilize two properties of trace: $\mathrm{Tr}(\mathbf{A}+\mathbf{B}) = \mathrm{Tr}(\mathbf{A}) + \mathrm{Tr}(\mathbf{B})$ and $\mathrm{Tr}(\mathbf{AB}) = \mathrm{Tr}(\mathbf{BA})$ [10].

The second term in Equation (4) attempts to model web page-web page relationships, which forces intent indicators of two web pages are similar if they are close to each other in terms of web page affinity subgraph $\mathbf{Y}$. Similarly, we can rewrite it into trace form as follows:

$$\begin{aligned}&\sum_{i,j=1}^{|\mathcal{P}|} Y_{ij} \cdot \|\mathbf{F}_{\mathcal{P}i} - \mathbf{F}_{\mathcal{P}j}\|_2^2 \\ =\ & 2\,\mathrm{Tr}\left(\mathbf{F}_{\mathcal{P}}^T\mathbf{D}^{(T)}\mathbf{F}_{\mathcal{P}} - \mathbf{F}_{\mathcal{P}}^T\mathbf{Y}\mathbf{F}_{\mathcal{P}}\right) = 2\,\mathrm{Tr}\left(\mathbf{F}_{\mathcal{P}}^T\mathbf{L}^{(T)}\mathbf{F}_{\mathcal{P}}\right),\end{aligned} \tag{6}$$

where $\mathbf{D}^{(T)}$ is defined as $D_{ii}^{(T)} = \sum_{j=1}^{|\mathcal{P}|} Y_{ij}$ and $\mathbf{L}^{(T)} = \mathbf{D}^{(T)} - \mathbf{Y}$ is the graph Laplacian matrix of $\mathbf{Y}$ [2].

As described in Section 4.1, web page-concept relationships have been transformed into concept-based relationships between web pages. Minimizing the third term in Equation (4) forces two web pages to have similar intent indicators if concept-based relationship between them is strong. Similarly we can define degree matrix $\mathbf{D}^{(\mathcal{E})}$ where $D_{ii}^{(\mathcal{E})} = \sum_{j=1}^{|\mathcal{P}|} E_{ij}$ and $\mathbf{L}^{(\mathcal{E})} = \mathbf{D}^{(\mathcal{E})} - \mathbf{E}$, and rewrite the term as follows:

$$\sum_{i,j=1}^{|\mathcal{P}|} E_{ij} \cdot \|\mathbf{F}_{\mathcal{P}i} - \mathbf{F}_{\mathcal{P}j}\|_2^2 = 2 \cdot \mathrm{Tr}\left(\mathbf{F}_{\mathcal{P}}^T\mathbf{L}^{(\mathcal{E})}\mathbf{F}_{\mathcal{P}}\right). \tag{7}$$

By substituting Equations (5), (6) and (7) into the objective function of Equation (4), the graph-based soft-clustering optimization problem is transformed equivalently as follows:

$$\begin{aligned}&\min_{\mathbf{F}_{\mathcal{Q}},\mathbf{F}_{\mathcal{P}}} \mathcal{L}(\mathbf{F}_{\mathcal{Q}},\mathbf{F}_{\mathcal{P}}) \\ =\ & \lambda_{\mathcal{QP}} \cdot \mathrm{Tr}\left(\mathbf{F}_{\mathcal{Q}}^T\mathbf{F}_{\mathcal{Q}} + \mathbf{F}_{\mathcal{P}}^T\mathbf{F}_{\mathcal{P}} - 2\cdot\mathbf{F}_{\mathcal{Q}}^T\mathbf{C}\mathbf{F}_{\mathcal{P}}^T\right) \\ & +2\lambda_T \cdot \mathrm{Tr}\left(\mathbf{F}_{\mathcal{P}}^T\mathbf{L}^{(T)}\mathbf{F}_{\mathcal{P}}\right) + 2\lambda_{\mathcal{E}} \cdot \mathrm{Tr}\left(\mathbf{F}_{\mathcal{P}}^T\mathbf{L}^{(\mathcal{E})}\mathbf{F}_{\mathcal{P}}\right) \\ \text{s.t.}\ & \mathbf{F}_{\mathcal{Q}} \in [0,1]^{|\mathcal{Q}|\times k}, \quad \mathbf{F}_{\mathcal{P}} \in [0,1]^{|\mathcal{P}|\times k},\end{aligned} \tag{8}$$

With the definition of augmented intent indicator $\mathbf{F} = [\mathbf{F}_{\mathcal{Q}}^T, \mathbf{F}_{\mathcal{P}}^T]^T$, Equation 8 can be further rewritten into a more concise form:

$$\min_{\mathbf{F}} \mathcal{L}(\mathbf{F}) = \mathrm{Tr}(\mathbf{F}^T\mathbf{L}\mathbf{F}) \quad \text{s.t.} \quad \mathbf{F} \in [0,1]^{(|\mathcal{Q}|+|\mathcal{P}|)\times k}, \tag{9}$$

where $\mathbf{L}$ is the global graph Laplacian matrix:

$$\mathbf{L} = \begin{bmatrix} \lambda_{\mathcal{QP}} \cdot \mathbf{D}^{(\mathcal{Q})} & -\lambda_{\mathcal{QP}} \cdot \mathbf{C} \\ -\lambda_{\mathcal{QP}} \cdot \mathbf{C}^T & \lambda_{\mathcal{QP}}\mathbf{D}^{(\mathcal{P})} + 2\lambda_{\mathcal{T}}\mathbf{L}^{(\mathcal{T})} + 2\lambda_{\mathcal{E}}\mathbf{L}^{(\mathcal{E})} \end{bmatrix}. \quad (10)$$

## 4.3 The Learning Algorithm

Directly solving the soft clustering problem in Equation (9) is not easy, since the objective function is non-convex and non-continuous. Similar to spectral clustering [8], we propose an efficient algorithm to approximately solve Equation (9) which first embeds each object into a $k$-dimensional intent space, and then clusters the objects based on the embedding intent features.

First, by relaxing $\mathbf{F}$ to $\mathbf{U} \in \mathbb{R}^{(|\mathcal{P}|+|\mathcal{Q}|)\times k}$ and imposing constraint on $\mathbf{U}$, we can learn an optimal graph embedding $\mathbf{U}$ similar to Laplacian eigenmaps [2], which encodes all types of relationships into a $k$-dimensional intent space as follows:

$$\min_{\mathbf{U}} \mathrm{Tr}(\mathbf{U}^T\mathbf{L}\mathbf{U}) \quad \text{s.t.} \quad \mathbf{U}^T\mathbf{M}\mathbf{U} = \mathbf{I}_k, \quad (11)$$

where $\mathbf{I}_k$ is identity matrix and $\mathbf{M}$ is global degree matrix defined as

$$\mathbf{M} = \begin{bmatrix} \lambda_{\mathcal{QP}} \cdot \mathbf{D}^{(\mathcal{Q})} & 0 \\ 0 & \lambda_{\mathcal{QP}}\mathbf{D}^{(\mathcal{P})} + 2\lambda_{\mathcal{T}}\mathbf{D}^{(\mathcal{T})} + 2\lambda_{\mathcal{E}}\mathbf{D}^{(\mathcal{E})} \end{bmatrix}. \quad (12)$$

The constraint $\mathbf{U}^T\mathbf{M}\mathbf{U} = \mathbf{I}_k$ in Equation (11) is imposed to remove arbitrary scaling of $\mathbf{U}$ where the degree matrix $\mathbf{M}$ provides a global measure on variance of $\mathbf{U}$ [2]. From Equation (11) we can see $\mathbf{L}$ is a positive semi-definite matrix. Optimal intent features $\tilde{\mathbf{U}}$ can be computed by $k$ generalized eigenvectors corresponding to $k$-smallest eigenvalues of the generalized eigenvalue problem $\mathbf{LU} = \lambda\mathbf{MU}$ (excluding the one with zero eigenvalue). In particular, we will show shortly (see Section 4.5) that Lanczos algorithm [10] can be used to iteratively compute the smallest $k$ generalized eigenvectors, which largely increase the efficiency by avoiding solving all eigenvalues.

With intent features $\tilde{\mathbf{U}} = [\tilde{\mathbf{U}}_{\mathcal{Q}}^T, \tilde{\mathbf{U}}_{\mathcal{P}}^T]^T$ for both queries and web pages, we derive intent features for concepts based on Equation (3), *i.e.*, $\tilde{\mathbf{U}}_{\mathcal{E}k} = \mathbf{P}_{\mathcal{E}\cdot k}^T \cdot \tilde{\mathbf{U}}_{\mathcal{P}}$, for $k = 1, 2, \ldots, |\mathcal{E}|$. Therefore, various soft clustering methods can be adopted on $\tilde{\mathbf{U}}_{\mathcal{Q}}$, $\tilde{\mathbf{U}}_{\mathcal{P}}$ and $\tilde{\mathbf{U}}_{\mathcal{E}}$ to learn search intent indicators $\mathbf{F}_{\mathcal{Q}}$, $\mathbf{F}_{\mathcal{P}}$ and $\mathbf{F}_{\mathcal{E}}$ simultaneously. In this work, we adopt the widely known fuzzy c-means [3], which optimizes the intent features as follows:

$$\{\tilde{\mathbf{O}}, \tilde{\mathbf{\Theta}}\} = \operatorname*{argmin}_{\mathbf{O},\mathbf{\Theta}} \sum_{i=1}^{|\mathcal{Q}|+|\mathcal{P}|+|\mathcal{E}|} \sum_{j=1}^{k} O_{ij}^2 \cdot \|\tilde{\mathbf{\Pi}}_i - \mathbf{\Theta}_j\|_2^2 \quad (13)$$

where $\tilde{\mathbf{\Pi}} = [\tilde{\mathbf{U}}_{\mathcal{Q}}^T, \tilde{\mathbf{U}}_{\mathcal{P}}^T, \tilde{\mathbf{U}}_{\mathcal{E}}^T]^T$ is augmented intent features for all objects and $\mathbf{\Theta}_j$ is the center of $j$-th cluster. Details of the fuzzy c-means algorithm is in [3]. Finally, we can obtain the intent indicators for queries, web pages and concepts by $\tilde{\mathbf{O}} = [\tilde{\mathbf{F}}_{\mathcal{Q}}^T, \tilde{\mathbf{F}}_{\mathcal{P}}^T, \tilde{\mathbf{F}}_{\mathcal{E}}^T]^T \in [0,1]^{(|\mathcal{Q}|+|\mathcal{P}|+|\mathcal{E}|)\times k}$.

## 4.4 Generalization for Intent Prediction

In practice, users continuously issue new queries and look for new web pages to satisfy their search requirements. Thus, we desire an algorithm with generalization ability which can predict search intents for unseen queries and web pages. In this section, we propose a modified algorithm for newly emerged objects based on the linear model, which is closely related to locality preserving projection [14].

Specifically, we impose linear models on intent features $\mathbf{U} = [\mathbf{U}_{\mathcal{Q}}^T, \mathbf{U}_{\mathcal{P}}^T]^T$ as follows:

$$\mathbf{U}_{\mathcal{Q}} = \mathbf{QW} \quad \text{and} \quad \mathbf{U}_{\mathcal{P}} = \mathbf{PV}, \quad (14)$$

where $\mathbf{W} \in \mathbb{R}^{|\mathcal{Q}|\times m}$ and $\mathbf{V} \in \mathbb{R}^{|\mathcal{P}|\times n}$ are parameters for the linear models. $\mathbf{Q} \in \mathbb{R}^{|\mathcal{Q}|\times n}$ is the term feature vector (weighted by TF-IDF) for queries and $n$ is the dimensionality of query term space. Suppose we have $\boldsymbol{\beta} = [\mathbf{W}^T, \mathbf{V}^T]^T$ as augmented parameters, $\mathbf{X} = \begin{bmatrix} \mathbf{Q} & 0 \\ 0 & \mathbf{P} \end{bmatrix}$ as augmented content feature, $\tilde{\mathbf{L}} = \mathbf{X}^T\mathbf{L}\mathbf{X}$ as global graph Laplacian and $\tilde{\mathbf{M}} = \mathbf{X}^T\mathbf{M}\mathbf{X}$ as global degree matrix, by substituting Equation (14) into Equation (11), a linear extension of originally intent learning problem can be derived as follows:

$$\min_{\boldsymbol{\beta}} \mathrm{Tr}(\boldsymbol{\beta}^T\tilde{\mathbf{L}}\boldsymbol{\beta}) \quad \text{s.t.} \quad \boldsymbol{\beta}^T\tilde{\mathbf{M}}\boldsymbol{\beta} = \mathbf{I}_{m+n}, \quad (15)$$

Similarly, the solution of above optimization problem can be computed by $k$ generalized eigenvector corresponding to $k$-smallest eigenvalues of $\tilde{\mathbf{L}}\boldsymbol{\beta} = \lambda\tilde{\mathbf{M}}\boldsymbol{\beta}$. With estimated parameters $\tilde{\boldsymbol{\beta}} = [\tilde{\mathbf{W}}^T, \tilde{\mathbf{V}}^T]^T$, we can further calculate the intent features $\tilde{\mathbf{F}}_{\mathcal{Q}}$ and $\tilde{\mathbf{F}}_{\mathcal{P}}$ by Equation (14), $\tilde{\mathbf{F}}_{\mathcal{E}}$ by Equation (3), and learn intent indicator following the same process as that in Section 4.2. Given a new query or web page $d$ and its content feature $\mathbf{p_d}$, we can predict its search intent by Equation (14) based on learned linear model parameters.

Finally, we summarize the entire procedure of the heterogeneous graph-based soft-clustering (HSoC) method for learning unified search intents in Algorithm 1.

**Algorithm 1** Unified Search Intent Learning by HSoC

**Input:** Adjacency matrices $\{\mathbf{C}, \mathbf{Y}, \mathbf{P}_{\mathcal{E}}\}$, textual features $\{\mathbf{Q}, \mathbf{P}\}$, parameters $\{\lambda_{\mathcal{QP}}, \lambda_{\mathcal{T}}, \lambda_{\mathcal{E}}\}$, number of intents $k$

**Output:** Intent features $\{\tilde{\mathbf{U}}_{\mathcal{Q}}, \tilde{\mathbf{U}}_{\mathcal{P}}, \tilde{\mathbf{U}}_{\mathcal{E}}\}$, intent indicators $\{\tilde{\mathbf{F}}_{\mathcal{Q}}, \tilde{\mathbf{F}}_{\mathcal{P}}, \tilde{\mathbf{F}}_{\mathcal{E}}\}$,

1: Derive adjacency matrix of concept-based affinity subgraph $\mathbf{E}$ based on $E_{ij} = \mathbf{P}_{\mathcal{E}i}\mathbf{P}_{\mathcal{E}j}^T$

2: Calculate matrices $\tilde{\mathbf{L}} = \mathbf{X}^T\mathbf{L}\mathbf{X}$ and $\tilde{\mathbf{M}} = \mathbf{X}^T\mathbf{M}\mathbf{X}$ using $\mathbf{X} = \begin{bmatrix} \mathbf{Q} & 0 \\ 0 & \mathbf{P} \end{bmatrix}$, $\mathbf{L}$ defined in Equation (10), and $\mathbf{M}$ defined in Equation(12)

3: Use Lanczos algorithm to get $k$ generalized eigenvectors $\tilde{\boldsymbol{\beta}}$ corresponding to $k$ smallest eigenvalues (excluding 0) of eigen-problem in Equation (15)

4: Compute intent features $\tilde{\mathbf{U}}_{\mathcal{Q}}$, $\tilde{\mathbf{U}}_{\mathcal{P}}$ and $\tilde{\mathbf{U}}_{\mathcal{E}}$ based on Equations (14) and (3), respectively

5: Use fuzzy c-means in Equation (13) to learn intent indicators $\tilde{\mathbf{F}}_{\mathcal{Q}}$, $\tilde{\mathbf{F}}_{\mathcal{P}}$ and $\tilde{\mathbf{F}}_{\mathcal{E}}$

## 4.5 Computational Complexity Analysis

In this section, we will analyze the computational complexity of proposed algorithm using the term *flam* [10].

For construction of heterogeneous graph, the cost for ESA is around $|\mathcal{P}|dt + |\mathcal{P}|t\log t$ flam given the built inverted index where $t$ is average number of indexed concepts for a term ($t \ll |\mathcal{E}|$) and $d$ is average number of terms in a web page ($d \ll n$) [9]. Constructing $\mathbf{Y}$ costs around $|\mathcal{P}|^2 d + 4|\mathcal{P}|d + |\mathcal{P}|^2 \log|\mathcal{P}|$ flam and similarly, constructing $\mathbf{E}$ costs around

Table 1: Statistics of two click graphs

| Data sets | AOL | Commercial |
|---|---|---|
| # of unique queries | 144,004 | 103,689 |
| # of unique URLs | 103,509 | 231,232 |
| # of edges | 266,954 | 363,753 |
| # of query words | 34,103 | 38,016 |
| # of page words | 50,810 | 60,177 |
| Total click count | 64,295k | 20,740k |

$|\mathcal{P}|^2 e + 4|\mathcal{P}|e + |\mathcal{P}|^2 \log |\mathcal{P}|$ flam where $e$ is average number of concepts related to a web page ($e \ll |\mathcal{E}|$).

For graph embedding, the calculation of sparse matrix $\tilde{\mathbf{L}} = \mathbf{X}^T\mathbf{L}\mathbf{X}$ requires around $|\mathcal{Q}|r + 2|\mathcal{Q}|rc + 2|\mathcal{P}|nd + |\mathcal{P}|d + 2|\mathcal{P}|Kd + 2|\mathcal{P}|md$ flam where $c$ is average number of clicks from a query ($c \ll |\mathcal{P}|$). Similarly, calculation of sparse matrix $\tilde{\mathbf{M}} = \mathbf{X}^T\mathbf{M}\mathbf{X}$ requires around $|\mathcal{Q}|r + 3|\mathcal{P}|d$ flam where $r$ is average number of terms in a query ($r \ll m$). Using Lanczos algorithm, eigen-problem in Equation (15) can be solved using $lk(m+n)(c+2K)$ flam where $l$ is number of iterations for Lanczos ($l \approx 20$) [10].

For clustering, Equations (3) and (14) costs in total $|\mathcal{Q}|kr + |\mathcal{P}|kd + |\mathcal{E}|ke$ flam and fuzzy c-means costs around $(|\mathcal{Q}| + |\mathcal{P}| + |\mathcal{E}|)k^3v$ where $v$ is number of iterations ($v \approx 30$). Overall, the total time complexity for Algorithm 1 is

$$\mathcal{O}\Big(|\mathcal{P}|^2(d + e + \log |\mathcal{P}|) + k^3 v(|\mathcal{Q}| + |\mathcal{P}| + |\mathcal{E}|)\Big).$$

# 5. EXPERIMENTS

In this section, we evaluate the effectiveness of intent features using search ranking and test the performance of the unified search intent learning method on object co-clustering. Two different search datasets are used for evaluation: commercial search data set and AOL search data set.

## 5.1 Data Preparation

Two real click-through data sets are used for building click graphs in our experiments: AOL search data and one week click-through data collected from a commercial search engine. Statistics of two data sets are shown in Table 1.

### *5.1.1 Click Graphs*

The AOL search data consists of about 20 million query entries collected from about 650k users over three months, which contains 4,811,651 unique queries (after converting to lower case and removing special characters such as punctuation), and 1,632,789 unique URLs (after normalization). We filtered out queries with objectionable content such as pornography and hate speech, and pruned potentially navigational queries (click ratio to a certain URL is more than 0.9). We only keep the links between queries and web pages if the click count is more than 4 since it is more popular and important to study [18], leading to 144,004 queries and 103,509 web pages (URLs) remaining.

For the commercial search log, it originally contained about 4 million entries spread over a week, including 2,111,378 unique queries and 1,897,130 unique URLs. A similar preprocessing procedure is applied to this data except that we set the minimum click frequency to be 20 since the average click count of each query in this data set is much larger than that of AOL data set. Finally we obtained 103,689 unique queries and 231,232 unique web pages (URLs).

### *5.1.2 Text-Based Web Page Subgraphs*

We crawled the page content for each URL and dropped those URLs which have no useful content information, resulting in about 101k URLs remained for AOL data and about 228k URLs remained for the commercial data set. To obtain textual features, we first extracted words from queries and web pages' content, removed stop words and normalized white space. Next, we represented each query or web page as a bag-of-word vector using TF-IDF weighting. We finally obtained 34,103 unique words for queries and 50,810 unique words for web pages in the AOL data set. From the commercial data set, we collected 38,016 unique words for queries and 60,177 unique words for web pages. A text-based KNN graph $G_{\mathcal{P}}$ was then constructed based on the method mentioned in Section 3.

Table 2: Statistics of two web page subgraphs

| Data sets | AOL | Commercial |
|---|---|---|
| # of unique concepts | 2,329,443 | 2,640,984 |
| # of edges in **E** | 419,332 | 1,252,184 |
| # of edges in **Y** | 513,326 | 1,239,856 |

### *5.1.3 Concept-Based Web Page Subgraphs*

We implemented the ESA algorithm following [9] and extracted top-300 relevant Wikipedia concepts for each web page. Empirically we found the performance of our method does not noticeably change when the number of related concepts is larger than 300. The concept-based web page subgraph **E** is then constructed based on the method mentioned in Section 4.1. Statistics of the two kinds of web page subgraphs for the two datasets are shown in Table 2.

### *5.1.4 Evaluation Sets*

To generate ground-truth data set, we manually judged a subset of query-page pairs into five different levels including "Perfect", "Excellent", "Good", "Fair" and "Bad". For AOL data set, we labeled 1,350 queries and 10.3 associated web pages on average. For the commercial data set, we labeled 2,260 queries and 13.2 associated web pages per query. Each ground-truth data set is split into three parts randomly and we used 1/3 as a validation set for tuning parameters, and 2/3 as a testing set for evaluations.

Similarly, we also labeled ground-truth data for query-concept pairs, including 1,080 queries with 8,652 concepts for AOL data set, and 2,120 queries with 10,241 concepts for the commercial data set.

In the rest of this section, we will present our experimental results on both data sets under two different tasks, search ranking and object co-clustering.

## 5.2 Search Ranking

In this section, we evaluate the effectiveness of the intent features, which are derived from the proposed heterogeneous graph embedding (HGE) method, in terms of search ranking. Given a query, the search ranking problem aims to find pages that best meet the search intents behind the query.

### *5.2.1 Experimental Settings*

To study the usefulness of textual (bag-of-word) and conceptual (Wikipedia concepts) information, we considered four variations to the proposed method: 1) Only click and textual (bag-of-word) information is used; 2) Only click and concept information is used; 3) all types of information are used and 4) use the linear model along with all types of information. Details are listed below.

**HGE:** We applied heterogeneous graph embedding in the proposed algorithm to learn intent features for queries and

Table 3: **Search ranking performance comparisons on AOL dataset and the commercial dataset in terms of MRR (larger is better) and NDCG@1, 3, 5. We report the performance under two different feature dimensionality ($k = 200$ and 300) for the four variations of the proposed method.**

| Method | AOL data | | | | Commercial data | | | |
|---|---|---|---|---|---|---|---|---|
| | NDCG@1 | NDCG@3 | NDCG@5 | MRR | NDCG@1 | NDCG@3 | NDCG@5 | MRR |
| BM25 | 0.6545 | 0.7477 | 0.8108 | 0.3423 | 0.5929 | 0.6963 | 0.7743 | 0.4508 |
| RW | 0.7148 | 0.7892 | 0.8308 | 0.5980 | 0.6577 | 0.7905 | 0.8480 | 0.6072 |
| MCoC | 0.6964 | 0.7724 | 0.8354 | 0.3655 | 0.6348 | 0.7461 | 0.8073 | 0.4756 |
| M-PLS | 0.7667 | 0.8264 | 0.8468 | 0.5732 | 0.7711 | 0.8061 | 0.8490 | 0.5012 |
| HGE-200 | 0.7799 | 0.8306 | 0.8706 | **0.7415** | 0.8401 | 0.8459 | **0.8823** | 0.7197 |
| HGE-300 | 0.7748 | 0.8314 | 0.8715 | 0.7268 | **0.8423** | **0.8451** | 0.8820 | **0.7389** |
| $HGE_{CG}$-200 | 0.7956 | 0.8188 | 0.8594 | 0.6531 | 0.8030 | 0.8262 | 0.8671 | 0.6595 |
| $HGE_{CG}$-300 | 0.7891 | 0.8151 | 0.8532 | 0.6764 | 0.7987 | 0.8209 | 0.8624 | 0.6697 |
| $HGE_{EG}$-200 | 0.7933 | 0.8285 | 0.8651 | 0.6641 | 0.7962 | 0.8281 | 0.8700 | 0.6739 |
| $HGE_{EG}$-300 | **0.8014** | 0.8345 | 0.8698 | 0.6806 | 0.7931 | 0.8241 | 0.8684 | 0.7067 |
| $HGE_{Fea}$-200 | 0.7703 | 0.8522 | 0.8857 | 0.6126 | 0.8294 | 0.8398 | 0.8712 | 0.6606 |
| $HGE_{Fea}$-300 | 0.7992 | **0.8540** | **0.8865** | 0.6050 | 0.7965 | 0.8218 | 0.8707 | 0.6871 |

web pages. Query-web page similarity is then calculated by Euclidean distance between intent features. For parameters, we set $\lambda_{qp} = 0.1$, $\lambda_t = 0.05$ and $\lambda_e = 0.05$ based on our parameter study (see Section 5.4).

**$HGE_{CG}$** : By setting $\lambda_e = 0$ in HGE, we only consider click graph and text-based web page subgraph $\mathbf{Y}$. Other parameters are set to be the same as in HGE.

**$HGE_{EG}$** : By setting $\lambda_t = 0$ in HGE, we only consider click graph and concept-based web page subgraph. Other parameters are set to be the same as in HGE.

**$HGE_{Fea}$** : This method integrates linear models with HGE as that in Section 4.4. The same parameters are applied here.

For comparison, we also considered four state-of-the-art methods, which are described below.

**BM25:** BM25 is a purely content-based method. It computes similarity scores between textual features of queries and those of web pages. We use the default settings, *i.e.*, $k_1 = 2$, $b = 0.75$.

**RW:** Given a query, RW performs backward random walk on the click graph [7] and provides probabilistic ranking of web pages. The method contains two parameters: the self-transition probability $s$ and number of transition steps $t$. As suggestion by [7], we fixed $s = 0.9$ and tuned $t$ in the range of $\{1, ..., 20\}$. It is observed that when $t > 5$ the method achieved stable performance. Thus, we set $t = 5$.

**MCoC:** Multi-class co-clustering (MCoC) [22] aims to learn latent features from a bipartite graph through an embedding procedure. We adopted this method on our click graph and calculated the query-web page similarity by Euclidean distance between corresponding feature vectors. Feature dimension is empirically set to $d = 100$ as suggested in [22].

**M-PLS:** Multi-view partial least square (M-PLS) [25] uses both click graph and different types of features of queries and web pages to learn query-web page similarity. We consider only textual features $\mathbf{Q}$ and $\mathbf{P}$ in our experiments. Feature dimension is set to $d = 100$ to balance the computational cost and performance [25].

### 5.2.2 *Evaluation Metrics*

To evaluate the performance of different methods in the search ranking task, we employ NDCG@1, 3, 5 as our evaluation metrics. The human-judged labels are mapped to ratings 0-4 accordingly.

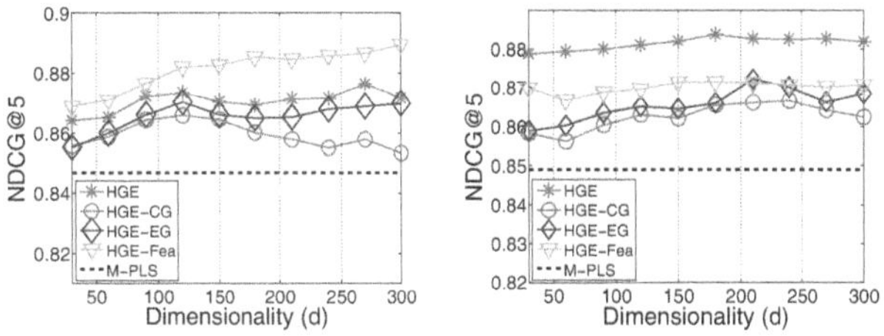


(a) NDCG@5 on AOL (b) NDCG@5 on Commercial

**Figure 2: Search ranking performance versus feature dimensionality ($k = \{30, 60, \ldots, 300\}$) of four alternative methods on AOL and the commercial datasets**

In order to evaluate different methods globally, we also calculated Mean Reciprocal Rank (MRR) over the entire data set, which is defined in Equation (16). Since MRR is only influenced by positive records, we treated "Perfect", "Excellent" and "Good" examples as positive.

$$\mathrm{MRR} = \frac{1}{|\mathcal{Q}_T|} \sum_{q_i \in \mathcal{Q}_T} \frac{1}{\mathrm{rank}(q_i)}, \quad (16)$$

where $\mathcal{Q}_T$ is the query set and $\mathrm{rank}(q_i)$ denotes the rank of first positive web page from the entire web page set.

### 5.2.3 *Results*

Table 3 summarizes the comparison results for search ranking on both data sets. All four variations of the heterogeneous graph embedding method outperform state-of-the-art algorithms. In particular, the HGE method obtains 24% improvement in MRR and 9.23% improvement in NDCG@1 compared to the best baseline, demonstrating the power of integrating multiple kinds of information.

There are also several interesting observations about the four variations of the proposed method. HGE consistently performs better than $HGE_{FEA}$ on the commercial data set while on AOL data set $HGE_{FEA}$ outperforms HGE in terms of NDCG@1, 3, 5. The difference may come from the quality difference between the textual features of the two data sets. AOL data set may contain richer textual information than that in the commercial data set, yielding less sparse textual features. We can also tell the usefulness of textual and concept information by comparing results of $HGE_{EG}$ with those of $HGE_{CG}$. It can be seen that $HGE_{EG}$ has better results than $HGE_{CG}$ in most cases, which leads to the conclusion that concepts bring richer information than textual content.

Moreover, HGE achieves significantly better MRR on both of the data sets, showing that its performance is stable in entire training set.

Figure 2 presents NDCG@5 of the four variations with respect to different intent space dimensionalities on both data sets. It can be seen that performances of these methods are not very sensitive to the dimensionality $d$. On the commercial data set, HGE always outperforms $HGE_{FEA}$ because of the sparsity issue of textual features. Also, HGE and $HGE_{FEA}$ always outperform $HGE_{CG}$ and $HGE_{EG}$ on all dimensionalities, showing that integrating information of the commercial data is helpful. However, we find NDCG@1 on AOL data is sensitive to the change of dimensionality, and $HGE_{CG}$ and $HGE_{EG}$ achieve better results when dimensionality is larger than 200. We believe this is due to the information conflict when merging textual and concept information.

## 5.3 Object Co-Clustering for Intent Learning

In this section, we evaluate the proposed heterogeneous graph-based soft-clustering method for search intent learning on AOL and the commercial datasets.

### 5.3.1 Experiment Setup

We compared the proposed method (HSoC) and its variation with the linear model (HSoC-Fea). We also conducted comparisons with several baselines including content-based methods and graph-based methods. Detailed introduction is shown below.

**TFIDF:** Uses unigrams with TF-IDF weighting to represent queries and web pages; calculates bag-of-word features for concepts based on Equation (3); employs fuzzy c-means clustering based on the Cosine similarity measure.

**PLSA:** Adopts probabilistic latent semantic analysis to co-cluster queries, web pages and concepts, by representing all objects with bag-of-word features. The number of topics are set to be the same as the number of clusters ($k$).

**BSGP:** Adopts bipartite spectral graph partition (BSGP) method [8] on the click graph and the web page-concept subgraph, respectively; We set the dimensionality $d = \lceil \log_2 k \rceil$ as suggested by [8].

**MCoC:** Uses Multi-class Co-clustering (MCoC) method [26] on the click graph and the web page-concept subgraph.

**HSoC:** Our proposed method for object co-clustering of queries, web pages and concepts. 1) Intent features are first learned; 2) Fuzzy c-means clustering method is adopted on the intent features to learn intent indicators.

**HSoC-Fea:** Adopt HSoC with the linear model.

### 5.3.2 Evaluation Metrics

Evaluation for the proposed method is different from traditional clustering evaluation methods because: 1) we cluster three types of objects collaboratively instead of a single type of objects; 2) we soft-cluster instead of assigning each object to single cluster. Thus, we evaluated the heterogeneous graph-based soft-clustering results by precision, recall, and $F_1$ score over pairs of objects including query-page pairs and query-pairs [13].

Specifically, we first generated binary judgements by treating pairs with "Perfect", "Excellent" and "Good" labels as positive examples, and those with "Bad" labels as negative ones. We define TP (true positive) as the number of positive objects pairs that are correctly assigned to same cluster, FP

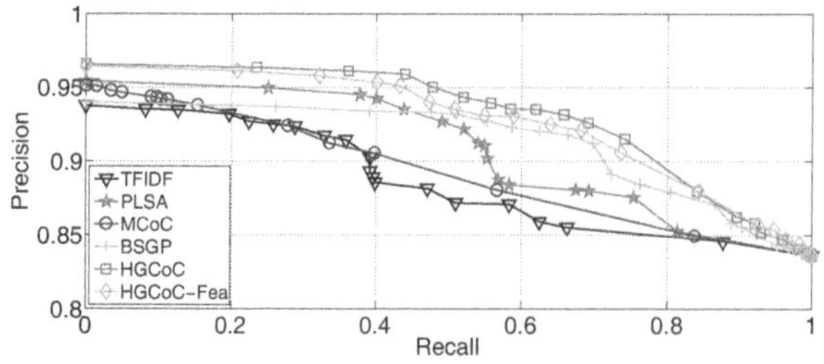


(a) AOL dataset

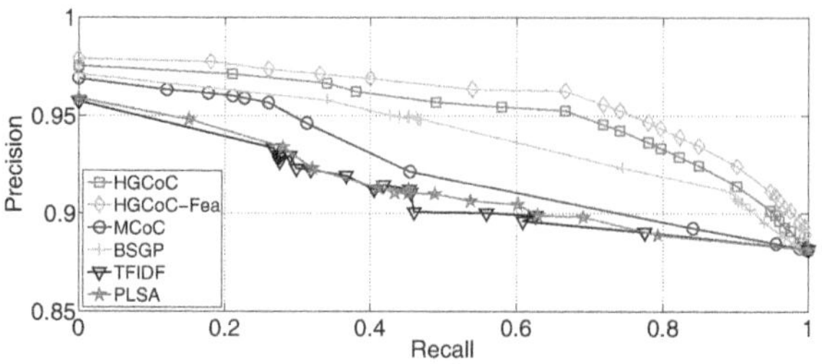


(b) The commercial dataset

**Figure 3: Precision-recall curves (plot by varying the number of intents, *i.e.*, dimensionality $k$) of HSoC, $HSoC_{Fea}$ and baselines for (a) the AOL and (b) the commercial datasets**

(false positive) as the number of negative object pairs that are assigned to the same cluster, TN (true negative) as the number of negative object pairs that are assigned to different clusters and FN (false negative) as the number of positive object pairs that are assigned to different clusters.

Precision (P) is calculated as the fraction of pairs correctly put in the same cluster (*i.e.*, P=TP/(TP + FP)), recall (R) is the fraction of similar pairs that were identified (*i.e.*, R=TP/(TP + FN)), $F_1$ score is the harmonic mean of precision and recall (*i.e.*, $F_1$ = 2PR/(P + R)). We also adopt the widely used clustering measure Rand index [21], defined as RI=(TP + TN)/(TP + FP + FN + TN).

### 5.3.3 Performance Comparisons

Since the ground-truth data set consists of binary-labeled object pairs, we propose to evaluate the soft-clustering methods (PLSA, MCoC and the proposed methods) by assigning each object to its 3 most confident intents in the intent indicator. For hard clustering methods (TFIDF and BSGP), each object is only assigned to single intent.

Table 4(a) and Table 4(b) show comparison results for 20 intents and 50 intents on both data sets. Each method is repeated for 10 trials for accurate clustering performance evaluation. We use bold number to highlight the best results on different metrics. The proposed HSoC and HSoC-Fea methods achieve significantly better results on Precision, Recall, $F_1$ score and Rand Index (RI), demonstrating the integration of different information in a unified framework does help the effectiveness of intent learning. In particular, we find content-based methods such as TFIDF outperform our methods and graph-based methods on Precision, but perform very poor on Recall and other metrics. This shows that content-based methods tend to generate purer but less complete clusters as intents while our methods generate intent clusters with better coverage. The reason may be because the unified optimization on heterogeneous graphs helps identify objects which share intents in a more comprehensive

Table 4: Object co-clustering performance comparisons on (a) AOL and (b) the commercial datasets in terms of Precision, Recall, $F_1$ and Rand index (RI). We set the number of intents to be 20 and 50 ($k = 20, 50$).

(a) The AOL dataset

| | performance on 20 clusters | | | | performance on 50 clusters | | | |
|---|---|---|---|---|---|---|---|---|
| Method | Precision | Recall | $F_1$ | RI | Precision | Recall | $F_1$ | RI |
| TFIDF | 0.8841±.01 | 0.4569±.07 | 0.5992±.06 | 0.4497±.07 | 0.8986±.01 | 0.3996±.07 | 0.5496±.07 | 0.4519±.04 |
| PLSA | **0.8978±.01** | 0.5756±.02 | 0.7013±.01 | 0.5904±.01 | **0.9085±.01** | 0.5551±.02 | 0.6889±.01 | 0.5812±.01 |
| BSGP | 0.8550±.00 | 0.8755±.00 | 0.8842±.00 | 0.7996±.00 | 0.8549±.00 | 0.8635±.00 | 0.8541±.00 | 0.7781±.00 |
| MCoC | 0.8870±.01 | 0.5267±.07 | 0.6582±.05 | 0.5476±.05 | 0.8823±.01 | 0.3169±.02 | 0.4054±.02 | 0.3658±.01 |
| HSoC | 0.8465±.00 | 0.9534±.01 | 0.8967±.00 | 0.8163±.00 | 0.8604±.01 | 0.8857±.01 | 0.8728±.00 | 0.7842±00 |
| $\text{HSoC}_{\text{Fea}}$ | 0.8417±.00 | **0.9776±.01** | **0.9045±.00** | **0.8275±.01** | 0.8614±.00 | **0.8880±.02** | **0.8743±.01** | **0.7868±.01** |

(b) The commercial dataset

| | performance on 20 clusters | | | | performance on 50 clusters | | | |
|---|---|---|---|---|---|---|---|---|
| Method | Precision | Recall | $F_1$ | RI | Precision | Recall | $F_1$ | RI |
| TFIDF | **0.9083±.00** | 0.4496±.04 | 0.6012±.03 | 0.4752±.02 | 0.9150±.00 | 0.4011±.04 | 0.5565±.03 | 0.4390±.03 |
| PLSA | 0.9052±.01 | 0.4881±.02 | 0.6352±.01 | 0.5060±.01 | 0.9105±.01 | 0.4527±.01 | 0.6047±.01 | 0.4728±.01 |
| BSGP | 0.9018±.00 | 0.9198±.00 | 0.9107±.00 | 0.8410±.00 | 0.9079±.00 | 0.8985±.00 | 0.9032±.00 | 0.8301±.00 |
| MCoC | 0.8822±.00 | 0.9258±.00 | 0.9036±.00 | 0.8365 ±.00 | 0.8926±.01 | 0.8311±.08 | 0.8589±.04 | 0.7632±.06 |
| HSoC | 0.8928±.00 | **0.9667±.01** | 0.9283±.00 | **0.8683±.00** | 0.9012±.00 | **0.9472±.00** | 0.9236±.00 | 0.8619±.00 |
| $\text{HSoC}_{\text{Fea}}$ | 0.9028±.01 | **0.9667±.00** | **0.9337±.00** | **0.8683±.00** | **0.9182±.01** | **0.9472±.00** | **0.9324±.00** | **0.8689±.00** |

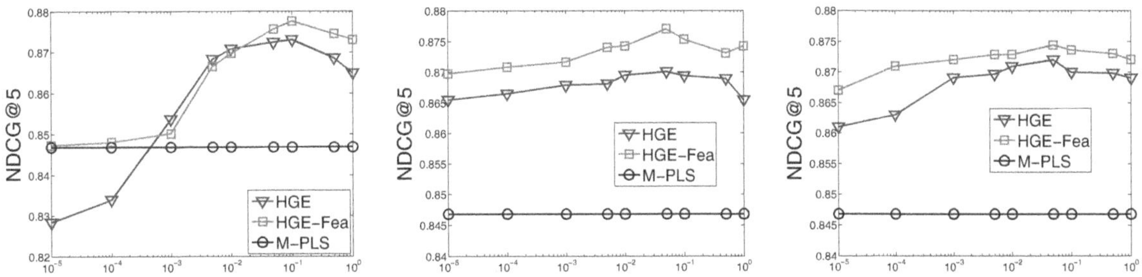


(a) Varing $\lambda_{\mathcal{QP}}$ (b) Varing $\lambda_{\mathcal{T}}$ (c) Varing $\lambda_{\mathcal{E}}$

**Figure 4: Parameter study for $\lambda_{\mathcal{QP}}$, $\lambda_{\mathcal{T}}$ and $\lambda_{\mathcal{E}}$ in terms of NDCG@5 on search ranking**

way. Also, we see that the $\text{HSoC}_{\text{Fea}}$ method outperforms HSoC in general, demonstrating the effectiveness of the linear model for the clustering problem.

To compare the performance with respect to the number of intents, we plot precision-recall curves in Figure 3 for both data sets by varying the number of cluster, $k$, from 1 to the number of objects in the ground-truth data set. First, the proposed HSoC and $\text{HSoC}_{\text{Fea}}$ methods clearly outperform baselines significantly, showing that unified optimization with three types of information helps. Also, we find that BSGP achieves similar performance as our methods when $k$ is small. This is probably because adding concept information does not help much in coarse level clustering.

### 5.3.4 *Case Study*

To provide a clearer look at the learned intents, we randomly selected 4 intent clusters to give as examples. For each intent cluster, we randomly picked 4 queries, 4 URLs and 4 concepts to show in Table 5.

First, we can see that the 4 randomly selected clusters cover 4 generic search intents from different domains. For example, cluster 19 is about software while cluster 43 is about music. This verifies that the proposed method is able to learn generic search intents which cover different domains. The queries "enterprise" (in cluster 8) and "office" (in cluster 19) indicate that the proposed method can handle ambiguous queries well. Also, we find the proposed method is able to handle queries with typos or shortenings such as "xboxx" in cluster 5 and "video2map3" in cluster 19, indicating that click-through and concept information are good complements for raw text. Finally, it can be observed that concepts from each intent cluster assist in intent interpretation, especially when the queries and URLs are hard to understand directly (see cluster 5 and 43 in Table 5).

## 5.4 Parameter Study

In this section we study the impact of three parameters (*i.e.*, $\lambda_{\mathcal{QP}}$, $\lambda_{\mathcal{T}}$ and $\lambda_{\mathcal{E}}$) in the proposed method. They control the information trade-off between query-page, text-based web page and concept-based web page relations, respectively. We studied the importance of these three relations on validation data sets by varying one of the parameter and fixing the other two parameters.

Figure 4 shows the search ranking performance in terms of NDCG@5 with respect to different parameter values on the AOL data set. We find the proposed method is more sensitive to $\lambda_{\mathcal{QP}}$ than the other two parameters, showing that query-web page relationship is more important to the search ranking performance. Also, increasing $\lambda_{\mathcal{E}}$ leads to larger performance enhancement than increasing $\lambda_{\mathcal{T}}$, which may be due to richer information from concepts.

## 6. CONCLUSION AND FUTURE WORK

In this paper, we study the problem of learning unified search intents for queries, web pages and Wikipedia concepts. The proposed method aims to leverage three types of objects together to tackle drawbacks from using only a single type of data source, yielding better understanding of intents. Also, bridging intents with concepts helps interpret intents

**Table 5: Examples of 4 randomly selected search intents (from 50 intent clusters) learned by $\text{HSoC}_{\text{Fea}}$ method. We randomly selected 4 queries, 4 URLs and 4 Wikipedia concepts from each of the selected intent cluster.**

| Queries | URLs | Concepts |
|---|---|---|
| | cluster ID: 5 (video games) | |
| pokemon | http://gamehouse.com/mahjong-games | crazy_taxi |
| daily jigsaw | http://gamestop.com/xbox360 | plants_vs._zombies |
| nickmom | http://freefishinggames.biz | call_of_duty_(video_game) |
| xboxx | http://freegamepick.com | the_sims |
| | cluster ID: 8 (car rentals) | |
| car rental | http://rentals.com | the_hertz_corporation |
| carmax | http://carmax.com/enus/car-search/new-cars.html | enterprise_tent-a-car |
| hertz car rental | http://enterprise.com/car_rental/contactus.do | budget_rent_a_car |
| enterprise | http://carmax.com | alamo_rent_a_car |
| | cluster ID: 19 (softwares) | |
| adobe flash player | http://adobe.com/products/reader.html | microsoft_office |
| video2map3 | http://freemake.com/free_youtube_converter | nuance_pdf_reader |
| office | http://support.microsoft.com/ph/14019 | windows_defender |
| google chrome | http://download.cnet.com/windows/activex | quest_software |
| | cluster ID: 43 (music) | |
| nicki minaj | http://youtubemusic.net | flo_rida |
| pitbull | http://en.wikipedia.org/wiki/john_mayer | linkin_park |
| adele | http://buzzworld.in/songs-pk | die_another_day_(song) |
| karaoke | http://pitbullmusic.com/us | pitbull_(rapper) |

when it is hard to understand queries and URLs. Technically, we cast this problem into a heterogeneous graph-based soft-clustering problem and develop an effective and efficient algorithm for solving it. Experimental results from search ranking demonstrate the effectiveness of the proposed intent features and the co-clustering results show significant improvement compared with state-of-the-art methods.

Interesting future work includes: 1) extending our method to automatically learn the importance of different types of relations; and 2) enabling our method to update the intent indicator in an online manner so that newly emerged search intents can be efficiently included.

# 7. ACKNOWLEDGEMENTS

The work was supported in part by the U.S. Army Research Laboratory under Cooperative Agreement No. W911NF-09-2-0053 (NS-CTA) and W911NF-11-2-0086 (Cyber-Security), the U.S. Army Research Office under Cooperative Agreement No. W911NF-13-1-0193, DTRA, MIAS, a DHS-IDS Center for Multimodal Information Access and Synthesis at UIUC, and U.S. National Science Foundation grants CNS-0931975, IIS-1017362, IIS-1320617, IIS-1354329.

# 8. REFERENCES

[1] L. M. Aiello, D. Donato, U. Ozertem, and F. Menczer. Behavior-driven clustering of queries into topics. In *CIKM*, 2011.

[2] M. Belkin and P. Niyogi. Laplacian eigenmaps and spectral techniques for embedding and clustering. In *NIPS*, 2001.

[3] J. C. Bezdek, R. Ehrlich, and W. Full. Fcm: The fuzzy c-means clustering algorithm. *Computers & Geosciences*, 10(2):191–203, 1984.

[4] I. Bordino, G. De Francisci Morales, I. Weber, and F. Bonchi. From machu_picchu to rafting the urubamba river: anticipating information needs via the entity-query graph. In *WSDM*, 2013.

[5] H. Cao, D. H. Hu, D. Shen, D. Jiang, J.-T. Sun, E. Chen, and Q. Yang. Context-aware query classification. In *SIGIR*, 2009.

[6] J. C. K. Cheung and X. Li. Sequence clustering and labeling for unsupervised query intent discovery. In *WSDM*, 2012.

[7] N. Craswell and M. Szummer. Random walks on the click graph. In *SIGIR*, 2007.

[8] I. S. Dhillon. Co-clustering documents and words using bipartite spectral graph partitioning. In *SIGKDD*, 2001.

[9] E. Gabrilovich and S. Markovitch. Computing semantic relatedness using wikipedia-based explicit semantic analysis. In *IJCAI*, 2007.

[10] G. H. Golub and C. F. Van Loan. *Matrix computations*, volume 3. JHU Press, 2012.

[11] Q. Gu and J. Zhou. Co-clustering on manifolds. In *SIGKDD*, 2009.

[12] Z. Guan, C. Wang, J. Bu, C. Chen, K. Yang, D. Cai, and X. He. Document recommendation in social tagging services. In *WWW*, 2010.

[13] M. Halkidi, Y. Batistakis, and M. Vazirgiannis. On clustering validation techniques. *Journal of Intelligent Information Systems*, 17(2-3):107–145, 2001.

[14] X. He and P. Niyogi. Locality preserving projections. In *NIPS*, 2003.

[15] J. Hu, G. Wang, F. Lochovsky, J. Sun, and Z. Chen. Understanding user's query intent with wikipedia. In *WWW*, 2009.

[16] Y. Hu, Y. Qian, H. Li, D. Jiang, J. Pei, and Q. Zheng. Mining query subtopics from search log data. In *SIGIR*, 2012.

[17] M. Ji, J. Yan, S. Gu, J. Han, X. He, W. V. Zhang, and Z. Chen. Learning search tasks in queries and web pages via graph regularization. In *SIGIR*, 2011.

[18] X. Li, Y. Wang, and A. Acero. Learning query intent from regularized click graphs. In *SIGIR*, 2008.

[19] J. Liu, C. Wang, J. Gao, and J. Han. Multi-view clustering via joint nonnegative matrix factorization. In *SDM*, 2013.

[20] F. Radlinski, M. Szummer, and N. Craswell. Inferring query intent from reformulations and clicks. In *WWW*, 2010.

[21] W. M. Rand. Objective criteria for the evaluation of clustering methods. *JSTOR*, 66(336):846–850, 1971.

[22] E. Sadikov, J. Madhavan, L. Wang, and A. Halevy. Clustering query refinements by user intent. In *WWW*, 2010.

[23] Y. Sun, Y. Yu, and J. Han. Ranking-based clustering of heterogeneous information networks with star network schema. In *SIGKDD*, 2009.

[24] X. Wang, D. Chakrabarti, and K. Punera. Mining broad latent query aspects from search sessions. In *SIGKDD*, 2009.

[25] W. Wu, H. Li, and J. Xu. Learning query and document similarities from click-through bipartite graph with metadata. In *WSDM*, 2013.

[26] B. Xu, J. Bu, C. Chen, and D. Cai. An exploration of improving collaborative recommender systems via user-item subgroups. In *WWW*, 2012.

[27] T. Yamamoto, T. Sakai, M. Iwata, C. Yu, J. Wen, and K. Tanaka. The wisdom of advertisers: mining subgoals via query clustering. In *CIKM*, 2012.

[28] X. Yin and S. Shah. Building taxonomy of web search intents for name entity queries. In *WWW*, 2010.

[29] H. Zeng, Q. He, Z. Chen, W. Ma, and J. Ma. Learning to cluster web search results. In *SIGIR*, 2004.

[30] X. Zhu, J. Guo, X. Cheng, and Y. Lan. More than relevance: high utility query recommendation by mining users' search behaviors. In *CIKM*, 2012.

# Exploiting User Disagreement for Web Search Evaluation: an Experimental Approach

Thomas Demeester[1], Robin Aly[2], Djoerd Hiemstra[2], Dong Nguyen[2], Dolf Trieschnigg[2], Chris Develder[1]

[1] Ghent University - iMinds, Belgium

[2] University of Twente, The Netherlands

tdmeeste@intec.ugent.be, {r.aly, d.hiemstra}@utwente.nl
{d.nguyen, d.trieschnigg}@utwente.nl, cdvelder@intec.ugent.be

## ABSTRACT

To express a more nuanced notion of relevance as compared to binary judgments, graded relevance levels can be used for the evaluation of search results. Especially in Web search, users strongly prefer top results over less relevant results, and yet they often disagree on which are the top results for a given information need. Whereas previous works have generally considered disagreement as a negative effect, this paper proposes a method to exploit this user disagreement by integrating it into the evaluation procedure.

First, we present experiments that investigate the user disagreement. We argue that, with a high disagreement, lower relevance levels might need to be promoted more than in the case where there is global consensus on the top results. This is formalized by introducing the User Disagreement Model, resulting in a weighting of the relevance levels with a probabilistic interpretation. A validity analysis is given, and we explain how to integrate the model with well-established evaluation metrics. Finally, we discuss a specific application of the model, in the estimation of suitable weights for the combined relevance of Web search snippets and pages.

## Categories and Subject Descriptors

H.3.3 [**Information Search and Retrieval**]: Miscellaneous

## Keywords

User disagreement, graded relevance, evaluation.

## 1. INTRODUCTION

Search engine evaluation uses relevance judgments of assessors to measure the effectiveness of search algorithms. Traditionally, a single assessor makes binary judgments about the relevance of documents based on a description of the information need at hand. Voorhees [22] showed that system comparisons are stable even for large disagreement among assessors. Because the research community agrees that relevance is in reality more complex than a binary label, modern evaluation measures consider graded relevance levels [18], groupings of documents into classes of the same type of content to evaluate the diversity of a ranking [25], and the ambiguity of search requests. Given the wide variety of users and internet content, we propose that in the Web context, it becomes increasingly questionable whether the judgments from one assessor lead to stable evaluation results. In this paper we investigate the disagreement of users on graded relevance levels, on two very different test collections: one with a large set of crowd-sourced Web search assessments, and one with less, but high-quality, judgments of both result snippets and result pages in a federated Web search setting.

Disagreement among users is an important aspect of search engine evaluation. Many works have investigated the influence of disagreement on search evaluation, (e.g., [4, 2, 22]). These works have been mainly based on binary relevance labels. The common approach to assess the disagreement is by measuring its amount, for example with the Jaccard coefficient or the kappa statistic, and to determine its influence by assessing the ranking of systems that the different judgment versions generate. Therefore, these works consider disagreement as a negative effect of including different judges, and test what the consequences of these unwanted effects are. In this paper we propose that disagreement should be seen as a reality that contains useful information, e.g., to estimate the relative importance of different levels of relevance. In Section 3 we will show that the overlap between judgments of top relevance for realistic Web data is rather low. Yet, Kekäläinen and Järvelin [15] propose that Web search evaluation should strongly favor documents of top relevance in the evaluation measure. This has been confirmed by Huang and Efthimiadis [12], as users tend to reformulate queries, rather than looking far down the result list. In that context, disagreement among users potentially has a strong effect on system evaluations. One of the key problems with integrating disagreement into evaluation measures is that there are no available models for disagreement. In this paper we propose one, referred to as the User Disagreement Model (UDM), for the disagreement in relevance judgments among users, and describe how the model's parameters can be accurately estimated with a limited number of queries judged by pairs of assessors.


*WSDM'14*, February 24–28, 2014, New York, New York, USA.

http://dx.doi.org/10.1145/2556195.2556268.

Current evaluation measures based on graded relevance either lack a motivation for the weights they are using, e.g., in the normalized Discounted Cumulative Gain (nDCG) measure [13], or, for probabilistically motivated models, the parameters are difficult to estimate, e.g., for the Graded Average Precision (GAP) measure [18]. We will use the UDM, based on the relevance opinion of multiple users, to make existing evaluation metrics for graded relevance more realistic.

In summary, this paper makes the following contributions to the field of search engine evaluation:

- We provide insight into user disagreement phenomena, with experimental results based on two test collections (Section 3).
- We propose a probabilistic model for user disagreement on relevance (Section 4).
- We show how our model can be used with existing graded relevance-base evaluation metrics to better reflect the real-world conditions of disagreeing users (Section 5).
- We indicate which parameters influence the robustness of our model (Section 6).
- We show how our model can be used to calculate suitable relevance weights for combined (snippet, page) relevance levels in Web search evaluation (Section 7).

## 2. RELATED WORK AND BACKGROUND

This section describes the relation of our disagreement model with other, well-established, aspects of search engine evaluation.

The evaluation of search engines usually involves modeling the following aspects: (i) the *label type* upon which the measure is based, (ii) a *user model* that describes how users process search results, (iii) *erroneous judgments* or *assessor bias*, and finally (iv) *evaluation metrics* that define the search effectiveness based on its input. We will now discuss these aspects in detail.

The *label types* for traditional evaluation metrics are limited to binary relevance, which is assumed to hold for all users having a well-defined information need. More recently, several works have improved upon this simplistic assumption, mainly into the following three directions: (i) capturing diversity by defining equivalence classes of documents [25, 7], (ii) capturing the ambiguity of queries by intent labels [1], and (iii) assuming that documents can have multiple grades of relevance [18, 13]. Compared to label types, the contribution in this paper is a different aspect of search engine evaluation. Instead of investigating how to assign different label types to documents that are valid over all users, our work acknowledges the fact that the labels naturally vary between users, and we define a model for user disagreement.

*User models* describe how users process ranked lists of search results. For example, Yilmaz et al. [23] proposed a probabilistic user model, where users read until reaching a random relevant document. The model by Moffat and Zobel [16] assumes that users stop reading a ranked list at a random rank. Such user models therefore also consider multiple users similar to our disagreement model. However, they focus on the reading behavior of users and assume that users agree on the same label for the same document. Our model is independent from the user's reading behavior and addresses the distribution of labels that different users might have. Another existing model that has a number of aspects in common with the UDM, is the user model underlying the GAP metric, by Robertson et al. [18], where one user is assumed to consider a result relevant, as soon as it has its relevance level at or above a specific cut-off level, with a specific distribution over the user population. However, estimating suitable collection-specific weights for these levels is not obvious, whereas it is automatically done by the UDM. Note that, where our model is simple and only based on relevance judgments, more complex user models have been proposed successfully, e.g., by Yilmaz et al. [24], based on the click data of real search sessions.

Investigating *judgment errors* and *assessor bias* is important, e.g., for assessors that are not trained or not motivated. In a recent study, Carterette and Soboroff [5] showed how different types of errors affect evaluation metrics and proposed strategies to compensate for errors, e.g., by selecting certain results for rejudging. These issues have in common with our model that they accept that the annotated labels are not necessarily 'true'. However, in contrast to previous research, we assume that the assessors are representative for the actual users and that an observed mismatch between annotation labels represents a form of user disagreement: we do not aim to "correct" it. For example, for highly erroneous assessments, the UDM-based relevance weights will be automatically adapted to large variations in relevance judgments for the same document. In an ideal scenario, however, judgment errors and bias would first be filtered from the assessments, upon which the UDM could provide suitable relevance weights for the remaining user disagreement.

The *evaluation metric* is a function defined on a label type and a user model and calculates the search effectiveness of a ranking to the current query. We see the main role of disagreement models in the adoption of strong existing evaluation measures, thereby providing relevance weights with a probabilistic interpretation, to incorporate the user disagreement in these measures.

In recent years, a lot of research on search evaluation has been done. Due to length constraints, we only mention a few more recent contributions that need to be explicitly mentioned in relation with the current paper. Some research on more advanced solutions than the traditional majority voting for aggregating multiple judgments has been done, e.g., by Hosseini et al. [11], who concurrently modeled the relevance of documents and the accuracy of assessors in a crowdsourcing setting. Our work instead models the disagreement among users, based on multiple judgments. Smucker and Clarke [20] already argued that it is essential for evaluation metrics to model variation between users, else the effect size of differences between retrieval systems would be overestimated. They proposed a suitable extension to the time-biased gain (TBG) metric. In relation to the combined snippet-based and page-based relevance weights given in Section 7, we acknowledge the work from Turpin et al. [21], on strategies to encorporate the snippet relevance into existing evaluation metrics.

# 3. EXPERIMENTAL INVESTIGATION OF USER DISAGREEMENT

In the following paragraphs, some properties of the relevance assessments for two different data collections will be investigated, focusing on issues related to the disagreement among assessors. The goal of this experimental analysis is to provide insights that are used to develop the user disagreement model (see Section 4).

## 3.1 Data

For the experiments presented in this paper, the relevance assessments for two publicly available datasets are used. The first is a crowd-sourced set of judgments for the TREC 2010 Relevance Feedback Track [3], and the second is a test collection composed in 2012 for research in federated Web search [17]. We will refer to these datasets as, respectively, the RelFeedback10 and the FedWeb12 data. Despite major differences, the relevance assessments for both datasets have three aspects in common, which are fundamental for the current work: (i) they both deal with Web data, (ii) use graded relevance levels, and (iii) contain independent relevance labels from different users. Some characteristics of the data, important for the remainder of this paper, are given below.

### 3.1.1 RelFeedback10 Data

The ground truth data for the RelFeedback10 data was created by means of mechanical Turk workers on English Web pages from the ClueWeb09 collection[1], for English search queries from the TREC 2009 Million Query Track [6]. Some of the documents also have prior 'gold' labels by NIST. The relevance levels are non-relevant (Non), relevant (Rel), and highly relevant (HRel). From the 20,232 judged results, we will focus on those 2,738 that contain 6 or more labels (making no distinction between the crowd and gold labels).

### 3.1.2 FedWeb12 Data

The FedWeb12 collection contains a large amount of sampled data from over a hundred diverse online search engines. It also contains relevance judgments by dedicated assessors, for both snippets and pages, of the first 10 results returned by each of these search engines. The test topics were taken from the TREC 2010 Web Track [8]. For the result snippets, the judgments for the perceived relevance (i.e., the estimate of page relevance, based on the snippet alone) are No, Unlikely, Maybe, and Sure, and for the pages, the levels are Non, relevant Rel, HRel, Key, and Nav. Only for some of the test topics (i.e., the navigational queries), the label Nav applied, and therefore in the current paper we merged it with the Key label. We will focus on the 15 test topics, that were entirely judged by two different assessors. More detailed information on the test topics, relevance judgments, and relevance distributions can be found in [9].

## 3.2 Tendencies in User Disagreement

The crowdsourced relevance judgments from the RelFeedback10 data are very noisy, such that there is a high disagreement among the assessors. For example, only 39% of the crowd assessments agree with the gold label. However, there is a trend toward higher labels for some documents, and lower labels for others, and this observation forms the starting point for the current paper. If we observe the label from one assessor for a particular result to be high, it can be expected that the other labels for that result tend to be high, too. We would like to quantify this effect, and therefore introduce $p_{\mathsf{HRel}|\bullet}$, the conditional probability of observing the highest label HRel, given the observation of a particular relevance label (denoted by •) by another user. One of the goals of this section, is to show that an estimation of $p_{\mathsf{HRel}|\bullet}$ based on only 2 relevance labels per document, approximates a more precise estimate based on a higher number of labels per document.

[1]http://lemurproject.org/clueweb09/

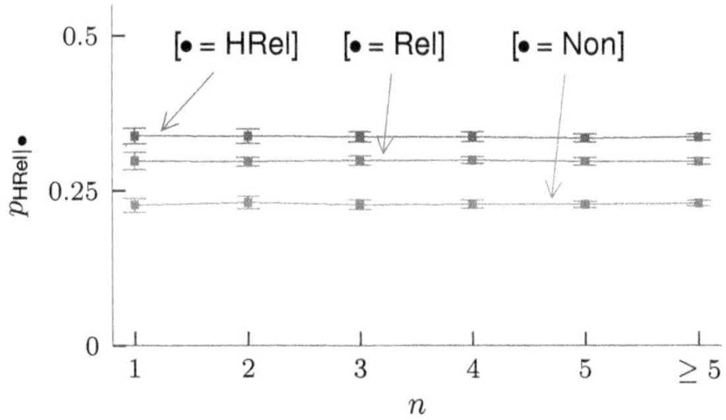


**Figure 1: The probability $p_{\mathsf{HRel}|\bullet}$ of a HRel label, given an observed label • (for • = HRel, Rel, and Non), estimated from $n$ judgments per document, showing the mean (±1 std.) over all documents in the RelFeedback10 data with at least 6 labels.**

In order to estimate, e.g., $p_{\mathsf{HRel}|\mathsf{Rel}}$, we conceived the following experiment. We went through all documents with at least 6 labels, randomly selected one of the labels, and if it was Rel, we calculated the fraction of HRel results among a random subset of $n$ from the remaining labels. Averaging these values over the included documents, yielded our estimate of $p_{\mathsf{HRel}|\mathsf{Rel}}$. In order to verify the influence of which documents were included in the estimation (depending on the random choice of a single label), we repeated this procedure 50 times and calculated the mean and standard deviation of $p_{\mathsf{HRel}|\mathsf{Rel}}$. The results, with indication of the mean and one standard deviation above and below the mean, are shown in Fig. 1, with $n$ varying from 1 to 5. The results are as intuitively expected: $p_{\mathsf{HRel}|\mathsf{HRel}} > p_{\mathsf{HRel}|\mathsf{Rel}} > p_{\mathsf{HRel}|\mathsf{Non}}$, and the estimates tend to be more precise (lower standard deviation) for increasing $n$. Yet, more importantly, the average is already fairly accurate even for $n = 1$: this is a support for our approach taken in Section 4, where we will only use double judgments to estimate similar parameters.

For IR evaluation purposes, finding a suitable choice for the weights of the different relevance levels is typically a problem. As mentioned before, Web search users are mostly interested in top results, i.e., the HRel results for the RelFeedback10 judgments. However, it seems that the weight for a result labeled Non should be almost as high as for a result labeled Rel, given that the average probability that a random other user would assign it the top label HRel, is not much lower. On the one hand, this demonstrates that care is required when relying on these noisy crowd judgments without further filtering. On the other hand, it leads to the following important insight: for a robust evaluation in the case of a large user disagreement, lower relevance levels might have to be promoted more than in the case where all assessors would agree upon the top results. This will be formalized in Section 4, with the introduction of the user disagreement model.

## 3.3 User Disagreement vs. Intra-Judge Inconsistency

Consistency in terms of relevance assessments is often investigated with the purpose of asserting that a test collection is trustworthy for evaluation purposes. We actually want to use the extra information hidden in the user disagreement to our advantage, to obtain intuitive weights for the different relevance labels. In this section we analyze the FedWeb12 relevance judgments, focusing in detail on the consistency in terms of the highest relevance level, i.e., the Key results. We need both inter- and intra-assessor consistency to verify that the user disagreement is really disagreement among users, and distinguishable from inconsistency within a single user's assessments[2].

### *3.3.1 Overlap between users*

Experiments done by Voorhees in [22] gave an average overlap in terms of relevant documents from two sets of binary relevance judgments ranging from 0.42 to 0.49, in the case of expert assessors judging topics on rather homogeneous datasets and a relevance cut-off level corresponding to our Rel level. However, at the top relevance level, different users tend to disagree more often. For the FedWeb12 judgments, the overlap for general Web search engines on Key results is only 0.36, and even lower for the other verticals. In fact, the level up to which the assessors agree can be used to estimate the practical upper limit of precision and recall on the performance of retrieval systems that are evaluated with the assessed test topics. For the TREC-4 data [22], there appeared to be a limit of 65%, whereas it is below 50% for Key relevance on the FedWeb12 data. For a less strict relevance level like Rel (see [9]), the results on the FedWeb12 data appeared comparable to those reported by Voorhees, but then again, in the Web search context, users strongly prefer top relevance.

### *3.3.2 Self-consistency vs. cross-user consistency*

In the following paragraphs, we will demonstrate for the (high-quality) FedWeb12 relevance assessments, that variations in opinion between users dominate the inconsistencies in the judgments. Actually, for this type of relevance judgments we can identify at least three important sources of inconsistencies: (i) judgment errors, (ii) uncertainty for each judge in assigning relevance (also called intra-judge reliability, see [19]), and (iii) inter-user disagreement (elsewhere in this paper shortly called user disagreement), reflected by inter-judge differences. The least important type are plain mistakes. These happen at random with all assessors, and can be due to a sudden drop in concentration, hitting the wrong key when assigning a specific relevance level, etc. However, we observe inconsistencies between judgments from the same assessors, with variations that are too large to stem solely from such random mistakes. Users especially seem to inconsistently assign different adjacent relevance levels, in the case of graded relevance assessments. In the following paragraphs, we will answer two research questions. How important is the intra-judge inconsistency with respect to inter-user disagreement, and can we make a distinction in user disagreement between different relevance levels despite the intra-judge inconsistencies?

[2]However, the *origin* of that user disagreement (e.g., different background knowledge, or even a completely different intent), does not affect the validity of the user disagreement model, introduced in Section 4.

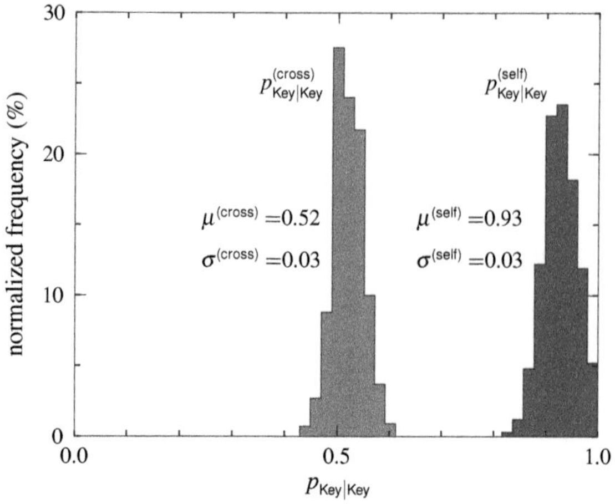


**Figure 2: Normalized histograms of the probability for results labeled Key in one judgment to receive label Key in another, by a different user ('cross'), respectively, the same user ('self').**

The first question we address is to establish self- vs. cross-user inconsistencies. We devised an experiment to obtain a better view on the influence of the self-inconsistency on the apparent difference in opinions between assessors, based on the FedWeb12 data. The resources used for FedWeb12 include several large Web search engines, implying an important overlap in their results for the test topics. From those test topics entirely judged by two assessors, we selected the pages corresponding to those URLs that appeared at least two times per topic, and whose multiple occurences were judged independently by the same judge. We found on average around 3 independent judgments by each of both users for the 387 selected URLs. We used a bootstrap sampling setup to visualize the variance in labels over multiple judgments by the same user for the same result. Assuming that each of the judgments effectively given by one user to a particular result is equally likely, we sampled the sets of judgments to generate single judgment lists for both of the users, which we then used to estimate the parameters $p_{Key|Key}$. A first result is shown in Fig. 2. It shows normalized histograms over 1000 such samples for the probability $p_{Key|Key}$ that Key relevance is assigned in one assessment, given Key relevance from another. The case where both assessments come from the same user, has an average probability $\mu^{(self)} = 0.92$, whereas for different users we get $\mu^{(cross)} = 0.52$. The standard deviation of the histograms reflects the self-inconsistency of one assessor (including possible random errors), and the separation between both histograms corresponds to the difference in opinion between different assessors. Clearly this difference in opinion between users overshadows the uncertainty a single user has.

The second issue to be addressed is whether the assessors' self-inconsistency does not prevent us from making a clear distinction between parameters $p_{Key|\bullet}$ for different relevance levels $\bullet$. Figure 3 shows histograms for $p_{Key|Non}$, $p_{Key|Rel}$, and

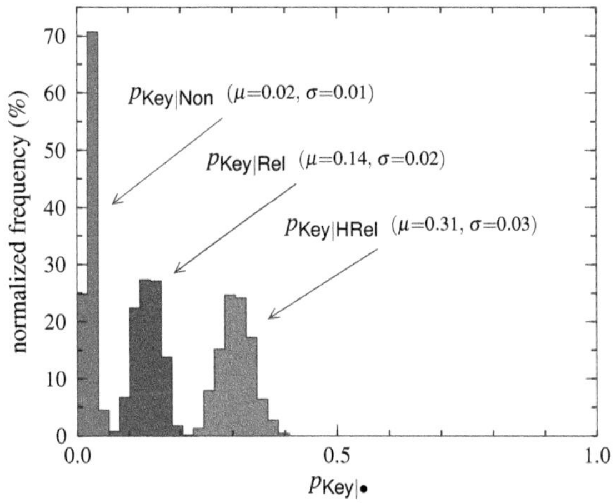


**Figure 3: Influence of self-inconsistency on $p_{\mathsf{Key}|\bullet}$ (for $\bullet$ =HRel, Rel, and Non), the probability that one assessor judges a result Key, given that another assessor judged it with another relevance level.**

$p_{\mathsf{Key|HRel}}$, based on the same set of samples as used for Fig. 2, indicating $\mu$, the mean value of $p_{\mathsf{Key}|\bullet}$, and its standard deviation $\sigma$. These $\mu$ and $\sigma$ lead us to observe that, despite the assesors' self-inconsistencies, we can distinguish the various $p_{\mathsf{Key}|\bullet}$ probabilities very well from each other.

Note that the $p_{\mathsf{Key|Non}}$ estimates are very low for the FedWeb12 data. Hence, we propose to neglect them, when we use the parameters $p_{\mathsf{Key}|\bullet}$ in the context of the UDM (see the next section). The validity of this approximation is further motivated by the fact that the estimated $p_{\mathsf{Key|Non}}$ from our data is an overestimation (related to the fact that only a particular subset of the non-relevant pages were judged, i.e., those with snippet label above No, see [9] for details). Most likely some of the few cases where one user assigns Key relevance to a result that another finds completely non-relevant, are due to the aforementioned random mistakes. Clearly, we do not want that random error to impact global relevance metrics, where large amounts of non-relevant results would erroneously contribute a small but non-neglible amount of relevance (proportional to the non-zero $p_{\mathsf{Key|Non}}$).

# 4. USER DISAGREEMENT MODEL

This section describes the proposed User Disagreement Model (UDM). Based on the experiments from Section 3, we first outline the context and goals for the model. Then we provide a somewhat naive illustration to explain the intuition behind UDM. This is followed by the description of the model itself, together with a verification using the RelFeedback10 data. Finally, we discuss certain subtleties of the model, specific for the FedWeb12 data.

## 4.1 Context and Goal

The UDM is proposed in a Web search context, where we adopt the notion that many users strongly prefer results of the highest relevance level, and are no longer satisfied with partially relevant results, from Kekäläinen and Järvelin [15] and Huang and Efthimiadis [12]. However, there is a significant disagreement on top relevance among assessors, as illustrated by the RelFeedback10 data and the FedWeb12 data in Sections 3.2, respectively, 3.3. It was also shown for the FedWeb12 data that this disagreement among assessors is more important than the uncertainty from a single assessor. We hence propose that the inconsistency among assessors is a *fundamental* difference, also present among actual users (assuming the assessors are representative for these users). The reason for the inter-assessor disagreement can be found partly in the insufficient description of the information need. However, even with a very detailed and unambiguous description, there would always be a difference in opinion, due to a different background knowledge, education, culture, personal taste, etc. Note that, for assessments with a very large variation in relevance (like the RelFeedback10 data), the observed disagreement might be mainly determined by the noisy judgments. However, the validity of the UDM model does not depend on the actual source of disagreement.

The main goals of the UDM are the following. We would like to have an evaluation system that is robust with respect to variations in assessments because of the aforementioned user disagreement. Indeed, search engines would prefer to predict the top-relevant documents for the complete user base, not just a single user (the assessor). Thus, we want to infer what documents would be considered a top result by, e.g., at least 1 out of 4 users, even though we only have, e.g., a single assessor's judgments available.

In the context of evaluation, we designed the UDM as a means to match the weights from graded relevance metrics to the collection under evaluation and the intended users. For example, if relevance assessments obtained by crowdsourcing are highly variable, the relevance levels below top might need a higher weight, in order to fairly take into account those results that would be judged top by many other users, but not the considered assessor. Alternatively, for relevance assessments based on highly precise information needs, the disagreement would be lower, and the relevance levels below top should be given a lower impact, because almost no users with such needs would consider them top.

## 4.2 Intuition

Consider the simple (artifical) configuration sketched in Fig. 4, where a collection of 8 documents is shown with the relevance opinions by 4 users over 4 relevance levels (indicated with different colors) for a particular query. We assume that each user is only interested in results with the top relevance level (indicated with a thick box), in this case corresponding to the relevance label Key. The figure shows a strong variation in assigned relevance grades among the users, which we refer to as the user disagreement. Now, assume that we only have one assessor (indicated with an asterisk), user 3, from whom we can observe the relevance labels. However, if we only return document $d2$ (considered top by the assessor), the other users are not satisfied. Yet, if we are aware of existing user disagreement in general (i.e., not for the specific given query), we could try to please them all, e.g., by returning documents at least one of them considers top. For each of the judgments from the assessor, we want to estimate the probability that one or more users would find the corresponding document a top result. We observe that for results labeled HRel, that probability can be estimated as 1/2 (because in half of the cases where the assessor indicated HRel, at least one of the others labeled it with Key), and for those labeled Rel (slightly relevant), it is only 1/3. As seen from Fig. 4, no one assigns top relevance to

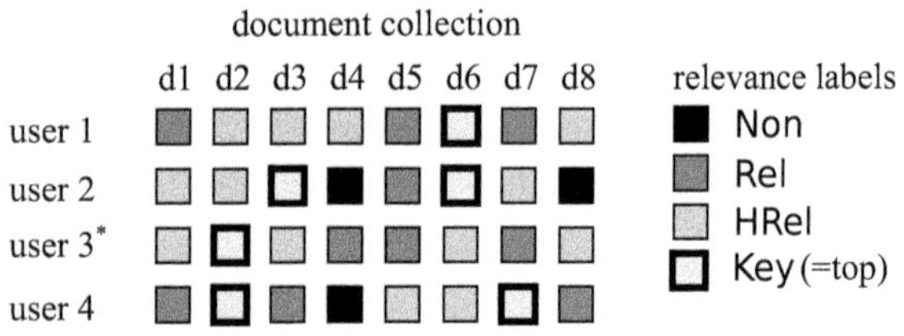


**Figure 4: Illustration of user disagreement for a specific query, with the different colors indicating the graded relevance levels, and the thick black boxes the top results per user.**

a result if another would label it Non, and the corresponding probability is 0. For results labeled Key by the assessor, we already know at least one of the users consider it top, hence the corresponding probability is 1. We can use these probabilities as weights for the respective relevance levels. Going over all the labels from the assessor, we can add these up to count the *effective* number of top results, which turns out to be 4, the number of documents considered top by at least one judge. In order to estimate the required probabilities, we used the relevance opinion of all other users, which in reality are not known. It will turn out that, if we assume all users to have a similar disagreement amongst them, we only need to know which documents one other user considers top.

Now that we have outlined the basic rationale of the UDM, we will more formally address the model details.

## 4.3 UDM Description

Consider a group of users that each want to retrieve top results, but the individual opinions on what results are top, vary amongst them. We define the total set of results considered relevant according to the UDM, as those that would receive the top relevance label $T$ by at least $M$ out of $N$ users (for example, at least one out of three). The parameter that defines the UDM is the probability that a document with one observed label $i$ ($i = 1, \dots, T$) is relevant in that sense, where the assessor belongs to the $N$ considered users. More specifically, this parameter is written $P_{T|i}^{(M/N)}$, and denotes the probability that at least $M$ out of $N$ randomly selected users consider it a top result, given the relevance label $i$ from one of these $N$ users. We call $P_{T|i}^{(M/N)}$ the UDM-based *relevance weight* for level $i$.

We consider $M$ and $N$ to be design parameters, depending on the purpose of the evaluation. For example, for small $M$ and large $N$, the effective number of top results (i.e., according to the UDM) would be higher than the number of top results indicated by a single user, smoothing out differences in opinion among users and effectively leading to a more robust and less strict relevance criterion. The relevance weights can for instance be used to calculate the expected number of relevant results in a result list (with the UDM notion of relevance introduced above), or as the probability of relevance for each result (again, following the UDM), which allows creating an ideally ranked result list as a reference for evaluation.

## 4.4 Estimation of UDM Relevance Weights

Consider the basic scenario with two users, $A$ (the assessor) and $R$ (a random user), and the case $M = 1$ and $N = 2$. For each result, we want to estimate the probability that at least one of these two users labels it top, given the assessor label $i_A$,

$$P_{T|i}^{(1/2)} = Pr\left[i_A = T \vee i_R = T | i_A = i\right]. \quad (1)$$

It turns out that

$$\begin{aligned} P_{T|i}^{(1/2)} &= 1, \quad & i = T, \\ &= p_{T|i}, \quad & i < T. \end{aligned} \quad (2)$$

where $i_R$ is the relevance label assigned by random user, and $i < T$ denotes that level $i$ is below the top level. The parameter $p_{T|i}$ is the probability that we will observe the label $T$ from one user, if we observed the label $i$ from another user, as introduced and investigated in Section 3.2. As shown in Fig. 1, this parameter can be estimated accurately using judgments from only two assessors. Other dependencies, e.g., on the test topics, will be discussed in Section 6.2.

The result described above is trivial, but it can be used to describe more general cases. First, consider the case of $M = 1$, and $N \geq 2$, where we want to estimate the probability that at least one among $N$ users judges the considered document top. We find

$$\begin{aligned} P_{T|i}^{(1/N)} &= 1, \quad & i = T, \\ &= 1 - (1 - p_{T|i})^{N-1}, \quad & i < T, \end{aligned} \quad (3)$$

For the case $i < T$, we assumed the same disagreement behavior and independence between the users. The probability that at least one out of $N$ users considers a result top, given that one of them already assigned level $i$ below top, is the complement of the probability that the $N - 1$ remaining users also consider it below top, and directly leads to (3). Before turning to the more general case, (3) allows making the following observations on the behavior of the relevance model. The probability that at least one out of $N$ users assigns top relevance to a result judged lower by the assessor, goes to one if $N$ is large enough and $p_{T|i} > 0$ (which means there is disagreement among the users, and the considered relevance level is above total non-relevance). If the different judges would always agree on the top relevance level, $P_{T|i}^{(1/N)}$, ($i < T$) would go to zero, and the relevance model would become binary relevance on the top level. These observations agree with our intuition and the prescribed idea of the UDM.

In the most general case, with $0 \leq M \leq N$, we find

$$P_{T|T}^{(M/N)} = \sum_{m=M-1}^{N-1} \binom{N-1}{m} (p_{T|T})^m (1 - p_{T|T})^{N-1-m}, \quad (4)$$

$$P_{T|i}^{(M/N)} = \sum_{m=M}^{N-1} \binom{N-1}{m} (p_{T|i})^m (1 - p_{T|i})^{N-1-m}, \quad i < T(5)$$

These formulas can be derived by summing the probabilities for each allowed configuration (with $M$ or more top results, taking into account the observed label), over all possible combinations of the labels. Alternatively, they can be written down directly from the binomimal cumulative distribution, with the Bernoulli parameter $p_{T|i}$. Using the binomial theorem, it can be easily verified that for the case $M = 1$, expression (5) leads to (3), and (4) becomes 1.

One property of $P_{T|T}^{(M/N)}$ should be mentioned here. If $M > 1$ and there is no perfect agreement on top relevance, $P_{T|T}^{(M/N)} < 1$. This means, for instance, that a result assigned top relevance by the assessor would contribute less than 1

**Table 1: Comparison between experimental values for $P^{(M/N)}_{\mathsf{HRel|Rel}}$, and those predicted with eq. (5), using the RelFeedback10 data.**

| | $P^{(M/N)}_{\mathsf{HRel|Rel}}$ | |
|---|---|---|
| $M$ / $N$ | experimental | prediction |
| 1 / 3 | 0.49 | 0.51 |
| 2 / 3 | 0.10 | 0.09 |
| 2 / 4 | 0.23 | 0.21 |
| 2 / 5 | 0.35 | 0.35 |

to the expected number of relevant results, according to the UDM relevance model with this particular choice of parameters $M$ and $N$. This leads to an effectively even stricter relevance cut-off than the highest relevance level $T$. This may be undesirable in some cases. For example, the expected precision for a set of results all assessed to be top relevant would be below 1, in which case the GAP metric (see Section 5) could not be used for evaluation. By conditioning on more than a single assessment, this problem could be avoided, but in that case, the model would require more than 2 judgment sets for the training topics. Note that the choice of using a single observed relevance judgment in the definition of the UDM is no inherent limitation, although it keeps the model simple. However, we assume that only for a few test topics, we can afford to gather double judgments[3]. For a more complicated model, e.g., with 2 observed labels, the number of parameters to be estimated becomes the square of the number of relevance levels, and too many three-fold judgments would be required to obtain good estimates for these. We therefore focus on the case $\alpha = 1/N$, $N \geq 2$.

## 4.5 Verification

Since the RelFeedback10 relevance assessments contain multiple labels per document, we can easily verify the validity of the prediction formulas for the relevance weights. During the experiment on the RelFeedback10 data described in Section 3.2, we recorded the fraction of cases in which at least $M$ out of the $N$ considered labels were HRel. The resulting estimates for $P^{1/N}_{\mathsf{HRel|Rel}}$ and $P^{1/N}_{\mathsf{HRel|Non}}$ are shown as rectangular markers in Fig. 5, with indication of the error (plus or minus one standard deviation) depending on the chosen sample of documents. The full lines and dotted lines respectively show the values predicted by (3), and the potential error due to inaccuracies in the estimation of $p_{\mathsf{HRel|Rel}}$, respectively, $p_{\mathsf{HRel|Non}}$. Note that these predictions are only valid for integer values of $N$, but were drawn as continuous lines for clarity. There is a clear correspondence, although the experimental values for smaller fractions $1/N$ are slightly lower than the predicted behavior. As a verification of the general formula 5, Table 1 provides a comparison between the experimental and the predicted values for different $M$ and $N$, with again a good correspondence.

[3]Alternative strategies are possible, e.g., by using crowdsourcing techniques to harvest large amounts of cheap but noisy judgments, and filtering out the least trustworthy ones.

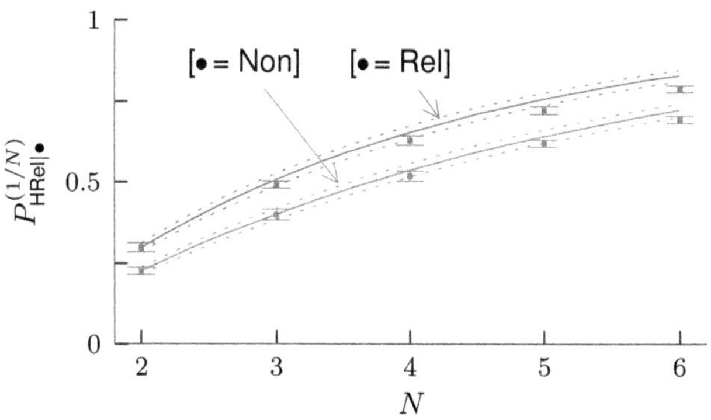


**Figure 5: Comparison between experimental values for $P^{(1/N)}_{\mathsf{HRel|Rel}}$ and $P^{(1/N)}_{\mathsf{HRel|Non}}$ (as the mean ± 1 std., with markers), and those predicted with eq. (3) (full lines), using the RelFeedback10 data.**

# 5. GRADED RELEVANCE METRICS AND THE UDM

This section describes possible ways to incorporate the UDM into the existing graded relevance evaluation metrics nDCG and GAP.

nDCG is a flexible measure, in the sense that it allows the user to define a suitable gain function for weighting the relevance level $i_k$ at position $k$, and a discount function that reflects how fast the contribution of relevant items ranked lower in the result list should decrease. In general, it can be written as follows

$$\mathrm{nDCG}^{(\mathrm{gain})}_{\mathrm{discount}} = \frac{1}{Z}\sum_k \mathrm{gain}(i_k)\,\mathrm{discount}(k) \qquad (6)$$

where $Z$ is a normalization constant that ensures a value of 1 for the ideal ranking. A popular gain function is the exponential $(2^{i_k} - 1)$, which promotes the highest relevance levels, and a typical discount function is the the logarithmic discount $1/\log_2(k+1)$ or the zipfian discount $1/k$. Further information can be found in [14]. These functions are well-chosen heuristics, and we propose to use the relevance weight $P^{(1/N)}_{i_T|i_k}$ of the result at rank $k$ as gain$(i_k)$. Note that the measure still remains inherently heuristic.

GAP is a highly informative and discriminative measure, which has a theoretical foundation and a nice probabilistic interpretation. However, because of these properties we must be careful when incorporating the UDM. The user model on which GAP is based, assumes that each user has a fixed cut-off relevance level, and considers results from any level equal to or higher than this cut-off level as relevant. The relevant parameters for the model are $q_i$, the probability that a user finds a result with relevance level $i$ or higher relevant[4], whereby $q_T = 1$ (for the top relevance level $T$).

[4]The original formulation by Robertson et al. [18] introduces the fundamental parameters $g_i$, the probability that a user finds *only* results with relevance level $i$ or higher relevant, which form a probability distribution over the space of users (with $\sum_{i=1}^{T} g_i = 1$). The parameters $q_i$ introduced above form the corresponding cumulative distribution function, $q_i = \sum_{j=1}^{i} g_j$, and are more convenient to make the link with the UDM.

For a ranked list of $K$ results, GAP is now defined as

$$\text{GAP} = \frac{\sum_{k=1}^{K} \frac{1}{k} \sum_{\kappa=1}^{k} q_{\min(i_\kappa, i_k)}}{\sum_{i=1}^{T} R_i\, q_i} \tag{7}$$

in which $R_i$ is the number of results with relevance level $i$ in the result list. It can be shown that the denominator of this expression represents the expected number of relevant results in the list, based on the probabilistic user model. In the special case where all users would have their relevance cut-off at the highest level ($q_i = 0$, $\forall i < T$), the denominator becomes the number of top results, and GAP becomes the average precision measure based on binary relevance at highest level $T$.

To our knowledge, the UDM cannot be directly translated into the user model underlying GAP, because the former is defined over different relevance opinions for a *result*, whereas the latter is based on varying user opinions for each *relevance level*. Nevertheless, all required parallels are there to apply the UDM to GAP. To do so, we only need to replace $q_i$ in (7) by the UDM relevance weights $P_{T|i}^{(1/N)}$. The denominator then denotes the expected number of top results according to the probabilistic UDM, and if all users had the same opinion, the GAP would also become the average precision at the top level. A similar derivation of GAP as in [18] could be done based on the UDM (whereby the cumulative user disagreement probability distribution to start from would be the ordered series of $P_{T|i}^{(1/N)}$ parameters), but would be somewhat artificial and is left out due to length restrictions. We however propose that the interesting fundamental properties of GAP remain valid even when based on the UDM.

# 6. ROBUSTNESS OF THE UDM

## 6.1 UDM-based Evaluation

We propose that UDM-based evaluation is more robust than when based on a single set of relevance judgments, and motivate it with following experiment. We again consider the double-judged test topics from the FedWeb12 dataset. The evaluation is considered robust, if two different relevance judgment sets for a particular test topic yield similar results. We use a leave-one-out cross-validation setting, whereby we present the average and standard deviation of a number of metrics over each of the test topics, based on the parameters estimated from the others. For the considered test topic, we used one judgment set as the reference, and the other as the 'retrieved' set (creating a ranked set by ranking according to descending relevance levels). The first metric considered is average precision (AP), based on binary Key relevance. We also consider $\text{GAP}^{(1/N)}$ for $N$ values of 2, 3, and 4. Finally, we report $\text{nDCG}_d^{(g)}$ for different gains $g$ and discount functions $d$. For the gain, (exp) denotes the traditional exponential gain, whereas $(1/N)$ means the coefficients $P_{\text{Key}|\bullet}^{(1/N)}$ are used as gain function. As discount functions, we report results for the logarithmic $(1/\log_2 n)$ and zipfian $(1/n)$ case. The results are shown in Table 2. The listed metrics would all be one if both judges had agreed upon Key relevance. A lower value indicates a larger difference between both baselines for the considered metric, and will lead to a larger dependency on the particular baseline when the metric is applied to a candidate ranking. The AP

**Table 2: Mutual evaluation of paired judgment sets with different evaluation metrics (mean ± 1 std.).**

| | |
|---|---|
| AP | 0.48 ± 0.28 |
| $\text{GAP}^{(1/2)}$ | 0.65 ± 0.18 |
| $\text{GAP}^{(1/3)}$ | 0.69 ± 0.16 |
| $\text{GAP}^{(1/4)}$ | 0.71 ± 0.16 |
| $\text{nDCG}_{\text{zipf}}^{(\text{exp})}$ | 0.70 ± 0.23 |
| $\text{nDCG}_{\log}^{(\text{exp})}$ | 0.86 ± 0.09 |
| $\text{nDCG}_{\log}^{(1/2)}$ | 0.84 ± 0.11 |
| $\text{nDCG}_{\log}^{(1/3)}$ | 0.87 ± 0.09 |
| $\text{nDCG}_{\log}^{(1/4)}$ | 0.89 ± 0.07 |

metric appears to be the least robust. The reported AP value of 0.48 means that an AP of 0.48 is the maximum value that can be used to compare retrieval algorithms (if one wants to judge on the strict notion of Key relevance), because the judges only agree up to this level. Whereas the AP corresponds to taking a single user's opinion into account, the GAP results (which consider those results relevant that would be judged Key by at least one out of $N$ users) increase for higher $N$, leading to a more robust evaluation. This effectively means that the below-top relevance levels get a higher weight. A similar behavior is observed for the nDCG measures $\text{nDCG}_{\log}^{(1/N)}$, based on the same weights. The fact that this metric appears to be much more robust than GAP, is due to the logarithmic discount function, where exchanging a Key result in the top with a lower result on a lower rank is penalized less heavily than for nDCG with the zipfian discount function, or GAP.

## 6.2 Parameter Dependencies

In previous sections we assumed that the parameters $p_{T|i}$ are constant over the considered collection. For the RelFeedback10 experiments from Section 3.2, they were calculated by sampling over all documents. Sometimes, however, better choices should be made due to the inhomegeneous character of the test collection, as is the case for the FedWeb12 data. Two sources of inhomogeneity will be shortly discussed in the following paragraphs: the type of test topics, and the origin of the results.

For test topics with an information need description in the sense of '*The user is looking for information about ...*' (as is mostly the case for the topics used in the FedWeb12 judgments), the $p_{i_T|i_t}$ will probably be higher than for cases where the information need is described in finer detail. The test topics were originally designed for the TREC 2010 Web Track that focused on result diversity, and can be divided into ambiguous topics (with multiple distinct interpretations), or faceted (with different possible aspects of the same interpretation), see [8]. Among our twice judged topics, 7 are ambiguous and 8 are faceted. The comparison of the parameters $p_{\text{Key}|\bullet}$ estimated separately for the different types of topics, see Table 3 shows that for the ambiguous queries there is a higher chance that assessors strongly disagree ($p_{\text{Key}|\text{Rel}}$ is larger), whereas for the faceted topics the distinction between both highest relevance levels is less clear ($p_{\text{Key}|\text{HRel}}$ is higher). In this paper, we do not make any further distinction between both types of topics and use the parameter estimates for all test topics together. However, different parameter sets could be used for evalution scenar-

Table 3: **Dependency of the parameters $p_{T|i}$ on the test topics (ambiguous vs. faceted), result list quality, and result ranks (top 5 vs. top 10).**

| # results | top 5 | | top 10 | | top 10 | |
|---|---|---|---|---|---|---|
| test topics | all | | all | | ambig. | facet. |
| high-quality | no | yes | no | yes | yes | |
| $p_{\mathsf{Key}\|\mathsf{Rel}}$ | 0.03 | 0.16 | 0.02 | **0.15** | 0.18 | 0.13 |
| $p_{\mathsf{Key}\|\mathsf{HRel}}$ | 0.09 | 0.25 | 0.06 | **0.23** | 0.22 | 0.26 |

ios where a distinction is needed. In future work, we will study the influence of the test topics with the much larger FedWeb13 test collection, for which the test topics are less homogeneous (see Demeester et al. [10]).

The judged results can be grouped as lists of 10 results per query and per resource (i.e., the top 10 results for that query from each of a wide variety of search engines). A large fraction of the search engines produced only non-relevant results for most queries. However, some search engines (e.g., general Web search engines) provided high-quality result lists. We can, for example, expect the following: when we only consider the low-quality resources, the probability that one user would give a Key label for a result labeled Rel by another, will probably be much lower than when we only look at result lists from strong search engines. Using an overall average for $p_{T|i}$ would hence lead to a value effectively too low for the test results of interest (i.e., those that originate from potentially interesting resources). In our experimental setting, we made a distinction between low- and high-quality result lists. Those with at least one Key result are considered high-quality lists, and the others low-quality. Table 3 displays $p_{\mathsf{Key}|\mathsf{Rel}}$ and $p_{T|i}$, calculated separately for both groups of result lists (indicated with 'high-quality' in the table). The difference is very large, as expected. For the current paper, we decided to only use the high-quality result lists to estimate these parameters (indicated in bold in Table 3). This implicates that the evaluation of the higher relevance grades is more accurate, whereas the over-estimated influence of the lower relevance levels is still small. For example, with GAP, the influence of lower ranked results is discounted rapidly, and therefore the potentially long tail of results with a low relevance hardly contributes to the final score, despite an over-estimated weight of $p_{\mathsf{Key}|\mathsf{low}}$.

For other search scenarios, other choices are possible. For example, for a single ranked result list in general (i.e., not in the federated search context), one might consider only the top-$k$ results for all doubly judged test queries, especially in combination with a metric that is calculated up to a rank $k$. As a demonstration that the considered position in the ranked list does influence our parameters, we estimated them from the top-5, respectively from the top-10, of each result list (see Table 3). The estimated $p_{i_T|i_t}$ values are consistently but only moderately higher for the lists with the higher average quality, i.e., the top-5 lists.

The above analysis has brought up some clear difficulties in estimating the parameters in a consistent way. It should be noted that most of these issues could be translated into similar issues within the probabilistic user model that Robertson et al. [18] proposed, where the required parameters are assumed constant as well.

# 7. APPLICATION

In Demeester et al. [9] it is demonstrated that the perceived relevance based on the snippet is often not in line with the actual page relevance, and that ideally a Web IR system should be evaluated based on the relevance experienced by the user, when the snippet and page relevance are combined. This means, e.g., that top pages behind bad snippets should be penalized when ranked at the top. One straightforward way to do that, is by creating combined relevance levels consisting of all combinations between relevance levels for pages and snippets. Examples are (Maybe, HRel), or (Sure, Rel), where we first mention the snippet level, followed by the page level. The experienced top relevance level in this context is defined as the combination of the top levels for snippets and pages separately, i.e., (Sure, Key).

A direct application of metrics like nDCG or GAP is difficult, because these would require an ordering according to relevance of these combined relevance levels. Yet, from the viewpoint of the user, should (Maybe, HRel) be the higher label, or rather (Sure, Rel)? We apply the UDM to find relevance weights with a probabilistic interpretation. The results are shown in Table 4, for $M/N = 1/3$. Each row presents a possible combined relevance level, and the rows are ordered for decreasing values of $P^{(1/3)}_{(\mathsf{Sure},\mathsf{Key}|\mathsf{L}_{\mathsf{snippet}},\mathsf{L}_{\mathsf{page}})}$, where $\mathsf{L}_{\mathsf{snippet}}$ and $\mathsf{L}_{\mathsf{page}}$ denote the different snippet, respectively, page relevance levels. For example, $P^{(1/3)}_{(\mathsf{Sure},\mathsf{Key}|\mathsf{Maybe},\mathsf{HRel})} = 0.31$ means that there is a 31% chance that at least one out of three users would assign the top relevance level (Sure, Key) to a result, given that we observed one of them assigning the snippet label Maybe and the page label HRel. For comparison, the relevance weights based on page relevance alone, are given as well. It appears that a snippet judgment below Sure leads to a degradation of the combined relevance, with respect to the corresponding relevance weight for the page relevance alone.

There are many combined relevance levels, and given a limited number of twice judged topics, we can therefore doubt the accuracy of all calculated parameters. For example, we only found 36 cases where one assessor judged a result as (No, HRel), and only in five of those cases the other assessor assigned top relevance to the same result. The result of 0.26 for $\alpha = 1/3$ is therefore most likely a poor estimate of the actual probability. Those relevance levels for which less than 50 cases were present in the data (an arbitrarily chosen boundary), are indicated between brackets, as being not accurate. However, the less accurate such an estimate becomes, the less often these cases appear in the collection, and the less influence possible variations of the estimates have on global evaluation scores. For the cases that often occur, the estimate is more accurate, and these most strongly influence the evaluation results. For example, there were 372 occurences of (Maybe, HRel) in our twice judged topics, with 87 matching top judgments by the other judge.

# 8. CONCLUSIONS

We introduced the probabilistic User Disagreement Model, which models fundamental differences in opinion on relevance among users. Empirical results were given based on two recent test collections (the TREC'10 Relevance Feedback judgments, and the FedWeb12 collection), and we provided insights into issues related to user disagreement, such

**Table 4: Relevance weights for combined (snippet, page) relevance levels, and for page levels alone (with brackets indicating where less than 50 judgments were found).**

| $L_{snippet}$ | $L_{page}$ | $P^{(1/3)}_{(Sure,Key \mid L_{snippet},L_{page})}$ | $P^{(1/3)}_{Key \mid L_{page}}$ |
|---|---|---|---|
| Sure | Key | 1 | 1 |
| Maybe | Key | 0.42 | |
| Sure | HRel | 0.41 | 0.41 |
| Unlikely | Key | (0.38) | |
| No | Key | (0.34) | |
| Maybe | HRel | 0.31 | |
| Sure | Rel | 0.29 | 0.28 |
| No | HRel | (0.26) | |
| Maybe | Rel | 0.20 | |
| Unlikely | HRel | (0.13) | |
| Unlikely | Rel | 0.13 | |
| No | Rel | 0.12 | |
| (any) | Non | 0 | 0 |

as the influence of intra-assessor inconsistencies, and the robustness of the UDM-based probability estimations. It was also shown how the model could be incorporated into the graded relevance metrics nDCG and GAP, as such allowing these measures to take into account user disagreement. As an illustration, the model was used to estimate the required relevance weights for the combined evaluation of snippet and page relevance in a federated Web search context.

This paper's main contributions are theoretical, and in future contributions we will reap the benefits in more tangible results, by evaluating actual retrieval results.

## 9. ACKNOWLEDGMENTS

This work was funded by Ghent University - iMinds in Belgium, by the EU Project AXES (FP7-269980), the Netherlands Organization for Scientific Research (NWO), grants 639.022.809 and 640.005.002 (FACT), and the Dutch national project COMMIT.

## 10. REFERENCES


[1] R. Agrawal, S. Gollapudi, A. Halverson, and S. Ieong. Diversifying search results. In *WSDM '09*, pages 5–14. ACM, 2009.

[2] P. Bailey, N. Craswell, I. Soboroff, P. Thomas, A. P. de Vries, and E. Yilmaz. Relevance assessment: are judges exchangeable and does it matter. In *SIGIR '08*, pages 667–674. ACM, 2008.

[3] C. Buckley, M. Lease, and M. D. Smucker. Overview of the TREC 2010 Relevance Feedback Track. In *TREC*, 2010.

[4] R. Burgin. Variations in relevance judgments and the evaluation of retrieval performance. *Information Processing & Management*, 28(5):619 – 627, 1992.

[5] B. Carterette and I. Soboroff. The effect of assessor error on IR system evaluation. In *SIGIR'10*, pages 539–546. ACM, 2010.

[6] B. Carterette, V. Pavlu, H. Fang, and E. Kanoulas. Million Query Track 2009 Overview. In *TREC*, 2009.

[7] C. L. A. Clarke, M. Kolla, and O. Vechtomova. An effectiveness measure for ambiguous and underspecified queries. In *ICTIR'09*, volume 5766, pages 188–199. Springer, 2009.

[8] C. L. A. Clarke, N. Craswell, I. Soboroff, and G. V. Cormack. Overview of the TREC 2010 Web Track. *TREC*, pages 1–9, 2010.

[9] T. Demeester, D. Nguyen, D. Trieschnigg, C. Develder, and D. Hiemstra. What Snippets Say about Pages in Federated Web Search. In *AIRS'12*, pages 250–261, 2012.

[10] T. Demeester, D. Trieschnigg, D. Nguyen, and D. Hiemstra. Overview of the TREC 2013 Federated Web Search Track. *TREC*, 2013.

[11] M. Hosseini, I. J. Cox, N. Milić-frayling, G. Kazai, and V. Vinay. On Aggregating Labels from Multiple Crowd Workers to Infer Relevance of Documents. *ECIR'12*, pages 182–194, 2012.

[12] J. Huang and E. N. Efthimiadis. Analyzing and Evaluating Query Reformulation Strategies in Web Search Logs. *CIKM'09*, pages 77–86. ACM, 2009.

[13] K. Järvelin and J. Kekäläinen. Cumulated gain-based evaluation of ir techniques. *ACM Trans. Inf. Syst.*, 20 (4):422–446, 2002.

[14] E. Kanoulas and J. A. Aslam. Empirical Justification of the Gain and Discount Function for nDCG. In *CIKM'09*, pages 611–620, 2009.

[15] J. Kekäläinen and K. Järvelin. Using Graded Relevance Assessments in IR Evaluation. *Journal of the American Society for Information Science and Technology*, 53(13):1120–1129, 2002.

[16] A. Moffat and J. Zobel. Rank-biased precision for measurement of retrieval effectiveness. *ACM Trans. Inf. Syst.*, 27(1):2:1–2:27, 2008.

[17] D. Nguyen, T. Demeester, D. Trieschnigg, and D. Hiemstra. Federated Search in the Wild: the Combined Power of over a Hundred Search Engines. In *CIKM'12*, pages 1874–1878. ACM, 2012.

[18] S. E. Robertson, E. Kanoulas, and E. Yilmaz. Extending Average Precision to Graded Relevance Judgments. In *SIGIR'10*, pages 603–610, 2010.

[19] F. Scholer, A. Turpin, and M. Sanderson. Quantifying test collection quality based on the consistency of relevance judgements. In *SIGIR'11*, pages 1063–1072. ACM, 2011.

[20] M. D. Smucker and C. L. A. Clarke. Modeling User Variance in Time-Biased Gain. *HCIR'12*, 2012.

[21] A. Turpin, F. Scholer, K. Järvelin, M. Wu, and J. S. Culpepper. Including Summaries in System Evaluation. *SIGIR'09*, pages 508-515. ACM, 2009.

[22] E. Voorhees. Variations in relevance judgments and the measurement of retrieval effectiveness. *Information Processing and Management*, 36:697–716, 2000.

[23] E. Yilmaz, J. A. Aslam, and S. Robertson. A new rank correlation coefficient for information retrieval. In *SIGIR'08*, pages 587–594. ACM, 2008.

[24] E. Yilmaz, M. Shokouhi, N. Craswell, and S. E. Robertson. Expected browsing utility for web search evaluation. *CIKM'10*, pages 1561-1564. ACM, 2010.

[25] C. X. Zhai, W. W. Cohen, and J. Lafferty. Beyond independent relevance: methods and evaluation metrics for subtopic retrieval. In *SIGIR'03*, pages 10–17. ACM, 2003.

# Improving Search Relevance for Short Queries in Community Question Answering

Haocheng Wu*
University of Science and Technology of China
Hefei, China
ustcwhc@outlook.com

Wei Wu
Microsoft Research
No. 5 Danling Street, Haidian District
Beijing, China
wuwei@microsoft.com

Ming Zhou
Microsoft Research
No. 5 Danling Street, Haidian District
Beijing, China
mingzhou@microsoft.com

Enhong Chen
University of Science and Technology of China
Hefei, China
cheneh@ustc.edu.cn

Lei Duan
Microsoft
1020 Enterprise Way
SunnyVale, CA, US
Lei.Duan@microsoft.com

Heung-Yeung Shum
Microsoft Research
One Microsoft Way
Redmond, WA, US
hshum@microsoft.com

## ABSTRACT

Relevant question retrieval and ranking is a typical task in community question answering (CQA). Existing methods mainly focus on long and syntactically structured queries. However, when an input query is short, the task becomes challenging, due to a lack information regarding user intent. In this paper, we mine different types of user intent from various sources for short queries. With these intent signals, we propose a new intent-based language model. The model takes advantage of both state-of-the-art relevance models and the extra intent information mined from multiple sources. We further employ a state-of-the-art learning-to-rank approach to estimate parameters in the model from training data. Experiments show that by leveraging user intent prediction, our model significantly outperforms the state-of-the-art relevance models in question search.

## Categories and Subject Descriptors

H.3.3 [**Information Storage and Retrieval**]: Information Search and Retrieval—*Retrieval models*

## Keywords

community question answering, question search, short query, user intent

## 1. INTRODUCTION

In the last decade, many community question answering (CQA) archives such as Yahoo! Answers, Quora, and Baidu Knows have emerged and accumulated a large number of questions, answers, and users. Many question-answer pairs on these sites are of high quality, attracting more and more attention on how to leverage historical content to answer new queries.

One way to leverage content in CQA archives is for the system to search the existing questions when users submit their queries and reuse the answers for relevant questions. Many studies have been conducted along this line [28, 26, 29, 15]. Existing methods usually focus on long and syntactically structured queries. However, we have found that when searching CQA archives, users influenced by web search are used to issuing short queries. For example, we collected a one-day search log of Yahoo! Answers and found that 24% of queries were shorter than 4 words and incomplete sentences. Basically speaking, for many users, organizing their information needs via long queries is more difficult than simply typing several keywords. Therefore, besides long queries, considering short queries in CQA question search is also important. On the other hand, on many CQA sites, the search results are not satisfactory when an input query is short. For example, we found that in Yahoo! Answers, the first result for the query "surface battery" was irrelevant to the new "Microsoft Surface Tablet", although most likely the user making the query expected to see questions about the battery performance of the new product[1]. The bad performance of search engines on popular CQA sites further demonstrates the importance and challenge of improving search relevance for short queries.

In this paper, we examine how to improve search relevance for short queries in CQA question search. One big challenge for short query search in CQA is how to understand the underlying search intent in short queries. On the one hand, understanding user search intent is the key to improving search relevance. For example, in the log of Yahoo! Answers, we found that someone issued a query "bad esn", browsed several search results, and finally clicked on the question, "How to fix a bad ESN number?" For this query, people usually want to see something about "fixing the bad

*The work is done when the author is an intern at Microsoft Research Asia

[1]The first returned question was "How long should my laptop have lasted? Is this worth complaining to customer care over?" before we submit the draft.


*WSDM'14*, February 24–28, 2014, New York, New York, USA.

http://dx.doi.org/10.1145/2556195.2556239.

esn issue on their cell phones", and thus results like "how to fix a bad esn number" should be highly ranked. However, without an understanding of the intent, it is hard to achieve this goal. On the other hand, understanding the underlying search intent in short queries is quite difficult, because short queries usually convey less information. More seriously, signals in CQA data that can facilitate search intent understanding are very sparse, which makes the task even more challenging. For example, unlike web pages, there is little anchor information in CQA data.

In this paper, we propose a model for improving the search relevance of short queries in CQA. To the best of our knowledge, we are the first to study this problem. Specifically, we mine search intent from question descriptions in CQA archives, web query logs, and web search results. Different types of sources provide us different types of signals and reveal user intent from different perspectives. From question descriptions, we obtain some specific and question-oriented intent; from web search logs, we gain an understanding of the pervasive preference of common web users; and from the top web search results, we further distill some of the popular topics related to the short queries. With the intent prediction, we propose a new intent-based language model. The model measures the relevance between a short query and a candidate question based on not only the query itself but also the underlying intent hidden behind the query. The final relevance is calculated as a linear combination of the similarity from the original query and the similarity from the associated intent. To further improve the model, we employ LambdaMART [6], which is a state-of-the-art learning to rank approach, to learn the parameters in the model from training data. With all the extra sources and supervision, our model can select highly relevant questions that match the information needs of short queries.

We conducted our experiments with data sets from Yahoo! Answers and Quora for short queries with an average length of 1.94. Yahoo! Answers is the largest and the most popular CQA site in the English world, while Quora is a rapidly growing CQA site and famous for its high quality content [25]. We compared our model with a number of state-of-the-art relevance models in CQA question search. The experimental results showed that our model significantly improves the performance of question ranking for short queries over the baseline methods.

Our contributions in this paper are 3-fold: (1) a proposal for improving search relevance for short queries in CQA; (2) a proposal for an intent-based language model by leveraging search intent that is mined from CQA, web search logs, and web search results; (3) the empirical verification of the efficacy of the proposed method on data from two popular CQA sites, Yahoo! Answers and Quora.

The rest of the paper is organized as follows. Section 2 introduces related work. Section 3 describes the methods of search intent mining. Section 4 provides the specifics of our model. Section 5 presents the experiments and finally Section 6 concludes the paper.

# 2. RELATED WORK

## 2.1 Question Search

Burke, et al. [7] retrieved semantically similar questions from frequently asked questions (FAQ) using a WordNet dictionary and a maker-passing algorithm [22]. In recent years, most retrieval models are based on language models [23]. Translation-based language models were proposed by interpolating translation probabilities into language models. The translation probabilities, including word-to-word translation probability [15] and phrase-to-phrase translation probability [29], are learnt from question-question pairs [15], question-description pairs [18], and question-answer pairs [28]. In addition to translation-based models, Cao, et al. [8] proposed a language model with leaf category smoothing in which they considered leveraging category information specified by users to improve search relevance. Duan, et al. [12] proposed a mixture model to extract topic and focus from questions and incorporated the information into language models. Wang, et al. [26] developed a tree kernel-based syntactic tree matching method to find similar questions. These work provides different ways to retrieve relevant questions from CQA archives. However, none of them considers the question retrieval problem for short queries.

Recently, Liu, et al. [19] proposed predicting web searcher satisfaction with question-answers from CQA. They extracted features that measure query clarity, query-question matching, and answer quality, and learned a regression model to predict how a question-answer pair in CQA could satisfy a web searcher's information needs. Compared with their work, we focus on understanding intent behind short queries and leveraging query expansion techniques to match query and questions in CQA, which goes beyond keyword matching as in Liu, et al.'s work.

## 2.2 User Intent Mining

User intent can be mined from a variety of sources. In CQA archives, in order to make their information needs clear, askers sometimes supply descriptions for their questions. These descriptions specify the askers' requests and thus can be used to mine the askers' information needs. Li, et al. [18] treated questions and the corresponding question descriptions as source-target pairs and employed a translation model to predict the askers' intent for ambiguous questions. In web search, user behavior when searching and clicking reflects their preference for particular search results. Therefore, user behavior implicitly indicates their search intent. Hu, et al. [13] leveraged web query logs and represented search intent in queries by subtopics mined from co-clicked queries and documents, where each subtopic was represented by a cluster of query expansions and clicked URLs. In addition to question descriptions in CQA and web search logs, search results can also be utilized to mine user intent for queries. For example, Wang, et al. [27] extracted text fragments containing query terms from the search results and clustered them into subtopics. In this paper, we have leveraged user intent mined from various sources to improve the relevance of short queries in CQA question search. Recently, Chen, et al. [10] proposed improving question search relevance with user intent. There is a stark difference between our work and theirs. We focus on short queries, while they deal with long questions.

## 2.3 Relevance Ranking

Relevance ranking is one of the key components of web search. Given a query, documents[2] are retrieved and ordered according to their relevance to the query. The relevance between a query and a document can be measured by relevance

[2]In this work, the documents are questions.

models. Traditional relevance models, such as BM25 [24], Language Model for Information Retrieval [16, 23], and dependency model [2, 3] based on Markov Random Field [21], are hand-crafted with a few parameters left for manually tuning. Recently, a supervised learning approach, namely learning-to-rank, has proven to be very affective at the automatic construction of relevance models for web search [17, 20]. In this paper, we also employ a learning-to-rank approach to learn the parameters of a model particularly designed for short query search in CQA.

# 3. USER INTENT MINING

Understanding user intent is the key to improving the relevance of a short query in a CQA question search due to the heterogeneity of query and question. It is common for one short query to relate to multiple candidate questions. On the other hand, searchers are usually only interested in questions whose content matches their intent. In this paper, we aim to select questions that match a user's main search intent hidden behind short queries. Search intent can be represented via subtopics of queries, and the subtopics can be discovered by tracking user behavior from various sources. Basically speaking, after issuing a short query, most question searchers expect to see results that relate to two aspects of the query: (1) the most interesting or the most important aspect of the query. For example, "pyramids", "history", and "ancient" for query "egypt". (2) The most popular subtopic of the query. For example, "brotherhood" and "revolution" for "egypt". The two types of intent represent different user preferences related to their queries, and it is hard to mine them from a single source.

We mine user intent from three different sources: question descriptions in CQA archives, web search logs, and the top search results from a commercial search engine. Basically speaking, data from the three different sources contains different aspects of a query: the intent signals mined from descriptions reveal an asker's specific needs for a question; the web search log conveys common preferences about the query; and the top search results displayed by popular search engines such as Google, Bing, and Yahoo contain popular subtopics related to the query. For each type of intent, we extract several keywords and assign each keyword a weight.

## 3.1 Intent Mining from CQA Archives

In CQA archives, askers are allowed to supply supplementary descriptions to their questions. The descriptions further clarify the askers' information needs in addition to the questions. For example, for the question "Why do you love Baltimore?", the words "Maryland" and "Charm City" in the description are quite useful to distinguish which Baltimore city is asking about, since there are more than 10 cities named "Baltimore"[3]. Therefore, descriptions are particularly useful for discovering an asker's specific intent.

To extract intent from the descriptions, we treat the questions as sources and the corresponding descriptions as targets, and train a term-to-term translation model. We employ the method proposed by [18] to predict user intent for short queries. Formally, given a short query Q, we rank terms by $P_{cqa}(t|q)$, where $P_{cqa}(t|q)$ is defined as

$$P_{cqa}(t|q) = \varepsilon \sum_{w \in q} P_{tp}(t|w) P_{ml}(w|q) + (1-\varepsilon) P_{ml}(t|C). \quad (1)$$

[3] `http://en.wikipedia.org/wiki/Baltimore_(disambiguation)`

In Equation (1), $P_{tp}(t|w)$ represents the translation probability from term $w$ in query $q$ to term $t$. $P_{ml}(w|q)$ is the maximum likelihood for term $w$ estimated from query $q$, and $P_{ml}(t|C)$ is the smoothing item estimated from a large corpus $C$. $0 \le \varepsilon \le 1$ is the parameter for a trade-off between the translation based likelihood and the smoothing item. In practice, we have found $\varepsilon = 0.3$ gives the optimal results.

With Equation (1), we rank the terms and select those with high probabilities as defined by $P_{cqa}(t|q)$ to represent the hidden intent. By this means we get the intent word set $W = \{(t, \varphi)\}$ from CQA archives, where $t$ is the intent term and $\varphi$ is the weight as defined by $P_{cqa}(t|q)$.

## 3.2 Intent Mining from Query Log

Most question searchers are also web users. Many searchers are accustomed to submitting their queries to search engines and browsing web pages before they search for answers in a CQA archive [11]. Therefore, user behavior tracked by a search engine or browser is another valuable source for understanding search intent in short queries.

In this paper, in addition to descriptions of questions, we also leverage large-scale query logs to mine user intent for short queries. Compared with those mined from question descriptions, intent mined from query logs represents more general information needs of common searchers. For example, for the query "beijing", the top intent mined from the query log is "travel". Therefore, we can guess that most searchers of "beijing" are interested in travel guides. On the other hand, the top intent mined from question descriptions is "olympics", which means that most askers would like to know something about the 2008 Summer Olympics in Beijing.

We mine user intent from a query log of a commercial search engine. Specifically, we employ the method proposed by Hu, et al. [13] and represent search intent behind short queries with subtopics. Given a query, the method collects queries that share the same suffix or prefix and aggregates the co-clicked URLs of these queries. After that, queries and URLs are clustered based on word overlap and the similarity of co-click patterns. Each cluster represents one subtopic of the original query and thus can be used to mine user intent. We extract intent from both the queries and URLs in the top subtopic cluster, since the top cluster represents a user's primary intent. For queries, we weight each suffix or prefix with click numbers and select the terms with high click numbers; For URLs, we first remove stop words and conduct stemming and then we calculate term frequencies and select the terms with high frequencies. After individual normalization of the numbers, we merge the terms from queries and URLs to get the intent word set $W = \{(t, \varphi)\}$, where $t$ is the intent term and $\varphi$ is the weight from queries or URLs. In this way, we leverage both the related queries and clicked documents to predict the pervasive intent of searchers.

## 3.3 Intent Mining from Web Search Results

With question descriptions in CQA archives and query logs, it is easy for us to mine some interesting subtopics related to short queries. However, the intent of some queries is time-sensitive. For these queries, understanding the current context of the intent is more important but hard to achieve with the sources mentioned above. For example, for the query "xbox", since Microsoft just announced the new console "Xbox ONE", questions about the new product may

**Algorithm 1:** Intent Mining from Web Search Results

**Input**: Query $q$, top $M$ search results $R$, window size $l$, weight parameters $\eta, \sigma, \tau$

**Output**: Intent term set $W = \{(t, \varphi)\}$

```
H ← titles of documents in R;
S ← snippets of documents in R;
U ← URLs of documents in R;
A ← concatenate T,S and U as a single string;
L ← length of A;
F ← {(t, f)} = ∅;
for i: 1 to L do
  if A[i] ∈ q then
    for j: −l to l do
      if F contains key A[i + j] then
        F[A[i + j]] ← F[A[i + j]] + 1;
      else
        F ← F ∪ (A[i + j], 1);
W ← {(t, φ)} = ∅;
for each (t, φ) ∈ F do
  φ ← 0;
  for each h ∈ H do
    φ+ = η · BM25(t, h, H);
  for each s ∈ S do
    φ+ = σ · BM25(t, s, S);
  for each u ∈ U do
    φ+ = τ · BM25(t, u, U);
  φ ← φ · f;
  W ← W ⋃{(t, φ)};
rank W in descending order of φ;
return W;
```

be more attractive than those about "Xbox 360". The intent "Xbox ONE" can be mined from the top search results (particularly, news about the Xbox), but it is hard to discern from query logs and question descriptions, since the Xbox 360 still dominates these sources.

Mining user intent from web search results has been studied by several researchers [1, 27]. The existing work adopts offline processing on web pages and thus is not able to capture the timely evolution of search intent on web pages. In this paper, we propose an online method to extract popular intent for short queries from the top search results.

Given a query, we crawl the newest search results from a commercial search engine and parse URLs, titles, and snippets of the top $M$ documents. For each query term, we calculate the frequency of co-occurrence terms within a fixed window size in URLs, titles, and snippets, and then collect these terms and their frequencies to form an intent candidate set. For each term in the candidate set, we calculate its BM25 scores with the URLs, the titles, and the snippets. We heuristically set a weight for each field (URL/title/snippet) and define a final score as a weighted linear combination of BM25 scores in the three fields. Each term in the candidate set is ranked based on the final score, and we pick terms with high scores as user intent mined from web search results.

Algorithm 1 shows the pseudo code for mining intent that is currently relevant for short queries from top search results. We heuristically set $\{\eta, \sigma, \tau, M, l\} = \{0.4, 0.2, 0.1, 10, 3\}$ in experiments.

Table 1 gives examples of user intent mined from question descriptions, query logs, and top search results. From the examples, we can see that intent mined from the three sources are quite different. Take "usain bolt" for instance. The intent mined from descriptions is more specific and it shows that askers on CQA website care more about his characteristics, such as being the fastest man in the world, a world record owner, and an Olympic star. Intent mined from search logs is more general and shows that search engine users care more about personal information, such as his biography, twitter account, and his girlfriend. The intent mined from the search engine shows the recent achievements of Usain Bolt, such as wining three gold medals at the 2013 Moscow World Championship.

# 4. MODELS

We incorporate the intent mined from the three sources into language models and propose a new model to improve the search relevance for short queries in CQA.

## 4.1 Language Model for Information Retrieval

In recent years, the language model for information retrieval (LMIR) [23] has proven to be effective at question retrieval. Formally, given a query $q$ and a candidate question $Q$, LMIR measures the relevance between $q$ and $Q$ through

$$P(q|Q) = \prod_{w \in q} [(1 - \lambda) P_{ml}(w|Q) + \lambda P_{ml}(w|C)], \quad (2)$$

where $P_{ml}(w|Q)$ represents the maximum likelihood of term $w$ estimated from $Q$, and $P_{ml}(w|C)$ is a smoothing item that is calculated as the maximum likelihood in a large corpus $C$. The smoothing item avoids zero probability, which stems from the terms appearing in the candidate question but not in the query. $\lambda \in (0, 1)$ is a parameter that acts as a trade-off between the likelihood and the smoothing item.

LMIR performs well when there is a great deal of overlap between a query and a candidate question, but when the two present similar meanings with different words, LMIR fails to capture their similarity.

## 4.2 Translation-based Language Model

LMIR cannot measure the similarity between a query and a candidate question when there are lexical gaps. For example, when a query is "How do I get knots out of my cat's fur?" and a candidate question is "How can I remove a tangle in my cat's fur?", LMIR gives a very low similarity score. To address this issue, a translation-based language model [4] is proposed. Translation-based language models improve traditional LMIR by learning term-term or phrase-phrase translation probability from question-description or question-answer pairs and incorporating the information into maximum likelihood. Formally, given a query $q$ and a candidate question $Q$, translation-based language is defined as

$$P_{trb}(q|Q) = \prod_{w \in q} [(1 - \lambda) P_{mx}(w|Q) + \lambda P_{ml}(w|C)], \quad (3)$$

where

$$P_{mx}(w|Q) = \alpha P_{ml}(w|Q) + \beta P_{tr}(w|Q)$$
$$P_{tr}(w|Q) = \sum_{v \in Q} P_{tp}(w|v) P_{ml}(v|Q).$$

Table 1: Examples of query intent words mined from three sources

| Query | Intent words from CQA | Intent words from query log | Intent words from search results |
|---|---|---|---|
| usain bolt | fastest, world, record, olympics | biography, twitter, girlfriend | 2013, gold, moscow, championship |
| superbowl | patriots, steelers, giants, nfl | story, history, 2012, ticket, xlvi | ticket, 2013, nfl, history, commercial |
| egypt | cairo, country, arabic, pyramids | morsi, election, ancient, history | revolution, brotherhood, police |

Here $\lambda$, $\alpha$, and $\beta$ are parameters, satisfying $\alpha + \beta = 1$. $P_{tp}(w|v)$ represents the translation probability from term $v$ in Question $Q$ to term $w$.

Xue, et al. [28] further considered the likelihood from answers and proved some improvement when interpolating a translation-based language model with an extra answer likelihood term $P_{ml}(w|a)$ from the answer $a$ of question $Q$. The model is defined as

$$P_{trba}(q|Q) = \prod_{w \in q} [(1-\lambda)P_{mx}(w|Q,a) + \lambda P_{ml}(w|C)], \quad (4)$$

where

$$P_{mx}(w|Q,a) = \alpha P_{ml}(w|Q) + \beta P_{tr}(w|Q) + \gamma P_{ml}(w|a).$$

$\gamma$ is an extra parameter satisfying $\alpha + \beta + \gamma = 1$.

The existing models work well for long question queries. However, when an input query is short, these models cannot accurately measure the relevance between the query and the candidates due to the lack of intent information.

## 4.3 Intent-based Language Model

We are aiming for improved relevance of short queries in CQA question search. To this end, given a query $q$, we mine different types of search intent from various sources, as presented in the previous section. Each type of intent is represented as a series of terms associated with weights. We rank the terms in a descending order based on their weights and pick the top $N$ terms for creating an intent-based language model. Formally, suppose that intent from source $i$ is $W_i = \{(t_{ij}, \varphi_{ij})\}$, $1 \leqslant i \leqslant 3$, $1 \leqslant j \leqslant N$, where $t_{ij}$ is the term, and $\varphi_{ij}$ is the weight. Our intent-based language model is defined as

$$P_{ib}(q|Q) = \pi_0 P_{trba}(q|Q) + \sum_{i=1}^{3} \pi_i \sum_{j=1}^{N} \varphi_{ij} P_{trba}(t_{ij}|Q), \quad (5)$$

where $P_{trba}$ represents the translation-based language model plus answer language model. $\{\pi_i\}_{0 \leq i \leq 3}$ are parameters that can be learned from training data. $\varphi_{ij}$ is the weight of intent word $t_{ij}$ in intent word set $W_i$ from the source $i$. Equation (5) means that the relevance between a query $q$ and a candidate $Q$ is determined by not only the query itself, but also the underlying user intent hidden behind the query. The final model is a linear combination of the relevance from the original query and the relevance from the intent of the query.

Note that there is stark difference between our model and the one proposed by [10]. They focus on long question queries with clear information needs and their intent means different types of questions (objective/subjective/opinion), while we are addressing the relevance issue for short queries and therefore have to first predict what the possible intent is for the queries and then take the predictions into account when calculating relevance.

# 5. EXPERIMENT

We conducted experiments to test the mined intent and the intent-based language model.

## 5.1 Experiment Setup

### 5.1.1 CQA Data Preparation

We crawled a large number of questions associated with descriptions and answers from Yahoo! Answers using a public API[4] and from Quora.com using the approach described in [25].

Table 2 presents overviews of the two CQA data sets. 81% of the questions in Yahoo! Answers and 58% of the questions in Quora have descriptions and the average number of answers in the two data sets are 7.0 and 2.7, respectively. Besides the two large-scale CQA data sets, we also collected a one-year query log from a commercial search engine and randomly sampled 1,782 queries. 94.2% of the sampled queries were shorter than 4 words and the average length of the queries was 1.94. In other words, we considered the retrieval task of short queries in our experiments. Table 3 gives the length distribution of the sampled queries.

We separately indexed the crawled questions from Yahoo! Answers and Quora using an open source Lucene.Net System[5]. For each sampled query, we retrieved several candidate questions from the indexed data based on the inline-ranking algorithm in Lucene.Net and created two subsets. One subset consisted of query-question pairs with questions coming from Yahoo! Answers, and the other contained candidate questions from Quora. Each question was associated with its description and answers as metadata. Table 4 gives the statistics of the two subsets.

We recruited human judges to label the relevance of the candidate questions regarding the queries and compared different methods for the labeled data[6]. Specifically, we hired two judges. Each judge followed our guidelines and labeled a question with one of four levels: "Excellent", "Good", "Fair", and "Bad". If the judges disagreed on a question, we invited a third expert to make the final decision. Table 5 presents the specifics of our labeling guideline and label distributions. We randomly split each of the two labeled data sets into a training set, a validation set, and a test set with a ratio 2:1:1. We learned the parameters in the intent-based language model on the training set, tuned the parameters of the learning to rank algorithm on the validation set and tested the performance of our model and other baseline models on the test set. The training set and the validation set are also used for tuning parameters in baseline models.

To evaluate the performance of different models, we calculated NDCG [14] at positions 1, 3, and 5.

[4]`http://developer.yahoo.com/answers/`

[5]`http://lucenenet.apache.org/`

[6]The labeled data from Yahoo! Answers is available at `http://home.ustc.edu.cn/~ustcwhc/`

Table 2: Overview of two CQA data sets

| Statistics | Yahoo | Quora |
|---|---|---|
| Question # | 127,787,139 | 649,843 |
| Description # | 103,605,696 | 375,829 |
| Answer # | 894,855,746 | 1,743,259 |

Table 3: Length distribution of the labeled queries

| Total | Query Length | | | | Avg. |
|---|---|---|---|---|---|
| | 1 | 2 | 3 | ≥4 | Length |
| 1782 | 658 | 732 | 289 | 103 | 1.94 |

### 5.1.2 Data Sources for Intent Mining

There are three different sources for intent mining: question descriptions in CQA, query logs, and the top search results of a web search engine. We first employed the method in [18] and trained two translation models using the crawled 103.6M and 375.8K question-description pairs of Yahoo! Answers and Quora, respectively. Secondly, we collected one-year (May 1st, 2012 - April 30th, 2013) query logs from a commercial search engine and employed the method in [13] to mine user intent. Finally, for the online intent prediction from web search results, we used Bing API[7], crawled top 10 documents for each query, and distilled user intent following Algorithm 1. In the experiments on both Yahoo data and Quora data, we used the same intent signals from search logs and search results, and individual intent signals from each question-description translation model. For each source, we selected the top intent words, which were three times as the length of the input query.

### 5.1.3 Baselines

We first employed four variants of language models as baseline methods: the traditional language model for information retrieval (LMIR) given by Equation (2) [23], translation model (TR) [4] given by Equation (3), translation-based language model (TBL) [15], and translation-based language model plus answer language model (TAL) given by Equation (4) [28]. For the translation-based models (TR, TBL, TAL), we individually trained question-answer translation models on Yahoo! Answers and Quora with the pooled approach proposed by Xue, et al. [28], which creates a parallel corpus from both question-to-answer pairs and answer-to-question pairs. To enhance efficiency, we sampled 10% of the pairs from Yahoo data in the translation model learning. The total number of pairs were 179M for Yahoo! Answers and 3.4M for Quora.

In addition to these models, we also considered the method proposed by Li, et al. [18] as a baseline, as it is among the state-of-the-art methods leveraging user intent in question retrieval. This method measures question-question similarity with an LDA-based model [9]. In this method, the description of a query question and a user's information needs are concatenated along text denoted as $D_i$, while the description of a candidate question is denoted as $D_j$. Question similarity is defined as the similarity of $D_i$ and $D_j$ calculated using a KL divergence on topic distributions. In our experiments, we concatenated each question and its description as a document. We trained LDA models [5] on 6.4M sampled documents from Yahoo! Answers and the whole 650K documents from Quora using GibbsLDA++[8], and heuristically set the topic number in the training to be 26 and other parameters to be default for both data sets.

[7]http://datamarket.azure.com/dataset/bing/search

Table 4: Overview of two labeled data sets

| Statistics | Yahoo | Quora |
|---|---|---|
| Queries # | 1,782 | 1,782 |
| Questions # | 12,947 | 13,739 |
| Quesitons #/query | 7.27 | 7.71 |

Table 5: Labeling guideline and label distribution

| Label | Yahoo | Quora |
|---|---|---|
| **Excellent** | 15.1% | 1.4% |
| Meaning: the question is quite related to the query, and would have pleased the searcher or made him or her want to follow up or explore further. | | |
| **Good** | 29.2% | 33.7% |
| Meaning: the question is related to the query, and the searcher is likely to have found it interesting. | | |
| **Fair** | 42.2% | 51.8% |
| Meaning: the question is related to the query, but is not likely to be interesting to the searcher. | | |
| **Bad** | 13.3% | 13.1% |
| Meaning: the question is not related to the query. | | |

For a fairer comparison, we linearly combined the top-performing language model TAL and the LDA-based model and denoted the model as TAL+LDA. The combination weights were learnt from training data using LambdaMART [6].

### 5.1.4 Parameter Tuning

Language models have smoothing parameters (e.g., $\{\lambda, \alpha, \beta, \gamma\}$ in TAL). We selected the best parameters in {0, 0.1, 0.2,..., 1} from training and validation sets. We found that the optimal parameter combinations of TAL are {0.7, 0.1, 0.1, 0.8} on Yahoo data and {0.3, 0.1, 0.5, 0.4} on Quora data.

We used RankLib[9] to train a LambdaMART [6] for learning parameters in both TAL+LDA and our intent-based language model. There are four parameters in LambdaMART: $\{nt, nl, lr, mil\}$, which stand for the number of trees, the number of leaves, the learning rate, and the minimum instances per leaf, respectively. We chose $nt$ from {10, 50, 100}, $nl$ from {2, 4, 16}, $lr$ from {0.1, 0.2, 0.3, 0.4}, and $mil$ from {10, 50, 100} for each model on the validation data.

## 5.2 Results

We denote our intent-based language model given by Equation (5) as IBLM. Table 6 reports the experimental results on the two data sets. From Table 6 we can see that IBLM outperformed all the baseline methods on both Yahoo data and Quora data for all metrics, and the improvements were statistically significant(sign-test, p value $< 0.01$). The results demonstrate both the usefulness of the intent mined from various sources and the efficacy of the proposed model on leveraging the mined intent for improving search relevance of short queries.

[8]http://sourceforge.net/projects/gibbslda/
[9]http://people.cs.umass.edu/~vdang/ranklib.html

Table 6: Evaluation results on Yahoo data and Quora data

| | Yahoo data | | | Quora data | | |
|---|---|---|---|---|---|---|
| | NDCG@1 | NDCG@3 | NDCG@5 | NDCG@1 | NDCG@3 | NDCG@5 |
| LDA[18] | 63.35 | 69.91 | 72.50 | 55.72 | 61.03 | 65.74 |
| LMIR[23] | 67.02 | 73.83 | 76.07 | 60.72 | 68.06 | 72.39 |
| TR[4] | 68.27 | 73.84 | 75.98 | 60.52 | 67.87 | 71.97 |
| TBL[15] | 68.13 | 73.89 | 76.37 | 60.97 | 68.28 | 72.46 |
| TAL[28] | 69.44 | 74.95 | 76.53 | 61.96 | 67.11 | 72.48 |
| TAL+LDA | 70.03 | 74.02 | 75.92 | 62.71 | 68.54 | 72.93 |
| IBLM | **71.33** | **77.12** | **77.70** | **64.04** | **69.98** | **74.14** |

Table 8: Evaluation results of different intent models

(a) Yahoo data

| | NDCG@1 | NDCG@3 | NDCG@5 |
|---|---|---|---|
| TAL [28] | 69.44 | 74.95 | 76.53 |
| TAL+TAL($W_{cqa}$) | 70.33 | 75.55 | 76.85 |
| TAL+TAL($W_{log}$) | 70.25 | 75.60 | **77.23** |
| TAL+TAL($W_{web}$) | **71.14** | **75.94** | 77.17 |

(b) Quora data

| | NDCG@1 | NDCG@3 | NDCG@5 |
|---|---|---|---|
| TAL [28] | 61.96 | 67.11 | 72.48 |
| TAL+TAL($W_{web}$) | 63.31 | 69.21 | 73.51 |
| TAL+TAL($W_{log}$) | 63.70 | 69.00 | **73.73** |
| TAL+TAL($W_{cqa}$) | **64.02** | **69.24** | 73.65 |

## 5.3 Discussions

We investigated the reasons why IBLM can outperform baseline methods. Table 7 gives an example. The query "priceline" represents a commercial web site that provides users discount rates for travel-related purchases such as airline tickets and hotel stays[10]. For this query, questions about hotels or tickets are more relevant than others. Therefore, given two questions "Is Priceline the cheapest way to buy hotel rooms online?", and "Why did Priceline acquire Kayak for $1.8 billion?", it is better to rank the former in a higher position than the latter. The best performing baseline TAL is not aware of the underlying intent in the query and thus cannot do a good job of ranking. In contrast, our model can leverage the intent mined from different sources and successfully identity the searcher's preference.

### *5.3.1 Comparison between Intent from Different Sources*

We also studied the different effects of intent mined from different sources. In this paper, we mined user intent from question descriptions in CQA archives, query logs, and web search results. To compare different intents, we calculated TAL models using the intent words mined from an individual source and linearly combined them with the original TAL model. The combination weights were learned using LambdaMART on training data, and the parameters of LambdaMART were tuned in the same way with IBLM. We denoted the three individual intent models as TAL+TAL($W_{cqa}$), TAL+TAL($W_{log}$) , and TAL+TAL($W_{web}$) , which means using intent mined from CQA archives, query logs, and web search results, respectively. Table 8 reports the results of individual intent models. We can see that all individual models improved the original TAL model and the improvement was statistically significant (sign test, $p < 0.01$).

TAL+TAL($W_{cqa}$) leverages intent mined from question descriptions. The intent reflects askers' specific needs when asking questions about a short query. Query 1 in Table 9 gives an example that demonstrates the effect of considering intent mined from question descriptions. The query "Baltimore" refers to more than 10 cities and therefore was ambiguous[11]. On the other hand, many askers were interested in Baltimore, Maryland, which is the most famous Baltimore and expressed their specific needs through descriptions after their questions. We mined the intent and took it into account in our model. Therefore, our model TAL+TAL($W_{cqa}$) can successfully rank the question about Baltimore in Maryland in a high position and fulfill the user's information needs.

TAL+TAL($W_{log}$) makes use of intent mined from query logs. User intent is represented by query subtopics and co-clicked URLs that reflect searchers' pervasive preference towards a short query. Query 2 in Table 9 gives an example. "Gangnam style" was a popular song in 2012, and many users searched for "gangnam style video" and "psy gangnam style" on search engines. Therefore, questions about videos for Gangnam Style or the singer of Gangnam Style may attract more attention from searchers. We mined this common intent from query logs and with the information our model successfully ranked the question "What meaning is intended to be conveyed by the different scenes in the Gangnam Style **video**?" with the label "Excellent" in a high position.

The TAL+TAL($W_{web}$) model leverages the top search results from a search engine to predict user intent. Modern search engines usually mix recent material such as news and general content such as Wikipedia pages in the top retrieval results. The diverse search results allowed us to mine both recent aspects and general aspects related to a short query. This makes intent mined from web search results particularly useful for improving the search relevance of time-sensitive queries such as sports events and new products. Query 3 in Table 9 gives an example. Every year, the Superbowl is the most popular sporting event for football fans in America, and every year there are new things happening in at that year's Superbowl. When a user issues this query, it is very likely that he or she would like to see questions about the most recent or upcoming superbowl rather than those about historical superbowls. Our model captured this information need (i.e., superbowl 2013) from top search results and pro-

[10] http://www.priceline.com/

[11] http://en.wikipedia.org/wiki/Baltimore_(disambiguation)

**Table 7: Example for comparison between IBLM and the best performing baseline TAL**

| Query 1 | priceline | | | |
|---|---|---|---|---|
| Intent Words | From three sources: ***hotel***, ***cheap***, ***bid***, flight, ticket | | | |
| Label | TAL | IBLM | Question | Answer |
| Excellent | Rank 3 | Rank 1 | Is Priceline the ***cheapest*** way to buy ***hotel*** rooms online? | It's a very good way to get a good rate if you have the time/patience to do re-***bids*** and have the flexibility in location of your stay......don't know the exact ***hotel*** you're getting...suppose you want a 5* ***hotel*** in Beverly Hills...that LAX doesn't have a 5* ***hotel*** |
| Fair | Rank 1 | Rank 3 | Why did Priceline acquire Kayak for $1.8 billion? | ...joint industry relations for better air and ***hotel*** deals... |

vided question searchers with the most recent and relevant results[12].

It is interesting to note that TAL+TAL($W_{web}$) performs best on Yahoo! Answers data (See Table 8(a)), while on Quora data the best performing model is TAL+TAL($W_{cqa}$) (See Table 8(b)). On the one hand, Yahoo! Answers is the largest CQA website, and there are a large number of active users on it. It is easier for recent content to emerge on Yahoo! Answers. Therefore using a mixture of recent intent and general intent mined from web search results can lead to the best performance on Yahoo data. On the other hand, data in Quora has higher quality than data in Yahoo! Answers. Users in Quora are better educated and more capable of presenting their questions, descriptions, and answers in clear statements [25]. Therefore, there is less noise in descriptions in the Quora data, which leads to better intent understanding through question-description translation. Thus, it is reasonable that the TAL+TAL($W_{cqa}$) model would achieve the best performance on Quora data.

### *5.3.2 Unsupervised Intent-based Model*

In our intent-based language model (see Equation (5)), each intent word is used to calculate a new TAL model and the final model is a linear combination of all the TAL models. An alternative for leveraging the intent could be concatenating the intent words with the original query and performing retrieval using the new, longer query in TAL. This renders an unsupervised intent-based language model. An interesting question is whether the unsupervised model performs as well as or even better than IBLM. In this section, we compared the unsupervised alternative with the supervised model and the best performing baseline, TAL model.

Figure 1 presents a comparison of the supervised model, the unsupervised model, and the baseline model across intent mined from all three sources. We denote the unsupervised alternative as TAL(Q+$W_{cqa}$), TAL(Q+$W_{log}$), and TAL(Q+$W_{web}$). From the experimental results, we can see that the unsupervised intent-based models performed the worst. This may stem from the fact that in the unsupervised models all intent words and the original query were equally weighted and the concatenation drifts the topic of a user's query and makes its intent more ambiguous. On the other hand, the supervised models can leverage the labeled data and calibrate the effect of different intent words in measuring the relevance between the original query and candidate questions.

[12]We conducted the experiments when Superbowl 2013 was still ongoing.

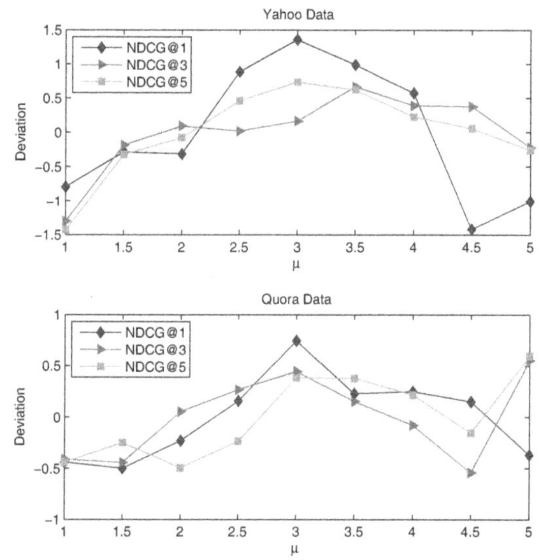


**Figure 2: The influence of $\mu$ on the performance of IBLM**

### *5.3.3 Influence of Intent Word Number*

In our experiments, we fixed the number of intent words at three times the length of the input query. In practice, it is worth understanding the influence of the intent word number to the final relevance. Intuitively, too few intent words may lack the power of disclosing underlying search intent while too many intent words may bring noise. To verify this intuition, we defined a parameter $\mu$ as the ratio of intent word number and query length and selected it from $\{1, 1.5, 2, 2.5, ..., 5\}$ . Figure 2 reports the performance of IBLM with different numbers of intent words on the two data sets. Note that in Figure 2, the vertical axis represents the deviation of the NDCG@i, which is defined as NDCG@i - Avg(NDCG@i). We employed this measure to highlight the gradual change of NDCG with respect to $\mu$. The experimental results verified our intuition and indicated that $\mu = 3$ is the best choice for the number of intent words.

Table 9: Examples for comparison between three variants of IBLM and TAL model

| | | | | |
|---|---|---|---|---|
| Query 1 | baltimore | | | |
| Intent Words | From question-description tranlsation model: ***maryland***, ***city***, ***area***, raven, harbor | | | |
| Label | TAL | TAL + TAL($W_{cqa}$) | Question | Answer |
| Excellent | Rank 3 | Rank 1 | What do people like about Baltimore? | ...most affordable truly urban ***areas*** in the United States...the cheapest "big" ***city*** in the north east corridor...in many ways by the ***Maryland*** Institute College of Art and its alumni...you would pay in another major ***city***... |
| Fair | Rank 1 | Rank 4 | Is Baltimore considered in the North or the South? | Being right near the border, Baltimore gets some of both: northern charm and southern efficiency. |
| Query 2 | gangnam style | | | |
| Intent Words | From query search log: youtube, ***video***, ***psy***, oppa, lyrics, dance | | | |
| Label | TAL | TAL + TAL($W_{log}$) | Question | Answer |
| Excellent | Rank 4 | Rank 1 | What meaning is intended to be conveyed by the different scenes in the Gangam Style ***video***? | ... The ***video*** is a satire about Gangnam...I think a lot of what ***Psy*** is pointing out is...The Subversive Message Within South Korea's Music ***Video*** Sensation... |
| Fair | Rank 1 | Rank 7 | What are some similarities and differences between Gangam Style and Kolaveri Di? | Blind following!! |
| Query 3 | superbowl | | | |
| Intent Words | From web search engine: ticket, ***2013***, ***nfl***, ***history***, commercial | | | |
| Label | TAL | TAL + TAL($W_{web}$) | Question | Answer |
| Good | Rank 3 | Rank 1 | As of January 14, ***2013***, which teams do you predict for the Superbowl ***2013*** and who will win it? | ...one of the ***NFL***'s deadliest weapons...The most complete team in the ***NFL*** is going to destroy Atlanta if they...three most explosive single-season offenses in ***NFL History***. |
| Fair | Rank 1 | Rank 9 | Which member of the QB class of 2012 will win a SuperBowl first? | Put me down for Russell Wilson. I think Andrew Luck is still likely to have the best career of the three,... |

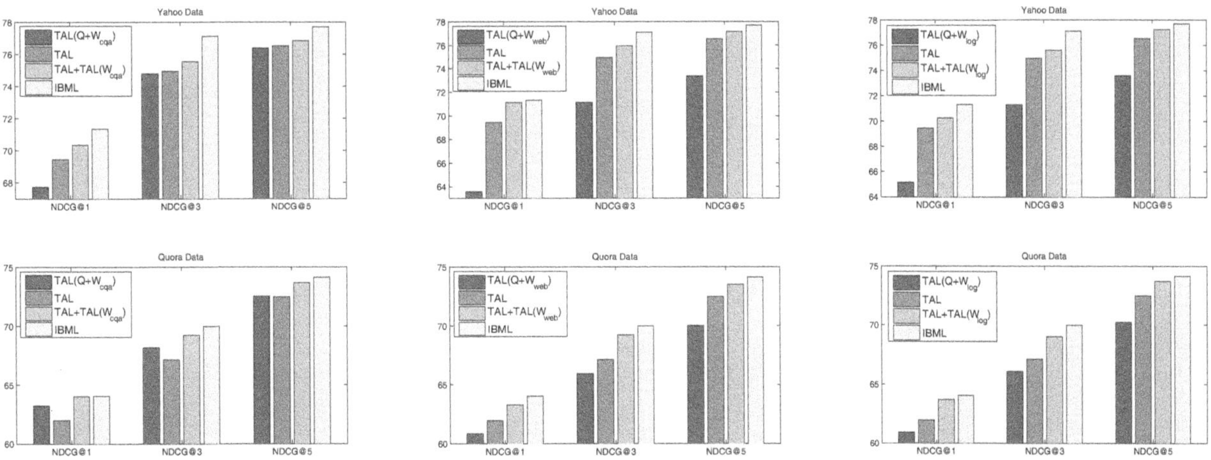


Figure 1: Comparisons between unsupervised IBLM, TAL and supervised IBLM

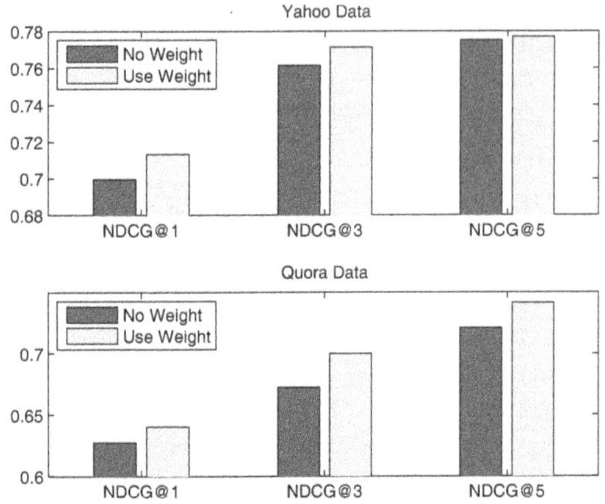


**Figure 3: The influence of intent word weight on the performance of IBLM**

### *5.3.4 Influence of Intent Word Weight*

In Equation (5), we not only leverage the content of intent but also consider the weight of different intent words. An interesting question is whether the intent word weight really contributes to the final relevance. In this section, we set each weight $\varphi_{ij}$ as 1 and compared it with IBLM.

Figure 3 shows the results when using and not using intent word weight. We can see that weighted IBLM performs better over all the metrics. This is because the weight encodes user behavior such as click numbers and thus can provide extra information other than intent content.

## 6. CONCLUSION

In this paper, we have investigated the problem of question retrieval for short queries in community question answering. We propose an intent-based language model that takes advantage of both the state-of-the-art question retrieval models and the extra intent information mined from three data sources. The parameters of the model are automatically learned with a state-of-the-art learning-to-rank approach. We empirically study the efficacy of the proposed model on data sets from Yahoo! Answers and Quora. The evaluation results show that with user intent prediction, our model can significantly improve state-of-the-art relevance models on question retrieval for short queries.

## 7. ACKNOWLEDGMENT

We would like to thank Fengze Jiang for his help in drawing the figures.

## 8. REFERENCES


[1] Bandyopadhyay, A., Ghosh, K., Majumder, P., and Mitra, M. Query expansion for microblog retrieval. *IJWS 1*, 4 (2012), 368–380.

[2] Bendersky, M., Metzler, D., and Croft, W. B. Learning concept importance using a weighted dependence model. In *WSDM* (2010), pp. 31–40.

[3] Bendersky, M., Metzler, D., and Croft, W. B. Parameterized concept weighting in verbose queries. In *SIGIR* (2011), pp. 605–614.

[4] Berger, A. L., Caruana, R., Cohn, D., Freitag, D., and Mittal, V. O. Bridging the lexical chasm: statistical approaches to answer-finding. In *SIGIR* (2000), pp. 192–199.

[5] Blei, D. M., Ng, A. Y., and Jordan, M. I. Latent dirichlet allocation. In *NIPS* (2001), pp. 601–608.

[6] Burges, C. From ranknet to lambdarank to lambdamart: An overview. *Microsoft Research Technical Report* (2010).

[7] Burke, R. D., Hammond, K. J., Kulyukin, V. A., Lytinen, S. L., Tomuro, N., and Schoenberg, S. Question answering from frequently asked question files: Experiences with the faq finder system. *AI Magazine 18*, 2 (1997), 57–66.

[8] Cao, X., Cong, G., Cui, B., Jensen, C. S., and Zhang, C. The use of categorization information in language models for question retrieval. CIKM '09, ACM, pp. 265–274.

[9] Celikyilmaz, A., Hakkani-Tur, D., and Tur, G. Lda based similarity modeling for question answering. In *NAACL HLT Workshop on Semantic Search* (2010), pp. 1–9.

[10] Chen, L., Zhang, D., and Levene, M. Question retrieval with user intent. In *SIGIR* (2013), pp. 973–976.

[11] Dror, G., Maarek, Y., Mejer, A., and Szpektor, I. From query to question in one click: suggesting synthetic questions to searchers. In *WWW* (2013), pp. 391–402.

[12] Duan, H., Cao, Y., Lin, C.-Y., and Yu, Y. Searching questions by identifying question topic and question focus. In *ACL* (2008), pp. 156–164.

[13] Hu, Y., nan Qian, Y., Li, H., Jiang, D., Pei, J., and Zheng, Q. Mining query subtopics from search log data. In *SIGIR* (2012), pp. 305–314.

[14] Järvelin, K., and Kekäläinen, J. Ir evaluation methods for retrieving highly relevant documents. In *SIGIR* (2000), pp. 41–48.

[15] Jeon, J., Croft, W. B., and Lee, J. H. Finding similar questions in large question and answer archives. In *CIKM* (2005), pp. 84–90.

[16] Lafferty, J. D., and Zhai, C. Document language models, query models, and risk minimization for information retrieval. In *SIGIR* (2001), pp. 111–119.

[17] Li, H. A short introduction to learning to rank. *IEICE Transactions 94-D*, 10 (2011), 1854–1862.

[18] Li, S., and Manandhar, S. Improving question recommendation by exploiting information need. In *ACL* (2011), pp. 1425–1434.

[19] Liu, Q., Agichtein, E., Dror, G., Gabrilovich, E., Maarek, Y., Pelleg, D., and Szpektor, I. Predicting web searcher satisfaction with existing community-based answers. In *SIGIR* (2011), pp. 415–424.

[20] Liu, T.-Y. *Learning to Rank for Information Retrieval.* Springer, 2011.

[21] Metzler, D., and Croft, W. B. A markov random field model for term dependencies. In *SIGIR* (2005), pp. 472–479.

[22] Minsky, M. L. *Semantic Information Processing.* The MIT Press, 1969.

[23] Ponte, J. M., and Croft, W. B. A language modeling approach to information retrieval. In *SIGIR* (1998), pp. 275–281.

[24] Robertson, S. E., and Walker, S. Some simple effective approximations to the 2-poisson model for probabilistic weighted retrieval. In *SIGIR* (1994), pp. 232–241.

[25] Wang, G., Gill, K., Mohanlal, M., Zheng, H., and Zhao, B. Y. Wisdom in the social crowd: an analysis of quora. In *WWW* (2013), pp. 1341–1352.

[26] Wang, K., Ming, Z., and Chua, T.-S. A syntactic tree matching approach to finding similar questions in community-based qa services. In *SIGIR* (2009), pp. 187–194.

[27] Wang, Q., nan Qian, Y., Song, R., Dou, Z., Zhang, F., Sakai, T., and Zheng, Q. Mining subtopics from text fragments for a web query. *Inf. Retr. 16*, 4 (2013), 484–503.

[28] Xue, X., Jeon, J., and Croft, W. B. Retrieval models for question and answer archives. In *SIGIR* (2008), pp. 475–482.

[29] Zhou, G., Cai, L., Zhao, J., and Liu, K. Phrase-based translation model for question retrieval in community question answer archives. In *ACL* (2011), pp. 653–662.

# Struggling or Exploring? Disambiguating Long Search Sessions

Ahmed Hassan, Ryen W. White, Susan T. Dumais, and Yi-Min Wang
Microsoft Research
Redmond, WA 98052 USA
{hassanam, ryenw, sdumais, ymwang}@microsoft.com

## ABSTRACT

Web searchers often exhibit directed search behaviors such as navigating to a particular Website. However, in many circumstances they exhibit different behaviors that involve issuing many queries and visiting many results. In such cases, it is not clear whether the user's rationale is to intentionally explore the results or whether they are struggling to find the information they seek. Being able to disambiguate between these types of long search sessions is important for search engines both in performing retrospective analysis to understand search success, and in developing real-time support to assist searchers. The difficulty of this challenge is amplified since many of the characteristics of exploration (e.g., multiple queries, long duration) are also observed in sessions where people are struggling. In this paper, we analyze struggling and exploring behavior in Web search using log data from a commercial search engine. We first compare and contrast search behaviors along a number dimensions, including query dynamics during the session. We then build classifiers that can accurately distinguish between exploring and struggling sessions using behavioral and topical features. Finally, we show that by considering the struggling/exploring prediction we can more accurately predict search satisfaction.

## Categories and Subject Descriptors

H.3.3 [**Information Search and Retrieval**]: Information Storage and Retrieval: *search process*, *selection process*.

## Keywords

Exploratory search; Exploring vs. struggling.

(a) A *struggling* session

(b) An *exploring* session

**Figure 1. Examples of *struggling* and *exploring* sessions.**

## 1. INTRODUCTION

Web search engines are a primary mechanism by which people seek information and solve problems. When searchers experience difficulty in finding information, their struggle may be evident in their search behavior via indicators such as issuing numerous search queries or visiting many results within a search session [2]. However, these same search behaviors may also be indicative of *exploratory* search activity, whereby people actively try to learn a topic and discover new information [24][29]. Accurately distinguishing between struggling and exploring is an important issue for search engines. For example, during post-hoc analysis of search logs, the ability to distinguish between these two situations can help to more accurately identify underperforming scenarios, signaling user frustration or unhappiness. In addition, predictive models could be applied to provide appropriate system support if the search situation can be discerned, e.g., providing a revised experience for exploratory searches such as a guided tour through related topics [13][34]. Since searchers may be reluctant to describe their situation explicitly to the search engine it is be desirable to predict this automatically from observed search activity.

There is a need to develop methods to automatically identify struggle and exploration from search behavior. Research on leveraging implicit feedback [9][14] has shown that we can learn when users are dissatisfied based on features of their search activity such as short landing-page dwell times and post-click query reformulation. Previous work on behavioral analysis has shown that multiple query refinements and multiple search-result clicks are associated with users experiencing difficulty [2], frustration [7], and to events such as search engine switching [31]. However, more querying is not necessarily a negative indicator if the user is learning and consuming content on their journey [27], and searchers can benefit from the information that they are exposed to as they search [32].

To illustrate the challenge of distinguishing between struggling and exploring automatically, let us present an example of user behavior with a single search session. Figure 1 (a) shows an example of a search session where the user is seeking information on tax software. We can see that in this session the searcher issued many related queries and clicked on many results (four queries and five results in total), providing some evidence that they are exploring. However, the queries are closely related, and the inter-query time is relatively short for some queries (suggesting impatience). This provides stronger evidence that the user is in fact struggling to find relevant information pertaining to the annual purchase of specific


*WSDM'14*, February 24–28, 2014, New York, New York, USA.

http://dx.doi.org/10.1145/2556195.2556221

tax software. In Figure 1 (b), we see an example of a user exploring different aspects of a topic "career development" and issuing multiple queries and having multiple clicks. While the difference between the two types of sessions may be discernible to human judges, existing automatic methods may be unable to perform this distinction using limited information such as the number of queries in the session or session duration. To date, researchers have not developed methods to *automatically* distinguish between struggling and exploring. Such mechanisms would have utility for a range of applications, including, as we demonstrate later in the paper, enhancing search satisfaction models, e.g., [12]. We address this shortcoming with the research presented in this paper.

We use behavioral data gathered from a large commercial Web search engine and consensus judgments about the type of session from external human assessors. Through our analysis, we show clear behavioral differences between struggling and exploring, and use these insights to develop machine-learned models capable of accurately distinguishing between the two situations. Specifically, we make the following three research contributions with this work presented in this paper:

- Characterize differences in the search behavior associated with struggling and exploring.
- Build predictive models to distinguish between struggling and exploring given behavioral data.
- Integrate the prediction into model of search satisfaction and demonstrate gains in prediction accuracy by considering whether the searcher is struggling or exploring.

The remainder of this paper is structured as follows. In Section 2, we describe related work in areas such as search satisfaction and searcher frustration. Section 3 defines struggling versus exploring and describes the labeled data that we use in our analysis. In Section 4 we compare and contrast search behavior for each of search situations. Section 5 describes the predictive model and we provide the findings of our experiments in Section 6. We discuss the implications and limitations in Section 7, and conclude in Section 8.

## 2. RELATED WORK

There is relevant related work in four main areas: (1) search satisfaction, (2) task difficulty, (3) searcher frustration, and (4) exploratory search and multi-query analysis. We address each area in turn.

### 2.1 Search Satisfaction

There is significant literature on estimating task success or failure from online search behavior. Methods that have been used include correlating search behavior, such as search-result clicks and dwell time for clicks, with either self-reported success or labels of success provided by expert judges. Fox et al. [9] used an instrumented browser to determine whether there was an association between explicit ratings of satisfaction and implicit measures of searcher interest and identified the measures that were most strongly associated with user satisfaction. They found that there was a relationship between user activity and search satisfaction ratings, and that click-through, dwell time, and session termination activity combined to make good predictors of satisfaction for Web pages. Fox et al. found that short dwell times and clicking numerous (four or more) search results for a query were both indicators of dissatisfaction.

Behavioral patterns have also been used to predict user satisfaction for search sessions in addition to individual queries. Huffman and Hochster [15] found a relatively strong linear correlation between session satisfaction and the relevance of the first three results returned for the first query in a search task, whether the information need was navigational, and the number of events in the session. Hassan et al. [12] developed models of user behavior to accurately estimate search success on a session level, independent of the relevance of documents retrieved by the search engine. Ageev et al. [1] propose a formalization of different types of success for informational search, and presented a scalable game-like infrastructure for crowdsourcing search behavior studies, specifically targeted towards capturing and evaluating successful search strategies on informational tasks with known intent. They show that their model can predict search success effectively on their data and on a separate set of logs comprising search engine sessions. Later in the paper, we will show that by considering evidence of struggling or exploring, we can improve the performance of search satisfaction models such as that described in previous work [12].

### 2.2 Task Difficulty

One explanation for why users struggle is the difficulty of the task being attempted. A study by Aula and colleagues [2] examined the behavior of searchers engaged in challenging closed informational search tasks, where the answer was difficult to find. They examined users' search behavior in two studies—a usability study and an online study—and showed that there were differences in search behavior when searchers were experiencing difficulty in finding relevant information. Specifically, searchers applied more advanced operators, spent longer on the search result page, and issued the longest search query toward the middle of the search session. We explore the role of these and related behavioral signals in the analysis described later in the paper.

Other research on the effects of task difficulty on search behavior has shown that beyond queries, there are other behavioral signals that correlate with task difficulty. For example, as task difficulty increases, the number of results viewed increases and average dwell time on landing pages also increases [22], as does the number of pages retained for later inspection (e.g., via bookmarking [20]). Gwizdka and Spence [11] showed that the number of unique web pages visited, the time spent on each page, the degree of deviation from the optimal path, and the degree of the navigation path's linearity, were good predictors of subjective task difficulty. Beyond behaviors, studies have also shown that signals of task difficulty are mediated by domain knowledge, and that should be considered when interpreting those signals [23]. Information about domain expertise is typically unavailable to search engines, but it could be estimated from signals such as topical interests and estimates of the reading difficulty of viewed Web pages [21].

### 2.3 Searcher Frustration

Users experiencing difficulty in finding the information they seek may experience frustration that can manifest in search behavior and other signals (including physiological indicators). While satisfaction and frustration are closely related, they are distinct. Searchers can ultimately satisfy their information need, but still be quite frustrated in the process [4]. We may therefore need to consider frustration separately in developing models of user behavior.

Although others have studied frustration from an information science perspective (e.g., [19]) they have not attempted to model frustration in a way that could be utilized directly by search engines. Feild et al. [7] developed methods to predict user frustration from behavioral signals gathered during the search process. They assigned users difficult information seeking tasks and monitored their degree of frustration via behavioral logs and physical sensors. They showed that behavioral features such as the total duration of the session and query complexity were good predictors of search frustration. These aligned with features that were shown to be useful in predicting another behavior, search engine switching, defined as the voluntary transition between different search engines. White and Dumais [31] showed that there are behavioral patterns such as a sequence of queries with no intervening clicks that could help predict engine switching.

## 2.4 Exploratory Search

As described earlier, during exploratory search users are focused on learning about a topic and gathering information [24]. This may be associated with searchers seeking different opinions on a topic, exploring or discovering aspects of a topic, or trying to ascertain an overview of a topic. Research on exploratory search has focused on characterizing the exploratory search process and the types of support that are required to help people perform exploratory searches [29]. For example, if it can be determined that the user is engaged in a complex search task then support can be offered to help them within the current session using tours or trails [13][34], tailored search support [3], or even across multiple search sessions with the ability to preserve and restore search state [25].

Other research has used within-session query reformulation for evaluation purposes, as well as supporting various aspects of the search process. Kanoulas and colleagues [19] proposed measures for evaluating search systems across multiple queries. Radlinski and Joachims [26] proposed the use of query chains of connected query reformulations, independent of exploring or struggling, to improve the ranking of search results. Recent research has studied intrinsically-diverse search tasks that typically require multiple user searches on different aspects of the same information need [27]. The authors proposed an approach that could alter the rankings presented to the user, to also provide them information on aspects of the task for which the user will search in the future.

The research presented in this paper extends previous work in a number of ways. First, we focus specifically on the important problem of *automatically* identifying exploring and struggling behavior, and distinguishing between the two situations even though they appear similar given coarse analysis of search behavior such as query reformulation counts or session duration. Second, we developed a labeling methodology to capture possible explanations for observed session behavior from external assessors. Using this approach we gather a large labeled set of struggling and exploring sessions from the logs of the Microsoft Bing search engine, labeled based on the consensus judgments of those assessors. Third, we characterize the key behavioral differences between struggling and exploring that help to inform feature generation in our predictive models. Finally, we develop predictive models and use the predictions to improve the performance of established models of search satisfaction.

# 3. STRUGGLING VS. EXPLORING

We begin by outlining the two different search scenarios and how we define them for the purposes of this study. We then describe the process by which we obtained labels on a sample of sessions taken from search engine logs.

## 3.1 Definitions

We focus our effort in this paper on studying long topically-coherent sessions (i.e., cases where users are observed pursuing information related to a common subject area). The behavior in these sessions could reflect either exploring or struggling. We adopt the following definitions for each of these concepts:

**Definition:** *Exploring sessions* are those where users are engaged in an open-ended and multi-faceted information-seeking task to foster learning and discovery.

**Definition:** *Struggling sessions* are those where users are experiencing difficulty locating the required information. Note that struggling may not necessarily result in failure (i.e., failing to locate the required information).

The challenge is in distinguishing between these types of sessions. In practice, users who are exploring or struggling issue multiple queries that share a common subject area.

In exploring sessions, multiple queries are intended to address different aspects of a topic and provide users with a combination of sought information and direction for future exploration. Because of the open-ended nature of such search sessions, the information goal is likely to be satisfied with information encountered during the search. Hence, multiple search queries can provide relevant information, reflecting increased engagement in the topic of interest.

In contrast, during struggling sessions, multiple queries are likely an indication of trouble in locating the required information. In such cases, people may have a well-defined information need and are trying to locate specific information, with little or no success.

Intuitively, both exploring and struggling sessions are topically coherent but they can have either multiple facets (exploring) or a single facet (struggling). In addition, both types of sessions are, by definition, long. A single-query session cannot be an exploring session because a single query cannot cover multiple facets of the search task. A single-query session cannot be a struggling session either because there is insufficient evidence that the user is experiencing difficulty in finding the information that they seek. Note, however, that a single-query session can be unsuccessful (e.g., a user who just gives up after a single query). We will elaborate on the difference between struggling and failure in Section 3.3.

## 3.2 Mining Search Sessions from Log Data

Our data consists of a sample of hundreds of thousands of search sessions from the logs of the Bing search engine. We analyzed a total of four weeks of interaction logs from March 2013. Log entries include a unique user identifier, and a timestamp for all queries and clicked Web pages. Intranet and secure (https) URL visits were excluded at the source. Any personally identifiable information was removed from the logs prior to analysis. In order to remove variability caused by geographic and linguistic variation in search behavior, we only include entries generated in the English speaking United States locale. Every session began with a query and could contain further queries or Web page visits. A session ended if the user was idle for more than 30 minutes. Similar criteria have been used in previous work to demarcate search sessions, e.g., [6][31].

To mine sessions that could potentially be related to exploring or struggling, we extract long sessions that exhibit topical coherence. To find sessions that meet these criteria, we do the following:

1. **Filter navigational queries:** Before we identify sessions. We start by collapsing all duplicate queries and removing the top 250 frequent navigational queries (e.g., facebook, amazon, etc.). Due to their navigational nature, we declare that these queries cannot be part of exploring or struggling sessions.
2. **Segment sessions into topically-coherent sub-sessions:** Since search sessions are segmented using a time threshold, it is likely that single sessions may contain multiple tasks [18] with unrelated information needs. To ensure that sessions are topically coherent, we predict two consecutive queries as belonging to the same topically-coherent session if they are no longer than 10 minutes apart and if one of the following conditions apply: (i) the two queries share at least one non-stop word terms, (ii) the two queries share at least one top ten search results, or (iii) the two queries share at least one domain name in their top ten results. Frequent domains that are not topically coherent (e.g., Wikipedia) were excluded.

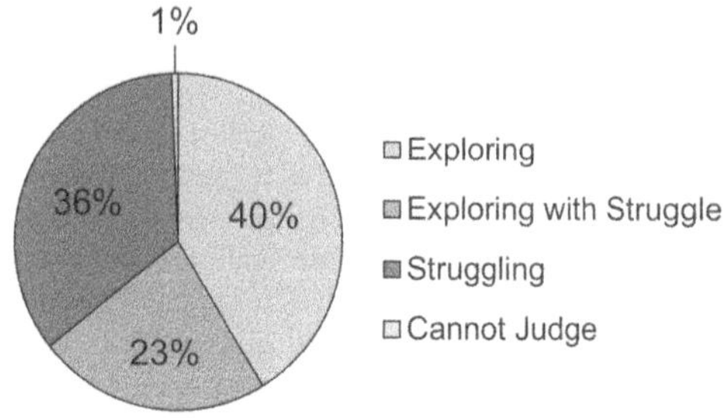


**Figure 2. Session type distribution as labeled by judges.**

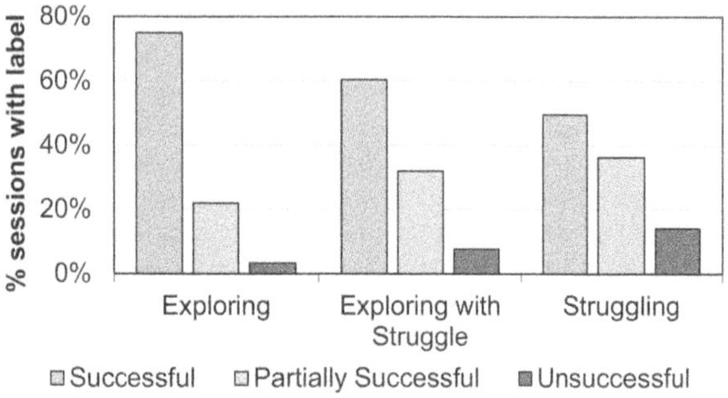


**Figure 3. Session success distribution as labeled by judges.**

3. **Filter short sessions:** After removing navigational queries and segmenting the logs into topically coherent sessions, we exclude sessions with less than three unique queries since these are unlikely to be exploring or struggling sessions.

We applied these criteria to identify long topically-coherent sessions because there are sessions in which users are likely to show exploring or struggling behavior. There were many thousands of such sessions in our data. We sampled 3000 of them and instructed external human judges to examine each session, try to understand the user's experience, and identify the reason for the observed behavior. We now describe the process by which the labels were collected from external judges.

## 3.3 Labeling Exploring and Struggling

Judges were recruited from the crowdsourcing service Clickworker.com, which provided access to crowd workers under contract. Judges resided in the United States and were fluent in English. Judges were shown sessions such as those illustrated in Figure 1. The interface was similar to Figure 1, and showed all queries, result clicks, and timestamps of all actions in the search session. They were instructed to examine the queries, the results pages (by clicking the "Query" text), the clicked pages, and to label the sessions as: *exploring*, *exploring with struggle*, or *struggling*. They were shown the definitions of exploring and struggling sessions using the same text as in the definitions provided in Section 3.1. Additionally, the following definition for *exploring with struggle sessions* was provided to judges:

**Definition:** *Exploring with struggle sessions* are exploring sessions where the user had experienced some difficulty in locating information about one or more of the facets being explored.

Judges were also instructed to label sessions with completely unrelated queries or sessions in a foreign language as "*cannot judge*". Figure 2 shows the distribution of labels collected from the judges. Judges excluded only 1% of the sessions as having unrelated queries or queries in a foreign language. Around 40% of the sessions were labeled as *exploring*, 23% as *exploring with struggle*, and the remaining 36% as *struggling* sessions. In total, the data set consisted of 3000 sessions with 17,117 queries, 13,168 distinct queries, and 13,780 result clicks.

We also asked the judges to assess the success of each session using the following labels:

- **Successful:** Sessions where searchers were able to locate the required information.
- **Partially Successful:** Sessions were searchers failed to locate some of the required information.
- **Unsuccessful:** Sessions where searchers failed to locate the required information.

Note that struggling is a characterization of the search process while success is a characterization of its outcome. Hence it is possible for a user who has difficulty locating the required information (struggling) to end up locating it (success). It is also possible for a user to fail in locating the required information without struggling (e.g., submit a single unsuccessful query then give up).

The distribution of success labels across session types is shown in Figure 3. The figure shows that most of the exploring sessions are successful (more than 75%) or partially successful (more than 20%). This agrees with our definition of exploring sessions, which are open-ended and multi-faceted in nature. Hence, failing to locate the required information is likely to prevent exploring early on in the session and in the cases when exploring does happen, the session is typically either successful or partially successful. Struggling sessions have a different success profile, with fewer sessions being successful (less than 50%) and more than 15% being unsuccessful.

The Cohen's kappa ($\kappa$) of inter-rater agreement is 0.59 for the exploring vs. struggling label, and 0.62 for the successful vs. unsuccessful label, signifying good agreement according to [8]. In both cases, we considered binary labels with *exploring* and *exploring with struggle* belonging to one class and *struggling* in the other. For the success label, *successful* was treated as one class and *partially successful* and *unsuccessful* were treated as another class. We use the same binary labels in the prediction task described later.

# 4. CHARACTERIZING EXPLORING AND STRUGGLING BEHAVIOR

In this section, we examine several characteristics of exploring and struggling sessions focusing on queries, result clicks, and topical dimensions.

## 4.1 Query Characteristics

At the outset of our analysis, we examine a number of different aspects of the session queries: (1) the number of unique queries, (2) similarity between queries, and (3) the nature of query transitions.

**Number of unique queries:** As described earlier, both exploring and struggling sessions are long by definition. One interesting question is whether exploring or struggling leads to longer sessions. If this was the case, then session length could be employed to discriminate between exploring and struggling. To answer this question, we compute the distribution over the number of unique queries for both types of session. We used unique queries to avoid counting the same query multiple times when the user refreshes the search page or hits the back button. The average number of unique queries per session was 4.50 and 4.36 for the exploring and struggling sessions respectively. The difference between the numbers of unique queries in the two search situations is not statistically significant at the 0.05 level according to a two-tailed $t$-test, suggesting that this is unlikely to be a distinguishing factor.

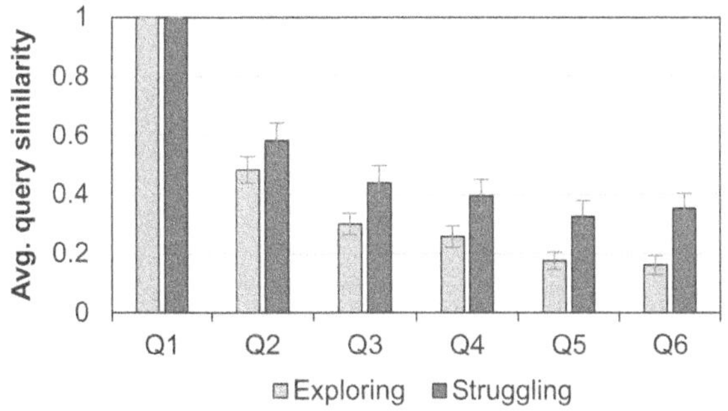


**Figure 4. Average similarity between all queries to the first query in exploring and struggling sessions (±SEM).**

**Query similarity:** Another interesting characteristic of exploring and struggling sessions may be the diversity of queries within the session. We might expect exploring sessions to contain less overlap as people revise their queries to explore alternatives. To examine this, we measure the similarity between every query in the session and the first query in the session. Our objective here is to assess how queries evolve as the user moves further into the session in both cases. If the user is struggling we might expect much of the initial query to still be present in future queries, but with terms being added or removed as the session proceeds.

To measure the similarity between pairs of queries in the session, we begin by performing standard text normalization where we lowercase the query text, replace all runs of whitespace characters with a single space, remove leading or trailing spaces, and remove stop words. Thus every query is represented as a bag of non-stop word terms. The similarity between any two queries $Q_i$ and $Q_j$ is computed as follows:

$$\frac{|Q_i \cap Q_j|}{|Q_i| + |Q_j| - |Q_i \cap Q_j|}$$

where $|Q_i|$ is the number of terms in query $Q_i$, and $|Q_i \cap Q_j|$ is the number of matched terms in $Q_i$ and $Q_j$.

To calculate the number of matches in $Q_i$ and $Q_j$ ($Q_i \cap Q_j$), we consider two terms matched if any of the following criteria are met:

1. **Exact Match:** The two terms match exactly.
2. **Approximate Match:** To capture spelling variants and misspelling, we allow two terms to match if the Levenshtein edit distance between them is less than two.
3. **Lemma Match:** Lemmatization is the process of reducing an inflected spelling to its lexical root or lemma form. We match two terms if the lemmas of their tokens match.
4. **Semantic Match:** To capture semantic variants, we match two terms if their similarity according to the WordNet Wu and Palmer measure (wup) is greater than 0.5. The Wu and Palmer measure [33] calculates relatedness by considering the depths of the two synsets in the WordNet taxonomies, along with the depth of the Least Common Subsumer (LCS). The measure is computed as follows:

$$wup(t_i, t_j) = \frac{2 * depth(LCS)}{depth(t_i) + depth(t_j)}$$

where the depth of any synset in WordNet is the length of the path connecting it to the root node plus one.

Figure 4 show the average similarity between all queries to the first query in every session for exploring and struggling sessions ± the standard error of the mean (SEM). Query similarity was calculated as described earlier where exact, approximate, lemma, and semantic matching is taken into consideration. A similarity value of one indicates a perfect match while a similarity value of zero indicates no matched terms in the two queries. We notice from the figure that as users move through an exploring session the queries get less similar to the first query. This is different from struggling sessions where queries remain quite similar to the initial query. All differences reported in Figure 4 are statically significant at the 0.05 level according to a two-tailed t-test. This aligns with previous work [2], which also found that when people are engaged in difficult search tasks that query reformulations closely resemble their initial search.

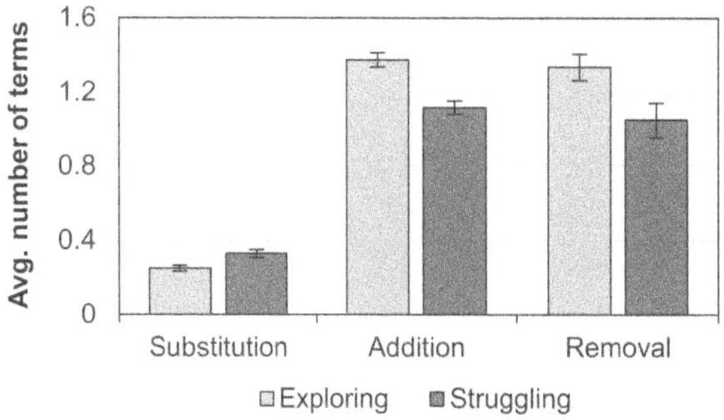


**Figure 5. Average number of term addition, removal and substitution in exploring and struggling sessions (±SEM).**

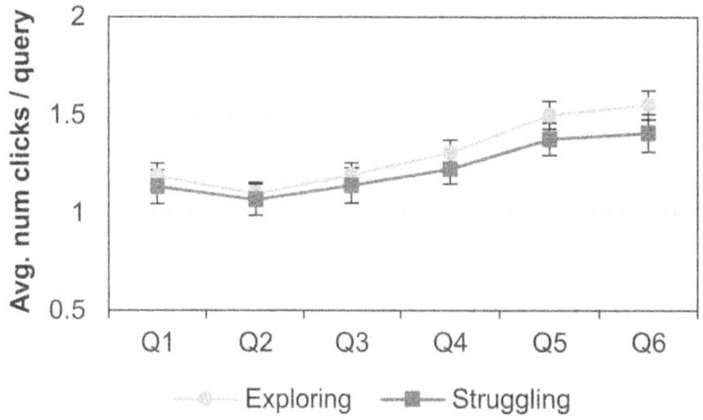


**Figure 6. Average number of clicks per query for exploring and struggling sessions (±SEM).**

**Transition between queries:** In addition to number of unique queries and similarity between queries, we also consider the strategies employed by the user when they transition from one query to another. There are multiple strategies for moving between queries. For simplicity, we consider the following three approaches, once again focusing on the relationship with the first query:

1. **Term Addition:** ≥ 1 words are added to first query.
2. **Term Removal:** ≥ 1 words removed from first query.
3. **Term Substitution:** This occurs when ≥ 1 words are substituted with a lexically or semantically matching terms. We treat one term is a substitution of another term if the two terms can be matched. Term matching is done by either exact, approximate, lemma, or semantic matching as described earlier.

Figure 5 compares the average number of term additions, removals and substitutions for exploring and struggling sessions. It is worth mentioning that our estimate of substitutions is clearly an underestimate because of the limited coverage of WordNet-based measures of synonyms. We notice from the figure that term addition and

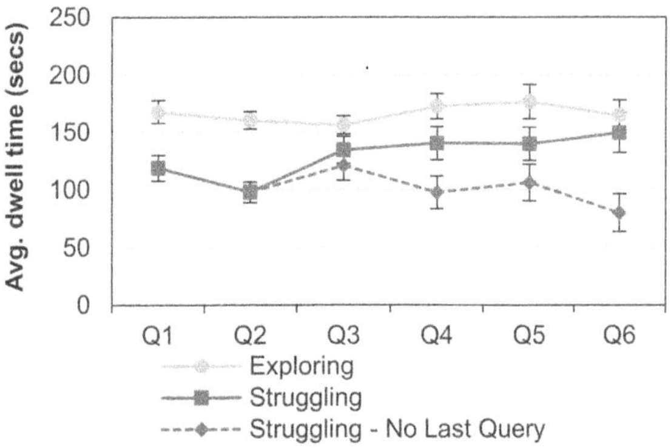


**Figure 7. Average dwell time per query for exploring and struggling search sessions (±SEM).**

removal are more popular reformulation strategies in exploring sessions (difference is statically significant at the 0.05 level according to a two-tailed *t*-test), while term substitution occurs somewhat more frequently in struggling sessions although this difference is not statistically significant at the 0.05 level. This aligns with our findings from the query similarity experiments which showed that struggling users are cycling as they attempt to conceive the correct query to locate a certain piece of information. Exploring users are more likely to remove old concepts and introduce new concepts as they progress in their search.

## 4.2 Click Characteristics

In addition to exploring properties of the queries that people issue, we also examine the characteristics of the search results they click. Clicks provide additional information about search intentions and the information that is encountered on the landing page can shape future search interactions.

**Number of clicks:** We suspected that exploring sessions might have more clicks than struggling sessions since struggling users are experiencing difficulty locating information. In our dataset, we have access to all clicks performed by the user during the search session. We excluded all non-result clicks (e.g., clicks on advertisements), as well as clicks that lead to another search result page (e.g., related search clicks, search vertical clicks, etc.). We then computed the average number of clicks for different query positions in the session for both exploring and struggling sessions. Computing the number of clicks at different points in the session allows us to observe changes in intentions and interests as the session proceeds. The result of this analysis is shown in Figure 6.

The figure shows that queries in exploring sessions contain more clicks compared to struggling sessions. The difference is small initially, and not statically significant up to Q3, and becomes larger later in the session, and statistically significant at the 0.05 level using a two-tailed t-test. Having multiple clicks in exploring sessions is expected since users are exploring multiple facets and hence are more likely to click on multiple results to locate information about these facets. Interestingly, the figures shows that struggling users tend to click on many results too, yet they still cannot locate the required information. The reason why they click may be related to the difference between the perceived relevance and the actual relevance of results. As shown in previous work [16][17], people tend to click on highly ranked results even if they are not relevant (position bias) and on results with good captions (caption bias) [5][35].

**Dwell time:** Another interesting question related to click characteristics is the difference in dwell time on clicked results in exploratory and struggling sessions. Dwell time reflects the time spent by

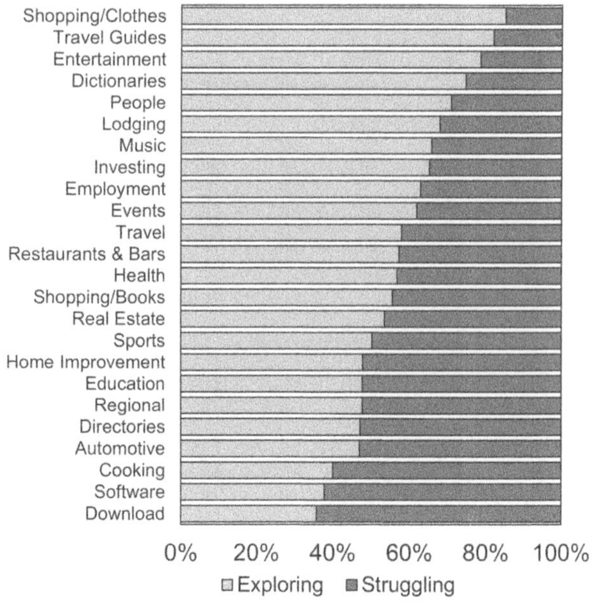


**Figure 8. Likelihood for exploring and struggling for different search topics.**

the user examining the clicked documents. The amount of time that people spend on pages can be an important indicator of whether they are satisfied with the content they encounter [9]. Dwell time can be estimated from click logs by computing the time between the click and the next seen click or query on the search engine.

We calculated the dwell time for every click in our dataset then we calculated the dwell time per query averaging the dwell time of all clicks corresponding to a single query. The average dwell time per query for both types of sessions is shown in Figure 7. The figure shows that clicks in struggling sessions increases during the session. However, it is much less than the dwell time for exploring sessions. The gap between the two types of sessions gets smaller as users progress through the sessions; especially in longer sessions. All difference are statically significant at the 0.05 level using a two-tailed t-test except for Q3 and Q6.

To understand the effect of the dwell time for clicks in the last query for the session, we remove the clicks of the last query before computing the average. This is important because many struggling sessions end up being successful and success typically occurs at the last query. Hence, the click dwell time of the last query in struggling sessions is likely different from other queries. There was no noticeable effect for removing the clicks of the last query in exploratory sessions. On the other hand, the average dwell time drops as users progress through struggling sessions if we ignore the last query. This shows that dwell time of clicks for the last query accounts for a large proportion of the total dwell time. This agrees with our earlier finding that many struggling sessions end up being successful or partly successful. Recall that in struggling sessions, users are typically trying to locate some information and, if successful, they typically find it at the last query and stop after finding it. Long dwell time has been shown to correlate with success in identifying the required information [9]. This explains the increase in dwell time for the last query in struggling sessions.

## 4.3 Topical Characteristics

Topical information has been used extensively to model search tasks and to capture users' intent. We wanted to understand the relationship between search situation and query topic. This may help us to understand whether there are particular topics, where searchers are experiencing difficulty, and identify those where exploring may be most important. To do so, we assigned a topic to each search session and calculated the likelihood of a session being exploring or struggling given its topic (proportion of exploring/struggling sessions for each topic). The topic of every session is the most common topic assigned to the visited documents in this session. To assign topics to documents, we used the Open Directory Project (ODP, dmoz.org) ODP category labels. ODP is an open Web directory maintained by a community of volunteer editors. It uses a hierarchical scheme for organizing URLs into categories and subcategories. Many previous studies of Web search behavior have used ODP to assign topics to URLs, e.g., [28][32].

Given the large number of URLs in our set we needed to label them automatically. We performed automatic classification of URLs into ODP categories similar to [32]. URLs in the directory were directly classified according to the corresponding categories. Missing URLs were incrementally pruned one level at a time until a match was found or a miss declared. We used the top two levels of the ODP hierarchy as topic labels.

Figure 8 shows the likelihood of exploring vs. struggling for the most frequent topics in the dataset. Topics are given abbreviated names (e.g., Home/Cooking → Cooking, Reference/Dictionaries → Dictionaries) due to space considerations. The figures show exploration is much more likely in particular, topics compared to others. For example, some popular exploration topics are Shopping, Travel, Entertainment, People (e.g., Celebrities), etc. In contrast, searches in Local, Technical (e.g., Computer Software), Downloads, etc. topics are less likely to be exploratory. The strong association between exploring and the Dictionaries topic may be attributable to users researching the meaning of related concepts.

## 4.4 Summary

In this section, we have characterized some key aspects of struggling and exploring. We have shown that although there are no significant differences in basic behaviors such as number of queries (an important demonstration of the need for this research), there are behaviors (primarily queries rather than clicks) and topical differences that do differ between the two motivations. In the next section, we describe a model that leverages these features and others to distinguish between struggling and exploring search sessions.

# 5. PREDICTING SESSION TYPE

We begin by formally defining our prediction task and then introducing the features used for prediction.

## 5.1 Problem Definition

As stated earlier, we study long sessions on a common subject area and hypothesize that searchers are engaged in either exploring sessions or struggling sessions. Given a session with more than two queries on a common subject area, as described in Section 3.1, our objective is to predict whether the current search session is exploring or struggling. For every session, we have all queries submitted by the user and all clicks, with a timestamp associated with every query or click action.

## 5.2 Features

Our predictive model used the following five groups of features:

**Query Features:** These are the features that describe general characteristics of the queries in the session such as the number of queries, query length and how the queries were issued (manual vs. clicked). If the source of a query is a click on a related search, this may suggest that the user is more likely to be exploring.

**Table 1. Features used to distinguish between exploring and struggling sessions. Features marked with an "*" had three versions corresponding to the minimum, maximum and average values per query/click.**

| Name | Description |
|---|---|
| **Query Features** | |
| NumQueries | Number of queries issued in session |
| CharQueryLen* | Query length in number of characters |
| WordQueryLen* | Query length in number of words |
| TimebetQueries* | Time between queries |
| PercManualQueries | Percentage of manually typed queries |
| PercSuggQueries | Percentage of clicked queries (e.g., query suggestions) |
| **Query Transition Features** | |
| AvgQuerySim* | Similarity between queries (see Section 4.1) |
| ExactMatch* | Number of terms that exactly match the previous query |
| AddTerms* | Number of added terms |
| DelTerms* | Number of removed terms |
| SubsTerms* | Number of substituted terms (see Section 4.1) |
| NumQGeneralizations | Number of queries where 1+ terms are removed from the previous query |
| NumQSpecifications | Number of queries where 1+ terms are added to the previous query |
| **Click Features** | |
| NumClicks | Total number of clicks in session |
| ClicksPerQuery | Average number of clicks per query |
| AbandonedQuerirs | Percentage of queries with no clicks |
| TotalDwellTime | Total dwell time in session |
| DwellTimePerClick* | Dwell time per click |
| DwellTimePerQuery* | Dwell time per query |
| TimeFirstClick* | Time to first click |
| UniqUrls | Percentage and number of unique clicked URLs |
| UniqDomains | Percentage and number of unique clicked domains |
| **Search History Features** | |
| QueryFreq* | Number of query impressions |
| QueryCTR* | Query clickthrough rate |
| QuerySuccessCTR* | Query success (dwell time > 30 sec) clickthrough rate |
| QueryQBCTR* | Query quickback (dwell time < 15 sec) clickthrough rate |
| QueryClickEntropy* | Entropy of click distribution |
| **Topic Features** | |
| Topic | Binary variable for every visited URL topic (see Section 4.3) |
| TopicRichness | Total number of unique topics per session |
| TopicEntropy | Topic distribution entropy |

**Query Transition Features:** The second group of features characterizes the way in which queries evolve as users progress in the session. These features included the number of added terms, substituted terms, and removed terms as users transitioned between queries. It also had features for the number of query generalizations and specifications in the session. See Section 4.1 for details on how we measure query similarity, added terms, substituted terms, etc.

**Click Features:** Click features were meant to describe the click behavior of the user during the session. They included features representing the number of clicks, their dwell time ,and features to capture whether the user was clicking on the same documents or documents from the same domain multiple times, perhaps indicative of difficulty locating a particular resource.

**Table 2. Performance of predicting exploring vs. struggling sessions. * indicates statistical significance at $p < 0.05$ using paired t-tests compared to the *First Query Text* baseline. A majority baseline has a 64% accuracy.**

| | Accuracy | Exploring F1 | Struggling F1 | AUC |
|---|---|---|---|---|
| *First Query Text* | 73.64 | 76.45 | 70.21 | 78.88 |
| *After 1st Query* | 74.22 | 76.63 | 71.28 | 79.90 |
| *After 2nd Query* | 75.72* | 77.85* | 73.20* | 80.90* |
| *After 3rd Query* | 80.41* | 82.02* | 78.51* | **85.34*** |
| *End of Session* | **81.67*** | **83.68*** | **79.17*** | 84.84* |

**Table 3. Performance of predicting successful sessions. * indicates statistical significance at $p \leq 0.05$ using paired t -tests compared to the baseline.**

| | Accuracy | F1 | AUC |
|---|---|---|---|
| *Baseline* | 70.75 | 72.97 | 76.80 |
| *+ Explore/Struggle (Predicted)* | 74.14* | 75.82* | 82.47* |
| *+ Explore/Struggle (Truth)* | **76.82*** | **77.51*** | **84.43*** |

**Search History Features:** The next group of features summarizes the behavior of other users who have submitted this query (e.g., clickthrough rate, frequency, and click entropy). The rationale behind including these features was that prior aggregate behavior may reveal something about the nature of search tasks of this type or engine performance on these queries (e.g., low clickthrough rate or low fractions of successful clicks).

**Topic Features:** The last group of features describes the topical characteristics of the session. Every visited URL in the session was mapped to an ODP category as described in Section 4.3. Given these topic labels, we compute a binary label for the presence and absence of each of the topics present in the session, topic richness, and topic entropy. As we see in Figure 8, there are differences in the nature of the search situation for different topics.

A summary of the features used for prediction is shown in Table 1. We now describe the experiments performed and the results of comparisons against a number of different baselines.

# 6. EXPERIMENTS AND RESULTS

In this section we describe the experimental setup and the results for the prediction experiments. We also include a detailed analysis of the performance of the features that were used in the prediction experiment, as well as an application of our predictive model for improving the performance of search satisfaction models.

## 6.1 Experimental Setup

We performed several experiments to study the performance of our approach. We conducted experiments using the data described in section 3 which had approximately 3000 sessions and 13100 queries. We train classifiers to distinguish between *exploring* and *struggling* sessions. We treat both *exploring* and *exploring with struggle* sessions as one class and *struggling* sessions as another class. Combining the two exploring classes has two advantages: (1) since we are adding a noisier behavioral signal to the exploring class, we can be more conservative in our estimates of the prediction performance, and (2) we can cover 99% of the labeled search sessions, with the remaining 1% as "Cannot Judge" (see Figure 2).

The model that we evaluate uses the full session behavior to predict whether the session comprises struggling or exploring, referred to as "End of Session". We also experiment with several other baselines that have access to no user behavior at all (i.e., by only considering the text of the first query, its topic, etc.) or have access to limited user behavior (e.g., behavior of the user on the first query, first two queries, etc.). This allows us to understand the effect of different features on the performance and to assess the extent to which user behavior is required to make accurate predictions. This can be useful for applications where we are interested in distinguishing between the two search situations earlier in the session. We compare our approach to four different baselines:

1. **First Query Text:** The first baselines has access to the text of the first query in the session only with no access to any behavior information forcing the classifier to use only the topical and the search history features.
2. **After 1st Query:** The second baseline has access to the behavior associated with the first query plus the topical and search history information.
3. **After 2nd Query:** The third baseline resembles the previous baseline but has access to behavior from the first two queries.
4. **After 3rd Query:** This baseline has access to all behavior information for the first three queries. It also has access to the topical and search history features.

We used 10-fold cross validation for all experiments and Multiple Additive Regression Trees (MART) for classification [10]. The advantages of MART include model interpretability (e.g., a ranked list of features is generated), facility for rapid training and testing, and robustness against noisy labels and missing values. We experimented with other classifiers (specifically logistic regression and SVM), and they yielded similar or worse performance than MART, hence we only report the results of MART here.

## 6.2 Results

We now present the results of the prediction experiment. Table 2 presents the results of the *exploring* vs. *struggling* experiment. We report the performance of the five classifiers described in Section 6.1 (our predictive model plus four baselines). For every classifier we report accuracy, F1 measure of the positive class (exploring), F1 measure of the negative class (struggling), and area under the curve (AUC). We also compare the performance against the majority baseline that always predicts the label of the dominant class.

Using no user behavior information and relying on the query text only yields better results than simply using marginal class distributions (64% accuracy). This shows the predictive power of the topic and search history features. This can be explained by the analysis in Section 4.3 where we showed that exploring is more likely to occur in certain topics (e.g., Shopping, Entertainment, etc.). Search history features are also important for identifying struggling sessions since low clickthrough rate and low success clickthrough rate (success clicks are clicks with dwell time longer than 30 seconds) are likely to be correlated with queries that lead to struggle.

As more behavioral features are included, we start noticing improvement in performance. After including the behavior associated with the first query, we notice a small improvement, albeit not statically significant at the 0.05 level according to a paired t-test. Given the behavior on only one query, we only have click signals (e.g., number of clicks, click dwell time). Query transition features are still missing though. Apparently click features, especially when limited to the first query only) do not help much in terms of performance. As the classifier obtains access to more behavioral features, the performance improves. We get the best predictive performance when the classifier has access to the entire session.

## 6.3 Feature Analysis

We now turn our attention to the features that contribute most to the prediction task. In order to assess the importance of the proposed features, we compute the information gain of all features. We do that by computing the error reduction for each feature at each node split using the squared loss function. We then aggregate the error reduction at all splits for every feature and use that as a measure of feature gain. We do not report feature gains at the individual feature level for the five classifiers here for space considerations. Instead, we report feature importance at the feature group level. We assigned a score from 0 to 10 to each feature. The feature is assigned a 10 if it is ranked first according to feature gain, 9 if it is ranked second, and so on. Features that do not appear in the top 10 list are assigned 0. Every feature group is assigned a rank. The rank of any feature group is the rank of its best performing feature according to feature gain. We also tried to assign every group the average of the ranks of all its features and obtained similar results.

In Figure 9, we show the feature importance for every feature group for every classifier. We notice that query features are moderately important at the beginning when no behavior is available, they quickly lose their influence though as more behavior is made available to the classifier. Click features are not available at the beginning when only query text is available, but once the classifier gets access to user behavior, the importance of the click features quickly increases. It drops again though as more user behavior is available, yet remains moderately important. Topic features and search history features behave similarly. When limited behavior is available, they dominate all other features and are constantly ranked at the first positions. As more behavior becomes available, their importance drops quickly and they remain at the bottom of the list of the top features. Query transition features behave in exactly the opposite way to topic and search history features. At the beginning, they are not available to the classifier. However, as the classifier obtains access to more user behavior, they quickly climb up the list and eventually dominate all other features.

## 6.4 Application: Search Success Prediction

Finally, we study the effect of identifying exploring vs. struggling sessions on success prediction. Traditionally, multiple related queries in a session have been regarded as a sign of a searcher experiencing difficulty in locating required information. This is correct for struggling sessions, but for exploring sessions multiple related queries are not only not a sign of failure, but also a sign on increased engagement which can be regarded as a sign of search success.

To assess the effect of identifying session type on success prediction, we train a success prediction classifier following the work of Hassan and colleagues [12][14]. In that work, they represent every session as sequence of actions (i.e., queries and clicks). They show that the bigrams extracted from these sequences (e.g., Q-Click, Q-END, etc.) are very strong predictors of success. We use these features to train a Multiple Additive Regression Trees (MART) classifier using 10-fold cross validation. The performance of this classifier ("Baseline") is reported in Table 3. We compare this baseline to two other classifiers. The first uses the same features as the baseline in addition to another feature representing the session type (Exploratory or struggling) as predicted by the classifier described earlier. The second is just like the first but uses the truth session type label (from the human judges) as an oracle label instead of the predicted one. Results show significant improvement in performance due to adding the session type feature. We also observe that the gains get us a good way to the performance of an oracle model that was truth aware (56-74% of the maximum possible gain with our labeled data). The session type feature had the highest feature level information gain for the success prediction task.

# 7. DISCUSSION AND IMPLICATIONS

Search engines aim to understand whether they are meeting searchers' needs, and if and when they need to improve their engine or intervene to help improve the search process. Struggling and exploration behaviors may appear similar, but the situations have radically different experiences for the searchers involved. Searchers who are struggling may be dissatisfied and frustrated, whereas searchers who are exploring may be satisfied and content. Distinguishing between these two scenarios across a broad range of users and information needs is important for search engines in understanding search success and in providing search support. In this paper, we showed that we can build a classifier to accomplish this effectively, using features of recorded search interactions including query and topic dynamics. We also demonstrate an important application of our classifier: improving the accuracy of models of search satisfaction by considering struggling and exploring.

Although our paper shows that our method has strong potential, there are at least two limitations that we should acknowledge. The first is the nature of the labels that we applied to the data. The labels were assigned by third-party judges based on their consensus opinion of the nature of the sessions. While using the consensus may improve the reliability of the label, the fact that the judges were not those searching may lead to unforeseen issues with the labels, or for the system to simply learn what was important to the judges in making their predictions, rather than the true situation that the searcher faced. Ways to address this shortcoming to include soliciting judgments from searchers in-situ at the time of the search. This can be intrusive; however, previous work has shown that there are ways to accomplish such data capture practically, e.g., [9]. Another limitation is the way in which the struggling/exploring signal was integrated into the satisfaction model used as an example application. In our implementation, the additional signal was added as a feature – however, a potentially more powerful way would be to build separate models for success prediction for different session types that uses both general behavior patterns as well as session type specific information.

The application scenario that we have focused on in this paper has been the retrospective prediction of the rationale behind observed search behavior given the full session. We also studied how we can do such predictions at different points in the session to understand how the feature contributions evolve. While this form of retrospective prediction can have value for satisfaction analysis such as that presented in this paper and other applications, there is also potential benefit from applying this classifier in real time as the session proceeds. A real time classifier could estimate when the user is struggling or exploring and intervene to improve their experience by adapting it to suit the current need. For example, if they appear to be struggling, alternative queries could be suggested that have been shown to help searchers with similar needs. Additionally, hard-to-find resources could be presented if there is evidence that they have been sought and found in prior similar sessions [29]. If they are exploring, additional results or a new interface could be presented to help them discover and synthesize information more effectively.

# 8. CONCLUSIONS

There are two main reasons that searchers issue many queries during a session: (a) they are experiencing difficulty in finding required information, or (b) they are engaged in an exploratory search. Although being able to distinguish between these situations is important for improving search accuracy and experience, the behaviors associated with the situations are similar in terms of the number of queries and session duration. A more sophisticated analysis of search behavior is required to distinguish these search situations. In this paper, we have presented such methods and associated analysis. We have shown that there are differences in behavioral attributes such as query transitions and result clicks, as well as topic dynamics that can be useful in distinguishing struggling from exploring. We have also developed classifiers that have shown we can perform this prediction accurately. Future work involves the expansion of our research in this area to consider the real-time prediction of the search situation, as well as other applications of the predictor such as selecting query suggestions to bypass common areas of difficulty and get people to answers faster.

## REFERENCES


[1] Ageev, M., Guo, Q., Lagun, D., and Agichtein, E. (2011). Find it if you can: A game for modeling different types of web search success using interaction data. *Proc. SIGIR*, 345–354.

[2] Aula, A., Khan, R., and Guan, Z. (2010). How does search behavior change as search becomes more difficult? *Proc. SIGCHI*, 35–44.

[3] Bron, M., Gorp, J., Vishneuski, A., Nack, F., Leeuw, S., and De Rijke, M. (2012). A subjunctive exploratory search interface to support media studies researchers. *Proc. SIGIR*, 425–434.

[4] Ceaparu, I., Lazar, J., Bessiere, K., Robinson, J., and Shneiderman, B. (2004). Determining causes and severity of end-user frustration. *Intl. J. of HCI*, 17(3): 333-356.

[5] Clarke, C.L.A., Agichtein, E., Dumais, S. and White, R.W. (2007). The influence of caption features on clickthrough patterns in web search. *Proc. SIGIR*, 135–142.

[6] Downey, D., Dumais, S., Liebling, D., and Horvitz, E. (2008). Understanding the relationship between searchers' queries and information goals. *Proc. CIKM*, 449–458.

[7] Feild, H., Allan, J., and Jones, R. (2010). Predicting searcher frustration. *Proc. SIGIR*, 34–41.

[8] Fleiss, J.L. (1981). *Statistical Methods for Rates and Proportions* (2nd edition). New York: John Wiley.

[9] Fox, S., Karnawat, K., Mydland, M., Dumais, S.T., and White, T. (2005). Evaluating implicit measures to improve the search experience. *ACM TOIS*, 23(2): 147–168.

[10] Friedman, J.H., Hastie, T., and Tibshirani, R. (1998). *Additive Logistic Regression: A Statistical View of Boosting*. Technical Report, Stanford University.

[11] Gwizdka, J. and Spence, I. (2006). What can searching behavior tell us about the difficulty of information tasks? A study of web navigation. *Proc. ASIST*, vol. 43: 1–22.

[12] Hassan, A., Jones, R., and Klinkner, K.L. (2010). Beyond DCG: User behavior as a predictor of a successful search. *Proc. WSDM*, 221–230.

[13] Hassan, A. and White, R.W. (2012). Task tours: helping users tackle complex search tasks. *Proc. CIKM*, 1885–1889.

[14] Hassan, A. (2012). A semi-supervised approach to modeling web search satisfaction. *Proc. SIGIR*, 275–284.

[15] Huffman, S. and Hochster, M. (2007). How well does result relevance predict session satisfaction? *Proc. SIGIR*, 567–574.

[16] Joachims, T. (2002). Evaluating search engines using clickthrough data. *Proc. SIGKDD*, 133–142.

[17] Joachims, T., Granka, L., Pan, B., Hembrooke, H., and Gay, G. (2005). Accurately interpreting clickthrough data as implicit feedback. *Proc. SIGIR*, 154–161.

[18] Jones, R. and Klinkner, K.L. (2008). Beyond the session timeout: Automatic hierarchical segmentation of search topics in query logs. *Proc. CIKM*, 699-708.

[19] Kanoulas, E., Carterette, B., Clough, P.D., and Sanderson, M. (2011). Evaluating multi-query sessions. *Proc. SIGIR*, 1053–1062.

[20] Kim, J. (2006). Task difficulty as a predictor and indicator of web searching interaction. *Proc. SIGCHI*, 959–964.

[21] Kim, J.Y., Collins-Thompson, K., Bennett, P.N., and Dumais, S.T. (2012). Characterizing web content, user interests, and search behavior by reading level and topic. *Proc. WSDM*, 213–222.

[22] Liu, J., Liu, C., Gwizdka, J., and Belkin, N.J. (2010). Can search systems detect users' task difficulty? Some behavioral signals. *Proc. SIGIR*, 845–846.

[23] Liu, C., Liu, J., Cole, M., Belkin, N.J., and Zhang, X. (2012). Task difficulty and domain knowledge effects on information search behaviors. *Proc. ASIST*, 49(1): 1–10.

[24] Marchionini, G. (2006). Exploratory search: From finding to understanding. *CACM*, 49(4): 41–46.

[25] Morris, D., Morris, M.R., and Venolia, G. (2008). SearchBar: A search-centric web history for task resumption and information refinding. *Proc. SIGCHI*, 1207–1216.

[26] Radlinski, F. and Joachims, T. (2005). Query chains: Learning to rank from implicit feedback. *Proc. SIGKDD*, 239–248.

[27] Raman, K., Bennett, P.N., and Collins-Thompson, K. (2013). Toward whole session relevance: Exploring intrinsic diversity in web search. *Proc. SIGIR*, 463–472.

[28] Shen, X., Dumais, S., and Horvitz, E. (2005). Analysis of topic dynamics in web search. *Proc. WWW*, 1102–1103.

[29] White, R.W. and Chandrasekar, R. (2010). Exploring the use of labels to shortcut search trails. *Proc. SIGIR*, 811–812.

[30] White, R.W. and Roth, R.A. (2009). *Exploratory Search: Beyond the Query-Response Paradigm*. Morgan Claypool.

[31] White, R.W. and Dumais, S.T. (2009). Characterizing and predicting search engine switching behavior. *Proc. CIKM*, 87–96.

[32] White, R.W. and Huang, J. (2010). Assessing the scenic route: Measuring the value of search trails in web logs. *Proc. SIGIR*, 587–594.

[33] Wu, Z. and Palmer, M. (1994). Verb semantics and lexical selection. *Proc. ACL*, 133–138.

[34] Yuan, X. and White, R.W. (2012). Building the trail best traveled: Effects of domain knowledge on web search trailblazing. *Proc. SIGCHI*, 1795–1804.

[35] Yue, Y., Patel, R., and Roehrig, H. (2010). Beyond position bias: Examining result attractiveness as a source of presentation bias in clickthrough data. *Proc. WWW*, 1011–1018.

# Democracy is Good for Ranking: Towards Multi-view Rank Learning and Adaptation in Web Search

Wei Gao
Qatar Computing Research Institute
Qatar Foundation
Doha, Qatar
wgao@qf.org.qa

Pei Yang
Department of Computer Science
South China University of Technology
Guangzhou, China
yangpei@scut.edu.cn

## ABSTRACT

Web search ranking models are learned from features originated from different views or perspectives of document relevancy, such as query dependent or independent features. This seems intuitively conformant to the principle of multi-view approach that leverages distinct complementary views to improve model learning. In this paper, we aim to obtain optimal separation of ranking features into non-overlapping subsets (i.e., views), and use such different views for rank learning and adaptation. We present a novel semi-supervised multi-view ranking model, which is then extended into an adaptive ranker for search domains where no training data exists. The core idea is to proactively strengthen view consistency (i.e., the consistency between different rankings each predicted by a distinct view-based ranker) especially when training and test data follow divergent distributions. For this purpose, we propose a unified framework based on listwise ranking scheme to mutually reinforce the view consistency of target queries and the appropriate weighting of source queries that act as prior knowledge. Based on LETOR and Yahoo Learning to Rank datasets, our method significantly outperforms some strong baselines including single-view ranking models commonly used and multi-view ranking models that do not impose view consistency on target data.

## Categories and Subject Descriptors

H.3.3 [**Information Storage and Retrieval**]: Information Search and Retrieval

## Keywords

Multi-view rank learning; rank adaptation; view consistency

## 1. INTRODUCTION

The capability of combining a large number of features in an optimal way is highly desirable for search engines [29]. Learning to rank or rank learning for Information Retrieval (IR) aims to learn how to combine the predefined relevance features properly for better ranking search results.

Typically, ranking features consist of hundreds of relevance scores derived from various retrieval relevance models, each of which corresponds to a permutation of search results from some particular perspective. For example, query dependent features, such as frequencies of the query terms in the document and BM25, are constructed from the perspective of query-document relevancy, while query independent features, such as PageRank and HostRank, are provided by link analysis algorithms depending on the connectivity of documents only. It can be expected that these distinct views of features, although possibly redundant sometimes, if combined correctly, may afford strong complementarity to each other and result in considerable improvement for ranking.

Such natural feature partition seems intuitively conformant to the philosophy of multi-view learning [6, 1, 41]. It was found that having multiple representations instead of combining all features into one view can improve classification performance when many unlabeled examples are available in addition to the labeled ones. For instance, the idea of co-training [6] is to train one learner on each view of the labeled data, and then each learner iteratively labels the unlabeled subsets of data where it has the highest confidence in its prediction. Since the views are independent, the newly labeled examples by one learner can give the other learner novel information for improving its model parameters.

Moreover, rank learning requires large training set that is very expensive or time-consuming to obtain. Co-training follows semi-supervised fashion where it needs only partially labeled data, and unlabeled data can also participate in training. In the competitive Web search market, it would be much desirable to quickly deploy ranking models into other search domains to support different verticals or search in the market of different languages where training data are rarely available. As a result, we need to extend in-domain ranking to rank adaptation for good out-of-domain performance by bridging domain gap [23, 13, 39, 12, 21, 22]. The semi-supervised nature of co-training-based algorithms makes them naturally extendible to cross-domain setting.

Although classification methods based on co-training are common [16, 17, 7, 32], the study of multi-view rank learning is almost absent. Existing multi-view classifiers hardly could be applied for ranking directly because (1) the concentration of ranking is on the order of a list of documents rather than their absolute class labels; (2) the confidence measure of a ranker and the consistency between rankers on distinct views are radically different from that of classifiers,


*WSDM'14*, February 24–28, 2014, New York, New York, USA.
Copyright 2014 ACM 978-1-4503-2351-2/14/02 ...$15.00.
http://dx.doi.org/10.1145/2556195.2556267.

which may require estimating the permutation probability of output rankings; (3) there is no explicit view boundary or feature definition provided in most ranking benchmark data sets. In addition, multi-view methods assume that different view-based learners give compatible predictions on the same instance with certain probability [6], but such view consistency assumption is largely violated in a cross-domain setting where training and test data are drawn from different distributions. All these render multi-view approach for rank learning and adaptation practically challenging.

In this paper, we investigate a novel and effective solution to tackle these challenges based on typical listwise ranking scheme [9, 40, 34, 36, 42], specifically ListMLE [40]. We extend an automatic feature decomposition approach for co-training [15], by which we simultaneously obtain the optimal feature split and exploit such multiple views for rank learning and adaptation. Different from [15] which is focused on class conditionally independent assumption, we argue that enhancing view consistency across domains can improve the adaptation effectiveness for multi-view ranking algorithms. We propose a unified ranking framework that incorporates listwise loss, listwise view consistency on target queries and the appropriate weighting of source queries. To deal with the lack of view agreement in adaptation setting, our method adopts an iterative procedure to mutually reinforce the view consistency of ranking on target queries and the weighting of source queries. Intuitively, since transferrable source queries likely have better view consensus in both domains, imposing view consensus on target queries may result in a stronger model being helpful to weigh out those transferrable source queries that can be used to further improve view consistency in target domain. With LETOR3.0 and Yahoo Learning to Rank datasets, experimental results show that our method makes significant improvements over the baselines.

The rest of this paper is organized as follows: Section 2 reviews the related work; Section 3 gives the preliminaries of using multiple views for ranking and adaptation; Section 4 presents the proposed multi-view ranking method; Section 5 descries experiments and discusses results; Section 6 draws conclusion and looks ahead to future work.

## 2. RELATED WORK

In this section, we briefly review ranking, domain adaptation, multi-view learning and how they were related.

### 2.1 Rank Learning and Adaptation

Rank learning is to optimize a ranking function given data consisting of queries, the retrieved documents and their relevance judgements. Given a new query, the learned function is used to predict the order of retrieved documents. Based on input spaces, three categories of approaches have been proposed, namely pointwise, pairwise and listwise approach. Listwise scheme [9, 40, 34, 36, 42] addresses ranking by considering the entire list of documents associated with the same query as instance and considers positional information in the loss function which intuitively makes more sense with the nature of ranking [29]. Our algorithm is listwise. A comprehensive survey on learning to rank is in [29].

It is worth mentioning that for saving labeling cost of ranking data, some studies explored semi-supervised rank learning with only partially labeled data in transductive [18] or inductive [2] manner. Multi-view approach is inherently semi-supervised and can be practiced in either way.

Domain adaptation [5, 24, 25, 27, 43] aims to save in-domain labeling expense by using out-of-domain training data, and tries to bridge the dataset shift [31] between distributions of two domains by using their common information. It is difficult to directly use classifier adaptation for ranking as rank adaptation is comparatively more challenging [23]. Therefore, rank adaptation received more and more attention recently [23, 13, 39, 12, 21, 22, 8]. In [13], the Gradient Boosting Tree structure of ranker learned from source data was adjusted using some target labeled data. In [23], prior knowledge was learned from source domain and the similarity of parameters between two domains was considered when training the target ranker. Both instance-based and feature-based adaptation were conducted for ranking with the help of a few target training data in [12]. Rank adaptation was also dealt with in [39] by bridging heterogeneous domains via some shared latent space. In [21], rankers were learned from two domains separately and then interpolated for a stronger model. Various instance-weighting schemes were proposed in [22] for adaptation with a more relaxed setting where no target ranking data is labeled. More recently, active selection of target queries was studied by [8] for improving rank adaptation performance. All these rank adaptation methods are of single view.

### 2.2 Multi-view Learning

Multi-view learning is a semi-supervised framework that utilizes the consensus among learners trained on independent views of the same problem to improve the model's overall performance. It holds two basic assumptions, i.e., conditional independence assumption and view consistency assumption. Early approaches include co-training [6] and its variants [41, 16]. Then the idea was widely explored or extended later on [1, 3, 17, 7, 32]. For example, the unnecessarily strong view-independence assumption was relaxed in [1], which then suggested that the disagreement rate of two independent hypotheses upper bounds the error rate of either hypothesis. It was also proved that a weaker expanding property called $\epsilon$-expandability on the multi-view data distribution is sufficient for co-training to work [3].

Co-training also assumes that all labels on the examples with non-zero probability are consistent with both hypotheses of each view [6]. Under this view consistency assumption, some algorithms impose consensus constraint between the predictors, each trained from one view of data, to improve the learning performance [35, 19, 20, 28]. A co-regularization approach [35] was proposed to learn a multi-view classifier from partially labeled data using a view-consensus-based regularization term. A supervised algorithm named SVM-2K [19] was proposed which imposed a similarity constraint between two distinct view-based SVMs. A two-view transductive SVM [28] was constructed by extending the work of [19] for utilizing the large set of unlabeled data available. A two-view learning algorithm [20] was studied by using stochastic agreement regularization based on a constrained EM. An automatic feature decomposition algorithm [15] was presented for pseudo multi-view learning where the original data has only one view.

All these methods deal with classification problem and treat distinct domains indiscriminately. We are focused on multi-view rank learning problem and our setting is more general where training and test data can come from related but different domains.

## 2.3 Hybrid Approach

The combination of multi-view learning and adaptation is potentially powerful but not well studied. Ganchev et al. [20] applied the proposed two-view semi-supervised learner to cross-domain sentiment classification, but they did not consider bridging domain gap explicitly in the model. Chen et al. [14] presented a variant of co-training for domain adaptation based on two logistic regression classifiers, and feature correlation between two domains was employed for feature selection that aimed to bridge the gap, but view consistency factor was not considered. Zhang et al. [44] integrated multi-view learning and transfer learning with a large margin approach, where source training data were used to learn a large margin classifier and the data from both domains were used to impose consistencies among multiple views. However, they did not co-relate domain gap to view consistency in the model which is important to adaptation. All these algorithms are based on classification models.

Multi-view semi-supervised learning was explored for ranking multilingual documents [37] where each view corresponds to one language. But it was for bipartite ranking and its feature space adopted bag-of-words representation, which is equivalent to classification. Adaptation was not considered.

Our method combines multi-view learning, ranking and adaptation in a unified framework to boost cross-domain ranking performance. There are significant distinctions from existing work: (1) we work on multi-view ranking which differs radically from classification; (2) we attempt to co-relate the factors of domain commonality and view consistency, and focus on mutually reinforcing the two components to improve rank transfer. To our knowledge, there is no previous work based on multi-view approach for rank adaptation.

# 3. PRELIMINARIES

Let rank training set contain $n$ queries $Q = \{q_i\}_{i=1}^n$, and each $q_i$ is associated with a list of documents represented by feature vectors $\mathbf{x}_i = \{\vec{x}_{ij}\}_{j=1}^{m_i}$ and a list of rank labels $\mathbf{y}_i = \{y_{ij}\}_{j=1}^{m_i}$ (each corresponds to a document), where $m_i$ is the number of documents of $q_i$, $\vec{x}_{ij} \in R^N$ is a feature vector consisting of $N$ pre-defined rank features of document $ij$, and $y_{ij}$ is its relevance judgement (e.g., highly relevant, relevant or irrelevant). The goal is to optimize a ranking function $f : \mathbf{x}_i \rightarrow \pi_i$ that maps the input document list $\mathbf{x}_i$ into a permutation $\pi_i$ of documents given $q_i$.

Ranking features typically can be expressed by query-dependent and query-independent relevance scores, being a natural split for distinct views, which inspires us to explore multi-view approach for rank learning. Nevertheless, possible decomposition of features is not limited to such an explicit split but can be optimized automatically, especially when feature definitions are unknown, which is not uncommon in the typical ranking dataset. Without loss of generality, we assume two views here for easy presentation.

## 3.1 View Consistency

Multi-view learning such as co-training [6] holds view consistency assumption that encourages the models on different views to give compatible predictions on the same instance with certain probability. In a ranking problem, given an input space $X = \{\mathbf{x}_i\}_{i=1}^n = \{(\mathbf{x}_i^1, \mathbf{x}_i^2)\}_{i=1}^n$, where $\mathbf{x}_i^1$ and $\mathbf{x}_i^2$ correspond to the two views of the same list of documents of $q_i$ (e.g., $\mathbf{x}_i^1 = \{\vec{x}_{ij}^1\}_{j=1}^{m_i}$ where $\vec{x}_{ij}^1$ is the first view of document $ij$), the view consistency assumption hypothesizes that for each $q_i$, all permutations of its documents with non-zero probability on $\mathbf{x}_i \in X$ agree with some target function on $\mathbf{x}_i^1$, i.e., $f_1 : \mathbf{x}_i^1 \rightarrow \pi_i$, and also agree with some target function on $\mathbf{x}_i^2$, i.e., $f_2 : \mathbf{x}_i^2 \rightarrow \pi_i$. However, this assumption seems too strong in most cases. In practice, some algorithms relaxed this assumption and tried to impose consensus constraint on the two view-based models directly with unlabeled examples [35, 19, 20, 28], which has been shown helpful to classification.

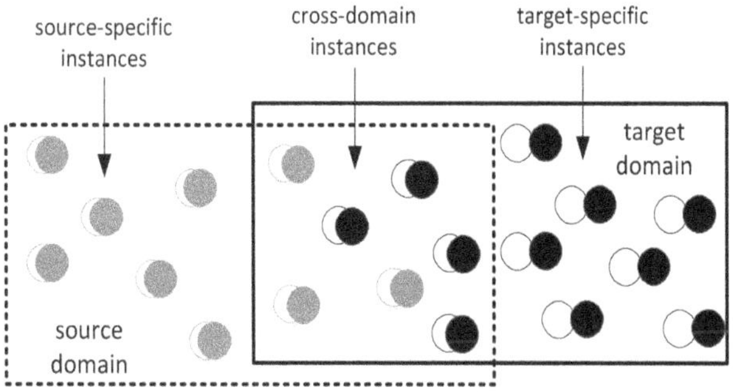


**Figure 1: A conceptual illustration of view consistency under dataset shift**

## 3.2 View Consistency under Dataset Shift

View consistency assumption would be more likely violated when training and test data come from different distributions or domains which is known as dataset shift [31]. Figure 1 conceptually illustrates the problem with a high-level representation of two related domains. In this figure, an instance[1] is represented using an hollowed circle and a filled circle coupled together, each corresponding to one view of the instance. The distance between the two coupled circles indicates the degree of agreement on that instance between the two models each learned from one view. The grey circle pairs are source domain instances and the dark pairs are of target domain. The instances intersecting two domains are called cross-domain instances that encode some general cross-domain commonality. And the other two regions that fall apart only encode specific knowledge of their own domains, referred to as domain-specific instances. Under dataset shift, the joint distribution of feature and relevance varies greatly between training and test data. Suppose we have two rankers each trained on one view using source training data. If we blindly apply them to target documents, their agreement on document rankings would be weakened, which is shown by the relatively larger distance between the coupled circles, due to the distribution gap of two domains.

Basically, the cross-domain instances from source domain would be helpful for learning target ranking model, and also, strengthening view consensus on target instances would be conducive to weighing out cross-domain source instances that are expected important to the success of adaptation, and vice versa.

[1]Note that in ranking, the instances may be documents, document pairs or queries depending on the specific scheme used. Here an instance corresponds to a query as we use listwise approach.

## 4. MULTI-VIEW RANKING APPROACH

Two views lacking of prediction consistency are subject to inferior ranking performance when they are combined. Our idea is to purposefully identify those important cross-domain instances from source data that can be used to boost target ranking performance by improving view consistency on target instances with a co-training-like procedure. As a result, the enhanced view consistency of target ranker can be expected helpful for selecting those informative cross-domain knowledge from the rest of source training data in a sense that the ranking of cross-domain source instances predicted by the target ranker would be better than that of source-specific instances. Therefore, some positive feedback would be resulted from the enhanced view consistency.

In this section, we describe the proposed multi-view ranking approach in semi-supervised as well as adaptation settings. First, we will introduce ListMLE, a state-of-the-art listwise ranking algorithm; Then, we will describe how it is extended and optimized by a multi-view approach.

### 4.1 ListMLE

Although listwise approach is natural and more effective, it is usually difficult to optimize a list-based loss directly because the performance measure on a document list is based on the result of a sort function. ListMLE employs a likelihood loss as the surrogate since it has nice properties [40]. Given the training data, it minimizes the sum of negative likelihood with respect to the ground-truth permutation of documents over all the training queries in $\{q_i\}_{i=1}^n$:

$$\min_{\vec{w}} L(\vec{w}) = \sum_{i=1}^{n} L_{q_i}(\vec{w}) = \sum_{i=1}^{n} -\log\left(P(\pi_{y_i}|\vec{w}, \mathbf{x}_i)\right) \quad (1)$$

where $\vec{w}$ is the weight vector to estimate, $P(\pi_{y_i}|\vec{w}, \mathbf{x}_i)$ is the permutation probability based on the ground truth $y_i$ of the documents of $q_i$, which is defined by Plackett-Luce model [30]:

$$P(\pi|\vec{w}, \mathbf{x}_i) = \prod_{j=1}^{m_i} \frac{\exp\left(f(\vec{w}, x_{\pi^{-1}(j)})\right)}{\sum_{k=j}^{m_i} \exp\left(f(\vec{w}, x_{\pi^{-1}(k)})\right)} \quad (2)$$

where $\pi^{-1}(j)$ is the index of document ranked at the $j$-th position of permutation $\pi$, and $f(\cdot)$ is the specific expression of ranking function $f$.

The advantage of ListMLE also lies in its efficiency in training where one only needs to compute the probability of a single permutation based on ground truth but not all the permutations, and its objective function is easy to minimize using gradient-based optimizers.

### 4.2 Semi-supervised CoListMLE

Let $\vec{w}_1 = [w_l^1]_{l=1}^N$ and $\vec{w}_2 = [w_l^2]_{l=1}^N$ be the weight vectors of the ranking model for view $\mathbf{x}^1$ and $\mathbf{x}^2$, respectively, where $N$ is the dimension of entire feature space, and $\mathbf{x}^1$ and $\mathbf{x}^2$ denote a non-overlapping separation of features according to $\vec{w}_1$ and $\vec{w}_2$. Let $Q_L = \{q_i\}_{i=1}^n$ and $Q_U = \{q_i\}_{i=1}^{n'}$ be the sets of (labeled) training queries and (unlabeled) test queries, respectively. Here we present a generalized semi-supervised framework for multi-view ranking called CoListMLE, inspired by the variant of co-training-based classification in [15].

Our objective is to minimize the combined likelihood rank loss of the two views on the labeled instances while maximizing the rank agreement between them on the unlabeled instances. Meanwhile, there are two critical issues for co-training to work: (1) the two view-based learners are trained on different subsets of features where each feature only can be used by one of the rankers; (2) the two view-based learners must be able to teach each other for boosting up learning performance, meaning that there should be sufficient number of unlabeled examples, on which only one of the learners can make confident prediction. The first condition constrains how to split the features, and the second was addressed by the $\epsilon$-expanding rule in [3]. Our co-training-based ListMLE model named as CoListMLE is formulated as follows:

$$\min_{(\vec{w}_1, \vec{w}_2)} \sum_{i=1}^{n} \left[L_{q_i}(\vec{w}_1) + L_{q_i}(\vec{w}_2)\right] + \lambda \cdot D_{Q_U}(\vec{w}_1, \vec{w}_2) \quad (3)$$

subject to:

(1) View splitting: $\sum_{l=1}^{N} \left[w_l^1 \cdot w_l^2\right]^2 = 0$

(2) $\epsilon$-expandability:

$$\sum_{i=1}^{n'} \left[c_{\vec{w}_1}(q_i)\bar{c}_{\vec{w}_2}(q_i) + \bar{c}_{\vec{w}_1}(q_i)c_{\vec{w}_2}(q_i)\right]$$

$$\geq \epsilon \min\left[\sum_{i=1}^{n'} \left[c_{\vec{w}_1}(q_i)c_{\vec{w}_2}(q_i)\right], \sum_{i=1}^{n'} \left[\bar{c}_{\vec{w}_1}(q_i)\bar{c}_{\vec{w}_2}(q_i)\right]\right]$$

Note that different from [15, 14], the first term of Equation 3 is the sum of likelihood-based rank loss of two views over all the labeled data, $\lambda$ is a control coefficient, and the second term $D_{Q_U}(\cdot,\cdot)$ is newly introduced to capture listwise view disagreement estimated by the difference between two permutation probability distributions over all the unlabeled instances:

$$D_{Q_U}(\vec{w}_1, \vec{w}_2) = \sum_{i=1}^{n'} \left[\log\left(P(\pi_i^{(k-1)}|\vec{w}_1, \mathbf{x}_i^1)\right) - \log\left(P(\pi_i^{(k-1)}|\vec{w}_2, \mathbf{x}_i^2)\right)\right]^2 \quad (4)$$

where $\pi_i^{(k-1)}$ is the permutation output by the model to the documents of $q_i$ during the $(k-1)$-th round of iteration. The reason we have to use the previous permutation is that the permutation of current (i.e., the $k$-th) round is the function of $\vec{w}_1$ and $\vec{w}_2$, which are yet to be computed. Though enhancing view consistency is straightforward in classification, it remains challenging to do so for view-based rankers. It is hard to optimize the correlation between two predicted permutations directly in the objective due to the position-based, non-continuous and non-differentiable nature of most IR evaluation measures. Thus, we use the discrepancy between two permutation probabilities here as a surrogate.

The constraint (1) of Equation 3 controls the decomposition of features to be non-overlapping. In constraint (2) as to $\epsilon$-expandability, $c_{\vec{w}_1}(q_i)$ or $c_{\vec{w}_2}(q_i)$ is a confidence indicator function of the corresponding view-based ranker regarding the prediction on query $q_i$, which is defined as:

$$c_{\vec{w}_1}^{(k)}(q_i) = \begin{cases} 1, & \text{if } P(\pi_i^{(k-1)}|\vec{w}_1, \mathbf{x}_i) > \tau; \\ 0, & \text{otherwise} \end{cases} \quad (5)$$

where probability threshold $\tau$ can be set empirically. Also, $\bar{c}(q) = 1 - c(q)$ indicates that the ranker is not confident about $q$. The constraint (2) ensures that the number of queries in $Q_U$ that exactly one ranker is confident about is larger than the the number of queries which both rankers are confident about or both are not, so that both of the ranks can utilize those instances they are not confident about to learn from the other ranker that is confident on them [15].

This generalized framework allows us to use different ranking models and train the model in a semi-supervised fashion with automatically splitted views. Such objective function is non-convex [14] and non-smooth. We smooth the constraints using approximation and resort to augmented Lagrangian method [4] to transform it into an unconstrained problem[2]. Then locally optimal solution is obtained using the standard conjugate gradient descent.

## 4.3 AdaCoListMLE for Rank Adaptation

We assume a typical unsupervised adaptation setting, where all rank labels exist in source data, and there is no labeled data but reasonable amount of unlabeled data in target domain. Rank adaptation requires finding the most informative cross-domain knowledge from source domain as training materials to guide the transfer of ranking knowledge. As discussed in Section 3.2, the cross-domain source instances can carry some important commonality knowledge related to the target domain. Such kind of information will be identified for use to train the target ranker. If identified, presumably it can be leveraged to strengthen view consistency on target instances. Once the ranking on target domain is getting improved, the ranker becomes more target-leaning, then it will have more discriminant power to differentiate the cross-domain instances from source-specific ones. Therefore, we come up with a reinforcement process where the weighting of source queries and the degree of view consistency on target queries will be mutually enhanced in a unified framework, which is referred to as AdaCoListMLE:

$$\min_{(\vec{w}_1,\vec{w}_2)} \left\{ \sum_{i=1}^{n_s} W_{q_i} \cdot [L_{q_i}(\vec{w}_1) + L_{q_i}(\vec{w}_2)] \; + \right. \tag{6}$$

$$\left. \lambda \cdot \sum_{i=1}^{n_t} \left[ \log\left( P(\pi_i^{(k-1)} | \vec{w}_1, \mathbf{x}_i^1) \right) - \log\left( P(\pi_i^{(k-1)} | \vec{w}_2, \mathbf{x}_i^2) \right) \right]^2 \right\}$$

where $W_{q_i}$ is the importance weight of source query $q_i$, and $n_s$ and $n_t$ are the number of source and target queries, respectively, and the same constraints of view splitting and $\epsilon$-expandability are imposed like in Equation 3.

### 4.3.1 *Source query weighting*

Now the problem is how to weigh out the cross-domain source queries based on the ranking model obtained thus far. The intuition is that if the retrieved documents of a source query can be ranked well by a target ranking model, it implies that the rank knowledge of this query is more suitable for the target ranking task, thus should be deemed as more informative. Otherwise, this source training query may be not a good choice. Therefore, the importance of a source query can be measured by the performance of target ranking model on this query. We weigh a source training query $q$ by directly using Normalized Discounted Cumulative Gain (NDCG) [26] obtained on it:

$$W_q = \frac{1}{Z_m} \sum_{j=1}^{m} \frac{2^{r(j)} - 1}{\log(1+j)} \tag{7}$$

[2]The derivation is not difficult which is omitted here due to space limit

---

**Algorithm 1** AdaCoListMLE: iterative reinforcement rank adaptation algorithm based on CoListMLE

---

**Input:**
$Q_s$: Training queries in source domain, $|Q_s| > 0$
$Q_t$: Unlabeled queries in target domain, $|Q_t| > 0$
$\lambda$, $\epsilon$, $\tau$, $\kappa$: The free parameters
**Output:**
Target ranking model $M$;
1: Initialize the weights of queries in $Q_s$ as 1;
2: Initialize the permutation output $\pi^{(0)}$ using ListMLE trained on $Q_s$;
3: **repeat**
4: Solve optimization problem in Equation 6 and obtain ranking model $M$ with weight vectors $\vec{w}_1$, $\vec{w}_2$;
5: Use function $f = (\vec{w}_1 + \vec{w}_2) \cdot \mathbf{x}$ to rank the documents of target queries in $Q_t$;
6: Move $\kappa$ most confident target queries from $Q_t$ to $Q_s$;
7: Train a target ranking model $M'$ with the predicted target data in step 5;
8: Use $M'$ to re-weigh the source queries using Equation 7;
9: **until** Converged (no more prediction is confident);
10: **return** Target ranking model $M$;

---

where $r(j)$ denotes the rank label of the $j$-th document in the ranked list of $q$, $m$ is the $m$-th top position in the list and $Z_m$ is a normalization constant which is chosen so that the perfect list gets score of 1. Here we adopt NDCG@10.

### 4.3.2 *Reinforcement training procedure*

The iterative reinforcement procedure for query weighting and view consistency enhancement is given in Algorithm 1. Step 1-2 initializes the weights of source training queries and the permutation output; Step 4 optimizes the objective function to obtain the two view-based rankers; Step 5 ranks the documents of target queries using the model learned thus far; Step 6 moves some most confident target queries to the source training set so that the model can be re-trained with the expanded dataset in next iteration; Step 7 trains a different ranker using the predicted target data in step 6, which is used to re-weigh the source queries using Equation 7 in step 8. The iteration continues until convergence is reached.

Note that step 7 trains target ranking model $M'$ using the predicted target data independent of current model $M$ for re-weighing source queries. Actually, another seemingly straightforward solution is to re-weigh the source queries by letting $M$, which is trained using the mixture of source training queries and most-confidently predicted target queries, rank the source documents. Both solutions have pros and cons: $M'$ uses pure target data but is trained with the ranks predicted by $M$ which may not be sufficiently accurate; $M$ is trained with more accurate ranks, but most of the training examples are from source domain, rendering its prediction on source queries source-leaning, and moreover, moving around queries from $Q_t$ to $Q_s$ in step 6 may not always lead to improved effectiveness as the confidence of ranker depends on how different two domains are at large. Therefore, using $M$ to re-weigh source queries is liable to some obvious risk. On the other hand, the predictive power of $M$ on target data may directly reflect the strengthened view agreement. Using the predicted target queries to train $M'$ will make sense provided that certain target ranking accuracy by $M$ could be reached. In fact, we conducted experiments using both of the solutions and found that source query weighting using $M'$ consistently outperformed using $M$. Therefore, we adopted $M'$ for re-weighing source queries.

# 5. EXPERIMENTS AND RESULTS

Since semi-supervised ranking is a special case of rank adaptation, we put emphasis on adaptation experiments. In-domain semi-supervised experiments are only conducted on one of the data sets.

## 5.1 Data Sets

We used two data sets for experiments: LETOR3.0[3] and Yahoo Learning to Ranking Challenge[4] data sets.

LETOR3.0 was constructed from the collections of TREC 2003 and 2004 Web track. The raw data were preprocessed into the standard format for learning to rank [33]. Each query-document pair is represented as 64 features, including both low-level features such as term frequency, inverse document frequency and document length, and high-level features such as BM25, language-modeling, PageRank and HITS. The relevance judgments take binary relevance values. Three query tasks were defined, namely Home Page Finding (HP), Named Page Finding (NP) and Topic Distillation (TD) [38]. HP aims to return the homepage of the specific organization or person. NP is required to return the page whose name is exactly the query. TD is to return a list of entry points of good websites that contain the contents relevant to the topic, and its focus is to return entry pages of good websites rather than the pages containing the relevant contents themselves. We can treat each query task as a separate domain like [12, 23, 22], which is only available in the 3.0 edition of LETOR data.

Yahoo dataset provides two sets of rank training data of search engines each from a different country and language. The original data include a large set (Set1) with 29,921 queries and a small set (Set2) with 6,330 queries. Each dataset is divided into 3 sets for training, validation and test. There are 700 features in this data, but their definition is not provided explicitly. Some features are defined in source or target domain only while some others are defined in both domains. We simply expanded the feature space to include all features of both domains where the missing features were put as 0. The relevance judgment takes 5 different levels from 0 (irrelevant) to 4 (perfectly relevant).

Since HP and NP are rather similar tasks but TD is different, we conducted experiments across TD and the other two tasks to examine adaptation performance. For Yahoo dataset, we use the training data of Set1 as source domain, and the test data of Set2 as target domain. We do not use any relevance label of target data during adaptation training. We also conducted in-domain training by using the training part of Set2 to examine single domain ranking performance. Table 1 shows statistics of the data sets used.

**Table 1: Statistics of the two data sets with different domains used for experiments**

| Data set | Domains | # queries | # docs/query |
|---|---|---|---|
| LETOR | NP04 | 75 | 1,000 |
| | HP04 | 75 | 1,000 |
| | TD04 | 75 | 1,000 |
| | TD03 | 50 | 1,000 |
| Yahoo | Set1-train | 19,944 | 27.5 |
| | Set2-train | 1,266 | 27.5 |
| | Set2-test | 3,798 | 27.2 |

## 5.2 Setup

Our multi-view algorithms are compared with three *single-view* baselines: (1) `naiveList`: A ListMLE trained in source domain is naively applied to target domain; (2) `dsList`: ListMLE that is trained by using domain-separator-based weighting method described in [22] for source query weighting, which is state-of-the-art rank adaptation based on instance weighting; (3) `wList`: This is a variant of `dsList` using our proposed query weighting technique, i.e., the weights of source queries are updated iteratively with Equation 7 by the ranker trained on the predicted target queries. It is also a single-view version of AdaCoListMLE descried in Algorithm 1.

The proposed multi-view algorithms are examined under four configurations: (1) `CoList` ($\lambda = 0$): CoListMLE with no view-consistency term in Equation 3, which equals to the ranking version of [15]; (2) `CoList`: CoListMLE with consistency term imposed in Equation 3; (3) `AdaCoList` ($\lambda = 0$): AdaCoListMLE with no view-consistency term in Equation 6 (but with query weighting); (4) `AdaCoList`: AdaCoListMLE with consistency term imposed in Equation 6 (i.e., with both query weighting and view consistency).

The free parameter $\lambda$ was tuned using the validation set of source data. We empirically set parameters $\epsilon = 1.0$, $\tau = 0.8$, and $\kappa = 5\%$.

The performance was measured by NDCG@1,3,5,10 [26] and Expected Reciprocal Rank (ERR) [10]. NDCG of a single query was given by Equation 7. ERR of a query is computed as $ERR = \sum_{i=1}^{m} \frac{1}{i} R(r_i) \prod_{j=1}^{i-1}(1 - R(r_j))$, where $r_i$ is the relevance level of document ranked at the $i$-th position, $R(r) = \frac{2^r - 1}{2^{r_{max}}}$ is a mapping from relevance level to probability of relevance ($r_{max}$ is the maximum relevance level), and $m$ is the length of the ranked list. We then take the average value of the measure over all test queries.

## 5.3 Results and Discussions

### 5.3.1 *Effectiveness of view decomposition*

The principle of multi-view algorithms is that the redundancy and complementarity between different decompositions of features help view-based learners teach each other so as to boost up overall learning performance. Therefore, it is necessary to show that this basic hypothesis holds for ranking by examining how the view decomposition can exert influence to ranking compared to a single-view baseline and different decomposition schemes.

We use `naiveList` as baseline and compare to `CoList` ($\lambda = 0$) using two different splitting methods: (1) natural split (`natural`), which exploits explicit views, i.e., query-dependent and query-independent features. For this, we resort to the feature definition given in LETOR dataset [33], where 52 features in the categories "Q" and "Q-D" are considered as query-dependent, and 12 features of category "D"

[3]`http://research.microsoft.com/en-us/um/beijing/projects/letor/`

[4]`http://learningtorankchallenge.yahoo.com/datasets.php`

**Table 2: The effectiveness of different view decomposition compared with single-view baseline: naive – NaiveListMLE; natural – Natural split; auto – Automatic split. The best performance is bolded, and † indicates significantly better than naive at 95% confidence level based on paired two-tailed t-test**

| | Methods | TD04-HP04 | TD04-NP04 | TD03-HP04 |
|---|---|---|---|---|
| NDCG1 | naive | 0.356 | 0.289 | 0.453 |
| | natural | 0.222 | 0.333 | 0.444 |
| | auto | **0.422** | **0.467**† | **0.471** |
| NDCG3 | naive | 0.539 | 0.562 | 0.547 |
| | natural | 0.567 | 0.479 | 0.572 |
| | auto | **0.642**† | **0.620**† | **0.584**† |
| NDCG5 | naive | 0.561 | 0.603 | 0.582 |
| | natural | 0.601 | 0.519 | 0.606 |
| | auto | **0.668**† | **0.630** | **0.622**† |
| NDCG10 | naive | 0.599 | 0.641 | 0.630 |
| | natural | 0.625 | 0.561 | 0.642 |
| | auto | **0.692**† | **0.686**† | **0.662**† |
| ERR | naive | 0.247 | 0.237 | 0.280 |
| | natural | 0.221 | 0.230 | 0.282 |
| | auto | **0.292**† | **0.293**† | **0.293**† |

as query-independent; (2) automatic split (`auto`), which resorts to the constraint (1) for automatic feature decomposition (see Equation 3). For fair comparisons, we just make CoListMLE perform in an unsupervised adaptation fashion and let two views trained with only one iteration of co-training not allowing further model updates. This aims to show whether feature decomposition is advantageous over the usual single-view treatment.

As shown in Table 2, the automatic split always outperforms `naive` and in most cases `auto` is significantly better, indicating that proper feature decomposition is in general more advantageous. The explicit views based on query dependency do not seem to be an effective feature decomposition scheme since the performance of `natural` varies greatly and is not significantly different from that of `naive`. This implies that using optimization techniques for good decomposition is crucial. Also, this is not the only reason why we use automatic split. Oftentimes, there is no specific feature definition provided in ranking benchmark datasets, in which case one has to decompose features in a principled way to work with multi-view ranker.

### 5.3.2 *Effectiveness of rank adaptation on LETOR*

In this experiment, we compare our approach with single-view and multi-view baselines using LETOR dataset. We conducted cross-domain ranking in two adaptation settings: TD04-NP04 and TD04-HP04. Figure 2 shows the performance. Paired two-tailed t-test results are detailed in Table 3, where we show p-values between `AdaCoList` and all other methods, and also p-values between the basic multi-view configuration `CoList` ($\lambda = 0$) and other multi-view configurations.

We have the following findings and discussions based on these results:

— Multi-view rankers generally performed better than traditional single-view rankers, indicating that splitting ranking features into views is the right direction for ranking. What really unleash the power of different views is the addition of view consistency factor imposed in our objective. We find that the performance clearly worsens when view consistency term is removed, i.e., $\lambda$ is set to zero in `CoList` and `AdaCoList`. This suggests that strengthening the agreement of view-based rankers on target queries is the key to the success of rank adaptation. Such an improvement owes to the cooperation between the $\epsilon$-expandability constraint and the view consistency term: The $\epsilon$-expandability ensures to capture those informative target instances, with which two view-based rankers can learn from each other. As a result, their ranking consensus could be gradually improved and explicitly captured by the view consistency term.

— Another crucial factor to adaptation is the appropriate weighting of source queries. Our weighting scheme is simple yet very effective, evidenced by the improvement of ranking not only when used in multi-view case but also in the single-view approach `wList`. `wList` always outperforms `dsList` in large margin, while the latter does not appear robust and sometimes is even worse than `naiveList`. Weighting scheme used by `dsList` is based on the so-called domain separator approach where the weight values are derived from the classification hyperplane of two domains, which although representing domain relatedness in some extent, cannot reflect the importance of source training queries in terms of ranking performance measure like our weighting scheme.

— Clearly, the two factors, one for strengthening view consistency on target queries and the other for appropriate weighting of source queries, can mutually reinforce each other in our proposed framework. This is reflected by the fact that `AdaCoList` significantly outperforms `CoList` and `AdaCoList` ($\lambda = 0$) in accordance with most of performance measures. The reason is straightforward: enhanced view agreement on target queries will lead to a better target-leaning ranker, which in return can help weigh out those cross-domain source queries since they receive higher ranking scores (in terms of NDCG@10) predicted by model $M'$.

— As shown in the left bottom part of Table 3, only imposing view consistency or only using source query weighting cannot ensure significant improvement over the multi-view baseline `CoList` ($\lambda = 0$). For example, on TD04-NP04, the NDCG@3,5,10 obtained may not necessarily significantly different. But combining the two components in the ultimate model makes them effectively reinforced.

### 5.3.3 *Effectiveness of rank adaptation on Yahoo data*

We conducted adaptation experiments on Yahoo dataset. Based on `AdaCoList`, we studied the sensitivity of coefficient $\lambda$ that is used to control the extent of view consistency in the model, for which we examined different values of $\lambda$ to show how ERR changed with it. Meanwhile, we also studied the trend of ranking performance varying with iteration. Both results are displayed in Figure 3[5].

We observe that large $\lambda$ typically results in poor adaptation performance, and $\lambda$ between 0 and 1 can give reasonably good results, and the best is achieved when $\lambda = 1$. This implies that the view consistency factor should be carefully chosen to avoid its side effect: (1) if weak view consistency is imposed due to very small $\lambda$, the magnitude of consistency term would be too weak to influence the loss to lean towards target direction; (2) if its magnitude is very large such as when $\lambda = 1000$, the consistency part will dominate the entire rank loss, making the model hard to keep certain level of accuracy, which means the two views being frequently and consistently wrong. Therefore, setting an appropriate value to $\lambda$ is helpful. But overall, the extent of performance vari-

[5] We stopped training after 10 iterations in the cases of $\lambda > 1$ due to their obviously poor performance

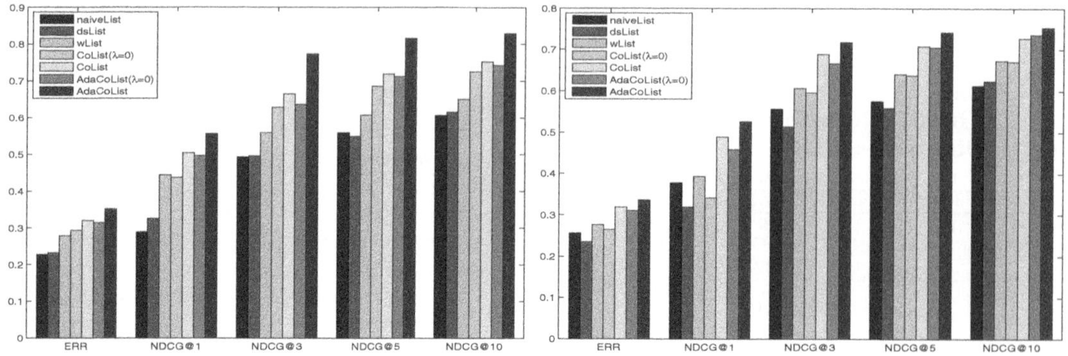


(a) TD04-NP04 adaptation results

(b) TD04-HP04 adaptation resutls

**Figure 2: The comparison of different algorithms for ranking adaptation using LETOR3.0 dataset. The source domain is Topic Distillation (TD) task in TREC-2004 (TD04) and the target domains are Named Page finding task (NP04) and Home Page finding task (HP04). `naiveList`: A single-view ListMLE ranker trained on source domain is naively applied to target domain; `dsList`: A single-view semi-supervised ListMLE using domain-separator based source query weighting described in [22]; `wList`: A variant of `dsList` using our proposed query weighting technique and equal to single-view version of AdaCoListMLE; `CoList` ($\lambda = 0$): CoListMLE w/o view consistency (i.e., ranking version of [15]); `CoList`: CoListMLE with view consistency; `AdaCoList` ($\lambda = 0$): AdaCoListMLE w/o view consistency; `AdaCoList`: AdaCoListMLE with view consistency**

**Table 3: Results of paired two-tailed t-test (p-values) between different algorithms and configurations**

| | TD04-NP04 | | | | | TD04-HP04 | | | | |
|---|---|---|---|---|---|---|---|---|---|---|
| | NDCG1 | NDCG3 | NDCG5 | NDCG10 | ERR | NDCG1 | NDCG3 | NDCG5 | NDCG10 | ERR |
| | AdaCoList | | | | | | | | | |
| naiveList | $\ll 0.01$ | $\ll 0.01$ | $\ll 0.01$ | $\ll 0.01$ | $\ll 0.01$ | 0.03 | 0.01 | $< 0.01$ | $< 0.01$ | $< 0.01$ |
| dsList | $\ll 0.01$ | $\ll 0.01$ | $\ll 0.01$ | $\ll 0.01$ | $\ll 0.01$ | $< 0.01$ | $\ll 0.01$ | $\ll 0.01$ | $< 0.01$ | $\ll 0.01$ |
| wList | 0.04 | $\ll 0.01$ | $\ll 0.01$ | $\ll 0.01$ | $< 0.01$ | 0.02 | 0.03 | 0.03 | $< 0.05$ | $< 0.01$ |
| CoList ($\lambda = 0$) | 0.01 | $< 0.01$ | $< 0.01$ | $< 0.01$ | $< 0.01$ | $< 0.01$ | $< 0.01$ | $< 0.01$ | $< 0.01$ | $\ll 0.01$ |
| CoList | 0.09 | $< 0.01$ | $< 0.01$ | $< 0.01$ | 0.01 | 0.13 | 0.11 | 0.04 | 0.04 | $< 0.05$ |
| AdaCoList ($\lambda = 0$) | 0.10 | $< 0.01$ | $< 0.01$ | $< 0.01$ | 0.02 | 0.07 | 0.09 | 0.05 | 0.05 | 0.04 |
| | CoList ($\lambda = 0$) | | | | | | | | | |
| CoList | 0.02 | 0.11 | 0.13 | 0.08 | 0.01 | 0.01 | $< 0.01$ | 0.01 | 0.02 | $< 0.01$ |
| AdaCoList ($\lambda = 0$) | 0.03 | 0.34 | 0.07 | $< 0.05$ | $< 0.01$ | 0.01 | 0.01 | $< 0.01$ | $\ll 0.01$ | $\ll 0.01$ |
| AdaCoList | 0.01 | $< 0.01$ | $< 0.01$ | $< 0.01$ | $< 0.01$ | $< 0.01$ | $< 0.01$ | $< 0.01$ | $< 0.01$ | $\ll 0.01$ |

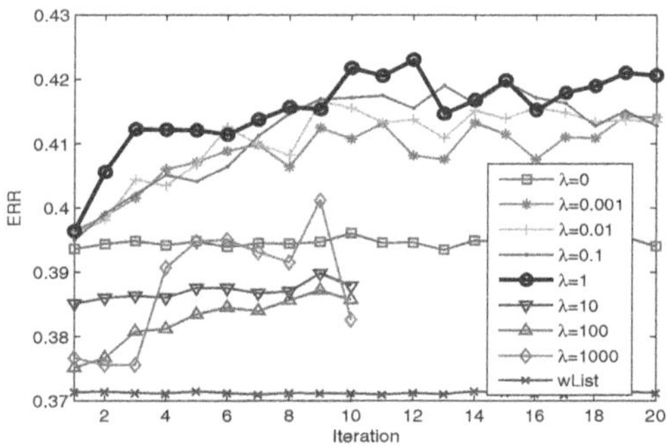


**Figure 3: Rank adaptation performance of `AdaCoList` varies with iterations and $\lambda$ based on Yahoo dataset**

ation, being within a magnitude of 0.1, can be considered not sensitive to $\lambda$.

Typically, iteration improves adaptation when $\lambda > 0$, indicating that view consistency and source query weighting are mutually strengthened. The curve remains flat when $\lambda = 0$, meaning that source query weighting does not work alone if without the view consistency imposed on target data. This is because such a case forms some pointless loop, where the algorithm iterates between a purely source-trained ranker and a target ranker trained with inaccurate rank predictions, and there is no any boosting point. Note that unlike on LETOR data, here we skip performing step 6 in Algorithm 1 because it was found that the move of queries worsened performance gradually. This may be due to the large domain gap of Yahoo data that came from search engines of different languages [11], and inappropriately using target queries may introduce considerable noise into source domain. Therefore, no target queries are selected into source domain during iteration. And we yet did not find reliable way to select these $\kappa$ target queries. We will leave it for future work.

The comparison of rank adaptation performance on Yahoo dataset is shown in Figure 4. We can see the similar trend of performance gain as using LETOR data. T-test indicates that `AdaCoList` is significantly better than all other methods and configurations (p-value<0.01). This again justifies our method is effective.

A different trend is that `wList` is not obviously better than other single-view baselines. This is simply because our weighting method has to rely on the improvement of the predictive power of current ranking model to give a better

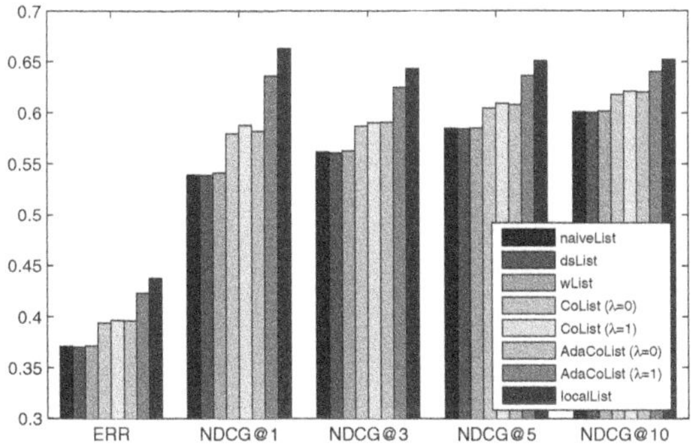


**Figure 4: Rank adaptation performance on Yahoo dataset, where `localList` is the performance of ListMLE trained locally on target domain**

**Table 4: The comparison of ranking performance in single domain based on Yahoo Set2. * indicates significantly better than baseline ListMLE at 99% confidence level according to paired two-tailed t-test**

| Metric | ListMLE | `CoList` ($\lambda$=0) | `CoList` ($\lambda$=1) |
|---|---|---|---|
| ERR | 0.437 | **0.445***  | 0.440* |
| NDCG@1 | 0.663 | **0.684*** | 0.662 |
| NDCG@3 | 0.643 | **0.660*** | 0.646 |
| NDCG@5 | 0.651 | **0.665*** | 0.656* |
| NDCG@10 | 0.652 | **0.664*** | 0.657* |

ranking prediction on target data. As discussed previously, because no target query was moved to source domain, there is no any boosting point for improving the current model as shown by the flat curve of `wList` also in Figure 3. Similarly, we found that introducing target queries to source domain based on confidence is harmful on this dataset, also probably due to the large distribution gap between two domains as described in [11].

Two strategies may improve the case. One is to exploit the presented multi-view approach by incorporating view consistency to work together with query weights which has demonstrated salient gains as shown in Figure 4. The other is to consider some reliable way for selecting and moving those target queries really useful to source domain in our future work.

### *5.3.4 In-domain ranking performance on Yahoo data*

We also studied the performance of the proposed multi-view approach for ranking in a single domain of Yahoo data. We trained the model using Set2-train and tested it on the Set2-test. The results are displayed in Table 4.

It can be observed that the two multi-view rankers both outperform the baseline ListMLE. T-test shows that `CoList` ($\lambda = 0$) is significantly better in terms of all the performance measures (p-value<0.01), and `CoList` is significantly better based on ERR and NDCG@5,10 (p-value<0.01). This verifies the effectiveness of multi-view approach for ranking in a single domain.

It is noted that in contrast to the performance in adaptation setting, using view consistency term worsens the in-domain ranking performance a little than not considering consistency-based loss. However, there is no significant difference between these two variants of `CoList`. The reason of performance drop is that when consistency-based loss on the data from same distribution is added, it will necessarily dilute the rank loss portion of the objective function, which may result in some degradation of ranking accuracy. Therefore, enhancing view consistency is less important for in-domain ranking. But it seems vital for adaptation since improving target ranking accuracy relies on effective query weighting which can benefit from enhanced view consistency.

## 6. CONCLUSION AND FUTURE WORK

We present a novel and effective ranking framework based on the principle of multi-view learning and listwise ranking approach. Our method is motivated by the description of ranking features from different perspectives which is conformant to the nature of multi-view learning paradigm. The idea is to strengthen the view consistency of rankings on the unlabeled data with a co-training-like procedure where the two view-based rankers can iteratively boost each other. Then our method is generalized to the typical rank adaptation scenario where training and test data follow different distributions and no target training data is available. To overcome the lack of view consensus due to distribution gap, it aims to mutually reinforce the view consistency of ranking for target queries and the weighting of source queries. The rationale is that imposing view consistency on target queries improves the target ranker which in return can help weigh out those cross-domain source queries that can be used to further strengthen the view consistency. Our method results in significant improvement over some strong single-view and multi-view baselines by rank adaptation on LETOR and Yahoo learning to rank datasets, and is also shown effective for in-domain rank learning on Yahoo dataset.

Our framework is generic that can accommodate various ranking and adaptation approaches. Existing single-view ranking algorithms can be upgraded using our multi-view scheme with reasonably small amount of effort. Also, for scalability aspect, extending our method to more than two views will be fairly straightforward, for example, by incorporating more pairwise consistency terms in the objective function resulting from the additional views.

There are a few more interesting directions to follow in our future work: we plan to investigate reliable ways of moving useful target queries to source domain to improve adaptation; we can try different ranking schemes and rank correlation measures in objective function; there also remain interesting theoretical issues regarding this topic worth of further study.

## 7. REFERENCES

[1] S. Abney. Bootstrapping. In *ACL*, pp. 360–367, 2002.

[2] M.-R. Amini, T.-V. Truong, and C. Goutte. A boosting algorithm for learning bipartite ranking functions with partially labeled data. In *SIGIR*, pp. 99–106, 2008.

[3] M. F. Balcan, A. Blum, and K. Yang. Co-training and expansion: Towards bridging theory and practice. In *NIPS*, pp. 87–96, 2004.

[4] D. P. Bertsekas, W. W. Hager, and O. L. Mangasarian. *Nonlinear programming*. Athena Scientic Belmont, MA, 1999.

[5] J. Blitzer, R. Mcdonald, and F. Pereira. Domain adapation with structural correspondce learning. In *EMNLP*, pp. 120–128, 2006.
[6] A. Blum and T. Mitchell. Combining labeled and unlabeled data with co-training. In *COLT*, pp. 92–100, 1998.
[7] U. Brefeld and T. Scheffer. Co-EM support vector learning. In *ICML*, pp. 121–128, 2004.
[8] P. Cai, W. Gao, A. Zhou, and K.-F. Wong. Relevant knowledge helps in choosing right teacher: Active query selection for ranking adaptation. In *SIGIR*, pp. 115–124, 2011.
[9] Z. Cao, T. Qin, T.-Y. Liu, M.-F. Tsai, and H. Li. Learning to rank: From pairwise approach to listwise approach. In *ICML*, pp. 129–136, 2007.
[10] O. Chapelle, D. Metzler, Y. Zhang, and P. Grinspan. Expected reciprocal rank for graded relevance. In *CIKM*, pp. 621–630, 2009.
[11] O. Chapelle and Y. Chang. Yahoo! learning to rank challenge overview. In *JMLR Workshop and Conference Proceedings*, 14:1–24, 2011.
[12] D. Chen, Y. Xiong, J. Yan, G.-R. Xue, G. Wang, and Z. Chen. Knowledge transfer for cross domain learning to rank. *Information Retrieval*, 13(3):236–253, 2009.
[13] K. Chen, R. Lu, C. Wong, G. Sun, L. Heck, and B. Tseng. Trada: Tree based ranking function adaptation. In *CIKM*, pp. 1143–1152, 2008.
[14] M. Chen, K. Q. Weinberger, and J. Blitzer. Co-training for domain adaptation. In *NIPS*, pp. 271–278, 2011.
[15] M. Chen, K. Q. Weinberger, and Y. Chen. Automatic feature decomposition for single view co-training. In *ICML*, pp. 953–960, 2011.
[16] M. Collins and Y. Singer. Unsupervised models for named entity classification. In *EMNLP*, pp. 100–110, 1999.
[17] S. Dasgupta, M. L. Littman, and D. McAllester. PAC generalization bounds for co-training. In *NIPS*, pp. 375–382, 2001.
[18] K. Duh and K. Kirchhoff. Learning to rank with partially-labeled data. In *SIGIR*, pp. 251–258, 2008.
[19] J. Farquhar, D. Hardoon, H. Meng, J. Shawe-Taylor, and S. Szedmak. Two view learning: SVM-2K, theory and practice. In *NIPS*, 2006.
[20] K. Ganchev, J. Graça, J. Blitzer, and B. Taskar. Multi-view learning over structured and non-identical outputs. In *UAI*, pp. 204–211, 2008.
[21] J. Gao, Q. Wu, C. Burges, K. Svore, Y. Su, N. Khan, S. Shah, and H. Zhou. Model adaptation via model interpolation and boosting for web search ranking. In *EMNLP*, pp. 505–513, 2009.
[22] W. Gao, P. Cai, K.-F. Wong, and A. Zhou. Learning to rank only using training data from related domain. In *SIGIR*, pp. 162–169, 2010.
[23] B. Geng, L. Yang, C. Xu, and X.-S. Hua. Ranking model adaptation for domain-specific search. *IEEE Transactions on Knowledge and Data Engineering*, 24(4):745–758, 2010.
[24] H. Daumé III. Frustratingly easy domain adaptation. In *ACL*, pp. 256–263, 2007.
[25] H. Daumé III and D. Marcu. Domain adaptation for statistical classifiers. *Journal of Artificial Intelligence Research*, 26(1):101–126, 2006.
[26] K. Jarvelin and J. Kekalainen. IR evaluation methods for retrieving highly relevant documents. In *SIGIR*, pp. 41–48, 2000.
[27] J. Jiang and C. Zhai. Instance weighting for domain adaptation in nlp. In *ACL*, pp. 264–271, 2007.
[28] G. Li, S. C. H. Hoi, and K. Chang. Two-view transductive support vector machines. In *SIAM SDM*, pp. 235–244, 2010.
[29] T.-Y. Liu. Learning to rank for information retrieval. *Foundations and Trends in Information Retrieval*, 3(3):225–331, 2009.
[30] J. Marden. *Analyzing and Modeling Rank Data.* Champman and Hall/CRC, 1995.
[31] J. Q. nero Candela, M. Sugiyama, A. Schwaighofer, and N. Lawrence. *Dataset Shift in Machine Learning.* MIT Press, Cambridge, 2009.
[32] K. Nigam and R. Ghani. Analyzing the effectiveness and applicability of co-training. In *CIKM*, pp. 86–93, 2000.
[33] T. Qin, T.-Y. Liu, J. Xu, and H. Li. LETOR: A benchmark collection for research on learning to rank for information retrieval. *Information Retrieval*, 13(4):346–374, 2010.
[34] T. Qin, X.-D. Zhang, M.-F. Tsai, D.-S. Wang, T.-Y. Liu, and H. Li. Query-level loss functions for information retrieval. *Information Processing and Management*, 44:838–855, 2008.
[35] V. Sindhwani, P. Niyogi, and M. Belkin. A co-regularized approach to semi-supervised learning with multiple views. In *ICML Workshop on Learning with Multiple Views*, 2005.
[36] M. Taylor, J. Guiver, S. Robertson, and T. Minka. Softrank: Optimising non-smooth rank metrics. In *WSDM*, pp. 77–86, 2008.
[37] N. Usunier, M.-R. Amini, and C. Goutte. Multiview semi-supervised learning for ranking multilingual documents. In *ECML-PKDD*, pp. 443–458, 2011.
[38] E. M. Voorhees. Overview of TREC 2004. In *TREC*, pp. 1–12, 2004.
[39] B. Wang, J. Tang, W. Fan, S. Chen, Z. Yang, and Y. Liu. Heterogeneous cross domain ranking in latent space. In *CIKM*, pp. 987–996, 2009.
[40] F. Xia, T.-Y. Liu, J. Wang, W. Zhang, and H. Li. Listwise approach to learning to rank – theory and algorithm. In *ICML*, pp. 1192–1199, 2008.
[41] D. Yarowsky. Unsupervised word sense disambiguation rivaling supervised methods. In *ACL*, pp. 189–196, 1995.
[42] Y. Yue, T. Finley, F. Radlinski, , and T. Joachims. A support vector method for optimizing average precision. In *SIGIR*, pp. 271–278, 2007.
[43] B. Zadronzny. Learning and evaluating classifiers under sample selection bias. In *ICML*, pp. 114–121, 2004.
[44] D. Zhang, J. He, Y. Liu, L. Si, and R. D. Lawrence. Multi-view transfer learning with a large margin approach. In *SIGKDD*, pp. 1208–1216, 2011.

# Relative Confidence Sampling for Efficient On-Line Ranker Evaluation

Masrour Zoghi, Shimon Whiteson, Maarten de Rijke
ISLA, University of Amsterdam
Amsterdam, The Netherlands
m.zoghi, s.a.whiteson, derijke@uva.nl

Remi Munos
INRIA Lille - Nord Europe
Villeneuve d'Ascq, France
remi.munos@inria.fr

## ABSTRACT

A key challenge in information retrieval is that of *on-line ranker evaluation*: determining which one of a finite set of rankers performs the best in expectation on the basis of user clicks on presented document lists. When the presented lists are constructed using *interleaved comparison methods*, which interleave lists proposed by two different candidate rankers, then the problem of minimizing the total *regret* accumulated while evaluating the rankers can be formalized as a *K-armed dueling bandits problem*. In this paper, we propose a new method called *relative confidence sampling* (RCS) that aims to reduce cumulative regret by being less conservative than existing methods in eliminating rankers from contention. In addition, we present an empirical comparison between RCS and two state-of-the-art methods, *relative upper confidence bound* and *SAVAGE*. The results demonstrate that RCS can substantially outperform these alternatives on several large learning to rank datasets.

## Categories and Subject Descriptors

H.3.3 [**Information Storage and Retrieval**]: Information Search and Retrieval

## Keywords

Evaluation; implicit feedback; on-line learning

## 1. INTRODUCTION

An important challenge in information retrieval is that of *ranker evaluation*: determining which of a finite set of rankers performs best in expectation. In *off-line* ranker evaluation, which goes back to the early Cranfield experiments [8], rankers are assessed based on a fixed set of queries and documents manually judged by human assessors. Unfortunately, obtaining such judgments is expensive and error prone. Because the assessors typically did not formulate the queries on which they judge documents, their assessments may not accurately reflect how well those documents meet the needs of real users.


*WSDM'14*, February 24–28, 2014, New York, New York, USA.

ACM 978-1-4503-2351-2/14/02 ...$15.00.
http://dx.doi.org/10.1145/2556195.2556256.

These difficulties can be addressed by *on-line* ranker evaluation, in which rankers are assessed using click feedback from actual users. A common approach is to use *interleaved comparison methods* [6, 7, 13, 15, 19, 26, 28], in which the document lists proposed by two candidate rankers for a given query are interleaved and the resulting list presented to the user, whose clicks are used to infer a noisy preference for one ranker over the other. Recently, interleaving methods have been successfully applied in large-scale settings [6, 7].

The use of interleaved comparison methods gives rise to a key challenge in ranker evaluation: how to efficiently determine the best ranker from a set using only pairwise comparisons. This challenge can be formalized as a *K-armed dueling bandits* problem [37], wherein the best ranker is defined as the one that in expectation wins an interleaved comparison with each other ranker.

In the *explore-then-exploit* setting [37], the algorithm's goal is defined with respect to a fixed period of time called the *horizon*, at the end of which the algorithm must report what it thinks the best ranker is. Performance is then evaluated according to both the *accuracy* with which it picks the best ranker and the cumulative *regret* it accrues during that period. Regret is a measure of the suboptimality, with respect to the best ranker, of the rankers selected for interleaving. Several algorithms have been proposed for this setting, including *interleaved filter* (IF) [37], *beat the mean* (BTM) [36], and *sensitivity analysis of variables for generic exploration* (SAVAGE) [32].

By contrast, in the *ongoing regret minimization* setting [23], no horizon is specified in advance and the goal is to minimize cumulative regret for *all* horizons. The *relative upper confidence bounds* (RUCB) [38] algorithm was recently proposed for this setting.

In this paper, we propose and evaluate a new method for evaluating rankers, called *relative confidence sampling* (RCS). To determine which rankers to interleave at each iteration, RCS proceeds in two phases. First, it uses the results of the comparisons conducted so far to simulate a round-robin tournament among the rankers. Second, the champion of this tournament is compared against a challenger deemed to have the best chance of beating it. As more comparisons are conducted, the best ranker is increasingly likely to be selected as both champion and challenger, causing regret to fall steeply over time.

To validate RCS, we evaluate its performance on large Microsoft and Yahoo! learning to rank datasets using both the explore-then-exploit and the ongoing regret minimization settings. Our results show that RCS significantly and substantially outperforms both SAVAGE, the state of the art in the explore-then-exploit setting, and RUCB, the state of the art in ongoing regret minimization.

The main contributions of this paper are thus:

1. We evaluate two existing $K$-armed dueling bandits algorithms on online ranker evaluation using two large learning to rank datasets, and
2. We propose and evaluate a new $K$-armed dueling bandits algorithm that performs better than existing state-of-the-art algorithms for online ranker evaluation.

In Section 2, we detail our problem setting and in Section 3 we discuss existing methods for ranker evaluation. Section 4 details relative confidence sampling, our new method for online ranker evaluation. Section 5 details our experimental setup and Section 6 presents our experimental results and discusses our findings. Section 7 contains our conclusions.

## 2. PROBLEM SETTING

One approach to ranker evaluation is to use manual expert annotations in a TREC-like setting [34]. However, collecting the necessary annotations is expensive and, because they are not based on real users, such annotations may not reflect real users' actual information needs. An attractive alternative is thus to evaluate rankers *on-line* using feedback from real users. One way to obtain such feedback is to measure the *click-through rate* [17, 18]. However, such feedback is often unreliable, since click-through rates can have substantial variance, particularly across users and topics [20, 21, 28, 29].

Fortunately, on-line feedback can also be obtained using *interleaved comparison methods*, which give *relative* feedback about how one ranker compares to another and has been shown to be more reliable [6, 26]. To compare two rankers on a given query, an interleaved comparison constructs a ranking that is an amalgamation of the rankings proposed by the two rankers for that query. Schemes for constructing the amalgamation include *balanced interleave* [19], *team draft* [28], *document constraints* [13], *probabilistic interleave* [15], and *optimized interleave* [27].

However, since interleaved comparison methods require feedback from real users, each comparison has significant real-world costs, i.e., if either of the compared rankers is poor, the interleaved ranking may also be poor, leaving the user dissatisfied. An important question is thus how to find the best ranker in a way that minimizes these costs.

This problem can be formalized as a *K-armed dueling bandits* problem [37], which is itself an extension of the *K-armed bandits* problem [2]. In the $K$-armed bandits problem, there are $K$ rankers, $\{\rho_1, \ldots, \rho_K\}$. At each *time step*, a ranker $\rho_i$ can be tried, generating a *reward* drawn from an unknown stationary distribution with expected value $\mu_i$, which might be a quantity like click-through rate [5].

The $K$-armed *dueling* bandits problem is a variation that models the relative feedback available in settings like ranker evaluation with interleaved comparison methods. The problem is defined by a matrix of comparison probabilities $\mathbf{P} = [p_{ij}]$. At each *time step*, two rankers $(\rho_i, \rho_j)$ are compared, e.g., using an interleaved comparison method, and with probability $p_{ij}$ ranker $\rho_i$ beats $\rho_j$. In this paper, we assume that there exists a *Condorcet winner* [32]: a ranker, which without loss of generality we label $\rho_1$, such that $p_{1i} > \frac{1}{2}$ for all $i > 1$. In other words, when interleaved with any other ranker, the Condorcet winner is expected to win.

The Condorcet winner is different in a subtle but important way from the *Borda winner* [32], which is a ranker $\rho_b$ that satisfies

$$\sum_j p_{bj} \geq \sum_j p_{ij}, \text{ for all } i = 1, \ldots, K.$$

In other words, when averaged across all other rankers, the Borda winner is the ranker with the highest probability of winning a given comparison.

To better understand the distinction between these two types of winners, consider an example from the world of sports. Suppose we wish to use a $K$-armed dueling bandit method to efficiently identify the world's best tennis player. In addition, suppose that Rafael Nadal is likely to win, say with probability 0.55, a match against the other top players since, according to The New York Times (June 9, 2013) "Nadal is also the only member of the so-called Big Four to have a head-to-head edge over all the other members of that club: [Novak] Djokovic, Roger Federer and Andy Murray." Finally, suppose also that, though Federer loses in expectation to Nadal, he has a 0.75 probability of beating Djokavic and Murray. Thus, Nadal is the Condorcet winner but Federer is the Borda winner.

It is not immediately obvious which player should be considered the best. While Nadal is the only undominated player, a gambler who could only bet on one player before the start of a tournament should pick Federer. However, in ranker evaluation, the Condorcet winner is the more suitable choice. The reason is that, although Federer is more likely than Nadal to win a given match, the goal of ranker evaluation is not to win interleaved comparisons but to identify and use the best ranker. Interleaving is thus only a means to an end, whereas in tennis the match is an end in itself. Choosing anything other than the Condorcet winner as the best ranker is suboptimal because it means that by definition another ranker exists that would beat the chosen ranker. More precisely, given a distribution over user-query pairs encountered by the retrieval system and a ranker $\rho_i$ other than the Condorcet winner $\rho_1$, then $\rho_1$ is morely likely to win an interleaved comparison against $\rho_i$ for a given user-query pair than vice-versa. In Section 3, we compare the Condorcet assumption, i.e., the assumption of the existences of a Condorcet winner, with the typically much stronger assumptions made by other $K$-armed dueling bandits algorithms.

The goal of an algorithm for the $K$-armed dueling bandits problem can be formalized in several ways. In this paper, we consider two standard settings:

1. *Explore-then-exploit* [37]: In this setting, the algorithm is told in advance the exploration *horizon*: the number of time steps that the evaluation process is given to *explore* before it has to produce a single ranker as the best, which will be *exploited* thenceforth. The algorithm is assessed on its *accuracy*, the probability that a given run of the algorithm reports the Condorcet winner as the best ranker, as well as the amount of *regret* accumulated during the exploration phase, where regret for each time step is defined as follows: if rankers $\rho_i$ and $\rho_j$ were chosen for comparison at time $t$, then regret at that time is set to be

$$r_t := \frac{\Delta_{1i} + \Delta_{1j}}{2}, \tag{1}$$

with $\Delta_{1k} := p_{1k} - \frac{1}{2}$ for all $k \in \{1, \dots, K\}$. Thus, regret measures the average advantage that the Condorcet winner has over the two interleaved rankers. Given our assumption on the probabilities $p_{1k}$, this implies that $r = 0$ if and only if the best ranker is interleaved with itself.

2. *Ongoing regret minimization* [23]: In this setting, no horizon is specified and the evaluation process continues indefinitely. Thus, it is no longer sufficient for the algorithm to maximize accuracy and minimize regret after a single horizon is reached. Instead, it must minimize regret across *all* horizons by rapidly decreasing the frequency of interleaved comparisons involving suboptimal rankers, particularly those that fare worse in comparison to the best ranker. This goal can be formulated as minimizing the cumulative regret over time, rather than with respect to a fixed horizon.

As we describe below in Section 3, most existing $K$-armed dueling bandits methods target the explore-then-exploit setting. However, we contend that the ongoing regret minimization setting better captures the key challenges of ranker evaluation on a deployed retrieval system for the following reason: explore-then-exploit methods require a horizon as input and behave differently for different horizons. This poses a practical problem because it is typically difficult to know in advance how many comparisons are required to determine the best ranker with confidence and thus how to set the horizon. If the horizon is set too long, the algorithm is too exploratory, increasing the number of evaluations needed to find the best ranker. If it is set too short, the best ranker remains unknown when the horizon is reached and the algorithm must be restarted with a longer horizon.

# 3. RELATED WORK

In this section, we briefly survey existing methods for the $K$-armed dueling bandits problem, considering both explore-then-exploit and ongoing regret minimization methods.

## 3.1 Explore-then-Exploit Methods

To our knowledge, the first method for the $K$-armed dueling bandits problem that was designed for an explore-then-exploit scenario is *interleaved filter* (IF) [37], which proceeds as follows: a ranker $\hat{\rho}$ is randomly chosen to be compared against all other rankers in sequence; these comparisons are repeated until another ranker $\rho'$ either loses to or beats $\hat{\rho}$ by a wide margin, i.e., the winner scores so many more wins over the loser that one can conclude with a high level of certainty that the loser can be eliminated. If $\hat{\rho}$ is the winner, then $\rho'$ is eliminated from the pool of rankers and is not compared against any other rankers. If $\hat{\rho}$ is the loser, then it is eliminated from the pool of rankers and $\rho'$ becomes the new $\hat{\rho}$. This process continues until either all but one of the rankers is eliminated or the horizon is reached. A variation of the algorithm eliminates not just $\hat{\rho}$ when it loses badly to $\rho'$, but also any other ranker that has lost to $\hat{\rho}$ on average (not necessarily by a wide margin).

More recently, the *beat the mean* (BTM) algorithm has been shown to perform better than IF [36]. BTM works by focusing exploration on the rankers that have been involved in the fewest comparisons. When it determines that a ranker fares on average too poorly in comparison to the remaining rankers, it removes it from consideration. More precisely, BTM considers the performance of each ranker against the *mean ranker* by averaging the ranker's scores against all other rankers and uses these estimates to decide which ranker should be eliminated.

IF and BTM require the comparison probabilities $p_{ij}$ to satisfy conditions that are difficult to verify without specific knowledge about the dueling bandits problem at hand. Specifically, IF and BTM require a *total ordering* $\{\rho_1, \dots, \rho_K\}$ of the rankers to exist such that $p_{ij} > \frac{1}{2}$ for all $i < j$. In Section 6, we show that, in the datasets we consider, the probability of a total ordering existing decreases quickly as the number of rankers increases, due to cyclical relationships among rankers other than the Condorcet winner.

Moreover, in addition to this total ordering, these two algorithms require a form of *stochastic transitivity*. In particular, IF requires *strong stochastic transitivity*: for any triple $(i, j, k)$, with $i < j < k$, the following condition is satisfied:

$$p_{ik} \geq \max\{p_{ij}, p_{jk}\},$$

BTM requies the less restrictive *relaxed stochastic transitivity*: there exists a number $\gamma \geq 1$ such that for all pairs $(j, k)$ with $1 < j < k$, we have

$$\gamma p_{1k} \geq \max\{p_{1j}, p_{jk}\}.$$

As pointed out in [36], strong stochastic transitivity is often violated in practice, a phenomenon also observed in our experiments: half of the $K$-armed dueling bandits on which we experimented require $\gamma > 1$.

BTM permits a broader class of $K$-armed dueling bandits problems, but it requires $\gamma$ to be explicitly passed to it as a parameter, which poses substantial difficulties in practice. If $\gamma$ is underestimated, the algorithm can in certain circumstances be misled with high probability into choosing the Borda winner instead of the Condorcet winner, e.g., when the Borda winner has a larger average advantage over the remaining arms than the Condorcet winner, as in the Nadal-Federer example. On the other hand, though overestimating $\gamma$ does not cause the algorithm to choose the wrong ranker, it nonetheless results in a severe penalty: if $\gamma$ is multiplied by $\theta$, then the number of interleaved comparisons required to eliminate suboptimal rankers from further consideration is multiplied by $\theta^4$. Hence, overestimating $\gamma$ by a factor of 2 means requiring 16 times as many comparisons, which can substantially affect the amount of regret accumulated.

By contrast, the algorithm we propose in Section 4 makes only the Condorcet assumption, which is implied by the total ordering assumption of IF and BTM. However, we show in Section 6.1 that there are many $K$-armed dueling bandits problems that satisfy the Condorcet assumption but do not have a total ordering.

Sensitivity Analysis of VAriables for Generic Exploration (SAVAGE) [32] is a recently proposed algorithm that outperforms both IF and BTM by a wide margin when the number of rankers is of moderate size. Moreover, one version of SAVAGE, which we call *Condorcet SAVAGE*, makes only the Condorcet assumption and performed the best experimentally [32]. Condorcet SAVAGE compares pairs of rankers uniformly randomly until there exists a pair for which one of the rankers beats the other by a wide margin, in which case the loser is removed from the pool of rankers under consideration. So far, the performance of Condorcet SAVAGE in the context of online learning to rank has not been evaluated on large-scale datasets. We show in this paper that our proposed algorithm for ranker evaluation substantially outperforms Condorcet SAVAGE on such datasets.

## 3.2 Ongoing Regret Minimization Methods

To our knowledge, the recently proposed *relative upper confidence bound* (RUCB) [38] is the only existing $K$-armed dueling bandits method that explicitly targets the ongoing regret minimization objective. RUCB is based on a well-known method for the $K$-armed bandit problem, called the *upper confidence bound* (UCB) algorithm [2], which maintains optimistic estimates of the mean reward for each ranker and selects the ranker with the largest optimistic estimate. By doing so, UCB ensures adequate exploration of the rankers to avoid fixating on the wrong ranker and accumulating regret indefinitely.

In a similar fashion, RUCB maintains both optimistic and pessimistic estimates of each $p_{ij}$ and uses them to choose which rankers to compare against each other. More specifically, it proceeds in two stages. First, it determines which rankers have a very low chance of being the best ranker by optimistically comparing each ranker against the rest: if they lose despite this optimism, they are omitted; one of the remaining rankers is chosen at random as the *champion*. Second, a pessimistic estimate is computed of how this purported champion would do against all possible opponents. The most formidable opponent is then selected as the *challenger*. Finally, the champion and the challenger are compared, i.e., the rankers are interleaved.

RUCB has a parameter $\alpha$ that controls how exploratory it is. If $\alpha > \frac{1}{2}$, then the regret accumulated by RUCB is proven to grow at most logarithmically with high probability [38]. In addition, it has been shown empirically to accumulate orders of magnitude less regret than BTM. Moreover, RUCB makes only the Condorcet assumption.

So far, the performance of RUCB in the context of online learning to rank has not been evaluated on large-scale datasets. We show that our proposed algorithm for ranker evaluation substantially outperforms RUCB on such datasets.

# 4. RELATIVE CONFIDENCE SAMPLING

In this section, we propose the *relative confidence sampling* (RCS) algorithm, which aims to reduce cumulative regret by being less conservative than the existing methods about eliminating rankers from contention. Though designed for the ongoing regret minimization setting, RCS is also easily adapted to the explore-then-exploit setting, and we show in Section 6 that it substantially outperforms the state-of-the-art methods in both settings.

While RCS is related to RUCB, which is also designed for the ongoing regret minimization setting, it differs in one crucial respect: the use of *sampling* when conducting a round-robin tournament to select a champion. The goal in doing so is to exploit one of the key lessons that has been learned in the study of regular $K$-armed bandits: that much better performance can be obtained by maintaining posterior distributions over the expected value of each ranker and sampling from those posteriors to determine which ranker to select. This is evidenced by the superior performance of Thompson Sampling [1, 22, 31], a $K$-armed bandit method that employs such sampling, over various UCB algorithms [5, 22]. Unlike UCB algorithms, which rely on estimates of the expected value that can be far off, sampling-based methods rely on posteriors that tend not to gravitate toward the extremes, leading to more appropriate choices more often.

**Algorithm 1** Relative Confidence Sampling (RCS)

**Input:** A set of rankers $\rho_1, \dots, \rho_K$ and an oracle that can take a pair of rankers and return one as the winner (e.g., an interleaved comparison method)

1: Choose $\alpha > \frac{1}{2}$
2: $\mathbf{W} \leftarrow \mathbf{0}_{K \times K}$ // *2D array of wins:* $\mathbf{W}_{ij}$ *is the number of times* $\rho_i$ *beat* $\rho_j$
3: **for** $t = 1, 2, \dots$ **do**
4: // **I**: *Run a simulated "tournament":*
5: $\boldsymbol{\Theta}(t) \leftarrow \frac{\mathbf{1}_{K \times K}}{2}$
6: **for** $i, j = 1, \dots, K$ with $i < j$ **do**
7: $\boldsymbol{\Theta}_{ij}(t) \sim \text{Beta}(\mathbf{W}_{ij} + 1, \mathbf{W}_{ji} + 1)$
8: $\boldsymbol{\Theta}_{ji}(t) = 1 - \boldsymbol{\Theta}_{ij}(t)$
9: **end for**
10: Pick $c$ such that $\boldsymbol{\Theta}_{cj}(t) \geq \frac{1}{2}$ for all $j$. If no such ranker exists, pick the ranker that has been chosen champion least often.
11: // **II**: *Run UCB in relation to* $c$:
12: $\mathbf{U}(t) = \frac{\mathbf{W}}{\mathbf{W}+\mathbf{W}^T} + \sqrt{\frac{\alpha \ln t}{\mathbf{W}+\mathbf{W}^T}}$ // *All operations are element-wise, with* $\frac{x}{0} := 1$ *for any* $x$.
13: $\mathbf{U}_{ii}(t) \leftarrow \frac{1}{2}$ for each $i = 1, \dots, K$.
14: $d \leftarrow \arg\max_j \mathbf{U}_{jc}(t)$
15: // **III**: *Update* $\mathbf{W}$
16: Compare rankers $\rho_c$ and $\rho_d$ and increment either $\mathbf{W}_{cd}$ if $\rho_c$ beat $\rho_d$ or $\mathbf{W}_{dc}$ otherwise.
17: **end for**

As we show in the experiments in Section 6, the advantage of sampling from the posterior distribution also appears in ranker evaluation and is in fact even more pronounced. RUCB tends to be very conservative in its choice of a potential champion, so unless it is highly confident that a ranker $\rho_i$ is inferior to another ranker, it will go on considering $\rho_i$ as a potential champion. By contrast, RCS is less timid in its choices: the more a ranker beats the rest, the greater its chances of being chosen as a champion to be compared against the rest.

The RCS algorithm, described in Algorithm 1, takes as input a set of rankers and an oracle such as an interleaved comparison method that can compare these rankers and return a noisy estimate of which is the winner. As it is horizonless, RCS does not have an output: as time goes by it chooses the best ranker more and more frequently. RCS has one parameter $\alpha$ (Line 1), which controls how exploratory the algorithm's behavior is: the higher the value of $\alpha$, the more slowly the algorithm settles on a single ranker. RCS maintains a *scoresheet* $\mathbf{W}$ (Line 2), in which it records the comparison results and proceeds in two phases:

- **I**: A tournament is simulated based on the current scoresheet, i.e., samples $\boldsymbol{\Theta}_{ij}$ are collected for each pair of rankers $(i, j)$ with $i > j$, from the posterior Beta distribution maintained on $p_{ij}$; Since $p_{ji} = 1 - p_{ij}$, RCS sets $\boldsymbol{\Theta}_{ji} = 1 - \boldsymbol{\Theta}_{ij}$ (Lines 6-9). Also, RCS sets $\boldsymbol{\Theta}_{ii} = \frac{1}{2}$ for each ranker $i$, since $p_{ii} = \frac{1}{2}$ and thus its posteriors are all concentrated at $\frac{1}{2}$ (Line 5). Given these sampled results, ranker $i$ beats ranker $j$ in the simulated tournament if $\mathbf{\Theta}_{ij} > \frac{1}{2}$ for $i \neq j$. There are two possibilities at this stage (Line 10):

1. There is a champion ranker $c$ that beats all other rankers in this tournament, i.e., $\mathbf{\Theta}_{cj} > \frac{1}{2}$ for all $j \neq c$.
2. No ranker beats all other rankers, in which case RCS sets $c = \text{argmin}_i N_i$, where $N_i$ is the number of times ranker $i$ was previously chosen as champion. In other words, $c$ is the ranker that has been the champion least often.

Eventually, once the Condorcet winner has been compared against the rest of the rankers often enough, its superiority over the rest will cause their elimination in this phase of the algorithm. So, as times goes by, $c$ will be the Condorcet winner more and more often.

**II**: The UCB algorithm is applied to the $K$-armed bandit problem with means $\{p_{1c}, \dots, p_{Kc}\}$ (Lines 12-14). In other words, for each $j \in \{1, \dots, K\}$, we calculate the optimistic estimate

$$u_{jc} := \frac{\mathbf{W}_{jc}}{\mathbf{W}_{jc} + \mathbf{W}_{cj}} + \sqrt{\frac{\alpha \ln t}{\mathbf{W}_{jc} + \mathbf{W}_{cj}}},$$

where the first term is our estimate of the comparison probability $p_{jc}$ and the second term is a confidence radius that is added to ensure adequate exploration by allowing the other rankers to compare themselves against $c$ optimistically. RCS picks the ranker $d$ for which $u_{dc}$ is higher than all other $u_{jc}$.

Finally, rankers $c$ and $d$ are compared against each other using a real interleaved comparison and $\mathbf{W}$ is updated accordingly (Line 16).

To better understand the rationale behind RCS, consider our Nadal-Federer example from Section 2. There, a key danger is that a $K$-armed dueling bandits algorithm may mistakenly conclude that Federer is the champion and stop comparing him against other players, most importantly Nadal. RCS avoids this pitfall in two ways. First, if Nadal has not been compared against the others enough times, then $\mathbf{\Theta}_{NF}$, where $N$ is Nadal and $F$ is Federer, will have high variance so that in Phase **I**, Federer will have difficulty beating the others in the simulated tournament in order to be chosen as the champion. In cases where no player beats everyone in the simulated tournament, RCS ensures that everyone gets a chance at being the champion, including Nadal. This ensures that our posterior belief in Nadal's chance of beating all other players will further concentrate above 0.5, making it even more likely that he will win future simulated tournaments. Second, even in cases where Federer does win the simulated tournament in Phase **I**, the fact that Nadal and Federer have not been compared often means that the upper bound $\mathbf{U}_{NF}$ will very likely be above $\mathbf{U}_{FF} = \frac{1}{2}$, hence preventing a fruitless comparison between Federer and himself. Instead, Federer will be compared to Nadal, ensuring that Nadal's superiority is eventually discovered.

RCS can be easily adapted to the explore-then-exploit setting: when the horizon is reached, it picks any ranker that beats the greatest number of other rankers according to the final scoresheet. We call this modification RCS also, since it is clear from context which version is meant.

# 5. EXPERIMENTAL SETUP

We seek to answer the following questions:

**RQ1** How often does the Condorcet assumption hold in comparison to the total ordering assumption?

**RQ2** How do SAVAGE and RCS perform at ranker evaluation on large-scale learning to rank datasets in the explore-then-exploit setting?

**RQ3** How do RUCB and RCS perform on these datasets in the ongoing regret minimization setting?

**RQ4** How does RUCB perform when the parameter $\alpha$ is too small for its theoretical guarantees to hold? Moreover, how does RCS perform in the same range?

**RQ5** How do RUCB and RCS scale as the number of rankers grows?

We address these questions using an experimental setup built on two large-scale learning to rank datasets: the Microsoft Learning to Rank (MSLR) and the Yahoo! Learning to Rank Challenge (YLR) datasets. The latter consists of two distinct subsets, Set 1 and Set 2, both of which we use. The specifics of these datasets are described in Table 1.

Table 1: The specifics of the datasets used.

| Datasets | Queries | URLs | Features | Reference |
|---|---|---|---|---|
| MSLR-WEB30K | 31,531 | 3,771,125 | 136 | [24] |
| YLR Set 1 | 19,944 | 473,134 | 519 | [4] |
| YLR Set 2 | 1,266 | 34,815 | 596 | [4] |

Using these datasets, we create a finite set of rankers, each of which corresponds to a ranking feature provided in the dataset, e.g., PageRank or BM25, and from this set we choose a subset to test our algorithms on. The ranker evaluation task thus corresponds to determining which single feature constitutes the best ranker.

The subsets were chosen by listing the rankers by their numbers and sorting them *alphabetically* and then taking the first $K$ rankers: given the fact that, at least with the features in the MSLR dataset, nearby features tend to be similar to each other,[1] this way of picking rankers ensures that not all the selected rankers are extremely similar to each other but there are nonetheless some similar rankers in the selected set. Consequently, some diversity is introduced without making the problem too easy, as would be the case if the rankers were picked completely randomly.

To compare a pair of rankers, we use *probabilistic interleave* (PI) [14], though any other interleaved comparison method could be used instead. To model the user's click behavior on the resulting interleaved lists, we employ a probabilistic user model [9, 14] that uses as input the manual labels (classifying documents as relevant or not for given queries) provided with both datasets. Queries are sampled randomly and clicks are generated probabilistically by conditioning on these assessments using a user model that resembles the behavior of an actual user [11, 12]. This approach follows an experimental paradigm that has previously been used for assessing the performance of rankers [13–16].

[1]We assume that a similar phenomenon also holds for the Yahoo! datasets, but there is no specific list of features for them that we could use to verify that claim.

Because we use probabilistic interleave, which already introduces noise into the interleaved comparison, we employ the *perfect click model* in our experiments. While another click model that injects additional noise, such as the *navigational click model* or the *informational click model* [15], could be used instead, doing so would only shift each $p_{ij}$ closer to 0.5. As a result, all methods would need more time to identify the best ranker, making our experiments take even longer to run.

We use two evaluation metrics, corresponding to the two objectives outlined in Section 2. We use *accuracy* (or best ranker rate) and *cumulative regret*, both of which are used in the explore-then-exploit setting, while only the latter is used for the ongoing regret minimization objective. Cumulative regret is the total amount of regret encountered by the algorithm until a given time, where regret at each time step is as defined in (1). A ranker evaluation algorithm accumulates regret when it makes a suboptimal choice, meaning that it does not interleave the best ranker with itself. The more suboptimal the rankers in the interleaved comparisons, the higher the accumulated regret. Thus, according to the ongoing regret minimization objective, the goal of the ranker evaluation algorithm is to increase the frequency with which it chooses the best ranker as soon as possible; doing so results in lower regret curves: the flatter the curve, the lower the frequency of picking poor rankers.

In most of our experiments, we set $\alpha = 0.501$ for both RUCB and RCS, as this ensures that RUCB's theoretical results apply without it being too exploratory. However, in one experiment, in order to address **RQ4**, we set $\alpha = 0.1$. In the experiments addressing **RQ2**–**RQ4**, the number of rankers that we consider is set to 10. In the addressing **RQ5**, we contrast the performance of RUCB and RCS with sets of 10, 20, 30 and 40 rankers.

# 6. RESULTS AND DISCUSSION

In this section, we present and discuss results concerning each of our research questions.

## 6.1 The Condorcet Assumption

RCS, like RUCB and Condorcet SAVAGE, relies on the Condorcet assumption. Other methods such as IF and BTM, rely on the even stronger assumption of total ordering, among others. Therefore, it is of interest to know to what extent these assumptions hold in learning to rank datasets. In order to address **RQ1**, we consider the 136 feature rankers in the MSLR-WEB30K dataset.

Using the full matrix of comparison probabilities $\mathbf{P}$, which was estimated by carrying out 80,000 interleaved comparisons between each pair of feature rankers, and a simple combinatorial calculation, we determined that the probability that a random subset of these features satisfies the Condorcet assumption is always above 0.91. For small and large subsets, the probability is even higher.

The probability that the total ordering assumption holds was estimated using a sampling approach: for each $K = 1, \ldots, 136$, we randomly sampled 10,000 sets of $K$ feature rankers and used the proportion of these subsets that satisfy total ordering as an approximation to the probability that total ordering holds for a subset of the given size $K$.

Figure 1 shows these probabilities as a function of the size of the subset of features considered: the blue curve shows the probability that the Condorcet assumption is satisfied for a

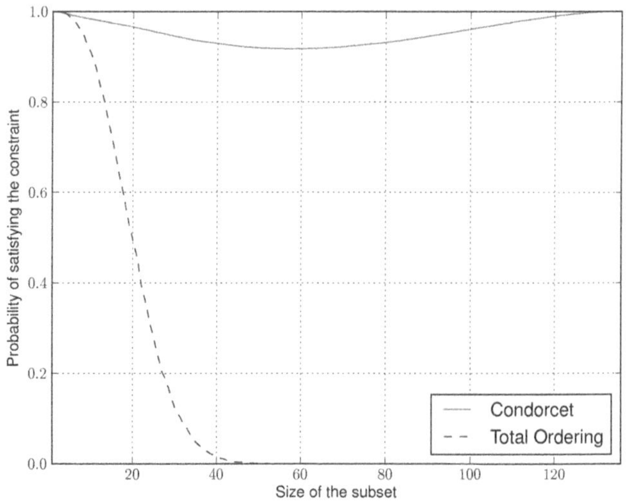


Figure 1: The probability that the Condorcet and the total ordering assumptions hold for subsets of the feature rankers in the MSLR-WEB30K dataset. The probability is shown as a function of the size of the subset.

subset of given size, while the red curve shows the same for the total ordering assumption. In the case of the Condorcet assumption, these probabilities are slightly smaller for intermediate subset sizes, since it is harder for larger subsets to avoid cycles in the *superiority graph* (the directed graph that has an edge from $i$ to $j$ if $p_{ij} > 0.5$), while for very large subsets, the total number of possible subsets is relatively small, so the probability becomes large again. By contrast, the larger the subset of rankers under consideration, the more likely it is to include a cycle, causing the probability of a total ordering existing to fall quickly.

One source of difficulty in this analysis are probabilities $p_{ij}$ that are very close or equal to 0.5. Even with 80,000 comparisons between each pair of rankers, our estimate of the preference matrix might contain fake loops that are simply due to the natural variance in frequentist estimates of such probabilities. This can lead to a reversal of the edges in the superiority graph. Indeed, for many cycles of size three in this graph, the "weakest link" is extremely close to 0.5, making it difficult to state with certainty that a cycle exists. However, the same variance can also break real cycles, and so these two phenomena should cancel each others' effects. Moreover, there are also many cycles whose edges are strong enough to deduce a genuine cycle.

## 6.2 Explore-then-Exploit Results

The performance of RCS in the explore-then-exploit setting was compared against Condorcet SAVAGE, which is the state of the art in this setting [32]. Recall from Section 2 that this setting considers both the accuracy and the cumulative regret of these algorithms at a given horizon. The top row of plots in Figure 2 compares the accuracy of RCS and Condorcet SAVAGE at 10 different horizons on three 10-armed bandits obtained from the three different datasets by considering 10 of the feature rankers. Note that the horizontal axis is in log scale and accuracy is the percentage of the runs that correctly produced the best ranker as the winner at the given horizon.

Note that, because Condorcet SAVAGE requires the horizon as input, the algorithm must be rerun from scratch for

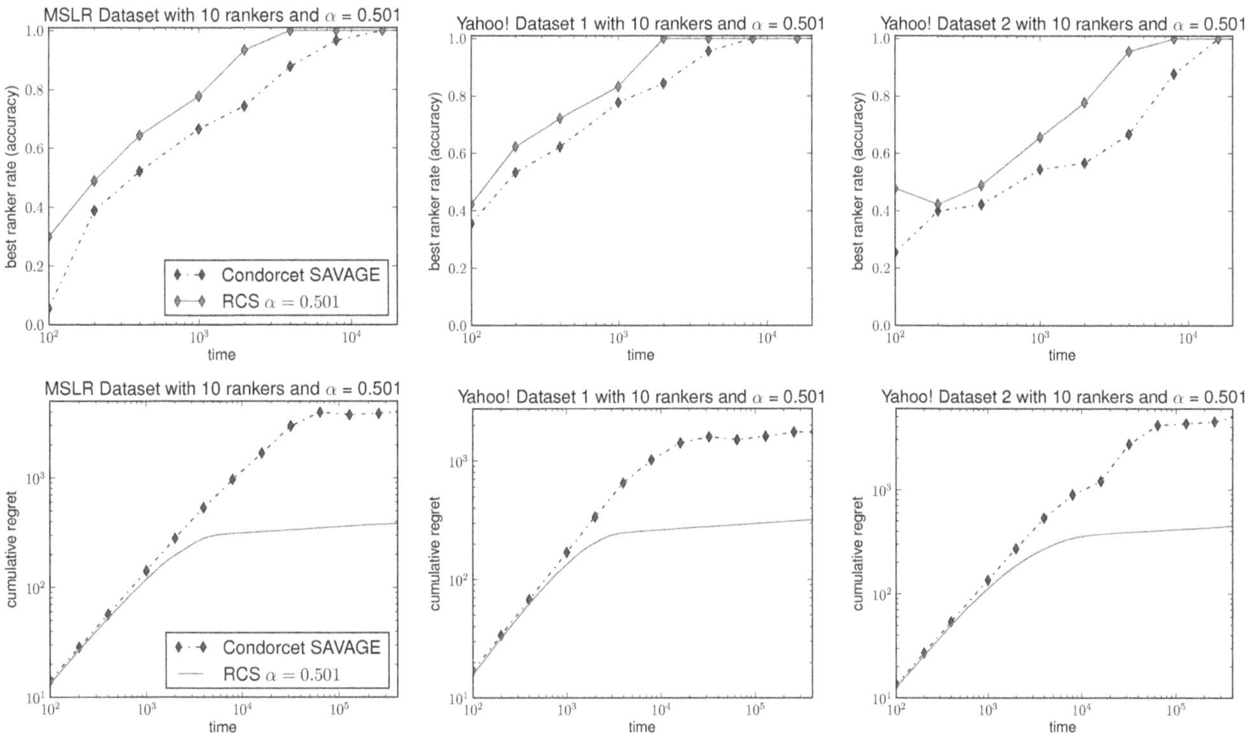


Figure 2: Accuracy (best ranker rate) and average cumulative regret over 90 runs; in top row of plots, the x-axis uses a log scale; in the bottom plots, both axes use log scales. Log scales were used for the x-axes to make the accuracy plots easier to read and in the y-axes of the regret plots since the regret accumulated by Condorcet SAVAGE is an order of magnitude higher than that of RCS.

each horizon. Thus, to obtain the plotted results, we conducted independent runs for each of the 10 horizons considered. By contrast, since RCS is a horizonless algorithm, we simply ran it until the longest horizon and then measured its accuracy at each of the 10 horizons.

Concerning **RQ2**, these results show that RCS has consistently higher accuracy than Condorcet SAVAGE on all datasets. This is a particularly striking result because RCS does not have any parameters optimized for the specific horizons in these experiments. Condorcet SAVAGE, by contrast, has the advantage that it receives the horizon as input and can thus adapt its behavior accordingly. Nonetheless, RCS outperforms Condorcet SAVAGE according to the metric for which Condorcet SAVAGE was designed. Though the lines appear close in the graph due to the log scale, the learning speed actually differs substantially: RCS reaches the same level of accuracy almost twice as quickly as Condorcet SAVAGE. For example, on the Yahoo! Set 1, RCS achieves an accuracy of 0.8 after 1000 steps while SAVAGE achieves it only after 2000 steps.

The other objective of the explore-then-exploit setting, which is to minimize the regret accumulated by the horizon, is addressed in the bottom row of plots in Figure 2. Note that these plots are in log-log scale. As with the accuracy plots, these plots select the performance of separate runs conducted at each horizon for Condorcet SAVAGE, while each RCS run was used to measure regret at all horizons. As is clear from these plots, RCS dramatically outperforms Condorcet SAVAGE despite being ignorant of the predetermined horizon. In fact, in each experiment, by the time Condorcet SAVAGE reaches 100% accuracy, it has accumulated at least 3 times as much regret as when RCS achieves that same accuracy.

The superior performance of RCS over Condorcet SAVAGE according to both accuracy and regret is due to related phenomena: the main advantage of RCS over Condorcet SAVAGE is that, instead of comparing pairs of rankers uniformly randomly, it rapidly focuses on comparing the Condorcet winner against the rest, thereby reducing regret, because one of the summands in the definition of regret (cf. (1)) is now zero and, more importantly, doing so leads to much better estimates of the probabilities $p_{1j}$, and thus greater confidence in the supremacy of the best ranker. This in turn leads to more frequent comparisons between the best ranker and itself, further reducing regret and increasing accuracy.

We also tested RUCB in the explore-then-exploit setting and found higher accuracy for RCS than RUCB, though the difference was relatively small. There was, however, a substantial difference in the regret performances of RUCB and RCS, as demonstrated in the next section. We omitted the accuracy curves for RUCB in order to increase readability.

## 6.3 Ongoing Regret Minimization Results

Turning now to the other method for evaluating $K$-armed dueling bandits algorithms, Figure 3 shows the expected cumulative regret obtained when applying RUCB and RCS to three 10-armed dueling bandits problems obtained from the three different datasets. For both RCS and RUCB, the parameter $\alpha$ is set to be 0.501 so that RUCB's theoretical guarantees [38] hold. The curves in the plots show the mean cumulative regret over 90 independent runs of each algorithm. The plots show results on the first 50,000 time steps, using linear scales on both axes.

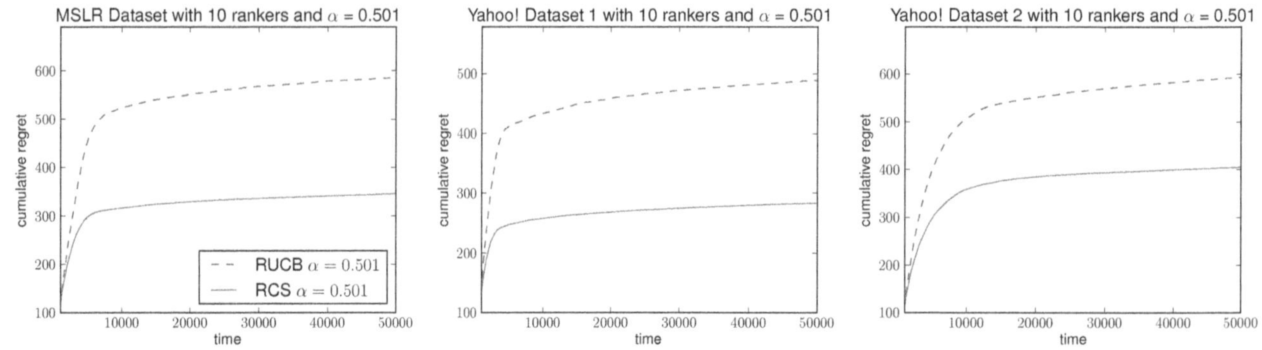


Figure 3: Cumulative regret averaged over 90 runs on the three datasets. All plots use axes with linear scale, since the two curves are much closer to each other than the ones in the regret plots in Figure 2.

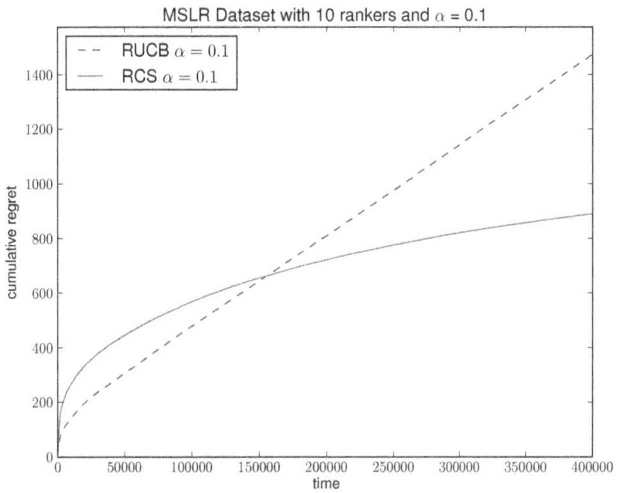


Figure 4: Cumulative regret averaged over 30 runs.

Regarding **RQ3**, the plots in Figure 3 clearly demonstrate that RCS accumulates substantially less regret than RUCB, with the former accumulating roughly a third less regret than latter. In other words, not only does RCS find the best ranker more quickly than RUCB, it also makes less severe errors in the process of doing so. In more concrete terms, the difference in the regret levels at which the two algorithms plateau is on the order of 200 in these three datasets, which roughly translates to an extra 2000 interleaved comparisons involving suboptimal rankers: this is because the probability with which the Condorcet winner beats the remaining arms is around 0.6. Needless to say, this performance difference can have a great impact on user satisfaction and engagement. Thus, these results highlight the benefits of a sampling-based approach to exploration.

Moreover, given the qualitative similarity between the performances of RUCB and RCS when $\alpha > 0.5$, we strongly suspect that similar regret bounds as those proven for RUCB [38] also hold for RCS. However, the use of sampling would necessitate a more intricate theoretical argument that we leave as future work.

Finally, in these experiments both algorithms had similar variance across runs; the best performing run of RUCB had a higher regret curve than the average regret curve of RCS.

## 6.4 Stability of RUCB and RCS

The improved performance of RCS over RUCB in the previous section can be attributed to the fact that RCS engages in less unnecessary exploration. Since lowering $\alpha$ makes both RCS and RUCB less exploratory, an important question, as posed in **RQ4**, is whether regret can be even further reduced by setting $\alpha$ to values below 0.5.

To address this question, we investigate the stability of RUCB and RCS by setting $\alpha = 0.1$, which lies outside the range permitted by RUCB's theoretical results. Figure 4 shows the cumulative regret results averaged over 30 runs of both RUCB and RCS on the MSLR dataset: fewer runs were used in this case to illustrate how easily RUCB can misbehave when $\alpha$ is below 0.5. These results show that the average cumulative regret for RUCB grows linearly, which was due to two of the runs never reaching the point where they keep interleaving the best ranker with itself. By contrast, though RCS accumulates almost twice as much regret at $\alpha = 0.1$ than $\alpha = 0.501$, the performance degradation is much less severe than for RUCB, with RCS's cumulative regret curve flattening much more. Similar results were also observed with the other datasets, but are not included here due to space constraints.

The performance difference is due to the fact that reducing $\alpha$ results in shrinking the confidence intervals maintained by RUCB, which results in the tournament phase of the algorithm not being exploratory enough. Hence, RUCB focuses prematurely on a single arm that has a temporary advantage over the others, preventing it from getting better estimates of the comparison probabilities between the Condorcet winner and the rest, which is necessary for the Condorcet winner to be chosen by the tournament. This, however, is not a stumbling block for RCS because there are no confidence intervals in the tournament phase, which relies on sampling instead. Figure 4 demonstrates that these samples ensure enough exploration to avoid getting stuck with a suboptimal ranker. Thus, while lower values of $\alpha$ are not beneficial to either algorithm, RCS remains stable while RUCB can experience the catastrophic negative performance associated with linear regret.

## 6.5 Size of the Set of Rankers

In order to study the issue of scalability, we compare RCS to RUCB on problems with 20, 30 and 40 rankers, all extracted from the MSLR dataset. See Figure 5.

Regarding **RQ5**, these results show that the cumulative regret curve of RCS flattens much sooner than that of RUCB. Thus, RCS starts focusing on the best ranker more quickly than RUCB: more specifically, where the two curves cross, RUCB was spending on average 6 to 9 times more iterations interleaving non-optimal rankers than RCS. For instance, in

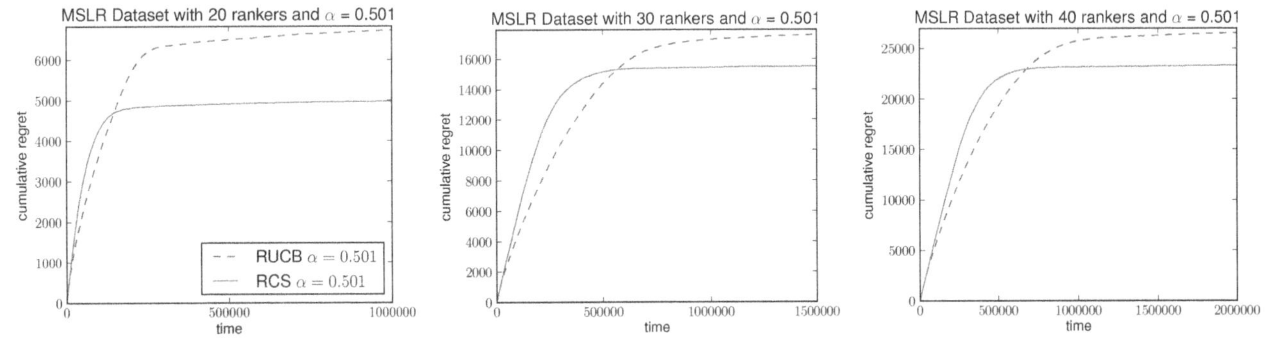


Figure 5: Cumulative regret averaged over 90 runs on the MSLR-WEB30K dataset, with 20, 30, 40 rankers. For comparison, the plot for 10 rankers is the leftmost plot in Figure 3; note that the scales differ between the four plots, which is necessary in order to illustrate the non-asymptotic portion of all of the results.

the experiments with 20 rankers, in the vicinity of the crossing point, 3.6% of RCS's comparisons involved subptimal rankers, whereas 27% of RUCB's did; the same quantities for the 30 and 40 ranker experiments are 1.9% vs. 17% and 3.3% vs. 21%. On the other hand, at time $T = \frac{T_0}{2}$, where $T_0$ is the time at which the two average regret curves cross, these differences are much smaller with the same numbers being 31% vs. 33%, 31% vs. 36% and 44% vs. 45% for the 20, 30 and 40 ranker experiments, respectively.

Note that this more rapid convergence to the best ranker requires more aggressive exploration early on. This can be deduced from the fact that, before plateauing, the red curves for RCS have slightly steeper slopes than the green curves for RUCB during the same period. This is due to the fact that RCS abstains from removing any rankers from consideration until it became clear which ranker is the best, whereas RUCB stops comparing poorer rankers earlier in the process. Nevertheless, RCS starts interleaving the best ranker with itself in substantially fewer iterations and thus accumulates much less regret in the long run. For instance, at time $T = 2T_0$, where $T_0$ is the time at which the two average regret curves cross, the average cumulative regret of RUCB is 30%, 12.3% and 12.6% higher than that of RCS for 20, 30 and 40 ranker experiments, respectively.

Moreover, the regret curves for RCS are much flatter after they plateau than those of RUCB, which means that, once the best ranker is identified, RCS is more likely to avoid futile interleaved comparisons with suboptimal rankers. More precisely, at time $T = 2T_0$, the percentage of comparisons RUCB devotes to suboptimal arms is still roughly 8 times higher than that of RCS, e.g., 2% and 0.3%, respectively, for the 20 ranker experiment.

# 7. CONCLUSIONS

We have proposed and experimentally evaluated a new method for addressing the problem of on-line ranker evaluation. Our method, *relative confidence sampling* (RCS), was evaluated against the existing methods on large scale learning to rank datasets, in two settings: explore-then-exploit and ongoing regret minimization. RCS significantly outperforms the existing state-of-the-art methods under both settings. In particular, given the need in online ranker evaluation scenarios to identify and compare the best ranker as quickly as possible, RCS has a large advantage over all existing algorithms, since when asked to return the best ranker in the explore-then-exploit setting, it has a higher probability of returning the best ranker, while minimizing the number of queries wasted on comparing suboptimal rankers (as evidenced by the lower regret curves for RCS), without requiring prior knowledge of the length of the evaluation or imposing restrictive assumptions such as a total ordering.

In future work, we aim to obtain theoretical guarantees for RCS, which require a considerably more delicate argument than that of RUCB because the use of sampling in RCS introduces a new dimension of uncertainty in the tournament phase of the algorithm.

Another important question is to design ranker evaluation algorithms that can deal with even larger (possibly infinite) numbers of rankers, without requiring convexity assumptions such as those in [35]. In general, one major technical difficulty facing interleaved comparisons, as opposed to approaches using click-through rate, is that the number of comparisons required to deal with a $K$-armed dueling bandits problem is of the order $K^2$, since every ranker needs to be compared against every other ranker. Some algorithms, such as Beat the Mean, get around this hurdle by averaging the comparisons between each arm and the rest. However, in order for these algorithms to find the Condorcet winner, the suboptimal arms need to satisfy a total ordering condition that is difficult to verify and is often violated in practice, as shown in Section 6.1. One potential remedy for dealing with this difficulty is to use correlation information between rankers and make use of continuous armed bandits algorithms [3, 10, 25, 30, 33], although both the algorithm and the theoretical analysis would be considerably more intricate in this setting, since the goal is not simply to find the maximum of a continuous function.

As explained in Section 5, we based our experiments on the *perfect* click model; in future experimental work we will confirm our experimental findings with alternative click models [15]. We expect such experiments to produce qualitatively similar results, since changing the click model simply makes the interleaved comparisons noisier without affecting whether a ranker beats another on average, i.e., the probability of one ranker beating the other is shifted closer to 0.5 without crossing it. This in turn will make the experiments take longer before finding the best ranker without affecting to which ranker the algorithms converge.

Finally, we remarked in Section 6.2 that RCS manages to beat Condorcet SAVAGE in the performance metrics that the latter was designed for. Thus, another possibility for future work is to investigate whether it is possible to further improve the performance of RCS (and RUCB, for that matter) by taking the horizon into account.

**Acknowledgments.** This research was supported by the European Community's Seventh Framework Programme (FP7/2007-2013) under grant agreement nr 288024 (LiMoSINe project), the Netherlands Organisation for Scientific Research (NWO) under project nrs 640.004.802, 727.011.005, 612.001.116, HOR-11-10, the Center for Creation, Content and Technology (CCCT), the QuaMerdes project funded by the CLARIN-nl program, the TROVe project funded by the CLARIAH program, the Dutch national program COMMIT, the ESF Research Network Program ELIAS, the Elite Network Shifts project funded by the Royal Dutch Academy of Sciences (KNAW), the Netherlands eScience Center under project number 027.012.105 and the Yahoo! Faculty Research and Engagement Program.

# REFERENCES

[1] S. Agrawal and N. Goyal. Analysis of Thompson sampling for the multi-armed bandit problem. In *Conference on Learning Theory*, pages 1–26, 2012.

[2] P. Auer, N. Cesa-Bianchi, and P. Fischer. Finite-time analysis of the multiarmed bandit problem. *Machine Learning*, 47(2-3):235–256, 2002.

[3] S. Bubeck, R. Munos, G. Stoltz, and C. Szepesvari. X-armed bandits. *Journal of Machine Learning Research*, 12:1655–1695, 2011.

[4] O. Chapelle and Y. Chang. Yahoo! learning to rank challenge overview. *Journal of Machine Learning Research-Proceedings Track*, 14:1–24, 2011.

[5] O. Chapelle and L. Li. An empirical evaluation of Thompson sampling. In *NIPS*, 2011.

[6] O. Chapelle, T. Joachims, F. Radlinski, and Y. Yue. Large-scale validation and analysis of interleaved search evaluation. *ACM Trans. Inf. Syst.*, 30(1): 6:1–6:41, 2012.

[7] A. Chuklin, A. Schuth, K. Hofmann, P. Serdyukov, and M. de Rijke. Evaluating aggregated search using interleaving. In *CIKM 2013*. ACM, October 2013.

[8] C. W. Cleverdon, J. Mills, and M. Keen. Factors determining the performance of indexing systems. In *ASLIB Cranfield project*. 1966.

[9] N. Craswell, O. Zoeter, M. Taylor, and B. Ramsey. An experimental comparison of click position-bias models. In *WSDM '08*, pages 87–94, 2008.

[10] N. de Freitas, A. Smola, and M. Zoghi. Exponential regret bounds for Gaussian process bandits with deterministic observations. In *ICML*, 2012.

[11] F. Guo, L. Li, and C. Faloutsos. Tailoring click models to user goals. In *WSCD '09*, pages 88–92, 2009.

[12] F. Guo, C. Liu, and Y. M. Wang. Efficient multiple-click models in web search. In *WSDM '09*, pages 124–131, New York, NY, USA, 2009. ACM.

[13] J. He, C. Zhai, and X. Li. Evaluation of methods for relative comparison of retrieval systems based on clickthroughs. In *CIKM '09*, pages 2029–2032, 2009.

[14] K. Hofmann, S. Whiteson, and M. de Rijke. A probabilistic method for inferring preferences from clicks. In *CIKM '11*, pages 249–258, USA, 2011.

[15] K. Hofmann, S. Whiteson, and M. de Rijke. Fidelity, soundness, and efficiency of interleaved comparison methods. *ACM Trans. Inf. Syst.*, 31(4), 2013.

[16] K. Hofmann, S. Whiteson, and M. de Rijke. Balancing exploration and exploitation in listwise and pairwise online learning to rank for information retrieval. *Information Retrieval*, 16(1):63–90, 2013.

[17] S. Ji, K. Zhou, C. Liao, Z. Zheng, G.-R. Xue, O. Chapelle, G. Sun, and H. Zha. Global ranking by exploiting user clicks. In *SIGIR '09*, pages 35–42, 2009.

[18] T. Joachims. Optimizing search engines using clickthrough data. In *KDD '02*, pages 133–142, 2002.

[19] T. Joachims. Evaluating retrieval performance using clickthrough data. In J. Franke, G. Nakhaeizadeh, and I. Renz, editors, *Text Mining*, pages 79–96. 2003.

[20] S. Jung, J. L. Herlocker, and J. Webster. Click data as implicit relevance feedback in web search. *Information Processing & Management*, 43(3):791–807, 2007.

[21] J. Kamps, M. Koolen, and A. Trotman. Comparative analysis of clicks and judgments for IR evaluation. In *WSCD'09*, pages 80–87, 2009.

[22] E. Kauffmann, N. Korda, and R. Munos. Thompson sampling: an asymptotically optimal finite time analysis. In *ALT'12*, pages 199–213, 2012.

[23] T. Lai and H. Robbins. Asymptotically efficient adaptive allocation rules. *Advances in Applied Mathematics*, 6(1):4–22, 1985.

[24] Microsoft Learning to Rank Datasets, 2012. `http://research.microsoft.com/en-us/projects/mslr/default.aspx`.

[25] R. Munos. Optimistic optimization of a deterministic function without the knowledge of its smoothness. In *NIPS*, 2011.

[26] F. Radlinski and N. Craswell. Comparing the sensitivity of information retrieval metrics. In *SIGIR '10*, pages 667–674, 2010.

[27] F. Radlinski and N. Craswell. Optimized interleaving for online retrieval evaluation. In *WSDM '13*, 2013.

[28] F. Radlinski, M. Kurup, and T. Joachims. How does clickthrough data reflect retrieval quality? In *CIKM '08*, pages 43–52, 2008.

[29] F. Scholer, M. Shokouhi, B. Billerbeck, and A. Turpin. Using clicks as implicit judgments: expectations versus observations. In *ECIR'08*, pages 28–39, 2008.

[30] N. Srinivas, A. Krause, S. M. Kakade, and M. Seeger. Gaussian process optimization in the bandit setting: No regret and experimental design. In *ICML*, 2010.

[31] W. Thompson. On the likelihood that one unknown probability exceeds another in view of the evidence of two samples. *Biometrika*, pages 285–294, 1933.

[32] T. Urvoy, F. Clerot, R. Féraud, and S. Naamane. Generic exploration and k-armed voting bandits. In *ICML*, 2013.

[33] M. Valko, A. Carpentier, and R. Munos. Stochastic simultaneous optimistic optimization. In *ICML*, 2013.

[34] E. M. Voorhees and D. K. Harman. *TREC: Experiment and Evaluation in Information Retrieval*. MIT Press, 2005.

[35] Y. Yue and T. Joachims. Interactively optimizing information retrieval systems as a dueling bandits problem. In *ICML*, 2009.

[36] Y. Yue and T. Joachims. Beat the mean bandit. In *ICML*, 2011.

[37] Y. Yue, J. Broder, R. Kleinberg, and T. Joachims. The K-armed dueling bandits problem. *Journal of Computer and System Sciences*, 78(5):1538–1556, Sept. 2009.

[38] M. Zoghi, S. Whiteson, R. Munos, and M. de Rijke. Relative upper confidence bound for the $k$-armed dueling bandits problem. Techn. Report arXiv:1312.3393, 2013.

# Adapting Deep RankNet for Personalized Search

[1]Yang Song, [2]Hongning Wang, [1]Xiaodong He

[1]Microsoft Research,
One Microsoft Way,
Redmond, WA 98052, USA
{yangsong, xiaohe}@microsoft.com

[2]Department of Computer Science
University of Illinois at Urbana-Champaign
Urbana IL, 61801 USA
{wang296}@cs.uiuc.edu

## ABSTRACT

RankNet is one of the widely adopted ranking models for web search tasks. However, adapting a generic RankNet for personalized search is little studied. In this paper, we first continue-trained a variety of RankNets with different number of hidden layers and network structures over a previously trained global RankNet model, and observed that a deep neural network with five hidden layers gives the best performance. To further improve the performance of adaptation, we propose a set of novel methods categorized into two groups. In the first group, three methods are proposed to properly assess the usefulness of each adaptation instance and only leverage the most informative instances to adapt a user-specific RankNet model. These assessments are based on KL-divergence, click entropy or a heuristic to ignore top clicks in adaptation queries. In the second group, two methods are proposed to regularize the training of the neural network in RankNet: one of these methods regularize the error back-propagation via a truncated gradient approach, while the other method limits the depth of the back propagation when adapting the neural network. We empirically evaluate our approaches using a large-scale real-world data set. Experimental results exhibit that our methods all give significant improvements over a strong baseline ranking system, and the truncated gradient approach gives the best performance, significantly better than all others.

## Categories and Subject Descriptors

H.3.3 [**Information Storage and Retrieval**]: Information Search and Retrieval—*Internet search*; H.3.0 [**Information Storage and Retrieval**]: General—*Web search*

## General Terms

Measurement,Experimentation

## Keywords

personalized search, deep learning, ranking adaptation


*WSDM'14,* February 24–28, 2014, New York, New York, USA.

http://dx.doi.org/10.1145/2556195.2556234.

## 1. INTRODUCTION

Search engine personalization, or otherwise known as personalized search, is getting more and more attention from the information retrieval community in recent years [24, 2, 5, 17, 18, 22, 23, 16]. In general, in order to better serve their users, search engines often record certain user activities such as queries and search-result clicks, and leverage such information to improve the relevance of the returned documents. To perform personalization, search engines try to match the user behaviors from the target users to others who have similar search behaviors and then aggregate the information from others to estimate the target user's search intent. Essentially, many of the existing works act fairly close to the collaborative filtering method [24, 22], where the user similarity is defined by considering their queries [22, 23], tasks [24], and etc.

In this paper, we address the personalized search problem from a model adaptation perspective. We adapt a generic RankNet model [3] that is trained on a user-independent data set to each individual user based on his/her search history and result preference. In literature, little has been studied on this direction until very recently, where the authors in [21] demonstrated competitive adaptation performance of RankNet when comparing with RankSVM and LambdaMART for personalized model adaptation. Interestingly, in their framework, the authors only used a RankNet without hidden layers which is mathematically equivalent to a logistic regression model. With the recent advance of leveraging deep learning models for information retrieval [9, 15, 11], we believe that, a well-trained deep RankNet with multiple layers of non-linear representations can offer an even better performance in training personalized models.

Our motivation of using deep learning for adaptation comes from two aspects. First and foremost, existing approaches on ranking model adaptation mainly focus on adapting from a source domain to a few number of target domains [8, 7] due to efficiency concern. It would be prohibitively expensive to adapt a generic model to each individual user using the current methods. Therefore, our proposal takes a model-based approach. i.e., we first train a user-independent ranker, and then for each individual user, we update the parameters of the global ranking model accordingly. Since a typical user's search history is short, adapting the global model becomes much more efficient than re-training the entire ranker.

Secondly, deep learning framework naturally constructs a semantic/abstract representation from the inputs. This property is desirable for model adaptation. Existing feature-based model adaptation methods, for example the CLRank algorithm in [4], maps both the source and target domains into a lower-dimensional space to learn a common feature representation. However, finding a reduced dimension, e.g., using SVD, is prohibitively expensive. Instead, deep learning automatically constructs reduced feature spaces from increasingly more compact representations of the network and achieves semantic representations at higher levels.

However, there are many challenges in using deep learning for personalized search. One of the biggest concerns in personalized search is the data sparsity issue, where each user only has a handful of queries in their search histories and therefore limits the learning capability of the personalization algorithms. Despite the recent advances via using probabilistic models [17] and model adaptation frameworks [21], little has been explored on the relationship between data sparsity and model performance in personalized search. Also, issues like model complexity and overfitting in personalized ranking model adaptation remain to be discussed.

Specifically, our paper makes the following contributions:

1. We use a deep learning framework for personalized ranking adaptation. This framework works by first training a deep RankNet as a global ranking model from user-independent label data. We then adapt the global model to each user by training individual models based on the user's search history. We train a variety of RankNets with different numbers of hidden layers and network structures on a per-user basis, and observed that a deep neural network with five hidden layers gives the best performance.

2. To further improve the performance of adaptation, we introduce several novel ideas including re-weighting adaptation data and regularizing back-propagation. Among all of the five proposals, we observe that a truncated gradient approach performs the best.

3. We empirically analyze the issue of model complexity and how it affects model training and the overfitting issue, on a large-scale data set from a commercial search engine's logs. We discover that overfitting can indeed happen if the adaptation data is not sufficient, or early-stopping is not performed properly.

4. We investigate the relationship between data sparsity and model performance by sampling users with different search frequencies. We observe that the adaptation performance often increases with more user search history data. On the other hand, when adaptation data is limited, regularizing back-propagation becomes important.

The remainder of the paper is organized as follows: Section 2 describes related work in personalized search and deep learning for ranking; Section 3 describes the data set used in this paper; Section 4 presents our adaptation framework; Section 5 shows the empirical results; Section 6 concludes our work with discussion and future work.

## 2. RELATED WORK

We will be discussing two relevant areas of related work in this section: (1) personalized search and (2) deep learning for IR.

(**Personalized Search**) There have been many researches on personalized search and we will highlight a few that is considered interesting and representative. In [23], White et al. leveraged short-term user behavior signals such as browser history, query history, as well as desktop information to re-rank the search results and predict the user search interests in the future. In particular, they built a predictive model leveraging the contextual information by representing user interests as a list of Open Directory Project (ODP) categories so that the model is capable of scaling up to a quarter million users with billions of URLs.

In [17], Sontag et al. proposed to learn user profiles from user's long-term search history. The authors introduced a generative probabilistic model to infer the search relevance of URLs. Two models were introduced: the first probabilistic model built directly on the user history without considering any background models; the second model, on the other hand, considered the topic distribution of documents which is incorporated into the personalized models to further improve the predictive performance.

Shen et al. [16] introduced a context-sensitive method by leveraging implicit user feedback for re-ranking. Their model used both click-through information and contextual queries as implicit signals from users. Specifically, the authors proposed to enhance the KL-divergence based retrieval model by incorporating the context-sensitive information into language models. They empirically analyzed the performance by constructing a test set from TREC AP data set, the result of which indicated an improved retrieval performance than the baseline methods.

Recently, White et al. [24] introduced a novel model by modeling the search task behavior among search users. Comparing to previous work that often model user similarity based on queries, the authors were among the first to introduce a novel concept of task where a task is considered as an atomic user information need, often containing several queries and search-result clicks. The task information was used to group users together to cohorts for generating click features for a particular set of users in consideration. Results indicated that task-based user grouping outperforms query-based and session-based groupings significantly.

From the model adaptation perspective, Wang et al. [21] brought this concept to personalized search from domain adaptation. They introduced a general framework for adaptation by first training a global ranking model on a user-independent data set and then adapting models to each individual user. To reduce the parameter size, feature grouping based on linear transformations such as scaling and shifting is proposed. The authors then applied their general framework to three popular ranking models: RankSVM, RankNet and LambdaRank. Note that in the realization of the RankNet model, no hidden layers are considered concerning the feature grouping complexity, and therefore it could result a suboptimal performance of RankNet.

Dou et al. [5] conducted a large-scale evaluation on several personalized search algorithms, by using a 12-day query log from MSN. They divided personalization into person-level re-ranking and group-level re-ranking, and compared five different variants. They employed two metrics for evaluation, namely web page ranking score and average rank. Experiments indicated that all personalized methods significantly outperformed the default ranking algorithm. It also revealed that personalized search has different effectiveness on different types of queries. For example, they observed that for queries with small click entropy, the performance gain was not that obvious comparing to those with large entropy.

(**Deep Learning for IR**) In recent years, the deep learning technique has been introduced to domains such as speech and image recognition with great success. In information retrieval, Hinton et al. [9] first introduced the idea of using neural networks for dimensionality reduction. In their work, they leveraged the representation of deep belief network (DBN) to initialize the deep network structure, and then used a deep auto-encoder to reconstruct the input data. Their results indicated that the variables on the top layer were able to give a better representation of each document, so that semantically similar documents are mapped to a closer position to each other.

Mirowski et al. [15] presented a novel algorithm for topic modeling and information retrieval based on a deep auto-encoder architecture. The objective of auto-encoder in general is to minimize the reconstruction error of the input instance. In their work, the authors leveraged a deep structure which produces increasingly more compact representations of the document vector space to reduce the dimensionality so that semantic representation can be achieved at higher level of the network. Besides minimizing the reconstruction error, their framework also minimized a weighted cross-entropy loss between word histograms concurrently. Experimental results on the NIPS article data set demonstrated a lower perplexity score than Latent Dirichlet Allocation (LDA).

Recently, Huang et al. [11] leveraged this technique to improve web search. In particular, the authors tried to bridge the lexical gaps between queries and documents via semantic matching using deep learning framework. In their model, queries and documents were treated as bag-of-words vectors as the input of the neural network, the model then learnt several layers of deep non-linear projections and outputted a vector in the semantic space. During the learning phases, each query is given the title of a URL that is clicked by users along with several un-clicked URLs, where clicked URLs are assumed to be relevant. The learning objective is to minimize the relevance loss of query titles on the sematic space, where the relevance is computed using cosine similarity between the query semantic space and URL semantic space. Experimental results on a large-scale data set indicated significant improvement over the traditional tf-idf based model as well as deep auto-encoder models.

Similarly, Wang et al. [20] addressed the issue of data sparsity in social media question-answering application. Due to the small length of both questions and answers, traditional ways of modeling their relationship turned out to be suboptimal. Instead, the authors leveraged deep learning to address the semantic relationship between them, by using two deep belief networks to model the semantic relevance. Experiments on a Chinese forum corpora indicated better performance than traditional methods.

# 3. DATA COLLECTION

We collect two sources of data for (1) global ranking model training, and (2) personalized model adaptation, respectively. Both of these data sets are sampled from the logs of a large-scale commercial search engine. Since the focus of this paper is Web document ranking, we filtered the logs to remove non-Web vertical records. In this study, we limit the scope to be English queries within the US search market.

We first randomly sampled a set of 456,238 queries from the logs, between April 2011 and October 2011. For each of the queries, we collected 10 to 30 top URLs returned by the search engine and asked human judgers to assess their relevance. The total query-URL pairs to judge is 5,578,881. The judgers were given 5 choices to annotate each query-URL pair: Perfect, Excellent, Good, Fair and Bad. Each pair is judged by three different assessors. Majority voting is used to determine the final label of each pair.

| | Users | Queries | URLs |
|---|---|---|---|
| Training Set | - | 456,238 | 5,578,881 |
| Adaptation Set | 3,000 | 48,238 | 479,923 |

**Table 1: Statistics of training and annotation sets.**

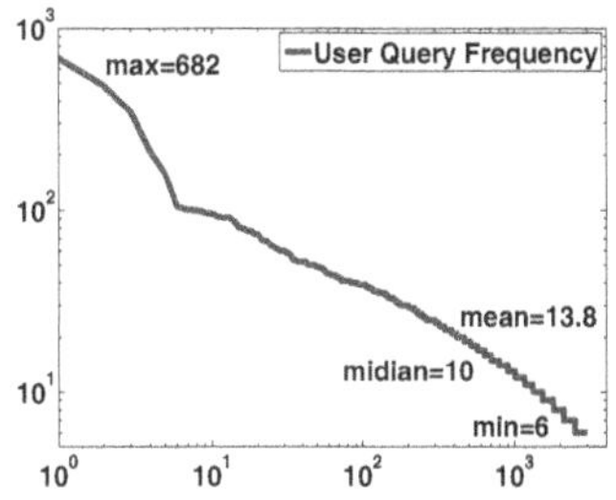


**Figure 1: The distribution of user query frequency.**

On the other hand, to generate user-specific data, we randomly selected 10,000 unique users based on their user id in the logs, between Jan 2013 and March 2013, a total of 60 days. User session information such as queries, clicked URLs, clicked positions are collected. For model adaptation purpose, we require a user to have at least 6 queries at minimum (2 for training, 2 for validation and 2 for testing). We further filtered out users with insufficient search history. Finally, we randomly sampled from the filtered set and gathered a total of 3,000 users. Table 1 summarizes the statistics of these two data sets. Figure 1 plots the user query frequency distribution, where the most frequent user had 682 queries and many users only had 6 queries.

# 4. METHODOLOGY

In this section, we introduce our deep learning framework for personalized model adaptation.

## 4.1 Preliminary

We first briefly review the RankNet model [3]. Unlike the traditional neural network framework, where each training instance first forward propagates the weights to the top layer, and then adjust the weights of individual neurons by back propagating the errors computed from the difference between the true label and the predicted label, RankNet works by considering query-URL pairs. Given a query $q$, each pair of URLs, say $U_i$ and $U_j$, is considered as a training pair if they have different relevance labels. Given these training pairs, the model learns a scoring function $f(\cdot)$ for each of such pair, $s_i = f(x_i)$ and $s_j = f(x_j)$, where $x$ represents the feature vector of the URL $U$. $s_i$ and $s_j$ are then mapped to probabilities using a logistic function

$$P_{ij} \equiv P(U_i \succ U_j) \equiv \frac{1}{1+e^{-(s_i - s_j)}}, \tag{1}$$

where $U_i \succ U_j$ denotes a preference relationship of $U_i$ over $U_j$. The model applies cross entropy as its cost function to penalize the deviation of the predicted probabilities from the true probabilities obtained from the labels. Denoting $\overline{P}_{ij}$ as

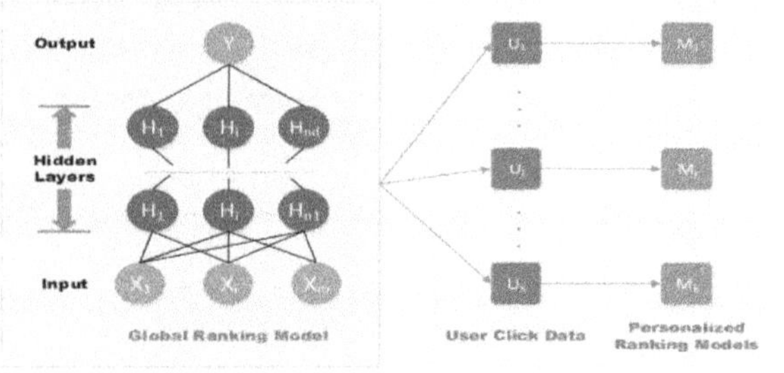


**Figure 2: Deep learning framework for personalized ranking adaptation.**

the true probability, the cost function can be written as

$$C_{ij} = -\overline{P}_{ij} \log P_{ij} - (1 - \overline{P}_{ij}) \log(1 - P_{ij}). \quad (2)$$

Taking the gradient of the above function, we have

$$\frac{\partial C}{\partial s_i} = -\frac{1}{1 + e^{s_i - s_j}} \quad (3)$$

for $U_i \succ U_j$. The gradient is used during the back propagation of the RankNet to update the weights of each neuron:

$$w_k \to w_k - \eta \frac{\partial C}{\partial w_k} = w_k - \eta \left( \frac{\partial C}{\partial s_i} \frac{\partial s_i}{\partial w_k} + \frac{\partial C}{\partial s_j} \frac{\partial s_j}{\partial w_k} \right), \quad (4)$$

with $\eta$ denoting learning rate. The RankNet can be further speed up by accumulating the gradient for each URL to perform a mini-batch update [3], where the speed up if often close to quadratic.

## 4.2 Deep RankNet for Personalized Model Adaptation

In this section we detail our framework of using deep RankNet for personalized search. Our framework can be divided into two stages: (1) training a global ranking model, and (2) adapting the global model to each individual user.

Specifically, we leverage the human labeled data to first train a deep RankNet, where each input URL $U_i$ is represented by its feature vector $X_i \in \mathbb{R}^m$ that has $m$ dimensions. The network consists of $d$ hidden layers $\{H_1, ...H_d\}$, where each layer can have different number of neurons. The output layer $Y$ is a scalar value that calculates the predicted value of each URL, which is used to update the weights of neurons during the back propagation step as in eq. (4). The hyper-parameter space of the deep RankNet includes the number of hidden layers, the number of neurons in each layer, the learning rate during back propagation, the number of iterations in training, as well as the weights of each neuron. So far in the deep learning community, these parameters are often set empirically. For example, a held-out validation set is often used to determine whether to increase or decrease the learning rate, or when to perform early stop of the training. On the other hand, greedy layer-wise pre-train is often used to initialize the weights of neurons, which has shown some improvement over random initialization [9]. We will discuss the choices of these parameters in our empirical study.

To adapt the global model to each user, we first need to construct user preference data. Since each user's information need is hidden from the search logs, it is not realistic to rely on human assessors to label the data. Therefore, we leverage the user clicks to construct user preference data. Specifically, we denote a preference pair $U_i \succ U_j$ if $U_i$ receives a click from the users and $U_j$ does not, given the same query. Additionally, in order to address the issue of positional bias, we also employed two click feedback strategies from [12], namely *Click > Skip Above* and *Click > No Click Next*, where the first one constructs pairs from the clicked URL and all the skipped URLs that are ranked above that URL. The second method constructs one pair if the current URL gets a click and the immediate URL ranked below does not receive any click.

Figure 2 illustrates our framework. In general, we perform *continue-train* on the global model for each individual user. E.g., we update the global model using the adaptation data from each user until model converges. Comparing to retraining the whole model by adding user preference data to the training set, the benefit of continue-train is two-fold. First, this strategy avoids revisiting the general user-independent training data, and thus is more efficient. Second, as illustrated in Figure 1, users often have only a handful of queries. Thus adding this small amount of data into millions of user-independent training samples may only incur subtle changes to the entire ranking model. In contrast, continue-train will refresh the model solely on the user preference data, and therefore can adapt the global model more effectively.

Despite the potential benefits, there are two issues we need to consider when performing continue-training. First, unlike the user-independent training data which are annotated by professionals, the user-preference data only contains click information, which is very noisy. Second, the amount of user-preference data is usually very limited, and therefore over-fitting becomes a critical issue. In order to address the first issue, we propose a variety of methods to estimate how informative the adaptation samples are, and update the model according to the data that mostly reflects the user-specific preference. In order to address the second issue, we regularize the back-propagation based training of the neural network in various ways. In the first method, inspired by the truncated gradient learning [13], we update the weight only when the corresponding gradient is significant, e.g., the absolute value is above certain threshold. In another method, we follow the techniques in [10, 25], by constraining the back-propagation to only the top layer. In the following sections, we describes the proposed techniques in details.

## 4.3 Strategy 1: Controlling Adaptation Data

The first strategy we use in adaptation is to properly estimate the weight of user data according to their importance. Take the query *amazon* for example, if a user issued this query and clicked on *www.amazon.com*, then re-training on this data point is most likely to have minimum effect on learning user preference since the majority of other users would also do so. However, if the user instead clicked on *wikipedia.org/amazon/* or *geography.about.com/amazonriver*, then we know that the user probably has a different intent than others, and the global ranking model should be adjusted by taking these clicks into account.

The above example is from a user's perspective. On the other hand, from a query's perspective, if the click concentration of a query is very low, i.e., different users tend to click on different returned documents of that query, it might also be a good indicator that the query needs to be treated with higher weight due to its ambiguity.

| Models | Training Pair Error | Validation Pair Error | Training NDCG@3 | Validation NDCG@3 |
|---|---|---|---|---|
| 50 50 | 0.14390 $\pm$ 0.0222 | 0.17383 $\pm$ 0.0492 | 0.6931 $\pm$ 0.0529 | 0.5678 $\pm$ 0.0503 |
| 100 100 100 | 0.20890 $\pm$ 0.0326 | 0.22909 $\pm$ 0.0329 | 0.6738 $\pm$ 0.0292 | 0.5211 $\pm$ 0.0322 |
| 100 100 20 20 | 0.17445 $\pm$ 0.0305 | 0.19694 $\pm$ 0.0684 | 0.687 $\pm$ 0.0690 | 0.5299 $\pm$ 0.0440 |
| 100 100 50 50 20 | 0.14375 $\pm$ 0.0653 | 0.16828 $\pm$ 0.0685 | 0.7033 $\pm$ 0.0295 | 0.5682 $\pm$ 0.0281 |

**Table 2: Training and validation results of several deep RankNets. Each model was repeated five times with random split data of 1:1 ratio between two sets. The best performed model is highlighted.**

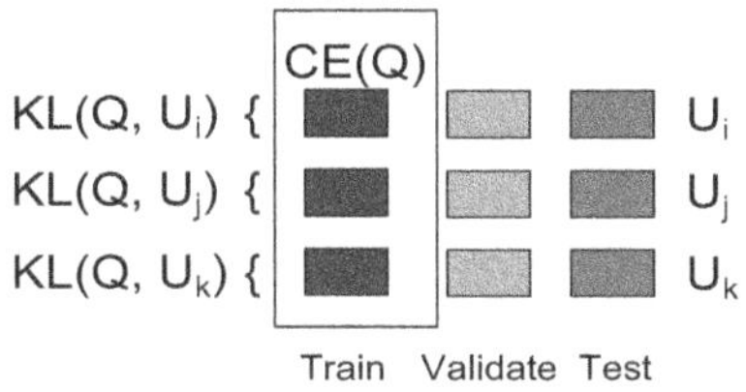


**Figure 3: An illustration of how query weights are calculated based on KL and CE, where KL is estimated on a per-user basis and CE is estimated from the entire training set.**

Therefore, we propose three heuristics here to assess the importance of adaptation queries.

**Heuristic 1: local query weighting via Kullback-ŰLeibler (KL) divergence.** Given a particular user $u$ and all his/her queries in training $\{q_1^{(u)}, ..., q_n^{(u)}\}$, consider each query $q_i^{(u)}$ to have a click distribution $P_u(q_i^{(u)})$ for user $u$ and $P_{\neg u}(q_i^{(u)})$ for the remaining users, normalized to be probability distributions. Its weight is determined by the KL divergence of these two probability distributions:

$$W_{KL}(P_u(q_i^{(u)})||P_{\neg u}(q_i^{(u)})) = \sum_j \log P_u(q_i^{(u)}, j) \left( \frac{P_u(q_i^{(u)}, j)}{P_{\neg u}(q_i^{(u)}, j)} \right), \quad (5)$$

so that the more similar user $u$'s click pattern on $q_i^{(u)}$ to the remaining users' pattern, the lower that $q_i^{(u)}$ will be weighted. When the two click patterns are exactly the same, that query will receive zero weight and therefore not used for adaptation.

**Heuristic 2: global query weighting via click entropy (CE) measurement.** In this method, we do not consider individual user but to aggregate all clicks for a particular query $q_i$ across all users. The weight of $q_i$ is then calculated as:

$$W_{CE}(q_i) = -\sum_j P(q_i, j) \cdot \log P(q_i, j), \quad (6)$$

where $P(q_i, j)$ is the probability of document $j$ being clicked given query $q_i$ (regardless of users). This heuristic is inspired by previous research [19]. According to the authors, queries with higher click entropies are more useful for personalization rather than lower ones.

Figure 3 briefly shows the difference between the KL and CE measurements. Each user's adaptation data is first divided into three parts, for training, validation and testing purposes. The KL measurement calculates individual query's weight on a per-user basis using only the training data, while CE leverages the entire training part to estimate the global weight for each query.

Lastly, we propose a heuristic that ignores queries for which a user clicked on the top-1 returned results, on a per-user basis:

**Heuristic 3: remove queries with top-one result clicks from the training set.** The reason for this heuristic is quite straight-forward: search engines have already learnt to present the results in descending order of their relevance, having the user clicked on the top result brings few information to help learn a better personalized model.

## 4.4 Strategy 2: Regularizing Back Propagation

In this section, we address how to regularize the back propagation step to prevent model overfitting. Generally, from a regularization perspective, we hope to update the weight of a neuron only if the neuron is not certain about a particular adaptation example. From a semantic point of view, each neuron is trained to explore certain portion of the feature space for decision making, e.g., topic distribution in IR [15], edge detector in vision [14]. Thus, when a new training example exhibits different feature distribution than previous ones, the algorithm should take it into account and update the corresponding neurons accordingly. In machine learning, such technique is often referred to as $L_1$-regularized subgradient, or truncated gradient [13], or otherwise known as confidence-weighted learning [6]. In principle, our proposed technique mimics these methods but with a notable difference: our truncation is enforced on each neuron, while previous methods often truncate feature weights. In our study, we introduce a regularization method by leveraging the statistics from a held-out validation set.

To be specific, each neuron's output is computed using its activation function, often in the form of sigmoid, i.e., $a(z) = \frac{1}{1+e^{-z}}$. During adaptation, we update the weights of each neuron $k$ using the truncated gradient as follows:

$$w_k \rightarrow w_k - \eta T_1 \left( \frac{\partial C}{\partial w_k}, a(k), \theta \right), \quad (7)$$

where $a(k)$ is the output of neuron $k$, $C$ is the cost function defined in eq. (2) and $T_1$ is defined as follows:

$$T_1(v, a, \theta) = \begin{cases} \max(0, v - a) & \text{if } v \in [0, \theta] \\ \min(0, v + a) & \text{if } v \in [-\theta, 0] \\ v & \textit{otherwise} \end{cases}$$

Figure 4 shows two examples of the truncated gradient with $a(k) = 3$, $\theta = 3$ and $a(k) = 1.5$, $\theta = 3$. For the first case, when $v$ falls into the range of $[-\theta, \theta]$, $T_1$ is always pushed to zero. In the second case which is less aggressive, only when $v$ is between $[-\alpha, \alpha]$, the gradient is rounded to zero. Otherwise, $T_1$ outputs the same value as $v$ for $v > \theta$.

It has been show in [13] that this version of truncated gradient $T_1$ outperforms direct rounding algorithm (i.e.,

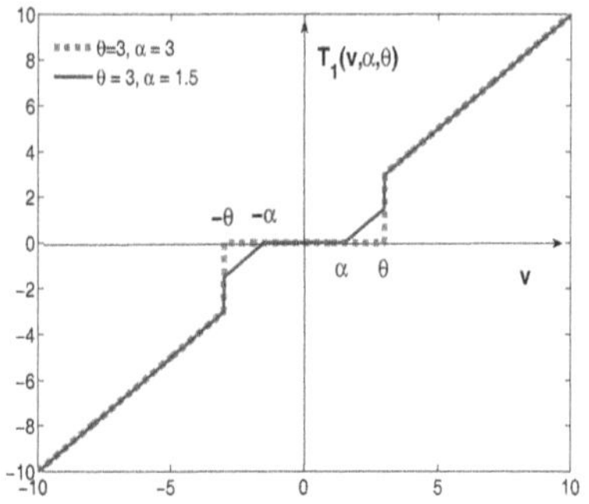


**Figure 4: An illustration of the truncated gradient with different values of $\alpha$ and $\theta$. X-axis is the value of $v$ and Y-axis the value of gradient.**

$T_0(v,\theta) = 0$ if $|v| \leq \theta$) in most scenarios with a proper choice of $\theta$. Consequently, we propose a variance-truncation heuristic in our RankNet framework:

**Heuristic 4: perform truncated gradient on adaptation using a validation set**. Given a validation set $\{v_1, ..., v_n\}$, for each neuron $k$, calculate the output of each validation example as $\{a_k(v_1), ...a_k(v_n)\}$. We assume that the outputs follow a Normal distribution $\mathcal{N} \sim (\mu_k, \sigma_k^2)$. For each adaptation example, update the model weight using truncated gradient with parameter $\theta = \mu_k + \sigma_k$.

Specifically, after the model converges in training, we run a set of held-out data through the network, without performing back propagation, and store the output (activation) values for all held-out examples at each neuron. During adaptation, if the output $\alpha$ of a new example at a specific neuron falls into the range of the mean plus one standard deviation of the validation set, we will truncate the gradient using $T_1$, to propagate a smaller value of error term to the next layer.

In another way, from the model structure perspective of view, we can also consider training and adaptation to be two different learning tasks but share the same network structure, i.e., they share the same input layer, hidden layers but not the output layer due to a different objective function. Indeed, this scenario has been explored in speech adaptation for cross-lingual model transfer [10]. To be concrete, the authors propose to back propagate only to the top hidden layer and fix the rest hidden layers during adaptation. Semantically, the top layer contains the most abstract features which is more likely to be applicable to different domains than those concrete features at bottom layers. Therefore, when the adaptation data is sparse, it could be beneficial for the model to only adapting the top layer. And therefore we have the following heuristic:

**Heuristic 5: back propagate to the highest layer only**. During the adaptation stage, we fix the neuron weights of the remaining hidden layers but only perform back propagation to the highest layer of the network and update its neuron's weight accordingly.

## 5. EMPIRICAL ANALYSIS

In this section, we present a comprehensive empirical study on the real-world data set introduced in Section 3. Although our focus is on the adaptation performance, we will first discuss the results from training global ranking models.

### 5.1 Global Ranking Model Performance

For each training instance in the 5,578,881 query-URL pair collection, we first extract top-400 most discriminative features which are used by the commercial search engine. These features include query-level features such as query term number, URL-level features such as domain rank, and query-URL features such as BM25 and so on. The reason for only using top-400 features for global model training is due to efficiency concern. Since the main focus on this paper is on adaptation rather than tuning a best deep RankNet for generic ranking purpose, we choose to use a limited set of features to speed up training. Later, we show that even with this limited set of features, the adaptation performance of deep RankNet can still significantly outperform a generic ranker which is trained using thousands of ranking features. We then divided the data into training set and validation set at a 1:1 ratio based on queries, ending up with roughly 228,119 queries in each set. We experiment with different configuration of the RankNet, from very shallow ones to deep ones that have five hidden layers. For each of the configuration, we repeat the data splitting and training for five times and report on the average results. We set the initial learning rate for each configuration to be fairly large $\eta = 1e^{-2}$. We empirically reduce the learning rate (at a step length of 5, $\eta \leftarrow \eta/5$) after an iteration when the validation performance becomes worse — in our scenario, the trigger condition is either that the pair-wise error goes up by more than 2%, or the validation NDCG@3 reduces by more than 1%. The minimum learning rate is controlled to be no less than $1e^{-6}$. The maximum number of training iteration is set to be 2,000. However, we often terminate training earlier if we observe the model has already converged, i.e., when the change of validation NDCG@3 is less than 0.01%.

We tested a total of over 20 different configurations of RankNet. Due to space limitation, Table 2 only lists the results of several typical models that have different numbers of hidden layers. Note that here model "50 50" means a RankNet model with two hidden layers (in addition to the input and output layers), each of which has 50 neurons. The most complex model we have trained is a model with five hidden layers where each one has 100 neurons. Overall, the best performance was achieved by the model "100 100 50 50 20", followed by a very simple configuration with only two hidden layers, "50 50". In general, adding more hidden layers does seem to help improve the ranking performance on average, as can be seen from the table that complex models often outperform simple ones. However, we have also observed that larger models tend to have higher variance than smaller ones, which means that they are more likely to be trapped into local minimums during back-propagation.

### 5.2 Adaptation Performance

In this section, we focus on reporting the adaptation performance based on two of the most well-performed models in the previous section due to space concern, i.e., "50 50" and "100 100 50 50 20". From now on, we refer them as 2-layer and 5-layer models, respectively.

#### *5.2.1 Data preparation and evaluation metrics*

As described in Section 4.2, the user-dependent adaptation data is constructed based on user click feedback. However, since the click signal is binary, it becomes inappropriate to use NDCG for evaluation. Therefore, we measure the ranking quality by using mean average precision (MAP) and mean reciprocal rank (MRR), where MAP is defined as the average precision scores on all queries, and MRR is the average reciprocal ranks of all results, defined as $MRR = \frac{1}{N}\sum_i \frac{1}{rank_i}$, with $rank_i$ being the rank of the *first* relevant URL in the list. For details of the metrics, readers can refer to [1].

Unlike the user-independent data used for training global models which we can randomly split into training and validation sets according to queries, user-specific data comes in chronological order where queries have time dependencies. Therefore, a rigorous way for performance evaluation is to split the user queries by their timestamps, use the first part for training, second part for validation and the latest queries for testing purposes. We uniformly set the ratios to be $\frac{1}{3}:\frac{1}{3}:\frac{1}{3}$ in our experiments.

### 5.2.2 Baseline Ranking Performance

We compare with three baselines. The first baseline is the performance of the production ranking system which uses much more training data than our data set, with more features (over 3,000 features) than our model (400 features). The second and third baselines are the results without performing adaptation. i.e., we directly use the two global RankNet models trained using user-independent data and check their performance on the user-specific portion testing data. Finally, we adapt the two global models to the user data by performing continue-train on the 1/3 portion training data. We monitor the adaptation performance using the validation data. Parameter settings and the early stopping criteria for adaptation are the same as training stage described in Sec. 5.1.

Table 3 lists the results. We see that without adaptation, deep RankNet models perform worse than the baseline system, which is quite expected since the production system leverages many more training data and features. With adaptation conducted, the ranking performance is improved quite drastically. Both models were able to improve the MAP and MRR scores by more than 6%, while reducing the average user-click position by more than 0.2, when compared to the production system. Paired t-test shows that both improvements are significant with *p-value* less than 0.05, comparing to the baseline production ranking. Comparatively, the 5-layer adaptation model slightly beats the 2-layer one, but insignificantly with a *p-value* around 0.2.

We further analyze the adaptation performance of the 5-layer model by randomly selecting two users from the adaptation set. One of the users is considered as a heavy user of the search engine who has issued over 300 queries during the two months, while the other user uses the search engine much less frequently and only had 20 queries during that period. The purpose is to study how likely the data sparsity issue could cause model overfitting. Figure 5 plots their training and validation errors over 2,000 iterations. From the figure, it becomes quite clear that the model adapted for the heavy user is much less immune to overfitting, since the validation error keep decreasing. On the other hand, with only less than 10 queries for training, the model adapted for the light user greatly suffered from the overfitting issue, whose validation error continues to rise after approximately 500 iterations and never decreases again. This illustration demonstrates the importance of early stopping. Note that for illustration purpose, we deliberately allow overfitting to happen in this case. During the actual adaptation stage, the process is stopped earlier before the overfitting happens.

| Model | MAP | MRR | Avg. Click Position |
|---|---|---|---|
| Production System | 0.5782 | 0.5783 | 1.83928 |
| Baseline (2-layer) | 0.5017 | 0.5102 | 2.46839 |
| Baseline (5-layer) | 0.5092 | 0.5132 | 2.40555 |
| 2-layer adaptation | 0.6311 | 0.6325 | 1.55006 |
| 5-layer adaptation | 0.6421 | 0.6494 | 1.54805 |

**Table 3: Per-user basis performance comparison between three baselines and two adaptation models.**

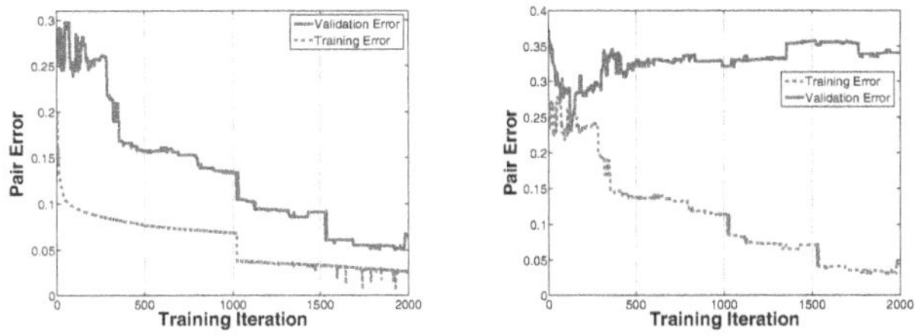


(a) A heavy user (b) A light user

**Figure 5: Performance of two users, (a) is considered a frequent user and (b) is an infrequent user.**

### 5.2.3 Do Adaptation Strategies Help?

Next, we evaluate the performance of the five heuristics for different types of users. To be concrete, we sort users based on their query numbers, which follows a power-law distribution as shown in Figure 1. We separate the users evenly into three categories, each of which has roughly 1,000 users, namely heavy, medium and light users.

(**Strategy 1 Performance**) We first compare the three heuristics in strategy 1 with the baseline adaptation performance. Overall, all three heuristics achieve performance improvement over the baseline adaptation, with 0.6506, 0.6977 and 0.6524 MRR scores for KL divergence (KL), Click Entropy (CE) and Drop Top Click (DT) for the 2-layer framework. Comparatively, the 5-layer RankNet improved even more with the heuristics, which in general outperforms the 2-layer model in terms of MRR scores by increasing roughly 0.15. Among all heuristics, CE has the best improvement while KL improves the least. In Figure 6, we plot the MRR scores in each category of users from the output of the 5-layer RankNet, along with their standard deviations. Most improvement comes from heavy users, where CE improves the MRR for more than 8%, and KL for 2.5% on average. However, for low-frequency users, we observe that KL performs even worse than the baselines, while DT has marginal gains and CE still shows significant improvement. We attribute the reason of different performance improvement to the fact of their query coverage, i.e., how many queries are affected by each heuristic. Since CE measures the global weight of the query, its coverage is always 100%. Meanwhile, KL means user-specific query weights, which requires a query to be issued by both the current user and at least once by one of the remaining users according to eq. (5), and therefore has a much lower coverage. DT, on the oth-

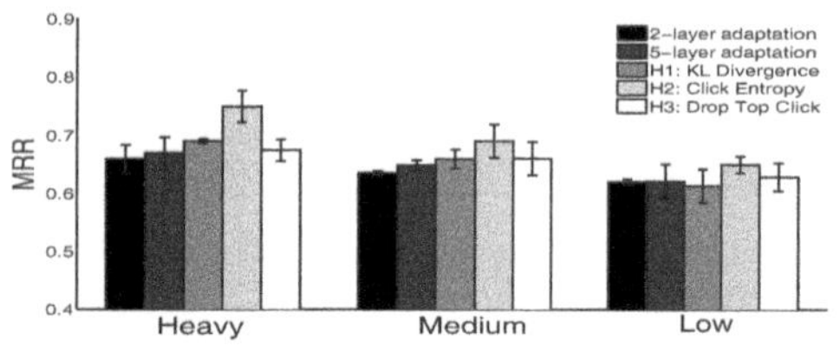


**Figure 6: Comparison of three heuristics in strategy 1 with baseline adaptations in terms of MRR scores, divided by three user groups.**

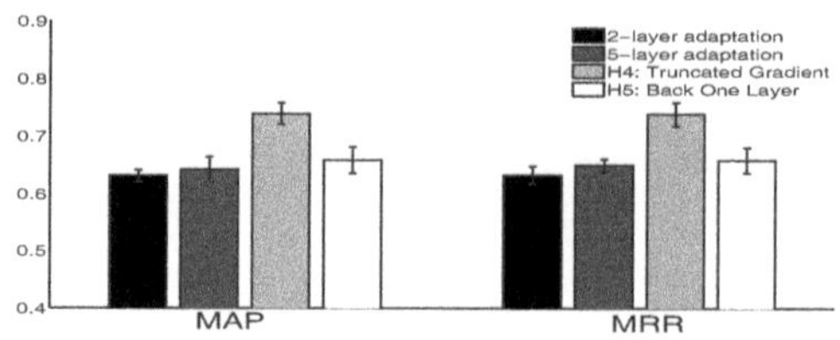


**Figure 7: Comparison of two heuristics in strategy 2 with baseline adaptations in terms of MAP and MRR scores.**

| Coverage | Heavy | Medium | Low |
|---|---|---|---|
| H1: KL Divergence | 43% | 25% | 6% |
| H2: Click Entropy | 100% | 100% | 100% |
| H3: Drop Top Click | 44% | 31% | 18% |

**Table 4: Percentage of queries re-weighted by three heuristics. Note in DT, re-weighting means setting the query weight to 0 and drop from training.**

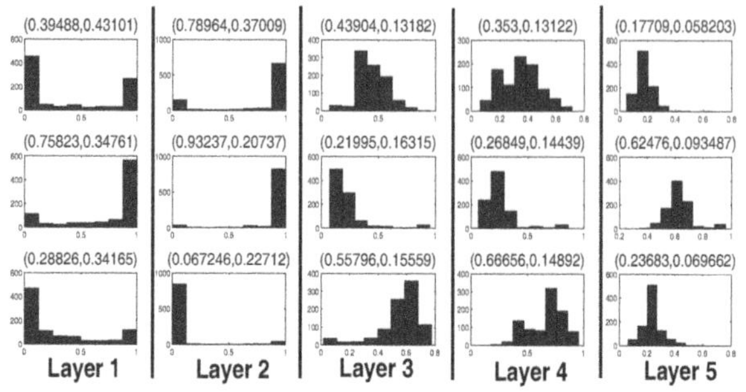


**Figure 8: Example of neuron outputs for the validation set on different hidden layer of RankNet. Title indicates (mean, std) of each neuron. Higher-layer neuron generally has less output variances.**

er hand, is also a user-specific weighting heuristic, which is determined by the percentage of top-1 clicks of the users.

The statistics from Table 4 confirms our hypothesis. Clearly, we can infer the reason why KL does not perform as well as CE. In general, KL has much lower query coverage than CE. Even for the heavy users, only 43% of the queries are found common among different users, while for low-frequency users, only 6% of queries can benefit from the re-weighting by KL divergence. On the other hand, DT continues to drop more queries when the user type becomes less frequent. In particular, for low-frequency users, DT drops as much as 82% of all queries. We analyzed the logs for a few of low-frequency users, and found out that indeed, those users have a much higher percentage of navigational queries like *amazon* and *yahoo email* than heavy users. Clicks of these queries are mostly on the first results, and therefore filtered from adaptation. In summary, the three re-weighting mechanisms review that heuristics with a high query coverage is critical to achieve good adaptation performance.

**(Strategy 2 Performance)** We now turn to analyzing heuristics of strategy 2, where the focus is more on the regularization of back propagation. Figure 7 plots the overall MRR and MAP scores of the two heuristics comparing with two baseline adaptation methods. The Truncated Gradient (TG) method expresses very compelling performance, which substantially improves the metrics from around 0.63 to 0.73, a 16% relative increase. However, the other heuristic, Back One Layer (BO), does not perform as well. BO only has a marginal 1% increase over the baselines, which are not statistically significant (*p-value* $\approx 0.12$).

For a deep understanding of layer-wise performance, we randomly sampled three neurons from each layer of the 5-layer model, and plotted the histograms of the output values given the validation set. Figure 8 shows the results. Note that here Layer 1 is the first/bottom layer of the network and Layer 5 the highest/top layer. The pattern looks quite consistent for neurons within each layer. In general, lower-layer neurons tend to have larger variances than neurons at high layers, which causes less updates to happen in the lower layers since more gradients are truncated during back propagation. From the statistics of over 2 million validation query-URL pairs, the gradients of neurons on layer 5 are truncated roughly 23% of all adaptation pairs, while the gradients of the first-layer neurons are truncated over 79% of the time.

Table 5 shows the comprehensive results of the heuristics performance along with the baseline. From the overall performance as well as user-category specific performance, we can observe that Truncated Gradient outperforms all other heuristics with significance. The results also suggest that applying heuristics on deep network (5 hidden layers) has better effect than shallow ones (2 hidden layers).

### *5.2.4 Repeated/non-repeated Query Performance*

In this section, we analyze the ranking performance by using different criteria in terms of queries. Table 6 lists the fairly comprehensive results of the five heuristics. We only report the performance of the 5-layer adaptation due to space limit. First, we separate queries in the test set into either repeated queries and new queries for each user, where repeated queries were previously seen in that user's adaptation query set while new queries not. We see that for all methods, most gains come from the repeated queries, which agrees with previous research results in [21]. For new queries, however, unlike in [21] where sometimes the results got worse than baselines, all our five heuristics are still able to increase the MRR scores comparing to the baselines. Compared to the 5-layer baseline (0.5602), Truncated Gradient has the largest improvement (0.6082), followed by Click Entropy (0.5827), both of which are statistically significant, followed by marginal improvements of the remaining ones.

Next, we compare the individual query performance to the baseline production ranking. Our criteria is to look at

| Model | MAP | MRR | Avg. Click Position | MRR For User Category | | |
|---|---|---|---|---|---|---|
| | | | | Heavy | Medium | Low |
| 2-layer Adaptation | 0.6311 | 0.6325 | 1.55006 | 0.6587 | 0.6348 | 0.6198 |
| 5-layer Adaptation | 0.6421 | 0.6494 | 1.54805 | 0.6693 | 0.6483 | 0.6210 |
| KL(2-layer) | 0.6541 | 0.6506 | 1.51197 | 0.6893 | 0.6593 | 0.6129 |
| Entropy(2-layer) | 0.6982 | 0.6977 | 1.45615 | 0.7494 | 0.6894 | 0.6492 |
| Drop Top(2-layer) | 0.6582 | 0.6524 | 1.50758 | 0.6739 | 0.6598 | 0.6284 |
| Truncated Gradient(2-layer) | 0.7389 | 0.7382 | 1.41913 | 0.7789 | 0.7385 | 0.7194 |
| Back One Layer(2-layer) | 0.6583 | 0.6582 | 1.44059 | 0.6878 | 0.6589 | 0.6283 |
| KL(5-layer) | 0.6672 | 0.6649 | 1.43849 | 0.6928 | 0.6679 | 0.6230 |
| Entropy(5-layer) | 0.7046 | 0.7085 | 1.41837 | 0.7589 | 0.6978 | 0.6589 |
| Drop Top(5-layer) | 0.6691 | 0.6692 | 1.47823 | 0.6819 | 0.6683 | 0.6375 |
| Truncated Gradient(5-layer) | 0.7473 | 0.7497 | 1.38973 | 0.7859 | 0.7508 | 0.7239 |
| Back One Layer(5-layer) | 0.6696 | 0.6673 | 1.42974 | 0.6928 | 0.6700 | 0.6359 |

**Table 5: Overall performance of all heuristics compared to baseline. The performance for different categories of users are also shown. Both RankNet frameworks with heuristics outperform adaptation without heuristics.**

the combination of MRR, MAP and click position to see whether a particular query gets improved or worsen, and then calculate the percentage for each heuristic. Table 6 also shows these two comparisons in column 4 and 5. Note that the majority of the queries remain the same performance so these two columns do not add up to 100%. Similarly, Truncated Gradient and Click Entropy improve more queries than other heuristics.

Another similar criterion we used is to see how many test queries are pushed to top rank after adaptation, while how many top-ranked queries are dropped down from the No.1 ranking position. Column 6 and 7 in Table 6 demonstrate that Truncated Gradient and Drop Top push more queries to No.1 than others, while Back One Layer and Truncated Gradient drop less number of top-ranked queries to lower positions than the remaining heuristics.

Finally, we separate the test queries into navigational and informational queries based on user intent. We use a rough classification method here: if more than 75% of all clicks for a query is on the same hyperlink, we classify the query as navigational. Otherwise the query is informational. Our classifier is by no means the state-of-the-art, but is sufficient for our task here to observe performance by different query types. We notice that in general, navigational queries have a much higher MRR scores than informational queries, for both baseline methods and all five heuristics. In comparison, Truncated Gradient still exhibits the most impressive performance, with both categories of queries improved noticeably from the baselines.

### 5.3 Model Comparison

We conclude our experiments with the performance comparison of the five proposed heuristics. To show the relative strength, we simply average their MAP and MRR scores for each pair of the methods in comparison, i.e., $Score(H_i|H_j) = \frac{1}{2}\left(\frac{MAP(H_i)}{MAP(H_j)} + \frac{MRR(H_i)}{MRR(H_j)}\right)$, which indicates the relative performance of $H_i$ compared to $H_j$. Figure 9 plots the heatmap of their scores, where each cell can be read, from y-axis to x-axis, as $H_i$ vs. $H_j$.

Overall, we observe that TG performs best among all, while KL performs the worst. Other than the case that CE outperforms BO, in general, strategy 2 outperforms strategy 1, which suggests that regularizing back-propagation

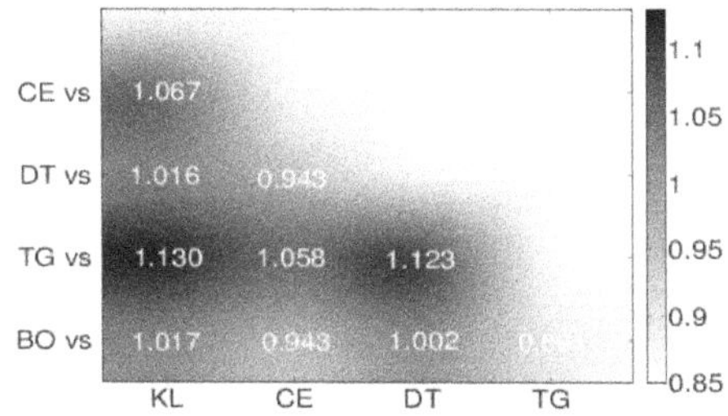


**Figure 9: Comparison of the 5 heuristics used in this paper in terms of MAP and MRR scores. Higher values indicate better comparative performance.**

can potentially lead better performance gain than adding constraints directly to the adaptation instances. The result also suggests that keeping as much data as possible for adaptation seems better than dropping some portion of the data which we assumed would not help adaptation. A global weighting mechanism for queries in general beats user-specific query weighting, as can be seen by the comparison between CE and KL. Finally, regularizing the gradient for each individual neuron (TG) seems to outperform a layer-wise treatment (BO) in back propagation. In summary, the relative strength of the 5 methods is: $TG > CE > BO > DT > KL$.

## 6. CONCLUSIONS AND FUTURE WORK

In this paper, we presented a large-scale study of personalized search adaptation, from a deep learning perspective. We proposed to use deep RankNet to first train a global ranking model, and then adapted to each individual user via continue-train. We proposed two strategies to improve the performance of adaptation. Strategy 1 focused on reweighting the user-specific adaptation data so that more important adaptation instances would be assigned higher importance weights. Strategy 2 emphasized on regularizing the back propagation stage, where we introduced the usage of truncated gradient when updating the neuron weights. We then empirically evaluated our framework on a real-world data set. The results indicated that a deep RankNet with 5 hidden layers in general outperformed a shallow RankNet

| Model | Repeated Q MRR | New Q MRR | % Query Improves | % Query Worsen | % Q Push to Rank 1 | % Rank-1 Q Drop Down | Nav Q MRR | Info Q MRR |
|---|---|---|---|---|---|---|---|---|
| 2-layer | 0.6893 | 0.5538 | 10.30% | 6.87% | 2.30% | 0.82% | 0.7283 | 0.5489 |
| 5-layer | 0.6913 | 0.5602 | 10.89% | 6.41% | 2.26% | 0.78% | 0.7385 | 0.5512 |
| H1: KL | 0.7093 | 0.5603 | 10.99% | 6.35% | 2.37% | 0.65% | 0.7483 | 0.5389 |
| H2: CE | 0.7243 | 0.5827 | 12.83% | 6.68% | 2.44% | 0.44% | 0.7531 | 0.5523 |
| H3: DT | 0.7033 | 0.5786 | 11.17% | 6.13% | 2.45% | 0.67% | 0.7392 | 0.5493 |
| H4: TG | 0.7483 | 0.6082 | 13.27% | 4.19% | 2.62% | 0.49% | 0.7592 | 0.5747 |
| H5: BO | 0.7034 | 0.5793 | 11.01% | 6.17% | 2.07% | 0.43% | 0.7804 | 0.5486 |

**Table 6: (5-layer RankNet) Performance breakdown of the five heuristics by different query criteria.**

with 2 hidden layers. Among the 5 heuristics we proposed to improve adaptation, the truncated gradient method performed the best, followed by the click entropy method that re-weighted adaptation instances.

There are several future work that we want to explore. We saw that click entropy has one of the best performance in all heuristics. Nevertheless, calculating click entropy for all queries is quite expensive in practice. The system needs to constantly update the weights of all queries whenever new user clicks become available, which is impractical for a production system. We therefore think of coming up with some approximation methods that can easily get the query weights without going back to the search logs constantly. Same for the truncated gradient heuristic, we want to approximate the truncation values more efficiently. On the other hand, since we observed that most performance gain came from heavy users rather than users with fewer queries, one way to improve the performance of light users is to group users together and use other similar users' search information to compensate for the short search history for light users.

## 7. ACKNOWLEDGEMENTS

We thank Jianfeng Gao for the insightful discussion on deep learning architecture. We thank Lihong Li and Ming-Wei Chang for their suggestions on tuning back propagation.

## 8. REFERENCES


[1] R. A. Baeza-Yates and B. Ribeiro-Neto. *Modern Information Retrieval.* Addison-Wesley Longman Publishing Co., Inc., Boston, MA, USA, 1999.

[2] P. N. Bennett, F. Radlinski, R. W. White, and E. Yilmaz. Inferring and using location metadata to personalize web search. In *Proc. of SIGIR '11*, pages 135–144. ACM, 2011.

[3] C. Burges, T. Shaked, E. Renshaw, A. Lazier, M. Deeds, N. Hamilton, and G. Hullender. Learning to rank using gradient descent. In *Proc. of ICML '05*, pages 89–96, 2005.

[4] D. Chen, Y. Xiong, J. Yan, G.-R. Xue, G. Wang, and Z. Chen. Knowledge transfer for cross domain learning to rank. *Inf. Retr.*, 13(3):236–253, June 2010.

[5] Z. Dou, R. Song, and J.-R. Wen. A large-scale evaluation and analysis of personalized search strategies. In *Proc. of WWW '07*, pages 581–590. ACM, 2007.

[6] M. Dredze, K. Crammer, and F. Pereira. Confidence-weighted linear classification. In *Proc. of ICML '08*, pages 264–271. ACM, 2008.

[7] J. Gao, Q. Wu, C. Burges, K. M. Svore, Y. Su, N. Khan, S. Shah, and H. Zhou. Model adaptation via model interpolation and boosting for web search ranking. In *EMNLP*, pages 505–513. ACL, 2009.

[8] B. Geng, L. Yang, C. Xu, and X.-S. Hua. Ranking model adaptation for domain-specific search. In *Proc. of CIKM '09*, pages 197–206. ACM, 2009.

[9] G. E. Hinton and R. R. Salakhutdinov. Reducing the dimensionality of data with neural networks. *Science*, 313(5786):504–507, 2006.

[10] J.-T. Huang, J. Li, D. Yu, L. Deng, and Y. Gong. Cross-language knowledge transfer using multilingual deep neural network with shared hidden layers. ICASSP 2013.

[11] P.-S. Huang, X. He, J. Gao, L. Deng, A. Acero, , and L. Heck. Learning deep structured semantic models for web search using clickthrough dat. In *Proc. of CIKM '13*, 2013.

[12] T. Joachims, L. Granka, B. Pan, H. Hembrooke, and G. Gay. Accurately interpreting clickthrough data as implicit feedback. In *Proc. of SIGIR '05*. ACM, 2005.

[13] J. Langford, L. Li, and T. Zhang. Sparse online learning via truncated gradient. *J. Mach. Learn. Res.*, 10:777–801, 2009.

[14] Q. Le, M. Ranzato, R. Monga, M. Devin, K. Chen, G. Corrado, J. Dean, and A. Ng. Building high-level features using large scale unsupervised learning. In *International Conference in Machine Learning*, 2012.

[15] P. Mirowski, M. Ranzato, and Y. LeCun. Dynamic auto-encoders for semantic indexing. In *Proc. of the NIPS 2010 Workshop on Deep Learning*, 2010.

[16] X. Shen, B. Tan, and C. Zhai. Context-sensitive information retrieval using implicit feedback. In *Proc. of SIGIR '05*, pages 43–50. ACM, 2005.

[17] D. Sontag, K. Collins-Thompson, P. N. Bennett, R. W. White, S. Dumais, and B. Billerbeck. Probabilistic models for personalizing web search. In *Proc. of WSDM '12*, pages 433–442. ACM, 2012.

[18] J. Teevan, S. T. Dumais, and E. Horvitz. Personalizing search via automated analysis of interests and activities. In *Proc. of SIGIR '05*, pages 449–456, 2005.

[19] J. Teevan, S. T. Dumais, and D. J. Liebling. To personalize or not to personalize: modeling queries with variation in user intent. In *Proc. of SIGIR '08*, pages 163–170, 2008.

[20] B. Wang, B. Liu, X. Wang, C. Sun, and D. Zhang. Deep learning approaches to semantic relevance modeling for chinese question-answer pairs. *ACM Transactions on Asian Language Information Processing*, 10(4), Dec. 2011.

[21] H. Wang, X. He, M.-W. Chang, Y. Song, R. W. White, and W. Chu. Personalized ranking model adaptation for web search. In *Proc. of SIGIR '13*, pages 323–332. ACM, 2013.

[22] R. W. White, P. Bailey, and L. Chen. Predicting user interests from contextual information. In *Proc. of SIGIR '09*, pages 363–370. ACM, 2009.

[23] R. W. White, P. N. Bennett, and S. T. Dumais. Predicting short-term interests using activity-based search context. In *Proc. of CIKM '10*, pages 1009–1018. ACM, 2010.

[24] R. W. White, W. Chu, A. Hassan, X. He, Y. Song, and H. Wang. Enhancing personalized search by mining and modeling task behavior. In *Proceedings of WWW '13*, pages 1411–1420, 2013.

[25] D. Yu, K. Yao, H. Su, G. Li, and F. Seide. Kl-divergence regularized deep neural network adaptation for improved large vocabulary speech recognition. ICASSP 2013, 2013.

# Search Engine Click Spam Detection Based on Bipartite Graph Propagation

Xin Li, Min Zhang, Yiqun Liu, Shaoping Ma, Yijiang Jin, Liyun Ru
State Key Lab of Intelligence Technology and Systems
Tsinghua National Laboratory for Information Science and Technology
Department of Computer Science and Technology, Tsinghua University, Beijing, 100084, China P.R.
x-l08@163.com, {z-m,yiqunliu,msp,yjjin}@tsinghua.edu.cn, lyru@vip.sohu.com

## ABSTRACT

Using search engines to retrieve information has become an important part of people's daily lives. For most search engines, click information is an important factor in document ranking. As a result, some websites cheat to obtain a higher rank by fraudulently increasing clicks to their pages, which is referred to as "Click Spam". Based on an analysis of the features of fraudulent clicks, a novel automatic click spam detection approach is proposed in this paper, which consists of 1. modeling user sessions with a triple sequence, which, to the best of our knowledge, takes into account not only the user action but also the action objective and the time interval between actions for the first time; 2. using the user-session bipartite graph propagation algorithm to take advantage of cheating users to find more cheating sessions; and 3. using the pattern-session bipartite graph propagation algorithm to obtain cheating session patterns to achieve higher precision and recall of click spam detection. Experimental results based on a Chinese commercial search engine using real-world log data containing approximately 80 million user clicks per day show that 2.6% of all clicks were detected as spam with a precision of up to 97%.

## Categories and Subject Descriptors

H.3.3 [**Information Storage and Retrieval**]: Information Search and Retrieval

## General Terms

Experimentation, Algorithms, Performance

## Keywords

Click Spam; Label Propagation; User Session Model; Frequent Sequential Patterns

## 1. INTRODUCTION

Search engines are very important in current network environment, which have become one of the major channels for people to access information on the Internet in recent years. After a query is submitted to a search engine, many relevant Web pages will be found. The search engine will rank the results based on a series of relevant ranking features, including textual information [18], link structure [20] and so on. According to the tasks of Yahoo! Labs Learning to Rank Challenge[1], hundreds of ranking features are used in current commercial search engines. Among the features, click information and relevant features have drawn much attention recently. Joachims [13] believes that click information can be used as a relevance feedback feature to rank the search results. Click model (such as cascade model [5], CCM [7], DBM [4] and so on) related works show that user click information plays an important role in ranking the search results.

According to the researches on search user behaviors [17], most users only pay attention to the top search results. So it is obvious that if a website can obtain a higher rank among all the related results, users will be more likely to click the site, and thus, the site traffic will increase. As a result, to raise the rankings of the results by forging user clicks has become the main channel for the illegal web page authors to improve user traffic and gain more economic benefits [6, 15, 24, 3]. Studies on cheating clicks show that various kinds of bots are used to issue queries and clicks automatically to search engines, which not only consume a great amount of capacity for the search engines but also affect the rankings of search results.

An increasing number of researchers focus on the task of anti-spam. Gyöngyi et al. [8] propose the algorithm of TrustRank, which is able to semi-automatically separate reputable, good pages from spam. They start from selecting a small set of reputable seed pages and discover other pages that are likely to be good with the link structure of the web. Their results show that based on a good seed set of less than 200 sites, spam from a significant fraction of the web can be effectively filtered out. Krishnan et al. [16] introduce the Anti-Trust Rank algorithm. Similar to the Trust Rank algorithm, they select a manually labeled seed set of pages and their experiments on the WebGraph dataset show that their approach is effective at detecting spam pages from a small seed set.

At present, user behavior information has been introduced into search engines [1, 17], and thus, search engines will adjust the rankings of search results according to user reactions. As a result, new cheating methods, called "click spam", that aim to exploit user behavior analysis have arisen. A

[1]http://learningtorankchallenge.yahoo.com/index.php


*WSDM'14*, February 24–28, 2014, New York, New York, USA.
Copyright 2014 ACM 978-1-4503-2351-2/14/02 ...$15.00.
http://dx.doi.org/10.1145/2556195.2556214.

typical example of click spam is "Google bombing"[2], which refers to raising the rank of a specific result in a search engine maliciously. Another two examples of click spam are the user sessions shown in Table 1, which are extracted from the real-world click logs of a popular Chinese commercial search engine. In the session shown in (a), after submitting a query, the user clicks on the same URL repeatedly. In the session shown in (b), the user submits different queries and clicks on the web pages with the same domain repeatedly. Both sessions may raise the rankings of the search results that the users click, which makes their websites easier to be clicked by other search engine users fraudulently. Obviously, click spam not only undermines the fairness among search results but also degrades user experience. For this reason, search engines are in urgent need of click spam detection techniques.

**Table 1: Two examples of click spam**

| user IP | query | isclick | clicked URL |
|---|---|---|---|
| 211.143.91.98 | 9999pp.com | 0 | |
| 211.143.91.98 | 9999pp.com | 1 | http://369ii.com/ |
| 211.143.91.98 | 9999pp.com | 1 | http://369ii.com/ |
| 211.143.91.98 | 9999pp.com | 1 | http://369ii.com/ |
| 211.143.91.98 | 9999pp.com | 1 | http://369ii.com/ |
| 211.143.91.98 | 9999pp.com | 1 | http://369ii.com/ |

(a)

| user IP | query | isclick | clicked URL |
|---|---|---|---|
| 219.135.43.71 | China | 0 | |
| 219.135.43.71 | China | 1 | http://www.zzyzzy .cn/html/322.html/ |
| 219.135.43.71 | Shanghai | 0 | |
| 219.135.43.71 | Shanghai | 1 | http://www.zzyzzy .cn/html/151.html/ |
| 219.135.43.71 | software | 0 | |
| 219.135.43.71 | software | 1 | http://www.zzyzzy .cn/html/188.html/ |
| 219.135.43.71 | summit | 0 | |
| 219.135.43.71 | summit | 1 | http://www.zzyzzy .cn/html/56.html/ |
| 219.135.43.71 | industry | 0 | |
| 219.135.43.71 | industry | 1 | http://www.zzyzzy .cn/html/220.html/ |

(b)

Click spam is a new method of cheating search engine rankings and involves user behavior, so it is difficult to distinguish normal and abnormal user reactions. In this paper, we propose a novel, automatic, click spam detection approach, which is, to the best of our knowledge, the first work to introduce the objective of user actions and time interval between actions into user session modeling for click spam detection. The proposed approach shows both effectiveness and efficiency at detecting click spam in a real commercial search engine. The approach uses the following procedure: 1. Model user session with a triple sequence; 2. Construct user-session bipartite graph and pattern-session bipartite graph to describe the relation between users and sessions as well as the relation between patterns and sessions; 3. Based on the seed cheating session modes, detect a large amount of click spam with a label propagation algorithm on the bipartite graph.

The rest of this paper is organized as follows: after a discussion of the related work in next section, we introduce the detection of cheating on single click record in Section 3. The modeling of user sessions is described in Section 4. Section 5 introduces the recognition of session-level click spam. Section 6 presents the evaluation and discussion of our approach, and finally, Section 7 concludes the paper.

## 2. RELATED WORK

Over the last decade, there has been a growing interest in detecting click fraud. Jansen [11] introduces intentional clicks on sponsored links with the purpose of gaining undue monetary returns or harming a particular content provider, which is called "Click Fraud". He also presents several countermeasures, such as strengthening the monitoring of click fraud, improving automated filters to identify and prevent click fraud, and changing the charging mode from pay-per-click to pay-per-action. Metwally et al. [19] present three forms of click fraud and methods to detect it. They find that several websites can cooperate with each other to create fraudulent clicks and thus advance their commercial interests. They develop an algorithm, called streaming-rules, to report association rules with tight guarantees on errors, using limited processing per element and minimal space, in order to detect fraud in advertising networks. The above previous work is related to the detection of click fraud. However, there are many differences between click spam for general search results and click fraud for sponsored advertisement links. Click fraud aims to increase the number of clicks on the advertisement links so as to gain more money from the websites that display the ads, while the goal of click spam is to make more clicks on the website to obtain a higher rank in the search results. Besides the detection of click fraud only needs to examine the IPs of the users that click on the ads, while the detection of click spam requires detailed analysis of click logs of the search engine. Consequently, the methods mentioned above cannot be directly applied to our work.

Radlinski [22] analyzes click spam from a utility standpoint. He finds that click spam plays an important role in the rankings of search results, which is harmful to search engines. He addresses malicious noise through partitioning the user population and suggests that personalizing search results can improve the robustness to click spam when using a simple ranking algorithm. Kang et al. [14] propose a semi-supervised learning algorithm for distinguishing program (bot) generated web search traffic from that of genuine human users. They first use the CAPTCHA technique to extract a large set of samples from the data logs as training data, and then develop a semi-supervised learning algorithm to take advantage of the unlabeled data to improve the classification performance. From their evaluation, the semi-supervised learning approach that they propose performs significantly better than the supervised learning algorithms.

All the above studies show that the analysis of features of single click records contribute to the detection of click spam. Other researchers focus on session-level click spam recognition. Sadagopan and Li [23] argue that it is important to identify typical and atypical user sessions in clickstreams. They model user session with a sequence of user actions. They classify user actions into 5 categories: page request, web click, sponsored click, next click and other click. They

[2]http://en.wikipedia.org/wiki/Google_bombing

then use a Markov chain model to represent user sessions and compute the transition probability as its likelihood score. A lower session score indicates a greater likelihood that the session is atypical. Their results show that their approach can identify typical and atypical sessions with a precision of about 89% and that filtering out the atypical sessions reduces the uncertainty of the mean CTR by about 40%.

To summarize, in the field of click spam detection, most research focuses on single click spam record detection, while few studies focus on session-level click spam recognition. However, click spam is user-level behavior. For example, if a user session is detected as a fraudulent session, all the actions of the user during the session should be regarded as fraudulent as well. Therefore, it is more important to detect click spam on a session level. Our approach focuses on session-level click spam recognition and is similar to the work of Sadagopan and Li; however, we also take into consideration the information about the action objective and the time interval between actions when modeling user sessions, and we adopt a bipartite graph propagation algorithm to further detect cheating sessions.

# 3. SINGLE CLICK SPAM RECORD DETECTION

The data used in our work consists of real click logs from a popular Chinese commercial search engine. There are about 80 million randomly sampled records in the click log per day with an anonymous ID and time information as well as submitted query, click type and clicked URL data. We selected the click logs from December 2011 for our experiment, which consist of 2.4 billion records in total.

Each time a user makes a click on the result page, the search engine will make a record of it in the click log. The record consists of the clicked URL, the type of the click, and so on. The type of the click is an important term in the click log. For example, the types of the clicks on two different general search results are the same. While the type of a click on a general search result and the type of a click on "Next Page" are different. For a legal record in the click log, the type of the click is representative of the clicked URL.

In the click log, tag represents the type of click. For example, tag of "image" indicates that the user clicks on the "Image Search" tab. For normal users, a tag of the click should be consistent with the true action of the user. When conflict is found, click spam can be detected. As an example, if the tag is "video", but the clicked URL comes from a general search result but not video search result, the spam is indicated.

In total there are 40,130 different tags from one day sampled log data (2011.12.7), which can be divided into 53 categories according to the prefix of the tags. For 20 of these tag categories, the clicked URLs share the same characteristic. Based on the analysis above, for a click record, if its tag is missing, or the clicked URL does not match the tag, we believe that this click record is suspicious of cheating. By this method, experiments have been made and the results are shown in Table 2.

As shown in the table, in total 443,415 click spam records out of 82,113,889 click records are detected in this way, which take up 0.54% of all the click records (except for the above listed 11,716,766 records, there are more clicks that cannot be recognized by this method). We also run the experiment on two other days, and the ratio is 0.55% and 0.52% respectively, which keeps stable by our detection methods.

The detection of the single click spam is quite precise (with 100% precision), but only handles the simplest spam techniques. Hence it can be used as part of the seeds to find more complicated click spams in our model (details are shown in Section 5).

**Table 2: Result of single click spam record detection**

| click type | #cheating clicks | #total clicks | spam ratio |
|---|---|---|---|
| –(missing tag) | 285,449 | 285,449 | 100% |
| query recommendation | 32,348 | 3,330,407 | 0.97% |
| next page | 3,105 | 2,209,056 | 0.14% |
| page number | 21,909 | 2,068,008 | 1.06% |
| sponsored search | 12,092 | 2,200,346 | 0.55% |
| Snapshot | 22,514 | 520,956 | 4.32% |
| Video | 5,051 | 342,363 | 1.48% |
| Picture | 4,844 | 246,900 | 1.96% |
| leftcolumn | 9,957 | 122,421 | 8.13% |
| Music | 4,841 | 113,434 | 4.27% |
| News | 5,028 | 49,622 | 10.1% |
| Maps | 9,737 | 33,917 | 28.7% |
| knowledge | 7,128 | 33,440 | 21.3% |
| previous page | 106 | 25,604 | 0.41% |
| searchForm | 2,452 | 11,075 | 22.1% |
| web help | 2,521 | 5,285 | 47.7% |
| Other | 14,333 | 118,483 | 12.1% |
| Total | 443,415 | 11,716,766 | 3.78% |

# 4. MODELING USER SESSIONS

The general idea of our work is to model user sessions with action sequences so that we can detect spam by judging whether the user session matches abnormal sequence modes. In previous works, generally a symbolic definition of a single action is given (e.g. [23]) without taking into consideration the time interval between actions or the semantic meanings of the action (for example, the action is to submit the same query as a previous one or to submit a new query). The innovation of our work lies in these two points. Consequently, the key points of modeling the user session are 1. to define actions with semantic meanings and 2. to introduce time as a factor into the model.

## 4.1 Action definitions

We derive user sessions based on a widely-used method: two consecutive actions (queries or clicks) are segmented into two sessions if the time interval between them exceeds 30 minutes. In the click log of a single day, more than 50 million user sessions can be generated by this method. During a user session, after the user submits a query, he may browse the result page, click on the search results, click on the tabs and so on, or he may reform his query and continue his interaction with the search engine. In our work, we define 6 kinds of user actions:

- $Qi$: Submit a query, in which $i$ is used to distinguish different queries (in a session, each time a new query is submitted, we assign a new ID)
- $Wi$: Click on web results, in which $i$ is used to distinguish different web clicks
- $Oi$: Click on sponsored results, in which $i$ is used to distinguish different sponsored clicks
- $N$: Load a new page, including clicking on the next page, the previous page or specific page numbers
- $T$: Scroll the page
- $Ai$: Perform other clicks, including clicks on tabs such as "Video" and "Music"

Thus the user actions in a user session can be divided into 6 categories. Unlike earlier studies, we assign different IDs for different queries and clicks on different links, which is able to distinguish action objectives. That is reasonable because it can be regarded as a normal behavior if a user clicks on 10 different web results after submitting a query. But if he clicks on the same web result 10 times after submitting a query, he is suspicious of cheating. In earlier studies, the 2 sessions are modeled as the same action sequence. While in our work, we can distinguish them according to the IDs of the actions.

## 4.2 Time interval

After defining the possible actions in a user session, we introduce the time interval information into our model. In a user session, there should be a reasonable time interval between actions. For example, after a user submits a query to the search engine, he takes time to read the search result page and then makes a click on one of the search results. He also takes time to read the landing page and then clicks on another search result. As a result, if the actions in a user session is excessive frequent, it is likely that the session is performed by a bot (a piece of program) and the user is suspicious of cheating. So it is important to take the time interval between actions into consideration when modeling user sessions. However, if we use the value of the time interval directly, the data will be too sparse because each different second of time interval means a different action. Instead, we need to segment the time interval. We analyse the time interval distributions of the 6 actions (the time interval of an action is the time interval between this action and the previous action, if this is the first action of the user session, the time interval is 0), which is shown in Figure 1.

As shown in Figure 1, the time interval distributions of the 6 actions are similar, so we apply the same segmentation strategy to the 6 actions. We segment the timeline into 4 parts with zero point and two inflection points according to the time interval distribution. To be specific, let $t$ be the time interval value (in seconds) and $\tau$ be the ID of the segment, then the segmentation is defined like this:

- $t = 0, \tau = 0$
- $0 < t \leq 10, \tau = 1$
- $10 < t \leq 30, \tau = 2$
- $t > 30, \tau = 3$

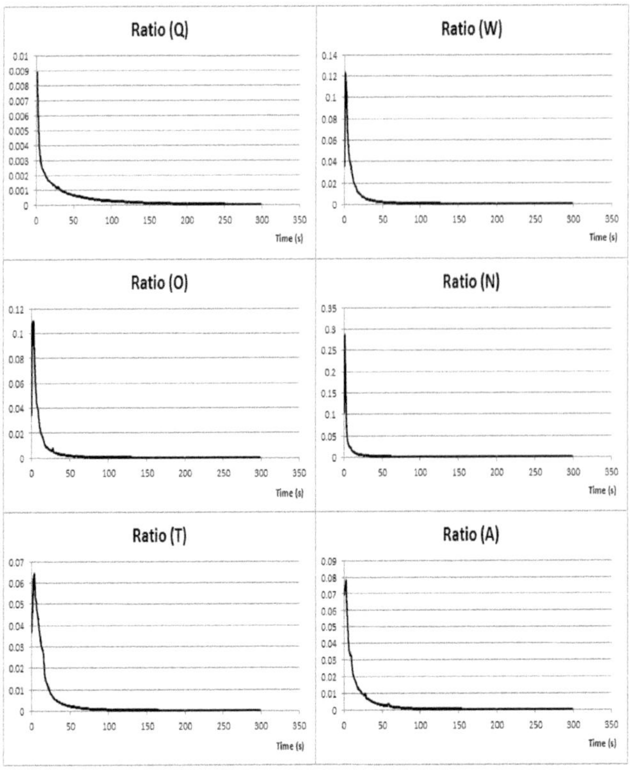


**Figure 1: Time interval distribution of the 6 actions**

Based on the analysis above, we are able to model user sessions involving action objective and time interval between actions. For each event in a session, we represent it with a triple $(S, i, \tau)$, where $S \in \{Q, W, O, N, T, A\}$, which represents an action, in which $i$ is used to distinguish different action objectives, and $\tau \in \{0, 1, 2, 3\}$, which represents the time interval. Thus each session can be represented by a triple sequence which starts with $(Q0, 0)$, since each session starts from a user submitting a query to the search engine with no time interval. Below is an example of a modeled user session:

$(Q0,0)$,$(T,1)$,$(Q0,1)$,$(Q0,0)$,$(W2,1)$,$(Q1,3)$,$(Q1,1)$,$(Q1,0)$, $(W2,1)$,$(T,2)$,$(Q1,1)$,$(Q1,0)$,$(W2,1)$,$(Q1,2)$,$(Q1,0)$,$(T,1)$

It means that the user submits a query $(Q0, 0)$, scrolls the page a short time later $(T, 1)$, re-submits the same query after a short time $(Q0, 1)$, submits the same query again immediately $(Q0, 0)$, and clicks on the third web result after a short time interval $(W2, 1)$....

# 5. SESSION-LEVEL CLICK SPAM RECOGNITION

## 5.1 Detection of cheating sessions based on Markov transition probability

We first use the approach proposed in [23] as a baseline experiment. The main idea behind the approach is that within a session, the next event is largely affected by the previous one, which leads to a Markov Chain Model for user sessions. The state space of the Markov Chain Model consists every action that occurs in user sessions. The transition probability $Pr(i,j)$ from state $i$ to $j$ is estimated as follows:

$$Pr(i,j) = \frac{Q_{i,j}}{Q_i}$$

where $Q_{i,j}$ is the number of instances where state $i$ is followed by state $j$, and $Q_i = \sum_j Q_{i,j}$.

Each user session can then be assigned a likelihood score by multiplying the probability of the individual state transitions in the session. Thus a session with a high likelihood score can be associated with normal behavior, while a session with a low likelihood score can be associated with rare behavior. Since the likelihood score is obtained by multiplying the probability of the individual state transitions, a user session with a longer sequence will get a smaller score. To avoid that case, they take a log of the likelihood score and normalize it by the length of the user session sequence to obtain the average Markovian LoglikeHood ($\text{MLH}_{avg}$). Consequently, a lower $\text{MLH}_{avg}$ score indicates a greater likelihood that the session is atypical. Thus cheating sessions can be detected from the tail of the $\text{MLH}_{avg}$ score distribution.

We use the approach of Sadagopan and Li to test our modeled user sessions from one day of click log data (2011.12.7), which consists of more than 50 million user sessions. We count the transition probability between states in user sessions and compute the $\text{MLH}_{avg}$ score of each session. The distribution of $\text{MLH}_{avg}$ scores is shown in Figure 2.

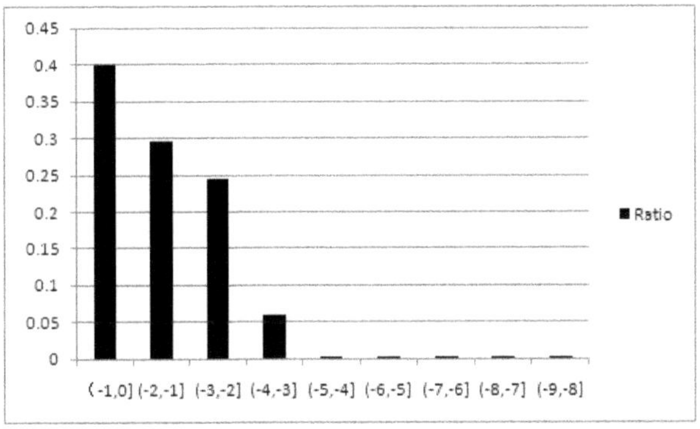


**Figure 2: Distribution of $\text{MLH}_{avg}$ scores**

From the figure we can see that for 99.6% of the user sessions, the $\text{MLH}_{avg} \in (-4, 0]$, which can be regarded as normal sessions. We detect the user sessions with score lower than $-4$ as cheating sessions. The evaluation of precision of the approach and the comparison with our methods will be given in Section 6.

## 5.2 Discovering seed cheating session modes

The main idea of our work is to first find a small set of seed cheating sessions, and then detect cheating users and sequential patterns with a label propagation algorithm on the user-session bipartite graph and pattern-session bipartite graph, which will help detect more cheating sessions and improve the precision and recall of our work. To find the seed cheating sessions, we discover the modes used by these sessions with the detected single click spam records above. We analyze the sessions that contain these records because these sessions are more likely to be cheating sessions. We model these sessions with the method described in Section 4 and discover the modes that many of these sessions share. We discover 5 cheating session modes in total and represent them by regular expressions, their characteristics are described as below.

- $(QAi)*$: Submit different queries and click on the websites with the same domain repeatedly (as shown in Table 1 (b)), where $i$ means the domains of the websites clicked by the user are the same.

- $(QiT)*$: Submit the same query and scroll the page repeatedly, where $i$ means the queries submitted by the user are the same.

- $(Qi)*$: Submit the same query repeatedly in order to increase the frequency of a certain keyword, where $i$ means the queries submitted by the user are the same.

- $Q(Wi)*$: After submitting a query, click on a web page after a short time interval repeatedly, where $i$ means the web pages clicked by the user are the same.

- $Q(Ai)*$: After submitting a query, click on a website with the same domain after a short time interval repeatedly, where $i$ means the domains of the websites clicked by the user are the same.

We use one day of click log data (2011.12.7) to evaluate the precision of the session modes above. We model the user sessions and obtain the sessions that match the 5 modes like this: if the length of the subsequence of a session that matches the mode exceeds 50% of the length of the session (only the actions of which the time interval is 0 or 1 are considered), we determine that the session matches the cheating mode. Here we do not consider the actions of which the time interval is 2 or 3 because we believe the actions in a cheating session are usually with a shorter time interval so that the user can perform more cheating actions during the same period of time. For each of the 5 modes, we extract 100 sessions that match the mode randomly for manual annotation and evaluation the precision. The number and precision of the sessions are shown in Table 3.

**Table 3: Click ratio and precision of the 5 seed cheating modes**

| mode | #session | #click | %click | precision |
|---|---|---|---|---|
| $(QAi)_{0-1}*$ | 11,981 | 143,214 | 0.226% | 100.0% |
| $(QiT)_{0-1}*$ | 3,964 | 36,964 | 0.058% | 98.0% |
| $(Qi)_{0-1}*$ | 17,258 | 14,956 | 0.024% | 95.0% |
| $Q(Wi)_{0-1}*$ | 2,069 | 36,097 | 0.057% | 100.0% |
| $Q(Ai)_{0-1}*$ | 4,079 | 82,843 | 0.130% | 100.0% |
| total | 39,351 | 314,074 | 0.495% | 98.6% |

In Table 3, the first column is the cheating mode, the second column is the number of the sessions that match the corresponding mode, the third column shows the number of actions (queries and clicks) in the sessions and the fourth column is the ratio between the actions in the sessions and all the actions in the one day click log, the last column is the precision of the corresponding mode. From the table we can see that the precision of the 5 cheating modes are rather high (98.6%) so that the detected 39,351 sessions can be used as seed cheating sessions.

## 5.3 User-session bipartite graph propagation algorithm

The user-session bipartite graph propagation algorithm is based on the assumption that if a certain number of a user's sessions are cheating sessions, the other sessions of this user are likely to be cheating sessions as well. According to that assumption, we start from the seed cheating sessions and find cheating users based on the cheating sessions, and then find more cheating sessions based on the cheating users that we have found. We repeat this process several times to detect a large number of cheating sessions to improve the precision and recall of our work. In order to complete that process, we construct the relationship between users and session sequences. In a search engine, a user may initiate sessions with different sequences, and the same session sequence may be made by different users. Their relationship forms the user-session bipartite graph, as shown in Figure 3. In the click log data of one day, there are nearly 40 million users and 1 million session sequences.

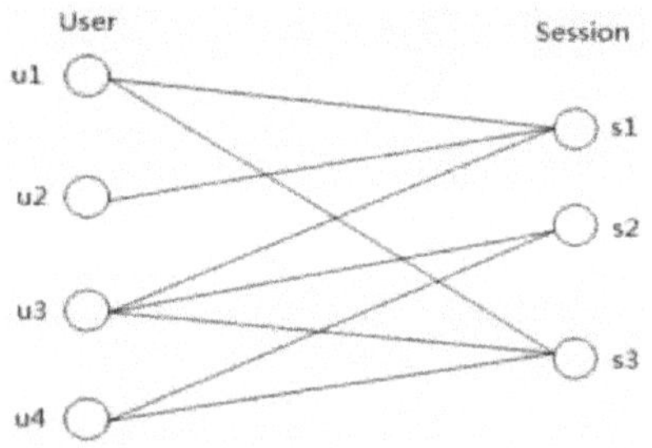


**Figure 3: User-session bipartite graph**

Based on the assumption and analysis, we propose the user-session bipartite graph propagation algorithm. First, we assign a score for each session. Specifically, for the sessions that match the cheating modes identified above, we assign an initial score of 1, and all other sessions are assigned a score of 0. Then, for each user, we update the score with the weighted average of the scores of the sessions that the user makes. For each session, we update the score with the weighted average of the scores of users who make the session to finish the first iteration. This process is repeated until the scores of the sessions between two iterations change little. A description of the algorithm is shown in Algorithm 1, where $w_{ij}$ is the frequency of user $i$ making session $j$.

**Algorithm 1** User-session bipartite graph propagation algorithm

**Require:**
The set of cheating session sequences, $C$;
The set of users, $U$;
The set of session sequences, $S$;
The user-session weight matrix, $W$;
The threshold to end the iteration, $\epsilon$;

**for** each $s_j$ in $S$ **do**
  $sscore(s_j) = 0$
**end for**
**for** each $s_j$ in $C$ **do**
  $sscore(s_j) = 1$
**end for**
$n = 1$
**while** $|sscore_n - sscore_{n-1}| > \epsilon$ **do**
  **for** each $u_i$ in $U$ **do**
    $uscore(u_i) = \sum_i w_{ij} \times sscore(s_j)$
  **end for**
  **for** each $s_j$ in $S$ **do**
    **if** $s_j$ in $C$ **then**
      $sscore(s_j) = 1$
    **else**
      $sscore(s_j) = \sum_j w_{ij} \times uscore(u_i)$
    **end if**
  **end for**
  $n = n + 1$
**end while**

## 5.4 Pattern-session bipartite graph propagation algorithm

From the user-session bipartite graph propagation algorithm, we can obtain a list of cheating users and cheating session sequences. However, our goal is to discover all the cheating sequential patterns so that we can detect the cheating sessions that match these patterns. The pattern-session bipartite graph propagation algorithm is based on the assumption that if a certain number of sessions that match a sequential pattern are cheating sessions, other sessions that match the sequential pattern are likely to be cheating sessions as well. The main idea of the pattern-session bipartite graph propagation algorithm is to find frequent sequential patterns from the modeled user sessions and to diffuse the cheating score of the seed sessions on the pattern-session bipartite graph in order to obtain a list of cheating sequential patterns.

First, we introduce the definition of *frequent sequential patterns*, which is given by [2]. An item set $I = \{i_1, i_2, ..., i_k\}$ is the set of all the items. A sequence $\alpha = \langle t_1, t_2, ..., t_m\rangle (t_i \subseteq I)$ is an ordered list of item subsets. A sequence $\langle a_1, a_2, ..., a_n\rangle$ *is contained in* another sequence $\langle b_1, b_2, ..., b_m\rangle$ if there exist integers $i_1 < i_2 < ... < i_n$ such that $a_1 \subseteq b_{i_1}, a_2 \subseteq b_{i_2}, ..., a_n \subseteq b_{i_n}$. Given a sequence database $D = \{s_1, s_2, ..., s_n\}$, the *support for a sequence* $\alpha$ is defined as the number of sequences in $D$ that contain $\alpha$. If the support for a sequence $\alpha$ is larger than $\theta|D|$ ($\theta$ is the user-specified threshold), $\alpha$ is called the *frequent sequential pattern*.

A variety of algorithms for finding frequent sequential patterns in very large sequential databases have been developed over the years, such as FreeSpan [9], PrefixSpan [10, 21], CloSpan [25] and so on. We use the PrefixSpan approach proposed in [10, 21] to mine frequent sequential patterns from the modeled user sessions. PrefixSpan works through divide and conquer. The complete set of sequential patterns is partitioned into different subsets according to different prefixes, and corresponding projected databases are constructed and frequent sequential patterns are mined recursively. Based on the mined frequent sequential patterns, we construct the pattern-session bipartite graph. Since each sequential pattern may be matched by different session sequences and each session sequence may match different sequential patterns, their relationship forms the pattern-session bipartite graph. We use the same algorithm with the user-session bipartite graph propagation to diffuse the cheating score of the seed sessions and obtain the cheating sequential patterns, as shown in Algorithm 2.

**Algorithm 2** Pattern-session bipartite graph propagation algorithm

**Require:**

The set of cheating session sequences, $C$;
The set of frequent sequential patterns, $P$;
The set of session sequences, $S$;
The pattern-session weight matrix, $W$;
The threshold to end the iteration, $\epsilon$;

**for** each $s_j$ in $S$ **do**
  $sscore(s_j) = 0$
**end for**
**for** each $s_j$ in $C$ **do**
  $sscore(s_j) = 1$
**end for**
$n = 1$
**while** $|sscore_n - sscore_{n-1}| > \epsilon$ **do**
  **for** each $p_i$ in $P$ **do**
    $pscore(p_i) = \sum_i w_{ij} \times sscore(s_j)$
  **end for**
  **for** each $s_j$ in $S$ **do**
    **if** $s_j$ in $C$ **then**
      $sscore(s_j) = 1$
    **else**
      $sscore(s_j) = \sum_j w_{ij} \times pscore(p_i)$
    **end if**
  **end for**
  $n = n + 1$
**end while**

The frequent sequential patterns do not require the actions in a session to be continuous, which effectively reduce the influence of the noise. The high robustness of the algorithm increases the recall of click spam detection.

# 6. EVALUATIONS AND DISCUSSIONS

In this section, we report the performance of the user-session bipartite graph propagation algorithm and pattern-session bipartite graph propagation algorithm using the click logs from a popular Chinese commercial search engine. We compare our approaches with the baseline method on precision and recall of detecting cheating sessions. We evaluate the effects of click spam on search results by comparing the NDCG value of search results before and after filtering out the detected cheating sessions.

## 6.1 Performance of the user-session bipartite graph propagation algorithm

We use the user-session bipartite graph propagation algorithm to experiment on the sampled click logs of one week, which contain about 80 million click records per day. From the raw click logs, we extract user sessions as described in Section 4 and more than 50 million user sessions can be generated by this method per day.

First we evaluate the performance of the algorithm using the click log of a single day (2011.12.7). In Algorithm 1, each session sequence receives a score after the iteration completes. Obviously the score of each session sequence is between 0 and 1. We calculate the number and *click ratio* of the sessions for different score ranges. Here, the *click ratio* of the sessions is defined as the ratio between the number of actions (queries and clicks) of the sessions in a specific score range and the number of actions of all the sessions. Since the scores of most (more than 80%) sessions are 0 because only a small set of sessions can be diffused from the seed cheating sessions by the algorithm, we only consider the sessions within the score range of (0,1]. The click ratios for different score ranges are shown in Figure 4.

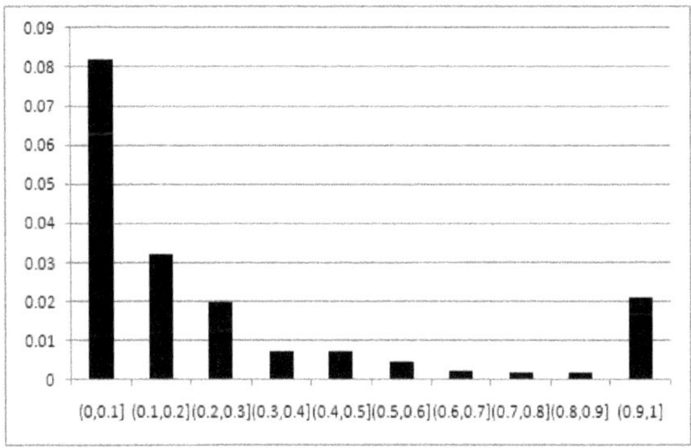


**Figure 4: Click ratios for different score ranges on one day with the user-session bipartite graph propagation algorithm**

As shown in Figure 4, most of the diffused sessions get a lower score while a relatively large percentage of sessions get a score between 0.9 and 1. From the algorithm we know that a higher score indicates that the session is closer to the seed cheating sessions on the bipartite graph and it is more likely that the session is cheating, so we evaluate the precision of the detected sessions with a higher score. For the sessions with a score larger than 0.5, we randomly sample 200 sessions for manual annotation to evaluate the precision, and the results are shown in Table 4.

**Table 4: Precision in the different score ranges**

| range | #session | #correct | precision |
|---|---|---|---|
| (0.9,1] | 59 | 57 | 0.966102 |
| (0.8,0.9] | 15 | 13 | 0.866667 |
| (0.7,0.8] | 22 | 19 | 0.863636 |
| (0.6,0.7] | 28 | 22 | 0.785714 |
| (0.5,0.6] | 76 | 55 | 0.723684 |
| total | 200 | 166 | 0.83 |

From the table we can see that the sessions in a higher score range get a higher precision to be cheating sessions, which meets our expectation. As the detection of click spam requires high precision, we take the sessions within the score range of (0.9,1] as cheating sessions, which make up 2.1% of the number of queries and clicks in all the sessions. We define *click spam ratio* as the click ratio of the sessions within the score range of (0,9,1]. As shown in Table 3, the click spam ratio of the seed sessions is 0.495% with a precision of 98.6%. In this case, the click spam ratio by our algorithm is 2.1% with a precision of 96.6%.

We also run the same experiment on one week's sampled data (2011.12.1 - 2011.12.7), which contains 550 million click records in total. We evaluate the performance of our algorithm with the click logs of separate days. We calculate the numbers and click ratios for different score ranges on separate days in a week and compare the click spam ratios of different days. The results are shown in Figure 5.

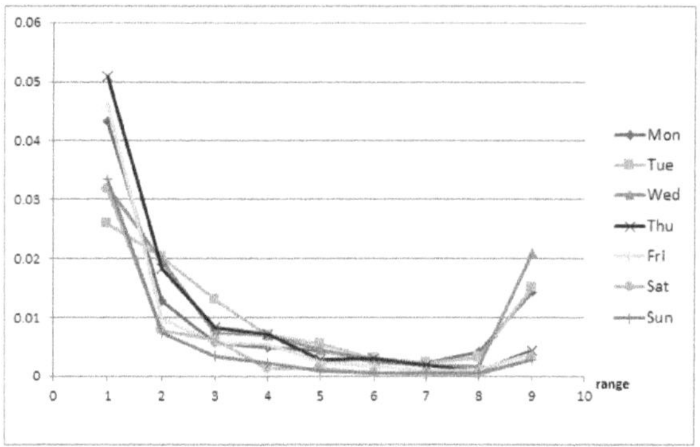


**Figure 5: Click ratios for different score ranges on separate days in a week with the user-session bipartite graph propagation algorithm**

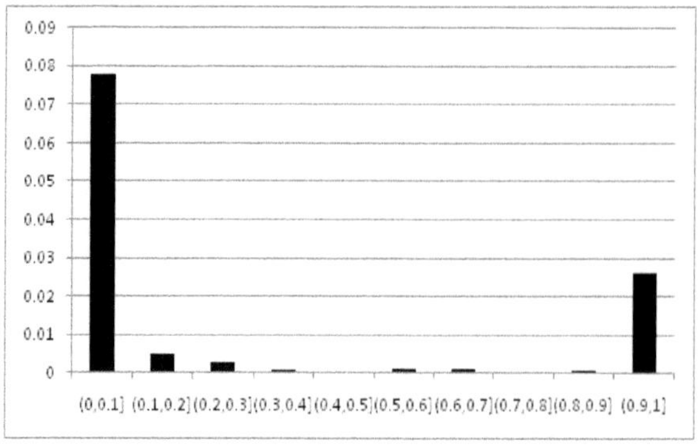


**Figure 6: Click ratio in different score ranges with the pattern-session bipartite graph propagation algorithm**

As shown in Figure 5, the number of cheating sessions detected is larger from Monday to Wednesday than from Thursday through Sunday. Perhaps it is because the cheating users or company are more active at the beginning of the week. So the detection of click spam should be more concentrated at the beginning of each week.

## 6.2 Performance of the pattern-session bipartite graph propagation algorithm

As mentioned in Section 5.4, to obtain frequent sequential patterns, we need to determine the support threshold $\theta$. To select the proper support threshold $\theta$ for mining frequent sequential patterns, we use a range of 0.005 to 0.01 for $\theta$ and test the sampled one-day log data using the pattern-session bipartite graph propagation algorithm and compute the click spam ratio. From the results for each $\theta$, we randomly sample 100 sessions within the score range of (0.9, 1] for manual annotation to evaluate the precision. The click spam ratio and precision for each $\theta$ are shown in Table 5.

**Table 5: Click spam ratio and precision for each $\theta$**

| support threshold $\theta$ | click spam ratio | precision |
|---|---|---|
| 0.01 | 0.026172068 | 97% |
| 0.009 | 0.026976257 | 92% |
| 0.008 | 0.027539188 | 93% |
| 0.007 | 0.028182539 | 92% |
| 0.006 | 0.028665052 | 91% |
| 0.005 | 0.028986728 | 91% |

These results indicate that with the decrease of $\theta$, the click spam ratio increases while the precision decreases. This is because with the decrease of $\theta$, more frequent sequential patterns can be mined and more sessions that match the patterns can be detected as cheating sessions, while some normal but frequent patterns may be mined and lower the precision of the detection. To ensure the precision of the detection of click spam, we set $\theta$ to be 0.01. The click ratio in different score ranges is shown in Figure 6.

The figure shows that the click spam ratio reaches 2.6%, which is higher than the 2.1% for the user-session bipartite graph propagation algorithm, thus proving the high robustness of the pattern-session bipartite graph propagation algorithm.

To compare the difference of time interval distribution between normal and cheating sessions, we count the number of the 4 segments of time interval in normal and cheating sessions respectively. The ratio of the 4 segments of time interval in normal and cheating sessions is shown in Figure 7 (the first action of each session is not considered since all the session sequences start with $(Q0, 0)$).

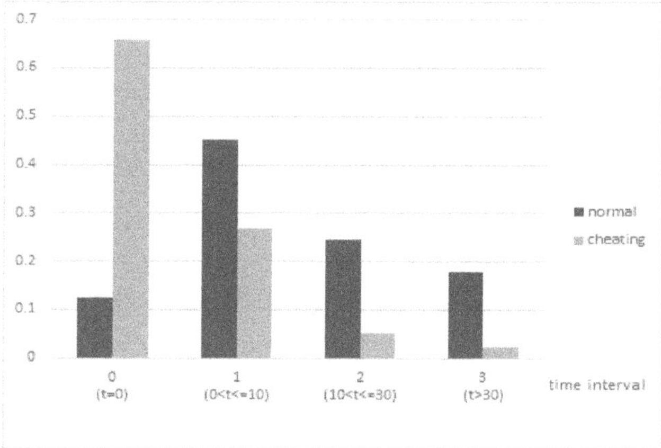


**Figure 7: Comparison of the ratio of the 4 segments of time interval between normal and cheating sessions**

The figure shows that the time interval between actions in cheating sessions is much shorter than normal sessions. This is reasonable because spammers make clicks on the search results without actually reading the landing pages, they can make clicks more frequently than normal users. As a result, a shorter time interval between actions enables them to perform more click spams in a certain period of time.

## 6.3 Comparison of the three approaches

We compare the performance of our algorithm with the traditional click spam detection approach [23]. For the baseline approach, we consider sessions with scores lower than -4 to be cheating sessions and randomly sample 100 sessions to evaluate the precision. The click spam ratio and precision of the three approaches are shown in Table 6.

The table shows that our approaches outperform the baseline method for both precision and recall because in our

Table 6: Comparison of the three approaches

| | click spam ratio | precision |
|---|---|---|
| Baseline[23] | 1.7% | 90% |
| User-session bipartite graph propagation algorithm | 2.1% | 97% |
| Pattern-session bipartite graph propagation algorithm | 2.6% | 97% |

model we take into consideration the action objectives and time interval between actions, thus introducing more information into our model. While maintaining high precision, the pattern-session bipartite graph propagation algorithm is able to detect more cheating sessions than the user-session bipartite graph propagation algorithm. This is because the frequent sequential patterns do not require the actions in a session to be continuous, which effectively reduce the influence of the noise.

## 6.4 Effects of click spam on search results

We evaluate the effects of click spam on search results by examining whether the relevance of the search results gets better after filtering out the detected cheating sessions. We use the NDCG metric to evaluate the relevance of the search results.

The Normalized Discounted Cumulative Gain (NDCG, [12]) is an important metric to evaluate the relevance of the search results. The NDCG at position $p(NDCG@p)$ is computed as:

$$DCG@p = \sum_{i=1}^{p} \frac{2^{rel_i} - 1}{log_2(1+i)}$$

$$NDCG@p = \frac{DCG@p}{IDCG@p}$$

where $rel_i$ is the manual label of the i-th document, and $IDCG@p$ represents an ideal DCG value obtained when sorting the documents by relevance. The formula indicates that the relevance of higher-ranking results is more important than that of lower-ranking results. For example, if a low relevance result is ranked high, the NDCG value will become relatively small and the ranking results will be less satisfactory. We filter out the detected cheating sessions and use NDCG metric to evaluate the changes.

We extract the queries in which the number of clicks is larger than 1000 and the click spam ratio is higher than 10% from the sampled one-day log data. These queries involve large number of click spam records, and we would like to evaluate whether our approach of click spam detection helps the search engine perform better. For each query, we rank the URLs by click-through rate (CTR) before and after filtering out the cheating sessions. Here CTR is computed as below:

$$CTR = \frac{Clicks}{Impressions} \times 100\%$$

where $Clicks$ is the number of clicks on the URL when searching the query and $Impressions$ is the number of which the query is searched. Since the detected cheating sessions involve large number of clicks on some of the results, these results will rank lower after we filter out the cheating sessions. We label the top 20 URLs for each query according to their relevance to the query and compute the NDCG value. We compare the average NDCG@5, NDCG@10 and NDCG@20 of the queries, and the results are shown in Figure 8.

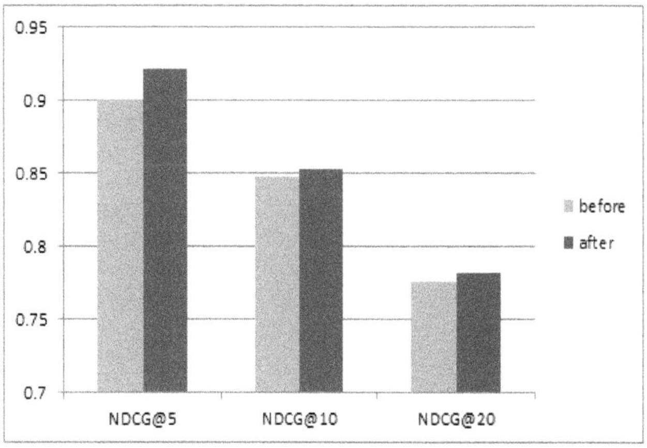


**Figure 8: Comparison of NDCG before and after filtering out the cheating sessions**

The figure shows that after filtering out the cheating sessions, the NDCG@5 gets a relatively larger increase. While the NDCG@10 and NDCG@20 values increase little. This result indicates that the detected click spammers tended to succeed in placing their websites at a higher position ($\leq$5) in search results. Our method of detecting click spam is able to improve the relevance of the search results and help the search engine perform better.

## 7. CONCLUSIONS

Previous studies show that click spam has a large influence on the performance of search engines. In this paper, we propose a novel automatic session-level click spam detection approach. We first model user sessions with a triple sequence that accounts for the action objective and the time interval between actions. Then, we construct the user-session bipartite graph and the pattern-session bipartite graph to describe the relations between users and sessions as well as patterns and sessions. Finally, based on the detected seed cheating sessions, we diffuse the cheating score on the bipartite graph and improve the precision and recall of our work. The approaches that we propose perform better than the traditional session-level click spam detection method, as our approach can detect 2.6% of all the queries and clicks as spam with a precision of 97%. After filtering out the cheating sessions that we have detected, the NDCG of the search results increases, which indicates that the search engine performs better.

## Acknowledgments

This work was supported by Natural Science Foundation (61073071) and National High Technology Research and Development (863) Program (2011AA01A205) of China. Part of the work has been done at the Tsinghua-NUS NExT Search Centre, which is supported by the Singapore National Research Foundation & Interactive Digital Media R&D Program Office, MDA under research grant (WBS:R-252-300-001-490).

## 8. REFERENCES


[1] E. Agichtein, E. Brill, and S. Dumais. Improving web search ranking by incorporating user behavior information. In *Proceedings of the 29th annual international ACM SIGIR conference on Research and development in information retrieval*, pages 19–26. ACM, 2006.

[2] R. Agrawal and R. Srikant. Mining sequential patterns. In *Data Engineering, 1995. Proceedings of the Eleventh International Conference on*, pages 3–14. IEEE, 1995.

[3] L. Becchetti, C. Castillo, D. Donato, S. Leonardi, and R. A. Baeza-Yates. Link-based characterization and detection of web spam. In *AIRWeb*, pages 1–8, 2006.

[4] O. Chapelle and Y. Zhang. A dynamic bayesian network click model for web search ranking. In *Proceedings of the 18th international conference on World wide web*, pages 1–10. ACM, 2009.

[5] N. Craswell, O. Zoeter, M. Taylor, and B. Ramsey. An experimental comparison of click position-bias models. In *Proceedings of the 2008 International Conference on Web Search and Data Mining*, pages 87–94. ACM, 2008.

[6] G. Gu, R. Perdisci, J. Zhang, W. Lee, et al. Botminer: Clustering analysis of network traffic for protocol-and structure-independent botnet detection. In *USENIX Security Symposium*, pages 139–154, 2008.

[7] F. Guo, C. Liu, A. Kannan, T. Minka, M. Taylor, Y.-M. Wang, and C. Faloutsos. Click chain model in web search. In *Proceedings of the 18th international conference on World wide web*, pages 11–20. ACM, 2009.

[8] Z. Gyöngyi, H. Garcia-Molina, and J. Pedersen. Combating web spam with trustrank. In *Proceedings of the Thirtieth international conference on Very large data bases-Volume 30*, pages 576–587. VLDB Endowment, 2004.

[9] J. Han, J. Pei, B. Mortazavi-Asl, Q. Chen, U. Dayal, and M.-C. Hsu. Freespan: frequent pattern-projected sequential pattern mining. In *Proceedings of the sixth ACM SIGKDD international conference on Knowledge discovery and data mining*, pages 355–359. ACM, 2000.

[10] J. Han, J. Pei, B. Mortazavi-Asl, H. Pinto, Q. Chen, U. Dayal, and M. Hsu. Prefixspan: Mining sequential patterns efficiently by prefix-projected pattern growth. In *proceedings of the 17th international conference on data engineering*, pages 215–224, 2001.

[11] B. J. Jansen. Click fraud. *Computer*, 40(7):85–86, 2007.

[12] K. Järvelin and J. Kekäläinen. Cumulated gain-based evaluation of ir techniques. *ACM Transactions on Information Systems (TOIS)*, 20(4):422–446, 2002.

[13] T. Joachims. Optimizing search engines using clickthrough data. In *Proceedings of the eighth ACM SIGKDD international conference on Knowledge discovery and data mining*, pages 133–142. ACM, 2002.

[14] H. Kang, K. Wang, D. Soukal, F. Behr, and Z. Zheng. Large-scale bot detection for search engines. In *Proceedings of the 19th international conference on World wide web*, pages 501–510. ACM, 2010.

[15] A. Karasaridis, B. Rexroad, and D. Hoeflin. Wide-scale botnet detection and characterization. In *Proceedings of the first conference on First Workshop on Hot Topics in Understanding Botnets*, volume 7. Cambridge, MA, 2007.

[16] V. Krishnan and R. Raj. Web spam detection with anti-trust rank. In *AIRWeb*, volume 6, pages 37–40, 2006.

[17] Y. Liu, R. Cen, M. Zhang, S. Ma, and L. Ru. Identifying web spam with user behavior analysis. In *Proceedings of the 4th international workshop on Adversarial information retrieval on the web*, pages 9–16. ACM, 2008.

[18] M. Marchiori. The quest for correct information on the web: Hyper search engines. *Computer Networks and ISDN Systems*, 29(8):1225–1235, 1997.

[19] A. Metwally, D. Agrawal, and A. E. Abbadi. Using association rules for fraud detection in web advertising networks. In *Proceedings of the 31st international conference on Very large data bases*, pages 169–180. VLDB Endowment, 2005.

[20] L. Page, S. Brin, R. Motwani, and T. Winograd. The pagerank citation ranking: bringing order to the web. 1999.

[21] J. Pei, J. Han, B. Mortazavi-Asl, J. Wang, H. Pinto, Q. Chen, U. Dayal, and M.-C. Hsu. Mining sequential patterns by pattern-growth: The prefixspan approach. *Knowledge and Data Engineering, IEEE Transactions on*, 16(11):1424–1440, 2004.

[22] F. Radlinski. Addressing malicious noise in clickthrough data. In *Learning to Rank for Information Retrieval Workshop at SIGIR*, volume 2007, 2007.

[23] N. Sadagopan and J. Li. Characterizing typical and atypical user sessions in clickstreams. In *Proceedings of the 17th international conference on World Wide Web*, pages 885–894. ACM, 2008.

[24] T. Schluessler, S. Goglin, and E. Johnson. Is a bot at the controls?: Detecting input data attacks. In *Proceedings of the 6th ACM SIGCOMM workshop on Network and system support for games*, pages 1–6. ACM, 2007.

[25] X. Yan, J. Han, and R. Afshar. Clospan: Mining closed sequential patterns in large datasets. In *Proc. 2003 SIAM Intąŕl Conf. Data Mining (SDMąŕ03)*, pages 166–177, 2003.

# Sampling Dilemma: Towards Effective Data Sampling for Click Prediction in Sponsored Search

Jun Feng
Tsinghua University
feng-j13@mails.tsinghua.edu.cn

Jiang Bian
Microsoft Research
jibian@microsoft.com

Taifeng Wang
Microsoft Research
taifengw@microsoft.com

Wei Chen
Microsoft Research
wche@microsoft.com

Xiaoyan Zhu
Tsinghua University
zxy-dcs@tsinghua.edu.cn

Tie-Yan Liu
Microsoft Research
tyliu@microsoft.com

## ABSTRACT

Precise prediction of the probability that users click on ads plays a key role in sponsored search. State-of-the-art sponsored search systems typically employ a machine learning approach to conduct click prediction. While paying much attention to extracting useful features and building effective models, previous studies have overshadowed seemingly less obvious but essentially important challenges in terms of data sampling. To fulfill the learning objective of click prediction, it is not only necessary to ensure that the sampled training data implies the similar input distribution compared with the real world one, but also to guarantee that the sampled training data yield the consistent conditional output distribution, i.e. click-through rate (CTR), with the real world data. However, due to the sparseness of clicks in sponsored search, it is a bit contradictory to address these two challenges simultaneously. In this paper, we first take a theoretical analysis to reveal this sampling dilemma, followed by a thorough data analysis which demonstrates that the straightforward random sampling method may not be effective to balance these two kinds of consistency in sampling dilemma simultaneously. To address this problem, we propose a new sampling algorithm which can succeed in retaining the consistency between the sampled data and real world in terms of both input distribution and conditional output distribution. Large scale evaluations on the click-through logs from a commercial search engine demonstrate that this new sampling algorithm can effectively address the sampling dilemma. Further experiments illustrate that, by using the training data obtained by our new sampling algorithm, we can learn the model with much higher accuracy in click prediction.

## Categories and Subject Descriptors

H.3.3 [**Information Search and Retrieval**]: Information Search and Retrieval; H.3.5 [**On-line Information Services**]: Web-based services


*WSDM'14*, February 24–28, 2014, New York, New York, USA.
Copyright 2014 ACM 978-1-4503-2351-2/14/02 ...$15.00.
http://dx.doi.org/10.1145/2556195.2556242.

## General Terms

Algorithms, Experimentation, Performance

## Keywords

Online Advertising, Sponsored Search, Click Prediction, Data Sampling

## 1. INTRODUCTION

As an online advertising system, sponsored search [8] [10] has been one of the most important business models for commercial Web search engines. It contributes most of the revenue for search engines by presenting to users sponsored search results, i.e., advertisements (ads), along with organic search results. To deliver right ads to right users, a sponsored search system consists of a couple of technical components, including query-to-ad matching [1], click prediction for matched ads [6] [9], filtration of the ads according to thresholds for relevance and click probability, and auction to determine the ranking, placement, and pricing of the remaining ads [7]. In today's industry, generalized second price auction (GSP) [7] is the most widely-used auction mechanism, in which the price that an advertiser has to pay depends on the predicted click probability of his/her own ad as well as the bid price and predicted click probability of the ad ranked in the next position. As click prediction has been widely used in the filtration, ranking, placement, and pricing of the ads, accurate prediction of click probability becomes an essential problem in sponsored search.

State-of-the-art sponsored search systems typically employ a machine learning approach to predict the probability that a user clicks on an ad. As a general machine learning process, there are a couple of key components that could influence the accuracy of click prediction, including data sampling for training, feature extraction, and model selection. Many of previous studies have spent their efforts in discovering important features for accurate click prediction. For example, as shown in previous work [6] [2] [9], the historical click information for each ad are shown to be effective for predicting the future click probability of the ad. In practical sponsored search systems, however, there are many ads without adequate historical click-through data (even after aggregation at different levels, e.g., campaign, advertiser, and query levels). To tackle this data sparseness issue, some relevance features have been investigated to improve the accuracy of click prediction, and this type of features is mostly based on the similarity between query and ad, and the quality of the ad [5] [14] [16] [15] [13] [19]. Some efforts have also focused on model selection for click prediction. For example, many previous studies employ the maximum entropy model [15] since its strength in formulating the click probability by combining diverse forms of features, while other works apply the Bayesian framework [18] for click prediction as it is more effective to incorporate temporal and positional information. One of most recent works [17] takes advantage of continuous conditional random fields based model for click prediction which succeeds in modeling relational information between different ads.

The attention paid to feature extraction and model selection for click prediction, however, have overshadowed seemingly less obvious but essentially important challenges in terms of data sampling. A commercial search engine can obtain billions of users' impressions on sponsored search results everyday. Such huge size of real world data requires extensive resource cost involved in the storage of data as well as significant time cost spent in the training of click prediction model. Hence, it has necessitated the need for collecting a sample of sponsored search logs in order for training and updating the click prediction model both effectively and efficiently. Typically, in order to obtain precise click prediction model, effective data sampling requires that the sampled data should yield the similar input data distribution as the original whole data. Beyond that, in the context of click prediction for sponsored search, there is another important requirement for the data sampling. In particular, as the goal of click prediction in sponsored search is to predict the probability that a user clicks an ad given a query, the learning objective of click prediction model is optimizing the click probability towards the click-through rate (CTR) with respect to the same ⟨query, ad⟩ pair. To this end, it requires the sampled data yield the consistent conditional output distribution, i.e. CTR, as the original whole data. However, due to the sparseness of click in sponsored search, it is generally a bit contradictory to fulfill these two requirements simultaneously.

From one hand, some judiciously chosen sampling practice, e.g. random sampling, is widely used to obtain the sampled training data for click prediction, as it is effective to retain the distribution of each input data, i.e. the ⟨query, ad⟩ pair, in the sample data. Unfortunately, because of the sparseness of clicks in sponsored search, random sampling can cause a big difference in terms of conditional output distribution between sampled data and original whole data, which means that the CTR of one ⟨query, ad⟩ pair computed based on sampled training data is quite different from that computed based on whole real world data. For example, assuming that one ⟨query, ad⟩ pair generates totally $10,000$ impressions in the whole real world data during a certain period and 10 of these impressions cause clicks (i.e. the CTR is $0.1\%$), if we plan to take $1\%$ random sampling for each ⟨query, ad⟩ pair to obtain training data, we are not able to let this pair yield the same CTR in the sampled data as in the whole data, no matter how many clicks are included in the sampled data. In this paper, a thorough data analysis will be presented to reveal how severe this problem is by using the judiciously chosen random sampling method.

On the other hand, in order to retain the ⟨query, ad⟩ pair's CTR in the sampled data, one straightforward method is to distribute different sampling ratios to various ⟨query, ad⟩ pairs based on their CTRs in the real world data. Specifically, those ⟨query, ad⟩ pairs with lower real CTRs can yield a bit higher sampling ratios while those with higher real CTRs can be sampled with lower ratios. For example, for the ⟨query, ad⟩ pair which has totally $10,000$ impressions and 10 of them are clicks, we could raise the sampling ratio to $10\%$. Then, it is more likely that we sample 1000 impressions with 1 click in it, which yields the same CTR to that of this pair in the whole data. This straightforward method, unfortunately, may cause that many ⟨query, ad⟩ pairs contribute very different relative volumes of traffic in the sampled data compared with those in the whole data. Consequently, the input data distributions reflected by the sampled data are quite different from the real data distributions in the whole data, which also prevents from achieving accurate click prediction.

To address this sampling dilemma between input data distribution and conditional output distribution, in this paper, we first formulate these challenges from a theoretical perspective, then we propose a new sampling algorithm which can balance the trade-off between these two factors so as to collect effective training data in order for achieving accurate click prediction. In this paper, we will conduct a large scale evaluation on the effectiveness of this new sampling algorithm based on the click-through logs from a commercial search engine. Experimental results demonstrate that, the click prediction model which is learned using the training data sampled by our new sampling algorithm can reach much better performance than the model learned using randomly sampled training data. Further experimental analysis also prove that our new sampling method is effective to balance the trade-off between keeping the similar input data distribution and keeping the consistent conditional output distribution (i.e. CTR) in the sampled data as in the real world whole data.

To sum up, the contributions of our work include:

- A comprehensive theoretical analysis to reveal the dilemma between retaining similar input data distribution and keeping consistent conditional output distribution during data sampling for learning the click prediction model.
- A thorough empirical analysis to illustrate that judiciously chosen random sampling is not effective at balancing the sampling dilemma for click prediction.
- An effective sampling algorithm for collecting training data in order for accomplishing accurate click prediction
- A large scale evaluations demonstrating that the new sampling algorithm can effectively balance the sampling dilemma and lead to the click prediction model with higher performance.

The remainder parts of this paper are organized as follows. In Section 2, we present our theoretical analysis to reveal the sampling dilemma in click prediction as well as the data analysis to illustrate the problem caused by judiciously chosen random sampling method. Section 3 formulates the problem of data sampling for click prediction and introduces our new sampling algorithm. After briefly introducing the click prediction modeling in Section 4, we present our experimental setup and results in Section 5. At last, we conclude the paper and discuss the future work in Section 6.

## 2. MOTIVATION AND DATA ANALYSIS

As mentioned above, click prediction in sponsored search is typically a machine learning process. In this section, we will first introduce the learning objective of click prediction and formulate the sampling dilemma for achieving accurate click prediction from the theoretical perspective. To gain more understanding on why effective data sampling plays an important role in click prediction, we will conduct a large scale data analysis on real sponsored search data, which will demonstrate that the judiciously chosen random sampling method may cause a critical problem in addressing the sampling dilemma between keeping input data distribution and keeping conditional output distribution (i.e. CTR).

## 2.1 Sampling Dilemma for Click Prediction

In this subsection, we give detailed formulation of click prediction as a supervised machine learning task, and show how the data sampling strategy influence the performance of the learned click prediction model, followed by which we formulate the sampling dilemma for click prediction.

In the problem of click prediction, the input data are a set of ⟨query, ad⟩ pairs, denoted as $\{\langle q_i, a_i\rangle; i = 1, 2, \cdots, n\}$, and each $\langle q_i, a_i\rangle$ can be represented as a vector of features, denoted as $\{x_i = \phi(q_i, a_i) \in \mathcal{X}; i = 1, 2, \cdots, n\}$. In general, the feature space $\mathcal{X}$ is infinite. In this work, to describe the problem more clearly, we assume that $\mathcal{X}$ is finite, i.e. $\mathcal{X} = \{z_1, z_2, \cdots, z_K\}$, with an underlying probability $P : p_k; k = 1, ..., K$ where $K$ is the size of feature space $\mathcal{X}$. Note that our description below can be naturally extended to the infinite feature space. The output consists of clicks or non-clicks on ads, denoted as $\{c_i \in \{0, 1\}; i = 1, \cdots, n\}$, which is generated from the underlying conditional probability $P(c = 1|x_i)$.

As the size of sampled data for learning click prediction is fairly large, we assume that, for each element in the ⟨query, ad⟩ space, there will be at least one sample. Thus, we re-form the data as follows: $\{(x_k, c_{k,j}); k = 1, \cdots, K; j = 1, \cdots, n_k\}$. We denote the frequency of a ⟨query, ad⟩ pair $x_k$ as $\hat{p}_k = \frac{n_k}{\sum_{k=1}^{K} n_k}$ and the empirical CTR for ad $x_k$ as $\hat{\text{CTR}}(x_k) = \frac{\sum_{j=1}^{n_k} c_{k,j}}{n_k}$.

Our objective is to learn a click prediction model $f : \mathcal{X} \to [0, 1]$ which can minimize the following expected loss:

$$\mathbb{E}L(f) = \sum_{k=1}^{K} p_k \left| f(x_k) - P(c = 1|x_k) \right|. \quad (1)$$

However, the underlying distributions $p_k$ and $P(c = 1|x_k)$ are unknown. Therefore, after conducting data sampling, we can just optimize the empirical loss on the sampled data set $D$.

$$\hat{L}(f; D) = \sum_{k=1}^{K} \hat{p}_k \left| f(x_k) - \hat{\text{CTR}}(x_k) \right|. \quad (2)$$

To further investigate the influence of the sampling, we describe the distance between the empirical distribution and underlying distribution in terms of *input distribution* and *conditional output distribution*. To be specific, we denote the distance in terms of *input distribution* as

$$\eta_D = \max_k |\hat{p}_k(D) - p_k| \quad (3)$$

and the distance in terms of *conditional output distribution* as

$$\gamma_D = \max_k |\hat{\text{CTR}}(x_k; D) - P(c = 1|x_k)|. \quad (4)$$

Note that the distance in terms of *conditional output distribution* implies that in terms of CTR. Then, it is easy to have the following proposition:

PROPOSITION 1. *Consider data set $D$, for $\forall f \in \mathcal{F}$, we have*

$$\mathbb{E}L(f) \leq \left(1 + \frac{\eta_D}{\min_k n_k(D)}\right) \hat{L}(f; D) + K\left(\eta_D + \gamma_D + \eta_D\gamma_D\right).$$

This proposition explains how the distance between empirical distribution of the sampled data and the underlying distribution influence the distance between empirical loss and the expected loss. When the size of sampled data approaches infinity, all the distance vanish, and empirical loss approaches expected loss; however, if the total sampling number is limited, in order to minimize the empirical loss, there is a trade-off between $\eta$ and $\gamma$, which indicates a dilemma between the *input distribution* and the *conditional output distribution*. We formulate it as a *Sampling Dilemma* for click prediction:

> **Sampling Dilemma**: *In the task of sampling a collection of data for learning click prediction, if the sample size is limited, in order to minimize the distance between empirical loss and the expected loss, smaller distance between the empirical distribution and underlying distribution in terms of input distribution, i.e. $\eta$, indicates higher distance between the empirical distribution and underlying distribution in terms of conditional output distribution, i.e. $\gamma$, and vice versa.*

Previous studies usually rely on some judiciously chosen sampling practice, e.g. random sampling. This method is easy to ensure a low distance between the empirical distribution and underlying distribution in terms of input distribution, which, unfortunately, indicates that this method may cause a big problem in retaining the consistent conditional output distribution, i.e. CTR, between the sampled data and the real world. In the following of this section, we will provide a large scale data analysis to demonstrate that random sampling could give rise to a big difference between the CTRs computed based on sampled data and those computed based on the whole real data.

## 2.2 Data Settings

All of our data used in this work are collected from a commercial search engine. In this analysis, we first collect the whole data from the sponsored search during one week. Then, based on this whole data, we conduct random sampling to generate a sample data.

**Dataset 1 - Whole data**: In order to obtain the real CTR for each ⟨query, ad⟩ pair, we collect the entire set of queries with all the ads displayed under them from the sponsored search logs during one week in July, 2012. Then, we compute the CTR of each ⟨query, ad⟩ pair based on its corresponding impressions and clicks in this whole data. To ensure the reliability of obtained CTR, we filter those ⟨query, ad⟩ pairs with less than $\mathcal{N}$ impressions. According to the results of cross-validation, we set $\mathcal{N}$ as 50 in this paper. Finally, we collect about 184M queries and the total number of impressions of all associated ⟨query, ad⟩ pairs is about 3.5B.

**Dataset 2 - Random sampled data**: In order to investigate if random sampling can retain the real CTR in the sample data, we take a random sampling on the **Whole data** with ratio 0.5%. Thus, the total number of impressions under this sample data is 0.5% of that under the **Whole data**. Finally, we collect 2M queries and the total number of impressions of all associated ⟨query, ad⟩ pairs in this sample

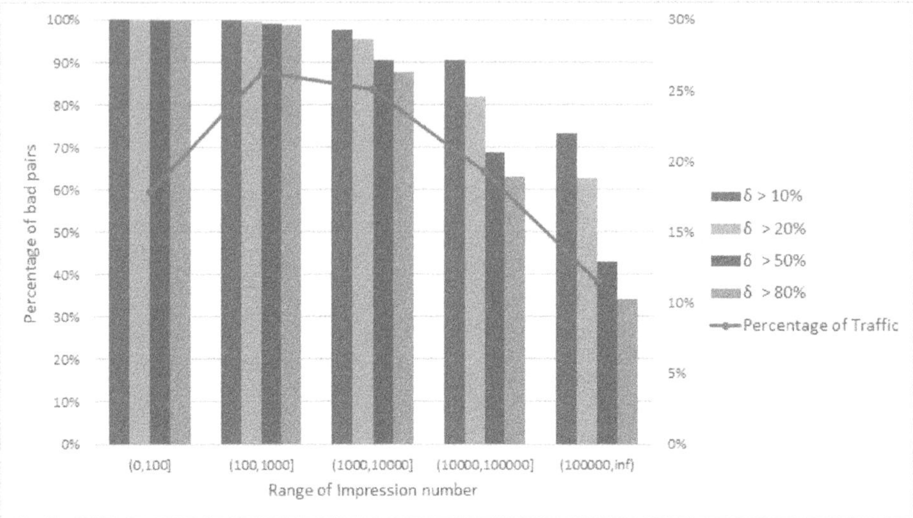


**Figure 1: Respective percentage of *bad* pairs over all unique ⟨query, ad⟩ pairs in the Random sample data, where the threshold of *bad* pairs is set with multiple values. All unique ⟨query, ad⟩ pairs are separated into several bucket according to their impressions. We also illustrate the respective percentage of traffic for each bucket, shown as the line in this figure.**

data is about 20.9M. We also compute CTR for each ⟨query, ad⟩ pair based on its corresponding impressions and clicks this sample data. In the next subsection, we will show that whether such CTRs are quite different with those computed based on the **Whole data**.

## 2.3 Inconsistency of CTR Caused by Random Sampling

In sponsored search, one of important characteristics is the extreme sparseness in terms of clicks, which makes click prediction in sponsored search be quite different with traditional machine learning process. Consequently, random data sampling may cause that the CTR of one ⟨query, ad⟩ pair computed based on randomly sampled data is quite different from that computed based on whole real world data, especially when the number of clicks on this pair is relatively very small. For example, assuming that one ⟨query, ad⟩ pair yields totally $100,000$ impressions in the **Whole data** and 10 of these impressions cause clicks. Thus, the CTR of this pair in the **Whole data** is 0.1%. However, after taking random sampling with ratio 0.1%, the CTR of this pair in the **Random sample data** could only be one of {0,, 1%, 2%, $\cdots$, 10% }, which cannot be consistent with the CTR in the **Whole data**.

To measure the CTR's changing for one one ⟨query, ad⟩ pair, we compute the relative difference:

$$\Delta_{\langle q_i, a_i \rangle} = \frac{|\mathrm{CTR}_i^{\mathrm{W}} - \mathrm{CTR}_i^{\mathrm{S}}|}{\mathrm{CTR}_i^{\mathrm{W}}}$$

where $\mathrm{CTR}_i^{\mathrm{W}}$ represents the CTR of $\langle q_i, a_i \rangle$ computed based on its impressions and clicks in the **Whole data**, and $\mathrm{CTR}_i^{\mathrm{S}}$ represents the CTR of $\langle q_i, a_i \rangle$ computed based on its impressions and clicks in the **Random sample data**. If such relative difference, $\Delta_{\langle q_i, a_i \rangle}$, is larger than a threshold, $\delta$, we call this pair a *bad* one caused by random sampling.

To investigate how random sampling will result in inconsistency of CTR, we conduct experiments to see how many *bad* pairs will be generated in the **Random sample data**. Note that the CTR of any ⟨query, ad⟩ pair, which has no click in the *Whole data*, will remain 0 in both **Whole data** and **Random sample data**. Accordingly, in this experiment, we filter out those ⟨query, ad⟩ pairs with no click in the **Whole data**. Figure 1 demonstrates the percentage of *bad* pairs over all unique ⟨query, ad⟩ pairs in the **Random sample data**. To examine the effects of varying number of impressions in the **Whole data** of different pairs, we separate all ⟨query, ad⟩ pairs into several buckets based on their impressions in the **Whole data** and compute the respective percentage of *bad* pairs. In addition, we compare the respective percentage of *bad* pairs against different settings of the threshold of the *bad* pair, i.e. $\delta$.

From this figure, we can find that, random sampling can result in a significant inconsistency of CTR for those ⟨query, ad⟩ pairs with relatively small impressions in the **Whole data**. For example, no matter how to set the threshold of the *bad* pair, i.e. $\delta$, the percentage of bad pairs reaches more than 95% for those pairs who have less than $1,000$ impressions in the **Whole data**. And, from the figure, we can find that all of these pairs comprise of about 45% of the whole traffic. For those ⟨query, ad⟩ pairs having more impressions, i.e. larger than $1,000$, the percentage of bad pairs declines with increasing number of impressions in the **Whole data**. Unfortunately, for those ⟨query, ad⟩ pairs with more than $100,000$ impressions, random sampling still generate a large portion of bad pairs even the threshold $\delta$ is set with a high value. For example, when setting the threshold $\delta$ as 50%, there are still more than 40% bad pairs in the **Random sample data** caused by random sampling.

As the predicted click probability is usually used to help rank ads in the sponsored search results, we conduct further experiments to examine if random sampling can retain the order of CTRs for ⟨query, ad⟩ pairs under the same query. Specifically, for one query $q_i$, we compute the respective CTR for each pair associated with this query in the **Whole data**, and rank all ads associated with this query based on their respective CTRs. Then, we compute another ranking of ads under the same query based on their respective CTRs obtained from the **Random sample data**. After that, for each query, we compare these two rankings to see whether they have overlaps among the top ranked ads. Figure 2 demonstrates the percentage of queries which have different top-$k$ rankings based on these two ranking results. From this figure, we can find that random sampling can result in a big difference in terms of the CTR orders under the same query.

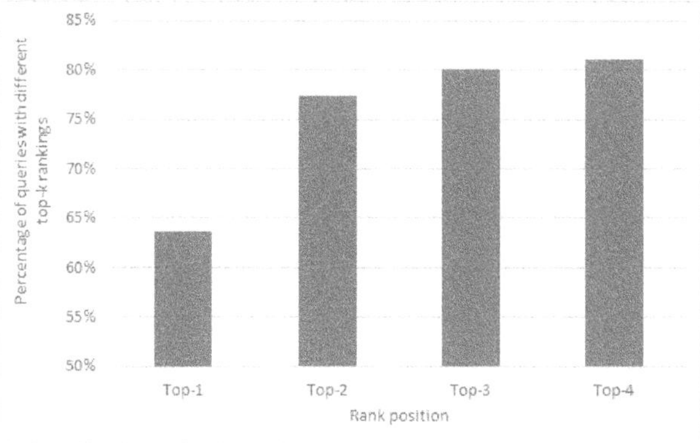


**Figure 2: Percentage of queries which have different top-$k$ rankings based on CTRs computed by the Whole data and the Random sample data, respectively.**

Based on all these studies, we can conclude that random sampling is likely to cause significant inconsistency of CTR for ⟨query, ad⟩ pairs, which implies a big influence on the learning objective for click prediction. Therefore, it is quite difficult to obtain an accurate click prediction model based on the training data generated via random sampling. To address this challenge, in the next section, we will formulate the sampling for click prediction as an optimization problem and further propose a new sampling algorithm which succeeds in balancing the difference in terms of input distribution and that in terms of conditional output distribution (i.e. CTR).

# 3. BALANCED SAMPLING FOR CLICK PREDICTION

As a general machine learning process, click prediction necessitates the need for sampling sponsored search data in order for training and updating the click prediction model in an effective and efficient way. However, as discussed in Section 2, judiciously chosen sampling method, especially random sampling, fails to address the *sampling dilemma*. Specifically, while random sampling can keep the similar input distribution between the whole data and the sampled data, it leads to inconsistency of the conditional output distribution, i.e. CTR, for click prediction. In this section, we will formulate this task as an optimization problem, the goal of which is to conduct data sampling with balancing the two aspects in the *sampling dilemma*, one of which is minimizing the distance between the whole data and the sampled data in terms of *input distribution*, while the other of which is minimizing the distance between the whole data and the sampled data in terms of *conditional output distribution* (i.e. CTR). Then, we propose a new balanced sampling algorithm which can achieve effective data sampling with addressing the two constraints in this problem.

## 3.1 Problem Statement

The general problem of data sampling for learning click prediction model in sponsored search can be formulated as follows.

First, we are given an entire collection of sponsored search logs during a certain period $(t_{\text{start}}, t_{end})$, which is defined as the *full set*.

Definition 1. **Full set:** *a full list of tuples,*

$$\mathcal{F} = \{\langle q_i, a_i, t_i, c_i\rangle | i = 1, 2, \cdots\}$$

*where $q, a$, and $t$ represent one user submitted query $q$ to the search engine and see a presented ad $a$ at time $t$ ($t \in (t_{\text{start}}, t_{end})$), and $c$ is set as 1 if the user click the ad $a$ or 0 otherwise.*

Based on this definition of *full set*, we can compute the *full relative traffic* and the *full CTR* for each $\langle q, a\rangle$ included in the *full set*.

Definition 2. **Full relative traffic:** *for each $\langle q, a\rangle$ included in the full set, assuming the whole list of its associated tuples in the full set is*

$$L^{\text{f}}_{\langle q,a\rangle} = \{\langle q, a, t_i, c_i\rangle | i = 1, 2, \cdots \wedge \langle q, a, t_i, c_i\rangle \in \mathcal{F}\}$$

*its full relative traffic is defined as*

$$\text{TF}^{\text{f}}_{\langle q,a\rangle} = \frac{|L^{\text{f}}_{\langle q,a\rangle}|}{|\mathcal{F}|}$$

Definition 3. **Full CTR:** *for each $\langle q, a\rangle$ included in the full set, assuming the whole list of its associated tuples in the full set is $L^{\text{f}}_{\langle q,a\rangle}$ defined as above, its full CTR is computed as*

$$\text{CTR}^{\text{f}}_{\langle q,a\rangle} = \frac{|\{\langle q, a, t_i, c_i\rangle | \langle q, a, t_i, c_i\rangle \in L^{\text{f}}_{\langle q,a\rangle} \wedge c_i = 1\}|}{|L^{\text{f}}_{\langle q,a\rangle}|}$$

Our goal for data sampling is to collect a subset of the *full set* with a certain sample ratio $\rho$, which is defined as the *sample set*.

Definition 4. **Sample set:** *a list of tuples which comprise of a subset of the full set,*

$$\mathcal{S} = \{\langle q_j, a_j, t_j, c_j\rangle | j = 1, 2, \cdots \wedge \langle q_j, a_j, t_j, c_j\rangle \in \mathcal{F}\}$$

*the sample ratio of which, $\rho$, is defined as $\rho = \frac{|\mathcal{S}|}{|\mathcal{F}|}$*

Based on this definition of *sample set*, we can compute the *sample relative traffic* and the *sample CTR* for each $\langle q, a\rangle$ included in the *sample set*.

Definition 5. **Sample relative traffic:** *for each $\langle q, a\rangle$ included in the full set, assuming the whole list of its associated tuples in the sample set is*

$$L^{\text{s}}_{\langle q,a\rangle} = \{\langle q, a, t_j, c_j\rangle | j = 1, 2, \cdots \wedge \langle q, a, t_j, c_j\rangle \in \mathcal{S}\}$$

*its sample relative traffic is defined as*

$$\text{TF}^{\text{s}}_{\langle q,a\rangle} = \frac{|L^{\text{s}}_{\langle q,a\rangle}|}{|\mathcal{S}|}$$

Definition 6. **Sample CTR:** *for each $\langle q, a\rangle$ included in the sample set, assuming the whole list of its associated tuples in the sample set is $L^{\text{s}}_{\langle q,a\rangle}$ defined as above, its sample CTR is computed as*

$$\text{CTR}^{\text{s}}_{\langle q,a\rangle} = \frac{|\{\langle q, a, t_j, c_j\rangle | \langle q, a, t_j, c_j\rangle \in L^{\text{s}}_{\langle q,a\rangle} \wedge c_j = 1\}|}{|L^{\text{s}}_{\langle q,a\rangle}|}$$

We now state our problem of more formally:

> **Problem:** (*Data sampling for learning click prediction model*) Given a *full set* $\mathcal{F}$ and a sample ratio $\rho$, generate a *sample set* $\mathcal{S}$ which yields $|\mathcal{S}| = \rho|\mathcal{F}|$ and can minimize both the aggregated difference between *full relative traffic* and *sample relative traffic* of each $\langle q, a\rangle$ and the aggregated difference between aggregated *full CTR* and *sample CTR* of each $\langle q, a\rangle$.

We can formalize this problem into an optimization problem with the objective:

$$\min_{\mathcal{S}\subset\mathcal{F}\wedge|\mathcal{S}|=\rho|\mathcal{F}|} \sum_{\langle q,a\rangle} |\mathrm{CTR}^{\mathrm{s}}_{\langle q,a\rangle} - \mathrm{CTR}^{\mathrm{f}}_{\langle q,a\rangle}| + \lambda|\mathrm{TF}^{\mathrm{s}}_{\langle q,a\rangle} - \mathrm{TF}^{\mathrm{f}}_{\langle q,a\rangle}| \tag{5}$$

where $|\mathrm{CTR}^{\mathrm{s}}_{\langle q,a\rangle} - \mathrm{CTR}^{\mathrm{f}}_{\langle q,a\rangle}|$ corresponds to the distance between the whole data and sampled data in terms of *conditional output distribution*, while $|\mathrm{TF}^{\mathrm{s}}_{\langle q,a\rangle} - \mathrm{TF}^{\mathrm{f}}_{\langle q,a\rangle}|$ corresponds to the distance between the whole data and sampled data in terms of *input distribution*, and $\lambda$ can be used to control this trade-off. This data sampling problem can be naturally viewed as a subset selection problem, which is typically NP-complete. Hence, in this paper, we propose a greedy balanced algorithm to address this problem.

## 3.2 Balanced Sampling Algorithm

Despite that there is one given sampling ratio for the whole sample set, we can greedily apply different sampling ratio to different $\langle q, a\rangle$ pairs, which is decided based on the corresponding CTR and number of impressions for each $\langle q, a\rangle$ pair.

Assuming that there are $N$ unique $\langle q, a\rangle$ pairs in the full set $\mathcal{F}$,

$$\{\langle q_1, a_1\rangle, \langle q_2, a_2\rangle, \cdots, \langle q_N, a_N\rangle\},$$

the *full CTRs* of them are respectively denoted as

$$\{\mathrm{CTR}^{\mathrm{f}}_1, \mathrm{CTR}^{\mathrm{f}}_2, \cdots, \mathrm{CTR}^{\mathrm{f}}_N\},$$

and the numbers of impressions for each pair are denoted as

$$\{\mathrm{Imp}^{\mathrm{f}}_1, \mathrm{Imp}^{\mathrm{f}}_2, \cdots, \mathrm{Imp}^{\mathrm{f}}_N\}.$$

In our new sampling algorithm, we will decide the respective number of impressions we target to sample and include in the sample set for each $\langle q, a\rangle$ pair, which are denoted as

$$\{\mu_1, \mu_2, \cdots, \mu_N\},$$

where, given a specific sampling ratio, $\rho$, the sum of the impressions we target to sample for each pair should be subject to $\sum_{i=1}^{N} \mu_i \leqslant \rho|\mathcal{F}|$. Then, we propose our balanced algorithm, as shown in Alg 1, to decide $\{\mu_1, \mu_2, \cdots, \mu_N\}$. After that, we could apply random sampling to each $\langle q_i, a_i\rangle$ to sample the associated tuples according to the sample ratio of $\frac{\mu_i}{\mathrm{Imp}^{\mathrm{f}}_i}$.

In this algorithm, $\alpha$ and $\beta$ are used together to trade-off the consistency between the input distribution and conditional output distribution. Specifically, if we set $\beta$ as a lower value, this algorithm requires more $\langle q, a\rangle$ pairs keep the consistent CTR, which indicates more emphasis on conditional output distribution. However, to satisfy the limited size of sample set, $\alpha$ has to be set with a higher value. On the other hand, if we set $\alpha$ as a lower value, which implies more emphasis on consistent input distribution, this algorithm requires us increase $\beta$ to satisfy the limited size of sample set. Therefore, $\alpha$ and $\beta$ collaboratively play the role of $\lambda$ in Eq. 5.

**Algorithm 1 Balanced Data Sampling Algorithm for Learning Click Prediction Model**

**Input:**
- $\mathcal{F}$: the full set with $N$ unique $\langle q, a\rangle$ pairs, i.e. $\{\langle q_1, a_1\rangle, \langle q_2, a_2\rangle, \cdots, \langle q_N, a_n\rangle\}$
- $\{\mathrm{CTR}^{\mathrm{f}}_1, \mathrm{CTR}^{\mathrm{f}}_2, \cdots, \mathrm{CTR}^{\mathrm{f}}_N\}$: the full CTRs of each $\langle q, a\rangle$ pair
- $\{\mathrm{Imp}^{\mathrm{f}}_1, \mathrm{Imp}^{\mathrm{f}}_2, \cdots, \mathrm{Imp}^{\mathrm{f}}_N\}$: the number of full impressions of each $\langle q, a\rangle$ pair
- $K = \rho|\mathcal{F}|$: the upper bound of the size of sample set.
- $\alpha$: the threshold for retaining input distribution.
- $\beta$: the threshold of the least precision of CTR, which is used for retaining conditional output distribution (i.e. CTR).

**Output:**
- $\{\mu_1, \mu_2, \cdots, \mu_N\}$: the number of impressions we target to sample and include in the sample set for each $\langle q, a\rangle$ pair

**Algorithms:**

1 Sort all the $\langle q, a\rangle$ pairs based on their full impression number in descending order.

2 To retain the full CTR, we should ensure that the sampled impression is large enough to include at least one click for each $\langle q_i, a_i\rangle$ pair. Thus, we compute the minimum of sampled impression, denoted as $\pi_i$, for each $\langle q_i, a_i\rangle$ pair as:

$$\pi_i = \begin{cases} \frac{1}{\mathrm{CTR}^{\mathrm{f}}_i}, & \text{if } \mathrm{CTR}^{\mathrm{f}}_i \geq \beta \\ 0, & \text{if } \mathrm{CTR}^{\mathrm{f}}_i < \beta \end{cases}$$

3 Initiate $\{\mu_1, \mu_2, \cdots, \mu_N\}$ as

$$\mu_i = \rho \cdot \mathrm{Imp}^{\mathrm{f}}_i$$

4 Scan the sorted list of all $\langle q, a\rangle$ pairs one by one, for each one (e.g $\langle q_i, a_i\rangle$):
- **if** $\mu_i > \pi_i$, $\mu_i$ has already met the condition and will not changed at this time
- **else**

  **for** $j = 1$ **to** $i - 1$ **:**

  **while**$(\frac{\mathrm{Imp}^{\mathrm{f}}_j}{\mathrm{Imp}^{\mathrm{f}}_{j+1}} - \frac{\mu_j}{\mu_{j+1}} < \alpha \wedge \mu_j > \pi_j \wedge \mu_i < \pi_i)$:

  $\mu_i = \mu_i + 1$

  $\mu_j = \mu_j - 1$

  **end while;**

  **if** $\mu_i > \pi_i$, **break;**

  **end for;**

The time complexity of this algorithm is $O(N^2)$ where $N$ is the number of data rows. But, most of the time, the algorithm is efficient and takes less than $O(N^2)$ because not all the $\langle q, a\rangle$ need to be adjusted.

# 4. CLICK PREDICTION MODELING

After sampling the training data, in this section, we will select a specific machine learning approach for click prediction modeling. As discussed above, given a query $q$ and an ad $a$, the problem of click prediction is to compute the probability of click $p(c|q, a)$. Therefore, the maximum entropy model [3] is well suited for this learning task since its strength in combining diverse forms of contextual information, and formulates the click probability for a ⟨query, ad⟩ pair as follows:

$$p(c|q,a) = \frac{1}{1+\exp(\sum_{j=1}^{d} \omega_j f_j(q,a))}$$

where $f_j(q, a)$ represents the $j$-th feature derived for ⟨query, ad⟩ pair $(q, a)$ and $\omega_j \in \mathbf{w}$ is the associated weight. Given the training set $\mathcal{D}_{\text{train}}$, the maximum entropy model learns the weight vector $\mathbf{w}$ by maximizing the likelihood of exponential models as:

$$\mathbf{w} = \max(\sum_{i=1}^{n} \log(p(c_i|q_i, a_i)) + \log(p(\mathbf{w})))$$

where the first part represents the likelihood function and the second part utilizes a Gaussian prior on the weight vector $\mathbf{w}$ to smooth the maximum entropy model. There are many approaches available in the literature [11] to solve this kind of optimization problems including iterative scaling and its variants, quasi-Newton algorithms, and conjugate gradient ascent. Given the large collection of samples and high dimensional feature space, we use a nonlinear conjugate gradient algorithm [12].

An accurate maximum entropy model relies greatly on the design of features. According to the state-of-the-art works in click prediction, there are majorly two kinds of features, which are relevance features and historical click features. In this work, we use some representative features according to previous work [4] [15]:

- For relevance features we employed edit distance of ad and query, edit distance of ad and bid keyword, cosine similarity between ad and query, the category matching between ad and query, etc.
- For historical features we employed history COEC (position normalized CTR) for ⟨query, ad⟩ pair, query, and ad, respectively, smoothed COEC according to query term, ad term, etc.

# 5. EXPERIMENTS

In this section, we first describe the settings of our experiments and then report the experimental results.

## 5.1 Experimental Settings

### 5.1.1 Data set

In our experiment, we would like to examine if our proposed balanced sampling algorithm can generate the training data which is more effective to learn the click prediction model with higher accuracy in sponsored search. We use the click through logs of a commercial search engine during a half month period in July 2012 as our experimental dataset. We divide this dataset into two parts, each of which contains the data of one week. Then, we use the first week's data as the full set. Note that, this full set is the **Whole data** we use for data analysis in Section 2.2. To learn the click prediction model, we will sample the training set from this full set. In our experiments, we first randomly sample query events from the original traffic as the baseline random sampled training set. Specifically, we randomly sample about 0.5% ad impressions from logs of the first week. Note that, this random sampled set is the **Random sampled data** we use for data analysis in Section 2.2. Then, we employ our proposed new balanced sampling algorithm to sample a new training set. Detailed statistics of these two training datasets can also be found in Table 1. After collecting training set, we use the second week's data to test the performance of the model. Table 1 also shows the detailed statistics of this test data set.

### 5.1.2 Compared Methods

As mentioned in Section 4, we employ maximum entropy modeling to training the click prediction model. In our experiments, we will use different sampling methods to obtain different training sets. Then, we will compare the performance of different click prediction models learned based on their respective training sets. Specifically, we compare the following click prediction models:

- **Random**: We use Random Sampling method to collect the training set and apply this data to learn the click prediction model.
- **Balanced**: We employ our proposed Balanced Sampling algorithm to obtain the training set and use this data to learn the click prediction model.

### 5.1.3 Parameters Setting

As discussed in Section 3.2, there are two parameters to set in our new Balanced Sampling algorithm, including the threshold for retaining the input distribution, i.e. $\alpha$, and the threshold for keeping the CTR precision, i.e. $\beta$. As introduced before, these two parameters are used to balance the trade-off between the consistence in terms of input distribution and that in terms of CTR. Therefore, before conducting the further evaluations, we run a cross-validation to find the best setting for these two parameters. According to the results of cross validation, we set the best parameter values as $\alpha = 0.001$ and $\beta = 0.005$. And, we will take more detailed discussions about the effects of different parameters settings in the experimental results.

### 5.1.4 Evaluation Metrics

In our work, the Maximum Entropy modeling is applied to predict click probability for every ad impression. We use recorded user actions, i.e. click or non-click, in the log data as labels. To evaluate the overall performance for the model, we employ average Relative Information Gain(RIG) [9] as the evaluation metric. The RIG is calculated as:

$$\text{RIG} = \frac{\text{CE} + \mathcal{H}(\tilde{p})}{\mathcal{H}(\tilde{p})}$$

where CE represents the empirical cross entropy and is computed as

$$\text{CE} = \frac{1}{N}\sum_i y_i \log \hat{p} + (1-y_i)\log(1-\hat{p})$$

where $N$ is the total number of ⟨query, ad⟩ pairs in the testing set, $y_i = 1$ if the $i$-th pair is labeled as *click* otherwise $y_i = 0$, $\hat{p}$ denotes the probability of click predicted by the model; and, $\mathcal{H}(\tilde{p})$ represents the entropy of CTR, which is calculated as

$$\mathcal{H}(\tilde{p}) = -(\tilde{p}\log\tilde{p} + (1-\tilde{p})\log(1-\tilde{p}))$$

where $\tilde{p}$ denotes the total CTR and is computed as $\tilde{p} = \frac{1}{N}\sum_i y_i$. Since $\mathcal{H}(\tilde{p})$ is the maximally attainable value of information gain, i.e. $\text{CE} + \mathcal{H}(\tilde{p})$, it quantifies the information gain relative to the source entropy.

Table 1: Statistics of the datasets.

| | Total impressions | # of unique ad | # of unique query | # of unique $\langle q, a \rangle$ pair |
|---|---|---|---|---|
| All 1st week data | 3.51B | 39.14M | 183.9M | 1.20B |
| All 2nd week data | 3.32B | 38.79M | 176.1M | 1.14B |
| Random sampled set | 20.9M | 0.23M | 1.04M | 10.8M |
| Balanced sampled set | 20.8M | 0.21M | 0.68M | 8.3M |

## 5.2 Experimental Results

In the following of this section, we will present several large-scale experiments. These experiments are used to demonstrate that (1) our new Balanced Sampling method succeeds in balancing the consistent between the sampled data and the whole data in terms of both input distribution and conditional output distribution (i.e CTR); (2) the accuracy of click prediction in sponsored search can be significantly improved by using the new Balanced Sampling method to generate the training set; (3) the new Balanced Sampling method can improve the click prediction model's robustness to the limited sampling ratio.

### *5.2.1 Consistency of CTR*

As discussed in Section 2.3, one of the most important problem caused by random sampling is the inconsistency between the whole data and the sampled data in terms of CTR. We first perform experiments to examine whether our new Balanced Sampling algorithm can address this problem. In particular, we use the same **Whole data** as described in Section 2.2, based on which we apply our new Balanced Sampling algorithm to obtain a new sample data with the same sampling ratio 0.5%. Thus, this new sample data, denoted as **New sample data**, yields the similar total impressions compared with the old **Random sample data** described in Section 2.2.

Similar to the analysis in Section 2.3, we investigate how many *bad* pairs will be generated in the **New sample data**. Figure 3 demonstrates the percentage of *bad* pairs over all unique ⟨query, ad⟩ pairs in the **New sample data**. Similar to our previous analysis, we separate all ⟨query, ad⟩ pairs into several buckets based on their impressions in the **Whole data** and compute the respective percentage of *bad* pairs. In addition, we compare the respective percentage of bad pairs against different settings of the threshold, i.e. $\delta$.

Based on the comparison between Figure 3 and Figure 1, we can find that our new sampling method can significantly alleviate the inconsistency between whole data and sample data in terms of CTR. In particular, despite of various settings of $\delta$, there is nearly zero percentage of *bad* ones for those ⟨query, ad⟩ pairs who have less than $1,000$ impressions or more than $100,000$ impressions in the **Whole data**. And, even for those pairs yielding impressions between $1,000$ and $100,000$ in the **Whole data**, there is a substantial reduction in the percentage of *bad* ones. For example, if we pay attention to ⟨query, ad⟩ pairs having impressions between $10,000$ and $100,000$, when setting $\delta$ as 50%, the percentage of *bad* pairs caused by our new sampling algorithm is only about 5%, which is a more than ten times reduction compared with about 68% of *bad* pairs caused by old random sampling. Note that, if $\delta$ is set as 10%, the percentage of *bad* pairs can still reach around 20% to 40% for those pairs having impressions between $1,000$ and $100,000$ in the **Whole data**. It indicates that our new sampling algorithm sacrifices a little consistency in terms of CTR to retain the consistency in terms of input distribution over all ⟨query, ad⟩ pairs.

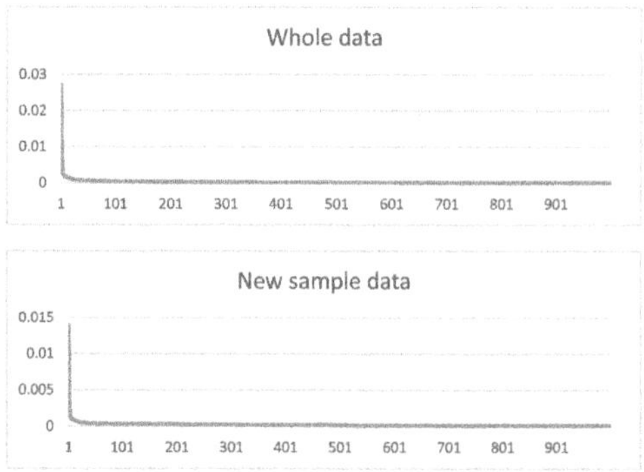


**Figure 4: Relative impressions of the top 1000 pairs in both Whole data and New sample data.**

### *5.2.2 Consistency of Input Distribution*

Besides the consistency of CTR, we conduct further experiment to examine whether our new sampling algorithm can retain the consistent input distribution between the whole data and the sampled data. In particular, we first rank all ⟨query, ad⟩ pairs in the descending order based on their impressions in the **Whole data**. Figure 4 illustrates the relative impressions of the top 1000 pairs. Similarly, we rank all ⟨query, ad⟩ pairs in the descending order based on their impressions in the **New sample data** and plot top 1000 pairs' relative impressions in Figure 4. Since our algorithm has constrained that the relative difference between two consecutive pairs should be less than a threshold, i.e. $\frac{\text{Imp}^{\text{f}}_j}{\text{Imp}^{\text{f}}_{j+1}} - \frac{\mu_j}{\mu_{j+1}} < \alpha$, these two figures have the same set of 1000 pairs which also yield the same ordering in both figures. From these two figures, we can observe that the new sample data have the similar input data distribution as the whole data. We also demonstrate the relative data size of several top pairs in both **Whole data** and **New sample data** in Table 2. From this table, we can observe that our new sampling algorithm sacrifices the consistency in terms of input data distribution on those ⟨query, ad⟩ pairs with very high impressions, but, fortunately, their CTRs in the new sample data will be remained consistent with that in the whole data since there are still enough impressions of them in the new sample data. On the other hand, we can also find that, more than 99% of ⟨query, ad⟩ pairs, e.g. those ranked beyond 200, still yield the consistent input data distribution.

### *5.2.3 Performance of Click Prediction*

After using Random Sampling method and our proposed Balanced Sampling algorithm to collect the training sets, respectively, we compare the performance of the two click prediction models trained by these two data sets separately. Table 3 demonstrates the RIG of **Balanced** model and **Random** model. From this table, we can find that our new Balanced Sampling algorithm can lead to more accurate click prediction model over the baseline random sampling. In particular, in terms of RIG, there is about 5.8% relative

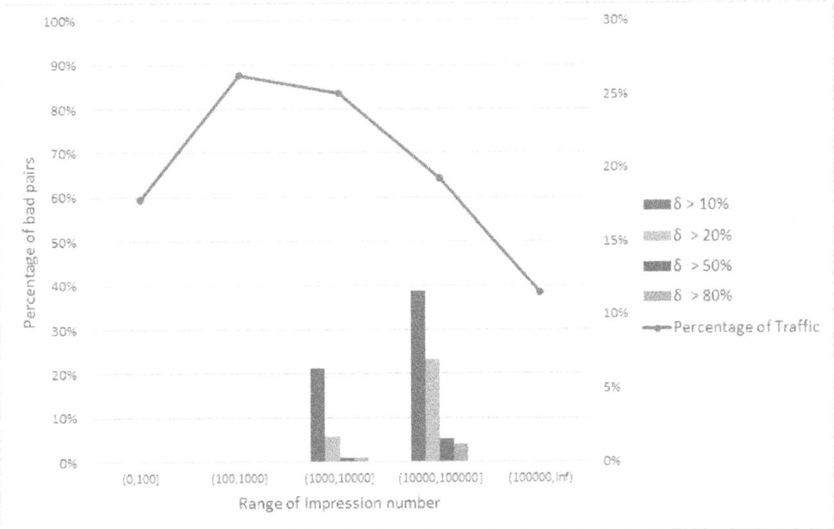


**Figure 3: Respective percentage of *bad* pairs over all unique ⟨query, ad⟩ pairs in the New sample data, where the threshold of *bad* pairs is set with multiple values. All unique ⟨query, ad⟩ pairs are separated into several bucket according to their impressions. We also illustrate the respective percentage of traffic for each bucket, shown as the line in this figure.**

**Table 2: Relative traffic size of the top ⟨query, ad⟩ pairs in both whole data and new sample data.**

| ⟨query, ad⟩ index | Whole data | New sample data |
|---|---|---|
| 1 | 2.72% | 1.40% |
| 2 | 0.70% | 0.36% |
| 3 | 0.59% | 0.31% |
| 4 | 0.27% | 0.15% |
| 5 | 0.22% | 0.12% |
| ... | ... | ... |
| 101 | 0.0407% | 0.0313% |
| 102 | 0.0406% | 0.0313% |
| 103 | 0.0404% | 0.0309% |
| 104 | 0.0403% | 0.0309% |
| 105 | 0.0403% | 0.0309% |
| ... | ... | ... |
| 201 | 0.0278% | 0.0276% |
| 202 | 0.0276% | 0.0275% |
| 203 | 0.0276% | 0.0275% |
| 204 | 0.0275% | 0.0275% |
| 205 | 0.0275% | 0.0275% |
| ... | ... | ... |

improvement when using the Balanced Sample algorithm to obtain training set rather than the Random Sampling . Actually, in real sponsor search system, increasing 1% on

**Table 3: Performance of click prediction in terms of RIG by using Balanced Sampling compared with using Random Sampling.**

| Sampling Method | RIG | Relative Gain |
|---|---|---|
| Balanced | 0.1516 | +5.8% |
| Random | 0.1434 | - |

the click prediction accuracy is already a big improvement. According to [7], 1% accuracy improvement will drive additional hundreds of million revenue per month. In this sense, 5.8% relative improvement is really significant in click prediction.

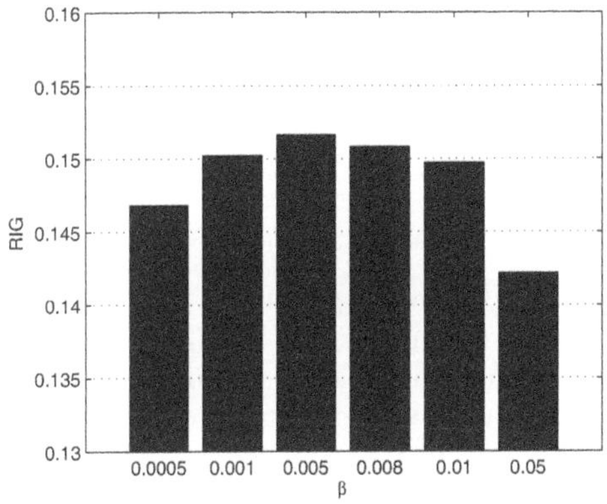


**Figure 5: RIG of the Balanced model against different $\beta$ during sampling.**

### 5.2.4 *Effects of Trade-off Between CTR and Traffic Distribution*

In this experiment, we examine the effects of different settings of the parameter $\beta$, i.e. the least precision of CTR in Balanced Sampling, on the final performance of click prediction. Specifically, we conduct a comparison study by varying the value of $\beta$. Note that, under each setting of $\beta$, we are able to find a best value for the threshold of keeping input distribution, i.e. $\alpha$, to optimize the performance of click prediction. Due to the limited size of sample set, the best setting of $\alpha$ will decreases with increasing value of $\beta$, and vice versa.

Figure 5 reports the performance of click prediction by using the **Balanced** model with varying $\beta$ during sampling. From this figure, we can find that, it is unable to achieve good performance of click prediction either when $\beta$ reaches a high value or when $\beta$ is set as a very low one. The higher $\beta$ implies that we pay more attention to keep the consistency of CTR even for those ⟨query, ad⟩ pairs without enough impressions. Therefore, it is necessary to distribute more sampling

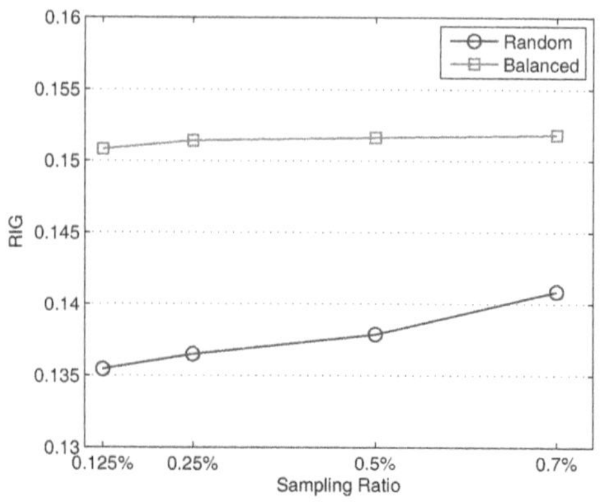


**Figure 6: RIG of the Balanced model compared with the Random model against different sampling ratio.**

quotes from high impressions ⟨query, ad⟩ pairs to those with low impressions, which will lead to a big difference in terms of input distribution between the whole data and the sample data. On the other hand, small $\beta$ indicates that we can obtain the sample data with consistent input distribution compared to the whole data. However, it will give rise to more ⟨query, ad⟩ pairs with inconsistent CTR between the whole data and the sample data. According to our definition in Eq. 5, higher $\beta$ leads to smaller $\sum_{\langle q,a\rangle} |\mathrm{CTR}^{s}_{\langle q,a\rangle} - \mathrm{CTR}^{f}_{\langle q,a\rangle}|$ but higher $\sum_{\langle q,a\rangle} |\mathrm{TF}^{s}_{\langle q,a\rangle} - \mathrm{TF}^{f}_{\langle q,a\rangle}|$, and vice versa. Therefore, the setting of the parameters $\beta$ and $\alpha$ implies our tradeoff between these two factors in sampling dilemma.

### 5.2.5 *Effects of Sampling Ratio*

We now explore the influence of the sampling ratio on the effectiveness of the sampled data. Figure 6 demonstrates the RIG of the **Balanced** model compared with the **Random** model against different sampling ratio $\rho$. Under each sampling ratio, we leverage cross validation to find the best parameters setting of **Balanced** model. From this figure, we can see that RIG of **Random** model decreases drastically with descending sampling ratio while **Balanced** model is more robust to the limited sampling ratio, which also indicates that our new sampling algorithm is more robust to the sparseness of clicks in building click prediction model.

Note that, although increasing sampling ratio can lead to better performance of **Random** model, it will give rise to more time complexity for model training. To achieve the same accuracy of click prediction, our new sampling algorithm can leverage smaller set of data with much fewer training time compared to random sampling.

## 6. CONCLUSION AND FUTURE WORK

In this paper, we point out that data sampling is an essentially important challenge in building click prediction model in sponsored search. Through a thorough theoretical and data analysis, we find that, due to the sparseness of clicks in sponsored search, there exists a sampling dilemma between retaining similar input distribution and consistent conditional output distribution, and the straightforward random sampling method fails to address this problem. Accordingly, we propose a new sampling algorithm to balance these two aspects. Large scale evaluations on the click-through logs from a commercial search engine demonstrate that the accuracy of click prediction can be improved significantly by using the training data obtained based on this new sampling approach.

According to our findings in this paper, input distribution and conditional output distribution comprise of a dilemma for achieving effective click prediction model. In this paper, we make an effort to address this dilemma from the perspective of data sampling. In future, we plan to conduct more investigation of this dilemma from the other perspectives, such as feature engineering and modeling, and take further attempts to address it through these new perspectives.

## 7. REFERENCES


[1] V. Abhishek and K. Hosanagar. Keyword generation for search engine advertising using semantic similarity between terms. In *Proc. of EC*, 2007.

[2] J. Attenberg, S. Pandey, and T. Suel. Modeling and predicting user behavior in sponsored search. In *Proc. of KDD*, 2009.

[3] A. Berger and V. Pietra. A maximum entropy approach to natural language processing. In *Computational Linguistics*, 1996.

[4] H. Cheng and E. Cantu-Paz. Personalized click prediction in sponsored search. In *Proc. of WSDM*, 2010.

[5] C. Clarke, E. Agichtein, S. Dumais, and R. White. The influence of caption features oh clickthrough patterns in web search. In *Proc. of SIGIR*, 2007.

[6] K. Dembczynski, W. Kotlowski, and D. Weiss. Predicting ads click-through rate with decision rules. In *Workshop on Targeting and Ranking in Online Advertising*, 2008.

[7] B. Edelman, M. Ostrovsky, and M. Schwarz. Internet adverstising and the generalized second-price auction: selling billions of dollars worth of keywords. In *The American Economic Review*, 2007.

[8] D. Fain and J. Pedersen. Sponsored search: a brief history. In *Proc. of 2nd Workshop on Sponsored Search Auctions*, 2006.

[9] T. Graepel, J. Candela, T. Borchert, and R. Herbrich. Web-scale bayesian click-through rate prediction for sponsored search advertising in microsoft's bing search engine. In *Proc. of ICML*, 2010.

[10] B. Jansen and T. Mullen. Sponsored search: an overview of the concept, history, and technology. In *International Journal of Electric Business*, 2008.

[11] T. P. Minka. A comparison of numerical optimizers for logistic regression. In *Technical report, Microsoft*, 2003.

[12] A. Mordecai. *Nonlinear Programming: Analysis and Methods*.

[13] F. Radlinski, A. Broder, P. Ciccolo, E. Gabrilovich, V. Josifovski, and L. Riedel. Optimizing relevance and revenue in ad search: a query substitution approach. In *Proc. of SIGIR*, 2008.

[14] H. Raghavan and R. Iyer. Evaluating vector-space and probabilistic models for query to ad matching. In *Proc. of SIGIR Workshop on Information Retrieval for Advertising*, 2008.

[15] M. Richardson, E. Dominowska, and R. Ragno. Predicting clicks: estimating the click-through rate for new ads. In *Proc. of WWW*, 2007.

[16] B. Shaparenko, O. Cetin, and R. Iyer. Data-driven text features for sponsored search click prediction. In *Proc. of ADKDD*, 2009.

[17] C. Xiong, T. Wang, W. Ding, Y. Shen, and T.-Y. Liu. Relational click prediction for sponsored search. In *Proc. of WSDM*, 2012.

[18] W. Xu, E. Manavoglu, and E. Cantu-Paz. Temporal click model for sponsored search. In *Proc. of SIGIR*, 2010.

[19] W. Zhang, X. He, B. Rey, and R. Jones. Query rewriting using active learning for sponsored search. In *Proc. of SIGIR*, 2007.

# Exploiting Contextual Factors for Click Modeling in Sponsored Search

Dawei Yin[†] * Shike Mei[⊣] * Bin Cao[S] Jian-Tao Sun[S] Brian D. Davison[†]
[†]Dept. of Computer Science and Engineering, Lehigh University, Bethlehem, PA, USA
[⊣]Dept. of Computer Science, University of Wisconsin-Madison, Madison, WI, USA
[S]Microsoft Research Asia, Beijing, China
[†]{day207, davison}@cse.lehigh.edu [⊣]mei@cs.wisc.edu [S]{bincao, jtsun}@microsoft.com

## ABSTRACT

Sponsored search is the primary business for today's commercial search engines. Accurate prediction of the Click-Through Rate (CTR) for ads is key to displaying relevant ads to users. In this paper, we systematically study the two kinds of contextual factors influencing the CTR: 1) In micro factors, we focus on the factors for mainline ads, including ad depth, query diversity, ad interaction. 2) In macro factors, we try to understand the correlations of clicks between organic search and sponsored search. Based on this data analysis, we propose novel click models which harvest these new explored factors. To the best of our knowledge, this is the first paper to examine and model the effects of the above contextual factors in sponsored search. Extensive experiments on large-scale real-world datasets show that by incorporating these contextual factors, our novel click models can outperform state-of-the-art methods.

**Categories and Subject Descriptors:** H.3.3 [**Information Storage and Retrieval**]: Information Search and Retrieval;

**Keywords:** CTR prediction, Click Through Rate, Ad CTR prediction, Sponsored search, Click model

## 1. INTRODUCTION

Sponsored search is the primary business for today's commercial search engines. Pay-per-click (PPC) is an advertising model that has been adopted by the sponsored search markets. Under the PPC model, advertisers are charged when their advertisements are clicked by search engine users. More clicks bring more revenue to search engine companies [6]. However, since showing too many ads on search result pages may hurt the user experience, search engine companies have to be conservative in the number of ads shown and try to display those that earn the most money which is a function of click-through rate (e.g., bid×CTR). Therefore, estimating the click-through rate of a search ad is an important problem for commercial search engines.

To better understand the challenges and difficulties of estimating click-through rate in sponsored search, examine the results of the search query "iPad deal" in Figure 1. We see that when a user issues a query, both a list of web pages (organic search) and two lists of ads (sponsored search) are displayed. Clearly, to estimate the click-through rate of a target ad, there are many factors to explore. Focusing on the mainline ads (top ads), we have the following the micro factors: ad depth (the total number of the ads displayed), the interaction between the target ad and query, and the interaction between the target and the adjacent ads. For macro factors, there may be interactive influences between sponsored search and organic search results [13].

As previous studies have shown, user clicks contain various biases [22, 8, 17, 12], which is both true in organic search and sponsored search [39]. But unlike organic search, sponsored search has additional biases and characteristics. For example, many people tend to skip ads and they are reluctant to click ads even if they are related to the query. Previous Cascade Click Models [12] assume that the top position is certainly examined by user ($P(E_1) = 1$) and is thus not suitable for modeling user click behavior in sponsored search. Intuitively, the probability of a user examining the sponsored search results is related to two factors: the depth of the ads (the number of ads displayed) and the commercial intent of a query. For the depth of the ads, the more ads that are shown at the same time, the larger the ad area is, the more attention from users is attracted. However, the search engine usually should not simply show too many ads due to the poor user experience. For the second feature, we notice that for some queries with a high commercial intent, ads usually are more likely to be interesting to users. This indicates that the examination probability is likely to be query dependent. The effects of both factors on examination and click-through rate are still not clear and have not been systematically investigated. Another key factor is interactive influence between the target ad and its context (e.g., query and adjacent ads). Previous research into mutual influence between similar ads [33] shows that there exists a mutually exclusive relationship between similar ads. However, in general, the mutual relationship between ads is not necessarily exclusive and negative, but could also be positive [34]. Unfortunately, the relational click model [33] fails to model positive effects between the ads. Xu et al. [34] study the cases of the relationship between two ads displayed together, but the case of more ads (e.g., 3 or 4 ads) is still unknown. No previous research has investigated the interaction between the target ad and its context, including both query and adjacent ads.

Beyond the factors within ads, the relationship between organic search and sponsored search is also a major factor influencing CTR and yet has not been systematically explored. Statistical analysis shows that about 80% of clicks go to organic search while approx-

*Equal contribution


*WSDM'14*, February 24–28, 2014, New York, New York, USA.
Copyright 2014 ACM 978-1-4503-2351-2/14/02 ...$15.00.
http://dx.doi.org/10.1145/2556195.2556237 .

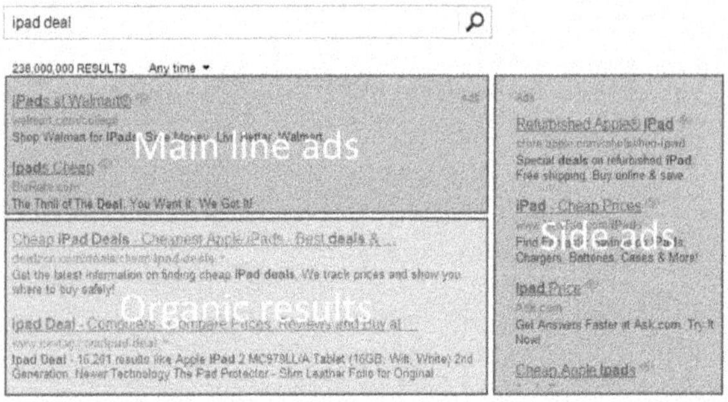


**Figure 1: Example: The returned results for a query include ads and search results. The ads can be displayed on the left side (mainline-ads) as well as the right side (side-ads)**

imately 5% go to ads [9], which is an order of magnitude smaller.[1] Moreover, the clicks also follow a power law distribution with respect to queries and ads. That is to say, most queries and ads fall into the "long tail" region and thus suffer from a limited number of user clicks. The sparsity problem and the long tail distribution introduce intrinsic difficulties to obtaining accurate CTR prediction results. Previous studies tried to solve the sparsity problem by exploring the rich features of ads, queries, and their relationships [18, 14, 33]. The hierarchical information on ads is leveraged and collaborative filtering techniques are utilized to smooth the model [27]. However, most current CTR prediction models are still limited by using the data within the ad domain. However, we have observed that exclusively depending on the ad domain is not ideal since most users seldom click on ads. Also, the information reflected by user behavior in organic search results is relatively richer and can potentially help ad click prediction. This phenomenon has also been observed in a recent study in [13], which shows there is a competitive relationship between search and ads in navigational queries. However, the question of how to leverage user behavior in organic search to address the sparsity problem in CTR prediction is still an under-explored research problem.

In this paper, we focus on analyzing mainline ads and systematically study the contextual factors which have not been well explored. We start with data analysis to understand the user clicks in sponsored search. For micro factors, we first investigate a number of contextual factors including ad depth, query diversity, ad interaction. Based on our analysis, we incorporate these factors into a novel click model. Experimental results show that the model with these new contextual factors can outperform three state-of-the-art methods. We then perform data analysis to understand the click correlations between organic search and ads (i.e., the macro factors), which illustrates the possibility of transferring the knowledge from the rich data in organic search to the ad CTR prediction problem. Our method jointly models user responses to sponsored ads and organic search results. The knowledge contained in the organic search log is utilized and transferred to the ad domain. We further discovered that the correlations between clicks in ads and organic search are query-dependent. To the best of our knowledge, this is the first paper to examine the effects of the above contextual factors in sponsored search together.

## 2. RELATED WORK

There are two major assumptions in click models: the Examination Hypothesis and the Cascade Model. The examination hypothesis assumes that if a displayed URL is clicked, it must be both examined and relevant [30, 37, 8, 12, 17, 26, 25, 32]. They have been compared by O'Chapelle [8] and experimentally found to be outperformed by the cascade model [12], which assumes that the user views search results from top to bottom and decides whether to click each url. Once a click is issued, documents below the clicked result are not examined regardless of the position. Then the dependent click model [20] generalizes the cascade model to allow multiple clicks within a single session. The click chain model [19] and dynamic Bayesian network [8] (which is inferred through Infer.NET [28]) provide a further generalization by allowing the user to abandon examination of more results. The general click model [39] treats all relevance and examination effects in the model as random variables. In addition to the above methods, there have been several click models following the above two assumptions but apply them in different contexts, such as the task centric click model [38], and the position normalized click model [10]. However, the above methods are mainly designed for understanding user click behavior in organic search. They fail to explore the specific properties in sponsored search as discussed earlier.

Recently, Xu et al. investigated relational click behavior [34], but their method can only be applied in cases with two ads. They fail to model the more general cases (e.g., 3, 4 or more ads) or handle new ads and queries. Xiong et al. [33] showed the mutually exclusive influence between similar ads, but their model fails to include positive effects between the ads. Also, they do not take examination bias into account. Additionally, there has been some research that addresses the relationship between organic search and sponsored advertising [35, 13]. However, Danescu-Niculescu-Mizil et al. [13] only considered the global correlation between clicks in search and advertising. Yang and Ghose [35] only consider this problem on a very restricted set of ads.

Generally speaking, previous studies [15, 18, 1, 14, 30, 29, 37, 11] mainly focus on building a linear model based on features extracted from a query and its ads. On the other hand, the ad CTR prediction problem can be also formulated as a recommendation problem and collaborative filtering (CF) techniques can be applied [27]. As shown in several recent competitions (e.g., the Netflix Prize and KDDCUP 2011 , collaborative filtering (CF) techniques, especially matrix factorization models, are very effective for recommendation problems [24, 4, 16]. In contrast to general recommendation tasks such as movie or music recommendations, the data of ad CTR prediction is far more sparse. Menon et al. [27] proposed using a matrix factorization model for ad CTR prediction and achieved state-of-the-art performance. However, we argue that, even with the help of auxiliary information, the ad CTR prediction problem still cannot be well-solved due to the limited number of user clicks we obtain from users. By incorporating other related domains into the model, we can exploit the inherent relationships across domains and help either or both domains.

Recently, Ashkan et al. [3, 2] conduct a preliminary study on the factors for click analysis in sponsored search: in [2], they study query commercial intent effects in sponsored search; in [3], they introduce query-bias into the click model. However, effects of other contextual factors still remain unknown and have not been modeled effectively, such as ad depth, interactive influence between ads and correlations between organic search and sponsored search. In this paper, we will focus on analyzing and modelling these factors.

## 3. MICRO FACTORS ANALYSIS

In this section, we verify our intuitions and conjectures for mainline ads in sponsored search. We collected one month of data from a commercial search engine. In total, there are 127,230,609 query

[1]The summation is not 1 because clicks could also go to other links such as query suggestions.

**Table 1: Average ad CTR at different positions and depths.**

| | pos. 1 | pos. 2 | pos. 3 | pos. 4 | Depth Avg. |
|---|---|---|---|---|---|
| depth 1 | 0.1298 | | | | 0.1298 |
| depth 2 | 0.1568 | 0.0450 | | | 0.1009 |
| depth 3 | 0.2158 | 0.0511 | 0.0306 | | 0.0992 |
| depth 4 | 0.2479 | 0.0711 | 0.0430 | 0.0341 | 0.0990 |
| Pos. Avg. | 0.1586 | 0.0547 | 0.0382 | 0.0341 | |

sessions, where a session consists of an input query, a list of sponsored search results and a list of clicked positions with time stamps.

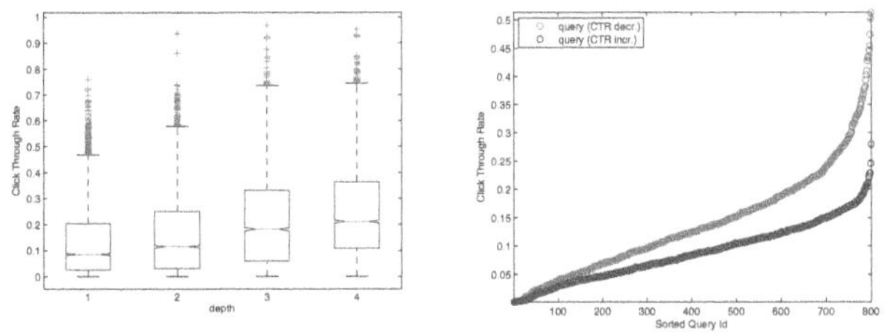

(a) CTR on position 1 as a function of depth (b) Depth changed from 1 to 3

**Figure 2: Representative analyses**

## 3.1 Depth Analysis

We first try to answer the following question: is ad CTR related to the number of ads displayed? Table 1 shows the average CTR at different positions and depth of mainline ad block. From the bottom line, we can see that the relationship between CTR and position is consistent with previous studies [30, 12]. Ads in the top positions usually receive higher CTR. We can also make some interesting observations about the relationship between CTR and depth: the CTR at the same position increases along with the depth. That is, as Figure 2(a) shows, the CTR of position 1 and depth 4 is significantly larger than the CTR of position 1 and depth 3, and CTR of position 1 and depth 3 is also larger than the CTR of position 1 and depth 2, etc. And these patterns also exist for position 2 and position 3.

We conjecture that these observations, shown in Table 1 and Figure 2(a), may be the result of four factors: first, greater ad depth typically means a larger ad area, which attracts more user attention. Therefore, ads in a larger ad area have a higher probability of user examination and higher CTRs should be expected. Second, the probability of user examining higher position might be greater than the lower position. Third, after a user examines all the ads, that user tends to click on the most relevant one. More relevant ads absorb more user clicks. The bottom ads actually play a supporting role, which has positive effects on the top ads. Finally, larger depth may imply higher commercial intent of query and higher relevance of the ads in the top position. To verify the conjectures, in Section 4, we incorporate these factors into the click model and the experiments in Section 5 show their contributions on CTR prediction.

We also notice that the average CTR decreases as the depth increases (from the right column of Table 1). This indicates that more ads being displayed may dilute the CTR of specific ads. However, note that the total click yield (the CTR summation of all ads for a given depth) becomes larger: for instance, the click yield of depth 4 is $0.099 \times 4$, which is much larger than depth 1.

## 3.2 Query Analysis

Query commercial intent has been well explored elsewhere [3, 2]. Here we conduct some experiments which [3, 2] does not cover.

In Section 3.1, we considered the effect of depth on click through rate: From Table 1, the average CTR over all positions (also averaged over ads and queries) slightly decreases when the depth increases. If we consider micro factors on queries, this may not be always true. For example, for some queries, the average CTR of the larger depth is greater than of the shorter depth. To find the properties of these queries, here we treat the average CTR of the query as the commercial intent of the query (higher average CTR means higher commercial intent), and investigate the relationship between the depth and the query's commercial intent. In our experiments, we change the depth from 1 to 3, and collected queries that achieve higher CTRs and queries that achieve lower CTRs. In Figure 2(b), we plot the queries whose average CTRs increase in blue and the queries whose average CTRs decrease in red. We see that queries with an increasing CTR have lower commercial intent while queries with a decreasing CTR have higher commercial intent. We perform a two sample t-test on the two groups of CTRs, and the $p$-value is 3.4710e-43 which is highly significant. This indicates that for queries with higher commercial intent, a single ad has a higher probability of matching user intent, and the user will more likely click this ad. However, when we show more ads, the average CTR decreases. This is consistent with the analysis by Xiong et al. [33]. Similar ads shown together will have exclusive effects and the CTR can be diluted by adjacent ads. On the other hand, for queries with lower commercial intent, if we show more ads at the same time, we achieve higher average CTRs. We conjecture that for these queries, the effects across ads are positive rather than exclusive or negative. In [33], the authors neglect to consider and model the positive cases.

**Table 2: CTRs of ads appearing in different depths**

| No. of ads | depth 1 | depth 2 | depth 3 | depth 4 |
|---|---|---|---|---|
| 588,619 | 0.0679 | 0.0736 | 0.0895 | 0.1161 |

## 3.3 Ad Analysis

In this section, we analyze the CTR from the perspective of ads. For ads that appear at different depths, we calculate their average CTR at different depths (dropping the ads that only appear in one depth). Table 2 shows that in our data sets, there are 588,619 ads that appear in at least two different depths. As the depth increases, the CTR (averaged over queries) also grows. This observation is consistent with the results in Section 3.1. We then further investigate the averaged CTR changes in specific positions and depths for these ads. The results are shown in Table 3. Take the first line as an example. There are 464,633 ads that appear at both depth 1 and depth 2. For these ads, if we show them alone, the click through rate was 0.0589. When they are shown at depth 2, their CTRs are 0.0676 and 0.0469 at position 1 and position 2, respectively. Similarly, the results of changing the depth from 1 to 3 and 4 are also shown. We can see that if the ad is in position 1, it achieves a higher CTR than when shown alone, but for position 2 and 3, a lower CTR occurs on these ads. However, we also notice that when the depth changes from 1 to 4, the ad CTR of all four positions at depth 4 are greater than the CTR at depth 1, even for the bottom position.

Next, to find ads with mutual influences, we perform a similarity analysis for ads that are shown together. Figure 3 presents the results. The similarity is calculated the same as Xiong et al. [33]. The X-axis indicates the similarity buckets. The Y-axis measures the difference $CTR_{sim} - CTR_{avg}$. In this box plot, the results are similar to [33]. As the similarity becomes higher, it shows negative effects. However, we also notice that for the majority of cases (similarity between 0 and 0.4), this negative effect is almost trivial. The median shows that the positive influence was also in half of the cases. We cannot only consider the exclusive influence between the targeted ad and the adjacent ads, even for highly similar ads. In

Table 3: CTRs of ads appearing in multiple positions

| Depth | No. ads | shown alone | pos 1 | pos 2 | pos 3 | pos 4 |
|---|---|---|---|---|---|---|
| 1→2 | 464,633 | 0.0589 | 0.0676 | 0.0469 | | |
| 1→3 | 117,625 | 0.0609 | 0.0862 | 0.0558 | 0.0441 | |
| 1→4 | 80,198 | 0.0547 | 0.1056 | 0.0778 | 0.0628 | 0.0555 |

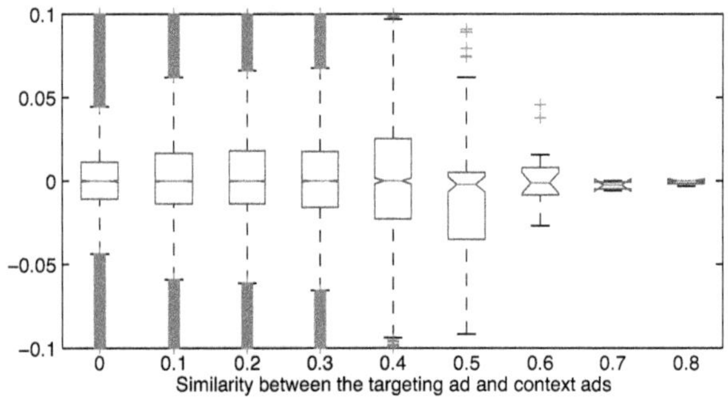


**Figure 3: ΔCTR against Similarity**

Section 5, we will clearly see the improvement of our interaction model, which can model both cases.

# 4. CLICK MODEL FOR MAINLINE ADS

We have seen some properties of ad context for predicting click through rate in sponsored search. In this section, we propose the Click Model for Mainline Ads to verify their effectiveness. Let us first define the notation. The records are presented by $\mathbf{S} = (q_m, \mathbf{a}_m, \mathbf{c}_m)_{m=1}^{M}$. For the single click log $(q, \mathbf{a}, \mathbf{c}) \in \mathbf{S}$, $q$ means the query in the record, $\mathbf{a}$ means the list of ads $\mathbf{a} = \{a_1, a_2, \cdots, a_{|a|}\}$ and $|\mathbf{a}|$ is the ad depth of this record. $i$ is the position of the list of ads $\mathbf{a}$, and $\mathbf{c}$ means the corresponding clicks $\mathbf{c} = \{c_1, c_2, \cdots, c_{|a|}\}$, where $c_i = 1$ for clicked position $i$, otherwise $c_i = 0$.

We have already seen some hints that for some queries, the probability of users being attracted by a specific number of ads is different. Here we introduce a new variable, $E_{(q,\mathbf{a})}$ to model the event that given a query $q$ and the displayed ads list $\mathbf{a}$, users will examine the ad area. Then following the classical examination hypothesis, we have the model assumption: for a record $(q, \mathbf{a}, \mathbf{c}) \in \mathbf{S}$,

$$\begin{aligned} c_i = 1 &\Leftrightarrow E_i = 1, E_{(q,\mathbf{a})} = 1, N_{i,(q,\mathbf{a})} = 1 \\ E_{(q,\mathbf{a})} = 0 &\Rightarrow E_i = 0 \\ E_i = 0 &\Rightarrow c_i = 0 \end{aligned}$$

where $E_i$ is the event that the user will examine the ad at position $i$ and $N_{i,(q,\mathbf{a})}$ is the event that the user is interested in the $i$th ad, given the context $(q, \mathbf{a})$. $N_{i,(q,\mathbf{a})}$ can also be considered as the variable of relevance. For a record $(q, \mathbf{a}, \mathbf{c}) \in \mathbf{S}$, the click is generatoted as

$$\begin{aligned} P(c_i = 1) &= P(c_i = 1|E_i = 1, E_{(q,\mathbf{a})} = 1) \\ &\quad P(E_i = 1|E_{(q,\mathbf{a})} = 1)P(E_{(q,\mathbf{a})} = 1) \end{aligned}$$

The probability of examining position $i$ $P(E_i = 1|E_{(q,\mathbf{a})} = 1)$ is well studied and can be formulized as the existing versatile position bias model, such as cascade models [19, 20, 12] and the examination hypothesis [17, 32]. In this work, we will not focus on investigating position bias and employed Position Model [32, 31]. We will however study the context-related hypotheses: the examination model for ad area $P(E_{(q,\mathbf{a})})$ and the relevance model $P(c_i = 1|E_i = 1, E_{(q,\mathbf{a})} = 1)$.

## 4.1 Examination Models

In this section, we discuss several possible types of examination hypothesis in modeling sponsored search clicks.

**Constant Examination (CE).** A simple method for modeling the probability of examining ad area $P(E_{(q,\mathbf{a})})$ is assuming $P(E_{(q,\mathbf{a})})$ is independent and does not depend on either query or ad depth. Then we have $P(E_{(q,\mathbf{a})} = 1) = \delta$, where $\delta$ is a corpus level parameter and shared by all queries and ad lists. Under this assumption, we might notice that $P(E_i = 1|E_{(q,\mathbf{a})} = 1)P(E_{(q,\mathbf{a})} = 1) = \delta \cdot \gamma_i$. Clearly, the two parameters can be merged. That is, the effects of the new parameter $\delta$ can be absorbed by $\gamma_i$ without changing prediction performance. Actually, this model is equivalent to the position model [32, 31]. $P(E_i = 1, E_{(q,\mathbf{a})} = 1) = \beta_i \equiv \delta \cdot \gamma_i$

**Depth Dependent Examination (DDE).** In Section 3, we analyzed the effects of ad depth on click through rate. As the analysis showed, a longer ad list displayed usually meant there was a higher probability of the ad area being examined. Following the intuition that the probability of examining the ad area is highly related to the depth of the ad list, we assume that the probability of examining the ad area $P(E_{(q,\mathbf{a})} = 1)$ is a depth dependent variable. That is $P(E_{(q,\mathbf{a})} = 1) = \delta_{|\mathbf{a}|}$, where $\delta_{|\mathbf{a}|}$ is discriminated by each different depth. Then we have the joint probability: $P(E_i = 1|E_{(q,\mathbf{a})} = 1)P(E_{(q,\mathbf{a})} = 1) = \delta_{|\mathbf{a}|} \cdot \gamma_i$. Alternatively, as in Constant Examination, we can also merge the two parameters. $P(E_i = 1, E_{(q,\mathbf{a})} = 1) = \beta_{i|\mathbf{a}|} \sim \delta_{|\mathbf{a}|} \cdot \gamma_i$ The merged model, which can be considered as a depth-position bias model with parameter $\beta_{i|\mathbf{a}|}$, actually has freer properties than the original one. However, this depth dependent examination model still cannot capture the query effects on the probability of examining the ad area.

**Query-Depth Dependent Examination (QDDE).** As in Section 3, we discussed that like depth effects, for queries with different commercial intent, the ad area may also receive different examination probability. Following this intuition, we propose a more delicate model, where we assume the $P(E_{(q,\mathbf{a})} = 1)$ is related to both queries and the depth of ad list. Similarly, $P(E_i = 1|E_{(q,\mathbf{a})} = 1)P(E_{(q,\mathbf{a})} = 1) = \delta_{q|\mathbf{a}|} \cdot \gamma_i$. Alternatively, as in the above section, we could also merge the two parameters. $P(E_i = 1, E_{(q,\mathbf{a})} = 1) = \beta_{iq|\mathbf{a}|} \sim \delta_{q|\mathbf{a}|} \cdot \gamma_i$ Similarly to the Depth Dependent Examination, the merged model with parameter $\beta_{iq|\mathbf{a}|}$ has freer properties than the original $\delta_{q|\mathbf{a}|} \cdot \gamma_i$. For every query $q$, we have a depth-position bias model. Although the two factors, query and depth are modeled here, one potential problem of this model is overfitting, due to the large number of parameters behind this model and sparseness of the ad data. We will test this method in the following experiments on the real data.

## 4.2 Relevance Models

In this section, we will describe the possible methods for the relevance model $P(c_i = 1|E_i = 1, E_{q|\mathbf{a}|} = 1) = \alpha_{i,(q,\mathbf{a})}$.

*Non-Informational Relevance*

As with previous methods [17, 32, 12, 39] for the click model, the relevance model can be trivially set to informational constraint on $\alpha_{i,(q,\mathbf{a})}$, that is, $\alpha_{i,(q,\mathbf{a})} \sim \mathcal{U}(0, 1)$, where $\alpha_{i,(q,\mathbf{a})}$ can be valued from uniform distribution in the range zero to one, in order to serve as the Bernoulli parameter of $P(c_i = 1|E_i = 1, E_{q|\mathbf{a}|} = 1)$. The major drawbacks of this model are three factors: first, since there is no informational constraints on $\alpha$, the model will more easily become overfitted to training data. Second, it cannot determine the hidden interactions across query, user, and ads. Finally, it cannot handle cold starts.

*Informational Relevance*

To overcome the problems in the non-information relevance model, we could add some informational constraints on the Bernoulli parameter $\alpha$. Let $f_{i,(q,\mathbf{a})}$ be the informational constraints, calculated from multiple resources of the context. By placing Gaussian noise, we have $\alpha_{i,(q,\mathbf{a})} \sim \mathcal{N}(\Phi(f_{i,(q,\mathbf{a})}), \sigma^2)$, where $\alpha_{i,(q,\mathbf{a})}$ follows univariate gaussian distribution with mean $\Phi(f_{i,(q,\mathbf{a})})$ and variance $\sigma^2$ and the link function $\Phi(x)$ could be Sigmoid function or Gaussian cumulative distribution function. Next, we will discuss several possible models for informational constraints $f_{i,(q,\mathbf{a})}$.

**Latent Bias (LBM):** One straightforward intuition is that whether the ad is clicked or not depends on the average click rate: $f_{i,(q,\mathbf{a})} = \mu_{a_i}$ where $\mu_{a_i}$ is the click through rate of the target ad across all contexts. We can extend this basic estimation by incorporating a wider bias from the context: Query bias $\mu_q$, relevance position bias $\mu_i$, ad list bias $\mu_{\mathbf{a}}$ and global average bias $\mu_0$. Then we have $f^{(1)}_{i,(q,\mathbf{a})} = \mu_0 + \mu_{a_i} + \mu_q + \mu_i + \mu_{\mathbf{a}}$

**Feature Model (FM):** Another relevance model is linear estimation, which predicts relevance by a linear combination of features. For a search session, we could collect the features of the ads and their contexts: Let $\mathbf{x}_{a_i}$ be the feature vector of the target ad $a_i$, which can be extracted from the terms of the shown title and body of the ad, click over expected clicks (COEC) [37] or latent topic distribution of the ad content. Let $\mathbf{x}_{(q,\mathbf{a})}$ be the feature vector of the context of the target ad $a_i$, which can be the terms of query and the titles of the adjacent ads, user profiles, the depth of the ad list, etc. $f^{(2)}_{i,(q,\mathbf{a})} = \mathbf{b}_1^T \mathbf{x}_{a_i} + \mathbf{b}_2^T \mathbf{x}_{(q,\mathbf{a})}$, where $\mathbf{b}_1$ and $\mathbf{b}_2$ are coefficients to be learned from the training set. Here, we further place a zero mean Gaussian prior or Laplace prior on the coefficient $\mathbf{b}$, corresponding to the $L_1$ and $L_2$ regularization respectively.

**Interactive Influence (IM):** Although linear models are efficient, they are usually over simplified and cannot capture interaction between the ad and the elements (e.g., query and adjacent ads) of the context. To model the interactions between the target ad and the context, we use two interaction matrices $\mathbf{Q} \in \mathbb{R}^{n\times m}$ and $\mathbf{A} \in \mathbb{R}^{n\times n}$, where $m$ is the number of queries and $n$ is the number of ads. The entry $Q_{a_i q}$ of $\mathbf{Q}$ represents the interaction between the target ad $a_i$ and query $q$, and the entry $A_{a_i,a_j}$ represents the interaction between the target ad $a_i$ and its adjacent ad $a_j$. $f^{(3)}_{i,(q,\mathbf{a})} = Q_{a_i q} + \sum_{j\neq i, j\leq|\mathbf{a}|} A_{a_i a_j}$ The interaction matrix $\mathbf{Q}$ and $\mathbf{A}$ are unknown and their entries could be either positive or negative. We treat them as latent variables to be learned from the data set. However, the model has two serious problems: the observed pair $(a_i, q)$ and $(a_i, a_j)$ in the training data is extremely sparse, and the majority of entries in the interaction matrix cannot be learned effectively. The second problem is that without any constraints on the interaction matrix, this model may cause overfitting. To avoid these two problems, we place low-rank constraints on the interaction matrix $\mathbf{Q}$ and $\mathbf{A}$. The low-rank approximation is widely used in recommender systems [23, 7, 36, 5]: $\mathbf{A} \approx \mathbf{\Theta}^T\tilde{\mathbf{\Theta}}$ and $\mathbf{Q} \approx \mathbf{\Theta}^T\mathbf{\Psi}$. Let $k$ be the dimensionality of the latent factor vector. $\mathbf{\Theta} \in \mathbb{R}^{k\times n}$ is the latent factor matrix for the target ads, $\tilde{\mathbf{\Theta}} \in \mathbb{R}^{k\times n}$ is the latent factor matrix for the adjacent ads. Because the ads can act as both the target ad and the adjacent ad, for each ad, there will be two latent factor vectors representing the ad's two roles (the target ad and adjacent ad) respectively. Similarly, $\mathbf{\Psi} \in \mathbb{R}^{k\times m}$ is the latent factor matrix for queries. Plug Equation 4.2 back into the interaction model, and we get

$$f^{(3)}_{i,(q,\mathbf{a})} = \boldsymbol{\theta}^T_{a_i}\psi_q + \sum_{j\neq i, j<|\mathbf{a}|} \boldsymbol{\theta}^T_{a_i}\tilde{\boldsymbol{\theta}}_{a_j}$$

**Table 4: Data sets**

| | April 2012 | May 2012 | total |
|---|---|---|---|
| Impressions | 29,722,684 | 13,160,289 | 42,882,973 |
| Context $(q, \mathbf{a})$ | 112,084 | 52,814 | 135,445 |
| Ads | 62,423 | 34,214 | 72,959 |
| Queries | 49,483 | 26,104 | 53,730 |

As with the coefficients in the Feature Model, the latent factor vectors of ads and queries $\boldsymbol{\theta}_{a_i}, \psi_q, \tilde{\boldsymbol{\theta}}_{a_j}$ can be assumed to be generated from Gaussian or Laplace priors, corresponding to $L_2$ or $L_1$ regularization respectively. In this paper, we assume the latent factors follow zero mean multi-variate gaussian distribution.

**Combined Models (CM):** It is straightforward to consider combining the three models LBM, FM and IM. Thus in the combined model, different parts of the model will explain a variety of the ads and contexts. The combined model could be simply: $f_{i,(q,\mathbf{a})} = f^{(1)}_{i,(q,\mathbf{a})} + f^{(2)}_{i,(q,\mathbf{a})} + f^{(3)}_{i,(q,\mathbf{a})}$ Obviously, the combination could also be any two of the three aspects.

## 4.3 Inference

To learn the parameters, we adopt Maximum a Posteriori (MAP). Let $\mathbf{\Lambda} = \{\boldsymbol{\alpha}, \boldsymbol{\beta}, \boldsymbol{\mu}, \mathbf{b}, \mathbf{\Theta}, \tilde{\mathbf{\Theta}}, \mathbf{\Psi}\}$ represent all model parameters. Assuming independent contexts, we get

$$p(\mathbf{S}|\mathbf{\Lambda}) = \prod_{(q,\mathbf{a},\mathbf{c})\in\mathbf{S}} p(\mathbf{c}|\mathbf{\Lambda}) = \prod_{(q,\mathbf{a},\mathbf{c})\in\mathbf{S}} \prod_i p(c_i|\mathbf{\Lambda})$$

$$= \prod_{(q,\mathbf{a},\mathbf{c})\in\mathbf{S}} \prod_i \left[(\alpha_{i,(q,\mathbf{a})} \cdot \beta_{iq|\mathbf{a}|})^{c_i} \cdot (1 - \alpha_{i,(q,\mathbf{a})} \cdot \beta_{iq|\mathbf{a}|})^{1-c_i}\right]$$

With the assumption of independent $\alpha$, we also have $p(\boldsymbol{\alpha}|\boldsymbol{\mu}, \mathbf{b}, \mathbf{\Theta}, \tilde{\mathbf{\Theta}}, \mathbf{\Psi}) = \prod_{i,(q,\mathbf{a})} p(\alpha_{i,(q,\mathbf{a})}|\boldsymbol{\mu}, \mathbf{b}, \mathbf{\Theta}, \tilde{\mathbf{\Theta}}, \mathbf{\Psi})$. As we describe above, we placed zero mean Gaussian prior on the parameter $\mathbf{b}$, $\mathbf{\Psi}$, $\mathbf{\Theta}$ and $\tilde{\mathbf{\Theta}}$ (L2 regularization). We employ EM algorithms to solve the model, treating examination $E$ as a latent variable.[2]

# 5. MAINLINE AD EXPERIMENTS

We use the data of Section 3 as training data, and further capture an additional two weeks of traffic as our test data. The data statistics are shown in Table 4.

Since the train/test data are split temporally, this evaluation is more instructive for real applications. The major measurement for performance evaluation is log likelihood, which is widely used in the CTR prediction problem [11]. Additionally, we also report Relative Information Gain (RIG) [18]. In our experiments, the dimension of latent factors for queries and ads is set at 10.

## 5.1 Analysis of Click Model for Mainline Ads

We conduct experiments to analyze the performance of the variations of our context aware CTR prediction model. First, we check the examination hypotheses by setting the relevance to Non-Informational Relevance (NIR). The results are shown in Table 5. We can see that Depth-Dependent Examination (DDE) outperforms the Constant Examination (CE) as we expected. However, we also notice that the performance of the query-dependent model QDDE is slightly worse than DDE. After examining the relevant data, we find that more than half of the queries do not hold complete depth records, and so, for these queries, some specific depths data are not applicable in the training data while they may appear in test

[2]We use SGD in M-step, so the learning algorithm is very efficient and the training time is linear in data size. Materials showing how to solve the model are available upon request.

Table 5: Model Analysis

| Examin. | Relev. | LL | RIG |
|---|---|---|---|
| CE | NIR | -0.4206 | 0.0250 |
| DDE | NIR | -0.4081 | 0.0539 |
| QDDE | NIR | -0.4123 | 0.0442 |
| DDE | LBM | -0.3789 | 0.1215 |
| DDE | LBM+FM | -0.3783 | 0.1229 |
| DDE | CM | **-0.3543** | **0.1787** |
| CE | CM | -0.3633 | 0.1578 |
| DDE | CM | **-0.3543** | **0.1787** |
| QDDE | CM | -0.3712 | 0.1395 |

data. In these cases, QDDE cannot make a better prediction and a more advanced model that can effectively handle query dependent parameters is necessary.

By using Depth Dependent Examination as our examination model, we can try different relevance models. From Table 5, we can see that if we only use the Latent Bias Model (LBM), we get better results than NIR. After adding features to the model (LBM+FM), the performance gets slightly better in both tasks too, but the improvement is negligible. By using more delicate features such as Click Over Expected Clicks (COEC) [37] or latent topic distribution of the ad, a larger improvement may be possible. Next, we use Combined Model, which combines the three models: LBM, FM, and IM. As expected, the model achieve the best performance. The improvement over LBM is much larger than FM. We also test different examination models with the combined relevance model, and the experiments show similar results, the Depth Dependent Model is always better than CE and QDDE. We also check convergence of the EM algorithms and it converges quickly, achieving a saddle point within 100 iterations. Next, we will employ the combined relevance model (CM) and Depth Dependent Examination model (DDE) to compare with other baselines.

## 5.2 Comparison with Existing Methods

We name our method CMMA for Click Model for Mainline Ads and compare our model with three existing methods on both Description Oriented Evaluation and Prediction Oriented Evaluation: **User Browsing Model (UBM)** is the baseline method and a classical click model [17]. We adopt EM inference process for parameter $\alpha$ and $\beta$. To avoid infinite values in log-likelihood, $\alpha$ is truncated into the range $(0.0001, 0.9999)$. **Matrix Factorization Click Model (MFCM)** is proposed by Shen et al. [31].[3] The dimensionality of the latent factor vector is also set at 10 for a fair comparison. **Relational click model (CRF)** is proposed by Xiong et al. [33]. They adopt Conditional Random Field (CRF) to model the exclusive effects between similar ads that are shown together in the same impression. The reason we choose these three methods is that UBM is a classical click model while MFCM and CRF are very recent state-of-the-art methods.

Table 6: Comparing with the baselines

| | UBM | CRF | MFCM | CMMA |
|---|---|---|---|---|
| Log Likelihood | -0.4227 | -0.39654 | -0.38464 | **-0.3543** |
| RIG | 0.0201 | 0.08086 | 0.10844 | **0.1787** |

The overall results are shown in Table 6. We see that CRF achieves much better results than UBM. As discussed, UBM cannot handle new query, ads or even the new pair query-ads with the existing query and ad. Thus, CRF which is designed for prediction

[3]In this paper, we do not focus on the personalized model. Personalization could be a factor of the ads contexts, and easily plugged into our framework.

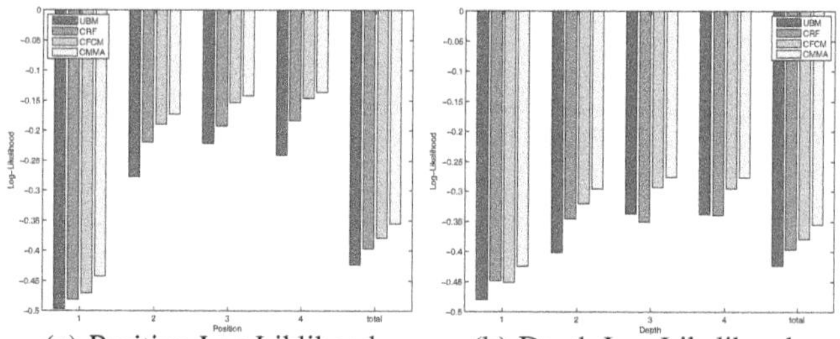


(a) Position-Log Liklihood (b) Depth-Log Likelihood

Figure 4: Comparing CMMA with baselines

tasks, outperforms UBM. For MFCM, we also consistently find that MFCM also outperforms UBM significantly as shown in [31]. Our method outperforms all three baselines. Similarly, we also show the results on positions in Figs. 4(a) and the results on depths in Figs. 4(b). For the cases of Position 1 and depth 1, the performance of all four methods is worse than other cases. Because the number of the cases of Position 1 and depth 1 are always much larger than other cases, they have a greater variance on CTR which increases the difficulty of predicting CTR. In all cases, our methods outperform all three other methods. The improvement on RMSE over MFCM is more than 10%.

# 6. MACRO FACTORS ANALYSIS

In previous section, we have already seen the effects of micro factors, including ad depth and interactive influence between query and ads and among ads. However, whether there are correlations or co-effects between ads and webpages is still not clear. In this section, our major objective is to leverage the relationship between ads and organic results to obtain better performing CTR prediction for ads. To study the relationship between their CTRs, we first introduce two factors. One is *Externality*, which means how competitory the sponsored search and organic search are. For example, when an ad is shown with a more attractive webpage, the attention given to the ad will be distracted [33]. The other is *Similarity*, which means how similar the sponsored search and organic search are in content. When a set of ads and webpages are too similar in content, the attention given to each individual ad/webpage may all be decreased or increased.

Since we target the relationship between mainline ads and organic results, we only consider search results displaying mainline ads. We examine data from a commercial search engine containing about 65 million search result page views (SERPs), about 200,000 unique queries, and 200,000 mainline ads. Each SERP can be represented by a triple consisting of (query, ad, organic results), where organic results is a ranked list of organic search results.

## 6.1 Overall Externality between Mainline Ads and Organic Results

To study the externality between mainline ads and organic results, we first define a *SERP group* as SERPs with the following criteria. 1. They contain the same ad in the same position. 2. They contain the same query 3. They contain the same organic results. Note that different SERP groups may have overlapping SERPs because one SERP may contain more than one mainline ad. We denote a mainline ad and the organic results in group $g$ as $A_{q,g}$ and $O_{q,g}$, respectively, where $q$ represents the query. To make the statistics meaningful, we only consider the groups shown in at least 15 SERPs. We define the CTR of ad $A_{q,g}$ (denoted as $\mathrm{CTR}_{A_{q,g}}$)

as the ratio of total clicks for the ad to the number SERPs in $A_{q,g}$: $\text{CTR}_{A_{q,g}} = \frac{\#Click_{A_{q,g}}}{|A_{q,g}|}$. The way to compute the CTR for organic results, denoted as $\text{CTR}_{O_{q,g}}$, of set $O_{q,g}$, is similar. After obtaining the CTRs, we can analyze the relationship between the CTR of mainline ads and organic results. To show the externality visually, we plot each SERP group as a point with coordinates of the two CTRs and get a density graph as shown in Figure 5(a).

Figure 5(a) shows that organic results' CTR does correlate to mainline ads' CTR. The increase of organic results' CTR accompanies the decrease of mainline ads' CTR, which shows these two CTRs are negatively correlated. Note that this observation is slightly different from [13], which can be attributed to several reasons. First, the setting of their data analysis is different from ours. They consider the relationship between a single ad and a single organic result while we consider the relationship to the complete organic result set. Second, they only show the average mainline ads' CTR for fixed organic results' CTR while we display the density graph, which shows more detailed information.

## 6.2 Externality between Mainline Ads and Organic Results on Query Level

The above analysis considers the externality with respect to overall CTRs. To better understand externality, we would like to consider externality on query level, which could help to remove the influence of relevance. We define a query group as a set of SERPs groups with the same ad and query. Within a query group, the relevance is the same and the relationship between the CTR of the ad and organic results can be mainly attributed to externality. For the statistical significance of our analysis, query groups with less than 10 SERP groups are discarded. After the preprocessing, we had 7,961 different query groups that covered about 21 million SERPs (including possible overlaps) for our externality study.

For each query group, we plot the points with coordinate $(\text{CTR}_{A,q,g}, \text{CTR}_{O,q,g})$ for each SERP group. To see the correlation between ad clicks and organic result clicks, we use linear function $y = \alpha + \beta x$ to fit the points. The slope $\beta$ expresses the sign and strength of the externality. To measure the fitness of the linear model, we further estimate the coefficient of determination $R^2$, which is the proportion of variability of data which can be explained by the linear regression function. The $R^2$ value of two random variables $X$ and $Y$ for the linear function model is defined by $R^2_{XY} = \frac{(\sum_i (x_i-\bar{x})(y_i-\bar{y}))^2}{\sum_i (x_i-\bar{x})^2 \sum_i (y_i-\bar{y})^2}$, where $x_i$ is the $i^{th}$ sample of $X$ and $\bar{x}$ is the mean of the samples for $X$, similarly for $y_i$ and $\bar{y}$.

We then plot the distributions of the slope and $R$ value for different query groups[4] in Figure 5(b) and Figure 5(c). There are a significant number of queries that have nonzero correlations ($|\beta| > 0$) between ad CTR and organic CTR, which is strong evidence that we should not treat them as independent and model them separately. Specifically, a major portion of the correlation coefficients fall into the interval $[-5, 0]$, indicating that a negative correlation dominates the relationship between ad clicks and organic clicks. This is also consistent with our previous analysis from a global perspective. At the same time, we can still observe a significant number of query groups (29.4%) that have positive correlations. The standard deviation of $\beta$ is 1.1282, showing that the slope varies widely between different query groups. The $R$ value can be seen as a confidence value of the linear dependency. We consider query groups with $R \in [0.5, 1]$ as high confidence groups. We find that 21.8% query groups have high confidence and 9.8% of these high confidence query groups have positive correlation.

[4]We plot $R$ instead of $R^2$ value because the approximately linear relationship of $R$ is easier to observe.

To better understand the results, we also conducted some case studies. We randomly drew two query groups with positive correlation and two query groups with negative correlation from the high confidence groups. We present the raw data and the fitting line, as well as the query of the query group in Figure (6). The two negative query groups both have navigational queries and the two positive query groups both are commercial but non-navigational queries. A non-navigational query means the user usually does not have strong intent when searching the query. This result is also consistent with [13]. However, they divided the query as navigational and non-navigational without considering the externality at the query level. We can see that the degree of correlations, measured by the slope of the line, is different for different queries.

In conclusion, the overall correlation between ads and organic results is negative. Yet, the correlation varies according to the query and the positive correlation cannot be neglected.

## 6.3 Similarity Analysis

In the previous section we showed the correlation between the CTR of ads and organic search results. In this section we study how similarity of content between ads and organic results influences their CTRs. We focus on the most clicked ads (denoted as $a^*_{q,g}$) in each set $A_{q,g}$ for query $q$, which is assumed to be the most popular ads in this group. We then find the most clicked organic results in the same group (denoted as $o^*_{q,g}$). If $a^*_{q,g}$'s URL and $o^*_{q,g}$'s URL share the same URL domain, we assume their content is similar to some extent and regard such a pair $(a^*_{q,g}, o^*_{q,g})$ as a similar pair. For each similar pair we find the control group where $o^*_{q,g}$does not appear and the experimental group where they both appear, by which we exclude the influence of other factors to the greatest extent. Then we estimate $\Delta\text{CTR}_{q,g}$, defined as, $\Delta\text{CTR}_{q,g} = \text{CTR}_{o^*_{q,g},q,g} - \text{CTR}_{o^*_{q,g},q,j}|a^*_{q,g}$, which means the difference in CTR on $o^*_{q,g}$ caused by the existence and absence of $a^*_{q,g}$.[5] We calculate the average difference for all similar pairs in a query and plot the distribution of the average value for each query in Figure 5(d). The resulting values are mainly positive, which fits the intuition that similar ads to organic results will distract attention from organic results . This phenomenon may be explained in that users have limited attention for one SERP, which makes it necessary to choose between ads and organic results based on their content. When the mainline-ads have similar content, it is likely that some clicks are distracted from organic results. This explanation implies that we should take the similarity of ads and organic results into consideration in CTR prediction. It further motivates us to prefer diversity when displaying ads and organic results.

# 7. CROSS-DOMAIN CLICK MODEL

We have already seen the correlations between organic search and sponsored search. To further verify the effects of correlations, we build a cross-domain model based on the results of the data analysis. Major parameters for this model are listed in Table 7. Note that for description convenience, we redefine some notations used in this sections. For the ad and organic search domains, we obtain two matrix factorization (MF) models as,

$$\begin{aligned} r_{qa} &\sim \boldsymbol{\theta}_q^{(a)} \cdot \boldsymbol{\psi}_a + \mathbf{b}^{(a)} \cdot \mathbf{x}_{qa} + \epsilon_a, \quad \epsilon_a \sim \mathcal{N}(0, (\sigma^{(a)})^2) \\ r_{qo} &\sim \boldsymbol{\theta}_q^{(o)} \cdot \boldsymbol{\psi}_o + \mathbf{b}^{(o)} \cdot \mathbf{x}_{qo} + \epsilon_o, \quad \epsilon_o \sim \mathcal{N}(0, (\sigma^{(o)})^2) \end{aligned} \tag{1}$$

[5]It would be better to have the setting the other way around. However, it is hard to do so offline and the current setting is meaningful in that it helps reveal the relationship between ads and organic results.

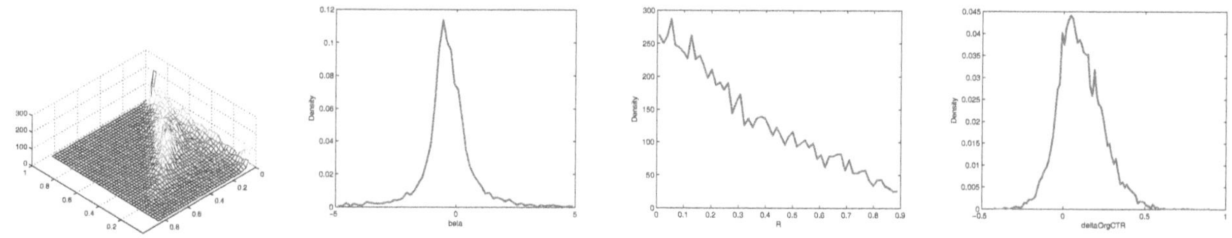

(a) Global externality. (b) Distribution of $\beta$. (c) Distribution of R value. (d) Distribution of similarity.

**Figure 5: Experimental results**

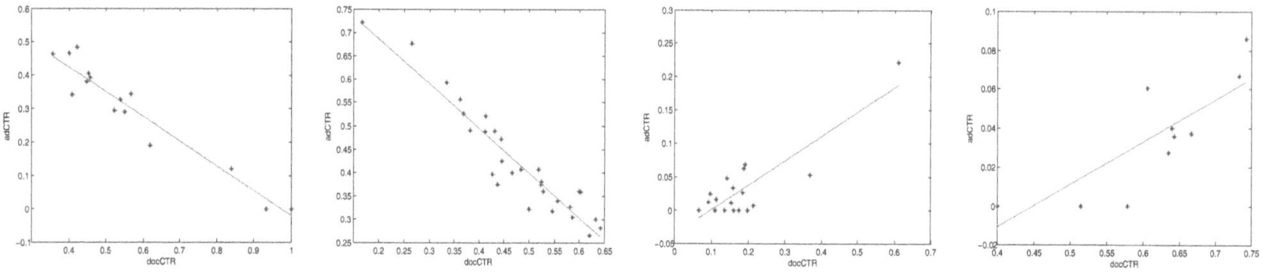

(a) "tdameritrade.com" (b) "freetaxusa" (c) "elmo" (d) "university of hawaii"

**Figure 6: Case studies.**

**Table 7: Notations used in model**

| Symbol | Description |
|---|---|
| $K$ | The dimension of latent feature vector |
| $\boldsymbol{\Omega}^q$ | The correlation between $\boldsymbol{\theta}_q^{(a)}$ and $\boldsymbol{\theta}_q^{(o)}$ |
| $\boldsymbol{\theta}_q^{(a)}$ | Latent feature vector representing query q in ad domain |
| $\boldsymbol{\theta}_q^{(o)}$ | Latent feature vector representing query q in organic domain |
| $\boldsymbol{\psi}_{a_i}$ | Latent feature vector representing ad $a_i$ |
| $\boldsymbol{\psi}_{o_j}$ | Latent feature vector representing organic result $o_j$ |
| $\mathbf{b}^{(a)}$ | Weights for explicit features in ad domain |
| $\mathbf{b}^{(o)}$ | Weights for explicit features in organic domain |
| $r_{qa}$ | User click/non-click response for ad $a$ given query $q$ |
| $r_{qo}$ | User click/non-click response for organic result $o$ given query $q$ |

where $\boldsymbol{\psi}_a$ and $\boldsymbol{\psi}_o$ are the latent representations of ad and organic results. $\boldsymbol{\theta}_q^{(a)}$ and $\boldsymbol{\theta}_q^{(o)}$ are the latent representations of the query in the ad and the organic domain. When we constrain the length of the vector to be 1 (then it degenerates to scalar) and fix the $\boldsymbol{\psi}_a$ and $\boldsymbol{\psi}_o$ as the element vector, model (1) becomes a multi-task linear regression model.

The factor for query $q$ appears in both MF models. According to our previous analysis, they should be correlated. To model the relationship between ads and organic search, we put a matrix-variate normal distribution [21] on the $\boldsymbol{\theta}_q^{(a)}$ and $\boldsymbol{\theta}_q^{(o)}$, which represent the latent factor of a query for ads and organic results, respectively. That means we use $\boldsymbol{\Omega}^q$ to characterize query-specific relationship between two domains based on the latent factors. Formally:

$$\mathbf{U}_q \sim \mathcal{MN}_{K\times 2}(\mathbf{0}_{K\times 2}, \mathbf{I}_K \otimes \boldsymbol{\Omega}_q) \quad (2)$$

where $\mathbf{U}_q$ is the $K \times 2$ matrix representation for query $q$ and $\mathbf{U}_q = [\boldsymbol{\theta}_q^{(a)}, \boldsymbol{\theta}_q^{(o)}]$.

In Eq (2), $\mathcal{MN}_{a\times b}(\mathbf{M}, \mathbf{A}\otimes\mathbf{B})$ denotes a matrix-variate normal distribution with mean $\mathbf{M} \in \mathbb{R}^{a\times b}$, row covariance matrix $\mathbf{A} \in \mathbb{R}^{a\times a}$ and column covariance matrix $\mathbf{B} \in \mathbb{R}^{b\times b}$.

The probabilistic density function of matrix-variate normal distribution is

$$\mathcal{MN}_{a\times b}(\mathbf{M}, \mathbf{A}\otimes\mathbf{B}) = \frac{\exp(-\frac{1}{2}\mathbf{tr}(\mathbf{A}^{-1}(\mathbf{X}-\mathbf{M})\mathbf{B}^{-1}(\mathbf{X}-\mathbf{M})^T))}{(2\pi)^{ab/2} \mid \mathbf{A} \mid^{b/2} \mid \mathbf{B} \mid^{a/2}} \quad (3)$$

where $\mathbf{tr}(\cdot)$ and $|\cdot|$ denote the trace and determinant, respectively, of a square matrix. Since $\mathbf{B}$ represents the covariance for columns, $\boldsymbol{\Omega}^q$ is the covariance for query $q$'s latent factors in two different domains. That is, $\boldsymbol{\Omega}^q$ is the parameter to describe the relationship between ads and organic search. Due to the scale of our problem, we use stochastic gradient descent (SGD) to solve the problem, which is an efficient algorithm for matrix factorization.

# 8. CROSS-DOMAIN EXPERIMENTS

In this section, we will present our experimental results based on our large real-world dataset. We try to answer two questions. Firstly, can the click information of organic results benefit the prediction of ad CTR? Secondly, can similarity information improve the performance of cross-domain CTR prediction?

The dataset we used in the following experiments is the same as the one introduced in Section 6. We do not use queries less then 30 SERPs because queries with few SERPs are not enough to build a good model for clicks of organic results, not to mention to transfer the knowledge for ad CTR prediction. For the purpose of this evaluation, we split the dataset into a training set, of which 85% is the data and the remaining 15% is the test set. The data was separated according to time information to avoid using future data to predict the past. We extract 19 features such as query bias, ad bias, ad URL, ad title, ad position, search result position, search result URL, time, as well as user bias and location and browser as the feature set.

We further group the queries in the test set according to the query frequency. The detailed information with the distribution of query frequency is listed in Table 8. The top query set, which consists of queries appearing more than 30,000 times in the training data, is discarded. This is because the top queries are relatively easy and the classical linear model [18] could already handle them well.

## 8.1 Methods

Here we compare our approach with two baseline methods. The first method is AdOnly, the classical linear regression model does not use the information of organic results. The second method is AdSim, the same algorithm as AdOnly, but some features used

Table 8: Details of Experiment Data

| Interval | Frequency | #Query | #SERP | #Entry |
|---|---|---|---|---|
| Freq 1 | $10^{1.5} \sim 10^{2}$ | 94,907 | 7,718,620 | 13,168,273 |
| Freq 2 | $10^{2} \sim 10^{2.5}$ | 48,547 | 10,376,698 | 19,184,516 |
| Freq 3 | $10^{2.5} \sim 10^{3}$ | 16,381 | 10,936,742 | 20,062,092 |
| Freq 3 | $10^{3} \sim 10^{3.5}$ | 4,220 | 8,934,949 | 15,686,684 |
| Freq 3 | $10^{3.5} \sim 10^{4}$ | 1,307 | 8,644,470 | 13,516,733 |
| Freq 3 | $10^{4} \sim 10^{4.5}$ | 309 | 6,340,607 | 9,031,495 |

**Table 9: Overall Performance of Different Models under Log Likelihood and Relative Information Gain**

| Model | AdOnly | AdSim | AdOrg | AdOrgSim | AdOrgSimMF |
|---|---|---|---|---|---|
| LL | -0.421 | -0.418 | -0.411 | -0.401 | **-0.391** |
| RIG | -0.330 | -0.322 | -0.308 | -0.279 | **-0.236** |

in [13] to describe the relationship between the ad and organic result, such as the edit distance between the ad's URL domain and the organic result's URL domain, are added as features. There could be more sophisticated ad CTR prediction baselines that use more information such as [27]. However, we did not include them because of two reasons. Firstly, due to the speciality of the problem, there is no benchmark dataset available and it is not possible to obtain the same data or even same feature set for fair comparisons. Secondly, our focus in this paper is to show the effect of combining organic search and sponsored search, rather than integrating all possible data sources to reach the best performance. Therefore, we only compare to the above two baselines.

Our proposed models also have three versions. The first version is AdOrg, our multi-task linear model that introduces correlated query bias. This model does not use similarity information used by AdSim . The second version is AdOrgSim, our multi-task linear model that considers the influence of similarity in the same way as in AdSim. The features used are exactly the same as AdSim. The third version is AdOrgSimMF, our multi-task matrix factorization models in section 7 that also consider similarity by utilizing features in AdSim. AdSim is designed to show that the introduction of the similarity features can improve the performance of ad CTR prediction. The AdOrg is expected to show that the multi-task linear regression model is a better way to model the interactions between ads and organic results. The AdOrgSim model is expected to further improvements over the AdOrg model by incorporating similarity. The AdOrgSimMF is expected to improve on the AdOrgSim model by exploiting the correlation between domains at the latent factor level. Like in Section 5, we also set $K$= 10 for the AdOrgSimMF model below.

## 8.2 Results

We evaluated the performance based on queries of all 6 frequency intervals and on queries of different correlation coefficient intervals, which we learned in the multi-task linear model.

### *8.2.1 Overall performance*

The overall performances of the five models are shown in Table 9. Note that we do not report the variance of the experiment results. This is because our dataset is large enough to be highly confident in the results even with one run. Based on the results, we can make the following observations: 1) The AdSim model, which considers the organic information with the similarity between ads and organic results as side information, outperforms AdOnly. This result is consistent with our data analysis that similarity is an important factor influencing the CTR. 2) By comparing AdOrg and

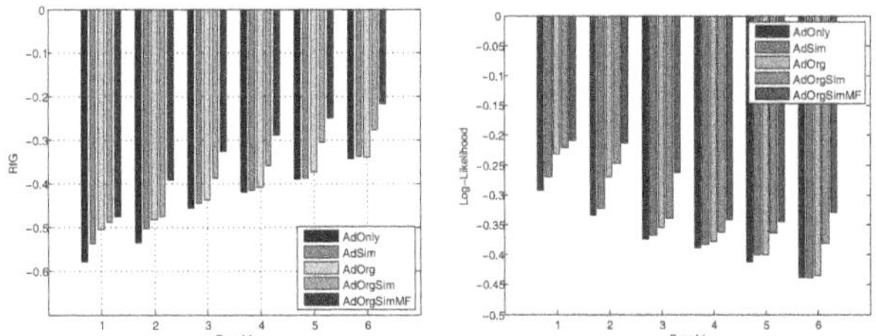


(a) RIG (b) Log Likelihood

**Figure 7: Experiment result for queries with different frequency**

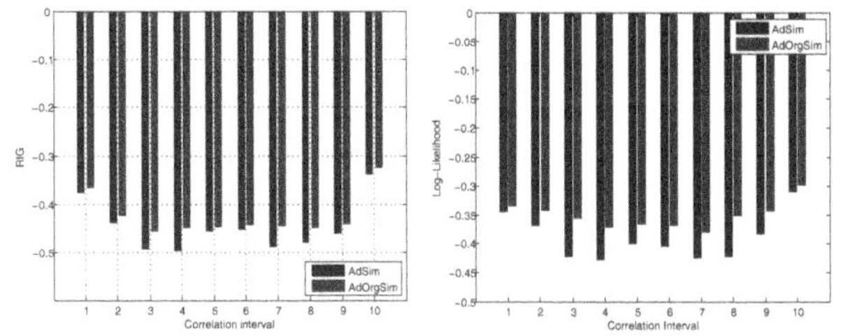


(a) RIG (b) Log Likelihood

**Figure 8: Experiment result for different value of $\rho_q$**

AdOnly, which use the same set of explicit features in the ad domain, we find that AdOrg significantly outperforms AdOnly. This observation is consistent with our analysis that AdOrg can predict the ad CTR better than AdSim by exploiting the relationship between ads and organic results. 3) The comparison between AdOrg and AdSim is more interesting. We find that the AdOrg model outperforms the AdSim model, though it uses fewer features than AdSim. This result indicates that only considering organic results as features is not enough. Instead, we should model the organic results in more principled method, as AdOrg achieves better performance through joint modeling. 4) We find that AdOrgSim has better performance than ArOrg and achieves significant improvements over the state-of-the-art AdSim model, which uses the information from organic results as side information. 5) Finally, we find the AdOrgSimMF model achieves the best performance and improves AdOrgSim, which shows that the factorization term in the model can better exploit the relationship among ads and organic results.

### *8.2.2 Queries with different frequency*

To study the influence of query frequency on performance, we present the detailed performance of the five models with different query frequency intervals in Figure 7. The results show that the improvements of AdOrg and AdOrgSim over AdOnly and AdSim are more significant for less frequent queries. On "tail queries," which appear only a few times (Freq 1$\sim$ Freq 3), AdOrg and AdOrgSim achieve the largest improvements over the baselines. The observations support our hypothesis that by exploiting the interaction between ad and organic results via a multi-task linear model, the proposed model alleviates the sparsity problem in ad CTR prediction. By carefully comparing the results of AdSim and AdOrg, we find the improvement is most significant for query intervals of Freq 2 and Freq 3. Queries of Freq 1 may give insufficient information to learn the relationship between ad and organic results. In conclusion, modeling the correlations between ad and organic search is more effective on tail queries and slightly more information gives us greater improvement.

### 8.2.3 *Performance over correlation coefficients*

In this section, we check the query-dependent correlations, which are modeled as the correlation parameter $\rho_q$ for each query in our AdOrgSim model, and its influence on the prediction of CTR.

$\rho_q$ can represent the correlation between ads and organic results and is guaranteed to be within the range $[-1, 1]$. A positive value means a positive correlation between ads and organic results and vice versa. The larger the absolute value is, the stronger the correlation is. We divide $[-1, 1]$ to 10 intervals with equal length, and compute the RIG and log likelihood for queries in each interval for model AdSim and AdOrgSim. The results are shown in Figure 8. As we can see, in the middle of Figure 8, which are the results for interval [-0.2,0] and [0,0.2], the average improvement is the smallest. However, when the absolute value of $\rho_q$ becomes larger, the improvement is much more significant. The results can be explained by the intuition that, when the correlation is weak, the advantage of jointly modeling the ad and organic result is small. When the correlation is stronger, the improvement becomes more significant. Figure 8 also proves that we can learn the correlations via the multi-task model.

## 9. CONCLUSION

We have studied the contextual factors of click-through rate for sponsored search in two aspects: for micro factors, we analyze the factors for mainline ads, such as ad depth, query bias and interactive influence between ads displayed together. For macro factors, we explored the correlation factor between sponsored search and organic search in terms of externality and similarity. We have incorporated these factors into click models and found that they play important roles in understanding and predicting user clicks on ads. Our extensive experiments based on large-scale real-world data sets show that our two proposed models (based on micro and macro factors) can outperform state-of-the-art methods.

However, we also notice that although our models verify the effectiveness of these contextual factors and provide some hints for future research in sponsored search, in this paper, we did not incorporate all factors together into a unified model, due to the complexity of modeling. We leave that as future work.

## 10. REFERENCES


[1] D. Agarwal, A. Z. Broder, D. Chakrabarti, D. Diklic, V. Josifovski, and M. Sayyadian. Estimating rates of rare events at multiple resolutions. In *KDD*, 2007.

[2] A. Ashkan and C. L. Clarke. Characterizing commercial intent. In *CIKM*, 2009.

[3] A. Ashkan and C. L. A. Clarke. Modeling browsing behavior for click analysis in sponsored search. In *CIKM*, 2012.

[4] R. Bell, Y. Koren, and C. Volinsky. The BellKor solution to the Netflix Prize A factorization model. *KorBell Teams Report to Netflix*, 2007.

[5] G. Bouchard, D. Yin, and S. Guo. Convex collective matrix factorization. In *AISTATS*, 2013.

[6] R. Briggs and N. Hollis. Advertising on the web: Is there response before click-through? In *Journal of Advertising Research*, 1997.

[7] B. Cao, D. Shen, K. Wang, and Q. Yang. Clickthrough log analysis by collaborative ranking. In *AAAI*, 2010.

[8] O. Chapelle and Y. Zhang. A dynamic bayesian network click model for web search ranking. In *WWW*, 2009.

[9] W. Chen, Z. Ji, S. Shen, and Q. Yang. A whole page click model to better interpret search engine click data. In *AAAI*, 2011.

[10] Y. Chen and T. W. Yan. Position-normalized click prediction in search advertising. In *KDD*, 2012.

[11] H. Cheng and E. Cantú-Paz. Personalized click prediction in sponsored search. In *WSDM*, 2010.

[12] N. Craswell, O. Zoeter, M. Taylor, and B. Ramsey. An experimental comparison of click position-bias models. In *WSDM*, 2008.

[13] C. Danescu-Niculescu-Mizil, A. Z. Broder, E. Gabrilovich, V. Josifovski, and B. Pang. Competing for users' attention: on the interplay between organic and sponsored search results. In *WWW*, 2010.

[14] K. S. Dave and V. Varma. Learning the click-through rate for rare/new ads from similar ads. In *SIGIR*, 2010.

[15] K. Dembczynski, W. Kotlowski, and D. Weiss. Predicting ads' click-through rate with decision rules. *Workshop on Targeting and Ranking in Online Advertising*, 2008.

[16] G. Dror, N. Koenigstein, and Y. Koren. The Yahoo! Music Dataset and KDD-Cup'11. *KDD-Cup*, 2011.

[17] G. E. Dupret and B. Piwowarski. A user browsing model to predict search engine click data from past observations. In *SIGIR*, 2008.

[18] T. Graepel, J. Q. Candela, T. Borchert, and R. Herbrich. Web-scale bayesian click-through rate prediction for sponsored search advertising in microsoft's bing search engine. In *ICML*, 2010.

[19] F. Guo, C. Liu, A. Kannan, T. Minka, M. Taylor, Y.-M. Wang, and C. Faloutsos. Click chain model in web search. In *WWW*, 2009.

[20] F. Guo, C. Liu, and Y. M. Wang. Efficient multiple-click models in web search. In *WSDM*, 2009.

[21] A. K. Gupta. *Matrix Variate Distributions*. Chapman & Hall/CRC, Oct. 1999.

[22] T. Joachims, L. Granka, B. Pan, H. Hembrooke, and G. Gay. Accurately interpreting click through data as implicit feedback. In *SIGIR*, 2005.

[23] Y. Koren. Factor in the neighbors: Scalable and accurate collaborative filtering. *ACM TKDD*, 4(1):1–24, January 2010.

[24] Y. Koren and R. Bell. Matrix factorization techniques for recommender systems. *IEEE Computer*, 42(8), 2009.

[25] C. Liu, F. Guo, and C. Faloutsos. Bbm: bayesian browsing model from petabyte-scale data. In *KDD*, 2009.

[26] C. Liu, F. Guo, and C. Faloutsos. Bayesian browsing model: Exact inference of document relevancfe from petabyte-scale data. *ACM Trans. Knowl. Discov. Data*, 4(4):19:1–19:26, Oct. 2010.

[27] A. K. Menon, K.-P. Chitrapura, S. Garg, D. Agarwal, and N. Kota. Response prediction using collaborative filtering with hierarchies and side-information. In *KDD*, 2011.

[28] T. Minka, J. Winn, J. Guiver, and A. Kannan. A click through model - sample code. `http://research.microsoft.com/en-us/um/cambridge/projects/infernet/docs/Click%20through%20model%20sample.aspx` , 2009.

[29] M. Regelson and D. Fain. Predicting click-through rate using keyword clusters. In *Proceedings of the Second Workshop on Sponsored Search Auctions*, volume 9623, 2006.

[30] M. Richardson, E. Dominowska, and R. Ragno. Predicting clicks: estimating the click-through rate for new ads. In *WWW*, 2007.

[31] S. Shen, B. Hu, W. Chen, and Q. Yang. Personalized click model through collaborative filtering. In *WSDM*, 2012.

[32] R. Srikant, S. Basu, N. Wang, and D. Pregibon. User browsing models: relevance versus examination. In *KDD*, 2010.

[33] C. Xiong, T. Wang, W. Ding, Y. Shen, and T.-Y. Liu. Relational click prediction for sponsored search. In *Proceedings of WSDM*, 2012.

[34] W. Xu, E. Manavoglu, and E. Cantu-Paz. Temporal click model for sponsored search. In *SIGIR*, 2010.

[35] S. Yang and A. Ghose. Analyzing the Relationship Between Organic and Sponsored Search Advertising: Positive, Negative, or Zero Interdependence? *Marketing Science*, 30(1), Apr. 2010.

[36] D. Yin, S. Guo, B. Chidlovskii, B. D. Davison, C. Archambeau, and G. Bouchard. Connecting comments and tags: Improved modeling of social tagging systems. In *WSDM*, 2013.

[37] W. V. Zhang and R. Jones. Comparing click logs and editorial labels for training query rewriting. In *Query Log Analysis: Social And Technological Challenges. A workshop at WWW 2007*.

[38] Y. Zhang, W. Chen, D. Wang, and Q. Yang. User-click modeling for understanding and predicting search-behavior. In *KDD*, 2011.

[39] Z. A. Zhu, W. Chen, T. Minka, C. Zhu, and Z. Chen. A novel click model and its applications to online advertising. In *WSDM*, 2010.

# Predicting Response in Mobile Advertising with Hierarchical Importance-Aware Factorization Machine

Richard J. Oentaryo
Living Analytics Research Centre
Singapore Management University
80 Stamford Road, Singapore
roentaryo@smu.edu.sg

Ee-Peng Lim
Living Analytics Research Centre
Singapore Management University
80 Stamford Road, Singapore
eplim@smu.edu.sg

Jia-Wei Low
Living Analytics Research Centre
Singapore Management University
80 Stamford Road, Singapore
jwlow@smu.edu.sg

David Lo
Living Analytics Research Centre
Singapore Management University
80 Stamford Road, Singapore
davidlo@smu.edu.sg

Michael Finegold
Department of Statistics
Carnegie Mellon University
229K Baker Hall, Pittsburgh, PA
mfinegol@andrew.cmu.edu

## ABSTRACT

Mobile advertising has recently seen dramatic growth, fueled by the global proliferation of mobile phones and devices. The task of predicting ad response is thus crucial for maximizing business revenue. However, ad response data change dynamically over time, and are subject to cold-start situations in which limited history hinders reliable prediction. There is also a need for a robust regression estimation for high prediction accuracy, and good ranking to distinguish the impacts of different ads. To this end, we develop a *Hierarchical Importance-aware Factorization Machine* (HIFM), which provides an effective generic latent factor framework that incorporates importance weights and hierarchical learning. Comprehensive empirical studies on a real-world mobile advertising dataset show that HIFM outperforms the contemporary temporal latent factor models. The results also demonstrate the efficacy of the HIFM's importance-aware and hierarchical learning in improving the overall prediction and prediction in cold-start scenarios, respectively.

## Categories and Subject Descriptors

H.3.3 [**Information Storage and Retrieval**]: Information Search and Retrieval; H.4 [**Information Systems Applications**]: Miscellaneous

## General Terms

Algorithms, Experimentation

## Keywords

Factorization machine, hierarchy, importance weight, mobile advertising, response prediction


*WSDM'14*, February 24–28, 2014, New York, New York, USA.

http://dx.doi.org/10.1145/2556195.2556240.

## 1. INTRODUCTION

The proliferation of mobile phones and devices has made mobile advertising an effective means for businesses to target the desired market on the fly. Global mobile advertising revenue is projected to hit $11.4 billion by 2013, creating new opportunities in many countries [7]. A mobile advertising ecosystem is typically governed by an *ad network*, which mediates all transactions between advertisers and content publishers. The *advertiser* plans a budget, provides ads, and agrees on commission for customer actions (e.g., clicking an ad, or bidding in an auction). The *publisher* contracts with the ad network to display ads on their (web)pages, and earns commission based on the traffic driven to the advertisers.

The most popular monetary paradigm in mobile advertising is the *cost-per-click* (CPC) scheme. An advertiser places a bid for an ad to be placed on some publisher's webpage, and pays the bid amount to the publisher only if the ad is displayed (i.e., an *exposure*) and chosen by a user (i.e., a *click*). Among the competing ads, the publisher chooses to display the ad with the highest *expected revenue*, which is the ad's bid price times the probability it is clicked. This probability is known as *clickthrough rate* ($CTR$), and accurately estimating it is important for maximizing revenue. The task of estimating $CTR$ (or similar metrics such as conversion rate) falls under the term *response prediction* [11, 15].

Response prediction tasks present several challenges. First, ad response data are dynamic and change over time. There is a need for a method that can account for the *temporal aspects* of the data. Second, most ads have limited or no past history in a page–also known as the *cold-start* issue. That is, the response estimation is highly unreliable if we have very low ad exposures. Robust estimation in cold-start cases is important for the advertisers, as it provides a means to measure/explore the potential of investing in new pages and ads. To increase robustness, we can plausibly leverage on prior knowledge in the form of *hierarchical structure* of pages and ads. Such hierarchy contains useful information about correlations between responses at various levels, which can smoothen the estimation for limited historical data.

From the modeling standpoint, response prediction tasks involve two requirements: good *regression* and good *ranking* performances [16]. In real-time auctions for mobile advertising, ads are often ranked based on $bid \times CTR$. It is thus important that $CTR$ gives good ranking that distinguishes the impacts of different ads. Also, ads are usually priced via a next-price auction, i.e., the price of a click on an ad at rank $i$ is based on the ad's expected $bid \times CTR$ at the next lower rank [3]. In this, the $CTR$ (regression) estimates must be as accurate as possible, especially for ads that are displayed many times. That is, high *importance weights* should be assigned to ads with high exposures, as the cost of inaccurately predicting the response of such ads is high.

To address all the above challenges and requirements, we present in this paper a novel latent factor model for response prediction, termed *Hierarchical Importance-aware Factorization Machine* (HIFM). Our HIFM is built upon the state-of-the-art factorization machines (FM) [12, 13], with new extensions to utilize importance weights and hierarchical knowledge for handling temporal/dynamic ad response data. We summarize our key contributions as follows:

- We develop a new latent factor framework that utilizes *importance-aware* and *hierarchical learning* for handling *temporal* ad response data. These two ideas help improve response prediction by putting priorities based on ads' exposures and by making more informative prediction in cold-start cases, respectively. Deviating from the existing approaches, which are often very specialized (e.g., only works for dyads) and not able to cater for temporal data, HIFM offers a generic approach to simultaneously address importance weight, hierarchical knowledge, and temporal dynamics.

- We adapt and generalize two learning algorithms, the *stochastic gradient descent* (SGD) and *coordinate descent* (CD), to facilitate importance-aware and hierarchical learning in HIFM. We adopt roulette wheel sampling strategy and weighted least square update to cater for the importance weight in SGD and CD respectively, while hierarchical learning is achieved in both SGD and CD by means of hierarchical fitting and regularization. For each algorithm, we develop several variants with (the same) linear runtime complexity. These extensions in turn facilitate comprehensive studies for evaluating different methods.

- Extensive experiments on real-world mobile advertising data show that HIFM outperforms contemporary temporal latent factor models. We also find statistically significant improvements due to the HIFM's importance-aware and hierarchical learning, in terms of the overall (weighted) prediction and prediction for cold-start cases, respectively. This shows the applicability of HIFM in complex response prediction tasks.

## 2. RELATED WORK

Traditionally, the data mining approaches to ad response prediction broadly fall into two camps: *feature-based* and *maximum likelihood-based* [11]. In feature-based methods, prediction models are constructed based on explicit features of a page and/or an ad. These features–also termed as *side information*–may include textual content of an ad, its placement on the (web)page, etc. Feature-based methods typically utilize prediction models from logistic regression family [8, 15]. However, constructing these models requires extensive manual intervention or domain knowledge. On the other hand, maximum likelihood-based methods try to smoothen the response estimation using statistical models of ad clicks and exposures, e.g., the Gamma-Poisson model [1, 2]. These methods, however, are based on simple linear models and lack the ability to capture rich latent structure in data.

**Table 1: Global count statistics**

| Entity | Minimum exposure ($e_{min}$) | | | |
|---|---|---|---|---|
| | 1 | 10 | 100 | 1000 |
| #records | 24,172,134 | 10,535,658 | 3,587,160 | 931,032 |
| #(web)pages | 244,341 | 138,351 | 55,260 | 16,374 |
| #publishers | 3,945 | 3,539 | 2,654 | 1,643 |
| #countries | 243 | 239 | 226 | 199 |
| #channels | 8 | 8 | 8 | 8 |
| #ads | 23,500 | 18,365 | 15,600 | 10,877 |
| #advertisers | 1,989 | 1,406 | 1,245 | 1,124 |
| #banner types | 5 | 4 | 3 | 3 |

In this light, Menon *et al.* [11] proposed a hybrid approach by combining matrix factorization (MF) with explicit page and ad features as well as hierarchical information about pages and ads. This method learns a set of latent features from data through MF, and at the same time allows side information–typical of traditional feature-based methods–to be incorporated for improving the prediction. However, the MF representation used in this method is only restricted to dyadic relations (e.g., page vs. ad), and does not cater for higher-order relations such as those that include temporal dynamics (e.g., page vs. ad vs. day). Similar hierarchical MF methods were proposed in [23, 18], but like [11] all of them assume a restrictive dyadic representation.

On the other hand, several time-aware factorization approaches have been proposed, which take into account the temporal dynamics in data. Comon *et al.* presented a tensor factorization method trained using an alternative least square algorithm [5]. Koren developed TimeSVD++ to address temporal dynamics via specific parameterization with factors drifting from a central time [9]. More recently, Shen *et al.* [19] proposed a tensor factorization model to address the issue of personalization in click modeling. Other models have been developed that combine MF and Kalman filter to simultaneously model the spatial and temporal patterns in data [10, 21]. Regardless, all these methods use restrictive representation and cannot be easily extended to augment side information such as hierarchical prior knowledge.

Recently, Rendle [12, 13] proposed a generic factorization machine (FM) framework, which can efficiently handle arbitrary relationships (i.e., dyad, triad, etc.). The approach can thus be used to address temporal data and can easily incorporate side information. As noted in [13], the FM approach can mimic many state-of-the art factorization models (e.g., pairwise tensor factorization, TimeSVD++, attribute-aware models, and neighborhood models), and exhibits good performances on many competitive tasks [13]. Nonetheless, the current FM does not yet cater for hierarchical structure and/or instance importance in its model. In light of response prediction task, we extend and generalize the FM framework in this work by combining importance-aware learning and hierarchical fitting and regularization.

## 3. PROBLEM FORMULATION

### 3.1 Dataset

In our study, we use the data provided by our industry partner, a global mobile advertising network based in Sin-

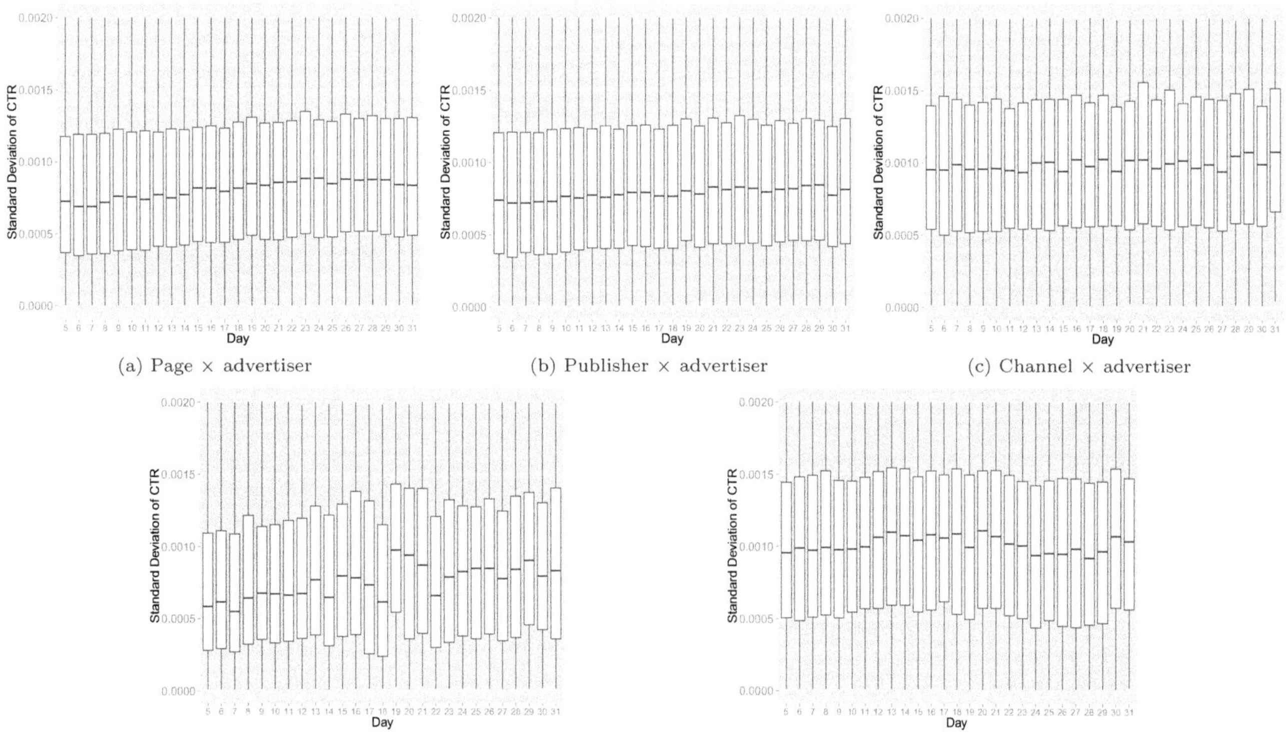


(a) Page × advertiser (b) Publisher × advertiser (c) Channel × advertiser

(d) Publisher × ad (e) Channel × ad

**Figure 1: Temporal distribution of click-through rates grouped at various hierarchy levels**

gapore. The supplied data consist of a *campaign* table and an *ad click* table. The latter contains records of clicks and exposures for various (web)pages and ads at different days. The data were taken from a 27-day period, 05-31 October 2012, and have 24,172,134 records. In this period, there are over 17 billion ad exposures and over 42 million ad clicks.

The ad click table has several fields: `day` (yyyy-mm-dd format), `page` (page ID), `publisher` (publisher ID), `ad` (ad campaign ID), `channel` (publisher's channel type), and `numclick` and `numexpose` (number of clicks and exposures for a page-ad pair at a given day, respectively). Each record in the table is uniquely identified by a (`page`, `ad`, `day`) triplet. There are five (i.e., `channel`) types, each denoting the publisher category (e.g., adult sites, entertainment and lifestyle, glamour and dating, etc.). From `numclick` and `numexpose`, we can then estimate $CTR = \frac{\texttt{numclick}}{\texttt{numexpose}}$, though precaution needs to be exercised when `numexpose` is low. Also note that all records in the ad click table have `numexpose` $\geq 1$.

The campaign table, on the other hand, complements the ad click table and comprises several fields: `ad` (as with the ad click table), `advertiser` (advertising company of the ad), and `bannertype` (type of ad banners). That is, the table maintains a list of ads with their corresponding advertisers and banner types; the latter involve five categories: $\{image, remote, splash, tablet, text\}$. It is also worth noting that all fields (except for *day*) in the ad click and campaign tables are anonymized for security protection.

Table 1 summarizes the count statistics derived from the ad click and campaign tables. It shows the counts of various entities as the minimum exposure threshold $e_{min}$ is varied from 1 to 1000. Here the number of records refers to that of (`page`, `ad`, `day`) triplets in the ad click table. As $e_{min}$ gets increased, we can see rather drastic reductions in the counts (except for `channel` and `bannertype`), suggesting a heavy-tail distribution where most pages have small number of ad exposures and thus low-confidence $CTR$ estimates.

## 3.2 Response Prediction

We now formulate our response prediction task: *Given a pair of page p and ad a at a specific day d, we predict the click probability CTR.* That is, we wish to compute the probability $P_{p,a,d} = Pr(Click|Exposure, p, a, d)$, where $p$, $a$ and $d$ denote a particular page, ad, and day respectively.

A simple solution to this task is to use the maximum likelihood estimate (MLE) [11], i.e., $P^{MLE}_{p,a,d} = \frac{c_{p,a,d}}{e_{p,a,d}}, \forall e_{p,a,d} > 0$, where $c_{p,a,d}$ and $e_{p,a,d}$ are the numbers of ad clicks and exposures respectively. However, when $e_{p,a,d}$ is very small, the MLE estimate would be highly noisy. For instance, if an ad has been exposed 3 times on a page and received no click, a $CTR$ estimate of 0 would make no sense. As this extreme case is common in practice, we need an alternative estimate $\hat{P}$ that smoothens the MLE so as to make it more reliable.

As advocated in [11], a good predictive model for estimating $\hat{P}$ should fulfill several criteria. First, it should provide smoothened estimates in the face of very few exposures $e_{p,a,d}$. Second, it should output meaningful probabilities, within the range $[0, 1]$. Finally, the MLE should be consistent, meaning that as $e_{p,a,d} \to \infty$, $\hat{P}_{p,a,d} \to P^{MLE}_{p,a,d}$. In other words, when the number of exposures is large enough, any estimator $\hat{P}$ should converge to the MLE.

## 3.3 Page and Ad Hierarchies

Further investigations on the ad click and campaign tables reveal that page and ad hierarchies exist in the data. That is, a **page** is associated with a **publisher**, and a **publisher** belongs to a unique **channel**. Similarly, an **ad** belongs to an **advertiser**. Hierarchical structure encodes useful prior knowledge for improving $CTR$ estimation when we have little data at granular level. For instance, if a (**page**, **ad**) pair has only very small **numexpose**, but the siblings of the **ad** has large **numexpose**, we can increase the confidence of its estimate by leveraging the siblings' estimates. This allows a "back-off" mechanism for borrowing data from coarse level to smoothen the estimation at the granular level [11].

For our hierarchy analysis, we compute the $CTR$ distribution for different pairs (Cartesian products) of entities in the page and ad hierarchies: **page** × **advertiser**, **publisher** × **ad**, **channel** × **ad**, **publisher** × **advertiser**, and **channel** × **advertiser**. Figure 1 shows the box plots of the $CTR$ variations (i.e., first quantile, median, and third quantile) for each entity pair over 27 days. To obtain Figure 1(a), for instance, we first group each **ad** by the **advertiser**, and then look at the $CTR$ variation under the **page-advertiser** pair for a given day. Specifically, we calculate the standard deviation of the CTR for each **page-advertiser** pair, which measures the homogeneity of the $CTR$ under the group. We repeat the procedure for the remaining (four) combinations, the results of which are shown in Figures 1(b)-(d).

From these plots, we can make several observations. First, the $CTR$ values vary across different days, which justifies the need to model temporal dynamics. Second, comparing Figure 1(a)-(c) and 1(d)-(e), we can see that the CTR variability increases as we go up in the hierarchy, implying that the $CTR$ values are less (more) homogeneous at the higher (lower) level. This suggests the feasibility of the "back-off" mechanism, i.e., when a child node lacks data, we can leverage on the estimates from its parent(s), and then those from its grandparent(s), and so on.

# 4. FACTORIZATION MACHINE

The HIFM model we proposed to predict $CTR$ is built upon a generic latent factor model called *factorization machine* (FM) [12, 13]. We first describe the basic FM in this section, and then new extensions that we develop in-house for HIFM in Section 5, based on different importance-aware learning methods and use of page and ad hierarchies.

## 4.1 Model Overview

The FM takes as its inputs a real-valued feature matrix (also called *design matrix*) $X \in \mathbb{R}^{N\times J}$. For an input vector $\mathbf{x}_i$ ($i \in \{1,\dots,N\}$, $\mathbf{x}_i \in \mathbb{R}^J$), the output $\hat{y}_i$ of an (order-2) FM is defined in (1):

$$\hat{y}(\mathbf{x}_i) = w_0 + \sum_{j=1}^{J} w_j x_{i,j} + \underbrace{\sum_{j=1}^{J}\sum_{j'=j+1}^{J} x_{i,j}x_{i,j'}\sum_{k=1}^{K} v_{k,j}v_{k,j'}}_{=\hat{p}(\mathbf{x}_i)} \tag{1}$$

where $K$ is the dimensionality of the interaction factors, and the model parameters $\Theta = \{w_0, w_1, \dots, w_J, v_{1,1}, \dots, v_{K,J}\}$ consist of $w_o \in \mathbb{R}$, $\mathbf{w} \in \mathbb{R}^J$, and $\mathbf{V} \in \mathbb{R}^{K\times J}$.

According to [12], we can efficiently compute the term $\hat{p}(\mathbf{x}_i)$ in (1) based on its equivalent formulation (2):

$$\hat{p}(\mathbf{x}_i) = \frac{1}{2}\sum_{k=1}^{K}\left[\left(\sum_{j=1}^{J} v_{k,j}x_{i,j}\right)^2 - \sum_{j=1}^{J} v_{k,j}^2 x_{i,j}^2\right] \tag{2}$$

This makes it possible to quickly process all $N$ instances of a design matrix $X$ in linear time $O(KN_z(X))$, where $N_z(X)$ is the number of non-zero entries in $X$.

## 4.2 Multilinearity Property

The FM has an appealing *multilinearity* trait: for each model parameter $\theta \in \Theta$, the FM output $\hat{y}(\mathbf{x}_i)$ is a linear combination of two functions $r_\theta(\mathbf{x})$ and $g_\theta(\mathbf{x})$, as per (3):

$$\hat{y}(\mathbf{x}_i) = r_\theta(\mathbf{x}_i) + \theta g_\theta(\mathbf{x}_i), \quad \forall \theta \in \Theta \tag{3}$$

where $g_\theta(\mathbf{x}_i)$ corresponds to the gradient term (4):

$$g_\theta(\mathbf{x}_i) = \frac{\partial \hat{y}(\mathbf{x}_i)}{\partial \theta} = \begin{cases} 1 & \text{if } \theta = w_0 \\ x_{i,j} & \text{if } \theta = w_j \\ x_{i,j}\,(q_{i,k} - v_{k,j}x_{i,j}) & \text{if } \theta = v_{k,j} \end{cases} \tag{4}$$

and $q_{i,k} = \sum_{j=1}^{J} v_{k,j}x_{i,j}$ is the inner-product term that can be precomputed (cached) for efficient learning (cf. Section 5.3). Note that in our learning procedures, the residual term $r_\theta(\mathbf{x}_i)$ need not be computed; we only use the term $g_\theta(\mathbf{x}_i)$.

# 5. THE PROPOSED HIFM FRAMEWORK

We extend the basic FM model to incorporate importance weights and hierarchical structure for response prediction tasks, which results in the proposed HIFM model. We first discuss how importance weights and hierarchy can be incorporated into our model in Sections 5.1 and 5.2, respectively. Section 5.3 then presents our several variants of optimization algorithm for learning the HIFM's model parameters.

## 5.1 Importance-Aware Loss Functions

We consider the problem of predicting the click probability $\hat{y}_i(\mathbf{x}|\Theta) \in [0,1]$ (i.e., CTR), given a design matrix $X$ and model parameters $\Theta$. The goodness-of-fit between the predicted and actual probabilities can be expressed using the two objective functions in (5) and (6):

$$L_{square}(\Theta) = \sum_{i=1}^{N} e_i\left(\frac{c_i}{e_i} - \hat{y}(\mathbf{x}_i|\Theta)\right)^2 + \Omega(\Theta) \tag{5}$$

$$L_{logistic}(\Theta) = -\sum_{i=1}^{N}(c_i \log \sigma(\hat{y}(\mathbf{x}_i|\Theta)) + (e_i - c_i)\log(1 - \sigma((\hat{y}(\mathbf{x}_i|\Theta))) + \Omega(\Theta)) \tag{6}$$

where $c_i \geq 0$ and $e_i \geq 1$ denote the numbers of observed ad clicks and exposures (impressions) for the $i^{th}$ instance $\mathbf{x}_i \in X$, respectively, $\hat{y}_i(\mathbf{x}|\Theta) \in [0,1]$ is the click probability to be predicted by FM, $\Omega(\Theta)$ is the regularization term, and $\sigma(x) = \frac{1}{1+e^{-x}}$ is the logistic function. These formulae are also known as the *weighted square* and *weighted logistic* loss functions, using $e_i$ as the importance weights.

The regularization term $\Omega(\Theta)$ is useful to reduce the risk of data overfitting, due to a large number of model parameters $\Theta$ (especially when $K$ is large). Typically, L2 regularization is used [20] as given in (7):

$$\Omega(\Theta) = \frac{1}{2}\sum_{\theta\in\Theta} \lambda_\theta \theta^2 \tag{7}$$

which is equivalent to imposing a Gaussian prior on $\theta$, i.e., $\theta \sim \mathcal{N}(0, \lambda_\theta^{-1})$. This regularization essentially tries to penalize model parameters that have large (squared) norm, thus driving the parameter values to be small.

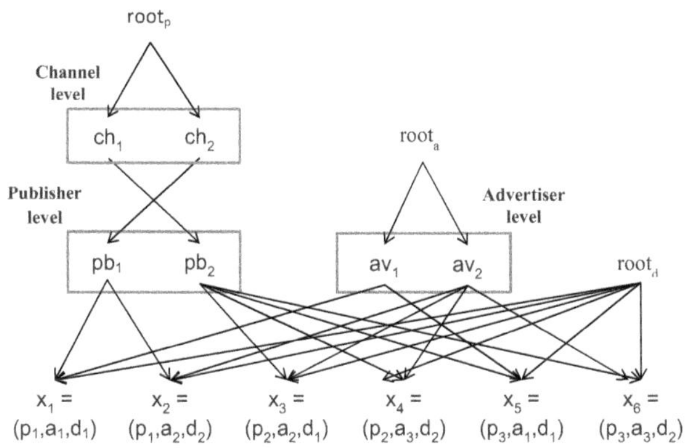


**Figure 2: Example of page and ad hierarchies**

## 5.2 Hierarchical Learning

Inspired by [11, 18], we utilize hierarchical information in our FM model via two ways: *hierarchical fitting* and *regularization*. For illustration, we consider the page and ad hierarchies in Figure 2. There are six instances at the bottom level, each corresponding to a page-ad-day ($p$, $a$, $d$) triplet. For the page hierarchy, each page belongs to a publisher node ($pb$) and then a publisher belongs to a unique channel ($ch$). Meanwhile, for the ad hierarchy, each ad belongs to an advertiser node ($av$). We implement the hierarchies as a *directed graph* (DG). It should be noted that the hierarchy structure need not be a tree; the DG representation allows us to work with non-tree hierarchy as well.

To incorporate hierarchical constraints into FM, we let every node in the hierarchy to possess its *own* latent factors (i.e., $\{w_j\}$ and $\{v_{k,j}\}$). Using this setup, we impose *hierarchical regularization* on the latent factors, so that each factor has a prior that makes it more similar to its parent in expectation. This is expressed in (8):

$$\theta_0 \sim \mathcal{N}(0, \lambda_{\theta_0}^{-1}), \forall \theta_0 \in \mathcal{H}^{root} \quad (8)$$

$$\theta_j \sim \mathcal{N}(\bar{\theta}_{Par}, \lambda_{\theta_j}^{-1}), \forall \theta_j \in \mathcal{H} - \mathcal{H}^{root} \quad (9)$$

where $\bar{\theta}_{Par}$ is the average of the parents' latent factors as defined in (10):

$$\bar{\theta}_{Par} = \frac{1}{|Par(\theta)|} \sum_{\theta_p \in Par(\theta)} \theta_p \quad (10)$$

where $Par(\theta)$ is the set of all parents of $\theta$.

The resulting hierarchical regularization is given in (11):

$$\Omega(\Theta) = \begin{cases} \frac{1}{2}\sum_\theta \lambda_\theta \left(\theta - \bar{\theta}_{Par}\right)^2 & \text{if } \theta \in \mathcal{H} - \mathcal{H}_{root} \\ \frac{1}{2}\sum_\theta \lambda_\theta \theta^2 & \text{if } \theta \in \mathcal{H}_{root} \end{cases} \quad (11)$$

where $\mathcal{H}$ is the set of all nodes in the hierarchy, and $\mathcal{H}_{root}$ is the set of root nodes sitting at the top of the hierarchy (i.e., with no incoming edges). In other words, *every* node is expected to be similar to its parents (if any). Note that our regularization approach is more general than that in [11, 18], which is only restricted to dyads (pages and ads in this case) and does not model temporal dynamics. Also, in our approach, the interactions between pages, ads (and days) are governed by shared latent factors $V_{k,j}$, instead of separate latent factors for pages and ads as in [11, 18]. Together with hierarchical regularization, this enables our method to handle sparse data more effectively.

| Importance weight | Page | | | Ad | | | Day | | Publisher | | Channel | | Advertiser | | Roots | | | Target | |
|---|---|---|---|---|---|---|---|---|---|---|---|---|---|---|---|---|---|---|---|
| $e_i$ | $p_1$ | $p_2$ | $p_3$ | $a_1$ | $a_2$ | $a_3$ | $d_1$ | $d_2$ | $pb_1$ | $pb_2$ | $ch_1$ | $ch_2$ | $av_1$ | $av_2$ | $root_p$ | $root_a$ | $root_d$ | CTR | |
| 100 | 1 | 0 | 0 | 1 | 0 | 0 | 1 | 0 | 0 | 0 | 0 | 0 | 0 | 0 | 0 | 0 | 0 | 0.0010 | page × ad × day |
| 200 | 1 | 0 | 0 | 0 | 1 | 0 | 1 | 0 | 0 | 0 | 0 | 0 | 0 | 0 | 0 | 0 | 0 | 0.0020 | |
| 100 | 0 | 1 | 0 | 0 | 1 | 0 | 1 | 0 | 0 | 0 | 0 | 0 | 0 | 0 | 0 | 0 | 0 | 0.0025 | |
| 100 | 0 | 1 | 0 | 0 | 0 | 1 | 0 | 1 | 0 | 0 | 0 | 0 | 0 | 0 | 0 | 0 | 0 | 0.0013 | |
| 200 | 0 | 0 | 1 | 1 | 0 | 0 | 0 | 1 | 0 | 0 | 0 | 0 | 0 | 0 | 0 | 0 | 0 | 0.0008 | |
| 100 | 0 | 0 | 1 | 0 | 0 | 1 | 0 | 1 | 0 | 0 | 0 | 0 | 0 | 0 | 0 | 0 | 0 | 0.0010 | |
| 100 | 0 | 0 | 0 | 1 | 0 | 0 | 1 | 0 | 1 | 0 | 0 | 0 | 0 | 0 | 0 | 0 | 0 | 0.0010 | publisher × ad × day |
| 200 | 0 | 0 | 0 | 0 | 1 | 0 | 1 | 0 | 1 | 0 | 0 | 0 | 0 | 0 | 0 | 0 | 0 | 0.0020 | |
| 100 | 0 | 0 | 0 | 0 | 1 | 0 | 1 | 0 | 0 | 1 | 0 | 0 | 0 | 0 | 0 | 0 | 0 | 0.0025 | |
| 200 | 0 | 0 | 0 | 0 | 0 | 1 | 0 | 1 | 0 | 1 | 0 | 0 | 0 | 0 | 0 | 0 | 0 | 0.0012 | |
| 200 | 0 | 0 | 0 | 1 | 0 | 0 | 0 | 1 | 0 | 1 | 0 | 0 | 0 | 0 | 0 | 0 | 0 | 0.0008 | |
| 100 | 0 | 0 | 0 | 1 | 0 | 0 | 1 | 0 | 0 | 0 | 0 | 1 | 0 | 0 | 0 | 0 | 0 | 0.0010 | channel × ad × day |
| 200 | 0 | 0 | 0 | 0 | 1 | 0 | 1 | 0 | 0 | 0 | 0 | 1 | 0 | 0 | 0 | 0 | 0 | 0.0020 | |
| 100 | 0 | 0 | 0 | 0 | 1 | 0 | 1 | 0 | 0 | 0 | 1 | 0 | 0 | 0 | 0 | 0 | 0 | 0.0025 | |
| 200 | 0 | 0 | 0 | 0 | 0 | 1 | 0 | 1 | 0 | 0 | 1 | 0 | 0 | 0 | 0 | 0 | 0 | 0.0008 | |
| 200 | 0 | 0 | 0 | 1 | 0 | 0 | 0 | 1 | 0 | 0 | 1 | 0 | 0 | 0 | 0 | 0 | 0 | 0.0010 | |
| 100 | 0 | 0 | 0 | 1 | 0 | 0 | 1 | 0 | 0 | 0 | 0 | 0 | 0 | 0 | 1 | 0 | 0 | 0.0010 | $root_p$ × ad × day |
| 300 | 0 | 0 | 0 | 0 | 1 | 0 | 1 | 0 | 0 | 0 | 0 | 0 | 0 | 0 | 1 | 0 | 0 | 0.0022 | |
| 100 | 0 | 0 | 0 | 0 | 0 | 1 | 0 | 1 | 0 | 0 | 0 | 0 | 0 | 0 | 1 | 0 | 0 | 0.0008 | |
| 200 | 0 | 0 | 0 | 1 | 0 | 0 | 0 | 1 | 0 | 0 | 0 | 0 | 0 | 0 | 1 | 0 | 0 | 0.0010 | |
| 100 | 1 | 0 | 0 | 0 | 0 | 0 | 1 | 0 | 0 | 0 | 0 | 0 | 1 | 0 | 0 | 0 | 0 | 0.0010 | page × advertiser × day |
| 200 | 1 | 0 | 0 | 0 | 0 | 0 | 1 | 0 | 0 | 0 | 0 | 0 | 0 | 1 | 0 | 0 | 0 | 0.0020 | |
| 100 | 0 | 1 | 0 | 0 | 0 | 0 | 1 | 0 | 0 | 0 | 0 | 0 | 0 | 1 | 0 | 0 | 0 | 0.0025 | |
| 100 | 0 | 1 | 0 | 0 | 0 | 0 | 0 | 1 | 0 | 0 | 0 | 0 | 0 | 1 | 0 | 0 | 0 | 0.0013 | |
| 200 | 0 | 0 | 1 | 0 | 0 | 0 | 0 | 1 | 0 | 0 | 0 | 0 | 1 | 0 | 0 | 0 | 0 | 0.0008 | |
| 100 | 0 | 0 | 1 | 0 | 0 | 0 | 0 | 1 | 0 | 0 | 0 | 0 | 0 | 1 | 0 | 0 | 0 | 0.0010 | |
| 300 | 1 | 0 | 0 | 0 | 0 | 0 | 1 | 0 | 0 | 0 | 0 | 0 | 0 | 0 | 0 | 1 | 0 | 0.0013 | page × $root_a$ × day |
| 100 | 0 | 1 | 0 | 0 | 0 | 0 | 1 | 0 | 0 | 0 | 0 | 0 | 0 | 0 | 0 | 1 | 0 | 0.0025 | |
| 100 | 0 | 1 | 0 | 0 | 0 | 0 | 0 | 1 | 0 | 0 | 0 | 0 | 0 | 0 | 0 | 1 | 0 | 0.0013 | |
| 300 | 0 | 0 | 1 | 0 | 0 | 0 | 0 | 1 | 0 | 0 | 0 | 0 | 0 | 0 | 0 | 1 | 0 | 0.0087 | |

- The remaining combinations ...

**Figure 3: Example of feature representation for FM**

While hierarchical regularization alone can help constrain the parameters of the nodes, the final derived priors may not conform directly to the underlying click and exposure data. More informative priors can be obtained by fitting the data directly, that is, by *agglomerating* the click/expose data over various pages and ads. As an example, for a publisher node $pb$, we agglomerate the clicks/exposures of all page-ad-day triplets $(p, a, d)$ where $p$ belongs to publisher. In this way, a reasonable prior for the children's latent factors can be learned. Formally, the aggregated clicks and exposures of a *non-leaf* node $u$ in the hierarchy are defined in (12):

$$c_u = \sum_{v:u \in Par(v)} c_v, e_u = \sum_{v:u \in Par(v)} e_v \quad (12)$$

The base case is when $v$ is the leaf node, such that $c_u$ (or $e_u$) is the standard click (or expose) value $c_i$ (or $v_i$).

Figure 3 illustrates the FM-compatible feature representation for the example in Figure 2. We use binary categorical features to represent various entities in the hierarchy. Each row represents a data instance, and is associated with a target response ($CTR$) and importance weight (exposures) $e_i$. The base instances (i.e., `page` × `ad` × `day`) correspond to the first six rows. In the next level `publisher` × `ad` × `day`, we aggregate the exposures $e_i$ (and similarly the clicks $c_i$), yielding the next five rows. We repeat this for the remaining combinations to obtain the full design matrix $X$ for FM.

One may notice from Figure 3 that, due to the agglomeration process, the exposures and clicks of the base cases `page` × `ad` × `day` will be outweighed by the ones in the parent level (e.g., publisher × ad × day). As our model is weighted by the exposures, the contribution of the base cases would be "ignored" in our HIFM training. To remedy this, we rescale the importance weights of all *non-base* cases using (13):

$$e_i \leftarrow \frac{e_i}{2} \frac{\sum_{p \in \texttt{page} \times \texttt{ad} \times \texttt{day}} e_p}{\sum_{q \notin \texttt{page} \times \texttt{ad} \times \texttt{day}} e_q}, \forall i \notin \texttt{page} \times \texttt{ad} \times \texttt{day} \quad (13)$$

That is, we rescale based on the ratio of the sum of exposures of the base cases over that of the non-base cases.

## 5.3 Optimization Algorithms

To support hierarchical and importance-aware learning in HIFM, we develop two classes of efficient iterative methods: *stochastic gradient descent* (SGD) and *coordinate descent* (CD), as described in Sections 5.3.1 and 5.3.2 respectively.

### 5.3.1 Stochastic Gradient Descent

The standard, unweighted SGD update for a specific model parameter $\theta$ is given in (14):

$$\theta \leftarrow \theta - \eta \left[ \frac{\partial l(y_i, \hat{y}(\mathbf{x}_i|\Theta))}{\partial \theta} + \frac{\partial \Omega(\Theta)}{\partial \theta} \right] \quad (14)$$

where $y_i$ is the target value of the $i^{th}$ instance, and $l(a,b) = (b-a)^2$ for square loss or $l(a,b) = -a\log(\sigma(b)) - (1-a)\log(1-\sigma(b))$ for logistic loss. The (sub)gradients of the square and logistic losses translate to (15)-(16) respectively:

$$\frac{\partial l_{square}(y_i, \hat{y}(\mathbf{x}_i|\Theta))}{\partial \theta} = (\hat{y}(\mathbf{x}_i|\Theta) - y_i)\, g_\theta(\mathbf{x}_i) \quad (15)$$

$$\frac{\partial l_{logistic}(y_i, \hat{y}(\mathbf{x}_i|\Theta))}{\partial \theta} = (\sigma(\hat{y}(\mathbf{x}_i|\Theta)) - y_i)\, g_\theta(\mathbf{x}_i) \quad (16)$$

A simple way to incorporate importance weights is to oversample the instances as many as the number of exposures $e_i$. However, for large $e_i$, the oversampled data would be much larger than the original data, leading to inefficient computation. Another tempting approach is to multiply the gradient term $g_\theta(\mathbf{x}_i)$ by $e_i$. However, such approach violates the principle that an instance $\mathbf{x}_i$ with importance weight $e_i$ should be treated as if it appears $e_i$ times in the data.

**Algorithm 1** Importance-aware SGD with regularization

**Input:** Design matrix $X$, targets $\mathbf{y} = \{y_i\}$, regularization parameters $\{\lambda_\theta\}$, initial width $\sigma$, learning rate $\eta$
**Output:** Model parameters $\Theta$

$w_0 \leftarrow 0$; $\mathbf{w} \leftarrow (0, \ldots, 0)$; $V \sim N(0, \sigma^2)$
**repeat**
**for** $i \in \{1, \ldots, N\}$ **do**
$i \leftarrow$ *RouletteWheelSelection*()
$w_0 \leftarrow w_0 - \eta \left( \frac{\partial l(\hat{y}(\mathbf{x}_i|\Theta), y_i)}{\partial w_0} + \frac{\partial \Omega(\Theta)}{\partial w_0} \right)$
**for** $j \in \{1, \ldots, J\} \wedge x_j \neq 0$ **do**
$w_j \leftarrow w_j - \eta \left( \frac{\partial l(\hat{y}(\mathbf{x}_i|\Theta), y_i)}{\partial w_j} + \frac{\partial \Omega(\Theta)}{\partial w_j} \right)$
**for** $k \in \{1, \ldots, K\}$ **do**
$v_{k,j} \leftarrow v_{k,j} - \eta \left( \frac{\partial l(\hat{y}(\mathbf{x}_i|\Theta), y_i)}{\partial v_{k,j}} + \frac{\partial \Omega(\Theta)}{\partial v_{k,j}} \right)$
**end for**
**end for**
**end for**
**until** stopping criterion is met

In light of these drawbacks, we propose to use a simple roulette wheel selection mechanism [4]. That is, the probability of selecting instance $\mathbf{x}_i$ with importance weight $e_i$ is given by $p(\mathbf{x}_i) = \frac{e_i}{\sum_{i'=1}^{N} e_{i'}}$, and subsequently a random sampling (with replacement) is carried out according to $p(\mathbf{x}_i)$ until $N$ instances are obtained[1]. In this way, we can avoid explicitly oversampling the data, while achieving asymptotically the same effect of presenting an instance $e_i$ times, given sufficient number of iterations. Note that, for each instance, the runtime complexity of our importance-aware SGD remains the same as the original SGD, i.e., $O(KN_z(X))$.

Our importance-aware SGD method (with generic regularization term) is summarized in Algorithm 1. With respect to the different regularizations (7) and (11), the term $\frac{\partial \Omega(\Theta)}{\partial \theta}$ evaluates to (17) and (18) respectively:

$$\frac{\partial \Omega(\Theta)}{\partial \theta} = \lambda_\theta \theta \quad (17)$$

$$\frac{\partial \Omega(\Theta)}{\partial \theta} = \lambda_\theta \left( \theta - \bar{\theta}_{Par} \right) \quad (18)$$

where we have a special case $\bar{\theta}_{Par} = 0$ if $\theta \in \mathcal{H}_{root}$.

Finally, in cold-start situations, we perform a special procedure when dealing with a new column $j$ in unseen (test) data. Specifically, whenever we have hierarchy information, we augment our prediction using the latent factors of the ancestors. This is realized via the "back-off" formula (19):

$$w_j \leftarrow \sum_{j' \in Path(j) - \{j\}} w_{j'}, \; v_{k,j} \leftarrow \sum_{j' \in Path(j) - \{j\}} v_{k,j'} \quad (19)$$

where $Path(j)$ refers to the path from the root node to node $j$ in the hierarchy. For a non-tree hierarchy, we utilize the average latent factor of the parent nodes level by level.

### 5.3.2 Coordinate Descent

The basic idea of the CD algorithm is to start with an initial (random) guess of $\Theta$, and then iterate over and update each model parameter $\theta \in \Theta$, assuming all the other parameters are fixed. We propose an extended importance-aware CD with generic regularization. For the weighted square loss in (5), the importance-aware CD algorithm performs an update of the form (20):

$$\theta = \arg\min_\theta \left( \sum_{i=1}^{N} e_i (\hat{y}(\mathbf{x}_i|\Theta) - y_i)^2 + \Omega(\Theta) \right) \quad (20)$$

Note that, for logistic loss, there is no closed-form solution for the update, so we focus only on square loss in this paper.

Consequently, the update steps for the regularization in (17) and (18) are given by (21) and (22) respectively:

$$\theta \leftarrow \frac{\theta \sum_{i=1}^{N} e_i g_\theta^2(\mathbf{x}_i) + \sum_{i=1}^{N} e_i g_\theta(\mathbf{x}_i) r_i}{\sum_{i=1}^{N} e_i g_\theta^2(\mathbf{x}_i) + \lambda_\theta} \quad (21)$$

$$\theta \leftarrow \frac{\theta \sum_{i=1}^{N} e_i g_\theta^2(\mathbf{x}_i) + \sum_{i=1}^{N} e_i g_\theta(\mathbf{x}_i) r_i + \lambda_\theta \bar{\theta}_{Par}}{\sum_{i=1}^{N} e_i g_\theta^2(\mathbf{x}_i) + \lambda_\theta} \quad (22)$$

where $r_i = y_i - \hat{y}(\mathbf{x}_i|\Theta)$ is the residual term and, again, $\bar{\theta}_{Par} = 0$ if $\theta \in \mathcal{H}_{root}$. The update for standard (L2) regularization is thus a special case of (22), where $Par(\theta) = \emptyset$. In the case of a cold-start column such that all $g_\theta(\mathbf{x}_i) = 0$, hierarchical regularization gives us $\theta \leftarrow \bar{\theta}_{Par}$, which should lead to a more informative prediction.

Algorithm 2 outlines our importance-aware CD method with generic regularization. Here, linear-time learning can

[1]The standard, unweighted SGD refers to a special case of roulette wheel selection with uniform probability $p(\mathbf{x}_i) = \frac{1}{N}$

**Algorithm 2** Importance-aware CD with regularization

**Input:** Design matrix $X$, targets $\mathbf{y} = \{y_i\}$, regularization parameters $\{\lambda_\theta\}$, initial width $\sigma$

**Output:** Model parameters $\Theta$

$w_0 \leftarrow 0$; $\mathbf{w} \leftarrow (0, \ldots, 0)$; $V \sim N(0, \sigma^2)$<br>
**repeat**<br>
$\hat{\mathbf{y}} \leftarrow$ predict all instances $X$<br>
$\mathbf{r} \leftarrow \mathbf{y} - \hat{\mathbf{y}}$<br>
Update $w_0$ using (21) or (22)<br>
Update cache $\mathbf{r}$ using (25)<br>
**for** $j \in \{1, \ldots, J\}$ **do**<br>
Update $w_j$ using (21) or (22)<br>
Update cache $\mathbf{r}$ using (25)<br>
**end for**<br>
**for** $k \in \{1, \ldots, K\}$ **do**<br>
Initialize cache $\mathbf{q}_{\cdot,k}$ using (24)<br>
**for** $j \in \{1, \ldots, J\}$ **do**<br>
Update $v_{k,j}$ using (21) or (22)<br>
Update cache $\mathbf{r}$ using (25)<br>
Update cache $\mathbf{q}$ using (26)<br>
**end for**<br>
**end for**<br>
**until** stopping criterion is met

be achieved using *r-cache* and *q-cache*, which store the results of (pre)computing the residuals $\{r_i\}$ and inner-product terms $\{q_{i,k}\}$. They are given in (23) and (24) respectively:

$$r_i = y_i - \hat{y}(\mathbf{x}_i|\Theta) \tag{23}$$

$$q_{i,k} = \sum_{j=1}^{J} v_{k,j} x_{i,j} \tag{24}$$

After each update of model parameter $\theta$, we update the $e$-cache accordingly. Similarly, for every update of $V_{k,j}$, we update the $q$-cache. The cache update steps are summarized in (25) and (26) respectively:

$$r_i \leftarrow r_i - \left(\theta^{new} - \theta^{old}\right) g_\theta(\mathbf{x}_i) \tag{25}$$

$$q_{i,k} \leftarrow q_{i,k} + \left(v_{k,j}^{new} - v_{k,j}^{old}\right) x_{i,j} \tag{26}$$

Referring to (22), the bulk of the CD computations lies on two terms: $\sum_{i=1}^{N} e_i g_\theta^2(\mathbf{x}_i)$ and $\sum_{i=1}^{N} e_i g_\theta(\mathbf{x}_i) r_i$. By caching residuals $\{r_i\}$ and inner-products $\{q_{i,k}\}$, each full iteration over all $\theta \in \Theta$ can be done quickly in $O(KN_z(X))$.

We also note that Algorithm 2 actually corresponds to the *cyclic coordinate descent*, which traverses all columns $j$ in a fixed order (i.e., from $j = 1$ to $j = J$). In a similar vein to [17], we also develop a stochastic variant called *stochastic coordinate descent*, which iterates over the columns in a random order instead. In our experiments, we found that this stochastic version exhibits faster convergence, albeit producing similar overall prediction quality (cf. Section 6.3).

# 6. EXPERIMENTS

## 6.1 Setup

We conducted 10 runs of experiments to evaluate our algorithms, based on the ad response dataset supplied by our partner for the period of 05-31 October 2012 (cf. Section 3). For each run, we take 9 days and split the data by time into a training set (7 days) and a test set (2 days). For our evaluations, we use the average and standard deviation of the prediction results on the 10 test sets. Table 2 summarizes the configuration of our training and test sets.

**Table 2: Experiment setup**

| Evaluation | Training period | Test period |
|---|---|---|
| Trial 1 | 05-11 October | 12-13 October |
| Trial 2 | 07-13 October | 14-15 October |
| Trial 3 | 09-15 October | 16-17 October |
| Trial 4 | 11-17 October | 18-19 October |
| Trial 5 | 13-19 October | 20-21 October |
| Trial 6 | 15-21 October | 22-23 October |
| Trial 7 | 17-23 October | 24-25 October |
| Trial 8 | 19-25 October | 26-27 October |
| Trial 9 | 21-27 October | 28-29 October |
| Trial 10 | 23-29 October | 30-31 October |

For all algorithms, we set the number of interaction factors as $K = 5$, as we find it gives good overall results. We also fix the regularization parameters as $\lambda_\theta = 0$ for $\theta = w_0$, and $\lambda_\theta = 0.001$ for $\theta = w_j$ or $\theta = V_{k,j}$. As our stopping criterion, we fix a total number of iterations for each algorithm. For the SGD algorithm, we set the total iterations to 100, while we use 10 for the CD algorithm (since CD generally requires fewer iterations than SGD to reach convergence).

## 6.2 Evaluation Metrics

As mentioned in Section 1, a desirable model for response prediction should give good regression and ranking results. Accordingly, we evaluate the prediction performances of our algorithms using several regression and ranking metrics. For regression, we use weighted root mean square error (wRMSE) and weighted negative log likelihood (wNLL), as defined in (27) and (28) respectively, for a test set with $N$ instances:

$$wRMSE = \sqrt{\frac{\sum_{i=1}^{N} e_i \left(y_i - \hat{y}_i\right)^2}{\sum_{i=1}^{N} e_i}} \tag{27}$$

$$wNLL = -\frac{\sum_{i=1}^{N} e_i (y_i \log \sigma(\hat{y}_i) + (1 - y_i) \log (1 - \sigma(\hat{y}_i))}{\sum_{i=1}^{N} e_i} \tag{28}$$

Here $y_i$ and $\hat{y}_i$ denote the target and predicted outputs respectively, and (again) $e_i$ is the number of exposures. The $wRMSE$ and $wNLL$ can be thought as complementary metrics quantifying the importance-weighted "distance" between predicted and actual probabilities. They also correspond to the loss functions (5) and (6) respectively.

For ranking, on the other hand, we use the weighted area under the receiver-operating characteristic curve (wAUC) [6]. Essentially, this metric reflects the probability that a predictive model will rank a randomly chosen positive instance higher than a randomly chosen negative one. In this, we treat the problem as a binary classification task, where a click (no click) indicates a positive (negative) instance. For example, if the number of exposures $e_i = 10$ and the number of clicks $c_i = 3$ (i.e., $CTR = y_i = 0.3$), we treat this as 3 positive instances and 7 negative instances. By "unrolling" all $CTR$ entries this way, we can compute AUC weighted by ad exposures so as to measure the ranking quality.

## 6.3 Overall Results

The overall prediction results, evaluated using the three performance metrics, are summarized in Tables 3, 4 and 5,

**Table 3: Consolidated results averaged over 10 trials for $e_{min} = 10$**

| Method | Type | Importance | Hierarchy | wRMSE | wNLL | wAUC |
|---|---|---|---|---|---|---|
| TensorALS | - | - | - | 0.0245347 ± 0.0006238 | 0.1141281 ± 0.0031088 | 0.5 ± 0.0 |
| TimeSVD++ | - | - | - | 0.0230917 ± 0.0005482 | 0.0369275 ± 0.0009549 | 0.7046705 ± 0.0101725 |
| FM-SGD | Square | No | No | 0.0105449 ± 0.0040673 | 0.0190836 ± 0.0033935 | 0.7600722 ± 0.0348881 |
| | | No | Yes | 0.0092290 ± 0.0034284(*) | 0.0190393 ± 0.0040543 | 0.7588117 ± 0.0426068 |
| | | Yes | No | 0.0043385 ± 0.0003909(*) | 0.0139876 ± 0.0021322(*) | 0.8263158 ± 0.0327539(*) |
| | | Yes | Yes | 0.0044152 ± 0.0006106(*) | 0.0143682 ± 0.0024797(*) | 0.8240209 ± 0.0343667(*) |
| FM-SGD | Logistic | No | No | 0.0067266 ± 0.0003933 | 0.0154207 ± 0.0013011 | 0.7730542 ± 0.0314904 |
| | | No | Yes | 0.0068068 ± 0.0008265 | 0.0149345 ± 0.0014383(*) | 0.7804171 ± 0.0339882(*) |
| | | Yes | No | 0.0052925 ± 0.0001996(*) | 0.0139813 ± 0.0014130(*) | 0.8136070 ± 0.0334504(*) |
| | | Yes | Yes | 0.0048635 ± 0.0001841(*) | 0.0136824 ± 0.0014207(*) | 0.8152107 ± 0.0340372(*) |
| FM-CD | Cyclic | No | No | 0.0061768 ± 0.0001934 | 0.0145682 ± 0.0015581 | 0.7617378 ± 0.0441938 |
| | | No | Yes | 0.0063543 ± 0.0001996 | 0.0151101 ± 0.0013793 | 0.7629488 ± 0.0455320 |
| | | Yes | No | 0.0044806 ± 0.0002127(*) | 0.0135587 ± 0.0017265(*) | 0.8262493 ± 0.0283374(*) |
| | | Yes | Yes | 0.0047210 ± 0.0001874(*) | 0.0141638 ± 0.0021363 | 0.8212097 ± 0.0321086(*) |
| FM-CD | Stochastic | No | No | 0.0062104 ± 0.0001935 | 0.0146287 ± 0.0015349 | 0.7617537 ± 0.0441836 |
| | | No | Yes | 0.0063543 ± 0.0001996 | 0.0151101 ± 0.0013793 | 0.7629527 ± 0.0455303 |
| | | Yes | Yes | 0.0044815 ± 0.0002135(*) | 0.0135992 ± 0.0017595(*) | 0.8255169 ± 0.0290100(*) |
| | | Yes | Yes | 0.0047006 ± 0.0001915(*) | 0.0138494 ± 0.0021000 | 0.8233171 ± 0.0326712(*) |

(*) indicates statistically significant improvements over the baseline based on Wilcoxon signed-rank test at significance level of 0.01

**Table 4: Consolidated results averaged over 10 trials for $e_{min} = 100$**

| Method | Type | Importance | Hierarchy | wRMSE | wNLL | wAUC |
|---|---|---|---|---|---|---|
| TensorALS | - | - | - | 0.0148571 ± 0.0007870 | 0.0898490 ± 0.0033757 | 0.5 ± 0.0 |
| TimeSVD++ | - | - | - | 0.0133219 ± 0.0009000 | 0.0300316 ± 0.0011584 | 0.7104049 ± 0.0104965 |
| FM-SGD | Square | No | No | 0.0066994 ± 0.0039766 | 0.0159641 ± 0.0030365 | 0.7906827 ± 0.0399742 |
| | | No | Yes | 0.0063514 ± 0.0036174 | 0.0155720 ± 0.0030424 | 0.7947463 ± 0.0436061 |
| | | Yes | No | 0.0035637 ± 0.0002817(*) | 0.0136790 ± 0.0022342(*) | 0.8263953 ± 0.0345580(*) |
| | | Yes | Yes | 0.0036013 ± 0.0003965(*) | 0.0143439 ± 0.0028064(*) | 0.8216659 ± 0.0377304(*) |
| FM-SGD | Logistic | No | No | 0.0052633 ± 0.0006386 | 0.0144573 ± 0.0013365 | 0.7831293 ± 0.0378750 |
| | | No | Yes | 0.0048462 ± 0.0009245 | 0.0139555 ± 0.0014297(*) | 0.7940811 ± 0.0385131(*) |
| | | Yes | No | 0.0048071 ± 0.0002476(*) | 0.0137598 ± 0.0014451(*) | 0.8085024 ± 0.0353346(*) |
| | | Yes | Yes | 0.0043588 ± 0.0002261(*) | 0.0134459 ± 0.0014542(*) | 0.8119756 ± 0.0355739(*) |
| FM-CD | Cyclic | No | No | 0.0052848 ± 0.0002765 | 0.0139085 ± 0.0017059 | 0.7725149 ± 0.0481081 |
| | | No | Yes | 0.0054034 ± 0.0002760 | 0.0141956 ± 0.0015021 | 0.7735657 ± 0.0484978 |
| | | Yes | No | 0.0035659 ± 0.0002768(*) | 0.0131528 ± 0.0016376(*) | 0.8246543 ± 0.0288612(*) |
| | | Yes | Yes | 0.0037860 ± 0.0002213(*) | 0.0134757 ± 0.0020551 | 0.8253329 ± 0.0321349(*) |
| FM-CD | Stochastic | No | No | 0.0053125 ± 0.0002773 | 0.0139288 ± 0.0016660 | 0.7725211 ± 0.0481107 |
| | | No | Yes | 0.0054034 ± 0.0002760 | 0.0141957 ± 0.0015021 | 0.7735673 ± 0.0484932 |
| | | Yes | Yes | 0.0035798 ± 0.0002810(*) | 0.0131411 ± 0.0016117(*) | 0.8248637 ± 0.0276094(*) |
| | | Yes | Yes | 0.0037806 ± 0.0002244(*) | 0.0133138 ± 0.0019167 | 0.8262658 ± 0.0313433(*) |

(*) indicates statistically significant improvements over the baseline based on Wilcoxon signed-rank test at significance level of 0.01

**Table 5: Consolidated results averaged over 10 trials for $e_{min} = 1000$**

| Method | Type | Importance | Hierarchy | wRMSE | wNLL | wAUC |
|---|---|---|---|---|---|---|
| TensorALS | - | - | - | 0.0105002 ± 0.0011214 | 0.0698346 ± 0.0037189 | 0.5 ± 0.0 |
| TimeSVD++ | - | - | - | 0.0093541 ± 0.0012304 | 0.0244543 ± 0.0009942 | 0.7066218 ± 0.0113939 |
| FM-SGD | Square | No | No | 0.0035179 ± 0.0006461 | 0.0140867 ± 0.0031550 | 0.8032424 ± 0.0479115 |
| | | No | Yes | 0.0033768 ± 0.0005637 | 0.0141022 ± 0.0031252 | 0.8029501 ± 0.0465531 |
| | | Yes | No | 0.0027669 ± 0.0003007(*) | 0.0127455 ± 0.0023743(*) | 0.8253467 ± 0.0383887(*) |
| | | Yes | Yes | 0.0027779 ± 0.0002821(*) | 0.0136180 ± 0.0027904 | 0.8191953 ± 0.0401579(*) |
| FM-SGD | Logistic | No | No | 0.0041532 ± 0.0003815 | 0.0133235 ± 0.0014580 | 0.7802751 ± 0.0425936 |
| | | No | Yes | 0.0035746 ± 0.0004055(*) | 0.0128660 ± 0.0014666(*) | 0.7920499 ± 0.0432757(*) |
| | | Yes | No | 0.0043950 ± 0.0003841 | 0.0130108 ± 0.0015346(*) | 0.7984587 ± 0.0402334(*) |
| | | Yes | Yes | 0.0038005 ± 0.0003306(*) | 0.0126841 ± 0.0015381(*) | 0.8057917 ± 0.0396685(*) |
| FM-CD | Cyclic | No | No | 0.0043290 ± 0.0004144 | 0.0131398 ± 0.0022141 | 0.7795976 ± 0.0543661 |
| | | No | Yes | 0.0044521 ± 0.0003917 | 0.0129831 ± 0.0016401 | 0.7811009 ± 0.0542086(*) |
| | | Yes | No | 0.0025551 ± 0.0003352(*) | 0.0124212 ± 0.0017798(*) | 0.8232776 ± 0.0334076(*) |
| | | Yes | Yes | 0.0027313 ± 0.0002812(*) | 0.0123107 ± 0.0018302(*) | 0.8268533 ± 0.0333732(*) |
| FM-CD | Stochastic | No | No | 0.0043391 ± 0.0004133 | 0.0129884 ± 0.0020158 | 0.7797752 ± 0.0543298 |
| | | No | Yes | 0.0044521 ± 0.0003917 | 0.0129832 ± 0.0016401 | 0.7811113 ± 0.0542079(*) |
| | | Yes | Yes | 0.0025507 ± 0.0003444(*) | 0.0124773 ± 0.0018751(*) | 0.8223575 ± 0.0337542(*) |
| | | Yes | Yes | 0.0027390 ± 0.0002842(*) | 0.0123266 ± 0.0018478(*) | 0.8262701 ± 0.0335686(*) |

(*) indicates statistically significant improvements over the baseline based on Wilcoxon signed-rank test at significance level of 0.01

for different minimum exposures $e_{min} = 10, 100$ and 1000, respectively. For our SGD algorithm, we employ two variants that optimize for square and logistic loss functions respectively. Similarly, we utilize the cyclic and stochastic variants of our CD algorithm. For comparison, we also experiment with two popular time-aware factorization algorithms: TensorALS [5] and TimeSVD++ [9], which should serve as good reference methods. For fairness, similar configurations were used in these methods, e.g., 5 latent factors ($K = 5$) and 100 training iterations (as with our SGD).

To investigate the effects of importance-weighted and hierarchical learning, we conduct experiments by turning on and off the importance weight and hierarchy, resulting in four configurations for each algorithm variant. Subsequently, to see how significant the result improvements are due to importance weight and/or hierarchy, we use the non-parametric Wilcoxon signed-rank statistical test[2] [22]. All the tests were performed at a significance level of 1%, with the baseline being the "no importance weight and no hierarchy" case.

Several observations can accordingly be made based on the overall prediction results in Tables 3, 4 and 5:

- All our FM-based algorithms outperform the TensorALS and TimeSVD++ methods, in terms of both regression and ranking results. (Separate Wilcoxon tests using TensorALS and TimeSVD++ as baselines also show that all our algorithms are significantly better.) Note also that TensorALS gives "flat" predictions on the test set (where all the time indices never appear in the training set), leading to a constant $wAUC = 0.5$.

- As the minimum exposure threshold $e_{min}$ increases, we see improvements in all performance metrics. This is expected, since a higher $e_{min}$ implies a higher confidence in the $CTR$ estimation and thus cleaner data for training and testing (recall that $CTR = \frac{\texttt{numclick}}{\texttt{numexpose}}$).

- We observe large improvements when we incorporate importance weights (i.e., importance-aware learning), while incorporating hierarchical information does not necessarily improve the overall prediction results. This is reasonable nonetheless, since we can expect that hierarchical learning helps in (near) cold-start cases, which would likely have small importance weights in our (weighted) evaluation on the test data. Further investigation on the performance of our methods in cold-start scenarios is presented in Section 6.4.

- In general, the CD algorithm produces similar performance to the SGD procedure, though the former needs fewer iterations to converge and has fewer user parameters (i.e., no learning rate $\eta$). Comparing the square and logistic SGD variants, we observe that the former generally exhibits better results in terms of $wRMSE$ and $wAUC$, while the latter is superior in terms of $wNLL$, which is expected. Meanwhile, the cyclic and stochastic CD variants yield very similar performances, though the stochastic approximation in the latter is expected to give faster training convergence.

## 6.4 Cold-Start Results

We carried out further studies on how hierarchical learning in our HIFM approach can help address the cold-start situations. In this study, we concentrate on the extreme cold-start scenarios whereby we deal with new pages *and* ads. We define new pages and ads as those that only appear in the test data, and never in the training set. We conducted the experiments as before, and averaged the results for these cold-start cases over 10 trials. We can expect that, when no hierarchical regularization or fitting takes place, our algorithms will produce a "flat' prediction (i.e., $wAUC = 0.5$). In this case, we may obtain reasonably good regression performance, but the ranking produced will be meaningless. Due to this reason (and space constraint), we shall focus on evaluating the ranking performance (i.e., $wAUC$) here.

[2]The Wilcoxon test can be used as an alternative to the t-test for matched pairs, or the t-test for dependent samples when they cannot be assumed to be normally distributed.

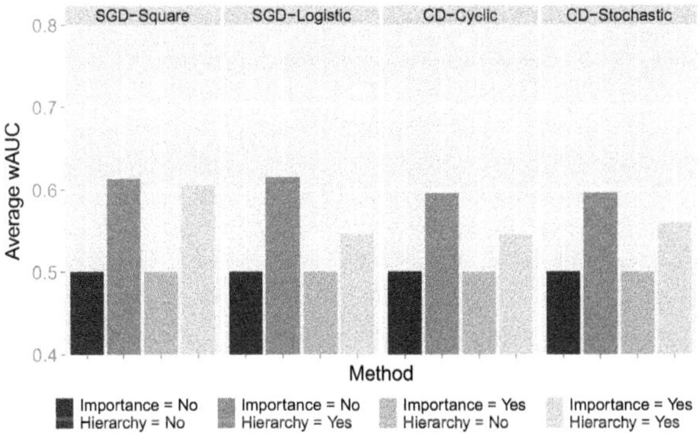


(a) Minimum exposure $e_{min} = 10$

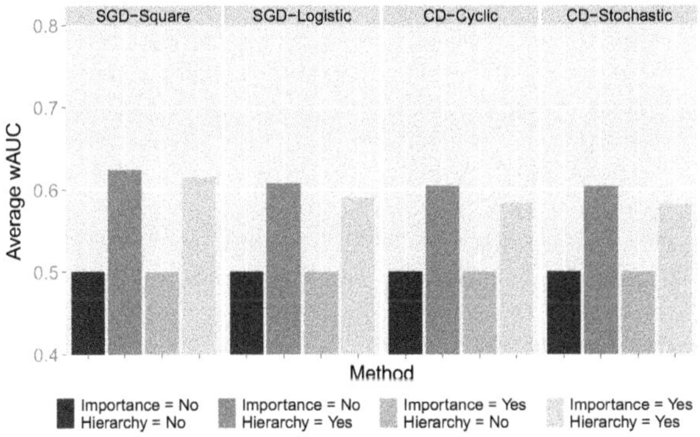


(b) Minimum exposure $e_{min} = 100$

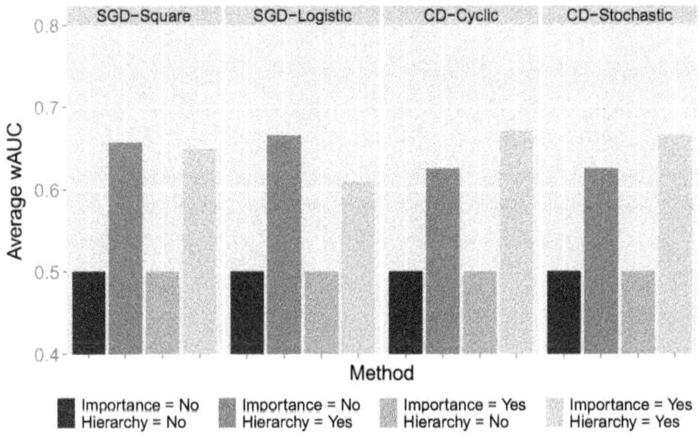


(c) Minimum exposure $e_{min} = 1000$

**Figure 4: Results for cold-start cases**

Our experimental results are presented in Figure 4, with the minimum exposure $e_{min}$ varied from 10 to 1000. It can be seen that the ranking results always improve as we incorporate hierarchy information in our algorithms. In addition, we observe that the result improvements get amplified as $e_{min}$ is increased, which can (again) be attributed to the higher confidence in the $CTR$ estimates (i.e., cleaner data). It is also worth noting that, for these cold-start cases, the results of importance-aware learning and those of unweighted learning are not directly comparable. In fact, the cold-start cases tend to have low exposures in the training data, for which the importance-aware learning would give lower priority. Nevertheless, the results illustrate that the importance-aware learning and hierarchy information are complementary in handling complex response prediction tasks.

# 7. CONCLUSION

In this paper, we put forward a latent factor model, termed the *Hierarchical Importance-Aware Factorization Machine* (HIFM), for predicting dynamic ad response. Using the factorization machine as the base generic framework, we develop new importance-aware and hierarchical learning mechanisms to improve the model's predictive abilities in complex response prediction tasks where cost-varying instances and cold-start cases are ubiquitous. Several variants of efficient learning methods have been developed to explore different ways of incorporating importance weight and hierarchy information in HIFM. The efficacy of our HIFM model has been exemplified through extensive empirical studies on real-world mobile advertising data from a global ad network.

Moving forward, we consider several avenues for future research. First, there is a need to further scale up the HIFM for large datasets, either by means of parallelization or a more efficient data representation (e.g., [14]). Second, we can further enhance the HIFM's predictive power by incorporating hierarchical Bayesian learning on top of a deep, multi-layer representation. Last but not least, we wish to explore the applicability of the HIFM in other task domains, such as temporal item adoption or rating prediction.

## Acknowledgment

This research is supported by Singapore National Research Foundation under its International Research Centre @ Singapore Funding Initiative and administered by the IDM Programme Office, Media Development Authority (MDA).

# 8. REFERENCES

[1] D. Agarwal, R. Agrawal, R. Khanna, and N. Kota. Estimating rates of rare events with multiple hierarchies through scalable log-linear models. In *Proceedings of the ACM SIGKDD Knowledge Discovery and Data Mining*, pages 213–222, 2010.

[2] D. Agarwal, B.-C. Chen, and P. Elango. Spatio-temporal models for estimating click-through rate. In *Proceedings of the International World Wide Web Conference*, pages 21–30, New York, NY, 2009.

[3] G. Aggarwal, A. Goel, and R. Motwani. Truthful auctions for pricing search keywords. In *Proceedings of the ACM Conference on Electronic Commerce*, pages 1–7, 2006.

[4] T. Bäck. *Evolutionary algorithms in theory and practice: evolution strategies, evolutionary programming, genetic algorithms.* Oxford University Press, Oxford, UK, 1996.

[5] P. Comon, X. Luciani, and A. L. F. de Almeida. Tensor decompositions, alternating least squares and other tales. *Journal of Chemometrics*, 23:393–405, 2009.

[6] T. Fawcett. ROC graphs: Notes and practical considerations for researchers. Technical report, 2004.

[7] Gartner. Gartner says worldwide mobile advertising revenue to reach $11.4 billion in 2013. Available: http://www.gartner.com/newsroom/id/23062152013.

[8] T. Graepel, J. Q. Candela, T. Borchert, and R. Herbrich. Web-scale Bayesian click-through rate prediction for sponsored search advertising in Microsoft's Bing search engine. In *Proceedings of the International Conference on Machine Learning*, 2010.

[9] Y. Koren. Collaborative filtering with temporal dynamics. In *Proceedings of the ACM SIGKDD International Conference on Knowledge Discovery and Data Mining*, pages 447–456, New York, NY, 2009.

[10] Z. Lu, D. Agarwal, and I. S. Dhillon. A spatio-temporal approach to collaborative filtering. In *Proceedings of the ACM conference on Recommender systems*, pages 13–20, 2009.

[11] A. K. Menon, K.-P. Chitrapura, S. Garg, D. Agarwal, and N. Kota. Response prediction using collaborative filtering with hierarchies and side-information. In *Proceedings of the ACM SIGKDD International Conference on Knowledge Discovery and Data Mining*, pages 141–149, 2011.

[12] S. Rendle. Factorization machines. In *Proceedings of the IEEE International Conference on Data Mining*, Sydney, Australia, 2010.

[13] S. Rendle. Factorization machines with libFM. *ACM Transactions on Intelligent Systems and Technology*, 3:57:1–57:22, 2012.

[14] S. Rendle. Scaling factorization machines to relational data. In *Proceedings of the International Conference on Very Large Data Bases*, pages 337–348, 2013.

[15] M. Richardson. Predicting clicks: Estimating the click-through rate for new ads. In *Proceedings of the International World Wide Web Conference*, pages 521–530, 2007.

[16] D. Sculley. Combined regression and ranking. In *Proceedings of the ACM SIGKDD International Conference on Knowledge Discovery and Data Mining*, pages 979–988, New York, NY, USA, 2010.

[17] S. Shalev-Shwartz and A. Tewari. Stochastic methods for l1 regularized loss minimization. In *Proceedings of the International Conference on Machine Learning*, pages 929–936, 2009.

[18] H. Shan, J. Kattge, P. B. Reich, A. Banerjee, F. Schrodt, and M. Reichstein. Gap filling in the plant kingdom–trait prediction using hierarchical probabilistic matrix factorization. In *Proceedings of the International Conference on Machine Learning*, Edinburgh, 2012.

[19] S. Shen, B. Hu, W. Chen, and Q. Yang. Personalized click model through collaborative filtering. In *Proceedings of the ACM International Conference on Web Search and Data Mining*, pages 323–332, 2012.

[20] N. Srebro, J. D. M. Rennie, and T. S. Jaakola. Maximum-margin matrix factorization. In *Proceedings of the Advances in Neural Information Processing Systems*, volume 17, pages 1329–1336, 2005.

[21] J. Z. Sun, K. R. Varschney, and K. Subbian. Dynamic matrix factorization: A state space approach. In *Proceedings of the IEEE International Conference on Speech and Signal Processing*, pages 1897–1900, Kyoto, Japan, 2012.

[22] F. Wilcoxon. Individual comparisons by ranking methods. *Biometrics Bulletin*, 1(6):80–83, 1945.

[23] E. Zhong, W. Fan, and Q. Yang. Contextual collaborative filtering via hierarchical matrix factorization. In *Proceedings of the SIAM International Conference on Data Mining*, pages 744–755, 2012.

# Partner Tiering in Display Advertising

Anand Bhalgat[*]
Facebook Inc
bhalgat@fb.com

Nitish Korula
Google Research
nitish@google.com

Hennadiy Leontyev
Google Inc
leontyev@google.com

Max Lin
Google Inc
whilin@google.com

Vahab Mirrokni
Google Research
mirrokni@google.com

## ABSTRACT

Display ads on the Internet are often sold by publishers to advertisers in bundles of thousands or millions of impressions over a particular time period. The ad delivery systems assign ads to pages on behalf of publishers to satisfy these contracts, and at the same time, try to maximize the overall quality of assignment. This is usually modeled in the literature as an online allocation problem, where contracts are represented by overall delivery constraints.

However an important aspect of these contracts is missed by the classical formulation: a majority of these contracts are not between advertisers and publishers; a set of publishers is typically represented by a middle-man and advertisers buy inventory from the middle man. As publishers vary in quality and importance, advertisers prefer these publishers differently. Similarly, as the inventory of ads is limited, ad-delivery engine needs to prefer a high-quality publisher over a low quality publisher for supplying ads. We formulate this problem as a hierarchical online matching problem where each incoming impression has a level indicating its importance, and study its theoretical properties. We also design practical solutions to this problem and study their performance on real data sets.

## Categories and Subject Descriptors

F.2.m [**Theory of Computation**]: Analysis of Algorithms and Problem Complexity—*Miscellaneous*; H.4.m [**Information Systems Applications**]: Miscellaneous

## Keywords

Display Ads Allocation; Partner-Tiering; Online Matching

## 1. INTRODUCTION

Worldwide online advertising revenues are estimated to exceed US $118 billion in 2013, with recent annual growth rates of 15% [1]. Motivated by practical problems in search and display advertising, recent years have seen the development of a rich theory of online allocation problems and algorithms. As the online advertising industry has evolved, research focus has shifted from search advertising [15, 10, 8] to contract-based display advertising [12, 13, 11, 6, 7] and auction-based advertising exchanges [4, 14, 5]. In the study of many of these models, an implicit assumption has been a *relative scarcity of advertising opportunities* (the supply of user-generated impressions), compared to a relative surplus of demand by advertisers. When this is not the case, for example, the standard budgeted allocation model [15, 10, 8] representing search advertising is not interesting: If there were a significant surplus of user queries / advertising opportunities, all advertisers will eventually spend their entire budgets, regardless of the allocation algorithm used. In this paper, we consider a problem motivated by an increasing availability of online advertising inventory in several applications, including in-app mobile advertising, web-based display advertising, and also video advertising for TV content creators. In the following, we elaborate on these motivating applications in more details.

We begin with the *in-app mobile advertising*. Given an unprecedented increase in popularity of smart-phones in recent past and ever-growing amount of time spent on them (according to mobile apps analytic firm Flurry, US consumers now spend over two and a half hours per day on mobile devices, almost the same as time spent watching television [2]), the in-app advertisers have an increasingly large available inventory to which they can target their ads. However, with the large number of apps that are advertsing inventory sources, (the Google Play store lists over a million apps, and Apple's iTunes App Store offers a similar number), it is clearly infeasible for advertisers to reach individual agreements with the creators of each app. This gives rise to the existence of platforms such as Velti or Millennial Media, which act as middlemen. These platforms *partner* with a number of advertising inventory sources; in this case, app creators. In the rest of the paper, we refer to an individual advertising inventory source in the platform as the *partner*.

Advertisers can approach the platform and create a single advertising campaign with a unified budget and other properties, but have their ads appear on the apps of many different partners. This nature of contracts introduces new challenges: From the perspective of an advertiser, not all inventory supplied by the platform is equally good; advertisers often value premium inventory (corresponding to users of apps such as the New York Times or the Economist) much

[*]Work done while interning at Google NYC.


*WSDM'14,* February 24–28, 2014, New York, New York, USA.
ACM 978-1-4503-2351-2/14/02.
http://dx.doi.org/10.1145/2556195.2556258.

more than other inventory sources (such as users of some gaming apps). However, it may not be possible for advertisers to explicitly list their preferences among all the different inventory sources, or to accurately estimate what fraction of inventory will come from different sources. In this situation, advertisers must rely on the platform (which implicitly or explicitly ranks inventory sources) to give them an appropriate share of premium inventory. From the platform's perspective, the advertising demand is constrained; and it makes business sense to match ads to premium partners over lower quality partners:

(a) If the platform satisfies as much demand as possible with inventory from premium partners, then the advertisers are more likely to return to the platform.

(b) If the *fill rate* for a premium partner (the fraction of impressions for a partner to which the platform assign an ad) is higher, then the premium partner sees more revenue and is more likely to stick with the platform. It is important for a platform to keep the premium partners in its inventory, as this helps attract and retain advertisers.

A similar problem occurs in web-based display advertising. In the past, advertisers made contracts with individual publishers such as the Wall Street Journal, reserving a certain number of impressions, and an ad serving platform (e.g. OpenX, DoubleClick, 24/7 Real Media) assigns ads to publisher's impressions at run-time. However, it is increasingly difficult for advertisers to reach agreements with more than a few top publishers, leading to the rise of various online exchanges (such as Google AdExchange or Yahoo! Right Media) that act as central clearinghouses or platforms where publishers can sell their remaining unallocated inventory. It is important to note, the *ads served under advertiser-publisher reservation contracts are premium ads, commanding a significantly higher CPM than the price a publisher gets for his leftover inventory on the exchanges.*

In this new business model of programmatic contracts, advertisers want to create a single unified campaign with the platform, which decides how to satisfy this advertising demand from different (contract-based as well as exchange-based) partner sources. One natural objective for the platform is to satisfy the demand in a way which maximizes the advertiser value (typically measured in number of clicks or conversions). In addition, the platform may also wish to ensure a high fill rate for higher-priority or premium partners, because this directly affects platform revenue and gives premium partners more incentive to stay with the platform.

Finally, a similar problem is faced by content creators, such as CBS, and this content is viewed by consumers on websites, such as YouTube, that serves as distribution partners. Here, the content creator plays the role of the middleman, making contracts with advertisers to show ads when their content is played on any partner website. Each distribution partner may have a different business relationship and revenue sharing arrangement with the creator, and so the ad serving platform should prefer to display ads on higher-value partners to generate more revenue for the content creator. Products such as MRM from FreeWheel solve this problem for content creators.

## 1.1 Our Contributions

Our first contribution is to provide a formal model of the common problem faced in all the applications above, and provide a *benchmark* to compare the performance of algorithms for this setting. Second, we design algorithms for both the offline and online settings and prove guarantees on their performance (with respect to the benchmark matching) for some cases of the problem. In particular, we observe that the exact optimum solution can be computed in polynomial-time for unweighted graphs, and present a constant-factor approximation algorithm for weighted graphs. Moreover, we show that one of our efficient heuristic online algorithms provide an improved approximation algorithm for the problem in the online stochastic arrival model. Finally, we study several efficient heuristics (`DUAL-SCALE` and `EW-SCALE`) for the problem and analyze their performance on real data-sets from a leading online advertising corporation. Our empirical study shows that the `DUAL-SCALE` algorithm performs better compared to the `EW-SCALE` algorithm.

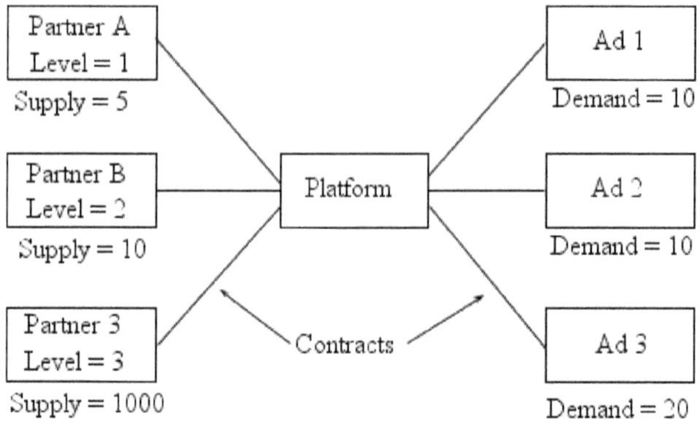


**Figure 1: Three partners at different levels represented by a single platform. Supply at level 1 and 2 is constrained, however the overall supply exceeds the demand.**

We next discuss these aspects in detail; we begin with describing the overall model.

**The Model:** There are multiple partners that are represented by a common platform. Each partner is associated with a priority level reflecting the general value of its inventory. Advertisers demand inventory from the platform that can be satisfied by partners at different levels. In general, there is a surplus of inventory from the partners, however the supply of premium inventory (high priority levels) is constrained compared to advertisers' demands. See Fig. 1 for an illustration.

**Platform Objectives:** Next we discuss the multiple objectives of the platform: First, it must satisfy the demand of the advertisers. Second, it should ensure a higher *fill-rate* for higher-level or premium partners: This may be to increase platform revenue, advertiser happiness, or long-term platform benefits by ensuring the continued association of premium partners. Third, in some applications, inventory may have different values for different advertisers (based on click probabilities, for instance) independent of the level of its source; in these settings, an additional objective is to maximize the total value of the allocated impressions.

Note that given the surplus of inventory, we do not expect that all (or even a large fraction of) inventory will be assigned to advertisers. Thus, the second objective is important: the platform needs to ensure that the premium inventory is not left unassigned. Often, these platform goals are contradictory and it is not clear which assignment is optimal;

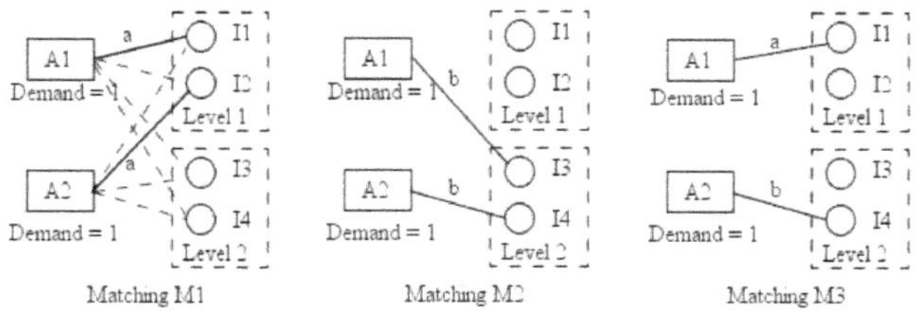


**Figure 2: The set of possible matchings in Example 1.1**

we illustrate with an example, where different matchings are optimal in this case based on different platform objectives:

**Example 1.1** *There are two advertisers $\mathcal{A}_1$ and $\mathcal{A}_2$. Both advertisers have demand* 1. *There are two partners: $P_1$ and $P_2$, at priority levels* 1 *and* 2 *respectively. Each partner supplies two impressions; the weight (CTR) of each impression from partner* 1 *for both advertisers is $a$ and weight (CTR) of each impression from partner* 2 *is $b$ for both advertisers; further we have $a < b$. The example and some of possible matchings in this case are illustrated in Fig. 1.1.*

In this example,

- The matching $M_1$ is optimal when the platform wants to maximize the fill rate for the premium inventory; however it is sub-optimal in terms of total number of clicks generated by the platform for its advertisers.
- The matching $M_2$ maximizes the total number of clicks; however the fill rate achieved for the premium impressions is nil.
- The matching $M_3$ does not achieve the maximum possible fill rate for premium impressions, and it does not generate maximum number of clicks. However, it is more fair to both objectives compared to $\mathcal{M}_1$ and $\mathcal{M}_2$.

Thus different platform goals lead to different optimal matchings. Even if one were to assume that the platform's final objective can be represented as a utility function over these contradictory goals, such function can be arbitrarily complex; and it is even unrealistic to expect that the utility function is known entirely (even to the platform) or can be completely expressed. Typically, the platform may be able to give his choice between a pair of matchings.

**Benchmark:** Given the complexities in defining the platform's utility function, we take a worst case approach and compare the matching against a set of $L$ distinct matchings ($L$: #(impression levels)) that serves as a benchmark. The $\ell$th matching in this set is an optimal off-line matching, considering impressions *only in levels* 1 through $\ell$; we indicate this matching (as well as its weight) by $\text{OPT}_\ell$. Given any matching $\mathcal{M}$, we denote the weight of $\mathcal{M}$ considering impressions in first $\ell$ levels by $W_i(\mathcal{M})$, and let $\alpha_\ell(\mathcal{M}) = \frac{W_\ell(\mathcal{M})}{\text{OPT}_\ell}$. We represent the performance of $\mathcal{M}$ by its approximation factor $(\alpha_1(\mathcal{M}), \alpha_2(\mathcal{M}), ..., \alpha_L(\mathcal{M}))$. Thus the benchmark serves as an indicator for the quality of a matching in absence of quantitative importance of impressions at various levels, which as discussed earlier in the section, may not exist.

**Previous Work.**

Our work is related to online ad allocation problems, including the *Display Ads Allocation (DA)* problem [12, 11, 3, 17, 6], and the *AdWords (AW)* problem [15, 10]. In both of these problems, the platform must assign online impressions to an inventory of ads, optimizing efficiency or revenue of the allocation while respecting pre-specified contracts. Both of these problems have been studied in the competitive adversarial model [15, 12, 8] and the stochastic random-arrival model [10, 11, 3, 17, 16]. We briefly summarize these two models. In a DA problem, advertiser $\mathcal{A}_i$ has capacity of $N(i)$ impressions; the platform allocates impressions to advertisers in order to maximize the total weight of matching (i.e. number of clicks) subject to each advertiser's capacity constraint. Whereas, in the AW problem, $\mathcal{A}_i$ has a budget $B(i)$ on the total spend and assigning impression $j$ to $\mathcal{A}_i$ consumes $w(i,j)$ units of $\mathcal{A}_i$'s budget.

Both the DA problem (because of the standard free-disposal assumption) and the AW problem can be seen as *supply-constrained*, i.e., the complexity of the problem is based on a limited supply of impressions with the platform compared to the advertiser demand. To illustrate this more clearly, recall that in the case of the AW problem, if there is a significant surplus of user queries / advertising opportunities, all advertisers will eventually spend their entire budgets, regardless of the allocation algorithm used. In comparison, the partner-tiering problem is *demand-constrained*: the platform has a large supply of impressions, but the advertising demand is limited, hence the platform must intelligently ensure a higher fill-rate for higher-priority inventory.

**Organization:** We formally define the model and provide important definitions in 2. Then we describe our results for offline and online setting in Sections 3 and 4 respectively. Finally, we highlight important empirical observations in Section 5.

## 2. PRELIMINARIES

We already discussed our basic model in Section 1.1. Here we describe the notation behind the abstract model that we will use throughout the paper. There is a set of advertisers $\mathcal{A}_1, \mathcal{A}_2, ..., \mathcal{A}_n$. Advertiser $\mathcal{A}_i$ wants $N(i)$ impressions. There are $m$ partners $P_1, P_2, \ldots, P_m$ represented by a platform (a middleman). Each partner (specifically, the set of impressions from a partner) is associated with a priority level between 1 and $L$. We denote $P_i$'s priority level by $\mathcal{L}(P_i)$.

In an *online-arrival setting*, impressions arrive online one-by-one; we denote the $j^{th}$ impression in the arrival sequence by $\mathcal{I}_j$. Each impression belongs to one partner and it inherits the partner's priority level. We denote $\mathcal{I}_j$'s priority level by $\mathcal{L}(j)$. When impression $\mathcal{I}_j$ arrives, the set of advertisers interested in it is revealed. We denote the weight(CTR) of assignment between $\mathcal{A}_i$ and $\mathcal{I}_j$ by $w(i,j)$.

We mainly consider the problem in the online arrival model, but in order to understand the underlying optimization problem, and for completeness, we also consider an offline variant of the problem: in an *off-line setting*, all impressions and their edge weights are known upfront to the algorithm.

In this paper, we consider *un-weighted* as well as *weighted* settings: in the un-weighted setting, $w(i,j) \in \{0,1\}$, where 0 indicates the absence of an edge and 1 indicates the presence of an edge. The weighted setting has no such restriction and arbitrary non-negative edge weights are allowed.

# 3. ALGORITHMS IN OFF-LINE SETTING

In this section, we develop algorithms to compute (approximately) optimal solutions to partner-tiering in the offline setting. As discussed earlier, even though the online settings is the focus of this paper, understanding the complexity and approximability of the problem in offline setting is important in understanding the problem in the online setting. We establish our result for the un-weighted case in Theorem 1, and follow it with our results for the weighted case (Theorem 2).

**Theorem 1** *For unweighted graphs in the off-line setting, there exists a matching that is an optimal matching, i.e.,* $(1, 1, \ldots, 1)$*-approximation. Further, there is a polynomial-time algorithm to compute such an optimal matching.*

PROOF. We give a proof sketch: Let $m$ be the total number of impressions in the sequence. We assign a weight to each edge in the graph as follows: the weight of an edge between an impression at level $\ell$ and an (interested) advertiser is $1 + \frac{L-1-\ell}{mL}$. It can be easily shown that the maximum-weight matching in this graph is a $(1, 1, \ldots, 1)$-approximation. □

### Weighted Graphs.

Next, we address the question of computing the optimal matching for a weighted graph in the offline setting. We first establish shortcomings of the standard free disposal assumption; we follow it with a relaxed definition for free disposal and establish theoretical results under this assumption.

**Free Disposal Assumption:** The DisplayAds problem is known to be inapproximable (to compute the maximum weight matching) without the free disposal assumption [12]. This assumption states that giving an advertiser more impressions than his demand does not decrease his value. In other words, advertiser $\mathcal{A}_i$ can be assigned more impressions than his demand $N(i)$; when we consider his value in the weight of the matching, we count the $N(i)$ impressions of highest weight and (freely) dispose of the remaining impressions.

We establish in the next example, that the standard free disposal assumption fails to capture the complexities when there are multiple layers of impressions and the partner-tiering problem remains inapproximable. We then introduce a *tier-based free disposal assumption*; and establish useful results under this assumption.

**Example 3.1** *There is one advertiser* $\mathcal{A}_i$ *with demand* $N(i)$*. There are* $L$ *levels of impressions. Each level* $\ell$ *has* $N(i)$ *impressions; the weight of an impression in level* $\ell$ *is* $k^\ell$ *for some large constant* $k > 1$*. All impressions are in* $\mathcal{A}_i$*'s target set. Given any assignment of impressions to* $\mathcal{A}_i$*; it can be easily seen that no fixed set of* $N(i)$ *impressions is simultaneously competitive against* $\text{OPT}_1$ *through* $\text{OPT}_\ell$*.*

**Tier-based Free Disposal Assumption:** Under this assumption, we are allowed to over-deliver impressions, however we *do not need to fix* the set of impressions to be disposed of when an advertiser is over-delivered. While computing the performance for advertiser $\mathcal{A}_i$ from the first $\ell$ levels, we can choose the $N(i)$ highest-weight impressions in the first $\ell$ levels. Thus, the set of impressions that count towards the objective can be a function of the level.

We illustrate the implications of this assumption in case of Example 3.1: here, we assign $N(i)$ impressions from each level to $\mathcal{A}_i$. When we measure the quality of this matching for first $\ell$ levels, the best $N(i)$ impressions in first $\ell$ levels are $N(i)$ impression from level $\ell$ each of weight $k^\ell$. Thus, the assignment is a $(1, 1, 1, \ldots, 1)$-approximate matching.

We next give an algorithm to compute an approximately optimal matching in this setting (Theorem 2), and show existence of instances which do not permit $(1, 1, \ldots, 1)$-approximate matchings (Example 3.2). We leave the question of computing tight upper bounds in this case as future work.

**Theorem 2** *For weighted graphs in the offline setting, there exists a matching that is a* $(1 - 1/e, 1 - 1/e, \ldots, 1 - 1/e)$*-approximation, under the* tier-based free-disposal assumption.

PROOF. We highlight the main ideas of the proof and defer the complete proof to the full version of the paper. We order impressions according to their priority levels, where impressions in level $\ell$ appear before impressions in level $\ell+1$, for each $\ell$. We then solve the DisplayAds instance assuming this order of impression arrival using the PD-Exp algorithm by Feldmen *et al* [12], neglecting impression levels. It can be shown that the matching computed in this process is a $(1 - 1/e, 1 - 1/e, \ldots, 1 - 1/e)$-approximate matching under the *tier-based free disposal* assumption. The crucial idea in the proof is that under the new free disposal assumption, the matching computed for a prefix of a sequence does not loose its value by subsequent insertion of impressions. □

**Example 3.2** *There are two levels of impressions and two advertisers, each with demand* $N$*. There are* $N$ *impressions in each level. Impressions in the first level have edge weights of* 0.1 *and* 0.2 *for* $\mathcal{A}_1$ *and* $\mathcal{A}_2$ *respectively; and the edge weights for the second level impressions are* 0.3 *and* 0.4 *respectively. Clearly, the optimal matching considering only the first-level impressions assigns all impressions to* $\mathcal{A}_2$*; whereas the optimal matching considering both levels assigns the first-level impressions to* $\mathcal{A}_1$ *and the second-level impressions to* $\mathcal{A}_2$*. Further, it can be easily seen that no matching is a* $(1, 1)$*-approximate matching.*

# 4. ALGORITHMS IN ONLINE SETTING

In this section, we develop practical algorithms for partner-tiering when impressions arrive online, and establish useful theoretical guarantees in online adversarial and online stochastic models. These algorithms are inspired by the dual-based techniques developed in past for online matching (in absence of impressions' levels); see e.g. [12, 6]. We begin with the *dual scaling* (`DUAL-SCALE`) algorithm.

## 4.1 Dual Scaling

In this algorithm, we are given a discount factor $\beta \in [0, 1]$ that is used to scale the value of dual in a dual-based algorithm, depending upon the level of an incoming impression and the prior assignment to an advertiser. We illustrate the details: let $\texttt{weight}(i, \ell)$ be the total weight of impressions in level $j$ assigned to advertiser $\mathcal{A}_i$ so far. For an incoming impression at level $\ell$, his scaled dual $\gamma(i, \ell)$ (for level $\ell$) is defined as

$$\gamma(i, \ell) = \frac{\sum_{l \leq \ell} \texttt{weight}(i, l) + \beta \times \left(\sum_{l > \ell} \texttt{weight}(i, l)\right)}{N(i)}$$

**Impression Assignment:** The incoming impression $\mathcal{I}_j$ at level $\ell$ is assigned to an advertiser that maximizes the marginal with respect to the scaled dual, i.e.

$$\text{argmax}_i\{w(i,j) - \gamma(i,\ell)\}$$

The $\beta$ serves as a *knob* that indicates *the importance of higher level impressions over the overall delivery quality.* Its value can be chosen statically; or one can also use online-adaptive techniques (such as PID-control).

*Implementation details for computing dual variables*: For each advertiser $\mathcal{A}_i$, we need to store up to top $N(i)$ impressions at each level. When $N(i)$ or the number of levels is large, the overhead can be reduced by storing the distribution over edge-weights at each level for an advertiser (at a small loss in accuracy).

The two extreme cases of this algorithm are:

When $\beta = 0$, the dual variable for $\mathcal{A}_i$ at level $\ell$ completely ignores impressions assigned to him in levels $\ell + 1$ and lower.

When $\beta = 1$, all impressions assigned to an advertiser are considered identical while computing his dual particular to a level. In this case, the algorithm degenerates to the PD-Avg algorithm from [12].

We next establish useful theoretical guarantees of the DUAL-SCALE algorithm for un-weighted graphs at these two extremes in an online arrival model.

### *Un-weighted Graphs:* $\beta = 0$.

We establish theoretical guarantees on the performance of the DUAL-SCALE algorithm for $\beta = 0$ in *adversarial* as well as *stochastic* arrival model. Interstingly, the approximation ratio of the algorithm is very different for these two arrival models: in the adversarial arrival model, its performance drop to $o(1)$ as the number of levels increases (Example 4.1); whereas it performs very well in a stochastic arrival model (Theorem 3). Further, in contrast to its guarantees in the adversarial arrival model, we observe that the DUAL-SCALE algorithm performs very well on real data sets for small values of $\beta$ (see Section 5).

**Example 4.1** *Consider an instance with $n + \sqrt{n}$ advertisers. Each advertiser has demand $t$. There are $n$ levels of impressions, each level has $t$ impressions, and the impressions in level $i$ are eligible for advertisers $i$ and $n+1$ through $n + \sqrt{n}$. Clearly the optimal matching considering impressions in all levels has weight $nt$ whereas the matching generated by the* DUAL-SCALE *algorithm has weight $2\sqrt{n}t$.*

**Stochastic Arrival Model:** We next define the stochastic arrival model considered in our study. We are given a set of impression-types $\mathcal{T}_1, \mathcal{T}_2, \ldots, \mathcal{T}_m$. Each incoming impression is *infinitesimally small* and belongs to one of the types. All impressions belonging to the same type are identical for an advertiser, and we use $\mathcal{N}(\mathcal{T}_j)$ to indicate the set of advertisers that are interested in impressions of type $\mathcal{T}_j$. Each impression type is associated with a non-zero arrival rate (per unit time), represented as the fraction of all incoming impressions in a unit time. The problem of online matching has been extensively studied in this model; see e.g. [9]. We note, this arrival model is different than the random-permutation-arrival model studied in past [10, 11, 3, 17].

We further assume that all impressions of a given type come from the same partner and hence have the same priority level. Next, (Theorem 3), we establish the approximation guarantee of the DUAL-SCALE algorithm for $\beta = 0$; we then show the tightness of this guarantee in Example 4.2.

**Theorem 3** *For un-weighted graphs and the stochastic arrival model, the approximation ratio of the* DUAL-SCALE *algorithm for $\beta = 0$ is $(1, 3/4, 13/18, \ldots, 1 - 1/e)$.*

PROOF. Due to space constraints, we briefly outline the central ideas and defer the complete proof to the full version of the paper.

As each impression-type is associated with a per unit-time arrival rate, we associate temporal aspect with impressions' arrival. We use 0 and $t_{end}$ to indicate the start and the end time of the impressions' arrival. Further, for any intermediate time $t$, we use $t_+$ and $t_-$ to indicate the time $\lim_{t' \to t_+} t'$ and $\lim_{t' \to t_-} t'$ respectively.

Given any impression type $\mathcal{T}_j$, let $\delta(i,j,t)$ be the rate of assignment of $\mathcal{T}_j$ to advertiser $\mathcal{A}_i$ at time $t$, let $\gamma(i,\ell,t)$ be the value of $\gamma(i,\ell)$ at time $t$. We next state important invariants of the algorithm; its proof follows by induction on $t$ and $\ell$.

**Lemma 4.1** *Given an arbitrary impression type $\mathcal{T}_j$, let $\ell$ be its priority level, then for each advertiser $\mathcal{A}_i \in \mathcal{N}(\mathcal{T}_j)$:*

- *For each $t > 0$, either (a) $\delta(i,j,t) = \delta(i,j,t_-)$ and $\gamma(i,\ell,t) < 1$ or (b) $\delta(i,j,t) = 0$ and $\gamma(i,\ell,t) = 1$.*
- *If $\delta(i_1,j,0_+) \neq 0$, and $\delta(i_2,j,0_+) \neq 0$, then $\gamma(i_1,\ell,t) = \gamma(i_2,\ell,t)$ for each $t > 0$.*
- *If $\mathcal{A}_{i_1}, \mathcal{A}_{i_2} \in \mathcal{N}(\mathcal{T}_j)$ and $\delta(i_1,j,0_+) > 0, \delta(i_2,j,0_+) = 0$, then for each $t > 0$, $\gamma(i_1,l,t) \le \gamma(i_2,l,t)$*

For the purpose of analysis of the approximation factor, we consider a bipartite graph, with advertisers on one side and impression types on the another side. The edges in the graph are from advertisers to impressions-types in their target set. The vertices in the graph have weights, indicating their demands (in case of advertisers) or supply (in case of impression types). Further, we consider a (weighted) matching induced on this graph by the impressions' assignment up to time $t_{end}$; the weight on each edge in this matching is the volume of assignment between a given advertiser-impression type pair. We now prove our claim for the first level.

**Lemma 4.2** *The matching computed by the* DUAL-SCALE *algorithm for $\beta = 0$ is optimal for the first level.*

PROOF. We note, impressions at level $\ge 2$ can be completely ignored for the purpose of this proof.

Consider any impression type $\mathcal{T}_j$ belonging to level 1 such that $\exists \mathcal{A}_i \in \mathcal{N}(\mathcal{T}_j)$ with $\delta(i,j,0_+) > 0$ and $\gamma(i,1,t) = 1$ at some $t < t_{end}$ (i.e. impressions from $\mathcal{T}_i$ are assigned to at least one advertiser whose complete demand is met before the end of the algorithm). It suffices to show that no augmenting paths beginning at $\mathcal{T}_j$ exists in the matching computed by the DUAL-SCALE algorithm. Using Lemma 4.1, for each $\mathcal{A}_k \in \mathcal{N}(\mathcal{T}_j)$, we have $\gamma(k,1,t) = 1$. Further, applying this argument recursively, we get that any alternating path beginning in $\mathcal{T}_j$ does not end at $\mathcal{A}_l$ with $\gamma(l,1,t_{end}) < 0$, implying that there are no augmenting paths in the matching computed by the algorithm. This establishes the lemma. □

The proof for higher levels is more involved and is deferred to the full version of the paper. We explain the main ideas behind the proof using level 2 as an example: for level 2 impressions, the matching graph at the end of the algorithm does not have any augmenting paths that use only one level (either level 1 or 2) of impressions. However, such path may begin with a level 2 impression and end with an advertiser whose demand is not completely met, and this path will have intermediate level 1 impressions (and no level 2 impressions). The main challenge is to bound the total volume of these paths. Towards this purpose, we use the following key property: when we trace any potential augmenting path and consider a sequence of advertisers on this path in the same order, then a non-decreasing fraction of advertiser's demand is met with level 1 impressions. Hence, the terminating advertiser on this path always has a greater fraction of his demand met through level 1 impressions than the first (and hence over-allocated) advertiser on this path. We then bound the volume of these augmenting paths by establishing important structural properties.

**Example 4.2** *Consider an instance with $n$ advertisers and $n$ impression types; $t \to \infty$ impressions of each type arrive and the capacity for each advertiser is $t$. Impressions of type $\mathcal{T}_1$ are eligible for all advertisers, $\mathcal{T}_2$ for first $n-1$ advertisers, $\mathcal{T}_3$ for first $n-2$ advertisers,and so on. Further, impressions of type $\mathcal{T}_j$ belong to level $j$ for each $j$. The* `DUAL-SCALE` *algorithm divides the impressions of each type equally among eligible advertisers. Thus, the weight of the matching achieved by the* `DUAL-SCALE` *algorithm is exactly $(t, 6t/4, 33t/18, \dots, nt(1-1/e))$; whereas the weight of the optimal matching is $(t, 2t, 3t, \dots, nt)$.*

### *Un-weighted Graphs for $\beta = 1$.*

For un-weighted graphs, the dual-scaling algorithm for $\beta = 1$ assigns an incoming impression to the advertiser with maximum unsatisfied demand (as a fraction of his total demand). Thus the impression remains unassigned when all interested advertisers have met their entire demand. We show that a slight modification to this algorithm has an interesting theoretical guarantee.

We refine the assignment of the algorithm when all eligible advertisers have completely used their demand: in this case, for an incoming impression $\mathcal{I}_j$ at level $\ell$, let $k \in [\ell, L]$ be the largest integer such that, there exists an advertiser $\mathcal{A}_i$ who has been assigned less than $N(i)$ impressions in first $k$ levels. Then, we assign the impression to $\mathcal{A}_i$. If no such $k$ exists, then the impression is left unassigned.

We note two invariants maintained by the algorithm; as a corollary, we get Lemma 4.3.

- For each level $\ell < L$, and for each prefix of $j$ incoming impressions; the matching generated by the algorithm is maximal, considering the impressions in first $\ell$ levels.
- For level $L$ and for each prefix of $j$ incoming impressions, the matching generated by the algorithm is $(1-1/e)$-approximate: this follows as the algorithm always assigns according to the dual based algorithm that treats all levels equally.

**Lemma 4.3** *For $\beta = 1$, the dual scaling algorithm is a $(1/2, 1/2, \dots, 1/2, 1-1/e)$-approximation.*

## 4.2 Edge-Weight Scaling

This is an additional heuristic that we consider in our empirical study. In the edge-weight scaling (`EW-SCALING`) algorithm, we are given scaling factors $\texttt{sc}_1 \geq \texttt{sc}_2 \geq \dots \texttt{sc}_L$: when an impression at level $\ell$ arrives, its weight is scaled by a factor $\texttt{sc}_\ell$. We define the dual variable $\gamma(i)$ for advertiser $\mathcal{A}_i$ as the average scaled weight of impressions assigned to him. The incoming impression $\mathcal{I}_j$ at level $\ell$ is assigned to the advertiser that maximizes:

$$argmax_i(\texttt{sc}_\ell \times w(i,j) - \gamma(i))$$

Different scaling factors can be used based on the delivery constraints and relative importance of the higher level impressions. When scaling factors are all 1, it is equivalent to treating all levels equally.

# 5. EXPERIMENTAL EVALUATION

**Dataset:** We study the performance of our algorithms on display ads data for a set of 3 anonymous 'publishers' (each representing multiple partners) working with a leading display ads serving corporation. We collect the entire set of impressions for a period of one week for each publisher. The number of impressions in a data set ranges from $200K$ to $3M$. For each incoming impression, the information about the set of interested advertisers, their (predicted) CTR values and the impression type is available. Further, the delivery contracts for each advertiser are also available.

The impressions do not reveal the partner-source (and hence their level); however we have information about the impression type (which represents the advertisers' targeting criteria for the impression). Hence, we generate synthetic values of priority levels for impressions based on their types. We associate each impression a priority level between 1 and 10 using three different techniques, giving us three types of data sets for each publisher.

- Method A: We statically associate each impression type with a priority level. When an impression arrives, this information is used to generate its priority level.
- Method B: For each incoming impression, we associate it a priority level based on its type with 80% probability and choose a uniformly random priority level between 1 and 10 otherwise.
- Method C: Each incoming impression is given a uniformly random priority level between 1 and 10.

We note, these three data sets represent three different types of workloads: The first data set represents a workload with little overlap in the impressions' types across partners, and hence an advertiser's target set of impressions is concentrated at one (or few) level(s); the second data-set corresponds to a scenario where there is a partial overlap in impressions' types across partners; and the third data-set represents a situation where an advertiser's target set of impression is equally distributed across various levels. In the rest of the section, we refer to the publisher data set of generated using method A (similarly B and C) as data-set A (similarly B and C).

### *Performance Metrics.*

We next illustrate the key metrics used to measure the performance of various algorithms.

**Fill Rate:** Given priority level $\ell$, the fill-rate for a publisher at level $\ell$ is the fraction of impressions at level $\ell$ that are assigned an advertisement. As we discussed in the introduction, the publisher wants to keep the fill rate as high as possible for high-priority partners. This is the most important metric for measuring the performance of an algorithm.

**Under-delivery:** It is the total unmet demand summed over all advertisers, expressed as a fraction of total advertiser demand. In order to satisfy contracts, it is important to keep the under-delivery as small as possible.

**Over-delivery:** We say that an advertiser is *over-delivered* when he has been assigned more impressions than his demand. We note, no additional revenue is generated by overserving an advertiser. Since a publisher can *delegate unassigned impressions* at run-time to other advertising markets (such as Google AdExchange, Yahoo! Right Media) to generate additional revenue, it is imperative to keep the over-delivery as low as possible.

We measure the over-delivery as the total number of over-delivered impressions summed over all over-delivered advertisers, expressed as the fraction of total advertisers' demand.

**Total Weight of Matching (Demand Capped):** We associate the CTR for an impression-advertiser pair as the weight on the edge between them. Thus the total weight of the matching represents the total number of clicks generated for advertisers. Modulo other constraints, the publisher prefers to keep the total weight of the matching as high as possible, as the advertisers' welfare is typically measured in terms for clicks generated for them.

We measure the *demand capped* weight of the matching; i.e. we only consider the top $N(i)$ edges for advertiser $\mathcal{A}_i$ towards the total matching weight.

### *Algorithms and Their Parameters.*

We perform exhaustive experimental analysis of various algorithms to measure their performance; we next enlist various algorithms and the set of parameters in each algorithm used in the experimental analysis.

`DUAL-SCALE`: The different values of $\beta$ used in the `DUAL-SCALE` algorithm are $\{0, 0.1, 0.2, 0.5, 0.9, 1.0\}$.

`EW-SCALE`: We use four different sets of scaling factors for the `EW-SCALE` algorithm. We illustrate the scaling factor for an impression at level $\ell$ in these sets:

**Set 1**: The scaling factor is $(1-0.1*(\ell-1))$ (*linear scaling*).

**Set 2**: The scaling factor is $(2-0.1*(\ell-1))$ (*linear scaling*).

**Set 3**: The scaling factor is $0.9^{\ell-1}$ (*exponential scaling*).

**Set 4**: The scaling factor is $0.8^{\ell-1}$ (*exponential scaling*).

**Use Both Techniques Simultaneously**: We also run experiments where we run both techniques simultaneously on an impression: when an impression at level $\ell$ arrives, we scale its weight according to the edge-weight scaling parameter; we then use the dual-scaling technique to compute the value of the dual for each advertiser.

**Baseline**: We use the PD-Avg algorithm by [12] as the baseline algorithm. This algorithm ignores impressions' levels, each advertiser's dual is the average weight of impressions assigned to him so far, and each incoming impression is assigned to an advertiser that maximizes the marginal between the edge-weight and his dual.

## 5.1 Experiments and Observations

### *Experiment 1: Comparison of Various Algorithms.*

We first compare the performance of all four algorithms; for the `DUAL-SCALE` algorithm, we use $\beta = 0.5$, and for the `EW-SCALE` algorithm, we use scaling set 3. Experimental results are given in Figures 5 (fill rates) and 3 (overall delivery metrics). We note salient observations; we begin with the `DUAL-SCALE` algorithm.

*For each publisher and its each data-set, the* `DUAL-SCALE` *algorithm has less under-delivery and more over-delivery than the baseline algorithm. Further, for each publisher, its under-delivery decreases from data-set A to data-set C; and the opposite is true for over-delivery.*, For example, in the case of publisher 2, the under-delivery decreases from 21 to 19.5 to 18 (from data-set A to C), whereas the over-delivery increases from 12.5 to 14.5 to 16. We next illustrate the reasons for these observations: let $\mathcal{I}_j$ be an incoming impression and its level is $\ell$. Before $\mathcal{I}_j$'s arrival, assume that the `DUAL-SCALE` algorithm and the baseline algorithm have assigned the same set of impressions to advertiser $\mathcal{A}_i$; let this set be $S_i$. As the dual scaling algorithm discounts the weight of impressions in level below $\ell$, we get:

$$\gamma(i, \ell) \leq \gamma(i, L)$$

Thus, the marginal gain for assignment to $\mathcal{A}_i$ in the dual scaling algorithm $(w(i,j) - \gamma(i,\ell)))$ dominates the same in the baseline algorithm $(w(i,j) - \gamma(i,L))$. Hence, the `DUAL-SCALE` algorithm will always assign an impression which would have been assigned by the baseline algorithm (assuming identical earlier assignment to all advertisers). However, its converse is not true: the `DUAL-SCALE` algorithm can also allocate impressions when the advertiser is fully allocated and the incoming impression is no better (in terms of its weight) compared to the average assignment to the advertiser. Thus the algorithm is prone to over-deliver (and, hence has lower under-delivery) compared to the baseline algorithm. Further, as we go from data-set A to data-set C, the target set of impressions for an advertiser is more evenly distributed across various levels. As a result, *we expect this effect to amplify.* This results in the observed patterns in under-delivery and over-delivery across data-sets for a single publisher. We also note, as a side-effect of less under-delivery, we see an increase in the number of clicks from data-set A to data-set C (with exception of publisher 2).

We observe an exact opposite pattern for the `EW-SCALE` algorithm. *The* `EW-SCALE` *algorithm always has more under-delivery and less over-delivery than the baseline algorithm for each publisher. Further, for each publisher, its under-delivery increases from data-set A to data-set C and the opposite is true for over-delivery.* We illustrate the reasons for these observations: the algorithm scales down the edge-weights for lower level impressions (compared to higher level impressions). Hence, even when an advertiser has unmet demand and the average weight of impressions assigned to him is lower than the edge-weight for an incoming impression, the impression may remain unassigned as it may now have negative marginal gain after edge-weight scaling; in comparison, this impression would have qualified for assignment in the baseline algorithm. As a result, we see more under-delivery and less over-delivery in the `EW-SCALE` algorithm compared to the baseline algorithm. Further, as an advertiser's target set is more evenly distributed, we expect this effect to

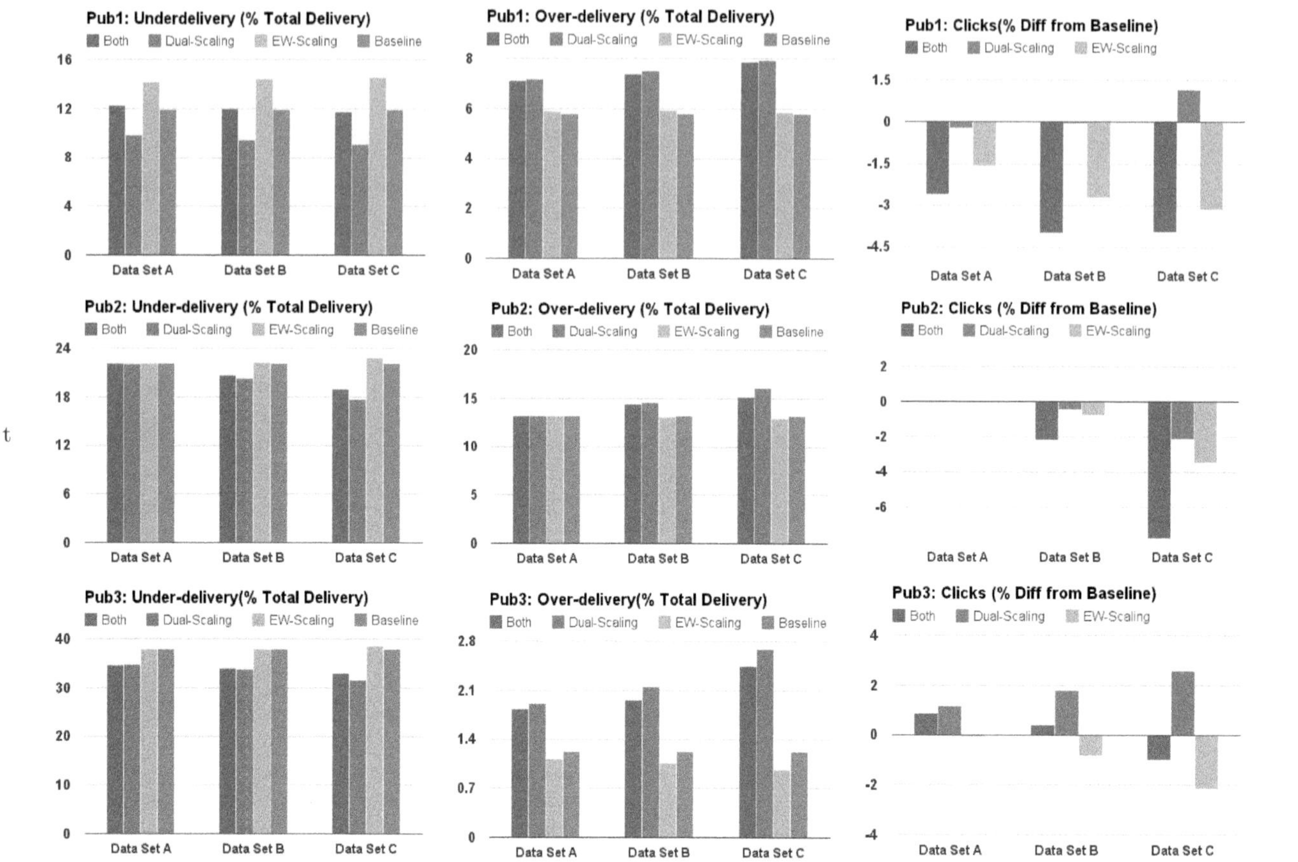


Figure 3: Overall Delivery Guarantees for Various Algorithms and Each Publisher: The plots in the $i$th row are under-delivery, over-delivery and total number of clicks observed in data-sets $A$ through $C$ for publisher $i$. We plot the over-delivery and the under-delivery as a fraction of total delivery; and the number of clicks are represented as percentage difference from the baseline algorithm.

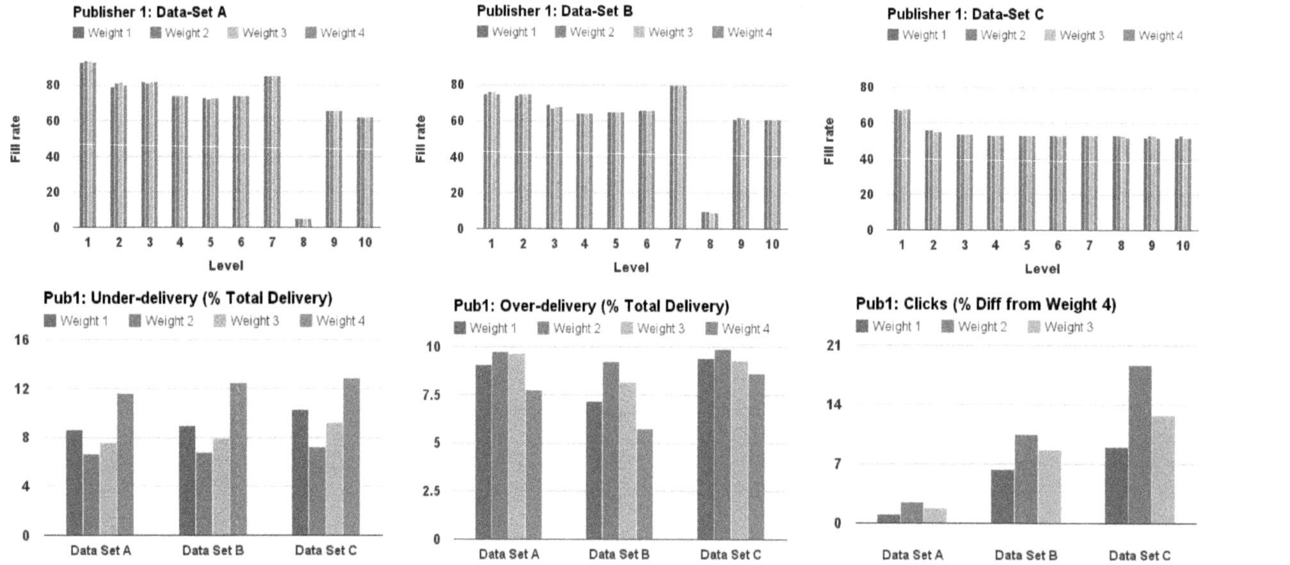


Figure 4: Scaling Factors in EW-SCALE: The plots in the first row are fill-rates for various scaling factors in the EW-SCALE algorithm for one publisher. In the second row, we study their impact on over-all quality metrics, such as under-delivery, over-delivery and number of clicks.

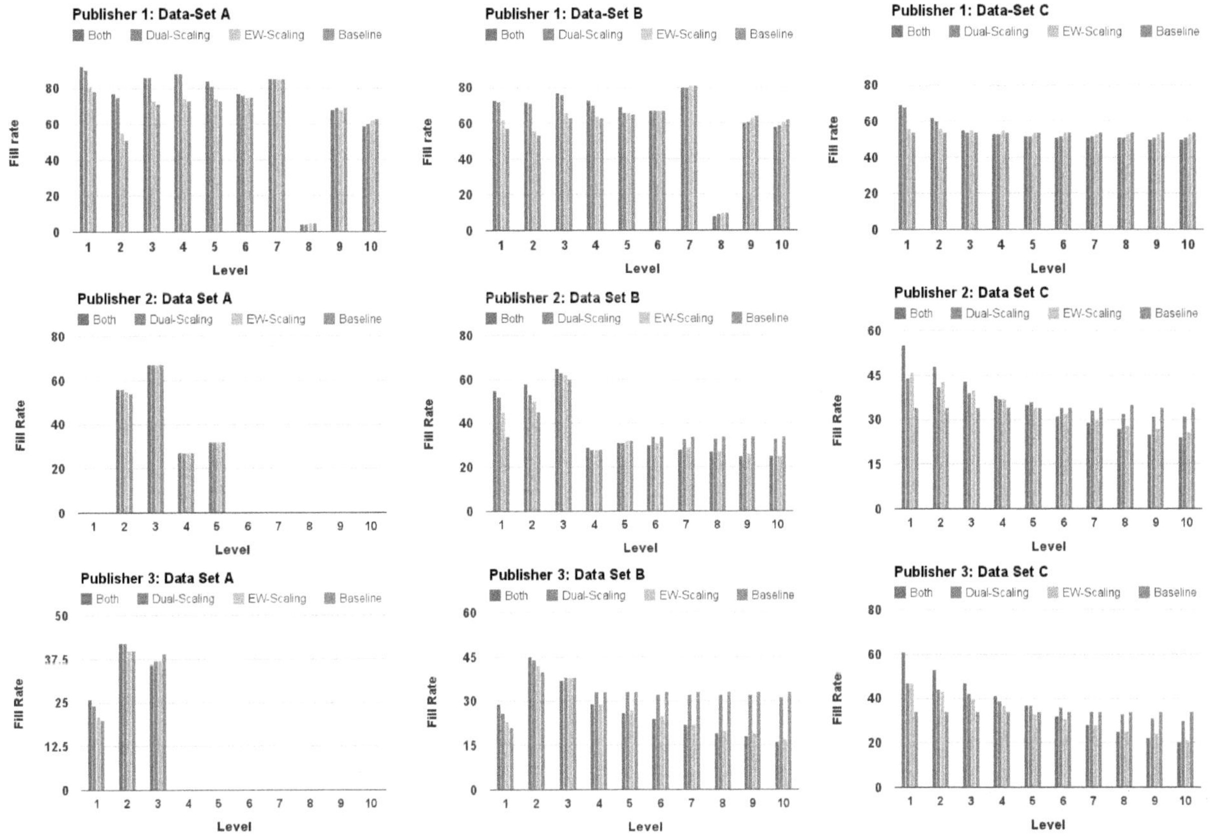


Figure 5: Fill Rates for Various Algorithms for Each Publisher: The plots in the $i$th row are fill-rates observed in data-sets $A$ through $C$ for publisher $i$. The fill-rates are represented at the percentage of impressions at a level that are assigned ads.

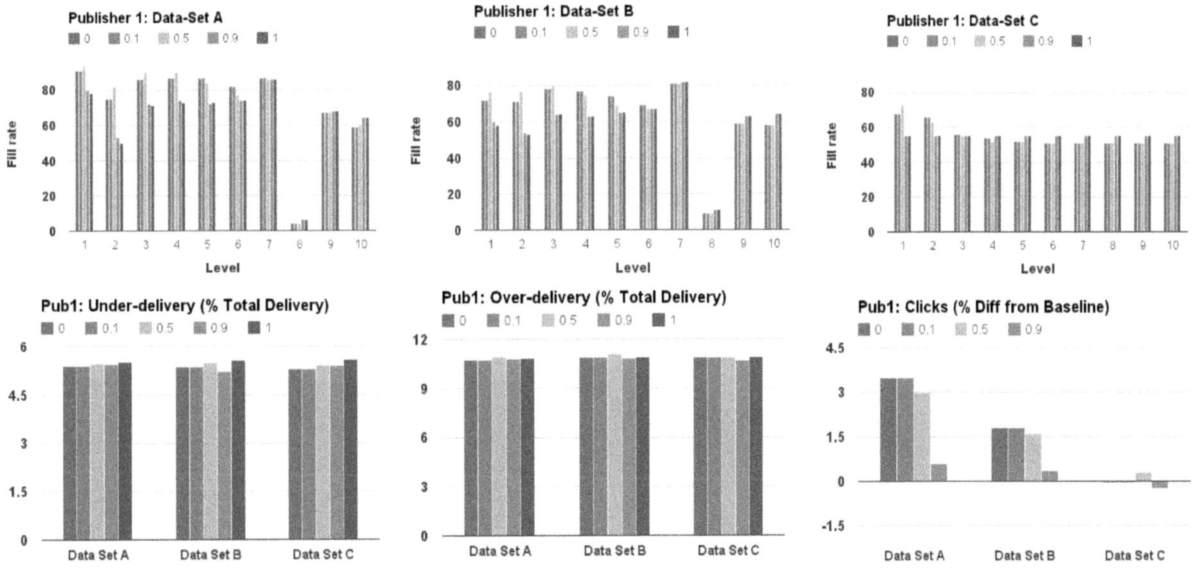


Figure 6: Effect of $\beta$ on DUAL-SCALE: The plots in the first row are fill-rates for various values of $\beta$ for three data-sets generated for a publisher. In the second row, we plot over-all quality metrics, such as under-delivery, over-delivery and number of clicks as a function of $\beta$.

amplify. As a result, we get the said patterns in the over-delivery and the under-delivery across data sets for any given publisher. Also, as a result of increased under-delivery, the number of clicks reduces from data-set A to data-set C.

We next discuss the observations in fill rates for various algorithms: we see that the fill rates at higher levels are significantly superior for the DUAL-SCALE algorithm compared to the EW-SCALE algorithm (with an exception of publisher 2 for data-set C where the EW-SCALE algorithm is slightly superior). Further, we see that the fill rates at lower levels for the EW-SCALE algorithm are significantly lower than the DUAL-SCALE algorithm; the reduced delivery at lower levels in the EW-SCALE algorithm is associated with the increased under-delivery of the EW-SCALE algorithm (discussed earlier). In comparison, the reduction in the fill rates at lower levels in the DUAL-SCALE algorithm (compared to the baseline algorithm) is less; and the algorithm is overall more *robust.*

We also note, using both techniques simultaneously gives a marginal benefit in terms of fill rates at higher levels compared to the DUAL-SCALE algorithm; however the penalty in terms of increased under-delivery far outweighs the gain.

### *Experiment 2: Scaling Factors in* EW-SCALE.

We next measure the impact of choice of edge-weight scaling factors on the key performance metrics of the EW-SCALE algorithm. Experimental observations for one publisher are given in Figure 4; other publishers yield similar results.

We note, among the four scaling factor sets, the set 4 (approximately) gives the highest bias to higher levels compared to lower levels, followed by set 1, set 3 and set 2 (in that order). We see that the under-delivery decreases (and the over-delivery increases) in the same order across all data sets for each publisher. This happens as a result of the delivery property of the EW-SCALE algorithm discussed in experiment 1: we expect the said effect to increase with increase in scaling bias, which is consistent with experimental observations.

We also observe that the total weight of matching increases in the order opposite of bias; this is related to the reduction in under-delivery in that order. We note, the experiments do not reveal any significant improvement in terms of fill rates at higher levels for a stronger bias.

### *Experiment 3: Effect of $\beta$ on* DUAL-SCALE.

We next measure the performance of the DUAL-SCALE algorithm for various values of $\beta$. We discard the real edges weights in this experiment and consider an edge-weight to be 1, when an impression is in the advertiser's target set, and 0 otherwise. This relates to the scenario where the advertising contracts have significantly higher priority than the clicks generated for the advertisers. Experimental observations for one publisher are given in Figure 6. Note, for $\beta = 1$, the algorithm degenerates to baseline.

Salient observations: the under-delivery improves from $\beta = 1$ to $\beta = 0$; further, for smaller $\beta$, it improves as we go from data-set A to data-set C. This happens due to the delivery property of the DUAL-SCALE algorithm discussed in experiment 1. As a result of reduced under-delivery, we also see an increase in the number of clicks as the value of $\beta$ is reduced. In terms of fill rates, we observe that the fill rates at higher levels reduce as we increase $\beta$ from 0.5 to 1.0. Curiously, we get better fill rates for $\beta = 0.5$ over $\beta = 0.0$. This happens as these algorithms are not implemented in isolation; they are implemented in a framework that simulates all complexities of a real system that handles live traffic and optimizes from various different perspectives.

## 6. REFERENCES


[1] emarketer. `http://www.emarketer.com/Article/Digital-Account-One-Five-Ad-Dollars/1009592`, 2013.

[2] Flurry Five-Year Report: It's an App World. The Web Just Lives in It. `http://blog.flurry.com/bid/95723/`, 2013.

[3] S. Agrawal, Z. Wang, and Y. Ye. A dynamic near-optimal algorithm for online linear programming. Working paper at http://www.stanford.edu/ yyye/.

[4] S. Balseiro, J. Feldman, V. S. Mirrokni, and S. Muthukrishnan. Yield optimization of display advertising with ad exchange. In *ACM-EC*, 2011.

[5] S. R. Balseiro, O. Besbes, and G. Y. Weintraub. Yield optimization of display advertising with ad exchange. In *ACM-EC*, 2013.

[6] A. Bhalgat, J. Feldman, and V. Mirrokni. Online allocation of display ads with smooth delivery. In *KDD*, 2012.

[7] V. Bharadwaj, P. Chen, W. Ma, C. Nagarajan, J. Tomlin, S. Vassilvitskii, E. Vee, and J. Yang. Shale: an efficient algorithm for allocation of guaranteed display advertising. In *KDD*, 2012.

[8] N. Buchbinder, K. Jain, and J. Naor. Online Primal-Dual Algorithms for Maximizing Ad-Auctions Revenue. In *Proc. ESA*, page 253. Springer, 2007.

[9] D. F. Ciocan and V. Farias. Model predictive control for dynamic resource allocation. In *Mathematics of Operations Research*, 2012.

[10] N. Devanur and T. Hayes. The adwords problem: Online keyword matching with budgeted bidders under random permutations. In *ACM EC*, 2009.

[11] J. Feldman, M. Henzinger, N. Korula, V. Mirrokni, and C. Stein. Online stochastic packing applied to display ad allocation. In *ESA*, 2010.

[12] J. Feldman, N. Korula, V. Mirrokni, S. Muthukrishnan, and M. Pal. Online ad assignment with free disposal. In *WINE*, 2009.

[13] A. Ghosh, P. McAfee, K. Papineni, and S. Vassilvitskii. Bidding for representative allocations for display advertising. In *WINE*, pages 208–219, 2009.

[14] K. Lang, J. Delgado, D. Jiang, B. Ghosh, S. Das, A. Gajewar, S. Jagadish, A. Seshan, C. Botev, M. Bindeberger-Ortega, S. Nagaraj, and R. Stata. Efficient online ad serving in a display advertising exchange. In *WSDM*, 2011.

[15] A. Mehta, A. Saberi, U. Vazirani, and V. Vazirani. Adwords and generalized online matching. In *FOCS*, 2005.

[16] B. Tan and R. Srikant. Online advertisement, optimization and stochastic networks. *CoRR*, abs/1009.0870, 2010.

[17] E. Vee, S. Vassilvitskii, and J. Shanmugasundaram. Optimal online assignment with forecasts. In *ACM EC*, 2010.

# Estimating Ad Group Performance in Sponsored Search

Dawei Yin[†] Bin Cao[S] Jian-Tao Sun[S] Brian D. Davison[†]
[†]Dept. of Computer Science and Engineering, Lehigh University, Bethlehem, PA, USA
[S]Microsoft Research Asia, Beijing, China
[†]{day207, davison}@cse.lehigh.edu [S]{bincao, jtsun}@microsoft.com

## ABSTRACT

In modern commercial search engines, the pay-per-click (PPC) advertising model is widely used in sponsored search. The search engines try to deliver ads which can produce greater click yields (the total number of clicks for the list of ads per impression). Therefore, predicting user clicks plays a critical role in sponsored search. The current ad-delivery strategy is a two-step approach which first predicts individual ad CTR for the given query and then selects the ads with higher predicted CTR. However, this strategy is naturally suboptimal and correlation between ads is often ignored under this strategy. The learning problem is focused on predicting individual performance rather than group performance which is the more important measurement.

In this paper, we study click yield measurement in sponsored search and focus on the problem—predicting group performance (click yields) in sponsored search. To tackle all challenges in this problem—depth effects, interactive influence, cold start and sparseness of ad textual information—we first investigate several effects and propose a novel framework that could directly predict group performance for lists of ads. Our extensive experiments on a large-scale real-world dataset from a commercial search engine show that we achieve significant improvement by solving the sponsored search problem from the new perspective. Our methods noticeably outperform existing state-of-the-art approaches.

## Categories and Subject Descriptors

H.3.3 [**Information Storage and Retrieval**]: Information Search and Retrieval; H.2.8 [**Database Management**]: Database applications—*Data Mining*

## Keywords

Sponsored search, CTR, Click yield, Ad clicks

## 1. INTRODUCTION

In modern commercial search engines, the pay-per-click (PPC) advertising model is widely used in sponsored search. Search engines try to deliver ads which can produce greater click yields (the total number of clicks for the list of ads per impression) for more revenue. Therefore, predicting user clicks plays a critical role in online services, which helps the system to serve items with high CTRs.

Current ad-delivery strategies are two-step approaches, and work as follows. The system first predicts individual ad click-through rates (CTRs) for the given query. Based on the estimated CTRs, the system selects the ads with high predicted CTR, subject to some conditions such as user utility and advertiser ROI [4]. The underlying assumption is that the rewards of ads are independent and clicks on the ads in a list is additive. However, this assumption does not hold in reality. For example, two similar ads in the same list could reduce the CTRs of each [39]. Moreover, this strategy is naturally suboptimal. The learning problem is focused on predicting individual performance rather than group performance which is selecting the best list of ads to maximize overall payoff. Under this scheme, the overall performance (e.g., click yield—the total number of clicks for the list of ads per impression) becomes another important measurement for ad selection in sponsored search. In this work, we consider click yield as the measure of group performance. The motivation behind the proposal to change the objective is based on nontrivial observations. That is, two systems that have similar precision on predicting individual performance could behave very differently on group performance. For example, we can have two models having the same CTR prediction accuracy. However, the ads selected by the two models have huge differences on the clicks obtained. Moreover, since the overall click yields are based on the delivered ad list and the CTRs are not independent, the results could be suboptimal even when the individual ad CTR prediction is perfect. In fact, it is not necessary to know accurately the CTRs of each individual ad, as long as we can select the best lists. Sometimes estimating CTRs of all ads may be an even more challenging problem due to the problem of sparsity.

Here, we challenge the traditional strategy for predicting group performance based on CTR prediction. We propose a novel framework that could directly predict the click yield for a ranked list of ads which has rarely been studied but is an important measurement for ad delivery. The problem is essentially a ranking problem since we would like to judge which lists of ads are better. However, unlike the problem of learning to rank that ranks single documents, here we rank sets of ads. Additionally, we leverage a special constraint on the problem. That is, the number of ads shown on a page is usually limited to a small number, (e.g., four mainline ads in a typical commercial search engine). Still, it is not realistic to explore all possible combination of ads. Therefore, we simplify the problem to rank historically presented ad lists only (that is, the ad lists which have been shown before).


*WSDM'14,* February 24–28, 2014, New York, New York, USA.
Copyright 2014 ACM 978-1-4503-2351-2/14/02 ...$15.00.
http://dx.doi.org/10.1145/2556195.2556257 .

However, solving the click yields prediction/ranking problem is still nontrivial for several reasons. At first, unlike organic search, sponsored search has its own bias and characteristics. The probability of a user examining sponsored search results is related to two major factors: the depth of the ads (the number of ads displayed) and the commercial intent of a query. For the depth of the ads, usually the more ads are shown at the same time, the larger the ad area is and the more attention from users is attracted. Moreover, with too many ads displayed together, the overall effects on click yields may not be always positive. On the other hand, for some queries with high commercial intent, ads usually are interesting to users, while for other queries, showing ads may annoy users. Secondly, interactive influences between query and ad lists and across ads/positions are also important factors to the click yields problem. Some preliminary work [32, 39] on CTR prediction has shown the existence of these interaction effects. However, these studies have focused on independent ads, and the effects of interactive influences and position correlation on total click yield are still not clear. Thirdly, cold start problems (new ads) also occur frequently in sponsored search [30, 36]. To model and utilize the content of the ad is critical when tackling this problem, but few investigations of ad content (short and sparse texts) have been conducted.

To estimate the ad group performance in sponsored search and tackle these challenging problems, we combine heterogenous types of information into the learning model. We first investigate several effects including latent biases, contextual features, interactive influence and correlation over positions. We find that a unified model can achieve the best performance. To best leverage the text features and solve the sparseness issue in text information and cold start on ads, we embed the topic coding model into our framework to learn the topic information of short ad text. We also discuss the effects of various loss functions. We find that ranking loss is preferred for this problem. Finally, we conduct extensive experiments on a large-scale real-world dataset from a commercial search engine. Our methods achieve significant improvement by solving the sponsored search problem from this new perspective.

We summarize our contributions as follow,

- We introduce a novel perspective for sponsored search—click yield—which measures the group performance of ads displayed together.
- To solve the click yield prediction problem, we propose a Click Yield Prediction framework which incorporates multiple factors, such latent bias, textual features, interactive influences, and position correlation.
- Our experiments, based on a large-scale real-world dataset, show our methods make noticeable improvements and outperform state-of-the-art methods based on the traditional strategy.

The paper is organized as follows: Section 2 discusses related work and we then present preliminary data analysis in Section 3. Section 4 presents the proposed model, followed by describing an efficient and scalable approach developed for estimating the model parameters. Section 6 presents the empirical evaluations of the proposed approach on a large real-world data set. Section 7 concludes the paper.

## 2. RELATED WORK

Related work is primarily in three topics: the users' click model, sponsored search and learning to rank techniques.

The bias in user click behaviors during search was first studied through eye-tracking [20]. There are two major assumptions in click models: the Examination Hypothesis [13, 24, 23, 33] and the Cascade Model. The examination hypothesis assumes that if a displayed url is clicked, it must be both examined and relevant [30]. Following the examination hypothesis, there are three basic models: the click over expected clicks (COEC) model [42], the examination model [6] and the logistic model [10]. They are compared in [6] and experimentally demonstrated to be outperformed by the cascade model, proposed by Craswell et al. [10, 16], which assumes that the user views search results from top to bottom and decides whether to click each url. Once a click is issued, documents below the clicked result are not examined regardless of the position. The click chain model [15] and dynamic Bayesian network [6] which is inferred through [27] made a further generalization by allowing the user to abandon examination of more results. The general click model [46] treats all relevance and examination effects in the model as random variables. In addition to the above methods, there have been several click models following the above two assumptions but apply them in different contexts, such as federated search [7], the task centric click model [43], and the position normalized click model [8]. However, the above methods are mainly designed for understanding users' click behaviors on organic search. They fail to explore the specific properties in sponsored search as discussed above. Moreover, they cannot solve the click yield problem.

For modeling sponsored search and predicting ad click through rate, Thore et al. [14] describe a Bayesian model which is based on a probit regression model. Richardson et al. [30] present a method based on logistic regression, where they extract features in four aspects: term CTR, ad quality, order specificity and external sources. In [42], Zhang and Jones introduce the Clicks Over Expected Clicks (COEC) model. Cheng et al. [9] develop user-specific and demographic-based features that reflect the click behaviors of individuals and groups to improve accuracy over the baseline model. Menon et al. [26] view the CTR prediction problems as a problem of matrix completion. Shen et al. [32] propose a personalized model. Recently, Xu et al. investigate the relational click behaviors [40]. They fail to model the more general cases (e.g., 3 or 4 ads) and handle new ads and queries. Xiong et al. [39] shows the mutually exclusive influence between similar ads. These methods are focused on predicting the click-through rate of ads. Although they have been used in selecting ads to display for specific query sessions, they are essentially two-step approaches and do not directly estimate ad group performance.

Another area of related work is learning to rank techniques. In Information Retrieval (IR), a generic task is to construct a ranked list of documents relevant to a query issued by a user. Although ranking is a fundamental problem in IR and has been studied for decades, it still remains challenging. Recent methods are summarized in [25]. In the standard Learning to Rank setting, a typical training set consists of queries with their associated documents represented by feature vectors as well as corresponding relevance judgements. A machine learning algorithm is employed to learn the ranking model, which can predict the ground truth label in the training set as accurately as possible in terms of a loss function. In the test phase, when a new query comes in, the learned model is applied to sort the documents according to their relevance to the query, and return the corresponding ranked list to the user as the response to the query. Depending on different hypotheses, input spaces, output spaces and loss functions, approaches to LtoR can be loosely grouped into three categories [25]: point-wise, pairwise, and list-wise [28].

# 3. PRELIMINARIES

In this section, we conduct some exploratory experiments to verify our intuitions and formalize the problem definition. We collect data from a commercial search engine in the U.S. English market in April 2012. In total, there are 127,230,609 query sessions, where a query session consists of an input query, a list of sponsored search results and a list of clicked ads with time stamps. Since click data are noisy, we filter out low frequency queries and ads to remove some noise and use the more confident click data for analysis.

## 3.1 Group Performance

Compared to individual performance, (e.g., individual ad CTR), ad group performance is much closer to the real system performance. For instance, in sponsored search, given a query, we can decide which group of ads to display, according to the estimated group performance.

### 3.1.1 *Click Yield*

We define the concept of *click yield* (CY) as follows. Given a query $q$ and an ad list $\mathbf{a} = \{a_1, a_2, \cdots, a_{|\mathbf{a}|}\}$, the click yield is the ratio of the total number of clicks on the ads in **a** over the total number of impressions:[1]

$$y_{q,\mathbf{a}} = \frac{\sum_{i=1}^{|\mathbf{a}|} \text{Click}(q, a_i)}{\text{Impr}(q, \mathbf{a})}$$

where $\text{Click}(q, a_i)$ denotes the total number of clicks on the ad $a_i$, with issued query $q$ and $\text{Impr}(q, \mathbf{a})$ denotes the number of times showing the ad group $\mathbf{a}$, with issued query $q$. The concept of click yield differs from the click-through rate (CTR) in that it measures the overall performance of ad lists rather than single ads. We see that unlike the click-through rate of an individual ad, $y_{q,\mathbf{a}}$ might be larger than one.

### 3.1.2 *Problem Definition*

With the definition of group performance, we formalized the problem as follows: the records are presented by $\mathcal{D} = (q_m, \mathbf{a}_m, y_m)_{m=1}^{M}$. For a single click log entry $(q, \mathbf{a}, y) \in \mathcal{D}$, $q$ is the query in the record, **a** is the list of ads $\mathbf{a} = \{a_1, a_2, \cdots, a_{|\mathbf{a}|}\}$ and $|\mathbf{a}|$ refers to the number of ads (i.e., depth). $y$ means the corresponding click yield. In this work, we will try to solve the following problem: given a query $q$ and a collection of available ad lists $\mathcal{D}_q$, we predict the click yields of the ad lists or rank the ad lists and find the best ad list out of $\mathcal{D}_q$ that has the highest click yield.

## 3.2 Click Yields Analysis

A commercial search engine typically adopts a two-step approach. That is, the search engine first predicts the click-through rate of ads given the query. Then, it selects the ads with higher predicted CTR to display. However, this approach is suboptimal even when the CTR prediction is perfect since it assumes the CTR of individual ads are independent of each other and clicks are additive. In the following analysis we will see this assumption does not hold in reality.

Fig. 1 shows the average click yields of specific depths (number of ads displayed together) over all queries. We can see that as the depth grows, the increase in click yield slows. For instance, the click yield of depth 1 is 0.1798, but the the click yields of

[1]The definition of click yield is slightly different from the one used in some other papers [18], where it is defined by the total number of clicks divided by the total number of search result page views. In Hillard et al. [18], the click yield is only a global metric while in this paper it is a metric for ad lists.

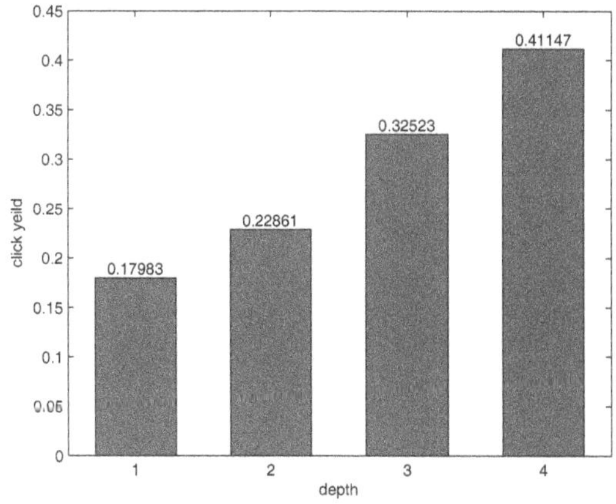


**Figure 1: Average Click Yields**

depth 2 is only 27% more than depth 1. This shows that with more ads displayed the clicks on individual ads may be diluted. As we can see, the average click yield becomes larger with increasing depth. However, showing more ads does not *always* get the best click yields. We find many examples like the one in Table 1: for query "worldofwatches", if we only display a single ad "http://WorldofWatches.com", the click yield is 0.2096, while if we display this ad with two other watch-related ads, the click yield of those ads is only 0.1428, which is even lower than the single ad. That is because with query "worldofwatches", although the users are interested in watches, the users' intent is quite clear and exactly want the website "http://WorldofWatches.com". Showing more ads may annoy users, and they are more likely to skip the ads area. In the case that some specific ad exactly matches the user's intent, it appears that less is more.

We further investigate the effects of the query's commercial intent on click yield and CTR. We treat the average CTR of the query as the measurement for commercial intent of the query (higher average CTR means higher commercial intent), and investigate the relationship between the depth and query commercial intent. In our experiments, we let the depth change from 1 to 3 and then test whether the commercial intent affects the changes of CTR or CY. We categorize the queries by two metrics, CTR and CY. Then, we obtain queries of four types: CTR increasing query, CTR decreasing query, CY increasing query, and CY decreasing query. For the majority of queries, with a larger depth, the average CTR of queries are diluted while the click yields increase, but for some special queries, the average CTR of a large depth is greater than a small depth, or the click yields of a small depth can be larger than that of a large depth. In Figures 2(a) and 2(b), we see that the majority of queries have higher commercial intent (average CTR). In our experiments, there are around 1/10 queries whose average CYs decrease when changing depth from 1 to 3. We see that the commercial intents of these queries are relatively low. Note that even if the average CY of a query increases when changing depth 1 to 3, the gain still may not be linear; that is, one cannot simply use additive CTRs to estimate CY. On the other hand, unfortunately, another type of the unusual cases—CTR increasing (CY increasing obviously) queries—also shares the same property (low commercial intent). That means, we cannot simply use average CTR of ads to decide the number of ads displayed together. A more sophisticated model is necessary to solve this problem. These factors are

**Table 1: An example of query "worldofwatches"**

| |
|---|
| Ad list 1 (Click Yields 0.2096) |
| **world of watches** (*http://WorldofWatches.com*)<br>Up To 80% Off On The World's Finest Watches. Free Shipping, Shop Now! |
| Ad list 2 (Click Yields 0.1428) |
| **world of watches** (*http://WorldofWatches.com*)<br>Up To 80% Off On The World's Finest Watches. Free Shipping, Shop Now!<br>**Ashford - Luxury for Less** (*http://Ashford.com/Watches_Sale*)<br>Shop Top Brand Watches. Free Shipping. 100%Authentic w/Warranty.<br>**Invicta up to 90% off** (*http://www.nextdaywatches.com*)<br>Authorized Invicta Dealer. Large Selection. Free, Next Day Delivery. |

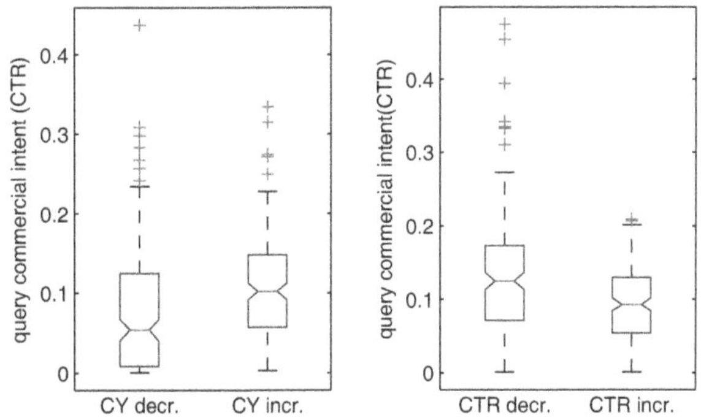


**Figure 2: Depth changed from 1 to 3**

rarely studied and in the following sections, we will directly study overall performance in ad delivery procedure.

# 4. PREDICTING CLICK YIELDS

Estimating ad group performance (click yield) is a more complicated problem than individual ad performance, due to extra factors: the number of ads, interactive influences between query and ads, interactive influences across ads. In this section, we will propose a unified model for predicting the click yield of $\mathbf{a}$, given query $q$. $y_{q,\mathbf{a}}$ represents the click yield. $f_{q,\mathbf{a}}$ the relevance score which can be used for estimating click yield or ranking the ad lists.

## 4.1 Estimation Model

**Latent Bias (LB):** One straightforward intuition is that whether the ad is clicked or not depends on the average click rate of the ads: $f(q, \mathbf{a}) = \sum_{i=1}^{k} \mu_{a_i}$ where $\mu_{a_i}$ is the CTR of the target ad across all other factors. Certainly, this estimation is too coarse and inaccurate, because as we mentioned before, the majority of ads are not clicked and multiple contextual factors of the ads are not incorporated. We can extend this basic estimation by incorporating wider biases from multiple factors: 1) Positional Query bias, because for each query, the average CTRs on specific positions are different. Given a query $q$, for each position $i$, one has a latent bias $\mu_q^{(i)}$. The latent bias of query $q$ can be expressed in a vector form $\boldsymbol{\mu}_q = \left[\mu_q^{(1)}, \mu_q^{(2)}, \cdots, \mu_q^{(d)}\right]^T$ where $d$ denotes the max depth of the ads area (the maximum number of ads shown in ads area). 2) For ad list $\mathbf{a}$, the average CTR of a specific ad depends on the both the position of the ad and the ad itself. Similarly, one has a positional bias for an ad list, $\boldsymbol{\mu}_\mathbf{a} = \left[\mu_{a1}^{(1)}, \mu_{a2}^{(2)}, \cdots, \mu_{ad}^{(d)}\right]^T$, where $\mu_a^{(i)}$ denotes the bias of ad $a$ on position $i$. To compose the final bias of a pair $(q, \mathbf{a})$, an indicator $\mathcal{I}_\mathbf{a}$ is also necessary. $\mathcal{I}_\mathbf{a}$ points out the positions which are filled by ad list $\mathbf{a}$. We define $\mathcal{I}_\mathbf{a} = \left[I_\mathbf{a}^{(1)}, I_\mathbf{a}^{(2)}, \cdots, I_\mathbf{a}^{(d)}\right]^T$ the position indicator vector of $\mathbf{a}$, where $I_\mathbf{a}^{(i)} = 1$ if some ad appears on position $i$ otherwise $I_\mathbf{a}^{(i)} = 0$. For instance, if $d = 4$ and $|\mathbf{a}| = 2$ which means the first two positions are filled by two ads, then $\mathcal{I}_\mathbf{a} = [1, 1, 0, 0]^T$. Then the latent bias is

$$f_{q,\mathbf{a}}^{LB} = \mu_0 + \mathcal{I}_\mathbf{a}^T \boldsymbol{\mu}_q + \mathcal{I}_\mathbf{a}^T \boldsymbol{\mu}_\mathbf{a}$$

where $\mu_0$ is the global bias. Note that these biases are the latent variables to be learned from the data sets. However, this model is appealing since no extra information is needed for learning, besides requiring indicators.

**Feature Model (FM):** A more powerful model than the bias model is the feature model, which predicts the relevance and harvests the information of features by a linear function of features. For a search session, we could extract the features of the ads and their contexts. Given a record $(q, \mathbf{a})$ and click yields $y_{q,\mathbf{a}}$, the feature vector can be extracted from two aspects:

- **Query Features:** Let $\mathbf{x}_q$ be the feature vector of query $q$, which can be extracted from the terms of the query or latent topic distribution of the query.
- **Ad Features:** Let $\mathbf{x}_{a_i}$ be the feature vector of ad $a_i$, which can be extracted from the terms of the shown title and body of the ad, the historical click over expected clicks (COEC) [42] or latent topic distribution of the ad content.

Like the latent bias model, with position and depth information, we define $\mathbf{x}_\mathbf{a} = \left[I_\mathbf{a}^{(1)}\mathbf{x}_{a_1}^T, I_\mathbf{a}^{(2)}\mathbf{x}_{a_2}^T, \cdots, I_\mathbf{a}^{(d)}\mathbf{x}_{a_d}^T\right]^T$. A simple linear combination of query features and ad features can be defined as:

$$f_{q,\mathbf{a}}^{FM} = \mathbf{b}_q^T \mathbf{x}_q + \mathbf{b}_\mathbf{a}^T \mathbf{x}_\mathbf{a}$$

$\mathbf{b}_q$ and $\mathbf{b}_\mathbf{a}$ are coefficients to be learned from the training set. The model is essentially equivalent to the one where ad feature and context features are combined into a single feature vector $\mathbf{x} = [\mathbf{x}_q^T, \mathbf{x}_\mathbf{a}^T]^T$ and a coeffecient $\mathbf{b} = [\mathbf{b}_q^T, \mathbf{b}_\mathbf{a}^T]^T$. Here, we further place a zero mean Gaussian prior or Laplace prior on the values of coefficient $\mathbf{b}$, corresponding to the $L_2$ and $L_1$ regularization, respectively. With the Gaussian prior, we have: $\mathbf{b} \sim \mathcal{N}(0, \lambda_\mathbf{b}^{-1}\mathbf{I})$

**Interactive Influence (IM):** Although linear models are efficient, they are usually over-simplified and cannot capture interactions between queries and ads. The interaction between the query and ads are studied in Xiong et al. [39]. However, their methods did not consider to model the interaction across ads. Moreover, their models still are designed for CTR prediction rather than click yield prediction. Similar to Rendle [29], we model interactions of click yields of a query-ad list pair $(q, \mathbf{a})$ through an additive function of ad positions. Let $\mathbf{G}^{(i)} \in \mathbb{R}^{N_a \times N_q}$ be the interaction matrix on position $i$. The interaction can be modeled as follows.

$$f_{q,\mathbf{a}}^{IM} = \sum_{i=1}^{d} I_\mathbf{a}^{(i)} G_{a_i q}^{(i)} \qquad (1)$$

The interaction matrix $\mathbf{G}^{(i)}$ is query-position-ad dependent, which is unknown and their entries could be either positive or negative. We treat them as the latent variables to be learned from the data set. However, the model has two issues: the observed pairs $a_i, q$ in training data are extremely sparse, meaning that the majority of entries of the interaction matrix cannot be learned effectively. The second problem is that without any constraints on the interaction matrix, this model may overfit due to the large number of parameters. To avoid these two problems, we place low-rank constraints on the interaction matrix $G$. The low-rank approximation is widely used in recommender systems [21, 5, 41, 3]:

$$\mathbf{G}^{(i)} \approx \mathbf{Q}^{(i)^T}\mathbf{A} \quad (2)$$

Let $k$ be the dimensionality of the latent factor vectors. $\mathbf{Q}^{(i)} \in \mathbb{R}^{k\times N_q}$ is the latent factor matrix for the queries on position $i$, $\mathbf{A} \in \mathbb{R}^{k\times N_a}$ is the latent factor matrix for the ads. Plugging Equation 2 back into the interaction model, we get

$$f^{IM}_{q,\mathbf{a}} = \sum_{i=1}^{d} I^{(i)}_{\mathbf{a}} \mathbf{Q}^{(i)^T}_{\cdot q} \mathbf{A}_{\cdot a_i} \quad (3)$$

Like the coefficients in Feature Model, the latent factor vectors of ads and queries $\mathbf{Q}^{(i)}_{\cdot q}$ and $\mathbf{A}_{\cdot a_i}$ could be assumed to be generating from a Gaussian prior,

$$\begin{aligned} \mathbf{Q}^{(i)}_{\cdot q} &\sim \mathcal{N}(0, \lambda_Q^{-1}\mathbf{I}),\ i = 1, \cdots, d \quad (4) \\ \mathbf{A}_{\cdot a_i} &\sim \mathcal{N}(0, \lambda_A^{-1}\mathbf{I}) \end{aligned}$$

**Correlations:** However, the above model still fails to capture the connections across positions/ads. To learn the relationships between different positions/ads, we place a matrix-variate normal distribution [17] on $\mathbf{Q} = \left[\mathrm{vec}(\mathbf{Q}^{(1)}), \mathrm{vec}(\mathbf{Q}^{(2)}), \cdots, \mathrm{vec}(\mathbf{Q}^{(d)})\right]$ where $\mathrm{vec}(\cdot)$ denotes the operator which converts a matrix into a vector in a column-wise manner. Then,

$$p(\mathbf{Q}|\mathbf{\Omega}) = \mathcal{MN}_{N_q k\times d}(\mathbf{Q}|\mathbf{Q}', \mathbf{I}_{N_q k} \otimes \mathbf{\Omega})$$

where $\mathbf{Q}'$ is the mean matrix (e.g., zero mean $\mathbf{Q}' = \mathbf{0}_{N_q k\times d}$), $\mathcal{MN}_{u\times v}(\mathbf{X}|\mathbf{M}, \mathbf{U}, \mathbf{V})$ denotes a matrix-variate normal distribution with mean $\mathbf{M} \in \mathbb{R}^{u\times v}$, row covariance matrix $\mathbf{U} \in \mathbb{R}^{u\times u}$ and column covariance matrix $\mathbf{V} \in \mathbb{R}^{v\times v}$. The probability density function of the matrix-variate normal distribution is defined as

$$p(\mathbf{X}|\mathbf{M}, \mathbf{U}, \mathbf{V}) = \frac{\exp(-\frac{1}{2}\mathrm{tr}(\mathbf{U}^{-1}(\mathbf{X}-\mathbf{M})\mathbf{V}^{-1}(\mathbf{X}-\mathbf{M})^T))}{(2\pi)^{uv/2}|\mathbf{U}|^{v/2}|\mathbf{V}|^{u/2}}$$

where $\mathrm{tr}(\cdot)$ and $|\cdot|$ denote the trace and determinant, respectively, of a matrix. More specifically, here the row covariance matrix $\mathbf{I}_{N_q k}$ models the relationships between query latent features, and the column covariance matrix $\mathbf{\Omega}$ models the relationships between different $\mathbf{Q}^{(i)}$'s. In other words, $\mathbf{\Omega}$ models the relationships between positions. We can see that if $\mathbf{Q}' = \mathbf{0}_{N_q k\times d}$ and $\mathbf{\Omega} = \lambda_Q^{-1}\mathbf{I}$, the model $p(\mathbf{Q}|\mathbf{\Omega})$ is equivalent to Eq. 4.

**Combined Models (CM):** It is straightforward to combine the three models LB, FM and IM. The combined model could be simply:

$$f_{q,\mathbf{a}} = f^{LB}_{q,\mathbf{a}} + f^{FM}_{q,\mathbf{a}} + f^{IM}_{q,\mathbf{a}}$$

Obviously, the combined model is more expressive than any single model. With more flexibility, there is also risk of overfitting using the combined model. Therefore, regularization is more important for the combined model.

## 4.2 Historical CTR Regularization

Instead of using a zero-mean prior of matrix $\mathbf{Q}$, that is $\mathbf{Q}' = \mathbf{0}_{N_q k\times d}$, we can incorporate historical CTR of pair query $q$ and ad $a$ into the prior information. Here, all positional query latent factors $\mathbf{Q}^{(i)}_{\cdot q}$ are generated from the same corresponding query latent factor $\tilde{\mathbf{Q}}_{\cdot q}$.

$$\mathbf{Q}^{(i)}_{\cdot q} \sim \mathcal{N}(\tilde{\mathbf{Q}}_{\cdot q}, \lambda_Q^{-1}\mathbf{I}),\ i = 1, \cdots, d$$

We call $\tilde{\mathbf{Q}}_{\cdot q}$ query latent factors and $\mathbf{Q}^{(i)}_{\cdot q}$ query positional latent factors. Then, we can place the matrix variate gaussian distribution on the $\mathbf{Q}^{(i)}_{\cdot q}$. We duplicate $\mathrm{vec}(\tilde{\mathbf{Q}})$ for $d$ times $\mathbf{Q}' = [\mathrm{vec}(\tilde{\mathbf{Q}}), \cdots, \mathrm{vec}(\tilde{\mathbf{Q}})]$, such that it can be shaped into the same form of $\mathbf{Q}$. Similarly, we can further assume query latent factors $\tilde{\mathbf{Q}}$ is generated from a Gaussian prior. With query latent factors $\tilde{\mathbf{Q}}$ and ad latent factors $\mathbf{A}$, the click-through rate can be incorporated into an optimization framework through traditional collaborative filtering techniques [22],

$$\mathrm{CTR}_{(q,a)} \sim \mathcal{N}(\tilde{\mathbf{Q}}^T_{\cdot q}\mathbf{A}_{\cdot a}, \lambda_c^{-1}\mathbf{I})$$

With the historical CTR regularization, we update the optimization problem as follows,

$$\begin{aligned} \mathrm{O}_c = & \sum_{q,\mathbf{a}} \ell(y_{q,\mathbf{a}}, f_{q,\mathbf{a}}) + \lambda_{\mathbf{b}}\|\mathbf{b}\|_2^2 + \lambda_{\tilde{\mathbf{Q}}}\|\tilde{\mathbf{Q}}\|_2^2 + \lambda_{\mathbf{A}}\|\mathbf{A}\|_2^2 \\ & + kN_q \ln|\mathbf{\Omega}| + \mathrm{tr}((\mathbf{Q}-\mathbf{Q}')\mathbf{\Omega}^{-1}(\mathbf{Q}-\mathbf{Q}')^T) \\ & + \lambda_c \sum_{q,a}(\mathrm{CTR}_{(q,a)} - \tilde{\mathbf{Q}}^T_{\cdot q}\mathbf{A}_{\cdot a})^2 + \mathrm{const} \end{aligned}$$

## 4.3 Optimization

With the proposed prediction models, we can formalize the click yield prediction problem into an optimization framework. The discrepancy between the estimation $f_{q,\mathbf{a}}$ and the true value $y_{q,\mathbf{a}}$ can be measured by a loss function. We can formalize the problem as an optimization problem as follows

$$\begin{aligned} \mathrm{O}_c = & \sum_{q,\mathbf{a}} \ell(y_{q,\mathbf{a}}, f_{q,\mathbf{a}}) + \lambda_{\mathbf{b}}\|\mathbf{b}\|_2^2 + \lambda_{\mathbf{A}}\|\mathbf{A}\|_2^2 + kN_q \ln|\mathbf{\Omega}| \\ & + \mathrm{tr}(\mathbf{Q}\mathbf{\Omega}^{-1}\mathbf{Q}^T) + \mathrm{const} \end{aligned}$$

The choice of the loss function $\ell(\cdot)$ is also critical to the performance. We will discuss several possible choices for the click yield problem in this section and show the performance comparison of these loss functions on click yield.

### *4.3.1 Regression loss:*

One straightforward method is to treat the problem as a regression problem, where we could use the following pointwise loss functions.

**Squared error loss (Gaussian):** $\ell(y_{q,\mathbf{a}}, f_{q,\mathbf{a}}) = (y_{q,\mathbf{a}} - f_{q,\mathbf{a}})^2$, which is also known as Gaussian response in regression problems.

**Huber loss (Huber):**

$$\ell(y_{q,\mathbf{a}}, f_{q,\mathbf{a}}) = \begin{cases} \frac{1}{2}(y_{q,\mathbf{a}} - f_{q,\mathbf{a}})^2 & \text{if} |y_{q,\mathbf{a}} - f_{q,\mathbf{a}}| < \delta \\ \delta(|y_{q,\mathbf{a}} - f_{q,\mathbf{a}}| - \delta/2) & \text{otherwise} \end{cases}$$

This function is quadratic for small values of $|y_{q,\mathbf{a}} - f_{q,\mathbf{a}}|$, and linear for large values, with equal values and slopes of the different sections at the two points where $|y_{q,\mathbf{a}} - f_{q,\mathbf{a}}| = \delta$

**$\epsilon$-insensitive loss (SVR):**

$$\ell(y_{q,\mathbf{a}}, f_{q,\mathbf{a}}) = \begin{cases} 0 & \text{if} |y_{q,\mathbf{a}} - f_{q,\mathbf{a}}| < \epsilon \\ |y_{q,\mathbf{a}} - f_{q,\mathbf{a}}| - \epsilon & \text{otherwise} \end{cases}$$

This loss function is used by support vector regression [11]. It has no penalty on any training data whose prediction is close enough to the ground truth (within a threshold $\epsilon$).

### *4.3.2 Rank loss*

The problem of click yields prediction is essentially to find the $\mathbf{a}$ which can generate maximum click yields given a query $q$. From this perspective, learning to rank methods are much preferable to the regression method.

**Margin ranking criterion (MRC):**

$$\ell^M(\mathbf{a}_1, \mathbf{a}_2) = \sum_{y_{q,\mathbf{a}_1} > y_{q,\mathbf{a}_2}} \max[0, 1 - f_{q,\mathbf{a}_1} + f_{q,\mathbf{a}_2}]$$

MRC considers all pairs of $y_{q,\mathbf{a}_1} > y_{q,\mathbf{a}_2}$, and assign each a cost if the negative label $f_{q,\mathbf{a}_2}$ is larger or within a "margin" of 1. This loss function has a problem that all pairwise violations are considered equally if they have the same margin violation, independent of their position in the list. For this reason the margin ranking loss might not optimize precision at k very accurately.

**Weighted Approximately Ranked Pairwise loss (WARP):** This loss, proposed in Usunier et al. [34], has been successfully applied in image retrieval tasks [37] and IR tasks [38]. The idea of WARP is to focus more on the top of the ranked list where the top k positions are those we care about, comparing to MRC where no notion of ranked list is introduced. By using the precision at k measure, one can weigh the pairwise violations depending on their position in the ranked list. WARP is defined as an error function as follows:

$$\text{WARP} = \sum_{q,\mathbf{a}} error(f_{q,\mathbf{a}}, y_{q,\mathbf{a}}) = \sum_{q,\mathbf{a}} L(rank(f_{q,\mathbf{a}})) \quad (5)$$

where $rank(f_{q,\mathbf{a}})$ is the rank of the ads list $\mathbf{a}$, given by $rank(f(q,\mathbf{a})) = \sum_{a' \in \mathcal{S}^-_{q,\mathbf{a}}} \mathbb{I}[f_{q,\mathbf{a}'} > f_{q,\mathbf{a}}]$, where $\mathbb{I}$ is the indicator function, $\mathcal{S}^-_{q,\mathbf{a}} = \{\mathbf{a}' | y_{q,\mathbf{a}'} < y_{q,\mathbf{a}}\}$. Here, rank measure $L(\cdot)$ is the function which transforms the rank to a loss:

$$L(k) = \sum_{j=1}^{k} \alpha_j, \text{with } \alpha_1 \geq \alpha_2 \geq \cdots \geq 0.$$

The idea of the rank function is to compute the violations where negative instances are ranked higher than the positive ones and the $L$ function is to transform the violations into loss. Different choices of $\alpha$ define different importance of the relevance position: for $\alpha_j = 1, \forall i$, we have the same AUC optimization as margin ranking criterion. For $\alpha_j = 1$ and $\alpha_{j>1} = 0$, the precision at 1 is optimized and similarly for $\alpha_{j<N} = 1$ and $\alpha_{j \geq N} = 0$, the precision at N is optimized. For $\alpha_i = 1/i$, a smooth weighting over position is given, where most weight is given to the top position. It is also shown to be superior to other schemes of $\alpha$ and yields state-of-the-art performance [34]. In this work, we will also adopt this setting $\alpha_i = 1/i$.

From Eq. 5, we notice that it is difficult to directly optimize WARP due to the discrete nature of indicator functions. In addition, since the number of negative instances is significantly larger than positive instances, the rank function is inefficient to be calculated. As in [37], Eq. 5 can be readily re-written as

$$\text{WARP} = \sum_{q,\mathbf{a}} \frac{L(rank(f_{q,\mathbf{a}})) \sum_{a' \in \mathcal{S}^-_{q,\mathbf{a}}} \mathbb{I}[f_{q,\mathbf{a}'} > f_{q,\mathbf{a}}]}{rank(f_{q,\mathbf{a}})}$$

with the convention 0/0=0 when the correct label $y$ is top-labeled. WARP can be approximated by the hinge loss $\max(0, 1 - f(q,\mathbf{a}) + f(q,\mathbf{a}'))$ instead of the indicator function, to make the loss function continuous [37]. To perform stochastic gradient descent (SGD) updates, another difficulty is that the rank function is still unknown without computing $f_{q,\mathbf{a}}$ for all $q, \mathbf{a}$. In order to approximate the rank function, for a given pair $q, \mathbf{a}$, one draws negative instances until one is found which violates the indicator function. Thus, the approximate $rank(f_{q,\mathbf{a}})$ by using $\lfloor \frac{D^- - 1}{N} \rfloor$ where $\lfloor \cdot \rfloor$ is the flow function, $D^-$ is the number of items in $\mathcal{S}^-_{q,\mathbf{a}}$ and $N$ is the number of trials of sampling until a violating pair is found. This approximation only requires local knowledge of negative instances, making it possible for SGD style updating rule.

#### *4.3.3 An Efficient Implementation*

To solve the problem, we adopt a hybrid optimization approach which mixes stochastic gradient descent and co-ordinate descent. In each iteration, we first perform stochastic gradient descent on $\mathbf{b}, \mathbf{Q}, \mathbf{A}, \tilde{\mathbf{Q}}$. Then, we update $\mathbf{\Omega}$ by the rule $\mathbf{\Omega} \leftarrow \frac{1}{N_q k}(\mathbf{Q} - \mathbf{Q}')^T(\mathbf{Q} - \mathbf{Q}')$ which is obtained by taking the derivative $\mathcal{O}_c$ with respect to $\mathbf{\Omega}$ and setting it to 0. Thus, for each iteration, the time complexity is $O(dkM)$, where $d$ denotes max depth, $k$ denotes the dimensions of latent factors and $M$ is the number of records. In practice, $d$ and $k$ usually are very small (e.g. $d = 4$, $k = 10$), and can be treated as constants. Then, the time complexity for a single iteration will be $O(M)$. Assuming the algorithms need $z$ iterations for convergence, the total time complexity will be $O(zM)$ which allows the algorithms to handle large-scale data.

## 5. HARVESTING THE TEXTUAL INFORMATION OF ADS

Although the click yield optimization framework proposed in the previous section could utilize many features for the prediction task, there are still issues with leveraging the content features, because the term representation of ad content is extremely sparse. Usually, an ad body only contains around 10 to 20 words. Bag-of-words features (e.g., term frequency or TFIDF) cannot effectively capture the underlying semantics. On the other hand, a latent factor model does not explicitly incorporate ad content, such that it cannot handle cold start ads (the ads do not exist in the training data), which frequently occur in real systems. Topic models [2, 45, 19] have been developed to learn the latent semantics of texts. A number of approaches, such as LDA [2] and sparse topical coding [45], could be used in our problem. In this work, we adopt the topical coding model [45] to incorporate ad content into our click yield optimization framework. The reasons for using topical coding are as follows: 1) the topical coding model is a non-probabilistic formulation of topic models for discovering latent representations of large collections of data. It can easily fit into our optimization framework. 2) it can directly control the sparsity of inferred representation by using an appropriate regularizer. 3) the integrated model can be solved efficiently. We treat the content of each ad as a document. For simplicity, we use $a$ as the index of an ad. Let $V = \{1, ..., N_v\}$ be the vocabulary with $N_v$ words. Then $w_{an}$ represents the raw word count of term $n$ in ad $a$. Let $\theta_a \in \mathbb{R}^k$ represent the document code, playing a similar role as $P(z|\theta)$ in traditional topic models like probabilistic latent semantic analysis (PLSA) [19] or latent Dirichlet allocation (LDA) [2]. Similarly, let $\beta \in \mathbb{R}^{k \times N}$ be a dictionary with $k$ bases, which can be treated as $P(z|w)$ in LDA or PLSA.

For $\theta$, due to the connection with the click yield model, we can place either Gaussian prior $p(\theta) \propto \exp(-\lambda_\theta \|\theta\|_2^2)$ or Laplace prior $p(\theta) \propto \exp(-\lambda_\theta \|\theta\|_1)$ for $L_2$ and $L_1$ regularization respectively rather than Dirichlet prior. Then let $\mathbf{\Theta} = \{\theta_a\}_{a=1}^{N_a}$ denote the codes for a collection of ads $\{\mathbf{w}_a\}_{a=1}^{N_a}$. We learn the parameter by maximimum a posteriori (MAP) estimation. Unlike [45], since we only use ad level topical coding in our methods, we remove word level coding. Then we have

$$\mathcal{O}_t = \min_{\boldsymbol{\theta},\beta} \sum_{a,n} - \log Poiss(w_{an}; \theta_a^T \beta_{.n} + \delta \cdot \beta_n^b) + \lambda_\theta \sum_d \|\boldsymbol{\theta}_d\|_2^2$$
$$\text{s.t. } :\theta_a \geq 0, \forall a; \beta_k \in \mathcal{P}, \forall k, \delta > 0, \beta^b \in \mathcal{P},$$

where $\ell(\theta_a, \beta)$ is Poisson loss, and alternatively we can place a background topic $\beta_n^b$.

$$\begin{aligned}\ell(\theta_a, \beta) &= -\log Poiss(w_{an}; \theta_a^T \beta_{\cdot n} + \delta \cdot \beta_n^b) \\ &= -w_{an} \log(\theta_a^T \beta_{\cdot n} + \delta \cdot \beta_n^b) + \theta_a^T \beta_{\cdot n} + \delta \cdot \beta_n^b\end{aligned}$$

The optimization problem can be solved efficiently due to three facts: 1) the property of multilinearity [29], which means that the model is linear with respect to each model parameter when others are fixed, 2) Proposition 1 in [45] states that the optimal value of a single parameter when others are fixed is the maximum between zero and the value obtained by a non-constrained version of the same problem. 3) Efficient methods [12] exist to project real-valued vectors onto the simplex.

To incorporate the topical coding into our click yields model, we explore two methods: one through features and the other through latent factors.

## 5.1 Topical Coding Through Features

In this form, we put the topical coding of ads into ad features and the new ad features become $\tilde{\mathbf{x}}_a = [\mathbf{x}_a^T, \theta_a^T]^T$. With the shared model parameter $\theta$, we connect the two optimization problem $\mathcal{O}_c$ and $\mathcal{O}_t$. This form is similar to the supervised topic model [1] and MedLDA [44]. The final optimization problem is

$$\mathcal{O}_c + \lambda \cdot \mathcal{O}_t$$

where $\lambda$ is a weight parameter for $\mathcal{O}_t$. Then, we perform stochastic gradient descent to update $\theta$, referring to the total optimization.

When passing a sample of click $y_{q,\mathbf{a}}$ and $a \in \mathbf{a}$, we have the following updates

$$\theta_a \leftarrow \mathcal{P}\left\{\theta_a - \eta \frac{\partial \mathcal{O}_c(y_{q,\mathbf{a}})}{\partial \theta_a}\right\}$$

Similarly, when passing a sample of word count $w_{an}$, we have

$$\theta_a \leftarrow \mathcal{P}\left\{\theta_a - \eta \frac{\partial \mathcal{O}_t(w_{an})}{\partial \theta_a}\right\}$$

where $\mathcal{P}\{\cdot\}$ is the projection function which truncates $\theta_a$ and guarantees $\theta_a \geq 0$

## 5.2 Topical Coding Through Latent Factors

An alternative method that can incorporate topical coding of ads is through latent factors. Without constraints, the latent representations of an ad learned from $\mathcal{O}_c$ and $\mathcal{O}_t$ are different. To connect the two problems, we can place constraints on the two latent representations of ads, such that the information of ad content can be incorporated into click yields optimization. One natural approach to require the two latent factors be the same:

$$\theta_a = \mathbf{A}_{\cdot a}, \forall a$$

In this method, the objective function will be $\mathcal{O}_c + \lambda \cdot \mathcal{O}_t$ that is the same as the one in Sec. 5.1 and similar optimization methods (e.g., stochastic gradient descent) can be used to solve the problem. Another more flexible approach is to use a regularizer to keep the two latent factors similar rather than identical, as:

$$\lambda_{\theta\mathbf{A}} \|\theta_a - \mathbf{A}_{\cdot a}\|_2^2, \forall a$$

The objective function will be $\mathcal{O}_c + \lambda_{\theta\mathbf{A}} \sum_a \|\theta_a - \mathbf{A}_{\cdot a}\|_2^2 + \lambda \cdot \mathcal{O}_t$. We can also view one latent factor as a sample drawing from a multivariate normal distribution with the mean of the other latent factor: $\mathbf{A}_{\cdot a} \sim \mathcal{N}(\theta_a, \lambda_{\theta\mathbf{A}}^{-1}\mathbf{I})$. This will produce the formalism in Wang and Blei's work [35]. Also, the SGD-style optimization can be used to solve the problem. In our studies, we find the performances of the two methods are comparable and we will use the first one in the following experiments.

**Table 2: Data sets**

| | April 2012 | May 2012 | total |
|---|---|---|---|
| Impressions | 29,722,684 | 13,160,289 | 42,882,973 |
| $(q, \mathbf{a})$ | 112,084 | 52,814 | 135,445 |
| Ads | 62,423 | 34,214 | 72,959 |
| Queries | 49,483 | 26,104 | 53,730 |

# 6. EXPERIMENTS

In this section, we analyze variations of the proposed model and compare our model with the state-of-the-art methods.

## 6.1 Experiment Setting

We collected the search log data from a commercial search engine in the U.S. market in April 2012 and the first two weeks of May 2012. The dataset in April 2012 is the same one as we used in Section 3. We filter out the low frequency queries and ads to remove the noise. In this work, we focus on head queries for three reasons: 1) Head queries hold the majority of the search traffic which is more important to the search engine. 2) Due to high traffic of head queries, user behaviors are usually consistent and we can mine the patterns of user behaviors effectively. 3) In this work, since we investigate ad list effects rather than individual ads, we do not have enough data to analyze tail queries. Finally, the April 2012 data set contains 29,722,684 impressions and the May 2012 data set contains 13,160,289 impressions. The other data statistics are shown in Table 2. We used April 2012 dataset as training set, and the May 2012 dataset as the test set. Since the train/test data are split temporally rather than randomly, we avoid the problem of predicting the past using future data. This evaluation is more consistent with a real application scenario. At the same time, the cold start problem becomes serious.

To evaluate the performance of click yields prediction, we report the standard ranking measurements—Mean Average Precision (MAP) and Precision@N for references.

By using our click yield prediction framework, with an issued query, we can reselect the group of ads to display with the higher predicted click yields, and it will improve the performance of current search engine. Solving this mathematical problem in runtime may not be affordable when the number of ad candidates is large. Therefore, we can only do it for the popular queries in off-line mode. We argue that these queries take the majority of the ad clicks in the traffics. To evaluate this relative improvement, we present a novel evaluation metric, referred to as Relative Gain of Click Yields (RGCY). The overall click yield of the current system is $\underline{\text{CY}} = \frac{1}{\text{Imp}} \sum_q \sum_{\mathbf{a}} y_{q,\mathbf{a}} \cdot \text{Imp}(q, \mathbf{a})$. Given a query $q$, ideally, if we know the optimal $\mathbf{a}$, which can generate the maximum click yield, that is for all impressions of $q$, one can always show this optimal result $\mathbf{a}_{opt(q)}$ which is defined $\mathbf{a}_{opt(q)} \in \{\mathbf{a}' | \forall \mathbf{a}, y_{q,\mathbf{a}'} \geq y_{q,\mathbf{a}}\}$. The maximum click yield which the system could have is $\overline{\text{CY}} = \frac{1}{\text{Imp}} \sum_q \tilde{y}_q \sum_{\mathbf{a}} \text{Imp}(q, \mathbf{a})$ where $\tilde{y}_q = y_{q,\mathbf{a}_{opt(q)}}$ denotes the optimal click yield for query $q$.

Given a query $q$ and its ranked ad lists $l_q = \{\mathbf{a}_{(1)}, \mathbf{a}_{(2)}, \cdots, \mathbf{a}_{(n)}\}$ where $f_{q,\mathbf{a}_{(1)}} \geq f_{q,\mathbf{a}_{(2)}} \cdots \geq f_{q,\mathbf{a}_{(n)}}$, $\text{CY@}N = \frac{1}{\text{Imp}} \sum_q \hat{y}_q \sum_{\mathbf{a}} \text{Imp}(q, \mathbf{a})$ where $\hat{y}_q$ is the average click yield of top N ad lists for query $q$, $\hat{y}_q = \frac{1}{N} \sum_{i=0}^{N} y_{q,\mathbf{a}_{(i)}}$. We define the relative gain of click yield to be

$$\text{RGCY@}N = \frac{\text{CY@}N - \underline{\text{CY}}}{\overline{\text{CY}} - \underline{\text{CY}}}$$

It is trivial to see that $\overline{\text{CY}} \geq \text{CY@}N \geq \underline{\text{CY}}$. The RGCY@$N$ actually measures the gap with the maximum click yield. More specifically, RGCY@1 is more critical to the system since it can generate the maximum click yield.

## 6.2 Model Analysis

In this section, we detail the anatomy of the proposed model and systematically analyze the contributions and effects of each part.

**Estimation Model Analysis:** We first test the scoring model. The results are shown in Figure 3(a). In this experiment, the performance is evaluated by PREC@1 and MAP, and the loss function is WARP. We can see that the performances are consistent in terms of PREC@1 and MAP. The bias model performs the worst on the left. With the feature model added, the model performs better. When we further incorporate the interaction model into the system, the model achieve the best performance in both PREC@1 and MAP.

**Convergence Check:** We also show the learning curve of the combined in Figure 3(b), where two loss functions are tested: Gaussian response and WARP. The convergence of the two loss functions can be achieved after 100 iterations. We can also see that the performance of the ranking loss (WARP) is much better than the regression loss (Gaussian response).

**Position Correlation Analysis:** Matrix $\boldsymbol{\Omega}$ is shown in Figure 3(c). We can see from the figure that position 1 is positively correlated to the position 4, while position 1 is negatively correlated to position 2 and position 3. This results are consistent with our intuitions: if the ads in position 2 and position 3 are similar to the ads in the top position, users are more likely to skip the ads due to information redundancy, which may decrease click yields. On the other hand, the ads at the bottom position (position 4) are positively correlated with position 1. One possible reason is that position 4 is far apart from the top position, and similarity between them is insensitive such that the click yields might increase.

**Loss Function:** From Figure 3(b), we have already seen the performance differences between different loss functions (WARP and Gaussian). In this experiment, all five loss functions in Section 4.3 are systematically compared. The results are shown in Table 3. For pointwise regression loss, we can see that the least square loss and $\epsilon$-insensitive loss (SVR) can generate comparable performance. Huber loss, which is quadratic for small errors and linear for large errors, can achieve slightly better performance than the two other pointwise regression losses in this problem. On the other hand, for pairwise ranking loss, WARP can be treated as a weighted version of MRC, which emphasizes the top positions weight. From Table 3, we can see that the overall performance (MAP) of WARP is similar to MRC, while the performance of WARP on the RGCY@1 which only evaluates the accuracy of top position (RGCY@1 can be considered as the weighted version of MRC) is much better than MRC. Overall, comparing with the pointwise regression losses, the two pairwise rank losses are preferable in click yield prediction in all three evaluations (PREC@1, MAP and RGCY@1).

## 6.3 Side Information

For the topical coding model, we explore how topics are learned. The dictionary $\boldsymbol{\beta}$ can be interpreted as a topic matrix as in standard topic models. We can describe topics as in other topic models by ranking terms in probabilities. We show some example topics in Table 4. We can see that these topics can be easily recognized. Moreover, modeling ad content is not only useful for explanatory analysis, it indeed improves the prediction tasks. From Table 3, we can see that by incorporating the topical coding of ads, we get further improvement on RGCY@1.

**Table 3: Predictive results of Click Prediction**

| Side | loss | PREC@1 | MAP | RGCY@1 |
|---|---|---|---|---|
| N/A | Gaussian | 0.5683 | 0.6792 | 0.6475 |
| CTR | Gaussian | 0.5689 | 0.6796 | 0.6510 |
| CTR,TCF | Gaussian | 0.5789 | 0.6894 | 0.6592 |
| CTR,TCL | Gaussian | 0.5771 | 0.6887 | 0.6701 |
| N/A | Huber | 0.5694 | 0.6811 | 0.6617 |
| CTR | Huber | 0.5695 | 0.6811 | 0.6618 |
| CTR,TCF | Huber | 0.5714 | 0.6834 | 0.6627 |
| CTR,TCL | Huber | 0.5730 | 0.6854 | 0.6679 |
| N/A | $\epsilon$-Insensitive | 0.5785 | 0.6886 | 0.6365 |
| CTR | $\epsilon$-Insensitive | 0.5787 | 0.6889 | 0.6401 |
| CTR,TCF | $\epsilon$-Insensitive | 0.5824 | 0.6925 | 0.6402 |
| CTR,TCL | $\epsilon$-Insensitive | 0.5833 | 0.6941 | 0.6416 |
| N/A | MRC | 0.5839 | 0.6930 | 0.6641 |
| CTR | MRC | 0.5848 | 0.6932 | 0.6661 |
| CTR,TCF | MRC | 0.5849 | 0.6936 | 0.6697 |
| CTR,TCL | MRC | 0.5859 | 0.6946 | 0.6732 |
| N/A | WARP | 0.5841 | 0.6923 | 0.6685 |
| CTR | WARP | 0.5845 | 0.6924 | 0.6782 |
| CTR,TCF | WARP | 0.5851 | 0.6936 | 0.6829 |
| CTR,TCL | WARP | 0.5859 | 0.6943 | 0.6882 |

**Table 4: Examples of topics are shown. The terms are top ranked terms in each topic. The topic names shown in bold are given by the authors**

| **Shopping** | **Video** | **Travel** | **Finance** | **Game** |
|---|---|---|---|---|
| low | tv | book | online | games |
| free | order | hotels | credit | play |
| order | free | rates | apply | store |
| shop | time | price | card | online |
| shipping | watch | insurance | get | free |
| quality | college | car | university | today |
| today | live | parts | gift | guarantee |
| orders | 24 | hotel | degree | official |
| high | take | great | website | fun |
| prices | like | best | back | enjoy |
| supplies | sears | auto | earn | favorite |
| site | movies | low | college | kids |
| state | community | quotes | magazine | better |
| official | episodes | deals | cash | toys |

Next, we examine the effects of two side information: historical CTR regularization and topical modeling of ad content. The results are shown in Table 3, where CTR represents historical CTR regularization, TCF represents topical model incorporated through features, TCL represents topical model incorporated through latent factors. We see that the performances improve slightly across all loss functions when adding historical CTR regularization into the system. When adding topical information, we see that the performance becomes much better than the original model, due to alleviating the cold-start and sparseness problems. We notice that WARP loss with CTR regularization and incorporated topical coding through latent factors achieve relative better performance than other combinations (although MRC is slightly better than WARP for MAP under CTR,TCL). In the following section, we will use it to compare with the other existing methods.

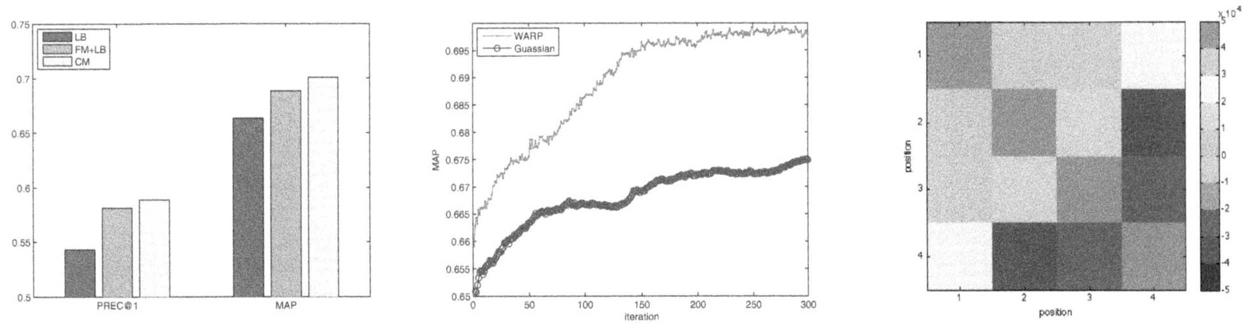


(a) Model Analysis (b) WARP vs. Gaussian (c) Co-relation across positions

**Figure 3: Experimental results for model analysis**

## 6.4 Comparison with existing methods

In this section, we name our methods CYP for Click Yield Prediction. Although there is no previous work on the click yield prediction problem, some models could be easily adapted to solve the problem. We compare our model with four existing methods:

- **Probabilistic Matrix Factorization (PMF)** is a popular method [31] in collaborative filtering. Here, we treat queries as the users and ads as the items to be recommended for users. CTR is the response in this framework.
- **User Browsing Model (UBM)** is the baseline method and a classical click model [13]. We adopt the EM inference process for parameter $\alpha$ and $\beta$. To avoid infinite values in log-likelihood, $\alpha$ is truncated into the range $(0.0001, 0.9999)$.
- **Matrix Factorization Click Model (MFCM)** is proposed by Shen et al. [32]. The model incorporates collaborative filtering techniques into the click model.
- **Relational click model (CRF)** proposed by Xiong et al. [39]. They adopt Conditional Random Fields (CRF) to model the exclusive effects between similar ads which are shown together in the same impression.

We choose these four methods to compare to various alternative methods to solve this problem. PMF is a classical recommender method, UBM is a classical click model while CFCM and CRF are very recent methods and the state-of-the-arts in modeling clicks. All four methods follows the classical two-step approach, that is, predicting CTR of individual ad at first and then compose the click yields for ad lists and rank them. The comparison results (on precision, RGCY and MAP) are shown in Table 5. We notice that the performances across five evaluations are consistent: the two classical methods—PMF and UBM—show similar performance on this problem, and they are relatively worse than the two recent click models—MFCM, CRF. MFCM which incorporates examination hypothesis into matrix factorization, can get slightly better results than matrix factorization. CRF is the first click model which tries to model the relational ad clicks on the ads displayed together. The performance of CRF is much better than other three baselines which only focus on modeling clicks on single ad. However, for the click yield prediction problem, because all these four methods are two-step approaches and not designed to optimize click yield directly, our method outperforms all these methods noticeably. Especially, on RGCY@1, our methods can achieve 0.6882 which almost improves the click yield 10% absolutely, comparing to 0.5975—the value of the second best method, CRF.

**Table 5: Comparison with existing methods**

| Model | PREC@1 | PREC@5 | MAP | RGCY@1 | RGCY@5 |
|---|---|---|---|---|---|
| CYP | **0.5859** | **0.7428** | **0.6943** | **0.6882** | **0.7438** |
| PMF | 0.5251 | 0.6828 | 0.6450 | 0.4991 | 0.5597 |
| UBM | 0.5338 | 0.6845 | 0.6647 | 0.4519 | 0.5015 |
| MFCM | 0.5553 | 0.6985 | 0.6754 | 0.5830 | 0.6293 |
| CRF | 0.5760 | 0.7320 | 0.6887 | 0.5975 | 0.7175 |

# 7. CONCLUSION

In this paper, we have studied ad group performance—click yield, which is a important measurement for ad delivery. Compared to traditional methods, we provide a new perspective to measure group performance of ads displayed together. We systematically explored different aspects: bias model, features, interactive influence, depth, and correlation across positions. Additionally, to best leverage the text features and solve the sparseness issue in textual information and cold starts on ads, we incorporate a topic coding model into our framework to learn the topic information of short texts for ads in two ways—through features and through latent factors. Finally, various loss functions are also studied. We find that ranking loss is preferred for this problem.

We collected a large-scale real world dataset from a commercial search engine to conduct experiments. Our experiments show that directly predicting click yields achieves noticeable improvement compared to state-of-the-art two-step approaches.

Several interesting points remain to be explored in the future: first, research beyond the prediction of group performance in sponsored search would be valuable. A more interesting problem is, given a query, find the best depth and the ad list that can generate the best click yields for search engines. This is a much harder problem, similar to a combinatorial optimization problem. Second, although we mainly study top queries in this work, studying tail queries is also interesting and necessary as future work.

# 8. REFERENCES

[1] D. M. Blei and J. D. McAuliffe. Supervised topic models. In *NIPS*, 2007.

[2] D. M. Blei, A. Y. Ng, and M. I. Jordan. Latent Dirichlet allocation. *Journal of Machine Learning Research*, 3:993–1022, January 2003.

[3] G. Bouchard, D. Yin, and S. Guo. Convex collective matrix factorization. In *Proceedings of AISTATS 2013*.

[4] A. Broder and V. Josifovski. Introduction to computational advertising, 2011. Retrieved from http://www.stanford.edu/class/msande239/.

[5] B. Cao, D. Shen, K. Wang, and Q. Yang. Clickthrough log analysis by collaborative ranking. In *AAAI*, 2010.

[6] O. Chapelle and Y. Zhang. A dynamic bayesian network click model for web search ranking. In *WWW '09*.

[7] D. Chen, W. Chen, H. Wang, Z. Chen, and Q. Yang. Beyond ten blue links: enabling user click modeling in federated web search. In *Proceedings of WSDM '12*, 2012.

[8] Y. Chen and T. W. Yan. Position-normalized click prediction in search advertising. In *Proceedings of KDD '12*.

[9] H. Cheng and E. Cantú-Paz. Personalized click prediction in sponsored search. In *Proceedings of WSDM '10*.

[10] N. Craswell, O. Zoeter, M. Taylor, and B. Ramsey. An experimental comparison of click position-bias models. In *WSDM '08*.

[11] H. Drucker, C. J. C. Burges, L. Kaufman, A. J. Smola, and V. Vapnik. Support vector regression machines. In *NIPS*, pages 155–161, 1996.

[12] J. Duchi, S. Shalev-Shwartz, Y. Singer, and T. Chandra. Efficient projections onto the l1-ball for learning in high dimensions. In *Proceedings of ICML '08*, 2008.

[13] G. E. Dupret and B. Piwowarski. A user browsing model to predict search engine click data from past observations. In *SIGIR '08*.

[14] T. Graepel, J. Q. Candela, T. Borchert, and R. Herbrich. Web-scale bayesian click-through rate prediction for sponsored search advertising in microsoft's bing search engine. In *ICML '10*.

[15] F. Guo, C. Liu, A. Kannan, T. Minka, M. Taylor, Y.-M. Wang, and C. Faloutsos. Click chain model in web search. In *WWW '09*.

[16] F. Guo, C. Liu, and Y. M. Wang. Efficient multiple-click models in web search. In *Proceedings of WSDM '09*, 2009.

[17] A. K. Gupta and D. K. Nagar. *Matrix Variate Distributions*. Chapman & Hall, 2000.

[18] D. Hillard, S. Schroedl, E. Manavoglu, H. Raghavan, and C. Leggetter. Improving ad relevance in sponsored search. In *Proceedings of WSDM '10*

[19] T. Hofmann. Unsupervised learning by probabilistic latent semantic analysis. *Machine Learning*, 42(1-2):177–196, January-February 2001.

[20] T. Joachims, L. Granka, B. Pan, H. Hembrooke, and G. Gay. Accurately interpreting click through data as implicit feedback. In *Proceedings of SIGIR '05*, 2005.

[21] Y. Koren. Factor in the neighbors: Scalable and accurate collaborative filtering. *ACM Transactions on Knowledge Discovery from Data*, 4(1):1–24, January 2010.

[22] Y. Koren, R. Bell, and C. Volinsky. Matrix factorization techniques for recommender systems. *Computer*, 42(8):30–37, 2009.

[23] C. Liu, F. Guo, and C. Faloutsos. Bbm: bayesian browsing model from petabyte-scale data. In *KDD '09*, 2009.

[24] C. Liu, F. Guo, and C. Faloutsos. Bayesian browsing model: Exact inference of document relevancfe from petabyte-scale data. *ACM Trans. Knowl. Discov. Data*, 4(4):19:1–19:26, Oct. 2010.

[25] T.-Y. Liu. Learning to rank for information retrieval. *Found. Trends Inf. Retr.*, 3(3):225–331, Mar. 2009.

[26] A. K. Menon, K.-P. Chitrapura, S. Garg, D. Agarwal, and N. Kota. Response prediction using collaborative filtering with hierarchies and side-information. In *KDD '11*.

[27] T. Minka, J. Winn, J. Guiver, and A. Kannan. A click through model - sample code. `http://research.microsoft.com/en-us/um/cambridge/projects/infernet/docs/Click%20through%20model%20sample.aspx`, 2009.

[28] T. Moon, A. Smola, Y. Chang, and Z. Zheng. Intervalrank: isotonic regression with listwise and pairwise constraints. In *WSDM '10*.

[29] S. Rendle. Factorization machines with libFM. *ACM Trans. Intell. Syst. Technol.*, 3(3):57:1–57:22, May 2012.

[30] M. Richardson, E. Dominowska, and R. Ragno. Predicting clicks: estimating the click-through rate for new ads. In *WWW '07*.

[31] R. Salakhutdinov and A. Mnih. Probabilistic matrix factorization. In *NIPS 21*, pages 1257–1264. 2008.

[32] S. Shen, B. Hu, W. Chen, and Q. Yang. Personalized click model through collaborative filtering. In *WSDM '12*.

[33] R. Srikant, S. Basu, N. Wang, and D. Pregibon. User browsing models: relevance versus examination. In *KDD '10*.

[34] N. Usunier, D. Buffoni, and P. Gallinari. Ranking with ordered weighted pairwise classification. In *ICML '09*.

[35] C. Wang and D. M. Blei. Collaborative topic modeling for recommending scientific articles. In *KDD '11*, 2011.

[36] X. Wang and et al. Click-through prediction for sponsored search advertising with hybrid models. In *KDDCUP 2012*, 2012.

[37] J. Weston, S. Bengio, and N. Usunier. Large scale image annotation: learning to rank with joint word-image embeddings. *Mach. Learn.*, 81(1):21–35, Oct. 2010.

[38] J. Weston, C. Wang, R. Weiss, and A. Berenzweig. Latent collaborative retrieval. In *ICML*, 2012.

[39] C. Xiong, T. Wang, W. Ding, Y. Shen, and T.-Y. Liu. Relational click prediction for sponsored search. In *Proceedings of WSDM '12*, 2012.

[40] W. Xu, E. Manavoglu, and E. Cantu-Paz. Temporal click model for sponsored search. In *SIGIR '10*, 2010.

[41] D. Yin, S. Guo, B. Chidlovskii, B. D. Davison, C. Archambeau, and G. Bouchard. Connecting comments and tags: Improved modeling of social tagging systems. In *Proceedings of WSDM '13*.

[42] W. V. Zhang and R. Jones. Comparing click logs and editorial labels for training query rewriting. In *Query Log Analysis: Social And Technological Challenges. A workshop at WWW 2007*.

[43] Y. Zhang, W. Chen, D. Wang, and Q. Yang. User-click modeling for understanding and predicting search-behavior. In *KDD '11*.

[44] J. Zhu, A. Ahmed, and E. P. Xing. Medlda: maximum margin supervised topic models for regression and classification. In *Proceedings of ICML '09*, 2009.

[45] J. Zhu and E. Xing. Sparse topical coding. In *UAI '11*, 2011.

[46] Z. A. Zhu, W. Chen, T. Minka, C. Zhu, and Z. Chen. A novel click model and its applications to online advertising. In *WSDM '10*, 2010.

# Scalable Hierarchical Multitask Learning Algorithms for Conversion Optimization in Display Advertising


Amr Ahmed *
Google
amra@google.com

Abhimanyu Das *
Microsoft Research
abhidas@microsoft.com

Alexander J. Smola *
Carnegie Mellon University
and Google
alex@smola.org



## ABSTRACT

Many estimation tasks come in groups and hierarchies of related problems. In this paper we propose a hierarchical model and a scalable algorithm to perform inference for multitask learning. It infers task correlation and subtask structure in a joint sparse setting. Implementation is achieved by a distributed subgradient oracle and the successive application of prox-operators pertaining to groups and subgroups of variables. We apply this algorithm to conversion optimization in display advertising. Experimental results on over 1TB data for up to 1 billion observations and 1 million attributes show that the algorithm provides significantly better prediction accuracy while simultaneously being efficiently scalable by distributed parameter synchronization.


## Categories and Subject Descriptors

G.3 [**Mathematics of Computing**]: Probability and Statistics; I.2.6 [**Artificial Intelligence**]: Learning

## 1. INTRODUCTION

In many cases data inference problems do not arise in isolation. That is, we usually encounter a range of *related* problems and there is considerable benefit in solving them jointly. This insight has been exploited repeatedly and it has led to algorithms commonly known as multitask learning techniques [1, 22, 12, 7, 18]. Applications, e.g. to massively multitasked spam filtering [20] show its practical importance. The key idea is that by solving related tasks we are able to learn more about an individual task.

In this paper we study the problem of conversion maximization in display advertising. That is, we focus on maximizing the occurrence of commercially relevant actions such as purchases, account creation, mailing list signups, etc. This involves estimating a user's propensity to perform such actions and to identify generally susceptible populations of users. The challenge here is that we have both a broad range of different advertisers and also a range of subtasks (views, clicks, conversions) that we wish to maximize.

As is to be expected in computational advertising, the amount of data can be quite significant. Moreover, the data is not necessarily homogeneous. Tasks have wildly varying sizes, commensurate with the financial stake of the advertisers and the popularity of their product. Likewise, attributes are sparse and many occur only in a small number of contexts. This requires an effective inference approach.

Our work builds on well known multiple kernel learning [19] and collaborative filtering techniques namely that of effectively imposing a hyperprior on the regularization term. In doing so it is possible to cast multitask learning as a nontrivial convex optimization problem. See e.g. [23] for details. This strategy is then combined with a hierarchical model over task and subtask specific parameters. Furthermore, we impose structured sparsity along the lines of [5].

To solve the problem in practice we rely on a distributed subgradient oracle. Load-balancing is achieved by using consistent hashing for task distribution over processors and distributed variable aggregation to mitigate the latency and task restarts otherwise required in Hadoop MapReduce. That is, we use the variable distribution of [13] for storage. Subsequently we invoke a sequence of prox operators [5] to synchronize efficiently between local and global penalties. To summarize, our contributions are the following:

- We formulate the joint conversion, click and unattributed-conversion modeling problem in behavioral targeting as a large-scale hierarchical multitask learning problem and show that the convex multitask learning approach of [23] can be adapted to this setting.
- We design an efficient distributed implementation of the above algorithm that scales to Terascale data.
- Using a real-world, web-scale display advertising targeting data set and two smaller public datasets, we show the ability of our algorithm to significantly improve on the baseline modeling performance obtained by traditional single-task inference systems.

### 1.1 Challenges in Conversion Maximization

Recent trends in behavioral targeting and display advertising emphasize the importance of commercially relevant actions. That is, rather than user clicks, advertisers aim to maximize the number of conversions they receive. Conversions stand for purchases, account creation, or any other relevant action that an advertiser sees as particularly desirable. To obtain good performance, publishers tend to instrument

*work done while the authors were at Yahoo! Research



*WSDM'14*, February 24–28, 2014, New York, New York, USA.



http://dx.doi.org/10.1145/2556195.2556264.

their websites with embedded code which allows third parties to capture user transactions and generate user segments that are of high value for a particular advertiser [1]. These segments primarily contain users that are actually inclined to perform a transaction as opposed to a casual visit to the web site through an accidental click.

Conversions on an advertiser's web site are either "attributed" to their corresponding display ads based on advertiser-specific rules, such as the amount of time elapsed between the conversion time and the time that the ad was last shown to the user, or they are "unattributed" if they cannot be tied to a specific display ad. Past work [3] has shown the superiority of targeting platforms maximizing for attributed conversions to traditional solutions maximizing for clicks.

For conversion-oriented behavioral targeting the traditional approach has been to only consider attributed conversions. The corresponding inference problem for each advertising campaign is then solved independently, for instance, by fitting a Support Vector Machine or Logistic Regression model. This generates separate models based on user data for each campaign. However, a typical behavioral targeting platform optimizing for attributed conversions, henceforth simply referred as conversions, faces two core issues:

- There is a large volumes of user histories that need to be processed in a periodic fashion in order to perform inference over attributed conversions for a large number of ad campaigns. Processing activities of billions of users on a daily basis imposes many challenges such as how to build user profiles in an efficient way, and how to optimize multiple campaigns at the same time;
- When optimizing for each campaign separately we are likely to do poorly for infrequent campaigns. We therefore need to design algorithms that can deal with sparseness of attributed conversions in many campaigns. The absence of a sufficient number of labeled data for the inference tasks creates a major bottleneck against achieving tangible targeting performance improvement.

## 1.2 Multitask Learning

For each advertising campaign, we can formulate several other related inference tasks apart from conversion modeling: we can attempt to infer the likelihood of a click (which is typically a prerequisite for conversion) and to model the likelihood of unattributed conversions (the latter helps to identify similar users). These different inference problems of each campaign are likely to be correlated. Hence modeling them jointly should improve estimation performance.

Additionally, it is quite likely that there is significant correlations between inference tasks across different advertising campaigns. For example, if there exists advertising campaigns corresponding to different brands of cars, the conversion or click models for all these campaigns might be quite similar to each other. Thus, performing a joint inference over all these potentially-correlated tasks together might lead to better performance than solving these inference tasks separately. This is the basic premise of multitask learning.

The key difference to conventional multitask learning is that in our case there exists a *hierarchy* between tasks. That is, we expect that all tasks for a given campaign (e.g. selling car insurance for a particular company) have related specificity in terms of their user demographic. Hence it is only reasonable that the sets of features and preferences are shared between them. It is to be expected that joint feature selection should improve the performance of each estimator.

Strictly speaking, we have two somewhat related goals — one is to do well for *all* tasks, i.e. click, conversion, and unattributed conversion estimation. This is a symmetric setting where the goal is to use the task correlations to simultaneously improve the prediction performance of all the tasks. The other task is to perform well for conversion prediction while using the remaining data as *side information*. This is an asymmetric setting. While both tasks are rather related, they are subtly different in their performance criteria and in terms of the estimation problem.

In this paper, we formulate two different hierarchical multitask models for these settings: a *hierarchical* model for the symmetric setting, and an *attachment* model for the asymmetric setting. In the hierarchical model, we first define an inter-campaign correlation matrix on a root-level set of feature weights for each campaign. This is then used to derive feature weights for its conversions, clicks and unattributed conversions locally. In the attachment model, the inter-campaign correlation matrix is applied directly on the feature weights for the conversion model of each campaign.

There is ample literature covering the subject of multitask learning. However, in the context of our behavioral targeting problem, there are two objectives that a multitask learning algorithm should satisfy: it should be easily distributable and scale to thousands of campaigns and millions of features; it should extend to a multi-level task hierarchy. This makes the setting rather nontrivial in terms of efficient inference.

## 1.3 Approach

In this paper, we use a convex formulation approach for multitask learning. Its basic idea is described in several variants e.g. in the context of multitask learning [23], matrix inference [16] and multiple kernel learning [14]. Essentially, one imposes a penalty over the covariance matrices governing correlation between attribute vectors. This way we can ensure that primarily similar attribute sets and related attribute vectors are chosen.

In terms of conversion maximization this means that we use an inter-campaign covariance matrix to model the relationships between the various campaigns. Moreover, intra-campaign covariance matrices are used to model the relationships between clicks, conversions and unattributed conversions of each campaign. A matrix-variate normal prior is imposed on these covariance matrices. A joint optimization objective can be formulated for all the tasks by obtaining a maximum likelihood estimate of the covariance matrices and the per-task feature weights for all the tasks. As we will show later, this objective is convex. It can be solved in a distributed fashion using proximal subgradient methods, such as the Fast Iterative Shrinkage algorithm (FISTA) [6].

For both models, we use a scalable alternating subspace descent method for simultaneous inference of both the task correlation matrices and the feature weights. A key tool for achieving scalability will be to use a cluster of machines as a distributed subgradient oracle [17]. Since iterative thresholding algorithms like FISTA require a significant number of gradient computations (e.g. [6] report 100 steps), our platform must preserve state and data locality between iterations. This makes it unsuitable to a naive Hadoop MapReduce implementation. Instead, we employ a consistent hashing based synchronization algorithm. We apply our dis-

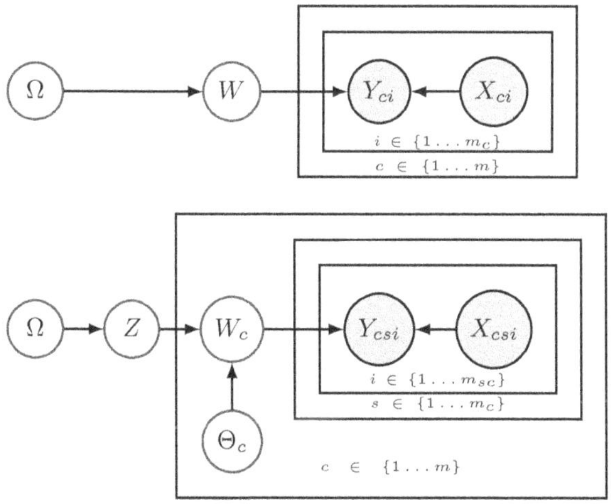


**Figure 1: Top: Standard multitask learning using a Matrix-Variate distribution. Observations $X_{ci}$ for campaign $c$ receive labels $Y_{ci}$. These are assigned using campaign-specific weight vectors $W_c$. The latter are exchangeable but not independent, hence jointly drawn from some distribution $p(W|\Omega)$. Bottom: Hierarchical multitask learning. After drawing task specific parameters $Z_c$ from an exchangeable but not independent distribution we draw subtask specific parameters $W_s$ using a joint parameter $\Theta_c$ and $Z_c$. The rest remains unchanged.**

tributed multitask learning framework to the conversion modeling problem described in [1] and we show how our system can improve the AUC performance significantly, when compared to individual conversion modeling of each ad-campaign.

# 2. MULTITASK LEARNING

## 2.1 Notation

We now cast the problem of campaign-specific estimation as a multitask learning problem. That is, we treat each campaign $c$ as a task. In each such case we observe covariates (patterns) $x_{ci}$ and our goal is to infer labels $y_{ci}$. For simplicity we assume that $x_{ci} \in \mathcal{X} = \mathbb{R}^d$ consists of $d$-dimensional vectors and moreover that $y_{ci} \in \mathcal{Y}$ are either binary $\mathcal{Y} = \{\pm 1\}$ for classification or real-valued $\mathcal{Y} = \mathbb{R}$ for regression. At a later stage (in section 3) we will assume that each campaign contains a number of subtasks $s$. The table below gives an overview of the symbols used:

| | |
|---|---|
| $\mathcal{X}$ | domain of observations (usually $\mathcal{X} = \mathbb{R}^d$) |
| $\mathcal{Y}$ | domain of labels (usually $\mathcal{Y} = \{\pm 1\}$ or $\mathcal{Y} = \mathbb{R}$) |
| $c$ | campaign index ($c \in \{1 \ldots m\}$) |
| $s$ | sub-campaign index ($s \in \{1 \ldots n\}$) |
| $j$ | observation index ($j \in \{1 \ldots m_c\}$ or $j \in \{1 \ldots m_{cs}\}$) |
| $x$ | observation ($x_{cj}$ or $x_{csj}$) |
| $X_c$ | set of observations for campaign $c$ |
| $y$ | observation ($y_{cj}$ or $y_{csj}$) |
| $Y_c$ | set of labels for campaign $c$ |
| $w$ | parameter vectors ($w_c$ or $w_{cs}$) |
| $W$ | stacked parameter vectors $W = \{\ldots w_c \ldots\}$ |
| $z$ | parameter vectors $z_c$ for top level hierarchy |
| $Z$ | stacked parameter vectors $Z = \{\ldots z_c \ldots\}$ |

Figure 1 captures the formal structure of the multitask learning problem. To capture interaction between covariates $x_{cj}$, campaigns $c$ and associated labels $y_{cj}$, e.g. whether a particular user converted on an ad in a particular campaign at a particular occasion, we consider the issue of estimating $y|x, c$ for a large range of campaigns simultaneously. We denote by $m$ the total number of campaigns and by $m_c$ the number of observations per campaign. Formally we consider sets of covariates and labels indexed by a campaign $c$, denoted by $X^c = \{x_1^c, \ldots, x_{n^c}^c\} \subseteq \mathcal{X}$ and $Y^c = \{y_1^c, \ldots, y_{n^c}^c\} \subseteq \mathcal{Y}$. Here each pair $(x_{cj}, y_{cj})$ is drawn from some distribution $p(x, y|c) = p(y|x, c)p(x|c)$ of covariates and labels respectively. Finally, we denote by $csi$ the combination of task, subtask, and coordinate, and by $\cdot$ the entire vector in the associated dimension. E.g. $w_{c \cdot i}$ denotes the vector over all subtasks $s$ associated with $c$ for coordinate $i$.

## 2.2 Objective

The inference problem is expressed either of risk minimization whenever we want to find a classifier which makes a small number of mistakes, or as one of maximizing the data likelihood. In the latter case we want to find parameters $W = \{w_1, \ldots w_m\}$ such that the maximizes label likelihood:

$$p(Y|X, W) = \prod_{c=1}^{m} p(Y_c|X_c, w_c) = \prod_{c=1}^{m} \prod_{j=1}^{m_c} p(y_{cj}|x_{cj}, w_c) \quad (1)$$

Choices for $y_{cj}|x_{cj}, w_c$ are e.g.

$$p(y_{cj}|x_{cj}, w_c) = (2\pi\sigma^2)^{-\frac{1}{2}} e^{-\frac{1}{2\sigma^2}(y_{cj} - \langle x_{cj}, w_c \rangle)^2} \quad (2)$$

$$p(y_{cj}|x_{cj}, w_c) = \frac{1}{1 + e^{-y_{cj}\langle x_{cj}, w_c \rangle}} \quad (3)$$

for regression and classification respectively. A naive maximization of the conditional response likelihood $p(Y|X, W)$ leads to overfitting unless the model complexity is overly small or unless a suitable prior is used. Multitask learning models aim to address this problem by imposing a suitable prior distribution $p(W)$ on $W$ which favors simple models and which exploits *correlation* between tasks. Consequently, instead of maximizing (1) one aims to find the Maximum-a-Posteriori (MAP) estimate of $W$ via

$$\underset{W}{\text{maximize}}\, p(W) \prod_{c=1}^{m} p(Y_c|X_c, w_c) \quad (4)$$

The challenge is now to define models of $p(W)$ that are both computationally tractable and statistically meaningful. This hierarchical modeling imperative leads to multitask learning.

## 2.3 Multitask Prior

Our working assumption is that $W$ is drawn from a matrix-variate distribution in such a way as to exploit correlations between the tasks, such as assuming that the tasks are more concentrated in a lower dimensional subspace. This is a reasonable assumption since there is no inherent order in which the tasks are laid out. One option is to choose a normal distribution as follows:

$$W \sim \mathcal{N}(0, \mathbf{1}_d \otimes \Omega) \text{ or equivalently } w_{\cdot i} \sim \mathcal{N}(0, \Omega) \quad (5)$$

for all coordinates $i$. The likelihood of $W|\Omega$ is given (up to constants) by

$$-\log p(W|\Omega) = \operatorname{tr} W \Omega^{-1} W^\top + d \log |\Omega| + c \quad (6)$$

It is straightforward to modify this by including a conjugate Wishart hyperprior on $\Omega$. Unfortunately, the outcome is concave in $W$.

An alternative is to replace the log-barrier arising from a conjugate prior on $\Omega$ by a trace constraint and a positive semidefiniteness constraint. That is, we replace $\log|\Omega|$ by $\Omega \succeq 0$ and $\operatorname{tr}\Omega = 1$. This is used, e.g. in [23]. Such a modification leaves the eigenspace of the $W$-dependent part of the optimization problem unchanged. This leads to the following alternative:

$$\underset{W,\Omega}{\text{minimize}} \sum_c -\log p(Y_c|X_c, w_c) + \lambda \operatorname{tr} W\Omega^{-1}W^\top \tag{7a}$$

$$\text{subject to } \Omega \succeq 0 \text{ and } \operatorname{tr}\Omega = 1 \tag{7b}$$

The above formulation is convex in both $W$ and $\Omega$ and can be solved using an efficient algorithm based on alternating subspace descent. For fixed $\Omega$ minimize (7) with respect to $W$. Subsequently, for fixed $W$, find the minimizer with respect to $\Omega$. A simple constrained optimization problem shows that this can be found via

$$\hat{\Omega} = \frac{\left[W^\top W\right]^{-\frac{1}{2}}}{\operatorname{tr}\left[W^\top W\right]^{-\frac{1}{2}}} \tag{8}$$

This approach forms the baseline relative to which we will compare our proposed method.

## 3. HIERARCHICAL MULTITASK LEARNING

While the flat models presented in Section 2 can learn the correlation structure between tasks, they are not so easily amenable for distributed optimization because of the squared dependency between all the tasks. Fortunately, many large scale multitask problems possess a hierarchical structure that allows us to decompose them into tasks and subtasks. For example, in display advertising each advertiser can be regarded as a task (a campaign) within which we can define three subtasks as follows:

- Conversion prediction: estimate if the user will convert, i.e. perform a commercially relevant action, on the current display ad.
- Click prediction: predict if the user will click on the currently displayed ad.
- Unattributed conversion: historical data of users who converted on previous advertisements of the advertiser.

We use $s$ to index the subtask. That is, rather than $c$ we now use the tuple $cs$ to index task and associated subtask, such as `(Coca Cola, clicks)`. All remaining notation is unchanged relative to the previous section.

In a nutshell we have two options for dealing with the hierarchical structure: firstly, we estimate the *joint* model for all tasks, subtasks and all campaigns. A second strategy is to solve the model for the primary subtask of conversion estimation exclusively and to use the associate (secondary) subtasks only as side-information. We will refer to the former as a *hierarchical* model and to the latter as *attachment* model. The key difference is in the following assumption:

- **Hierarchical Model:** We assume that for each task group there exists some parameter vector $z_c$, with $Z = \{z_1, \ldots z_m\}$ that specifies preferences per task

  $$Z \sim \mathcal{N}(0, \mathbf{1}_d \otimes \Omega) \text{ or equivalently } z_{\cdot i} \sim \mathcal{N}(0, \Omega) \tag{9}$$

  Moreover, within each task, the distribution over subtasks is given by

  $$w_{c \cdot i} \sim \mathcal{N}(1 \cdot z_{ci}, \Theta_c). \tag{10}$$

  This assumes that correlations within subgroups are decoupled.

- **Attachment Model:** Denote by $s = 1$ the primary subtask (conversion estimation). Instead of using $z_c$ as an intermediary we couple the models directly via $w_{c1}$ and use a hierarchical model on the remaining parameters. This amounts to

  $$w_{\cdot 1i} \sim \mathcal{N}(0, \Omega) \text{ and } w_{c \cdot i} \sim \mathcal{N}(1 \cdot w_{c1i}, \Theta_c) \text{ for } s > 1.$$

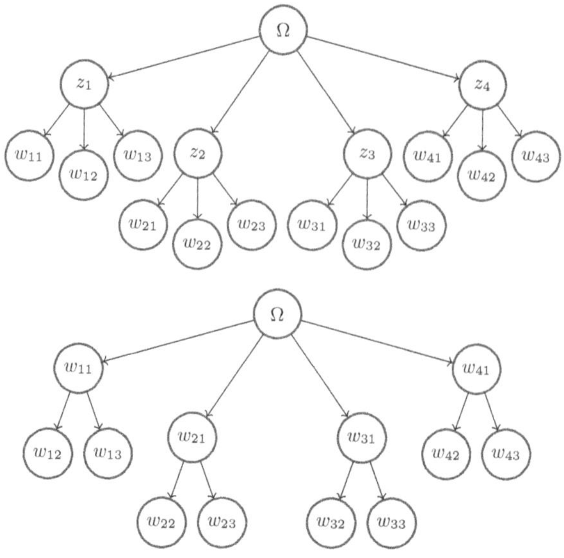


**Figure 2: Top: Hierarchical dependency structure over parameter vectors for multitask learning. The intermediate parameter vector $z_c$ encapsulates commonalities per task. Bottom: Attachment model. Here the conversion-specific parameters are directly coupled. For simplicity of the diagram we omitted $\Theta_c$ in both cases.**

The diagram in Figure 2 describes the difference between both approaches for a rather simplistic structure of 4 tasks (in reality we may have millions of such tasks).

As previously discussed in Section 2, we again resort to a reformulation that uses a trace constraint and positive semidefiniteness rather than the log-barrier to restrict $\Omega$ and $\Theta_c$. That is, instead of

$$\begin{aligned} & -\log p(W, Z|\Omega, \Theta) \qquad (11) \\ = & \sum_c \frac{1}{2} \operatorname{tr}(w_{c\cdot} - 1 \cdot z_c)^\top (w_{c\cdot} - 1 \cdot z_c)\Theta_c^{-1} + m_{cs} \log|\Theta_c| \\ & + \frac{1}{2} \operatorname{tr} Z^\top \Omega^{-1} Z + m_c \log|\Omega| + c \end{aligned}$$

for the hierarchical model and analogous setting for the attachment model, we use the following objectives $L(W, Z, \Omega, \Theta)$:

$$L_{\text{hier}}(W, Z, \Omega, \Theta) \tag{12}$$
$$= \sum_c \frac{1}{2} \operatorname{tr}(w_{c\cdot} - 1 \cdot z_c)^\top (w_{c\cdot} - 1 \cdot z_c)\Theta_c^{-1} + \frac{1}{2} \operatorname{tr} Z^\top \Omega^{-1} Z$$

subject to $\operatorname{tr}\Theta_c \succeq 0$ and $\operatorname{tr}\Theta_c = 1$ and $\operatorname{tr}\Omega \succeq 0$ and $\operatorname{tr}\Omega = 1$ for the hierarchical model. Moreover, for the attachment model:

$$L_{\text{attach}}(W, \Omega, \Theta) \tag{13}$$
$$= \frac{1}{2} \operatorname{tr} w_{c\cdot}^\top w_{c\cdot} \Theta_c^{-1} + \frac{1}{2} \sum_i w_{\cdot 1i} \Omega^{-1} w_{\cdot 1i}^\top$$

subject to the same constraints as for $L_{\text{hier}}$. The only real difference is that we eliminated $z$ and instead, we attach the model to $w_{c1}$ directly. In either case this detaches the subtasks from the problem of joint task inference.

## 3.1 Structured Sparsity

A second aspect of multi-task learning is to use structured sparsity [5] to select relevant variables for an entire block of terms jointly rather than eliminating terms for each task individually. This is achieved by adding a mixed norm on the parameters $W$ and $Z$ to the optimization problem. We need some more notation first. the $p$ norm of a vector $x \in \mathbb{R}^d$:

$$\|x\|_p^p := \sum_i |x_i|^p \text{ for } p < \infty \text{ and } \|x\|_\infty := \max_i |x_i|.$$

Moreover, the mixed norm of a matrix $X$, where we apply sparsity row-wise, is defined for $p, q \geq 1$ via

$$\|X\|_{p,q} := \left\| \|X_{1\cdot}\|_p, \ldots \|X_{d\cdot}\|_p \right\|_q. \tag{14}$$

Of particular interest is the $\|X\|_{2,1}$ norm, which attempts to eliminate entire rows of $X$ at a time. Finally, we use the abbreviation $\|X\|_1 := \|X\|_{1,1}$ to denote the sum over absolute values in $X$. This leads to the following sparsity penalties for the hierarchical and attachment models respectively:

$$S_{\text{hier}}(W, Z) = \lambda_1 \|Z\|_1 + \lambda_2 \|Z\|_{2,1} + \lambda_1 \|W\|_1 + \lambda_2 \sum_c \|W_c\|_{2,1} \tag{15}$$

$$S_{\text{attach}}(W) = \lambda_1 \|W\|_1 + \lambda_2 \|W\|_{2,1} + \lambda_2 \sum_c \|W_c\|_{2,1} \tag{16}$$

The coefficients $\lambda_1$ and $\lambda_2$ govern the trade-off between generic sparsity and group sparsity. That is, for $\lambda_2$ there will be no correlation in sparsity patterns beyond what is obtained from data. For $\lambda_1 = 0$ we can assume that whenever any given $W_{csi} \neq 0$ then also all related $W_{cs'i}$ will not vanish.

## 3.2 Optimization Problems

We conclude this section by stating the two optimization problems that we will solve subsequently. The key ingredients are a likelihood function $-\log p(Y|X, W)$ which depends on the specific problem to solve, a simplified multitask learning penalty as defined by $L_{\text{hier}}(W, Z, \Omega, \Theta)$ and $L_{\text{attach}}(W, \Omega, \Theta)$ respectively, and a sparsity penalty as in $S_{\text{hier}}(W, Z)$ and $S_{\text{attach}}(W)$. We have the following for the hierarchical multitask model:

$$\begin{aligned} \underset{W,Z,\Omega,\Theta}{\text{minimize}} \; & \sum_{csj} -\log p(y_{csj}|x_{csj}, w_{cs}) + \frac{1}{2} \operatorname{tr} Z^\top \Omega^{-1} Z \\ & + \sum_c \frac{1}{2} \operatorname{tr}(w_{c\cdot} - 1 \cdot z_c)^\top (w_{c\cdot} - 1 \cdot z_c)\Theta_c^{-1} \\ & + \lambda_1 \|Z\|_1 + \lambda_2 \|Z\|_{2,1} \qquad (17a) \\ & + \lambda_1 \|W\|_1 + \sum_c \lambda_2 \|W_c\|_{2,1} \end{aligned}$$

$$\text{subject to } \Omega, \Theta_c \succeq 0 \text{ and } \operatorname{tr}\Omega = \operatorname{tr}\Theta_c = 1. \tag{17b}$$

Moreover, the attachment multitask model yields:

$$\begin{aligned} \underset{W,\Omega,\Theta}{\text{minimize}} \; & \sum_{csj} -\log p(y_{csj}|x_{csj}, w_{cs}) \qquad (18a) \\ & + \frac{1}{2} \sum_c \operatorname{tr} w_{c\cdot}^\top w_{c\cdot} \Theta_c^{-1} + \frac{1}{2} \sum_i w_{\cdot 1i} \Omega^{-1} w_{\cdot 1i}^\top \\ & + \lambda_1 \|W\|_1 + + \lambda_2 \|W\|_{2,1} + \sum_c \lambda_2 \|W_c\|_{2,1} \end{aligned}$$

$$\text{subject to } \Omega, \Theta_c \succeq 0 \text{ and } \operatorname{tr}\Omega = \operatorname{tr}\Theta_c = 1. \tag{18b}$$

# 4. INFERENCE

The optimization problems (17) and (18) are jointly convex in $(W, Z, \Omega, \Theta)$ and $(W, \Omega, \Theta)$ respectively. For practical optimization we resort to a Gauss-Southwell [15] approach of minimizing blocks of parameters at a time. In practice this means that we alternate between minimizing with respect to $W, Z$ and $\Omega, \Theta$. This is known to converge to the globally optimal solution (albeit slowly on occasion). Issues of problem distribution and parallelization will be discussed in the next section.

## 4.1 Covariance Updates

Assume that we are given $W, Z$. In this case we may find optimal values for the psd matrices $\Omega, \Theta_c$ using the derivation in (8) as follows:

$$\Omega = (\operatorname{tr} O)^{-1} O \tag{19}$$

$$\text{where } O = (ZZ^\top)^{-\frac{1}{2}} \quad \text{(hierarchical)}$$

$$O = \left[\sum_i w_{\cdot 1i} w_{\cdot 1i}^\top\right]^{-\frac{1}{2}} \quad \text{(attachment)}$$

Likewise, for $\Theta_c$ we have the updates

$$\Theta_c = (\operatorname{tr} T)^{-1} T \tag{20}$$

$$\text{where } T = \left[\sum_i (w_{c\cdot i} - z_{ci})(w_{c\cdot i} - z_{ci})^\top\right]^{-\frac{1}{2}} \quad \text{(hierarchical)}$$

$$T = \left[\sum_i w_{c\cdot i} w_{c\cdot i}^\top\right]^{-\frac{1}{2}} \quad \text{(attachment)}$$

This means that we can compute $T$ entirely with only access to all subtask specific parameters $s$ for a given campaign $c$. Hence, as long as it is possible to have all such data available on a single machine, we need not communicate the lower level of the hierarchy outside the machine.

## 4.2 Optimization with Sparsity Penalty

Next we need to discuss update steps in terms of $W$ and $Z$. Recall that we imposed a mixed norm penalty on both terms such that we obtain group sparsity. Our strategy borrows from [5], and [10, Proposition 1]. Recall the structure of the penalties imposed by $\|\cdot\|_{2,1}$ and $\|\cdot\|_1$. They constitute a *hierarchy* over nonzero terms in $W$ and $Z$ respectively — the $(2,1)$-norm attempts to zero out the entire set of contributions for a given coordinate and the 1-norm ensures that even if we use an attribute, we only use it sparingly.

Given $\Omega, \Theta$ the remainder of the problem is a convex *unconstrained* optimization problem. One of the algorithms recently proposed are of a structure resembling FISTA (Fast Iterative Successive Thresholding) [6]. In it one interleaves a gradient descent step with regard to the convex differentiable part of the objective with a thresholding step with regard to the sparsity penalty. That is, for the problem:

$$\underset{a}{\text{minimize}}\, f(a) + \lambda\Omega[a] \tag{21}$$

one performs the following steps (after initializing $a_0$)

$$b_{t+1} := a_t - \eta_t \partial_a f(a_t) \text{ and} \tag{22}$$

$$a_{t+1} = \underset{a}{\text{argmin}}\, \frac{1}{2t_t}\|a - b_{t+1}\|^2 + \lambda\Omega[a] \tag{23}$$

Here (22) is essentially a gradient descent step in $f$. The step (23) is commonly referred to as a prox-operator. The step size $t_i$ is chosen such that $t_i^{-1}$ majorizes the Lipschitz constant of $\partial_a f(a)$.

We discuss computing gradients with respect to the objective in Section 4.3 for the hierarchical model (the attachment model follows similarly). In this context we mean by $\mathcal{F}[Z,W]$ either the first two lines of (17) or of (18) with $\Omega$ and $\Theta$ fixed at this point. For now note that in our case $\Omega[a]$ decomposes into penalties applied per task. That is

$$\Omega[W,Z] = \sum_c \lambda_1 \left[\|z_c\|_1 + \sum_s \|w_{cs}\|_1\right] + \tag{24}$$
$$\lambda_2 \left[\|z_c\|_2 + \sum_s \|w_{cs}\|_2\right]$$

Solving (23) can be carried out for each task $c$ and for each $z_c$ and $w_c$ individually, hence it is amenable to easy distribution. Using [10, Proposition 1] one can see that performing successive prox operations with respect to the $\ell_1$ norm and subsequently with respect to the $\ell_2$ norm lead to an exact solution of (23). For instance, for $z_c$ this means that we perform the following steps

$$z_c \leftarrow z_{ci} - t_i \partial_{z_c}\mathcal{F}[Z,W] \tag{25}$$
$$z_{ci} \leftarrow \operatorname{sgn} z_{ci} \max(0, |z_{ci}| - t_i\lambda_1) \tag{26}$$

and subsequently we threshold the entire vector via

$$z_c \leftarrow \frac{z_c}{\|z_c\|_2}\max(0, \|z_c\| - t_i\lambda_2) \tag{27}$$

In other words, first we perform gradient descent. Then all coefficients that are individually too small are eliminated and the remainder is shrunk. Finally, we perform shrinkage of the remainder in the direction of their unit vector. The objective is either that of the hierarchical or of the attachment model. Updates with respect to $W$ are entirely analogous and therefore omitted.

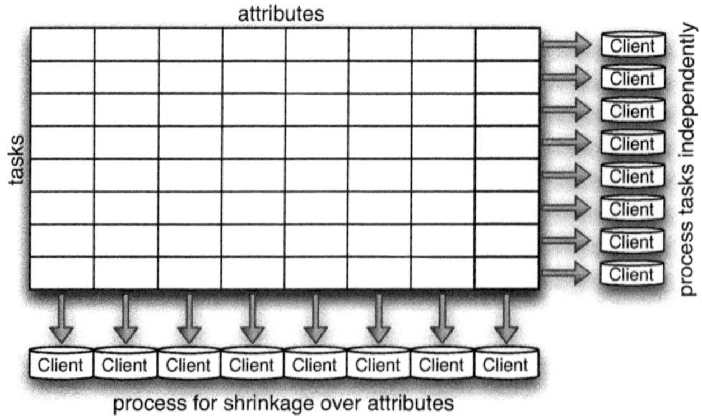


**Figure 3: The parameter matrices $W$ and $Z$ are of size $\mathbb{R}^{d\times m}$. For gradient computation we need to have access to all parameters for a given task $c$ on a given machine, hence the row-wise split. Subsequently, to perform shrinkage over attributes, we need all parameters pertaining to a feature (for all tasks) on a given machine. Load balancing for both of these tasks is achieved by consistent hashing.**

## 4.3 Gradients

We complete our overview of optimization by discussing the gradient in terms of $W$ and $Z$. As before, we limit ourselves to a discussion of the hierarchical model of (17). Since the reasoning required for (18) is essentially identical, we omit the details. Straightforward calculation yields

$$\partial_{z_{ci}}\mathcal{F}[Z,W] = \left[\Omega^{-1}Z_{\cdot i}\right]_c + \Theta_c^{-1}(1\cdot z_{ci} - w_{c\cdot i}) \tag{28}$$

$$\partial_{w_{csi}}\mathcal{F}[Z,W] = \sum_j \partial_{w_{csi}} - \log p(y_{csj}|x_{csj}, w_{cs}) \tag{29}$$
$$+ \Theta_c^{-1}(w_{c\cdot i} - 1\cdot z_{ci})$$

As can be seen, again all gradients decompose in terms of tasks and subtasks respectively. We will exploit this for distributed optimization. The exact form of the gradient for $p(y_{csj}|x_{csj}, w_{cs})$ is straighforward to compute for both the regression and classification problem given the form of the conditional probability in (2) and (3) respectively.

# 5. DISTRIBUTED OPTIMIZATION

We now discuss how to implement a distributed optimization algorithm efficiently on a cluster of commodity workstations. As discussed previously, invoking steps (22) and (23), and updating $\Omega$ and $\Theta$ requires the following operations:

1. Compute partial subgradients of $\mathcal{F}[Z,W]$ for all campaigns with respect to $Z$ and $W$.
2. Aggregate subgradients obtained from all instances and apply it to the model parameters.
3. Distribute coordinates (or subsets $S \in \mathcal{S}$ thereof) of the subgradients (or rather updated coordinates) to clients for application of the prox operator.
4. Invoke the prox operator.
5. Redistribute the results to the machines holding the campaign-specific data.

Since this is an iterative procedure with two barriers per iteration (send subgradients, return values) this sounds as if it were a good fit for MapReduce. Unfortunately, this approach suffers from inefficiencies inherent in the Hadoop implementation of MapReduce: context in the mappers is not preserved between iterations. Moreover, Hadoop communicates primarily via file I/O. Since the proposed algorithm can take tens of iterations and since we need to communicate parameters repeatedly, this means significant waste of resources by repeatedly having to initialize the state of the mappers. Hence we resort to a method discussed in [13, 2], namely to allocate the machines using Hadoop and then to establish an overlay communication network.

**Algorithm 1** Distributed Optimization

```
for all i = 1···p parallel do
  read data blocks from disk
  for all campaigns with m(c) = i do
    compute subgradient g_c
  end for
  write g_c to (key,value) store according to m(i)
end for
reach a barrier
for all i = 1···p parallel do
  read g_c from (key,value) store according to m(i)
  for all coordinates with m(j) = i do
    solve the prox operator
  end for
  write to the (key,value) store according to m(c)
  Compute contribution to sufficient statistics of Ω and
  write it back to shared memory.
end for
reach a barrier
Read sufficient statistics of Ω and compute new value.
```

## 5.1 Data and Task Distribution

In the following we assume that we have $p$ machines to process data. Recall that $d$ denotes the number of attributes, i.e. $x_{csi} \in \mathbb{R}^d$ and that $m$ denotes the number of campaigns. We use randomized load-balancing to determine which machine receives which portion of the data in both the data-bound and the parameter-bound part of the optimization procedure. This is achieved, e.g. by consistent hashing [11]:

$$m(c) = \operatorname*{argmin}_{m \in \mathcal{M}} h(m, c) \text{ and } m(i) = \operatorname*{argmin}_{m \in \mathcal{M}} h(m, i) \quad (30)$$

to assign machines from a machine pool $\mathcal{M}$ for campaigns $c$ and coordinates $i$ respectively.

Finally, data exchange is carried out in the form of a distributed (key,value) store. For reasons of practicality we used `memcached` as our reference implementation. This follows the design pattern of [21, 13] and it avoids file I/O for synchronization. Such a strategy is much more efficient than repeated invocations of Hadoop MapReduce.

## 5.2 Distributed Subgradient Oracle

By design, the subgradients of $\mathcal{F}[Z, W]$ and $\mathcal{F}[W]$ decompose into terms that are easily computable in a campaign-specific manner (terms related to the negative log-likelihood) and terms that are easily computable in a coordinate-specific manner (the penalties in terms of $\Omega, \Theta$ and the sparsity penalties). Furthermore, only the former requires direct access to data, whereas the latter requires access to a given coordinate across all tasks. This means that we can compute gradients in two stages: a pass over data, as performed by the workers that have the data, a reshuffle of parameters, and a finalizing pass (plus prox step) in a coordinate-specific fashion.

**Likelihood gradients:** Since data is partitioned according to tasks $c$, subgradients with regard to $w_{cs}$ are easily computed via

$$g_{cs} = \sum_{j=1}^{n_{cs}} \partial_{w_{cs}} - \log p(y_{csj} | x_{csj}, w_{cs}). \quad (31)$$

Next we compute gradients with respect to $\frac{1}{2} \sum_s w_{cs}^\top \Theta_c^{-1} w_{cs}$, i.e. we add $\Theta_c^{-1} w_{c\cdot}$ to $g_{cs}$. The analogous reasoning holds for $\sum_s (w_{oo} - z_c)^\top \Theta_c^{-1} (w_{cs} - z_c)$. These gradients are then redistributed according to Figure 3 such that all $g_{csi}$ for a given coordinate $i$ (ranging over all tasks and subtasks) are available on the same machine.

**Multitask gradients:** At this point we can compute coordinate specific parts as arising from the $\Omega$-dependent terms on a per-coordinate basis. For this purpose we only need $Z_{\cdot i}$ or $w_{\cdot 1i}$, depending on whether we chose the hierarchical or attachment model respectively. We only need to read the weights corresponding to non-zero entries in $\Omega^{-1}$.

## 5.3 Distributed Prox Operator and Covariance Estimation

The final step required is to solve the prox operator related to the $\|\cdot\|_1$ and $\|\cdot\|_{2,1}$ norms as these enforce sparsity. Whenever we have a fully hierarchical setting, Proposition 1 of [10] applies and we can simply perform prox steps bottom up in the process. Whenever this assumption is not satisfied, we may still iterate the prox operator to obtain a suboptimal solution. This suffices as a descent step, since optimization in $Z$ and $W$ is just a subroutine in the overall optimization scenario involving $\Theta$ and $\Omega$. Note that the prox operator can be carried out in linear time — we only require computing norms of vectors and rescaling them.

The data exchange is completely analogous to the gradient computation, except that we now work on attributes rather than campaigns. After the prox operation we redistribute parameters back into a (key,value) storage. As before, this requires a barrier to ensure that up-to-date values are available on all workers for another pass through the data. Similar to the gradient computation phase, the read and write steps can be performed in parallel.

Finally we note that estimating $\Theta$ can be done locally in each worker however the sufficient statistics required to compute $\Omega$ (see 19) is distributed on a per-attribute basis. Thus we overlay this step with the prox-operator step. Each worker computes its contribution to the sufficient statistics using its assigned attributes. For example in the hierarchical model this reduces to computing a $C \times C$ matrix $\sum_{i \in m(i)} z_i z_i^\top$. After reaching a barrier, worker 0 then reads those partial sums and computes the new value for $Z$ using (8) and then writes $\Omega$ back to a shared memory to be read by each worker for the next iteration. Alternatively each worker can read the sufficient statistics of $\Omega$ and compute the new value deterministically. Moreover, instead of using (8), we could use the graphical lasso estimation of [9] to get a sparse inverse covariance estimation of $\Omega^{-1}$ from its sufficient statistics. This sparse inverse covariance is desirable In distributed settings to minimize parameter movements when computing the multi-task gradient as it depends on the non-zero elements of the inverse covariance (i.e. $\Omega^{-1}$).

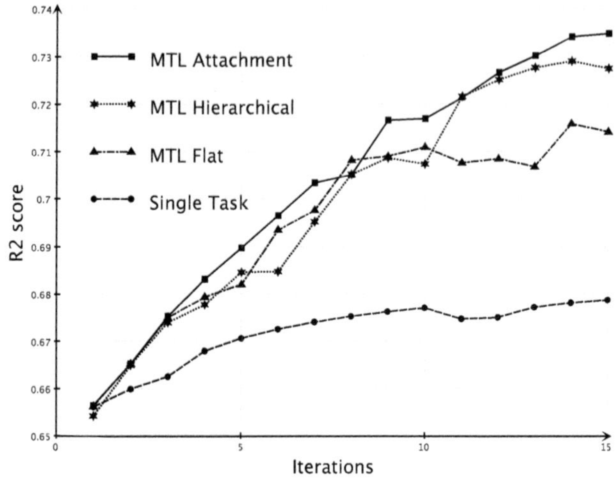


**Figure 4: School Data: $R^2$ Performance for various multitask learning algorithms. Note the faster convergence and better performance of ATT-MTRL.**

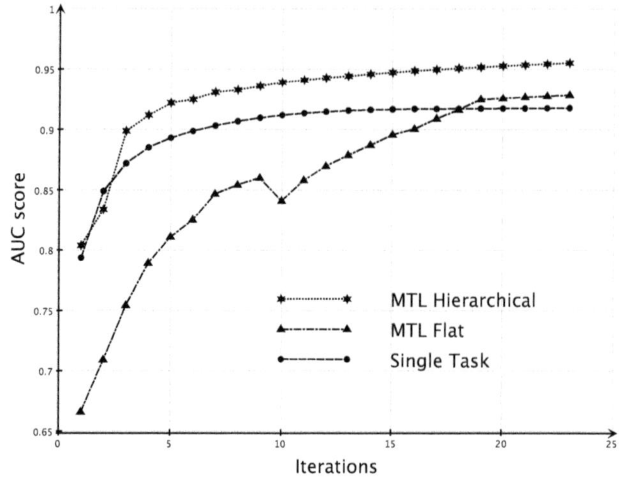


**Figure 5: 20-newsgroup MTL: AUC Performance for various multitask learning algorithms. The hierarchical MTL algorithm starts off better than the flat algorithm and it consistently outperforms both single task and flat multitask learning.**

# 6. EXPERIMENTS ON PUBLIC DATA

To establish the efficacy of our approach we report results on both two public datasets and one proprietary dataset. We make this choice since we are unable to share proprietary and financially relevant data outside Yahoo, yet at the same time we wish to provide the reader with some means of gaining insight into the working of the proposed algorithm. In other words, we show that the proposed algorithm improves on the state of the art and simultaneously that it scales to substantial problem sizes.

In terms of public datasets we choose two standard datasets: estimation of examination scores for students attending secondary schools in London and multi-task classification of the 20-newsgroup dataset. The algorithms we compare are the Hierarchical MTL (HIE-MTRL) and Attachment MTL (ATT-MTRL) algorithms, along with two baselines: the first one is the Single-task Learning (STL) algorithm which does not use multitask learning, and optimizes all the tasks independently. The second baseline is the Flat MTL (F-MTRL) algorithm of [23] that uses a matrix-variate normal prior on the task correlation matrix. This algorithm performs multitask learning, however it does not account for the hierarchical task and subtask structure. It "flattens" the task hierarchy and treats (task, subtask) as individual tasks and learns a joint covariance structure.

## 6.1 Student score estimation

This dataset has been used widely for studying multitask regression[1]. It consists of the exam scores of 15,362 students from 139 secondary schools in London during 1985, 1986 and 1987. Originally, the input consists of the year of the exam, four school-specific and three student-specific attributes. The goal is to estimate the exam scores for the students. Several papers [23, 4] evaluate multitask learning by treating the school-ids as attributes, but one could arguably treat this dataset as specifying a hierarchical task/subtask structure, where the school ID refer to tasks and the exam years for each school correspond to the subtasks of the school ID. Thus, there are a total of 139 tasks, with up to 3 subtasks for each task. We note that several tasks have only 2 tasks in the dataset.

We replace each categorical attribute with one binary variable for each possible attribute value as in [4] but remove the attributes corresponding to the exam years. As a result of this preprocessing, we have a total of 24 input attributes. We use a 66/34 split of the dataset to use as training instances and test instances, and report the average (over all years and schools) performance of our algorithms, on the test set. For our performance measure, we use the normalized inner product between the input score vector and the predicted score vector. This measure is proportional to the squared multiple correlation coefficient $R^2$, a normalized version of the regression error, defined as

$$R^2 := 1 - \frac{\sum_i (y_i - f_i)^2}{\mathrm{Var}[y]}. \quad (32)$$

That is, it is the ratio between explained variance and total variance. See e.g. [8] for further details.

For F-MTRL, HIE-MTRL and ATT-MTRL we use 5-fold cross validation to determine the optimal value of the appropriate regularization constants and learning rate. Figure 6.1 plots the $R^2$ performance of the algorithms as optimization progresses. As can be seen in the graph, and as also reported by [23, 4], multitask learning provides a significant performance improvement. F-MTRL improves over the baseline by around 5%. However, by using the task-subtask hierarchy, our HIE-MTRL and ATT-MTRL obtain a further improvement from a score of around 0.71 (for F-MTRL) to almost 0.73. The performance for ATT-MTRL was slightly better than HIE-MTRL in this dataset.

## 6.2 Multi-Task Classification

The task at hand is multi-task classification of the 20-newsgroup dataset[2]. The goal here is to predict the newsgroup of a given post. The 20 news groups are arranged into a two-level hierarchy. The first level comprises 5 categories:

[1] http://www0.cs.ucl.ac.uk/staff/A.Argyriou/code

[2] http://qwone.com/ jason/20Newsgroups/

Table 1: **20-newsgroup analysis: AUC performance for single task and multitask algorithms on varying percentages of the data.**

| Fraction of data | STL | F-MTRL | HIE-MTRL |
|---|---|---|---|
| 20% | 0.755 | 0.775 | **0.827** |
| 40% | 0.821 | 0.839 | **0.881** |
| 60% | 0.875 | 0.893 | **0.910** |
| 80% | 0.899 | 0.917 | **0.932** |
| 100% | 0.918 | 0.931 | **0.957** |

politics, religion, recreational, science, and computers. Each category has 2-5 subcategories in the second level. We map categories to tasks and sub-categories to sub-tasks. The dataset comprises 18k documents and we followed the standard test/train split. We removed stop words and words appearing less than 10 times. Five-fold cross validation is used to determine the values of the regularization parameters for all models.

We measure classification accuracy using the AUC measure. Since in this dataset we do not have the notion of an anchor task, we only use the symmetric HIE-MTRL formulation. In Figure 5 we compare the performance of HIE-MTRL against the state of the art algorithm in [23] F-MTRL and against single-task baseline STL. As evident from figure HIE-MTRL improves over the F-MTRL baseline by around 2% points and the improvement was statistically significant. Moreover HIE-MTRL outperforms all other competing algorithms in terms of speed of convergence.

To see the effect of varying the training set size, we select different fractions of the data for each task to form the training set while keeping the test set fixed. As can be seen in Table 1 HIE-MTRL outperforms all other competing algorithms for a range of different sample sizes. Moreover, the improvement of HIE-MTRL over competing algorithms is more apparent when the training data size is small (a 5% improvement over the F-MTRL baseline using a 20% fraction of the training data).

# 7. OPTIMIZING DISPLAY ADVERTISING

## 7.1 Data

We collected 4 weeks of advertising data, i.e. impressions, clicks, and conversions, for a total of 1,468 advertising campaigns.[3] Each campaign is treated as a separate targeting task. 66% of the data is used for training, while the remaining 34% is used for scoring. The train/test split is performed using a reference time stamp (impressions before that time stamp used for training and afterwards impression for testing). Since the user profiles span 56 days of user history, each training/scoring example is preceded by at least 4 weeks of user events. This benchmark data set enables us to perform rigorous offline experiments. We count users based on the unique number of browser cookies (see table below).

| days | users | features | campaigns | dataset size |
|---|---|---|---|---|
| 56 | $10^9$ | 934,000 | 630 | 1.4TB |

We study the performance of our techniques compared to the baseline system developed in [3]. We mainly compare modeling performance in terms of the area under the ROC curve (AUC). Unless otherwise specified, all metrics are measured as conversion-weighted average of AUC across all campaigns in the benchmark set. We denote the conversion-weighted average of AUC as *Weighted AUC*.

We represent each user using features from both *active* and *passive* observations. Passive observations include viewing ads and visiting pages in which an action is not specifically required upon seeing the page. Active observations include issuing search queries and clicking ads in which users actually perform an action on the page.

Each advertising campaign has three subtasks:

- **Predicting conversions:** This sub task contains data that shows whether users converted on a given campaign. That is, it contains information whether they performed an advertiser-specified action such as purchasing a product or filling a form.
- **Predicting clicks:** This subtask contains data that shows whether users clicked on the ad of this campaign or not.
- **Prediction on auxiliary (unattributed conversion) data:** This subtask contains data that shows whether users converted on historic data on related campaigns of the same advertiser. This data is supplied by the advertiser.

We define the feature weight for a given user-(sub)campaign example to be the number of days (before showing the user the campaign ad) in which the feature appears. Our platform experiences a large variance of feature weights across our feature types thus making it hard to set a single count-threshold below which we consider the feature to be irrelevant. We thus rely on the learning algorithm to perform joint conversion optimization and feature selection.

## 7.2 Results

All experiments reported in this section were performed using 300 machines. We assess the performance both in terms of AUC accuracy and scalability of the algorithms. The attachment multitask learning algorithm (ATT-MTRL) significantly outperforms flat multitask and single task learning. Moreover, the results for hierarchical multitask learning (HIE-MTRL) were only slightly inferior to ATT-MTRL (thus we omit them for space limitations). This finding is consistent with our findings of Section 6.1. Note that ATT-MTRL also performs multitask feature selection, which is essential here due to the large feature space. We compare our performance with the baseline Single-task Learning, which optimizes for all the tasks and subtasks separately. We omit comparing with the F-MTRL for this task since the flat MTL requires flattening the task-subtask structure ( 2k tasks) which results in massive weight vector movements across machines and as such does not scale to this dataset (though in Table 4 we show the effect of introducing task and subtask covariance on the overall performance).

The parameters for all models were tuned on a validation set. In Table 2 we report the overall performance of the model against the baseline. As we can see, our model clearly outperforms the baseline. All improvements of our models over the baselines are statistically significant. Note that the task of conversion prediction is very difficult since positive examples are very rare.

Secondly, we quantify the effect of feature selection. For this purpose we select the top 10k, 30k and 50k features (using mutual-information measure) and use them in the STL. For comparison we run ATT-MTRL using conservative

[3]We note here that data from users that opted out of behavioral targeting were not collected.

Table 2: **Attachment multitask performance.**

| AUC | STL | ATT-MTRL |
|---|---|---|
| all subtasks | 0.658 | **0.674** |
| conversions | 0.629 | **0.653** |
| auxiliary (unattributed) | 0.677 | **0.714** |
| clicks | 0.662 | **0.671** |

**Table 3: Feature selection effectiveness:**

| | Conversion AUC | features |
|---|---|---|
| STL + $\ell_2$ + top features | 0.606 | 10,000 |
| STL + $\ell_2$ + top features | 0.609 | 30,000 |
| STL + $\ell_2$ + top features | 0.607 | 50,000 |
| ATT-MTRL (aggressive) | 0.631 | 3,992 |
| ATT-MTRL (conservative) | **0.653** | 17,789 |

**Table 4: Ablation study for ATT-MTRL.**

| AUC | conversions | all sub-tasks |
|---|---|---|
| L1 | 0.621 | 0.642 |
| L1+L12 | 0.629 | 0.658 |
| L1+L12+Θ | 0.641 | 0.663 |
| L1+L12+Θ+Ω | **0.653** | **0.674** |

($\lambda_1 = 0.4, \lambda_2 = 10$) and aggressive ($\lambda_1 = 0.4, \lambda_2 = 25$ ) feature selection parameters. The results in Table 3 are reported in terms of the weighted average AUC measure.

Finally, in table 4 shows the contributions of the various components of the ATT-MTRL algorithm towards the learning performance. $\Omega$ refers to the task-correlation regularization, $\Theta$ refers to the sub-task correlation regularization, and $L1$ and $L12$ refer to per-campaign and multitask feature selection respectively. As seen from the figure, using multitask feature selection($L12$) leads to only a marginal improvement over single task feature selection($L1$). However, adding the multitask learning components lead to a significant improvement over using just $L1$ and $L12$ regularization. These results clearly show the importance of leveraging cross-campaign and cross-campaign-subtask information to improve the performance of campaigns with very few conversions, as opposed to the baseline techniques.

# 8. CONCLUSION

In this paper we addressed the problem of hierarchical multitask learning when tasks are organized in a hierarchy. We presented two convex formulations to this problem and showed that models that exploit the hierarchical structure outperformed flat models. Furthermore, we showed how to scale our models to a tera-scale advertising task. An advantage of our hierarchical formulation is the utilization of the task substructure for efficient parameter distribution that reduces parameter movements across machines. We validated our models on both public and private datasets with favorable performance.

# 9. REFERENCES


[1] A. Ahmed, M. Aly, A. Das, A. Smola, and T. Anastasakos. Web-scale multi-task feature selection for behavioral targeting. In *CIKM*, 2012.

[2] A. Ahmed, M. Aly, J. Gonzalez, S. Narayanamurthy, and A. Smola. Scalable inference in latent variable models. In *Web Science and Data Mining (WSDM)*, 2012.

[3] M. Aly, A. Hatch, V. Josifovski, and V. K. Narayanan. Web-scale user modeling for targeting. In *WWW*, 2012.

[4] A. Argyriou, T. Evgeniou, and M. Pontil. Convex multi-task feature learning. *Machine Learning*, 73(3):243–272, 2008.

[5] F. Bach, R. Jenatton, J. Mairal, and G. Obozinski. Optimization with sparsity-inducing penalties. *Foundations and Trends in Machine Learning*, 4(1):1–106, 2012.

[6] A. Beck and M. Teboulle. A fast iterative shrinkage-thresholding algorithm for linear inverse problems. *SIAM Journal on Imaging Sciences*, 2(1):183–202, 2009.

[7] R. Caruana. Multitask learning. *Machine Learning*, 28:41–75, 1997.

[8] N. R. Draper and H. Smith. *Applied Regression Analysis.* John Wiley and Sons, New York, NY, 1981.

[9] J. Friedman, T. Hastie, and R. Tibshirani. Sparse inverse covariance estimation with the graphical lasso. *Biostatistics*, 9(3):432–441, 2008.

[10] R. Jenatton, J. Mairal, G. Obozinski, and F. Bach. Proximal methods for hierarchical sparse coding. *Journal of Machine Learning Research*, 12:2297–2334, 2011.

[11] D. Karger, E. Lehman, T. Leighton, M. Levine, D. Lewin, and R. Panigrahy. Consistent hashing and random trees: Distributed caching protocols for relieving hot spots on the world wide web. In *Symposium on the Theory of Computing STOC*, pages 654–663, New York, May 1997. Association for Computing Machinery.

[12] T. R. Shultz and F. Rivest. Using knowledge to speed learning: A comparison knowledge-based cascade-correlation and multi-task learning. In *Proc. Intl. Conf. Machine Learning*, pages 871–878. Morgan Kaufmann, San Francisco, CA, 2000.

[13] A. J. Smola and S. Narayanamurthy. An architecture for parallel topic models. In *Very Large Databases (VLDB)*, 2010.

[14] S. Sonnenburg, G. Rätsch, C. Schäfer, and B. Schölkopf. Large scale multiple kernel learning. *Journal of Machine Learning Research*, 7:1531–1565, 2006.

[15] W. H. Southwell. Fitting data to nonlinear functions with uncertainties in all measurement variables. *Comput. J.*, 19(1):69–73, 1976.

[16] N. Srebro and A. Shraibman. Rank, trace-norm and max-norm. In P. Auer and R. Meir, editors, *Proc. Annual Conf. Computational Learning Theory*, number 3559 in Lecture Notes in Artificial Intelligence, pages 545–560. Springer-Verlag, June 2005.

[17] C. Teo, Q. Le, A. J. Smola, and S. V. N. Vishwanathan. A scalable modular convex solver for regularized risk minimization. In *Proc. ACM Conf. Knowledge Discovery and Data Mining (KDD)*. ACM, 2007.

[18] S. Thrun and J. O'Sullivan. Discovering structure in multiple learning tasks: the TC algorithm. In *Proc. Intl. Conf. Machine Learning*, pages 489–497. Morgan Kaufmann, 1996.

[19] M. Varma and B. R. Babu. More generality in efficient multiple kernel learning. In A. P. Danyluk, L. Bottou, and M. L. Littman, editors, *ICML*, volume 382 of *ACM International Conference Proceeding Series*, page 134. ACM, 2009.

[20] K. Weinberger, A. Dasgupta, J. Attenberg, J. Langford, and A. J. Smola. Feature hashing for large scale multitask learning. In L. Bottou and M. Littman, editors, *International Conference on Machine Learning*, 2009.

[21] J. Ye, J. Chow, J. Chen, and Z. Zheng. Stochastic gradient boosted distributed decision trees. In *CIKM*. ACM, 2009.

[22] K. Yu, V. Tresp, and A. Schwaighofer. Learning gaussian processes from multiple tasks. In *Proceedings of the 22nd International Conference on Machine Learning*, volume 119, pages 1012–1019. ACM, 2005.

[23] Y. Zhang and D.-Y. Yeung. A convex formulation for learning task relationships in multi-task learning. In *Uncertainty in Artificial Intelligence*, 2010.

# An Efficient Framework for Online Advertising Effectiveness Measurement and Comparison

Pengyuan Wang
Yahoo Labs
701 1st Ave, Sunnyvale
California 94089
pengyuan@yahoo-inc.com

Yechao Liu
Yahoo Inc.
11 West 19th Street
New York, NY 10011
yechao@yahoo-inc.com

Marsha Meytlis
Yahoo Inc.
11 West 19th Street
New York, NY 10011
mmeytlis@yahoo-inc.com

Han-Yun Tsao
Yahoo Labs
701 1st Ave, Sunnyvale
California 94089
hanyun@yahoo-inc.com

Jian Yang
Yahoo Labs
701 1st Ave, Sunnyvale
California 94089
jianyang@yahoo-inc.com

Pei Huang
Yahoo Inc.
11 West 19th Street
New York, NY 10011
peih@yahoo-inc.com

## ABSTRACT

In online advertising market it is crucial to provide advertisers with a reliable measurement of advertising effectiveness to make better marketing campaign planning. The basic idea for ad effectiveness measurement is to compare the performance (e.g., success rate) among users who were and who were not exposed to a certain treatment of ads. When a randomized experiment is not available, a naive comparison can be biased because exposed and unexposed populations typically have different features. One solid methodology for a fair comparison is to apply inverse propensity weighting with doubly robust estimation to the observational data. However the existing methods were not designed for the online advertising campaign, which usually suffers from huge volume of users, high dimensionality, high sparsity and imbalance. We propose an efficient framework to address these challenges in a real campaign circumstance. We utilize gradient boosting stumps for feature selection and gradient boosting trees for model fitting, and propose a subsampling-and-backscaling procedure that enables analysis on extremely sparse conversion data. The choice of features, models and feature selection scheme are validated with irrelevant conversion test. We further propose a parallel computing strategy, combined with the subsampling-and-backscaling procedure to reach computational efficiency. Our framework is applied to an online campaign involving millions of unique users, which shows substantially better model fitting and efficiency. Our framework can be further generalized to comparison of multiple treatments and more general treatment regimes, as sketched in the paper. Our framework is not limited to online advertising, but also applicable to other circumstances (e.g., social science) where a 'fair' comparison is needed with observational data.


*WSDM'14,* February 24–28, 2014, New York, New York, USA.
Copyright 2014 ACM 978-1-4503-2351-2/14/02 ...$15.00.
http://dx.doi.org/10.1145/2556195.2556235.

## Categories and Subject Descriptors

G.3 [**PROBABILITY AND STATISTICS**]: Statistical Computing; J.1 [**ADMINISTRATIVE DATA PROCESSING**]: Business, Marketing

## Keywords

Advertising, Causal Inference, Propensity Score, Gradient Boosting Trees, Feature Selection, Subsampling, Parallel Computing

## 1. INTRODUCTION

As the online advertising industry has evolved into an age of diverse ad formats and delivery channels, the market increasingly demands a reliable measurement and a sound comparison of ad effectiveness. A metric is needed to show change in brand interest independent of variables that characterize online users that enable us to isolate the effect of the campaign from the effect of other variables. The use cases for such a metric could be: 1) performance assessment of a single campaign, e.g., a website takeover, and 2) synergy effect of multiple campaigns, e.g., the effect of a website takeover on top of a targeted display campaign; 3) performance comparison of different campaigns, e.g., a website takeover versus a targeted display campaign. [1]

The basic idea for ad effectiveness measurement is to compare the performance (e.g. success rate[2]) of users who were and who were not exposed to a certain treatment of ads. In a randomized experiment, i.e., an A/B test, the direct comparison between the success rates of the two groups is unbiased. However in an advertising campaign, we rarely have opportunities to assign random treatments to the users. In such cases, the direct comparison may pro-

[1]Targeted campaigns are those campaigns that only serve ads to a specific group of users, e.g. users who visited the advertiser's website in past 30 days. Website takeover is an ad format that serves mainly for branding purposes. It's usually not targeted in a sense that users visiting the website during the flight will all get to see the takeover. Synergy effect refers to the fact that users exposed to multiple channels of campaigns will have a higher conversion rate than users exposed to a single channel.

[2]A success is an action favored by the campaign, such as click, search or site visitation. Success rate is the percentage of unique users who take a success action. In this paper we use success and conversion interchangeably.

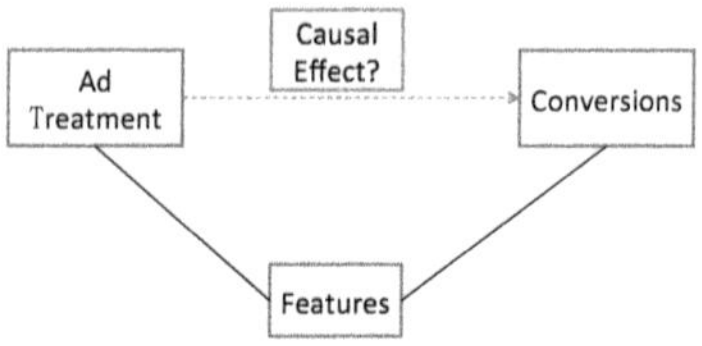


Figure 1: Confounding Effect of Features

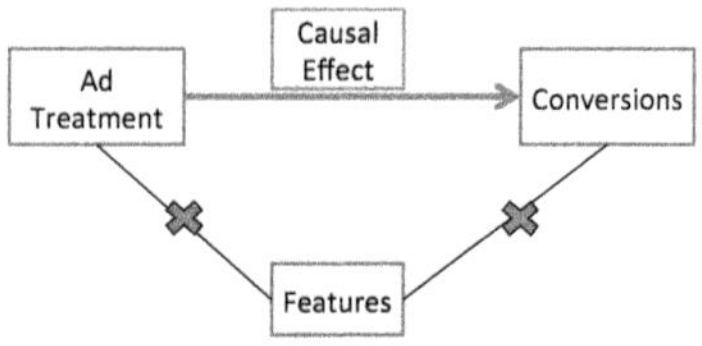


Figure 2: Causal Inference

duce selection biases if each of the groups has a different probability to be exposed to an ad. For example, imagine an auto campaign where all of exposed users are males and all of the non-exposed users are females. If the males generally have a larger conversion rate than females, the effectiveness of the campaign could be overestimated because of the confounding effect of the user features, in this case, gender: It might just be that males are more likely to be exposed and convert. Hence the relationship between the ad treatments and conversions is not causal without eliminating the selection bias. The intuition behind this argument can be seen from Figure 1, where the ad effect on conversion is confounded by the features (which is gender in this example). The causal inference is aiming to establish a causal connection between the ads treatment and the campaign performance, eliminate the impact of features as in Figure 2, and hence estimate the real impact of ads on conversions. We introduce causal inference in Section 2.1 in details.

A straightforward approach attempting to eliminate the impact of user features on the outcome (conversion or non-conversion) is to adjust the outcomes with a set of user-level covariates using regressions, for example, including them as independent variables in a regression as well as indicators of treatments to fit the individual outcomes. However the features of the users receiving each treatments may have complex correlations with the outcomes, and hence the causal effect of the treatment is difficult to estimate by adjusting the outcome with the covariates directly.

To address this problem, Rosenbaum and Rubin [27] established the causal inference in observational studies with propensity score as the major instrument for binary treatments. Defining the subjects of two treatments as 'control' and 'exposed' subjects respectively, the propensity score is defined as the estimated probability for a subject to be exposed, given a set of observed pre-treatment covariates. It is aiming to control for the difference between the groups of subjects receiving different treatments. Linear logistic regression [28, 29] was proposed and then widely used as a standard approach for the propensity score estimation. Other estimation approaches were also proposed, for example semiparametric regression (semiparametric single index and semiparametric binary quantile regression models [20]), and non-parametereic regression (kernal-based matching and local linear regression in [12], boosted regression in [22]). More robust result is reached via doubly robust (DR) estimator [25, 30], which is proven to have a smaller asymptotic variance.

The method rapidly becomes popular in various fields, including economics ([13]), epidemiology [10], longitudinal data [2], health care [4], social science [18], politics [15], online behavior study [8] and advertising [5, 21, 31, 7, 3]. Specifically in the online advertising area, [21] showed that observational data may lead to incorrect estimates, [31] explored the benefits of estimating several other parameters of interest and another method targeted maximum likelihood estimation (TMLE)),[7] used causal inference for a multi-attribution problem, and[3] used it in an experimental circumstance.

The above mentioned approaches were not specifically designed for industrial advertising campaign data with huge volume, high dimensionality and extremely sparse conversion. To the best of our knowledge, we are the first to construct an efficient framework to handle these challenges, which often exist for typical online advertising dataset. In this paper, we propose a novel approach that takes into account the characteristics of real, live campaigns. Our contribution can be summarized as follows:

1. We propose to employ gradient boosting stumps [14] for feature selection, and then gradient boosting trees (GBT) [9, 24] to model ad exposure probability and conversion probability, which selects a small yet sufficient set of features for causal inference and achieves substantially better out-of-sample performance than logistic regressions.

2. We develop a novel subsampling-and-backscaling approach to deal with extremely sparse (few successes) dataset, which significantly improves the out-of-sample performance of the probability models.

3. We devise a new parallel computation scheme to deal with large industrial data sets and combine it with the subsampling-and-backscaling approach to reach computation efficiency and robustness.

Chan et al. [5] also considered the industrial advertising data, but with moderate size. Our framework applies to a much larger dataset with sparser conversion, which is typical for industrial banner ads. The efficient calculation is enabled by the above contributions.

The rest of the paper is organized as follows. In Section 2, we briefly illustrate the intuition behind causal inference, and review the inverse propensity weighting (IPW) with DR estimation. In Section 3, we introduce gradient boosting stumps for feature selections and then GBT for propensity score and success rate modeling. The method is combined with a novel subsampling-and-backscaling approach that deals with extremely sparse conversion data in Section 4. To address the high volume of data, we propose a parallel computing algorithm in Section 5 for computation efficiency. In Section 6 we describe the marketing campaign data of a major auto insurance company used in this study and the procedure for data collection. In Section 7 we apply the proposed method to the dataset. We assess the model performance in Section 7.1, and further validate the causal inference with irrelevant conversion test in Section 7.2. Results in Section 7.2 verifies several aspects of our framework, including the features collection, feature selection scheme and choice of GBT model. In Section 8 we report the results on the whole dataset. In Section 9, we outline how to generalize the framework to multi-treatment cases and more general treatment regimes, where the treatment can be continuous and/or multi-dimensional. We conclude in Section 10.

As a roadmap, the algorithms are summarized in Table 1 to 4. Table 4 is the parallel computation (Section 5) algorithm, within which the subsampling-and-backscaling (Section 4) algorithm (Table 2 and 3) is embedded. The algorithm 2 further contains the IPW (Section 2.2) and DR (Section 2.3) estimation with GBT and feature selection (Section 3) algorithm as in Table 1.

## 2. A PRIMER ON CAUSAL INFERENCE

### 2.1 Intuitive Behind Causal Inference

Imagine the outcomes under the alternative treatments that may not have been observed. For example to evaluate the performance of a single campaign, one may consider, if no advertising campaign is running, what would happen? Would there be less conversions? If the campaign reaches every user, would there be more conversions? If the conversion rates in the two cases are the same, this campaign is not effective, i.e., it does not cause conversions. Only if there is a change in conversions under different treatments, should we be able to claim the campaign as effective. The same idea also works for causal inference on synergy effect of multiple campaigns. Imagine that in one situation all the subjects[3] see impressions from both of the two placements (takeover and targeted display) while in another situation the subjects only see impressions from the targeted display placement. The difference or ratio of the conversion rates under the two situations indicates the causal effect of the additional placement. In this section we focus on binary treatment, but the framework is readily generalizable to multiple or more treatment regimes as sketched in Section 9.

Usually the causal effect is measured by comparing a specific treatment (exposure) toward another (control) [4]. For example in the case where the performance of a single campaign needs to be evaluated, 'exposure' treatment is campaign impressions while 'control' treatment is no campaign impression. In the case where we measure the effect of a website takeover on top of a targeted display campaign, 'exposure' treatment is impressions from both placements while 'control' treatment is impressions only from the targeted display placement. In our case, the ad effectiveness is defined as the treatment effect of the exposure. Formally, we define conversions as the desired outcomes of advertising campaign. Each subject has two potential outcomes $Y_c$ and $Y_e$ under control and exposure treatments, respectively. The difference or ratio of the expectations ($E(Y_e) - E(Y_c)$ or $E(Y_e)/E(Y_c)$, respectively) can be used to evaluate the effectiveness of exposure. In reality, either $Y_c$ or $Y_e$ is observed for each subject and hence $E(Y_e)$ and $E(Y_c)$ need to be estimated.

Suppose that the control (e.g. no ad impression) and exposure (e.g. ad impressions) treatments are applied to two groups of subjects with no overlaps, indicted by $z_i = 0$ or $1$ for subject $i = 1, 2, ..., N$, and hence the subjects are divided into exposed group ($z_i = 1$) and control group ($z_i = 0$). The success metric (such as conversion), is indicated by $y_i = 0$ or $1$. A naive way to estimate $E(Y_e)$ and $E(Y_c)$ is to calculate the average success rates of the two groups, respectively, as in Equations 1 and 2.

$$r_{naive,exposed} = \frac{1}{\sum_i z_i} \sum_i z_i y_i; \quad (1)$$

$$r_{naive,control} = \frac{1}{\sum_i (1 - z_i)} \sum_i (1 - z_i) y_i. \quad (2)$$

Hence naive estimators (difference and ratio[5]) of the exposure effectiveness are defined as in Equations 3 and 4.

$$D_{naive} = r_{naive,exposed} - r_{naive,control}; \quad (3)$$

$$R_{naive} = r_{naive,exposed} / r_{naive,control}. \quad (4)$$

[3]In this advertising study, the subjects are online users.

[4]Another method is the difference-in-difference approach [26, 32].

[5]In the rest of the paper we will use amplifier to indicate the ratio of the conversion rates of the exposed and control groups.

The naive estimators are unbiased if the control and exposed groups of users are randomly sampled from the population. However in an advertising campaign, we rarely have opportunities to assign random treatments to the users. In many of the cases, the ad treatments are highly related to user features, such as network activity, website visitation, demographics, etc. In such cases, the estimated $r_{naive,exposed}$ and $r_{naive,control}$ cannot represent the whole population. In other words, it does not ensure the comparison of the two groups is on equal footing. The test in Section 7.2 verifies that for online advertising, the naive estimator can be severely biased.

Another straightforward approach to eliminate the impact of user features on the outcome, as mentioned in Section 1, is to adjust the outcomes with a set of user-level covariates $X_i$ as well as treatment indicators, i.e. fit a model $y_i \sim f(X_i, z_i)$. However the estimated effect of $z_i$ may not necessarily imply causal effect, since the model may not correctly address the relationship between $z_i$ and $X_i$. We test such an approach in Section 7.2, and the result shows that, it may mistakenly 'detect' ad effectiveness while actually no effect should exist.

The basic idea to address the differences of the control and exposed groups is to consider the treatment $z_i$ as a random variable depending on a set of pre-treatment covariates $X_i$ for each subject $i$. Causal inference tries to balance the features of different treatment groups, and the methods introduced in this section rely on two assumptions.

Assumption 1: Stable unit treatment value assumption. "The (potential outcome) observation on one unit should be unaffected by the particular assignment of treatments to the other units" [6]. This assumption allows us to model the outcome of one subject independent of another subject's treatment status, given the covariates.

Assumption 2: Strong ignorability of treatment assignment (also called "Unconfoundedness")[27]. Given the covariates $X$, the distribution of treatment assignments is independent of the potential outcomes. This assumption allows us to model the treatment with respect to the covariates, independent of the outcome. It means all the features that are related to both the treatment assignment and the success have been included in the model.

Ignoring the above assumptions may result in misspecification of the causality model, and hence result in biases in the estimation. In the methodology elaboration part we assume these two assumptions are satisfied. In the application, we check the causality model misspecification with an irrelevant response test as in Section 7.2.

In the rest of this section, we briefly review the IPW approach that addresses the selection bias, and DR estimator, which further improves the robustness of the result. More details can be found in [27], [25] and [30].

### 2.2 IPW

Assuming a feature vector $X_i$ is available for each subject $i$ with features collected before each subject's exposure, propensity score is defined as the probability $\hat{p}_i = P(z_i = 1|X_i), \forall i$. Using $X$ to indicate features and $z$ to indicate treatment without specifying a particular user, ideally, the exposed and control groups will be balanced in terms of propensity score, i.e. $P(z = 1|X, exposed) = P(z = 1|X, control)$. This can be reached in a randomized experiment, in which case the naive estimators in Equations 3 and 4 are unbiased. However in observational data, this assumption is usually violated.

Usually $\hat{p}_i$ is estimated by fitting a model $\hat{P}(X)$ to estimate probability to be exposed with respect to the covariate $X$. Specifically we model $\hat{p}_i \sim \hat{P}(X_i)$ where $z_i = 1$ with probability $\hat{p}_i$. The basic idea is to use the estimated $\hat{p}_i$ to match the two groups, rather than to match the multi-dimensional $X$. In this paper we choose to use GBT with feature selection as in Section 3 to fit the model, with features chosen as in Section 6.

The IPW method proposes that each control subject is weighted by $1/(1-\hat{p}_i)$ and the exposed subjects is weighted by $1/\hat{p}_i$. [6] Hence the weighted success rates of the control and exposed groups are defined as in Equations 5 and 6.

$$r_{ipw,exposed} = \frac{1}{N}\sum_i z_i y_i/\hat{p}_i; \tag{5}$$

$$r_{ipw,control} = \frac{1}{N}\sum_i (1-z_i)y_i/(1-\hat{p}_i). \tag{6}$$

The IPW estimation of ad effectiveness (difference and amplifier) are then defined in Equations 7 and 8.

$$D_{ipw} = r_{ipw,exposed} - r_{ipw,exposed}; \tag{7}$$

$$R_{ipw} = r_{ipw,exposed}/r_{ipw,exposed}. \tag{8}$$

The above weighting strategy is to estimate the average exposure effect over the whole population. We are also interested in the average exposure effect on the subpopulation of subjects who actually got exposed. This is called the treatment on treated effect (TTE). For this estimation, the control subjects are weighted by $\hat{p}_i/(1-\hat{p}_i)$ and the exposed subjects are not weighted. Hence the TTE with IPW is calculated as in Equations 9 to 12.

$$r_{ipw,tte,exposed} = \frac{1}{\sum_i z_i}\sum_i z_i y_i; \tag{9}$$

$$r_{ipw,tte,control} = \frac{1}{\sum_{control}\hat{p}_i/(1-\hat{p}_i)}\sum_i (1-z_i)y_i\hat{p}_i/(1-\hat{p}_i). \tag{10}$$

$$D_{ipw,tte} = r_{ipw,tte,exposed} - r_{ipw,tte,control}; \tag{11}$$

$$R_{ipw,tte} = r_{ipw,tte,exposed}/r_{ipw,tte,control}. \tag{12}$$

## 2.3 DR Estimation

Based on IPW, [25] suggested further improvement of the estimator for robustness, i.e. smaller variance, which requires estimation of the probability to succeed under exposure and control treatments respectively.

Fit success model $\hat{M}_0(X)$ and$\hat{M}_1(X)$ to estimate probability to convert with respect to the covariate $X$ under control and exposed treatments respectively, and we can estimate each subject's success probabilities under exposed and control conditions as $\hat{m}_{1i}$ and $\hat{m}_{0i}$. Specifically $\hat{M}_1$ is fitted with the observed exposed subjects and their features, where $\hat{m}_{i1} \sim \hat{M}_1(X_i)$, and $y_i = 1$ with probability $\hat{m}_{i1}$. The model $\hat{M}_0$ is fitted similarly with control user data. In this paper we again choose to use GBT with feature selection as in Section 3 to fit the model, with features chosen as in Section 6. Define $\delta_{i,exposed}$ and $\delta_{i,control}$ to be the adjusted observations "augmented" with cross terms $-\hat{m}_{1i}(z_i - \hat{p}_i)$ and $\hat{m}_{0i}(z_i - \hat{p}_i)$ and $r_{dr,exposed}$ and $r_{dr,control}$ to be the adjusted estimation of the success rates of exposed and control groups respectively as below.

$$\delta_{i,exposed} = \frac{z_i y_i - \hat{m}_{1i}(z_i - \hat{p}_i)}{\hat{p}_i}; \tag{13}$$

$$\delta_{i,control} = \frac{(1-z_i)y_i + \hat{m}_{0i}(z_i - \hat{p}_i)}{1-\hat{p}_i}, \tag{14}$$

$$r_{dr,exposed} = \frac{1}{N}\sum_i \delta_{i,exposed}; \tag{15}$$

$$r_{dr,control} = \frac{1}{N}\sum_i \delta_{i,control}. \tag{16}$$

Hence the DR estimators of the advertising effectiveness is defined as

$$D_{dr} = r_{dr,exposed} - r_{dr,control}; \tag{17}$$

$$R_{dr} = r_{dr,exposed}/r_{dr,control}. \tag{18}$$

The TTE is estimated similarly:

$$r_{exposed,tte} = \frac{1}{\sum_i \hat{p}_i}\sum_i \delta_{i,exposed}\hat{p}_i; \tag{19}$$

$$r_{control,tte} = \frac{1}{\sum_i \hat{p}_i}\sum_i \delta_{i,control}\hat{p}_i. \tag{20}$$

$$D_{dr,tte} = r_{exposed,tte} - r_{control,tte}; \tag{21}$$

$$R_{dr,tte} = r_{exposed,tte}/r_{control,tte}. \tag{22}$$

The idea in DR estimator is to "augment" the observed outcomes with a correction $-\hat{m}_{1i}(z_i - \hat{p}_i)$ ( or $\hat{m}_{0i}(z_i - \hat{p}_i)$). The correction terms are products of the estimators from success model and the propensity score model. Intuitively if the error of either estimator is 0, the product of the two errors is 'zeroed out'. In fact [25] proved that, the estimation is unbiased if either the propensity model or the success model is correctly specified. The IPW with DR estimator algorithm is illustrated as in Table 1.

# 3. GBT WITH FEATURE SELECTION

The methodology described in section 2.2 and 2.3 requires to model the propensity score and success probability under control and exposure treatments with covariate $X$. In our dataset each internet user has thousands of features. To account for the large number of features, for the propensity model, we perform feature selection by fitting gradient boosting stumps [14] and choose the features with non-zero influence. We then feed the chosen features to GBT (with logistic loss) for propensity score model $\hat{P}$ [22]. Similar feature selection scheme and GBT model are applied to obtain the success model $\hat{M}_1$ and $\hat{M}_0$.

A comparison of the GBT and the standard logistic regression is presented in Section 7.1.2, which shows uniform superiority of GBT over logistic regression. The test in Section 7.2 verifies that the feature selection scheme captures sufficient features for causal inference while greatly reduces the number of features, and the estimated $\hat{p}_i$ by GBT can represent the characteristics of subjects.

The computation is conducted based on R ([23]) with gbm package ([11]) for GBT fitting.

# 4. SUBSAMPLING AND BACK-SCALING

The banner ad dataset typically has extremely sparse conversions. In order to better capture the pattern of the data, we propose a two-stage strategy for propensity score and success model fitting, consisting of a subsampling stage and a back-scaling stage. In the subsampling stage, we sample the converters with a higher sampling rate than the non-converters. The success rates of the two

[6] The basic intuition is that, a control subject belongs to its group with probability $1-\hat{p}_i$, and hence it is weighted by the inverse of this probability to infer the situation of the population. Similarly for the exposed subjects. See [25] for proofs.

Table 1: Algorithm of IPW with DR estimator

| | |
|---|---|
| Input: | $y_i$, $X_i$, $z_i$ for $i = 1, 2, ...N$. |
| Output: | $r_{dr,exposed}$, $r_{dr,control}$, $D_{dr}$, $R_{dr}$. |
| Step 1: | Fit the propensity score model. With users in the dataset, fit a model $\hat{P}(X)$ to estimate probability to be exposed with respect to the covariates $X$. |
| Step 2: | Estimate propensity score $\hat{p}_i = \hat{P}(X_i)$ for each user $i$. |
| Step 3: | Fit the success model for exposed users. With users in exposed group, fit model $\hat{M}_1(X)$ to estimate probability to succeed with respect to the covariate $X$. Estimate the success probability of each user in the population under exposed treatment $\hat{m}_{1i} = \hat{M}_1(X_i)$. |
| Step 4: | Fit the success model for control users. With users in control group, fit model $\hat{M}_0(X)$ to estimate probability to succeed with respect to the covariate $X$. Estimate the success probability of each user in the population under control treatment $\hat{m}_{0i} = \hat{M}_0(X_i)$. |
| | Whole Population Effect: |
| Step 7: | Calculate the adjusted success rates as in Equations 13 to 16. |
| Step 8: | Calculate the difference or amplifier as in Equations 17 or 18. |
| | TTE: |
| Step 7': | Calculatethe adjusted success rates as in Equations 19 and 20. |
| Step 8': | Calculate the TTE difference or amplifier as in Equations 21 or 22. |

groups within the subsample are estimated as in Table 1. The subsample success rates are then back-scaled according to the sampling rates to estimate the population-level success rates in the back-scaling stage. The two-stage procedure is laid out as in Table 2 and 3.

The procedure applies to both population level effect and TTE. Numerical results are provided in section 7.1 to show substantial improvement of out-of-sample predictions by utilizing this strategy.

## 5. PARALLEL COMPUTING

The online ad dataset usually contains large volumes of users, and the computation time is substantially shortened by utilizing parallel computing. We propose to divide the whole dataset into subsamples, and conduct the subsampling-and-backscaling strategy as in Section 4. The computation on each of the subsamples yields an estimation of ad effectiveness, and the point estimation and variation of the population-level ad effectiveness are summarized from the collected subsample estimations. The algorithm is summarized in Table 4.

The parallel computation strategy is implemented on Hadoop (Apache$^{TM}$ Hadoop® project) with an in-house package.

## 6. DATA

We apply our framework to a marketing campaign of a major auto insurance company, which consists of a specific website takeover and a direct response banner. The study is to measure the effectiveness of the website takeover on top of the direct response banner. The exposed group is defined as the users who were exposed to both the website takeover and the banner ads during a 10-day analysis period, while the control group subjects are only exposed to the banner ads. The control subjects must also have visited at least one of the websites visited by the exposed group,

Table 2: Algorithm of Subsamping

| | |
|---|---|
| Input: | $y_i$, $X_i$, $z_i$ for $i = 1, 2, ...N$. |
| Output: | $r_{e,sub}$, $r_{c,sub}$, $SP_{e,s}$, $SP_{e,ns}$, $SP_{c,s}$, $SP_{c,ns}$. |
| Step 1: | From the whole dataset, obtain a subsample such that the number of success users and non-success users are balanced in the subsample. |
| Step 2: | Count the number of subjects in each of the four groups (exposed & success, exposed & non-success, control & success, control & non-success) in the subsample as $n_{e,s}$, $n_{e,ns}$, $n_{c,s}$ and $n_{c,ns}$ respectively. (Subscripts "e" and "c" are short for "exposed" and "control", and "s" and "ns" are for "success" and "non-success", respectively.) |
| Step 3: | Count the number of subjects in each of the four groups in the population as $N_{e,s}$, $N_{e,ns}$, $N_{c,s}$ and $N_{c,ns}$ respectively.. |
| Step 4: | Calculate the sampling probability of the four groups: $SP_{e,s} = n_{e,s}/N_{e,s}$, $SP_{e,ns} = n_{e,ns}/N_{e,ns}$, $SP_{c,s} = n_{c,s}/N_{c,s}$, $SP_{c,ns} = n_{c,ns}/N_{c,ns}$. |
| Step 5: | Calculate the estimated success rates of the exposed and control groups $r_{e,sub}$ and $r_{c,sub}$ with the sampled dataset, as in Table 1. |

Table 3: Algorithm of Back-Scaling

| | |
|---|---|
| Input: | $r_{e,sub}$, $r_{c,sub}$, $SP_{e,s}$, $SP_{e,ns}$, $SP_{c,s}$, $SP_{c,ns}$ from algorithm in Table 2. |
| Output: | $r_d$, $r_c$, $D$, $R$. |
| Step 1: | Estimate the population-level success rates. $r_e = \frac{r_{e,sub}/SP_{e,s}}{r_{e,sub}/SP_{e,s}+(1-r_{e,sub})/SP_{e,ns}}$, $r_c = \frac{r_{c,sub}/SP_{c,s}}{r_{c,sub}/SP_{c,s}+(1-r_{c,sub})/SP_{c,ns}}$. |
| Step 2: | Calculate the population-level ad effectiveness $D = r_e - r_c$ and $R = r_e/r_c$ (difference and amplifier respectively). |

Table 4: Algorithm of Parallel Computing

| | |
|---|---|
| Input: | $y_i$, $X_i$, $z_i$ for $i = 1, 2, ...N$. |
| Output: | The estimated ad effectiveness and its variation. |
| Step 1: | Extract all the converters ($y_i = 1$) within the dataset. |
| Step 2: | Split the rest of the dataset into $K$ chunks. |
| Step 3: | For each chunk $k = 1, 2, ..., K$, do steps 3.1 to 3.5: |
| Step 3.1: | Combine the chunk with all the converted users or a sample of them, such that the number of success users and non-success users are balanced in the sample dataset.. |
| Step 3.3: | Compute $r_{e,sub}$ and $r_{c,sub}$ within this chunk, as in Table 2. |
| Step 3.4: | Scale $r_{e,sub}$ and $r_{c,sub}$ back to population level to obtain $r_e$ and $r_c$ and compute the ad effectiveness (difference and amplifier), as in Table 3. |
| Step 4: | Gather the results from each chunk together and observe the mean estimation and variation (SD). |

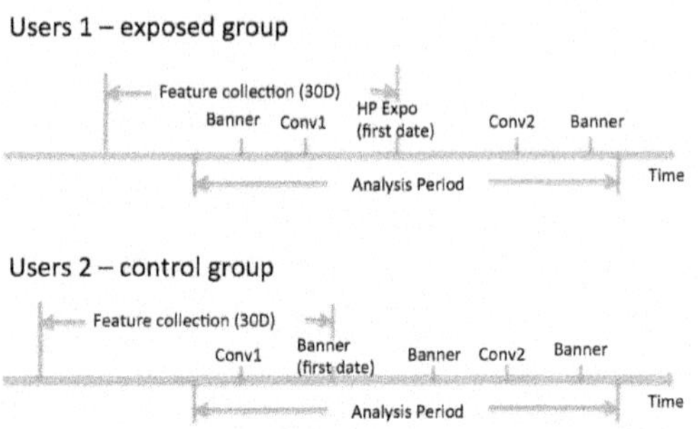


Figure 3: Timeline of Data Collection

and must have at least one feature that are available for the exposed group. These restrictions are to insure that the control and exposed subjects have common website visits and features.

The features are captured in a fixed length of time period (30 days) before the ad treatment. For each user of the exposed group, the features are captured in a 30-day time period before his/her first exposure to the website takeover in the analysis time period. For each user of the control group, the features are captured before his/her first exposure to the banner ads in the analysis time period. The timeline is illustrated in Figure 3.

The collected dataset[7] contains about 2.8 million users (2.0 million control and 0.8 exposed) with 11.7 thousand converters (8.4 thousand control and 3.3 thousand exposed). The dataset is extremely imbalanced since only 0.4% of the users converted. Each user is labeled with an exposure flag and a success flag (defined as a price quote of auto insurance on the advertiser's website). The features of each user, including website visitation, ad exposure, demographic information, market interest, etc., are collected repeatedly on a daily basis. They are then summarized by a weighted summation with a exponential time-decay factor, i.e. for a specific feature, the value observed $d$ days before the advertising treatment is weighted by $\alpha^d$ where $0 < \alpha < 1$ . We choose 1000 features which are most populated (i.e. least missing data) for the analysis. A sample of the features and corresponding values are shown in Table 5 for illustration. The features of the two groups show significant differences, and as an example, the network activity[8] of the exposed and control groups are shown in Figure 6(a) and (b).

According to the 'unconfoundedness' assumption as in Section 2.1, one must include all the important features that are related to both the treatment assignment and the success in the model, and one way to validate the choice of features is to conduct an irrelevant conversion test as in Section 7.2. The result shows that the features we suggest to collect in this section capture user's characteristics related to ad impression and success.

In this marketing campaign project, we focus on the TTE amplifier estimator.

[7]The reported dataset and results are deliberately incomplete and subject to anonymization, and thus do not necessarily reflect the real portfolio at any particular time.

[8]Network activity is a general indicator of how active across the web a user is and in this paper is defined as the summation of the feature scores for all the online activities, e.g. website visitation, banner impressions. etc.

Table 5: Sample Features

<table>
<tr><th>Feature</th><th>Value</th></tr>
<tr><td>Demographic | Gender | Male</td><td>0</td></tr>
<tr><td>Demographic | Gender | Female</td><td>1</td></tr>
<tr><td>Demographic| Age</td><td>27</td></tr>
<tr><td>Demographic| Family Size</td><td>1</td></tr>
<tr><td>...</td><td></td></tr>
<tr><td>Interest | Celebrities</td><td>0.01</td></tr>
<tr><td>Interest | Auto | New</td><td>0.23</td></tr>
<tr><td>Interest | Auto | Used</td><td>0.65</td></tr>
<tr><td>...</td><td></td></tr>
<tr><td>Site Visitation | Finance</td><td>67.4</td></tr>
<tr><td>Site Visitation | Movies</td><td>1.3</td></tr>
<tr><td>Site Visitation | Sports</td><td>0.0</td></tr>
<tr><td>...</td><td></td></tr>
<tr><td>Ad Impression | Auto | Company 1</td><td>7.24</td></tr>
<tr><td>Ad Impression | Insurance | Company 2</td><td>9.43</td></tr>
<tr><td>...</td><td></td></tr>
</table>

# 7. MODEL PERFORMANCE AND VALIDATION

We evaluate and validate the model from two aspects. Section 7.1 focuses on the performance of the propensity score model and success model fitting. However these performance assessment does not provide information for the causality model misspecification which might be because of important feature missing. We validate the causal inference with an irrelevant conversion test in Section 7.2, which verifies various aspects of the framework.

## 7.1 Model Performance

The proposed procedure is applied to a sample (about 0.5% data) from the marketing campaign dataset. When fitting the propensity score model and the success models with GBT, we always use 50% of the data as training dataset and the rest as test dataset to choose the best number of trees.

### *7.1.1 Balance of the Two Groups*

The IPW successfully balances the propensity score and hence the features of the users. The propensity scores of the control and exposed groups in the sample dataset before and after the weighting are summarized in Figure 4. Since the propensity score is the probability to be exposed, the figures suggest that after the weighting, the adjusted groups have similar probabilities to be exposed.

The QQ-plot of the propensity scores before and after the weighing (Figure 5) further shows that the weighing balances the propensity scores of the two groups.

As an example of the user features, the network activities before and after the weighting are summarized in Figure 6 and QQ-plot Figure 7. Both of the figures show significant improvement in the network activity balance. Similar phenomena are observed for other important features, such as auto purchase intention, which implies balance between the adjusted control and exposed groups.

### *7.1.2 GBT with Feature Selection Performance*

Through the feature selection with gradient boosting stumps , the percentage of chosen features varies for the propensity score and success rate models, ranging from 10% to 30%. The selection greatly reduces the number of features to be fed into GBT and hence the computation time. Yet the performance is similar to that of GBT on the full set of features (less than 1% difference in out-of-sample mean squared error (MSE).)

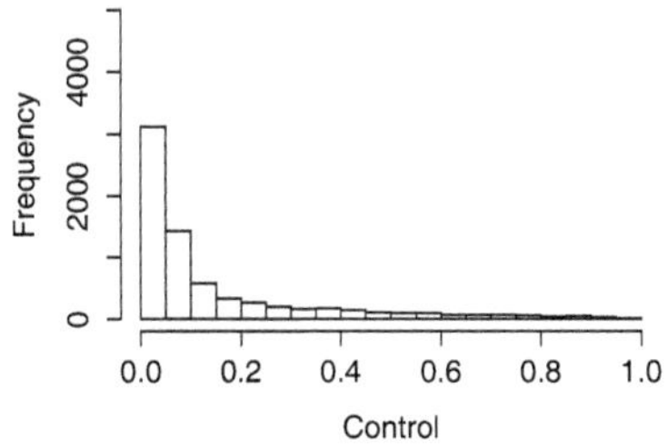


(a) Control, Before

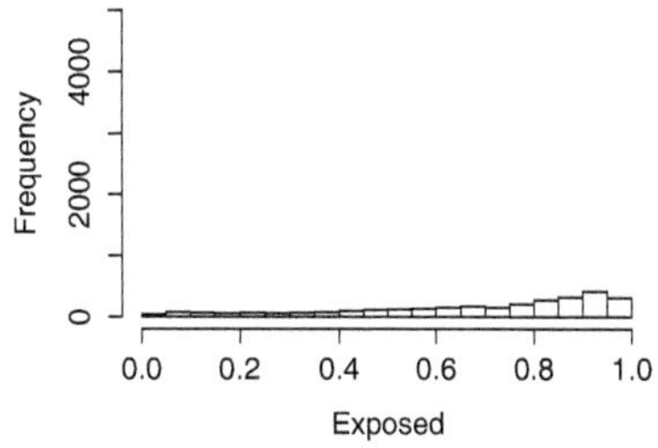


(b) Exposed, Before

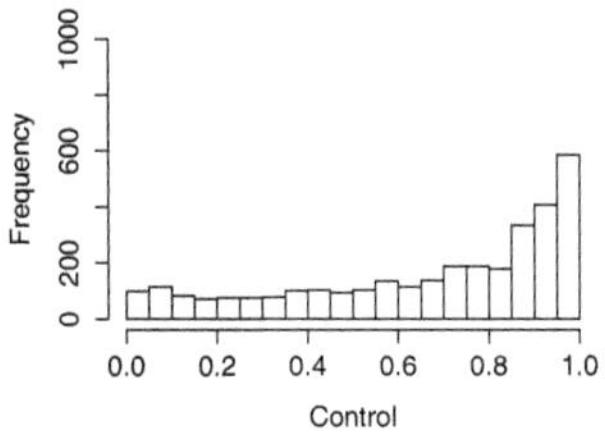


(c) Control, After

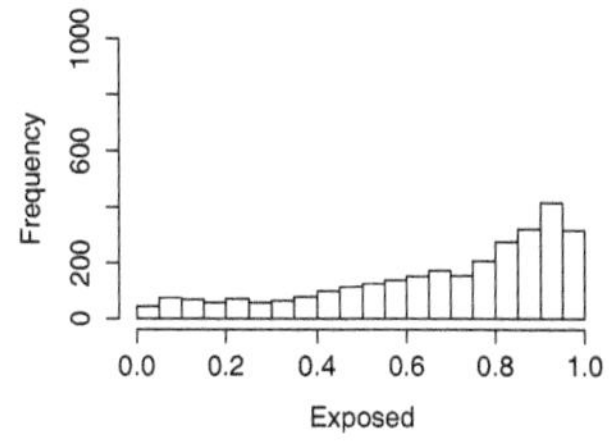


(d) Exposed, After

Figure 4: Propensity Score Before (a, b for control and exposed groups respectively) and After (c, d for control and exposed groups respectively) the Weighting

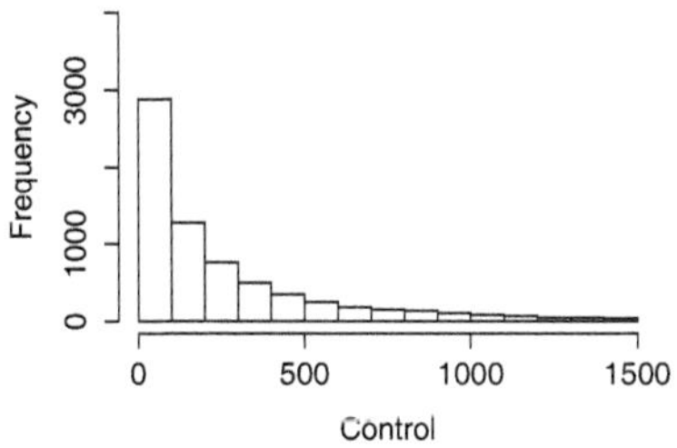


(a) Control, Before

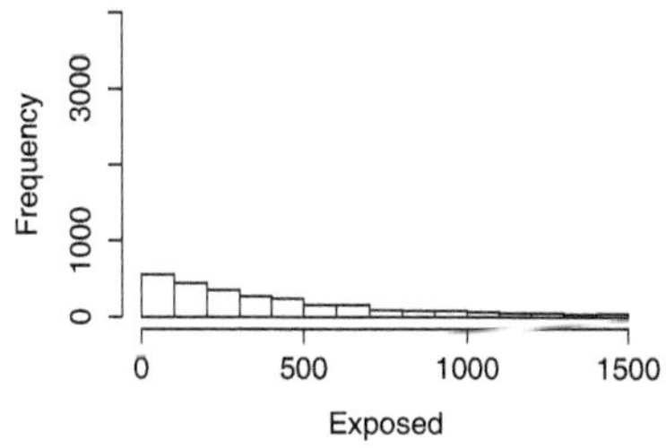


(b) Exposed, Before

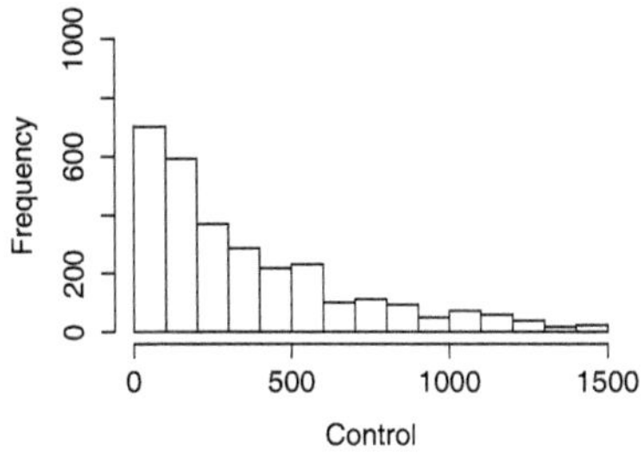


(c) Control, After

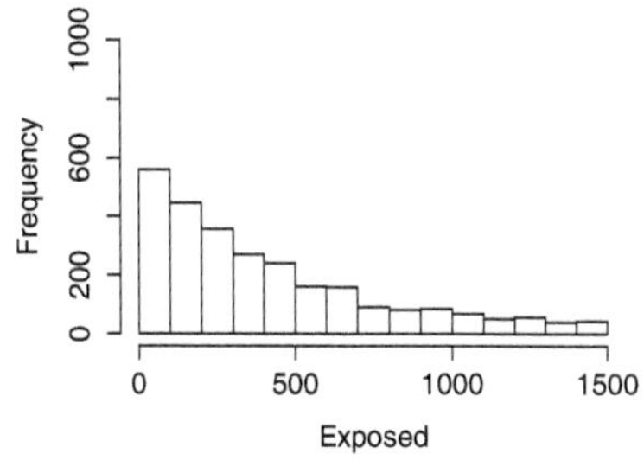


(d) Exposed, After

Figure 6: Network Activities Before (a, b for control and exposed groups respectively) and After (c, d for control and exposed groups respectively) the Weighting

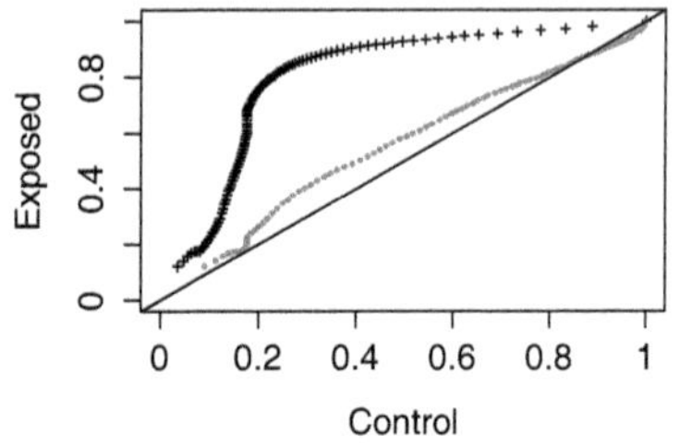


Figure 5: QQ Plot of Propensity Scores Before (cross mark) and After (dot mark) Weighting

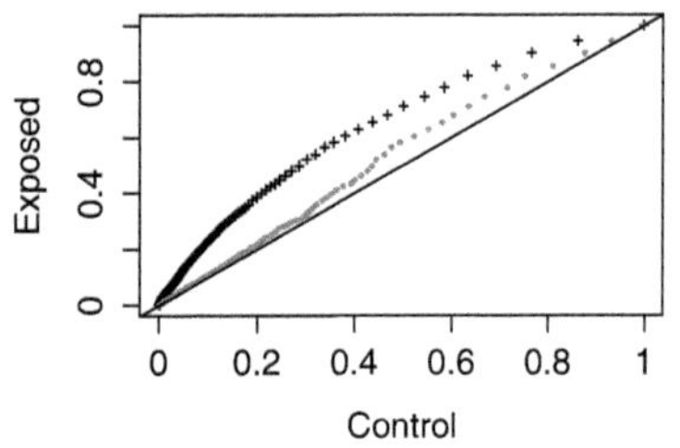


Figure 7: QQ Plot of Network Activity Before (cross mark) and After (dot mark) Weighting

We compare the performance of GBT with feature selection and the standard logistic regression by considering out-of-sample predictions. The MSE of GBT is 47% lower than the logistic regression. The out-of-sample ROC curve in Figure 8 further shows the advantage of the GBT approach.

In causal inference, the model has to not only fit the data well, but also represent and hence balance the features of the control and exposed groups well. One way to validate this point is to conduct an irrelevant conversion test as in Section 7.2. The test result suggests that our feature selection scheme chooses a small fraction of features, but the chosen ones are still sufficient for the causal inference. It also suggests that the GBT model constructs the propensity scores that can represent the high-dimensional user features.

### *7.1.3 Subsampling Performance*

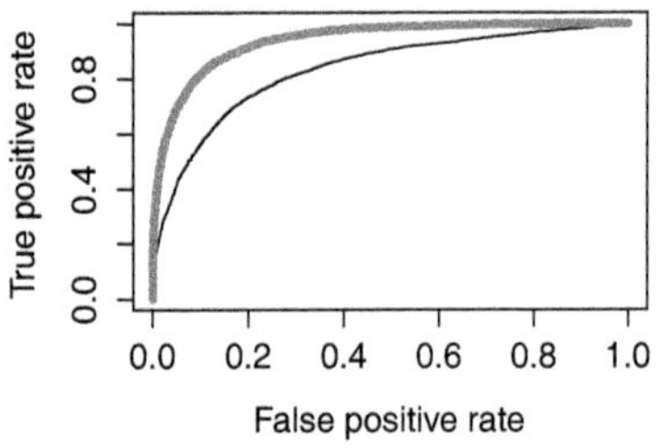


Figure 8: ROC of GBT (thick line) and Logit Regression (thin line)

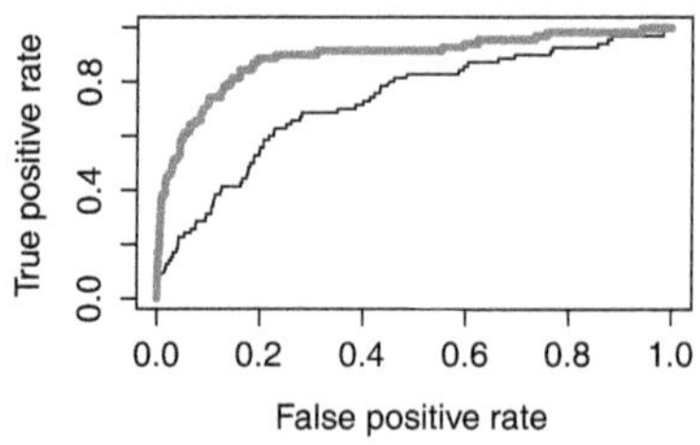


Figure 9: ROC with (thick line) and without (thin line) Subsampling

The two-stage strategy of subsampling and back-scaling in Section 4 improves the out-of-sample model prediction for the success models. As an example, we display the ROC curve of the success model within control group in Figure 9, which shows uniform superiority of the subsampling strategy.

## 7.2 Model Validation and Irrelevant Conversion Test

In the calculation, we observe less than 2% of the subjects with weights larger than 5, which suggests that the calculation is not sensitive to a small fraction of subjects and hence the robustness of the result.

We also calculate the effective sample sizes ($(\sum_j w_j)^2/\sum_j w_j^2$, where $w_j$ is the weight for subject $j$ in the sample, as suggested in [17]) of the two groups. The effective sample size of the control group is about 47% of the actual control sample size, and 60% for the exposed group. It results in about 2.0 controls per exposed user, and shows sufficient control sample size.

The above methods suggest validation and robustness of the result, but are not sufficient to provide information about causality model misspecification. As suggested in [26], one way to test the misspecification of the causality model is to use irrelevant outcomes, i.e. outcome not related to the treatment. Specifically, one may compose a dataset where the success flag is from a completely different business from the ad treatment, and hence is irrelevant to this particular advertising campaign. If the model successfully matches the control and exposed groups, the estimated ad effectiveness on the irrelevant conversion should be null. To be formal, it is a test with $H_0 : R = 1$ and $H_a : R \neq 1$, where $R$ is the estimated amplifier for irrelevant conversion.

In this irrelevant conversion test, we flag the treatment according to an auto insurance ad impression while the conversion is flagged according to purchases of a consumer electronics brand. The naive amplifier is 0.714 with a bootstrap standard error 0.013, while the adjusted amplifier is 0.974 with a bootstrap standard error 0.075. Another irrelevant conversion test where the conversion is flagged according to purchase of an IT brand reveals similar results.

Before the adjustment, the estimated amplifier is different from 1 statistically significantly, which shows the invalidation of the direct comparison of the success rates. After the adjustment with the causal inference, we accept the null hypothesis that the ad has no effect on an irrelevant conversion, which means our method successfully captures and balances the differences between observed control and exposed groups, and hence conducts a fair comparison.

The result provides validation to multiple aspects in our framework: 1) The effect that the model 'drags' the amplifier toward 1 verifies that GBT captures the differences of the control and ex-

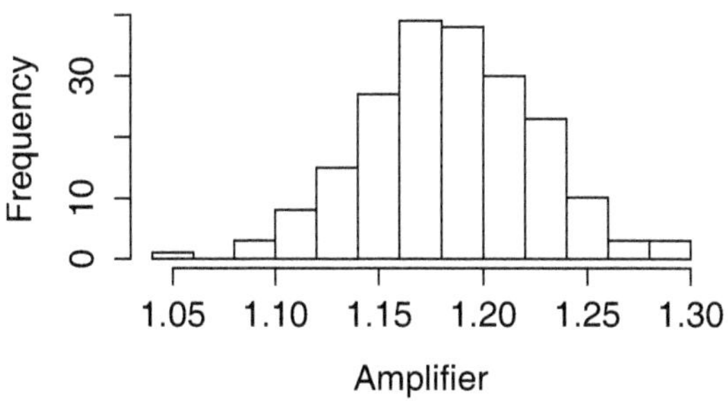


Figure 10: Histogram of TTE Amplifiers

posed groups, and the propensity scores estimated by GBT is a good representation of the user features. 2) The feature selection scheme chooses the features that are sufficient for causal inference while reducing the number of features substantially. 3) The features we suggest in Section 6 cover the major characteristics of online users that are related to ad exposures and conversions.

To show that directly fitting a model with features $X_i$ and exposure indicator $z_i$ may not necessarily work, we fit a logistic regression model and a GBT model for the irrelevant conversion with $X_i$ and $z_i$. In the logistic regression model, the coefficient of $z_i$ has a p-value nearly 0. In the GBT model, the exposure indicator $z_i$ shows substantial influence. Both of the models mistakenly 'detect' the ad effect on irrelevant conversion, which should not exist.

# 8. MARKETING CAMPAIGN EFFECTIVENESS RESULTS

The naive amplifier (as in Equation 4) of the campaign summarized from the whole dataset is 0.94. According to the test in Section 7.2, the naive amplifier may be biased by the different characteristics of the control and exposed groups. With our proposed framework , we reach a population level TTE amplifier 1.184, i.e. the webpage takeover lift the conversion rate by 18.4% on top of the direct response banner ad. The collected amplifier estimations from each chunk have standard deviation 0.041, which suggest small variation in the results for different sub-datasets. The histogram (Figure 10) of the subsample amplifiers shows good robustness of the results. It also shows symmetry and uni-mode, which suggests that the average of the amplifiers from each chunk is a good representation of the amplifier of the population.

# 9. GENERALIZATION

In many of the cases, there are multiple advertising treatments that require fair comparison. For example ads with multiple designs (e.g. text, video and figure), or from multiple serving pipelines (e.g. banner, search and email). In such cases, it is straightforward to generalize this framework to multiple treatment situation, where the treatment indicator $z_i = t$ for user $i$ where $t = 1, 2, ..., T$ indicates the treatment the user received. The key step is to modify the formula to estimated the success rate of each treatment group. Specifically, Equations 1 , 2, 5, 6, 15 and 16 need to be changed.

In the IPW approach, Equations 5 and 6 need to be changed to

$$r_{ipw,t} = \frac{1}{N} \sum_i I_{z_i=t} y_i / \hat{p}_i^t, \tag{23}$$

Table 6: Basic Algorithm of Propensity Function with Subclassification

| | |
|---|---|
| Input: | $y_i$, $X_i$, treatment $Z_i$ that might be continuous and/or multi-dimensional for $i = 1, 2, ...N$. |
| Output: | Estimated treatment effect. |
| Step 1: | Instead of propensity score which is probability of one treatment (exposure), one fits propensity functions $\hat{P}(X)$ with the pre-treatment covariates. It is a sufficient statistic for the distribution of treatments, namely $Z_i \perp X_i \vert P(X_i)$ and could be supported on the real line and be multi-dimensional. |
| Step 2: | Sub-classify the subjects with similar propensity functions together and forms $S$ subclasses. |
| Step 3: | Within each subclass $s$, calculate the number of subjects $n_s$ and estimate the treatment effect $D_s$ or $R_s$. |
| Step 4: | Gather the results from each subclass and calculate the population treatment effect as a weighted average of $D_s$ or $R_s$, where the weight is proportional to $n_s$. |

where $\hat{p}_i^t$ is the estimated probability for user $i$ to be exposed to treatment $t$, and hence $r_{ipw,t}$ is the estimated success rate for users of treatment t. A popular way to estimate $\hat{p}_i^t$ for multiple treatments is Multinomial Logistic Regression (MLR) [19]. Other approaches, such as GBT may also be applied.

For the DR approach, Equations 13 to 16 need to be changed to

$$\delta_{i,t} = \frac{I_{z_i=t} y_i - \hat{m}_i^t (I_{z_i=t} - \hat{p}_i^t)}{\hat{p}_i^t}; \tag{24}$$

$$r_{dr,t} = \frac{1}{N} \sum_i \delta_{i,t}, \tag{25}$$

where $\hat{m}_i^t$ is the estimated conversion probability for user $i$ if he/she receives treatment $t$, and $r_{dr,t}$ is the estimated success rate under treatment $t$.

Besides weighting, another set of causal inference approaches is based on classifications, where one subclassifies similar subjects together, estimates the treatment effect within each subclass, and calculates the final treatment effect as a weighted average of the treatment effects within each subclass. By utilizing this approach, this framework can be further generalized to general treatment regimes through the concept propensity functions [16], where the treatments could be continuous and/or multi-dimensional. The basic algorithm is summarized in Table 6.

An example where the treatment could be multi-dimensional and non-binary is that, for a specific banner ad, considering the number of impressions per day and number of days with impression separately. Then $Z_i$ = (# impressions/day, # days with impression), where $Z_i$ is multi-dimensional and the elements of $z_i$ are integer numbers rather than binary indicators. By the algorithm specified in Table 6, one can draw causal effect of two aspects of banner ads: the frequency of ads per day, and the frequency of days with impressions. These two aspects are usually considered together as the total number of impressions in a time period, but they may have different impacts if modeled separately.

# 10. CONCLUSIONS

In this paper, we propose a novel causal inference framework employing IPW and DR estimator. We advocate to fit the models (propensity score model and success models) with GBT with a feature selection by gradient boosting stumps, and embed the approach in a subsampling-and-backscaling strategy to deal with extremely sparse conversions, thus better capture the pattern in the data. To deal with large volume of data, we devise a new parallel computing plan that provides the estimation of the mean ad effectiveness and the variation. We apply our framework to a real-world advertising dataset, which shows efficiency and robustness of the method.

Through the generalization discussions in Section 9, our framework is readily generalizable to multi-treatment cases and general treatment regimes, which can be used to compare multiple advertising treatments, multiple aspects of an ad simultaneously, and other general ad treatments. Also, this paper focuses on measuring the effectiveness of online ads, but the framework is readily applicable to other cases (e.g. social science) when a fair comparison needs to be conducted from observational data.

## 11. REFERENCES


[1] Apache™ hadoop® project. *http://hadoop.apache.org*.

[2] H. Bang and J. M. Robins. Doubly robust estimation in missing data and causal inference models. *Biometrics*, 61(4):962–973, 2005.

[3] J. Barajas, J. Kwon, R. Akella, A. Flores, M. Holtan, and V. Andrei. Marketing campaign evaluation in targeted display advertising. In *Proceedings of the Sixth International Workshop on Data Mining for Online Advertising and Internet Economy*, page 5. ACM, 2012.

[4] A. Basu, D. Polsky, and W. G. Manning. Use of propensity scores in non-linear response models: the case for health care expenditures. Technical report, National Bureau of Economic Research, 2008.

[5] D. Chan, R. Ge, O. Gershony, T. Hesterberg, and D. Lambert. Evaluating online ad campaigns in a pipeline: causal models at scale. In *Proceedings of the 16th ACM SIGKDD international conference on Knowledge discovery and data mining*, pages 7–16. ACM, 2010.

[6] D. R. Cox. Planning of experiments. 1958.

[7] B. Dalessandro, C. Perlich, O. Stitelman, and F. Provost. Causally motivated attribution for online advertising. In *Proceedings of the Sixth International Workshop on Data Mining for Online Advertising and Internet Economy*, page 7. ACM, 2012.

[8] A. Dasgupta, K. Punera, J. M. Rao, X. Wang, J. Rao, and X.-J. Wang. Impact of spam exposure on user engagement. In *USENIX Security*, 2012.

[9] J. H. Friedman. Stochastic gradient boosting. *Computational Statistics & Data Analysis*, 38(4):367–378, 2002.

[10] M. J. Funk, D. Westreich, C. Wiesen, T. Stürmer, M. A. Brookhart, and M. Davidian. Doubly robust estimation of causal effects. *American journal of epidemiology*, 173(7):761–767, 2011.

[11] Greg Ridgeway with contributions from others. *gbm: Generalized Boosted Regression Models*, 2013. R package version 2.0-8.

[12] S. Guo and M. W. Fraser. Propensity score analysis. *Statistical methods and applications*, 2010.

[13] J. J. Heckman, H. Ichimura, and P. Todd. Matching as an econometric evaluation estimator. *The Review of Economic Studies*, 65(2):261–294, 1998.

[14] R. C. Holte. Very simple classification rules perform well on most commonly used datasets. *Machine learning*, 11(1):63–90, 1993.

[15] K. Imai. Do get-out-the-vote calls reduce turnout? the importance of statistical methods for field experiments. *American Political Science Review*, 99(2):283–300, 2005.

[16] K. Imai and D. A. Van Dyk. Causal inference with general treatment regimes. *Journal of the American Statistical Association*, 99(467), 2004.

[17] L. Kish. Survey sampling. new york: J. *Wiley & Sons*, 643:16, 1965.

[18] M. Lechner. Earnings and employment effects of continuous gff-the-job training in east germany after unification. *Journal of Business & Economic Statistics*, 17(1):74–90, 1999.

[19] J. Ledolter. Multinomial logistic regression. *Data Mining and Business Analytics with R*, pages 132–149.

[20] S. F. Lehrer and G. Kordas. Matching using semiparametric propensity scores. *Empirical Economics*, 44(1):13–45, 2013.

[21] R. A. Lewis, J. M. Rao, and D. H. Reiley. Here, there, and everywhere: correlated online behaviors can lead to overestimates of the effects of advertising. In *Proceedings of the 20th international conference on World wide web*, pages 157–166. ACM, 2011.

[22] D. F. McCaffrey, G. Ridgeway, A. R. Morral, et al. Propensity score estimation with boosted regression for evaluating causal effects in observational studies. *Psychological methods*, 9(4):403–425, 2004.

[23] R Development Core Team. *R: A Language and Environment for Statistical Computing*. R Foundation for Statistical Computing, Vienna, Austria, 2008. ISBN 3-900051-07-0.

[24] G. Ridgeway. Generalized boosted models: A guide to the gbm package. *Update*, 1:1.

[25] J. M. Robins, A. Rotnitzky, and L. P. Zhao. Analysis of semiparametric regression models for repeated outcomes in the presence of missing data. *Journal of the American Statistical Association*, 90(429):106–121, 1995.

[26] P. R. Rosenbaum. *Observational studies*. Springer, 2002.

[27] P. R. Rosenbaum and D. B. Rubin. The central role of the propensity score in observational studies for causal effects. *Biometrika*, 70(1):41–55, 1983.

[28] P. R. Rosenbaum and D. B. Rubin. Reducing bias in observational studies using subclassification on the propensity score. *Journal of the American Statistical Association*, 79(387):516–524, 1984.

[29] P. R. Rosenbaum and D. B. Rubin. Constructing a control group using multivariate matched sampling methods that incorporate the propensity score. *The American Statistician*, 39(1):33–38, 1985.

[30] D. O. Scharfstein, A. Rotnitzky, and J. M. Robins. Adjusting for nonignorable drop-out using semiparametric nonresponse models. *Journal of the American Statistical Association*, 94(448):1096–1120, 1999.

[31] O. Stitelman, B. Dalessandro, C. Perlich, and F. Provost. Estimating the effect of online display advertising on browser conversion. *Data Mining and Audience Intelligence for Advertising (ADKDD 2011)*, 8, 2011.

[32] P. Wang, M. Traskin, and D. S. Small. Robust inferences from a before-and-after study with multiple unaffected control groups. *Journal of Causal Inference*, pages 1–26, 2013.

# LASER: A Scalable Response Prediction Platform For Online Advertising

Deepak Agarwal
LinkedIn Inc.
dagarwal@linkedin.com

Bo Long
LinkedIn Inc.
blong@linkedin.com

Jonathan Traupman
LinkedIn Inc.
jtraupman@linkedin.com

Doris Xin
LinkedIn Inc.
dxin@linkedin.com

Liang Zhang
LinkedIn Inc.
lizhang@linkedin.com

## ABSTRACT

We describe LASER, a scalable response prediction platform currently used as part of a social network advertising system. LASER enables the familiar logistic regression model to be applied to very large scale response prediction problems, including ones beyond advertising. Though the underlying model is well understood, we apply a whole-system approach to address model accuracy, scalability, explore-exploit, and real-time inference. To facilitate training with both large numbers of training examples and high dimensional features on commodity clustered hardware, we employ the Alternating Direction Method of Multipliers (ADMM). Because online advertising applications are much less static than classical presentations of response prediction, LASER employs a number of techniques that allows it to adapt in real time. LASER models can be divided into components with different re-training frequencies, allowing us to learn from changes in ad campaign performance frequently without incurring the cost of retraining larger, more stable sections of the model. Thompson sampling during online inference further helps by efficiently balancing exploration of new ads with exploitation of long running ones. To enable predictions made with the most recent feature data, we employ a range of techniques, including extensive caching and lazy evaluation, to permit real time, low latency scoring. LASER models are defined using a configuration language that ties together the training, validation, and inference pieces and permits even non-programming analysts to experiment with different model structures without modifications to code or interruptions to running servers. Finally, we show via extensive offline experiments and online A/B tests that this system provides significant benefits to prediction accuracy, gains in revenue and CTR, and reductions in system latency.

## Categories and Subject Descriptors

H.3.3 [**Information Search and Retrieval**]: Retrieval models; I.2.6 [**Artificial Intelligence**]: Learning; H.5.3 [**Information Systems**]: Web-based Interaction


*WSDM'14*, February 24–28, 2014, New York, New York, USA.

http://dx.doi.org/10.1145/2556195.2556252.

## Keywords

Machine learning, response prediction, logistic regression, scalability, computational advertising

## 1. INTRODUCTION

Online advertising is a multi-billion dollar business and forms a large swath of the internet economy. It is practiced in various forms like sponsored search advertising, contextual advertising and display advertising [5]. These are highly automated systems that auction ad space for user visits on various publisher pages. The auction entails ranking eligible ads as a function of advertiser bid and ad click-through rates (CTR). The advertiser payoff is often determined through a second-price auction where the winner pays the minimum price required to win the auction. For performance based advertising, such a payment is only made when a user clicks on an ad or performs some advertiser specified post-click action.

Large scale online advertising systems rely heavily on machine learned models that can accurately predict CTR. This is a difficult learning problem due to the curse of dimensionality and data sparseness, but such methods have been studied extensively in the last few years in the machine learning and data mining communities. However, deploying such methods for large scale online advertising systems in a reliable and cost-effective fashion involves non-trivial challenges, beyond fitting machine learning models to large data.

An ideal system should allow for scalable model training using standard and well understood commodity clustered hardware to reduce maintenance cost; it should be easy to test a new model on live traffic without much effort on coding; offline metrics that are indicative of online performance should be available to terminate below-par models quickly; the system should also provide a mechanism for exploration to avoid ad starvation; finally, runtime computations should scale under latency constraints. The main theme of this paper is to provide such an end-to-end holistic solution. We argue that building machine learning models without consideration to all such issues is not the right approach in practice for advertising systems. Machine learning methods should not be only tied to out-of-sample predictive accuracy. Careful attention to all such practical issues is important.

**Background** We begin with a brief background of an online advertising system. To simplify the exposition, we assume the pay-per-click model where an advertiser pays only when a user clicks on an ad. The flow works as follows: an ad server receives a request when a user visits some publisher page. Depending on the application, we may have information about the user and also the context in which the request was made. For instance, in sponsored search the user specified query is a necessary and important context to match ads, while user attributes might be helpful but of secondary importance. For display advertising, context information includes the device, the ad placement information, and other information about how and where the ad is shown. In this setting, user attribute information plays a more important role since user intent is typically weak. For a given request, we rank the set of eligible ads based on some function of advertiser bid and CTR (e.g., the product of bid and CTR). Such ranking has to be done for thousands of ads under tight latency constraints (tens of milliseconds).

Our **contributions** are as follows. We introduce LASER, a holistic end-to-end machine learning solution to deploy response prediction models based on logistic regression to large online advertising system. We partition the logistic regression model into a purely feature based *cold-start* component and an ad-campaign-specific *warm-start* component. The *cold-start* component is trained on commonly available commodity clustered hardware running MapReduce using the scatter-and-gather Alternating Direction Method of Multipliers (ADMM) algorithm [4], whereas the *warm-start* component learns residual campaign-level variation through frequent retraining. LASER also supports explore-exploit via Thompson sampling [19], which is an easy-to-implement yet powerful algorithm that draws samples from the posterior distribution of warm start coefficients. To permit low-latency computations at runtime, we introduce a range of techniques that take advantage of extensive caching and lazy evaluation. Our models are defined through a flexible configuration language that ties training, validation and inference pieces together, enabling testing new models without change to production code. Our system has been fully deployed on a large social media site, and we illustrate our method through extensive experiments using both offline data and online A/B tests in a real online advertising system.

## 2. RELATED WORK

Significant work have been done on machine learning models to accurately predict CTR for advertising applications [16, 17, 10, 1, 6, 11, 20]. However, these papers only focus on improving offline model training to improve out-of-sample predictive accuracy; scalable model training and good feature construction are the primary focus. We make a new contribution to this area by providing a scalable model fitting approach through ADMM that can scale on standard MapReduce infrastructure. Explore/exploit via Thompson sampling for advertising was recently studied by [6] but in a simulation and replay framework; no A/B test results on a live system were reported as we do in this paper. The issue of scaling runtime computations has been addressed by some papers separately through predictive indexing [2, 9], where the main idea is to perform pre-computations to do fast retrieval in an approximate fashion. Our approach is to reduce the generality of the model class (we confine ourselves to generalized linear models) but take a more general approach from a systems perspective, leveraging lazy evaluation and extensive caching for scalability. Unlike all the previous papers, to the best of our knowledge, this is the first paper that provides an end-to-end solution to deploy sophisticated machine learning models for a large scale online advertising system in an efficient, reliable and cost-effective fashion. The closest work that is similar in spirit to ours is [16], but they mainly provide an extensive summary of experience and issues when fitting large scale machine learning models in an offline fashion. The focus of that paper is building an efficient and robust offline training pipeline to minimize out-of-sample predictive accuracy metrics; issues like agile model deployment and efficient runtime computations are not the focus.

## 3. OUR MODEL

In this section we describe the components of the logistic regression model used by LASER. This is followed by a description of our scalable model fitting procedure and our explore/exploit strategy via Thompson sampling.

### 3.1 Model Description

**Notations**. Throughout the paper, we will use index $i$ to denote user $i$, index $j$ to denote item $j$ (e.g. ad campaigns), and index $t$ to denote context $t$ (e.g. time of day, day of week, where the item was shown, etc). The binary response (click or non-click) for a user $i$ on an item $j$ for context $t$ is denoted as $y_{ijt}$. Since the users, items, and contexts can all have features, we denote the features for user $i$ as $x_i$, the features for item (campaign) $j$ as $c_j$, and the features for context $t$ as $z_t$.

**Model**. Since the response $y_{ijt}$ is binary, it is natural to assume a Bernoulli model with logistic link function

$$y_{ijt} \sim \text{Bernoulli}(p_{ijt}), \quad (1)$$

where

$$p_{ijt} = \frac{1}{1+\exp(-s_{ijt})}. \quad (2)$$

We model the log-odds $s_{ijt}$ as

$$\begin{aligned} s_{ijt} &= \omega + s^{1,c}_{ijt} + s^{2,c}_{ijt} + s^{2,w}_{ijt}, & (3)\\ s^{1,c}_{ijt} &= x_i'\alpha + c_j'\beta + z_t'\gamma, & (4)\\ s^{2,c}_{ijt} &= x_i'Ac_j + x_i'Cz_t + z_t'Bc_j, & (5)\\ s^{2,w}_{ijt} &= \delta_j + x_i'\eta_j + z_t'\xi_j. & (6) \end{aligned}$$

Here, $\omega$ is the global intercept, $s^{1,c}_{ijt}$ consists of all first order interactions or main effects, $s^{2,c}_{ijt}$ consists of all second order interactions among features. The parameters $\omega$, $\alpha$, $\beta$, $\gamma$, $A$, $B$ and $C$ are global coefficients that are shared across all events. We call this set of unknown coefficients $\mathbf{\Theta_c} = \{\omega, \alpha, \beta, \gamma, A, B, C\}$ the **cold-start** component, because for a new user or ad campaign, we can still use features to obtain a reasonable estimate of CTR through $s^{1,c}$ and $s^{2,c}$.

Since the number of ad-campaigns is relatively small compared to the number of users, there is heterogeneity in the sample size available across campaigns. For campaigns with large data, one could estimate residual campaign specific idiosyncrasies by adding a **warm-start** component $s^{2,w}$ in equation (3). The warm-start parameters would be denoted by $\mathbf{\Theta_w} = \{\delta_j, \eta_j, \xi_j\}, j = 1, \cdots, J$. This component provides a mechanism to learn campaign-specific corrections and smoothly transition from cold start to warm start based on the sample sizes of campaigns. Such a transition is possible by allowing for regularization/shrinkage on coefficients, obtained by constraining them through prior distributions that we describe below.

**Priors**. Since the feature set is often high-dimensional, especially for second-order interaction terms in cold-start and per-campaign coefficients in warm-start, proper shrinkage and regularization of coefficients are required to avoid over-fitting. We use Gaussian priors for all the parameters $\mathbf{\Theta} = \{\omega, \alpha, \beta, \gamma, A, B, C, \delta_j, \eta_j, \xi_j\}$. Specifically, for scalars $\omega$ and $\delta_j$, the priors become $\omega \sim N(0, \sigma_\omega)$, and $\delta_j \sim N(0, \sigma_\delta)$. For coefficient vectors such as $\alpha$, $\beta$, $\gamma$, $\eta_j$, and $\xi_j$, we let $\alpha \sim MVN(0, \sigma_\alpha I)$, $\eta_j \sim MVN(0, \sigma_\eta I)$ and so forth. For coefficient matrices $A$, $B$ and $C$, we assume entries are i.i.d.

Gaussian with mean 0 and variance $\sigma_A$, $\sigma_B$ and $\sigma_C$ respectively. We estimate the prior variance through cross-validation using a tuning set. Also, for simplicity, in our own implementation we assume $\alpha, \beta, \gamma, A, B$, and $C$ all share the same prior variance, the $\delta_j$'s have the same prior variance, and $\eta_j$'s and $\xi_j$'s share the same prior variance for all campaigns.

## 3.2 Large Scale Model Fitting

**Model fitting on a single machine**. When the data size is relatively small and can be loaded into the memory of a standard machine, the model fitting proceeds by using routine methods available to fit a logistic regression with Gaussian priors ($L_2$ regularization).

Posterior mode of $(\boldsymbol{\Theta}_c, \boldsymbol{\Theta}_w)$ can be obtained via any convex optimization algorithm like conjugate gradient, L-BFGS [22], trust region [15], and others. The model can be trained frequently to rapidly update the warm-start coefficients.

### *3.2.1 Model Training with Large Data*

For large online advertising systems where training data with hundreds of millions of observations and hundreds of thousands of coefficients (if not more) is routine, fitting logistic regression is challenging. In our system, it is also desirable to have a model fitting procedure that runs on standard distributed computing infrastructure like Hadoop. This simplifies the production workflow and provides a more reliable system.

Since the coefficient $\boldsymbol{\Theta}_c$ is more stable and changes slowly relative to $\boldsymbol{\Theta}_w$, we can have different training frequencies for cold-start and warm-start components. For the slow-changing $\boldsymbol{\Theta}_c$, we have found weekly or bi-weekly training cycles for this component to be adequate in practice. The warm-start coefficients $\boldsymbol{\Theta}_w$ needs to be re-trained more frequently since it is time sensitive and changes with the activation and termination of ad campaigns. We have found that re-training this component as frequently as possible (e.g., on the order of minutes to hours) is important.

Note that for known cold-start coefficients, the warm-start coefficients can be computed independently for each ad campaign. Thus, we are able to decompose a big logistic regression into several small logistic regressions that can be trained independently of each other. This can be done routinely on Hadoop by splitting the data using campaign id as key in the map phase, and running independent per campaign regression in the reduce phase. To train the cold-start component, we adopt the ADMM algorithm that scales through a scatter-and-gather approach. It partitions data and runs an independent regression on each partition, but obtains a consensus estimate by combining estimates across partitions after each iteration. A few iterations of such a scatter-and-gather approach are enough for convergence, provided we are careful in how we initialize and adjust the step size of the algorithm across iterations.

### *3.2.2 Estimating Cold-Start Coefficients on Hadoop*

Traditional logistic regression model fitting approaches such as conjugate gradient or trust region require many iterations (e.g. at least in the order of 100s) to converge; running them on a Map-Reduce infrastructure like Hadoop usually introduces significant I/O overhead. This is mainly because each iteration is a new Map-Reduce job, and since the input and output of mappers and reducers are through disk, popular Map-Reduce infrastructures like Hadoop are not suitable for iterative algorithms that require large number of iterations. Although new infrastructures, such as Spark [21], have emerged recently that are more efficient for iterative machine learning algorithms, their development is still in an early stage; full integration to the Hadoop system in a production environment could have considerable costs in terms of stability, multi-user resource management, and software compatibility.

In our LASER system, we adopt the Alternating Direction Method of Multipliers (ADMM) algorithm [4] to obtain cold-start coefficient estimates, and our implementation is developed to work with the widely adopted Hadoop Map-Reduce infrastructure. ADMM can be shown to converge to the posterior mode obtained by fitting logistic regression to the entire data on a single machine. Compared to other popular fitting algorithms, such as conjugate gradient or trust region, ADMM requires significantly fewer outer iterations (i.e. Map-Reduce jobs) to converge. After applying a few modifications, like better initialization and step size selection, we have found 5-10 outer iterations of ADMM provides good predictive performance in practice. The number of inner iterations required to fit smaller logistic regression to each partition is still significant, but that does not involve I/O overhead, hence is efficient on Hadoop.

### *3.2.3 The ADMM Algorithm to Fit $L_2$ Regularized Logistic Regression*

Suppose we partition the data randomly into $R$ partitions. For each partition $r$, denote the data as $d_r$ and coefficient as $\boldsymbol{\Theta}_r$. Also denote the logistic loss function (i.e. negative log-likelihood) for each partition $r$ as $\mathscr{L}_r(\Theta_r; d_r)$, and the $L_2$ penalty function on $\Theta$ as $\mathscr{P}(\Theta)$. The main idea of ADMM is to assume each partition $r$ has its own coefficient $\boldsymbol{\Theta}_r$, and assume our interest is to obtain a global consensus estimate $\boldsymbol{\Theta}$, obtained by imposing a constraint $\boldsymbol{\Theta}_r = \boldsymbol{\Theta}$ for all $r = 1 \dots R$. The optimization problem is formally given by

$$\min \sum_{r=1}^{R} \mathscr{L}_r(\boldsymbol{\Theta}_r; d_r) + \mathscr{P}(\boldsymbol{\Theta}), \quad (7)$$

subject to

$$\boldsymbol{\Theta}_r - \boldsymbol{\Theta} = 0, r = 1 \dots R. \quad (8)$$

The ADMM algorithm for large scale logistic regression can be described as follows: At iteration $l+1$, the estimate for $\boldsymbol{\Theta}_r$ which is denoted by $\boldsymbol{\Theta}_r^{l+1}$ can be fitted independently and in parallel by

$$\boldsymbol{\Theta}_r^{l+1} = \text{argmin}_{\boldsymbol{\Theta}_r} \mathscr{L}_r(\boldsymbol{\Theta}_r; d_r) + \rho/2 \left\| \boldsymbol{\Theta}_r - \boldsymbol{\Theta}^l + \boldsymbol{u}_r^l \right\|^2 \quad (9)$$

where $\rho$ is the step size (learning rate) that controls the convergence rate, $\boldsymbol{\Theta}^l$ is the consensus estimate of $\boldsymbol{\Theta}$ at iteration $l$, and $\boldsymbol{u}_r^l$ intuitively is a measure of the partition-specific bias of the coefficients. When $\boldsymbol{\Theta}_r^{l+1}$ for all $r = 1 \dots R$ are obtained through a Map-Reduce job, we aggregate the results and compute the mean of $\boldsymbol{\Theta}_r^{l+1}$ for all $r = 1 \dots R$ as $\bar{\boldsymbol{\Theta}}^{l+1}$, and the mean of $\boldsymbol{u}_r^l$ for all $r = 1 \dots R$ as $\bar{\boldsymbol{u}}^l$. The consensus estimate at $l+1$, $\boldsymbol{\Theta}^{l+1}$ can be estimated by

$$\boldsymbol{\Theta}^{l+1} = \text{argmin}_{\boldsymbol{\Theta}} \mathscr{P}(\boldsymbol{\Theta}) + (R\rho/2) \left\| \boldsymbol{\Theta} - \bar{\boldsymbol{\Theta}}^{l+1} - \bar{\boldsymbol{u}}^l \right\|^2 \quad (10)$$

and

$$\boldsymbol{u}_r^{l+1} = \boldsymbol{u}_r^l + \boldsymbol{\Theta}_r^{l+1} - \boldsymbol{\Theta}^{l+1} \quad (11)$$

**Expediting convergence of ADMM**. In our use ADMM we have found two ways to improve the empirical convergence rate. First, we observed that the convergence of ADMM is sensitive to the initialization of the consensus $\boldsymbol{\Theta}^0$. We found a simple initialization approach that improves the convergence of ADMM significantly. The idea is to run independent logistic regression on each partition and use the mean of the parameters from the $R$ partitions as the initialization of $\boldsymbol{\Theta}^0$ to start ADMM.

Second, we observed that the convergence and performance of ADMM is quite sensitive to the step size $\rho$. One possible way to improve is to adaptively change the step size $\rho$ over iterations. In general, a larger step size pushes the partition parameters more towards the current estimate of the global consensus; on the other hand, a smaller step size gives each partition more freedom to explore their own data to estimate partition parameters. With the consensus initialization, we have a good starting point for the global parameter. Hence, it will be meaningful to strongly force each partition's coefficients to be close to the current global consensus at the beginning. After a couple of iterations, reducing the step size to let each partition explore more may further boost the performance. Based on this idea, we found empirically that with consensus initialization, the exponential decay of $\rho$ over iterations is a good choice which balances the global convergence with exploration within the partitions. Specifically, we adaptively adjust $\rho$ as follows,

$$\rho^{(l+1)} = \rho^{(0)} e^{-\tau l} \tag{12}$$

where $\rho^{(0)}$ is the base learning rate, $\tau$ is the decay the rate, and $l$ is the number of iterations.

Combining the two approaches, we are able to significantly reduce the number of iterations until convergence of ADMM. The empirical results of how the two approaches improve the ADMM convergence on our data can be found in Section 5.2.

### *3.2.4 Fitting Algorithm: Putting It All Together*

Our algorithm for fitting the cold start and warm start components at different frequencies is described in Algorithm 1. We note that:

- Since $\Theta_c$ is purely feature driven, it changes slowly and needs to be trained less frequently (e.g., once every few days or few weeks) but since $\Theta_w$ captures fast-changing item specific behaviors, it has to be updated quickly (e.g., every few minutes/hours).
- By treating $\Theta_c$ as a known offset in the model, $\Theta_w$ can either be obtained via running independent logistic regression for each item based on a moving window, or independent online logistic regression for each item learned on data that are split in batches. Our approach to online logistic regression utilizes the dynamic state space concept by using the posterior from the previous batch process as priors for the current batch to transition into a new state. In our current LASER system we adopt the moving window approach for simplicity. We plan to test the online logistic regression approach in the future.
- Although it may appear redundant to include $\Theta_w$ when estimating $\Theta_c$ using ADMM, this detail is in fact critical since without including $\Theta_w$ in the fitting of $\Theta_c$, we will introduce bias when estimating $\Theta_c$, especially when the clicks are sparse in the data (i.e. CTR is small).

## 3.3 Explore-Exploit with Thompson Sampling

The goal in online advertising is to estimate CTR to maximize revenue; improving out-of-sample predictive accuracy is not our main objective. This is an explore/exploit problem, and there is a positive utility associated with serving ads that have low empirical means but high variances. We exploit ads that are known to be good based on current knowledge for near term gains, but also explore those that could be potentially good for longer-term gains.

Several explore/exploit schemes have been used in the literature. Examples include epsilon-greedy, the upper confidence bound approach (UCB) [3, 14], Gittins index [8] and Thompson sampling [19, 18, 6]. Of these, Thompson sampling works well when the posterior distribution of parameters is available. [6] showed that Thompson sampling is better than other schemes like epsilon-greedy, UCB, and exploit-only approaches through simulation studies conducted on an advertising application. They however did not test it on a real advertising system. In our LASER system, we adopt Thompson sampling and find it to work well in practice.

**Algorithm 1** LASER Model Fitting Algorithm

```
for every D days do
  Obtain the most recent data and use ADMM to fit Θ_c and Θ_w
  simultaneously by treating item-id as features.
  for every M minutes do
    Obtain the most recent data
    Split the data by item id
    for each item j in parallel do
      Treat Θ_c as a given offset and fit (or update) {δ_j, η_j, ξ_j}
      (i.e. Θ_w for item j)
    end for
  end for
end for
```

The main idea of Thompson sampling is to draw a sample from the posterior of parameters $(\Theta_c, \Theta_w)$, and compute CTR based on the drawn sample instead of using the posterior mode. Intuitively, this introduces more exploration for ad campaigns that have high posterior variances due to small sample sizes. Since $\Theta_c$ is estimated using large amounts of data, we assume the posterior is peaked and always use the mode as a plug-in estimate. However, we do obtain the posterior of $\Theta_w$ and draw samples from it at serving time. We assume this posterior is Guassian centered around the estimated mean and posterior covariance. For simplicity and fast runtime computation, the posterior covariance matrix is assumed to be diagonal.

## 3.4 Efficient Computation of Interaction Terms

For computing CTR according to model described in Equation (3), we have to compute quadratic terms of the form $x_i' A c_j$, where $x_i$ and $c_j$ are feature vectors and $A$ is a matrix of coefficients. Computing these interaction terms at runtime can be expensive. We reduce this cost by pre-computing

$$\tilde{A}_j = A c_j$$

or the equivalent product with $x_i$. In general, the number of ads is smaller than number of users, hence it is more beneficial to compute $\tilde{A}_j$.

At the time of inference, the scoring system only computes the inner product $x_i' \tilde{A}_j$, saving considerable computation. This technique is particularly effective when the set of all $c_j$ is much smaller than the set of all $x_i$, since the offline pre-computation is not too costly and the set of $\tilde{A}_j$ coefficients can be effectively cached. The full set of $\tilde{A}_j$ values only needs to be computed when the original coefficients $A$ are updated, but new and changed items will need their $\tilde{A}_j$ values re-computed, either on demand or on a frequent schedule.

# 4. CONFIGURATION AND INFERENCE

In addition to achieving high performance on the typical metrics used to benchmark click prediction systems, the LASER system is designed to satisfy additional requirements needed for deployment in a web-scale advertising system. In the previous section, we described using ADMM to scale training on commodity cluster systems. In this section, we present our solutions to two additional challenges posed by our application: flexible configuration and real-time inference.

## 4.1 Flexible Configuration

Models rarely stay constant: we are always working to improve performance, introduce new features, and accommodate changes in the training data. To facilitate rapid model experimentation, LASER specifies the feature construction and transformation structure using a JSON-based [7] configuration language that drives both the training process and online inference. The model's feature processing is expressed through the arrangement of three types of components: *sources*, *transformers*, and *assemblers*, whose configurations can be changed and refined without code modifications or service restarts. We have developed a rich library of components that can be used without modification as well as standard interfaces for the implementation of application-specific functionality.

### *4.1.1 Sources*

Source components translate features from external sources into a numeric feature vector representation. The specification for sources is deliberately left rather vague: features can come from almost anywhere and be originally in any conceivable format. So long as the component can translate these features into a numerical vector, it can be used as a feature source.

For ad click prediction, we created sources for the user, ad campaign, and context features as described Section 3. The user and ad sources pull features off of the user profile and ad copy respectively, including both standardized features, like known entities, and less structured features, like the text of an ad. The context source encodes all information we have about where and when the ad is displayed, such as the time of the request, the page where it is to be shown, the displayed size, and the formatting of the ad.

The actual implementations of these sources are clearly specific to a given environment, but can often be reused widely within a site. For example, our user profile features are standardized across many applications and generated in a common format, so we can use the user source built for ad click models in all response prediction tasks that use user profile data as an input.

### *4.1.2 Transformers*

Like sources, transformers emit feature vectors; however, they are further constrained to only consume other feature vectors in the system as input (i.e. feature vector outputs from sources or other transformers). Transformers implement vector-to-vector functions that modify the feature vectors into a form that is more useful for a specific prediction task. Because they both consume and emit a common datatype, transformers are even more easily reused than sources.

Some examples of the basic transformers included in the LASER system are:

**Subset transformer**. Sources are typically written for maximum reuse, so they often include features that may not be useful in a given application. The subset transformer allows the modeler to specify exactly which features are needed (usually based on feature selection results), so that the dimensionality of the feature space can be reduced.

**Bucketing transformer**. Sometimes discretizing a numerical feature into several categorical features can provide better model performance. For example, we might have the time of a request encoded as seconds since midnight, but it's more useful to encode it as one of eight discrete 3 hour day parts. The bucketing transformer allows the model writer to specify how to encode a real valued feature into set of ordinal or categorical binary features, each representing a range of the original real value.

**Disjunction transformer**. The disjunction transformer combines several fine-grained binary features into a single coarser binary feature using the logical-OR operation.

**Interaction transformer**. The interaction transformer operates on a pair of inputs and computes their outer product. As a practical implementation matter, the interaction transformer also performs a subset operation using results from feature selection, since it is rare that all interaction features in the outer product are useful, and it is far less expensive to never compute them than to subset them in a subsequent transformer.

**Function transformer**. The function transformer applies a user-specified function to its input vector. Among other applications, this permits feature linearization and basis expansions.

### *4.1.3 Assembler*

The final component in the LASER feature transformation pipeline is the assembler. Unlike the other types, there is typically only a single assembler in the end of a model configuration file. The assembler takes inputs from each transformer or source output that is to be used in the model, and packages them together into a single block feature vector that is then used for model training, validation and inference.

### *4.1.4 Example Model*

In Figure 1 we provide a simple example of a LASER model with two feature sources and three transformers. This model obtains its input features from the user and the ad campaign sources. The feature vectors produced by each of these sources are fed through subset transformers, where we keep the country and occupation features from the user, and the title and body text features from the ad campaign. These vectors then become the input to an interaction transformer that creates interaction terms between the user's country and occupation and the ad campaign's title and body text. The assembler finally gathers the output feature vectors from the subset and interaction transformers and packages them for training and inference.

Should we wish to modify what feature terms are used in this model or how they are generated — e.g. by adding a third source, changing the features kept by the subset transformers, or modifying how feature vectors flow through the pipeline — we only need to change this JSON file. Extensive model changes can thus be made without modifying code in either the training or inference systems.

## 4.2 Real-time Inference

Given a trained model, predicting the CTR for a new event may appear trivial, but performing such inference in real-time at web scale presents a host of challenges. Each user visit generates one or more requests to LASER to score and rank between several hundred and a few thousand ads, with each request requiring features for the user, context and each ad. LASER must gather these features and score these requests quickly — typically within 10-20 milliseconds — to prevent delays in dependent systems.

```
{
  objects: [{
    "name": "user_source",
    "class": "org.laser.source.UserSource",
    "parameters": { ... }
  }, {
    "name": "ad_source",
    "class": "org.laser.source.AdSource",
    "parameters": { ... }
  }, {
    "name": "user_subset",
    "class": "org.laser.transformer.Subset",
    "parameters": {
      "input": "user_source",
      "features": ["country", "occupation"]
    }
  }, {
    "name": "ad_subset",
    "class": "org.laser.transformer.Subset",
    "parameters": {
      "input": "ad_source",
      "features": ["title", "body"]
    }
  },{
    "name": "user_ad_int",
    "class": "org.laser.transformer.Interaction",
    "parameters": {
      "inputs": [ "user_subset", "ad_subset" ],
      "interactions": [["country", "occupation"], ["title", "body"]]
    }
  }, {
    "name": "assembler",
    "class": "org.laser.assembler.Assembler",
    "parameters": {
      "inputs": ["user_subset", "ad_subset", "user_ad_int"]
    }
  }]
}
```

**Figure 1: A simple LASER model**

### *4.2.1 "Better Wrong Than Late"*

It often takes time to compute a feature vector. For example, the ad and user sources must retrieve feature data from a remote data store that may not be able to respond within the time window LASER has to process a request, particularly if we have to query for many items. The same situation would arise in the case of a transformer that has to perform a computationally expensive operation on its input.

One advantage of the logistic regression models we use is that they degrade gracefully when features are missing. Offline, we can compute the mean of each term in the model using an unbiased sample of impressions. Then if features are missing for a given term, we can substitute this expected value as a reasonable approximation to the term. LASER exploits this mechanism to ensure that scoring remains quick by treating as missing any features that are not immediately available.

We call this approach the "better wrong than late" philosophy, since slightly less accuracy is preferable to not being able to generate a prediction because data takes too long to arrive. Any component in a LASER model that expects to block or take excessively long to compute its output vector (typically, but not always, sources) is written such that it returns an empty value if the actual vector is not immediately available. When these empty values reach the assembler, the system will interpret them using the missing values for that part of the model. Processing of these vectors proceeds in a background thread and upon completion, the created feature vector is stored in a cache for instant lookup on subsequent requests that need the same data.

### *4.2.2 Caching And Lazy Evaluation*

All terms in a LASER model take the form of a dot product between a coefficient vector and a feature vector, both of which may be indexed by one or more of the entities present in the request being scored. A typical model has 10 or more such terms. We often observe that these terms recur unchanged across different items that are being scored. For example, in a single request, we may be asked to score multiple items for the same user $i$, so the term $x_i'\alpha$ can be reused. Or we may have a popular item $j$ that we need to score for all users visiting the site during a given period of time; in this case the term $c_j'\beta$ can be shared across all the users from different requests.

**Partial Results Cache.** We can save considerable time by caching the scalar values of each of these terms. Subsequent requests can use these cached values, saving the overhead of repeatedly computing the dot product. We call the structure that manages this operation the *Partial Results Cache (PRC)*, as it stores pieces of the final score. The entries in the PRC, which are simply these scalar dot products, are referenced using keys that uniquely identify the feature and coefficient vectors in the term. Because both the keys and values are small — unlike the feature vectors and coefficients — the PRC can be made very large, improving its effectiveness.

**Keyed Feature Vectors.** In order to index into the PRC, all sources and transformers emit *keyed feature vectors*, a combination of a string key and the actual feature vector. These keys obey the following two constraints:

1. For each component, the output vector's key must be computed from only information passed in on the request and/or the *keys*, but not the actual content, of any input vectors.
2. If two keyed feature vectors have equal keys, they must also have equal values.

Keyed feature vectors are implemented using *lazy evaluation* [12]. On each request, LASER components generate only the keys, which can be computed very quickly. The vector content is a *thunk* [13]: a function that can compute the actual vector on demand. On a PRC hit, the thunk is never evaluated so we do not pay the cost of constructing the actual feature vector.

How the sources and transformers obey these constraints is up to the implementor. In our application, we construct keys by combining the unique name of the source or transformer with identifying informatiom about the vector, such as the ID of the underlying item in the case of sources or the value of the input keys in transformers.

**Using the PRC for real-time inference.** To illustrate how the PRC helps with real-time inference, consider the user main effect term, $x_i'\alpha$, in the example model from Figure 1. Upon receiving a request, LASER passes request information into the pipeline, causing the user source to emit a keyed feature vector with a fully constructed key, which takes a form like "user_source:$i$". Provided all objects in the pipeline follow similar naming conventions, this form of key obeys the necessary constraints: because source and transformer names are unique, no other component will generate the same key for a different vector even if they refer to the same user $i$. Likewise, the keyed feature vectors for two different users will be different due to their different values of $i$. Finally, this form of key does not require any information other than what is available from the request.

This keyed feature vector then passes to the user subset transformer, which emits its own keyed feature vector. This vector has the key, "user_subet:user_source:$i$", which again follows the constraints by relying on the uniqueness of both the transformer name and input key to guarantee uniqueness of the output key. At this time, neither the user source nor the user subset transformer has done any computation to create the actual vector values.

When scoring this section of the model, the inference engine will use the keyed feature vector's key and a key that identifies the coefficient vector[1] to look up the scalar value of the term in the PRC.

[1] Because coefficients do not flow through an abitrary transformer pipeline, keying them is considerably easier. In our implementation, we simply use the identity of the coefficient term, $\alpha$ in this case, along with an identifier of the model, such as a unique name or version number.

If the PRC contains that value, then no further work needs to be done: all scoring for this section has been reduced to some tiny string manipulations and a cache lookup.

On a PRC miss, we first execute the thunk in the keyed feature vector produced by the user subset transformer. This thunk performs the actual subset computation, but first needs the original user feature vector, which it obtains by evaluating the thunk in the user source's keyed feature vector. Once all the lazy computations complete, the inference engine can use the final vector value along with the coefficients to compute the dot product, which it then puts into the PRC for reuse.

**PRC effectiveness** Figure 2(a) demonstrates the effectiveness of these techniques using a LASER model with around 20K binary features in the cold-start section. The number of features in the warm-start section depends on the total number of campaigns we train. We typically see 20-100 non-sparse entries in the feature vector for a single item in a request. For this test, we took a single instance of LASER running in a production ad serving environment and disabled the Partial Results Cache for a period of about 30 minutes. During this test, we saw response times leap 49% from a baseline of 9.4ms to a peak of 14.0ms. Upon reactivating the caches, performance immediately dropped back to pre-test levels. Below, we show the marginal cost of scoring an item using LASER with the PRC is approximately 6$\mu$s, so the additional 5.6ms latency is equivalent to scoring an additional 930 items. During this test, we were scoring 927 items on average, so disabling the PRC is equivalent to doubling the size of the request. Despite only caching computation — slow, off-process communication is handled by additional caching layers — the PRC is a major contribution to LASER's speed and scalability.

#### *4.2.3 Performance Evaluation*

To evaluate the scalability of the LASER system, we gathered one week's worth of performance data at two hour increments from an instance serving live ad traffic. Figure 2(b) plots LASER's average time to score a request against the number of requests received per second. As the request volume increases, LASER's latency is largely unaffected: we observe no significant correlation between the number of requests per second and the time it takes to process each one. This is not surprising since there are no explicit dependencies between requests (i.e. LASER inference is "embarrasingly parallel"), so additional requests can be handled easily up until machine resources are exhausted or lock contention on shared caches becomes an issue. In our experience, this tipping point occurs at around 300-350 requests per second per server with existing hardware, beyond which latencies rise dramatically.

Figure 2(c) shows LASER's time per request against the average number of items being scored per request. This graph shows a very clear ($R^2 = 0.98$) linear correlation between items scored and response time: each additional item adds about 6$\mu$s to the request time. LASER can thus easily be scaled to rank thousands of items per request while still maintaining real-time responsiveness. If the number of items increases to the point that latency becomes an issue, it is usually straightforward to break them apart so that they can be serviced by separate threads or even servers.

## 5. EXPERIMENTS

In this section we describe our experimental results on the following aspects: (a). A convergence study of ADMM comparing the original ADMM to the improved version that includes better initialization and adaptive selection of step size $\rho$. (b). An offline experiment that compares the full model in Equation (1) - (3) with a couple of baseline models. (c). An online A/B test result showing the performance of our LASER models with and without Thompson sampling.

We denote the models considered in our experiments as follows:

- CONTROL is a per-campaign CTR counting model that gets updated per 15 minutes. For each item (campaign) $j$, it obtains the number of clicks $NC_j$ and number of views $NV_j$ from the entire campaign history, and the predicted CTR is equal to $NC_j/NV_j$.
- COLD-ONLY is the cold-start-component-only model that models $s_{ijt}$ by

$$s_{ijt} = \omega + s_{ijt}^{1,c} + s_{ijt}^{2,c}. \tag{13}$$

- LASER is the full model that is specified in Equation (1) - (3) that contains both the cold-start component and the warm-start component. At serving time LASER uses the posterior mean of $\Theta_w$ to score, which means for new campaigns with no data in the previous batches, all the warm-start coefficients are 0.
- LASER-EE is the LASER model that uses Thompson sampling in the serving time. To be conservative we adjust the posterior variance of $\Theta_w$ by 0.1. We note that the adjustment of the posterior variance in Thompson sampling is a common practice that may provide better performance [6].

### 5.1 The Data

Our data for offline experiments consist of 45 days of advertising event logs for a major social network site from July 16 to August 29, 2012. We use the first 30 days of data as training and the last 15 days data as test. To fit models, we down-sampled the negatives but re-adjusted the probabilities to obtain CTR estimates on the original scale. After downsampling, both the training and test sets consist of hundreds of millions of events.

We use thousands of features for $x_i$ and $c_j$ for both user and item (ad campaign), and hundreds of features for the context feature $z_t$. For instance, the ad campaign features include n-grams, categories, advertiser characteristics, among others. The context features include time of day, day of week, the page id that the ad is shown, and the format id that the ad is placed with. We use mutual information and the minimum support criteria to do feature selection on these features and the two-way interactions between all pairs. Finally we obtain a cold-start feature set that contains roughly 20K binary features. We note that 20K is just the dimensionality of the cold-start features; the total number of warm-start features that occur in the model depends on the total number of campaigns. To predict CTR for a user, campaign and context triplet, roughly 20-100 such binary features occur per example.

### 5.2 The Study of ADMM Convergence

In Figure 3 we compare the convergence speed of the original ADMM algorithm [4] with the improved ADMM algorithm using the two variations described in Section 3.2: the initialization of the consensus $\Theta^0$ at the first iteration, and an exponential decay of step size $\rho$ over iterations. In Figure 3 the average test log-likelihood versus the number of iterations is shown. We use ADMM to denote the original algorithm, ADMM-M to denote the ADMM algorithm with only the consensus initialization but without adaptive $\rho$ and ADMM-MA to denote the ADMM algorithm with both consensus initialization and adaptive $\rho$. We note that the consensus initialization significantly boosts the convergence rate of ADMM in terms of the test log-likelihood. With consensus initialization, the test log-likelihood of the first iteration of ADMM-M is close to the test

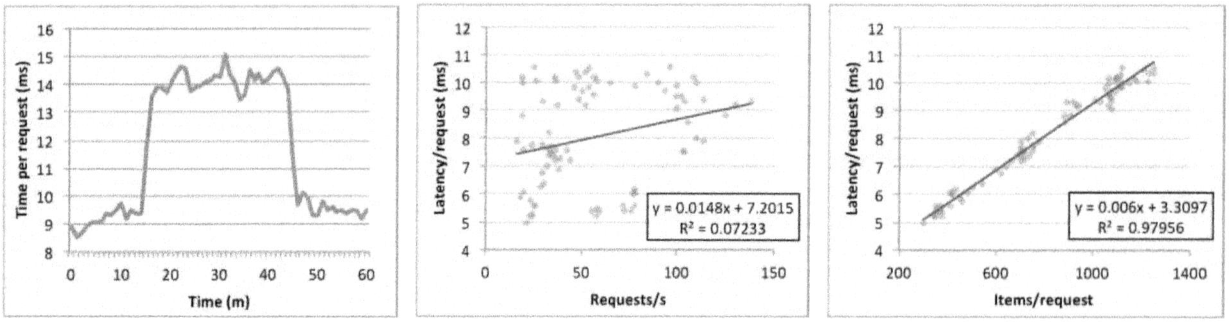


(a) Effect of disabling PRC (b) Latency versus request frequency (c) Latency versus request size

**Figure 2: LASER performance tests**

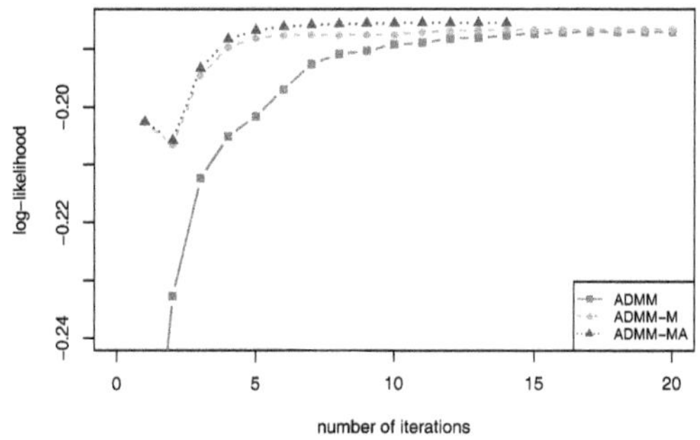


**Figure 3: Convergence of the original ADMM compared to ADMM with initialization and adaptive $\rho$.**

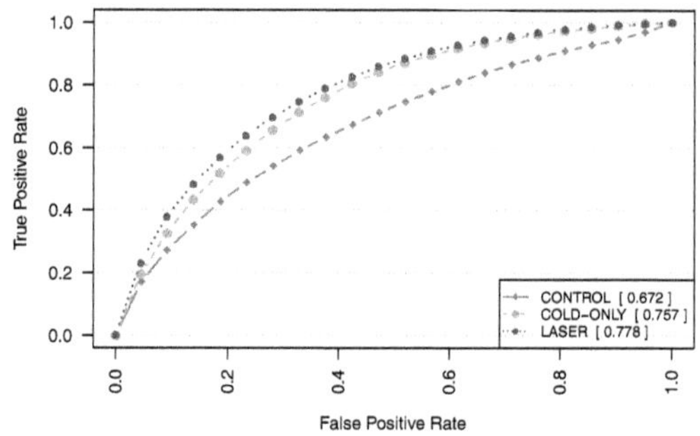


**Figure 4: Offline AUC of the LASER model compared to CONTROL and COLD-ONLY baseline models.**

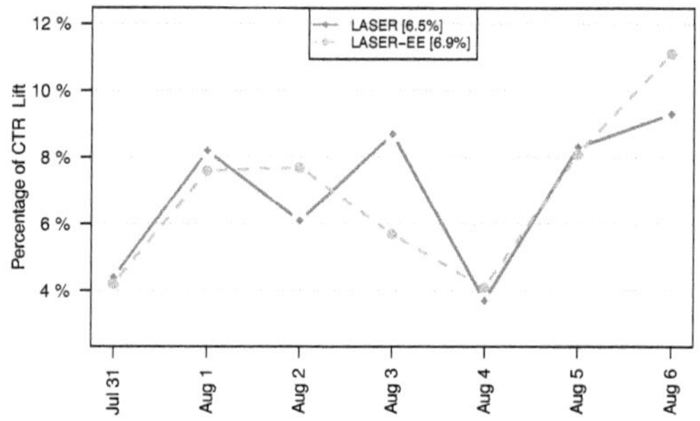


**Figure 5: Percent improvement in CTR for LASER and LASER-EE versus CONTROL, Jul. 31–Aug. 6.**

log-likelihood from the 6th iteration of ADMM. Making $\rho$ to adaptively evolve across iterations makes the convergence even faster. Figure 3 shows that it only takes ADMM-MA 6 iterations to reach the same log-likelihood that ADMM takes 20 iterations to reach. The two modifications to ADMM above reduced the model training time by approximately 70% for our data.

## 5.3 Offline Experiments

Using the data described in Section 5.1 we compare the performance of our LASER model to two baselines: the CONTROL model which only uses the campaign-CTR as the score (i.e. similar to warm-start only model), and the COLD-ONLY model which only contains the cold-start component. The ROC curves along with the AUC values (numbers in the legend of the figure) for the three models are shown in Figure 4. It is obvious that our LASER model that consists of both cold start and the warm start components provide the best performance in terms of the predictive accuracy.

## 5.4 Online A/B Test Results

In this section we show the result of an online A/B test experiment that was run from July 31 to August 6, 2013 in the advertising system of a major social network site. The site traffic is split randomly by user id into three buckets: CONTROL (10%), LASER (85%) and LASER-EE (5%). In general, we routinely run several such tests in our system and ramp new models that perform better than the status quo.

**Overall performance**. In this example, the daily performance lifts over CONTROL for LASER and LASER-EE in terms of two major business-related metrics CTR and CPM (cost per impression) are shown in Figure 5 and 6 (The overall improvements are shown in the figure legends). We note that for both metrics, LASER and LASER-EE are significantly and consistently better than CONTROL (more than 6.5% CTR lift and more than 10.5% CPM lift over the 7 days). On the other hand, the overall performance of LASER and LASER-EE are similar. This is interesting, since one would intuitively expect the latter to be inferior due to the exploration cost, because both models share the same training data.

**Segmented analysis by campaign warmness**. To better understand the difference between LASER and LASER-EE, we split the observed data into 8 different segments based on the "degree of warmness" of the campaigns. The **degree of warmness** for a campaign at a given time is defined as the number of training samples in the training data before the specified time that contain the campaign. We are unable to reveal the actual splitting criteria of the segments, but they are obtained through logarithmic binning on campaign sample size. We also note that segment #1 contains

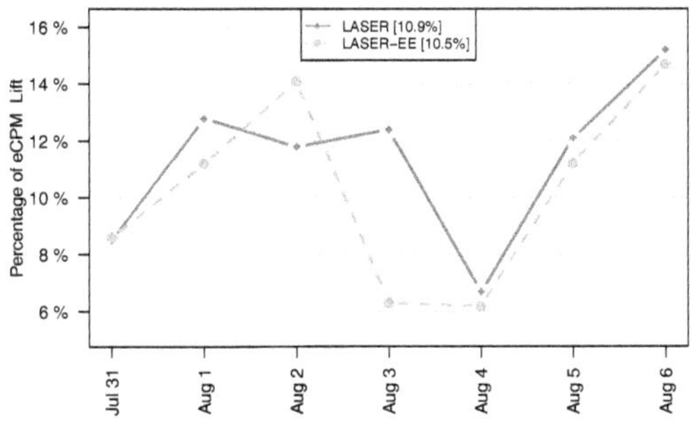


**Figure 6: Percent improvement in CPM for LASER and LASER-EE versus CONTROL, Jul. 31–Aug. 6.**

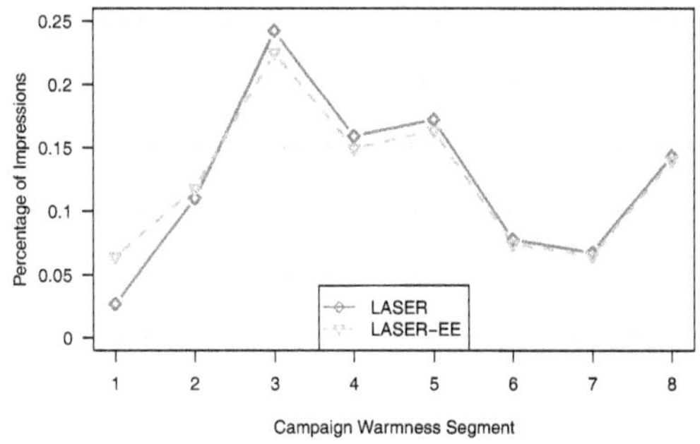


**Figure 7: Fraction of impressions served by LASER-EE and LASER for the 8 campaign warmness segments.**

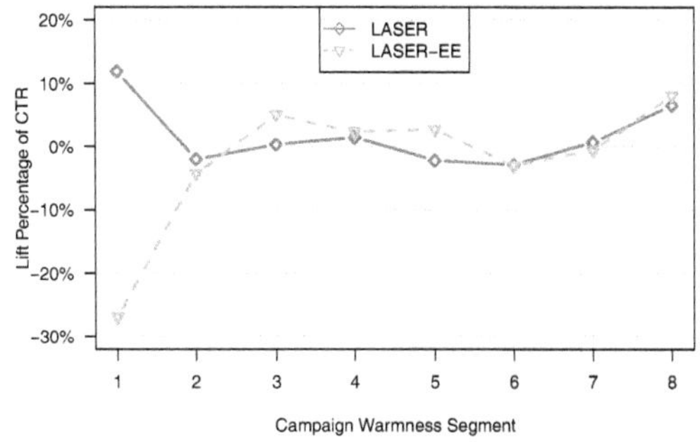


**Figure 8: Percent improvement in CTR for LASER and LASER-EE versus CONTROL by campaign warmness segment.**

the campaigns with almost no data in training, while segment #8 consists of campaigns that are served most heavily in the previous batches so that their CTR can be estimated quite accurately. The distributions of the number of impressions over the 8 segments served by LASER and LASER-EE are shown in Figure 7, and the CTR and CPM lifts of LASER and LASER-EE over CONTROL for the 8 campaign warmness segments are shown in Figure 8 and 9. From these figures we note the following interesting points:

- For the "cold-start" campaigns that have very little data to learn from (i.e. segment #1), the CTR and CPM performance of LASER-EE are significantly worse than LASER model and CONTROL due to its exploration property. Due to the same reason, more impressions are also served in this segment for LASER-EE relative to LASER, due to higher posterior variances of the warm-start coefficients.

- For segment #1 LASER is much better than CONTROL. This is because the cold-start features are helpful in providing a good CTR estimate for relatively new campaigns. The fact that cold-start features help is also corroborated by the AUC numbers in offline experiments.

- LASER-EE provides significantly better performance for both CTR and CPM than LASER in segments #3 to #5, and from the impression distribution plot it is clear that these three segments are the segments with the largest amount of traffic. This is expected since winners in these segments were able to win despite the optimism Thompson sampling provided to new campaigns that were participating in these auctions, hence only the best would win. This is not the case for LASER where the cold-start campaigns use an average CTR estimate. It is interesting to note that for LASER-EE the losses due to exploration are compensated by the increased performance in these segments.

**Number of campaigns served.** Although from our A/B test experiments LASER-EE does not provide better performance than LASER in terms of overall CTR and CPM, it provides valuable exploration data that can be used by the exploit-only model LASER. It also adds more diversity in terms of number of campaigns served to a user segment, which is good for the long-term marketplace health. This can be seen in Figure 10, the percentage increase in the number of campaigns served by LASER-EE over LASER. Note that the bucket size of LASER-EE is only 5% while LASER's bucket size is 85%. For a fair comparison we did 20 bootstraps within the LASER bucket to obtain 20 sampled 5% buckets. We then take an average of the number of campaigns and the number of impressions served over the 20 bootstrap samples for each campaign warmness segment for LASER. It is obvious from the figure that for almost all segments LASER-EE is serving significantly more campaigns than LASER, in every campaign segment.

Although it is difficult to compare LASER-EE and LASER since the latter learns from exploration data generated by the former, the results above show that in our system, LASER-EE, with an explore/exploit scheme built-in, is better than its exploit-only counterpart. In general, we recommend running Thompson sampling and its exploit only counterpart together and analyzing the explore/exploit behavior. It is worthwhile to start with the explore/exploit model on a relatively smaller fraction (e.g. 5%-10%) and gradually ramp up, based on performance.

**Observed vs expected ratio.** Another offline metric that we have found very useful before launching a new model on live traffic is the ratio of observed versus expected number of clicks (o/e ratio). The observed number of clicks is simply the number of clicks in the data and the expected number of clicks can be computed by the sum of the predicted CTR for each impression. Since in serving time only the top-ranked campaigns are served for each impression and there are often thousands of campaigns to be ranked in the auction, selection bias tends to choose campaigns with over-estimated CTR (also referred to as winner's curse). Therefore, a good CTR prediction model should have lower curse, reflected in an o/e ratio that is close to unity. In Figure 11 we show such ratios for LASER, LASER-EE and CONTROL. It is obvious that LASER and LASER-EE in general have a much better o/e ratio than CONTROL, and it is also not surprising that LASER-EE has the worst o/e ratio for the segment #1 ("cold-start") since it is mainly exploring there. We have found this offline metric to be a better indicator of online model performance than standard out-of-sample predictive accuracy metrics like AUC and log-likelihood that are used to measure quality of a supervised learning algorithm.

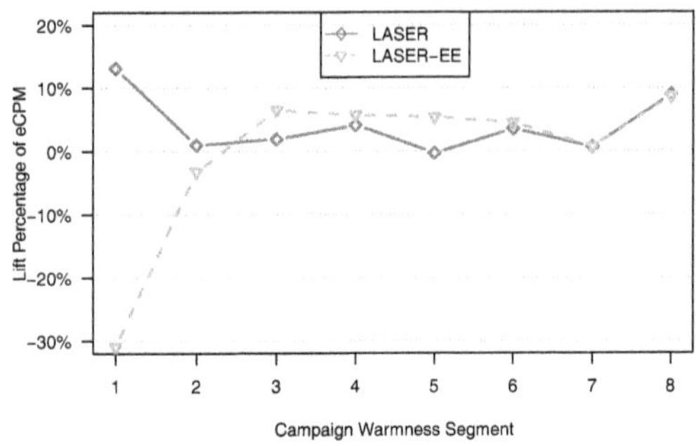


**Figure 9: Percent improvement in eCPM for LASER and LASER-EE versus CONTROL by campaign warmness segment.**

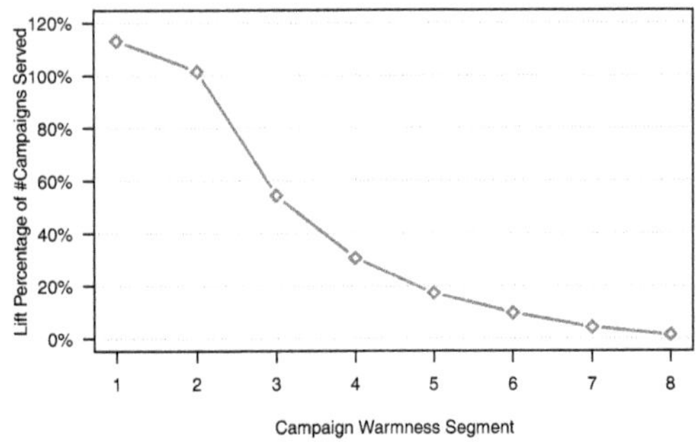


**Figure 10: Increase in number of campaigns served by LASER-EE versus LASER by campaign warmness segment.**

# 6. CONCLUSION

We introduced LASER, a scalable response prediction platform used as a part of a social network advertising system. Although the logistic regression model we used is standard, the major contribution of this paper comes from integrating several key components to obtain a scalable, reliable and accurate end-to-end system. These include: a large-scale model fitting algorithm that uses ADMM with modifications, a novel system design that enables flexible configuration and fast inference with low latency, and an explore-exploit serving scheme using Thompson sampling with interesting insights illustrated through A/B tests on a live system.

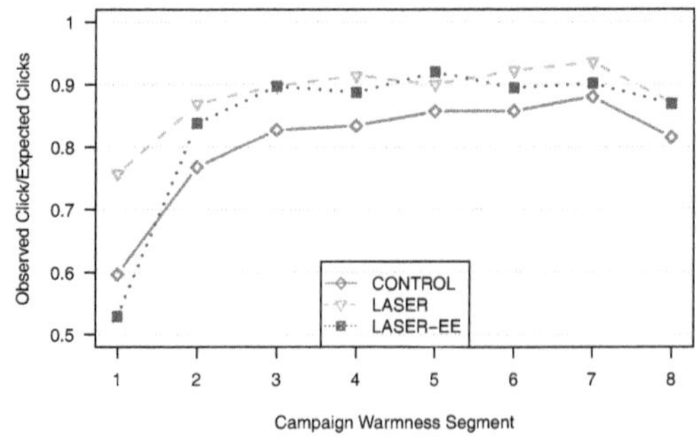


**Figure 11: Ratio of observed to expected clicks served by LASER-EE and LASER by campaign warmness segment.**

# 7. REFERENCES


[1] D. Agarwal, R. Agrawal, R. Khanna, and N. Kota. Estimating rates of rare events with multiple hierarchies through scalable log-linear models. In *KDD*, pages 213–222. ACM, 2010.

[2] D. Agarwal and M. Gurevich. Fast top-k retrieval for model based recommendation. In *WSDM*, pages 483–492, 2012.

[3] P. Auer, N. Cesa-Bianchi, and P. Fischer. Finite-time analysis of the multiarmed bandit problem. *Machine learning*, 47(2-3):235–256, 2002.

[4] S. Boyd, N. Parikh, E. Chu, B. Peleato, and J. Eckstein. Distributed optimization and statistical learning via the alternating direction method of multipliers. *Foundations and Trends® in Machine Learning*, 3(1):1–122, 2011.

[5] A. Broder. Computational advertising. In *SODA*, pages 992–992, 2008.

[6] O. Chapelle and L. Li. An empirical evaluation of thompson sampling. In *NIPS*, pages 2249–2257, 2011.

[7] D. Crockford. RFC 4627: The application/json media type for JavaScript object notation (JSON), June 2006.

[8] J. C. Gittins. Bandit processes and dynamic allocation indices. *Journal of the Royal Statistical Society. Series B (Methodological)*, pages 148–177, 1979.

[9] S. Goel, J. Langford, and A. L. Strehl. Predictive indexing for fast search. In *NIPS*, pages 505–512, 2008.

[10] T. Graepel, J. Q. Candela, T. Borchert, and R. Herbrich. Web-Scale Bayesian Click-Through rate Prediction for Sponsored Search Advertising in Microsoft's Bing Search Engine. In *ICML'10*, pages 13–20, 2010.

[11] D. Hillard, S. Schroedl, E. Manavoglu, H. Raghavan, and C. Leggetter. Improving ad relevance in sponsored search. In *WSDM*, pages 361–370, 2010.

[12] P. Hudak. Conception, evolution, and application of functional programming languages. *ACM Computing Surveys*, 21(3):359–411, September 1989.

[13] P. Ingerman. Thunks: a way of compiling procedure statements with some comments on procedure declarations. *Communications of the ACM*, 4(1):55–58, January 1961.

[14] L. Li, W. Chu, J. Langford, and R. E. Schapire. A contextual-bandit approach to personalized news article recommendation. In *WWW*, pages 661–670. ACM, 2010.

[15] C.-J. Lin, R. C. Weng, and S. S. Keerthi. Trust region newton method for logistic regression. *JMLR*, 9:627–650, 2008.

[16] H. B. McMahan, G. Holt, D. Sculley, M. Young, D. Ebner, J. Grady, L. Nie, T. Phillips, E. Davydov, D. Golovin, S. Chikkerur, D. Liu, M. Wattenberg, A. M. Hrafnkelsson, T. Boulos, and J. Kubica. Ad click prediction: a view from the trenches. In *KDD*, 2013.

[17] M. Richardson, E. Dominowska, and R. Ragno. Predicting clicks: estimating the click-through rate for new ads. In *WWW*, 2007.

[18] S. L. Scott. A modern bayesian look at the multi-armed bandit. *Applied Stochastic Models in Business and Industry*, 26(6):639–658, 2010.

[19] W. R. Thompson. On the likelihood that one unknown probability exceeds another in view of the evidence of two samples. *Biometrika*, 25(3/4):285–294, 1933.

[20] K. Weinberger, A. Dasgupta, J. Langford, A. Smola, and J. Attenberg. In *ICML*, pages 1113–1120, 2009.

[21] M. Zaharia, M. Chowdhury, M. J. Franklin, S. Shenker, and I. Stoica. Spark: cluster computing with working sets. In *Proceedings of the 2nd USENIX conference on Hot topics in cloud computing*, pages 10–10, 2010.

[22] C. Zhu, R. H. Byrd, P. Lu, and J. Nocedal. Algorithm 778: L-bfgs-b: Fortran subroutines for large-scale bound-constrained optimization. *ACM Transactions on Mathematical Software (TOMS)*, 23(4):550–560, 1997.

# Discovering Common Motifs in Cursor Movement Data for Improving Web Search

Dmitry Lagun
Emory University
dlagun@mathcs.emory.edu

Mikhail Ageev *
Moscow State University
mageev@yandex.ru

Qi Guo *
Microsoft
qiguo@microsoft.com

Eugene Agichtein
Emory University
eugene@mathcs.emory.edu

## ABSTRACT

Web search behavior and interaction data, such as mouse cursor movements, can provide valuable information on how searchers examine and engage with the web search results. This interaction data is far richer than traditional search click data, and can be used to improve search ranking, evaluation, and presentation. Unfortunately, the diversity and complexity inherent in this interaction data make it more difficult to capture salient behavior characteristics through traditional feature engineering. To address this problem, we introduce a novel approach of *automatically discovering* frequent subsequences, or motifs, in mouse cursor movement data. In order to scale our approach to realistic datasets, we introduce novel optimizations for motif discovery, specifically designed for mining cursor movement data. As a practical application, we show that by encoding the motifs discovered from thousands of real web search sessions as features, enables significant improvements on result relevance estimation and re-ranking tasks, compared to a state-of-the-art baseline that relies on extensive feature engineering. These results, complemented with visualization and qualitative analysis, demonstrate that our approach is able to automatically capture key characteristics of mouse cursor movement behavior, providing a valuable new tool for search behavior analysis.

## Keywords

Web search behavior mining; mouse cursor movement analysis; web search ranking and evaluation

## 1. INTRODUCTION

Millions of users interact with Web search engines daily. These interaction patterns contain valuable information, which could be useful for search engines to improve user experience, and for site designers to improve website layout and usability [2, 11, 6, 32]. Recently, studying fine-grained user behavior such as eye-gaze movements [16, 11, 7] and mouse cursor movements [38, 18, 27] have become an active area of research, as these interactions provide additional insights into searcher behavior compared to coarser models of clicks alone. In particular, recent work has demonstrated the coordination between eye gaze position and mouse cursor movements [38, 19, 25] and showed that both gaze and cursor interactions indicate user preferences [7, 27, 20]. Search engine companies also began investigating and modelling the cursor movement data to improve understanding of search result examination patterns [38], ranking of search results [26, 43], understanding of search result abandonment [27], and evaluation of content layout and noticeability [36].

While the importance of analyzing mouse cursor data for search is now evident, it often involves intensive manual effort [7, 20, 25] to gain insights about the data, and to make use of it for practical applications. For example, video recordings (or, similarly, a series of snapshots) from online analytic services, typically allow the replay of visitor interactions in great detail, but the process of viewing the replays is time-consuming – it is virtually impossible to view all the replays even for a relatively small site with thousands of daily visits, not to mention for larger web sites with millions of visitors. The alternative approach of visualizing areas of high cursor activity by using "heatmaps", that use different colors to indicate different levels of activity, provides a more complete view of the user behavior data in aggregate, but suffers from loss of detail about the sequences of interactions of individual users.

In this paper, we propose a novel technique to *automatically* and *efficiently* extract common patterns from search result and landing page examination data, obtained via mouse cursor tracking. Our method, based on frequent subsequence mining, is able to capture common user- and location-invariant sequences from the mouse cursor data, some of which would be difficult to identify or describe by manual inspection or feature engineering. In data mining literature, such frequent sub-sequences have been called *motifs* [34] because of the analogy to their discrete counterparts in computational biology. For the rest of the paper, we adapt the term *motif* to refer to a frequent pattern, representing a group of similar subsequences derived from the the mouse cursor movement data. We will define mouse cursor motifs more precisely in Section 3.

An example of a common motif extracted from the mouse cursor data is shown in Figure 1. This motif corresponds to the common search behavior of "following" examination behavior (identified by Rodden et al. [38]). In this example, the user appears to examine the second and third search results, before returning to click on the first result. This behavior could be used to infer that a user has examined the second and third results and judged them to be non-relevant, providing valuable additional information to augment the click data.

*Work done at Emory University.


*WSDM'14*, February 24–28, 2014, New York, New York, USA.

http://dx.doi.org/10.1145/2556195.2556265.

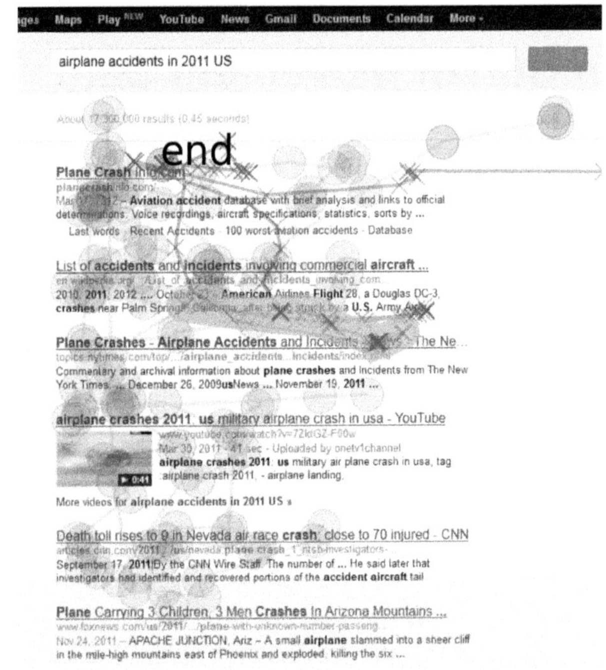


Figure 1: An example automatically discovered motif from mouse cursor data (shaded in green), corresponding to the common "follow" searcher behavior, where gaze (red circles) briefly follows the mouse cursor (blue crosses). The "end" label indicates the result click.

As searchers examine results and pages at different rates, it is difficult to find exact matches between mouse cursor movements across different users. For this reason, we adapt a more robust distance measure, namely Dynamic Time Warping (DTW), that is capable to identify similar mouse cursor trajectories. However, discovering such motifs from large cursor movement datasets is computationally expensive, and is not feasible with existing motif mining techniques. To address this problem, we propose novel optimizations for motif discovery, specifically designed for cursor movement data, based on spatial indexing and learning-based similarity metrics. These optimizations enable an order of magnitude speed-up in motif discovery on realistic datasets. As a practical application, the cursor movement motifs discovered by our approach can then be used as *features* for more accurate estimation of search result relevance and for significantly improving the quality of search result ranking.

Specifically, our contributions are threefold:

- A new scalable method for automatically discovering frequent patterns, or motifs, from cursor movement data (Section 3).
- The first empirical study of common mouse cursor motifs discovered from real web search examination data (Section 4).
- A practical demonstration of using the discovered mouse cursor motifs as features, resulting in significant improvements on search relevance estimation and re-ranking tasks (Section 5).

Next, we describe related work, in order to place our contributions in context.

## 2. RELATED WORK

The related work spans several areas of research, namely web search behavior and interaction mining, time series mining, and fast similarity search.

**Mouse Cursor Data in Web Search**: Modeling searcher attention and interest has wide-ranging applications in web search ranking, evaluation, and interface design. while traditionally most of the experimental work on user attention relied on infrared eye tracking which allows tracking eye movement on computer screen at great detail, however recently, mouse cursor tracking emerged as more accessible and scalable proxy for user's attention (e.g., [19] and [25]). One of the earliest studies of mouse cursor and eye gaze alignment in search was reported by Rodden et al. [38], where the authors discovered the coordination between a user's eye movements and mouse movements when scanning a web search results page, and identified three patterns of active mouse usage: *following the eye vertically with the mouse*, *following the eye horizontally with the mouse*, and *using the mouse to mark a promising result*. Guo and Agichtein [19] extended this work to predict eye-mouse coordination (i.e., whether the mouse cursor is in close proximity to eye gaze at any given point in time) by modeling mouse movements. This work was further extended by Huang et al. [25] to directly predict the gaze position from mouse cursor movement. These efforts solidify the evidence that a user's attention in web search can be approximated by using mouse cursor movement and other interaction data.

In addition to studying user attention, mouse cursor data have been used for more practical tasks. Goecks and Shavlik [15] modeled user actions such as mouse activity to infer user's interest in web pages. Shapira [41] studied several mouse cursor-based implicit interest indicators and found that the ratio of mouse movement to reading time was a good indicator of the explicit page rating. Guo and Agichtein [17] modeled mouse cursor movement and other interactions for inferring general search intent such as *navigational* vs. *informational*, as well as other intent categories, allowing for more accurate future ad clickthrough prediction [18]. Huang et al. [27] found that hovering over a search result provides indication of relevance in addition to result clickthrough. Huang et al. [26] also developed models to predict result clickthrough by incorporating mouse hovering and scrolling information. White and Buscher [43] proposed a method that uses text selections as implicit feedback. Guo and Agichtein [20] proposed a *Post Click Behavior (PCB)* model to estimate the "intrinsic" relevance by engineering a wide array of features to capture post-click behavior such as mouse cursor movements and scrolling, resulting in substantial improvements in estimating personalized search relevance and re-ranking search results. Recently, Ageev et al. [1] demonstrated that cursor data collected on search result landing pages can also be used to improve quality of search result summaries, or "snippets".

Unfortunately, mouse cursor activity is complex and noisy, and often specific to each user (e.g., [43]) – making it difficult to effectively discover robust predictive features. Previous approaches, therefore, relied on extensive feature engineering (e.g., [20] and [23]) to manually craft features applicable a specific task (e.g. relevance prediction). In contrast, we propose to *automatically* discover common mouse cursor movement patterns, by adapting time series analysis techniques from the data mining literature, to complement manual feature engineering used in prior research.

**Time Series Mining**: Research on mining time series databases included several directions: constructing low cardinality symbolized representations such as *iSAX* [42], Piecewise Aggregate Approximation [13] or other types of representations, such as discrete Fourier Transform or Discrete Wavelet Transform, for more comprehensive review consult [42]. Principle Component Analysis (PCA) [28] is another popular dimensionality reduction technique employed for indexing and fast search in time series data bases. Despite the efficiency benefits offered by dimensionality reduction techniques, they only provide approximate search with respect to the original representation, hence potentially degrading the accuracy of retrieval and thus potentially missing important patterns.

Taking a different tack, exact search in time series databases can also be significantly sped-up by various pruning strategies. The most well-known pruning strategies rely on some sort of a lower bound, after calculating which, one can decide whether exact distance calculation is needed or it can be abandoned. Such lower bounds include LB_Kim [31], LB_Yi [45], LB_Keogh [29] and LB_Improved [33]. Among them, LB_Keogh, introduced by Keogh [29], exhibited excellent performance, and was successfully used in many time series applications [29]. Recently, Mueen et al.[35] introduced an efficient exact motif discovery algorithm, known as the KM algorithm.

Recall, that in order to account for the high variability between users' examination speeds and different page layouts, we would like to use a more flexible distance measure, such as Dynamic Time Warping (DTW). DTW [39] was initially introduced for spoken word recognition, but since then, DTW has been applied to a variety of applications including hand writing recognition, information retrieval, image recognition, shape matching for security purposes. We refer an interested reader to the comprehensive review[29, 33, 30]. DTW allows matching two time series with possibly different lengths by computing the closest warping path between them. Thus, it is a flexible distance measure that is able to tolerate a web surfer's own pace of mouse cursor movement, allowing us to discover common cursor movements across different users. Unfortunately, the KM algorithm [35] was specifically designed for finding motifs under Euclidian Distance, for which triangle inequality holds, and is therefore not appropriate for pattern discovery with DTW as the distance measure.

More recently, there has been an effort in mining predictive subsequences, called *shapelets*, from labeled data [44] or un-labeled [46] time series data. Unfortunately, in applications with large amounts of data, where coverage of the extracted motifs is important (e.g., for asking questions such as "how many users perform a particular mouse cursor movement?"), previous approaches do not scale up to large datasets. That is, in our setting we are interested in finding *all occurrences* of a common motif, and not merely a single re-occurrence of a given pattern.

**Similarity Search**: The most common approach to speed-up search for similar objects is to construct an index that allows pruning far objects without computation of similarity measure for each object in index. The main idea for pruning similarity search is to prune far objects using triangle inequality [47]. For Euclidean distance in a low-dimensional space there are efficient indexing techniques such as R-Tree [4], approximation trees [40], and $k$-d Tree [9]. But the DTW distance measure does not satisfy triangle inequality [33], and a heuristic approach is required to build an efficient index for a specific application [12]. Similarity measure learning has received significant attention in machine learning community, primarily in clustering applications [5, 10, 3]. Surprisingly, to the best of our knowledge, learning-based similarity measures have not yet been applied to optimize similarity search in time series databases.

In summary, prior work on using cursor data for implicit feedback heavily relied on manually engineering cursor movement features in order to capture specific aspects of the cursor movement. This process can be tedious and time-consuming, and has to be re-done for each application. Our work proposes a general approach that *automatically* and *efficiently* discovers common mouse cursor motifs, which are not easily described by manual feature engineering. To accomplish this, our work builds upon the state-of-the art in time series mining, allowing for efficient motif extraction at scale, specifically optimized for mining cursor movement data.

# 3. MOTIF MINING FROM CURSOR DATA

This section describes our pattern (motif) extraction system. First, we define mouse cursor motifs more precisely, and state the problem more formally. Then, we describe, in turn, the key components of our solution, that involves first generating and pre-processing many possible candidate subsequences, and then efficiently computing the similarity between them to find the groups of similar subsequences to discover the frequent motifs. Thus, the steps are, respectively, *Candidate Generation and Pre-Processing* (Section 3.2), *Similarity Computation* (Section 3.4) and *Efficient Computation of a Distance Measure* (Section 3.5), which together comprise our frequent motif discovery method.

## 3.1 Problem Statement

We start with introducing the necessary notation to define a motif and our problem. Intuitively, we first need to define what constitutes a non-trivial *match* between subsequences in cursor movement data, and then use this definition to define frequent subsequences (or motifs), and in turn state our motif discovery problem more precisely.
**Match**: Given a positive real number $R$ as the range, or maximum distance, and a dataset of time series of cursor movements containing subsequences $A$ and $B$, then $B$ is called a matching subsequence of $A$, if $Dist(A, B) \leq R$, and $A$ and $B$ were recorded from *different* page visits. Here $Dist(\cdot, \cdot)$ a generic distance measure, such as Euclidian Distance or Dynamic Time Warping (DTW), defined below. The reason to insist on different page visits is to avoid "trivial" matches, most notably where $A$ and $B$ significantly overlap.
**Motif**: For a set of two dimensional time series $T = \{(x_i, y_i)\}_{i=1}^N$, and a subsequence length $n$, a *motif* $M$ is defined as the subsequence $M$ in $T$ that has at least $min\_count$ matches, as defined above.
**Cursor Motif Discovery Problem**: Given a set of two-dimensional time series representing mouse cursor movements $T = \{(x_i, y_i)\}_{i=1}^N$, the range $R$, the subsequence length $n$, and a threshold $min\_count$, *find all motifs* with match count higher than ($min\_count$) and the distance $Dist(\cdot, \cdot)$ between each two of them is at least $R$.

## 3.2 Candidate generation and pre-processing

At this step our system creates all possible motif candidates that will be matched against each other in the similarity search. The candidate motifs are generated by maintaining a sliding window of a given length and shifting it for every example in the database. Every shift of the time window creates a motif candidate. In our experiments we used a sliding window of 5 seconds. We experimented with different values during development, and chose 5 seconds as long enough to capture interesting behavior patterns, and yet short enough to be able to capture short-term page visits. Other parameter values might be possible, to be explored further in future work.

After a candidate sequence has been generated, we normalize the values by subtracting the means of the $x$ and $y$ coordinates for that given candidate. This step is crucial as it allows us to match subsequences in different regions of the page, focusing on the their *shape similarity* instead of mining sub-sequences that occur in the same region area of screen. We do not otherwise rescale the values: in our development experiments with eye-gaze data, *z-score* normalization (suggested by Keogh et al. [37]) resulted in poor matches, as it leads to matching sub-sequences with large range to small oscillations of eye-gaze within the fixation.

## 3.3 Distance Measure

A distance measure defines the similarity between different motif candidates for grouping. As discussed above, we adapted a robust distance measure, namely *Dynamic Time Warping (DTW)* [29]. DTW method calculates the smallest possible distance between two

**Algorithm 1** FindMotifs

**function** FindMotifs($candidates, R, min\_count$)
  $motifs \leftarrow \{\emptyset\}$
  **for** $i = 1$ ***to*** length(candidates) **do**
    $similar \leftarrow FindSimilar(candidates, i, R)$
    $distinct \leftarrow DeDuplicate(similar, R)$
    **if** length $(distinct) \geq min\_count$ **then**
      $motifs \leftarrow motifs \cup \{i\}$
    **end if**
  **end for**
  **return** $motifs$
**end function**

time series by aligning one time series with another, such that, distance between them is minimized. The example shown in Figure 2 motivates the choice of DTW for mining mouse cursor data. Figure 2 plots the $x$ coordinates of a discovered cursor motif (shown in blue) along with similar, but not identical, cursor movements (shown in different colors). While all movements exhibit similar periodic behavior, each individual movement peaks at different point in time, making it impossible for a simple distance measure, e.g., Euclidean distance, to identify the common similarity between them. In contrast, DTW allows to warp the series in time, such that they are best aligned. The flexibility of DTW comes with an expense – the

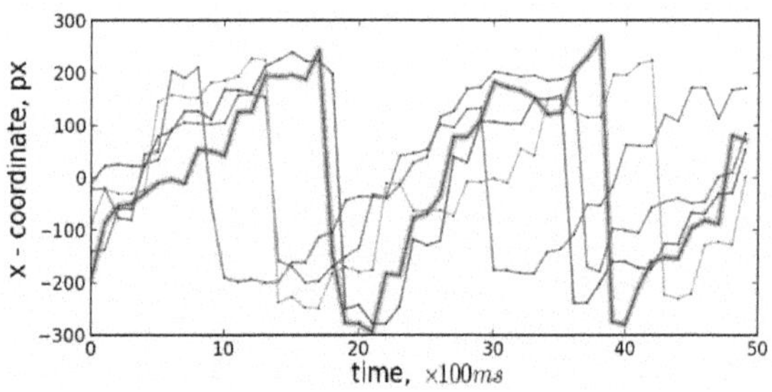


Figure 2: The $x$ coordinate of an example motif (shown in blue) together with similar cursor movements recorded for different users (shown in different colors).

time required to compute DTW is $O(n^2)$, as opposed to $O(n)$ for Euclidean distance. To reduce the computation time, constrained version of DTW [39] is often used in practice. Constrained DTW disallows warping (aligning) points that are farther than $W$ time steps from each other. In our system we employ DTW constrained with Sakoe-Chiba band [39] with $W = n/2$, where $n$ is time series length. Finally, the distance between two cursor movements is defined as the *sum* of DTW distances on the $x$ and $y$ dimensions.

## 3.4 Candidate Similarity Computation

As the number of motif candidates can grow large (e.g., for even a small realistic dataset we use for experiments, there are several millions of candidate motifs and tens of millions of time series objects), we need an efficient way to search among the candidates to find similar objects. We employ *early abandonment* and *lower bounding* techniques, described below, that are commonly used in time series mining applications [37] which allow us to speed up the similarity search significantly. Algorithm 1 describes our FindMotifs algorithm more precisely. The algorithm starts with initially empty set of motifs and considers each motif candidate one-by-one. For each candidate $FindSimilar$ function computes the raw number of matches, i.e. number of sub-sequences from the time series database that are similar (have distance smaller than a $R$) to the candidate. As motif candidates may match large number of overlapping subsequences, the match count computed by $FindSimilar$ can be overestimated. To circumvent this problem, we only count matches that are distinct, i.e. are outside of $R$ range from each other. Finally, if motif frequency defined as number of distinct matches exceeds $min\_count$ threshold the candidate is added to the set of discovered motifs. Note that exact implementation of $FindSimilar$ depends on particular pruning strategy and is discussed below.

## 3.5 Scaling Up Motif Discovery

In order to scale up motif discover to realistic datasets, we adapt a number of optimization techniques, some well known, and some novel, combining them to speed up motif discovery by an order of magnitude.

**Lower bounding**: The idea of lower bounding has already become a standard technique to eliminate needless distance computations. In order to do that, one needs to compute a relatively cheap lower bound to see if DTW computation can be omitted. It is important to ensure that lower bound is exact, that is, it does not prune candidates in proximity of the distance threshold. Among several known lower bounds for DTW, the LB_Keogh lower bound is the commonly used solution due to its good pruning power and relatively fast computation time. LB_Keogh is calculated by computing Euclidian distance between "envelope" time series, hence it is $O(n)$. We implemented LB_Keogh as suggested and outlined in [37] and supporting web page of the *UCR-Suite*[1]. Other lower bounds are either more computationally expensive [33] or produce looser lower bounds, making pruning less efficient [31].

**Early Abandoning:** During the computation of either DTW or LB_Keogh, if our current value of lower bound measure exceeds a given distance threshold, we can safely abandon the computation for the remaining candidates at that point, since the resulting lower bound value will be higher than the distance threshold. Similar idea can be implemented for DTW. As this idea comes with no additional computation cost we employ it in multiple places in our code. For example, due to the nature of mouse tracking data we can early abandon after LB_Keogh or DTW values exceeded on either x or dimension.

**Distance Measure Learning (Novel Optimization):** As an alternate way to speed up similarity search directly, one can consider reducing dimensionality of time series data by either obtaining symbol representation such as *iSAX* [42] or Principal Component Analysis (PCA [28]). Neither of these approaches directly address the inaccuracy of time series measure calculated in the feature space caused by the reduction. Instead, we employ the idea of *learning* the distance metric, which was previously investigated by a number of authors [5, 10, 3]. Note that DTW is not a metric, and triangular inequality does not hold for it [33]. However, it is possible to approximate DTW by the Euclidian metric in the feature space. More specifically, feature space comprised of simple time series statistics such as standard deviation and range of x and y coordinates may well differentiate time series that are not similar and eliminate the need to compute the lower bound. In our experiments we use five features: standard deviation and ranges of x and y coordinates, respectively, and the mean squared speed of cursor movement. The intuition is that we can expect distinct mouse gestures to have different shape characteristics such as ranges, and speed, thus being sufficiently separated in the simplified feature space. To learn the feature weights directly from the data, we construct training and test data sets by sampling a large number of time series candidates, and computing the exact DTW for pairs of these time series. To obtain

[1]UCR-Suite: http://www.cs.ucr.edu/ eamonn/UCRsuite.html

the weights of the features, such that the error between the feature-based Euclidian metric and the true DTW of the original time series is minimized, we solve the following minimization problem:

$$\underset{w}{\text{minimize}} \quad \sum_{i,j} \left( y_{ij}^2 - \sum_{k=1}^{d} w_k \left( x_i^{(k)} - x_j^{(k)} \right)^2 \right)^2 \qquad (1)$$

where $x \in \mathbb{R}^d$ and $d$ is the number of time series features; $i$ and $j$ are index i-th and j-th time series example in the training data, $y_{ij}$ is the DTW for pair of these time series and indices $i$ and $j$ enumerate all the training examples. Since it is an unconstrained optimization problem, we can derive an efficient gradient descent-based method to find the feature weights $w$ that minimize the error between the feature-based Euclidian metric and DTW on the original pair of time series. The resulting distance measure is referred as $DM$ throughout the paper. As the reduced feature space dimensionality is smaller than the typical length of time series we are interested in, such a measure allows us to index time series efficiently using any of the available spatial data structures, and subsequently pruning candidates that are unlikely to be similar at much smaller computational cost.

**R-Tree Indexing (Novel Optimization):** For efficient query processing and effective candidate pruning we employ spatial indexing using the R-Tree data structure. The R-Tree [24] is one of the most popular index structure for large multidimensional databases. Data in the R-tree is organized in a tree, where each node contains a bounding box of all entries in the corresponding subtree, and the leaf nodes store the data required for each child. In our case, the entries are points in five-dimensional space of similarity features described above.

To search the R-tree for similar subsequences, the "query" is a five-dimensional hypercube, a $\delta$-environment of a given sequence. The search recursively traverses the tree starting from the root node. When a leaf node that overlaps with the query is reached, all entries in that node are tested against the distance measure to a query point. If the distance is less then $\delta$, then the candidate point is returned.

It is known [4] that R-Tree performance degrades in high-dimensional spaces, where $d > 16$. In our case, the dimensionality is 5, allowing us to effectively reduce search space of candidates for the exact computation of DTW measures.

**Combining Pruning Strategies:** Clearly, combining several pruning techniques may speed up our algorithm. In this paper we consider four system variations depending on the pruning utilized. Table 2 summarizes the pruning strategies enabled for each of the system variations we have tested. The combined system, which we call **DM-RTree** in the remainder of the paper, is expected to scale well to large datasets.

We analyze the expected complexity of the approximate DM distance measure, using the notation in Table 1. The exact computation of DTW for a single query point requires $O(k^2)$ time, so the computation of all $\epsilon$-neighbors for all instances will take $O(N^2k^2)$ time. The computation of LB_Keogh lower bound requires $O(k)$ time for a single point, so adoption of LB_Keogh pruning requires $N^2$ LB_Keogh computations, plus the time for computation of exact DTW for all selected points, a total of

$$O\left(N^2k + \tau_{\text{LB\_Keogh}}(\epsilon)N^2k^2\right)$$

time, which is better than exhaustive DTW computation, but also quadratic over the the number of sequences in the database. Using DM gives $\frac{d}{k}$ speedup at the pruning stage, and $\frac{\tau_{\text{LB\_Keogh}}(\epsilon)}{\tau_{\text{DM}}(\delta)}$ difference in DTW computation stage. Using R-Tree index allows us to eliminate $N^2$ multiplier in pruning stage. The height of R-Tree is $O(\log N)$, and for a sufficiently small $\delta$, the R-Tree search time

| Notation | Description |
|---|---|
| $N$ | the number of sequences in the database |
| $k$ | average time sequence length |
| $\epsilon$ | distance threshold for DTW similarity |
| $\delta$ | Euclidean distance threshold for DM |
| $\tau_{\text{DM}}(\delta)$ | pruning factor for DM, the average ratio of instances in $\delta$-neighborhood of a query point |
| $\tau_{\text{LB\_Keogh}}(\epsilon)$ | pruning factor for LB_Keogh |
| $\text{PP} = 1 - \tau_*$ | pruning power of DM and LB_Keogh pruning |
| $d = 5$ | dimension of approximate distance function |

Table 1: Notations for Complexity Analysis

| System Name | LB_Keogh | DM | DM-RTree |
|---|---|---|---|
| Exact | | | |
| LB_Keogh | ✓ | | |
| DM | ✓ | ✓ | |
| DM-RTree | ✓ | ✓ | ✓ |

Table 2: Pruning strategies considered for each system.

depends on output size as $O(\tau_{DM}(\delta)N \log N)$, so the complexity of our algorithm is:

$$O\left(\tau_{DM}(\delta)N^2\left(d\log N + k^2\right)\right)$$

Thus, DM-RTree is expected to perform better than LB_Keogh pruning, if the pruning factor $\tau_{DM}(\delta) \ll 1$, as we verify experimentally in the next section.

# 4. SCALABLE MOTIF DISCOVERY

This section demonstrates feasibility of our approach for large scale mouse cursor dataset, and evaluates its efficiency along with currently known techniques.

## 4.1 Experimental Setup and Dataset

We experiment with a dataset of mouse cursor movement collected "in the wild" using the EMU browser plugin [22] from over 5,000 real users of a university library. The EMU plugin recorded time-stamped events of user actions or changes in the web browser state, including url change, mouse cursor movements, clicks, page rendering and page content change events. The dataset contains 52,378 search engine result page (SERP) views, and 48,345 landing page views, resulting from over 31,860 queries. From this data, 100,723 cursor movement trajectory subsequences were extracted, comprising the sequence dataset for the experiments in the rest of this section. We use this dataset for empirical performance comparisons between LB_Keogh and our approach (Section 4.3), and to mine common motifs (Section 4.4) for subsequent relevance experiments.

## 4.2 Evaluating Distance Measure Learning

To verify the feasibility of effective distance measure learning we constructed the training and test data splits by randomly sampling a large number of time series pairs and calculating DTW for these pairs. Overall, our data set contains nearly 500,000 pairs and associated DTW distance values. The test and training datasets are split in equal proportions of 50%. We experimented with the five similarity features described above. We obtain the feature weights $w$ by minimizing the objective function from Equation 1. Stochastic gradient descent is used to perform the optimization, converging in fewer than 10 iterations.

We now verify that we do not prune the truly similar candidates within $\epsilon$-proximity of the query candidate. In other words, we inves-

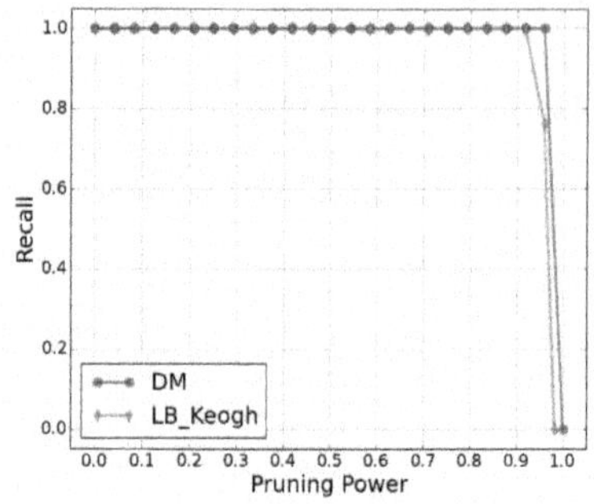


(a) $\epsilon < 300$

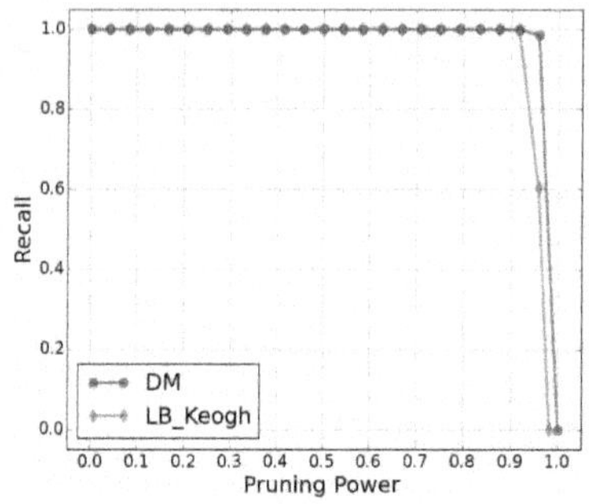


(b) $\epsilon < 500$

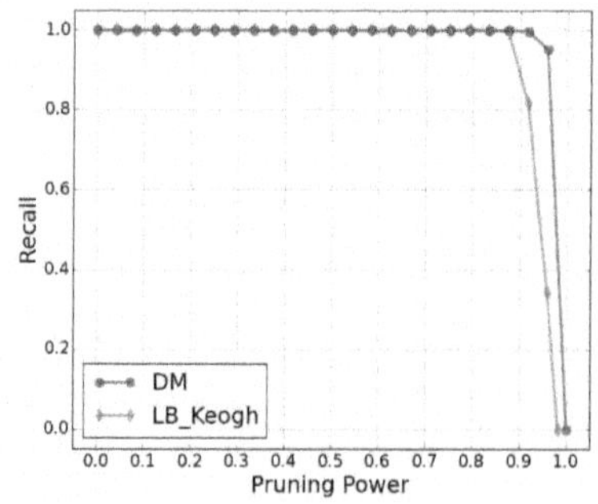


(c) $\epsilon < 1000$

Figure 3: Recall of finding similar motifs vs. Pruning Power for LB_Keogh and DM methods, shown for representative values of $\epsilon$.

tigate the "Recall" of our distance measure, vs. the corresponding "pruning power". Here, Recall is defined as the number of candidates found by our algorithm in $\epsilon$-vicinity, divided by a total number of true positives according to exact DTW computation. *Pruning power* is defined as fraction of candidates pruned away early by our algorithm, and therefore eliminated from the (expensive) exact distance computation. By increasing the parameter $\delta$, defined in Section 3.5, one can achieve better Recall, but lower Pruning Power, as more candidates are retained for exact distance computation. In our experiments we set the $\delta = 135$ resulting in desirable Recall of 95%. Figure 3 shows the Recall vs. Pruning Power curves for DM and LB_Keogh methods, with sub-figures corresponding to different values of $\epsilon$. DM outperforms LB_Keogh exhibiting higher pruning power with 100% Recall, while significantly decreasing the computation cost.

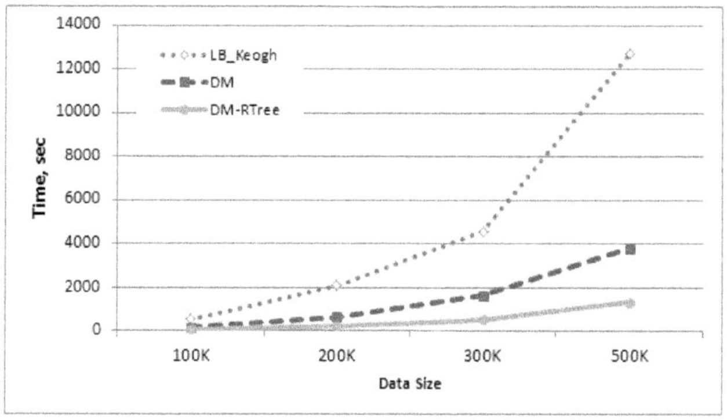


Figure 4: Comparison of running time for LB_Keogh, DM and DM-RTree systems.

## 4.3 Runtime Performance Results

In order to compare the performance of our final system DM-RTree (defined in Section 3.5), we performed benchmark tests for the three systems, using the dataset described above. Specifically, we compared: LB_Keogh, which uses pruning based on the lower bound; DM, our system based on distance measure with linear search among all candidates; and our DM-RTree system. We do not report the runtimes of the exact DTW computation, as it is 17 times slower than LB_Keogh, and more than 100 times slower than DM-RTree, and takes over several days to run for larger datasets. All experiments we performed on Intel Xeon CPU E5-2630 2.30GHz with 20 cores. Figure 4 reports the time performance for the systems as the size of the data is increased. Notably, DM-RTree system exhibits the lowest computation time, while growing at the slowest rate as the data size increases. The DM-RTree system outperforms the state-of-the art LB_Keogh by nearly an order of magnitude (8 - 9.5 times speedup), for different data sizes, without degrading Recall below 95%. Note that the speed-up factor increases with the data size, as the R-Tree index becomes more efficient in pruning candidates, compared to linear scanning performed by other systems. The benchmark test was repeated 10 times. For datasets greater than 200K, the differences in running times are significant with $p < 0.01$.

## 4.4 Discovered Cursor Motifs

To demonstrate that our approach is not only efficient, but also effective in discovering meaningful motifs, we focus on the motifs extracted from the large dataset described above. At the same time, we investigate – whether common cursor motifs vary between search results pages and landing pages with possibly arbitrary layout. While applying motif extraction to a large dataset may result in finding hundreds of motifs, we focus on the top 5 frequent motifs. Figure 5 reports the top 5 most frequent motifs (out of 127) discovered from the cursor movement data on the search result pages, or SERPs. Figure 6 reports top five most frequent motifs (out of 157), extracted from cursor data on the landing (clicked results) pages. In both figures, the mouse traces are annotated with arrows pointing in the direction of cursor movement, and shading of the circles indicates lower speed of cursor movement, or higher density of cursor positions. The common motifs extracted from SERPs correspond to previously (heuristically) identified patterns of cursor usage by Rodden et al. [38], such as marking of promising search results (a and d), and using mouse as a reading aid while following along a line of text (b), or interacting with the search query box (c), and following the attention vertically (e). Similarly, the discovered motifs on landing pages appear to indicate patterns of marking important information on page (a, b and d), and vertical movement (c) – potentially indicating the rapid shift of the user's attention downward, and directing the mouse cursor to click on a link (e), corresponding to heuristically identified patterns of cursor movement on landing pages in Guo et al. [20]. We emphasize that both SERP and landing page motifs above were discovered automatically, without changing the algorithm for the different page types. As we demonstrate in the next section, the motifs automatically discovered using our approach provide valuable information about the user's interactions with the result pages, and are effective for relevance estimation and ranking.

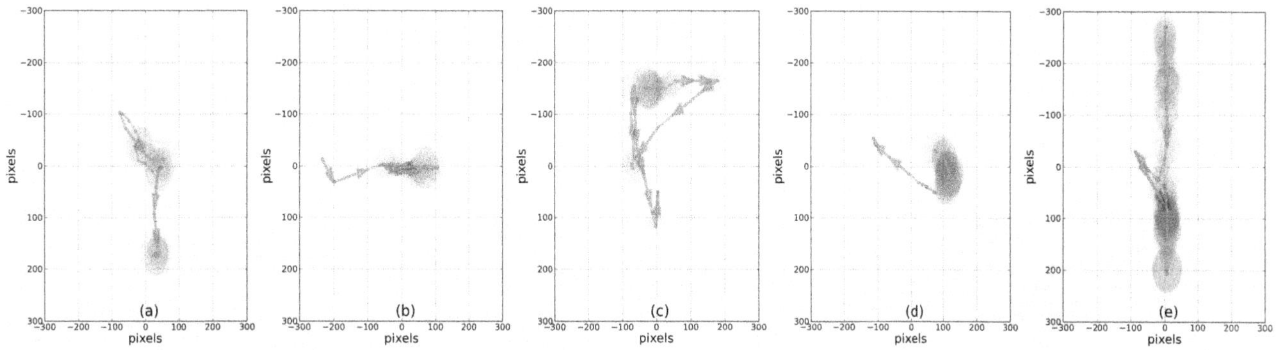


Figure 5: Top frequent motifs discovered from mouse traces recorded on search result pages (SERPs).

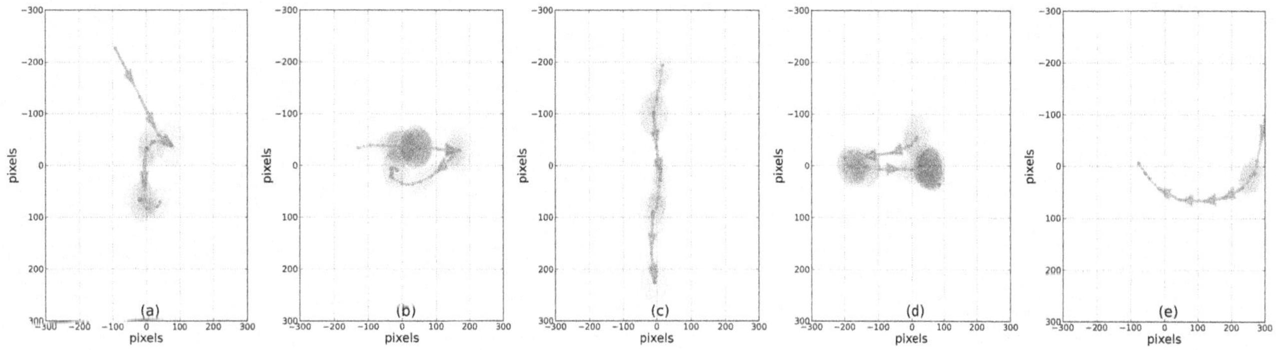


Figure 6: Top frequent motifs discovered from mouse traces recorded on landing pages (non-SERPs).

# 5. USING MOTIFS FOR RELEVANCE PREDICTION AND RANKING

Estimation of document relevance from large scale user behavior data is of critical importance to Web search engines. In this sections we demonstrate how automatically discovered mouse cursors motifs can be used to improve estimation of search result relevance and ranking. To ensure proper comparison with prior work of Huang et al. [27] and Guo et al. [20], we adhere to the same evaluation metrics: Pearson correlation coefficient and Normalized Discounted Cumulative Gain (NDCG). In the rest of the section, we describe how motif-based features can be incorporated into the existing *PCB* model and significantly improve the quality of personalized relevance prediction.

## 5.1 Experimental Setup and Dataset

Our test dataset, also referred to as **D1** in subsequent experiments, was constructed in a user study with 21 participants, following the methodology described by Feild et al. [14]. The dataset contains 566 queries and corresponding 1,340 page views, including search engine result pages (SERPs), with dwell times of at least 5 seconds. Each user was asked to provide a relevance rating for the web page (on five point scale), immediately prior to navigating to the next web page. Mouse cursor position recording was stopped prior to showing the rating interface, thus the data was not "polluted" by extraneous cursor movements. The subjects were only asked to provide their ratings on landing pages (non-SERP). This allowed us to analyze mouse movements performed by a user on the landing page and relate them to the explicit relevance rating given by the very same user. Overall, there were 854 relevance judgments provided by user study participants. We use these relevance judgments in the relevance estimation and re-ranking experiments of Section 5.3.

## 5.2 Motif-based Relevance Prediction System

We now describe our system for predicting relevance of a document using our automatically discovered motifs as features, as a standalone system *Motifs*. We also compare *Motifs* against a state-of-the-art relevance prediction system, *PCB*, using manually engineered features [20], and the combination of the two feature sets, as *PCB+Motifs*. The specific features used are described below.

**PCB Features** The features or predictors of the *PCB* model include the document viewing time – also known as dwell time, the characteristics of mouse cursor movements and scrolling behavior, such as ranges of mouse cursor movements for $x$ and $y$, cursor movement speed, scrolling direction and frequencies, hovering certain area of interest on a web page by mouse cursor and various click statistics. These features aim to capture the searcher engagement with the examined document and viewing patterns such as "reading" and "skimming", which are shown to be indicative of document relevance [20]. The complete list of *PCB* features, and other model details can be found in reference [20].

**Motif Features** All of the motifs discovered from the user study dataset were encoded as *features*. We only considered mouse cursor data from landing pages, as relevance judgements are not defined for search result pages. Each document was then represented with a vector of features, each feature corresponding to one motif. The feature values were computed as the minimum distances between a motif and the observed mouse cursor trajectory, using the following formula:

$$\mathrm{MinDist}(motif, mouse) = \min_{0<t<T-w} \mathrm{DTW}(motif, mouse[t, t+w]) \quad (2)$$

where $T$ is the mouse cursor trajectory length, $w$ is the motif length

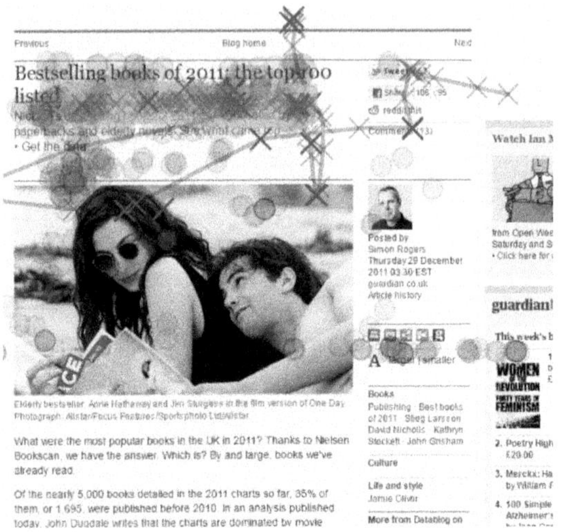


Figure 7: Example match of a "follow" motif (shaded green) to cursor trace (blue crosses) on a relevant landing page for a query "best selling books of 2011". For reference, eye gaze positions are marked as light red circles.

(5000 ms in our case) and $DTW(\cdot,\cdot)$ is the Dynamic Time Warping distance between the motif and sub-sequence. Therefore, the smaller the minimum distance in the Equation 2, the higher the match between the motif and the mouse trajectory (and corresponding feature value). In fact, if the motif perfectly matches any subsequence of a page view, $MinDist$ is equal to zero. This is analogous to a bag-of-words document representation that is widely used in information retrieval, except that in our case the "words" represent the common mouse cursor movements represented as motifs that occur in a page examination time series (analogous to a "document"), and the value interpretations are reversed (lower is better). Figure 7 illustrates this idea by highlighting the best match between the cursor trace, and a discovered "follow" motif, also seen in Figure 5(d). The figure plots the cursor positions (shown as blue crosses) and eye gaze positions (shown as light red circles), and overlays the best match of the motif (shaded in green). The user searched for book bestsellers of 2011, and has subsequently judged this page as relevant, as it contains the list of top-20 book best sellers at the bottom of the page (full page snapshot cropped due to lack of space).

## 5.3 Relevance Prediction

We now report the performance of the different systems on predicting document relevance. As evaluation metric, we use the Pearson correlation coefficient $\rho$, between the predicted and the true relevance labels, defined as:

$$\rho_{f,y} = \frac{\sum_{(x,y)\in D}(f(x)-\mu_f)(y-\mu_y)}{(|D|-1)\sigma_f\sigma_y}$$

where $\mu$ is the observed sample mean and $\sigma$ is the observed sample standard deviation. Pearson correlation is the evaluation metric of choice in previous work [20, 27], thus appropriate for comparison to previously proposed methods, namely *PCB* and cursor hover [27].

**Predicting Relevance**: We formulate the prediction problem as regression, and conduct 10-fold cross validation. The regression algorithm we used is Ridge Linear Regression, which is a variant of Multiple Linear Regression. Ridge linear regression is reported to be more robust against predictor collinearity and overfitting.

**Results:** Table 3 summarizes the performance of four regression models with distinguished with different feature subsets. As we can

| Feature Group | Pearson correlation [2] | p-value |
|---|---|---|
| *Hover* [27] | 0.12 | $p < 0.001$ |
| *PCB [20]* | 0.392 (n/a) | $p < 0.001$ |
| *Motifs* | 0.394 (+0.5%) | $p < 0.001$ |
| *PCB + Motifs* | **0.468 (+19.4%)** | $p < 0.001$ |

Table 3: Pearson correlation between the actual relevance judgments and the predicted ratings for *PCB*, *Motifs* and *PCB+Motifs* models on Dataset D1.

see, the best performing model results from combining the automatically extracted motifs and the *PCB* predictors (*PCB + Motifs*), achieving the correlation of 0.468 between the actual personally judged relevance and the estimated relevance. Our model improved the prediction effectiveness over the state-of-the-art *PCB* model by over 19%. The system using the automatically extracted motifs alone (*Motifs*) correlated with the actual relevance judgments at 0.394, which is comparable with the *PCB* model. This demonstrates that our approach indeed enables discovery of valuable patterns that are not easily identifiable through manual effort. To compare with prior work of Huang et al. [27] reported as *Hover*, we calculated Pearson correlation between cursor the hover rate and the explicit labels provided by the participants. We have not found a substantial correlation between hover rate and relevance labels measured for all participants. However, correlation coefficient calculated for each participant separately, varies from -0.23 to 0.27, which explains the small correlation across the users. In our comparison we report average absolute value for all participants, thus giving an advantage to *Hover*. Nevertheless, it provides little correlation, and is outperformed by *PCB* and *Motif* models by a substantial margin.

## 5.4 Result Ranking

We now turn to the other practical application of motif discovery, result ranking. As in the relevance prediction experiments, we compare four models: *Hover* [27], *Motifs*, *PCB* and the combined *PCB+Motifs*. For consistency, we use the same Linear Ridge Regression as for the experiments above. We perform cross validation stratified *by user*: that is, for each run we hold out documents seen by a single user, and train the model on the rest of the data. The same motifs are used as before, as they were discovered on a disjoint, unlabeled dataset described in section 5.3. We repeat the training and testing procedure for each of 21 users in our dataset and report the ranking performance averaged across all the users, resulting in a leave-one-out form of cross validation. Specifically, as a metric we use Normalized Discounted Cumulative Gain (NDCG), widely accepted for assessing the quality of Web search results ranking.

**Normalized Discounted Cumulative Gain at K (NDCG@$k$)** is parametrized by cutoff position $k$, that is, to calculate NDCG@$k$ we consider only top k results. NDCG@$k$ is defined as:

$$NDCG@k = \frac{DCG@k}{IDCG@k}, DCG@k = \sum_{i=1}^{k} \frac{2^{rel_i}-1}{\log_2(i+1)}$$

where $IDCG@k$ is the $DCG@k$ value of the ideal document ranking according to the relevance labels, and $rel_i$ is relevance score for a $i$-th document. $DCG@k$ penalizes ranking with relevant documents appearing at lower position in the list with logarithmic discount. The $NDCG@k$ value of 1.0 indicates a perfect ranking. At test stage we compute relevance scores for the held out documents and calculate $NDCG@k$ based on the actual relevance labels.

**Results:** Figure 8 reports $NDCG@k$ for the values of $k$ ranging from 1 to 50. Interestingly, despite similar performance measured

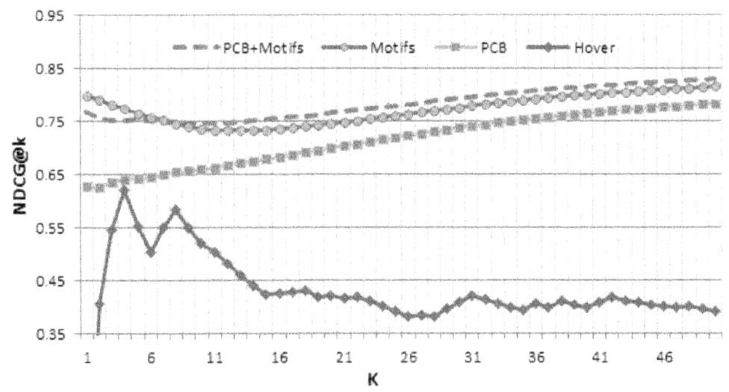


Figure 8: NDCG@K of result rankings based on *Hover*, *PCB*, and motif models (*Motifs* and *PCB+Motifs*), on dataset D1.

by Pearson correlation, ranking based on motif features behaves differently from the ranking based on the *PCB* model. Specifically, the motif model has significantly higher NDCG values at positions 1 through 10 (with the improvement on NDCG@1 over the original *PCB* model of 27%, p-value < 0.001). However, this improvement decreases with higher values of $k$. The combined *PCB+Motifs* model outperforms both *PCB* and *Motifs* at lower rank positions with relative improvements from 13% at rank 10 decreasing to 6% at rank 30. By comparison, *Hover* model alone performs consistently poorly, especially at lower ranks.

## 5.5 Most predictive motifs

To gain a better understanding of the motif features, we conducted feature importance analysis using the weights assigned to the features by the linear ridge regression algorithm. The distribution of feature weights is reported in Figure 9. Note that the majority of the feature weights are concentrated near zero, suggesting that the motif feature set could potentially be further pruned by applying standard feature selection algorithms. Ridge regression also naturally supports the interpretation of motif correlation directions through the signs of the feature weights. That is, the motif features with positive weights are positively correlated with the relevance label, while motif features with negative weights are anti-correlated with relevance labels. Figures 10 and 11 show two examples of motifs with high absolute weights. In Figure 10, the example motif has a high positive weight, suggesting a high level of user interest and engagement with the page content, in turn, indicating high document relevance. In Figure 11, the example motif has relatively large negative weight, corresponding to the pattern of link pointing or other types of page navigation (e.g., clicking the "Back" button to leave the current page), indicating the viewed page to be non-relevant. Note that these, and other most predictive motifs such as "follow", are not captured by the *PCB* model, and in fact would be difficult to capture by manually engineered features. Thus, motif discovery provides a powerful way of building a dictionary of complex behavior features, with minimal application-specific effort.

# 6. DISCUSSION AND CONCLUSIONS

Our relevance prediction and ranking experiments demonstrated that the automatically extracted motifs are helpful for improving Web search result ranking, and provide additional clues about document relevance, over previously discovered patterns developed by manual examinations. We believe that these findings can facilitate the research and development of the mouse cursor movement data, especially at large scale.

For exploratory applications, researchers and practitioners may, for example, choose to only look at search queries accompanied with extensive "skimming" behavior, as search results for these queries are more likely to be poor and require more attention. Similarly, search result documents with substantial "reading" behavior may be more relevant than those without. For example, we have shown that by using motif presence (as feature values) as predictors, search result ranking can be substantially and significantly improved. Generally speaking, with our approach, one may construct a dictionary of mouse cursor motifs, and use them to predict various user metrics, e.g., affect, satisfaction, frustration, or user interest and engagement with web pages, not necessarily only search results. And, since our motif discovery approach is completely automatic and application-independent, no application-specific feature engineering is required.

This work opens a number of future research directions. While our proposed technique are page- and user-independent, the behavioral patterns may vary for different users, page layouts or tasks. For example, while the extracted motifs are prevalent across users, some of the patterns may be more dominant for particular users. Therefore, modeling individual characteristics may be helpful for segmenting and targeting different user groups (e.g., more active users vs. more passive users [8]), which would further improve the relevance prediction models. Our approach can also be naturally extended to touch screen devices that do not use mouse cursor, but provide other interaction features such as swiping and zooming (requiring novel features and models, such the recent work by Guo et al. [21]), and is a promising direction for future work.

In summary, we introduced a novel technique for automatically and efficiently extracting frequent mouse-cursor movement patterns (motifs) from web search examination data. To enable motif mining on realistic datasets, we introduced novel optimizations, using spatial indexing and learning distance measures, which resulted in an order of magnitude improvement in runtime performance. As a result, meaningful motifs such as reading, marking, and skimming a page were discovered from the search behavior data of real users, The discovered motifs were shown to be valuable for estimating document relevance for improving Web search result ranking, enabling over 19% improvement in relevance estimation and over 27% improvement in result ranking over the state-of-the-art baselines. Thus, our novel techniques provide a general, robust, and scalable method for analyzing search behavior data, while enabling significant improvements on practical search tasks.

**ACKNOWLEDGMENTS** This work was supported by the National Science Foundation grant IIS-1018321, the DARPA grant D11AP00269, and the Yahoo! Faculty Research Engagement Program.

# 7. REFERENCES

[1] M. Ageev, D. Lagun, and E. Agichtein. Improving search result summaries by using searcher behavior data. In *Proc. of SIGIR*, 2013.

[2] E. Arroyo, T. Selker, and W. Wei. Usability tool for analysis of web designs using mouse tracks. In *CHI extended abstracts*, 2006.

[3] H. Becker, M. Naaman, and L. Gravano. Learning similarity metrics for event identification in social media. In *Proc. of WSDM*, 2010.

[4] N. Beckmann, H.-P. Kriegel, R. Schneider, and B. Seeger. The r*-tree: an efficient and robust access method for points and rectangles. In *Proc. of SIGMOD*, 1990.

[5] M. Bilenko, S. Basu, and R. J. Mooney. Integrating constraints and metric learning in semi-supervised clustering. In *Proc. of ICML*, 2004.

[6] G. Buscher, E. Cutrell, and M. R. Morris. What do you see when you're surfing?: using eye tracking to predict salient regions of web pages. In *Proc. of CHI*, 2009.

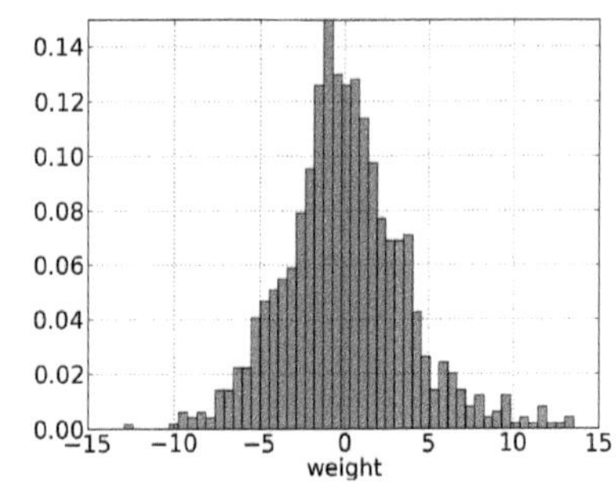


Figure 9: Distribution of motif feature weights.

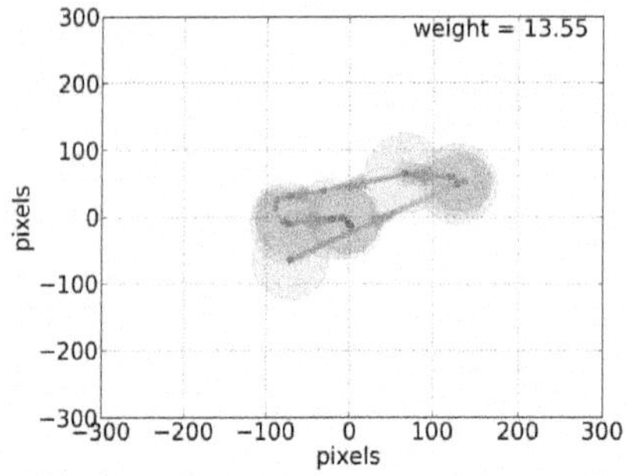


Figure 10: Most predictive positive motif.

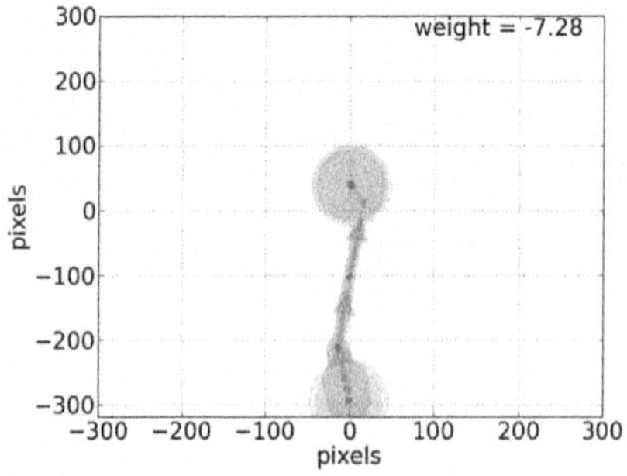


Figure 11: Most predictive negative motif.


[7] G. Buscher, A. Dengel, and L. van Elst. Query expansion using gaze-based feedback on the subdocument level. In *Proc. of SIGIR*, 2008.

[8] G. Buscher, R. W. White, S. Dumais, and J. Huang. Large-scale analysis of individual and task differences in search result page examination strategies. In *Proc. of WSDM*, 2012.

[9] E. Chávez, G. Navarro, R. Baeza-Yates, and J. L. Marroquín. Searching in metric spaces. *ACM Comput. Surv.*, Sept. 2001.

[10] S. Chopra, R. Hadsell, and Y. LeCun. Learning a similarity metric discriminatively, with application to face verification. In *Proc. of CVPR*, 2005.

[11] E. Cutrell and Z. Guan. What are you looking for?: an eye-tracking study of information usage in web search. In *Proc. of CHI*, 2007.

[12] P. Esling and C. Agon. Time-series data mining. *ACM Comput. Surv.*, 2012.

[13] C. Faloutsos, M. Ranganathan, and Y. Manolopoulos. *Fast subsequence matching in time-series databases*. 1994.

[14] H. A. Feild, J. Allan, and R. Jones. Predicting searcher frustration. In *Proc. of SIGIR*, 2010.

[15] J. Goecks and J. Shavlik. Learning users' interests by unobtrusively observing their normal behavior. In *Proc. of IUI*, 2000.

[16] L. A. Granka, T. Joachims, and G. Gay. Eye-tracking analysis of user behavior in WWW search. In *Proc. of SIGIR*, 2004.

[17] Q. Guo and E. Agichtein. Exploring mouse movements for inferring query intent. In *Proc. of SIGIR*, 2008.

[18] Q. Guo and E. Agichtein. Ready to buy or just browsing?: detecting web searcher goals from interaction data. In *Proc. of SIGIR*, 2010.

[19] Q. Guo and E. Agichtein. Towards predicting web searcher gaze position from mouse movements. In *Proc. of CHI*, 2010.

[20] Q. Guo and E. Agichtein. Beyond dwell time: estimating document relevance from cursor movements and other post-click searcher behavior. In *Proc. of WWW*, 2012.

[21] Q. Guo, H. Jin, D. Lagun, S. Yuan, and E. Agichtein. Mining touch interaction data on mobile devices to predict web search result relevance. In *Proc. of SIGIR*, 2013.

[22] Q. Guo, R. P. Kelly, S. Deemer, A. Murphy, J. A. Smith, and E. Agichtein. EMU: the emory user behavior data management system for automatic library search evaluation. In *Proc. of JCDL'09*, 2009.

[23] Q. Guo, D. Lagun, and E. Agichtein. Predicting web search success with fine-grained interaction data. In *Proc. of CIKM*, 2012.

[24] A. Guttman. R-trees: a dynamic index structure for spatial searching. *SIGMOD Rec.*, 14(2), June 1984.

[25] J. Huang, R. White, and G. Buscher. User see, user point: gaze and cursor alignment in web search. In *Proc. of CHI*, 2012.

[26] J. Huang, R. W. White, G. Buscher, and K. Wang. Improving searcher models using mouse cursor activity. In *Proc. of SIGIR*, 2012.

[27] J. Huang, R. W. White, and S. Dumais. No clicks, no problem: using cursor movements to understand and improve search. In *Proc. of CHI*, 2011.

[28] I. Jolliffe. *Principal component analysis*. Wiley Online Library, 2005.

[29] E. Keogh and C. Ratanamahatana. Exact indexing of dynamic time warping. *Knowledge and information systems*, 7(3):358–386, 2005.

[30] E. Keogh, X. Xi, L. Wei, and C. A. Ratanamahatana. The ucr time series classification/clustering homepage, 2006.

[31] S.-W. Kim, S. Park, and W. W. Chu. An index-based approach for similarity search supporting time warping in large sequence databases. In *Proc. of ICDE*, 2001.

[32] L. Leiva. Automatic web design refinements based on collective user behavior. In *CHI Extended Abstracts*, 2012.

[33] D. Lemire. Faster retrieval with a two-pass dynamic-time-warping lower bound. *Pattern recognition*, 42(9):2169–2180, 2009.

[34] L. Lonardi, Jessica, K. Eamonn, Stefano, and P. Patel. Finding motifs in time series. In *Proc. of the 2nd Workshop on Temporal Data Mining*, 2002.

[35] A. Mueen, E. Keogh, Q. Zhu, S. Cash, and B. Westover. Exact discovery of time series motifs. In *Proc. of SIAM International Conf. on Data Mining*, 2009.

[36] V. Navalpakkam and E. Churchill. Mouse tracking: measuring and predicting users' experience of web-based content. In *Proc. of CHI*, 2012.

[37] T. Rakthanmanon, B. Campana, A. Mueen, G. Batista, B. Westover, Q. Zhu, J. Zakaria, and E. Keogh. Searching and mining trillions of time series subsequences under dynamic time warping. In *Proc. of KDD*, 2012.

[38] K. Rodden, X. Fu, A. Aula, and I. Spiro. Eye-mouse coordination patterns on web search results pages. In *Proc. of CHI*, 2008.

[39] H. Sakoe and S. Chiba. Dynamic programming algorithm optimization for spoken word recognition. *Acoustics, Speech and Signal Processing, IEEE Transactions on*, 26(1), 1978.

[40] Y. Sakurai, M. Yoshikawa, S. Uemura, H. Kojima, et al. The a-tree: An index structure for high-dimensional spaces using relative approximation. In *Proc. of the VLDB*, 2000.

[41] B. Shapira, M. Taieb-Maimon, and A. Moskowitz. Study of the usefulness of known and new implicit indicators and their optimal combination for accurate inference of users interests. In *Proc. of ACM SAC*, 2006.

[42] J. Shieh and E. Keogh. i sax: indexing and mining terabyte sized time series. In *Proc. of KDD*, 2008.

[43] R. W. White and G. Buscher. Text selections as implicit relevance feedback. In *Proc. of SIGIR*, 2012.

[44] L. Ye and E. Keogh. Time series shapelets: a new primitive for data mining. In *Proc. KDD*, 2009.

[45] B.-K. Yi, H. Jagadish, and C. Faloutsos. Efficient retrieval of similar time sequences under time warping. In *Proc. of ICDE*, 1998.

[46] J. Zakaria, A. Mueen, and E. Keogh. Clustering time series using unsupervised-shapelets. In *Proc. of ICDM*, 2012.

[47] P. Zezula, G. Amato, V. Dohnal, and M. Batko. *Similarity Search: The Metric Space Approach*. Springer, 2010.

# Modeling Dwell Time to Predict Click-level Satisfaction

Youngho Kim[1]*, Ahmed Hassan[2], Ryen W. White[2], and Imed Zitouni[2]
[1] University of Massachusetts, 140 Governors Drive, Amherst, MA 01003, USA
[2] Microsoft, One Microsoft Way, Redmond, WA 98052, USA
yhkim@cs.umass.edu, {hassanam, ryenw, izitouni}@microsoft.com

## ABSTRACT
Clicks on search results are the most widely used behavioral signals for predicting search satisfaction. Even though clicks are correlated with satisfaction, they can also be noisy. Previous work has shown that clicks are affected by position bias, caption bias, and other factors. A popular heuristic for reducing this noise is to only consider clicks with long dwell time, usually equaling or exceeding 30 seconds. The rationale is that the more time a searcher spends on a page, the more likely they are to be satisfied with its contents. However, having a single threshold value assumes that users need a fixed amount of time to be satisfied with any result click, irrespective of the page chosen. In reality, clicked pages can differ significantly. Pages have different topics, readability levels, content lengths, etc. All of these factors may affect the amount of time spent by the user on the page. In this paper, we study the effect of different page characteristics on the time needed to achieve search satisfaction. We show that the topic of the page, its length and its readability level are critical in determining the amount of dwell time needed to predict whether any click is associated with satisfaction. We propose a method to model and provide a better understanding of click dwell time. We estimate click dwell time distributions for SAT (satisfied) or DSAT (dissatisfied) clicks for different click segments and use them to derive features to train a click-level satisfaction model. We compare the proposed model to baseline methods that use dwell time and other search performance predictors as features, and demonstrate that the proposed model achieves significant improvements.

## Categories and Subject Descriptors
H.3.3 [**Information Storage and Retrieval**]: Search Process.

## Keywords
Dwell time analysis; User behavior; Click satisfaction.

## 1. INTRODUCTION
Implicit measures of user behavior are important for enhancing web search quality [14][42]. Since obtaining explicit feedback from users is prohibitively expensive and challenging to implement in real-world Information Retrieval (IR) systems, commercial search engines have exploited implicit feedback signals derived from user activity (e.g., search result clickthrough statistics). Previous work has extensively studied implicit feedback measures

**Table 1: Click examples. Label means whether a click is satisfied (SAT) or dissatisfied (DSAT)**

| No. | Query | Label | Dwell Time | Readability Level |
|---|---|---|---|---|
| 1 | *abdominal aortic aneurysm* | DSAT | 55s | Difficult |
| 2 | *what to serve for dinner along with chicken parm* | SAT | 19s | Easy |

(e.g., mouse scrolling, gaze tracking, physiological signals, etc.), and verified their effectiveness in predicting search satisfaction (or dissatisfaction) (e.g., [6][13][14][16][20][31]).

Among many implicit measures, *click dwell time* (i.e., the time that the user spends on a clicked result) is one of the most important features because it is clearly correlated with result-level satisfaction or document relevance [6][10][14]. Longer dwell time on a clicked page has traditionally been used to identify satisfied (SAT) clicks. While clickthrough statistics can be sometimes misleading due to order and caption biases, click dwell time is a more robust measure. Click dwell time has been successfully used in a number of retrieval applications (e.g., implicit relevance feedback [42], re-ranking [2], and query expansion [6]). In those applications, SAT clicks are simply identified by some predefined time threshold (i.e., a click is SAT if its dwell time equals or exceeds that threshold). A dwell time equaling or exceeding 30 seconds, as proposed in [14], has typically been used to identify clicks with which searchers are satisfied. However, the dwell time depends on page content and has been shown to vary based on other factors such as search task and user [32]. A more robust interpretation of click dwell time is therefore needed to more accurately predict SAT (or DSAT (dissatisfaction)) clicks. We address this important challenge with the research presented in this paper. Note that we use the terms "dwell time" and "click dwell time" interchangeably to refer to the time spent on a search result.

We assume that the dwell time required by a given user to locate the required information on a landing page varies depending on factors such as query type, page topic, page content, and page readability level. We refer to these factors as the *query-click attributes*. For example, longer dwell time would be required when the user clicks on pages related to technical topics, even if the pages are not relevant. Table 1 shows two click examples drawn from our experiments where one click is dissatisfied with a long dwell time and the other is satisfied with a short dwell time. In the first example, the query is on a medical topic, and the contents of the clicked page have a high readability level. In contrast, the clicked page in the second example is related to food, and the user can easily comprehend this page in less time. In both examples, the 30-second threshold typically used in previous work (e.g., [6][42]) appears ineffective in determining whether a click is satisfied.

* This work was conducted while interning at Microsoft Research


*WSDM'14*, February 24–28, 2014, New York, New York, USA.

http://dx.doi.org/10.1145/2556195.2556220

To better understand click dwell time, we propose a method to model it given query-click attributes (e.g., readability level, search topics, etc.). This model helps to identify dwell time distributions of SAT and DSAT clicks for different segments of clicks. From this, we address the following important research questions:

**RQ1**. How can we model $p(t|\text{SAT}, att)$ (where $t$ and $att$ denote dwell time and query-click attributes, respectively)?

**RQ2.** How can $p(\text{SAT}|t, att)$ or $p(\text{DSAT}|t, att)$ be calculated?

**RQ3**. How can SAT dwell time thresholds be identified for particular queries, topics, or reading levels?

To model click dwell time, we collect click instances and label them as either SAT or DSAT. We then generate query and click attributes for each instance, and use them to identify different click segments (i.e., groups of clicks). Given these attributes, we could have used every attribute as a click segment (e.g., query type is "navigational"). However, some of these attributes are very broad and can result in general dwell time models that are similar to global models derived from all data. To address this problem, we apply a data mining approach for identifying attribute associations, and each association serves as a click segment. Once segments are identified, we derive distributions to model dwell time of SAT and DSAT clicks from each segment using Maximum Likelihood Estimation (MLE).

After deriving dwell time distributions, we develop an estimator to predict SAT and DSAT dwell time distributions for new (unseen) clicks. Since the generated segments may not cover all possible clicks, this estimator is required to expand the coverage of our method. The estimator is then used to devise a classification model to predict click satisfaction. This model includes dynamic dwell time features which identify probabilistic distances of a click instance to SAT and DSAT distributions, and we show that these features can significantly improve prediction performance.

The remainder of the paper is structured as follows. Section 2 describes relevant related work in the areas of implicit feedback analysis, search satisfaction, and search performance prediction. In Section 3, we describe how we generate and label the click data used for our method. Section 4 proposes our method to model click dwell time and provides dwell time analysis. In Section 5, we describe a click satisfaction model. We present experimental results in Section 6 and conclude in Section 7.

# 2. RELATED WORK

There are three main areas of related work that are relevant to the research presented in this paper: (1) implicit feedback, where inferences about intentions and relevance can be made from search behavior; (2) search satisfaction modeling, where search behavior is used to estimate user satisfaction, and; (3) search performance prediction, where estimates are made about result quality in advance of querying the search engine, or in some cases based on the results returned. We cover each of these areas in turn.

## 2.1 Implicit Feedback Analysis

The utility of implicit feedback as a relevance estimator has been extensively studied. Early research [29] found that implicit feedback is useful for inferring relevance. Kelly and Belkin [32] demonstrated a correlation between the amount of time spent examining a document and its relevance.

Implicit feedback based on search-result clicks has also been used to infer search preferences [3]. Radlinski et al. [39] showed that interleaving the results of two ranking functions and presenting the interleaved results to users can serve as a good predictor of relative search engine performance. In their analysis, they discovered that metrics including abandonment and reformulation did not predict relative performance as accurately as interleaving. Another way to use implicit feedback is to provide training data for learning-to-rank algorithms. Joachims [26] presented one of the earliest studies on using clickthrough data for optimizing learning to rank algorithms. Agichtein et al. [2] showed that incorporating behavior data can significantly improve the relevance of the top results in Web search. Other forms of feedback such as eye gaze and cursor movements have also been used for estimating document relevance [6][16].

Beyond search result interactions, other researchers have tried to understand browsing behavior by examining time spent on pages [35]. This work was not limited to Web search and did not differentiate between visits to useful pages and other non-relevant pages. In this work, we focus on predicting click-level satisfaction using dwell time as an implicit feedback signal. This work differs from previous research in this area by moving beyond the use of clicks or dwell time as signals to richer models of click dwell time that take contextual, topical, and content information into consideration.

Most recently, Yin et al. [44] used dwell time to capture user's voting actions for recommending social media content. They interpreted longer dwell time on the content as "pseudo votes", and improved recommendation performance by modeling the user's expectation levels that cause viewing and voting behaviors.

## 2.2 Search Satisfaction Modeling

There is significant literature on predicting satisfaction from user behavior. Proposed methods include correlating search behavior, such as clicks and dwell time, with satisfaction labels collected either first hand from users or using third-party judges.

Recent work has targeted behavioral modeling and using behavior to construct models of user satisfaction [1][19][20][22]. Fox et al. [14] found a strong correlation between search activity and user satisfaction labels gathered in-situ via a browser plugin. They modeled explicit satisfaction ratings provided by searchers using features such as clickthrough rate, click dwell time, and features associated with session termination. Hassan et al. [20] developed models of user behavior to accurately estimate search success on a task level, independent of the relevance of documents retrieved by the search engine. Hassan [19] proposed another satisfaction prediction model that can learn from both labeled and unlabeled data. Ageev et al. [1] proposed a formalization of different types of success for informational search, and presented a scalable game-like infrastructure for crowdsourcing studies of search behavior, specifically targeting the capture and evaluation of successful search strategies on informational tasks with known intent. Their model can predict search success effectively on their data and on a separate set of logs comprising search engine sessions.

Rather than relying on explicit search satisfaction labels, Huffman and Hochster [25] used a different approach where they studied the correlation between user satisfaction and simple relevance metrics. They reported a fairly strong correlation between user satisfaction and linear models encompassing the query-document relevance of the first three results for the first query in the search task.

In this work, we focus on *click level satisfaction* as opposed to task or session level satisfaction. Previous work on satisfaction prediction has focused on user action sequences and on generating a prediction for the full task. However, we argue that being able to determine satisfaction at the individual click level is important for a number of applications, such as ranking, where satisfied clicks are used. As stated earlier, to date, work on click level satisfaction has employed a fixed threshold on dwell time to distinguish satisfied and dissatisfied clicks, with the most popular threshold being 30 seconds [14]. This is a crude estimate that ignores many factors that can affect dwell time. We show that with our method we can attain more accurate satisfaction estimates than with dwell time alone.

## 2.3 Search Performance Prediction

Another related line of work is research on search performance prediction. Several search performance predictors have been proposed in the literature (e.g., query clarity [12], inverse collection term frequency [23], and weighted information gain [46]). These predictors do not require relevance judgments and can be applied at query time to generate an estimate of how the search engine will perform, and hence how likely the user is to be satisfied. These predictors mostly utilize features derived from query information, except [17] which examines the effectiveness of interaction information (e.g., clickthrough statistics). Query clarity proposed in [12] measures relative entropy between query and collection models, i.e., how query terms are discriminant from the search collection. He and Ounis [23] examined several pre-retrieval features (e.g., query scope, query length) and found that inverse collection term frequency and (simplified) query clarity are strongly correlated with precision. Leskovec et al. [34] leveraged graphical properties recognized from the link structure of search results to predict the quality of the results. Zhou and Croft [46] proposed a weighted information gain approach which combines term probability and proximity features. Although their approach is more effective in predicting the quality of top retrieved documents, the proposed predictor requires additional query classification because their method is adapted for specific query types (i.e., named page finding or content-based). Guo et al. [17] utilized user-behavior information for predicting query performance, and found that interaction features mined from search log data can significantly improve prediction performance. Most recently, Kim et al. [33] proposed a method to generate association rules by combining topical and lexical features from the query, and showed that the generated rules are effective for predicting query performance. Continuing this line of work, we use multiple query attributes and also page attributes with the new objective of building better models of click dwell time and estimating click-level search satisfaction rather than query performance.

We now describe our methods and the experiments that we conducted to evaluate their performance. We begin with the data acquired to provide labels from which to characterize SAT and DSAT dwell times and train our models to learn more accurate satisfaction estimates for individual clicks.

# 3. DATA ACQUISITION

## 3.1 Human-Labeled Data

Our data was sampled from 10 days of search logs from a large commercial Web search engine. Each log entry contains a query, URLs of every clicked page, and the timestamps of the query and the clicks. The click dwell time was calculated by measuring the time between the click time and the next seen click or query. From this data, we randomly sampled 7,500 queries and their clicks, and asked human assessors to review the search session and estimate the satisfaction associated with every observed click.

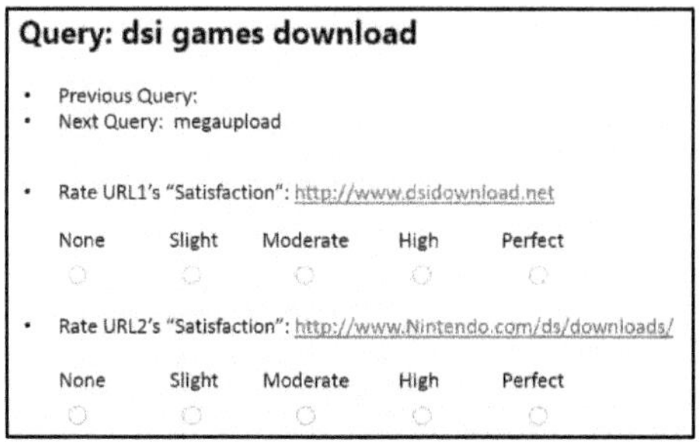


**Figure 1: An example of the judgment interface from which we obtained the click-level satisfaction judgments in HLD.**

Judges were shown the query, along with the previous and the next query to help them identify the context. For every click, the judges were asked to examine the query and the content of the clicked URL and then rate user satisfaction with the click on a five-point scale with the following response options: *none*, *slight*, *moderate*, *high*, *perfect*. To derive a binary satisfaction score from these multi-point ratings, clicks labeled as *high* or *perfect* were considered as satisfied (SAT); otherwise, the clicks were labeled as dissatisfied (DSAT). Figure 1 shows a screenshot of the judgment interface.

To obtain a ground truth satisfaction estimate for each click, we first collected the judgment results from two annotators. If the two annotators agreed at the binary label, then we use that label. If they disagreed, we ask another judge to label the instance and we use the majority label among the three judges as the satisfaction estimate.

Once every click was judged, we initially identified that 82.8% of all clicks are SAT. This skewness is not surprising because typically most queries end up being satisfied [1][19]. However, such imbalanced data is more challenging to deal with from a statistical learning point of view because the model trained by an imbalanced data would be biased to the majority class (i.e., SAT) and less effective for the minority class (i.e., DSAT). To alleviate this problem, we randomly downsample the majority class to obtain a 50/50 balanced dataset. The final dataset includes 3,204 click instances (1,602 instances are SAT and the others are DSAT). Throughout the paper, we refer to this as the Human-Labeled Data (HLD). This data set is used for evaluating the SAT click prediction model (described in Section 5.2). In addition to this dataset, we will describe a "pseudo labeled" data set in the next subsection that leverages post-click interaction behaviors to estimate click satisfaction. Due to the relatively small size of the human labeled data, we used the pseudo-labeled data to derive probability distributions of click dwell time across click segments as will be described later in the paper.

## 3.2 Pseudo-Labeled Data

Our method relies on partitioning the set of clicked URLs into smaller segments and learning the dwell time distribution for SAT and DSAT clicks for every segment. If we only partition the human labeled data into segments, we end up with a small number of instances in each segment and hence we may have insufficient data to reliably estimate the dwell time distributions in each segment. To resolve this problem, we build a pseudo-labeled dataset from the search logs and use it to estimate the dwell time distribution. Note that the pseudo labeled data set is only used for training purposes, not for testing; all evaluations are conducted on the human labeled dataset (HLD) only.

To generate the pseudo-labeled dataset, we randomly extracted hundreds of thousands of query impressions from the query logs of the same search engine that provided the data for the HLD assessment. To assign pseudo satisfaction labels to clicks, we assume that a click followed by a query reformulation is a dissatisfied click, while a click not followed by a query reformulation is a satisfied click. A query reformulation is the act of submitting a follow up query to modify a previous search query in hope of retrieving better results. Post-click query reformulation has been used as a predictor of search satisfaction in previous work [21]. The intuition here is that dissatisfied users will reformulate their queries, while satisfied users will not. This is a crude estimate of click satisfaction but it allows us to easily generate large numbers of pseudo labeled instances without leveraging any information about the click itself (which could lead to confounding). We will show later that these pseudo labels can be used to significantly improve click success prediction as measured on the HLD.

To identify query reformulations we use a method similar to that described in [5], where features of query similarity (e.g. edit distance, word overlap, etc.) and time between queries are used to identify query reformulations. Using these assumptions, we randomly collected 104,000 click instances from the search logs of the engine described earlier from March 2013. The data contains the same number of SAT and DSAT instances and does not overlap with any of the human labeled data. We refer to this data set as the Pseudo-Labeled Data (PLD), and randomly divide it into two sets: mining (training) and validation. The mining set contains 91,000 instances, and is used to model click dwell time (Section 4) and training an estimator for dwell time distributions (Section 5.1). Besides, the validation set includes the rest of the data and is used for optimizing the parameters of learning algorithms for SAT click prediction (described in Section 5.2). Note that both data sets are balanced such that there an equal number of SAT and DSAT instances.

# 4. CLICK DWELL TIME MODEL

In this section, we present our method to model click dwell time. We first identify segments (groups) of clicks, each of which effectively characterizes some of the click instances (Section 4.1). After that, we derive probabilistic models of SAT and DSAT dwell times for each click segment (Section 4.2).

## 4.1 Click Segment Generation

We generate click segments (i.e., groups of labeled click instances) using query-click attributes (e.g., query types, search topics, readability levels, etc.). In this paper, we assume that these attributes would affect the user's dwell time on a clicked result, and simply each attribute can form a click segment. However, some of these attributes are very broad (e.g., query type is "navigational"). This could result in dwell time models that are too general (similar to the global model which can be derived without the attributes). To avoid this problem, we mine click segments by associating important query-click attributes (e.g., reading difficulty of the text is high and the search topic is "drugs & medicines"). Specifically we first generate many query-click attributes for each click instance. After that, we identify associations of the attributes using decision tree learning. These groups of attributes are used to characterize the click segments.

### *4.1.1 Attribute Generation*

For each click instance, we know the text of the search query, the URL of clicked result, and the downloaded content of the URL. To characterize each instance, we generate the following attributes:

**Query Topic Attributes:** Open Directory Project (ODP, dmoz.org) provides a Web hierarchy that lists topically similar pages in the same category (predefined) including sub-categories. ODP has been widely used for topical classification of query text (e.g., [4]) or web pages (e.g., [43]). We use the query-based ODP classifier, proposed in [4], to assign topic labels to queries. The classifier used query text and clicked pages associated with every query from aggregated historic search data from the search engine to assign a topic label to each query (see [4] for more details about performance and coverage of the classifier). For each instance, the classifier assigns the five most likely categories with their associated probabilities, and we use the categories whose probabilities are higher than 0.5 (empirically set) as attributes.

**Query Type Attributes**: Query type classification has been the subject of various research efforts with the objective of understanding search intent (e.g., homepage finding task [28]). We leverage such query-type categories to characterize query-click instances. To do this, we train text classifiers that can label a query as query-type categories, and use them as binary attributes. It is worth noting that the classifiers are trained using human-labeled query examples since such human involvement can help to improve the accuracy of the classification.

**Page Topic Attributes**: We use the ODP categories to assign topic labels to every clicked page. Given the large number of pages in our set we need to label them automatically. We perform automatic classification of pages into ODP categories using an approach similar to [41], which involves looking up the URL for each page in ODP and backing off on the URL path as necessary. URLs in the directory are directly classified according to their corresponding categories. Missing URLs are incrementally pruned one level at a time until a match is found in the ODP or a miss declared. The top two levels of the ODP hierarchy are used as topic labels.

**Reading Level Attributes**: Given a document, the automatic identification of its reading difficulty has been studied in [11]. The reading difficulty of each document is represented on a 12-point scale mapped to American school grade levels. The reading level predictor we use adopts a language modeling approach using a multinomial naïve Bayes classifier, proposed in [11], and this approach has been shown to be effective, as reported in [30]. For each click instance, we first download the content of the page, and the classifier then predicts the reading level of the content.

Overall, we use 600 attributes (219 query-based ODP categories + 363 URL-based ODP categories + 6 query types + 12 reading levels) as binary attributes for mining click segments.

### *4.1.2 Click Segment Mining*

To generate click segments, we can use various algorithms leveraged for data mining (e.g., decision tree learning [38], k-means clustering [36], etc.). We selected decision tree learning because of its simplicity (e.g., clustering approaches need to define a similarity between examples) and efficiency in applying decision rules to instances (i.e., additional computation to identify a membership of a new instance is not necessary). Click segments (i.e., decision rules) are mined as follows. We are given a set of SAT and DSAT click instances, each of which contains 600 binary attributes, and a binary decision tree can be trained using this data to classify an instance into either SAT or DSAT (i.e., the non-leaf nodes in the tree contain any of the 600 attributes). Once a decision tree is learned, we can extract decision rules (where each rule is formed by the path from the root to a leaf node). Each decision rule contains an association of the attributes (e.g., Shopping $\wedge$ Computer)

**ALGORITHM:** Iterative Decision Tree Learning

**INPUT:**

- Set of labeled click instances, $C = \{c_1, c_2, \dots, c_n\}$ where the label of $c$ is $DSAT$ or $SAT$, i.e., $L(c) \in \{\text{DSAT}, \text{SAT}\}$
- Set of attributes $A = \{a_1, a_2, \dots, a_d\}$
- Min. number of examples in a leaf node, $m$.

**OUTPUT:** A set of segment rules

**PROCESS:**

1) Initialize $R = \{\}, T = \{\}, R' = \{\}$
2) Do
3)   $N = |R|$
4)   $A \leftarrow A - T$
5)   Train a binary decision tree, $DT$ which uses $A$ as features and C as examples where $L(q)$ indicates a label of $c \in C$ and the minimum number of examples in a leaf node is set as $m$
6)   For each leaf node
7)     Generate $P$ the set of nodes (features) in the path from the root to the leaf node in $DT$
8)     $R \leftarrow R \cup \{P\}$
9)   End For
10)   $T \leftarrow T \cup \{a_t\}$ where $a_t$ is the root node of $DT$
11)   $N' = |R|$
12) While $N \neq N'$
13) For each rule $r$ in $R$
14)   Generate $r'$ by excluding the attribute associated with negation in $r$
15)   $R' \leftarrow R' \cup \{r\}$
16) End For
17) Return $R'$

**Figure 2: Iterative decision tree learning algorithm.**

and can form a click segment. To extend the rule coverage, we ignore negated attributes (e.g., ¬Recreation).

To mine more segments, we devise an iterative learning algorithm that iteratively learns multiple decision trees with different attribute sets. Specifically, we first learn a decision tree using all attributes (defined in Section 4.1.1), and extract all rules from the learned tree. In the next iteration, we identify the root node (i.e., top attribute) of the previous tree and exclude it from the current learning iteration. In other words, the decision tree learned from the current iteration does not generate the rules containing the root node. By doing this, we can discover new rules that are not extracted from the previous iteration because every previously-mined rule contains the top attribute (root node) of the previous decision tree. This process is repeated until no new rules can be extracted. Figure 2 describes this algorithm. In that, we control the number of examples in a click segment by $m$ (i.e., the minimum number of examples in a leaf node). A value of $m$ that is too small is less effective because it causes the learning process to take a long time and results in rules with a small number of clicks. A small number of examples for each rule (segment) would be insufficient to derive a probabilistic model (Section 4.2). Besides, too large an $m$ is inappropriate since only a few attributes are selected and the number of generated rules would be insufficient.

In experiments, we used the C4.5 algorithm implemented in [18], and ran our iterative learning algorithm on the mining set of PLD (Section 3.2) by setting $m$ as $100, 200, \dots, 1000$. We obtained 269 rules (segments). Table 2 shows some examples of the rules. From that, we can identify how each segment is characterized by the query-click attributes, e.g., QueryTopic(Business) ∧ RLV(12)

**Table 2: Segment examples. #SAT and #DSAT indicate the number of SAT and DSAT click examples, respectively.**

| Segment (Rule) | #SAT | #DSAT |
|---|---|---|
| PageTopic (Computers/Companies) | 1,423 (46%) | 1,659 (54%) |
| QueryTopic(Business) ∧ RLV(12) | 916 (58%) | 652 (42%) |

means that the queries of the corresponding clicks are related to "business" topics and their clicked pages are difficult to understand (i.e., their readability level is 12).

## 4.2 Model Fitting

Now we describe how to fit a probability distribution to the SAT and DSAT examples of each segment. The Gamma distribution has been frequently used to model waiting time [24]. In this paper, we assume that the Gamma distribution can govern the amount of time that the user dwells at each clicked page, and the dwell times of the same-segment clicks would follow the same distribution. The distribution includes two parameters: a shape, $k$ and scale, $\theta$, and the probability density function (PDF) is given as:

$$p(t|k,\theta) = \frac{t^{k-1}}{\Gamma(k)\theta^k}\exp\left(-\frac{t}{\theta}\right) \quad (1)$$

where $k > 0, \theta > 0$ and $t$ is a click dwell time where $t \epsilon (0, \infty)$.

Given a click segment, we first collect SAT and DSAT examples that belong to the segment, and generate two lists of dwell times from the SAT and DSAT examples. For each dwell time list $\{t\}_1^n$, we estimate the parameter values to fit the distribution by Maximum Likelihood Estimation (MLE) as follows.

The log-likelihood for $n$ i.i.d. dwell time samples are given as:

$$\ell(k,\theta) = (k-1)\sum_{i=1}^{n} \ln t_i - \frac{1}{\theta}\sum_{i=1}^{n} t_i - n \ln \Gamma(k) - nk \ln \theta \quad (2)$$

The maximum of $\theta$ is found by taking the derivative of Eq. (2).

$$\hat{\theta} = \frac{1}{kn} \cdot \sum_{i=1}^{n} t_i \quad (3)$$

Substituting Eq. (3) into Eq. (2) gives:

$$\ell = (k-1)\sum_{i=1}^{n} \ln t_i - kn - n \ln \Gamma(k) - nk \ln\left(\frac{\sum_{i=1}^{n} t_i}{kn}\right) \quad (4)$$

To find the maximum of $k$, we take the derivate of Eq. (4) as:

$$\ln k - \psi(k) = \ln\left(\frac{1}{n}\sum_{i=1}^{n} t_i\right) - \frac{1}{n}\sum_{i=1}^{n} \ln t_i \quad (5)$$

where $\psi$ is the digamma function.

A numerical solution for Eq. (5) is introduced in [9] which gives the Newton-Raphson iteration as:

$$\frac{1}{k^{(t+1)}} \leftarrow \frac{1}{k^{(t)}} + \frac{\ln k^{(t)} - \psi(k^{(t)}) - s}{(k^{(t)})^2\left(1/k^{(t)} - \psi'(k^{(t)})\right)} \quad (6)$$

where $s = \ln\left(\frac{1}{n}\sum_{i=1}^{n} t_i\right) - \frac{1}{n}\sum_{i=1}^{n}(\ln t_i)$, $\psi'$ denotes the trigamma function, and $k^{(t)}$ is the $t$-th update of $k$.

More details of the derivation are described in [37], and by the equations above we can estimate two parameter sets, i.e., $\langle \hat{k}_{\mathrm{SAT}}, \hat{\theta}_{\mathrm{SAT}} \rangle$ and $\langle \hat{k}_{\mathrm{DSAT}}, \hat{\theta}_{\mathrm{DSAT}} \rangle$. For each parameter set, its goodness is determined using the Kolmogorov-Smirnov test (K-S test) [27] which is typically used for evaluating the goodness of an estimation. The Kolmogorov-Smirnov statistic measures a probabilistic distance between the empirical Cumulative Distribution Function (eCDF) of a sample and the CDF of a reference distribution (i.e., one-sample K-S test). In our case, the reference distribution is the Gamma distribution, and the null hypothesis is that the sample (dwell times of click instances) is drawn from the Gamma distribution. We reject the null hypothesis at the 5% significance level ($p < 0.05$), and an estimated parameter set is rejected if its testing result is rejection. In which case, the rule (segment) is discarded. In experiments, we initially extracted 269 segments (rules), and accordingly the same number of SAT or DSAT parameter sets were obtained. After testing every parameter set, we removed a segment if its SAT or DSAT estimation is rejected. As a result, 56 segments are discarded, and 213 segments are retained.

## 4.3 Dwell Time Analysis

In this section, we provide an empirical analysis of SAT and DSAT dwell times using our dwell time distributions. For each attribute or segment, we extract corresponding instances from mining the PLD, estimate SAT and DSAT parameters, and plot their PDFs. From this, we can understand the difference between SAT and DSAT dwell times across attributes or segments. Note that for each estimation the K-S test is performed and the estimation is rejected if it could not pass the test.

We first analyze SAT and DSAT dwell times by different reading levels. Figure 3, 4, and 5 show the PDFs estimated by SAT and DSAT examples whose reading levels are 2 (easy), 6 (moderate), and 12 (difficult), respectively. In each figure, a click which belongs to the corresponding reading level is likely to be SAT if its dwell time is placed within the region where SAT probability is higher than DSAT probability; otherwise, the click is likely to be DSAT. Based on this interpretation, we empirically mark the dwell-time threshold where a click is likely to be SAT if its dwell time is longer than that (i.e., (1)). For the easy reading level, such threshold is found at around 160 seconds, the threshold of the moderate reading level is slightly increased (i.e., recognized at around 175 seconds), and the difficult reading level requires more than 200 seconds before a satisfied determination can be made. This suggests that the user requires different dwell times to examine clicked pages according to their reading difficulty. Moreover, in each figure, we can identify the dwell time when its DSAT probability is maximized (i.e., the highest DSAT probability). In the easy reading level, the shorter dwell time a click has, the more likely to be DSAT. However, in the medium reading level, about 30 seconds can maximize the DSAT probability whereas in the difficult reading level, such maximum point moves to over 50 seconds. That is, a longer dwell time is required for more complex pages even if their clicks are DSAT.

Next, we provide a similar analysis focused on different topics and rules other than reading level. Figure 6 plots the SAT and DSAT PDFs estimated by an ODP category of "Reference/Knowledge Management". Since this category generally contains "technical" topics (e.g., knowledge discovery, knowledge retrieval, etc.), the dwell time threshold (i.e., (1)) is quite increased, and the highest DSAT probability is obtained when the dwell time is about 70 seconds (similar to that of the difficult reading level).

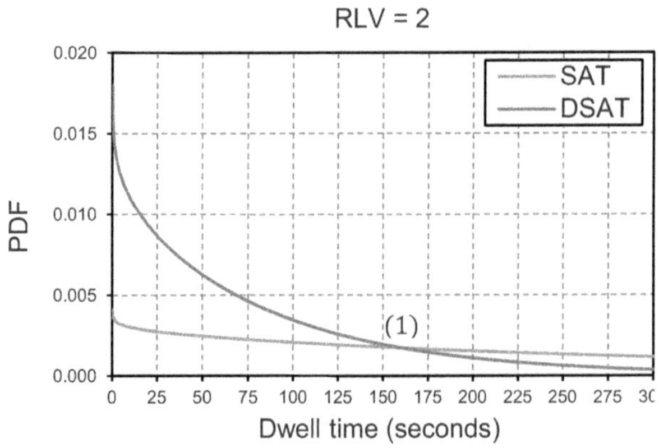


**Figure 3: SAT and DSAT PDFs of RLV = 2 (easy).**

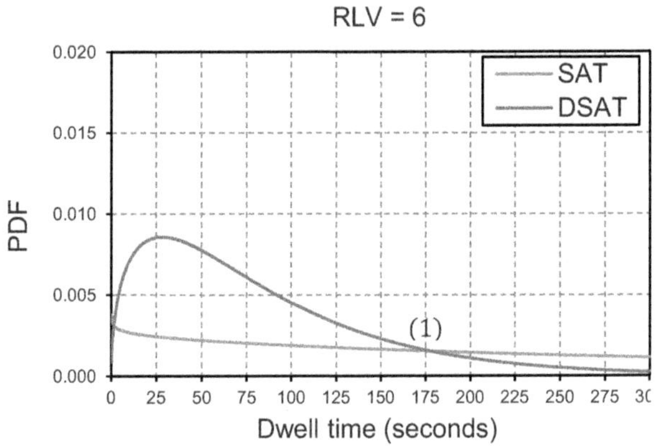


**Figure 4: SAT and DSAT PDFs of RLV = 6 (moderate).**

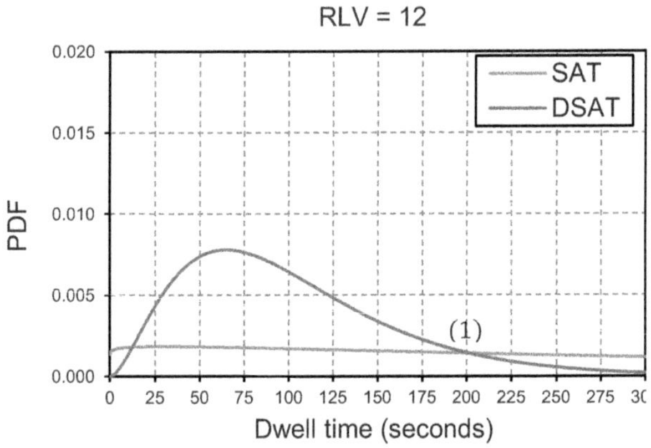


**Figure 5: SAT and DSAT PDFs of RLV = 12 (difficult).**

Regarding click segments, Figure 7 and 8 show the PDFs generated from two sample segments. The first segment contains the instances related to "Computer/Companies" (from Page Topic) and "Technical Help" (among query types), which form a "technical" segment. Again, the dwell time threshold is high (about 210 seconds) because the searches in this segment relate to technical topics and searchers may require longer to determine content value. Different from this, the clicks from the second segment (i.e.,) are related to less-technical topics (i.e., "shopping") and its dwell time threshold is much shorter than that of the first segment (i.e., technical topics).

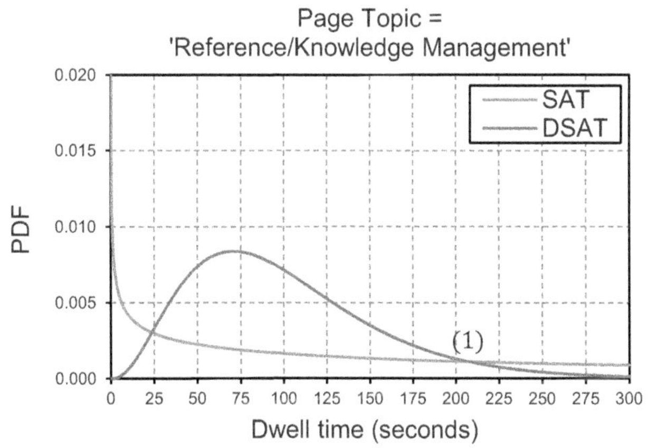


**Figure 6: SAT and DSAT PDFs of a sample attribute.**

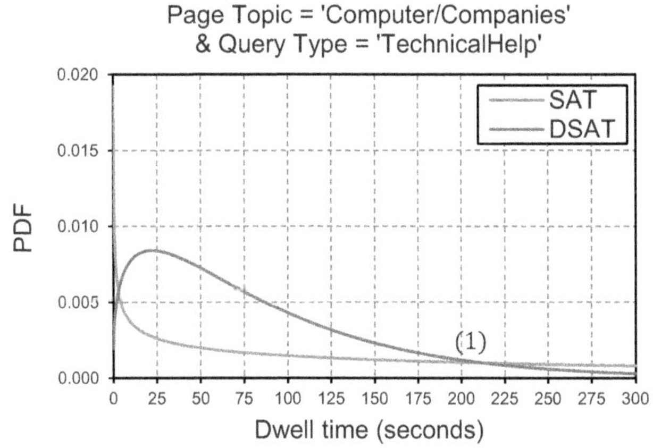


**Figure 7: SAT and DSAT PDFs of a "technical" segment.**

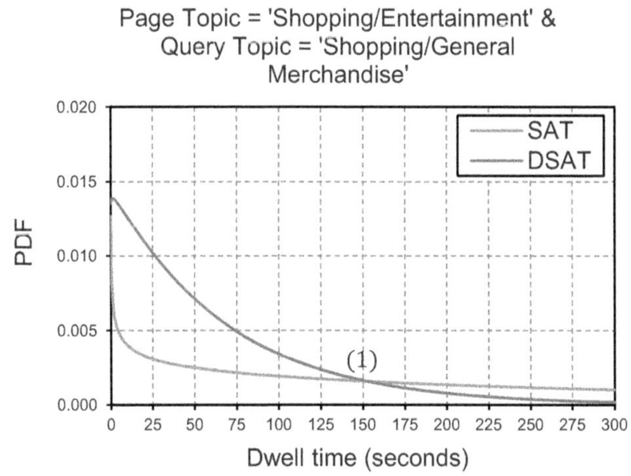


**Figure 8: SAT and DSAT PDFs of a "shopping" segment.**

It is clear from the findings presented in this section that there are differences in the SAT and DSAT dwell times associated with attributes of the clicked page, such as complexity and topic. This demonstrates that a single satisfaction threshold across all pages may be insufficient. In the next section we describe a click satisfaction model that leverages these dwell time distributions.

# 5. CLICK SATISFACTION MODEL

In this section, we describe a click-level satisfaction model exploiting our dwell time distributions. In Section 5.1, we describe how to estimate SAT and DSAT dwell time distributions for unseen click instances, and Section 5.2 provides a classification model to predict SAT clicks based on the estimated distributions.

**Table 3: Features for estimating dwell time distribution [35].**

| Feature | Description |
|---|---|
| **PageSize** | Size (in bytes) of the clicked page |
| **PageLength** | # of words in the clicked page |
| **RenderTime** | Time to render the clicked page |
| **HTML Tag** | The frequency distribution of the 93 HTML tags (see http://www.quackit.com) |
| **QueryTopic** | Query topic (as described in Section 4.1) |
| **PageTopic** | Page topic (as described in Section 4.1) |
| **Readability** | Page readability level (as described in Section 4.1) |

## 5.1 Estimating Dwell Time Distributions

Given a click instance, we would like to use the SAT and DSAT distributions described in Section 4 to determine whether the click is SAT. Although we generate many segments using a large-scale data set, we still have some unseen clicks that do not belong to any generated segments. Hence, some statistical method is required to estimate the SAT and DSAT dwell time distributions for these unseen clicks.

To estimate SAT and DSAT dwell time distributions for unseen instances, we develop a regression model to predict the parameters of each distribution. The formal definition of this model is given as follows. Suppose that $S = \{s_1, s_2, \dots, s_n\}$ is a set of $n$ click segments and $\Pi = \{\pi_1, \pi_2, \dots, \pi_n\}$ is a list of estimated parameter sets from each segment. Each parameter set contains the parameters for SAT and DSAT distributions, i.e., $\pi_i = \{y_i^{\mathrm{SAT}}, y_i^{\mathrm{DSAT}}\}$ where $\pi_i$ includes the corresponding parameters for $s_i$. In our case, each $y$ involves a shape and scale values because we use the Gamma distribution for model fitting. In addition, for each segment, we have labeled instances used for estimating the parameters, which are expressed as $\{x_i^{\mathrm{SAT}}, x_i^{\mathrm{DSAT}}\}$ where $x_i^{\mathrm{SAT}}$ is the set of instances used for estimating$y_i^{\mathrm{SAT}}$. Then, we train regression models using SAT and DSAT instances, i.e., $T_{\mathrm{SAT}} = \{(\phi(x_i^{\mathrm{SAT}}), y_i^{\mathrm{SAT}})\}_{i=1}^{n}$ and$T_{\mathrm{DSAT}} = \{(\phi(x_i^{\mathrm{DSAT}}), y_i^{\mathrm{DSAT}})\}_{i=1}^{n}$ where $\phi$ is a feature function and $y_i$ is a target regression value for $x_i$. Note that in experiments, we generate four different regressors since each $y$ in our case includes two parameter values (see Section 6.1). The regression function $f: \phi(x) \mapsto \Re$ maps a feature vector to a real value, and the model is trained to minimize a loss function defined by the difference between the mapped value and the target regression value ($y$) of every training example. To generate a feature vector for each instance, we leverage the features described in Table 3. These features have been shown to correlate with browsing time such as page length, the distribution of HTML tags, etc. [35]. In addition to these features, we use the query-click attributes (described in Section 4.1) and the segment rules (described in Section 4.2) as features because the clicks would follow the same distribution if they have some common attributes or belong to the same segment.

## 5.2 Predicting SAT Clicks

We now describe our method to predict click-level satisfaction. In that, we classify a click instance into either SAT or DSAT, i.e., a binary classification. As shown in Section 4.3, our dwell time model (i.e., SAT and DSAT dwell time distributions) can help to

Table 4: Dynamic dwell time features. $M_{SAT}$ is the SAT Gamma distribution estimated by the regressor in Section 5.1, $t$ is the dwell time of a click instance, $k_{SAT}$ and $\theta_{SAT}$ are the shape and scale parameter values for $M_{SAT}$, respectively.

| No. | Definition | Description |
|---|---|---|
| F1 | $k_{SAT} - k_{DSAT}$ | Difference between SAT and DSAT shape values |
| F2 | $\theta_{SAT} - \theta_{DSAT}$ | Difference between SAT and DSAT scale values |
| F3 | $\mu_{SAT} = k_{SAT}\theta_{SAT}$ | Mean of SAT distribution |
| F4 | $\mu_{DSAT} = k_{DSAT}\theta_{DSAT}$ | Mean of DSAT distribution |
| F5 | $\mu_{SAT} - \mu_{DSAT}$ | Diff. between $\mu_{SAT}$ and $\mu_{DSAT}$ |
| F6 | $\lvert t - \mu_{SAT} \rvert$ | Time distance to $\mu_{SAT}$ |
| F7 | $\lvert t - \mu_{DSAT} \rvert$ | Time distance to $\mu_{DSAT}$ |
| F8 | $p(t \mid M_{SAT})/p(t \mid M_{DSAT})$ | Ratio of the SAT likelihood to the DSAT likelihood |
| F9 | $\ln p(t \mid M_{SAT})$ | Log-likelihood to SAT |
| F10 | $\ln p(t \mid M_{DSAT})$ | Log-likelihood to DSAT |
| F11 | $\ln p(t \mid M_{SAT}) - \ln p(t \mid M_{DSAT})$ | Difference between log-likelihoods of SAT and DSAT |

dynamically determine dwell time thresholds according to attributes and segments, and provide better interpretations of the dwell time of a click. As an example, given a dwell time, the likelihoods to SAT and DSAT distributions can be calculated. Therefore, our click satisfaction model can include more elaborate dwell time features based on the SAT and DSAT dwell time distributions estimated by the regression models described in Section 5.1.

Table 4 shows our dynamic dwell time features to facilitate the click classification. F1, F2, F3, F4, and F5 are calculated only using the distribution parameters estimated by the regression models, and the dwell time of each instance (i.e., $t$) is not necessary. On the other hand, F6, F7, F8, F9, F10, and F11 require $t$ for calculating each feature value, but those features may provide better understanding of $t$ for classification algorithms. In other words, F6, F7, F8, F9, F10, and F11 would be useful in that they indicate how much each instance is likely to be a SAT or DSAT click. Additionally, we use the segment rules mined by decision trees (Section 4.1) as binary features because those rules contain discriminative attributes to identify SAT or DSAT clicks.

Using the features described above, we train a classification model using labeled click instances, and the formal definition of this is given as follows. Given a set of $n$ labeled examples, $\{x_1, x_2, \dots, x_n\}$, we generate a feature vector of each $x_i$, i.e., $\phi(x_i)$, and the label of each $x_i$ is indicated by $L(x_i)$. A set of training examples is given as $\Phi = \{(\phi(x_i), L(x_i))\}_{i=1}^{n}$, and a classification function map a feature vector to a SAT or DSAT label, i.e., $f: \phi(x) \mapsto \{1,0\}$ where 1 and 0 denote SAT and DSAT, respectively. The model is learned by minimizing the disagreement between a mapped label and original label, $L(q_i)$ for every training example.

# 6. EXPERIMENTS

## 6.1 Estimating Dwell Time Distributions

In this section, we discuss the performance in estimating SAT and DSAT dwell time distributions, which is significant for the SAT click prediction. To identify an appropriate regression method, we test various algorithms for our SAT and DSAT distribution estimation (described in Section 5.1). We employ Poisson regression [7], Stochastic Gradient Descent (SGD) [5], and Multiple Additive Regression Trees (MART) [15]. Since a Gamma distribution includes two parameters (i.e., $k$ (shape) and $\theta$ (scale)), we generate four regressors for each parameter of $\{k_{SAT}, \theta_{SAT}, k_{DSAT}, \theta_{DSAT}\}$. We measure the Root Mean Square (RMS) error for each method. For evaluation, we can use the mining set from PLD (Section 3.2), which contains 91,000 click examples (45,500 instances are SAT and the others are DSAT) because this data set is used for deriving dwell time distributions (Section 4.2) and accordingly corresponding regression values for each example are already calculated. Note that in this experiment the SAT or DSAT label of each instance is not used since we only test our regression model. We run each algorithm 10 times and for each run, 10-fold cross-validation is performed with random partitioning.

Table 5: RMS error by regression method. A significant improvement is marked using the first letter of each method. The Wilcoxon rank sum test is performed with $p < 0.01$.

| Method | $k_{SAT}$ | $\theta_{SAT}$ | $k_{DSAT}$ | $\theta_{DSAT}$ |
|---|---|---|---|---|
| Poisson [7] | 0.224 | 813.968 | 0.166 | 111.205 |
| SGD [5] | $0.159^{P}$ | $56.876^{P}$ | $0.083^{P}$ | $10.740^{P}$ |
| MART [15] | $0.014^{PS}$ | $8.905^{PS}$ | $0.012^{PS}$ | $0.762^{PS}$ |

Table 5 shows the regression results using the three different algorithms. We report an average value of the RMS error over every testing example. Note that the evaluation metric denotes a numerical error where a smaller value indicates a better performance. It is quite clear that MART can significantly outperform the others in every regression. In the next series of experiments, we use MART as a learning algorithm of the regression model for dwell time distributions.

## 6.2 SAT Click Classification

We now describe the experiments that we performed to predict whether observed clicks were satisfied. We begin by describing the experimental setup (including baseline features), and then present the classification results comparing the different methods.

### *6.2.1 Experimental Setup*

We conduct experiments to evaluate our SAT click classification model. For this evaluation, we use HLD (described Section 3.1) that contains 3,204 human-labeled click instances (where the half of them are SAT and the others are DSAT). To each instance, we apply the MART regressors (trained using the mining set of PLD; see Section 6.1) for estimating its dwell time distributions. To learn the classification model, we use MART boosted decision trees [15]. We also conducted the experiment with another classification algorithm, i.e., Linear Support Vector Machine (SVM) [8] using baseline features (described below), and MART performed significantly better than SVM (we omit the results due to space limitation). The classifier was run 10 times, and for each run, 10-fold cross-validation is performed using random partitioning.

**Baselines:** For a baseline, the dwell time of each click can be used. As analyzed in [14], dwell time (the time spent on a clicked result) is significantly correlated with click satisfaction, and this feature is used as Baseline 1. In addition, we use the attributes described in Section 4.1.1 and the features from previous work on predicting search performance [12][23]. Since dwell time can be influenced by reading difficulty, topics, and query types, these attributes may help to identify the satisfaction of each click. Besides, search performance predictors (e.g., [12][23]) are effective in estimating search quality which would be related to click satisfaction. We choose to use the query clarity score [12], inverse collection term frequency [23], and query term length, which can be easily implemented and effectively work as much as other predictors (e.g., [45][46]).

Table 6: Classification Results on Human-Labeled Data. Baseline 1 contains only the dwell time of each click instance, Baseline 2 includes the search performance predictors [12][23] and the click attributes described in Section 4.1, and Baseline 3 is the combination of Baseline 1 and 2. D and R denote dynamic dwell time features (see Section 5.2) and click segment rules (Section 4.1), respectively. In each column, a significant improvement over each baseline is marked by its number, e.g., B12 indicates an improvement over Baseline 1&2, and a * indicates a significant improvement of each Baseline + D + R over the Baseline + D (i.e., the effectiveness of R for each Baseline + D). The Wilcoxon rank sum test is performed with $p < 0.01$, and the best result in each column is marked in bold.

| Method | SAT Precision | SAT Recall | SAT F1 | DSAT Precision | DSAT Recall | DSAT F1 | Accuracy |
|---|---|---|---|---|---|---|---|
| Baseline 1 | 0.5758 | 0.5180 | 0.5453 | 0.5620 | 0.6184 | 0.5888 | 0.5682 |
| Baseline 1 + D | 0.7103 B1 | 0.6736 B1 | 0.6915 B1 | 0.6897 B1 | 0.7253 B1 | 0.7071 B1 | 0.6995 B1 |
| *vs. Baseline 1* | *+23.36%* | *+30.04%* | *+26.81%* | *+22.72%* | *+17.29%* | *+20.08%* | *+23.10%* |
| Baseline 1 + D + R | 0.7278 B1* | 0.6967 B1* | 0.7119 B1* | 0.7092 B1* | 0.7395 B1* | 0.7240 B1* | 0.7181 B1* |
| *vs. Baseline 1* | *+26.40%* | *+34.50%* | *+30.55%* | *+26.18%* | *+19.57%* | *+22.95%* | *+26.38%* |
| Baseline 2 | 0.7564 B1 | 0.6979 B1 | 0.7260 B1 | 0.7196 B1 | 0.7753 B1 | 0.7464 B1 | 0.7366 B1 |
| Baseline 2 + D | **0.8178** B123 | **0.7951** B123 | **0.8062** B123 | **0.8006** B123 | **0.8228** B123 | **0.8115** B123 | **0.8089** B123 |
| *vs. Baseline 2* | *+8.11%* | *+13.93%* | *+11.06%* | *+11.26%* | *+6.13%* | *+8.73%* | *+9.82%* |
| Baseline 2 + D + R | 0.8168 B123 | 0.7901 B123 | 0.8032 B123 | 0.7968 B123 | 0.8227 B123 | 0.8095 B123 | 0.8064 B123 |
| *vs. Baseline 2* | *+7.98%* | *+13.22%* | *+10.64%* | *+10.73%* | *+6.12%* | *+8.46%* | *+9.48%* |
| Baseline 3 | 0.7570 B1 | 0.7116 B1 | 0.7336 B1 | 0.7279 B1 | 0.7715 B1 | 0.7491 B1 | 0.7416 B1 |
| Baseline 3 + D | 0.8149 B123 | 0.7933 B123 | 0.8039 B123 | 0.7986 B123 | 0.8199 B123 | 0.8091 B123 | 0.8066 B123 |
| *vs. Baseline 3* | *+7.66%* | *+11.47%* | *+9.59%* | *+9.71%* | *+6.26%* | *+8.01%* | *+8.76%* |
| Baseline 3 + D + R | 0.8174 B123 | 0.7933 B123 | 0.8051 B123 | 0.7992 B123 | 0.8227 B123 | 0.8108 B123 | 0.8080 B123 |
| *vs. Baseline 3* | *+7.98%* | *+11.47%* | *+9.75%* | *+9.79%* | *+6.63%* | *+8.23%* | *+8.96%* |

To estimate the inverse collection term frequency, we use term probabilities obtained from the Web N-Gram services [40]. We calculate the sum, standard deviation, ratio of the maximum to the minimum, maximum, arithmetic mean, and geometric mean among the term probabilities of all query terms. Therefore, Baseline 2 contains 600 binary attributes (see Section 4.1.1) and eight search performance predictors. To develop more robust baseline, we combine the features from Baselines 1 and 2 to form Baseline 3. Note that the features for estimating dwell time distributions (i.e., Table 3&4) are not used in any baselines.

### 6.2.2 *Classification Results*

We now evaluate our SAT click prediction model that contains dynamic dwell time features (proposed in Section 5.2). With each baseline, we incorporate the dynamic dwell time features, and the combined model would perform better if the proposed features are effective to identify SAT and DSAT clicks. Besides, we additionally test with the segment rules (Section 4.1) as binary features for expecting further improvements. We measure precision, recall, and F1 for each class, and accuracy (i.e., weighted precision) is measured to verify overall classification performance.

Table 6 shows the classification results on HLD. First, the features in Baseline 2 seem to be more effective than Baseline 1. Baseline 2 and 3 including the search performance predictors and query-click attributes can significantly outperform the Baseline 1 containing only dwell time. However, no significant difference is observed between the results of Baseline 2 and 3. Second, the proposed features can significantly improve every baseline. This means that our dynamic dwell time features are quite effective for predicting SAT and DSAT click examples. In particular, only dwell time (Baseline 1) appears somewhat less important (i.e., its overall accuracy is only 0.5682), but combining it with the dynamic dwell time features, the performance is dramatically improved, i.e., +23.10% in accuracy. Third, we can only observe the further improvement achieved by segment rules when combining with Baseline 1 (dwell time only), marked by an asterisk in Table 6. This is because Baselines 2 and 3 already contain the attributes used for generating the segment rules (i.e., a segment rule is an association of discriminant attributes).

## 7. CONCLUSIONS

Current methods to estimate search satisfaction use a single dwell time threshold applied to all result clicks. In this paper, we proposed a method to model dwell time distributions of SAT and DSAT clicks related to specific query-click attributes, i.e., reading difficulty of clicked pages, search topics, and query types. Our dwell time model can provide better interpretations of a click dwell time, e.g., the likelihood of the click to be associated with SAT or DSAT. In addition, we identified changes in SAT or DSAT dwell times according to the attributes, e.g., more dwell time is required for pages which have sophisticated content (high reading level) although its click is DSAT. To the best of our knowledge, this is the first study to identify and characterize the effect of query-click attributes on click dwell time. Based on the dwell time model, we also proposed regression models that estimate SAT and DSAT dwell time distributions for new clicks. Using these regressors, we could generate dynamic dwell time features for predicting SAT clicks, which resulted in significant improvements in prediction performance. For future work, we will explore other techniques to determine dwell time (e.g., client side monitoring rather than server side as reported here), study other factors that may affect click dwell time (e.g., pages revisited by the same user may lead to lower dwell times given increased familiarity with the page), and analyze the impact of these variations on the performance of our click-level satisfaction predictor. We will also explore the use of the satisfaction predictions as more reliable implicit feedback in applications such as search result ranking.

## REFERENCES


[1] Ageev, M., Guo, Q., Lagun, D., and Agichtein, E. (2011). Find it if you can: a game for modeling different types of web search success using interaction data. *Proc. SIGIR*, 345-354.

[2] Agichtein, E., Brill, E., and Dumais, S. (2006). Improving web search ranking by incorporating user behavior information. *Proc. SIGIR*, 19-26.

[3] Agichtein, E., Brill, E., Dumais, S.T., and Ragno, R. (2006). Learning user interaction models for predicting web search result preferences. *Proc. SIGIR*, 3-10.

[4] Bennett, P.N., Svore, K., and Dumais, S.T. (2010). Classification-enhanced ranking. *Proc. WWW*, 111-120.

[5] Boldi, P., Bonchi, F., Castillo, C., Donato, D., Gionis, A., and Vigna, S. (2008). The query-flow graph: model and applications. *Proc. CIKM*, 609-618.

[6] Buscher, G., van Elst, L., and Dengel, A. (2009). Segment-level display time as implicit feedback: a comparison to eye tracking. *Proc. SIGIR*, 67-74.

[7] Cameron, A.C. and Trivedi, P.K. (1998). *Regression Analysis of Count Data*. Cambridge University Press.

[8] Chang, C.-C. and Lin, C.-J. (2011). LIBSVM: a library for support vector machines. *ACM Transactions on Intelligent Systems and Technology*, 2(27): 1-27.

[9] Choi, S.C. and Whette, R. (1969). Maximum likelihood estimation of the parameters of the gamma distribution and their bias. *Technometrics*, 11(4): 683-690.

[10] Claypool, M., Le, P., Wased, M., and Brown, D. (2001). Implicit interest indicators. *Proc. IUI*, 33-40.

[11] Collins-Thompson, K. and Callan, J. (2004). A language modeling approach to predicting reading difficulty. *Proc. HLT*, 193-200.

[12] Cronen-Townsend, S., Zhou, Y., and Croft, W.B. (2002). Predicting query performance. *Proc. SIGIR*, 299-306.

[13] Feild, H., Allan, J., and Jones, R. (2010). Predicting searcher frustration. *Proc. SIGIR*, 34-41.

[14] Fox, S., Karnawat, K., Mydland, M., Dumais, S., and White, T. (2005). Evaluating implicit measures to improve web search. *ACM TOIS*, 23(2): 147-168.

[15] Friedman, J.H. (2001). Greedy function approximation: a gradient boosting machine. *The Annals of Statistics*, 29(5): 1189-1232.

[16] Guo, Q. and Agichtein, E. (2012). Beyond dwell time: estimating document relevance from cursor movements and other post-click searcher behavior. *Proc. WWW*, 569-578.

[17] Guo, Q., White, R.W., Dumais, S.T., Wang, J., and Anderson, B. (2010). Predicting query performance using query, result, and user interaction features. *Proc. RIAO*, 198-201.

[18] Hall, M., Frank, E., Holmes, G., Pfahringer, B., Reutemann, P., and Witten, I.H. (2009). The WEKA data mining software: an update. *SIGKDD Explorations*, 11(1): 10-18.

[19] Hassan, A. (2012). A semi-supervised approach to modeling web search satisfaction. *Proc. SIGIR*, 275-284.

[20] Hassan, A., Jones, R., and Klinkner, K.L. (2010). Beyond DCG: user behavior as a predictor of a successful search. *Proc. WSDM*, 221-230.

[21] Hassan, A., Shi, X., Craswell, N., and Ramsey, B. (2013). Beyond clicks: query reformulation as a predictor of search satisfaction. *Proc. CIKM*, 2019-2028.

[22] Hassan, A., Song, Y., and He, L. (2011). A task level user satisfaction model and its application on improving relevance estimation. *Proc. CIKM*, 125-134.

[23] He, B. and Ounis, I. (2006). Query performance prediction. *Information System*, 31(7): 585-594.

[24] Hogg, R. V., McKean, J., and Craig, A.T. (2012). *Introduction to Mathematical Statistics*. Pearson, 7th Ed.

[25] Huffman, S. and Hochster, M. (2007). How well does result relevance predict session satisfaction? *Proc. SIGIR*, 567-574.

[26] T. Joachims. (2002). Optimizing search engines using clickthrough data. *Proc. SIGKDD*, 132-142.

[27] Justel, A., Peña, D., and Zamar, R. (1997). A multivariate Kolmogorov-Smirnov test of goodness of fit. *Statistics & Probability Letters*, 35(3): 251-259.

[28] Kang, I.-H. and Kim, G. (2003). Query type classification for web document retrieval. *Proc. SIGIR*, 64-71.

[29] Kelly, D. and Teevan, J. (2003). Implicit feedback for inferring user preference: a bibliography. *SIGIR Forum*: 37(2).

[30] Kidwell, P., Lebanon, G., and Collins-Thompson, K. (2009). Statistical estimation of word acquisition with application to readability prediction. *Proc. EMNLP*, 900-909.

[31] Kelly, D. and Belkin, N.J. (2001). Reading time, scrolling, and interaction: exploring implicit sources of user preferences for relevance feedback. *Proc. SIGIR*, 408-409

[32] Kelly, D. and Belkin, N.J. (2004). Display time as implicit feedback: understanding task effects. *Proc. SIGIR*, 377-384.

[33] Kim, Y., Hassan, A., White, R.W., and Wang, Y.-M. (2013). Playing by the rules: mining query associations to predict search performance. *Proc. WSDM*, 133-142.

[34] Leskovec, J., Dumais, S., and Horvitz, E. (2007). Web projections: learning from contextual sub graphs of the web. *Proc. WWW*, 471-480.

[35] Liu C., White, R.W., and Dumais, S. (2010). Understanding web browsing behaviors through Weibull analysis of dwell time. *Proc. SIGIR*. 379-386.

[36] Lloyd, S.P. (1982). Least squares quantization in PCM. *IEEE Transactions on Information Theory*, 28(2): 129-137.

[37] Minka, T.P. (2002). *Estimating a Gamma Distribution*. Microsoft Research Technical Report.

[38] Quinlan, J.R. (1993). *C4.5: Programs for Machine Learning*. Morgan Kaufmann Publishers.

[39] Radlinski, F., Kurup, M. and Joachims, T. (2008). How does clickthrough data reflect retrieval quality? *Proc. CIKM*, 43-52.

[40] Wang, K., Thrasher, C., Viegas, E., Li, X. and Hsu, P. (2010). An overview of Microsoft web n-gram corpus and applications. *NAACL HLT Demo Session*, 45-48.

[41] White, R.W. and Huang, J. (2010). Assessing the scenic route: measuring the value of search trails in web logs. Proc. *Proc. SIGIR*, 587-594.

[42] White, R. W. and Kelly, D. (2006). A study on the effects of personalization and task information on implicit feedback performance. *Proc. CIKM*. 297-306.

[43] Xue, G.-R., Xing, D., Yang, Q., and Yu, Y. (2008). Deep classification in large-scale text hierarchies. *Proc. SIGIR*, 619-626.

[44] Yin, P., Luo, P., Lee, W.-C., and Wang, M. (2013). Silence is also evidence: interpreting dwell time for recommendation from psychological perspective. *Proc. KDD*, 989-997.

[45] Zhou, Y., and Croft, W.B. (2006). Ranking robustness: a novel framework to predict query performance. *Proc. CIKM*, 567-574.

[46] Zhou, Y. and Croft, W.B. (2007). Query performance prediction in web search environments. *Proc. SIGIR*, 543-550.

# User Modeling in Search Logs via a Nonparametric Bayesian Approach

Hongning Wang[1], ChengXiang Zhai[1], Feng Liang[2]
[1]Department of Computer Science
[2]Department of Statistics
University of Illinois at Urbana-Champaign
Urbana IL, 61801 USA
{wang296,czhai,liangf}@illinois.edu

Anlei Dong, Yi Chang
Yahoo! Labs
701 First Avenue, Sunnyvale CA, 94089 USA
{anlei,yichang}@yahoo-inc.com

## ABSTRACT

Searchers' information needs are diverse and cover a broad range of topics; hence, it is important for search engines to accurately understand each individual user's search intents in order to provide optimal search results. Search log data, which records users' search behaviors when interacting with search engines, provides a valuable source of information about users' search intents. Therefore, properly characterizing the heterogeneity among the users' observed search behaviors is the key to accurately understanding their search intents and to further predicting their behaviors.

In this work, we study the problem of user modeling in the search log data and propose a generative model, dpRank, within a non-parametric Bayesian framework. By postulating generative assumptions about a user's search behaviors, dpRank identifies each individual user's latent search interests and his/her distinct result preferences in a joint manner. Experimental results on a large-scale news search log data set validate the effectiveness of the proposed approach, which not only provides in-depth understanding of a user's search intents but also benefits a variety of personalized applications.

## Categories and Subject Descriptors

H.4 [**Information Systems Applications**]: Miscellaneous

## Keywords

User modeling, search log mining, nonparametric Bayesian

## 1. INTRODUCTION

Among various ways of mining search engine logs, such as studying the distribution of queries and query categories that users frequently search for [11] and recognizing temporal dynamics of search topics [15], identifying individual user's search intent from search logs is of particular importance. Given the huge diversity of search engine users' information needs, accurate understanding of a user's search interests and preferences is arguably one of the most critical research challenges in information retrieval studies [9, 24, 26]. It is, however, impractical to ask users to give explicit feedback about their search intents; and thus studying how to effectively mine such diverse information needs of users from the search logs becomes a valuable research direction.

Search log mining has drawn a considerable amount of attention in research. White and Drucker investigated the variability in people's search behaviors, and suggested two typical types of searchers: navigators and explorers, whose search interaction pattern is highly consistent or highly variable [26]. The studies in [1, 13] showed that implicit feedback extracted from the aggregated users' clickthroughs is reasonably accurate to interpret the generic ranking preferences over the retrieved documents. Although much effort has been devoted to mining general search behaviors of users, little attention has been paid to identifying individual user's search preferences from the search log data. Liu et al. [16] profiled a user's search interest by classifying his/her queries into predefined categories and tailored the ranking model for each individual user accordingly. Sontag et al. [23] proposed a probabilistic model to estimate topic-based profiles for both documents and users, and used such profiles to calibrate the relevance estimation of retrieved documents for each individual user, i.e., search personalization.

A major limitation of existing work is that the analysis of a user's query distribution and that of his/her associated click behaviors are *isolated*. We should note that both queries and clickthroughs convey useful clues about a user's search intent. Taking news search as an example, a user who frequently issues celebrity queries has distinct search interest from another user who often searches for the past political news events. Such difference can be captured by modeling the query distributions of different users and be used to adjust the search results. However, it is insufficient to only model a user's query distribution. For example, even for the same celebrity query, some users tend to click on the most recent news exhibiting his/her unique preference on the latest report about the celebrities, while other users might only click on the reports from authority sources. Therefore, in order to provide a comprehensive understanding of a user's search intent, we must capitalize on the following two aspects simultaneously: 1) user's search interest, i.e., the distribution of queries a user frequently enters; 2) user's unique result ranking preference, i.e., the probability of observing a particular click pattern from the user. Such a joint analysis, however, is missing in the previous work.


*WSDM'14*, February 24–28, 2014, New York, New York, USA.
Copyright 2014 ACM 978-1-4503-2351-2/14/02 ...$15.00.
http://dx.doi.org/10.1145/2556195.2556262.

In this paper, we study the problem of user modeling in search logs, and develop a generative model, dpRank, in the non-parametric Bayesian framework to enable *joint* modeling of query distributions and clickthrough patterns in each individual user. To capture the heterogeneity among all search users, we introduce a novel concept of *latent user groups*. In detail, each latent user group possesses a unique distribution over the queries: for instance, in news search, one group of users may frequently issue celebrity queries, while another group may only look for breaking news events. Meanwhile, the click preference of each latent user group is portrayed by the corresponding relative importance of the ranking features, which leads to distinct click patterns over the returned documents. For example, for the same input query, some group of users may want high authority websites (i.e., larger weight on the pagerank score), while the other groups may prefer the documents better matched with their queries (e.g., larger weight on the relevance features such as BM25). In order to characterize the heterogeneity among the queries and clickthroughs in a single user's search history, we model each user's search intent as a mixture over those latent user groups, where the mixing proportion governs each user's unique search behavior pattern.

By postulating such generative assumptions, homogeneity of users' aggregated search behaviors is captured by the latent user groups, while the variability of individual user's interaction patterns is captured by modeling each user as a mixture over the latent user groups. As a mixture model, the number of mixture components, which is usually manually set, determines the granularity of the model. However, due to the dynamic nature and scale of search logs, it is infeasible for us to manually exhaust the optimal number of the latent user groups. An appealing alternative is to adopt a fully data-driven approach, i.e., postulating Dirichlet process priors [8] over the mixture components, to exploit the clustering property of users' search behaviors. In dpRank, we assume the parameters characterizing each latent user group are drawn from a shared Dirichlet process; accordingly, the mixing proportion in each user over the latent groups is drawn from another Dirichlet process to accommodate such infinite number of components. As a result, the number of latent user groups can be automatically determined based on the data characteristics.

Knowledge discovered by dpRank from the search logs can be useful for many applications. Characteristics of latent user groups, such as those different criteria for document ranking, provide an in-depth understanding of search engine users. The estimated mixing proportion of latent user groups in each user can be used as a proxy to measure similarity between users for collaborative filtering based tasks, or for many other personalized applications.

To investigate the effectiveness of the proposed dpRank model for user modeling in search logs, we collected a large collection of search logs from a commercial news search engine. Experimental results validated our basic hypothesis that joint modeling of users' search behaviors, i.e., their queries and clicks, in search logs provides a more comprehensive and accurate understanding of users' search intents than those isolated modeling approaches. And the mined knowledge about users can benefit a variety of applications, e.g., search result ranking, collaborative query recommendation, and document re-ranking, to improve task performance. In addition, the proposed dpRank model is general; and thus it can be directly applied to many other types of search logs, e.g., web search and blog search logs.

## 2. RELATED WORK

A great amount of effort has been devoted to turning the massive search usage data in search engine logs into actionable knowledge: Jansen et al. [11] explored search logs to analyze the types of information users search for and how people do search within a web search engine; Kulkarni et al. studied the dynamics of search topics over time [15]; White and Drucker investigated variability in people's search interaction behaviors [26]. A comprehensive survey of research about search log mining can be found in [22].

While many studies have been performed on mining general interests of users from search logs, little work has been done on discovering knowledge about individual users. The related work in this direction can be summarized into two major categories.

One type of studies focuses on the semantic interpretation of queries. Liu et al. [16] categorized a user's queries into a set of ODP categories and tailored the ranking results for each individual user according to such identified search interest. Rose and Levinson [19] grouped the queries from the same user into search tasks, in which the user exhibits consistent information need.

Another type of work aims at accurately modeling and interpreting a user's ranking preferences from their click feedback. Joachims et al. [13] and Agichtein et al. [1] analyzed the reliability of implicit feedback generated from clickthrough data and designed a set of click heuristics to extract relative search result preferences from clicks in the search logs. Probabilistic click models [5, 7, 28] have been proposed for modeling user click behaviors and extracting intrinsic relevance information from the clickthroughs.

However, the aforementioned work isolated the analysis of query distribution in a user and that of associated click behaviors. Our approach extends the previous work to enable *joint* modeling of the queries and click behaviors of individual users. By postulating generative assumptions about a user's search behaviors, the proposed dpRank model identifies each individual user's latent search interests and his/her distinct ranking preferences in a unified way, which is necessary to capture subtle preference variations of user interests.

In terms of methodology, the most similar work to ours is Bian et al.'s "divide-and-conquer" approach for web search [3] and Giannopoulos et al.'s method for learning to rank user intent [10], although they isolated the analysis of users' query distribution and click patterns. In [3], Bian et al. represented the queries by the aggregated ranking features from pseudo-feedback documents, and clustered the queries into groups by the $k$-means algorithm. Within each identified query group, a separate RankSVM [12] model was trained to satisfy the group-specific ranking requirement. Giannopoulos et al. [10] took a similar procedure to cluster queries and estimate independent RankSVM models for each query group. In particular, they represented the queries by the weight vectors from RankSVM models learned in each query. However, in both of these two methods, query is the major focus of study, and they grouped the queries either by the derived query features or click patterns. But neither of them model the users, who generated the queries and clicks.

## 3. METHOD

In this work, we propose a generative model, dpRank, to enable *joint* modeling of users' queries and clicks in search logs. Given a collection of search logs, including the queries from users, documents returned by a search engine, and the corresponding clicks from the users, dpRank aims to identify each individual user's latent search interests and their distinct ranking preferences in a unified way. An efficient Markov chain Monte Carlo sampling algorithm is developed to estimate the posterior distribution of latent variables in the proposed dpRank model.

## 3.1 Problem Definition

Denote a collection of users as $U = \{u_1, u_2, \ldots, u_n\}$ in the given search log data, in which each user $u_i$ is associated with a set of queries $Q^{u_i} = \{q_1^{u_i}, q_2^{u_i}, \ldots, q_m^{u_i}\}$. Each query $q_j^{u_i}$ is represented by a $T$-dimensional vector of query features, e.g., query length and query frequency in the collection; and $q_j^{u_i}$ is associated with a list of retrieved documents together with user clicks $D_j^{u_i} = \{(d_{j1}^{u_i}, y_{j1}^{u_i}), (d_{j2}^{u_i}, y_{j2}^{u_i}), \ldots, (d_{jl}^{u_i}, y_{jl}^{u_i})\}$, where $d_{jl}^{u_i}$ is a $V$-dimensional vector of ranking features describing the relevance quality of document $d_{jl}^{u_i}$ to query $q_j^{u_i}$, and $y_{jl}^{u_i}$ indicates if the document $d_{jl}^{u_i}$ is clicked by user $u_i$ (e.g., 1 for the clicked documents and 0 for the skipped ones).

The problem of user modeling in search log data is to characterize different users' search intents by analyzing the association patterns of their issued queries and corresponding clicks. Using the language of probabilistic models, one needs to estimate the joint distribution of queries and click preferences in user $u$, i.e., $p(Q, D, u)$. In-depth knowledge about individual users can then be discovered by posterior inference on various conditional distributions. For example, $p(Q|u)$ reveals a user's search interest via his/her query distribution; and $p(D|Q, u)$ reflects a user's unique ranking preferences over the returned documents.

## 3.2 Generative Story in dpRank

The basic idea behind the proposed dpRank model is to define the joint probability $p(Q, D, u)$ in a generative way. To model the diversity among different users' search interests (i.e., heterogeneity among the distribution of queries) and ranking preferences (i.e., heterogeneity among users' clicks in search engine returned documents), we introduce the concept of latent user groups. We assume that to issue a query to the search engine, the user would first select a particular user group he/she belongs to, from which he/she would then pick a query according to its generation probability within this group. Once the search engine returns a list of documents for the input query, the user will carefully examine those documents, and selectively click the ones that match his/her result preferences for this type of queries specified in the latent user group. As a result, by modeling each individual user's search intents as a mixture over those latent user groups, patterns of users' search behaviors can be automatically identified.

## 3.3 User Modeling via dpRank

In dpRank, each latent user group indexed by $c$ refers to a homogeneous generative model for $p(q, D)$. Within the user group $c$, we employ a $T$-dimensional multivariate Normal distribution to model the generation of queries, i.e., $p(q_j^{u_i}) \sim N(\mu_c, \sigma_c^2 \mathbf{I})$, where we assume a diagonal covariance matrix. It is known that users' clicks may be biased by the displayed ranking positions [5, 7, 28], but the relative preferences of clicked documents over skipped ones are reasonably accurate [1, 13]. Therefore, to learn a user's result ranking preference reflected in his/her clicks, we employ a pairwise preference model on the returned document list, i.e., $p(D_j^{u_i}|q_j^{u_i}) = \prod_{y_{js}^{u_i} > y_{jt}^{u_i}} p(y_{js}^{u_i} > y_{jt}^{u_i} | d_{js}^{u_i}, d_{jt}^{u_i})$. Specifically, we use a logistic function to model such pairwise ranking preferences as,

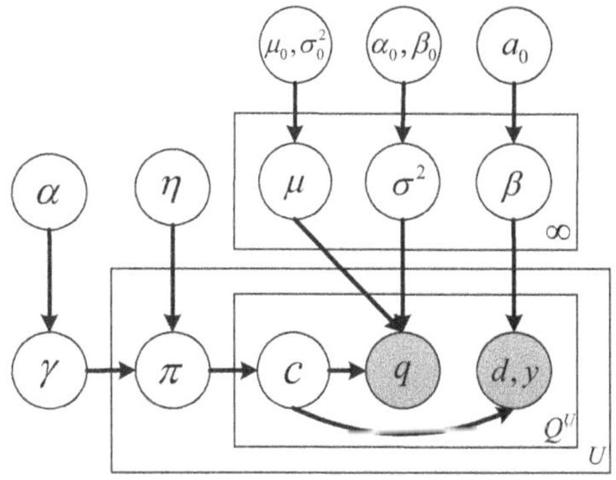


**Figure 1: Graphical model representation of dpRank. Light circles denote the latent random variables, and shadow circles denote the observed random variables. The outer plate indexed by $U$ denotes the users in the given search log, the inner plated indexed by $Q^U$ denotes the queries and the associated documents and clicks from user $u$, and the upper plate denotes the parameters for the countably infinite number of latent user groups in the collection.**

$$p(y_{js}^{u_i} > y_{jt}^{u_i} | d_{js}^{u_i}, d_{jt}^{u_i}, \beta_c) = \frac{1}{1 + \exp\left(-\beta_c^{\mathsf{T}}(d_{js}^{u_i} - d_{jt}^{u_i})\right)} \quad (1)$$

where $\beta_c$ is a $V$-dimensional weight vector indicating the relative importance of ranking features in latent group $c$.

Based on these specifications, each latent user group can be fully characterized by a set of parameters, $\theta_c = (\mu_c, \sigma_c^2, \beta_c)$. The joint distribution of query $q_j^{u_i}$ and corresponding clickthroughs in $D_j^{u_i}$ is thus modeled as,

$$p(q_j^{u_i}, D_j^{u_i} | \theta_c) = p(q_j^{u_i} | \mu_c, \sigma_c^2) \prod_{y_{js}^{u_i} > y_{jt}^{u_i}} p(y_{js}^{u_i} > y_{jt}^{u_i} | d_{js}^{u_i}, d_{jt}^{u_i}, \beta_c) \quad (2)$$

given that they are generated from a particular user group $c$. Note that we do not model the generation of returned documents for query $q_j^{u_i}$, but just the corresponding click preferences conditioned on them, since the documents are returned by the search engine and thus are independent of the users given the query (i.e., without considering the personalization feature in search engines).

To construct a fully generative model, we need to specify the generation of the parameter $\theta_c$ for each latent user group. In dpRank, in order to avoid manually specifying the configuration of $\theta_c$, e.g., how many unique $\theta_c$ should be used for a given collection, we assume $\theta_c$ itself is also a random variable and is drawn from a Dirichlet process (DP). A Dirichlet process $DP(G_0, \alpha)$ with a base distribution $G_0$ and a scaling parameter $\alpha$ is a distribution over distributions [8]. An important feature of the DP is that draws from a DP often share some common values, and therefore naturally form clusters. The number of unique draws, i.e., the number of clusters, varies with respect to the data and therefore is random, instead of being pre-specified.

As a result, in dpRank, the global distribution of queries and corresponding clicks in a given collection of search logs distributes as a DP, and it can then be expressed using a stick-breaking representation [21]:

$$p(Q^U, D^U) = \sum_{k=1}^{\infty} \gamma_k \delta_{\theta_k} \tag{3}$$

where $\theta_k \sim G_0$, $\delta_\theta$ is a distribution of $(Q^U, D^U)$ concentrated at $\theta$ and $\gamma = (\gamma_k)_{k=1}^{\infty} \sim Stick(\alpha)$ represents the global distribution of mixture components in the whole collection. The stick-breaking process $Stick(\alpha)$ for $\gamma$ is defined as: $\gamma'_k \sim Beta(1, \alpha), \gamma_k = \gamma'_k \prod_{t=1}^{k-1}(1-\gamma'_t)$. Specifically, we further assume that each dimension of parameters for generating the query features, i.e., $(\mu_k, \sigma_k^2)$, and each dimension of the linear weights for the ranking features, i.e., $\beta_k$, are independently drawn from their corresponding prior distributions defined in $G_0$: for $t = 1 \dots T$, $\mu_{kt} \sim N(\mu_0, \sigma_0^2)$, $1/\sigma_{kt}^2 \sim Gamma(\alpha_0, \beta_0)$ and for $v = 1 \dots V$, $\beta_{kv} \sim N(0, a_0^2)$.

The global distribution defined in Eq (3) captures the homogeneity of users' search behaviors for the whole population (characterized by the group parameter $\boldsymbol{\theta}$), but tells us little about each individual user. Therefore, we need to inject the information about the variabilities of individual users to the dpRank model.

Because the global distribution defined in Eq (3) only has finite supports at the points of $\theta = \{\theta_k\}_{k=1}^{|Q^U|}$, the distribution of mixture components in each user will only have support at those points as well. Based on Eq (2), the joint probability of queries and clicks in user $u_i$ can be naturally modeled as,

$$p(q_j^{u_i}, D_j^{u_i}) = \sum_{k=1}^{\infty} \pi_{u_i k} p(q_j^{u_i}, D_j^{u_i} | \theta_k) \tag{4}$$

where $\pi_{u_i} = (\pi_{u_i k})_{k=1}^{\infty} \sim DP(\gamma, \eta)$, i.e., we introduce another layer of DP with the global proportion $\gamma$ as the base distribution for modeling the mixing of latent user groups in each user.

The benefit of such an approach is two-fold. From a modeling aspect, this modeling approach reveals the information of users both at the aggregated level (i.e., the shared latent user groups) and also at the individual level (i.e., the user-specific mixing proportions). From a learning aspect, it allows information sharing across different users, and therefore makes learning more efficient.

Based on the above discussions, we can formalize the generation process of queries and clickthroughs in search logs defined in dpRank using the language of probabilistic graphical models in Figure 1.

## 3.4 Posterior Inference

To apply the proposed model for user modeling in search logs, we need to calculate the posterior distribution of latent variables. In dpRank, the latent variables of interest are: $(\mu, \sigma^2)$ that characterize the generation of queries in a latent user group; $\beta$ that depicts a user's relative emphasis over the ranking features in a latent user group; and $\pi$ that profiles an individual user's search intent over the global latent user groups.

Following the sampling scheme proposed in [17, 25], we develop an efficient Markov chain Monte Carlo (MCMC) algorithm, or more precisely, a Gibbs sampler, to perform the posterior inference for dpRank. To facilitate later description of the employed sampling scheme, we assume that at a particular sampling step, there are in total $K$ active components (i.e., components that associate with data instances), and by permuting the indices, we can index them from 1 to $K$. We define $\gamma_e = 1 - \sum_{k=1}^{K} \gamma_k$ to be the total mixing proportion for the remaining inactive components.

The key to perform Gibbs sampling is to derive the full conditional distribution for each latent variable. In the following, we will discuss about detailed derivation of the conditional posterior distributions of interest.

• **Sampling $c_{uj}$:** Given user $u$, the conditional distribution of $\mathbf{c}_u$ and $\pi_u$ is given by

$$\begin{aligned} & p(\pi_u, \mathbf{c}_u | \gamma, \boldsymbol{\theta}, q^u, D^u, G_0, \alpha, \eta) \\ \propto\ & p(\pi_u|\gamma, \eta) \prod_j p(q_j^u, D_j^u | \theta_{c_{uj}}) p(c_{uj}|\pi_u) \end{aligned} \tag{5}$$

To sample the latent user group assignment $c_{uj}$ for a particular query $q_j^u$ from user $u$, we can integrate over $\pi_u$ in Eq (5) analytically because of the conjugacy between the Dirichlet distribution $p(\pi_u|\gamma, \eta)$ and the multinomial distribution $p(c_{uj}|\pi_u)$, and get the conditional probability of $c_{uj}$ given $\gamma$ and $\eta$ as:

$$p(c_{uj}|\gamma, \eta) = \frac{\Gamma(\eta)}{\Gamma(\eta + m_u)} \prod_{k=1}^{K} \frac{\Gamma(\eta\gamma_k + m_{uk})}{\Gamma(\eta\gamma_k)} \tag{6}$$

where $m_u$ is the number of queries user $u$ has and $m_{uk}$ is the number of queries in user $u$ assigned to group $k$.

As a result, the conditional probability of $c_{uj} = k$ given query $q_j^u$, corresponding clicks in $D_j^u$ and other latent variables is,

$$p(c_{uj} = k | q_j^u, D_j^u, \boldsymbol{\theta}, \gamma, \eta) \propto (\eta\gamma_k + m_{uk}^{-uj}) p(q_j^u, D_j^u | \theta_k) \tag{7}$$

where $k$ takes values in $\{1, \dots, K, e\}$, $m_{uk}^{-uj}$ is the number of queries from user $u$ assigned to group $k$ except the current query $q_j^u$, and $\theta_e$ is an auxiliary component drawn from the base distribution $G_0$.

If the sampling result of $c_{uj}$ makes an active component associate with no observations, we need to remove it from the list of active components, set $K = K - 1$ and update $\gamma_e$ accordingly; and if the sampling result of $c_{uj}$ is $e$, we need to append $\theta_e$ to the list of active components, and draw a new global proportion $\gamma_{K+1}$ for it. To achieve so, we sample $b \sim Beta(1, \alpha)$ and set $\gamma_{K+1} = b\gamma_e$, $\gamma_e = (1-b)\gamma_e$.

• **Sampling $\gamma$:** Following the sampling scheme introduced in [25], we employ the same auxiliary variable method for sampling the global mixture proportion $\gamma$.

By expanding the ratios of Gamma functions in Eq (6) and including the Stick-breaking prior for $\gamma$, we get the posterior distribution for $\gamma$ conditioned on the auxiliary variable $\mathbf{h}$ as:

$$p(\gamma|\alpha, \mathbf{h}) \propto \gamma_e^{\alpha-1} \prod_{k=1}^{K} \gamma_k^{\sum_{i=1}^{n} h_{u_i k} - 1} \tag{8}$$

where $h_{u_i k}$ is a random variable based on the occurrence of group $k$ in user $u_i$, which takes value from 1 to $m_{u_i k}$. And the corresponding distribution of $\mathbf{h}$ given $\mathbf{c}$ and $\gamma$ is,

$$p(h_{u_i k} = h | \mathbf{c}, \gamma) \propto s(m_{u_i k}, h)(\eta\gamma_k)^h \tag{9}$$

where $s(m, h)$ is the unsigned Stirling numbers of the first kind.

Due to the conjugacy between $\gamma$ and $\mathbf{c}$, the posterior distribution of $\gamma$ given $\mathbf{h}$ still follows a Dirichlet distribution with parameters of $\alpha$ and $\mathbf{h}$ in Eq (8); and $h_{u_i k}$ acts as an estimated number of occurrence of group $k$ in user $u_i$ in Eq (9) (more explanation of $\mathbf{h}$ can be found in [25]). Based on Eq (8) and Eq (9), iterative sampling between $\gamma$ and $\mathbf{h}$ is performed to get the posterior samples for $\gamma$.

• **Sampling $\boldsymbol{\theta}$:** Conditioned on the group assignments $\mathbf{c}$ of all the users in the collection, the posterior distributions of $\boldsymbol{\theta}$ are determined by the queries (from all users) assigned to each group, namely,

$$p(\theta_k|\mathbf{c}, \mathbf{Q}, \mathbf{D}, G_0) \propto p(\theta_k|G_0) \prod_{c_j^u=k} p(q_j^u, D_j^u|\theta_k) \tag{10}$$

Because of the Normal-Normal and Normal-Gamma conjugacy, the posterior distributions for $\mu_k$ and $\sigma_k^2$ can be analytically calculated. Since we have assumed each dimension of $\mu_k$ and $\sigma_k$ is independently drawn from the priors, we can calculate the posteriors of them separately. To simplify the notations, we denote $n_k$ as the total number of queries assigned to group $k$ given $\mathbf{c}$, and $\lambda_{kt} = 1/\sigma_{kt}^2$, i.e., the precision of a Normal distribution. As a result, we have,

$$p(\mu_{kt}|\mathbf{c}, \mathbf{q}) = N(\mu_{n_k t}, \sigma_{n_k t}^2) \tag{11}$$

where $\sigma_{n_k t}^2 = \frac{1}{\frac{n_k}{\sigma_{kt}^2} + \frac{1}{\sigma_0^2}}$ and $\mu_{n_k t} = \sigma_{n_k t}^2 (\frac{\mu_0}{\sigma_0^2} + \frac{\sum_{c_j^u=k} q_{jt}^u}{\sigma_{kt}^2})$.
And,

$$p(\lambda_{kt}|\mathbf{c}, \mathbf{q}) = Gamma(\alpha_{n_k t}, \beta_{n_k t}) \tag{12}$$

where $\alpha_{n_k t} = \alpha_0 + \frac{n_k}{2}$ and $\beta_{n_k t} = \beta_0 + \frac{1}{2}\sum_{c_j^u=k}(q_{jt}^u - \mu_{kt})^2$.

Based on the posterior distributions specified in Eq (11) and Eq (12), iterative sampling is performed for the posterior update of $\mu_k$ and $\sigma_k^2$ in each user group.

However, because there is no proper conjugate prior for the linear weight $\beta$ in the click preference modeling module as defined in Eq (1), the posterior distribution of Eq (10) with respect to $\beta$ cannot be analytically calculated. In this work, we appeal to the Metropolis Hasting sampling algorithm with Hamiltonian dynamics [18] to perform $\beta$'s posterior update. Briefly, this sampling scheme uses Hamiltonian dynamics to produce proposals for the Metropolis Hasting algorithm. Because the proposal is generated based on the gradient of energy function defined by the target distribution (as in Eq (10)), it provides faster exploration of the state space comparing to simple random-walk proposals.

• **Gibbs sampling procedure:** the Gibbs sampling for the proposed dpRank model can be performed by alternating the sampling steps for $\mathbf{c}$, $\gamma$ and $\boldsymbol{\theta}$ described above iteratively. We should note that the sampling of $\mathbf{c}$ is performed for every query from the users in the given collection, and the samplings of $\gamma$ and $\boldsymbol{\theta}$ are performed for the whole collection given the newly updated latent user group assignments $\mathbf{c}$. As an MCMC algorithm, samples from the sampling chain are usually correlated with nearby samples. To collect independent samples, we only kept the samples from every five iterations, i.e., thinning the sampling chain. Besides, samples from the beginning of the sampling chain (i.e., the burn-in period) may not accurately represent the desired distribution. We only kept the posterior samples after the burn-in period (in our experiment, we discarded the first 20% of samples).

## 3.5 Discussion

Compared to the two-step query-clustering-based ranking methods introduced in [3, 10], the proposed dpRank model is user-centric and for the first time enables the joint modeling of a user's search query distribution and corresponding click behaviors. As explicitly expressed in Eq (7), the assignment of latent user group for a particular query $q^u$ in user $u$ is determined by two factors: 1) the current proportion of the latent user groups in $u$; and 2) the likelihood of observing the given query and corresponding clicks in a candidate user group. As a result, the chosen user group for query $q^u$ in user $u$ should not only well explain both of the query $q^u$ and clicks in $D^u$, but also closely align with his/her general search interest, i.e., the proportion of user group assignments in his/her rest queries. In [3, 10], no user-specific information is considered for clustering the queries, and those clusterings are solely determined by either the queries or clickthrough patterns independently. In [3], only the characteristics of queries were modeled based on the derived query features. As a result, users who issued the same query but clicked on different documents will be assumed to have the same search intent and served with the same ranking result. In [10], to capture users' distinct click preferences, independent ranking models are estimated for each query. But the same user's click preference in different queries cannot be modeled, and sparsity becomes a serious issue for estimating ranking models in each individual query.

In dpRank, by inferring the posterior distribution of the latent variables in a given collection of search logs, important knowledge about a user's search intent can be discovered. First, the posterior distribution of parameter $\theta = (\mu, \sigma^2, \beta)$ reveals the distribution of queries and clickthrough patterns in a particular user group. For instance, by analyzing $\beta$, we can understand users' relative emphasis of the ranking features in each user group. Based on such knowledge, we can directly influence the general ranking model training (e.g., create new ranking features for each user group) or estimate a separate ranking model if the ranking criterion in this specific group is very different from that in the global ranking model. Second, the posterior distribution of latent user group assignments in user $u$, i.e., $p(\pi_u|q^u, D^u, \gamma, \eta)$, summarizes an individual user's search intent in history. This distribution can serve as a compact user profile for many personalized applications. For example, we can compute the similarity between users based on it for collaborative query recommendation and document re-ranking [20].

Besides, the proposed user modeling method can be flexibly applied in the real dynamic search environment, where new users or new queries keep emerging. As it is a Bayesian model, we do not need to re-estimate the model for the whole data set, but just to perform the posterior update discussed in Section 3.4 on the newly arrived data. This property renders dpRank a wider application scenario in practice.

# 4. EXPERIMENTAL RESULTS

To evaluate the proposed method for user modeling in search logs, we conducted experiments on a large-scale search log data set. First, we qualitatively demonstrated the knowledge discovered by dpRank from the search logs, e.g., distribution of queries in the identified user groups and the corresponding result ranking preferences. Then, we performed a series of quantitative evaluations to validate our main hypothesis in this work that joint modeling of users' search behaviors could provide a more comprehensive and accurate understanding of users' search intents than those isolated approaches in a variety of scenarios.

## 4.1 Data Set

A large set of search logs are collected from Yahoo! news search engine[1] in a two-months period, from late May to late July 2011. During this period, a subset of users are randomly selected and all their search activities are collected, including the anonymized user ID, query string, timestamp,

[1] http://news.search.yahoo.com

top 10 returned documents and the corresponding user clicks. In this data set, each document is represented by 65 basic ranking features, such as document age, website authority, and query matching in document title and body.

Since we are modeling users in a per-user basis, we must ensure every user has his/her own training and testing queries in our evaluation. To achieve so, we ordered the queries in each user by their timestamps, and used the first 60% queries for training and the rest 40% for testing in each user.

Simple pre-processing is applied on this data set: 1) filter out the queries without clicks; 2) discard the users with less than two queries; 3) normalize the ranking features by their mean and standard deviation estimated in the training queries, i.e., $z$-score. After the pre-processing steps, there are 42,642 users with 288,786 queries selected in this collection, among which 189,757 queries are used for training and 99,029 queries for testing. The basic statistics about this evaluation search log set are summarized in Table 1.

**Table 1: Basic statistics of evaluation search log set.**

| | | | |
|---|---|---|---|
| #user | 42,642 | #query | 288,786 |
| #document | 2,483,486 | query/user | 6.77±6.21 |
| click/query | 1.22±0.57 | uni-user/query | 17.9±121.7 |

However, in this data set, there is no predefined query feature. We appealed to the method proposed in [3] to create query features from the search engine returned documents. In detail, we computed the mean vector of ranking features in the documents associated with the given query as its query feature representation.

In dpRank, there is a set of hyper-parameters to be determined in the prior distribution $G_0$. *Uninformative prior* is often used in Bayesian models when the number of observations is large. In our experiments, we found that the performance of dpRank was not sensitive to the setting of such hyper-parameters due to the large volume of observations we have. Therefore, in the following experiments, we fixed the hyper-parameters in $G_0$: $\mu_0 = 0$, $\sigma_0^2 = 0.5$, $\alpha_0 = 1.0$, $\beta_0 = 0.5$, $a_0 = 1.0$, $\alpha = 1.0$, $\eta = 0.1$. And we set the total number of Gibbs sampling iterations to be 1000.

## 4.2 Qualitative Evaluation

The posterior distribution of latent variables in dpRank reveals in-depth knowledge about a user's information need buried in the search log data. In this experiment, we qualitatively illustrate some interesting findings from dpRank in our news search log data set.

By averaging the group assignment $c$ for each training query $q$ in the posterior samples, we can estimate the posterior distribution of queries within each user group as,

$$p(q|c=k) \propto \sum_{s\in S'}\sum_{u\in U}\delta(c_{uq}^{s}=k) \tag{13}$$

where $S'$ is a set of effective posterior samples and $c_{uq}^{s}$ is the sampling result of group assignment for query $q$ from user $u$ in $s$-th effective sample. Because in dpRank the number of user groups might change during the sampling iterations (i.e., generating/removing groups), we only collected samples after the sampling chain is stabilized in this estimation.

From one run of Gibbs sampling, 47 different user groups were created for our training set. Due to space limit, in Table 2, we only list the top 5 most probable queries from 10 selected user groups. We reassigned the IDs of these selected groups in the table for illustration purpose.

**Table 2: Top 5 most probable queries under 10 selected latent user groups.**

| Group | Top Ranked Queries |
|---|---|
| 1 | iran, china, libya, vietnam, syria |
| 2 | selena gomez, lady gaga, britney spears, jennifer aniston, taylor swift |
| 3 | fake tupac story, pbs hackers, alaska earthquake, southwest pilot, arizona wildfires |
| 4 | joplin missing, apple icloud, sony hackers, google subpoena, ford transmission |
| 5 | casey anthony trial, casey anthony jurors, casey anthony, crude oil prices, air france flight 447 |
| 6 | tree of life, game of thrones, sonic the hedgehog, world of warcraft, mtv awards 2011 |
| 7 | the titanic, the bachelorette, cars 2, hangover 2, the voice |
| 8 | los angeles lakers, arsenal football, the dark knight rises, transformers 3, manchester united |
| 9 | miami heat, los angeles lakers, liverpool football club, arsenal football, nfl lockout |
| 10 | today in history, nascar 2011 schedule, today history, this day in history |

As shown in Table 2, the query distributions in the automatically identified user groups are quite meaningful. The queries in groups 1 and 2 are mostly the names of countries and celebrities. Those queries account for the users' constant interest of obtaining the latest update about these countries and celebrities over time. The queries in groups 3 to 5 are mainly for breaking news events in the summer of 2011, e.g., "alaska earthquake" and "casey anthony trial." Queries in groups 6 and 7 are entertainment-focused, and those in groups 8 and 9 are sports related. We should note that we did not utilize any external knowledge, e.g., entity lexicon or taxonomy, about the queries in our query feature representation, but the proposed model automatically discovered such meaningful association among the queries by exploring the users' search behaviors.

One thing we want to emphasize is that the query distribution within each user group as illustrated in Table 2 is not solely determined by the query features, but also governed by the users' click preferences. Therefore, it is interesting to further investigate how different the users' ranking preferences are in those seemly distinct groups. In dpRank, the posterior distribution of linear weight $\beta$ reflects a user's relative emphasis over the ranking features, and thus can be used to analyze users' ranking preferences in each group. In Figure 2, we visualized the corresponding posterior mean of $\beta$s from the same user groups as shown in Table 2. For comparison purpose, we also included the linear weights estimated by a globally trained RankSVM model and named it as Group 0. To make the scale of those linear weights comparable across different groups, we followed the approach used in [10] to normalize the weight vectors by $l_2$ norm. After normalization, we computed the variance in the linear weights of those features across different groups and selected the top 20 features with the largest variance for illustration. In particular, the first 4 features in the figure are *document age*, *query match in title*, *proximity in title*, and *site authority*.

Comparing to the globally estimated feature weights, users in different groups exhibit distinct ranking requirements. The users belonging to groups 1, 2, 8 and 9 highly emphasize the freshness quality of the returned documents, i.e., document age. And for those in groups 4, 5 and 6, they not

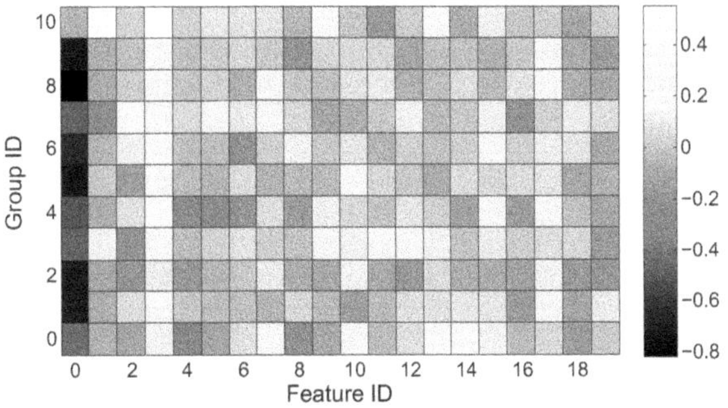


**Figure 2: Heat map visualization of 20 selected feature weights in 11 different user groups (including a global RankSVM as group 0). Features are ordered by the variance of the estimated weights across different groups in descending order.**

only prefer the latest news reports, but also emphasize the relevance quality of the documents, i.e., higher weight on query document matching. One interesting group of users identified by dpRank is group 10: they repeatedly issued the queries of "today in history." They did not mind the freshness of results, but stressed the query-document matching quality and site authority. In this sense, their search intent is more like navigational web search, rather than news search.

From the above results, it is evident that users' search intents are distinct, and dpRank captures such diversity and properly groups them by jointly modeling the users' issued queries and corresponding clicks in the search logs.

## 4.3 Quantitative Evaluation

In this section, we performed quantitative evaluation to test the main hypothesis in our work: the joint modeling of users' queries and clicks is better than those isolated modeling approaches. To test this, we compared our dpRank model with several state-of-the-art methods, which take separated steps for modeling the queries and clicks in the search logs, on the tasks of document ranking, collaborative query recommendation and document re-ranking.

Due to the randomness of sampling-based inference, the performance of dpRank varies across different runs of Gibbs sampler. In the following experiments, we report the average performance of dpRank over 5 different runs of sampling.

### 4.3.1 Baselines

As we discussed in Section 2, the two query-clustering-based ranking approaches [3, 10] analyzed the queries and clicks in an isolated manner. To test our hypothesis, we employed them as our major baselines for comparison.

Bian et al. proposed Topical RankSVM (TRSVM) for separating the training corpus into query-specific groups [3]. RankSVM models are trained on each of the identified groups. In TRSVM, $k$-means algorithm is used to cluster queries into groups based on the aggregated ranking features from pseudo-feedback documents for each query. In addition, to incorporate the knowledge of feature's importance in ranking, they weighted each dimension of query features by the weight vector from a global RankSVM model. To predict the ranking scores of documents in a new query, they assembled the independent RankSVM models' output by,

$$f(q,d) = \sum_{k=1}^{K} p(c=k|q) f_k(d) \tag{14}$$

where $f_k(d)$ is the output of RankSVM in the $k$-th group. The ensemble weight $p(c=k|q)$ is calculated by $p(c=k|q) \propto \exp(-||q-\bar{q}_k||^2)$, in which $\bar{q}_k$ is the mean feature vector of cluster $k$ given by the $k$-means algorithm.

Giannopoulos et al. performed similar procedures to cluster queries and estimate RankSVM models for each query group [10]. But they represented queries by the linear weights from RankSVM models learned in each query, and assumed it reflected users' search intents. We will refer to this method as Intent RankSVM (IRSVM). In the original IRSVM, the ensemble weight $p(c=k|q)$ for a new testing query is estimated by the assignments of query groups in its similar training queries. But the authors did not clearly explain how to define such similarity between queries, and whether the model's performance is sensitive to such similarity metric. In our experiment, we estimated this ensemble weight by averaging the query group assignments in the same user's training queries,

$$p(c=k|u) \propto \sum_{q} \delta(c_{uq}=k) \tag{15}$$

We randomly sampled 20% training queries and performed 5-fold cross-validation to select the best performing cluster size $K$ in TRSVM and IRSVM (according to MAP metric for document ranking). As a result, we fixed $K$ in TRSVM and IRSVM to be 30 and 20 in the following experiments.

### 4.3.2 Document Ranking

In dpRank, a document's ranking score $\mathbf{s}$ for a given query in user group $c$ can be calculated by the inner product between the linear weight vector $\beta_c$ and document's ranking features, i.e., $\mathbf{s}(q^u_j, d^u_{jt}|c) = \beta_c^{\mathsf{T}} d^u_{jt}$. To rank documents for a testing query, we can compute the expectation of document $d^u_{jt}$'s ranking score $\mathbf{s}$ for query $q^u_j$ in user $u$, and order the documents by the descending order of such scores,

$$\mathbf{s}(d^u_{jt}, q^u_j) = \frac{1}{|S|}\sum_{s\in S}\sum_{k} p(c^{(s)}=k|q^u)\beta_k^{(s)\mathsf{T}} d^u_{jt} \tag{16}$$

where $S$ is a set of posterior samples for the testing query $q^u_j$ after burn-in period; the group index $k$ takes value in $\{1,\dots,K^{(s)},e\}$, and $K^{(s)}$ is the number of active groups in the $s$-th sample; and $p(c^{(s)}=k|q^u) \propto p(q^u|\mu_k^{(s)},\sigma_k^{(s)2})p(c^{(s)}=k|\pi_u^{(s)})$ is the posterior group assignment for the new query $q^u_j$ estimated by the $s$-th sample.

We also included two standard baselines for comparison: 1) a global RankSVM model is estimated based on all the training queries; 2) a set of independent RankSVM models are estimated for each user based on his/her own training queries, and applied to their testing queries accordingly. We named these two baselines as GRSVM and URSVM.

To quantitatively compare different models' ranking performance, we employed a set of standard IR evaluation metrics: by treating all the clicked documents as relevant, we calculated Mean Average Precision (MAP), Precision at 1 (P@1), Precision at 3 (P@3) and Mean Reciprocal Rank (MRR). Definitions of these metrics can be found in [2].

The ranking performance of different models is listed in Table 3, in which the proposed dpRank outperformed all the baseline methods. As we have demonstrated in Section 4.2, users' search intents are diverse, the global ranking model, i.e., GRSVM, failed to satisfy such divergent ranking requirements by using the one-size-fits-all ranking strategy. On the other hand, estimating separate ranking models for each individual user did not work as well. Because of the

Table 3: Comparison of ranking performance.

| | MAP | P@1 | P@3 | MRR |
|---|---|---|---|---|
| URSVM | 0.4865 | 0.2979 | 0.2195 | 0.5010 |
| GRSVM | 0.6161 | 0.4464 | 0.2826 | 0.6315 |
| TRSVM | 0.6223 | 0.4585 | 0.2825 | 0.6378 |
| IRSVM | 0.6165 | 0.4492 | 0.2814 | 0.6318 |
| dpRank | **0.6424*** | **0.4854*** | **0.2897*** | **0.6578*** |

*$p$-value<0.05 under paired t-test against TRSVM

sparsity of training queries in each user (on average each user only has 4 training queries in this data set), URSVM cannot get accurate estimation of model parameters. For the same reason, IRSVM did not perform well either, since it depends on the ranking models estimated on each single query to perform the grouping. TRSVM and dpRank addressed the problems of diversity and sparsity by clustering the queries/users. But in TRSVM no user-related information is explored in query clustering, and thus the same queries from users with distinct ranking preferences will be ranked in the same way. dpRank solves this limitation by jointly exploring user-specific heterogeneity in their search behaviors (as shown in Eq (7)), which provides more accurate ranking for each individual user.

As having been demonstrated in Table 3, dpRank alone can already provide promising ranking performance. We want to further explore the merit of such joint modeling approach in helping general ranking model training. In this experiment, we chose LambdaMART [27] as our base ranking model. LambdaMART is one of the best performing learning-to-rank algorithms [4], which estimates a set of boosted regression trees to directly optimize IR-related metrics, e.g., MAP or MRR.

A set of additional ranking features are created based on dpRank's output for all the query-document pairs in the collection. In detail, beside the dpRank's output ranking score for a particular query-document pair (as defined in Eq (16)), we also treated the product of a document's predicted ranking score $\mathbf{s}(q^u_j, d^u_{jt}|c)$ in each user group and the corresponding posterior weight of this group inferred in the given query as a new ranking feature:

$$\tilde{f}_k(d^u_{jt}, q^u_j) \triangleq \frac{1}{|S'|}\sum_{s\in S'} p(c^{(s)} = k|q^u)\beta^{(s)\mathsf{T}}_k d^u_{jt} \quad (17)$$

where $p(c^{(s)} = k|q^u)$ is the group assignment solely estimated on query $q^u$ (the same as in Eq (16)) and $S'$ is a set of effective posterior samples collected in the same way as in Eq (13) to avoid the change of number of user groups during Gibbs sampling. As a result, $K+1$ additional ranking features are introduced by dpRank. We did not include the auxiliary user group $\theta_e$, because its prediction is random across different documents.

Similar procedures can be applied to TRSVM and IRSVM to extract corresponding ranking features. We computed the new query-group-based ranking features by,

$$\tilde{f}_k(d^u_{jt}, q^u_j) \triangleq p(c = k|q^u_j)f_k(d_{jt}) \quad (18)$$

where $f_k(d_{jt})$ and $p(c = k|q^u_j)$ are RankSVM's output and the ensemble weight as defined in TRSVM and IRSVM.

These newly introduced ranking features are appended to the original 65 relevance-driven ranking features, and fed into LambdaMART together. We used the implementation in RankLib [6] with the default parameter settings (500 regression trees with 20 nodes in each tree), and MAP was chosen to be optimized during training. To avoid overfitting, we held out 25% training queries as validation set, and applied the best performing model from validation set to the testing queries. The ranking performance of LambdaMART with different features is shown in Table 4.

Table 4: Comparison of LambdaMART performance with ranking features derived by different methods.

| Features | MAP | P@1 | P@3 | MRR |
|---|---|---|---|---|
| original | 0.6643 | 0.5142 | 0.2975 | 0.6797 |
| +TRSVM | 0.6620 | 0.5108 | 0.2974 | 0.6774 |
| +IRSVM | 0.6361 | 0.4767 | 0.2872 | 0.6516 |
| +dpRank | **0.6696*** | **0.5212** | **0.2989*** | **0.6833*** |

*$p$-value<0.05 under paired t-test against original

As we can notice in the results, only the features generated by dpRank improved LambdaMART's ranking performance against the original features. To investigate the contribution of the new features introduced by dpRank, we computed the relative feature importance in the estimated LambdaMART model according to the method used in [14]. The top 10 important features are listed in Table 5. The most important feature selected by LambdaMART is dpRank's predicted document ranking score, which has already been proved to be highly correlated with users' click preferences by the results shown in Table 3. In addition, many features newly derived by dpRank were also considered as important, i.e., predicted document ranking score in different clusters, which correspond to coherent user groups, e.g., those who keep searching for celebrity or breaking news. As a result, the features from dpRank provide informative signals about each user's search intents and unique ranking preferences that enhance LambdaMART.

Table 5: Relative feature importance determined by LambdaMART.

| Feature | Relative Importance |
|---|---|
| dpRank-score | 1.000 |
| $c_{12}$-score | 0.464 |
| $c_0$-score | 0.250 |
| query match in body | 0.235 |
| document age | 0.228 |
| perplexity in body | 0.221 |
| $c_{13}$-score | 0.220 |
| $c_4$-score | 0.163 |
| query match in title | 0.141 |
| site authority | 0.135 |

### 4.3.3 *Collaborative Filtering*

The distribution of user group assignment $\pi_u$ in each user naturally serves as a profile of user's search intent. It can be used as a proxy to measure similarity between the users. To study the quality of such user profile generated by our join modeling approach, we test it in the applications of collaborative query recommendation and document re-ranking.

The basic idea of collaborative filtering based method is to promote the items from users who share similar interest as the target user [20]. Therefore, the quality of employed similarity metric between users is crucial for this type of algorithms. In dpRank, we defined user similarity based on the posterior distribution of $\pi_u$ as,

$$sim(u_i, u_j) = 1 - \frac{1}{2}\left[KL(\pi_{u_i}||\pi_{u_j}) + KL(\pi_{u_j}||\pi_{u_i})\right] \quad (19)$$

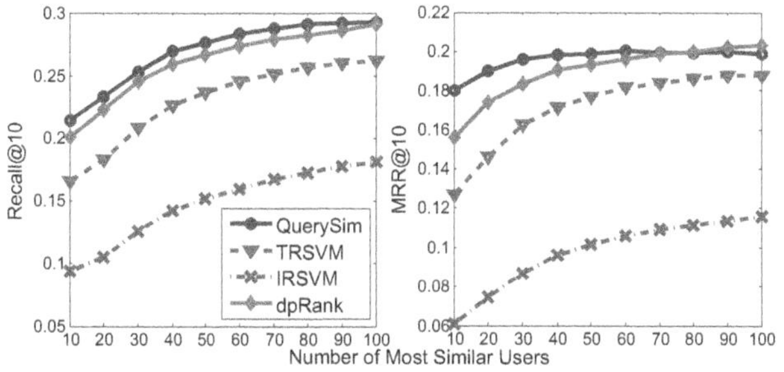


**Figure 3: Comparison of collaborative query recommendation performance.**

No user profiles can be directly extracted from TRSVM or IRSVM, because neither of them explicitly model the individual users. To make them applicable in this experiment, we used the same approach defined in Eq (15) to estimate the proportion of query groups in each user as his/her profile. In addition, we smoothed the estimation in Eq (15) by the global query group distributions in TRSVM and IRSVM to avoid zero probabilities. Based on this derived user profile, similarity between users is computed in the same way as defined in Eq (19) for TRSVM and IRSVM.

• **Collaborative Query Recommendation.** A good user profile for query recommendation should capture a user's specific search interest. To perform collaborative query recommendation, we calculated the weighted frequency of a candidate query in the $M$ most similar users of the target user $u$, and selected the top 10 queries as recommendation. In detail, we only used the testing queries in each user for recommendation, since the training queries have already been used for creating the user's profile. Each candidate query $q$'s recommendation score in user $u$ is computed as,

$$r(q,u) = \sum_{u_i \in N(u,M)} sim(u,u_i)\delta(q,u_i) \qquad (20)$$

where $N(u, M)$ is the set of $M$ most similar users to the target user $u$, and $\delta(q, u_i) = 1$ if the candidate query $q$ occurs in $u_i$'s testing query set.

In addition, we included a baseline method that only uses the vector of queries from a user's training query set as user profile. The similarity between users was measured by the cosine similarity between the query vectors of two users. We named this baseline as QuerySim.

To evaluate the recommendation performance, we treated the testing queries in the target user as relevant, and computed Recall (percentage of relevant queries occurred in the recommendation query set) and MRR as the performance metrics. We did not measure the precision of recommended queries, because in our setting it is uncertain whether the users did not like the recommended query or they just did not know about it when they did the search.

We varied the setting of $M$ from 10 to 100 and summarized different methods' performance in Figure 3.

The user profile generated by dpRank outperformed those from TRSVM and IRSVM, because neither of these baselines explicitly model the distribution of queries in different users; but it was worse than QuerySim. We examined the recommendation results and found that a large portion of users tend to repeat their queries over time, e.g., celebrity queries. QuerySim captured such property by directly exploring a user's issued queries in history; while the granularity of profiles generated by dpRank is too coarse to capture such details of a user's search interest (user-group level v.s. query level). However, because QuerySim relies on strictly query matching for measuring user similarities, its coverage is limited: it cannot align the users with too few queries or those who shared the same search interest but issued different queries (e.g., vocabulary gap).

**Table 6: Query recommendation performance with combined user profile (M=100).**

| | Recall@10 | MRR@10 |
|---|---|---|
| QuerySim | 0.2929 | 0.1991 |
| QuerySim+TRSVM | 0.3133 | 0.2262 |
| QuerySim+IRSVM | 0.2763 | 0.2001 |
| QuerySim+dpRank | **0.3280*** | **0.2365*** |

*$p$-value<0.05 under paired t-test against QuerySim

Since dpRank does not suffer from such a coverage issue as QuerySim, it would be beneficial to take advantage of both types of profiles for better query recommendation performance. In Table 6, we list the recommendation performance given by the combined user profiles with $M = 100$. In particular, we linearly interpolated the similarity scores given by dpRank and QuerySim, and gave QuerySim a higher weight (0.8 versus 0.2) due to the scale difference between cosine similarity and KL distance. We applied similar procedures on TRSVM and IRSVM for comparison purpose.

We can find that by combining the profiles from QuerySim all the model-based profiles, i.e., those generated by TRSVM, IRSVM and dpRank, achieved improved recommendation performance. And the combined profiles from TRSVM and dpRank further outperformed QuerySim profiles, and between them dpRank got better improvement.

• **Collaborative Document Re-ranking.** An effective user profile for collaborative document re-ranking should precisely reflect a user's result ranking preference. Similar procedure as we used in collaborative query recommendation can be applied here: given a list of documents ordered by a global ranking model, we promote the documents that have been clicked by the users who share similar profile as the target user. In particular, we define the collaborative ranking score for document $d$ under query $q$ in user $u$ as,

$$r(d,q,u) = \sum_{u_i \in N(u,M)} sim(u,u_i)\delta(d,q,u_i) \qquad (21)$$

where $\delta(d, q, u_i) = 1$ if user $u_i$ has clicked document $d$ under query $q$.

The re-ranking procedure is performed as follows: given a list of documents ordered by a global model, we give extra credit to the documents that have been clicked by the target user's most similar peers ($u_i \in N(u, M)$) according to the score defined in Eq (21); for documents that have not been clicked by the target user's peers, we will keep their original ranking. For the same consideration as in the collaborative query recommendation, we only performed such re-ranking in each user's testing queries.

In this experiment, we also included a simple baseline method by re-ranking the documents according to its click-through rate (CTR) in all the users *except* the target user. We named this method as GlobalCTR.

Table 7 lists the re-ranking performance based on different user profiles, where the global ranking order is given by GRSVM and we computed the recommendation score in 100 most similar users, i.e., $M = 100$ in $N(u, M)$.

The profile generated by the user's queries in history (i.e., QuerySim) performed much worse than the simple GlobalCTR baseline. This result validates our hypothesis that

**Table 7: Performance comparison of collaborative document re-ranking with different user profiles.**

| | MAP | P@1 | P@3 | MRR |
|---|---|---|---|---|
| GRSVM | 0.6161 | 0.4464 | 0.2826 | 0.6315 |
| GlobalCTR | 0.6444 | 0.4832 | 0.2945 | 0.6601 |
| QuerySim | 0.6360 | 0.4738 | 0.2908 | 0.6521 |
| TRSVM | 0.6461 | 0.4861 | 0.2953 | 0.6619 |
| IRSVM | 0.6455 | 0.4855 | 0.2951 | 0.6614 |
| dpRank | **0.6539*** | **0.5016*** | **0.2957** | **0.6711*** |

*$p$-value<0.05 under paired t-test against GlobalCTR

only modeling a user's queries alone cannot well explain his/her search intent, and one also needs to capture the factors that affect the user's clicks on the retrieved documents. Comparing to TRSVM and IRSVM, which performed very similarly as the GlobalCTR baseline, profile generated by dpRank performed significantly better than GlobalCTR. Because we are evaluating in the news search log data, where new documents keep emerging. Only a small number of users who issued the same query will have overlap on the returned documents. As a result, the number of effective peers where we can collect click statistics for the target user is very limited; and thus the final performance is very sensitive to the quality of similarity metric between the users. In dpRank, the identified latent user groups explicitly encode different users' click preferences, so that when we weight the clicks from similar users by such profiles, we can get more accurate click predictions for the target user.

## 5. ACKNOWLEDGMENTS

Hongning Wang is supported by a Google Ph.D. Fellowship. This work is partly supported by the National Science Foundation under Grant Number CNS-1027965.

## 6. CONCLUSIONS

In this work, we studied the problem of joint modeling of users' queries and clicks in the search log data, and proposed a generative model, dpRank, to enable such a joint modeling. By introducing the concept of latent user groups and modeling each individual user's search intent as a mixture over such latent user groups, dpRank effectively identifies each individual user's search interests and their distinct ranking preferences in a unified way. Experimental results on a large-scale news search log data set validate our hypothesis that joint modeling of user's search behaviors provides a more comprehensive and accurate understanding of users' search intents, and the mined knowledge about the users is beneficial for a variety of personalized applications, e.g., document ranking and collaborative query recommendation.

The proposed modeling approach is general, and thus can be easily applied to many other types of search logs, e.g., web search and blog search. Besides, the current model only considers the users' logged search behaviors, but it would be interesting to incorporate more information about the users, e.g., gender, location, and social networks, to explore a more comprehensive understanding of users' search intents.

## 7. REFERENCES

[1] E. Agichtein, E. Brill, S. Dumais, and R. Ragno. Learning user interaction models for predicting web search result preferences. In *SIGIR'06*, pages 3–10. ACM, 2006.

[2] R. Baeza-Yates and B. Ribeiro-Neto. *Modern information retrieval*, volume 463. ACM press New York, 1999.

[3] J. Bian, X. Li, F. Li, Z. Zheng, and H. Zha. Ranking specialization for web search: a divide-and-conquer approach by using topical ranksvm. In *WWW'2010*, pages 131–140. ACM, 2010.

[4] O. Chapelle and Y. Chang. Yahoo! learning to rank challenge overview. *Journal of Machine Learning Research-Proceedings Track*, 14:1–24, 2011.

[5] O. Chapelle and Y. Zhang. A dynamic bayesian network click model for web search ranking. In *WWW'09*, pages 1–10. ACM, 2009.

[6] V. Dang. Ranklib-v2.1. `http://people.cs.umass.edu/~vdang/ranklib.html`.

[7] G. E. Dupret and B. Piwowarski. A user browsing model to predict search engine click data from past observations. In *SIGIR'08*, pages 331–338. ACM, 2008.

[8] T. Ferguson. A bayesian analysis of some nonparametric problems. *The annals of statistics*, pages 209–230, 1973.

[9] R. Fidel and M. Crandall. Users' perception of the performance of a filtering system. In *SIGIR'97*, pages 198–205. ACM, 1997.

[10] G. Giannopoulos, U. Brefeld, T. Dalamagas, and T. Sellis. Learning to rank user intent. In *CIKM'2011*, pages 195–200. ACM, 2011.

[11] B. Jansen, A. Spink, and T. Saracevic. Real life, real users, and real needs: a study and analysis of user queries on the web. *Information processing & management*, 36(2):207–227, 2000.

[12] T. Joachims. Optimizing search engines using clickthrough data. In *KDD'02*, pages 133–142. ACM, 2002.

[13] T. Joachims, L. Granka, B. Pan, H. Hembrooke, and G. Gay. Accurately interpreting clickthrough data as implicit feedback. In *SIGIR'05*, pages 154–161. ACM, 2005.

[14] A. C. König, M. Gamon, and Q. Wu. Click-through prediction for news queries. In *SIGIR'09*, pages 347–354. ACM, 2009.

[15] A. Kulkarni, J. Teevan, K. Svore, and S. Dumais. Understanding temporal query dynamics. In *WSDM'11*, pages 167–176. ACM, 2011.

[16] F. Liu, C. Yu, and W. Meng. Personalized web search by mapping user queries to categories. In *CIKM'02*, pages 558–565. ACM, 2002.

[17] R. Neal. Markov chain sampling methods for dirichlet process mixture models. *Journal of computational and graphical statistics*, 9(2):249–265, 2000.

[18] R. Neal. Mcmc using hamiltonian dynamics. *Handbook of Markov Chain Monte Carlo*, 54:113–162, 2010.

[19] D. Rose and D. Levinson. Understanding user goals in web search. In *WWW'04*, pages 13–19. ACM, 2004.

[20] B. Sarwar, G. Karypis, J. Konstan, and J. Riedl. Item-based collaborative filtering recommendation algorithms. In *WWW'2001*, pages 285–295. ACM, 2001.

[21] J. Sethuraman. A constructive definition of dirichlet priors. *Statistica Sinica*, 4:639–650, 1994.

[22] F. Silvestri. Mining query logs: Turning search usage data into knowledge. *Foundations and Trends in Information Retrieval*, 4(1-2):1–174, 2010.

[23] D. Sontag, K. Collins-Thompson, P. N. Bennett, R. W. White, S. Dumais, and B. Billerbeck. Probabilistic models for personalizing web search. In *WSDM'12*, pages 433–442. ACM, 2012.

[24] J. Teevan, S. Dumais, and D. Liebling. To personalize or not to personalize: modeling queries with variation in user intent. In *SIGIR'08*, pages 163–170. ACM, 2008.

[25] Y. W. Teh, M. I. Jordan, M. J. Beal, and D. M. Blei. Hierarchical dirichlet processes. *Journal of the American Statistical Association*, 101(476):1566–1581, 2006.

[26] R. W. White and S. M. Drucker. Investigating behavioral variability in web search. In *WWW'07*, pages 21–30. ACM, 2007.

[27] Q. Wu, C. Burges, K. Svore, and J. Gao. Adapting boosting for information retrieval measures. *Information Retrieval*, 13(3):254–270, 2010.

[28] Y. Zhang, W. Chen, D. Wang, and Q. Yang. User-click modeling for understanding and predicting search-behavior. In *KDD'2011*, pages 1388–1396. ACM, 2011.

# The Last Click: Why Users Give up Information Network Navigation

Aju Thalappillil Scaria*
Google, Inc.
Mountain View, California
aju@google.com

Rose Marie Philip*
Facebook, Inc.
Menlo Park, California
rosephilip@fb.com

Robert West
Stanford University
Stanford, California
west@cs.stanford.edu

Jure Leskovec
Stanford University
Stanford, California
jure@cs.stanford.edu

## ABSTRACT

An important part of finding information online involves clicking from page to page until an information need is fully satisfied. This is a complex task that can easily be frustrating and force users to give up prematurely. An empirical analysis of what makes users abandon click-based navigation tasks is hard, since most passively collected browsing logs do not specify the exact target page that a user was trying to reach. We propose to overcome this problem by using data collected via *Wikispeedia,* a Wikipedia-based human-computation game, in which users are asked to navigate from a start page to an explicitly given target page (both Wikipedia articles) by only tracing hyperlinks between Wikipedia articles. Our contributions are two-fold. First, by analyzing the differences between successful and abandoned navigation paths, we aim to understand what types of behavior are indicative of users giving up their navigation task. We also investigate how users make use of back clicks during their navigation. We find that users prefer backtracking to high-degree nodes that serve as landmarks and hubs for exploring the network of pages. Second, based on our analysis, we build statistical models for predicting whether a user will finish or abandon a navigation task, and if the next action will be a back click. Being able to predict these events is important as it can potentially help us design more human-friendly browsing interfaces and retain users who would otherwise have given up navigating a website.

## Categories and Subject Descriptors

H.5.4 [**Information Interfaces and Presentation**]: Hypertext/Hypermedia—*navigation*; H.1.2 [**Models and Principles**]: User/Machine Systems—*human information processing*

## General Terms

Experimentation, Human Factors

*Research done as graduate students at Stanford University.


*WSDM'14,* February 24–28, 2014, New York, New York, USA.

http://dx.doi.org/10.1145/2556195.2556232.

## Keywords

Navigation, browsing, information networks, abandonment, Wikipedia, Wikispeedia

## 1. INTRODUCTION

Finding information on the Web is a complex task, and even expert users often have a hard time finding precisely what they are looking for [19]. Frequently, information needs cannot be fully satisfied simply by issuing a keyword query to a search engine. Rather, the process of locating information on the Web is typically incremental, requiring people to follow hyperlinks by clicking from page to page, backtracking, changing plans, and so forth. Importantly, click-based navigation is not simply a fall-back option to which users resort after query-based search fails. Indeed, it has been shown that users frequently prefer navigating as opposed to search-engine querying even when the precise search target is known [12], one of the reasons being that useful additional information can be gathered along the way [18].

The complexity of such incremental navigation tasks can be frustrating to users and often leads them to give up before their information need is met [5]. Understanding when this happens is important for designing more user-friendly information structures and better tools for making users more successful at finding information. However, an empirical analysis of what makes users give up click-based navigation tasks is complicated by the fact that most browsing logs, as collected by many search-engine providers and website owners, contain no ground-truth information about the exact target pages users were trying to reach. As a result, in most previous analyses, targets had to be inferred from the queries and from post-query click behavior. For these reasons researchers have typically made heuristic assumptions, e.g., that the information need is captured by the last search result clicked, or the last URL visited, in a session [6]. Other researchers have avoided such assumptions by classifying information needs in broader categories, such as informational versus navigational [20], while ignoring the exact information need.

Furthermore, since passively collected browsing data contain no ground-truth information about the target the user is trying to reach, it is also very hard to determine why the user stopped browsing at any particular point. On one extreme, she could have found the information she was looking for and abandoned the session simply because the information need was satisfied. Or, on the other extreme, it could be that the user abandoned the search process precisely because she could *not* locate the desired information and

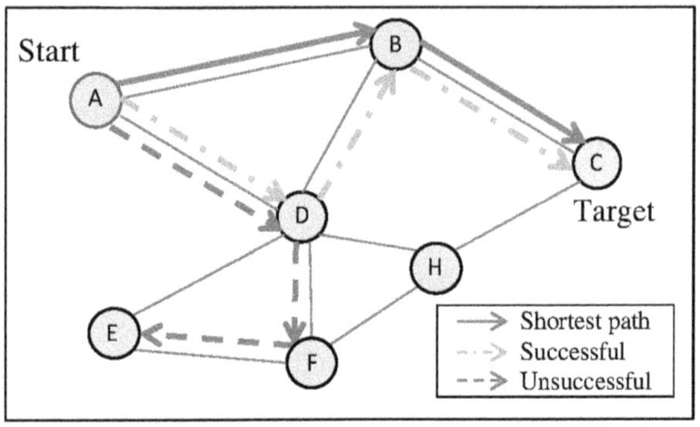


**Figure 1: An example navigation mission from start *A* to target *C*. The *gray arrows* represent an optimal 2-click navigation, the *green arrows* illustrate a successful 3-click navigation, and the *red arrows* show an unsuccessful, abandoned 3-click navigation, where the user did not reach the target *C*.**

gave up. Thus, abandonment in Web search and navigation is not always a sign of giving up [9].

In this paper, we address these two issues by leveraging data collected from *Wikispeedia* [17], a Wikipedia-based online human-computation game. In this game, users are given explicit navigation tasks, which we also refer to as *missions* (Fig. 1). Each mission is defined by a *start* and a *target article,* selected from the set of Wikipedia articles, and users are asked to navigate from the start article to the known target in as few clicks as possible, using exclusively hyperlinks encountered in the Wikipedia articles along the way.

Using this dataset alleviates both of the problems we have discussed earlier: First, the goal of the navigation mission (i.e., the target page) is explicitly known and need not be inferred. Second, since the task can by definition only be solved by reaching the target, abandonment can always be interpreted as giving up (although we acknowledge that, next to failure, boredom could also be a reason for giving up; we address this point later, when introducing the dataset). An additional advantage of our setup is that each page is a Wikipedia article and therefore has a well-defined content, comparable to other pages by standard text-mining measures such as TF-IDF cosine.

We believe that these factors enable a more controlled analysis of the reasons causing users to give up click-based navigation tasks than most previous log-based studies. In particular, our work makes two main contributions:

1. We empirically analyze differences and commonalities between finished and abandoned navigation tasks. We also analyze back clicks, a frequently employed means to back off from unsuccessful strategies.

2. We apply our findings by building statistical models for predicting whether users are about to give up on a navigation task, and whether they will hit the back button next.

Regarding the first point, our analysis shows that some missions are intrinsically harder than others, but also that, even when controlling for intrinsic hardness, some users manage to find better strategies and are thus also less likely to give up. We observe that it is typically easy to make progress at the beginning of navigation paths, whereas there is much more variability later on, when users are trying to home in on the target page. Sometimes users make bad moves, taking them further away (in a shortest-path sense) from the target than they already were, and in these cases, we note an increased likelihood of back clicks—a sign that users typically have a sense for whether they have made progress towards the target article or not. However, users who are to eventually give up are worse at doing so. They click back despite having made progress towards the target much more frequently than successful users do. In other words, not only are unsuccessful users worse at making progress, they are also worse at realizing it once they do make progress.

Concerning the second contribution, our predictive models could potentially be the basis for mechanisms serving to improve websites in an interactive manner. For instance, if we can reliably predict whether a user is about to give up navigating, i.e., to leave the site, we could take actions to retain that user, e.g., by displaying a support phone number or a chat window. The features we use in our models are based on the insights drawn from the analysis of successful and unsuccessful missions, and predict well if users are going to quit their navigation.

## 2. RELATED WORK

Related work may be divided into three broad areas: query abandonment, click-trail analysis, and decentralized search.

*Query abandonment,* as studied in the information retrieval community, analyzes queries that are not followed by a search-result click. Li et al. [9] distinguish 'bad' and 'good' abandonment. The former occurs when the information need could not be met (e.g., because no relevant results were returned), the latter, when the information need could be satisfied even without clicking a search result. Good abandonment occurs surprisingly often (17% of abandoned queries on PCs, 38% on mobile devices), which confirms the need for controlling for abandonment type, as we attempt to do. Diriye et al. [5] strive to understand more deeply and on a larger scale what causes users to abandon queries, thus eliciting useful indicators which they subsequently use to build a predictive model of query abandonment. Das Sarma et al. [4] focus on bad abandonment and offer a method to reduce it by learning to re-rank results. In these works, abandonment is usually defined as 'zero clicks'. We, on the contrary, adopt a broader definition, by considering as abandoned also those searches in which the user has already made some clicks but gives up before reaching the final target. Note that this is possible only because the exact target is explicitly known in our setup. Also, our setup involves only click-based navigation and no search queries, which allows us to analyze human navigation behavior in isolation, thus avoiding conflating users' navigation skills with their query formulation skills.

*Click-trail analysis* primarily studies the click paths on which users embark, starting from search-engine result pages. In early fundamental work, Chi et al. [3] invent the notion of 'information scent', operationalized by Olston and Chi [11] in a system for supporting users by combining query- and click-based navigation strategies. We have already mentioned the work of White and Huang [18], who establish that click trails add value to the information contained in the ultimate target page, and of Teevan et al. [12], who show that users frequently prefer click-based navigation to querying. Downey et al. [6] investigate the benefits of navigating versus querying further, finding that navigating is particularly useful when the information need is rare. Finally, White and Singla's [20] work is relevant in that it explores how different trail topologies (such as stars, trees, and linear chains) are observed in different search scenarios (informational versus navigational). Our work extends these ideas. For instance, while White and Singla [20] manually assign topologies to paths, we devise an automatic method for doing so. Further, while they must heuristically assume that the last observed page is the target page, we have ground-truth target information, which allows for a much refined analysis.

Some very relevant work was done by Ageev et al. [1]. They, too, have developed a human-computation game for collecting data, in which users are asked to find the answers to as many factual questions (e.g., 'What is the highest peak in the Western Hemisphere?') as possible within a given amount of time, using Web search queries that may optionally be followed by click-based navigation. There, too, the goal is explicitly known, but not in the form of a specific target page but rather in the form of a specific answer string. Ageev et al.'s setup has the advantages of a more realistic search scenario, since both querying and navigating are allowed, and of a more realistic browsing environment (the Web rather than Wikipedia only). On the flip side, our approach allows for several types of analysis that are impossible in their setup. For instance, each Wikipedia page has a clearly defined topic, with the target being exactly one page (rather than an answer string that might be gleaned from several pages), such that it is straightforward to quantify how related a page along the click path is to the target. Moreover, the network topology is known entirely in our case.

*Decentralized search* is rooted in Milgram's seminal small-world experiment [10], which asked participants to forward a letter to a friend such that it could finally reach a predestined target person. The game through which our data was collected is similar to this task in that a target must be reached in the absence of prior information about the underlying network. It is different in that our setup has the same user staying in control from the start all the way to the target, whereas, in the small-world experiment, every step is executed by a new, autonomous participant. Kleinberg [8] investigated the algorithmic aspects of the small-world problem, showing that efficient search is only possible when the probability of long-range link decays with a specific exponent. Much research has followed in Kleinberg's wake, so we focus on the most directly related pieces of work: datasets such as ours were previously analyzed by West and Leskovec, who characterize human strategies in successful navigation tasks [16] and train machine-learning models capable of navigating automatically [15], and by Trattner et al. [13], who explore heuristic navigation algorithms based on hierarchical knowledge representations. The present paper extends previous work by considering abandoned navigation paths in addition to successful ones.

# 3. DATASET

In this section, we introduce the data collection procedure and the dataset we used. We also make the data available online.[1]

**Data collection.** We analyze navigation paths collected through the Wikipedia-based human-computation game *Wikispeedia*[2] [17] (see Fig. 2 for screenshots). The rules are simple: A user arriving at the site is given a mission (Fig. 1), consisting of a start and a target article sampled randomly from the set of all articles in the strongly connected core component of Wikipedia's hyperlink graph, to ensure that there is a path between the two. Alternatively, the user can specify a mission herself, or choose from a list of 5 randomly sampled missions solved previously by other users. Given a mission, the task is to navigate from the start to the target article, exclusively by following hyperlinks, in as few clicks as possible. Backtracking via the browser's back button is allowed, and forward clicks that were later undone this way, as well as the back clicks themselves, are not counted when ranking users in high-score tables. Many Wikipedia articles are about obscure topics few people know about, but having a clear idea of the target and its context is crucial for solving navigation tasks. Therefore, users have the option to read the contents of the target article before starting to navigate.

A condensed and curated version of Wikipedia[3] is used, containing 4,600 articles and around 120,000 links. We consider a set of around 32,000 navigation paths. The data has been collected since August 2009, when the Wikispeedia website was launched. Participation has been completely voluntary and open to all Web users, with no reward offered, other than the fun inherent in the game.

Of the 32,000 recorded paths, only 49% were completed successfully. Indeed, it is this surprisingly low number that triggered our investigation into what causes users to give up. It is, however, important to note that, while Wikispeedia produces data that is well suited for studying user abandonment, the site was not specifically designed for this purpose.

In addition to the navigation paths, the site also logs if a task ended (1) because the session expired (after 30 minutes of inactivity; 38% of abandoned missions), or (2) because the user decided to give up on the current task and start a new one (62%). Upon restarting, the user is presented with a different start–target pair.

**Data preprocessing.** Several factors might play a role in giving up: (1) Users might be unable to solve the navigation task, or (2) they might have become bored, disinterested, or distracted, switching their attention to something else. We are interested in giving up due to failure (reason 1) rather than disinterest or distraction. As the Wikispeedia interface does not ask abandoning users why they gave up, we cannot know which missions where given up because of reason 1. Instead, we filter our data the following way. First, we think it is reasonable to assume that the tasks abandoned after a very small number of clicks (in the extreme case without a single click) were given up not because the users were unable to solve the task, but rather because they got bored, disinterested, or distracted. Hence, we consider only missions in which at least 3 clicks were made. Second, we argue that timeouts tend to be caused by boredom, disinterest, or distraction, whereas quitting the current mission and starting a new one is much more likely to be a sign of failure to find a path to the target article. Therefore, we restrict the set of abandoned missions to those that the user gave up in order to start a new one.

Not all start–target pairs can be solved in the same optimal number of steps, so another potential confounding factor becomes immediately clear: missions with longer optimal solutions are intrinsically harder, which is likely to increase the probability of giving up, independent of any other factors. To control for this effect, we further constrain our analysis to missions with an optimal solution length of exactly 3 clicks. This does not decrease our sample size by too much, due to the fact that the Wikipedia hyperlink graph constitutes a tightly connected 'small world', with a mean/median/maximum shortest-path length of 3.18/3/9, across all node pairs. After these filtering steps, the final dataset we study consists of about 16,000 paths (10,000 finished, 6,000 unfinished).

# 4. DYNAMICS OF GIVING UP

Previous work showed that, at every single step in our setting, there is roughly a 10% chance of the user dropping out [16]. In this section, we investigate the reasons *why* users give up while navigating to find some specific piece of information. We break our analysis into two parts. First, we investigate the intrinsic hardness of navigation tasks, as hard missions are more likely to be aban-

[1] `http://snap.stanford.edu/data/wikispeedia.html`
[2] `http://www.wikispeedia.net`

[3] `http://schools-wikipedia.org` (accessed 08/2008)

(a) Before navigation starts (b) During navigation (c) After successful navigation

**Figure 2: Screenshots of Wikispeedia, the human-computation game used for data collection (cf. Section 3).**

| Property | Finished | Unfinished |
|---|---|---|
| TF-IDF distance | 0.971 | 0.977 |
| Target in-degree | 62.8 | 28.6 |
| Target PageRank | $4.77 \times 10^{-4}$ | $2.33 \times 10^{-4}$ |
| Source out-degree | 32.4 | 31.1 |

**Table 1: Means of start and target properties for finished versus unfinished navigation paths. Two-tailed $t$-tests yielded highly significant differences ($p < .0005$) for all pairs.**

doned. Second, we analyze the user behaviors that are indicative of successful or unsuccessful[4] navigation, respectively.

While we think the way we preprocessed our data eliminated the most obvious confounding factors, the question of intrinsic mission hardness remains: even if all missions can be optimally solved in 3 clicks, solutions may be easier to find for some missions than others. Hence, we structure the present analysis into two parts: (1) We analyze what features of the start and target pages (beyond mere shortest-path length) make a mission intrinsically hard, and (2) we look into how successfully finished navigation paths differ from prematurely abandoned ones, in terms of features of the click paths rather than features of just the start and target articles.

**Intrinsic mission hardness.** To elicit the factors that make a mission hard independent of any user-dependent features, we compare properties of the start and target articles for finished versus unfinished missions. Note that we only consider start–target pairs that can be reached in exactly 3 clicks. The results are summarized in Table 1. We make the following observations:

- The textual distance between the source and target articles (measured as one minus the TF-IDF cosine of the article contents) in successful and unsuccessful missions are significantly different (the numbers are so close because all TF-IDF distances tend to be close to 1). This means that it is less frustrating to find paths between start and target articles that are conceptually more related.
- The in-degree and PageRank of target articles in unsuccessful missions are only about half as large as in successful ones. Both of these measures capture how easy it is to reach the target article (in-degree in a local, and PageRank in a global sense), so we conclude that missions with hard-to-find targets are more likely to be abandoned. While at first glance this might seem trivial, it is important to note that PageRank is based on a random-walker model [2], whereas humans do not navigate randomly; they have vast amounts of background knowledge, which might well allow them to find paths that are hard to find for an uninformed random walker. So the fact that the simplistic notion of PageRank is a good indicator of whether a mission will be abandoned is in fact nontrivial and of practical importance (e.g., later on in this paper, when we use it as a feature for predicting abandonment).
- The out-degree of start nodes is similar in finished and unfinished paths. This means that the starting phase of missions is less important than the final phase. Even if the start article offers only few outgoing links, the chance of giving up are not much affected. Thus, properties of the source are not indicative of user abandonment. It is only the properties of the target that determine the success rate of a mission. We hypothesize this is caused by the small-world structure of the network: there are some hub nodes (such as UNITED STATES) that are easily reached from all over the network (even from low-out-degree nodes) and that link to many distinct parts of it, so they often serve as transition points between an easy 'getting-away' and a harder 'homing-in' phase [16].

In summary, even when the optimal path length is held fixed, the intrinsic hardness of missions varies widely as a function of both content- and network-related properties of the start and target articles. To gain additional insights, we will later further control for mission hardness by only considering all the instances of particular start–target pairs (e.g., BRAIN to TELEPHONE).

**Navigation in successful versus unsuccessful paths.** Another way to understand why people give up is to analyze properties of articles along the path they took. We compare how different article properties evolve along navigation paths both for successful and unsuccessful missions. The results to be discussed next are depicted in Fig. 3. Plots in the left column were computed based on finished missions, and those on the right based on unfinished ones. Even though all missions had a shortest-path length (SPL) from start to target of 3 clicks (cf. Section 3), the actual paths can consist of any number of clicks, depending on the choices made by the user. As a result, we draw a separate curve for each path length, grouping all paths of the same length together. The $x$-axes show the path position (in terms of the number of clicks made from the start article), and the $y$-axes, the mean of the respective property. Thus, each curve may be thought of as representing the average value of the property—running from left to right—for the respective path length. Since the last node is always the target in finished paths,

[4]We use the word groups *finished/successful* and *unfinished/ unsuccessful/abandoned/given up* interchangeably.

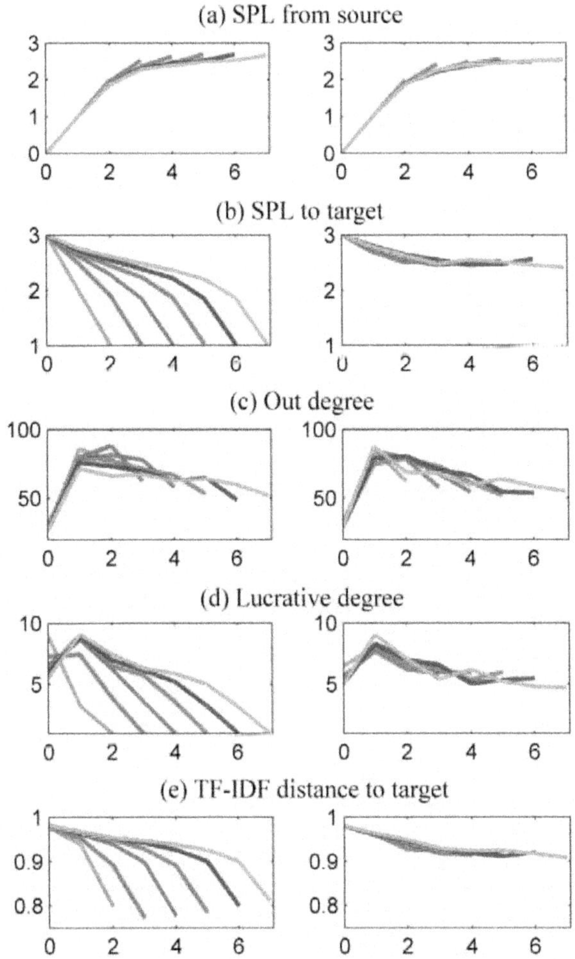


**Figure 3: Comparison between finished *(left)* and unfinished *(right)* navigation missions. Paths of the same length are grouped in the same curve and have the same color. The $x$-axes show the path position (defined as the number of clicks from source), and the $y$-axes, the mean of the respective property. The last node along the path (the target in the case of finished paths) is omitted from all plots. See text for description of properties.**

this would in many cases distort the $y$-axes, so we do not plot it. To be consistent, we also omit the last node from all unfinished paths.

One of our early hypotheses for explaining why people abandon navigating was that they might have traveled very far from both the start and the target node—in other words that they might have gotten 'lost' in the network. However, as the top two rows of Fig. 3 show, the average SPL (shortest-path length) with respect to both the start and the target article always remains less than 3, even for unfinished paths. We further see that the average SPL from the source (row 1) looks very much the same when compared to successful navigation tasks. Successful and unsuccessful missions also have in common that the SPL to the target (row 2) decreases with the first click. However, while in successful missions, users make on average continuous progress towards the target, this is not the case in abandoned missions, where it stays at a constant level of around 2.5. The same pattern of initial progress with ensuing stagnation is exposed by the plot of TF-IDF distance to the target (row 5).

So, while straying very far from either source or target is not a big danger—since everything tends to be close to everything else in small-world networks—unsuccessful users seem to be unable to make the crucial click that finally lets them 'gravitate' towards the target. Therefore, instead of 'getting lost', the analogy for unsuccessful navigation should rather be 'orbiting' at a constant distance from the target, which can be frustrating, thus causing users to give up.

This reinforces a point we have already briefly touched upon in our discussion of intrinsic hardness: making progress is easy in the beginning. SPL and TF-IDF distance to the target drop initially even for unfinished missions, but the crucial difference to finished missions is that users in finished missions continue to make progress, while those in unfinished missions do not.

As mentioned before, West and Leskovec [16] have argued that the initial progress might stem from clicking to a high-degree hub node. This is confirmed by Fig. 3, rows 3 and 4, which show that out-degree and lucrative degree (defined as the number of outgoing links that decrease the SPL to the target) spike after one click. We see that a hub-based strategy is pursued even by users who are to eventually give up, another indicator that the opening is not as crucial as the later phase in determining whether a navigation task will be finished.

**The case of paths with more than 8 clicks.** Note that Fig. 3 is based on missions of a maximum of 8 clicks. It is also interesting to look at longer missions, the question being: If a successful mission consists of many clicks, is it that the user made steady progress throughout the mission and just took longer to find the target, or did they rather stumble upon the target by luck after trying a lot of different options?

To answer this question, Fig. 4 repeats some of the plots of Fig. 3 for longer missions (10, 15, and 20 clicks), comparing them with missions of length 5. We find that the distinction between successful and abandoned missions is much diminished for paths of many clicks, except that there is a brief final phase of 'gravitating into the target' in the case of successful missions. It looks more as though in these cases the successful users found a way to the target not so much via a straightforward strategy but rather by luck, having 'orbited' around the target for a long time, as typical also for abandoned missions. The other properties show similar trends and we omit them for space reasons.

**Controlling for intrinsic hardness.** Since certain features of start and target articles can make missions intrinsically harder, a critical reader might object that mixing missions of all levels of intrinsic hardness together (as we do in Fig. 3 and 4) might induce a potential confounding factor: as harder missions are *a priori* more likely to be abandoned, the differences observed in our previous analysis might indeed be caused by the skewed levels of hardness in finished versus unfinished missions, rather than by more versus less successful strategies. To rule this out, we repeated our analysis for 4 *fixed* pairs of start and target articles for which an increased number of samples were collected, thus controlling for intrinsic hardness. The resulting figures are qualitatively very similar to those shown, and all our findings still hold. We nonetheless show the figures based on all missions, as they are based on more samples and therefore more reliable.

# 5. BACK-CLICKING PATTERNS

Given that navigating information networks is a complex task, it is quite natural for users to backtrack while navigating to locate a specific target. *A priori,* it is not clear if backtracking is rather a sign of successful or of unsuccessful missions: On one hand, a mission might be successful because the user extensively explored

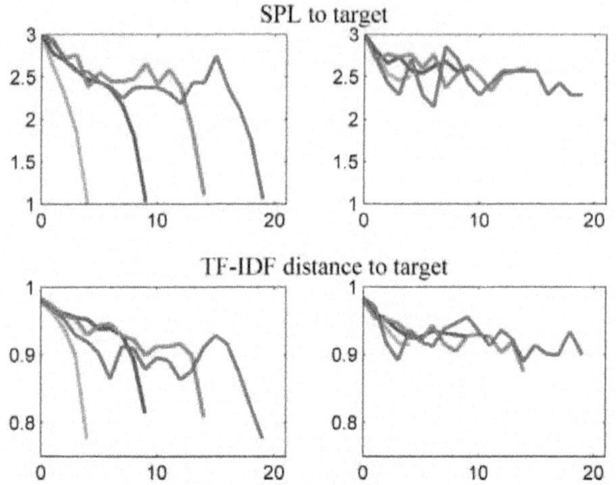


**Figure 4: Analogous to Fig. 3 (b and e), but for a wider range of path lengths (*left:* finished; *right:* unfinished).**

| | Finished | | | Unfinished | | |
|---|---|---|---|---|---|---|
| | − | = | + | − | = | + |
| SPL | .242 | .102 | .033 | .233 | .153 | .116 |
| TF-IDF dist. | .189 | .096 | .049 | .253 | .161 | .111 |

**Table 2: Back-click probability conditional on progress: (+) progress, i.e., property decreased with last click; (−) regress, i.e., property increased; (=) neither progress nor regress (in the case of TF-IDF, taken as a relative change of $< 10\%$).**

the network via back clicks, but on the other hand, backtracking might be a sign of the users being at a loss.

The data favors the second alternative, with backtracking being more common in unsuccessful missions: 20.3% of abandoned paths contained at least one back click (average of 2.48 back clicks per mission), while this percentage is only 16.4% (2.24 back clicks per mission) for finished paths.

Next, to dig deeper, we consider the following two questions: First, when do users typically backtrack? Second, what are the most common backtracking patterns?

**When do users typically backtrack?** We conjectured that users are inclined to backtrack when they feel they might have navigated too far away from the target article. To test this hypothesis, we observe how the probability of backtracking varies depending on whether progress towards the target was made with the previous click. Here we measure progress in two ways: (1) Did the SPL to the target decrease? (2) Did the conceptual distance to the target (measured as one minus TF-IDF cosine similarity of article texts) decrease? The findings are summarized in Table 2. Note that backtracking is least likely when progress was made with the previous click, most likely when the opposite of progress was achieved (i.e., when SPL or TF-IDF distance to the target increased), and on a middle ground when neither of these two extremes is the case. Furthermore, the probability of backtracking after making progress is considerably higher in unsuccessful than in successful paths (11.6% vs. 3.3% for SPL, and 11.1% vs. 4.9% for TF-IDF distance). We draw two conclusions from these observations. First, even though the underlying network structure is unknown, both successful and unsuccessful users have an intuition whether a click choice they have just made was good or bad. Second, successful users are better at forming these intuitions, whereas unsuccessful users are three times more likely to undo a useful click, which in fact took them closer to the target. This is similar to a finding by Ageev et al. [1], who show that successful users are better at identifying relevant documents on search engine result pages.

**What are the most common backtracking patterns?** Given that backtracking is important in distinguishing finished from abandoned navigation paths, we wanted to go beyond simply counting paths with at least one back click and move to a more topological analysis of how back-click patterns are arranged in paths. We started by adopting a methodology similar to White and Singla's [20] and manually inspected graphical representations of navigation paths (such as in Fig. 5), finding that one main dimension of variability is the 'star-likeness' of paths. A path from start to target is more star-like when all back clicks lead back to the same node, which serves as a hub for exploring its neighborhood (cf. Fig. 5(d) for an extreme example).

Whereas White and Singla stick to hand-labeling, we strive to automatically analyze the tens of thousands of paths we have at our disposal. To this end, we introduce a novel but simple measure, which we call *star score.* Intuitively, a path is maximally star-like if all back clicks return to the same hub, and least so if every back click leads to a different previously visited node. More formally, the star score should be high if the distribution of back-click targets is highly peaked. Additionally, when this distribution is equal for two paths, we want a path with a larger number of back clicks to receive a higher star score. Formally, the *star score* of a path $p$ is defined as

$$S(p) = (1 - G(p)) \cdot N, \qquad (1)$$

where $N$ is the total number of back clicks on the path, and $G(p) = 1 - \sum_{i=1}^{n} f_i^2$ is the Gini impurity of the back-click distribution. The Gini index measures how even or uniform a given distribution is ($f_i$ is the fraction of back clicks to node $i$ and $n$ is the number of nodes in the path).[5] The star score is defined for paths with at least one back click and always lies between 1 and $N$.

Fig. 5 shows the plot of the paths taken by some users as directed graphs, alongside the corresponding star scores. Clearly, the graphs with denser star-like patterns have higher star scores.

Initially, we hypothesized that unsuccessful missions would be more likely to show star-like patterns because users keep exploring new ways and then backtrack from them without achieving success. However, we were unable to discern any noticeable differences in the distribution of star score in successful versus unsuccessful paths. We think that the reason is that exploring in a star-like fashion is not necessarily a sign of failure—indeed, as argued in the beginning of this section, it might even contribute to a better understanding of the local graph neighborhood and thus increase the chances of success. Still, navigation paths with very high star scores (greater than 6), even though few in number, all ended up being abandoned.

Moreover, it seems that not all nodes are equally suited for backtracking. Backtracking may be the manifestation of a change of strategy, so we hypothesized that users are more likely to return to hub nodes, i.e., nodes of high out-degree, which are best suited for 'teleporting' to a different part of the network. To investigate this issue, we found, for each path involving a back click, the node receiving the highest number of back clicks and computed its rank in the list of all nodes on the path sorted by out-degree. The results are presented in Fig. 6. In 30% of unfinished, and around 20% of finished missions, the node receiving most back clicks is also the node of highest out-degree on the path. Also, the likelihood of a node re-

[5] A user might visit the same article more than once even without a back click, through a series of clicks, which we consider equivalent to a back click.

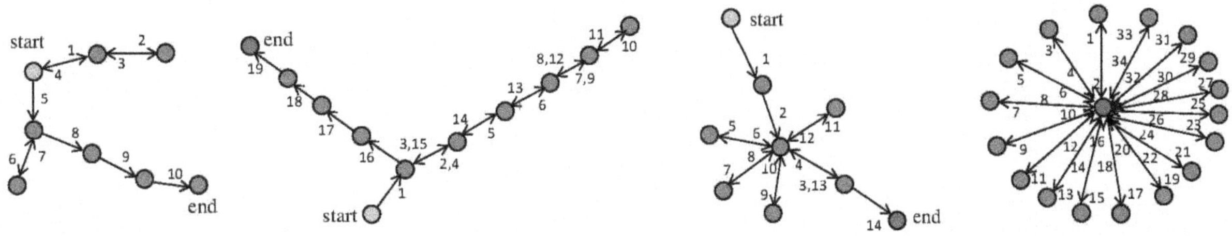


(a) Star score = 1.0 (3) (b) Star score = 1.57 (7) (c) Star score = 5.0 (5) (d) Star score = 17.0 (17)

**Figure 5: Examples of navigation paths, illustrating our star score metric. The numbers within brackets are the numbers of back clicks on the paths. Users navigate from the start node to the end node (i.e., the target for finished, and the last visited node for unfinished, paths). The numbers along the edges indicates the ordering of clicks. In (d), the start and end nodes are the same.**

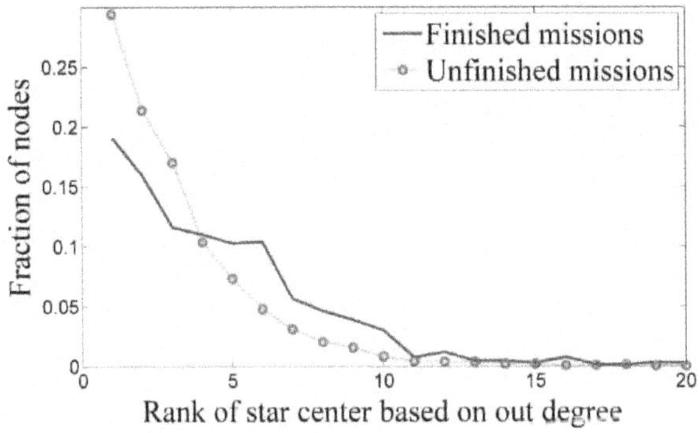


**Figure 6: Centers of stars are hubs.**

ceiving most back clicks shrinks with decreasing out-degree rank. It is also interesting to note that users in unfinished missions have a higher inclination to backtrack to hub nodes.

We have focused on star-like patterns here, but for future work, it might be interesting to explore a wider variety of topological navigational structures, using more advanced graph techniques from the data visualization community (e.g., [14, 7]).

# 6. PREDICTING ABANDONMENT AND BACK CLICKS

In the earlier sections, we have analyzed the reasons why some navigation paths end up abandoned, and also in what situations users decide to backtrack. Our next goal is to apply the lessons learnt, in order to develop models for predicting three navigation events, based only on the first few clicks:

1. Will the user abandon the mission before finishing it?
2. Will the user backtrack with the next click?
3. Will the user give up without making any additional clicks?

We formulate binary classification tasks and apply logistic regression with a set of features based on the observations made earlier. The model learns weights for each feature and makes a prediction of the likelihood of the event given a new example. Since the model outputs a probability value, the effectiveness of the system depends on the threshold (or confidence) above which we declare a sample to belong to the positive class. As the choice of threshold affects the accuracy of the task, we decided instead to plot ROC curves and use the area under the curve (AUC), which does not require choosing a threshold, as our performance measure. Since our models are trained on actual human navigation trajectories, they learn characteristic features of human behavior.

Applications of such models have already been alluded to in the introduction. They include tracking the progress of a website user to understand if he is about to stop his navigation, or is lost in the network of pages, so that we could incentivize him to stay by offering phone or chat support, or by offering special bargain deals.

## 6.1 Description of Prediction Tasks

We first give details about each of the three prediction tasks. Then we describe the features used, and finally we present the results. For each of the tasks, we created a balanced dataset consisting of equal numbers of positive and negative examples (by randomly sampling from the class with more examples) and used 70% of the data for training and 30% for testing.

**Task 1: Will the user abandon the mission before finishing it?** Here, we predict if a user will complete or abandon a mission with known start and target, based on only the first few clicks. The number of clicks given as input to the classifier, which we refer to as the *window size* $W$, is a parameter that can be chosen, and we build separate models for $W = 1, \ldots, 4$. We restrict ourselves to missions with a SPL from start to target of at least 3. The negative examples consist of unfinished paths of at least $W$ clicks. Regarding the positive examples, we took additional care: In Fig. 4, we saw that for very long paths, the differences between successful and unsuccessful instances vanish, so for each path, we included it only if it was finished within 5 additional clicks, compared to the optimum (i.e., compared to the SPL from start to target). For instance, if the SPL from start to target was 3, we allow up to 8 clicks; and for SPL of 4, up to 9, and so on. We define this value as the *tolerance* allowed in positive samples (in this case, the tolerance is 5). Further, Fig. 3 shows that finished paths differ a lot from unfinished ones in the last couple of clicks. We want to prevent the learning algorithm from 'cheating' (by simply learning these typical endgame patterns), so, for window size $W$, we consider only paths of at least $W+2$ clicks.

**Task 2: Will the user backtrack with the next click?** The dataset we used for this task is same as in the previous one. We again exclude the last two clicks from consideration, for the same reasons outlined above. In the previous task, each input path was represented by the first $W$ clicks. However, since in the present task we are trying to predict a local event (Will the next click be a back click?), we extract features from a sliding window of $W$ clicks. For example, for $W = 3$, in a path with 8 clicks, 3 samples may be constructed: one to predict click 4 (whether it will be a back click or not) from clicks 1, 2, and 3; another to predict click 5 from clicks 2, 3, and 4; and so on. Positive examples are those in which the last click in the window was followed by a back click, and the rest, negative examples.

**Task 3: Will the user give up after the current click?** We extend the model used for predicting back clicks to also predict if the person is going to quit navigating immediately after the current click, without making any additional clicks. Here, too, we use a sliding window, similar to the model for predicting back clicks.

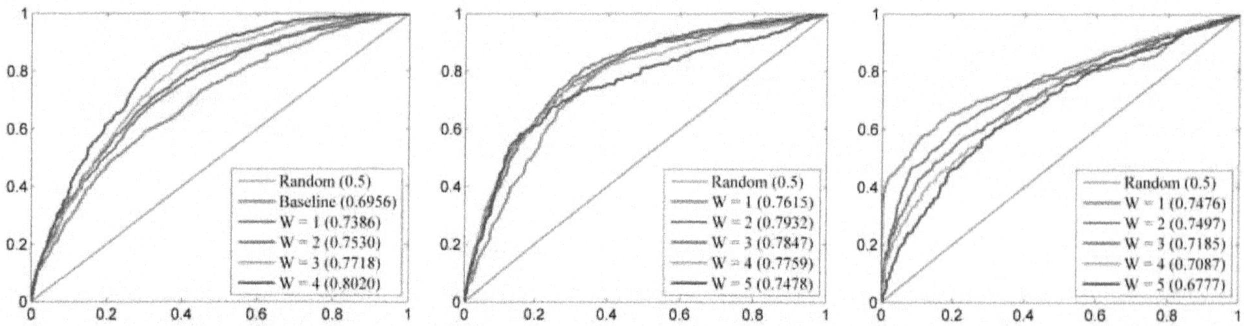


(a) Task 1: Giving up before finishing (b) Task 2: Backtracking with next click (c) Task 3: Giving up after current click

**Figure 7: ROC curves for the 3 prediction tasks; AUC in parentheses; $W$ is a window-size parameter (see text for description).**

| | Tolerance w.r.t. SPL | | |
|---|---|---|---|
| | 3 | 4 | 5 |
| AUC | 0.958 | 0.8304 | 0.802 |

**Table 3: Variation in AUC of classifier for predicting abandonment with tolerance in path length of positive samples (for windows size $W = 4$). See text for description.**

Positive examples are those in which the last node in the window is also the last node on the path, and the rest are negative examples.

## 6.2 Features Used for Learning

The features we use in all three tasks are based on the insights drawn by comparing the properties of finished and unfinished missions. In each of the prediction tasks, given $W$ clicks (or $W+1$ nodes), we use the following features:

- *Properties of start and target nodes:* SPL from start to target; lucrative degree (as defined in Section 4) and lucrative ratio (defined as the fraction of out-links of a node that decrease SPL to target) of start node; PageRank of target; in-degree of target; TF-IDF distance of start and target.
- *For each adjacent node pair:* TF-IDF distance; relative change in lucrative degree and lucrative ratio.
- *For each node:* lucrative degree; lucrative ratio; TF-IDF distance to target; SPL to target; indicator variable: Was a back click done although SPL to target decreased compared to previous node (inspired by Table 2)?

For some tasks, we use additional features, which will be introduced as we are discussing the results for the respective task.

## 6.3 Experimental Results

Next, we present the results of our predictive models on each of the three tasks.

**Results for Task 1.** For the task of predicting if a path is going to be finished successfully or not (Fig. 7(a)), we built a baseline model that uses only properties of start and target to make a prediction. This model yields an AUC of 0.70. Considering that random guessing would give an AUC of 0.5, this baseline model performs rather well, which supports our argument from the Section 4 that some navigation tasks are intrinsically harder than others. Fig. 7(a) further shows that, as expected, a larger window size $W$ results in better predictions; specifically, for $W = 4$, the AUC increases to 0.80, a 14% relative improvement over the start–target baseline.

We also wanted to see how sensitive our results were to the choice of the tolerance of path length allowed in positive samples (set to 5, for the plots in Fig. 7(a)). So, we repeated the evaluation for tolerances of 3 and 4 (and $W = 4$), with the result that, the lesser the tolerance, the higher the AUC (cf. Table 3). This is expected: as we raise the quality of finished paths (by reducing the tolerance), the differences between finished and unfinished navigation paths becomes more obvious.

**Results for Task 2.** For this task, we used two additional features apart from the ones used for Task 1: the number of clicks made so far on the path, and the fraction of back clicks in the path till now. The number of pages visited is important because people could have a different rate of quitting depending on how far into the path they are, and we want to capture this. The performance for various choices of the window size $W$, visualized in Fig. 7(b), lie between 0.75 and 0.79. Performance goes up as we increase $W$ from 1 to 2 and then goes down as we increase it further. We assume this is the case because backtracking is a local event that is done mainly when users feel they have made bad choices in the last one or two clicks. As a result, beyond $W = 2$, the larger context size increases the noise, while adding only little signal.

**Results for Task 3.** Here we use the same features as in Task 2. The results are plotted in Fig. 7(c). The performance of predicting whether the user is going to leave after the current click turns out to be harder than Task 1, in which we predicted whether the user will abandon *at any later point*. Even if someone has made up their mind to leave the mission, it could still be the case that they make one or two more clicks, simply out of curiosity or to see if they get closer to the target by luck. This kind of behavior is difficult to predict and could be a reason why our model performance is slightly lower than that on the other two tasks. Even so, we still achieve an AUC between 0.68 and 0.75, depending on $W$.

## 6.4 Analysis of Learned Predictive Models

Our models use around 30 features. In this section, we describe our method to find the features that are most important and analyze the results. We performed 10-fold cross validation on the training set, in combination with backward feature selection, starting with the set of all features and progressively discarding features that contributed least to the AUC score until the AUC score began to drop. The following list of features was found to be most powerful for Task 1, alongside explanations why these features might matter:

- *SPL from last node in input to target:* If a user has not made much progress towards the target in the first few clicks, he has more ground to cover and there is a higher chance that he might get frustrated and give up.

- *TF-IDF distance between last two nodes in input and target:* The same reasoning applies.
- *In-degree of target:* The fewer in-links the target has, the more difficult it is to find in the network, making the mission intrinsically harder (cf. Table 1).
- *Indicator whether a back click was made despite having made progress:* As we saw in Table 2, users who give up are worse at identifying that they have made progress.
- *TF-IDF distance between adjacent nodes:* Making abrupt changes in terms of article content seems to be an indicator of frustration or confusion.

The same features were prominent in Tasks 2 and 3, with the addition that the two features used specifically in those two tasks (number of clicks already made so far, and fraction of back clicks) were also found to be important.

# 7. DISCUSSION AND CONCLUSION

In this paper, we investigate why and when users abandon click-based navigation tasks in a given information network. Even though billions of navigation paths are given up when browsing websites or navigating Wikipedia, the navigational patterns that lead to task abandonment have largely remained underexplored. Many previous empirical analyses of navigation behavior have suffered from shortcomings imposed by the datasets studied. The target pages users attempted to reach were not explicitly known, so it was not clear whether they stopped navigating because the target was already found or because, on the contrary, they were unable to find it. In contrast, by studying navigation paths from a human-computation experiment in which users are navigating Wikipedia by clicking from page to page, we overcome this obstacle. Since users are explicitly told what they are supposed to find, the target of the navigation task is known and can be factored into the analysis.

Our analysis demonstrates that some missions are intrinsically harder than others, determined primarily by factors dependent on the navigation target and not the source. However, since the target is explicitly known, we can control for this intrinsic mission hardness and focus on which kinds of navigation strategies are more likely to result in success than others.

We find that it is easier to make progress at the beginning of paths. In both successful and unsuccessful missions, users navigate through high-degree hub nodes. However, it is homing in on the target that makes the difference. Unsuccessful users keep orbiting around the target and eventually get frustrated, leading to abandonment, whereas, successful users manage to find the crucial link that lets them gravitate into the target.

We also find that backtracking plays an important role and is employed in both successful as well as unsuccessful paths. In some cases, it could be used by people who are gathering useful information by exploring the local neighborhood, aiding their navigation, whereas, in other cases, it could indicate that the user is confused and is desperately trying to find a way to the target. In both successful and unsuccessful missions, users prefer backtracking to hubs of high out-degree, which serve as landmarks from which many different parts of the graph can be explored. Interestingly, both successful and unsuccessful users prefer backtracking after making a bad click, i.e., one that increases the shortest-path length or TF-IDF distance to the target. However, a distinctive difference between the two types of user is that successful navigators are better at realizing when they have made progress. Unsuccessful users are three times more likely to backtrack after making progress towards the target.

Building on these insights, we formulate predictive models for three tasks, showing that our analytic findings can be applied to predict user behavior. Our models have the potential to be useful in practice, such as aiding website owners to improve navigability, or user experience in general. However, applying the models to build real-world tools also poses unique challenges. For example, some of our features depend on the target, which is explicitly known in our case, but which is normally unknown in real use cases. Thus, an advantage and at the same time also the limitation of our current approach and model is that the target of the navigation is explicitly known ahead of time. However, we argue that target prediction could be treated as an orthogonal problem and then be combined with the method we introduce here. For instance, West and Leskovec [16] propose an algorithm for target prediction, given only a few initial clicks.

Our user experiments were conducted entirely within the Wikipedia hyperlink network. This enables more powerful analyses, compared to log-based analyses of users browsing the 'wild Web', since in our setup, each page has a clearly defined topic, and since the full network topology is known. On the flip side, constraining the navigation environment to Wikipedia poses a *caveat* to the generalizability of our results, since the placement of hyperlinks in Wikipedia follows rather well defined rules, making it easier, and possibly qualitatively different, for users to find their way on Wikipedia than on the 'wild Web'.

Further, real navigation settings tend to involve additional actions beyond clicking from page to page, such as search engine queries. Rather than beginning on a page that is unrelated to the navigation target (as in our data), users will typically use a search engine to be 'teleported' to a page that is more or less related to the final target, followed by some click-based navigation to zero in on the exact target page [1, 6, 12]. When this fails, query reformulation offers yet another recovery mechanism, in addition to the backtracking strategies we study in this work. On the one hand, it is an advantage of our experimental setup that it lets us study click-based navigation in isolation, without confounding users' pathfinding skills with their query formulation skills. On the other hand, we anticipate opportunities for highly interesting future research in extending our analysis of abandonment to more holistic settings involving both query- and click-based navigation, in order to understand the interplay between these two modes of information search.

In summary, we have made contributions towards understanding what causes users to give up navigating towards a target in information networks. We hope that future work will draw on our insights to build tools to help users navigate websites more easily to find what they are looking for.

# ACKNOWLEDGMENTS

This research has been supported in part by NSF IIS-1016909, CNS-1010921, CAREER IIS-1149837, IIS-1159679, ARO MURI, Docomo, Boeing, Allyes, Volkswagen, Intel, Alfred P. Sloan Fellowship and the Microsoft Faculty Fellowship. Robert West acknowledges support by a Stanford Graduate Fellowship and a Facebook Graduate Fellowship.

# 8. REFERENCES

[1] M. Ageev, Q. Guo, D. Lagun, and E. Agichtein. Find it if you can: A game for modeling different types of Web search success using interaction data. In *SIGIR*, 2011.

[2] S. Brin and L. Page. The anatomy of a large-scale hypertextual Web search engine. *Computer Networks and ISDN Systems*, 30(1), 1998.

[3] E. H. Chi, P. Pirolli, K. Chen, and J. Pitkow. Using information scent to model user information needs and actions and the Web. In *CHI*, 2001.

[4] A. Das Sarma, S. Gollapudi, and S. Ieong. Bypass rates: Reducing query abandonment using negative inferences. In *KDD*, 2008.

[5] A. Diriye, R. W. White, G. Buscher, and S. Dumais. Leaving so soon? Understanding and predicting Web search abandonment rationales. In *CIKM*, 2012.

[6] D. Downey, S. Dumais, D. Liebling, and E. Horvitz. Understanding the relationship between searchers' queries and information goals. In *CIKM*, 2008.

[7] M. Harrigan, D. Archambault, P. Cunningham, and N. Hurley. EgoNav: Exploring networks through egocentric spatializations. In *AVI*, 2012.

[8] J. Kleinberg. The small-world phenomenon: An algorithmic perspective. In *STOC*, 2000.

[9] J. Li, S. Huffman, and A. Tokuda. Good abandonment in mobile and PC Internet search. In *SIGIR*, 2009.

[10] S. Milgram. The small world problem. *Psychology Today*, 2, 1967.

[11] C. Olston and E. H. Chi. ScentTrails: Integrating browsing and searching on the Web. *TCHI*, 10(3), 2003.

[12] J. Teevan, C. Alvarado, M. S. Ackerman, and D. R. Karger. The perfect search engine is not enough: a study of orienteering behavior in directed search. In *CHI*, 2004.

[13] C. Trattner, D. Helic, P. Singer, and M. Strohmaier. Exploring the differences and similarities between hierarchical decentralized search and human navigation in information networks. In *i-KNOW*, 2012.

[14] T. von Landesberger, M. Gorner, and T. Schreck. Visual analysis of graphs with multiple connected components. In *VAST*, 2009.

[15] R. West and J. Leskovec. Automatic versus human navigation in information networks. In *ICWSM*, 2012.

[16] R. West and J. Leskovec. Human wayfinding in information networks. In *WWW*, 2012.

[17] R. West, J. Pineau, and D. Precup. Wikispeedia: An online game for inferring semantic distances between concepts. In *IJCAI*, 2009.

[18] R. W. White and J. Huang. Assessing the scenic route: Measuring the value of search trails in Web logs. In *SIGIR*, 2010.

[19] R. W. White and D. Morris. Investigating the querying and browsing behavior of advanced search engine users. In *SIGIR*, 2007.

[20] R. W. White and A. Singla. Finding our way on the Web: Exploring the role of waypoints in search interaction. In *WWW*, 2011.

# Lessons from the Journey: A Query Log Analysis of Within-Session Learning

Carsten Eickhoff
Data Analytics Lab
ETH Zurich
Switzerland
c.eickhoff@acm.org

Jaime Teevan, Ryen White,
Susan Dumais
Microsoft Research, WA, USA
{sdumais, teevan, ryenw}
@microsoft.com

## ABSTRACT

The Internet is the largest source of information in the world. Search engines help people navigate the huge space of available data in order to acquire new skills and knowledge. In this paper, we present an in-depth analysis of sessions in which people explicitly search for new knowledge on the Web based on the log files of a popular search engine. We investigate within-session and cross-session developments of expertise, focusing on how the language and search behavior of a user on a topic evolves over time. In this way, we identify those sessions and page visits that appear to significantly boost the learning process. Our experiments demonstrate a strong connection between clicks and several metrics related to expertise. Based on models of the user and their specific context, we present a method capable of automatically predicting, with good accuracy, which clicks will lead to enhanced learning. Our findings provide insight into how search engines might better help users learn as they search.

## Categories and Subject Descriptors

H.3.3 [**Information Search & Retrieval**]: Search Process;
I.2.6 [**Learning**]: Knowledge Acquisition;
H.1.2 [**User-Machine Systems**]: Human Factors

## Keywords

User Modeling, Domain Expertise, Information Search, Search Intent

## 1. INTRODUCTION

With size estimates of 30 to 50 billion indexed pages on commercial web search engines [10], the Internet is a very large collection of information. Empowered by affordable and easily available Internet connections, searching for information on-line has become a natural step in the knowledge acquisition process for modern society [12]. The wealth of available information makes tools such as Web search engines indispensable in identifying and accessing information.


*WSDM'14*, February 24–28, 2014, New York, New York, USA.

http://dx.doi.org/10.1145/2556195.2556217.

In recent years, search systems have employed representations of the user's preferences, current context, and recent behavior to more accurately model user interests and intentions [33]. This allows systems to better address the specific needs of individual searchers rather than considering only the dominant search intent across all users. However, even with such advanced retrieval technology, exploratory and open-ended information needs can be challenging to satisfy, especially when the searcher is unfamiliar with the domain in question [11]. Previous work [36] has shown that searchers acquire domain knowledge by means of web search. Continued exposure to and interaction with information appears to influence the users domain expertise over time. This increase in expertise is a byproduct of the actual search process. This observation is of particular interest with regard to modern relevance models. State-of-the-art search algorithms attempt to maximise the relevance of a list of results retrieved for an expressed information need. Commercial search engines often assess relevance using explicit judgments and click-through statistics, considering long dwell times as a proxy for searcher satisfaction. Following this paradigm of the shortest path to the goal, the searcher might not be exposed to additional, relevant information [37].

In this paper, we study the development of expertise at the session level in order to better understand the value that the journey towards the final result, as opposed to just that result in isolation, holds for the searcher.

Our work makes three major contributions over the state of the art in knowledge acquisition: (1) We present an investigation of explicit knowledge seeking sessions dedicated to finding procedural or declarative information. Based on such sessions, we examine changes in domain expertise within search sessions and show how these changes are sustained across session boundaries. (2) We investigate factors related to changes in domain expertise by studying the connection between page visits and the subsequent development of expertise and searcher behavior. (3) Finally, we present an automatic means of predicting the potential for learning from page visits.

The remainder of this paper is structured as follows: Section 2 provides an overview of related work in the areas of Web search personalization, search intent frameworks, domain expertise, and exploratory search. In Section 3, we identify web search sessions in which people explicitly seek to acquire knowledge and characterize different knowledge acquisition intent types seen in the log files of a popular Web search engine. Section 4 studies how domain expertise develops within a session and how it is sustained across sessions. Section 5 investigates the reasons that underly the previously observed learning. In Section 6, based on page-level features, we predict which page visits are most likely to help the users in expanding their domain expertise. Sections 7 and 8 present a discussion of our findings and their implications on future research, and practical applications in Web search.

## 2. RELATED WORK

The work presented in this paper is situated at the intersection of several areas of related prior work: Search personalization, investigations of domain expertise, search intent classification schemes and exploratory search and their respective roles in information retrieval applications. We will discuss each of these in turn.

Search engine providers employ a wide array of personalization techniques and large-scale resources such as previous interactions or external resources to accurately determine the relevance of documents to a query for individual searchers [26, 34]. Personalization is often applied in a re-ranking step following the original global ranking. Examples of such efforts include topical user profiles based on previous browsing or search activity [29]. Teevan et al. [33] re-ordered the top 50 search results based on previous user profiles, finding that full-text models outperformed selective keyword models. Li et al. [20] proposed a dynamic graph adaptation scheme to account for changes in the user's short term browsing behavior. Bennett et al. [5] investigated trade-offs between long- and short-term usage histories for search personalization. Eickhoff et al. [11] investigated personalizing atypical sessions in which searchers seek unfamiliar topics that would not benefit from their general search history.

Recent work has considered the searcher's familiarity with the topic domain as a ranking criterion. White et al. [36] discovered differences in the Web search behavior of domain experts and novices. Experts displayed significantly higher search success for their topic of expertise, and found evidence that domain expertise increases as searchers spent several sessions on the same topic. White et al. identified several factors associated with differences in behaviors between experts and novices, including query terms, the diversity of sites visited, the time spent reading, and search strategies. Zhang et al. [40] used behavioral features in order to predict users' domain expertise. Liu et al. [21] studied the evolution of knowledge across multiple sessions of the same overarching task. Based on a lab-based user study, the authors find a general tendency for knowledge to increase with each successive search session. Wildemuth [38] studied the connection between domain expertise and search strategies, finding that domain novices converge towards the same search patterns as experts as they are exposed to the topic and learn more. Previous work primarily focused on the long-term, cross-session dynamics of domain expertise, typically measured over the course of an academic semester. To the best of our knowledge, there has not yet been an investigation of domain expertise at the session level. In this paper, we close this gap by studying the within-session development of domain expertise and its connection to sustained learning across sessions.

The complexity of content has also been shown to be related to domain expertise. Tan et al. [32] measure reading level and comprehensibility of content on the community question answering portal Yahoo! Answers. Depending on the user's domain expertise, simple vs. more technical answers, respectively, were ranked higher. Collins-Thompson et al. [9] factor readability into Web search personalization, showing that accommodating for users' preferences in document complexity can significantly improve rankings. Kim et al. [16] connect user, complexity and topic, and show that personalized readability models perform even better when considering the topic-specific distribution of complexity. Our work is inspired by these previous findings on expertise as a function of users, topics and content complexity. As such, we will further investigate expertise as a constantly evolving notion, rather than a static property that could be attributed to a user-topic pairing.

There is an extensive body of work on understanding and describing the intentions and motivations that underly the search process. Belkin et al. [4] describe the phenomenon of the *Anomalous State of Knowledge* (ASK) whereby searchers may lack a clear mental representation of their own information needs. Broder [7] proposed a ternary classification of informational, navigational and transactional queries. Following on Broder's work, a multitude of different search intent classification schemes have been presented. Rose and Levinson [27] expand Broder's classification with a number of sub-categories such as directed, undirected or advice intents under the informational needs category. Baeza-Yates et al. [3] identify two fundamental intent dimensions, topic and goal, each of which can take one of a number of different values. Alternative frameworks and criteria have been proposed, including for example the user's intent to buy products [2] or the concrete data types and formats [31] that were searched for. Our work investigates two different knowledge acquisition intents grounded in psychology and cognitive science literature on procedural and declarative memory in order to characterize different learning goals.

Exploratory search is closely related to the knowledge acquisition scenario that we investigate in this paper. Marchionini [22] describes exploratory search as an information seeking scenario where the primary goal is broadly learning about a given topic. As we will see in Section 3, this matches the definition of *declarative information needs*, one of the knowledge acquisition intent classes that we consider. The existing literature on exploratory search focuses primarily on alternative user interfaces and technologies to best support this interaction paradigm. Examples include the use of faceted search interfaces [18], collaborative and multi-user interfaces [13] and topic summarization systems [25]. In this work, we will focus on studying different knowledge acquisition intents and their characteristics based on the log files of a popular Web search engine. Rather than designing a search system to cater for one particular intent class, we aim at furthering our understanding of knowledge acquisition in general.

## 3. DATA SET & METHODOLOGY

Previous work [36] showed that searchers can, over time, acquire domain expertise as they are exposed to domain-related information. We believe that learning happens all the time when people interact with information items. However, for the sake of this study, we try to select the clearest and most explicit examples of sessions where learning is likely to occur.

## 3.1 Identifying Example Sessions

Jones et al. [15] suggest that search sessions are often task-driven and dedicated to a satisfying a single overarching information need. We follow the established approach of drawing session boundaries after an inactivity of at least 30 minutes and begin by identifying those web search sessions targeted at knowledge acquisition. To do this we draw on psychological literature which distinguishes between two fundamental types of knowledge: *procedural knowledge* and *declarative knowledge*. Procedural knowledge refers to knowing **how to do** something, whereas declarative knowledge refers to knowing **about** something [1]. In the context of web search we seek to identify search sessions in which people explicitly search for how to do something or to find out about something. These are sub-categories of Broder's informational sessions.

To identify procedural and declarative search sessions, we use a simple 4-step heuristic:

(1) We start by identifying popular procedural and declarative resources. We use `http://ehow.com`, a site that offers more than 2 million tutorial articles and videos to several million visitors daily, as the procedural source. And, we use `http://wikipedia.org`, a site contains more than 4 million encyclopedia pages in English, as the declarative information source. We then identify all queries, $Q_p$, for which the last click in a session is on `http://ehow.com`, and all those queries, $Q_d$, for which the last click in a session is on `http://wikipedia.org`.

(2) From these two query sets, we build variable length n-gram language models $LM_p$ and $LM_d$ as described by Niesler and Woodland [24]. We also build a general collection model, $LM_G$, which we describe in more detail below.

(3) Following the approach used by Tomokiyo and Hurst [35], we determine the point-wise KL-divergence between the general collection model and each of the knowledge acquisition intent-specific models. Equation 1 shows how we compute the KL divergence for each n-gram $t$. This method lets us identify those n-grams that occur more frequently in the knowledge acquisition intent query pools than in the overall query log. Table 1 shows the top 10 query terms for the two knowledge acquisition intents after removing domain-specific terms such as "wiki" or "ehow" from the candidate list. Intuitively, the term lists are reasonable and they reflect our intended separation between learning how to do something and learning about something.

(4) On the basis of these 10 term sets, we create experimental datasets $D_{proc}$ and $D_{decl}$, defined as those sessions that contained at least one of the indicator terms. If terms from both lists were present in the session, we assigned the class with the greatest query term coverage. The remainder of our corpus that was not found to be either procedural or declarative will be addressed as $D_{other}$. Table 2 gives two typical examples of procedural and declarative search sessions obtained from our log files.

## 3.2 Dataset

Our investigation is based on the log files of a popular web search engine. The data sample used for this study covers the period between February 1st and 28th, 2013. In order to reduce variability introduced by the highly multilingual nature of the Internet and its users, we focus on the English-speaking US market. To concentrate on informational search intent, we remove all purely navigational sessions based on the output of a proprietary query classifier. After this step, we are left with 26.4 million sessions issued by 2.1 million unique users. About 3% of these sessions have an explicit knowledge acquisition intent, falling into either $D_{proc}$ or $D_{decl}$.

**Table 1: Knowledge acquisition intent cue words.**

| Rank | Procedural | Declarative |
|---|---|---|
| 1 | to | what |
| 2 | how | what is |
| 3 | how to | who |
| 4 | how do | list of |
| 5 | to make | syndrome |
| 6 | how to make | biography |
| 7 | how do I | what is a |
| 8 | computer | about |
| 9 | can you | is the |
| 10 | change | history of |

**Table 2: Procedural / declarative session examples.**

| Procedural | | |
|---|---|---|
| # | Query | Clicked URL |
| 1 | Weak wireless signal | - |
| 2 | How to expand wifi range | http://www.repeaterstore.com/.../fg24008.php |
| 3 | Wifi repeater how to | - |
| 4 | Wifi repeater tutorial | http://forum.ubnt.com/showthread.php?t=13735 |
| 5 | How to boost wifi signal | http://www.ehow.com/...boost-wifi-signal.html |

| Declarative | | |
|---|---|---|
| # | Query | Clicked URL |
| 1 | What do sponges look like | a-z-animals.com/animals/sponge/ |
| 2 | What do sponges feed on | tolweb.org/treehouses/?treehouse$_id = 3431$ |
| 3 | Sponges as pets | http://www.buzzle.com/articles/sponge-facts.html |
| 4 | How do sponges reproduce | http://answers.yahoo.com/...127140016AANRe91 |
| 5 | Where do sponges live | http://en.wikipedia.org/wiki/Sponge |

$$KL_{LM_i,LM_G}(t) = P_{LM_i}(t) log \frac{P_{LM_i}(t)}{P_{LM_G}(t)} \quad (1)$$

Closer inspection of the "knowledge acquisition intent" collections showed a high precision despite the simplicity of our method. We manually labeled a sample of 300 $D_{proc}$ and $D_{decl}$ sessions and found that 87% of the selected instances indeed identified procedural or declarative knowledge seeking intents. Since only about 3% of sessions have a clear knowledge acquisition intent, manual labelling efforts to identify additional knowledge acquisition intents were not practical. Instead, we used the existing high-precision collections as bootstrap resources and create expanded collections $D_{proc-ext}$ and $D_{decl-ext}$ by including all sessions in which the URLs clicked in the high-precision sets also appeared.

Table 3 gives an overview of key properties of these five data sets. $D_{proc}$ and $D_{decl}$ show a generally greater tendency for content exploration. For these sets, sessions are longer, and users issue more queries, dwell longer on each result, visit lower-ranked results, and move beyond the first result page more often. We also see a greater topical diversity than was observed for $D_{other}$. The expanded data sets closely follow the overall behavior of the background collection.

We conducted all experiments described in this paper with the two expanded collections $D_{proc-ext}$ and $D_{decl-ext}$ as well as the two high-precision collections $D_{proc}$ and $D_{decl}$. The results for $D_{proc-ext}$ and $D_{decl-ext}$ were nearly identical to those for the general background collection. Thus our at-

Table 3: Comparison of experimental data sets.

| Dataset | # sessions | queries per session | median dwell time | median session duration | topics/ SERP | max page no | lowest rank clicked | query length |
|---|---|---|---|---|---|---|---|---|
| $D_{other}$ | 25.6m | 1.7 | 10 sec | 43 sec | 3.1 | 1.07 | 1.3 | 2.2 |
| $D_{proc}$ | 443k | 4.1 | 185 sec | 603 sec | 4.5 | 1.20 | 3.2 | 5.8 |
| $D_{decl}$ | 355k | 6.3 | 287 sec | 1003 sec | 6.2 | 1.28 | 4.1 | 4.5 |
| $D_{proc-ex}$ | 3.8m | 2.1 | 17 sec | 123 sec | 3.4 | 1.09 | 1.5 | 3.1 |
| $D_{decl-ex}$ | 4.1m | 2.4 | 20 sec | 147 sec | 3.7 | 1.09 | 1.7 | 2.8 |

tempt to expand knowledge acquisition sessions seems to have resulted in more noise than useful knowledge acquisition sessions. For the sake of brevity, we will not discuss these two collections further in this paper. Instead we focus on the two high-precision collections of procedural and declarative knowledge acquisition intents as well as $D_{other}$, the remainder of the original 26.4m sessions.

## 3.3 Metrics

As the starting point for our investigation, we consider a set of six metrics that have previously been used to describe domain expertise and search behavior:

**Domain Count.** White et al. [36] found that domain experts encountered different and more diverse domains than domain novices. They measured diversity by the number of unique domains present on the result pages (SERPs), and we use this measure as well. We also consider two measures of topical diversity (focus and entropy), as described below.

**Focus.** Focus is concerned with how narrow the topical space is that the user explores. We measure focus as the proportion of entries on the result page that fall into the most frequent observed topical category. We use the output of a text classifier that assigns ODP category labels based on the textual content of web pages. To achieve a degree of detail that has been previously found appropriate, we follow Shen et al. [28] and use the second level of the ODP taxonomy.

**Entropy.** Where focus describes the degree to which the SERP is covered by just a single topic, entropy is concerned with how diverse the entire topic distribution on the result page is. The higher the entropy, the more diverse is the range of topics on the result page.

**Branchiness.** Branchiness describes how often the searcher returns to a previously visited point (e.g., a search engine result page or other hub page) and follows a previously unexplored link from there on. We use branchiness to measure how broadly the user explores the available content. Previous work [36] has shown that domain experts have more branchy search paths than domain novices.

**Display Time.** The amount of time a user spends on average to read retrieved documents has previously been considered an indicator of domain expertise. White et al. [36] found that experts generally spend less time per retrieved web page than novices. They hypothesised that domain experts may be more adept at reading technical content and locating the desired information than domain novices.

**Query Complexity.** Content complexity is a traditional and intuitive indicator of domain knowledge which manifests in the form of technical jargon or other highly specialized vocabulary unknown to novices. Because our collection covers so many different technical domains it was impractical to collect domain-specific thesauri as others have done for restricted domains such as medicine. Instead we chose to use reading level metrics to characterize changes in the complexity of query terms. Traditional reading level metrics require longer coherent text samples and are not very effective when applied to very short texts. Kuperman et al. [19] compiled a listing of more than 30,000 English words along with the age at which native speakers typically learn the term. The higher this score, the harder and more specialized a term is assumed to be. In order to measure the complexity of queries, we report the maximum age of acquisition across all query terms.

# 4. WITHIN-SESSION LEARNING

The central goal of our work is to better understand how users acquire new knowledge while they are searching the Web. Previous work on domain expertise investigated long term developments of knowledge across the course of several months worth of search activity [36] or throughout the course of an academic semester during which students were exposed to lecture material [39]. In this section, we start to address a previously unstudied problem by investigating domain expertise at much finer granularity; at the session level.

## 4.1 Metric Changes Within Sessions

Figure 1 compares within-session changes of all six metrics for our three experimental corpora for 5-query sessions. The same tendencies hold for other lengths, but are omitted for space reasons. We partition the data by session length to rule out external effects such as different dynamics of short and long sessions. All scores are relative to the score observed for the first query in each session.

We observe that focus rises initially but tends to fall quickly for $D_{proc}$ and $D_{decl}$, evidencing broader exploration than in $D_{other}$ where scores level out. After initial increases, topical entropy decreases for all corpora. Especially for $D_{proc}$ scores plummet dramatically, which we take as evidence for the user narrowing down the topical space when approaching the desired resource. This is further supported by display time scores which rise most dramatically towards the end of procedural sessions. This suggests that the user found the desired information and now studies a single document in depth, potentially replicating its instructions on the spot. Branchiness of sessions tends to fall, with only $D_{decl}$ as an exception which shows the broadest exploration of content.

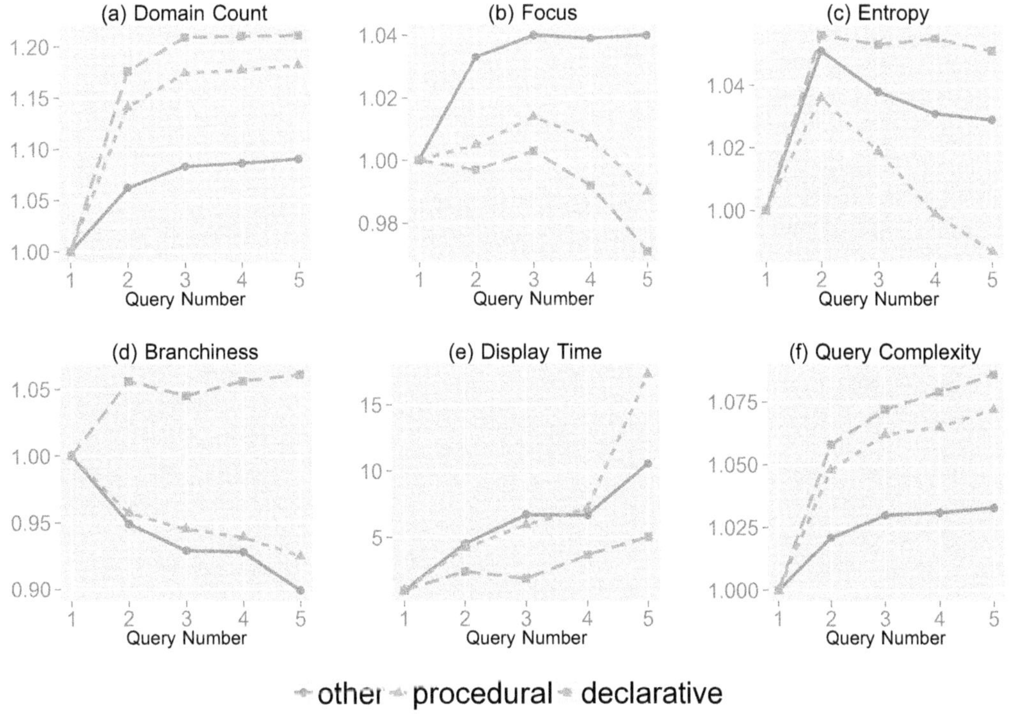


**Figure 1: Within-session development of domain count (a), focus (b), entropy (c), branchiness (d), display time (e) and query complexity (f) for sessions of length 5. Scores are relative to the first query per session.**

At the same time, the domain count rises for all session types with strongest increases among knowledge acquisition sessions. Query complexity gradually increases for all sessions but knowledge acquisition sessions show much steeper gradients than others. To summarize, for focus, domain count and complexity, knowledge acquisition sessions ($D_{proc}$ and $D_{decl}$) show strong differences from the remaining collection. Consistently, declarative search sessions show tendencies towards broader, less focused exploration as evidenced by higher entropy, domain count and branchiness.

## 4.2 Persistence of Learning

Previously, we demonstrated how expertise development can be observed at the session level. We now study how domain expertise acquired within a session is sustained across session boundaries. As a first step in this direction, we investigate how much knowledge is carried over from within-session learning to the following session. We examine this by comparing sessions $S_i$ based on whether or not the directly preceding session $S_{i-1}$ showed a within-session increase in the respective metric. All scores in this comparison are relative to the user's previous average score for this information need. To rule out the effects of task-specific variance, we only compare those sessions that belong to the same task. This condition is ensured by requiring sessions to share at least a 50% overlap in query terms. E.g., if a user has 5 sessions in the task and we find a metric gain in Session 3, we compare the onset (first query) of Session 4 with the average across Sessions 1 - 3. Results of this analysis are shown in Figure 2. The coherence metrics (focus and entropy) show somewhat greater (but not statistically significant) gains for post-gain sessions. For domain count and complexity, the tendencies are more pronounced and we observe significantly greater increases for post-gain sessions. Statistical significance was determined by means of a Wilcoxon signed-rank test with $\alpha \leq 0.01$.

Finally, we move beyond the onset of post-gain sessions and investigate evidence of expertise across several sessions within the same overarching task. To do this, we study the cross-session development of expertise for sessions that follow a session in which within-session learning was detected. We contrast these sessions with a sample following on sessions without learning. Figure 3 shows the results of this comparison. As we found for session onsets, focus and entropy show small insignificant changes as a function of whether metrics increased in the previous session. Domain count and query complexity, however, show significantly larger increases for sessions on the same task after within-session increases.

# 5. PAGE VISITS AS LEARNING CATALYST

Previously, we observed within-session increases of domain expertise that were sustained across session boundaries. In this section, we try to find the cause for these developments.

## 5.1 Page Visits Change Behavior

To gain a better understanding of the effects and dependencies at play within a search session, we conduct a qualitative analysis of different sub-samples of our experimental

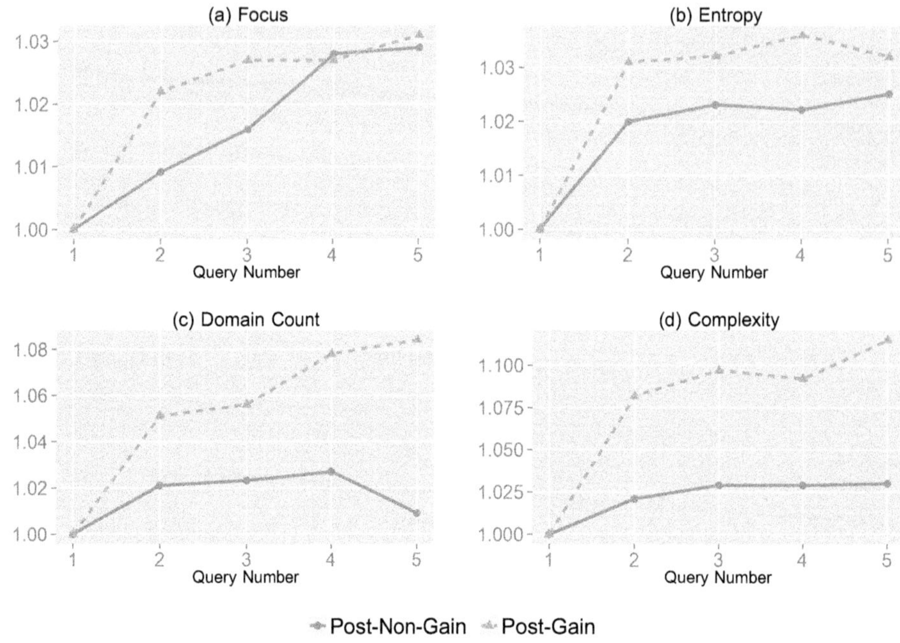


**Figure 3: The development of focus (a), entropy (b), domain count (c) and query complexity (d) as a consequence of within-session learning. All numbers are relative to the first session per task.**

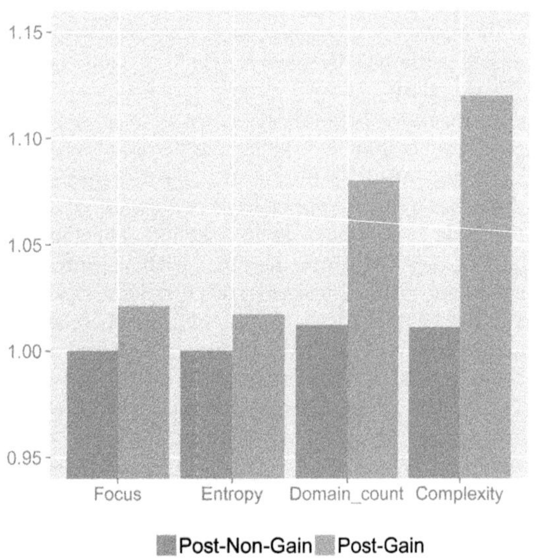


**Figure 2: Comparison of domain expertise onset between post-gain sessions and post-non-gain sessions.**

corpus. For each of the six metrics, we select the 200 search sessions with the strongest change in the respective metric from the overall dataset $D$. These sets are contrasted with six sets of 200 randomly sampled sessions in which no significant gains or losses were observed. The first author manually analysed the query log entries for the 2400 selected sessions, trying to identify reasons for the observed changes. From this sample, we note that **(1)** Sessions with clear increases in branchiness contain many medical queries as well as queries related to construction and DIY. **(2)** Procedural sessions tend to show the most pronounced increases in dwell time. This can be explained by the particular mode of interaction that is typical for procedural information. The user searches for a useful resource (e.g., a how-to), once the right resource is located, they will follow the instructions on the page step by step, which may take considerable amounts of time. **(3)** Finally, we observed that there were two major reasons for changes in query complexity. The first is task switching. When the user tries to satisfy different information needs there can be large topic-dependent changes in complexity. More interestingly, however, we noted that within the confines of the same task, page visits often resulted in a change in the complexity of subsequent queries.

## 5.2 Page Visits and Query Reformulations

It appears that page visits have significant influence on the vocabulary of subsequent queries as users are exposed to new information which they use to modify their queries. To verify this hypothesis, we investigate the origin of newly added query terms. We inspect the proportion of query term additions that can be explained based on snippets or page content of clicked pages. Table 4 shows the proportion of

**Table 4: The origin of newly added query terms. Measured in terms of recall of newly added query terms among different resources.**

| | Snippet | Short page visits | Long page visits ($t \geq 30$ sec) | None |
|---|---|---|---|---|
| $D_{other}$ | 0.27 | 0.13 | 0.41 | 0.52 |
| $D_{proc}$ | 0.23 | 0.12 | 0.44 | 0.49 |
| $D_{decl}$ | 0.26 | 0.10 | 0.45 | 0.49 |

new query terms that were found among the snippets shown on the previous result page or on clicked pages. It also reports the share of newly added terms that were not found in any of the previous resources. The numbers do not sum to 100% per row because the same term could occur in snippets as well as on clicked pages. SERP snippets account for approximately one quarter of all new additions. Nearly half of all newly added terms could be found on pages that the user visited directly before the query reformulation. Long page visits (dwell time $\geq$ 30 seconds) contain about 4 times as many term additions as short visits. Our results confirm the general findings of previous work by Stamou and Kozanidis [30]. In our dataset, the influence of page content is significantly higher than reported previously. This may be due to the fact that earlier work only considered visited pages (not snippet content), or that they considered only 18 selected users.

## 5.3 Page Visits and Metrics

Finally, let us quantify the impact that page visits have on the various coherence and expertise metrics. At this point, we work on the basis of the full collections $D_{proc}$, $D_{decl}$ and $D_{other}$ rather than just the qualitative 200-session samples. For each metric $m$, we compute the posterior probability of its score increasing by more than one standard deviation $P_{m,+}(.)$, falling by more than one standard deviation $P_{m,-}(.)$ or staying stable $P_{m,=}(.)$. We partition the data by whether the previous result page $SERP_{i-1}$ received no clicks, only short clicks, or at least one long click, represented by its click condition $c \in \{no\ click, short, long\}$.

$$P_{m,+}(c) = \frac{Count(m(SERP_i)>m(SERP_{i-1})+\sigma_m, c)}{Count(c)}$$

$$P_{m,-}(c) = \frac{Count(m(SERP_i)<m(SERP_{i-1})-\sigma_m, c)}{Count(c)}$$

$$P_{m,+}(c) = \frac{Count(m(SERP_{i-1})+\sigma_m \geq m(SERP_i) \geq m(SERP_{i-1})-\sigma_m, c)}{Count(c)}$$

In order to reduce the influence of task switching during sessions, we require all result page pairs ($SERP_{i-1}, SERP_i$) to be dedicated to the same overarching task. We measure this by requiring them to be adjacent in time (i.e., there was no other query in between any pair $SERP_{i-1}, SERP_i$) and to share at least a 50% overlap in query terms. Table 5 shows the results of this comparison. In order to interpret the scores, we have to compare analogous changes across click conditions. E.g., $P_{m,+}(c = non)$ to $P_{m,+}(c = short)$ in order to see how short clicks influence the likelihood of a subsequent increase in $m$ as compared to unclicked SERPs. Statistically significant changes with respect to unclicked SERPs are denoted by the $\triangle$ character for increases and the $\blacktriangledown$ character for decreases. Statistical significance was tested by means of a Wilcoxon signed-rank test at $\alpha \leq 0.01$-level. We observe a number of fundamental tendencies: (1) Topical diversity tends to increase as the result of a click ($P_+$ falls while $P_=$ and $P_-$ rise). Similarly, the entropy in the topic distribution increases ($P_+$ and $P_=$ increase while $P_-$ falls with respect to unclicked search result pages). This suggests that exposure to new information offered on visited pages diversifies subsequent queries by introducing new influences. (2) The number of unique domains per SERP also tends to increase in response to a click ($P_+$ and $P_=$ increase, $P_-$ falls). This finding supports the diversifying effect observed in topical space. (3) After a click, the complexity of subsequent queries increases more than it does for unclicked SERPs ($P_+$ and $P_=$ increase, $P_-$ falls).

The findings are largely consistent across collections, with $D_{other}$ showing less pronounced tendencies than $D_{proc}$ and $D_{decl}$. For most metrics, there were no significant differences between long and short page visits. It seems that even short visits introduce sufficient amounts of new information to influence subsequent queries. It should be noted that the tendencies shown for branchiness and page display time (both increase most dramatically after an unclicked search result page) are necessarily biased since both metrics depend on clicks. E.g., there is no chance for a display time of 0 in the case of an unclicked result page to still fall.

At this point, our experiments can be expected to include a moderate amount of chance variance. Especially in $D_{other}$ we observe seemingly arbitrary drops and increases in various metrics that influence the resulting aggregates in Table 5. This can be attributed to chance drops in metrics as a consequence of e.g., exchanging synonymous query terms or visiting near duplicates of previously seen results which blur our observations. In order to mitigate such effects, we further restrict our analysis by considering only sustained changes in metrics. This means, that only those sessions in which changes are sustained throughout the whole session, contribute to the computation of posterior probabilities. Take for example a query complexity increase from a score of 5.4 to 7.1 between $SERP_{i-1}$ and $SERP_i$. Where previously, we would have directly counted this towards $P_+$, now, we only do so if the respective score never falls below 7.1 for all further result pages $SERP_{i+1}, SERP_{i+2} \ldots R_I$. The normalization component $Count(c)$ is adjusted to this new definition accordingly. Table 6 shows the outcome of this altered experimental setup. We observe the same general tendencies, but the differences between clicked and unclicked SERPs are more pronounced.

# 6. PREDICTING CLICK IMPORTANCE

In the previous sections, we showed evidence of within-session learning and its continuation across session boundaries. In an effort to explain the observed domain expertise gains, we found a connection between page visits and subsequent learning. In the final experimental contribution of this paper, we now predict which page visits are most likely to advance a user's domain expertise. To this end, we begin with a brief description of the features used to represent Web documents:

**Text length** The overall amount of Web page text has been previously reported as an indicator for resource complexity [23]. We measure text length as the overall number of words on the page.

**Sentence length** Similarly, long sentences were found to indicate content complexity [23]. Sentence length is measured as the average number of words per sentence.

Table 5: Post-click trends.

| | | Focus | | | Entropy | | | Branchiness | | | Display Time | | | Domain Count | | | Complexity | | |
|---|---|---|---|---|---|---|---|---|---|---|---|---|---|---|---|---|---|---|---|
| | | $P_+$ | $P_=$ | $P_-$ | $P_+$ | $P_=$ | $P_-$ | $P_+$ | $P_=$ | $P_-$ | $P_+$ | $P_=$ | $P_-$ | $P_+$ | $P_=$ | $P_-$ | $P_+$ | $P_=$ | $P_-$ |
| $D_{other}$ | Non | 0.25 | 0.45 | 0.30 | 0.24 | 0.47 | 0.29 | 0.44 | 0.56 | 0.00 | 0.65 | 0.35 | 0.00 | 0.29 | 0.36 | 0.35 | 0.17 | 0.66 | 0.17 |
| | Short | $0.16^\blacktriangledown$ | $0.60^\triangle$ | $0.24^\blacktriangledown$ | $0.29^\triangle$ | $0.59^\triangle$ | $0.12^\blacktriangledown$ | $0.25^\blacktriangledown$ | $0.24^\blacktriangledown$ | $0.51^\triangle$ | $0.31^\blacktriangledown$ | 0.35 | $0.34^\triangle$ | $0.22^\blacktriangledown$ | $0.56^\triangle$ | $0.22^\blacktriangledown$ | $0.21^\triangle$ | $0.60^\blacktriangledown$ | $0.19^\triangle$ |
| | Long | 0.23 | $0.49^\triangle$ | 0.28 | $0.30^\triangle$ | 0.49 | $0.21^\blacktriangledown$ | $0.28^\blacktriangledown$ | $0.25^\blacktriangledown$ | $0.47^\triangle$ | $0.18^\blacktriangledown$ | 0.34 | $0.48^\triangle$ | $0.33^\triangle$ | 0.37 | $0.30^\blacktriangledown$ | $0.23^\triangle$ | 0.67 | $0.10^\blacktriangledown$ |
| $D_{proc}$ | Non | 0.34 | 0.32 | 0.34 | 0.30 | 0.35 | 0.35 | 0.43 | 0.57 | 0.00 | 0.69 | 0.31 | 0.00 | 0.38 | 0.16 | 0.46 | 0.33 | 0.37 | 0.30 |
| | Short | $0.30^\blacktriangledown$ | $0.35^\triangle$ | 0.35 | 0.31 | $0.39^\triangle$ | $0.30^\blacktriangledown$ | $0.24^\blacktriangledown$ | $0.21^\blacktriangledown$ | $0.55^\triangle$ | $0.25^\blacktriangledown$ | $0.35^\triangle$ | $0.40^\triangle$ | $0.43^\triangle$ | 0.17 | $0.40^\blacktriangledown$ | 0.35 | $0.42^\triangle$ | $0.23^\blacktriangledown$ |
| | Long | $0.31^\blacktriangledown$ | $0.35^\triangle$ | 0.34 | $0.33^\triangle$ | 0.37 | $0.30^\blacktriangledown$ | $0.21^\blacktriangledown$ | $0.27^\blacktriangledown$ | $0.52^\triangle$ | $0.19^\blacktriangledown$ | $0.37^\triangle$ | $0.44^\triangle$ | $0.46^\triangle$ | 0.15 | $0.39^\blacktriangledown$ | $0.38^\triangle$ | 0.37 | $0.25^\blacktriangledown$ |
| $D_{decl}$ | Non | 0.36 | 0.30 | 0.34 | 0.31 | 0.35 | 0.34 | 0.41 | 0.59 | 0.00 | 0.71 | 0.29 | 0.00 | 0.38 | 0.15 | 0.47 | 0.32 | 0.36 | 0.32 |
| | Short | $0.31^\blacktriangledown$ | $0.33^\triangle$ | 0.36 | 0.31 | $0.38^\triangle$ | $0.31^\blacktriangledown$ | $0.24^\blacktriangledown$ | $0.20^\blacktriangledown$ | $0.56^\triangle$ | $0.31^\blacktriangledown$ | $0.35^\triangle$ | $0.44^\triangle$ | $0.43^\triangle$ | $0.17^\triangle$ | $0.40^\blacktriangledown$ | $0.36^\triangle$ | $0.40^\triangle$ | $0.24^\blacktriangledown$ |
| | Long | $0.30^\blacktriangledown$ | $0.35^\triangle$ | 0.35 | $0.34^\triangle$ | $0.38^\triangle$ | $0.28^\blacktriangledown$ | $0.27^\blacktriangledown$ | $0.25^\blacktriangledown$ | $0.48^\triangle$ | $0.18^\blacktriangledown$ | $0.37^\triangle$ | $0.45^\triangle$ | $0.44^\triangle$ | 0.16 | $0.40^\blacktriangledown$ | $0.37^\triangle$ | 0.37 | $0.26^\blacktriangledown$ |

Table 6: Sustained post-click trends.

| | | Focus | | | Entropy | | | Branchiness | | | Display Time | | | Domain Count | | | Complexity | | |
|---|---|---|---|---|---|---|---|---|---|---|---|---|---|---|---|---|---|---|---|
| | | $P_+$ | $P_=$ | $P_-$ | $P_+$ | $P_=$ | $P_-$ | $P_+$ | $P_=$ | $P_-$ | $P_+$ | $P_=$ | $P_-$ | $P_+$ | $P_=$ | $P_-$ | $P_+$ | $P_=$ | $P_-$ |
| $D_{other}$ | Non | 0.28 | 0.44 | 0.28 | 0.23 | 0.49 | 0.28 | 0.43 | 0.57 | 0.00 | 0.71 | 0.29 | 0.00 | 0.29 | 0.36 | 0.35 | 0.21 | 0.67 | 0.12 |
| | Short | $0.11^\blacktriangledown$ | $0.59^\triangle$ | 0.30 | $0.29^\triangle$ | $0.56^\triangle$ | $0.15^\blacktriangledown$ | $0.25^\blacktriangledown$ | $0.22^\blacktriangledown$ | $0.53^\triangle$ | $0.28^\blacktriangledown$ | $0.35^\triangle$ | $0.37^\triangle$ | $0.32^\triangle$ | $0.50^\triangle$ | $0.18^\blacktriangledown$ | $0.25^\triangle$ | $0.62^\blacktriangledown$ | 0.13 |
| | Long | $0.20^\blacktriangledown$ | 0.46 | $0.34^\triangle$ | $0.32^\triangle$ | 0.49 | $0.19^\blacktriangledown$ | $0.28^\blacktriangledown$ | $0.21^\blacktriangledown$ | $0.51^\triangle$ | $0.17^\blacktriangledown$ | $0.32^\triangle$ | $0.51^\triangle$ | $0.37^\triangle$ | $0.44^\triangle$ | $0.19^\blacktriangledown$ | $0.27^\triangle$ | 0.65 | $0.08^\blacktriangledown$ |
| $D_{proc}$ | Non | 0.35 | 0.33 | 0.32 | 0.29 | 0.34 | 0.37 | 0.44 | 0.56 | 0.00 | 0.74 | 0.26 | 0.00 | 0.42 | 0.18 | 0.40 | 0.31 | 0.39 | 0.30 |
| | Short | $0.25^\blacktriangledown$ | 0.32 | $0.43^\triangle$ | $0.32^\triangle$ | $0.37^\triangle$ | $0.31^\blacktriangledown$ | $0.21^\blacktriangledown$ | $0.22^\blacktriangledown$ | $0.57^\triangle$ | $0.28^\blacktriangledown$ | $0.34^\triangle$ | $0.38^\triangle$ | 0.44 | 0.19 | $0.37^\blacktriangledown$ | $0.35^\triangle$ | $0.42^\triangle$ | $0.23^\blacktriangledown$ |
| | Long | $0.18^\blacktriangledown$ | $0.35^\triangle$ | $0.47^\triangle$ | $0.34^\triangle$ | $0.39^\triangle$ | $0.27^\blacktriangledown$ | $0.22^\blacktriangledown$ | $0.26^\blacktriangledown$ | $0.52^\triangle$ | $0.22^\blacktriangledown$ | $0.34^\triangle$ | $0.44^\triangle$ | $0.46^\triangle$ | 0.19 | $0.35^\blacktriangledown$ | $0.36^\triangle$ | $0.44^\triangle$ | $0.20^\blacktriangledown$ |
| $D_{decl}$ | Non | 0.36 | 0.30 | 0.34 | 0.34 | 0.36 | 0.30 | 0.47 | 0.53 | 0.00 | 0.68 | 0.32 | 0.00 | 0.41 | 0.16 | 0.43 | 0.31 | 0.38 | 0.31 |
| | Short | $0.30^\blacktriangledown$ | $0.33^\triangle$ | $0.37^\triangle$ | 0.36 | $0.38^\triangle$ | $0.26^\blacktriangledown$ | $0.24^\blacktriangledown$ | $0.21^\blacktriangledown$ | $0.55^\triangle$ | $0.26^\blacktriangledown$ | 0.35 | $0.39^\triangle$ | $0.44^\triangle$ | 0.17 | $0.39^\blacktriangledown$ | $0.36^\triangle$ | $0.40^\triangle$ | $0.24^\blacktriangledown$ |
| | Long | $0.27^\blacktriangledown$ | $0.34^\triangle$ | $0.39^\triangle$ | $0.37^\triangle$ | 0.36 | $0.27^\blacktriangledown$ | $0.33^\blacktriangledown$ | $0.27^\blacktriangledown$ | $0.40^\triangle$ | $0.18^\blacktriangledown$ | $0.37^\triangle$ | $0.45^\triangle$ | $0.45^\triangle$ | $0.19^\triangle$ | $0.36^\blacktriangledown$ | 0.32 | $0.42^\triangle$ | $0.26^\blacktriangledown$ |

**Term length** Long words are an indicator for specific and complex vocabulary [23]. We measure term length as the average number of characters as well as the average number of syllables per term on the page.

**Coverage of query terms in title** The presence or absence of query terms in the page title may give an insight in the nature of the page. I.e., does the page only mention the topic (low expected learning potential) or is it centrally concerned with the topic (high expected learning potential)?

**Distribution of query terms** Following a similar intuition, we measure the distribution of query terms on the page. Concentrated term occurrences may signal that the query topic is only one of many aspects of the page, whereas when query terms are spread across the whole page they may represent the page's core topic. To this end, we measure the proportion of page text that lies between the first and the last occurrence of query terms as well as the median distance between query terms.

**POS distribution** The syntactic structure of the page may give clues about its intention and complexity [8]. To reflect this, we include four features representing the relative share of page texts falling into the Parts-of-speech *noun*, *verb*, *adjective*, or *other*.

**Page complexity** One of the most direct indications of page complexity can be achieved by measuring the age of acquisition across all terms on the page. Similarly, Kuperman et al. [19] offer statistics of the percentage of adult native speakers that know each corpus term. The lower this number, the more specific and complex is the language that was used. We report page-wide averages for both figures.

**Page complexity vs. query complexity** All previous features treated page complexity in isolation. We assume, however, that the relative complexity with regard to the user's current state of knowledge will have strong influences on the learning potential. To account for this, we report the ratio of page complexity to query complexity.

Our investigation is based on a balanced sample of 50,000 data points. For 50% of the data subsequent learning was detected. The remaining half shows no evidence of learning. A stratified sample of 10,000 instances is withheld as a test set. Each instance represents a page visit and is annotated with whether or not the visit was immediately followed by an increase in both query complexity and domain count. We evaluated several state-of-the-art classifiers. The overall best performance of $F_1 = 0.76$ and an area under ROC curve of 0.81 is achieved by a Support Vector Machine (SVM) with Pearson Universal kernel ($\omega = 1.2, \sigma = 1.0, \epsilon = 10^{-12}, c = 1.0$). The parameter settings were determined by means of a greedy parameter sweep. To further understand the separation between those clicks that lead to an increase in expertise metrics and those that do not, we compare the mutual information between each of the above features and the class label. We find the strongest connection in features that contrast page and query complexity, effectively expressing how close the complexity of the user's produced vocabulary is to that of the page. We generally find the highest learning potential for pages that are slightly more complex than the user's observed active vocabulary.

On the basis of our classifier, we now analyze the distribution of learning potential across the ranks of search result pages. Ideally, for knowledge acquisition sessions we would require the documents with the highest likelihood of advancing the user's state of knowledge to be ranked highest. Note that we have to rely on predictor output for this experiment since log-based examples of learning can only be observed as a consequence of clicks. Clicks in turn have been frequently reported to be affected by position biases [14]. Figure 4 shows the distribution of predicted learning potential across SERP ranks. We note only a weak correlation between search result page ranks and learning potential.

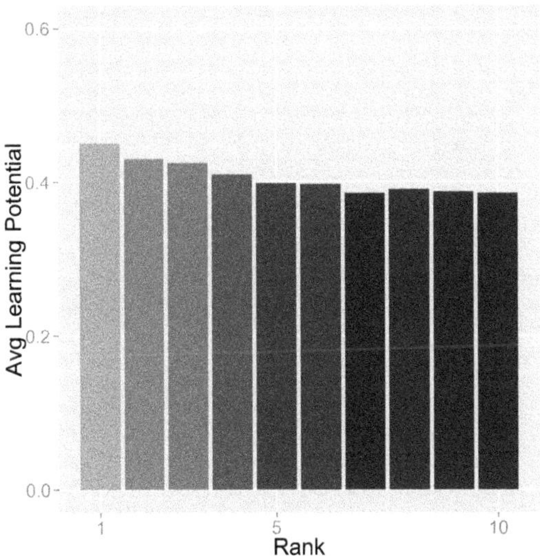


**Figure 4: Distribution of predicted learning potential across the ranks of the search result page.**

Integration of our classifier as a ranking criterion might help to optimize the learning potential of result lists.

## 7. DISCUSSION

We have seen that people's behavior changes over the course of a search session in a way that suggests they learn as they search, and observed that what they learn appears to persist across sessions. Further, it is possible to predict which clicks and sessions will result in the greatest change in behavior. In this section we discuss the ways these findings can be used to support users and optimize the search experience to promote knowledge acquisition.

By recognizing the different stages of learning in a search session we can reinforce existing knowledge acquisition behavior. For example, we observe that the number of domains on a search result page increases over the course of a session, particularly for procedural and declarative queries. We could reinforce this outcome by encouraging greater search result diversity for queries later in a session when it does not happen naturally. Likewise, we see that the query terminology gets more sophisticated as a session progresses. The query suggestions offered to users could, when a user first embarks on a new topic, start out simple and increase in complexity over time. Because people often use terms from the search result snippets in their queries as they search, the best query suggestions may be ones that are biased towards including terms that occurred in the snippets of results that are visited and dwelt on.

These approaches could be applied to all search sessions, since many of the changes we observed were true for general queries. However, we also saw that it was possible to automatically identify queries that indicate procedural or declarative information needs, and that these sessions exhibit particularly strong and sometimes unique learning behavior. For example, while search result entropy increases for most queries, it drops sharply towards the end of a session for procedural queries. Rather than encouraging topical diversity later in a session for such queries, it may make sense instead to help the user converge and enforce greater consistency among the search results.

In addition to reinforcing observed behavior, our findings could also be used to promote faster learning, helping people get to the information that will change their search behavior earlier than they might otherwise. For example, we found that we could easily and accurately identify results that promote learning. This information could be used to re-rank the search results so that the top ranked results promote learning. This may be particularly useful early in a search session and for new topics that the searcher engages with, as an increase in knowledge acquired early on may encourage future learning in subsequent queries and sessions.

It may also be possible to promote faster learning by augmenting the search interface. We saw that it is possible to identify terms that will be important to the user because they appear in the clicked search result snippets. These terms could be defined on the search result page to help improve the vocabulary available to the searcher. Additionally, rather than requiring a user to actually visit a page that will help improve their ability to search on a topic, valuable information could be extracted from those pages and provided alongside the results. The approach used by Bernstein et al. [6] to extract short answer text for in-line search result answers could be applied in this case.

As search engines get better, and people are able to find what they are looking for with less need to hunt around, there is a risk that they will also learn less during the search process. Our findings can be used to ensure this does not happen. In addition to providing the end content, search engines can provide important, intermediate information like the clicked results studied in Section 4.

## 8. CONCLUSION

In this paper, we investigated evidence of users' within-session knowledge acquisition based on the log files of a popular Web search engine. During several qualitative and quantitative analyses, we made the following observations: **(1)** Information seeking sessions can be divided into procedural and declarative sessions, both of which show significant differences from sessions without explicit knowledge acquisition intent as well as from each other. Many information seeking sessions do not fall into either of these categories. They do, however, represent a high-precision set of cases in which people are explicitly seeking to acquire knowledge. As such, they allow us to observe knowledge acquisition via Web search in great detail. **(2)** Based on an automatically extracted set of procedural and declarative search sessions, we studied the development of domain expertise and find evidence of within-session learning that is sustained across sessions as well. **(3)** We gained initial insights into the reason for the observed learning. By tracking the origin of query reformulations, we show that significant proportions of newly added query terms had been previously present on result page snippets and recently visited pages. This suggests that the search process, not just the final result, contributes towards expanding the user's domain knowledge. **(4)** Finally, we develop a classifier based on document and session-level features that was able to accurately predict the knowledge acquisition potential of Web pages for a given user.

There are several promising directions for future work on Web search-driven knowledge acquisition. Firstly, it will be interesting to investigate the potential of using information about the user's knowledge acquisition intent for ranking purposes. Evidence such as the output of the predictor that was presented in Section 6 may be able to improve the ranking quality of knowledge search sessions. Similarly, we will investigate how confirmed knowledge acquisition intents can be supported on an interface level by providing dedicated tools appropriate for the intent in question. This could, for example, include providing high-level overviews and summaries of relevant concepts in the domain in the case of declarative information needs which are often exploratory in nature. Finally, in Section 4, we showed that future query terms are often present on previously visited pages. In this paper, we have no means of knowing whether the searcher actually saw the term on the page or whether it has another origin. A dedicated eye-tracking study of query reformulation can be expected to create much further insight into this interesting question.

# 9. REFERENCES


[1] John R Anderson. *Language, Memory, and Thought.* Earlbaum, 1976.

[2] Azin Ashkan, Charles LA Clarke, Eugene Agichtein, and Qi Guo. Classifying and characterizing query intent. In *ECIR 2009.*

[3] Ricardo Baeza-Yates, Liliana Calderón-Benavides, and Cristina González-Caro. The intention behind web queries. In *SPIRE 2006.*

[4] Nicholas J Belkin, Robert N Oddy, and Helen M Brooks. Ask for information retrieval: Part i. background and theory. *Journal of documentation*, 1982.

[5] Paul N Bennett, Ryen W White, Wei Chu, Susan T Dumais, Peter Bailey, Fedor Borisyuk, and Xiaoyuan Cui. Modeling the impact of short-and long-term behavior on search personalization. In *SIGIR 2012.*

[6] Michael S Bernstein, Jaime Teevan, Susan Dumais, Daniel Liebling, and Eric Horvitz. Direct answers for search queries in the long tail. In *SIGCHI 2012.*

[7] Andrei Broder. A taxonomy of web search. In *ACM SIGIR Forum 2002.*

[8] Jamie Callan and Maxine Eskenazi. Combining lexical and grammatical features to improve readability measures for first and second language texts. In *NAACL HLT 2007.*

[9] Kevyn Collins-Thompson, Paul N Bennett, Ryen W White, Sebastian de la Chica, and David Sontag. Personalizing web search results by reading level. In *CIKM 2011.*

[10] Maurice de Kunder. Daily estimated size of the world wide web. http://www.worldwidewebsize.com/, 2013.

[11] Carsten Eickhoff, Kevyn Collins-Thompson, Paul N. Bennett, and Susan T. Dumais. Personalizing atypical web search sessions. In *WSDM 2013.*

[12] Carsten Eickhoff, Pieter Dekker, and Arjen P de Vries. Supporting children's web search in school environments. In *IIiX 2012.*

[13] Gene Golovchinsky, John Adcock, Jeremy Pickens, Pernilla Qvarfordt, and Maribeth Back. Cerchiamo: a collaborative exploratory search tool. *Proceedings of Computer Supported Cooperative Work (CSCW)*, 2008.

[14] Thorsten Joachims, Laura Granka, Bing Pan, Helene Hembrooke, and Geri Gay. Accurately interpreting clickthrough data as implicit feedback. In *SIGIR 2005.*

[15] Rosie Jones and Kristina Lisa Klinkner. Beyond the session timeout: automatic hierarchical segmentation of search topics in query logs. In *CIKM 2008.*

[16] Jin Young Kim, Kevyn Collins-Thompson, Paul N Bennett, and Susan T Dumais. Characterizing web content, user interests, and search behavior by reading level and topic. In *WSDM 2012.*

[17] Aris Kosmopoulos, Eric Gaussier, Georgios Paliouras, and Sujeevan Aseervatham. The ecir 2010 large scale hierarchical classification workshop. In *ACM SIGIR Forum*, 2010.

[18] Bill Kules, Robert Capra, Matthew Banta, and Tito Sierra. What do exploratory searchers look at in a faceted search interface? In *2009 ACM/IEEE-CS joint conference on Digital libraries.*

[19] Victor Kuperman, Hans Stadthagen-Gonzalez, and Marc Brysbaert. Age-of-acquisition ratings for 30,000 english words. *Behavior Research Methods*, 2012.

[20] Lin Li, Zhenglu Yang, Botao Wang, and Masaru Kitsuregawa. Dynamic adaptation strategies for long-term and short-term user profile to personalize search. In *Advances in Data and Web Management.* 2007.

[21] Jingjing Liu, Nicholas J Belkin, Xiangmin Zhang, and Xiaojun Yuan. Examining usersï£¡ knowledge change in the task completion process. *Information Processing & Management*, 2012.

[22] Gary Marchionini. Exploratory search: from finding to understanding. *Communications of the ACM*, 2006.

[23] G Harry McLaughlin. Smog grading: A new readability formula. *Journal of Reading*, 1969.

[24] Thomas R Niesler and PC Woodland. A variable-length category-based n-gram language model. In *ICASSP 1996.*

[25] Brendan O'Connor, Michel Krieger, and David Ahn. Tweetmotif: Exploratory search and topic summarization for twitter. In *ICWSM*, 2010.

[26] James Pitkow, Hinrich Schütze, Todd Cass, Rob Cooley, Don Turnbull, Andy Edmonds, Eytan Adar, and Thomas Breuel. Personalized search. *Communications of the ACM*, 2002.

[27] Daniel E Rose and Danny Levinson. Understanding user goals in web search. In *WWW 2004.*

[28] Dou Shen, Jian-Tao Sun, Qiang Yang, and Zheng Chen. A comparison of implicit and explicit links for web page classification. In *WWW 2006.*

[29] Mirco Speretta and Susan Gauch. Personalized search based on user search histories. In *2005 IEEE/WIC/ACM International Conference on Web Intelligence.*

[30] Sofia Stamou and Lefteris Kozanidis. Impact of search results on user queries. In *International Workshop on Web Information and Data Management 2009.*

[31] Shanu Sushmita, Benjamin Piwowarski, and Mounia Lalmas. Dynamics of genre and domain intents. In *Information Retrieval Technology.* 2010.

[32] Chenhao Tan, Evgeniy Gabrilovich, and Bo Pang. To each his own: personalized content selection based on text comprehensibility. In *WSDM 2012.*

[33] Jaime Teevan, Susan T Dumais, and Eric Horvitz. Personalizing search via automated analysis of interests and activities. In *SIGIR 2005.*

[34] Jaime Teevan, Susan T Dumais, and Eric Horvitz. Potential for personalization. *ACM TOCHI 2010.*

[35] Takashi Tomokiyo and Matthew Hurst. A language model approach to keyphrase extraction. In *Proceedings of the ACL 2003 workshop on Multiword expressions: analysis, acquisition and treatment-Volume 18.*

[36] Ryen W. White, Susan T. Dumais, and Jaime Teevan. Characterizing the influence of domain expertise on web search behavior. In *WSDM 2009.*

[37] Ryen W White and Jeff Huang. Assessing the scenic route: measuring the value of search trails in web logs. In *SIGIR 2010.*

[38] Barbara M Wildemuth. The effects of domain knowledge on search tactic formulation. *JASIST 2004.*

[39] Zahide Yildirim, M Yasar Ozden, and Meral Aksu. Comparison of hypermedia learning and traditional instruction on knowledge acquisition and retention. *The Journal of Educational Research*, 2001.

[40] Xiangmin Zhang, Michael Cole, and Nicholas Belkin. Predicting users' domain knowledge from search behaviors. In *SIGIR 2011.*

# Scalable K-Means by Ranked Retrieval*

Andrei Broder
Google
1600 Amphitheater Parkway
Mountain View, CA 94043
broder @google.com

Lluis Garcia-Pueyo
Google
1600 Amphitheater Parkway
Mountain View, CA 94043
lgpueyo@google.com

Vanja Josifovski
Google
1600 Amphitheater Parkway
Mountain View, CA 94043
vanjaj@google.com

Sergei Vassilvitskii
Google
1600 Amphitheater Parkway
Mountain View, CA 94043
sergeiv@google.com

Srihari Venkatesan
xAd
440 North Wolfe Road
Sunnyvale, CA 94085

## ABSTRACT

The `k-means` clustering algorithm has a long history and a proven practical performance, however it does not scale to clustering millions of data points into thousands of clusters in high dimensional spaces. The main computational bottleneck is the need to recompute the nearest centroid for every data point at every iteration, a prohibitive cost when the number of clusters is large. In this paper we show how to reduce the cost of the `k-means` algorithm by large factors by adapting ranked retrieval techniques. Using a combination of heuristics, on two real life data sets the wall clock time per iteration is reduced from 445 minutes to less than 4, and from 705 minutes to 1.4, while the clustering quality remains within 0.5% of the `k-means` quality.

The key insight is to invert the process of point-to-centroid assignment by creating an inverted index over all the points and then using the current centroids as queries to this index to decide on cluster membership. In other words, rather than each iteration consisting of "points picking centroids", each iteration now consists of "centroids picking points". This is much more efficient, but comes at the cost of leaving some points unassigned to any centroid. We show experimentally that the number of such points is low and thus they can be separately assigned once the final centroids are decided. To speed up the computation we sparsify the centroids by pruning low weight features. Finally, to further reduce the running time and the number of unassigned points, we propose a variant of the WAND algorithm that uses the results of the intermediate results of nearest neighbor computations to improve performance.

*Work done while the authors were at Yahoo! Research


*WSDM'14*, February 24–28, 2014, New York, New York, USA.

http://dx.doi.org/10.1145/2556195.2556260 .

## Categories and Subject Descriptors

H.3.3 [**Information Search and Retrieval**]: Clustering

## Keywords

k-means;WAND

## 1. INTRODUCTION

The web abounds in high-dimensional "big" data: for example, collections such as web pages, web users, search clicks, and on-line advertising transactions. A common way to mitigate Bellman's infamous "curse of dimensionality" [9] is to *cluster* these items: for example, classifying users according to their interests and demographics. Among popular approaches to clustering, the classic `k-means` algorithm remains a standard tool of practitioners despite its poor theoretical convergence properties [4, 34]. However, when clustering $n$ data points into $k$ clusters, each iteration of the `k-means` method requires $O(kn)$ distance calculations, making it untenable for clustering scenarios requiring a partition of millions of points each with hundreds of non-null coordinates into thousands of clusters. While parallel programming techniques alleviate this cost by distributing the computation across many machines, with web scaled datasets, even massively parallelized implementation based on Hadoop (e.g. [16]) might take thousands of CPU-hours to converge on current hardware.

Approaches optimizing the `k-means` running time generally fall into two categories: Some assume that the data is contained in a low dimensional space and use $kd$-trees and other geometric data structures to reduce the number of distance computations [21, 28, 29]; Others (e.g. [19, 30]) assume that the number of points per cluster is large, and subsample the data to deal with scale. Unfortunately when both the data dimensionality is high and the average number of points per cluster is small, both of the approaches above fail to provide significant speed ups. This is precisely the situation we address in this paper: we show how to reduce the cost of the `k-means` algorithm by large factors by adapting ranked retrieval techniques. Using a combination of heuristics, on two real-world data sets the wall clock time per iteration is reduced from 445 minutes to less than 4, and from 705 minutes to 1.4, without affecting quality or convergence speed—after 13 phases the algorithm has converged to within 0.5% of the `k-means` quality with the same number of phases.

To reduce the cost of the `k-means` algorithm we use nearest neighbor data structures, optimized for retrieving the top $\ell$ closest points[1] to a query point. Specifically, we use inverted indexes and a novel variant of the WAND ranked retrieval algorithm [12] to speed up the nearest centroid computations at the core of the `k-means` method.

The `k-means` algorithm uses an iterative refinement technique where each iteration consists of two steps: the *assignment step* where the points are assigned to the closest centroid, and the *update step* where the centroids are recalculated based on the last assignment. The latter phase can be performed in a linear scan over the assigned points and is the less expensive of the two. Thus, we focus on the use of indexing to speed up point assignment. But what should we index? The natural choice is to index the centroids, and then run a query for each data point, retrieving the closest centroid. This approach would exactly implement the `k-means` algorithm, but since the centroids change in each iteration, this method requires both rebuilding the index and evaluating $n$ queries at each iteration. In addition, as the centroids have many non-zero elements, they correspond to dense documents for which top-$\ell$ nearest neighbor retrieval algorithms are not particularly efficient.

In this work we propose the converse approach. Instead of indexing the centroids and using the points as queries, we propose indexing the *points* and using *centroids* as queries. This approach has several benefits. First, we do not need to rebuild the index between iterations since the points are stationary and only the centroids move from one iteration to the next. Second, the number of queries per iteration is significantly smaller ($k$ rather than $n$) since we only pose one query per centroid.

By retrieving only the top $\ell$ points closest to each centroid, we run the risk of leaving some points unassigned to any centroid. We show experimentally that the number of such points is low and thus they can be separately assigned once the final centroids are decided. In any case, these points are precisely the outliers in the dataset (they are far away from all known cluster centers), thus the setting of the parameter $\ell$ allows a tradeoff between the clustering speed and the acceptable number of outliers. Finally, in many applications, such as web search and ad selection, the application *per se* requires indexing the items of interest, thus large scale clustering of these items can be done without requiring significant additional infrastructure.

To speed up the computation we begin by sparsifying the centroids by pruning low weight features: we show experimentally that this pruning brings significant improvements in efficiency while not changing the clustering performance at all. We then delve into the details of the WAND algorithm [12], and modify it to remember all of the points that were ranked in the top $\ell$ list during the retrieval. Again, our experimental evaluation over two datasets from realistic practical scenarios shows that the proposed approaches are efficient and scale well with the number of clusters $k$, while having virtually no impact on the quality of the results. Indeed, in some cases, the new approaches produce clusters of slightly better quality than the standard `k-means` algorithm possibly by reducing the confusing effect of outliers.

The techniques presented in this paper can be used in a single-machine setting, or at individual nodes in partitioned implementations. In both cases, the proposed method reduces the processing time and resource use by one to two orders of magnitude, while resulting in a negligible loss in clustering quality.

In summary the contributions of this paper are as follows:

- We describe an implementation of the `k-means` algorithm that is over 100 times faster than the standard implementation on realistic datasets by using an inverted index over all the points and then using the current centroids as queries into this index to decide on cluster membership.
- We show experimentally that selectively re-assigning in each iteration only the subset of the points that are "close enough" to the current centroids and sparsifying the centroids does not materially change the quality of the final clustering.
- For retrieval in the index above, we modify the WAND algorithm for similarity search to remember the runner-ups in the current iteration and the radius of each cluster in the previous one, thus making significant efficiency gains.

## 2. BACKGROUND

We follow the standard vector space model. Let $T = \{t_1, t_2, \ldots, t_m\}$ be a collection of $m$ terms, and $D$ be a collection of $n$ documents over the terms, $D = \{d_1, d_2, \ldots, d_n\}$. We treat each document $d \in D$ as a vector lying in $m$-dimensional term space, and use $d(i)$ to denote the $i$-th coordinate. To judge the similarity between a pair of documents, we use the cosine similarity metric: for two documents $d, d' \in D$:

$$\textsc{cossim}(d, d') = \frac{d \circ d'}{\|d\| \|d'\|},$$

where $\circ$ denotes the vector dot product, and $\|\cdot\|$ the vector's length. Note that since the COSSIM measure is a function of the angle between the vectors $d$ and $d'$, it is invariant under scaling of its inputs. For any constants $\alpha, \beta > 0$:

$$\textsc{cossim}(d, d') = \textsc{cossim}(\alpha d, \beta d').$$

Thus we can assume without loss of generality that all of the documents $d \in D$ are normalized to have unit length, $\|d\| = 1$.

Recall that, the COSSIM of any pair of documents is always between 0 and 1, and $f(d, d') = 1 - \textsc{cossim}(d, d')$ defines a metric: that is, it is non-negative, symmetric and satisfies the triangle inequality.

Our goal is to find a partition of the documents in $D$ into $k$ non-overlapping clusters, $\mathcal{C} = \{C_1, C_2, \ldots, C_k\}$ each with a representative point $c_i$ that maximizes the average cosine similarity between a document and its closest (under

[1]we use the term *top-$\ell$* instead of *top-$k$* to avoid confusion between the number of retrieved points and the number of clusters in `k-means` clustering.

$f$) representative. We will refer to the points $c_i$ as centers of individual clusters. Formally, we want to find a partition $\mathcal{C}$ which maximizes:

$$\psi(D, \mathcal{C}) = \sum_{d \in D} \max_{c \in \mathcal{C}} \text{COSSIM}(c, d).$$

## 2.1 The k-means algorithm

The `k-means` algorithm is a widely used clustering method [24]. In its usual formulation, the algorithm is given a point set $X \subset \mathbb{R}^d$, and a desired number of clusters $k$. It returns a set $\mathcal{C}$ of $|\mathcal{C}| = k$ cluster centers $\{c_1, \ldots, c_k\}$ that forms a local minimum for a potential function

$$\phi(X, \mathcal{C}) = \sum_{x \in X} \min_{c \in \mathcal{C}} \|x - c\|^2.$$

In other words, it attempts to find a set of centers that minimizes the sum of squared distances between each point and its nearest cluster center.

The algorithm is a local search method that minimizes $\phi$ by repeatedly (1) assigning each point to its nearest cluster center and (2) recomputing the best cluster centers given the point assignment.

### *K-means for Cosine Similarity*

We adapt the `k-means` algorithm to maximize the average cosine similarity, $\psi$. The assignment phase remains identical—we assign each point to the cluster center with the maximal cosine similarity. Next we show how to compute the optimal center given a set of points. To preserve the structure of the algorithm, we show below that selecting the (normalized) mean of the points as the center, maximizes the average similarity of a cluster. A similar observation has previously been made by Strehl et al. [32].

LEMMA 1. *For a set of $n$ vectors $D = \{d_1, d_2, \ldots, d_n\}$, the unit length vector $c = \frac{\sum_i d_i}{\|\sum_i d_i\|}$ maximizes*

$$\sum_{d \in D} \text{COSSIM}(c, d).$$

PROOF. We want to find a unit length vector $c$ that maximizes:

$$\sum_{d \in D} \text{COSSIM}(c, d) = \sum_{d \in D} \frac{c \circ d}{\|c\|\|d\|} = \sum_{d \in D} c \circ d = c \circ \sum_{d \in D} d$$

The vector $c$ that maximizes the dot product with vector $\bar{D} = \sum_{d \in D} d$ must be parallel to $\bar{D}$, setting

$$c = \frac{1}{\|\bar{D}\|} \sum_i d_i$$

ensures that it is parallel to $\bar{D}$ and is of unit length. □

Given the lemma, we can conclude that the `k-means` method will converge to a local optimum.

PROPOSITION 2. *Given a set of documents $D = \{d_1, \ldots, d_n\}$, the k-means method which assigns each document to its most similar cluster, and recomputes the cluster center as the mean of the documents assigned to it converges to a local maximum of the objective function:*

$$\psi(D, \mathcal{C}) = \sum_{d \in D} \max_{c \in \mathcal{C}} \text{COSSIM}(d, c_i)$$

.

## 2.2 Ranked retrieval

Inverted indexes have become a de facto standard for evaluation of similarity queries across many different domains due to their very low latency and good scalability properties [35]. In an inverted index, each term $t \in T$ has an associated *postings list* which contains all of the documents $d \in D$ that contain $t$ (those with $d \cap t \neq \emptyset$). For each such document $d$, the list contains an entry called a *posting*. A posting is composed of the document id (DID) of $d$, and other relevant information necessary to evaluate the similarity of $d$ to the query. In this paper we denote that additional information with $d(t)$, and assume that it represents a weight for the particular term in the document. Such weights can be derived using variety of IR models [6] and in this work we chose to use the *tf-idf* weighting framework, but other methods are equally well applicable with our approach. The postings in each list are sorted in increasing order of DID. Often, B-trees or skip lists are used to index the postings lists, which facilitates searching for a particular DID within each list [35].

Inverted indexes are optimized for retrieving most similar documents for a query under an additive scoring model. Formally, a query $q$ is a subset of terms, $q \subseteq T$, each with a given weight $q(t)$. In this manner, a query can be seen as another document. Given a similarity function $g$, the score of a document for a query, is $\sum_{t \in d \cap q} g(q(t), d(t))$. When working with cosine similarity, the score is $q \circ d$, with both $q$ and $d$ normalized to be unit length.

Broder et al. [12] describe WAND, a method that allows for fast retrieval of the top-$\ell$ ranked documents for a query. We choose WAND due to its ability to scale well with the number of features in the query, as reported in [15]. Additionally, this is a method where we can use information from previous rounds to further improve the retrieval time. A major difference in our setting is the fact that queries, representing centroids in `k-means`, are dense. We take special measures to sparsity the vectors, nevertheless, in our work queries are still substantially longer than the average search query of approximately 3 words.

The main intuition behind the WAND algorithm (presented in Algorithm 1) is to use an upper bound of the similarity contribution of each term to eliminate documents that are too dissimilar from the query to make it into the top-$\ell$ list. WAND works by keeping one pointer called a *cursor* for each of the query terms (dimensions) that points at a document in the corresponding posting list. During the evaluation, the algorithm repeatedly choses a cursor to be moved, and advances this cursor as far as possible in order to avoid examining unnecessary documents. To find the optimal cursor and improve the efficiency, the cursors are kept sorted by the DID they point to.

At initialization time, for each term $t \in T$, WAND first fetches the upper bound $\text{UB}_t$ of the document weights across all documents in the posting list of $t$. $\text{UB}_t$ is query independent and is computed and stored during the index building phase at no extra cost. Next, all cursors are initialized by pointing at the first posting in their corresponding posting lists (the one with the minimum DID). The outer loop of the algorithm repeatedly retrieves the next (in order of DID) document that qualifies for the top-$\ell$ list.

During the evaluation, the algorithm maintains a heap of highest scoring top-$\ell$ documents among those examined so far. The minimum score in this heap, or the score of the current $\ell$-th best result, is denoted by $\theta$. The key property of WAND is that it does not fully score every document, but skips the ones that have no chance in making it in the top-$\ell$ list. Intuitively, if we can determine that the score of a an unexamined document cannot be higher than $\theta$, then we can forego any further evaluation of this document and skip to the next DID that has a chance at success. The first document that has the property of having upper bound of its score higher than $\theta$ is known as the *pivot* document. We present the pivot finding subroutine as Algorithm 2.

The subroutine relies on two helper functions. The first, `findPivotTerm`, returns the earliest term, $t^*$, in the list, such that the sum of the score upper bounds, $\text{UB}_t$ for all terms $t$ preceding $t^*$ is at least $\theta$. Given the pivot document, we then check whether the cursors in the first and $t^*$-th position point to the same document. Since the cursors are sorted by DID, if the two cursors point to different documents, the one pointed to by the first cursor cannot possibly make it to the top-$\ell$ list. and we advance the cursors (Lines 15-18). The function `PickCursor` selects a cursor to advance to the first document with DID at least $d^*$ (Line 17).

On the other hand, If both the first cursor and the cursor at $t^*$ point to a posting with the same DID, the similarity of that document is fully evaluated (Line 12).

In the description we have simplified the algorithm by not dealing with some of the stopping conditions and end of postings list issues. The WAND algorithm is fully described in [12]. We have also described a basic version of the WAND algorithm for simplicity: several modifications are possible to improve the efficiency of the processing both for on-disk and in-memory scenarios [15].

**Algorithm 1** WAND

**Input:** Centroid query $C$
  Index $I$
**Output:** Heap $H$ with the top $\ell$ points most similar to $C$
**for** $t \in dimensions(C)$ **do**
  fetch $\text{UB}_t$
  Cursors[t].DID = first DID in posting_list(t);
**end for**
Initialize empty heap $H$ of size $\ell$;
**while** true **do**
  sort Cursors by Cursors[t].DID (ascending)
  $\theta = minSimilarity(H)$
  $(candidate, sim) = FindCandidate(Cursors, \theta)$;
  **if** $candidate == LastDID$ **then**
    break;
  **end if**
  $replaceMinElement(H, candidate, sim)$;
**end while**
**return** $H$;

**Algorithm 2** FindCandidate

1: **Input:** Query: $q$
  `Cursors[1..|q|]`: array of cursors over the posting lists used in the query,
  Threshold: $\theta$
2: **Output:** Next feasible document, its similarity
3: **loop**
4: {Find pivot cursor}
5: pivotTerm ← findPivotTerm(Cursors,$\theta$)
6: **if** pivotTerm == Null **then**
7: **return** *NoMoreDocs*
8: **end if**
9: pivotDoc ← Cursors[pivotTerm].DID
10: **if** Cursors[0].DID == pivotDoc **then**
11: {Evaluate pivot document}
12: **if** COSSIM($q$,pivotDoc) $\geq \theta$ **then**
13: **return** pivotDoc, COSSIM($q$, pivotDoc)
14: **end if**
15: **else**
16: {Advance Cursors}
17: dim ← PickCursor(Cursors[0..pivotTerm])
18: Cursors[dim].advance(pivotDoc)
19: **end if**
20: **end loop**

## 3. ALGORITHMS

In this Section we describe our main approach of using an inverted index to speed up `k-means` computations. As we mentioned previously, the main bottleneck in getting `k-means` to work on millions of points and thousands of clusters in multi-thousand dimensional spaces is the fact that at every iteration we must find the nearest cluster center to every one of the data points. The naive implementation requires $O(nkd)$ time per round. Previous work has focused on reducing this complexity either by sampling ([19, 30]), which does not work well when the number of points per cluster is relatively small, or by employing kd-trees and other data structures ([21, 28, 29]) which are only efficient in low dimensional spaces.

A simple approach to reduce the amount of time to compute the nearest cluster center for every point would be to build a nearest neighbor data structure on the cluster centers, and then issue a query for each data point to find the nearest neighbor. Unfortunately since the cluster centers move at every iteration this would force us to rebuild the index at every iteration, the cost of which would outweigh any potential savings. Instead we perform the converse. We build a nearest neighbor data structure on the *points* and then use the current *centroids* as queries to find the points closest to the centroids. Since the points do not move from one iteration to the next, we only have to build the index once, thereby amortizing the cost across the iterations of `k-means`. Furthermore, often, inverted indexes of the points are build for other applications and can be reused for the computation of the clusters, using the algorithms described in this section.

This approach has an additional benefit: it automatically detects outliers. Intuitively, the outlier points are precisely those points that are far away from all of the centers, and with this method these are exactly the points that are never returned by the nearest neighbor data structure. It is well known [18] that outliers present a problem for `k-means` and can skew the position of the final clusters. In our algorithm, the outliers are never be retrieved as part of the top-$\ell$ list for any of the centroids, therefore they do not impact the computation, rather we assign them to clusters in a post processing step. The value of the parameter $\ell$ allows us to control the rank (number of closer points) that classifies a point into an outlier.

## 3.1 WAND Based k-means

We present a progression of algorithms that incorporate the nearest neighbor index into `k-means`.

### *WAND for point assignment*

The first algorithm we explore uses standard WAND to perform the point assignment as described in Section 2. Instead of the nested loop computing the distances for all pairs of centroids and points, as in regular `k-means`, we invoke the WAND algorithm to find the top-$\ell$ closest points to each centroid. The WAND operator returns a set of $\ell$ points along with their similarity to the cluster.

Although these are the most similar $\ell$ documents to the center, a single document $d$ may be in the top-$\ell$ lists for a number of different centroids. Thus we have to maintain the id of the centroid that is closest to $d$. We proceed by using an assignment table $A$ which is a map with the document id, DID, as the key and whose payload contains the id of the most similar center and the corresponding similarity. Each point returned by the WAND operator is then checked against this table. If it is already in the table with a similarity larger than the one returned for the current cluster, the result is ignored. Otherwise it is added to the table with the new similarity, potentially replacing an existing entry associated with a previously evaluated centroid. The assignment table is reset at the beginning of each iteration.

### *Using the assignment table within WAND*

Instead of using the assignment table $A$ to post-process the results returned by WAND, we may instead modify the WAND algorithm to use the table $A$ directly. The corresponding similarity value in $A$ then serves as a lower bound on the similarity a point must achieve in order to be returned by WAND. TWe omit the full specification of this algorithm for brevity.

### *Warm start of thresholds*

The WAND algorithm works by comparing the partial score of documents to the score of the $\ell$-th best result. In the naive implementation as in Algorithm 2, this threshold, $\theta$ is initialized to 0 at every iteration. This has the effect that the first $\ell$ documents are always fully evaluated, since their similarity is guaranteed to be at least 0.

We can improve the performance by keeping track of intermediate information across the `k-means` iterations. Specifically, for each cluster $c_i$ we remember the threshold, $\theta_i^t$, used by WAND when executed with $c_i^t$ as the query at time $t$ (this is identical to the similarity to the $\ell$-th closest point considered by WAND). Let $\sigma_i^t$ denote the similarity between the center of cluster $i$ at time $t$ and that at time $t-1$. Then if we set the threshold in the following iteration to $\theta_i^{t+1} = \theta_i^t - \sigma_t^i$, we can guarantee that all of the points returned by WAND in iteration $t$ would also qualify for iteration $t+1$. (A similar approach was used by Elkin [14] to reduce the number of distance computations performed by `k-means`.) This follows by the fact that $1 - \text{COSSIM}$ forms a metric, thus for any point $d$:

$$\begin{aligned}\text{COSSIM}(d, c_i^{t+1}) &\geq \text{COSSIM}(d, c_i^t) - \text{COSSIM}(c_i^{t+1}, c_i^t)\\ &\geq \theta_i^t - \sigma_i^t = \theta_i^{t+1}\end{aligned}$$

In practice, we find that setting $\theta_i^{t+1} = \theta_t^i$ works equally well and is more efficient, since we can forgo the computation of $\sigma_i^t$.

### *Expanded use of the assignment table*

By pushing the assignment table into the WAND subroutine, the caller only has access to the final $D_i$ documents returned. However, during the course of computing the top-$\ell$ documents most similar to $c_i$, the full similarity is computed for many more documents. There are two reasons why this similarity may not be preserved. First, a document may be reassigned to an even closer center in the assignment table, $A$. However, it could also be the case that a document $d$ lies in the Voronoi cell of a particular centroid $c_i$ (that is it is closer to $c_i$ than to any other centroid), but it is not one of the top-$\ell$ documents closest documents. If such a document $d$ has a low DID then it will be fully scored, and temporarily placed on the heap in WAND, only to be replaced by an even closer document later on.

As we show below, this situation is far from rare, and remembering the assignment and similarity information for such documents allows the algorithm designer to set a lower threshold $\ell$ to achieve the same effect. Therefore it pays to remember this information and incorporate it when computing the centroids. The final version of the `wand-k-means` algorithm, shown in Algorithm 3

## 3.2 Analysis

The key idea behind the algorithms presented thus far is to consider only the $\ell$-closest points to the cluster center when executing the assignment phase of `k-means`. To find the $\ell$ closest points, the WAND algorithm gains added efficiency by giving up on the distance computation as soon as one can safely conclude that the point is further away than the desired threshold. Nevertheless, during the typical course of its operation, the exact distance is computed for more than $\ell$ points. We formally analyze the number of such points and show it to be significantly higher than $\ell$.

Consider a point set $D = \{d_1, d_2, \ldots, d_n\}$, a center $c$ and let the elements of $D$ be examined in a random order. The question we consider is how many elements of $D$ are ever included in the top-$\ell$ list. Call such an element $d \in D$ *fully-examined.*

LEMMA 3. *If $D$ is examined in a random order, the expected number of fully examined points is $\ell(1+\log\frac{n}{\ell})+o(\frac{\ell}{n})$.*

PROOF. A point $d_i \in D$ is fully examined if and only if it is one of the $\ell$-closest points to $c$ among those in $\{d_1, d_2, \ldots, d_i\}$. Let $Y_i$ be an indicator variable which is set to 1 if the point in position $i$ is fully examined and 0 otherwise and let $p_i$ denote the probability that $y_i$ is set to 1. Then the expected number of fully examined points is $\sum_i \mathbb{E}[Y_i] = \sum_i p_i$.

**Algorithm 3** wand-k-means

```
wand-k-means:
    Input: D = Set of documents, k
    Output: Centroids, C = {c_1, ..., c_k}
φ = ∞
C ← InitializeCentroids
θ[1..k] ← 0
repeat
    φ* ← φ, φ ← 0, A ← ∅
    for all c_i ∈ C do {Find Nearby Documents}
        ⟨A, θ_i⟩ ← WAND(c_i, i, A, ℓ, θ_i)
    end for
    for 1 ≤ i ≤ k do {Compute Assignment}
        C_i ← {d ∈ D : A[d].clust = i}
    end for
    for 1 ≤ i ≤ k do {Recompute Centers}
        c_i ← (1/|C_i|) Σ_{d∈C_i} d
        for all d ∈ C_i do {Update Cost Function}
            φ ← φ + A[d].sim
        end for
    end for
until φ = φ*
return C = {c_1, ..., c_k}
```

```
WAND
    Input: query q, cluster id i, table A, ℓ, threshold θ_i
    Output: updated table A
for all i ∈ q do
    Cursors[i].init
end for
H ← Heap of size ℓ
while true do
    θ_i ← max(θ_i, min(H))
    ⟨d, sim⟩ ← WAND-Next(Cursors, θ_i)
    if d == null then
        return A
    end if
    if (A[d] == null or A[d].sim < sim) then
        A[d].sim ← sim, A[d].clust ← i
        H.add(sim)
    end if
end while
```

Since the first $\ell$ points are always examined, for $1 \leq i \leq \ell$ we have $p_i = 1$. Now consider a point in position $j > \ell$, it will be fully examined only if it is one of the $\ell$ closest points among those in positions $1, 2, \ldots, j$. Since we assumed that the elements arrived in random order, $p_j = \frac{\ell}{j}$.

Therefore,

$$\sum_{i=1}^{n} p_i = \ell + \sum_{i=\ell+1}^{n} p_i = \ell + \sum_{i=\ell+1}^{n} \frac{\ell}{i} = \ell(1 + H_n - H_\ell)$$

$$= \ell(1 + \log n - \log \ell + o(\frac{1}{n}))$$

$$= \ell(1 + \log \frac{n}{\ell}) + o(\frac{\ell}{n})$$

□

In practice the order of the documents in $D$ is not random, but we can use the intuition given by the Lemma to show that even when looking for the $\ell$ closest points, the algorithm will compute the distances to far more than $\ell$ points, which in turn allows us to use WAND with a smaller value of $\ell$, improving its performance.

#### *3.2.1 Convergence*

The original `k-means` algorithm increases the overall similarity in every step—both when assigning each point to its most similar center, and when recomputing the centers. Therefore, it is well known that it will converge to a locally optimum solution, although such convergence may take an exponential number of steps [34]. Since the `wand-k-means` algorithm potentially examines only the closest $\ell$ points in each iteration, the same analysis no longer holds. To ensure convergence, we compute the cost of assigning *all* of the points every 50 iterations, and stop if no progress is made on this objective. As we will show, in practice the algorithm keeps all of the convergence properties of `k-means`: it converges to a locally optimum solution after just a handful of iteration, see Section 4 for more details.

### 3.3 Sparsification

The majority of time in any implementation of the `k-means` algorithm is spend computing the cosine similarity between two points. As we saw in the previous section, we can leverage the infrastructure initially designed for nearest neighbor retrieval to improve the speed of `k-means`. The inverted index data structure that we use for nearest neighbor retrieval is especially efficient in the case that the query itself is sparse, i.e. contains few non-zero entries.

In the applications we consider, the points (or documents) lie in a very high dimensional space: for example, the datasets in our experiments consist of 26 million and 7 million features respectively. Although an individual document typically has a small number of features (we find the average number of features per document to be around 100), the number of features in the cluster center $c_i$ tends to be very large, since the cluster center almost surely has a non-zero value for *every* feature present in the individual documents. As an additional optimization, we consider sparsifying each cluster center after computing it, effectively only keeping the top $p$ features with the highest absolute value. A similar performance improvement was previously suggested in [30], the combination of sparse clusters with inverted indexing further improves the performance gained by this approach.

## 4. EXPERIMENTAL EVALUATION

In this Section we present the results of the empirical evaluation of the algorithms on two real-world datasets. We begin by describing the datasets, and then evaluate the effect of each of the parameters.

We use two datasets from a real world textual advertising system. In Dataset 1, each point (item) represents a textual ad (encompassing both sponsored search and content match) from a production version of a large internet search engine in 2008. The point features are extracted from the combination of the ad creative (the body, title, display url) and the list of keywords that the advertisers have associated with the ad. Clustering of similar ads is used in a variety of textual advertising tasks, for example to predict the clickthrough rate of previously unseen ads. Dataset 2 is composed of web search queries that are expanded with features of the web search results returned by a search engine. It is well known that the brevity of the queries poses a challenge in query analysis and it is beneficial to expand them. Such an approach has been shown to work well for classification [11]. The queries in Dataset 2 were chosen by a stratified sampling of web queries by volume. The main statistics of the two datasets are provided in Table 1.

| | Dataset 1 | Dataset 2 |
|---|---|---|
| Number of Documents | 974,738 | 933,761 |
| Number of Features | 26,013,163 | 7,126,669 |
| Average Features per Document | 95.6 | 98.9 |

**Table 1: Dataset statistics.**

#### *4.0.1 Initialization*

There are two initialization tasks that must be performed before running the `wand-k-means` algorithm, building the index and selecting the initial centers. Building the index took approximately 54 minutes on both of the datasets above. In order to make for a fair comparison between methods, we computed an initial seed set for both datasets and then used the same initial seeds in all of the algorithms and baselines. We used `k-means++` [5] as the initialization method, as it has been proven to perform significantly better than a simple random assignment both in theory and in practice. We chose to cluster the data into $k = 1000$ clusters for the majority of the experiments. We report on scalability experiments separately in Section 4.4.

## 4.1 Number of documents retrieved

The overall results are shown in Table 2, where we evaluate all the average similarity, $\psi$ for all of the methods at iteration 13. The average similarity is computed after assigning *all* of the documents to their nearest center. As we can see, decreasing $\ell$ has a negligible effect on the final clustering similarity, but tremendously speeds up the iteration time. The effect of using *all* of the documents fully examined by WAND is apparent as well, even the setting of $\ell = 1$ performs very well, owning to the fact that many more documents are examined during the WAND iteration.

In addition, smaller values of $\ell$ allow `wand-k-means` to converge to a slightly better optimum than the vanilla `k-means` method. We conjecture that this is due to the fact that outliers are automatically detected and ignored during the execution of the algorithm (since they are not part of the top $\ell$ elements).

By changing the value of $\ell$ we do not affect the rate of convergence to the final solution. In Figure 1(a) we plot the average similarity as a function of the number of iterations. Here, we only compute the similarity for those documents that are assigned to some cluster at each iteration, but as we will see later (Section 4.2) the total number of unassigned documents is rather small. The rate of convergence to a solution does not change as a function of $\ell$, and examining fewer points has no detrimental effects on the quality of the clustering. In Figure 1(b) we plot the average time per iteration. It is clear that by reducing the value of $\ell$ we reduce the per iteration running time of `k-means` more than five-fold.

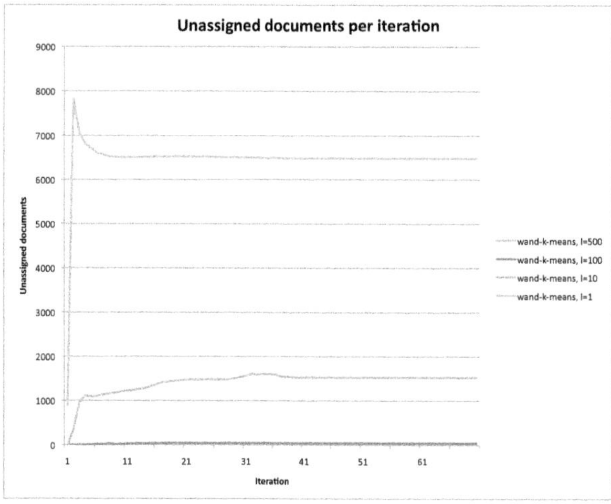


**Figure 3: The number of unassigned documents in Dataset 1 as a function of the number of iterations for different values of $\ell$.**

## 4.2 Outliers

We further explore the trade-off between the setting of the parameter $\ell$ and the number of documents marked as unassigned by the algorithm. Recall, the unassigned documents are those that do not appear in the top-$\ell$ list any cluster center during the execution of WAND. We plot the number of unassigned documents as a function of the iteration in Figure 3. There are two interesting observations. First, as expected, reducing $\ell$ allows `wand-k-means` to label more points as outliers, and the algorithm does take advantage of this new freedom. Moreover, the set of outliers remains very small, even the 6,500 outliers at $\ell = 1$, represent less than 1% of the overall dataset.

## 4.3 Sparsification

In this section we investigate the effect of the sparsification parameter $p$ on the algorithm's performance. We present the overall results, showing the average similarity of *all* documents at the end of iteration 13 in Table 3. Note that, while generally decreasing $p$ slowly decreases the quality of the clustering, high values of $p$ perform much better than having no sparsification at all. Again, we conjecture that this is because sparsification allows the algorithm to focus its performance on the critical features and ignore the contributions of outliers to the centroids.

The effect of $p$ on the running time is even larger than that obtained by restricting $\ell$. By insisting that the centroid have at most 500 non-zero features reduces the running time by a factor of 7 for dataset 1, and over a factor of 60 for dataset 2. The performance increase is much bigger for dataset 2, because the average similarity is low, and thus WAND is less effective at pruning out far away documents.

To study the effect of sparsification on convergence, we again plot the per iteration quality and running time in Figure 2(a) and 2(b) respectively. (Here too we only compute

| System | $\ell$ | Dataset 1 Similarity | Dataset 1 Time | Dataset 2 Similarity | Dataset 2 Time |
|---|---|---|---|---|---|
| `k-means` | — | 0.7804 | 445.05 | 0.2856 | 705.21 |
| `wand-k-means` | 100 | 0.7810 | 83.54 | 0.2858 | 324.78 |
| `wand-k-means` | 10 | 0.7811 | 75.88 | 0.2856 | 243.9 |
| `wand-k-means` | 1 | 0.7813 | 61.17 | 0.2709 | 100.84 |

**Table 2: The average point to centroid similarity at iteration 13 and average iteration time (in minutes) as a function of $\ell$**

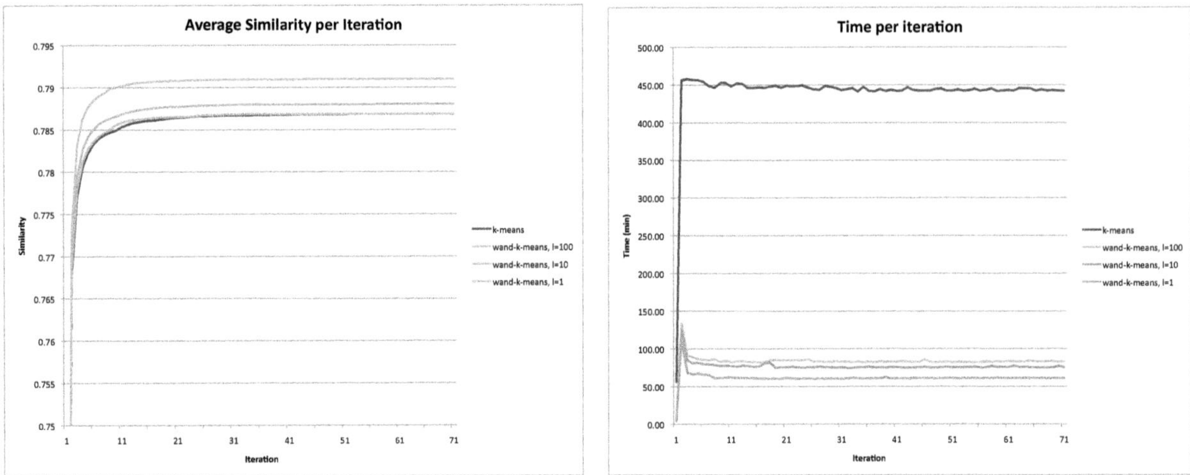


(a) (b)

**Figure 1: Evaluation of `wand-k-means` on Data 1 as function of different values of $\ell$: (a) The average point to centroid similarity at each iteration (b) The running time per iteration.**

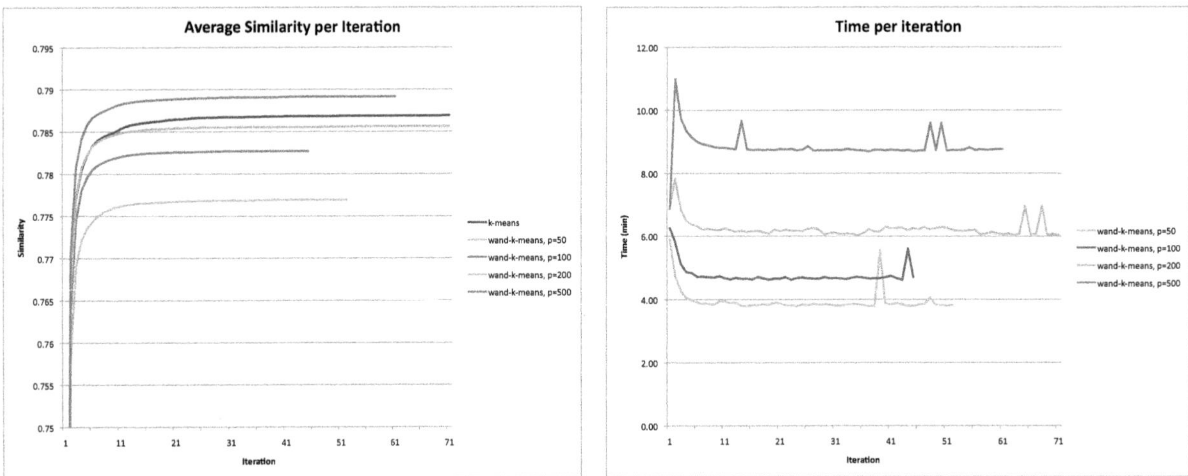


(a) (b)

**Figure 2: Evaluation of `wand-k-means` on Dataset 1 as a function of different values of $p$: (a) The average point to centroid similarity at each iteration (b) The running time per iteration. Note that we de not display the running time of `k-means` in part (b) since it is over 50 times slower.**

the similarity for those documents that are assigned to some cluster at each iteration.) Note that we removed the running time of `k-means` from Figure 2(b) since it is almost two orders of magnitude worse than all of the other methods.

## 4.4 Number of Clusters

Next we investigate the performance of the algorithm as we increase the number of clusters, $k$ beyond to 3,000 and 6,000.

| System | p | $\ell$ | Dataset 1 Similarity | Dataset 1 Time | $\ell$ | Dataset 2 Similarity | Dataset 2 Time |
|---|---|---|---|---|---|---|---|
| k-means | — | — | 0.7804 | 445.05 | — | 0.2858 | 705.21 |
| wand-k-means | — | 1 | 0.7813 | 61.17 | 10 | 0.2856 | 243.91 |
| wand-k-means | 500 | 1 | 0.7817 | 8.83 | 10 | 0.2704 | 4.00 |
| wand-k-means | 200 | 1 | 0.7814 | 6.18 | 10 | 0.2855 | 2.97 |
| wand-k-means | 100 | 1 | 0.7814 | 4.72 | 10 | 0.2853 | 1.94 |
| wand-k-means | 50 | 1 | 0.7803 | 3.90 | 10 | 0.2844 | 1.39 |

**Table 3: Average point to centroid similarity and iteration time (minutes) at iteration 13 as a function of $p$ .**

We observe the same qualitative behavior: the average similarity of `wand-k-means` is indistinguishable from `k-means`, while the running time is faster by an order of magnitude.

## 5. RELATED WORK

**Clustering.** The `k-means` clustering algorithm remains a very popular method of clustering over 50 years after its initial introduction by Lloyd [24]. Its popularity is partly due to the simplicity of the algorithm and its effectiveness in practice. Although it can take an exponential number of steps to converge to a local optimum [34], in all practical situations it converges after 20-50 iterations (a fact confirmed by the experiments in Section 4). The latter has been partially explained using smoothed analysis [3, 5] to show that worst case instances are unlikely to happen.

Although simple, the algorithm has a running time of $O(nkd)$ per iteration, which can become large as either the number of points, clusters, or the dimensionality of the dataset increases. The running time is dominated by the computation of the nearest cluster center to every point, a process taking $O(kd)$ time per point. Previous work, [14, 20] used the fact that both points and clusters lie in a metric space to reduce the number of such computations. Other authors [28, 29] showed how to use kd-trees and other data structures to greatly speed up the algorithm in low dimensional situations.

Since the difficulty lies in finding the nearest cluster for each of the data points, we can instead look for nearest neighbor search methods. The question of finding a nearest neighbor has a long and storied history. Recently, locality sensitive hashing, LSH [2] has gained in popularity. For the specific case of document retrieval, inverted indices [6] are the state of the art. We note that a straightforward application of both of these approaches would require rebuilding the data structure and querying it $n$ times during every iteration, thereby negating most, if not all, of the savings over a straightforward naive implementation.

The well known data deluge lead several groups of researchers to investigate the `k-means` algorithm in the regime when the number of points, $n$ is very large. Guha et al. [17] show how to solve $k$-clustering problems in a data stream setting where points arrive incrementally one at a time. Their analysis for the related k-median problem was further refined and improved by [13, 25] and most recently by [10, 31]. However, all of these methods scale poorly with $k$, which is the problem we tackle in this work.

As parallel algorithms have reemerged in their popularity these methods were adapted to speeding up `k-means` as well, [1, 7]. In fact the `k-means` method is implemented in Mahout [16], a popular machine learning package for MapReduce. The all point similarity algorithm proposed in [8] also uses indexing but focuses on savings achieved by avoiding the full index construction, rather than repeatedly using the same index in multiple iterations.

Yet another approach has been suggested by Sculley [30], who showed how to use a sample of the data to improve the performance of the `k-means` algorithm. Similar approaches were previously used by Jin et al. [19]. Unfortunately this, and other subsampling methods break down when the average number of points per cluster is small, requiring large sample sizes to ensure that no clusters are missed. Finally our approach is related to subspace clustering [27] where the data is clustered on a subspace of the dimensions with a goal to shed noisy or unimportant dimensions. In our approach we perform the dimension selection based on the centroids and in an adaptive manner, while executing the clustering approach. In our current work we are exploring more the relationship between our approach and some of the reported subspace clustering approaches.

**Indexing.** A recent survey and a comparative study of in-memory Term at a time (TAAT) and document at a time (DAAT) algorithms was reported in [15]. A large study of known TAAT and DAAT algorithms was conducted by [22] on the Terrier IR platform with disk-based postings lists using TREC collections They found that in terms of the number of scoring computations, the Moffat TAAT algorithm [26] had the best performance, though it came at a tradeoff of loss of precision compared to naive TAAT approaches and the TAAT and DAAT *MAXSCORE* algorithms [33]. In this paper we did not evaluate approximate algorithms such as Moffat TAAT [26]. We leave this study as future work. Finally, a memory-efficient TAAT query evaluation algorithm was proposed in [23].

## 6. CONCLUSION

In this work we showed that using centroids as queries into a nearest neighbor data structure built on the data points can be very effective in reducing the number of distance computations needed by the `k-means` clustering method. Additionally, we showed that using the full information from the WAND algorithm, and sparsifying the centroids further improves performance. Our experimental evaluation over two real world data sets shows that the approach proposed in this paper is viable in practice, with up to a 20x reduction in the computation time, especially for large values of $k$.

## 7. REFERENCES


[1] N. Ailon, R. Jaiswal, and C. Monteleoni. Streaming k-means approximation. In Y. Bengio, D. Schuurmans,

J. Lafferty, C. K. I. Williams, and A. Culotta, editors, *NIPS 22*. 2009.

[2] A. Andoni and P. Indyk. Near-optimal hashing algorithms for approximate nearest neighbor in high dimensions. *Commun. ACM*, 51(1):117–122, Jan. 2008.

[3] D. Arthur, B. Manthey, and H. Röglin. Smoothed analysis of the k-means method. *J. ACM*, 58(5):19, 2011.

[4] D. Arthur and S. Vassilvitskii. How slow is the *k*-means method? In *Symposium on Computational Geometry*, 2006.

[5] D. Arthur and S. Vassilvitskii. K-means++: the advantages of careful seeding. In N. Bansal, K. Pruhs, and C. Stein, editors, *SODA*. SIAM, 2007.

[6] R. A. Baeza-Yates and B. Ribeiro-Neto. *Modern Information Retrieval*. Addison-Wesley Longman Publishing Co., Inc., Boston, MA, USA, 1999.

[7] B. Bahmani, B. Moseley, A. Vattani, R. Kumar, and S. Vassilvitskii. Scalable k-means++. *PVLDB*, 5(7):622–633, 2012.

[8] R. J. Bayardo, Y. Ma, and R. Srikant. Scaling up all pairs similarity search. In *Proceedings of the 16th international conference on World Wide Web*, WWW '07, 2007.

[9] R. E. Bellman. *Dynamic Programming*. Princeton University Press, Princeton, NJ, USA, 1957.

[10] V. Braverman, A. Meyerson, R. Ostrovsky, A. Roytman, M. Shindler, and B. Tagiku. Streaming k-means on well-clusterable data. In *Proceedings of the Twenty-Second Annual ACM-SIAM Symposium on Discrete Algorithms*, SODA '11, pages 26–40. SIAM, 2011.

[11] A. Broder, M. Fontoura, E. Gabrilovich, A. Joshi, V. Josifovski, and T. Zhang. Robust classification of rare queries using web knowledge. In *SIGIR'07*, 2007.

[12] A. Z. Broder, D. Carmel, M. Herscovici, A. Soffer, and J. Y. Zien. Efficient query evaluation using a two-level retrieval process. In *CIKM*, 2003.

[13] M. Charikar, L. O'Callaghan, and R. Panigrahy. Better streaming algorithms for clustering problems. In L. L. Larmore and M. X. Goemans, editors, *STOC*. ACM, 2003.

[14] C. Elkan. Using the triangle inequality to accelerate k-means. In *ICML*, pages 147–153, 2003.

[15] M. Fontoura, V. Josifovski, J. Liu, S. Venkatesan, X. Zhu, and J. Y. Zien. Evaluation strategies for top-k queries over memory-resident inverted indexes. *PVLDB*, 4(11), 2011.

[16] A. S. Foundation, I. Drost, T. Dunning, J. Eastman, O. Gospodnetic, G. Ingersoll, J. Mannix, S. Owen, and K. Wettin. Apache mahout, 2010. `http://mloss.org/software/view/144/`.

[17] S. Guha, N. Mishra, R. Motwani, and L. O'Callaghan. Clustering data streams. In *FOCS*, 2000.

[18] V. Hautamäki, S. Cherednichenko, I. Kärkkäinen, T. Kinnunen, and P. Fränti. Improving k-means by outlier removal. In *SCIA*, 2005.

[19] R. Jin, A. Goswami, and G. Agrawal. Fast and exact out-of-core and distributed k-means clustering. *Knowl. Inf. Syst.*, 10(1):17–40, July 2006.

[20] T. Kanungo, D. M. Mount, N. S. Netanyahu, C. D. Piatko, R. Silverman, and A. Y. Wu. An efficient k-means clustering algorithm: Analysis and implementation. *IEEE Trans. Pattern Anal. Mach. Intell.*, 24(7), 2002.

[21] T. Kanungo, D. M. Mount, N. S. Netanyahu, C. D. Piatko, R. Silverman, and A. Y. Wu. A local search approximation algorithm for k-means clustering. *Comput. Geom.*, 28(2-3), 2004.

[22] P. Lacour, C. Macdonald, and I. Ounis. Efficiency comparison of document matching techniques. In *Efficiency Issues in Information Retrieval Workshop; European Conference for Information Retrieval*, 2008.

[23] N. Lester, A. Moffat, W. Webber, and J. Zobel. Space-limited ranked query evaluation using adaptive pruning. In *WISE*, 2005.

[24] S. P. Lloyd. Least squares quantization in pcm. *IEEE Transactions on Information Theory*, 28, 1982.

[25] A. Meyerson. Online facility location. In *FOCS*, 2001.

[26] A. Moffat and J. Zobel. Self-indexing inverted files for fast text retrieval. *ACM Transactions on Information Systems*, 14(4), 1996.

[27] L. Parsons, E. Haque, and H. Liu. Subspace clustering for high dimensional data: a review. *SIGKDD Explor.*, 6(1), 2004.

[28] D. Pelleg and A. Moore. Accelerating exact k-means algorithms with geometric reasoning. In *Proceedings of the fifth ACM SIGKDD international conference on Knowledge discovery and data mining*, KDD '99, pages 277–281, New York, NY, USA, 1999. ACM.

[29] D. Pelleg and A. Moore. X-means: Extending k-means with efficient estimation of the number of clusters. In *In Proceedings of the 17th International Conf. on Machine Learning*, pages 727–734. Morgan Kaufmann, 2000.

[30] D. Sculley. Web-scale k-means clustering. In *WWW*, 2010.

[31] M. Shindler, A. Wong, and A. W. Meyerson. Fast and accurate k-means for large datasets. In J. Shawe-Taylor, R. Zemel, P. Bartlett, F. Pereira, and K. Weinberger, editors, *Advances in Neural Information Processing Systems 24*, pages 2375–2383. 2011.

[32] A. Strehl, J. Ghosh, and R. J. Mooney. Impact of similarity measures on web-page clustering. In *Proc. AAAI Workshop on AI for Web Search (AAAI 2000), Austin*, pages 58–64. AAAI/MIT Press, July 2000.

[33] H. R. Turtle and J. Flood. Query evaluation: Strategies and optimizations. *Information Processing and Management*, 31(6), 1995.

[34] A. Vattani. *k*-means requires exponentially many iterations even in the plane. *Discrete & Computational Geometry*, 45(4):596–616, 2011.

[35] J. Zobel and A. Moffat. Inverted files for text search engines. *ACM Computing Surveys*, 38(2), 2006.

# Taxonomy Discovery for Personalized Recommendation

Yuchen Zhang
UC Berkeley
Berkeley, CA, USA
yuczhang@berkeley.edu

Amr Ahmed, Vanja Josifovski
Google Inc
Mountain View, CA, USA
{amra,vanjaj}@google.com

Alexander Smola
Carnegie Mellon University
Pittsburgh, PA, USA
alex@smola.org

## ABSTRACT

Personalized recommender systems based on latent factor models are widely used to increase sales in e-commerce. Such systems use the past behavior of users to recommend new items that are likely to be of interest to them. However, latent factor model suffer from sparse user-item interaction in online shopping data: for a large portion of items that do not have sufficient purchase records, their latent factors cannot be estimated accurately.

In this paper, we propose a novel approach that automatically discovers the taxonomies from online shopping data and jointly learns a taxonomy-based recommendation system. Out model is non-parametric and can learn the taxonomy structure automatically from the data. Since the taxonomy allows purchase data to be shared between items, it effectively improves the accuracy of recommending tail items by sharing strength with the more frequent items. Experiments on a large-scale online shopping dataset confirm that our proposed model improves significantly over state-of-the-art latent factor models. Moreover, our model generates high-quality and human readable taxonomies. Finally, using the algorithm-generated taxonomy, our model even outperforms latent factor models based on the human-induced taxonomy, thus alleviating the need for costly manual taxonomy generation.

## Categories and Subject Descriptors

H.1 [**Information Systems**]: Models and Principles; G.3 [**Mathematics of Computing**]: Probability and Statistics

## General Terms

Algorithms, Theory, Experimentation

## Keywords

Recommender System, Latent Factor Model, Taxonomy


*WSDM'14,* February 24–28, 2014, New York, New York, USA.
ACM 978-1-4503-2351-2/14/02.
http://dx.doi.org/10.1145/2556195.2556236.

## 1. INTRODUCTION

Personalized recommender systems are used widely to increase sales and customer satisfaction in e-commerce. These systems use past behavior of users to recommend new items that are likely to be of interest to them. One of the most extensively studied techniques are latent factor models and related variants [1, 8, 9, 10]. These models project users and items into a lower-dimensional space of latent factors. Then, the similarity between a particular user and an item is computed via the inner product of their latent factors and the most similar items are recommended to the user.

Despite substantial success in the Netflix contest [3, 8], in tag recommendation [15] and other applications, the latent factor model approach encounters specific challenges in product recommendation for online shopping: on a typical retail website we observe a long tail effect both in terms of users and in terms of items. This means that not only most users only buy a small number of items, but also that the majority of items are only infrequently purchased. On our data users typically purchase 2.4 items and 85% of the items are purchased by less than 10 users. This sparsity of user-item interactions makes it difficult to learn latent factors.

In order to resolve the sparsity problem in online shopping, Kanagal et al. [7] use a human-induced taxonomy that attaches every item to a node in the category tree. Their proposed taxonomy-aware latent factor model assumes that the latent factor associated with each tree node is sampled from its parent node, thus generalizing the purchase data from an individual item to items belonging to the same category. Experimental studies show that this significantly improves the performance for online shopping data. Other related work includes Mnih et al. [12] and Menon et al. [11] who use the taxonomy to measure biases in music recommendation, and earlier works by Ziegler et al. [17] and Weng et al. [16] who incorporates the taxonomy in alternative recommender systems besides latent factor models.

Unlike previous work that requires an existing taxonomy, we propose in this paper a novel approach that automatically discovers the taxonomy from online shopping data and jointly learns a taxonomy-based recommendation system from raw data. This has several benefits:

1. Many online shopping datasets don't have an associated human-induced taxonomy since it may be too expensive to create a hand-crafted taxonomy and attach every item to the category. In contrast, for our algorithm it is sufficient to obtain the textual description text of items (whenever available) and purchase records. Both sources are much easier to collect.

2. Human-created taxonomies are static and they do not evolve with a change in user demographics or product inventory. Our method adaptively handles incremental data. This makes it capable of dynamically updating the tree structure.
3. Human labelings are noisy and not optimized for learning latent factor models. For example, in our reference taxonomy, video game software and video game consoles are categorized into two different top-level departments: "Software" and "Electronics". In reality, they are usually bought together and thus have similar latent factors. Our method combines categorization with latent factor optimization so that items having similar latent factors tend to have common ancestors in the tree, which allow them to share purchase data.

We use a nonparametric generative procedure which we refer to as a hierarchical latent factor model (HF Model). It generates a tree structure for categories and items by means of a nested Chinese Restaurant Process (nCRP) [4]. Then, the item's descriptions are generated via a language model and the user purchase data is generated by a latent factor model. We propose an inference algorithm to jointly optimize the tree structure and the latent factors. Thereby the HF model constructs a taxonomy that depends on both the item's description and on the user's purchase data.

Recent work of Mnih et al. [13] clusters items a binary tree by their latent factors in order to reduce the computation complexity of inference. Agarwal et al. [1] propose a regression-based latent factor model that uses meta-information to help tail items. We found that building a dynamic taxonomy based on both descriptions and purchase data performs considerably better than these models.

We report comprehensive experiments that compare the HF model with state-of-the-art latent factor models on a large-scale online shopping dataset. There the HF model significantly improves on existing models. We also compare the HF model to the latent factor model that relies on human-induced taxonomy. We find that although the HF model requires no human effort, it outperforms the human dependent model. An extensive study shows that the HF model generates high-quality and human-readable taxonomies.

The rest of this paper is organized as follow. In Section 2, we describe related works and baseline models. In Section 3, we define the hierarchical latent factor model with its learning algorithm described in Section 4. In Section 5, we present experiments that compare the HF model with state-of-the-art latent factor models. In Section 6, we illustrate how the HF model interacts with human-induced taxonomy, and conduct empirical studies to illustrate its advantage over methods that directly use the human-induced taxonomy as a priori.

## 2. RELATED WORKS

We give a brief overview of four state-of-the-art latent factor models for personalized recommendation, since we will compare their performance to the HF model empirically.

### 2.1 Latent Factor Models

A latent matrix factorization model (MF) assumes that there is a factor associated with each user and each item. We denote the factor for user $u$ and item $i$ by $v_u, v_i \in R^d$ respectively. Each item is associated with a bias term $b_i$ that models the relative popularity of the item (we need no such bias for users since we recommend items to users rather than the converse). The model defines an affinity score $x_{ui}$ between user $u$ and item $i$ by an inner product, that is:

$$x_{ui} = \langle v_u, v_i \rangle + b_i.$$

When the observed user-item interaction is in the form of an implicit feedback where we only have access to positive interactions between users and items, we adopt the Bayesian Personalized Ranking (BPR) criterion as described in [14]. BPR adopts a preference ranking approach by ranking items that the user liked (or bought) higher than items that the user did not interact with. For items $i$ and $j$ we denote by $R_{uij}$ the event of user $u$ preferring $i$ to $j$. In this case

$$P(R_{uij}|v_u, v_i, v_j) = \sigma(x_{ui} - x_{uj}) \text{ with } \sigma(x) = \frac{1}{1+e^{-x}}.$$

We denote the set of model parameters (item and user factors, biases) by $\Theta$ and we summarize the pairwise relations by $R$. Based on the above model the likelihood of the dataset factorizes via

$$P(R|\Theta) = \prod_{u \in U} \prod_{i \in B_u} \prod_{j \notin B_u} P(R_{uij}|v_u, v_i, v_j).$$

Here $U$ is the set of all users and $B_u$ is the set of items that user $u$ purchases. If we further assume that every entry in $\Theta$ is independently sampled from a normal distribution $\mathcal{N}(0, 1/\lambda)$, then the log-posterior distribution of parameters given the data is represented by

$$\log P(\Theta|R) = \sum_{u \in U} \sum_{i \in B_u} \sum_{j \notin B_u} \log \sigma(x_{ui} - x_{uj}) - \lambda \|\Theta\|_2^2. \quad (1)$$

The Bayesian Personalized Ranking (BPR) method estimates $\Theta$ by minimizing the negative log posterior (1) via stochastic gradient descent (SGD). For each iteration, a user $u$, a purchased item $i$ and an unpurchased item $j$ are sampled. The gradient of the associated log-posterior contribution is calculated and the parameters are updated via SGD.

### 2.2 Collaborative Item Selection Model

The collaborative item selection model (CIS) [13] organizes items in a binary tree, where the leaf nodes represent items and the internal nodes represent intermediate categories. Let $n$ be a node of the tree and $C(n)$ be the set of its children. The CIS model assumes that for user $u$, the probability of moving from node $n_p$ to node $n_c$ on a root-to-leaf tree traversal is given by

$$P(n_c|n_p, u) = \frac{\exp(U_u^\top Q_{n_c} + b_{n_c})}{\sum_{m \in C(n_p)} \exp(U_u^\top Q_m + b_m)} \text{ if } n_c \in C(n_p).$$

Here $Q_n$ and $b_n$ are factors and biases of node $n$, and $U_u$ is the factor vector of user $u$. The probability of selecting item $i$ is then given by the product of the probabilities of the decisions leading from the root to the leaf containing $i$:

$$P(i|u) = \prod_{j=1}^{L_i} P(n_j^i | n_{j-1}^i, u).$$

Here $n_j^i$ represents the $j$-th node in the path from the root to item $i$. Given a tree over items, the CIS model can be trained using stochastic gradient ascent in log-likelihood, updating parameters after each user/item pair. Mnih et al. [13] also propose an approximate algorithm to learn the structure of the tree. Their approach assumes that the latent factors are known. It then learns individual levels of the tree iteratively from top to bottom by maximizing log-likelihood. The model is trained in a three-stage procedure. First, we train a CIS model based on a random balanced binary tree, then extract the user vectors learned by the model and use them to learn a better tree from the data. Finally, we train a CIS model based on the learned tree, updating all the parameters, including the user vectors.

## 2.3 Regression-based Latent Factor Model

The regression-based latent factor model (RLFM) [1] maps features of items and users into a lower dimensional factor space and then defines the affinity between users and items using these latent factors. Concretely, let $v_{uj}$, $w_u$ and $z_i$ be dyadic, user and item feature vectors, then the affinity score $x_{ui}$ is given by

$$x_{ui} = b^\top v_{ui} + w_u^\top g + d^\top z_i + w_u^\top G^\top D z_i$$

where the parameters of the model are the vectors $b, g$ and $d$, and matrices $G$ and $D$. Given affinity scores, [1] defined a set of response functions to model the observed data and learn the model parameters by maximizing the log-likelihood of the observed data. However since in our problem we are only given implicit feedback, i.e. only positive interaction, we adopt the BPR objective function as in Section 2.1 in training the RLFM. For simplicity of notation we will refer to this BPR-modified variant as RLFM throughout the paper, since all models except CIS are trained using the BPR objective. We learn the RLFM model parameters by maximizing log-likelihood through stochastic gradient ascent. Note that within feature vectors $w_u$ and $z_i$, we always include the unique IDs of the user and the item. If there are other meta-information associated with either user or item, we concatenate them to the feature vector.

## 2.4 Taxonomy-aware Latent Factor Model

To address prediction accuracy issues related to cold-start for new items and the problem of sparsity, taxonomy-based models were proposed. The main idea is to utilize the categorical information in a human-induced taxonomy to share statistical strength between frequently purchased items and tail items.

In the taxonomy-aware latent factor model (TF) [7], a latent variable is associated with each user $u$, each item $i$, and each category $k$. Specifically, we use $w_u$, $w_i$ and $w_k$ to represent the corresponding factors. Given an item or a category $i$, let $\pi(i)$ indicate the parent of $i$ in the taxonomy tree. Then, the latent factor for item $i$ is defined recursively

$$v_i = \begin{cases} w_i & i \text{ is the root.} \\ w_i + v_{\pi(i)} & \text{otherwise.} \end{cases}$$

In other words, the effective factor associated with node $i$ is the sum of all latent factors associated with nodes along the path from (and including) $i$ to the root. The affinity score between user $u$ and node $i$ is consequently defined by:

$$x_{ui} = \langle w_u, v_i \rangle + b_i.$$

As above, the BPR objective is used for model estimation.

**Table 1: Notation used for the HF model.**

| | |
|---|---|
| $u$ | User |
| $i, j$ | Item |
| $v_u, v_i$ | Latent factor for user $u$ or items $i$ |
| $x_{ui}$ | Affinity score between user $i$ and item $i$ |
| $y, z$ | Internal nodes of the categorization tree |
| $\pi(z)$ | Parent of node $z$ |
| $C(y)$ | Children of node $z$ |
| $\phi_z, \varphi_z$ | Multinomial distribution associated with $z$ |
| $n_z$ | Number of items belonging to category $z$ |
| $\alpha$ | Chinese Restaurant Process parameter |
| $\beta, \eta$ | Dirichlet distribution parameter |
| $D_i, A_i$ | Description of item $i$ (a set of terms) |
| $t, a$ | Term in the description |
| $q_i$ | Popularity measure of item $i$ |
| $\sigma^2, \tau^2$ | Variance for generating latent variables. |

# 3. HIERARCHICAL LATENT FACTOR MODEL

Our goal in designing a hierarchical latent factor model (HF) is to automatically generate a hierarchical categorization for all items based on their descriptions and their purchase data, so that we can learn the item/user latent factors jointly. Our model has the following features:

- It arranges the items in a taxonomy with infinite (adaptive) depth and width using a non-parametric prior [2].
- In addition to purchase data it can use side-information such as item descriptions to infer the taxonomy.
- It smoothes the model parameters over the induced taxonomy and as such combats data sparsity.
- It can utilize a partial (or full) human-induced taxonomy when available (we defer details to section 6).

Table (1) summarizes the notation used in the paper.

## 3.1 Taxonomy Generation

We now describe a non-parametric prior over trees with infinite depth and width. This is similar to the nested Chinese restaurant process in [2, 4]. In a nutshell, to organize items in a tree, one needs to generate a path for each item over the tree. A path can be conceptually viewed as a *nested* set of decisions. Starting from the root, a child is selected and the process continues until a termination condition is satisfied. These choices can be modeled using a Chinese Restaurant Process (CRP) where at each node the probability of selecting a child is proportional to the child's frequency.

Consider an arbitrary item $i$ that we want to attach to the category tree. For this to happen we generate a path in the tree from the root to the leaf node that represents $i$. Starting from node $v$, the probability of selecting an existing (or new) child is

$$P(y \to z) = \begin{cases} \frac{n_z}{n_y+\alpha} & \text{if } z \in C(y) \\ \frac{\alpha}{n_y+\alpha} & \text{for a new node} \end{cases} \quad (2)$$

Recall that $n_y$ is the number of items belongs to category $y$ and $n_z$ is the number of items that belongs to $z$. The parameter $\alpha$ controls the probability of creating a new child for $y$, i.e. the probability that the item belongs to a new category under $y$.

Once a child node is selected, the process is repeated until a full path is defined. To ensure finite paths we need to allow for the probability of termination at a vertex. Here, we define that the process terminates at category $z$ if $z$ is the first child of its parent. This strategy is in complete analogy to Ghahramani et al. [6] — we treat the probability of terminating at a vertex in complete analogy to that of generating a special child.

### 3.2 Parameter Cascade

The nCRP process gives a distribution over trees. However, we still need to assign parameters to each node in the tree and tie these parameters in a manner that is consistent with the semantic of the tree, i.e. nodes close in the tree should have similar parameters. We endow each internal node $z$ with two latent variables: a latent factor $v_z$ and a multinomial distribution over terms $\phi_z$. These parameters are cascaded over the tree as follows:

$$v_z \sim \begin{cases} \mathcal{N}(0, \sigma^2 \mathbf{1}) & w \text{ is the root node} \\ \mathcal{N}(v_{\pi(z)}, \sigma^2 \mathbf{1}) & \text{otherwise} \end{cases} \quad (3)$$

and the multinomial is sampled by a Dirichlet distribution:

$$\phi_z \sim \begin{cases} \text{Dir}(\beta) & z \text{ is the root node} \\ \text{Dir}(\eta\phi_{\pi(z)}) & \text{otherwise} \end{cases} \quad (4)$$

### 3.3 Generating item data

After we generate the tree with its associated parameters, we need to generate data associated with item $i$: an item description, an item latent factor and item bias. Item latent factors are sampled from its parent's latent factors via

$$v_i \sim \mathcal{N}(v_{\pi(i)}, \sigma^2 \mathbf{1}).$$

We generate the item description according to the multinomial distribution associated with its parent. In particular, for each term $t$ in the description of item $i$, it is sampled by a multinomial distribution:

$$t \sim \text{Mult}(\phi_{\pi(i)}). \quad (5)$$

Every item also maintains a popularity measure $q_i$. A high $q_i$ indicates that the item attracts customer regardless of the customer's latent factor. The popularity measure is generated by a normal distribution

$$q_i \sim \mathcal{N}(0, \tau^2). \quad (6)$$

The generative procedure for items and categories is complete by combining (2)-(6) appropriately.

### 3.4 Generating User Purchase Preferences

Given items and their features obtained in Section 3.3, we can then generate the purchase preference $R_{uij}$ for any particular user $u$ and item pairs $i, j$ via the BPR model. For an arbitrary item $i$, we define the affinity score between $u$ and $i$ to be

$$x_{ui} = \langle v_u, v_i \rangle + [q_i]^+$$

Here, $v_u$ and $v_i$ are user and item latent factors, $q_i$ is the popularity measure that we define in Section 3.3. The notation $[q_i]^+ = \max(q_i, 0)$ indicates that we force the contribution from the popularity measure to be non-negative. We impose this constraint because $[q_i]^+$ behaves like a bias term in the latent factor model. Consequently, its value is strongly correlated to the frequency that item $i$ is purchased in the user log data. Without the $[\cdot]^+$ operator, infrequently purchased items will always have negative biases, which makes

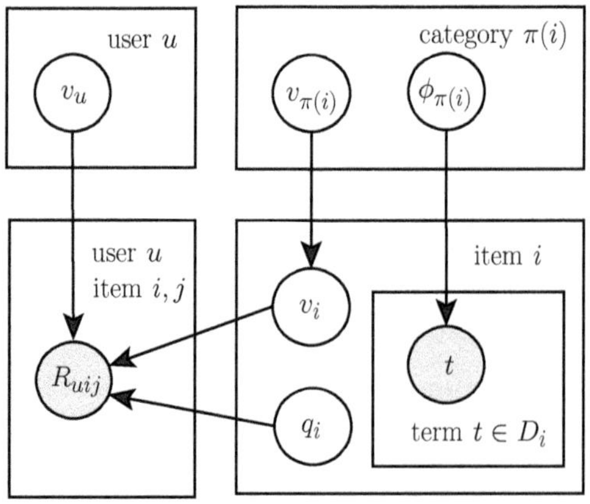


**Figure 1: Graphical model representation of the H-F model. White nodes represent random variables and shaded nodes represent observations. $R_{uij}$ is the event that user $u$ prefers item $i$ over item $j$. Large plates indicate parts of the graph that are repeated. Graphical model omits some dependencies to avoid cluttering the display. For example the hidden variable $\pi(i)$ is sampled from nCRP process. Moreover, dependencies between categories and subategories latent variables $\phi$ and $v$ are omitted for clarity. See Section 3 for a full description.**

them unlikely to be recommended to any customer. Since a large percentage of items are infrequent, this makes the personalized recommendation ineffective. By adopting the non-negative constraint on $q_i$, it promotes frequent items but does not penalize infrequent items. This allows the model to recommend tail items to specific groups of target customers as long as their latent factors match. This yields

$$R_{uij} \sim \text{Bernoulli}(\sigma(x_{ui} - x_{uj})).$$

An alternative means of deriving $R_{uij}$ is as follows: Given the affinity $x_{ui}$, the probability that $u$ selects $i$ is given by

$$P(i|u) = \frac{\exp(x_{ui})}{\sum_j \exp(x_{uj})}.$$

By this definition, for two items $i$ and $j$ available to $u$, the probability that the user chooses $i$ over $j$ is

$$P(i > j|u) = \frac{\exp(x_{ui})}{\exp(x_{ui}) + \exp(x_{uj})} = \sigma(x_{ui} - x_{uj}) \quad (7)$$

Note that the conditional probability (7) is consistent with the BPR optimization criterion [14]. Figure 1 shows a simplified summary of the HF model.

## 4. INFERENCE

We observe item descriptions and purchase data. The goal of learning is to infer the tree structure, category parameters and latent factors. We use a collapsed Gibbs sampler and we integrate out multinomial variables $\phi$ to improve mixing. Our goal is thus to infer the posterior $P(\Theta, T|D, R)$, where $T$ denotes the tree structure, $\Theta$ denotes the remaining latent variables (factors and biases for items and categories), $D$ denotes item description and $R$ purchase preferences. We alternate until convergence between two steps: sampling a path for each item over the tree and then optimizing the latent factors of items and categories while keeping the tree structure fixed. The following sections describe each step.

## 4.1 Sampling Hierarchical Categories

Sampling a tree structure $T$ amounts to sampling a path for each item $i$ over the tree. Collectively the set of item paths defines the tree. We denote by $p_i = (p_{i0}, p_{i1}, \cdots)$ the path of item $i$, where $p_{i0}$ is the root, $p_{i1}$ is a child of the root selected by item $i$, etc.; In general $p_{i,k} \in C(p_{i,k-1})$. If $l(p_i)$ denotes the length of the path, then $p_{i,l(p)}$ is the parent category of item $i$. The probability that the path is sampled is given by:

$$P(p_i|D_i, v_i, \text{rest}) = P(p_i|\text{rest})P(v_i, D_i|p_i, \text{rest}) \quad (8)$$

where rest denotes all other hidden variables. The first component defines the prior probability of the path, while the second component defines the likelihood of item description and latent variable given this path selection. The prior probability of a path $p_i$ is given by the nCRP process as follows $P(p_i|\text{rest}) = \prod_{k=0}^{l(p_i)-1} P(p_{i,k} \to p_{i,k+1})$, where each factor is determined by (2).

Unfortunately this is very costly, since the space of possible paths scales as $O(N)$, where $N$ is the number of nodes in the tree. Therefore we resort to a greedy approximation following [2] which works well in practice. In this approximation we use a level-wise strategy: assume that we are at level $k$ and that $p_{i,k} = y$, then we can descend the tree as follows:

1. Stay on the current node $y$ — i.e. pick child 0, and set $p_{i,k+1} = 0$.
2. Move to a child node $z$ of $y$ other than child 0, and set $p_{i,k+1} = z$.
3. Create a new child node of node $y$ and move to it, and set $p_{i,k+1}$ accordingly.

The probability of each choice shares a similar form:

$$P(p_{i,k+1} = z|p_{i,k} = y, \text{rest})P(D_i, v_i|p_{i,k+1} = z, \text{rest}) \quad (9)$$

Here the first probability is

$$P(p_{i,k+1} = z|p_{i,k} = y, \text{rest}) = P(y \to z) \quad (10)$$

as defined in (2).

The second term is essentially the probability of the item data given a choice of the parent $z$ under consideration in the path which can be decomposed into two components: the probability of the item description $P(D_i \,|\, p_{i,k+1} = z, \text{rest})$ , and the probability of the item factor given its parent's factor $P(v_i \,|\, p_{i,k+1} = z, \text{rest})$. The latter probability is simply normally distributed:

$$P(v_i \,|\, p_{i,k+1} = z, \text{rest}) = \mathcal{N}(v_z, \sigma) \quad (11)$$

Since we integrated out the multinomial distributions $\phi$, computing $P(D_i \,|\, p_{i,k+1} = z, \text{rest})$ amounts to a standard Dirichlet-multinomial integration, that is:

$$P(D_i \,|\, p_{i,k+1} = z, \text{rest}) = \prod_{t \in D_i} \frac{\overline{m}_{z,t}^{-i}}{\overline{m}_z^{-i}}. \quad (12)$$

where the notation $\overline{m}_{z,t}^{-i}$ indicates the *regularized* occurrence of term $t$ in the item descriptions under category $z$ (excluding item $i$). In particular, we have

$$\overline{m}_{z,t}^{-i} = \begin{cases} m_{z,t}^{-i} + \beta & v \text{ is the root node.} \\ m_{z,t}^{-i} + \eta \cdot m_{y,t} & \text{otherwise} \end{cases} \quad (13)$$

where $m_{z,t}^{-i}$ is the exact occurrence of term $t$ under category $z$ (excluding item $i$). The two coefficients $\beta$ and $\eta$ are defined in equation (4). The quantity $\overline{m}_z^{-i}$ represents the sum of $\overline{m}_{z,t}^{-i}$ over all possible term $t$, which serves as a normalizer in equality (12). Similarly, if $z$ is a new node, then

$$P(D_i \,|\, p_{i,k+1} = z, \text{rest}) = \begin{cases} \prod_{t \in D_i} \frac{\eta+1}{|V|+|D_i|} & y \text{ is the root node.} \\ \prod_{t \in D_i} \frac{\eta \cdot m_{y,t}+1}{\eta \cdot m_y + |D_i|} & \text{otherwise} \end{cases} \quad (14)$$

where $V$ is the vocabulary that contains all possible terms.

The complexity of this sampling procedure is $O(LC)$ for each item, where $L$ is the depth of the tree and $C$ is the average number of children per node. Comparing to the naive implementation, the approximate sampling procedure is exponentially faster for a balanced tree.

## 4.2 Estimating Model Parameters

Given the tree structure, we estimate the latent factors and the popularity measures for categories and items. The parameter estimation model is based on BPR and the optimization is implemented via stochastic gradient ascent.

At each iteration, we sample a user $u$, a purchased item $i$ and an unpurchased item $j$. Suppose that $i_0 \to i_1 \to \cdots i_{L_i} = i$ represents the path from the root node to $i$. We define the same notation for item $j$. Given the conditional probability (7), the log-posterior of the observation that user $u$ prefers item $i$ over item $j$ is given by

$$L_{uij} = \log\sigma(x_{ui} - x_{uj}) - \sum_{k=0}^{L_i-1} \frac{\|v_{i_k} - v_{i_{k+1}}\|^2}{2\sigma^2} - \frac{q_i^2}{2\tau^2} - \sum_{k=1}^{L_j} \frac{\|v_{j_k} - v_{j_{k-1}}\|^2}{2\sigma^2} - \frac{q_j^2}{2\tau^2},$$

We update the parameters in this local objective function by stochastic gradient ascent. The first step is to compute the local derivatives. Let $c_{uij}$ denote the quantity $1-\sigma(x_{ui}-x_{uj})$. Then we find that

$$\frac{\partial L_{uij}}{\partial v_u} = c_{uij}(v_i - v_j) - \frac{v_u}{\sigma^2}. \quad (15)$$

For latent factors, we update the difference between every latent factor $v_{i_k}$ to its parent $v_{i_{k-1}}$. Then all latent factors are implicitly updated once their differences to the parent are updated. Let $w_{i_k} = v_{i_k} - v_{i_{k-1}}$ be such a shorthand notation, then we have

$$\frac{\partial L_{uij}}{\partial w_{i_k}} = c_{uij} v_u - \frac{v_{i_k}}{\sigma^2} \quad k = 1, \ldots, L_i; \quad (16)$$

$$\frac{\partial L_{uij}}{\partial w_{j_k}} = -c_{uij} v_u - \frac{v_{j_k}}{\sigma^2} \quad k = 1, \ldots, L_j. \quad (17)$$

For popularity measures $q_i$ and $q_j$, since they are part of a non-smooth operator $[\cdot]^+$, we first approximate the operator by a differentiable function

$$g(x) = \delta\log(1 + \exp(x/\delta))$$

**Table 2: Metadata used in experiments.**

| | |
|---|---|
| description | Description of the item (string) |
| brand | Brand of the item (string) |
| price | Discretized price of the item |

for some small constant $\delta$ and then compute the partial derivatives by

$$\frac{\partial L_{uij}}{\partial q_i} = \frac{c_{uij} e^{q_i/\delta}}{1 + e^{q_i/\delta}} - \frac{q_i}{\tau^2}, \quad (18)$$

$$\frac{\partial L_{uij}}{\partial q_j} = -\frac{c_{uij} e^{q_j/\delta}}{1 + e^{q_j/\delta}} - \frac{q_j}{\tau^2}. \quad (19)$$

According to equations (15)-(19), we update the parameters $\theta \in \{v_u, w_{i_k}, w_{j_k}, q_i, q_j\}$ via stochastic gradient ascent:

$$\theta \leftarrow \theta + \epsilon \frac{\partial L_{uij}}{\partial \theta}. \quad (20)$$

where $\epsilon$ is the stepsize. The update terminates when all parameters of the model converge.

# 5. EXPERIMENTS

In this section, we present experimental evaluations for the hierarchical latent factor model. We compare the HF model with three state-of-the-art latent factor models: the classical latent factor model (MF), the collaborative item selection model (CIS) and the regression-based latent factor model (RLFM).

## 5.1 Dataset

We used a log of user online transactions obtained from a major search engine, email provider and online shopping site. The dataset contains information about the historical purchases of users over a period of 3 months. We fully anonymize the users by dropping the original user identifier and assigning a new, sequential numbering of the records. As a result, we have about 14 million anonymized users with an average of 2.4 purchases per user and 3.28 million individual products.

We also group items with respect to their frequencies (number of purchases in the log data) and summarize the result in Figure 2. As Figure 2(a) shows, the majority of all items have frequency of at most 10. However, as Figure 2(b) shows, a majority of all purchases occur with high-frequency items (item of frequency greater than 100). In other words, most of the items in the dataset don't have sufficient purchases for estimating their parameters. This unbalanced distribution of data characterizes the challenge of our task.

We partition the purchase history of each user into two parts: training and testing. The first part contains 1/2 of the purchased items and the second part contains the remaining 1/2. Then, we take the first part as the training data and second part as the test data. In particular, if the user bought only one item, then we assign it to the training set. This results in about 18.6 million purchases for training and about 14.8 million purchases for testing.

If we examine the data distribution in Figure 2(a) and Figure 2(b), we find that purchases on the top 2% most frequent items actually occupy more than 60% of the overall purchases. This unbalanced data distribution makes the gap between different approaches small, because even for the simplest latent factor model (such as MF), as long as it achieves good performance on the top-frequency items, it achieves good overall performance. We construct a sparse data set that tests the models' capability of learning from all items. In particular, we remove those "trivial" users that only buy popular items and keep those "non-trivial" users that have bought at least one tail item (item with frequency $1-10$). As shown in Figure 2(c), it makes training and recommendation more challenging since infrequent items have more weight in the sparse dataset. By this construction, we obtain 3.5 million users and 12.4 million purchases. We employ the same strategy as in the previous paragraph to partition the training set and the test set which gives us 6.1 million purchases for training and 6.3 million purchases for testing. The sparse dataset contains about 37% users in the original full dataset.

In our implementation, every user and every item is represented by a unique id. The item id and user id are used by all models to construct latent factors. Besides using purchase data, we leverage three types of meta-information to help recommendation. These meta-information, which we summarize in Table 2, are used by the RLFM model and the HF model. In particular, the RLFM model uses all three types of meta-information. The HF model uses the item description information. Note that it is possible to modify the HF model's specification in Section 3 to allow it accepting brand and price features. We don't do it in this paper since we want the model specification to be concise as possible and only using the description information turns out to achieve good performance.

## 5.2 Implementation Details

We developed a multi-core implementation of all five models in C++. In latent factor models, we choose the factor dimensions $d \in \{10, 20, 40, 60, 80\}$ where $d = 20$ is the default setting. The latent factors are initialized by multivariate Gaussian $\mathcal{N}(0, 0.1 \times \mathbf{1})$. For stochastic gradient descent, we control the gradient stepsize using the adaptive gradient method [5]. For all experiments, we use regularization coefficients obtained by cross validation. The constant $\delta$ that approximates the operator $[\cdot]^+$ is set to be 0.2.

## 5.3 Evaluation

We use the AUC (Area under the ROC curve) metric to compare the performance of models. AUC is a widely used metric for testing recommender systems and latent factor models [14, 1, 7]. Let $X$ be the set of all products. Given a user $u$, we suppose that $r(u,i)$ is the numerical rank of item $i \in X$ provided by some model $\mathcal{M}$. Let $T_u$ be the set of items the user $u$ purchased in the test set, the formula to compute AUC is given by: (Here $\delta(x)$ is the indicator function that returns 1 if $x$ is true or 0 otherwise):

$$\text{AUC}_u = \frac{1}{|T_u||X \backslash T_u|} \sum_{i \in T_u,\ j \in I \backslash T_u} \delta(r(u,i) < r(u,j))$$

The AUC on the overall test set is the average individual user's AUC weighted by the size of their purchases, that is

$$\text{AUC} = \frac{\sum_u |T_u| \text{AUC}_u}{\sum_u |T_u|}$$

It is straightforward to see that AUC is a value in the range of $[0,1]$. A greater AUC indicates a better ranking quality provided by the model $\mathcal{M}$.

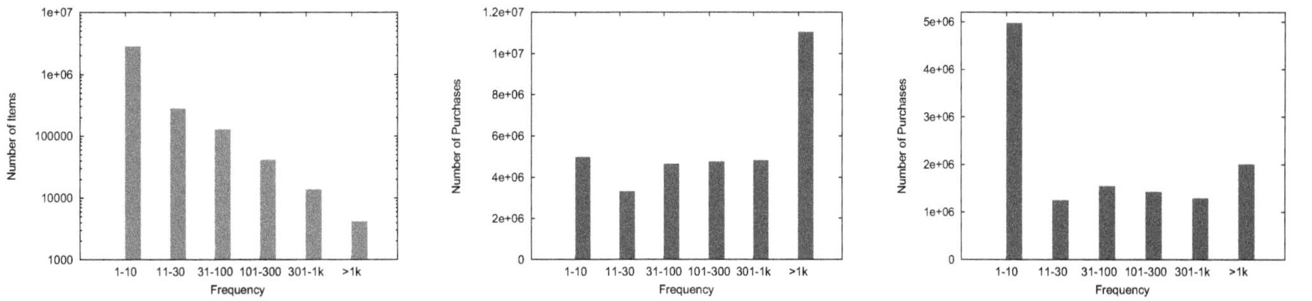


(a) Item distribution (b) Purchase distribution on full data (c) Purchase distribution on sparse data

**Figure 2: The figures show the distribution of items and purchases in the dataset. (a) Distribution of items in each frequency group. (b) Distribution of purchases in each frequency group. (c) Distribution of purchases in the sparse dataset. For the sparse dataset, we keep users that have bought at least one infrequent item.**

**Table 3: Comparing models on the full set with AUC metric. Bold numbers indicate the best performance and the star indicates statistical significance (p-value $< 0.01$).**

| Item Frequency | 1 - 10 | 11 - 30 | 31 - 100 | 101 - 300 | 301 - 1000 | > 1000 | Overall |
|---|---|---|---|---|---|---|---|
| MF | 0.453 | 0.878 | 0.961 | 0.987 | 0.996 | 0.9996 | 0.899 |
| CIS | 0.444 | 0.860 | 0.948 | 0.982 | 0.995 | 0.9996 | 0.893 |
| RLFM | 0.529 | 0.863 | 0.957 | 0.987 | 0.996 | 0.9995 | 0.908 |
| HF | **0.617*** | **0.891*** | **0.965*** | **0.989** | **0.997** | **0.9996** | **0.925*** |

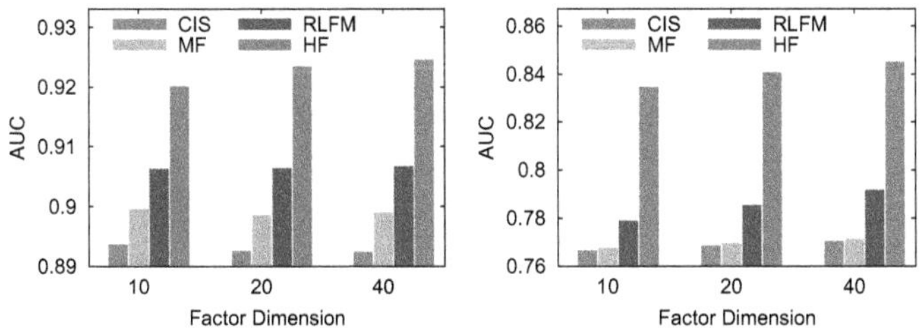


(a) On full data (b) On sparse data

**Figure 3: Comparing latent factor model performances with factor dimensions $d \in \{10, 20, 40, 60, 80\}$. The HF model outperforms the MF, CIS and RLFM models.**

## 5.4 Comparing Latent Factor Models

In this section, we compare the performance of latent factor models on full dataset and sparse dataset. The evaluation results are summarized in Figure 3(a) and Figure 3(b).

Among the four models, the MF model and the CIS model have similar performances, and the RLFM model is slightly better. The HF model yields significantly better performance than the three baseline methods. Note that the HF model uses only a subset of meta-information that is used by the RLFM model. It suggests that the hierarchical structure in the HF model organizes the meta-information in a more efficient way than in the RLFM model's regression approach.

In order to examine more carefully the evaluation results, we pay more attention to the setting of $d = 60$ (best results for most models) and we partition the test set into six frequency groups to evaluate performances on each individual group. The results are reported in Table 3 and Table 4. From these tables, we find that the biggest performance gaps are among the low-frequency groups. For items that have frequency of $1-10$, the RLFM model, which leverages meta-information, is better than the MF model and the CIS model that only use user purchase data. Furthermore, the HF model which maintain structural categorization of items is much better than the RLFM model. It confirms that hierarchical categorization is especially helpful to low-frequency items.

Finally, as plots and tables suggest, the HF model's improvement is more significant on the sparse dataset. One reason is that the sparse dataset is harder for training since the user-item interaction is insufficient. The HF model, which allows sharing purchase data among infrequent items under hierarchical categorization, is more robust to sparsity. This intuition is confirmed by Table 3 and Table 4's column for frequency $1-10$, where the performance gap between HF and RLFM is greater on the sparse data (12% for sparse data versus 9% for full data). On the other hand, the sparse dataset is also more challenging for testing since the low-frequency items occupy more weight as suggested by Figure 2(c). This makes the HF model's improvement over low-frequency items to be more noticeably reflected in the overall performance. As a comparison, the HF model is at least 1.7% better than the baseline models on the full dataset, and at least 5.1% better on the sparse dataset.

## 5.5 An Example of Algorithm-generated Taxonomy

In Figure 4, we present a portion of the hierarchical categories discovered by the HF model. Besides the top-ranked terms in each category, we also manually labeled the category names to make them more readable. As Figure 4 shows, the HF model is capable of constructing a high-quality hierarchical structure of categories. Categories in higher level represent broader concepts, and their sub-categories represents more refined range of products. For example, the taxonomy in Figure 4 clustered clothing items together, and refines the category by jeans, dresses and polos. It also divide the jeans category into two smaller sub-categories separating men's jeans and women's jeans, which is in analogy to the taxonomy that is created by human. Note that the hierarchical tree used by the HF model is automatically generated and dynamically updated. Thus, unlike the static

Table 4: Comparing models on the sparse dataset with AUC metric. For this dataset, we keep users that have bought at least one infrequent item. Bold symbols indicate best performance and the star indicates the statistical significance (p-value $< 0.01$).

| Item Frequency | 1 - 10 | 11 - 30 | 31 - 100 | 101 - 300 | 301 - 1000 | > 1000 | Overall |
|---|---|---|---|---|---|---|---|
| MF | 0.479 | 0.707 | 0.913 | **0.983** | **0.995** | **0.9993** | 0.772 |
| CIS | 0.472 | 0.720 | 0.916 | 0.978 | 0.993 | 0.9993 | 0.771 |
| RLFM | 0.544 | 0.741 | 0.904 | 0.976 | 0.994 | 0.9992 | 0.796 |
| HF | **0.662*** | **0.798*** | **0.923*** | 0.981 | 0.994 | 0.9992 | **0.847*** |

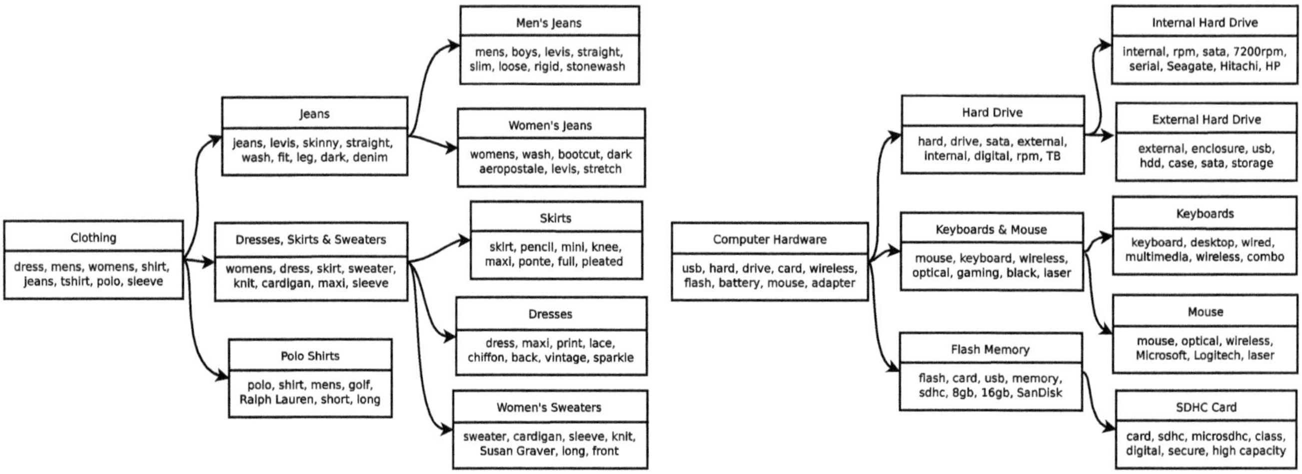


**Figure 4: A portion of hierarchical categories discovered by the HF model. The diagram shows two categories and a subset of their sub-categories. Each block shows the top ranked terms in the category and a manual labeling of the category's name based on the terms.**

human-induced taxonomy, the algorithm-generated taxonomy is adaptive to incremental data as more items and more users arrive.

# 6. USING HUMAN-INDUCED TAXONOMY

In this section, we assume that the human-induced taxonomy is available to the recommendation system. We study approaches that incorporate the human-induced taxonomy into the HF model. We also compare the HF model with the taxonomy-aware latent factor model (TF), which is the state-of-the-art latent factor model based on human-induced taxonomies. Even without using the human-induced taxonomy, we find that the HF model consistently outperforms the TF model. Incorporating human-induced taxonomy further improves the HF model's accuracy to make it achieving the best performance in our comparison.

We begin with describing the human-induced taxonomy that we use in this section. In this reference taxonomy, products are organized by a tree-structured taxonomy that has 20 top-level categories and 5140 internal nodes. The average depth of the tree is 4.4. Each items is attached to exactly one internal node of the tree.

## 6.1 Including Human-induced Taxonomy in Generative Model

When a human-induced taxonomy is available to the HF model, we can include it as a part of the HF model. More specifically, we assume that these taxonomies are also generated by the underlying hierarchical model described in Section 3. Then, by observing the human-induced taxonomy as long as the item descriptions and user purchase data, we use the technique in Section 4 to infer the model structure and the model parameters.

Let $A_i$ be the set of ancestors of item $i$ in the human-induced taxonomy tree. $A_i$ can be seen as a collection of terms, which provides another description to the item. For every category node in the HF model, we maintain another multinomial distribution that is used for generating such descriptions. When a new category node $w$ is generated, we sample the multinomial distribution by

$$\varphi_w \sim \begin{cases} \mathrm{Dir}(\beta') & w \text{ is the root node} \\ \mathrm{Dir}(\eta' \varphi_{\pi(w)}) & \text{otherwise} \end{cases}$$

and when an item $i$ is generated, we sample each term $a$ in the associated set $A_i$ by the multinomial distribution

$$a \sim \mathrm{Mult}(\varphi_{\pi(i)}).$$

By setting hyper-parameters $\beta'$ and $\eta'$, we can control the weight of the human-induced taxonomy in the global objective function. A smaller value of $\beta'$ or $\eta'$ indicates that the human-induced taxonomy is more strictly followed when the hierarchical structure is constructed. In practice, we set the values of $\beta'$ or $\eta'$ using cross validation.

The inference for this modified HF model still follows the approximation algorithm described in Section 4. In equation (9), we multiply an additional term describing the likelihood of the observed description $A_i$, whose computation is in complete analoge to the likelihood term for $D_i$ using equations (12-14). We omit the mathematical details here due to space limitations.

**Table 5: Number of internal nodes, entropies and their mutual information for three categorizations. In this table, $T_{human}$ is the taxonomy created by human, $T_{HF(D)}$ and $T_{HF(D+T)}$ are taxonomies generated by the HF(D) model and the HF(D+T) model.**

| Categorization | # Nodes | Entropy | Mutual Information |
|---|---|---|---|
| $T_{human}$ | 5140 | 5.976 | - |
| $T_{HF(D)}$ | 7424 | 8.247 | - |
| $T_{HF(D+T)}$ | 7356 | 8.182 | - |
| $T_{human}$, $T_{HF(D)}$ | - | - | 3.957 |
| $T_{human}$, $T_{HF(D+T)}$ | - | - | 5.162 |

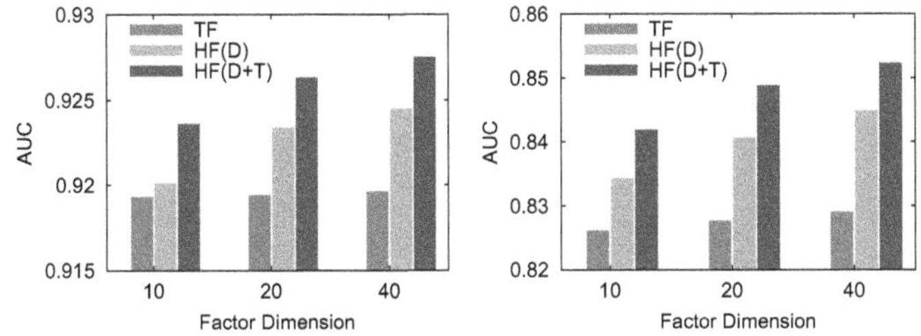


(a) On full data (b) On sparse data

**Figure 5: Using only item descriptions, the HF(D) model outperforms the TF model which relies on human-induced taxonomy. The HF(D+T) model achieves the best performance.**

We rename the two variants of the HF model by HF(D) and HF(D+T), indicating that the model relies on only the item description or relies on both the description and the human-induced taxonomy. In next section, we compare the taxonomy generated by HF(D) or HF(D+T) to the taxonomy induced by human.

## 6.2 Comparing Taxonomies induced by Human and by Algorithm

To measure the connection between taxonomies that the HF model generates and the taxonomy induced by human, we compute the entropy of each taxonomy and their mutual information. Let $C$ be the set of categories in taxonomy $T$. Let $p_c$ be the portion of items belonging to category $c \in C$. Then, the entropy of $T$ is defined by

$$H(T) = \sum_{c \in C} -p_c \log(p_c).$$

For two taxonomies $T_1$ and $T_2$, their joint entropy is calculated based on the Cartesian product of their category set $C_1 \otimes C_2$, and their mutual information is defined by

$$I(T_1, T_2) = H(T_1) + H(T_2) - H(T_1, T_2).$$

A high mutual information indicates that two taxonomies are strongly correlated. As Table 5 shows, taxonomies generated by the HF model have the similar number of internal nodes and entropies as the human-induced taxonomy. The HF(D) model is capable of producing categories that has high mutual information with the human-induced taxonomy (equals 3.957). When human-induced taxonomy is incorporated to form the HF(D+T) model, the mutual information increases to 5.162, which means that the resulting taxonomy preserves most of the information induced by human.

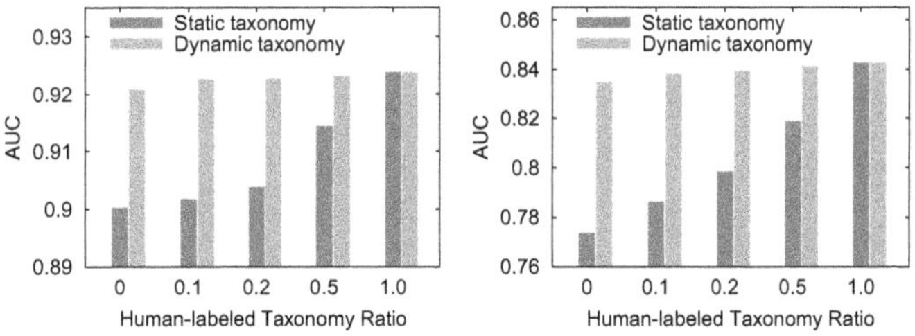


(a) On full data (b) On sparse data

**Figure 6: When human-induced taxonomy is partially available, the dynamic taxonomy generated by the HF model leads to robust recommendation performance.**

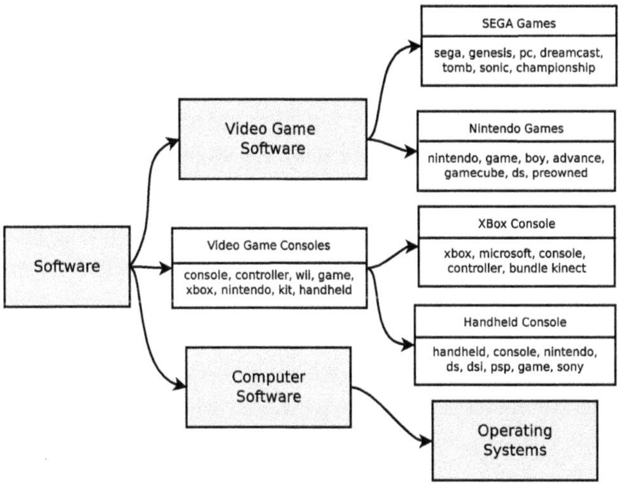


**Figure 7: A portion of dynamic taxonomy generated by the HF model for $r = 0.1$. The shaded box represents human-created categories. The white box represents automatically generated categories with top-ranked terms and manually labeled category names.**

Next, we compare the three taxonomies in recommender systems. As Figure 5(a) and Figure 5(b) shows, the HF(D) models, though only relying on the raw data, consistently outperforms the TF model which relies on human labels. The HF(D+T) model outperforms all other models on both datasets. The HF(D+T) model's improvement over the TF model is 0.9% on the full data and 2.4% on the sparse data, both are statistically significant. The experiment results confirm our intuition that the HF model has advantage over the TF model in recommendation accuracy, since it combines categorization and parameter estimation together and optimize both jointly. In contrast, the human-induced taxonomy used by the TF model is not optimized for learning latent factor models.

## 6.3 Dynamically Evolving Human-induced Taxonomy

In this section, we consider a scenario when the human-induced taxonomy is taken as the ground truth, but it is not fully available. That means, some of the items are categorized by human and others remains uncategorized. This commonly happens when new source of items are added to the database or when new types of products appear in the market. In this case, the recommender doesn't want to completely reconstruct the taxonomy that is already labeled by editors. Instead, he/she desires a dynamic hierarchy: old items keep their positions in the existing taxonomy, new items are automatically added to the taxonomy, and new categories are inserted when necessary.

The HF model is capable of maintaining such a dynamic taxonomy. In particular, In section 4.1 we initialize the tree with the human-induced taxonomy so that existing items always belong to their human-induced categories. When new items arrive, they are assigned to existing categories or assigned to new categories according to the sampling algorithm in Section 4.1.

We simulate a partial human-induced taxonomy in experiment by taking a ratio $r \in \{0, 0.1, 0.2, 0.5, 1\}$ of items categorized by the human-induced taxonomy, and keeping the remaining items uncategorized. We compare the HF model with static tree where uncategorized items are directly attached to the root, and the HF model with the dynamic tree described above. According to the experiment results, the dynamic taxonomy appears to be very robust to incomplete categorization. As Figure 6 shows, when using a static tree, the latent factor model's performance dramatically decreases as the ratio $r$ goes down, but with the dynamic tree, the performance always retains at a high level. It suggests that in reality the human editor only need to label a small portion of items, then the algorithm will complete the remaining part.

In Figure 7, we present a portion of the dynamic tree to illustrate how the taxonomy envolves. In this example, the HF model adds sub-categories to the "Video Game Software" node to further refine the categorization. Interestingly, it also creates a "Video Game Consoles" category that does not belong to the original taxonomy. Although the game consoles are literally not software, they are indeed closely related to the game software purchase, which makes the resulting taxonomy a reasonable priori for recommendation.

## 7. CONCLUSIONS

In this paper we addressed the problem of inferring a taxonomy for recommender systems. Smoothing latent factor models over a taxonomy combats sparsity and allows for sharing statistical strength between items. However, in many situations a human-induced taxonomy is not available, for example when new items arrive, when a new merchant is added to the system (possibly with items from a different culture/language), or when users do not supply categories for new items (as in youtube videos). Luckily, it is always possible to obtain a textual description of items. We described an unsupervised non-parametric method that jointly learns taxonomy structure over items and item factors in a recommender system from both items' textual description and purchase data. We showed that the performance of our model compares favourably with several state of the art baselines and even with the performance of a human-induced taxonomy when available. Furthermore, we showed that our model can utilize and improve upon a partial human-induced taxonomy if available. In the future we plan to apply our taxonomy induction to the regression latent factor model in [1]. Moreover, we plan to investigate user clustering when users' meta data is available.

## 8. REFERENCES


[1] D. Agarwal and B.-C. Chen. Regression-based latent factor models. In *Proceedings of the 15th ACM SIGKDD International Conference on Knowledge Discovery and Data Mining*, pages 19–28. ACM, 2009.

[2] A. Ahmed, L. Hong, and A. Smola. The nested chinese restaurant franchise process: User tracking and document modeling. *Proceedings of the 30th International Conference on Machine Learning*, 2013.

[3] J. Bennett and S. Lanning. The netflix prize. In *Proceedings of KDD cup and workshop*, volume 2007, page 35, 2007.

[4] D. M. Blei, T. L. Griffiths, and M. I. Jordan. The nested chinese restaurant process and bayesian nonparametric inference of topic hierarchies. *Journal of the ACM*, 57(2):7, 2010.

[5] J. Duchi, E. Hazan, and Y. Singer. Adaptive subgradient methods for online learning and stochastic optimization. *Journal of Machine Learning Research*, 12:2121–2159, 2010.

[6] Z. Ghahramani, M. I. Jordan, and R. P. Adams. Tree-structured stick breaking for hierarchical data. In *Advances in Neural Information Processing Systems*, pages 19–27, 2010.

[7] B. Kanagal, A. Ahmed, S. Pandey, V. Josifovski, J. Yuan, and L. Garcia-Pueyo. Supercharging recommender systems using taxonomies for learning user purchase behavior. *Proceedings of the VLDB Endowment*, 5(10):956–967, 2012.

[8] Y. Koren. Factorization meets the neighborhood: a multifaceted collaborative filtering model. In *Proceedings of the 14th ACM SIGKDD International Conference on Knowledge Discovery and Data Mining*, pages 426–434. ACM, 2008.

[9] Y. Koren. Collaborative filtering with temporal dynamics. *Communications of the ACM*, 53(4):89–97, 2010.

[10] Y. Koren, R. Bell, and C. Volinsky. Matrix factorization techniques for recommender systems. *Computer*, 42(8):30–37, 2009.

[11] A. K. Menon, K.-P. Chitrapura, S. Garg, D. Agarwal, and N. Kota. Response prediction using collaborative filtering with hierarchies and side-information. In *Proceedings of the 17th ACM SIGKDD International Conference on Knowledge Discovery and Data Mining*, pages 141–149. ACM, 2011.

[12] A. Mnih. Taxonomy-informed latent factor models for implicit feedback. 2011.

[13] A. Mnih and Y. W. Teh. Learning label trees for probabilistic modelling of implicit feedback. In *Advances in Neural Information Processing Systems*, pages 2825–2833, 2012.

[14] S. Rendle, C. Freudenthaler, Z. Gantner, and L. Schmidt-Thieme. Bpr: Bayesian personalized ranking from implicit feedback. In *Proceedings of the 25th Conference on Uncertainty in Artificial Intelligence*, pages 452–461. AUAI Press, 2009.

[15] S. Rendle and L. Schmidt-Thieme. Pairwise interaction tensor factorization for personalized tag recommendation. In *Proceedings of the 3rd ACM international Conference on Web Search and Data Mining*, pages 81–90. ACM, 2010.

[16] L.-T. Weng, Y. Xu, Y. Li, and R. Nayak. Exploiting item taxonomy for solving cold-start problem in recommendation making. In *Proceedings of the 20th IEEE International Conference on Tools with Artificial Intelligence*, volume 2, pages 113–120. IEEE, 2008.

[17] C.-N. Ziegler, G. Lausen, and L. Schmidt-Thieme. Taxonomy-driven computation of product recommendations. In *Proceedings of the 13th ACM International Conference on Information and Knowledge Management*, pages 406–415. ACM, 2004.

# Who likes it more?
# Mining Worth-Recommending Items from Long Tails by Modeling Relative Preference

Yu-Chieh Ho
Dept. of Computer Science and Information Engineering, National Taiwan University
Taipei, Taiwan
yuchieh.ho@gmail.com

Yi-Ting Chiang
Institute of Information Science, Academia Sinica
Taipei, Taiwan
yitingchiang@gmail.com

Jane Yung-Jen Hsu
Dept. of Computer Science and Information Engineering, National Taiwan University
Taipei, Taiwan
yjhsu@csie.ntu.edu.tw

## ABSTRACT

Recommender systems are useful tools that help people to filter and explore massive information. While the accuracy of recommender systems is important, many recent research indicated that focusing merely on accuracy not only is insufficient to meet user needs, but also may be harmful. Other characteristics such as novelty, unexpectedness and diversity should also be taken into consideration. Previous work has shown that more the sales of long-tail items could be more beneficial to both customers and some business models. However, the majority of collaborative filtering approaches tends to recommend popular selling items.

In this work, we focus on long-tail item promotion and aggregate diversity enhancement, and propose a novel approach which diversifies the results of recommender systems by considering "recommendations" as resources to be allocated to the items. Our approach increases the quantity and quality of long-tail item recommendations by adding more variation into the recommendation and maintains a certain level of accuracy simultaneously. The experimental results show that this approach can discover more worth-recommending items from Long Tails and improves user experience.

## Categories and Subject Descriptors

H.3 [**Information Systems**]: INFORMATION STORAGE AND RETRIEVAL

## Keywords

Recommendation Diversity, Recommender System, Aggregate Diversity, Long Tail, Collaborative Filtering


*WSDM'14*, February 24–28, 2014, New York, NY, USA.

http://dx.doi.org/10.1145/2556195.2566589 .

## 1. INTRODUCTION

Recommender systems [26], as a filter and guide for users when dealing with huge volume of information, were expected to predict the user preference based on his/her profiles or previous behaviours. Most works and competition such as Netflix Prize aims to construct accurate recommender systems (i.e. minimize the difference between the predicted rating values and the real rating values). Although accuracy is one of the most important metric for recommender system evaluation, many recent research indicated that focusing merely on accuracy not only is insufficient to meet user needs, but also may be harmful. Other characteristics such as novelty, unexpectedness and diversity should also be taken in to consideration [11, 19, 27].

Long-tail items, or Long Tails are items located in the tail of the sales distribution [3]. Although different manufacturers and retailers may have diverse business strategies in driving sales toward the head or the tail of the sales distribution [6], more sales of long-tail items could be beneficial to both customers and some business models [5, 9]. For example, one of the most crucial niche of online book stores is the availability of books hidden in Long Tails and it is also a good way to develop customer loyalty by helping the user to discover more long-tail items that he/she does not know yet. In addition, "uniqueness" could be the key concern in clothing selection and [5] showed that providing more diverse recommendations increases the sales on long tail items. On the other hand, one study in the domain of people to people recommendation indicated that in the context of online dating, expression of interests (EOI) sent to unpopular users got higher success rate [23]. Another study also indicates that promoting less popular candidates can improves user success rates, while only recommending popular candidates results in a decreased rate [16].

However, the majority of collaborative filtering (CF) based algorithms tends to recommend popular items because the popular items, on average, are likely to get higher predicted ratings than less popular ones from both memory-based and model-based techniques for rating prediction [2][7]. Therefore, the long-tail items have very little chance to be seen by the users, while popular items occupy the majority of the recommendations, if the system generates recommendations that only depends on the predicted rating values. This disproportion can get worse and worse, and more items will be trapped in the long tail.

Aggregate diversity, which is a measurement of the distribution of recommendations over all items, has been considered as one of the important aspects of recommender system, since it has been shown that recommender systems which utilizes aggregate diversity are able to significantly associate recommendations with the sales of long-tail items [5, 7, 20].

In this work, we focus on long-tail item promotion and aggregate diversity enhancement, and propose a novel approach which diversifies the results of recommender systems by considering "recommendations" as resources to be allocated to the items. Compared to the classical framework of a recommender system (Figure 1a), where the results of recommendation depend only on the ordering of predicted rating values, our framework (Figure 1b) allows the service providers to re-organize the recommendations according to their strategies. In our framework, the preference prediction acts as the first step instead of being the final step of a recommender system. A good predicting algorithm can guarantee the accuracy, by acting as the role of rating predictor in Figure 1a and 1b. In the proposed approach, predicted rating values are also used in the recommendation organizer, showed in Figure 1b, which can guarantee the degree of aggregated diversity by allocating the "resources" (i.e. recommendations) based on the given allocation strategy and current user-item interactions (i.e. user rating values and predicted rating values). Our approach increases the quantity and quality of long-tail item recommendations by adding more variation into the recommendation approach and maintains a certain level of accuracy simultaneously.

The structure of the rest of the paper is as follows. We start with a review of related work on recommendation diversity and the matrix factorization technique for recommender systems in Section 2. Then, we describe the intuitive idea and the detailed methodology of our approach in Section 3. Section 4 presents and discusses the evaluation results on five metrics: average prediction (accuracy), coverage, gini coefficient, the quantity and quality of long-tail item recommendations that our system generated. Finally, we conclude our contributions and address potential directions for future work in Section 5.

## 2. RELATED WORK

In the following section, we review the matrix factorization technique which we used for rating value prediction, and several related work in the field of recommendation diversity.

### 2.1 Matrix Factorization

Matrix factorization (MF) is an effective model based CF approach in terms of rating value prediction and is famous for its success in Netflix Prize competition [14]. Given a $m \times n$ user-item matrix constructed by user rating records, MF technique captures the interactions between users and items by factorizing (decomposing) the user-item matrix into a $m \times k$ user-factor matrix and an $k \times n$ item-factor matrix where $k$ is the number of latent factors. It characterizes both items and users by vectors of factors inferred from existing rating patterns and predict the unknown rating values by computing the inner product of those factors (i.e. user-factor matrix and item-factor matrix). MF is more accurate and more memory- efficient than the classical memory based CF approaches [15].

### 2.2 Recommendation Diversity

The diversity of recommendations has become one of the key dimensions in the research of recommender systems. Many researchers had worked on generating more diverse recommendations [4, 30, 29, 17, 12, 18, 2, 1, 16] and several studies on human factors and recommender systems [13, 19, 24] also suggested that it is necessary to maintain a certain level of diversity in the results of a recommender system even at the risk of accuracy loss. Generally speaking, we can classify the research on recommendation diversity into two categories: individual diversity and aggregate diversity.

The researches on individual diversity [4, 30, 29, 17] focused on the dissimilarity of items within a recommendation list to the individuals. [30] diversified the results of content based recommender systems by transforming the problem into a constrained optimization problem in quadratic form. The authors controlled the trade-off between similarity (to the user query) and diversity of the recommendation lists by a single parameter and proposed a solution for solving the optimization problem. [17] enhanced the individual diversity and novelty by building informative user profiles from user-item interactions and designing a hybrid mechanism which consists of accuracy-orientated, diversity-orientated, and novelty-orientated algorithms.

On the other hand, aggregate diversity focus on the coverage and the distribution of total recommendations among all items, especially the long-tail items with only few ratings. [22] and [21] improved the predictive accuracy and increased the recommendation of long-tail items by clustering the items according to their similarity on several derived variables (e.g. average rating values, number of ratings, etc) and computing the predictive rating values within each cluster. Different from most of the recommender systems which are triggered by the customers, [18] and [12] proposed an item-triggered recommendation approach to identify potential customers for long-tail items, which increases the recommendations on those cold sellers. This approach computes customer lists, ordered by the probability that the customers are willing to buy given items by solving a rare-class classification problem. In addition, [16] proposed a decision tree based approach to promoting the less popular candidates and showed that recommending less popular candidates can improve user success (the sender get reply from the message receiver) rates on online dating websites. Furthermore, [28] challenged the Long Tail Recommendation problem with a random walk based algorithm. The authors defined the concept of *absorbing time* to capture the longtailness of items and the relevance between users and items. Finally, [2] improved the aggregate diversity by re-ranking the item list according to given ranking strategies (e.g. the popularity of items and the average ratings of items), and [1] proposed a graph-theoretic approach which maximizing aggregate recommendation diversity by solving maximum flow or maximum bipartite matching problems.

In this work, we re-organize the recommendation lists by resource allocation, where recommendations are considered as resources, after the rating value estimation. We chose [2] and [1] as our benchmarks because their system share similar work flows and goals with our approach.

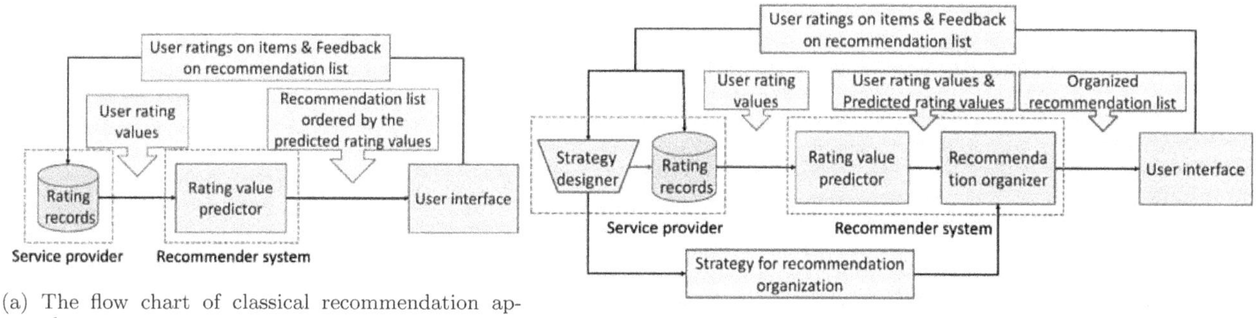


(a) The flow chart of classical recommendation approach.



(b) The flow chart of proposed approach. The red lines indicate the differences between the two approaches.

Figure 1: The framework of classical recommender system and the proposed approach.

# 3. METHODOLOGY

## 3.1 Game of Colors

The core idea behind our approach is "exploring individual users' unique taste" and we would like to give an intuitive analogy to our approach before digging into the technical details.

In this section, we make an analogy between item recommendation and pigment distribution in a painting class. Imagine that you are a teacher, and you want each of your student to complete a painting with the colors which show his/her unique taste. You design a game of colors to determine those colors and the two steps of this game are just a simplified version of approaches in Section 3.2.1 and Section 3.2.2.

First, every student gives a score between one and five to 36 colors. Next, you buy some color pigments. The quantity of each color is according to the ratings given by the students, the higher the ratings the more you purchase, and a minimum of one bottle for each color. (The idea of Section 3.2.1)

The purchased color pigments is then distributed to the students. In order to emphasize the uniqueness of each student, the distribution of the pigments will depend on comparison with the overall rating in the whole class. For example, suppose that the total amount of blue pigments and green pigments that you purchased are about the same, and one of the student has the score of 3.5 for blue and 3.7 for green. Although the student rates blue lower than green, the student will nevertheless receive more blue pigments than green pigments, if most of the other students rates higher than 3.7 for green, and lower than 3.5 for blue. Because in this case, blue is a more representative color regarding his/her unique taste.(The idea of Section 3.2.2)

After all 36 colors are distributed to each student, each student then sort their color pigments according to the amount they have received in descending order. Finally, the students can start to paint with only the top six colors, and can ask for more pigments if necessary.(top-N recommendation)

Therefore, this method of distribution depends on two factors:

1. The total amount of pigments in this color, which depends on the popularity of this color.

2. How much does the student like the color, compare with the others.

The first factor is decided by the ratings given to each color by the students in the first step, and the second factor is decided by comparing individual students' rating to the overall rating of the whole class. This color distribution will produce more diverse and individualized paintings than those that considers only the highest ratings given by the students.

## 3.2 Proposed Approach

The goal of our approach is to diversify the recommendations and maintain a reasonable level of accuracy by mining worth-recommending items from Long Tails. To achieve our goal, we compute a score named *5D-score* for each user-item pair, and the scores are used for re-organizing the recommendation lists. The role of 5D-score in our approach is just like the quantity of the color pigments that a student receives in the game of colors. We named it the "5D-score" because it is computed by considering the five "dimensions" that are critical to the evaluation of aggregate diversity and long-tail item promotion. The five dimensions are as follows:

1. Accuracy: the average predicted rating values of all recommended items.

2. Balance: the distribution of recommendations among all items after a round of recommendation (providing a top-N recommendation for each user).

3. Coverage: the percentage of recommended items among all items after a "round" of recommendation.

4. Quantity of long-tail item recommendation: the ratio of long-tail items among all recommended items.

5. Quality of long-tail item recommendation: the average predicted rating values of those recommended long-tail items.

Just like the "game of colors", our approach includes two sequential phases: the resource allocation phase and the recommendation phase (Figure 2). In the first phase, we consider the "opportunity of being recommended" as resources, and allocate them among all items according to some allocation strategies. In the second phase, each user receives a certain amount of resources from each item depending on how much the user likes a specific item, and the top-N recommendation list for a specific user is generated by the ranking of the amount of the resource he/she receives from each item.

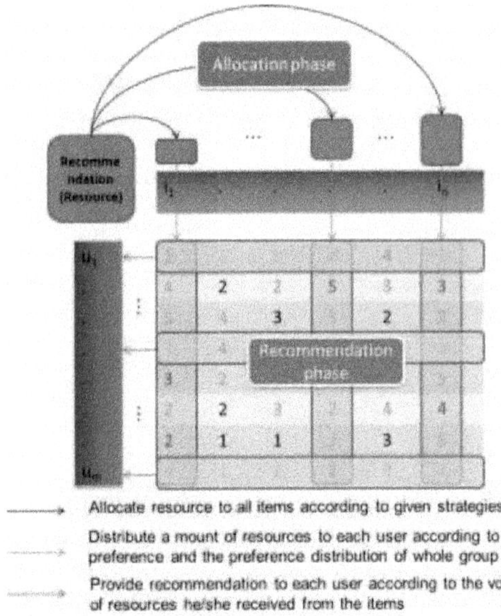


Figure 2: The diagram of allocation phase and recommendation phase.

The following section describe the details of the proposed approach and we summarize some notations here:

- $U = \{u_1, \ldots, u_m\}$: The set of users.
- $I = \{i_1, \ldots, i_n\}$: The set of items.
- $I_u$: The set of items rated by the user $u$.
- $R_u = \{r_{u,1}, \ldots, r_{u,n}\}$: The set of ratings. Where $r_{u,i}$ is the predicted or real rating of user $u$ on item $i$.

### 3.2.1 *Resource Allocation Phase*

In the first phase, we would like to allocate certain quantity of resources on all items with the following objectives:

1. Items with higher rating values shall receive more resources (opportunity of being recommended) to guarantee the quantity of recommendations on those items with good reputations.
2. The allocation shall follow the first objective but in a balanced way. That is, non-popular items shall also receive reasonable amount of resources to keep their chance of being recommended.

Our approach begins with a complete $m \times n$ user-item matrix (Figure 2) where all the elements are filled by either ratings from the users (the black numbers) or predicted ratings (the blue numbers) computed by a recommendation algorithm (e.g. matrix factorization). We formulate the resource allocation approach as the following maximization problem:

$$\operatorname{argmax}_{X=\{x_1,\ldots,x_n\}} \prod_{i \in I} x_i^{\text{allocation}(i)}, \tag{1}$$

where $x_1 + \ldots + x_n = k$, $k > n$ and $x_i \geq q > 0$.

allocation$(i)$ is the allocation strategy to be plugged into the objective function and we want to find the $n$ dimensional vector $X$ (resource allocation among all items) which maximizes the objective function given an allocation strategy. We leverage the series multiplication as the fundamental form of our objective function because we would like to allocate the resources in a more balanced fashion (objective 2): Allocating all the resource to a single variable $x_j$ would not be a proper solution for Equation 1 even when allocation$(j)$ is larger than all the other indexes.

We define the allocation strategy as a function of $i$ for flexibility and one can define his/her own function to facilitate other context. In this work, the allocation strategy is defined as:

$$\text{allocation}(i) = \sum_{u \in U} \frac{r_{u,i} - \overline{R_u}}{\sigma_u}, \forall i \in I, \tag{2}$$

where $\sigma_u$ is the standard deviation of $R_u$ and $\overline{R_u} = \frac{1}{n}\sum_i r_{u,i}$.

For each item $i$, Equation 2 is the summation of the normalized rating values and predicted rating values of each users (the $z$-scores of those ratings). As a result, allocation$(i)$ models the preferences of all users on item $i$, and allocation$(1)$, $\ldots$, allocation$(n)$ model the distribution of preferences of all users over all items. By plugging this allocation strategy into Equation 1, the maximization process would assign larger values to the variables with larger indexes, which means the items with higher rating records will receive more (but not extreme) resources as we expected (objective 1).

### 3.2.2 *Recommendation Phase*

In the recommendation phase, we would like to distribute those resources that we have allocated on the items to each user according to their *relative preferences*, and then provide recommendations based on the results of distribution (i.e. 5D-scores.). The approach is designed to achieve the following objectives:

1. Improve the aggregate diversity by emphasizing the unique taste of individuals: The user who likes a specific item more than the other shall receive more resources (higher 5D-score) from this item.
2. Promote the long-tail items by giving them more chance to be seen by the user who likes them: When a user have similar preference on a popular item and a long-tail item, he/she is more likely to receive more resources from the latter.

The ratings and predicted ratings can represent users' preference, but they may contain rating bias. Therefore, we have to eliminate the rating bias by normalizing the rating values before the comparison. For example, although a movie was rated as three (out of five) points by a user named John, it could be a negative rating if John never gave a score lower than 3.5 to any movie. On the other hand, a rating of three points in John's rating record may denote a positive preference on that movie if he is very critical and most of his ratings are lower than 2.5. Equation 3 calculates the z-scores of the rating values of each user (row by row calculation on the user-item matrix) and models the preferences of all user on all items.

$$Z(u,i) = \frac{r_{u,i} - \overline{R_u}}{\sigma_u} \tag{3}$$

As mentioned in the beginning of section 3.2.2, we would like to distribute the resource according to the *relative preferences* of users on each item. The next step is to calculate the 5D-score (Equation 4) based on the normalized preferences computed by Equation 3.

$$5\mathrm{D}(u,i) = \frac{Z(u,i) - \overline{Z(U,i)}}{\sigma_{Z(U,i)}} \times x_i, \quad (4)$$

where $\overline{Z(U,i)}$ and $\sigma_{Z(U,i)}$ are the mean value and the standard deviation of $Z(u_1,i),\ldots,Z(u_m,i)$ respectively. We use $\frac{Z(u,i)-\overline{Z(U,i)}}{\sigma_{Z(U,i)}}$ as the *relative preference* in this work.

Equation 4 is a "column by column" calculation on the user-item matrix. When we observe the 5D-scores within a single column $j$, they actually modeled the distribution of preferences from all users on item $j$. By Equation 3 and 4, we transformed the user preferences to *relative preferences* among all users and distributed the resources from items to users by calculating the product of those *relative preferences* and the quantity of resources $(x_1,\ldots,x_n)$ each item received. Finally, by sorting the items according to $\{5\mathrm{D}(u,1),\ldots,5\mathrm{D}(u,n)\}$, we generate the top-N recommendation for a user $u$.

Compared to the top-N lists generated merely according to the predicted rating values which are accurate but narrow and unbalanced, 5D-scores can help to promote the worth-recommending items in Long Tails and provide more diverse recommendations with sufficient accuracy.

The distribution of 5D-scores can help to promote the long-tail items (objective 2) because it tends to assign a higher value for a user from a cold seller (long-tail item) instead of a superstar (popular item) when this user has similar preference on the two items. Note that two z-scores with the same value (say $Z(u,i)$ and $Z(u,j)$) could have different meanings given that item $i$ is a cold seller and item $j$ is a superstar. For example, even user $u$ have the same preference on the two items ($Z(u,i) = Z(u,j)$), $5\mathrm{D}(u,i)$ could still be higher than $5\mathrm{D}(u,j)$ because $Z(u,i)$ is relatively high among $\{Z(1,i),\ldots,Z(m,i)\}$ and relatively low when considering others' preferences on item $j$. In addition, this characteristic of 5D-scores also helps to diversify the recommendations because our approach emphasizes the unique taste of the users on the long-tail items (objective 1).

### 3.2.3 *Accuracy Enhancement Algorithms*

Providing recommendations according to 5D-scores can improve aggregate diversity and keep reasonable level of accuracy simultaneously. However, in some situations, we may need to keep a higher level of average predicted rating value. We have designed two algorithms which allow the user to balance the trade-off between accuracy and diversity. We will describe the two algorithms in this section.

The Rank by Rankings Algorithm, described in Algorithm 1, takes the advantages of two ranking strategies (original predicted rating values and 5D-scores). The algorithm ranks the items according to both strategies and generates two ranking results, then combines the ranking results together.

In line 5, we combine the two ranking results of predicted rating values and 5D-scores by multiplying two ranking indexes on each item and sort the items according to those products. Recall that for any two values $v_1 + v_2 = V$, we have $(\frac{V}{2})^2 \geq v_1 \times v_2$. This property helps us to capture those items with at least one extreme high ranking instead of those with two average rankings.

The goal of the Accuracy Filtering algorithm (Algorithm 2) is to pick the first N items that have higher predicted rating values than a threshold T from a list ranked by the 5D-score (or other ranking strategy). If there are less than N items that can fulfill this requirement, the algorithm will fill up the list with items that have the next-highest 5D-scores(line 3).

**Algorithm 1:** Rank by Rankings

**Input** : $a$: the active user.
$\{r_{a,i_1},\ldots,r_{a,i_n}\}$: $R_u$.
$\{5\mathrm{D}(a,i_1),\ldots,5\mathrm{D}(a,i_n)\}$: the 5D-scores.
$N$: length of recommendation list.

**Output**: Top-N recommendations for user $a$, $N \leq n$.

**Data**: $i.\mathrm{idx}_r$: raking index of item $i$ according to $R_u$.
$i.\mathrm{idx\_5D}$: ranking index of item $i$ according to 5D-scores.

1. Sort the items by $\{r_{a,i_1},\ldots,r_{a,i_n}\}$ in descending order.
2. Assign $i.\mathrm{idx}_r$ for each item $i$ according to the current order.
3. Sort the items by $\{5D(a,i_1),\ldots,5\mathrm{D}(a,i_n)\}$ in descending order.
4. Assign $i.\mathrm{idx\_5D}$ for each item $i$ according to the current order.
5. Sort the items by $\{1.\mathrm{idx}_r \times 1.\mathrm{idx\_5D},\ldots,n.\mathrm{idx}_r \times n.idx\_5D\}$ in ascending order, and let the result be $\{i_{rr_1},\ldots,i_{rr_n}\}$.
`// New items are those items not in` $I_a$.
6. Top-N recommendations for user $a$ is The top $N$ new items in $\{i_{rr_1},\ldots,i_{rr_n}\}$.

**Algorithm 2:** Accuracy Filtering

**Input** : $\{i_1,\ldots,i_n\}$: sorted items (according to a given ranking strategy like 5D-scores or the results of Algorithm 1).
$\{r_{a,i_1},\ldots,r_{a,i_n}\}$: the real and predicted rating.
$a$: the active user.
$T$: the threshold of predicted rating value.
$N$: length of recommendation list.

**Output**: $L_{\text{Top-N}}$: Top-N recommendations for the active user, $N \leq n$.

1. Collect 2 sets of items $I_c$ and $I_r$ from $\{i_1,\ldots,i_n\}$, where $I_c = \{i|r_{a,i} \geq T, i \notin I_a\}$ and $I_r = \{i|r_{a,i} < T, i \notin I_a\}$ without loss the order.
2. If $|I_c| \geq N$, insert top $N$ items of $I_c$ into $L_{\text{Top-N}}$.
3. If $|I_c| < N$, insert $I_c$ and top $(N - |I_c|)$ items of $I_r$ into $L_{\text{Top-N}}$.

## 4. EXPERIMENTS

We conducted several experiments on MovieLens dataset [10] to show the effectiveness of our methods. We adopted three metrics: prediction, coverage, and gini coefficient to evaluate *accuracy*, *coverage* and *balance* of the recommendation results, and two metrics: long-tail recommendation and prediction on long-tail items to evaluate *quantity* and *quality* of the recommended long-tail items. All the experimental results are computed under the setting of top-N recommendation. That is, the recommendation approaches will generate $N$ best items for each user.

## 4.1 Datasets and Data Preprocessing

The MovieLens dataset is a public-domain dataset collected by the GroupLens lab in the Department of Computer Science and Engineering at the University of Minnesota. We conducted the experiments on MovieLens 100k (ML-100k) and MovieLens 1M (ML-1M)datasets, where ML-100k contains 100000 ratings (values from 1 to 5) from 943 users on 1682 movies and ML-1M contains 1,000,209 ratings from 6040 users on 3952 movies. In addition to the ratings, brief demographic information of the users is also available in the dataset. Researchers in the GroupLens lab have cleaned up the dataset and removed the users who rated less than 20 movies or have no complete demographic information.

We employed libFM [25] to predict the rating values of all the unrated movies based on the real rating values in the datasets.

## 4.2 The Metrics

Five metrics were adopted in our experiments. To begin with, we employed the prediction-in-top-N metric (in short, prediction) from [1] to evaluate the level of accuracy. This metric is defined as

$$\text{prediction-in-top-}N = \frac{\sum_{u\in U}\sum_{i\in L_N(u)} r^*_{u,i}}{\sum_{u\in U}|L_N(u)|},$$

where $U$ is the set of users and $L_N(u)$ is the top-N recommended list for user $u$. $r^*_{u,i}$ is the predicted rating value that user $u$ may rate on item $i$. A high prediction value indicates that the recommended items matched the user preferences.

We also evaluated coverage, which denotes the proportion of recommended items among all items. This metric was used to show the degree of diversity of the top-$N$ item set generated by recommender systems. In this work, we defined coverage as

$$\text{Coverage} = \frac{|I_R|}{|I|},$$

where $I$ is the set of items, and $I_R$ is the set of recommended items. A higher coverage means that more items were recommended by the recommender system.

Furthermore, we employed the well-known Gini coefficient [8], which is used to measure the income distribution of a nation's residents, as our metric to measure the balance of recommendations among all items. Therefore, the balance of recommendations is essentially the recommendation frequency distribution of the items after the top-N recommendation are provided to each user.

In addition, in order to evaluate the degree of opportunity that the long-tail items can be recommended in a recommender system, we defined a metric named long-tail recommendation. In our work, long-tail items are items which were rated by less than $L$ users and the long-tail recommendation was defined as

$$\text{long-tail} = \frac{\sum_{u\in U}|\,\text{longtail}(L_N(u))|}{\sum_{u\in U} L_N(u)},$$

where $\text{longtail}(L_N(u))$ is the set of long-tail items in $L_N(u)$.

Finally, since the quality of these recommended long-tail items should also be taken into consideration, we also computed the prediction on long-tail items to evaluate their quality.

## 4.3 Benchmarks and Our Approaches

We compared our approaches with three benchmarks. We first implemented four recommendation approaches as our approaches: **5D**, **5D_RR**, **5D_ACC**, and **5D_RR_ACC**, which are based on the 5D-score and the combination of rank by rankings (RR) algorithm and accuracy filtering (ACC) algorithm.

In addition, we implemented two approaches proposed in [1] and [2] as the benchmarks. The approach proposed in [1] is based on graph theory, so it is called **GBA** in our experiment. Similarly, the approaches adopted from [2] are called **RBT** approaches since they are based on ranking techniques. Moreover, the classical approach which simply selects top-N items according to the predicted rating values generated by MF was also implemented as a **baseline** benchmark.

In [2], several ranking methods were used to examine the ranking-based technique. We adopted the item popularity and the item average rating as the ranking methods and implemented two benchmarks, **RBT with itemPop** and **RBT with AvgRating**. We chose these two ranking methods because the item average rating method outperformed the others in respect of coverage and precision loss on MovieLens dataset in [2], and the experiment in [2] also showed that item popularity generated more long-tail recommendations on MovieLens dataset than the other methods.

[1] and [2] introduced *ranking-threshold* $T_R \in [T_H, T\text{max}]$ to control the trade-off between accuracy and diversity of the recommendations. The ranking-threshold plays the same role as the threshold $T$ in our accuracy filtering (ACC) algorithm. The main difference between our work and [1] [2] is the way we sort the items before generating the recommendation list. RBT and GBA sort the items according to the predicted rating values while our approaches sort the items according to the 5D-scores. Therefore, the items within the interval of $[T_H, T_R)$ can never ranked higher than those within $[T_R, T\text{max}]$ by RBT. In our approaches, those items have better opportunities to achieve higher ranking because 5D-scores consider not only popularity of items but also relative preference of users. Similarily, although GBA maximizes the coverage by recommending maximum number of different items within $[T_R, T\text{max}]$, it has difficulty in improving the quantity of long-tail recommendation.

## 4.4 Parameters and Experimental Results

We compared the results of recommendation methods with our approach under different threshold settings. $T_H$ and $T\text{max}$ were set to 3.5 and 5 in [1] and [2]. In our experiments, they were set to 2 and 5 respectively, and $T_R$ was set to $[4.2, 3.8, ..., 2.2]$ for ML-100k and $[5, 4.8, ..., 3]$ for ML-1M. We decided the range of $T_R$ by considering the average of median rating of each user (ML-100k: 2.148; ML-1M: 3.15), and the average of their 99th percentile(ML-100k) and 99.5th percentile(ML-1M) (ML-100k: 4.249; ML-1M: 4.727). This threshold was also applied to 5D_ACC and 5D_RR_ACC. The parameter $k$ and $q$ in equation 1 were set to $3N$ and 1, and $\text{allocation}(i)$ was normalized to [0,1]. Finally, the value $N$ of the top-N setting was set to 3, 5, and 10 respectively in this experiments.

In order to define the Long Tails, we analysed the distribution of ratings in the ML-100k and ML-1M datasets. There are about 70% of items were rated by less than 50(5%) users in ML-100k dataset and about 70% of items were rated by less than 250(4%) users in ML-1M dataset. Therefore, in our experiments, long-tail items are those items have less than 50/250 real ratings.

We first present the patterns of all approaches under all thresholds on three metrics: prediction, coverage and long-tail recommendation on ML-100k dataset in Figure 3.

We noticed an interesting phenomenon in Figure 3a: the prediction-in-top-N of our approaches with ACC had the best performance when the threshold was close to 2.8. The reason is that ACC took both 5D-scores and predicted rating values into consideration and thus retained the prediction-in-top-N, however, in the situations of higher threshold (system failed to find enough ($N$) items) or lower threshold (too many candidate items), the predicted rating values were ignored. As a result, prediction-in-top-N decreases.

In addition, the baseline approach showed its weakness in coverage (Figure 3b), since it only recommended best-rating items. RBT approaches performed worse than the baseline approach when $T_R \leq 2.4$, which is surprising. The reason may be that these approaches recommended only high-ranked items (according item popularity or item average rating) when the threshold value was small.

Finally, Figure 3c shows the results of long-tail recommendation. Comparing with the RBT with ItemPop approach, our approaches recommended more long-tail items in large threshold values and RBT with ItemPop outperformed ours in small threshold values.

In the following section, we show the average performances (under all thresholds) of 8 approaches on 5 Metrics over two datasets.

Figure 4 shows the result of the prediction. The baseline benchmark (the 6th bar), which only recommended items with high predicted rating values, maximized the prediction. 5D (the 1st bar)sacrificed considerable amount of prediction, but the prediction values significantly improved in 5D_RR (the 2nd bar)and 5D_RR_ACC (the 4th bar) with the help of RR and ACC algorithms. Comparing to ACC, RR would be a better choice to improve prediction-in-top-N.

According to Figure 5, GBA (the 5th bar) had the best performance on coverage and our approaches performed stably in this metric as well. Although we can see that 5D_RR and 5D_RR_ACC are outperformed by 5D and 5D_ACC (the 3rd bar)in most cases, all of our approaches surpassed the RBT approaches(the 7th and 8th bars) and the performances increased significantly with the increasing of $N$.

Figure 6 displays the Gini coefficient of the recommendations generated by these approaches. (Note that a smaller Gini coefficient means a more balanced recommendation set, which is preferred.) The results on Gini coefficient were similar to coverage. Firstly, RBT approaches and the baseline approaches performed badly in Gini coefficient. On the other hand, GBA showed its effectiveness in this metric. Moreover, 5D and 5D_ACC performed better than 5D_RR and 5D_RR_ACC again. Note that when $N$ increased, GBA's advantage became less-significant. Our approaches outperformed GBA when $N = 10$.

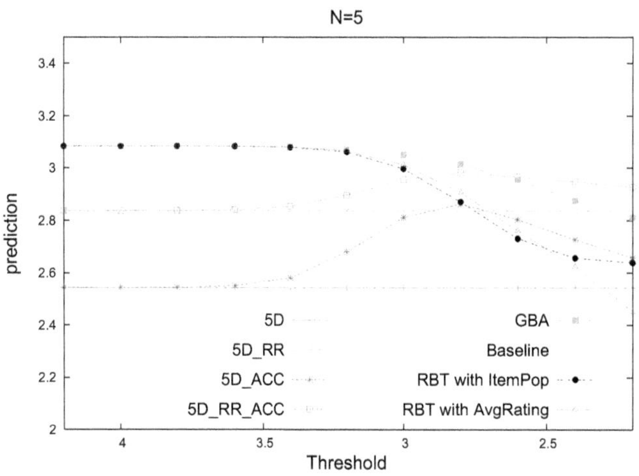


(a) Prediction@5

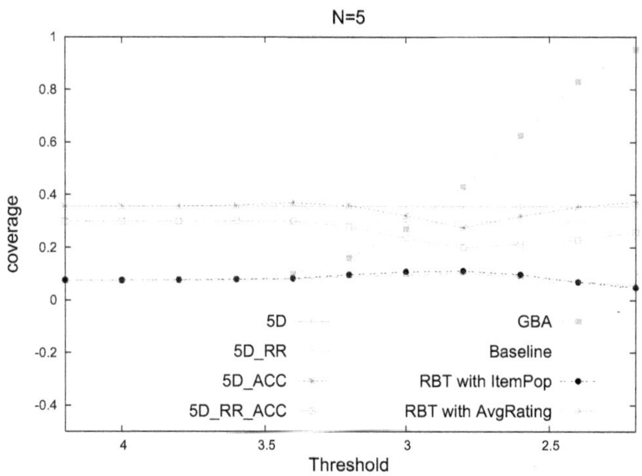


(b) Coverage@5

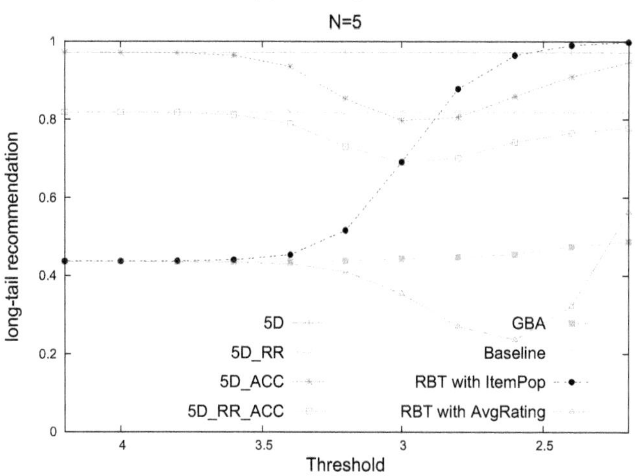


(c) Long-tail recommendation@5

Figure 3: The results of prediction, coverage and long-tail recommendation in Top 5 on MovieLens 100k.

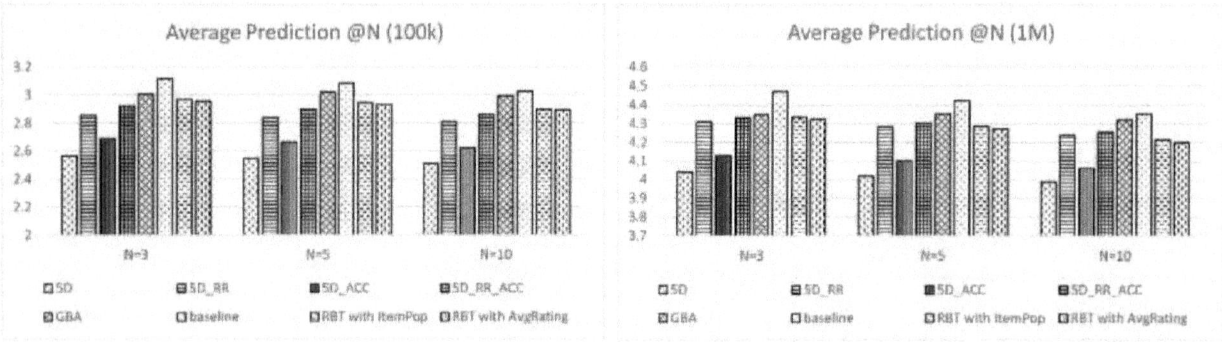


(a) (b)

Figure 4: The results of average prediction-in-Top-$N$ over MovieLens 100k( 4a) and MovieLens 1M( 4b)

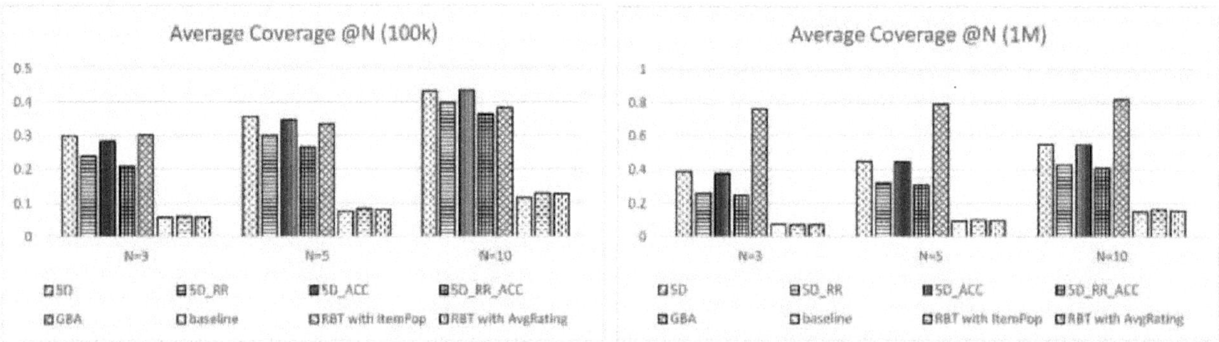


(a) (b)

Figure 5: The results of average coverage-in-Top-$N$ over MovieLens 100k( 5a) and MovieLens 1M( 5b)

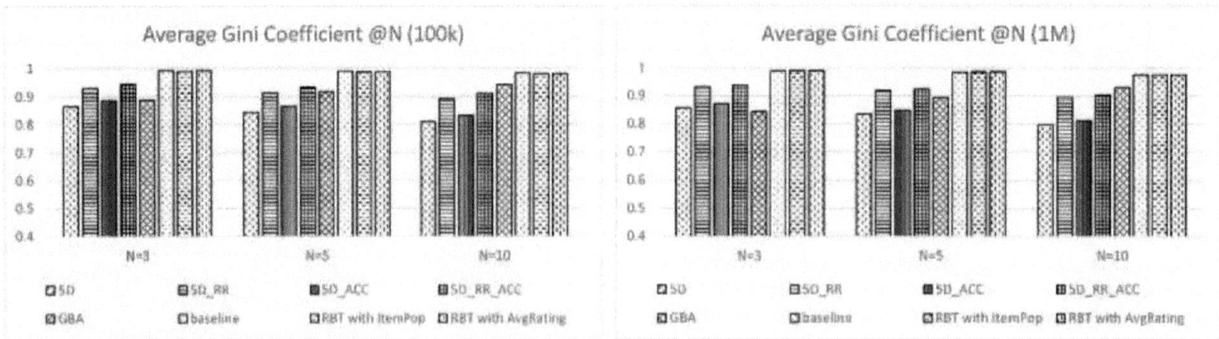


(a) (b)

Figure 6: The results of average Gini coefficient-in-Top-$N$ over MovieLens 100k( 6a) and MovieLens 1M( 6b)

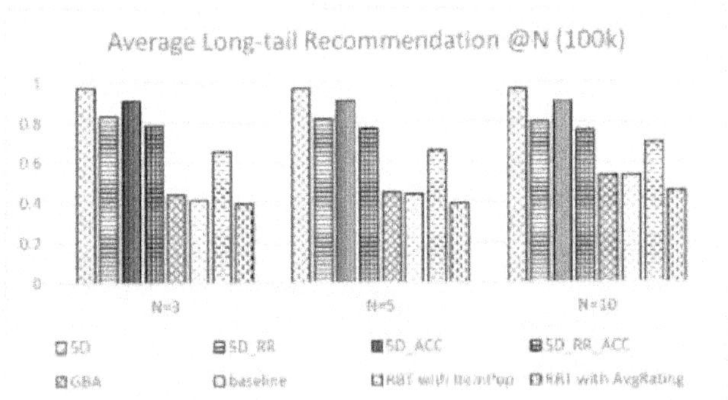


(a)

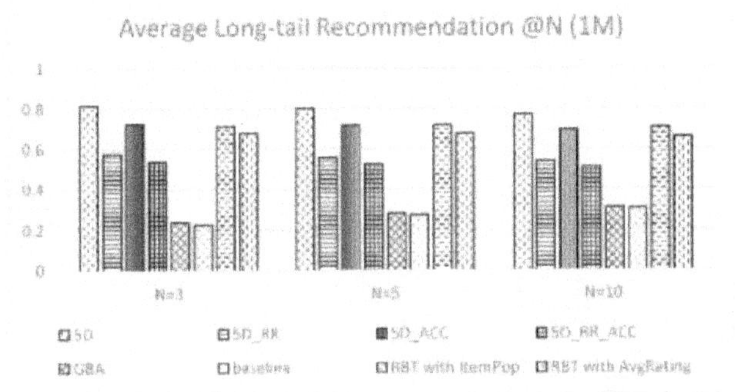


(b)

Figure 7: The results of average long-tail recommendtion-in-Top-$N$ over MovieLens 100k( 7a) and MovieLens 1M( 7b)

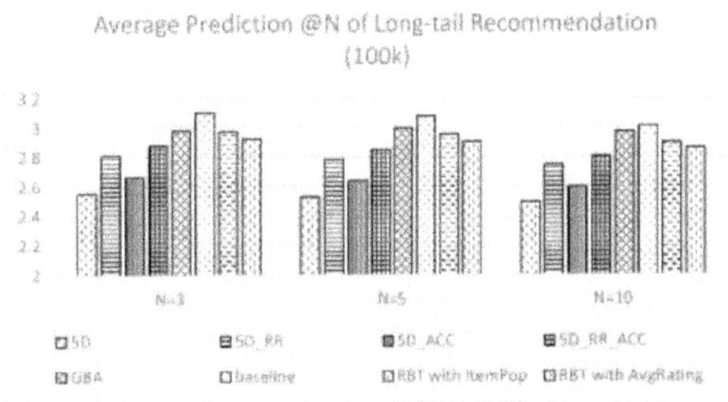


(a)

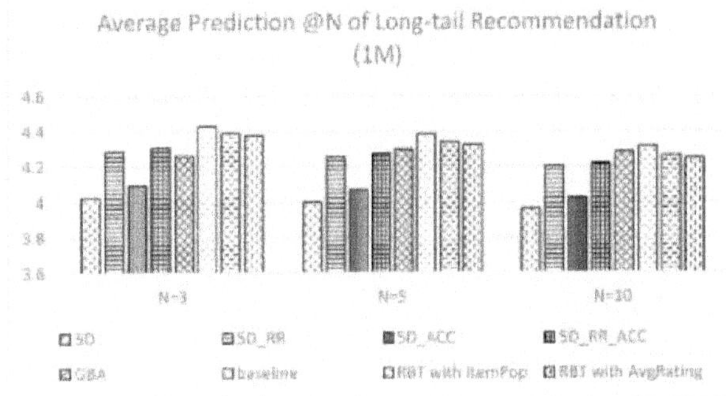


(b)

Figure 8: The results of average prediction-in-Top-$N$ of long-tail recommendation over MovieLens 100k( 8a) and MovieLens 1M( 8b)

Finally, the results of long-tail recommendation are shown in Figure 7 and the prediction on long-tail items are shown in Figure 8. In Figure 7, we can find that RBT with item-Pop outperformed RBT with AvgRating, which is consistent with the result given in [2]. GBA had difficulty in recommending long-tail items since this approach does not focus on recommending items in Long Tails. Our approaches have significant advantage over the baseline approach and GBA and showed similar performance with RBT approaches on these two metrics.

To summarize, our approaches can improve long-tail recommendation and coverage/balance simultaneously. While other benchmarks performed well in either coverage/balance (GBA) or long-tail recommendation (RBT) only; our approach improve current recommendation results.

## 5. CONCLUSIONS AND FUTURE WORK

In this work, we designed a recommender system to promote long-tail items and enhance aggregate diversity. We proposed the concept of 5D-scores which takes accuracy, coverage, balance, the quantity of the recommended items, and the quality of the recommended items into consideration.

Our approach includes two sequential phases: the resource allocation phase and the recommendation phase. In the resource allocation phase, we re-distributed "the chance of being recommended" to all items. This distribution reserves some opportunities for the long-tail items to be recommended and keeps some privilege for the popular items with good reputations, thus guaranteeing a balance between the diversity and the accuracy of recommendations. In the recommendation phase, we further improve the aggregate diversity and promote long-tail items by considering the *relative preferences* of the users and the resource allocation from the resource allocation phase. Note that we consider not only the quantity, but also the quality of the long-tail items in our recommendations. The whole approach follows the idea of "exploring individual users' unique taste" and aims at discovering worth-recommending long-tail items which can attract the users and emphasize their individual taste.

As shown in the experiments, our approach can generate highly divergent and balanced recommendations with little amount of prediction loss. Moreover, our approach excels in promoting long-tail items on quantity as well as quality. Although we believe that our approach is data-independent, it would be interesting to conduct further experiments on public datasets to investigate the generality of our approach. Moreover, the application of our approach on an on-line recommendation system and user study would likely improve our understanding of the usability of our approach in more practical settings.

Last but not least, it would also be interesting to combine our approach with people-to-people recommender system. It has been shown that expression of interests (EOI) sent to unpopular users on online dating websites gets higher success rate [23] and promoting less popular users also improves the success rates [16]. We believe that our approach may able to help to discover more worth-recommending candidates for the users of online dating websites.

## 6. REFERENCES


[1] G. Adomavicius and Y. Kwon. Maximizing aggregate recommendation diversity: A graph-theoretic approach. In *Proceedings of workshop on novelty and diversity in recommender systems*, pages 3–10, 2011.

[2] G. Adomavicius and Y. Kwon. Improving aggregate recommendation diversity using ranking-based techniques. *Knowledge and Data Engineering, IEEE Transactions on*, 24(5):896–911, 2012.

[3] C. Anderson. *The long tail: Why the future of business is selling less of more*. Hyperion Books, 2008.

[4] K. Bradley and B. Smyth. Improving recommendation diversity. In *Proceedings of the Twelfth National Conference in Artificial Intelligence and Cognitive Science (AICS-01)*, pages 75–84, 2001.

[5] E. Brynjolfsson, Y. J. Hu, and D. Simester. Goodbye pareto principle, hello long tail: The effect of search costs on the concentration of product sales. *Management Science*, 57(8):1373–1386, Aug. 2011.

[6] E. Brynjolfsson, Y. J. Hu, and M. D. Smith. Research commentary - long tails vs. superstars: The effect of information technology on product variety and sales concentration patterns. *Information Systems Research*, 21(4):736–747, 2010.

[7] D. M. Fleder and K. Hosanagar. Blockbuster culture's next rise or fall: The impact of recommender systems on sales diversity. *Management Science*, 55(5):697–712, 2009.

[8] C. Gini. Measurement of inequality of incomes. *The Economic Journal*, 31(121):124–126, 1921.

[9] D. G. Goldstein and D. C. Goldstein. Profiting from the long tail. *Harvard Business Review*, 84(6):24–28, June 2006.

[10] J. L. Herlocker, J. A. Konstan, A. Borchers, and J. Riedl. An algorithmic framework for performing collaborative filtering. In *Proceedings of the 22nd annual international ACM SIGIR conference on Research and development in information retrieval*, SIGIR '99, pages 230–237, New York, 1999. ACM.

[11] J. L. Herlocker, J. A. Konstan, L. G. Terveen, and J. T. Riedl. Evaluating collaborative filtering recommender systems. *ACM Transactions on Information Systems*, 22(1):5–53, January 2004.

[12] H.-s. Huang, K.-l. Lin, J. Y.-j. Hsu, and C.-n. Hsu. Item-triggered recommendation for identifying potential customers of cold sellers in supermarkets. In *Workshop on the Next Stage of Recommender Systems Research, in conjunction with the 2005 International Conference on Intelligent User Interfaces*, 2005.

[13] N. Jones and P. Pu. User Technology Adoption Issues in Recommender Systems. In *Proceedings of the 2007 Networking and Electronic Commerce Research Conference*, pages 379–394, Riva del Garda, 2007.

[14] Y. Koren. Factorization meets the neighborhood: a multifaceted collaborative filtering model. In *Proceedings of the 14th ACM SIGKDD international conference on Knowledge discovery and data mining*, KDD '08, pages 426–434, New York, 2008. ACM.

[15] Y. Koren, R. Bell, and C. Volinsky. Matrix factorization techniques for recommender systems. *Computer*, 42(8):30–37, August 2009.

[16] A. Krzywicki, W. Wobcke, X. Cai, M. Bain, A. Mahidadia, P. Compton, and Y. S. Kim. Using a critic to promote less popular candidates in a people-to-people recommender system. In *Proceedings of the Twenty-Fourth Conference on Innovative Applications of Artificial Intelligence*. AAAI, 2012.

[17] A. Lacerda and N. Ziviani. Building user profiles to improve user experience in recommender systems. In *Proceedings of the sixth ACM international conference on Web search and data mining*, WSDM '13, pages 759–764, New York, NY, USA, 2013. ACM.

[18] K.-L. Lin. *Item-triggered Recommendation*. PhD thesis, National Taiwan University, 2005.

[19] S. M. McNee, J. Riedl, and J. A. Konstan. Being accurate is not enough: how accuracy metrics have hurt recommender systems. In *CHI'06 Extended Abstracts on Human Factors in Computing Systems*, CHI EA'06, pages 1097–1101, New York, NY, USA, 2006. ACM.

[20] G. Oestreicher-Singer and A. Sundararajan. Recommendation networks and the long tail of electronic commerce. *MIS Quarterly*, 36(1):65–84, March 2012.

[21] Y.-J. Park. The adaptive clustering method for the long tail problem of recommender systems. *Knowledge and Data Engineering, IEEE Transactions on*, 25(8):1904–1915, 2013.

[22] Y.-J. Park and A. Tuzhilin. The long tail of recommender systems and how to leverage it. In *Proceedings of the 2008 ACM conference on Recommender systems*, RecSys '08, pages 11–18, New York, NY, USA, 2008. ACM.

[23] L. Pizzato, T. Rej, J. Akehurst, I. Koprinska, K. Yacef, and J. Kay. Recommending people to people: the nature of reciprocal recommenders with a case study in online dating. *User Modeling and User-Adapted Interaction*, 22:1–42, 2012.

[24] P. Pu, L. Chen, and R. Hu. Evaluating recommender systems from the user's perspective: survey of the state of the art. *User Modeling and User-Adapted Interaction*, 22(4-5):317–355, 2012.

[25] S. Rendle. Factorization machines with libFM. *ACM Transactions on Intelligent Systems and Technology*, 3(3):1–22, May 2012.

[26] P. Resnick and H. R. Varian. Recommender systems. *Communications of the ACM*, 40(3):56–58, Mar. 1997.

[27] G. Shani and A. Gunawardana. Evaluating recommendation systems. In F. Ricci, L. Rokach, B. Shapira, and P. B. Kantor, editors, *Recommender Systems Handbook*, pages 257–297. Springer US, 2011.

[28] H. Yin, B. Cui, J. Li, J. Yao, and C. Chen. Challenging the long tail recommendation. *Proc. VLDB Endow.*, 5(9):896–907, May 2012.

[29] M. Zhang. Enhancing diversity in top-n recommendation. In *Proceedings of the third ACM conference on Recommender systems*, RecSys '09, pages 397–400, New York, NY, USA, 2009. ACM.

[30] M. Zhang and N. Hurley. Avoiding monotony: improving the diversity of recommendation lists. In *Proceedings of the 2008 ACM conference on Recommender systems*, RecSys '08, pages 123–130, New York, NY, USA, 2008. ACM.

# On Building Entity Recommender Systems Using User Click Log and Freebase Knowledge

Xiao Yu[†*], Hao Ma[‡], Bo-June (Paul) Hsu[‡], Jiawei Han[†]
[†]University of Illinois at Urbana-Champaign [‡]Microsoft Research
[†]{xiaoyu1, hanj}@illinois.edu [‡]{haoma, paulhsu}@microsoft.com

## ABSTRACT

Due to their commercial value, *search engines* and *recommender systems* have become two popular research topics in both industry and academia over the past decade. Although these two fields have been actively and extensively studied separately, researchers are beginning to realize the importance of the scenarios at their intersection: providing an integrated search and information discovery user experience. In this paper, we study a novel application, *i.e.*, personalized entity recommendation for search engine users, by utilizing user click log and the knowledge extracted from Freebase.

To better bridge the gap between search engines and recommender systems, we first discuss important heuristics and features of the datasets. We then propose a generic, robust, and time-aware personalized recommendation framework to utilize these heuristics and features at different granularity levels. Using movie recommendation as a case study, with user click log dataset collected from a widely used commercial search engine, we demonstrate the effectiveness of our proposed framework over other popular and state-of-the-art recommendation techniques.

## Categories and Subject Descriptors

H.3.3 [**Information Search and Retrieval**]: Search Process, Information Filtering

## Keywords

Entity Recommendation; Entity Graph; Personalization; Search Click Log; User Behavior Analysis

## 1. INTRODUCTION

In order to meet web users' ever-increasing information needs, search engines are shifting their focus from the top-10-blue-link query answering paradigm to information discovery. Instead of passively matching users' queries to web documents, today's search engines are striving to proactively provide valuable and related information to users. Inspired by this paradigm change, many techniques have been proposed to help users explore web content, *e.g.*, query suggestion [3] and website recommendation [16] [28]. However, such efforts are conducted on a relatively coarse granularity. For example, though website recommender systems suggest websites of potential interest to users, they treat sites as black boxes without considering the content, and thus they cannot present detailed information to users directly.

With the active study and rapid evolution of semantic web techniques, entity graphs which contain entities, attributes, relationships as well as other structural data become widely accessible. Most recently, several commercial search engines have enhanced their search experience by displaying related entity information from entity graphs along with web search results. For example, when answering a query like "skyfall", besides traditional web search results and the entity attributes of this movie, as shown in Figure 1, search engines also suggest "related movies" or display "people also search for" results. These features take an important step forward in unifying search and information discovery experience, as the recommendations are now generated at the entity level.

**Figure 1: Related entity suggestion feature on major search engines**

**Figure 2: Personalized entity recommendation scenario studied in this paper. When a user types movie related queries in a search engine, like "movies", "skyfall", we show movie recommendations for this user based on his/her past user log.**

*The research was performed during an internship of the first author at Microsoft Research.


*WSDM'14*, February 24–28, 2014, New York, New York, USA.

http://dx.doi.org/10.1145/2556195.2556233.

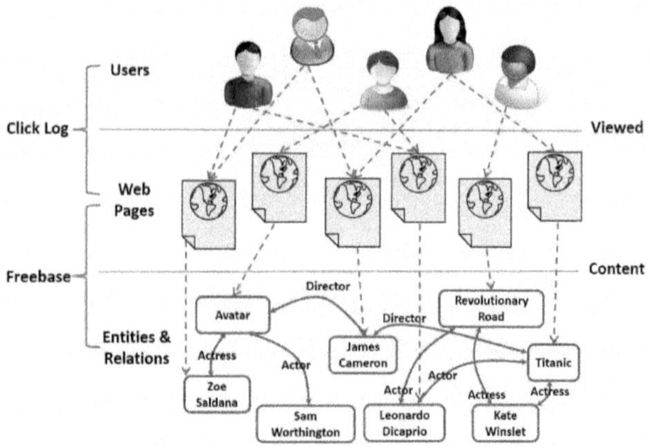


**Figure 3: Heterogeneous relations between users, web pages and entities**

However, to our best knowledge, no existing search engine currently provides personalized entity recommendations based on users' past behaviors. To further enhance user search experience and improve information recommendation quality in search engines, we study personalized entity recommender systems for search engine users in this paper.

By taking advantage of user click log and knowledge extracted from Freebase[1], the proposed framework analyzes users' preferences and interests, and then recommends entities of interest to search engine users during search sessions. By deploying such a system, when a user searches for movie-related web content, in addition to suggesting "related movies", we present personalized movie recommendations as well, illustrated in Figure 2. Notice that in this work, personalized entity recommendations may not directly depend on the queries. Instead, we use the search queries only to determine the domain of recommendation.

In order to build such a system, we are facing many technical as well as data related challenges, including but not limited to:

- How to map users' clicked URLs to specific entities in the knowledge base.
- How to take advantage of entity relationships and different types of attributes in the user log and knowledge base when defining recommendation models.
- How to model users' drift of interests over time.
- How to utilize users' non-entity related click logs.

Aiming to solve the problems mentioned above, we first explore heuristics and features which are critical to the entity recommendation problem, such as different types of entity relationships in the knowledge base, the consistency and drift of users' interests, and cross-domain correlations. Then we propose a global recommendation model which utilizes the aforementioned heuristics and features. We apply the same global recommendation model to different user click logs to achieve personalized recommendation results for different users. We then propose personalized recommendation models for different users to further distinguish users' behaviors at the model level. Empirical studies and analysis in Section 5 demonstrate the effectiveness of the proposed framework over traditional entity recommendation techniques.

[1] `http://www.freebase.com/`

The major contributions of this paper are summarized as follows:

- **Conceptual**: In order to improve user information discovery experience, we study a novel application, *i.e.*, personalized entity recommender system for search engine users, which requires good understanding on both user click log and the Freebase knowledge base.
- **Modeling**: We design a general learning framework which can model different features from both user click log and Freebase entity graph at different granularity levels.
- **Experimental**: We conduct experiments on user click data extracted from a commercial search engine. The results demonstrate the effectiveness of our proposed framework in comparison with several popular recommendation algorithms.

The remainder of this paper is organized as follows. Section 2 introduces the background and preliminaries of this paper. Section 3 discusses features and heuristics in user click log and the Freebase entity graph. Section 4 introduces the proposed entity recommender framework. Experiments and results are discussed in Section 5. Related work, conclusions and future works are presented at the end of the paper.

# 2. BACKGROUND AND PRELIMINARIES

In this section we present background and preliminaries of this paper, including input data format and the definition of the entity recommendation problem of our study.

## 2.1 User Click Log

User click log contains the web pages users visited when using search engines. For each user, a user log sequence can be collected by sequentially connecting web pages this user visited following an ascending timestamp order. We denote user click log sequence for user $u$ as

$$L^u = \langle e_1^u, e_2^u, ..., e_t^u, ..., e_T^u \rangle,$$

where $e_t^u$ is the web page $u$ visited at timestamp $t$. Attributes including timestamp, language of the web page, dwelling time of the visiting event, time of day, *etc.*, may be utilized for entity recommendation task as well.

Additionally, we use $L_t^u$ to represent the user log history of user $u$ from timestamp 1 to $t-1$, *i.e.*, $L_t^u = \langle e_1^u, e_2^u, ..., e_{t-1}^u \rangle$. We name timestamp $T$, the most recent timestamp in the user log sequence of $u$, the *target timestamp*. When evaluating recommendation results, we use $L_T^u$ as input and recommend potential entities of interest to user $u$ at timestamp $T$. We define $e_T^u$ as the entity page that $u$ actually visited at $T$, and use this entity page as the ground truth when comparing different recommender systems in Section 5.

The top two layers ("Users" and "Web Pages") in Figure 3 illustrate the relationship between users and web pages in user click log.

## 2.2 Freebase Entity Graph

Freebase [1] is a large collaborative knowledge base consisting of entities and relationships composed mainly by its community members. It now contains 1.9 billion instances of relationships between 40 million entities. Freebase is widely used in academia and industry in many research problems and applications [14] [19].

Each entity in Freebase are associated with some URLs that are related to this entity. For example, for the movie entity "Jobs"[2], by utilizing the relationships "/common/topic/

[2] `http://www.freebase.com/m/0j7j4ls`

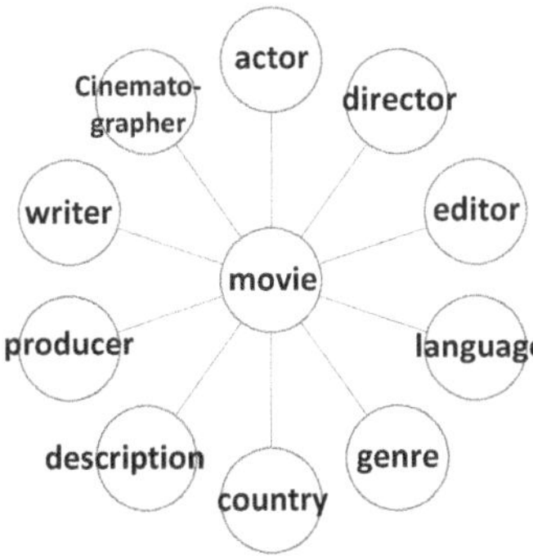

**Figure 4: Partial movie related entity graph schema**

official_website" and "/common/topic/topic_equivalent_webpage", we can obtain this movie's official site, IMDb pages as well as Wikipedia pages. Moreover, we can also get other types of entities related to this movie, including actors, directors, genres, producers, *etc.*

Formally, a Freebase entity graph is a heterogeneous information network [23], which contains multi-typed entities, relationships and attributes collected from different domains. Similar to an entity-relation diagram in relational databases, we use an abstract graph to represent the entity and relationship type restrictions in Freebase, which is usually referred to as the *entity graph schema*, denoted as $G_T = (\mathcal{A}, \mathcal{R})$. An example of a partial entity graph schema for the movie domain can be found in Figure 4.

The bottom two layers ("Web Pages" and "Entities & Relations") in Figure 3 present the relationship between web pages and Freebase entity graph. Moreover, in this paper, we use the phrases "Freebase", "knowledge base" and "entity graph" interchangeably.

## 2.3 Mapping URLs to Entities

With the definitions in Section 2.1 and Section 2.2, we can now map users' clicked URLs in user log to the corresponding entities in Freebase, as demonstrated in Figure 3. A user's interests can now be represented by a set of entities and web pages this user visited before. The visited entities and web pages as well as various relationships between these entities can be utilized for making personalized recommendation for this user.

## 2.4 Problem Definition

With the definitions of user click log and Freebase entity graph, we define entity recommendation problem for search engine users as follows:

Given a set of user click log sequences $L$, the Freebase entity graph $G$, and a specific click log sequence $L_T^u$ of user $u$, an entity recommendation model for search engine users should be able to recommend potential entities of interest to user $u$ at timestamp $T$. We denote this recommendation result as $\hat{e}_T^u$.

Important notations used in the rest of the paper can be found in Table 1.

# 3. EXPLORING THE DATA

In this section, we discuss features and heuristics in search engine user click log and the Freebase entity graph, which can be advantageous when building entity recommender systems for search engine users.

## 3.1 Consistency and Drift of User Interest

Modeling user interests is crucial in building entity recommender systems. For a specific user, his or her interests usually cover only a small number of topics over a certain time period. A user may be interested in "X-Files" related information this week, and then begins to search for romantic movie related web pages the next week. Recommending related entities in a timely manner can assist the information gathering process of this user.

**Table 1: Notations**

| Notation | Description |
|---|---|
| $e_t^u$ | entity page user $u$ visited at timestamp $t$ |
| $L$, $G$ | user log and entity graph |
| $w_t(\cdot,\cdot)$ | temporal similarity of two page visiting events |
| $w_u(\cdot,\cdot)$ | similarity between two user log sequences |
| $\hat{e}_T^u$ | recommended entity to user $u$ at timestamp $T$ |
| $L_t^u$ | user log sequence of $u$ from timestamp 1 to $t-1$ |
| $N(\cdot)$ | user log subsequence neighbors |
| $S(\cdot,\cdot)$ | a user log or entity graph pairwise feature |
| $\theta$ | parameters for recommendation models |

One possible way of recommending entities to users with this motivation is to estimate conditional probabilities (*a.k.a* co-click or co-occurrence) between entities in recent user click log. With learned conditional probabilities, given a user log sequence $L_T^u$, recommendation score for certain entity $\hat{e}_T^u$ can be calculated as follows:

$$r(\hat{e}_T^u, L_T^u) \propto \sum_{e_t^u \in L_T^u} P(\hat{e}_T^u | e_t^u). \quad (1)$$

Conditional probability between entities is easy to estimate and can be very effective with sufficient training data. However, such approach can only recommend entities that have previously been observed in the user log before, hence it suffers from the *cold start* problem for newly introduced entities.

Although user interests might follow one theme or topic in a certain time period, eventually they change over time. We demonstrate this phenomenon by measuring similarities between entities (using pairwise shortest distance-based method in entity graph) from different days in the same user log sequence. In Figure 5(a), we sum up user log similarities of all users for each day and plot the accumulated similarity difference between days with a heat map (both axes represent date, 0 is March 1st, 1 is March 2nd, *etc*). Red color indicates high similarity while blue indicates dissimilarity. One can observe that the accumulated user log similarity is higher when the two dates are closer. Notice that the heat map possesses a 7-day periodic pattern, which is caused by users' weekly behavior repeat.

To eliminate such periodic patterns, we aggregate similarity differences between days and plot it against day difference (1 means the entity similarities are one day apart) (Figure 5(b)). The scale of y-axis has been removed to comply with the company's non-disclosure policy. In both plots, users' interests stay relatively consistent when the time interval is small (1 or 2 days), but change dramatically when the time interval is big (2 weeks).

In order to provide satisfying recommendation results, an entity recommender system should model both the consistency and the drift of user interest simultaneously. When recommending entities, the recommender system should rely more on recent behaviors, less on the old behaviors and age user log with a time decay function accordingly.

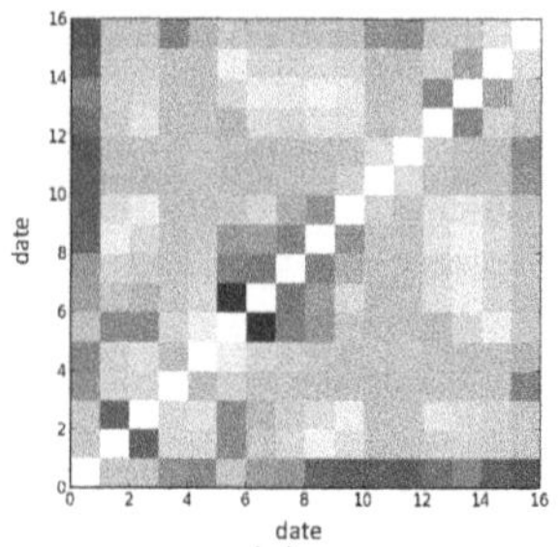

(a)

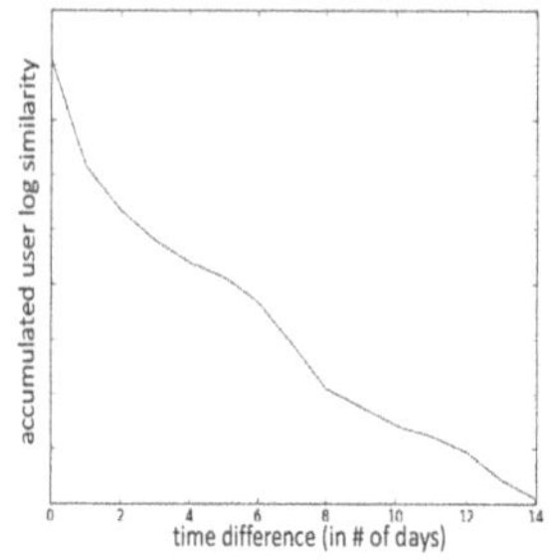

(b)

**Figure 5: User interests drift over time ((a) is the user interest similarity heat map and (b) is the aggregated user interest similarity plot again time difference)**

**Table 2: Cross-Domain Correlation Example**

| Rank | comicbookresources.com | ruelala.com |
|---|---|---|
| 1 | The Avengers | Magic Mike |
| 2 | Spider-Man | The Avengers |
| 3 | The Dark Knight Rises | Prometheus |
| 4 | Prometheus | Moonrise Kingdom |
| 5 | Men In Black 3 | Ted |
| 6 | Iron Man 2 | Snow White and Huntsman |
| 7 | Superman : The Man of Steel | Savages |
| 8 | Thor | Hunger Games |
| 9 | Snow White and huntsman | Rock of Ages |
| 10 | Battleship | The Best Exotic Marigold Hotel |

## 3.2 Entity Relationships in Entity Graph

The entity relationship heterogeneity of the Freebase entity graph provides possibilities of measuring entity similarities from different perspectives. Taking the movie entity graph schema in Figure 4 as an example, we can claim two movies are similar if they share the same genres (*movie-genre* relation), cast (*movie-actor* relation), or directors (*movie-director* relation). Additionally, previous studies [13] [23] introduced approaches to quantitatively measure entity similarities in entity graphs, and suggested that entities which are connected by different types of paths could be similar for different reasons. Entity relationships and similarity measurements can help capture users' different interests when defining entity recommendation models.

## 3.3 Cross-Domain Correlation

When building recommendation models in one domain, *e.g.*, movie recommendation, certain seemingly irrelevant information can also contribute (*e.g.*, users' preferences in books and music). In order to demonstrate this cross-domain correlation heuristic, we calculate the conditional probabilities between movie entities and two non-movie websites with user click log from summer 2012. The top 10 movies correlated with each website can be found in Table 2.

We first observe that the two ranking lists are substantially different. Comic Book Resources[3] users are mostly interested in comic book based sci-fi movies, including Spider-Man, Superman, Thor, *etc.* Rue La La[4] users, however, prefer romantic movies, *e.g.*, Magic Mike, Moonrise Kingdom, and Rock of Ages. Based on the above observation, we believe by incorporating cross-domain information when defining recommendation models, the quality of the recommendation results could be potentially improved. Most importantly, it can also greatly alleviate the cold start problem. When we know nothing about a user in a target domain, cross-domain information becomes critical in personalizing recommendation process.

[3]comicbookresources.com, a comic book discussion website

[4]ruelala.com, a fashion boutique with mostly female customers

**Table 3: Representative Features**

| | |
|---|---|
| Entity Graph Path Features | |
| movie–actor–movie | movies with the same actors |
| movie–director–movie | movies with the same directors |
| movie–producer–movie | movies with the same producers |
| movie–star–movie | movies with the same stars |
| movie–writer–movie | movies with the same writers |
| movie–genre–movie | movies with the same genres |
| movie–language–movie | movies with the same language |
| Entity Graph Binary Features | |
| is_prequel | *movie1* is a prequel of *movie2* |
| is_sequel | *movie1* is a sequel of *movie2* |
| actor–movie | actor appears in the movie |
| director–movie | director directs the movie |
| producer–movie | producer produces the movie |
| Entity Graph Content Features | |
| release date | two movie with close release dates |
| description similarity | text similarity in movie descriptions |
| User Log Features | |
| co-click | conditional probability between entities |
| global popularity | movie popularity of all time |
| local popularity | movie popularity today |
| cross-domain | cross-domain correlation |

## 3.4 Feature Calculation

Based on the above discussion, in Table 3, we present representative features generated from both user click log and Freebase, which can be potentially useful in building movie recommendation models. We group these features into four categories: entity graph path features which measure similarities between movies using the PathSim method [23]; entity graph binary features which are defined with important entity graph relationships; entity graph content features which utilize content based attributes to measure entity similarities; user log features which are generated from user click log following different heuristics.

Entity graph path features are defined along different types of paths in entity graph. We use the entity types on paths to represent the path types when there is no ambiguity (*e.g.*, movie–actor–movie). If two entities are linked together by paths following one certain path type, following [23], we can calculate the similarity score between these two entities with Equation 2:

$$S_{\mathcal{P}}(e_i, e_j) = \frac{2 \times |\{p_{e_i \rightsquigarrow e_j} : p_{e_i \rightsquigarrow e_j} \in \mathcal{P}\}|}{|\{p_{e_i \rightsquigarrow e_i} : p_{e_i \rightsquigarrow e_i} \in \mathcal{P}\}| + |\{p_{e_j \rightsquigarrow e_j} : p_{e_j \rightsquigarrow e_j} \in \mathcal{P}\}|} \quad (2)$$

where $\mathcal{P}$ represents the path type. $p_{e_i \rightsquigarrow e_j}$ is a path between $e_i$ and $e_j$, $p_{e_i \rightsquigarrow e_i}$ is a path between $e_i$ and $e_i$, and $p_{e_j \rightsquigarrow e_j}$ is a path between $e_j$ and $e_j$.

Entity graph binary features are defined with the existence of certain entity relationship. Entity graph content features are defined based on the content type. For example, we use exponential decay function to define the movie release date similarity and cosine similarity to measure movie description similarity.

All features we used in this project are normalized to the range of [0, 1]. One may notice that, although most of the features are pairwise features defined between two entities, point-wise features like popularity can facilitate the recommendation as well. In order to incorporate such point-wise features into the recommendation model, we rewrite such features in a pairwise format $S(e_j) = S(\cdot, e_j)$. For such a pseudo-pairwise functions, no matter what the first parameter is, they always return the point-wise function value based on $e_j$.

# 4. RECOMMENDATION FRAMEWORK

With the features and heuristics discussed in Section 1 and 3, we present the proposed entity recommendation framework in this section.

## 4.1 Global Recommendation Model

With features generated from user click log and the Freebase dataset, considering the consistency and drift of user interest over time, we propose the following global entity recommendation model (Equation 3):

$$r(\hat{e}_T^u; L_T^u, \theta) = \sum_{e_t^u \in L_T^u} w_t(\hat{e}_T^u, e_t^u) \sum_{k=1}^{K} \theta_k S_k(\hat{e}_T^u, e_t^u), \quad (3)$$

where $w_t(e_T, e_t)$ is the temporal similarity function between two entity page visiting events, defined as $w_t(e_T, e_t) = \beta e^{-\alpha(T-t)}$. Intuitively, if timestamp $T$ and $t$ are nearby, $w_t$ will assign a high similarity to these two events. However, if $T$ and $t$ are two remote timestamps, $w_t$ will be small, which means $e_t^u$ will have less effect on the recommendation results at $T$.

$S(\cdot, \cdot)$ are pairwise features as defined in the previous section, and $K$ is the total number of features. $\theta$ are the parameters for the global model, representing different weights of these features. With the global recommendation model, given a user log sequence $L_T^u$, we can assign recommendation scores to possible entities and return the entities with high scores to user $u$ as the recommendation results.

To estimate $\theta$ in global recommendation model, we first denote the margin between the ground truth entity $e_T^u$ (the entity $u$ actually visited at $T$) and the entity with the highest recommendation score besides $e_T^u$, as follows:

$$g(e_T^u; L_T^u, \theta) = r(e_T^u; L_T^u, \theta) - r(e_m^u; L_T^u, \theta), \quad (4)$$

where $e_m^u = argmax_{e \neq e_T^u} r(e; L_T^u, \theta)$. As explained above, $e_m^u$ is the entity with the highest recommendation besides $e_T^u$. $\theta$ can be estimated by minimizing the following objective function:

$$O_g(\theta) = -\sum_u g(e_T^u; L_T^u, \theta) + \frac{\lambda}{2} \|\theta\|_2^2, \quad (5)$$

where $\lambda$ controls $L_2$ regularization to prevent over-fitting.

Objective function defined in Equation 5 is one possible way to estimate global model parameters. One can adopt other margin measures when defining $g$, like hinge loss, or kernel based similarity. Moreover, we can also directly optimize ranking-based metrics like reciprocal rank (Equation 12) by defining the margin as follows:

$$g\prime(e_T^u; L_T^u, \theta) = RR(e_T^u; L_T^u, \theta) - RR(e_m^u; L_T^u, \theta), \quad (6)$$

where $RR(e; L_T, \theta)$ is the reciprocal rank score of entity $e$ given $\theta$ and $L_T$. However, due to scalability consideration, we need to choose the most computational efficient method. Equation 4 only requires the calculation of the recommendation scores of $e_T^u$ and $e_m^u$. While to utilize Equation 6, we need to calculate the recommendation scores of all possible entities and rank them accordingly. Preliminary evaluation on a small dataset yields similar recommendation results from these two methods, suggesting that Equation 4 can achieve similar effectiveness as Equation 6. Hence, in this paper, we use Equation 4 as the margin definition.

Global recommendation model takes advantage of various features from both user click log and the Freebase entity graph. However, when recommending entities to search engine users, we apply the same model to all the users, which may not be sufficient to capture user interest diversity.

## 4.2 Personalized Recommendation Model

In reality, search engine users have different interests and preferences. Moreover, they may like the same entities for different reasons. Some users may like comedy movies while others may prefer movies with famous actors. Even for the same movie, *e.g.*, "The Dark Knight Rises", some users are interested in this movie due to the superhero theme while other viewers might be the fans of the director. With the global model, the recommender system cannot distinguish users' different preferences properly, which may lead to unsatisfying recommendation results. To better model search engine users' interests and preferences, we propose a personalized recommendation model as follows:

$$r(\hat{e}_T^u; L_T^u, \theta_T^u) = \sum_{e_t^u \in L_T^u} w_t(\hat{e}_T^u, e_t^u) \sum_{k=1}^{K} S_k(\hat{e}_T^u, e_t^u) \theta_k^u. \quad (7)$$

Different from Equation 3, personalized recommendation model requires a set of parameters $\theta^u$ for each user.

When learning personalized models, directly maximizing margins between $e_T^u$ and $e_m^u$ as we did when learning the global model might not be as effective. Due to the data sparsity issue, we do not have sufficient data from one user to learn a personalized ranking model (we demonstrate this claim in Section 5). To alleviate such problem, when learning personalized models, we use both the user log history $L_T^u$ of the target user, as well as other "similar" user log sequences, namely the *neighbors* of $L_T^u$, denoted by $N(L_T^u)$. We provide the formal definition of *neighbors* as well as an efficient approach to generate neighbors in Section 4.3.

Based on this philosophy, we propose the following per-user objective function to estimate parameters for the personalized models:

$$\begin{aligned} O_u(\theta^u) = \; & - \sum_{t=1}^{T} w_t(e_T^u, e_t^u) g(e_t^u; L_t^u, \theta^u) + \\ & \lambda_1 \sum_{L_{T\prime}^{u\prime} \in N(L_T^u)} w_u(L_{T\prime}^{u\prime}, L_T^u) g(e_{T\prime}^{u\prime}; L_{T\prime}^{u\prime}, \theta^u) + \\ & \tfrac{1}{2}\lambda_2 \; \|\theta^u - \theta_g\|_2^2, \end{aligned} \quad (8)$$

where $w_t(\cdot, \cdot)$ measures the temporal similarity of two visiting events, and $w_u(\cdot, \cdot)$ measures the similarity between two user log sequences, the definition of which is given in Equation 10. We use $\theta_g$ to represent the previous learned global model.

The personalized objective function $O_u$ contains three terms. The first term in Equation 8 models the consistency and drift of user interest (Section 3.1). The personalized model parameters are learned to make predictions at $T$ for each target user. We use these parameters to predict target user's past behavior at a previous timestamp ($t$, from 1 to $T$) given the corresponding user log sequence $L_t^u$. The expected accuracy of such prediction is controlled by $w_t(\cdot, \cdot)$, *i.e.*, $\theta^u$ should provide a more accurate prediction if the visiting events happened more recently. The second term ($\lambda_1$) models the similarity between the target user log sequence and the neighbor sequences. We use parameters of $u$ at $T$ to predict the neighbors' behaviors at their corresponding target timestamp $T\prime$. Similarly, the expected accuracy of such prediction is controlled by $w_u(\cdot,\cdot)$, *i.e.*, $\theta^u$ should explain the neighbor's behavior more accurately if the neighbor and $L_T^u$ are more similar. The third term ($\lambda_2$) defines the $L_2$ regularization between personalized models and the global model to prevent over-fitting.

The aforementioned data sparsity issue not only complicates parameter estimation process, but may also compromise the quality of the recommendations. With insufficient user log history, even with personalized models, the final recommendation results could be biased or unsatisfying. With the neighbor definition available for $L_T^u$, we revisit the personalized recommendation model proposed in Equation 7 and propose a new neighborhood based personalized recommendation model in Equation 9:

$$r_n(\hat{e}_t^u; L_T^u, \theta^u) = r(\hat{e}_t^u; L_T^u, \theta^u) + \lambda_1 \sum_{L_{T\prime}^{u\prime} \in N(L_T^u)} w_u(L_{T\prime}^{u\prime}, L_T^u) r(\hat{e}_t^u; L_{T\prime}^{u\prime}, \theta^u). \tag{9}$$

In this neighborhood based recommendation function, besides personalized recommendation function defined in Equation 7, we also use neighbor log sequences of $L_T^u$ to facilitate recommendation. Neighbors contribute to the recommendation score differently based on the similarity between a neighbor log sequence and the log sequence of the target user $L_T^u$. $\lambda_1$ controls the percentage of the neighborhood recommendation score. When $L_T^u = \emptyset$, *i.e.*, for a new user with no user log history, the first term of $r_n(\cdot)$ becomes zero, and the recommendation score will be decided by only its neighbors. In this situation, the $w_u(\cdot,\cdot)$ function will be 1 for all users in the dataset, *i.e.*, all users are neighbors of $L_T^u$ with the same neighbor similarity. Thus this personalized model degeneralizes to the global model defined in Equation 3. When the log history of the target user is long and dense (active users), the recommendation score will mostly rely on the user's previous behavior and the impact from the neighbors will be lessened accordingly.

Discussion and performance comparison between Equation 7 and Equation 9 are presented in Section 5.

## 4.3 User Log Sequence Neighbors

As stated above, due to data sparsity, we may not have enough data from one user to learn a personalized recommendation model. Also insufficient personal user log sequence $L_T^u$ may compromise recommendation results. To alleviate this issue, we define similar user log sequences of $L_T^u$ as neighbors of the target sequence, denoted by $N(L_T^u)$. We first define user log sequence similarity function as follows:

$$w_u(L_T^u, L_{t\prime}^{u\prime}) = \frac{r(E; L_T^u, \theta_g) \cdot r(E; L_{t\prime}^{u\prime}, \theta_g)}{\|r(E; L_T^u, \theta_g)\| \|r(E; L_{t\prime}^{u\prime}, \theta_g)\|}, \tag{10}$$

where $r(E;\cdot)$ represents the corresponding recommendation score vector over the entire entity space given certain user log $L$ and the global model $\theta_g$. $\|\cdot\|$ calculates the $L_2$ norm of the recommendation score vectors.

When searching for neighbors, we use user log subsequences $L_t = \langle e_1, e_2, ..., e_{t-1}\rangle$ as neighbor candidates. Based on the above definition, traditional *K-NN* method takes $O(N^2)$ to find the nearest neighbors for all user log sequences. However, by employing random projection based locality sensitive hashing, we can estimate the nearest neighbors of all user log sequences in $O(N)$. Details of this method can be found in [26].

With the learned personalized recommendation models for search engine users, for a target user $u$, the recommender system can now assign recommendation scores to potential entities of interest based on the user log history and the neighborhood information. By presenting the top-$K$ entities when $u$ searches for related web content in search engines, the proposed system can facilitate user's information discovery process and further improve the overall user experience of the search engines.

## 4.4 Parameter Estimation

In Equation 4, we utilize the margins between $e_T^u$, the target entity, and $e_m^u$, the entity with the highest score besides $e_T^u$ given a certain $\theta$. Notice that the entity ranking order changes with $\theta$, thus $e_m^u$ changes accordingly, which makes $g$ in Equation 4 non-continuous and both objective functions (Equations 5 and 8) non-convex. Non-convex optimization methods, *e.g.*, Powell's method, are mostly computationally intractable. Considering the size of the training dataset (commercial search engine user log and the Freebase entity graph), we use the following method to approximate the results.

Although Equations 5 and 8 are non-convex during the entire optimization process, when fixing $e_m^u$, both functions will become convex and differentiable. Due to the limitation of space, we here only give the partial derivative of Equation 4 with a fixed $e_m^u$ as follows. The gradients of the two objective functions can be obtained accordingly:

$$\frac{\partial g}{\partial \theta_k} = \sum_{e_t^u \in L_T^u} w_t(e_T^u, e_t^u)\Big(S_k(e_T^u, e_t^u) - S_k(e_m^u, e_t^u)\Big). \tag{11}$$

With this observation, we can now employ the well-studied and efficient iterative convex optimization techniques to estimate the models. In each iteration, given the current $\theta$, we first calculate and fix $e_m^u$, and then compute the gradient of the objective function accordingly. Similar optimization methods have been employed before in [5], and it is known that such approximation may lead to a local minimum. One possible way to overcome this issue is to execute the optimization process multiple times with randomly initialized $\theta$, and choose the parameters which produce the best results. We compared Powell's method and this method on a small dataset. Similar results are generated separately, which suggests the proposed objective function can be approximately estimated in this way. With the approximated gradient, we use L-BFGS to finally estimate the recommendation models.

# 5. EXPERIMENTS

In this section, we implement both global and personalized entity recommendation models proposed in Section 4 along with several popular and state-of-the-art recommendation methods which fit in the problem definition of this study. We apply these methods on a user log dataset collected from a commercial search engine, and the entity graph extracted from Freebase. We then perform a series of experiments to demonstrate the effectiveness of the proposed models. We present experimental results with discussion and performance analysis in this section.

## 5.1 Datasets

Although the proposed recommendation framework is generic, we take movie related entity recommendation as a case study in the following experiments. We use three months user click log collected from a commercial search engine in 2012 as the user log dataset. We then extracted the corresponding subgraph from Freebase. Note that this extracted Freebase dataset not only contains movie entities, but also contains other related entities as well as the relationships be-

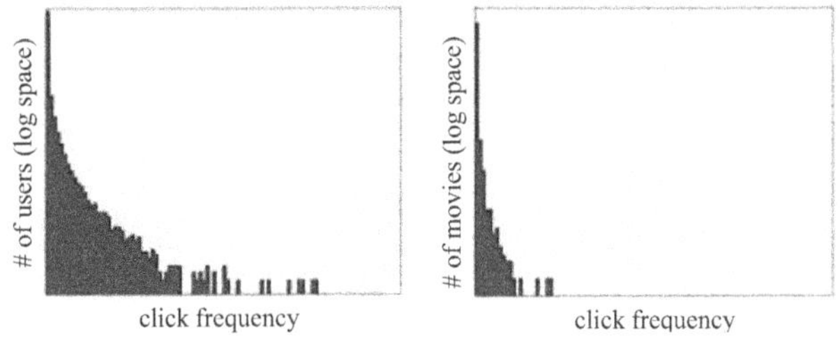


**Figure 6: User Log Distribution**

tween these entities, including actors, directors, producer, *etc.* Moreover, the URLs related to those movie entities can also obtained in order to map users' clicked URLs to movie related entities. Finally, after jointing the collected user click log and the Freebase entity graph, we sampled approximately 1,000,000 users with at least one movie related entity page visiting activity in the dataset. Data distribution of the movie entity related user log dataset can be found in Figure 6.

To comply with the company's non-disclosure policy, we hide both axis scales of the plots. The first plot is users' entity page visiting frequency (number of users *v.s.* visit frequency) distribution, which follows a power law distribution. One can notice that most users only visited a small number of movies related entity pages in the dataset. Similarly, the second plot, movies' entity page visiting frequency distribution (number of movies *v.s.* visit frequency) is also a power law distribution. From this plot, we can observe that the majority of movie related entity pages have only been visited for a small number of times while only a very small number of movies have been viewed frequently. These two plots demonstrate the sparsity issue of the user log dataset.

## 5.2 Performance Test

We partition the entire user log dataset into two sets: 10,000 users with their corresponding user log sequences are sampled as the test dataset, and the rest user log data are used as the training dataset. As described in problem definition, we adopt the *leave-one-out* validation method to evaluate the performance, *i.e.*, given the user log sequence $L_T^u$, which contains entity pages $u$ visited from timestamp 1 to $T-1$, we attempt to predict the entity $u$ visited at $T$. We call this entity $e_T^u$ the ground truth entity. We use top-10 *mean reciprocal rank* (MRR) as the evaluation metric:

$$MRR = \frac{1}{|D_{test}|}\sum_{i=1}^{|D_{test}|}\frac{1}{rank(e_T^u)}, \tag{12}$$

where $|D_{test}|$ is the size of the test dataset and $rank(e_T^u)$ represents the rank of the ground truth entity $e_T^u$ with certain recommendation function. $rank(e_T^u)$ will be 0 if the recommendation model can not rank $e_T^u$ in the top-10 results. Notice that a larger MRR indicates better performance.

Models proposed in this paper are implemented as follows:

- Global recommendation model: estimate global recommendation model $\theta_g$ using Equation 5 and recommend entities with Equation 3;
- Personalized recommendation model without neighbor data: estimate personalized recommendation model $\theta_T^u$ with Equation 8 and recommend entities with Equation 7. We abbreviate this method as *PRM*;
- Personalized recommendation model with neighbor data: estimate personalized recommendation model $\theta^u$ with Equation 8 and recommend entities using Equation 9. We abbreviate this method as *PRM-KNN*.

**Table 4: Experiment Results**

| Method | MRR |
|---|---|
| Global Popularity | 0.024 |
| Local Popularity | 0.043 |
| Cross Domain | 0.039 |
| Matrix Factorization | 0.160 |
| Co-Click | 0.340 |
| Global Model | 0.354 |
| PRM | 0.361 |
| PRM-KNN | 0.451 |

We implement the following popular recommendation approaches besides the proposed methods. Features and models of all methods are learned in the training dataset and MRRs are calculated based on the recommendation performances in test dataset.

- Global Popularity: recommend the most popular (most frequently visited) movies in the entire user log training dataset;
- Local Popularity: recommend the most popular movies of the day;
- Cross-Domain: recommend movies based on users' non-movie web page visiting log;
- Co-Click: estimate conditional probabilities between entities and recommend movies using Equation 1;
- Implicit binary matrix factorization: build binary user-entity implicit feedback matrix with test user log dataset, and apply the matrix factorization method presented in [6], to recommend entities to users.

To make a fair comparison, we apply the same feature set to all three proposed recommendation models. All methods are able to generate a recommendation score given a user log sequence $L_T^u$ and the target entity $e_T^u$. Ideally we should evaluate all entities with each method and rank these entities accordingly, which can be, however, very time consuming. Also as presented in Figure 6, most users are only interested in a small number of entities, which makes evaluating all entities for each user unnecessary and excessive. For simplicity and efficient reasons, each method will only rank a set of most promising candidates, which are pooled by different features. With this evaluation process, the MRR scores reported in this paper are the lower bounds of the actual performances of these methods. Performance results of all the recommendation approaches are presented in Table 4.

In Cross-Domain method, we estimate the conditional probabilities of movie entities with 3,000 popular websites. This method gives a similar performance of the popularity based methods. Among these three single feature methods, local popularity approach performs the best with $MRR = 0.043$. Binary matrix factorization method reaches $MRR = 0.160$ in the dataset. Although matrix factorization performs well in traditional recommendation problem, it could not fully take advantage of the heuristics and features generated from user click log and the entity graph. In order to thoroughly evaluate matrix factorization based recommender systems, we also implemented technique proposed in [11], which utilizes temporal information during matrix factorization process, but the performance does not change as much. One possible explanation is that matrix factorization method heavily depends on the learned user and item factors, $U$ and $V$; if these two matrices are not accurately learned due to the noises or the data sparsity, adding other factors like temporal information, or other contextual information may not achieve significantly better performance as expected.

Co-Click model (conditional probability between entities) outperforms all baseline methods, which makes it the strongest baseline method for this problem. As stated in Section 4, with a sufficient amount of data (approximately 1 million users' log), co-click can be very effective and provide satisfying recommendation results.

The proposed global recommendation model takes advantage of pairwise similarity features extracted from both entity graph and user log. In our experiments, parameters are estimated with *L-BFGS* with a randomly sampled 5,000 user log sequences. Regularization term $\lambda$ in Equation 5 is set to 0.2 which is determined by cross validation.

Personalized recommendation framework, different from global recommendation model, assigns a different recommendation model to each user. Parameters in each personalized recommendation model are estimated with the target user log sequence $L_T^u$ as well as the neighborhood data. With personalized parameters, users' behaviors and interests patterns can be better interpreted. In this experiment, we use the same set of features when defining personalized models as in the global model. We use $\theta_g$ from global recommendation model in the regularization term of Equation 7 as well as neighbor similarity function (Equation 10). Neighborhood similarity threshold in Equation 10 is set to 0.5. In neighbor similarity definition, $E$ represents the entire entity space. For simplicity reason, we only use partial entity space (5,000 entities) to estimate neighborhood similarity. This estimation could damage the performance of both personalized recommendation methods (PRM and PRM-KNN).

For computational efficiency, we set the upper bound of neighborhood size of each user to 80, *i.e.*, if the random projection of user log $L_T^u$ is "popular" and a large number of similar neighbors are found, we only randomly sample 80 neighbors when estimating personalized models. Two regularization parameters ($\lambda_1$ and $\lambda_2$) in Equation 8 are set to 0.05 and 0.1 respectively and similar to global recommendation model, these two parameters are estimated with cross validation. We use the global temporal similarity function $w_t(\cdot,\cdot)$ in personalized recommendation models although later experiments suggest personalized temporal similarity function may lead to better performance, since the rates of user interest drift are different.

As discussed in previous section, when recommending entities using personalized models, we can either include neighbor data or only use the target user's click log history. Based on experiment results, when only using target user log, the improvement of performance is not as significant compared to global recommendation model (1.98% improvement on MRR). But when including neighbor data during recommendation, a much more significant performance boost can be achieved (27.4%). Analysis and discussions of the personalized recommendation models are presented in the next subsection.

## 5.3 Personalized Recommendation Model Performance

In the following experiments, we analyze the performance change of the proposed personalized recommendation framework in different scenarios.

### *5.3.1 With Different Entity Frequencies*

We first study the correlation between performance of the personalized recommendation method and the frequency of the target movie. We split the test dataset based on the frequency of the target movies and apply personalized recommendation models on each group. The results of this experiment can be found in Figure 7(a). Based on the results, one can notice that popular movies (movies which appear frequently in the user log dataset) are easier to predict than other movies. Two reasons may be able to explain this performance change. First, features in recommendation models favor popular movies, e.g., global and local popularity. The co-click feature provides more accurate prediction with popular movies considering the frequency of these movies in the training dataset. Second, with sufficient training data for popular movies, high quality recommendation models can be learned in such scenarios, thus MRR will be increased accordingly.

### *5.3.2 With Different Neighborhood Sizes*

The second experiment we conducted on analyzing personalized recommendation framework is to study the correlation between recommendation performance and the number of neighbors that locality sensitive hashing technique can find for different user log sequences. Results are presented in Figure 7(b). From the plot one can notice that the more neighbors each user log sequence has, the better recommendation results our framework can provide. Two reasons might be able to explain this phenomenon. First, based on Equation 8, more neighbors indicate more data during parameter estimation, so that a higher quality recommendation model can be obtained in this situation. Second, user log sequences with more neighbors, *a.k.a.*, the "popular" user log sequences, are usually associated with popular movie entities. Based on the previous experiment, user log sequences with more neighbors are usually easier to model which leads to a better recommendation results.

### *5.3.3 With Different Sequence Lengths*

The third performance analysis experiment we conducted is to study whether any correlation exists between personalized recommendation performance and the length of the user log sequences. Similar to the two previous experiments, we split the test users into groups based on the lengths of their user log sequences, and apply personalized recommendation models on each group. The results of this study can be found in Figure 7(c). The result plot indicates that the performance of the proposed method peaks when lengths of user log sequences are from 3 to 5. Shorter and longer user log sequences lead to compromised performances. When a user log sequence is too short (red circle in the plot), not enough data are available when estimating parameters, which could damage the quality of the personalized models. When a user log sequence is too long (green circle in the plot), user's interests may drift overtime severely, and such information varying can be hard to capture with a global temporal similarity function. Another possible explanation for the compromised performance when user log sequence is long, is the existence of Internet-addict users. These users visit a large number of entity pages with a broad interests, which makes building personalized recommendation model for these users very challenging.

One might argue that, since performance peaks when user log sequence length is in the range of 3 to 5, old visiting events might not help as much as the most recent 3 to 5 web page visiting events. To verify this hypothesis, we chop all user log sequences to length 3 (only preserve the most recent 3 web page visiting events) and apply personalized recommendation method on this dataset. MRR dropped to

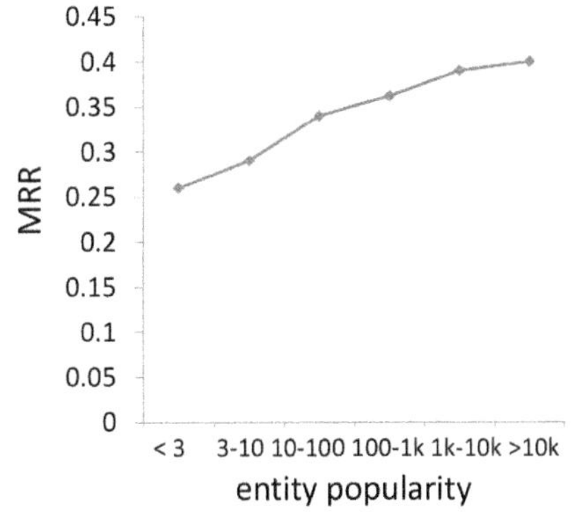

(a) Entity Popularity

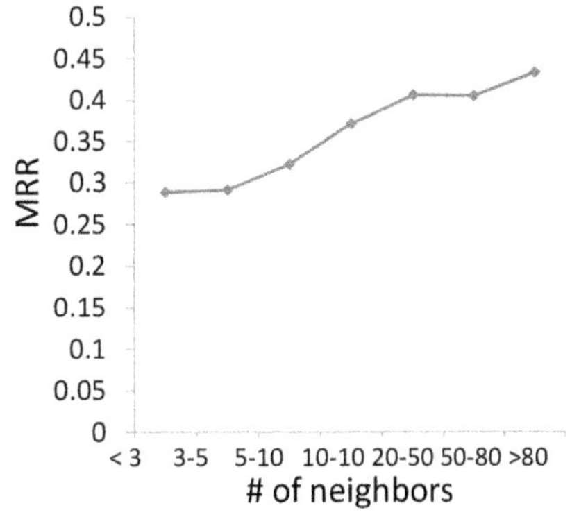

(b) Number of Neighbors

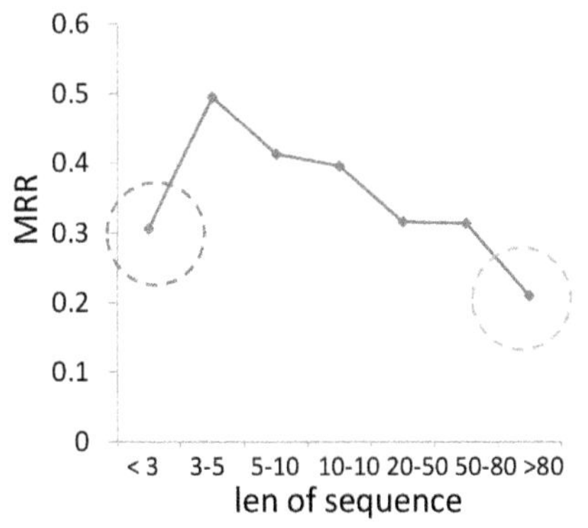

(c) Length of Sequence

**Figure 7: Personalized Framework Performance Analysis**

0.114 which is much lower than the best performance we can obtain when using all user web page visiting events. This experiment demonstrates that previous behavior does help entity recommendation in the near future. As we stated before, personalized temporal similarity function might be able to capture the each user's interest drift more accurately, with which recommendation performance can be improved.

This performance analysis experiment also explains the performance improvement of personalized recommendation method when using neighborhood data during recommendation. As discussed above, the compromised performance in red circle in Figure 7(c) is due to lack of data, and as shown in Figure 6, the majority of users only have a very limited number of web page visiting events so these users belong to the red circle. Adding neighborhood data during recommendation helps lessen the data sparsity problem so that it can improve the performance for most users resulting the significant result improvement in Table 4.

# 6. RELATED WORKS

In this section, we review two related research areas, which are (1) the existing recommender systems, and (2) the information network analysis methods.

## 6.1 Recommender Systems

Recommender systems have received increasing attention and have been actively studied in recent years due to the various applications in E-commerce and other Web applications. Collaborative filtering techniques, which includes neighbor-based approaches and model-based approaches, are popular and widely applied. Neighbor-based methods usually study similarity calculation methods among users (user-based) [2] [20] or items (item-based) [15] [22]. User-based collaborative filtering methods provide recommendation to target users by first finding similar users and then collecting and analyzing neighbor ratings to further predict items that target users would be interested in. Similarly, item-based collaborative filtering methods take advantage of rating information of similar items.

Model-based collaborative filtering methods try to fit user-item rating data into different models (Bayesian Network [27], matrix factorization [12] [21], or clustering models [25] *etc*) and use the learned models to recommend items to users in unseen scenarios. Matrix factorization techniques gain rising attention in both explicit and implicit feedback applications. Using low-rank approximation to represent user-item rating matrix suits the need of handling large scale datasets nicely. Many studies have been done using this technique to interpret different heuristics in user-item rating datasets [10]. In [6], Hu et al. propose to model implicit feedback as positive and negative preferences with different confidence levels with a matrix factorization based approach. Koren et al. incorporate temporal information in matrix factorization models to further improve the recommendation quality [11].

Besides traditional recommender systems, researchers proposed hybrid approaches to incorporate both user-item rating dataset as well as other contextual information in different scenarios, including social network information, time information, *etc.* For instance, social trust or friend aware recommender approaches model trustworthiness or similarities of users [7] [17] [27]. Koren in [11] proposed a time-aware collaborative filtering method that can effectively incorporate time information into the matrix factorization framework. Middleton et al. propose to use ontological user profiling technique to build recommendation system [18]. Notice that ontology is substantially different from the entity graph we employed in this study. An ontology usually summarizes the concept levels of certain domains, *e.g.*, "text classification" is a subtopic of "machine learning", and the size of which is usually small. Entity graph is built with real world entities. The size of entity graphs can be of very large-scale. Yu et al. [30] [31] introduced meta-path concept into hybrid recommender systems. However, these works usually focus on the heterogeneous entity relationships, and can not fully take advantage of the rich features in user click log and Freebase.

The proposed framework in this paper belongs to hybrid recommender system category. Different from previous works, our work models various features and heuristics generated from user click log and Freebase, which suits the application better than transitional methods, thus can achieve more promising performances.

## 6.2 Information Network Analysis

Heterogeneous information networks which contain multi-typed entities and links are the general data format of entity graphs. Information network analysis and mining have gained wide attention in both academia and industry. Many researchers believe that the heterogeneity and rich-relation nature make information network a good data representation in many scenarios. A lot of information network mining and learning tasks have been done in the past couple of years, including clustering [24], classification [9], and link prediction [29] *etc.* Studies regarding entity similarity measurements, as a fundamental technique, have been actively engaged in many research works as well [4] [8] [23]. Researchers also discover that certain similarity measurements could be defined along paths in information network, and such path compatible measurements could capture different similarity semantic meanings and can be used in different applications [13] [23]. These works also motivated user guided data mining and analysis with information networks [24].

# 7. CONCLUSION AND FUTURE WORKS

In this paper, we study to bridge the gap between search engines and recommender systems. We propose the entity recommendation problem by utilizing user click log and the Freebase entity graph. We present a generic entity recommendation framework which utilizes various pairwise similarity features extracted from both user log dataset and the entity graph. The proposed recommendation framework takes advantage of the consistency and drift natures of user interest, different types of entity relationships as well as several other heuristics, which are crucial to build such a recommendation system. During empirical studies, we compared our proposed methods with several existing popular and state-of-the-art recommendation approaches and demonstrate the effectiveness of our method. We also analyze the performance of our methods under different scenarios, explain the philosophies behind the proposed models and discuss possible revisions to improve performances in special cases.

With the fast development of search engines and recommender systems, studies on bridging these two popular systems as does this paper could benefit both applications and vastly improve user experience when employing such hybrid system. Interesting future studies include recommender techniques which can incorporate users' feedback on-the-fly, systematic pairwise and non-pairwise feature generation given a new domain, as well as a revised on-line version of the framework in which parameters can be estimated efficiently in almost real time.

## Acknowledgments

The work was supported in part by the U.S. Army Research Laboratory under Cooperative Agreement No. W911NF-09-2-0053 (NS-CTA) and U.S. National Science Foundation grants CNS-0931975, IIS-1017362, IIS-1320617, IIS-1354329.

# 8. REFERENCES

[1] K. Bollacker, C. Evans, P. Paritosh, T. Sturge, and J. Taylor. Freebase: a collaboratively created graph database for structuring human knowledge. In *Proceedings of the 2008 ACM SIGMOD international conference on Management of data*, SIGMOD '08, pages 1247–1250, Vancouver, Canada, 2008.

[2] J. S. Breese, D. Heckerman, and C. Kadie. Empirical analysis of predictive algorithms for collaborative filtering. In *Proceedings of the Fourteenth conference on Uncertainty in artificial intelligence*, UAI'98, pages 43–52, San Francisco, CA, USA, 1998.

[3] H. Cao, D. Jiang, J. Pei, Q. He, Z. Liao, E. Chen, and H. Li. Context-aware query suggestion by mining click-through and session data. In *Proceedings of the 14th ACM SIGKDD international conference on Knowledge discovery and data mining*, KDD '08, pages 875–883, Las Vegas, Nevada, USA, 2008.

[4] S. Chakrabarti. Dynamic personalized pagerank in entity-relation graphs. In *Proceedings of the 16th international conference on World Wide Web*, WWW '07, pages 571–580, Banff, Alberta, Canada, 2007.

[5] Q. Gu and J. Zhou. Subspace maximum margin clustering. In *Proceedings of the 18th ACM conference on Information and knowledge management*, CIKM '09, pages 1337–1346, Hong Kong, China, 2009.

[6] Y. Hu, Y. Koren, and C. Volinsky. Collaborative filtering for implicit feedback datasets. In *Proceedings of the 2008 Eighth IEEE International Conference on Data Mining*, ICDM '08, pages 263–272, 2008.

[7] M. Jamali and M. Ester. Trustwalker: a random walk model for combining trust-based and item-based recommendation. In *Proceedings of the 15th ACM SIGKDD international conference on Knowledge discovery and data mining*, KDD '09, pages 397–406, Paris, France, 2009.

[8] G. Jeh and J. Widom. Simrank: a measure of structural-context similarity. In *Proceedings of the eighth ACM SIGKDD international conference on Knowledge discovery and data mining*, KDD '02, pages 538–543, Edmonton, Alberta, Canada, 2002.

[9] M. Ji, J. Han, and M. Danilevsky. Ranking-based classification of heterogeneous information networks. In *Proceedings of the 17th ACM SIGKDD international conference on Knowledge discovery and data mining*, KDD '11, pages 1298–1306, San Diego, California, USA, 2011.

[10] Y. Koren. Factorization meets the neighborhood: a multifaceted collaborative filtering model. In *Proceedings of the 14th ACM SIGKDD international conference on Knowledge discovery and data mining*, KDD '08, pages 426–434, Las Vegas, Nevada, USA, 2008.

[11] Y. Koren. Collaborative filtering with temporal dynamics. In *Proceedings of the 15th ACM SIGKDD international conference on Knowledge discovery and data mining*, KDD '09, pages 447–456, Paris, France, 2009.

[12] Y. Koren, R. Bell, and C. Volinsky. Matrix factorization techniques for recommender systems. *Computer*, 42(8):30–37, 2009.

[13] N. Lao and W. Cohen. Relational retrieval using a combination of path-constrained random walks. *Machine learning*, 81(1):53–67, 2010.

[14] T. Lin, P. Pantel, M. Gamon, A. Kannan, and A. Fuxman. Active objects: actions for entity-centric search. In *Proceedings of the 21st international conference on World Wide Web*, WWW '12, pages 589–598, Lyon, France, 2012.

[15] G. Linden, B. Smith, and J. York. Amazon.com recommendations: Item-to-item collaborative filtering. *Internet Computing, IEEE*, 7(1):76–80, 2003.

[16] H. Ma, C. Liu, I. King, and M. R. Lyu. Probabilistic factor models for web site recommendation. In *In Proceedings of SIGIR*, 2011.

[17] H. Ma, D. Zhou, C. Liu, M. R. Lyu, and I. King. Recommender systems with social regularization. In *Proceedings of the fourth ACM international conference on Web search and data mining*, WSDM '11, pages 287–296, Hong Kong, China, 2011.

[18] S. E. Middleton, N. R. Shadbolt, and D. C. De Roure. Ontological user profiling in recommender systems. *ACM Trans. Inf. Syst.*, 22(1):54–88, Jan. 2004.

[19] M. Mintz, S. Bills, R. Snow, and D. Jurafsky. Distant supervision for relation extraction without labeled data. In *In Proceedings of ACL*, 2009.

[20] M. Pazzani. A framework for collaborative, content-based and demographic filtering. *Artificial Intelligence Review*, 13(5):393–408, 1999.

[21] J. D. M. Rennie and N. Srebro. Fast maximum margin matrix factorization for collaborative prediction. In *Proceedings of the 22nd international conference on Machine learning*, ICML '05, pages 713–719, Bonn, Germany, 2005.

[22] B. Sarwar, G. Karypis, J. Konstan, and J. Riedl. Item-based collaborative filtering recommendation algorithms. In *Proceedings of the 10th international conference on World Wide Web*, WWW '01, pages 285–295, Hong Kong, Hong Kong, 2001.

[23] Y. Sun, J. Han, X. Yan, S. P. Yu, and T. Wu. PathSim: Meta Path-Based Top-K Similarity Search in Heterogeneous Information Networks. In *Proceedings of the 37th international conference on Very large data bases*, VLDB '11, 2011.

[24] Y. Sun, B. Norick, J. Han, X. Yan, P. S. Yu, and X. Yu. Integrating meta-path selection with user-guided object clustering in heterogeneous information networks. In *Proceedings of SIGKDD'12*.

[25] L. Ungar and D. Foster. Clustering methods for collaborative filtering. In *AAAI Workshop on Recommendation Systems*, number 1, 1998.

[26] S. Vempala. *The random projection method*, volume 65. Amer Mathematical Society, 2005.

[27] Y. Wang and J. Vassileva. Bayesian network-based trust model. In *Proceedings of the 2003 IEEE/WIC International Conference on Web Intelligence*, WI '03, 2003.

[28] R. W. White, P. Bailey, and L. Chen. Predicting user interests from contextual information. In *Proceedings of SIGIR*, 2009.

[29] X. Yu, Q. Gu, M. Zhou, and J. Han. Citation prediction in heterogeneous bibliographic networks. In *SDM*, 2012.

[30] X. Yu, X. Ren, Q. Gu, Y. Sun, and J. Han. Collaborative filtering with entity similarity regularization in heterogeneous information networks. In *IJCAI HINA*, 2013.

[31] X. Yu, X. Ren, Y. Sun, B. Sturt, U. Khandelwal, Q. Gu, B. Norick, and J. Han. Entity recommendation in heterogeneous information networks with implicit user feedback. In *RecSys*, 2013.

# Improving Pairwise Learning for Item Recommendation from Implicit Feedback

Steffen Rendle*
University of Konstanz
78457 Konstanz, Germany
steffen.rendle@uni-konstanz.de

Christoph Freudenthaler
University of Konstanz
78457 Konstanz, Germany
chr.freudenthaler@gmail.com

## ABSTRACT

Pairwise algorithms are popular for learning recommender systems from implicit feedback. For each user, or more generally context, they try to discriminate between a small set of selected items and the large set of remaining (irrelevant) items. Learning is typically based on stochastic gradient descent (SGD) with uniformly drawn pairs. In this work, we show that convergence of such SGD learning algorithms slows down considerably if the item popularity has a tailed distribution. We propose a non-uniform item sampler to overcome this problem. The proposed sampler is context-dependent and oversamples informative pairs to speed up convergence. An efficient implementation with constant amortized runtime costs is developed. Furthermore, it is shown how the proposed learning algorithm can be applied to a large class of recommender models. The properties of the new learning algorithm are studied empirically on two real-world recommender system problems. The experiments indicate that the proposed adaptive sampler improves the state-of-the art learning algorithm largely in convergence without negative effects on prediction quality or iteration runtime.

## Categories and Subject Descriptors

I.2.6 [**Artificial Intelligence**]: Learning—*Parameter learning*

## General Terms

Algorithms, Experimentation, Measurement, Performance

## Keywords

Item Recommendation; Recommender Systems; Matrix Factorization; Factorization Model

*Current affiliation: Google Inc.


*WSDM'14*, February 24–28, 2014, New York, New York, USA.
Copyright 2014 ACM 978-1-4503-2351-2/14/02 ...$15.00.
http://dx.doi.org/10.1145/2556195.2556248.

## 1. INTRODUCTION

Recommender systems have become an important feature in modern websites, e.g. in Amazon, Netflix, or Flickr. Click rates, revenues and other measures of success may be increased by the application of effective recommender systems. The difficult task is to identify relevant items even if they are generally unpopular. Recommender systems leverage available context such as user information, time, location, etc. to filter relevant items. Thereby, also items from the tails of the popularity distribution are successfully recommended.

In practice, often only implicit feedback is available to learn a recommender system. Examples for implicit feedback are clicks, watched movies, played songs, purchases or assigned tags. A characteristic of implicit feedback is that it is one-class, i.e. only positive observations are available. For example, a website logs that a user has bought an item on a specific day or chosen a tag for a specific resource. A common approach in recommender systems to deal with this data is to assume that everything that has not been selected is of less interest for the user in this situation. This idea results in a pairwise ranking loss that tries to discriminate between a small set of selected items and a very large set of all remaining items. Due to the very large number of pairs, learning algorithms are usually based on sampling pairs (uniformly) and applying stochastic gradient descent (SGD). This optimization framework is also known as Bayesian Personalized Ranking (BPR) [14]. Many recent published recommender systems use BPR for learning, including tensor factorization models for tag recommendation [15], relation extraction [17], sequential shopping recommender with taxonomies [8], focused matrix factorization for advertisement [7], hierarchical latent factor models [1] or co-factorization machines [5].

In this paper, it is shown that uniform sampling pairs results in slow convergence, especially if the pool of items is large and the overall item-popularity is tailed. Both properties are common to most real-world data sets. We argue that most SGD updates have no effect because the gradient vanishes. The reason is that a uniformly sampled negative item is very likely to be ranked correctly below a (random) observed item and thus the gradient of the pair is near 0. Empirically, we show that simple oversampling by global popularity is not sufficient to solve this problem. We propose a non-uniform sampling distribution that adapts both to the context and the current state of learning. An efficient sampling algorithm with constant amortized runtime complexity is developed to sample from the proposed distribution. Experiments on two real-world recommender applications indicate that the proposed adaptive sampler improves the state-of-the art learning algorithm largely in convergence without negative effects on prediction quality or iteration runtime. Finally, we show how to generalize the algorithm to a large class of factorization models.

# 2. PROBLEM STATEMENT

First the problem of recommending items from implicit feedback data is described. Then pairwise learning with BPR [14] is shortly recapitulated. The novel contribution of this section is to show that convergence of BPR algorithms slows down due to uniform sampling of negative items.

## 2.1 Ranking from Implicit Feedback

Let $S \subset C \times I$ be a set of observed actions, where $C$ is a set of context and $I$ a set of items. For instance, $C$ could be a set of users, $I$ a set of movies and $S$ states which movies a user has watched, i.e. user-movie pairs. More complex examples can also be handled, e.g. $C$ might hold additional variables like location, mood, time, sequences or attributes; also $I$ might be described by additional variables, e.g. attributes or taxonomies (see section 4.2).

The task of item recommendation is to find a ranking $\hat{r}$ of items for each context. We formulate this by a bijective[1] function $\hat{r} : I \times C \to \{1, \ldots, |I|\}$, where $\hat{r}(i|c)$ is the rank of item $i$ for a given context $c$. The ranking function is usually modeled by a scoring function $\hat{y}(i|c)$ which is itself parametrized by a set of model parameters $\Theta$. E.g. matrix factorization (MF) is a common choice for the scoring model $\hat{y}$ if $i$ and $c$ are categorical variables[2]. Ranking with any scoring model can be done by computing scores for all items (given a context $c$) and sorting the items by scores (for each context). The formal link between the rank $\hat{r}$ and the scoring function $\hat{y}$ can be defined as

$$\hat{r}(i|c) := |\{j : \hat{y}(j|c) \geq \hat{y}(i|c)\}|. \quad (1)$$

E.g. for the top item (i.e. rank 1) there is only one item (the item itself) that is as large or larger. For the item at rank 2 there are only 2 items where the score is as large or larger, etc.

The ranking itself is uniquely (up to ties) specified by the values of the model parameters $\Theta$ – through the scoring function $\hat{y}$.

## 2.2 Pairwise Learning from Implicit Feedback

The values of the model parameters $\Theta$ are learned from the implicit feedback data $S$. A popular approach to learn the model parameters $\Theta$ is based on pairwise learning. The idea is to discriminate for each context $c \in C$ between the selected items $I^+(c) := \{i : (i, c) \in S\}$ and the remaining items $I \setminus I^+(c)$. An item $i$ is preferred over an item $j$ under a context $c$ (notation $i \succ_c j$), if and only if $i$ but not $j$ was selected under context $c$:

$$i \succ_c j \Leftrightarrow i \in I^+(c) \land j \in I \setminus I^+(c). \quad (2)$$

The set of all pairwise preferences $D_S \subseteq C \times I \times I$ can be defined as

$$(c, i, j) \in D_S :\Leftrightarrow i \in I^+(c) \land j \in I \setminus I^+(c). \quad (3)$$

[1]Bijective in $I$.

[2]Note that MF is just an example and the following presentation is not restricted to MF.

The link from pairwise preference to the model/ scoring function $\hat{y}$ is established by

$$p(i \succ_c j) := \sigma(\hat{y}(i|c) - \hat{y}(j|c)) \quad (4)$$

where $\sigma(x) = 1/(1+\exp(-x))$. The goal is to maximize the likelihood of correctly ordering the preferences

$$\operatorname*{argmax}_{\Theta} \prod_{(c,i,j) \in D_S} p(i \succ_c j), \quad (5)$$

which is equivalent to minimizing the negative log likelihood (NLL)

$$\text{NLL} := - \sum_{(c,i,j) \in D_S} \ln \sigma(\hat{y}(c, i) - \hat{y}(c, j)). \quad (6)$$

### *SGD Learning.*

The gradient of an arbitrary model parameter $\theta \in \Theta$ is

$$\frac{\partial \text{NLL}}{\partial \theta} = \sum_{(c,i,j) \in D_S} (1 - \sigma(\hat{y}(c, i) - \hat{y}(c, j))) \frac{\partial(\hat{y}(c, i) - \hat{y}(c, j))}{\partial \theta}. \quad (7)$$

As the number of pairs $|D_S|$ is very large[3], learning algorithms typically are based on stochastic gradient descent (SGD). A pair $(c, i, j) \in D_S$ is sampled uniformly and a stochastic gradient descent step is performed:

$$\theta \leftarrow \theta - \eta \underbrace{(1 - \sigma(\hat{y}(c, i) - \hat{y}(c, j)))}_{=:\Delta_{c,i,j}} \frac{\partial}{\partial \theta}(\hat{y}(c, i) - \hat{y}(c, j)). \quad (8)$$

where $\eta$ is the learning rate and has to be chosen small enough to ensure that the step is done in the right direction – i.e. the gradient is only (approximately) correct within a small region around $\theta$. Note the difference between implicit feedback $S \subseteq C \times I$ and training pairs $D_S \subseteq C \times I \times I$.

Sampling a preference $(c, i, j) \in D_S$ uniformly can be done without explicitly storing $D_S$, by first sampling $(c, i) \in S$ and then sampling a negative item $j \in I \setminus I^+(c)$. See figure 2 for the full algorithm. The whole framework of a pairwise loss between selected and all remaining items, as well as the SGD algorithm using uniform sampling was proposed for item recommendation in [14] under the name *Bayesian Personalized Ranking* (BPR).

## 2.3 Issues in Tailed Item Distributions

Even though BPR has been successfully applied in numerous recommender applications and for a variety of models, in the following it is shown that convergence slows down considerably if the pool of items $I$ is large and the item popularity is non-uniform distributed.

### *Gradient Magnitude.*

Learning model parameters with BPR is done by looping over eq. (8). As it can be seen, each gradient step has a multiplicative scalar

$$\Delta_{c,i,j} := (1 - \sigma(\hat{y}(c, i) - \hat{y}(c, j))) = (1 - p(i \succ_c j)). \quad (9)$$

[3]Approximately $\mathcal{O}(|S|\,|I|)$ because the number of selected items $I^+(c)$ in a context $c$ is much smaller than the number of all items $I$.

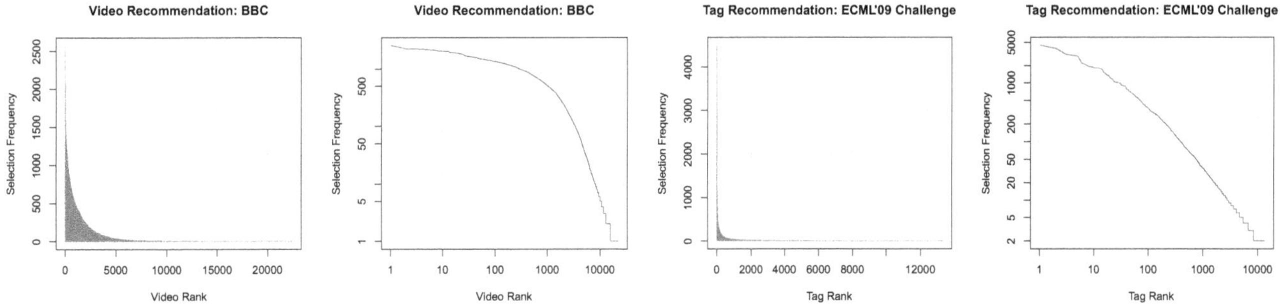


**Figure 1: Item popularity in two example datasets (see section 5.1) plotted in raw and log-log scales. Popularity in both datasets is tailed.**

```
1: procedure LEARNBPR(η, S)
2:     Randomly initialize Θ
3:     repeat
4:         Draw (c, i) ∈ S uniformly
5:         Draw j ∈ I \ I⁺(c) uniformly
6:         for θ ∈ Θ do
7:             Update θ with eq. (8).
8:         end for
9:     until convergence
10:    return Θ
11: end procedure
```

**Figure 2: BPR – a stochastic gradient descent algorithm that learns to discriminate observed selections $(c, i) \in S$ from all remaining items $j \in I \setminus I^+(c)$.**

This quantity depends on how the scoring model (using the current model parameters $\Theta$) would discriminate between the positive item $i$ and the negative item $j$ under context $c$. The quantity $\Delta_{c,i,j}$ is obviously a probability and is close to 0 if $i$ is correctly assigned a larger score than $j$. It is close to 1 if $j$ is falsely assigned a larger score than $i$. This means, $\Delta_{c,i,j}$ can be read as how much influence a pairwise preference $(c, i, j)$ has for improving $\Theta$. If $\Delta_{c,i,j}$ is close to 0, nothing can be learned from the case $(c, i, j)$ because its gradient vanishes, i.e. $\theta$ is not changed by the update step (eq. 8). Thus, in the remainder $\Delta_{c,i,j}$ is called the *gradient magnitude* of a sampled case $(c, i, j)$. Note that $\Delta_{c,i,j}$ depends on the model parameters $\Theta$ and thus $\Delta_{c,i,j}$ changes while learning.

### *Tailed Item Distributions.*

In recommender systems, item popularity is typically non-uniform distributed and some items are in general more popular than others. Figure 1 shows two item popularity distributions for a movie and a social tagging dataset – see section 5.1 for details about the datasets. Both figures show that most items are rarely selected overall[4].

As discussed before, SGD algorithms cannot learn from samples $(c, i, j)$ where the magnitude $\Delta_{c,i,j}$ is close to zero. $\Delta_{c,i,j}$ is supposed to be small when $i$ is correctly ranked over $j$ – i.e. $\Delta_{c,i,j}$ is smaller the larger the difference $\hat{y}(c, i) - \hat{y}(c, j)$ is. Because $(c, i)$ is a positive observation (and overall positive observations are tailed distributed as in fig. 1) and $j$ is uniformly drawn, it is very likely that the model score $\hat{y}(c, i)$ is also larger than $\hat{y}(c, j)$ and thus the gradient magnitude is small. Figure 3 shows the probability that a sample $(c, i, j)$ has a gradient magnitude smaller than 0.01, 0.1 and 0.5 respectively. It can be seen that already after a few training epochs (one epoch includes $10 \cdot |S|$ many single BPR updates), almost all samples have very small magnitudes and therefore most of the samples are useless in the SGD algorithm – i.e. an update (eq. 8) does not change the value. It should be noted that this does not mean that the loss is inappropriate, but that the *good* samples have just not been seen by the algorithm yet. E.g. under a given context, a positive item might be estimated on rank 10 instead of 1, which means there are 9 very informative samples while the vast majority of the remaining |I| - 10 items are mainly non-informative. If $|I|$ is large, uniform sampling is very likely to need many iterations before finding some of these 9 samples and in the meantime the algorithm spends a lot of time applying updates on useless samples.

In the remainder of this work, non-uniform samplers are proposed that exchange the negative item sampler in the BPR algorithm (see fig. 2, line 5) to overcome this issue.

[4]However, keep in mind that recommender systems target at personalizing, i.e. overall unpopular items might be preferred by some users and should be ranked high.

## 3. IMPROVED ITEM SAMPLING

In this section, non-uniform samplers for negative items are proposed to speed up convergence. The sampling distribution for negative items will be denoted as $p(j|c)$. First, sampling according to the global item popularity is presented as a baseline. Then an adaptive, context-aware sampling distribution that follows the belief of the ranking model $\hat{y}$ is proposed.

### 3.1 Static & Global Sampling

In section 2.3, the uniform sampling assumption ($p(j|c) \propto 1$) of pairwise learning was identified as the main reason of slow convergence of SGD learning. This resulted in mostly uninformative pairs which are trivial to rank in the right order.

A simple approach to increase the fraction of difficult pairs is to oversample popular items. The empirical popularity/selection frequency (see fig. 1) can be used directly to define the sampling distribution

$$p(j|c) \propto |\{(c', j') \in S : j = j'\}|. \tag{10}$$

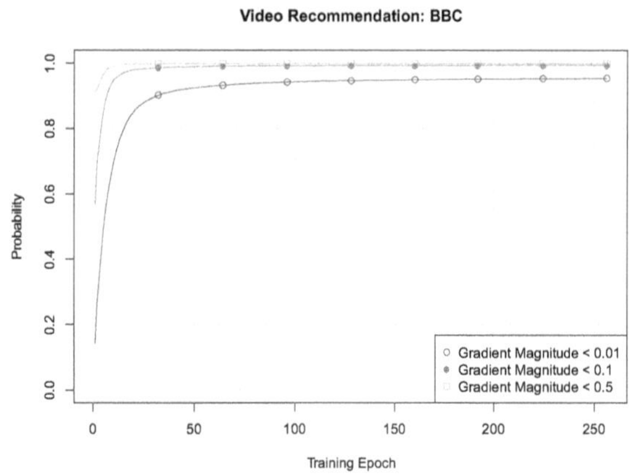


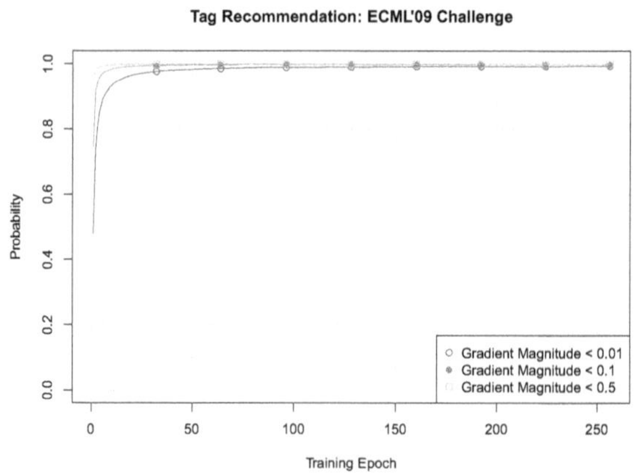


**Figure 3: Gradient magnitude (eq. 9) measures how much influence ([0,1] interval) a training case has on the current learning process. The three curves depict how many magnitudes are smaller than 0.01, 0.1 and 0.5 when uniform sampling (BPR) is used. After only a few training epochs almost all magnitudes are smaller than 0.1 and most are smaller than 0.01. Training cases with near zero magnitudes slow down learning because the corresponding SGD update step won't change the model parameters but requires computational time. See fig. 6 for the development of the average gradient and section 5.1 for details on the experimental setup.**

A sampler from this distribution is trivial to implement: an observation $(c', j)$ is drawn uniformly from the observations $S$, then $c'$ is discarded and $j$ is used as the negative item.

Alternatively a parametric sampling can be used. Typically, the empirical distribution follows approximately an analytical law, e.g. a Geometric or Zipf distribution (see fig. 1). E.g. for the Geometric distribution[5]

$$p(j|c) = \gamma (1-\gamma)^{r(j)}, \quad \gamma \in (0,1) \tag{11}$$

or equivalently in another notation/ parametrization

$$p(j|c) \propto \exp(-r(j)/\lambda), \quad \lambda \in \mathbb{R}^+, \tag{12}$$

where $r(j)$ is the rank of item $j$ according to global popularity ranking. The expected rank in the distribution of eq. (12) is identified by the parameter $\lambda$.

Whether to choose the empirical distribution (eq. 10) or its parametric counterpart results in approximately the same results. In practice, the empirical distribution might be easier to implement and we use it in the evaluation. However, the more complex models proposed later use a parametric approach and thus, it facilitates readability to discuss the parametric counterpart already here.

*Properties.*
The presented sampling distribution has two important properties:

1. **Global**: The item distribution is independent of the context, i.e. for different context, the distribution is the same.

2. **Static**: The distribution does not change while model parameters are learned.

[5]For readability, throughout the paper all ideas are illustrated with the Geometric distribution. It is straightforward to exchange the Geometric distribution (eqs. 12, 14, 21) by another analytic distribution.

*Algorithm.*
Because the distribution is global and static, sampling from the parametric item distribution (eq. 12) is simple: First, a rank $r$ is sampled from the Geometric distribution[6] in $\mathcal{O}(1)$. Second, the item ranked on position $r$ of the global popularity list[7] is returned in $\mathcal{O}(1)$.

In total, sampling from eq. (12) can be done without increasing the computational complexity of the original BPR algorithm.

*Discussion.*
The motivation for developing a sampler is to select for a given context $c$ an item $j$ such that the pair $(i, j)$ is informative at the current state of learning (i.e. for the current values of $\Theta$). The proposed popularity based sampler does not reflect this in two aspects: (1) It is static and thus does not take into account that the estimated rank $\hat{r}(j|c)$ of an item $j$ changes during learning. E.g. an item might be ranked high in the beginning but after several steps of learning it is ranked low. (2) The sampler is global and does not reflect, that it depends on the context how informative an item is. E.g. one item might be interesting for one group of persons but not for another one. Both aspects can also be seen in the gradient magnitude $\Delta_{c,i,j}$, which depends on $c$ and changes during learning.

## 3.2 Adaptive & Context-dependent Sampling

In the following a fine-grained sampler is developed that adapts both to the context and the current belief (i.e. to $\hat{y}$ through $\Theta$) of the model. Analogously to the global item popularity (eq. 10) one could define a static context-specific popularity distribution

$$p(j|c) \propto |\{(c', j') \in S : c = c', j = j'\}| = \delta((c, j) \in S) \tag{13}$$

[6]With the parametrization of eq. (12), an exponential sampler can be used: $r \sim \lfloor \text{Exp}(1/\lambda) \rfloor$.
[7]This (static) list can be precomputed once.

However, this distribution has two drawbacks: (1) it is defined on very few samples, i.e. for a given context $c$, there exists only a small subset $I^+(c)$ of selected items, where typically none is selected multiple times. This would make the item distribution a step function where the negative items are indistinguishable. (2) it does not take the current belief (i.e. $\Theta$) into account.

Instead we propose to use the scoring function $\hat{y}$ to define the sampling distribution. Intuitively, when a negative item $j$ for a given observation $(c, i) \in S$ should be sampled, the closer $j$ is to the top (the smaller the rank $\hat{r}(j|c)$), the more informative is $j$. This can also be seen in the gradient magnitude $\Delta_{c,i,j}$: if $(c, i)$ is given, we should choose $j$ s.th. $\hat{y}(j|c)$ is *large* because it will increase $\Delta_{c,i,j}$. Instead of using the notion of a *large* score, it is better to formalize a small predicted rank $\hat{r}(j|c)$ because largeness of scores is relative w.r.t. other items but ranks are an absolute value. This allows to formulate an adaptive and context-aware sampling distribution

$$p(j|c) \propto \exp(-\hat{r}(j|c)/\lambda), \quad \lambda \in \mathbb{R}^+. \tag{14}$$

### *Properties.*

The item distribution (eq. 14) depends on $\hat{r}(j|c)$. Remind that $\hat{r}(j|c)$ is the rank of item $j$ among all items $I$ using the score model $\hat{y}(j|c)$ for ordering items. Thus the proposed sampler is:

1. **Context-dependent**: The sampling probability depends on the context because $\hat{r}(j|c)$ is the estimated rank of item $j$ for a given context $c$. The more the model $\hat{y}$ can distinguish different context, the more context-aware is the ranking and thus the sampler.

2. **Adaptive**: The sampler changes while model parameters $\Theta$ are learned because changes in $\Theta$ result consecutively in changes in the scoring model $\hat{y}$, the ranking $\hat{r}$ and sampler.

### *Trivial Algorithm.*

The sampler for the negative item $j$ given a positive observation $(c, i) \in S$ can be implemented by: First, sample a rank $r$ from the Geometric distribution in $\mathcal{O}(1)$. Second, return the item $j$ which is currently ranked on the $r$-th position, i.e. find $j$ s.th. $\hat{r}(j|c) = r$ or $j = \hat{r}^{-1}(r|c)$. A trivial implementation of the second step would be to compute $\hat{y}(j|c)$ for all $j \in I$, then sort the items $j$ by their score and finally return the item at place $r$. This algorithm has a complexity of $\mathcal{O}(|I| \cdot T_{\text{pred}} + |I| \log(|I|))$ where $T_{\text{pred}}$ is the time for predicting a score. Note that this sampler should replace line 5 in algorithm 2 and would increase the runtime of BPR by a factor of $\mathcal{O}(|I| \cdot T_{\text{pred}} + |I| \log(|I|))$. This is clearly not feasible in practice.

## 4. EFFICIENT SAMPLING ALGORITHM

In the following it is shown how approximative sampling from eq. (14) can be implemented efficiently in amortized constant time for a broad class of factorization models. First the basic idea is shown for matrix factorization and then a generalization to factorization machines [13] is shown.

### 4.1 Matrix Factorization (MF)

Assume that the context $C$ and items $I$ are represented by categorical variables, i.e. $C = \{c_1, c_2, \ldots\}$ and $I = \{i_1, i_2, \ldots\}$ respectively. For example, each context $c$ could correspond to a user in a personalization setting. Let the scoring model $\hat{y}$ be a matrix factorization (MF)

$$\hat{y}(l|c) := \sum_{f=1}^{k} v_{c,f}\, v_{l,f}, \quad V \in \mathbb{R}^{(C \cup I) \times k}. \tag{15}$$

where $k \in \mathbb{N}$ is the latent dimension and the factors $V$ are the model parameters $\Theta$. Scoring one item with MF (eq. 15) is clearly in $\mathcal{O}(k) =: T_{\text{pred}}$.

In the following, a fast adaptive and context-dependent sampling algorithm is derived which approximates the sampler from eq. (14) in amortized constant time. The idea is to formalize eq. (14) as a mixture of ranking distributions over normalized factors. The mixing probability is derived from a normalized version of the MF scoring function eq. (15). Note that the final sampler works with any MF model and no transformation has to be performed explicitly however the transformation is necessary to derive the algorithm.

### *Rank-Invariant Normalization.*

First, a transformation $\hat{y}^*$ of $\hat{y}$ is defined

$$\hat{y}^*(l|c) := \sum_{f=1}^{k} p(f|c)\, \text{sgn}(v_{c,f})\, v^*_{l,f} \tag{16}$$

where $p(f|c)$ is the probability function

$$p(f|c) :\propto |v_{c,f}|\, \sigma_f \tag{17}$$

and $v^*_{l,f}$ are standardized item factors

$$v^*_{l,f} = \frac{v_{l,f} - \mu_f}{\sigma_f} \tag{18}$$

with the empirical mean and variance over all item factors

$$\mu_f = E(v_{\cdot,f}), \quad \sigma_f^2 = \text{Var}(v_{\cdot,f}). \tag{19}$$

LEMMA 4.1 (RANK INVARIANCE). *Ranking $\hat{r}^*$ generated from scoring $\hat{y}^*$ results in the same ranking as $\hat{r}$ from $\hat{y}$.*

PROOF. First, the scoring function can be rewritten as:

$$\begin{aligned}
\hat{y}(l|c) &= \sum_{f=1}^{k} v_{c,f}\, v_{l,f} = \sum_{f=1}^{k} |v_{c,f}|\, \text{sgn}(v_{c,f})\, (\sigma_f\, v^*_{l,f} + \mu_f) \\
&= \sum_{f=1}^{k} |v_{c,f}|\, \text{sgn}(v_{c,f})\, \sigma_f\, v^*_{l,f} + \sum_{f=1}^{k} |v_{c,f}|\, \text{sgn}(v_{c,f})\, \mu_f \\
&= \hat{y}^*(l|c) + \underbrace{\sum_{f=1}^{k} |v_{c,f}|\, \text{sgn}(v_{c,f})\, \mu_f}_{=:b(c)}
\end{aligned}$$

The additional term $b(c)$ is independent of the item $l$. Thus $\hat{y}(l|c)$ is a linear transformation[8] of $\hat{y}^*(l|c)$. In general, linear transformations are rank-invariant because

$$\begin{aligned}
\hat{y}(i|c) \geq \hat{y}(j|c) &\Leftrightarrow a(c)\, \hat{y}(i|c) \geq a(c)\, \hat{y}(j|c) \\
&\Leftrightarrow a(c)\, \hat{y}(i|c) + b(c) \geq a(c)\, \hat{y}(j|c) + b(c) \\
&\Leftrightarrow \hat{y}^*(i|c) \geq \hat{y}^*(j|c)
\end{aligned}$$

[8] I.e. there exist a positive constant $a(c)$ and an arbitrary constant $b(c)$, s.th. $\hat{y}(l|c) = a(c)\, \hat{y}^*(l|c) + b(c)$.

From this follows the lemma. □

This means, if we are interested in the ranks generated by $\hat{y}$, we can also work with $\hat{y}^*$. Even though $\hat{y} \neq \hat{y}^*$, the generated rankings are equal, $\hat{r} = \hat{r}^*$.

*Rank Mixture.*
The representation $\hat{y}^*$ has the advantage that $p(f|c)$ can be read as a mixing probability over standardized item factors. I.e. the larger $p(f|c)$, the more important the dimension $f$ for the specific context $c$. This allows to define the sampling distribution as the mixture:

$$p(j|c) := \sum_{f=1}^{k} p(f|c)\, p(j|c,f) \qquad (20)$$

Due to the standardization of $v^*_{\cdot,f}$, it is reasonable to define $p(j|c,f)$ analogously to eq. (14)

$$p(j|c,f) \propto \exp(-\hat{r}^*(j|c,f)/\lambda), \qquad (21)$$

where the ranking $\hat{r}^*(j|c,f)$ is generated from the context- *and* factor-dependent scoring function $\hat{y}^*(j|c,f)$. Following eq. (16), this scoring function can be defined as

$$\hat{y}^*(l|c,f) := \operatorname{sgn}(v_{c,f})\, v^*_{l,f}. \qquad (22)$$

We can get rid of the standardization of $v^*_{l,f}$ and use a rank-invariant[9] but simpler function

$$\hat{y}(l|c,f) := \operatorname{sgn}(v_{c,f})\, v_{l,f}. \qquad (23)$$

Note that $\hat{y}(l|c,f)$ depends on the original parameters $V$ and not on their normalization. The scoring function $\hat{y}(l|c,f)$ has a very simple relation to its ranking $\hat{r}(l|c,f)$: the item on rank $r$ has the $r$-th largest factor $v_{l,f}$ – if $\operatorname{sgn}(v_{c,f})$ is positive otherwise it has the $r$-th largest negative factor.

*Sampling from Rank Mixture.*
The formalization of the sampling distribution as a mixture model (eq. 20), results in a simple sampling algorithm for negative items:

1. Sample a rank $r$ from a Geometric distribution.
2. Sample a factor dimension $f$ from $p(f|c)$ (eq. 17).
3. Sort items according to $v_{\cdot,f}$, which is equivalent to an inverse ranking function $\hat{r}^{-1} : \mathbb{N} \times \{1,\ldots,k\} \to I$.
4. Return the item $j$ on position $r$ in the sorted list, i.e. $\hat{r}^{-1}(r|f)$ if $\operatorname{sgn}(v_{c,f}) = 1$, or $\hat{r}^{-1}(|I| - r + 1|f)$ if $\operatorname{sgn}(v_{c,f}) = -1$.

Steps 1 and 4 can be performed in $\mathcal{O}(1)$, step 2 including the computation of $p(f|c)$ in $\mathcal{O}(k) = T_{\text{pred}}$. The only computational intensive step is 3, where the factors are sorted in $O(|I| \log |I|)$.

In order to further reduce the complexity, we propose to precompute the ordering $\hat{r}^{-1}(\cdot|f)$ for each of the $k$ factor dimensions and recompute it every couple of stochastic updates. After a single gradient step, the ranking $\hat{r}^{-1}(\cdot|f)$ changes only little and many update steps are necessary

[9] The proof of invariance of $\hat{y}(l|c,f)$ and $\hat{y}^*(l|c,f)$ follows from the fact that $\hat{y}(l|c,f)$ is a linear transformation of $\hat{y}^*(l|c,f)$.

**procedure** LEARNADAPTIVEOVERSAMPLING($\eta$, $S$)
  Randomly initialize $\Theta$, $q = 0$
  **repeat**
    $q \leftarrow q + 1$
    **if** $q \,\%\, |I| \log |I| = 0$ **then** ▷ every $|I| \log |I|$ draws
      **for** $f \in \{1,\ldots,k\}$ **do**
        Compute $\hat{r}^{-1}(\cdot|f)$ ▷ $\mathcal{O}(|I| \log |I|)$
        Compute $\sigma_f^2$ and $\mu_f$ ▷ $\mathcal{O}(|I|)$
      **end for**
    **end if**
    Draw $(c,i) \in S$ uniformly
    Draw $r$ from $p(r) \propto \exp(-r/\lambda)$ ▷ $\mathcal{O}(1)$
    Draw $f$ from $p(f|c) \propto |v_{c,f}|\, \sigma_f$ ▷ $\mathcal{O}(k)$
    $j \leftarrow \begin{cases} r^{-1}(r|f), & \text{if } \operatorname{sgn}(v_{c,f}) = 1 \\ r^{-1}(|I| - r + 1|f), & \text{else} \end{cases}$ ▷ $\mathcal{O}(1)$
    **for** $\theta \in \Theta$ **do**
      Update $\theta$ with eq. (8).
    **end for**
  **until** convergence
  **return** $\Theta$
**end procedure**

**Figure 4: BPR with adaptive and context-dependent oversampling of negative items for matrix factorization.**

to change the precomputed ranking considerably. We propose to recompute the $k$ rankings every $|I| \log |I|$ iterations which gave also good results in the evaluation. The described precomputation strategy has an amortized runtime of $\mathcal{O}(k)$ because every $|I| \log |I|$ iterations there is an effort of $\mathcal{O}(k\,|I| \log |I|)$. Moreover, the precomputation takes $k|I|$ additional memory for storing all $\hat{r}^{-1}(\cdot|f)$.

In total, the sampling algorithm has an amortized runtime of $\mathcal{O}(k)$ for drawing an item which is the same as the costs for a single gradient step of a MF model ($= T_{\text{pred}}$). As there is one sample for each gradient step, the computational complexity of the original SGD algorithm does not increase. Figure 4 sketches pseudocode of the improved learning algorithm.

## 4.2 Complex Factorization Models

In this section, it is shown how to modify the efficient algorithm in fig. 4 to learn the generic factorization machine (FM) model[10].

Let $\mathbf{x}_i \in \mathbb{R}^{p_I}$ be an arbitrary feature vector that describes item $i$ with $p_I$ real-valued variables and $\mathbf{x}_c \in \mathbb{R}^{p_C}$ be a feature vector that describes context $c$ with $p_C$ variables. This flexible representation allows to describe many different data including attributes, temporal or sequential context as well as their combinations [13]. A second order factorization machine (FM) over a feature vector $\mathbf{x} \in \mathbb{R}^p$ – here $\mathbf{x} = (\mathbf{x}_c, \mathbf{x}_i)$ and $p = p_C + p_I$ – is defined as

$$\hat{y}(\mathbf{x}) = w_0 + \sum_{l=1}^{p} w_l\, x_l + \sum_{l=1}^{p} \sum_{l'>l}^{p} x_l\, x_{l'}\, \langle \mathbf{v}_l, \mathbf{v}_{l'} \rangle \qquad (24)$$

where $w_0, w_1, \ldots, w_p, v_{1,1}, \ldots, v_{p,k}$ are the model parameters $\Theta$. The complexity of computing the scoring function (eq. 24) is $T_{\text{pred}} = \mathcal{O}(k\,(N_Z(\mathbf{x}))$, where $N_Z(\mathbf{x})$ is the number of

[10] See [13] for details about how FM can mimic other factorization models.

non-zero values in $\mathbf{x}$. Also a SGD step has this complexity [13]. In the following, it is shown how to sample a negative item in amortized $T_{\text{pred}}$ time.

### *Rank-Invariant Translation.*

To derive an efficient sampling algorithm, first define for each context and item a $k+1$ dimensional factor vector $\mathbf{v}'$

$$v'_{c,f} := \sum_{l=1}^{p_C} v_{l,f}\, x_{c,l},$$
$$v'_{c,0} := 1,$$
$$v'_{i,f} := \sum_{l=1}^{p_I} v_{l+p_C,f}\, x_{i,l},$$
$$v'_{i,0} := \sum_{l=1}^{p_I} w_{l+p_C}\, x_{i,l} + \sum_{l=1}^{p_I}\sum_{l'>l}^{p_I} x_{i,l+p_C}\, x_{i,l'+p_C}\, \langle \mathbf{v}_{l+p_C}, \mathbf{v}_{l'+p_C}\rangle. \quad (25)$$

The transformed factors $\mathbf{v}'$ can be used to define a matrix factorization model

$$\hat{y}(i|c) := \sum_{f=0}^{k} v'_{c,f}\, v'_{i,f}. \quad (26)$$

This model is rank-invariant to the FM of eq. (24) and thus all the derivations from the MF section can be applied here (now on $\mathbf{v}'$ instead of $\mathbf{v}$). The proof of rank invariance follows directly from inserting the definition of $\mathbf{v}'$ into eq. (26) which is equal to eq. (24) except for a constant (rank-independent) term.

### *Efficient Algorithm.*

For sampling negative items from a FM scoring model, the algorithm for matrix factorization (see fig. 4) has to be adapted slightly: The factor dimension $f \in \{0, \ldots, k\}$ is sampled from $p(f|c) \propto |v'_{c,f}|\, \sigma_f$, where $V'$ are the translated vectors according to eqs. (25). Second, the ordering of items $r^{-1}$ is generated not on raw factors $V$ but on translated ones $V'$ as well.

Note that the transformed representation $V'$ is only used for sampling negative items. The SGD parameter learning should still be done on the original parameters $\mathbf{w}, V$.

# 5. EVALUATION

The properties of the proposed oversampling algorithm are studied on two real world recommender tasks. The convergence behavior of prediction quality and gradient magnitudes are investigated.

## 5.1 Experimental Setup

### *Dataset & Model.*

A video dataset from the BBC[11] with play events (user-movie pairs) and the social tagging dataset from the ECML PKDD 2009 Discovery challenge[12] with tagging events (user-article-tag triples) are used. For BBC, the context is the user; for ECML'09, the context is a user-article pair. For the BBC dataset, all activities from randomly selected 100,000 users are picked. From the resulting set, one activity is randomly selected per user (only for users with at least 10 activities) into a test set $S_{\text{test}}$ and the remaining activities form the training set $S$. The hyperparameters (learning rate, regularization and sampling rate) are tuned on a second random subset of 100,000 users that has been generated by the same protocol as described above. For the ECML'09 dataset, we use the official split from the challenge.

For the dyadic BBC dataset, a matrix factorization model is used. For the ternary ECML'09 dataset, the winning pairwise interaction tensor factorization (PITF) model [15] is applied. In total, both the simple MF model as well as a complex model (PITF) are investigated. Pairwise learning (see sec. 2.2) is used to learn the model parameters.

### *Compared Sampling Methods.*

The negative item sampler is varied:

1. *Uniform sampling*: equivalent to the common BPR algorithm [14], (fig. 2).
2. *Static oversampling*: the algorithm described in section 3.1, which samples negative items from the global popularity distribution.
3. *Adaptive oversampling*: the proposed sampling distribution of section 3.2 with the algorithm of figure 4, which samples negative items with respect to the estimated ranking for this context.

### *Measures & Protocol.*

The recommendation quality is evaluated on the test set $S_{\text{test}}$. For each context in the test dataset, a ranking is generated and it is measured on which ranks the items in the test set appear. The average measure over all test context is reported where the selected measures are: average precision (MAP) with a cutoff of 1000 and the half-life utility (HLU) [2]. The influence of the sampled pairs is measured by the average gradient magnitude. The gradient magnitude (eq. 9) is measured for each sampled pair and the average magnitude over a training epoch is reported. A training epoch is defined as $10 \cdot |S|$ single SGD update steps.

### *Experimental Reproducibility.*

All reported results use a factorization dimension of $k = 64$. Results for $k = 16, 32, 128$ show similar behavior but are omitted for space reasons. The hyperparameters for BBC are: learning rate $\eta = 0.05$, random Gaussian initialization $\mathcal{N}(0, 0.01)$, regularization of 0.01 for oversampling and 0.001 for uniform sampling, $\lambda = 500$ for the Geometric distribution and 256 training epochs. The hyperparameters for ECML'09 differ in the regularization, which is 0.005 for oversampling and 0.00005 for uniform sampling, and the number of epochs is 2000. The source code of the learning algorithms can be obtained from our website[13].

## 5.2 Prediction Quality

Figure 5 shows the prediction quality as a function of training epochs. For comparison a non-personalized, most-popular baseline model is shown which ranks items by global popularity in the observed data $S$. All three personalized

[11] http://www.bbc.co.uk/

[12] http://www.kde.cs.uni-kassel.de/ws/dc09/, task 2

[13] http://www.libfm.org/

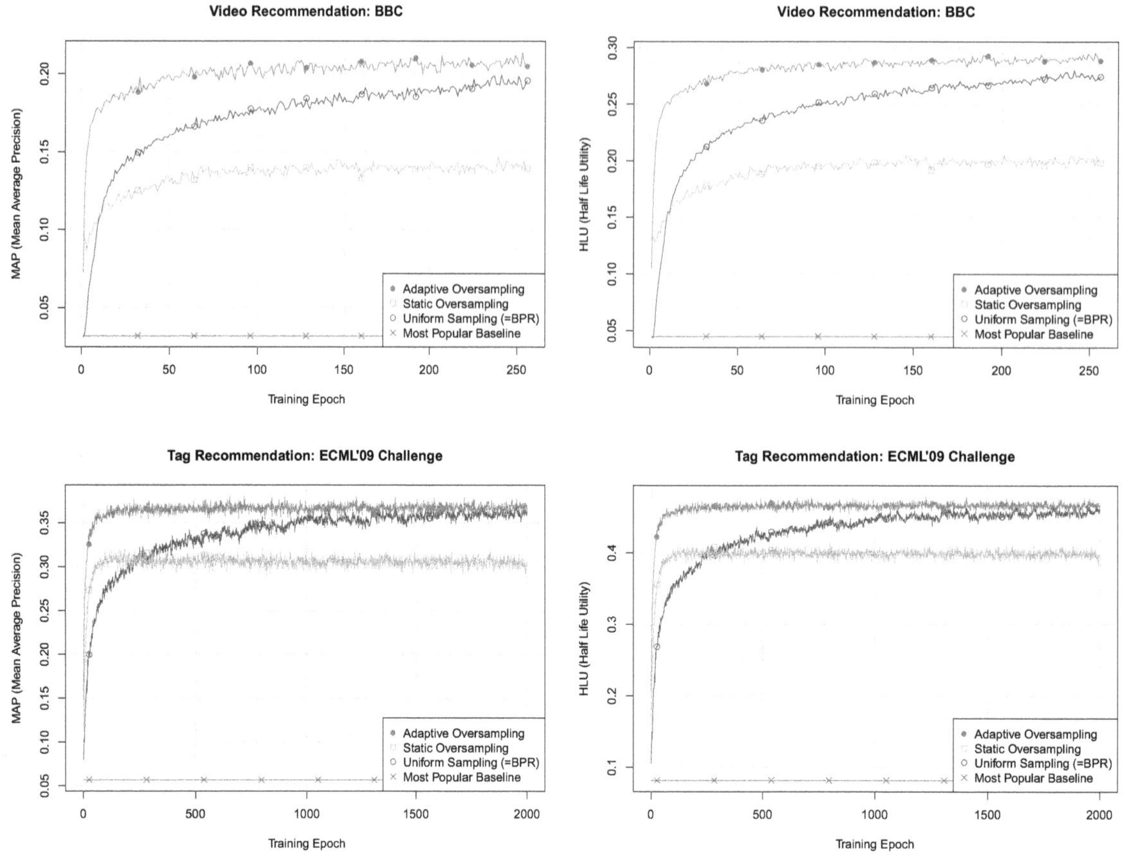


**Figure 5: Quality as a function of training epochs for standard BPR with uniform sampling of negative items, static oversampling and the proposed adaptive oversampling algorithm (see fig. 4). Adaptive oversampling converges much faster than the common BPR algorithm.**

models (independently of the sampling algorithm) outperform this baseline.

*Adaptive Oversampling vs. Uniform Sampling (BPR).*
On both datasets and both measures, the proposed adaptive oversampling has a much faster convergence and better prediction quality than the BPR algorithm. The much steeper learning curve confirms that oversampling improves learning. On both datasets, adaptive oversampling achieves after very few iterations the same accuracy as BPR achieves after hundreds of iterations. E.g. for ECML'09 the MAP of adaptive oversampling after about 50 iterations is comparable to the quality of BPR after 1000 iterations. Also for BBC, the quality of adaptive oversampling after 10 iterations is already better than BPR with 100 iterations. On the long run (esp. on the 2000 iterations for ECML'09), BPR slowly catches up with adaptive oversampling which emphasizes that uniform sampling (BPR) generates many useless training pairs.

*Static Oversampling.*
A second observation is that simple static oversampling using the global item distribution does not result in competitive quality. In the very first iterations, static oversampling seems to work well and outperforms standard BPR. However, convergence stops too early and on all datasets and measures, a much worse final quality than BPR or adaptive oversampling is achieved. This indicates that the oversampling distribution should adapt to the model parameters/ scoring function during learning. Adaptive oversampling shows that it is possible to sample meaningful negative items throughout training.

*Runtime.*
The empirical runtime on the BBC dataset for one training epoch increases from 12 seconds for BPR to 16 seconds for adaptive oversampling. This confirms that adaptive oversampling does not increase computational complexity and that the empirical overhead is only marginal.

## 5.3 Gradient Magnitude

Figure 6 shows the average gradient magnitudes. The first observation is that both oversampling methods are successful in increasing the gradient magnitudes, i.e. the sampled pairs result in SGD updates that actually change model parameters (eq. 8). E.g. on BBC, the average gradient of adaptive oversampling is 0.034 after 256 iterations whereas for BPR it is 0.004 – an increase of 8.5 times. For ECML'09 the numbers are 0.016 after 2000 iterations for adaptive oversampling and 0.0005 for BPR – an increase of 32 times.

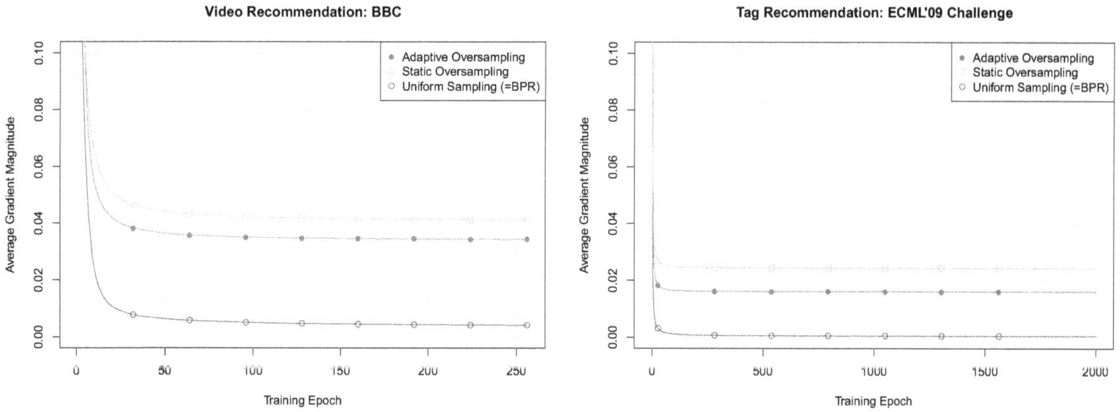


**Figure 6: Average gradient magnitude as a function of training epochs. Oversampling increases the average gradient magnitude by a large factor and thus SGD updates result in faster change of model parameters. Static oversampling generates pairs with large gradient magnitudes but the pairs are not as informative as with adaptive oversampling (see figure 5).**

Comparing static oversampling with adaptive oversampling, static oversampling has even a larger average gradient magnitude than adaptive oversampling throughout all epochs. However, the qualitative results in figure 5 show that static oversampling has worse prediction quality than adaptive oversampling and even than uniform sampling (on the long run). This indicates that a large gradient magnitude alone is not enough but the sampled pairs also should be informative. The qualitative results (fig. 5) indicate that adaptive oversampling fulfills both requirements.

## 6. RELATED WORK

Factorization models play a central role in modern recommender systems. The popular matrix factorization model (e.g. [16]), has been extended for many recommender scenarios, e.g. using implicit information [10, 18], time [11], neighborhood information [10] or attributes [20]. For context-aware settings, tensor factorization approaches have been applied (e.g. [9, 13]). Whereas these works solve the rating prediction task (i.e. regression), our work deals with item recommendation (i.e. ranking) from implicit (one-class) feedback. The item recommendation task is much harder because the optimization target is not directly observed. Hu et al. [6] and Pan et al. [12] investigate item recommendation from implicit feedback and propose to cast the one-class problem into a two class problem by imputing all non-observed values with 0 and to apply regression. This is similar to standard (algebraical) singular value decomposition (SVD) but includes confidence weights and L2 regularization. Weimer et al. [21] optimize a matrix factorization model for the ranking measure NDCG. This approach is mainly designed for data where ratings (or other ordering information on user feedback) is present. Recently, CLiMF [19] has been proposed for optimizing a matrix factorization model using implicit feedback datasets for the reciprocal rank measure. Bayesian personalized ranking (BPR) [14] is a generic optimization framework (not restricted to matrix factorization) for learning recommender systems from implicit feedback. BPR has been applied among others to matrix factorization and nearest-neighbor [14], tensor factorization for tag recommendation [15], factorized markov chains for sequential basket recommendation with taxonomy-awareness [8], social update streams [4] and relation extraction [17]. All these works on BPR use the uniform sampling assumption and thus are supposed to suffer from slow convergence. Our proposed adaptive sampler has the potential to improve all existing recommender systems that are based on BPR learning.

Gantner et al. [3] extend BPR with non-uniform sampling where the sampling probabilities for negative items are a priori given weights resulting from the problem description. In our work, the sampling probabilities are not fixed, but are generated from the current model. In the WARP algorithm [22], negative items (='annotations') are drawn repeatedly until the score of a drawn item is large enough. This algorithm increases the runtime because up to $N \leq |I|$ samples are drawn and their score is computed each time (in $\mathcal{O}(N\,T_{\text{pred}})$) before an SGD update (costs $\mathcal{O}(T_{\text{pred}})$) is performed. Moreover, within the rejection sampler, the negative items are sampled uniformly in WARP, which might need a large number of draws $N$ before finding an item that is not in the tail.

## 7. CONCLUSION

In this paper, we have shown how to increase convergence of BPR-style learning algorithms. The motivation is that uniform sampling of negative items results in mostly non-informative updates. An adaptive and context-dependent sampling distribution for negative items is proposed which oversamples top ranked items. An efficient approximative sampling algorithm is developed for MF and a broad class of factorization machine models, including PITF, attribute-aware MF or sequential MF. The proposed algorithm has an amortized constant runtime. Empirically, the computational overhead over common BPR was about 33%. On two real-world datasets, the proposed sampler improves convergence by a large factor – in our experiments about 10 and 20 times faster. We expect our improved algorithm also to be valuable for existing recommender systems that are based on the BPR algorithm, such as [17, 8, 7, 1, 5].

## 8. ACKNOWLEDGMENTS

We would like to thank Chris Newell from the BBC for providing us with the anonymized video recommendation dataset. This work was supported by the DFG Research Training Group GK-1042 'Explorative Analysis and Visualization of Large Information Spaces', University of Konstanz.

## 9. REFERENCES

[1] A. Ahmed, B. Kanagal, S. Pandey, V. Josifovski, L. G. Pueyo, and J. Yuan. Latent factor models with additive and hierarchically-smoothed user preferences. In *Proceedings of the sixth ACM international conference on Web search and data mining*, WSDM '13, pages 385–394, New York, NY, USA, 2013. ACM.

[2] J. S. Breese, D. Heckerman, and C. Kadie. Empirical analysis of predictive algorithms for collaborative filtering. In *Proceedings of the Fourteenth Conference on Uncertainty in Artificial Intelligence (UAI-98)*, pages 43–52, San Francisco, 1998. Morgan Kaufmann.

[3] Z. Gantner, L. Drumond, C. Freudenthaler, and L. Schmidt-Thieme. Personalized ranking for non-uniformly sampled items. *Journal of Machine Learning Research Workshop and Conference Proceedings*, 2012.

[4] L. Hong, R. Bekkerman, J. Adler, and B. D. Davison. Learning to rank social update streams. In *Proceedings of the 35th international ACM SIGIR conference on Research and development in information retrieval*, SIGIR '12, pages 651–660, New York, NY, USA, 2012. ACM.

[5] L. Hong, A. S. Doumith, and B. D. Davison. Co-factorization machines: modeling user interests and predicting individual decisions in twitter. In *Proceedings of the sixth ACM international conference on Web search and data mining*, WSDM '13, pages 557–566, New York, NY, USA, 2013. ACM.

[6] Y. Hu, Y. Koren, and C. Volinsky. Collaborative filtering for implicit feedback datasets. In *IEEE International Conference on Data Mining (ICDM 2008)*, pages 263–272, 2008.

[7] B. Kanagal, A. Ahmed, S. Pandey, V. Josifovski, L. Garcia-Pueyo, and J. Yuan. Focused matrix factorization for audience selection in display advertising. In *Data Engineering (ICDE), 2013 IEEE 29th International Conference on*, pages 386–397, 2013.

[8] B. Kanagal, A. Ahmed, S. Pandey, V. Josifovski, J. Yuan, and L. G. Pueyo. Supercharging recommender systems using taxonomies for learning user purchase behavior. *PVLDB*, 5(10):956–967, 2012.

[9] A. Karatzoglou, X. Amatriain, L. Baltrunas, and N. Oliver. Multiverse recommendation: n-dimensional tensor factorization for context-aware collaborative filtering. In *RecSys '10: Proceedings of the fourth ACM conference on Recommender systems*, pages 79–86, New York, NY, USA, 2010. ACM.

[10] Y. Koren. Factorization meets the neighborhood: a multifaceted collaborative filtering model. In *KDD '08: Proceeding of the 14th ACM SIGKDD international conference on Knowledge discovery and data mining*, pages 426–434, New York, NY, USA, 2008. ACM.

[11] Y. Koren. Collaborative filtering with temporal dynamics. In *KDD '09: Proceedings of the 15th ACM SIGKDD international conference on Knowledge discovery and data mining*, pages 447–456, New York, NY, USA, 2009. ACM.

[12] R. Pan, Y. Zhou, B. Cao, N. N. Liu, R. M. Lukose, M. Scholz, and Q. Yang. One-class collaborative filtering. In *IEEE International Conference on Data Mining (ICDM 2008)*, pages 502–511, 2008.

[13] S. Rendle. Factorization machines with libFM. *ACM Trans. Intell. Syst. Technol.*, 3(3):57:1–57:22, May 2012.

[14] S. Rendle, C. Freudenthaler, Z. Gantner, and L. Schmidt-Thieme. BPR: Bayesian personalized ranking from implicit feedback. In *Proceedings of the 25th Conference on Uncertainty in Artificial Intelligence (UAI 2009)*, 2009.

[15] S. Rendle and L. Schmidt-Thieme. Pairwise interaction tensor factorization for personalized tag recommendation. In *WSDM '10: Proceedings of the third ACM international conference on Web search and data mining*, pages 81–90, New York, NY, USA, 2010. ACM.

[16] J. D. M. Rennie and N. Srebro. Fast maximum margin matrix factorization for collaborative prediction. In *ICML '05: Proceedings of the 22nd international conference on Machine learning*, pages 713–719. ACM, 2005.

[17] S. Riedel, L. Yao, B. M. Marlin, and A. McCallum. Relation extraction with matrix factorization and universal schemas. In *Joint Human Language Technology Conference/Annual Meeting of the North American Chapter of the Association for Computational Linguistics (HLT-NAACL '13)*, June 2013.

[18] R. Salakhutdinov and A. Mnih. Probabilistic matrix factorization. In *Advances in Neural Information Processing Systems*, volume 20, 2008.

[19] Y. Shi, A. Karatzoglou, L. Baltrunas, M. Larson, N. Oliver, and A. Hanjalic. Climf: learning to maximize reciprocal rank with collaborative less-is-more filtering. In *Proceedings of the sixth ACM conference on Recommender systems*, RecSys '12, pages 139–146, New York, NY, USA, 2012. ACM.

[20] D. H. Stern, R. Herbrich, and T. Graepel. Matchbox: large scale online bayesian recommendations. In *Proceedings of the 18th international conference on World wide web*, WWW '09, pages 111–120, New York, NY, USA, 2009. ACM.

[21] M. Weimer, A. Karatzoglou, Q. V. Le, and A. J. Smola. Cofi rank - maximum margin matrix factorization for collaborative ranking. In J. Platt, D. Koller, Y. Singer, and S. Roweis, editors, *Advances in Neural Information Processing Systems 20*, pages 1593–1600, Cambridge, MA, 2008. MIT Press.

[22] J. Weston, S. Bengio, and N. Usunier. Wsabie: scaling up to large vocabulary image annotation. In *Proceedings of the Twenty-Second international joint conference on Artificial Intelligence - Volume Volume Three*, IJCAI'11, pages 2764–2770. AAAI Press, 2011.

# Personalized Entity Recommendation: A Heterogeneous Information Network Approach

Xiao Yu[†], Xiang Ren[†], Yizhou Sun[‡], Quanquan Gu[†],
Bradley Sturt[†], Urvashi Khandelwal[†], Brandon Norick[†], Jiawei Han[†]
[†]University of Illinois at Urbana-Champaign, Urbana, IL, USA
[†]{xiaoyu1, xren7, qgu3, sturt1, khndlwl2, bnorick, hanj}@illinois.edu
[‡]Northeastern Univeristy, Boston, MA, USA
[‡]yzsun@ccs.neu.edu

## ABSTRACT

Among different hybrid recommendation techniques, network-based entity recommendation methods, which utilize user or item relationship information, are beginning to attract increasing attention recently. Most of the previous studies in this category only consider a single relationship type, such as friendships in a social network. In many scenarios, the entity recommendation problem exists in a *heterogeneous information network* environment. Different types of relationships can be potentially used to improve the recommendation quality. In this paper, we study the entity recommendation problem in heterogeneous information networks. Specifically, we propose to combine heterogeneous relationship information for each user differently and aim to provide high-quality personalized recommendation results using user implicit feedback data and personalized recommendation models.

In order to take full advantage of the relationship heterogeneity in information networks, we first introduce meta-path-based latent features to represent the connectivity between users and items along different types of paths. We then define recommendation models at both global and personalized levels and use Bayesian ranking optimization techniques to estimate the proposed models. Empirical studies show that our approaches outperform several widely employed or the state-of-the-art entity recommendation techniques.

## Categories and Subject Descriptors

H.3.3 [**Information Search and Retrieval**]: Information Filtering

## Keywords

Hybrid Recommender System; Information Network

## 1. INTRODUCTION

Entity recommendation, as one of the most effective and widely used information filtering and discovery methods, has been actively studied in the past decade in both industry and academia. Among different recommendation techniques, hybrid recommender systems, which combine user feedback data (explicit ratings or implicit user log) and additional information of users or items, can achieve better recommendation results in certain scenarios, based on recent studies [6] [20].

In many recommendation applications, additional information regarding users and items can be obtained, *e.g.*, user demographic attributes, product specifications, or user social network information. Moreover, the entity recommendation problem often exists in a heterogeneous information network environment with different types of attributes and relationships of users, items, and other entities available. An illustration of a movie recommendation problem in a heterogeneous information network can be found in Figure 1. In this example, besides users and movies and the user-movie interaction relationships, other types of entities can be found and linked to the movie recommendation problem, such as actors, directors, and genres. Different types of relationships between users (*e.g.*, friendship) and entities (*e.g.*, director directed a movie) can be potentially utilized in hybrid recommender systems.

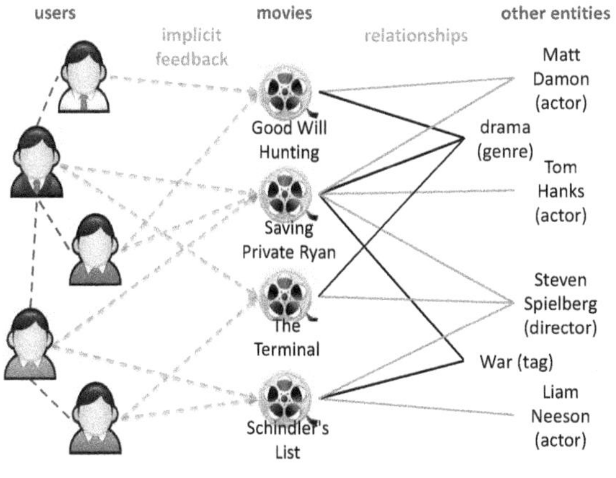


**Figure 1: A heterogeneous information network snippet with users, movies, actors, directors and tags as entities and the corresponding relationships between these entities**

Previous studies suggest that by utilizing additional user or item relationship information, the quality of the recommender systems can be improved. Our study falls in the category of such hybrid recommender systems. The difference between our work and other link-based hybrid methods is that most previous studies only utilize a single type of relationship, *e.g.*, trust relationship [10], friend relationship [19],


*WSDM'14*, February 24–28, 2014, New York, New York, USA.
Copyright 2014 ACM 978-1-4503-2351-2/14/02 ...$15.00.
http://dx.doi.org/10.1145/2556195.2556259.

or user membership [31]. We propose to study entity recommendation problem in the aforementioned heterogeneous network environment, aiming to take advantage of different types of relationship information at the same time.

Previous studies [29] [30] on link-based hybrid recommender systems apply the same recommendation models to all the users when recommending items. They rely on the personal ratings or user feedback data to achieve recommendation personalization. However, such approaches cannot fully distinguish user interests and preferences, and thus may lead to unsatisfying results. For example, Alice and Bob watched the movie "Pacific Rim". Alice watched this movie because she likes robot / monster stories (genre and story of the movie) while Bob watched this movie because his friends watched the same movie. If we apply the same recommendation model (*e.g.*, social network-based collaborative filtering) to both users without understanding or differentiating their motives and interests, the recommendation results may not satisfy the information discovery needs of different users.

In this paper, we introduce a novel entity recommendation framework in heterogeneous information networks using implicit feedback data. We combine user feedback with different types of entity relationships in a collaborative filtering way. We personalize recommendation results by both considering personal user implicit feedback data and building personalized recommendation models for different users.

To take advantage of the relationship heterogeneity of the information network, we first diffuse the observed user implicit feedback along different meta-paths to generate possible recommendation candidates, under the corresponding user interest semantic assumptions. We apply matrix factorization techniques on the diffused user preferences to calculate latent representations for users and items accordingly. We then combine these latent features and define a global recommendation model. To further distinguish user interests, we propose to build recommendation models at personalized level, *i.e.*, *we build different entity recommendation models for different users.* We adopt a Bayesian ranking optimization technique for model estimation. Empirical studies in two real world datasets, IMDb-MovieLens-100K and Yelp, have shown that the proposed recommendation models outperform several state-of-the-art implicit feedback recommendation systems.

The contributions of this paper are summarized as follows:

1. We study personalized entity recommendation with implicit user feedback in heterogeneous information networks.

2. To take advantage of the relationship heterogeneity, we propose to diffuse user preferences along different meta-paths in information networks to generate latent features for users and items.

3. The proposed framework generates personalized recommendation models for different users effectively and efficiently.

4. Empirical studies in two real-world datasets, IMDb-MovieLens-100K and Yelp, demonstrate the power of our methodology.

The remainder of this paper is organized as follows. The preliminaries for this study are introduced in Section 2. The meta-path-based latent features and the global recommendation model are presented in Section 3. We propose the personalized recommendation framework in Section 4 and parameter estimation techniques in 5. Experiments and analysis are in Section 6. Finally, we discuss related work in Section 7 and conclude the study in Section 8.

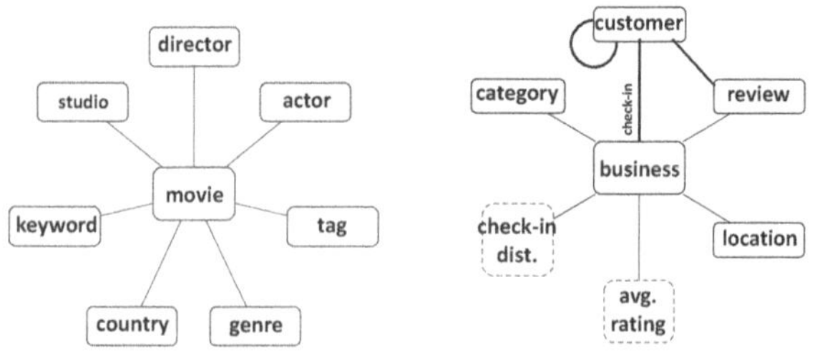

(a) IMDb Network Schema (b) Yelp Network Schema

**Figure 2: Information network schemas (solid rectangles represent entity types and dashed rectangles represent attribute types)**

**Table 1: Notations**

| Notation | Description |
|---|---|
| $u$, $e$ | user, item (or entity) |
| $R$ | implicit feedback matrix |
| $G$, $G_T$ | heterogeneous information network and schema |
| $A$, $R$ | entity type and relationship type |
| $\mathcal{P}$, $p$ | meta-path and path |
| $\tilde{R}^{(q)}$ | diffused user preferences along the $q$-th meta-path |
| $U$, $V$ | low rank representations of users and items |
| $C$ | user clusters |
| $\theta$, $\theta^{\{\cdot\}}$ | global and hidden local model parameters |

## 2. BACKGROUND AND PRELIMINARIES

In this section, we present the background and preliminaries of this study. Detailed problem definition is included at the end of this section.

### 2.1 Binary User Feedback

With $m$ users $\mathcal{U} = \{u_1, ..., u_m\}$ and $n$ items $\mathcal{I} = \{e_1, ..., e_n\}$, we define the user implicit feedback matrix $R \in \mathbb{R}^{m \times n}$ as follows:

$$R_{ij} = \begin{cases} 1, & \text{if } (u_i, e_j) \text{ interaction is observed;} \\ 0, & \text{otherwise.} \end{cases}$$

Notice that the value 1 in $R$ represents interactions between users and items, *e.g.*, users watched a movie or users browsed a restaurant website. The value 1 in the implicit feedback data does not mean that users like the items. A user buys a movie ticket because she or he is interested in the movie but this user might dislike the movie after watching it. Similarly the value 0 in $R$ does not mean that the users dislike the items, but are a mixture of negative feedback (the users are not interested in the items) and unobserved interactions (the users are not aware of these items for now). Several previous studies have additional assumptions about the implicit feedback data, *e.g.*, user-item interaction frequency, or the dwelling time of each interaction. Not to digress from the purpose of this study, we use binary user feedback in its original form as defined above. However, additional information as mentioned can be added into the factorization process of the proposed models accordingly.

### 2.2 Heterogeneous Information Network

Similar to [24], we define information networks as follows:

DEFINITION 1 (INFORMATION NETWORK). *An information network is defined as a directed graph $G = (V, E)$ with an entity type mapping function $\phi : V \to \mathcal{A}$ and a link type mapping function $\psi : E \to \mathcal{R}$. Each entity $v \in V$ belongs to* *an entity type $\phi(v) \in \mathcal{A}$, and each link $l \in E$ belongs to a relation type $\psi(l) \in \mathcal{R}$.*

We call an information network a *heterogeneous information network* when $|\mathcal{A}| > 1$ or $|\mathcal{R}| > 1$. To be consistent with recommender system terminology, we refer to the entities in the information network which are being recommended as *items*.

Similar to an entity-relation diagram in a relational database, we use an abstract graph (*i.e.*, *network schema*) to represent the entity and relation type restrictions in heterogeneous information networks, denoted by $G_T = (\mathcal{A}, \mathcal{R})$. Examples of heterogeneous information networks and partial network schemas can be found in Figure 2.

## 2.3 Matrix Factorization for Implicit Feedback

Matrix factorization techniques have been used to interpret implicit user feedback in previous studies [5] [9], by learning the low-rank matrix representations for users and items. More specifically, factorization methods seek to approximate the implicit feedback matrix $R$ with the product of the low-rank matrices as follows:

$$R \approx UV^T \quad (1)$$

where $U \in \mathbb{R}^{m \times d}$ are the latent features representing users and $V \in \mathbb{R}^{n \times d}$ are the latent features representing items, with $d < \min(n, m)$.

The recommendation score between $u_i$ and $e_j$ can be computed with the estimated low-rank matrices as $r(u_i, e_j) = U_i V_j^T$, where $U_i$ denotes the $i$-th row of the matrix $U$ and $V_j$ denotes the $j$-th row of $V$. By sorting items with their recommendation scores, we can return the top-$k$ items which $u_i$ has not interacted with before as the recommendation results.

To solve Equation (1), the non-negative factorization techniques (NMF) discussed in [5] can be directly employed. More advanced methods [9] [6] [19] have been studied recently to incorporate additional information in order to further improve the performance.

In our proposed recommendation models, when defining user item features, we rely on matrix factorization methods to derive low-rank representations of users and items under different semantics. One should notice that our proposed models are orthogonal to factorization techniques, *i.e.*, one can extend the proposed models easily with advanced factorization techniques. In this study, aiming to propose a generic recommendation framework, we use the basic NMF method in [5] when defining features and models. By utilizing advanced factorization methods, the performance of the our methods can be improved accordingly due to the aforementioned orthogonality.

## 2.4 Problem Definition

We define the recommendation problem which we study in this paper as follows:

DEFINITION 2 (PROBLEM DEFINITION). *Given a heterogeneous information network $G$ with user implicit feedback $R$, for a user $u_i$, we aim to build personalized recommendation model for $u_i$, and recommend a ranked list of items that are of interest to $u_i$ accordingly.*

Notations which are used in the rest of the paper can be found in Table 1.

# 3. META-PATH-BASED LATENT FEATURES

In this section, aiming to utilize the rich yet under-discovered information network, we present a user preference diffusion-based feature generation approach, which combines user implicit feedback and heterogeneous entity relationships. We then define a recommendation function with the latent features at a global level at the end of this section. Notice that we use the term "global" to represent the process of applying the same recommendation model to all users. We still utilize personal user implicit feedback data during recommendation with the global recommendation model. We introduce personalized recommendation models in Section 4. We discuss the learning algorithms for the recommendation models in Section 5.

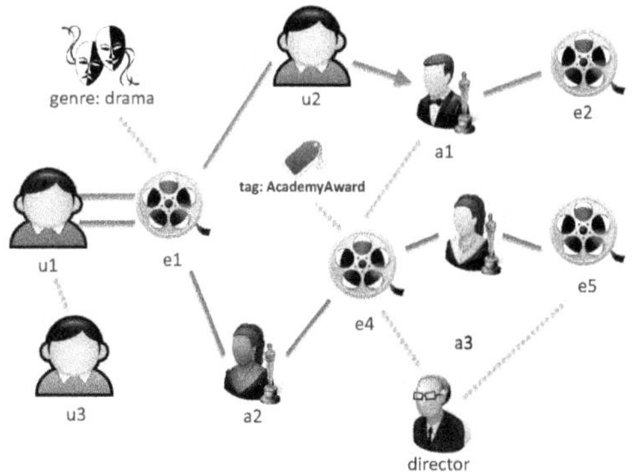


**Figure 3: User preference discussion along different meta-paths (Example 1)**

## 3.1 Meta-Path

From the information network point of view, the entity recommendation problem is to seek certain connectivity between users and items. In heterogeneous information networks, two entities can be connected via different paths (see Figure 3 for examples). Due to the multiplicity of entity and relationship types in the information networks, these paths may contain different entity types, relationship types in different orders and they can have various lengths. In order to describe path types in heterogeneous information network, we introduce the definition of *meta-path* proposed in [24]. Meta-paths are defined in the scope of information network schemas, and describe how two entity types could be connected via different types of paths.

DEFINITION 3 (META-PATH). *A meta path $\mathcal{P} = A_0 \xrightarrow{R_1} A_1 \xrightarrow{R_2} \ldots \xrightarrow{R_k} A_k$ is a path in a network schema $G_T = (\mathcal{A}, \mathcal{R})$, which defines a new composite relation $R_1 R_2 \ldots R_k$ between type $A_0$ and $A_k$, where $A_i \in \mathcal{A}$ and $R_i \in \mathcal{R}$ for $i = 0, \ldots, k$, $A_0 = dom(R_1) = dom(\mathcal{P})$, $A_k = range(R_k) = range(\mathcal{P})$ and $A_i = range(R_i) = dom(R_{i+1})$ for $i = 1, \ldots, k-1$.*

where $dom(\cdot)$ defines the domain of certain relationship and $range(\cdot)$ defines the range.

We use $p$ to denote the paths in information networks and $\mathcal{P}$ to denote meta-paths. Based on the above definition, one can notice that meta-paths are the types for paths in information networks. Previous studies suggest that meta-paths can be used to facilitate entity similarity or proximity measurement and similarity semantic disambiguation [24] [28]. We use the following example to demonstrate the intuition of utilizing meta-paths in entity recommendation problem.

EXAMPLE 1 (DIFFERENT META-PATHS IN IMDB). *With the graph schema of IMDb defined in Figure 2(a), we can derive a number of meta-paths which connect users with movies. We show two possible meta-paths as follows:*

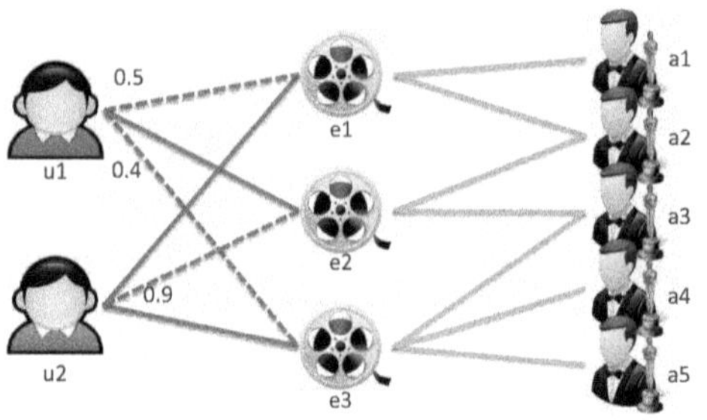


**Figure 4: User preference diffusion score calculation (Example 2). The solid red links represent observed user implicit feedback while the purple doted links represent diffused user preferences.**

- $\mathcal{P}_1$: $user \xrightarrow{Viewed} movie \xrightarrow{Viewed^{-1}} user \xrightarrow{Follows} actor \xrightarrow{StarredIn} movie$
- $\mathcal{P}_2$: $user \xrightarrow{Viewed} movie \xrightarrow{StarredIn^{-1}} actor \xrightarrow{StarredIn} movie \xrightarrow{StarredIn^{-1}} actor \xrightarrow{StarredIn} movie$

*We give two path examples of the two meta-paths in Figure 3 (the solid blue line represents meta-path $\mathcal{P}_1$ and the solid red line represents meta-path $\mathcal{P}_2$). These two meta-paths connect users and movies under different semantic assumptions. $\mathcal{P}_1$ explores the social relationships of other users who watched movies in common with the target user, while $\mathcal{P}_2$ utilizes movie-actor links to build relationships between users and movies. By measuring proximity between users and movies along different meta-paths, we may be able to make movie recommendations to users from different semantic perspectives in information networks.*

When representing longer meta-paths, relationship types can be ignored when doing so does not cause ambiguity. The recursive parts of the meta-paths can be compressed with exponentiation notation. For example, we use **user** $-($**movie** $-$ **actor** $-$ **movie**$)^2$ to represent meta-path $\mathcal{P}_2$ in the above example.

## 3.2 User Preference Diffusion

With the implicit user feedback data defined in Section 2 and meta-path defined above, we introduce the the user preference diffusion process along meta-paths. As mentioned before, implicit feedback represents user item interactions. the value 1 in implicit feedback indicates that users are more interested in the corresponding items than the rest of the items. We use the term *user preference* to represent the user interests in implicit feedback data. Intuitively, if we can understand the semantic meanings of user preferences and find similar items to the ones that the users were interested in, following the discovered semantics, we can make entity recommendations to these users accordingly.

Based on this observation and the problem definition presented in Section 2, in this paper, we focus on meta-paths in the format of **user** $-$ **item** $- * -$ **item** when building recommendation models. The intuition is we want to diffuse the observed users preferences in implicit feedback data along different meta-paths so that users can be connected with other items. By defining a user preference diffusion score between the target user and all possible items along different meta-paths, we can now measure the possibility of an unobserved user-item interaction in the information network under different semantic assumptions.

Given a meta-path $\mathcal{P} = R_1R_2...R_k$ with $dom(\mathcal{P}) =$ **user** and $range(\mathcal{P}) =$ **item**, let $\mathcal{P}' = R_2...R_k$ with $dom(\mathcal{P}') =$ **item** and $range(\mathcal{P}') = range(\mathcal{P}) =$ **item**. We define the user preference diffusion score between user $i$ and item $j$ along $\mathcal{P}$ by extending PathSim measurement proposed in [24] as follows:

$$s(u_i, e_j|\mathcal{P}) \tag{2}$$
$$= \sum_{e \in \mathcal{I}} \frac{2 \times R_{u_i,e} \times |\{p_{e \rightsquigarrow e_j} : p_{e \rightsquigarrow e_j} \in \mathcal{P}'\}|}{|\{p_{e \rightsquigarrow e} : p_{e \rightsquigarrow e} \in \mathcal{P}'\}| + |\{p_{e_j \rightsquigarrow e_j} : p_{e_j \rightsquigarrow e_j} \in \mathcal{P}'\}|}$$

where $p_{e \rightsquigarrow e_j}$ is a path between $e$ and $e_j$, $p_{e \rightsquigarrow e}$ is a path between $e$ and $e$, and $p_{e_j \rightsquigarrow e_j}$ is a path between $e_j$ and $e_j$.

The user preference diffusion score between user $u_i$ and item $e_j$ contains two parts: (1) the observed user-item interactions associated with $u_i$, and (2) the connectivity between the items that $u_i$ is interested in and potential items of interest, which are represented by $e_j$ in Equation (2). Notice the connectivity between items is defined as the number of paths between these items following meta-path $\mathcal{P}$ and normalized by the visibility of the items so the diffusion score does not overly favor popular items. We demonstrate the user preference diffusion process with a toy example as in Figure 4.

EXAMPLE 2 (USER PREFERENCE DIFFUSION SCORE). *In this toy example, we use a small information network which contains two users ($u_1$ and $u_2$), three movies ($e_1$, $e_2$ and $e_3$), and 5 actors ($a_1$, ..., $a_5$). These entities are interconnected as shown in Figure 4 (The solid red links represent observed user implicit feedback while the purple doted links represent the diffused user preferences). We use **user** $-$ **movie** $-$ **actor** $-$ **movie** as meta-path $\mathcal{P}$ when calculating the diffusion score. Based on implicit feedback data $R$, we know that $u_1$ watched movie $e_2$. Based on the information network structure, there is 1 path between $e_1$ and $e_2$ following the aforementioned meta-path, 2 paths between $e_1$ and $e_1$ and 2 paths between $e_2$ and $e_2$. By plugging the implicit feedback data and the numbers of paths described above into Equation (2), we can get that the user preference diffusion score under meta-path $\mathcal{P}$ from $u_1$ to $e_1$ is 0.5. Other diffusion scores in this example can be calculated accordingly.*

By measuring the diffusion scores between all users and all items along meta-path $\mathcal{P}$, we can generate a diffused user preference matrix $\tilde{R} \in \mathbb{R}^{m \times n}$. $\tilde{R}_i$ represents the possible preferences of user $u_i$ if he or she explores the network for new content following meta-path $\mathcal{P}$ ($u_i$ watches movies with certain genres or $u_i$ watches movies from certain directors). By repeating this process, with $L$ different meta-paths, we can calculate $L$ different diffused user preference matrices accordingly. We denote these user preference matrices as $\tilde{R}^{(1)}, \tilde{R}^{(2)}, ..., \tilde{R}^{(L)}$.

This process propagates user preferences along different meta-paths in the heterogeneous information networks, and it mimics users' information discovery process. The diffusion score indicates the possibility of certain user-item interaction under certain meta-path semantic. The diffusion scores can be used to define recommendation models.

## 3.3 Global Recommendation Model

We denote $\tilde{R}^{(q)}$ as the diffused user preference matrix along the $q$-th meta-path. Following the intuition and principle of matrix factorization-based recommendation methods, we can derive low-rank user and item matrices from each diffused preference matrix accordingly. These low-rank matrices are the latent representations of users and items, under the semantic meaning of the corresponding meta-path. With low-rank matrix factorization technique, we can factorize the diffused matrix $\tilde{R}^{(q)}$ as follows:

$$(\hat{U}^{(q)}, \hat{V}^{(q)}) = \text{argmin}_{U,V} \|\tilde{R}^{(q)} - UV^T\|_F^2 \quad (3)$$
$$\text{s.t.} \quad U \geq 0, \quad V \geq 0,$$

where $\hat{U}^{(q)} \in \mathbb{R}^{m \times d}$ represents users and $\hat{V}^{(q)} \in \mathbb{R}^{n \times d}$ represents items, with $d < \min(n, m)$. $\hat{U}_i^{(q)}$ is the latent feature for user $u_i$ along the $q$-th meta-path and $\hat{V}_j^{(q)}$ is the latent feature for $e_j$ along the $q$-th meta-path respectively.

As discussed in Section 2, we apply the generic NMF method to solve Equation (3), although more advanced factorization techniques can be used instead. By repeating the above process for all $L$ diffused user preference matrices, we can now generate $L$ pairs of representations of users and items $(\hat{U}^{(1)}, \hat{V}^{(1)})$, ..., $(\hat{U}^{(L)}, \hat{V}^{(L)})$. Each low-rank feature pair represents users and items under a specific relationship semantic due to the user preference diffusion process. When defining recommendation models with these latent-features, different feature pairs may have different importance. For example, users are more likely to follow certain actors when choosing movies rather than consider which movie studios these movies are made. With this observation, following [30], we define a global recommendation model as follows:

$$r(u_i, e_j) = \sum_{q=1}^{L} \theta_q \cdot \hat{U}_i^{(q)} \hat{V}_j^{(q)T} \quad (4)$$

where $\theta_q$ is the weight for the $q$-th user and item low-rank representation pair. Based on the non-negative property of the features, we add $\theta_q \geq 0$ as an optimization constraint.

With the recommendation model in Equation (4), given a user, we can now assign recommendation scores to all items, and then rank these items accordingly. We return the top-$K$ results as the recommendation results. We will discuss how to estimate the parameters in the recommendation model in Section 5.

# 4. PERSONALIZED RECOMMENDATION MODEL

We proposed to diffuse user preferences along different meta-paths in heterogeneous information networks, and calculate latent features for users and items under various semantic assumptions with matrix factorization techniques. We then defined the global recommendation model with these latent features, which essentially combines the observed implicit feedback from users and different types of relationships in the information network together. During recommendation, we apply the global model to all users and utilize users' personal feedback to generate recommendation results. However, such a solution does not distinguish user interests or behavior patterns at the model level. For example, the learned global model may suggest that majority users watch popular movies featuring famous actors, but this rule might not be true for all individuals.

In this section, we extend the proposed global recommendation model to a finer level of granularity. Rather than learn one recommendation model for all the users, we aim to calculate different recommendation models for different users to better capture user preferences and interests. The straightforward way of learning personalized models is to estimate the recommendation model defined in Equation (4) with each user's own implicit feedback data. However, the number of feedback per user follows power law distribution (we demonstrate this claim in Section 6), which means we do not have enough feedback data to learn personalized models for most of the users.

Although users may have different behaviors from each other, a subgroup of users can share similar interests and preferences from certain perspectives. For example, comic fans are interested in super-hero, fantasy and adventure movies while fans of Steven Spielberg follow movies directed by him. Motivated by this observation, we propose to first cluster users based on their interests, and then learn a recommendation models within each cluster. Notice that one user can belong to different user clusters (one can be comic fan and Spielberg fan at the same time). When recommending, we first calculate the personalized recommendation model for the target user by combining the recommendation models of the related user clusters, and then calculate the recommendation results with the personalized model of the target user. We define the personalized recommendation function for user $u_i$ as follows:

$$r^*(u_i, e_j) = \sum_{k=1}^{c} sim(C_k, u_i) \sum_{q=1}^{L} \theta_q^{\{k\}} \cdot \hat{U}_i^{(q)} \hat{V}_j^{(q)T} \quad (5)$$

where $C$ represents user clusters related to target user $u_i$ and function $sim(\cdot, \cdot)$ defines the cosine similarity between the center of cluster $C_k$ and $u_i$. $\theta_q^{\{k\}}$ represents the recommendation model defined in cluster $C_k$. We define $\theta^{\{\cdot\}} = \theta^{\{1\}}, ..., \theta^{\{c\}}$ as the recommendation model parameters for this approach.

Compared with $L$ parameters in the global recommendation model (Equation (4)), the personalized recommendation approach has a total $c \times L$ parameters, where $c$ is the number of clusters. With a relatively larger parameter space, now we can generate personalized recommendation models efficiently and represent different user interests or behavior patterns effectively. We discuss the user clustering and the model learning algorithm in details in Section 5.

After estimating recommendation models for all the user clusters $\theta^{\{\cdot\}}$, when recommending items for $u_i$, we first find the clusters that $u_i$ is related to (has a high similarity to the cluster center), and then combine the related user clustering parameters following Equation (5). With the calculated personalized recommendation model, we can assign recommendation score to each item for $u_i$. Recommendation can be made by sorting all items with their recommendation scores and returning the top-$k$ items.

The number of clusters could be essential to this method. If the cluster number $c$ is too small, we may not be able to distinguish user interests well. If the cluster number is too big, the number of users in each cluster becomes very small. In this case, we may not have enough training data to learn the recommendation models. A good estimation of the optimal number of clusters can be achieved by cross-validation using training data. We discuss the performance change with different parameter $c$ in Section 6.5.

# 5. MODEL LEARNING WITH IMPLICIT FEEDBACK

In this section, we introduce learning algorithms for both global and personalized recommendation models. We first discuss parameter estimation method for global recommendation model (Equation (4)) and then extend the learning algorithm to personalized recommendation models.

Recommendation models proposed in this paper take advantage of the heterogeneous entity relationships in information networks. More specifically, we combine network diffusion-based latent features with parameters indicating the importance of the corresponding meta-path in the recommendation process. To learn the importance of the latent features, we use user implicit feedback as training data. As discussed in Section 2, the value 1 in implicit feedback data represents positive feedback (users are interested in such items) while the value 0 represents a mixture of negative feedback (users are not interested in such items) and unobserved potential interactions (users are not aware of such items). Traditional learning methods adopt classification or learning-to-rank objective functions and usually treat 1s in training dataset as positives and 0s as negatives. As we discussed, such methods do not fit in the definition of implicit feedback data and they cannot generate high quality recommendation models.

Motivated by [21], we employ a different learning approach by considering the correct item pair orders. We define an objective function to order 1 values before 0 values for each user. The assumption behind this objective function is that users are more interested in the items with value 1 in $R$ than the rest of the items, which is a weaker and more plausible assumption compared with the traditional approaches.

## 5.1 Bayesian Ranking-Based Optimization

We use $p(e_a > e_b; u_i|\theta)$ to denote the probability that user $u_i$ prefers $e_a$ over $e_b$. The Bayesian formulation of the optimization criterion is to maximize the posterior probability as follows:

$$p(\theta|R) \propto p(R|\theta)p(\theta), \tag{6}$$

where $\theta = \{\theta_1, ..., \theta_L\}$ represents the global model parameters, and $p(R|\theta)$ represent the probability that all item pairs can be ranked correctly for all users according to $R$, *i.e.*, for each user, items with feedback 1 can be ranked before items with feedback 0.

With the assumption that both user preferences and ordering of the item pairs are independent, we can expand the likelihood function $p(R|\theta)$ as follows:

$$\begin{aligned} p(R|\theta) &= \prod_{u_i \in \mathcal{U}} p(R_i|\theta) \qquad (7) \\ &= \prod_{u_i \in \mathcal{U}} \prod_{(e_a > e_b) \in R_i} p(e_a > e_b; u_i|\theta) \end{aligned}$$

where $(e_a > e_b) \in R_i$ represent all item pairs with the correct orders in the observed implicit feedback of $u_i$.

We define $p(e_a > e_b; u_i|\theta)$ as:

$$p(e_a > e_b; u_i|\theta) = \sigma(r(u_i, e_a) - r(u_i, e_b)), \tag{8}$$

where $\sigma$ is the logistic sigmoid function $\sigma(x) = \frac{1}{1+e^{-x}}$.

We assume that $p(\theta)$ is a Gaussian distribution with zero mean and variance-covariance matrix $\Sigma_\theta = \lambda I$. With the probability and the likelihood defined above, we can derive the objective function as follows:

$$\begin{aligned} O &= -\ln p(\theta|R) = -\ln p(R|\theta)p(\theta) \qquad (9) \\ &= -\sum_{u_i \in \mathcal{U}} \sum_{(e_a > e_b) \in R_i} \ln p(e_a > e_b; u_i|\theta) + \lambda\|\theta\|_2^2 \\ &= -\sum_{u_i \in \mathcal{U}} \sum_{(e_a > e_b) \in R_i} \ln \sigma(r(u_i, e_a) - r(u_i, e_b)) + \lambda\|\theta\|_2^2 \end{aligned}$$

where $\lambda\|\theta\|_2^2$ is a data dependent $L_2$ regularization term.

By minimizing $O$ in Equation (9), we can estimate the recommendation parameter $\theta$ from the implicit feedback data.

## 5.2 The Optimization Algorithm

Notice that Equation (9) is differentiable, many optimization techniques (e.g., SGD [2], BFGS-B method [3]) can be utilized to estimate parameter $\theta$. The gradient of Equation (9) with respect to $\theta$ can be calculated as follows:

$$\begin{aligned} \frac{\partial O}{\partial \theta} &= -\sum_{u_i \in \mathcal{U}} \sum_{(e_a > e_b) \in R_i} \frac{\partial}{\partial \theta} \sigma(r_{i,ab}) + \frac{\lambda}{2} \frac{\partial}{\partial \theta} \|\theta\|_2^2 \\ &= -\sum_{u_i \in \mathcal{U}} \sum_{(e_a > e_b) \in R_i} \frac{e^{-r_{i,ab}}}{1 + e^{-r_{i,ab}}} \frac{\partial}{\partial \theta} r_{i,ab} + \lambda\theta, \end{aligned}$$

where $r_{i,ab} = r(u_i, e_a) - r(u_i, e_b)$.

Considering the data size of the real-world recommender systems, with the above gradient, we employed the stochastic gradient descent (SGD) method [2] to estimate the parameters in our empirical studies. Notice that the time complexity of this proposed learning process is $O(mn^2)$ where $m$ is the number of users and $n$ is the number of items. In large datasets this can be overwhelming. With SGD, we only need to estimate the gradient with a very small subset ($10^{-5}$ sample rate) of training pairs sampled from $R$ at each iteration. We discuss sample rate selection for parameter estimation in Section 6.

## 5.3 Learning Personalized Recommendation Models

As discussed in Section 4, the proposed global recommendation model failed to distinguish individual interests and behavior differences, and thus the quality of the results may not be satisfying. We observed that although users may have different interests from each other, a subgroup of users can share similar interests or behavior patterns. Instead of learning one global model, which cannot represent user individuality, or learning personalized models directly, which can be time consuming and may cause model over-fitting, we propose to learn recommendation models for user subgroups. With recommendation models for user subgroups, when making recommendations, we can calculate the personalized recommendation model for a target user by combining the recommendation models he or she is most related to, and generate recommendation results accordingly.

In order to learn recommendation models for user subgroups, we first need to cluster users based on their interests and preferences, by examining the user implicit feedback data. Considering the sparsity of $R$, we first learn low-rank representation for users by applying non-negative matrix factorization on $R$ directly. With the low dimension user matrix $U$, we apply the well-studied *k-means* algorithm with a cosine function as similarity measurement between users, to finally cluster users into subgroups. For each cluster, we apply the techniques we discussed above to learn a recommendation model. The learning algorithm of personalized recommendation models can be found in Algorithm 1.

After estimating parameters of the recommendation models, given a target user, we can calculate the corresponding personalized recommendation model with Equation (5), and make personalized entity recommendation by using both the personalized recommendation model and his or her personal feedback data accordingly.

# 6. EMPIRICAL STUDY

We present the empirical studies of the proposed recommendation framework in this section. We implemented both global and personalized recommendation models proposed in Section 3 and 4 along with several popularly deployed or the state-of-the-art implicit feedback recommendation techniques. We applied these methods on two real-world datasets and performed a series of experiments to demonstrate the effectiveness of the proposed approach. We present both experimental results and discussion with analysis.

**Algorithm 1:** Learning Personalized Recommendation Models

`// input: implicit feedback and information network`
`// output: recommendation models for user clusters`
**Input**: $R$, $G$
**Output**: $\theta^{\{\cdot\}}$
Prepare $L$ meta-paths in the format of **user** $-$ **item** $- * -$ **item**
`// User preference diffusion along meta-paths`
**for** $q \leftarrow 1$ ***to*** $L$ **do**
  **foreach** $u_i$ *and* $e_j$ **do**
    $\tilde{R}^{(q)}_{u_i,e_j} = s(u_i, e_j | \mathcal{P}^{(q)})$ (Equation (2))
  **end**
  Calculate latent features $\hat{U}^{(q)}, \hat{V}^{(q)}$ with $\tilde{R}^{(q)}$ (Equation (3))
**end**
`// Clustering users into subgroups`
Factorize $R$ and derive $U$, $V$
$C$ = k-means($U$)
`// Learn recommendation models`
**foreach** $C_k$ *in* $C$ **do**
  Optimize $\theta^{\{k\}}$ with implicit feedback in user subgroup $C_k$ (Equation (9))
**end**

| Name | #Items | #Users | #Ratings | #Entities | #Links |
|---|---|---|---|---|---|
| IM100K | 943 | 1360 | 89,626 | 60,905 | 146,013 |
| Yelp | 11,537 | 43,873 | 229,907 | 285,317 | 570,634 |

(a) Datasets Description

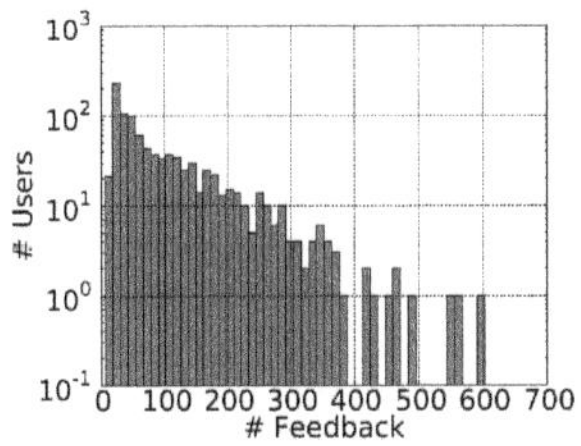


(b) IMDb Feedback Distribution

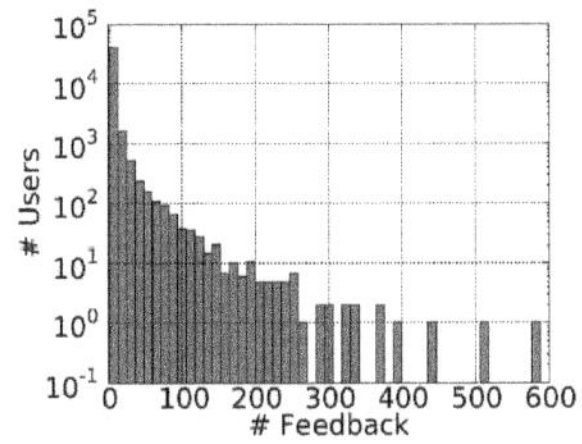


(c) Yelp Feedback Distribution

**Figure 5: IM100K and Yelp Datasets**

## 6.1 Data

To demonstrate the effectiveness of the proposed recommendation framework, we choose two datasets from different domains (movie and local business) for empirical studies. The first dataset is built by combining the popular MovieLens-100K dataset and the corresponding IMDb dataset together. We name this dataset IMDb-MovieLens-100K (IM100K). We use MovieLens user ratings as user feedback and we build a corresponding heterogeneous information network from the IMDb dataset. If users watched a certain movie and wrote a review about this movie, no matter whether they liked the movie or not, we say we observed the user-item interaction and we set this feedback as 1, otherwise, we set as 0. When building this dataset, we mapped two datasets using titles and release date of the movies, which could be erroneous on certain movies so the results we presented below are lower-bound of the actual performances.

**Table 2: Meta-path examples (we set $n = 1$ and 2. "biz" is short for "local business")**

| Network | Meta-Path |
|---|---|
| IM100K | user$-$(movie$-$tag$-$movie)$^n$ |
| | user$-$(movie$-$director$-$movie)$^n$ |
| | user$-$(movie$-$genre$-$movie)$^n$ |
| | user$-$movie$-$plot$-$movie |
| Yelp | user$-$(biz$-$category$-$movie)$^n$ |
| | user$-$(biz$-$customer$-$biz)$^n$ |
| | user$-$biz$-$checkin$-$biz |
| | user$-$biz$-$location$-$biz |

The second dataset is the Yelp challenge dataset[a]. This dataset contains both user reviews and local business information (an information network). When a user wrote a review for a restaurant, we set the feedback as 1, otherwise it would be set to 0. We summarize these two datasets in Figure 5(a) and the schema of which can be found in Figure 2. Notice that the Yelp dataset is much sparser than the IM100K dataset, so the performances of all methods decline accordingly. The distributions of the user feedback can be found in Figure 5.

Both datasets have timestamps with each user item interaction. We split the feedback matrix $R$ of both datasets for each user into training and test based on timestamps, *i.e.*, we use 80% of the "past" feedback to predict 20% of "future" feedback. In Yelp dataset, we have to filter out all the users who only have 1 review since we can not create training and test data for such users.

## 6.2 Competitors and Evaluation Metrics

We implement several widely deployed or the state-of-the-art recommendation approaches as comparison methods as follows:

- **Popularity:** Recommend the popular items to users.
- **Co-Click:** Estimate conditional probabilities between items and recommend items with an aggregated conditional probability calculated using the training data of the target user.
- **NMF:** Non-negative matrix factorization on $R$, details of which is discussed in Section 2.3
- **Hybrid-SVM:** Use SVM-based ranking function [13] to learn a global recommendation model with user implicit feedback and meta-paths based similarity measures [24].

We use *HeteRec-g* to denote the proposed global recommendation model and *HeteRec-p* to represent the personalized recommendation models derived from user subgroup recommendation models. We utilize 10 different meta-paths in each information network, including the most simple meta-path *user* $-$ *item*, which means user preferences can only be propagated to items with observed positive feedback. We list some other meta-paths and / or attribute similarity measures in Table 6.1. For explicit feedback recommendation evaluation, measures like *root mean square error* (RMSE) are the standard evaluation metric. However, these metrics do not suit the definition of implicit feedback problem. In this study, we test all methods as ranking models and use the well-studied information retrieval metrics including precision-at-position and top-10 *mean reciprocal rank* (MRR, Equation (10)) to evaluate and compare the performance of these methods.

$$\mathrm{MRR}_K = \frac{1}{m}\sum_{i=1}^{m}\left(\sum_{e \in test(u_i)} \frac{1}{rank(u_i, e)}\right) \qquad (10)$$

[a]`http://www.yelp.com/dataset_challenge/`

**Table 3: Performance Comparison**

| Method | IM100K | | | | Yelp | | | |
|---|---|---|---|---|---|---|---|---|
| | Prec1 | Prec5 | Prec10 | MRR | Prec1 | Prec5 | Prec10 | MRR |
| Popularity | 0.0731 | 0.0513 | 0.0489 | 0.1923 | 0.00747 | 0.00825 | 0.00780 | 0.0228 |
| Co-Click | 0.0668 | 0.0558 | 0.0538 | 0.2041 | 0.0147 | 0.0126 | 0.01132 | 0.0371 |
| NMF | 0.2064 | 0.1661 | 0.1491 | 0.4938 | 0.0162 | 0.0131 | 0.0110 | 0.0382 |
| Hybrid-SVM | 0.2087 | 0.1441 | 0.1241 | 0.4493 | 0.0122 | 0.0121 | 0.0110 | 0.0337 |
| HeteRec-g | 0.2094 | 0.1791 | 0.1614 | 0.5249 | 0.0165 | 0.0144 | 0.0129 | 0.0422 |
| HeteRec-p | **0.2121** | **0.1932** | **0.1681** | **0.5530** | **0.0213** | **0.0171** | **0.0150** | **0.0513** |

## 6.3 Performance Comparison

The performance of all 6 methods in the two datasets can be found in Table 3.

Based on Figure 5, user feedback data follow power law distribution, *i.e.*, a very small number of items have interaction with a large number of users. Due to this property, recommending the popular items to users has a decent performance (MRR=0.1923 in IM100K). Co-click method, as one of the most widely deployed technique, achieves MRR = 0.2041 in IM100K and has a similar performance as the NMF method in Yelp (MRR=0.0371).

We implemented the NMF as the CF baseline (details of this method can be found in Section 2.3). We set the dimensionality of the low-rank representations $d = 20$ in IMD100K and $d = 60$ in Yelp with cross validation in training dataset. We use the same method and settings in the diffusion-based latent feature generation method for the proposed approaches. With parameter tuning and additional information (*e.g.*, [9]), NMF may perform better than the results in Table 3. However, the same performance improvement can be achieved in our methods accordingly by replacing the NMF solver in Equation (3) with a more advanced technique. As presented in Table 3, NMF achieved MRR = 0.4938 and Prec1 = 0.2061 in IM100K dataset and MRR = 0.0382 and Prec1 = 0.0162 in Yelp dataset. This method outperforms other baselines methods in both datasets.

Hybrid-SVM method is a hybrid recommendation approach which uses the same amount of information as our proposed methods. This method combines both implicit feedback and heterogeneous relationship information following the intuitions of our study. However, it adopts an SVM based ranking framework [13] and uses PathSim [24] measures as features when defining the recommendation model. Without the proposed diffusion-based feature generation method, the learning algorithm and the recommendation model personalization, Hybrid-SVM can not fully take advantage of the feedback data and the heterogeneity of the information network. This method can only achieve MRR = 0.4493 in IM100K (compared to 0.4938 with NMF) and MRR = 0.0337 (compared to 0.0371 with Co-Click method). The low-performance of the Hybrid-SVM method proves the effectiveness of the proposed framework.

Our proposed global recommendation model (HeteRec-g), which takes advantage of both user feedback and the related information network, and users the same amount of information as Hybrid-SVM, beats all baseline methods in both datasets. It improves MRR by 6.1% compared to NMF in IM100K and 10.4% in Yelp dataset. This proves our assumption that adding information network as external knowledge with the proposed approach can alleviate the data sparsity issue and improve the recommendation quality. Morever, HeteRec-g produces much more accurate recommendation results compared to Hybrid-SVM (in IM100K, MRR of HeteRec-g is 0.5249 while MRR of Hybrid-SVM is only 0.4493). Both methods utilize the same set of meta-paths, and use the same sample rate during training. Both methods define "global" recommendation models since they apply the same model to all the users. The performance increase of HeteRec-g proves the effectiveness of our diffusion-based latent feature generation method. Another interesting observation is that the MRR gain of HeteRec-g compared with NMF in the relatively dense IM100K dataset is less than it is in the sparer Yelp dataset (6.1% v.s. 10.4%), which fits our intuition that when feedback dataset is sparser, the informative network-based recommendation approach can improve the performance even more. When training, we employ a uniform sample rate $10^{-5}$ in SGD and we apply the same rate to all supervised approaches in this experiment. Parameter tuning of the sample rate is discussed later this section.

HeteRec-p as the personalized recommendation approach can further improve the performance in both datasets. HeteRec-p method clusters users based on their interests and utilizes personalized model parameters when recommending. This approach can distinguish user behaviors while HeteRec-g treats all users as the same. We use $c = 10$ in IM100K dataset and $c = 100$ in Yelp dataset. We discuss the strategy of choosing the correct granularity later this section. Compared with the global recommendation model (HeteRec-g), personalized models can provide higher quality recommendation results in both datasets. It improves Prec5 by 7.9% and MRR by 5.4% in IM100K, and improves Prec1 by 29% and MRR by 21.5% in Yelp. This verifies that different users indeed have different interests and behavior patterns. Applying global recommendation model to all users can not distinguish user differences properly. Recommendation models which are learned within user subgroups can represent user interests and behaviors at a finer granularity level, and thus HeteRec-p can generates better results. Compared with baseline methods which only utilize user feedback data, HeteRec-p surpasses NMF by 12.0% in terms of MRR in IM100K and beats the MRR score of Co-Click by 38.3% in Yelp dataset.

Overall, the proposed recommendation models outperform all comparison methods in both IM100K and Yelp datasets. The experiments verify that using heterogeneous information networks in recommender systems can improve recommendation quality. Personalized recommendation models can better distinguish user interests and behaviors, and thus can lead to personalized and more accurate recommendation results.

## 6.4 Performance Analysis

We analyze the performance of Co-Click, NMF, HeteRec-g and HeteRec-p in different recommendation scenarios. We ran the following analytical experiments on both datasets and observed similar performance change in both datasets. Due to the page limitation, we only present these findings with IM100K dataset.

We first study the correlation between the performance of different recommendation methods and the training feedback data size of each user. We split all users into 6 groups based on their individual training data size. Users in group 1 provided very limited number of feedback (average size is 13) while users in group 6 provided the most amount of

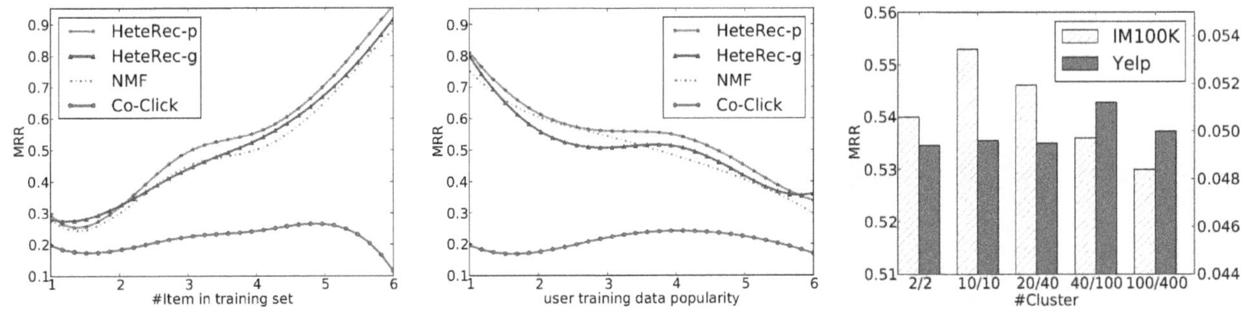


(a) Performance Change with User Feedback Number (b) Performance Change with User Feedback Popularity (c) Local Model Cluster Number Tuning

**Figure 6: Performance Analysis and Parameter Tuning**

feedback (average size is 224). We apply all 4 methods in each group. The results of this study can be found in Figure 6(a). One can notice that overall HeteRec-p outperforms all the other methods for users with different feedback sizes. When the user feedback size is small, *i.e.*, the data sparsity issue is severe, the performances of all methods are bad. When the feedback size of each user increases, the performances increase accordingly. The performance of Co-Click however does not change as much among different groups. This proves that all CF based methods could be affected when data are sparse. When feedback data are insufficient, it is critical to utilize information network as external knowledge to alleviate this issue.

We then study the correlation between performances of the 4 methods and the popularity of the items that users interacted in the feedback dataset. We split users into 6 groups based on the average popularity of the movies they interacted with in the training dataset. Users in group 1 prefer less popular movies (average popularity of items is 71) whle users in group 6 prefer the most popular movies (average popularity is 281). The results of this study can be found in Figure 6(b). Similar to the previous study, overall HeteRec-p outperforms all the other methods for different user groups. Interestingly, all CF based methods perform better for users who prefer unpopular movies. This finding may be counter-intuitive. It would seem like popular movies are easier to handle since the related data are sufficient. However, users who prefer popular movies usually do not have specific interests (they watch anything popular without considering genres, stories or any other types of information). Recommending movies to such users is always challenging. One possible way of handling this problem is to identify such users and use popularity based methods for the recommendation.

## 6.5 Parameter Tuning

The proposed methods have several additional parameters compared with other methods.

In Equation (9), $\lambda$ controls $L_2$ regularization of the function. We cross-validated this parameter and set it to 0.1 when optimizing objective function. Another parameter is the sampling rate in SGD when estimating parameters. As mentioned in Section 5, with the proposed objective function, the scale of the training dataset is $O(mn^2)$ which can be overwhelming in large datasets (this number in Yelp dataset is approximately $10^{12}$). Instead of using the entire dataset, we only sample a subset during training. We study the relationship between the sample rate and the performance of HeteRec-g in IM100K (Figure 7).

Notice the x-axis in Figure 7 is at log scale. When sample rate is more than $10^{-5}$, the performance of the global

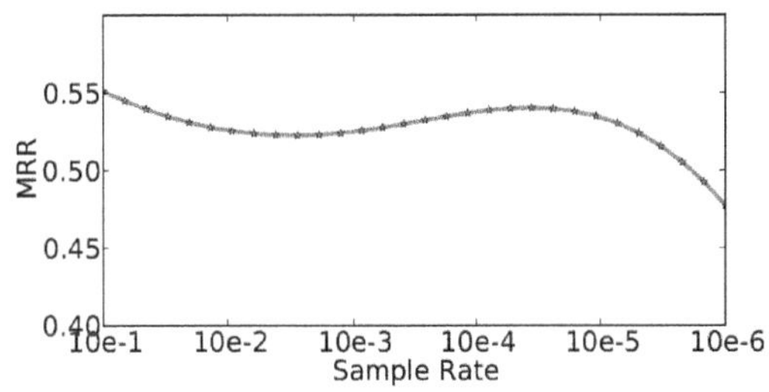


**Figure 7: Sample Rate Tuning**

model is relatively stable which means we do not need all the data to learn a high quality model with the proposed approach. However, inefficient training data size could harm the performance when we only supply $10^{-6}$ or less training data.

Another parameter for HeteRec-p is the number of user clusters. As presented in Figure 6(c), although not very sensitive to this parameter, HeteRec-p does perform differently with different numbers of clusters. It peaks at $c = 10$ in IM100K and $c = 100$ in Yelp dataset compared with other parameters tested. When the number of clusters is small, HeteRec-p could not distinguish users behavior very well while a large cluster number could lead to training data deficiency for each subgroup model, and thus lead to performance decreasing.

# 7. RELATED WORK

## 7.1 CF Based Hybrid Recommender Systems

As one of the most popular recommendation approaches, collaborative filtering techniques have been extensively studied from different perspectives[23] [8]. Among different techniques, matrix factorization-based models [22, 14] are widely employed in many systems due to their good performances [15].

Recent studies on collaborative filtering turn to leveraging different types of external information so that data sparsity problem can be addressed and better recommending performance can be achieved. [20, 6, 1] incorporate item or user profiles (e.g., user demographic and item attributes) into collaborative filtering framework, leading to content-based collaborative filtering.

In contrast to content-based information, knowledge extracted from relational data are attracting increasing interest. In particular, several works leverage different social relationships in social network such as trust relationship [18,

10], friend relationship [19, 7], and user membership [31]. to boost collaborative filtering since it provides user's like-minded neighbors. Yu *et al.* [29] suggest the utilization of graph Lapalacian regularization to exploit entity similarity measurements defined along different meta-paths.

To the best of our knowledge, existing relation-based collaborative filtering focuses on extracting knowledge from single or multiple homogeneous networks, *i.e.*, networks with single type of nodes and links. Our work discusses leverage external knowledge extracted from heterogeneous information networks for collaborative filtering boosting at a personalized level.

On the other hand, regarding data characteristics, most existing methods handle user's explicit feedback like item ratings. Recently there has been increasing interest on usage of user implicit feedback to conduct collaborative filtering [9, 21], which are much easier to be collected.

## 7.2 Information Network Analysis

Heterogeneous information networks which contain multi-typed entities and links are the general data format of knowledge graphs. Information network analysis and mining have gained wide attention in both academia and industry [27]. Many researchers believe that the heterogeneity and rich-relation nature make information network a better data representation in many scenarios. A lot of information network mining and learning tasks have been done in the past couple of years, including clustering [25] [26], classification [12], and link prediction [28] [16], *etc.* Studies regarding entity similarity measurements, as a fundamental technique, have been actively engaged in many research works as well [4] [11] [24]. Researchers also discover that certain similarity measurements could be defined along paths in information networks, and such path compatible measurements could capture different similarity semantic meanings and can be used in different applications [17] [24]. These papers also motivated user guided or personalized data mining and analysis with information networks [25].

# 8. CONCLUSION AND FUTURE WORK

In this paper, we study recommendation in the scope of heterogeneous information networks. We propose a generic recommendation framework for implicit feedback dataset by taking advantage of different types of entity relationships in heterogeneous information networks. We define recommendation models at both global and personalized levels. Personalized recommendation models can be efficiently generated on the fly, and this approach can provide high quality personalized recommendation results compared to other recommendation methods. A Bayesian ranking process is utilized to estimate the weights of the recommendation models. We compared the proposed approaches with several widely employed or state-of-the-art implicit feedback recommendation techniques, and empirical study demonstrates the effectiveness of our methods. We also analyzed the performance of these methods under different scenarios and explained the reasons of the performance drift. Interesting future work includes on-line recommendation model update with users providing model feedback, large scale recommendation model in information networks as well as approximate learning process with low time complexity.

## Acknowledgments

The work was supported in part by the U.S. Army Research Laboratory under Cooperative Agreement No. W911NF-09-2-0053 (NS-CTA) and W911NF-11-2-0086 (Cyber-Security), the U.S. Army Research Office under Cooperative Agreement No. W911NF-13-1-0193, DTRA, DHS, and U.S. National Science Foundation grants CNS-0931975, IIS-1017362, IIS-1320617, IIS-1354329.

# 9. REFERENCES

[1] J. Basilico and T. Hofmann. Unifying collaborative and content-based filtering. In *ICML*, 2004.

[2] L. Bottou. Large-scale machine learning with stochastic gradient descent. In *COMPSTAT*. 2010.

[3] R. H. Byrd, P. Lu, J. Nocedal, and C. Zhu. A limited memory algorithm for bound constrained optimization. *SIAM Journal on Scientific Computing*, 16(5):1190–1208, 1995.

[4] S. Chakrabarti. Dynamic personalized pagerank in entity-relation graphs. In *WWW*, 2007.

[5] C. H. Ding, T. Li, and M. I. Jordan. Convex and semi-nonnegative matrix factorizations. *PAMI*, 2010.

[6] Q. Gu, J. Zhou, and C. Ding. Collaborative filtering: Weighted nonnegative matrix factorization incorporating user and item graphs. In *SDM*, 2010.

[7] I. Guy, N. Zwerdling, D. Carmel, I. Ronen, E. Uziel, S. Yogev, and S. Ofek-Koifman. Personalized recommendation of social software items based on social relations. In *RecSys*, 2009.

[8] T. Hofmann. Collaborative filtering via gaussian probabilistic latent semantic analysis. In *SIGIR*, 2003.

[9] Y. Hu, Y. Koren, and C. Volinsky. Collaborative filtering for implicit feedback datasets. In *ICDM*, 2008.

[10] M. Jamali and M. Ester. A matrix factorization technique with trust propagation for recommendation in social networks. In *SIGKDD*, 2010.

[11] G. Jeh and J. Widom. Simrank: a measure of structural-context similarity. In *SIGKDD*, 2002.

[12] M. Ji, J. Han, and M. Danilevsky. Ranking-based classification of heterogeneous information networks. In *SIGKDD*, 2011.

[13] T. Joachims. Training linear svms in linear time. In *SIGKDD*, 2006.

[14] Y. Koren. Factorization meets the neighborhood: a multifaceted collaborative filtering model. In *SIGKDD*, 2008.

[15] Y. Koren, R. Bell, and C. Volinsky. Matrix factorization techniques for recommender systems. *Computer*, 42(8):30–37, 2009.

[16] T.-T. Kuo, R. Yan, Y.-Y. Huang, P.-H. Kung, and S.-D. Lin. Unsupervised link prediction using aggregative statistics on heterogeneous social networks. In *SIGKDD*. ACM, 2013.

[17] N. Lao and W. Cohen. Relational retrieval using a combination of path-constrained random walks. *Machine learning*, 2010.

[18] H. Ma, I. King, and M. R. Lyu. Learning to recommend with social trust ensemble. In *SIGIR*, 2009.

[19] H. Ma, H. Yang, M. Lyu, and I. King. Sorec: social recommendation using probabilistic matrix factorization. In *CIKM*, 2008.

[20] P. Melville, R. J. Mooney, and R. Nagarajan. Content-boosted collaborative filtering for improved recommendations. In *AAAI*, 2002.

[21] S. Rendle, C. Freudenthaler, Z. Gantner, and L. Schmidt-Thieme. Bpr: Bayesian personalized ranking from implicit feedback. In *UAI*, 2009.

[22] J. D. Rennie and N. Srebro. Fast maximum margin matrix factorization for collaborative prediction. In *ICML*, 2005.

[23] B. Sarwar, G. Karypis, J. Konstan, and J. Riedl. Item-based collaborative filtering recommendation algorithms. In *WWW*, 2001.

[24] Y. Sun, J. Han, X. Yan, S. P. Yu, and T. Wu. PathSim: Meta Path-Based Top-K Similarity Search in Heterogeneous Information Networks. In *VLDB*, 2011.

[25] Y. Sun, B. Norick, J. Han, X. Yan, P. S. Yu, and X. Yu. Integrating meta-path selection with user guided object clustering in heterogeneous information networks. In *KDD*, 2012.

[26] Y. Sun, Y. Yu, and J. Han. Ranking-based clustering of heterogeneous information networks with star network schema. In *KDD*, 2009.

[27] M. Szell, R. Lambiotte, and S. Thurner. Multirelational organization of large-scale social networks in an online world. *Proceedings of the National Academy of Sciences*, 107(31):13636–13641, 2010.

[28] X. Yu, Q. Gu, M. Zhou, and J. Han. Citation prediction in heterogeneous bibliographic networks. In *SDM*, 2012.

[29] X. Yu, X. Ren, Q. Gu, Y. Sun, and J. Han. Collaborative filtering with entity similarity regularization in heterogeneous information networks. In *IJCAI HINA*, 2013.

[30] X. Yu, X. Ren, Y. Sun, B. Sturt, U. Khandelwal, Q. Gu, B. Norick, and J. Han. Entity recommendation in heterogeneous information networks with implicit user feedback. In *RecSys*, 2013.

[31] Q. Yuan, L. Chen, and S. Zhao. Factorization vs. regularization: fusing heterogeneous social relationships in top-n recommendation. In *RecSys*, 2011.

# Social Collaborative Retrieval

Ko-Jen Hsiao
University of Michigan
Ann Arbor, MI, USA 48109
coolmark@umich.edu

Alex Kulesza
University of Michigan
Ann Arbor, MI, USA 48109
kulesza@umich.edu

Alfred O. Hero III
University of Michigan
Ann Arbor, MI, USA 48109
hero@umich.edu

## ABSTRACT

Socially-based recommendation systems have recently attracted significant interest, and a number of studies have shown that social information can dramatically improve a system's predictions of user interests. Meanwhile, there are now many potential applications that involve aspects of both recommendation and information retrieval, and the task of *collaborative retrieval*—a combination of these two traditional problems—has recently been introduced. Successful collaborative retrieval requires overcoming severe data sparsity, making additional sources of information, such as social graphs, particularly valuable. In this paper we propose a new model for collaborative retrieval, and show that our algorithm outperforms current state-of-the-art approaches by incorporating information from social networks. We also provide empirical analyses of the ways in which cultural interests propagate along a social graph using a real-world music dataset.

## Categories and Subject Descriptors

H.3.3 [**Information storage and retrieval**]: Information Search and Retrieval; I.2.6 [**Artificial Intelligence**]: Learning

## General Terms

Algorithms, Experimentation

## Keywords

collaborative filtering, information retrieval, social networks

## 1. INTRODUCTION

Collaborative filtering (CF) and related recommendation techniques, which aim to automatically predict the interests of users and make personal recommendations of music, movies, products, or other items, have been both intensively studied by researchers and successfully deployed in industry during the past decade [3, 9, 18, 21]. Recently, Weston et al. [24] proposed extending CF to a setting termed collaborative retrieval (CR), in which recommendations are made with respect to a particular *query context*; for instance, a user might be looking for music in a particular genre or movies similar to a recent favorite. In these situations, otherwise accurate recommendations will become irrelevant. Similarly, a shopping website might want to deliver a list of recommended items to a user based on their browsing history. In this case the recently viewed pages act as a sort of query, and we would like recommendations that are specific both to the query and to the user. Weston et al. [24] proposed the first algorithm to solve CR problems, called latent collaborative retrieval (LCR).

However, several important issues remain. While it is well-known that CF models typically contend with data sparsity problems since a large number of user-item pairs must be judged for compatibility based on a relatively small dataset, CR problems suffer even more severely from sparsity, since the range of possible queries multiplies the number of judgments to be made. Viewed as a matrix completion problem, traditional CF requires filling out a user $\times$ item matrix, where each entry indicates the relevance of a specific item to a specific user; this is often done using techniques like singular value decomposition and non-negative matrix factorization (NMF) [19]. In the same light, CR can be seen as a tensor completion problem, where the goal is to fill out a much larger query $\times$ user $\times$ item tensor. Recent work has begun to extend matrix factorization techniques for CF to tensor models of this type [6, 22, 25, 26]; however, these methods typically do not accommodate the ranking losses used for CR, and sparsity remains an important concern. In this work, we propose to deal with data sparsity in CR by incorporating an additional (but often readily available) source of information: a social graph.

In recent years social networking sites have become extremely popular, producing significant insights into the ways in which people connect themselves and interact. Information derived from these networks can be used to help address the sparsity problem faced by recommender systems, for instance by propagating information from a user's social connections to fill in gaps in the recommendation matrix. A variety of CF models augmented with social information have recently been proposed [5, 7, 8, 10, 12, 16]; these include state-of-the-art methods like Collaborative Topic Regression with social matrix factorization [16], which is based on LDA [2], and Probabilistic Matrix Factorization (PMF) [10, 17]. There has also been interest in so-called *trust-aware*


*WSDM'14*, February 24–28, 2014, New York, New York, USA.

ACM 978-1-4503-2351-2/14/02 ...$15.00.
http://–enter the whole DOI string from rightsreview form confirmation.

recommendation methods [1, 11, 13, 14, 15], which are similar in spirit but inherently limited compared with using real social networks [12]. However, social information has not yet been made to work for collaborative retrieval, which arguably stands to benefit even more. In this paper we set out to fill this gap.

We propose an approach we call social collaborative retrieval (SCR), which builds on the latent collaborative retrieval (LCR) model of Weston et al. [24] by integrating social networking data. Notice that this work is different from researches in collaborative information seeking (CIS). CIS is a popular field of research that studies methods and systems for people working in collaborative group for information seeking. In [20], CIS is defined as "a process of collaboratively seeking information that is defined explicitly among the participants, interactive, and mutually beneficial." CIS can be viewed as an active process and is quite different from collaborative filtering. While our work is more related to collaborative filtering, our SCR model connects users via their social network in addition to their passive involvements (e.g., listening to similar music artists).

As in LCR, our algorithm sets out to optimize the top-ranked items retrieved for a given user and query, but we incorporate a regularization penalty that encourages the low dimensional embedding of each user to be similar to those of the user's nearest social neighbors. On a collaborative retrieval task using real-world artist ratings from the Last.fm music dataset, our proposed algorithm significantly outperforms LCR, as well as baseline CF methods based on non-negative matrix factorization and singular value decomposition, particularly when a smaller training set leads to increased data sparsity.

The rest of this paper is organized as follows. In Section 2 we provide a brief introduction to latent collaborative retrieval (LCR) [24], followed by the details of our proposed SCR algorithm. Section 3 presents an empirical analysis of the Last.fm social networking dataset, and we present experimental results evaluating the performance of SCR in Section 4.

## 2. COLLABORATIVE RETRIEVAL

The goal of collaborative retrieval is to produce a ranked list of items that are of interest to a particular user given a particular query. While one approach might be to simply filter a set of unconstrained CF recommendations for the specified user using the query—or, conversely, to filter a set of generic search results for the query using the user's profile—these pipeline approaches fail to account for interactions between the query and the user. For instance, two users might have very different interpretations of the query "jazz", despite having broadly similar preferences among artists. CR attempts to obtain more informative results through a unified approach.

We thus formalize the problem by defining a single score function $f(q, u, a)$ to represent the relevance of a given item $a$ with respect to both a query $q$ and a user $u$. If we enumerate all users, queries, and items, we can think of this score function as specifying the values of a rating tensor $\mathbf{R} \in \mathbb{R}^{|\mathcal{Q}|\times|\mathcal{U}|\times|\mathcal{A}|}$, where $\mathcal{Q}$ is the set of all queries, $\mathcal{U}$ is the set of users, and $\mathcal{A}$ is the set of items. However, in practice we usually only care about the top $k$ items retrieved (for some small constant $k$) for a given user and query, and our evaluation metrics will share this property as well. (We discuss specific error measures in Section 2.3.) Thus, learning a score function that can correctly *rank* items for a given user-query pair is more important than learning one which can correctly approximate the full set of entries in $\mathbf{R}$. The objectives that we use to learn the parameters of the score function will therefore involve a measure of error on such top-$k$ ranked lists.

We next briefly review the existing latent collaborative retrieval model for this problem, and then introduce our model using social information. Finally, we discuss the optimization needed to learn the parameters of the model.

### 2.1 Latent collaborative retrieval

Latent collaborative retrieval (LCR) [24] was the first algorithm proposed to solve collaborative retrieval problems. The central idea is to embed users, queries, and items in a common $n$-dimensional space in which they can be compared using linear operations. ($n$ is a hyperparameter that is typically tuned on a validation set.) Formally, LCR is parameterized by matrices $S \in \mathbb{R}^{n\times|\mathcal{Q}|}$, $V \in \mathbb{R}^{n\times|\mathcal{U}|}$, and $T \in \mathbb{R}^{n\times|\mathcal{A}|}$, which give the low-dimensional representations of queries, users, and items, respectively. Additionally, for each user $u$ a matrix $U_u \in \mathbb{R}^{n\times n}$ encodes the user-specific relationship between queries and items. The scoring function $f$ is then defined as

$$f(q, u, a) = S_q^\top U_u T_a + V_u^\top T_a \ , \tag{1}$$

where $S_q$ is the column of $S$ corresponding to query $q$, $T_a$ is the column of $T$ corresponding to item $a$, and $V_u$ is the column of $V$ corresponding to user $u$. Intuitively, the first term in Equation 1 measures the similarity between the query and the item in the low-dimensional space under a linear transformation that is dependent on the user. The second term is independent of the query and can be viewed as a bias term which models user preferences for different items. Since for a given instance of a CR task the query and user are held fixed, there is no need for the scoring function to include a term like $S_q^\top V_u$, which would measure the compatibility of a user and a query. However, interactions between the user and the query that pertain to actual item recommendations can be expressed in the first term. If there are significant non-user-specific aspects of the compatibility between queries and items (i.e., a $S_q^\top T_a$ term), these can simply be absorbed into the first term and need not appear separately.

The parameters of the LCR scoring function are learned by optimizing a chosen error metric over a training set; we discuss some such metrics and other details in Section 2.3.

To aid in generalization, and to avoid the potentially prohibitive enumeration of queries, Equation 1 can be generalized using features. In this case $\Phi_Q(q)$, $\Phi_U(u)$ and $\Phi_A(a)$ are vector-valued feature maps for queries, users, and items, respectively, and $S$, $T$, and $V$ are linear maps from feature vectors to the embedded $n$-dimensional space. The feature-based scoring function is given by

$$f(q, u, a) = \Phi_Q(q)^\top S^\top U_u T \Phi_A(a) + \Phi_U(u)^\top V^\top T \Phi_A(a) \ . \tag{2}$$

If the feature maps are simple characteristic vectors, with a unique feature for each query, user, and item, then we recover the simpler form of Equation 1. Features of this type can also be used for content-based recommendation models (see [24]). For our purposes, we simply note that this feature-based formulation can be easily extended to SCR, but for simplicity we focus on the form in Equation 1 going forward.

## 2.2 Social collaborative retrieval

In the real world, people often turn to their friends for recommendations of musics, movies, or products. Here, we apply this intuition to improve the performance of CR techniques on tasks where social information is available. Our approach, which we refer to as social collaborative retrieval (SCR), learns a scoring function using a combination of *behavioral* and *relational* error measures.

Behavioral measures encourage the model to respect implicit similarities between users, items, and queries that are revealed by the training data. For instance, the preferences of one user may be useful for recommending items to another user if the two users have expressed similar preferences in the past. This is the traditional mode of operation for collaborative filtering, as well as for CR.

Relational measures, on the other hand, take account of explicitly labeled connections that (hopefully) reveal underlying similarities. In this work, we employ a relational measure that encourages the scoring function to be smooth with respect to a social graph; that is, we assume that users who are social neighbors should, on average, have more similar preferences than those who are not. (We validate this assumption empirically in Section 3.) The hope is that this relational measure term provides complementary guidance to the system when little is known about the behavior of a user.

For simplicity, and to make the fairest comparisons later, we use the same parameterization of the scoring function as LCR (Equation 1); we have $n$-dimensional representations of queries, users, and items in matrices $S$, $V$, and $T$, respectively, as well as user-specific transformations $U_u \in \mathbb{R}^{n \times n}$. We additionally assume that a social graph $G$ is available, where $G(i,j) = 1$ whenever users $i$ and $j$ are linked, and $G(i,j) = 0$ otherwise. We will sometimes refer to users who are linked as "friends", though of course the social graph may encode relations with varying semantics. To bias the preferences of friends toward each other, SCR introduces the social error measure

$$\text{err}_{\text{social}}(V, G) = \sum_{i,j,G(i,j)=1} \|\sigma(V_i^T V_j) - 1\|^2 , \qquad (3)$$

where $\sigma(\cdot)$ is the sigmoid function

$$\sigma(x) = \frac{1}{1 + e^{-cx}} \qquad (4)$$

and $c$ is a hyperparameter. This measure can be seen as a regularization penalty that is minimized when friends have identical, high-norm representations in $V$. Notice that we do not penalize similarity among non-friends, since users may have similar tastes even though they are not friends. Importantly, although we encourage friends to have similar representations $V_u$, we do not introduce such regularization for $U_u$ matrices, as this would tend to force friends to always receive the same results. Intuitively, we expect that friends are likely to have similar taste in items, but we allow each their own particular querying "style".

Combining the relational measure in Equation 3 with a behavioral measure $\text{err}_{\text{behavior}}$ that depends on the scoring function $f$ and the training set $X$ yields the SCR learning objective to be minimized:

$$\text{err}_{\text{behavior}}(f, X) + w_s \text{err}_{\text{social}}(V, G) , \qquad (5)$$

where $w_s$ is a regularization hyperparameter. In the following subsection we will discuss choices for $\text{err}_{\text{behavior}}$, as well as optimization techniques used to find the parameters in practice.

Similarity-based error measures related to Equation 3 have been proposed by others, typically based not on a social graph but instead on measured similarities between users. For example, the measured Pearson correlation of item ratings can be used as a similarity measure $Sim(i,j)$ between users $i$ and $j$, and this can be incorporated using a measure such as [12]:

$$\sum_{i=1}^{|\mathcal{U}|} \left\| V_i - \frac{\sum_{j,G(i,j)=1} Sim(i,j) \times V_j}{\sum_{j,G(i,j)=1} Sim(i,j)} \right\|_2^2 . \qquad (6)$$

However, accurately estimating similarities from data is often unreliable due to sparsity, especially in the CR setting. Moreover, such measures make it difficult to easily recommend items to newer users; without a long history of ratings, we cannot know which established users they are similar to. On the other hand, SCR requires an external source of information in the form of a social graph. But social networks are increasingly ubiquitous, and, since they are by nature centralized, can often be reliable even when extensive training data for a specific CR task is not yet available.

SCR can be viewed as a blend of social networking, collaborative filtering, and information retrieval. As a side benefit, in addition to providing improved recommendations for users under particular query contexts, SCR can potentially be used in the inverse to recommend new social links between users with similar preferences. In this way SCR can strengthen the social network and improve its own predictions in the future.

## 2.3 Learning

The goal of SCR learning is to (efficiently) find parameters $S$, $V$, $T$, and $U_u$ that minimize the objective in Equation 5. In this section we describe the formal learning setup, the specific behavioral measures used in our experiments, and the algorithm used to optimize the model parameters.

We assume we are given a training set $X$ containing $N$ training examples:

$$X = \{(q_i, u_i, a_i, w_i)\}_{i=1,2,\ldots,N} , \qquad (7)$$

where $q_i \in \mathcal{Q}$ is a query, $u_i \in \mathcal{U}$ is a user, $a_i \in \mathcal{A}$ is an item, and $w_i \in \mathbb{R}_{>0}$ is a measure of relevance for the item $a_i$ given the user $u_i$ and the query $q_i$. Importantly, we assume that the weights $w_i$ always have a positive connotation; that is, triples $(q, u, a)$ that do not appear in the training set implicitly have a weight of zero, and are therefore dispreferred to triples that do appear. For instance, in our experiments, $w_i$ will be derived from the number of times a user listens to a particular musical artist.

The behavioral part of the objective, which measures the compatibility of the scoring function $f$ (defined by the model parameters) with the training set $X$, can take a variety of forms depending on the setting. As noted earlier, we will focus on top-$k$ ranking losses that optimize the most important aspects of the model, rather than, say, filling out all entries of the tensor $\mathbf{R}$.

Following Weston et al. [24] we define the vector $\bar{f}(q,u)$, which contains predictions for all items in the database given query $q$ and user $u$. The $a^{th}$ entry of $\bar{f}(q,u)$, denoted $\bar{f}_a(q,u)$, is equal to $f(q,u,a)$.

With this notation, we can define the *Weighted Approximate-Rank Pairwise (WARP) Loss*, introduced in [23]:

$$\mathrm{err}_{\mathrm{WARP}}(f,X) = \sum_{i=1}^{N} L\left(\mathrm{rank}_{a_i}\left(\bar{f}(q_i,u_i)\right)\right) . \tag{8}$$

Here $\mathrm{rank}_{a_i}\left(\bar{f}(q_i,u_i)\right)$ is the margin-based rank of item $a_i$,

$$\mathrm{rank}_{a_i}\left(\bar{f}(q_i,u_i)\right) = \sum_{b \neq a_i} \mathbb{I}[1 + \bar{f}_b(q_i,u_i) \geq \bar{f}_{a_i}(q_i,u_i)] , \tag{9}$$

where $\mathbb{I}[\cdot]$ is the indicator function, and $L$ is a loss function:

$$L(k) = \sum_{i=1}^{k} \alpha_i \tag{10}$$

$$\alpha_1 \geq \alpha_2 \geq \alpha_3 \geq \cdots \geq 0 , \tag{11}$$

with the values of $\alpha_r$ determining the additional penalty for each successive reduction in rank. We choose $\alpha_r = 1/r$, which gives a smooth weighting over positions while assigning large weights to top positions and rapidly decaying weights to lower positions.

Intuitively, the WARP loss prefers that the item $a_i$ is always ranked highest. For each training example $i = 1, \ldots, N$, the positive item $a_i$ is compared pairwise with all other (negative) items in the database. If the score of another item is less than a margin of one from the score of $a_i$, this pair incurs a cost. The WARP loss determines this cost based on the corresponding items' ranking positions and the choice of $\alpha$ parameters.

We use the WARP loss in our experiments for comparison with prior work. However, in our setting it ignores the relevance scores $w_i$ that are part of the training set; this can be inefficient, since the optimization cannot focus on the most important training examples. We thus propose a modified behavioral measure that we refer to as the weighted WARP loss:

$$\mathrm{err}_{\mathrm{weighted}}(f) = \sum_{i=1}^{N} w_i L\left(\mathrm{rank}_{a_i}\left(\bar{f}(q_i,u_i)\right)\right) , \tag{12}$$

where rank and $L$ are defined as before. In our results, we refer to models learned under this loss as SCR-weighted, while models trained under the standard WARP loss are referred to simply as SCR. We will derive the optimization procedure for the weighted WARP loss, since the standard WARP loss is a special case.

To minimize Equation 5, we employ stochastic gradient descent, choosing at each iteration a single training instance $i$ uniformly at random from the training set. We then seek to optimize the objective for this single example; that is, we minimize

$$w_i L\left(\mathrm{rank}_{a_i}\left(\bar{f}(q_i,u_i)\right)\right) + w_s \sum_{v, G(u_i,v)=1} \|1 - \sigma(V_{u_i}^{\top} V_v)\|^2 . \tag{13}$$

Because it is expensive to compute the exact rank of an item $a_i$ when the total number of items is very large, the optimization procedure includes a sampling process at each step, as introduced in [23]. For the training sample $i$ chosen at the current iteration, negative items $b$ are sampled uniformly at random from $\mathcal{A}$ until a pairwise violation is found—that is, until $1 + f(q_i,u_i,b) > f(q_i,u_i,a_i)$. If $K$ steps are required to find such a $b$, then the rank of $a_i$ can be approximated as

$$rank_{a_i}(\bar{f}(q_i,u_i)) \approx \left\lfloor \frac{|\mathcal{A}| - 1}{K} \right\rfloor , \tag{14}$$

where $\lfloor \cdot \rfloor$ is the floor function.

Following Weston et al. [23], the single-instance objective becomes

$$w_i L\left(\left\lfloor \frac{|\mathcal{A}| - 1}{K} \right\rfloor\right) \cdot |1 - f(q_i,u_i,a_i) + f(q_i,u_i,b)| + w_s \sum_{v, G(u_i,v)=1} \|1 - \sigma(V_{u_i}^{\top} V_v)\|^2 . \tag{15}$$

Rewriting Equation 15, we have

$$C_i(1 + (S_{q_i}^{\top} U_{u_i} + V_{u_i}^{\top})(T_b - T_{a_i})) + w_s \sum_{v, G(u_i,v)=1} \|1 - \sigma(V_{u_i}^{\top} V_v)\|^2 , \tag{16}$$

where $C_i = w_i \cdot L(\lfloor \frac{|\mathcal{A}|-1}{K} \rfloor)$. To speed up each gradient step, we only update the variables associated with the current violation pair; that is, we only update $S_{q_i}$, $V_{u_i}$, $T_{a_i}$, $T_b$, and $U_{u_i}$. (In particular, we do not update the representations $u_i$'s friends $V_v$ for $G(u_i,v) = 1$.) Now we can simply take the gradient of (16) to perform an update.

The update for user $u_i$'s low-dimensional embedding is

$$V_{u_i} \leftarrow V_{u_i} - \eta \Bigg( C_i(T_b - T_{a_i}) + w_s \sum_{v, G(u_i,v)=1} \left(-2c\sigma(V_{u_i}^T V_v)\left(1 - \sigma(V_{u_i}^T V_v)\right)^2\right) \cdot V_j \Bigg) , \tag{17}$$

or equivalently

$$V_{u_i} \leftarrow V_{u_i} - \eta C_i(T_b - T_{a_i}) + w_s' \sum_{v, G(u_i,v)=1} b_v \cdot V_v , \tag{18}$$

where $b_v = 2c\sigma(V_{u_i}^T V_v)(1 - \sigma(V_{u_i}^T V_v))^2 > 0$, $w_s' = \eta w_s$, and $\eta$ is a learning rate parameter. (Recall that $c$ is a hyperparameter for the sigmoid function.) Thus at each gradient step, the user's low-dimensional embedding is updated toward the weighted mean of his or her friends' embeddings.

Similarly, we can derive updates for the remaining parameters:

$$S_{q_i} \leftarrow S_{q_i} - \eta \left( C_i(U_{u_i}(T_b - T_{a_i})) \right) \tag{19}$$

$$T_{a_i} \leftarrow T_{a_i} - \eta \left( C_i(-U_{u_i}^T S_{q_i} - V_{u_i}) \right) \tag{20}$$

$$T_b \leftarrow T_b - \eta \left( C_i(U_{u_i}^T S_{q_i} + V_{u_i}) \right) \tag{21}$$

$$U_{u_i} \leftarrow U_{u_i} - \eta \left( C_i \left( S_{q_i}(T_b - T_{a_i})^T \right) \right) . \tag{22}$$

Finally, we constrain the parameters using

$$\|S_i\|_2 \leq C_S \ , \quad i \in \{1, \ldots, |Q|\} \tag{23}$$
$$\|T_i\|_2 \leq C_T \ , \quad i \in \{1, \ldots, |A|\} \tag{24}$$
$$\|V_i\|_2 \leq C_V \ , \quad i \in \{1, \ldots, |\mathcal{U}|\} \tag{25}$$

and project the parameters back on to the constraints at each step.

# 3. SOCIAL DATA ANALYSIS

Before showing results that compare our proposed approach to existing state-of-the-art methods, we first experimentally validate the fundamental assumption that friends, on average, have more in common than non-friends.

## 3.1 Last.fm dataset

In our experiments we use a real-word music dataset obtained from the Last.fm music website, *hetrec2011-lastfm-2k* [4]. In this dataset each user is described by his or her listen counts for all musical artists in the database (items, in our setting), as well as any artist tags that might have been provided by each user.

While the data contain more than ten thousand unique tags across all users, the vast majority of tags are used by only one user. Typically these tags appear to be personal "notes" rather than widely used genre distinctions. To remove this noisy information, we throw out tags that are less frequent, keeping only the top 30 most common tags. These tags were all used by at least 165 unique users, and generally correspond to genres of music; for example, the top 5 most popular tags are *"rock"*, *"pop"*, *"alternative"*, *"electronic"* and *"indie"*. The Last.fm dataset contains listening histories for 1892 users and 17632 music artists. A social graph is also included; on average each user has 13.44 friends.

## 3.2 Shared musical interests

Do friends share more preferences than non-friends? This is a key question for our approach. If the answer is no, it may not be useful to include social networks as a predictor variable in recommendation systems. To estimate the similarity between two users' tastes for music, we compute the *listened artists overlap ratio*, defined as

$$Sim(i,j) = \frac{|A_i \cap A_j|}{|A_i \cup A_j|} \in [0,1] \quad \forall\, i,j \ , \tag{26}$$

where $A_i$ is the set of artists listened to by user $i$.

The overlap ratios are computed for all $\binom{|\mathcal{U}|}{2}$ user pairs. We then divide the range [0, 1] of possible ratios evenly into 100 intervals, and calculate the fraction of the user pairs falling in each interval that are linked in the social graph. Intuitively, we hope that users with greater similarity are more likely to be friends. The result is shown in Figure 1 (a). The percentage of realized *friend* relations increases sharply as the artist overlap ratio increases.

To reinforce this analysis, we also compute the average similarity between each user $i$ and his or her friends, as well as the average similarity between user $i$ and all other non-friend users, denoting the two numbers as $\beta^i_{friend}$ and $\beta^i_{non-friend}$. Figure 1 (b) shows the values of $\beta^i_{friend}$ and $\beta^i_{non-friend}$ averaged over the set of users with a given number of friends; this number varies on the horizontal axis. We can see that, no matter how many friends a user has, on average the user has more in common with his or her friends

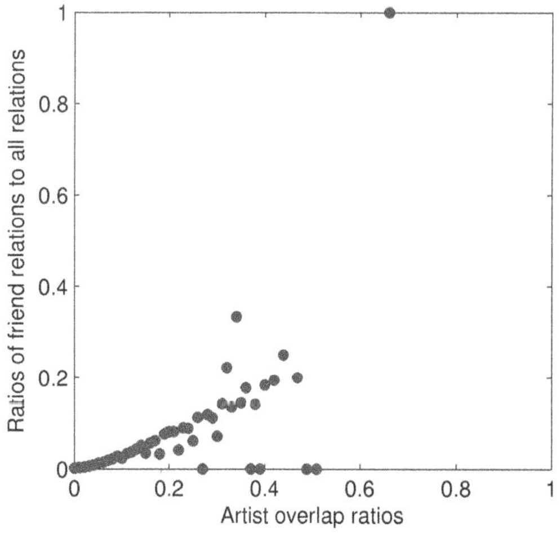


(a)

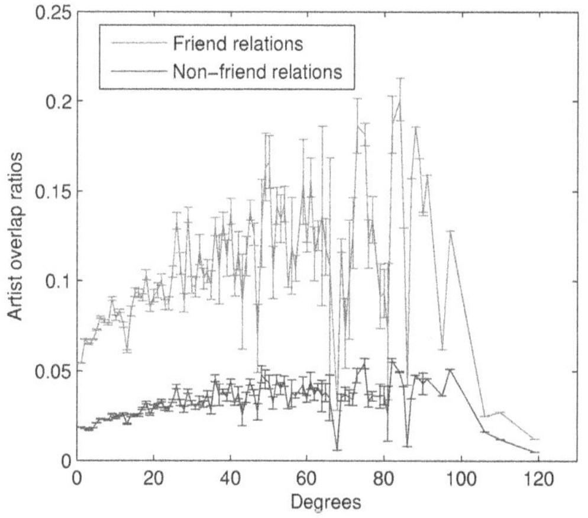


(b)

Figure 1: (a) For user pairs having listened artist overlap ratios within the same interval, the proportion of friend relations among these pairs is shown. (b) Average artist overlap ratios among friends (red) and non-friends (blue) for users having different numbers of friends (degree).

than with non-friends; moreover, the size of this effect increases for users with more friends. Overall, these analyses support our assumptions regarding the use of social networks for recommendation and retrieval tasks on this dataset.

# 4. EXPERIMENTS

We next compare the SCR approach with other state-of-the-art algorithms. For the Last.fm dataset described in the previous section, a *query* × *user* × *item* triple corresponds to a *genre* × *user* × *artist*, where genres are obtained from the set of filtered user tags.

We preprocess the data set in two ways to obtain listening counts for each such triple. First, if a user $u$ has listened to an artist $a$ and assigned multiple genres, for example *rock* and *indie*, then $u$'s listening counts for $a$ are evenly distributed to triples (*rock*, $u$, $a$) and (*indie*, $u$, $a$). If the user has not assigned any genre to an artist, the genres of $a$ are

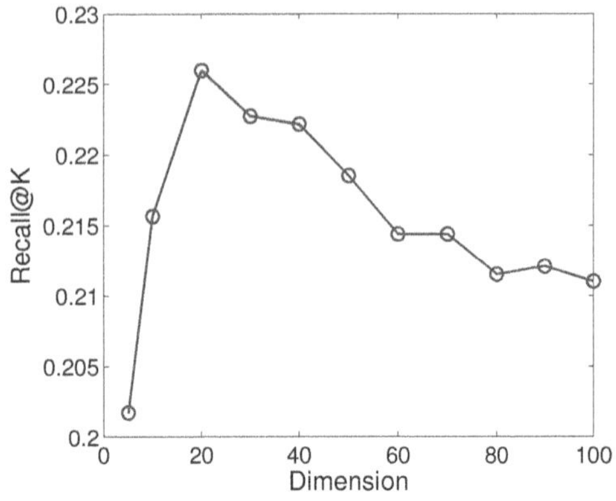


(a)

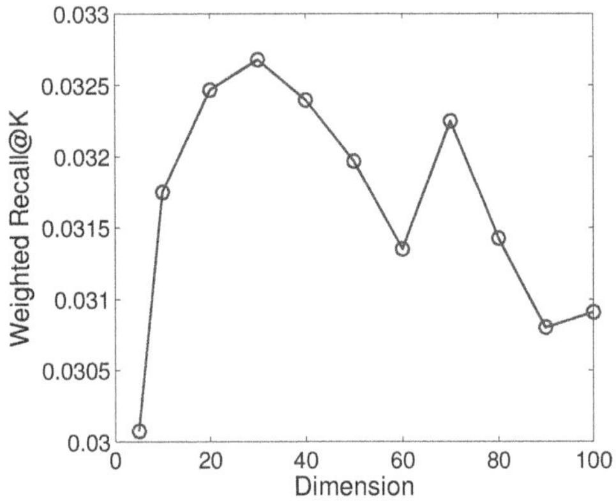


(b)

Figure 2: (a) Recall@30 of SCR-weighted using different embedding dimensions. (b) Weighted Recall@30 of SCR-weighted using different embedding dimensions.

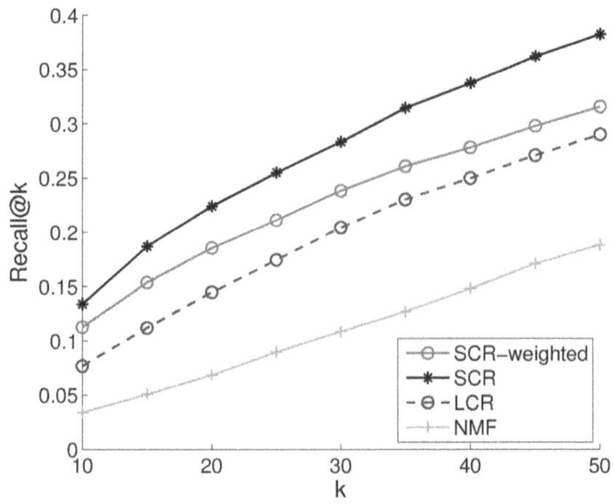


(a)

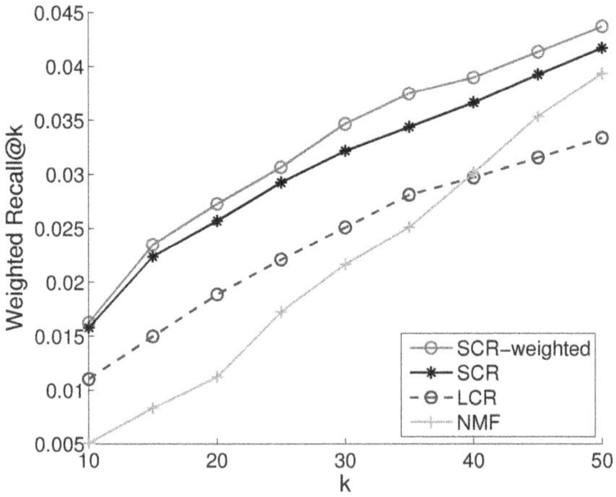


(b)

Figure 3: (a) Recall at different values of k. (b) Weighted recall at different values of k.

those assigned to $a$ by other users, and the listening count of $a$ is distributed to each triple according to how frequently the genre appears. If no user has ever assigned any genre to $a$, the genres of $a$ are defined as the genres used by $u$ for any artist, and the listening count is again prorated to the triples.

Second, since we are interested in ranking artists given a particular user and query, we normalize listening counts of triples having the same $u$ and $q$ so that their weights sum to 1. In the end we have 389,405 data points of the form $(q, u, a, w)$, where $w$ is the normalized listen count of artist $a$ by user $u$ in genre $q$.

Since our main goal is to show how social information can help compensate for data sparsity in a collaborative retrieval task, we identify a series of subsets of the Last.fm data that correspond to increasingly less compact social networks. We use a standard implementation of hierarchical clustering on the complete social adjacency matrix to select subsets of users that exhibit significant internal social structure; the number of users in these sets varies from 200 to 1000 (see Table 1). For each user set, the corresponding set of items contains all artists listened to by one or more of the selected users. In this way, the number of artists grows organically with the number of users. As in Section 3, we use the 30 most frequent genre tags as our query set.

The resulting datasets are referred to as Compact-*lastfm-N*, where $N$ denotes the number of users in the dataset. Their statistics are shown in Table 1. By construction, users in the smaller datasets have higher average numbers of within-set friends. This means that the smaller sets are more tightly connected, which may make them more amenable to social regularization. Conversely, the larger datasets are sparser and may be more representative of large-scale social networks. Note that the *density* of social links falls with the number of users even if the average number of within-set friends stays constant, thus the largest datasets are in fact quite a bit more sparse than the smallest ones. We will show how the relative performance of SCR changes as these qualities are varied.

## 4.1 Evaluation

To evaluate the performance of each algorithm, for a given test sample $(q, u, a, w)$ we first compute $f(q, u, i)$ for $i =$

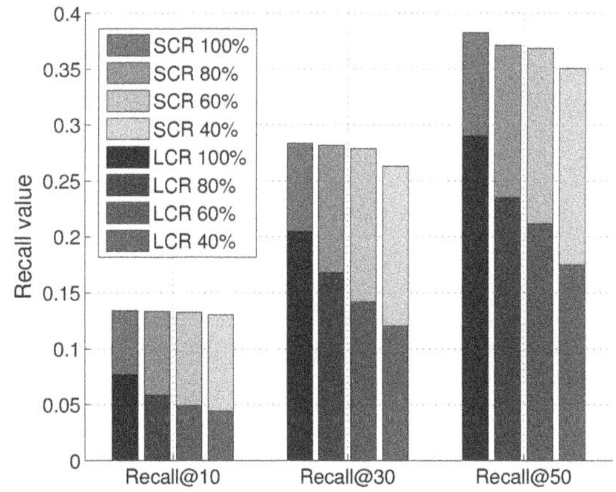


(a)

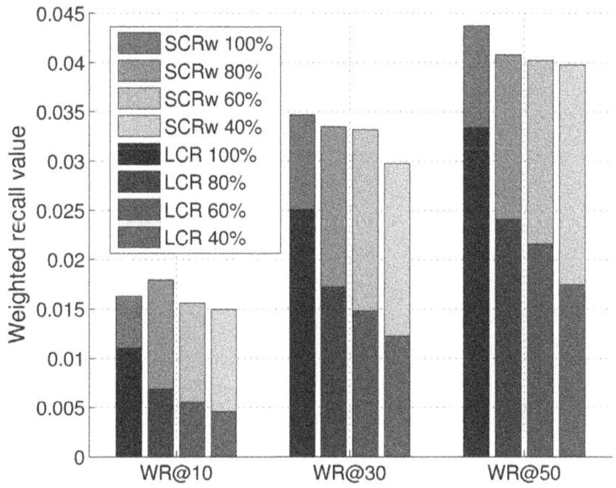


(b)

Figure 4: (a) Recall for training data of different reduced sizes. (b) Weighted Recall for training data of different reduced sizes.

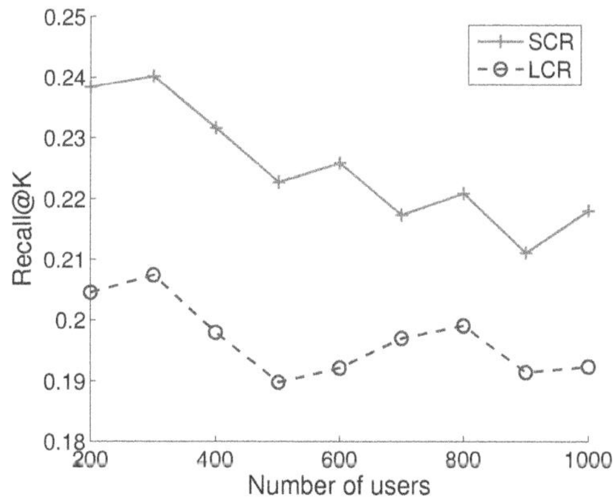


(a)

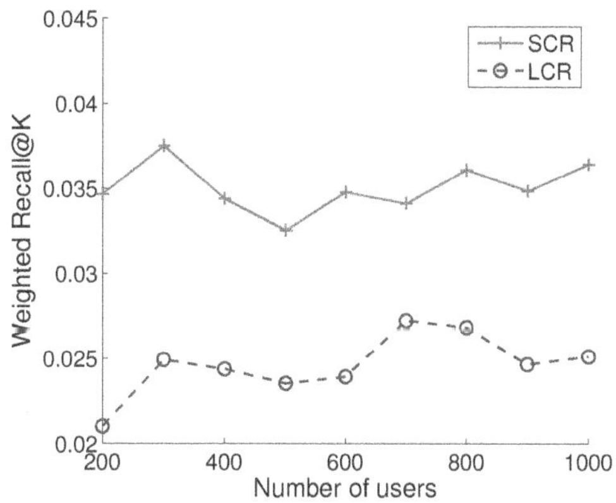


(b)

Figure 5: (a) Recall@30 for datasets of different sizes. (b) Weighted Recall@30 for datasets of different sizes.

$1, \dots, |\mathcal{A}|$ and sort the artists in descending order of score. We then measure recall@$k$, which is 1 if artist $a$ appears in the top $k$, and 0 otherwise, and report the mean recall@$k$ over the whole test dataset. As a secondary measure we report *weighted* recall@$k$, which is $w$ if artist $a$ appears in the top $k$, and 0 otherwise. Mean weighted recall@$k$ thus not only measures how many triples are ranked in the top $k$, but the quality of these test triples.

## 4.2 Results

We compare SCR with state-of-the-art algorithms used for collaborative retrieval as well as traditional collaborative filtering. Popular matrix factorization methods such as SVD and NMF are often used for collaborative filtering; these methods optimize the deviation of the rating matrix from entries supplied in the training set. However, standard SVD and NMF techniques are not directly applicable to tensors. Instead, we perform NMF on the $|\mathcal{Q}|$ different user $\times$ artist matrices to compute the rank of $a$ among all artists given $q$ and $u$. We also compare to latent collaborative retrieval (LCR).

The dimension of the embeddings for all methods is chosen to be 30; as shown in Figure 2, this choice yields approximately optimal performance for SCR-weighted; however, the results are not qualitatively different for other choices of embedding dimension. The hyperparameters $w_s$, $\eta$, and $c$, along with constraint parameters $C_S$, $C_S$ and $C_V$, are chosen separately for each method (as applicable) using the validation set. Since matrix factorization approaches are not specially designed for tensors and typically show worse performance than LCR [24], we only present results for NMF, which performed the best. We use the NMF implementation from `http://www.csie.ntu.edu.tw/~cjlin/nmf/`. For each experiment, 60% of the samples are used for training (or less; see below), 20% are used for validation, and 20% are used for testing.

We begin with results for the smallest datasat, Compact-*lastfm-200*, which is small enough to be practical for all methods. The resulting recall@$k$ and weighted recall@$k$ for different $k$ are shown in Figure 3. SCR (weighted or unweighted) outperforms the baselines on this top $k$ ranking problem; note that SCR-weighted outperforms SCR under

| Dataset | users | items (artists) | queries (tags) | samples | Average # of friends |
|---|---|---|---|---|---|
| *lastfm-2k* | 1892 | 17632 | 11946 | 186479 | 13.44 |
| Compact-*lastfm-200* | 200 | 2392 | 30 | 29850 | 28.54 |
| Compact-*lastfm-300* | 300 | 3299 | 30 | 44318 | 29.79 |
| Compact-*lastfm-400* | 400 | 4091 | 30 | 58098 | 29.10 |
| Compact-*lastfm-500* | 500 | 4928 | 30 | 72125 | 27.81 |
| Compact-*lastfm-600* | 600 | 5765 | 30 | 85522 | 26.32 |
| Compact-*lastfm-700* | 700 | 6454 | 30 | 98367 | 24.90 |
| Compact-*lastfm-800* | 800 | 7071 | 30 | 111062 | 23.57 |
| Compact-*lastfm-900* | 900 | 7782 | 30 | 124005 | 22.23 |
| Compact-*lastfm-1000* | 1000 | 8431 | 30 | 137518 | 21.01 |

Table 1: Last.fm dataset statistics

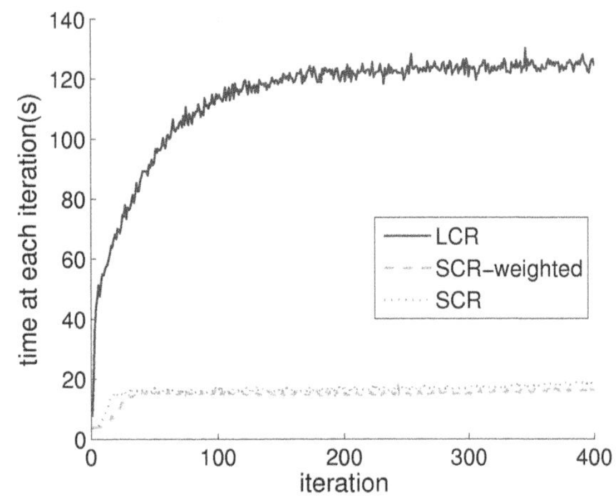


Figure 6: Runtime required for each training iteration of LCR and two versions of SCR on the Compact-*lastfm-200* dataset.

the weighted recall criterion, which makes sense since it incorporates relevance scores in the loss function.

Since we expect social information to be particularly useful when data are sparse, we also show results of recall@$k$ and weighted recall@$k$ for different amounts of training data (100%, 80%, 60% and 40% of the total training data) in Figure 4. Notice that the performance gap between SCR-weighted and LCR becomes larger as the number of available training examples is reduced, suggesting that our proposed algorithm can be especially useful for predicting the interests of new users or infrequent users when social network information is available.

Moving to the larger datasets, computation time increasingly becomes an issue for the matrix factorization approaches, so we focus on only two algorithms: SCR-weighted and LCR. Figure 5 shows recall results for all of the compact datasets. Note that the performance gap between SCR and LCR narrows slightly but remains significant even as the size of system becomes larger and the density of social links decreases. It may be counterintuitive that performance decreases (at least for unweighted recall) as the size of the dataset grows; however, since the number of artists grows with the number of users, the prediction problem is becoming more difficult at the same time. These results suggest that, while a dense social network may improve the relative performnce of SCR, it retains significant advantages even in larger, sparser settings.

Finally, we show in Figure 6 the runtimes for each stochastic gradient training iteration of SCR and LCR on the Compact-*lastfm-200* dataset; SCR is dramatically faster, despite using essentially similar optimization techniques. This is because the runtime is dominated by the sampling procedure used to estimate the rank function. LCR promotes the observed items to high positions quickly, thus making subsequent iterations quite slow. SCR, on the other hand, has additional regularization that appears to prevent this situation. Combined with the performance improvements discussed above, this is a significant practical advantage.

## 5. CONCLUSIONS AND FUTURE WORK

We proposed a new model that blends social networking, information retrieval, and collaborative filtering. Our SCR model uses social networks to improve performance on collaborative retrieval problems, which we believe are rapidly becoming important in practice. The proposed method outperforms state-of-the-art CR and CF approaches, and shows that users tend to share interests with friends. We believe the combination of recommendation and retrieval using social information will become increasingly useful; going forward we hope to develop a two-pass version of the SCR algorithm that helps predict interest commonalities between friends, and can be used to prune out edges on the social graph that may work against achieving good performance.

## References

[1] Punam Bedi, Harmeet Kaur, and Sudeep Marwaha. Trust based recommender system for semantic web. In *proceedings of the 2007 International Joint Conferences on Artificial Intelligence*, pages 2677–2682, 2007.

[2] David M Blei, Andrew Y Ng, and Michael I Jordan. Latent dirichlet allocation. *the Journal of machine Learning research*, 3:993–1022, 2003.

[3] John S Breese, David Heckerman, and Carl Kadie. Empirical analysis of predictive algorithms for collaborative filtering. In *Proceedings of the Fourteenth conference on Uncertainty in artificial intelligence*, pages 43–52. Morgan Kaufmann Publishers Inc., 1998.

[4] Ivan Cantador, Peter Brusilovsky, and Tsvi Kuflik. Second workshop on information heterogeneity and fusion in recommender systems (hetrec2011). In *Proceedings of the fifth ACM conference on Recommender systems*, pages 387–388. ACM, 2011.

[5] David Carmel, Naama Zwerdling, Ido Guy, Shila Ofek-Koifman, Nadav Har'El, Inbal Ronen, Erel Uziel, Sivan Yogev, and Sergey Chernov. Personalized social search based on the user's social network. In *Proceedings of the 18th ACM conference on Information and knowledge management*, pages 1227–1236. ACM, 2009.

[6] Alexandros Karatzoglou, Xavier Amatriain, Linas Baltrunas, and Nuria Oliver. Multiverse recommendation: n-dimensional tensor factorization for context-aware collaborative filtering. In *Proceedings of the fourth ACM conference on Recommender systems*, pages 79–86. ACM, 2010.

[7] Henry Kautz, Bart Selman, and Mehul Shah. Referral web: combining social networks and collaborative filtering. *Communications of the ACM*, 40(3):63–65, 1997.

[8] Ioannis Konstas, Vassilios Stathopoulos, and Joemon M Jose. On social networks and collaborative recommendation. In *Proceedings of the 32nd international ACM SIGIR conference on Research and development in information retrieval*, pages 195–202. ACM, 2009.

[9] Greg Linden, Brent Smith, and Jeremy York. Amazon. com recommendations: Item-to-item collaborative filtering. *Internet Computing, IEEE*, 7(1):76–80, 2003.

[10] Hao Ma, Haixuan Yang, Michael R Lyu, and Irwin King. Sorec: social recommendation using probabilistic matrix factorization. In *Proceedings of the 17th ACM conference on Information and knowledge management*, pages 931–940. ACM, 2008.

[11] Hao Ma, Irwin King, and Michael R Lyu. Learning to recommend with social trust ensemble. In *Proceedings of the 32nd international ACM SIGIR conference on Research and development in information retrieval*, pages 203–210. ACM, 2009.

[12] Hao Ma, Dengyong Zhou, Chao Liu, Michael R Lyu, and Irwin King. Recommender systems with social regularization. In *Proceedings of the fourth ACM international conference on Web search and data mining*, pages 287–296. ACM, 2011.

[13] Paolo Massa and Paolo Avesani. Trust-aware collaborative filtering for recommender systems. In *On the Move to Meaningful Internet Systems 2004: CoopIS, DOA, and ODBASE*, pages 492–508. Springer, 2004.

[14] Paolo Massa and Paolo Avesani. Trust-aware recommender systems. In *Proceedings of the 2007 ACM conference on Recommender systems*, pages 17–24. ACM, 2007.

[15] John O'Donovan and Barry Smyth. Trust in recommender systems. In *Proceedings of the 10th international conference on Intelligent user interfaces*, pages 167–174. ACM, 2005.

[16] Sanjay Purushotham, Yan Liu, and C-C Jay Kuo. Collaborative topic regression with social matrix factorization for recommendation systems. *arXiv preprint arXiv:1206.4684*, 2012.

[17] Ruslan Salakhutdinov and Andriy Mnih. Probabilistic matrix factorization. *Advances in neural information processing systems*, 20:1257–1264, 2008.

[18] Badrul Sarwar, George Karypis, Joseph Konstan, and John Riedl. Item-based collaborative filtering recommendation algorithms. In *Proceedings of the 10th international conference on World Wide Web*, pages 285–295. ACM, 2001.

[19] D Seung and L Lee. Algorithms for non-negative matrix factorization. *Advances in neural information processing systems*, 13:556–562, 2001.

[20] Chirag Shah. Lessons and challenges for collaborative information seeking (cis) systems developers. *Group*, 2009.

[21] Xiaoyuan Su and Taghi M Khoshgoftaar. A survey of collaborative filtering techniques. *Advances in Artificial Intelligence*, 2009:4, 2009.

[22] Panagiotis Symeonidis, Alexandros Nanopoulos, and Yannis Manolopoulos. Tag recommendations based on tensor dimensionality reduction. In *Proceedings of the 2008 ACM conference on Recommender systems*, pages 43–50. ACM, 2008.

[23] Jason Weston, Samy Bengio, and Nicolas Usunier. Large scale image annotation: learning to rank with joint word-image embeddings. *Machine learning*, 81 (1):21–35, 2010.

[24] Jason Weston, Chong Wang, Ron Weiss, and Adam Berenzweig. Latent collaborative retrieval. In *Proceedings of the 29th International Conference on Machine Learning (ICML-12)*, pages 9–16, 2012.

[25] Liang Xiong, Xi Chen, Tzu-Kuo Huang, Jeff Schneider, and Jaime G Carbonell. Temporal collaborative filtering with bayesian probabilistic tensor factorization. In *Proceedings of SIAM Data Mining*, volume 2010, 2010.

[26] Vincent W Zheng, Bin Cao, Yu Zheng, Xing Xie, and Qiang Yang. Collaborative filtering meets mobile recommendation: A user-centered approach. In *Proceedings of the 24rd AAAI Conference on Artificial Intelligence*, 2010.

# Transferring Heterogeneous Links across Location-Based Social Networks

Jiawei Zhang
University of Illinois at Chicago
Chicago, IL, USA
jzhan9@uic.edu

Xiangnan Kong
University of Illinois at Chicago
Chicago, IL, USA
xkong4@uic.edu

Philip S. Yu
University of Illinois at Chicago
Chicago, IL, USA
psyu@cs.uic.edu

## ABSTRACT

Location-based social networks (LBSNs) are one kind of online social networks offering geographic services and have been attracting much attention in recent years. LBSNs usually have complex structures, involving heterogeneous nodes and links. Many recommendation services in LBSNs (e.g., friend and location recommendation) can be cast as link prediction problems (e.g., social link and location link prediction). Traditional link prediction researches on LBSNs mostly focus on predicting either social links or location links, assuming the prediction tasks of different types of links to be independent. However, in many real-world LBSNs, the prediction tasks for social links and location links are strongly correlated and mutually influential. Another key challenge in link prediction on LBSNs is the data sparsity problem (i.e., "new network" problem), which can be encountered when LBSNs branch into new geographic areas or social groups. Actually, nowadays, many users are involved in multiple networks simultaneously and users who just join one LBSN may have been using other LBSNs for a long time. In this paper, we study the problem of predicting multiple types of links simultaneously for a new LBSN across partially aligned LBSNs and propose a novel method TRAIL (TRAnsfer heterogeneous lInks across LBSNs). TRAIL can accumulate information for locations from online posts and extract heterogeneous features for both social links and location links. TRAIL can predict multiple types of links simultaneously. In addition, TRAIL can transfer information from other aligned networks to the new network to solve the problem of lacking information. Extensive experiments conducted on two real-world aligned LBSNs show that TRAIL can achieve very good performance and substantially outperform the baseline methods.

## Categories and Subject Descriptors

H.2.8 [**Database Management**]: Database Applications-Data Mining


*WSDM'14*, February 24–28, 2014, New York, New York, USA.

http://dx.doi.org/10.1145/2556195.2559894.

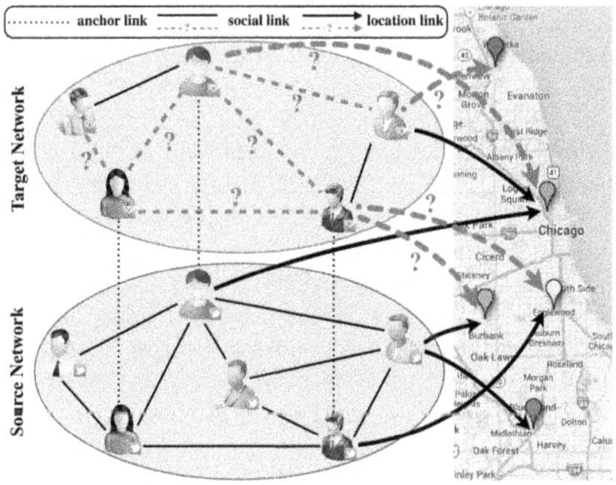


**Figure 1: Example of collective link transferring across two aligned location-based social networks.**

## Keywords

Location-Based Social Networks, Link Prediction, Transfer Learning, Data Mining

## 1. INTRODUCTION

Location-based social networks (LBSNs) are one kind of online social networks that can provide geographic services, e.g., location check-ins and posting reviews, and have been attracting much attention in recent years [20, 16, 19, 5, 21]. LBSNs usually have very complex structures, including multiple kinds of nodes (e.g., users, locations, etc.) and different types of links among these nodes (e.g., social links among users and location links between users and locations). For example, Foursquare[1] is a mainstream LBSN. It involves millions of users and locations. Foursquare users can add friends, check in at different locations with cellphones, write reviews and share with others.

Link prediction, which aims at predicting whether two entities have certain relationships, has become a hot topic in recent years [3, 12, 7, 15, 18, 14, 9]. Many important services offered by LBSNs can be cast as link prediction problems. For example, friend recommendation involves predicting social links among users; location recommendation aims at predicting location links between users and locations. LBSNs can benefit a lot from the high-quality social link and location link prediction results. The reason is that well-established social ties can improve user's engagement in so-

[1]https://foursquare.com

Table 1: Summary of related problems.

| Property | Transferring Heterogeneous Links across LBSNs | Collective Link Prediction across Multi-Domains [4] | Collaborative Recommendation for Networks[12, 7] | Predicting Social Links across Aligned Networks [22] | Inferring Anchor Links across Networks [11] |
|---|---|---|---|---|---|
| # networks | multiple | multiple | single | multiple | multiple |
| network type | heterogeneous | bipartite graph | heterogeneous | heterogeneous | heterogeneous |
| network aligned? | partially aligned | no | no | fully aligned | fully aligned |
| predicted links | multiple kinds (social and location links) | multiple kinds | multiple kinds | single kind (social link) | single kind (anchor link) |
| settings | transfer learning | transfer learning | unsupervised learning | transfer learning | transfer learning |
| knowledge to transfer | network structure through anchor links | network structure via task similarities | n/a | network structure through anchor links | network structure through anchor links |

cial networks [13]. Meanwhile, in location-based social networks, high-quality predicted location links can enhance the value of the location services of the networks.

Conventional link prediction researches on LBSNs mostly focus on predicting either social links [16, 19] or location links [21, 5] and usually assume that the prediction tasks of different types of links to be independent. However, in many real-world LBSNs, the link prediction tasks for social links and location links are strongly correlated and mutually influential. For example, if two users are friends with each other, they are more likely to check-in at similar locations. Thus the performance of location recommendation can be significantly improved if we could make accurate friendship predictions. Similarly, if two users often check-in at similar locations, they are more likely to know each other and have friend links in real life. The performance of friend recommendation can be greatly improved if we could make accurate location-link predictions.

Another major challenge in link prediction for LBSNs is the information sparsity problem, where the linkage information within the network can be very sparse. Conventional link prediction methods usually assume that there are sufficient links within the network to compute features (e.g., common neighborhoods) between each pair of nodes. However, LBSNs often encounter "new network" problems when they branch into new geographic areas or social groups. For example, when a LBSN decides to extend services in a new geographic area (e.g., Foursquare's expansion into Chinese market), the linkage information within the area (both social links and location links) can be very sparse. Similarly, when a LBSN decides to promote in a new group of users (e.g., Facebook's expansion from college students to white collar), the linkage information within the social group can be largely missing. The constituent of a LBSN is not quite connected to the existing members, and it can be considered to be a "new network".

In order to solve the "new network" problems, we need to utilize additional information sources to facilitate the link prediction process. Actually, nowadays, many people are involved in multiple LBSNs to enjoy specific services offered by different ones. Users who just joined one LBSN may have been using other LBSNs for a long time. For example, in Figure 1, we have two LBSNs. The LBSN on the top is a new network, e.g., Foursquare, and the social links and location links in it are very sparse. However, some users have joined another LBSN that has already existed in the geographic area or social group for a long time with abundant linkage information. We refer such users as "anchors" and the link between the two accounts of the same user as an "anchor link". For simplicity, the new network is called the *target network* and the developed network is called the *source network*.

In this paper, we study the collective link prediction problem for a new network across aligned LBSNs and the links to be predicted include both social links and location links. This problem has not been studied before. Meanwhile, it is also very challenging to solve in the following aspects:

1. *Collective link prediction.* The first challenge mainly lies in the fact that social links and location links in LBSNs are correlated instead of being independent. The prediction tasks on social links and location links should be considered at the same time. Many existing works focus on predicting one single type of links in LBSNs [16, 19, 21, 5], which do not consider the correlation between different link prediction tasks.

2. *Lack of information in the target network.* The target network is a new network, information in which is quite rare. We need to overcome the information sparsity problem in the target network. Existing works on link prediction mainly focus on one single network [16, 19, 21, 5, 12, 7]. In real-world LBSNs, the anchor users between two networks can serve as a bridge to transfer information from one LBSN to the other LBSN. Such knowledge transfer can benefit the link prediction for both social links and location links.

A more detailed comparison with previous works is shown in Table 1.

In this paper, we propose a supervised collective linkage transferring method, TRAIL, to address the above challenges. TRAIL can accumulate auxiliary information for locations from online posts which have check-ins at them and can extract heterogeneous features for both social links and location links. TRAIL can predict social links and location links simultaneously. In addition, TRAIL can use both information in the target network and that transferred from the aligned source network at the same time.

## 2. PROBLEM FORMULATION

### 2.1 Location-Based Social Networks

A location-based social network (LBSN) can be modeled as a heterogeneous network $G = (V, E, W)$, where $V = \bigcup_i V_i$ is the union of different types of nodes and $V_i, i \in \{1, 2, \cdots, |V|\}$ is the set of nodes of the $i_{th}$ type. $E = \bigcup_j E_j$ is the union of link sets among nodes in $V$ and $E_j, j \in \{1, 2, \cdots, |E|\}$ is the set of links of the $j_{th}$ type, $W : E \rightarrow \mathbb{R}$ denotes the weight of links in $E$.

Specially, for a LBSN, node set $V = \mathcal{U} \cup \mathcal{L} \cup \mathcal{T} \cup \mathcal{W}$ is the union of node sets of users, locations, time and words.

The link set $E = E_s \cup E_l \cup E_t \cup E_w$ is the union of link sets consisting of social relationships, location check-ins, active time and published words of users, $W$ denotes the weight of links in $E$.

## 2.2 Aligned LBSNs

Based on the definition of heterogeneous network, the aligned LBSNs can be definied as $\mathcal{G} = (G_{set}, A_{set})$, where network set $G_{set} = \{G^1, G^2, \cdots, G^{|G_{set}|}\}$ is the set of $|G_{set}|$ different LBSNs, anchor link set $A = \{A^{1,2}, A^{1,3}, \cdots, A^{1,|G_{set}|}, A^{2,1}, \cdots, A^{|G_{set}|,|G_{set}|-1}\}$ contains the directed *anchor links* between pairwise networks in $G_{set}$. $A^{i,j} \subseteq \mathcal{U}^i \times \mathcal{U}^j$ is the set of directed *anchor links* from network $G^i$ to $G^j$, where $\mathcal{U}^i$,$\mathcal{U}^j$ are the sets of users in network $G^i$ and $G^j$. Link $(u^i_m, u^j_n) \in A^{i,j}$ is an *anchor link* between $G^i$ and $G^j$ iff. $(u^i_m \in \mathcal{U}^i) \wedge (u^j_n \in \mathcal{U}^j) \wedge (u^i_m$ and $u^j_n$ are accounts owned by the same user in $G^i$ and $G^j)$.

Given two aligned heterogeneous networks $G^i$ and $G^j$, if all user accounts in one network are related to accounts in the other network by anchor links mutually, then $G^i$ and $G^j$ are *fully aligned*, in which case $|\mathcal{U}^i| = |\mathcal{U}^j| = |A^{i,j}|$ and the anchor links in $A^{i,j}$ have an inherent *one-to-one* property [2]. While, if some users in $G^i$ do not have the corresponding accounts in $G^j$ or some users in $G^j$ do not have the corresponding accounts in $G^i$, then $G^i$ and $G^j$ are *partially aligned* and $|A^{i,j}| \leq \min\{|\mathcal{U}^i|, |\mathcal{U}^j|\}$.

## 2.3 Collective Link Prediction

Fully aligned social networks merely exist in the real world. In this paper, we are predicting multiple kinds of links for new networks across two *partially aligned* LBSNs. Let $\mathcal{G} = (\{G^t, G^s\}, \{A^{t,s}, A^{s,t}\})$ be the networks studied in this paper, where $G^t$ is the target network, which is very new, and $G^s$ is the aligned well-established source network, $A^{t,s}$, $A^{s,t}$ are the sets of directed *anchor links* between $G^t$ and $G^s$. The set of users and locations in $G^t$ are denoted as $\mathcal{U}^t$ and $\mathcal{L}^t$, while the sets of existing social links and location links in $G^t$ are represented as $E^t_s$ and $E^t_l$. What we want to predict are a subset of potential social links among users in $G^t$: $\boldsymbol{L}^t_s \subset (\mathcal{U}^t \times \mathcal{U}^t - E^t_s)$ and a subset of potential location links in $G^t$: $\boldsymbol{L}^t_l \subset (\mathcal{U}^t \times \mathcal{L}^t - E^t_l)$. In other words, we want to build a mapping: $f: \{\boldsymbol{L}^t_s, \boldsymbol{L}^t_l\} \to \{-1, 1\}$ to decide whether potential links in $\{\boldsymbol{L}^t_s, \boldsymbol{L}^t_l\}$ exist or not and a confidence score function $P: \{\boldsymbol{L}^t_s, \boldsymbol{L}^t_l\} \to [0, 1]$ denoting their existence probabilities.

# 3. PROPOSED METHODS

In this section, we will introduce the supervised collective link transferring method, TRAIL, in details.

## 3.1 Information Accumulation and Feature Extraction

TRAIL is based on a supervised setting, as a result, we need to extract features for both social links and location links using the heterogeneous information in the network. Before introducing the extracted features, we will introduce a method to accumulate information for locations at first.

### 3.1.1 *Information Accumulation for Locations*

Locations are represented as $(latitude, longitude)$ pairs in our problem, which possess no auxiliary information except location links with users in the network. As a result, we will

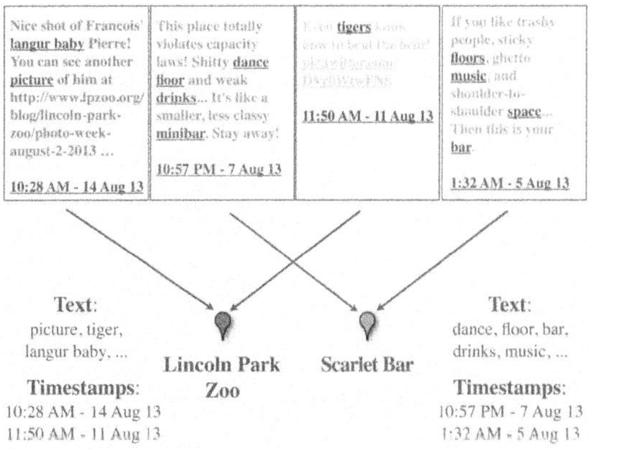


**Figure 2: Example of information accumulation for locations from online posts.**

confront problems of lacking auxiliary information when extracting heterogeneous features for location links. Actually, we notice users can publish online posts at the locations. And we propose to accumulate the text and timestamps information of the online posts checked in at a certain location as the auxiliary information possessed by that location.

From a statistical point of view, information from posts published at a certain location, including both timestamps and text contents, can reveal some properties of the location. For example, the timestamps of most posts published at nightlife sites are after 6:00 PM. While, those of posts published at restaurants serving brunch are during the daytime. Posts published at national parks can contain some phrases depicting the scenes, while posts published at basketball court may be mostly talking about games, teams and players. So, we can know more about the locations from the information accumulated from online posts.

For example, in Figure 2, we have two totally different locations: the Lincoln Park Zoo[2] and Scarlet Bar[3]. The Lincoln Park Zoo is the largest free zoo in Chicago and is open during 10:00 AM - 5:00 PM. The Scarlet Bar is one of the most famous bar in Chicago, where people can drink with friends, dance to enjoy their night life, and it is open during 8:00 PM - 2:00 AM.

We also have 4 online posts published by people at these two places in either Foursquare or Twitter. From the content of these posts, we find that people usually publish words about animals, pictures and the scene at the Lincoln Park Zoo. However, people who visit the Scarlet Bar mainly talk about the atmosphere in the bar, the drinks, the dance floor and the music there. So, users who frequently talk about animals in daily life can be interested in the Lincoln Park Zoo, while those who usually post words about the drinks may like the Scarlet Bar more. Meanwhile, we can also accumulate the timestamps of posts published at these two places. The timestamps of posts published at the Lincoln Park Zoo are mostly during the daytime, while those of posts published at the Scarlet Bar are at night. So, users who are usually active in the daytime can be more likely to visit the Lincoln Park Zoo, while people who are active during the night may prefer the Bar.

[2]http://www.lpzoo.org

[3]http://www.scarletbarchicago.com

Table 2: Features extracted from vector $x$ and $y$

| Features | Descriptions |
|---|---|
| Extended Degree Count (EDC) | $\|\|\boldsymbol{x}\|\|_1, \|\|\boldsymbol{y}\|\|_1$ |
| Extended Degree Ratio (EDR) | $\|\|\boldsymbol{x}\|\|_1 / \|\|\boldsymbol{y}\|\|_1$ |
| Extended Common Neighbour (ECN) | $\boldsymbol{x} \cdot \boldsymbol{y}$ |
| Extended Jaccard's Coefficient (EJC) | $\frac{\boldsymbol{x} \cdot \boldsymbol{y}}{\|\|\boldsymbol{x}\|\|_1 \cdot \|\|\boldsymbol{y}\|\|_1}$ |
| Extended Preferential Attachment (EPA) | $\|\|\boldsymbol{x}\|\|_1 \cdot \|\|\boldsymbol{y}\|\|_1$ |
| Euclidean Distance (ED) | $(\sum_k (x_k - y_k)^2)^{1/2}$ |
| Cosine Similarity (CS) | $\frac{\boldsymbol{x} \cdot \boldsymbol{y}}{\|\|\boldsymbol{x}\|\|_2 + \|\|\boldsymbol{y}\|\|_2}$ |

### 3.1.2 Heterogeneous Features

In this part, we will extract 4 different categories of features for both social links and location links from the heterogeneous information in the network networks, which include *social features*, *spatial distribution features*, *text usage features* and *temporal distribution features*. A summary of frequently used features is available in Table 2, where $||\boldsymbol{x}||_p = (\sum_{i=1}^{|\boldsymbol{x}|} |x_i|^p)^{1/p}$ is the $L^p$-norm of vector $\boldsymbol{x}$.

- **Features of Social Links:** For a certain social link $(u_i, u_j)$, we can get their followers from the network: $\Gamma(u_i)$ and $\Gamma(u_j)$. Based on $\Gamma(u_i)$, we can construct the social link weight vector $\tilde{s}(u_i)$ for $u_i$, where $\tilde{s}(u_i) = (p_{1,i}, p_{2,i}, \cdots, p_{k,i}, \cdots, p_{n,i})^T, n = |\mathcal{U}|$ is the size of user set and $p_{k,i}$ is the weight of social link $(u_k, u_i), \forall u_k \in \mathcal{U}$: if $u_k \in (\mathcal{U} - \Gamma(u_i))$, $p_{k,i} = 0.0$; if $u_k \in \Gamma(u_i)$ and link $(u_k, u_i)$ exists originally, then $p_{k,i} = 1.0$; otherwise, $p_{k,i}$ is the existence probability of link $(u_k, u_i)$. Similarly, we can construct vector $\tilde{s}(u_j)$ for user $u_j$, which is of the same length as $\tilde{s}(u_i)$. From $\tilde{s}(u_i)$ and $\tilde{s}(u_j)$, we extract 7 different *social features* for social link $(u_i, u_j)$, which are summarized in Table 2.
  In a similar way, for a certain social link $(u_i, u_j)$, we can get the set of locations visited by user $u_i$ and $u_j$: $\Phi(u_i)$ and $\Phi(u_j)$, from which we can obtain their location link weight vectors: $\tilde{l}(u_i)$ and $\tilde{l}(u_j)$. From the timestamps of posts published by users, we can obtain the users' active patterns. Each day is divided into 24 slots and the ratio of online posts published by user $u$ in each hour is saved in a temporal distribution vector $\tilde{t}(u)$, whose length is 24. For social link $(u_i, u_j)$, we can construct the temporal distribution vectors: $\tilde{t}(u_i)$ and $\tilde{t}(u_j)$ for $u_i$ and $u_j$. In addition, we transform the words used by two users $u_i$ and $u_j$ into two text usage vectors: $\tilde{w}(u_i)$ and $\tilde{w}(u_j)$ weighted by TF-IDF, which are of the same length. From these vectors, we can extract the *spatial distribution features*, *temporal distribution features* and *text usage features* similar to the social link features summarized in Table 2 for social link $(u_i, u_j)$.

- **Features of Location Links:** Similarly, we can obtain the set of users who have visited a location and regard them as the "neighbours" of that location. And for a location link $(u_i, l_j)$, we can get the sets of neighbours of $u_i$ and $l_j$: $\Gamma(u_i)$ and $\Psi(l_j)$, from which we can construct the social link weight vectors: $\tilde{s}(u_i)$ and $\tilde{s}(l_j)$. From the accumulated text and timestamps information of locations and the auxiliary information owned by users, we can also constract the temporal distribution vectors: $\tilde{t}(u_i)$ and $\tilde{t}(l_j)$ and the text usage vectors: $\tilde{w}(u_i)$ and $\tilde{w}(l_j)$ for location link $(u_i, l_j)$.
  From these vectors, we can extract the *social features*, *temporal distribution features* and *text usage features* for location link $(u_i, l_j)$.
  In addition, according to previous definitions, we can get the locations that user $u$ has visited in the past: $\Phi(u)$ and the location link weight vector of $u$: $\tilde{l}(u)$ as well as the neighbors of a location $l$: $\Psi(l)$ and its social link weight vector: $\tilde{s}(l)$. For a certain location link $(u_i, l_j)$, we extract 3 spatial distribution features from the network:

  (1) average weighted geographic distance between locations in $\Phi(u_i)$ and $l_j$

$$\frac{\sum_{l_k \in \Phi(u_i)} GeoD(l_k, l_j) \cdot \tilde{l}(u_i)_{l_k}}{||\tilde{l}(u_i)||_1 \cdot |\Phi(u_i)|}$$

  where, $GeoD(l_k, l_j)$ is the geographic distance of $l_k$ and $l_j$ and $\tilde{l}(u_i)_{l_k}$ is the weight of location link $(u_i, l_k)$ saved in $u_i$'s location link weight vector $\tilde{l}(u_i)$.

  (2) weighted number of users who have visited both locations in $\Phi(u_i)$ and $l_j$

$$\sum_{l_k \in \Phi(u_i)} \tilde{s}(l_k) \cdot \tilde{s}(l_j) \cdot \tilde{l}(u_i)_{l_k}$$

  (3) average weighted number of users who have visited both locations in $\Phi(u_i)$ and $l_j$

$$\frac{\sum_{l_k \in \Phi(u_i)} \tilde{s}(l_k) \cdot \tilde{s}(l_j) \cdot \tilde{l}(u_i)_{l_k}}{||\tilde{l}(u_i)||_1 \cdot \sum_{l_k \in \Phi(u_i)} ||\tilde{l}(s_k)||_1}$$

## 3.2 Collective Link Predictions

In this section, we will analyze and formulate the correlation between the social link prediction task and the location link prediction task.

### 3.2.1 Correlation Between Different Tasks

When predicting a link, the classifiers will give a score within range $[0, 1]$ to show its existence probability. Newly predicted social links will update the social link existence probability information in the network, which can affect other location link prediction tasks. For example, these updated social link existence probabilities can change the extended common neighbours of a location and a user. Similarly, the location link prediction task can also influence the social link prediction result.

For example, in Figure 3, we show an example of different link prediction methods. Figure 3(a) is the input aligned networks, in which there are 4 users and some existing social links $(u_3, u_4)$, $(u_1, u_4)$ and location links $(u_2, l_1)$, $(u_3, l_1)$, $(u_1, l_2)$, $(u_1, l_3)$ as well as many other potential links to be predicted. Based on the information in the network, including social information (e.g., common neighbours), location information (e.g., co-checkins) and other auxiliary information, traditional link prediction methods can predict social links and locate links independently. Figure 3(b) shows the result of independent social link prediction result, in which social link $(u_2, u_3)$ and $(u_1, u_3)$ are predicted to be existent, while social link $(u_1, u_2)$ and $(u_2, u_4)$ are predicted to be nonexistent. Figure 3(c) shows the independent location link prediction result and in the result, location links $(u_2, l_2)$, $(u_1, l_1)$, $(u_4, l_3)$ are predicted to be existent, while $(u_2, l_3)$ and $(u_3, l_3)$ is predicted to be nonexistent.

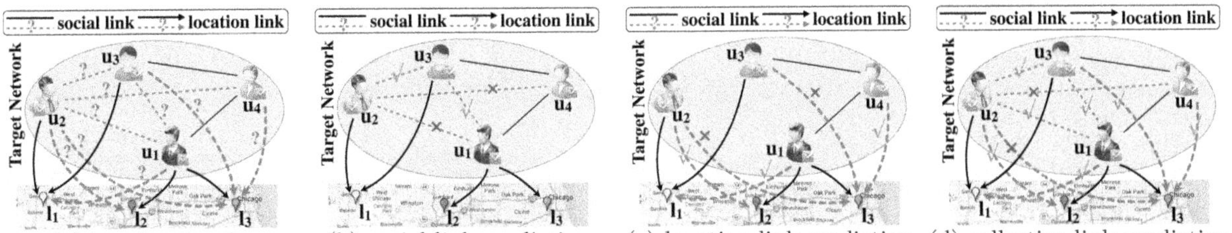


(a) input network (b) social link prediction (c) location link prediction (d) collective link prediction

**Figure 3: An example of different link prediction methods. (a) is the input network. (b)-(c) is independent social link and location link prediction result. (d) shows the collective link prediction result.**

From the results in Figures 3(b) and 3(c), we can find some problematic phenomena. For example, user $u_2$ and $u_1$ are predicted to have visited locations $l_1, l_2$ and they are also predicted to share a common neighbour: $u_3$. Based on the result, it is highly likely that the potential social link $(u_2, u_3)$ will be predicted to be existent. However, it is predicted to be nonexistent in Figure 3(b). Another example is that many neighbours of user $u_3$, both the originally existing $u_4$ and the newly predicted $u_1$ both have visited or are predicted to have visited $l_3$. By using Friend-based Collaborative Filtering (FCF) [21], $u_3$ is highly likely to be predicted to have visited $l_3$. However, the location link between $u_3$ and $l_3$ is predicted to be nonexistent in Figure 3(c).

If we consider the correlation between these two link prediction tasks and predict social links and location links simultaneously, the predicted results of social link $(u_1, u_2)$ and location link $(u_3, l_3)$ are highly likely to be predicted as existent. In Figure 3(d), we show a potential result of collective link prediction methods.

### 3.2.2 *Collective Link Prediction*

We formulate the sets of potential social links and potential location links to be predicted as $\boldsymbol{L}_s^t \subset (\mathcal{U}^t \times \mathcal{U}^t - E_s^t)$ and $\boldsymbol{L}_l^t \subset (\mathcal{U}^t \times \mathcal{L}^t - E_l^t)$ in the problem formulation section. For links $l_s^t \in \boldsymbol{L}_s^t$ and $l_l^t \in \boldsymbol{L}_l^t$, the supervised models built with the existing information in the network will give them the predicted labels: $y(l_s^t)$ and $y(l_l^t)$, as well as the existence probability scores: $P(y(l_s^t) = 1)$ and $P(y(l_l^t) = 1)$. Traditional methods predicting social links and location links independently aims at finding the set of labels achieving the maximum probability scores for each kind of links. In other words, let $\hat{\mathcal{Y}}_s^t \subset \{-1, 1\}^{|\boldsymbol{L}_s^t|}$, $\hat{\mathcal{Y}}_l^t \subset \{-1, 1\}^{|\boldsymbol{L}_l^t|}$ be the sets of optimal labels

$$\hat{\mathcal{Y}}_s^t = arg \max_{\mathcal{Y}_s^t} P(\mathbf{y}(\boldsymbol{L}_s^t) = \mathcal{Y}_s^t)$$

$$\hat{\mathcal{Y}}_l^t = arg \max_{\mathcal{Y}_l^t} P(\mathbf{y}(\boldsymbol{L}_l^t) = \mathcal{Y}_l^t)$$

where, $P(\mathbf{y}(\boldsymbol{L}_s^t) = \mathcal{Y}_s^t)$ and $P(\mathbf{y}(\boldsymbol{L}_l^t) = \mathcal{Y}_l^t)$ denote the probability scores achieved when links in $\boldsymbol{L}_s^t$ and $\boldsymbol{L}_l^t$ are assigned with labels in $\mathcal{Y}_s^t$ and $\mathcal{Y}_l^t$.

However, considering connections between these two link prediction tasks, the inferred social link or location link information should all be used in other link prediction tasks. The optimal selection of label sets $\hat{\mathcal{Y}}_s^t$ and $\hat{\mathcal{Y}}_l^t$ will be

$$\hat{\mathcal{Y}}_s^t, \hat{\mathcal{Y}}_l^t = arg \max_{\mathcal{Y}_s^t, \mathcal{Y}_l^t} P(\mathbf{y}(\boldsymbol{L}_s^t) = \mathcal{Y}_s^t | \mathbf{y}(\boldsymbol{L}_l^t) = \mathcal{Y}_l^t) \times P(\mathbf{y}(\boldsymbol{L}_l^t) = \mathcal{Y}_l^t | \mathbf{y}(\boldsymbol{L}_s^t) = \mathcal{Y}_s^t)$$

## 3.3 Collective Linkage Transfer across LBSNs

### 3.3.1 *Supervised Link Prediction*

Traditional supervised link prediction methods by using one single network implicitly or explicitly assume that information in the target network itself is enough to build effective link prediction models. These methods use the extracted features of existing links in the traget network to train classifiers, which will be applied to predict other potential links. For example, we want to predict the existence probability of a social link $(u_i^t, u_j^t)$ in the target network $G^t$, which is:

$$P(y(u_i^t, u_j^t) = 1 | G^t)$$

where $y(u_i^t, u_j^t)$ is the label of link $(u_i^t, u_j^t)$. From $G^t$, we can extract a set of heterogeneous features for social link $(u_i^t, u_j^t)$. Then

$$P(y(u_i^t, u_j^t) = 1 | G^t) = P(y(u_i^t, u_j^t) = 1 | \boldsymbol{x}(u_i^t, u_j^t))$$

where $\boldsymbol{x}(u_i^t, u_j^t) = [x(u_i^t, u_j^t)^1, x(u_i^t, u_j^t)^2, \cdots, x(u_i^t, u_j^t)^n]^T, n = |\boldsymbol{x}(u_i^t, u_j^t)|$ and $x(u_i^t, u_j^t)^k, k \in \{1, 2, \cdots, n\}$ is the $k_{th}$ feature extracted from the target network for social link $(u_i^t, u_j^t)$. Usually, feature $x(u_i^t, u_j^t)^k$ can be the summarized properties of social link $(u_i^t, u_j^t)$, e.g., extended common neighbours.

Similarly, for a certain location link $(u_i^t, l_j^t)$ in $G^t$, we can also use the extracted features for it from the target network, $\boldsymbol{x}(u_i^t, l_j^t)$, to predict its existence probability.

$$P(y(u_i^t, l_j^t) = 1 | G^t) = P(y(u_i^t, l_j^t) = 1 | \boldsymbol{x}(u_i^t, l_j^t))$$

If the target network is quite new, the features vectors extracted for both social links and location links can be very sparse, which can hardly build good link prediction models. Next, we will transfer information from the aligned source network to solve the problem.

### 3.3.2 *Linkage Transfer across LBSNs*

With the *anchor links*, we can locate users' corresponding accounts in the aligned source network, information in which can be transferred to the target network. Suppose, for instance, we want to predict a potential social link $(u_i^t, u_j^t)$ by using information in both networks. By taking advantages of the *anchor links*, we can obtain the corresponding

**Algorithm 1** TRAIL

**Input:** two aligned heterogeneous LBSNs, $G^s$, $G^t$.
existing social links and location links: $E_s^t$, $E_l^t$
anchor links between $G^t$ and $G^s$: $A^{t,s}$, $A^{s,t}$
potential social links and location links: $L_s^t$, $L_l^t$
**Output:** the inferred labels and existence probabilities of links in $L_s^t$ and $L_l^t$: $\hat{\mathcal{Y}}_s^t, \hat{\mathcal{P}}_s^t, \hat{\mathcal{Y}}_l^t, \hat{\mathcal{P}}_l^t$

construct training sets, test sets with $E_s^t$, $E_l^t$, $L_s^t$ and $L_l^t$.
$converge \leftarrow False$
**while** $converge$ is $False$ **do**
  extract features $\boldsymbol{x}^t(E_s^t)$ and $\boldsymbol{x}^t(L_s^t)$ for social links in $E_s^t$ and $L_s^t$ from $G^t$.
  extract features $\boldsymbol{x}^s(E_s^t)$ and $\boldsymbol{x}^s(L_s^t)$ for social links in $E_s^t$ and $L_s^t$ from $G^s$ by utilizing anchor links in $A^{t,s}$.
  $C_s \leftarrow$ **train**($[\boldsymbol{x}^t(E_s^t)^T, \boldsymbol{x}^s(E_s^t)^T, y^s(E_s^t)]^T, y^t(E_s^t)$)
  $\hat{\mathcal{Y}}_s^t, \hat{\mathcal{P}}_s^t \leftarrow C_s$.**classify**($[\boldsymbol{x}^t(L_s^t)^T, \boldsymbol{x}^s(L_s^t)^T, y^s(L_s^t)]^T$)
  update $G^t$ with $\hat{\mathcal{Y}}_s^t, \hat{\mathcal{P}}_s^t$
  Accumulate information for locations
  extract features $\boldsymbol{x}^t(E_l^t)$ and $\boldsymbol{x}^t(L_l^t)$ for location links in $E_l^t$ and $L_l^t$ from $G^t$.
  extract features $\boldsymbol{x}^s(E_l^t)$ and $\boldsymbol{x}^s(L_l^t)$ for location links in $E_l^t$ and $L_l^t$ from $G^s$ by utilizing anchor links in $A^{t,s}$.
  $C_l \leftarrow$ **train**($[\boldsymbol{x}^t(E_l^t)^T, \boldsymbol{x}^s(E_l^t)^T, y^s(E_l^t)]^T, y^t(E_l^t)$)
  $\hat{\mathcal{Y}}_l^t, \hat{\mathcal{P}}_l^t \leftarrow C_l$.**classify**($[\boldsymbol{x}^t(L_l^t)^T, \boldsymbol{x}^s(L_l^t)^T, y^s(L_l^t)]^T$)
  update $G^t$ with $\hat{\mathcal{Y}}_l^t, \hat{\mathcal{P}}_l^t$
  **if** $\hat{\mathcal{Y}}_s^t, \hat{\mathcal{P}}_s^t, \hat{\mathcal{Y}}_l^t, \hat{\mathcal{P}}_l^t$ all converge **then**
    $converge \leftarrow True$
  **end if**
**end while**
Return $\hat{\mathcal{Y}}_s^t, \hat{\mathcal{P}}_s^t, \hat{\mathcal{Y}}_l^t, \hat{\mathcal{P}}_l^t$

accounts of $u_i^t$ and $u_j^t$ in the aligned source network: $u_i^s$ and $u_j^s$. If $u_i^s$ and $u_j^s$ both exist in $G^s$, then we will only transfer information related to the corresponding social link $(u_i^s, u_j^s)$ in the aligned source network to the target network, which is represented as a feature vector extracted from $G^s$ for link $(u_i^s, u_j^s)$: $\boldsymbol{x}(u_i^s, u_j^s)$. We notice that the existence information of link $(u_i^s, u_j^s)$ in the aligned source network, $y(u_i^s, u_j^s)$, is very useful, which is defined as *pseudo label* of link $(u_i^t, u_j^t)$.
**Definition 1** (Pseudo Label): Let $(n_i^t, n_j^t)$ be a link in $G^t$, where $n_i^t, n_j^t$ are nodes in it and they can be users, locations, etc., the corresponding link of $(n_i^t, n_j^t)$ in the aligned source network $G^s$ will be $(n_i^s, n_j^s)$. The existence indicator of link $(n_i^s, n_j^s)$ in $G^s$: $y(n_i^s, n_j^s)$ is defined as the *pseudo label* of link $(n_i^t, n_j^t)$.

The *pseudo label* is used as an extra feature added to the extended feature vector, obtained by merging feature vectors extracted from $G^t$ and $G^s$.

$$P(y(u_i^t, u_j^t) = 1 | G^t, G^s)$$
$$= P\left(y(u_i^t, u_j^t) = 1 | \left[\boldsymbol{x}(u_i^t, u_j^t)^T, \boldsymbol{x}(u_i^s, u_j^s)^T, y(u_i^s, u_j^s)\right]^T\right)$$

Similarly, for a certain location link $(u_i^t, l_j^t)$, we have

$$P(y(u_i^t, l_j^t) = 1 | G^t, G^s)$$
$$= P\left(y(u_i^t, l_j^t) = 1 | \left[\boldsymbol{x}(u_i^t, l_j^t)^T, \boldsymbol{x}(u_i^s, l_j^s)^T, y(u_i^s, l_j^s)\right]^T\right)$$

Actually, we can also use *pseudo label* as the prediction result of link $(n_i^t, n_j^t)$ in $G^t$ and the method is called the NAIVE, which will be used as a baseline in our experiment.

**Table 3: Properties of the Heterogeneous Social Networks**

| | property | network: Twitter | network: Foursquare |
|---|---|---|---|
| # node | user | 5,223 | 5,392 |
| | post | 9,490,707 | 48,756 |
| | location | 297,182 | 38,921 |
| # link | follow | 164,920 | 31,312 |
| | write | 9,490,707 | 48,756 |
| | locate | 615,515 | 48,756 |

### 3.3.3 Collective Linkage Transfer across LBSNs

By using two aligned networks, the optimization equation will be revised as follows

$$\hat{\mathcal{Y}}_s^t, \hat{\mathcal{Y}}_l^t = arg \max_{\mathcal{Y}_s^t, \mathcal{Y}_l^t} P(\mathbf{y}(\boldsymbol{L}_s^t) = \mathcal{Y}_s^t | G^t, G^s, \mathbf{y}(\boldsymbol{L}_l^t) = \mathcal{Y}_l^t)$$
$$\times P(\mathbf{y}(\boldsymbol{L}_l^t) = \mathcal{Y}_l^t | G^t, G^s, \mathbf{y}(\boldsymbol{L}_s^t) = \mathcal{Y}_s^t)$$

For the given optimization equation, there are many different solutions. In this part, we will give an iterative method, TRAIL, to approach it, which can predict the social links and location links iteratively until convergence. Let $\tau$ be the $\tau_{th}$ iteration and the optimal label sets of social links and location links achieved in the $\tau_{th}$ iteration be $\hat{\mathcal{Y}}_s^{t(\tau)}$ and $\hat{\mathcal{Y}}_l^{t(\tau)}$, then

$$\hat{\mathcal{Y}}_s^{t(\tau)} = arg \max_{\mathcal{Y}_s^t} P(\mathbf{y}(\boldsymbol{L}_s^t) = \mathcal{Y}_s^t | G^t, G^s, \mathbf{y}(\boldsymbol{L}_s^t) = \hat{\mathcal{Y}}_s^{t(\tau-1)},$$
$$\mathbf{y}(\boldsymbol{L}_l^t) = \hat{\mathcal{Y}}_l^{t(\tau-1)})$$
$$\hat{\mathcal{Y}}_l^{t(\tau)} = arg \max_{\mathcal{Y}_l^t} P(\mathbf{y}(\boldsymbol{L}_l^t) = \mathcal{Y}_s^t | G^t, G^s, \mathbf{y}(\boldsymbol{L}_s^t) = \hat{\mathcal{Y}}_s^{t(\tau)},$$
$$\mathbf{y}(\boldsymbol{L}_l^t) = \hat{\mathcal{Y}}_l^{t(\tau-1)})$$

The pseudo code of TRAIL is available in Algorithm 1.

## 4. EXPERIMENTS

To testify the effectiveness of TRAIL in dealing with real-world aligned LBSNs, in this section, we will conduct extensive experiments on two real-world network datasets: Foursquare and Twitter.

### 4.1 Datasets Description

The networks used in this paper are: Foursquare, a famous LBSN, and Twitter, the hottest micro-blogging social network. Users play the key roles in both networks and they can follow/make friends with others, write posts online. Foursquare is constructed mainly around locations and can offer many location-related services, e.g., location check-ins and posting online reviews. Affected by the success of LBSNs, Twitter also starts to offer location-related services, e.g., online tweets can attach location check-ins. The locations in both of these social networks are represented as (latitude, longitude) pairs.

1. **Foursquare**: Users together with their online tips are crawled from Foursquare, whose numbers are 5,392 and 94,187 respectively. All these tips can attach location check-ins and the total number of locations crawled

from Foursquare is 38,921. The bidirectional friend link in Foursquare is decomposed into two unidirectional follow link and the original follow links are preserved. Detailed information about the Foursquare network is available in Table 3.

2. **Twitter**: Similarly, 5,223 users and all their online tweets are crawled from Twitter. The number of tweets crawled by us is 9,490,707, among which 615,515 tweets contain location check-ins and they account about 6.5% of all the tweets. The total number of locations obtained from the tweets is 297,182. The numbers of follow link among users, write link between users and tweets and the location link between tweets and locations are available in Table 3.

Both of these two networks are obtained from the webpages crawled with a shell script during the November, 2012. Meanwhile, if users display their Twitter accounts on their Foursquare homepages, we treat the connections between the accounts of Foursquare and Twitter as the anchor links between these two social networks. So, the anchor links are obtained by crawling the users' twitter IDs from their Foursquare homepages by using a shell script and the number of anchor links crawled is 3,388.

## 4.2 Experiment Settings

In this section, we will talk about the comparison methods, the evaluation measures and setups of the experiments in details.

### 4.2.1 *Comparison Methods*

To show that TRAIL can work well and outperform other state-of-art link prediction methods, we will compare TRAIL with many comparison methods, which can be divided into two categories: (1) supervised methods; (2) unsupervised methods.

- **TRAIL**: Method TRAIL is the link prediction method proposed in this paper. TRAIL is a supervised method and it can extract different categories of features for social links and location links from the heterogeneous networks. TRAIL can predict social links and location links simultaneously and can utilize both information in the target network and that transferred from the aligned source network.

- **Supervised Methods**: To show that predicting multiple kinds of links collectively can achieve better performance than predicting each kind of links independently, we compare TRAIL with SCAN (Supervised Cross Aligned Networks link prediction) [22], which is a supervised methods and can predict each kind of link independently across aligned networks. To demonstrate that using information in two aligned networks at the same time can achieve better performance than using one single network, we compare TRAIL with collective link prediction methods TRAILS (TRAnsfer heterogeneous lInks for LBSNs with Source network), TRAILT (TRAnsfer heterogeneous lInks for LBSNs with Target network) and compare SCAN with SCANS (Supervised Cross Aligned Link Prediction with Source network), SCANT (Supervised Cross Aligned Link Prediction with Target network). Methods TRAILT and SCANT utilize information in the target network only, while TRAILS and SCANS only use that transferred from the aligned source network.

- **Unsupervised Methods**: Some traditional unsupervised social link prediction methods are also used as the baseline methods to be compared with TRAIL, which include Common Neighbour (*CN*) [10]: $CN(x,y) = |\Gamma(x) \cap \Gamma(y)|$, Jaccard Coefficient (*JC*) [10]: $JC(x,y) = \frac{|\Gamma(x) \cap \Gamma(y)|}{|\Gamma(x) \cup \Gamma(y)|}$ and Adamic/Adar (*AA*) [1]: $AA(x,y) = |\Gamma(x)|\,|\Gamma(y)|$, where $\Gamma(x), \Gamma(y)$ are sets of neighbours of user $x$ and $y$. A traditional unsupervised location recommendation method: *FCF* (Friend based Collaborative Filtering) [21]: $r_{i,j} = \frac{\sum_{u_k \in \Gamma(u_i)} r_{k,j} w_{i,k}}{\sum_{u_k \in \Gamma(u_i)} w_{i,k}}$ is used as the location link prediction baseline method, where $r_{i,j}$ is the rating of user $u_i$ on location $l_j$ and $w_{i,k}$ is the similarity of user $u_i$ and $u_k$. NAIVE introduced before is used as a baseline method.

### 4.2.2 *Evaluation Methods*

To measure the effectiveness of these methods in predicting links, we will use two evaluation methods to assess their performance, which include AUC (Area Under ROC Curve) and *Accuracy*. Traditional unsupervised socal link and location link prediction methods *CN*, *JC*, *AA* and *FCF* can only output scores of potential links and their results are assessed by AUC only. Meanwhile, NAIVE can only produce labels of potential links and its performance is evaluated by *Accuracy* only. All other methods are evaluate by both AUC and *Accuracy*.

### 4.2.3 *Setups*

In the experiment, Foursquare is used as the target network and Twitter is used as the aligned source network. Existing social links and location links in Foursquare are used as the ground-truth.

We delete all the users' reposted tweets in Twitter about users' activities in Foursquare. Then, we group existing social links and location links in the target network as the positive social link set and positive location link set. Considering that users can visit a certain place multiple times which can , we delete all the duplicated location links and preserve on one copy. Sets of non-existent social links and location links collected from the target network are used as the negative social link set and negative location link set, which are of the same size as the positive sets. All these link sets are partitioned into two subsets by the 5-fold cross validation partitioned by links. To show that TRAIL can work well when the training pairs are quite limited, we use 1 fold as the training set and the remaining 4 folds as the test set. The target network studied in this paper is a new network and to simulate the different degrees of newness of it, we randomly sample a proportion of information in it to use under the control of parameter *remaining information rate* $\sigma$, which can include temporal activities, words used, locations visited etc. For example, if $\sigma = 0.1$, then the network is very new and only 10% of the information in original the network is available; if $\sigma = 0.8$, then the network is not that new as 80% of the information exists. To control the existence of *anchor links* between these two aligned social networks, we use another parameter: *anchor link sample rate* $\rho \in [0, 1.0]$ in the experiment. If $\rho = 0.0$, then these two networks are totally independent and have no anchor links between them; if $\rho = 1.0$, then these two networks are

Table 4: Performance comparison of different methods for inferring social and location links for Foursquare of different remaining information rates. The anchor link sample rate $\rho$ is set as 1.0.

| | | | remaining information rates $\sigma$ | | | | | | |
|---|---|---|---|---|---|---|---|---|---|
| link | measure | methods | 0.1 | 0.2 | 0.3 | 0.4 | 0.5 | 0.6 | 0.7 |
| social | AUC | TRAIL | **0.810±0.012** | **0.824±0.009** | **0.837±0.008** | **0.844±0.009** | **0.832±0.003** | **0.852±0.009** | **0.847±0.009** |
| | | TRAILT | 0.691±0.040 | 0.684±0.039 | 0.704±0.033 | 0.729±0.006 | 0.718±0.020 | 0.732±0.005 | 0.730±0.008 |
| | | TRAILS | 0.572±0.007 | 0.578±0.007 | 0.580±0.004 | 0.575±0.012 | 0.580±0.011 | 0.583±0.009 | 0.578±0.009 |
| | | SCAN | 0.772±0.050 | 0.788±0.004 | 0.811±0.009 | 0.830±0.005 | 0.809±0.004 | 0.825±0.008 | 0.824±0.012 |
| | | SCANT | 0.524±0.023 | 0.559±0.008 | 0.559±0.017 | 0.554±0.044 | 0.630±0.008 | 0.599±0.007 | 0.627±0.004 |
| | | SCANS | 0.583±0.005 | 0.579±0.003 | 0.583±0.010 | 0.562±0.005 | 0.579±0.004 | 0.585±0.003 | 0.584±0.003 |
| | | *CN* | 0.494±0.002 | 0.500±0.015 | 0.504±0.006 | 0.496±0.012 | 0.495±0.018 | 0.491±0.015 | 0.489±0.018 |
| | | *JC* | 0.497±0.003 | 0.503±0.004 | 0.501±0.002 | 0.502±0.010 | 0.496±0.008 | 0.496±0.019 | 0.492±0.008 |
| | | *AA* | 0.494±0.002 | 0.499±0.014 | 0.501±0.006 | 0.494±0.012 | 0.492±0.018 | 0.489±0.015 | 0.493±0.022 |
| | Accuracy | TRAIL | **0.855±0.002** | **0.849±0.004** | **0.850±0.008** | **0.854±0.005** | **0.850±0.003** | **0.851±0.001** | **0.852±0.004** |
| | | TRAILT | 0.622±0.046 | 0.627±0.036 | 0.655±0.022 | 0.676±0.009 | 0.674±0.019 | 0.677±0.004 | 0.679±0.008 |
| | | TRAILS | 0.548±0.004 | 0.551±0.006 | 0.552±0.004 | 0.549±0.000 | 0.551±0.002 | 0.553±0.003 | 0.544±0.001 |
| | | SCAN | 0.747±0.003 | 0.752±0.007 | 0.748±0.000 | 0.754±0.008 | 0.746±0.005 | 0.745±0.007 | 0.747±0.003 |
| | | SCANT | 0.512±0.009 | 0.522±0.002 | 0.520±0.001 | 0.537±0.006 | 0.554±0.008 | 0.542±0.003 | 0.567±0.007 |
| | | SCANS | 0.557±0.002 | 0.547±0.006 | 0.553±0.002 | 0.545±0.006 | 0.552±0.007 | 0.551±0.002 | 0.551±0.004 |
| | | NAIVE | 0.525±0.014 | 0.526±0.006 | 0.525±0.008 | 0.526±0.007 | 0.525±0.013 | 0.525±0.009 | 0.525±0.013 |
| location | AUC | TRAIL | **0.848±0.005** | **0.856±0.010** | **0.870±0.010** | **0.878±0.007** | **0.899±0.007** | **0.886±0.022** | **0.887±0.009** |
| | | TRAILT | 0.839±0.006 | 0.850±0.003 | 0.857±0.009 | 0.866±0.008 | 0.862±0.005 | 0.871±0.005 | 0.869±0.003 |
| | | TRAILS | 0.631±0.003 | 0.632±0.002 | 0.631±0.001 | 0.634±0.001 | 0.634±0.002 | 0.634±0.002 | 0.635±0.001 |
| | | SCAN | 0.712±0.010 | 0.757±0.002 | 0.758±0.009 | 0.770±0.005 | 0.775±0.005 | 0.784±0.004 | 0.792±0.003 |
| | | SCANT | 0.676±0.009 | 0.711±0.005 | 0.730±0.005 | 0.749±0.003 | 0.756±0.001 | 0.763±0.005 | 0.769±0.003 |
| | | SCANS | 0.633±0.003 | 0.633±0.003 | 0.633±0.001 | 0.636±0.001 | 0.637±0.000 | 0.633±0.001 | 0.634±0.001 |
| | | *FCF* | 0.598±0.008 | 0.638±0.015 | 0.638±0.005 | 0.654±0.012 | 0.664±0.007 | 0.661±0.007 | 0.664±0.010 |
| | Accuracy | TRAIL | **0.719±0.004** | **0.736±0.001** | **0.749±0.006** | **0.754±0.003** | **0.753±0.002** | **0.760±0.002** | **0.761±0.002** |
| | | TRAILT | 0.674±0.009 | 0.697±0.004 | 0.706±0.005 | 0.709±0.001 | 0.717±0.006 | 0.716±0.007 | 0.717±0.002 |
| | | TRAILS | 0.536±0.003 | 0.527±0.001 | 0.537±0.005 | 0.553±0.003 | 0.560±0.002 | 0.565±0.000 | 0.566±0.001 |
| | | SCAN | 0.658±0.000 | 0.670±0.002 | 0.682±0.001 | 0.697±0.003 | 0.699±0.003 | 0.723±0.003 | 0.723±0.007 |
| | | SCANT | 0.610±0.001 | 0.623±0.001 | 0.631±0.001 | 0.647±0.001 | 0.653±0.002 | 0.671±0.003 | 0.676±0.002 |
| | | SCANS | 0.536±0.025 | 0.531±0.008 | 0.535±0.002 | 0.547±0.004 | 0.557±0.004 | 0.565±0.001 | 0.566±0.001 |
| | | NAIVE | 0.536±0.014 | 0.536±0.002 | 0.536±0.001 | 0.537±0.008 | 0.536±0.012 | 0.536±0.009 | 0.537±0.019 |

fully aligned; otherwise they are partially aligned. From the networks, different categories of features are extracted for each kind of pairs in the training set and test set. To solve the problem of lacking information in the target network, we transfer information from the aligned to the target network via the *anchor links*. The feature vectors obtained from both the target network and the aligned source network together with the *pseudo label* are merged into an expended feature vector to make use of information in both networks simultaneously. We train and classify social links and location links with iterative update until convergence or meet a certain maximum iteration number, which is set as 10 in our experiment.

## 4.3 Experiment Results

Experiment results are available in Table 4, which is under the setting that *anchor link sample rate* $\rho$ is set as 1.0 and the *remaining information rate* $\sigma$ changes from 0.1 to 0.8, and in Table 5, which is under the setting that *remaining information rate* $\sigma$ is set as 1.0 and the *anchor link sample rate* $\rho$ changes from 0.0 to 1.0 with an increasing step of 0.2. The results in these two tables can be divided into two parts: the first part is about the social links and the seciond part is about the location links, whose performance are evaluated by AUC and *Accuracy*.

In Table 4, compared with traditional unsupervised methods, like *FCF*, *CN*, *JC* and *AA*, supervised method TRAIL can substantially outperform them under the evaluation metric. For example, when $\sigma = 0.5$, the evaluation metric (AUC) of TRAIL is over 60% higher than that of *CN*, *JC*, *AA* and the evaluation metric (*Accuracy*) achieved by TRAIL is about 34% higher than that *FCF*. And compared with NAIVE, TRAIL can also perform far better, e.g., the evaluation metric (*Accuracy*) is over 40% higher than that of NAIVE when $\sigma = 0.5$ in Table. 4 By comparing TRAIL with SCAN, TRAILS with SCANS, TRAILT with SCANT in predicting both social links and location links, we can find that the methods predicting links collectively with iterative update can achieve better performance consistently than methods predicting each type of links independently. By comparing TRAIL with TRAILS and TRAILT, we can find that TRAIL using information in both the target network and the aligned source network can achieve better performance than using information in one single network, which can also be obtained by comparing SCAN with SCANS and SCANT. Similar results can be obtained in Table 5 as the *anchor link sample rate* $\rho$ changes.

So, TRAIL can outperform all these state-of-art supervised baseline methods and traditional unsupervised methods for networks of different *remaining information rate* and different *anchor link sample rate* in Table 4 and Table 5, when the training cases is very limited under the evaluation of AUC and *Accuracy*.

In addition, the prediction result of method TRAIL can also converge very quickly. In Figure 4, we show the social and location link prediction results of TRAIL evaluated by *Accuracy* and AUC. Figures 4(a)- 4(d) are the results obtained by TRAIL when $\sigma = 0.5$ and $\rho = 1.0$. While, Figures 4(e)- 4(h) show the results obtained by TRAIL when $\sigma = 1.0$ and $\rho = 0.5$. We can find that all the results can converge quickly in less than 5 iterations.

# 5. RELATED WORK

Link prediction first proposed by D. Liben-Nowell et al. [14] has become a significant research topic in social network studies in recent years. M. A. Hasan et al. [9] are the first to study the link prediction problem as a supervised problem. However, their method is based on a homogeneous

Table 5: Performance comparison of different methods for inferring social and location links for Foursquare of different anchor link sample rates. The remaining informaiton rate $\sigma$ is set as 1.0.

| link | measure | methods | anchor link sample rates $\rho$: 0.0 | 0.2 | 0.4 | 0.6 | 0.8 | 1.0 |
|---|---|---|---|---|---|---|---|---|
| social | AUC | TRAIL | **0.712±0.004** | **0.733±0.019** | **0.761±0.017** | **0.782±0.007** | **0.821±0.012** | **0.855±0.008** |
| | | TRAILT | 0.712±0.012 | 0.711±0.007 | 0.711±0.012 | 0.711±0.010 | 0.712±0.014 | 0.712±0.005 |
| | | TRAILS | 0.500±0.000 | 0.507±0.005 | 0.524±0.005 | 0.555±0.036 | 0.577±0.028 | 0.583±0.015 |
| | | SCAN | 0.603±0.020 | 0.621±0.036 | 0.539±0.022 | 0.664±0.026 | 0.748±0.027 | 0.827±0.002 |
| | | SCANT | 0.603±0.009 | 0.603±0.014 | 0.603±0.016 | 0.603±0.027 | 0.603±0.006 | 0.604±0.011 |
| | | SCANS | 0.500±0.000 | 0.496±0.001 | 0.513±0.013 | 0.515±0.015 | 0.570±0.060 | 0.572±0.007 |
| | | *CN* | 0.525±0.000 | 0.525±0.008 | 0.524±0.013 | 0.525±0.005 | 0.525±0.013 | 0.525±0.007 |
| | | *JC* | 0.527±0.008 | 0.527±0.011 | 0.527±0.010 | 0.528±0.002 | 0.527±0.016 | 0.528±0.009 |
| | | *AA* | 0.493±0.006 | 0.490±0.006 | 0.490±0.012 | 0.490±0.009 | 0.493±0.013 | 0.490±0.006 |
| | Accuracy | TRAIL | **0.654±0.014** | **0.746±0.009** | **0.756±0.009** | **0.764±0.008** | **0.768±0.012** | **0.839±0.002** |
| | | TRAILT | 0.655±0.004 | 0.653±0.008 | 0.655±0.014 | 0.655±0.008 | 0.655±0.008 | 0.655±0.005 |
| | | TRAILS | 0.500±0.000 | 0.501±0.003 | 0.535±0.009 | 0.529±0.006 | 0.535±0.004 | 0.545±0.014 |
| | | SCAN | 0.554±0.028 | 0.567±0.009 | 0.563±0.007 | 0.605±0.014 | 0.656±0.011 | 0.748±0.012 |
| | | SCANT | 0.553±0.002 | 0.553±0.004 | 0.553±0.003 | 0.554±0.002 | 0.553±0.001 | 0.553±0.003 |
| | | SCANS | 0.500±0.000 | 0.498±0.003 | 0.515±0.008 | 0.529±0.003 | 0.536±0.003 | 0.541±0.005 |
| | | NAIVE | 0.500±0.000 | 0.508±0.001 | 0.514±0.006 | 0.517±0.002 | 0.519±0.003 | 0.526±0.000 |
| location | AUC | TRAIL | **0.871±0.020** | **0.876±0.011** | **0.891±0.006** | **0.881±0.028** | **0.916±0.016** | **0.925±0.007** |
| | | TRAILT | 0.871±0.015 | 0.872±0.004 | 0.872±0.013 | 0.872±0.003 | 0.872±0.017 | 0.872±0.014 |
| | | TRAILS | 0.500±0.000 | 0.492±0.002 | 0.479±0.004 | 0.504±0.002 | 0.580±0.001 | 0.652±0.003 |
| | | SCAN | 0.745±0.005 | 0.746±0.011 | 0.773±0.010 | 0.788±0.012 | 0.796±0.016 | 0.797±0.009 |
| | | SCANT | 0.745±0.021 | 0.744±0.011 | 0.745±0.025 | 0.744±0.020 | 0.743±0.011 | 0.744±0.010 |
| | | SCANS | 0.500±0.000 | 0.490±0.002 | 0.481±0.002 | 0.504±0.001 | 0.578±0.005 | 0.651±0.005 |
| | | *FCF* | 0.682±0.006 | 0.683±0.002 | 0.682±0.007 | 0.683±0.002 | 0.683±0.006 | 0.682±0.003 |
| | Accuracy | TRAIL | **0.734±0.008** | **0.754±0.005** | **0.765±0.006** | **0.775±0.003** | **0.789±0.008** | **0.797±0.010** |
| | | TRAILT | 0.735±0.002 | 0.734±0.007 | 0.734±0.007 | 0.734±0.006 | 0.735±0.004 | 0.735±0.004 |
| | | TRAILS | 0.500±0.000 | 0.509±0.003 | 0.514±0.006 | 0.511±0.001 | 0.533±0.000 | 0.569±0.001 |
| | | SCAN | 0.731±0.002 | 0.753±0.001 | 0.754±0.002 | 0.755±0.002 | 0.767±0.002 | 0.777±0.003 |
| | | SCANT | 0.732±0.013 | 0.732±0.010 | 0.732±0.016 | 0.732±0.009 | 0.732±0.004 | 0.732±0.004 |
| | | SCANS | 0.500±0.000 | 0.511±0.002 | 0.516±0.006 | 0.517±0.005 | 0.534±0.001 | 0.568±0.002 |
| | | NAIVE | 0.500±0.000 | 0.509±0.001 | 0.517±0.001 | 0.517±0.005 | 0.525±0.010 | 0.536±0.004 |

network and many networks are heterogeneous nowadays. Y. Sun et al. [17] propose a meta path-based prediction model to predict co-author relationship in the heterogeneous bibliographic network.

As the Location-based social networks (LBSNs) are becoming more and more popular in recent years, many works have been done on such kind of social networks. M. Ye et al. [20] study the semantic annotation of locations in location-based social networks. Meanwhile, some works have also been done on predicting links for LBSNs. S. Scellato et al. [16] predict social links by using heterogeneous information in the network. D. Wang et al. [19] try to predict social links by utilizing the moving pattern of users. These works are all predicting social links and some other works focus on predicting location links. M. Ye et al. [21] study location recommendation problem by using friend-based collaborative filtering method. E. Cho et al. [5] regard the location recommendation problem as a supervised link prediction problem. Y. Zheng et al. propose to mine interesting locations and travel sequences from GPS trajectories in [23].

Most existing works focus on predicting one single type of link but some other works can predict multiple kinds of links simultaneously. I. Konstas et al. [12] propose to use collaborative filtering method to recommend multiple kinds of links for networks. While, F. Fouss et al. [7] use a traditional method: random walk to predict multiple kinds of links. B. Cao et al. [4] propose to predict links in different domains simultaneously with transfer learning. Some works propose to combine link prediction with other classification tasks. For example, M. Bilgic et al. [3] propose to do collective classification and link prediction for networks simultaneously.

All these works are based on one single network but many researchers start to shift their attention to multiple networks. Tang et al. [18] focus on inferring the type of links over multiple heterogeneous networks. Z. Lu et al. [15] propose to do supervised link prediction by using multiple information sources. Y. Dong et al. [6] propose to predict links across heterogeneous social networks. To deal with the differences in information distributions of multiple networks, G. Qi et al. [8] propose to use biased cross-network sampling to predict links across networks.

When studying multiple social networks, the first problem will be how to construct the bridges between networks to transfer information across them. X. Kong et al. [11] propose a method to infer the links between the accounts owned by the same users in different social networks and they are the first one to introduce the concepts of "anchor links" and "multiple aligned heterogeneous networks". J. Zhang et al. propose to predict social links for new users with information transferred from aligned source network through anchor links to solve the cold start problem in [22] and they are the first one to propose to transfer information across "aligned networks" through "anchor links".

## 6. CONCLUSION

In this paper, we study the collectively link prediction problem for new networks across aligned LBSNs and the links to be predicted in this paper include both social links and location links. We propose method TRAIL to deal with the challenges and solve the problem. TRAIL can accumulate information for locations and can extract different categories of features for both social links and location links from the networks. By taking advantage of the *anchor links*, TRAIL can utilize the information transferred from the aligned source network to ease the information sparsity problem. TRAIL can predict social links and location links by iterative updating the network with newly predicted re-

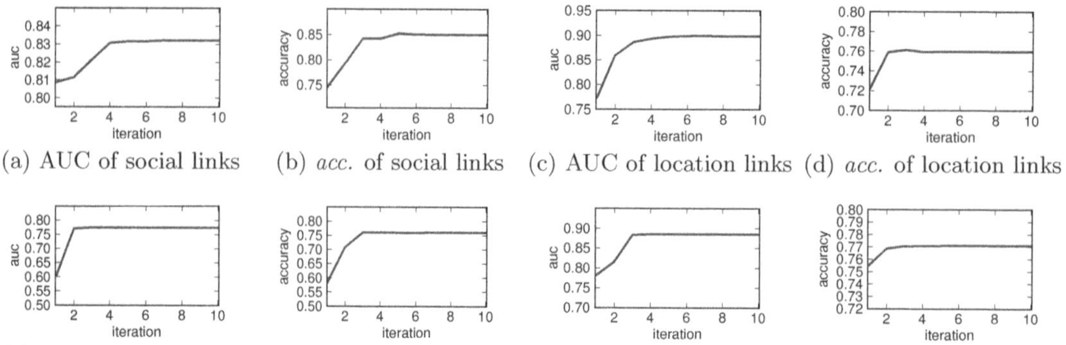


(a) AUC of social links (b) *acc.* of social links (c) AUC of location links (d) *acc.* of location links

(e) AUC of social links (f) *acc.* of social links (g) AUC of location links (h) *acc.* of location links

**Figure 4: Social link and location link prediction results of each iteration under the evaluation of AUC and *Accuracy*. (a)-(d) are the results when $\sigma = 0.5$ and $\rho = 1.0$; (e)-(h) are the same results when $\sigma = 1.0$ and $\rho = 0.5$, where $\sigma$ is the remaining information rate and $\rho$ is the anchor link sample rate.**

sults. Extensive experiments conducted on two real-world data sets demonstrate that TRAIL can achieve good prediction result for the target network of different degrees of newness and different anchor link sample rates.

## 7. ACKNOWLEDGMENTS

This work is supported in part by NSF through grants CNS-1115234, DBI-0960443, and OISE-1129076, US Department of Army through grant W911NF-12-1-0066, and Huawei Grant.

## 8. REFERENCES

[1] L. Adamic and E. Adar. Friends and neighbors on the web. *Social Networks*, pages 211–230, 2001.

[2] A. E. Aladağ and C. Erten. Spinal: scalable protein interaction network alignment. Bioinformatics, pages 917–924, 2013.

[3] M. Bilgic, G. M. Namata, and L. Getoor. Combining collective classification and link prediction. In *ICDMW*, pages 381–386, 2007.

[4] B. Cao, N. Liu, and Q. Yang. Transfer learning for collective link prediction in multiple heterogenous domains. In *ICML*, pages 159–166, 2010.

[5] E. Cho, S. Myers, and J. Leskovec. Friendship and mobility: user movement in location-based social networks. In *KDD*, pages 1082–1090, 2011.

[6] Y. Dong, J. Tang, S. Wu, J. Tian, N. Chawla, J. Rao, and H. Cao. Link prediction and recommendation across heterogeneous social networks. In *ICDM*, pages 181–190, 2012.

[7] F. Fouss, A. Pirotte, J. Renders, and M. Saerens. Random-walk computation of similarities between nodes of a graph with application to collaborative recommendation. *TKDE*, pages 355–369, 2007.

[8] C. Aggarwal G. Qi and T. Huang. Link prediction across networks by biased cross-network sampling. In *ICDE*, pages 793–804, 2013.

[9] M. Hasan, V. Chaoji, S. Salem, and M. Zaki. Link prediction using supervised learning. In *SDM*, pages 71–83, 2006.

[10] M. A. Hasan and M. J. Zaki. A survey of link prediction in social networks. In *Social Network Data Analytics*, pages 243–275. Springer, 2011.

[11] X. Kong, J. Zhang, and P. Yu. Inferring anchor links across multiple heterogeneous social networks. In *CIKM*, pages 179–188, 2013.

[12] I. Konstas, V. Stathopoulos, and J. M. Jose. On social networks and collaborative recommendation. In *SIGIR*, pages 195–202, 2009.

[13] H. Kwak, C. Lee, H. Park, and S. Moon. What is twitter, a social network or a news media? In *WWW*, pages 591–600, 2010.

[14] D. Liben-Nowell and J. Kleinberg. The link prediction problem for social networks. In *CIKM*, pages 556–559, 2003.

[15] Z. Lu, B. Savas, W. Tang, and I. Dhillon. Supervised link prediction using multiple sources. In *ICDM*, pages 923–928, 2010.

[16] S. Scellato, A. Noulas, and C. Mascolo. Exploiting place features in link prediction on location-based social networks. In *KDD*, pages 1046–1054, 2011.

[17] Y. Sun, R. Barber, M. Gupta, C. Aggarwal, and J. Han. Co-author relationship prediction in heterogeneous bibliographic networks. In *ASONAM*, pages 121–128, 2011.

[18] J. Tang, T. Lou, and J. Kleinberg. Inferring social ties across heterogenous networks. In *WSDM*, pages 743–752, 2012.

[19] D. Wang, D. Pedreschi, C. Song, F. Giannotti, and A. Barabasi. Human mobility, social ties, and link prediction. In *KDD*, pages 1100–1108, 2011.

[20] M. Ye, D. Shou, W. Lee, P. Yin, and K. Janowicz. On the semantic annotation of places in location-based social networks. In *KDD*, pages 520–528, 2011.

[21] M. Ye, P. Yin, and W. Lee. Location recommendation for location-based social networks. In *GIS*, pages 458–461, 2010.

[22] J. Zhang, X. Kong, and P. Yu. Predicting social links for new users across aligned heterogeneous social networks. In *ICDM*, pages 1289–1294, 2013.

[23] Y. Zheng, L. Zhang, X. Xie, and W. Ma. Mining interesting locations and travel sequences from gps trajectories. In *WWW*, pages 791–800, 2009.

# Customized Tour Recommendations in Urban Areas

Aristides Gionis
HIIT and Aalto University
aristides.gionis@aalto.fi

Theodoros Lappas
Stevens Institute of Technology
tlappas@stevens.edu

Konstantinos Pelechrinis
University of Pittsburgh
kpele@pitt.edu

Evimaria Terzi
Boston University
evimaria@cs.bu.edu

## ABSTRACT

The ever-increasing urbanization coupled with the unprecedented capacity to collect and process large amounts of data have helped to create the vision of intelligent urban environments. One key aspect of such environments is that they allow people to effectively navigate through their city. While GPS technology and route-planning services have undoubtedly helped towards this direction, there is room for improvement in intelligent urban navigation. This vision can be fostered by the proliferation of location-based social networks, such as `Foursquare` or `Path`, which record the physical presence of users in different venues through *check-ins*. This information can then be used to enhance intelligent urban navigation, by generating customized path recommendations for users.

In this paper, we focus on the problem of recommending customized tours in urban settings. These tours are generated so that they consider (a) the different types of venues that the user wants to visit, as well as the order in which the user wants to visit them, (b) limitations on the time to be spent or distance to be covered, and (c) the merit of visiting the included venues. We capture these requirements in a generic definition that we refer to as the TourRec problem. We then introduce two instances of the TourRec problem, study their complexity, and propose efficient algorithmic solutions. Our experiments on real data collected from `Foursquare` demonstrate the efficacy of our algorithms and the practical utility of the reported recommendations.

## Categories and Subject Descriptors

H.4 [**Information Systems Applications**]: Miscellaneous; H.2.8 [**Database Management**]: Database Applications—*Data Mining*

## Keywords

urban computing; tour recommendations


*WSDM'14,* February 24–28, 2014, New York, New York, USA.

http://dx.doi.org/10.1145/2556195.2559893.

## 1. INTRODUCTION

Based on a recent report from the United Nations, more than 50% of the world's population currently lives in cities. This percentage is projected to increase to 70% by the year 2050 [2]. These facts have motivated the concept of *smart cities* [16], that will provide intelligent services to significantly enhance the quality of urban life. One of the critical services within smart cities is *urban navigation*. While GPS technology has undoubtedly improved people's capability to move easily through a city, intelligent urban navigation goes *beyond* shortest paths. In this paper, we study how we can utilize contextual information to provide customized *tour recommendations* for advanced urban navigation.

In order to accomplish our goal we exploit information provided by a new class of applications: *location-based social networks*. These applications enable users to share their locations through *check-ins* to specific *venues* (e.g., restaurants, bars, parks, museums etc.). This interaction captures the user's physical presence within a city and results in rich datasets that encode real-world activities.

One of the main functionalities currently offered by location-based social networks is the recommendation of *venues* or *location-specific activities*, based on user preferences. For example, `Foursquare`, the largest location-based social network to date, with more than 30 million users, is positioning itself as a location-recommendation engine, used to recommend venues to users based on their own check-in history, as well as that of their friends [1].

A key characteristic of such recommendation systems [8, 25, 33] is that they evaluate each venue *independently*. The result of this evaluation is a personalized probability that a specific user likes the venue, or a general value representing the venue's quality or reputation. The venues with the top-$k$ highest scores are then recommended to the user. The main drawback of such ranking schemes is their inability to evaluate venues in *groups*, and deliver *tour recommendations* that obey certain thematic and spatial constraints.

As an example, consider the scenario shown in Figure 1. A user must travel for business in an unfamiliar part of the megacity in which she lives (e.g., NYC). After her work is completed, she wants to explore this area further. In particular, she is interested in taking a "stroll" to visit an outdoor relaxing spot, (e.g., a nice park — Type A in the figure), before heading to a nice restaurant for lunch (Type B). From there, she wants to go to a popular place for a happy-hour drink (Type C) and then return to her initial point (marked by the bulls-eye in the figure) so she can go back home. Since

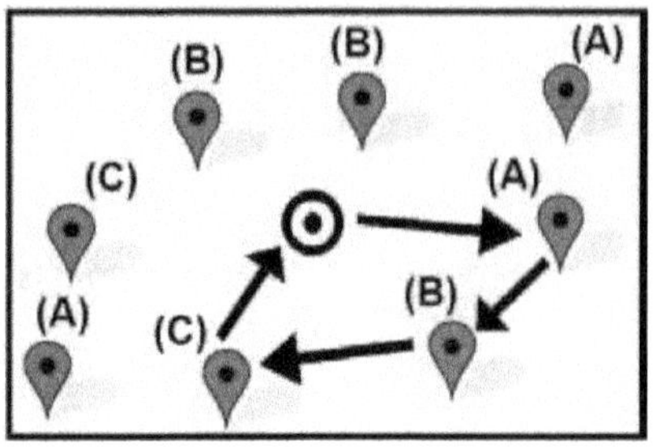


Figure 1: An example of the Tour Recommendation setting.

there are different venues from each type scattered across the map, there are multiple potential tours that respect the given type order (such as the one marked in the figure). The tour-recommendation problem becomes even more complex if we also want to keep the total distance within a given budget, and also maximize the overall merit of the venues included in the tour, as we do in this paper.

Even though a number of tour-recommendation approaches have been recently proposed [14, 23, 27, 34] (for a review see Section 5), those approaches suffer from a number of limitations. These include the dependence on training data in the form of past tours or trajectories, the assumption that all venues belong to the same type and thus service the same user need, and the inability to cater to the user who wants to cover different needs in a specific order during the tour.

In this paper, we develop a framework that addresses these shortcomings by delivering tour recommendations that take into account: (*i*) the different types of venues, as well as the order in which the user wants to visit them; (*ii*) budget constraints expressed in terms of the total distance that the user is willing to traverse (or the total time the user is willing to spend); and (*iii*) the satisfaction that each venue can provide to the user, if included in the tour. In our work, we propose and study the computational and the qualitative effect of two alternative definitions for user satisfaction.

We capture and formalize the above requirements in our definition of the TOURREC problem, which asks for a group of venues that adheres to the user constraints and also maximizes the expected user satisfaction. Depending on the way user satisfaction is measured, we define two variants of the TOURREC problem: the first variant assumes a (personalized or general) expected satisfaction score for every venue, and asks for the tour with the maximum total satisfaction. The second variant captures the scenario where each venue *covers* certain attractions (e.g., nearby city landmarks, current location-specific events). The goal is then to find a tour that respects the constraints and covers the maximum number of distinct attractions. We study the complexity of both variants and propose efficient algorithmic solutions.

At a high level, the TOURREC problem is related to variants of the traveling-salesman problem (e.g., TSP, prize-collecting TSP, orienteering). However, the partitioning of the venues into types, the ordering constraints, as well as the characteristics of our objective functions, necessitate customized algorithms for our problem. In our experiments, we demonstrate the superiority of our methods over competitive baselines via an extensive evaluation on real datasets collected from `Foursquare` for three major cities.

**Roadmap:** The rest of the paper is organized as follows: we start with the formal definition of our problems in Section 2. The algorithms we design for the different variants of the problems are described in Section 3 and they are experimentally evaluated in Section 4. We review the related work in Section 5 and conclude the paper in Section 6.

## 2. PROBLEM DEFINITION

Next, we introduce our notation, define the TOURREC problem and its variants, and discuss their complexity.

### 2.1 Preliminaries

Throughout our discussion, we use the term *venue* to refer to locations, landmarks, restaurants, museums etc. We assume that there are $n$ venues $V = \{v_1, ...., v_n\}$, and a function $\text{Dist}(\cdot)$ that measures the physical distance between any two venues. Our assumption is that every venue is associated with a *type*. Indicative types are: museum, gallery, cinema, restaurant, etc. For venue $v$, we use $T(v)$ to denote its type. We assume that each venue is associated with one type and that there are $m$ *venue types* $\mathcal{T} = \{T_1, \ldots, T_m\}$.

We assume a function $f(v)$ that returns a custom value for a given venue $v$. The value represents the expected satisfaction of the user, if the user visits the particular venue. We assume that higher values of $f(v)$ correspond to higher satisfaction levels. In principle, different users get different satisfaction levels from different venues and therefore the values of $f(v)$ are personalized. Although obtaining accurate estimates of such personalized values is an important problem that is beyond the scope of this paper, when such an estimation function is available (e.g., using the algorithms proposed by Bao et al. [6]) it can be incorporated as it is in our framework. In our implementation we estimate expected user satisfaction using intuitive proxies, such as the total number of check-ins or the average review score.

Our goal is to find a *tour* $\mathcal{R}$ that maximizes the satisfaction of the user and obeys a set of user-specified constrains. A tour is a *sequence* of venues. For example, $\mathcal{R}$ may be equal to $\mathcal{R} = \langle v_1, v_3, v_5 \rangle$, which means that the user is recommended to visit venue $v_1$, then venue $v_3$ and, finally, venue $v_5$. We use the notation $\mathcal{R}(i)$ to refer to the $i$-th venue in the tour. In addition to the sequence of venues, the tour includes a starting point $s$ and ending point $t$, which are specified by the user and can be arbitrary locations on the map. We refer to the number of venues in the tour (excluding the source and the destination) as the *size* of the tour.

We consider the following constraints:

**Ordering constraints:** We assume that the user provides a *type order* $\pi$, which expresses precedence constraints in the order in which the user wants to visit venues of different types. The order $\pi$ is a total order over the types in $\mathcal{T}$ and we say that $T_i \prec_\pi T_j$ if the user expresses a preference of visiting venues of type $T_i$ *before* venues of type $T_j$. Although in Section 3.3 we discuss how these total order constraints can be relaxed, for now we assume that a tour $\mathcal{R}$ is *consistent with type order* $\pi$ if for every $1 \leq i \leq |\mathcal{R}| - 1$ we have that if $v = \mathcal{R}(i)$ and $v' = \mathcal{R}(i+1)$, then $T(v) \prec_\pi T(v')$.

The order constraint is motivated by the observation that daily human activities are correlated with the time of the day. For example, people typically have coffee in the morning and visit restaurants in the afternoon and early evening (lunch and dinner times). Also they cannot visit a museum in the evening since it will be most probably closed. This intuition has been repeatedly studied and verified in relevant literature [26, 15, 22, 17, 3], where it is found that tourists have a very specific opinion on when is the best time within the day for each type of activity or attraction.

In Section 3.3, we show how to extend our framework to address *partial orders on types*, *super types* and *type skips*, in which there is flexibility in the visiting order of venues.

**Budget constraints:** The budget constraints enable users to specify the total distance $D$ they are willing to cover. In Section 3.3, we discuss how temporal or other types of constraints can also be incorporated. For now, we consider the total distance $\textsc{ShortestPath}(\mathcal{R})$ of a tour $\mathcal{R}$ that starts at $s$, traverses the venues in $\mathcal{R}$ in order, and ends in $t$.

**Multiplicity bounds:** The multiplicity bounds allow users to specify the number of venues of a particular type that they want to visit. This number is expressed as an interval. That is, the users provide a lower and an upper bound, $L_i$ and $U_i$, on the number of venues of type $T_i$ they are willing to visit. The set of lower and upper bounds over all venue types is denoted by $B = \{(L_i, U_i)\}_{i=1}^m$.

A tour $\mathcal{R}$ is *consistent with multiplicity bounds* $B$ if for every type $T_i$ the number of venues of type $T_i$ in $\mathcal{R}$ are more than or equal to $L_i$ and less than or equal to $U_i$.

**User satisfaction:** We use a generic *satisfaction function* $F(\mathcal{R})$ to measure the expected satisfaction of the user with respect to a candidate tour $\mathcal{R}$. We define two variants of this satisfaction function: the *additive* and *coverage* functions, denoted by $\mathcal{A}$dd and $\mathcal{C}$ov, respectively. Each function evaluates $\mathcal{R}$ in a different way as we discuss below.

*The additive satisfaction function* $\mathcal{A}$dd*:* $\mathcal{A}$dd assumes that there is a benefit $b(v)$ associated with every venue $v$.[1] This benefit may be generic or a personalized probability that a particular user will like the venue. Given such venue-specific benefits, the additive satisfaction function evaluates the overall satisfaction of a tour $\mathcal{R}$ as $\mathcal{A}dd(\mathcal{R}) = \sum_{v \in \mathcal{R}} b(v)$.

*The coverage satisfaction function* $\mathcal{C}$ov*:* This function is appropriate when each venue is associated with a set $S(v)$ that includes attractions that located in the vicinity of the venue (or even activities that the user can perform within or near the venue). Then, the coverage of a path $\mathcal{R}$ is defined as $\mathcal{C}ov(\mathcal{R}) = |\cup_{v \in \mathcal{R}} S(v)|$, and represents the total number of **distinct** attractions or activities that the user will have the chance to visit or perform during the tour.

Conceptually, $\mathcal{A}dd(\mathcal{R})$ is appropriate when the user wants to maximize the quality or the personalized relevance of the venues in the tour. On the other hand, $\mathcal{C}ov(\mathcal{R})$, is appropriate for more *diverse* routes that offer a wide range of associated attractions and activities.

## 2.2 The TourRec problem

Given the above notation, our goal is to solve the following generic problem.

Problem 1 (TourRec). *Given a type order $\pi$, a distance budget $D$, multiplicity bounds $B$, and starting and ending locations $s$ and $t$, find a a tour $\mathcal{R}$ such that:*

*(i) it is consistent with the order $\pi$ and type bounds $B$;*

*(ii) it starts at location $s$ and ends at location $t$;*

*(iii) the total covered distance is less than $D$, i.e., $\textsc{ShortestPath}(\mathcal{R}) \leq D$;*

*(iv) it maximizes the user satisfaction $F(\mathcal{R})$.*

[1] $b(v)$ is essentially a specific instantiation of the $f(v)$ function mentioned earlier.

The different variants of the $F$ function give rise to different variants of the TourRec problem. For example, when the total benefit is measured by $\mathcal{A}$dd, then we call the underlying problem the AdditiveTour problem; when the total benefit is measured by $\mathcal{C}$ov, then we refer to the resulting problem as the CoveringTour problem.

We have the following NP-hardness results for the complexity of these two problems.

Lemma 1. *The* AdditiveTour *problem is* **NP**-*hard.*

For the proof of the above lemma it is sufficient to observe that AdditiveTour contains the Traveling Salesman Problem (TSP) [19]: let us consider the decision version of AdditiveTour, defined as follows: given $V$, $\mathcal{T}$, $B$, $s$, $t$, $D$ and a satisfaction bound $M$, is there a tour $\mathcal{R}$ that satisfies all the constraints, has total distance cost at most $D$ and $\mathcal{A}dd(\mathcal{R}) \geq M$? We can show that TSP can be reduced to this decision version of AdditiveTour. Indeed, consider a TSP instance on a graph $G = (V, E)$ with distance bound $D$. We then define an instance of the decision AdditiveTour problem as follows. We consider a graph with the same edge distances and a single type of venues $\mathcal{T} = \{T\}$. We also set $|T| = |V| = n$, $L_T = U_T = n$, $s = t$, $b(v) = 1$ for all venues $v \in V$, $M = n$, and distance bound $D$ (the same as in the TSP instance). It is easy to see that the TSP instance has a solution if and only if the transformed instance of the decision AdditiveTour problem has a solution.

Similarly, for CoveringTour we have the following.

Lemma 2. *The* CoveringTour *problem is* **NP**-*hard.*

The proof of Lemma 2 relies on the fact that the CoveringTour problem when there is a single type of venues $\mathcal{T} = \{T\}$ such that $|T| = |V| = n$, $B = \{(L, U)\}$ with $L = U = k$, and $s = t$ then our problem is identical to the $k-$Maximum Coverage problem [19]. In fact, we can show that the CoveringTour problem is NP-hard even when $L_i = U_i = 1$ for every type $i$ and $D = \infty$. In this case, CoveringTour is identical to the Maximum Coverage with Group BudgetConstraints problem [10].

# 3. ALGORITHMS

We begin this section by describing our algorithms for AdditiveTour. Then, we demonstrate how these can be adapted for solving CoveringTour.

## 3.1 Algorithms for AdditiveTour

First, we consider the version of the AdditiveTour problem where we specify a total order $\pi$ over the venue types and we want to have *exactly* one venue from every type in our tour. For this case, we have the following result:

Lemma 3. *When $\pi$ is a total order, and $L_i = U_i = 1$ for all types $T_i \in \mathcal{T}$, then the* AdditiveTour *problem can be solved optimally in time $\mathcal{O}(n^2 D)$.*

Proof. This version of the AdditiveTour problem can be solved via dynamic programming. More specifically, we define the table $B(v,d)$ to denote the maximum value of the $\mathcal{A}dd$ function one can achieve with a walk consistent with $\pi$, which starts at $s$, ends at $v$, and covers a total distance which is at most $d$. Clearly, for $n$ venues and maximum distance $D$, the size of the table $B$ is $(n+2) \times D$.

First, we sort the venue types according to the order $\pi$ — the ordering of the venues within each type does not matter and can be arbitrary. Then, for every $v \in T_k$ we can evaluate $B(v,d)$ by following recursion

$$B(v,d) = \max_{v' \in T_{k-1}} \{B(v', d - \text{Dist}(v,v')) + b(v)\}. \qquad (1)$$

The time required for evaluating Equation (1) is $\mathcal{O}(n^2 D)$. Thus, the dynamic-programming algorithm is pseudo polynomial. For the special case where all the venues are on a graph with unit edge weights, the time required for the above recursion is polynomial in $n$. □

We refer to the dynamic-programming algorithm that implements recursion (1) as the `Rel-DP` algorithm.

In addition to the exact pseudo-polynomial `Rel-DP` algorithm, we can also have a fully polynomial-time approximation scheme (FPTAS) for the problem. This scheme firsts scales down the instance of the input problem so that all distances are polynomial in $n$. It then runs the `Rel-DP` algorithm on the scaled-down instance and returns the solution. In more detail, given a parameter $\epsilon$, we define $K = \frac{\epsilon D}{n}$. We then scale down every distance by $\text{Dist}'(v,v') = \lfloor \frac{\text{Dist}(v,v')}{K} \rfloor$, and we run the `Rel-DP` algorithm with distances $\text{Dist}'$ and distance bound $D' = \lfloor \frac{D}{K} \rfloor$. The resulting dynamic-programming table has dimensions $(n+2) \times \lfloor \frac{n}{\epsilon} \rfloor$ and thus the running time of the algorithm is $\mathcal{O}(n^2 \lfloor \frac{n}{\epsilon} \rfloor)$. It is also easy to see that the returned solution is a $(1-\epsilon)$-approximation to the optimal solution.[2] Summarizing, we have:

LEMMA 4. *When $\pi$ is a total order and $L_i = U_i = 1$ for all types $T_i \in \mathcal{T}$, for any $\epsilon > 0$ the* ADDITIVETOUR *problem be approximated within factor $(1-\epsilon)$ in time $\mathcal{O}(n^2 \lfloor \frac{n}{\epsilon} \rfloor)$.*

**Efficiency consideration:** The $O(n^2 D)$ running times of the `Rel-DP` algorithm is a worst-case estimates. In practice, the running time of depends on the distribution of venues into types as well as the binning of $D$, i.e., the size of the step we adopt for distances when we construct the dynamic-programming tables. Our experiments show that appropriate binning can lead to very efficient algorithms.

## 3.2 Algorithms for COVERINGTOUR

Again, we consider the version of the COVERINGTOUR problem in which the user wants to visit *exactly one* venue from each type. We can solve this version of COVERINGTOUR by modifying Recursion (1) as follows:

$$C(v,d) = \max_{v' \in T_{k-1}} \{C(v', d - \text{Dist}(v',v)) + \mathcal{C}ov(v \mid \mathcal{R}_{v', d-\text{Dist}(v',v)})\}, \qquad (2)$$

where $C(v,d)$ keeps the best coverage of a path that ends in $v$ and has total shortest path $d$, and $\mathcal{R}_{v',d}$ denotes the actual path that ends in $v'$ and is within the distance budget $d$.

We refer to the dynamic-programming algorithm that implements Recursion (2) as the `Cover-DP` algorithm. The time complexity of evaluating Recursion (2) is the same as the time complexity for evaluating Recursion (1), i.e., $O(n^2 D)$. Note that the speedups discussed in the previous paragraph can be also applied here.

[2]Keep in mind that we are dealing with a maximization problem.

## 3.3 Extensions

In this section we present different extensions to our framework. We extend the applicability of our work and address intuitive scenarios that can emerge in urban settings.

**Relaxing the total order constraint:** Although the above discussion assumed a total order on the venue types, our algorithms can be easily modified for arbitrary partial type orders. In this section we provide three different ways to relax the total-order constraint: *partial orders of types*, *super types*, and *type skips*.

*Partial orders.* The first way to relax the total-order constraint is to allow the venue types to satisfy any partial order. In this scenario, our goal is to find a tour which visits venues in a way that respects a user-submitted partial order. we assume that a user provides a partial order, and the aim is to find a tour for which the ordering of the venues in the tour satisfies the partial order. A simple solution to this problem is to consider all *linear extensions* of the given partial order. Recall that a linear extension of a partial order is a total order that is consistent with the partial order. Therefore, we can enumerate all those total orders, solve the recommendation problem in each total order, and pick the best solution. Even though in the general case the number of linear extensions can be exponentially large, in our setting, we expect that a user specifies a small number of venue types (less than 5), so given a partial order it is possible to try all consistent total orders. Our results in Section 4.2 indicate that each total order instance can be computed very fast. Furthermore, the total number of distinct venue types in our dataset is 9, hence, the number of consistent total orders for any query is relatively small as well. In addition, each consistent total order can be evaluated independently, allowing for a naturally parallelizable implementation.

In practice, we should not expect from users to be familiar with the concept of partial orders in order to be able to specify their constraints. However, it is possible to design a system in which users specify their constraints as pair-wise precedence constraints via a simple user interface, and the constraints are represented internally as a partial order.

*Super-types.* An alternative family of ordering constraints, simpler than partial orders, are *bucket orders*, or as we call them in our setting, *super-types*. In this case, users can specify that they could visit *any* type of venues among a given subset. For example, users can specify that they are interested in visiting a museum OR a gallery OR a landmark and then go for lunch to a restaurant OR to a cafe. Those type groupings are called super-types. Our algorithms can then be applied directly to satisfy any such order. The idea is to simply consider super-types as types and apply the algorithms we developed in the previous sections.

The concept of super-types, coupled with allowing to specify multiple venues from each type, which we will discuss shortly, increases the flexibility of the user by a great deal. For example, a user may specify a super-type consisting of 4 types and asking for a recommendation that contains at most 3 venues from this super-type, and the same individual type can be repeated.

*Type skips.* Another way to relax the total order is to allow types to be skipped. So far we have assumed that exactly one venue from every type must be included in the recommended tour (i.e., $L_i = U_i = 1$). However, our methods can be generalized to find tours that are allowed to skip some types. For the ADDITIVETOUR problem, this is captured by the following lemma.

LEMMA 5. *Consider the* ADDITIVETOUR *problem where* $L_i, U_i \in \{0, 1\}$ *(with* $L_i \leq U_i$*) for all types* $T_i \in \mathcal{T}$. *In this case, the* ADDITIVETOUR *problem can be solved optimally in time* $\mathcal{O}(n^3 D)$.

PROOF. We are using the same benefit table $B$ of dimension $(n+2) \times D$ and the same ordering of venues as in the previous proof. However, Recursion (1) is modified to the following recursive evaluation:

$$B(v,d) = \max_{\substack{k'=1\ldots k-1 \\ v' \in T_{k'}}} \{B(v', d - \text{Dist}(v,v')) + \mathcal{A}\text{dd}(v)\}. \quad (3)$$

The main difference between Recursion (1) and (3) is that in the latter when forming the tour that ends in venue $v \in T_k$, all tours ending in venues of all types that precede type $T_k$ are examined (as opposed to only the tours that end in venues of type $T_{k-1}$). □

The complexity of recursion (3) is $O(n^3 D)$. A similar modification can be used to allow types to be skipped in the COVERINGTOUR problem.

**Multiple venues per type:** Lemmas 3 and 5 assume that *exactly* and *at most* one venue from each venue type will be added in the final tour, respectively. For the ADDITIVETOUR problem, the variant where multiple venues of the same type are required (i.e., $U_k > 1$) can be handled by extending the dynamic programming recursion of Equation (1). This can be done as follows: consider again the dynamic programming table $B(v,d)$ that stores the maximum benefit solution ending at $v$ of type $T_k$ and having total cost at most $d$. Then for every $v \in T_k$ we can evaluate $B(v,d)$ as follows:

$$B(v,d) = \max_{\substack{v' \in T_{k-1} \\ d' \leq d}} \{B(v', d - d') + \text{Path}(v', v, d - d')\}. \quad (4)$$

In the above equation, $\text{Path}(v', v, x)$ is the benefit achieved by the best path that starts at $v'$ ends at $v$, has cost at most $x$ and visits the required a number of places in $T_k$. Computing $\text{Path}(v', v, x)$ is in fact the orienteering problem [30] and therefore known algorithms for this problem [11] can be applied as a subroutine to the above recursion.

For the COVERINGTOUR problem, we can allow for multiple venues per type by creating copies of all the venues of category $T_i$ and treating every copy as a different category. Observe that, for this problem, picking the same venue will not improve the coverage function, while it will increase the cost of the path. Therefore, the algorithm will always prefer to pick new venues.

**Time budget and venue delays:** In practice, users may have an upper bound on the time that they are willing to allocate to their tour, instead of on the distance that they are willing to cover. In this case, we can transform distance into time by multiplying with the appropriate velocity (e.g., walking speed). The pairwise distance between venues can then be measured in time units without affecting our algorithms. In addition, the time-based formulation allows us to consider the expected duration of a visit to a particular venue. For example, a visit to MoMA (Museum of Modern Art) in New York City could last a lot longer than a visit to a small local gallery. Our algorithms can be easily extended to account for this, by adding the temporal cost associated with each venue $v$ to the existing cost of transitioning from $v$ to any other venue $v'$.

**Multiple transportation types:** In practice, the user may have different options from moving from one place to another, e.g., walking, taking a taxi, metro etc. Each such option would incur a different time cost. This can be modeled by considering different types of edges connecting every pair of two venues. Then the dynamic-programming recursions would simply have to iterate over all possible types of edges. This would increase the computational complexity of all the above algorithms by a factor of $L$ — where $L$ is the maximum number of transportation options that can be observed between two nodes.

Table 1: Statistics for the **NYC**, **SF** and **London** datasets.

| | **NYC** | **SF** | **London** |
|---|---|---|---|
| # Check-ins | 322 504 | 91 887 | 47 916 |
| # Venues | 12 728 | 3 903 | 2 740 |

# 4. EXPERIMENTS

Our experiments with real data from `Foursquare` demonstrate the practical utility of our formulations and the corresponding algorithms.

## 4.1 Experimental setup

**The `Foursquare` datasets:** We obtain an initial set of venues using the publicly available dataset of Cheng et al. [13], which includes geo-tagged, user-generated content that was pushed to Twitter's public feed from Sept 2010 to Jan 2011. From this dataset, we select tweets related to `Foursquare` check-ins into popular venues (with at least 10 check-ins). Our final dataset consists of 6 699 516 check-ins.

The classification of venues to types in `Foursquare` is hierarchical. In our experiments, we use the upper level of this classification and thus each one of our venues can belong to one of the following 9 types: *Arts & Entertainment*, *College & University*, *Food*, *Professional & Other Places*, *Nightlife Spots*, *Great Outdoors*, *Shop & Service*, *Travel & Transport* and *Residence*. The original dataset did not include the category information for the venues, so we did the mapping of venues to types by crawling `Foursquare.com`.

From this dataset, we generate three smaller datasets, which correspond to venues in three large cities, New York City (**NYC**), San Francisco (**SF**) and London (**London**). Each one of these datasets contains all the check-ins that took place within a 10-mile radius from the corresponding city center. Table 1 shows the statistics of these datasets.

In all three datasets, we consider the venues that belong to the category *Great Outdoors* to be the attractions/activities that one wants to cover in the COVERINGTOUR problem. Hence, we use the rest 8 categories as the (ordinary) venue types for both the ADDITIVETOUR and COVERINGTOUR problems. For our experiments, we compute a universal relevance score $b(v)$ for every venue $v$. This is computed as the fraction of check-ins for venue $v$ over the total number of check-ins in

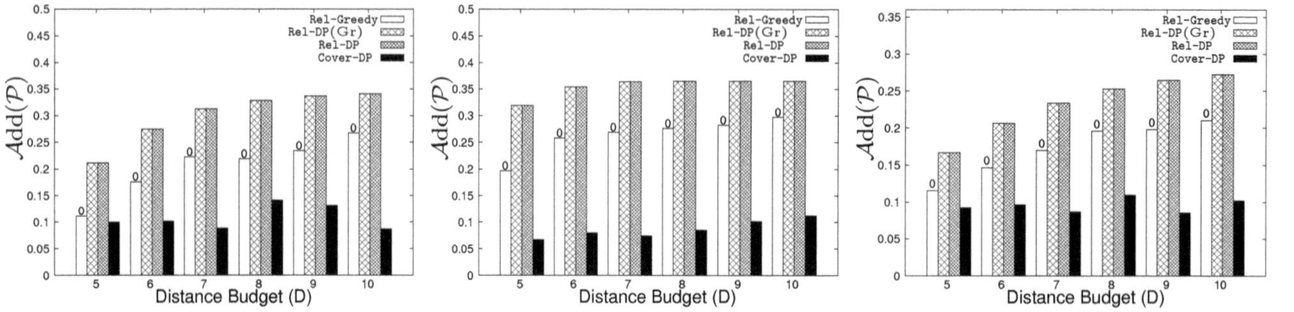


(a) **NYC** (b) **SF** (c) **London**

Figure 2: The value of $\mathcal{A}dd(\mathcal{R})$ for tours $\mathcal{R}$ output by the different algorithms for distance bounds $D \in \{5, 6, 7, 8, 9, 10\}$ (in miles) for all three datasets.

venues of type $T(v)$. Similarly, for venue $v$, we compute the set of nearby activities, denoted by $S(v)$ as the set of venues of type *Greater Outdoors* that are within 1 mile from $v$.

**Baseline heuristics:** We compare our algorithms with a `Greedy` baseline adopted from the operations research literature [29]. This `Greedy` algorithm is iterative: at step $t$, it picks a venue from the $t$-th type $T_t$ in the order $\pi$. More specifically, among all venues $v_t$ in $T_t$ it identifies the four venues with the highest value of the ratio of the objective function divided by the distance $\text{Dist}(v_t, w_{t-1})$, where $w_{t-1}$ is the venue picked at the $t-1$ step. Then one of these four venues is finally chosen at random with probability proportional to the corresponding value of the ratio. The algorithm proceeds until it reaches the destination or it runs out of distance budget. If the algorithm terminates before reaching the destination, it reports a *failure*. In all our experiments, we repeat the above process for 100 times and we report the solution with the highest value of the objective function. We refer to the `Greedy` algorithm that uses the $\mathcal{A}dd$ (resp. $\mathcal{C}ov$) objective as the `Rel-Greedy` (resp. `Cov-Greedy`) algorithm.

## 4.2 Quality evaluation

Using the above set up we evaluate the quality of the various algorithms for solving the AdditiveTour and the CoveringTour problems respectively. When evaluating the quality of our algorithms for AdditiveTour, we measure the $\mathcal{A}dd$ of the proposed tours, while when we evaluate the algorithms for the CoveringTour problem, we measure the $\mathcal{C}ov$ or the output tours. In all cases, higher values of the objective mean better-quality results.

In all the experiments we present we have $L_i = U_i = 1$ for all types. We evaluate our algorithms with regard to the distance budget ($D$) that a user is willing to walk and the number of venue types ($k$) of the requested tour. In all cases the trends are similar: the `Rel-DP` and the `Cover-DP` algorithms are clearly the best algorithms for AdditiveTour and CoveringTour respectively. In addition to giving lower-quality solutions, the `Greedy` heuristics often fail to find a solution, even if one exists.

**Varying the distance budget $D$:** In this experiment, we study the effect of the distance bound $D$ on the results reported by each algorithm. We generate 10 random type orders. Each type order includes 6 (distinct) types chosen randomly from the set of available ordinary types (i.e., $k = 6$). We evaluate our algorithms for each value of $D \in \{5, 6, 7, 8, 9, 10\}$ (in miles) over all generated orders.

Figures 2 and 3 show the average value achieved by the algorithms for the $\mathcal{A}dd$ and $\mathcal{C}ov$ objectives, respectively. Observe that all values are averages over the 10 different type orders. Although the dynamic programming algorithms always report a solution if one exists, the greedy approaches may fail to find a solution. In such cases the reported average is taken over the type orders for which the algorithm successfully reported a tour. The number on top of the bar corresponding to a greedy algorithm represents the number of instances (out of 10) for which the algorithm reported a failure. For a fair comparison, we also report the average value of $\mathcal{A}dd$ achieved by the dynamic programming algorithms over the instances for which the greedy baselines actually found a solution (the `Rel-DP`(Gr) and `Cover-DP`(Gr) bars for the $\mathcal{A}dd$ and $\mathcal{C}ov$ objectives, respectively). The plots also include the $\mathcal{A}dd$ value achieved by `Cover-DP` and the $\mathcal{C}ov$ value achieved by `Rel-DP`. Our goal is to verify that a customized approach is required for each objective function.

As can be seen in Figure 2, `Rel-DP` finds a solutions for all instances and for all values of $D$. The same is also true for `Rel-Greedy` (and hence, `Rel-DP` and `Rel-DP`(Gr) match). However, with respect to the objective function ($\mathcal{A}dd$), `Rel-DP` consistently outperforms `Rel-Greedy`. Another observation is that the optimal benefit (reported by `Rel-DP`) peeks after the distance bound has been sufficiently relaxed, and stops increasing after that point (which differs among cities). The results for the $\mathcal{C}ov$ objective are shown in Figure 3. While the general trends are very similar to the ones we made for $\mathcal{A}dd$, the figure motivates additional observations. First, we observe that `Cov-Greedy` fails to report a solution for a significant number of order types. For example, for the **NYC** dataset, the `Cov-Greedy` failed to find a solution for 5 out of 10 instances for $D = 10$. In fact, `Cov-Greedy` failed to report *any* solutions (e.g., for the $D \in \{5, 6\}$ for **London** or for $D = 5$ for Pnyc). Due to this failures, the `Cover-DP` bar differs from the `Cover-DP`(Gr) bar — recall that the latter is the performance of `Cover-DP` over the instances for which `Cov-Greedy` was able to deliver a solution. Nevertheless, in all cases, both `Cover-DP` and `Cover-DP`(Gr) outperform `Cov-Greedy`. This demonstrates the inability of `Cov-Greedy` to leverage the overlap among the sets of attractions covered by the various venues.

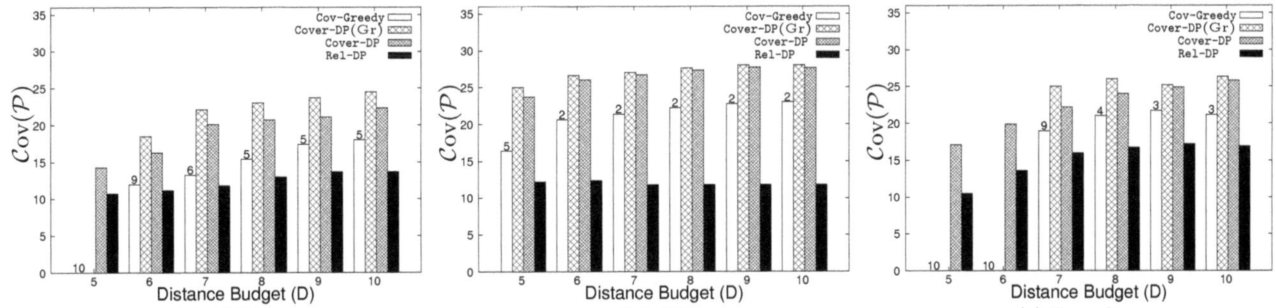


(a) **NYC** (b) **SF** (c) **London**

Figure 3: The value of $\mathcal{C}ov(\mathcal{R})$ for tours $\mathcal{R}$ found by the different algorithms for distance bounds $D \in \{5, 6, 7, 8, 9, 10\}$ (in miles) for all three datasets.

Finally, we observe that `Cover-DP` and `Rel-DP` failed to achieve high values for the objectives functions that they were not customized for ($\mathcal{A}dd$ and $\mathcal{C}ov$ respectively). In fact, they were even outperformed by the greedy baselines in those tasks. This verifies our intuition that both problems are non-trivial, and require customized algorithms.

**Varying the Tour size $k$:** In this experiment, we evaluate the effect of the size of the tour $k$ (i.e., the number of venue types in the tour) on the performance of the algorithms. We set $D = 6$ miles, and generate 10 random permutations of $k$ (distinct) types, for $k \in \{2, 3, 4, 5, 6, 7, 8\}$, emulating the process that we followed in the previous experiment. The results for the **NYC** dataset for both the $\mathcal{A}dd$ and $\mathcal{C}ov$ objectives are shown in Figure 4.[3]

The `Rel-DP` and `Cover-DP` algorithms outperform the greedy baselines for the $\mathcal{A}dd$ and $\mathcal{C}ov$ objectives, respectively. This demonstrates that our algorithms are able to include additional venues and improve their respective objectives, while respecting the distance bound. On the other hand, the values of the greedy approaches may only increase trivially or even decrease, as $k$ becomes larger and more types are added to the tour. In fact, for the $\mathcal{C}ov$ objective, `Cov-Greedy` often fails to find a solution, especially for larger values of $k$.

**Binning of distances:** As we have already discussed in Section 3, the running time of both the `Rel-DP` and `Cover-DP` depends on the granularity of the bins that we use to break the distance budget $D$. We expect that finer granularity gives better results in terms of the objective functions, yet is computationally more expensive. Tables 2 and 3 show the values of the objective functions $\mathcal{A}dd(\mathcal{R})$ and $\mathcal{C}ov(\mathcal{R})$ as well as the corresponding running times of the `Rel-DP` and the `Cover-DP` algorithms for bins of sizes $b = 0.1$ and $b = 0.01$ miles. For the results reported here we set $D = 10$. From the two tables we observe that bins of size 0.1 of miles achieve the same values of the objectives while they result in 10 times faster algorithms. Observe that the running time of `Cover-DP` is larger than the running time of `Rel-DP`. The reason for that is that the former needs to evaluate a more complex objective — which in every step requires the evaluation of the intersection of two sets: the set of already-covered activities and the activities introduced by any newly-considered venue.

[3]The results for the other two datasets were very similar and omitted due to space constraints as well.

Table 2: Value of $\mathcal{A}dd(\mathcal{R})$ and running times achieved by `Rel-DP` for bin sizes $b = 0.1$ or 0.01 miles and $D = 10$ miles.

| | $\mathcal{A}dd(\mathcal{R})$ | | Running time (ms) | |
|---|---|---|---|---|
| | $b = 0.01$ | $b = 0.1$ | $b = 0.01$ | $b = 0.1$ |
| **London** | 0.27 | 0.27 | 976.9 | 103.7 |
| **SF** | 0.36 | 0.36 | 1176.7 | 125.4 |
| **NYC** | 0.34 | 0.34 | 1072.5 | 139.3 |

Table 3: Value of $\mathcal{C}ov(\mathcal{R})$ and running times achieved by `Rel-DP` for bin sizes $b = 0.1$ or 0.01 miles and $D = 10$ miles.

| | $\mathcal{C}ov(\mathcal{R})$ | | Running time (ms) | |
|---|---|---|---|---|
| | $b = 0.01$ | $b = 0.1$ | $b = 0.01$ | $b = 0.1$ |
| **London** | 24.7 | 24.7 | 4587.6 | 384.8 |
| **SF** | 26.5 | 26.5 | 6596.1 | 547.6 |
| **NYC** | 21.3 | 21.3 | 4612.8 | 445.5 |

## 4.3 Anecdotal evaluation

Here, we use visualization in order to provide some further insight on the tours output by the different algorithms as solutions to the AdditiveTour and CoveringTour problems. Due to lack of space we show here the results for a request of a tour in London — results in other cities convey similar intuition. The query we consider requires a tour of size $k = 4$ (i.e., four venue types) and the input type order is $\pi = \{1, 3, 6, 5\}$, where types *1,3,6,5* correspond to the `Foursquare` types *"Arts & Entertainment"*, "*Food*", "*Shop & Services*" and "*Nightlife Spot*" respectively. For the results we report here we assume that both the starting and the ending point of the tour is London's city center.

Solving the AdditiveTour problem for London with a distance bound $D = 6$ miles, gives the tours presented on the maps at Figure 5; `Rel-DP` reports the solution depicted on the left, while `Rel-Greedy` reports the solution on the right. The point labeled "0" is the starting and ending point of the tour, while the red point-marks correspond to the venues recommended and are labeled with their type number. We also report the total benefit obtained from the two algorithms (top left corner of each map), and the benefit of each individual venue. While both tours begin with the

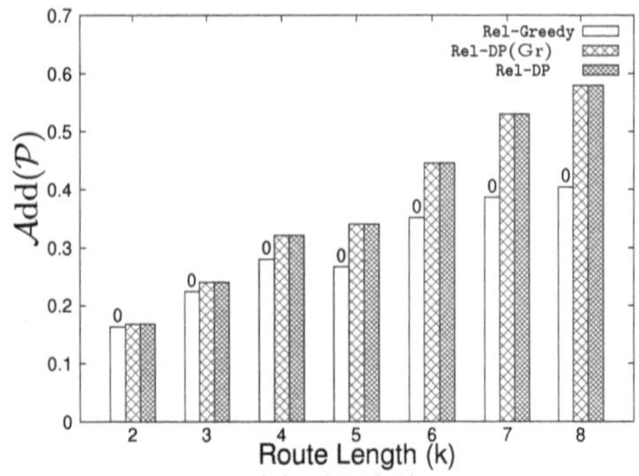


(a) $\mathcal{A}dd(\mathcal{R})$

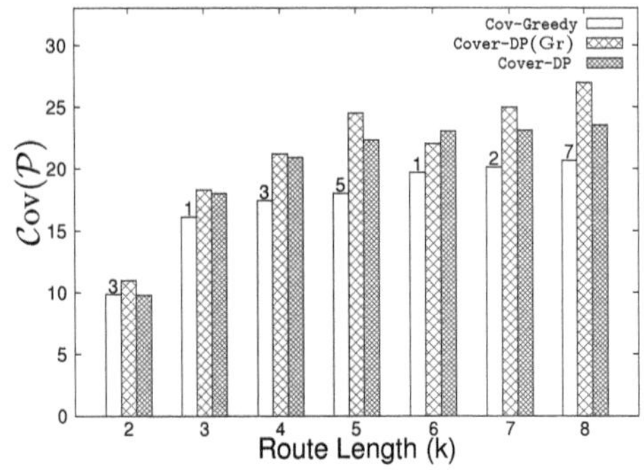


(b) $\mathcal{C}ov(\mathcal{R})$

Figure 4: The $\mathcal{A}dd(\mathcal{R})$ and $\mathcal{C}ov(\mathcal{R})$ for tours $\mathcal{R}$ output by the different algorithms for the **NYC** dataset and varying the tour size $k \in \{2, 3, 4, 5, 6, 7, 8\}$.

same venue (the Tate Museum of Modern Arts),[4] they proceed to include different venues, thus leading to different $\mathcal{A}dd$ values. In fact, the value achieved by `Rel-DP` is almost two times greater than that achieved by `Rel-Greedy`.

Solving the CoveringTour problem for London with the same parameters gives the tours presented on the maps at Figure 6. `Cover-DP` reports the solution depicted on the left, while `Cov-Greedy` reports the solution on the right. We now present with a dotted circle centered at each venue, the area that the latter *covers* with respect to locales of type "Greater Outdoors", which as aforementioned are the attractions for our CoveringTour problem. Furthermore, the actual attractions covered are shown on the map as blue mark-points. As one can see, the tours that are provided by the two algorithms are completely different in this case. For instance, `Cover-DP` recommends Alice to start her tour from the British Museum, while `Cov-Greedy` recommends the Tate Museum of Modern Arts. However, again `Cover-DP` clearly outperforms `Cov-Greedy`, since the number of "blue nodes" covered by the former is 20, as compared to the 14 attractions covered by the `Cov-Greedy`.

## 5. RELATED WORK

The proliferation of location-based systems has given rise to literature on spatial recommendations, which is clearly relevant to our work. Related to our study are also combinatorial problems that deal with finding tours on graphs. We review this work below.

**Spatial recommendations:** The rapid proliferation of location-based social networks has motivated a volume of work that focuses on methods for personalized location (or venue) recommendations [8, 25, 33] to social-network users. These methods, deploy collaborative-filtering techniques [33], geometric embeddings [8] or they even incorporate features present in the users' social network [25] in order to associate every venue with a score, which encodes the probability of a user liking (or visiting) a particular venue recommendation. Contrary to our own work, all these approaches evaluate each venue independently of the rest. Thus, venues are not considered as groups or as stops in a tour and therefore thematic redundancy or spatiotemporal constraints cannot be taken into consideration. This is the key difference between our work and all these described above.

Motivated by the limitation of the above methods, recent work has focused on recommending *tours* of locations. For instance, De Choudhury et al. [14] focus on segmenting streams of spatiotemporally tagged photos into paths, and then assembling these paths into itineraries. Similar works are those by Kurashima et al. [24] and Yoon et al. [34], who utilize spatiotemporal traces (e.g., photo streams, GPS trajectories) to recommend spatiotemporally affordable tours In addition to being applicable only in the presence of training sequences of spatiotemporally tagged photographs (or other similar traces), these approaches cannot handle multiple types of venues that cater to different user needs. This limitation is also shared by the relevant works on interactive tour recommendation [27, 18, 23], which iteratively personalize or improve a tour based on user feedback. Clearly, by not allowing for venues of multiple types, all of these approaches can also not support the user's requirement to satisfy her needs in a particular order.

The support for multiple types of venues is considered by Ardissono et al. [5]. However, the proposed system expects the user to *manually* select a venue from each desired type. A tour traversing the selected venues is then proposed. Finally, in a recent demo paper, Xie et al. [32] describe a single-type system for tour-recommendations, and briefly describe how this could be extended to handle multiple types. The proposed method is not comparable to ours, since it does not allow the user to specify the order in which the user wants to visit the different types. In addition, even though no experimental evaluation is provided, the authors suggest that multiple venues can be combined to form a spatiotemporally efficient tour via a simple greedy approach. However, our experiments on real data demonstrate the inadequacies of the greedy approach in practical scenarios.

Further, approaches that focus on reconstructing and recommending routes based on existing location trajectories (e.g., [31, 12]) are complementary to our work; the output of our methods can be used as input to such approaches.

**Tours in operations research:** At a high level, there is a connection between our problems and the orienteering problem (OP) [30] studied in operations-research and theoretical computer science. In OP the input consists of a set of locations with an associated benefit for each location, and a cost for the traversal of an edge between two locations. The goal is to visit a set of locations such that the benefit is maximized, while the total distance covered is within a bound $D_{max}$. The first difference between our problem and

[4]We defer from mentioning commercial venues for the rest of the types.

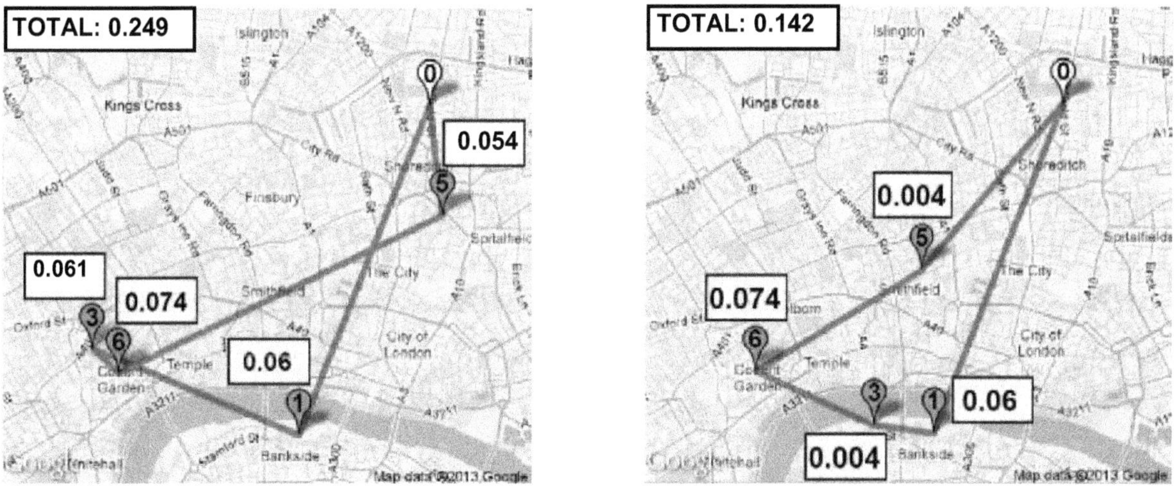


(a) `Cover-DP` (b) `Cov-Greedy`

Figure 5: Anecdotal results for the **London** dataset when tours are obtained as solutions to the AdditiveTour problem; distance budget $D = 6$ miles, $\pi = \{$*Arts & Entertainment (1), Food (3), Shop & Services (6), Nightlife Spot (5)*$\}$.

the OP is that our locations (which we call venues) are associated with types, and only a certain number of each type can be included in the tour. In addition, the user-specified ordering constraints over these types are also absent from OP. Thus, the OP-specific heuristics [11, 21, 28] are not directly applicable to our problem.

The connection between our problems and the Traveling Salesman Problem (TSP) [4] and its prize-collecting versions [7, 9] is equally abstract. The TSP problem considers a set of cities and distances between them and asks for the shortest possible tour that visits each city exactly ones and returns to the original city. The prize-collecting version of the same problem assumes that there is a benefit associated with visiting every city and the goal is to maximize the total benefit by visiting cities, divided by the total distance covered by the tour. The consideration of multiple venue types, the ordering constraints and the freedom to not visit all the venues (but only some from every type) make our problems distinct from all the above formulations. Moreover, the CoveringTour version of our problem is very distinct from any prize-collecting problem that has appeared in relevant literature, since the benefit induced by every venue does not depend solely on the venue itself, but also on the rest of the venues included in the tour. In short, the existing algorithms for the different TSP versions are not applicable for solving the problems that we study in our work.

**Travel package recommendations:** Tangential to the spatial recommendation problems, is that of travel package recommendations, where the goal is to recommend vacation packages (i.e., destination, hotels and organized activities). Although these studies (e.g., [20]) also fall into the general realm of - group - recommendation systems, they are distinct from our work. First, their focus is on creating combinatorial packages that satisfy different constraints, rather than on the concept of creating ordered routes which is essential to our work. We consider such systems to be complementary to ours: once a user is in a given urban area, possibly picked by one of the package-recommendation approaches discussed above, our work provides a system that is able to provide a customized tour based on her preferences.

# 6. CONCLUSIONS

We have presented two alternative instantiations of a framework for generating customized tour recommendations as a paradigm of an intelligent urban navigation service. The first one, AdditiveTour, assigns a benefit to each location and retrieves the sequence of venues with the maximum total benefit, constrained by a given distance budget and a preferred visitation order for the types of venues in the tour. The second formulation, CoveringTour, assigns to each venue a set of associated attractions *covered* by it (i.e., are within range). The goal is to maximize the total number of attractions covered, under the same set of constraints. We study the complexity of these problems and provide efficient algorithmic solutions. Furthermore, we evaluate our methods on a large dataset from `Foursquare`, the largest location-based social network to date. The results demonstrate the practical utility of the proposed formulations and the efficacy of the proposed algorithms.

## Acknowledgments

This research was partially funded by NSF grants III 1218437 and CAREER 1253393 and gifts from Microsoft and Google.

# 7. REFERENCES

[1] Foursquare as a recommendation engine: https://foursquare.com/about/.
[2] United nations-world urbanization prospects: The 2011 revision – highlights: http://esa.un.org/unup.
[3] A. M. W. Alan A. Lew, C. Michael Hall. *A Companion to Tourism.* Wiley, 2004.
[4] D. Applegate, R. Bixby, V. Chvátal, and W. Cook. *The Traveling Salesman Problem: A Computational Study.* 2006.
[5] L. Ardissono, A. Goy, G. Petrone, M. Segnan, and P. Torasso. Intrigue: Personalized recommendation of tourist attractions for desktop and hand held devices. *Applied Artificial Intelligence*, 17(8-9), 2003.

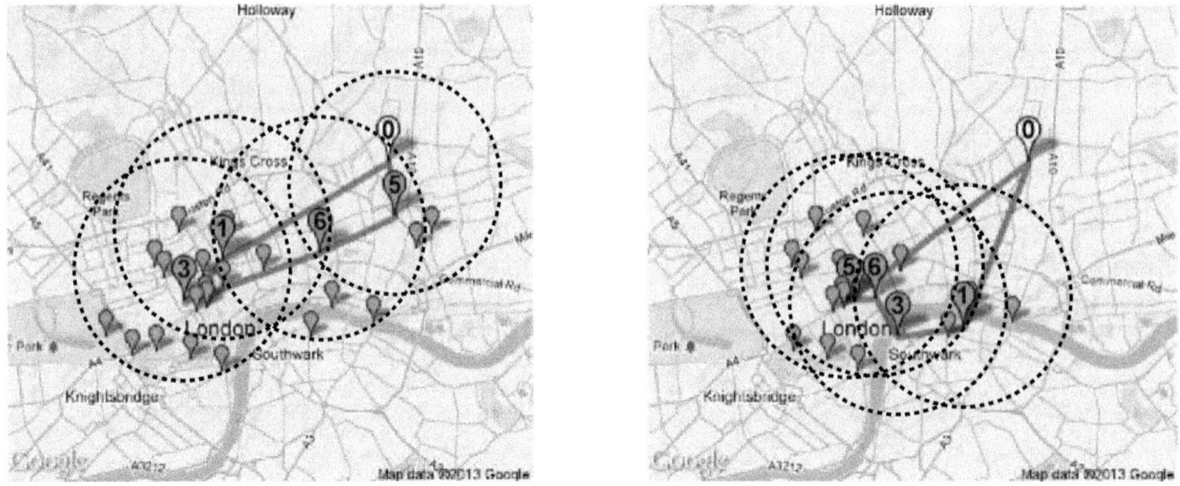


(a) `Cover-DP` (b) `Cov-Greedy`

Figure 6: Anecdotal results for the **London** dataset when tours are obtained as solutions to the CoveringTour problem; distance budget $D = 6$ miles, $\pi = \{$*Arts & Entertainment (1), Food (3), Shop & Services (6), Nightlife Spot (5)*$\}$.


[6] J. Bao, Y. Zheng, and M. Mokbel. Location-based and preference-aware recommendation using sparse geo-social networking data. In *ACM SIGSPATIAL GIS*, 2012.

[7] R. Bar-Yehuda, G. Even, and S. Shahar. On approximating a geometric prize-collecting traveling salesman problem with time windows. *Journal of Algorithms*, 55(1), 2005.

[8] B. Berjani and T. Strufe. A recommendation system for spots in location-based online social networks. In *SNS*, 2011.

[9] D. Bienstock, M. X. Goemans, D. Simchi-Levi, and D. P. Williamson. A note on the prize collecting traveling salesman problem. *Math. Program.*, 59, 1993.

[10] C. Chekuri and A. Kumar. Maximum coverage problem with group budget constraints and applications. In *APPROX-RANDOM*, 2004.

[11] C. Chekuri and M. Pál. A recursive greedy algorithm for walks in directed graphs. *IEEE FOCS*, 2005.

[12] Z. Chen, H. Chen, X. Zhou, Y. Zheng, and X. Xie. Searching trajectories by locations: An efficiency study. In *ACM SIGMOD*, 2010.

[13] Z. Cheng, J. Caverlee, K. Lee, and D. Sui. Exploring millions of footprints in location sharing services. In *ICWSM*, 2011.

[14] M. De Choudhury, M. Feldman, S. Amer-Yahia, N. Golbandi, R. Lempel, and C. Yu. Automatic construction of travel itineraries using social breadcrumbs. In *HT*, 2010.

[15] B. Dellaert, A. Borgers, and H. Timmermans. A day in the city: Using conjoint choice experiments to model urban tourists' choice of activity packages. *Tourism Management*, 16(5):347 – 353, 1995.

[16] P. Doherty. Smart cities: How to build sustainable and resilient environments in an increasingly urbanized world. In *McGraw Hill Financial Global Institute White Paper*, 2013.

[17] D.Scott. Exploring time patterns in people's use of a metropolitan park district. In *Leisure Sciences*, 1997.

[18] S. Dunstall, M. Horn, P. Kilby, M. Krishnamoorthy, B. Owens, D. Sier, and S. Thièbaux. An automated itinerary planning system for holiday travel. In *Journal of IT and Tourism*, 2003.

[19] M. Garey and D. S. Johnson. *Computers and Intractability: A Guide to the Theory of NP-Completeness.* W.H. Freeman, 1979.

[20] Y. Ge, Q. Liu, H. Xiong, A. Tuzhilin, and J. Chen. Cost-aware travel tour recommendation. In *KDD*, 2011.

[21] B. Golden, L. Levy, and R. Vohra. The orienteering problem. In *Naval Research Logistics*, 1987.

[22] N. Grinberg, M. Naaman, B. Shaw, and G. Lotan. Extracting diurnal patterns of real world activity from social media. In *AAAI ICWSM*, 2013.

[23] K. Kim, H. Kim, and J. Ryu. Triptip: a trip planning service with tag-based recommendation. In *CHI (Extended abstract)*, 2009.

[24] T. Kurashima, T. Iwata, G. Irie, and K. Fujimura. Travel route recommendation using geotags in photo sharing sites. In *CIKM*, 2010.

[25] A. Noulas, S. Scellato, N. Lathia, and C. Mascolo. A random walk around the city: New venue recommendation in location-based social networks. In *SocialCom*, 2012.

[26] D. G. Pearce. Tourist time-budget. *Annals of Tourism Research*, 15(1):106 – 121, 1988.

[27] S. Roy, G. Das, S. Amer-Yahia, and C. Yu. Interactive itinerary planning. In *ICDE*, 2011.

[28] W. Souffriau, P. Vansteenwegen, J. Vertommen, G. V. Berge, and D. V. Oudheusden. A personalized tourist trip design algorithm for mobile tourist guides. In *Applied Artificial Intelligence*, 2008.

[29] T. Tsiligirides. Heuristic methods applied to orienteering. In *The Journal of Operational Research Society*, 1984.

[30] P. Vansteenwegen, W. Souffriau, and D. V. Oudheusden. The orienteering problem: A survey. In *European Journal of Operational Research*, 2011.

[31] L.-Y. Wei, Y. Zheng, and W.-C. Peng. Constructing popular routes from uncertain trajectories. In *ACM KDD*, 2012.

[32] M. Xie, L. Lakshmanan, and P. Wood. Comprec-trip: a composite recommendation system for travel planning. In *ICDE (demo)*, 2011.

[33] M. Ye, Y. Peifeng, and W.-C. Lee. Location recommendation for location-based social networks. In *SIGSPATIAL GIS*, 2010.

[34] H. Yoon, Y. Zheng, X. Xie, and W. Woo. Social itinerary recommendation from user-generated digital trails. In *Personal and Ubiquitus Computing*, 2012.

# Detecting Cohesive and 2-mode Communities in Directed and Undirected Networks

Jaewon Yang, Julian McAuley, Jure Leskovec
Stanford University
{jayang, jmcauley, jure}@cs.stanford.edu

## ABSTRACT

Networks are a general language for representing relational information among objects. An effective way to model, reason about, and summarize networks, is to discover sets of nodes with common connectivity patterns. Such sets are commonly referred to as *network communities*. Research on network community detection has predominantly focused on identifying communities of densely connected nodes in undirected networks.

In this paper we develop a novel overlapping community detection method that scales to networks of millions of nodes and edges and advances research along two dimensions: the connectivity structure of communities, and the use of edge directedness for community detection. First, we extend traditional definitions of network communities by building on the observation that nodes can be densely interlinked in two different ways: In *cohesive* communities nodes link to each other, while in *2-mode* communities nodes link in a bipartite fashion, where links predominate *between* the two partitions rather than inside them. Our method successfully detects both 2-mode as well as cohesive communities, that may also overlap or be hierarchically nested. Second, while most existing community detection methods treat directed edges as though they were undirected, our method accounts for edge directions and is able to identify novel and meaningful community structures in both directed and undirected networks, using data from social, biological, and ecological domains.

**Categories and Subject Descriptors:** H.2.8 [**Database Management**]: Database Applications – *Data mining*
**General Terms:** Algorithms, theory, experimentation.
**Keywords:** Network communities, Overlapping community detection, 2-mode communities.

## 1. INTRODUCTION

Networks are a powerful way to model relational information among objects from social, natural, and technological domains. Networks can be studied at various levels of resolution ranging from whole networks to individual nodes. Arguably the most useful level of resolution is at the level of groups of nodes. Studying groups of nodes allows us to identify and analyze modules or components of networks. For example, understanding the organization of networks at the level of groups helps us to discover functional roles of proteins in protein-protein interaction networks [36], political factions in a network of bloggers [1], social circles in online social networks [31], or even topics in word association networks [2].

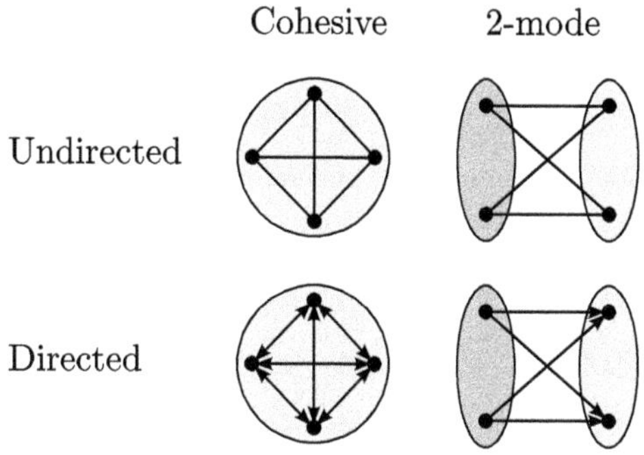


**Figure 1: Two types of networks (directed and undirected) and two types of communities (cohesive and 2-mode). While research has predominantly focused on undirected-cohesive communities (top left), we develop a method that can detect cohesive as well as 2-mode communities in both directed and undirected networks.**

One way to understand networks at the level of groups is to identify sets of nodes with similar connectivity patterns. Traditional methods aim to find network *communities*, which are defined as groups of nodes with many connections among the group's members, but few to the rest of the network [2, 11, 14, 34]. However, dense communities are but one kind of group structure in networks, and there may be other structures that help us to understand networks better. For example, consider a Twitter follower network and the "community" of candidates in the 2012 U.S. presidential election. This community is not densely interlinked, in the sense that the candidates do not follow each other; thus we would not be able to find this community if we were to use traditional methods that search for densely connected sets of nodes. However, such communities can be identified because they form around nodes whose edges have similar endpoints. Continuing our example, presidential candidates form a community in Twitter not because they follow each other but because a common set of "fans" follows them.

Thus communities can be characterized by the connectivity structure between the members *and also* by the connectivity structure of the members to the rest of the network. We refer to these communities as *2-mode communities*. For example, in case of "fans" linking to "celebrities" members of a community may be linked to the same set of endpoints, even if they do not link to each other. Similar examples also exist beyond social networks; for example, in protein-protein interaction networks, some protein complexes act


*WSDM'14*, February 24–28, 2014, New York, New York, USA.
Copyright 2014 ACM 978-1-4503-2351-2/14/02 ...$15.00.
http://dx.doi.org/10.1145/2556195.2556243.

as bridges or regulators, *i.e.*, they do not interact among themselves but regulate/interact with the same set of proteins [36].

Another common assumption made by many present community detection methods is that networks are *undirected* [34, 43]. This implies that relationships between connected nodes are symmetric or reciprocal. However, in directed networks relationships are asymmetric, as with our previous example about "fans" who follow "celebrities". Even though methods can often be adapted to handle directed networks, this is often done in an ad-hoc fashion (*e.g.*, by treating directed edges as though they were undirected) and can lead to unexpected or undesirable results [14, 26, 39]. Moreover, by ignoring edge directedness important information may be lost, especially if relationships are predominantly non-reciprocal as in predator-prey networks [26] or in social networks like Twitter.

**Present work: Detecting cohesive and 2-mode communities in directed and undirected networks.** Here we consider new notions of community linking structure that go beyond thinking of communities as internally well-connected sets of nodes. Our work stems from social network literature on structural equivalence [9], where it has been noted that social homogeneity (*i.e.*, social communities) arises not only between nodes that link to each other (*i.e.*, *internal group connectivity*), but also between nodes that link to the rest of the network in a coordinated way (*i.e.*, *external group connectivity*). In particular, we consider different notions of "communities" that are depicted in Figure 1. We differentiate between *cohesive* communities (Fig. 1, Cohesive) and *2-mode* communities (Fig. 1, 2-mode) where nodes link in a bipartite fashion with links predominantly appearing between partitions rather than inside them.

While existing community detection methods typically focus on Undirected-Cohesive or Directed-Cohesive communities [11, 14, 26, 34, 43], the focus of our paper is on developing methods that can detect communities of all four different types depicted in Figure 1. By modeling each of these definitions in concert, we are able to capture the complex structure present in networks.

**Present work: Communities through Directed Affiliations.** We present *CoDA (Communities through Directed Affiliations)*, a method for overlapping community detection that scales to networks with millions of nodes and tens of millions of edges. CoDA exhibits the following three properties: (1) It naturally detects both cohesively connected as well as 2-mode communities. (2) CoDA allows cohesive and 2-mode communities to overlap or be hierarchically nested. (3) CoDA naturally allows for community detection in directed as well as undirected networks.

We develop our community detection method by first presenting a generative model of networks where edges arise from affiliations of nodes to cohesive and 2-mode communities. Then we fit the model to a given network and thus discover communities.

Our model starts with a bipartite affiliation graph [25, 43, 45, 47], where nodes of the underlying network represent one 'layer' of the bipartite graph and communities represent the other. Edges between network-nodes and community-nodes in the affiliation graph represent memberships of nodes to communities. However, our approach has a simple but critical innovation: while memberships of nodes to communities have previously been modeled as undirected, we model the memberships as *directed*.

Though simple on the surface, this modification leads to substantial changes in the modeling capability of affiliation network models. In particular, a directed affiliation between a node and a community models whether the node *sends* or *receives* (or both) links to other members of the community. Directed affiliations allow us to simultaneously model cohesive as well as 2-mode communities. In cohesive communities node affiliations are bidirectional (a node both sends *and* receives links from other members); 2-mode communities are modeled with unidirectional memberships where some members mostly send/create links (*i.e.*, fans) while others mostly receive them (*i.e.*, celebrities).

Having defined the node-community affiliation model we then develop a method to fit the model to a given network. Our model fitting procedure builds on that of the BigCLAM community detection method [45]. Although we solve a more complex problem than BigCLAM (*i.e.*, we find both 2-mode as well as cohesive communities), we employ similar approximation techniques. Until recently, methods for overlapping community detection could only process networks with up to around 10,000 nodes [16]. In contrast, CoDA can easily handle networks that are two orders of magnitude larger: millions of nodes, tens of millions of edges. Moreover, CoDA can be easily parallelized which further increases the scalability.

**Present work: Experimental results.** We evaluate CoDA on a number of networks from various domains. We consider social, biological, communication, and ecological networks. We test CoDA on networks with explicitly labeled ground-truth communities [31, 44] as well as on networks where communities can be manually examined.

Experiments demonstrate that CoDA's ability to detect 2-mode as well as cohesive communities leads to improved performance over the existing state-of-the-art. For example, when detecting social circles in the Google+ online social network, CoDA gives a relative improvement in accuracy of 36% over Link clustering [2] (28% over MMSB [3], 25% over clique percolation [34] and 21% over DEMON [11]).

More importantly, CoDA facilitates novel discoveries about the community structure of networks. For example, we find that 2-mode communities in foodwebs of predatory relations between organisms correspond to groups of predators who rely on similar groups of prey. Interestingly we find that in scientific paper citation networks, protein-protein interaction networks, as well as web graphs, the majority of detected communities are 2-mode. However, in social networks where edges signify reciprocal friendships, cohesive communities are more frequent. In Twitter or Google+, where relationships are asymmetric, 2-mode communities represent a significant portion of the network (20% in Twitter and 30% in Google+).

**Further related work.** While there exist a number of different definitions of network communities [14], traditionally, communities have been thought of as densely connected sets of nodes [2, 12, 34, 37]. In contrast, the notion of structural equivalence suggests that nodes with similar connectivity patterns may be considered a community even if they do not link to each other [9, 17, 23]. Our work here builds on both notions of network communities and attempts to resolve them by using a single, unified model.

Detecting communities of densely connected sets of nodes is an extensively researched area [14, 30, 35, 42] with a plethora of different algorithms and heuristics. For example, separate methods have been proposed for detecting communities in undirected networks that are disjoint [4, 13, 21, 38, 40], overlapping [3, 6, 11, 34, 43], or hierarchically nested [2, 44]. On the other hand, detection of 2-mode communities has been much less researched. An exception here is *Trawling* [23], which is a method for extracting 2-mode communities in large directed networks. The critical difference with our work here is that Trawling only identifies *complete* bipartite subgraphs of a given directed network. In contrast, our method is able to identify cohesive as well as bipartite communities in directed as well as undirected networks.

Conceptually CoDA is related to existing work on *block models*, which are in principle capable of detecting cohesive as well as 2-mode communities [3, 16, 18]. Our work differs from such approaches in terms of how communities overlap and are hierarchically nested. We also emphasize the scalability of CoDA compared to these approaches.

CoDA is an example of an affiliation network model [25, 43, 45, 47]. While existing affiliation network models can only model undirected cohesive communities, the crucial difference here is our ability to model *directed* networks and *2-mode* communities.

The rest of the paper is organized as follows. Section 2 defines the affiliation network model and Section 3 discusses the model fitting procedure. We present experimental results in Sections 4 and 5, and conclude in Section 6.

## 2. DIRECTED COMMUNITY AFFILIATIONS

We start by presenting a stochastic generative model of networks in which the probability of an edge appearing between a pair of nodes depends on the community affiliations of thise nodes. We then develop an efficient model fitting procedure which allows for detecting community affiliations of nodes in a given network.

We describe our model in the context of directed networks and then show how it can straightforwardly be adapted to undirected networks. Our model builds upon BigCLAM, an affiliation model for overlapping network communities [45]. However, whereas BigCLAM focuses on finding only *cohesive* communities in *undirected* networks, our work here aims to find 2-mode communities *as well as* cohesive communities in both directed and undirected networks.

**Directed Affiliation Network Model.** We begin with the intuition that a desirable model of communities in directed networks should exhibit two properties. First, communities should be modeled not only in terms of their internal connectivity, but also in terms how members connect to non-members. Second, the model should account for asymmetries, *i.e.*, directedness, of edges between nodes. We later demonstrate that accounting for these two properties is important. Perhaps surprisingly, our method gives improved performance even when modeling communities in *undirected* networks. This is due to the fact that when edge directions are not explicit, relationships in the network may still be (implicitly) asymmetric, and identifying such asymmetries leads to improved performance.

We proceed by formulating a simple conceptual model of networks that we refer to as a *Directed Affiliation Network Model*. Our work builds on a family of affiliation network models [8], however, existing affiliation models are typically designed to handle cohesive communities in undirected networks [25, 43, 45, 47]; here we extend such models in order to capture cohesive as well as 2-mode communities in directed as well as undirected networks.

To represent node community memberships, we consider a bipartite affiliation graph where the nodes of the network (bottom layer) connect to communities (top layer) to which they belong (Figure 2(a)). Edges of the underlying network (Figure 2(b)) then arise due to shared community affiliations of nodes.

Consider for a moment an undirected network; when a node belongs to a community in such a network it typically means that the node has (undirected) edges to other members of the community. This type of community affiliation can be modeled using a bipartite graph of nodes and communities where undirected affiliations are formed between nodes and communities [25, 43, 45, 47].

In directed networks, however, we need a richer notion of community affiliation (Figure 2(a)): a node may *create* edges *to* other members of a community, and it also *receive* edges *from* other members of the community, or both. Therefore, we assume that nodes in directed networks can have two "types" of community affiliation: "Outgoing" affiliations from nodes to communities mean that in the network the node *sends* edges to other members of the community. And, "incoming" affiliations from communities to nodes mean that nodes *receive* edges from other community members. We model this using *directed* memberships between nodes and communities: outgoing memberships and incoming memberships.

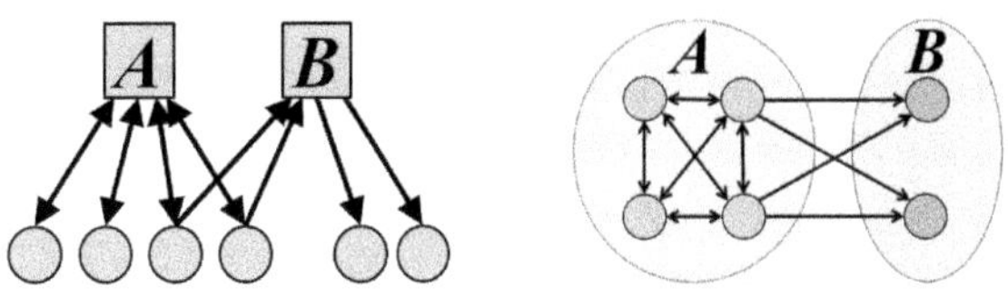


(a) Node community affiliations (b) Network $G$

**Figure 2: (a) Directed node community affiliation graph. Squares: communities, Circles: nodes of network $G$. Affiliations from nodes to communities indicate that nodes *create* edges to other members in those communities, while affiliations from communities to nodes indicate that nodes *receive* edges from others. Community $A$ is cohesive, while $B$ is a 2-mode community. (b) Network $G$ corresponding to model in (a).**

Formally, we denote a bipartite affiliation graph as $B(V, C, M)$, where $V$ is the set of nodes of the underlying network $G$, $C$ the set of communities, and $M$ a set of directed edges connecting nodes $V$ and communities $C$. An outgoing membership edge of node $u \in V$ to community $c \in C$ is denoted as $(u, c) \in M$ and, and an incoming membership is denoted as $(c, u) \in M$.

Now, given the affiliation graph $B(V, C, M)$, we need to specify a process that generates the edges $E$ of the underlying directed network $G(V, E)$. To this end we consider a simple parameterization where we assign a single parameter $p_c$ to every community $c \in C$. The parameter $p_c$ models the probability of a directed edge forming from a member node $u$ with an *outgoing* membership to community $c$ to another member $v$ of $c$ with an *incoming* membership. In other words, we generate a directed edge between a pair of nodes with probability $p_c$ if they are connected in $B$ with a 2-step directed path via community $c$. Each community $c$ creates edges independently. However, if two nodes are connected by more than one community, duplicate edges are not included in the graph $G(V, E)$.

DEFINITION 1 (DIRECTED AFFILIATION NETWORK MODEL). *Let $B(V, C, M)$ be a directed bipartite graph where $V$ is a set of nodes, $C$ is a set of communities, and $M$ is a set of directed edges between $V$ and $C$. Also, let $\{p_c\}$ be a set of probabilities for all $c \in C$. Given $B(V, C, M)$ and $\{p_c\}$, the model generates a directed graph $G(V, E)$ by creating a directed edge $(u, v)$ from node $u \in V$ to node $v \in V$ with probability $p(u, v)$:*

$$p(u, v) = 1 - \prod_{k \in C_{uv}} (1 - p_k), \tag{1}$$

*where $C_{uv} \subset C$ is a set of communities through which $u$ has a 2-step directed path to $v$ ($C_{uv} = \{c|(u, c), (c, v) \in M\}$). If $C_{uv} = \varnothing$ then we set $p(u, v) = 1/|V|$.*

Our Directed Affiliation Network Model and the underlying generated network are illustrated in Figure 3. Directed affiliations are able to explain the overlapping nature of cohesive as well as 2-mode communities. For example, imagine a Twitter network among a community of music fans ($A$), a community of movie fans ($B$),

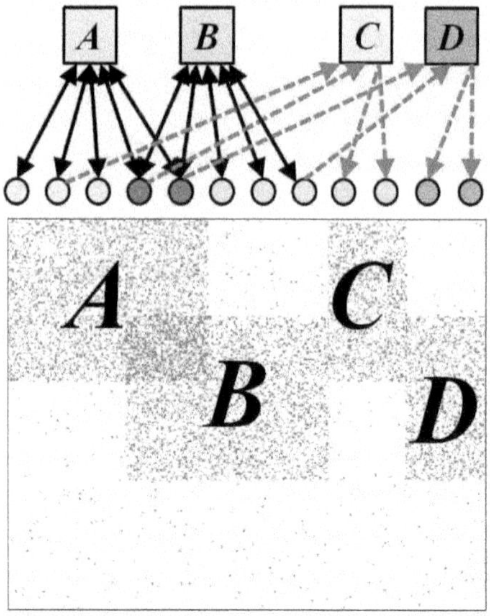


**Figure 3: Affiliation graph (top) of the Directed Affilation Network Model that corresponds to the network adjacency matrix (bottom). It contains two overlapping cohesive ($A$, $B$) and two overlapping 2-mode ($C$, $D$) communities. Black edges in the affiliation graph denote bidirectional community memberships and red edges denote unidirectional memberships.**

a group of famous singers ($C$), and a group of famous actors ($D$). Members in communities $A$ and $B$ build bi-directional social relationships inside their respective communities. Some nodes may belong to both communities $A$ and $B$ as they are interested in both movies and music. As for one-directional relationships, we can easily see that music fans would follow singers ($C$) and movie fans would follow actors ($D$). Together, these relations would form the adjacency matrix at the bottom of Figure 3. Our model captures this complex community structure very naturally, as shown in the community affiliation graph above the adjacency matrix, where green nodes represent music fans ($A$), blue nodes are movie fans ($B$), red nodes are fans of both movies and music, ivory nodes are singers ($C$), and purple nodes are actors ($D$). Affiliations between nodes and cohesive communities $A$ and $B$ flow in both directions because members of those communities have reciprocal relationships with each other, whereas fans and celebrities belonging to 2-mode communities $C$ and $D$ have edges flowing in only one direction (fans follow celebrities, celebrities are followed by fans).

More generally, our model has two important advantages over existing approaches [25, 43, 45, 47]: First, CoDA can model natural overlaps between communities. It has been shown that community affiliation models for undirected networks [43] can model community overlaps accurately, which traditional models of overlapping communities fail to capture [2, 3, 34]. The model also captures realistic community overlaps because its modeling power *generalizes* that of other community affiliation models for undirected networks, *i.e.*, CoDA can model overlaps between cohesive communities *in addition to* 2-mode communities. The second advantage of our model is its ability to model 2-mode communities. By modeling such communities, we can better capture the interaction between groups of nodes. This is a significant improvement over current methods that model only interactions *within* communities.

# 3. COMMUNITY DETECTION

Given an unlabeled, directed network $G(V, E)$, our goal is to identify cohesive as well as 2-mode communities. We achieve this by fitting our *Directed Affiliation Network Model* to $G(V, E)$, *i.e.*, by finding an affiliation graph $B$ and parameters $\{p_c\}$ that maximize the data likelihood. For now, we assume that the number of communities $K$ is given; we will later discuss how to automatically determine $K$. We aim to solve the following Maximum Likelihood Estimation problem:

$$\underset{P,\{p_c\}}{\text{argmax}} \sum_{(u,v)\in E} \log p(u,v) + \sum_{(u,v)\notin E} \log(1 - p(u,v)), \quad (2)$$

where the edge probability $p(u, v)$ is defined in Eq. 1.

Eq. 2 leads to a challenging optimization problem. Specifically, it involves a combinatorial search over all possible affiliation graphs $B$ [43]. Therefore, we develop an approximate algorithm for optimizing Eq. 2. We achive this by relaxing the original problem by changing binary memberships into real-valued memberships.

We build on the intuition from the BigCLAM [45] optimization procedure and begin by introducing variables to represent the memberships of the nodes. As noted earlier, we distinguish nodes' incoming memberships and outgoing memberships. In particular, let $M_{uc}$ indicate whether the node $u$ belongs to community $c$ with an outgoing membership, and $L_{vc}$ indicate whether node $v$ has an incoming membership for $c$. Now Eq. 1 can be represented as:

$$p(u,v) = 1 - \prod_{c\in C_{uv}} (1 - p_c) = 1 - \prod_c (1 - p_c)^{M_{uc}L_{vc}},$$

By applying the change of variables $1 - p_c = \exp(-\alpha_c)$ with $\alpha_c \geq 0$, the equation becomes linear in $M$, $L$, and $\alpha_c$:

$$p(u,v) = 1 - \exp(-\sum_c M_{uc}\alpha_c L_{vc}).$$

We then further simplify the equation by letting $\tilde{M}_{uc} = \sqrt{\alpha_c} M_{uc}$ and $\tilde{L}_{vc} = \sqrt{\alpha_c} L_{vc}$.

$$p(u,v) = 1 - \exp(-\sum_c \tilde{M}_{uc}\tilde{L}_{vc}).$$

So far, we have not used any approximations and the problem is still combinatorial since the variables remain restricted: $\tilde{M}_{uc} \in \{\sqrt{\alpha_c}, 0\}$ and $\tilde{L}_{vc} \in \{\sqrt{\alpha_c}, 0\}$.

However, note that we can interpret $\tilde{M}_{uc}$ as the strength of the membership of node $u$ to community $c$. Thus the condition $\tilde{M}_{uc} \in \{\sqrt{\alpha_c}, 0\}$ simply means that if node $u$ belongs to $c$, it would be connected to other member nodes in $c$ with the factor $\sqrt{\alpha_c}$, which determines $p_c$. The same argument also applies to $\tilde{L}_{vc}$.

Now we replace $\tilde{M}_{uc}$ and $\tilde{L}_{vc}$ with *nonnegative continuous* valued memberships $F_{uc}$ and $H_{vc}$, respectively. The advantage here is that now each node can pick the "strength" of its membership to a given community: A high value of $F_{uc}$ means that the node $u$ has many outgoing edges towards other members of $c$, while high $H_{vc}$ means that node $v$ has many incoming edges from other members of $c$. Now we ca write:

$$p(u,v) = 1 - \exp(-F_u H_v^T).$$

And we transformed Eq. 2 into a continuous optimization problem:

$$\{\hat{F}, \hat{H}\} = \underset{F,H\geq 0}{\text{argmax}}\, l(F, H) \quad (3)$$

where

$$l(F,H) = \sum_{(u,v)\in E} \log(1 - \exp(-F_u H_v^T)) - \sum_{(u,v)\notin E} F_u H_v^T.$$

In other words, in order to detect network communities we fit our model by estimating non-negative affiliation matrices $\hat{F}, \hat{H} \in \mathbb{R}^{N \times K}$ that maximize the likelihood $l(F, H) = \log P(G|F, H)$.

**Solving the optimization problem.** To solve the problem in Eq. 3, we adopt a block coordinate ascent approach: We update $F_u$ for each $u$ with $H$ fixed and update $H_v$ for each $v$ with $F$ fixed, *i.e.*, we update either incoming or outgoing memberships of one node while fixing the other type of memberships. This approach has the advantage that each subproblem of updating $F_u$ and $H_v$ is convex. For brevity we describe only how to update $F_u$. Updating $H_v$ is analogous. For each $u$ we solve:

$$\underset{F_{uc} \geq 0}{\operatorname{argmax}}\, l(F_u), \tag{4}$$

where

$$l(F_u) = \sum_{v \in \mathcal{N}(u)} \log(1 - \exp(-F_u H_v^T)) - \sum_{v \notin \mathcal{N}(u)} F_u H_v^T,$$

where $\mathcal{N}(u)$ is a set of neighbors of $u$. To solve this convex problem, we use projected gradient ascent with the following gradient:

$$\nabla l(F_u) = \sum_{v \in \mathcal{N}(u)} H_v \frac{\exp(-F_u H_v^T)}{1 - \exp(-F_u H_v^T)} - \sum_{v \notin \mathcal{N}(u)} H_v$$

We compute the step size using backtracking line search. After each update, we project $F_u$ into a space of nonnegative vectors by setting $F_{uc} = \max(F_{uc}, 0)$.

Naive computation of $\nabla l(F_u)$ takes time $O(|V|)$. However, we reduce the computational complexity to the *degree* of $u$, $O(|\mathcal{N}(u)|)$, which significantly increases the scalability of our approach. We achieve this by computing the second term $\sum_{v \notin \mathcal{N}(u)} H_v$ in $O(|\mathcal{N}(u)|)$ by storing/caching $\sum_v H_v$:

$$\sum_{v \notin \mathcal{N}(u)} H_v = (\sum_v H_v - H_u - \sum_{v \in \mathcal{N}(u)} H_v).$$

Given that real-world networks are extremely sparse ($|\mathcal{N}(u)| \ll N$), we can update $F_u$ for a single node $u$ in *near-constant* time. The update rule for $H_v$ can be similarly derived and takes near-constant time $O(|\mathcal{N}(v)|)$. In practice, we iteratively update $F_u, H_u$ for each $u$ and stop iterating once the likelihood does not increase (by 0.01%) after we update $F_u, H_u$ for all $u$.

**Determining community affiliations of nodes.** From the real-valued $\hat{F}, \hat{H}$ that we estimate, we want to determine "hard" community affiliations of nodes. We achieve this by thresholding $F_{uc}$ and $H_{uc}$ with a constant $\delta$, *i.e.*, we regard $u$ has an outgoing membership to community $c$ if $F_{uc} \geq \delta$, and an incoming membership from $c$ if $H_{uc} \geq \delta$.

We choose the value of $\delta$ so that every pair of members in community $c$ has edge probability higher than the background edge probability $1/|V|$ (see Eq. 1):

$$\frac{1}{|V|} \leq 1 - \exp(-\delta^2)$$

This inequality leads to $\delta = \sqrt{-\log(1 - 1/|V|)}$. We note that we also experimented with other values of $\delta$ and found that this choice for $\delta$ works well in practice.

**Algorithm initialization.** To initialize $F, H$, we employ *locally minimal neighborhoods*, which provide good seed-sets for community discovery [15]. A neighborhood $N(u)$ of a node $u$ is a set consisting of the node $u$ and its neighbors, and $N(u)$ is said to be "locally minimal" if $N(u)$ has lower conductance score than $N(v)$ for any other neighbor $v$ of $u$ [15]. For a node $u'$ belonging to such a locally minimal neighborhood $k$, we initialize $F_{u'k} = 1$ if $u'$ has an outgoing edge (or $F_{u'k} = 0$ otherwise), and set $H_{u'k} = 1$ if $u'$ has an incoming edge (or $H_{u'k} = 0$ otherwise).

**Choosing the number of communities.** To automatically determine the number of communities $K$, we follow the approach proposed in [3]. We divide all node pairs into 80% training and 20% test set. Varying $K$, we fit CoDA with $K$ communities on the training pairs and measure the likelihood for the test pairs. We then select $K$ with the highest test set likelihood. For a small networks with fewer than 100 edges, we find that a different criterion works better in practice. Here we choose $K$ so as to achieve the smallest value of the Bayesian Information Criterion:

$$BIC(K) = -2l(\hat{F}, \hat{H}) + NK \log |E|.$$

**Parallelization and implementation details.** Our approach also naturally allows for *parallelization*, which further increases scalability of CoDA. When updating $F_u$ for each node $u$ (Eq. 4), we observe that each subproblem is *separable* since all other variables in Eq. 4 ($H$) remain fixed. That is, updating the value of $F_u$ for a specific node $u$ does not affect updates of $F_v$ for all other nodes $v$. In the parallelized version of CoDA, we solve Eq. 4 for multiple nodes in parallel. This parallelization does not affect the final result of the method. Updating $H_u$ for each node $u$ can be parallelized in the same way. As we show in Section 4, parallelization on a single shared memory machine boosts the speed of CoDA by a factor of 20 (the number of threads) used when analyzing a 300,000 node network. Last, we also experimented with other optimization techniques such as the cyclic coordinate descent method (CCD) [19] which optimizes $F_{uc}$ for each $u$ and each $c$ by Newton's method, but we found that block coordinate ascent converges the fastest.

A parallel C++ implementation of CoDA is publicly available at `http://snap.stanford.edu`.

**CoDA for undirected networks.** So far, we have discussed CoDA under the context of directed networks. However, CoDA can easily be applied to undirected networks as well. We make a simple observation: undirected networks model symmetric relationships and thus an undirected relationship is equivalent to two directed relationships, one each way. Thus, given an undirected network, we simply convert the network into a directed one by regarding every edge as reciprocal, and then apply CoDA to detect communities.

Now, CoDA will easily detect cohesive communities in this converted network as edges in cohesive communities are reciprocal. Detecting 2-mode communities is also simple. Consider the case where we are given an undirected 2-mode community $X$ where nodes in group $A$ are connected to nodes in group $B$. Once we convert $X$ into a directed network with reciprocal edges between $A$ and $B$, CoDA will estimate two 2-mode communities from this community $X$: $\hat{X}_1$ for edges from $A$ to $B$, and $\hat{X}_2$ for edges from $B$ to $A$. Thus, CoDA is able to correctly discover $X$, with the caveat that it discovers it twice (both $\hat{X}_1$ and $\hat{X}_2$ correspond to $X$).

## 4. EXPERIMENTS

We evaluate the performance of CoDA and compare it to state-of-the-art community detection methods on a range of directed as well as undirected networks. We measure the quality of community detection by computing the detection accuracy based on gold-standard ground-truth communities. We also evaluate the scalability of the methods by measuring runtime as network size increases.

### 4.1 Dataset Description

We begin by briefly describing the networks that we consider in this study. Overall, we consider 5 undirected and 9 directed net-

| Method | $F_1$ score Google+ | Twitter | Facebook | Jaccard similarity Google+ | Twitter | Facebook | Average |
|---|---|---|---|---|---|---|---|
| MMSB [3] | 0.324 (0.033) | 0.262 (0.005) | 0.374 (0.042) | 0.214 (0.026) | 0.169 (0.004) | 0.266 (0.036) | 0.268 |
| Clique percolation [34] | 0.331 (0.036) | 0.246 (0.006) | 0.429 (0.051) | 0.240 (0.032) | 0.163 (0.005) | 0.342 (0.050) | 0.292 |
| Link clustering [2] | 0.304 (0.016) | 0.334 (0.003) | 0.372 (0.027) | 0.226 (0.016) | **0.238 (0.003)**[2] | 0.275 (0.024) | 0.291 |
| BigCLAM [43] | 0.324 (0.017) | 0.344 (0.005) | 0.442 (0.042) | 0.217 (0.014) | 0.234 (0.004) | 0.325 (0.038) | 0.315 |
| DEMON [11] | 0.343 (0.029) | 0.308 (0.005) | 0.418 (0.046) | 0.255 (0.027) | 0.210 (0.005) | 0.311 (0.041) | 0.307 |
| NMF [29] | 0.333 (0.019) | 0.318 (0.004) | 0.406 (0.038) | 0.242 (0.026) | 0.221 (0.004) | 0.301 (0.050) | 0.303 |
| **CoDA**, undirected | **0.414 (0.027)**[1] | **0.348 (0.005)**[2] | **0.470 (0.042)**[1] | **0.314 (0.026)**[1] | 0.237 (0.004) | **0.357 (0.039)**[1] | **0.357**[2] |
| **CoDA**, directed | **0.406 (0.025)**[2] | **0.363 (0.005)**[1] | **0.470 (0.042)**[1] | **0.314 (0.024)**[1] | **0.250 (0.004)**[1] | **0.357 (0.039)**[1] | **0.360**[1] |

**Table 2: Performance on Facebook, Google+, and Twitter. Higher is better. Standard errors are shown in parentheses. The best and second best methods are annotated as '1' and '2'.**

| Dataset | Directed | $N$ | $E$ | $C$ | $S$ | $A$ |
|---|---|---|---|---|---|---|
| Google+ | ✓ | 250,469 | 30,230,905 | 437 | 143.51 | 0.25 |
| Twitter | ✓ | 125,120 | 2,248,406 | 3,140 | 15.54 | 0.39 |
| Facebook | ✗ | 4,089 | 170,174 | 193 | 28,76 | 1.36 |
| Enron | ✓ | 45,266 | 185,172 | 4,572 | 63.93 | 6.46 |
| LiveJournal | ✗ | 3,997,962 | 34,681,189 | 287,512 | 22.31 | 1.59 |
| Youtube | ✗ | 1,134,890 | 2,987,624 | 8,385 | 13.50 | 0.10 |

**Table 1: Dataset statistics. Directed: Yes/no, $N$: number of nodes, $E$: number of edges, $C$: number of ground-truth communities, $S$: average ground-truth community size, $A$: ground-truth community memberships per node. Further datasets used in this study are described in Table 5.**

works from a wide spectrum of domains. We consider social, communication, information, biological and ecological networks.[1]

**Networks with ground-truth communities.** For the experiments in this section, we consider a subset of 6 publicly available networks where we have explicit *ground-truth* memberships of nodes to communities [44]. The availability of ground-truth allows us to quantify the quality of community detection methods *quantitatively*. Table 1 shows the statistics of the networks and the ground-truth communities. The networks come from three different domains: The first three networks are the collection of ego-networks from online social networks of Facebook, Twitter and Google+ [31], the Enron email communication network [22], and LiveJournal and Youtube social networks [33]. We describe the nature of ground-truth communities in each of these datasets in more detail later.

## 4.2 Experimental Setup

**Baselines.** For comparison we consider the following baseline methods: *MMSB* (Mixed Membership Stochastic Blockmodels) [3], which can detect both cohesive and 2-mode communities in undirected networks and is extremely slow; *Clique Percolation*, [34] *Link Clustering* [2], *BigCLAM* [43, 45] are state of the art overlapping cohesive community detection techniques for undirected networks; *DEMON* [11] is a scalable local community detection method for directed networks; *NMF* [29] is a state-of-the-art non-negative matrix factorization approach which can be used for directed networks. We use publicly available implementations of each of the methods.

Some methods require input parameters. MMSB and NMF requires the number of communities $K$. We use the Bayes information criterion suggested by the authors [3] to choose $K$. DEMON requires $\varepsilon$, the threshold value for merging two communities. As there exists no standard criterion for $\varepsilon$, we set $\varepsilon$ so that DEMON detects the same number of communities as CoDA does.

[1]We use the publicly available data from the Stanford Large Network Collection: `http://snap.stanford.edu`.

Last, we note that the above baselines represent the current state-of-the-art in community detection. However, we also considered other baselines, including those that make use of node features [20], network topology [39], or both [5, 31]; however experiments demonstrate that none of these alternatives outperforms CoDA.

**Evaluation.** To evaluate the performance of the above methods we quantify the degree of correspondence between the ground-truth and the detected communities. To compare a set of ground-truth communities $C^*$ to a set of predicted communities $C$, we adopt an evaluation procedure previously used in [43, 45], where every detected (ground-truth) community is matched with its most similar ground-truth (detected) counterpart community:

$$\frac{1}{2|C^*|}\sum_{C_i^* \in C^*} \max_{C_j \in C} \delta(C_i^*, C_j) + \frac{1}{2|C|}\sum_{C_j \in C} \max_{C_i^* \in C^*} \delta(C_i^*, C_j),$$

where $\delta(C_i^*, C_j)$ is some measure of the similarity between the communities $C_i^*$ and $C_j$. We consider two standard measures of the similarity between sets, namely the $F_1$ score and the Jaccard similarity. Thus, we obtain a value between 0 and 1, where 1 indicates perfect recovery.

## 4.3 Detecting Social Circles

First we consider the problem of discovering users' social circles [31]. Circles (or 'lists' in Facebook and Twitter) give users a means of categorizing their immediate neighbors, or in the case of directed networks, the users whom they follow. Thus the problem of automatically identifying users' social circles can be posed as a community detection problem on each user's ego-network [31].

In Table 2 we evaluate the performance of CoDA and baselines on social circle detection. Across all three datasets and both evaluation metrics, CoDA (the last row) is the best or second-best performer. On average, CoDA outperforms MMSB by 34%, Clique percolation by 23%, Link clustering by 24%, BigCLAM by 14%, DEMON by 17%, and NMF by 19%.

The 3 data sets possess very different reasons for community (*i.e.*, social circle) formation: Facebook is an undirected network and in Facebook circles are driven by dense mutual friendships among users with homogeneous backgrounds [31]; therefore, we would expect cohesive communities in Facebook. Google+ and Twitter are directed networks and as such circles are not necessarily based on friendship, because edges in these networks denote *follower* relationships: The fraction of reciprocated edges is only 29% in Google+ and 54% in Twitter. For example, a social circle in Twitter might consist of authors who publish in the same genre, or candidates in the same election. As we will see later in Section 5, many social circles in Google+ and Twitter follow such 2-mode structure.

Regardless of very different nature of the data sets, CoDA is the best performing method in each of them. This result means that CoDA recovers 2-mode circles in Google+ or Twitter *as well as*

| Method | $F_1$ score | Jaccard similarity | Average |
|---|---|---|---|
| MMSB | N/A | N/A | N/A |
| Clique percolation | N/A | N/A | N/A |
| Link clustering | 0.195 | 0.294 | 0.245 |
| BigCLAM | 0.478 | 0.358 | 0.418 |
| DEMON | 0.464 | 0.350 | 0.407 |
| NMF | N/A | N/A | N/A |
| CoDA, undirected | 0.538 | 0.431 | 0.485 |
| CoDA, directed | 0.617 | 0.516 | 0.567 |

**Table 3: Performance of recipient discovery on the Enron network. Algorithms that do not scale to the size of the dataset are labeled as "N/A".**

cohesive circles in Facebook, *i.e.*, CoDA can detect *both* kinds of communities more accurately than the baselines.

**Directed vs. undirected networks.** To further examine the performance out method on directed and undirected networks we perform an experiment with the goal of understanding whether CoDA is still able to recover 2-mode communities even when edge directions are dropped and networks are considered as undirected. To test this, we convert the directed networks of Twitter and Google+ into undirected by removing the edge directions. Then we apply CoDA (CoDA, undirected, the second to last row in Table 2). Surprisingly, CoDA achieves similar performance even without explicit edge directions in the network. Based on this evidence we conclude CoDA is capable of accurately finding 2-mode communities even in undirected networks.

## 4.4 Discovering Recipient Lists in Email Networks

We also define a task of automatically discovering recipient lists in the the email communication network. The idea is that such lists exhibit a distinct structural pattern in the network as the recipient lists may have 2-mode community structure as a set of users who receive the same email may not necessarily email each other [32].

We consider all Enron emails [22] with 20 or more recipients. This gives us a set of 4,572 unique recipient lists in the Enron dataset, which we treat as ground-truth communities (Table 1). Now we are given an unlabeled directed Enron email communication network, where an edge $i \rightarrow j$ means that $i$ sent at least one mail to $j$, and the goal is to discover email recipient lists.

We then apply CoDA as well as the baselines to this network and in Table 3 we measure how accurately the communities detected by CoDA correspond to these ground-truth email recipient lists. We report both the $F_1$ score and Jaccard similarity (for methods that do not scale to networks of this size, we report N/A). Table 3 shows that CoDA outperforms other methods by a significant margin. CoDA outperforms Link clustering by 131%, DEMON by 39%, and BigCLAM by 36%.

## 4.5 Experiments on Large Networks

Last, we also examine two real-world social networks with millions of nodes in which nodes explicitly declare their community memberships [44]. We consider the LiveJournal and Youtube social networks, and regard user-created groups as ground-truth communities. We ignore groups containing fewer than 10 nodes, yielding 71,093 communities in LiveJournal and 2,078 in Youtube.

Of the baselines previously mentioned, only BigCLAM could scale to both networks and DEMON could scale to the Youtube network. Therefore, we also consider two large-scale graph partitioning methods as baselines for this experiment: Metis [21] and Graclus [13]. For all methods we set the number of communities $K$ to be the number of ground-truth communities.

| | Relative $F_1$ score | | Absolute $F_1$ score | |
|---|---|---|---|---|
| Method | LiveJournal | Youtube | LiveJournal | Youtube |
| Metis | 100% | 200% | 0.12 | 0.028 |
| Graclus | 100% | 185.7% | 0.12 | 0.026 |
| BigCLAM | 121.0 % | 278.1 % | 0.14 | 0.039 |
| DEMON | N/A | 100% | N/A | 0.014 |
| CoDA | 129.4% | 307.1% | 0.15 | 0.043 |

**Table 4: Relative accuracy (compared to the worst performing method) of detected communities on large scale social networks.**

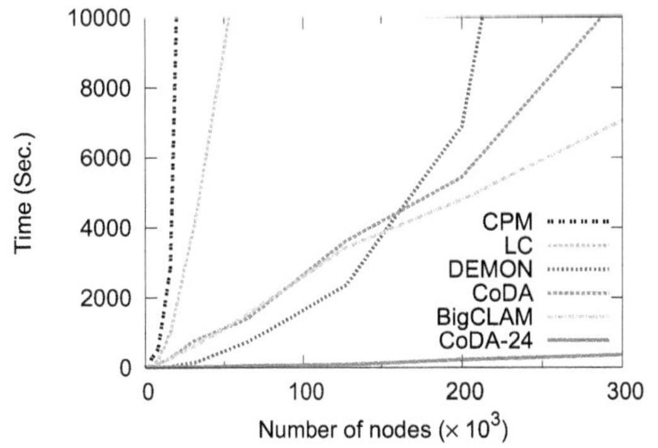


**Figure 4: Algorithm runtime.**

Table 4 shows the results. For this experiment we focus on the score relative to that of the worst-performing baseline in each network (so that the worst-performing baseline has a score of 100%). We compute the relative score because the networks are only partially labeled and the overall performance is thus artificially low (as methods discover many unlabeled communities). We find that CoDA outperforms its nearest competitor by 8.4% on LiveJournal and 29% on Youtube.

## 4.6 Scalability

Last, we evaluate the scalability of CoDA by measuring its running time on synthetic networks with increasing size. We generate synthetic networks using the Forest fire model [27] with the forward and backward probabilities set to 0.36 and 0.32, respectively. Since CoDA is easily parallelizable as described in Section 3, we also consider a singe machine parallel implementation running with 24 threads (CoDA-24).

Scalability results are shown in Figure 4. Link Clustering and Clique Percolation scale to networks of at most a few thousand nodes. DEMON is a fast and scalable overlapping community detection method. DMEON tends to be faster than CoDA (single-threaded implementation) for networks up to 100,000 nodes, however, once the network becomes larger, CoDA becomes much faster.

When comparing single-threaded implementations we also note that BigCLAM is the fastest method in our experiments. However, we note that CoDA takes only 30% more time than BigCLAM while it is also solving a more complicated problem, namely detecting cohesive as well as 2-mode communities.

Last, we also measure a parallelized version of CoDA (CoDA-24). Using 24 threads on a single machine, we achieve nearly 24x speedup. Ultimately, CoDA takes just 6 minutes to process a 300,000 node network.

| Dataset | Directed | $N$ | $E$ | $C$ | $S$ | $A$ |
|---|---|---|---|---|---|---|
| PPI-Y2H | ✗ | 1,647 | 2,518 | 40 | 90.75 | 2.20 |
| PPI-LC | ✗ | 1,213 | 2,556 | 40 | 42.08 | 1.39 |
| web-Stanford | ✓ | 281k | 2,312k | 19k | 70.63 | 4.59 |
| web-Google | ✓ | 875k | 5,105k | 39k | 41.79 | 1.86 |
| cit-HepTh | ✓ | 27k | 353k | 2,000 | 70.00 | 5.04 |
| cit-HepPh | ✓ | 34k | 422k | 4,976 | 51.52 | 7.42 |
| Florida Bay | ✓ | 121 | 1,745 | 6 | 45.33 | 2.25 |
| Chesapeake | ✓ | 33 | 72 | 5 | 9.20 | 1.39 |

**Table 5: Dataset statistics. Directed: Whether the network is directed or not, $N$: number of nodes, $E$: number of edges, $C$: number of detected communities, $S$: average size of detected communities, $A$: community memberships per node.**

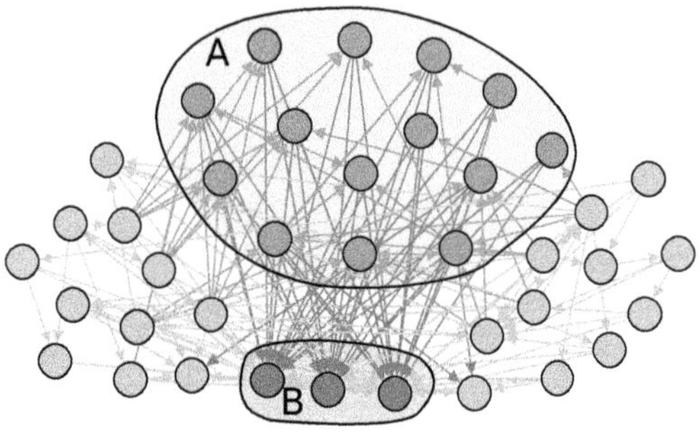


**Figure 5: Two detected communities in a Foodweb (Chesapeake Bay). Among other communities, CoDA identifies sets of nodes with similar predators ($A$, blue nodes) and with similar prey ($B$, red nodes), both of which have low internal connectivity.**

# 5. COMMUNITY DISCOVERY

So far we have demonstrated that CoDA can reliably detect both cohesive and 2-mode communities in directed as well as undirected networks. In the following section, we shall demonstrate that 2-mode communities take an important role in networks. We shall use CoDA to perform a qualitative study of various networks in order to determine the extent to which community structures vary across real-world networks from various domains.

**Network data.** In addition to the datasets already introduced, we also analyze biological networks, foodwebs, web graphs, and citation networks (Table 5). For biological networks, we consider the protein-protein interaction network of *Saccharomyces cerevisiae*: yeast two-hybrid (PPI-Y2H) and literature-curated (PPI-LC) [2]. We also consider the Chesapeake and Florida Bay foodwebs [41], the web graph of Stanford University web pages (web-Stanford), the web graph released by Google in 2002 (web-Google) [28], and the arXiv citation networks from high-energy physics phenomenology (cit-HepPh) and theory (cit-HepTh) [27] all available from `http://snap.stanford.edu`.

## 5.1 Biological and Foodweb Communities

We first present 2-mode communities in foodwebs, where nodes represent organisms and an edge from a node $u$ to $v$ means that $u$ is preyed upon by $v$. We apply CoDA on the Chesapeake Bay foodweb network shown in Figure 5, and display an induced subgraph of detected 2-mode communities in Figure 6.

In foodweb networks, we find 2-mode communities of groups of predators who rely on similar groups of prey (Figure 6). The blue 2-mode community ($B$-$D$) represents predators and prey in the the Chesapeake Bay sands: *nereis*, *macoma spp.*, and *mya arenaria* (in $B$) are small, sand-dwelling clams and worms that are fed on by fish (in $D$). Alternately, the red community ($A$-$C$) shows predator-prey relationships among fish: small fish ($A$) are eaten by bigger fish ($C$). CoDA also discovers the *overlap* between two predator groups where *white perch* and *spot* prey on both fish and clams.

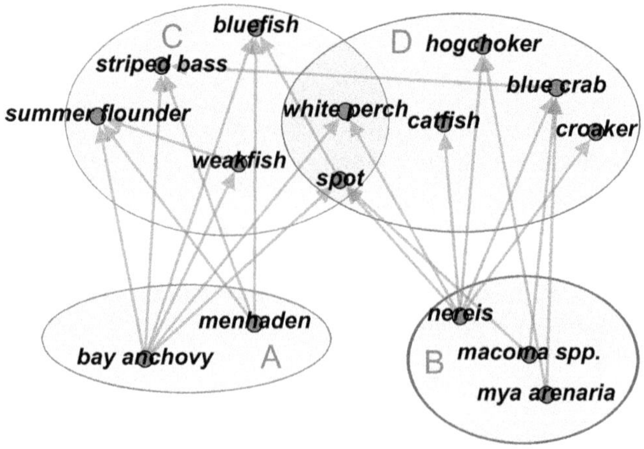


**Figure 6: Examples of overlapping 2-Mode communities detected by our method in the Chesapeake bay foodweb network. See main text for the explanation of community structure.**

CoDA also allows us to gain insights into biological PPI networks. Interestingly, CoDA discovers many 2-mode communities in the undirected protein-protein interaction network determined by yeast two-hybrid screening (PPI-Y2H). For example, Figure 8 displays the induced subgraph of two communities that CoDA detects. 2-mode communities detected by CoDA clearly reveal the interaction between different protein groups. For example, proteins in group $C$ of Figure 8 heavily interact with proteins in group $A$, even though these proteins do not interact within the same group (with $A$ or within $C$).

To further analyze the role of these communities, we used gene ontologies to identify relevant terms/functions of proteins in $A$, $B$, $C$, and $D$ using the GO Term Finder [7]. The proteins in the large groups ($C$, $D$) are generally associated with catalytic activity and ion binding ($p$-value $\sim 10^{-4}$).

However, these proteins are regulated by different protein groups ($A$, $B$) which have different functions. Proteins in $A$ (*e.g.*, YLR347C and YNL189W) are protein transporters, whereas proteins in $B$ (*e.g.*, YLR291C) are regulators. Perhaps more interestingly, YPL070W belongs to both $A$ and $B$ and regulates both $C$ and $D$. However, its role is not yet known. But based on known functions of proteins in groups $A$ and $B$ we can extrapolate the function of YPL070W. This example shows how network analysis and community detection in particular can provide research directions for experimental biology [10].

## 5.2 2-mode vs. Cohesive Communities

Since CoDA can detect both cohesive and 2-mode communities, we can use it to measure the extent to which real network data exhibits cohesive and 2-mode behavior. This analysis allows us to characterize the mesoscale structure of real-world networks as the proportion of 2-mode versus cohesive communities can be used to gain further insights into community structure of networks.

**Experimental setup.** For this experiment, we consider 12 networks from 6 domains in order to characterize their different community structures. We consider ego networks (Twitter, Google+) and social networks (LiveJournal, Youtube) from Section 4. We also include 8 networks from 4 different domains: Biological networks,

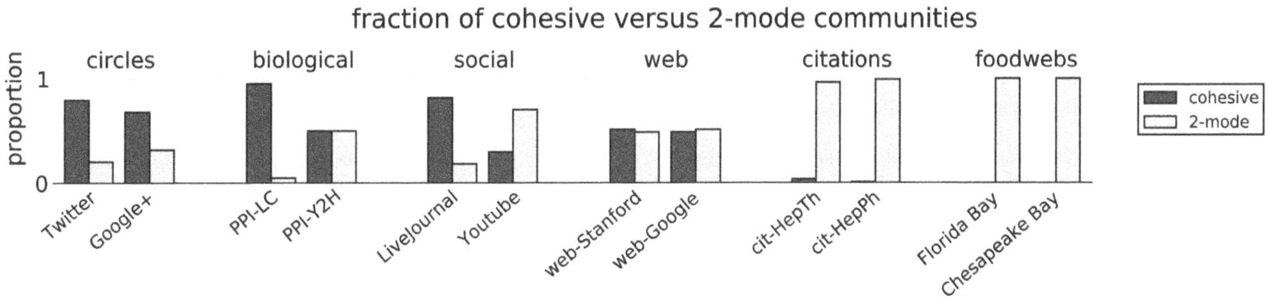


**Figure 7: Fraction of 2-Mode communities and cohesive communities in six different types of networks.**

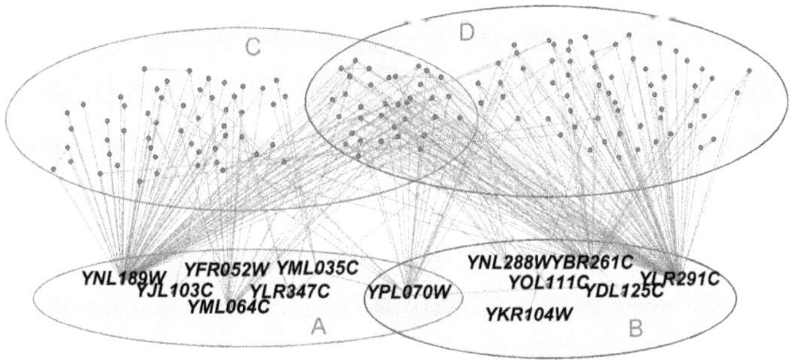


**Figure 8: Overlapping 2-Mode communities detected by our method in a Protein-Protein interaction network. See main text for the explanation of community structure.**

web graphs, foodwebs, and citation networks among research papers from Table 5.

To classify whether a detected community is 2-mode or cohesive, we measure the Jaccard similarity $J(c) = \frac{|O(c) \cap I(c)|}{|O(c) \cup I(c)|}$ between the set of member nodes with outgoing memberships $O(c)$, and the set of member nodes with incoming memberships $I(c)$. In a completely cohesive community, this Jaccard similarity is 1 because two sets of members are identical, whereas it is 0 in a completely 2-mode community. We regard a community $c$ as 2-mode if $J(c)$ is lower than some threshold $\gamma$ or as cohesive otherwise ($J(c) \geq \gamma$). We use $\gamma = 0.2$ as this setting gives the most interpretable results.

**Experimental results.** Figure 7 shows the fraction of 2-mode and cohesive communities in 12 networks described above. Ego networks (Twitter and Google+) exhibit a relatively high fraction of cohesive communities and as noted earlier Facebook ego networks (not shown) have an even higher fraction (over 95%) of cohesive communities. This result is in line with [11] where the authors show that Facebook ego networks can be easily divided into cohesive communities. However, it is important to note that a significant fraction of Twitter (20%) and Google+ (30%) communities exhibit 2-mode structure.

Literature-curated protein-protein interaction networks (PPI-LC) practically have only cohesive communities (and no 2-mode). On the other hand, in PPI networks generated based on yeast two-hybrid screening (PPI-Y2H) about 50% of the communities are 2-mode. This difference is interesting and confirms a previous study of PPI networks [46], which provided the following explanation: Edges of PPI-LC are extracted from scientific papers that report experimentally validated interactions. However, current biological experiments have mainly been guided by research on cohesive communities and thus it seems as though most interactions that have been explored take place in "cohesive" communities [46]. On the other hand, the PPI-Y2H network is created by a noisy automatic process and more faithfully represents the interaction network. In this case many 2-mode communities emerge [46].

In social networks we also find interesting results. In LiveJournal, communities are more cohesive, which can be explained by the fact that edges in LiveJournal indicate "friendships" (*i.e.*, sharing private blog content). On the other hand, Youtube communities are predominantly 2-mode. Youtube differs from other social networks in one important way: Edges in Youtube are essentially "subscriptions" for content rather than mutual friendships; consequently, high degree nodes tend to connect to low degree nodes [33].

Web graphs are of interest because Kumar et al. [23] used the existence of 2-mode communities as indicators or signatures for cohesive communities. Our results nicely suggest the co-existence of cohesive communities and 2-mode communities by showing that web graphs have an equal proportion of 2-mode and cohesive communities.

Finally, foodwebs as well as citation networks consist almost entirely of 2-mode communities. These results are natural as reciprocal and cohesive relationships are extremely unlikely in these networks. In foodwebs, for example, few species prey upon each other. Citation networks are directed acyclic graphs and reciprocal citation is impossible by definition. Intuitively, cohesive communities in directed networks contain some number of bidirectional edges among their members, therefore a lack of such reciprocal edges naturally leads to the dominance of 2-mode communities, as we observe in Figure 6.

# 6. CONCLUSION

An accurate notion of a *community* is critical when studying the mesoscale structure of networks. Traditional models consider 'communities' to be sets of densely connected nodes. In addition, here we also consider *2-mode* communities, which are groups of nodes who may not link to each other but link in a coordinate way to the other nodes in the network.

We have presented CoDA, a community detection method which naturally detects both densely connected and 2-mode communities. CoDA can capture overlapping and hierarchical structure among communities, and handles both directed and undirected networks. Our experimental findings reveal that CoDA outperforms the current state-of-the-art in detecting ground-truth communities. Moreover, CoDA also reveals how 2-mode and cohesive communities co-exist in real networks.

The versatility of CoDA to detect both cohesive and 2-mode communities accurately in directed and undirected networks raises many interesting avenues of future work. For example, understanding the interaction between 2-mode communities and cohesive communities is a fruitful direction. Inferring the role of nodes from their community affiliations would also be useful. Another idea is to extend CoDA to find important nodes in each community. This could be achieved by the fact that CoDA estimates real-valued membership strengths ($F_{uc}$ and $H_{uc}$) of each node to each community. From the values of $F_{uc}$ and $H_{uc}$ for node $u$ and community $c$, we could determine which nodes are most important and have the "heaviest" membership to a given community $c$.

**Acknowledgements.** This research has been supported in part by NSF IIS-1016909, CNS-1010921, CAREER IIS-1149837, IIS-1159679, ARO MURI, DARPA GRAPHS, ARL AHPCRC, Okawa Foundation, Docomo, Boeing, Allyes, Volkswagen, Intel, Alfred P. Sloan Fellowship, and the Microsoft Faculty Fellowship.

## 7. REFERENCES

[1] L. Adamic and N. Glance. The political blogosphere and the 2004 U.S. election: divided they blog. In *LinkKDD '05*, 2005.
[2] Y.-Y. Ahn, J. Bagrow, and S. Lehmann. Link communities reveal multi-scale complexity in networks. *Nature*, 2010.
[3] E. Airoldi, D. Blei, S. Fienberg, and E. Xing. Mixed membership stochastic blockmodels. *JMLR*, 2007.
[4] R. Andersen and K. Lang. Communities from seed sets. In *WWW '06*, 2006.
[5] R. Balasubramanyan and W. Cohen. Block-LDA: Jointly modeling entity-annotated text and entity-entity links. In *SDM '11*, 2011.
[6] B. Ball, B. Karrer, and M. Newman. Efficient and principled method for detecting communities in networks. In *Phys. Rev. E*, 2011.
[7] E. Boyle et al. GO::TermFinder—open source software for accessing gene ontology information and finding significantly enriched gene ontology terms associated with a list of genes. *Bioinformatics*, 2004.
[8] L. Breiger. The duality of persons and groups. *Social Forces*, 1974.
[9] R. Burt. Cohesion versus structural equivalence as a basis for network subgroups. *Sociological Methods and Research*, 1978.
[10] D. Carney, B. Davies, and B. Horazdovsky. Vps9 domain-containing proteins: activators of Rab5 GTPases from yeast to neurons. *Trends in Cell Biology*, 2006.
[11] M. Coscia, G. Rossetti, F. Giannotti, and D. Pedreschi. Demon: a local-first discovery method for overlapping communities. In *KDD '12*, 2012.
[12] L. Danon, J. Duch, A. Diaz-Guilera, and A. Arenas. Comparing community structure identification. *J. of Stat. Mech.: Theory and Experiment*, 2005.
[13] I. Dhillon, Y. Guan, and B. Kulis. Weighted graph cuts without eigenvectors: A multilevel approach. *IEEE PAMI*, 2007.
[14] S. Fortunato. Community detection in graphs. *Physics Reports*, 2010.
[15] D. Gleich and Seshadhri. Neighborhoods are good communities. In *KDD '12*, 2012.
[16] P. Gopalan, D. Mimno, S. Gerrish, M. Freedman, and D. Blei. Scalable inference of overlapping communities. In *NIPS '12*, 2012.
[17] K. Henderson, B. Gallagher, T. Eliassi-Rad, H. Tong, S. Basu, L. Akoglu, D. Koutra, C. Faloutsos, and L. Li. Rolx: structural role extraction & mining in large graphs. In *KDD*, 2012.
[18] P. W. Holland, K. B. Laskey, and S. Leinhardt. Stochastic blockmodels: First steps. *Social Networks*, 1983.
[19] C.-J. Hsieh and I. S. Dhillon. Fast coordinate descent methods with variable selection for non-negative matrix factorization. In *KDD '11*, 2011.
[20] S. Johnson. Hierarchical clustering schemes. *Psychometrika*, 1967.
[21] G. Karypis and V. Kumar. Multilevel k-way partitioning scheme for irregular graphs. *J. of Parallel and Distributed Computing*, 1998.
[22] B. Klimt and Y. Yang. Introducing the enron corpus. In *CEAS '04*, 2004.
[23] R. Kumar, P. Raghavan, S. Rajagopalan, and A. Tomkins. Trawling the web for emerging cyber-communities. *Computer Networks*, 1999.
[24] H. Kwak, C. Lee, H. Park, and S. Moon. What is twitter, a social network or a news media? In *WWW '10*, 2010.
[25] S. Lattanzi and D. Sivakumar. Affiliation networks. In *STOC '09*, 2009.
[26] E. Leicht and M. E. Newman. Community structure in directed networks. *Phys. Rev. Lett.*, 2008.
[27] J. Leskovec, J. Kleinberg, and C. Faloutsos. Graphs over time: densification laws, shrinking diameters and possible explanations. In *KDD '05*, 2005.
[28] J. Leskovec, K. J. Lang, A. Dasgupta, and M. W. Mahoney. Community structure in large networks: Natural cluster sizes and the absence of large well-defined clusters. *Internet Mathematics*, 2009.
[29] C-J. Lin. Projected Gradient Methods for Nonnegative Matrix Factorization. *Neural Computation*, 2007.
[30] F. Malliaros and M. Vazirgiannis. Clustering and Community Detection in Directed Networks: A Survey. *Physics Reports*, 2013.
[31] J. McAuley and J. Leskovec. Learning to discover social circles in ego networks. In *NIPS '12*, 2012.
[32] A. McCallum, X. Wang, and A. Corrada-Emmanuel. Topic and role discovery in social networks with experiments on enron and academic email. *JAIR*, 2007.
[33] A. Mislove, M. Marcon, K. P. Gummadi, P. Druschel, and B. Bhattacharjee. Measurement and analysis of online social networks. In *IMC '07*, 2007.
[34] G. Palla, I. Derényi, I. Farkas, and T. Vicsek. Uncovering the overlapping community structure of complex networks in nature and society. *Nature*, 2005.
[35] S. Papadopoulos, Y. Kompatsiaris, A. Vakali, and P. Spyridonos. Community detection in social media. *DMKD*, 2011.
[36] S. Pinkert, J. Schultz, and J. Reichardt. Protein interaction networks—more than mere modules. *PLoS CompBio*, 2010.
[37] F. Radicchi, C. Castellano, F. Cecconi, V. Loreto, and D. Parisi. Defining and identifying communities in networks. *PNAS*, 2004.
[38] M. Rosvall and C. Bergstrom. An information-theoretic framework for resolving community structure in complex networks. *PNAS*, 2007.
[39] M. Rosvall and C. T. Bergstrom. Maps of random walks on complex networks reveal community structure. *PNAS*, 2008.
[40] V. Satuluri and S. Parthasarathy. Scalable Graph Clustering using Stochastic Flows: Applications to Community Discovery. *KDD '09*, 2009.
[41] R. Ulanowicz, C. Bondavalli, and M. Egnotovich. Network analysis of trophic dynamics in south florida ecosystem, fy 97: The florida bay ecosystem. *Ref. CBL98-123. Chesapeake Biological Laboratory*, 1998.
[42] J. Xie, S. Kelley, and B. K. Szymanski. Overlapping community detection in networks: the state of the art and comparative study. *ACM Computing Surveys*, 2013.
[43] J. Yang and J. Leskovec. Community-affiliation network model for overlapping community detection. In *ICDM '12*, 2012.
[44] J. Yang and J. Leskovec. Defining and evaluating network communities based on ground-truth. In *ICDM '12*, 2012.
[45] J. Yang and J. Leskovec. Overlapping community detection at scale: A non-negative factorization approach. In *WSDM '13*, 2013.
[46] H. Yu, P. Braun, M. A. Yildirim, I. Lemmens, K. Venkatesan, J. Sahalie, T. Hirozane-Kishikawa, F. Gebreab, N. Li, N. Simonis, and et al. High-quality binary protein interaction map of the yeast interactome network. *Science*, 2008.
[47] E. Zheleva, H. Sharara, and L. Getoor. Co-evolution of social and affiliation networks. In *KDD '09*, 2009.

# FENNEL: Streaming Graph Partitioning for Massive Scale Graphs

Charalampos E. Tsourakakis[1] Christos Gkantsidis [2] Bozidar Radunovic[2] Milan Vojnovic[2]
[1] Aalto University [2]Microsoft Research
Espoo, Finland Cambridge, UK

## ABSTRACT

Balanced graph partitioning in the streaming setting is a key problem to enable scalable and efficient computations on massive graph data such as web graphs, knowledge graphs, and graphs arising in the context of online social networks. Two families of heuristics for graph partitioning in the streaming setting are in wide use: place the newly arrived vertex in the cluster with the largest number of neighbors or in the cluster with the least number of non-neighbors.

In this work, we introduce a framework which unifies the two seemingly orthogonal heuristics and allows us to quantify the interpolation between them. More generally, the framework enables a well principled design of scalable, streaming graph partitioning algorithms that are amenable to distributed implementations. We derive a novel one-pass, streaming graph partitioning algorithm and show that it yields significant performance improvements over previous approaches using an extensive set of real-world and synthetic graphs.

Surprisingly, despite the fact that our algorithm is a one-pass streaming algorithm, we found its performance to be in many cases comparable to the *de-facto* standard offline software METIS and in some cases even superiror. For instance, for the Twitter graph with more than 1.4 billion of edges, our method partitions the graph in about 40 minutes achieving a balanced partition that cuts as few as 6.8% of edges, whereas it took more than $8\frac{1}{2}$ hours by METIS to produce a balanced partition that cuts 11.98% of edges. We also demonstrate the performance gains by using our graph partitioner while solving standard PageRank computation in a graph processing platform with respect to the communication cost and runtime.

## Categories and Subject Descriptors

H.2.4 [**Database Systems**]: [Distributed databases]; D.2.8 [**Software Engineering**]: Metrics—*complexity measures, performance measures*; G.2.2 [**Mathematics of Computing**]: [Graph Algorithms]


*WSDM'14*, February 24–28, 2014, New York, NY, USA.

http://dx.doi.org/10.1145/2556195.2556213 .

## Keywords

Streaming; Balanced Graph partitioning; Distributed Computing

## 1. INTRODUCTION

The scale of graph data that needs to be processed in the context of online services is massive. For example, the Web graph amounts to at least one trillion of links, Facebook recently reported more than 1 billion of users and 140 billion of friend connections, and, in 2009, Twitter reported more than 40 million of users and about 1.5 billion of social relations [21]. A standard approach for scalable computation on massive scale input graph data is to partition an input graph into smaller partitions and then use a large distributed system to process them. The partition sizes have to be balanced to exploit the speedup of parallel computing over different partitions. Furthermore, it is critical that the number of edges between distinct partitions is small, in order to minimize the communication cost incurred due to messages that are exchanged between different partitions. Many popular graph processing platforms such as Pregel [23] that builds on MapReduce [7], and its open source cousin Apache Giraph, PEGASUS [13] and GraphLab [22] use as a default partitioner Hash Partition of vertices, which corresponds to assigning each vertex to one of the $k$ partitions uniformly at random. This heuristic is efficient for balancing the number of vertices over different clusters, but ignores entirely the graph structure. In fact, the expected fraction of edges cut by a random partition of vertices into $k \geq 1$ clusters is equal to $1 - 1/k$. Given the fact that real-world graphs tend to have sparser cuts [4], it is important to discover methods that are computationally efficient, practical, and yet yield high quality graph partitioning.

The problem of finding a balanced graph partition that minimizes the number of edges cut is known as the *balanced graph partitioning* problem, which has a rich history in the context of theoretical computer science. This problem is known to be NP-hard [19] and several approximation algorithms have been derived in previous work, which we review in Section 2. In practice, systems aim at providing good partitions in order to enhance their performance, e.g., [23, 27]. It is worth emphasizing that the balanced graph partitioning problem appears in various guises in numerous other domains, e.g., see [16].

Another major challenge in the area of big graph data is efficient processing of dynamic graphs. For example, new accounts are created and deleted every day in online services such as Facebook, Skype and Twitter. Furthermore, graphs

| | Fennel | | Best competitor | | Hash Partition | | METIS | |
|---|---|---|---|---|---|---|---|---|
| # Clusters ($k$) | $\lambda$ | $\rho$ | $\lambda$ | $\rho$ | $\lambda$ | $\rho$ | $\lambda$ | $\rho$ |
| 2 | 6.8% | 1.1 | 34.3% | 1.04 | 50% | 1 | 11.98% | 1.02 |
| 4 | 29% | 1.1 | 55.0% | 1.07 | 75% | 1 | 24.39% | 1.03 |
| 8 | 48% | 1.1 | 66.4% | 1.10 | 87.5% | 1 | 35.96% | 1.03 |

**Table 1: Fraction of edges cut $\lambda$ and the normalized maximum load $\rho$ for Fennel, the previously best-known heuristic (linear weighted degrees [29]) and hash partitioning of vertices for the Twitter graph with approximately 1.5 billion edges. Fennel and best competitor require around 40 minutes, METIS more than $8\frac{1}{2}$ hours.**

created upon post-processing datasets such as Twitter posts are also dynamic, see for instance [2]. It is crucial to have efficient graph partitioners of dynamic graphs. For example, in the Skype service, each time a user logs in, his/her online contacts get notified. It is expensive when messages have to be sent across different graph partitions since this would typically involve using network infrastructure. The balanced graph partitioning problem in the dynamic setting is known as *streaming graph partitioning* [29]. Vertices (or edges) arrive and the decision of the placement of each vertex (edge) has to be done "on-the-fly" in order to incur as little computational overhead as possible.

It is worth noting that the state-of-the-art work on graph partitioning seems to roughly divide in two main lines of research. Rigorous mathematically work and algorithms that do not scale to massive graphs, e.g., [20], and heuristics that are used in practice [16, 26, 29]. Our work contributes towards bridging the gap between theory and practice.

**Summary of our Contributions.** Our contributions can be summarized in the following points:

- We introduce a general framework for graph partitioning that relaxes the hard cardinality constraints on the number of vertices in a cluster [3, 20]. Our formulation provides a unifying framework that subsumes two of the most popular heuristics used for streaming balanced graph partitioning: the folklore heuristic of [26] which places a vertex to the cluster with the fewest non-neighbors, and the degree-based heuristic of [29], which serves as the current state-of-the-art method with respect to performance.
- Our framework allows us to define formally the notion of interpolation between between the non-neighbors heuristic [26] and the neighbors heuristic [29]. This provides improved performance for the balanced partitioning problem in the streaming setting. Moreover, for a special case of our framework, we provide a $O(\frac{\log(k)}{k})$ approximation algorithm, where $k$ is the number of clusters.
- We evaluate our proposed streaming graph partitioning method, Fennel, on a wide range of graph datasets, both real-world and synthetic graphs, and show that it produces high quality graph partitions. For example, Table 1 shows the performance of Fennel versus the best previously-known heuristic, which is the linear weighted degrees [29], and the baseline Hash Partition of vertices. We observe that Fennel achieves, simultaneously, significantly smaller fraction of edges cut and balanced cluster sizes.
- We compare Fennel to Hash Partition, the default partitioner of various major large-scale graph processing platforms. Specifically, we demonstrate significant performance gains with respect to the communication cost and the runtime while running Pagerank over a distributed graph in the graph processing platform Apache Giraph.

**Structure of the Paper.** The remainder of the paper is organized as follows. Section 2 discusses the related work. Section 3 introduces our graph partitioning framework and presents our main theoretical result. Section 4 presents a scalable, streaming algorithm. Section 5 evaluates our method versus the state-of-the-art work on an extensive set of real-world and synthetic graphs. Section 6 illustrates that Fennel is a choice for achieving fast and high-quality partitioning in a real system, by performing a baseline comparison to Hash Partition in Apache Giraph. Finally, Section 7 concludes the paper.

## 2. RELATED WORK

Balanced graph partitioning is an NP-hard problem [10]. It is a fundamental problem in every parallel and distributed application since data placement typically affects significantly the execution efficiency of jobs [17]. The goal of balanced graph partitioning is to minimize an application's overall runtime. This is achieved by assigning to each processor/machine an equal amount of data and concurrently minimizing the parallel/distributed overhead by minimizing the number of edges cut by the corresponding partition. Formally, the $(k,\nu)$-balanced graph partitioning asks to divide the vertices of a graph in components each of size less than $\nu\frac{n}{k}$, for some given positive integer $k$ and $\nu \geq 1$. The case $k=2, \nu=1$ is equivalent to the *minimum bisection problem*, an NP-hard problem [10]. Several approximation algorithms and heuristics exist for this problem, see, e.g., [9] and [18] respectively. When $\nu = 1+\epsilon$ for any desired but fixed $\epsilon > 0$ there exists a $O(\epsilon^{-2}\log^{1.5} n)$ approximation algorithm [19]. When $\nu = 2$ there exists an $O(\sqrt{\log k \log n})$ approximation algorithm based on semidefinite programming (SDP) [20]. Due to the practical importance of $k$-paritioning there exist several heuristics, among which METIS [15] and its parallel version [28] stands out for its good performance. For this reason, METIS is used in many existing systems, e.g. [14]. Recently, it was shown that label propagation [31] is efficient and effective. An extensive summary of existing heuristics can be found in [1].

Online graph partitioning was introduced by Stanton and Kliot [29]. The online setting is also well adapted to dynamic graphs, where offline methods incur an expensive computational cost, requiring to repartition the entire graph. Moreover, the newly obtained partitioning can significantly differ from the old one. This in turn implies a large reshuffle of the data, which is very expensive in a distributed system. Currently the most advanced online partitioning algorithm is by Stanton and Kliot [29], against which we extensively compare our approach.

# 3. PROPOSED FRAMEWORK

**Notation.** Let $G(V, E)$ be a simple undirected graph, where $|V| = n, |E| = m$. For a subset of vertices $S \subseteq V$, let $e(S, S)$ be the set of edges with both end-vertices in $S$, and let $e(S, V \setminus S)$ be the set of edges across the cut $(S, V \setminus S)$. For a given vertex $v$ let $t_S(v)$ be the number of triangles $(v, w, z)$ such that $w, z \in S$. We define a *vertex partition* $\mathcal{P} = (S_1, \ldots, S_k)$ to be a family of pairwise disjoint vertex sets whose union is $V$. We refer to each $S_i, i = 1, \ldots, k$, as a *cluster* of vertices. Let $\partial e(\mathcal{P})$ to be the set of edges that cross partition boundaries, i.e. $\partial e(\mathcal{P}) = \cup_{i=1}^{k} e(S_i, V \setminus S_i)$. Finally, we refer to $|\partial e(\mathcal{P})|$ as the *edge-cut size.*

**Graph Partitioning Framework.** We formulate a balanced graph partitioning framework that is based on accounting for the cost of internal edges and the cost of edges cut by the vertex partition in a single global objective function.

*The size of individual clusters.* We denote with $\sigma(S_i)$ the size of the cluster of vertices $S_i$, where $\sigma$ is a mapping to the set of positive real numbers. Special instances of interest are (a) *edge cardinality* where the size of the cluster $i$ is proportional to the total number of edges with at least one end-vertex in the set $S_i$, i.e. $|e(S_i, S_i)| + |e(S_i, V \setminus S_i)|$, (b) *interior-edge cardinality* where the size of cluster $i$ is proportional to the number of internal edges $|e(S_i, S_i)|$, and (c) *vertex cardinality* where the size of partition $i$ is proportional to the total number of vertices $|S_i|$. The edge cardinality is a measure of cluster size that is of interest in some applications, e.g. iterative computations on input graph data where the computational complexity within a cluster is linear in the number of edges with at least one vertex in the given cluster. The vertex cardinality is a standard measure of the size of a cluster and for some graphs, e.g., of bounded degree, may serve as a proxy for the edge cardinality.

*The global objective function.* We define a global objective function that consists of two elements: (1) the inter-partition cost $c_{\mathrm{OUT}} : \mathbb{N}^k \to \mathbb{R}_+$ and (2) the intra-partition cost $c_{\mathrm{IN}} : \mathbb{N}^k \to \mathbb{R}_+$. These functions are assumed to be increasing and super-modular (or convex, if extended to the set of real numbers). For every given partition of vertices $\mathcal{P} = (S_1, S_2, \ldots, S_k)$, we define the global cost function as

$$f(\mathcal{P}) = c_{\mathrm{OUT}}(|e(S_1, V \setminus S_1)|, \ldots, |e(S_k, V \setminus S_k)|) + c_{\mathrm{IN}}(\sigma(S_1), \ldots, \sigma(S_k)).$$

It is worth mentioning some particular cases of interest. Special instance of interest for the inter-partition cost is the linear function in the total number of cut edges $|\partial e(\mathcal{P})|$. This instance is of interest in cases where an identical cost is incurred per each edge cut, e.g. in cases where messages are exchanged along cut edges and these messages are transmitted through some common network bottleneck. For the intra-partition cost, a typical goal is to balance the cost across different partitions and this case is accommodated by defining $c_{\mathrm{IN}}(\sigma(S_1), \ldots, \sigma(S_k)) = \sum_{i=1}^{k} c(\sigma(S_i))$, where $c(x)$ is a convex increasing function such that $c(0) = 0$. In this case, the intra-partition cost function, being defined as a sum of convex functions of individual cluster sizes, would tend to balance the cluster sizes since the minimum is attained when sizes are equal.

We formulate the graph partitioning problem as follows.

**Optimal $k$-Graph Partitioning**

Given a graph $G = (V, E)$, find a partition $\mathcal{P}^* = \{S_1^*, \ldots, S_k^*\}$ of the vertex set $V$, such that $f(\mathcal{P}^*) \geq f(\mathcal{P})$, for all partitions $\mathcal{P}$ such that $|\mathcal{P}| = k$.

We refer to the partition $\mathcal{P}^*$ as the optimal $k$-graph partition of the graph $G$.

*Streaming setting.* The streaming graph partitioning problem can be defined as follows. Let $G = (V, E)$ be an input graph and let us assume that we want to partition the graph into $k$ disjoint subsets of vertices. The vertices arrive in some order, each one with the set of its neighbors. We consider three different stream orders, as in [29].

- Random: Vertices arrive according to a random permutation.
- BFS: This ordering is generated by selecting a vertex uniformly at random and performing breadth first search starting from that vertex.
- DFS: This ordering is identical to the BFS ordering, except that we perform depth first search.

A $k$-partitioning streaming algorithm has to decide whenever a new vertex arrives to which cluster it is going to be placed. A vertex is never moved after it has been assigned to a cluster. Finally, it is worth mentioning that even if we focus on vertex balanced partitions in Section 5, FENNEL also works for edge balanced paritions as well, see [29].

**Application to Classical Balanced Partitioning.** Classical balanced graph partitioning problem is the most common special case of our framework, in which the inter-partition cost is equal to the total number of edges cut, and the intra-partition cost is defined in terms of the vertex cardinalities. We will next explain the intuition behind our framework in this important case, and how to derive appropriate cost functions.

The starting point in the literature, e.g., [19, 20], is to impose hard cardinality constraints, namely $|S_i^*| \leq \nu \frac{n}{k}$ for some small constant $\nu$, $i = 1, \ldots, k$. This set of constaints makes the problem significantly hard. Currently, the state-of-the-art work depends on the Arora-Rao-Vazirani barrier [3] which results in a $O(\sqrt{\log n})$ approximation factor. The typical formulation is the following:

$$\begin{array}{rl} \text{minimize}_{\mathcal{P}=(S_1,\ldots,S_k)} & |\partial e(\mathcal{P})| \\ \text{subject to} & |S_i| \leq \nu \frac{n}{k}, \ \forall i \in \{1, \ldots, k\} \end{array}$$

The idea behind our approach is to *relax* the hard cardinality constraints by introducing a term in the objective $c_{\mathrm{IN}}(\mathcal{P})$ whose minimum is achieved when $|S_i| = \frac{n}{k}$ for all $i = 1, 2, \ldots, k$. Therefore, our framework is based on a well-defined global graph partitioning objective function, which allows for a principled design of approximation algorithms and heuristics as shall be demonstrated. Our graph partitioning method is based on solving the following optimization problem:

$$\text{minimize}_{\mathcal{P}=(S_1,\ldots,S_k)} \quad |\partial e(\mathcal{P})| + c_{\mathrm{IN}}(\mathcal{P}) \tag{1}$$

*Intra-partition cost.* With the goal in mind to favor balanced partitions, we may define the intra-partition cost function by $c_{\text{IN}}(\mathcal{P}) = \sum_{i=1}^{k} c(|S_i|)$ where $c(x)$ is an increasing function choosen to be *super-modular*, so that the following increasing returns property holds $c(x+1) - c(x) \geq c(y+1) - c(y)$, for every $0 \leq y \leq x$.

We focus on the following family of functions $c(x) = \alpha x^\gamma$, for $\alpha > 0$ and $\gamma \geq 1$. By the choice of the parameter $\gamma$, this family of cost functions allows us to control how much the imbalance of cluster sizes is accounted for in the objective function. In one extreme case where $\gamma = 1$, we observe that the objective corresponds to minimizing the number of cut-edges, thus entirely ignoring any possible imbalance of the cluster sizes. On the other hand, by taking larger values for the parameter $\gamma$, the more weight is put on the cost of partition imbalance, and this cost may be seen to approximate hard constraints on the imbalance in the limit of large $\gamma$. Parameter $\alpha$ is also important. We advocate a principled choice of $\alpha$ independently of whether it is suboptimal compared to other choices. Specifically, we choose $\alpha = m\frac{k^{\gamma-1}}{n^\gamma}$. This provides us a proper scaling, since for this specific choice of $\alpha$, our optimization problem is equivalent to minimizing a natural normalization of the objective function $\frac{\sum_{i=1}^{k} e(S_i, V \setminus S_i)}{m} + \frac{1}{k}\sum_{i=1}^{k}\left(\frac{|S_i|}{\frac{n}{k}}\right)^\gamma$.

*An equivalent maximization problem.* We note that the optimal $k$-graph partitioning problem admits an equivalent formulation as a maximization problem which makes a connection with the concept of graph modularity [24]. For a graph $G = (V, E)$ and $S \subseteq V$, we define the function $h : 2^V \rightarrow \mathbb{R}$ as:

$$h(S) = |e(S, S)| - c(|S|)$$

where $h(\emptyset) = h(\{v\}) = 0$ for every $v \in V$. Given $k \geq 1$ and a partition $\mathcal{P} = \{S_1, \ldots, S_k\}$ of the vertex set $V$, we define the function $g$ as

$$g(\mathcal{P}) = \sum_{i=1}^{k} h(S_i).$$

Now, observe that maximizing the function $g(\mathcal{P})$ over all possible partitions $\mathcal{P}$ of the vertex set $V$ such that $|\mathcal{P}| = k$ corresponds to the $k$-graph partitioning problem. Indeed, this follows by noting that

$$\begin{aligned} g(\mathcal{P}) &= \sum_{i=1}^{k} |e(S_i, S_i)| - c(|S_i|) \\ &= m - (\sum_{i=1}^{k} |e(S_i, V \setminus S_i)|) - c(|S_i|)) \\ &= m - f(\mathcal{P}). \end{aligned}$$

Thus, maximizing function $g(\mathcal{P})$ corresponds to minimizing function $f(\mathcal{P})$, which is precisely the objective of our $k$-graph partitioning problem.

*Modularity.* We note that when the function $c(x)$ is taken from the family $c(x) = \alpha x^\gamma$, for $\alpha > 0$ and $\gamma = 2$, our objective has a special combinatorial interpretation. Specifically, our problem is equivalent to maximizing the function

$$\sum_{i=1}^{k} [|e(S_i, S_i)| - p\binom{|S_i|}{2}]$$

where $p = 2\alpha$. In this case, each summation element corresponds to the difference between the realized and the expected number of edges within each cluster under the null-hypothesis that the graph is an Erdős-Rényi random graph with probability $p$. This is intimately related to the concepts of graph modularity [11] and quasi-cliques [30].

*Approximation guarantees.* For the special case of $\gamma = 2$ we can derive an approximation algorithm with provable guarantees. We design a semi-definite programming algorithm for a shifted version of our objective. Specifically, the objective is shifted by $\alpha\binom{n}{2}$ to ensure that the optimal objective value is non-negative, a necessary condition for designing multiplicative approximation algorithms. Given that a typical real-world graph is sparse, e.g., $m = O(n)$ or $m = O(n\text{polylog}(n))$, the objective is dominated by the main $O(n^2)$ term. Therefore, the shifted objective guarantees performance at least as good as Hash Partitioning due to the main term and then optimizes a second order term which is $O(m) = o(n^2)$. Our approximation guarantee provides an imrovement of $O(\log k)$ over hash partitioning, see Theorem 1.

THEOREM 1. *There exists a polynomial time algorithm which provides an $\Omega(\frac{\log k}{k})$-approximation guarantee for the shifted by $\alpha\binom{n}{2}$ Optimal $k$-Graph Partitioning.*

The proof and algorithm along with the discussion about when the incurred additive error due to shifting does not render the algorithm useless will appear in an extended version of this work. An interesting research direction is to pursue additive rather than multiplicative guarantees for maximizing $g(\mathcal{P})$.

## 4. ONE-PASS STREAMING ALGORITHM

**General design.** We derive a streaming algorithm by using a greedy assignment of vertices to clusters as follows: assign each arriving vertex to a partition such that the objective function of the $k$ graph partitioning problem, defined as a maximization problem, is increased the most. Formally, given that current vertex partition is $\mathcal{P} = (S_1, S_2, \ldots, S_k)$, a vertex $v$ is assigned to partition $i$ such that

$$\begin{aligned} & g(S_1, \ldots, S_i \cup \{v\}, \ldots, S_j, \ldots, S_k) \\ \geq \; & g(S_1, \ldots, S_i, \ldots, S_j \cup \{v\}, \ldots, S_k), \text{ for all } j \in [k]. \end{aligned}$$

Defining $\delta g(v, S_i) = g(S_1, \ldots, S_i \cup \{v\}, \ldots, S_j, \ldots, S_k) - g(S_1, \ldots, S_i, \ldots, S_j, \ldots, S_k)$, the above greedy vertex assignment naturally suggests the following streaming algorithm.

**Greedy vertex assignment**

- Assign vertex $v$ to partition $i$ such that $\delta g(v, S_i) \geq \delta g(v, S_j)$, for all $j \in [k]$

**Application to Classical Balanced Partitioning.** We treat the important special case of balancing edge-cuts and vertex cardinality in more detail, since we evaluate it experimentally in Section 5. In this case, $\delta g(v, S_l) = |N(v) \cap S_l| - \delta c(|S_l|)$, where $\delta c(x) = c(x+1) - c(x)$, for $x \in \mathbb{R}_+$, and $N(v)$ denotes the set of neighbors of vertex $v$. The two summation terms in the greedy index $\delta g(v, S_l)$ account for the two underlying objectives of minimizing the number of cut edges and balancing of the partition sizes. Notice that the component $|N(v) \cap S_i|$ corresponds to the number of neighbours of vertex $v$ that are assigned to partition $S_i$. In other words, this corresponds to the degree of vertex $v$ in the subgraph induced by $S_i$. On the other hand, the component $\delta c(|S_i|)$ can be interpreted as the marginal cost of increasing the partition $i$ by one additional vertex.

For our special family of cost functions $c(x) = \alpha x^\gamma$, we have $\delta c(x) = \alpha\gamma x^{\gamma-1}$. For $\gamma = 1$, the greedy index rule corresponds to assigning a new vertex $v$ to partition $i$ with the largest number of neighbours in $S_i$, i.e $|N(v) \cap S_i|$. This is one of the greedy rules considered by Stanton and Kliot [29], and is a greedy rule that may result in highly imbalanced partition sizes.

On the other hand, in case of quadratic cost $c(x) = \frac{1}{2}x^2$, the greedy index is $|N(v) \cap S_i| - |S_i|$, and the greedy assignment corresponds to assigning a new vertex $v$ to partition $i$ that minimizes the number of *non-neighbors* of $v$ inside $S_i$, i.e. $|S_i \setminus N(v)|$. Hence, this yields the following heuristic: *place a vertex to the partition with the least number of non-neighbors* [26]. This assignment accounts for both the cost of cut edges and the balance of partition sizes.

Finally, we outline that in many applications there exist very strict constraints on the load balance. Despite the fact that we investigate the effect of the parameter $\gamma$ on the load balance, one may apply the following algorithm, which enforces to consider only machines whose load is at most $\nu \times \frac{n}{k}$. This algorithm for $1 \leq \gamma \leq 2$ amounts to interpolating between the basic heuristics of [29] and [26]. The overall complexity of our algorithm is $O(n + m)$.

**Greedy vertex assignment with threshold $\nu$**

- Let $I_\nu = \{i : \mu_i \leq \nu\frac{n}{k}\}$. Assign vertex $v$ to partition $i \in I_\nu$ such that $\delta g(v, S_i) \geq \delta g(v, S_j)$, for all $j \in I_\nu$

# 5. EXPERIMENTAL EVALUATION

In this section we present our experimental findings. Specifically, Section 5.1 describes the experimental setup. Sections 5.2 and 5.3 present our findings for synthetic and real-world graphs respectively.

## 5.1 Experimental Setup

The real-world graphs used in our experiments are shown in Table 2. Multiple edges, self loops, signs and weights were removed, if any. Furthermore, we considered the largest connected component from each graph in order to ensure that there is a non-zero number of edges cut. All graphs are publicly available on the Web. All algorithms have been implemented in JAVA, and all experiments were performed on a single machine, with Intel Xeon CPU at 3.6GHz, and 16GB of main memory. Wall-clock times include only the algorithm execution time, excluding the required time to load the graph into memory.

In our synthetic experiments, we use two random graph models. The first model is the hidden partition model [6]. It is specified by four parameters parameters: the number of vertices $n$, the number of clusters $k$, the intercluster and intracluster edge probabilities $p$ and $q$, respectively. First, each vertex is assigned to one of $k$ clusters uniformly at random. We add an edge between two vertices of the same (different) cluster(s) with probability $p$ ($q$) independently

| | Nodes | Edges | Description |
|---|---|---|---|
| amazon0312 | 400 727 | 2 349 869 | Co-purchasing |
| amazon0505 | 410 236 | 2 439 437 | Co-purchasing |
| amazon0601 | 403 364 | 2 443 311 | Co-purchasing |
| as-735 | 6 474 | 12 572 | Auton. Sys. |
| as-Skitter | 1 694 616 | 11 094 209 | Auton. Sys. |
| as-caida | 26 475 | 53 381 | Auton. Sys. |
| ca-AstroPh | 17 903 | 196 972 | Collab. |
| ca-CondMat | 21 363 | 91 286 | Collab. |
| ca-GrQc | 4 158 | 13 422 | Collab. |
| ca-HepPh | 11 204 | 117 619 | Collab. |
| ca-HepTh | 8 638 | 24 806 | Collab. |
| cit-HepPh | 34 401 | 420 784 | Citation |
| cit-HepTh | 27 400 | 352 021 | Citation |
| cit-Patents | 3 764 117 | 16 511 740 | Citation |
| email-Enron | 33 696 | 180 811 | Email |
| email-EuAll | 224 832 | 339 925 | Email |
| epinions | 119 070 | 701 569 | Trust |
| Epinions1 | 75 877 | 405 739 | Trust |
| LiveJournal1 | 4 843 953 | 42 845 684 | Social |
| p2p-Gnutella04 | 10 876 | 39 994 | P2P |
| p2p-Gnutella05 | 8 842 | 31 837 | P2P |
| p2p-Gnutella06 | 8 717 | 31 525 | P2P |
| p2p-Gnutella08 | 6 299 | 20 776 | P2P |
| p2p-Gnutella09 | 8 104 | 26 008 | P2P |
| p2p-Gnutella25 | 22 663 | 54 693 | P2P |
| p2p-Gnutella31 | 62 561 | 147 878 | P2P |
| roadNet-CA | 1 957 027 | 2 760 388 | Road |
| roadNet-PA | 1 087 562 | 1 541 514 | Road |
| roadNet-TX | 1 351 137 | 1 879 201 | Road |
| Slashdot0811 | 77 360 | 469 180 | Social |
| Slashdot0902 | 82 168 | 504 230 | Social |
| Slashdot081106 | 77 258 | 466 661 | Social |
| Slashdot090216 | 81 776 | 495 661 | Social |
| Slashdot090221 | 82 052 | 498 527 | Social |
| usroads | 126 146 | 161 950 | Road |
| wb-cs-stanford | 8 929 | 2 6320 | Web |
| web-BerkStan | 654 782 | 6 581 871 | Web |
| web-Google | 855 802 | 4 291 352 | Web |
| web-NotreDame | 325 729 | 1 090 108 | Web |
| web-Stanford | 255 265 | 1 941 926 | Web |
| wiki-Talk | 2 388 953 | 4 656 682 | Web |
| Wikipedia-20051105 | 1 596 970 | 18 539 720 | Web |
| Wikipedia-20060925 | 2 935 762 | 35 046 792 | Web |
| Twitter | 41 652 230 | 1 468 365 182 | Social |

**Table 2: Datasets used in our experiments.**

of the other edges. We denote this model as $\mathsf{HP}(n, k, p, q)$. The second model we use is a standard model for generating random power law graphs. Specifically, we first generate a power-law degree sequence with a given slope $\delta$ and use the Chung-Lu random graph model to create an instance of a power law graph [5]. The model $\mathsf{CL}(n, \delta)$ has two parameters: the number of vertices $n$ and the slope $\delta$ of the expected power law degree sequence.

We evaluate our algorithms by measuring two quantities from the resulting partitions. In particular, for a fixed partition $\mathcal{P}$ we use the measures of the *fraction of edges cut* $\lambda$ and the *normalized maximum load* $\rho$, defined as

$$\lambda = \frac{\#\text{ edges cut by } \mathcal{P}}{\#\text{ total edges}} = \frac{|\partial e(\mathcal{P})|}{m}, \text{ and}$$

$$\rho = \frac{\text{maximum load}}{\frac{n}{k}}.$$

Notice that $k \geq \rho \geq 1$ since the maximum load of a cluster is at most $n$ and there always exists at least one cluster with at least $\frac{n}{k}$ vertices.

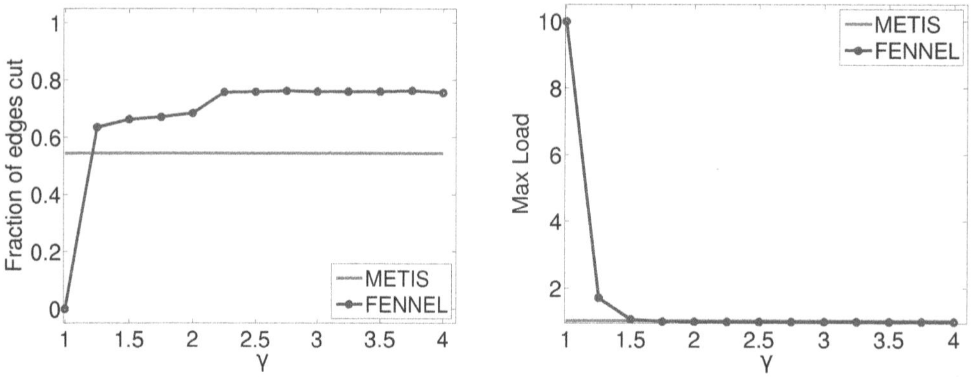


**Figure 1: Fraction of edges cut $\lambda$ and maximum load normalized $\rho$ as a function of $\gamma$, ranging from 1 to 4 with a step of 0.25, over five randomly generated power law graphs with slope 2.5. The straight lines show the performance of METIS.**

| | BFS | | Random | |
|---|---|---|---|---|
| Method | $\lambda$ | $\rho$ | $\lambda$ | $\rho$ |
| H | 96.9% | 1.01 | 96.9% | 1.01 |
| B [29] | 97.3% | 1.00 | 96.8% | 1.00 |
| DG [29] | 0% | 32 | 43% | 1.48 |
| LDG [29] | 34% | 1.01 | 40% | 1.00 |
| EDG [29] | 39% | 1.04 | 48% | 1.01 |
| T [29] | 61% | 2.11 | 78% | 1.01 |
| LT [29] | 63% | 1.23 | 78% | 1.10 |
| ET [29] | 64% | 1.05 | 79% | 1.01 |
| NN [26] | 69% | 1.00 | 55% | 1.03 |
| Fennel | 14% | 1.10 | 14% | 1.02 |
| METIS [16] | 8% | 1.00 | 8% | 1.02 |

**Table 3: Performance of various existing methods on amazon0312 ($k = 32$).**

| | | Fennel | | METIS | |
|---|---|---|---|---|---|
| $m$ | $k$ | $\lambda$ | $\rho$ | $\lambda$ | $\rho$ |
| 7 185 314 | 4 | 62.5 % | 1.04 | 65.2% | 1.02 |
| 6 714 510 | 8 | 82.2 % | 1.04 | 81.5% | 1.02 |
| 6 483 201 | 16 | 92.9 % | 1.01 | 92.2% | 1.02 |
| 6 364 819 | 32 | 96.3% | 1.00 | 96.2% | 1.02 |
| 6 308 013 | 64 | 98.2% | 1.01 | 97.9% | 1.02 |
| 6 279 566 | 128 | 98.4 % | 1.02 | 98.8% | 1.02 |

**Table 4: Fraction of edges cut $\lambda$ and normalized maximum load $\rho$ for Fennel and METIS [16] averaged over 5 random graphs generated according to the HP(5 000, k, 0.8, 0.5) model.**

In Section 5.2, we use the greedy vertex assignment without any threshold. Given that we are able to control the ground truth, we are mainly interested in understanding the effect of the parameter $\gamma$ on the tradeoff between the fraction of edges cut and the normalized maximum load. In Section 5.3, the setting of the parameters we use throughout our experiments is $\gamma = \frac{3}{2}$, $\alpha = \sqrt{k}\frac{m}{n^{3/2}}$, and $\nu = 1.1$. Despite the fact that one can choose $\gamma$ based on the how skewed the degree sequence is in order to obtain superior performance, see Section 5.2, we use the same value $\gamma$ for all graphs. This choice of $\gamma$ is reasonable in the light of our findings in Section 5.2. The choice of $\alpha$ is based on the related discussion in Section 3. Finally, $\nu = 1.1$ is a small enough load balancing factor for any practical purposes.

For competitors, we consider the state-of-the-art heuristics. Specifically, in our evaluation we consider the following heuristics from [29], which we briefly describe here for completeness. Let $v$ be the newly arrived vertex, then place $v$ to a cluster $S_i$ with

- Balanced (B): minimum cardinality $|S_i|$.
- Hash partitioning (H): $S_i$ choosen uniformly at random.
- Deterministic Greedy (DG): maximum $|N(v) \cap S_i|$.
- Linear Weighted Deterministic Greedy (LDG): maximum $|N(v) \cap S_i|(1 - |S_i|/(n/k))$.
- Exponentially Weighted Deterministic Greedy (EDG): maximum $|N(v) \cap S_i|(1 - \exp(|S_i| - n/k))$.
- Triangles (T): maximum $t_{S_i}(v)$.
- Linear Weighted Triangles (LT): maximum $t_{S_i}(v)(1 - |S_i|/(n/k))$.
- Exponentially Weighted Triangles (ET): maximum $t_{S_i}(v)(1 - \exp|S_i| - n/k))$.
- Non-Neighbors (NN): minumum $|S_i \setminus N(v)|$.

In accordance with [29], we observed that LDG is the best performing heuristic. Even if Stanton and Kliot do not compare with NN, LDG outperforms it also. Non-neighbors typically have very good load balancing properties, as LDG as well, but cut significantly more edges. Table 3 shows the typical performance we observe across all datasets. Specifically, it shows $\lambda$ and $\rho$ for both BFS and random order for amazon0312. DFS order is omitted since qualitatively it does not differ from BFS. We observe that LDG is the best competitor, Fennel outperforms all existing competitors and is inferior to METIS, but of comparable performance. In the following, the best competitor is LDG unless otherwise mentioned.

## 5.2 Synthetic Datasets

In this section we present result that support the following main findings: (a) The value $\gamma = \frac{3}{2}$ achieves good performance for all graphs considered. (b) The effect of the stream order is minimal on the results. Specifically, when $\gamma \geq \frac{3}{2}$ all orders result in the same qualitative results. When $\gamma < \frac{3}{2}$

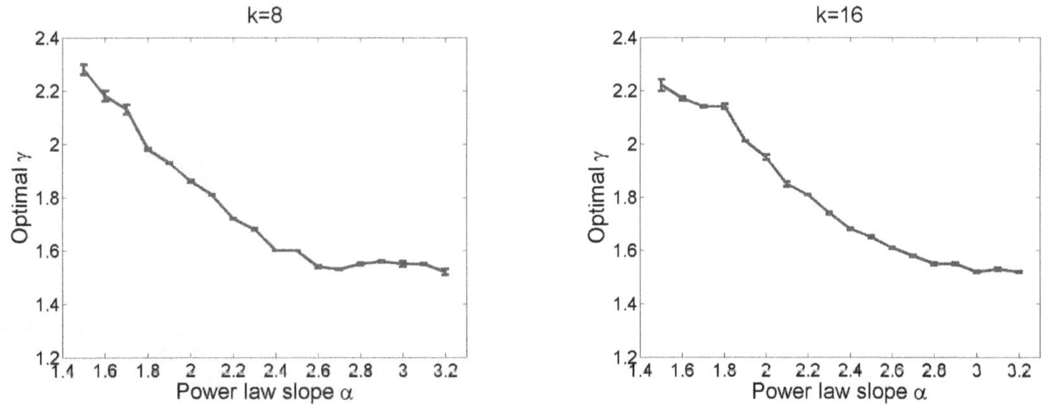


**Figure 2: Figure plots the average optimal value $\gamma^*$ by ranging the power-law exponent in the interval $[1.5, 3.2]$ using a step of 0.1 over twenty generated graphs (for each exponent) that results in the smallest possible fraction of edges cut $\lambda$ conditioning on a maximum normalized load $\rho = 1.2$ versus the power-law exponent of the degree sequence. Error bars indicate the variance around the average optimal value $\gamma^*$. Strong concentration around the average is observed. (a) $k = 8$ (b) $k = 16$.**

BFS and DFS orders result in the same results which are worse with respect to load balancing –and hence better for the edge cuts– compared to the random order. (c) FENNEL's performance is comparable to METIS. (d) It is possible to compute easy graph statistics such as the power-law exponent of the degree sequence of a power-law graph to fine-tune the choice of $\gamma$.

*Hidden Partition:* We report averages over five randomly generated graphs according to the model $\mathsf{HP}(5000, k, 0.8, 0.5)$ for each value of $k$ we use. We study (a) the effect of the parameter $\gamma$, which parameterizes the function $c(x) = \alpha x^\gamma$, and (b) the effect of the number of clusters $k$.

We range $\gamma$ from 1 to 4 with a step of 1/4, for six different values of $k$ shown in the second column of Table 4. For all $k$, we observed consistently the following behavior: for $\gamma = 1$, $\lambda = 0$ and $\rho = k$, which means that one cluster receives all vertices. For any $\gamma$ greater than 1, we obtain good load balancing with $\rho$ ranging from 1 to 1.05, and the same fraction of edges cut with METIS up the the first decimal digit. It is noteworthy that this behavior was not expected a priori, since in general we expect the edge-cut $\lambda$ to increase and $\rho$ to decrease as $\gamma$ grows. Given the insensitivity of FENNEL to $\gamma$ in this setting, we present our findings for $\gamma$ fixed to $\frac{3}{2}$, in Table 4. For each $k$ shown in the second column we generate five random graphs. The first column shows the average number of edges. Notice that despite the fact that we have only 5,000 vertices, we obtain graphs with several millions of edges. The four last columns show the performance of FENNEL and METIS. As we see, their performance is comparable and in one case (k=128) FENNEL clearly outperforms METIS.

*Power Law:* It is well known that power law graphs have no good cuts [12], but power-law graphs are commonly observed in practice so we consider them. We examine the effect of parameter $\gamma$ for $k$ fixed to 10. In contrast to the hidden partition experiment, we observe the expected tradeoff between $\lambda$ and $\rho$ as $\gamma$ changes. We generate five random power law graphs CL(20 000,2.5), since this value matches the typical slope of real-world networks [24]. Figure 1 shows the tradeoff when $\gamma$ ranges from 1 to 4 with a step of 0.25 for the random stream order. The straight line shows the performance of METIS. As we see, when $\gamma < 1.5$, $\rho$ assumes a value that may be considered unacceptably large for real-world applications. When $\gamma = 1.5$ we obtain essentially the same load balancing performance with METIS. Specifically, $\rho_{\text{Fennel}} = 1.02$, $\rho_{\text{METIS}} = 1.03$. The corresponding cut behavior for $\gamma = 1.5$ is $\lambda_{\text{Fennel}} = 62.58\%$, $\lambda_{\text{METIS}} = 54.46\%$. Furthermore, we experimented with the random, BFS and DFS stream orders. We observe that the only major difference between the stream orders is obtained for $\gamma = 1.25$. For all other $\gamma$ values the behavior is identical. For $\gamma = 1.25$ we observe that BFS and DFS stream orders result in significantly worse load balancing properties. Specifically, $\rho_{\text{BFS}} = 3.81$, $\rho_{\text{DFS}} = 3.73$, $\rho_{\text{Random}} = 1.7130$. The corresponding fractions of edges cut are $\lambda_{\text{BFS}} = 37.83\%$, $\lambda_{\text{DFS}} = 38.85\%$, and $\lambda_{\text{Random}} = 63.51\%$.

Finally, we explore the graph-specific parameter selection. Specifically, we consider the degree sequence as an easy-to-compute graph statistic and we generate for a realistic range of power-law exponents [8] twenty random power-law graphs on 3000 vertices. The number of vertices is chosen to be large enough in order to ensure that for large power-law exponents the graphs have sufficiently many edges to guarantee concentration of our findings. For each exponent, we compute the average optimal value $\gamma^*$ in the range $[1.5, 3.2]$ using a step of 0.1 over twenty generated graphs that results in the smallest possible fraction of edges cut $\lambda$ conditioning on a maximum normalized load $\nu = 1.2$. Figure 2 shows the resulting error bars for 8 and 16 clusters respectively. The variance for each power-law exponent is very small compared to the square of the average, indicating a strong concentration around the mean as the error bars show. We observe that $\gamma^*$ tends to be non-increasing function with the power-law slope $\alpha$. Also, by comparing Figures 2(a),(b) we observe that $\gamma^*$ is less sensitive to $k$, with a general trend of a decreasing $\gamma^*$ as $k$ increases. Understanding these functions and exploiting them for increasing systems' performance is an interesting problem for future work.

## 5.3 Real-World Datasets

We summarize our main findings as follows: (a) FENNEL *is superior to existing streaming partitioning algorithms.*

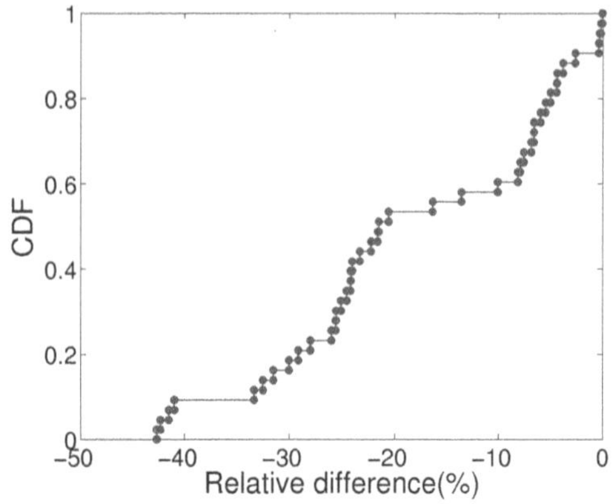


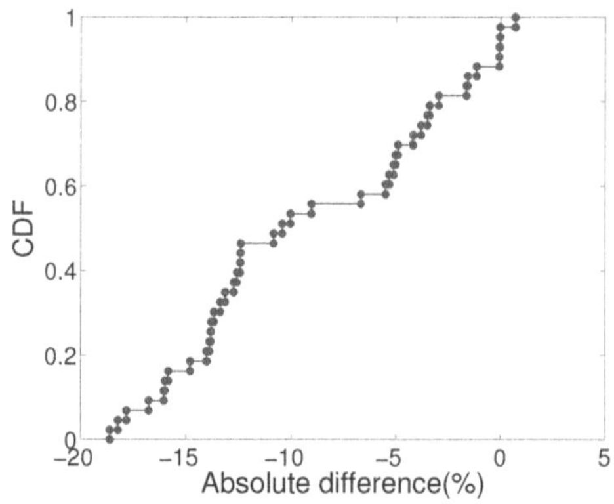


**Figure 3: (Left) CDF of the relative difference $(\frac{\lambda_{\mathbf{Fennel}}-\lambda_{\mathbf{c}}}{\lambda_{\mathbf{c}}}) \times 100\%$ of percentages of edges cut of our method and the best competitor for all graphs in our dataset. (Right) Same but for the absolute difference $(\lambda_{\mathbf{Fennel}} - \lambda_{\mathbf{c}}) \times 100\%$.**

| $k$ | Relative Gain | $\rho_{\text{Fennel}} - \rho_c$ |
|---|---|---|
| 2 | 25.37% | 0.47% |
| 4 | 25.07% | 0.36% |
| 8 | 26.21% | 0.18% |
| 16 | 22.07% | -0.43% |
| 32 | 16.59% | -0.34% |
| 64 | 14.33% | -0.67% |
| 128 | 13.18% | -0.17% |
| 256 | 13.76% | -0.20% |
| 512 | 12.88% | -0.17% |
| 1024 | 11.24% | -0.44% |

**Table 5: The relative gain $(1 - \frac{\lambda_{\mathbf{Fennel}}}{\lambda_{\mathbf{c}}}) \times 100\%$ and load imbalance, where subindex $c$ stands for the best competitor, averaged over all datasets in Table 1 as a function of $k$.**

Specifically, over a wide range of $k$ values and over all datasets FENNEL consistently outperforms the current state-of-the-art. FENNEL achieves excellent load balancing with significantly smaller edge cuts. (b) For smaller values of $k$ (less or equal than 64) the observed gain is more pronounced. (c) FENNEL *is fast*. Our implementation scales well with the size of the graph. It takes about 40 minutes to partition the Twitter graph which has more than 1 billion of edges.

*Twitter Graph.* Twitter graph is the largest graph in our collection of graphs, with more than 1.4 billion edges. This feature makes it the most interesting graph from our collection, even if, admittedly, it is a graph that can be loaded into the main memory of a state-the-art personal computer. The performance of FENNEL on this graph is remarkably good. Specifically, Table 1 shows the performance of FENNEL, the best competitor LDG, the baseline Hash Partition and METIS for $k = 2, 4$ and 8. All methods achieve balanced partitions, with $\rho \leq 1.1$. FENNEL, is the only method that always attains this upper bound. However, this reasonable performance comes with a high gain for $\lambda$. Specifically, we see that FENNEL achieves better performance of $k = 2$ than METIS. Furthermore, FENNEL requires 42 minutes whereas METIS requires $8\frac{1}{2}$ hours. Most importantly, FENNEL outperforms LDG consistently. Specifically, for $k = 16, 32$ and 64, FENNEL achieves the following results $(\lambda, \rho) = (59\%, 1.1)$, $(67\%, 1.1)$, and $(73\%, 1.1)$, respectively. Linear weighted degrees (LDG) achieves $(76\%, 1.13)$, $(80\%, 1.15)$, and $(84\%, 1.14)$, respectively. Now we turn our attention to smaller bur reasonably-sized datasets.

In Figure 3, we summarize the results of comparison results of FENNEL and all other heuristics that we consider on all graphs from our dataset in Table 2. In that figure, we show the distribution of the difference of the fraction of edges cut of our method and that of the best competitor, conditional on that the maximum observed load is at most 1.1. This distribution is derived from the values observed by partitioning each input graph from our set averaged over a range of values of parameter $k$ that consists of values $2, 4, \ldots, 1024$. These results demonstrate that the fraction of edges cut by our method is smaller than that of the best competitor in *all cases*. Moreover, we observe that the median absolute difference (relative difference) is in the excess of 20% (15%), thus providing significant performance gain.

Furthermore, in Table 5, we present the average performance gains conditional on the number of partitions $k$. These numerical results amount to an average relative reduction of the fraction of edges cut in the excess of 18%. Moreover, the performance gains observed are consistent across different values of parameter $k$, and are more pronounced for smaller values of $k$.

*Bicriteria.* In our presentation of experimental results so far, we focused on the fraction of edges cut by conditioning on the cases where the normalized maximum load was smaller than a fixed threshold. Figures 4(a), (b) provide a closer look at both criteria and their relation. Specifically, we consider the difference of the fraction of edges cut versus the difference of normalized maximum loads of the best competitor and our method. We observe that in all the cases, the differences of normalized maximum loads are well within 10% while the fraction of edges cut by our method is significantly smaller. These results confirm that the observed reduction of the fraction of edges cut by our method is not at the expense of an increased maximum load.

*Speed of partitioning.* We comment on the efficiency of our method with respect to the run time to partition a graph. Our graph partitioning algorithm is a one-pass streaming algorithm, which allows for fast graph partitioning. In order to support this claim, in Figure 5, we show the run time

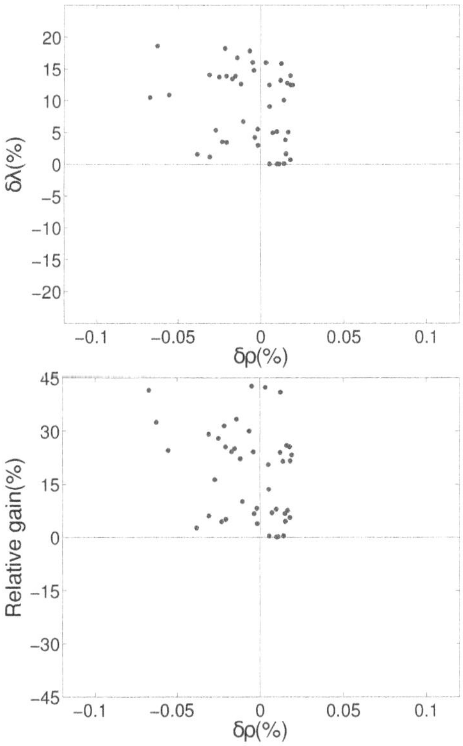


**Figure 4: Absolute difference $\delta\lambda$ and relative gain versus the maximum load imbalance $\delta\rho$.**

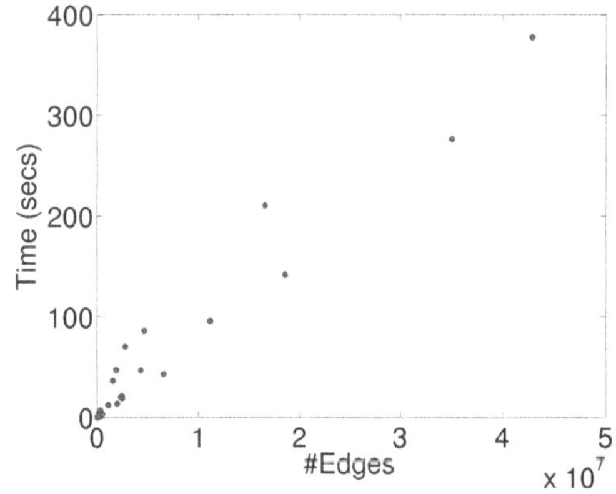


**Figure 5: Elapsed running time for FENNEL versus number of edges.**

it took to partition each graph from our dataset versus the graph size $m$. We observe that few minutes suffice to partition large graphs of tens of millions of edges. As we also mentioned before, partitioning the largest graph from our dataset collection took about 40 minutes.

# 6. SYSTEM EVALUATION

Evaluating a partitioning algorithm is a non-trivial task from a systems perspective, since it depends on system characteristics. For instance, in a large-scale production data center, it may be more important to balance the traffic across clusters than the traffic or the amount of computation executed within a cluster. However, in a small-scale cluster consisting of few tens of nodes, rented by a customer from a large cloud provider such as Amazon's Elastic MapReduce, for example, it may be more important to well balance the computation load on each node. Given this diversity of scenaria, a detailed evaluation is out of the scope of this work. Here, we perform a basic experiment to verify the superiority of our proposed method versus the standard approach load balancing approach of hash partitioning with respect to speeding up a large-scale computation.

We consider Pagerank as the computational task. Notice, that an advantage of Fennel is that it gives a flexibility in choosing a suitable objective that accomodates the needs of the specific application. We demonstrate the efficiency and flexibility of Fennel with the typical Elastic MapReduce scenario in mind. We set up a cluster and we vary the number of nodes to 4, 8 and 16 nodes. Each node is equipped with Intel Xeon CPU at 2.27 GHz and 12 GB of main memory. On the cluster we run Apache Giraph, a graph processing platform that runs on top of Hadoop. We implemented a PageRank algorithm on Giraph and run it on Live Journal graph data [1].

Since the complexity of PageRank depends on the number of edges and not vertices, we use a version of Fennel objective (eq. 1) that balances the number of edges per cluster with $\gamma = 1.5$ We compare with hash partitioning, the default partitioning scheme used by Giraph, with respect to the following two metrics. The first metric is the average duration of an iteration of the PageRank algorithm. This metric is directly proportional to the actual run time and incorporates both the processing and the communication time. The second metric is the average number of Megabytes transmitted by a cluster node in each iteration. This metric directly reflects the quality of the cut and is proportional to the incurred network load.

The results are shown in Table 6. We see that Fennel has the best run time in all cases. This is because it achieves the best balance between the computation and communication load. Hash partitioning takes 25% more time than Fennel and it also has a much higher traffic load.

# 7. CONCLUSION

In this work we provide a novel perspective on a recent line of research [25, 29] for the balanced graph partitioning problem, which results in state-of-the-art performance in terms of *speed* and *quality*. Despite the fact that FENNEL performs a single pass over the graph, it achieves performance comparable to METIS, see also [25]. Furthermore, our general framework is particularly suitable for dynamic graph data. Also, it allows us to quantify the notion of interpolation between the two state-of-the-art heuristics [26, 29] for streaming partitioning. Specifically, we evaluate our proposed framework extensively both on synthetic and real-world graphs. We verify consistently over a wide range of number of clusters, the superiority of our method compared to existing ones. Finally, we demonstrate the benefits of the method in the graph processing platform Apache Giraph.

An interesting research problem is to derive hard approximation guarantees for the class of algorithms defined by FENNEL. We provide initial results in this direction for

[1]At the time of the evaluation, the Twitter graph was too large for a 16-node Giraph cluster.

| | Run time [s] | | Communication [MB] | |
|---|---|---|---|---|
| # Clusters ($k$) | Hash | FENNEL | Hash | FENNEL |
| 4 | 32.27 | **25.49** | 321.41 | **196.9** |
| 8 | 17.26 | **15.14** | 285.35 | **180.02** |
| 16 | 10.64 | **9.05** | 222.28 | **148.67** |

**Table 6: The average duration of a step and the average amount of MB exchanged per node and per step during the execution of PageRank on LiveJournal data set.**

the special case related to the concept of graph modularity. However, additive error guarantees appear to be more suitable for our objective. Second, it would be of interest to understand on a firm mathematical ground, the function shown in Figure 2. Potentially, this understanding can lead to choosing optimally the parameter values based on simple graph characteristics, such as the exponent of the degree distribution for a power-law graph.

## 8. REFERENCES


[1] `http://staffweb.cms.gre.ac.uk/~wc06/partition/`.

[2] A. Angel, N. Sarkas, N. Koudas, and D. Srivastava. Dense subgraph maintenance under streaming edge weight updates for real-time story identification. *VLDB*, 2012.

[3] S. Arora, R. Satish, and U. Vazirani. Expander flows, geometric embeddings and graph partitioning. In *STOC*, pages 222-231, 2004.

[4] D. Blandford, G. Blelloch, and I. Kash. An experimental analysis of a compact graph representation. In *ALENEX*, 2004.

[5] F. R. K. Chung and L. Lu. The average distance in a random graph with given expected degrees. *Internet Mathematics*, 1(1):91–113, 2003.

[6] A. Condon and R. M. Karp. Algorithms for graph partitioning on the planted partition model. In *RANDOM-APPROX*, pages 221–232, 1999.

[7] J. Dean and S. Ghemawat. Mapreduce: simplified data processing on large clusters. *Commun. ACM*, 51(1):107–113, January 2008.

[8] Sergey N Dorogovtsev and Jose FF Mendes. Evolution of networks. *Advances in physics*, 51(4):1079–1187, 2002.

[9] U. Feige and R. Krauthgamer. A polylogarithmic approximation of the minimum bisection. *SIAM J. Comput.*, 31(4), 2002.

[10] M. R. Garey, D. S. Johnson, and L. Stockmeyer. Some simplified np-complete problems. In *STOC*, 1974.

[11] M. Girvan and M. E. J. Newman. Community structure in social and biological networks. *Proceedings of the National Academy of Sciences*, 99(12):7821–7826, 2002.

[12] J. Gonzalez, Y. Low, H. Gu, D. Bickson, and C. Guestrin. Powergraph: Distributed graph-parallel computation on natural graphs. In *OSDI*, 2012.

[13] U. Kang, C. E. T., and C. Faloutsos. Pegasus: A peta-scale graph mining system. In *ICDM*, 2009.

[14] T. Karagiannis, C. Gkantsidis, D. Narayanan, and A. Rowstron. Hermes: Clustering users in large-scale e-mail services. In *Cloud Computing*, 2010.

[15] G. Karypis and V. Kumar. Parallel multilevel graph partitioning. In *IPPS*, pages 314–319, 1996.

[16] G. Karypis and V. Kumar. A fast and high quality multilevel scheme for partitioning irregular graphs. *SIAM J. Sci. Comput.*, 20(1):359–392, December 1998.

[17] Q. Ke, V. Prabhakaran, Y. Xie, Y. Yu, J. Wu, and J. Yang. Optimizing data partitioning for data-parallel computing. In *HotOS XIII*, May 2011.

[18] B. W. Kernighan and S. Lin. An efficient heuristic procedure for partitioning graphs. *Bell Syst. Tech. J.*, 49(2):291–307, February 1970.

[19] A. Konstantin and H. Räcke. Balanced graph partitioning. In *SPAA '04*, pages 120–124, 2004.

[20] R. Krauthgamer, J. (S.) Naor, and R. Schwartz. Partitioning graphs into balanced components. In *SODA '09*, pages 942–949, 2009.

[21] H. Kwak, C. Lee, H. Park, and S. Moon. What is twitter, a social network or a news media? In *Proceedings of the 19th international conference on World wide web*, WWW '10, pages 591–600, New York, NY, USA, 2010. ACM.

[22] Y. Low, J. Gonzalez, A. Kyrola, D. Bickson, C. Guestrin, and J. M. Hellerstein. Graphlab: A new framework for parallel machine learning. In *UAI*, pages 340–349, 2010.

[23] G. Malewicz and et al. Pregel: a system for large-scale graph processing. In *SIGMOD '10*, pages 135–146, 2010.

[24] M. E. J. Newman. The structure and function of complex networks. *SIAM review*, 45(2):167–256, 2003.

[25] J. Nishimura and J. Ugander. Restreaming graph partitioning: Simple versatile algorithms for advanced balancing. In *ACM KDD*, 2013.

[26] V. Prabhakaran and et al. Managing large graphs on multi-cores with graph awareness. In *USENIX ATC'12*, 2012.

[27] J. Pujol and et al. The little engine(s) that could: Scaling online social networks. In *ACM SIGCOMM 2010*, 2010.

[28] K. Schloegel, G. Karypis, and V. Kumar. Parallel static and dynamic multi-constraint graph partitioning. *Concurrency and Computation: Practice and Experience*, 14(3):219 – 240, 2002.

[29] I. Stanton and G. Kliot. Streaming graph partitioning for large distributed graphs. In *ACM KDD*, pages 1222–1230, 2012.

[30] C.E. Tsourakakis, F. Bonchi, A. Gionis, F. Gullo, and M. Tsiarli. Denser than the densest subgraph: Extracting optimal quasi-cliques with quality guarantees. In *KDD'13*, 2013.

[31] Johan Ugander and Lars Backstrom. Balanced label propagation for partitioning massive graphs. In *WSDM '13*, pages 507–516, 2013.

# Finding HeavyPaths in Weighted Graphs and a Case-Study on Community Detection

Mohammad Khabbaz
Department of Computer Science
University of Calgary
mohammmad@gmail.com

## ABSTRACT

A heavy path in a weighted graph represents a notion of connectivity and ordering that goes beyond two nodes. The heaviest path of length $\ell$ in the graph, simply means a sequence of nodes with edges between them, such that the sum of edge weights is maximum among all paths of length $\ell$. It is trivial to state the heaviest edge in the graph is the heaviest path of length 1, that represents a heavy connection between (any) two existing nodes. This can be generalized in many different ways for more than two nodes, one of which is finding the heavy weight paths in the graph. In an influence network, this represents a highway for spreading information from a node to one of its indirect neighbors at distance $\ell$. Moreover, a heavy path implies an ordering of nodes. For instance, we can discover which ordering of songs (tourist spots) on a playlist (travel itinerary) is more pleasant to a user or a group of users who enjoy all songs (tourist spots) on the playlist (itinerary). This can also serve as a hard optimization problem, maximizing different types of quantities of a path such as score, flow, probability or surprise, defined as edge weight. Therefore, if one can solve the Heavy Path Problem (HPP) efficiently, they can as well use HPP for modeling and reduce other complex problems to it.

More precisely, we aim at finding $k$ heaviest (top-$k$) paths of a given length $\ell$. The weight of a path is defined as a monotone aggregation of individual edge weights using functions such as sum or product. We argue finding simple paths is way more practical than finding paths with cycles in applications such as: routing, playlist recommendation, itinerary planning and influence maximization. Avoiding cycles results in lists without repeated items and with better diversity. Simple paths are also expected to have a higher utility in practice. This makes HPP NP-hard and inapproximable. We propose an efficient algorithm that despite its *exponential* (theoretical) *worst case* running time, achieves the exact answer of the NP-hard problem in many useful cases and study the problem from different perspectives.

We compare our main algorithm, Repeated Sorted Access (RSA), against baseline and state-of-the-art algorithms. We show with experiments that following our approach is significantly more scalable than existing algorithms for solving HPP. We conduct a comprehensive set of experiments on four graphs that inherit characteristics of real life applications. This supports our arguments regarding scalability of RSA in practice. We make all of our implementations as well as graphs publicly available to enable reproducibility of our experiments. Our focus is on solving the technical problem in the first segment of the paper. Following our technical presentation, we provide a novel case study on community detection to illustrate the usefulness of solving HPP with a novel application.


*WSDM'14,* February 24–28, 2014, New York, New York, USA.

http://dx.doi.org/10.1145/2556195.2559897.

## 1. INTRODUCTION

Graphs are convenient data structures for modeling real life data such as social networks, citation networks, the web, phone call and email histories, purchase/transaction records and user actions [1]. It is easy to model data with graphs. However, we need sophisticated tools to make sense of such data. In order to do so, we need to study notions such as connectivity [1], centrality [23] and density [8]. Graph algorithms are at the core of community detection, for discovering various types of groups based on previous interactions of individuals [7]. Random walk based methods have been used in many mining and graph applications. Mining interesting multi-relational patterns is solved as discovering maximal pseudo cliques in k-partite graphs [3].

A problem that has received relatively less attention in the *research community* is that of finding $k$ cycle-free heaviest paths of length $\ell$ in a weighted graph (HPP). Sum and product are examples of monotone aggregation functions that define the aggregate weight of a path. Generating lists of items of interest is a great practical example. Suppose edge probability $w_{(u,v)} = P(v|u)$, the conditional transition probability that a random user would like to listen to $u$ (as next song) given that $v$ is the current song. Also assume there is equal probability for any user to like any song. Using product as aggregation function, the weight of a path is directly proportional to the probability that a cycle free *"chain"* of songs appears one after another in a listening session. A heavy path in such graph, represents a playlist with high overall transition probability between songs. The graph can be created according to user(s) listening history. We can imagine other kinds of lists such as reading lists of books or papers that show flows of ideas through publications.

In influence networks, recently there have been attempts for sparcification [20]. A path with high probability is a highway for spreading influence in an influence network with transition probabilities on edges. A more principled approach takes into account only heavy paths rather than technicalities and complex problem definitions. A complete study of all of HPP applications goes beyond the scope of this paper. We need the preliminary work done in this paper, in order to aim at creating a toolbox that uses heavy paths for network analysis. Here, we show a possible novel application for community detection in research communities in a co-authorship network. We use maximal frequent sub-paths in top-$k$ heavy paths in order to discover the *cores* and further *"grow"* each core with peripheral nodes using existing edges in top paths. We enhance our observations with meta-data, and show that the core communities found using our approach unanimously report highly influential researchers.

We make the following contributions in the subsequent sections:

- We formalize and motivate the HPP problem and show it is NP-hard and inapproximable. We discuss four exact algorithms, and provide a comparison of classical vs. novel algorithms for solving HPP. We provide a comprehensive experimental study of HPP algorithms presented in Section 7.
- We present a case study to discover small but influential networks of people in research communities. We do this analysis on a sub-graph of DBLP co-authorship graph, and report the results in Section 6.
- We show how a well studied top-$k$ query processing problem in the database literature can be converted to HPP on graphs where there is no database. We solely focus on algorithmic aspects, and propose a more scalable algorithm that overcomes the shortcommings of the Rankjoin [12] algorithm.

## 2. TECHNICAL PROBLEM DEFINITION

The most similar well studied problem to HPP in the literature is finding top-$k$ heavy paths on directed $\ell$-partite graphs. A nice example is *$k\ell$-Stable Clusters* problem [2]. Absence of cycles makes the studied problem considerably simpler than HPP. Furthermore, practical applications of HPP are not limited to $\ell$-partite graphs as described in Section 1. We show HPP is NP-hard and propose a practical algorithmic framework for solving it in the general case. It is common to use exponential time but efficient algorithms for mining purposes. Great examples are ***Apriori*** and ***FP-Growth*** [13], that is used for frequent item-set mining. Heavy paths also represent lists of highly connected items that can be used in similar ways to frequent item-sets and also for ordering of the items in the set.

Given a weighted graph $G(V, E, W)$, where weight $w_{(u,v)}$ represents the edge weight between $u$ and $v$, we aim at finding the $k$ heaviest simple paths of length $\ell$, with highest overall path weights. We call this the *Heavy Path Problem (HPP)*.

A simple path of length $\ell$ is a sequence of nodes $(v_0, \ldots, v_\ell)$ such that $(v_i, v_{i+1}) \in E$, $0 \leq i < \ell$, and there are no cycles, i.e., the nodes $v_i$ are distinct. Unless otherwise specified, in the rest of the paper, we use the term path to mean simple path. We focus on sum and product, as aggregation functions that define the weight of a path. For simplicity of presentation and practical considerations, we present using sum. We define weight of $P = (v_0, ..., v_\ell)$, as $P.weight = \sum_{j=0}^{\ell-1} w_{(j,j+1)}$. Furthermore, we know we can convert product to sum using log values and this does not change the order of the list of top-$k$ heaviest paths.

Finding the heaviest path for a given parameter $\ell$ is equivalent to the $\ell$-TSP problem, defined as follows: Given a weighted graph, find a path of ***minimum*** weight that passes through any $\ell + 1$ nodes. It is easy to see that for a given length $\ell$, a path $P$ is a solution to $\ell$-TSP iff it is a solution to HPP (with $k = 1$) on the same graph but with edge weights modified as follows: let $w_{(u,v)}$ be the weight of an edge $(u, v)$ in the $\ell$-TSP instance; then the edge weight in the HPP instance is $w'_{(u,v)} = C - w_{(u,v)}$, where $C$ is any constant. This reduction works in both ways given that we use the same constant $C$. We are not concerned with negative edge weights since we deal with paths without cycles; but, we focus on cases where edges are either all negative or all positive for simplicity. *It is well known that $\ell$-TSP is NP-hard (as a version of TSP).* Furthermore, $\ell$-TSP does not have any bounded approximation in the general case i.e. no triangle inequality on edge weights etc [5, 4].

**PROPOSITION** 1. *HPP does not have any bounded approximation in polynomial time.*

PROOF. We know $\ell$-TSP is not approximable. Remember the $C-w$ reduction between $\ell$-TSP($G1$) and HPP ($G2$) introduced earlier. Suppose $C = 0$ and $k = 1$, if $P$ is the answer to HPP (the heaviest path) on $G2$, it is the answer to $\ell$-TSP on $G1$ after $-w$ transformation on edge weights. The weight of $P$ in $G1$ ($-W_{max}$) is the negative of its weight in $G2$ ($W_{max}$). If we find an $\alpha$ ($0 < \alpha < 1$) approximation to $P$ on $G2$ as a result of finding path $Q$ in polynomial time we have $Q.W \geq \alpha \times W_{max}$. On $G1$ graph equivalently we can say, $-Q.W \leq \alpha \times -W_{max}$. Since $-W_{max}$ is the optimal answer on $G1$ graph (i.e. minimum weight among all paths), it is guaranteed that $-Q.W$ is in the range $-W_{max} \leq -Q.W \leq \alpha \times -W_{max}$ and is a true approximate answer to $\ell$-TSP. We know $\ell$-TSP is not approximable. According to the above argument, approximability of HPP results in approximability of $\ell$-TSP. This is in contradiction with the known fact that $\ell$-TSP and TSP are not approximable in the general case. □

In Figure 1(a), the heaviest simple path of length 4, is obtained by visiting the nodes in the order 6–1–2–3–4 and has a weight of 3.35. In contrast, a different permutation of the nodes 4–3–6–1–2 has a weight of 3.08. The higher weight of a path can represent a sequence with more strength or better quality. Different permutations result in paths with different weights simply because paths consist of different edges most likely with different edge weights.

## 3. ALGORITHMS

### 3.1 Baselines

An obvious algorithm for finding the heaviest paths of length $\ell$ is performing a depth-first search (DFS) from each node, with the search limited to a depth of $\ell$, while maintaining the $k$ heaviest paths and avoiding cycles. This is an exhaustive algorithm and is not expected to scale. A somewhat better approach is dynamic programming. Held and Karp [10] proposed a dynamic programming algorithm for TSP which we adapt to HPP as follows. Since path lengths required in our problem are typically much smaller than the total number of nodes in the graph, we replace the notion of "allowed nodes" with "avoiding nodes". The idea is to find the heaviest $J$-avoiding path of length $\ell - 1$ that ends in one of the neighbors of $J$. We can repeat this recursively during

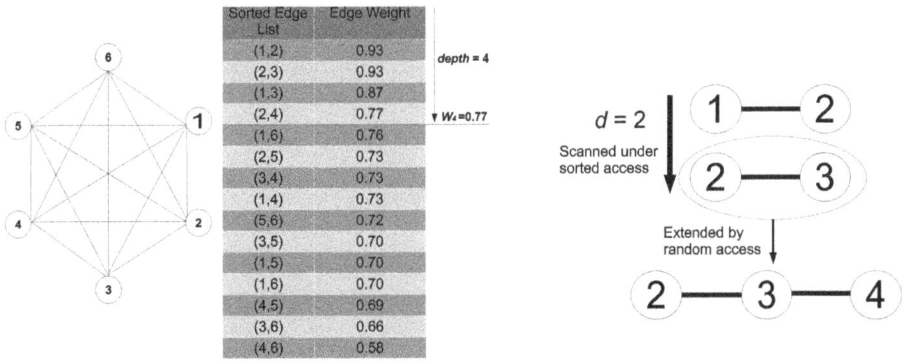


(a) (b)

**Figure 1:** (a) A complete graph with 6 nodes and sorted list of edges. (b) An example of random access is shown on the right.

the execution using smaller path lengths and larger avoidance sets as parameters. The base case is where the input parameter assigned to length is 1, in which we only need to consider the paths created by extending the current path by one hop, making sure we do not extend by any nodes that belong to the $(\ell - 1)$ size avoidance set. The rest is similar to DFS. We repeat this for every node($J$) and keep track of the heaviest path. Dynamic Programming algorithm aggregates and discards many short path segments early on by choosing the heaviest one that ends at a certain node. Both DFS and Dynamic Programming can be easily generalized to report top-$k$ paths which is not the focus of this paper.

## 3.2 Sorted Access Algorithm (SAA) for HPP

The methods discussed in the previous section lack the ability to prune the search space using edge weights. It may be more promising to first look at those parts of the graph with heavier edge weights. If they connect, they can create heavy paths. This way, we solve HPP only for a smaller sub-graph or at least explore the search space more efficiently. This can make a considerable difference to the exponentially increasing running time of the problem using smaller input size. There exists a body of work on top-$k$ algorithms in the database community started by Fagin et al. [6]. These algorithms aim at finding top-$k$ items without searching the whole search space using *sorted access*. The framework is such that partial item scores from multiple sorted lists $(l_1 ... l_\ell)$, are aggregated using a monotone aggregation function. Following their idea more aggressive top-$k$ algorithms were proposed in order to extend their framework with probabilistic guarantees such as [18]. We can argue the weight of a path (item), is the aggregation of several partial item scores (edges). This makes following top-$k$ query processing ideas promising for solving HPP. In particular, in Rank Join [11, 21] problem, partial scores in $l_1$ can join more than one partial scores in $l_2$. For instance, suppose $l_1$ provides a sorted list of movie theaters and $l_2$ provides a sorted list of restaurants sorted by their popularity score. One may be interested in watching a movie and going to a restaurant in the same neighborhood. The score of a combination is defined using the sum of the individual scores and items of interest are (movie theater, restaurant) combinations. There may be many movie theaters and restaurants in the same neighborhood.

***Problem Conversion:*** *Define a tripartite graph. The first column of nodes is a single dummy node (dummy1) as well as the third column(dummy3). Every node in the middle column represents a neighborhood (such as downtown). Every movie theater ($l_1$), is modeled as an edge that connects dummy1 to its neighborhood with a directed edge. Every restaurant ($l_2$), is modeled as a directed edge that connects its neighborhood to dummy3. Edge weight is defined as item score. Heaviest paths of length 2 are top combinations. Rankjoin can be converted to heavy path on a tripartite graph.*

We design an adaptation of Rankjoin that works with self-joins (i.e. all $l_i$ are identical) for solving HPP on general graphs. Direct usage of Rankjoin results in creating many paths with cycles that need to be pruned later on. SAA (Algorithm 1), avoids creating cycles early on. SAA algorithm scans the sorted list of edges and reads one edge at a time. Once a new edge ($e$) is read under sorted access, it is joined with the list of heavier edges (ScannedEdges) $\ell - 1$ times. The *Join* operation used in line 8, takes two input parameters: 1) a list of paths of length $i$, $P^i$; 2) a list of edges, *ScannedEdges*. It extends all paths of length $i$ in $P^i$ with matching edges in *ScannedEdges* (i.e. smaller search space) and ensures no cycles are created. This results in paths of length $i+1$. In case $P^{i+1}$ is empty because there are no matching nodes to join without cycles, naturally, no path will be created. For instance no path of length $l > 1$ is created after joining the heaviest edge and the empty set of scanned edges. This is how *Join* is defined as an operation. Join is one of the operations defined in Relational Algebra. Therefore, it is not scary to use *Join*, it has been used in practice as part of the DBMS operations for a long time. We do an enhanced implementation for self-joins that prunes cycles as well. Paths of length

**Algorithm 1** SAA $(E, \ell, k)$

**Input:** Sorted edge list $E$, path length $\ell$, number of paths $k$
**Output:** top-$k$ heaviest paths of length $\ell$

1: $topKBuffer$ = // empty sorted set
2: $\theta = \ell \times W_{max}$ // edge weights $\in [0, 1]$
3: $ScannedEdges$ = // empty hash table
4: $e = E.getNextEdge()$
5: **while** $topKBuffer.BottomScore < \theta$ **do**
6: $P^1 = e$
7: **for** $l = 1$ to $\ell - 1$ **do**
8: $P^{i+1} = Join(P^i, ScannedEdges)$ // avoid cycles
9: $Update(topKBuffer, P^\ell)$
10: $\theta = e.w + (\ell - 1) \times W_{max}$
11: $ScannedEdges.put(e.start, e)$
12: $ScannedEdges.put(e.end, e)$
13: $e = E.getNextEdge()$
14: **return** $topKBuffer$

$\ell$ will be created after enough edges are scanned in sorted order. This operation is repeated $\ell - 1$ times, until all possible paths of length $\ell$ including $e$ and heavier edges are produced. At this point (line 10), SAA knows that no path can be created during the rest of execution which is heavier than $\theta = e.w + (\ell - 1) \times W_{max}$. Therefore, if we have already constructed $k$ paths heavier than $\theta$, we know that these are the correct top-$k$ paths of length $\ell$. In order to speed up the *Join* operation, *ScannedEdges* is maintained as a hash table that maps nodes (keys) to edges (values). Consider the example graph in Figure 1(a). Suppose we are interested in the heaviest path of length 3. The SAA algorithm proceeds by scanning the edge list in sorted order of the edge weights. After reading 4 edges at depth $d = 4$, the edge weight ($w_4$) is 0.77 and $w_{max} = 0.93$. We can calculate the threshold (upperbound) as: $\theta(2.63) = 0.77 + (3 - 1) * 0.93$. At depth 5, SAA is able to construct the path (6,1,2,3) and $\theta(2.62) = 0.76 + 2 * 0.93$. Since $\theta$ is equal to the weight of (6,1,2,3), we know it is at least one of the heaviest paths in the graph and can terminate without processing the rest of the edges in the sorted list. This is what we call *search space pruning by Sorted Access.*

## 4. LIMITATIONS OF *SAA* AND OPTIMIZATIONS

**LIMITATION** 1. *Let $P$ be a path of length $\ell$ and suppose e is the lightest edge on $P$, i.e., its weight is the least among all edges in $P$. Then until e is seen under sorted access, the path $P$ will not be constructed by SAA.*

Limitation 1, simply follows the fact that paths are created using *only* sorted access to the list of edges. If we run SAA on the graph of Fig. 2, we won't create the heaviest path (a,b,c,d) until the edge (c,d) is scanned. However, (c,d) is the lightest edge in the graph. This means following only sorted access, may delay the construction of the heaviest path until many irrelevant paths are created and discarded. This observation motivates the following optimization for finding heaviest paths.

**OPTIMIZATION** 1. *We should try to avoid delaying the production of a heavy path of a certain length until the lightest edge on the path is seen under sorted access. One possible way of making this happen is via random access. However, random accesses have to be done with care in order to keep the overhead low.*

In the example of Fig. 2, suppose we have constructed (a,b,c) and know it is the heaviest path of length 2. It may be a good heuristic to extend (a,b,c) with new edges such as (c,d) and create paths of length 3. Since (a,b,c) is the heaviest path of length 2, it is very likely to create heavy paths of length 3 by extending (a,b,c). Making access to graph edges such as (c,d), regardless of where they appear on the sorted list of edges, is what we refer to as *"**random access**"*. An example of random access is presented by Figure 1(b). Making random access to the edge list simply means reading an edge without caring about where the edge is located on the sorted list of edges (through the adjacency matrix). This can help produce *heavy paths* containing *low weight* edges earlier. Our case study in Section 6, shows one practical example where a *low weight* edge on a heavy path, can have

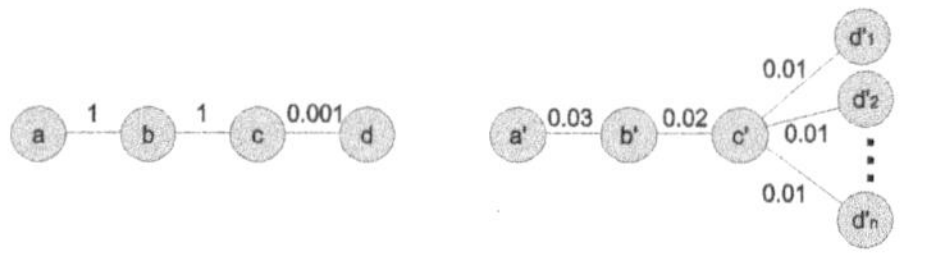


**Figure 2: Example instance of HPP. Graph has one heavy path and $n$ lighter paths.**

a meaningful interpretation. The discussion is provided in Section 6, for *Gui-Rong Xue's* edges with others. Following this optimization, suppose we use random accesses to find "matching" edges with which to extend heaviest paths of length $\ell - 1$ to length $\ell$. This way we won't delay the creation of heavy paths until their lightest edge is visited under sorted access. However, this may not be enough for early termination of the algorithm. Another decisive factor in early termination is the upperbound threshold ($\theta$) value on weight of paths we have not created yet using the *ScannedEdges*.

**LIMITATION** 2. *SAA threshold is conservative compared to what can be easily obtained during the execution.*

SAA stops when $\theta$ gets smaller than the weight of the heaviest path of length $\ell$ discovered so far. Suppose there is an instance in which the heaviest path of length $\ell$ is lighter than $w_{min} + (\ell - 1) \times w_{max}$. In this case, SAA will produce every path of length $\ell$ before reporting the heaviest path, resulting in no pruning. In Fig. 1(a), this happens when trying to find the heaviest path of length 4 and in Fig. 2, when trying to find the heaviest path of length 3. The following lemma highlights a natural possibility during the execution of SAA for obtaining a tighter threshold that results in earlier termination.

**LEMMA** 1. *Let $P$ be the heaviest path of length $\ell$. When SAA terminates, every path of length $\ell - 1$ that has weight no less than $P.weight - w_{max}$, will be created. This includes the heaviest path of length $\ell - 1$.*

PROOF. Suppose SAA finds $P$ at depth $d$. This means $P.weight \geq w_d + (\ell - 1) \times w_{max}$, and, $P.weight - w_{max} \geq w_d + (\ell - 2) \times w_{max}$. Notice that $P.weight - w_{max}$ is a lower bound on the weight of the heaviest path of length $\ell - 1$. Therefore, if there is a path of length $\ell - 1$ that is heavier than $P.weight - w_{max}$, it will be produced by SAA by depth $d$. □

One way of making the threshold tighter is by keeping track of shorter paths. For example, if we know $P$ is a heaviest path of length $\ell - 1$, we can infer that the heaviest path of length $\ell$ cannot be heavier than $P.weight + w_{max}$, a bound often much tighter than $w_d + (\ell - 1)w_{max}$.

For this, we need to keep track of the heaviest paths of length $\ell - 1$ one by one to lower the threshold more aggressively, gradually and smoothly. Pursuing this idea recursively leads to a framework where we maintain and release heaviest paths of each length $i$, $2 \leq i \leq \ell$, at the right time and make the next threshold tighter. More precisely, we can perform the following optimization. For this purpose, we can use Buffers as sorted sets (priority queue) in order to store (insert) and release heavy paths (remove top). Figure 3 schematically describes the idea of using buffers for different path lengths. Buffer $B_1$ is the sorted edge list for the graph in Figure 2. Buffers $B_2$ and $B_3$ store paths of length 2 and 3 respectively. When random accesses are performed to extend paths of length $l - 1$ to those of length

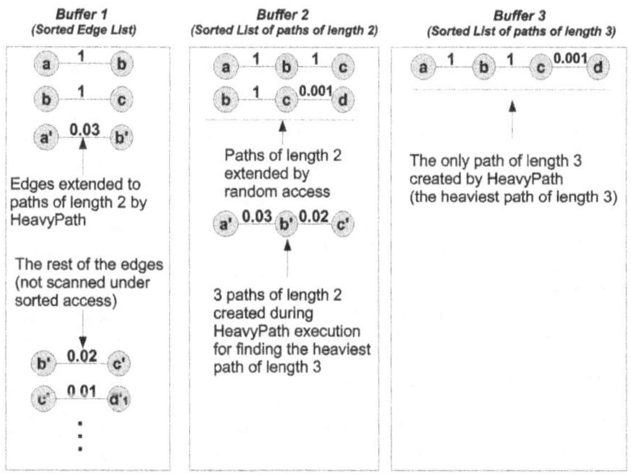


**Figure 3:** RSA example for finding the heaviest path of length 3 on graph of Figure 2

**Algorithm 2** RSA $(E, \ell, k)$

**Input:** Sorted edge list $E$, path length $\ell$, number of paths $k$
**Output:** top-$k$ heaviest paths of length $\ell$

```
for l = 2 to ℓ do
    B_l ← ∅ // empty sorted set
    θ_l = w_max × l
topPaths ← ∅ // empty sorted set
while | topPaths |< k do
    topPaths ← topPaths ∪ NextHeavyPath (E, ℓ)
```

$l$, the buffers can be used to store these intermediate paths. For instance, when the heaviest path of length 1 is seen, say edge $(a, b)$ is seen, it can be extended to paths of length 2 by accessing edges connected to its end points, as represented by $B_2$ in Figure 3. Similarly, the heaviest path of length 2 can be extended by an edge using random access to obtain path(s) in buffer $B_3$. Obviously, we do not extend all shorter path segments and extend only the one that is known to be the next heaviest path of shorter length in its own buffer. We describe this framework in more detail when we present the final algorithm next.

**LIMITATION** 3. *SAA tends to produce the same sub-path multiple times. For example, when SAA is required to produce the heaviest path of length 3 for the graph in Figure 2, for paths $(a', b', c', d'_i)$, $i \in [1, n]$, it produces the length 2 sub-path $(a', b', c')$ $n$ times as it does not maintain shorter path segments. This results in more edge reads and significantly increases the running time.*

## 5. REPEATED SORTED ACCESS(RSA) ALGORITHM

We start this section by providing an outline of our main algorithm for solving HPP. Our algorithm maintains a buffer $B_i$ for storing paths of length $i$ explored and not released ($P.w < \theta$), where $2 \leq i \leq \ell$. Let threshold $\theta_i$ denote an upper bound on the weight of any path of length $i$ that has never been inserted into $B_i$. Algorithm 2 describes the overall approach. It takes as input a list of edges $E$ sorted in non-increasing order of edge weights, and parameters $\ell$ and $k$. It calls the NextHeavyPath method (Algorithm 3) repeatedly until the top-$k$ heaviest paths of length $\ell$ are found.

**Algorithm 3** NextHeavyPath $(E, l)$

**Input:** Sorted list of edges $E$, and path length $l$
**Output:** Next heaviest path of length $l$

```
1: if l = 1 then
2:     P^1 ← ReadEdge(E)
3:     θ_2 = 2 × P^1.weight
4:     return P^1
5: while B_l.topScore ≤ θ_l do
6:     P^{l-1} ← NextHeavyPath (E, l − 1) // recursion
7:     s, t ← EndNodes(P^{l-1})
8:     for all y ∈ V | (y, s) ∈ E do
9:         B_l ← B_l ∪ ((y, s) + P^{l-1}) // avoiding cycles
10:    for all z ∈ V | (t, z) ∈ E do
11:        B_l ← B_l ∪ (P^{l-1} + (t, z)) // avoiding cycles
12: P^l ← RemoveTopPath(B_l)
13: if l < ℓ then
14:     θ_{l+1} = max(B_l.topScore, θ_l) + w_max
15: return P^l
```

Algorithm 3[1] describes the NextHeavyPath method. It takes as input a list of edges $E$ sorted in non-increasing order of edge weights, and the desired path length $l$, $l \geq 2$. It is a recursive algorithm that produces heaviest paths of shorter lengths on demand, and extends them with edges to produce paths of length $\ell$. The base case for this recursion is when $l = 1$ and the algorithm reads the next edge from the sorted list of edges. The ReadEdge method returns the heaviest unseen edge in $E$ (sorted access, line 2). If $l < \ell$, the path of length $l$ obtained as a result of the recursion is extended by one hop to produce paths of length $l + 1$. Specifically, a path of length $l < \ell$ is extended using edges (random access, lines 8 and 10) that can be appended to either one of its ends (returned by method EndNodes). The "+" operator for appending an edge to a path is defined in a way that guarantees no cycles are created. The threshold $\theta_l$ is updated aggressively when the next heaviest path of length $l - 1$ is released from $B_{l-1}$. This is done by calling the method RemoveTopPath for buffer $B_{l-1}$ and returning the resulting path. If there is no path already in the buffer that beats $\theta_{l-1}$, this results in more recursion using smaller $l$, until this condition becomes true at some point during the execution. At any point during the execution if $i < \ell$ and the next heaviest path of length $i$ (P) has been obtained ($B_i.topScore > \theta_i$), $\theta_{i+1}$ is more intuitively updated as $\theta_{i+1} = P.W + W_{max}$ [2].

**THEOREM** 1. *Algorithm* RSA *correctly finds top-k heaviest paths of length $\ell$.*

Proof. The proof is by induction. The base case is for going from edges to paths of length 2. Given that all of the edges above depth $d$ are extended, the heaviest path that can be created from them is already in $B_2$. The weight of the heaviest path that can be created from lighter edges is at most $2 \times w_d$. If the heaviest path in $B_2$ is heavier than $2 \times w_d$, then it must be the heaviest path of length 2. Assuming the heaviest paths of length $l$ are produced correctly in sorted order, we show the heaviest path of length $l + 1$ is found correctly. Suppose $P$, the heaviest path of length $l + 1$, is created for the first time by extending $Q$, which is the $n^{th}$ heaviest path of length $l$. The next heaviest path of length $l$ is either already in $B_l$ or has not been created yet. Therefore, $\max(\theta_l, B_l.topScore)$ is an upper bound on the next heaviest path of length $l$ that has not been identified yet. Any such path can be extended by an edge of weight at most $w_{max}$. Suppose when the $m^{th}$ heaviest path of length $l$ is seen, $\max(\theta_l, B_l.topScore) + w_{max}$ is updated to a value smaller than $P.weight$. It is guaranteed that $P$ is already in $B_{l+1}$ and has the highest weight in that buffer. In other words, when the threshold

[1] In order to avoid StackOverflow we do a non-recursive implementation. We use the recursive pseudo code because it is more intuitive.
[2] We use a bound tighter threshold, line 14 of Algorithm 3.

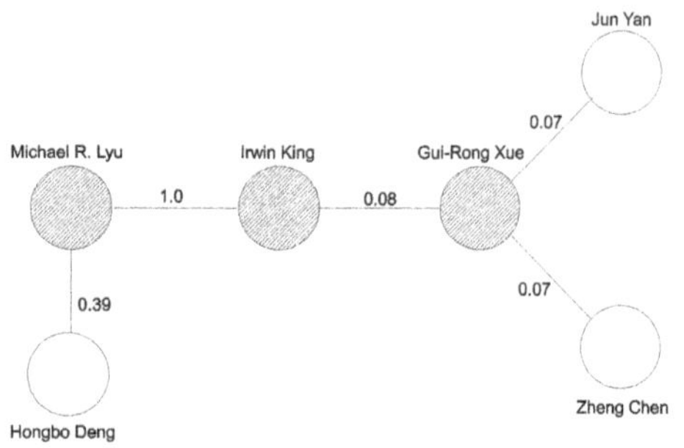


(a) Community 1 (Chinese University of Hong Kong, Aliyun.com, MSRA)

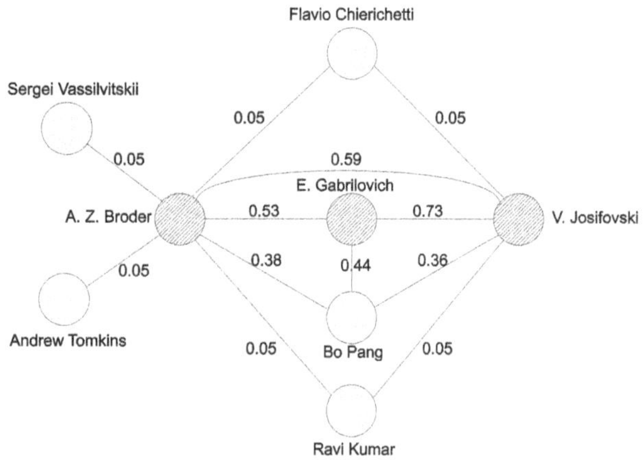


(b) Community 2 (Yahoo!, Google)

**Figure 4: Two sample communities along with their cores, found using parameters $\ell = 5$, $k = 100$ and support = 10.**

is smaller than $P.weight$, the difference between the weight of $P$ and next heaviest path of length $l$ is more than $w_{max}$. Now, paths of length $l + 1$ that can be created from heavier paths of length $l$ are already in the buffer, and no unseen path of length $l$ can be extended to create a path heavier than $P$. Therefore, $P$ is guaranteed to be the heaviest path. The preceding arguments hold for top-$k$ heaviest paths where $k > 1$. □

# 6. COMMUNITY DETECTION CASE-STUDY

Suppose we have a co-authorship graph that connects researchers according to their publications. The edge weight is defined as the sum of *"pairwise collaboration credits"* that researchers get from each paper they publish together. Pairwise collaboration credit for a pair of authors in a paper, is $1/authorNum$. Where $authorNum$ is the number of authors of a paper. Given a collection of publications, we define an edge between two researchers if they have published at least one paper together. Then use the sum of *"pairwise collaboration credits"* they get from all of the papers they have published together as the edge weight. Single author papers do not contribute to edge weights. We further normalize edge weights by the maximum so that they are all in $[0, 1]$. Using this graph, and given parameters $\ell$ and $k$ and a *popularity* [3] parameter, we do the following,

1. Find top-$k$ heaviest paths of length $l$
2. Finding ***cores*** of communities: Find all ***maximal*** frequent sub-paths in top-$k$ paths. Frequent sub-paths are those that appear in more number of paths than the *popularity* parameter.
3. Aggregate top-$k$ paths and form the *aggregate graph of top paths*
4. Given a ***core*** and the *aggregate graph of top paths*, do the following: add any edges that connect any other researchers in the aggregate graph of top paths to the core. This shapes a community of *core* researchers that appear on many heavy paths. It also adds those other researchers who are strongly connected to the core community.
5. Communities can grow using larger values for $k$ that adds more nodes to the picture. In a way, $k$ can be used to zoom in and zoom out of communities.

Using DBLP data [14], we constructed this graph using papers published between 2008 and 2011 (inclusive), presented in the main program one of these conferences: "SDM", "PKDD", "ICDM", "SIGKDD", "CIKM", "SIGIR", "ICML", "NIPS", "WWW" and "WSDM". Figure 4, shows two of the communities we find using parameters $l = 5$, $k = 100$ and $popularity = 10$. We provide this graph (DBLPG), and the top-100 paths of length 5, to enable the reader to reproduce the communities described [4]. We notice that the core of community 1 (Figure 4(a)) contains the pair of researchers with the highest edge weight in the graph. This shows a long lasting collaboration. We did a quick google search about each of the core communities in DBLPG. Irwin King and Michael R. Lyu work for the Chinese University of Hong Kong. They are connected to Gui-Rong Xue who is the senior director at Aliyun.com and he is connected to a principal researcher from Microsoft research Asia (Zheng Chen).

Most of the researchers in community 2 (Figure 4(a)) have worked for Yahoo! Research Labs, including the three researchers in the core. Andrei Z. Broder is currently a distinguished scientist at Google. He has previously worked at Yahoo!, IBM and Altavista. We also found on his Wikipedia page that he is the inventor of MinHash locality sensitive hashing. Evgeniy Gabrilovich, is a senior staff research scientist at Google who also used to have a central role at Yahoo! research. Vanja Josifovski apparently still works for Yahoo! and is a Principal Research Scientist and the Lead of the Performance Advertising Group at Yahoo! Research. Most of the other researchers in community 2 work for yahoo! as their emails appear on their publications. Some may have moved to Google recently!

It is worth noting that we discovered three other cores as well in our output. Due to space limitations, we only report the cores: *core 3* = {Andrei Z. Broder, Evgeniy Gabrilovich, Xuerui Wang }(weight = 0.73), *core 4* = {Shuicheng Yan, Ning Liu, Jun Yan, Zheng Chen } and *core 5* = {Ning Liu,

[3] Same as support in frequent pattern mining

[4] http://ucalgary.ca/~mkhabbaz/DBLPG.zip

Jun Yan, Zheng Chen, Weizhu Chen }. Xuerui Wang is also a scientist at Yahoo! labs. Cores 4 and 5 have size 4. We notice that a sub-path of length 3 is shared between these two, with all researchers from Microsoft Research Asia. Community 1 is connected to two of these three researchers through Gui-Rong Xue. This shows a potential for collaboration between these two *cores* in the future! who are the Chinese University of Hong Kong and Microsoft Research Asia. Changing the parameters $l$, $k$ and *popularity*, changes the output in the form presented in Figure 6. It can also help with creating a visualization tool that adapts its output with the current parameter values and be used for visualizing hierarchies and relationships of communities at different scales. Such a tool needs to run RSA repeatedly with different parameter values in order to change its view. This highlights the importance of scalability and efficiency for HPP problem. We leave the continuation and implementation of this idea to our future work.

The case study presented in this section, is also an example of an application where finding the exact solution is required. This is because we focus on 100 heaviest paths and frequent pattern mining in order to discover the cores of communities. Heuristic or any sort of approximate solutions may result in paths that do not necessarily go through the cores that form the top communities. *Top-k heaviest paths, rely on their cores to be heavy!*

# 7. EXPERIMENTAL ANALYSIS

## 7.1 Reproducibility

We use four graphs in our experiments. We create graphs using Cora[5], last.fm[6] and DBLP datasets. **Cora(70 nodes-1580 edges):** nodes represent research topics and edge weights are defined using the average fraction of citations between the two topics. **Last.fm(40k nodes-183k edges)**: we crawled the existing collection of playlists. Nodes represent songs and edges represent co-occurrence in playlists. Edge weight is defined using the Dice coefficient[7]. **BAY(321k nodes-400k edges)**: it represents the road network in San Francisco Bay area[8]. For this graph we perform the $C-W$ (C=1) transformation described in Section 2, and solve $\ell$-TSP because distance minimization makes more sense for road networks. **DBLPG(4.5k nodes-9k edges)**: Section 6 describes how the graph is created. In all cases, the graph we work with has edge weights in $[0-1]$ and the input graph is a text file that stores one edge per line in this format: "source destination weight". You can access a .zip file containing all the preprocessed graphs[9]. We do not use graphs with millions of edges since the problem is NP-hard and we focus on finding exact answers. On the other hand, all of the graphs we use in experiments deal with practical real life applications. One interesting fact we discovered in our experiments is that the smallest of the graphs (Cora) we use, is one of the most challenging scenarios. This is due to the fact that its average node degree is higher than others and this results in an exponentially larger number of longer paths when $\ell$ increases. We do not report any results regarding the DFS algorithm because it is inferior to Dynamic Programing in all cases. Source code of all algorithms, along with instructions for running can be downloaded[10]. All experiments were performed on a Linux machine with 64GB of main memory and 2.93GHz-8Mb Cache CPU. To be consistent, we allocated 12GB of memory for each run. In all of the cases where RSA[11] runs out of memory, other algorithms either also run out of the 12GB allocated memory, or do not terminate after running for a couple of days. Our implementation is in Java. For all algorithms other than RSA, we provide implementation such that the time spent on Garbage Collection can be measured accurately using the *Jstat* tool[12]. All of the figures that present running time use log scale on Y-axis. We further analyzed GC time and found it is negligible compared to the total running time in all cases as supposed to be since Java is one of the most reliable programming languages.

## 7.2 Empirical Evaluation

Figure 5(a-c) show the running time for finding the top-1 path of various lengths for Cora, last.fm and Bay graphs. Average node degree plays a key role in the empirical hardness of HPP. This is due to the fact that the complexity of the problem increases exponentially with node degree.

The running time increases with $\ell$ for all algorithms, as supposed to be. SAA does not manage to go beyond short path lengths in most cases, the reasons being those limitations mentioned in Section 4. Beyond some depth down the sorted edge list, SAA becomes inefficient due to the increasing complexity of the problem and the fact that it either does not manage to construct heavy paths early on or the fact that the threshold decays slowly. For shorter path lengths SAA terminates earlier than Dynamic Programing because it does pruning and uses a threshold for termination while Dynamic Programing explores a larger search space. RSA performs considerably more efficient than other algorithms except for one case on Cora graph for $\ell = 3$ where it is slightly less efficient than SAA. We believe this is due to the fact that RSA uses a combination of sorted and random access. Random access results in fundamental improvements in the running time as we see in most cases. However, in some rare cases SAA may get lucky because it avoids random access and also the edge weights are such that result in fast termination. Albeit, at the cost of losing all the other experiments. All in all, our findings show that RSA is a way more scalable and reliable algorithm. Dynamic Programing behaves consistently and manages to achieve pruning by aggregating shorter path segments early on. However, it finds the heaviest path ending at every node and although it scales to longer lengths, it is orders of magnitude slower than RSA. We would like to highlight again that we use log scale on Y-axis and the difference in the running times is considerable. All in all, there is no question about the surprising scalability of RSA in all experiments.

Figures 5(d-f), compare the running times of SAA and RSA for varying $k$ and fixed $\ell = 4$, since these two are the algorithms designed to work as top-$k$ algorithms. In all cases, RSA is more efficient and it spends a smaller marginal run-

[5] http://www.cs.umass.edu/~mccallum/data

[6] www.last.fm

[7] $\text{dice}(i,j) = \frac{2|i \cap j|}{|i|+|j|}$

[8] http://www.dis.uniroma1.it/

[9] http://ucalgary.ca/~mkhabbaz/Graphs.zip

[10] http://ucalgary.ca/~mkhabbaz/HPPCase.zip

[11] We use the name HeavyPath for our implementation of the algorithm.

[12] Java does garbage collection automatically using GC algorithms. http://docs.oracle.com/javase/1.5.0/docs/tooldocs/share/jstat.html

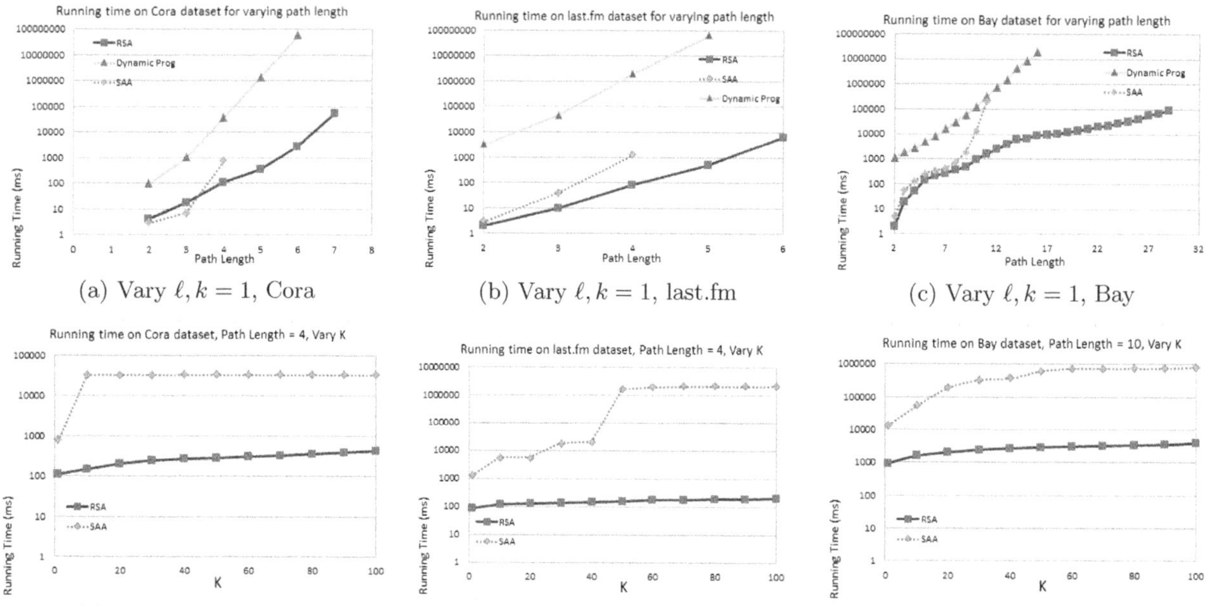


(a) Vary $\ell, k = 1$, Cora (b) Vary $\ell, k = 1$, last.fm (c) Vary $\ell, k = 1$, Bay

(d) $\ell = 4$, vary $k$, Cora (e) $\ell = 4$, vary $k$, last.fm (f) $\ell = 10$, vary $k$, Bay

**Figure 5: Running time comparisons for exact algorithms with different parameter settings.**

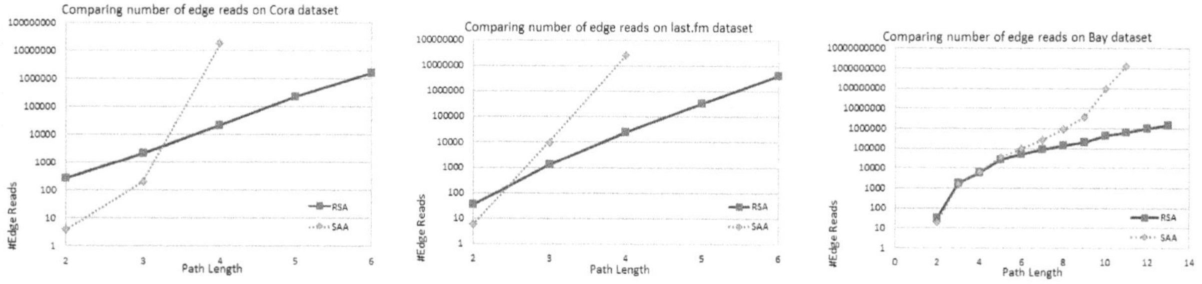


(a) Vary $\ell, k = 1$, Cora (b) Vary $\ell, k = 1$, last.fm (c) Vary $\ell, k = 1$, Bay

**Figure 6: Comparing the number of edge reads between SAA and RSA for different $\ell$**

ning time compared to SAA for finding top-$k$. We observe sudden jumps in the running time of SAA when $k$ changes while RSA continues to work reliably for values of $k$ less than 100 in these experiments and scales more smoothly.

We further compare the number of edge reads of SAA and RSA in Figure 6, that is a system independent notion of the running time. We observe patterns very similar to Figures 5(a-c). This highlights the fact that the number of edges read during the execution is the main factor determining the running time. We observe in some cases (for small $\ell$), SAA reads fewer edges but spends slightly more time for execution. This is due to the fact that RSA is performing random access using the adjacency matrix of the graph to construct longer paths. However, SAA performs the *Join* operation and looks up edges in a hash table which itself requires few milliseconds of time overall.

Finally, Figure 7 shows the running times and the number of edge reads on the DBLPG graph for finding the heaviest paths of different lengths. We notice on this Graph, SAA algorithm performs more poorly compared with the Dynamic Programming algorithm. Of course, RSA beats all algorithms in all cases and finds the exact solution almost 10 times faster than the rest. Figures 7(b) and 8, illustrate this.

# 8. DISCUSSIONS

Our theoretical results prove that HPP is np-hard and inapproximable in the general case. While it makes sense to seek more tractable problem definitions by adding constraints, still we show experimentally that we can achieve scalability practical enough for our main algorithm to be used in a real time fashion and be used in smart software technologies. We use a *branch and bound* solution for finding the exact solution, inspired by top-k algorithms. We use a constraint $\ell$, on edge weights and this makes our comparison for finding heavy paths, representing significantly important sequences in the graph more fair. Comparing path weights of paths with different lengths may not make enough sense in the general case. We show exact solution even for small $\ell$, if obtained, can be used in practice effectively, while other algorithms fail to report even for small $\ell$ in a timely manner. It is obviously nice to scale to longer paths and this requires smarter strategies for reducing $\theta$ during the execution that leads to faster search space pruning. We make a proposal for designing a network visualization tool-box with zoom-in and zoom-out functionalities with changing $k$. We find our presented case study practical but obviously as mentioned in Section 1, applications are not restricted to this and there are other applications such as those in bioinformatics. We can use high probability sequences in order to fix technology

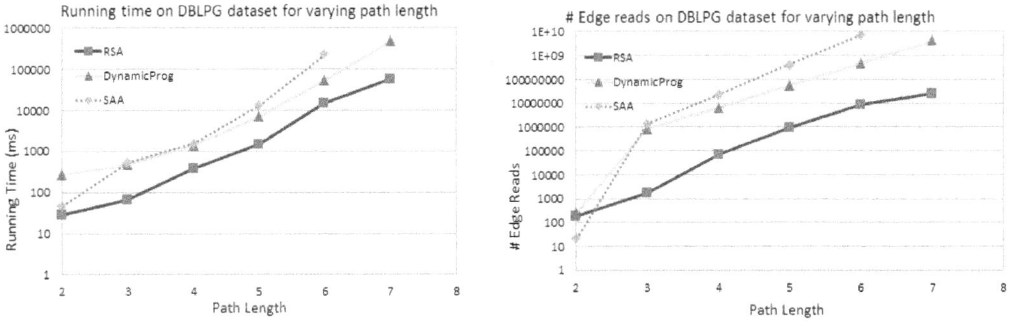


(a) Vary $\ell, k = 1$, DBLPG: Running Time(ms) (b) Vary $\ell, k = 1$, DBLPG: Number of Edge Reads

**Figure 7:** **Scalability results on DBLPG dataset**

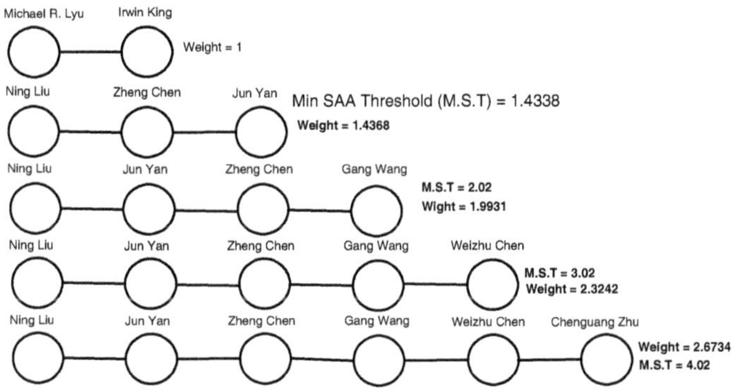


**Figure 8:** **Heaviest paths of $\ell = 1$ to $\ell = 5$ on DBLPG Graph. SAA terminates for $\ell = 2$ before processing all edges at depth 28 (out of 9060 edges). The minimum threshold value when SAA terminates is 1.4338 and smaller than the weight of the heaviest path of $\ell = 2(1.4388)$. For $\ell > 2$, SAA can not terminate without processing all edges i.e. almost equivalent to the DFS algorithm. As can be seen in Figure 7, SAA terminates earlier than Dynamic Programing for $\ell = 2$ but when $\ell > 2$, Dynamic Programing becomes more efficient since SAA behaves as naive as DFS.**

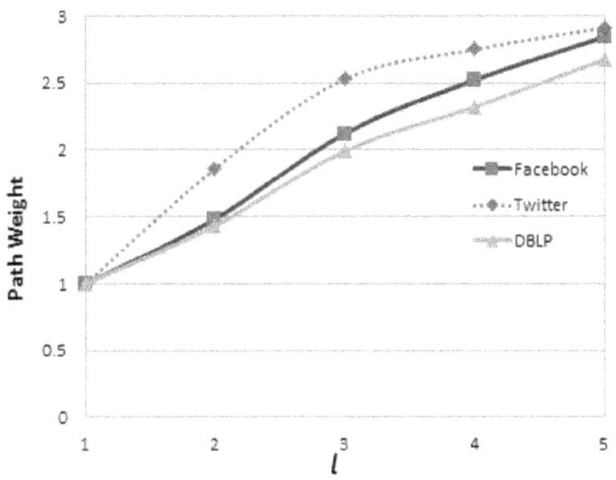


**Figure 9:** **Heaviest path weights of $\ell = 1$ to $\ell = 5$ for Twitter, Facebook and DBLPG using Egonetwork circles.**

related errors such as replacing inaccurate or suspicious entries or filling in missing values in biological sequences. We can also use these high probability sequences for feature extraction from DNA which is an extremely long sequence of symbols in bioinformatics for classification and other learning tasks. One reason we choose visualizing bibliographic networks is presenting interpretable results for computer science audience. While there is a variety of solutions to be used in these applications, we want to propose a solution to a well-defined problem in computer science similar to TSP, that can be significantly leveraged for creating technologies in software industry. Another way to add constraints to the problem and make pruning more possible is through designing reliable heuristic algorithms with constraints on the distribution of edge weights. Of course, this requires careful testing for estimating distributions and we can focus on this extension in the future.

Recently, there have been advancements in the field of social networks described as Egonetworks [13]. Egonetworks are typically presented as groups of people involved in different *"circles"*. Our bibliographic network described in Section 6, is similar to the notion of circles in Egonetwork where each list of authors represents a circle. In an extreme scenario there may be many nodes involved in each circle in domains such as concrete social networks. Any problem definition for discovering dense or significant subgraphs according to such networks can result in finding significant sub-structures. We propose an effective approach for constructing such a graph. Based on the data available we prefer to make no judgement about the significance of individuals. Our proposed solution based on finding top-k heavy paths is proven to be scalable by experiments. On the other hands we can manage to change the output using simple parameters such as $k$, that enables us to zoom-in and zoom-out. Our argument for reliability of our output is the following observation. We notice many heavy paths share the same exact shorter sub-paths. This emphasizes the importance of some collaborations in the bibliographic network around which an important and successful research community is formed. This led to our definition of community detection approach that makes use of maximal frequent subpaths for discovering such frequent short paths shared among many top-k heavy paths. We follow the same approach for constructing graphs from Facebook and Twitter Egonetworks. In particular, we only use circles and convert mutual presence of nodes in circles to define edges. We find the same exact method described in Section 6, in order to define edge weights. Figure 8, reports the heaviest path weights of $\ell = 1$ to $\ell = 5$, and compares them with those obtained from DBLP data. We use the union of all circles first and then construct the graph. Since edge weights are all scaled to $(0 - 1)$, we expect heaviest paths of different length to be in the same range for all datasets.

[13] `http://snap.stanford.edu/data/index.html`

In comparison, we notice in Figure 9, that all graphs follow a similar curve for increasing $\ell$. We notice that the slope decreases with $\ell$, and it is quite likely path weight converges quickly for large $\ell$. This increases the chances of finding reliable heuristic algorithms with output close enough to the exact answer of the np-hard problem. Facebook and Twitter datasets result in paths with slightly heavier weights and we believe this is because in real life networks people with strong connections belong to many active networks while researchers may not be as socially active as ordinary people. Although the difference in path weights is small and almost negligible. The most notable facts to highlight are the similar shape of curves as well as the decreasing slope.

## 9. RELATED WORK

In [9], Hansen and Golbeck make a case for recommending playlists and other collections of items. The AutoDJ system of Platt et al. [15] is one of the early works on playlist generation that uses acoustic features of songs rather than a graph based representation. Random walk methods were used in [22], in order to generate lists of videos in a co-view graph. We formalized and presented our view of generating lists using random walks in introduction for recommending lists as an ordered package of items to users.

The HPP in a special case was studied recently by [2] and they defined a notion of *Stable Clusters* for the specific application of finding persistent chatter in the blogosphere. Unlike our setting, the graph associated with their application is $\ell$-partite and acyclic. Absence of cycles makes their technical problem more tractable than ours. The most efficient algorithm presented in their work is a BFS based method that follows a dynamic programming approach. We followed dynamic programming algorithm that also avoids cycles and found this approach extremely inefficient compared to RSA.

Rankjoin was first proposed by Ilyas et al. [11, 12, 17, 16, 19] to produce top-$k$ join tuples in a relational database. We show how to convert Rankjoin to HPP. Furthermore, no one has studied Rankjoin with self-joins to the best of our knowledge. In [21], authors provide a comprehensive summary of this algorithm and do optimality analysis as done in the theoretical database literature. Their conclusion is that beyond $\ell = 2$, we can not guarantee any optimality results for Rankjoin. This also matches our results regarding HPP being np-hard and inapproximable.

## 10. CONCLUSIONS AND FUTURE WORK

Finding the top-$k$ heaviest paths in a graph is an interesting problem with many practical applications. We discuss the hardness of this problem. We focus on developing practical exact algorithms for this problem. We use an innovative top-$k$ query processing algorithm. We motivate the problem from several different perspectives and discuss possible applications. We present a case study on core community detection. Our findings suggest that our case study can be further extended to a community detection tool that discovers the key influential people in a network represented by a weighted graph. Our future work will focus on more applications of RSA, specially those in network analysis, community detection, recommender systems and bioinformatics. We would also like to investigate more scalable algorithms and threshold update strategies within the same framework. We also intend to design probabilistic and robust heuristic algorithms that work under memory and other types of constraints such as edge distribution.


## 11. ACKNOWLEDGEMENTS

I would like to thank my family for supporting me. All of the professors at the University of British Columbia with whom I had discussions about this problem and provided positive feedback. I would also like to thank WSDM 2014 SPC member, Silvio Lattanzi, for guiding me through the revision process, and Dr. Jon Rokne at the University of Calgary for helping me to continue my research.


## 12. REFERENCES


[1] F. M. P. R. S. R. R. S. A. T. J. W. Andrei Broader, Ravi Kumar. Graph structure in the web. *Computer Networks*, 2000.

[2] N. Bansal, F. Chiang, N. Koudas, and F. W. Tompa. Seeking stable clusters in the blogosphere. In *VLDB*, 2007.

[3] T. D. B. Eirini Spyropoulou. Interesting multi-relational patterns. In *ICDM*, 2011.

[4] N. G. et al. a 2-approximation for the k-mst problem in graphs. In *STOC*, 2005.

[5] N. G. et al. S. arora and g. karakostas. a 2 + epsilon approximation algorithm for the k-mst problem. In *Math. Prog.*, 2006.

[6] R. Fagin, A. Lotem, and M. Naor. Optimal aggregation algorithms for middleware. *J. of Comp. Sys. Sc.*, 66, 2003.

[7] S. Fortunato. Community detection in graphs. *Physics Reports*, 2009.

[8] D. Gibson, R. Kumar, and A. Tomkins. Discovering large dense subgraphs in massive graphs. In *VLDB*, 2005.

[9] D. L. Hansen and J. Golbeck. Mixing it up: recommending collections of items. In *CHI*, 2009.

[10] M. Held and R. M. Karp. A dynamic programming approach to sequencing problems. 10(1), 1962.

[11] I. F. Ilyas, W. G. Aref, and A. K. Elmagarmid. Supporting top-$k$ join queries in relational databases. In *VLDB*, 2003.

[12] I. F. Ilyas, R. Shah, W. G. Aref, J. S. Vitter, and A. K. Elmagarmid. Rank-aware query optimization. In *SIGMOD*, 2004.

[13] Y. Y. Jiawei Han, Jian Pei. Mining frequent patterns without candidate generation. In *SIGMOD*, 2000.

[14] L. Y. J. L. L. Z. Jie Tang, Jing Zhang and Z. S. ArnetMiner. Extraction and mining of academic social networks. In *SIGKDD*, 2008.

[15] S. S. C. W. A. Z. John C. Platt, Christopher J. C. Burges. Learning a gaussian process prior for automatically generating music playlists. In *NIPS*, 2001.

[16] N. P. Jonathan Finger. Robust and efficient algorithms for rank join evaluation. In *SIGMOD*, 2009.

[17] C. Li, K. C.-C. Chang, I. F. Ilyas, and S. Song. RankSQL: Query algebra and optimization for relational top-$k$ queries. In *SIGMOD*, 2005.

[18] R. S. M. Theobald, Gerhard Weikum. Top-k query evaluation with probabilistic guarantees. In *VLDB*, 2004.

[19] D. Martinenghi and M. Tagliasacchi. Cost-aware rank join with random and sorted access. *TKDE*, 2011.

[20] C. C. A. G. A. U. Michael Mathioudakis, Francesco Bonchi. Sparsification of influence networks. In *KDD*, 2011.

[21] K. Schnaitter and N. Polyzotis. Optimal algorithms for evaluating rank joins in database systems. *TODS*, 2010.

[22] D. S. Y. J. J. Y. S. K. D. R. M. A. Shumeet Baluja, Rohan Seth. Video suggestion and discovery for youtube: taking random walks through the view graph. In *WWW*, 2008.

[23] J. S. H. T. U Kang, Spiros Papadimitriou. Centralities in large networks: Algorithms and observations. In *SDM*, 2011.

# A Few Good Predictions: Selective Node Labeling in a Social Network

Gaurish Chaudhari
IIT Bombay
gsc.chaudhari@gmail.com

Vashist Avadhanula
IIT Bombay
vas1089@gmail.com

Sunita Sarawagi
IIT Bombay
sunita@iitb.ac.in

## ABSTRACT

Many social network applications face the following problem: given a network $G = (V, E)$ with labels on a small subset $\mathcal{O} \subset V$ of nodes and an optional set of features on nodes and edges, predict the labels of the remaining nodes. Much research has gone into designing learning models and inference algorithms for accurate predictions in this setting. However, a core hurdle to any prediction effort is that for many nodes there is insufficient evidence for inferring a label.

We propose that instead of focusing on the impossible task of providing high accuracy over all nodes, we should focus on *selectively* making the few node predictions which will be correct with high probability. Any selective prediction strategy will require that the scores attached to node predictions be well-calibrated. Our evaluations show that existing prediction algorithms are poorly calibrated. We propose a new method of training a graphical model using a conditional likelihood objective that provides better calibration than the existing joint likelihood objective. We augment it with a decoupled confidence model created using a novel unbiased training process. Empirical evaluation on two large social networks show that we are able to select a large number of predictions with accuracy as high as 95%, even when the best overall accuracy is only 40%.

## Categories and Subject Descriptors

I.2.6 [**Artificial Intelligence**]: Parameter Learning

## Keywords

well calibrated probabilities; graphical models; high confidence predictions

## 1. INTRODUCTION

The problem of predicting labels for users in a partially labeled social network has many applications. For example, in the Twitter follower network, a recent problem [17, 9, 12, 10, 22] is predicting a user location starting from a small 1–2% known locations obtained from users who allow geo-tagging their tweets. These predictions are used to improve user experience through location based services like recommendations, advertisements, and automatic language selection. As another example consider a friendship network like Facebook, where a small subset of users provide profile attributes such as age, gender, education, and, hobbies. A problem of recent interest [28, 19, 31] is to predict the missing attributes of other users based on known attributes of their friends.

A core problem faced by all prediction algorithms is that for most users there is just not sufficient signal to infer their labels. For example, existing efforts on location prediction of Twitter users report accuracy in the range of 50–60% [17, 9, 12, 10]. This means that almost half of the predicted locations are wrong, leading to misplaced recommendations sometimes bordering on to downright absurd. Our goal is to abstain from making such prediction. Our motto is *pauca sed matura*[1] — make a few predictions but ensure that they are correct with high probability. More formally, our problem statement is as follows.

Given a social network $G = (V, E)$, known labels for a small subset $\mathcal{O} \subset V$, and a confidence threshold $\sigma$, predict the labels of the largest possible $V$ such that the predictions are correct with at least $\sigma$ probability. Equivalently, attach a *well-calibrated* probability $p_u$ with the predicted label of each node $u$ where well-calibrated $p_u$ values have the property that the accuracy over nodes $u$ with $p_u \geq \sigma$ is at least $\sigma$.

Such a selective labeling problem is well-motivated in large social networks settings because such networks exhibit very high diversity in accuracy in different regions arising out of differences in the level of connectivity of users, the degree of homophily of the predicted labels, and the fraction of known labels. A node labeling algorithm just needs to translate the diversity to correctness probability of the predicted label. Algorithms for labeling nodes in a partially labeled graph have been extensively researched across multiple communities (see [24, 21, 16, 3, 14] for a survey). Many techniques have been harnessed, including, iterative classification [5, 15, 24], Markov Random Fields (MRFs) [29, 4, 27], random walks [2, 25], label propagation [26], semi-supervised learning [6, 32], communities [19] and co-citations [3]. When we compared many of these on their ability to provide well-calibrated probabilities, we found that labeling probabilities were poorly calibrated in all methods, including MRF-based methods which create a joint distribution over labels in a

[1] *few but ripe .... Carl Friedrich Gauss*


*WSDM'14*, February 24–28, 2014, New York, New York, USA.

http://dx.doi.org/10.1145/2556195.2556241 .

graph. While many studies [24, 16, 18, 21] have compared methods on overall accuracy, ours is the first comparison on calibration quality.

In this paper we propose a method for labeling nodes in a partially labeled graph and attaching well-calibrated probabilities to the predicted label. Our approach is based on MRFs, chosen because of their popularity in the graph labeling community and their elegant modeling of the joint distribution over all labels in a graph. We make two key modifications to MRFs to make them better calibrated.

First, we propose a novel training objective: *maximize likelihood of each known label conditioned on every other known label.* This objective is more directly linked to our calibration goal than the conventional objective: *maximize joint likelihood of all known labels.* Also, it is both theoretically and empirically superior to another popular objective: *maximize pseudo-likelihood.* We address the computational challenge of training our objective through a theoretically sound graph pruning algorithm that guarantees an $\epsilon$ approximation on trees. Second, we propose a decoupled stage of confidence estimation based on marginals obtained from inference on the MRF. A challenge in training such two stage models is providing unbiased labeled data to both stages without hard partitioning the data across them. We propose a novel leave one out inference strategy on graphs to tackle this problem and provide an efficient algorithm for implementing the strategy.

Experiments on two large social networks show that our two-stage strategy is much better calibrated than any of the existing techniques and provides a practical solution to the selective prediction problem on graphs. On a one million node Twitter location prediction problem, with only 2% observed locations (a typical situation on the real Twitter dataset), the best overall accuracy by any graph prediction algorithm was only 30% whereas our method could select 60,000 users with accuracy over 80%. The best existing approach could select only one-fifth of this number.

The rest of the paper is organized as follows. Section 2 sets up the problem and notations. Section 3 discusses existing algorithms. Section 4 describes our approach. Theoretical results on pruning are in Section 5. Empirical comparisons appear in Section 6 and conclusions in Section 7.

## 2. PROBLEM SETUP AND NOTATIONS

Let $G = (V, E)$ be our social network where $V$ is the set of $n$ users and $E$ the set of pairwise homophilic relationships among them. Let $\mathcal{O} \subset \{1, \ldots, n\}$ denote the set of $k$ users each of whose label is known and let $R = V - \mathcal{O}$. Without loss of generality assume $\mathcal{O} = \{1, \ldots, k\}$. Let $\mathcal{Y}$ denote the space of possible labels, and $c_u \in \mathcal{Y}$ for each $u \in \mathcal{O}$ denote user $u$'s label. Let $\mathbf{c}$ denote the vector $c_1, \ldots, c_k$, and $m$ denote the cardinality $|\mathcal{Y}|$.

In general, each node and edge in $G$ is associated with a set of features which is either user-provided (e.g. the education of a user may help predict age) or derived from properties of $G$ (e.g, the strength of an edge may depend on the log(degree) of its endpoints). We use $\mathbf{f}(\ell, u)$ to denote the vector of node features when user $u$ takes label $\ell$, and $\mathbf{f}(\ell, \ell', u, v)$ to denote the edge feature vector on edge $(u, v)$ when label of $u$ is $\ell$ and $v$ is $\ell'$. Often the node feature vector is empty, and the edge features may only depend on whether $\ell$ and $\ell'$ are equal. We do not consider features over larger subsets of variables, for example a node and all its neighbors, because most such features can be rewritten as sum of edge features.

Our goal is to infer a label $\hat{c}_u$ for each remaining user $u \in V - \mathcal{O}$ based on $G$ and the features, and attach a probability $p_u$ that the prediction is correct. Typically, this task is performed in two steps. First we *train* parameters of a model using observed labels. We will generically call these parameters as $\mathbf{w}$. Second, we *deploy* the trained model to get $(\hat{c}_u, p_u)$ for each $u \in R$.

In this paper we use bold-faced symbols for vectors (e.g. $\mathbf{c}, \boldsymbol{\mu}_j$) and normal font for their members indexed either as a subscript (e.g. $c_i$) or as an argument (e.g. $\mu_j(i)$).

## 3. EXISTING/RELATED APPROACHES

We consider two types of existing solutions to this problem: iterative classification based (Section 3.1) and graphical model based (Section 3.2). Readers familiar with these approaches can directly skip to our approach in Section 4. We do not consider methods based on random walks [2, 25], label propagation [6, 26], and other pure inference algorithms [19] because these either do not support learning with both node and edge features, or are subsumed by the graphical model based approach. Another promising approach based on Gaussian Markov Models is Copula Latent Markov models [30]. These do not fit our setup because they require the labels to be binary and do not model features on edges. Our datasets span thousands of labels and heavily depend on edge features.

**Algorithm 1** Framework: training and deployment

**Input:** $G = (V, E), \mathbf{f}, \mathcal{O}, \mathbf{c}$
**Initialize** $\mathbf{w}$.
**while** $\mathbf{w}$ not converged **do**
  **E-step** Call inference($G, \mathbf{w}, \mathbf{c}$) and obtain prediction $\hat{c}_u$ and marginals $\mu_u(\ell)$ for $u \in R, \ell \in \mathcal{Y}$.
  **M-step** Re-estimate $\mathbf{w}$ using $(\hat{c}_u, \boldsymbol{\mu}_u)$ for each $u \in R$ and $c_u$ for each $u \in \mathcal{O}$.
**end while**
**Deployment** Call inference($G, \mathbf{w}, \mathbf{c}$) to get $(\hat{c}_u, \mu_u(\hat{c}_u))$ for $u \in R$.

### 3.1 Iterative classification

This popular approach from relational learning [5, 15, 24, 20] consists of repeatedly creating a classifier to predict a node's label using features of the node and labels of its neighbors in the graph, only some of which may be observed. In Algorithm 1 we present a common framework to describe the many existing variants of this approach. The first step is to initialize the parameters $\mathbf{w}$ of the classifier by training on only the observed node and its observed neighbors. Next, we enter a EM kind of loop that trains the classifier $\Pr(x_u|\mathbf{c}_{N(u)}, \hat{\mathbf{c}}_{N(u)}, \boldsymbol{\mu}_{N(u)})$ which predicts $x_u$ conditioned on known label $c_v$, or predicted label $\hat{c}_v$ and/or distribution $\boldsymbol{\mu}_v$ over possible labels of each neighbor $v$ of $u$. The loop consists of two steps:

**E-step:** First, using the existing parameters $\mathbf{w}$ infer the unknown labels $\hat{c}_u$ and marginal probability $\mu_u(\ell)$ that an unobserved node $u$ takes label $\ell$. We call this the *inference* step. Inference is also iterative and is known by several names, including ICM, relaxation labeling, and mean field inference [21].

**M-step:** Second, we retrain the classifier so as to maximize likelihood of the observed nodes conditioned on the (re)estimated labels/marginals of all its neighbors. This is like normal classifier training except features are aggregate over predicted/true labels/marginals of neighbors.

We compare with four variants: the ICA method that ignores the marginals $\boldsymbol{\mu}_{N(u)}$ in $\Pr(x_u|\mathbf{c}_{N(u)}, \hat{c}_{N(u)}, \boldsymbol{\mu}_{N(u)})$ and the ICA-Soft method that includes them and ignores the hard predictions $\hat{c}_{N(u)}$, the ICA-NoLoop method which after initialization, skips the training loop; and the LR method that uses only the observed nodes for both training and deployment and is thus a simple logistic regression classifier.

## 3.2 Graphical model based approach

The repeated classification approach does not create a consistent global distribution, and expresses variable dependence in ad hoc terms. An undirected graphical model or a Markov Random Field provides a more principled joint distribution among interacting variables in a graph and has served as another popular choice for label prediction in social networks [29, 4, 27, 24]. Let $\mathbf{x} = x_1, \ldots, x_n$ be variables denoting the labels of all $n$ users and let $\mathbf{F}(\mathbf{x})$ denote the sum of the feature vectors over the entire graph, that is

$$\mathbf{F}(\mathbf{x}) = \sum_{i}^{n} \mathbf{f}(x_i, i) + \sum_{(i,j)\in E} \mathbf{f}(x_i, x_j, i, j) \quad (1)$$

A graphical model expresses the joint distribution as

$$\Pr(x_1, \ldots, x_n|\mathbf{w}) = \frac{1}{Z(\mathbf{w})} e^{\mathbf{w}.\mathbf{F}(x_1,\ldots,x_n)} \quad (2)$$

where $Z(\mathbf{w})$ is a normalizer called the partition function and is equal to $\sum_{x_1,\ldots,x_n} e^{\mathbf{w}.\mathbf{F}(x_1,\ldots,x_n)}$

Many different methods have been proposed to train $\mathbf{w}$. We discuss one of the most popular of these: the joint likelihood method. This method maximizes the joint probability of all observed labels as follows

$$\begin{aligned} &\max_{\mathbf{w}} \log \Pr(\mathbf{x}_{\mathcal{O}} = \mathbf{c}|\mathbf{w}) \\ &= \max_{\mathbf{w}} \log \sum_{\mathbf{x}_R} e^{\mathbf{w}.\mathbf{F}(\mathbf{c},\mathbf{x}_R)} - \log Z(\mathbf{w}) \end{aligned} \quad (3)$$

The objective is not convex when $R$ is non-empty because of the summation within the log. Therefore, typically the EM algorithm is used for finding a local optima.

**E-step:** The E-step computes marginal probability of each node and edge conditioned on the observed labels. That is, for each node compute $\mu_u(\ell) = \Pr(x_u = \ell|\mathbf{x}_{\mathcal{O}} = \mathbf{c}, \mathbf{w})$ and for each edge compute $\mu_{u,v}(\ell, \ell') = \Pr(x_u = \ell, x_v = \ell'|\mathbf{x}_{\mathcal{O}} = \mathbf{c}, \mathbf{w})$ by marginalizing the joint distribution in Equation 2. These can be computed simultaneously for all nodes and edges using one of the many existing algorithms for inference in graphical models [13]. However, on general graphs, exact inference is intractable, and many approximations exist, including Gibbs Sampling, Mean-field, Belief Propagation (BP) and its convergent variants such as TRWS [13].

**M-step:** The M-step solves for the expected log likelihood of the observed node which becomes

$$\begin{aligned} &\mathbf{w}.E_\mu(\mathbf{F}(\mathbf{c}, \mathbf{x}_R)) - \log Z(\mathbf{w}) \\ &\text{where } E_\mu(\mathbf{F}(\mathbf{c}, \mathbf{x}_R) = \\ &\sum_{(i,j)\in E,\ell,\ell'} \mu_{ij}(\ell,\ell')\mathbf{f}(\ell,\ell',i,j) + \sum_{i\in V,\ell} \mu_i(\ell)\mathbf{f}(\ell,i) \end{aligned} \quad (4)$$

This objective is convex in $\mathbf{w}$ and can be solved using gradient descent. However, a new challenge is that computation of $\log Z(\mathbf{w})$ is intractable and approximate inference via methods like BP or sampling does not guarantee a convergent gradient descent loop. Recent research [23, 11] provides an elegant solution to this problem by approximating $\log Z(\mathbf{w})$ as a convex optimization over message variables and jointly solving for the message variables and $\mathbf{w}$ as one convergent program.

After training parameters $\mathbf{w}$, a final inference step (same as in the E-step of training) is used to compute the marginals $\mu_u(\ell) = \Pr(x_u = \ell|\mathbf{x}_{\mathcal{O}} = \mathbf{c}, \mathbf{w})$ for each $u \in R, \ell$ and predict label $\hat{c}_u = \text{argmax}_\ell \mu_u(\ell), \quad \forall u \in R$. The confidence $p_u$ of the prediction is just $\mu_u(\hat{c}_u)$.

Since the confidence is marginal probability of a distribution trained via a statistically sound training objective, we expected the confidence values to be well-calibrated. But, when we deployed them on two real-life social networks, we did not find that to be the case at all. Therefore, in the next section we present the steps we took to solve this problem.

# 4. OUR APPROACH

We address the problem of getting well-calibrated probabilities through fixes on two fronts. First, we link the graphical model training objective more directly to our calibration goal (Section 4.1). Second, we decouple the confidence estimation problem from label prediction and develop a method of collecting an unbiased labeled set for training a well-calibrated estimator of confidence (Section 4.2).

## 4.1 Modified training of graphical models

We observed an impedance mismatch in the graphical model approach (Section 3.2) between the training objective of maximizing *joint probability of all observations* $\Pr(\mathbf{x}_{\mathcal{O}} = \mathbf{c}|\mathbf{w})$, and the predicted *single variable marginals conditioned on all observation* $\Pr(x_u = \hat{c}_u|\mathbf{x}_{\mathcal{O}} = \mathbf{c})$. We propose to fix this mismatch through a training objective that maximizes conditional likelihoods where for each observed label $c_i$ we maximize its probability conditioned on all other observed labels. Our revised training objective then becomes:

$$\begin{aligned} &\max_{\mathbf{w}} \log \prod_{i\in\mathcal{O}} \Pr(x_i = c_i|\mathbf{x}_{\mathcal{O}-i} = \mathbf{c}_{-i}, \mathbf{w}) \\ &= \max_{\mathbf{w}} \sum_{i\in\mathcal{O}} \log \sum_{\mathbf{x}_R} e^{\mathbf{w}.\mathbf{F}(\mathbf{c},\mathbf{x}_R)} - \log \sum_{\mathbf{x}_{R\cup\{i\}}} e^{\mathbf{w}.\mathbf{F}(\mathbf{c}_{-i},\mathbf{x}_{R\cup\{i\}})} \end{aligned}$$

where the condition $\mathbf{x}_{\mathcal{O}-i} = \mathbf{c}_{-i}$ implies that we are fixing the labels of all observed nodes except the $i$th one. We call this the node conditional likelihood method or NCL in short. Likewise, we use the short form JL for the Joint Likelihood method. We next elaborate on the steps required for solving this objective efficiently. This objective is also non-convex but this is only due to the first term which is the same as in JL (except for being repeated $k$ times). Therefore we use the same EM framework to solve for a local optimum.

**E-step:** Same as in JL.

**M-step:** The M-step is different because of difference in the second term. We need to solve for expected conditional likelihood of each observed node which becomes:

$$\sum_{i} \mathbf{w}.E_\mu(\mathbf{F}(\mathbf{c}, \mathbf{x}_R)) - \log \sum_{\mathbf{x}_{R\cup\{i\}}} e^{\mathbf{w}.\mathbf{F}(\mathbf{c}_{-i},\mathbf{x}_{R\cup\{i\}})} \quad (5)$$

where $E_\mu(\mathbf{F}(\mathbf{c}, \mathbf{x}_R))$ is same as in Equation 4. The second term looks like a partition function and we denote it as $\log Z(\mathbf{w}|\mathbf{c}_{-i})$. In order to compute $\log Z(\mathbf{w}|\mathbf{c}_{-i})$ we need to separately run inference for each observed node because the conditioning variables are different for each $i$. There is no easy way to reuse computation across different $i$ values and requires inference on the full graph $k$ times for each optimization loop. We propose an approximation to reduce this cost. For computing $\Pr(x_i = c_i|\mathbf{x}_{\mathcal{O}-i} = \mathbf{c}_{-i}, \mathbf{w})$ (henceforth denoted as $\Pr(c_i|\mathbf{c}_{-i})$) we select a mini-graph $G_i$ from $G$ such that the approximate probability $\Pr_{G_i}(c_i|\mathbf{c}_{-i})$ computed only using features of variables in $G_i$ is within a user-given tolerance $\epsilon$ of $\Pr(c_i|\mathbf{c}_{-i})$. In Section 5 we present how such mini-graphs are selected. Let $R_i$ denote the subset of $R$ in $G_i$ and let $\mathbf{F}_{G_i}(\mathbf{x})$ denote the sum of features over nodes and edges in $G_i$. The modified M-step now becomes:

$$\sum_i \mathbf{w}.E_\mu(\mathbf{F}_{G_i}(\mathbf{c}, \mathbf{x}_R)) - \log \sum_{\mathbf{x}_{R_i \cup \{i\}}} e^{\mathbf{w}.\mathbf{F}_{G_i}(\mathbf{c}_{-i}, \mathbf{x}_{R\cup\{i\}})}$$

Computationally, this objective for each $i$ is not too different from the M-step of joint likelihood except that it is performed over a smaller graph $G_i$. As in the joint likelihood case, even though the objective is convex, the computation of $\log Z(\mathbf{w}|\mathbf{c}_{-i})$ is intractable on arbitrary $G_i$s. Therefore, here also we rely on the convex approximation of [23, 11]. This provides us an efficient and convergent M-step.

After training parameters $\mathbf{w}$, we use inference to compute $(\hat{c}_u, \mu_u(\hat{c}_u))$ $\forall u \in R$ exactly as in JL.

#### 4.1.1 Asymptotic statistical guarantees

We can prove that like JL, the NCL objective is also consistent. This means that if the model is faithful to the true data distribution, and if labeled data is infinite, then the NCL objective will find the true parameters. We skip a proof due to lack of space but the broad steps are the same as in Theorem 20.3 of [13]. Also, our EM-algorithm is guaranteed to find a locally optimum solution as in JL. This is easy to see because EM only modifies the first non-convex term in the NCL objective and this term is identical to the first term of JL up to a positive multiplicative constant.

#### 4.1.2 Relationship to other training objectives

Some readers might find our NCL objective similar to another popular training objective [29, 13] called Pseudo-likelihood (PL). PL is based on approximating the joint probability $\Pr(x_1, \ldots, x_n)$ as $\prod_{u=1}^n \Pr(x_u|\mathbf{x}_{N_u})$, the product of node-level probability conditioned on the node's neighbors. When all neighbors are known, PL is identical to NCL since $\Pr(x_i = c_i|\mathbf{x}_{\mathcal{O}-i} = \mathbf{c}_{-i}, \mathbf{w}) = \Pr(x_i = c_i|\mathbf{x}_{N_i} = \mathbf{c}_{N_i}, \mathbf{w})$. However, for the general case with unknown neighbors, the only known extension of PL we are aware of is the PL-EM method of [29] which is very different from NCL. PL-EM proposes an approximate EM-based solution of the PL objective where in the E-step mean-field inference is used to compute the marginals $\boldsymbol{\mu}_u$ for each $u \in R$. The M-step then solves the following convex objective:

$$\sum_{i\in\mathcal{O}} \sum_{\mathbf{x}_{R_i^N}} \prod_{u\in R_i^N} \mu_u(x_u) \log \Pr(x_i|\mathbf{x}_{R_i^N}, \mathbf{x}_{\mathcal{O}_i} = \mathbf{c}_{\mathcal{O}_i}, \mathbf{w}) \quad (6)$$

where $R_i^N$ denotes the unobserved neighbors of node $i$ and $\mathcal{O}_i$ denote the observed neighbors of $i$. Unlike our approach, PL-EM is not statistically consistent because its M-step attempts to maximize expected likelihood with respect to the *mean field distribution* which is not guaranteed to match the true distribution. We will also contrast the two approaches empirically in Section 6.

### 4.2 Decoupled confidence estimation

We now describe a second step that we took to better calibrate the confidence of predictions $\hat{c}_u$ from inference on the graphical model. While the marginals $\mu_u(\hat{c}_u)$ of NCL are better calibrated than of JL, our experiments show that they are still not good enough for selective node labeling. Both methods tended to provide overly inflated values of $\mu_u(\hat{c}_u)$ for immediate neighbors of observed nodes, and there was no easy way to offset that while also ensuring effective label propagation in the graph. We therefore chose to train a decoupled model $\mathcal{C}$ that works on $\hat{c}_u$ and marginals $\mu_u(.)$ produced by the graphical model and outputs a confidence $p_u$ of the prediction $\hat{c}_u$ being correct for each $u \in R$.

Assume that we know true labels of a subset of nodes $D \subset R$ that does not overlap with $\mathcal{O}$. Then $\mathcal{C}$ can be a probabilistic binary classifier, like a logistic regression model trained using $D$ as follows. For each $j \in D$, create an instance with a label $y_j = 1$ if $\hat{c}_j = c_j$ and $y_j = 0$ otherwise, and a set of features $\mathbf{z}_j$ derived from observed and predicted labels/marginals in $j$'s neighborhood. Examples of such features include, the smoothed fraction of $j$'s neighbors that have label $\hat{c}_j$, the marginal $\mu_j(\hat{c}_j)$, the largest fraction of nodes having a label other than $\hat{c}_j$ in $j$. The complete list of features we used can be found in [7].

A major shortcoming of the above method is that we need a labeled set $D$ to train $\mathcal{C}$ in addition to the set $\mathcal{O}$ for prediction. Since our goal is to maximize the number of nodes correctly predicted, we want $\mathcal{O}$ to be as large as possible. Setting aside a portion of $\mathcal{O}$ as $D$ will compromise this goal, and/or could lead to a poorly trained $\mathcal{C}$.

We propose a novel method of creating an unbiased training set for $\mathcal{C}$ without any additional labeled data. When we perform inference on the full graph to get predictions $\hat{c}_u$ on the unobserved set $R$, the labels of nodes in $\mathcal{O}$ are pinned to $\mathbf{c}$, and therefore get no predicted label. Our key idea is to use the mini-graphs created during NCL training, to run inference on each $G_i$ with all but the $i$th observed label $\mathbf{c}_{-i}$ in $G_i$ to obtain marginals $\bar{\mu}_u^i(\ell) = \Pr(x_u = \ell|\mathbf{c}_{-i}, \mathbf{w})$, and prediction $\bar{c}_u^i = \text{argmax}_\ell \bar{\mu}_u^i(\ell)$ for each $i \in \mathcal{O}$ and $u \in \{i\} \cup N(i)$. Note, we used a different symbol for these marginals computed without $c_i$ to distinguish from the marginal obtained using all of $\mathbf{c}$. This step is efficient because $G_i$ is small and in Section 5 we will show how to obtain such a $G_i$. Now, for each $i \in \mathcal{O}$ create a labeled instance with label $y_i = 1$ if $\bar{c}_i^i = c_i$ else $y_i = 0$, and features $\mathbf{z}_i$ created as above. The $y_i$ labels of the observed nodes can also be used to create additional features such as the fraction of wrongly predicted observed nodes in a node's neighborhood.

Algorithm 2 presents our overall approach.

#### 4.2.1 Related work on confidence estimation

The use of a decoupled binary model to get confidence with predictions is not new, for example, [4] uses one such for selecting nodes for active labeling. The novelty of our approach is in the way we create an unbiased labeled dataset for training while using the same data for predictions. In contrast, [4] assumes a separate labeled dataset. We show in Section 6.3.1 how that impacts selective accuracy.

**Algorithm 2** Our approach.

**Input:** $G = (V, E), \mathcal{O}, \mathbf{c}$
$\mathbf{w}$ = Trained parameters using NCL (Section 4.1).
Call inference($G, \mathbf{w}, \mathbf{c}$) and get $(\hat{c}_u, \boldsymbol{\mu}_u)$ for $u \in R$
**for** $i \in \mathcal{O}$ **do**
  $G_i$ = Prune $G$ to approximate $\Pr(c_i|\mathbf{c}_{-i})$ (Section 5)
  Call inference($G_i, \mathbf{w}, \mathbf{c}_{-i}$), get $(\bar{c}^i_u, \bar{\boldsymbol{\mu}}^i_u)$ $u \in \{i\} \cup N(i)$
  $\mathbf{z}_i$ = Make_ Features($\bar{c}^i_i, \bar{\boldsymbol{\mu}}^i_i, \bar{\mathbf{c}}^i_{N(i)}, \bar{\boldsymbol{\mu}}^i_{N(i)}, \mathbf{c}_{N(i)}$)
  $y_i = 1$ if $\bar{c}^i_i = c_i$, $y_i = 0$ otherwise.
**end for**
$\mathcal{C}$ = logistic model trained using $\{(\mathbf{z}_i, y_i) : i \in \mathcal{O}\}$
**for** $u \in R$ **do**
  $\mathbf{z}_u$ = Make_ Features($\hat{c}_u, \boldsymbol{\mu}_u, \hat{c}_{N(u)}, \boldsymbol{\mu}_{N(u)}, \mathbf{c}_{N(u)}$)
  $p_u = \mathcal{C}(\mathbf{z}_u)$
**end for**
**return** $\{(u, p_u) : u \in R\}$

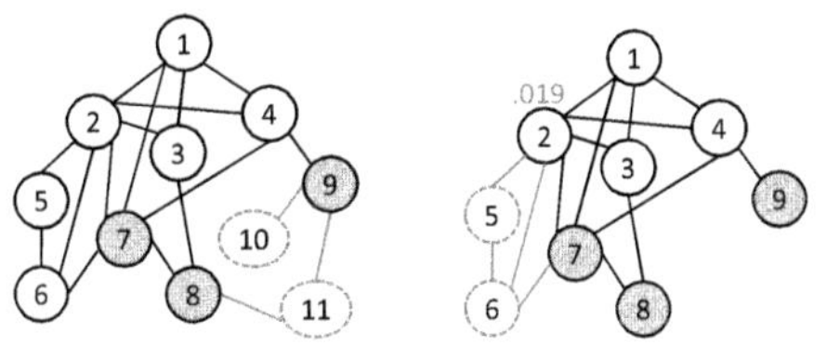


Figure 1: An example of graph pruning to obtain $\Pr(c_1|\mathbf{c}_{-1})$. The shaded nodes are observed. The dotted nodes in the left are nodes pruned via the Markov condition. The dotted nodes in the right are nodes pruned using $\epsilon = 0.02$ via the method of Section 5.3.

# 5. PRUNING THE GRAPHICAL MODEL

We show how to select a sub-graph $G_i$ of $G$ such that the approximate probability $\Pr_{G_i}(c_i|\mathbf{c}_{-i})$ computed only using $G_i$ is within $\epsilon$ of $\Pr(c_i|\mathbf{c}_{-i})$. First, based on the Markov property of graphical models, we can prune any node $u$ from $G$ all of whose paths to $i$ are through observed nodes without modifying $\Pr(c_i|\mathbf{c}_{-i})$. For example, in Figure 1, we can prune nodes 10 and 11 when $i = 1$ because for both of them the only paths to node 1 are through observed nodes (shown shaded). Call the pruned graph $G_i$. $G_i$ might still be large and we present recipes for pruning further nodes from it while maintaining an $\epsilon$ approximation. For ease of notation, we will drop the subscript $i$, use $G$ instead of $G_i$, assume $i = 1$, $c_i = 1$, and assume that the nodes in $G$ are numbered $1, \ldots, n$. Also, we denote the node potentials as $\psi_u(x_u)$ and define $\psi_u(x_u) = e^{\mathbf{w}.\mathbf{f}(x_u,u)}$ for $u \in (R \cap G_i) \cup \{i\}$, $\psi_u(x_u) = M$ if $u \in (\mathcal{O} - i) \cap G_i, x_u = c_u$ and $\psi_u(x_u) = 1$ otherwise where $M \gg 1$ is a large constant. We denote edge potentials as $\psi_{uv}(x_u, x_v) = e^{\mathbf{w}.\mathbf{f}(x_u,x_v,u,v)}$. We assume that edge features $\mathbf{f}(x_u, x_v, u, v)$ depend only on whether $x_u = x_v$. Therefore, they can be expressed as $\psi_{uv}(x_u, x_v) = (\alpha_{uv}$ if $x_u = x_v, 1$ else$)$ where $\alpha_{uv}$ is a constant. Further, since we assume homophily, $\alpha_{uv} \geq 1$. Let $\alpha$ be an upper bound on the values of $\alpha_{uv}$. During parameter training when the potentials are unknown, we assume that the user can guess a suitably tight bound for $\alpha$ as pruning is performed in terms of $\alpha$. This is not too difficult in our experience, particularly since the penalty for over-estimate is just reduced pruning.

With these notations we can cast the conditional probability $\Pr(x_1 = 1|\mathbf{x}_{\mathcal{O}-1} = \mathbf{c}_{-1})$ as this marginal probability

$$\Pr(x_1^1) = \frac{\sum_{x_2,\ldots,x_n:x_1=1} \prod_u \psi_u(x_u) \prod_{(u,v)} \psi_{uv}(x_u, x_v)}{\sum_{x_1,x_2,\ldots,x_n} \prod_u \psi_u(x_u) \prod_{(u,v)} \psi_{uv}(x_u, x_v)}$$

where we use the shorthand $x_1^1$ for $x_1 = 1$. We introduce a convenient normalization operator $\mathcal{N}(\mathbf{z})$ that when applied on a vector $\mathbf{z}$ normalizes its entries so they sum to one. Using this, we can write

$$\Pr(x_1 = \ell) = \mathcal{N}(\sum_{x_2,\ldots,x_n} \prod_u \psi_u(x_u) \prod_{(u,v)} \psi_{uv}(x_u, x_v))(\ell)$$

Our goal is to remove nodes from $G$ so as to approximate $\Pr(x_1^1)$ within a given $\epsilon$ of the unpruned value. We develop the method in three stages: first assume that $G$ is a chain with $x_1$ at one end, then generalize to the case when $G$ is a tree, and finally to arbitrary graphs.

The proofs in the rest of the section are quite technical and assume knowledge of message-based computations in graphical models. Readers unfamiliar with the topic can skip the proofs and just see the main pruning results in Theorems 5.1, 5.2, and 5.3.

## 5.1 Single chain

Assume the chain of nodes is $x_1, \ldots, x_n$ with an edge between each $x_u$ and $x_{u+1}$. In a chain if we remove a node $x_t$, all nodes $x_j$ for $j > t$ are also removed. Let $P(x_1|\psi_{1\ldots t})$ denote the marginal calculated with potentials up to node $t$. Then $P(x_1|\psi_{1\ldots t}) =$

$$\mathcal{N}\left(\psi_1(x_1) \sum_{x_2,\ldots,x_t} \prod_{u=2}^{t} \psi_u(x_u)\psi_{u-1,u}(x_{u-1}, x_u)\right) \qquad (7)$$

Thus, our task reduces to identifying an index $t$ such that $|P(x_1^1|\psi_{1\ldots n}) - P(x_1^1|\psi_{1\ldots t})| \leq \epsilon$. For a chain, the impact of all potentials on node 1 after $t$ can be expressed as a simplex message, say $\boldsymbol{\theta}_t$ that node $t+1$ sends to $t$ and we can rewrite $P(x_1^1|\psi_{1\ldots n}) = P(x_1^1|\psi_{1\ldots t}, \boldsymbol{\theta}_t)$. The principle we follow for pruning is to find the maximum swing in this value over all possible values of $\boldsymbol{\theta}_t \in \Delta^m$, the $m$ dimensional simplex. Let $\hat{\boldsymbol{\theta}}$ and $\check{\boldsymbol{\theta}}$ denote the two extreme values of $\boldsymbol{\theta}_t$ that maximize this difference, that is, $(\hat{\boldsymbol{\theta}}, \check{\boldsymbol{\theta}}) =$

$$\text{argmax}_{\hat{\boldsymbol{\theta}}',\check{\boldsymbol{\theta}}' \in \Delta^m} \left|P(x_1^1|\psi_{1\ldots t}, \hat{\boldsymbol{\theta}}') - P(x_1^1|\psi_{1\ldots t}, \check{\boldsymbol{\theta}}')\right|$$

Now, we will derive what $(\hat{\boldsymbol{\theta}}, \check{\boldsymbol{\theta}})$ should be and for what $t$ will the difference be $\leq \epsilon$. We first introduce some notations. Let $\hat{\mathbf{M}}^t_r$ denote a message at distance $r$ from node 1, when a message $\hat{\mathbf{M}}^t = \hat{\boldsymbol{\theta}}$ is injected from node $t+1$ to $t$. Likewise define $\check{\mathbf{M}}^t_r$ with message $\check{\boldsymbol{\theta}}$ from $t+1$ and $\bar{\mathbf{M}}^t_r$ with message $\boldsymbol{\theta}_t$ from $t+1$. Let $h(\boldsymbol{\psi}, \alpha, \mathbf{M})$ denote the outgoing message at a node with node potential $\boldsymbol{\psi}$ when a message $\mathbf{M}$ is injected into it via an edge with Potts potential $\alpha$. That is,

$$h(\boldsymbol{\psi}, \alpha, \mathbf{M}) = \mathcal{N}(\boldsymbol{\psi\gamma}) \text{ where } \boldsymbol{\gamma} = (\alpha - 1)\mathbf{M} + \mathbf{1}_m, \qquad (8)$$

where $\mathbf{1}_m$ is a length $m$ vector of all ones. Using this we can express $\bar{\mathbf{M}}^t_r$, recursively as follows:

$$\bar{\mathbf{M}}^t_r = h(\boldsymbol{\psi}_r, \alpha, \bar{\mathbf{M}}^t_{r+1}), \text{ if } r < |t|, \quad \bar{\mathbf{M}}^t_t = \boldsymbol{\theta}_t, \qquad (9)$$

and similarly $\check{\mathbf{M}}^t, \hat{\mathbf{M}}^t$. From the above, it is easy to see that $P(x_1^1|\psi_{1\ldots t}, \boldsymbol{\theta}_t) = \bar{M}^t_1(1)$.

First, we assume no node potentials and derive a closed form expression for $\Pr(x_1 = \ell|\psi_{1\ldots t}, \boldsymbol{\theta}_t)$.

**Lemma 5.1** If $G$ is a chain, $\alpha_{uv} = \alpha$, $\psi_u(\ell) = 1\ \forall u, \ell$, then

$$\Pr(x_1 = \ell | \psi_{1\ldots t}, \boldsymbol{\theta}_t) = \frac{\theta_t(\ell) - 1/m}{(\frac{m}{\alpha - 1} + 1)^{t-1}} + \frac{1}{m} \quad (10)$$

PROOF. When node potential is 1 for all labels, Equations 8 and 9 gives that $\bar{M}^t_{r-1}(\ell) = \frac{(\alpha-1)\bar{M}^t_r(\ell)+1}{m+\alpha-1}$. To get $\bar{M}^t_1(\ell)$ which is equal to $\Pr(x_1 = \ell|\psi_{1\ldots t}, \boldsymbol{\theta}_t)$ we repeatedly apply this formula $t$ times. After simplifying the result, we get the RHS.

A corollary from the above that we will find useful is:

**Corollary 5.1** If $\alpha_{uv} \leq \alpha \quad \forall (u, v) \in E$ (other conditions same as in Lemma 5.1), then

$$\Pr(x_1 = \ell|\psi_{1\ldots t}, \boldsymbol{\theta}_t) - \left[\frac{\theta_t(\ell) - 1/m}{(\frac{m}{\alpha-1} + 1)^{t-1}} + \frac{1}{m}\right] \leq 0 \text{ if } \theta_t(\ell) \geq \frac{1}{m}$$
$$\geq 0 \text{ otherwise.}$$

**Theorem 5.1** If $G$ is a chain, $t > \frac{\log \frac{1}{\epsilon}}{\log(\frac{m}{\alpha-1}+1)}$, $\alpha_{uv} \leq \alpha$ $\psi_u(\ell) = 1 \quad \forall u, \ell$ then $|P(x_1^1|\psi_{1\ldots n}) - P(x_1^1|\psi_{1\ldots t})| \leq \epsilon$. In other words, pruning potentials $\psi_{t,t+1}\ldots, \psi_{n-1,n}$ changes $\Pr(x_1^1)$ by at most $\epsilon$.

PROOF.

$$\begin{aligned}
&|P(x_1^1|\psi_{1\ldots n}) - P(x_1^1|\psi_{1\ldots t})| \\
&\leq \max_{\hat{\boldsymbol{\theta}}, \check{\boldsymbol{\theta}} \in \Delta^m} \left|P(x_1^1|\psi_{1\ldots t}, \hat{\boldsymbol{\theta}}) - P(x_1^1|\psi_{1\ldots t}, \check{\boldsymbol{\theta}})\right| \\
&\leq \max_{0 \leq \check{\theta}(1) \leq 1/m \leq \hat{\theta}(1) \leq 1} \left|\frac{\hat{\theta}(1) - \check{\theta}(1)}{(\frac{m}{\alpha-1} + 1)^{t-1}}\right| \quad \text{(Corollary 5.1)} \\
&\leq \frac{1}{(\frac{m}{\alpha-1} + 1)^{t-1}} \leq \epsilon
\end{aligned}$$

Now let us extend the result to include node potentials. Recall that since training is not over, we do not know the value of the node potentials. Unlike edge potentials, it is difficult to bound their values and without those we cannot obtain a closed form expression for $\Pr(x_1)$ in terms of $\boldsymbol{\theta}_t$ unlike what we did earlier. So, we take an alternative approach and bound the difference between the upper and lower bound of label 1 in the message at stage $r$ $\hat{M}^t_r(1) - \check{M}^t_r(1)$ in terms of the corresponding difference $\hat{M}^t_{r+1}(1) - \check{M}^t_{r+1}(1)$ at stage $r + 1$. The following lemma gives the bound.

**Lemma 5.2** $\hat{M}^t_r(1) - \check{M}^t_r(1) \leq \kappa(m, \alpha)(\hat{M}^t_{r+1}(1) - \check{M}^t_{r+1}(1))$ where

$$\kappa(m, \alpha) = \frac{(\alpha - 1)(m + \alpha - 1)}{\alpha(m + \alpha - 1) + 3m + \alpha - 5} \quad (11)$$

PROOF. The proof is involved and we provide a brief sketch. Let $\boldsymbol{\psi}_r$ denote the unknown node potential at $r$. Since,

$$\begin{aligned}
\hat{M}^t_r(1) - \check{M}^t_r(1) &= h(\boldsymbol{\psi}_r, \alpha, \hat{\mathbf{M}}^t_{r+1})(1) - h(\boldsymbol{\psi}_r, \alpha, \check{\mathbf{M}}^t_{r+1})(1) \\
&\leq \max_{\boldsymbol{\psi}} h(\boldsymbol{\psi}, \alpha, \hat{\mathbf{M}}^t_{r+1})(1) - h(\boldsymbol{\psi}, \alpha, \check{\mathbf{M}}^t_{r+1})(1)
\end{aligned}$$

We prove in [1] that the solution $\boldsymbol{\psi}^*$ for the optimization problem above is

$$\psi^*(1) = \frac{\sqrt{(1 - \hat{\gamma}_1)(1 - \check{\gamma}_1)}}{\sqrt{(1 - \hat{\gamma}_1)(1 - \check{\gamma}_1)} + (m - 1)\sqrt{\hat{\gamma}_1\check{\gamma}_1}}, \ \psi^*(l > 1) = \frac{1 - \psi^*(1)}{m - 1}$$

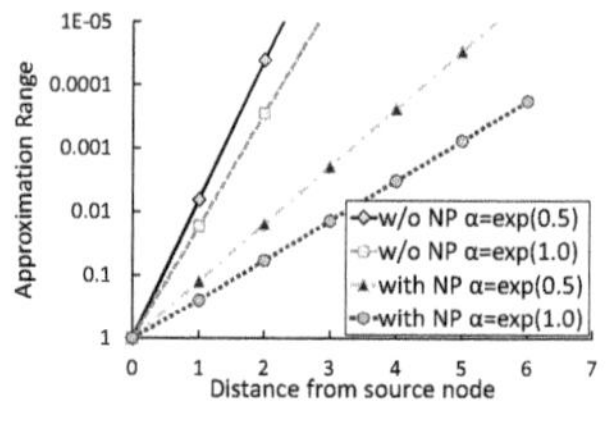


Figure 2: Error bounds (log scale) vs distance $t$ for $m = 100$

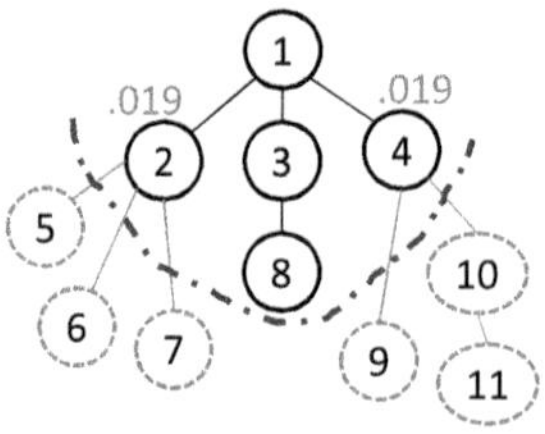


Figure 3: An example tree. Pruned nodes are dotted: $\epsilon = 0.05, m = 100, \alpha = e^{0.5}$.

where $\hat{\gamma}_1 = \frac{(\alpha-1)\hat{M}^t_{r+1}(1)+1}{m+\alpha-1}$ and likewise $\check{\gamma}_1$. Plugging in this solution we can show that:

$$\max_{\boldsymbol{\psi}} h(\boldsymbol{\psi}, \alpha, \hat{\mathbf{M}}^t_{r+1})(1) - h(\boldsymbol{\psi}, \alpha, \check{\mathbf{M}}^t_{r+1})(1) =$$
$$= \frac{\hat{\gamma}_1 - \check{\gamma}_1}{2\sqrt{(1 - \hat{\gamma}_1)(1 - \check{\gamma}_1)\hat{\gamma}_1\check{\gamma}_1} + \hat{\gamma}_1(1 - \check{\gamma}_1) + \check{\gamma}_1(1 - \hat{\gamma}_1)}$$

Next, we use a set of inequalities to show that this expression can be upper bounded by $\kappa(m, \alpha)(\hat{M}^t_{r+1}(1) - \check{M}^t_{r+1}(1))$. The details of this can be found in [1].

**Theorem 5.2** If $G$ is a chain where $\alpha_{uv} \leq \alpha$ and $t > \frac{\log \epsilon}{\log(\kappa(m,\alpha))} + 1$, then $|P(x_1^1|\psi_{1\ldots n}) - P(x_1^1|\psi_{1\ldots t})| \leq \epsilon$.

PROOF. The proof follows by repeatedly applying Lemma 5.2 $t-1$ times until we get that $|P(x_1^1|\psi_{1\ldots t}, \hat{\boldsymbol{\theta}}) - P(x_1^1|\psi_{1\ldots t}, \check{\boldsymbol{\theta}})| = \hat{\mathbf{M}}^t_1(1) - \check{\mathbf{M}}^t_1(1) \leq \max_{\hat{\boldsymbol{\theta}}, \check{\boldsymbol{\theta}}} \kappa(m, \alpha)^{t-1}(\hat{\theta}(1) - \check{\theta}(1)) = \kappa(m, \alpha)^{t-1}$.

In Figure 2 we plot the worst case bound on $|\Pr(x_1^1|\psi_{1\ldots n}) - \Pr(x_1^1|\psi_{1\ldots t})|$ on a chain when we prune nodes after distance $t$ from node 1 for $\alpha = e^{0.5}, m = 100$ and $\alpha = e$ and for the two cases: without node potentials (Theorem 5.1) and with node potentials (Theorem 5.2). The bounds are tighter without node potentials but in all cases we achieve good approximation within a small $t$. With $\alpha = e^{0.5}$, a typical value in our datasets, we approximate to within 0.0001 and 0.019 respectively at $t = 2$.

## 5.2 Tree

Now consider the case where $G$ is a tree rooted at $x_1$. Pruning now amounts to choosing a frontier of $G$ so that the size of the pruned tree is smallest while ensuring that the maximum swings in the potentials outside the frontier do not impact $\Pr(x_1^1)$ by more than $\epsilon$.

Suppose we decide to prune all nodes below a node $x_t$ with parent $p$. The contribution of all potentials under $x_t$ (inclusive of its own node potential) in computing $\Pr(x_1^1)$ can be expressed as a message $\mathbf{M}_t$ from $t$ to $p$. We compute what happens to $\mathbf{M}_t$ along the path $\mathcal{P}(t)$ to $x_1$. Unlike for chains, the path has incoming messages from other children of intermediate nodes. For example, in Figure 3 $\mathbf{M}_9$ has to multiplied with when the message from node 10 passes through node 4 to node 1. During message passing, all incoming messages at a node $u$ are multiplied with the node potential at $u$, so the messages can be treated as a modified node potential. Our bounds in the previous section assumed the most adverse node potentials. These same bounds can be used unchanged on the path ignoring all other branches on the path, we only have to modify Equation 9 to work with non-continuous indices along a path $\mathcal{P}(t)$. We use notation $\hat{\mathbf{M}}^{\mathcal{P}(t)}$ instead of $\hat{\mathbf{M}}^t$ therefore.

Thus, we know how to compute message bounds for single path in the tree. If we prune below a frontier of multiple nodes, we can simply add the bounds for each frontier node because our per-path bounds are with respect to the worst effect of messages from the rest of the tree. The final theorem for pruning a tree based on frontier of nodes appears below (We skip a formal proof due to lack of space).

**Theorem 5.3** Let $G$ be a tree rooted at 1 with potentials as per Theorem 5.2. If $G_T$ is a subset of $G$ obtained by removing all nodes below a frontier $T = t_1, \dots, t_f$ such that $\sum_j \kappa(m, \alpha)^{|\mathcal{P}(t_j)|} \le \epsilon$ then $|P(x_1^1|\psi_G) - P(x_1^1|\psi_{G_T})| \le \epsilon$.

An example of a pruned tree obtained by using $\alpha = e^{0.5}, m = 100$ and $\epsilon = 0.05$ is shown in Figure 3. The weights on a node $t$ is $\kappa(m, \alpha)^{|\mathcal{P}(t)|}$ and the frontier is $T = 2, 4$.

## 5.3 Arbitrary graph

For arbitrary graphs, inference is intractable and it is difficult to efficiently bound the influence that a message from some node $u$ has on node 1 when there are multiple paths between them. Recently, [8] addressed this problem by choosing the shortest path between two nodes to bound this influence. We follow the same strategy. Let $\mathcal{SP}(t)$ denote the shortest path from node $t$ to 1. Define the frontier nodes of a pruned graph $G' \subset G$ as the set of unobserved nodes in $G'$ with at least one pruned neighbor. We choose $G'$ with frontier nodes $T = t_1, \dots, t_f$ such that $\sum_j \kappa(m, \alpha)^{|\mathcal{SP}(t_j)|} \le \epsilon$. For example, the right graph in Figure 1 is obtained by pruning with $\epsilon = 0.02$. Node 2 is the only frontier node here; node 7 is not a frontier node because it is observed.

Unlike for trees, we have no approximation guarantees on $\Pr(x_1^1)$ with this pruning but since inference algorithms on general graphs are also not exact, we cannot hope to do much better. Empirically, we will show in Section 6.3.3 that our pruning method is effective.

# 6. EXPERIMENTS

We present an evaluation of different methods on their ability to do selective node prediction and an analysis of our method along different dimensions.

## 6.1 Social Networks

Our experiments were performed on two large real-life social networks, Twitter and Pokec, each with more than one million nodes. We summarize their key statistics in Table 1.

**Twitter:** We crawled 82 million geo-tagged tweets from all over the world over four weeks in June and July 2012. We extracted from these 3.5 million geo-tagged users and assigned to each his most frequent tweet location. We then crawled for followers of users. We removed users with more than 1000 neighbors because these are typically celebrity or media accounts, and not useful for location prediction. This left us with 3 million users. The raw user locations were in (latitude, longitude) format. Since our focus is discrete prediction, we mapped these to one of 2,113 top-populated world cities using Google's Geo-coding API[2]. Users outside these 2113 cities were removed giving rise to our final graph of 1.07 million users and 3.86 million edges.

[2]developers.google.com/maps/documentation/geocoding

| | Twitter | Pokec |
|---|---|---|
| # Nodes | 1,071,254 | 1,136,049 |
| # Edges | 3,863,698 | 10,773,722 |
| % Uni-directional edges | 42.87 | 61.24 |
| # Labels($m$) | 2,113 | 10 |

Table 1: Twitter and Pokec graph statistics

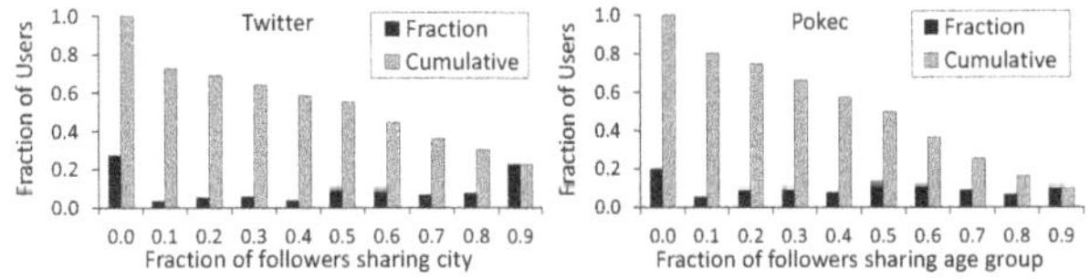


Figure 4: Histograms of fraction of followers of a user sharing his label for Twitter(left) and Pokec(right). Blue (darker) bars are for histogram and red (lighter) bars for cumulative probabilities.

**Pokec:** As a representative of the attribute prediction problem in a friendship network, we used the publicly[3] available Pokec social network (crawled in May 2012), a popular social network in Slovakia. Each user has a profile in Slovak spanning attributes like gender, age, hobbies, marital status, children, profession, and education. Our task is to predict a user's age, available in only 68% user profiles. We retained these 68% users, giving rise to a graph of 1.13 million nodes and 10.8 million edges. We segmented age into bins of five years, obtaining 10 age groups.

## 6.2 Setup and Methods

We compared eight methods: four methods from the iterative classification family (Section 3.1): LR, ICA-NoLoop, ICA, and ICA-Soft; three methods based on graphical models: JL trained on joint likelihood (Section 3.2) and PL-EM trained on pseudo likelihood (Section 4.1.2), and NCL trained on node conditional likelihood (Section 4.1); and finally our two stage method NCL+Conf that uses the decoupled training of Section 4.2. The base classifier for LR, ICA-NoLoop, ICA, and ICA-Soft was a multi-class linear logistics regression model. Methods JL and NCL used BP during deployment and convergent TRWS during training.

For both our datasets an edge could be bi-directional or uni-directional. We designed a set of nine edge features based on intuitive clues such as edges between high degree nodes indicate less homophily, bi-directional edges are stronger, and high entropy of observed labels implies less homophily. These are summarized in Table 2 and fire only for the case when $x_u = x_v$. Thus all our edge potentials are Potts. For Pokec we experimented with node features derived from a user's profile attributes like education and marital status which seemed indicative of age. However, we obtained no gain in accuracy from them. One reason could be that these were both highly unstructured text fields. Our best effort at picking high signal phrases provided little gain. In contrast, we found that our edges were highly homophilic. We ascertain this via Histograms in Figure 4 where X-axis is the fraction $s_u$ of a user's neighbors that have the same label, bucketed into steps of 0.1, and Y-axis is the proportion of users with $s_u$ fraction co-labeled friends. On Twitter, for more than 55% of the users, majority of their graph neighbors share his label; and for Pokec it is 51%. The edge

[3]http://snap.stanford.edu/data/soc-pokec.html

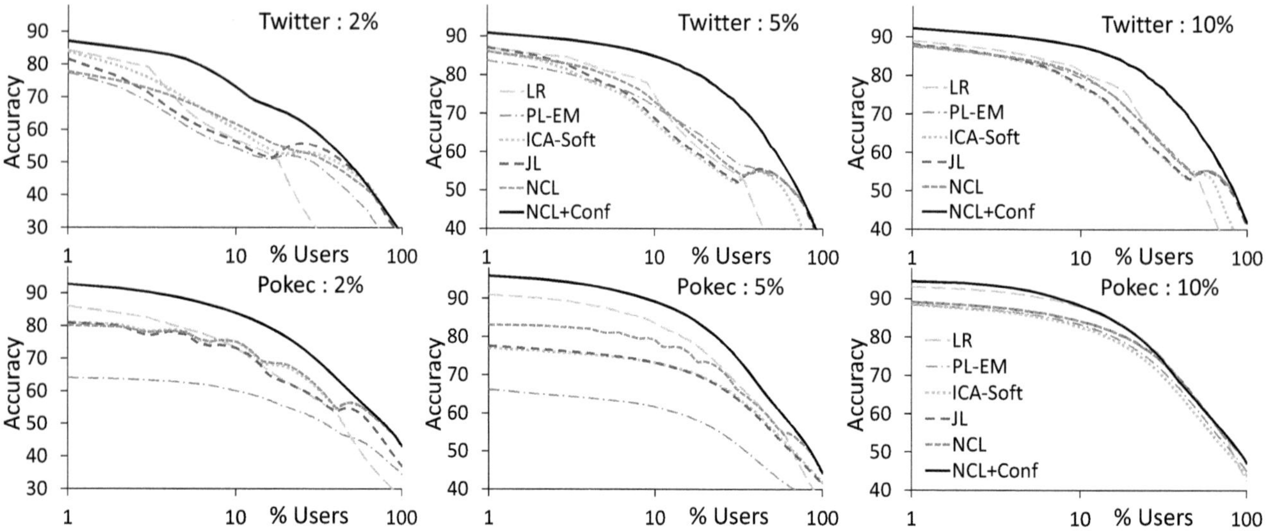


Figure 5: Precision-recall curves comparing different methods on Twitter(up) and Pokec(below) for $k$ = 2% (left), 5% (middle), 10% (right). The legend is the same for all charts and dropped in some charts to reduce clutter. [Best seen in color]

| | |
|---|---|
| $f_0(u,v) =$ | 1 (This is a bias feature) |
| $f_1(u,v) =$ | 1 if edge $(u,v)$ is bi-directional |
| $f_2(u,v) =$ | $\frac{1}{\log(\#\text{followers}(u)+1)}$ if $u$ has a follower $v$ |
| $f_3(u,v) =$ | $\frac{1}{\log(\#\text{followees}(v)+1)}$ if $u$ follows $v$ |
| $f_4(u,v) =$ | $\frac{1}{\log(\text{degree}(u)+1)} + \frac{1}{\log(\text{degree}(v)+1)}$ |
| $f_5(u,v) =$ | $\frac{1}{\log(\#\text{followers}(u)+1)} + \frac{1}{\log(\#\text{followers}(v)+1)}$ ... if $u$ and $v$ are follower-followee |
| $f_6(u,v) =$ | $\frac{1}{\log(\#\text{followees}(u)+1)} + \frac{1}{\log(\#\text{followees}(v)+1)}$ ... if $u$ and $v$ are follower-followee |
| $f_7(u,v) =$ | 1 if u or v is observed node |
| $f_8(u,v) =$ | 2 - $\frac{\text{entropy}(\ell^O_{N(u)}) - \text{entropy}(\ell^O_{N(v)})}{\log m}$ where $\ell^O_{N(i)}$ are labels of $i$'s observed neighbors |

Table 2: Edge features used by our models. The label argument is missing because they only fire when $u, v$ get the same label.

affinity values as defined in [19] for the two datasets are 7.7 and 2.8 respectively, which compares favorably to affinities in other social networks [19]. Thus, both our datasets were trained on the nine edge features alone. The parameter vector **w** represents weight of these nine features trained via different methods. For methods from the iterative classifier family, the features at a node $u$ were a sum of features in Table 2 over all neighbors $v$ of $u$. Thus, all our methods used the same set of features and were trained with L2 regularization.

We select various subsets $\mathcal{O}$ of observed nodes in a clustered manner to simulate homophily in the level of privacy that a user prefers. Starting from a random node, we select its neighbor with probability $\beta$ and teleport to some other node with probability 1-$\beta$. We set $\beta$ as 0.85. We found that relative performance was not too sensitive to $\beta$ and even for $\beta$ as small as 0.5 we got similar curves. To select a set $\mathcal{O}$ of size $k$, we take $k$ steps in this random walk. We used $k$ values for 2%, 5% and 10% of the graph size. For each $k$, we select 10 random $\mathcal{O}$ sets and average over these 10 runs. We measure statistical significance using a student's t-test over the 10 seeds and accuracy at the top-p% most confident predictions for p=1,2,...,10%. Since our focus is accuracy at the top, we do not consider larger p.

## 6.3 Results

In Figure 5 we plot the PR curves for six[4] methods for Twitter on the first row and Pokec on the second and for $k$ = 2% on the left, $k$ = 5% in the middle, and $k$ = 10% on the right. The Y-axis is the accuracy on the top-X% predictions sorted on the confidence $p_u$ output by each method. We used a log scale on the X-axis because our focus is accuracy on the top-few most confident predictions. The overall accuracy of a method is the Y-axis value when X-value is 100%. We make the following observations from these plots.

1. The overall accuracy of different methods ranges from 26%–41% for Twitter and 27–47% for Pokec. The variation in the overall accuracy of different methods is not of consequence because even the maximum is too low to be useful in practice.
2. If we focus on accuracy among the top 1% to 20% predictions we get a more positive story. Many methods provide high accuracy in this selected set, which touches 95% with the top 1–3% predictions. As we compare graphs from left to right for increasing $k$, we see that the top accuracy increases with $k$.
3. The best selective accuracy is provided by our decoupled approach NCL+Conf. In all cases, NCL+Conf dominates all other methods for top-20% predictions even though its overall accuracy is the same. For example, with 5% observed nodes if our goal is 85% accuracy we can find *four* and *2.1* times more predictions than any other method on Twitter and Pokec respectively. The gain of NCL+Conf is statistically significant with p-value $< 10^{-27}$ for all six cases.
4. Between the two graphical model approaches, NCL provides better calibration than JL, even though the

[4]The ICA-NoLoop and ICA methods were superseded by ICA-Soft and LR and were not plotted to reduce clutter.

| $\mathcal{O}$ % | NCL+Conf | NCL | ICA-Soft | LR |
|---|---|---|---|---|
| | | *Twitter* | | |
| 2 | **0.0/6.0** | 0.0/0.6 | 0.0/1.4 | 0.0/1.2 |
| 5 | **1.5/18.1** | 0.0/5.1 | 0.08/3.5 | 0.15/4.6 |
| 10 | **4.3/24.8** | 0.0/10.2 | 0.2/7.7 | 0.3/10.1 |
| | | *Pokec* | | |
| 2 | **3.5/15.3** | 0.0/0.1 | 0.0/2.6 | 0.0/4.6 |
| 5 | **8.8/23.1** | 0.0/7.0 | 0.0/0.03 | 2.1/14.4 |
| 10 | **8.0/23** | 0.02/18.7 | 0.02/14.4 | 6.8/22.6 |

Table 3: % of nodes selected at accuracy 90% (above the slash) & at accuracy 80% (below the slash) for Twitter and Pokec.

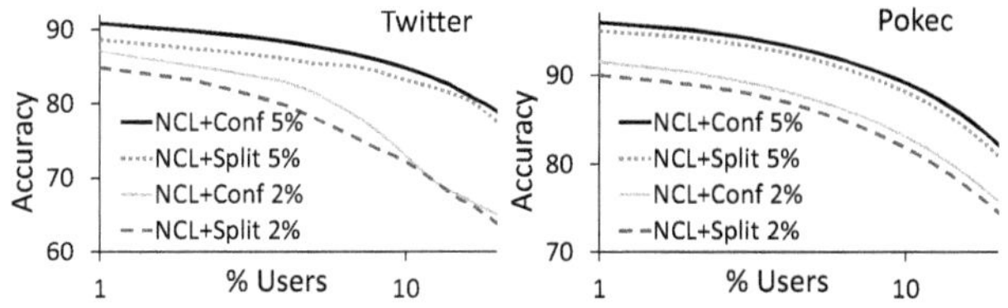


Figure 7: Comparing two different methods of training the second stage model: (1) our leave one out strategy (NCL+Conf) and (2) 70-30 split of labeled data across the two stages (NCL+Split) for $k$=5% and 2%.

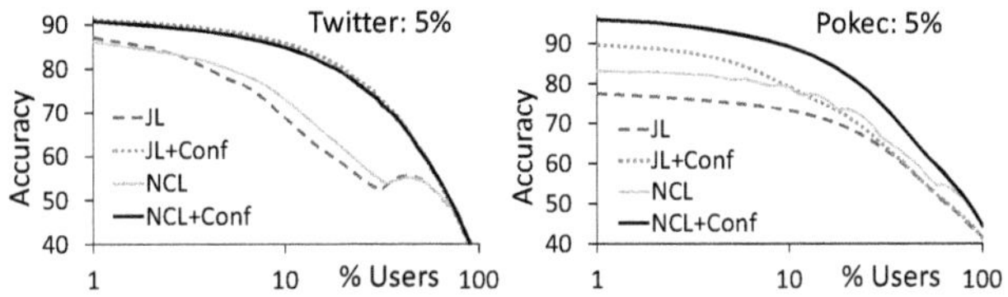


Figure 6: PR curves to compare gain of second stage on JL and NCL on Twitter and Pokec datasets with $k = 5\%$.

| Method | 2% Twitter | | 5% Twitter | | 5% Pokec | |
|---|---|---|---|---|---|---|
| | *Learn* | *Infer* | *Learn* | *Infer* | *Learn* | *Infer* |
| LR | 0.1 | 42.9 | 0.2 | 48.4 | 0.2 | 42.1 |
| ICA-Soft | 601 | 3971 | 19 | 216 | 163 | 14717 |
| PL-EM | 16 | 1265 | 3416 | 4380 | 4533 | 13115 |
| JL | 227 | 2378 | 69 | 2749 | 198 | 14621 |
| NCL | 846 | 4584 | 696 | 4994 | 5334 | 909 |
| NCL+Conf | 1414 | 4627 | 2701 | 5042 | 11771 | 950 |

Table 4: Learning and inference time in seconds.

overall accuracies are comparable. See for example, Pokec 5%. This confirms that conditional likelihood is a better objective for selective prediction. The gain of NCL over JL is statistically significant with p-value $< 10^{-4}$ in all cases except Pokec-10% where it is 0.04.

5. The method closest to NCL from the existing literature, PL-EM, does not provide good calibration for $k = 2, 5\%$ but is okay for larger $k$, corroborating the conclusion of [29] that PL-EM is good with many observed nodes. On overall accuracy PL-EM is competive with JL as observed in [29], but on the top-10% accuracy, JL scores over PL-EM in all cases.
6. Among the iterative classification methods, ICA-Soft that conditions on marginal probability provides steadily better results than ICA that conditions on hard predictions. ICA-Soft is comparable to JL — slightly better than it for 2% but worse for 5% and 10%. ICA-Soft is worse than NCL in most cases.
7. The LR method is good in a narrow range but degrades rapidly, particularly for 2% observations. This is because for the few nodes with many observed neighbors the classifier is able to assign high confidence. But, there is no generalization beyond this narrow set.

As further evidence of the effectiveness of NCL+Conf for selective prediction, in Table 3 we show the fraction of nodes selected at two target accuracy values (80% and 90%) via four methods for 2, 5, and 10% observed nodes. We see that NCL+Conf is able to make selective predictions on significantly more nodes than others, particularly when size of $\mathcal{O}$ is small. For example, on Pokec 2% when the target accuracy is 90%, we are able to select 3.5% nodes whereas none of the other approach can select any node. For a target accuracy of 80%, NCL+Conf can select between $2k$ and $7k$ nodes where $k$ is the size of $\mathcal{O}$.

### 6.3.1 *Efficacy of our confidence estimator*

Since our main gain is from the second stage confidence model, we perform two experiments to analyze this stage further. First, we check whether the lift in top-accuracy of NCL due to the second stage, holds for other methods too, e.g. JL. In Figure 6 we show PR curves for JL and JL+Conf for Twitter and Pokec with $k = 5\%$. We observe that JL+Conf is indeed much better than JL although on Pokec it continues to be worse than NCL+Conf because on that dataset even JL is much worse than NCL. Second, we check the gain due to our specific method of creating an unbiased training set over *all* observed nodes through our novel mini-graph inference method. We compare with the standard practice of splitting the observed nodes over the two stages. In Figure 7 we measure accuracy of NCL+Conf with NCL+Split which uses 70% of $\mathcal{O}$ as observed nodes for NCL inference and 30% for training the second stage. We observe that NCL+Conf shows a statistically significant gain over NCL+Split for both $k = 2\%$ and 5%.

### 6.3.2 *Running time*

In Table 4 we show the time taken for learning and inference using various methods on a sequential program on a 2.5 GHz Intel Xeon linux server with 8 GB RAM. As expected, the plain LR model is the fastest because it only looks at the small number of observed nodes during training. The running time for all graphical model-based methods show a lot of variability because the convergence of inference is dependent on the potentials, the observed nodes, and edge density. Roughly, learning+inference on Twitter takes an hour, whereas on Pokec it is three hours. The training time for NCL+Conf is two to four times more than NCL and most of it goes in computing the mini-graph instances. However, this part of the code is trivially parallelizable.

### 6.3.3 *Pruning efficiency*

In this section we analyze the running time versus accuracy trade offs due to our pruning strategy. In Figure 8 we plot average error in the probability of the true label and average inference time (log-scale) over hundred nodes for increasing sizes of the mini-graph. The X-axis varies from a minigraph size of 5 nodes to the full graph. We observe that

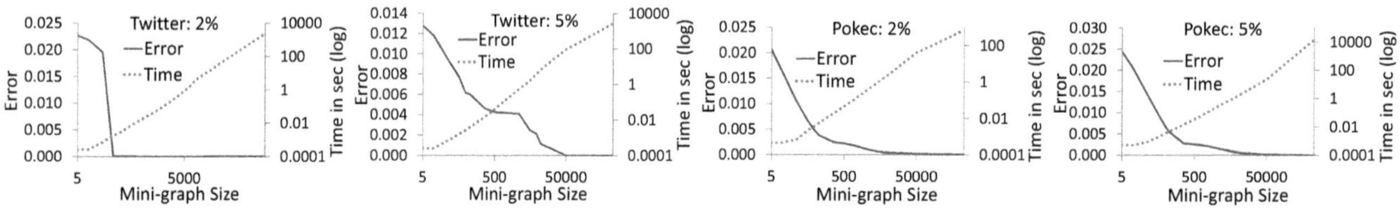


Figure 8: Error and inference time for increasingly pruned graph for Twitter and Pokec with 2% and 5% observed nodes.

the running time drops by several orders of magnitude when we prune mini-graphs so that the error is $\leq 0.002$. This shows that our pruning strategy is effective for the leave one out inference needed for well-calibrated probabilities.

# 7. CONCLUSION AND FUTURE WORK

In this paper we defined and motivated the problem of selective prediction of labels in a social network. Our study over two large social networks revealed that existing graph-based prediction algorithms do not provide well-calibrated probabilities — a pre-requisite for selective prediction. We proposed a new node conditional likelihood objective for training a graphical model-based prediction algorithm, and a decoupled model for confidence estimation based on a novel unbiased training process. We provided theoretically sound graph pruning strategies for training the new objective. These ideas together provide an accurate and practical mechanism for selective predictions in social networks.

An important outcome of our work is that it raises even graver privacy concerns, than the ones raised in earlier studies based on overall accuracy [31]. An interesting area of future work is understanding the relationship between information blurring models and selective prediction models.

# 8. REFERENCES


[1] V. Avadhanula. Selective node labeling in social networks. Master's thesis, IIT Bombay, 2013.

[2] A. Azran. The rendezvous algorithm: Multiclass semi-supervised learning with markov random walks. In *ICML*, 2007.

[3] S. Bhagat, G. Cormode, and S. Muthukrishnan. Node classification in social networks. In *SNDA*. 2011.

[4] M. Bilgic and L. Getoor. Effective label acquisition for collective classification. In *Proc. ACM SIGKDD*, 2008.

[5] S. Chakrabarti, B. Dom, and P. Indyk. Enhanced hypertext categorization using hyperlinks. *SIGMOD Rec.*, 27(2):307–318, 1998.

[6] O. Chapelle, B. Schölkopf, and A. Zien, editors. *Semi-Supervised Learning.* MIT Press, 2006.

[7] G. Chaudhari. High confidence predictions in social networks. Master's thesis, IIT Bombay, 2013.

[8] A. Chechetka and C. Guestrin. Focused belief propagation for query-specific inference. *JMLR*, 9:89–96, 2010.

[9] Z. Cheng, J. Caverlee, and K. Lee. You are where you tweet: a content-based approach to geo-locating twitter users. In *CIKM*, 2010.

[10] J. Eisenstein, B. O'Connor, N. A. Smith, and E. P. Xing. A latent variable model for geographic lexical variation. In *Proc. EMNLP*, 2010.

[11] T. Hazan and R. Urtasun. A primal-dual message-passing algorithm for approximated large scale structured prediction. In *NIPS*, 2010.

[12] L. Hong, A. Ahmed, S. Gurumurthy, A. J. Smola, and K. Tsioutsiouliklis. Discovering geographical topics in the twitter stream. In *Proc WWW*, 2012.

[13] D. Koller and N. Friedman. *Probabilistic Graphical Models: Principles and Techniques.* MIT Press, 2009.

[14] D. Koutra, T.-Y. Ke, U. Kang, D. H. Chau, H.-K. K. Pao, and C. Faloutsos. Unifying guilt-by-association approaches: Theorems and fast algorithms. In *ECML/PKDD (2)*, 2011.

[15] Q. Lu and L. Getoor. Link-based classification. In *Machine Learning, ICML*, pages 496–503, 2003.

[16] S. A. Macskassy and F. J. Provost. Classification in networked data: A toolkit and a univariate case study. *JMLR*, 8:935–983, 2007.

[17] J. Mahmud, J. Nichols, and C. Drews. Where is this tweet from? inferring home locations of twitter users. In *Proc. ICWSM*, 2012.

[18] L. K. McDowell, K. M. Gupta, and D. W. Aha. Cautious collective classification. *JMLR*, 10:2777–2836, 2009.

[19] A. Mislove, B. Viswanath, P. K. Gummadi, and P. Druschel. You are who you know: inferring user profiles in online social networks. In *WSDM*, 2010.

[20] J. Neville and D. Jensen. Relational dependency networks. *Journal of Machine Learning Research*, 8, 2007.

[21] J. Neville and F. Provost. Predictive modeling with social networks. ICWSM, Tutorial, 2009.

[22] A. Sadilek, H. Kautz, and J. P. Bigham. Finding your friends and following them to where you are. In *WSDM*, 2012.

[23] A. G. Schwing, T. Hazan, M. Pollefeys, and R. Urtasun. Efficient structured prediction with latent variables for general graphical models. In *ICML*, 2012.

[24] P. Sen, G. Namata, M. Bilgic, L. Getoor, B. Gallagher, and T. Eliassi-Rad. Collective classification in network data. *AI Magazine*, 29(3):93–106, 2008.

[25] M. Szummer and T. Jaakkola. Partially labeled classification with markov random walks. In *NIPS*, 2001.

[26] P. P. Talukdar, J. Reisinger, M. Pasca, D. Ravichandran, R. Bhagat, and F. Pereira. Weakly-supervised acquisition of labeled class instances using graph random walks. In *EMNLP*, 2008.

[27] B. Taskar, E. Segal, and D. Koller. Probabilistic classification and clustering in relational data. In *IJCAI*, 2001.

[28] U. Weinsberg, S. Bhagat, S. Ioannidis, and N. Taft. Blurme: inferring and obfuscating user gender based on ratings. In *RecSys*, 2012.

[29] R. Xiang and J. Neville. Pseudolikelihood em for within-network relational learning. In *ICDM*, 2008.

[30] R. Xiang and J. Neville. Collective inference for network data with copula latent markov networks. In *WSDM*, 2013.

[31] E. Zheleva and L. Getoor. To join or not to join: the illusion of privacy in social networks with mixed public and private user profiles. In *Proc. WWW*, 2009.

[32] D. Zhou, O. Bousquet, T. N. Lal, J. Weston, and B. Schölkopf. Learning with local and global consistency. In *NIPS*, 2003.

# Active Learning for Networked Data Based on Non-progressive Diffusion Model

Zhilin Yang
Department of Computer Science and Technology
Tsinghua University
kimiyoung@yeah.net

Jie Tang and Bin Xu
Department of Computer Science and Technology
Tsinghua University
{jietang, xubin}@tsinghua.edu.cn

Chunxiao Xing
Department of Computer Science and Technology
Tsinghua University
xingcx@tsinghua.edu.cn

## ABSTRACT

We study the problem of active learning for networked data, where samples are connected with links and their labels are correlated with each other. We particularly focus on the setting of using the probabilistic graphical model to model the networked data, due to its effectiveness in capturing the dependency between labels of linked samples.

We propose a novel idea of connecting the graphical model to the information diffusion process, and precisely define the active learning problem based on the non-progressive diffusion model. We show the NP-hardness of the problem and propose a method called MaxCo to solve it. We derive the lower bound for the optimal solution for the active learning setting, and develop an iterative greedy algorithm with provable approximation guarantees. We also theoretically prove the convergence and correctness of MaxCo.

We evaluate MaxCo on four different genres of datasets: Coauthor, Slashdot, Mobile, and Enron. Our experiments show a consistent improvement over other competing approaches.

## Categories and Subject Descriptors

H.2.8 [**Database Management**]: Database Applications—*Data Mining*; I.2.6 [**Artificial Intelligence**]: Learning

## General Terms

Algorithms, Experimentation

## Keywords

Active learning, Non-progressive model, Factor graph model

## 1. INTRODUCTION

One challenge for a machine learning task is how to collect sufficient labeled samples for training an accurate classification model. Active learning is a method to alleviate this problem by actively querying experts to obtain the desired labels of a few samples. For example, Hoi et al. [12] studied active learning on text categorization problem. Cohn et al. [5] proposed two methods: mixtures of Gaussians and locally weighted regression for efficiently selecting samples in neural networks. Settles et al. [22] provided a survey for various sample selection strategies. The underlying idea for most of these methods is to measure the informativeness of each unlabeled sample and finally select an "informative" sample to query each time. The problem becomes more difficult with the increase of the complexity of the input data. First, the samples in the input data may be connected and correlated with each other (i.e., networked data), which implies that selecting the most informative (but isolated sample) may be not that helpful for classifying the other samples. Second, in practice, to avoid frequently querying the experts, it is usually desirable to select a set of samples and query the users in a batch mode.


*WSDM'14,* February 24–28, 2014, New York, New York, USA.

http://dx.doi.org/10.1145/2556195.2556223.

In this paper, we try to systematically address the above questions. The problem can be formally defined as follows:

*Definition 1.* **Batch Mode Active Learning for Networked Data.** Given a network $G = (V_U, V_L, \mathbf{y}_L, E, \mathbf{X})$, where $V_U$ denotes a set of unlabeled samples, $V_L$ denotes a set of labeled samples, $\mathbf{y}_L$ corresponds to labels of the labeled samples, $E$ is the set of edges between samples in the network $G$, and $\mathbf{X}$ is an $(|V_U| + |V_L|) \times d$ attribute matrix in which each row $\mathbf{x}_i$ represents the vector of attributes for sample $v_i$, our goal is to query a subset of $k$ unlabeled samples so as to maximize the following utility function:

$$\max_{V_S \subseteq V_U} Q(V_S), \text{ with } \quad |V_S| \leq k \tag{1}$$

In the formulation, the utility function $Q(V_S)$ is a general definition on the subset $V_S$, and can be instantiated in different ways. Such a definition of active learning for networked data has been extensively used in the literature [2, 23, 31].

To model the correlation between labels of linked samples, we consider the probabilistic graphical model. In the setting of graphical model, we connect the active learning problem to the theory of non-progressive diffusion [8], and develop an instantiation model for the above problem. The active learning problem based on non-progressive diffusion is proved to be NP-hard. We present an efficient method named MaxCo to solve the problem with provable approximation guarantee. Theoretically, we prove the convergence and correctness of the proposed method and also provide its approximation ratio.

Empirically, we verify the proposed method on four different genres of datasets: Coauthor, Slashdot, Mobile, and

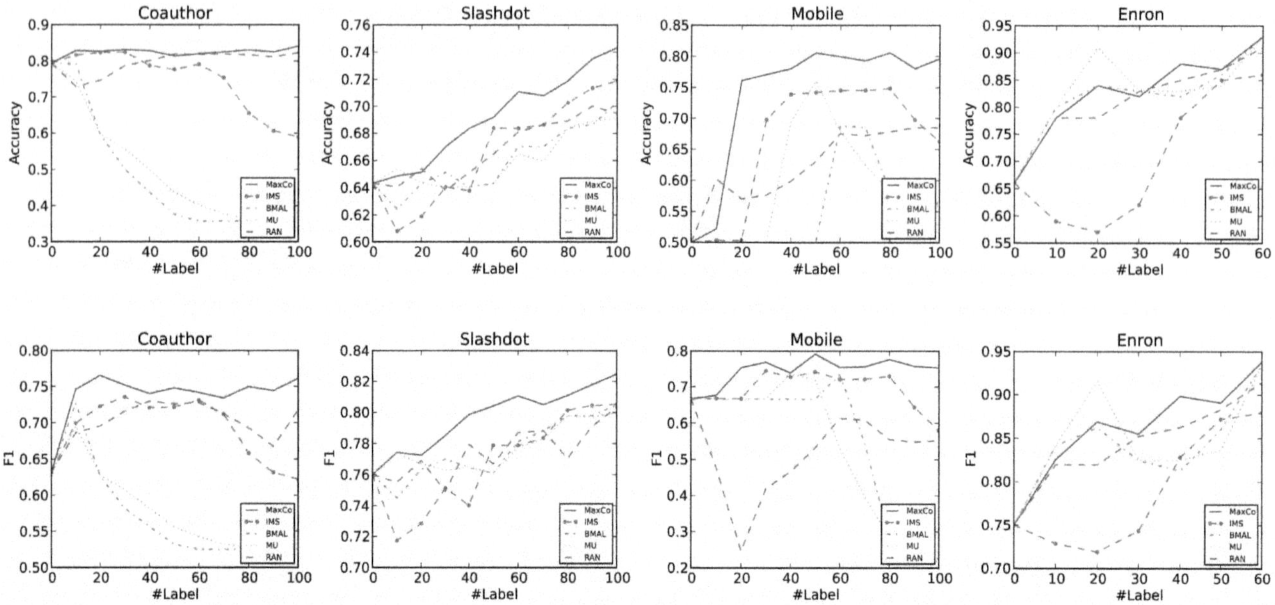


**Figure 1: Performance Comparison: Five algorithms on four datasets with accuracy and F1 measure. X-axis denotes the number of labeled samples while y-axis represents the measure score.**

Enron. We compare MaxCo with several competing methods (Cf. §5 for definitions of the competing methods). The experimental results indicate that the proposed method can significantly improve the active learning performance over the other methods. Figure 1 shows the performance comparison of the comparison methods on the four datasets. On average, our method MaxCo outperforms the other methods by 5%-10% in terms of F1 (t-test, $p$-value $< 0.01$).

To summarize, the major contribution of this work lies in the following aspects:

- Precisely define the problem of active learning for networked data via the non-progressive diffusion model, which provides an elegant way to model the diffusion probabilities from the available labeled samples to the unlabeled samples.
- Prove the NP-hardness of the problem and develop an efficient algorithm with provable approximation guarantee to solve the problem.
- Theoretically analyze the proposed algorithm, prove its convergence and correctness, and provide an upper bound and a lower bound of the proposed algorithm.
- Empirically evaluate the proposed algorithm on several real-world datasets to demonstrate the effectiveness of our algorithm.

**Organization.** Section 2 presents the factor graph framework and instantiates the problem in the settings of non-progressive diffusion model; Section 3 proposes the algorithm; Section 4 provides the theoretical analysis; Section 5 evaluates the algorithm; Section 6 discusses related work, and finally Section 7 concludes the work.

## 2. MODEL

The first question we want to address is how to leverage the link information to improve the effectiveness of active learning. In a network setting, for example a social network, users are connected with each other and their behaviors are strongly correlated. To deal with this, we consider the probabilistic graphical model as our basic framework. We utilize Loopy Belief Propagation (LBP) [17] to learn parameters in the probabilistic graphical model.

For active learning, a frequently used method is to select the most informative samples [23, 31]. However, they do not consider the fact that in the graphical model learning process, an instance classified to have label $y_i$ after iteration $\tau$ may be classified to have label $y_j$ after the next iteration $\tau + 1$. To this end, we propose a novel idea of connecting message passing in LBP to the theory of non-progressive diffusion and instantiate the active learning problem based on non-progressive diffusion model.

### 2.1 Factor Graph Model

Factor graph is one type of probabilistic graphical models. It leverages factorization of probabilistic distribution to capture dependency and correlation among random variables.

In particular, we consider a partially labeled setting for the factor graph model, denoted as $G = (V_L, V_U, \mathbf{y}_L, E, \mathbf{X})$, which is consistent with our definition in active learning problem for networked data. We associate each sample $v_i \in V_U \cup V_L$ with a random variable $y_i$ taking value in a discrete space $\mathcal{Y}$. Basically, there are two categories of nodes in a factor graph, variable nodes and factor nodes. If a factor function is defined over a clique, a factor node will be added into the graph and all variable nodes in the clique will be connected to the factor node respectively. Given this, let $V = V_U \cup V_L$, we can define the joint probability over all the labeled and unlabeled samples:

$$P(\mathbf{y}|\mathbf{y}_L;\Theta) = \frac{1}{Z}\exp\left\{\sum_{v_i \in V}\theta_i f(y_i,\mathbf{x}_i) + \sum_{(v_i,v_j)\in E}\theta_{i,j} g(y_i,y_j)\right\} \quad (2)$$

where $f(y_i, \mathbf{x}_i)$ represents the factor function defined on variable node $y_i$ with attribute vector $\mathbf{x}_i$ and $g(y_i, y_j)$ denotes the factor function defined on a factor node that connects $y_i$ and $y_j$; $\Theta = (\{\theta_i\}, \{\theta_{ij}\})$ are parameters to be estimated and $Z$ is a normalization factor.

**Model Learning.** Given a training dataset, we aim to estimate the parameter $\Theta$ in the factor graph model. One challenge here is how to leverage unlabeled data for parameter estimation. When training the parameter, we maximize the likelihood of labeled samples by summing up all possible distributions over the unlabeled samples. For the sake of simplicity, we first rewrite the conditional probability (Eq. 2) as follows:

$$P(\mathbf{y}|\mathbf{y}_L;\Theta) = \frac{1}{Z}\exp\{\Theta^T\mathbf{S}(\mathbf{y})\} \quad (3)$$

where $\mathbf{S}(\mathbf{y})$ denotes all the factor functions defined on the graph $G$ related to variable $\mathbf{y}$. For maximum likelihood estimation, the log-likelihood objective function can be written as:

$$\begin{aligned}\mathcal{O} &= P(\mathbf{y}_L|G) \\ &= \log\sum_{\mathbf{y}|\mathbf{y}_L}\exp\{\Theta^T\mathbf{S}(\mathbf{y})\} - \log Z\end{aligned} \quad (4)$$

where $\mathbf{y}|\mathbf{y}_L$ indicates a label configuration inferred from the available labels $\mathbf{y}_L$. Then we can write the gradient of the objective function w.r.t. to the parameter $\Theta$:

$$\begin{aligned}\frac{\partial\mathcal{O}}{\partial\Theta} &= \frac{\partial}{\partial\Theta}\log\sum_{\mathbf{y}|\mathbf{y}_L}\exp\{\Theta^T\mathbf{S}(\mathbf{y})\} - \frac{\partial}{\partial\Theta}\log\sum_{\mathbf{y}}\exp\{\Theta^T\mathbf{S}(\mathbf{y})\} \\ &= \frac{\sum_{\mathbf{y}|\mathbf{y}_L}\exp\{\Theta^T\mathbf{S}(\mathbf{y})\}\cdot\mathbf{S}(\mathbf{y})}{\sum_{\mathbf{y}|\mathbf{y}_L}\exp\{\Theta^T\mathbf{S}(\mathbf{y})\}} - \frac{\sum_{\mathbf{y}}\exp\{\Theta^T\mathbf{S}(\mathbf{y})\}\cdot\mathbf{S}(\mathbf{y})}{\sum_{\mathbf{y}}\exp\{\Theta^T\mathbf{S}(\mathbf{y})\}} \\ &= \mathbb{E}_{p(\mathbf{y}|\mathbf{y}_L;\Theta)}\mathbf{S}(\mathbf{y}) - \mathbb{E}_{p(\mathbf{y};\Theta)}\mathbf{S}(\mathbf{y})\end{aligned} \quad (5)$$

We can apply gradient descent method to solve the objective function. However, $\mathbb{E}_{p(\mathbf{y}|\mathbf{y}_L;\Theta)}$ and $\mathbb{E}_{p(\mathbf{y};\Theta)}$ are intractable when the graph contains cycles [29]. A state-of-the-art approximate solution is Loopy Belief Propagation(LBP)[17].

**Loopy Belief Propagation.** LBP utilizes message passing to calculate marginal probability. More specifically, for each iteration, message passing is performed according to the following update rules.

$$\begin{aligned}\mu^{\tau}_{y_i\to f}(\mathbf{x}_i) &= \prod_{f^*\in NB(y_i)\backslash f}\mu^{\tau-1}_{f^*\to y_i}(\mathbf{x}_i) \\ \mu^{\tau}_{f\to y_i}(\mathbf{x}_i) &= \sum_{\sim y_i} f(\mathbf{x}_f)\prod_{y_j\in NB(f)\backslash\{y_i\}}\mu^{\tau-1}_{y_j\to f}(\mathbf{x}_j)\end{aligned} \quad (6)$$

For iteration $\tau$, $\mu^{\tau}_{y\to f}$ represents the message passed from a variable node $y$ to a factor node $f$, while $\mu^{\tau}_{f\to y}$ denotes the message passed in the reverse direction. $NB(y)$ is the set of neighbor factor nodes of a variable node $y$. $f(\mathbf{x}_f)$ denotes the factor function associated with certain factor node $f$. $\sum_{\sim y_i}$ means to sum up the factor function over all variables except $y_i$. After LBP converges to a fixed point, the belief probability of each variable node $y_i$ can be obtained as the product of all messages passing toward $y_i$.

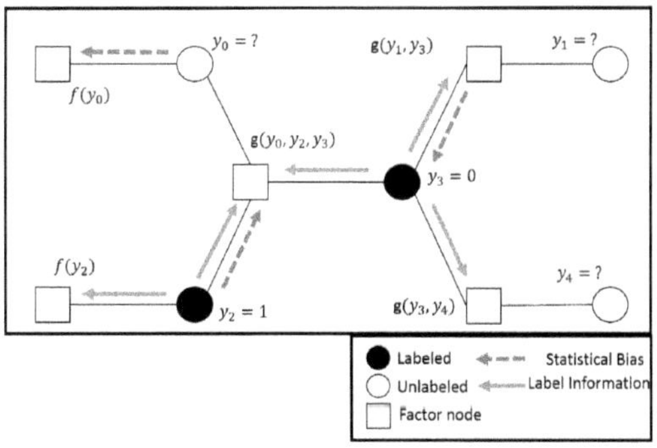


**Figure 2: Modeling LBP with information diffusion: Streams of label information are diffused from labeled samples while flows of statistical bias are intrinsically distributed in the network.**

## 2.2 Active Learning on Non-progressive Diffusion Model

We propose a novel idea of connecting the LBP process to the information diffusion model and develop an instantiation model for the active learning for networked data.

In the information diffusion theory, there are two state-of-the-art diffusion models: linear threshold model and independent cascaded model [13]. We consider the linear threshold model, where a sample will be activated as long as the number of its active neighbors exceeds its threshold. According to the diffusion process, the linear threshold model can be further classified into two categories: progressive model and non-progressive model.

In the progressive model, a node in the network can only be activated once and remains its status in the following diffusion process. More formally, let $f_\tau(v)$ denote the status of node $v$ at time $\tau$. If $f(v) = 1$ then $v$ is activated, otherwise not. Let $NB(v)$ denote the neighbor set of $v$, the formal definition of $f$ is as follows.

$$f_\tau(v) = \begin{cases} 1 & \text{if } \sum_{u\in NB(v)} f_{\tau-1}(u) \geq t(v) \text{ or } f_{\tau-1}(v) = 1 \\ 0 & \text{if } \sum_{u\in NB(v)} f_{\tau-1}(u) < t(v) \text{ and } f_{\tau-1}(v) = 0 \end{cases}$$

In the non-progressive model, a node in the network can reverse its status in both directions, i.e., either from active to inactive, or vice versa, depending on the status of its neighbors at the last time step. More formally,

$$f_\tau(v) = \begin{cases} 1 & \text{if } \sum_{u\in NB(v)} f_{\tau-1}(u) \geq t(v) \\ 0 & \text{if } \sum_{u\in NB(v)} f_{\tau-1}(u) < t(v) \end{cases}$$

Which model is more suitable for modeling the message passing process in an LBP? As illustrated in figure 2, we can imagine that there are two types of information diffusing across the social network. One is statistical bias, which may be caused by insufficiency of labeled data, imbalance of labeled data or redundancy of selected features. This kind of information is distributed randomly and intrinsically in the given network and may cause overfitting of the factor graph model. The other type is labeled information, which indicates the ground truth, counterbalances the statistical bias and thus enhances the capability of generalization of factor graph model. Suppose statistical bias and labeling information are spreading across the network simultaneously, our goal is to maximize the influence of labeling information and minimize the side effects of statistical bias. In this perspective, as for an uncertain variable node, whose "belief" is around 0.5, it may be alternatively influenced by statistical bias and labeling information, and thus sway its "belief" probability between 0.49 and 0.51. For this reason, during LBP message passing, except the initially labeled nodes, a node predicted to have label $y_i$ after iteration $\tau$ will be probably predicted to have label $y_j$ after the next iteration $\tau + 1$. Therefore, apparently, it is more acceptable to select non-progressive model because a variable node in the factor graph, as we demonstrated above, can reverse its status in both directions.

Now we utilize non-progressive linear threshold model to instantiate the utility function in Eq. 1.

*Problem 1.* **Active Learning on Non-progressive Diffusion Model.** Given a factor graph model trained on the partially labeled network $G = (V_L, V_U, \mathbf{y}_L, E, \mathbf{X})$, the threshold values and uncertainty values for each sample, denoted as $\{t(v)|v \in V_L \cup V_U\}$ and $\{\mu(v)|v \in V_L \cup V_U\}$, and a budget $k$, we aim to query a subset of $k$ unlabeled samples, such that the performance of factor graph model will be best improved. Suppose the uncertainty of variable $v$ grows as $\mu(v)$ increases, the utility function can be defined as:

$$\max_{V_S \subseteq V_U} \{\max_{V_T \subseteq V_U} |V_T|\}, \quad |V_S| \leq k$$

with the constraints:

$$f_0(v) = 1 \iff v \in V_S \tag{7}$$

$$\exists \tau_M \text{ s.t. } \forall v \in V_T \; \forall \tau > \tau_M \; f_\tau(v) = 1 \tag{8}$$

$$\forall v \in V_U \backslash V_T, \forall u \in V_T, \mu(v) \leq \mu(u) \tag{9}$$

$$f_\tau(v) = 1 \iff \sum_{u \in NB(v)} f_{\tau-1}(u) \geq t(v) \tag{10}$$

Here we interpret the constraints we made above. Constraint (7) indicates that we initially label all samples in $V_S$. By constraint (8) we require all samples in $V_T$ to be eventually activated, because we assume that only an activated sample can be effectively influenced by label information. By constraint (9), we also require $V_T$ is made up of top $k$ uncertain nodes in $V_U$, instead of simply counting the number of eventually infected nodes. In this way of definition we are only interested in those samples that lie on the edge of right and wrong, which is the key point to the active learning problem, rather than treating every unlabeled sample equally. Constraint (10) indicates that we consider the active learning problem under non-progressive diffusion model. Because there may be more than one $V_T$ satisfying the constraints, we select the maximum one in the utility function.

## 3. ALGORITHMS

In this section, we solve problem 1 by two steps. First we reduce the problem to Minimum Source Set problem. Second we give an approximate solution to Minimum Source Set problem.

### 3.1 Reduction

In problem 1, we fix the number of source set $V_S$ and try to maximize the size of target set $V_T$. However, in this section, we define a Minimum Source Set problem where we fix the number of target set $V_T$ and aim to minimize the number of queried samples.

*Problem 2.* **Minimum Source Set** Given a factor graph model trained on the networked data $G = (V_L, V_U, \mathbf{y}_L, E, \mathbf{X})$, the threshold values for each sample, denoted as $\{t(v)|v \in V_L \cup V_U\}$, and the target set $V_T \subseteq V_U$, we aim to find a minimal source set $V_S \subseteq V_U$ to eventually activate all samples in $V_T$, i.e.,

$$\min |V_S|$$

with the constraints that if $f_0(v) = 1$ for all $v \in V_S$, then $\exists \tau_M$ s.t. $f_t(v) = 1$ for all $v \in V_T$ and $t > \tau_M$. The samples in the graph are updated with the non-progressive rule:

$$f_\tau(v) = 1 \iff \sum_{u \in NB(v)} f_{\tau-1}(u) \geq t(v)$$

We are now to introduce the equivalence of problem 1 and problem 2.

*Theorem 1.* The problem of Active Learning on Non-progressive Diffusion Model(problem 1) and Minimum Source Set problem(problem 2) are equivalent.

PROOF. First, we introduce a reduction from problem 1 to problem 2. For problem 1, given $|V_S| = k$, we aim to find an instance of $V_S$ to maximize $|V_T|$. We build a family of instances of problem 2 to solve problem 1. We enumerate $|V_T|$ from its maximum possible value $|V_U|$ and count down until $|V_T|$ can be achieved with $|V_S| \leq k$. We build an instance of problem 2 to find out the optimal solution $V_{S,\text{opt}}$ given $|V_T|$. If $|V_{S,\text{opt}}| \leq k$, then we can quit the algorithm and $V_{S,\text{opt}}$ is the optimal solution for the problem 1, with which the maximum size of $|V_T|$ is the one being enumerated, denoted as $|V_T|_m$.

Now we prove the reduction above by contradiction. Suppose that there exists another solution $V_S^*$ such that $|V_S^*| \leq k$ and $|V_T^*| > |V_T|_m$, where $V_T^*$ is the target set corresponding to $V_S^*$. Therefore, when we build an instance of problem 2 with $|V_T^*|$, the optimal solution $V_{S,\text{opt}}$ will satisfy $|V_{S,\text{opt}}| \leq |V_S^*| \leq k$. Thus, the algorithm will quit and $|V_T|_m$ will not be enumerated, which leads to contradiction. Therefore, the reduction above gives optimal solution to problem 1.

Next, we prove that problem 2 can be reduced to problem 1. For problem 2, given $|V_T| = l$, we aim to find a smallest source set $V_S$ to eventually activate all samples in $V_T$. Similar to the reduction in the reverse direction, we can enumerate the value of $|V_S|$ in this case. Because we want to minimize $|V_S|$, we enumerate $|V_S|$ from 0 and count upwards until $V_T$ can be activated by $V_S$. Again we leverage an instance of problem 1 to find the maximum size of target set $|V_T|_m$ with source set of size $|V_S|$. If $|V_T|_m \geq l$, we terminate the algorithm and the optimal solution is the one returned by problem 1, denoted as $V_{S,\text{opt}}$.

Now we prove the reduction above by contradiction. Suppose that there exists another solution $V_S^*$ such that $|V_S^*| < |V_{S,\text{opt}}|$ and the size of eventually activated sample set

**Algorithm 1:** MaxCo Algorithm part 1: Reduction

**Input**: $G = (V_U, V_L, \mathbf{y}_L, E, \mathbf{X})$, $k$, threshold function $t$
**Output**: $V_S$: the selected set of nodes to be labeled.

$l \leftarrow$ min value for $|V_T|$
$r \leftarrow$ max value for $|V_T|$
$V_{S,\text{opt}} \leftarrow \emptyset$
**while** $l < r$ **do**
  $|V_T| \leftarrow \frac{l+r}{2}$
  $V_S \leftarrow \text{MinimumSourceSet}(G, |V_T|)$
  **if** $|V_S| \leq k$ **then**
    $l \leftarrow |V_T| + 1$
    $V_{S,\text{opt}} \leftarrow V_S$
  **else**
    $r \leftarrow |V_T|$
**return** $V_{S,opt}$

$|V_T^*| \geq l$. When we enumerate $|V_S^*|$, we can leverage an instance of problem 1 to obtain a target set $V_T$ with $|V_T| \geq l$. Therefore, $|V_{S,\text{opt}}|$ will not be enumerated, which contradicts the assumption.

It follows two problems are equivalent. □

LEMMA 1. *For problem 2, if either $\mu(v_1) < \mu(v_2)$ or $\mu(v_2) < \mu(v_1)$ $\forall v_1, v_2 \in V_U \cup V_L$ and $v_1 \neq v_2$, $|V_{S,opt}|$ is monotonically non-decreasing with respect to $|V_T|$.*

PROOF. To prove the lemma, we only need to prove that for two target sets $V_{T1}$ and $V_{T2}$ and their optimal solutions $V_{S1}$ and $V_{S2}$, if $|V_{T1}| > |V_{T2}|$, then we have $|V_{S1}| \geq |V_{S2}|$.

According to the definition of minimum source set problem, the target set should be top-$l$ uncertain nodes. Because samples can be strictly ordered with respect to uncertainty, we can infer $V_{T2} \subset V_{T1}$ from the assumption that $|V_{T1}| > |V_{T2}|$.

Suppose $|V_{S1}| < |V_{S2}|$. Because $V_{S1}$ can activate all samples in $V_{T1}$ and $V_{T2} \subset V_{T1}$, $V_{S1}$ can activate all samples in $V_{T2}$ as well. It contradicts the assumption that $V_{S2}$ is the optimal solution for $V_{T2}$. Therefore, $|V_{S1}| \geq |V_{S2}|$. □

In practice, we can force any two uncertainty values to be strictly ordered even if they are arithmetically equal. For example, we can assume that $v_i$ is uncertain than $v_j$ if $\mu(v_i) = \mu(v_j)$ but $i > j$. Therefore, because $|V_{S,\text{opt}}|$ is monotonically non-decreasing with respect to $|V_T|$, we can apply bisection method to optimize the reduction algorithm introduced in the proof of theorem 1. When reducing from problem 1 to problem 2, instead of enumerating the value of $|V_T|$ one by one, we can leverage bisection method to bisect the interval and select a subinterval recursively, which will largely speed up the algorithm from $\mathcal{O}(n)$ to $\mathcal{O}(\log n)$, where $n$ indicates the size of domain of $|V_T|$. The complete procedure for reduction from problem 1 to problem 2 is illustrated in algorithm 1.

## 3.2 Threshold and Uncertainty

Because the problem of Active Learning on Non-progressive Diffusion Model can be reduced to Minimum Source Set problem in polynomial time, we now focus on solving the Minimum Source Set problem.

Before we solve Minimum Source Set problem, we need to give a definition of threshold function $t(v)$.

**Threshold Definition.** The threshold value of a sample reflects how sensitive it is to the status of its neighbors. In the factor graph model, if the "belief" probability of a sample $v$ is quite close to $\frac{1}{|\mathcal{Y}|}$, i.e., variable node $v$ is very uncertain, then it is easily activated by the messages passed from its neighbors. For this reason, samples with higher uncertainty should obtain a lower threshold. Moreover, because a sample with high degree will receive a great number of messages, which may contain both labeling information and statistical bias, its threshold should be relatively high. Considering both degree and uncertainty factors, we define the threshold function as follows.

$$t(v) = \min\{\lceil \eta(\mu\text{max} - \mu(v))d(v) \rceil, d(v)\} \tag{11}$$

where $d(v)$ is the degree, $\mu\text{max}$ is the maximum value of uncertainty measure and $\eta$ is a global constant factor to adjust the distribution of thresholds. We apply ceiling operation to the expression to avoid some extreme cases where $t(v) = 0$. Also, of course, the value $t(v)$ should not be greater than $d(v)$, otherwise $v$ will never be activated whatsoever.

Given Eq. 11, it is a nontrivial job to tune the parameter $\eta$ because it varies in a wide range in different data sets. To have a unified representation, we further define $\eta$ to be

$$\eta = \frac{\gamma}{\text{Avg}(\mu\text{max} - \mu)} \tag{12}$$

where *Avg* means the average value over the given data set, and $\gamma$ is a constant factor. Under the definition, we can instead tune $\gamma$ between 0 and 1, which is relatively irrelevant to the specific data set.

**Uncertainty Definition.** Now what remains to be defined is an uncertainty function. There are several measures corresponding to the uncertainty of a variable node in a factor graph. One is to define it as the sum of difference between expected belief and calculated belief of each class [21].

$$\mu(v) = -\sum_{y \in \mathcal{Y}} \left| \mathcal{B}_v(y) - \frac{1}{|\mathcal{Y}|} \right| + 2\left(1 - \frac{1}{|\mathcal{Y}|}\right) \tag{13}$$

where $\mathcal{B}_v(y)$ is obtained by LBP, indicating the "belief" probability that $v$ is classified to have label $y$. We add a constant term to ensure that $\mu(v)$ is always nonnegative.

Another extensively used measure of uncertainty is entropy(aka TTE in [22]). More formally,

$$\mu(v) = \sum_{y \in \mathcal{Y}} \mathcal{B}_v(y) \log \frac{1}{\mathcal{B}_v(y)} \tag{14}$$

We reserve two ways of definition here and judge them through experiments in § 5.

## 3.3 MinSS

After defining the threshold function and uncertainty function, in this section, we aim to solve Minimum Source Set problem.

First we claim that Minimum Source Set is an NP-hard problem, which will be proved in § 4. We design an approximate algorithm MinSS to find the source set $V_S$ iteratively and greedily.

**Algorithm 2:** MaxCo Algorithm part 2: MinSS

**Input**: $G = (V_U, V_L, \mathbf{y}_L, E, \mathbf{X})$, $k$, threshold function $t$
**Output**: $V_S$: the selected set of nodes to be labeled.
1 calculate $\mathcal{B}_v(y)$ and $\mu(v)$ by LBP
2 $V_\tau \leftarrow V_T \leftarrow$ {top $k$ uncertain nodes in $V_U$}
3 $V_S \leftarrow \emptyset$
4 **while** $V_S = \emptyset$ **do**
5   $V_P \leftarrow V_U \backslash V_\tau$
6   sort nodes in $V_P$ in descending order of $t(v)$ as $v_1, v_2, ..., v_p$
7   **foreach** $v \in V_\tau$ **do**
8     $w(v) \leftarrow 0$
9   **for** $i \leftarrow 1$ **to** $p$ **do**
10     **if** $w(u) < d(u) - t(u)\ \forall u \in NB(v_i) \cap V_\tau$ **then**
11       **foreach** $u \in NB(v_i) \cap V_\tau$ **do**
12         $w(u) \leftarrow w(u) + 1$
13       $V_P \leftarrow V_P \backslash \{v_i\}$
14   **if** $V_P = \emptyset$ **then**
15     sort nodes in $V_\tau$ in ascending order of $d(v)$ as $v_1, v_2, ..., v_m$
16     **foreach** $v \in V_\tau$ **do**
17       $w(v) \leftarrow 0$
18     **foreach** $i \leftarrow 1$ **to** $m$ **do**
19       **if** $\exists u \in NB(v_i) \cap V_\tau$ *st.* $w(u) = d(u) - t(u)$ **then**
20         $V_S \leftarrow V_S \cup \{v_i\}$
21       **else**
22         **foreach** $u \in NB(v_i) \cap V_\tau$ **do**
23           $w(u) \leftarrow w(u) + 1$
24   $V_\tau \leftarrow V_\tau \cup V_P$
25 **return** $V_S$

**MinSS.** The basic idea of MinSS is to find an extended target set $V_\tau$. An extended target set should satisfy two constraints. First, $V_\tau$ is a superset of $V_T$. Second, $V_\tau$ can be eventually activated if we initially label a subset of $V_\tau$. MinSS is an iterative algorithm. In each iteration, we greedily select samples to expand the size of $V_\tau$ until $V_\tau$ satisfies the constraints made above.

The procedure of MinSS is illustrated in Algorithm 2. We first select top k uncertain nodes in $V_U$ to form the target set $V_\tau$. Here we may define the uncertainty with either Eq. 13 or Eq. 14. Then we expand the target set $V_\tau$ iteratively. For each iteration, we sort all unselected samples $v \in V_P$ in descending order of threshold value because a smaller threshold value indicates less active neighbor samples required. From line 9 to line 13, we greedily remove samples from $V_P$ with large threshold value while satisfying the constraint that each node $v \in V_\tau$ have at least $t(v)$ neighbors in $V_\tau \cap V_P$. In line 14, if $V_P = \emptyset$, then $V_\tau$ is an extended target set. This time we greedily remove samples from $V_\tau$ with small degree and all samples left form the source set $V_S$, which is done from line 15 to line 23. In algorithm 2, $w(v)$ is used to count the unselected neighbors of sample $v$.

So far, we solve the problem of Active Learning on Non-progressive Diffusion Model by two steps. First, the problem is reduced to Minimum Source Set problem. Second, we solve Minimum Source Set problem by algorithm MinSS. We combine these two steps and refer to the algorithm as MaxCo.

# 4. THEORETICAL ANALYSIS

In this section, we theoretically analyze the problems defined in § 2 and the MinSS algorithm proposed in § 3.

## 4.1 NP-hardness

Now we introduce the tools for proofs in this section.

LEMMA 2. *Suppose $V_{S,opt}$ is an optimal solution for problem 2, if $\alpha|V_U| \leq |V_{S,opt}|$ for every bipartite graph $H$, then $\alpha|V_U| \leq |V_{S,opt}|$ for every graph $G$.*

LEMMA 3. *Minimum Source Set problem is NP-hard when $V_T = V_U$.*

The proofs of lemma 2 and lemma 3 could be found in [8]. It is trivial to show that Minimum Source Set problem is NP-hard.

LEMMA 4. *Minimum Source Set problem is NP-hard.*

PROOF. The theorem follows directly from lemma 3 because the problem in lemma 3 is a special case of Minimum Source Set problem. □

COROLLARY 1. *The problem of Active Learning on Non-progressive Diffusion Model is NP-hard.*

PROOF. By lemma 4 and theorem 1, the conclusion follows. □

## 4.2 Convergence and Correctness

Now we analyze the convergence issue for MinSS algorithm.

LEMMA 5. ***Convergence.*** *The MinSS algorithm will converge within $\mathcal{O}(|V_U| - |V_T|)$ time.*

PROOF. Denote $V_\tau$ after each round of iteration as a sequence $V_{\tau 0}, V_{\tau 1}, ..., V_{\tau\gamma}$. For each iteration $i$, if $V_P = \emptyset$, the loop of iteration will be terminated since $V_S$ will be a non-empty set. Therefore, if $i < \gamma$, then $V_P \neq \emptyset$. It follows that $|V_{\tau i+1}| > |V_{\tau i}|$ for $i \in \{0, 1, ..., \tau - 1\}$. That is, $|V_{\tau i}|$ is strictly monotonically increasing.

It is trivial to show that $|V_{\tau i}| \leq |V_U|$ and $|V_{\tau 0}| = |V_T|$. Therefore, the length of sequence $\{V_{\tau i}\}_{i=0}^{\gamma}$ is finite. More precisely, $|\gamma| \leq |V_U| - |V_T|$, which yields the conclusion. □

Then we formally prove that MinSS algorithm will return a feasible solution once it converges.

*Theorem 2.* **Correctness.** If MinSS algorithm converges, $V_S$ is a feasible solution. That is, if we initially label all samples in $V_S$, there exists a $\tau_H$ such that $f_\tau(v) = 1$ for all $v \in V_T$ and $\tau \geq \tau_H$.

PROOF. The MinSS algorithm converges if and only if $V_P = \emptyset$. In addition, after each iteration, $v \in V_P$ iff $\exists u \in \text{NB}(v) \cap V_\tau$ st. $w(u) \geq d(u) - t(u)$. At the end of the algorithm, because $V_P$ is empty, we have $w(v) < d(v) - t(v)$ for all $v \in V_\tau$. That is,

$$|\text{NB}(v) \cap V_\tau| \geq t(v) \text{ for all } v \in V_\tau$$

Now we prove $f_\xi(v) = 1$ for all $v \in V_\tau$ and $\xi \geq 1$ by induction. For $\xi = 1$, since $w(v) < d(v) - t(v)$ for all $v \in V_\tau$, $\sum_{u \in \mathrm{NB}(v)} f_0(u) \geq t(v)$. Therefore, $f_1(v) = 1$ for all $v \in V_\tau$. For $\xi > 1$,

$$\sum_{u \in \mathrm{NB}(v)} f_{\xi-1}(u) \geq \sum_{u \in \mathrm{NB}(v) \cap V_\tau} f_{\xi-1}(u)$$

By induction hypothesis, $f_{\xi-1}(v) = 1$ for all $v \in V_\tau$. Therefore, for all $v \in V_\tau$,

$$\sum_{u \in \mathrm{NB}(v)} f_{\xi-1}(u) > |\mathrm{NB}(v) \cap V_\tau| \geq t(v)$$

Then we have $f_\xi(v) = 1$ for all $v \in V_\tau$. Because $V_T \subseteq V_\tau$, the conclusion follows. □

## 4.3 Approximation Ratio

Now we show a lower bound for the optimal solution to problem 2 when $V_T = V_U$.

*Theorem 3.* **Lower Bound.** Let $D(V) = \sum_{v \in V} d(v)$, $T(V) = \sum_{v \in V} t(v)$, and suppose $t(v) \leq \beta d(v)$ for all $v \in V$. If $2T(V_U) - D(V_U) > 0$ and $V_T = V_U$, we have an lower bound for optimal solution $\left|V_{S,\mathrm{opt}}\right|$ to problem 2.

$$\left|V_{S,\mathrm{opt}}\right| \geq \frac{2T(V_U) - D(V_U)}{\beta\Delta} \tag{15}$$

The proof of Theorem 3 is given in the appendix. Because MinSS is an approximate algorithm, we give an upper bound for it as follows. We denote $\Delta$ as the maximum degree among nodes in the graph $G$.

*Theorem 4.* **Upper Bound.** Suppose $t(v) \leq \beta d(v)$ for all $v \in V$, we can derive an upper bound for MinSS algorithm.

$$|V_S| \leq \frac{\beta\Delta}{1 - \beta + \beta\Delta}|V_U|$$

The detailed proof of Theorem 4 is given in the appendix. With an upper bound and a lower bound, we can prove an approximation ratio when $V_T = V_U$.

COROLLARY 2. ***Approximation Ratio.*** *Let $V_{S,g}$ denote the solution given by MinSS algorithm, $V_{S,opt}$ represent the optimal solution and $\Delta$ be the maximum degree in the graph. Suppose $t(v) \leq \beta d(v)$ for all $v \in V$, if $V_T = V_U$ and $2T(V_U) > D(V_U)$, we have*

$$\frac{|V_{S,g}|}{\left|V_{S,opt}\right|} \leq \frac{(\beta\Delta)^2}{(1 - \beta + \beta\Delta) \cdot Avg[2t(v) - d(v)]} \tag{16}$$

*where Avg[.] represents the expectation over all samples in the network.*

PROOF. By Theorem 3, we have

$$\left|V_{S,\mathrm{opt}}\right| \geq \frac{2T(V_U) - D(V_U)}{\beta\Delta} = \frac{\mathrm{Avg}[2t(v) - d(v)]}{\beta\Delta}|V_U| \tag{17}$$

By Theorem 4, we have

$$|V_{S,g}| \leq \frac{\beta\Delta}{1 - \beta + \beta\Delta}|V_U| \tag{18}$$

Dividing (18) by (17) yields the conclusion. □

The approximation ratio given in equation (16) depends on two variables $\beta$ and $\mathrm{Avg}[2t(v) - d(v)]$. Both of them will be affected if we adjust the value of $\eta$ given in equation (11). To optimize the approximation ratio, we need to tune $\beta$ as small as possible and set $\mathrm{Avg}[2t(v) - d(v)]$ as large as possible. However, it is contradictory. Suppose we tune up the value of $\eta$, then according to definition of threshold value, in general, $\beta$ and $\mathrm{Avg}[2(v) - d(v)]$ will both be tuned up. And for another thing if we tune down $\eta$, both $\beta$ and $\mathrm{Avg}[2t(v) - d(v)]$ will be tuned down as well. Thus, for practical application, we need to carefully choose the value of $\eta$ such that we can balance the effects of $\beta$ and $\mathrm{Avg}[2t(v) - d(v)]$. This issue will be further discussed in § 5 by experiments.

# 5. EXPERIMENTAL RESULTS

The proposed active learning framework is general and can be applied to arbitrary networked data. In this section, we evaluate the proposed algorithm (MaxCo) and compare with existing methods. All codes and datasets used in this paper can be found at `http://arnetminer.org/maxco/`.

## 5.1 Datasets and Comparison Methods

We consider four social network datasets in our evaluation: Coauthor, Slashdot, Mobile and Enron. In all these datasets, we aim to infer the type of social relationships in the different networks. Regarding the partially labeled factor graph model, we use the implementation from [28, 31].[1] In the factor graph model, we view each relationship as a variable node and define factor functions according to the specific properties of each network.

- Coauthor. The dataset is a subgraph extracted from ArnetMiner [27]. In this dataset, we aim to infer advisor-advisee relationship from the given network. The factor graph built upon this dataset consists of 6096 variable nodes and 24468 factor nodes.

- Slashdot. The dataset is crawled from Slashdot website. We try to infer friendship on this network. The factor graph built upon this network contains 370 variable nodes and 1686 factor nodes.

- Mobile. This dataset contains logs of call, blue tooth scanning and location collected by mobile applications on 107 phones in a span of 10 months. We aim to infer friendship on this dataset. The factor graph built upon the data consists of 314 variable nodes and 513 factor nodes.

- Enron. The dataset consists of 136,329 emails among 151 Enron employees. We aim to infer manager subordinate relationship from the network. The factor graph model built has 100 variable nodes and 236 factor nodes.

We the compare our algorithm (MaxCo) with the following methods for the problem of batch mode active learning for networked data.

- Random(RAN). In this method, each time we randomly select given number of samples to label.

[1]The source code is available at http://keg.cs.tsinghua.edu.cn/jietang/software/OpenCRF_PartiallyLabeledFGM.rar

Table 1: Factor Graph Size

| Data | #Variable Node | #Factor Node |
|---|---|---|
| Coauthor | 6,096 | 24,468 |
| Slashdot | 370 | 1,686 |
| Mobile | 314 | 513 |
| Enron | 100 | 236 |

Table 2: Average Accuracy(%)

| Data | IMS | MaxCo | MU | RAN | BMAL |
|---|---|---|---|---|---|
| Coauthor | 74.24 | **82.70** | 46.99 | 79.72 | 44.92 |
| Enron | 71.17 | 85.33 | **85.67** | 83.67 | 84.67 |
| Slashdot | 66.95 | **69.62** | 66.11 | 67.00 | 66.16 |
| Mobile | 67.83 | **76.15** | 59.68 | 63.73 | 55.86 |

- Maximum Uncertainty (MU). This method greedily selects samples with great entropy(Eq. 14).
- Batch Mode Active Learning (BMAL). This method is proposed by [23], which aims to maximize the following quality function of selected sample set $V_S$.

$$Q(V_S) = \alpha C(V_S) + (1-\alpha)H(V_S), 0 \le \alpha \le 1$$

where the definition of $H(V_S)$ and $C(V_S)$ is as follows.

$$H(V_S) = \sum_{i \in V_S} H(i)$$

$$C(V_S) = \sum_{i \in V_U} (H(i))^{\beta} \left( \max_{j \in V_L \cup V_S} w_{ij} \right)^{1-\beta}$$

Here $H(i)$ is the entropy of a variable node $i$ and $\beta$ is a constant parameter; $w_{ij}$ denotes the similarity between variable $i$ and $j$, and can be calculated by $e^{-\frac{\|\mathbf{x}_i - \mathbf{x}_j\|^2}{\sigma^2}}$, where $\mathbf{x}$ represents an attribute vector for each variable.

- Influence Maximization Selection (IMS). IMS is proposed by [31], which also utilizes information diffusion model to solve the active learning problem. However, it is based on progressive diffusion model.
- Maximum Coverage (MaxCo). We use entropy to measure uncertainty and empirically set $\gamma = 0.7$(Eq. 12).

For each dataset, we randomly label 10 samples to form $\mathbf{y}_L$ at the beginning. Then we iteratively apply the active learning algorithm, by selecting 10 samples to query each time. After each round, we train the factor graph to test the accuracy and F1 score.

## 5.2 Performance Analysis

Table 3: Average F1-score(%)

| Data | IMS | MaxCo | MU | RAN | BMAL |
|---|---|---|---|---|---|
| Coauthor | 69.55 | **76.15** | 59.68 | 63.73 | 55.86 |
| Enron | 79.50 | **87.94** | 86.30 | 85.85 | 85.59 |
| Slashdot | 76.90 | **80.04** | 77.85 | 77.60 | 77.74 |
| Mobile | 69.51 | **75.31** | 51.23 | 50.17 | 53.57 |

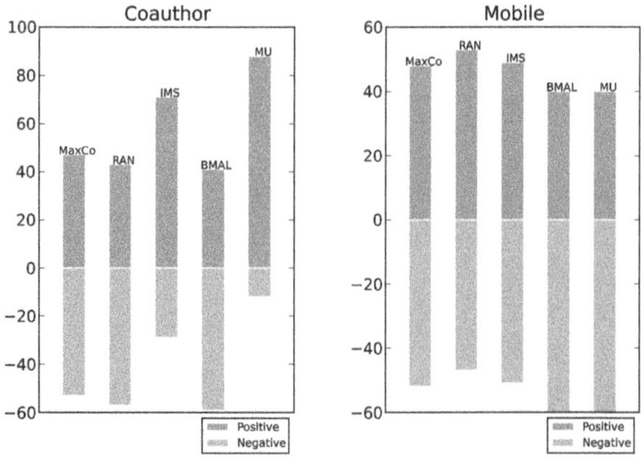


(a) Coauthor: #Label=100 (b) Mobile: #label=100

**Figure 3: Labeled Data Balance: Blue bars above 0 represent the number of positive selected samples and red bars below 0 indicate the number of negative selected samples with different active learning strategies.**

Figure 1 shows F1-score and accuracy performance of each algorithm on each dataset. We also calculate the average accuracy performance and F1 score for all selection strategies, which is shown in Table 2 and Table 3 respectively.

**Performance Comparison.** According to Figure 1 and Table 2 and 3, we see that MaxCo significantly outperforms other competing methods on the four datasets. In Coauthor, MaxCo is better than the random selection method by 2.98% and 12.42% improvements in terms of average accuracy and F1 score. Other methods such as MU and BMAL seems to amplify the side effects of label imbalance, which will be discussed later. In Enron, MaxCo is 0.43% worse than MU by average accuracy, but 1.64% better in terms of average F1. These two methods strongly outperform other methods. In Slashdot and Mobile, MaxCo achieves outstanding performance while other methods perform relatively closely to each other.

**Imbalance of Labeled Data.** From the results, we found a phenomenon: for some active learning strategies, performance will decrease as the number of labels grows. By further investigation, we discover that the phenomenon is related to labeled data imbalance. From figure 1 we can see that, Coauthor and Mobile datasets are relatively more sensitive to the balance of labeled data. For these two datasets, the curves representing MU and BMAL turn down sharply as the number of labeled instances increases. When the number of labeled data comes to 100, the F1 score falls to around 50% in the Coauthor data and 30% in the Mobile data, the accuracy performance also suffers sharp decrease. We observe the ratio of positive and negative instances and find that the ineffectiveness of these two models in this case is correlated to imbalance of labeled data.

Figure 3 plots the number of positive and negative labeled samples when the number of labeled samples is 100. Figure 3(a) is for the Coauthor dataset and figure 3(b) is for the Mobile dataset. On the Coauthor dataset, IMS and MU tend to label positive instances while BMAL labels significantly more negative instances. On the Mobile dataset, also, BMAL and MU suffer from labeled data imbalance,

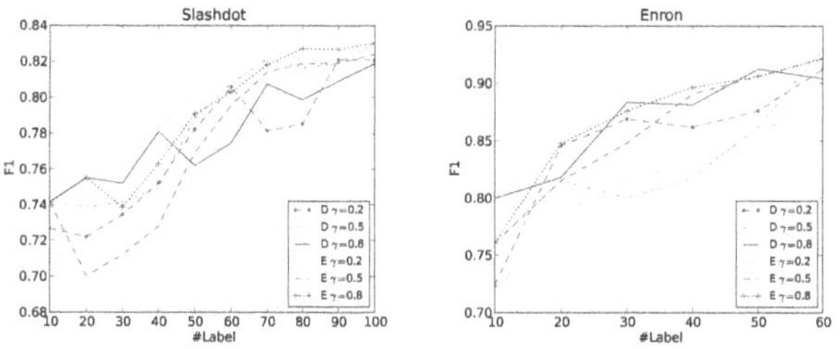


(a) Slashdot (b) Enron

**Figure 4: Parameter Sensitivity: D denotes distance measure of uncertainty and E represents entropy measure; $\gamma$ is the constant factor in threshold function.**

where negative instances take up to 60 percent of all labeled samples. The results show that for some datasets, the performance of factor graph model will be influenced by the balance of labeled samples. The results also demonstrate that MaxCo can produce relatively balanced results.

**Significance Test.** We perform significance test for the results of the comparison methods. Pairing the measure scores(F1 or accuracy) of two models with the same number of labeled instances on a dataset, we assume that the difference of the two models is random and symmetric around the median. Therefore, we can perform Wilcoxon signed-rank test [24] to demonstrate the significance level of the difference between the two models. The result shows that $p$-value is less than 0.01, which indicates that the improvements of MaxCo over the competing methods are statistically significant.

**Parameter Sensitivity.** We further study the parameter sensitivity of $\gamma$ in MaxCo. We also consider the effects of uncertainty definition. According to § 3, we compare distance measure (Eq. 13) with entropy measure (Eq. 14). We repeat our experiment with different ways of threshold definition and uncertainty definition. The results are plotted in Figure 4. We can see that MaxCo is insensitive to the threshold parameter and uncertainty definition. Entropy measure is slightly better than distance measure, with a relatively larger $\gamma$.

# 6. RELATED WORK

Active learning is a very important topic in the study of social network and web mining because of exponentially growing size of data and high cost of data labeling. Settles et al. [22] surveyed query selection strategies for sequence models and proposed novel algorithms. There have been several works designing active learning algorithms to specific problems. For example, Arasu et al. [1] present novel algorithms for the problem of record matching packages. Hoi et al. [12] studied active learning on text categorization problem. Different from existing methods, we propose a general framework, which can be applied to different problems. There are also several works based on specific models. Martinez et al. [16] formulated the active learning problem under for the conditional random field (CRF) model. Golovin et al. [10] developed a greedy algorithm for Bayesian active learning with noisy observations. A similar work [31] by Zhuang et al. also studied active learning problem on factor graph model. However, they utilize progressive information diffusion to solve the problem, which is demonstrated to be less effective than non-progressive one in this paper. In [23], Shi et al. proposed a general framework on batch mode active learning. They used three criteria for instance selection. We also compare to their algorithm in §5. Also, extensive literature focused on active learning on social network [15, 14, 2, 20].

Our work is also related to information diffusion model. In [13], Kempe et al. solved the influence maximization problem on progressive diffusion model and show a reduction to non-progressive one. However, their definition of non-progressive model cannot be applied to the active learning problem. There are several works studying the spread of social influence with various propagation models [9, 18, 30, 6]. Besides, the diffusion models are widely used in real-world applications such as viral marketing [19, 7]. Progressive diffusion models have been extensively studied in the literature [25, 4, 11, 3, 26]. Fazli et al. [8] proposed a greedy algorithm for non-progressive model and proved approximation ratio on power law graph. However, their works cannot be directly applied to active learning problem for the network data.

# 7. CONCLUSION

In this paper, we study the problem of batch mode active learning for networked data, which aims to query $k$ unlabeled samples in a network such that we can achieve best performance improvement. We utilize factor graph model as our basic framework so as to leverage link formation of networked data. We leverage Loopy Belief Propagation to learn the parameter in factor graph model. We propose a novel idea of connecting the graphical model to the information diffusion process. Therefore, we precisely instantiate the active learning problem on a non-progressive diffusion model.

We solve the problem of active learning on non-progressive diffusion model by MaxCo, which includes two steps. First we prove a reduction to Minimum Source Set problem and then we propose an iterative greedy algorithm MinSS to solve the Minimum Source Set problem. We theoretically show the NP-hardness of our problem, analyze the convergence and correctness of MinSS, and finally provide approximation guarantees for our algorithm with an upper bound and a lower bound. We empirically evaluate MaxCo algorithm in comparison with several baseline methods on several datasets. The experimental results demonstrate that our approach significantly outperforms the competing methods.

**Acknowledgements.** The work is supported by National Basic Research Program of China (No. 2011CB302302) and Natural Science Foundation of China (No. 61222212, No. 61073073), and a research fund supported by Huawei Inc.

# 8. REFERENCES

[1] A. Arasu, M. Götz, and R. Kaushik. On active learning of record matching packages. In *SIGMOD'10*, pages 783–794, 2010.

[2] M. Bilgic, L. Mihalkova, and L. Getoor. Active learning for networked data. *ICML*, pages 79–86, 2010.

[3] C. Chang and Y. Lyuu. Spreading messages. *Theor Comput Sci*, 410:2714–2724, 2009.

[4] W. Chen, C. Wang, and Y. Wang. Scalable influence maximization for prevalent viral marketing in large-scale social networks. In *KDD'10*, pages 1029–1038, 2010.

[5] D. A. Cohn, Z. Ghahramani, and M. I. Jordan. Active learning with statistical models. *J. Artif. Int. Res.*, 4(1):129–145, Mar. 1996.

[6] Z. Dezsö and A. Barabási. Halting viruses in scale-free networks. *Phys Rev*, 2002.

[7] P. Domingos and M. Richardson. Mining the network value of customers. In *KDD'01*, pages 57–66, 2001.

[8] M. Fazli, M. Ghodsi, J. Habibi, P. J. Khalilabadi, V.Mirrokni, and S. S. Sadeghabad. On the non-progressive spread of influence through social networks. *LATIN 2012: Theoretical Informatics*, 7256:315–326, 2012.

[9] L. Freeman. *The development of social network analysis.* Empirical Press Vancouver, British Columbia, 2004.

[10] D. Golovin, A. Krause, and D. Ray. Near-optimal bayesian active learning with noisy observations. *CoRR*, 2010.

[11] A. Goyal, F. Bonchi, and L. V. Lakshmanan. Learning influence probabilities in social networks. In *WSDM'10*, pages 241–250, 2010.

[12] S. C. H. Hoi, R. Jin, and M. R. Lyu. Large-scale text categorization by batch mode active learning. In *WWW'06*, pages 633–642, 2006.

[13] D. Kempe, J. Kleinberg, and E. Tardos. Maximizing the spread of influence through a social network. In *KDD'03*, pages 137–146, 2003.

[14] M. Kimura, K. Satio, R. Nakano, and H. Motoda. Extracting influential nodes on a social network for information diffusion. *DMKD*, 20:70–97, 2010.

[15] A. Kuwadekar and J. Neville. Relational active learning for joint collective classification models. In *ICML'11*, pages 385–392, 2011.

[16] O. Martinez and G. Tsechpenakis. Integration of active learning in a collaborative crf. In *CVPRW'08*, pages 1–8, 2008.

[17] K. P. Murphy, Y. Weiss, and M. I. Jordan. Loopy belief propagation for approximate inference: An empirical study. In *UAI'99*, pages 467–475, 1999.

[18] R. Pastor-Satorras and A. Vespignani. Epidemic spreading in scale-free networks. *Phys Rev*, 65, 2002.

[19] M. Richardson and P. Domingos. Mining knowledge-sharing sites for viral marketing. In *KDD'02*, pages 61–70, 2002.

[20] N. Roy and A. McCallum. Toward optimal active learning through sampling estimation of error reduction. *ICML*, pages 441–448, 2001.

[21] T. Scheffer, C. Decomain, and S. Wrobel. Active hidden markov models for information extraction. In *CAIDA'01*, pages 309–318, 2001.

[22] B. Settles and M. Craven. An analysis of active learning strategies for sequence labeling tasks. In *EMNLP*, pages 1070–1079, 2008.

[23] L. Shi, Y. Zhao, and J. Tang. Batch mode active learning for networked data. *ACM Transactions on Intelligent Systems and Technology (TIST)*, 2011.

[24] Siegel and Sidney. *Non-parametric statistics for the behavioral sciences.* New York: McGraw-Hill, 1956.

[25] J. Tang, J. Sun, C. Wang, and Z. Yang. Social influence analysis in large-scale networks. In *KDD'09*, pages 807–816, 2009.

[26] J. Tang, S. Wu, and J. Sun. Confluence: Conformity influence in large social networks. In *KDD'13*, pages 347–355, 2013.

[27] J. Tang, J. Zhang, L. Yao, J. Li, L. Zhang, and Z. Su. Arnetminer: Extraction and mining of academic social networks. In *KDD'08*, pages 990–998, 2008.

[28] W. Tang, H. Zhuang, and J. Tang. Learning to infer social ties in large networks. In *ECML/PKDD'11*, pages 381–397, 2011.

[29] M. J. Wainwright and M. I. Jordan. Graphical models, exponential families, and variational inference. *Found. Trends Mach. Learn.*, 1(1-2):1–305, Jan. 2008.

[30] D. Wilson. Levels of selection: An alternative to individualism in biology and the human sciences. *Soc Networks*, 11:257–272, 1989.

[31] H. Zhuang, J. Tang, W. Tang, T. Lou, A. Chin, and X. Wang. Actively learning to infer social ties. *Data Mining and Knowledge Discovery*, 25(2):270–297, 2012.

# APPENDIX

# A. PROOFS

## A.1 Proof of Theorem 3

PROOF. First, suppose $G = (X, Y)$ is a bipartite graph. Let $e_A$ denote the number of edges in $A$ and $e_{AB}$ denote the number of edges across $A$ and $B$. Let $B_X = V_S \cap X$, $B_Y = V_S \cap Y$ and $W = V_U \backslash V_S$. Following the lemma in [8], we have

$$e_{WB_X} + e_W \leq \sum_{v \in B_X \cup W} (d(v) - t(v))$$

$$e_{WB_Y} + e_W \leq \sum_{v \in B_Y \cup W} (d(v) - t(v))$$

Because $\sum_{v \in W} d(v) = 2e_W + e_{WB_X} + e_{WB_Y}$, it follows

$$\sum_{v \in W} d(v) \leq \sum v \in V_U(d(v) - t(v)) + \sum_{v \in W} (d(v) - t(v))$$

Therefore,

$$T(W) \leq D(V_U) - T(V_U)$$

Because $T(V_S) = T(V_U) - T(W)$, we have

$$T(V_S) \geq T(V_U) - (D(V_U) - T(V_U)) = 2T(V_U) - D(V_U)$$

Because $t(v) \leq \beta d(v)$ for each $v \in V$, we can derive

$$T(V_S) \leq \beta D(V_S) \leq \beta \Delta |V_S|$$

Therefore, it yields

$$\left| V_{S,\text{opt}} \right| \geq \frac{2T(V_U) - D(V_U)}{\beta \Delta}$$

By Lemma 2, the inequality holds as well for any general graph G. □

## A.2 Proof of Theorem 4

PROOF. Let $Q = \{v | w(v) = d(v) - t(v) \land v \in V_U\}$, and $W = V_U \backslash V_S$. By definition we have,

$$\sum_{v \in Q} (d(v) - t(v)) \leq \sum_{v \in W} d(v)$$

Therefore,

$$(1 - \beta) \sum_{v \in Q} d(v) \leq \sum_{v \in W} d(v)$$

Referring to the procedure of MinSS algorithm, a sample $v$ is inserted into $V_S$ if and only if $\text{NB}(v) \cap Q \neq \emptyset$. Because for $v \in Q$, $w(v) = d(v) - t(v)$, we have

$$|V_S| \leq \sum_{v \in Q} t(v) \leq \beta \sum_{v \in Q} d(v) \leq \frac{\beta}{1 - \beta} \sum_{v \in W} d(v) \leq \frac{\beta}{1 - \beta} \Delta |W|$$

Because $|W| = |V_U| - |V_S|$, it follows,

$$|V_S| \leq \frac{\beta \Delta}{1 - \beta + \beta \Delta} |V_U| \quad \square$$

# Learning Latent Representations of Nodes for Classifying in Heterogeneous Social Networks


Yann Jacob, Ludovic Denoyer, Patrick Gallinari

Sorbonne Universites, UPMC Univ Paris 06, UMR 7606, LIP6, F-75005, Paris, France
CNRS, UMR 7606, LIP6, F-75005, Paris, France

firstname.lastname@lip6.fr



## ABSTRACT

Social networks are heterogeneous systems composed of different types of nodes (e.g. users, content, groups, etc.) and relations (e.g. social or similarity relations). While learning and performing inference on homogeneous networks have motivated a large amount of research, few work exists on heterogeneous networks and there are open and challenging issues for existing methods that were previously developed for homogeneous networks. We address here the specific problem of nodes classification and tagging in heterogeneous social networks, where different types of nodes are considered, each type with its own label or tag set. We propose a new method for learning node representations onto a latent space, common to all the different node types. Inference is then performed in this latent space. In this framework, two nodes connected in the network will tend to share similar representations regardless of their types. This allows bypassing limitations of the methods based on direct extensions of homogenous frameworks and exploiting the dependencies and correlations between the different node types. The proposed method is tested on two representative datasets and compared to state-of-the-art methods and to baselines.



## Categories and Subject Descriptors

I.2 [**Artificial Intelligence**]: Learning; E.1 [**Data**]: Data Structures—*Graphs and networks*

## Keywords

Machine learning; Classification; Social networks


## 1. INTRODUCTION

Social Media on the Web are most often complex heterogeneous networks with nodes and relations between nodes of different types, corresponding to different objects, concepts and relationships. Classical examples include user content networks like Flickr where nodes correspond to users, photos, comments, tags, and relations to friendship or authorship, or bibliographic networks like DBLP with nodes corresponding to authors, papers, venues, terms and relations to citations, co-authorship, proceedings, contained in, etc. Heterogeneous networks also frequently occur in other domains like e-commerce sites with users, items, comments and reviews, or recommendation sites such as TripAdvisor. Modeling and analyzing such complex networks has recently been explored for generic data mining tasks such as classification [2], clustering [22], link prediction [5] or influence analysis [16] and is still largely an open area.

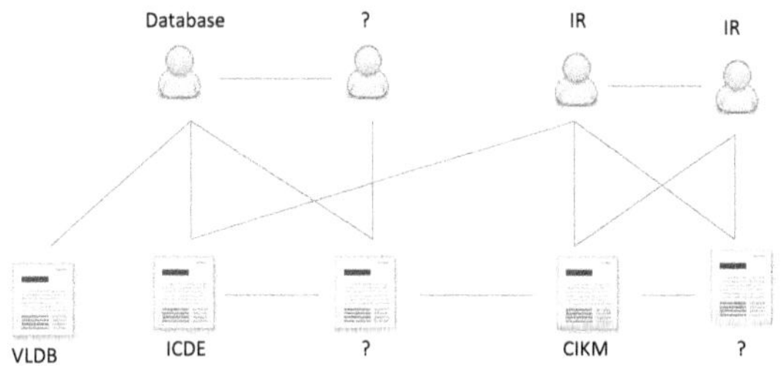


**Figure 1: Bibliographic heterogeneous network with authors and articles connected. Authors are labeled with topic names (IR = Information Retrieval), while articles are labeled with conference venue names.**

In this article, we consider the task of node classification in heterogeneous networks composed of different types of nodes, each node type beging associated with its own set of labels. For instance, in a bibliographic network, authors and papers might be labeled respectively by their research topic and conference name (see Figure 1), while in the Flickr, network users and photos might be respectively labeled by subscribed groups reflecting their topic interests and visual tags. Much work has been devoted to classification for homogeneous networks composed of a single node type, e.g. [3, 17, 19, 27] to cite a few. Classification in heterogeneous networks, representative of real world media, is much more recent with only a few attempts for now. Many of them rely on the idea of mapping an heterogeneous network onto an homogeneous network so that classical relational techniques are then used [8, 10, 14, 2]. They do not fully exploit the correlations between the different node labels or characteristics. Moreover, many of these methods also make strong



*WSDM'14*, February 24–28, 2014, New York, New York, USA.



ACM 978-1-4503-2351-2/14/02 ...$15.00.
http://dx.doi.org/10.1145/2556195.2556225.

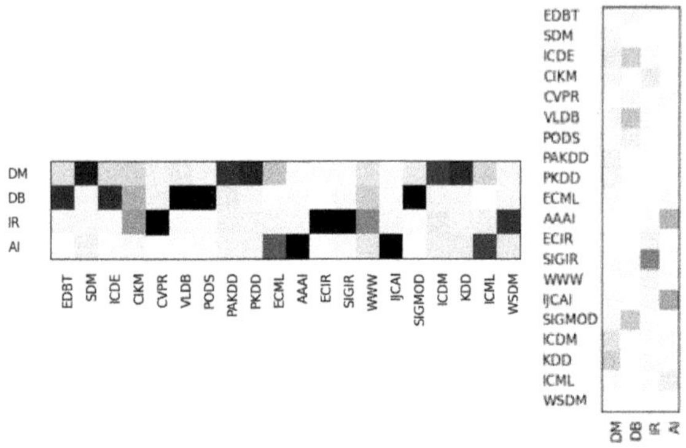


**Figure 2: Two matrices illustrating the inter-dependencies between labels of connected nodes of different types for DBLP data. Left matrix corresponds to $P(Author - topic|Article - conference)$ while right matrix illustrates $P(Article{-}conference|Author{-}topic)$. The darker the square is, the higher the probability value. Both matrices show strong correlations between the *topics* of an author and the *conference* names.**

hypothesis on the nature of the task that is not realistic for real world situations.

The assumption we make in the paper is **that nodes of different types do influence each other**, so that labels of the different node types will be inter-dependent; modeling this dependence between different node types is thus important for accurate node classification or labeling and cannot be achieved via classical homogeneous network formulations. For example, in a Flickr network, the groups a user belongs to will be related to the tags the user has been using or the comments he has posted and vice versa. This assumption is illustrated in Figure 2 which shows some statistics computed over a heterogeneous bibliographic network extracted from DBLP. The DBLP graph is composed of authors and scientific articles connected through an *authorship* relation[1]. Authors are labeled with 4 different topics — *IR = Information retrieval, DB = Database, DM = Data Mining, AI = Artificial Intelligence* — while articles are labeled with 20 possible conferences they have been published in. The left side of Figures 2 (left) shows the values of the probability $P(Author - topic|Article - conference)$ i.e. the probability that an author node has the label *topic* given that one of its neighboring article nodes has the label *conference*. Similarly, the right side of Figure 2 (right) illustrates the probability $P(Article - conference|Author - topic)$. Figure 2 exhibits strong correlations between the two label sets and confirms that the correlation between the labels of different nodes may be used for classification.

We propose a new algorithm for learning to label nodes in an heterogeneous network to exploit dependencies on label sets and node characteristics and relationships between different node types. The proposed algorithm operates in the transductive setting and makes use of a regularization framework. It can be used for labeling nodes of different types with different label sets, and with any graph structure. It is designed to learn the dependencies between the label sets associated to the different node types, and to infer the labels associated to a node by exploiting both global graph properties and local node neighborhood characteristics.

It is important to mention that the proposed algorithm learns a latent representation of the network nodes so that all nodes, irrespectively of their type, will share a common latent space. Such representation will then be effectively used to infer the categories. Unlike unsupervised relational data projection methods [23, 4], our method is semi-supervised so that the projection space exploits both the relational structure and the labeled information. In other words, the algorithm makes use of the heterogeneous training labels to constrain the projection, by encouraging nodes with the same labels to have close latent representations. Moreover, it takes the correlations between the labels of different node types into account when learning the latent representation. Consequently, the model learns simultaneously a metric associated to the heterogeneous classification problem and a way to label the nodes given this metric space. Additionally, the same formulation can be naturally extended to modeling node attributes, such as content information associated to the nodes in our context, by simply considering these attributes as specific nodes.

The main contributions are: (i) (i) an effective method for mapping nodes representtions onto a common lateent space: This mapping exploits the dependencies on the node label sets, and relationships between these labels sets and the node characteristics. This new method allows a simple formulation of the classication problem in an heterogeneous setting; (ii) An algorithm to solve the general classication problem in heterogeneous networks under a general assumption about the node classes or the relations between nodes. In particular it can handle the challenging case of non intersecting label sets between the different node types. All the dependencies are learned directly from the data without necessitating a user-defined or a heuristic pre-processing procedure to perform graph projection.

The paper is organized as follows: Section 2 presents the notations, and introduces some background concerning classical graph labeling models for homogeneous networks. Section 3 describes the proposed algorithm and an extension for incorporating node content information to the model. Section 4 presents experimental results on two datasets, and a qualitative analysis of the latent representations learned by the model. Section 5 provides a synthesis of the related literature.

## 2. BACKGROUND AND NOTATIONS

### 2.1 Notations

A heterogeneous network will be modeled as an undirected weighted graph with a node type associated to each node.

Let us denote by $\mathcal{T} = 1, 2, \ldots, T$ the set of $T$ possible nodes types. Nodes are denoted $x_i$, and edges $w_{i,j} \in \mathbb{R}$, where $w_{i,j}$ is the weight of the relation between $x_i$ and $x_j$. $w_{i,j} = 0$ if there is no link between $x_i$ and $x_j$, the number of nodes is $N$. We will denote $t_i \in \mathcal{T}$ the node type $x_i$, $\mathcal{Y}^t$ the set of categories associated to the type of node $t$, and $C^t$ the cardinality of $\mathcal{Y}^t$. We consider a transductive context where the network is composed of $\ell < N$ labeled nodes $(x_1, \ldots, x_\ell)$ with $\forall i \in \{1 \ldots \ell\}, y_i \in \mathbb{R}^{C^{t_i}}$, and $N - l$ unlabeled nodes.

[1]The dataset is described in Section 4.1.

The component $j$ of $y_i$, denoted by $y_i^j$, is defined as $y_i^j = +1$ if $x_i$ belongs to category $j$, and $y_i^j = -1$ otherwise.

## 2.2 Homogeneous Label Propagation Model

When there is only one type of node i.e. $T = 1$, classical transductive models exploit the manifold assumption where *two connected nodes tend to have the same labels*. Let us denote by $\hat{y}_i$ the vector of scores for the categories predicted at any node $x_i$ in the network. Transductive learning in graph models often uses a loss function with the following form [1, 27, 28]:

$$(\hat{y_1}, \ldots, \hat{y_N}) = \underset{\tilde{y_1}, \ldots, \tilde{y_N}}{\text{argmin}} \sum_{i=1}^{\ell} \Delta(\tilde{y_i}, y_i) + \lambda \sum_{i,j} w_{i,j} ||\tilde{y_i} - \tilde{y_j}||^2 \tag{1}$$

where $\Delta$ corresponds to the cost of predicting scores $\tilde{y_i}$ instead of true categories $y_i$ for labeled nodes and $||\tilde{y_i} - \tilde{y_j}||^2$ is a regularization term that encourages connected nodes to have the same score. $\lambda$ is an hyper-parameter that corresponds to the smoothness one wants to obtain on the network structure. Many variations of this formulation have been proposed with different prediction and regularization losses. Different techniques can be used to minimize this function such as plain or stochastic gradient-descent algorithm, coordinate descent methods and random walks.

## 2.3 Extending the homogeneous setting to heterogeneous networks

The homogeneous framework can be extended in multiple ways to handle the case of heterogeneous networks [11, 8, 2]. Our claim is that such extensions do not allow one to fully benefit from the information present in the heterogeneous network and in particular from the correlations and dependencies between the different node labels.

As an illustration, let us consider the case of a graph composed of two types of nodes 1 and 2 with label sets $\mathcal{Y}^1$ and $\mathcal{Y}^2$ — see Figure 3 (a). It is not possible to make a direct propagation of labels from $\mathcal{Y}^1$ to $\mathcal{Y}^2$ since the two label sets are different and correspond to different label semantics. A common solution is to map the heterogeneous graph onto one or more homogeneous graphs as illustrated in Figure 3 (b) and (c) and to perform label propagation on the different graphs. This mapping may be defined either explicitly through graph projections or implicitly through the algorithm like in [2, 14] for example. It has two drawbacks: (i) Dependencies between the two types of labels are lost, since the labels predicted for one node are only dependent of the labels of its neighbors **of the same type**. For example, a relation like *users labeled as "old" are connected to pictures labeled as "flowers"* cannot be preserved by such projection. The more node types there are, the more this loss of information is important. (ii) Extending this idea to more complex graphs could be problematic, and the corresponding semantic can become complex. Consider for example the case of multiple (more than 2) node types. There are multiple ways to define such mappings, paths joining two nodes of the same type could be of different lengths with different node types on the path. What could then be the semantic of a link between two nodes of a given type? How to weight these links?

These are main reasons why such extensions are often limited by simplifying assumptions on the nature of the graphs, the label sets or the relations. A simple example is provided in Figure 3 (c), where there are multiple possible projections to an homogeneous graph for the photos. One can connect the photos published by the same user (giving a graph with multiple components). Or one can connect the photos published by the same user or published by friend users. Therefore, different homogeneous graphs can be obtained by projection for nodes of the same type. We promote here that the dependencies might be learned in an unified way and directly from the data under general and non restrictive hypothesis. This is made possible by a change of paradigm w.r.t. conventional approaches which is implemented here by using a latent representation space common to all the node types in the network.

# 3. MODEL

## 3.1 Learning latent node representations

We first introduce the method for the case where no attribute (content) is associated to graph nodes and then describe in Section 3.2 a natural extension for incorporating node content. The underlying ideas of the method are as follows:

- Each node will be mapped onto a latent representation in a vectorial space $\mathbb{R}^Z$. The latent space is common to all node types.
- The new metric developed on this latent representation space $\mathbb{R}^Z$ is such that two connected nodes will tend to have similar representations (*this is an extension of the smoothness assumption to heterogeneous networks*).
- For each node type, a classification function will be learned. It takes as input a latent node representation and computes associated class label. A linear function will be used here to ensure smoothness in the classification decision while avoiding overfitting the new space.

The latent projection space is learned according to two constraints: smoothness and class separability of the projections. If one considers nodes of the same type, the smoothness constraint tends to group nodes that are linked by a path in the graph, whatever the nature of the path is (homogeneous or heterogeneous). The strength of this constraint decreases with the length of the path. This is an extension of the classical smoothness hypothesis on homogeneous graphs. On the other hand, if one considers nodes of different types, their projections will be close if they share multiple connections in the graph. This will happen for example if the classes in two node types are correlated (see for example Figure 5). This is also how dependencies or correlations between the different label sets are captured. Besides smoothness, the separability imposes an additional constraint on the latent projections. It is defined on the labeled nodes, but also operates on the unlabeled nodes representations through the diffusion mechanism. An alternative approach would be to learn a separate latent space for every pair of node types. This would be, however, too costly and not allow exploiting multiple dependencies between label sets. Note that exploiting node types pairs dependencies has been proposed by some authors [8, 11] for the case where all types of nodes share the same labels set.

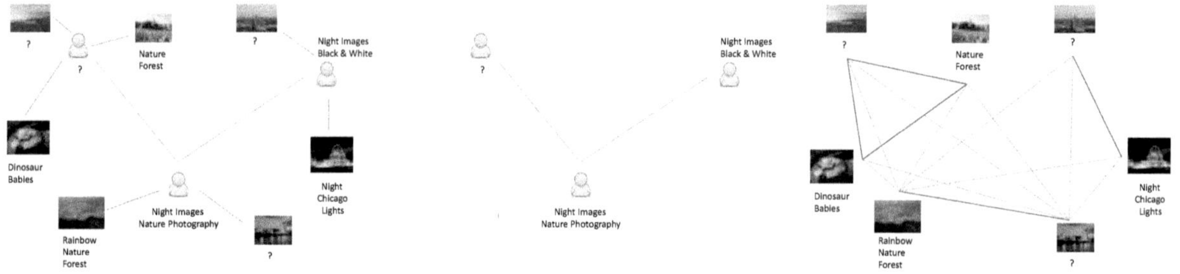


(a) Original Heterogeneous graph

(b) Homogeneous graph of users

(c) Homogeneous graph of photos built using two different projection methods: connecting photos published by the same author (purple relation) and connecting photos published by friend authors (green relation)

**Figure 3: (a) An heterogeneous network that can be mapped to different homogeneous networks (b), (c). Using Homogeneous models for classification of such a network is not trivial since several projection methods exist as shown in (c).**

### *3.1.1 Transductive classification model*

Let us denote by $z_i \in \mathbb{R}^Z$ the latent representation of node $x_i$. In order to capture the graph metric in the latent space, we impose the following loss which embodies the metric smoothness constraint and forces correlated nodes to have similar representations:

$$\sum_{i,j/w_{i,j}\neq 0} w_{i,j}||z_i - z_j||^2 \quad (2)$$

We are using an $L_2$ norm in the latent space, but other metrics could be used as well. This term is similar to the smoothness term for Equation 1 except that it is defined in the latent space and not in the label space as in Equation 1. The mapping onto the latent space is learned so that the labels for each type of node can be predicted from the latent representations. For that, we consider a linear classification function for each type of node $k$ denoted by $f_\theta^k$. This function takes as input a node representation and outputs the predicted label(s). The $f$-functions can be learned by minimizing a loss on labeled data as follows:

$$\sum_{i=1}^{\ell} \Delta(f_\theta^{t_i}(z_i), y_i) \quad (3)$$

where $\Delta(f_\theta^{t_i}(z_i), y_i)$ is the loss of predicting labels $f_\theta^{t_i}(z_i)$ instead of observed labels $y_i$. The final objective loss of our model combines the classification and regularization losses 3 and 2:

$$L(z,\theta) = \sum_{i=1}^{\ell} \Delta(f_\theta^{t_i}(z_i), y_i) + \lambda \sum_{i,j/w_{i,j}\neq 0} w_{i,j}||z_i - z_j||^2 \quad (4)$$

The minimization of this loss is performed both on the $\theta$ parameters and on the $z_i$ representations. It aims at finding a trade-off between the smoothness over the latent representations of correlated nodes $\mathcal{Z}$ and the predicted observed labels in $\mathcal{Y}_k$. Optimizing this loss will allow us to learn:

- The projection $z_i$ of each node $x_i$ in the latent space.
- The classification functions $f_\theta^k$ for each nodes type $k$ which transforms the latent space to category scores.

### *3.1.2 Learning*

Learning consists in minimizing the loss function defined in Equation 4. Different optimization methods can be considered. We have used a Stochastic Gradient Descent Method. The algorithm is detailed in Algorithm 1.

**Algorithm 1** Stochastic Gradient Descent Algorithm

1: **procedure** LEARNING($x, w, \epsilon, \lambda$)
2:   **for** A fixed number of iterations **do**
3:     Choose a $(x_i, x_j)$ at random with $w_{i,j} > 0$.
4:     **if** $i \leq \ell$ **then** ▷ if $x_i$ is labeled
5:       $\theta \leftarrow \theta + \epsilon \nabla_\theta \Delta(f_\theta^{t_i}(z_i), y_i)$
6:       $z_i \leftarrow z_i + \epsilon \nabla_{z_i} \Delta(f_\theta^{t_i}(z_i), y_i)$
7:     **end if**
8:     **if** $j \leq \ell$ **then** ▷ if $x_j$ is labeled
9:       $\theta \leftarrow \theta + \epsilon \nabla_\theta \Delta(f_\theta^{t_j}(z_j), y_j)$
10:       $z_j \leftarrow z_j + \epsilon \nabla_{z_j} \Delta(f_\theta^{t_j}(z_j), y_j)$
11:     **end if**
12:     $z_i \leftarrow z_i + \epsilon\lambda \nabla_{z_i} ||z_i - z_j||^2$
13:     $z_j \leftarrow z_j + \epsilon\lambda \nabla_{z_j} ||z_i - z_j||^2$
14:   **end for**
15: **end procedure**

The algorithm chooses iteratively a pair of connected nodes and then makes a gradient update over the parameters of the model. If one of the chosen nodes is labeled, the algorithm first performs an update according to the first term of Equation 3. This update – lines 5-6 and 9-10 – consists in successively modifying the parameters of the classification function $\theta$ and of the latent representations $z_i$ and $z_j$ so as to minimize the classification loss term. Note that this step not only modifies the classifier parameter $\theta$, but also the node representation $z$. Then, the model updates node representation $z$ w.r.t the smoothness term of Equation 2 – lines 12-13. If the node is unlabeled, only the later step will be performed. Nevertheless, the classification constraint will propagate to these unlabeled nodes via their connection to labeled ones.

Note that, while we use a stochastic gradient descent, other methods like minibatch gradients or batch algorithms could be used as well. Here, $\epsilon$ is the gradient step, and $\lambda$

is the trade-off between the classification and smoothness terms.

In our implementation, we have used an hinge-loss function for $\Delta$:

$$\Delta(f_\theta^t(z), y) = \sum_{k=1} max(0; 1 - y^k f_\theta^{t,k}(z)) \quad (5)$$

where $y^k$ is the desired score of category $k$ for node $x$ ($-1$ or $+1$) and $f_\theta^{t,k}(z)$ is the predicted score of category $k$ by the model. Here again other loss functions, e.g. logistic could be used.

### *3.1.3 Complexity*

At each step of the algorithm, one has to make two updates over the latent representation – lines 12-13 – and, zero, one or two additional updates if the chosen nodes are labeled. These updates have to be repeated several times, over all pairs of connected nodes. Let us denote by $E$ the number of edges in the network, the complexity algorithm is thus $\mathcal{O}(E + \ell)$. The learning time thus scales linearly with regard to the number of edges which is the same complexity than classical homogeneous models.

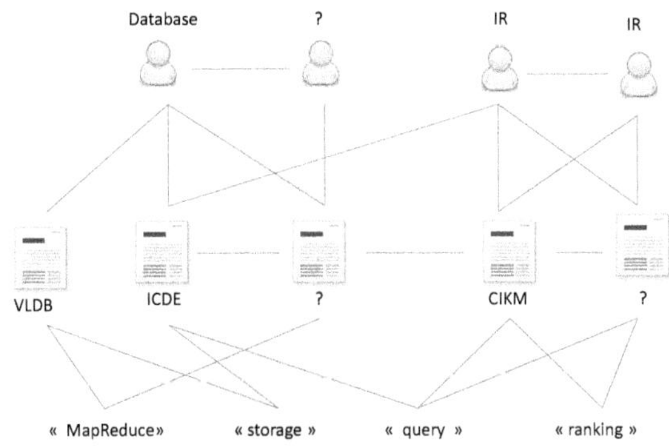


**Figure 4: Bibliographic heterogeneous network with content modeled as word nodes.**

## 3.2 Heterogeneous model and content

The objective function in Equation 4 only considers the graph structure through its weight matrix and node labels. Often, attributes are associated to nodes (e.g. textual content for comments or visual content for images). Let us consider as an example the case of textual attributes (the description is similar for any other discrete set of attributes or features associated to a node type). The above formulation allows to easily integrate this information into the model by associating each term to a new node like in [11] and a weighted link between this term and any node containing it. The weight of the relation may be defined according to any relevant measure (e.g. word frequency).

This solution is illustrated in Figure 4. In that case, the model jointly learns a latent representation of all the elements of the network – users, documents, words. Documents and their content words will then tend to have close latent representations, so will words appearing in the same documents or documents sharing similar words, even if they are not directly connected in the network. Nodes associated to words are special in the sense that they do not have associated labels and that in most real applications they do not share direct connections - except if one makes use of some term ontology for example, in which case this information could again be naturally incorporated in the model. Their representation does not appear in the classification loss term in Equation 4, but only in the smoothing term.

# 4. EXPERIMENTS

## 4.1 Datasets

Experiments have been performed on two datasets respectively extracted from DBLP and Flickr. For the former, the task is monolabel classification, and for the latter multilabel classification. For DBLP two families of experiments - without and with content words have been performed. They are respectively denoted by *DBLP No Content* and *DBLP With Content* hereafter. For the Flickr experiments, no additional node characteristics has been considered. The two datasets are introduced below.

The **DBLP** dataset is a bibliographic network composed of authors and papers. This dataset was published in [22], where the task was heterogeneous classification with the authors and papers sharing the same set of labels (their research domain). The task studied here considers two different sets of labels: authors are labeled with their research domain (4 different domains) while papers are labeled with the name of the conference where they were published (20 labels). Authors and papers are connected through a *authorship* relation. The version without content is composed of two types of nodes and the graph is bipartite with one relation type. The version with content has three types of nodes – authors, papers and words – where each paper is connected to the nodes of its title – as shown in Figure 4. Classification is monolabel on papers and authors. General statistics about this corpus are given in Table 1.

The **Flickr** corpus is a dataset of photos and users. The photo labels correspond to different possible tags while the user labels are their subscribed groups. The classification problem is multi-label: images and users may belong to more than one category. Photos are related to users through an *authorship* relation, while users are related to other users through a *friendship* relation. This dataset is illustrated in Figure 3 (a) and statistics are given in Table 1. We have kept the image tags that appear in at least 500 images, and user categories that appear also at least 500 times in the dataset resulting in 21 possible labels for photos and 42 for authors[2].

## 4.2 Models

We have compared the proposed approach denoted by **LSHM** (Latent Space Heterogeneous Model) with two other models representative of the main-stream families of algorithms. The first one transforms the heterogeneous classification problem into multiple homogeneous problems. The second one performs an unsupervised projection of the heterogeneous network onto a latent space and then applies a multi-class classification algotirhm on this space. Both models are state of the art approaches. Note that except for [2, 14] there does not exist any algorithm that handles the relational classification problem on heterogeneous networks with disjoint label sets. More precisely, the first model, de-

[2]The dataset is available at http://www-poleia.lip6.fr/~jacoby/Research/research_en.html

| | | Type | Nb. Nodes | Nb. Labeled Nodes | Nb. Labels |
|---|---|---|---|---|---|
| DBLP No content | Nodes | Paper | 14,376 | 14,376 | 20 |
| | | Author | 14,475 | 4,057 | 4 |
| | Edges | **Type** | **Nb. Edges** | | |
| | | Author→Paper | 41,794 | | |
| DBLP With Content | Nodes | Paper | 14,376 | 14,376 | 20 |
| | | Author | 14,475 | 4,057 | 4 |
| | | Words | 8,920 | 0 | |
| | Edges | Author→Paper | 41,794 | | |
| | | Paper→Word | 114,624 | | |
| Flickr | Nodes | Photos | 46,926 | 8,766 | 21 |
| | | User | 4,760 | 3,476 | 42 |
| | Edges | User←User | 175,779 | | |
| | | User←Photo | 46,926 | | |

**Table 1: Statistics on the three datasets**

| Model | Type of node | Training Size 10% | 30% | 50% |
|---|---|---|---|---|
| MTH | Author | 58.8 | 65.0 | 69.2 |
| | Paper | 28.2 | 32.7 | 34.8 |
| ULS | Author | 27.0 | 27.7 | 27.6 |
| | Paper | 11.0 | 12.4 | 12.5 |
| LSHM (no Content) | Author | **64.9** | **75** | **83** |
| | Paper | **30.4** | **34.5** | **37.2** |
| LSHM (with Content) | Author | **67** | **82** | **87.1** |
| | Paper | **30.6** | **35.6** | **37.9** |

**Table 2: Accuracy over the DBLP datasets with a latent space of size 30.**

| Model | Type of node | Training Size 10% | 30% | 50% |
|---|---|---|---|---|
| MTH | User | 42 | **46.8** | 48.7 |
| | Photo (Same Author) | 35.6 | 59.4 | 65.5 |
| | Photo (Author are friends) | 19.3 | 21.7 | 22 |
| | Photo (Author are same or friends) | 22.4 | 31.3 | 32.4 |
| ULS | User | 26.1 | 28.0 | 28.3 |
| | Photo | 9.8 | 9.8 | 9.9 |
| LSHM | User | **42.9** | 45.7 | **49.1** |
| | Photo | **43.3** | **61.6** | **68.1** |

**Table 3: P@1 over the Flickr datasets with a latent space of size 200**

noted by **Mapping to Homogeneous Model (MTH)**, uses multiple homogeneous graphs, one for each node type, to represent the heterogeneous network. For each homogeneous problem, we use the model proposed in [6] that minimizes the loss in Equation 1. It does not make use of the correlations between labels of nodes types.

The homogeneous graphs have been built as follows:

- For the DBLP corpus, the graph of authors is built by connecting two co-authors; the graph of papers is built by connecting two papers written by the same author.
- For Flickr, the graph of users is built by connecting two friends. Different graphs of photos are possible:
  - The **Same author** graph is built by connecting two photos that have the same author.
  - The **Author are friends** graph is built by connecting two photos that have been published by two friends.
  - The **Author are same or friends** graph is built by connecting two photos that have been published by the same user of by two friends.

Note that for these tests, the model "Same author" where two images are linked through an intermediate author node, shares similarities with the Graffiti model [2] which uses a 2 hops random walk for connecting nodes of the same type linked by a path of length 2 and separated by a node from another type.

The second model we have compared with, denoted by **ULS** (Unsupervised Latent Space), learns a latent representation for each node of the graph without using the labels and learns to predict the labels based on the latent representations. We use a variant of the model proposed in [4] for learning embeddings of knowledge databases. This model learns unsupervised projections of relational knowledge bases with a specific metric for each relation type. Here we used only one metric for all relations. Compared to our model, the main difference is that the latent space is built in an unsupervised way – the objective is to keep the graph structure in the latent space – while our method aims at finding "the best" representations for a particular classification problem.

Experiments were performed with 10 random training labeled sets and the reported performance was obtained by averaging those obtained over the 10 runs. Different configurations were tested:

- Experiments were performed with different training sizes: 10%, 30%, 50%. The training size refers to **the proportion of labeled nodes** used in the training set. For example, in the DBLP No Content dataset, a training set of 10% means that 1,437 papers over 14,376 and 405 users over 4,050 labeled users were considered. Note that for this dataset, all papers are labeled whereas only 4,050 users over 14,475 are labeled. Unlabeled nodes will only appear in the smoothing term of Equation 4. The evaluation was performed on the labeled nodes not used during training.
- The gradient descent step for LSHM was fixed to 0.1 – similar performance in terms of accuracy was obtained at the price of a lower convergence speed.

- The dimension of the projection spaces for ULS and LSHM is 30 was chosen that yields good performance for both models in our experiments.

- Since there are much more links among users than between users and photos in the Flickr dataset, the weights of the relations have been normalized in order to avoid that the *user* → *user* relations have more influence than the *user* → *photo* relations. Weight for *user* → *photo* relations is 1 while weight for *user* → *user* has been set to 0.1.

## 4.3 Evaluation measures

*Mono-Label Datasets:* . In the case of mono-label datasets (DBLP with and without content), we consider that the predicted category is the category with the highest score. We make use of an *accuracy* measure which is the ratio between the number of good classification and the number of total testing nodes.

*Multi-Label Dataset:* . For multi-label datasets, after predicting the scores of the different categories, one has to decide which subset of categories to assign to any node of the network. For the evaluation, we have considered two different evaluation measures: The **Precision at 1 (P@1)** measures the percentage of nodes for which the category with the highest score is a relevant category. The **Precision at k (P@k)** is the proportion of correct labels in the set of k labels with the highest predicted scores. For each evaluation node, $k$ is artificially chosen to be the number of relevant categories. This measure is an optimistic measure of the capacity of a model to correctly rank the $k$ relevant categories of any node.

## 4.4 Results

### 4.4.1 Quantitative evaluation

Tables 2 and 3 show the performance obtained on the different datasets for different training set sizes. The evaluation of the models is separately made on two different types of nodes – paper and author for DBLP, user and photo for Flickr. Globally, our model is able to outperform the other models. For example, for the DBLP dataset without content, at a training size of 10%, our model obtains 64.9% accuracy on the author nodes and 30.4% on the paper nodes while the MTH model obtains 58.8% for the authors and 28.2% for the papers. The ULS model only obtains 27% for the authors and 11% for the papers. This is due to the fact that the latent representations are learned independently of the classifiers, without using training labels[3]. When using the graph with content – i.e. when words are integrated into the heterogeneous network – our model obtains even better results and outperforms the heterogeneous model without content, showing the ability of our method to handle not only different types of nodes, but also content information. Compared to the MTH model performance increase is important for author nodes, and smaller for paper nodes. This is probably because there are far less labeled authors than papers so that the classification task on authors is more difficult and the simpler models fail. It is also more important when the proportion of labeled is increased (e.g. increase of 18% for 50% of labeled nodes). Here our more sophisticated LSHM model is able to take advantage of the additional information provided by these labels.

For Flickr, we compared LSHM model with different projected graphs for the photos in the MTH model, as described in section 2. The performance for $P@1$ and $P@k$ are given in Table 5. The performance increase is much smaller here than with DBLP, which is probably due to the pre-eminence of "friend" and "same author" relations respectively for users and photos. Said otherwise, for this Flickr dataset, much of the information is present in these two types of relations only. On the other hand, the proposed model allows us to reach best performance without testing for many graph projections.

[3]The ULS results have been obtained in a latent space of size 30. We have tested many different sizes, and only the best results are reported here.

| Training Size | $Z$ | Acc. Author | Acc. Paper |
|---|---|---|---|
| 10% | MTH | 58.8 | 28.2 |
| | ULS | 27.0 | 11.0 |
| | 10 | 63.4 | 28.8 |
| | 20 | 62.6 | 29.1 |
| | 30 | **64.9** | **30.4** |
| | 50 | 62.5 | 29.7 |
| | 100 | 62.3 | 29.1 |
| 30% | MTH | 65.0 | 32.7 |
| | ULS | 27.7 | 12.4 |
| | 10 | 74.3 | 33.9 |
| | 20 | 74.6 | 33.6 |
| | 30 | **75** | **34.5** |
| | 50 | 72.8 | 33.5 |
| | 100 | 72.7 | 33.4 |
| 50% | MTH | 69.2 | 34.8 |
| | ULS | 27.6 | 12.5 |
| | 10 | **83.6** | 37 |
| | 20 | 82.6 | **37.2** |
| | 30 | 83 | **37.2** |
| | 50 | 80.6 | 36 |
| | 100 | 78.8 | 36 |

**Table 4: (a) Accuracy on DBLP No Content depending on the representation size $Z$.**

### 4.4.2 Influence of the Representation size

Let us now examine how performance varies depending on the size of the latent space $Z$ – Tables 4 and 5. For the DBLP corpus, using a space of 30 dimensions often gives the best results for all training sizes. When the number of dimensions is too small, the model is unable to find good representations, while when it is too large, the model is overfitting, resulting in a loss of performance. Concerning the Flickr corpus for which the graph topology is more complex, a latent space of 200 dimensions allows one to obtain good performance on both photos and users. When restricting the dimensions of this space to 20, the model seems to concentrate more on users than on photos. This is probably due to the fact that users are connected through direct relations, while photos are connected through paths of minimum size 2: when the model does not have enough representation capacity, it tends to better propagate on close nodes, and is not able to model longer propagations.

| Training Size | $Z$ | P@1/P@k Photo | P@1/P@k User |
|---|---|---|---|
| 10% | MTH | 35.6/35.4 | 42/33.4 |
| | ULS | 26.1/21.3 | 9.8/10.5 |
| | 20 | 38.4/33.8 | **46.5**/**33.5** |
| | 50 | 41.3/38 | 39.7/29.6 |
| | 100 | **43.3**/40.4 | 39.8/30.5 |
| | 200 | 43.1/**41.7** | 42.9/30.6 |
| 30% | MTH | 59.4/56.3 | 46.8/**36.2** |
| | ULS | 28.0/23.2 | 9.8/10.6 |
| | 20 | 48.8/46.4 | **47.6**/33.7 |
| | 50 | 55/53.9 | 46.3/33.7 |
| | 100 | 60.4/58 | 45.6/33.5 |
| | 200 | **61.6**/**58.2** | 45.7/33.5 |
| 50% | MTH | 65.5/63.7 | 48.7/36.0 |
| | ULS | 28.3/23.5 | 9.9/10.8 |
| | 20 | 50.3/48.7 | **49.2**/30.5 |
| | 50 | 57.4/57.3 | 47.3/**36.4** |
| | 100 | 67.6/**64.8** | 48.3/35.1 |
| | 200 | **68.1**/64.7 | 49.1/34.6 |

**Table 5: P@1 and P@k on Flickr depending on the representation size $Z$ w.r.t MTH and ULS.**

### *4.4.3 Qualitative results*

In order to visualize the latent representations, we have performed a PCA over these representations for both articles and authors on the DBLP dataset for testing nodes. A 2 dimensional PCA projection corresponding to the first 2 axis is illustrated in Figure 5. The right figure shows all the labeled nodes in the latent space (after PCA dimension reduction) - different shapes correspond to different types of nodes (large diamond shapes for authors, small diamonds for conferences), and different colors correspond to different labels. PCA projection shows that the proposed model is able to map nodes with the same labels onto the same parts of the latent space. The left part of the figure shows the average latent representation projection for each label. The four diamonds correspond to the centroid of the four authors research domains, while the 20 smaller star points correspond to the centroids of the papers published at each of the 20 conferences. One can see that, for any particular research domain corresponding to the author classes, the model is able to find a latent representation which is close to the conferences that are related to this domain, showing the ability of the model to find correlation between the labels of the different types of nodes.

## 5. RELATED WORK

Graph node classification has motivated a lot of work during the last decade and different models have been proposed. Two main families of models can be distinguished:
(i) Collective classification techniques are extensions of inductive learning to relational data. They consider both node attributes, labels and their dependencies. The classification problem is formulated as an optimal assignment of labels to the vertices of a graph. Since exact algorithms cannot be used in general for this combinatorial problem, approximate iterative algorithms have been developed. Sen et al. [19] provide a general introduction and a comparison of these models. They distinguish between local and global models. The former such as *Iterative Classification* [19] and its variants like SICA [18], *Gibbs Sampling* [17], or *Stacked Learning* [15], make use of local classifiers taking as input the node attributes and statistics on the neighbors labels. The latter attempt to optimize a global function using graphical models, e.g. Markov Random Fields trained for example using loopy belief propagation. In practice, they advocate the use of simple local models which offer similar performance as more complex graphical models and do not suffer from convergence problems exhibited by the latter. All these methods have been proposed for homogeneous networks whereas heterogeneous classification was explicitly mentioned as an open problem.
(ii) The second family of models consists of semi-supervised and transductive regularized models – [28], [3] and [27] – which are based on the minimization of an objective function that encourages connected nodes to have the same labels. This family of models has been initially proposed for pure relational classification (no content associated to nodes) and for homogeneous networks. It has been extensively used in many different contexts. Extensions for handling node content information have been developed with applications to social network labeling [6] and Web-spam detection [1]. Several extensions have been proposed for dealing with more complex networks. For example, algorithms have been developed for multi-relational graphs, where nodes are all of the same type, but can be connected through multiple relations which will have different influences on the label propagation. These methods can learn from the data the weights of the different relations, and the multi-graph is then reduced to a simple graph by combining the different types of relations –[25, 12, 9]. Note that besides node classification, other methods have been proposed for other tasks like link-prediction [7] for example
Mining heterogeneous networks is a much more recent domain and different tasks have been addressed: classification of nodes [11, 10, 8, 2], link prediction [5],[24], influence analysis [16], clustering [20], entity similarity search [26], [21]. We will concentrate here on classification which has been addressed in a few papers.

Most of the proposed models are extensions of algorithms developed for homogeneous models. Typical of the transductive regularized models extensions is the work by Ji et al. [11] which is inspired by the homogeneous model of Zhou et al. [27]. For each couple of node types, they consider the weight matrix of the bipartite subgraph corresponding to the edges linking the two node types. The objective function is then a linear combination of the smoothness constraints defined over each of these matrices. For instance in an heterogeneous network of authors and papers like DBLP, this model will consider three relation types: author-author, paper-paper and author-paper and as many weight matrices. Instead of one smoothing term in the homogeneous case, the number of smoothing loss terms is proportional to the square of the number of node types ($n(n-1)/2$ if there are $n$ node types) and of course there are as many regularization coefficients to set up which might become problematic for complex networks. Note that in these approaches, the authors do not make the choice of an a priori graph projections but consider all possible binary relationships between node types. An extension of this work [10] is proposed for a ranking problem: the objects in each class are ranked according to their class relevance. A very similar formulation is proposed in [8] which is also a direct extension of the algorithm in [27]. Again, multiple weight matrices between node type

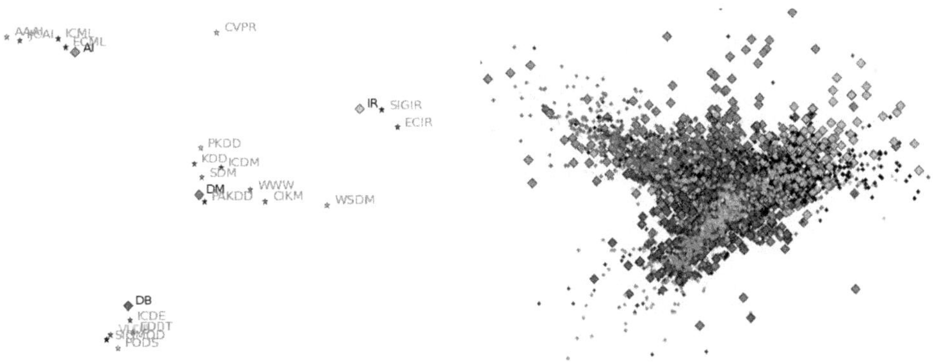


(a) Centroid of different authors and papers labels (unlabeled nodes)

(b) All nodes

**Figure 5: PCA on the DBLP corpus computed over the latent representation of the testing nodes projection when using 10% nodes for training.**

sets are introduced and linearly combined in a loss function. All these extensions consider that the different types of nodes share the same set of categories. In our model, the latent space formulation allows to bypass this limitation.

Some authors have proposed extensions of the collective classification methods [19]. In a series of papers, Kong, Yu and colleagues [14, 13] make use of the notion of meta-path for extending the *Iterative Classification* technique to heterogeneous networks both for mono-label and multi-label classification. A meta-path is a path in an heterogeneous graph that links two nodes through an heterogeneous path. For instance in a bibliographic network, the meta-path "Paper $\xrightarrow{cite^{-1}}$ Author $\xrightarrow{cite}$ Paper" connects two papers with the same author. All the possible non-redundant meta-paths shorter than a chosen length are used. Their algorithm first extracts a certain number of relevant meta paths and considers the nodes linked by such paths as neighbors. Then it applies the ICA algorithm to the corresponding graph. Only one type of nodes is considered for a classification task since relevant meta path may differ from one type to another. In their experiments, they consider meta paths joining two nodes of the same type. Heuristics for limiting the number of meta paths are used. This is equivalent to defining a projection graph for each class based on these meta paths and then doing collective classification. These methods consider both the relational structure and node characteristics, and make use of the latter to initialize the node class probabilities. Here again the proposed method relies on heuristics for defining the paths, and does not directly exploit inter-node types dependencies.

To our knowledge, the only existing model addressing directly heterogeneous network classification with different label sets per node type is [2]. The algorithm is based on a random walk method, where, in addition to simple jumps to neighboring nodes which could be of any type, 2-hop jumps between nodes of the same type are allowed. Nodes of the same type can then be connected by a path of size 2 where the intermediate node is of a different type. Labels propagate among nodes of the same type. Paths joining nodes of the same type and longer than 2 are ignored. However the propagation mechanism allows the diffusion of labels on longer paths with a decreasing influence when the path length increases. This algorithm makes use of node characteristics in order to initialize node class distributions. Although the exact correspondence with our algorithm is difficult to analyze, this method intuitively corresponds to a random walk on an extended graph where connections corresponding to two hops between nodes of the same type define the connection graph. Compared to this approach, our model is able to consider the correlations between the labels of connected nodes of different types through the latent space projection which is not the case in their model. It also learns directly a discriminant function instead of propagating initial label distributions modulated by node class authority.

# 6. CONCLUSION

We have proposed a new model able to label nodes of heterogeneous networks where the nodes are of different types, each type corresponding to a particular set of possible categories. Our method is able to use the correlation between the labels of two connected nodes of different types, and thus to use the complex structure of the graph for labeling. Our algorithm is based on the idea of computing a latent representation of nodes in a space that is common to all the possible types of nodes, and to assume that two connected nodes tend to have close latent representations. The labels are then deduced from these representations. Our experiments on three datasets show that the proposed model outperforms classical approaches, and qualitative analysis show that the proposed method effectively captures the inter-dependencies between the labels of different types of nodes. Different extensions of this model are currently being investigated: the first one is to deal with multi-relational heterogeneous networks – i.e. heterogeneous networks where two nodes can be connected with more than one relation – and dynamic heterogeneous networks. We are also working on an extension which allows one to learn sparse representation of nodes in the graph.

# 7. ACKNOWLEDGMENTS

This work has been partially supported by the REMI FUI project and the ANR (French National Research Agency) MLVIS project

## 8. REFERENCES


[1] Jacob Abernethy, Olivier Chapelle, and Carlos Castillo. Witch: A new approach to web spam detection. In *In Proceedings of the 4th International Workshop on Adversarial Information Retrieval on the Web (AIRWeb)*, 2008.

[2] Ralitsa Angelova, Gjergji Kasneci, and Gerhard Weikum. Graffiti: graph-based classification in heterogeneous networks. *World Wide Web*, 15(2):139–170, 2012.

[3] Mikhail Belkin, Partha Niyogi, and Vikas Sindhwani. Manifold regularization: A geometric framework for learning from labeled and unlabeled examples. *J. Mach. Learn. Res.*, 7:2399–2434, December 2006.

[4] A. Bordes, J. Weston, R. Collobert, and Y. Bengio. Learning structured embeddings of knowledge bases. In *AAAI*, 2011.

[5] Darcy Davis, Ryan Lichtenwalter, and N.V. Chawla. Multi-Relational Link Prediction in Heterogeneous Information Networks. In *ASONAM*, 2011.

[6] Ludovic Denoyer and Patrick Gallinari. A ranking based model for automatic image annotation in a social network. In *ICWSM*, 2010.

[7] Sheng Gao, Ludovic Denoyer, and Patrick Gallinari. Link pattern prediction with tensor decomposition in multi-relational networks. In *CIDM*, 2011.

[8] Taehyun Hwang and Rui Kuang. A heterogeneous label propagation algorithm for disease gene discovery. In *SDM*, page 12, 2010.

[9] Yann Jacob, Ludovic Denoyer, and Patrick Gallinari. Classification and annotation in social corpora using multiple relations. In *CIKM*, pages 1215–1220, 2011.

[10] Ming Ji, Jiawei Han, and Marina Danilevsky. Ranking-based classification of heterogeneous information networks. In *KDD*, pages 1298–1306. ACM, 2011.

[11] Ming Ji, Yizhou Sun, Marina Danilevsky, Jiawei Han, and Jing Gao. Graph regularized transductive classification on heterogeneous information networks. In *ECML PKDD*, volume 53, pages 570–586, 2010.

[12] T. Kato, H. Kashima, and M. Sugiyama. Integration of multiple networks for robust label propagation. In *SIAM Conf. on Data Mining*, pages 716–726, 2008.

[13] Xiangnan Kong, Bokai Cao, and Philip S. Yu. Multi-label classification by mining label and instance correlations from heterogeneous information networks. KDD '13, pages 614–622, 2013.

[14] Xiangnan Kong, Philip S. Yu, Ying Ding, and David J. Wild. Meta path-based collective classification in heterogeneous information networks. In *CIKM*, pages 1567–1571, 2012.

[15] Zhenzhen Kou. Stacked graphical models for efficient inference in markov random fields. In *In Proc. of the 2007 SIAM International Conf. on Data Mining*, 2007.

[16] Lu Liu, Jie Tang, Jiawei Han, and Meng Jiang. Mining topic-level influence in heterogeneous networks. In *CIKM*, 2010.

[17] Sofus A. Macskassy and Foster Provost. A simple relational classifier. In *Proceedings of the Second Workshop on Multi-Relational Data Mining (MRDM-2003) at KDD-2003*, pages 64–76, 2003.

[18] Francis Maes, Stephane Peters, Ludovic Denoyer, and Patrick Gallinari. Simulated iterative classification a new learning procedure for graph labeling. *Proceedings of the European Conference on Machine Learning and Knowledge Discovery in Databases Part II*, II:47–62, 2009.

[19] Prithviraj Sen, Galileo Namata, Mustafa Bilgic, Lise Getoor, Brian Gallagher, and Tina Eliassi-Rad. Collective classification in network data. *AI Magazine*, 29(3):93–106, 2008.

[20] Yizhou Sun, Charu C. Aggarwal, and Jiawei Han. Relation strength-aware clustering of heterogeneous information networks with incomplete attributes. *PVLDB*, 5(5):394–405, 2012.

[21] Yizhou Sun, Jiawei Han, Xifeng Yan, Philip S. Yu, and Tianyi Wu. Pathsim: Meta path-based top-k similarity search in heterogeneous information networks. *PVLDB*, 4(11):992–1003, 2011.

[22] Yizhou Sun, Yintao Yu, and Jiawei Han. Ranking-based clustering of heterogeneous information networks with star network schema. In *KDD*, pages 797–806, 2009.

[23] Lei Tang, Xufei Wang, and Huan Liu. Community detection via heterogeneous interaction analysis. *Data Min. Knowl. Discov.*, 25(1):1–33, 2012.

[24] Chi Wang, Rajat Raina, David Fong, Ding Zhou, Jiawei Han, and Greg J. Badros. Learning relevance from heterogeneous social network and its application in online targeting. In *SIGIR*, pages 655–664, 2011.

[25] Meng Wang, Xian-Sheng Hua, Richang Hong, Jinhui Tang, Guo-Jun Qi, and Yan Song. Unified video annotation via multigraph learning. *Circuits and Systems for Video Technology, IEEE Transactions on*, 19(5):733 –746, may 2009.

[26] Xiao Yu, Yizhou Sun, Brandon Norick, Tiancheng Mao, and Jiawei Han. User guided entity similarity search using meta-path selection in heterogeneous information networks. CIKM '12, pages 2025–2029, New York, NY, USA, 2012. ACM.

[27] Dengyong Zhou, Olivier Bousquet, Thomas Navin Lal, Jason Weston, and Bernhard Schölkopf. Learning with local and global consistency. In Sebastian Thrun, Lawrence Saul, and Bernhard Schölkopf, editors, *Advances in Neural Inform. Process. Systems 16*. 2004.

[28] Dengyong Zhou, Jiayuan Huang, and Bernhard Schölkopf. Learning from labeled and unlabeled data on a directed graph. In *Proc. of the 22nd intern. conf. on Mach. learn.*, ICML '05, pages 1036–1043, 2005.

# Prediction in a Microblog Hybrid Network Using Bonacich Potential

Shanchan Wu
HP Labs Palo Alto
1501 Page Mill Road, Palo Alto, CA, 94304
shanchan.wu@hp.com

Louiqa Raschid
University of Maryland Institute for Advanced Computer Studies College Park, MD 20742
louiqa@umiacs.umd.edu

## ABSTRACT

Microblogs such as Twitter support a rich variety of user interactions using hashtags, urls, retweets and mentions. Microblogs are an exemplar of a hybrid network; there is an explicit network of followers, as well as an implicit network of users who retweet other users, and users who mention other users. These networks are important proxies for influence. In this paper, we develop a comprehensive behavioral model of an individual user and her interactions in the hybrid network. We choose a focal user and predict those users who will be influenced by her, and will retweet and/or mention the focal user, in the near future. We define a potential function, based on a hybrid network, which reflects the likelihood of a candidate user being influenced by, and having a specific type of link to, a focal user, in the future. We show that the potential function based prediction model converges to the Bonacich centrality metric. We develop a fast unsupervised solution which approximates the future hybrid network and the future Bonacich potential. We perform an extensive evaluation over a microblog network and a stream of tweets from Twitter. Our solution outperforms several baseline methods including ones based on singular value decomposition (SVD) and a supervised Ranking SVM.

**Categories and Subject Descriptors:** H.2.8 [**Database Management**]: Database Applications —Data mining
**Keywords:** Link Prediction; Social media; Social networks

## 1. INTRODUCTION

Microblogs such as Twitter support a rich variety of user interactions. One can follow a user and read her tweets. One can search for keywords or hashtags or follow trending tweets. A user can initiate a new topic by creating a new tweet or hashtag, often including a url in the tweet to refer to more detailed articles. One can interact with another user by mentioning them. One can also participate in the diffusion of a topic by retweeting. All of these interactions create a dynamic and rich social network for diffusion of information and to establish the influence of a user. In addition to the rich communication platform, microblogs have the advantage that it is simple to monitor the media stream due to the brevity of microblogs. Hashtags and urls enhance the stream with richer content and links.


*WSDM'14,* February 24–28, 2014, New York, New York, USA.
Copyright 2014 ACM 978-1-4503-2351-2/14/02 ...$15.00.
http://dx.doi.org/10.1145/2556195.2556247.

More important, diffusion can be easily monitored through retweets and mentions and both retweets and mentions have been identified as an important proxy for influence [4].

All the above factors increase the importance of monitoring social media. Our motivation for this research is to develop models and tools to exploit the power of this medium, as follows: A first step is monitoring to build behavioral models at the level of the individual user and her interactions. The next step is developing accurate prediction models of future actions and interactions in social media streams. The final step is to make personalized recommendations that combine the individual level behavioral model with predictions of future social media interactions. Our objective is thus to develop a behavioral model that can capture the richness and complexity of microblogs. We use this to make predictions about the future at the level of an individual focal user, i.e., given a focal user, we want to predict the other users who will be influenced by her and will interact with her.

An example application for this research is monitoring for personalized and interactive brand management. A brand manager has the objective of monitoring conversations about a brand, to track relevant topics and sentiment, and to identify potentially negative conversations. While aggregate statistics, e.g., a trending topic about the brand, or an increase in negative sentiment, is important, social media also provides a platform for personalized and interactive brand management.

Suppose a brand manager knows which user $u$ is likely to talk about her brand, either in a positive or negative way. It will be useful if she could determine if $u$ is influential, as well as other users $v$ who will be influenced by $u$. With this knowledge, the brand manager could perhaps take a proactive action such as engaging in a conversation with $u$.

However, a user $u$ who is an expert on a brand (topic) and is influential may not be willing or interested in engaging directly with a brand manager. The brand manager may then decide to engage with other users $v$ who are in turn influenced by $u$. The richness of social media also allows one to make diverse recommendations, e.g., to target yet another user $w$ who has not previously tweeted about the brand but who has several friends with an interest in the brand and who have engaged in creating or diffusing relevant content.

There are many diffusion and influence models for social networks. For example, the Linear Threshold Model and the Independent Cascade Model have been widely studied [8, 15]. For the Linear Threshold Model, in each step, a user will be activated (influenced) if the total weight of her active neighbors is greater than a threshold. For the Independent Cascade Model, each active user has a single opportunity with some probability to activate each of her inactive neighbors.

These prior models have limitations when applied to microblogs. One limitation is that these prior models capture behavior at the aggregate level, e.g. at the level of a topic [24]. One popular aggregate level influence challenge is the influence maximization problem. It was first formulated as a discrete optimization problem in [15] and has been studied by others [5]. The target of influence maximization is to select an initial set of users who eventually influence the largest number of people in the network. Predicting the degree of influence has also been studied; for example, a regression model was used to predict the influence of a user [1].

Another limitation is that both the Linear Threshold Model and the Independent Cascade Model typically assume that one can only influence her immediate neighbors. The definition of neighbors is that there are edges in the network between these users. The edges are concrete and observable. For example, in a friendship network, one can only influence her friends. In a disease spread network, some diseases can only spread through direct contact with a user. Our observation for microblogs is that influence is not limited to the immediate neighborhood, i.e., influence can spread outside the friendship network of microblogs. One can retweet or mention users who are not one's friends. For example, in our experimental dataset (described in Section 5), more than 40% of the mentions are from outside the Follower network.

Most other research consider diffusion or prediction for a single homogeneous network. However, Twitter is an example of a *hybrid network* composed of multiple networks. There is an explicit Follower network. Retweet actions and mention actions also reflect key interactions between users; hence, Retweet and Mention networks can be constructed. Prior research typically considered the evolution of a single network, typically the equivalent of the Follower network of Twitter. However, given a hybrid network of microblogs, we expect all three networks to evolve as a result of the influence of the user. For example, if $u$ is retweeted a lot, she may attract additional followers $f$, and that in turn may lead to even more retweets and mentions from the followers of each $f$ who recently joined the Follower network of $u$. This is an example of the Retweet network causing an evolution of the Follower network, which in turn results in an evolution of the Retweet and Mention networks, respectively. We further note that our prediction method relies primarily on network features. The evolution of the three networks makes predicting the future network, while using network based features, more challenging.

To summarize, microblogs exhibit complex user interactions over a hybrid network. Influence is not limited to the immediate followers and it can be measured through the characteristics of the three networks. Further, the impact of influence may result in the evolution of all three networks. We wish to develop a prediction model at the level of the individual user, to predict those users who are most influenced by the focal user, and will retweet or mention the focal user, in the future.

Our contributions approach can be summarized as follows:

- We define a hybrid network made up of a Follower Retweet and Mention network. We define two prediction problems at the level of the individual focal user: the future retweet prediction and the future mention prediction.
- We define a potential function over the hybrid network that reflects the likelihood of a candidate user being influenced by, and having a specific type of link in the future to a focal user.
- We show that the potential function converges to the Bonacich centrality metric in the hybrid network. This is consistent with prior research that showed this metric was a good proxy for influence.
- We develop a fast unsupervised solution that approximates the future hybrid network and the future Bonacich potential. We perform an extensive evaluation over a microblog network and a stream of tweets from Twitter. Our model can provide high quality personalized recommendations of future interactions, at the level of individual behavioral interactions, with a surprisingly high degree of accuracy.
- We outperform several baseline methods including one based on singular value decomposition (SVD) and a supervised Ranking SVM based method.

The rest of the paper is organized as follows: Section 2 discusses related work; Section 3 formally formulates the problem and proposes the prediction model and solution; Section 4 explains how to choosing parameters; 5 describes the evaluation dataset and metrics and data properties; Section 6 presents evaluation results on our methods. Finally, Section 7 concludes our work.

## 2. RELATED WORK

Cha et al. in [4] have studied measuring user influence in a microblog, i.e., Twitter. They found that retweets and mentions are more important than the Follower network to determine influence. Predicting the most influential users in a microblog has been addressed in [23]. Beyond microblogs, future link prediction in the blogosphere has been addressed in [27]. Gomez-Rodriguez et al. in [9] proposed an approach to infer networks of diffusion and influence. They tried to reconstruct the network over which contagions propagate. So their target is to build the historical network where there is rich information in the history when the network was built. Our target is to predict future relationship where the information in the future is unknown when the relationship will be built.

Hong et al. in [11] proposed Matrix Co-Factorization to model user interests and to predict individual decisions in Twitter. Given a specific tweet, they predict if a focal user will retweet it. Peng et al. in [22] used Conditional Random Fields and Yang et al. in [28] proposed a semi-supervised framework on a factor graph model to solve a similar problem. While this problem is related to our problem of retweet prediction, their problem targets a specific tweet, where the content of the tweet is known a priori. Thus, content based features plan a very important in their prediction. Our prediction task is targeted on a specific user, where the contents of his/her future tweets is not known. Our research has to use both content and network based features. We note that the supervised learning approach of Hong et al. [11] has good accuracy and we compare the datasets and evaluation results in a later section.

Retweet and mention prediction can be formalized as a link prediction problem. Link prediction has been studied in various applications including social networks, relational datasets, labeled entity-relationship graphs, etc. An array of topological methods for link prediction were studied by Liben-Nowell and Kleinberg [19] who evaluated them on co-authorship networks. Machine learning approaches have also been applied to link prediction. Solution approaches include spectral transformation [17], the heat diffusion kernel [12], Markov Random Field Model [26], collective classification [25] and ranking SVM [27] etc. We note that previous link prediction research has not considered a hybrid network, where there may be different types of links between two nodes.

The most similar work on a prediction model based on a composite network [21] has been applied to predict the adoption of mobile apps. The authors collected different social networks using built-in

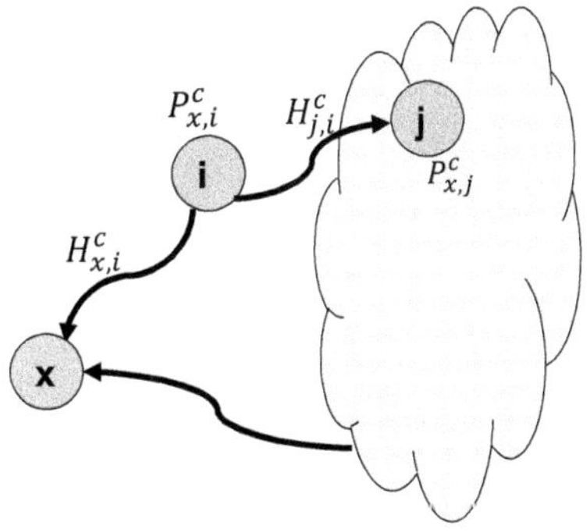


**Figure 1: Prediction model. $P_{x,i}^c$ or $P_{x,j}^c$ is the potential of $i$ or $j$ having a type $c$ link to $x$ in the future. $H_{x,i}^c$ and $H_{x,j}^c$ are the weights of the hybrid network edges.**

sensors, including Bluetooth proximity network, call log network, etc. Their model is based on the assumption that the adoption decision is influenced by neighbors in the composite network. They solved an optimization problem to create the composite network; however, there are scalability challenges in applying their work since they only consider a few hundred users. Further, unlike our link prediction problem, where future links reflect the evolution of the composite network, the adoption of mobile apps is not a link prediction problem; app adoption does not impact the composite network.

# 3. PROBLEM FORMULATION AND SOLUTION

## 3.1 Problem Definition

DEFINITION 1. ***Future Retweet Prediction:*** *Given a focal microblog user $u$ at a specific time point $T$, identify $K$ microblog users $S_T^u$ who will retweet one (or more) future tweet(s) of user $u$ in the near future.*

DEFINITION 2. ***Future Mention Prediction:*** *Given a microblog user $u$ at a specific time point $T$, identify $K$ microblog users $S_T^u$ who will mention microblog user $u$ one (or more) times in the near future.*

## 3.2 Prediction Model

Our objective is to exploit historical knowledge and the corresponding hybrid network to accurately predict future links. Let $G^1, \cdots, G^M$ represent the $M$ relationship networks constructed using history; for Twitter $M$=3 corresponding to the three networks: Follower, Mention and Retweet. The corresponding relationship networks in the future time period are denoted $Y^1, \cdots, Y^M$. Our objective is to infer an optimal composite network $H^c$ from $G^1, \cdots, G^M$ to predict each $Y^c$, $1 \leq c \leq M$. To be optimal, the hybrid network $H^c$ should be customized to each network $Y^c$.

Let $G_{i,j}^m$ represent the weight associated with the edge from node $j$ to node $i$ in some network $G^m$. Let $H_{i,j}^c$ represent the weight associated with the edge from $j$ to $i$ in the hybrid network $H^c$.

We define the hybrid network $H^c$ for each $Y^c$ as follows:

$$H_{i,j}^c = \sum_m \omega_m^c G_{i,j}^m \quad \text{where } \forall m, \omega_m^c \geq 0. \tag{1}$$

A potential function $P_{x,i}^c$ defined over each hybrid network $H^c$ reflects the likelihood of a candidate node $i$ having a link of type $c$ in the future to a focal node $x$. It reflects if $i$ is influenced by $x$. We define this potential function $P_{x,i}^c$ as follows:

$$P_{x,i}^c = \beta H_{x,i}^c + \alpha \sum_j P_{x,j}^c H_{j,i}^c \quad \text{where } \alpha \geq 0, \beta \geq 0. \tag{2}$$

For a focal node $x$, we consider several factors contributing to the potential from node $i$. The first factor is the weight of the hybrid network edge from node $i$ to node $x$. The second factor is the potential of the neighbors $j$ of node $i$ to focal node $x$. The third factor is the weight of the hybrid network edges from node $i$ to its neighbors $j$. Figure 1 is the visualization of these factors towards the potential function.

We can finally define a conditional probability to determine whether node $i$ will have a type $c$ link to node $x$ in the future, based on the potential of node $i$. Similar to [21], we adopt an exponential probability distribution to determine this function. We define our conditional probability as follows:

$$Prob(Y_{x,i}^c > 0 \mid G^m, 1 \leq m \leq M) = 1 - \exp(-s - P_{x,i}^c) \tag{3}$$

$Y_{x,i}^c$ is the weight of a future type $c$ edge from node $i$ to node $x$. If the value is greater than zero, it means that such a future edge exists. In the right side of the equation, $s$ is a parameter. Parameter $s$ will not change the ranking of the probabilities, but it will help to adjust the probability values and make the values more meaningful, especially when a probability threshold needs to be picked up.

The exponential function of $f(x) = exp(-x)$ has the monotonic and concave properties and matches the recent research [3] which suggests that the probability of adoption increases at a decreasing rate with increasing external network signals [21].

We note that this is a linear mixture model for creating the hybrid network. There are potentially other models for creating the hybrid network. For example, we could add more terms such as $\sum_{m_1,m_2} \omega_{m_1,m_2}^c G_{i,j}^{m_1} G_{i,j}^{m_2}$ to equation (1) to consider a quadratic model. Different models for the hybrid network will not affect the way we define a potential function. However, different models would have different complexity to determine an optimal set of parameter values. We choose the linear model since it straightforward to obtain the optimal set of parameter values. Further, the linear model captures the essence of the hybrid network.

**Convergence of our solution:**

In equation (2), $H_{x,i}^c$ is the weight of the hybrid network edge from node $i$ to node $x$, $H_{j,i}^c$ is the weight of the hybrid network edge from node $i$ to node $j$, and $\alpha$ and $\beta$ are two parameters. Here we have potential values on both sides of the equation. By solving a group of these equations, we can represent the potential by other factors and parameters rather than having potential variables on the right side. By applying equation (1) to equation (2), we have the following formula:

$$P_{x,i}^c = \beta \sum_m (\omega_m^c \cdot G_{x,i}^m) + \alpha \sum_j \left\{ P_{x,j}^c \sum_m (\omega_m^c \cdot G_{j,i}^m) \right\} \tag{4}$$

By recursively replacing $P_{x,j}^c$ with its expression in equation (4), we have the following expression of $P_{x,i}^c$.

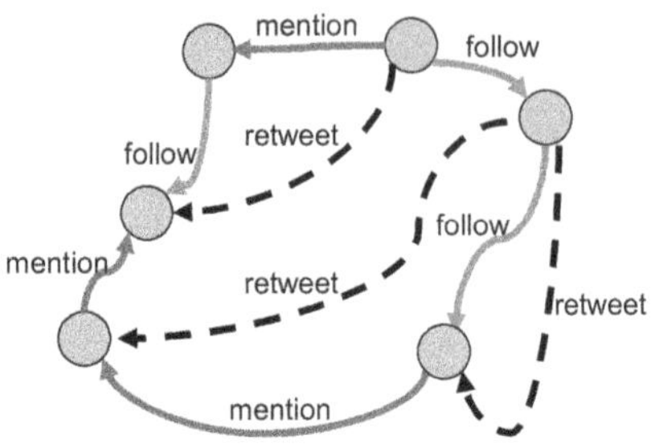


**Figure 2: Microblog networks.**

$$
\begin{aligned}
P^c_{x,i} =& \beta \sum_m \left(\omega^c_m \cdot G^m_{x,i}\right) \\
&+\beta\alpha \sum_j \left\{ \sum_m \left(\omega^c_m \cdot G^m_{x,j}\right) \sum_m \left(\omega^c_m \cdot G^m_{j,i}\right) \right\} \\
&+\beta\alpha^2 \sum_j \sum_{j_1} \left\{ \sum_m \left(\omega^c_m G^m_{x,j_1}\right) \sum_m \left(\omega^c_m G^m_{j_1,j}\right) \right. \\
&\left. \sum_m \left(\omega^c_m G^m_{j,i}\right) \right\} \\
&+ \cdots\cdots
\end{aligned} \tag{5}
$$

In equation (5), the first factor is the impact of the paths of length 1 to the potential, and the second factor is the impact of the paths of length 2 to the potential, and so on. The expression contains infinite factors. The expression is the generalization of the Bonacich metric [2]. The original Bonacich metric only considers one type of path whereas we consider hybrid paths.

*Bonacich centrality* is a generalization of Katz's metric [14]. *Katz* measures the status of a node by the total number of paths linking it to other nodes in the graph; an exponential discount is used as the path length increases. *Bonacich centrality* also reflects the total number of paths originating from a node and uses an attenuation factor $\alpha$ to discount indirect links and $\beta$ to discount direct links. *Katz* has been shown to be one of the best topological methods in [19] and *Bonacich* metric was shown to outperform metrics like *Jaccard* and *CommonNeighbors* in [27]. Previous work has shown Bonacich to be a good proxy for influence.

## 3.3 Representing Microblog Networks

Figure 2 illustrates user interactions in Twitter. We define the following adjacency matrices for the Retweet, Mention and Follower networks:

- $M$: Mention network adjacency matrix; the value of $M_{i,j}$ is the number of mentions from user $j$ of user $i$. Note that in the previous subsections, we have also used $M$ to denote the number of networks. In this subsection and any of the following sections, $M$ will only denote mention network adjacency matrix or mention network.
- $R$: Retweet network adjacency matrix; the value of $R_{i,j}$ is the number of retweets by user $j$ of tweets from user $i$.
- $F$: Follower network adjacency matrix; $F_{i,j}$ is equal to 1 if user $j$ is a follower of user $i$; else $F_{i,j}$ is equal to 0.

We define $F^*$ to be an adjusted follower network adjacency matrix reflecting the popularity factor of each follower. $F^*_{i,j}$ is a weighted value if user $j$ is a follower of user $i$; otherwise $F_{i,j}$ is equal to 0. If user $j$ is a follower of user $i$, the weighted value of $F^*_{i,j}$ is affected by the number of friends of that user $j$. We calculate $F^*_{i,j}$ as follows:

$$F^*_{i,j} = \frac{\overline{D}}{D_j}$$

$\overline{D}$ is the average of number of friends over all users; $D_j$ is the number of friends of user $j$. The intuition is that if a user $j$ has a lot of friends, then her attention will be divided among those friends, and she will pay less attention to user $u$. Consequently, user $u$ has a lower influence on user $j$, if $j$ has a lot of friends.

## 3.4 Solution Using the Hybrid Network: hybridBON

For this approximate solution, we first estimate the weights of different networks to create the hybrid (composite) network. We discuss choosing parameters for estimating weights in Section 4. After we create the composite network, for the focal user $x$, we can calculate the potential values of all candidate users according to equation (5), with respect to the likelihood of having type $c$ link to $x$ in the future. Since we already know the weights of different networks, we can simplify the equation (5) by using equation (1) as:

$$P^c_{x,i} = \beta H^c_{x,i} + \beta\alpha(H^c \cdot H^c)_{x,i} + \beta\alpha^2(H^c \cdot H^c \cdot H^c)_{x,i} + \cdots\cdots \tag{6}$$

The formula (6) has the same format as the *Bonacich centrality* [2].

Let $A$ be the adjacency matrix. Recall that each node in the link graph is a user. Suppose $T$ is the time when the prediction is to be made. Thus, we consider all historical links prior to $T$. We set the value of the element $A_{i,j}$ in the adjacency matrix $A$ is the number of direct links of some type pointing from node $j$ to node $i$ that exist in history before time $T$. Then, the value of $(A^n)_{i,j}$ is equal to the number of paths of length $n$ from node $j$ to node $i$ in history. Bonacich centrality is computed as follows:

$$
\begin{aligned}
C(\alpha, \beta) &= (\beta A + \beta\alpha A \cdot A + ... + \beta\alpha^n A^{(n+1)} ...) \\
&= \beta A(1 - \alpha A)^{(-1)}
\end{aligned}
$$

This equation holds while $\alpha < 1/\mu$, where $\mu$ is the largest characteristic root of A [6]. For $\alpha = \beta$, this measure reduces to the Katz score.

Unlike $A$ in the above equation, where the value of each element is the number of links from a node to another node, for matrix $H^c$ of a composite network, the value of each element is a real number which represents the weight of the edge from a node to another node. Then, rather than being equal to the number of paths of length $n$ from node $j$ to node $i$, the value of $(H^n)_{i,j}$ can represent the weight of the path of length $n$ from node $j$ to node $i$. Let $P$ be the matrix of all potential values $\{P^c_{x,i}\}$. According to formula (6), we can calculate the score matrix $P$ as following:

$$
\begin{aligned}
P &= (\beta H^1 + \beta\alpha H^2 + ... + \beta\alpha^n H^{(n+1)} ...) \\
&= \beta H(1 - \alpha H)^{(-1)}
\end{aligned} \tag{7}
$$

In this equation, we refer to $H^c$ as $H$ since we use the superscript $n$ in $H^n$ to refer to the power matrix expression for the matrix representation of each $H^c$. Then $P$ can be used for prediction, and we label this method as **hybridBON**.

# 4. CHOOSING PARAMETERS

For the approximation approach *hybridBON*, where we want to first create a composite network, $H^c = r \cdot R + m \cdot M + f \cdot F^*$, we consider two factors for the weights $r$, $m$, $f$. We first scale the matrices so that no matrix can dominate the others. We then use the ground truth from the training data to calibrate the influence of each network $R$, $M$, $F^*$ with respect to retweet prediction and mention prediction.

## 4.1 Scale Factor

The scale of each of the matrices may be different, e.g., the distribution of the values. This can result in one matrix dominate another.

We define a scale factor $\gamma$. Given a matrix $B$, then $\gamma(A, B)$ will scale matrix $A$ with respect to $B$. For retweet prediction, $R$ is the matrix that has the greatest influence and is used as a standard. We use the summation of the weights (values) of $R$, $\sum_{i,j} R_{i,j}$, to determine $\gamma$ for retweet prediction. The scale factors for the three different networks with respect to retweet prediction are formally calculated as follows:

$$\gamma(R,R) = 1,\ \gamma(M,R) = \frac{\sum_{i,j} R_{i,j}}{\sum_{i,j} M_{i,j}},\ \gamma(F^*,R) = \frac{\sum_{i,j} R_{i,j}}{\sum_{i,j} F^*_{i,j}}$$

The meaning of using retweet network as standard is that there are some total number of retweets among the users in the training period. Scaling other network to this standard is to mimic the retweet relationship but with somewhat different distribution.

Similarly, the scale factors for the three different networks with respect to mention prediction are formally calculated as follows:

$$\gamma(R,M) = \frac{\sum_{i,j} M_{i,j}}{\sum_{i,j} R_{i,j}},\ \gamma(M,M) = 1,\ \gamma(F^*,M) = \frac{\sum_{i,j} M_{i,j}}{\sum_{i,j} F^*_{i,j}}$$

## 4.2 Penalty Factor

We define penalty factors to lessen the weight of the networks which have lower prediction ability. Intuitively, for retweet prediction, the matrix $R$ (which matches the retweet ground truth from training data) is the most important. If another network $M$ or $F^*$ deviates from $R$ then a penalty factor must be imposed. We assign the penalty factors to other networks according to their correlation with the ground truth network in the training data, i.e., the network in the history with the same type of link to predict in the future.

We use average Spearman's rank correlation coefficient as the metric of how two adjacency matrices are correlated. A high correlation means a low deviation. For two rank sets $X$, $Y$, suppose $x_i$ and $y_i$ are the ranks of the values of $X_i$ and $Y_i$ in $X$ and $Y$ respectively, and the number of elements in $X$ and $Y$ are both $n$, Spearman's rank correlation coefficient is calculated as:

$$\rho(X,Y) = 1 - \frac{6\sum(x_i - y_i)}{n(n^2-1)}$$

The closer $\rho$ is to +1 or -1, the stronger the correlation is. A perfect positive correlation will have a $\rho$ value +1 and a perfect negative correlation will have a $\rho$ value -1. We only consider the positive correlation. The penalty factor should be related to the correlation. The lower the correlation, the penalty will be stronger, i.e., the penalty factor should be lower. We define a penalty factor to be a function with respect to $\rho$ as $\rho^\varepsilon$. Figure 3 shows the curves of $\rho^\varepsilon$ with respect to different $\varepsilon$ values. When $\rho$ is in the range of (0,+1], $\rho^\varepsilon$ will also be in the range of (0,+1]. When $\varepsilon$ is greater than 1, $\rho^\varepsilon$ has lower value than $\rho$. The bigger value of $\varepsilon$, the stronger penalty is applied with the same correlation value.

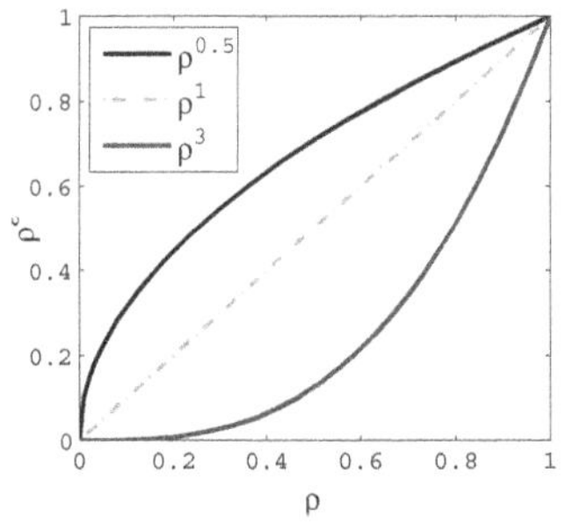


**Figure 3: Function $\rho^\varepsilon$.**

The penalty factors for the three different networks with respect to retweet prediction are formally calculated as follows:

$$\varphi(R,R) = 1, \varphi(M,R) = \left\{\frac{1}{N}\sum_i \rho(M_i, R_i)\right\}^\varepsilon, \quad \varphi(F^*,R) = \left\{\frac{1}{N}\sum_i \rho(F^*_i, R_i)\right\}^\varepsilon \tag{8}$$

where $\rho(M_i, R_i)$ is the Spearman's rank correlation of the $i$th row of $M$ and the $i$th row of $R$, $\rho(F^*_i, R_i)$ is the Spearman's rank correlation of the $i$th row of $F^*$ and the $i$th row of $R$, and $N$ is the number of rows.

Similarly, the penalty factors for the three different networks with respect to mention prediction are as follows:

$$\varphi(R,M) = \left\{\frac{1}{N}\sum_i \rho(R_i, M_i)\right\}^\varepsilon, \varphi(M,M) = 1, \quad \varphi(F^*,M) = \left\{\frac{1}{N}\sum_i \rho(F^*_i, M_i)\right\}^\varepsilon \tag{9}$$

For two variable sets, to calculate the Spearman's rank correlation coefficient, identical values (value duplicates) are assigned a rank equal to the average of their positions in the ascending order. By this way, even if most of the entries of two matricies are 0, the rank correlation would not be dominated by the sparseness of the matricies. For two corresponding rows in two matrices, if the numbers of the zero values are different, the ranks for the zero values in the two rows would be different. Table 1 is an example to show the different rank values for the zero values for two variable set $X$ and $Y$, where zero value is the least value for both of the two variable sets.

## 4.3 Merging Parameters

Next we consider the merging parameters to create the composite network; they combine the scale factors and penalty factors. We label them as $r$, $m$, $f$, for simplicity, and note that they refer to the weights $\omega^c_m$ in equation (1).

For retweet prediction,

$$r = \gamma(R,R) \cdot \varphi(R,R),\ m = \gamma(M,R) \cdot \varphi(M,R),$$

$$f = \gamma(F^*,R) \cdot \varphi(F^*,R)$$

**Table 1: Example of the rank value of tie values**

| Variable $X_i$ | Position in the ascending order | Rank $x_i$ |
|---|---|---|
| 0 | 1 | $\frac{1+2+3}{3} = 2$ |
| 0 | 2 | $\frac{1+2+3}{3} = 2$ |
| 0 | 3 | $\frac{1+2+3}{3} = 2$ |
| 2 | 4 | 4 |
| 4 | 5 | 5 |

| Variable $Y_i$ | Position in the ascending order | Rank $y_i$ |
|---|---|---|
| 0 | 1 | $\frac{1+2}{2} = 1.5$ |
| 0 | 2 | $\frac{1+2}{2} = 1.5$ |
| 2 | 3 | 3 |
| 8 | 4 | 4 |
| 12 | 5 | 5 |

For mention prediction,

$$r = \gamma(R, M) \cdot \varphi(R, M),\ m = \gamma(M, M) \cdot \varphi(M, M),$$

$$f = \gamma(F^*, M) \cdot \varphi(F^*, M)$$

The composite network $H^c$ is created by merging the hybrid networks as

$$H^c = r \cdot R + m \cdot M + f \cdot F^*$$

# 5. EVALUATION DATASET AND METRICS

## 5.1 Data Collection

There have been several successful efforts to construct a proxy graph that characterizes the structure of a real network [7, 18]. For this experiment, our objective was different. It was to construct a dataset that reflected a comprehensive history of user interaction and tweet content, over an extended period, for a significant number of active users, given the strict limitations imposed by the Twitter API. We constructed a network of 15,000 users, as well as all their follower (friend) associations within this subnetwork. In choosing these 15,000 users, we focused on active users. Our premise is that the active users generate the most content and have the greatest influence. Thus, following the largest number possible (15,000) of active users provided us with a dataset that captured a majority of the activity that would have had an influence on these 15,000 users. We note that had we constructed a 15,000 user dataset to reflect the typical distribution of users in the network, we may have been severely limited in our ability to capture a majority of the relevant activity.

We used the Twitter API to construct the network in the following way: Starting from a seed *active* user, we expanded her follower network and added further active users until we reached 15,000 active users. The test for an active user was as follows based on their most recent 100 tweets: (1) The user should have an average minimum tweet frequency of one tweet per day in this time period. (2)There was at least one retweet in the most recent 100 tweets. We used the twitter streaming API to collect all tweets published by the 15K active users between April 25, 2011 and June 25, 2011.

Retweeting is identified by the use of *RT @username* in tweets. Mentioning is identified by *@username* in the tweet content, after excluding *RT @username* . We built up the retweet and mention network by extracting users being retweeted or mentioned in each tweet. Hashtags identified by *#hashtag* and URLs were also extracted. Since username and hashtag are case insensitive, we transformed all usernames and hashtags to lowercase.

**Table 2: Statistics of the twitter experiment data set**

| | |
|---|---|
| Time range | 04/25/11–06/25/11 |
| Number of active users | 15,000 |
| Number of tweets for the active users | 10,979,278 |
| Number of edges of following relationship within the 15K active users | 3,293,840 |
| Number of retweets by and of the 15K active users, excluding to-self retweets | 147,970 |
| Number of mentions by and of the 15K active users, excluding to-self mentions | 584,597 |
| Number of appearances of hashtags | 3,616,614 |
| Number of distinct hashtags | 302,628 |
| Number of appearances of URLs | 3,622,992 |
| Number of distinct URLs | 2,611,550 |

**Test Dataset and Training Dataset:**

We used the first month data (from April 25th to May 25th) as the training dataset and we obtained the ground truth from the second month data (from May 26 to June 25) and used it as the test dataset. We picked the sets of microblog users who had ground truth in the test dataset for evaluation. 4257 users had retweet ground truth and 7296 users had mention ground truth. The average number of ground truth (retweeters) for the 4257 users is 4.56, and the average number of ground truth (mentioners) for the 7296 users is 8.12.

For tuning the parameters, we selected those microblog users that contain ground truth from May 15 to May 25 as focal training users. The networks for training were collected in the preceding time interval from April 25 to May 15. There was no overlap between the training and testing time interval. Similarly there was no overlap in the time interval for the collection of training networks and to obtain the training ground truth.

## 5.2 Metrics and Parameters

Mean Average Precision (MAP) is widely used for evaluating ranking methods; it provides a single-figure measure of quality across recall levels. MAP has been shown to have especially good discrimination and stability [20] and we report on the values of MAP. We also use Normalized Discounted Cumulative Gain (NDCG) [10] for evaluation. NDCG is also a measure commonly used for evaluating the results of ranking methods. The NDCG value of a ranking list at position $i$ is calculated as:

$$NDCG@i = Z_i \sum_{j=1}^{i} \frac{2^{r(j)} - 1}{log(1 + j)}$$

where $r(j)$ is the rating for the $jth$ item and $Z_i$ is a normalization constant. $Z_i$ is chosen so that the NDCG score for a perfect ranking is 1. In our experiments we measured NDCG at the positions of 5 and 10.

We report on a sensitivity analysis for the choice of parameters in the next section. Here we report on specific parameter choices as follows:

$K = 20$, where $K$ is used in the definition of Retweet and Metion Prediction in Section 3.1.

$\alpha = 0.00005$ and $\beta = 1.0$, where $\alpha$ and $\beta$ are parameters in equations (2), (4), (5), (6) and (7).

$\varepsilon = 3.5$, where $\varepsilon$ is a parameter in equations (8) and (9).

For methods **SVD** and **SVD+BON**, in equation (10), $s$ is set to be

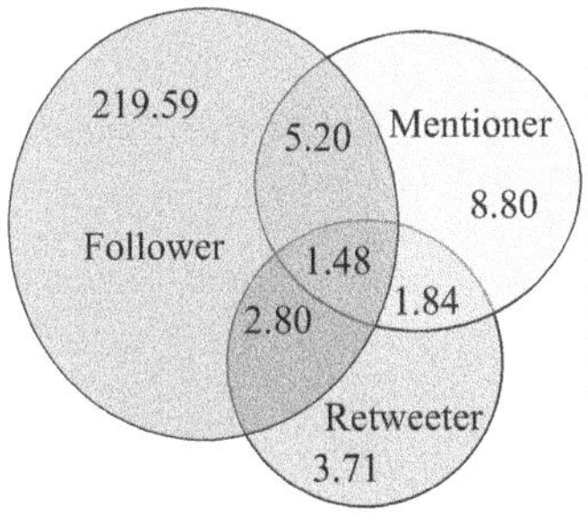


**Figure 4: Average numbers of followers, retweeters, mentioners from the 15K users and the 2-month dataset for each twitterer (excluding to-self).**

**Table 3: Correlation to retweet network adjacency matrix**

| | $R$ | $M$ | $F^*$ | $RR$ | $MM$ | $F^*F^*$ |
|---|---|---|---|---|---|---|
| $R$ | 1.000 | 0.653 | 0.222 | 0.638 | 0.495 | 0.073 |
| | $RM$ | $MR$ | $RF^*$ | $F^*R$ | $MF^*$ | $F^*M$ |
| $R$ | 0.621 | 0.526 | 0.601 | 0.130 | 0.443 | 0.116 |

5227 for retweet prediction and 6997 for mention prediction; again these are the best values for the dataset.

## 5.3 Network Properties

Figure 4 reports on the average numbers of followers, retweeters, mentioners for each twitterer, and the average numbers of their overlaps. The figure shows that the average number of followers for each twitterer is 219.59, the average number of retweeters is 3.71, and the average number of mentioners is 8.80. And it also shows the intersections of the retweeters, mentioners and followers. From the intersections, we can calculate that for a user, 1.3% of her followers retweet her tweets in the 2-month dataset, 2.4% of her followers mention her in the 2-month dataset, and 0.7% of her followers both retweet her tweets and mention her in the 2-month dataset. From these statistics, we can see that simply picking up one's followers would not solve the prediction problem.

Figure 5 reports on the follower network degree distribution within the 15K active users. Figure 5(a) is on log-linear scale, while Figure 5(b) is on log-log scale. The distribution has an approximately straight-line form on the log-linear scale for majority part of the data, while it only shows part of straight-line form on the log-log scale (in the beginning and the tail), which means that the follower network within the 15K active users is more close to an exponential degree distribution in general, but for degree less than 100 or greater than 3000 it is more close to a power-law degree distribution. Figure 6 reports on the retweet network degree distribution and Figure 7 reports on the mention network degree distribution within the 15K active users in the 2-month period. Both retweet network and mention network have a power-law degree distribution (note the log-log scales used in Figure 6 and Figure 7).

## 5.4 Hybrid Network Correlation

We know that there are some correlation between different types of networks. As discussed in section 4, we used the metric of average Spearman's rank correlation coefficient to evaluate their correlation. For two network adjacency matrices $A$ and $B$, we calculated the Spearman's rank correlation coefficients of the corresponding rows of the two matrices, and then used the average value to represent the correlation of the two matrices.

**Table 4: Correlation to mention network adjacency matrix**

| | $R$ | $M$ | $F^*$ | $RR$ | $MM$ | $F^*F^*$ |
|---|---|---|---|---|---|---|
| $M$ | 0.653 | 1.000 | 0.222 | 0.578 | 0.475 | 0.076 |
| | $RM$ | $MR$ | $RF^*$ | $F^*R$ | $MF^*$ | $F^*M$ |
| $M$ | 0.571 | 0.489 | 0.535 | 0.128 | 0.444 | 0.120 |

Table 3 reports on the average Spearman's rank correlation of different types of networks to the retweet network constructed from the first 30-day training data. Table 4 reports on the average Spearman's rank correlation of different types of networks to the mention network constructed from the first 30-day training data. From the two tables, we can see that a network adjacency matrix has the highest correlation to itself and the matrices of different paths (or networks) show different correlations to the retweet adjacency matrix $R$ and mention adjacency matrix $M$. This indicates that different paths (or networks) should be given different credits for the prediction task. Furthermore, most of the correlation values are not shown to be close to 1, which demonstrates that this correlation metric would not be dominated by the sparseness of the network adjacency matrices. If they are dominated by the sparseness of the matrices, the correlation values should be very close to 1. We also have the following observations and indications:

- The correlation between $R$ and $M$ is stronger than the correlation between $R$ and $F^*$, and stronger than correlation between $M$ and $F^*$. This indicates that to predict retweeters, the feature of mentioners are more important than the feature of followers; similarly to predict mentioners, the feature of retweeters is more important than the feature of followers.

- The correlation between $R$ and $RF^*$ is stronger than the correlation between $R$ and $F^*R$. This indicates that for a user, the followers of his retweeters are more likely to retweet him than the retweeters of his followers.

- The correlation between $R$ and $MF^*$ is stronger than the correlation between $R$ and $F^*M$. This indicates that for a user, the followers of his mentioners are more likely to retweet him than the mentioners of his followers.

- The correlation between $M$ and $RF^*$ is stronger than the correlation between $M$ and $F^*R$. This indicates that for a user, the followers of his retweeters are more likely to mention him than the retweeters of his followers.

- The correlation between $M$ and $MF^*$ is stronger than the correlation between $M$ and $F^*M$. This indicates that for a user, the followers of his mentioners are more likely to mention him than the mentioners of his followers.

# 6. EVALUATION RESULTS

## 6.1 Baseline Methods

**NaiveHybrid**: This baseline method is to combine $R$, $M$, $F^*$ unweighted and calculate *Bonacich* metric at this combined network.
**BON:** This baseline method computes the Bonacich metric over the Retweet network and the Mention network, $R$ and $M$, for retweet prediction and mention prediction respectively.
**SVD:** This is a baseline method that is based on matrix factorization. *SVD* has been popularly applied for large sparse applications and recommender systems [16]. Specifically, suppose the singular value decomposition (SVD) of the adjacency $A$ is given by

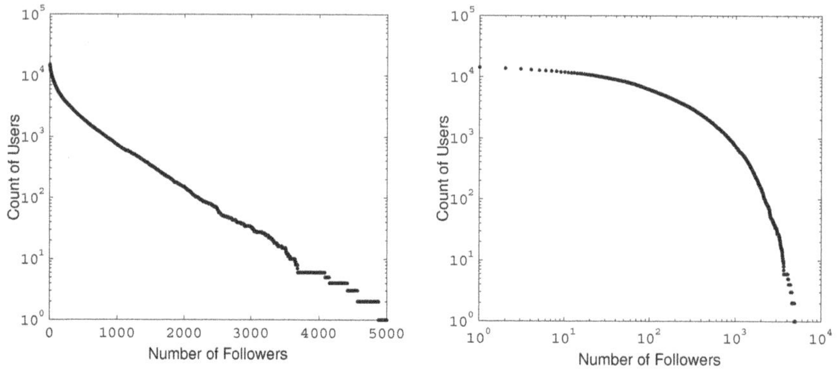


(a) log-linear scale (b) log-log scale

**Figure 5: Follower network degree distribution within the 15K active users. X axis is the number of followers; Y axis is the number of users that have the number of followers greater than or equal to the corresponding value on X axis.**

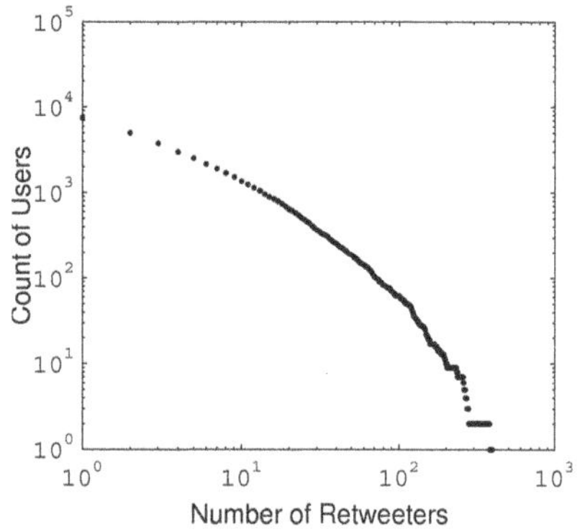


**Figure 6: Retweet network degree distribution within the 15K active users. X axis is the number of Retweeters; Y axis is the number of users that have the number of Retweeters greater than or equal to the corresponding value on X axis.**

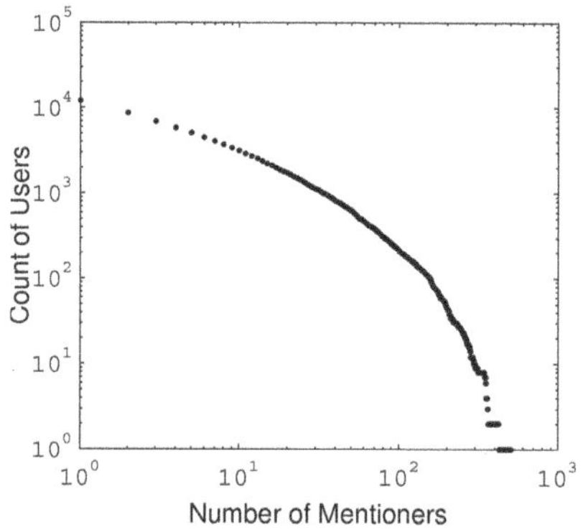


**Figure 7: Mention network degree distribution within the 15K active users. X axis is the number of mentioners; Y axis is the number of users that have the number of mentioners greater than or equal to the corresponding value on X axis.**

$A = U\Sigma V^T$, where $U$ and $V$ are orthogonal matrices, and $\Sigma$ is a diagonal matrix of singular values of $\delta_1 > \delta_2 ... > \delta_L > 0$. Let

$$A' = U_s \Sigma_s V_s^T \tag{10}$$

where $U_s$ and $V_s$ are created by the first $s$ columns of $U$ and $V$ and $\Sigma_s$ is the $s \times s$ principal submatrix of $\Sigma$. Then $A'$ is the matrix of scores for predicting future links.

For retweet prediction, $A$ will be set to the retweet adjacency matrix $R$. For mention prediction, $A$ will be set to the mention adjacency matrix $M$.

**SVD+BON:** This baseline method will apply the Bonacich metric to the score matrix $A'$ generated by the *SVD*.

**RankingSVM:** Finally, we consider a supervised learner. Ranking SVM [13] learns a ranking function from partial ranking training data. We provide several network based features to the SVM including the adjacency matrices of retweet counts, mention counts, and the edge weights of the adjusted follower network $F^*$.

## 6.2 Comparison wth Baseline Methods

Figure 8 reports on the MAP, NDCG@5 and NDCG@10 for retweet prediction. Figure 9 reports on the results for mention prediction. Both Figures 8 and 9 show that *hybridBON* has the best prediction accuracy. It dominates *NaiveHybrid* and *BON*. It also outperforms *SVD* and *SVD+BON*. *SVD+BON* does not show improvement over *BON*, which means that applying Bonacich metric to the score matrix from the output of *SVD* rather than the original matrix does not help.

Finally, *hybridBON* also outperforms a supervised learner *rankingSVM* using network based features. This demonstrates that our proposed solution *hybridBON*, inspired by the Bonacich metric based potential function and the hybrid network, can improve prediction accuracy. Further, while *hybridBON* is an unsupervised method that only estimates the future Bonacich potential and future hybrid network, it still has the best accuracy.

The performance accuracy appears to be higher for retweet prediction compared to mention prediction. We note that retweets reflect the influence of both a topic and a focal user, and this may explain the improved prediction accuracy.

To evaluate the running time of the solutions, we ran the Matlab code on Red Hat Enterprise Linux with Intel Core2 Quad Q8400, 4 cores and 12GB memory. Table 5 shows the running time for the methods except *RankingSVM*. *SVD* took around 11 hours; *BON* and *NaiveHybrid* took around 10 minutes; *SVD+BON* took more than 11 hours; *hybridBON* took around 30 minutes. To summarize, *hybridBON* and *BON* and *NaiveHybrid* are much more efficient than *SVD* and *SVD+BON*. We did not include the running time for *RankingSVM* in the table since it was not implemented in Matlab and hence it is not a good way to put them together. For *RankingSVM* it

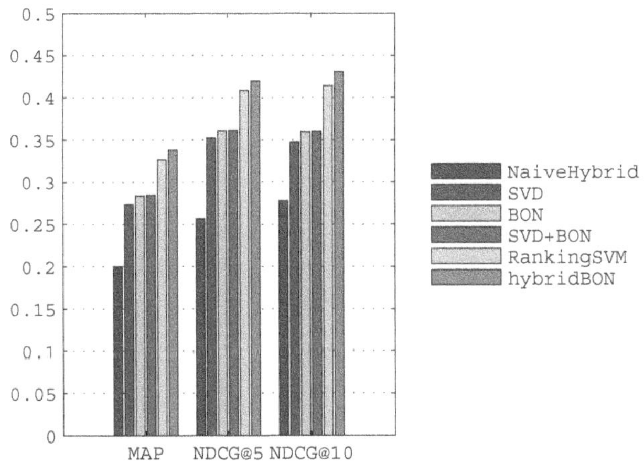


**Figure 8: The performance of the methods *NaiveHybrid*, *SVD*, *BON*, *SVD+BON*, *RankingSVM* and *hybridBON* for retweet prediction.**

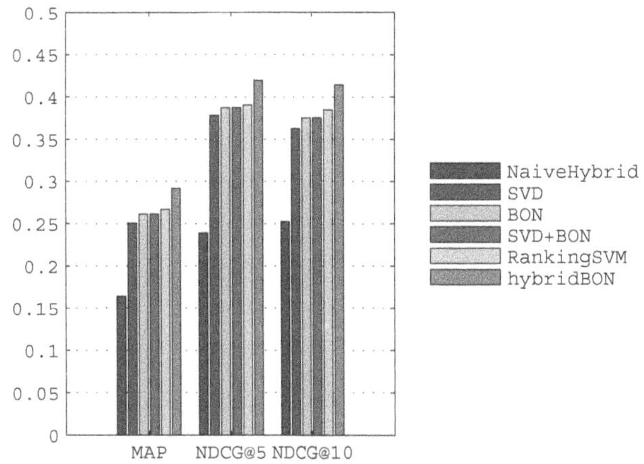


**Figure 9: The performance of the methods *NaiveHybrid*,*SVD*, *BON*, *SVD+BON*, *RankingSVM* and *hybridBON* for mention prediction.**

took us less than half an hour to train a model with a fixed trade-off parameter $C$. To tune the trade-off parameter $C$ for *RankingSVM*, it took pretty many rounds and pretty much time..

To explain, SVD has complexity $O(C \cdot N^3)$, where C is a constant and N is the matrix size. The complexity of *BON* is the complexity of matrix inversion. Matrix inversion has complexity $O(C \cdot N^3)$. However, Strassen's method for inversion has complexity $O(C \cdot N^{log_2(7)}) = O(C \cdot N^{2.807\ldots})$ to calculate the inversion of a completely general matrix. Further, the constant $C$ for SVD is bigger than the constant for matrix inversion and there are additional optimized solutions for matrix inversion on sparse matrices. The complexity of *hybridBON* is the complexity of calculating the parameters which is $O(C \cdot N^2)$ plus the complexity of *BON*. Thus, *BON* and *hybridBON* is more efficient than *SVD*.

We note that the research in [11] addressed a similar problem: given a tweet, does a focal user retweet the tweet. They used a matrix co-factorization (*coFM*) based solution for the objective function (`http://www.libfm.org/`), and they used stochastic gradient descent (*SGD*) for learning. While they do not provide details of execution time, we note that the computation of the many (content and network based) features that they use is likely to be quite expensive. They report on high MAP scores for their prediction which is appropriate since they use supervised learning.

To summarize, *hybridBON* is a fast approximate solution with good accuracy. Despite *hybridBon* only estimating the future Bonacich potential and future hybrid network, it shows the superiority of the Bonacich metric and hybrid network as features for link prediction. It outperforms a state of the art unsupervised approach based on singular value decomposition (*SVD*) in both accuracy and efficiency. *hybridBON* is also more accurate than a supervised approach based on *ranking SVM* that uses three network based features. While a supervised learning approach *coFM+SGD* in [11] may have higher accuracy, it used a large number of features and is likely to be computationally more expensive; the higher accuracy is expected from a supervised approach. In future work, we plan to explore supervised solutions using the Bonacich based feature.

## 6.3 Parameter Analysis

For method *hybridBON*, there are three parameters: $\alpha$, $\beta$, and $\varepsilon$. If we look at Eqations (5), (6) and (7), we can see that $\beta$ will only have impact on the absolute score values of the nodes, but will not have impact on their rankings and prediction output. For simplicity, we set $\beta = 1.0$. We conducted experiments to test the impact of the parameters $\alpha$ and $\varepsilon$ to the method *hybridBON*.

**Table 5: Running time of the methods SVD, BON, SVD+BON and hybridBON**

| Method | time |
|---|---|
| *NaiveHybrid* | 0.2 hour |
| *SVD* | 11 hours |
| *BON* | 0.2 hour |
| *SVD+BON* | 11.2 hours |
| *hybridBON* | 0.5 hour |

Figure 10 reports on the MAP values of *hybridBON* with respect to different $\varepsilon$ values, while keeping $\alpha$ and $\beta$ fixed. The figure shows that when $\varepsilon$ is greater than 0, the MAP values are pretty stable. When $\varepsilon$ value is around 3.5, the MAP value shows highest, and when $\varepsilon$ is bigger than 3.5 it decreases slowly. This tells us that method *hybridBON* is not sensitive to the values of parameter $\varepsilon$.

Figure 11 reports on the MAP values of *hybridBON* with respect to different $\alpha$ values, while keeping $\varepsilon$ and $\beta$ fixed. The figure shows that when $\alpha$ is less than 0.0005 and greater than 0, the MAP has pretty stable high values. When $\alpha$ value is is greater than 0.0005, the MAP values show significant decrease. So as long as we keeps $\alpha$ values less than some small value, the method *hybridBON* is not sensitive to the values of parameter $\alpha$.

# 7. CONCLUSIONS

In this paper, we address the microblog prediction problem by utilizing the hybrid networks. Given a focal user, we predict who will retweet her tweets and who will mention her in the near future. We propose a general prediction model to utilize the hybrid networks for the prediction and propose an approximate approach *hybridBON* based on the prediction model. Our solution *hybridBON* is based on a potential function over a hybrid network. The potential function converges to the Bonacich metric.

We found that for a focal user, the followers of his retweeters are more likely to retweet him than the retweeters of his followers, and the followers of his mentioners are more likely to mention him than the mentioners of his followers, and other path patterns.

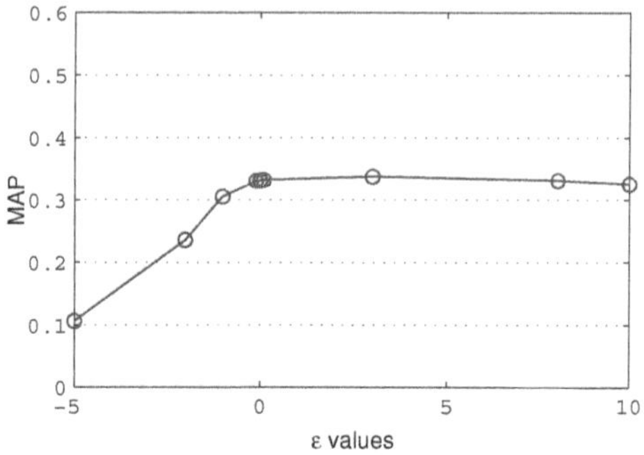


**Figure 10: The MAP values with respect to different $\varepsilon$ values for the *hybridBON* method for retweet prediction. Other parameters are fixed with $\alpha = 0.00005$ and $\beta = 1.0$.**

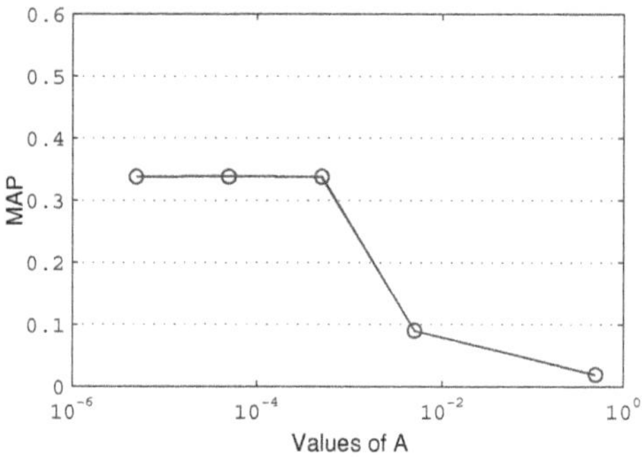


**Figure 11: The MAP values with respect to different $A$ values for the *hybridBON* method for retweet prediction. Other parameters are fixed with $\varepsilon = 3.5$ and $\beta = 1.0$.**

We demonstrate that *hybridBON* outperforms a state of the art baseline solution based on singular value decomposition *SVD*, and also outperforms *RankingSVM* with edge weight features of the networks. We note that *coFM-SGD* is a supervised approach using matric co-factorization and stochastic gradient based learning and has good accuracy on a similar problem.

Further, we note that there is little research on learning any centrality based objective function and in future work we will explore a supervised approach to *hybridBON*.

**Acknowledgements.** We thank Peratham Wiriyathammabhum for support on some experiments. This research is partially supported by NSF grant IIS1018361.

# 8. REFERENCES

[1] E. Bakshy, J. M. Hofman, W. A. Mason, and D. J. Watts. Everyone's an influencer: quantifying influence on twitter. In *WSDM*, 2011.

[2] P. Bonacich. Power and centrality: A family of measures. *The American Journal of Sociology*, 92(5):1170–1182, 1987.

[3] D. Centola. The spread of behavior in an online social network experiment. *Science*, 329(5996):1194–1197, 2010.

[4] M. Cha, H. Haddadi, F. Benevenuto, and K. Gummadi. Measuring user influence in twitter: The million follower fallacy. In *ICWSM*, 2010.

[5] W. Chen, C. Wang, and Y. Wang. Scalable influence maximization for prevalent viral marketing in large-scale social networks. In *SIGKDD*, 2010.

[6] W. L. Ferrar. Finite matrices. *Oxford Univ. Press*, 1951.

[7] M. Gjoka, M. Kurant, C. T. Butts, and A. Markopoulou. Walking in facebook: a case study of unbiased sampling of osns. In *INFOCOM*, 2010.

[8] J. Goldenberg, B. Libai, and E. Muller. Talk of the network: A complex systems look at the underlying process of word-of-mouth. *Marketing Letters*, 12(3):211–223, 2001.

[9] M. Gomez-Rodriguez, J. Leskovec, and A. Krause. Inferring networks of diffusion and influence. *ACM Trans. Knowl. Discov. Data*, 5(4):21:1–21:37, Feb. 2012.

[10] W. Hersh, C. Buckley, T. J. Leone, and D. Hickam. Ohsumed: an interactive retrieval evaluation and new large test collection for research. In *SIGIR*, 1994.

[11] L. Hong, A. S. Doumith, and B. D. Davison. Co-factorization machines: modeling user interests and predicting individual decisions in twitter. In *WSDM*, 2013.

[12] T. Ito, M. Shimbo, T. Kudo, and Y. Matsumoto. Application of kernels to link analysis. In *SIGKDD*, 2005.

[13] T. Joachims. Optimizing search engines using clickthrough data. In *SIGKDD*, 2002.

[14] L. Katz. A new status index derived from sociometric analysis. *Psychometrika*, 18:39–40, 1953.

[15] D. Kempe, J. Kleinberg, and E. Tardos. Maximizing the spread of influence through a social network. In *SIGKDD*, 2003.

[16] Y. Koren, R. Bell, and C. Volinsky. Matrix factorization techniques for recommender systems. *Computer*, 42(8):30–37, Aug. 2009.

[17] J. Kunegis and A. Lommatzsch. Learning spectral graph transformations for link prediction. In *ICML*, 2009.

[18] J. Leskovec and C. Faloutsos. Sampling from large graphs. In *SIGKDD*, 2006.

[19] D. Liben-Nowell and J. Kleinberg. The link prediction problem for social networks. In *CIKM*, 2003.

[20] C. Manning, P. Raghavan, and H. Schutze. *Introduction to Information Retrieval*. Cambridge University Press, 2008.

[21] W. Pan, N. Aharony, and A. Pentland. Composite social network for predicting mobile apps installation. In *AAAI*, 2011.

[22] H.-K. Peng, J. Zhu, D. Piao, R. Yan, and Y. Zhang. Retweet modeling using conditional random fields. In *ICDMW*, 2011.

[23] K. Subbian and P. Melville. Supervised rank aggregation for predicting influencers in twitter. In *SocialCom/PASSAT*, pages 661–665, 2011.

[24] J. Tang, J. Sun, C. Wang, and Z. Yang. Social influence analysis in large-scale networks. In *SIGKDD*, 2009.

[25] B. Taskar, M.-F. Wong, P. Abbeel, and D. Koller. Link prediction in relational data. In *NIPS*, 2003.

[26] C. Wang, V. Satuluri, and S. Parthasarathy. Local probabilistic models for link prediction. In *ICDM '07: Proceedings of the 2007 Seventh IEEE International Conference on Data Mining*, pages 322–331, 2007.

[27] S. Wu, L. Raschid, and W. Rand. Future link prediction in the blogosphere for recommendation. In *ICWSM '11: Proceedings of the International Conference on Weblogs and Social Media*, 2011.

[28] Z. Yang, J. Guo, K. Cai, J. Tang, J. Li, L. Zhang, and Z. Su. Understanding retweeting behaviors in social networks. In *CIKM '10: Proceedings of the 19th ACM International Conference on Information and Knowledge Management*, pages 1633–1636, 2010.

# Learning Social Network Embeddings for Predicting Information Diffusion

Simon Bourigault, Cedric Lagnier, Sylvain Lamprier, Ludovic Denoyer, Patrick Gallinari

Sorbonne Universités, UPMC Univ Paris 06, UMR 7606, LIP6, F-75005, Paris, France
CNRS, UMR 7606, LIP6, F-75005, Paris, France

firstname.lastname@lip6.fr

## ABSTRACT

Analyzing and modeling the temporal diffusion of information on social media has mainly been treated as a diffusion process on known graphs or proximity structures. The underlying phenomenon results however from the interactions of several actors and media and is more complex than what these models can account for and cannot be explained using such limiting assumptions. We introduce here a new approach to this problem whose goal is to learn a mapping of the observed temporal dynamic onto a continuous space. Nodes participating to diffusion cascades are projected in a latent representation space in such a way that information diffusion can be modeled efficiently using a heat diffusion process. This amounts to learning a diffusion kernel for which the proximity of nodes in the projection space reflects the proximity of their infection time in cascades. The proposed approach possesses several unique characteristics compared to existing ones. Since its parameters are directly learned from cascade samples without requiring any additional information, it does not rely on any pre-existing diffusion structure. Because the solution to the diffusion equation can be expressed in a closed form in the projection space, the inference time for predicting the diffusion of a new piece of information is greatly reduced compared to discrete models. Experiments and comparisons with baselines and alternative models have been performed on both synthetic networks and real datasets. They show the effectiveness of the proposed method both in terms of prediction quality and of inference speed.

## Categories and Subject Descriptors

I.2 [**Artificial Intelligence**]: Learning; E.1 [**Data**]: Data Structures—*Graphs and networks*

## Keywords

Machine learning; Information diffusion; Social networks


*WSDM'14*, February 24–28, 2014, New York, New York, USA.

ACM 978-1-4503-2351-2/14/02 ...$15.00.
http://dx.doi.org/10.1145/2556195.2556216.

## 1. INTRODUCTION

The emergence of Social Networks and Social Media sites has motivated a large amount of recent research. Various generic tasks, such as Social Network Analysis, Social Network annotation, Community Detection or Link Prediction, have been explored. An important research topic is the study of temporal propagation of information through this type of media. It aims at studying how interactions between users, such as sharing a link on Facebook or retweeting something on Twitter, effect the spread of items such as pictures, videos or gossip on the internet. While the study of this word-of-mouth phenomenon pre-dates the development of computer science, the amount of data made available by the growth of online social networks offers an unprecedented opportunity and has enabled new developments (see Section 4 for a review of related works). Most of the initial work in this area is derived from the literature on epidemiology or social science. Different propagation models such as the independent cascade models (IC) [7, 22] or the linear threshold models (LT) [13] have been developed or adapted to internet data. These models attempt to predict and understand the dynamic of observed propagation. Recently, works have also focused on prediction tasks such as *Buzz detection* - predicting whether a particular content will have an important impact over the network [20], *Opinion Leader identification*, detecting whether a node in a network will play an important role in content spread [13, 17], or *Diffusion prediction*, predicting which users (or nodes of the network) will be reached by a given piece of information in the future [19].

Most of the existing propagation models rely on a probabilistic modeling of information diffusion based on explicit relationships between nodes in the network. It has been shown that these models are well adapted when the underlying link structure is representative of the diffusion channels, but may suffer from different drawbacks when used on social networks extracted from the Web [19]. Since they rely on the structure of the network, these models assume that the information only propagates through links between users and usually aim at estimating propagation probabilities along these links. This limits their ability to explain future diffusion since the underlying process is much more complex : diffusion is the result of various interactions between heterogeneous users on several interleaving networks. Users interactions themselves are difficult to detect and quantify [25, 29]. Moreover, theses approaches, which usually come down to learning propagation paths along links of a graph, require a large amount of observations to avoid over-fitting.

Recently, various works have suggested to discover the implicit structure of diffusion from users' behaviours *before* modelling diffusion w.r.t. the extracted graph [29, 8, 25]. These works first find the graph structure that best explains observed diffusion under some hypothesis on the diffusion mechanics, and then use the extracted graph to perform prediction. These approaches are often grounded on a discrete cascading process - i.e., the information iteratively jumps from a user to another following some transfer probabilities on links. Such an iterative process implies successive decisions when inferring diffusion, which may lead to low performance results when mistakes are made at the early steps of the diffusion process. Moreover, inference by such models requires the use of expensive Monte-Carlo simulation techniques to predict the spread of information.

In this paper, we focus on modeling how information diffuses, with the goal of predicting which users will be contaminated by a particular content, knowing the user at the source of the diffusion. Instead of adopting a graph-based approach which would imply dealing with discrete structures, we propose to work in continuous spaces where we learn the temporal dynamics of diffusion from observations. Grounded on the heat diffusion theory, our approach consists in learning heat diffusion kernels that define, for each node of the network, its likelihood to be reached by the propagated information, given the initial source of diffusion. An advantage of this framework is that diffusion does not depend on a prior graph structure, and the model is directly built from observed diffusion cascades. Also, the use of a continuous space representation allows very fast inference when dealing with new cascades. The contribution of this paper is threefold:

- We present an original way to learn diffusion processes by embedding users in a continuous latent space.
- We propose an extension of the model allowing us to take into account the nature of the content being propagated, resulting in differentiated diffusion processes that depend on the features of the information that diffuses.
- We compare this approach with baseline and alternative methods on three corpora extracted from the Web and on synthetic datasets.

The paper is organized as follows: Section 2 defines the notations used throughout the paper, and presents our general approach and the models we propose. In Section 3, we compare our models to several baselines on real and artificial datasets. Section 4 reviews related work on the topic of diffusion in social networks. Finally, Section 5 concludes our works and gives some insight of possible future works.

## 2. NOTATIONS AND MODEL

Traditionally, diffusion on networks is represented with the notion of *cascade*. A cascade is a sequence of users infected by some information (for instance, it could be the list of users who "liked" a specific YouTube video). A cascade describes to whom and when an item spreads through the network, but not *how* diffusion happens: while it is easy to know *when* a user got infected by some content, it is usually not possible to know *who* infected him.

Given a social network composed of a set of $N$ users[1] $\mathcal{U} = (u_1, ...., u_N)$, cascades correspond to sets of users infected by the propagated information. Depending on the kind of network and the task in concern, the propagated information can for instance correspond to a given topic, a particular url, a specific tag, etc. In the following, we consider $\mathcal{C}$ to be a set of cascades over a given network, divided in two subsets of distinct cascades: $\mathcal{C}_\ell \subseteq \mathcal{C}$ the set of training cascades and $\mathcal{C}_t \subseteq \mathcal{C}$ the set of testing cascades. A cascade $c \in \mathcal{C}$ is defined as:

- A source $s^c \in \mathcal{U}$ which is the user at the source of the cascade - i.e, the first user that published the item concerned by the diffusion.
- A set of contaminated users $S^c \subset \mathcal{U}$ such that $u_i \in S^c$ means that $u_i$ has participated to the cascade $c$ - i.e., the user has performed some action (retweet, like, comment...) that is considered as an infection by $c$ (liking a video, publishing a tweet with a specific hashtag...); $\bar{S}^c$ is the set of users who have not participated in $c$.
- A contamination timestamp function defined over $S^c$ such that $t^c(u_i)$ corresponds to the timestamp at which $u_i \in S^c$ has first participated in the cascade. We consider that the contamination timestamp of the source is equal to 0.
- A feature vector $q_c \in \mathbb{R}^Q$ that characterizes the content of the cascade $c$, with $Q$ the size of the *content features space*[2]. This features vector is usually defined as the content of the publication.

### 2.1 Proposed Approach

The proposed models aim at predicting information diffusion. The central idea of these models is to map the observed information diffusion process into a heat diffusion process in a continuous (euclidean) space. To perform this, we learn diffusion kernels that capture the dynamics of diffusion from a set of training cascades. Let us denote $\mathcal{Z} = \mathbb{R}^n$ an euclidean space of $n$ dimensions - also called *latent space*[3]. Learning such a diffusion kernel comes down in our case to learning a mapping of each node of the network to a particular location in $\mathcal{Z}$ such that, for a given metric, the latent space explains the contamination timestamps observed in the training cascades. Figure 1 depicts a diffusion process where users have been projected in a latent space w.r.t. their timestamps of contamination in training cascades. This approach has several advantages:

- The learning problem is mapped to a continuous optimization problem that can easily be solved using classical optimization methods.
- The propagation model is learned directly from the observations, without the need of a graph structure, and without making strong assumptions about how information propagates.

[1]We talk about users throughout the paper, but the results remain valid for any other kinds of nodes.

[2]For example, when dealing with textual information, the feature vector $q_c$ may be a *tf-idf* vector.

[3]See Section 3 for a discussion concerning the choice of the dimension $n$

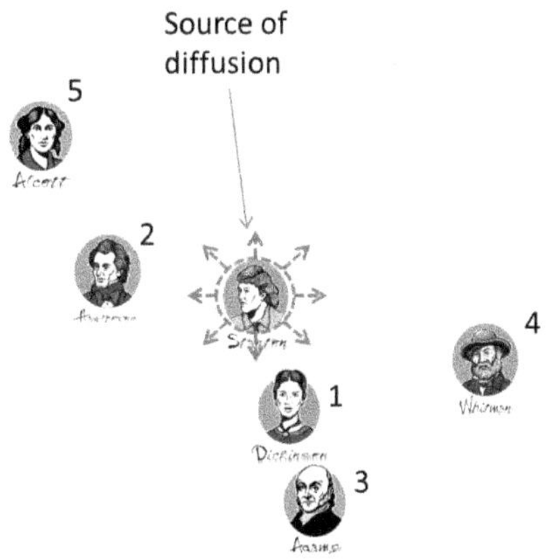


**Figure 1: Diffusion in a latent space: each user is associated with a location in this space. The source of the diffusion is at the center of the picture and information spreads uniformly from it in all directions. The numbers indicate the contamination order over the different users according to the modelized diffusion process: the closer a user is from the source, the sooner he is infected by information from the source.**

- The inference of the diffusion can be performed in the continuous space, which allows a very fast computation of the prediction without the need of an explicit discrete simulation. Simulation has an expensive processing cost and may lead to unreliable results, with a high variance between results of successive simulations of the same diffusion.
- Finally, the approach allows an easy integration of the content information by making the geometry of the latent space dependent on the information that spreads.

*Diffusion Kernel.*

Let us consider a geometric manifold $\mathcal{X}$. We define heat diffusion as a function $f(x,t) : \mathcal{X} \times \mathbb{R}^+ \rightarrow \mathbb{R}$ where $f(x,t)$ is the heat at location $x$ at time $t$. Such a process can be described by the following heat equations:

$$\begin{cases} \frac{\partial f}{\partial t} - \Delta f = 0 \\ f(x,0) = f_0(x) \end{cases} \quad (1)$$

where $f_0(x)$ is the initial condition of the process; $\Delta$ is the *Laplace operator.* The heat diffusion kernel is the fundamental solution to these heat diffusion equations in a specified domain with appropriate boundary conditions [11]. We define a diffusion kernel $K(t,y,x)$ such that $K : \mathbb{R}^+ \times \mathcal{X} \times \mathcal{X} \rightarrow \mathbb{R}$ computes the heat at location $x$ and time $t$ knowing that the heat source is $y$. It models the heat diffusion when an initial unit heat is positioned at location $y$ at time $t = 0$. This initial condition corresponds to:

$$K(0,y,x) = \delta(y - x) \quad (2)$$

where $\delta$ is the *dirac function.* In an Euclidean space of $n$ dimensions, the diffusion kernel can be written as:

$$K(t,y,x) = (4\pi t)^{-\frac{n}{2}} e^{-\frac{||y-x||^2}{4t}} \quad (3)$$

The diffusion kernel is at the root of our approach and will be used to model how information spreads between nodes of the network.

*Learning Diffusion Kernel in a Latent Space.*

While some works consider specific cases of heat diffusion based on the structure of the network [14, 17], we want our model to be independent from any predefined explicit network. For that we propose to model the information propagation in an Euclidean space using kernels as defined in equation 3 and to learn these kernels directly from observed cascades. The goal is thus to learn a representation of nodes in this latent space in a way that let the diffusion kernel explain the cascades observed in the training set. This can be seen as a problem of **learning the "best" diffusion kernel** w.r.t. a particular training set of cascades. Let us rewrite the diffusion kernel as a function $K(t, s^c, u_i)$ which returns a value corresponding to the contamination score of node $u_i$ at time $t$ knowing that the source of the contamination - the initial contaminated node - is $s^c$. We define $Z = (z_{u_1}, ..., z_{u_N})$ such that $z_{u_i} \in \mathbb{R}^n$ denotes the location of user $u_i$ in the latent space $\mathbb{R}^n$. The obtained diffusion kernel is:

$$K_Z(t, s^c, u_i) = (4\pi t)^{-\frac{n}{2}} e^{-\frac{||z_{s^c} - z_{u_i}||^2}{4t}} \quad (4)$$

The problem of modeling how information propagates corresponds to finding the optimal value of $Z$ according to every cascade $c \in \mathcal{C}$. The empirical risk of the model is then defined as:

$$\mathcal{L}(Z) = \sum_{c \in C_l} \Delta(K_Z(., s^c, .), c) \quad (5)$$

where $\Delta(K_Z(., s^c, .), c)$ is a measure of how much, given a source $s^c$, predictions performed by the diffusion kernel $K_Z$ differs from the observed diffusion in $c$. Different $\Delta$ functions can be defined and we focus on a particular case based on a ranking measure. The final learning problem is an optimization problem which consists in finding $Z^*$ such that:

$$Z^* = argmin_Z \mathcal{L}(Z) \quad (6)$$

*Learning Diffusion as a Ranking Problem.*

The diffusion kernel models the contamination propensity of *any* node at time $t$ given a particular information source. For learning the kernel function, there is however no full supervision available - this would correspond to a continuous time function giving the heat evolution at any point. The observations only provide the contamination time of the different nodes in a cascade. This partial supervision will be used to constrain the kernel to contaminate the different nodes **in their actual temporal order of infection**.

In practice, we will use the following constraints:

- Given two nodes $u_i$ and $u_j$ such that $u_i$ and $u_j$ are contaminated during cascade $c$ - i.e $u_i \in S^c$ and $u_j \in S^c$ - and respecting $t^c(u_i) < t^c(u_j)$, $K_Z$ must be defined such that $\forall t, K_Z(t, s^c, u_i) > K_Z(t, s^c, u_j)$
- Given two nodes $u_i$ and $u_j$ and a cascade $c$ such that $u_i$ is in $S^c$ and $u_j$ not in $S^c$, $K_Z$ must be defined such that $\forall t, K_Z(t, s^c, u_i) > K_Z(t, s^c, u_j)$

The constraints basically aim at finding embeddings such that users who are contaminated first are closer to the source of the contamination than users contaminated later (or not contaminated at all). With the expression of $K_Z$ given in equation 4, we can easily rewrite these two constraints as:

$$\begin{aligned}
&\forall (u_i, u_j) \in S^c \times S^c, \\
&\qquad t^c(u_i) < t^c(u_j) \Rightarrow ||z_{s^c} - z_{u_i}||^2 < ||z_{s^c} - z_{u_j}||^2 \\
&\forall (u_i, u_j) \in S^c \times \bar{S}^c, \\
&\qquad ||z_{s^c} - z_{u_i}||^2 < ||z_{s^c} - z_{u_j}||^2
\end{aligned} \tag{7}$$

By the use of classical hinge loss functions, these constraints can be handled by defining a ranking objective $\Delta_{rank}$ such as:

$$\begin{aligned}
&\Delta_{rank}(K_Z(., s^c, .), c) = \\
&\sum_{\substack{u_i, u_j \in S^c \times S^c \\ t^c(u_i) < t^c(u_j)}} max(0, 1 - (||z_{s^c} - z_{u_j}||^2 - ||z_{s^c} - z_{u_i}||^2)) \\
&+ \sum_{u_i, u_j \in S^c \times \bar{S}^c} max(0, 1 - (||z_{s^c} - z_{u_j}||^2 - ||z_{s^c} - z_{u_i}||^2))
\end{aligned} \tag{8}$$

## 2.2 Learning Algorithm

The final training objective is:

$$\mathcal{L}_{rank}(Z) = \sum_{c \in \mathcal{C}_\ell} \Delta_{rank}(K_Z(., s^c, .), c) \tag{9}$$

We name this model "Content diffusion Kernel" (CDK). Different methods can be used to optimize the objective function. We propose to use a classical stochastic gradient descent method, as illustrated in Algorithm 1, which iterates until a stop criterion is met (typically a number of iterations without significant improvement of the global loss). After having randomly initialized[4] all embeddings for users in $\mathcal{U}$ (line 3), the algorithm samples at each iteration a cascade $c$ from the training set $\mathcal{C}_\ell$ and two users $u_i$ and $u_j$ with $u_j$ a user that is either non-infected, or contaminated after $u_i$ in the diffusion process described by cascade $c$ (lines 6 to 8). If constraints defined in equation 7 are not respected with a sufficient margin[5] for this cascade $c$ and the pair of users $u_i$ and $u_j$, embeddings $z_{u_i}$, $z_{u_j}$ and $z_{s^c}$ are modified towards their respective steepest gradient direction with a learning rate $\alpha$ (lines 13 to 15) which is a decreasing function of the number of iterations.

### *Learning and Inference Complexity.*

Let $T$ be the number of iterations. The learning complexity is $O(T \times n)$, where $n$ is the size of the latent space. Once $Z$ has been learned, the inference process is simple. For a cascade $c \in C_t$, we just compute the distance between the user $s^c$ and every other user in $\mathcal{U}$. The inference complexity for every cascade is then $O(N \times n)$, where $N$ is the number of users. Considering that $n \ll N$, this turns out to be much smaller than the complexity of most alternative discrete methods. For instance, the inference step of the very famous Independant Cascade model[6], which is a probabilistic model where diffusion propabilities are defined on edges of the network's graph, requires to consider at each time step of the diffusion $t$ every possible infection situation at previous time $t-1$, which quickly becomes untractable. In practice, inference of graphical models is done by employing a Monte-Carlo approximation that consists in performing a high amount of simulations of the diffusion process starting from the source of the cascade and following the diffusion probabilities on links of the graph. The inference complexity of this approximation of IC is $O(r \times \hat{Succs} \times |\hat{S^c}|)$, where $|\hat{S^c}|$ is the average number of infected nodes in the performed simulations, $\hat{Succs}$ is their average outdegree and $r$ is the number of simulations used for the MCMC approximation. The weaker the probabilities defined on links are, the greater $r$ must be set to obtain a correct approximation of the distribution of final infection probabilities. More information about computation times are given in section 3.

[4]Different initialization strategies can be adopted. In our experiments, we used an uniform initialization between -1 and 1.

[5]As defined by the hinge loss function, see equation 8.

[6]We present details and results of this model in section 3

**Algorithm 1** Stochastic gradient descent algorithm

1: **procedure** SGD RANK DIFFUSION KERNEL LEARNING($\mathcal{U}, \mathcal{C}_\ell, T$)
2: $\quad\tau \leftarrow 0$
3: $\quad\forall u \in \mathcal{U}, z_u^{(\tau)} \leftarrow random$
4: $\quad$**while** $\tau < T$ **do**
5: $\quad\quad Z^{(\tau+1)} \leftarrow Z^{(\tau)}$
6: $\quad\quad$Sample $c \in \mathcal{C}_\ell$
7: $\quad\quad$Sample $u_i \in S^c$
8: $\quad\quad$Sample $u_j \in \mathcal{U}$ with $t^c(u_i) < t^c(u_j)$ or $u_j \in \bar{S}^c$
9: $\quad\quad d_i \leftarrow ||z_{s^c}^{(\tau)} - z_{u_i}^{(\tau)}||^2$
10: $\quad\quad d_j \leftarrow ||z_{s^c}^{(\tau)} - z_{u_j}^{(\tau)}||^2$
11: $\quad\quad \delta_d \leftarrow d_j - d_i$
12: $\quad\quad$**if** $\delta_d < 1$ **then**
13: $\quad\quad\quad z_{u_i}^{(\tau+1)} \leftarrow z_{u_i}^{(\tau)} + \alpha(\tau) \times 2(z_{s^c}^{(\tau)} - z_{u_i}^{(\tau)})$
14: $\quad\quad\quad z_{u_j}^{(\tau+1)} \leftarrow z_{u_j}^{(\tau)} + \alpha(\tau) \times 2(z_{u_j}^{(\tau)} - z_{s^c}^{(\tau)})$
15: $\quad\quad\quad z_{s^c}^{(\tau+1)} \leftarrow z_{s^c}^{(\tau)} + \alpha(\tau) \times 2(z_{u_i}^{(\tau)} - z_{u_j}^{(\tau)})$
16: $\quad\quad$**end if**
17: $\quad\quad \tau \leftarrow \tau + 1$
18: $\quad$**end while**
19: $\quad Z \leftarrow Z^{(\tau)}$
20: **end procedure**

## 2.3 Content-based Diffusion Kernel

We now propose an extension of the previous model able to take into account the content of each cascade by considering that different contents will propagate differently in the network. Our goal is thus to model different propagation schemes depending on the source and also on the content of the information that spreads. Our extension is based on the following ideas: (i) First, the propagation will still be modeled by a diffusion kernel in a latent space - each user corresponding to a particular location. (ii) Second, the content will influence **the metric** of the latent space - i.e instead of being isotropic around the source node projection for any content, propagation in the latent space will also depend on the content. Each possible content will then correspond to a specific metric in the latent space resulting in differentiated propagation schemes. The metrics and the users locations will be learned simultaneously from training cascades. In this work, the content metric has been developed in the way such that the content operates as an offset affecting the location of the source in the latent space[7] This model, named *Content-based Source Diffusion Kernel (CSDK)*, is described in the following.

We consider a parametrized function called *content embedding function* and denoted $f_\theta : \mathbb{R}^Q \rightarrow \mathbb{R}^n$. It will map any content information into a particular location in the latent space, $\theta$ being the set of parameters of this function[8]. The function will map two different contents $q_c$ and $q_{c'}$ to two different locations $f_\theta(q_c)$ and $f_\theta(q_{c'})$ in the latent space as illustrated in Figure 2. Let us define the new diffusion kernel as a function $K_{Z,\theta}^{CSDK}(q^c, t, s^c, u_i)$ which measures the contamination of user $u_i$ at time $t$ knowing that the source of the diffusion is $s^c$ and the content of the cascade is $q^c \in \mathbb{R}^Q$. In order to consider both the source of the contamination and the content that diffuses, based on the *content embedding function* $f_\theta$, we propose to model $K^{CSDK}$ such that:

$$K_{Z,\theta}^{CSDK}(q^c, t, s^c, u_i) = (4\pi t)^{-\frac{n}{2}} e^{-\frac{||z_{s^c} + f_\theta(q^c) - z_{u_i}||^2}{4t}} \quad (10)$$

The location of the source $z_{s^c} + f_\theta(q^c)$ now depends on both the latent representation of the source user $s^c$ and on the embedded content $f_\theta(q^c)$. Two different contents will thus correspond to two different initial locations, resulting in two different diffusion kernels - see Figure 2.

The content embedding function and the users locations will be learned simultaneously, resulting in learning problem that consists in minimizing on both $\theta$ and $Z$ the following objective function:

$$\mathcal{L}_{CSDK}(Z) = \sum_{c \in \mathcal{C}_\ell} \Delta_{rank}(K_{Z,\theta}^{CSDK}(q^c, ., s^c, .), c) \quad (11)$$

The final learning problem can thus be written as:

$$\Delta_{rank}(K_{Z,\theta}^{CSDK}(q^c, ., s^c, .), c) = \sum_{\substack{u_i \in S^c \\ u_j \in S^c \\ t^c(u_i) < t^c(u_j)}} max(0, 1 - (||z_{s^c} + f_\theta(q^c) - z_{u_j}||^2 - ||z_{s^c} + f_\theta(q^c) - z_{u_i}||^2)) + \sum_{\substack{u_i \in S^c \\ u_j \in \bar{S^c}}} max(0, 1 - (||z_{s^c} + f_\theta(q^c) - z_{u_j}||^2 - ||z_{s^c} + f_\theta(q^c) - z_{u_i}||^2)) \quad (12)$$

and is optimized using a stochastic gradient descent method similar to the one presented previously.

# 3. EXPERIMENTS

## 3.1 Datasets

We tested our models on several datasets from various online sources as well as artificial ones.

### *Real-world datasets.*

We have used three datasets extracted from the Web:

- The first dataset comes from the International AAAI Conference on Weblogs and Social Media 2009 (*ICWSM*) which published a corpus containing 44 millions blog posts collected over a 1-year period [4]. We consider each blog to be a "user" in the social network and cascades are composed of sets of posts which are linked to each other: each connected component of the posts graph is a cascade. A cascade is then represented by a set of users (authors of the posts composing the cascade) and by the timestamps at which they have been infected (timestamps of the posts). We also extracted an oriented graph using hyperlinks : if there is at least one link from a post of user $a$ to a post of user $b$ in the training set, we create a link $b \rightarrow a$. This graph is needed by some of the baseline models used in the experiments, but not by our models.

- The second dataset is extracted from *Memetracker* corpus described in [16]. This corpus contains articles from news websites and blogs, collected during the 2008 US presidential campaign. The corpus is built by tracing the flow of short phrases or *memes* through the web. This dataset is similar to ICWSM and we have defined users, cascades and the social graph the same way. The main difference is the lack of posts content, so we did not apply the CSDK model on this dataset.

- The third dataset is extracted from Digg, which is a collaborative news portal on which users can post links to *stories* (articles, blog posts, videos...). Other users can then "digg" these stories if they like it. Stories appear on the front page of Digg based on the amount of "diggs" they have. We use stories as cascades, each "digg" given by a user being considered as a user contamination. We used the Digg stream API to collect the *complete* Digg history (every single story posted, all diggs, and all comments) during a one month time window. We built a graph, which will be used by the IC and Graph diffusion baselines, in the following way:

[7]different possibilities have been tested and this one offered a good compromise

[8]We consider here that $f_\theta$ is a linear function

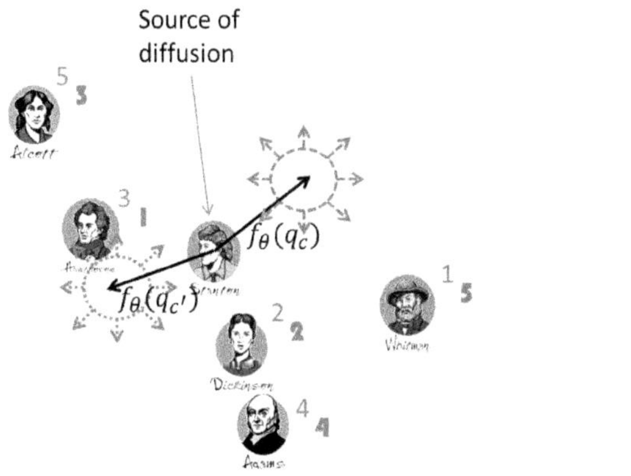


Figure 2: CDSK Diffusion model: The source of the diffusion is a translation of the source user by a vector $f_\theta(q^c)$ that depends on the content of the cascade. Here, two different contents $q_c$ and $q_{c'}$ spread from the source user and correspond to two different embedded locations $f_\theta(q_c)$ and $f_\theta(q_{c'})$. Even if they have the same source, these two cascades thus corresponds to two different source locations in the latent space. The two numbers near each user indicate the contamination order by the two contents.

for each user $a$ who has digged a post created by user $b$, we create a link $b \rightarrow a$ in the graph.

We filtered the users of each dataset to keep about 5000 users with the most posts. Table 1 gives some statistics about the datasets sizes.

*Synthetic Data.*

In order to better understand how the CSDK model handles the content information, we have also generated synthetic datasets for which we can control the correlation between the content information and the diffusion behavior. In order to generate such datasets, we consider that any cascade content is composed of *one* word $w$ in a set of $Q$ possible words. For each word, the diffusion follows a particular IC model denoted $E_w$ where $E_w$ is the transition matrix between nodes - i.e the diffusion probability. The $Q$ transitions matrices are generated randomly: 99 % of the values in these matrices are equal to 0 and, all remaining values are sampled between 0 and 0.01, resulting in sparse matrices. To generate a new cascade, we first randomly choose a source user $u$ and a content word $w$, and use the corresponding transition matrix $E_w$ to generate the cascade. By making the value of $Q$ higher, we obtain more complex propagation schemes. Note that if $Q = 1$, our generation method corresponds to a classical single IC model. In these datasets we have used 10000 cascades as training cascades, and 10000 cascades for test with a set of 1000 users.

## 3.2 Evaluation Measures

For each dataset the cascade set $C$ is divided in two subsets $C_\ell$ and $C_t$, for training and testing purposes. Our goal is to retrieve, for each cascade in the testing set, which user(s) will eventualy be infected. This can be seen as an Information Retrieval task, with cascades as "queries" and users as "documents". We evaluate the performance through Mean Average Precision (MAP) and Precision-Recall curves. For every cascade in the testing set, each model predicts a "contamination score" for each user in the testing set, indicating how likely that user is to be infected by this cascade. We then sort users in descending order and use Mean Average Precision to evaluate our performance as it is done in [6]. Let $\sigma_{c,k}$ be the rank of user $u_k$ for cascade $c$. Let $P_{c,k}$ be the precision at rank $k$ for cascade $c$, i.e. the percentage of infected users among the top k users in the ranking order. Mean Average precision is defined as:

$$MAP = \frac{1}{|C_t|} \sum_{c \in C_t} \frac{\sum_{u_k \in S^c} P_{c,\sigma_{c,k}}}{|S^c|}$$

We also use Precision-Recall curves to visualize performances. Most cascades do not reach more than 1 or 2 users leading to a small number of recall points. We then show the average precision at each recall point instead of precision at a recall value. Consequently, only a few cascades contain a lot of users and there is a higher variance for high recall points.

Note that each experiment has been done 10 times and the results are the average over the 10 different runs.

## 3.3 Baselines

We compare our models to several baselines and state-of-the-art models. We first used two naive baselines:

- **Nb_App**: For each user, we count the proportion of cascades in the training set he participates in. We then use that value as an infection score for that user in every cascade in the testing set. It corresponds to a propensity to be infected by any cascade.
- **Mean_rank**: In this model, the contamination score of any user $u_i$ is the inverse of the average rank of this user in the training cascades: the sooner $u_i$ tends to be infected by cascades in the training set, the higher his infection score for cascades from the testing set.

In addition to these baselines, we compare our approaches to state-of-the-art models:

- **IC model**: We implemented the classic independent cascade model (IC) which is usually used in the literature as a comparison method. IC uses the social graph, and works in a discrete way: when a user $u_i$ becomes infected at time step $t$, every neighbour $u_j$ of $u_i$ has a probability $p_{i,j}$ to become infected at time step $t + 1$. In the learning phase, all $p_{i,j}$ are learnt in an EM-fashion [22]. Since this is a stochastic model, it is hard to compute the actual probability for a user to become infected at some point in the process. We thus use a Monte-Carlo approximation: given an initialy infected user, we run a large number of simulations. The final contamination score of each user is equal to the number of simulations in which he was infected. Note that, temporal extensions of the IC model have been proposed, but since they did not allow better results in this experimental protocol [15] they were not been used in our experiments.
- **Netrate**: We show results for the *exponential* version of the NETRATE model described in [8]. NETRATE is used here as a state-of-the-art method which does not need the knowledge of the network structure to predict how information propagates, which is also the case of our approaches. Note that different variants of this model exists (*power law* and *rayleigh* - [8]) that obtain similar results. NETRATE is briefly described in Section 4.
- **Graph Diffusion**: At last, we also compare our methods with the model proposed in [17, 11] which is based on a graph diffusion kernel that shares some similarities with the methods we propose. In this model, instead of *learning the best kernel* as we do, the authors of the paper define a particular kernel over the structure of the network. This kernel models the fact that the temperature of any node in the graph diffuses equally on the different outgoing links. In comparison to our approach, the diffusion model is not learned over the set of training cascades, and clearly depends on the knowledge of the network structure.

We do not compare to models like [15] or [23] which also make use of the content because they need a user profile which is not available in our datasets.

## 3.4 Results

### 3.4.1 Models without content

Table 2 shows the mean average precision (MAP) for all models on the 3 real datasets. First, we can see that all other baselines models perform worse than the IC model.

| | Nb. of Users | Nb. of Links | Nb. of train Cascades | Nb. of test Cascades | Avg cascade size |
|---|---|---|---|---|---|
| meme | 5000 | 4372 | 2377 | 600 | 2.17 |
| icwsm | 5000 | 17746 | 19027 | 4711 | 2.22 |
| digg | 4751 | 71263 | 150000 | 66744 | 2.43 |

**Table 1: Some statistics about our real datasets.**

| Model | $n$ | Memetracker | ICWSM | Digg |
|---|---|---|---|---|
| CDK | 5 | 0,176 | 0,660 | 0.170 |
| | 10 | 0.257 | 0.721 | 0.212 |
| | 30 | 0.344 | 0.769 | 0.273 |
| | 50 | 0.355 | 0.774 | 0.285 |
| | 100 | 0.347 | 0.771 | 0.282 |
| | 200 | 0.357 | **0.776** | 0.302 |
| | 500 | 0.363 | 0.773 | 0.280 |
| CSDK | 5 | - | 0.605 | 0.255 |
| | 10 | - | 0.663 | 0.304 |
| | 30 | - | 0.714 | 0.348 |
| | 50 | - | 0.731 | **0.352** |
| | 100 | - | 0.744 | 0.352 |
| | 200 | - | 0.732 | 0.350 |
| | 500 | - | 0.748 | 0.351 |
| IC | | 0.372 | 0.712 | 0.197 |
| Netrate | | 0.287 | 0.187 | 0.162 |
| Graph Diff. | | **0.374** | 0.483 | 0.082 |
| Nb_App | | 0.180 | 0.112 | 0.077 |
| Mean_Rank | | 0.187 | 0.121 | 0.206 |

**Table 2: Results on 3 real datasets: *Memetracker*, *ICWSM* amd *Digg*. Results of CDK and CSDK are given for several values of $n$, the dimension of the latent space $\mathcal{Z}$.**

This is not surprising for *Nb_App* and *Mean_Rank* which are based on naive heuristics. The low performance of the NetRate model is due to the fact that the learning process it relies on requires too large amounts of training data to avoid over-training when used to predict information diffusion. At last, the Graph diffusion approach outperforms IC on the MemeTracker dataset but gives lower performance on the two other corpora showing that the assumptions it is based on are less adapted to the three datasets than the IC assumption concerning how information spreads.

If we compare our approach (CDK) with IC, we see that on the *Memetracker* and *ICWSM* datasets they both obtain similar results, and CDK clearly outperforms IC on the *Digg* dataset. Note, that, like NETRATE, our method is not based on any knowledge concerning the structure of the network meaning that this algorithm is able to do as well or better than IC, using less information. The performance of the CDK model also depends on the size of the latent space: a smaller space gives lower predictions quality, while a larger space can tend to overfit.

Concerning the inference times, the CDK model takes around 15 minutes to infer all scores for all cascades on the *Digg* dataset. In comparison, IC model needs more than 1 day and NETRATE model, which is one complexity degree above IC, takes a few days. All these experiments have been done on a standard desktop computer.

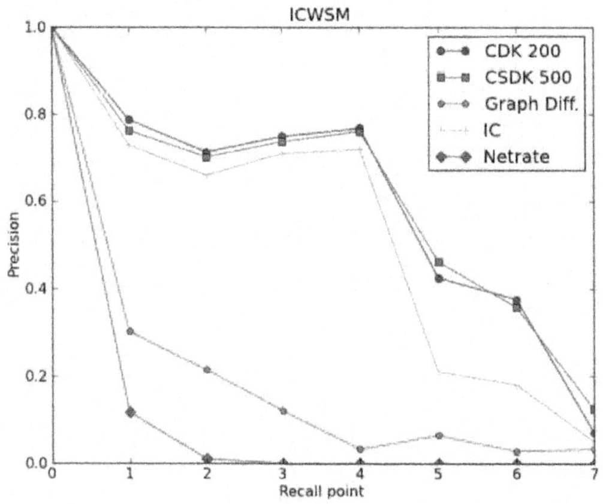


**Figure 3: Precision at recall points for the main models on the ICWSM dataset. Results of CDK and CSDK are given for specific latent space dimensionality.**

### 3.4.2 *Integration of content*

When comparing the Content based approach (CSDK) with the other models (Table 2), we can see that the integration of the content degrades the performance on the ICWSM dataset, but clearly increases the predictions quality over the Digg dataset. Actually, the quality of this model depends on the information given by the content of each cascade; in the case of ICWSM, the content is noisy due to the way it has been captured (using RSS feeds that only give part of the content of the blog posts), while the Digg content is clearly more informative since it is composed of the full content of news articles.

In order to further explore and better understand how the CSDK model depends on the quality of the content, we have performed experiments on synthetic datasets with different content sizes (see Table 3). First, one can see that the performance of all the algorithms degrades when the variance of the content (number of words considered) increases. The task becomes more and more complex when multiple content information is considered. CDSK degrades less than all other approaches and is still able to obtain good performance. It always outperforms state-of-the-art methods. These experiments show that CSDK is more robust to a complex content-dependent propagation scheme than classical approaches.

Finally, Figures 3 and 4 gives more details concerning the precision of each model at different recall points - we have only drawn the "best" versions of CDK and CSDK. On these curves, one can see that our methods obtain a better precision than classical methods, and that CSDK clearly outperforms CDK on the Digg dataset.

| Model | $n$ | 5 words | 10 words | 20 words | 30 words | 40 words | 50 words |
|---|---|---|---|---|---|---|---|
| CDK | 10 | 0.323 | 0.205 | 0.147 | 0.111 | 0.102 | 0.098 |
| | 30 | 0.422 | 0.301 | 0.207 | 0.146 | 0.128 | 0.121 |
| | 50 | 0.414 | 0.304 | 0.207 | 0.158 | 0.136 | 0.128 |
| | 100 | 0.430 | 0.304 | 0.210 | 0.155 | 0.140 | 0.126 |
| CSDK | 10 | 0.394 | 0.243 | 0.184 | 0.139 | 0.135 | 0.124 |
| | 30 | 0.605 | 0.442 | 0.301 | 0.218 | 0.200 | 0.179 |
| | 50 | 0.615 | 0.466 | **0.346** | 0.259 | 0.234 | 0.219 |
| | 100 | **0.631** | **0.469** | 0.343 | **0.271** | **0.248** | **0.228** |
| IC | | 0.482 | 0.317 | 0.211 | 0.163 | 0.125 | 0.111 |
| Netrate | | 0.289 | 0.150 | 0.175 | 0.137 | 0.017 | 0.017 |
| Graph Diff. | | 0.308 | 0.091 | 0.081 | 0.084 | 0.073 | 0.076 |
| Nb_App | | 0.118 | 0.101 | 0.088 | 0.085 | 0.079 | 0.081 |
| Mean_Rank | | 0.209 | 0.196 | 0.165 | 0.160 | 0.151 | 0.143 |

**Table 3: Results (MAP values) of our models and baselines n artificial datasets generated with different number of words. Results of CDK and CSDK are given for several values of $n$, the dimension of the latent space $\mathcal{Z}$.**

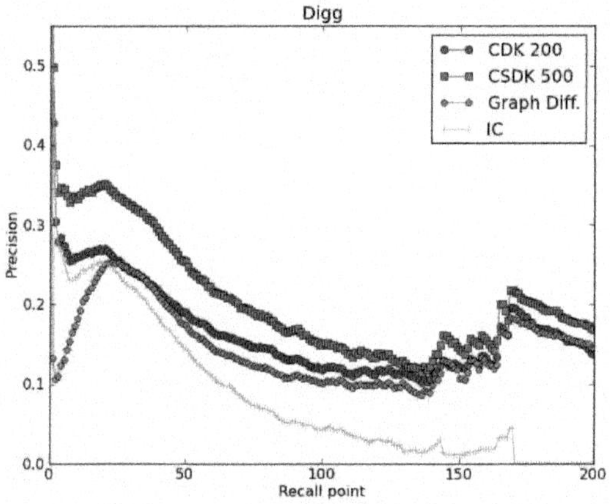


**Figure 4: Precision at recall points for the main models on the Digg dataset. Results of CDK and CSDK are given for specific latent space dimensionality.**

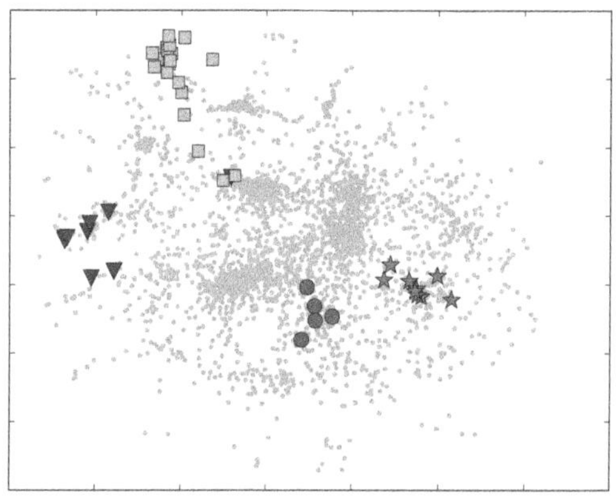

**Figure 5: The Digg dataset users in 2D. Light gray dots represent users, and groups of identical symbols represent four cascades from the testing set.**

## 3.5 Discussion

While information diffusion in social network is a widely studied topic (see next section), the concept has not been clearly defined. The phenomenon itself is quite rare: only a very small fraction of the information generated each day on the internet will become popular and "viral". In our datasets, most cascades only reach a small percentage of the user set (see table 1). Because of this sparsity, learning the dynamics of users interactions turns out to be quite difficult. In this paper, we project users in a euclidean space in which we use a distance to represent the diffusion. This gives our CDK model an important property: for any triplet of users $(u_i, u_j, u_k)$, we have the triangle inequality $||z_i - z_j||^2 \leq ||z_i - z_k||^2 + ||z_k - z_j||^2$. This means that if users $u_i$ and $u_j$ never interact each with the other in training but both interacts with some third user $u_k$, our model tends to set $u_i$ and $u_j$ to be relatively close. A model like IC is unable to learn such a property. In order to better visualize this ability to regroup users with similar activities, we have trained a CDK model with a latent space of size $n = 2$ on the Digg corpus and propose to visualize how users have been projected onto this space (Figure 5). We have highlighted users involved in different randomly chosen cascades extracted from the test set. From this figure, we can see that our model naturally tends to build clusters, each cluster corresponding to a group of users generally involved in the same cascades. We suppose that this ability to group users with the "same behavior" opens the door to other usages of our method, particularly concerning the use of CDK and CSDK for visualization softwares that could allow people to understand the different spreading schemes for a particular dataset. In the CDK model, using a distance also mean that we consider diffusion to be symetric, i.e. diffusion from $u_i$ to $u_j$ is identical to diffusion from $u_j$ to $u_i$. This is a strong hypothesis which has been recently discussed [3]. We are currently experimenting an extension of this work where users are projected at different locations of the space whether they are senders or receivers of the propagated content.

## 4. RELATED WORK

Historically, the diffusion process has been studied in the context of product adoption in [1]. In this work, the author models product adoption by consumers as a function of time with two parameters: the influence of word-of-mouth and the weight of a marketing campaign. In the early 2000s, the availability of large amount of internet data enabled researchers to suggest methods based on the social graph like the Independent Cascade model (IC) [7, 22] and the Linear Threshold models (LT) [13], both modeling a user-to-user contamination process. Since then, the rapid growth of social websites like Facebook or Twitter has triggered many new developments.
Several extensions of IC and LT have been proposed. For instance, [21] proposed an asynchronous extension of the IC model (ASIC) which enables IC to integrate the temporal dimension. In [17, 11], a heat diffusion process occurring on the social graph is used to model interactions between users. As we have seen in this paper, many cascades cannot be explained using only user interactions. In [23], the authors take users profiles into account to infer the probability of diffusion. [12] or [15] use information content and user profiles to infer the contamination. The same idea has been used in [26] which integrates the content of tweets to predict the probabilities of diffusion between users. It is important to note that all these models make the assumption that the graph on which the propagation occurs is known. This turns out to be a strong hypothesis: the social graph defined by an online social network (friends, followers, subscriptions...) is often incomplete, irrelevant [25] or unknown. To overcome this limitation, two main families of methods have been studied.

- A first family consists of link prediction methods: given an online social network population and a set of observations (shopping habits, movie reviews, hashtags usage...), the goal is to predict a set of links (followers, friends, influencers...) that best explains the observed user actions. These models have not been designed specifically for diffusion prediction, but they all model the propagation process to infer the most plausible links. NetInf [9] and then Connie [18] use a greedy algorithm to find a fixed number of links between users that maximize the likelihood of a set of observed diffusions under an IC-like diffusion hypothesis. A more general framework have been proposed in [8] where the Netrate model, used in our experiments as a baseline, is used to predict the user-to-user contamination. Netrate is a cascade model like IC: it aims at finding propagation probabilities between pairs of users. The first improvement with regard to IC is that they do not use the social graph, they directly infer probabilities from observed diffusions. Secondly, they use an exponential delay to infer the time after which the diffusion occurs. These works have later been extended in [10]. Recently, [25] used transfer entropy to compute the inter-user influence and infer a graph containing the most "predictive" links.

- The second family makes use of statistical learning instead of using graph-based approaches. One very simple yet efficient method is to study the relation between the number of infected users after a short period of time and after a longer period [24]. [29] predicts the volume of diffusion based on the infection time of a selected subset of users.

The models we have introduced in this article do not need any social graph and are based on a new approach where the propagation is modeled as a heat diffusion process in a continuous latent space. Heat diffusion processes, and particularly diffusion kernels, have been studied recently for different applications: classification [14], dimensionality reduction [27], and also to rank nodes [28]. The work that is closest to our is the one in [17] where the authors use a diffusion kernel to select marketing candidates. The main difference is that we learn the diffusion kernel from data when they use a predefined graph kernel.

At last, the idea of projecting discrete relational data onto a continuous space had already been proposed for different tasks. For example, in [5], the authors propose to learn embeddings for the nodes of a graph such that the resulting distances between vectors is "as close as possible" to the original distance between vertices in the graph. More recently, learning embeddings has also been used for coding relational databases [2].

## 5. CONCLUSION

We have presented a new family of information diffusion models based on the heat diffusion kernel. Their originality is to formulate diffusion as a process in a continuous space, built using an embedding of the nodes learned from observed cascades. These models have some interesting characteristics 1) they learn directly from the observations and therefore do not require a predefined diffusion graph structure which is often not available for social applications. 2) they run much faster (1 or 2 orders of magnitude) than classical discrete models due to the continuous context and 3) they allow an easy integration of the content by modifying the geometry of the latent space. Performance obtained on real-world and artificial datasets show the ability of these methods to model information spread, and to take into account the content information in the diffusion process. They are competitive with and sometimes better than state of the art reference models.

Two research directions are currently considered: the first one consists in developing alternative models for a better use of the content information. Particularly, we are studying **metric learning** paradigms that should offer new possibilities to incorporate this information in the geometry of the latent space. A second direction consists in applying these methods to other diffusion tasks not restricted to social networks.

## 6. ACKNOWLEDGMENTS

This work has been partially supported by the DIFAC FUI project and the ANR (French National Research Agency) MLVIS project

## 7. REFERENCES

[1] F. M. Bass. A new product growth for model consumer durables. *Management Science*, 15:215–227, 1969.

[2] A. Bordes, J. Weston, R. Collobert, and Y. Bengio. Learning structured embeddings of knowledge bases. In *AAAI*, 2011.

[3] R. Bosagh Zadeh, A. Goel, K. Munagala, and A. Sharma. On the precision of social and information networks. In *Proceedings of the first ACM conference on Online social networks*, pages 63–74. ACM, 2013.

[4] K. Burton, A. Java, and I. Soboroff. The icwsm 2009 spinn3r dataset. In *Proceedings of the Third Annual Conference on Weblogs and Social Media*, May 2009.

[5] M. Chen, Q. Yang, and X. Tang. Directed graph embedding. In *IJCAI*, pages 2707–2712, 2007.

[6] W. Feng and J. Wang. Retweet or not?: personalized tweet re-ranking. In *Proceedings of the sixth ACM international conference on Web search and data mining*, WSDM '13. ACM, 2013.

[7] J. Goldenberg, B. Libai, and E. Muller. Talk of the network: A complex systems look at the underlying process of word-of-mouth. *Marketing letters*, 12(3):211–223, 2001.

[8] M. Gomez-Rodriguez, D. Balduzzi, and B. Schölkopf. Uncovering the temporal dynamics of diffusion networks. In *Proceedings of the 28th International Conference on Machine Learning (ICML-11)*, ICML '11, pages 561–568. ACM, 2011.

[9] M. Gomez Rodriguez, J. Leskovec, and A. Krause. Inferring networks of diffusion and influence. In *Proceedings of the 16th ACM SIGKDD international conference on Knowledge discovery and data mining*, KDD '10, New York, NY, USA, 2010. ACM.

[10] M. Gomez-Rodriguez, J. Leskovec, and B. Schölkopf. Modeling information propagation with survival theory. In *ICML*, 2013.

[11] A. Grigoryan. *Heat Kernel and Analysis on Manifolds.* AMS/IP Studies in Advanced Mathematics. American Mathematical Society, 2009.

[12] A. Guille and H. Hacid. A predictive model for the temporal dynamics of information diffusion in online social networks. In *Proceedings of the 21st international conference companion on World Wide Web*, WWW '12 Companion. ACM, 2012.

[13] D. Kempe, J. Kleinberg, and E. Tardos. Maximizing the spread of influence through a social network. In *Proceedings of the ninth ACM SIGKDD international conference on Knowledge discovery and data mining*, KDD '03, pages 137–146. ACM, 2003.

[14] R. I. Kondor and J. Lafferty. Diffusion kernels on graphs and other discrete input spaces. In *ICML*, volume 2, pages 315–322, 2002.

[15] C. Lagnier, L. Denoyer, E. Gaussier, and P. Gallinari. Predicting information diffusion in social networks using content and user's profiles. In *European Conference on Information Retrieval*, ECIR '13, 2013.

[16] J. Leskovec, L. Backstrom, and J. Kleinberg. Meme-tracking and the dynamics of the news cycle. In *Proceedings of the 15th ACM SIGKDD international conference on Knowledge discovery and data mining*, KDD '09, pages 497–506, New York, NY, USA, 2009. ACM.

[17] H. Ma, H. Yang, M. R. Lyu, and I. King. Mining social networks using heat diffusion processes for marketing candidates selection. In *Proceedings of the 17th ACM conference on Information and knowledge management*, CIKM '08, pages 233–242, New York, NY, USA, 2008. ACM.

[18] S. A. Myers and J. Leskovec. On the convexity of latent social network inference. *CoRR*, abs/1010.5504, 2010.

[19] A. Najar, L. Denoyer, and P. Gallinari. Predicting information diffusion on social networks with partial knowledge. In *Proceedings of the 21st international conference companion on World Wide Web*, WWW '12 Companion, pages 1197–1204, New York, NY, USA, 2012. ACM.

[20] D. M. Romero, B. Meeder, and J. Kleinberg. Differences in the mechanics of information diffusion across topics: idioms, political hashtags, and complex contagion on twitter. In *Proceedings of the 20th international conference on World wide web*, pages 695–704. ACM, 2011.

[21] K. Saito, M. Kimura, K. Ohara, and H. Motoda. Generative models of information diffusion with asynchronous timedelay. *Journal of Machine Learning Research - Proceedings Track*, 13:193–208, 2010.

[22] K. Saito, R. Nakano, and M. Kimura. Prediction of information diffusion probabilities for independent cascade model. In *Proceedings of the 12th international conference on Knowledge-Based Intelligent Information and Engineering Systems, Part III*, KES '08, pages 67–75. Springer-Verlag, 2008.

[23] K. Saito, K. Ohara, Y. Yamagishi, M. Kimura, and H. Motoda. Learning diffusion probability based on node attributes in social networks. In M. Kryszkiewicz, H. Rybinski, A. Skowron, and Z. W. Ras, editors, *ISMIS*, volume 6804 of *Lecture Notes in Computer Science*, pages 153–162. Springer, 2011.

[24] G. Szabo and B. A. Huberman. Predicting the popularity of online content. *Communications of the ACM*, 53(8):80–88, 2010.

[25] G. Ver Steeg and A. Galstyan. Information-theoretic measures of influence based on content dynamics. In *Proceedings of the sixth ACM international conference on Web search and data mining*, WSDM '13, pages 3–12, New York, NY, USA, 2013. ACM.

[26] L. Wang, S. Ermon, and J. E. Hopcroft. Feature-enhanced probabilistic models for diffusion network inference. In *Proceedings of the 2012 European conference on Machine Learning and Knowledge Discovery in Databases - Volume Part II*, ECML PKDD'12, pages 499–514. Springer-Verlag, 2012.

[27] K. Q. Weinberger, F. Sha, and L. K. Saul. Learning a kernel matrix for nonlinear dimensionality reduction. In *Proceedings of the twenty-first international conference on Machine learning*, page 106. ACM, 2004.

[28] H. Yang, I. King, and M. R. Lyu. Diffusionrank: a possible penicillin for web spamming. In *Proceedings of the 30th annual international ACM SIGIR conference on Research and development in information retrieval*, pages 431–438. ACM, 2007.

[29] J. Yang and J. Leskovec. Modeling information diffusion in implicit networks. In *Proceedings of the 2010 IEEE International Conference on Data Mining*, ICDM '10, pages 599–608, Washington, DC, USA, 2010. IEEE Computer Society.

# Modeling Opinion Dynamics in Social Networks

Abhimanyu Das
Microsoft Research
Silicon Valley
abhidas@microsoft.com

Sreenivas Gollapudi
Microsoft Research
Silicon Valley
sreenig@microsoft.com

Kamesh Munagala
Dept. of Computer Science
Duke University
kamesh@cs.duke.edu

## ABSTRACT

Our opinions and judgments are increasingly shaped by what we read on social media – whether they be tweets and posts in social networks, blog posts, or review boards. These opinions could be about topics such as consumer products, politics, life style, or celebrities. Understanding how users in a network update opinions based on their neighbor's opinions, as well as what global opinion structure is implied when users iteratively update opinions, is important in the context of viral marketing and information dissemination, as well as targeting messages to users in the network.

In this paper, we consider the problem of modeling how users update opinions based on their neighbors' opinions. We perform a set of online user studies based on the celebrated conformity experiments of Asch [1]. Our experiments are carefully crafted to derive quantitative insights into developing a model for opinion updates (as opposed to deriving psychological insights). We show that existing and widely studied theoretical models do not explain the entire gamut of experimental observations we make. This leads us to posit a new, nuanced model that we term the BIASEDVOTERMODEL. We present preliminary theoretical and simulation results on the convergence and structure of opinions in the entire network when users iteratively update their respective opinions according to the BIASEDVOTERMODEL. We show that consensus and polarization of opinions arise naturally in this model under easy to interpret initial conditions on the network.

## 1. INTRODUCTION

Opinion formation among individuals and the resulting dynamics it induces in a social network has been widely studied, both from the perspective of analytic modeling as well as experimental psychology. It is known that there are several complementary influence processes that shape opinion formation [6] in society – these include group (or normative) influence, influence due to formation of stereotypes, and so on. One of these processes is termed *informational influence*[1], where users lacking necessary information seek the opinions of their neighbors in order to update their beliefs. Such a process is, for instance, common in opinion formation for fashion, consumer products, and music. Many celebrated theoretical models of opinion formation in networks use informational influence as the underlying premise [4, 17, 5, 16]. Specifically, these works model how an individual user updates her opinion in the face of information learned from her neighbors, and then use the model to characterize the evolution of opinions in the network in terms of convergence time, and the emergence of a consensus or polarization.

However, many of these theoretical models are inspired by processes in physics and biology, for instance, flocking behavior in birds [16], or cellular automata [4, 17, 18]. Though the natural processes inspiring these models are intuitively related to human behavior, it is conceivable that human behavior, even at the level of informational influence, is not as clean as these models make it out to be. In fact, there is scant literature that precisely connects *any* of these quantitative models to empirical human behavior.

We ask: *Do the existing theoretical models adequately explain how users update opinions when faced with opinions of their neighbors? If not, how do we gather empirical data, and can we posit a faithful model from this? And finally, can we understand the dynamics of opinion formation in a network when individuals iteratively update opinions using this model, in terms of convergence to a common opinion, polarization, and convergence time to these states?*

In this paper, we focus on the problem of modeling how users update opinions based on their neighbors' opinions. We begin by a preliminary analysis of opinions expressed by users on Twitter[2] to gain initial understanding into if and how a user's opinions are correlated with her neighborhood opinions. We show that such a correlation indeed exists, even when restricted to sentiments (positive or negative) about a particular topic, such as Hyundai Cars, Tim Cook, or Organic Food. (See Appendix A for details.) Though Twitter is a rich source of information, trying to derive a model of user behavior from such data is not feasible: First, sentiment analyzers we use are noisy and imprecise, producing mainly qualitative data; and secondly and more importantly, there are several competing influence processes


*WSDM'14,* February 24–28, 2014, New York, New York, USA.

http://dx.doi.org/10.1145/2556195.2559896.

[1]This is different from the information cascade and diffusion models proposed in [14, 20, 13, 11, 25]. See Sections 2.2 and 2.3 for more details.

[2]`http://www.twitter.com`

and group dynamics that operate in such a network, so that teasing out informational influence is a difficult problem.

We therefore perform a carefully designed set of user experiments in order to generate our insights into modeling. These experiments measure the shift in user opinions when exposed to the responses of other users, and are based on the celebrated conformity studies of Asch [1] and subsequent work. While the aim of their experiments was to derive qualitative psychological insights, we design ours carefully toward the end-goal of recovering a coarse *quantitative model* to explain the observations. In our experiments, we recover three distinct types of opinion update processes arising out of *stubbornness, compromise, and biased conformity.* Stubborn users do not change opinion; compromising users update their opinion to be a convex combination of their initial opinion and their neighbors' opinions; and conforming users simply take on the opinions of their neighbors, ignoring their own – the choice of neighbor biased by the closeness of their opinion to the user's own. We show, somewhat surprisingly, that these behaviors are not immutable – a user can take on different behaviors when faced with different amounts and types of information.

The above experiments motivate us to define a new analytic model of user behavior that we term the BIASEDVOTERMODEL. The model is surprisingly simple with only two parameters, one capturing the *stubbornness* in behavior, and the other capturing the *conformity bias* of the user. We study the dynamics that this simple model induces, both analytically as well as via simulations. We show that this model reaches a consensus under reasonable assumptions; however, it can take exponential time to converge to such a consensus, and the states in which it spends most time in transience can be heavily polarized. In this sense, it explains persistent disagreement in society even when users take into account *all* opinions in their neighborhood in their opinion formation process, something that we empirically observe. In contrast, to achieve polarization, existing models either require users to ignore opinions that are less related to their own in their opinion formation process, or require them to always be stubborn regardless of the information they receive – neither of these assumptions is faithful to the experimental data we observe.

## 2. PRIOR WORK

In this section, we present a brief survey of the commonly used theoretical models of opinion formation. We further survey experimental evidence from psychology and economics literature. In the discussion below, we will use the terms agent, user, node, and vertex interchangeably.

### 2.1 Theoretical Models

The broad research area of opinion formation is quite classical, and we refer the interested reader to [19] for a survey. The earliest work in this domain comes from the sociology and statistics literature [27, 5, 8].

#### *Averaging Models.*

One notable example in this setting is the DEGROOT model [9, 15, 5] which studies in a fixed network how consensus is formed when individual opinions are updated using the average of the neighborhood. Formally, suppose there are $n$ agents located in an undirected graph $G(V, E)$. The Link $(i, j) \in E$ has weight $w_{ij} = w_{ji}$, which captures homophily between agents $i$ and $j$. Let $N(i)$ denote the set of agents who have an edge to agent $i$. The opinions of the agents lie on a real line. At time $t$, let $\vec{z}(t) \in \Re^n$ denote the vector of the opinions of the agents. The update rule in this model is the following:

$$z_i(t+1) = \frac{w_{ii}z_i(t) + \sum_{j\in N(i)} w_{ij}z_j(t)}{w_{ii} + \sum_{j\in N(i)} w_{ij}} \quad (1)$$

We assume $w_{ii} \geq c \times \sum_{j\in N(i)} w_{ij}$, where $c$ is an absolute constant. We term $c$ the *relative weight* of the initial opinion of $i$. Typically instances of the DEGROOT model in the literature updated a user's opinion by averaging her opinion with the *mean of her neighboring opinions*. Therefore, for concreteness, we use DEGROOT for the setting where $c \geq 0.25$.

This model can be generalized easily to directed links, and it is easy to show using a contraction mapping argument that this model always reaches a consensus assuming the graph induced by links with $w_{ij} > 0$ is strongly connected.

In reality, consensus is rare in society, and opinions tend to typically be in a state of persistent disagreement, often in highly polarized states. The DEGROOT model was extended by Friedkin and Johnsen [10], to include both disagreement and consensus by associating with each node $i$ an innate opinion $s_i$ in addition to its expressed opinion. In this model, the dynamics becomes:

$$z_i(t+1) = \frac{w_{ii}s_i + \sum_{j\in N(i)} w_{ij}z_j(t)}{w_{ii} + \sum_{j\in N(i)} w_{ij}} \quad (2)$$

We note that averaging models predict persistent disagreement via two means: (1) Agents can be stubborn, *i.e.*, have $w_{ij} = 0$ for all neighbors, and (2) Agents can have different intrinsic opinions $s_i$.

#### *Flocking Models.*

It is folklore that opinion formation has a *conformity bias* [1, 23, 6], *i.e.*, agents assign more weight to opinions that already conform to their beliefs. This phenomenon is a special case of *flocking* behavior (or influence systems [3]).

Several classic opinion formation models combine averaging with flocking. In the popular *bounded confidence* model of Hegselmann and Krause [16] (HK model), opinions lie on a real line. Suppose agent $i$ has opinion $z_i$. For fixed $\epsilon$, the confidence region of an agent is captured by the set

$$S_i(\vec{z}) = \{j \mid |z_j - z_i| \leq \epsilon\} \quad (3)$$

Each agent $i$ iteratively updates its opinion by averaging the opinions of agents in $S_i(\vec{z})$. In the DW model of Weisbuch et al. [28], two random nodes $i$ and $j$ meet and update their opinions $z_i$ and $z_j$ to the average of the two opinions if these originally satisfied $|z_i - z_j| \leq \epsilon$.

There is also a large body of work (see [3, 24] and references therein) that has focused on characterizing the convergence of bounded confidence dynamics to either *absolute consensus* or some clustering (polarization).

#### *Voter Models.*

The voter model was independently proposed by Clifford and Sudbury [4], and by Holley and Liggett [17]. In this model, we have a strongly connected directed graph and opinions are discrete, typically coming from a small set [30]. At each step, a node is selected at random; this node chooses one of its neighbors uniformly at random (including itself) and adopts that opinion as its own. A modification is termed the Label Propagation Algorithm, where the node adopts the majority opinion in its neighborhood (breaking ties randomly). The former algorithm is termed the *voter algorithm*, and can be shown to reach a consensus. Techniques based on coalescing random walks [7] bound the convergence time and steady state distribution of this dynamics.

There are several variants of the voter model known. As a relevant example, Yildiz *et al.* [29] consider the modification where agents can be stubborn. Kempe *et al.* [21] propose a modification where the possible opinions (or types) define a graph, where two types are adjacent if they correspond to similar opinions. They restrict the neighborhood graph on the users to be a *complete graph*. At any step, every user picks a random other user whose type neighbors his own type, and adopts that opinion.

## 2.2 Asch's Experiments

We now move to experimental evidence to support models for opinion formation. Most of this research comes from social psychology, particularly the work of Asch [1], Deutsch and Gerard [6] and extensive followup research (see [2] for a survey). Asch, in his seminal conformity experiments, observed that a large fraction of his subjects could be swayed to essentially say "white is black" if everyone else in the group said the same. In Asch's experiments, the subject was placed in a room with several stooges who unanimously gave the false (binary) response to a question where the true answer was self-evident. Asch made several observations, the most relevant being the following: (1) The extent of conformity (percent of subjects who conform) depends on the size of the group; and (2) Even when one of the stooges gives the true response, that is sufficient to reduce conformity significantly.

Deutsch and Gerard argued that Asch's observations are the superposition of two types of conformity – *normative*, where subjects conform so as to gain social acceptance into a group, and *informational*, where subjects use the responses of others as evidence of reality, and adjust their beliefs accordingly. They ran similar experiments where the other responses shown to the subject were anonymous and fabricated (though the subject believed these responses were real), and observed similar behavior to Asch's experiments – in effect showing that Asch's observations happen even with purely informational influence and no group pressure, though to a slightly lesser extent. They therefore term Asch's experiments a study of informational influence as opposed to normative influence.

It is also well-known (see [26] for a survey) that there are other mechanisms for opinion formation that apply for medium to long-term interactions. The most widely accepted of these is the notion of stereotyping – subjects form a stereotype of themselves, as well as of others, and use these stereotypes to adopt the opinion of homophilous neighbors. This stereotype could itself be formed based on previous opinions expressed on possibly unrelated topics. Though these mechanisms are important in driving opinion formation, they involve the formation of implicit and explicit groups of users, which will not be the main focus of this paper.

## 2.3 Diffusion/Influence Models

We briefly mention work on diffusion, influence and information flows in networks that, though not directly relevant to our work, discuss models for the adoption or spread of ideas, rumors or content among online users. Well known models in this domain include Threshold [14] and Cascade models [12] that specify how a node adopts a particular idea or product based on the adoption pattern prevalent in its neighborhood. Subsequently, several papers studied, both theoretically [20] and empirically [11, 13, 25] the phenomenon of diffusion of ideas or content in a social network and the related problem of identifying influential nodes to seed in order to maximize adoption rates. The work in this space is not directly related to our problem since it is mainly concerned with the *dissemination* or the spread of information (in general) through the network while the focus of our work is on the *assimilation* of this information to form an opinion (with possibly a different value from the neighboring values) by a individual user in the network. This often leads to a much finer-grained opinion dynamic model for a single user, which is what we seek to model.

## 2.4 Our Contribution

In this paper, we focus on informational influence (defined in Section 2.2), which we believe will be the dominant mode of influence in short-term anonymous interactions, for instance on review boards or chat rooms. We analytically model opinion formation in social networks in the presence of informational influence using a model that we term BIASEDVOTERMODEL. Our model combines certain aspects of the flocking and the DEGROOT models, yet it is different from both. We base our model on several online user experiments that are modeled after the experiments of Deutsch and Gerard – in contrast with their experiments, our experiments do not have an easily discernible ground truth, and the responses are not binary (true/false). We note that binary outcomes can be consistent with several analytical models simultaneously – we therefore make the responses themselves continuous in our experiments, and carefully choose the neighborhood to tease out the modeling desiderata.

We study the response of the subjects not only as a function of the size of the neighborhood, but also as a function of the *distribution* of these opinions, and the *distance* of these opinions from the subject's own. Not only are our observations are consistent with prior work on binary opinions (and generalize them), but they also provide us sufficient qualitative and quantitative insights to postulate a model.

# 3. ONLINE USER STUDIES

We will now present experiments to distinguish all of the above models at a qualitative level. Our online user experiments are modeled after the anonymous experiments of Deutsch and Gerard [6]. The key differences are that we require continuous quantitative responses to questions whose ground truth is uncertain; and further, we ask questions from several different domains to check consistency of the findings. We will show that for these experiments, none of the DEGROOT, flocking, or the voter models consistently explains our data, motivating the need for the BIASEDVOTERMODEL model.

## 3.1 Experimental Setup

We used an interacting network of online users recruited from Amazon Mechanical Turk (mturk) and a personal survey website to host the experiments. Subjects were asked to take part in one of two online surveys hosted on the external website. The first survey corresponded to questions about estimating the number of dots in three images. The second survey asked questions about estimating the monthly sales volume of two car models (Hyundai and Ford) and two soda brands (Coke and Pepsi).

Each survey consisted of two sequential phases: In the first phase, for each question on the survey, the user was asked to enter her response to the question. The user did not know apriori there would be a second phase. Then, in the second phase, the user was shown a set of "neighboring opinions" that were synthetically generated (as described later) but were presented to the user as being the most recent answers from previous participants of the survey. The user was then asked to read these neighboring opinions and re-enter her answer to the question. The first answer of the user was used as her initial opinion, while the second answer which was provided by the user after having seen her neighboring opinions was treated as her final opinion.

SURVEY1 (DOTS): This survey consisted of three questions about three images, each containing 10000 5000, and 4000 dots respectively. The user was asked to guess the number of dots in each of the images. We varied the number of neighboring opinions shown for each question: 20 opinions for the first question, 10 for the second question, and 5 for the third question. In all three cases, the neighboring opinion distribution was generated using a (roughly) trimodal distribution with around 20% of the nodes clustered around the neighboring opinion closest to the user's initial opinion, and around 60% clustered around the opinion farthest from the user's initial opinion. We also repeated the entire survey for the case where the neighboring opinions were randomly permuted before being shown to a user, instead of being presented in sorted order.

SURVEY2(CARS AND CANS): This survey asked each user four questions about estimating the sales of car and soda brands (Coke, Pepsi, Ford Focus and Hyundai Elantra) during June 2014. The generation of neighboring opinions for each question was similar to that in the previous survey except for two differences: First, we fixed the number of neighboring opinions to be 20. Second, we used different neighboring opinion distributions: for the Coke and Hyundai questions, we used a Gaussian distribution with mean 0 and standard-deviations of 2000 and 300 respectively. For the Pepsi and Ford questions, we used a truncated Power-Law distribution, with exponent 2. In both cases, we then shifted the set of neighboring opinions (generated using the above distributions) by a constant that depends on the user's initial opinion, as described below.

For all our experiments, the set of neighboring opinions were generated such that they were either all smaller or all larger than the user's initial opinion. Figure 1 gives an illustration of the generation of neighboring opinions based on a user's initial opinion. We use $o_i$ to denote the user's initial opinion, $o_e$ denotes the neighboring opinion closest to $o_i$, $o_c$ denotes the median neighboring opinion, and $o_m$ denotes the neighboring opinion farthest from $o_i$. For the dots experiment, we generated the neighboring opinions such that the gap $|o_i - o_e|$ was set to 4000 if $o_i$ was less than 30000 and $o_i - 26000$ otherwise. Similarly, for the cars and soda experiments, the gap $|o_i - o_e|$ was set to 4000 if $o_i$ was less than 60000 and $o_i - 56000$ otherwise.

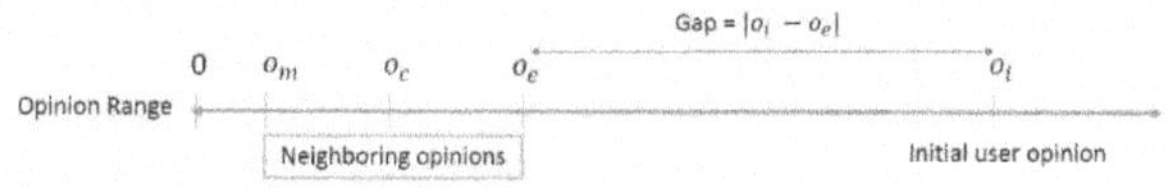


**Figure 1: Illustration of user/neighboring opinions for User Experiments**

Each survey was answered by around 200 online users. To ensure that the survey response quality was high, we restricted each user to participate in at most one survey.

## 3.2 Results and Interpretation

As mentioned above, we carefully construct the experiment so that it can qualitatively distinguish between the various models of opinion formation – DEGROOT, Flocking, and VOTER models.

### *3.2.1 DEGROOT versus VOTER model*

We begin with an experiment which shows that for large number of neighboring opinions, the VOTER model explains the opinion dynamics better compared to the DEGROOT model. We remind the reader of a user following the DEGROOT model [5] averages her opinion with the opinions of her neighbors. As mentioned before we assume for concreteness that such a user gives at least $c \geq 0.25$ relative weight to its own opinion. A user following the VOTER model chooses a neighboring opinion at random and moves to this opinion. Toward this end, we consider a large set of users whose initial opinions are *significantly far* from the set of neighboring opinions. We define these as follows:

DEFINITION 3.1. *Let $o_i$ denote the user's initial opinion. We define $o_i$ to be* significantly far *if* $|o_i - o_e| \geq 3|o_c - o_m|$.

The above definition ensures that we can make the following claim – if many users indeed follow the DEGROOT model, their final opinion should lie in between their initial opinion and the set of the neighboring opinions[3]. Note that this observation precludes the stubborn who do not change their opinions by much. To further make the distinction clear, we restrict our attention to experiments where the neighboring opinions are drawn from a Gaussian distribution with relatively small variance – the Hyundai and Coke experiments. This further ensures that variance in the neighboring opinions does not confuse the analysis. Thus, users whose final opinions lie within the relatively small range of neighboring opinions are likely to follow the VOTER model.

Based on the above, we categorize users based on the following quantity. Let $o_f$ denote the final opinion of the user. Let $s = \frac{|o_i - o_f|}{|o_i - o_e|}$. We define a user to be *stubborn* if $s < 0.1$; it follows the VOTER model if $s > 0.9$, and it follows DEGROOT if $s \in [0.1, 0.9]$. Fig. 2 illustrates this categorization of users. We note here that our results do not qualitatively change much even if we vary the $s$ threshold used for categorizing users into stubborn, DEGROOT and VOTER models slightly; this can be seen by observing in Figures 5(a) and

[3]While the constant 3 in Definition 3.1 is sufficient to ensure that we can distinguish between DEGROOT and VOTER models, our experimental results use even more conservative constants of around 8

5(b) that the distribution of users into the three categories is relatively stable to small perturbations in the $s$ thresholds.

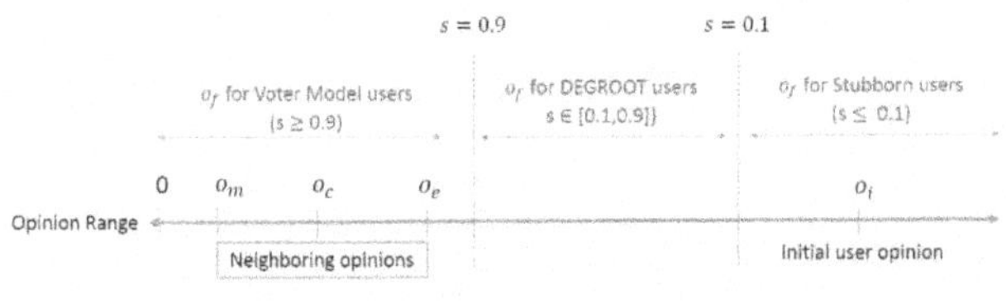


**Figure 2: Categorization of user into DEGROOT, Stubborn or VOTER model**

We restrict our attention to users whose initial and final opinions are at least 1000 and whose initial opinions satisfy Def. 3.1. In Fig. 3(a), we plot the histograms for the three buckets defined above for both the experiments. We observe that a overwhelming fraction of around 75% of the users indeed adopt their final opinion to be one of (or close to) the neighboring opinions consistent with the VOTER model. Furthermore, we observe that even the number of stubborn users (of around 15%) is larger than the remaining set we surmise to be following the DEGROOT model. This observation follows from the fact that the final opinions of all the DEGROOT user's lie in between their initial opinion and the set of neighboring opinions.

To make the conclusion more concrete, we focus on the Coke experiment. We filter on initial opinions at least $500K$. For such users, the corresponding neighboring opinions lie in a small range $[44K, 56K]$, with mean $50K$. The mean is factor 10 away from the initial opinion, so that a user performing DEGROOT with relative weight at least $c \geq 0.1$ to his own opinion and using 20 neighbors will be clearly separated from users who adopt an opinion close to their neighbors. We plot the histogram in Fig. 3(b). As before, at most 15% of users perform DEGROOT as opposed to more than 65% who follow the VOTER model. To complete the analysis, we expand the user set to include users with initial opinion at least 250K, and split the users with $s > 0.9$ (VOTER model) into three groups: Those for which $s \in (0.9, 1)$ (who adopt an opinion larger than $56K$), those whose final opinions is in $(54K, 56K]$, and those with final opinions at most $54K$. These are the third, fourth, and fifth buckets respectively, while the first two buckets, $s < 0.1$ and $s \in [0.1, 0.9]$ remain the same. We plot this histogram in Fig. 3(c). We note that more than 50% of users move to an opinion at most $56K$, while at most 15% have $s \in (0.1, 1]$, corresponding to an expanded definition of DEGROOT. Even within the former set of users, a vast majority move to an opinion at most $54K$, showing that they use the mean/median/mode of $50K$ in forming their opinion. This shows the predominance of users whose behavior is better modeled by the VOTER model.

### 3.2.2 *Bias in Opinion Choice*

The above experiment makes a case that the VOTER model is a more accurate model for the Coke and Hyundai experiments than DEGROOT. We now dig deeper into *which* neighboring opinion is adopted more frequently. Is it a an opinion chosen uniformly at random, or is it biased by the user's initial opinion? The Coke experiment (Fig. 3(c)) shows that users move to an easily discernible majority cluster – since the neighboring opinions are drawn from a Gaussian distribution, the users move to the mode of this distribution.

We consider the DOTS experiment where we show 20 neighboring opinions. We filter only users whose initial opinions lie in $[75K, 150K]$ (the upper bound is not critical and is mainly used to filter out users who we believe give arbitrary answers). For these users, the neighboring opinions lie in $[16K, 26K]$. However, the distribution of these opinions is tri-modal: There are 5 distinct opinions in $[25K, 26K]$, the median is $23.5K$, and the mode is $22K$, with 6 neighboring opinions taking this value. When the data is presented in sorted order, the mode is clearly identifiable.

As before, we bucket the users into stubborn ($s < 0.1$), DEGROOT ($s \in [0.1, 0.9)$), and VOTER model ($s \geq 0.9$). Within the third group, we create three sub-groups, one where $s \in [0.9, 1)$ (where the final opinion is larger than $26K$), the second where the final opinion is in $[26K, 25K]$, and the other where the final opinion is smaller than 25K. The histogram of final opinions is shown in Figure 4. We present two histograms, one where the neighboring opinions are shown in sorted order, and the other where they are shown in random order.

We find that around 40% of the users move to an opinion that is close to the extreme cluster around $26K$ – this includes users for which $s \geq 0.9$ and users whose final opinion is in $[25K, 26K]$. This shows that users give more weight to nearby opinions while forming their final opinion. However, note that there is a small but non-trivial fraction of users who perform DEGROOT (around 20%), and that move to an opinion below $25K$ (around 15%).

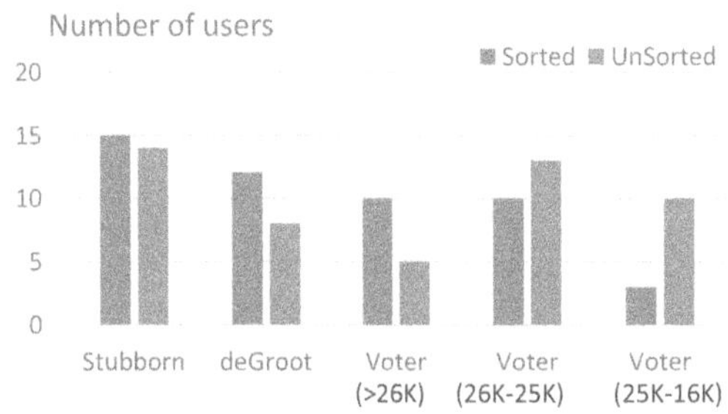


**Figure 4: DOTS experiment with 20 neighbors and initial opinions between 75K and 150K**

### 3.2.3 *Effect of Size of Neighborhood*

In the next set of experiments, we measure the effect of the number of neighboring opinions on the final opinion of the user. Toward this end, we considered a set of 20, 10, 5, and 1 neighboring opinions for the DOTS question. As Figures 6(a) and 6(b) shows, there are two effects that are observed. First, stubbornness reduces as users see more neighboring opinions. We observe that the fraction of stubborn nodes decreases from around 35% to 22% as the number of neighboring opinions changes from 1 to 20. This is a natural consequence of a user not seeing enough number of alternate opinions to sway her from her initial opinion, a phenomenon that was documented as early as Asch [1]. Second, we observe more users adopting the DEGROOT model as the number of neighboring opinions decrease. This could either be because users can easily compute averages over a small set of neighboring opinions, or because they are swayed less and adopt an intermediate response. The point we wish

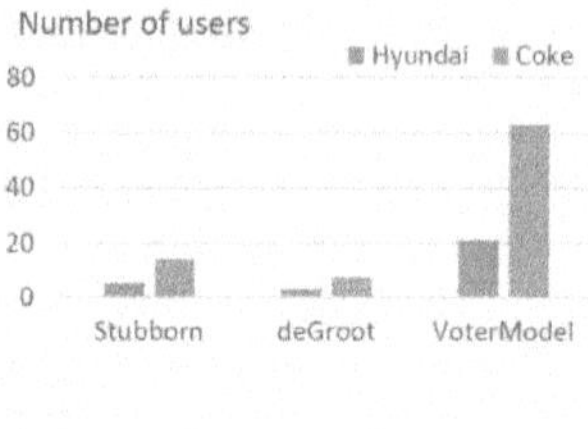


(a) Hyundai and Coke experiments with initial opinions *significantly far.*

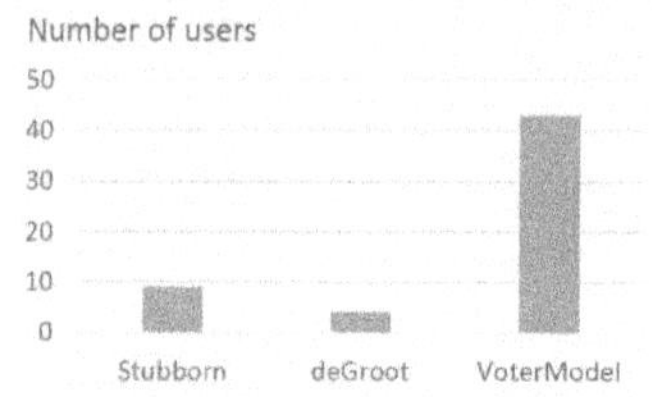


(b) Coke experiment with initial opinions at least $500K$, and neighboring opinions in $(44K, 56K)$.

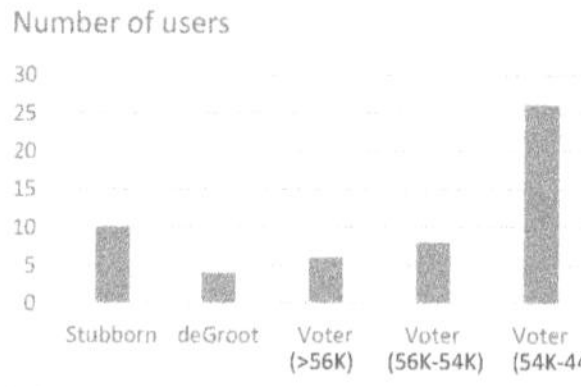


(c) Coke experiment with initial opinions at least $250K$ and finer-grained bucketing of final opinions.

**Figure 3: Coke and Hyundai Experiments**

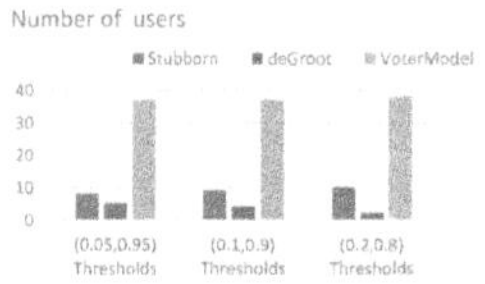

(a) Hyundai and Coke experiment.

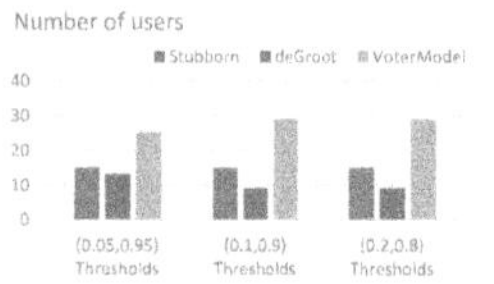

(b) DOTS experiment.

**Figure 5: Distribution of Stubborn, DEGROOT and VOTER users for various $s$-threshold values used for categorizing users into the three classes**

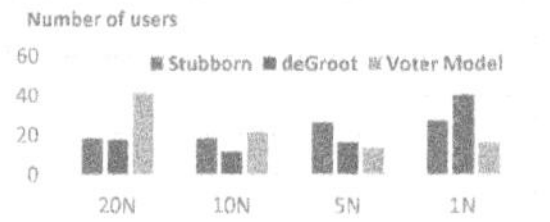

(a) Sorted neighboring opinions.

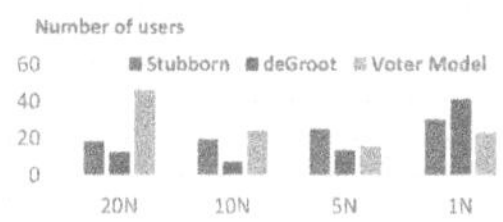

(b) Unsorted neighboring opinions.

**Figure 6: Effect of the number of neighboring opinions. This was measured using the DOTS experiment with significantly far initial opinions**

to make is that the pure VOTER model cannot capture the behavior of users when there are few neighboring opinions, since a significant fraction of them move to an opinion in between their initial opinion and the neighboring opinions.

### 3.2.4 Correlation in Responses

We finally study whether user behavior is consistent across questions – do stubborn users always give stubborn responses, and do conforming users always conform?

To address this, we first consider each user's behavior across all the answered by that user in a survey. We categorize users as *consistently stubborn* if the user is stubborn for all questions, and respectively *consistently* DEGROOT and *consistently* VOTER. We label a user as *mixed* if her behavior changes across questions. Figure 7 summarizes the distribution of these categories in our experiments, for both our Surveys. As seen in the Figure, around 63%(for the DOTS survey) and 55% (for the CARS AND CANS survey) of users exhibit consistent behaviors across the questions answered by them.

Next, we consider a more fine-grained consistency test to understand if user exhibit consistent behavior even within the DEGROOT and VOTER models in terms of selecting the averaging constant (for DEGROOT) or the choice of neighboring opinion to adopt (for VOTER). We consider two questions in the DOTS survey, that use 20 and 10 neighboring opinions respectively. The same user answers both these questions. As before, we restrict only to users whose initial opinions for *both* questions are *significantly far* according to Def. 3.1. We now construct one value $q$ from the responses of the user. We compute the quantity $s$ as before. Let $t = \max(0, \min(s, 1))$. Without loss of generality, assume $o_i$ is larger than all neighboring opinions. Sort the neighboring opinions as $w_1 \geq w_2 \geq \cdots \geq w_k$, so that $w_1$ is the closest opinion to $o_i$. Let $r$ denote the index of $o_f$ in this sorted order, where if $o_f > w_1$, the index is 0. Let $r' = 2r/k$. (For instance, if the user reports $o_f$ as the median $w_{k/2}$ of the neighboring opinions, then $r' = 1$.) Let $r'' = \min(r', 1)$. Then, we define $q = t + r''$. Therefore, $q$ is a number between 0 and 2. If $o_f \in (w_1, o_i]$, then $q = s$. If $o_f = w_1$, then $q = 1$; if $o_f = w_{k/2}$, then $q = 2$.

We compute the Pearson's correlation coefficient between the $q$ values for the 20 and 10 neighbors case for the DOTS experiment, restricted to *significantly far* initial responses for both questions. There are 90 such users. The correlation coefficient is 0.57 with p-value less than 0.001. We repeat the above computation for users answering both Hyundai and Ford questions, again restricting to both initial opinions being *significantly far.* We obtain a Pearson correlation coefficient of 0.4 with p-value less than 0.001.

## 4. DESIDERATA OF A NEW MODEL

We have shown above that by themselves, neither the DEGROOT model, the VOTER model, nor the Flocking model is a good qualitative model for our data; the DEGROOT model cannot explain the Coke and Hyundai experiment where users with large initial opinions move close to a neighboring opinion (nor can it explain Asch's observations); the VOTER Model cannot explain the Dots experiment with few neighboring opinions where users seem to be performing averaging, and the Flocking models cannot explain why users are not stubborn when their initial opinions are very divergent from their neighbors (nor can it explain why stubbornness should decrease with more neighboring opinions). In fact, we observe that users can be largely classified into three basic behavioral types *viz,*

**Stubborn Behavior:** Users do not change their opinions, regardless of how extreme their opinion is relative to the neighborhood, and how many neighbors they have;

**Compromising (DEGROOT) Behavior:** Users choose an opinion that is in between their initial opinion, and the average of the opinions in their neighborhood; and

**Biased Conforming Behavior:** Users move to an opinion chosen at random from their neighborhood, giving more weight to opinions that are closer by to their initial opinion. We remind the reader that the VOTER model corresponds to an unbiased conforming behavior.

Note that the same user can exhibit multiple types of behavior depending on the neighborhood (represented by the *mixed* category in Figure 7). While admitting all these behaviors, we would also like our model to gracefully handle the effects of the neighborhood size as well as a user's bias in opinion adoption we observed in our experiments.

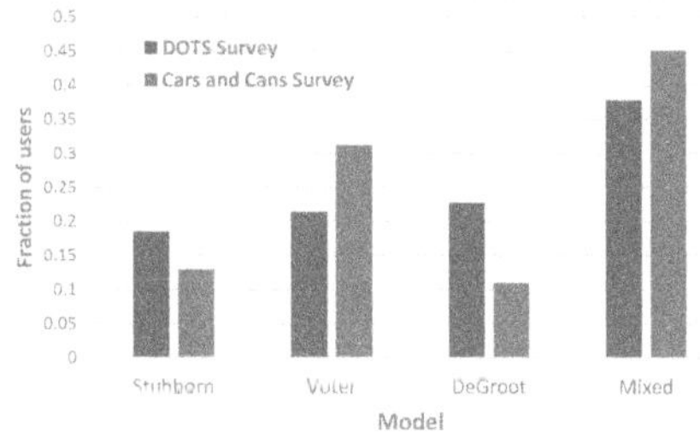


**Figure 7: Histogram of users following a certain type of behavior**

### *Effect of Size of Neighborhood.*

When there are a large number of neighboring opinions, the same user is much more likely to discount his own opinion a lot and simply adopt a neighboring opinion, much like the VOTER model. For small neighborhood size, we observe that the same users do indeed adopt average opinions reasonably frequently (much like DEGROOT). While we did not explicitly vary the number of opinions with time in our user-studies, users, in an online setting, are quite likely to see different number of opinions at different points in time. Therefore, the effect of varying neighboring opinions needs to be carefully modeled, something not addressed in all previous models.

### *Bias in Opinion Adoption.*

Asch's experiments show that conformity with a divergent majority dramatically reduces when there is one neighboring opinion that agrees with the user's own. This is in accordance with the classical Flocking models. However, unlike these models, we do not observe any "confidence interval" beyond which users are stubborn. In fact, we find that users move to the neighboring opinion even when they are arbitrarily far away, the choice of neighbor biased towards the user's own opinion.

We state that our goal of proposing a new model is not to fit our experimental data exactly, since human behavior, even on simple questions, is not likely to admit one simple model. Instead we aim to propose a simple extension to the VOTER model that admits the above desiderata. We observe that a geometric model captures the above findings reasonably well. Figure 8(a) illustrates the *bias* in the choice of neighboring opinions selected by users in our surveys. Clearly, we observe a significant decrease in the probability of choosing a neighbor's opinion further from a user's innate or initial opinion. In other words, as the index of the neighbor's opinion in the presented order increases. On the effect of *stubbornness*, we observe that a user's stubbornness is independent of the distance of neighboring opinions —in fact, it is relatively independent of the specific question in a given survey too. This observation is shown in Figure 8(b) which plots the average of $|s_i - \bar{s}_i|/k$ for all users following the DEGROOT model. Here $\bar{s}_i$ is the average $s$ of user $i$ across all the $k$ questions she participated in. Note that $s = 0$ denotes a stubborn user while a larger value indicates a user's willingness to conform. In the next section, we will describe our model incorporating both stubbornness and bias parameters.

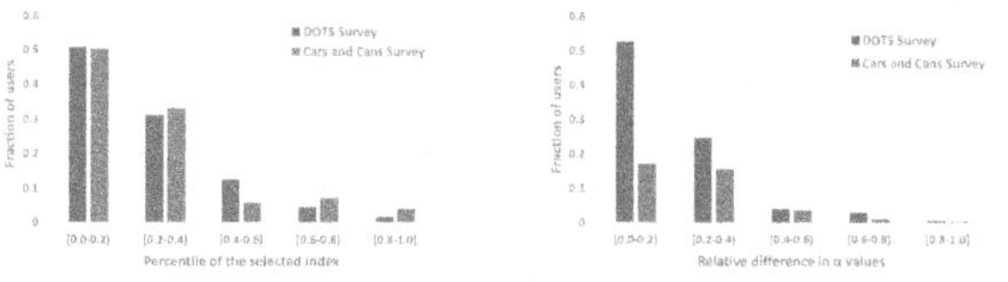

(a) Effect of the distance of a neighboring opinion on the likelihood of it getting selected.

(b) The stubbornness of user across multiple questions for a fixed number of neighboring opinions.

**Figure 8: Effect of key parameters of a candidate model**

## 5. THE BIASED VOTER MODEL

In this section, we propose a model that is more qualitatively consistent with our (and prior) observations that we noted in the previous section. Our model, which we term BIASEDVOTERMODEL, uses a combination of the DEGROOT model and the VOTER model. Formally, there is a directed graph $G(V, E)$ on the users. User $i$ has a set of neighbors $N(i)$, which is the set of users $i$ follows, and whose opinions $i$ potentially receives. We assume the opinion dynamics evolve over a sequence of discrete time steps. Let $z_i(t)$ denote the opinions of user $i$ at time step $t$, and let $S_i(t)$ denote the set of opinions of the neighbors of $i$ at time $t$. This is precisely the set of opinions $z_j(t)$ for $j \in N(i)$. Each user $i$ then sets $z_i(t+1)$ based on $z_i(t)$ and the set $S_i(t)$, as described by the BIASEDVOTERMODEL below;

User $i$ is parametrized by two innate quantities: we term these as the *bias parameter* $p_i$, and the *stubbornness parameter* $\alpha_i$. We start with a discrete type space $\mathcal{T} = \{1, 2, \ldots, k\}$ of opinions. The *distance* between two types $a, b \in \mathcal{T}$ is simply $|a - b|$, so that the type of 1 is an extreme opinion, and type of $k$ is the opposite extreme opinion.

Let $z_i(t) = q_0$. For set $S_i(t)$, sort the opinions in increasing order of distance from $q_0$; denote this multi-set of opinions as $\{q_1, q_2, \ldots, q_d\}$, where $d$ is the degree of user $i$.

Let $q^* = \text{argmin}_{q \in S}|q - q_0|$ be the "closest" neighboring opinion to $i$'s own. Then:

- With probability $p_i$, set $z_i(t+1) = q_1$; else with probability $p_i$, set $z_i(t+1) = q_2$, and so on.
- If the above step did not set $z_i(t+1)$, then:
  - With probability $\alpha_i$, set $z_i(t+1) = q_0$; and
  - With probability $1 - \alpha_i$ set $z_i(t+1) = q$, where $q \in [q_0, q^*]$ is chosen uniformly at random.

Note that this model is faithful to the experimental results: As $|S|$ increases, the user is more likely to conform to a neighboring opinion, and this opinion is more likely to be closer to the initial opinion. We further note that if all nodes update opinions each step, and if $p_i = 1/d_i$, where $d_i$ is the degree of $i$ in $G(V, E)$, then BIASEDVOTERMODEL reduces to the classical VOTER model [4, 17] since users choose a neighboring opinion (almost) uniformly at random.

## 5.1 Dynamics

In this section, we present some analytical results about the dynamics of the BIASEDVOTERMODEL, mainly focusing on the nature of stable equilibria, and the rate of convergence towards them. In all the results below, we assume $G(V, E)$ is strongly connected; if this assumption does not hold, the theorems hold in each strongly connected component. The proofs of these observations follow from standard Markov chain analysis techniques [7, 29], and we omit them.

In the results below, by *consensus*, we mean that all users adopt the same opinion. By a *stable equilibrium*, we mean that the opinions of all nodes have converged to some value from which it does not change further.

THEOREM 5.1. *In the* BIASEDVOTERMODEL, *the following are true:*

- *The frequencies of different opinions converges, though there may be no stable equilibria in the sense that the opinions of a individual user may not converge.*
- *If $\alpha_i, p_i < 1$ for all users $i$, then the only stable equilibria correspond to consensus.*

The most interesting of the above observations is that in the BIASEDVOTERMODEL, if every user compromises a little and there are no stubborn users with $\alpha_i = 1$, then this is enough to make each connected component reach a consensus. However, note that if there is a clique of size $k$ all of whose users have the same opinion, then it takes at least $1/(1-p)^k$ steps for any user in this set to adopt a different opinion. In a sense, it is easy to see that though consensus is the only stable equilibrium, there could be transient states that are polarized, and that are persistent in the sense that the system spends exponential time in these states. Such transience is likely to be pronounced if there are a lot of triadic closures in the graph. On the other hand, if there are stubborn users, consensus is not guaranteed and the opinions of users can oscillate; however the distribution of opinions reaches stability (see Figure 9).

We note that though our model can be viewed as a biased version of the VOTER model, the coalescing random walk techniques [7] for analyzing steady state properties in the VOTER model do not naturally extend to BIASEDVOTERMODEL. Developing new analysis techniques in this domain is an interesting open question. In the interim, we simulate this dynamics to understand the steady state behavior as a function of the stubbornness and bias parameters.

## 5.2 Simulations

We performed simulations to characterize the effect of stubbornness (parameter $\alpha_i$) and bias (parameter $p_i$) exhibited by a node on the dynamics underlying the discrete BIASEDVOTERMODEL. Toward this end, we generated graphs having both random and power law degree distributions. The number of nodes in the graph was set to 1000. The maximum degree in the random graph was set to 50 while the corresponding number in the power law graph was set to 200. We assume $k = 10$, so that every node takes on one of 10 opinions in $\{0, 1, 2, \ldots, 9\}$. We define a stubborn node $i$ as one with $\alpha_i = 1$ and $p_i = 0$. We fixed the stubborn nodes to assume one of the two extreme opinions, *viz.*, 0 and 9. The rest of the nodes have the corresponding values drawn uniformly at random. Finally, we note that all results are averaged over 10 runs.

Before we characterize the effect of both the parameters, we make an observation on the convergence of the dynamics. Theorem 5.1 shows that even in the presence of stubbornness and bias, the distribution of opinions in the BIASEDVOTERMODEL dynamics always converges, though the rate of convergence can be slower than in the VOTER model (where $p_i$ is small). While we observed the voter model converges to a consensus almost always within 3000 iterations on a 1000 node random graph, the corresponding behavior is different in the BIASEDVOTERMODELFirst, there presence of stubborn nodes results in no consensus at convergence. Second, the number of iterations taken to converge could be significantly higher. Figure 9 illustrates the latter for different choices of the fraction of stubborn nodes in the graph where we see that the number of users adopting any of the stubborn opinions (i.e. opinions 0 or 9) stabilizes after around 70,000 iterations.

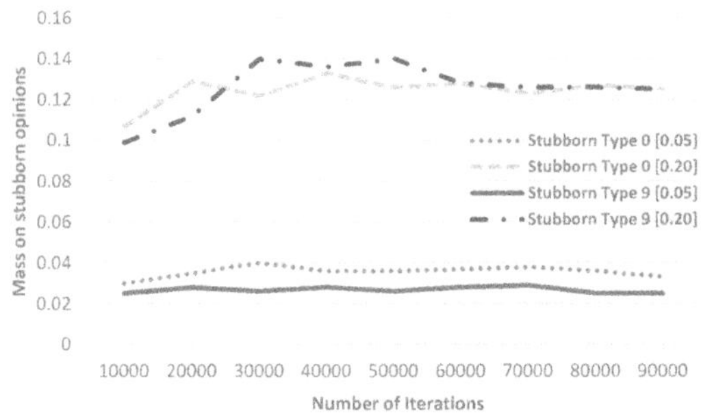


**Figure 9: Convergence of the BIASEDVOTERMODEL dynamics with different fraction (5% and 20%) of stubborn nodes with one of opinions 0 and 9. The bias parameter $p_i$ is uniformly distributed in [0,1].**

**Effect of Stubbornness:** We varied the fraction of nodes exhibiting stubbornness in the graph and measured the number of nodes adopting any of the stubborn opinions at the 10000th iteration in the dynamic. Figure 10 shows the total number of nodes adopting the stubborn opinions, i.e., 0 or 9 for starting configurations with different fraction of stubborn nodes. Clearly, if all nodes adopts one of the stubborn opinions, we can say that the network is polarized along these opinions. Any decrease in the number of stubborn nodes can only lead to more polarization possibly involving smaller groups and more opinions. Alternately, this can be viewed as a rate of convergence. In this context, we observe that the placement of the stubborn nodes plays a crucial role in the rate of convergence, i.e., the adoption of the stubborn opinions by rest of the graph. Clearly, the slowest rate of convergence is associated with the case when the stubborn nodes are the low degree nodes in the power law graph. On the other hand, when the stubborn users are placed on the high degree nodes in the power law graph, the graph almost immediately converges to the stubborn opinions even when the fraction of the stubborn users is as small as 10% in the graph. Not surprisingly, under uniform seeding of stubborn nodes, the power law graph converges faster compared to the dynamics on a random graph.

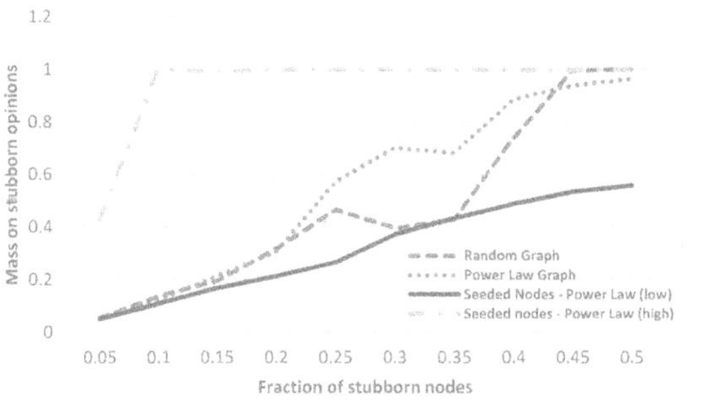


**Figure 10: The effect of the placement of the stubborn nodes on the fraction of nodes adopting the stubborn opinions at $t = 10000$. The bias parameter $p_i$ is uniformly distributed in [0,1].**

**Effect of Bias:** Next, we set the bias $p_i$ of every node to be the same and varied the value of this parameter in [0,1]. In the absence of any stubborn nodes, Theorem 5.1 gives us consensus (the dashed line in Figure 11(a) confirms this result). Keeping this in mind, we studied the extent of polarization and consensus in the network at the 10000th iteration. A transient behavior that arises with increase in the bias value is the breakdown of any consensus that existed for small values of $p_i$. This can be explained by the observation that as the propensity to select the nearest neighbor increases, users tend to quickly converge to smaller groups (having same opinion). Figure 11(a) illustrates this observation. This effect is more pronounced in the power-law graph. On the other hand, when there are stubborn nodes in the graph (see Figure 11(b)), we observe a different behavior. In the case of a random graph, there is hardly any consensus on the stubborn opinions regardless of the value of $p_i$. In the case of a power-law graph, we note that smaller values of $p_i$ are sufficient to break any consensus compared to the behavior observed in Figure 11(a). Indeed, this is precisely the behavior characteristic of the BIASEDVOTERMODEL wherein the presence of stubborn nodes as well as bias toward particular opinions in the neighborhood can have adverse effect on consensus formation in the network.

# 6. CONCLUSION

Our work is a preliminary attempt to posit an analytical model for opinion formation and informational influence, based on carefully designed online experiments. We first mention some caveats of our experiments and model, which we plan to resolve in future work. In the user experiments, we have shown neighboring opinions that are chosen in a structured fashion. We have not explored if this has any side effects on opinion formation. Secondly, the questions in this study have a hard to discern ground truth, and are chosen so that users do not have side information apriori. We do not know if this impacts the model for informational influence in a significant way.

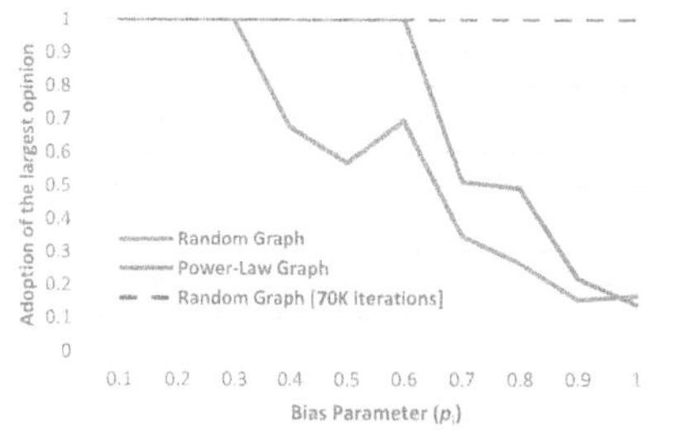


(a) No stubborn nodes

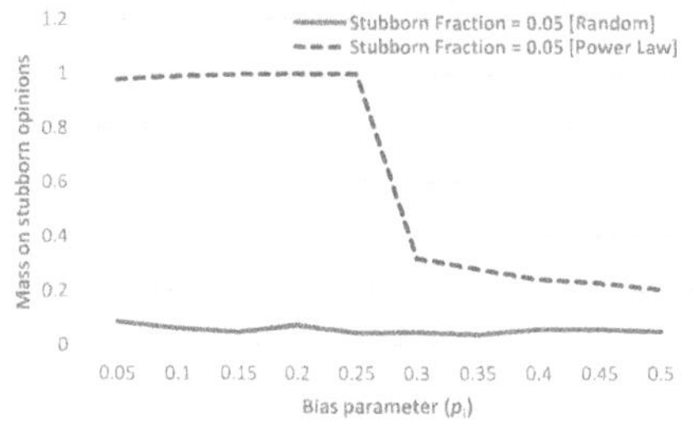


(b) The fraction of stubborn nodes is 5%.

**Figure 11: Effect of bias parameter $p_i$ on consensus formation after $t = 10000$ iterations.**

There are several avenues for future research. The BIASEDVOTERMODEL leads to interesting dynamics that needs to be analytically explored. In the presence of such dynamics, how can messages be targeted to users in the network so that the final set of opinions is close to a desired outcome? We have focused on informational influence and have ignored normative influence as well as stereotyping. How do the presence of these types of influence interact with informational influence?

**Acknowledgements.** Kamesh Munagala is supported by an award from Cisco, and by NSF via grants CCF-0745761, CCF-1008065, and IIS-0964560.

# 7. REFERENCES

[1] S. Asch. Opinions and social pressure. *Scientific American*, 193:35–40, 1955.

[2] R. Bond and P. B. Smith. Culture and conformity: A meta-analysis of studies using Asch's line judgment task. *Psychological Bulletin*, 119(1):111–137, 1996.

[3] B. Chazelle. Natural algorithms and influence systems. *Communications of the ACM*, 2012.

[4] P. Clifford and A. W. Sudbury. A model for spatial conflict. *Biometrika*, 60:581–588, 1973.

[5] M. H. DeGroot. Reaching a consensus. *J. American Statistical Association*, 69:118–121, 1974.

[6] M. Deutsch and H. B. Gerard. A study of normative and informational social influences upon individual judgement. *J. Abnormal and Social Psychology*, 51:629–636, 1955.

[7] R. Durrett and H. Kesten. *Random walks, Brownian motion, and interacting particle systems.* Birkhauser Verlag AG, 1991.

[8] J. Fowler and N. Christakis. Cooperative behavior cascades in human social networks. *PNAS*, 107(12):5334–8, 2010.

[9] J. R. P. French. A formal theory of social power. *Psychological Review*, 63:181–94, 1956.

[10] N. E. Friedkin and E. C. Johnsen. Social influence and opinions. *J. Mathematical Sociology*, 15(3-4):193–205, 1990.

[11] S. Goel, D. Watts, and D. Goldstein. The structure of online diffusion networks. In *ACM EC*, pages 623–638, 2012.

[12] J. Goldenberg, B. Libai, and E. Muller. Talk of the network: A complex systems look at the underlying process of word-of-mouth. *Marketing letters*, 12(3):211–223, 2001.

[13] M. Gomez Rodriguez, J. Leskovec, and A. Krause. Inferring networks of diffusion and influence. In *Proc. of the 16th ACM SIGKDD*, pages 1019–1028. ACM, 2010.

[14] M. Granovetter. Threshold models of collective behavior. *American journal of sociology*, pages 1420–1443, 1978.

[15] F. Harary. A criterion for unanimity in French's theory of social power. In D. Cartwright, editor, *Studies in Social Power*. Institute for Social Research, Ann Arbor, MI, 1959.

[16] R. Hegselmann and U. Krause. Opinion dynamics and bounded confidence models, analysis, and simulation. *Artificial Societies and Social Simulations*, 5(3), 2002.

[17] R. A. Holley and T. M. Liggett. Ergodic theorems for weakly interacting infinite systems and the voter model. *The Annals of Probability*, 3(4):643–663, 1975.

[18] P. Holme and M. E. J. Newman. Nonequilibrium phase transitions in the coevolution of networks and opinions. *Phys Rev E Stat Nonlin Soft Matter Phys*, 74:056108, 2006.

[19] M. O. Jackson. *Social and Economic Networks*. Princeton University Press, Princeton, NJ, USA, 2008.

[20] D. Kempe, J. Kleinberg, and É. Tardos. Maximizing the spread of influence through a social network. In *Proc. of the ninth ACM SIGKDD*, pages 137–146. ACM, 2003.

[21] D. Kempe, J. M. Kleinberg, S. Oren, and A. Slivkins. Selection and influence in cultural dynamics. In *ACM EC*, pages 585–586, 2013.

[22] Lexalytics. Salience engine - `http://www.lexalytics.com/technical-info/salience-engine-for-text-analysis`.

[23] C. G. Lord, L. Ross, and M. R. Lepper. Biased assimilation and attitude polarization: The effects of prior theories on subsequently considered evidence. *J. Personality and Social Psychology*, 37(11):2098–2109, 1979.

[24] J. Lorenz. Heterogeneous bounds of confidence: Meet, discuss and find consensus! *Complexity*, 15(4):43–52, 2010.

[25] S. A. Myers, C. Zhu, and J. Leskovec. Information diffusion and external influence in networks. In *Proc. of the 18th ACM SIGKDD*, pages 33–41. ACM, 2012.

[26] V. Price, L. Nir, and J. N. Cappella. Normative and informational influences in online political discussions. *Communication Theory*, 16(1):47–74, 2006.

[27] T. C. Schelling. Models of segregation. *American Economic Review*, 59(2):488–493, 1969.

[28] G. Weisbuch, G. Deffuant, F. Amblard, and J.-P. Nadal. Meet, discuss and segregate! *Complexity*, 7(3):55–63, 2002.

[29] E. Yildiz, D. Acemoglu, A. Ozdaglar, A. Saberi, and A. Scaglione. Discrete opinion dynamics with stubborn agents. *ACM EC*, 2013.

[30] M. E. Yildiz, R. Pagliari, A. Ozdaglar, and A. Scaglione. Voting models in random networks. In *Information Theory and Applications Workshop (ITA), 2010*, pages 1–7, 2010.

# APPENDIX

# A. OPINION CORRELATION ON TWITTER

We present empirical evidence on Twitter to show that for a wide range of topics, the sentiments that a user expresses are correlated with the sentiments in its neighborhood. We note that one cannot conclusively infer evidence of influence from such data, but the very existence of correlation even for sentiments of the *same* topic is motivation to study models of opinion formation and dynamics in social networks.

**Dataset:** Our dataset comprised of user opinions extracted from a large set of tweets corresponding to one of four topics: "Hyundai", "Tim Cook", "Organic food", and "Electric Cars". We considered all tweets related to these topics (using simple keyword-based classifiers) within a 6-month timeline from 12/1/2012 to 5/31/2013. The total number of tweets in each topic varied between 200000 and 4000000. We then ran each tweet through a commercial sentiment analyzer [22] software to obtain three categorical opinions value: negative, positive, and neutral. For each node (user) and topic, we associated a list of opinions ordered by their timestamps. Using the Twitter follow graph, we computed the induced subgraph over the nodes (across all topics) with around 2 million nodes and 300 million edges.

**Table 1: Experiment 1**

| Fraction of +/- opinions in +/- class | Hyundai | Tim Cook | Electric Cars | Organic Food |
|---|---|---|---|---|
| +ve opinion, +ve class | 0.706 | 0.584 | 0.430 | 0.832 |
| +ve opinion, -ve class | 0.553 | 0.550 | 0.347 | 0.733 |
| -ve opinion, -ve class | 0.331 | 0.420 | 0.594 | 0.206 |
| -ve opinion, +ve class | 0.260 | 0.409 | 0.529 | 0.138 |

**Table 2: Experiment 2**

| Distance between +/- user opinion and +/- nbr opinion | Hyundai | Tim Cook | Electric Cars | Organic Food |
|---|---|---|---|---|
| +usr, +nbr | 884 | 652 | 763 | 600 |
| -usr, +nbr | 1149 | 944 | 855 | 788 |
| -usr, -nbr | 1007 | 661 | 683 | 1324 |
| +usr, -nbr | 1428 | 928 | 851 | 1707 |

To unearth statistically-significant evidence of correlations between a user and her neighborhood, we analyze each user's list of opinions expressed in the 6-month window, and compare it with a list of all her neighboring users' opinions expressed in that same window. To alleviate the inherent noise in the opinion mining and sentiment extraction process, we ignore all neutral opinions in our experiments and only consider users that have expressed at least two (non-neutral) opinions. We then perform the following two experiments across each of the 4 topics:

**Experiment 1**: We categorize users into two classes: a positive (resp. negative) class and a non-positive (resp. non-negative) class, based on whether they have expressed at least one positive (resp. negative) opinion. For each class, we then consider the set of neighboring opinions of users of that class, and measure the overall fraction of positive (resp. negative) opinions in that set. We observe that this fraction is higher for the set of neighboring opinions corresponding to the positive (resp. negative) class, than for the non-positive (resp. non-negative) class. Table 1 illustrates these results. The difference between the two classes is statistically significant at p-value levels of much less than 0.001 using two-sample t-tests.

**Experiment 2**: Next, we measure the average distance (in time) from a positive opinion of a user to her closest neighboring positive opinion in the past, and compare this to the average distance from a negative opinion of a user to her closest neighboring positive opinion in the past. We observe (in Table 2) that the former distance (in units of seconds) is much smaller than the latter, which suggests that conditioned on her neighborhood expressing a positive opinion, a user is more likely to express a positive opinion than a negative opinion. Similar observations hold for negative opinions as well. As before, we validated that these differences are statistically significant at p-value levels of much less than 0.001 using two-sample t-tests.

# Fast Approximation of Betweenness Centrality through Sampling

Matteo Riondato
Dept. of Computer Science
Brown University
Providence, RI, USA
matteo@cs.brown.edu

Evgenios M. Kornaropoulos
Dept. of Computer Science
Brown University
Providence, RI, USA
evgenios@cs.brown.edu

## ABSTRACT

Betweenness centrality is a fundamental measure in social network analysis, expressing the importance or influence of individual vertices in a network in terms of the fraction of shortest paths that pass through them. Exact computation in large networks is prohibitively expensive and fast approximation algorithms are required in these cases. We present two efficient randomized algorithms for betweenness estimation. The algorithms are based on random sampling of shortest paths and offer probabilistic guarantees on the quality of the approximation. The first algorithm estimates the betweenness of all vertices: all approximated values are within an additive factor $\varepsilon$ from the real values, with probability at least $1 - \delta$. The second algorithm focuses on the top-K vertices with highest betweenness and approximate their betweenness within a multiplicative factor $\varepsilon$, with probability at least $1 - \delta$. This is the first algorithm that can compute such approximation for the top-K vertices. We use results from the VC-dimension theory to develop bounds to the sample size needed to achieve the desired approximations. By proving upper and lower bounds to the VC-dimension of a range set associated with the problem at hand, we obtain a sample size that is independent from the number of vertices in the network and only depends on a characteristic quantity that we call the vertex-diameter, that is the maximum number of vertices in a shortest path. In some cases, the sample size is completely independent from any property of the graph. The extensive experimental evaluation that we performed using real and artificial networks shows that our algorithms are significantly faster and much more scalable as the number of vertices in the network grows than previously presented algorithms with similar approximation guarantees.

## Categories and Subject Descriptors

G.2.2 [**Discrete Mathematics**]: Graph Theory—*Graph algorithms*; H.2.8 [**Database Management**]: Database Applications—*Data mining*

## Keywords

Betweenness centrality, graph mining, range set, sampling, social network analysis, VC-dimension, vertex diameter


*WSDM'14*, February 24–28, 2014, New York, New York, USA.

http://dx.doi.org/10.1145/2556195.2556224.

## 1. INTRODUCTION

Centrality indices are fundamental metrics for network analysis. They express the relative importance of a vertex in the network. Some of them, e.g., degree centrality, reflect local properties of the underlying graph, while others, like betweenness centrality, give information about the global network structure, as they are based on shortest path computation and counting [28]. In this work we are interested in *betweenness centrality* [3, 14], that is, for every vertex in the graph, the fraction of shortest paths that goes through that vertex (see Section 3 for formal definitions) . Betweenness centrality has been used to analyze social and protein interaction networks, to evaluate traffic in communication networks, and to identify important intersections in road networks [15, 28]. There exist polynomial-time algorithms to compute the exact betweenness centrality [8], but they are not practical for the analysis of the very large networks that are of interest these days. Graphs representing online social networks, communication networks, and the web graph have millions of nodes and billions of edges, making a polynomial-time algorithm too expensive in practice. Given that data mining is exploratory in nature, approximate results are usually sufficient, especially if the approximation error is guaranteed to be within user-specified limits. In practice, the user is interested in the relative ranking of the vertices according to their betweenness, rather than the actual value of the betweenness, so a very good estimation of the value of each vertex is sufficiently informative for most purposes. It is therefore natural to develop algorithms that trade off accuracy for speed and efficiently compute high-quality approximations of the betweenness of the vertices. Nevertheless, in order for these algorithms to be practical it is extremely important that they scale well and have a low runtime dependency on the size of the network (number of vertices and/or edges).

*Our contributions.* We present two randomized algorithms to approximate the betweenness centrality (and some of its variants) of the vertices of a graph. The first algorithm guarantees that the estimated betweenness values for all vertices are within an *additive* factor $\varepsilon$ from the real values, with probability at least $1-\delta$. The second algorithm focuses on the top-$K$ vertices with highest betweenness and returns a *superset* of the top-$K$, while ensuring that the estimated betweenness for all returned vertices is within a *multiplicative* factor $\varepsilon$ from the real value, with probability at least $1-\delta$. This is the first algorithm to reach such a high-quality approximation for the set of top-$K$ vertices. The algorithms are based on random sampling of shortest paths. The analysis to derive the sufficient sample size is novel and uses notions and results from VC-dimension theory. We define a range set associated with the problem at hand and prove strict bounds to its VC-dimension. The resulting sample size *does not depend on the size of the graph*, but only on the maximum number of vertices in a shortest path, a *characteristic quantity* of the graph that we call the *vertex-diameter*. For some networks, we show that the VC-dimension is actually at most a constant and so the sample size depends *only on the approximation parameters* and not on any property of the graph, a somewhat surprising fact that points out interesting insights. Thanks to the lower runtime dependency on the size of the network, our algorithms are *much faster and more scalable* than previous contributions [10, 15, 18], while offering the same approximation guarantees. Moreover, the amount of work performed by our algorithms per sample is also less than that of others algorithms. We extensively evaluated our methods on real graphs and compared their performances to the exact algorithm for betweenness centrality [8] and to other sampling-based approximation algorithms [10, 15, 18], showing that our methods achieve a huge speedup (3 to 4 times faster) and scale much better as the number of vertices in the network grows.

We present related work in Sect. 2. Section 3 introduces all the basic definitions and results that we will use throughout the paper. A range set for the problem at hand and the bounds to its VC-dimension are presented in Sect. 4. Based on these results we develop and analyze algorithms for betweenness estimation that we present in Sect. 5. Section 6 reports the methodology and the results of our extensive experimental evaluation.

## 2. RELATED WORK

Over the years, a number of centrality measures have been defined [28]. In this work we focus on betweenness centrality and some of its variants.

Betweenness centrality was introduced in the sociology literature [3, 14]. Brandes [9] presents a number of minor variants. A particularly interesting one, $k$-bounded-distance betweenness, limits the length of the shortest paths considered when computing the centrality [7, 9, 29]. This is not to be confused with $k$-path betweenness centrality defined by Kourtellis et al. [20], which considers simple random walks that are not necessarily shortest paths. Dolev et al. [12] present a generalization of betweenness centrality which takes into account routing policies in the network.

The need of fast algorithms to compute the betweenness of vertices in a graph arose as large online social networks started to appear. Brandes [8] presents the first efficient algorithm for the task, running in time $O(nm)$ on unweighted graphs and $O(nm + n^2 \log n)$ on weighted ones. The algorithm computes, for each vertex $v$, the shortest path to every other vertex and then traverses these paths backwards to efficiently compute the contribution of the shortest paths from $v$ to the betweenness of other vertices. For very large networks, the cost of this algorithm would still be prohibitive in practice, so many approximation algorithms were developed [4, 10, 15, 18, 23, 25]. The use of random sampling was one of the more natural approaches to speed up the computation of betweenness. Inspired by the work of Eppstein and Wang [13], Jacob et al. [18] and independently Brandes and Pich [10] present an algorithm that mimics the exact one, with the difference that, instead of computing the contribution of all vertices to the betweenness of the others, it only considers the contributions of some vertices sampled uniformly at random. To guarantee that all estimates are within $\varepsilon$ from their real value with probability at least $1 - \delta$, the algorithm from [10, 18] needs $O(\log(n/\delta)/\varepsilon^2)$ samples. The analysis for the derivation of the sample size uses Hoeffding bounds [17] and the union bound [26]. Geisberger et al. [15] noticed that this can lead to an overestimation of the betweenness of vertices that are close to the sampled ones and introduced different unbiased estimators that are experimentally shown to have smaller variance and do not suffer from this overshooting. Our algorithm is different from these because we sample, each time, a single random shortest path. This leads to a much smaller sample size and less work done for each sample, resulting in a much faster way to compute approximations of the betweenness with the same probabilistic guarantees. We delve more in the comparisons with these algorithms in Sect. 5.3 and 6.

A number of works explored the use of adaptive sampling, in contrast with the previous algorithms (and ours) which use a fixed sample size. Bader et al. [4] present an adaptive sampling algorithm which computes good estimations for the betweenness of high-centrality vertices, by keeping track of the partial contribution of each sampled vertex, obtained by performing a single-source shortest paths computation to all other vertices. Maiya and Berger-Wolf [25] use concepts from expander graphs to select a connected sample of vertices. They estimate the betweenness from the sample, which includes the vertices with high centrality. They build the connected sample by adding the vertex which maximizes the number of connections with vertices not already in the sample. Modified versions of this algorithm and an extensive experimental evaluation appeared in [23]. The algorithm does not offer any guarantee on the quality of the approximations. Compared to these adaptive sampling approaches, our methods ensure that the betweenness of all (or top-$K$) vertices is well approximated, while using a fixed, predetermined amount of samples. Sariyüce et al. [33] present an algorithm that pre-processes the network in multiple ways by removing degree-1 vertices and identical vertices, and splits it in separate components where the computation of betweenness can be performed independently and then aggregated. They do not present an analysis of the complexity of the algorithm.

In the analysis of our algorithm we use results from VC-dimension theory [34], a key component of statistical learning theory. We compute an upper bound to the VC-dimension of a range set defined on shortest paths. Kranakis et al. [21] present a number of results on the VC-dimension of various range sets for graphs (stars, connected sets of vertices, sets of edges), but do not deal with shortest paths. Abraham et al. [1] use VC-dimension to speed up shortest path computation but their range set is different from the one we use: their ground set is the set of vertices while ours is defined on shortest paths.

## 3. PRELIMINARIES

In this section we introduce the definitions and lemmas that we will use to develop and analyze our results throughout the paper.

### 3.1 Graphs and betweenness centrality

Let $G = (V, E)$ be a graph, where $E \subseteq V \times V$, with $n = |V|$ vertices and $m = |E|$ edges. The graph $G$ can be directed or undirected. We assume that there are no self-loops from one vertex to itself and no multiple edges between a pair of vertices. Each edge $e \in E$ has a non-negative weight $\mathsf{w}(e)$. Given a pair of distinct vertices $(u, v) \in V \times V$, $u \neq v$, a *path* $p_{uv} \subseteq V$ *from* $u$ *to* $v$ is an ordered sequence of vertices $p_{uv} = (w_1, \ldots, w_{|p_{uv}|})$ such that $w_1 = u$, $w_{|p_{uv}|} = v$ and for each $1 \leq i < |p_{uv}|$, $(w_i, w_{i+1}) \in E$. The vertices $u$ and $v$ are called the *end points* of $p_{uv}$ and the vertices in $\mathsf{Int}(p_{uv}) = p_{uv} \setminus \{u, v\}$ are the *internal vertices of* $p_{uv}$. The *weight* $\mathsf{w}(p_{uv})$ of a path $p_{uv} = (u = w_1, w_2, \cdots, w_{|p_{uv}|} = v)$ from $u$ to $v$ is the sum of the weights of the edges composing the path: $\mathsf{w}(p_{uv}) = \sum_{i=1}^{|p_{uv}|-1} \mathsf{w}((w_i, w_{i+1}))$. We denote with $|p_{uv}|$ the number of vertices composing the path and call this the *size of the path* $p_{uv}$. Note that if the weights are not all unitary, it is not necessarily true that $\mathsf{w}(p_{uv}) = |p_{uv}| - 1$. A special and degenerate path is the *empty path* $p_\emptyset = \emptyset$, which by definition has weight $\mathsf{w}(p_\emptyset) = \infty$, no end points, and $\mathsf{Int}(p_\emptyset) = \emptyset$.

Given two distinct vertices $(u, v) \in V \times V$, the *shortest path distance* $d_{uv}$ between $u$ and $v$ is the weight of a path with minimum weight between $u$ and $v$ among all paths between $u$ and $v$. If there is no path between $u$ and $v$, $d_{uv} = \infty$. We call a path between $u$ and $v$ with weight $d_{uv}$ a *shortest path between $u$ and $v$*. There can be multiple shortest paths between $u$ and $v$ and we denote the set of these paths as $\mathcal{S}_{uv}$ and the number of these paths as $\sigma_{uv} = |\mathcal{S}_{uv}|$. If there is no path between $u$ and $v$, then $\mathcal{S}_{uv} = \{p_\emptyset\}$[1]. We denote with $\mathbb{S}_G$ the union of all the $\mathcal{S}_{uv}$'s, for all pairs $(u, v) \in V \times V$ of distinct nodes $u \neq v$:

$$\mathbb{S}_G = \bigcup_{\substack{(u,v) \in V \times V \\ u \neq v}} \mathcal{S}_{uv} \ .$$

We now define a characteristic quantity of a graph that we will use throughout the paper.

*Definition 1.* Given a graph $G = (V, E)$, the *vertex-diameter* $\mathsf{VD}(G)$ *of* $G$ is the size of the shortest path in $G$ with maximum size:

$$\mathsf{VD}(G) = \max\{|p| \ : \ p \in \mathbb{S}_G\} \ .$$

The vertex-diameter is the maximum number of vertices among all shortest paths in $G$. If all the edge weights are unitary, then $\mathsf{VD}(G)$ is equal to $\mathsf{diam}(G) + 1$, where $\mathsf{diam}(G)$ is the number of edges composing the longest shortest path in $G$.

Given a vertex $v$, let $\mathcal{T}_v \subseteq \mathbb{S}_G$ be the set of all shortest paths that $v$ is *internal* to:

$$\mathcal{T}_v = \{p \in \mathbb{S}_G \ : \ v \in \mathsf{Int}(p)\} \ .$$

In this work we are interested in the *betweenness centrality* of the vertices of a graph.

*Definition 2.* [3, 14] Given a graph $G = (V, E)$, the *betweenness centrality of a vertex* $v \in V$ is defined as[2]

$$\mathsf{b}(v) = \frac{1}{n(n-1)} \sum_{p_{uw} \in \mathbb{S}_G} \frac{\mathbb{1}_{\mathcal{T}_v}(p)}{\sigma_{uv}} \ .$$

It is easy to see that $\mathsf{b}(v) \in [0, 1]$. Brandes [8] presented an algorithm to compute the betweenness centrality for all $v \in V$ in time $O(nm)$ for unweighted graphs and $O(nm + n^2 \log n)$ for weighted graphs.

A "local" variant of betweenness, called *$k$-bounded-distance betweenness*[3] only considers the contribution of shortest paths of size up to $k+1$ [7, 9]. For $k > 1$ and any pair of distinct vertices $u, v \in V$, $u \neq V$, let $\mathcal{S}_{uv}^{(k)} \subseteq \mathcal{S}_{uv}$ be the set of shortest paths from $u$ to $v$ of size at most $k+1$, with $\sigma_{uv}^{(k)} = |\mathcal{S}_{uv}^{(k)}|$, and let $\mathbb{S}_G^{(k)}$ be the union of all the $\mathcal{S}_{uv}^{(k)}$. Let $\mathcal{T}_v^{(k)} \subseteq \mathcal{T}_v$ be the set of all shortest paths *of size up to $k$* that $v$ is internal to, for each $v \in V$.

*Definition 3.* [7, 9] Given a graph $G = (V, E)$ and an integer $k > 1$, the *$k$-bounded-distance betweenness centrality of a vertex* $v \in V$ is defined as

$$\mathsf{bb}^{(k)}(v) = \frac{1}{n(n-1)} \sum_{p_{uw} \in \mathbb{S}_G^{(k)}} \frac{\mathbb{1}_{\mathcal{T}_v^{(k)}}(p)}{\sigma_{uw}^{(k)}} \ .$$

Other variants of centrality are presented in the extended version [31].

## 3.2 Vapnik-Chervonenkis dimension

The Vapnik-Chernovenkis (VC) dimension of a class of subsets defined on a set of points is a measure of the complexity or expressiveness of such class [34]. Given a probability distribution on the set of points, a finite bound on the VC-dimension of the class of subsets implies a bound on the number of random samples required to approximate the probability of each subset in the class with its empirical average. We outline here some basic definitions and results and refer the reader to the book by Mohri et al. [27] for an in-depth presentation.

Let $D$ be a domain and $\mathcal{R}$ be a collection of subsets from $D$. We call $\mathcal{R}$ a *range set on* $D$. Given $B \subseteq D$, the *projection of $\mathcal{R}$ on $B$* is the set $P_\mathcal{R}(B) = \{B \cap A \ : \ A \in \mathcal{R}\}$. We say that the set $B$ is *shattered* by $\mathcal{R}$ if $P_\mathcal{R}(B) = 2^B$.

*Definition 4.* The *Vapnik-Chervonenkis (VC) dimension of* $\mathcal{R}$, denoted as $\mathsf{VC}(\mathcal{R})$, is the cardinality of the largest subset of $D$ that is shattered by $\mathcal{R}$.

The main application of VC-dimension in statistics and learning theory is in computing the number of samples needed to approximate the probabilities of the ranges using their empirical averages as unbiased estimators. Formally, let $X_1^k = (X_1, \ldots, X_k)$ be a collection of independent identically distributed random variables taking values in $D$, sampled according to some distribution $\phi$ defined on the elements of $D$. For a set $A \subseteq D$, let $\phi(A)$ be the probability that a sample from $\phi$ belongs to the set $A$, and let the *empirical average* of $\phi(A)$ on $X_1^k$ be

$$\phi_{X_1^k}(A) = \frac{1}{k} \sum_{j=1}^{k} \mathbb{1}_A(X_j) \ .$$

The empirical average of $\phi(A)$ can be used as an *unbiased* estimator for $\phi(A)$.

*Definition 5.* Let $\mathcal{R}$ be a range set on $D$ and $\phi$ be a probability distribution on $D$. For $\varepsilon \in (0, 1)$, an *$\varepsilon$-approximation to $(\mathcal{R}, \phi)$* is a bag $S$ of elements of $D$ such that

$$\sup_{A \in \mathcal{R}} |\phi(A) - \phi_S(A)| \leq \varepsilon \ .$$

When an upper bound to the VC-dimension of $\mathcal{R}$ is available, it is possible to build an $\varepsilon$-approximation by sampling points of the domain according to the distribution $\phi$.

THEOREM 1 (THM. 2.12 [16] (SEE ALSO [22])). *Let $\mathcal{R}$ be a range set on a domain $D$ with $\mathsf{VC}(\mathcal{R}) \leq d$, and let $\phi$ be a distribution on $D$. Given $\varepsilon, \delta \in (0, 1)$ let $S$ be a collection of $|S|$ points from $D$ sampled according to $\phi$, with*

$$|S| = \frac{c}{\varepsilon^2}\left(d + \ln\frac{1}{\delta}\right) \qquad (1)$$

*where $c$ is an universal positive constant. Then $S$ is an $\varepsilon$-approximation to $(\mathcal{R}, \phi)$ with probability at least $1 - \delta$.*

The constant $c$ is approximately 0.5 [24]. It is possible to obtain *relative* guarantees on the approximation.

[1] Note that even if $p_\emptyset = \emptyset$, the set $\{p_\emptyset\}$ is not empty. It contains one element.

[2] We use the normalized version of betweenness as we believe it to be more suitable for presenting approximation results.

[3] Bounded-distance betweenness is also known as $k$-betweenness. We prefer the former denomination to avoid confusion with $k$-path betweenness.

*Definition 6.* Let $\mathcal{R}$ be a range set on $D$ and $\phi$ be a probability distribution on $D$. For $p, \varepsilon \in (0,1)$, a *relative $(p,\varepsilon)$-approximation to $(\mathcal{R},\phi)$* is a bag $S$ of elements from $D$ such that

- For any $A \in \mathcal{R}$ such that $\phi(A) \geq p$, we have
$$|\phi(A) - \phi_S(A)| \leq \varepsilon\phi(A) \ .$$
- For any $B \in \mathcal{R}$ such that $\phi(B) < p$, we have $\phi_S(B) \leq (1+\varepsilon)p$.

THEOREM 2 (THM. 2.11 [16]). *Let $\mathcal{R}$ be a range set on a domain $D$ with $\mathsf{VC}(\mathcal{R}) \leq d$, and let $\phi$ be a distribution on $D$. Given $\varepsilon, \delta, p \in (0,1)$ let $S$ be a collection of $|S|$ points from $D$ sampled according to $\phi$, with*

$$|S| \geq \frac{c'}{\varepsilon^2 p}\left(d \log\frac{1}{p} + \log\frac{1}{\delta}\right) \qquad (2)$$

*where $c'$ is an absolute positive constant. Then $S$ is a relative $(p,\varepsilon)$-approximation to $(\mathcal{R},\phi)$ with probability at least $1-\delta$.*

It is important to mention that if $\mathsf{VC}(\mathcal{R})$ and/or the upper bound $d$ do not depend on $|D|$ or on $|\mathcal{R}|$ neither do the sample sizes presented in Thm. 1 and 2. This will make our algorithms scale well as the size of the network increases.

# 4. A RANGE SET OF SHORTEST PATHS

We now define a range set of the shortest paths of a graph $G = (V,E)$, and present a strict upper bound to its VC-dimension. We use the range set and the bound in the analysis of our algorithms for estimating the betweenness centrality of vertices of $G$.

The range set $\mathcal{R}_G$ is defined on the set $\mathbb{S}_G$ of all shortest paths between vertices of $G$. It contains, for each vertex $v \in V$, the set $\mathcal{T}_v$ of shortest paths that $v$ is internal to:

$$\mathcal{R}_G = \{\mathcal{T}_v \ : \ v \in V\} \ .$$

LEMMA 1. $\mathsf{VC}(\mathcal{R}_G) \leq \lfloor \log_2(\mathsf{VD}(G) - 2)\rfloor + 1$.

PROOF. Let $\ell > \lfloor \log_2(\mathsf{VD}(G)-2)\rfloor + 1$ and assume for the sake of contradiction that $\mathsf{VC}(\mathcal{R}_G) = \ell$. From the definition of the VC-dimension there is a set $Q \subseteq \mathbb{S}_G$ of size $\ell$ that is shattered by $\mathcal{R}_G$. Let $p$ be an element of $Q$. There are $2^{\ell-1}$ non-empty subsets of $Q$ containing the path $p$. Let us label these non-empty subsets of $Q$ containing $p$ as $S_1, \ldots, S_{2^{\ell-1}}$, where the labelling is arbitrary. Given that $Q$ is shattered, for each set $S_i$ there must be a range $R_i$ in $\mathcal{R}_G$ such that $S_i = Q \cap R_i$. Since all the $S_i$'s are different from each other, then all the $R_i$'s must be different from each other. Given that $p$ belongs to each $S_i$, then $p$ must also belong to each $R_i$, that is, there are $2^{\ell-1}$ distinct ranges in $\mathcal{R}_G$ containing $p$. But $p$ belongs only to the ranges corresponding to internal vertices of $p$, i.e., to vertices in $\mathsf{Int}(p)$. This means that the number of ranges in $\mathcal{R}_G$ that $p$ belongs to is equal to $|p|-2$. But $|p| \leq \mathsf{VD}(G)$, by definition of $\mathsf{VD}(G)$, so $p$ can belong to at most $\mathsf{VD}(G)-2$ ranges from $\mathcal{R}_G$. Given that $2^{\ell-1} > \mathsf{VD}(G)-2$, we reached a contradiction and there cannot be $2^{\ell-1}$ distinct ranges containing $p$, hence not all the sets $S_i$ can be expressed as $Q \cap R_i$ for some $R_i \in \mathcal{R}_G$. Then $Q$ cannot be shattered and $\mathsf{VC}(\mathcal{R}_G) \leq \lfloor \log_2(\mathsf{VD}(G)-2)\rfloor + 1$. □

### *Unique shortest paths.*

In the restricted case when the graph is undirected and every pair of distinct vertices has either none or a unique shortest path between them, the VC-dimension of $\mathcal{R}_G$ reduces to a *constant.* This is a somewhat surprising result with interesting consequences. From a theoretical point of view, it suggests that there should be other characteristic quantities of the graph different from the vertex diameter that control the VC-dimension of the range set of shortest paths, and these quantities are constant on graph with unique shortest paths between vertices. From a more practical point of view, we will see in Sect. 5 that this result has an impact on the sample size needed to approximate the betweenness centrality of networks where the unique-shortest-path property is satisfied or even enforced, like road networks [15]. In particular, the resulting sample size will be *completely independent* from any characteristic of the network, and will only be a function of the parameters controlling the desired approximation guarantees. We are currently investigating whether this result can be extended to the case of directed graphs. Due to space constraints, we defer the proof to the extended online version of the paper [31].

LEMMA 2. *Let $G = (V,E)$ be an undirected graph with $|\mathcal{S}_{uv}| \leq 1$ for all pairs $(u,v) \in V \times V$. Then* $\mathsf{VC}(\mathcal{R}_G) \leq 3$.

### *Bounded-distance betweenness.*

For the case of $k$-bounded-distance betweenness, if we let $\mathcal{R}_G^{(k)} = \{\mathcal{T}_v^{(k)} \ : \ v \in V\}$, it is easy to bound $\mathsf{VC}(\mathcal{R}_G^{(k)})$ following the same reasoning as in Lemma 1.

LEMMA 3. $\mathsf{VC}(\mathcal{R}_G^{(k)}) \leq \lfloor \log_2(k-1)\rfloor + 1$.

## 4.1 Tightness

The bound presented in Lemma 1 is strict in the sense that for each $d \geq 1$ we can build a graph $G_d$ with vertex-diameter $\mathsf{VD}(G_d) = 2^d + 1$ and such that the range set $\mathcal{R}_{G_d}$ associated to the set of shortest paths of $G_d$ has VC-dimension exactly $d = \lfloor \log_2(\mathsf{VD}(G_d) - 2)\rfloor + 1$.

There is a class $\mathcal{G} = (G_d)_{d \geq 1}$ of graphs indexed by d, such that the graphs in $\mathcal{G}$ are the ones for which we can show the tightness of the bound to the VC-dimension of the associated range set. We call the graph $G_d \in \mathcal{G}$ the *d-th concertina graph.* Figure 1 shows $G_1$, $G_2$, $G_3$, and $G_4$. The generalization to higher values of $d$ should be straightforward. Each graph $G_d$ has $3(2^{d-1}$ vertices and vertex-diameter $d$.

LEMMA 4. $\mathsf{VC}(\mathcal{R}_{G_d}) = d$.

Due to space constraints, we defer the proof to the extended online version of the paper [31].

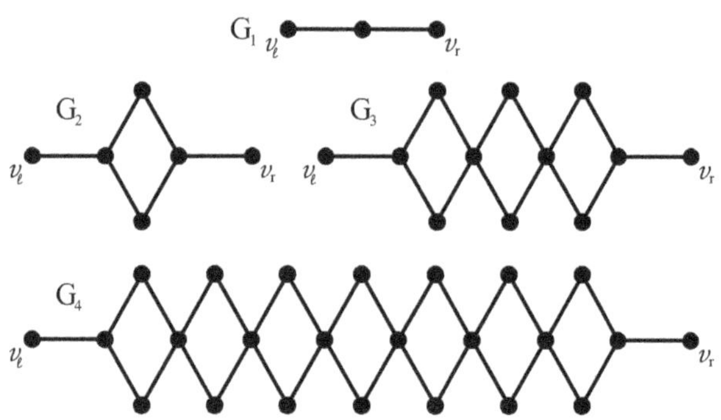


Figure 1: Examples of concertina graphs $G_d$ for $d = 1, 2, 3, 4$.

The upper bound presented in Lemma 2 for the case of unique shortest paths is also strict in the same sense. The proof can be found in the extended online version of the paper [31].

LEMMA 5. *There is a graph $G = (V, E)$ with $|\mathcal{S}_{uv}| \leq 1$ for all pairs $(u, v) \in V \times V$ such that the range set $\mathcal{R}_G$ associated to the shortest paths in $G$ has VC-Dimension exactly 3.*

# 5. ALGORITHMS

In this section we present our algorithms to compute a set of approximations for the betweenness centrality of the (top-$K$) vertices in a graph through sampling, with probabilistic guarantees on the quality of the approximations.

## 5.1 Approximation for all the vertices

The intuition behind the algorithm to approximate the betweenness values of all vertices is the following. Given a graph $G = (V, E)$ with vertex-diameter $\mathsf{VD}(G)$ and two parameters $\varepsilon, \delta \in (0, 1)$ we first compute a sample size $r$ using (1) with

$$d = \lfloor \log_2(\mathsf{VD}(G) - 2) \rfloor + 1 \ .$$

The resulting sample size is

$$r = \frac{c}{\varepsilon^2}\left(\lfloor \log_2(\mathsf{VD}(G) - 2)\rfloor + 1 + \ln\frac{1}{\delta}\right) \ . \qquad (3)$$

This is sufficient to achieve the desired accuracy (expressed through $\varepsilon$) with the desired confidence (expressed through $1-\delta$). The algorithm repeats the following steps $r$ times: *1.* it samples a pair $u, v$ of distinct vertices uniformly at random, *2.* it computes the set $\mathcal{S}_{uv}$ of all shortest paths between $u$ and $v$, *3.* it selects a path $p$ from $\mathcal{S}_{uv}$ uniformly at random, *4.* it increases by $1/r$ the betweenness estimation of each vertex in $\mathsf{Int}(p)$. Note that if the sampled vertices $u$ and $v$ are not connected, we can skip steps 3 and 4 because we defined $\mathcal{S}_{uv} = \{p_\emptyset\}$. Denoting with $S$ the set of the sampled shortest paths, the *unbiased* estimator $\tilde{\mathsf{b}}(w)$ for the betweenness $\mathsf{b}(w)$ of a vertex $w$ is the sample average

$$\tilde{\mathsf{b}}(w) = \frac{1}{r}\sum_{p\in S} \mathbb{1}_{\mathsf{Int}(p)}(w) = \frac{1}{r}\sum_{p\in S} \mathbb{1}_{\mathcal{T}_w}(p) \ .$$

There are two crucial steps in this algorithm: the computation of $\mathsf{VD}(G)$ and the sampling of a path uniformly at random from $\mathcal{S}_{uv}$. We first deal with the latter, and then present a linear-time constant-factor approximation algorithm for $\mathsf{VD}(G)$. Algorithm 1 presents the pseudocode of the algorithm, including the steps to select a random path. The `computeAllShortestPaths(u,v)` on line 8 is a call to a modified Dijkstra's (or BFS) algorithm to compute the set $\mathcal{S}_{uv}$, with the same modifications as [8]. The `getDiameterApprox()` procedure computes an approximation for $\mathsf{VD}(G)$.

### *Unique shortest paths.*

When, for each pair $(u, v)$ of vertices of $G$, either there is a unique shortest path from $u$ to $v$ or $v$ is unreachable from $u$, then one can apply Lemma 2 and obtain a smaller sample size

$$r = \frac{c}{\varepsilon^2}\left(3 + \ln\frac{1}{\delta}\right)$$

to approximate the betweenness values of all the vertices. This is an interesting result: the number of samples needed to compute a good approximation to all vertices is a *constant* and completely *independent from G*. Intuitively, this means that the algorithm is extremely fast on graphs with this property. Unique shortest paths are common or even enforced in road networks by slightly perturbing the edge weights or having a deterministic tie breaking policy [15].

### *Bounded-distance betweenness.*

For the case of $k$-bounded-distance betweenness, the sample size on line 6 of Alg. 1 can be reduced to

$$r = \frac{c}{\varepsilon^2}\left(\lfloor \log_2(k - 1)\rfloor + 1 + \ln\frac{1}{\delta}\right)$$

and the computation of the shortest paths on line 8 can be stopped after we reached the vertices that are $k$ "hops" far from $u$.

### *Sampling a shortest path.*

Our procedure to select a random shortest path from $\mathcal{S}_{uv}$ is inspired by the dependencies accumulation procedure used in Brandes' exact algorithm [8]. Let $u$ and $v$ be the vertices sampled by our algorithm (Step 7 of Alg. 1). We assume that $u$ and $v$ are connected otherwise the only possibility is to select the empty path $p_\emptyset$. Let $y$ be any vertex belonging to at least one shortest path from $u$ to $v$. Following Brandes [8], we can compute $\sigma_{uy}$ and $\mathcal{S}_{uy}$ while we compute the set $\mathcal{S}_{uv}$ of all the shortest paths from $u$ to $v$. We can then use this information to select a shortest path $p$ uniformly at random from $\mathcal{S}_{uv}$ as follows. For each vertex $w$ let $P_u(w)$ be the subset of neighbors of $w$ that are *predecessors* of $w$ along the shortest paths from $u$ to $w$. Let $p^* = \{v\}$. Starting from $v$, we select one of its predecessors $z \in P_u(v)$ using weighted random sampling: each $z \in P_u(v)$ has probability $\sigma_{uz}/\sum_{w\in P_u(v)}\sigma_{uw}$ of being sampled. We add $z$ to $p^*$ and then repeat the procedure for $z$. That is, we select one of $z$'s predecessors from $P_u(z)$ using weighted sampling and add it to $p^*$, and so on until we reach $u$. Note that we can update the estimation of the betweenness of the internal vertices along $p^*$ (the only ones for which the estimation is updated) as we compute $p^*$.

LEMMA 6. *The path $p^*$ built according to the above procedure is selected uniformly at random among the paths in $\mathcal{S}_{uv}$.*

PROOF. The probability of sampling $p^* = (u, z_1, \ldots, z_{|p^*|-2}, v)$ equals to the product of the probabilities of sampling the vertices internal to $p^*$, hence

$$\Pr(p^*) = \frac{\sigma_{uz_{|p^*|-2}}}{\sigma_{uv}}\frac{\sigma_{uz_{|p^*|-3}}}{\sigma_{uz_{|p^*|-2}}}\cdots\frac{1}{\sigma_{uz_2}} = \frac{1}{\sigma_{uv}}$$

where we used [8, Lemma3] which tells us that for $w \neq u$,

$$\sigma_{uw} = \sum_{j\in P_u(w)} \sigma_{uj}$$

and the fact that for $z_1$, which is a neighbor of $u$, $\sigma_{uz_1} = 1$. □

### *Approximating the vertex-diameter.*

The algorithm presented in the previous section requires the value of the vertex-diameter $\mathsf{VD}(G)$ of the graph $G$ (line 4 of Alg. 1). Computing the exact value of $\mathsf{VD}(G)$ could be done by solving the All Pair Shortest Paths (APSP) problem, and taking the shortest path with the maximum size. Algorithms for exactly solving APSP problem such as Johnson's which runs in $O(V^2 \log V + VE)$ or Floyd-Warshall's ($\Theta(V^3)$), would defeat our purposes: once we have all the shortest paths for the computation of the diameter, we could as well compute the betweenness of all the vertices exactly. Given that Thm. 1 (and Thm. 2) only requires an upper bound to the VC-dimension of the range set, an approximation of the vertex-diameter would be sufficient for our purposes. Several refined algorithms for approximating the diameter are known [2, 6, 32], with various running times and quality of approximations. We briefly present a well-known and simple approximation algorithm that has the right balance of accuracy and speed for our purposes.

**Algorithm 1:** Computes approximations $\tilde{\mathsf{b}}(v)$ of the betweenness centrality $\mathsf{b}(v)$ for all vertices $v \in V$.

**Input** : Graph $G = (V, E)$ with $|V| = n$, $\varepsilon, \delta \in (0, 1)$
**Output**: A set of approximations of the betweenness centrality of the vertices in $V$

1 **foreach** $w \in V$ **do**
2     $\tilde{\mathsf{b}}(v) \leftarrow 0$
3 **end**
4 $\mathsf{VD}(G) \leftarrow$`getVertexDiameter`$(G)$
5 $r \leftarrow (c/\varepsilon^2)(\lfloor \log_2(\mathsf{VD}(G) - 2) \rfloor + \ln(1/\delta))$
6 **for** $i \leftarrow 1$ *to* $r$ **do**
7     $(u, v) \leftarrow$`sampleUniformVertexPair`$(V)$
8     $\mathcal{S}_{uv} \leftarrow$`computeAllShortestPaths`$(u, v)$
9     **if** $\mathcal{S}_{uv} \neq \{p_\emptyset\}$ **then**
        `//Random path sampling and estimation update`
10         $j \leftarrow v$
11         $s \leftarrow v$
12         $t \leftarrow v$
13         **while** $t \neq u$ **do**
14             sample $z \in P_s(t)$ with probability $\sigma_{uz}/\sigma_{us}$
15             **if** $z \neq u$ **then**
16                 $\tilde{\mathsf{b}}(z) \leftarrow \tilde{\mathsf{b}}(z) + 1/r$
17                 $s \leftarrow t$
18                 $t \leftarrow z$
19             **end**
20         **end**
21     **end**
22 **end**
23 **return** $\{(v, \tilde{\mathsf{b}}(v)), v \in V\}$

Let $G = (V, E)$ be an *undirected* graph where *all the edge weights are equal*. It is a well-known result that one can obtain a 2-approximation $\widetilde{\mathsf{VD}}(G)$ of the vertex-diameter $\mathsf{VD}(G)$ of $G$ in time $O(V + E)$ in the following way: 1. select a vertex $v \in V$ uniformly at random, 2. compute the shortest paths from $v$ to all other vertices in $V$, and 3. finally take $\widetilde{\mathsf{VD}}(G)$ to be the sum of the lengths of the two shortest paths with maximum size (which equals to the two longest shortest paths) from $v$ to two distinct other nodes $u$ and $w$. In case we have multiple connected components in $G$, we compute an upper bound to the vertex diameter of each component separately by running the above algorithm on each component, and then taking the maximum. The connected components can be computed in $O(n+m)$ by traversing the graph in a Breadth-First-Search (BFS) fashion starting from a random $v$. The time complexity of the approximation algorithm in the case of multiple connected components is again $O(n + m)$ since the sum of the vertices of individual components is $n$ and the sum of edges is $m$.

The use of the above 2-approximation in the computation of the sample size from line 6 of Alg. 1 results in at most $c/\varepsilon^2$ additional samples than if we used the exact value $\mathsf{VD}(G)$. The computation of $\widetilde{\mathsf{VD}}(G)$ does not affect the running time of our algorithm: for the construction of the first sample we can reuse the shortest paths from the sampled vertex $v$ that we used to obtain the approximation. Specifically, we can sample a new vertex $u \neq v$ and then choose with uniform probability one of the (already computed) shortest paths between $v$ and $u$.

If the graph is directed and/or not all edge weights are equal, the computation of a good approximation to $\mathsf{VD}(G)$ becomes more problematic. In particular, notice that there is no relationship between $\mathsf{VD}(G)$ and $\mathsf{diam}(G)$ when $G$ is weighted, as the shortest path with maximum size may not be the shortest path with maximum weight. In these cases, one can use the size (number of vertices) of the largest Weakly Connected Component (WCC), as a loose upper bound to $\mathsf{VD}(G)$. The WCC's can again be computed in $O(n + m)$ using BFS. This quantity can be as high as $n$ but for the computation of the sample size we use its logarithm, mitigating the crudeness of the bound. In this case our sample size is comparable to that proposed by Brandes and Pich [10]. Nevertheless the amount of work done per sample by our algorithm is still much smaller (see Sect. 5.3 and 6 for more details). In practice, it is possible that the nature of the network suggests a much better upper bound to the vertex-diameter of the graph, resulting in a smaller sample size.

*Analysis.*

Algorithm 1 offers probabilistic guarantees on the quality of all approximations of the betweenness centrality.

LEMMA 7. *With probability at least $1 - \delta$, all the approximations computed by the algorithm are within $\varepsilon$ from their real value:*

$$\Pr\left(\exists v \in V \text{ s.t. } |\mathsf{b}(v) - \tilde{\mathsf{b}}(v)| > \varepsilon\right) < \delta \ .$$

PROOF. For each $p_{uv} \in \mathbb{S}_G$ let

$$\pi_G(p_{uv}) = \frac{1}{n(n-1)} \frac{1}{\sigma_{uv}} \ .$$

It is easy to see that $\pi_G$ is a probability distribution and $\pi_G(p_{uv})$ is the probability of sampling the path $p_{uv}$ during an execution of the loop on line 6 in Alg. 1, given the way that the vertices $u$ and $v$ are selected and Lemma 6.

Consider the range set $\mathcal{R}_G$ and the probability distribution $\pi_G$. Let $S$ be the set of paths sampled during the execution of the algorithm. For $r$ as in (3), Thm. 1 tells us that the sample $S$ is a $\varepsilon$-approximation to $(\mathcal{R}_G, \pi_G)$ with probability at least $1 - \delta$. Suppose that this is indeed the case, then from Def. 5 and the definition of $\mathcal{R}_G$ we have that

$$\left|\pi_G(\mathcal{T}_v) - \frac{1}{r}\sum_{p \in S} \mathbb{1}_{\mathcal{T}_v}(p)\right| = \left|\pi_G(\mathcal{T}_v) - \tilde{\mathsf{b}}(v)\right| \leq \varepsilon, \forall v \in V \ .$$

From the definition of $\pi_G$ we have

$$\pi_G(\mathcal{T}_v) = \frac{1}{n(n-1)} \sum_{p_{uw} \in \mathcal{T}_v} \frac{1}{\sigma_{uw}} = \mathsf{b}(v),$$

which concludes the proof. □

## 5.2 High-quality approximation of the top-$K$ betweenness vertices

Very often in practice one is interested only in identifying the vertices with the highest betweenness centrality, as they are the "primary actors" in the network. We present here an algorithm to compute a very high-quality approximation of the set $\mathsf{TOP}(K, G)$ of the top-$K$ betweenness vertices in a graph $G = (V, E)$. Formally, let $v_1, \ldots, v_n$ be a labelling of the vertices in $V$ such that $\mathsf{b}(v_i) \geq \mathsf{b}(v_j)$ for $1 \leq i < j \leq n$. Then $\mathsf{TOP}(K, G)$ is defined as the set of vertices with betweenness at least $\mathsf{b}(v_K)$:

$$\mathsf{TOP}(K, G) = \{(v, \mathsf{b}(v)), \ : v \in V \text{ and } \mathsf{b}(v) \geq \mathsf{b}(v_K)\} \ .$$

Note that $\mathsf{TOP}(K, G)$ may contain more than $K$ vertices.

Our algorithm works in two phases. Each phase is basically a run of the algorithm for approximating the betweenness of all vertices. The two phases differ in the way they compute the number of paths to sample and the additional operations at the end of each phase. In the first phase, we compute a lower bound $\ell'$ to $\mathsf{b}(v_K)$. In the second phase we use $\ell'$ to compute the number of samples $r$ needed to obtain a relative $(\ell', \varepsilon)$-approximation to $(\mathcal{R}_G, \pi_G)$. We use $r$ samples to approximate the betweenness of all vertices again, and return a collection of vertices that is, with high probability, a superset of $\mathsf{TOP}(K, G)$.

Let $\widetilde{\mathsf{VD}}(G)$ be an upper bound to the vertex-diameter of $G$. Given $\varepsilon, \delta \in (0,1)$, let $\delta', \delta''$ be two positive reals such that $(1-\delta')(1-\delta'') \geq (1-\delta)$. Let

$$r' = \frac{c}{\varepsilon^2}\left(\lfloor \log_2(\widetilde{\mathsf{VD}}(G) - 2)\rfloor + 1 + \log\frac{1}{\delta'}\right) .$$

Let $\tilde{\mathsf{b}}'_k$ be the $K$-th highest estimated betweenness obtained using Algorithm 1 where $r = r'$, and let $\ell' = \tilde{\mathsf{b}}_K - \varepsilon$, and

$$r'' = \frac{c'}{\varepsilon^2 \ell'}\left((\lfloor \log_2(\widetilde{\mathsf{VD}}(G) - 2)\rfloor + 1)\log\frac{1}{\ell'} + \log\frac{1}{\delta''}\right) .$$

We run Algorithm 1 with $r = r''$ and let $\tilde{\mathsf{b}}''_K$ be the so-obtained $K$-th highest estimated betweenness. Let $\ell'' = \min\{\tilde{\mathsf{b}}''(v)/(1+\varepsilon) : v \in V \text{ s.t. } \tilde{\mathsf{b}}''(v) \geq \tilde{\mathsf{b}}''_K\}$. We return the collection $\widetilde{\mathsf{TOP}}(K, G)$ of vertices $v$ such that $\tilde{\mathsf{b}}''(v) * (1+\varepsilon)/(1-\varepsilon) \geq \ell''$:

$$\widetilde{\mathsf{TOP}}(K, G) = \left\{ v \in V : \tilde{\mathsf{b}}''(v)\frac{1+\varepsilon}{1-\varepsilon} \geq \ell'' \right\} .$$

LEMMA 8. *With probability at least* $1 - \delta$,

1. $\mathsf{TOP}(K, G) \subseteq \widetilde{\mathsf{TOP}}(K, G)$, *and*
2. *for all* $v \in \mathsf{TOP}(K, G)$ *we have* $|\tilde{\mathsf{b}}''(v) - \mathsf{b}(v)| \leq \varepsilon \mathsf{b}(v)$, *and*
3. *no vertex* $u \in \widetilde{\mathsf{TOP}}(K, G) \setminus \mathsf{TOP}(K, G)$ *has an estimated betweenness greater than* $\ell'(1+\varepsilon)$.

We refer the reader interested in the proof to the extended online version of the paper [31].

The advantage of using our algorithm to approximate the collection of top-$K$ betweenness vertices consists in the very high-quality approximation of the betweenness values for the returned set of vertices: they are all within a multiplicative factor $\varepsilon$ from their exact values. By reverse-sorting them according to the approximated betweenness, one can obtain a ranking that is very similar to the original exact one. Previous algorithms could not achieve such a good ranking as they were only able to approximate the betweenness values to within an additive error $\varepsilon$. The cost of computing the high quality approximation for the top-$K$ vertices is the cost of an additional run of our algorithm to compute good approximations for all the vertices.

## 5.3 Discussion

Jacob et al. [18] and independently Brandes and Pich [10] present a sampling-based algorithm to approximate the betweenness centrality of all the vertices of the graph. The algorithm (which we call BP) creates a sample $S = \{v_1, \ldots, v_r\}$ of $r$ vertices drawn uniformly at random and computes all the shortest paths between each $v_i$ to all other vertices in the graph. Their estimation $\tilde{\mathsf{b}}_{\mathsf{BP}}(u)$ for $\mathsf{b}(u)$ is

$$\tilde{\mathsf{b}}_{\mathsf{BP}}(u) = \frac{1}{(n-1)r}\sum_{v_i \in S}\sum_{\substack{w \neq v_i \\ w \neq u}}\sum_{p \in \mathcal{S}_{v_i w}} \frac{\mathbb{1}_{\mathsf{Int}(p)}(u)}{|\mathcal{S}_{v_i w}|} .$$

As it was for Algorithm 1, the key ingredient to ensure a correct approximation for the betweenness centrality is the computation of the sample size $r$. Inspired by the work of Eppstein and Wang [13], Brandes and Pich [10] prove that, to obtain good (within $\varepsilon$) estimations for the betweenness of all vertices with probability at least $1-\delta$, it must be

$$r \geq \frac{1}{2\varepsilon^2}\left(\ln n + \ln 2 + \ln\frac{1}{\delta}\right) .$$

From this expression it should be clear that this sample size is usually much larger than ours, as in practice $\mathsf{VD}(G) \ll n$. For the same reason, this algorithm would not scale well as the network size increases (see also Sect. 6).

Another interesting aspect in which our algorithm and BP differ is the *amount of work done per sample*. Our algorithm computes a single set $\mathcal{S}_{uv}$ for the sampled pair of vertices $(u, v)$: it performs a run of Dijkstra's algorithm (or of BFS) from $u$, stopping when $v$ is reached. BP instead computes all the sets $\mathcal{S}_{uw}$ from the sampled vertices $u$ to all other vertices, again with a single run of Dijkstra or BFS, but without the "early-stopping condition" that we have when we reach $v$. Although in the worst case the two computations have the same time complexity[4], in practice we perform many fewer operations, as we can expect $v$ not to always be very far from $u$ and therefore we can terminate early. This fact has a huge impact on the running time. Our algorithm also touches *many fewer* edges than BP. The latter can touch all the edges in the graph *at every sample*, while our computation exhibits a much higher *locality*, exploring only a neighborhood of $u$ until $v$ is reached. The results of our experimental evaluation presented in Sect. 6 highlights this and other advantages of our method over the one from [10, 18]. In the future, we plan to investigate the possibility of using *bidirectional A* search* [19, 30] to further speed up the computation for each sample of our algorithms.

# 6. EXPERIMENTAL EVALUATION

We conducted an experimental evaluation of our algorithms, with two major driving goals in mind: study the behavior of the algorithms presented in this paper and compare it with that of other related algorithms [8, 10, 15, 18], in terms of accuracy of the estimation, execution time, work performed, and scalability as function of the network size. Due to space limitations, we only report a subset of our results and refer the reader to the extended online version of the paper [31].

### *Implementation and environment.*

We implemented our algorithms, the one presented in [10, 18] and the linear scaling version from [15] in C, by extending the implementation of the exact algorithm [8] contained in igraph [11][5]. The implementations are similarly engineered, given that they are based on the same subroutines for the computation of the shortest path (Dijkstra's algorithm for weighted graphs, BFS for unweighted ones), and they received similar amounts of optimization. We exposed our implementations through Python 3.3.1, which was used for running the simulations. We run the experiments on a quad-core AMD Phenom™II X4 955 Processor with 16GB of RAM, running Debian *wheezy* with a Linux kernel version 3.2.0.

[4]It is a well-known open problem whether there is an algorithm to perform a single $s, t$-shortest path computation between a pair of vertices with smaller worst-case time complexity than the Single Source Shortest Path computation.

[5]The implementations are available at `http://cs.brown.edu/~matteo/centrsampl.tar.bz2`.

| Graph | Graph Properties $\lvert V\rvert$ | $\lvert E\rvert$ | VD($G$) | $\frac{\text{Time}_{BP}}{\text{Time}_{VC}}$ diam-2approx min | max |
|---|---|---|---|---|---|
| oregon1-010331 | 10,670 | 22,002 | 9 | 4.39 | 4.75 |
| oregon1-010526 | 11,174 | 23,409 | 10 | 4.26 | 4.73 |
| ca-HepPh | 12,008 | 237,010 | 13 | 3.06 | 3.33 |
| ca-AstroPh | 18,772 | 396,160 | 14 | 3.26 | 3.76 |
| ca-CondMat | 23,133 | 186,936 | 15 | 3.75 | 4.08 |
| email-Enron | 36,692 | 421,578 | 12 | 3.60 | 4.16 |

(a) Undirected graphs

| Graph | Graph Properties $\lvert V\rvert$ | $\lvert E\rvert$ | VD($G$) | $\frac{\text{Time}_{BP}}{\text{Time}_{VC}}$ diam-exact min | max | diam-UB min | max |
|---|---|---|---|---|---|---|---|
| wiki-Vote | 7,115 | 103,689 | 7 | 3.35 | 3.69 | 1.05 | 1.27 |
| p2p-Gnutella25 | 22,687 | 54,705 | 11 | 5.45 | 5.78 | 1.94 | 2.09 |
| cit-HepTh | 27,770 | 352,807 | 14 | 3.58 | 3.83 | 1.39 | 1.61 |
| cit-HepPh | 34,546 | 421,578 | 12 | 4.91 | 5.01 | 1.60 | 1.71 |
| p2p-Gnutella30 | 36,682 | 88,328 | 10 | 5.02 | 5.46 | 2.08 | 2.22 |
| soc-Epinions1 | 75,879 | 508,837 | 13 | 4.20 | 4.25 | 1.35 | 1.38 |

(b) Directed graphs

Figure 2: Graph properties and running time ratios.

*Datasets.*

In our evaluation we used a number of graphs from the Stanford Large Network Dataset Collection[6]. These are all real world datasets including online social networks, communication (email) networks, scientific citation and academic collaboration networks, road networks, Amazon frequent co-purchased product networks, and more. Basic information about the graphs we used are reported in the two leftmost columns of Figs. 2b and 2a. We refer the reader to the SLNDC website for additional details about each dataset. To evaluate scalability we also created a number of artificial graphs of different sizes (1,000 to 100,000 vertices) using the Barabási-Albert model [5] as implemented by igraph [11].

*Diameter approximation.*

As we discussed in the previous sections the number of samples that the proposed algorithm requires depends on the vertex-diameter of the graph. For the computation of the vertex-diameter in case of undirected graphs we used the 2-approximation algorithm that we briefly described in Sect. 5. We denote this as "diam-2-approx" when reporting results in this section. For directed graphs, we computed the number of samples using both the exact value of the vertex-diameter (indicated as diam-exact) as well as the trivial upper bound $|V| - 2$ (indicated as diam-UB).

## 6.1 Accuracy

Our theoretical results from Sect. 5 guarantee that, with probability at least $1 - \delta$, all estimations of the betweenness values for all vertices in the graph are within $\varepsilon$ for their real value. We run Algorithm 1 five times for each graph and each value of $\varepsilon$ in $\{0.01, 0.015, 0.02, 0.04, 0.06, 0.08, 0.1\}$. The parameter $\delta$ was fixed to 0.1 and we used $c = 0.5$ in (1) to compute the sample size, as suggested by Löffler and Phillips [24]. As far as the *confidence* is concerned, we report that in all the hundreds of runs we performed, the guarantee on the quality of approximation was *always* satisfied, not just with probability $1 - \delta$ $(= 0.9)$. We evaluated how good the estimated values are by computing the average *estimation error* $(\sum_{v\in V} |\mathsf{b}(v) - \tilde{\mathsf{b}}(v)|)/|V|$ across five runs of our algorithm and taking the average and the standard deviation of this measure, for different values of $\varepsilon$. We also compute the maximum error $|\mathsf{b}(v) - \tilde{\mathsf{b}}(v)|$ overall. The results are reported in Fig. 3a for the directed graph p2p-Gnutella30, and in Fig. 3b for the undirected graph email-Enron. Results for other graphs are similar [31]. It is evident that the maximum error is an error of magnitude smaller than the guaranteed value of $\varepsilon$ and that the average error is almost two orders of magnitude smaller than the guarantees, and the `Avg+Stddev` points show that the estimation are quite concentrated around the average. We can conclude that in practice the algorithm performs even *better than guaranteed*, achieving higher accuracy and confidence than what the theoretical analysis indicates. This is due to a number of factors, like the fact that we use an *upper bound* to the VC-dimension of the range set.

[6]`http://snap.stanford.edu/data/index.html`

## 6.2 Runtime

We compared the running time of Algorithm 1 (denoted in the following as VC to that of the algorithm from [10, 15, 18] (denoted as BP), and to that of the exact algorithm [8]. As VC and BP give the same guarantees on the accuracy and confidence of the computed estimations, it makes sense to compare their running times to evaluate which is faster in achieving the goal. The performances of the algorithm proposed in [15] takes the same time as BP, because it follows the same sampling approach and only differs in the definiton of the estimator for the betweenness, so we do not report those. The algorithms VC and BP take parameters $\varepsilon$ and $\delta$ and compute the sample size accordingly. We run each experiments five times for each value of $\varepsilon$, and measured the average running time across the runs. The results are presented in Figs. 2 and 4. In Fig. 2a we report the minimum and the maximum ratio of the running time of BP over VC, taken over the ratios obtained by running the algorithms with the different values of $\varepsilon$. As it can be seen from this table our algorithm performs significantly faster, more than 300%. Similar results are reported for directed graphs in Fig. 2b. The diam-UB and the diam-exact values can be seen as the two extremes for the performance of Algorithm 1 in terms of runtime. In the case of the diam-exact we have as few samples as possible (for VC) since we use the exact value of the vertex-diameter, whereas in the case of diam-UB we have as many samples as possibles because we use the worst case estimation for the vertex-diameter of the graph. From Fig. 2a we can see that the value for the vertex-diameter that we consider in the case of diam-UB ($|V| - 2$) is many orders of magnitudes greater than the actual value, which translates in a significant increase of the number of samples. But even in the case of this crude vertex-diameter approximation (diam-UB), the VC algorithm performs uniformly faster than BP. In the case where the exact value of the diameter was used, we can see that our algorithm computes an estimation of the betweenness that satisfies the desired accuracy and confidence guarantees *3 to 5 times faster* than BP. In Fig. 4a we study the directed graph p2p-Gnutella30 and we present the measurements of the average running time of the algorithms for different values of $\varepsilon$, using the exact algorithm from [8] as baseline. The VC algorithm requires significantly less time than the BP algorithm. The figure also shows that there are values of $\varepsilon$ for which BP takes more time than the exact algorithm, because the

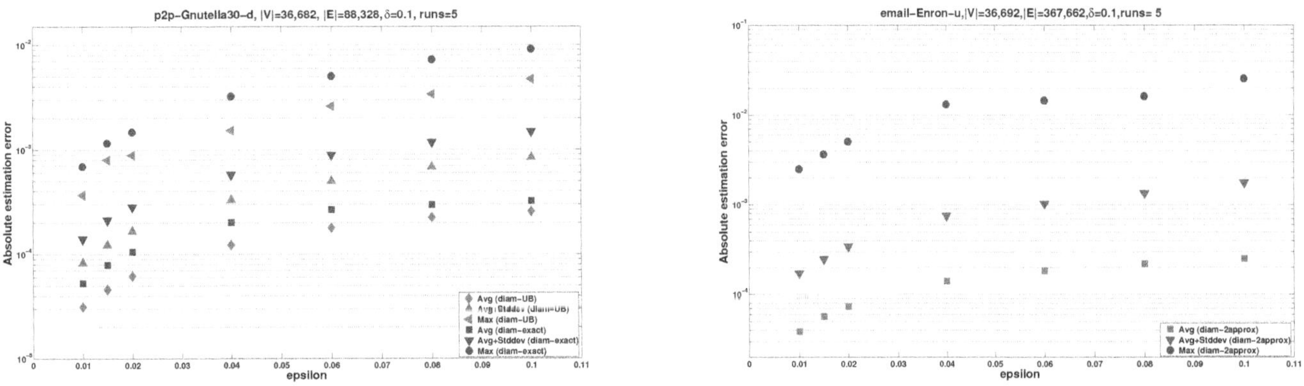


(a) p2p-Gnutella30 (directed)

(b) email-Enron (undirected)

Figure 3: Betweenness estimation error $|\tilde{\mathsf{b}}(v) - \mathsf{b}(v)|$ evaluation for directed and undirected graphs

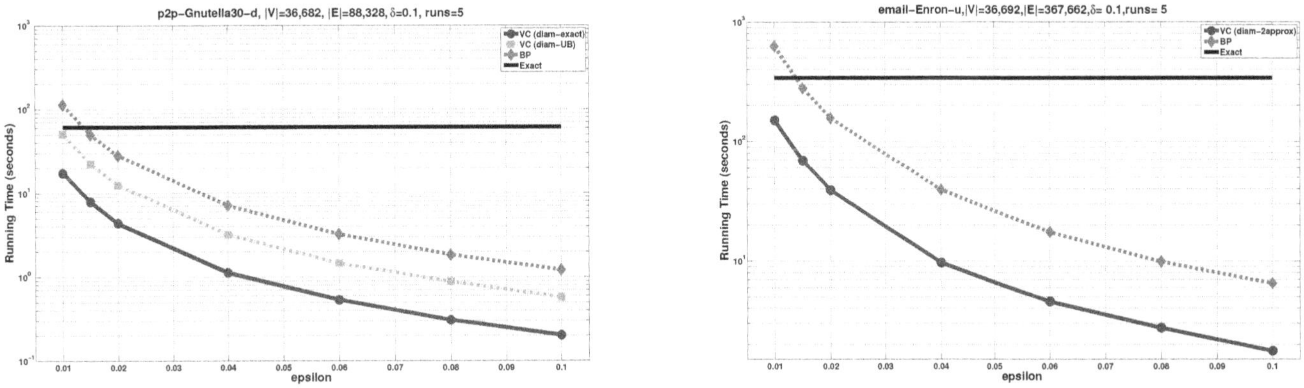


(a) p2p-Gnutella30 (directed)

(b) email-Enron (undirected)

Figure 4: Running time (seconds) comparison between VC, BP, and the exact algorithm.

resulting sample size is larger than the graph size. Given that VC uses fewer samples and does fewer operations per sample, it can be used with lower $\varepsilon$ than BP, while still saving time compared to the exact computation. Figure 4b shows the average running time of the algorithms for the undirected graph email-Enron. The behavior is similar to that for the undirected case. Algorithm 1 is faster than BP for two reasons, both originating from from our use of results from the VC-dimension theory: 1) we use a significantly smaller amount of samples and 2) VC performs the same amount of computations *per sample* as BP only in the worst case. Indeed our algorithm needs only to find the shortest path between a sampled pair of vertices, whereas the algorithms from [10, 15] need to compute the shortest paths between a sampled source and all the other vertices. In our experimental evaluation we found out that the running time of the algorithms is directly proportional to the number of edges touched during the shortest path computation. The use of bidirectional $A^*$ search [19, 30] can help in lowering the number of touched edges for VC and therefore the runtime of our algorithm (BP would not benefit from this improvement). We plan to explore this in future work.

## 6.3 Scalability

In Sect. 5.3 we argued about the reasons why Algorithm 1 is more scalable than BP, while still offering the same approximation guarantees. To evaluate our argument in practice, we created a number of graphs of increasing size (1,000 to 100,000 vertices) using the Barabási-Albert [5] and run the algorithms on them, measuring their running time. We report the results in Fig. 5. The most-scalable algorithm would be completely independent from the size (number of vertices) of the graph, corresponding to a flat (horizontal) line in the plot. Therefore, the less steep the line, the more independent from the network size would be the corresponding algorithm. From the figure, we can appreciate that this is the case for VC, which is much more scalable and independent from the size of the sample than BP. This is very important, as today's networks are not only huge, but they also grow rapidly, and algorithms to mine them must scale well with graph size.

# 7. CONCLUSIONS

In this work we presented two random-sampling-based algorithms for accurately and efficiently estimate the betweenness centrality of the (top-$K$) vertices in a graph, with high probability. Our algorithms are based on a novel application of VC-dimension theory, and therefore take a different approach than previous ones achieving the same guarantees [10, 15, 18]. The number of samples needed to approximate the betweenness with the desired accuracy and confidence does not depend on the number of vertices in the graph, but rather on a characteristic quantity of the network that we call *vertex-diameter*. In some cases, the sample size is completely independent from any property of the graph. Our algorithms per-

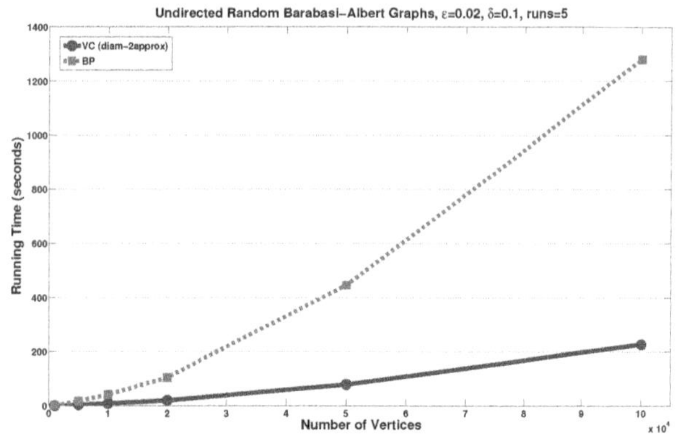


Figure 5: Scalability on random [5] graphs.

form much less work than previously presented methods. As a consequence, they are much faster and scalable, as verified in the extensive experimental evaluation using many real and artificial graphs. In future work we would like to explore the possibility of using bidirectional A* search [19, 30] to further speed up our algorithms.

*Acknowledgements.* This project was supported, in part, by the National Science Foundation under award IIS-1247581. We are thankful to Eli Upfal for his guidance and to the anonymous reviewers whose comments helped us improving this work.

## 8. REFERENCES

[1] I. Abraham et al. VC-dimension and shortest path algorithms. ICALP'11, 2011.

[2] D. Aingworth et al. Fast estimation of diameter and shortest paths (without matrix multiplication). *SIAM J. on Comput.*, 28(4):1167–1181, 1999.

[3] J. M. Anthonisse. The rush in a directed graph. TR BN 9/71, Stichting Mathematisch Centrum, Amsterdam, Netherlands, 1971.

[4] D. A. Bader et al. Approximating betweenness centrality. WAW'07, 2007.

[5] A.-L. Barabási and R. Albert. Emergence of scaling in random networks. *Science*, 286(5439):509–512, 1999.

[6] K. Boitmanis et al. Fast and simple approximation of the diameter and radius of a graph. WEA'06, 2006.

[7] S. P. Borgatti and M. G. Everett. A graph-theoretic perspective on centrality. *Soc. Net.*, 28(4):466–484, 2006.

[8] U. Brandes. A faster algorithm for betweenness centrality. *J. Math. Sociol.*, 25(2):163–177, 2001.

[9] U. Brandes. On variants of shortest-path betweenness centrality and their generic computation. *Soc. Net.*, 30(2):136–145, 2008.

[10] U. Brandes and C. Pich. Centrality estimation in large networks. *Intl. J. Bifurc. and Chaos*, 17(07):2303–2318, 2007.

[11] G. Csárdi and T. Nepusz. The igraph software package for complex network research. *InterJournal*, Complex Sys.:1695, 2006. URL `http://igraph.sf.net`.

[12] S. Dolev et al. Routing betweenness centrality. *J. ACM*, 57 (4):25:1–25:27, May 2010.

[13] D. Eppstein and J. Wang. Fast approximation of centrality. *J. Graph Alg. and Appl.*, 8(1):39–45, 2004.

[14] L. C. Freeman. A set of measures of centrality based on betweenness. *Sociometry*, 40:35–41, 1977.

[15] R. Geisberger et al. Better approximation of betweenness centrality. ALENEX'08, 2008.

[16] S. Har-Peled and M. Sharir. Relative $(p, \varepsilon)$-approximations in geometry. *Discr. & Comput. Geom.*, 45(3):462–496, 2011.

[17] W. Hoeffding. Probability inequalities for sums of bounded random variables. *J. Am. Stat. Assoc.*, 58(301):13–30, 1963.

[18] R. Jacob et al. Algorithms for centrality indices. *LNCS*, 3418: 62–82, 2005.

[19] H. Kaindl and G. Kainz. Bidirectional heuristic search reconsidered. *J. Artif. Intell. Res.*, 7:283–317, 1997.

[20] Kourtellis et al. Identifying high betweenness centrality nodes in large social networks. *Soc. Net. Analysis and Mining*, pages 1–16, 2012.

[21] Kranakis et al. The VC-dimension of set systems defined by graphs. *Discr. Appl. Math.*, 77(3):237–257, 1997.

[22] Y. Li et al. Improved bounds on the sample complexity of learning. *J. Comp. and Sys. Sci.*, 62(3):516–527, 2001.

[23] Y.-s. Lim et al. Online estimating the k central nodes of a network. NSW'11, 2011

[24] M. Löffler and J. M. Phillips. Shape fitting on point sets with probability distributions. ESA'09, 2009.

[25] A. Maiya and T. Berger-Wolf. Online sampling of high centrality individuals in social networks. PAKDD'10, 2010.

[26] M. Mitzenmacher and E. Upfal. *Probability and Computing: Randomized Algorithms and Probabilistic Analysis*. Cambridge University Press, 2005.

[27] M. Mohri et al. *Foundations of Machine Learning*. The MIT Press, 2012.

[28] M. E. J. Newman. *Networks - An Introduction*. Oxford University Press, 2010.

[29] J. Pfeffer and K. M. Carley. k-centralities: local approximations of global measures based on shortest paths. WWW'12, 2012.

[30] I. Pohl. *Bidirectional Heuristic Search in Path Problems*. PhD thesis, Stanford University, 1969.

[31] M. Riondato and E. M. Kornaropoulos Fast Approximation of Betweenness Centrality through Sampling. (extended version) `http://cs.brown.edu/~matteo/papers/RiondatoKornarop-BetweennessSampling.pdf`, 2013.

[32] L. Roditty and V. V. Williams. Approximating the diameter of a graph. *CoRR abs/1207.3622*, 2012.

[33] A. E. Sariyüce et al. Shattering and compressing networks for betweenness centrality. SDM'13, 2013.

[34] V. N. Vapnik and A. J. Chervonenkis. On the uniform convergence of relative frequencies of events to their probabilities. *Theory of Prob. and its Appl.*, 16(2):264–280, 1971.

# Effective Co-betweenness Centrality Computation

Mostafa Haghir Chehreghani
Department of Computer Science, KU Leuven
Celestijnenlaan 200a - box 2402
3001 Leuven, Belgium
Mostafa.HaghirChehreghani@cs.kuleuven.be

## ABSTRACT

*Betweenness centrality* of vertices is essential in the analysis of social and information networks, and *co-betweenness centrality* is one of two natural ways to extend it to sets of vertices. Existing algorithms for co-betweenness centrality computation suffer from at least one of the following problems: *i*) their applicability is limited to special cases like sequences, sets of size two, and *ii*) they are not efficient in terms of time complexity. In this paper, we present efficient algorithms for co-betweenness centrality computation of any set or sequence of vertices in weighted and unweighted networks. We also develop effective methods for co-betweenness centrality computation of sets and sequences of edges. Results of this paper, provide a clear and extensive view about the complexity of co-betweenness centrality computation for vertices and edges in weighted and unweighted networks. Finally, we perform extensive experiments on real-world networks from different domains including social and information, to show the empirical efficiency of the proposed method.

## Categories and Subject Descriptors

G.2.2 [**Discrete Mathematics**]: Graph Theory—*Graph algorithms, Path and circuit problems*; E.1 [**Data**]: Data structures—*Graphs and networks*

## General Terms

Theory

## Keywords

Social networks, network analysis, centrality, betweenness centrality, co-betweenness centrality, algorithm, complexity.

## 1. INTRODUCTION

*Centrality* is a structural property of vertices in a network which determines the importance of a vertex (or a set of vertices) within the network [14]. *Betweenness centrality* of a vertex, introduced by Linton Freeman [13], is defined as the number of shortest paths (geodesic paths) from all vertices to all others that pass through that vertex. He used it as a measure for quantifying the control of a human on the communication between other humans in a social network [13].

There are several applications which benefit from a definition of centrality used for sets of vertices rather than individual vertices [12]. Betweenness centrality of vertices is extended to betweenness centrality of sets of vertices in two ways:

- *group betweenness centrality* of a set [12], which is defined as the number of shortest paths that pass through at least one of the vertices in the set, and
- *co-betweenness centrality* of a set [20], which is defined as the number of shortest paths that pass through all vertices in the set.

It has been shown that these two notions are intimately related [20]. The focus of this paper is *co-betweenness centrality*. In [20], the authors illustrated the utilization of co-betweenness centrality of sets of vertices in different social and communication networks and showed its interesting features in different real world networks. They also showed that co-betweenness centrality allows one to identify certain vertices which act as important actors in the relaying and destinating information in the network.

The following computation problems are defined for co-betweenness centrality.

PROBLEM 1. *Vertex co-betweenness centrality computation: given an unweighted graph (network)* $\mathbf{G}$ *and a set* $K \subseteq V(\mathbf{G})$*, compute co-betweenness centrality of* $K$.

Parameters of Problem 1 are $n$, $m$ and $|K|$, where $n$ and $m$ are the number of vertices and the number of edges of the network, respectively.

PROBLEM 2. *Edge co-betweenness centrality computation: given an unweighted graph (network)* $\mathbf{G}$ *and a set* $W \subseteq E(\mathbf{G})$*, compute co-betweenness centrality of* $W$.

Similar to Problem 1, parameters of Problem 2 are $n$, $m$ and $|W|$. The problems can be defined similarly, for sequences (where the order in which vertices in $K$ (or edges in $W$) must be met by shortest paths is fixed), as well as for sets and sequences in weighted (valued) graphs.

Recently, a number of complexity results have been reported for co-betweenness centrality computation. For example,

- In [20], the authors presented an algorithm for vertex co-betweenness centrality computation. However, their method works only for sets of size 2 and its worst case time complexity is a $O(n^3)$.


*WSDM'14*, February 24–28, 2014, New York, New York, USA.
Copyright 2014 ACM 978-1-4503-2351-2/14/02 ...$15.00.
http://dx.doi.org/10.1145/2556195.2556263.

- The authors of [32], as a part of their algorithm for computing successive group betweenness centrality of sets of vertices, showed that co-betweenness centrality of a sequence consisting of two vertices is computable in $O(mn)$ time.

- In [11], the authors introduced the Routing Betweenness Centrality (RBC) index, which is a generalization of betweenness centrality. In this work, they studied complexity of RBC computation of sequences.

However, several problems like co-betweenness centrality computation of vertices, co-betweenness centrality computation of edges and co-betweenness centrality computation in weighted graphs, either have not been studied yet, or complexity of proposed algorithms is too high. In this paper [1]:

- We present an $O(nm-|K|m+n|K|\log|K|-|K|^2\log|K|)$ time algorithm for co-betweenness centrality computation of a set $K$ of vertices in unweighted graphs. We show that it is possible to compute co-betweenness centrality of $K$ in weighted graphs in $O(nm-|K|m+n^2\log n-|K|n\log n)$ time.

- We show that co-betweenness centrality of a sequence $K$ of vertices is computable in $O(nm-|K|m)$ time in unweighted graphs and in $O(nm-|K|m+n^2\log n-|K|n\log n)$ time in weighted graphs.

- We present an $O(nm+n|W|\log|W|)$ time algorithm for co-betweenness centrality computation of a set $W$ of edges in unweighted graphs. We show that it is possible to compute co-betweenness centrality of $W$ in weighted graphs in $O(nm+n^2\log n)$ time.

- We show that co-betweenness centrality of a sequence $W$ of edges is computable in $O(nm)$ time in unweighted graphs and in $O(nm+n^2\log n)$ time in weighted graphs.

- We perform extensive experiments on real-world networks from different domains including social, information, and collaboration, and show the empirical efficiency of the proposed method.

We show that both vertex co-betweenness centrality computation and edge co-betweenness centrality computation can reduce to betweenness centrality computation of a single vertex. As a result, increasing the size of the set does not necessarily increase complexity of co-betweenness centrality computation, and for sequences, computation of co-betweenness centrality for larger sequences is always easier than smaller ones.

A shortcoming of our proposed algorithms is that unlike the Brandes algorithm [7] which can calculate betweenness centrality of all vertices simultaneously, they need the set of vertices/edges as an input. However, we think this shortcoming is not important since checking all sets of vertices is usually needed when someone wants to find the minimum set of vertices with the highest betweenness centrality. While finding such a *prominent set* is crucial for group betweenness centrality [32], it is not of high importance for co-betweenness centrality. The reason is that as the size of the set increases, co-betweenness centrality decreases so that betweenness centrality of single vertices is always higher than co-betweenness centrality of their super-sets. In practice, rather than considering all sets of vertices, it might be more desirable to compute co-betweenness centrality of only a few sets, like core vertices of communities in social/information networks, or hubs in communication networks.

The rest of this paper is organized as follows. In Section 2, preliminaries and definitions related to co-betweenness centrality computation are given. In Section 3, we present an efficient algorithm for computing co-betweenness centrality of a set (or a sequence) of vertices in unweighted and weighted graphs. In Section 4, we investigate complexity of edge co-betweenness centrality computation for sets and sequences in weighted and unweighted networks. We empirically study the proposed methods in Section 5. In Section 6, we have a brief overview on related work. Finally, in Section 7, the paper is concluded.

## 2. PRELIMINARIES

In this section, we present definitions and notations widely used in the paper. We assume that the reader is familiar with basic concepts in graph theory. Throughout the paper, $\mathbf{G}$ refers to a graph (network). For simplicity, we assume that $\mathbf{G}$ is a connected graph without multi-edges. In Sections 3-3.1, $\mathbf{G}$ points to an unweighted graph and in Section 3.2, it points to a weighted graph with positive weights. $V(\mathbf{G})$ and $E(\mathbf{G})$ refer to the set of vertices and the set of edges of $\mathbf{G}$, respectively. Throughout the paper, $n$ points to $|V(\mathbf{G})|$ and $m$ points to $|E(\mathbf{G})|$. For an edge $e=(u,v)\in E(\mathbf{G})$, $u$ and $v$ are two end-points of $e$. A graph $G'$ is a *subgraph* of $G$ if $V(G')\subseteq V(G)$ and $E(G')\subseteq E(G)$. $G'$ is an *induced subgraph* of $G$, if $V(G')\subseteq V(G)$ and $E(G')$ contains all edges of $E(G)$ which have both end-points in $V(G')$.

A *shortest path* (also called a *geodesic path*) between two vertices $u,v\in V(\mathbf{G})$ is a path whose size is minimum, among all paths between $u$ and $v$. For two vertices $u,v\in V(\mathbf{G})$, we use $d_{\mathbf{G}}(u,v)$, to denote the size (the number of edges) of a shortest path connecting $u$ and $v$. By definition, $d_{\mathbf{G}}(u,u)=0$ and $d_{\mathbf{G}}(u,v)=d_{\mathbf{G}}(v,u)$. For $s,t\in V(\mathbf{G})$, $\sigma_{st}$ denotes the number of shortest paths between $s$ and $t$. $\sigma_{st}(v)$ denotes the number of shortest paths between $s$ and $t$ that also pass through $v$. $\sigma_{st}(K)$, $K\subseteq V(\mathbf{G})$, denotes the number of shortest paths between $s$ and $t$ that also pass through all vertices in $K$. We have $\sigma_s(v)=\sum_{t\in V(\mathbf{G})\setminus\{s,v\}}\sigma_{st}(v)$ and $\sigma_s(K)=\sum_{t\in V(\mathbf{G})\setminus\{s\}\setminus K}\sigma_{st}(K)$.

*Betweenness centrality* of a vertex $v$ is defined as:

$$\mathcal{B}(v)=\sum_{s,t\in V(G)\setminus\{v\}}\sigma_{st}(v) \tag{1}$$

*Co-Betweenness centrality* of a set $K\subset V(\mathbf{G})$ is defined as:

$$\mathcal{CB}(K)=\sum_{s,t\in V(G)\setminus K}\sigma_{st}(K) \tag{2}$$

We note that the number of shortest paths passing through a set of vertices can be exponential in terms of $n$.

A notion which is widely used for counting the number of shortest paths in a graph is the directed acyclic graph (DAG) containing all shortest paths starting from a vertex $s$ (see e.g. [7]). In this paper, we refer to it as the *shortest-path-DAG*, or *SPD* for short, rooted at $s$. For every vertex $s$ in a graph $G$, the *SPD* rooted at $s$ is unique, and it can be computed in $O(m)$ time for unweighted graphs and in $O(m+n\log n)$ time for weighted graphs [7]. In the SPD $D$ rooted at $s$, the *depth* of $v\in V(D)$, denoted $dep_D(v)$, is defined as $d_D(s,v)$.

[1]The definition of betweenness centrality and as a result co-betweenness centrality considered here is slightly different from the definition considered in [20] and [32]. While similar to [21] and [31], we define co-betweenness centrality as the *number* of shortest paths passing through a given set, in [20] and [32] it is defined as the *ratio* of shortest paths passing through a given set.

In [7], the authors introduced the notion of the *dependency score* of a vertex $s \in V(\mathbf{G})$ on a vertex $v \in V(\mathbf{G}) \setminus \{s\}$, which is defined as:

$$\delta_{s\bullet}(v) = \sum_{t \in V(\mathbf{G}) \setminus \{v,s\}} \sigma_{st}(v) \tag{3}$$

and then:

$$\mathcal{B}(v) = \sum_{s \in V(\mathbf{G}) \setminus \{v\}} \delta_{s\bullet}(v) \tag{4}$$

As discussed in [8], given the SPD rooted at $s$, $\delta_{s\bullet}(v)$ can be computed in $O(m)$.

## 3. COMPUTING CO-BETWEENNESS CENTRALITY OF A SET OF VERTICES

In this section, we study Problem 1. In [20], the authors introduced the problem and extended an $O(n^3)$ time algorithm for the special case of $|K| = 2$. We present a $O(nm)$ time algorithm for co-betweenness centrality computation of a set $K$ of vertices. $K$ can be a set of any size. First, in Lemma 1, we present a property for every SPD $D$ containing at least one shortest path which passes through all the vertices in $K$. Then, we present a *pruned* subgraph of $D$ with respect to $K$, called $\rho_K(D)$, and show that co-betweenness centrality computation of $K$ can be reduced to betweenness centrality computation of a single vertex in $\rho_K(D)$.

LEMMA 1. *Let $s \in V(\mathbf{G})$, $K \subseteq V(\mathbf{G}) \setminus \{s\}$, and $D$ be the SPD rooted at $s$. There exists a shortest path from $s$ to some vertex $t \in V(\mathbf{G}) \setminus \{s\} \setminus K$ passing through all vertices in $K$, if for any two vertices $u, v \in K$, either $u$ is an ancestor of $v$ or $v$ is an ancestor of $u$ in $D$.*

PROOF. Let $s \to t$ be a shortest path passing through all vertices in $K$ and without loss of generality, assume that in the SPD rooted at $s$, $s \to t$ passes through $u$ before $v$. Let $w$ be the vertex which is met by $s \to t$ after $u$. Obviously, $w$ can not be a parent of $u$. On the other hand, in every SPD, two vertices with the same distance from the root are not connected to each other. Therefore, $w$ is a child of $u$, and similarly, the next vertex will be a child of $w$, etc. After finite steps, $s \to t$ will reach $v$. Therefore, $v$ is a descendant of $u$. □

Lemma 1 expresses the necessary condition for a source vertex $s$, to have at least one shortest path to other vertices in the graph passing through all vertices in $K$. This condition applies a total ordering on the members of $K$ according to their distance from $s$ which can be expressed in terms of the $\alpha$ operator introduced in Definition 1.

*Definition 1.* The operator $\alpha : K \to \{1 \dots |K|\}$ is defined with respect to a SPD $D$ and maps an integer $i \in \{1 \dots |K|\}$ to a vertex $v \in K$, such that:

- $\forall i, j \in \{1, \dots, |K|\} : i \neq j \Leftrightarrow \alpha_{D,K}(i) \neq \alpha_{D,K}(j)$, and
- $\forall i, j \in \{1, \dots, |K|\} : i < j \Leftrightarrow \alpha_{D,K}(i)$ is an ancestor of $\alpha_{D,K}(j)$.

*Definition 2.* Let $D$ be the SPD rooted at $s \in V(\mathbf{G})$ and $K \subset V(\mathbf{G})$. A vertex $v \in V(\mathbf{G})$ is *markable* in $D$ if $v \notin K$ and at least one of the following conditions holds:

1. there exists a vertex $u \in K$ such that $dep_D(v) = dep_D(u)$,
2. if vertices satisfying condition (1) are removed from $\mathbf{G}$, in the resultant graph, $v$ and $s$ are not in the same component.

For example, in Figure 1.(b), vertices distinguished with a red '+' are *markable* vertices. Vertices '3', '7' and '15' are markable because they satisfy condition (1) of Definition 2, and vertices '6', '9', '10' and '11' are markable because they satisfy condition (2) of Definition 2.

*Definition 3.* Let $D$ be the SPD rooted at $s \in V(\mathbf{G})$ and $K \subset V(\mathbf{G})$. The *pruned DAG* of $D$ with respect to $K$, denoted by $\rho_K(D)$, is the subgraph of $D$ induced by $\{v \in V(D) | v \text{ is not markable}\}$.

Figure 1.(c) shows the pruned DAG of the SPD presented in 1.(b), with respect to $K = \{'2', '8', '14'\}$.

LEMMA 2. *Given a SPD $D$ rooted at $s \in V(\mathbf{G})$ and $K \subseteq V(\mathbf{G})$, $\rho_K(D)$ is computable in $O(m)$.*

The following properties can be shown for $\rho_K(D)$:

- if for a set $K$ of vertices, the condition of Lemma 1 is satisfied, none of the members of $K$ are markable, and therefore, $K \subseteq V(\rho_K(D))$.
- if for a set $K$ of vertices, the condition of Lemma 1 is satisfied, for every $i : 1 \leq i \leq |K|$, $\alpha_{D,K}(i) = \alpha_{\rho(D),K}(i)$. We sometimes write $\alpha_{D,K}(i)$ or $\alpha_{\rho(D),K}(i)$ simply as $\alpha_K(i)$.
- For $v \in V(D) \cap V(\rho(D))$, $dep_D(v) = dep_{\rho(D)}(v)$.

In the rest of this paper, we might talk about computing dependency scores either in a SPD $D$, or in its pruned form $\rho(D)$. To distinguish these two situations, we use $\delta_{s\bullet}(A, D)$ for dependency score computation in $D$ and $\delta_{s\bullet}(A, \rho(D))$ for dependency score computation in $\rho(D)$. $s$ is a vertex in the network and $A$ is either a 'vertex' or 'a set of vertices' or 'a sequence of vertices'.

LEMMA 3. *Let $s \in V(\mathbf{G})$, $K \subseteq V(\mathbf{G}) \setminus \{s\}$, and $D$ be the SPD rooted at $s$.*

1. *if members of $K$ are not in a single path of $D$, then: $\delta_{s\bullet}(K, D) = 0$*
2. *if all members of $K$ are in a single path of $D$, then:*

$$\delta_{s\bullet}(K, D) = \delta_{s\bullet}(\alpha_K(|K|), \rho(D)) \tag{5}$$

*i.e. $\delta_{s\bullet}(K, D)$ is equal to the number of shortest paths in $\rho(D)$ from $s$ to other vertices which pass through $\alpha_K(|K|)$.*

PROOF. Case (1) is directly resulted from Lemma 1. To prove case (2):

- First, we prove that for every shortest path in $D$ starting form $s$ and passing through all vertices in $K$, there exists a shortest path in $\rho(D)$ which starts from $s$ and passes through $\alpha_K(|K|)$. Let $S = s_1 s_2 \dots s_l$ be a shortest path from $s_1 (= s)$ to $s_l$ in $D$ which passes through all vertices in $K$. As a contradiction, for any $1 < i \leq l$, suppose $s_i \notin V(\rho_K(D))$. Let $s_j \in S$ be the ancestor of $s_i$ with the largest depth which belongs to $V(\rho_K(D))$. $s_j$ always exists because $s_1$ is an ancestor of $s_i$ and $s_1 \in V(\rho_K(D))$. $s_j$ is not equal to $s_l$ because otherwise, $S$ is a path in $\rho_K(D)$. Now, consider $s_{j+1}$. $s_{j+1}$ is not *markable* because:
  - there does not exist a $v \in K$ such that $dep_D(v) = dep_D(s_{j+1})$ because $S$ passes through all members of $K$ (and $S$ can not pass through two vertices with the same depth). Therefore the first condition of Definition 2 does not hold for $s_{j+1}$.

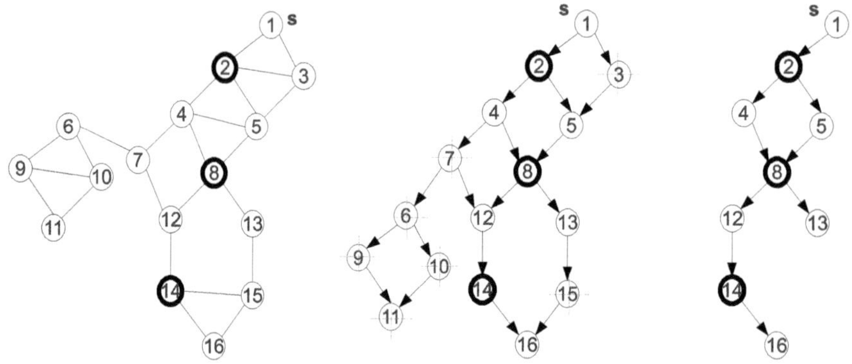


a) G b) The SPD $D$ rooted at $s$ c) $\rho(D)$

**Figure 1: Part (a) shows a network G. $K$ is $\{'2','8','14'\}$, which are depicted with bold circles. Part (b) shows the SPD rooted at $s='1'$. In this graph, vertices with red '+' are *markable* vertices with respect to $K$. We have: $\alpha(1)='2', \alpha(2)='8', \alpha(3)='14'$. Part (c) shows $\rho_K(D)$. As Lemma 3 says, the number of shortest paths in G starting from $s$ and passing through all $'2'$, $'8'$ and $'14'$, is equal to the number of shortest path in $\rho_K(D)$ starting from $s$ and passing through $'14'$.**

- $s_j$ is not markable (since it belongs to $V(\rho_K(D))$) and $s_{j+1}$ is connected to it, therefore, the second condition of Definition 2 does not hold for $s_{j+1}$.

Therefore, a contradiction occurs because $s_{j+1}$ is an ancestor of $s_i$ which belongs to $V(\rho_K(D))$ and $dep_D(s_{j+1}) > dep_D(s_j)$. So, $s_i$ belongs to $V(\rho_K(D))$.

- Second, we prove that for every shortest path $S$ in $\rho(D)$ which starts from $s$ and passes through $\alpha_K(|K|)$, there exists a shortest path in $D$ which starts form $s$ and passes through all vertices in $K$. Since $V(\rho_K(D)) \subseteq V(D)$, vertices of $S$ exist in $D$ and we only need to show that $S$ passes through all vertices in $K$. As a contradiction suppose that in $D$, $S$ does not pass through at least one vertex $v \in K$. Then, there will exist a vertex $u$ such that $u \notin K$, $dep_D(u) = dep_D(v)$ and $S$ passes through $u$. However, according to the first condition of Definition 2, $u$ is markable and it can not be in $\rho(D)$ and therefore, $S$ can not pass through it. □

□

Lemma 3 says that if we check the property expressed in Lemma 1 for $K$, and then, prune the network in the way defined in Definition 3, instead of co-betweenness centrality computation of $K$, we can compute betweenness centrality of a single vertex. This means that co-betweenness centrality computation of larger sets is not necessarily more difficult that co-betweenness centrality computation of smaller ones.

For example, in Figure 1, $K = \{'2','8','14'\}$, vertices $'2'$ ,$'8'$ and $'14'$ are in a single path of the SPD rooted at $s='1'$ and $\alpha_K(1)='2'$, $\alpha_K(2)='8'$ and $\alpha_K(3)='14'$. $\alpha_K(|K|)='14'$ and We have: $\delta_{'1'\bullet,D}(\{'2','8','14'\}) = \delta_{'1'\bullet,\rho(D)}('14')$.

Algorithm 1 shows the high level pseudo code for co-betweenness centrality computation of a set $K$. For a vertex $s \in V(\mathbf{G}) \setminus K$:

- First, the SPD $D$ rooted at $s$ is formed. Using e.g. the method of [7], this step can be done in $O(m)$ time.
- Second, it is checked whether members of $K$ are in a single path of $D$. To do so, the following steps are done:
  1. For every $v \in K$, $dep_D(v)$ is computed. This can be done in $O(m)$ time.
  2. Vertices in $K$ are sorted increasingly, according to their *depth* in $D$. Using sorting algorithms like *merge sort* [19], this step can be done in $O(|K| \log|K|)$ time.
  3. If two or more vertices have the same *depth*, they are not in a single path. Time complexity of this check is $O(|K|)$.
  4. Let $v_1 \ldots v_{|K|}$ be the members of $K$ which are sorted according to their *depth* in $D$. For every $j$, $1 \leq j \leq |K|-1$, the following procedure is performed: the subgraph of $D$ induced by

  $$\{v_j\} \cup \{u \in V(D) | u \textit{ is a descendant of } v_j\}$$

  is traversed in BFS, until either (*i*) $v_{j+1}$ is met or, (*ii*) the traversal is finished. In case (*i*), $v_{j+1}$ is a descendant of $v_j$ and the procedure is performed for $j+1$. In case (*ii*), $v_{j+1}$ is not a descendant of $v_j$ and therefore, all members of $K$ are not in a single path of $D$. Members of $K$ are in a single path of $D$, if and only if for all $j$, case (*i*) occurs. This procedure is done in $O(m)$ time.

  Therefore, it can be decided in $O(m + |K| \log|K|)$ time whether all members of $K$ are in a single path of $D$.
- Third, $\rho(D)$ is computed. As Lemma 2 says, it can be computed in $O(m)$.
- Forth, the dependency score of $s$ on $\alpha_{D,K}(|K|)$ in $\rho(D)$ is computed. Using e.g. the method of [7], this step can be done in $O(m)$ time.

The above mentioned procedure is performed for every $s \in V(\mathbf{G}) \setminus K$. Therefore, we have the following theorem.

THEOREM 1. *Algorithm 1 computes co-betweenness centrality of a set $K \subset V(\mathbf{G})$ in $O(nm - |K|m + n|K| \log|K| - |K|^2 \log|K|)$ time.*

**Algorithm 1** High level pseudo code of the algorithm of computing vertex co-betweenness centrality.

```
VERTEXCOBETWEENNESS
Require. A network (graph) G, a set K ⊆ V(G).
Ensure. The co-betweenness centrality of K.
CB ← 0;
for all s ∈ V(G) \ K do
    Generate the SPD D rooted at s;
    if all vertices in K are in a single path of D then
        Compute ρ(D)
        cb ← δ_{s,•}(α_{D,K}(|K|), ρ(D));
        CB ← CB + cb;
    end if
end for
return CB;
```

## 3.1 Computing co-betweenness centrality of sequences

In this section, we investigate how the algorithm proposed for computation of co-betweenness centrality of sets can be revised to compute co-betweenness centrality of sequences.

Let $K = v_1, \ldots, v_k$ be the sequence of vertices for which we want to compute co-betweenness centrality. Let $s \in V(\mathbf{G})$ and $D$ be the SPD rooted at $s$. There exists a shortest path from $s$ to some other vertex $t \in V(\mathbf{G}) \setminus \{s\} \setminus K$ passing through all vertices in $K$ in order (i.e. first $v_1$, second $v_2$ etc), if in addition to the condition presented in Lemma 1 (i.e. all $v_i$s are in a single path of $D$), the following holds:

$$\forall i \in \{1, \ldots, k\} \Rightarrow v_i = \alpha_{D,K}(i) \tag{6}$$

which means the order of vertices in $K$ corresponds to the order applied by the condition presented in Lemma 1. This condition makes computation of co-betweenness centrality easier; it is possible to check both conditions in $O(m)$ time as follows:

Let $D$ be the SPD rooted at $s \in V(\mathbf{G}) \setminus K$. For every $v_i$, $i \in \{1, \ldots, |K| - 1\}$, the subgraph of $D$ induced by $\{v_i\} \cup \{u \in V(D)$ : *u is a descendant of* $v_i\}$ is traversed in BFS, until either (*i*) $v_{i+1}$ is met, or (*i*) the traversal is finished. In case (*i*), $v_{i+1}$ is a descendant of $v_i$. In case (*ii*), $v_{i+1}$ is not a descendant of $v_i$, and therefore, the conditions do not hold. The conditions presented in Lemma 1 and Equation 6 hold if and only if for all $v_i$s, case (*i*) occurs. The procedure can be done in $O(m)$ time, therefore it is possible to decide in $O(m)$ time whether the conditions are satisfied. In fact, for sequences we do not need to compute the depth of vertices in $D$ and sort members of $K$ according to their depth.

Similar to sets, in order to compute co-betweenness centrality of a sequence $K$, for every $s \in V(\mathbf{G}) \setminus K$, the following steps are done:

1. Form the SPD $D$ rooted at $s$,
2. Check whether members of $K$ satisfy the conditions presented in Lemma 1 and Equation 6,
3. Compute $\rho_K(D)$ (if the conditions hold),
4. Calculate $\delta_{s\bullet}(v_k, \rho_K(D))$ (if the conditions hold).

Co-betweenness centrality of $K$ is the sum of the calculated dependency scores. All steps 1-4 can be done in $O(m)$ time, and they are performed for $n - |K|$ times, therefore, co-betweenness centrality of a sequence of vertices is computable in $O(nm - |K|m)$ time:

THEOREM 2. *Co-betweenness centrality of a sequence $K$ of vertices in an unweighted graph can be computed in $O(nm - |K|m)$ time.*

## 3.2 Computation of co-betweenness centrality in weighted graphs

Algorithms proposed for unweighted graphs can be used to compute co-betweenness centrality in weighted graphs. However, compared to unweighted graphs, time complexity of steps like forming SPDs, is higher for weighted graphs. As Corollary 4 of [7] says, for a weighted graph $\mathbf{G}$, given a source $s \in V(\mathbf{G})$, the number of all shortest paths to other vertices can be determined in time $O(m + n \log n)$.

For vertex co-betweenness centrality computation, this time complexity overcomes time complexity of checking whether all members of the set (or the sequence) are in a single path. This means that for weighted graphs, it is possible to compute co-betweenness centrality of a set (or sequence) $K$ of vertices in $O((n - |K|) \times (m + n \log n)) = O(nm - |K|m + n^2 \log n - |K|n \log n)$ time.

THEOREM 3. *For weighted graphs, co-betweenness centrality of a set (or a sequence) $K$ of vertices is computable in $O(nm - |K|m + n^2 \log n - |K|n \log n)$ time.*

# 4. CO-BETWEENNESS CENTRALITY COMPUTATION OF SETS OF EDGES

Betweenness of edges, defined in terms of the number of shortest paths passing through an edge, has many interesting applications in network analysis. For example, Girvan and Newman [16] used it to detect communities in complex networks. Very recently, Cuzzocrea et al. [10] proposed a new topology-control algorithm in wireless sensor networks, called edge betweenness centrality, which is based on edge betweenness centrality.

Co-betweenness centrality of a set or a sequence of edges (*edge co-betweenness centrality*), is a generalization of this notion to a set or a sequence of edges. It has several applications in traffic network analysis, social networks etc. For example, an important problem in traffic data analysis is finding *hot routes* in a road network. A *hot route* is a sequence of edges which share (almost) the same amount of traffic. This problem has applications in city planning, real estate developing, etc and allows city-holders to better direct traffic or analyze congestion resources. Efficient algorithms for addressing this problem cluster sets of edges based on the density of common traffic they share [25]. With the assumption that movements are done through shortest paths, the basic element of this problem is *edge co-betweenness centrality* computation. A weight can be assigned to every edge (road) to reflect the number of trajectories passing through that edge. In the rest of this section, we first briefly formulate edge co-betweenness centrality, and then, we discuss about effective edge co-betweenness centrality computation.

## 4.1 Edge co-betweenness centrality

For $e \in E(\mathbf{G})$, $\sigma_{st}(e)$ denotes the number of shortest paths between $s$ and $t$ that also pass through $e$. We note that in this definition, $s$ and $t$ are allowed to be an end-point of $e$. $\sigma_{st}(W)$, $W \subseteq E(\mathbf{G})$, denotes the number of shortest paths between $s$ and $t$ that also pass (in any order) through all members of $W$. We have

$$\sigma_s(e) = \sum_{t \in V(\mathbf{G}) \setminus \{s\}} \sigma_{st}(e)$$

and

$$\sigma_s(W) = \sum_{t \in V(\mathbf{G}) \setminus \{s\}} \sigma_{st}(W)$$

*Betweenness centrality* of an edge $e$ is defined as

$$\mathcal{B}(e) = \sum_{s,t \in V(G)} \sigma_{st}(e)$$

*Co-Betweenness centrality* of a set $W \subseteq E(\mathbf{G})$ is defined as:

$$\mathcal{CB}(W) = \sum_{s,t \in V(G)} \sigma_{st}(W)$$

We note that the number of shortest paths passing through a set of edges can be exponential in terms of $n$.

## 4.2 Computation of edge co-betweenness centrality

Lemma 4 expresses the necessary condition for a source vertex $s$, to have at least one shortest path to other vertices in the network which pass through all edges in $W$:

LEMMA 4. *Let $s \in V(\mathbf{G})$, $W \subseteq E(\mathbf{G})$ and $D$ be the SPD rooted at $s$. There exists at least one shortest path from $s$ to some other vertex in the network which pass through all edges in $W$, if vertices in $L$ are in a single path of $D$, where $L$ is*

$$\{v \in V(\mathbf{G}) \setminus \{s\} | v \text{ is an end-point of at least one } e \in W\} \quad (7)$$

PROOF. The proof is omitted because it is similar to the proof of Lemma 1. □

As a result of Lemma 4, we can define an ordering operator $\alpha$, in a way similar to Definition 1, which applies a total ordering on the members of $L$, and therefore, on the members of $W$. Dependency score of $s \in V(\mathbf{G})$ on $W \subseteq E(\mathbf{G})$, i.e. the number of shortest paths from $s$ to other vertices in the network which pass through all edges in $W$, is defined as $\delta_{s\bullet}(W) = \sum_{t \in V(\mathbf{G}) \setminus \{s\}} \sigma_{st}(W)$, and then $\mathcal{CB}(W) = \sum_{s \in V(\mathbf{G})} \delta_{s\bullet}(W)$.

Lemma 5 shows how 'edge co-betweenness centrality' of $W$ is related to 'betweenness centrality' of a single vertex in $L$.

LEMMA 5. *Let $s \in V(\mathbf{G})$, $W \subseteq E(\mathbf{G})$ and $D$ be the SPD rooted at $s$.*

1. *if $W \subseteq E(D)$ and members of $L$ are in a single path of $D$, then:*

$$\delta_{s\bullet}(W, D) = \delta_{s\bullet}(\alpha_L(|L|-1), \rho_L(D)) \quad (8)$$

*where $L$ is defined in Equation 7.*

2. *otherwise: $\delta_{s\bullet}(W, D) = 0$*

We note that in $\rho_L(D)$, $\alpha_L(|L|-1, \rho_L(D))$ has always exactly one child which is $\alpha_L(|L|, \rho_L(D))$ and $\alpha_L(|L|, \rho_L(D))$ has always exactly one parent which is $\alpha_L(|L|-1, \rho_L(D))$.

As an example, consider Figure 2. All members of $W$ which is $\{('1','2'), ('4','8'), ('12','14')\}$, are in a single path of the SPD $D$ rooted at $s$. Furthermore, $W \subseteq E(D)$. Therefore, $\delta_{s\bullet}(W, D) = \delta_{s\bullet}('12', \rho(D))$

Algorithm 2 shows the high level pseudo code of co-betweenness centrality computation for a set of edges. It differs from Algorithm 1 in two aspects. First, we need to check whether $W \subseteq E(D)$ (Line 7 of Algorithm 2). This step can be done in $O(|W|)$ time since we can check in $O(1)$ time whether there exists an edge between two vertices of a graph $G$. Second, we need to perform the different steps (generating SPDs, checking whether $W \subseteq E(D)$, checking whether all members of $K$ are in a single path of $D$, and computing dependency scores) for $n$ times (the loop in Lines 5-14). We note that the second case increases time complexity of edge co-betweenness centrality, compared to vertex co-betweenness centrality computation.

THEOREM 4. *Algorithm 2 computes co-betweenness centrality of a set $W \subset E(\mathbf{G})$ in $O(nm + n|W| \, log|W|)$ time.*

**Algorithm 2** High level pseudo code of the algorithm of computing co-betweenness centrality of a set of edges.

```
1: EDGECOBETWEENNESS
2: Require. A network (graph) G, a set W ⊆ E(G).
3: Ensure. The co-betweenness centrality of W.
4: CB ← 0;
5: for all s ∈ V(G) do
6:     Generate the SPD D rooted at s;
7:     if W ⊆ E(D) then
8:         {let L be {v ∈ V(G) \ {s}|v is an end-point of at least one e ∈ W}}
9:         if all vertices in L are in a single path of D then
10:            cb ← δs•(αD,L(|L| − 1), ρL(D));
11:            CB ← CB + cb;
12:        end if
13:    end if
14: end for
15: return CB;
```

Co-betweenness centrality of a sequence $W$ of edges can be computed, as the following. For every vetex $s$ in the graph:

1. form the SPD $D$ rooted at $s$,
2. check whether $W \subset E(D)$,
3. check whether members of $L$ are in a single path of $D$,
4. the condition expressed in item (3), applies a total ordering on the edges in $W$. Check whether this total ordering is consistent with the order of edges in the sequence.
5. calculate $\delta_{s\bullet}(\alpha_{D,L}(|L|-1), \rho_L(D))$, if the conditions hold ($L$ is defined in Equation 7).

Similar to our discussion for vertex co-betweenness centrality computation, we can show that every step 1-5 can be done in $O(m)$ time. Therefore, we have the following theorem:

THEOREM 5. *Co-betweenness centrality of a sequence $W$ of edges in an unweighted graph can be computed in $O(nm)$ time* [2].

Finally, for co-betweenness centrality computation of a set (or a sequence) of edges in weighted graphs, we present the following theorem, where the proof is omitted because it is similar to the case of vertex co-betweenness centrality computation in weighted graphs.

THEOREM 6. *For weighted graphs, co-betweenness centrality of a set (or a sequence) $W$ of edges is computable in $O(nm + n^2 \log n)$ time.*

[2] A sequence of edges is also the sequence of vertices composing the edges. What increases time complexity of co-betweenness centrality computation for edges is the number of source vertices used to form SPDs. According to the definitions, a shortest path starting with (or ending to) a member of a sequence of vertices does not contribute to the co-betweenness centrality of the sequence. However, a shortest path starting with (or ending to) an end-point of a member of a sequence of edges contributes to co-betweenness centrality of the sequence.

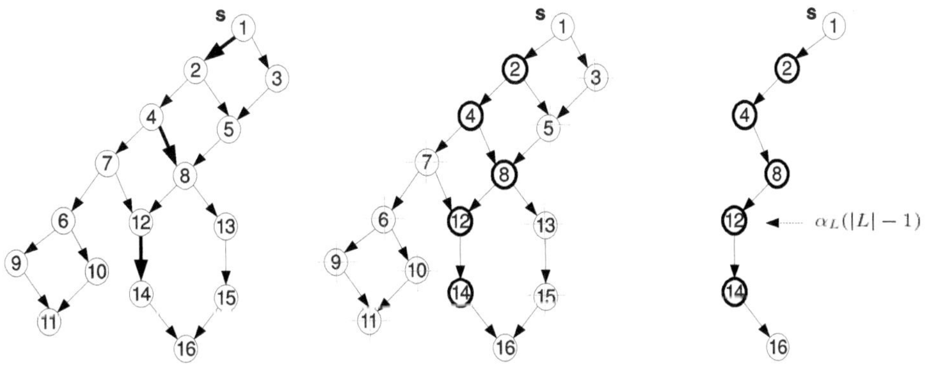


b) The SPD $D$ rooted at $s$ b) The SPD $D$ rooted at $s$ c) $\rho(D)$

**Figure 2: Part (a) shows the SPD rooted at $s='1'$. $W$ is $\{('1','2'),('4','8'),('12','14')\}$ which are distinguished with bold lines. In part (b), members of $L=\{'2','4','8','12','14'\}$ are distinguished with bold circles and vertices with red '+' are *markable* vertices with respect to $L$. We have: $\alpha(1)='2'$, $\alpha(2)='4'$, $\alpha(3)='8'$, $\alpha(4)='12'$, $\alpha(5)='14'$. Part (c) shows $\rho_L(D)$.**

**Table 1: Summary of real-world networks.**

| Dataset | # vertices | # edges | Reference |
|---|---|---|---|
| Advogato | 6,551 | 51,332 | [27] |
| ego-facebook | 2,888 | 2,981 | [28] |
| caida | 26,475 | 53,381 | [22] |
| CA-HepTh | 27,770 | 352,807 | [23] |
| Eva | 8,343 | 6,726 | [30] |
| Odlis | 2,909 | 18,419 | [34] |
| Dolphins | 62 | 159 | [26] |
| dblp | 12,591 | 49,793 | [24] |

# 5. EXPERIMENTAL RESULTS

We performed extensive experiments on real-world networks from different domains to assess the quantitative and qualitative behavior of the proposed algorithm. The experiments were done on one core of a single AMD Processor 270 clocked at 2.0 GHz with 8 GB main memory and $2\times 1$ MB L2 cache, running Ubuntu Linux 12.0. The program was compiled by the GNU C++ compiler 4.0.2 using optimization level 3. Table 1 summarizes specifications of our real-world networks.

Due to lack of space, we only report the results obtained for co-betweenness centrality computation of a set of vertices. The results obtained for other problems, e. g. a set of edges, are very similar to the results reported here for a set of vertices. In our experiments, for every dataset, we select a random set $P$ of vertices such that the subgraph induced by them is a path. Then, we start with a randomly chosen subset $K$ of $P$ (of size 2) and compute their co-betweenness centrality. Then, we add a randomly chosen vertex $v\in P\setminus K$ to $K$ and compute co-betweenness centrality of the vertices in $K$. Adding new vertices to $K$ is continued until co-betweenness centrality of all vertices in $P$ is computed. We note that if the subgraph induced by $K$ is a cyclic graph, its co-betweenness centrality will be 0.

Two well-known existing methods in the literature are the algorithm of Kolaczyk et. al. [20] and the algorithm of Dolev et. al. [11]. As mentioned earlier, the first one can only computes co-betweenness centrality of sets of size 2. On the other hand, the algorithm of Dolev et. al. can only compute co-betweenness centrality of sequences. Therefore, both algorithms are improper for our comparisons since they consider limited cases. Thus, we only report the results of our algorithm. Table 2 reports the empirical results.

The first dataset studied here is the *Advogato* network[3]. It is the trust network of the Advogato online community. Vertices are users of Advogato and edges represent trust relationships [27]. Clearly, by increasing the size of $K$, co-betweenness centrality decreases, i.e. for a subset $K'$ of $K$, co-betweenness centrality of $K'$ is not less than co-betweenness centrality of $K$. This is reflected in our experiments. On the other hand, over Advogato, as the size of $K$ increases, the time required to compute co-betweenness centrality decreases. It shows the efficiency of the SPDs pruning techniques.

The next dataset is the *ego-facebook* network[4]. This network contains Facebook user-user friendships. A vertex represents a user and an edge indicates a friendship relationship [28]. As depicted in Table 2, over this dataset, co-betweenness centrality always decreases as the size of $K$ increases. On the other hand, the running time usually decreases, as the size of $K$ increases. The only exception is that the time required to compute co-betweenness centrality of $\{428,10\}$ is less than the time required to compute co-betweenness centralities of $\{2897,428,10\}$ and $\{3428,2897,428,10\}$. In these situations, while compared to smaller sets, forming pruned SPDs with respect to larger sets is much more expensive, shortest path counting over pruned SPDs of larger sets is not much more efficient. In other words, the time required to prune SPDs dominates the speed-up resulted by counting shortest paths over pruned SPDs.

The next dataset comes from autonomous systems of the Internet[5]. The *caida* network is the undirected network of autonomous systems of the Internet connected with each other from the CAIDA project, collected in 2007. Vertices are autonomous systems (AS) and edges are communications [22]. Over this dataset, the running time does not stay consistent as the size of $K$ changes. For example, the running time increases when vertex 14835 is added to $\{3891,5379,81,1\}$. The next dataset is CA-HepTh[6]. This collaboration network covers scientific collaborations between authors papers submitted to High Energy Physics - Theory category. If an

[3]http://konect.uni-koblenz.de/networks/advogato
[4]http://snap.stanford.edu/data/egonets-Facebook.html
[5]http://snap.stanford.edu/data/as-caida.html
[6]http://snap.stanford.edu/data/ca-HepTh.html

**Table 2: Empirical results of our proposed algorithm on different datasets. $K$ contains the vertex identifiers of the chosen vertices.**

| Dataset | Vertices in the set $K$ | Running time (sec) | Co-betweenness centrality |
|---|---|---|---|
| **Advogato** | $\{428, 1\}$ | 822.643 | 662982499 |
| | $\{2209, 428, 1\}$ | 546.88 | 152106265 |
| | $\{5235, 2209, 428, 1\}$ | 533.351 | 76053118 |
| | $\{5234, 5235, 2209, 428, 1\}$ | 469.635 | 38026559 |
| **ego-facebook** | $\{428, 10\}$ | 238.184 | 1683935329 |
| | $\{2897, 428, 10\}$ | 500.259 | 23371727 |
| | $\{3428, 2897, 428, 10\}$ | 383.021 | 4475940 |
| | $\{3999, 3428, 2897, 428, 10\}$ | 349.836 | 106570 |
| | $\{4000, 3999, 3428, 2897, 428, 10\}$ | 361.781 | 85256 |
| | $\{4001, 4000, 3999, 3428, 2897, 428, 10\}$ | 307.447 | 63942 |
| | $\{4002, 4001, 4000, 3999, 3428, 2897, 428, 10\}$ | 303.489 | 42628 |
| | $\{4003, 4002, 4001, 4000, 3999, 3428, 2897, 428, 10\}$ | 302.32 | 21314 |
| **caida** | $\{5379, 81, 1\}$ | 6079.36 | 979172539 |
| | $\{3891, 5379, 81, 1\}$ | 5897.89 | 4198841 |
| | $\{14835, 3891, 5379, 81, 1\}$ | 6015.15 | 1050967 |
| | $\{14834, 14835, 3891, 5379, 81, 1\}$ | 5998.22 | 263472 |
| | $\{20972, 14834, 14835, 3891, 5379, 81, 1\}$ | 5237.81 | 16866 |
| **CA-HepTh** | $\{5622, 7907, 5784, 2930\}$ | 1836.33 | 3793691022 |
| | $\{3125, 5622, 79075784, 2930\}$ | 1284.3 | 3762578814 |
| | $\{9457, 3125, 5622, 7907, 5784, 2930\}$ | 1219.95 | 3306837476 |
| | $\{7289, 9457, 3125, 5622, 7907, 5784, 2930\}$ | 1071.67 | 2227068862 |
| | $\{840, 7289, 9457, 3125, 5622, 7907, 5784, 2930\}$ | 1046.52 | 1115518431 |
| **Eva** | $\{165, 0\}$ | 280.202 | 162635430 |
| | $\{159, 165, 0\}$ | 332.485 | 118993976 |
| | $\{2, 159, 165, 0\}$ | 220.67 | 8610082 |
| | $\{287, 2, 159, 165, 0\}$ | 201.197 | 158516 |
| | $\{4356, 287, 2, 159, 165, 0\}$ | 299.393 | 29440 |
| | $\{4853, 4356, 287, 2, 159, 165, 0\}$ | 314.575 | 7728 |
| | $\{4584, 4853, 4356, 287, 2, 159, 165, 0\}$ | 367.678 | 7544 |
| | $\{4859, 4584, 4853, 4356, 287, 2, 159, 165, 0\}$ | 380.485 | 5152 |
| | $\{4660, 4859, 4584, 4853, 4356, 287, 2, 159, 165, 0\}$ | 401.938 | 4600 |
| | $\{4554, 4660, 4859, 4584, 4853, 4356, 287, 2, 159, 165, 0\}$ | 302.847 | 920 |
| | $\{6239, 4554, 4660, 4859, 4584, 4853, 4356, 287, 2, 159, 165, 0\}$ | 407.922 | 368 |
| **Odlis** | $\{2530, 117\}$ | 116.878 | 233058 |
| | $\{2531, 2530, 117\}$ | 197.293 | 232872 |
| | $\{1541, 2531, 2530, 117\}$ | 238.806 | 230268 |
| | $\{1550, 1541, 2531, 2530, 117\}$ | 196.662 | 155310 |
| | $\{339, 1550, 1541, 2531, 2530, 117\}$ | 189.471 | 144336 |
| | $\{481, 339, 1550, 1541, 2531, 2530, 117\}$ | 54.8989 | 10602 |
| | $\{270, 481, 339, 1550, 1541, 2531, 2530, 117\}$ | 46.7788 | 4278 |
| | $\{155, 270, 481, 339, 1550, 1541, 2531, 2530, 117\}$ | 46.482 | 4092 |
| | $\{2025, 155, 270, 481, 339, 1550, 1541, 2531, 2530, 117\}$ | 48.6372 | 2790 |
| | $\{2430, 2025, 155, 270, 481, 339, 1550, 1541, 2531, 2530, 117\}$ | 51.9214 | 2604 |
| **Dolphins** | $\{40, 0\}$ | 0.0431 | 13348 |
| | $\{7, 40, 0\}$ | 0.033 | 355 |
| | $\{54, 7, 40, 0\}$ | 0.0308 | 233 |
| | $\{13, 54, 7, 40, 0\}$ | 0.0308 | 83 |
| | $\{32, 13, 54, 7, 40, 0\}$ | 0.0302 | 38 |
| **dblp** | $\{2, 135\}$ | 3812.74 | 3242271388 |
| | $\{2, 135, 1377\}$ | 3556.46 | 1823783366 |

author $i$ co-authored a paper with author $j$, an edge is drawn between vertices $i$ and $j$ [23]. Over this dataset, the running time always decreases, as the size of $K$ increases.

Eva is a prototype system for extracting, visualizing, and analyzing corporate ownership information as a social network. Applying the system to the telecommunications and media industries, Norlen et al. [30] constructed an ownership network with 6,726 relationships among 8,343 companies[7]. In this network, an edge from company $u$ to company $v$ is drawn iff the company $u$ is an owner of company $v$. Since we do not have ownership relationships for all companies, there will be companies without edges. Analysis shows that this network is highly clustered, with over 50% of all companies connected to one another in a single component. We tested our proposed algorithm over this ownership network. In this dataset, co-betweenness value of a set shows its impact on the ownership relations in the network. Our proposed algorithm scales well on this dataset, as sets with different sizes have close running times. By increasing the size of the set, its co-betweenness score decreases.

Odlis [34] is a hypertext reference system for users like library and information science professionals and university students and faculty. Users can add a new term to the system if they expect to encounter it in future or if they require to know its meaning. In the network representing this system, vertices are terms and an edge from term $u$ to term $v$ exists iff in the Odlis dictionary the term $v$ is used to describe the meaning of term $u$ [8]. As reflected in Table 2, over this network, in most cases, by increasing the size of the set the time required to compute its co-betweenness centrality decreases. In this network, the co-betweenness score of a set $K$ shows the number of pairs of terms which use all terms in $K$ to describe their meaning.

We also tested the proposed algorithm on a small dataset. The dolphins dataset [26] consists of an undirected graph of frequent associations between 62 dolphins in a community living off Doubtful Sound, New Zealand [9]. In this dataset, the co-betweenness value of a set $K$ of dolphins shows the importance of all members in $K$ with together in associations between dolphins. As depicted in Table 2, over this dataset, sets with different sizes have almost the same running time.

Finally, we performed experiments on the dblp dataset[10]. Each vertex in this network is a publication (paper, book, etc), and each edge represents a citation of a publication by another publication [24]. Using the proposed algorithm, we calculated co-betweenness scores of two sets of vertices $\{2, 135\}$ and $\{2, 135, 1377\}$. As presented in Table 2, it takes a shorter time to compute co-betweenness score of the larger set.

# 6. RELATED WORK

Betweenness centrality is widely used as a precise indicator for the information flow controlled by a vertex in social and information networks [35]. It assumes that information flow is done through shortest paths. Brandes [7] introduced new algorithms for computing betweenness centrality of a vertex, which is performed in $O(nm)$ and $O(nm + n^2 \log n)$ time for unweighted and weighted networks, respectively. Holme [17] showed that betweenness centrality of a vertex is highly correlated with the fraction of time that the vertex is occupied by the traffic of the network. Barthelemy [3] showed that many scale-free networks [1] have a power-law distribution of betweenness centrality. There are also several notions of betweenness centrality which are used to determine the structural prominence of Web pages [18] and [9].

There are several variations of betweennes centrality which are not designed for shortest path routing. *Flow betweenness* [15] equally considers all paths for routing. Borgatti [4] and [5] considered betweenness for all possible paths, as well as all possible trails, as well as walks (weighted inversely by length). He used numerical simulation to estimate the betweenness values. Newman [29] proposed *Random walk betweenness* which prefers shorter paths over the longer ones. In this work, Newman provided closed-form equations for the case of random traversal via walks. Borgatti [5] proposed a dynamic model-based view of centrality that focuses on the outcomes of vertices in a graph.

In [13], Freeman defined group betweenness centrality as a measure of homogeneity of betweenness of members. Everett and Borgatti [12] defined group betweenness centrality as a natural extension of betweenness centrality for sets of vertices. The other natural extension of betweenness centrality is *co-betweenness centrality* [20]. The authors of [20] presented an algorithm for individual co-betweenness centrality computation. However, this method works only for sets of size 2 and its time complexity is $O(n^3)$. Puzis et al. [32] proposed a $O(|K|^3)$ time algorithm for computation of successive group betweenness centrality. In [33], the authors presented two algorithms for finding the most prominent group. The first algorithm is based on heuristic search and the second is based on iterative greedy choice of vertices. In [11], the authors defined the Routing Betweenness Centrality (RBC) measure and presented algorithms for computing RBC of single vertices in the network and algorithms for computing group RBC of sets (or sequences) of vertices. Ballester et al. [2] discussed the importance of finding the key group in a criminal network. Borgatti elaborated in [6] on a Key Player Problem (KPP) that is strongly related to the cohesion of a network. He defined two problems: KPP-Pos and KPP-Neg. The solution of the first problem is a group maximally connected to all other vertices in a graph and the solution of the second is a group maximally disrupting the network.

**Table 4: Time complexity of edge co-betweenness centrality computation ($|W|$ is the size of the set (sequence)).**

| | Unweighted graphs | Weighted graphs |
|---|---|---|
| Set | $O(nm + n\|W\| \log\|W\|)$ | $O(nm + n^2 \log n)$ |
| Sequence | $O(nm)$ | $O(nm + n^2 \log n)$ |

# 7. CONCLUSION

In this paper, we developed efficient algorithms for vertex and edge co-betweenness centrality computation in different settings. Tables 3 and 4 summarize time complexity of the proposed methods. Our methods are based on reducing *vertex co-betweenness centrality* and *edge co-betweenness centrality* of a set (or a sequence) to *betweenness centrality* of a single vertex. They are not limited to special cases and they are more efficient than existing methods. We empirically evaluated the efficiency of the proposed methods and showed their high performance over different real-world networks.

# 8. REFERENCES

[1] A.-L. Barabasi and R. Albert, Emergence of scaling in random networks, Science, 286, 509-512, 1999.

[7] http://vlado.fmf.uni-lj.si/pub/networks/data/econ/Eva/Eva.htm

[8] http://vlado.fmf.uni-lj.si/pub/networks/data/dic/odlis/Odlis.htm

[9] http://www-personal.umich.edu/~mejn/netdata/

[10] http://konect.uni-koblenz.de/networks/dblp-cite

**Table 3: Time complexity of vertex co-betweenness centrality computation ($|K|$ is the size of the set (sequence)).**

| | Unweighted graphs | Weighted graphs |
|---|---|---|
| Set of vertices | $O(nm - \lvert K\rvert m + n\lvert K\rvert \log\lvert K\rvert - \lvert K\rvert^2 \log\lvert K\rvert)$ | $O(nm - \lvert K\rvert m + n^2 \log n - \lvert K\rvert n \log n)$ |
| Sequence of vertices | $O(nm - \lvert K\rvert m)$ | $O(nm - \lvert K\rvert m + n^2 \log n - \lvert K\rvert n \log n)$ |


[2] C. Ballester, A. C. Armengol and Y. Zenou, Who's who in networks. wanted: The key player, Econometrica, 74(5), 1403-1417, Sep. 2006.

[3] M. Barthelemy, Betweenness centrality in large complex networks. The Europ. Phys. J. B - Condensed Matter 38, 2(Mar.), 163-168, 2004.

[4] S. P. Borgatti, Types of network flows and how to destabilize terrorist networks, Sunbelt International Social Networks Conference, New Orleans, 2002.

[5] S. P. Borgatti, Centrality and network flow, Social Networks, 27(1), 55-71, 2005.

[6] S. P. Borgatti, Identifying sets of key players in a social network, Comput. Math. Organ. Theory, 12(1), 21-34, 2006.

[7] U. Brandes, A Faster Algorithm for Betweenness Centrality. Journal of Mathematical Sociology, 25(2), 163-177, 2001.

[8] U. Brandes, On variants of shortest-path betweenness centrality and their generic computation, Social Networks, 30(2), 136-145, May 2008.

[9] S. Brin, R. Motwani, L. Page and T. Winograd, What can you do with a web in your pocket? IEEE Bulletin of the Technical Committee on Data Engineering, 21(2), 37-47, 1998.

[10] A. Cuzzocrea, A. Papadimitriou, D. Katsaros and Y. Manolopoulos, Edgebetweenness centrality: A novel algorithm for QoS-based topology control over wireless sensor networks, Journal of Network and Computer Applications, 35(4), 1210-1217, July 2012.

[11] S. Dolev, Y. Elovici and R. Puzis, Routing betweenness centrality, J. ACM, 57(4), 2010.

[12] M. Everett and S. Borgatti. The centrality of groups and classes, Journal of Mathematical Sociology, 23(3), 181-201, 1999.

[13] L. C. Freeman, A set of measures of centrality based upon betweenness, Sociometry, 40, 35-41, 1977.

[14] L. C. Freeman, Centrality in social networks: Conceptual clarification. Social Networks, 1(3), 215-239, 1979.

[15] L. C. Freeman, S. P. Borgatti, and D. R. White, Centrality in valued graphs: A measure of betweenness based on network ïňĆow, Social Networks, 13(2), 141-154, 1991.

[16] M. Girvan and M. E. J. Newman, Community structure in social and biological networks, Proc. Natl. Acad. Sci. USA 99, 7821-7826, 2002.

[17] P. Holme, Congestion and centrality in traffic flow on complex networks, Adv. Complex Syst, 6(2), 163-176, 2003.

[18] J. M. Kleinberg, Authoritative sources in a hyperlinked environment, Journal of the Association for Computing Machinery, 46(5), 604-632, 1999.

[19] D. Knuth, Section 5.2.4: Sorting by Merging, Sorting and Searching. The Art of Computer Programming 3 (2nd ed.), Addison-Wesley, 158-168, 998.

[20] E. D. Kolaczyk, D. B. Chua and M. Barthelemy. Group-betweenness and co-betweenness: Inter-related notions of coalition centrality, Social Networks, 31(3), 190-203, 2009.

[21] S. Lammer, B. Gehlsen, D. Helbing. Scaling laws in the spatial structure of urban road networks. Physica A, 363(1), 89-95, 2006.

[22] J. Leskovec, J. Kleinberg and C. Faloutsos, Graphs over Time: Densification Laws, Shrinking Diameters and Possible Explanations, KDD, 2005.

[23] J. Leskovec, J. Kleinberg and C. Faloutsos, Graph Evolution: Densification and Shrinking Diameters, ACM Transactions on Knowledge Discovery from Data (ACM TKDD), 1(1), 2007.

[24] M. Ley, The DBLP computer science bibliography: Evolution, research issues, perspectives, In Proc. Int. Symposium on String Processing and Information Retrieval, 1-10, 2002.

[25] X. Li, J. Han, J.-G. Lee and H. Gonzalez, Traffic density-based discovery of hot routes in road networks, 10th Symposium on Spatial and Temporal Databases (SSTD), 441-459, 2007.

[26] D. Lusseau, K. Schneider, O. J. Boisseau, P. Haase, E. Slooten, and S. M. Dawson, The bottlenose dolphin community of Doubtful Sound features a large proportion of long-lasting associations, Behavioral Ecology and Sociobiology 54, 396-405, 2003.

[27] P.Massa, M. Salvetti and D. Tomasoni, Bowling alone and trust decline in social network sites, In Proc. Int. Conf. Dependable, Autonomic and Secure Computing, 658-663, 2009.

[28] J. McAuley and J. Leskovec, Learning to discover social circles in ego networks, NIPS, pages 548-556. 2012.

[29] M. E. J. Newman, A measure of betweenness centrality based on random walks, Social Networks, 27(1), 39-54, 2005.

[30] K. Norlen, G. Lucas, M. Gebbie and J. Chuang, EVA: Extraction, Visualization and Analysis of the Telecommunications and Media Ownership Network. Proceedings of International Telecommunications Society 14th Biennial Conference (ITS2002), Seoul Korea, August 2002.

[31] A. Perer, B. Shneiderman, Balancing systematic and flexible exploration of social networks, IEEE Transactions on Visualization and Computer Graphics, 12(5), 693-700, 2006.

[32] R. Puzis, Y. Elovici and S. Dolev. Fast algorithm for successive computation of group betweenness centrality, Phys. Rev. E, 76(5), 2007.

[33] R. Puzis, Y. Elovici and S. Dolev, Finding the most prominent group in complex networks, AI Commun. 20(4), 287-296, 2007.

[34] J. M. Reitz, ODLIS: Online Dictionary of Library and Information Science, 2002.

[35] G. Yan, T. Zhou, B. Hu, Z. Q. Fu, and B.-H. Wang, Efficient routing on complex networks. Phys. Rev. E, 73, 046108, 2006.

# Chinese-English Mixed Text Normalization

Qi Zhang, Huan Chen, Xuanjing Huang
Shanghai Key Laboratory of Intelligent Information Processing
School of Computer Science, Fudan University
825 Zhangheng Road, Shanghai, P.R.China
{qz, 12210240054, xjhuang}@fudan.edu.cn

## ABSTRACT

Along with the expansion of globalization, multilingualism has become a popular social phenomenon. More than one language may occur in the context of a single conversation. This phenomenon is also prevalent in China. A huge variety of informal Chinese texts contain English words, especially in emails, social media, and other user generated informal contents. Since most of the existing natural language processing algorithms were designed for processing monolingual information, mixed multilingual texts cannot be well analyzed by them. Hence, it is of critical importance to preprocess the mixed texts before applying other tasks. In this paper, we firstly analyze the phenomena of mixed usage of Chinese and English in Chinese microblogs. Then, we detail the proposed two-stage method for normalizing mixed texts. We propose to use a noisy channel approach to translate in-vocabulary words into Chinese. For better incorporating the historical information of users, we introduce a novel user aware neural network language model. For the out-of-vocabulary words (such as pronunciations, informal expressions and et al.), we propose to use a graph-based unsupervised method to categorize them. Experimental results on a manually annotated microblog dataset demonstrate the effectiveness of the proposed method. We also evaluate three natural language parsers with and without using the proposed method as the preprocessing step. From the results, we can see that the proposed method can significantly benefit other NLP tasks in processing mixed text.

## Categories and Subject Descriptors

H.3.3 [**Information Storage and Retrieval**]: Information Search and Retrieval - Information Search and Retrieval

## General Terms

Algorithms, Experimentation.

## Keywords

Words Normalization, Chinese-English Mixed Text, User Aware Neural Network Language Model


*WSDM'14*, February 24–28, 2014, New York, New York, USA.

http://dx.doi.org/10.1145/2556195.2556228.

## 1. INTRODUCTION

With the rapidly growing of Internet and the needs of globalization, exposure of individuals to multiple languages is becoming increasingly frequent. It promotes needs for people to acquire additional languages. Multilingual speakers have even outnumbered monolingual speakers [26]. Code-switching, which is the use of more than one language in the context of a single conversation, occurs frequently especially in informal texts. Due to the drastically increasing of social medias, the amount of user generated content (UGC) is extensively growing. Therefore, the mixed usages of more than one languages becomes a social phenomenon.

In Chinese, among all kinds of informal language phenomena, the mixed usage of Chinese and English is one the most frequent types. Through analyzing 210 million microblogs collected from Sina Weibo[1], which is one of the most popular website providing microblogging service in China, we find that over 14.8% microblogs contain at least one English word. Moreover, these English words include not only nouns but also adjectives, adverbs, and even verbs. For example, let us consider the following example:

帮我 ***book*** 一下会议室
(Please help me book a meeting room)

The speaker uses "*book*" instead of its Chinese translation "预订" to express his meaning.

Since existing natural language processing techniques (e.g. POS tagging, chunking, parsing, opinion mining, etc.) were designed for processing monolingual text, multilingual mixed texts cannot be well processed by these methods. Moreover, due to lack of annotated corpus for informal texts, the effectiveness of most state-of-the-art supervised models are high impacted in processing informal content. We evaluated the performances of Stanford Parser and Berkeley Parser, which both of are widely used for various applications, drop to 66.4% and 67.9% respectively in processing the POS of English words in the Chinese-English mixed microblogs. It also demonstrates the great importance of normalizing the mixed texts. Zhao et al. [36] have also noticed this issue and proposed to use dynamic features under sequence labeling framework to achieve POS tagging problem for mixed texts. However, their work only focused on a specific task, POS tagging, and can not be directly adopted to process other tasks. Moreover, creating training data for mixed texts or investigating novel algorithms specifically for different NLP tasks are all time-consuming and sometimes difficult to accomplish. We argue that this kind of approaches can be easily generalized.

[1]http://www.weibo.com.

Several existing works have been proposed to achieve the task from the perspective of normalizing general informal Chinese texts. Li and Yarowsky [16] proposed to use bootstrapping model to identify candidate informal phrases and use conditional log-linear model based on rule-based intuitions and data co-occurrence phenomena to rank candidates. Wang and Ng [33] introduced a beam-search decoder based normalization method for missing word recovery, punctuation correction, manually assembled dictionary based word correction, and resegmentation. However, these methods are mainly based on the assumption of frequent occurrence. According to our statistic based on microblogs collected from real online service, the occurrence of English words in mixed texts also follow Zipf's law. Therefore, lots of English words' frequency in the mixed texts are low. These infrequent English words cannot be well translated or categorized by these methods.

Although most Chinese-English mixed microblogs only contain a few of English words, this is still a very challenging task due to the following facts: 1) there are enormous number and various types of English words. According to our statistic, more than 149K distinct words are included in 2.6 million mixed microblogs. 2) the linguistic and syntactic usages of English words may different from their original one. Due to that these mixed texts usually follow the grammar of one language, Part-of-speech tags of some English words may even be changed.

In this paper, we take a normalization centric view of processing Chinese-English mixed texts. We propose a novel two-stage method to achieve the task. For in-vocabulary English words, we propose to translate them into Chinese. Out-of-vocabulary words (including , pronunciations, informal expressions, etc.) are classified into different categories, such as person name, organization name, and so on. With these steps, mixed texts can be processed by existing NLP methods with little additional efforts. The normalized texts are much more easily for monolingual speakers to understand. To the best of our knowledge, this is the first work focused on normalizing Chinese-English mixed texts.

We propose to use noisy-channel approach with neural network language model to translate in-vocabulary words. To capture the historical information of users, we propose a novel user aware neural network language model. For training the word-level translation model, we constructed a parallel corpus based on subtitles of movie and TV series. To categorize words, we propose to use a graph-based unsupervised method with a novel initialization technique. For evaluating the proposed method, we also manually constructed a labeled corpus. Experimental results show that the proposed method achieves better performances than state-of-the-art methods. The main contributions of this paper are as follows:

- We formalize the English word normalization problem in Chinese-English mixed text. At the extent of the authors knowledge, it is the first work focused on this topic.
- To incorporate the historical information of users, we propose a novel user aware neural network language model.
- We manually labeled a number of microblogs extracted from real-world microblogs for evaluation.

The remaining parts are organized as follows: Section 2 gives some brief descriptions of related works. In section 3, we describe the phenomena and analysis of mixed texts. Section 4 describes the proposed normalization methods. Experimental results and analyses are given in Section 5. Section 6 concludes the paper.

# 2. RELATED WORK

The research of text normalization can be traced back to the task of converting numbers, dates, etc. into the standard dictionary words. Along with the rapid increasing of user generated content, text normalization task has received much more attentions in recent years [1, 13, 16, 2, 18, 14, 10, 6]. In this paper we classify the related works into three categories: lexical normalization, named entity normalization and informal text processing.

## 2.1 Lexical Normalization

Aw et al. [1] treated the lexical normalisation problem as a translation problem from the informal language to formal English They also studied the differences among SMS normalization, general text normalization, spelling check and text paraphrasing. Based on the investigated phenomena of SMS messages, they adapted a phrase-based method to achieve the task.

Kobus et al. [13] studied the problem of normalizing the orthography of French SMS messages. They proposed machine translation based method and nondeterministic phonemic transduction based method.

Han and Baldwin [8] proposed a supervised method to detect ill-formed words and used morphophonemic similarity to generate correction candidates. Then, all candidates were ranked based on a number of features generated from noisy context and similarity between ill-formed words and candidates.

Liu et al. [18] proposed to use a broad coverage lexical normalization method consisting three components. They assumed that a set of letter transformation patterns were used by humans to decipher the nonstandard tokens and integrated three human perspectives, including enhanced letter transformation, visual priming, and string/phonetic similarity

Han et al. [9] introduced a dictionary based method and an automatically normalisation dictionary construction method. They assumed that lexical variants and their standard forms occur in similar contexts.

Derczynski et al. [6] also proposed to use dictionary based method to achieve the task. They created a set of mappings from OOV words to their IV equivalents, using slang dictionaries and manual examination of the training data.

Wang and Ng [33] focused on the problem of missing word recovery, punctuation correction, manually assembled dictionary based word correction, and resegmentation. They introduced a beam-search decoder based normalization method to do it.

Although these methods achieved significant improvement on processing SMS and UGCs, they only focused on the monolingual text. Hence, Chinese-English mixed text can not be directly processed by these methods.

## 2.2 Named Entity Normalization

Normalizing named entity abbreviations to their standard forms is also an important preprocessing task for UGCs. This task has also attracted lots of attentions [3, 23, 17, 16, 34, 35].

Chang and Teng [3] introduced an HMM-based single character recovery model to extract character level abbreviation pairs for textual corpus. Okazaki et al. [23] also used discriminative approach for this task. They formalized the abbreviation recognition task as a binary classification problem and used Support Vector Machines to model it.

Yang et al. [35] treated the abbreviation generation problem as a labeling task and used Conditional Random Fields (CRFs) to do it. They also proposed to rerank candidates by a length model and web information.

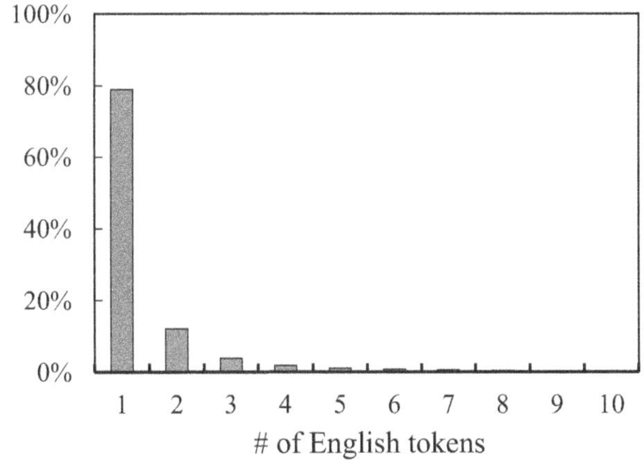


**Figure 1: Distribution of number of English tokens per microblog.**

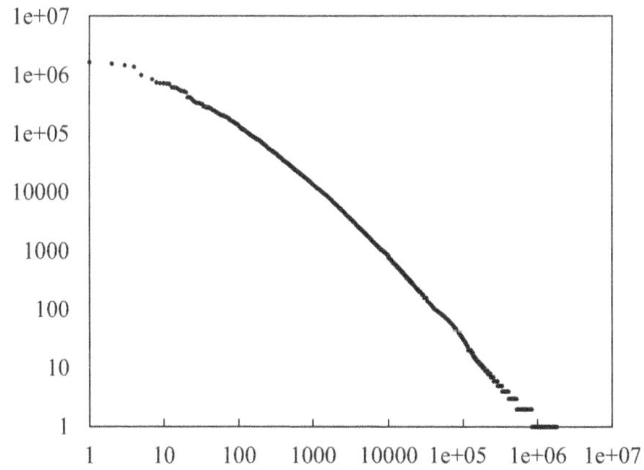


**Figure 2: English token frequency in Chinese-English mixed microblogs.**

Xie et al. [34] proposed to extract Chinese abbreviations and their corresponding definitions based on anchor texts. They constructed a weighted bipartite graph from anchor texts and applied co-frequency based measures to quantify the relatedness between two anchor texts.

Li and Yarowsky [17] proposed an unsupervised method extracting the relation between a full-form phrase and its abbreviation from monolingual corpora. They used data co-occurrence intuition to identify relations between abbreviation and full names. They also improved a statistical machine translation by incorporating the extracted relations into the baseline translation system.

Based on the data co-occurrence phenomena, Li and Yarowsky [16] also introduced a bootstrapping procedure to identify formal-informal relations in web corpora. They used search engine to extract contextual instances of the given informal phrase, and ranked the candidate relation pairs using conditional log-linear model.

## 2.3 Informal Text Processing

Despite the normalization based methods, a number of works have been proposed to directly process the informal texts [7, 19, 20, 30, 27, 36].

Freitag [7] studied the problem of performing information extraction from informal text. They showed the strategies of creating a term-space representation and exploiting typographic information in the form of token features. Minkov et al. [19] also introduced methods for extracting named entitles from informal texts and showed that informal text had different characteristics from formal text.

Mullen and Malouf [20] described statistical tests on a dataset of political discussion group postings. They concluded that traditional text classification methods would be inadequate to the task of sentiment analysis in this domain.

Thelwall et al. [30] focused on the task of detecting sentiment strength from informal texts. Through experimental results, they demonstrated incorporating decoding nonstandard spellings seemed to be one of factors of relative improvements given by their method.

Ritter et al. [27] experimental demonstrated that existing methods for POS tagging, Chunking and Named Entity Recognition performed quite poorly for processing Tweets. They presented a distantly supervised approach based LabeledLDA for Named Entity Classification problem on tweets.

Zhao et al. [36] proposed to use dynamic features under sequence labeling framework to process POS tagging problem for Chinese-English mixed texts. They extracted features from both local and non-local information and taked advantage of the characteristics of the mixed texts.

Previous works have been made to study the problem from various aspects. However, most works focused on specific tasks. Different with them, in this paper, we take a normalization centric view of processing Chinese-English mixed texts.

# 3. DATA ANALYSIS

For better understanding the phenomena of mixed usage of Chinese and English, in this section, we examine the dataset which contains about 210 millions microblogs crawled from Sina Weibo. We firstly describe the analyzing results from raw dataset. Then, we introduce the results acquired from manually categorized English words in these mixed texts. Since Chinese phonetic system and some informal usages are also represented by English alphabet letters, for clarification, we use *English token* to represent a sequence of English alphabet letters without any blank in between.

Firstly, the microblogs which contain at least one English token are extracted from the dataset. We observe that more than 14.8% microblogs are Chinese-English mixed texts. Figure 1 shows the distribution of number of English tokens per microblog in the Chinese-English mixed microblogs. We can observe that more than 94.6% microblogs contain less than 3 English tokens. About 78.8% mixed texts contain only one English token. It means that most English tokens are surrounding by Chinese characters. Hence, the linguistic usages of these English tokens may be different from their original ones. The part-of-speech tags of some tokens are even changed.

From the perspective of English token, we also look at the frequency of each token. Figure 2 shows a plot of English tokens frequency . The plot is in log-log coordinates. X-axile is the rank of a token in the frequency table. Y-axile is the total number of the token's occurrences. From the figure, we can observe that the frequency of English tokens also follow Zipf's law. It means that lots of tokens occur infrequently.

Table 1: Categories of English tokens in Chinese-English mixed texts. (English translations are in the brackets.)

| Category | Percent | Example |
|---|---|---|
| Vocabulary word[a] | 68.3% | 别忘记明天的*meeting* (Please don't forget tomorrow's meeting). |
| Abbreviation | 12.3% | *BBC*拍摄的《美丽中国》(Wild China produced by BBC). |
| Pronunciation | 4.0% | 发了几条*weibo* (Update several microblogs). |
| Slang | 7.8% | *Orz* (A posture emoticon representing a kneeling person). |
| Other | 7.6% | User ID, Chinese word followed by *ing*, misspelling, and so on. |

[a]The vocabulary is constructed based on the parallel corpus, which will be described in Section 4.1.

For investigating the types of these English tokens, we randomly selected 2,000 microblogs which contain at lest one English token and manually labeled categories of English tokens. The five categories we use to classify queries are listed in Table 1. Table 1 also shows examples and percentages of each category. From the table, we can observe that vocabulary words and abbreviations take part in 68.3% and 12.3% among all English tokens respectively. It means that the tokens which can be translated take great part in all mixed texts. Among all the five categories, tokens belonging to "Slang" and "Other" categories are most difficult to normalize. For example, "Orz" is originated from Japan and can be used to express various meanings in different context.

## 4. THE PROPOSED METHOD

In this section, we describe the proposed normalization method for English tokens in Chinese-English mixed texts. For the tokens which are vocabulary words, we propose to use noisy channel model with word embeddings to translate them. For the out-of-vocabulary words and other types of English tokens, a graph-based unsupervised method is introduced to categorize them. The following sections will describe the proposed methods.

### 4.1 Word Translation

Let $t$ represents the given mixed text. It contains a sequence of words $w_1 w_2 .... w_n$. Each word $w_i$ is either a Chinese word or an English word. For the mixed text $t$, the word translation method try to produce the normalization candidate $\hat{c}$ under the noisy channel model, which contain two components:

- A *language model* assigns a probability $p(c)$ for any sentence $c = w_1 w_2 .... w_n$ in Chinese.
- A *translation model* assigns a conditional probability $p(c|t)$ to any Chinese/Mixed-Text pair of sentences.

Given these two components of the model, following the general noisy-channel approach, the output of the translation model on a Chinese-English mixed sentence $t$ is:

$$\hat{c} = \arg\max_{c \in C} p(c) \times p(c|t), \tag{1}$$

where $C$ is the set of all sentences in Chinese.

For language model, motivated by recent great success achieved by neural language models [11], we also incorporate it in this work. To better capture the historical information of users, we propose a novel user-aware neural language model. The proposed model learns to discriminate the next word given a short word sequence (local context) and sentences the user wrote recently (user historical information). As shown in Figure 3, two scoring components are defined for the final score of a (word sequence, user historical information) pair. The scoring components are computed by two neural networks.

Following the framework proposed by Collobert and Weston [4], given a word sequence $c$ and user historical information $u$, our goal is to discriminate the correct last word in $c$ for other random words. $s(c, u)$ represents the scoring function modeled by neural networks. $c^w$ represents word sequence $c$ with the last word replaced by word $w$. Hence, the objective is that the margin between $s(c, u)$ and $s(c^w, u)$ is larger than 1, for any other word $w$ in the vocabulary. The object function is to minimize the ranking loss for for each $(c, u)$ in the training corpus:

$$L_{c,u} = \sum_{w \in V} \max\left(0, 1 - s(c, u) + s(c^w, u)\right) \tag{2}$$

Firstly, the word sequence $c = w_1 w_2 .... w_n$ is represented by an ordered list of vectors $x = (x_1, x_2, ..., x_n)$ where $x_i$ is the embedding of word $i$ in the sequence. $x_i$ is a column in the embedding matrix $E \in \mathbb{R}^{m \times |V|}$, in which $|V|$ denotes the vocabulary size. The embedding matrix $E$ will be learned and updated during the training procedure. $score_l$ is modeled by a neural network with one hidden layer:

$$\begin{aligned} a_1 &= f(W_1[x_1; x_2; ...; x_n] + b_1) && (3) \\ score_l &= W_2 a_1 + b_2, && (4) \end{aligned}$$

where $f$ is an element-wise activation function such as $tanh$; $a_1 \in \mathbb{R}^{h \times 1}$ is the activation of the hidden layer with $h$ hidden nodes; $W_1 \in \mathbb{R}^{h \times (mn)}$ is the first layer weights of the neural network; $W_2 \in \mathbb{R}^{1 \times h}$ is the second layer weights; $b_1$, $b_2$ are the biases of each layer.

Following the work done by Huang et al.[11], for representing user historical information, we also use the weighted average of all embeddings of words belonging to the user historical information. $u$ denotes the user historical information vector and is calculated as follows:

$$u = \frac{\sum_{i=1}^{m} f(w_i^u) x_i^u}{\sum_{i=1}^{m} w(w_i^u)}, \tag{5}$$

where $w_1^u, w_2^u, ...w_m^u$ represents the words of user historical information; $x_i^u$ denotes the embedding of $w_i^u$; $f(\cdot)$ captures the importance of the given word $w_i$. In this paper idf-weighting is used as the weighting function.

We also use a neural network with one hidden layer to compute the user historical information score, $score_u$ as follows:

$$\begin{aligned} a_1^u &= f(W_1^u[u; x_n] + b_1^u) && (6) \\ score_u &= W_2^u a_1^u + b_2^u, && (7) \end{aligned}$$

where $[u; x_n]$ is the concatenation of the weighted average user historical information vector and the vector of the last word in $t$; $a_1^u \in \mathbb{R}^{h^u \times 1}$ is the activation of the hidden layer with $h^u$ hidden

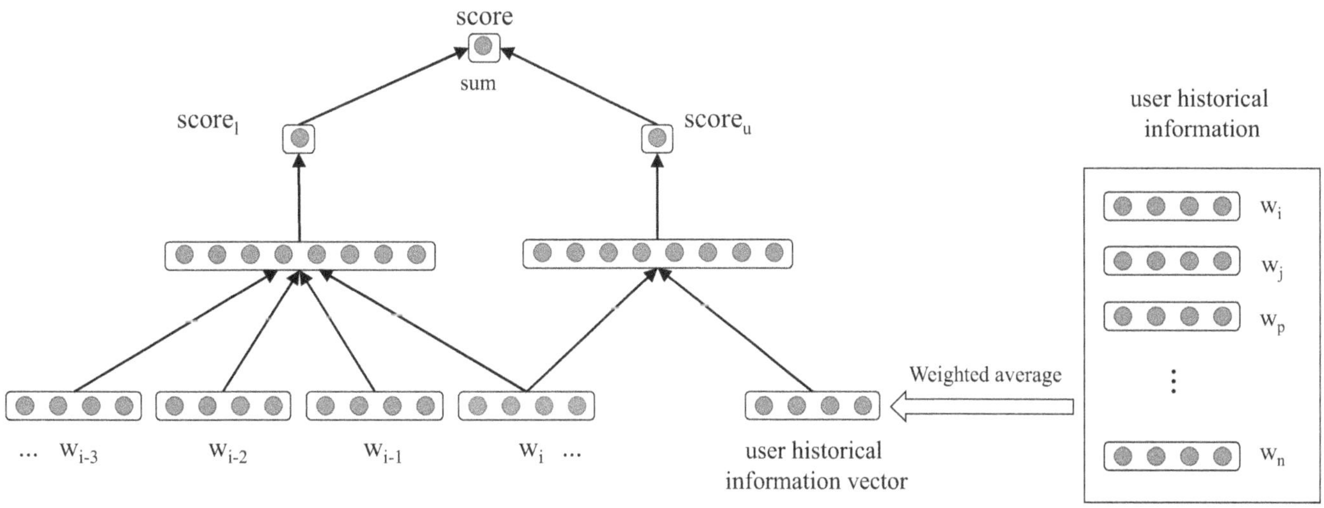


**Figure 3: Overview structure of the proposed user-aware neural language model.**

nodes; $W_1^u \in \mathbb{R}^{h^u \times (2m)}$ is the first layer weights of the neural network; $W_2^u \in \mathbb{R}^{1 \times h^u}$ is the second layer weights; $b_1^u$, $b_2^u$ are the biases of each layer.

The final score is the sum of score of local context and user historical information:

$$score = score_l + score_u \tag{8}$$

For training the parameters: weights of the neural network and the embedding matrix $E$, we also follow the corrupt example sampling method [4], and sample the gradient of the objective by randomly choosing a word from the dictionary as a corrupt example for each sequence-context pair, $(t, u)$. These weights are updated via back-propagation.

For the translation model $p(c|t)$, we make the following independence assumptions:

$$p(c|t) = \prod_{t_i \in Eng} p(c_i|t_i), \tag{9}$$

where $p(c|t)$ is the probability of generating Chinese word $c$ from English word $t$ and can be estimated by IBM Model 1 with parallel corpus.

Based on Eq.(8) and Eq.(9), the translation model Eq.(1) on a new Chinese-English mixed sentence $t$ can be reformulated as:

$$\begin{aligned} \hat{c} &= \arg\max_{c \in C} p(c) \times p(c|t) \qquad (10) \\ &\propto \arg\max_{c \in C} \prod_{i, t_i \in Eng} score(t_1 t_2..t_i, u) p(c_i|t_i) \end{aligned}$$

According to the statistic of the crawled corpus, we observe that more than 94.6% percent Chinese-English mixed texts contain less than 3 English words. Hence, in this work, the decoding problem can be efficiently solved.

## 4.2 Word Categorization

As described in Section 2, except in-vocabulary words, there are also a number of English tokens used as product name, informal expressions, and so on. For these tokens, we propose to use label propagation (LP) [37] to classify them into different categories. In this work, we try to classify English tokens into the following five categories: person name, product name, organization name, slang, and loanword.

From analyzing the dataset, we observe that (I) words belongs to the same categories tend to have similar contexts; (II) words and their corresponding category description words tend to have frequent co-occurrence relations. Previous researches also show that words with high context similarity tend to have similar semantic meanings [9]. Based on the observation, we propose to use context similarities to measure the edge weight of the graph. LP transfers labels from labeled data to unlabeled data through weighted graph. Based on the observation (II), we propose a novel label initialization method.

### 4.2.1 *Graph Construction*

We construct an undirected graph $G = (V, E)$ to represent the relations between English tokens. $V = \{v_1, ..., v_n\}$ denotes all the vertices in the graph. Vertices represent English tokens needed to be categorized. $E = \{e_{ij}, 1 \leq i, j \leq n\}$ represents the similarities between tokens. $e_{ij}$ represents the similarity between vertex $v_i$ and $v_j$. In order to reduce the computation cost of iteratively propagating, we also exclude edges whose value is less than threshold $\theta$ to prune the edges.

For calculating the similarities between tokens, we first extract all the context words in a predefined window (the windows size used in this work is 4) for each token. Context words are treated independently for each other. We use vector space model to construct context vector $\vec{f}$, of which each dimension is calculated by $tf \cdot idf$. Cosine measure is used to calculate the similarity between tokens:

$$e_{ij} = \cos(\vec{f_i}, \vec{f_j}) = \frac{\vec{f_i} \cdot \vec{f_j}}{\| \vec{f_i} \| \| \vec{f_j} \|} \tag{11}$$

### 4.2.2 *Label Propagation*

Label propagation method transfers the labels from labeled data to unlabeled data based on the constructed weighted graph. It has been successfully used for many tasks [21, 15, 32, 5, 29]. In this work, we also adopt LP to obtain the categories of English tokens.

From the observation (II), we know that words tend to have frequent co-occurrence with their category description words. For example, more than 1.98 billions documents can be retrieved using the query "iphone product" through Google. While, only 25 millions documents are returned using the query "iphone informal expressions". Based on the observation, we firstly construct a number of description words for each category. $cdw_{ij}$ represents $j$th description word of the $i$th category. Similar as SO-PMI-IR [31], we propose to use the following equation to measure the possibility of token $v_i$ in the category $z_j$:

$$\text{SO-P}(v_i, z_j) = \max_{k=1}^{m} \frac{\text{hits}(v_i \text{ NEAR } cdw_{jk})}{\text{hits}(v_i) \cdot \text{hits}(cdw_{jk})}, \quad (12)$$

where hits($query$) is the number of hits given the query $query$ and is returned by Bing; "NEAR" is used to restrict the distance between search phrases[2].

The label distribution of each vertex is initialized as follows:

$$q_i^0(z_j) = \begin{cases} 1 & if\ v_i \in V_s\ and\ v_i \in V_{s_j} \\ 0 & if\ v_i \in V_s\ and\ v_i \notin V_{s_j} \\ \dfrac{\text{SO-P}(v_i, z_j)}{\sum_{k=1}^{m} \text{SO-P}(v_i, z_k)} & otherwise \end{cases}, \quad (13)$$

where $q_i^k(i = 1...|V|)$ is the category distribution for vertex $v_i$ after $k$ propagation; $q_i^k(z_j)$ represents the weight of a category $z_j$ in $q_i^k$ ; $V_{s_j}$ is the set of seed words category for category $z_j$; $V_s = V_{s_1} \cup ... \cup V_{s_m}$ is the set of seed words of all categories.

With the initialization weights, label propagation method is used to iteratively update $q_i^k$ through weighted edges. In each iteration, the probability propagation is also under the condition that edges with higher similarities allow easier propagation. Category distributions for each vertex is updated as follows:

$$q_i^k(z_j) = \begin{cases} q_i^0(z_j) & if\ v_i \in V_s \\ \dfrac{\sum_{v_j \in N(v_i)} e_{ij} \cdot q_j^{k-1}(z_j)}{\sum_{v_j \in N(v_i)} e_{ij}} & otherwise \end{cases}, \quad (14)$$

where $N(v_i)$ is the set of vertices linking to $v_i$.

## 5. EXPERIMENTS

In this section, we describe the experimental evaluations of the proposed method. Firstly, we describe the collections used for evaluation and experimental setups. Secondly, the performances of word translation and categorization are presented respectively. Finally, we evaluate performances of three Chinese parsers with and without the proposed method as preprocessing step.

### 5.1 Collection

As described in Section 2, for analyzing the phenomena of Chinese-English mixed text, we collected 210 millions microblogs from Sina Weibo. For evaluating the effectiveness of the proposed methods, we used a subset of them as testing data. We randomly selected 1,000 microblogs from all Chinese-English mixed ones and manually labeled the translation or categories of all English tokens in these texts. The testing data contains 1,195 English tokens in total.

Three annotators were involved in the labeling task. Since most mixed texts contain only a small number of English tokens, the ambiguity problem is not serious. Annotators were firstly asked to provide translations for all tokens. To evaluate the quality of corpus, we validate the agreements of human annotations using Cohen's kappa coefficient. The average $\kappa$ among all annotators is 0.646. It indicates that the annotations of the corpus are reliable. Since some words have multiple translations, one of the annotator made the final decision to decide which translations should be included as the golden standards. For the word categorization, annotators were also asked to label categories for every words. If a category were labeled by more than two annotators for a word, the category is selected as the standard label of the word.

[2]We use the advanced keywords of Bing "near:10" to implement the NEAR constraint.

**Table 2: Word translation results of different methods.**

| Methods | Accuracy (%) | | |
|---|---|---|---|
| | Top-1 | Top-5 | Top-10 |
| D-LM † | 28.9 | 47.6 | 51.9 |
| D-NLM | 29.5 | 48.9 | 52.0 |
| D-NLM+U | 31.2 | 50.9 | 52.6 |
| PC-LM † | 60.3 | 80.7 | 84.0 |
| PC-NLM | 61.4 | 83.8 | 88.1 |
| PC-NLM+U | **64.6** | **86.2** | **91.5** |
| Li and Yarowsky[16] | 21.2 | 33.6 | 37.5 |
| Han et al.[9] | 19.6 | 27.2 | 31.3 |

† The in-vocabulary words based on online dictionary and parallel corpus take part in 66.3% and 67.6% respectively among all English tokens.

### 5.2 Experiment Configurations

For training the word translation model described in Section 3.1, we also collected 24,853 subtitles of movies and TV series from Shooter [3]. All these subtitles contain both Chinese and English text in single or separated files. Using these subtitles, we construct a parallel corpus, which contains more than 18.5 millions sentence pairs. For training the neural network language model, we randomly sampled 10 millions microblogs, due to the computation limited. We implement the proposed method based on the code of Huang et al. [11][4].

FudanNLP [25] is used for Chinese word segmentation. For training the word translation model, we use Giza++ toolkit [22] with the parallel corpus we constructed. For constructing the similarity graph, we implemented it using Hadoop 1.2.0 to handle massive computation. We also incorporate the proposed method as the preprocess step for three parsers: Stanford Parser 3.2 [28], Berkeley Parser 1.7 [12], and FudanNLP 1.57 [25].

For evaluating word translation, we adopt word-level n-best accuracy to evaluate the proposed methods. For each English token, the output is considered as correct if any of the corresponding golden standard words is among the top-$n$ returned results. Evaluation metrics used for word categorization throughout the experiments include: Precision, Recall, and F1-score.

### 5.3 Word Translation Results

For translation model, we compare the proposed parallel corpus based method with dictionary[5] based method.

- "D" represents dictionary based method, where all the translations given by the dictionary are selected as candidates.
- "PC" represents parallel corpus based method, where the translation probability is given by the toolkit Giza++.

[3]http://www.shooter.cn. It is one of the most popular websites which provide subtitles with Chinese translations.

[4]http://ai.stanford.edu/ ehhuang/

[5]In this paper, we use dict.cn as the dictionary. It is one of the biggest online dictionary website in China.

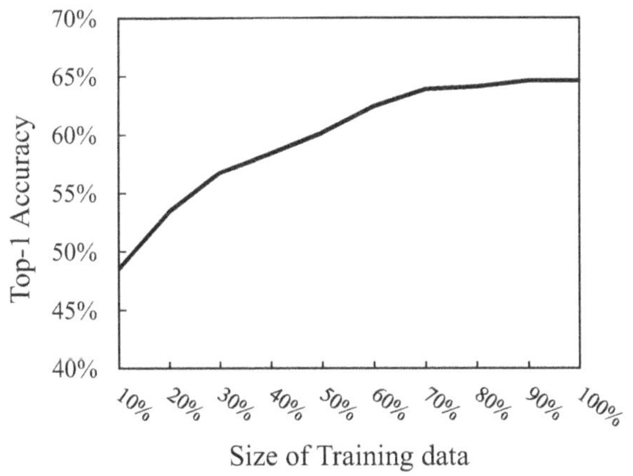


**Figure 4: Sensitivity of translation probability obtained by Giza++ to number of training Data.**

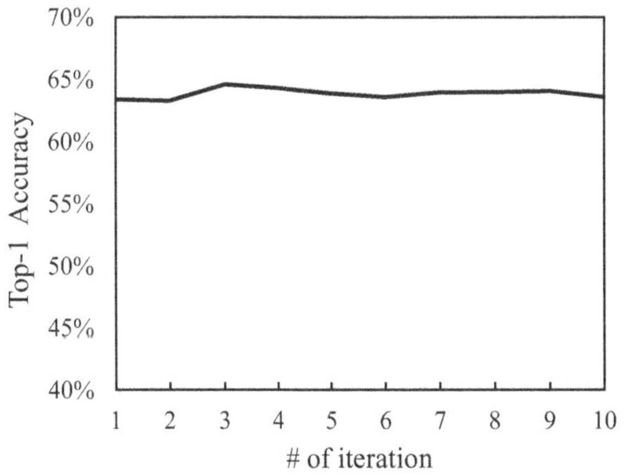


**Figure 5: The impact of number of iterations of user aware neural network language model.**

For language model, we compare the following methods:

- "LM" represents the traditional n-gram language model. In this work, we also use the toolkit Giza++ to train the model.
- "NLM" represents proposed by method proposed by Collobert and Weston [4].
- "NLM+U" represents the proposed user aware neural network language model.

Some existing works focused on constructing vocabularies for informal expressions can also be adapted for this task. In this work, we re-implemented works done by Han et al. [9] and Li and Yarowsky [16]. Since the string similarities between English tokens and their corresponding Chinese words are zero, the re-ranking part [9] is ignored. The window size is set to 3. Bi-gram is used to calculate the context similarity. For the method proposed by Li and Yarowsky [16], we used the data-driven hypothesis generation method and optimal weights in the log-liner model they used in their work. Vocabulary words generated based on parallel corpus are treated as the informal expressions.

The results of different word translation methods are shown in Table 2. From the results, we can observe that the proposed method, which incorporates noisy channel approach with neural network language model, achieve better performance than other methods. Comparing the results of dictionary based method with parallel corpus based method, we can see that the parallel corpus based method achieve better performance with all language models, although the two methods have the similar in-vocabulary words percentages. The main reason may be that movie and TV series have the similar language usages as social media. Comparing the results with different language models, we can observe that user aware neural network language model is better than neural network language model and n-gram language model. It demonstrates that the user historical information can benefit this task. Since the methods proposed by [16] and [9] mainly focus on frequent informal expressions, only English words with high frequency can be well processed by their work. However, these methods can process abbreviation, pronunciation, and some other kinds of English tokens.

For investigating the impact of training data used to estimate the word translation model, we showed the performance of PC+NLM+U with different number of training data for word translation model. Figure 4 shows the Top-1 accuracy with training data from 10% to 100% on the constructed parallel corpus. From the results, we can observe that the size of parallel corpus has a certain effect on the performance word translation model. We think that the increasing number of in-vocabulary words along with size of parallel corpus is one of main reasons.

To show the performance impact of the number of iterations of user aware neural network language model, we evaluate the accuracy of word translation method with different number of iterations. The results are shown in Fig. 5. From the figure, we can observe that it can achieve satisfactory accuracy with only one iteration. The top-1 accuracy achieved by user aware neural network language model with only one iteration is even better than the performance achieved by n-gram language models.

We also analyze the errors of the proposed method (PC-NLM+U) and find several types of words which cannot be well processed except the low frequency words. The first of these types are words which do not have Chinese translations in special context, for example, movie names, album names, etc. The second one are multiple words which should be translated as phrases. The third one are abbreviations which have multiple meanings. For example, "PE" can be used as the abbreviation of physical education, product engineering, private equity fund, and so on. We will leave these types of words for future work.

## 5.4 Word Categorization Results

Table 3 shows the word categorization results of different methods in five categories: person name, product name, organization name, informal expressions, and loanwords. We compare the following methods:

- "LP" represents the original label propagation without initialization method described in Eq.(12).
- "INIT" represents results of the method only based on Eq.(13).
- "INIT+LP/WS" denotes the proposed method with seed words.
- "INIT+LP/WOS" represents the proposed method without seed words.

Table 3: **Word categorization results of different methods.**

| Methods | Person Name | | | Product Name | | | Org. Name | | | Slang | | | Loanwords | | | Acc. |
|---|---|---|---|---|---|---|---|---|---|---|---|---|---|---|---|---|
| | P | R | F | P | R | F | P | R | F | P | R | F | P | R | F | |
| LP | 37.5 | 23.8 | 29.1 | **93.9** | 18.4 | 30.8 | **57.7** | 17.4 | 26.8 | 19.2 | 31.3 | 23.8 | 8.8 | **39.1** | 14.4 | 22.5 |
| INIT | 23.1 | **60.0** | **33.3** | 36.2 | 27.6 | 31.3 | 28.1 | 52.3 | 36.6 | 27.9 | 45.8 | 34.6 | 42.9 | 13.0 | 20.0 | 32.3 |
| INIT+LP/WOS | 80.3 | 10.0 | 17.2 | 84.9 | 36.8 | 51.4 | 34.4 | **89.5** | 49.7 | 40.3 | 56.3 | 47.0 | 50.0 | 4.4 | 8.0 | 42.9 |
| INIT+LP/WS | **90.9** | 19.2 | 31.7 | 86.4 | **58.6** | **69.8** | 39.0 | 84.9 | **53.4** | **48.7** | **75.0** | **59.0** | **57.1** | 17.4 | **26.7** | 55.8 |

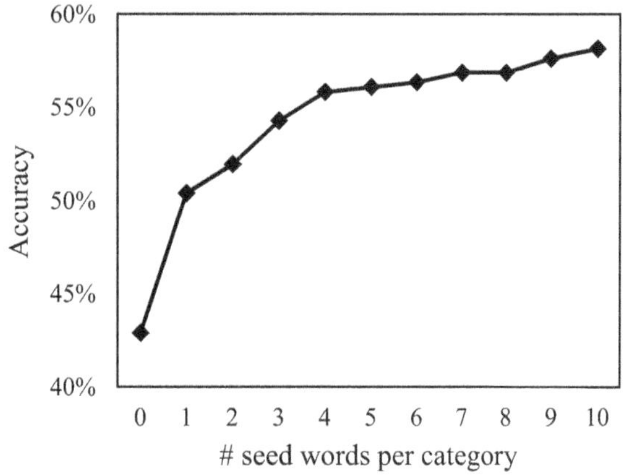


**Figure 6: The impact of number of seed words per category.**

For the methods INIT+LP/WS and LP, 4 seed words are used for each category. The total number of out-of-vocabulary words are 387, which takes about 32.3% percents among all English tokens.

From the results, we can observe that the propose method (INIT+LP/WS) achieves the best performances in four of the five categories. The accuracy of the proposed method is also significantly better than other methods. Comparing the results with and without the proposed initialization method (INIT+LP/WS v.s. LP), we can observe that initialization contributes a lot. The relative accuracy improvement is more than 148%. It demonstrates that the proposed method can achieve better performance with a small number of seed words.

From the Table 3, we also observe that all the methods cannot achieve satisfactory performances for the categories of person name and loanwords. We analyze the errors in these categories and find that lots of errors are caused by acronyms. Person names may be represented by acronyms. However, some of them are also used as the organization name. Since the number of webpages about a organization is usually larger than the number of webpages describing a person, most of them are classified into organization category. This is also one of the main reason of why all the methods achieve low precision in organization name category. These acronyms cannot be correctly classified without context information.

To show the performance impact of the number of seed words, we evaluate the accuracy of word categorization method with different number of seed words. The results are shown in Fig. 6. From the figure, we can observe that the accuracy is significantly improved with seed words comparing to the method without seed words. The accuracies are improving continuously along with the increasing the number of seed words. Although, when the number of seed words per category is more than 4 words, the performances increase slowly. We think that lack of context information is one of the main reasons.

**Table 4: The perfomances of POS tagging of English tokens by different parsers with/without the proposed method. "WP" and "WoP" represent the accuracy with and without normalization method respectively.**

| Methods | WoP | WP |
|---|---|---|
| Stanford Parser 3.2 | 66.4% | 84.7% |
| Berkeley Parser 1.7 | 67.9% | 83.9% |
| FudanNLP 1.57 | 54.0% | 79.6% |

## 5.5 Applications

To show the effectiveness of the proposed method as the preprocessing step for other NLP tasks, we evaluate our method with three Chinese parsers. In this work, we only focus on the relative changes caused by English tokens. We randomly select 100 microblogs from the whole evaluation set. The in-vocabulary words are translated into Chinese. The words which cannot be translated are replaced by their category names.

Table 4 shows the accuracy of POS tagging of English tokens with and without the proposed normalization method. From the results, we can observe that all three parsers benefit a lot from the proposed normalization method in processing mixed texts. The relative improvements are significant. Since features extracted from words play important rules in existing methods, lack of word information may highly impact their performances. For the methods which label all English tokens with a same tag [24], the proposed method can bring much more benefit for them.

# 6. CONCLUSIONS

In this paper, we focus on the task of normalizing the Chinese-English mixed texts. We firstly analyzed the phenomena of mixed usage in Chinese. Then, we propose to use word translation and categorization to achieve the task. For word translation, we use noisy-channel approach with neural network language model to translate in-vocabulary words. A novel user aware neural network language model is introduced to capture the useful historical information of users. For categorizing words, a graph-based unsupervised method is proposed . We also introduce a novel initialization technique to improve the effectiveness. Experimental results show that the top-5 word translation accuracy of proposed method achieves 86.2%. For word categorization, the propose method also achieves significant improvement over the baseline methods. The relative improvement over the original label propagation method is more than 148%. We also incorporate the proposed method as preprocessing steps for three different parsers. All of them benefit a lot from the proposed method.

## 7. ACKNOWLEDGEMENT

The authors wish to thank the anonymous reviewers for their helpful comments. This work was partially funded by National Natural Science Foundation of China (61003092, 61073069), National Major Science and Technology Special Project of China (2014ZX03006005), Shanghai Municipal Science and Technology Commission (No.12511504502), Key Projects in the National Science & Technology Pillar Program(2012BAH18B01) and "Chen Guang" project supported by Shanghai Municipal Education Commission and Shanghai Education Development Foundation(11CG05).

## 8. REFERENCES

[1] A. Aw, M. Zhang, J. Xiao, and J. Su. A phrase-based statistical model for sms text normalization. In *Proceedings of the COLING/ACL 2006 Main Conference Poster Sessions*, pages 33–40, Sydney, Australia, July 2006. Association for Computational Linguistics.

[2] R. Beaufort, S. Roekhaut, L.-A. Cougnon, and C. Fairon. A hybrid rule/model-based finite-state framework for normalizing sms messages. In *Proceedings of the 48th Annual Meeting of the Association for Computational Linguistics*, ACL '10, pages 770–779, Stroudsburg, PA, USA, 2010. Association for Computational Linguistics.

[3] J.-S. Chang and W.-L. Teng. Mining atomic chinese abbreviations with a probabilistic single character recovery model. *Language Resources and Evaluation*, 40(3-4):367–374, 2006.

[4] R. Collobert and J. Weston. A unified architecture for natural language processing: deep neural networks with multitask learning. In *Proceedings of the 25th international conference on Machine learning*, ICML '08, pages 160–167, New York, NY, USA, 2008. ACM.

[5] D. Das and S. Petrov. Unsupervised part-of-speech tagging with bilingual graph-based projections. In *Proceedings of the 49th Annual Meeting of the Association for Computational Linguistics: Human Language Technologies*, pages 600–609, Portland, Oregon, USA, June 2011. Association for Computational Linguistics.

[6] L. Derczynski, A. Ritter, S. Clark, and K. Bontcheva. Twitter part-of-speech tagging for all: Overcoming sparse and noisy data. In *Proceedings of the International Conference on Recent Advances in Natural Language Processing*. Association for Computational Linguistics, 2013.

[7] D. Freitag. Machine learning for information extraction in informal domains. *Machine Learning*, 39(2-3):169–202, 2000.

[8] B. Han and T. Baldwin. Lexical normalisation of short text messages: Makn sens a #twitter. In *Proceedings of the 49th Annual Meeting of the Association for Computational Linguistics: Human Language Technologies*, pages 368–378, Portland, Oregon, USA, June 2011. Association for Computational Linguistics.

[9] B. Han, P. Cook, and T. Baldwin. Automatically constructing a normalisation dictionary for microblogs. In *Proceedings of the 2012 Joint Conference on Empirical Methods in Natural Language Processing and Computational Natural Language Learning*, EMNLP-CoNLL '12, pages 421–432, Stroudsburg, PA, USA, 2012. Association for Computational Linguistics.

[10] B. Han, P. Cook, and T. Baldwin. Lexical normalization for social media text. *ACM Trans. Intell. Syst. Technol.*, 4(1):5:1–5:27, Feb. 2013.

[11] E. H. Huang, R. Socher, C. D. Manning, and A. Y. Ng. Improving word representations via global context and multiple word prototypes. In *Proceedings of the 50th Annual Meeting of the Association for Computational Linguistics: Long Papers - Volume 1*, ACL '12, pages 873–882, Stroudsburg, PA, USA, 2012. Association for Computational Linguistics.

[12] M. Johnson and A. E. Ural. Reranking the berkeley and brown parsers. In *Human Language Technologies: The 2010 Annual Conference of the North American Chapter of the Association for Computational Linguistics*, pages 665–668, Los Angeles, California, June 2010. Association for Computational Linguistics.

[13] C. Kobus, F. Yvon, and G. Damnati. Normalizing sms: are two metaphors better than one? In *Proceedings of the 22nd International Conference on Computational Linguistics - Volume 1*, COLING '08, pages 441–448, Stroudsburg, PA, USA, 2008. Association for Computational Linguistics.

[14] C. Li and Y. Liu. Improving text normalization using character-blocks based models and system combination. In *Proceedings of COLING 2012*, pages 1587–1602, Mumbai, India, December 2012. The COLING 2012 Organizing Committee.

[15] X. Li, Y.-Y. Wang, and A. Acero. Learning query intent from regularized click graphs. In *Proceedings of the 31st annual international ACM SIGIR conference on Research and development in information retrieval*, SIGIR '08, pages 339–346, New York, NY, USA, 2008. ACM.

[16] Z. Li and D. Yarowsky. Mining and modeling relations between formal and informal chinese phrases from web corpora. In *Proceedings of the Conference on Empirical Methods in Natural Language Processing*, EMNLP '08, pages 1031–1040, Stroudsburg, PA, USA, 2008. Association for Computational Linguistics.

[17] Z. Li and D. Yarowsky. Unsupervised translation induction for chinese abbreviations using monolingual corpora. In *Proceedings of ACL-08: HLT*, pages 425–433, Columbus, Ohio, June 2008. Association for Computational Linguistics.

[18] F. Liu, F. Weng, and X. Jiang. A broad-coverage normalization system for social media language. In *Proceedings of the 50th Annual Meeting of the Association for Computational Linguistics: Long Papers - Volume 1*, ACL '12, pages 1035–1044, Stroudsburg, PA, USA, 2012. Association for Computational Linguistics.

[19] E. Minkov, R. C. Wang, and W. W. Cohen. Extracting personal names from email: applying named entity recognition to informal text. In *Proceedings of the conference on Human Language Technology and Empirical Methods in Natural Language Processing*, HLT '05, pages 443–450, Stroudsburg, PA, USA, 2005. Association for Computational Linguistics.

[20] T. Mullen and R. Malouf. A preliminary investigation into sentiment analysis of informal political discourse. In *Proceedings of AAAI-2006 Spring Symposium on Computational Approaches to Analyzing Weblogs*, 2006.

[21] Z.-Y. Niu, D.-H. Ji, and C. L. Tan. Word sense disambiguation using label propagation based

semi-supervised learning. In *Proceedings of the 43rd Annual Meeting on Association for Computational Linguistics*, ACL '05, pages 395–402, Stroudsburg, PA, USA, 2005. Association for Computational Linguistics.

[22] F. J. Och and H. Ney. A systematic comparison of various statistical alignment models. *Comput. Linguist.*, 29(1):19–51, Mar. 2003.

[23] N. Okazaki, M. Ishizuka, and J. Tsujii. A discriminative approach to japanese abbreviation extraction. In *Proceedings of the Third International Joint Conference on Natural Language Processing (IJCNLP 2008)*, pages 889–894, 2008.

[24] X. Qian, Q. Zhang, X. Huang, and L. Wu. 2d trie for fast parsing. In *Proceedings of the 23rd International Conference on Computational Linguistics*, COLING '10, pages 904–912, Stroudsburg, PA, USA, 2010. Association for Computational Linguistics.

[25] X. Qiu, Q. Zhang, and X. Huang. Fudannlp: A toolkit for chinese natural language processing. In *Proceedings of ACL*, 2013.

[26] G. Richard. A global perspective on bilingualism and bilingual education. *Georgetown University Round Table on Languages and Linguistics 1999: Language in Our Time: Bilingual Education and Official English, Ebonics and Standard English, Immigration and the Unz Initiative Languages and Linguistics 1999*, page 332, 2001.

[27] A. Ritter, S. Clark, Mausam, and O. Etzioni. Named entity recognition in tweets: an experimental study. In *Proceedings of the Conference on Empirical Methods in Natural Language Processing*, EMNLP '11, pages 1524–1534, Stroudsburg, PA, USA, 2011. Association for Computational Linguistics.

[28] R. Socher, J. Bauer, C. D. Manning, and A. Y. Ng. Parsing with compositional vector grammars. In *Proceedings of ACL 2013*, June 2013.

[29] A. Tamura, T. Watanabe, and E. Sumita. Bilingual lexicon extraction from comparable corpora using label propagation. In *Proceedings of the 2012 Joint Conference on Empirical Methods in Natural Language Processing and Computational Natural Language Learning*, EMNLP-CoNLL '12, pages 24–36, Stroudsburg, PA, USA, 2012. Association for Computational Linguistics.

[30] M. Thelwall, K. Buckley, G. Paltoglou, D. Cai, and A. Kappas. Sentiment strength detection in short informal text. *Journal of the American Society for Information Science and Technology*, 61(12):2544–2558, 2010.

[31] P. D. Turney and M. L. Littman. Unsupervised learning of semantic orientation from a hundred-billion-word corpus. *(No. ERB-1094, NRC #44929): National Research Council of Canada*, 2002.

[32] L. Velikovich, S. Blair-Goldensohn, K. Hannan, and R. McDonald. The viability of web-derived polarity lexicons. In *Human Language Technologies: The 2010 Annual Conference of the North American Chapter of the Association for Computational Linguistics*, HLT '10, pages 777–785, Stroudsburg, PA, USA, 2010. Association for Computational Linguistics.

[33] P. Wang and H. T. Ng. A beam-search decoder for normalization of social media text with application to machine translation. In *Proceedings of the 2013 Conference of the North American Chapter of the Association for Computational Linguistics: Human Language Technologies*, pages 471–481, Atlanta, Georgia, June 2013. Association for Computational Linguistics.

[34] L.-X. Xie, Y.-B. Zheng, Z.-Y. Liu, M.-S. Sun, and C.-H. Wang. Extracting chinese abbreviation-definition pairs from anchor texts. In *Machine Learning and Cybernetics (ICMLC)*, volume 4, pages 1485–1491, 2011.

[35] D. Yang, Y.-C. Pan, and S. Furui. Vocabulary expansion through automatic abbreviation generation for chinese voice search. *Computer Speech & Language*, 26(5):321 – 335, 2012.

[36] J. Zhao, X. Qiu, S. Zhang, F. Ji, and X. Huang. Part-of-speech tagging for chinese-english mixed texts with dynamic features. In *Proceedings of the 2012 Joint Conference on Empirical Methods in Natural Language Processing and Computational Natural Language Learning*, EMNLP-CoNLL '12, pages 1379–1388, Stroudsburg, PA, USA, 2012. Association for Computational Linguistics.

[37] X. Zhu and Z. Ghahramani. Learning from Labeled and Unlabeled Data with Label Propagation. In *Technical Report CMU-CALD-02-107*. Carnegie Mellon University, 2002.

# Sentiment Analysis on Evolving Social Streams: How Self-Report Imbalances Can Help

Pedro Calais Guerra, Wagner Meira Jr.
Dept. of Computer Science
Universidade Federal de Minas Gerais (UFMG)
Belo Horizonte, MG, Brazil
{pcalais,meira}@dcc.ufmg.br

Claire Cardie
Dept. of Computer Science
Cornell University
Ithaca, NY 14853 USA
cardie@cs.cornell.edu

## ABSTRACT

Real-time sentiment analysis is a challenging machine learning task, due to scarcity of labeled data and sudden changes in sentiment caused by real-world events that need to be instantly interpreted. In this paper we propose solutions to acquire labels and cope with concept drift in this setting, by using findings from social psychology on how humans prefer to disclose some types of emotions. In particular, we use findings that humans are more motivated to report **positive** feelings rather than **negative** feelings and also prefer to report **extreme** feelings rather than **average** feelings.

We map each of these *self-report imbalances* on two machine learning sub-tasks. The preference on the disclosure of positive feelings can be explored to generate labeled data on *polarizing* topics, where a positive event for one group usually induces negative feelings from the opposing group, generating an imbalance on user activity that unveils the current dominant sentiment.

Based on the knowledge that extreme experiences are more reported than average experiences, we propose a feature representation strategy that focus on terms which appear at spikes in the social stream. When comparing to a static text representation (TF-IDF), we found that our feature representation is more capable of detecting new informative features that capture the sudden changes on sentiment stream caused by real-world events.

We show that our social psychology-inspired framework produces accuracies up to 84% while analyzing live reactions in the debate of two popular sports on Twitter – soccer and football – despite requiring no human effort in generating supervisory labels.

## Categories and Subject Descriptors

H.2.8 [**Database Management**]: Database Applications—*Data Mining*

## General Terms

Algorithms, Experimentation

## Keywords

Sentiment Analysis, Stream Data Mining, Social Media Analytics


*WSDM'14,* February 24–28, 2014, New York, New York, USA.

http://dx.doi.org/10.1145/2556195.2556261.

## 1. INTRODUCTION

One goal of a sentiment analysis system is to, given a text document, infer its polarity toward entities and events mentioned in the text [45, 32]. As social media platforms become the primary medium used by people to express their opinions and feelings about a multitude of topics that pop up daily on news media, the vast amount of opinionated data now available in the form of *social streams* gives us an unprecedented opportunity to build valuable applications that monitor public opinions and opinion shifts [24, 23]. For example, a sports web portal can track the crowd sentiment during live matches, something far more appealing than the relative number of mentions of each team, which is what most sports web sites currently offer. Creating such applications enrich the personal experience of watching live events on TV, and following the social media buzz simultaneously with live broadcasted events is becoming a joint experience, where watching not only the event itself, but how others react to it, is part of the experience.

The task of interpreting positive and negative feelings expressed on social streams exhibits a number of unique characteristics that are not present in the static and well-controlled domains on which sentiment analysis has focused in the last decade – mainly product and movie reviews [45, 37, 23]. On the downside, it faces two challenges that are common to many data stream classification tasks [33]: (i) the limited availability of labeled data and (ii) the need to deal with the evolving nature of the stream, which causes the target concept to change and requires learning models to be constantly updated – a problem known as *concept drift* [47]. Challenge (i) is a serious drawback because current sentiment analysis models are heavily based on supervised approaches [37, 45], and human constraints on generating a constant flow of labeled messages on streams remain high. The sparsity of language, the use of neologisms and word lengthening as an indicator of sentiment (e.g., "coooooooool!", "gooooooooaal!" [8]) also contribute to make the process of acquiring large labeled sets of pre-classified messages unfeasible [23]. Challenge (ii) arises in sentiment streams as it is necessary to deal with constant changes of vocabulary and sudden changes of sentiment in reaction to real-world events. For example, in a few minutes a positive sentiment of the fans of a soccer team commenting on Twitter or Facebook may vanish by a goal scored by the adversary team; such *sentiment drift* represents a great challenge for real-time sentiment tracking, since it requires the stream classifier to be capable of quickly identifying and adapting to the sudden change on the dominant sentiment [43].

Despite these important constraints and drawbacks, streams reflecting the society's immediate emotional reactions regarding a topic have an important property, which we seek to exploit in this work, namely, the flow of opinions from social networking services is inherently constrained to manifestations from individuals that have explicitly and deliberately *chosen* to post a message in reaction to some real-world event; thus, the distribution of positive and negative opinions is potentially quite different from the random samples obtained in traditional opinion polls and survey methodologies [31]. Although such *reporting bias* is usually perceived as a source of inaccuracy [28, 16], here we argue that the self-reporting nature of social media, when observed on large-scale social network data, may actually provide signals that ease the task of sentiment tracking in online environments, provided that we understand the **factors** that motivate people to publicly express their feelings. We build sentiment analysis models that exploit two factors widely described by substantive research from social psychology and behavioral economics that describe human preferences when disclosing emotion publicly:

> **Positive-negative sentiment report imbalance:** People tend to express positive feelings more than negative feelings in social environments [5, 12, 30, 25].
>
> **Extreme-average sentiment report imbalance:** People tend to express extreme feelings more than average feelings in social environments [2, 11, 10, 28].

We explore each of these two self-report imbalances to accomplish a different subtask in learning-based sentiment analysis. The first self-report factor, which we call **positive-negative sentiment report imbalance** throughout the paper, is employed to acquire labeled data that supports supervised classifiers. In the context of *polarizing groups* – a division of the population into groups of people sharing similar opinions in the context of a topic [3, 19], a positive event for one group tends to be negative to the other, and vice-versa. For example, while supporters of a football team are likely to be happy when their team scores, fans of the adversary team are expected to be upset when faced with the same event. Based on social psychology research that states that the disclosure of positive feelings is preferred, we can then make a prediction of the current dominant sentiment by simply counting how many members of each group, relative to group sizes, decided to post a message during the specified time frame. Since the social context information only holds during time frames when a significant real-world event happens, we adopt a probabilistic model that computes the uncertainty of the social context, and, at each time frame, generates a probabilistic sentiment label, which can then be incorporated into a range of content-based supervised classifiers.

The second self-report factor we explore is related to the human tendency to report extreme experiences more than average experiences [2, 11, 10, 28]. The **extreme-average sentiment report imbalance** implies an important consequence for real-time sentiment tracking: because extreme feelings stimulate reactions, spikes of activity in streams of opinionated text tend to contain highly emotional terms, which are precisely the features that are helpful for sentiment prediction. We propose a simple text representation strategy based on this observation, named *term arousal*, that maintains, for each term (or lexical unity, e.g., n-grams), a measure of how often it appears in high-volume time windows in the stream; we call these **high-arousal** terms. Our experimental studies demonstrate that these terms are better indicators of emerging and strong feelings than traditional static representations (e.g., TF-IDF), allowing the underlying classification model to adapt quicker to sudden sentiment drift induced by real-world events.

In summary, our main contributions in this paper are:

1. We raise awareness over the fact that opinions expressed on social media platforms are *not* a random sample of the online population, but are impacted by many social and psychological factors that need to be accounted for in order to build reliable and useful sentiment analysis systems;

2. We show that self-report imbalances create rich *social contexts* that can be leveraged to improve two key subtasks in the construction of a sentiment stream classifier – namely, the acquisition of labeled data and feature representation suitable to deal with sudden sentiment drifts.

We evaluated our social psychology-inspired framework on sports events heavily debated on Twitter; when instantiating our framework with a Multinomial Naive Bayes classifier, our results are comparable to what is typically obtained as an acceptable result for document-level sentiment analysis – between 80% and 85% of accuracy [45] – but, because the stream-based scenario imposes stricter and harder constraints, we believe they point to a promising option for sentiment classification on evolving social streams. In addition, our approach targets two generic sub-tasks for learning-based sentiment analysis – label acquisition and feature representation. As a result, our framework can be incorporated into sophisticated sentiment classifiers that make use of more powerful NLP models and features.

## 2. SOCIAL PSYCHOLOGY BACKGROUND

Psychologists classify emotions into two independent dimensions: pleasure (happiness or sadness) and activation (or arousal) [4]. The *self-report imbalances* we briefly presented in Section 1 are biases in the bidimensional emotion space caused by the fact that social media systems are *communicative* platforms; as a consequence, opinions and feelings expressed in online social environments are a result of opinion holders' explicit desire to make his friends or followers aware of his or her opinions. In other words, the communicative nature of social media makes social data a side effect of intentional and deliberate communication between users, rather than as a representation of some underlying activity [39, 31].

On the positive-negative dimension, the preference on the disclosure of positive feelings is caused by our need in being perceived as successful and happy persons [34, 40], and it causes a bias where everyone in online social environments perceives others as happier than they actually are [25]. In the case of opinions expressed over a polarizing topic, the preference on sharing positive news and opinions goes beyond the human's desire to improve his or her reputation: each group also gives preference to news and facts that favor their viewpoints, a result of many biases such as *confirmation bias* and *selective exposure* [20, 31]. Notice that the definition of a *positive* event is group-dependent: for rival supporters of a team or opposers of politicians in office, negative facts such as a conceded goal or a political scandal will be explored by them as "positive" – i.e., as a motivation to explore the fact to their benefit. Also, in some contexts, such as product reviews, the bias leans toward the disclosure of negative experiences [22]; our sentiment analysis framework is generalized to take advantage of the asymmetry on either direction.

On the arousal dimension, it was found that extreme emotions – angriness, anxiety, awe, excitement – are *high-arousal* emotions: they affect our body and put us in a state of activation and readiness for action [4, 5]. In social media, action means making private feelings public, what makes sentiment expressed on online media to be biased towards strong feelings and opinions.

In the next sections we will detail how we embed these biases on sentiment self-report in the analysis of feelings expressed on social streams.

## 3. ACQUIRING LABELED DATA

Differently from the majority of research on supervised sentiment analysis, which focus on batch processing of opinionated documents [37, 45], here we are interested in the setting where the data arrives as an infinite stream and reflects real-world unpredictable events. As we discussed in Section 1, in this setting a constant flow of labeled messages is required to build and update supervised sentiment models. Unfortunately, in textual streams characterized by sparse and time-changing content it is not feasible to manually obtain labeled data in significant amounts and in a timely manner [33].

To overcome this problem, we propose a method to acquire labeled messages by exploring the *positive-negative sentiment report imbalance* in the context of polarizing groups. We compare the strength of reactions of polarizing groups during each time span, moving from processing individual messages to processing groups of messages. These groups are obtained by dividing the social stream into a sequence of non-overlapping and contiguous time windows of equal duration (e.g., $\Delta t$ minutes), what gives us the capability of exploiting the **social context** induced by the set of users that expressed their sentiment w.r.t. topic $T$ during each time window $W_t$. Each window $W_t$ contains all messages sent during the time period $[t_i, t_i + \Delta t]$ ($W_0$ starts at $t_0$ and $t_{i+1} = t_i + \Delta t$) and is composed of a triple $(\mathcal{S}_t, \mathcal{D}_t, \mathcal{Y}_t)$:

- $\mathcal{S}_t$ is a multiset of group memberships of all users who posted a message during $W_t$. On a polarized domain, we assume that each user belongs to one of two groups, $G_A$ or $G_B$.[1] For instance, $\mathcal{S}_t = \{G_A, G_A, G_A, G_B, G_B\}$ indicates that 3 members of group $G_A$ and 2 members of group $G_B$ posted a message during $W_t$. Assigning users to groups is a task that can be accomplished by several community detection and graph mining techniques that explore the social ties among users, under the assumption that similar users are likely to connect to each other [1, 19].

- $\mathcal{D}_t$ is the sum vector of all feature vectors extracted from messages written during $W_t$;

- $\mathcal{Y}_{e,t} \in \{+, -\}$ indicates the ground-truth sentiment expressed during $W_t$ w.r.t. an entity $e$ in the context of topic T. Here, each $e$ is an individual or organization naturally linked to the polarizing group that supports it; for instance, if $G = \{\text{Democrats}\}$, than $e(G) = \{\text{Barack Obama}\}$, and $e(G) = \{\text{New York Giants team}\}$ if $G = \{\text{New York Giants fans}\}$.

Note that, instead of seeking for labels for individual messages, we label *all* the messages mentioning an entity $e$ in time window $W_t$ with the same polarity $\mathcal{Y}_{e,t}$. Although we do not expect every opinion expressed during a time window to follow the same polarity, we seek here to determine the *dominant* sentiment during $W_t$; furthermore, the probabilistic method we will detail next assigns a confidence on the label estimation, what can be interpreted as an estimate of the proportion of positive and negative messages written during a given $W_t$.

For now we ignore the content vector $\mathcal{D}_t$ and focus on $\mathcal{S}_t$ as an input to build a sentiment prediction function $f : \mathcal{S} \rightarrow \mathcal{Y}$. The fundamental principle we seek to exploit is that, on polarized discussions dominated by two opposing groups $G_A$ and $G_B$, in general $\mathcal{Y}_{e(G_A),t} = +$ implies that $\mathcal{Y}_{e(G_B),t} = -$, and vice-versa (we will relax this requirement in Section 4, by learning a content-based classifier based on labels provided by $\mathcal{S}_t$). A simple approach to predict $\mathcal{Y}_t$ based on $\mathcal{S}_t$ is to consider that each message is a "vote" toward the sentiment expected to drive more reactions and, thus, a majority-voting strategy is employed to predict the dominant sentiment at $W_t$. In the toy example $\mathcal{S}_t = \{G_A, G_A, G_A, G_B, G_B\}$, since we are supported by social theories that indicate preference toward the report of positive sentiment, we would predict 3 votes for labels ($\mathcal{Y}_{e(G_A),t} = +$, $\mathcal{Y}_{e(G_B),t} = -$) and 2 votes for labels ($\mathcal{Y}_{e(G_A),t} = -$, $\mathcal{Y}_{e(G_B),t} = +$). The only point of caution here is that normalizing by group sizes $|G_A|$ and $|G_B|$ is important to discount the effect of larger groups on $\mathcal{S}_t$.

Majority-voting is a simple and straight-forward approach, but it has an important limitation: it does not quantify the uncertainty on the information provided by the voters [42]. Since the labeling mechanism by social context is not perfect, capturing the degree of confidence on the correlation between $\mathcal{S}_t$ and $\mathcal{Y}_t$ is crucial if we will incorporate this information on learning models. In particular, the labeling scheme based on positive-negative report imbalance is error-prone due to two reasons:

1. $\mathcal{S}_t$ is likely to carry a significant correlation with the dominant sentiment only when a well-determined and relevant event happened during time window $W_t$, i.e., a goal or touchdown in a sports match, or some breaking news on the topic being followed. Most of the time, the positive-negative report imbalance will not be triggered at a sufficient strength, and an unreliable prediction will be generated.

2. Since we are modeling only user posting decisions in face of positive/negative events and abstracting from several other factors that influence the posting decision (as well as different individual posting probabilities), we are prone to deal with noise due to the many factors that motivate user reactions and that we are not accounting for.

Therefore, in order to make our approach reliable and more useful, it is desirable to associate with each predicted label $\mathcal{Y}_t$ a measure of confidence $P(\mathcal{Y}_t|\mathcal{S}_t)$ that captures the noisy nature of the multiset of group memberships $\mathcal{S}_t$. We instantiate a probabilistic model that assumes that on each time window $W_t$ a coin of bias $\theta_t$ is tossed to decide whether each message will be authored by a member of $G_A$ or $G_B$, and $|G_{A,t}|$ messages from members of $G_A$ and $|G_{B,t}|$ from members of $G_B$ are observed. A fair coin is expected to generate a number of heads ($G_A$) and tails ($G_B$) proportional to $\theta_{fair} = \frac{|G_A|}{|G_A|+|G_B|}$ and $1 - \theta_{fair}$, respectively, modeling the fact that members of both groups are reporting their sentiment with the same probability. Alternatively, a biased coin, whose $\theta_t$ is different from $\frac{|G_A|}{|G_A|+|G_B|}$ at some degree, means that members of one group are self-reporting their feelings at a higher rate than the other, indicating that its members are probably experiencing positive feelings in comparison to the other group.

A coin model is convenient because it naturally models the intuitive fact that spikes of activity in the social stream are more informative: in the same way that our confidence on the bias of a coin increases as we toss it more times, a time window $W_t$ which contains a large number of messages (and, consequently, a larger multiset $\mathcal{S}_t$) is more likely to carry a clear dominant sentiment, not only due to a larger sample, but because spikes of activity are likely to be associated with real-world events that trigger the positive-negative report imbalance. Our probabilistic model is divided into two steps:

1. Estimate the probability distribution on the latent variable $\theta_t$;

2. Estimate how far $\theta_t$ is from $\theta_{fair} = \frac{|G_A|}{|G_A|+|G_B|}$.

[1]In practice, a domain can be associated with more than two groups, i.e., N=20 groups of supporters are found on National Football League. However, at each event of interest (e.g., a football match), we focus on the two polarizing groups that have a direct interest on it.

We use Bayesian estimates in both steps. To estimate the uncertainty on $\theta_t$, we need to calculate the posterior predictive distribution $P(\theta_t|\mathcal{S}_t)$, i.e., the distribution over $\theta_t$ after observing the resulting multiset $\mathcal{S}_t$. In Bayesian inference, the posterior $P(\theta_t|\mathcal{S}_t)$ is proportional to a likelihood function $P(\mathcal{S}_t|\theta_t)$ and a prior distribution $P(\theta_t)$; we adopt the classical Beta-Binomial model: $P(\mathcal{S}_t|\theta_t)$ is computed from a binomial distribution $Bin(|W_t|, \frac{|G_{A,t}|}{|G_{A,t}|+|G_{B,t}|})$ and the prior follows a Beta distribution $Beta(a, b)$ ($a$ and $b$ are hyperparameters) [42, 7]. As a result of the conjugacy property of the Binomial and the Beta distributions, the posterior predictive distribution nicely follows a Beta distribution $Beta(|G_{A,t}|+a, |G_{B,t}|+b)$ that captures our uncertainty over $\theta_t$ [7].

It is still necessary to choose the hyperparameters $a$ and $b$ that govern the prior distribution $P(\theta_t)$ and capture the knowledge acquired from previous observed data streams over the noisy nature of the coin. To incorporate our prior knowledge that $\theta_t$ is expected to be proportional to group sizes, we want to find hyperparameters $a$ and $b$ in the form $a = \frac{K|G_A|}{|G_A|+|G_B|}$ and $b = \frac{K|G_B|}{|G_A|+|G_B|}$. $K$ can be understood as a smoothing parameter: the greater its value, the more confident the model is that $\theta_t$ is close to $\theta_{fair}$ and less importance will be given to the data. On the other hand, if we choose an uniform prior $Beta(1, 1)$, then we let the model rely totally on the observed data to judge how likely the tosses are coming from a coin of bias $\theta_t$; the expected value of the coin bias in this case is equivalent to the maximum likelihood estimate $\theta_t = \frac{|G_{A,t}|}{|G_{A,t}|+|G_{B,t}|}$ [7]. Such direct estimation of $\theta_t$ makes the unrealistic assumptions that tosses are generated i.i.d. from a noiseless coin.

We estimate $K$ from the streaming data by employing an Empirical Bayes approach[2]. To learn the extent to which the coin we are modeling is noisy, we take advantage of the data continuity in the stream: we observe a sequence of noisy estimates $(\theta_0, \theta_1, ..., \theta_t)$ of a different coin being tossed at each time window. The property we want to explore here is that we expect consecutive time windows $W_i$ and $W_{i+1}$ of *similar message volume* to share a similar $\theta$; large differences in $\theta$ between these windows should be attributed to noise, since no significant real-world event has happened (otherwise we would observe a large $||S_{i+1}| - |S_i||$). On the other hand, we would like to allow consecutive time windows with a large difference in message volume to exhibit a larger absolute difference $|\theta_{i+1} - \theta_i|$, since, according to our user behavior model, a spike of activity will trigger a bias either on $G_A$ or $G_B$.

We seek to find the value of $K$ that maximizes Equation 1. $\rho$ is the Pearson correlation coefficient, and $\Delta V$ and $\Delta\theta(K)$ are vectors containing the sequence of $||S_{i+1}| - |S_i||$ and $|\theta_{i+1} - \theta_i|$ observed on the stream. Note that we write $\Delta\theta(K)$ as a function of $K$, since the estimates of $\theta_t$ are affected by the prior distribution $P(\theta_t|K)$. The highest Pearson correlation will explain larger differences in $\theta$ through larger differences in time-window volume, and we estimate it by using a standard gradient descent method.

$$K = argmax(\rho(\Delta V, \Delta\theta(K))) \tag{1}$$

Recall that our goal is to estimate how far the latent variable $\theta_t$ is from $\theta_{fair} = \frac{|G_A|}{|G_A|+|G_B|}$, what indicates a bias in the posting decision of either $G_A$ or $G_B$. This value can be estimated by calculating the area under the curve of the distribution $Beta(|G_{A,t}| + a, |G_{B,t}| + b)$ at the decision threshold $x = \frac{|G_A|}{|G_A|+|G_B|}$. If $I_x(a, b)$ is the CDF of $Beta(a, b)$ in the interval $(0, x)$, then

$$\begin{aligned} conf(\theta_{fair}, \mathcal{S}_t) = \max(&I_{|G_A|/(|G_A|+|G_B|)}(|G_{A,t}| + a, |G_{B,t}| + b),\\ &1 - I_{|G_A|/(|G_A|+|G_B|)}(|G_{A,t}| + a, |G_{B,t}| + b)) \end{aligned} \tag{2}$$

where $I$ is the regularized incomplete Beta function and can be used to compute to the cumulative distribution function in a Beta distribution [42]. The value $1 - conf(\theta_{fair}, \mathcal{S}_t)$ gives us an estimate of how likely the predicted label is trustable given the observed social context $\mathcal{S}_t$, i.e., $P(\mathcal{Y}_t|\mathcal{S}_t)$.

## 3.1 Experimental Evaluation using Twitter data

We evaluate the predictive power of social contexts induced by the positive-negative report imbalance on the analysis of the reactions expressed on Twitter by fans of two popular sports that generate passionate debate on social media: soccer and (American) football. Sports competitions are among the topics that generate the largest fractions of audience both in broadcasting media [46] and social media [29]; however, most initiatives taken by content portals to turn the live game experience into an online social experience are still restricted to simple tools such as the display of the most popular tweets or plots on the variation of the relative number of mentions of the playing teams. Measuring the crowd sentiment during live matches is something far more appealing and may answer relevant questions such as "do the supporters still believe in a win, despite losing the match so far?".

Table 1 gives an overview of two datasets we obtained from the Twitter data collection API. The datasets comprise fans' debate on Brazilian Soccer League seasons (2010, 2011 and 2012) and NFL (2010/11, 2011/12 and 2012/13 seasons). We chose team names and specific words of each competition as keywords. More than 35.8 million tweets from 5.6 million users have been collected in the `SOCCER` dataset, and 23 million tweets from 4.2 million users in the case of the `NFL` dataset. While tweets on Brazilian soccer are mostly in Portuguese, NFL debate is dominated by English, what gives us the possibility to experiment our model in two languages, after we build a content-based stream classifier in Section 4.

Table 1: General overview of the datasets collected from Twitter.

| | Soccer | NFL |
|---|---|---|
| seasons | 10-11-12 | 10/11, 11/12, 12/13 |
| language | Portuguese | English |
| # of user groups (teams) | 12 | 20 |
| # of tweets | 35,834,453 | 23,094,280 |
| # of users | 5,638,906 | 4,230,731 |
| # of users w/ 1+ post/week | 35,121 | 58,981 |

Before performing any sentiment prediction, we need to segment the user base into polarizing groups. In the sports domain, the natural criterion for dividing users into polarizing groups is to reflect their team preference. Several community detection and graph mining approaches that leverage social ties and social interactions can be used to accomplish this task; we manually labeled a set of users with their team preference and then used the similarities in their retweet pattern to estimate the class of unlabeled users [20].

Due to the highly-dynamic nature of sporting events, we analyze sentiment and social contexts in 1-minute time windows; larger time frames may be suitable for less dynamic domains. To generate ground-truth sentiment labels, we examined the match facts and the evolving sentiments for a number of matches in the `SOCCER` and `NFL` dataset. In addition to the match score, we manually examined the content of tweets and also included cases where the match

[2]Empirical Bayes methods are approaches that estimate the prior distribution over a random variable from the data itself, rather than defining the distribution before observing any data, as on standard Bayesian inference [17].

score did not reflect the sentiment, as soccer matches that ended as null ties (0–0), but the result was enough to grant one of the teams the championship title. Although each time window is associated with a set of messages, we aim to determine the overall, global sentiment which dominates each time window, instead of individually trying to predict the polarity associated with each post.

Figure 1 shows the accuracy on the sentiment prediction task for the two datasets. On the $x$ axis, we grouped time windows according to its volume in relation to the average time window volume: $bin = i$ corresponds to time windows where the number of messages were between $i$ and $i + 1$ times the average.

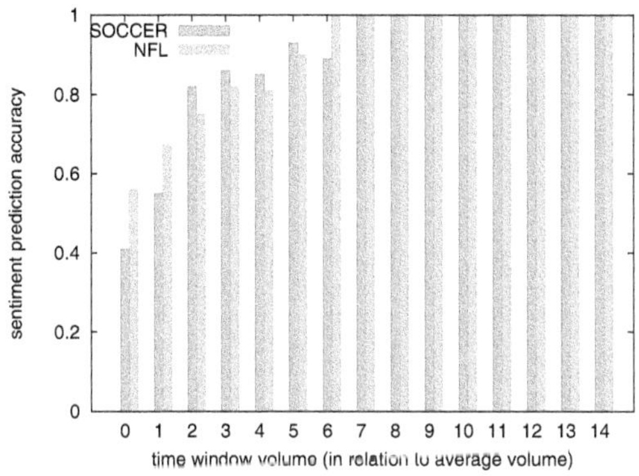


Figure 1: Accuracy on sentiment prediction on 1-minute time windows. We grouped time windows according to its volume in relation to the average time window volume. Social contexts based on positive-negative sentiment report imbalance are highly effective on sentiment prediction on large-volume time windows.

We observe that, for high-volume time windows, accuracy is very high: we could predict with more than 90% of accuracy the dominant sentiment on time windows whose volume of tweets were at least 5 times the average, despite not taking any textual content into account. This result validates the sociopsychological principle that motivated our method – positive and negative feelings are disclosed with different probabilities – and, confirms that, in the sports domain, sentiment report is biased toward the positive feeling.

We can also note from the histogram that accuracy decreases with the volume of tweets in the time-window; on time-windows whose volume is above average, accuracy is comparable to a random guesser, meaning that the induced social context is not relevant and the positive-negative report imbalance is not triggered in sufficient strength, and other factors are affecting the posting decisions' of members of $G_A$ and $G_B$.

Since the majority of the time windows are not voluminous, it is important to capture the uncertainty on the sentiment prediction made by social contexts. In order to instantiate the probabilistic measure of label uncertainty we presented in this section, we use the data to set hyperparameters $K_{soccer}$ and $K_{NFL}$ that capture the previous knowledge on the coin that control the relationship between messages and author's groups over time. We found $K_{soccer} = 12000$ and $K_{NFL} = 6000$ as the value that maximizes the Pearson correlation that relates $\Delta V$ and $\Delta\theta(K)$ (Equation 1). Figure 2 compares, for the SOCCER dataset, the theoretical label uncertainty prediction with the empirical accuracy obtained for each volume bin; the approximation is reasonable, and results are similar for the NFL dataset.

Figure 3 shows the convex shape of the Pearson correlation measure (Equation 1) as we increase the hyperparameter $K_{Soccer}$ in the coin model. On the red curve, we plot the absolute error between

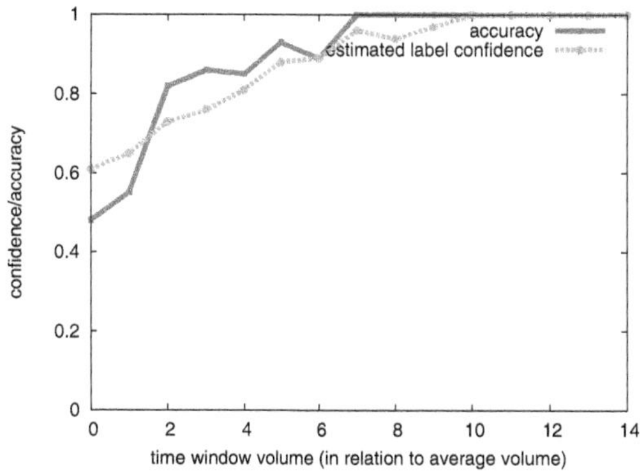


Figure 2: Difference between theoretical confidence estimate and empirical accuracy obtained for time windows of tweet volume = $x$ times the average.

the predicted and empirical accuracy for each value of $K_{soccer}$, to show that the maximum of the Pearson correlations coincides with the minimum of the absolute error curve. Results are similar for the NFL dataset, and demonstrate that exploring the sequence of time-windows to smooth the measure of the coin bias $\theta$ is a simple and effective strategy.

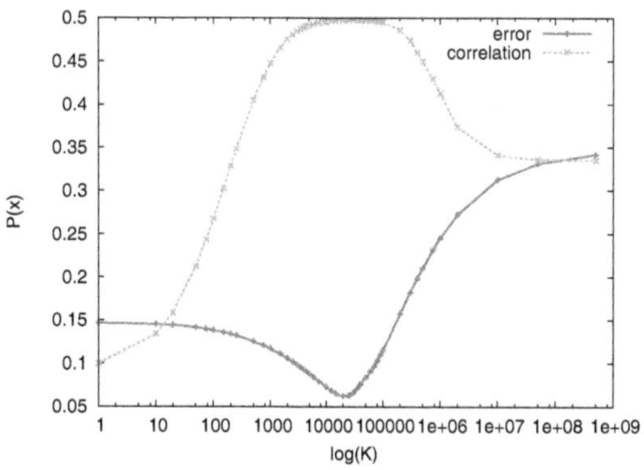


Figure 3: Choice of hyperparameter $K_{soccer}$ as the value that maximizes Equation 1; Pearson correlation maximum coincides with the best empirical measurement of uncertainty.

## 4. FEATURE REPRESENTATION

In the last section, we demonstrated the predictive power of social contexts induced by the positive-negative report imbalance and the segmentation of users into polarizing groups. In addition to the low accuracy on low-time volume windows, using just $\mathcal{S}$ and ignoring content $\mathcal{D}$ is restrictive due to two reasons:

1. Sentiment prediction does not improve over time, since knowledge from past time windows is not carried to recent time windows. Improving performance as more data is processed is a basic requirement for any machine learning approach;

2. It enforces that $\mathcal{Y}_{G_A,t} = + \rightarrow \mathcal{Y}_{G_B,t} = -$, what is generally acceptable, given the polarized nature of polarized debate, but is not capable of capturing more complex variations of sentiment, where members of $|G_A|$ and $|G_B|$ can share a similar sentiment at the same time, or different intensities of sentiment.

We take inspiration on the social psychology finding that describes how humans' decision on expressing their feelings is increased by the strength of the sentiment they are experiencing [2, 11, 10, 28] (which we call, for short, as **extreme-average report imbalance**) to devise a textual feature representation (and, hence, a feature selection strategy) specially designed to track sudden variations of sentiment on evolving and dynamic social streams and that makes use of the textual feature vector $\mathcal{D}_t$ to improve accuracy on sentiment prediction.

It is widely known that the underlying text representation impacts the performance of text mining and linguistics applications [21, 44]; different *feature definition* choices (part-of-speech features, bag-of-words, n-grams etc), *feature weighting* schemes (such as binary, TF and TF-IDF) and *feature selection* approaches can be suitable for different tasks – such as text classification, text clustering and search [44, 48]. When the textual data arrives as a stream, an adequate choice of text representation is even more critical:

- The potentially infinite size of the stream limits the storage of an ever growing high dimensional feature space, what increases the need for adequate feature representation/selection that keeps the feature space as compact as possible [26].
- Static text representations (such as TF-IDF) may not be optimized to nonstationary text streams, since they do not capture adequately the dynamic nature of the feature probability distribution [27, 21], which is strongly affected by emerging new topics and real-world events.

As explained in Section 3, $\mathcal{D}_t$ is the feature vector extracted from messages written during time window $W_t$:

$$\mathcal{D}_t = [w_{t1}, w_{t2}, ..., w_{tM}]$$

and $w_{tj}$ is the weight of the $j$-th feature in $\mathcal{D}_t$. Instead of adopting traditional term frequency (TF) or term-frequency-inverse document frequency (TF-IDF) as weights, we exploit the fact that time-windows have a varying volume of messages and, according to the extreme-average report imbalance, more people post a message when affected by an emotional, strong feeling. As a consequence, emotional content is likely to be concentrated on spikes of activity in social streams at a greater frequency than low-emotional terms. Let $\overline{W_t} = \frac{\sum_{k=0}^{t} ||W_t||}{N}$ be the average volume of messages sent in each time window up to the $t$-th time window and $\overline{W_{t,term}} = \frac{\sum_{k=0}^{t} ||W_k|term \in D_k||}{N_k}$ be the same measure, but considering only time windows that contain $term$. We then define $w_{t,term}$ as:

$$w_{t,term} = \frac{\overline{W_{t,term}}}{\overline{W_t}} \quad (3)$$

$w_{t,term}$ measures how the occurrence of $term$ between $[W_0, W_t]$ is correlated to high-volume time windows. $w_{t,term} = 1$ means that $term$ appears on time windows whose volume are, on average, equal to the average time window volume, and thus it indicates that the term is not expected to be associated with strong emotions (e.g., spikes). A term with $w_{t,term} = 5$ means that $term$, on average, appears on time windows whose volume are five times greater than the average. We name these terms as *high-arousal* terms, since they are associated with moments where the crowd being monitored felt motivated to react and express feelings and opinions, caused by the fact that highly emotional feelings *activate* people and drive them to action [4]).

Figure 4 provides empirical evidence that the arousal feature space is adequate to capture sentimental n-grams by correlating the arousal measure with two features commonly associated with sentiment – the use of word lengthening [8] (as on "cooooooooooooool") and the use of uppercase. The more arousal we associate with a term (n-gram), the greater is the chance it is written using one of these two linguistic indicators. In Tables 2 and 3, we display the top features in each dataset according to arousal and TF-IDF. In brackets, we show the value of arousal identified for each term; high-arousal n-grams are clearly more sentimental than TF-IDF.

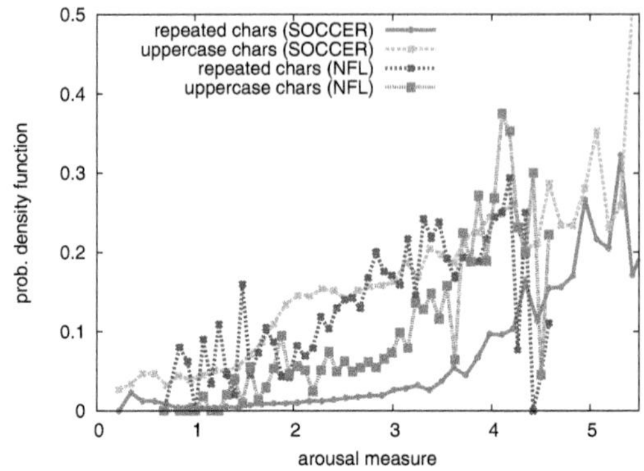


Figure 4: Indicators of excitement (use of uppercases and repeated characters) correlate with term arousal measure.

Table 2: Top 5 features for NFL dataset, according to *arousal* and TF-IDF representations. Arousal values are in brackets.

| arousal | TF-IDF |
|---|---|
| PACKERS_WIN_SUPERBOWL (3.54) | yu_know_what |
| SUPER_BOWL_CHAMPIONS!!! (3.53) | you_would_think |
| YEAH! (3.43) | your_quarterback_is |
| superbowl_xlv_champions (2.65) | you_lost_money |
| touchdown!! (2.34) | you_imagine_how |

Table 3: Top 5 features for SOCCER dataset, according to *arousal* and TF-IDF representations. Arousal values are in brackets.

| arousal | TF-IDF |
|---|---|
| great_goal (7.53) | win! |
| goooooooooooooool (6.80) | gol_from_team |
| he_scores(5.31) | an_equalizer |
| GOOOL (5.00) | go! |
| penalty_for_team (3.34) | he_shoots |

**High-arousal terms and concept drift.** There has been significant efforts to perform effective classification on text streams under concept drift environments; the most common strategy is to employ forgetting and weighting mechanisms that decrease the importance of old instances of data and force the stream classifier to focus on recent instances [49]. We follow a different strategy: instead of trying to restrict learning to recent examples, we design a dynamic feature space, where at any given time the feature space is defined by the useful terms selected using $arousal$ as a selection criterium. As a consequence, we are capable of quickly identifying, on spikes of activity, new features with high predictive power that may appear or gain importance over time (i.e., high values of *arousal*) that become important for sentiment classification.

When a spike occurs and (potentially) changes the dominant sentiment in the stream, due to a real world event which immediately affect users' happiness, adapting the model to such concept drift is challenging if the stream model is strongly built on past data [27]. Tackling concept drift at the feature representation stage has the advantage that unlike instance weighting and forgetting mechanisms, useful knowledge from the past is never discarded, what could harm classification perfomance [27]. In pratice, this means that we use information from old spikes to predict the sentiment at the current time window, what may be especially useful when the label is incorrectly predicted by the model we presented in Section 3.

## 4.1 Experimental Evaluation

We incorporate the textual feature vector $\mathcal{D}_t$ in a learning model by interpreting $P(\mathcal{Y}|\mathcal{S})$ estimates from Section 3 as *probabilistic labels* (or *soft labels*), which can then be incorporated into a variety of supervised learning algorithms [42, 36]. We have chosen to employ a version of Multinomial Naive Bayes extended to consider probabilistic labels [38]. We make this choice because of the easiness to extend Naive Bayes to incorporate probabilistic labels and its suitability for stream classification, since conditional term-class probabilities can be easily updated as more data is processed. Our features correspond to unigrams, bigrams and trigrams represented with term-arousal weights.

Figure 5 shows how accuracy varies, in the SOCCER dataset, as we vary the number of features we include in the model, considering both our term arousal representation and the traditional TF-IDF representation. We varied a threshold at the time window level, i.e., we included in the model the top K-ranked features on each time window. In addition to being more effective, the term arousal representation allows the sentiment model to be very compact, since the best accuracy were obtained by considering just the top 50 terms on each time window. Results are similar in the NFL dataset.

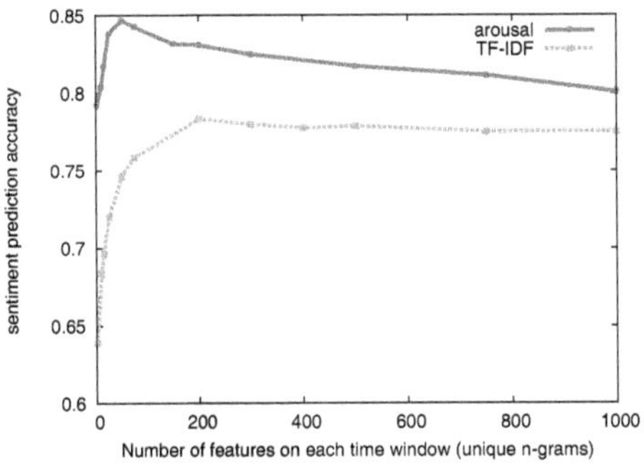


Figure 5: Accuracy vs top-K features comparing term-arousal and TF-IDF feature representation – SOCCER dataset.

In Figure 6 we show the increase on accuracy per volume bin, when adding textual features to the model. The increase on accuracy on lower-volume bins can be interpreted as the "transfer" of the reliable social context from spikes to the lower-volume time windows through the terms: when a high-arousal term is used on a low-volume time window, it contributes to the correct prediction of such time intervals.

## 4.2 Real-time sentiment tracking of live matches

To illustrate the usefulness and the utility of our combined label acquisiton/feature representation method, we now analyze the sentiment of the crowds expressed on Twitter during some interesting matches. For each match, we show the variation on the sentiment score over time in conjunction with the overall volume of tweets from each crowd. The scores are obtained by computing the ratios between the positive and negative probability estimates of the Naive Bayes classifier. Figure 7 shows the reactions of the supporters during SuperBowl 2011:

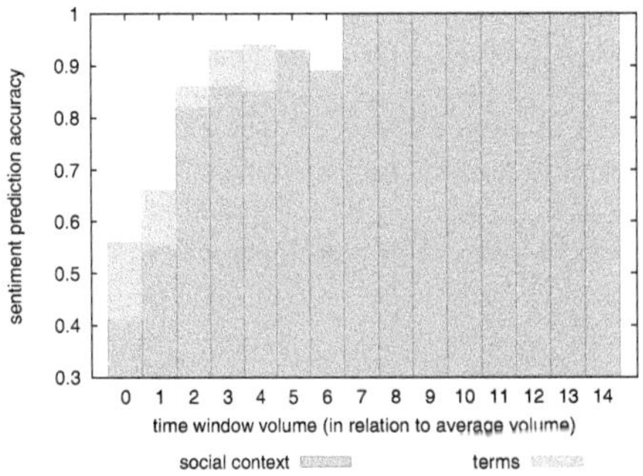


Figure 6: High-arousal n-grams carry the informative social contexts from the spikes to subsequent low-volume time windows – SOCCER dataset.

1. The Green Bay Packers score two touchdowns in the first quarter, reflected on the two spikes of happiness before 200'.
2. At 200' the Steelers scores a touchdown, and, after another touchdown at 240', the mood of Steelers' fans are better than Packers for a significant part of the match.
3. After a sequence of touchdowns from both teams between 320' and 350', the game comes to an end at 360' and Packers is proclaimed SuperBowl winners. Note that the majority of changes in the dominant sentiment of each crowd occur after a spike in the volume of messages, indicating that users are reacting to events. Note, also, that after the spike at 360' related to Packers' victory, our content-based classifier is capable of keeping track the positive sentiment towards Packers, in part because of high-arousal terms such as the ones shown in Table 2.

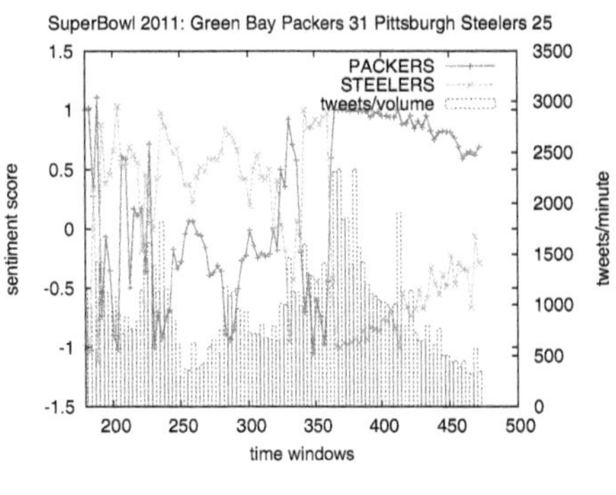


Figure 7: Sentiment variation during SuperBowl 2011 – Packers vs Steelers.

In the 2012 SuperBowl, played on February 5th, we also detected changes in crowd's humour, as shown in Figure 8:

1. The New York Giants started the game scoring 2-0 at 158' and 9-0 with a touchdown at 168'.

2. The Patriots scored two touchdowns in a row, at 224' and 265', reversing the expectations about the game outcome.

3. The Giants managed to score a touchdown in the last minute of the game and were proclaimed the 2012 SuperBowl champions at 298', generating a long period of happiness on their supporters, whereas Patriots supporters were upset.

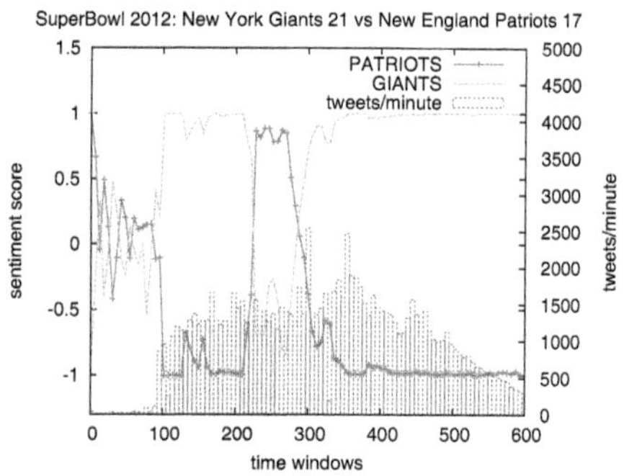


Figure 8: Sentiment variation during SuperBowl 2012 – Giants vs Patriots.

**Soccer.** We also illustrate our results with two matches of the last round of the 2011 Brazilian Soccer League. In Figure 9, team Cruzeiro comfortably beats his fierce rival Atletico by a surprising score of 6-1, scoring two goals in the early minutes of the match. Our model was able to correctly capture the positive reactions of Cruzeiro fans, and negative reactions of Atletico supporters. The second match, in Figure 10, showed a totally different pattern: Vasco and Flamengo played at the last round of the Brazilian 2011 Soccer League and Vasco needed to win in order to have any chance of winning the championship title:

1. At 149', Vasco scored, and our algorithm detected a sudden burst of positive sentiments for Vasco and negative sentiments for Flamengo.

2. At minute 199', however, Flamengo scores (note the spike in volume of tweets), vanishing any chances of Vasco winning the title. Our algorithm detected a sharp negative spike for Vasco in that moment. Even after conceding a goal, Vasco supporters were still upset, as expected; this illustrates the capacity of our algorithm in learning from spikes and using the learned term polarities on the subsequent time intervals.

3. Note that we have been able to track different supporters' reactions, even during "similar" events: although Atletico scored against Cruzeiro at 220', it was already losing by 5-0, what kept Cruzeiro supporters at a better mood. On the other hand, Flamengo's tie goal against Vasco was a much more important one, and, even though Vasco was not losing the game, that goal vanished their chances of winning the title.

# 5. RELATED WORK

Social media data has been successfully used to detect real-world events such as disease outbreaks [9], earthquakes [41] and recurring events such as goals and touchdowns in sports matches [29]. Most of these researches are not focused on the deviation between self-reported data and real data; it is implicitly assumed that the number of users who decide to react and comment on the events

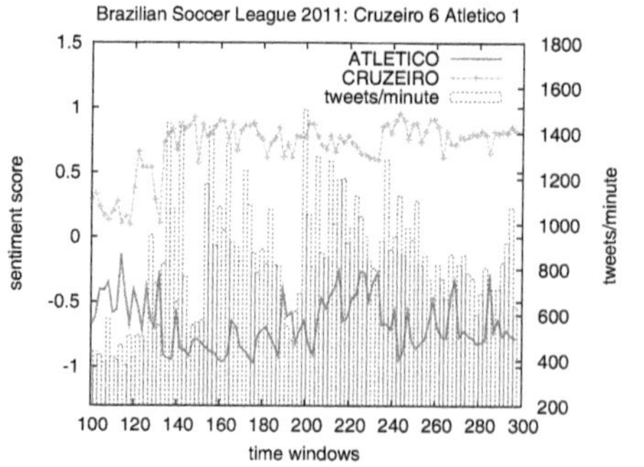


Figure 9: Sentiment variation during Brazilian Soccer League match – Cruzeiro vs. Atletico.

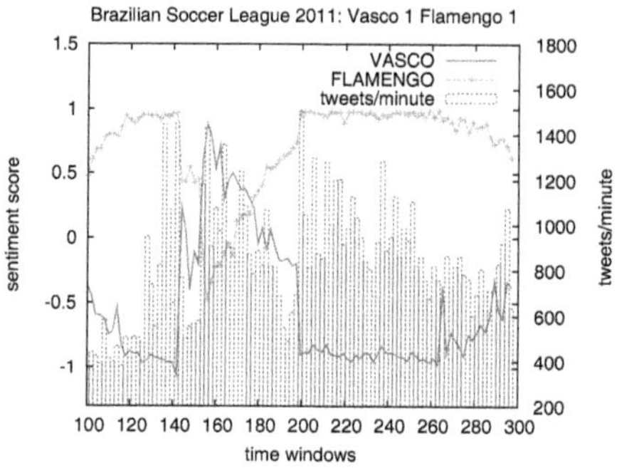


Figure 10: Sentiment variation during Brazilian Soccer League - Vasco vs. Flamengo.

being monitored will be large enough to allow detection. However, the self-reported nature of social media can strongly impact the observed social data, as observed by [28]: if we search in Twitter for the words "breathing" and "drinking water", we may end up (wrongly) concluding that people usually drink more water than breath in their daily lifes. Some recent works try to compensate these biases in analysis of political debate, by observing that a small fraction of people intensively self-report their political opinions, while a silent majority does not [35], what can dramatically change conclusions and statistics on political behavior. Differently from these works, we stress that we aim to use self-reporting bias and the social/temporal contexts it creates to our benefit, in the design of better opinion analysis models, rather than correcting its effects.

Our work is closely related to research that explores opinion holder biases' to perform sentiment analysis. Especially on the political domain, it is known that biases on opinion holders highly correlate to the type of opinion they express, and that social contexts based on groups of people with similar viewpoints provide useful signals for opinion analysis [20, 15, 31]. We add to these group-based social contexts a temporal perspective to explore the correlation between the real-world events taking place and the users currently reacting to what they are observing. To the best of our knowledge, this is the first attempt to detect positive and negative sentiment expressed on online media by capitalizing on the reasons that stimulate people to communicate more or less their feelings.

Sentiment analysis is still focused on static scenarios such as product reviews [37], on which lexicons of positive and negative words and traditional supervised machine learning techniques have been quite successful [45]. We are interested in sentiment analysis as a stream data mining task, a setting which requires learning algorithms to constantly update and refine data description models, in face of the time-changing characteristics of the data [14, 6]. The simultaneous presence of concept drift and lack of labeled data makes real-time sentiment analysis an even harder problem, since some standard solutions from one challenge make assumptions that do not hold in the other. The state-of-the art solution for coping with the scarcity of labeled data, *semi-supervised learning*, makes use of both labeled and unlabeled data for model generationand has also been applied to sentiment analysis [32]. However, due to the nonstationary characteristic of social streams, the usefulness of a few initially available labeled examples may be limited since they can become quickly outdated [13]. Conversely, the traditional approach for dealing with concept drift on nonstationary data is to incrementally update the model through fresh, recently-acquired labels that are provided by the stream [47], but this solution may not be feasible due to lack of labeled data. In terms of machine learning approaches, our algorithm is best related to *distant supervision* [18], which generate labeled data not by manual inspection of individual instances, but by applying some sort of heuristic/rule which output noisy labels. While distant supervision has considered emoticons as the source of labels, we take inspiration on social psychology patterns that guide people's reactions.

# 6. CONCLUSIONS

As a growing fraction of web content is generated in the form of social streams, there is a promising opportunity to build rich applications that track the emotional reactions of social media users during dynamically changing and potentially polarizing events such as sports matches, political debates and live breaking news. Traditional sentiment analysis, however, is not designed to operate on the stream setting, since the field has focused its attention on extracting opinions from static text such as product and movie reviews.

Real-time sentiment analysis is a difficult task; labeled data is usually not available to support supervised classifiers, and debate about monitored topics may turn into unpredictable discussions. We propose solutions to these challenges based on the different propensity users have on disclosing positive and extreme feelings, in comparison to negative and average feelings.

Since we mapped the usage of the social information on two machine-learning sub-tasks – acquisition of labeled data and feature representation – our work is orthogonal to current and future supervised models for real-time sentiment analysis. Depending on the characteristics of the domain and the social media platform, one or other sub-task may benefit more from our models.

We envisage a series of future research directions. In addition to experimenting our models on other domains (e.g, political debate and TV shows), we plan to enrich the social context we use to track sentiment by exploring the reaction patterns not only at group-level, but at user-level and on multi-group levels. At the user level, we can uncover different, more complex behavior of social media user posting patterns. Are there users which, in contrast to the dominant pattern, prefer to comment on negative experiences for their opposing sides than on positive events of their own side? At multi-group level, we may exploit the different relationships between polarized groups to generate more informative social contexts. For instance, supporters from rival teams are likely to follow and react whenever their rivals are being defeated, and that information could be embedded in the social context.

Another direction to improve our work is to better investigate the impact of time window sizes. In addition to automatically determine the optimal window size (or make it dynamic), analyzing effects of different window sizes in our models may unveil new patterns on how social media users react to real-world events.


## Acknowledgments

This work was supported by InWeb - National Institute of Science and Technology for the Web, CNPq, Fapemig, and by Google, through its 2013 Google Brazil Focused Research Grants Program.


# 7. REFERENCES


[1] L. A. Adamic and N. Glance. The political blogosphere and the 2004 U.S. election: divided they blog. In *LinkKDD '05: Proceedings of the 3rd international workshop on Link discovery*, New York, NY, USA, 2005. ACM.

[2] E. W. Anderson. Customer satisfaction and word of mouth. *Journal of Service Research*, 1(1):5–17, 1998.

[3] R. Balasubramanyan, W. W. Cohen, D. Pierce, and D. P. Redlawsk. Modeling polarizing topics: When do different political communities respond differently to the same news? In *ICWSM*. The AAAI Press, 2012.

[4] L. F. Barrett and J. A. Russell. The Structure of Current Affect: Controversies and Emerging Consensus. *Current Directions in Psychological Science*, 8(1):10–14, 1999.

[5] J. Berger. *Contagious: Why Things Catch On*. Simon & Schuster, 2013.

[6] A. Bifet and R. Kirkby. Data stream mining: a practical approach, August 2009.

[7] C. M. Bishop. *Pattern Recognition and Machine Learning (Information Science and Statistics)*. Springer-Verlag New York, Inc., Secaucus, NJ, USA, 2006.

[8] S. Brody and N. Diakopoulos. Cooooooooooooooollllllllllll!!!!!!!!!!!!!!: using word lengthening to detect sentiment in microblogs. In *Proc. of the Conf. on Empirical Methods in Natural Language Processing*, EMNLP '11, Stroudsburg, PA, USA, 2011. ACL.

[9] A. Culotta. Towards detecting influenza epidemics by analyzing twitter messages. In *Proceedings of the First Workshop on Social Media Analytics*, SOMA '10, pages 115–122, New York, NY, USA, 2010. ACM.

[10] C. Dellarocas and R. Narayan. A Statistical Measure of a Population's Propensity to Engage in Post-Purchase Online Word-of-Mouth. *Statistical Science*, 21(2):277–285, 2006.

[11] C. Dellarocas and C. A. Wood. The sound of silence in online feedback: Estimating trading risks in the presence of reporting bias. *Manage. Sci.*, 54(3):460–476, Mar. 2008.

[12] E. Diener, R. Emmons, R. Larsen, and S. Griffin. The satisfaction with life scale. *J Pers Assess*, 49(1):71–5, 1985.

[13] K. B. Dyer and R. Polikar. Semi-supervised learning in initially labeled non-stationary environments with gradual drift. In *IJCNN*, pages 1–9. IEEE, 2012.

[14] J. a. Gama, R. Sebastião, and P. P. Rodrigues. Issues in evaluation of stream learning algorithms. In *Proceedings of the 15th ACM SIGKDD international conference on Knowledge discovery and data mining*, KDD '09, New York, NY, USA, 2009. ACM.

[15] M. Gamon, S. Basu, D. Belenko, D. Fisher, M. Hurst, and A. C. Konig. Blews: Using blogs to provide context for news articles. In *In Proceedings of the 2nd Int'l AAAI Conference on Weblogs and Social Media (ICWSM)*, 2008.

[16] D. Gayo-Avello, P. T. Metaxas, and E. Mustafaraj. Limits of electoral predictions using twitter. In L. A. Adamic, R. A. Baeza-Yates, and S. Counts, editors, *ICWSM*. The AAAI Press, 2011.

[17] A. Gelman, J. Carlin, H. Stern, and D. Rubin. *Bayesian Data Analysis, Second Edition*. Chapman & Hall/CRC Texts in Statistical Science. Taylor & Francis, 2003.

[18] A. Go, R. Bhayani, and L. Huang. Twitter sentiment classification using distant supervision. Technical report, Stanford, 2009.

[19] P. H. C. Guerra, W. Meira, Jr, C. Cardie, and R. Kleinberg. A measure of polarization on social media networks based on community boundaries. In *7th Int'l AAAI Conf. on Weblogs and Social Media (ICWSM 2013)*, Boston, MA, 2013.

[20] P. H. C. Guerra, A. Veloso, W. Meira, Jr, and V. Almeida. From bias to opinion: A transfer-learning approach to real-time sentiment analysis. In *Proceedings of the 17th ACM SIGKDD Conference on Knowledge Discovery and Data Mining*, San Diego, CA, 2011.

[21] Q. He, K. Chang, E.-P. Lim, and J. Zhang. Bursty feature representation for clustering text streams. In *SDM*. SIAM, 2007.

[22] N. Hu, J. Zhang, and P. A. Pavlou. Overcoming the j-shaped distribution of product reviews. *Commun. ACM*, 52(10):144–147, Oct. 2009.

[23] X. Hu, L. Tang, J. Tang, and H. Liu. Exploiting social relations for sentiment analysis in microblogging. In *Proceedings of the sixth ACM international conference on Web search and data mining*, WSDM '13, 2013.

[24] B. J. Jansen, M. Zhang, K. Sobel, and A. Chowdury. Twitter power: Tweets as electronic word of mouth. *J. Am. Soc. Inf. Sci. Technol.*, 60:2169–2188, 2009.

[25] A. H. Jordan, B. Monin, C. S. Dweck, B. J. Lovett, O. P. John, and J. J. Gross. Misery Has More Company Than People Think: Underestimating the Prevalence of Others' Negative Emotions. *Personality and Social Psychology Bulletin*, 37(1):120–135, Dec. 2010.

[26] I. Katakis, G. Tsoumakas, and I. Vlahavas. On the utility of incremental feature selection for the classification of textual data streams. In *10th Panhellenic Conference on Informatics (PCI 2005)*. Springer-Verlag, 2005.

[27] I. Katakis, G. Tsoumakas, and I. Vlahavas. Dynamic feature space and incremental feature selection for the classification of textual data streams. In *in ECML/PKDD-2006 International Workshop on Knowledge Discovery from Data Streams. 2006*. Springer Verlag, 2006.

[28] E. Kiciman. OMG, i have to tweet that! a study of factors that influence tweet rates. In *ICWSM*. The AAAI Press, 2012.

[29] J. Lanagan and A. F. Smeaton. Using twitter to detect and tag important events in live sports. *Artificial Intelligence*, 2011.

[30] R. Larson, M. Csikszentmihalyi, and R. Graef. Time alone in daily experience: Loneliness or renewal? *Loneliness: A sourcebook of current theory, research and therapy*, 1982.

[31] Y.-R. Lin, D. Margolin, B. Keegan, and D. Lazer. Voices of victory: a computational focus group framework for tracking opinion shift in real time. In *Proceedings of the 22nd int'l conference on World Wide Web*, WWW '13, 2013.

[32] B. Liu. *Sentiment Analysis and Opinion Mining*. Synthesis digital library of engineering and computer science. Morgan & Claypool, 2012.

[33] M. M. Masud, C. Woolam, J. Gao, L. Khan, J. Han, K. W. Hamlen, and N. C. Oza. Facing the reality of data stream classification: coping with scarcity of labeled data. *Knowl. Inf. Syst.*, 33(1):213–244, 2011.

[34] D. Meshi, C. Morawetz, and H. R. Heekeren. Nucleus accumbens response to gains in reputation for the self relative to gains for others predicts social media use. *Frontiers in Human Neuroscience*, 7(439), 2013.

[35] E. Mustafaraj, S. Finn, C. Whitlock, and P. T. Metaxas. Vocal minority versus silent majority: Discovering the opinions of the long tail. In *SocialCom/PASSAT*. IEEE, 2011.

[36] Q. Nguyen, H. Valizadegan, and M. Hauskrecht. Learning classification with auxiliary probabilistic information. In *Proc. of the 11th IEEE Int'l Conf. on Data Mining*, ICDM '11, Washington, DC, USA, 2011. IEEE Computer Society.

[37] B. Pang and L. Lee. Opinion mining and sentiment analysis. *Foundations and Trends in Information Retrieval*, 2(1-2):1–135, 2008.

[38] G. Ramakrishnan, K. P. Chitrapura, R. Krishnapuram, and P. Bhattacharyya. A model for handling approximate, noisy or incomplete labeling in text classification. In *Proceedings of the 22nd international conference on Machine learning*, ICML '05, New York, NY, USA, 2005. ACM.

[39] M. Rost, L. Barkhuus, H. Cramer, and B. Brown. Representation and communication: challenges in interpreting large social media datasets. In *Proceedings of the 2013 conference on Computer supported cooperative work*, CSCW '13, New York, NY, USA, 2013. ACM.

[40] T. Ryan and S. Xenos. Who uses facebook? an investigation into the relationship between the big five, shyness, narcissism, loneliness, and facebook usage. *Computers in Human Behavior*, 27(5):1658 – 1664, 2011.

[41] T. Sakaki, M. Okazaki, and Y. Matsuo. Earthquake shakes twitter users: real-time event detection by social sensors. In *Proceedings of the 19th international conference on World wide web*, WWW '10, New York, NY, USA, 2010. ACM.

[42] V. S. Sheng, F. Provost, and P. G. Ipeirotis. Get another label? improving data quality and data mining using multiple, noisy labelers. In *Proceedings of the 14th ACM SIGKDD international conference on Knowledge discovery and data mining*, KDD '08, New York, NY, USA, 2008. ACM.

[43] I. S. Silva, J. Gomide, A. Veloso, W. Meira, Jr., and R. Ferreira. Effective sentiment stream analysis with self-augmenting training and demand-driven projection. In *Proc. of the 34th Int'l Conf. on Research and development in Information Retrieval (SIGIR)*, New York, USA, 2011. ACM.

[44] P. Soucy and G. W. Mineau. Beyond tfidf weighting for text categorization in the vector space model. In *Proceedings of the 19th international joint conference on Artificial intelligence*, IJCAI'05, San Francisco, CA, USA, 2005.

[45] P. D. Turney. Thumbs up or thumbs down? semantic orientation applied to unsupervised classification of reviews. In *ACL*, 2002.

[46] G. Whannel. Reading the sports media audience. *MediaSport*, pages 221–232, 1998.

[47] G. Widmer and M. Kubat. Learning in the presence of concept drift and hidden contexts. *Mach. Learn.*, 23(1):69–101, Apr. 1996.

[48] Y. Yang and J. O. Pedersen. A comparative study on feature selection in text categorization. In *Proc. of the 14th Int'l Conference on Machine Learning (ICML)*, 1997.

[49] I. Zliobaite, A. Bifet, G. Holmes, and B. Pfahringer. MOA concept drift active learning strategies for streaming data. *Journal of Machine Learning Research*, 17:48–55, 2011.

# Entity Linking at the Tail: Sparse Signals, Unknown Entities, and Phrase Models

Yuzhe Jin, Emre Kıcıman, Kuansan Wang, Ricky Loynd
Microsoft
One Microsoft Way, Redmond, WA 98052, USA
{yuzjin,emrek,kuansan.wang,riloynd}@microsoft.com

## ABSTRACT

Web search is seeing a paradigm shift from keyword based search to an entity-centric organization of web data. To support web search with this deeper level of understanding, a web-scale entity linking system must have 3 key properties: First, its feature extraction must be robust to the diversity of web documents and their varied writing styles and content structures. Second, it must maintain high-precision linking for "tail" (unpopular) entities that is robust to the existence of confounding entities outside of the knowledge base and entity profiles with minimal information. Finally, the system must represent large-scale knowledge bases with a scalable and powerful feature representation. We have built and deployed a web-scale unsupervised entity linking system for a commercial search engine that addresses these requirements by combining new developments in sparse signal recovery to identify the most discriminative features from noisy, free-text web documents; explicit modeling of out-of-knowledge-base entities to improve precision at the tail; and the development of a new phrase-unigram language model to efficiently capture high-order dependencies in lexical features. Using a knowledge base of 100M unique people from a popular social networking site, we present experimental results in the challenging domain of people-linking at the tail, where most entities have limited web presence. Our experimental results show that this system substantially improves on the precision-recall tradeoff over baseline methods, achieving precision over 95% with recall over 60%.

## Categories and Subject Descriptors

H.4 [**Information Systems Applications**]: Miscellaneous

## General Terms

Algorithm, experimentation

## Keywords

Web-scale system, tail entity linking, sparsity, unknown entity, phrase language model


*WSDM'14*, February 24–28, 2014, New York, New York, USA.

http://dx.doi.org/10.1145/2556195.2556230.

## 1. INTRODUCTION

Web search is undergoing a paradigm shift from keyword-based search to an entity-centric organization of web data. A core component of this transformation is our improved understanding of the contents of documents — replacing the shallow summarization of documents sketched out by keywords with a deeper association between documents and the entities mentioned in them. Together with other technologies to allow better understanding of searchers' intents, this enables powerful new user experiences, from search results that directly show key facts about people, places and things, to improved refinement interfaces that allow searchers to quickly locate web documents that mention only the specific people, places or other things they are looking for.

*Entity linking* is the process of matching the references to people, places and other entities in a document to specific instances in an entity knowledge base. Entity linking is a critical step in establishing entity-level understanding of web documents and subsequent entity-centric search experiences. An entity linking system must have three desired properties to be successful at web-scale. First, it must work with heterogeneous web documents that differ in content structure, writing style, vocabulary and editorial quality, enabling a unified approach to analyzing noisy personal blogs as well as professional news articles. The second desired property is robustly linking "tail" entities that, individually, are infrequently seen in web documents, but in aggregate make up a significant bulk of entity references on the web. Linking these "tail" or unpopular entities is challenging because the entity descriptions at the "tail" are more likely to contain minimal information, in contrast with the comprehensive articles written about more popular entities in Wikipedia. Furthermore, because of the sheer number of existent tail entities, the corresponding tail knowledge bases include an order of magnitude or more entities than Wikipedia and other head knowledge bases. As a result of its size, a tail knowledge base is more likely to include entities that match confounds, including unknown homonymous entities that are not contained in even the largest of today's knowledge bases. Finally, and crucially, the system must effectively represent the information in the knowledge base and web documents using scalable representations for web-scale deployment.

We present an unsupervised entity linking system that provides a complete solution to all of these desired properties. Our primary contribution is the presentation and evaluation of the three key components of our system. First, we achieve a unified approach to analyzing diverse web documents through sparse signal recovery. We use a sparse signal recovery technique, adapted with a novel probability-based distance metric, to efficiently determine the most discriminative features in a web document — and ignoring noisy and irrelevant features — regardless of the document's content structure or style. Secondly, we incorporate into our algorithms an explicit model of the entities outside of our knowledge base. This model improves the accuracy of "tail" entity linking by acting as a competing hypothesis that, in effect, dynamically adapts our decision criteria based on the statistical distributions of population features. Third, we capture higher-order dependencies among the lexical features in our web documents and knowledge base by replacing a token-based unigram language model with a phrase language model. This phrase language model maintains the same parameter complexity as a unigram language model, enabling efficient storage and access. While there is much existing research on entity recognition and linking, to our knowledge, no previous work has met all of these requirements for practically operating entity-linking in a web-scale environment with diverse document styles and structures and large-scale, tail-heavy knowledge bases. We have built and deployed our system for a commercial search engine, linking entity references in web documents with a large entity knowledge base.

We believe that entity linking at the tail is the core challenge that must be met for entity-linking systems to meet the requirements of next-generation web search and entity-centric applications, and previous entity linking works cannot provide web-scale solutions with desired requirements. In this paper, we use a knowledge base of 100 million unique people from a popular social networking site. We present experimental results in the challenging domain of people-linking at the tail, where most entities have many confounding and often unknown homonyms. We characterize this complexity, and demonstrate that our system substantially improves on the precision-recall tradeoff over baseline methods, achieving 96% precision with 62% recall. While it is not the focus of this paper, our quality reviews of our system's production deployment show that we achieve precision over 95% and recall over 80% on entity linking against Wikipedia entities, which consist of mainly "head" (popular) entities. We also test the performance of our parallelizable system, demonstrating that, with an average per-node processing capacity of 750 documents per second, it can be easily scaled to process tens of billions of web documents using existing distributed computing infrastructures.

The rest of the paper is organized as follows. Section 2 briefly reviews the necessary background on sparse signal recovery. Section 3 introduces our entity linking system in detail. Performance evaluation and algorithm complexity are analyzed in Section 4. We review related works in entity linking in Section 5. Section 6 concludes the paper.

## 2. SPARSE SIGNAL RECOVERY

Since the entity linking system exploits the recent developments in sparse signal recovery, we briefly review the model and techniques for finding sparse signals in this section as a technical preparation. Readers familiar with this area are free to skip this section without loss of understanding.

### 2.1 Model

Sparse signal recovery, also known as compressed sensing, has received much research attention [6, 11]. It studies how to represent a signal of interest (e.g., speech, image, video, text) by using only a few building elements (usually out of a dictionary with many building elements) and still capture the gist of the signal for an application. Mathematically, the goal is to approximate a signal $\mathbf{y}$ using a signal $\mathbf{x}$ under the constraint that $\mathbf{x}$ is *sparse*, which has only a few nonzero coefficients. Let $\mathcal{T}(\mathbf{x})$ be some transformation of $\mathbf{x}$ as the approximated signal. As a popular scenario, when $\mathcal{T}(\mathbf{x}) = A\mathbf{x}$ for a known matrix $A \in \mathbb{R}^{n\times m}$, the underlying signal model reduces to the linear model $\mathbf{y} = A\mathbf{x} + \mathbf{z}$, where $\mathbf{z}$ represents the fitting error. Let $\mathcal{D}(\mathcal{T}(\mathbf{x}), \mathbf{y})$ be a metric of the distance between the target signal $\mathbf{y}$ and the approximated signal $\mathcal{T}(\mathbf{x})$. For the linear model, $\mathcal{D}$ can be the Euclidean distance, i.e., $\mathcal{D}(A\mathbf{x}, \mathbf{y}) = \|A\mathbf{x} - \mathbf{y}\|_2^2$. Let $\mathcal{S}(\mathbf{x}) \geq 0$ measure the sparsity of the signal $\mathbf{x}$, i.e., a smaller $\mathcal{S}(\mathbf{x})$ indicates a sparser $\mathbf{x}$. Sparse signal recovery aims to find $\mathbf{x}$ according to the following generic optimization

$$\mathbf{x}^* = \arg\min_{\mathbf{x}} \mathcal{D}(\mathcal{T}(\mathbf{x}), \mathbf{y}) \text{ s.t. } \mathcal{S}(\mathbf{x}) \leq \epsilon \qquad (1)$$

where $\epsilon > 0$ is a pre-defined threshold on the sparsity level, and $\mathbf{x}^*$ is the estimate of the sparse signal.

### 2.2 Algorithms

There are mainly two classes of algorithms for finding sparse signals: joint recovery algorithms and sequential selection algorithms. Joint recovery algorithms jointly estimate all nonzero entries in $\mathbf{x}$ by materializing (1) or its variants. In the case of a linear model, a well known example is the Lasso algorithm [36], which employs the Euclidean distance and $\mathcal{S}(\mathbf{x}) = \|\mathbf{x}\|_1$, and solves for

$$\hat{\mathbf{x}}_{\text{Lasso}} = \arg\min_{\mathbf{x}\in\mathbb{R}^m} \|A\mathbf{x} - \mathbf{y}\|_2^2 + \lambda\|\mathbf{x}\|_1 \qquad (2)$$

where $\lambda \geq 0$ is a regularization parameter, which balances between fitting quality and sparsity of the solution vector.

Sequential selection algorithms do not materialize and solve (1) directly. Rather, they sequentially determine the nonzero entries of $\mathbf{x}$ one by one via a number of iterations. At each iteration, an algorithm of this class determines a nonzero entry whose addition into the signal $\mathbf{x}$ can most reduce the distance $\mathcal{D}$, and then updates the signal with the newly found nonzero element. The algorithm terminates using a stopping criterion, which guarantees the sparsity of $\mathbf{x}$ by limiting the number of iterations. A well known example for the linear signal model is the Matching Pursuit algorithm, which we briefly review as follows. As an initialization, let $\mathbf{y}^{(0)} = \mathbf{y}$ and $\mathcal{B}^{(0)} = \emptyset$. Consider the $k$-th iteration. There have been $(k-1)$ nonzero entries' locations recorded in $\mathcal{B}^{(k-1)}$ from the previous $(k-1)$ iterations. Now, Matching Pursuit finds among the remaining locations the column that best approximates the previous residual signal via the following optimization criterion

$$i^{(k)} = \arg\min_{i\in\{1,\ldots,m\}\setminus\mathcal{B}^{(k-1)}} \left[\min_{\alpha\in\mathbb{R}} \|\mathbf{y}^{(k-1)} - \alpha A_i\|_2^2\right] \qquad (3)$$

where $A_i$ denotes the $i$-th column vector of $A$. Note that the inner minimization finds the best fit to $\mathbf{y}^{(k-1)}$ using a given column $A_i$, whereas the outer minimization finds the best fit over all remaining columns. In effect, this step recovers a new nonzero entry that most reduces the matching error to the previous residual signal in Euclidean distance. Then, let $\mathcal{B}^{(k)} = \mathcal{B}^{(k-1)} \cup \{i^{(k)}\}$, and $\mathbf{y}^{(k)} = \mathbf{y}^{(k-1)} - \frac{A_{i^{(k)}} A_{i^{(k)}}^{\intercal}}{\|A_{i^{(k)}}\|_2^2} \cdot \mathbf{y}^{(k-1)}$. Matching Pursuit terminates as the number of iterations reaches a pre-defined threshold, or the approximation error is small enough. The final index set, denoted by $\mathcal{B}$, contains the indices corresponding to the locations of the nonzero entries. The values of the nonzero entries can be readily found by solving a least squares problem

$$\hat{\mathbf{x}}_{\mathcal{B}} = (A_{\mathcal{B}}^{\intercal} A_{\mathcal{B}})^{-1} A_{\mathcal{B}}^{\intercal}\mathbf{y}.$$

The full vector $\hat{\mathbf{x}}_{\text{MP}}$ can be determined by using the values of $\hat{\mathbf{x}}_{\mathcal{B}}$ at corresponding indices in $\mathcal{B}$ and setting zero to all other locations.

We will evaluate entity linking algorithm instances from both classes of algorithms in our experiments.

# 3. THE ENTITY LINKING SYSTEM

We present our web-scale entity linking system in this section. To assist the technical development, we present the following definitions and notations. Let $\mathcal{E}$ denote an entity knowledge base. For each entity $e \in \mathcal{E}$, the information is represented in the form of attribute-value pairs. Let $a_e$ denote an attribute of $e$, and $v_e$ denote the corresponding value of attribute $a_e$. We work with text-based (lexical) values, although, in general, the values can take on other forms such as image, audio, or video. Using this representation, the profile of an entity $e$ in the knowledge base can be characterized by $\{(a_e^{(k)}, v_e^{(k)})\}_{k=1}^{r}$, where $r$ is the number of attribute-value pairs available for entity $e$. For a given web document $D$, the goal of entity linking is to determine an entity $e \in \mathcal{E}$ so that $D$ mentions $e$ in its content. If no such entity exists, we claim that $D$ mentions an entity that is outside of $\mathcal{E}$, or simply an *unknown* entity.

## 3.1 Importance of Sparsity in Entity Linking

For web-scale entity linking, the system is required to be able to process heterogeneous web documents that significantly differ in edit quality, writing style, content structure, among other characteristics. It is inevitable that a web document usually contains information that is irrelevant to the entity of interest. The key realization that motivates the design of our system is that the most discriminative features in a web document for entity linking are usually only a few, and thus highly sparse compared with all the information presented in the document. As an example, below is an excerpt from a person Ryan Smith's home page.

"*Ryan Smith is a versatile, classically trained pianist from South Carolina. Ryan has performed solo and collaborative recitals across the Southeast. He has recently appeared at the Columbia Museum of Art, Piccolo Spoleto Festival, [Edit: other venues he played at.]*

*Ryan is a member of the Columbia Music Teachers Association. In 2007 Ryan was designated a Nationally Certified Teacher of Music (NCTM) by the National Music Teachers' Association. [Edit: continue to discuss his students.]*

*In addition to performing, [Edit: his other interests.]*"

Among the many lexical terms presented above, the salient lexical features leading to a confident entity linking can be "pianist", "South Carolina", and "Columbia Music Teachers Association", together with the person's name. The rest of the lexical components include (i) language components which are merely related to the entity, e.g., "a member of", "in addition to performing"; (ii) features that are less critical (and more ambiguous) once the most salient features are identified, e.g., "versatile", "Southeast", and the places loosely related to him due to his appearance at, e.g., "Columbia Museum of Art".

Note that the excerpt above (from a person's home page) can be regarded as a document with average editorial quality. The web documents generated by social media, such as social network pages, blogs, forums, are usually of lower editorial quality and more arbitrary content organization. Conceivably, in such documents, the most discriminative information for entity linking is even sparser due to the usage of free style writing and the nature of discussion.

In our system, we fully exploit the sparsity nature in entity linking by identifying a small amount of features with the most discriminative power. We designed a Bayesian sequential selection approach to select the most discriminative features one by one. The selection process is terminated as soon as a decision on entity linking can be confidently reached. This ensures that only a small set of features is selected, therefore guaranteeing sparsity. An accompanying novel aspect that distinguishes our system from virtually all other sparsity signal recovery systems is that we adopt the posterior probability as the distance metric, which is in sharp contrast to the dominant adoption of the Euclidean distance. The Bayesian framework naturally leads to the posterior probability as the distance metric. Our experiments show that much higher precision in entity linking can be achieved, which is a highly desirable property for novel entity search applications.

Now, let us start unveiling the system in mathematical details. Some details are intentionally left unexplained at present, and they will become clear as we progress into later sections.

Let $\mathcal{F}_e$ denote the set of lexical features for entity $e$. Let $\mathsf{P}(f|e)$ be the probability of seeing feature $f$ in a document that mentions entity $e$. A typical approach for estimating $\mathsf{P}(f|e)$ is to apply the maximum likelihood estimate, which translates into the normalized frequency of the occurrence of $f$ in $\mathcal{F}_e$. A smoothing method can be applied to improve the estimation [8]. Let $\mathsf{P}(e)$ denote the prior probability of the entity $e$.

For entity linking, it is often helpful to apply proper heuristics to reduce the search space to a set of entities that are most likely to contain the underlying entity. Let us work with a confined entity set, denoted by $\mathcal{E}_c$ with $\mathcal{E}_c \subseteq \mathcal{E}$, which is usually a much smaller subset of the entity knowledge base $\mathcal{E}$. For example, we might select an $\mathcal{E}_c$ such that each entity in the subset has a name or nickname that is at least a partial match with some name in the document.

To exploit the sparsity in entity linking, we develop the Posterior Probability Pursuit (PPP) algorithm, which is an instance of the sequential selection algorithms for sparse signal recovery. Given a document $D$ and its lexical feature set $\mathcal{G}$, PPP iteratively selects the most discriminative features, and it terminates with a confident entity linking decision using as few iterations as possible, resulting in a sparse set of features being selected. The algorithm is described in Algorithm 1.

---

**input** : $\mathcal{E}_c, \mathcal{G}, \mathsf{P}(f|e), \mathsf{P}(e), t \in (0,1); K \in \mathbb{N}$.
**output**: $e^*$
**begin**
  Initialization. $\mathcal{F}_0 = \emptyset, k = 1$;
  **while** $\mathcal{G} \backslash \mathcal{F}_k \neq \emptyset$ **do**
    Feature selection. Let

$$f_k = \arg \min_{g \in \mathcal{G} \backslash \mathcal{F}_{k-1}} \left[ \min_{e \in \mathcal{E}_c} - \log \mathsf{P}(e|\mathcal{F}_{k-1} \cup \{g\}) \right] \quad (\star)$$

    Set $\mathcal{F}_k = \mathcal{F}_{k-1} \cup \{f_k\}$;
    **if** $\max_{e \in \mathcal{E}_c} \mathsf{P}(e|\mathcal{F}_k) > t$ **or** $k = K$ **then**
      break;
    **end**
    $k \leftarrow k + 1$;
  **end**
  $e^* = \arg\min_e - \log \mathsf{P}(e|\mathcal{F}_k)$. $(\triangle)$
**end**

---

**Algorithm 1:** The Posterior Probability Pursuit algorithm.

The essence of PPP is to find the best features which can minimize the distance between the web document and *some* entity profile in the entity knowledge base. To this end, PPP adopts the sequential selection principle to augment the best feature set $\mathcal{F}$ over a number of iterations. At the beginning of each iteration, the most discriminative yet unselected lexical feature from $\mathcal{G}$ is found to maximally decrease the distance metric, which measures the agreement between an entity and the features selected from the web document thus far. Indeed, by letting $\mathcal{D}(D, e) = -\log \mathsf{P}(e|\mathcal{F})$ and $\mathcal{S}(\mathcal{F}) = |\mathcal{F}|$, this step of PPP resembles (3) in the Matching Pursuit algorithm. By enforcing an early termination, PPP encourages only a small amount of highly discriminative features to be utilized for resolving entities, which echoes the sparsity nature underlying the problem. At termination, the entity with the lowest distance to the web document is determined as the entity linking outcome. In particular, the distance metric, to be exact, is the negative log posterior probability, i.e., $-\log \mathsf{P}(e|\mathcal{F})$. This is a novel application of sparse signal recovery, which is different from the widely used Euclidean distance metric in this area but is shown later to be much more suitable for entity linking.

The PPP algorithm can be also interpreted as combining the Naive Bayes classifier with the sparse sequential selection principle. From a Bayesian viewpoint, PPP only uses a subset of features with the most discriminative power, which are determined *dynamically* for a given web document. This is different from the Naive Bayes classifier which bases its decision on all features.

## 3.2 Competing Hypothesis for Tail Entities

Web-scale entity knowledge bases significantly extend into the entities with limited web presence and popularity, which are colloquially termed as *tail* entities. As examples, many people entities on social networks such as LinkedIn and Facebook have limited web presence outside their profiles on the social network. Resolving tail entities are much more challenging due to the following reasons. First, the profile of a tail entity often contains much less information, i.e., smaller number of attribute-value pairs, and/or shorter value descriptions. This can be readily seen by comparing a random person's LinkedIn profile and, say, NBA player Michael Jordan's Wikipedia page. Another reason is the incomplete coverage of entity knowledge bases. The majority of tail entities are not been included in even the largest of today's entity knowledge bases. Ironically, however, while these knowledge bases are not large enough to contain the majority of tail entities, they are large enough to include some of the confounding, homonymous entities. The result is that, in practice, we discover that the out-of-knowledge-base entities indeed create a significant challenge for a robust entity linking system. If these unknown entities are not addressed in the model, a system will mistakenly assign an entity with the same name in the knowledge base to the web document, hurting the precision of the system and entity-centric experiences built upon it.

In our system, we adopt a simple and effective model for the out-of-knowledge-base entities, similar to the approach advocated in [18]. The essence of the model is to construct a profile of a special entity, which is designed to characterize all the entities outside the entity knowledge base. Thus, this artificially injected entity serves as a competing hypothesis that represents the tail entities outside the knowledge base and therefore cannot be linked yet.

To be concrete, let us formally define an *unknown entity*, denoted by $e_u$, to represent the out-of-knowledge-base entities. For $e_u$, we define

$$\mathsf{P}(f|e_u) = |\{e : f \in \mathcal{F}_e\}|/|\mathcal{E}|$$

for $f \in \cup_{e\in\mathcal{E}}\mathcal{F}_e$, which means that the probability of encountering feature $f$ in a document describing an out-of-knowledge-base entity is approximated by the probability of seeing $f$ in the feature set of a random entity from the knowledge base. Essentially, we assume that the knowledge base is representative of the greater, unknown population.

To employ the unknown entity in the PPP algorithm, we simply treat it as a regular entity and factor it into the equations. Specifically, in the computation of $(\star)$ in Algorithm 1, we use the Bayes rule as well as the conditional independence assumption to obtain

$$\mathsf{P}(e|\mathcal{F}) = \frac{\mathsf{P}(\mathcal{F}|e)\mathsf{P}(e)}{\sum_{e'\in\mathcal{E}_c\cup\{e_u\}}\mathsf{P}(\mathcal{F}|e')p(e')}$$

where

$$\mathsf{P}(\mathcal{F}|e) = \prod_{f\in\mathcal{F}} p(f|e), \quad e \in \mathcal{E}_c \cup \{e_u\}$$

and the prior probabilities of the entities are computed as follows

$$\mathsf{P}(e) = \frac{1}{M + |\mathcal{E}_c|}, \quad e \in \mathcal{E}_c$$

$$\mathsf{P}(e_u) = \frac{M}{M + |\mathcal{E}_c|}.$$

Note that the free parameter $M \in \mathbb{N}$ controls the prior probability of the unknown entity as well as the known entities.

Meanwhile, the $(\triangle)$ of the PPP algorithm should include the unknown entity as one possible outcome, as shown below.

---

Revised $(\triangle)$ in PPP: $e^* = \arg\min_{e\in\mathcal{E}_c\cup\{e_u\}} -\log \mathsf{P}(e|\mathcal{F}_k)$.

---

Similarly, this unknown entity model may also be integrated with Naive Bayes and other probabilistic methods.

## 3.3 Phrase Language Model

The last component of our system is the extraction of features $f$ from web documents and entities in our knowledge base for use in the PPP algorithm. Our system utilizes lexical features to build models for entities. All the (text-based) values (i.e., $v_e$'s) in the knowledge base serve as the source of lexical features. Traditionally, lexical features are exploited using a bag of words model or a unigram language model [7]. These models have proven effective in many information retrieval tasks [10, 33, 21, 3]. A major drawback of the unigram LM is its inability to model high-order dependencies among words. Higher order language models have been pursued to address this issue. However, such LMs require a much larger parameter space and hence are not suitable for web-scale entity linking with potential storage and processing feasibility constraints, despite the modest performance gains [7].

In our system, we employ a novel phrase unigram language model $\mathsf{P}(f|e)$, in which a lexical feature $f$ can be either a word or a phrase, where the latter can naturally preserve the dependencies among words [38, 26]. However, phrase boundaries are usually hidden, unlike those between words. Building a phrase unigram language model requires that phrases be systematically harvested from the text. Two phrase discovery approaches are explored.

The first approach relies on the observation that some attribute $a_e$ usually takes a phrase as its value $v_e$. For example, in the LinkedIn knowledge base, attributes such as "geographic area", "professional association", and "job title" typically have values which are by themselves phrases, e.g., "South Carolina", "Columbia Music Teachers Association", and "classical pianist", respectively. Using this heuristic, the value $v_e$ in its entirety can be extracted as a phrase.

The second approach algorithmically discovers phrases from free style texts, such as the main body of a Wikipedia article, a detailed review of a restaurant on Yelp, a summary of some person's professional experiences and qualifications on LinkedIn, and the biography of a movie director on IMDb. The phrases are extracted through application of a statistical language model, which models phrase boundaries as partially observable random variables. Punctuation marks provide some phrase boundaries, while other phrase boundaries are unobserved. A phrase segmentation is a set of contiguous phrases spanning a particular range of text. The procedure applies successive EM iterations. The first step of an iteration is to define new phrases. The second step is to re-segment the training corpus. The third step is to rebuild the model. The iterations are terminated when over-fitting is observed on a held-out data set.

In our system, we use both approaches for harvesting phrases from text. The advantages of a phrase unigram language model is that it effectively captures useful dependencies among words in a model that can be efficiently stored and accessed.

## 3.4 Discussion on Algorithmic Detail

### *3.4.1 Parameter Selection*

In PPP, the parameters $t$ and $K$ directly control the termination criteria. Obviously, $t$ takes values between $[0, 1]$. When $t$ is set closer to 1, the stopping criterion is more stringent. The effect is to require more lexical features for entity linking. Thus, it reduces the rate of falsely claiming a matching entity, at the expense of missing out entities that are actually mentioned in the web document. It is usually the requirement of the application that determines the operational performance tradeoff. The parameter $K$ can be a pre-defined threshold indicating the maximum number of iterations. Our experiences show that $K = 20$ usually suffices. The parameter $M$ determines the prior probability of all entities, and it can be interpreted as an estimate of the total amount of out-of-knowledge-base entities, which is itself difficult to estimate [15, 23].

### *3.4.2 Adaptive Feature Selection*

Note that PPP dynamically determines the most salient features from a web document. This is different from the existing feature selection techniques [17, 32] in which a set of feature dimensions with fixed weights are learned using the training data and then used for classification in all test cases. Essentially, our system adaptively selects the salient features on a per-test-case basis. Beside the benefit that no labeled data is required to perform the proposed techniques, the mechanism of dynamic feature selection represents an adaptation to leverage the sparse intersection between lexical features of the web document and the entities caused by various reasons including frequent updates to the knowledge base as well as different writing-styles, which are circumstances that systems with fixed weighting schemes cannot handle robustly [5].

# 4. EVALUATION

In our regular quality reviews of our commercial deployment, we find that our system's performance on "head" (Wikipedia) entities achieves a precision over 95% with recall over 80%. In this paper, we focus our performance evaluation on the more challenging, and we believe as yet unaddressed, task of entity linking for "tail" entities.

For this purpose, we use an entity knowledge base of 100M people profiles, gathered from a social networking site; and evaluate the quality of our entity linking on a selection of diverse web pages mentioning people. Note that our experiments focus on the entity linking task, and we assume that entity recognition (finding entity mentions, for example) is handled separately.

## 4.1 Entity Knowledge Base

The knowledge base is built upon the information from a popular online social network. It contains the profiles of about 100 million unique people entities. Most of the people entities are tail entities, which means that their web presences are limited. Each profile employs the attribute-value pair representation to store various aspects of information about a person. For the purpose of illustration, Table 1 presents an example profile of a people entity.

| Attribute | Value |
|---|---|
| Name | Ryan Smith |
| Location | Columbia, South Carolina |
| University | University of South Carolina |
| Degree | Doctor of Musical Arts |
| Work | South Carolina State University |
| Expertise | Taubman approach and physical aspects ... |

**Table 1: An example profile in the people knowledge base.**

## 4.2 Documents with Entity Labels

Building an independent set of web documents with entity labels requires one to determine whether some or none of the people entities in the knowledge base are mentioned in a document. Comprehensively labeling entities is particularly important for measuring the recall for linking tail entities. Overall, we obtained labels for 555 web documents with entity labels. Among them, 185 web documents are found to have matching people entities in the entity knowledge base. For the rest of the 370 web documents, our exhaustive search found no matching entities within the knowledge base, and hence they are labeled as out-of-knowledge-base, unknown entities. Specifically, the large portion (about 67%) of the documents with an unknown entity label clearly signals the severity of out-of-knowledge-base tail entities, even for a large KB with over 100M entities.

The detailed procedure is described as follows. We randomly selected 50 names from our people knowledge base. For each selected name, we collect a set of web pages that may mention some people entity with this name as follows. By using each name as a query, we first obtain the top 20 results in the SERP via a commercial search engine. Then, the following types of web pages are manually removed: (i) Directory page. A web document of this kind usually mentions many different people entities with the same or similar names. Common domains for such web pages are, for example, `pipl.com` and `www.spokeo.com`. (ii) Password-protected page, which requires log-in to access the actual information. (iii) Web pages directly from the social network which are used to build our entity knowledge base. Using this procedure, we obtain 555 web documents with potential people entity mentions. These web documents encompass a large variety of writing styles and editorial qualities. Only about 10% of the documents are news articles and online knowledge base articles which have decent editorial quality. The rest of the documents include (i) home pages of people with different professions; (ii) home pages of different small businesses; (iii) articles/conversations/reviews from blogs (e.g., WordPress), technical forums, YouTube, academic research listings, social networks, etc. For each web document $D$, the people entities with the name which is used as the query to retrieve $D$ comprise the confined entity set $\mathcal{E}_c$. The size of $\mathcal{E}_c$ ranges from only one to about 2,400, depending on the number of namesakes in the people knowledge base.

To obtain the ground-truth entity labels, we manually examined each web document and applied exhaustive search to determine whether a matching entity exists in the confined entity set $\mathcal{E}_c$. The detailed procedure is described as follows. First, by reading through a web document, we determine whether it is actually about any person with the specific name. There are occasions that the first name and the last name happen to co-occur in a web document without actually referring to any person with the specific name. Once we recognize such a situation, we determine that the web document refers to no entity in $\mathcal{E}_c$, or equivalently an unknown entity for our purpose. When the web document mentions some person with the specific name, we try to understand the information about the person by inspecting the content in the document. Then, we look for entities that matched the features on the web document from the people knowledge base. We declare a matching entity if we can find one from the inspection. Otherwise, we continue looking for the entity from the social networking site from which the knowledge base is built. Eventually, if a matching people entity still cannot be found, we declare that the web document mentions an unknown entity.

## 4.3 Baseline Methods

Our proposed approach for entity linking utilizes the lexical features in the documents as well as the knowledge base. Meanwhile, the people entity knowledge base in our experiment contains no direct relationships or interconnections among the people entities. Thus, it is impractical to compare with previous methods such as discussed in [9, 30, 29] due to their dependence on the structures and the interlinks in Wikipedia pages. Since lexical features are arguably the most important building block for text information processing tasks, we employ three baseline methods for entity linking that are all based on lexical features. Note that the confined entity set $\mathcal{E}_c$ is also employed by the baseline methods.

*Cosine similarity with tf-idf weights* (tf-idf). The vector space representation of the web document and the people entity profiles are formed using the tf-idf weights. The cosine similarity is calculated to determine the best matching people entity. To determine the unknown people entity, we preset a threshold on the cosine similarity. If the people entity with the highest cosine similarity does not exceed the threshold, an unknown entity will be claimed. This baseline method represents the lexical-features-based algorithmic component applied across a series of entity disambiguation techniques [2, 5, 9, 20].

*Naive Bayes* (NB). A Naive Bayes classifier with the additional unknown entity is constructed. The entity with the maximum posterior probability is linked to the people mention in the web document. The pre-defined parameter is the total number of unknown population $M$, which equivalently specifies the prior probabilities of the entities. This baseline method essentially reproduces the state-of-the-art technique developed in [18] without the name variation model, which has to be learned with information beyond lexical features.

*Lasso based entity linking* (Lasso). This method also exploits the sparsity in entity linking using sparse signal recovery. It is an instance of the joint recovery algorithms. It differs from PPP in three important aspects. First, it employs the Lasso algorithm to jointly select the discriminative features. Second, it adopts the Euclidean distance for measuring the closeness between the web document and entity profiles. Finally, it has to work with phrases by algorithmic nature: a phrase corresponds to a dictionary item, i.e., a columns of the matrix $A$. There are two parameters, one being $\lambda$ in (2), another being a threshold on the Euclidean distance for determining unknown entity. Note that the Lasso algorithm has been adopted to build the state-of-the-art web information processing applications [22].

## 4.4 Definitions of Precision and Recall

We define the performance metrics. Since an entity search application can only utilize the web documents with *known* entities, the performance metrics should emphasize the importance of the correct discovery of known entities over the correct claim of unknown, out-of-knowledge-base entities. By slightly abusing the terminologies in traditional information retrieval, we define the *precision* and *recall* as follows.

First, we define the following auxiliary quantities:

$n_1$: the number of documents for which the algorithm correctly determines the matching people entity in the knowledge base.

$n_2$: the number of documents which the algorithm determines as mentioning some people entity in the knowledge base.

$n_3$: the number of documents which have a matching people entity in the knowledge base, i.e., $n_3 = 185$ in this experiment.

Then, we define the performance metrics as

$$\textit{precision} \triangleq \frac{n_1}{n_2}, \qquad \textit{recall} \triangleq \frac{n_1}{n_3}.$$

To understand the metrics, consider the following examples. Suppose an additional web document mentions no entity in the knowledge base but the algorithm incorrectly determines a matching entity in the knowledge base. Then, it decreases the precision due to an increased $n_2$. As another example, suppose the algorithm correctly identifies an additional web document as mentioning an unknown entity. Then, $n_1, n_2$ stay unchanged so that both precision and recall are unaffected. This behavior reflects the downstream applications' need for web document with known entities, since their correct identifications can provide actual useful information to enrich the entity search experience.

Since different entity centric applications require different precision and recall in entity linking, it is incomplete and improper to use a single best performance metric (such as $F_1$) for evaluation. Instead, we compare the precision-recall tradeoffs offered by an algorithm. This methodology provides a comprehensive view of all the operational points of an algorithm.

## 4.5 Results

We first pivot the performance comparison on different perspectives to understand how the entity linking system requirements are met. The overall result is presented together in Fig.5 at the end of the section.

### *4.5.1 Usefulness of Sparsity*

We examine the usefulness of exploiting the sparsity nature of entity linking. In this section, we employ the bag of phrases model for all algorithms. First, we compare two baseline methods, tf-idf and Lasso. Their distance metrics are both based on the cosine similarity defined in the sense of Euclidean distance. The difference is that while the tf-idf approach uses all the lexical features, the Lasso based approach only uses a sparse subset of lexical features. Fig.1 shows the results. We see that the performance tradeoff of Lasso is relatively insensitive to the parameter $\alpha$ (or, $\lambda$). Obviously, at the same recall, the Lasso based approach achieves much higher precision than the tf-idf approach. The entire range of precision score for the tf-idf approach stays rather low. By enforcing sparsity in the selection of lexical features, Lasso achieves much more favorable performance.

Next, we compare PPP to the NB classifier. They are both developed under the Bayesian framework and equipped with posterior probability as the distance metric. The difference is that PPP works with only a few features whereas NB utilizes all of them. The results are presented in Table 2.

Note that varying the parameters $M$ and $t$ in the PPP algorithm delivers a tradeoff between precision (P) and recall (R). For a fixed $M$, NB can be viewed as a special case of PPP by using *all* the

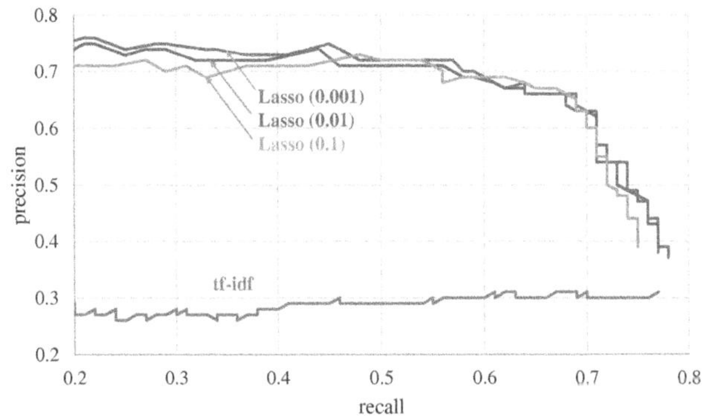


**Figure 1: Sparsity helps: tf-idf (non-sparse) vs. Lasso (sparse). For tf-idf, different points on the curve are obtained using different thresholds (from 0 to 1) on the cosine similarity for determining unknown entity. For Lasso, the value in the parenthesis indicates the parameter $\alpha$ (as used in the regularization parameter $\lambda = \alpha \|A^{\mathsf{T}}\mathbf{y}\|_\infty$ [13]). Different points on a Lasso curve correspond to different thresholds (from 0 to 1) for determining unknown entity.**

| | | PPP | | | | | | NB |
|---|---|---|---|---|---|---|---|---|
| $M$ | $t_0$ | 1 | 3 | 5 | 7 | 9 | 11 | |
| $10^8$ | P | 0.62 | 0.76 | 0.82 | **0.87** | **0.87** | **0.87** | 0.83 |
| | R | 0.79 | 0.78 | 0.77 | **0.76** | **0.73** | **0.73** | 0.70 |
| $10^{10}$ | P | 0.77 | 0.86 | 0.93 | 0.94 | 0.94 | **0.96** | 0.96 |
| | R | 0.66 | 0.65 | 0.65 | 0.63 | 0.62 | **0.62** | 0.58 |
| $10^{12}$ | P | 0.87 | 0.95 | 0.97 | 0.97 | **0.99** | **0.99** | 0.99 |
| | R | 0.57 | 0.56 | 0.54 | 0.52 | **0.52** | **0.52** | 0.48 |
| $10^{14}$ | P | 0.96 | 0.98 | 0.98 | **1** | **1** | **1** | 1 |
| | R | 0.47 | 0.44 | 0.44 | **0.43** | **0.43** | **0.42** | 0.38 |

**Table 2: Sparsity helps: NB (non-sparse) vs. PPP (sparse). For PPP, $t = 1 - 10^{-t_0}$.**

lexical features, which is algorithmically achieved by setting $t = 1$ (or, $t_0 = \infty$) and $K = \infty$ in PPP. From the P-R scores in boldface, PPP improves the recall at precisions no lower than its NB counterpart when $t$ is close to, but surely less than, one. Clearly, properly exploiting the sparsity nature enables performance improvement.

### 4.5.2 Effect of Distance Metric and Unknown Entity

For PPP (and NB), the posterior probability distance metric naturally incorporates the probabilistic unknown entity model as an entity class. For Lasso (and tf-idf), the Euclidean distance metric directly works with a threshold on the distance metric to determine unknown entities. The distance metric and the unknown entity model require mutual compatibility and should not be paired with arbitrary substitutes. Therefore, we examine their joint effect by studying the performance comparison between PPP and Lasso using the phrase language model. Fig.2 shows the performance.

Based on Fig.2, the precision-recall tradeoff of PPP over different $M$ is relatively insensitive to the parameter $t$. Obviously, the two sets of curves unveil the sharp difference between the performance tradeoffs of PPP and Lasso, respectively. PPP enjoys a much better precision-recall tradeoff, in which the precision can be greatly improved over the Lasso based approach at a given recall.

Next, we analyze the result from a different perspective. Note that, in effect, a mechanism for modeling unknown entity controls the degree of aggression in outputting unknown labels. Let us compare the tradeoff between the entity linking accuracy on the web documents mentioning a known people entity and the accuracy on the web documents mentioning an unknown people entity for PPP and Lasso, respectively, in Fig.3.

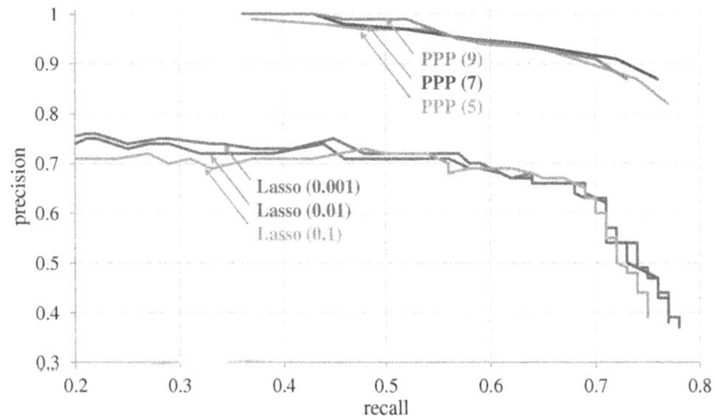


**Figure 2: PPP outperforms Lasso. For PPP, each curve corresponds to $t = 1 - 10^{-t_0}$ where $t_0$ is provided in the parenthesis; different points on a curve represent different $M$ (from $10^8$ to $10^{15}$), where higher precision corresponds to greater $M$.**

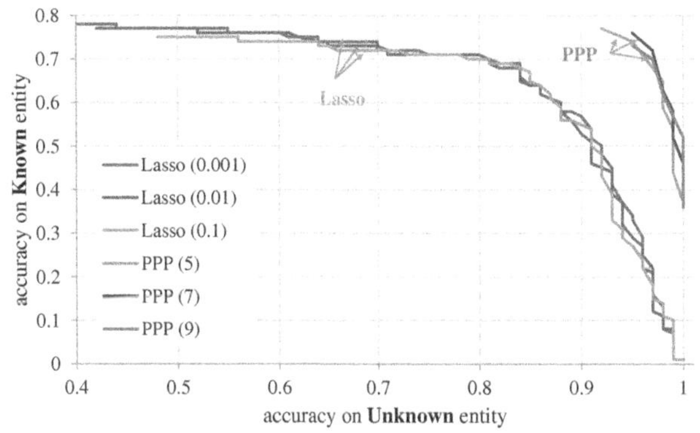


**Figure 3: How well an algorithm does in linking *known* entities vs. determining *unknown* entities?**

Note that within each set of curves (PPP and Lasso, respectively) in Fig.3, the performance tradeoffs are similar. At a given linking accuracy on the web documents mentioning known people entities, PPP offers much better linking accuracy on the web documents mentioning unknown people entities. From an algorithmic viewpoint, PPP employs a principled unknown entity model which is probabilistic in nature. In contrast, Lasso uses a simple threshold on the similarity measure, which is mainly an engineering solution to determining unknown entities. Since there is a nontrivial probability of encountering unknown entities (in this experiment, about 67%) as in web-scale applications with many tail entities, the unknown entity model introduced in Section 3.2 (adopted by PPP) delivers a much greater capability for determining whether a people entity is outside of the knowledge base.

Finally, we completely disable the unknown entity model by setting $M = 0$ in PPP. The threshold $t$ on the posterior probability is used to determine unknown entity. We found that the precision stays at a very low level, $27\% \pm 1\%$, at a recall of $84\% \pm 1\%$, for $t \in [0.5, 1 - 10^{-12}]$. (Similar results are also observed for NB with $M = 0$.) Clearly, the unknown entity model is critical for achieving high precision in entity linking.

### 4.5.3 Utility of Phrase Language Model

In this section, we examine the utility of the phrase unigram language model for entity linking. For ease of illustration, only PPP is considered. We plot the best precision-recall tradeoffs by using phrases (labeled as "PPP (phrase)") and using the traditional word unigram (labeled as "PPP (word)"), respectively, in Fig.4.

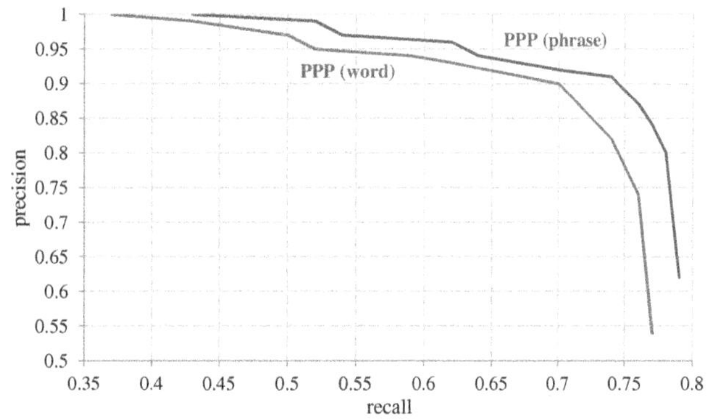


**Figure 4: Phrase LM improves performance.**

From Fig.4, we can clearly see a substantial improvement by using the phrase unigram language model in PPP. Especially, by including the phrases in the model, PPP can achieve much higher recall at the high precision region.

### 4.5.4 Overall Result

Finally, the best precision-recall tradeoff of each algorithm is shown in Fig.5. Overall, the sparsity-exploiting PPP algorithm with

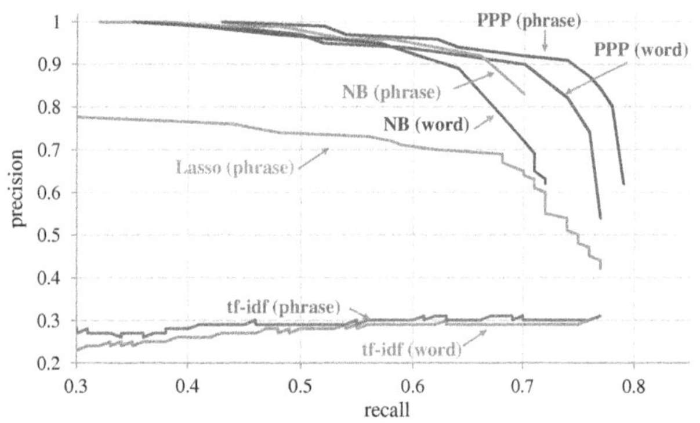


**Figure 5: Overall performance comparison. Our system (PPP with Phrase LM) achieves the best performance tradeoff.**

the phrase unigram language model, which is employed in our entity linking system, yields the best precision-recall tradeoff among all approaches in comparison.

## 4.6 Performance at Large-Scale

In this section, we analyze the time complexity of the system and demonstrate its feasibility for web-scale entity linking. We divide the system into three major stages and discuss their respective complexities.

*Phrase Discovery.* As a preprocessing step, this stage extracts phrases from free-style attribute values. Given an entity knowledge base, the phrase breaker routine finds a phrase segmentation which maximally reduces perplexity on a held-out portion of all free-style values in the knowledge base. For a knowledge base with 100 million entities, both of these procedures can be completed within one day using a single machine with 16 cores.

*Building Entity Feature Model.* In this stage, the system builds the phrase unigram language model, i.e., $\mathsf{P}(f|e)$, for every entity (including the unknown entity) in the knowledge base. We can build these models for 100 million entities in 20 minutes using a MapReduce cluster with thousands of nodes.

*Entity linking.* This stage invokes the PPP algorithm on web documents paired with the entity models. To obtain meaningful estimate of average complexity, we performed entity linking for more than 20 million documents and calculated the number of documents processed per node per second. On average, one node (with a single core) can process about 750 documents per second. In practice, we run thousands of nodes in parallel on a MapReduce cluster to process 10 billion web documents. In conclusion, the system is highly scalable for web-scale entity linking applications.

# 5. RELATED WORK

The major technique for disambiguating entity mentions in documents is to compare the contexts of both the mention in the document and an entity. Lexical features have proven very useful in previous entity linking and disambiguation works. In cross-document coreferencing, Bagga and Baldwin [2] compute the lexical similarity between the sentences extracted for each pair of documents based on a vector space model and threshold the similarity score to determine if two documents refer to the same entity. In addition to lexical features, during the past decade there has been much work that focused on the special structures available in an entity knowledge base. A representative example is Wikipedia, which not only contains texts describing the entities but also possesses rich structures such as redirect pages, disambiguation pages, categories, anchor texts and hyperlinks. These structures establish the relationships between entities, leading to systems built to exploit the correlations among entities [1, 5, 12, 25, 37, 30, 24, 19, 4]. Milne and Witten [30] consider the relatedness of the entities, which is measured in terms of the shared in-links to the entities' Wikipedia pages, in building a feature representation of the mentions to be revolved. Machine learning approaches are proposed to determine the weight among commonness, relatedness and context in the disambiguation module. The method reported in Medelyan et al. [28] computes the average semantic similarity between documents, which is also defined using the in-links structure in Wikipedia, and combine it with other features to resolve entity mentions. In Bunescu and Paşca's system [5], the context-article similarity, which is basically measured in the cosine similarity between the standard vector space models, and the taxonomy kernel, which essentially utilizes the Wikipedia categories to build feature vectors, are jointly exploited for designing a supervised learning approach for entity disambiguation using SVM. Hoffart et al. [20] models the popularity prior of entities, the context similarity between mentions and entities, and the coherence among entities. Then, a mention-entity graph is constructed with the edges representing the linear combination of the factors weighted by coefficients learned from a held-out data set. A dense subgraph is computed with each mention exactly linking with one entity, hence collectively disambiguate the entity mentions. These approaches build supervised learning systems to disambiguate entity mentions. However, unfortunately, it is infeasible to extend these supervised approaches for web-scale entity linking due to the size and the frequent updates of the knowledge bases, as well as the difficulty in obtaining high quality labeled data in the presence of vast ambiguity among entities.

Cucerzan [9] proposed an approach to solve the named entity disambiguation problem by optimizing the agreement between each of the mentions and the document in terms of contextual information as well as all pairwise agreements between mentions in terms of Wikipedia category information. Mihalcea and Csomai [29] considered linking mentions to the Wikipedia entities. In the link disambiguation process, they apply a knowledge-based approach which computes the contextual overlap between the entity definitions and the words to be disambiguated, and an approach that adopts features including part-of-speech, local contexts with specified locations, among others. A voting scheme is further devised based on these two orthogonal approaches to filter out incorrect predictions by seeking agreements between the two methods. Han et al. [19] consider a collective approach for disambiguate multiple entities in a web document using the Wikipedia knowledge base. Global interdependence between different entity disambiguations are modeled and a referent graph is constructed to jointly disambiguate the meanings of the entities in the web document by exploiting their semantic relatedness. Han and Sun [18] employs a generative entity-mention model for linking entity mentions to a knowledge base, which can incorporate the prior popularity of entities, name variations, and the context of the entity in the knowledge base. A Naive Bayes classifier is then employed based on the generative model to determine the best matching entity in the knowledge base. These techniques perform well on web documents with decent editorial quality, such as news or Wikipedia articles. However, for establishing entity mapping on the entire web, the heterogeneous edit qualities, various writing styles, and arbitrary content organizations present a new challenge beyond the capacity of existing systems.

The increasing popularity of social networks has attracted a series of research on entity recognition and disambiguation on social network data. In particular, entity linking in tweets against the Wikipedia entity knowledge base has become a fast growing research area [34, 27, 14, 16, 35]. In this setting, the tweets are viewed as very short and noisy "documents" unlike typical web documents which are generally longer and richer in useful context for disambiguating the entity mentions. To alleviate this problem, it is shown useful to consider a collection of tweets from one user and build a topical model that can draw the user's past tweeting preference to help understand new posts. Meanwhile, the relations among the entities, especially the categorical structures in Wikipedia, are commonly exploited to improve entity linking performance. Our work, in contrast, considers the entity linking at the tail. We focus on exploring the utility of lexical features only, since relations and connections among entities in a tail entity knowledge base may not exist or be poorly constructed.

Recently, web information processing has provided an emerging opportunity for the theories and algorithms of sparse signal recovery [6] to harness the large-scale data available on the web. In [22], Kasiviswanathan et al. apply the technique for sparse signal recovery to detect emerging topics in streaming user-generated contents. The novelty of a document can be characterized by the quality of a sparse representation. In [31], Min et al. utilize a low-rank and sparse matrix decomposition technique to separate the background topics from keywords on a set of documents. The topical background shared across multiple documents is modeled by a low-rank matrix, whereas the keywords specifically related to each individual document are captured by a sparse matrix. These works pioneered the exciting application of sparse signal recovery techniques to the web information processing. The techniques therein, however, are all based on the Euclidean distance as the metric for model fitting, which resides in the traditional sparse signal recovery regime. In contrast, our system employs a probabilistic distance metric, which is a highly innovative extension and a provably effective adaptation of sparse signal recovery to web information processing.

## 6. CONCLUSIONS

We built a web-scale entity linking system for tail entities on the web. At the core of the system is a posterior probability pursuit that exploits the sparse nature of entity linking, augmented by an unknown entity model characterizing the presence of out-of-knowledge-base entities, and the phrase unigram language model that effectively captures high-order dependencies among words. The system achieves the superior precision-recall tradeoff which is desired by many entity centric web applications.

For the past decade, the availability of Wikipedia, Freebase and other (head-focused) knowledge bases has enabled substantial advances in entity linking for popular, well-described entities. As that challenge comes closer to resolution, and new, large-scale, tail-focused knowledge bases — built from social networking and social media sites — become available, we believe focus will and must shift to linking tail entities in order to satisfy the breadth of requirements for next generation search and entity-centric applications. Our system is, to our knowledge, the first large-scale system to be designed for and demonstrate high performance entity linking at the tail.

## 7. REFERENCES


[1] S. F. Adafre and M. de Rijke. Discovering missing links in wikipedia. In *Proceedings of the 3rd International Workshop on Link Discovery*, 2005.

[2] A. Bagga and B. Baldwin. Entity-based cross-document co-referencing using the vector space model. In *Proceedings of ACL*, pages 79–85, 1998.

[3] D. Blei, A. Ng, and M. Jordan. Latent dirichlet allocation. *Journal of Machine Learning Research*, (3):993–1022, 2003.

[4] K. Bollacker, C. Evans, P. Paritosh, T. Sturge, and J. Taylor. Freebase: a collaboratively created graph database for structuring human knowledge. In *Proceedings of SIGMOD*, 2008.

[5] R. Bunescu and M. Pasca. Using encyclopedic knowledge for named entity disambiguation. In *Proceedings of EACL*, 2006.

[6] E. J. Candes. Compressive sampling. *Proc. Int. Congr. Mathematicians*, 2006.

[7] C.D.Manning, P. Raghavan, and H. Schutze. *Introduction to Information Retrieval*. Cambrige Univ. Press, 2008.

[8] S. F. Chen and J. Goodman. An empirical study of smoothing techniques for language modeling. *Harvard University, TR-10-98*, 1998.

[9] S. Cucerzan. Large-scale named entity disambiguation based on wikipedia data. In *Proceedings of EMNLP*, pages 708–716, June 2007.

[10] S. Deerwester, S. T. Dumais, G. W. Furnas, T. K. Landauer, and R. Harshman. Indexing by latent semantic analysis. *Journal of the American Society for Information Science*, 41(6):391–407, 1990.

[11] D. L. Donoho. Compressed sensing. *IEEE Trans. Inf. Theory*, 52(4):1289–1306, 2006.

[12] M. Dredze, P. McNamee, D. Rao, A. Gerber, and T. Finin. Entity disambiguation for knowledge base population. In *Proceedings of COLING*, 2010.

[13] M. Figueiredo, R. D. Nowak, and S. J. Wright. Gradient projection for sparse reconstruction: Application to

compressed sensing and other inverse problems. *IEEE JSTSP*, 1:586–597, 2007.

[14] A. Gattani, D. S. Lamba, N. Garera, M. Tiwari, X. Chai, S. Das, S. Subramaniam, A. Rajaraman, V. Harinarayan, and A. Doan. Entity extraction, linking, classification, and tagging for social media: a wikipedia-based approach. In *Proceedings of VLDB*, 2013.

[15] I. Good. The population frequency of species and the estimation of population parameters. *Biometrika*, 40(3):237–264, 1953.

[16] S. Guo, M.-W. Chang, and E. Kıcıman. To link or not to link? a study on end-to-end tweet entity linking. In *Proceedings of NAACL-HLT*, 2013.

[17] I. Guyon and A. Elisseeff. An introduction to variable and feature selection. *Journal of the Journal of Machine Learning Research*, 3:1157–1182, 2003.

[18] X. Han and L. Sun. A generative entity-mention model for linking entities with knowledge base. In *Proceedings of ACL-HLT*, pages 945–954, June 2011.

[19] X. Han, L. Sun, and J. Zhao. Collective entity linking in web text: A graph-based method. In *Proceedings of SIGIR*, pages 765–774, July 2011.

[20] J. Hoffart, M. A. Yosef, I. Bordino, H. Furstenau, M. Pinkal, M. Spaniol, B. Taneva, S. Thater, and G. Weikum. Robust disambiguation of named entities in text. In *Proceedings of EMNLP*, pages 782–792, 2011.

[21] T. Hofmann. Probabilistic latent semantic indexing. In *Proceedings of SIGIR*, 1999.

[22] S. Kasiviswanathan, P. Melville, A. Banerjee, and V. Sindhwani. Emerging topic detection using dictionary learning. In *Proceedings of CIKM*, 2011.

[23] S. Katz. Estimation of probabilities from sparse data for the language model component of a speech recognizer. *Ieee Transactions On Acoustics, Speech, And Signal Processing*, 35(3):400–401, 1987.

[24] S. Kulkarni, A. Singh, G. Ramakrishnan, and S. Chakrabarti. Collective annotation of wikipedia entities in web text. In *Proceedings of KDD*, 2009.

[25] X. Li, P. Morie, and D. Roth. Identification and tracing of ambiguous names: discriminative and generative approaches. In *Proceedings of the 19th national conference on Artificial intelligence*, 2004.

[26] D. Lin and X. Wu. Phrase clustering for discriminative learning. In *Proceedings of ACL and AFNLP*, 2009.

[27] X. Liu, Y. Li, H. Wu, M. Zhou, F. Wei, and Y. Lu. Entity linking for tweets. In *Proceedings of ACL*, 2013.

[28] O. Medelyan, I. Witten, and D. Milne. Topic indexing with wikipedia. In *Proceedings of WIKIAI*, pages 19–24, 2008.

[29] R. Mihalcea and A. Csomal. Wikify! linking documents to encyclopedic knowledge. In *Proceedings of CIKM*, 2007.

[30] D. Milne and I. H. Witten. Learning to link with wikipedia. In *Proceedings of CIKM*, 2008.

[31] K. Min, Z. Zhang, J. Wright, and Y. Ma. Decomposing background topics from keywords by principal component pursuit. In *Proceedings of CIKM*, 2010.

[32] A. Ng. Feature selection, l1 vs. l2 regularization, and rotational invariance. In *Proceeding of ICML*, 2004.

[33] J. Ponte and W. Croft. A language modeling approach to information retrieval. In *Proceedings of SIGIR*, 1998.

[34] A. Ritter, S. Clark, Mausam, and O. Etzioni. Named entity recognition in tweets: An experimental study. In *Proceedings of EMNLP*, 2011.

[35] W. Shen, J. Wang, P. Luo, and M. Wang. Linking named entities in tweets with knowledge base via user interest modeling. In *Proceedings of KDD*, 2013.

[36] R. Tibshirani. Regression shrinkage and selection via the LASSO. *J. R. Statist. Soc. B*, 58(1):267–288, 1996.

[37] Y. Zhou, L. Nie, O. Rouhani-Kalleh, F. Vasile, and S. Gaffney. Resolving surface forms to wikipedia topics. In *Proceedings of COLING*, 2010.

[38] M. Zhu, S. Shi, N. Yu, and J. Wen. Can phrase indexing help to process non-phrase queries? In *Proceedings of CIKM*, 2008.

# Latent Dirichlet Allocation based Diversified Retrieval for E-commerce Search

Jun Yu*
Oregon State University
yuju@eecs.orst.edu

Sunil Mohan
eBay Inc.
smohan@ebay.com

Duangmanee (Pew) Putthividhya
Google
pew@google.com

Weng-Keen Wong
Oregon State University
wong@eecs.orst.edu

## ABSTRACT

Diversified retrieval is a very important problem on many e-commerce sites, e.g. eBay and Amazon. Using IR approaches without optimizing for diversity results in a clutter of redundant items that belong to the same products. Most existing product taxonomies are often too noisy, with overlapping structures and non-uniform granularity, to be used directly in diversified retrieval. To address this problem, we propose a Latent Dirichlet Allocation (LDA) based diversified retrieval approach that selects diverse items based on the hidden user intents. Our approach first discovers the hidden user intents of a query using the LDA model, and then ranks the user intents by making trade-offs between their relevance and information novelty. Finally, it chooses the most representative item for each user intent to display. To evaluate the diversity in the search results on e-commerce sites, we propose a new metric, *average satisfaction*, measuring user satisfaction with the search results. Through our empirical study on eBay, we show that the LDA model discovers meaningful user intents and the LDA-based approach provides significantly higher user satisfaction than the eBay production ranker and three other diversified retrieval approaches.

## Categories and Subject Descriptors

H.3.3 [**Information Storage and Retrieval**]: Information Search and Retrieval

## Keywords

E-commerce search; diversified retrieval; Latent Dirichlet Allocation

*This work was done when the first author was an intern at eBay Search Science.


*WSDM'14*, February 24–28, 2014, New York, New York, USA.
Copyright 2014 ACM 978-1-4503-2351-2/14/02 $15.00.
http://dx.doi.org/10.1145/2556195.2556215.

## 1. INTRODUCTION

Online marketplaces such as eBay and Amazon globally connect buyers directly to sellers. Given the large and dynamic inventory, retrieving relevant products for the users' queries is a crucial task. Due to the extremely diverse inventory of products on these sites, many inexperienced users looking to purchase different products may express their intents in the same way, leading to ambiguity [2]. For example, the query *fossil* could refer to either the brand Fossil in the Fashion category or the antique fossils in the Collectible category. A user often has a hidden purchase intent before shopping online and considers different products as relevant; without the prior knowledge of their interests, it is better to show different types of products so that at least one of them will be relevant to the user's intent [20].

Information retrieval approaches, based on the probabilistic ranking principle [19], can not satisfy users with different purchase intents. The probabilistic ranking principle ranks documents by their probability of relevance to the query and relies on the assumption that the relevance of a document is evaluated independently from the other documents. This assumption does not hold in practice because the most relevant documents often contain highly similar contents, resulting in redundancy. This problem becomes more severe in online marketplaces where there exists a large number of highly similar listings in the inventory and users are allowed to create their own product description to advertise their listings. Using product search without optimizing for diversity results in a clutter of similar products being ranked in the top slots in the search result page and wastes valuable prime real estate that could be used to satisfy other purchase intents.

To tackle this problem, we investigate methodology that introduces diversity in the search results. Diversified retrieval has been studied in the context of web search assuming the existence of a taxonomy [1, 26, 27]. In the e-commerce setting, one is tempted to follow suit and use the product taxonomy to help select a set of diverse items that satisfy different user intents. In practice, however, the existing product taxonomy on many e-commerce sites are found to be too complex and noisy due to (a) overlapping subtrees which allow similar products to reside in different parts of the taxonomy, and (b) non-uniform granularity in different subtrees, i.e. a category may include one or multiple products. For example, all iPod products are within one giant category in the eBay product taxonomy. Thus diversified retrieval based on taxonomy can not further explore different products within the same category. While the product taxonomy works well to enhance inventory browsing experience, it is rendered useless for diversified retrieval purposes.

Unlike web search, diversified retrieval in product search must be able to accommodate dynamic inventory changes and fluctuating demand in real time. On eBay, there are hundreds of items listed and ended every second. The ability to perform fast scoring and ranking is essential in such a dynamic environment. In addition, user interests on e-commerce sites evolve quickly over time. For example, the latest generation of iPhone immediately becomes popular on eBay after its release. The model should be able to quickly adjust itself to the change of user interests over time.

To address these unique challenges in the e-commerce domain, we propose a Latent Dirichlet Allocation (LDA) [3] based diversified retrieval approach. The key idea is to choose diverse items based on the hidden user intents of a query. Our approach first discovers the user intents of a query by learning an LDA model, then ranks the uncovered user intents by making trade-offs between their popularity and information novelty, and finally selects the most representative item for each user intent to display. In addition, our approach can easily incorporate user feedback, e.g. Figure 1 shows two listings of query *keyboard* corresponding to two different user intents, "See more items like this" option can take user feedback and allow users to explore similar items within a particular user intent.

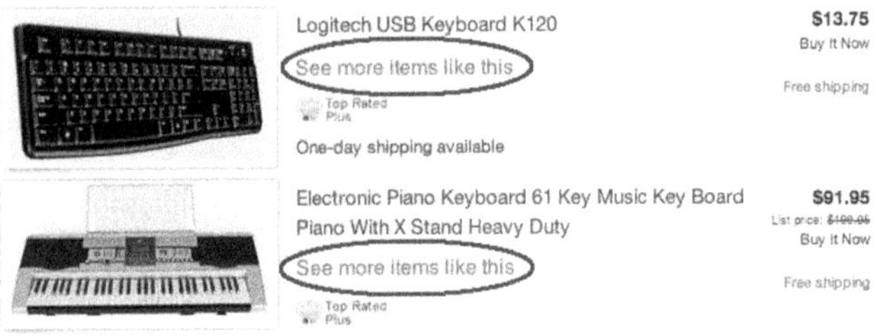


**Figure 1: Listings of query *keyboard* with "See more items like this" option.**

To evaluate the search results on e-commerce sites, we propose a novel offline metric, *average satisfaction*, to measure user satisfaction with the search results. Our empirical study on eBay data shows that the LDA model discovers meaningful user intents and the LDA-based approach provides significantly higher average satisfaction than the eBay production ranker and three other diversified retrieval approaches. The main contributions of this paper include:

- We identify the unique challenges for product search on e-commerce sites and propose an LDA-based diversified retrieval approach to address these challenges.

- We develop a variant of the standard LDA model, *Multivariate Bernoulli LDA*, that is more suitable for modeling short item titles without duplicated terms.

- We propose a new metric to evaluate user satisfaction with the search results and perform a detailed evaluation comparing different methods using the eBay data.

## 2. METHODOLOGY

To improve user satisfaction on e-commerce sites, it is important we understand different user intents associated with the same query [9]. Following this intuition, our approach consists of three steps: *discovering user intents*, *ranking user intents* and *selecting items for user intents*, which we describe in the following subsections.

### 2.1 Discovering user intents

The user behavior on the search result page often carries the information on a user's hidden purchase intent. For example, users with different purchase intents tend to click on different types of products on the search result page. Since most e-commerce sites collect user behavior data, this is plentiful and obtained with little extra cost. Then the challenge is how to discover the hidden user intents of a query from the user behavior data. In our approach, we uncover the hidden user intents using the Latent Dirichlet Allocation (LDA) model [3]. Latent Dirichlet Allocation is a probabilistic generative model, originally invented to uncover the underlying topics from a collection of documents. The idea behind the LDA model is that each document can be characterized by a mixture of topics where each topic defines its own probability distribution over a fixed vocabulary. The words in a document contain semantic information of its topic proportions and documents of similar topics tend to use a similar set of words.

To discover the hidden user intents of a query with the LDA model, we first generate the "corpus" for that query. Since the item title is the most descriptive, concise and relatively noise-free portion of an item on e-commerce sites, we generate the "corpus" of a query by collecting all the item titles from the user behavior data. Then we apply the LDA model on it and the discovered topics correspond to the hidden user intents for that query. Similarly, each user intent is characterized by its own multinomial distribution over the terms in the vocabulary. Terms that represent a user intent well are assigned with higher weight and the same term gets different weights in different user intents. From this point on, we use a topic and a user intent interchangeably.

Though an LDA model needs to be built for each query, we can reduce this overhead in practice. Firstly, only ambiguous queries need to be treated with diversified retrieval. Secondly, we can cluster similar queries and train a single LDA model for the group of similar queries. Finally, though training the LDA models is in general slow, it can be done offline and the hidden user intents are stored for real time scoring. In addition, recent developments in topic modeling have made inference in the LDA model very efficient and able to handle large amounts of data. For example, the parallel LDA [23] allows training the LDA model in distributed systems and the online LDA [12] allows us to easily incorporate the latest user behavior data coming in a stream and avoid the cost of retraining the model completely.

#### *The Multivariate Bernoulli LDA model.*

The LDA model assumes a word in a document is drawn from the multinomial distribution associated with its topic assignment. Under this assumption, the same term may occur multiple times in a document. In our application, however, the item titles are often short and do not contain duplicated terms. To better model this unique property of the data on e-commerce sites, we propose a variant of the LDA model, *Multivariate Bernoulli LDA*, in Figure 2.

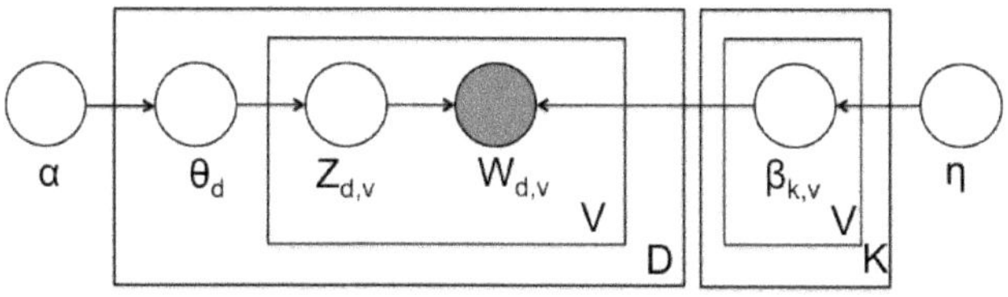


**Figure 2: Graphical model representation of the Multivariate Bernoulli LDA model.**

**for** *each topic* $k$ **do**
  **for** *each term* $v$ *in the vocabulary* **do**
    Draw probability of occurrence $\beta_{k,v} \sim Beta(\eta)$
  **end**
**end**
**for** *each document* $d$ **do**
  Draw topic proportion $\theta_d \sim Dirichlet(\alpha)$ **for** *each term* $v$ *in the vocabulary* **do**
    Draw topic assignment $Z_{d,v} \sim Multinomial(\theta_d)$
    Draw term occurrence $W_{d,v} \sim Bernoulli(\beta_{Z_{d,v},v})$
  **end**
**end**

**Algorithm 1:** Generative process of the Multivariate Bernoulli LDA model.

Assume we have $D$ documents in the corpus, a vocabulary of size $V$ and a predefined number of topics $K$. In the Multivariate Bernoulli LDA (MB-LDA) model, each topic is characterized by a multivariate Bernoulli distribution instead of a multinomial distribution. Each term $v$ in the vocabulary within a topic $k$ has its own Bernoulli distribution with parameter $\beta_{k,v}$. For a document $d$, the model first samples the topic assignment $Z_{d,v}$ for each term $v$ in the vocabulary and then samples the term occurrence $W_{d,v}$ from the Bernoulli distribution associated with its topic assignment $Z_{d,v}$. The generative process of the MB-LDA model is given in Algorithm 1. Since the occurrence of a term in a document is modeled as a binary random variable, a term can occur at most once in a document. Like the LDA model, the inference of the MB-LDA model is also computationally intractable. In this work we use the collapsed Gibbs sampling method [10] to learn the MB-LDA model and details of the collapsed Gibbs sampler are given in Appendix A. In the experiment, we compare both LDA models in ranking the eBay listings and show that the MB-LDA model provides better performance.

## 2.2 Ranking user intents

We rank the uncovered user intents of a query by trading off their relevance and information novelty. Though the user intents indicate different user information needs of a query, some user intents are similar and may correspond to the same high-level user intent (e.g. *Fossil men watch* and *Fossil women watch* are part of the high-level user intent *Fossil watch*). Given some similar user intents, choosing one of them downweights the information novelty of the others. To achieve better user satisfaction, we rank all user intents by making trade-offs between their relevance and information novelty. The relevance measures the importance of a user intent to a query and the information novelty measures the amount of extra information a user intent adds onto the user intents already selected.

In this paper, we adopt the Maximal Marginal Relevance approach [5] to rank all uncovered user intents. Maximal Marginal Relevance (MMR) ranks user intents by choosing the next one that maximizes the marginal relevance in Equation 1.

$$\lambda Rel_Q(T_i) - (1-\lambda) \max_{T_j \in S} Sim(T_i, T_j) \tag{1}$$

The marginal relevance is a linear combination of relevance and information novelty with the parameter $\lambda$ trading off these two factors. The first term $Rel_Q(T_i)$ measures the relevance of user intent $T_i$ to query $Q$. The relevance of a user intent can be measured using its popularity in the data. User intents associated with more user behavior data (e.g. the clicked items) are more popular and thus more relevant to the query. Since each item is characterized by a mixture of user intents, we calculate the popularity of a user intent $T_i$ by summing the proportion of that user intent over all the items in the data, i.e. $Rel_Q(T_i) = \frac{1}{D}\sum_{d=1}^{D} \theta_{d,i}$, where $\theta_{d,i}$ specifies the proportion of user intent $T_i$ in item $d$. As an equivalent of measuring the information novelty of a user intent, we measure its redundancy. The second term $\max_{T_j \in S} Sim(T_i, T_j)$ measures the redundancy of user intent $T_i$ with respect to the set of selected user intents $S$. The redundancy is low when the user intent is very different from any selected user intent. Since each user intent has its own distribution over the terms in the vocabulary, we measure the similarity between two user intents using the cosine similarity. The best value of parameter $\lambda$ is tuned on the validation data. Again, ranking user intents can be done offline and we save the ordering of user intents for real time ranking in the last step.

## 2.3 Selecting items for user intents

Finally, we select the most representative item for each user intent to display. The form of a user intent in the LDA model allows for fast scoring so that we can find the most representative item for a user intent very efficiently. Since a user intent is characterized by a multivariate Bernoulli distribution in the MB-LDA model, the parameters specifying the probability of term occurrence indicate the weight of a term within that user intent. To find the most representative item for a user intent, we score all the items in the inventory using the term weights of that user intent and choose the item with the maximum score.

Given the term weights within a user intent, we score each item by summing the weights of matching terms in the title using Equation 2.

$$Score(I_i, T_k) = \frac{\sum_{j=1}^{|I_i|} \beta_{k,W_{i,j}}}{max(AvgTitleLength_Q, |I_i|)} \tag{2}$$

where $W_{i,j}$ denotes the $j$th word in the title of item $I_i$ and $\beta_{k,W_{i,j}}$ specifies the weight of term $W_{i,j}$ in user intent $k$. In addition, we normalize the score by the max of the title length and the average title length of query $Q$. This normalization can help prevent title spamming[1] by penalizing listings with an unusually long title, and avoid showing

[1]The sellers put irrelevant terms in the title to get higher exposure.

listings with very short title since they are generally less informative.

## 3. AVERAGE SATISFACTION METRIC

Classical metrics (e.g. precision, recall and NDCG) can not be used to evaluate diversity in the search results because they do not take into account the correlation between items. In addition, studies [21, 14] have shown that accuracy metrics do not necessarily correlate with user satisfaction. Variants of classical metrics have been proposed to evaluate diversity in different settings [7, 1]. However, these metrics either require human judgement or rely on existing categories. In this section, we propose a new metric to evaluate diversity in the search results based on user satisfaction and justify its use in the e-commerce domain.

Recognizing that users with different purchase intents use the same query, the goal of ranking then becomes to capture the interests of as many users as possible and as quickly as possible. This can be expressed through risk minimization framework [27, 1]. The risk of a ranker is measured by the proportion of users that can not find any relevant items. Instead of measuring the risk, we can measure the user satisfaction. **Average Satisfaction (AS)** for query $Q$ is defined to be the user satisfaction with respect to the top $N$ items in the ranking list $R$, averaged across all the users $\mathbf{U_Q}$. Average satisfaction can be written as Equation 3 where $Satisfaction(U_j, R_N)$ specifies the satisfaction of user $U_j$ on the top $N$ items in a ranking list $R$. In addition, **Mean Average Satisfaction (MAS)** is defined to be the mean of the average satisfaction over the top $N$ rank positions shown in Equation 4.

$$AS_N(R,Q) = \frac{1}{|\mathbf{U_Q}|} \sum_{U_j \in \mathbf{U_Q}} Satisfaction(U_j, R_N) \quad (3)$$

$$MAS_N(R,Q) = \frac{1}{N} \sum_{n=1}^{N} AS_n(R,Q) \quad (4)$$

Average satisfaction takes into account both relevance and diversity based on user demands, making it a natural metric for the e-commerce domain. To show that, we use the simplified example on query *fossil*. Assume there are 10 users in which 5 users are interested in Fossil bag, 3 users are interested in Fossil watch and 2 users are interested in antique fossils. The satisfaction of a user is 1 if there exists at least one item matching his interest and 0 otherwise. Given the ranking results from three different rankers {Fossil bag, Fossil watch, antique fossils}, {Fossil watch, antique fossils, Fossil bag} and {Fossil bag, Fossil bag, Fossil watch}, the average satisfaction of these three ranking results at rank position $N$ from 1 to 3 are: {0.5, 0.8, 1.0}, {0.3, 0.5, 1.0} and {0.5, 0.5, 0.8}, where ranker 1 has the largest mean average satisfaction of 0.767. At $N = 3$, both ranker 1 and 2 satisfy all the users while ranker 3 dissatisfies 20% of the users. Ranker 3 orders items according to their probabilities of relevance, but includes similar items, resulting in redundancy. Meanwhile, ranker 1 is better than ranker 2, because it captures the user interests more quickly by ranking them according to their probabilities of relevance.

The utility function, $Satisfaction(U_j, R_N)$, is hard to measure directly on e-commerce sites due to their rapidly changing inventory. Since the clicked items of a user indicate the user's interest, we define this utility function to be the similarity between the clicked items of user $U_j$ and the most similar item on the ranking list $R_N$. The satisfaction of a user with multiple clicks can be calculated by averaging across all the clicked items. In practice, however, it is difficult to associate a clicked item with a user. Therefore, we treat each clicked item as if it is from a different user as an approximation. Finally, the average satisfaction of ranking $R$ on query $Q$ is shown in Equation 5 where $I_j$ denotes the $j$th clicked item in the set of all clicked items $C_Q$ for query $Q$ and $I_i$ denotes the $i$th item in the ranking list $R_N$.

$$AS_N(R,Q) = \frac{1}{|C_Q|} \sum_{I_j \in C_Q} \max_{I_i \in R_N} Sim(I_j, I_i) \quad (5)$$

We use the weighted cosine similarity function to measure the similarity between two items, where the weight of a term is query-dependent and reflects its relevance to the query. In our study, the weights are learned from a relevance model described in Section 4.

Given our definition of the utility function, average satisfaction and mean average satisfaction are monotonically increasing functions of $N$ as adding more items to the ranking list never reduces the user satisfaction. Our proposed metric is similar to the metric used in [17] except that their utility function is calculated using user feedback.

## 4. EVALUATION

### 4.1 Data description

We evaluate our approach using the data at eBay, one of the largest online marketplaces. eBay manages over 90 million active users worldwide, 200 million items for sale and 8 billion URL requests daily. Unlike web search, eBay works in a dynamic environment where about 10% of the items in the inventory are listed, expired or sold every day. Given a wide variety of products in the inventory, eBay maintains a very large and complex taxonomy, with more than 18,500 leaf categories. However, the design of different subtrees in the eBay product taxonomy depends on different expert knowledge. The large-scale data, the dynamic environment and the complex and noisy product taxonomy make diversified retrieval extremely challenging at eBay.

In our study, we randomly sample 120 queries from all the queries submitted to eBay in two weeks (excluding those extremely rare queries). These queries cover a wide spectrum of query frequencies with some queries having as many as 30,000 daily submissions and as few as 300 daily submissions. For each query, we collect two months of user clicked data where items with multiple clicks have multiple copies in the data. Then, we randomly sample 10,000 items for training, 10,000 items for evaluation and another 2,000 items as validation data for parameter tuning. To leverage the category of an item, we add the item category as an extra term to the item title. For example, the item *iPhone 4 black ATT 16GB* in category *Cell Phones and Smartphones* is converted into a bag of words with "cat-Cell Phones and Smartphones" added in as an extra term. Items in more than one category have multiple categorical terms added into the bag of words.

### 4.2 Experiment

One way to evaluate a model on e-commerce sites is to run the A/B testing and calculate the online metrics, e.g. click through rate (CTR). However, the online metrics in the A/B

| fossil | | basketball | | iPod | |
|---|---|---|---|---|---|
| *Fossil bag and purse* | "cat-Handbags and Purses" purse handbag bag leather tote shoulder key cross | *basketball* | "cat-Basketball" official size spalding ball 29.5 street | *iPod touch* | "cat-Portable Audio & Headphones" touch apple gb 8th generation |
| *Fossil men watch* | "cat-Wristwatches" watch men chronograph mens ch stainless steel fs | *basketball shoes* | "cat-Men's shoes" shoes nike size mens air black adidas | *iPod nano* | nano "cat-Portable Audio & Headphones" gb generation 8th model 4th |
| *Fossil women watch* | "cat-Wristwatches" watch es women stella relic gold dial by | *basketball card* | "cat-cards" card jordan lot michael auto rookie topps | *iPod case* | for case usb iPhone touch 4th new apple |
| *Fossil wallet* | wallet "cat-Wallets" leather clutch nwt brown new coin | *basketball shirt* | nike shirt shorts xl "cat-Men's Clothing" new jersey | *iPod charger* | for charger usb iPhone cable 4th mp 3rd |
| *antique fossils* | ammonite shark "cat-Shark Teeth" dinosaur "cat-Amphibian,Reptile and Dinosaur" "cat-Ammonites" tooth | *basketball hoop* | hoop "cat-Basketball" backboard rim nba portable in ground | *iPod classic* | "cat-Portable Audio & Headphones" classic apple 5th 30 gb black generation |

**Table 1: The user intents of query *fossil*, *basketball*, and *iPod* using the MB-LDA model with 5 topics.**

testing may not accurately capture the aspect of user satisfaction and the A/B testing itself requires many resources. Alternatively we evaluate our models using the offline metric *average satisfaction* defined in Section 3. In our experiment, we compare six different approaches in ranking the eBay inventory, including the eBay production ranker, Maximal Marginal Relevance (MMR), Probabilistic Latent Maximal Marginal Relevance (PLMMR), the category-based approach and two LDA-based approaches (LDA and MB-LDA).

**The eBay ranker** is a machine learning ranker with many features built in to improve sales on eBay. Since the eBay ranker scores each item independently, the diversity in the search results is introduced as a side-effect. We use the eBay ranker as our baseline and compare the other approaches against it.

**MMR** [5] takes the ranking from a relevance model and reranks the items by trading off their relevance and novelty. The relevance model used in eBay makes the bag-of-word assumption and learns the weight for each term in the vocabulary based on both clicked and skipped user data. In general, the weight of a term is proportional to the number of occurrences in the clicked data. However, a term may get a negative weight if it rarely occurs in the clicked data, but frequently in the skipped data[2]. The relevance model scores an item by summing the weight of the terms in its title and normalizing it by the average title length of the query. Given the output from the eBay relevance model, MMR reranks 500 most relevant items by greedily choosing the next item that maximizes the marginal relevance. The parameter $\lambda$, that makes trade-offs between relevance and novelty, is chosen from the set $\{0, 0.2, 0.4, 0.6, 0.8, 1\}$ and the best value of $\lambda$ is tuned on the validation data.

**PLMMR** [11] is a probabilistic latent version of MMR and takes into account the hidden user intents. Like our approach, PLMMR learns an LDA model for each query and then represents the document and the query as probability vectors of latent topics. The relevance term and novelty term are then calculated in the space of latent topics. In the experiment, the same LDA models learned in our approach are used in PLMMR.

[2]The skipped data is defined to be the items above the first clicked item on the search result page.

**The category-based approach** selects diverse items based on the eBay product taxonomy. First we estimate the weight of each leaf category for a query based on the user demands, sort them in decreasing order, and choose the top-ranked item by the relevance model within a category.

**The LDA-based approach** For each query, we first construct its vocabulary by removing the rare terms whose frequency is below 1% in the training data. For both the LDA model and the MB-LDA model, we set the number of topics to be 10, use the symmetric hyper parameter $\alpha$ and $\eta$ with value 0.1, and run collapsed Gibbs sampling for 5,000 iterations and check on the convergence. The trade-off parameter $\lambda$ is chosen from the set $\{0, 0.2, 0.4, 0.6, 0.8, 1\}$ and the best value of $\lambda$ is tuned on the validation data.

# 5. RESULTS AND DISCUSSION

## 5.1 Discovered user intents

First, we examine whether the LDA models discover semantically meaningful user intents for a query. We use queries *fossil*, *basketball* and *iPod* as our illustrative examples and more examples can be found in Appendix B. We run the MB-LDA model with 5 topics, and show the discovered user intents in Table 1.[3] The left column shows the manually interpreted labels of the user intents and the right column shows the terms of the largest probability of occurrence. The MB-LDA model indeed discovers meaningful user intents. Firstly, the MB-LDA model is able to distinguish different categories of a query and associate the terms with the corresponding category. For example in query *basketball*, the model is able to associate *spalding* and *ball* with category "Basketball", and *nike* and *shoes* with category "Men's shoes". Secondly, the discovered user intents are more expressive than the eBay product taxonomy. In query *iPod*, the MB-LDA model is able to further split all iPod products in one giant category "Portable Audio & Headphones" into more detailed user intents *iPod touch*, *iPod nano* and *iPod classic*, which better captures users' different information needs. Finally, the MB-LDA model is able

[3]We only show the results from the MB-LDA model due to space limitations, but the user intents discovered by the LDA model are similar.

to combine similar categories adaptively. The user intent *antique fossils* of query *fossil* includes three different categories of antique fossils. Given the relatively small user demands on antique fossils, combining different categories of antique fossils into one user intent helps save the space to show items for other popular user intents.

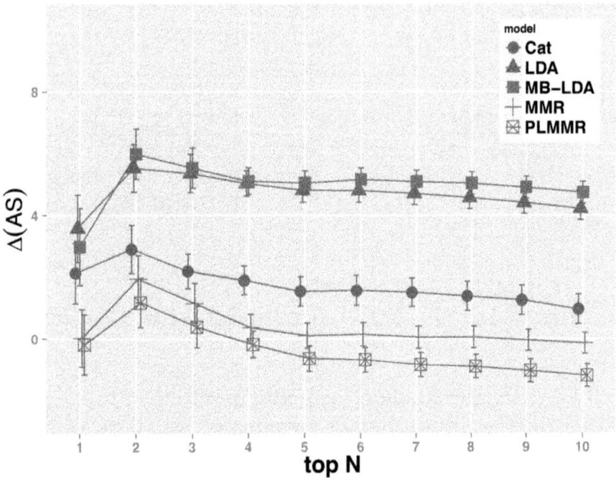


**Figure 3: The mean and 95% CI of the difference of average satisfaction for different approaches against the eBay ranker on all testing queries. The $X$ axis denotes the rank position $N$ and the $Y$ axis denotes the difference of average satisfaction.**

## 5.2 Performance against the eBay ranker

Next, we compare five different approaches against the eBay ranker. For each query, we rank the eBay inventory with different approaches, evaluate on the top 10 diverse items, and compute the difference of average satisfaction against the eBay ranker. In Figure 3, we show the mean and 95% confidence interval of the difference of average satisfaction on all testing queries. The paired t-test indicates only the LDA-based approaches and the category-based approach are statistically better than the eBay ranker across all top 10 rank positions and they improve the baseline by as much as 6% and 3% respectively. The MB-LDA model is better than the LDA model even though the difference is not statistically significant. In Table 2, we show the mean average satisfaction on top 10 items in the first row. The MB-LDA model shows the best overall performance and is more than 3% better than the category-based approach. Since both LDA models perform similarly with the MB-LDA model being slightly better. For the sake of clarity, we use the results of the MB-LDA model in the following analyses.

Both MMR and PLMMR do not work well. MMR fails to consider the user intents, thus the selected items may not represent user intents well and certainly can not cover all different user intents of a query. Though PLMMR considers the hidden user intents, it does not consider the length of an item title in computing the relevance and diversity, therefore it may choose items with either very short or very long titles, which are less informative. Since MMR and PLMMR are obvious less effective in improving user satisfaction, we focus on the comparison between the LDA-based approach and the category-based approach.

**Table 2: The mean average satisfaction at rank 10 on different types of queries. The approaches highlighted in bold indicate the best performer in that type of queries.**

| Query Type | eBay ranker | MMR | PL-MMR | Cat | LDA | MB-LDA |
|---|---|---|---|---|---|---|
| All | 68.1% | 68.7% | 68.2% | 69.8% | 73.2% | **73.7%** |
| High | 60.3% | 60.6% | 60.1% | 66.0% | 66.5% | **67.4%** |
| Low | 74.1% | 75.1% | 74.8% | 72.7% | **78.3%** | **78.3%** |

**Table 3: The queries that the MB-LDA based approach outperforms and underperforms the category-based approach the most. + indicates the MB-LDA model is better and - otherwise.**

| Query | Daily submissions | Ambiguity score | $\Delta(AS_3)$ |
|---|---|---|---|
| ipad 1st generation | 100 | 9.4 | +15.5% |
| verizon cell phones | 11K | 0.6 | +12.8% |
| nike 60 | 600 | 14.8 | +12.7% |
| iphone 4 | 1.3M | 7.2 | +12.2% |
| unlocked cell phone touch screen | 3.6K | 1.1 | +12% |
| ps 3 | 11K | 12.7 | +11.3% |
| porcelain doll | 800 | 21.9 | -4.2% |
| lego | 800 | 21.8 | -2.9% |
| coach | 23K | 25.9 | -2.7% |

To better understand the different behaviors of the LDA-based and the category-based approaches, we show the queries where these two models differ the most in ranking the top 3 items and their statistics in Table 3. The ambiguity score of a query describes how ambiguous the query is based on the distribution of user demands over different categories [16]. The LDA-based approach provides 10-15% more average satisfaction in the best case and only about 4% less in the worst case. Since the category-based approach heavily depends on the existing taxonomy, it becomes less effective when the granularity of the part in the eBay taxonomy is coarse. The LDA-based approach, however, discovers user intents based on item titles and is not affected much by the quality of the eBay taxonomy. As a result, the LDA-based approach works better on queries of low ambiguity. In queries where the LDA-based approach does worse, the item titles are often noisy and less informative, thus the LDA model can not discover meaningful and stable user intents. For example in query *lego*, the sellers use very different words in the title to describe similar products and there is a large variety of different lego products on the market. On the other hand, the eBay product taxonomy is well designed for this type of product and the category-based approach is able to achieve better performance on this type of queries.

## 5.3 Queries of different ambiguity

To further investigate the model performance, we run the same analysis on two groups of queries, one including queries of high ambiguity and the other one including queries of low ambiguity. In particular, we take 25% most and 25% least ambiguous testing queries based on their ambiguity scores for this analysis. The results are shown in Figure 4. The

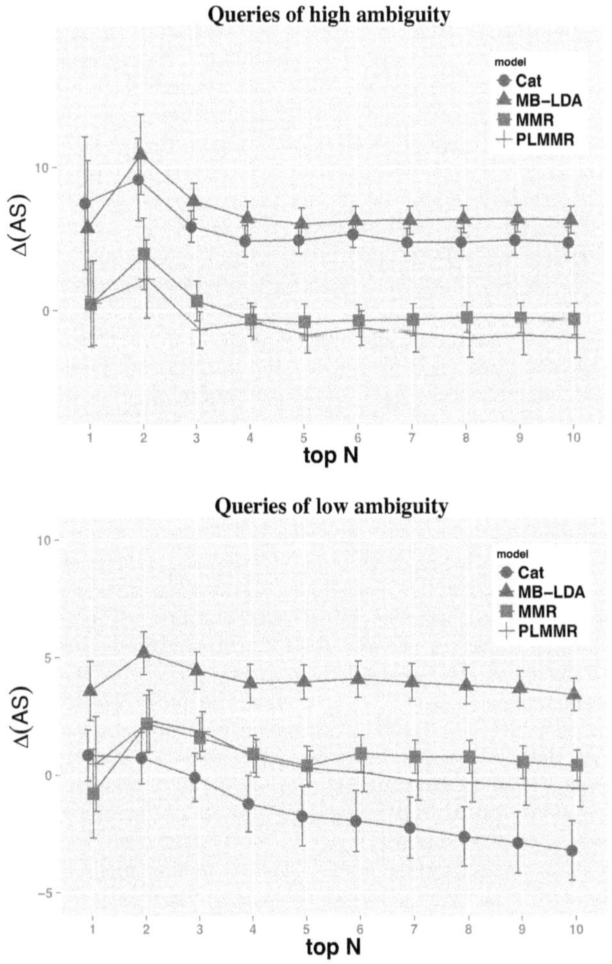


**Figure 4: The mean and 95% CI of the difference of average satisfaction for different approaches against the eBay ranker on queries of high ambiguity (top) and queries of low ambiguity (bottom).**

figure on the top shows the difference of average satisfaction on queries of high ambiguity. Both the LDA-based and the category-based approaches perform statistically better than the eBay ranker. Since there are often more different user intents associated with queries of high ambiguity, more items needs to be selected to cover all different user intents, resulting in lower mean average satisfaction (the second row in Table 2). Again, the MB-LDA model shows the best performance and is able to improve the eBay ranker by as much as 7% on mean average satisfaction.

The difference between the LDA-based and the category-based approaches becomes smaller on queries of high ambiguity. Since the granularity of the eBay taxonomy is often more refined on this type of queries, the category-based approach is able to capture most of the user intents based on the category information. However, the LDA-based approach is able to handle the correlations between categories and the overlapping subtrees in the taxonomy. For example, we show the top three items of query *fossil* selected by the eBay ranker, the category-based approach and the LDA-based approach in Table 4. All three items selected by the eBay ranker are bags and purses, showing very limited diversity. The category-based approach shows a bag, a watch and a purse. Though the bag and the purse are from different categories, they are actually similar due to the strong correlation between the categories *Handbags and Purses* and *Wallets*. The LDA-based approach selects a bag, a watch and a set of fossil teeth, and clearly shows the most diversity in the search results.

| | eBay ranker | Cat | MB-LDA |
|---|---|---|---|
| 1 |  |  |  |
| 2 | 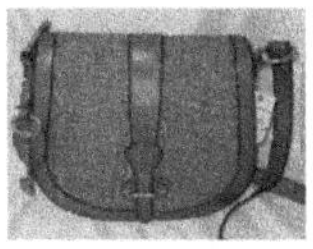 |  |  |
| 3 |  | 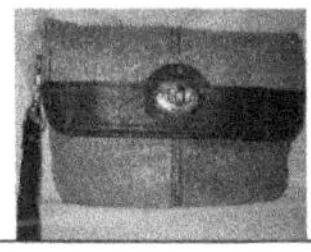 | 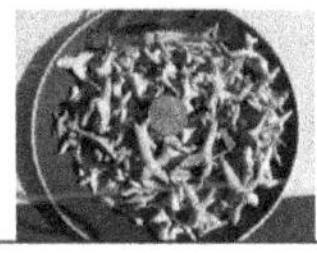 |

**Table 4: The top three items selected by the eBay ranker, the category-based approach and the LDA based approach for query *fossil*.**

The figure on the bottom in Figure 4 shows the difference of average satisfaction on queries of low ambiguity. As we expected, the difference of average satisfaction on this type of queries is smaller because they are in general less ambiguous. The category-based approach performs badly on this type of queries due to the coarse granularity of the subtrees in the eBay product taxonomy. The LDA-based approaches are still very effective in showing diverse items in the search results and is the only method that is statistically better than the eBay ranker. The third row in Table 2 shows the mean average satisfaction of different approaches on queries of low ambiguity, both the LDA model and the MB-LDA model perform the best and improve the eBay ranker by around 4% on mean average satisfaction.

## 5.4 The number of user intents

In our last analysis, we investigate how the number of user intents affects the performance of the LDA-based approach. We run the MB-LDA model with 10 and 20 topics and plot the difference of average satisfaction against the eBay ranker in Figure 5. The MB-LDA (K=10) model outperforms the MB-LDA (K=20) model early in the ranking, but becomes worse afterwards. The MB-LDA model with more topics discovers more specific user intents, but these user intents are sometimes too specific to users and are not as effective as more abstract user intents. For example in query *fossil*, it would be less effective to display a men watch and a women watch if only two slots are allowed to show diverse items. However, as we have more slots to show the diverse items in the search result page, more specific user intents become better in satisfying users with a particular interest. Depending on the number of slots we have to show the diverse items in the search result page, we can adjust the number of

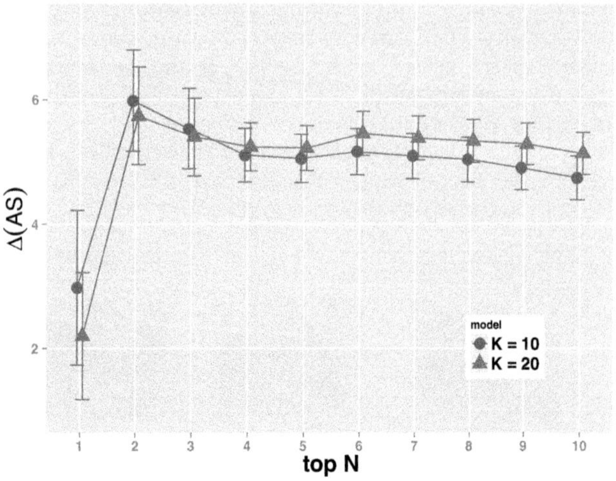


**Figure 5: The mean and 95% CI of the difference of average satisfaction for the MB-LDA model with 10 and 20 user intents on all testing queries.**

topics in the LDA model accordingly to achieve better user satisfaction.

Given the analyses we have done so far, we try to give some insights on when users benefit the most from introducing the diversity in the search results and which diversified retrieval approach we should apply. On queries of high ambiguity, introducing diversity in the search result page can improve user satisfaction significantly, while the gain is generally less on queries of low ambiguity. Out of all the queries we examine, there are about 15% queries where the LDA-based approach provides 10% or more average satisfaction than the eBay ranker, and there are only 5% queries where the LDA-based approach does worse. The LDA-based approach is preferred when the item titles of the query are descriptive and relatively noisy-free and the granularity of the subtrees in the product taxonomy associated with the query is coarse. On the other hand, the category-based approach is preferred when the product taxonomy is well designed and its granularity is fine-grained.

# 6. RELATED WORK

Carbonell and Goldstein [5] first looked into the problem of diversity in document summarization. They proposed the Maximal Marginal Relevance (MMR) approach where items are ranked by a linear combination of their relevance and novelty. Along this line of research, Zhang et al. [29] proposed different measures to compute redundancy in adaptive information filtering system. Guo and Sanner [11] derived a probabilistic latent view of the MMR that can balance relevance and diversity automatically. Instead of ranking items by the marginal function, [4, 6] maintain a probability of relevance conditioned on the previously selected documents and update it whenever a new document is selected. Bookstein [4] updated this probability of relevance using user feedback. Chen and Karger [6] proposed the *1-greedy* approach which updates the probability of relevance by treating all previously selected documents as irrelevant.

Another line of research used the Markov walk on a graph to select the diverse items. This approach first converts the problem into a graph where each item is a node in the graph and the edge, measuring the similarity between two items, defines the transition probability. Then the diverse items are selected based on different criterions, including the information richness [28], a reinforced random walk [15] and an absorbing random walk [30]. Instead of calculating the weight of the edge with some specific function, Dubey et al. [8] learned the edge weights from data and then selected the center nodes that maximize the entropy of the conductance between the center nodes and the rest of the graph.

The above approaches work without assuming an existing taxonomy of the data. Diversified retrieval based on an existing taxonomy has also been studied in different settings. Zhai et al. [26, 27] formalized the problem of diversity as subtopic retrieval where the goal is to find documents that cover many different subtopics of a query. Yue and Joachims [25] assumed the topic coverage of a document is unknown and proposed a structural SVM framework to learn a mapping from words in a document to the topic coverage. This approach penalizes low diversity in the loss function of the structural SVM. Li et al. [13] extended the structural SVM framework by explicitly adding constraints for diversity, coverage and balance respectively and learning a function to select a subset of sentences for document summarization. Ziegler et al. [31] applied topic diversification in book recommendation where they measured the similarity between two product sets based on the taxonomy and demonstrated that the users prefer diversified recommendations. Agrawal et al. [1] studied the problem of answering ambiguous web queries and proposed a greedy approach *IA-Select* to minimize the risk of dissatisfaction of the average user. Different from previous work, it takes into account both the importance of a category and the relevance of a document for a category. Welch et al. [24] proposed a search diversification algorithm where the users require multiple relevant documents to satisfy their needs.

Only a few approaches have addressed the diversity in online search engines. Gollapudi and Sharma [9] pointed out it is key to understand user intents in designing an effective ranking system in the search engine. They proposed a set of axioms for result diversification, provided three diversification objectives based on these axioms and demonstrated its effectiveness on semantic and product disambiguation. Radlinski and Dumais [17] used related search to address the diversity in personalized web search. Their approach first finds the related queries of the search query and then outputs a combination of the results from the related queries. Vee et al. [22] studied the problem of diversity in online shopping applications. They assumed each item is in the form of attribute-value pairs and the goal is to find an ordering of attributes to maximize diversity. Radlinski et al. [18] learned a diverse ranking of documents using multi-armed bandits. Their approach works in an online fashion where it requires user feedback in the form of clicks. Brandt et al. [9] proposed a dynamic ranking framework where the search engine dynamically generates the rankings based on user feedback.

# 7. CONCLUSION

We develop a Latent Dirichlet Allocation based diversified retrieval approach to address the unique challenges of product search on e-commerce sites. We also propose a Multivariate Bernoulli LDA model to target the short text without duplicates in the e-commerce data. To evaluate the quality of the search results, an offline metric *average satisfaction* is proposed to measure user satisfaction. Our empirical study on the eBay data shows that the LDA model can discover meaningful user intents and the LDA-based approach outperforms the eBay production ranker and three other diversified retrieval approaches. In particular, our approach can improve the eBay production ranker on average satisfaction by as much as 6% on average and more than 10% on the ambiguous queries. Finally, we shed light on when a diversified retrieval approach should be applied and which diversified retrieval approach we should use so that users can benefit the most from introducing the diversity in the search results on e-commerce sites.

For future work, we would like to extend the LDA model to include other item-level metadata and to train the LDA model on other types of user behavior data to further improve user satisfaction. In addition, we would like to evaluate user feedback on including the "See more items like this" option in the search result page.

## Acknowledgments

We would like to thank Daniel Miranda and Nadia (Ghamrawi) Vase for their helps on the eBay title relevance model.

## 8. REFERENCES

[1] R. Agrawal, S. Gollapudi, A. Halverson, and S. Ieong. Diversifying search results. In *WSDM*, pages 5–14, 2009.

[2] A. Anagnostopoulos, A. Z. Broder, and D. Carmel. Sampling search engine results. In *WWW*, pages 245–256, 2005.

[3] D. M. Blei, A. Ng, and M. Jordan. Latent dirichlet allocation. *JMLR*, 3:993–1022, 2003.

[4] A. Bookstein. Information retrieval: A sequential learning process. *Journal of the American Society for Information Science*, 34(5):331–342, 1983.

[5] J. Carbonell and J. Goldstein. The use of mmr, diversity-based reranking for reordering documents and reproducing summaries. In *SIGIR*, 1998.

[6] H. Chen and D. R. Karger. Less is more: probabilistic models for retrieving fewer relevant documents. In *SIGIR*, pages 429–436, 2006.

[7] C. L. Clarke, M. Kolla, G. V. Cormack, O. Vechtomova, A. Ashkan, S. Büttcher, and I. MacKinnon. Novelty and diversity in information retrieval evaluation. In *SIGIR*, pages 659–666, 2008.

[8] A. Dubey, S. Chakrabarti, and C. Bhattacharyya. Diversity in ranking via resistive graph centers. In *KDD*, pages 78–86, 2011.

[9] S. Gollapudi and A. Sharma. An axiomatic approach for result diversification. In *WWW*, pages 381–390, 2009.

[10] T. L. Griffiths and M. Steyvers. Finding scientific topics. *PNAS*, 101:5228–5235, 2004.

[11] S. Guo and S. Sanner. Probabilistic latent maximal marginal relevance. In *SIGIR*, pages 833–834, 2010.

[12] M. Hoffman, D. M. Blei, and F. Bach. Online learning for latent dirichlet allocation. In *NIPS*, pages 856–864, 2010.

[13] L. Li, K. Zhou, G.-R. Xue, H. Zha, and Y. Yu. Enhancing diversity, coverage and balance for summarization through structure learning. In *WWW*, pages 71–80, 2009.

[14] M. R. McLaughlin and J. L. Herlocker. A collaborative filtering algorithm and evaluation metric that accurately model the user experience. In *SIGIR*, pages 329–336, 2004.

[15] Q. Mei, J. Guo, and D. Radev. Divrank: the interplay of prestige and diversity in information networks. In *KDD*, pages 1009–1018, 2010.

[16] D. P. Putthividhya. ebay's internal report. 2011.

[17] F. Radlinski and S. Dumais. Improving personalized web search using result diversification. In *SIGIR*, pages 691–692, 2006.

[18] F. Radlinski, R. Kleinberg, and T. Joachims. Learning diverse rankings with multi-armed bandits. In *ICML*, pages 784–791, 2008.

[19] S. E. Robertson. Readings in information retrieval. chapter The probability ranking principle in IR, pages 281–286. Morgan Kaufmann Publishers Inc., 1997.

[20] J. Teevan, S. T. Dumais, and E. Horvitz. Characterizing the value of personalizing search. In *SIGIR*, pages 757–758, 2007.

[21] A. Turpin and F. Scholer. User performance versus precision measures for simple search tasks. In *SIGIR*, pages 11–18, 2006.

[22] E. Vee, U. Srivastava, J. Shanmugasundaram, P. Bhat, and S. A. Yahia. Efficient computation of diverse query results. In *ICDE*, pages 228–236, 2008.

[23] Y. Wang, H. Bai, M. Stanton, W.-Y. Chen, and E. Y. Chang. Plda: Parallel latent dirichlet allocation for large-scale applications. In *AAIM*, pages 301–314, 2009.

[24] M. J. Welch, J. Cho, and C. Olston. Search result diversity for informational queries. In *WWW*, pages 237–246, 2011.

[25] Y. Yue and T. Joachims. Predicting diverse subsets using structural svms. In *Proceedings of the 25th international conference on Machine learning*, pages 1224–1231, 2008.

[26] C. Zhai, W. Cohen, and J. Lafferty. Beyond independent relevance: Methods and evaluation metrics for subtopic retrieval. In *SIGIR*, pages 10–17, 2003.

[27] C. Zhai and J. Lafferty. A risk minimization framework for information retrieval. *Information Processing and Management*, 42(1):31–55, 2006.

[28] B. Zhang, H. Li, Y. Liu, L. Ji, W. Xi, W. Fan, Z. Chen, and W.-Y. Ma. Improving web search results using affinity graph. In *SIGIR*, pages 504–511, 2005.

[29] Y. Zhang, J. Callan, and T. Minka. Novelty and redundancy detection in adaptive filtering. In *SIGIR*, pages 81–88, 2002.

[30] X. Zhu, A. B. Goldberg, J. V. Gael, and D. Andrzejewski. Improving diversity in ranking using absorbing random walks. In *HLT-NAACL*, pages 97–104, 2007.

[31] C.-N. Ziegler, S. M. McNee, J. A. Konstan, and G. Lausen. Improving recommendation lists through topic diversification. In *WWW*, pages 22–32, 2005.

## APPENDIX

## A. THE COLLAPSED GIBBS SAMPLER FOR MULTIVARIATE BERNOULLI LDA

Assume we have $D$ documents in the corpus, a vocabulary of size $V$ and a predefined number of topics $K$. Associated with each term $v$ in document $d$, there exists a topic assignment $Z_{d,v}$ and a term occurrence $W_{d,v}$ indicating whether term $v$ appears in document $d$. The topic proportion $\theta_d$ specifies a multinomial distribution of topics associated with document $d$ and the probability of occurrence $\beta_{k,v}$ specifies a Bernoulli distribution of term $v$ in topic $k$. $\alpha$ and $\eta$ are the hyper parameters of the prior distributions where $\theta$ and $\beta$ are generated from. The joint probability of the MB-LDA model is written as follows.

$$P(W, Z, \theta, \beta; \alpha, \eta)$$
$$= \prod_{k=1}^{K}\prod_{v=1}^{V} P(\beta_{k,v}; \eta) \prod_{d=1}^{D} P(\theta_d; \alpha) \prod_{v=1}^{V} P(Z_{d,v}|\theta_d) P(W_{d,v}|\beta_{Z_{d,v},v})$$

The collapsed Gibbs sampler integrates out the hidden variables $\theta$ and $\beta$ so that the Gibbs sampling converges faster. After integrating out $\theta$ and $\beta$, we get the following marginal probability.

$$P(W, Z; \alpha, \eta) = \prod_{d=1}^{D} \frac{\Gamma(\sum_{k=1}^{K}\alpha_k)}{\prod_{k=1}^{K}\Gamma(\alpha_k)} \frac{\prod_{k=1}^{K}\Gamma(n_{d,k,\cdot}^{\cdot} + \alpha_k)}{\Gamma(\sum_{k=1}^{K} n_{d,k,\cdot}^{\cdot} + \alpha_k)}$$
$$\prod_{k=1}^{K}\prod_{v=1}^{V} \frac{\Gamma(\eta_1 + \eta_0)}{\Gamma(\eta_1)\Gamma(\eta_0)} \frac{\Gamma(n_{\cdot,k,v}^{1} + \eta_1)\Gamma(n_{\cdot,k,v}^{0} + \eta_0)}{\Gamma(n_{\cdot,k,v}^{1} + \eta_1 + n_{\cdot,k,v}^{0} + \eta_0)} \quad (6)$$

where $n_{d,k,v}^{1}$ is 1 when term $v$ occurs in document $d$ and has topic assignment $k$ and is 0 otherwise. 1 on the superscript specify the occurrence of term $v$ in document $d$. We use $\cdot$ to indicate that we sum over all configurations of that variable. For example, $n_{\cdot,k,v}^{0}$ is the number of documents where term $v$ does not occur and has topic assignment $k$.

The collapsed Gibbs sampler approximates the conditional distribution $P(Z|W; \alpha, \eta)$ by sampling the topic assignment iteratively. More specifically, it samples the topic assignment $Z_{a,b}$ for term $b$ in document $a$ from the conditional distribution $P(Z_{a,b}|Z_{\neg(a,b)}, W; \alpha, \eta)$ while keeping the other topic assignments $Z_{\neg(a,b)}$ fixed. For topic $k'$, the conditional probability $P(Z_{a,b} = k'|Z_{\neg(a,b)}, W; \alpha, \eta)$ is proportional to the marginal distribution in Equation 6. Finally, the collapsed Gibbs sampler for the MB-LDA model can be written in the following simple form.

$$P(Z_{a,b} = k'|Z_{\neg(a,b)}, W; \alpha, \eta)$$
$$\propto (n_{a,k',\cdot}^{\cdot,\neg(a,b)} + \alpha_{k'}) \frac{n_{\cdot,k',b}^{W_{a,b},\neg(a,b)} + \eta_{W_{a,b}}}{n_{\cdot,k',b}^{\cdot,\neg(a,b)} + \eta_1 + \eta_0}$$

Once the collapsed Gibbs sampler converges, we can estimate the parameters $\theta$ and $\beta$ using the hidden topic assignments.

$$\theta_{d,k} = \frac{n_{d,k,\cdot}^{\cdot} + \alpha_k}{\sum_{k'=1}^{K} n_{d,k',\cdot}^{\cdot} + \alpha_{k'}}$$

$$\beta_{k,v} = \frac{n_{\cdot,k,v}^{1} + \eta_1}{n_{\cdot,k,v}^{1} + \eta_1 + n_{\cdot,k,v}^{0} + \eta_0}$$

## B. USER INTENTS OF MORE QUERIES

**Table 5: The user intents of query *keyboard, hello kitty, mirror,* and *timberland* using the MB-LDA model with 4 topics.**

**keyboard**

| | |
|---|---|
| *computer keyboard* | usb "cat-Keyboards, Mice & Pointing" black new dell hp gaming |
| *silicone keyboard* | "cat-Keyboards, Mice & Pointing" silicone usb roll foldable computer |
| *musical keyboard* | "cat-Electronic Instruments" electronic electric piano key 61 casio music yamaha |
| *keyboard combo* | "cat-Keyboards, Mice & Pointing" mouse combo wireless bluetooth mini logitech |

**hello kitty**

| | |
|---|---|
| *hello kitty watch* | watch "cat-Watches" girl quartz pcs wrist gift new lady |
| *hello kitty case* | case for iPhone cover "cat-Cell Phone Accessories" 4th 3rd |
| *hello kitty purse and bag* | bad pure "cat-Women's Handbags & Bags" tote handbag shoulder |
| *hello kitty necklace* | "cat-Animation Characters" necklace crystal girl gift fashion bow |

**mirror**

| | |
|---|---|
| *wall mirror* | wall "cat-Home Decor" decorative decor new vintage large |
| *antique mirror* | antique "cat-Decorative Arts" vintage wood with gold |
| *motorcycle mirror* | "cat-Motorcycle Parts" harley motorcycle chrome for honda black |
| *car mirror* | side car "cat-Car Exterior" view power door left rear |

**timberland**

| | |
|---|---|
| *timberland shirt* | men shirt size "cat-Men's Clothing" jacket new nwt |
| *timberland men boots* | boots "cat-Men's Shoes" men wheat work waterproof |
| *timberland women boots* | boots "cat-Women's Shoes" women leather new size |
| *timberland shoes* | "cat-Men's Shoes" shoes classic boat men brown |

# Supervised $N$-gram Topic Model

Noriaki Kawamae
NTT Comware
1-6 Nakase, Mihama-ku, Chiba, Japan
Japan 261-0023
kawamae@gmail.com

## ABSTRACT

We propose a Bayesian nonparametric topic model that represents relationships between given labels and the corresponding words/phrases, as found in supervised articles. Unlike existing supervised topic models, our proposal, supervised $N$-gram topic model (SNT), focuses on both the number of topics and power-law distribution in the word frequencies for topic-specific $N$-grams. To achieve this goal, SNT takes a Bayesian nonparametric approach to topic sampling; it assigns a topic to each token using Chinese restaurant process (CRP), and generates a word distribution jointly with the given variable in textual order, and then forms each $N$-gram word as a hierarchy of Pitman-Yor process (PYP) priors. CRP can help SNT to automatically estimate the appropriate number of topics, which impacts the quality of topic specific words, $N$-grams, and observed value distribution. Since PYP recovers the exact formulation of interpolated Kneser-Ney, one of the best smoothing approaches for $N$-gram language models, it can allow SNT to generate more interpretable $N$-grams that the alternatives. Experiments on labeled text data show that SNT is useful as a generative model for discovering more phrases that better complement human experts than existing alternatives and provide more domain specific knowledge. The results show that SNT can be applied to various tasks such as automatic annotation.

## Categories and Subject Descriptors

I.7 [**DOCUMENT AND TEXT PROCESSING**]: Document analysis

## Keywords

Nonparametric Bayes models, Nonparametric Dirichlet process, Topic models, Latent variable models, Graphical models, Sentiment analysis, $N$-gram topic model


*WSDM'14*, February 24–28, 2014, New York, New York, USA.
Copyright 2014 ACM 978-1-4503-2351-2/14/02 ...$15.00.
http://dx.doi.org/10.1145/2556195.2559895.

## 1. INTRODUCTION

Our goal is to enhance supervised topic models though the incorporation of $N$-grams. Text mining methods are needed to develop superior web services since more and more people are expressing their opinions of products and services to the extent that the volume of such opinions now exceeds the analysis capabilities of any individual. Among these tasks, sentiment analysis, which captures customer's opinions as expressed in text data, is becoming an important knowledge discovery approach, and is one of the most useful applications of topic models. This task aims to classify a text as exhibiting positive, negative or neutral sentiments [29] by extracting sentiments on each aspect of a product and the corresponding rating. Automatically discovering these sentiments from documents increases both the quality and the quantity of information available for marketing, decision making, and purchase recommendations; it decreases both the time and the cost required to collect information.

In practice, capturing both topics and polarities simultaneously is critical for sentiment analysis based on topic models. These models provide useful descriptions for the generative process underlying various data and have been applied for information retrieval, social network analysis, and collaborative filtering. Following this approach, more focus is being placed on systems that produce fine-grained sentiment analysis of recent articles [6, 18] to extract the desired information automatically.

While previous works are designed to detect the aspects discussed in the review articles and predict the sentiment of the writer toward each product, they are based on the bag of words approach, or try to detect $N$-gram phrases first and then later associate them with given labels. In general, $N$-gram phrases are expected to carry more meaning than the sum of the individual words and meaning can depend on context. For example, the isolated rating prediction approach will rate the sentiment 'high' uniformly for the phrases 'high quality' and 'high price', even though 'high' expresses a positive opinion in 'high quality' but a negative opinion in 'high price'. Although introducing phrases would make the topic models complicated, it is essential for applications that need to capture sentiments and detect them in a unified model.

Motivated by the above observations, we propose a topic model called Supervised $N$-gram Topic Model (SNT) to model word co-occurrence patterns jointly with given labels from supervised text, and form $N$-grams by concatenating consecutive words. This model aims to represent $N$-grams as a tree structure by taking the Pitman-Yor process (PYP) [17] and the Chinese restaurant process (CRP) [1] as Bayesian nonparametric approaches in which parameters are endowed with distributions which may themselves introduce new parameters ad infinitum; a tree can be viewed as an $N$-gram with $N$ set to infinity [24]. Since PYP is a generalization of the Dirichlet process (DP) [4], and one of the best smoothing methods for $N$-gram language models, we introduce PYP as a prior of word distributions to handle parameters of infinite dimension that are hierarchically associated each topic. SNT leverages the observed value, (e.g., rating score that each reviewer gave to the referred item according to the reviewer's preference in each review article) to accurately capture sentiment words so that topic discovery is influenced by the rating information. SNT uses CRP as non-parametric approach in deciding the number of topics rather than learning it from the given corpus itself since the quality of the topic-specific tree hierarchy of an $N$-gram depends on the number of topics.

We discuss the key advantages of SNT in terms of its theoretical contribution and its practical contribution.

**Theoretical contribution**: We show how to build $N$-grams in topic models, and derive an inference algorithm for this model by leveraging both DP, PYP, and the supervised label. Since these processes have the practical property of exchangeability, which permits the use of standard sampling algorithms for inference, we design an inference algorithm that allows SNT to form topic specific $N$-grams just like assigning customers to tables in CRP. Because PYP transforms the word frequencies to recover Kneser-Ney [11], one of the best smoothing methods for $N$-gram language models, PYP allows SNT to better handle natural language expressions.

**Practical contribution**: Our approach is designed to detect phrases by modeling the joint distribution of words and their supervised value, and discretizing values such as rating, timestamps, and temperature; the conventional gradual approaches detect $N$-grams based on their frequencies or natural language tools, and then correlate them with these values. Since this task is done without using any prior knowledge or domain-specific dictionaries, our model is applicable to automatic rating annotation and rating-based item retrieval. Because new words continue to arise in consumer-generated content, the maintenance of dictionaries consumes time and manpower. SNT can be applied to capture meaningful phrases over the supervised labels of other continuous variables in a similar manner.

We demonstrate the efficacy of SNT through experiments and show that it can detect sentiment/temporal phrases in the articles, and thus well complement human experts and provide more domain specific knowledge.

# 2. PREVIOUS WORKS

## 2.1 Sentiment analysis

Sentiment analysis aims to extract customer attitudes and feeling from their unstructured reviews by distinguishing subjective information from the other information; it has become one of the most mature applications of supervised topic models. For example, Multi-grain Topic Model (MG-LDA) [23] extends the conventional topic model by using sliding windows to induce multi-grain topics. Latent Aspect Rating Analysis (LARA) [27] aims at analyzing opinions expressed in each review at the level of topical aspects to discover each reviewer's latent rating on each aspect as well as the relative importance weight on different aspects when forming the overall judgment. Latent Evaluation Topic model (LET) [8] focuses on the difference between writers' preferences to predict which item each writer will select and how he/she will evaluate it, based on reviews of like-minded consumers.

While these models consider a continuous value, some supervised topic models employ user supervision to discover relationships among hidden topics, and these labels [19]. Since $N$-gram phrases are much more crucial in determining the topics than their individual words, the models that consider $N$-grams would be more effective in information extraction applications. Brody and Elhadad [3] propose to detect aspect-specific opinion words by taking into account the influence of aspect on sentiment polarity. MaxEnt-LDA [30] tries to jointly capture both aspect and opinion words within topic models; it allows non-adjective opinion words.

## 2.2 Topic models

Bigram topic model (BTM) [25] incorporates the concept of topic into bigram models on the basis of the hierarchical Dirichlet language model [14]. By introducing a latent variable that denotes if a bigram can be formed with the previous token, Topical $N$-grams (TNG) model [28] extends BTM to $N$-grams and so reflects dependency on nearby context. Both models could be extended to support sentiment analysis by adding more variables and their relationships based on reasonable assumptions. Multi-Aspect Topic Model (MAS) [22] extends MG-LDA to aggregate sentiment texts for each rating aspect extracted from MG-LDA. Although these models discover co-occurrence information from the text, they do not explicitly separate aspect and opinion words, and fail to capture the power-law distribution in the frequencies of word tokens [5].

Supervised topic models are likely to be applicable to sentiment analysis by slightly modifying them. For example, Labeled LDA [19] constrains LDA by defining a one-to-one correspondence between its latent topics and observed labels to directly learn word-label correspondences. Identifying Sentiments over $N$-gram (ISN) [10] is an extension of both Switch Topics over Time (sTOT) [9] and TNG, and forms higher-order $N$-grams approximately by simply concatenating consecutive words (2-gram) based on dirichlet distributions, like previous $N$-gram models. However, these models fail to leverage an appropriate smoothing method to form $N$-grams ($N > 2$). One implementation problem is that these models require more available memory for a one machine to store $N$-grams (i.e., $\#words^N$ ) and higher computation costs to burn in the Gibbs sampling. Conventional topic models need to consider the appropriate smoothing methods to describe the gross statistical properties of linguistic data beyond the capacity of most human ability, while these models have advantages that improve themselves by including additional knowledge in a principled manner.

## 2.3 Nonparametric Bayesian Approach

By developing models that can generically exhibit power laws, it may be possible to create methods that can better identify the appropriate structure in text data. In this setting, it is natural to consider sets of Dirichlet processes (DP) [4], which provide a nonparametric prior for unknown probability distributions and the number of mixture components within each group in Bayesian nonparametric modeling. This process generates probability distributions, while the Dirichlet distribution generates multinomial parameter vectors and then a distribution over discrete categories. The Pitman-Yor process (PYP) is a two-parameter generalization of the DP. While Phrase Discovering LDA (PDLDA) [13] extends TNG by incorporating PYP hierarchy into the process of forming phrases, the change-point variable prevents this model from applying the nonparametric approach in learning the number of topics directly, and also requires more memory to store these variables.

SNT uses the Pitman-Yor process as prior distributions to represent a word distribution to capture both supervised labels and their corresponding words/phrases from labeled articles, while previous models use the Dirichlet-multinomial distributions. Consequently, SNT overcomes several inherent limitations and weaknesses of conventional topic models: how to select the appropriate number of topics and how to incorporate the power-law distribution in the word frequencies.

# 3. NONPARAMETRIC BAYESIAN STATISTICS

## 3.1 Chinese restaurant process (CRP)

The Chinese restaurant process (CRP) [1, 5], can be taken as a prior distribution over topics, as CRP is a stochastic process that generates partitions of integers and is used in nonparametric DP [15]. CRP is described using the metaphor of a restaurant with an infinite number of tables, each of which has infinite seating capacity. Assume that the tables are numbered in sequence, and $z_i$ indicates the table at which the $i$-th customer sits. The probability of choosing an occupied table is proportional to the number of people already sitting downi $n_*$, and the probability of choosing an unoccupied table is proportional to some constant parameter. That is, the first customer sits at the first table, $z_1$=1, and the $i$-th customer chooses a table according to the following distribution,

$$p(z_i = k|\mathbf{z}_{\backslash i}, \alpha) = \begin{cases} \frac{n_k}{i-1+\alpha}, \text{if } k \text{ is already occupied,} \\ \frac{\alpha}{i-1+\alpha}, \text{if } k \text{ is an adjoining unoccupied table,} \end{cases} \quad (1)$$

where $\mathbf{z}_{\backslash i}$ is the seating arrangement of the current $i$-1 customers, and $n_k$ is the number of current customers sitting at table $k$ in the current seating arrangement, and $\alpha$ $(0 \leq \alpha)$ is a parameter of the process that determines how "spread out" the customers become. Therefore, CRP can describe the marginal probabilities of DP in terms of a random partition obtained from a sequence of customers sitting at tables in a restaurant. After all customers select a table and sit down, we obtain a partition of integers, which exhibits the same clustering structures as drawn from a Dirichlet process [4]. The sequence generated by this process, $w_1, ...w_{n-1}$, is exchangeable, and is invariant to permutation of the order of the word sequence.

## 3.2 Pitman-Yor process (PYP)

A power law is a mathematical relationship between two quantities, and known as Zipf's law [31] in linguistics. For instance, the probability that word $w$ will occur with frequency $n_w$ in a sufficiently large corpus, $p(n_w)$, is given by

$$p(n_w) \propto n_w^{-k}, \quad (2)$$

where $k$ is a constant parameter. PYP defines the Dirichlet process, which performs nonparametric estimation in a Bayesian framework by defining a prior distribution on an infinite-dimensional parameter space (the set of probability measures over a given domain). This makes PYP$(\gamma, d, B)$ a distribution over distributions over a probability space, where $\gamma$, $d$, and $B$ are a concentration parameter $\gamma > -d$, a discount parameter that controls the power-law property of the distribution $0 \leq d < 1$, and a base distribution over a probability space and can be understood as a mean parameter of draws from PYP$(\gamma, d, B)$, respectively. For each word $w \in W$, let $G(w)$ be the estimated probability of $w$, and let $G = [G(w)]_{w \in W}$ be the vector of word probabilities. We place a PYP prior on $G_0$ and then obtain $G$:

$$G \sim PYP(\gamma, d, G_0), \quad w \sim G, \quad (3)$$

where $G_0(= [G_0(w)]_{w \in W})$ is the base probability measure of $G$; it is taken to be the mean of draws from $PYP(\gamma, d, G_0)$. When $d = 0$, it becomes the Dirichlet process. Teh [20] showed that interpolated Kneser-Ney [11]can be interpreted as a particular approximate inference scheme in the hierarchical Pitman-Yor language model.

The procedure of generating draws $G \sim PYP(\gamma, d, G_0)$ can be described using the CRP metaphor, like Eq (1). The newly introduced parameters $d$ and $\gamma$ show the effect of smoothing, and yield a power-law; that is, the first customer sits at the first table, $z_1$=1, and the $i-th$ customer chooses a table according to the following distribution,

$$p(z_i = k|\mathbf{z}_{\backslash i}, \gamma, d) = \begin{cases} \frac{n_k - d}{i-1+\gamma}, \text{if } k \text{ is already occupied,} \\ \frac{\gamma + dK}{i-1+\gamma}, \text{if } k \text{ is an adjoining unoccupied table,} \end{cases} \quad (4)$$

where $K$ is the current number of occupied tables; this process is also exchangeable like CRP. When the number of tables increases as many customers enter the restaurant with $d > 0$, this discount parameter yields a power-law. That is, PYP allows outcomes to obey a power-law distribution: a few outcomes have very high probability while most outcomes occur with low probability, where the probability of a set of outcomes is not affected by their ordering [1].

# 4. SUPERVISED $N$-GRAM MODELING

## 4.1 Overview

In this subsection, we describe SNT, it takes a Bayesian nonparametric approach and extends topic models by representing $N$-grams as a tree hierarchy of the context, Table 1 shows the notations used in this paper; Figure 1 shows a graphic model of SNT. Like other conventional topic models, SNT models each review text as a mixture of underlying topics and generates each word from one topic. Unlike those models, SNT considers word order, and the interdependency between specific words and specific rating in a

**Table 1: Notations used in this paper**

| SYMBOL | DESCRIPTION |
|---|---|
| $D(K, W)$ | number of documents (topics, words) |
| $N_j$ | number of word tokens in document $j$ |
| $v_j$ | the rating associated with document $j$ |
| $z_{ji}$ | the topic associated with the $i$th token in document $j$ |
| $w_{ji}$ | the $i$th token in document $j$ |
| $r_{ji}$ | the switch associated with the $i$th token in $j$ |
| $u$ | word sequence (phrase) $w_{1:n-1\|k} = w_{1\|k}, ..., w_{n-1\|k}$ |
| $\|u\|$ | the length of $u$ |
| $u\backslash$ | word sequence $w_{2:n-1\|k} = w_{2\|k}, ..., w_{n-1\|k}$ |
| $G_b$ | the word distribution of a given corpus |
| $G_k$ | the topic $k$ specific word distribution |
| $G_k^u$ | the $u$ specific word distribution in topic $k$ |
| $\theta_j$ | the document $j$ specific word distribution |
| $\alpha$ | the Dirichlet parameter:$\alpha \sim Gamma(a, b)$ |
| $\beta, \omega, \delta, \epsilon$ | the fixed parameters of symmetric Dirichlet priors of $(\phi, \varphi, \psi, \mu)$ |
| $d_n$ | the discount parameter:$d_n \sim Beta(e_n, f_n)$ |
| $\gamma_n$ | the concentration parameter: $\gamma_j \sim Gamma(g_j, h_j)$ |

text, to detect topic specific $N$-grams as subjective information. This is necessary as the same phrase could have a different meaning in different topics. For example, "small size" and "light weight" are positive aspects of mobile devices, although these phrases are negative aspects of fruits. To handle this difficulty, this model takes a Bayesian nonparametric approach to avoid the weakness of conventional topic models: the need to select an appropriate number of topics and the lack of power-law distribution in the word frequencies.

The motivation for modeling ideas in the nonparametric setting is the property of taking the building blocks provided by simple stochastic processes such as the Dirichlet process; it allows us to construct models that exhibit richer kinds of probabilistic structure. By placing this prior over a given word distribution recursively, SNT generates $N$-gram words as a tree hierarchy of Pitman-Yor process priors [20], where this model defines $N$-gram word probabilities over the current word given the various contexts formed by up to N-1 words. Additionally, SNT takes the non-parametric approach when learning the number of topics since the quality of topic-specific tree hierarchy of $N$-grams depends eventually on the number of topics.

## 4.2 ISN

ISN extends topic models to form $N$-grams through the concatenation of consecutive topics, where topic discovery is influenced by not only word co-occurrence but also rating information. This model incorporates $v_j$ in each token, empowers a switch variable $r_{ji}$ to handle more status in word generation and connect the current topic with the previous topic. For distinguishing these differences in word tokens, ISN defines $r$ as a switch for handling more kinds of statuses as follows. If $r_{ji}$=0 (1), ISN generates word $w_{ji}$ from the background word distribution $\phi_b$ (the document-specific word distribution $\phi_d$). If $r_{ji}$=2 (3), ISN selects topic $z_{ji}$ from the document-specific topic distribution $\theta_j$ (the previous topic $z_{ji-1}$ specific topic distribution $\psi_{\bar{z}}$), and then generates word $w_{ji}$ from topic-specific word distribution $\phi_z$ (this current topic and previous word-specific word distribution $\varphi_{w_{ji-1}z_{ji}}$). These approaches allow ISN to predict the absolute supervised value of a labeled text, and, conversely, the word/phrase distribution given a rating.

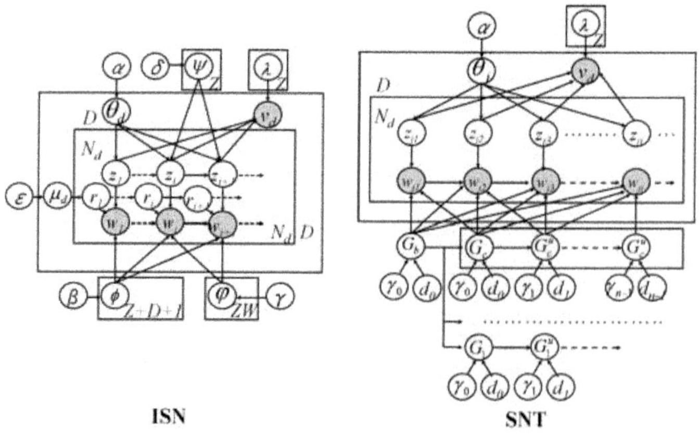


**Figure 1: Graphic Model of ISN and SNT: In this figure, shaded and unshaded variables indicate observed and latent variables, respectively. An arrow indicates a conditional dependency between variables and stacked panes indicate a repeated sampling with the iteration number shown. Intuitively, SNT is a unified probabilistic model that 1) captures the interdependency between rating $v$ and the corresponding word $w$ using $\lambda$ via $z$, and 2) handles the generating process of a word in each token, and then 3) generates both word and rating using the continuity between previous words and the current topic.**

## 4.3 SNT

### *4.3.1 Topic distributions using CRP*

For document $j$, SNT draws a mixing topic proportion $\theta_j$ from a Dirichlet with parameter $\alpha$. For $i$-th token in $j$, topic $z_{ji}$ is drawn from $\theta_j$, and word $w_{ji}$ is then drawn from $z_{ji}$ in proportional to $G_k^u$, $G_k$, or $G_b$. As was done for previous topic models, $\theta_j$ are analytically marginalized. That is, SNT represents the distribution over topics in each document by using CRP, which can partition the data into several clusters without requiring the number of clusters to be set in advance. This property means that our model determines the appropriate number of topics, and then samples each topic by Eq. (1).

We describe a generative process procedure analogous to CRP, which handles the marginal probabilities of DP in terms of a random partitioning obtained from a sequence of customers sitting at tables in a restaurant. That is, if $z_{ji}$ is the index of the table chosen by the $i$-th customer in restaurant $j$, then

$$p(z_{ji} = k|\mathbf{z}_{\backslash ji}, \alpha) = \begin{cases} (\frac{n_{jk\backslash ji}}{n_{j\backslash ji}+\alpha}), & \text{if } k \text{ is already occupied,} \\ (\frac{\alpha_j}{n_{j\backslash ji}+\alpha}), & \text{if } k \text{ is an adjoining unoccupied table} \end{cases} \quad (5)$$

where $n_{j\backslash ji}$ represents the number of all tokens in document $j$, except $w_{ji}$, $n_{jk\backslash ji}$ represents the number of tokens assigned to topic $k$ in document $j$, except $w_{ji}$. The hyper parameters, $\alpha$ in this equation can be estimated by auxiliary variable sampling [15], where $\alpha$ is a parameter of the process determining how "spread out" the customers have become.

Since we are interested in associating words/phrases with a given supervised value via each topic, SNT incorporates, for supervision, value $v$ on each topic by simply constraining the topic model to use only those topics that correspond to this value; supervised latent Dirichlet allocation (sLDA) [2], on the other hand, aims to relate words to this value via a sequence of topics. Here, SNT uses the beta distribution to describe rating $v$ in each document and associates this distribution with words on each topic, where all ratings are normalized to the range of 0 to 1; a Gaussian distribution would take a wider range. This distribution allows SNT to set both continuous and discrete values of articles on the topic level; discrete values can be easily converted into a beta distribution.

To simultaneously achieve dimensionality reduction in the presentation of words and the determination of its corresponding rating, we combine words and a given rating via topics using the beta distribution. Accordingly, the probability of rating $v_j$ on $z_{ji} = k$ is given by

$$p(v_j|\lambda_k) = \frac{v_j^{\lambda_k^1 - 1}(1-v_j)^{\lambda_k^2 - 1}}{B(\lambda_k^1, \lambda_k^2)}$$
$$\lambda_k^1 = (1 - \bar{v}_k)(\frac{\bar{v}(1-\bar{v}_k)}{s_k^2} - 1), \lambda_k^2 = \bar{v}_k(\frac{\bar{v}_k(1-\bar{v}_k)}{s_k^2} - 1) \quad (6)$$

where $B$ is the beta function with $k$ specific shape parameters $\lambda_k^1$ and $\lambda_k^2$, and $\bar{v}_k$ ($s_k^2$) is the sample mean (the biased sample variance) of the rating assigned to topic $k$.

### 4.3.2 Word distributions on Pitman-Yor

SNT places PYP as a prior distribution over the word probabilities, as PYP recovers the exact formulation of interpolated Kneser-Ney, one of the best smoothing methods for $N$-gram language models [20]. By placing this prior over a given word distribution recursively, SNT generates $N$-gram words by using the hierarchical Pitman-Yor topic process, where this model defines $N$-gram word probabilities over the current word given the various contexts yielded by up to $n$-1 words. To form $N$-gram, SNT samples a word hierarchically as follows: First, we consider unigram word distributions, $G_b$, using PYP as the prior and base distribution $G_0$. $G_b$ is the vector of probabilities over the current word without knowledge of prior information and is assigned to topic $k$=0, while $G_0$ is a uniform distributions over fixed vocabulary $W$ of $V$ words. By placing prior $G_0$ on $G_b(= [G_b(w)]_{w \in W})$, we can gain this distribution:

$$G_b \sim PYP(\gamma_0, d_0, G_0), \quad (7)$$

where $G_0$ is the global mean vector given a uniform value of $G_0(w) = 1/W$ for all $w \in W$. This is one new approach to introducing a base word distribution of a given review corpus; it distinguishes the role of words in each review and better detects sentiment phrases than existing schemes.

Given $G_b$ and current topic $k$, we obtain a topic specific unigram distribution over words $G_k$: By placing prior $G_b$ on $G_k$, we can gain $G_k(= [G_k(w)]_{w \in W})$:

$$G_k \sim PYP(\gamma_0, d_0, G_b). \quad (8)$$

SNT differs from PDLDA in that hierarchical PYP has a parent node $G_b$ that represents the background topic distribution instead of a uniform distribution over words, so $G_b$ can absorb words shared by various topics.

To form $N$-gram word distributions over each topic, we extend the Chinese restaurant franchise [21] by regarding each topic as the restaurant owner. For example, each $G_k^u$ has a corresponding restaurant indexed by (the sequence of words) $u$ and is managed by owner (topic) $k$, where $G_k^u$ is the conditional probability of $w$ following $u$ and $u$ is the sequence of the prior $n-1$ words in topic $k$, $w_{1:n-1|k} = w_{1|k}, ..., w_{n-1|k}$. Customers in the restaurant are drawn from $G_k^u$, tables are drawn from its base distribution $G_k^{u\backslash}$, and dishes are the values drawn from $W$, where $u\backslash$ is the sequence obtained by dropping the first word $w_{1|k}$ in $u$. By placing PYP as a prior distribution over the word probabilities, SNT defines each $N$-gram as being drawn from the same successive topic assignments in each document, and is terminated by $k$=0, a change of topic, or punctuation. By induction, we reach the distribution over current word given $N$-1 gram phrase $w_{1:n-1|k} = w_{1|k}, ..., w_{n-1|k}$ in topic $k$; $G_k^u(= [G_k^u(w)]_{w \in W})$ using the hierarchical Pitman-Yor process:

$$G_k^u \sim PYP(\gamma_{n-1}, d_{n-1}, G_k^{u\backslash}). \quad (9)$$

The concentration and discount parameters are functions of the length, $n-1$, of the phrase, $u\backslash$. Following this notion, we represent $\gamma_k$ ($\gamma_b$), and $d_k$ ($d_b$) with $\gamma_0$, and $d_0$, respectively, as the length of their $|u|$ is 0. In Eq (9), the mean vector is $G_k^{u\backslash}$, the vector of probabilities of the current word given all but the 1-st word in the phrase. By recursively placing a prior over $G_k^{u\backslash}$ using the Eq (9), we can gain $G_k^{u\backslash}$ with parameters $\gamma_{n-2}$, $d_{n-2}$, the base probability measure $G_k^{u\backslash\backslash}$ instead. This operation is repeated until we get background word distribution $G_b$ that corresponds $k = 0$; it is the vector of probabilities over the current word without knowledge of prior information, and is rating invariant. This setting of the prior structure supports the idea that both words appearing later in a context and their order play an important role in modeling the probability of the current word and so we should connect them to form an $N$-gram.

### 4.3.3 N-gram probability

SNT defines automatically the length of each $N$-gram by employing a document-token specific changepoint $r_{ji}$ that explicitly models where each $N$-gram starts and ends in each $j$, while TNG and PDLDA assume the probability of change point $c_i$ if the $i$-th token depends on the current topic $z_{ji}$ and the previous word $w_{ji-1}$ that indicates the bigram status. When $r_{ji} = 0$ and $z_{ji} = k$, $w_{ji}$ is drawn from a topic $k$ unigram distribution. When $r_{ji} = 1$, $z_{ji} = k$, and $w_{ji-1} = w$, $w_{ji}$ is drawn from a topic $k$ distribution conditioned on the previous word $w$. When $r_{ji} = |u|$, $z_{ji} = ... = z_{ji-u} = k$, $u(= w_{i-u:i-1|k} = w_{i-u|k}, ..., w_{i-1|k}$, $w_{ji}$ is drawn from a topic specific distribution conditioned on the previous word sequence $u$ and forms new word sequence $w_{i-u:i|k} = w_{i-u|k}, ..., w_{i|k}$. This is repeated until we get the start of a new $N$-gram (e.g. $r_{ji+1} = 0$ after $r_{ji} = |u|$) or the change of topic(e.g. $z_{ji+1} \neq z_{ji}$). Given a set of a sequences, each with up to $N$-1 words with consecutive numbers in the same topic, SNT forms an $N$-gram by concatenating these consecutive words.

For each $w$ and $u$, we define $c^k_{uwl}$, and $t^k_{uw}$ as the number of customers sitting at table $l$ and eating dish (word) $w$ in the restaurant $u$ managed by $k$ ($c^k_{uwl}$=0 if table $l$ does not serve dish $w$ in the restaurant $u$ run by $k$), and the number of tables serving dish $w$ in the same restaurant $u$ by $k$, respectively. Note that multiple tables may offer the same dish $w$. By denoting marginal counts by $\cdot$, $c^k_{u \cdot l}$ is the number of customers sitting at table $l$ in $u$ managed by $k$, $c^k_{uw\cdot}$ is the number of customers eating dish $w$ in $u$ run by $k$, $c^k_{u\cdot\cdot}$ is the number of customers in $u$ operated by $k$, and $t^k_{u\cdot}$ is the number of tables in $u$ owned by $k$.

Consequently, the next word $w$ drawn from $G^u_k$, $G_k$, and $G_b$ can be computed recursively as in

$$p^u_k(w) = \frac{C^k_{uw\cdot} - d_{n-1} t^k_{uw}}{C^k_{u\cdot\cdot} + \gamma_{n-1}} + \frac{\gamma_{n-1} + d_{n-1} t^k_{u\cdot}}{C^k_{u\cdot\cdot} + \gamma_{n-1}} p^{u\backslash}_k(w), \quad (10)$$

if $w$ appears after $N-1$ words in topic $k$ ($N$-gram)

$$p_k(w) = \frac{C^k_{\emptyset w\cdot} - d_0 t^k_{\emptyset w}}{C^k_{\emptyset\cdot\cdot} + \gamma_0} + \frac{\gamma_0 + d_0 t^k_{\emptyset\cdot}}{C^k_{\emptyset\cdot\cdot} + \gamma_0} p_b(w), \quad (11)$$

if $w$ appears in topic $k$ (>0) (unigram)

$$p_b(w) = \frac{C^b_{\emptyset w\cdot} - d_0 t^b_{\emptyset w}}{C^b_{\emptyset\cdot\cdot} + \gamma_0} + \frac{\gamma_0 + d_0 t^b_{\emptyset\cdot}}{C^b_{\emptyset\cdot\cdot} + \gamma_0} \frac{1}{W}, \quad (12)$$

if $w$ appears in background topic $k = 0$

where $C^k_{\emptyset w\cdot}$ represents the number of customers eating dish $w$ in restaurant $\emptyset$ (no previous word) managed by $k$, $C^b_{\emptyset w\cdot}$ represents the number of customers eating dish $w$ in $\emptyset$ (no previous word) managed in public restaurants, $C^k_{\emptyset\cdot\cdot}$ represents the number of customers in restaurant $\emptyset$ (no previous word) managed by $k$, and $C^b_{\emptyset\cdot\cdot}$ represents the number of customers in restaurant $\emptyset$ (no previous word) managed in public. Hyper parameters $\gamma_{n-1}$ ($\gamma_0$) and $d_{n-1}$ ($d_0$) in this equation can be estimated by auxiliary variable sampling [15]. Only a unigram is allowed at the beginning of a document, as this model can always generate a bigram depending on nearby context. Therefore, we use the next word ($i$>1) to constrain the topic assignment to be considered.

Note that $u$ is a sequence of ordered words and corresponds to topic $k$ in Eq (5). That is, the exchangeability of the PYP property holds good for $w$ on $u$ over the entire corpus; this property is effective over topic $k$ within each document.

Since each topic pattern and its rating value are assumed to have been generated conditional on topic $z$, the resulting beta and multinomial parameters will correspond. A rating score that has high probability under a certain topic, $z$, will likely contain the set of words that co-occurred with high probability in the same topic. Each new word/score is generated by again selecting from topic $z$ and repeating the entire process. Thus, we can view $z$ as a high level representation of the ensemble of word/rating pairs in terms of a probability distribution over the factors that each word/rating can be assembled from.

## 4.4 Inference in SNT

Approximate inferencing over hidden topic variables is performed by Gibbs sampling, as this sampling has been developed to handle large numbers of latent variables and parameters. As the graphical model shown in Figure 1, an overview of the generative procedure of SNT is as follows:

1. For each topic $k$ ($k = 1$ to $K$), draw $\lambda^1_z, \lambda^2_z$.
2. For each document $j$ ($j = 1$ to $D$), draw $z_{ji}$ using Eq (5) in each token ($i = 1$ to $N_j$)

If $z_{ji}$>K then $K+ = 1$ endif

increment counts $n_{jk}$ += 1; $n_k$ += 1;

- if $z_{ji}$=0 then draw $w_{ji}$ from Eq (12)
- elseif $z_{ji}$=$z_{j(i-1)}$ and $i > 1$ then draw $v_j$ from Eq (6) and draw $w_{ji}$ from Eq (10)
- else draw $v_j$ from Eq (6) and draw $w_{ji}$ from Eq (11)

increment counts $n_{kw}$ += 1;

update $C^b_{\emptyset w\cdot}$,$C^b_{\emptyset\cdot\cdot}$,$C^z_{\emptyset w\cdot}$,$C^z_{\emptyset\cdot\cdot}$,$C^z_{uw\cdot}$,$C^z_{u\cdot\cdot}$, $t^z_{bw}$,$t^z_{b\cdot}$,$t^z_{\emptyset w}$,$t^z_{\emptyset\cdot}$,$t^z_{uw}$, $t^z_{u\cdot}$, $\bar{v}_k$, and $\bar{s}^2_k$.

**Algorithm 1** Inference for SNT

// initialization
zero all count variables, $n_{jk}$,$n_k$,$C^k_{uwl}$,$t^k_{uw}$ and set $K$;
**for** $j = 1$ to $D$ **do**
  **for** $i = 1$ to $N_j$ **do**
    sample topic index $z_{ji} = k \sim Multinomial(1/K)$
    $n_{jk}$ += 1; $n_k$ += 1; $n_{kw}$ += 1;
  **end for**
**end for**
// Gibbs sampling over burn-in and sampling period
**for** iteration=1 to $N_{iteration}$ **do**
  **for** $j = 1$ to $D$ **do**
    **for** $i = 1$ to $N_j$ **do**
      // for the current assignment of $k$ in document $j$
      decrement counts $n_{jk}$ -= 1; $n_k$ -= 1;
      Call RemoveCustomer ($w$,$u$,$k$):
      // topic assignment
      draw $z_{ji}$ with probabilities proportional to
      $p(z_{ji} = k|\mathbf{z}_{\backslash ji}, \alpha) * p(v_j|\hat{\lambda}_{k1}, \hat{\lambda}_{k2})$
      $*\{p^u_k(w_{ji}), p_k(w_{ji}), p_b(w_{ji})\}$
      using Eq (5), (6), (10), (11), (12).
      // create a new topic
      **if** $k > K$ **then**
        $K = K + 1$
      **end if**
      Call AddCustomer ($w$,$u$,$k$):
      // for the new assignment of $k$ in document $j$
      increment counts $n_{jk}$ += 1; $n_k$ += 1;
    **end for**
    **for** $z = 1$ to $K$ **do**
      **if** $n_k$=0 **then**
        prune empty topic $k$
      **end if**
      update $\hat{\lambda}_{k1}, \hat{\lambda}_{k2}$ using $\bar{v}_k$, $s^2_k$, and Eq (6).
    **end for**
  **end for**
  update $\alpha$, $\gamma_n$, and $d_n$
**end for**

We can obtain a Gibbs sampler for SNT using CRP, where the seating arrangement for each restaurant consists of the number of customers, that of tables, the table where each customer sits, the dish served on each table, and the dish each customer eats. To facilitate the inference and realize it in as few iterations as possible while ensuring convergence, we consider only 1-gram at this stage.

As in the previous work [20], the sampler iterates over all customers in each restaurant, and resamples the table where each customer sits using two routines: RemoveCustomer and AddCustomer. The detail of the inference for SNT is shown

**Algorithm 2** Function: RemoveCustomer $(w,u,k)$ in Algorithm 1

**if** $k$=0 **then**
  decrement $C^b_{\emptyset w}$.
**else**
  remove a customer from $l-th$ table from $u$ with probabilities proportional to $C^k_{uwl}$ and decrement $C^k_{uwl}$
  **if** as a result the $l-th$ table becomes unoccupied **then**
    **if** $|u|$>0 **then**
      Call Remove customer $(w,u_{\setminus},k)$
    **else**
      decrement $C^b_{\emptyset w}$.
    **end if**
  **end if**
**end if**

**Algorithm 3** Function: AddCustomer $(w,u,k)$ in Algorithm 1

**if** $k_{new}$=0 **then**
  increment $C^b_{\emptyset w}$.
**else**
  sit a customer at $l-th$ table in $u$ with probability proportional to $max(0, C^k_{uwl}-d_{n-1})$ and increment $C^k_{uwl}$
  sit a customer at a new table $l_{new}$ serving $w$ in $u$ with probability proportional to $(\gamma_{n-1}+d_{n-1}t^k_{u\cdot})p^{u\setminus}_k(w)$ using Eq (10) and increment $t^k_{uw}$, and set $C^k_{uwl_{new}}=1$
  **if** $|u|$>0 **then**
    Call AddCustomer $(w,u_{\setminus},k)$
  **else**
    increment $C^b_{\emptyset w}$.
  **end if**
**end if**

in Algorithm (1), where we represent $C^k_{\emptyset wl}$, $\gamma_0$, $d_0$, $t^k_{\emptyset w}$, and $t^k_{\emptyset\cdot}$ with $C^k_{uwl}$, $\gamma_{n-1}$, $d_{n-1}$, $t^k_{uw}$, and $t^k_{u\cdot}$ for simplification. To reduce the number of iterations required to gain final convergence, we can sample a topic with the constraint of sampling only 1-grams until coverage is reached (2nd burn), and then form $N$-grams on a fixed topic assignment (e.g. skip topic assignment) in this inference.

# 5. EXPERIMENTS

## 5.1 Data sets

We focus here on the extraction of rating score/timestamps specific topics, and use the following data sets to evaluate against with previous models for quantitative evaluations using the metrics of mean absolute error(MAE).

Amazon review data[1]: This is the biggest public review data set currently available and is used often in sentiment analysis research [7, 12]. This data consists of 5686344 reviews and 3784413 unique words, where ALL denotes the entire data set, and DVD (Book, Music) denotes the data extracted using this item category from ALL.

Twitter data[2]: We selected tweets from 30/08/2012 to 29/01/2013, and gained a corpus consisting of 65,456,988 users and 321,513,597 tweets.

[1] Amazon Product Review Data (Huge): http://www.cs.uic.edu/~liub/FBS/sentiment-analysis.html
[2] Twitter: http://twitter.com

**Table 2: MAE comparison of sLDA, sTNG, sTOT, ISN, sPDLDA and SNT: Model based approaches (sLDA, LARA, sTNG, sTOT, sPDLDA and SNT) were learned with the number of topics $Z$ set at the optimal number learned by SNT and only unigram for a fair comparison. Results that differ significantly, t-test $p < 0.01$, $p < 0.05$, from ISN are marked with '**', '*' respectively.**

| sLDA | sTNG | sTOT | ISN | sPDLDA | SNT |
|---|---|---|---|---|---|
| DVD (Amazon) $Z=27$ | | | | | |
| 0.283 | 0.263 | 0.225 | 0.208 | 0.205 | 0.206 |
| Book (Amazon) $Z=35$ | | | | | |
| 0.245 | 0.253 | 0.206 | 0.193 | 0.185 | 0.178* |
| Music (Amazon) $Z=31$ | | | | | |
| 0.253 | 0.273 | 0.228 | 0.217 | 0.213 | 0.212* |
| ALL (Amazon) $Z=112$ | | | | | |
| 0.298 | 0.282 | 0.278 | 0.261 | 0.252 | 0.238* |
| Twitter $Z=125$ | | | | | |
| 0.363 | 0.327 | 0.312 | 0.321 | 0.310 | 0.311 |

In Amazon reviews, the rating score is a discrete value and varies from 1.0 to 5.0 in 0.5 increments. We normalized this value and assigned rating $v$ in the range [0,1] to each article, and then the timestamps, the, in the range [0,1] to each tweet in Twitter corpus. We split a string with all whitespace characters and non-word characters as delimiters, removed numbers, and the words that appeared less than five times in the corpus, as a preprocessing step.

We ran the experiments on 20 PCs with Dual Core 2.66 GHz Xeon processors and the number of Gibbs sampling iterations was set to 2000, where it takes less than an hour to run, and requires less than 200 iterations to burn (SNT requires 500 iterations additionally as a 2nd burn) in the sampler.

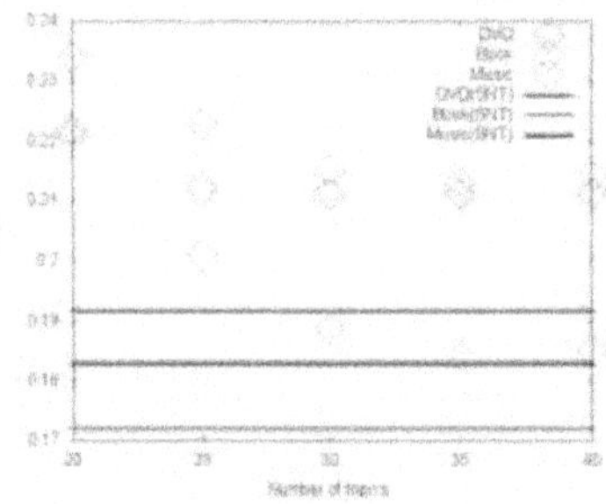

**Figure 2: MAE comparison of sPDLDA and SNT over 2-gram**

## 5.2 Quantitative Evaluation

The main goal of these experiments is to show that the $N$-gram phrases detected by our model are close to human-labeled phrases, and their quality improves as N is varied from 2 to 3.

First, we evaluated the rating prediction performance given the words/sentiment(temporal) words in a review. This evaluation aims to compare which model can infer the rating score most precisely from just the word distributions. In this case, we used 10-fold cross-validation which starts by partitioning; a single subsample is retained as the validation data for testing the models, and the remaining sub-

Table 3: MAE comparison of MR, sTNG, ISN, sPDLDA, rPDLDA, and SNT

| bigram | | | | | | trigram | | | | | |
|---|---|---|---|---|---|---|---|---|---|---|---|
| MR | sTNG | ISN | sPDLDA | rPDLDA | SNT | MR | sTNG | ISN | sPDLDA | rPDLDA | SNT |
| DVD | | | | | | | | | | | |
| 0.262 | 0.243 | 0.203 | 0.211 | 0.263 | 0.192* | 0.288 | 0.241 | 0.202 | 0.223 | 0.278 | 0.178** |
| Book | | | | | | | | | | | |
| 0,257 | 0.222 | 0.188 | 0.183 | 0.251 | 0.172** | 0.261 | 0.213 | 0.182 | 0.192 | 0.253 | 0.155** |
| Music | | | | | | | | | | | |
| 0.281 | 0.236 | 0.211 | 0.215 | 0.261 | 0.183** | 0.286 | 0.228 | 0.207 | 0.222 | 0.288 | 0.171** |
| ALL | | | | | | | | | | | |
| 0.293 | 0.277 | 0.275 | 0.268 | 0.295 | 0.197** | 0.295 | 0.282 | 0.287 | 0.272 | 0.302 | 0.191** |
| Twitter | | | | | | | | | | | |
| 0.313 | 0.221 | 0.203 | 0.211 | 0.286 | 0.166** | 0.327 | 0.198 | 0.182 | 0.215 | 0.316 | 0.152** |

samples are used as training data. This process is then repeated 10 times, with each of the 10 subsamples used exactly once as the validation data. Given a review (tweet), we predict its rating (timestamps) by choosing the discrete rating (timestamps) that maximizes the posterior, which is calculated by multiplying all the rating probabilities of word tokens/$N$-grams from a topic-wise Beta distribution over rating $v$ (timestamps $t$) $p(v(t)|\lambda_{k1}\lambda_{k2})$. As the baseline methods, we prepared supervised latent Dirichlet allocation (sLDA) [2], Topical $N$-grams (TNG) model [28], Switch Topics over Time (sTOT) [9], Phrasing Discovery LDA(PDLDA) [13], and Identifying Sentiments over $N$-gram (ISN) [10] as model-based approaches, and then measured the difference between the predicted v(t) and the correct value for all methods. In the experiment, TNG, ISN, and SNT were constrained in that no bigram was allowed for stop words or sentence/paragraph boundaries. As these models use the beta distribution over ratings, we normalized these values to lie in the range of 0 to 1. For the two stage approaches, we predicted $v(t)$ by using $argmax_{v(t)}$ $\prod_{i=1}^{n_{d_t}} p(v(t), w_{di}|\lambda_{k1}\lambda_{k2})$ for each test review $d_t$, where $p(v(t), w_{di}|\lambda_{k1}\lambda_{k2})$ and their parameters have already been learned from the training data. Although original TNG and PDLDA do not provide any rating score, we inserted this value in each token of TNG and PDLDA as the observed score $v_d$ that is conditioned on each topic k and can be sampled from the topic specific beta distribution ($v_d(t_d) \sim p(v(t), w_{di}|\lambda_{k1}\lambda_{k2})$, like sTOT and SNT, and call supervised TNG (sTNG) and supervised PDLDA (sPDLDA), so that both sTNG and sPDLDA predict the score. In our evaluation, the smoothing parameters of the previous models followed the previous setting ( [2, 9, 10, 28]). As simpler two stage approaches, we generated $N$-grams based on Mahout/PDLDA and then used ridge regression to predict ratings based on these $N$-grams (MR/rPDLDA).

As the number of topics is also one of the important aspects of our approaches, we changed the number of topics in sPDLDA. The comparison results are shown in Figure 2, where sPDLDA was learned by changing the number of topics. This table shows that sPDLDA offers the best precision performance when the number of topics is close to that automatically learned by SNT. This result leads us to set the number of topics of the baseline topic models to that of SNT.

As shown in Table 2, SNT achieves better precision than ISN, and provides an average reduction in MAE relative error of 5.3%. As SNT exactly supports $N$-gram using a suffix tree, the prediction power of our model increases with $N$-gram length, see Table 3. This result also indicates that manipulation of the background topic is essential for describing the generative process of review articles. Note that the difference between sTOT and sTNG is greater than that between SNT and sTOT. Although most background topic words are reused over almost all reviews regardless of content, referred item, and corresponding score, sTNG assigns background topic words to topics like other sentiment specific words. In previous models, "disappointed" is judged as a negative word, or this phrase is overwhelmed by the plurality of words generated under the bag of words assumption, while SNT detects the positive sentiment phrase "not disappointed". This defect weakens the predictive performance of the previous models. Strangely, the precision of sPDLDA is inversely proportional to the number of N over all data sets. Because the number of topics appeared in each document is too few [26], the change point of PDLDA tends to allow the same topic in succession over long tokens. It leads PDLDA to grow the $N$-gram suffix tree greedily and create trees with wide spread branches, that include too many $N$-grams of low frequency or forms the shape of the beta distribution gently. These results support the basis of SNT that our desired topic specific words/$N$-grams need both words/$N$-grams and observed variables to discover latent topics that would otherwise be missed, since the number of words/topics influenced by the observed variables is fewer than that of the others, and the number of $N$-grams associated with these values is also fewer than that of the others. For example, "words about star wars story" have 5 topics and 2314 unique words, while "word of positive aspects over this story" is only 1 topic and 152 unique words in this data.

## 5.3 Qualitative Evaluation

Table 4 an example of words of topics extracted by sTOT, SNT, sTNG. These selected topics have the highest probability in each category. In each category, we select one topic having a right skewed beta distribution from the topics learned by sTOT. For each selected topic, we pick up the most similar topic from topics learned by SNT, where we measure this similarity by KL divergence equation over the topic specific distribution over words. We then we choose N-grams from this selected topic. For comparison, we choose one topic and one $N$-gram topic learned by sTNG and have the most similar word distribution with selected topic learned by sTOT, as measured by KL divergence. For each topic, we list the top 10 words in decreasing order of topic-specific probability $G_{z_j}$ and $G_{z_{ji}}^{w_{n-2:n-1}}$.

**Table 4: Word distribution learned from the data set by sTOT, SNT and sTNG: We list top 5 words (bigram words) from sTOT, sTNG and SNT with high rating. The values in the columns are the corresponding probabilities.**

| sTOT | SNT | | sTNG | |
|---|---|---|---|---|
| $w_{ji}$ $\hat{\phi}_{z_{ji}w_{ji}}$ | $w_{ji}$ $G_{z_{ji}}$ | $w_{j(i-1)}w_{ji}$ $G_{zji}^{w_{n-2:n-1}}$ | $w_{ji}$ $\hat{\phi}_{z_{ji}w_{ji}}$ | $w_{j(i-1)}w_{ji}$ $\hat{\psi}_{w_{j(i-1)}z_{ji}w_{ji}}$ |
| | | DVD | | |
| great 0.037 | great 0.087 | effects good 0.083 | , 0.124 | people movie 0.062 |
| quality 0.023 | special 0.035 | high quality 0.071 | people 0.058 | george lucas 0.051 |
| enjoy 0.020 | quality 0.026 | return jedi 0.068 | star 0.053 | return jedi 0.048 |
| funny 0.018 | fans 0.022 | darth vader 0.057 | like 0.038 | empire strike 0.039 |
| special 0.018 | enjoy 0.018 | special effect 0.052 | movie 0.029 | people meet 0.037 |
| best 0.015 | star 0.018 | skywalker mark 0.025 | . 0.023 | people like 0.028 |
| | | Books | | |
| hogwarts 0.104 | potter 0.131 | good writer 0.076 | , 0.103 | harry potter 0.073 |
| young 0.050 | harry 0.081 | great deal 0.072 | book 0.084 | read book 0.072 |
| wizard 0.031 | hogwarts 0.073 | harry potter 0.071 | harry 0.077 | book series 0.071 |
| potter 0.030 | voldmort 0.035 | lord voldmort 0.052 | read 0.065 | ministry magic 0.062 |
| stories 0.025 | questions 0.031 | eagerly awaiting 0.048 | potter 0.062 | want know 0.055 |
| | | Music | | |
| ears 0.026 | better 0.079 | like best 0.092 | , 0.132 | linkin park 0.025 |
| weird 0.025 | listen 0.072 | really good 0.053 | album 0.065 | good song 0.018 |
| better 0.019 | hit 0.052 | perfect work 0.042 | listen 0.061 | music industry 0.016 |
| notes 0.018 | perfect 0.048 | worth money 0.038 | . 0.043 | music like 0.014 |
| hit 0.018 | quite 0.032 | linkin park 0.037 | just 0.032 | rock opera 0.012 |

In the DVD category, topics extracted by sTOT and SNT concatenate words associated with "star wars" DVD, while the sTNG topic includes generic words such as "people", "movie" and "think", those are detected as background words by SNT. More importantly, the difference of this word list impacts the formation of phrases and thus the quality of the bigram word list. For example, highly related phrases such as "effects good" are not ranked high but "people movie" are top ranked in the sTNG list, due to sTNG's partiality for common words. On the contrary, "effects good" is top ranked and "people movie" is not ranked in the SNT list. $N$-gram words learned by sTNG consist of the background words detected by sTOT and SNT, since sTNG can not distinguish these words and their appearance frequency is higher than those of the other words. In the other category, we can find similar phenomena as well. The sTNG topic also includes common words such as "read", "book" and "written", and these words are also detected as background words. On the other hand, sTOT and SNT do not rank these words and merely concatenates words associated with "harry potter" book. Consequently, common words do not appear in the phrases extracted by SNT, while these words appear as the expressions such as "read book" and "book series" in sTNG. This characteristic can be observed in the other topics and categories.

Since background words are highly probable in each topic and yield stronger co-occurrence patterns more easily than the other words, phrases containing these words appear more often than the other phrases and dampen the quality of phrases and rating prediction. The crucially important but buried words are extracted by SNT, as SNT assigns most of the common words to the background topic. Table 4 shows that $N$-gram phrases can be approximately modeled by concatenating consecutive words as is done by SNT, as discussed in the previous section. SNT could generate phrases containing general words by excluding $k$=0, although this might decrease the prediction quality. Thus, SNT can identify sentiment words that are specific to both topics and the corresponding rating. Both benefits are useful for predicting the rating of a given review article.

## 6. DISCUSSION

The main goal of SNT is to jointly model a given value with the corresponding words or phrases from supervised articles. In general, increasing the number of topics makes topic-specific word distributions clear and distinct. This is not possible with $N$-gram words that are conditioned on the previous words and topic. As these words are sampled from the combination of two different variables (previous word and current topic), increasing the number of topics expands the parameter dimension for $N$-gram word assignment. Because this reflects a kind of data sparseness, increasing the number of topics can not increase the number of meaningful sentiment phrases.

We discuss the computation cost and memory requirements of SNT. Two stage approaches require both lexicons and human supervision, unlike SNT, while SNT consumes more time than the two stage approaches require for learning. As new items are emerging and disappearing every day and user preferences change over time, these jobs may consume more time than learning. Consequently, the difference between them is not significant in view of the overall cost. Both TNG (sTNG) and ISN form $N$-grams by concatenating adjacent bigrams, and fail to yield accurate $N$-grams. However, SNT uses a hierarchical Pitman-Yor process prior over the predictive distributions that are conditioned on all previous $N-1$ words as each $N$-gram, and provides a compact representation of $N$-grams. Since the hierarchical Pitman-Yor process allows SNT to select an appropriate number of topics, and thus yield simplified structures, SNT offers more rapid learning due to the reduced number of sampling updates. That is, SNT stores only the numbers of customers, numbers of tables, and sizes of all tables in each layers, instead of the precise seating arrangement of each restaurant, using the metaphor of Chinese restaurant process. Memory requirements depend on both memory for data and memory for model parameters. This model takes $O(NW)$ time and requires $O(M)$ memory space per each iteration [24], where $NW$ is the product of the length of $N$-gram and number of unique words $W$, and $M$ is the sampling iteration of unique $N$-grams. sTNG requires $O(2KWW)$ memory, much more than SNT, as we implemented the $N$-gram suffix tree so that $M$ is much smaller than $2KWW$. Since this tree structure allows SNT to insert, search, and check $N$-grams in $O(N)$, the major time consuming part for inferencing is evaluating the conditional probability for Gibbs sampling. Through these experiments, SNT really converges at 50% fewer iterations than previous models, and consumes 90% less memory less. Consequently, SNT can process large text data sets faster than the others, with less memory requirements and computation cost than the others.

## 7. CONCLUSION

This paper introduced a topic model that detects topic-specific $N$-grams with supervised continuous value. Our contribution lies in building $N$-grams as a suffix tree and deriving an inference algorithm for this model by leveraging both DP, PYP, and supervised labels. Future work is to detect each aspect and then discover each individual reviewer's latent attitude to each aspect so that product recommendations are provided together with textual evidence.

## 8. REFERENCES


[1] D. Aldous. *Exchangeability and related topics*, volume 1117 of *Lecture Notes in Math.* Springer, Berlin, 1985.

[2] D. Blei and J. McAuliffe. Supervised topic models. In *NIPS*, pages 121–128, 2007.

[3] S. Brody and N. Elhadad. An unsupervised aspect-sentiment model for online reviews. In *HLT-NAACL*, pages 804–812, 2010.

[4] T. S. Ferguson. A bayesian analysis of some nonparametric problems. *The Annals of Statistics*, 1(2):209–230, Mar 1973.

[5] S. Goldwater, T. L. Griffiths, and M. Johnson. Producing power-law distributions and damping word frequencies with two-stage language models. *J. Mach. Learn. Res.*, 12(48):2335–2382, Jul 2011.

[6] M. Hu and B. Liu. Mining and summarizing customer reviews. In *KDD*, pages 168–177, 2004.

[7] N. Jindal and B. Liu. Opinion spam and analysis. In *WSDM*, pages 219–230, 2008.

[8] N. Kawamae. Predicting future reviews: Sentiment analysis models for collaborative filtering. In *WSDM*, pages 605–614, 2011.

[9] N. Kawamae. Trend analysis model: Trend consists of temporal words, topics, and timestamps. In *WSDM*, pages 317–326, 2011.

[10] N. Kawamae. Identifying sentiments over n-gram. In *WWW*, pages 541–542, 2012.

[11] R. Kneser and H. Ney. Improved backing-off for m-gram language modeling. In *ICASSP*, pages 181–184, 1995.

[12] E.-P. Lim, V.-A. Nguyen, N. Jindal, B. Liu, and H. W. Lauw. Detecting product review spammers using rating behaviors. In *CIKM*, pages 939–948, 2010.

[13] R. V. Lindsey, W. P. Headden, III, and M. J. Stipicevic. A phrase-discovering topic model using hierarchical pitman-yor processes. In *EMNLP-CoNLL*, pages 214–222, 2012.

[14] D. J. MacKay and L. C. B. Peto. A hierarchical dirichlet language model. *Natural Language Engineering*, 1:1–19, 1994.

[15] R. M. Neal. Markov chain sampling methods for dirichlet process mixture models. *JCGS*, 9(2):249–265, 2000.

[16] D. Newman, A. Asuncion, P. Smyth, and M. Welling. Distributed algorithms for topic models. *JMLR*, 10:1801–1828, dec 2009.

[17] J. Pitman and M. Yor. The two-parameter poisson-dirichlet distribution derived from a stable subordinator. *Annals of Probability*, 25(2):855–900, 1997.

[18] A. Popescu and O. Etzioni. Extracting product features and opinions from reviews. In *EMNLP*, pages 339–346, 2005.

[19] D. Ramage, D. Hall, R. Nallapati, and C. D. Manning. Labeled lda: a supervised topic model for credit attribution in multi-labeled corpora. In *EMNLP*, pages 248–256, 2009.

[20] Y. W. Teh. A hierarchical bayesian language model based on pitman-yor processes. In *Coling/ACL*, pages 985–992, 2006.

[21] Y. W. Teh, M. I. Jordan, M. J. Beal, and D. M. Blei. Hierarchical dirichlet processes. *JASA*, 101(476):1566–1581, 2006.

[22] I. Titov and R. McDonald. A joint model of text and aspect ratings for sentiment summarization. In *ACL*, pages 308–316, 2008.

[23] I. Titov and R. McDonald. Modeling online reviews with multi-grain topic models. In *WWW*, pages 111–120, 2008.

[24] E. Ukkonen. On-line construction of suffix trees. *Algorithmica*, 14(3):249–260, 1995.

[25] H. Wallach. Topic modeling: Beyond bag-of-words. In *ICML*, pages 977–984, 2006.

[26] H. Wallach, D. Mimno, and A. McCallum. Rethinking lda: Why priors matter. In *NIPS*, pages 859–872, 2009.

[27] H. Wang, Y. Lu, and C. Zhai. Latent aspect rating analysis on review text data: a rating regression approach. In *KDD*, pages 783–792, 2010.

[28] X. Wang, A. McCallum, and X. Wei. Topical n-grams: Phrase and topic discovery, with an application to information retrieval. In *ICDM*, pages 697–702, 2007.

[29] J. Wiebe. Learning subjective adjectives from corpora. In *AAAI*, pages 735–740, 2000.

[30] W. X. Zhao, J. Jiang, H. Yan, and X. Li. Jointly modeling aspects and opinions with a maxent-lda hybrid. In *EMNLP*, pages 56–65, 2010.

[31] G. Zipf. *Selective Studies and the Principle of Relative Frequency in Language*. Harvard University Press, Cambridge, MA, 1932.

# Going Beyond Corr-LDA for Detecting Specific Comments on News & Blogs

Mrinal Das† mrinal@csa.iisc.ernet.in
Trapit Bansal† trapit@csa.iisc.ernet.in
Chiranjib Bhattacharyya† chiru@csa.iisc.ernet.in

† Department of Computer Science and Automation, Indian Institute of Science, India

## ABSTRACT

Understanding user generated comments in response to news and blog posts is an important area of research. After ignoring irrelevant comments, one finds that a large fraction, approximately 50%, of the comments are very specific and can be further related to certain parts of the article instead of the entire story. For example, in a recent product review of *Google Nexus 7* in ArsTechnica (a popular blog), the reviewer talks about the prospect of "*Retina equipped iPad mini*" in a few sentences. It is interesting that although the article is on *Nexus 7*, but a significant number of comments are focused on this specific point regarding "*iPad*". We pose the problem of detecting such comments as *specific comments* location (SCL) problem. SCL is an important open problem with no prior work.

SCL can be posed as a correspondence problem between comments and the parts of the relevant article, and one could potentially use Corr-LDA type models. Unfortunately, such models do not give satisfactory performance as they are restricted to using a single topic vector per article-comments pair. In this paper we propose to go beyond the single topic vector assumption and propose a novel correspondence topic model, namely SCTM, which admits multiple topic vectors (MTV) per article-comments pair. The resulting inference problem is quite complicated because of MTV and has no off-the-shelf solution. One of the major contributions of this paper is to show that using stick-breaking process as a prior over MTV, one can derive a *collapsed Gibbs sampling* procedure, which empirically works well for SCL.

SCTM is rigorously evaluated on three datasets, crawled from *Yahoo! News* (138,000 comments) and *two blogs*, ArsTechnica (AT) Science (90,000 comments) and AT-Gadget (160,000 comments). We observe that SCTM performs better than Corr-LDA, not only in terms of metrics like *perplexity* and *topic coherence* but also discovers more unique topics. We see that this immediately leads to an order of magnitude improvement in F1 score over Corr-LDA for SCL.


*WSDM'14*, February 24–28, 2014, New York, New York, USA.

http://dx.doi.org/10.1145/2556195.2556231.

## Categories and Subject Descriptors

G.3 [**Probability and Statistics**]: Probabilistic algorithms; I.2.7 [**Artificial Intelligence**]: Natural Language Processing—*Text Analysis*

## Keywords

specific, correspondence, comments, news, blogs

## 1. INTRODUCTION

Comments on news and blogs naturally promote user participation and play a pivotal role in increasing the popularity of host websites. In this paper we investigate the correlation structure between the content, such as news or blog-postings, and user generated comments.

Consider the example in Figure 1 that shows an excerpt from the review on *Google Nexus 7*, dated July 31 2013[1]. It is one of the well commented recent reviews with more than 200 comments. Some comments are related to the entire article, like ... *good to see tablets are becoming cheaper* (black colored in Figure 1), which are *general comments*. Some comments are *irrelevant*, for example *I work on a laptop* (blue in Figure 1).

In the same article, in about 8% of the sentences, the author talks about retina display and compares with "*iPad*" (colored green in Figure 1). It was found that, leaving irrelevant comments, around 22% comments (colored green in Figure 1) are made only on that specific point. The fact of 22% comments on a topic covered in 8% of sentences, and those sentences being far different from the central theme of the article, is quite astonishing. These comments are not useless, rather they provide valuable user feedback. We call such comments as *specific comments*. Discovering *specific comments* and the associated part of the content which is specific to the comment will be called the *specific comment location* (SCL) problem.

Solving SCL will open up many opportunities such as accumulating user feedback, analysing market trends, improving user experience etc. There is no prior work related to SCL, furthermore there are no off-the-shelf techniques which could be adapted to solve this problem. Discriminative techniques are often accurate but require lot of labeled training data which in this case is not available. Past approaches such as [11] on comment understanding demonstrates that accuracy of discriminative approaches depend

[1]arstechnica.com/gadgets/2013/07/the-2013-nexus-7-review-meet-the-new-standard-for-android-tablets/

on cleverly crafted features. Keeping this in mind we pursue topic models, an unsupervised approach, to the SCL problem. Correspondence LDA (Corr-LDA) [1] is an interesting topic model which could be a potential candidate for SCL. Existing topic models, including Corr-LDA, assign a single topic vector to each document. This makes Corr-LDA more suitable for discovering general comments and as empirical evidence suggests it is not suitable for SCL. In this paper we address the issue of SCL and make the following contributions.

**Contributions:** We introduce *specific correspondence topic models* (SCTM), based on the notion of *multiple topic vectors* (MTV) as opposed to single topic vector in the state of the art models. Moreover, in order to handle wide variety of comments we enhance the diversity among topics through sparsity. The inference becomes non-standard due to MTV and sparsity. We explore a *stick-breaking process* (SBP) as a prior over MTV. One major contribution of this paper is a collapsed Gibbs sampling inference procedure for SCTM. The resultant algorithm converges fast and also leads to simple update equations which are easy to implement. Using three real world datasets, we evaluate the proposed approach in two aspects. (i) Using perplexity and topic coherence we show that SCTM models data better than the state of art. Then, we demonstrate that SCTM discovers more diverse set of topics and converges faster in terms of likelihood. (ii) Using precision-recall we compare SCTM with the baseline on the task of discovering specific comments as well as aligning them to the respective sentences in the article. Finally, we show various use cases of SCTM on some interesting practical applications.

The paper is organized as follows. We formulate the problem of SCL and discuss the challenges and related works in section 2. Then in section 3 we present the proposed model and the Gibbs sampling inference algorithm. We describe the algorithm for SCL in section 4. In section 5, we provide empirical evaluation. Finally, section 6 presents some use cases of SCL.

## 2. THE PROBLEM OF SPECIFIC COMMENT LOCATION

In this section we introduce the problem of specific comment location (SCL) and discuss the difficulties in resolving SCL. We begin by introducing relevant notation.

**Notation:** The set of element wise positive $d$ dimensional vectors will be denoted by $\mathbb{R}^d_+$. $\sim$ means "distributed as", $1_x$ is a $x$ dimensional vector with all entries as 1. $K$ is the number of topics and $V$ is the number of words in the vocabulary. $\beta_k$ is a $V$ dimensional vector such that $\sum_{j=1}^{V} \beta_{kj} = 1$, popularly called as a "topic". $x.y$ is element wise product of two vectors $x$ and $y$ of same dimension. *Dir* denotes Dirichlet distribution, $U$ denotes discrete uniform distribution and *mult* represents multinomial distribution. $[n] = \{1, 2, \ldots, n\}$ and $|R|$: cardinality of set $R$. $\tilde{x}$ means a set of variables of same type. $I[.]$ is the indicator function.

**Definition:** A news or a blog article $A_d$, indexed by $d$, is a collection of $S_d$ number of sentences. More explicitly $A_d = \{s_{da} | a \in [S_d]\}$, where each sentence is denoted by $s_{da} = \{w_{dai} | i \in [n_{da}]\}$. The $i$th word in the $a$th sentence

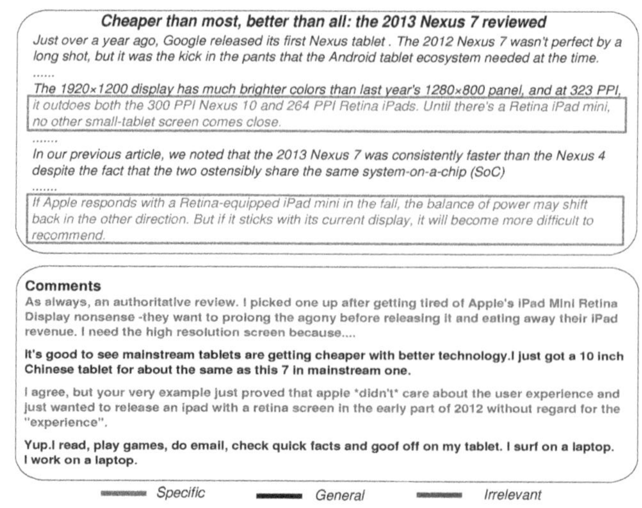


**Figure 1: Example from ArsTechnica. For specific comments (in green), the corresponding sentences in the article (in green, referred as $R_{de}$) are few and are not contiguous. The box shows *hot-spot* (most commented sentences). Irrelevant comment (in blue) does not have any corresponding sentence in the article, whereas general comments (in black) are related to the entire article.**

$s_{da}$ is denoted by $w_{dai}$ and the number of words in $s_{da}$ is denoted by $n_{da}$. Corresponding to each article, $A_d$ there is a set of comments denoted by $C_d = \{c_{dej} | j \in [n_{de}],\ e \in [E_d]\}$ where $c_{dej}$ is the $j$th word in the $e$th comment related to article $A_d$. Number of comments on $A_d$ is denoted by $E_d$ and $n_{de}$ is the number of words in the $e$th comment. Furthermore $w_{dai}, c_{dei} \in [V]$, where $V$ is the number of unique words in the entire corpus. Let $R_{de} \subseteq A_d$ denote the set of sentences related to the $e$th comment of $d$th article. In Figure 1 the boxes show the sentences indexed by $R_{de}$ for the green colored comment. The $e$th comment can be a general, irrelevant or specific comment depending on the size of $R_{de}$. It is a general comment when $|R_{de}|$ is *almost equal or equal* to $S_d$, and is an irrelevant comment when $R_{de}$ is empty. Comment $e$ is a specific comment if $0 < |R_{de}| \leq N_d$, where the parameter $N_d$ is preset by the user and determines the granularity of specific comments. Notice that general comments and irrelevant comments are two extreme cases.

**SCL formulation:** The problem of specific comment location can now be formulated as identifying $R_{de}$ given $A_d$ and the $e$th comment whenever $|R_{de}| \leq N_d$.

For a specific comment $e$, the set $R_{de}$ can be understood as *specific correspondence* between the comment and the article $A_d$. In this paper we concentrate on articles and comments but it is conceivable that similar problems exist in many other domains such as *technical paper and bibliography, image and tags* etc.

**The difficulty in resolving SCL:** It is not easy to discover $R_{de}$. Specific comments and general comments look very similar, and there are no distinguishing features such as length (number of words), presence of proper-nouns, or selection of words in comments. Absence of distinguishing features makes it impractical to apply rule based approaches.

In addition, due to lack of labeled data, supervised models are inapplicable. For example, [11] made an attempt to align comments to paragraphs in an article, however their method being supervised is restrictive and does not apply generally. An immediate alternative could be the use of *keyword* based searches.

*Very low textual overlap between specific comments and the article:* To measure the overlap in words between a specific comment and the main article, we define, $\Delta_{dae} = \frac{n_{dae}}{\sqrt{n_{da}}\sqrt{n_{de}}}$, where $n_{dae}$ is the number of words in common between $a^{th}$ sentence and $e^{th}$ comment for article indexed by $d$. $\Delta_{dae}$ can be interpreted as cosine distance or correlation coefficient which computes the normalized similarity between a sentence in the main article with a comment. $n_{da}$ and $n_{de}$ are as defined before. Let $D$ be the total number of $(A_d, C_d)$ pairs then the average textual overlap over all sentences and the articles can be measured by $\Delta = \frac{1}{D}\sum_d \frac{1}{E_d}\sum_e \frac{1}{|R_{de}|}\sum_{a\in\{a|s_{da}\in R_{de}\}} \Delta_{dae}$.

From our study based on ArsTechnica gold-standard (see section 5), we find the following. For specific comments, considering all sentences of the article (i.e. using $A_d$ instead of $R_{de}$ in $\Delta$ above), $\Delta$ is 0.07 and for non-specific comments it is 0.06. However, considering only the relevant sentences for the specific comments, the value of $\Delta$ is 0.08. Notice that, not only the value is very small but also they are very similar for both specific and non-specific comments. For example in Figure 1, "*iPad*" is the only word which probably can link but due to other words the overlap becomes low. This makes keyword based approaches difficult to apply.

**Topic models:** Over the last decade Topic modeling has become ubiquitous in text analysis. It is an unsupervised approach rooted in Bayesian modeling. In the following we review some of the related topic models and discuss their suitability for SCL. There has been an increasing interest in using topic models such as [9, 15, 6] for understanding user generated content. [6] considered the problem of finding episodic tweets about an event, tweets which are related to one of the segments of an event. Their model is similar in spirit to [15], where event and tweet are exchangeable. As noted in [1] these models [15, 6] are not suited for understanding the dependency between a news article and comments. MG-LDA [12] has been developed to model local topics. A set of sliding windows are used across the sentences in a document which uses local topics. MG-LDA is inappropriate because: (i) local topics scatter across the corpus which is not the case here, and (ii) every segment or a set of contiguous sentences may not correspond to a comment. Among the existing models the most suited seems to be Corr-LDA [1] and we will use it as a baseline.

**Review of Corr-LDA:** Corr-LDA [1] is a topic model for understanding correspondences. It was initially proposed for modeling annotations on images. Corr-LDA uses a bag-of-words and there is no notion of sentences, i.e. $S_d = 1$. The generative process of Corr-LDA is as follows.

For each $(A_d, C_d)$

- Sample a topic vector $\theta_d \sim Dir(\alpha 1_K)$
- For each word $w_{di}$, $i \in [n_d]$
  - sample topic $z_{di} \sim mult(\theta_d)$
  - sample word $w_{di} \sim mult(\beta_{z_{di}})$
- For each comment $e \in [E_d]$
  - For each word $i \in [n_{de}]$
    - sample topic $y_{dei} \sim U(\tilde{z}_d)$
    - sample word $c_{dei} \sim mult(\beta_{y_{dei}})$

Notice that comment topic indices are sampled uniformly at random from article topic indices. Hence, $y_{de}$ corresponds to the complete set $\tilde{z}_d$ and comment $e$ becomes related to the entire article $d$. This lacks the *specific correspondence* focus of the current paper. Using Algorithm 1 (to be described in section 4) Corr-LDA can be used for SCL.

**Limitations of Corr-LDA for SCL:** We summarize some major limitations of Corr-LDA for SCL as below.

*A.) Very low correspondence:* Corr-LDA models $R_{de}$ as the entire article, however $R_{de}$ is not known a priori and is very small for specific comments. Based on the gold-standard on ArsTechnica (see section 5), we observe that on average only 3% of the sentences in an article are related to a specific comment, i.e. $|R_{de}|$ is very small. In Figure 1, for the specific comment on "*iPad*", $\frac{|R_{de}|}{S_d}$ is 0.08.

*B.) Topical difference in $R_{de}$:* A specific comment $e$ is related to a small part $R_{de}$ and is less relevant to the rest of the article. Therefore, $R_{de}$ has a different topic proportion than the rest of the article. For example, in Figure 1, $R_{de}$ should have high probability for "*iPad*" topic, although that is a topic with low overall probability in the article.

Note that in Corr-LDA there is a single topic vector $\theta_d$ for document $d$. Hence topic proportions in $R_{de}$ is also $\theta_d$, i.e. probability of "*iPad*" topic, for example, in Figure 1 is also low in $R_{de}$. This is a major drawback which we address in our proposed model SCTM.

# 3. SCTM: A CORRESPONDENCE TOPIC MODEL

In this section we define *specific correspondence topic models* (SCTM) and the associated inference algorithm.

## 3.1 SCTM

**The need for multiple topic vectors (MTV):** As pointed out in the last section, existing correspondence topic models use a single topic vector $\theta_d$ for each pair of article and the associated comments. This makes the topic proportions constant throughout the article and comments. Though this maybe suitable for general comments, where one might have similar topic proportions, but specific comments have different proportion over topics than the main article. Precisely, a specific comment $e$ and $R_{de}$ should have similar topic proportions. It is thus clear that one needs to go beyond the single topic vector assumption to resolve SCL. To this end we introduce the novel concept of using multiple proportions over topics per article-comments pair to model *specific correspondence*.

**Modeling topical difference in $R_{de}$ using MTV:** Note that the challenge is that $R_{de}$ is not known a priori, so that we can extract $R_{de}$ from the main article and model the correspondence between $R_{de}$ and comment $e$ following Corr-LDA. We resolve this by introducing multiple topic proportions to be called as MTV (multiple topic vectors). Recently, [5] has used the concept of MTV in a different context to find subtle topics.

For each vocabulary term $v \in [V]$

- Sample $\kappa_v \sim Beta(\frac{\nu\lambda}{V}, \lambda)$

For each topic $k \in [K]$,

- For each term of the vocabulary $v \in [V]$
  - Sample word selector $\phi_{kv} \sim Bernoulli(\kappa_v)$
- Draw topic distribution $\beta_k \sim Dir(\eta 1_{V+1} . \phi_k)$

For each article-comments pair $(A_d, C_d)$, $d \in [D]$,

- For $j \in [J_d]$, draw $\theta_{dj} \sim Dir(\alpha 1_K)$
- For each article sentence $a \in [S_d]$,
  - Draw $\rho_{da} \sim stick(\tau, \iota)$
  - For each word $i \in [n_{da}]$,
    * Draw $b_{dai} \sim mult(\rho_{da})$
    * Draw $z_{dai} \sim mult(\theta_{db_{dai}})$
    * Draw word $w_{dai} \sim mult(\beta_{z_{dai}})$
- For each comment, $e \in [E_d]$
  - Sample $\pi_{de} \sim Beta(\varrho_1, \varrho_2)$
  - Sample $\epsilon_{de} \sim Beta(\varsigma_1, \varsigma_2)$
  - For each sentence $a$ of the article
    * Draw $\xi_{dea} \sim Bernoulli(\pi_{de})$
  - Set $\varphi_{de} = \{z_{dai}, \forall (a, i) \mid \xi_{dea} = 1\}$
  - For each comment word $i \in [n_{de}]$,
    * Draw $t_{dei} \sim Bernoulli(\epsilon_{de})$
    * If $t_{dei} = 1$, $y_{dei} = K+1$ (irrelevant topic)
    * Else $y_{dei} \sim U(\varphi_{de})$
    * Draw word $c_{dei} \sim mult(\beta_{y_{dei}})$

**Figure 2: Generative process of SCTM. $\theta_{dj}$: topic-proportion vector, $\rho_{da}$: distribution over topic-vectors, $b_{dai}$: topic-vector index, $z_{dai}$: topic assignment, $\xi_{dea}$: sentence selector, $t_{dei}$: irrelevant topic selector. *stick* refers to construction as in (1).**

Therefore, per article-comments pair there are $J_d \geq 1$ topic vectors denoted by $\{\theta_{dj}\}_{j=1}^{J_d}$. While generating a word in a sentence, one $\theta_{dj}$ is selected randomly. So, proportions over topics in each sentence can be different and a random selection of $R_{de}$ from article $d$ can have very different proportions over topics than that of article $d$. For example, even if "*iPad*" topic has low probability in the entire article in Figure 1, it may have high probability in some $R_{de}$.

**Choice of a suitable prior for MTV:** The choice of a suitable prior for MTV is an important question. The challenge is that, (i) in the SCL problem, it may occur that some topic has an extremely low probability in the entire document but might have a very high probability in a specific region and can be useful in detecting specific comments. (ii) Topic vectors should be shared across the sentences in an article because for a specific comment $e$ on article $d$, $R_{de}$ may span over multiple non-contiguous sentences. Important to note that, over-estimation of $J_d$ will try to model many general comments as specific in nature, whereas under-estimation will try to model specific comments as general ones. Nonparametric priors such as dependent Dirichlet process can mitigate this issue. One could potentially use hierarchical Dirichlet process (HDP) which is suited to share topics as required in (ii). However the difficulty with HDP is its *rich getting richer property* which tends to make a widely appearing topic vector highly probable in all the sentences, contradicting the requirement (i). We will explore SBP as an alternative prior which could address these issues.

**Stick-breaking process (SBP):** SBP[7] is defined as follows. Let $\tau, \iota \in \mathbb{R}_+^J$ and $\Gamma$ is a diffuse probability measure on a measurable space $(\Omega, \mathcal{B})$. A random probability measure $G$ on $(\Omega, \mathcal{B})$ is a stick-breaking prior if $G = \sum_{j=1}^{J} \rho_j \delta_{\theta_j}$, $\theta_j \overset{iid}{\sim} \Gamma$ and $(\rho_j)$ are constructed as

$$\rho_1 = v_1, \quad \rho_j = v_j \prod_{l=1}^{j-1} (1 - v_l), \; j > 1 \tag{1}$$

where $v_j \overset{iid}{\sim} Beta(\tau_j, \iota_j)$, $j < J$, and $v_J = 1$. To keep the exposition simple we assume $J$ to be finite. $\delta_{\theta_j}$ denotes an atomic distribution where the entire probability mass is concentrated at $\theta_j$. $\Gamma$ is a measure defined on vectors $\theta_j$, commonly referred as atoms of $G$. Furthermore by construction $\sum_{j=1}^{J} \rho_j = 1$. For each sentence $s_{da}$ in article $A_d$ we use a distribution $G_{da}$ with topic vectors $(\theta_{dj})$ as atoms. In our case the topic vectors are sampled from a Dirichlet prior $Dir(\alpha 1_K)$. For a fixed $d$ assume that $(\rho_{da})$ is defined as in equation (1) then

$$\theta_{dj} \overset{iid}{\sim} Dir(\alpha 1_K), \; G_{da} = \sum_{j=1}^{J_d} \rho_{da} \delta_{\theta_{dj}} \tag{2}$$

Notice that, the proportion over the topic vectors for a sentence does not depend on those of other sentences, nor does it depend on any document wide property. Unlike Dirichlet distribution, $J_d$ acts as an upper limit on number of topic vectors, where higher indexed topic vectors get lower prior probabilities. Thus SBP allows to provide high weight on a topic vector for some sentences, whereas for most of the sentences that topic vector has low probability. Unfortunately though SBP is suitable, as it is not commonly known in machine learning, makes the inference non-standard.

**Generation of $R_{de}$** We randomly select a set of sentences in article $A_d$ as $R_{de}$. Random selection of $R_{de}$ and use of MTV vary the topic proportions in $R_{de}$ making SCTM appropriate for SCL. Note that, alternatively, $R_{de}$ could be sampled first and then corresponding to each $R_{de}$ a topic vector could be used. But this has several problems: (i) even if $R_{de}$ is same for two comments it will have two different $\theta$, (ii) articles with large number of comments will create too many topic vectors, (iii) modeling article will become dependent on comments. So we have avoided this choice.

**Enhancing diversity in topics:** Note that, topics related to specific comments contain words which are very rare in the article. For example, "*iPad*" has rarely appeared in the article. Now considering a web scale data we need to consider a vast and diverse set of article-comments. Hence, it is required that we detect a diverse set of topics which have high probability for different sets of words.

We model this fact by modifying the definition of topic slightly. Instead of defining a topic over all the words in the vocabulary, similar to the selection of $R_{de}$ we randomly select a subset of words using $\phi$ and define a topic over that subset of words. $\phi$ is a Bernoulli random variable and when $\phi_{kv} = 0$, $\beta_{kv} = 0$ with probability one, where $\beta_{kv}$ is the probability of word indexed by $v$ in the $k^{th}$ topic. To avoid accidental situations, we use $\phi_k$ of length $V+1$, and set $\phi_{k,V+1} = I[\sum_{i=1}^{V} \phi_{ki} = 0]$. Similar concept has been explored by [13] for decoupling sparsity and smoothness in topics. Unlike [13], we have two parameters $\lambda$ and $\nu$, where $\lambda$ is a *repulsion parameter*. When $\lambda$ increases, diversity across $\phi$ increases, in turn increasing diversity across $\beta$, i.e. topics.

**Irrelevant topic:** Irrelevant topic is used for modeling comments to take care of words which generally appear in comments but not in main articles. These words are uninformative words, motivating the name of the topic. For example in Figure 1, "Yup" in the irrelevant comment is one such word. Irrelevant topic models a topic which is irrelevant to any type of correspondence between article and comment. It has been observed that irrelevant comments mostly contain this topic. Similar technique has been explored in [9].

## 3.2 Collapsed Gibbs sampling inference

In this section we describe an efficient and easy to implement Gibbs sampling based inference procedure for SCTM. In order to achieve accelerated convergence, we need to marginalize out the real valued random variables $\beta$, $\theta$, $\epsilon$, $\rho$, $\pi$ and $\kappa$, in the generative process (Fig. 2) and infer the latent variables $z$, $y$, $b$, $\xi$ and $\phi$. The major challenges are: (1) sampling $b$, due to SBP the inference becomes non-standard and (2) $\xi$, $\phi$ are binary random variables demanding novel inference mechanisms.

We address the first challenge by noting the relationship between *SBP* and *generalized Dirichlet distribution* $\mathcal{GD}$ [4], and conjugacy of $\mathcal{GD}$ with the multinomial distribution. That allows us to integrate out $\rho$, see appendix for details. We address the second challenge by integrating out the parameters using the Beta-Bernoulli conjugacy and directly sampling the binary random variables. Following counting notations will be used in the inference.

**Count notation:** (i) "dot" in the suffix represents marginalization at the corresponding index, (ii) $(-x)$ in the superscript means counting without $x$.

$\bar{m}_{kv}$ denotes number of times word $v$ is assigned to topic $k$, and $\bar{m}_{k.}$ is number of times topic $k$ has occurred. $\dot{m}_{deak} = \sum_{r=1}^{n_{da}} I[z_{dar} = k, \xi_{dea} = 1]$, i.e. number of times topic $k$ has occurred in the article considering only those sentences selected by $\xi_{dea}$. $\hat{m}_{djk}$ is number of times topic $k$ has been used from topic vector $j$ of article $d$. $\check{m}_{daj}$ is number of times topic vector $j$ has appeared in sentence $a$ in document $d$. $\mathring{m}_{dk} = \sum_{e=1}^{E_d} \sum_{i=1}^{n_{de}} I[y_{dei} = k]$ is the number of times topic $k$ has appeared across all the comments.

**Sampling $b$:** We compute the conditional probability $p(b_{dai} = j | b^{-dai}, \tau, \iota)$, for $j < J_d$, as

$$\frac{\tau_j + \check{m}_{daj}^{-dai}}{\tau_j + \iota_j + \sum_{r=j}^{J_d} \check{m}_{dar}^{-dai}} \prod_{l<j} \frac{\iota_l + \sum_{s=l+1}^{J_d} \check{m}_{das}^{-dai}}{\tau_l + \iota_l + \sum_{s=l}^{J_d} \check{m}_{das}^{-dai}} \tag{3}$$

& $p(b_{dai} = J_d | b^{-dai}, \tau, \iota) = 1 - \sum_{l=1}^{J_d - 1} p(b_{dai} = l | \tilde{b}^{-dai}, \tau, \iota)$. For any $j$ the above equation can be expressed as $u_j \prod_{l=1}^{j-1} (1 - u_l)$ for suitably defined $u$. The probability of $b_{dai} = j$ directly depends on probability of $b_{dai} \neq l, l < j$. This property is absent in standard priors e.g. finite dimensional Dirichlet distribution, nonparametric DP. Finally, $p(b_{dai} = j | \mathbf{b}^{-dai}, \mathbf{z})$ is computed as:

$$\begin{aligned} &\propto p(z_{dai} | b_{dai} = j, \tilde{z}^{-dai}) p(b_{dai} = j | \tilde{b}^{-dai}) \\ &= \frac{\alpha + \hat{m}_{dj z_{dai}}^{-dai}}{K\alpha + \hat{m}_{dj.}^{-dai}} \, p(b_{dai} = j | \tilde{b}^{-dai}) \end{aligned} \tag{4}$$

**Sampling $\phi$:** Note that, $\phi_{kv}$ is a binary selector, so if $\bar{m}_{kv} > 0$ then $\phi_{kv} = 1$ a.s., otherwise we compute $p(\phi_{kv} = 1 | \tilde{w}, \tilde{z}, \tilde{\phi}^{-kv})$ as below.

$$\begin{aligned} &\propto p(w | \phi_{kv} = 1, \tilde{z}, \tilde{\phi}^{-kv}) p(\phi_{kv} = 1 | \tilde{\phi}^{-kv}) \\ &= \frac{\Gamma(\sum_{u \neq v} \phi_{ku} \eta + \eta)}{\Gamma(\sum_{u \neq v} \phi_{ku} \eta + \eta + \bar{m}_{k.})} p(\phi_{kv} = 1 | \tilde{\phi}^{-kv}) \end{aligned} \tag{5}$$

where $p(\phi_{kv} = 1 | \tilde{\phi}^{-kv})$ can be computed as

$$\int d\kappa_v \, p(\phi_{kv} = 1 | \kappa_v) p(\kappa_v | \tilde{\phi}^{-kv}) = \frac{\frac{\nu\lambda}{V} + \sum_{j \neq k} \phi_{jv}}{\frac{\nu\lambda}{V} + \lambda + K} \tag{6}$$

**Sampling $\xi$:** The inference equation is derived from uniform (first part) and Beta Bernoulli conjugacy (second part). We compute $p(\xi_{dea} = 1 | \tilde{y}_{de}, \tilde{\xi}^{-dea}, \tilde{z}_d, \varrho)$ as below.

$$\begin{aligned} &\propto \prod_{i=1}^{n_{de}} p(y_{dei} | \tilde{z}_d, \xi_{dea} = 1, \tilde{\xi}^{-dea}) \;\; p(\xi_{dea} = 1 | \tilde{\xi}^{-dea}, \varrho) \\ &= \prod_{i=1}^{n_{de}} \frac{\dot{m}_{de.y_{dei}}^{-a} + \dot{m}_{dea y_{dei}}}{\dot{m}_{de..}^{-a} + \dot{m}_{dea.}} \;\; \frac{\varrho_1}{\varrho_1 + \varrho_2} \end{aligned} \tag{7}$$

**Sampling $z$:** Sampling topic indices $z$ follows from Dirichlet multinomial conjugacy as follows. $p(z_{dai} = k | \tilde{w}, \tilde{z}^{-dai})$ is computed as below.

$$\begin{aligned} \propto \;& p(w_{dai} | z_{dai} = k, \tilde{\phi}, \eta) p(z_{dai} = k | \tilde{z}^{-dai}, \tilde{b}, \alpha) \\ & \times p(\tilde{y}_d | \tilde{z}^{-dai}, z_{dai} = k) \\ = \;& \frac{\phi_{k w_{dai}} \eta + \bar{m}_{k w_{dai}}^{-dai}}{\sum_v \phi_{kv} \eta + \bar{m}_{k.}^{-dai}} \frac{\alpha + \hat{m}_{d b_{dai} k}^{-dai}}{\alpha K + \hat{m}_{d b_{dai} .}^{-dai}} \prod_{l \neq k} \dot{m}_{de.l}^{\mathring{m}_{dl}} (\dot{m}_{de.k} + 1)^{\mathring{m}_{dk}} \end{aligned} \tag{8}$$

**Sampling $y$:** Comment indices depend on topic-word Dirichlet-multinomial conjugacy (first part) and uniform distribution (second part) for the comments-article correspondence. We compute $p(y_{dei} = k | \tilde{c}, \tilde{y}^{-dei}, \tilde{z}_d, \tilde{\xi}_{de})$ as below.

$$\begin{aligned} &\propto p(c_{dei} | y_{dei} = k, \tilde{y}^{-dei}, \tilde{\phi}, \eta) \;\; p(y_{dei} = k | \tilde{y}^{-dei}, \tilde{z}_d, \tilde{\xi}_{de}) \\ &= \frac{\phi_{k c_{dei}} \eta + \bar{m}_{k c_{dei}}^{-dei}}{\sum_v \phi_{kv} \eta + \bar{m}_{k.}^{-dei}} \;\; \frac{\dot{m}_{de.k}}{\dot{m}_{de..}} \end{aligned} \tag{9}$$

**Inference algorithm:** Equations (4), (5), (7), (8) and (9) together form the inference algorithm. Inference of all variables depend on others, so we need to solve iteratively. The procedure starts by initializing the variables randomly.

**Relationship with other algorithms:** [7] and [5] have given two different algorithms for solving SBP. The algorithm in [7] samples $v$ explicitly, while the algorithm in [5] is similar to that used here. On the other hand, [13] uses a different mechanism for inducing sparsity over words, they do

**Algorithm 1** Classification & alignment

**Input:** $\mathbf{y}$, $\mathbf{z}$; thresholds: $t_{cos}, t'_{cos}, t_\xi$
Compute $\tilde{\mathbf{y}}$, $\tilde{\mathbf{z}}$ from $\mathbf{y}$, $\mathbf{z}$.
**for** $d \leftarrow 1, \ldots, D$ **do**
  Initialize $\Phi_d \leftarrow \{\}$, $\Psi_d \leftarrow \{\}$, $\Gamma_d \leftarrow \{\}$  ▷ empty
  **for** $e \leftarrow 1, \ldots, E_d$ **do**
    $R_{de} \leftarrow \{\}$, $S_{de} \leftarrow \{\}$  ▷ empty
    **for** $a \leftarrow 1, \ldots, S_d$ **do**
      $\Delta(a,e) \leftarrow \frac{\tilde{y}_{de}^T \tilde{z}_{da}}{\|\tilde{y}_{de}\| \|\tilde{z}_{da}\|}$,  ▷ cosine distance
      **if** $\Delta(a,e) \geq t_{cos}$ **then**
        $R_{de} \leftarrow R_{de} \cup \{a\}$  ▷ insert $a$
      **end if**
      **if** $\Delta(a,e) \geq t'_{cos}$ & $p(\xi_{dea}|y_{de}, z_d) \geq t_\xi$ **then**
        $S_{de} \leftarrow S_{de} \cup \{a\}$  ▷ insert $a$
      **end if**
    **end for**
    **if** $|R_{de}| == 0$ **then**  ▷ cardinality is 0
      $\Psi_d \leftarrow \Psi_d \cup \{e\}$  ▷ Irrelevant
    **else if** $|R_{de}| \leq N_d$ **then**
      $\Phi_d \leftarrow \Phi_d \cup \{e\}$  ▷ Specific
    **else** $\Gamma_d \leftarrow \Gamma_d \cup \{e\}$  ▷ General
    **end if**
  **end for**
**end for**
**Output:** $\Phi_d, \Psi_d, \Gamma_d, R_{de}, S_{de}$

not sample the binary random variables $\phi$ explicitly. The algorithm given here is novel and much simpler to implement, yet efficient. Use of $\xi$ has not been studied before.

# 4. ALGORITHM FOR SCL

In this section we propose an algorithm based on SCTM for SCL. The algorithm considers the inferred latent variables $z$, $y$ and $\xi$ obtained from SCTM inference procedure and uses them for labeling each comment as general, specific or irrelevant and recover the set $R_{de}$ for specific comments.

$\mathbf{z}$ and $\mathbf{y}$ are topic indices for the article and comment respectively [2] $\tilde{\mathbf{z}}$, $\tilde{\mathbf{y}}$ are topic frequency vectors[3] for article and comment respectively. Following the definition in section 2, we need to compute $R_{de}$ for each comment $e$ corresponding to article $d$. Computation of $R_{de}$ follows from cosine similarity, between the topic assignment counts of the comment $\tilde{\mathbf{y}}$ and the sentence $\tilde{\mathbf{z}}$, above a fixed threshold. The decision will depend on threshold $N_d$, i.e. specific if $|R_{de}| \leq N_d$. The details are given in Algorithm 1. For SCTM we can also use the posterior probability of $\xi$, i.e. $p(\xi_{dea} = 1|y_{de}, z_d)$, to improve the alignment to specific sentences. Thus, for SCTM, we have a separate set $S_{de}$ in the algorithm which is obtained by using this information .

**Selecting thresholds:** We set the threshold as $N_d = min(N_g, \lfloor 0.6 * S_d \rfloor)$. $N_g$ limits the threshold for very large documents. $N_g \in [6, 10]$ is found to work well.

# 5. EMPIRICAL EVALUATION

In this section we will evaluate the proposed model SCTM empirically on various aspects using real life datasets[4].

[2] $\mathbf{z} = \{\{z_{dai}|i \in [n_{da}], a \in [S_d]\}_{d=1}^D\}$
[3] $\tilde{\mathbf{z}} = \{\{\tilde{z}_{da}|a \in [n_{da}]\}_{d=1}^D\}$, $\tilde{z}_{da} = (\tilde{z}_{dak})_{k=1}^K \in \mathbb{R}^K, \tilde{z}_{dak} = \frac{1}{n_{da}} \sum_{i=1}^{n_{da}} I[z_{dai} = k]$, $\tilde{\mathbf{y}}$ is defined similarly
[4] Relevant resources at: mllab.csa.iisc.ernet.in/sctm

**Table 1: Properties of the datasets.**

| | AT-Science | AT-Gadgets | Yahoo! News |
|---|---|---|---|
| #(Articles) | 1,369 | 2,186 | 730 |
| #(Comments) | 90,654 | 160,761 | 138,538 |

## 5.1 Datasets

We show some basic properties of the datasets in Table 1 and provide a description below. Note that the data consists mostly of articles with a large number of comments which introduces further challenges in discovering specific comments as their number will be expected to be very small compared to the total comments.

**ArsTechnica Science (AT-Science):** The dataset consists of articles and comments crawled from Science section of the site ArsTechnica[5]. ArsTechnica is a science and technology blog whose writers consist mostly of academicians. Its articles and readership leads to opinionated discussions in the comments which makes it a perfect testbed for our problem. We crawled 1500 articles and their comments over approximately a two year timeline (June 2011 to March 2013) and removed articles with less than 5 comments.

*Gold-standard:* In order to quantitatively evaluate our model, we developed a gold standard by manually annotating articles over a one year timeline (March 2012 to March 2013) after filtering out articles which either had very few comments or had only general and irrelevant comments. For each of these article we manually labeled specific and non-specific comments and also created the alignment of specific comments to the relevant sentences. The gold standard consists of 501 articles with a total of 3176 comments, in which there are 1443 specific comments with an average of 2.9 specific comments per article.

**ArsTechnica Gadgets (AT-Gadgets):** The dataset consists of articles and comments crawled from Gadgets section of the site ArsTechnica[6]. This dataset consists mostly of product reviews on latest gadgets. We crawled about 2200 articles and their comments over a two year timeline (August 2011 to August 2013) and removed articles with less than 5 comments.

**Yahoo! News:** The dataset consists of articles and comments crawled from the most-commented[7] and archive section[8] of the site Yahoo! News, one of the most popular news site. We crawled about 1150 articles along with their comments, going chronologically backwards from 31 March 2013. We then removed all those articles in the dataset which had fewer than 5 lines or had fewer than 5 comments. We were left with 730 articles with more than 100,000 comments.

## 5.2 Experimental setup

We have used the same pre-processing of the dataset and exactly similar parameter settings for Corr-LDA as well as SCTM. We have removed stop words and transformed all

[5] arstechnica.com/science
[6] arstechnica.com/gadgets
[7] news.yahoo.com/all-sections-most-commented/most-popular
[8] news.yahoo.com/archive

Table 2: **Perplexity on test data (lower is better).**

| Model | AT-Science | AT-Gadgets | Yahoo! News |
|---|---|---|---|
| SCTM | **12,327** | 6,445 | **6,880** |
| Corr-LDA | 14,029 | 6,443 | 9,673 |

**Table 3: Topic coherence for top 50 topics (greater is better).**

| Model | AT-Science | AT-Gadgets | Yahoo! News |
|---|---|---|---|
| SCTM | **-52.08** | **-50.47** | **-65.83** |
| Corr-LDA | -88.22 | -87.27 | -93.68 |

**Table 4: Topic diversity (greater is better).**

| Model | AT-Science | AT-Gadgets | Yahoo! News |
|---|---|---|---|
| SCTM | **96.34** | **96.78** | **99.45** |
| Corr-LDA | 9.0 | 23.34 | 21.5 |

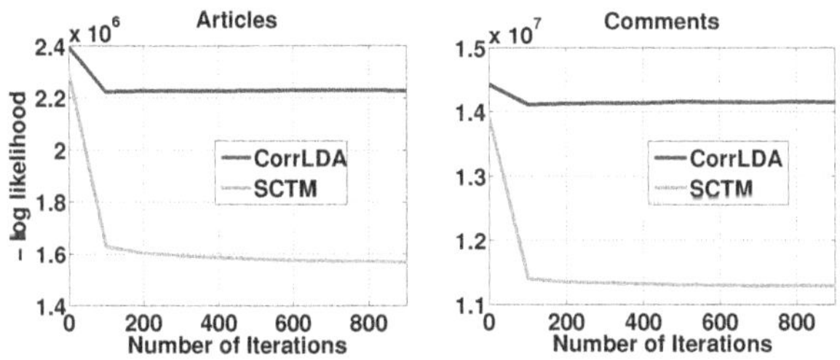


**Figure 3: Convergence of inference: change in negative log-likelihood with number of iterations of the sampling algorithm on Yahoo! News (lower is better). SCTM converges faster and better.**

characters into small case. Blank spaces are treated as the delimiter between words. However, we have not used stemmer or POS-taggers.

We used the following parameter setting: $\alpha = 1$, $\eta = 1$, $\tau_j = 0.01$, $\iota_j = 0.1$ $(\forall j)$, $\nu = 1$, $\lambda = 10$, $\varrho_1 = 1$, $\varrho_2 = 4$, and $J_d = S_d$. For $\alpha, \eta$ we use uninformative value. For other parameters specific to SCTM, low held-out data perplexity (Table 2) and high training likelihood (Figure 3) indicate that model is less sensitive to these hyperparameters. We used 300 topics and 20,000 vocabulary in our experiments.

**Evaluation criteria:** First we evaluate SCTM against Corr-LDA in terms of fitness to the dataset. We use perplexity, topic coherence, topic diversity on all three datasets and convergence of the algorithm on Yahoo! News. Then we focus on the main question of this paper, by evaluating the performance for SCL on AT-Science (subset with gold-standard) and a limited evaluation on Yahoo! News.

## 5.3 Comparison of SCTM and Corr-LDA

We quantitatively evaluate SCTM in the task of modeling article-comments dataset, comparing with the baseline Corr-LDA. For this task, we use perplexity, topic-coherence, diversity among discovered topics and convergence of the inference algorithm as evaluation metrics. The results are presented in Table 2, 3, 4 and Figure 3.

**Table 5: Precision, recall and F1 score for discovering specific comments.**

| Model | Precision | Recall | F1 |
|---|---|---|---|
| SCTM | **0.60** | **0.61** | **0.60** |
| Corr-LDA | 0.23 | 0.21 | 0.22 |

**Perplexity:** Perplexity is a standard quantitative measure in topic modeling literature to compare the performance of various topic models [2]. A lower value of perplexity indicates better generalizability of the topic model. As shown in Table 2, SCTM performs far superior than Corr-LDA.

**Topic coherence:** By approximating the user experience of *topic quality* on top $\sigma$ words of a topic, [10] proposed that topic coherence (TC) can be measured as: $TC(\sigma) = \sum_{i \le \sigma} \sum_{j<i} \log \frac{D(w_i, w_j)+\epsilon}{D(w_j)}$. $D(w)$ is the document frequency of any word $w$, and $D(w_i, w_j)$ is the document frequency of $w_i$ and $w_j$ together. $\epsilon$ is a small constant to avoid log zero. Values closer to zero indicate better coherence. We have used $\sigma = 5$ to compute coherence of a topic. Table 3 contains the comparison between SCTM and Corr-LDA which shows supremacy of the proposed approach.

**Topic diversity:** We want to evaluate the ability of SCTM in discovering diverse set of topics. We consider top 5 words for topics which have maximum probability for a word greater than 0.01. Then compute textual difference between topic $i$ and topic $j$ as $Tdiv_{ij} = 1 - |tw_i \cap tw_j|/5$, where $tw_i$ contains top 5 words for topic $i$. Averaging over all pairs we report in Table 4. Note that higher value of $Tdiv$ is better and empirical results show that SCTM is superior.

**Convergence of inference:** We plot negative log likelihood of SCTM and Corr-LDA against iterations in Figure 3. Note that SCTM mixes much better than Corr-LDA. Both the models, SCTM as well as Corr-LDA, converge almost in the same time. However, as fitness of Corr-LDA is worse, the likelihood of the dataset remains low throughout.

**Discussion:** Interestingly, SCTM outperforms Corr-LDA in modeling aspects commonly used in topic modeling literature. The main reason behind this is that SCTM finds more unique topics, whereas Corr-LDA finds relatively mixed topics by mixing up many unique topics. On the other hand, supremacy of SCTM over Corr-LDA in topic diversity is expected as that is explicitly ensured in the modeling. Low perplexity on held-out dataset and high likelihood on training data affirms that although SCTM is a far more complex model than Corr-LDA, it is able to learn from the dataset appropriately.

## 5.4 Accuracy of SCTM over Corr-LDA on SCL

We evaluate the main task of this paper in this section, i.e. the task of discovering specific comments. We use the manually annotated gold-standard from AT-Science dataset for evaluation. Using Algorithm 1 we classify comments into specific and non-specific (general and irrelevant) for both Corr-LDA and SCTM. Using the gold-standard we compute precision-recall and report them in Table 5. SCTM outperforms Corr-LDA significantly.

Table 6: **Precision, recall and F1 score for aligning specific comments to the sentences.**

| Model | Precision | Recall | F1 |
|---|---|---|---|
| SCTM | **0.365** | **0.442** | **0.400** |
| Corr-LDA | 0.019 | 0.038 | 0.025 |

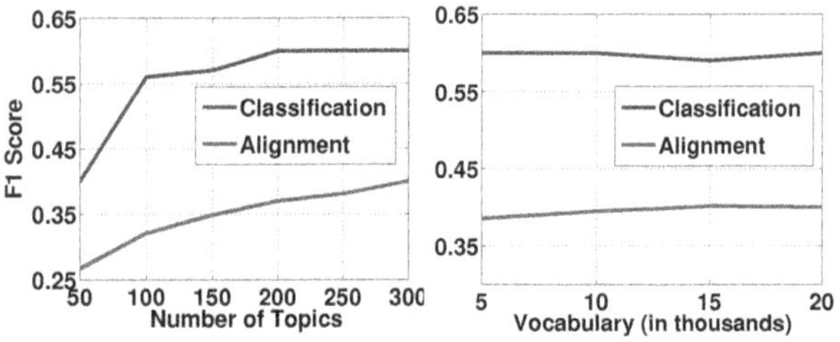


**Figure 4: Sensitivity analysis: F1 score variation with respect to number of topics and vocabulary size for SCTM.**

Similarly, from Algorithm 1 we get the article sentences corresponding to each specific comment detected by the models, for both Corr-LDA and SCTM. Then using gold-standard we compute precision, recall and F1. The results are reported in Table 6. SCTM is far superior than Corr-LDA.

We can see that Corr-LDA is unable to give any satisfactory result in discovering specific comments. This is due to the fact that there is one topic vector per article-comments pair which fails to model specific comments properly.

**Evaluation on Yahoo! News:** Due to the unavailability of ground-truths and the large number of comments in the dataset, we have done a limited evaluation on all articles which had upto 50 predicted specific comments (a total of 604 articles out of 730). Out of a total of 138,538 comments in the dataset, SCTM predicted 23,624 comments to be specific comments and the per document average accuracy is **63%**. In comparison, Corr-LDA discovers only a total of 4,704 comments in the dataset which is even less than 50% of the *correctly* discovered specific comments by SCTM.

**Sensitivity analysis of SCTM:** We analyse the sensitivity of SCTM towards number of topics and vocabulary size, two important hyperparameters, in Figure 4. F1 score is observed to be not sensitive to the vocabulary size, however it gets better with the number of topics and stabilizes gradually. This is justified as we expect to get large number of topics due to diversity across the articles and comments.

# 6. USE CASES OF SCL

Comments are a great source of public response. Whereas specific comments are more useful to mine information from comments. To demonstrate that SCTM is useful in a wide variety of applications, we do a detailed analysis of two specific articles. (i) Regarding *President Obama*'s visit to Middle-Eastern countries and (ii) a product review on *Google Nexus*. The first article was the *most commented* article in our Yahoo! News dataset and the second article was the most recent well commented article in ArsTechnica's Gadget section. The two articles demonstrate the efficacy of SCTM in the diverse scenarios of large and small number of comments, different categories of politics and product reviews and different hosting platforms of news and blogs. Note that, such analysis is subject to efficacy in SCL and hence is beyond the scope of the existing methods.

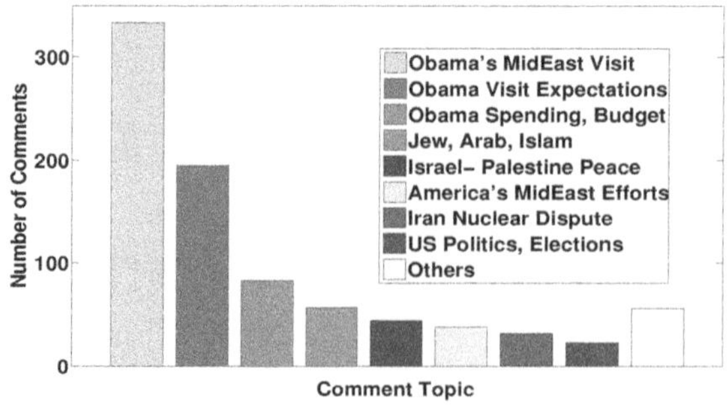


**Figure 6: Popularity of topics based on number of comments. The first topic (gray-colored) corresponds to general comments. Except that, all other topics correspond to specific comments and are missed by the state of the art methods.**

## 6.1 Analysing comments using topics discovered by SCTM

We analyse the comments on the news reporting *President Obama*'s visit to the Middle East during March 19-23, 2013[9]. The event was widely covered in the media and was highly commented upon. Figure 5 shows excerpts from one such article at Yahoo! News. At the time of crawling, the article had 1919 comments. Analysing the comments one can accumulate a survey of opinion.

Note that the article in example touches upon various issues like Iranian nuclear program, Syria etc in different segments of the article. The number of such issues covered in the article is large but the amount of text contributing to each of them is small. Interestingly, many comments focus on such issues minorly described in the article.

Figure 5 shows some of the topics discovered by SCTM on this event and the comments corresponding to those topics. Sentences, topics and the comments are color coded such that they signify a link among them. Note that, SCTM is able to discover fine topics like "*Obama's MidEast Visit*", "*Israel-Palestine Peace*" and "*Iran Nuclear Dispute*" where Corr-LDA mixes them together. SCTM is able to retrieve comments which are related to such topics described in specific parts of the article.

Using the ability to detect precise topics SCTM can analyze the public response quantitatively, on the basis of the topic being discussed in the comment. We categorize comments based on their major topic. Figure 6 shows the number of comments classified in this way into the different topics. As expected, we find that most of the comments are general and about the topic "*Obama's MidEast Visit*" (gray colored). The remaining comments are specific and related to other topics. Among the specific comments, the most discussed topic is "*Obama Visit Expectations*" (red colored) with 195 comments marking the "*hot-spot*" in the article (box in Figure 5).

[9]news.yahoo.com/obama-heads-middle-east-low-expectations.html

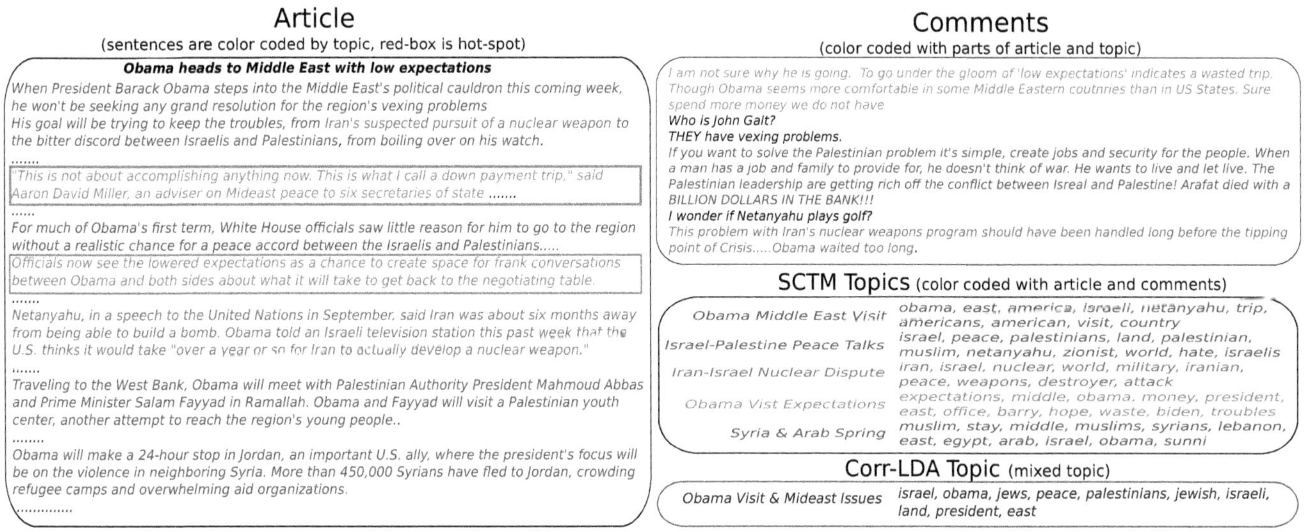


**Figure 5: An example from Yahoo! News. SCTM is able to find issues under-reported in the article and specific comments on them. SCTM also detects *hot-spot* (red box), although "*Obama-Visit-Expectations*" topic has appeared only in those two sentences, it has received the most number of comments leaving general ones. Corr-LDA finds only one mixed topic failing to analyse user response effectively.**

It is important to note that sentences in the main article related to a specific comment can be very few and may not be contiguous (which can be seen in Figure 5 and Figure 1). This demonstrates the elegance of SCTM in performing such a hard task of SCL.

## 6.2 Capturing surprising market trends

We analyse the comments on the review of a recently launched tablet, *Google Nexus 7*, published in AT-Gadget. An excerpt is given in Figure 1. This article is one of the well commented reviews in the recent times with 180 comments at the time of crawling. In review articles, the story generally covers a wide range of aspects and many of them will be less described. However, people might be sensitive to a certain aspect which is difficult to guess a priori.

The author discussed only in approximately 8% of the sentences the "screen display quality", or more precisely, the comparison with "*iPad* Retina display" and the future prospect of "*iPad mini*" equipped with such retina display. SCTM correctly found that this point received a great deal of attention from users with 22% of comments leaving the irrelevant ones. It is surprising because an article about a new *Google* tablet has attracted a large number of comments related to another tablet, "*iPad mini*", which has not even been released. Examples of such specific comments can be seen in Figure 1, all of these were correctly discovered by SCTM. We hope, this provides an important feedback to both *Google* as well as *Apple*. Note that none of the existing methods are capable to capture such trends.

## 6.3 Enhancing user satisfaction

We demonstrate two applications of SCL which can improve user experience. In these cases accuracy on SCL is critical and hence beyond the scope of the existing methods.

**Hot-spot detection:** A *hot-spot* is the set of sentences in the article which have received most attention in the comments. For example, in Figure 5 the portions in *red box* are the hot-spots discovered by SCTM. Similarly, in Figure 1 the portions in *green box* are the hot-spots in that article. SCL enables one to find such hot-spots in articles automatically. This can help in summarization, advertisements, better user engagement etc.

The ability of SCTM in categorizing comments into various issues covered in the article and connecting with the sentences in the article is key to discover hot-spots, where existing methods fail.

**Comment cleaning:** Comment cleaning is one of the important tasks today for online media sites. Being equipped with SCL, we propose a novel method of cleaning up irrelevant comments without using any external resource or supervision. Existing methods of comment cleaning focus on special features like presence of URL or certain keywords. However, even after filtering out such comments, there will be some comments which are absolutely irrelevant and in many cases indecent (see Figure 7). But it is difficult for existing methods to clean up such irrelevant comments as they look very much similar to the normal comments, many of them may contain words present in the article. Moreover, most of the existing methods are either supervised or semi supervised (refer to [8] for a complete review) or use text enrichment [14].

The algorithm for detecting irrelevant comments is in Algorithm 1. The comments shown in Figure 7 on two articles of AT-Science[10] are all examples of *irrelevant comments* correctly detected by SCTM, where existing methods failed.

We evaluated the performance of SCTM in finding irrelevant comments on 100 randomly selected articles from the Yahoo! News dataset. For each of these articles, the algorithm was applied to predict top 20 irrelevant comments

[10]arstechnica.com/science/2013/03/first-planck-results-the-universe-is-still-weird-and-interesting/, arstechnica.com/science/2013/03/voyager-probes-key-transition-remains-mysterious/

| Voyager over the "heliocliff," but Solar System transition mysterious | First Planck results: the Universe is still weird & interesting |
|---|---|
| - You sure?Maybe they were just clicking that "restart later" button every four hours... | - Yes.Of course you're right! Duh!Argh..newborn baby brain. Not think good with no sleep |
| - I propose calling it the "Frank Cliff" for all eternity. | - If you are a teacher, know a teacher, or can convince them you are a teacher |
| - If I ever have kids, this is what they're growing up to. Old McDonald had a cliff, e-i-e-i-o And on that cliff there was a Voyager, e-i-e-i-o ..... | - This may be the first and only time we can see tweets from astrophysicists that read "Busy plancking right now" |
| - I believe that was intended to be a pun. Heliocliff...Cliff Notes....Ha ha?... | - Your cell phone sensor doesn't detect microwaves, though. |

**Figure 7: Examples of irrelevant comments on two articles from AT-Science (showing only headline and irrelevant comments). Notice that these comments look normal and do not have any specific feature except lack of correspondence to the main article making it challenging for existing methods. These comments are correctly marked by SCTM to be irrelavnt, whereas the existing methods failed.**

which were manually annotated as correct or incorrect. The mean average precision at 20 (**MAP@20**) was found to be **0.87** which is quite high. Moreover, most of the mistakes that the model makes fall in a grey area, where humans will differ in their opinion of the comment being irrelevant.

## 7. CONCLUSION

In this paper we explored an interesting problem of specific comment location which is beyond the scope of the state of the art. A novel correspondence topic model, namely SCTM, has been proposed which admits an efficient collapsed Gibbs sampling algorithm. Following [3] the proposed inference can be easily modified to be scalable. On three real life datasets we evaluated SCTM against Corr-LDA to demonstrate efficacy of the proposed approach. Finally, we demonstrated four different use cases with practical importance. We believe similar study can be done using SCTM on other datasets like image-tag, paper-bibliography etc.

## 8. ACKNOWLEDGMENTS

We are thankful to all the reviewers for their valuable comments. The authors were partially supported by DST grant (DST/ECA/CB/1101).

## 9. REFERENCES

[1] D. M. Blei and M. I. Jordan. Modeling annotated data. In *SIGIR*, pages 127–134. ACM, 2003.

[2] D. M. Blei, A. Y. Ng, and M. I. Jordan. Latent Dirichlet allocation. *Journal of Machine Learning Research*, 3:993–1022, Jan. 2003.

[3] K. R. Canini, L. Shi, and T. L. Griffiths. Online inference of topics with latent Dirichlet allocation. In *AISTATS*, volume 5, 2009.

[4] R. J. Connor and J. E. Mosimann. Concepts of independence for proportions with a generalization of the Dirichlet distribution. *Journal of the American Statistical Association*, 64(325):194–206, 1969.

[5] M. Das, S. Bhattacharya, C. Bhattacharyya, and G. Kanchi. Subtle topic models and discovering subtly manifested software concerns automatically. In *ICML*, pages 253–261, 2013.

[6] Y. Hu, A. John, D. D. Seligmann, and F. Wang. What were the tweets about? Topical associations between public events and twitter feeds. In *ICWSM*, 2012.

[7] H. Ishwaran and L. F. James. Gibbs sampling methods for stick-breaking priors. *Journal of the American Statistical Association*, 96(453):161–173, 2001.

[8] R. Kant, S. H. Sengamedu, and K. S. Kumar. Comment spam detection by sequence mining. In *WSDM*, pages 183–192. ACM, 2012.

[9] Z. Ma, A. Sun, Q. Yuan, and G. Cong. Topic-driven reader comments summarization. In *CIKM '12*, pages 265–274. ACM, 2012.

[10] D. Mimno, H. M. Wallach, E. Talley, M. Leenders, and A. McCallum. Optimizing semantic coherence in topic models. In *EMNLP*, pages 262–272. Association for Computational Linguistics, 2011.

[11] D. K. Sil, S. H. Sengamedu, and C. Bhattacharyya. Supervised matching of comments with news article segments. In *CIKM*, pages 2125–2128. ACM, 2011.

[12] I. Titov and R. McDonald. Modeling online reviews with multi-grain topic models. In *WWW*, pages 111–120. ACM, 2008.

[13] C. Wang and D. Blei. Decoupling sparsity and smoothness in the discrete hierarchical Dirichlet process. In *NIPS*, pages 1982–1989. 2009.

[14] J. Wang, C. T. Yu, P. S. Yu, B. Liu, and W. Meng. Diversionary comments under political blog posts. In *CIKM*, pages 1789–1793. ACM, 2012.

[15] T. Yano, W. W. Cohen, and N. A. Smith. Predicting response to political blog posts with topic models. In *NAACL*, pages 477–485. ACL, 2009.

## APPENDIX

### *Collapsing SBP random vector $\rho$.*

From the relation between $SBP$ and $\mathcal{GD}$ [4] we get that, if $\rho_{da}$s are constructed as equation (1), then they are equivalently distributed as $\mathcal{GD}$ [7]. The density of $\rho_{da}$ is:

$$f_{\rho_{da}} = \prod_{j=1}^{J_d-1} \frac{\rho_{daj}^{\tau_j-1}(1-\sum_{l=1}^{j}\rho_{dal})^{\kappa_j}}{B(\tau_j,\iota_j)} \quad (10)$$

where $B(\tau_j,\iota_j) = \frac{\Gamma(\tau_j)\Gamma(\iota_j)}{\Gamma(\tau_j+\iota_j)}$. $\kappa_j = \iota_j - \iota_{j+1} - \tau_{j+1}$ for $j = 1,2,\ldots,J_d-2$ and $\kappa_{J_d-1} = \iota_{J_d-1} - 1$. Note that, $\rho_{daJ_d} = 1 - \sum_{l=1}^{J_d-1}\rho_{dal}$. Note that, by setting $\iota_{j-1} = \tau_j + \iota_j$, $2 \le j < J_d$, $\mathcal{GD}$ reduces to standard Dirichlet distribution.

Like Dirichlet distribution, $\mathcal{GD}$ is also conjugate to the multinomial distribution, and hence we can integrate out $\rho$'s and $v$'s. If $\rho_{da} \sim \mathcal{GD}_{J_d-1}(\tau_1,\ldots,\tau_{J_d-1},\iota_1,\ldots,\iota_{J_d-1})$, and $b_{daj}$s are sampled from $mult(\rho_{da})$, then the posterior distribution of $\rho_{da}$ given $(b_{dal})$s $(l \neq i)$ is again a $\mathcal{GD}$ with density $\mathcal{GD}_{J_d-1}(\bar{\tau}_1,\ldots,\bar{\tau}_{J_d-1},\bar{\iota}_1,\ldots,\bar{\iota}_{J_d-1})$, where $\bar{\tau}_j = \tau_j + \check{m}_{daj}^{-dai}$, $\bar{\iota}_j = \iota_j + \sum_{l=j+1}^{J_d}\check{m}_{dal}^{-dai}$.

# Nonparametric Bayesian Upstream Supervised Multi-Modal Topic Models

Renjie Liao
Department of Computer Science & Engineering
The Chinese University of Hong Kong
rjliao@cse.cuhk.edu.hk

Jun Zhu
State Key Lab of Intell. Tech & Sys.; TNLIST Lab
Dept. of Comp. Sci & Tech
Tsinghua University, Beijing, 100084, China
dcszj@mail.tsinghua.edu.cn

Zengchang Qin
Intelligent Computing and Machine Learning Lab
School of ASEE
Beihang University, Beijing, 100191, China
zcqin@buaa.edu.cn

## ABSTRACT

Learning with multi-modal data is at the core of many multimedia applications, such as cross-modal retrieval and image annotation. In this paper, we present a nonparametric Bayesian approach to learning upstream supervised topic models for analyzing multi-modal data. Our model develops a compound nonparametric Bayesian multi-modal prior to describe the correlation structure of data both within each individual modality and between different modalities. It extends the hierarchical Dirichlet process (HDP) through incorporating upstream supervised response variables and values of latent functions under Gaussian process (GP). Upstream responses shared by data from multiple modalities are beneficial for discriminatively training and GP allows flexible structure learning of correlations. Hence, our model inherits the automatic determination of the number of topics from HDP, structure learning from GP and enhanced predictive capacity from upstream supervision. We also provide efficient variational inference and prediction algorithms. Empirical studies demonstrate superior performances on several benchmark datasets compared with previous competitors.

## Categories and Subject Descriptors

G.3 [**Probability and Statistics**]: Nonparametric statistics; H.3.3 [**Information Search and Retrieval**]: Retrieval models; H.4 [**Information System Applications**]: Miscellaneous

## Keywords

Multi-modal Learning; Nonparametric Bayesian; Topic Model; Cross-modal Retrieval

## 1. INTRODUCTION

Nowadays, large collections of data on the web consist of various modalities, such as images, texts, and audio or video clips. Extracting useful knowledge from these growing multi-modal data has become increasingly important in many application areas. Multi-modal learning, sometimes referred to as multi-view learning [8] or multi-field learning [26], aims at modeling collections of such kind of data and making predictions when data of some modalities is missing. One typical example is to model pairs of images and associated texts (e.g., captions, paragraphs or articles), which lays the foundation of many valuable applications, including cross-modal retrieval, image annotation and so on. However, this multi-modal learning problem is rather challenging, since it requires analyzing not only the characteristics of data in single modality but also the relevances of data across different modalities.

Previous works in this area have primarily focused on looking for latent representations shared by the multi-modal data. Based on the different techniques they used, these works can be roughly divided into three categories: subspace learning, undirected probabilistic graphical models (PGMs), and directed PGMs. Representative works of the first class include canonical correlation analysis (CCA) and its variants [31, 28]. By maximizing the correlation between different modalities, it aims to find a low dimensional subspace representation for multi-modal data. Another ones are based on distance metric learning [33, 34] and hash function learning [39], which try to discover optimal nonlinear subspace endowed with an expected similarity measure. For the second class, Markov random fields (MRF) based methods have commonly been used. For example, the dual-wing harmonium model [35] describes the latent representations shared by images and texts through tying the latent variables of two basic harmonium models. The above two types of models are capable of effectively discovering the desired latent representations, but often lack intuitive explanations and do not perform well in terms of prediction.

The main line of the third class of work are multi-modal topic models (mmTM), such as multi-modal latent Dirichlet allocation (mmLDA) [2], correspondence latent Dirichlet allocation (CorrLDA) [2] and the multi-modal aspect model [22]. Most of them describe the single-modal data via standard topic models, like latent Dirichlet allocation (LDA) [4]. Thereafter, [36] extends the Dirichlet prior in mmTM by using a hierarchical Dirichlet process (HDP) [29] which is able to automatically choose the number of topics. These models introduce shared latent variables which either indicate the topic proportions as in mmLDA or the


*WSDM'14*, February 24–28, 2014, New York, New York, USA.
Copyright 2014 ACM 978-1-4503-2351-2/14/02 ...$15.00.
http://dx.doi.org/10.1145/2556195.2556238.

indexes of topics as in CorrLDA, thus enforcing strong correlations between topics from different modalities. This kind of strong correlation is inappropriate since usually data in one modality contains a considerable amount of modality-private information that is unrelated to the other. Therefore, relying on the logistic normal distribution adopted in correlated topic model (CTM) [3], authors in [26] relax this strong correlation and allow structure learning of the correlation matrix. Beyond that, the discrete infinite logistic normal (DILN) [23] distribution is utilized in [30] to further keep the private topics inside each modality. All the above mmTMs learn the latent representations of the multi-modal data in an unsupervised manner and are able to offer intuitive probabilistic interpretations.

Recently, upstream supervised response variables, like categorical labels, which are available in many scenarios, are utilized for enhancing the performance of prediction. Upstream supervised models are common for understanding scenes in computer vision community [11, 41], since image categories are cheaply accessible on the web. In contrast to downstream supervised models, like supervised topic model and its variants [5, 40], upstream ones assume that response variables are directly or indirectly involved in generating latent variables. In the setting of multi-modal learning, these supervised response variables are usually shared by data from different modalities, thus help describing the relation between data from different modalities precisely. Moreover, with this kind of supervised guidance, latent representations learned by the model are presumably more discriminative. For example, it has been shown in [24] that applying logistic regression to class label, is helpful for improving the predictive capacity of CCA in cross-modal retrieval. At the same time, similar categorical information has been exploited in [8, 7] to extend the MRF-based multi-view models through a supervised max-margin approach and boosted predictive results are also demonstrated.

In this paper, we propose a novel nonparametric Bayesian upstream supervised (NPBUS) multi-modal topic model by combining the above advantages of previous works. Specifically, our model first inherits the two merits of having an explicit probabilistic explanation and automatic determination of the number of topics from the HDP-based mmTM. Then our model introduces a Gaussian process (GP) [25] to flexibly capture correlation structures both within each individual modality and between multiple different modalities. Moreover, upstream supervised response variables shared by data from different modalities are incorporated into a normalized gamma representation of HDP, thus making our method possess remarkable predictive ability. We also derive an efficient variational inference algorithm for training. The proposed NPBUS model demonstrates superior experimental results than various competitors in the predictive tasks of cross-modal retrieval and image annotation.

The rest of the paper is structured as follows. Sec. 2 introduces the background works related to our model. Sec. 3 elucidates our NPBUS multi-modal topic model. Sec. 4.1 presents our variational inference and prediction algorithms. Sec. 5 presents our empirical results on cross-modal retrieval and image annotation. Finally, Sec. 6 concludes.

## 2. BACKGROUND WORKS

In this section, we review the hierarchical Dirichlet process (HDP) [29] based topic model for single-modal data and the discrete infinite logistic normal (DILN) distribution [23], which lays the foundation of our model to be presented later. Terminologies from text modeling, e.g. "words", "documents" and "vocabulary", are used throughout the paper, since they can be well generalized in modeling data of other modalities. For example, in the context of bag-of-words model for image classification, "words", also referred to as "visual words", are clustering centers of some low level visual descriptors (e.g. SIFT [19]), and "documents" correspond to images.

### 2.1 Hierarchical Dirichlet Process Topic Models

We first introduce latent Dirichlet allocation (LDA) [4] which assumes that documents are represented as mixtures of latent topics $\eta$ and words appearing in a document are drawn independently from their corresponding topics. Specifically, a topic mixing proportion $\theta$ for each document is first sampled from a Dirichlet prior and thereafter the topic for each word is chosen through sampling a topic index $z \sim Mult(\theta)$, where $Mult(\cdot)$ is a multinomial distribution. At last, word $x$ is drawn from its corresponding topic $\eta_z$ which is a multinomial distribution over the words in the vocabulary. Note that, in a fully Bayesian treatment, we may place a prior for topics $\eta$. To further model the topic mixing proportion, hierarchical Dirichlet process (HDP) [29], a nonparametric Bayesian prior, is widely adopted. Formally, HDP is a Dirichlet process (DP) [13] that has another Dirichlet process as its base probability measure. In this paper, we focus on two-level HDPs, though it may be extended to arbitrary levels. Its hierarchical representation is

$$\begin{aligned} G &\sim DP(\alpha G_0) \\ \tilde{G} &\sim DP(\beta G), \end{aligned} \tag{1}$$

where $G_0$ is the aforementioned Dirichlet prior for $\eta$, and $\alpha$ and $\beta$ are the first and second level concentration parameters respectively. The main advantage of HDP formulation is the automatical determination of the number of topics owing to its nonparametric nature. Moreover, due to the almost sure discreteness property of DP [1], the HDP prior enables the implicit sharing of atomic probability measures between the repeatedly sampled topic proportions $\theta$. And it will largely ease our work of specifying multiple priors, since there will be multiple different sets of topics in the multi-modal setting.

### 2.2 Discrete Infinite Logistic Normal (DILN) Distribution

Though HDP is a popular prior for modeling topic proportions, it is insufficient to capture the correlation structure between different topics since its construction is a random measure which means all random variables as well as all summations of subsets are independent. To overcome this weak point, discrete infinite logistic normal (DILN) model [23] is proposed. It takes advantages from both HDP and CTM, and offers an effective prior for structure learning of topics.

Specifically, DILN first introduces an auxiliary variable $\ell$ for each topic $\eta$. It can be interpreted as the latent location of a topic in some latent space. As $\ell$ and $\eta$ are associated, the base distribution used in the first level HDP is augmented as a product measure $G_0 \times L_0$, where $G_0$ is still the prior distribution for topics and $L_0$ is a distribution over latent locations. To construct DILN, a hierarchical sampling process is

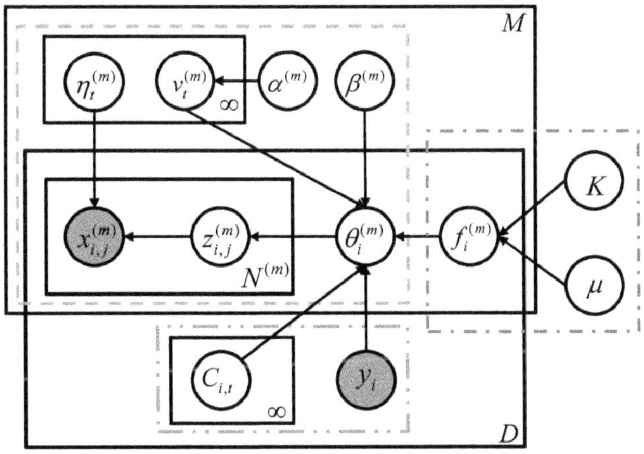


**Figure 1: A graphical illustration of our NPBUS model. The red rectangle (single dot dashed lines) indicates the part of GP, the green rectangle (dashed lines) indicates the part of HDP topic model and the blue rectangle (double dots dashed lines) indicates the part of upstream supervised response variable.**

implemented as HDP. In the first level, a random measure $G$ is drawn from Dirichlet process, $G \sim DP(\alpha G_0 \times L_0)$. And in the second level, a random measure $\tilde{G}$ is drawn from another DP, $\tilde{G} \sim DP(\beta G)$. Meanwhile, a random function $f(\ell)$ is drawn from a Gaussian process, $f(\ell) \sim GP(\mu(\ell), k(\ell, \ell'))$, where $f(\cdot)$ and $GP$ are defined on the latent location $\ell$, $\mu$ and $k$ are the mean function and kernel function respectively. Finally, a sample from DILN, i.e., the topic mixing proportion, is constructed via multiplying the random measure $\tilde{G}$ by the exponentiated value of the random function $f(\ell)$. Hence, a topic assignment $z$ could be drawn as,

$$z \sim \exp(f(\ell))\tilde{G}. \tag{2}$$

Since $\ell$ is explicitly correlated via a GP, topic proportions drawn from DILN are also correlated. And, due to the discreteness of $\tilde{G}$, the sampled topic mixing proportion is discrete.

# 3. NPBUS MULTI-MODAL TOPIC MODEL

We now develop the nonparametric Bayesian upstream supervised (NPBUS) multi-modal topic model and elaborate its merits in modeling multi-modal data. Without loss of generality, we focus on the two-modal dataset which contains collection of images and texts. We emphasize that the generalization to more and different modalities is straightforward. For clarity, we denote the two-modal observable dataset by $X = \{x_i^{(m)}, y_i | i = 1, 2, ..., D, m = 1, 2\}$, where $x_i^{(m)}$ and $y_i$ are the $i$th word of $m$th modality and $i$th response variable respectively, and $D$ is the size of the dataset. Note that in our problem setting, each pair of image and text shares an extra response variable which plays an supervision role. Here we highlight the key challenges dealing with such a type of dataset: (i) modeling correlations of topic proportions both within modality and between different modalities; and (ii) exploiting upstream supervising information of response variable. Then we will explain in detail our NPBUS model and how it tackles the above challenges.

## 3.1 Compound Nonparametric Bayesian Multi-Modal Prior

In the context of multi-modal learning, words in each modality are drawn independently from the modality-specific topic given their corresponding topic assignments. For the $i$th document of $m$th modality, we denote the vector of topic mixing proportion as $\theta_i^{(m)}$ and the probability of choosing the $t$th topic is thus $\theta_{i,t}^{(m)}$. The topic assignment of the $j$th word $x_{i,j}^{(m)}$ is defined as $z_{i,j}^{(m)}$ and the auxiliary variable of $t$th topic appeared in DILN is $f_{i,t}^{(m)}$. Note that, $f_{i,t}^{(m)}$ is the value of a random function modeled by GP and we omit its input latent location $\ell_t$ here and clarify the reason later.

Similar with HDP topic models, the first level Dirichlet process of our model is represented via a stick breaking process [27],

$$\begin{aligned} \eta_t^{(m)} &\sim G_0 \\ \tilde{v}_t^{(m)} &\sim Beta(1, \alpha^{(m)}) \\ v_t^{(m)} &= \tilde{v}_t^{(m)} \prod_{j=1}^{t-1} (1 - \tilde{v}_j^{(m)}) \\ G &= \sum_{t=1}^{\infty} v_t^{(m)} \delta_{\eta_t^{(m)}}, \end{aligned} \tag{3}$$

where $G_0$ is the Dirichlet prior for topics, $v_t^{(m)}$ is the stick proportion and $Beta(\cdot)$ is a beta distribution.

In the second level, we first draw a random measure $\tilde{G}$ from another Dirichlet process, $DP(\beta^{(m)}G)$. Note that we here focus on presenting our prior and leave the detailed construction of this DP in next section. As aforementioned, different topics are just weakly correlated owing to the normalization property of probability measure $\tilde{G}$. To capture flexible correlation structures, we then concatenate the auxiliary variables from each modality into an single vector, like below,

$$f_i = [f_{i,1}^{(1)}, ...f_{i,\infty}^{(1)}, f_{i,1}^{(2)}, ...f_{i,\infty}^{(2)}, ..., f_{i,1}^{(M)}, ..., f_{i,\infty}^{(M)}]. \tag{4}$$

Then we use a GP to model the whole vector $f_i$, which is similar with what [26] and [30] have done. Finally, as in DILN, we could multiply the samples from $G$ by the exponentiated value of $f_{it}^{(m)}$, which fulfills the introduction of correlation to topic proportions. Specifically, in the covariance matrix of GP, the diagonal blocks describe the correlation of topic proportions within the same modality, and off-diagonal ones describe the correlation of topic proportions between different modalities. Note that, to sample $f_{it}^{(m)}$, we merely need to sample $f_i$ and obtain $f_{it}^{(m)}$ immediately according to its position in the whole vector.

We now turn to model the upstream supervised response variable $y$ which can be categorical labels, rating scores and so on. Here we only consider the discrete case, i.e., $y \in \{1, 2, ..., \mathbb{K}\}$. Since these responses induce a supervised grouping of multi-modal data, we could conduct correlation structure learning within each group. Therefore, in this way, the whole multi-modal dataset would be modeled more precisely and the generated topic proportions would be more discriminative. Specifically, we introduce another random scaling factor $C_{i,t}$ which is drawn from a gamma distribution $Gamma(a_{t,y_i}, b_{t,y_i})$. Then we divide exponentiated value $\exp(f_{i,t}^{(m)})$ by $C_{i,t}$ to obtain a response dependent random scaling factor. By doing so, the compound nonparametric

Bayesian multi-modal prior distribution of topic proportions is formulated as,

$$\theta_i^{(m)} \propto \sum_{t=1}^{\infty} \frac{\exp(f_{i,t}^{(m)})}{C_{i,t}} \tilde{G}. \tag{5}$$

Now the correlation structures of multi-modal data is captured in the weight term $\exp(f_{i,t}^{(m)})$. And, multi-modal data within the same group, i.e., having the same value of $y_i$, would share the same hyperparameters $a_{t,y_i}$ and $b_{t,y_i}$. Thus the group specific random weight $C_{i,t}$ has introduced the upstream supervising information. As a result, with this prior at hand, we have solved the two challenges mentioned above.

## 3.2 Normalized Gamma Representation

Following the normalized gamma process construction of HDP in [23], we now develop a representation of our NPBUS multi-modal topic model. It will be clear that this kind of representation incorporates the correlation structure via the second parameter of gamma distribution and simplifies our posterior inference.

First of all, a normalized gamma process construction of the second level HDP could be expressed as,

$$\begin{aligned} \tilde{\theta}_{i,t}^{(m)} &\sim Gamma(\beta^{(m)} v_t^{(m)}, 1) \\ \theta_i^{(m)} &= \sum_{t=1}^{\infty} \frac{\tilde{\theta}_{i,t}^{(m)}}{\sum_{j=1}^{\infty} \tilde{\theta}_{i,j}^{(m)}} \delta_{\eta_t^{(m)}}. \end{aligned} \tag{6}$$

where the normalizing constant $\sum_{j=1}^{\infty} \tilde{\theta}_{i,j}^{(m)}$ is almost surely finite [23]. Building upon Eq. (6), a topic mixing proportion $\theta_i^{(m)}$ drawn from the second level of our prior could be constructed below,

$$\begin{aligned} f_{i,t}^{(m)} &\sim GP(\mu, K), \\ C_{i,t} &\sim Gamma(a_{y_i,t}, b_{y_i,t}), \\ \tilde{\theta}_{i,t}^{(m)} &\sim Gamma(\beta^{(m)} v_t^{(m)}, \exp(-f_{i,t}^{(m)})/C_{i,t}), \\ \theta_i^{(m)} &= \sum_{t=1}^{\infty} \frac{\tilde{\theta}_{i,t}^{(m)}}{\sum_{j=1}^{\infty} \tilde{\theta}_{i,j}^{(m)}} \delta_{\eta_t^{(m)}}. \end{aligned} \tag{7}$$

where the third line is derived by absorbing the scaling factor $\exp(f_{i,t}^{(m)})/C_{i,t}$ of Eq. (5) into the second parameter of gamma distribution.

Once the topic mixing proportion $\theta_i^{(m)}$ is obtained, we are capable to generate multi-modal data. The overall generative process of our model is summarized below:

- For each modality $m = 1, ..., M$
  - For each latent topic $t = 1, 2, ..., \infty$

    draw $\{v_t^{(m)}, \eta_t^{(m)}\}$ according to Eq. (3)
  - For each document $i = 1, 2, ..., D$

    draw $\theta_i^{(m)}$ according to Eq. (7)
    - For each word $j = 1, 2, ..., N^{(m)}$

      draw $z_{i,j}^{(m)} \sim Mult(\theta_i^{(m)})$

      draw $x_{i,j}^{(m)} \sim Mult(\eta_{z_{i,j}^{(m)}}^{(m)})$

Graphically, the PGM of our model is illustrated as in Fig. 1 in which we separately annotate the part of HDP topic model, the part of GP prior and the part of upstream supervised response variable. Here we omit the prior $G_0$ of topics and hyperparameters of $C_{i,t}$ in the figure for simplicity. As can be seen from the figure, both within modality and between modality correlation of topic proportions are captured and the upstream supervised response variable is also exploited.

## 3.3 The Correlation Structure

We now exploit the correlation structure of topic proportions in our model. Owing to the normalized gamma process representation above, we could analytically calculate the first two order central moments and the covariance of the unnormalized topic proportions (i.e., $\tilde{\theta}_{i,t}^{(m)}$). These moments essentially contain the desired correlation structures, since the correlation matrix can be obtained by merely normalizing the covariance matrix. The mean function $\mu$ of GP is assumed to be zero in deriving the following equations. After some integration procedures, we could obtain the results below,

$$\begin{aligned} &\mathbb{E}[\tilde{\theta}_{i,t}^{(m)}|\Theta] = \frac{\beta^{(m)} v_t^{(m)} a_{y_i,t}}{b_{y_i,t}} e^{K_{t,t}^{(m,m)}/2} \\ &\mathbb{V}[\tilde{\theta}_{i,t}^{(m)}|\Theta] = \\ &\frac{\beta^{(m)} v_t^{(m)} a_{y_i,t}}{b_{y_i,t}} e^{2K_{t,t}^{(m,m)}} \left[1 + \frac{\beta^{(m)} v_t^{(m)} a_{y_i,t}}{b_{y_i,t}} (1 - \frac{1}{e^{K_{t,t}^{(m,m)}}})\right] \\ &Cov[\tilde{\theta}_{i,t}^{(m)}, \tilde{\theta}_{i,s}^{(n)}|\Theta] = \\ &\frac{\beta^{(m)} \beta^{(n)} v_t^{(m)} v_s^{(n)} a_{y_i,t} a_{y_i,s}}{b_{y_i,t} b_{y_i,s}} e^{(K_{t,t}^{(m,m)} + K_{s,s}^{(n,n)})/2} (e^{K_{t,s}^{(m,n)}} - 1) \end{aligned} \tag{8}$$

where the conditional set is $\Theta = \{\beta^{(m)}, v_t^{(m)}, a_{t,y_i}, b_{t,y_i}, K | t = 1, 2, ..., \infty\}$. Recall that the diagonal block sub-matrices of $K$ denote the correlation of topic proportions within each modality and off-diagonal ones denote the correlation between different modalities. To make expressions clear, we use the superscripts of $K$ to denote the row and column indexes of block sub-matrices in $K$. For example, $K^{(1,1)}$ may denote the covariance matrix of topics from image modality, and $K^{(1,2)}$ may denote the covariance matrix between topics of image modality and text modality. Then we use the subscripts of $K$ to denote the row and column indexes in the corresponding sub-matrix.

Note that the correlation structures shown in the above equations are distinct from ones in [26] and [30]. As discussed in [23], the term $v_t^{(m)}$ indicates how sparsity is enforced in the first level DP. Moreover, in our model, it is clear that the covariance depends both on the kernel matrix $K$ of GP and hyperparameters $a_{t,y_i}$ and $b_{t,y_i}$ of gamma distribution. We could control the correlation structure flexibly through learning these parameters.

# 4. INFERENCE AND PREDICTION

In this section, we focus on the computational problems of our NPBUS model and present an efficient variational posterior inference algorithm and a corresponding prediction algorithm.

## 4.1 Variational Inference

To infer the posterior distributions of the latent variables, especially the unnormalized topic mixing proportions $\tilde{\theta}$, and to learn the model parameters, we employ a truncated mean-field variational inference algorithm, which has been shown to be effective in dealing with nonparametric Bayesian models [29]. First of all, we denote the previous set of observed variables as $X$ and the set of all latent variables as $V$. By introducing a variational distribution $q(V)$, we can write the general variational lower bound for the log evidence $\log p(X)$ as

$$\mathcal{L} = \mathbb{E}_q[\log p(V, X)] - \mathbb{E}_q[\log q(V)], \tag{9}$$

where $\mathbb{E}_q[\cdot]$ means the expectation is calculated with respect to the distribution $q$. According to the PGM in Fig. 1,

$$V = \{C_{i,t}, \alpha^{(m)}, \beta^{(m)}, v_t^{(m)}, \eta_t^{(m)}, z_{i,j}^{(m)}, \tilde{\theta}_{i,t}^{(m)}, f_{i,t}, \mu, K| \\ m = 1, 2, i = 1, ..., D, j = 1, ..., N^{(m)}, t = 1, ..., T\}, \tag{10}$$

where $N^{(m)}$ is the maximum number of words per document in $m$th modality. $T$ is the truncation level, which means $q(\tilde{v}_T^{(m)} = 1) = 1$, and $\tilde{v}_T^{(m)}$ is defined as in Eq. (3). The joint probability distribution $p(V, X)$ can be obtained according to the generative process mentioned before. As for the variational distribution $q(V)$, it can be factorized according to the mean-field assumption,

$$q(V) = \prod_{m=1}^{M} \prod_{i=1}^{D} \prod_{j=1}^{N^{(m)}} \prod_{t=1}^{T} q(\alpha^{(m)}) q(\beta^{(m)}) q(v_t^{(m)}) \\ q(\eta_t^{(m)}) q(C_{i,t}) q(z_{i,j}^{(m)}) q(\tilde{\theta}_{i,t}^{(m)}) q(f_i) q(\mu) q(K). \tag{11}$$

Note that here we exploit the variational distribution of $f_i$ for approximation. And $q(f_{i,t}^{(m)})$ thus can be obtained straightforwardly via marginalization of $q(f_i)$, due to the construction in Eq. (4). Next, distributions in the right hand side of Eq. (11) are further defined as,

$$\begin{aligned}
& q(\eta_t^{(m)}) \sim Dir(\pi_t^{(m)}), \\
& q(z_{i,j}^{(m)}) \sim Mult(\phi_{i,j}^{(m)}), \\
& q(f_i) \sim Normal(\tilde{\mu}_i, diag(\tilde{\sigma}_i)), \\
& q(C_{i,t}) \sim Gamma(\tilde{a}_{y_i,t}, \tilde{b}_{y_i,t}), \\
& q(\tilde{\theta}_{i,t}^{(m)}) \sim Gamma(\hat{a}_{i,t}^{(m)}, \hat{b}_{i,t}^{(m)}), \\
& q(\alpha^{(m)}) q(\beta^{(m)}) q(v_t^{(m)}) = \delta_{\alpha^{(m)}} \cdot \delta_{\beta^{(m)}} \cdot \delta_{v_t^{(m)}}, \\
& q(\mu) q(K) = \delta_\mu \cdot \delta_K,
\end{aligned} \tag{12}$$

where $\delta(\cdot)$ is the Kronecker delta function and is used for tractability of inference as in [17]. Moreover, $Dir(\cdot)$ and $Normal(\cdot)$ are the Dirichlet distribution and multivariate normal distribution respectively. Here $\tilde{\sigma}_i$ is a vector and $q(f_i)$ thus has a diagonal covariance matrix.

Now we have set up the variational lower bound, which up to a constant is equivalent to the negative Kullback-Leibler (KL) divergence of the true posterior of latent variables $p(V|X)$ from the approximated variational distribution $q(V)$ [15]. We now derive a coordinate ascent algorithm for maximizing the lower bound by taking derivatives of Eq. (9) with respect to variational parameters. Since our variational inference algorithm is partly related to the one given by [23], here we only list the different updates. Specifically, the update equation or gradients of variational parameters are listed as below:

$$\begin{aligned}
\frac{\partial L}{\partial \tilde{\mu}_i} &= \lambda_i - \gamma - K^{-1}(\tilde{\mu}_i - \mu) \\
\frac{\partial L}{\partial \tilde{\sigma}_{i,t}} &= -\frac{1}{2}(\lambda_{i,t} + K_{t,t}^{-1} - \frac{1}{\tilde{\sigma}_{i,t}}) \\
\frac{\partial L}{\partial a_{i,t}} &= \sum_{j=1}^{D} \delta(y_j = i)\{\log \frac{b_{y_j,t}}{\tilde{b}_{y_j,t}} + \psi(\tilde{a}_{y_j,t}) - \psi(a_{y_j,t})\} \\
b_{i,t} &= \frac{a_{i,t}\tilde{b}_{i,t}}{\tilde{a}_{i,t}} \\
\frac{\partial L}{\partial \tilde{a}_{i,t}} &= \sum_{j=1}^{D} \delta(y_j = i) \left\{1 - (\gamma_t + \tilde{a}_{y_j,t})\psi'(\tilde{a}_{y_j,t}) - \frac{b_{y_j,t}}{\tilde{b}_{y_j,t}} + \frac{\lambda_{y_j,t}}{\tilde{a}_{y_j,t}}\right\} \\
\frac{\partial L}{\partial \tilde{b}_{i,t}} &= \sum_{j=1}^{D} \delta(y_j = i) \left\{\frac{\gamma_t - \tilde{a}_{y_j,t} - \lambda_{y_j,t}}{\tilde{b}_{y_j,t}} + \frac{\tilde{a}_{y_j,t}}{\tilde{b}_{y_j,t}^2} b_{y_j,t}\right\},
\end{aligned} \tag{13}$$

where $\psi(\cdot)$ and $\psi'(\cdot)$ are the digamma function and trigamma function respectively. $\lambda_i$ is a vector which has the same size as $f_i$. And its $t$th element is given as,

$$\lambda_{i,t} = \exp(-\tilde{\mu}_{i,t} + \frac{1}{2}\tilde{\sigma}_{i,t}) \frac{\hat{a}_{y_i,t}\tilde{b}_{y_i,t}}{\tilde{b}_{y_i,t}\tilde{a}_{y_i,t}}. \tag{14}$$

$\gamma$ is a vector which is also of the same size as $f_i$ and similarly constructed as in Eq. (4),

$$\gamma = [\beta^{(1)} v_1^{(1)}, \ldots, \beta^{(1)} v_T^{(1)}, \ldots, \beta^{(M)} v_1^{(M)}, \ldots, \beta^{(M)} v_T^{(M)}]. \tag{15}$$

Based on above derivations, we thus are able to perform efficient gradient-based techniques, e.g. Newton-Raphson, stochastic gradient descent, to find the optimized variational parameters.

To update the parameters of GP, we maximize the marginal likehood, which provides equations of $\mu$ and $K$:

$$\begin{aligned}
\mu &= \frac{1}{D} \sum_{i=1}^{D} \tilde{\mu}_i \\
K &= \frac{1}{D} \sum_{i=1}^{D} \{(\tilde{\mu}_i - \mu)(\tilde{\mu}_i - \mu)^T + diag(\tilde{\sigma}_i)\},
\end{aligned} \tag{16}$$

We update the kernel matrix directly rather than the kernel function, since the latter one will increase the computational burden by inferring latent locations $\ell$ which are as many as latent topics of both image and text modality. Moreover, in this way, low rank approximations of the gram matrix $K$, like Nystrom approximation [25], could be applied for speeding up the inference.

## 4.2 Prediction

Prediction tasks under the upstream supervised multi-modal setting usually involve two objectives, (i) given testing multi-modal samples $\{\bar{x}_j^{(m)} | m = 1, 2, j = 1, ..., \mathbb{N}\}$, predicting their corresponding response variables $\{\bar{y}_j\}$; (ii) given testing samples of one modality $\{\bar{x}_j^{(1)}\}$, predicting samples of the missing modality $\{\bar{x}_j^{(2)}\}$ and the corresponding response variable $\{\bar{y}_j\}$. Here we focus on achieving the second objective, since (ii) is generally harder than (i) and is more closely related to the scenarios of cross-modal retrieval and image annotation.

Specifically, the aim of (ii) is to obtain the predictive posterior distribution $p(\bar{y}_j, \bar{x}_j^{(2)}|\bar{x}_j^{(1)}, X)$, where $X$ is the aforementioned set of training dataset. Relying on the Bayes theorem, the desired probability could be expressed as,

$$p(\bar{y}_j, \bar{x}_j^{(2)}|\bar{x}_j^{(1)}, X) = \int p(\bar{x}_j^{(2)}|\bar{x}_j^{(1)}, \bar{y}_j, V)p(\bar{y}_j)dp(V|X), \tag{17}$$

where $V$ is the set of all latent variables as in Sec. 4.1 and $p(\bar{y}_j)$ is the prior of response variable. Note that, in the training process, response variable is observable, whereas it is a latent variable to be inferred during testing. In our experiments, we just use the empirical distribution of $y$ in the training dataset. Analogous to the empirical approximation of MCMC sampling, we calculate the predictive distribution using variational posterior as,

$$p(\bar{y}_j, \bar{x}_j^{(2)}|\bar{x}_j^{(1)}, X) \approx E_{q^*}[p(\bar{x}_j^{(2)}|\bar{x}_j^{(1)}, \bar{y}_j, V)]p(\bar{y}_j), \tag{18}$$

where $q^*(V)$ stands for the approximated variational distribution inferred during training process according to Sec. 4.1.

To compute $E_{q^*}[p(\bar{x}_j^{(2)}|\bar{x}_j^{(1)}, \bar{y}_j, V)]$, we could first infer the topic mixing proportion vector $\theta_j^{(1)}$ and the vector of auxiliary latent variables $f_j^{(1)}$ through maximizing a lower bound as in Eq. (9). Then, based on the conditional expectation of multivariate Gaussian distribution, we can obtain the auxiliary variables for the missing modality as,

$$f_j^{(2)} = \mu^{(2)} + K^{(2,1)}(K^{(1,1)})^{-1}(f_j^{(1)} - \mu^{(1)}), \tag{19}$$

where $\mu^{(1)}$ and $\mu^{(2)}$ are factorized from $\mu$ according to the construction in Eq. (4), and superscripts of $K$ denote the row and column indexes of its block sub-matrices as in Sec. 3.3. With $f_j^{(2)}$ at hand, we now are capable to calculate the expectation.

Further more, if we are only interested in estimating $\bar{y}_j$, e.g. in the situation of cross-modal retrieval, we can integrate $\bar{x}_j^{(2)}$ from the predictive posterior distribution Eq. (18) which provides the maximum a posterior (MAP) estimation. When the prior for $\bar{y}_j$ is a uniform distribution, MAP is equivalent to the maximum likelihood estimation which is what common upstream models [11, 41] do. Therefore, we could make our prediction algorithm flexible and powerful by imposing a proper application dependent prior for response variable. In turn, $\bar{x}_j^{(2)}$ could be obtained in a similar manner for situations where $\bar{y}_j$ is less cared, like image annotation.

## 5. EXPERIMENTS

In this section, we present in detail the experiments for evaluating the performance of our NPBUS model in capturing correlation structures of multi-modal data and its predictive capacity.

### 5.1 Data & Experimental Settings

We evaluate the performance of our model on two predictive tasks—cross-modal retrieval and image annotation. For the first one, we use the public wiki dataset[1] contributed by N. Rasiwasia et al. [24]. The dataset consists of 2,866 image-text pairs which are collected from 2,700 articles selected and reviewed by Wikipedia, of which 2,173 pairs are randomly chosen to be the training set and the other 693 image-text pairs are chosen to be the test set. Moreover, a response variable of category label is offered for each training pair. These labels cover 10 semantic categories, like art, biology, music and so forth. For the experiments on image annotation we use the public Corel5K [10] as the benchmark dataset, which contains around 5,000 images that are only accompanied by 1 to 5 annotations of keywords. We use a fixed set of 499 images for testing and the rest for training, following the setup in [14]. Since there is no human labeled category information for training data, we cluster the tags through hierarchical Dirichlet process (HDP) topic model and automatically find 21 clusterings in total. Then the obtained clustering labels are regarded as response variables. Note that tags for each image are represented as a vector of words distribution on the vocabulary and response variable adopts 1-of-W vector representation. Besides, all visual features and ground-truth annotated text tags are available on the web[2].

### 5.2 Correlation Structure

We first investigate how our NPBUS model chooses topics and how topics learned by our model are correlated on the wiki dataset. First, we demonstrate the stick proportions $v_t^{(m)}$ obtained through inference. We notice that, in Fig. 2, the stick proportions of image vary differently with ones of text, which motivates our incorporation of separate HDPs for the modalities. Also, from Fig. 2, we see that the last stick proportions are close to zero which justifies the truncation level $T = 100$ is sufficient.

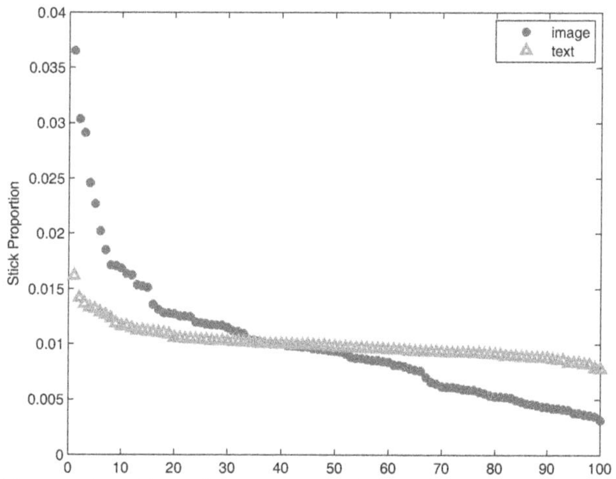


**Figure 2: Visualization of stick proportions learnt from our model for image modality (red ball) and text modality (green triangle).**

Next, we turn to illustrate the learned correlation structures of topics. For saving space, we only show the correlation matrix between topics of image modality and topics of text modality in Fig. 3. We can see that some correlation values are negative which may suggest absence of specific topics from the other modality. Moreover, only a few topics of image are strongly correlated with topics of text. This is as expected, since every pair of image and text in this wiki dataset is extracted owning to their close positions on the webpage which does not imply close similarity of their contents. To further inspect whether the correlation learned by

[1] http://www.svcl.ucsd.edu/projects/crossmodal/

[2] http://lear.inrialpes.fr/people/guillaumin/data.php

our model matches our own intuition, we are supposed to present the content of a pair of correlated topics. However, it is not intuitive for visualize the topics of image, since they are distributions over SIFT vocabulary. In order to overcome this problem, we adopt the same visual relevance measurement $\rho$ as in [30]. For each topic of text modality, $\rho$ is defined to be the mean value of absolute correlations with all image topics. Note that, this measurement captures the co-occurrences of text topics and combined image topics. Then we can rank topics according to its value of visual relevance. In Table. 1, ranked topics and their text contents are summarized. We see that topics with strong visual relevance, i.e., large values of $\rho$, contain clear and concrete visual counterparts. For example, the first topic is about birds and their living environments, which are easily depicted by pictures. Nevertheless, topics with weak visual relevance are difficult to be described by visual contents, like the fifth topic in the last row. Therefore, our NPBUS model does capture the correlation structures of multi-modal data.

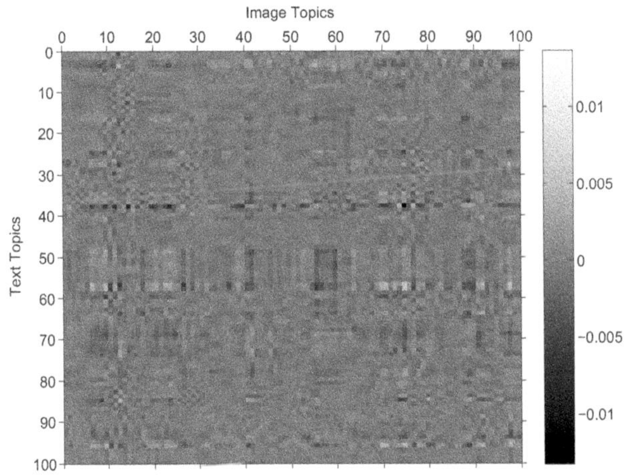


**Figure 3: Visualization of correlation structure between topics of image modality (columns) and topics of text modality (rows).**

## 5.3 Cross-Modal Retrieval

Table 2: MAP scores of cross-modal retrieval

| Method | Image Query | Text Query | Average |
|---|---|---|---|
| SCM [24] | 0.277 | 0.226 | 0.252 |
| GMA [28] | 0.272 | 0.232 | 0.253 |
| CMTC [38] | 0.293 | 0.232 | 0.266 |
| MLBE [39] | 0.381 | 0.496 | 0.439 |
| NPBUS | **0.408** | **0.544** | **0.476** |

We then conduct cross-modal retrieval which contains two sub-tasks—text retrieval through image queries and image retrieval through text queries. We first execute our variational inference algorithm for the training dataset. Then, given a query in one modality, we predict its corresponding response variable $y$ by the prediction algorithm mentioned in Sec. 4.2. Finally, we use the probability vector $p(y)$ to calculate the ranking of all retrieved data. More specifically, the response variables of training data are encoded in 1-of-$\mathbb{K}$ vector representation and here $\mathbb{K}$ equals 10

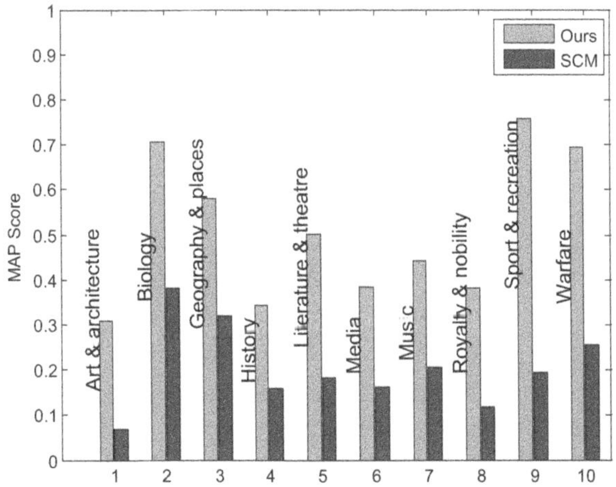


**Figure 4: MAP scores per category with text query.**

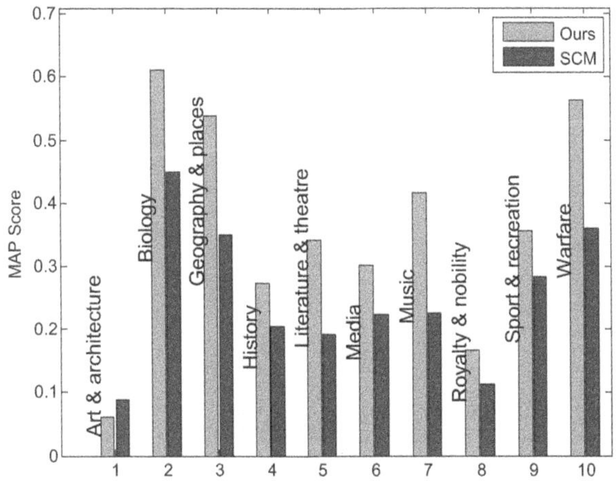


**Figure 5: MAP scores per category with image query.**

since there are 10 categories. Therefore, the distance between two response variables is established as distance of two vectors in vector space. Note that we experimented with different distance measures, including $L_1$, $L_2$, normalized correlation (NC) and chi-squared $\chi^2$ distance, and we found that the $L_1$ distance outperforms all others. To make the comparison fair, we take the same feature settings as in [24], that is, we use topic mixing proportions to represent text documents and use bag of SIFT features to represent images. In the training stage, we set the initial values of two concentration parameters in HDP as: $\alpha = 15$ and $\beta = 5$, and the truncation level as $T = 100$ for each modality. 34 and 66 topics are learnt automatically for training texts and images, respectively. We compare our NPBUS model with semantic correlation matching (SCM) [24], generalized multi-view analysis (GMA) [28], cross-modal topic correlations (CMTC) [38] and multi-modal latent binary embedding (MLBE) [39]. The performance is measured with mean average precision (MAP) which has good discrimination and stability and is widely used in the literature of information retrieval [9].

The overall MAP scores are reported in Table 2. It is clear from this table that our NPBUS outperforms other models

| Topics with top-5 visual relevances |
|---|
| population species north birds forest area males females found breeding trees year largest high conservation |
| film music production movie scene play musical studio role american sound hollywood pictures performance |
| ship navy fleet naval guns war sea british battleship royal squadron world hitler enemy iowa coast aircraft |
| king family george prince life wife duke earl father died royal princess marriage lord son daughter married |
| book works published novel story life writing critics stories popular characters literary history author volume |
| Topics with least-5 visual relevances |
| up base out hit second single two followed third cardinals left home inning pearl fly field down yankees |
| through wall sculpture neilston placed although models agricultural model turrets flight entire having computer |
| gold richard california order bangladesh nails amp due entire jews raised hotel videos 1976 far observer hours |
| canadian adams states united tournament international revolutionary gold winter world people old historical |
| people female eggs number american african minnesota many census 2001 chicks days rate around home life |

**Table 1: Visualization of topic contents. Each row of words indicates a topic. From top row to bottom row, the corresponding visual relevances are decreasing. Words from left to right in each topic are ranked in descending order according to their probabilities.**

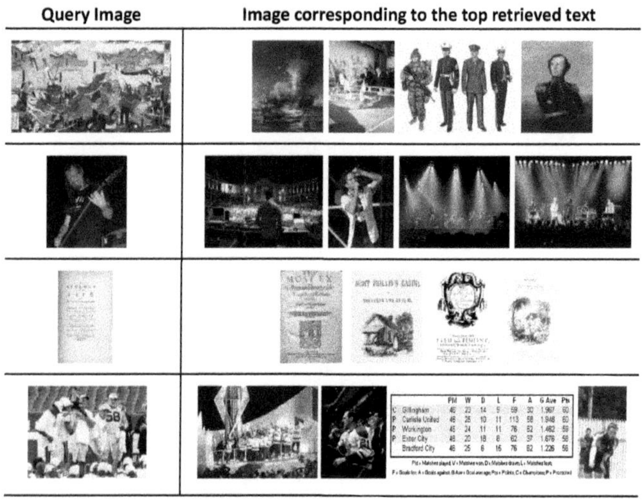


**Figure 6: Examples of cross-modal retrieval with image query. Images corresponding to retrieved texts with top-4 rank scores are shown.**

**Table 3: Comparison of performance for image annotation**

| Methods | $P$ | $R$ | $N+$ |
|---|---|---|---|
| CorrLDA [2] | 6 | 9 | 59 |
| CRM [16] | 16 | 19 | 107 |
| InfNet [21] | 17 | 24 | 112 |
| NPDE [37] | 18 | 21 | 114 |
| SML [6] | 23 | 29 | 137 |
| MBRM [12] | 24 | 25 | 122 |
| TGLM [18] | 25 | 29 | 131 |
| MSC [32] | 25 | 32 | 136 |
| JEC [20] | 27 | 32 | 139 |
| TagProp [14] | **33** | 42 | 160 |
| NPBUS | 29 | **44** | **187** |

in both sub-tasks on the wiki dataset. This improvement of performance validates the benefits of incorporating supervising information of semantic abstracts. Note that the boost of performance is larger in sub-task with text query than the one with image query. It is perhaps because that the SIFT feature is not expressive enough for generally describing visual objects with semantic meaning. Since only SCM published their per category MAP scores, we compare the histograms of both text query and image query with SCM in Fig. 4 and Fig. 5 respectively. And our NPBUS achieves better results for almost all categories. More instances of cross-modal retrieval are demonstrated in Fig. 6 and Fig. 7. We consider the top-4 ranked retrieved texts for image queries in Fig. 6. And in Fig. 7, we show the top-5 ranked images for text queries. Note that, for the ease of display, we only show the images corresponding to the retrieved texts in Fig. 6 and contents of text queries have been fragmented in Fig. 7.

## 5.4 Image Annotation

In experiments of image annotation, variational inference is first conducted to obtain the approximated variational distribution for training dataset. For testing images, we compute the desired conditional probability of tags given response variables and image feature according to the prediction algorithm. Following the aforementioned convention, captions with first 5 highest conditional probabilities are drawn as the final annotation results. As for image features, we exploit the same types of ones as in [14], and normalize them by their $L_1$ norm separately before the combination step. Since the overall features they used are of more than 30,000 dimensions, we reduce the dimension to 500 by principle component analysis (PCA) for computational efficiency. Moreover, 3 standard measures are adopted as in [6]: the mean precision per word (i.e., $P$), the mean recall per word (i.e., $R$) and number of keywords with non -zero recall value (i.e., $N+$). We compare our NPBUS with 10 other methods which publicly report their results on this dataset. The experimental comparisons are listed in Table 3. From this table, we can find that NPBUS ranks 2nd with respect to $P$ and achieves the best results in terms of $R$ and $N+$. The causes for less precision than the state-of-art may be the reduced-dimension visual features used in our experiments. Also, since some training images have too few attached tags, the topic model may not perform better compared to some simple model, like logistic regression in [14]. Finally, the supervising information obtained via unsupervised HDP clustering is somewhat limited.

On 31 January, the effort to retake the city began anew. The attack was launched at 08:30 hours, and was met by inaccurate Iraqi fire which knocked-out two Saudi V-150 wheeled vehicles.Stanton, p. 9, claims that two vehicles were destroyed, while Westermeyer, p. 31, claims that three were knocked-out. The 8th battalion of the Saudi brigade was ordered to deploy to the city by 10:00 hours, while 5th Battalion to the north engaged another column of Iraqi tanks attempting to reach the city. The latter engagement led to the destruction of around 13 Iraqi tanks and armored personnel carriers, and the capture of 6 more vehicles and 116 Iraqi soldiers, costing the Saudi battalion two dead and two wounded......

"Honoured members: the Hockey Hall of Fame", p. 91. On March 30, 1993, it was announced that Gil Stein, who at the time was the president of the National Hockey League, would be inducted into the Hall of Fame. There were immediate allegations that he had engineered his election through manipulation of the hall's board of directors. Due to these allegations, NHL commissioner Gary Bettman hired two independent lawyers, Arnold Burns and Yves Fortier, to lead an investigation. They concluded that Stein had "improperly manipulated the process" and "created the false appearance and illusion" that his nomination was the idea of Bruce McNall......

**Figure 7: Two examples of cross-modal retrieval with text query. Left parts are fragmented queries and right parts are corresponding retrieved images with top-5 rank scores. The content of the top text describes a war and the below one is about hockey.**

# 6. CONCLUSIONS

In this paper, we have presented a nonparametric Bayesian upstream supervised (NPBUS) multi-modal topic model. Our NPBUS model allows flexible learning of correlation structures of topics within individual modality and between different modalities. And it becomes more discriminative via incorporating upstream supervising information shared by multi-modal data. Last, it is capable to automatically determine the number of latent topics in each modality. We also devise efficient variational inference and prediction algorithms. Extensive experiments demonstrate the above advantages in terms of cross-modal retrieval and image annotation.

In future work, we intend to develop truncation free algorithms to improve our approximated inference, or utilize sampling methods, like MCMC. And we also will exploit low rank approximations to accelerate the kernel learning. Moreover, we will apply our model for mining more different kinds of multi-modal data, e.g., multi-lingual webpages, multi-source perception data of robotics.

# 7. ACKNOWLEDGMENTS

Jun Zhu is supported by the National Basic Research Program (973 Program) of China (Nos. 2013CB329403, 2012CB316301), and National Natural Science Foundation of China No. 61322308. Zengchang Qin is supported by the National Science Foundation of China No. 6130504.

# 8. REFERENCES

[1] D. Blackwell and J. MacQueen. Ferguson distributions via Pólya urn schemes. *The Annals of Statistics*, 1(2):353–355, 1973.

[2] D. Blei and M. Jordan. Modeling annotated data. In *ACM SIGIR*, pages 127–134, 2003.

[3] D. Blei and J. Lafferty. A correlated topic model of science. *The Annals of Applied Statistics*, pages 17–35, 2007.

[4] D. Blei, A. Ng, and M. Jordan. Latent Dirichlet allocation. *JMLR*, 3:993–1022, 2003.

[5] D. M. Blei and J. D. McAuliffe. Supervised topic models. In *NIPS*, 2007.

[6] G. Carneiro, A. Chan, P. Moreno, and N. Vasconcelos. Supervised learning of semantic classes for image annotation and retrieval. *IEEE Trans. Pattern Anal. Mach. Intell.*, 29(3):394–410, 2007.

[7] N. Chen, J. Zhu, F. Sun, and E. Xing. Large-margin predictive latent subspace learning for multiview data

analysis. *IEEE Trans. Pattern Anal. Mach. Intell.*, 34(12):2365–2378, 2012.

[8] N. Chen, J. Zhu, and E. Xing. Predictive subspace learning for multi-view data: A large margin approach. In *NIPS*, 2010.

[9] W. B. Croft, D. Metzler, and T. Strohman. *Search engines: Information retrieval in practice.* Addison-Wesley Reading, 2010.

[10] P. Duygulu, K. Barnard, J. De Freitas, and D. Forsyth. Object recognition as machine translation: Learning a lexicon for a fixed image vocabulary. In *ECCV*, pages 349–354. Springer, 2002.

[11] L. Fei-Fei and P. Perona. A Bayesian hierarchical model for learning natural scene categories. In *CVPR*, volume 2, pages 524–531. IEEE, 2005.

[12] S. Feng, R. Manmatha, and V. Lavrenko. Multiple Bernoulli relevance models for image and video annotation. In *CVPR*, volume 2, pages II–1002. IEEE, 2004.

[13] T. Ferguson. A Bayesian analysis of some nonparametric problems. *The Annals of Statistics*, pages 209–230, 1973.

[14] M. Guillaumin, T. Mensink, J. Verbeek, and C. Schmid. Tagprop: Discriminative metric learning in nearest neighbor models for image auto-annotation. In *ICCV*, pages 309–316. IEEE, 2009.

[15] M. Jordan, Z. Ghahramani, T. Jaakkola, and L. Saul. An introduction to variational methods for graphical models. *Machine Learning*, 37(2):183–233, 1999.

[16] V. Lavrenko, R. Manmatha, and J. Jeon. A model for learning the semantics of pictures. In *NIPS*, 2003.

[17] P. Liang, S. Petrov, M. I. Jordan, and D. Klein. The infinite PCFG using hierarchical Dirichlet processes. In *EMNLP/CoNLL*, 2007.

[18] J. Liu, M. Li, Q. Liu, H. Lu, and S. Ma. Image annotation via graph learning. *Pattern Recognition*, 42(2):218–228, 2009.

[19] D. G. Lowe. Distinctive image features from scale-invariant keypoints. *International journal of computer vision*, 60(2):91–110, 2004.

[20] A. Makadia, V. Pavlovic, and S. Kumar. A new baseline for image annotation. In *ECCV*, volume 8, pages 316–329, 2008.

[21] D. Metzler and R. Manmatha. An inference network approach to image retrieval. In *CIVR*, 2004.

[22] F. Monay and D. Gatica-Perez. Modeling semantic aspects for cross-media image indexing. *IEEE Trans. Pattern Anal. Mach. Intell.*, 29(10):1802–1817, 2007.

[23] J. Paisley, C. Wang, and D. M. Blei. The discrete infinite logistic normal distribution. *Bayesian Analysis*, 7(4):997–1034, 2012.

[24] N. Rasiwasia, J. Costa Pereira, E. Coviello, G. Doyle, G. Lanckriet, R. Levy, and N. Vasconcelos. A new approach to cross-modal multimedia retrieval. In *ACM Multimedia*, pages 251–260, 2010.

[25] C. Rasmussen and C. Williams. *Gaussian processes for machine learning*, volume 1. MIT press Cambridge, MA, 2006.

[26] K. Salomatin, Y. Yang, and A. Lad. Multi-field correlated topic modeling. *SIAM SDM*, 2009.

[27] J. Sethuraman. A constructive definition of Dirichlet priors. *Statistica Sinica*, 4:639–650, 1994.

[28] A. Sharma, A. Kumar, H. Daume, and D. Jacobs. Generalized multiview analysis: A discriminative latent space. In *CVPR*, pages 2160–2167. IEEE, 2012.

[29] Y. Teh, M. Jordan, M. Beal, and D. Blei. Hierarchical Dirichlet processes. *Journal of the American Statistical Association*, 101(476):1566–1581, 2006.

[30] S. Virtanen, Y. Jia, A. Klami, and T. Darrell. Factorized multi-modal topic model. In *UAI*, 2012.

[31] S. Virtanen, A. Klami, and S. Kaski. Bayesian CCA via group sparsity. In *ICML*, 2011.

[32] C. Wang, S. Yan, L. Zhang, and H. Zhang. Multi-label sparse coding for automatic image annotation. In *CVPR*, pages 1643–1650. IEEE, 2009.

[33] P. Wu, S. C.-H. Hoi, P. Zhao, and Y. He. Mining social images with distance metric learning for automated image tagging. In *WSDM*, pages 197–206. ACM, 2011.

[34] H. Xia, P. Wu, and S. C. Hoi. Online multi-modal distance learning for scalable multimedia retrieval. In *WSDM*, pages 455–464. ACM, 2013.

[35] E. Xing, R. Yan, and A. Hauptmann. Mining associated text and images with dual-wing harmoniums. In *UAI*, 2005.

[36] O. Yakhnenko and V. Honavar. Multi-modal hierarchical Dirichlet process model for predicting image annotation and image-object label correspondence. In *SIAM SDM*, 2009.

[37] A. Yavlinsky, E. Schofield, and S. Rüger. Automated image annotation using global features and robust nonparametric density estimation. In *CIVR*, 2005.

[38] J. Yu, Y. Cong, Z. Qin, and T. Wan. Cross-modal topic correlations for multimedia retrieval. In *ICPR*, 2012.

[39] Y. Zhen and D. Yeung. A probabilistic model for multimodal hash function learning. In *ACM SIGKDD*, 2012.

[40] J. Zhu, A. Ahmed, and E. P. Xing. Medlda: maximum margin supervised topic models. *Journal of Machine Learning Research*, 13:2237–2278, 2012.

[41] J. Zhu, L.-J. Li, L. Fei-Fei, and E. P. Xing. Large margin learning of upstream scene understanding models. In *NIPS*, pages 2586–2594, 2010.

# Spatial Compactness meets Topical Consistency: Jointly modeling Links and Content for Community Detection

Mrinmaya Sachan, Avinava Dubey, Shashank Srivastava, Eric P. Xing, Eduard Hovy
School of Computer Science
Carnegie Mellon University
{mrinmays, akdubey, shashans, epxing, hovy}@cs.cmu.edu

## ABSTRACT

In this paper, we address the problem of discovering topically meaningful, yet compact (densely connected) communities in a social network. Assuming the social network to be an integer-weighted graph (where the weights can be intuitively defined as the number of common friends, followers, documents exchanged, etc.), we transform the social network to a more efficient representation. In this new representation, each user is a bag of her one-hop neighbors. We propose a mixed-membership model to identify compact communities using this transformation. Next, we augment the representation and the model to incorporate user-content information imposing topical consistency in the communities. In our model a user can belong to multiple communities and a community can participate in multiple topics. This allows us to discover community memberships as well as community and user interests. Our method outperforms other well-known baselines on two real-world social networks. Finally, we also provide a fast, parallel approximation of the same.

## Categories and Subject Descriptors

H.2.8 [**Information Systems**]: Data Mining; G.3 [**Probability and Statistics**]: [Probabilistic Algorithms]

## Keywords

Community Detection, Social Networks, Graphical Models

## 1. INTRODUCTION

Social Networks allow users to stay in touch with friends, relatives and other acquaintances wherever they are in the world. At the same time, they unite users with common interests and/or beliefs through various groups and pages. These groups allow users to share ideas, pictures, posts, activities, events, etc. with other users. This makes them an invaluable source of heterogeneous data that can be exploited to discover relationships among groups of people. An important problem associated with discovering relationships among users in a social network is the automated discovery of communities. A community is a collection of users as a group such that there is a higher degree of 'similarity' among users in the group as against people across groups.

The notion of 'similarity' between users is subjective and has been addressed differently in previous works. Preliminary paradigms treated communities as densely connected components in the network. They postulated that real networks are not random, but display inhomogeneities leading to a high level of order and organization with high concentrations of edges within special groups of vertices (communities), and low concentrations between these groups [4]. This is often referred to as the notion of "compactness" in community structure. The notion of compactness is important as it reflects a higher level of interaction and social vicinity among members of a community and allows the interpretation of the global organization of the social network as the coexistence of their local structural sub-units (communities) associated with more highly interconnected parts. Such an interpretation is also desirable for explaining local cliques that people find themselves in their daily lives, for example in people's personal relationships, in corporate organizations and in scientific research activities.

Using this interpretation of communities, methods like cut-based graph partitioning[6], local agglomerative/divisive clustering[4], centrality based[7] and Clique percolation methods (CPM)[16] have been suggested to optimize different notions of compactness. While these works gained rapid popularity, a drawback in most of these models (with exceptions) is that they involve a hard partitioning of nodes, and do not allow users to have memberships in multiple communities. However, today, it is understood that users in a social network rarely belong to only one community: for instance the same individual usually has family, friend, and colleague affiliations in different social circles.

Further, in the context of social networks, communities have become synonymous to interest groups providing people interested in similar topics common forums. In fact, these ideas have now found explicit existence and dedicated nomenclature in Google+ "circles" or Facebook "smart lists". Finally, early works that only considered the underlying graph structure were also handicapped as they did not account for node properties such as user interests which can be easily gauged from the text associated with the network.

On the other end of the spectrum, there have been purely user-content based works to cluster users into communities like CUT[24]. In fact, neither information alone is satisfactory in determining the community memberships: the link


*WSDM'14,* February 24–28, 2014, New York, New York, USA.
Copyright 2014 ACM 978-1-4503-2351-2/14/02 ...$15.00.
http://dx.doi.org/10.1145/2556195.2556219.

information is often sparse and noisy and results in a poor partition of networks. On the other hand, the irrelevant content attributes significantly mislead the process of community detection. It is therefore important to combine link and content information for community detection in networks. At the same time it is also important to retain the notion of compactness as we wish to exploit the inhomogeneous structure of social networks and discover individuals contained in communities that are not just topically similar but are closely knit and share communications.

Several mixed-membership models for community discovery have been proposed to incorporate structural and/or user-interest information in social networks. A significant reason for the success of these models is that they enable us to incorporate domain knowledge by modeling a complex set of factors responsible for generating the data as latent variables. Inferring the posterior often allows the discovery of unseen structures and intricate relations between entities. For example, social network users are often modeled as having distributed membership over a set of communities or a set of topics (user-interests), and a community itself as a distribution over topics (community-interests).

Broadly, all of these models fall under one of two modeling paradigms. The first paradigm (MMSB[1], Link-PLSA-LDA[13], Topic-Link LDA[11] and RTM[3]) draws a vector of community memberships for the two candidate entities (documents or users) and typically makes a Bernoulli draw for a binary link between them using a notion of similarity between the community membership vectors. These methods directly model the adjacency matrix leading to a $\Omega(U^2)$ latent variables, where $U$ is the number of users (nodes) in the network. This can be too large for real-world social networks. The second paradigm (CART[17] and various TURCM models[19]) implicitly assumes a link between the sender and the recipients for every post in the social network and extends the author-topic model[18] to model community memberships for the sender-recipient pair for every message. This significantly increases the number of parameters to be estimated to $\Omega(U^2C)$ where $C$ is the number of communities. This too, can be large for real-world social networks.

Note that CUT[24] purely models content and MMSB[1] purely models linkage. CART[17] and TURCM models[19] claim to combine both but do not model compactness. [1]

Further, while the first paradigm assumes that users that are interconnected share similar interests, the second paradigm posits that users that actively talk about similar topics are connected with each other. Neither is always true in the real world. In real world social networks, there are users who are members of communities but do not actively contribute in them. Also, there are members who may be vocal about the same topics but may not be connected at all. As we will later see in our evaluations on real-world datasets, previously suggested latent variable models following the two paradigms do not conform to the notion of compactness in social networks. This often leads to cases when the individuals contained in a community may not share much communication and, as such, may not actually reflect a community in the 'traditional' sense. Finally, all the aforementioned latent variable models work on binary (link or no-link) networks.

In this paper, we propose a framework to use integer-valued weights in the networks. We believe that this is intuitive in a real-world setting where the strength of interaction between users can be measured as the number of common friends or followers, number/length of documents exchanged, number of comments or likes on same thread, etc. We represent the integer-weighted network efficiently as a bag of users; each user is herself represented as a bag of her neighbors. We use this representation to present a mixed membership model that can discover compact communities. Next, we extend both the representation and the model to incorporate the content information leading to compact yet topically consistent communities. We believe that with our approach, it would be possible to "zoom" into the network and uncover not only the communities but also the interests of the communities and its members. Hence, it would provide a tool to identify and interpret local organizations in large networks that are not only topologically compact (based on graph structure) but also semantically aligned (based on topics discovered). We show improvements over previous methods in terms of held-out perplexity, several compactness metrics and on a link prediction task.

As another contribution, we also provide a faster, efficient parallel implementation of the method and illustrate its speed-up over the sequential counterpart.

## 2. NOTATION

Let a (text associated) social network (TSN) be defined as a network where every edge is associated with a set of text documents. Let $\mathbf{U}$ be the set of users (nodes) in the TSN. Let $\mathbf{N_u}$ be the set of neighbors of user (sender) $u \in \mathbf{U}$. For a given user $u \in \mathbf{U}$ and its neighbor $r \in \mathbf{N_u}$, let $S_{ur}$ be the strength of interaction between $u$ and $r$ and $\mathbf{D_{ur}}$ be the set of documents sent by $u$ to $r$. Then, $\mathbf{D_u} = \cup_{r \in \mathbf{N_u}} \mathbf{D_{ur}}$ is the set of all documents authored by $u$. Let $\mathbf{W_d}$ be the multi-set of words in a given document $d$. We note that a document can be sent to multiple users (recipients) at the same time. Let $\mathbf{R_d}$ be the set of recipients for a given document $d$. Let the vocabulary set be $\mathbf{V}$. Also, let the cardinality of all these sets (in boldface) be represented by their corresponding capitalized symbols. Overall, let $\Delta_u$ be the (weighted) degree of node $u$ where $\Delta_u = \sum_{r \in \mathbf{N_u}} S_{ur}$. We experimented with various definitions of $S_{ur}$ as discussed before and found that $S_{ur} = D_{ur}$ i.e. setting strength of interaction as the number of documents exchanged between the users works best. Assume this setting henceforth.

## 3. NET-LDA: THE NETWORK MODEL

The idea of transforming the input representation for a better task-specific performance is not new[9]. A well-known example of this idea is the bag-of-words representation for a document, in which each document is seen as an exchangeable collection of words. This representation has proven to be effective in various NLP tasks such as topic modeling. We propose an alternate representation to model the link structure of a social network that explicitly takes into account the entire neighborhood of every user. By doing so, we can better model the inhomogeneity of structure in social networks and lead to more compact communities.

[1]Also note that other bayesian models like RTM[3], Link-PLSA-LDA[13] and Topic-Link LDA[11] have also been proposed for document networks (citation networks and co-authorship networks) but they are not directly extendable to social networks in their full generality.

As the name suggests, Net-LDA closely follows the modeling scheme in LDA [2] to model the network structure. To model neighborhoods in the underlying graph, we translate the network to a document corpus and argue that an LDA model on the newly constructed corpus discovers communities in the social graph just as LDA discovers topics in a document corpus. Each user in the network is represented by a document in this alternate representation and the list of all the users interacting with it forms the words in the document (replicated as many times as the integer weight of the edge connecting them). Formally, let every user $u$ be characterized by a network interaction footprint (NIF), a document representing all its interactions with other users in the network: $NIF(u) = \cup_{r \in \mathbf{N_u}} \{r, r, \ldots S_{ur} \ times\}$ and $\cup$ represents the multi-set union (i.e. each interacting user $r \in \mathbf{N_u}$ is represented $S_{ur}$ times in the NIF document). For example, in a dummy network where user $A$ sends two documents to user $B$, three documents to user $C$ (and no more documents to other users), the network interaction footprint of $A$ (document representing $A$) is $[B, B, C, C, C]$. Note that because of this transformation, we only need $\theta(\sum_u \Delta_u)$ space to represent the graph (instead of $\Omega(U^2)$).

The network interaction footprints of the users are represented as random mixtures over latent community variables. Each community is in turn defined as a distributions over the interacting users $r$. This idea is analogous to LDA where the network interaction footprint is a document, interactions are words in that document and communities are latent topics. Just as LDA clusters similar words into one topic, this extrapolation would cluster users with similar neighborhoods in one community. This can also be seen as soft clustering (e.g. Soft K-Means) on the adjacency matrix of the graph. This makes the communities detected by Net-LDA "compact". Technically, this occurs due to the sparsity induced by the Dirichlet prior. The sparsity through the user-community Dirichlet prior penalizes the model for using many topics for a document. This ensures that all the neighbors of a node have slightly higher odds to belong to the same community. This, in turn, makes the community structure spatially "compact". On the other hand, the sparsity induced by the community-neighbor Dirichlet ensures that the user (document) is assigned to only a few communities (topics). This conforms to real world scenarios where users are typically members of a small number of communities. Note that this model has $\theta(\sum_u \Delta_u)$ latent variables, which is much smaller than $U^2$ in models following paradigm 1 (e.g. MMSB) for real-world (sparse) networks. Further, this model has $\theta(UC)$ parameters which can be efficiently estimated and is a reduction over $\Omega(U^2)$ parameters as in models following Paradigm 2.

# 4. SN-LDA:THE SOCIAL NETWORK MODEL

In the social network literature, previous works[8] have shown success in combining local (node-based) features with neighborhood features for various graph mining tasks. In order to account for the spatial as well as topic-coherence of communities discovered, we represent the TSN as a collection of users, where each user is represented as a bag of one hop neighbors and a bag of documents authored by the user.

We further augment Net-LDA with content information. To achieve this, we associate every user with a multinomial distribution $\pi$ over communities. This distribution gives the membership of the user in every community. We define a topic to be a semantic theme represented as a multinomial distribution $\phi$ over words. We associate topics with the communities and hence model communities as a multinomial distribution $\theta$ over the topics of interest amongst users in the community. This can help us determine key topics prevailing in a community and can be useful in locating/searching communities on given themes and interests. Just as in Net-LDA, we represent the user as a distribution $\pi$ over the community space and communities as a distribution $\eta$ over the space of interacting users. The plate notation is given in Figure 1 and generative story below. Here $Dir_X(\alpha)$ denotes a X-dimensional symmetric Dirichlet with scalar parameter $\alpha$ and $Mult(.)$ denotes the discrete multinomial. The sender, neighbor (recipient) and words are observed. The communities and topics are latent.

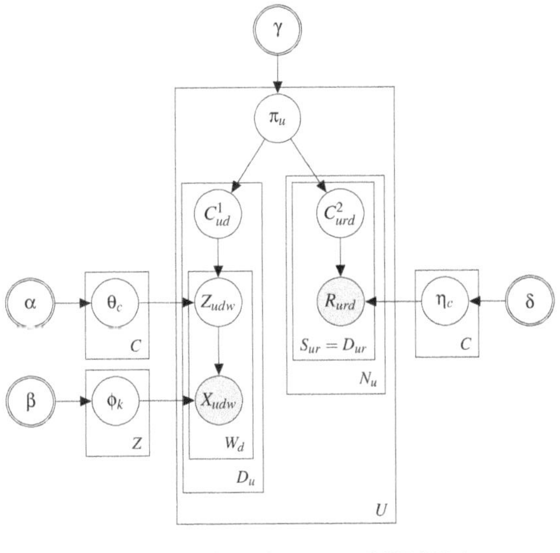


Figure 1: Plate diagram of SN-LDA

1. For each topic index, $1 \leq k \leq Z$, sample a $V$ dimensional multinomial, $\vec{\phi}_k \sim Dir_V(\beta)$.

2. For each community index, $1 \leq c \leq C$:

   (a) Sample a U dimensional multinomial $\vec{\eta}_c \sim Dir_U(\delta)$.

   (b) Sample a Z dimensional multinomial $\vec{\theta}_c \sim Dir_Z(\alpha)$.

3. For each user $u \in \mathbf{U}$, sample a $C$ dimensional multinomial, $\vec{\pi}_u \sim Dir_C(\gamma)$.

4. For each user $u \in \mathbf{U}$:

   (a) For each document $d \in \mathbf{D_u}$ sent by sender $u$:

      i. Draw community assignment $C^1_{ud} \sim Mult(\vec{\pi}_u)$.

      ii. For every word $w \in \mathbf{W_d}$:

      - Draw topic assignment $Z_{udw} \sim Mult(\vec{\theta}_{C^1_{ud}})$.
      - Draw word $X_{udw} \sim Mult(\vec{\phi}_{Z_{udw}})$.

   (b) For each neighbor $r \in \mathbf{N_u}$:

      i. For each document $d \in \mathbf{D_{ur}}$:

      - Draw community assignment $C^2_{urd} \sim Mult(\vec{\pi}_u)$.
      - Draw neighbor $R_{urd} \sim Mult(\vec{\eta}_{C^2_{urd}})$.

We hypothesize that while a document is assigned to a particular community, the recipients of the document might still belong to different communities. This necessitates the community variables for the document $c^1$ and the recipients $c^2$ to be separate. To test this hypothesis, we design another graphical model (we call it Naiive SN-LDA) where the community variable is only drawn once for each document. The generative story of Naiive SN-LDA can be obtained by replacing 4(b) with 4(a)-iii in SN-LDA as follows:

4(a)-iii. For each recipient $r \in \mathbf{R_d}$:

- Draw recipient (neighbor) $R_{urd} \sim Mult(\vec{\eta}_{C^1_{ud}})$.

We will see in our evaluations that Naiive SN-LDA doesn't do well in practice. This substantiates our hypothesis and justifies the aforementioned modeling choice.

## 4.1 Parameter Estimation

We sample the topic and community assignments from the conditional for the variable given the observations and other assignments using a Gibbs sampling procedure. Let $C^1_{ud}$, $C^2_{urd}$, $Z_{udw}$, $R_{urd}$ and $W_{udw}$ be the community, topic, recipient and word assignments for a given user, document and word, as appropriate. Let $\#^{B_1 \ldots B_v A}_{b_1 \ldots b_v a,-i}$ be the number of times $a, (1 \leq a \leq A)$ is generated along with the combination of variables $b_1 \ldots b_v$ in the model, $(1 \leq b_i \leq B_i, 1 \leq i \leq v)$ excluding the instance $i$. Also, $\#_{cz,ud}$ be the number of times topic $z$ is assigned to words in community $c$ for user $u$ in document $d$. The Gibbs sampling equations are given below.

$$P(C^2_{urd} = c^* | \mathbf{C^2_{-urd}}, -) \propto \left(\#^{UC^2}_{uc^*,-urd} + \#^{UC^1}_{uc^*} + \gamma\right) \frac{\#^{C^2R}_{c^*r,-urd} + \delta}{\Sigma_{r'} \#^{C^2R}_{c^*r',-urd} + U\delta} \quad (1)$$

$$P(C^1_{ud} = c^* | \mathbf{C^1_{-ud}}, -) \propto \left(\#^{UC^1}_{uc^*,-ud} + \#^{UC^2}_{uc^*} + \gamma\right) \times \frac{\prod_{z \in \mathbf{Z}} \prod_{i=0}^{\#_{c^*z,ud}} (\#^{C^1Z}_{c^*z,-ud} + \alpha + i)}{\prod_{i=0}^{W_d - 1} (\Sigma_{z'} \#^{C^1Z}_{c^*z',-ud} + Z\alpha + i)} \quad (2)$$

$$P(Z_{udw} = z^* | \mathbf{Z_{-udw}}, \mathbf{C^1_{ud} = c^*}, \mathbf{C^1_{-ud}}, -) \propto \frac{\#^{CZ}_{c^*z^*,-udw} + \alpha}{\Sigma_{z'} \#^{CZ}_{c^*z',-udw} + Z\alpha} \times \frac{\#^{ZW}_{z^*w,-udw} + \beta}{\Sigma_{w'} \#^{ZW}_{z^*w',-udw} + V\beta} \quad (3)$$

A single iteration of the sampler performs $\mathcal{O}(DC + WZ)$ computations to model the texts (Let $D$ be the total number of documents and $W$ be the total number of words in the TSN) and $\mathcal{O}(C \sum_u \sum_{r \in \mathbf{N_u}} S_{ur})$ computations to model the network. Hence, the sampler has a worst time complexity of $\mathcal{O}[(DC + WZ) + C \sum_u \sum_{r \in \mathbf{N_r}} S_{ur}]$. The complexity could be significantly high even for moderate size TSNs. Note that this is a longstanding drawback of latent variable models.

# 5. PARALLEL SN-LDA

The Gibbs Sampling procedure utilized by our model makes multiple passes at the data and hence, does not scale to real-world data sizes. An obvious solution to address this issue is to distribute the learning over multiple processors. Next, we provide a parallel implementation of SN-LDA that has

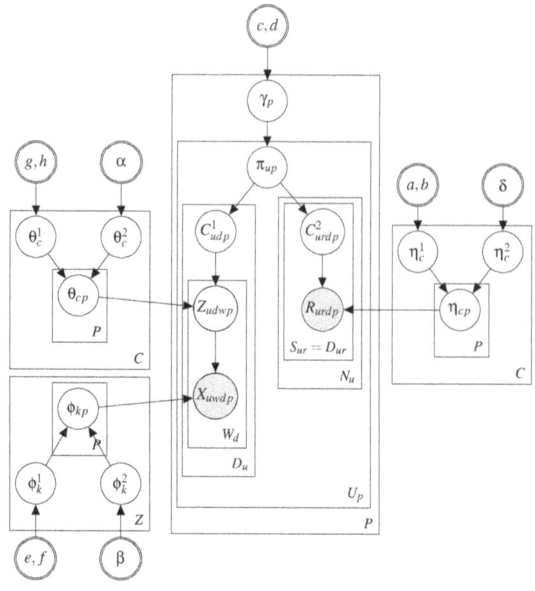


Figure 2: Plate diagram of Parallel SN-LDA

theoretical guarantees of convergence and also does well in practice.

The approach for the parallel variant (inspired from Distributed LDA[14]) is to split the data (social network) roughly equally into $P$ processors. Each processor is roughly (randomly) assigned $U/P$ users (along with their network interaction footprints and all the documents authored by the users). All the sufficient statistics in the previous Gibbs sampler ($\#^{B_1 \ldots B_v A}_{b_1 \ldots b_v a,-i} \forall a, b_j, A, B_j, i$) are also distributed with each processor keeping a local copy. Moreover, the parallel version also keeps a copy of the four distributions $\theta$, $\phi$, $\pi$ and $\eta$ on each processor. Appropriate priors are introduced to bind these distributions globally. For instance, a global hierarchy of word-topic distributions $\phi^2_k$ and a topic dependent strength parameter $\phi^1_k$ is placed over the local word topic distributions $\phi_{kp}$. Likewise, $\theta, \pi$ *and* $\eta$ are also distributed. The model on each processor essentially is an SN-LDA model. Figure 2 shows the Bayesian model reflecting this structure. The generative process for the model is:

$$\begin{array}{lll}
\eta^1_c \sim Gamma(a,b) & \eta^2_c \sim Dir(\delta) & \eta_{cp} \sim Dir(\eta^1_c \eta^2_c) \\
\theta^1_c \sim Gamma(g,h) & \theta^2_c \sim Dir(\alpha) & \theta_{cp} \sim Dir(\theta^1_c \theta^2_c) \\
\phi^1_k \sim Gamma(e,f) & \phi^2_k \sim Dir(\beta) & \phi_{kp} \sim Dir(\phi^1_k \phi^2_k) \\
\gamma_p \sim Gamma(c,d) & \pi_{up} \sim Dir(\gamma_p) & \\
C^1_{udp} \sim \pi_{up} & Z_{udwp} \sim \theta_{C^1_{udp}} & X_{udwp} \sim \phi_{Z_{udwp}} \\
C^2_{urdp} \sim \pi_{up} & R_{urdp} \sim \eta_{C^2_{urdp}} &
\end{array}$$

Pseudocode of Parallel SN-LDA is given in Algorithm 1. Processors concurrently perform Gibbs sampling on the local data partition followed by a global update of the counts. Local variables $C^1_{udp}$, $C^2_{urdp}$ and $Z_{udwp}$ are inferred locally and the global variables $\gamma_p$, $\theta^1_c$, $\theta^2_c$, $\eta^1_c$, $\eta^2_c$, $\phi^1_k$ and $\phi^2_k$ are then inferred globally after the local processing finishes on all processors. Here, we employ an auxiliary variable method [5] to sample both the local and global variables. Please refer to the appendix for the Gibbs sampling equations.

**Algorithm 1:** Parallel SN-LDA Implementation

Initialize: All Local and Global Variables;
**while** *!(Termination Condition)* **do**
  **for** *each processor p in parallel* **do**
    *Sample $c_1, c_2, z$ locally using the local data partition*
    *Sample $\gamma_p$ locally*;
  **end**
  *Synchronize*;
  *Sample global variables $\theta_c^1, \theta_c^2, \eta_c^1, \eta_c^2, \phi_k^1$ and $\phi_k^2$*;
  *Broadcast global variables $\theta_c^1, \theta_c^2, \eta_c^1, \eta_c^2, \phi_k^1$ and $\phi_k^2$*;
**end**

The average case time complexity of one iteration of the Gibbs sampler (both local and global updates) is $\mathcal{O}[(X + M)/P + M]$ where $X = DC + WZ + C\sum_u \sum_{r \in \mathbf{N_u}} S_{ur}$ and $M = ZW + CU + CZ$. This is an improvement over the sequential implementation when $P \geq \mathcal{O}(\frac{X+M}{X-M})$. Note that this is an average case analysis and assumes that all the processes run at the same speed and the data is uniformly (and roughly equally) divided across machines. Our evaluations show that the technique works well in practice.

# 6. EVALUATION

## 6.1 Datasets

In our experiments, we perform a comparative evaluation of Net-LDA and SN-LDA against baseline models (CUT, TUCM, TURCM-1, TURCM-2, Full TURCM, CART and MMSB) on two real-world datasets: first, is the publicly available Enron Email corpus[2] and secondly, a subset of the collection of tweets crawled from Twitter[3] over a 7 month period (June 1 - Dec 31, 2009). The Enron dataset contains email exchanges from about 150 employees, mostly senior management. On the other hand, Twitter is a social networking and micro blogging service where users communicate by short text messages (up to 140 characters) called 'tweets'. Follower relationships impose an underlying graph structure. The Twitter dataset used has 5405 nodes, 13214 edges and 23043 posts. The posts were preprocessed and stemmed appropriately. We choose these two datasets for the diversity and challenges they bring along with them. While Twitter imposes a restriction on the length of posts, the number of followers of a user can run into millions. In a social network, such nodes (users) are sometimes called 'star nodes'. This is a case when the graph is dense but the associated content is much smaller. On the other hand, while the Enron dataset has fewer nodes, emails can be arbitrarily long; case of a sparse graph but rich content. Scaling a technique that integrates both content and link to such diverse social networks is an important challenge.

## 6.2 Experimental Design

As we discussed before, our definition of communities lays emphasis on two criteria: how tightly users in a community are inter-connected and how strongly users in a community share interests. Hence, we firstly give a qualitative evaluation of the communities and try to argue how topics and links combine to produce communities effectively.

[2]http://www.cs.cmu.edu/ enron
[3]http://snap.stanford.edu/data/twitter7.html

We evaluate the strength of inter-connections in the community structure by computing various compactness metrics like normalized-cut[20] and fuzzy modularity [10] of the community structure discovered. Normalized-cut measures the degree of disassociation between groups by computing the cut cost as a fraction of the total edge connections to all the nodes in the graph. On the other hand, modularity [15] was specifically designed as a measure of compactness for community structure. It assumes that a good division of the network is one in which the number of edges between groups is smaller than expected. Since we perform a fuzzy partition of the network, we will instead use a fuzzy variant called Fuzzy Modularity $Q_f$ introduced in [10]. Along with these two measures, we will also use other community quality evaluation measures from the graph clustering literature such as Average link $J_{al}(C)$ and Rouben's measure $J_{rm}(C)$[23]. Next, we pick the task of link prediction and show improvements over baseline models. Finally, we demonstrate speed-up of the parallel variant of SN-LDA over its sequential counterpart in terms of various compactness measures, perplexity and link-prediction accuracy.

A key step in such parametric approaches is choosing the hyper-parameter values. A common heuristic is to pick the values that minimize held-out perplexity on a validation set. A quick investigation on the two datasets showed that setting the number of topics to 15 and number of communities to something between 10 to 12 roughly leads to optimality. Hence, we use the setting Z=15, C=12 in our experiments. In line with other topic modeling works, we set $\alpha = \frac{1}{Z}, \beta = \frac{50}{V}, \gamma = \frac{1}{C}$ *and* $\delta = \frac{10}{U}$ in our SN-LDA implementation. For Parallel SN-LDA, guided by the set-up in previous works[14] we set $a = \frac{U \times (P-1)}{PC}, b = 1, c = 2, d = 0.1, e = \frac{W \times (P-1)}{PZ}, f = 1, g = \frac{W \times (P-1)}{PC}, h = 1, \alpha = \frac{2}{C}, \beta = \frac{2}{Z}, \gamma = 0.1$ *and* $\delta = \frac{2}{C}$. Gibbs sampling was carried out by starting with a random assignment to all the latent variables and using the corresponding update equations to compute fresh values over a large burn-in period (first 1000 iterations). When this distribution stabilizes, sufficient number of samples were taken at regular intervals (every 5th iteration for next 4000 iterations) to avoid correlation.

## 6.3 Results

### 6.3.1 *Qualitative Analysis*

From our first analysis, we intend to qualitatively corroborate our intuition that communities are formed when users with similar interests aggregate together. We first give a view of top words for a few sample topics discovered by SN-LDA on the Enron corpus in Table 1. As many as 10 out of the 15 topics can be recognized as popular and sensible topics of discussion in Enron like power, gas, etc. Similar visualization is possible for the twitter datasets where we obtain topics like Internet, Stock Markets, Web, News, etc.

Next, we illustrate intuitively the utility of such a probabilistic model. For instance, we can compute the distribution over topics for a particular user showing the things that she is primarily interested in (See Figure 3a). [12] showed how one can discover social roles of people by associating words with users through their community memberships and the corresponding community-topic distribution. In Table 2 we give top words for a few roles using the Enron corpus. From these words we can see that social roles are nothing but work profiles for people working in Enron, like management, en-

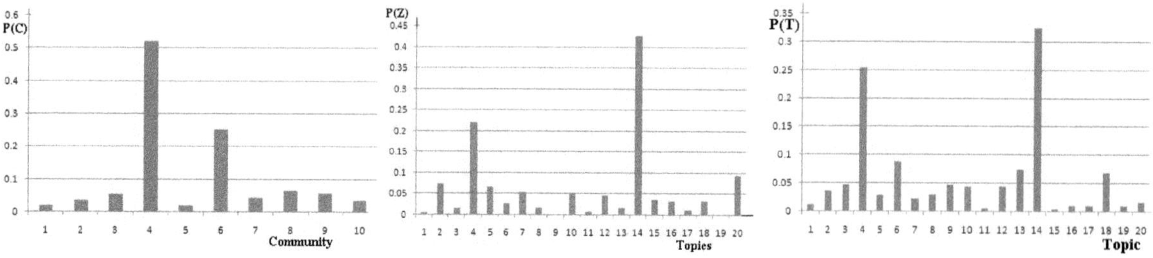


Figure 3: (a) Community Proportions for a given user, (b) Topic Proportions for a given Community and (c) Topic Proportions for a given user for Twitter dataset

| Email | Web | Stock Market | Gas Prices | California Power |
|---|---|---|---|---|
| message | mailto | pdx | enron | edison |
| subject | aol | nymex | gas | power |
| fw | hotmail | enronxgate | prices | energy |
| original | net | company | book | ect |
| mail | http | corp | dynergy | california |
| **Positions** | **Office** | **Power Crisis** | **Gas Trading** | **Gas Production** |
| analyst | backup | gas | city | enron |
| associate | plan | california | hou | energy |
| capacity | seat | power | gas | paso |
| california | business | ect | trading | ngcorp |
| company | work | energy | california | el |

Table 1: (Manually labeled) Topics for SN-LDA on Enron

| Management | Engineering | Analyst |
|---|---|---|
| contract | mailto | pdx |
| agreement | dynergy | california |
| meeting | electric | cash |
| corporation | psa | database |
| budget | calpx | meeting |

Table 2: Social Roles discovered by SN-LDA on Enron

gineering and analyst. These social roles can be confirmed against their true roles in Enron. For example, the roles of Sally Beck (Chief Operating Officer), Vincent Kaminski (Head of Quantitative Modeling Group) and Louise Kitchen (President of Enron Online) can be conveniently recognized as management and the role of William Williams III (Senior Analyst) can be recognized as an analyst. Interestingly, the social roles/departmental structures also have high degree of overlap with the community structure discovered.

In Figure 3a, we illustrate for the Twitter dataset that a particular user (user 93) has a membership in community 4 to a high degree in our SN-LDA model. Besides, the model also suggests that the user participates in community 6 to some extent. This analysis gives us an insight to the extent of participation of a user in various social groups. This probabilistic notion of membership has clear advantages in modeling user tastes and preferences to the hard clustering approach taken in many previous approaches for community discovery. Further, topical peaks for a community indicate the dominant topics for that particular community. For example, after looking at the topic proportions for community 4 (see Figure 3b), which is the primary community for user 93, it was found that topics 14 (Stock Markets) is the dominant topic in this community. Also topic 4 (Internet) is the dominant topic in community 6. Now that we know how to estimate community memberships and topical interest of

| | Enron Corpus | | | Twitter Corpus | | |
|---|---|---|---|---|---|---|
| | $N-Cut$ | $J_{al}$ | $J_{rm}$ | $N-Cut$ | $J_{al}$ | $J_{rm}$ |
| Net-LDA | 6.280 | 1.230 | 0.5753 | 7.432 | 1.189 | 0.698 |
| SN-LDA | **6.083** | **1.616** | **1.134** | **6.953** | **1.457** | **0.928** |
| TUCM | 10.563 | 0.672 | 0.413 | 9.112 | 0.657 | 0.442 |
| TURCM-1 | 9.584 | 0.695 | 0.441 | 9.938 | 0.623 | 0.425 |
| TURCM-2 | 8.235 | 0.701 | 0.452 | 8.887 | 0.729 | 0.461 |
| Full TURCM | 8.137 | 0.921 | 0.563 | 9.115 | 0.696 | 0.451 |
| CART | 11.375 | 0.694 | 0.481 | 10.976 | 0.605 | 0.410 |
| CUT | 10.122 | 0.705 | 0.456 | 10.785 | 0.627 | 0.422 |
| MMSB | 7.980 | 1.266 | 0.646 | 8.463 | 1.198 | 0.606 |
| Naiive SN-LDA | 13.184 | 0.296 | 0.280 | 10.847 | 0.418 | 0.416 |

Table 3: Network Quality Measures on Enron and Twitter

communities, we can also determine the topical interests of the users. Figure 3c shows the distribution over topics for the Twitter user (user 93). It shows that this user is primarily interested in topic 14 (Stock Markets) and also likes topics 4 (Internet). Recall that topics 14 and 4 were strong interests of the communities (community 4 and 6) the user had a high membership in). This analysis is useful in finding individual user's interests and tastes. This kind of analysis supports our hypothesis that users tend to communicate frequently over certain topics (based on interests) and form communities based on those interests. This also illustrates the power of SN-LDA over the plain Net-LDA model.

### 6.3.2 *Community Quality Analysis*

Next, we present our first quantitative results for evaluating the goodness of communities obtained on the compactness metrics previously defined and compare Net-LDA and SN-LDA against state-of-the-art methods. Tables 3 and 4 show the comparison on both datasets. To establish consistency of the method for various parameter values, table 4 shows the fuzzy modularity comparison for different numbers of communities (Z fixed to 15). Both NetLDA and SN-LDA show much better scores than the baselines, suggesting that our models have detected more spatially compact communities. Also, as expected SN-LDA shows an improvement over Net-LDA due to its additional power of accounting for user interests while discovering communities. It is interesting to note that Net-LDA shows an improvement over MMSB, another model for community detection using link structure in graphs, which suggests that our modeling scheme for networks models compactness in a better manner for integer-valued graphs. Naiive SN-LDA does not perform well. This substantiates our modeling choice for drawing separate community labels for content and link modeling.

To reiterate our argument, we visualize the community assignments for CART and our two methods on the Enron dataset in figure 4. We assign each user to his most probable community and rearrange so that all the users assigned to

| | Enron Corpus | | | | | Twitter Corpus | | | | |
|---|---|---|---|---|---|---|---|---|---|---|
| | **6** | **8** | **10** | **12** | **14** | **6** | **8** | **10** | **12** | **14** |
| Net-LDA | 0.619 | **0.542** | **0.463** | 0.340 | 0.421 | 0.413 | 0.442 | 0.462 | 0.471 | 0.463 |
| SN-LDA | **0.634** | 0.534 | 0.427 | **0.427** | **0.436** | **0.438** | **0.491** | **0.482** | **0.484** | **0.485** |
| TUCM | 0.148 | 0.243 | 0.291 | 0.287 | 0.246 | 0.167 | 0.263 | 0.321 | 0.313 | 0.262 |
| TURCM-1 | 0.198 | 0.271 | 0.339 | 0.331 | 0.283 | 0.168 | 0.261 | 0.309 | 0.287 | 0.241 |
| TURCM-2 | 0.203 | 0.278 | 0.346 | 0.337 | 0.289 | 0.166 | 0.265 | 0.324 | 0.309 | 0.261 |
| Full TURCM | 0.215 | 0.294 | 0.363 | 0.350 | 0.299 | 0.171 | 0.272 | 0.332 | 0.316 | 0.267 |
| CART | 0.152 | 0.249 | 0.302 | 0.294 | 0.255 | 0.157 | 0.227 | 0.243 | 0.235 | 0.196 |
| CUT | 0.133 | 0.231 | 0.266 | 0.278 | 0.227 | 0.159 | 0.244 | 0.299 | 0.285 | 0.237 |
| MMSB | 0.2601 | 0.3313 | 0.3745 | 0.375 | 0.362 | 0.226 | 0.274 | 0.289 | 0.291 | 0.284 |
| Naiive SN-LDA | 0.114 | 0.119 | 0.125 | 0.127 | 0.128 | 0.158 | 0.175 | 0.187 | 0.192 | 0.200 |

Table 4: Fuzzy Modularity Comparisons on Enron and Twitter Corpora as C is varied, Z=15

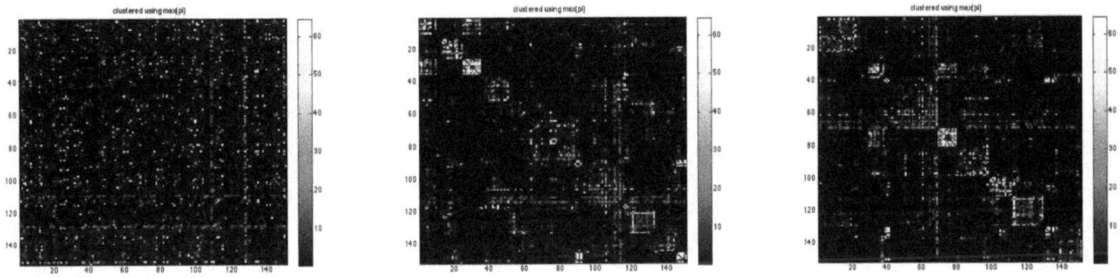

Figure 4: Visualizing the community assignments for (a) CART, (b) Net-LDA (c)SN-LDA on Enron Dataset

a particular community are stacked together. After this operation, the adjacency (strength) matrix is plotted for each model. We can observe that Net-LDA and SN-LDA roughly show a block diagonal structure reaffirming our argument that these methods detect compacter communities. Previous models (like CART), on the other hand, do not show a characteristic compactness structure.

### 6.3.3 Link prediction

Next, we illustrate performance on a supervised link prediction task. Link prediction is closely related to communities. In fact, community information is often included in similarity-based link prediction methods[21] with an implicit assumption that two nodes in the same community are more likely to be connected. However, we believe that this assumption would fail if the communities were not spatially compact. Hence, we provide performance on the link prediction task as another evaluation of our models. For this, we made a 60-40 split of all documents. We learnt our model parameters from the 60% training split and trained SVM to predict links (if there is a document exchange in Enron) between user pairs on the test-split, using user community-membership profiles as the feature vectors. Table 5 shows that both NetLDA and SN-LDA outperform the baselines on both datasets further confirming our hypothesis.

### 6.3.4 Parallel SN-LDA

As our final evaluation, we illustrate the speed-up of Parallel SN-LDA over its sequential counterpart. Herein, we are interested in two aspects of performance: the quality of the models learned measured by the compactness metrics, performance on the link prediction task and perplexity of held out data, and the time taken to learn the models.

To begin with, we compute held out perplexity. Perplexity is a measure used to evaluate language models. We compute perplexity using the harmonic mean method proposed in

| | Enron Corpus | | | Twitter Corpus | | |
|---|---|---|---|---|---|---|
| | **Prec.** | **Rec.** | **F1** | **Prec.** | **Rec.** | **F1** |
| Net-LDA | 0.708 | 0.467 | 0.563 | 0.648 | 0.547 | 0.593 |
| SN-LDA | 0.656 | 0.527 | **0.584** | 0.677 | 0.559 | **0.612** |
| TUCM | 0.583 | 0.403 | 0.476 | 0.542 | 0.428 | 0.478 |
| TURCM-1 | 0.528 | 0.329 | 0.405 | 0.526 | 0.401 | 0.455 |
| TURCM-2 | 0.512 | 0.367 | 0.427 | 0.582 | 0.449 | 0.507 |
| Full TURCM | 0.504 | 0.412 | 0.453 | 0.558 | 0.450 | 0.498 |
| CART | 0.565 | 0.332 | 0.418 | 0.538 | 0.388 | 0.451 |
| CUT | 0.513 | 0.304 | 0.382 | 0.515 | 0.353 | 0.419 |
| MMSB | 0.590 | 0.482 | 0.531 | 0.547 | 0.474 | 0.508 |
| Naiive SN-LDA | 0.512 | 0.286 | 0.367 | 0.505 | 0.326 | 0.396 |

Table 5: Link Prediction Results on Enron and Twitter

[22]. However, unlike topic models where data is just the set of words, here we want to evaluate how well our models do on learning the linkage structure as well as the text. Hence, we further compute the perplexity of observing links and text separately. The link and text perplexity can be computed using $S$ samples from independent chains of the posterior:

$$p(\mathbf{W_{test}}|.) = \sum_{u\in\mathbf{U}}\sum_{d\in\mathbf{D_u}} log\frac{1}{S}\left(\sum_{s}\sum_{c}\pi_{c|u}\prod_{w\in d}\sum_{z}\theta_{z|c}\phi_{w|z}\right)$$

$$p(\mathbf{R_{test}}|.) = \sum_{u\in\mathbf{U}}\sum_{r\in\mathbf{N_u}}\sum_{d\in\mathbf{D_{ur}}}\sum_{v\in\mathbf{V}} log\frac{1}{S}\left(\sum_{s}\sum_{c}\pi_{c|u}\eta_{r|c}\right)$$

$$\pi_{c|u} = \frac{\#^{UC^1}_{uc} + \#^{UC^2}_{uc} + \gamma}{\sum_c\left(\#^{UC^1}_{uc} + \#^{UC^2}_{uc} + \gamma\right)}, \theta_{z|c} = \frac{\#^{CZ}_{cz} + \alpha}{\sum_z(\#^{CZ}_{cz} + \alpha)}$$

$$\phi_{w|z} = \frac{\#^{ZW}_{zw} + \beta}{\sum_w(\#^{ZW}_{zw} + \beta)}, \eta_{r|c} = \frac{\#^{CR}_{cr} + \delta}{\sum_r(\#^{CR}_{cr} + \delta)}$$

$$Ppx(\mathbf{W}) = exp\left(\frac{-log\ p(\mathbf{W_{test}}|.)}{W_{test}}\right), Ppx(\mathbf{R}) = exp\left(\frac{-log\ p(\mathbf{R_{test}}|.)}{R_{test}}\right)$$

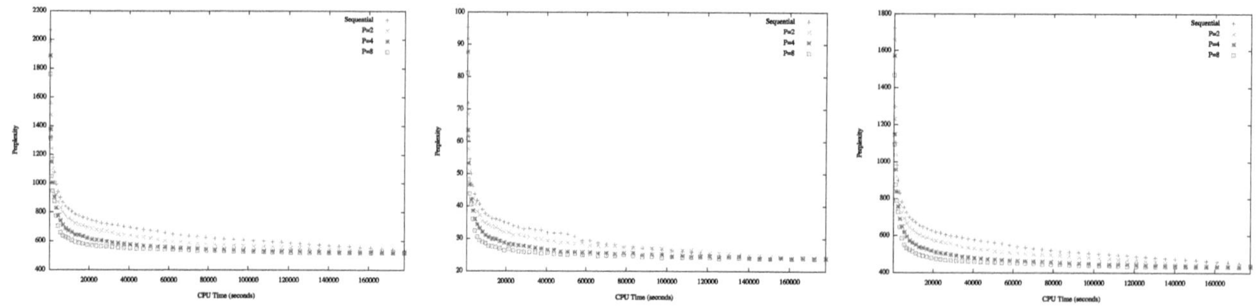

Figure 5: Perplexity Comparisons: Parallel SN-LDA and SN-LDA (a) Text, (b) Link, (c) Overall Perplexity on Enron

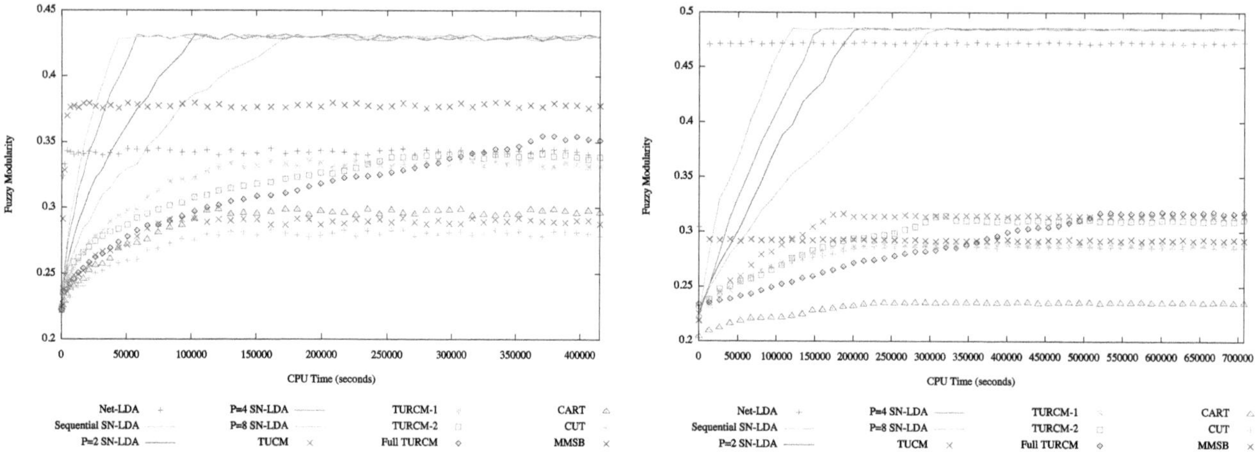


Figure 6: Speedup & Comparison of Fuzzy Modularity on (a) Enron, (b) Twitter

Figure 5 plots held out perplexity against runtime for parallel SN-LDA model (when number of processors is 2,4 and 8) and SN-LDA for the Enron dataset. Herein, it is easy to observe that Parallel SN-LDA shows a greater drop in both held-out perplexities as well as overall perplexities with time implying faster convergence. Both text and link perplexities fall monotonically. This implies that the model's predictive ability on both text and link improves with time. The drop becomes more and more steep as the number of processors increase. Please note that in the limit, the perplexity of the parallel algorithms matches the sequential algorithm. This pattern is independent of choice of Z and C. Similar pattern is seen on the Twitter dataset. In fact, the parallel model also improves with time on various compactness metrics at a greater rate than the sequential version as the number of processors is increased. Figure 6 shows the improvement on both datasets. A similar pattern was also seen in terms of link prediction in Figure 7. Also note that in our experiments, Parallel SN-LDA with just 4 processors converges faster that all the baselines with the exception of MMSB.

| | 100 | 500 | 2500 | 12500 |
|---|---|---|---|---|
| **P=2** | 0.613 | 0.593 | 0.599 | 0.592 |
| **P=4** | 0.607 | 0.594 | 0.593 | 0.568 |
| **P=8** | 0.602 | 0.593 | 0.575 | 0.564 |

Table 6: Efficiency Speed-ups by Parallel SN-LDA on Twitter datasets of various sizes

Finally, we compute the speed-up efficiency: fractional decease in training (cpu) time over the number of processors used ($\frac{T_1}{pT_p}$). All simulations have been done on the same architecture and platform. In all models, training is assumed to finish when the held-out likelihoods converge (change in likelihood over consecutive iterations falls below 0.1% of the likelihood in the previous iteration). We chose twitter datasets of various sizes (100, 500, 2500 and 12500 nodes, respectively) and compute the speed-ups with respect to the size of datasets for various number of processors used in Table 6. The consistency of speed-ups across data sizes makes us believe that it should be possible to scale up our technique to datasets of larger size with more processors.

## 7. CONCLUSION

We began by positing that communities are formed by users who communicate on topics of mutual interest, are connected to each other in the social graph and share frequent personal communication. We described a new representation for social networks and used it to propose a mixed-membership model which incorporates both text and link information for community detection in social networks that conforms to the notion of 'compactness'. When compared against existing methods, our experiments show significant improvements in terms of various compactness metrics and on the link prediction task. We also provide a fast, efficient parallel approximation of the model that scales well in terms of both memory and time. We believe that the scheme of modeling network information as described in Net-LDA can

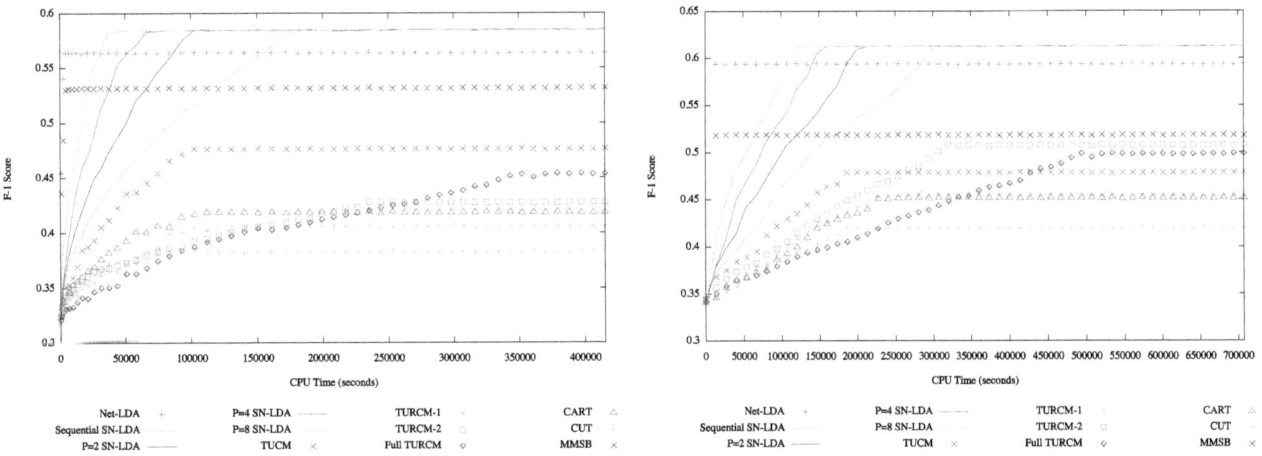


Figure 7: Speedup & Comparison of Link Prediction on (a) Enron, (b) Twitter

be employed to improve various latent variable models previously described in the literature.

# APPENDIX

**Gibbs Sampling for Parallel SN-LDA:**

For parallel SN-LDA the posterior of $Z_p, C_p^1, C_p^2$ given the global variables $\gamma_p, \theta_c^1, \theta_c^2, \eta_c^1, \eta_c^2, \phi_k^1, \phi_k^2$ has the same form as the posterior of $Z, C^1, C^2$ given $\gamma, \beta, \alpha, \delta$ for SN-LDA.

$$P(\mathbf{Z}_{\dots\mathbf{p}}, \mathbf{C^1}_{..\mathbf{p}}, \mathbf{C^2}_{\dots\mathbf{p}} | \gamma_p, \theta_c^1, \theta_c^2, \eta_c^1, \eta_c^2, \phi_k^1, \phi_k^2) \propto$$
$$\prod_{u \in \mathbf{U_p}} \left[ \frac{\Gamma(C\gamma_p)}{\Gamma(C\gamma_p + \#_{u.p}^{UC^1P} + \#_{u.p}^{UC^2P})} \prod_c \frac{\Gamma(\gamma_p + \#_{ucp}^{UC^1P} + \#_{ucp}^{UC^2P})}{\Gamma(\gamma_p)} \right]$$
$$\prod_c \left[ \frac{\Gamma(\theta_c^1)}{\Gamma(\#_{c.p}^{C^1ZP} + \theta_c^1)} \prod_z \frac{\Gamma(\#_{czp}^{C^1ZP} + \theta_c^1 \theta_{cz}^2)}{\Gamma(\theta_c^1 \theta_{cz}^2)} \right]$$
$$\prod_c \left[ \frac{\Gamma(\eta_c^1)}{\Gamma(\#_{c.p}^{C^2RP} + \eta_c^1)} \prod_r \frac{\Gamma(\#_{crp}^{C^2RP} + \eta_c^1 \eta_{cr}^2)}{\Gamma(\eta_c^1 \eta_{cr}^2)} \right]$$
$$\prod_z \left[ \frac{\Gamma(\phi_z^1)}{\Gamma(\#_{z.p}^{ZWP} + \phi_z^1)} \prod_w \frac{\Gamma(\#_{zwp}^{ZWP} + \phi_z^1 \phi_{zw}^2)}{\Gamma(\phi_z^1 \phi_{zw}^2)} \right]$$

Consequently, the sampling equation for the local variables are similar to that of SN-LDA given in equation 1-3 with $\gamma$ replaced by $\gamma_p$, $\alpha$ replaced by $\theta_c^1\theta_c^2$ and $\beta$ replaced by $\phi_k^1\phi_k^2$ and the counts replaced by counts for the given processor.

The auxiliary variable method used to sample the global variables $\gamma_p, \theta_c^1, \theta_c^2, \eta_c^1, \eta_c^2, \phi_k^1$ *and* $\phi_k^2$ here is explained in detail in [5] and [14]. We use the following expression:

$$\frac{\Gamma(a)}{\Gamma(a+n)} = \frac{1}{\Gamma(n)} \int_0^1 t^{a-1}(1-t)^{n-1} dt \qquad (4)$$
$$\frac{\Gamma(a+n)}{\Gamma(a)} = \sum_{s=0}^{n} S(n,s)(a)^s \qquad (5)$$

where, $S$ is the sterling number of the first kind.

**Sampling $\gamma_p$:**

$$P(\gamma_p|-) \propto \prod_{u \in \mathbf{U_p}} \left[ \frac{\Gamma(C\gamma_p)}{\Gamma(C\gamma_p + \#_{u.p}^{UC^1P} + \#_{u.p}^{UC^2P})} \prod_c \frac{\Gamma(\gamma_p + \#_{ucp}^{UC^1P} + \#_{ucp}^{UC^2P})}{\Gamma(\gamma_p)} \right] \gamma_p^{c-1} \exp(-d\gamma_p)$$

Using equations 4 and 5 :

$$P(\gamma_p, t, s|-) \propto \prod_{u \in \mathbf{U_p}} \left[ t_u^{C\gamma_p - 1}(1-t_u)^{\#_{u.p}^{UC^1P} + \#_{u.p}^{UC^2P}} \right] \times$$
$$\prod_{u \in \mathbf{U_p}} \prod_c \left[ S(\#_{ucp}^{UC^1P} + \#_{ucp}^{UC^2P}, s_{ucp}) \gamma_p^{s_{ucp}} \right] \gamma_p^{c-1} \exp(-d\gamma_p)$$

This leads to simultaneous sampling equations for $\gamma_p$, $t$ & $s$:

$$P(\gamma_p|t,s,-) \propto \prod_{u \in \mathbf{U_p}} t_u^{C\gamma_p} \left( \prod_{u \in \mathbf{U_p}} \prod_c \gamma_p^{s_{ucp}} \right) \gamma_p^{c-1} \exp(-d\gamma_p)$$
$$= Gamma\left( c + \sum_{u \in \mathbf{U_p}} \sum_c S_{ucp}; d - C \sum_{u \in \mathbf{U_p}} t_u \right) \quad (*)$$

$$P(t_u|\gamma_p, s-) \propto t_u^{C\gamma_p - 1}(1-t_u)^{\#_{u.p}^{UC^1P} + \#_{u.p}^{UC^2P}}$$
$$= Beta\left( C\gamma_p; \#_{u.p}^{UC^1P} + \#_{u.p}^{UC^2P} \right) \quad (*)$$

$$P(s_{ucp}|\gamma_p, t, -) \propto S(\#_{ucp}^{UC^1P} + \#_{ucp}^{UC^2P}, s_{ucp}) \gamma_p^{s_{ucp}}$$
$$= Antoniak\left( \#_{ucp}^{UC^1P} + \#_{ucp}^{UC^2P}, \gamma_p \right) \quad (*)$$

Note that both auxiliary variables can be sampled locally.

**Sampling $\eta_c^1$ *and* $\eta_c^2$:**

$$P(\eta_c^1, \eta_c^2|-) \propto \prod_c \left[ \frac{\Gamma(\eta_c^1)}{\Gamma(\#_{c.p}^{C^2RP} + \eta_c^1)} \prod_r \frac{\Gamma(\#_{crp}^{C^2RP} + \eta_c^1 \eta_{cr}^2)}{\Gamma(\eta_c^1 \eta_{cr}^2)} \right]$$
$$\left[ \prod_r \eta_{cr}^{2\ \delta-1} \right] \eta_c^{1\,a-1} \exp(-b\eta_c^1)$$

Using the same argument but different auxiliary variables:

$$P(\eta_c^1, \eta_c^2, t, s|-) \propto \eta_c^{1\,a-1} \left[ \prod_p t_{cp}^{\eta_c^1 - 1}(1-t_{cp})^{\#_{c.p}^{C^2RP} - 1} \right] \times$$
$$\left[ \prod_{p,r} S(\#_{crp}^{C^2RP}, s_{crp})(\eta_c^1 \eta_{cr}^2)^{s_{rcp}} \right] \left[ \prod_{c,r} \eta_{cr}^{2\ \delta-1} \right] \exp(-b\eta_c^1) \quad (*)$$

$$P(\eta_c^1|-) \propto Gamma\left[a + \sum_{p,r} s_{crp}; b - \sum_{p} \log(t_{cp})\right] \quad (*)$$

$$P(\eta_c^2|-) \propto Dirichlet\left[\delta + \sum_{p} s_{crp}\right] \quad (*)$$

$$P(t_{cp}|-) \propto Beta\left[\eta_c^1; \#_{c.p}^{C^2RP}\right] \quad (*)$$

$$P(s_{crp}|-) \propto Antoniak\left[\#_{crp}^{C^2RP}; \eta_c^1\eta_{cr}^2\right] \quad (*)$$

**Sampling for $\theta_c^1$, $\theta_c^2$, $\phi_k^1$ and $\phi_k^2$ is similar to $\eta_c^1$ and $\eta_c^2$.**

## Acknowledgments

Thanks to Qirong Ho, Kriti Puniyani, Keerthiram Murugesan and the anonymous reviewers for their valuable comments and suggestions to improve the quality of the paper.

## A. REFERENCES

[1] Edoardo M. Airoldi, David M. Blei, Stephen E. Fienberg, and Eric P. Xing. Mixed membership stochastic blockmodels. *J. Mach. Learn. Res.*, 9:1981–2014, June 2008.

[2] David M. Blei, Andrew Y. Ng, and Michael I. Jordan. Latent dirichlet allocation. *J. Mach. Learn. Res.*, 3:993–1022, March 2003.

[3] Jonathan Chang. Relational topic models for document networks. In *Proc. of Conf. on AI and Statistics (AISTATS)*, 2009.

[4] Aaron Clauset, M. E. J. Newman, and Cristopher Moore. Finding community structure in very large networks. *Phys. Rev. E*, 70(6):066111, 2004.

[5] Michael D. Escobar and Mike West. Bayesian density estimation and inference using mixtures. *Journal of the American Statistical Association*, 90:577–588, 1994.

[6] Gary William Flake, Steve Lawrence, C. Lee Giles, and Frans M. Coetzee. Self-organization and identification of web communities. *IEEE Computer*, 35:66–71, 2002.

[7] M. Girvan and M. E. J. Newman. Community structure in social and biological networks. *Proceedings of the National Academy of Sciences*, 99(12):7821–7826, 2002.

[8] Keith Henderson, Brian Gallagher, Lei Li, Leman Akoglu, Tina Eliassi-Rad, Hanghang Tong, and Christos Faloutsos. It's who you know: graph mining using recursive structural features. In *Proceedings of the 17th ACM SIGKDD international conference on Knowledge discovery and data mining*, KDD '11, pages 663–671, New York, NY, USA, 2011. ACM.

[9] Qirong Ho, Junming Yin, and Eric P. Xing. On triangular versus edge representations — towards scalable modeling of networks. In Peter L. Bartlett, Fernando C. N. Pereira, Christopher J. C. Burges, LÃl'on Bottou, and Kilian Q. Weinberger, editors, *NIPS*, pages 2141–2149, 2012.

[10] Jian Liu. Fuzzy modularity and fuzzy community structure in networks. *The European Physical Journal B*, 77:547–557, 2010.

[11] Yan Liu, Alexandru Niculescu-Mizil, and Wojciech Gryc. Topic-link lda: joint models of topic and author community. In *Proceedings of the 26th Annual International Conference on Machine Learning*, ICML '09, pages 665–672, New York, NY, USA, 2009. ACM.

[12] Andrew McCallum, Andrés Corrada-Emmanuel, and Xuerui Wang. Topic and role discovery in social networks. In *Proceedings of the 19th international joint conference on Artificial intelligence*, IJCAI'05, pages 786–791, San Francisco, CA, USA, 2005. Morgan Kaufmann Publishers Inc.

[13] Ramesh M. Nallapati, Amr Ahmed, Eric P. Xing, and William W. Cohen. Joint latent topic models for text and citations. In *Proceedings of the 14th ACM SIGKDD international conference on Knowledge discovery and data mining*, KDD '08, pages 542–550, New York, NY, USA, 2008. ACM.

[14] David Newman, Arthur Asuncion, Padhraic Smyth, and Max Welling. Distributed algorithms for topic models. *J. Mach. Learn. Res.*, 10:1801–1828, December 2009.

[15] M. E. J. Newman. Modularity and community structure in networks. *Proceedings of the National Academy of Sciences*, 103(23):8577–8582, 2006.

[16] Gergely Palla, Imre Derényi, Illés Farkas, and Tamás Vicsek. Uncovering the overlapping community structure of complex networks in nature and society, 2005.

[17] Nishith Pathak, Colin DeLong, Arindam Banerjee, and Kendrick Erickson. Social topics models for community extraction. In *Proceedings of the 2nd SNA-KDD Workshop*, 2008.

[18] Michal Rosen-Zvi, Thomas Griffiths, Mark Steyvers, and Padhraic Smyth. The author-topic model for authors and documents. In *Proceedings of the 20th conference on Uncertainty in artificial intelligence*, UAI '04, pages 487–494, Arlington, Virginia, United States, 2004. AUAI Press.

[19] Mrinmaya Sachan, Danish Contractor, Tanveer A. Faruquie, and L. Venkata Subramaniam. Using content and interactions for discovering communities in social networks. In *Proceedings of the 21st international conference on World Wide Web*, WWW '12, pages 331–340. ACM, 2012.

[20] Jianbo Shi and Jitendra Malik. Normalized cuts and image segmentation. *IEEE Trans. Pattern Anal. Mach. Intell.*, 22(8):888–905, August 2000.

[21] Sucheta Soundarajan and John Hopcroft. Using community information to improve the precision of link prediction methods. In *Proceedings of the 21st international conference companion on World Wide Web*, WWW '12 Companion, pages 607–608, New York, NY, USA, 2012. ACM.

[22] Hanna M. Wallach, Iain Murray, Ruslan Salakhutdinov, and David Mimno. Evaluation methods for topic models. In *ICML*, 2009.

[23] M.-S. Yang. A survey of fuzzy clustering. *Mathematical and Computer Modelling*, 18(11):1 – 16, 1993.

[24] Ding Zhou, Eren Manavoglu, Jia Li, C. Lee Giles, and Hongyuan Zha. Probabilistic models for discovering e-communities. In *Proceedings of the International Conference on World Wide Web*, 2006.

# Scalable Topic-Specific Influence Analysis on Microblogs


Bin Bi
UCLA
bbi@cs.ucla.edu

Yuanyuan Tian
IBM Almaden Research Center
ytian@us.ibm.com

Yannis Sismanis[◇]
Google
yannis@google.com

Andrey Balmin[*]
GraphSQL
andrey@graphsql.com

Junghoo Cho
UCLA
cho@cs.ucla.edu



## ABSTRACT

Social influence analysis on microblogs, such as Twitter, has been playing a crucial role in online advertising and brand management. While most previous influence analysis schemes rely only on the links between users to find key influencers, they omit the important text content created by the users. As a result, there is no way to differentiate the social influence in different aspects of life (topics). Although a few prior works do support topic-specific influence analysis, they either separate the analysis of content from that of network structure, or assume that content is the only cause of links, which is clearly an inappropriate assumption for microblog networks.

To address the limitations of the previous approaches, we propose a novel Followship-LDA (FLDA) model, which integrates both content topic discovery and social influence analysis in the same generative process. This model properly captures the content-related and content-independent reasons why a user follows another in a microblog network. We demonstrate that FLDA produces results with significantly better precision than existing approaches. Furthermore, we propose a distributed Gibbs sampling algorithm for FLDA, and demonstrate that it provides excellent scalability on large clusters. Finally, we incorporate the FLDA model in a general search framework for topic-specific influencers. A user freely expresses his/her interest by typing a few keywords, the search framework will return a ranked list of key influencers that satisfy the user's interest.


## Categories and Subject Descriptors

H.4 [**Information Systems Applications**]: Miscellaneous

## 1. INTRODUCTION

Microblogging services, such as Twitter (`twitter.com`), have gained tremendous popularity in recent years. Using these services, a user can publish a short message, called a *tweet*, and *follow* other users to keep up with their latest updates. The "follow" relationship (or *followship*) is directed, with information only flowing from the *followee* to the *follower*. A large amount of microblog data has been accumulated over time. For example, according to a March 2012 report, Twitter had over 500 million registered users creating over 340 million tweets daily [27].

The rich text and social information in microblogs has become a popular resource for marketing campaigns to monitor the opinions of consumers on particular products and to launch viral advertising. Identifying key influencers in microblogs is required for such marketing activities. Although a lot of work has been done on social influence analysis, most of these studies [8, 16, 17, 18, 9] infer influence only from the network structure, while ignoring the valuable text content that the users created. As a result, the learned influence of each user is only *global*, with no way to assess the influence in a particular aspect of life (topic). For example, no one can deny that President Obama is a key influencer in general. But his impact is most prominent in politics. In other subjects, like choosing digital cameras, he is unlikely to be influential. Clearly, *topic-specific* influence analysis provides a more detailed influence portfolio for a user, which is critical for effective marketing.

A number of PageRank-based methods, such as Topic-Sensitive PageRank [15] and TwitterRank [28], are able to compute per-topic influence ranks, but they require the topics to be already created either manually or by a topic modeling preprocess. As content and links are related to each other in a microblog network, the separation between the analysis on content and the analysis on the network structure usually leads to inferior performance, compared to those methods, like Link-LDA [10], which can detect topics and infer influences at the same time. However, Link-LDA, as originally designed for citation networks, assumes that the generation of links is purely based on the content. This assumption clearly does not apply to microblogs, since it is prevalent for a user to follow celebrities simply because of their fame and stardom, with nothing to do with what he/she actually tweets about.

To correctly model topic-specific influence on microblogs, we propose a new Bernoulli-Multinomial mixture model, called Followship-LDA (FLDA). This model contains two levels of mixtures: an upper-level Bernoulli mixture with one of the components being a Multinomial mixture. FLDA jointly models text and followship in the same generative process. Furthermore, it is able to differentiate the different reasons why a user follows another. Sometimes, A follows B because they tweet in similar topics. This type of followship is content-based. In other times, A follows B purely because B is a pop star. In this case, the followship is content-independent. Using FLDA, we can not only learn the per-user preference of following by content or not, but also remove the stardom effect when computing the topic-specific influence. Our empirical study on two popular microblog datasets, Twitter and Tencent Weibo, shows that

[◇*] This work was done while the authors were at IBM Almaden Research Center.



*WSDM'14*, February 24–28, 2014, New York, New York, USA.
Copyright 2014 ACM 978-1-4503-2351-2/14/02 ...$15.00.
http://dx.doi.org/10.1145/2556195.2556229.

the FLDA model produces significantly higher quality results than the prior arts.

Gibbs sampling is a widely used approach to approximate target distributions for LDA-like Bayesian models. To meet the computational challenge posed by rapid growing microblog data, we propose a *distributed* Gibbs sampling algorithm which significantly speeds up the Gibbs sampling process. For example, a sequential job that would take 21 days on a high end server can finish in 1.5 days using the distributed algorithm on a cluster of 27 commodity machines! We chose to implement the distributed Gibbs sampling on top of the Spark cluster computing framework [29]. Several alternative platforms [7, 3, 5] have been proposed to address the problem of machine-learning at scale. Spark is such a parallel programming framework, which supports efficient iterative algorithms on datasets stored in the aggregate memory of a cluster. We pick Spark as the underlying framework, because of its extreme flexibility as far as cluster programming is concerned. In addition to machine-learning algorithms, which were the main motivation behind the design of Spark, various data-parallel applications can be expressed and executed efficiently using Spark; examples include MapReduce, Pregel[20], HaLoop[7] and many others(see [29]).

Finally, we propose a general search framework for topic-specific key influencers, which can flexibly plug in various topic-specific influence methods, including FLDA, Link-LDA, Topic-Sensitive PageRank and TwitterRank. A user just needs to enter a set of keywords to describe his/her interest, the search framework will infer a topic distribution from the keywords and return a ranked list of influencers in the corresponding topic combination.

In particular, this paper makes the following contributions:

- We propose a new Bayesian Bernoulli-Multinomial mixture model, FLDA, to jointly model both content and links in the same generative process, while separating the various reasons why a user follows another in a microblog network.
- We discuss and implement a distributed Gibbs-sampling technique for training FLDA over large clusters.
- We propose a general search framework for finding topic-specific key influencers with various models (including FLDA, Link-LDA and PageRank variants).
- Through extensive experimentation with two large real datasets, we demonstrate (a) the substantial better precision achieved by FLDA than previous work, (b) the excellent scalability of the distributed Gibbs-sampling technique over large clusters and (c) various interesting insights gained from the real datasets.

The rest of this paper is organized as follows. In Section 2, we describe the related work. The FLDA model is introduced in Section 3. Section 4 presents the distributed Gibbs sampling algorithm for FLDA, while Section 5 provides an overview of the general search framework for topic-specific key influencers. In Section 6, we present our experimental results. Finally we conclude the paper in Section 7.

## 2. RELATED WORK

Much work has been done on influence analysis in social networks. Kempe et. al. pioneered the Linear Threshold Model and Independent Cascade Model to explain the spread of influence in a social network and abstracted the key influencer problem into a maximization problem [17]. Along with subsequent works, such as [18] and [9], these methods are only after the identification of *global*

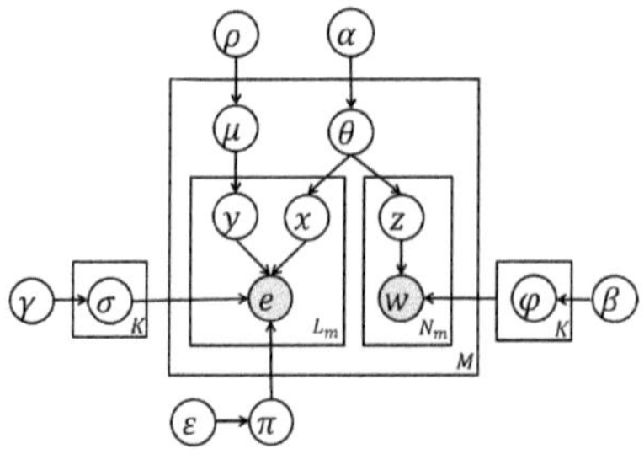


Figure 1: Followship-LDA

influencers instead of influencers for specific topics. Although Barbieri et. al. extended the Linear Threshold Model and Independent Cascade Model to be topic-aware [2], the topics are still obtained based on the network structure, while totally ignoring the valuable content information.

Given the popularity of PageRank [6], it is only natural to extend it for topical influence analysis. Topic-Sensitive PageRank (TSPR) [15] was such an extension for computing per-topic PageRank scores. TSPR biases the computation of PageRank by replacing the classic PageRank's uniform teleport vector with topic-specific ones. However, it requires a separate preprocess to create topics and provide per-topic teleport vectors. This preprocess can be done by either utilizing existing manually categorized topic hierarchies, such as suggested in [15], or applying well-known topic modeling methods like LDA [4] on the text content, as suggested in [28].

In [28], TwitterRank was proposed to find topic-level influencers on Twitter. A set of topics is first produced by LDA on the tweets. Then TwitterRank applies a method similar to TSPR to compute the per-topic influence rank. The transition probability between two users in TwitterRank is defined based on the number of tweets published by different followees and the topical similarity between the follower and the followee.

In the context of documents and citations (or hyperlinks), a mixed membership model was proposed in [10] to jointly model text and citations in the same generative process, which we will refer to as Link-LDA. In the generative process of Link-LDA, for a given document, a citation to another document is created in exactly the same way as a word is created, and they share the same per-document topic distribution. If we aggregate all the tweets for each user, and treat a user as a document and his/her followships to other users as citations, then Link-LDA can be applied to the microblog network, to learn the probability of each microblog user $u$ being followed by someone given a specific topic $t$. This probability can be used to measure $u$'s influence on the topic $t$. Link-PLSA-LDA [22] is an extension to Link-LDA, but also assumes that the cause of links is purely based on the text content.

In [26], Tang et al. proposed a Topical Affinity Propagation (TAP) model for topic-level social influence. But, similar to TSPR and TwitterRank, TAP requires a separate topic modeling approach to be applied first to derive a set of topics on the content.

In [24], Pal et. al. proposed to identify topical authorities by clustering users using 15 carefully selected features and then rank users within each cluster. Cognos [11] heavily relies on the manually curated Twitter "Lists" to infer topics of expertise and rank experts for different topics. Liu et al. introduced a graphical model to learn influence in the context of general heterogeneous networks [19].

## 3. FOLLOWSHIP-LDA

The existing works on topic-specific influence analysis can be categorized into two camps. The first camp, represented by TSPR and TwitterRank, completely detach the topic detection process

Table 1: Notations used in FLDA

| Notation | Description |
|---|---|
| $\theta$ | Per–user topic distribution |
| $\varphi$ | Per-topic word distribution |
| $\sigma$ | Per-topic followee distribution |
| $\pi$ | Multinomial distribution over followees |
| $\mu$ | Per-user Bernoulli distribution over indicators |
| $\alpha, \beta, \gamma, \epsilon, \rho$ | Parameters of the Dirichlet (Beta) priors on Multinomial (Bernoulli) distributions |
| $w$ | Word identity |
| $e$ | Followee identity |
| $z$ | Identity of the topic of a word |
| $x$ | Identity of the topic of a followee |
| $y$ | Binary indicator of whether a followship is related to the content of tweets |
| $M$ | Number of unique users |
| $V$ | Number of words in the vocabulary |
| $K$ | Number of unique topics |
| $N_m$ | Number of words in the tweets of user $m$ |
| $L_m$ | Number of followees for user $m$ |

Choose $\pi \sim Dirichlet(\varepsilon)$
For each topic $k = 1, \ldots, K$
    Choose $\varphi_k \sim Dirichlet(\beta)$
    Choose $\sigma_k \sim Dirichlet(\gamma)$
For each user $m = 1, \ldots, M$
    Choose $\theta_m \sim Dirichlet(\alpha)$
    For the $n^{th}$ word of the $m^{th}$ user, where $n \in \{1, \ldots, N_m\}$
        Choose a topic $z_{m,n} \sim Multinomial(\theta_m)$, where $z_{m,n} \in \{1, \ldots, K\}$
        Choose a word $w_{m,n} \sim Multinomial(\varphi_{z_{m,n}})$, where $w_{m,n} \in \{1, \ldots, V\}$
    Choose $\mu_m \sim Dirichlet(\rho)$
    For the $l^{th}$ link of the $m^{th}$ user, where $l \in \{1, \ldots, L_m\}$
        Choose a topic $x_{m,l} \sim Multinomial(\theta_m)$, where $x_{m,l} \in \{1, \ldots, K\}$
        Choose an indicator $y_{m,l} \sim Bernoulli(\mu_m)$, where $y_{m,l} \in \{0,1\}$
        If $y_{m,l} = 0$ then
            Choose a followee $e_{m,l} \sim Multinomial(\pi)$, where $e_{m,l} \in \{1, \ldots, M\}$
        Else if $y_{m,l} = 1$ then
            Choose a followee $e_{m,l} \sim Multinomial(\sigma_{x_{m,l}})$, where $e_{m,l} \in \{1, \ldots, M\}$

Figure 2: Generative process for Followship-LDA

from the influence analysis. As we will show later in this paper, thesc methods perform inferior to those approaches in the second camp that integrate text topic discovery and social influence analysis in the same model. Link-LDA represents the best prior work in the second camp. However, it was originally developed for citation and hyperlink networks. In Link-LDA, the topic assignments for words and for citations are drawn from the same topic distribution $\theta$, assuming that the content of a document is topically related to that of its cited documents. This is a very reasonable assumption for citation/hyperlink networks, since an author most definitely chooses the topically related documents to cite. But this assumption no longer applies to microblog networks. There are many reasons for a microblog user to follow another. Some are content-related (they tweet in similar topics) and others are not. For example, President Obama has a massive number of followers in Twitter, but some of them have never tweeted about politics at all. It is very common to see users follow celebrities, not because they share any topic of interest, but just because they are famous and popular. Clearly, Link-LDA is not able to capture these non-content related factors in the influence analysis.

To correctly model the topics and social influence in microblog networks, we propose **Followship-LDA**, abbreviated as FLDA. The graphical model for FLDA is depicted in Figure 1, with the notations described in Table 1. The generative process of a user's content and links/followees is summarized in Figure 2.

For the generation of content, each user is viewed as a mixture of latent topics from which words are drawn, similar to LDA. To be more specific, for the $m^{th}$ user, we first pick the per-user topic distribution $\theta_m$ from a Dirichlet prior with parameter $\alpha$. Then, to generate the $n^{th}$ word for the tweets of the user, a topic $z_{m,n}$ is first chosen from $\theta_m$. Finally, the word $w_{m,n}$ is picked from the per-topic word distribution $\varphi_{z_{m,n}}$.

On the other hand, the links of the $m^{th}$ user are generated by a much more complex three-stage stochastic process. First of all, every user has a unique preference of following others based on content or non-content reasons. The Bernoulli distribution $\mu_m$ characterizes this per-user preference. As a result, for the $l^{th}$ link/followee of the $m^{th}$ user, we first consult $\mu_m$ to decide on the value of the binary variable $y_{m,l}$. $y_{m,l} = 1$ indicates that the link creation is based on the user's content, whereas $y_{m,l} = 0$ means that content has nothing to do with the link. Now if $y_{m,l} = 1$, we use the same topic distribution $\theta_m$ to pick a topic $x_{m,n}$ of interest, just as in the content generation part of FLDA. Afterward, we choose a followee $e_{m,l}$ who well addresses the picked topic from the per-topic followee distribution $\sigma_{x_{m,l}}$. When $y_{m,l} = 0$, the user is following someone for non-content reasons. We use $\pi$ to capture this probability distribution. In particular, a followee $e_{m,l}$ is chosen from the Multinomial distribution $\pi$.

Note that FLDA is a much more complex mixture model than LDA and Link-LDA. We call it a Bernoulli-Multinomial mixture model, because the model consists of two levels of mixtures: an upper-level Bernoulli mixture that includes a Multinomial mixture underneath. More specifically, each followee $e$ of a user $m$ is drawn from a Bernoulli mixture of two components. One of the mixture components is a Multinomial distribution with parameter $\pi$, corresponding to the global popularity. The other component, however, is itself a mixture of $K$ Multinomial components, each corresponding to a topic. The distribution of followee $e$ of user $m$ is: $p(e|\mu, \pi, \theta, \sigma) = \mu_{m,0}\pi_e + \mu_{m,1}\sum_{k=1}^{K}\theta_{m,k}\sigma_{k,e}$, where $\mu$ are the outer mixing proportions, and $\theta$ are the inner mixing proportions.

The various probability distributions we can learn from the FLDA model characterize the different factors that affect the textual and social structures of a microblog network. For a user $m$, the probability $\theta_{z|m}$ represents the likelihood of $m$ tweeting about topic $z$, and $\mu_{y|m}$ is the probability of the reason indicator $y$ (content-related or not) why the user $m$ follows others. For content of tweets, $\varphi_{w|z}$ gives the probability of word $w$ belonging to topic $z$. In terms of links, $\sigma_{e|x}$ captures the likelihood of a user $e$ being followed by someone for a given topic $x$. This value essentially quantifies the influence of user $e$ on $x$ and is exactly the topic-specific influence score we want to compute. Finally, $\pi_e$ indicates the probability of a user $e$ being followed for any non-content reason. In some sense, $\pi_e$ is measuring the global popularity of $e$. We formally define:

*Topic-Specific Influence*: the influence of user $e$ on topic $x$ is measured by $\sigma_{e|x}$ which is the probability of $e$ being followed for topic $x$ in the FLDA model.

*Content-Independent Popularity*: the content-independent popularity of user $e$ is measured by $\pi_e$ which is the probability of $e$ being followed for any content-independent reason in the FLDA model.

## 3.1 Gibbs Sampling for FLDA

To learn the various distributions in the FLDA model, we use collapsed Gibbs sampling. However, the derivation of posterior distributions for Gibbs sampling in FLDA is complicated by the fact that followee distribution is a joint distribution of two-level mixtures. As a result, we need to compute the joint distribution of $x$ and $y$ in the Gibbs sampling process. The posterior distributions for Gibbs sampling in FLDA are given in the equations below. The detailed derivation of these equations is provided in the appendix.

$$p(z_{m,n}|z_{-(m,n)}, x, w, e, y, \alpha, \beta, \gamma, \varepsilon, \rho)$$
$$\propto \frac{(c_{z_{m,n},m,*}^{-(m,n)} + d_{z_{m,n},m,*,*} + \alpha_{z_{m,n}})(c_{z_{m,n},*,w_{m,n}}^{-(m,n)} + \beta_{w_{m,n}})}{c_{z_{m,n},*,*}^{-(m,n)} + \sum_{i=1}^{W}\beta_i} \quad (1)$$

$$p(x_{m,l}, y_{m,l} = 0 | y_{-(m,l)}, x_{-(m,l)}, w, z, e, \alpha, \beta, \gamma, \varepsilon, \rho)$$
$$\propto \quad (c_{x_{m,l},m,*} + d^{-(m,l)}_{x_{m,l},m,*,*} + \alpha_{x_{m,l}})(d^{-(m,l)}_{*,m,*,0} + \rho_0) \times \frac{d^{-(m,l)}_{*,*,e_{m,l},0} + \varepsilon_{e_{m,l}}}{d^{-(m,l)}_{*,*,*,0} + \sum_{i=1}^{M} \varepsilon_i} \tag{2}$$

$$p(x_{m,l}, y_{m,l} = 1 | y_{-(m,l)}, x_{-(m,l)}, w, z, e, \alpha, \beta, \gamma, \varepsilon, \rho)$$
$$\propto \quad (c_{x_{m,l},m,*} + d^{-(m,l)}_{x_{m,l},m,*,*} + \alpha_{x_{m,l}})(d^{-(m,l)}_{*,m,*,1} + \rho_1) \times \frac{d^{-(m,l)}_{x_{m,l},*,e_{m,l},1} + \gamma_{e_{m,l}}}{d^{-(m,l)}_{x_{m,l},*,*,1} + \sum_{i=1}^{M} \gamma_i} \tag{3}$$

In the above equations, $z_{m,n}$ denotes the topic of the $n^{th}$ word for the $m^{th}$ user, and $y_{m,l}$ is the reason indicator (content or non-content) of the $l^{th}$ link for the $m^{th}$ user. $w_{m,n}$, $x_{m,l}$ and $e_{m,l}$ follow similar definitions. Let $z_{-(m,n)}$ denote the topics for all words except $z_{m,n}$, and $y_{-(m,l)}$ and $x_{-(m,l)}$ follow an analogous definition. We define $c_{z,m,w}$ as the number of times word $w$ is assigned to topic $z$ for the $m^{th}$ user, and $d_{x,m,e,y}$ as the number of times link $e$ is assigned to topic $x$ for the $m^{th}$ user with indicator $y$. If any of the dimensions in above notations is not limited to a specific value, we use $*$ to denote. Essentially, $*$ represents an aggregation on the corresponding dimension. For example, $c_{z,*,w}$ is the total number of times word $w$ is assigned to topic $z$ in the entire document collection. Finally, let $c^{-(m,n)}_{z,m,w}$ be the same meaning of $c_{z,m,w}$ only with the $n^{th}$ word for the $m^{th}$ user excluded. Similarly, $d^{-(m,l)}_{x,m,e,y}$ is defined in the same way as $d_{x,m,e,y}$ only without the count for the $l^{th}$ link for the $m^{th}$ user.

After the sampling algorithm has run for an appropriate number of iterations (until the chain has converged to a stationary distribution), the estimates for the parameters of $\theta$, $\varphi$, $\mu$, $\sigma$ and $\pi$ can be obtained via the following equations:

$$\theta_{x|m} = \frac{c_{x,m,*} + d_{x,m,*,*} + \alpha_x}{c_{*,m,*} + d_{*,m,*,*} + \sum_{i=1}^{K} \alpha_i} \tag{4}$$

$$\varphi_{w|z} = \frac{c_{z,*,w} + \beta_w}{c_{z,*,*} + \sum_{i=1}^{W} \beta_i} \tag{5}$$

$$\mu_{y|m} = \frac{d_{*,m,*,y} + \rho_y}{d_{*,m,*,*} + \rho_0 + \rho_1} \tag{6}$$

$$\sigma_{e|x} = \frac{d_{x,*,e,1} + \gamma_e}{d_{x,*,*,1} + \sum_{i=1}^{M} \gamma_i} \tag{7}$$

$$\pi_e = \frac{d_{*,*,e,0} + \varepsilon_e}{d_{*,*,*,0} + \sum_{i=1}^{M} \varepsilon_i} \tag{8}$$

# 4. SCALABLE GIBBS SAMPLING FOR FLDA

The rapid growth of microblog data poses a significant challenge for influence analysis in terms of both computation time and memory requirements. Scalable solutions that can take advantage of the computation power and memory capacity of multiple computers are becoming more crucial. However, the Gibbs sampling updates of FLDA shown in equations (1)-(3) are inherently sequential, which makes it very difficult to parallelize the computation. However, given the abundance of words and the large number of links in a microblog dataset, the dependency between different topic assignments or indicator assignments in equations (1)-(3) is relatively weak. As a result, we can relax the sequential requirement of the Gibbs sampling updates and distribute the computation to a number of processes running in parallel. In fact, similar observations were used to develop approximate parallel/distributed Gibbs sampling algorithm for LDA in [23], [25] and [1]. We implemented our distributed FLDA Gibbs sampling algorithm on a distributed cluster computing framework called Spark [29]. Before the details of our distributed algorithm, we first provide a brief overview of Spark.

```
1  val baseRDD = sc.textFile ("hdfs://master/baseData.log")
2  val lowerRDD = lines.map(String.toLowerCase _ )
3  val regexB = sc.broadcast(REGEX)
4  val nMatches = sc.accumulator(0)
5  lowerRDD.foreach (s =>
6     if ( s.matches(regexB.value) )
7      nMatches += 1
8  )
9  println ("#Matches is:\%d".format(nMatches.value))
```

Listing 1: Sample Spark code.

## 4.1 Spark Overview

Spark is a large-scale distributed processing framework specifically targeted at machine-learning iterative workloads. It uses a functional programming paradigm, and applies it on large clusters by providing a fault-tolerant implementation of distributed data sets called Resilient Distributed Data (RDD). RDDs can either reside in the aggregate main-memory of the cluster, or in efficiently serialized disk blocks. Especially for iterative processing, the opportunity to store the data in main-memory can significantly speed up processing. An RDD contains immutable data; i.e. it cannot be modified, however, a new RDD can be constructed by transforming an existing RDD.

The Spark runtime consists of a single coordinator node and multiple worker nodes. The coordinator keeps track of how to re-construct any partition of the RDD when any of the workers fails.

Computation in Spark is expressed using functional transformations over RDDs. For instance, assume that we have a log file, and that we want to transform each string to lower case. Consider the first two lines of actual Spark code in Listing 1: The first line of code defines an RDD of strings, called `baseRDD`, over a file "baseData.log" stored in a Hadoop Distributed FileSystem; each text line of the log file, corresponds to a string of the RDD. The second line of code, uses the `map` function to transform each string in `baseRDD` through the function `String.toLowerCase`. The transformation happens in parallel on all the workers, and defines a new RDD, called `lowerRDD` that contains the lower-case string of each string in `baseRDD`.

Spark's programming model provides additionally two useful abstractions: broadcast variables and accumulators. Broadcast variables are initialized at the coordinator node, and made available to all worker nodes, through efficient network broadcast algorithms. Spark chooses a topology-aware network-efficient algorithm to disseminate the data. Line 3 in Listing 1 initializes a broadcast variable called `regexB` to a regular expression (called `REGEX`). In Line 6, this value is used inside the `foreach` loop to check if any of the lines in the RDD called `lowerRDD` matches that regular expression. Note that broadcast variables are immutable, read-only, objects and cannot be modified by the workers.

Similar to a broadcast variable, an accumulator is also a variable that is initialized on the coordinator node, and sent to all the worker nodes. However, unlike a broadcast variable, an accumulator is mutable and can be used to aggregate results of computations at worker nodes. Worker nodes may update the state of the accumulator (usually just by incrementing it, or by using computations such as count and sum). At the end of the RDD transformation, each worker node sends its locally-updated accumulator back to the coordinator node, where all the accumulators are combined (using either a default or user-supplied combine function) into a final result. In our example listing, `nMatches` is an accumulator that is locally incremented by all workers (line 7) before it is globally aggregated (through an implicit addition over all the partial results in line 9).

### 4.2 Distributed FLDA using Spark

We now describe how we use the Spark framework to implement the distributed Gibbs sampling algorithm for FLDA. In particular we discuss technical issues that distributed approaches encounter, and propose solutions and justify various implementation choices.

First, we define the notion of a *user object*. Each user object corresponds to a single user $m$, and holds information about the content (i.e. the actual words used by $m$) and the link structure (i.e. other users that $m$ is following). For each word $w$ and link $e$, the user object holds the last topic assignment, i.e. the corresponding latent variables $z$ and $x$. For each link additionally it holds the last binary state (i.e. content-related or content-independent) for the $y$ latent variable. Finally, each user object holds the *user-local* counters $d_{x,m,e,y}$, $c_{x,m,w}$, as well as all aggregates of these (like $d_{*,m,*,*}$) that show up in equations (1)-(3). Note that the corresponding local aggregates always have a $m$ index in the subscript. Such aggregates are entirely local to a user and need not be shared.

Note that in addition to the user-local counters and aggregates, equations (1)-(3) require *global* aggregates (like $d_{x,*,*,1}$) over all the users. Such global aggregates always have a $*$ instead of $m$ in the corresponding subscript index.

Based on previous work ([25]), the global aggregates are not stored in the user object, but are computed periodically and distributed to all workers through an accumulator. The idea is that such aggregates should change slowly and thus any inaccuracies (because of the periodic synchronization) shouldn't affect the quality of the final result. Although this assumption has been shown to work well in practice for basic LDA, it is not evidently clear whether it works for FLDA. A big difference is that the global aggregates, that distributed LDA periodically needs to synchronize, are only per document terms and thus their count is limited (especially after typical pre-processing, like stop-word removal or stemming). However, distributing FLDA requires the periodic synchronization of orders of magnitude more aggregates;not only per document terms but also per user terms (and typically there are many more users). In the experiments, we show that for real datasets with millions of users, distributing FLDA still works very well.

Second, we define a mapping function, `GibbsSampleMap`, which takes as input one such user object, runs Gibbs sampling once and returns a new user object. In particular, this function goes over all the words and links in the object and (a) "undoes" the effects of the last assignment to the latent variables $x$, $y$ and $z$ (by properly decreasing the corresponding counts $d_{x,m,e,y}$, $c_{x,m,w}$ as well as all the corresponding local and global aggregates), (b) computes the new probabilities for the latent variables $x$, $y$ and $z$ according to the equations (1)-(3), and finally (c) assigns new latent variables according to these probabilities, and increases the corresponding counts and all user-local and global aggregates.

Putting all these together, first we initialize an RDD of user objects by (a) properly parsing and co-grouping the content and the link structure for each user, (b) randomly initializing the latent variable assignments and (c) computing the corresponding user-local counters and aggregates based on these initial assignments. Then we run a number of iterations over the RDD, where each iteration maps all user objects (in parallel) to new user objects using the `GibbsSampleMap` function we defined above. At the beginning of each iteration we accumulate and broadcast the global aggregates. We note, that each worker has its each own copy of the global aggregates, that the mapping function modifies. Thus although each worker starts with the same global aggregates, as user objects are transformed through the mapping functions, the workers' copies of the global aggregates get "out-of-sync", until the start of the next iteration when new global aggregates are computed and broadcasted. Finally, when all the iterations are done, we use equations (4)-(8) to estimate the parameters $\theta$, $\varphi$, $\mu$, $\sigma$ and $\pi$ of the FLDA model.

### 4.3 Discussion

The distributed Gibbs sampling algorithm is quite generic and could be used to train other Bayesian models as well. We emphasize that the final result depends on the assumptions made in [23] and [25]. In particular, the global-aggregates change slowly and thus are not updated continuously, but only once every iteration (or even less often and asynchronously in the case of [25]). This choice does not seem to affect the final result of topic models like LDA. The literature shows that the quality of the result (in terms of perplexity or log-likelihood) is equivalent to that from a purely sequential implementation (where the global aggregates are always updated). We empirically show that the same holds for FLDA. We emphasize that it is not immediately clear whether this approach works for FLDA, since it requires the synchronization of order of magnitude more global aggregates. In Section 6 we compare the resulting user rankings produced by serial and distributed version of the algorithm and show virtually no difference. Finally we note that in the experiments with various real datasets, we observed that computing and synchronizing the global-aggregates just once every ten iterations doesn't seem to affect the quality of the results. It is an open problem exactly how infrequent such global updates can be.

Although Spark provides a lineage based fault-recovery mechanism, we chose to complement it using manual checkpoints for every ten iterations. The reason, is that replaying all the iterations from the beginning for every failed worker (although infrequent) takes quite some time. With the checkpoints, we guarantee that at most ten iterations will have to be replayed in case of failures. Our choice was also based on the fact that the cost of a checkpoint was negligible (a small fraction of the time required to do an iteration).

Finally, we took extra care for the correctness of the distributed Monte-Carlo simulation. Since multiple workers are spawned at roughly the same time, typical random-number generators are seeded with similar (or even exactly the same) seeds. This introduces correlations between the pseudo random numbers generated across the workers. In extreme cases, two workers could "see" exactly the same stream of pseudo-random numbers. Such correlation jeopardizes the quality of the returned results. To guarantee correctness of the distributed simulation, we use the technique discussed in [14] for generating multiple streams of uniform numbers that are provably independent. In particular, we assign a unique stream for each RDD block and iteration pair (i.e. if we have 100 RDD blocks and 500 iterations, we have $100 \times 500$ independent streams of random numbers). This approach guarantees not only the correctness of the simulation, but also repeatability; every time we run the simulation with the same initial seed we get exactly the same results, regardless of the number of workers or possible worker failures.

## 5. QUERYING TOPICAL INFLUENCERS

Finally, we propose a general search framework for topic-specific key influencers, called **SKIT**. Inspired by the popular search engine framework, SKIT allows a user to freely express his/her interests by typing a set of keywords. Then, SKIT returns an ordered list of key influencers by their influence scores that satisfy the user's intent.

SKIT flexibly allows plugging in different topical influence methods. All that it needs from the underlying influence analysis are (a) the derivation of interested topics from the query keywords, and

Table 2: Statistics of Experimental Datasets.

| Dataset | # users | # dist. words | # total words | # links |
|---|---|---|---|---|
| Twitter | 1.76 M | 159 K | 2363 M | 183 M |
| Weibo | 2.33 M | 714 K | 492 M | 51 M |

(b) the per-topic influence scores for every microblog user. More specifically, given a set of key words as a query $q$, SKIT first derives a weight $W(t, q)$ for each topic $t$ in the set of all topics $T$, indicating the likelihood of topic $t$ being represented by query $q$. Then, utilizing the learned per-topic influence score for each user INFL$(t, u)$, the final influence score INFL$(q, u)$ for a user $u$ given a query $q$ is computed as

$$\text{INFL}(q, u) = \sum_{t \in T} W(t, q) \cdot \text{INFL}(t, u). \quad (9)$$

Finally, the users are returned in decreasing order of their influence scores INFL$(q, u)$.

When our FLDA model is used as the underlying topic-specific influence analysis method, the probability distributions $\theta_{z|m}$ and $\sigma_{e|x}$ are produced as part of the results. Here, $\theta_{z|m}$ represents the probability of topic $z$ given user $m$, and $\sigma_{e|x}$ is the probability of user $e$ being followed by someone given topic $x$. If we treat a query $q$ as a new user, we can use the folding-in [13] or the variational inference [25] technique on FLDA to quickly learn $\theta_{z=t|m=q}$, the probability of topic $t$ given the query $q$, and use this value as $W(t, q)$ in Equation (9). On the other hand, the per-topic influence score INFL$(t, u)$ for each user can be quantified by $\sigma_{e=u|x=t}$.

Besides FLDA, our flexible SKIT search framework can also easily plug in Link-LDA, TSPR and TwitterRank. The folding-in and the variational inference techniques equally apply to Link-LDA and LDA, if LDA is used in the topic modeling preprocess for TSPR and TwitterRank, to compute $W(t, q)$. The definition of INFL$(t, u)$ for Link-LDA is the same as in FLDA. For both TSPR and TwitterRank, INFL$(t, u)$ is simply the PageRank score for user $u$ and topic $t$.

# 6. EXPERIMENTS

In this section, we start with evaluating the effectiveness of our FLDA model on two microblog datasets, Twitter and Tencent Weibo. On the Twitter dataset, we give examples of topics and influencers found by the FLDA model, then we use the Tencent Weibo dataset to systematically compare FLDA with a number of existing approaches including TSPR, TwitterRank and Link-LDA. Finally, we demonstrate the scalability of the distributed Gibbs sampling algorithm, and show that it produces results with indistinguishable quality as the sequential algorithm.

**Experiment Setup.** The sequential FLDA Gibbs sampling algorithm was run on an 4-core Intel Xeon (X5672) 64-bit 3.2GHz server with 192GB RAM. For distributed FLDA Gibbs sampling, we used a cluster of 27 IBM System x iDataPlex dx340 servers. Each server consisted of two quad-core Intel Xeon (E5540) 64-bit 2.5GHz processors, 32GB RAM, and interconnected using 1GB Ethernet. We reserved one server as the Spark coordinator, and use the remaining ones for workers. Each machine was configured to run up to 8 concurrent workers. By default, we used 200 workers for distributed FLDA.

## 6.1 Effectiveness on Twitter Dataset

We first evaluate our FLDA model on a Twitter dataset[1], crawled between October 2009 and January 2010. The raw dataset consists of roughly half a terabyte of text and link information. The basic statistics of this dataset are given in Table 2. We used the tokenizer from the TweetNLP project [12] in order to improve the accuracy of the recognized terms in the noisy text. We tried to further reduce the inherent noise of tweets, by removing terms that appear in less than 50 tweets. We set the number of topics to 100 and run the distributed FLDA Gibbs sampling for 500 iterations. All the priors were set to 0.1 except $\rho$ which was set to 1. These settings are fairly typical for LDA-based approaches and their tuning is beyond the scope of this paper.

Table 3 shows some of the resulting topics with their top keywords and influencers. We named these topics to simplify the presentation. Intuitively, it is clear that the influencers are very relevant to the corresponding topics. For example, one would expect O'Reily publishers, Gartner research, and popular software bloggers to be influential for an IT-related topic. Just as one would expect school age kids to be influenced by pop stars. Some of the findings are insightful. For example, Australians seem to be particularly influenced by comedians. While the first person in the list is Prime Minister of Australia (at the time of the crawl), the following three are comics.

FLDA separated the "globally" popular users from the content-specific influencers, and elected that 15% of all links were content-independent. In other words, 15% of the time, these popular users were followed regardless of what people tweet about. By comparison, the largest topic was associated with less than 2.5% of all links. The top five globally popular users detected by FLDA were: Pete Wentz (singer), Ashton Kutcher (actor), Greg Grunberg (actor, author of Yowza mobile app), Britney Spears (singer), and Ellen DeGeneres (comedian, TV host). In comparison, the top five most-followed Twitter accounts were: Barack Obama, Ashton Kutcher, Britney Spears, Ellen DeGeneres, Shaquille OŠNeal (basketball player). Although President Obama was most followed, we found his impact was most prominent in politics, which was topic-related. Similarly, the basketball star Shaquille O'Neal was mostly followed, due to his impact in basketball. FLDA can correctly identify topic-specific influence from the content-independent popularity.

There were a number of similar topics produced by both FLDA and Link-LDA. Table 4 compares the top five influencers from FLDA and Link-LDA for a few example topics. As shown from the table, FLDA produced dramatically better results than Link-LDA. For example, the "Jobs" topic produced by FLDA and Link-LDA had virtually the same top-10 keywords. The top five influencers identified by FLDA were all popular job-search websites, whereas the influencers found by Link-LDA were mostly tech bloggers. Upon inspection of their tweets it seems clear that the Link-LDA list was much less relevant to the job search topic. As another example, on the "Music" topic, FLDA successfully identified popular music media as influencers, whereas Link-LDA misidentified Club Ubuntu and a consultant as influencers in the music topic.

Naturally, such anecdotal evidence is very hard to generalize and quantify. Luckily, 2012 KDD Cup provided us with the data needed to objectively measure the quality of FLDA and other approaches, as we describe next.

## 6.2 Effectiveness on Tencent Weibo Dataset

In this section, we systematically evaluate the effectiveness of our FLDA model on a sample dataset from the popular Chinese microblog site – Tencent Weibo (`t.qq.com`).

This Tencent Weibo dataset is released by KDD Cup 2012[2]. The basic statistics of this dataset [3] are given in Table 2. A very nice feature of the Weibo dataset is the set of provided VIP users (also

[1]This dataset was crawled in a BSF manner with the top 1000 users in `twitterholic.com` as the seeds.

[2]`www.kddcup2012.org/c/kddcup2012-track1/data`

[3]In the Tencent Weibo dataset, for each user, the appearance of each word is

Table 3: A sample of FLDA topics and their influencers.

| Topic | Top-10 keywords | Top-5 influencers |
|---|---|---|
| "Information Technology" | data, web, cloud, software, open, windows, microsoft, server, security, code | Tim O'Reilly, Gartner Inc., Scott Hanselman (software blogger), Jeff Atwood (software blogger, co-founder of stackoverflow.com), Elijah Manor (software blogger) |
| "Food and drink" | food, chocolate, coffee, eat, chicken, lunch dinner, cheese, recipe, tea | Whole Foods (organic grocery chain), Foodimentary.com (food blog), WineTwits.com (wine community), Barack Obama, L.A. Times Food |
| "Cycling and running" | bike, ride, race, training, running, miles, team, workout, marathon, fitness | Lance Armstrong, Levi Leipheimer, George Hincapie (all 3, US Postal pro cycling team members), Johan Bruyneel (US Postal team director), RSLT (radioshackleopardtrek.com – pro cycling team) |
| "Advertiser's dream" | class, sleep, hate, bed, tired, movie, homework, finally, bored, ugh | Taylor Swift, Pete Wentz, Katy Perry (all 3 singers), Perez Hilton (celeb blogger), Lady Gaga |
| "Ppl can't spell" | ppl, dnt, nite, tht, jus, goin, lov, wat, abt, plz | Kim Kardashian, Kourtney Kardashian, Khloe Kardashian, Tila Tequila (all 4 reality TV stars), Ciara (singer) |
| "Down under" | travel, Australia, latest, Sydney, Melbourne fishing, Australian, trip, hotel, island | Kevin Rudd (Australian PM in 2010), Rove McManus, Dave Hughes, Wil Anderson (all three are Aussie comedians and TV hosts), Ruby Rose (Australian model and TV presenter) |

Table 4: A sample of the topics of FLDA and Link-LDA together with their influencers

| Topic | Model | Top-10 keywords | Top-5 influencers |
|---|---|---|---|
| "Job" | FLDA | business, job, jobs, management, manager, sales, services, company, service, hiring | job-hunt.org, jobsguy.com, integritystaffing.com/blog (Job Search Ninja), JobConcierge.com, careerealism.com |
| | Link-LDA | job, jobs, manager, business, sales, management, service, company, services, hiring | Paul Terry Walhus (web host developer and blogger), Wayne Sutton (startup advisor), Adam Glickman (tech professional), bloggersblog.com (blogging news), Mary Hodder (tech blogger) |
| "Music" | FLDA | listening, album, rock, band, song, john, black, top, tour, artists | pitchfork.com (music website), Trent Reznor (singer), Paste Magazine (music magazine), New Musical Express, Sub Pop Records |
| | Link-LDA | listening, rock, album, song, band, black, john, top, beatles, bob | Club Ubuntu, Nithin Jawali (tech enthusiast), Paul Shaffer (musician) Debra Zimmer (consultant), iheartquotes.com (a collection of quotes) |
| "Justice" | FLDA | police, court, case, law, report, death, story, arrested, woman, state | Barack Obama, CNN Breaking News, The New York Times, CanadaCool.com, BBC Breaking News |
| | Link-LDA | police, ap, law, court, report, press, case, death, reuters, state | Health Brand, 2humor.com (funny stuff), healthsmartme.tumblr.com Daniel Vega (lawyer), Multiplaza Shopping (shopping deals) |
| "Weather" | FLDA | snow, weather, rain, winter, high, nc, denver, storm, wind, county | CNN Breaking News, The Denver Post, NPR News, The Weather Channel, CBS Denver |
| | Link-LDA | snow, weather, atlanta, rain, high, nc, county, south, fire, north | DiningPerks.com, Georgia Aquarium, Atlanta Journal-Constitution (Atlanta newspaper), HelloNorthGeorgia.com, Q100 Atlanta (radio) |

called items in Weibo), which enables us to systematically evaluate the precision of various key influencer methods. These VIP users are manually labeled by Weibo administrators, and organized in hierarchical categories. An example hierarchical category is *science_and_technology.internet.mobile*, where categories in different levels are separated by a dot ".". In this dataset, categories are anonymized as integers, such as 1.4.2.3. There are 377 categories and on average each category contains 16.2 VIPs. According to Weibo, the VIP users are typically famous people and organizations. In other words, they are "key influencers" in their corresponding categories. As a result, the VIP users can be used as the "ground truth" for our empirical evaluation. While we don't expect VIP categories to have 100% precision or recall, they give us enough information to facilitate relative comparisons across different schemes.

Based on this information, we have set up the following experiment. For a given category, we use one VIP (i.e. all the words of this user) as the query, and observe how many of the fellow VIP users in the same category are identified as top influencers by the different schemes. In the following, we compare our FLDA model with TSPR, TwitterRank and Link-LDA. We maintain the number of topics at 100 for all the methods and run 500 iterations for LDA (used in TSPR and TwitterRank), Link-LDA and FLDA. The priors used are 1.0 for $\alpha$, 0.01 for $\beta$, $\gamma$ and $\epsilon$, and 0.1 for $\rho$.

Figure 3a and Figure 3b compare our FLDA model with TSPR, TwitterRank and Link-LDA on two of the largest categories in the Weibo dataset. For each category, we use every VIP user as a key influencer query and check how many of the top K returned users are the fellow VIP users. We report the average number of VIPs among the top K returned results across all the queries. As shown in both figures, our FLDA model consistently produces better precision results than the others by a significant margin. TSPR is usually the worst among all methods, followed by TwitterRank. Link-LDA performs slightly better than the two PageRank-based approaches.

To analyze the results across all categories we employ a standard Mean Average Precision (MAP) [21] metric. MAP for a set of queries is defined as the mean of the average precision scores ($AvgP$) for each query. $AvgP$ of a list of top-$k$ query results is defined as the average of precision values for all $k$ prefixes.

Figure 4 shows MAP of all the queries across all categories in the Weibo dataset. Again, FLDA produces significantly better results than the competing methods, more than 2 times better than TSPR and TwitterRank, and around 1.6 times better than Link-LDA. Interestingly, FLDA elected only 50% of Weibo links to be content-related. This explains the significant advantage of FLDA over Link-LDA, which assumes that all links are topic-specific.

As shown in Figure 3a, 3b and Figure 4, the distributed FLDA consistently produces result with quality almost identical to that of the sequential FLDA. This confirms the relaxed dependency assumption on which our distributed FLDA Gibbs sampling is based.

Throughout the experiments we measured the time taken by the on-line component of our SKIT search framework. On average, each query takes 1.7 sec to get the results, and this time does not depend on the off-line modeling scheme we use.

associated with a weight (usually $\leq 1.0$). We multiply this weight by 100 to approximate the underlying word frequency.

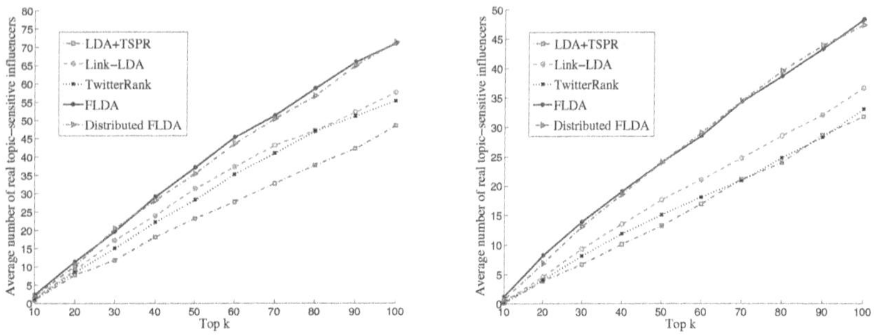


(a) category 1.6.2.1 (#VIPs in this category: 277) (b) category 1.6.2.2 (#VIPs in this category: 123)

Figure 3: Average number of returned VIPs

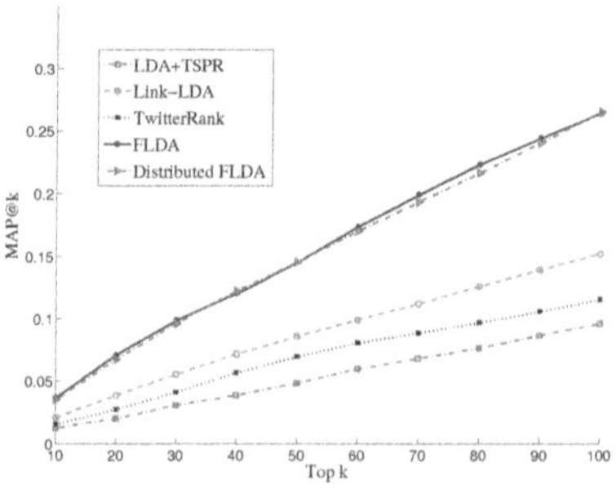


Figure 4: Mean Average Precision

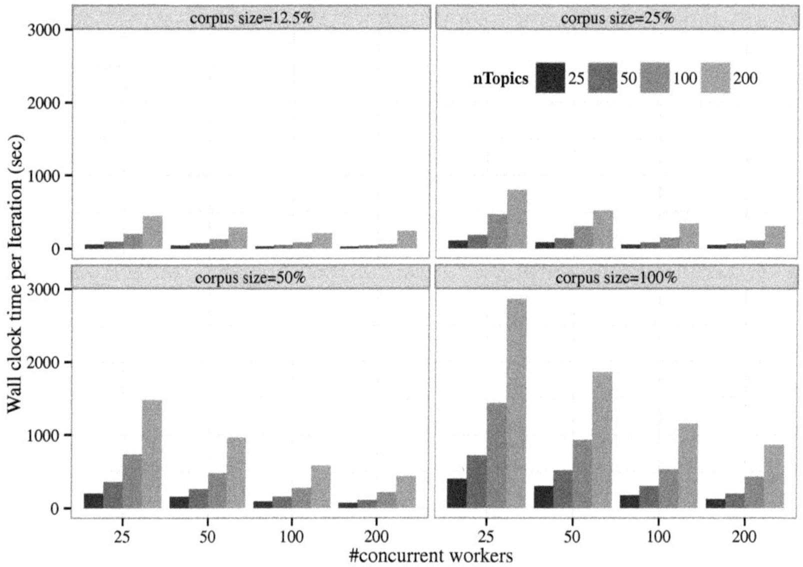


Figure 5: Speed-Up of Distributed FLDA on Twitter dataset.

## 6.3 Scalability

Before evaluating the scalability of our distributed FLDA Gibbs sampling algorithm, we first report the execution times for the sequential algorithm. For the KDD Weibo dataset, the sequential Gibbs sampling on a high-end server (192GB RAM, 3.2GHz processor) takes around 13 minutes per iteration, and for the Twitter dataset, it takes more than one hour per iteration. On Twitter dataset FLDA runs longer because there are many more words and links to sample. Running sequential Gibbs sampling for 500 iterations takes around 4.6 days for the KDD Weibo dataset, and would take 21 days for the Twitter dataset! This clearly motivates the need for a scalable solution.

Our distributed algorithm completes 500 iterations on Twitter data in about 36 hours, using 200 workers on 27 machines. Overall, the distributed FLDA in this instance is about 14 times faster than a sequential implementation running on single, large-memory server.

We tested the scalability of the distributed algorithm along three dimensions: data size, number of topics, and the number of concurrent workers. To obtain the scaled down dataset we performed uniform random sampling of users, for example to generate a 4 times smaller dataset we use a sampling rate of 25%. The results are summarized in Figure 5 where the scaled-down dataset is denoted as *corpus size* and is measured by the sampling rate used. We explore a wide range of sizes (from 12.5% all the way up to 100%), number of topics (from 25 to 200) and number of workers (from 25 to 200). The figure shows that the distributed FLDA scales well along all dimensions, given the limitations of our cluster. Our (older) CPU's were significantly oversubscribed with 8 workers per node, which was the case with 200 workers.

## 7. CONCLUSION

This paper addresses the problem of identifying topic-specific key influencers in microblog networks. To model the per-topic influence of each user, we introduce a novel Bernoulli-Multinomial mixture model called FLDA. FLDA incorporates the content of tweets and the network structure of microblogs into one unified model. Different from the previous work, such as Link-LDA, our FLDA model is specifically designed for microblogs in that it captures the fact that in reality a user sometimes follows another due to content-independent reasons. Moreover, in order to apply FLDA to a web-scale microblog network, we design a distributed Gibbs sampling algorithm for FLDA on the Spark distributed computing framework. Finally, the FLDA model is incorporated in a proposed general search framework for topic-specific key influencers, which provides a keyword search interface for users to freely query key influencers in different topic combinations.

Through experiments on two real-world microblog datasets, we demonstrate that FLDA significantly outperforms the state-of-the-art methods in terms of precision. Furthermore, the distributed Gibbs sampling algorithm for FLDA provides excellent speed-up to hundreds of workers.

# 8. REFERENCES


[1] A. Ahmed, M. Aly, J. Gonzalez, S. Narayanamurthy, and A. J. Smola. Scalable inference in latent variable models. In *WSDM'12*, pages 123–132, 2012.

[2] N. Barbieri, F. Bonchi, and G. Manco. Topic-aware social influence propagation models. In *Proceedings of the 2012 IEEE 12th International Conference on Data Mining*, ICDM '12, pages 81–90, 2012.

[3] D. Battré, S. Ewen, F. Hueske, O. Kao, V. Markl, and D. Warneke. Nephele/pacts: a programming model and execution framework for web-scale analytical processing. In *SoCC*, 2010.

[4] D. M. Blei, A. Y. Ng, and M. I. Jordan. Latent dirichlet allocation. *Journal of Machine Learning Research*, 3:993–1022, March 2003.

[5] V. R. Borkar, M. J. Carey, R. Grover, N. Onose, and R. Vernica. Hyracks: A flexible and extensible foundation for data-intensive computing. In *ICDE*, 2011.

[6] S. Brin and L. Page. The anatomy of a large-scale hypertextual web search engine. In *WWW'98*, pages 107–117, 1998.

[7] Y. Bu, B. Howe, M. Balazinska, and M. D. Ernst. Haloop: efficient iterative data processing on large clusters. *PVLDB*, 2010.

[8] D. Chakrabarti and C. Faloutsos. Graph mining: Laws, generators, and algorithms. *ACM COMPUTING SURVEYS*, 38(1):2, 2006.

[9] W. Chen, Y. Wang, and S. Yang. Efficient influence maximization in social networks. In *KDD '09*, pages 199–208, 2009.

[10] E. Erosheva, S. Fienberg, and J. Lafferty. Mixed-membership models of scientific publications. *Proceedings of the National Academy of Sciences*, 101:5220–5227, 2004.

[11] S. Ghosh, N. Sharma, F. Benevenuto, N. Ganguly, and K. Gummadi. Cognos: crowdsourcing search for topic experts in microblogs. In *SIGIR '12*, pages 575–590, 2012.

[12] K. Gimpel, N. Schneider, B. O'Connor, D. Das, D. Mills, J. Eisenstein, M. Heilman, D. Yogatama, J. Flanigan, and N. A. Smith. Part-of-speech tagging for twitter: Annotation, features, and experiments. In *ACL*, pages 42–47, 2011.

[13] M. Girolami and A. Kabán. On an equivalence between plsi and lda. In *SIGIR '03*, pages 433–434, 2003.

[14] H. Haramoto, M. Matsumoto, T. Nishimura, F. Panneton, and P. L'Ecuyer. Efficient Jump Ahead for 2-Linear Random Number Generators. *INFORMS Journal on Computing*, 20(3):385–390, 2008.

[15] T. H. Haveliwala. Topic-sensitive pagerank. In *WWW '02*, pages 517-526, 2002.

[16] A. Java, P. Kolari, T. Finin, and T. Oates. Modeling the spread of influence on the blogosphere. In *WWW 2006 Workshop on Weblogging Ecosystem: Aggregation, Analysis and Dynamics*, 2006.

[17] D. Kempe, J. Kleinberg, and E. Tardos. Maximizing the spread of influence through a social network. In *KDD '03*, pages 137–146, 2003.

[18] J. Leskovec, A. Krause, C. Guestrin, C. Faloutsos, J. VanBriesen, and N. Glance. Cost-effective outbreak detection in networks. In *KDD '07*, pages 420–429, 2007.

[19] L. Liu, J. Tang, J. Han, and S. Yang. Learning influence from heterogeneous social networks. *Data Mining and Knowledge Discovery*, 25:511–544, 2012.

[20] G. Malewicz, M. H. Austern, A. J. C. Bik, J. C. Dehnert, I. Horn, N. Leiser, and G. Czajkowski. Pregel: a system for large-scale graph processing. In *SIGMOD*, 2010.

[21] C. D. Manning, P. Raghavan, and H. Schtze. *Introduction to Information Retrieval*. Cambridge University Press, New York, NY, USA, 2008.

[22] R. Nallapati and W. W. Cohen. Link-plsa-lda: A new unsupervised model for topics and influence of blogs. In *Proceedings of the Second International Conference on Weblogs and Social Media*, 2008.

[23] D. Newman, A. Asuncion, P. Smyth, and M. Welling. Distributed algorithms for topic models. *J. Mach. Learn. Res.*, 10:1801–1828, Dec. 2009.

[24] A. Pal and S. Counts. Identifying topical authorities in microblogs. In *WSDM '11*, pages 45–54, 2011.

[25] A. Smola and S. Narayanamurthy. An architecture for parallel topic models. *PVLDB*, 3(1-2):703–710, Sept. 2010.

[26] J. Tang, J. Sun, C. Wang, and Z. Yang. Social influence analysis in large-scale networks. In *KDD '09*, pages 807–816, 2009.

[27] Twitter.com. Twitter turns six, 2012.

[28] J. Weng, E.-P. Lim, J. Jiang, and Q. He. Twitterrank: finding topic-sensitive influential twitterers. In *WSDM '10*, pages 261–270, 2010.

[29] M. Zaharia, M. Chowdhury, T. Das, A. Dave, J. Ma, M. McCauley, M. J. Franklin, S. Shenker, and I. Stoica. Resilient distributed datasets: a fault-tolerant abstraction for in-memory cluster computing. In *NSDI'12*, 2012.


# APPENDIX

The Gibbs sampling equation for latent variable $z$ can be derived in a similar way to Link-LDA. We omit its derivation due to space limitation. Let us derive the posterior probability of latent variables $x$ and $y$:

$$
\begin{aligned}
& p(x_{m,l}, y_{m,l} | y_{-(m,l)}, x_{-(m,l)}, w, z, e, \alpha, \beta, \gamma, \varepsilon, \rho) \\
& \propto p(x, y, w, z, e | \alpha, \beta, \gamma, \varepsilon, \rho) \\
& = \int\int\int\int\int p(x, y, w, z, e, \theta, \varphi, \sigma, \pi, \mu | \alpha, \beta, \gamma, \varepsilon, \rho) d\theta d\varphi d\sigma d\pi d\mu \\
& = \int\int\int\int\int p(x|\theta) p(y|\mu) p(w|z, \varphi) p(z|\theta) p(e|x, y, \sigma, \pi) \\
& \quad \times p(\theta|\alpha) p(\varphi|\beta) p(\sigma|\gamma) p(\pi|\varepsilon) p(\mu|\rho) d\theta d\varphi d\sigma d\pi d\mu
\end{aligned} \tag{10}
$$

As $p(e|x, y, \sigma, \pi) = p(e|x, \sigma)^y p(e|\pi)^{1-y}$, we get,

$$
\begin{aligned}
& = \int p(\theta|\alpha) p(z|\theta) p(x|\theta) d\theta \int p(\sigma|\gamma) p(e|x, \sigma)^y d\sigma \\
& \quad \times \int p(\varphi|\beta) p(w|z, \varphi) d\varphi \int p(\pi|\varepsilon) p(e|\pi)^{1-y} d\pi \int p(\mu|\rho) p(y|\mu) d\mu
\end{aligned} \tag{11}
$$

Let us derive the first two integrals in Equation (11).

$$
\begin{aligned}
& \int p(\theta|\alpha) p(z|\theta) p(x|\theta) d\theta \int p(\sigma|\gamma) p(e|x, \sigma)^y d\sigma \\
& = \int \prod_{j=1}^{M} p(\theta_j|\alpha) \prod_{j=1}^{M} \prod_{u=1}^{N_j} p(z_{j,u}|\theta_j) \prod_{j=1}^{M} \prod_{v=1}^{L_j} p(x_{j,v}|\theta_j) d\theta \\
& \quad \times \int \prod_{k=1}^{K} p(\sigma_k|\gamma) \prod_{j=1}^{M} \prod_{v=1}^{L_j} p(e_{j,v}|\sigma_{x_{j,v}})^{y_{j,v}} d\sigma
\end{aligned} \tag{12}
$$

Expand each probability formula based on its density,

$$
\begin{aligned}
& = \int \prod_{j=1}^{M} \frac{\Gamma(\sum_{k=1}^{K} \alpha_k)}{\prod_{k=1}^{K} \Gamma(\alpha_k)} \prod_{k=1}^{K} \theta_{j,k}^{\alpha_k - 1} \prod_{j=1}^{M} \prod_{u=1}^{N_j} \theta_{z_{j,u}} \prod_{j=1}^{M} \prod_{v=1}^{L_j} \theta_{x_{j,v}} d\theta \\
& \quad \times \prod_{k=1}^{K} \int \frac{\Gamma(\sum_{i=1}^{M} \gamma_i)}{\prod_{i=1}^{M} \Gamma(\gamma_i)} \prod_{i=1}^{M} \sigma_{k,i}^{\gamma_i - 1} \prod_{j=1}^{M} \prod_{v=1}^{L_j} \sigma_{x_{j,v}, e_{j,v}}^{y_{j,v}} d\sigma_k
\end{aligned} \tag{13}
$$

Replace the innermost products over words in a document $N_m$ by exponentiating to the sum of the counts, and do the same replacement for the products over users,

$$
\begin{aligned}
& = \prod_{j=1}^{M} \int \frac{\Gamma(\sum_{k=1}^{K} \alpha_k)}{\prod_{k=1}^{K} \Gamma(\alpha_k)} \prod_{k=1}^{K} \theta_{j,k}^{\alpha_k - 1} \prod_{k=1}^{K} \theta_{j,k}^{c_{k,j,*}} \prod_{k=1}^{K} \theta_{j,k}^{d_{k,j,*,*}} d\theta_j \\
& \quad \times \prod_{k=1}^{K} \int \frac{\Gamma(\sum_{i=1}^{M} \gamma_i)}{\prod_{i=1}^{M} \Gamma(\gamma_i)} \prod_{i=1}^{M} \sigma_{k,i}^{\gamma_i - 1} \prod_{i=1}^{M} \sigma_{k,i}^{d_{k,*,i,1}} d\sigma_k \\
& = \prod_{j=1}^{M} \int \frac{\Gamma(\sum_{k=1}^{K} \alpha_k)}{\prod_{k=1}^{K} \Gamma(\alpha_k)} \prod_{k=1}^{K} \theta_{j,k}^{\alpha_k + c_{k,j,*} + d_{k,j,*,*} - 1} d\theta_j \\
& \quad \times \prod_{k=1}^{K} \int \frac{\Gamma(\sum_{i=1}^{M} \gamma_i)}{\prod_{i=1}^{M} \Gamma(\gamma_i)} \prod_{i=1}^{M} \sigma_{k,i}^{\gamma_i + d_{k,*,i,1} - 1} d\sigma_k
\end{aligned} \tag{14}
$$

Multiply each term by a constant equal to one (consisting of two inverse fractions), and distribute the integral over the original constant Γ-function fraction for the priors,

$$= \prod_{j=1}^{M} \frac{\Gamma(\sum_{k=1}^{K}\alpha_k)\prod_{k=1}^{K}\Gamma(\alpha_k + c_{k,j,*} + d_{k,j,*,*})}{\prod_{k=1}^{K}\Gamma(\alpha_k)\,\Gamma(\sum_{k=1}^{K}\alpha_k + c_{k,j,*} + d_{k,j,*,*})}$$
$$\times \int \frac{\Gamma(\sum_{k=1}^{K}\alpha_k + c_{k,j,*} + d_{k,j,*,*})}{\prod_{k=1}^{K}\Gamma(\alpha_k + c_{k,j,*} + d_{k,j,*,*})} \prod_{k=1}^{K} \theta_{j,k}^{\alpha_k + c_{k,j,*} + d_{k,j,*,*} - 1} d\theta_j$$
$$\times \prod_{k=1}^{K} \frac{\Gamma(\sum_{i=1}^{M}\gamma_i)\prod_{i=1}^{M}\Gamma(\gamma_i + d_{k,*,i,1})}{\prod_{i=1}^{M}\Gamma(\gamma_i)\,\Gamma(\sum_{i=1}^{M}\gamma_i + d_{k,*,i,1})}$$
$$\times \int \frac{\Gamma(\sum_{i=1}^{M}\gamma_i + d_{k,*,i,1})}{\prod_{i=1}^{M}\Gamma(\gamma_i + d_{k,*,i,1})} \prod_{i=1}^{M} \sigma_{k,i}^{\gamma_i + d_{k,*,i,1} - 1} d\sigma_k \tag{15}$$

Note that both integrals are over the entire support of Dirichlet densities, so they both evaluate to 1, and hence drop out of the products,

$$= \prod_{j=1}^{M} \frac{\Gamma(\sum_{k=1}^{K}\alpha_k)\prod_{k=1}^{K}\Gamma(\alpha_k + c_{k,j,*} + d_{k,j,*,*})}{\prod_{k=1}^{K}\Gamma(\alpha_k)\,\Gamma(\sum_{k=1}^{K}\alpha_k + c_{k,j,*} + d_{k,j,*,*})}$$
$$\times \prod_{k=1}^{K} \frac{\Gamma(\sum_{i=1}^{M}\gamma_i)\prod_{i=1}^{M}\Gamma(\gamma_i + d_{k,*,i,1})}{\prod_{i=1}^{M}\Gamma(\gamma_i)\,\Gamma(\sum_{i=1}^{M}\gamma_i + d_{k,*,i,1})} \tag{16}$$

Eliminate constant terms that do not depend on the position $(m, l)$,

$$\propto \frac{\prod_{k=1}^{K}\Gamma(\alpha_k + c_{k,m,*} + d_{k,m,*,*})}{\Gamma(\sum_{k=1}^{K}\alpha_k + c_{k,m,*} + d_{k,m,*,*})} \times \prod_{k=1}^{K} \frac{\Gamma(\gamma_{e_{m,l}} + d_{k,*,e_{m,l},1})}{\Gamma(\sum_{i=1}^{M}\gamma_i + d_{k,*,i,1})} \tag{17}$$

Define $c^{-(m,l)}$ the same way as $c$, only without the counts for position $(m, l)$. Then, for counts that do not include position $(m, l)$, $c^{-(m,l)} = c$. For ones that do include $(m, l)$, $c^{-(m,l)} = c + 1$. $d^{-(m,l)}$ is defined in the same way. Also, using the fact that $\Gamma(x + 1) = x \times \Gamma(x)$, expand out the incremented terms depending on $(m, l)$,

$$= \frac{\prod_{k \neq x_{m,l}}\Gamma(\alpha_k + c_{k,m,*} + d_{k,m,*,*}^{-(m,l)})}{\Gamma(1 + \sum_{k=1}^{K}\alpha_k + c_{k,m,*} + d_{k,m,*,*}^{-(m,l)})}$$
$$\times \Gamma(\alpha_{x_{m,l}} + c_{x_{m,l},m,*} + d_{x_{m,l},m,*,*}^{-(m,l)})$$
$$\times (\alpha_{x_{m,l}} + c_{x_{m,l},m,*} + d_{x_{m,l},m,*,*}^{-(m,l)})$$
$$\times \prod_{k \neq x_{m,l}} \frac{\Gamma(\gamma_{e_{m,l}} + d_{k,*,e_{m,l},1}^{-(m,l)})}{\Gamma(\sum_{i=1}^{M}\gamma_i + d_{k,*,i,1})} \times \frac{\Gamma(\gamma_{e_{m,l}} + d_{x_{m,l},*,e_{m,l},1}^{-(m,l)})}{\Gamma(\sum_{i=1}^{M}\gamma_i + d_{x_{m,l},*,i,1}^{-(m,l)})}$$
$$\times \frac{\gamma_{e_{m,l}} + d_{x_{m,l},*,e_{m,l},1}^{-(m,l)}}{\sum_{i=1}^{M}(\gamma_i + d_{x_{m,l},*,i,1}^{-(m,l)})} \tag{18}$$

Refold the residual Γ-function terms back into their general products,

$$= \frac{\prod_{k=1}^{K}\Gamma(\alpha_k + c_{k,m,*} + d_{k,m,*,*}^{-(m,l)})}{\Gamma(1 + \sum_{k=1}^{K}\alpha_k + c_{k,m,*} + d_{k,m,*,*}^{-(m,l)})}$$
$$\times (\alpha_{x_{m,l}} + c_{x_{m,l},a,*} + d_{x_{m,l},m,*,*}^{-(m,l)})$$
$$\times \prod_{k=1}^{K} \frac{\Gamma(\gamma_{e_{m,l}} + d_{k,*,e_{m,l},1}^{-(m,l)})}{\Gamma(\sum_{i=1}^{M}\gamma_i + d_{k,*,i,1})} \times \frac{\gamma_{e_{m,l}} + d_{x_{m,l},*,e_{m,l},1}^{-(m,l)}}{\sum_{i=1}^{M}(\gamma_i + d_{x_{m,l},*,i,1}^{-(m,l)})} \tag{19}$$

Remove all the terms that do not depend on $x_{m,l}$ or $y_{m,l}$.

If $y_{m,l} = 0$, the last term $\frac{\gamma_{e_{m,l}} + d_{x_{m,l},*,e_{m,l},1}^{-(m,l)}}{\sum_{i=1}^{M}(\gamma_i + d_{x_{m,l},*,i,1}^{-(m,l)})}$ in Equation (19) does not exist,

$$\propto \alpha_{x_{m,l}} + c_{x_{m,l},m,*} + d_{x_{m,l},m,*,*}^{-(m,l)} \tag{20}$$

If $y_{m,l} = 1$,

$$\propto \frac{(\alpha_{x_{m,l}} + c_{x_{m,l},m,*} + d_{x_{m,l},m,*,*}^{-(m,l)})(\gamma_{e_{m,l}} + d_{x_{m,l},*,e_{m,l},1}^{-(m,l)})}{\sum_{i=1}^{M}(\gamma_i + d_{x_{m,l},*,i,1}^{-(m,l)})} \tag{21}$$

The third integral $\int p(\varphi|\beta)p(w|z,\varphi)d\varphi$ in Equation (11) is independent of both $x$ and $y$, so it can be safely canceled out. Let us turn to the forth integral in Equation (11).

$$\int p(\pi|\varepsilon)p(e|\pi)^{1-y}d\pi$$
$$= \int \frac{\Gamma(\sum_{i=1}^{M}\varepsilon_i)}{\prod_{i=1}^{M}\Gamma(\varepsilon_i)} \prod_{i=1}^{M} \pi_i^{\varepsilon_i - 1} \prod_{j=1}^{M}\prod_{v=1}^{L_j} \pi_{e_{j,v}}^{1-y_{j,v}} d\pi$$
$$= \int \frac{\Gamma(\sum_{i=1}^{M}\varepsilon_i)}{\prod_{i=1}^{M}\Gamma(\varepsilon_i)} \prod_{i=1}^{M} \pi_i^{d_{*,*,i,0}+\varepsilon_i - 1} d\pi$$
$$\propto \frac{\Gamma(\sum_{i=1}^{M}\varepsilon_i)}{\prod_{i=1}^{M}\Gamma(\varepsilon_i)} \times \frac{\prod_{i=1}^{M}\Gamma(d_{*,*,i,0} + \varepsilon_i)}{\Gamma(\sum_{i=1}^{M}d_{*,*,i,0} + \varepsilon_i)}$$
$$\propto \frac{\prod_{i \neq e_{m,l}}\Gamma(d_{*,*,i,0} + \varepsilon_i) \times \Gamma(d_{*,*,e_{m,l},0} + \varepsilon_{e_{m,l}})}{\Gamma(\sum_{i=1}^{M}d_{*,*,i,0} + \varepsilon_i)} \tag{22}$$

If $y_{m,l} = 0$, Equation (22) can be written as:

$$= \frac{\prod_{i \neq e_{m,l}}\Gamma(d_{*,*,i,0}^{-(m,l)} + \varepsilon_i) \times \Gamma(d_{*,*,e_{m,l},0}^{-(m,l)} + \varepsilon_{e_{m,l}} + 1)}{\Gamma(1 + \sum_{i=1}^{M}d_{*,*,i,0}^{-(m,l)} + \varepsilon_i)}$$
$$= \frac{\prod_i \Gamma(d_{*,*,i,0}^{-(m,l)} + \varepsilon_i)}{\Gamma(\sum_{i=1}^{M}d_{*,*,i,0}^{-(m,l)} + \varepsilon_i)} \times \frac{d_{*,*,e_{m,l},0}^{-(m,l)} + \varepsilon_{e_{m,l}}}{\sum_{i=1}^{M}d_{*,*,i,0}^{-(m,l)} + \varepsilon_i}$$
$$\propto \frac{d_{*,*,e_{m,l},0}^{-(m,l)} + \varepsilon_{e_{m,l}}}{\sum_{i=1}^{M}d_{*,*,i,0}^{-(m,l)} + \varepsilon_i} \tag{23}$$

If $y_{m,l} = 1$, Equation (22) can be written as:

$$= \frac{\prod_i \Gamma(d_{*,*,i,0}^{-(m,l)} + \varepsilon_i)}{\Gamma(\sum_{i=1}^{M}d_{*,*,i,0}^{-(m,l)} + \varepsilon_i)} \propto 1 \tag{24}$$

Finally, we derive the last integral in Equation (11).

$$\int p(\mu|\rho)p(y|\mu)d\mu$$
$$= \prod_{j=1}^{M} \int \frac{\Gamma(\sum_s \rho_s)}{\prod_s \Gamma(\rho_s)} \prod_s \mu_{j,s}^{\rho_s - 1} \prod_{j=1}^{M}\prod_{v=1}^{L_j} \mu_{j,y_{j,v}} d\mu_j$$
$$= \prod_{j=1}^{M} \int \frac{\Gamma(\sum_s \rho_s)}{\prod_s \Gamma(\rho_s)} \prod_s \mu_{j,s}^{d_{*,j,*,s}+\rho_s - 1} d\mu_j$$
$$\propto \prod_{j=1}^{M} \frac{\prod_s \Gamma(d_{*,j,*,s} + \rho_s)}{\Gamma(\sum_s d_{*,j,*,s} + \rho_s)}$$
$$= \prod_{j \neq m} \frac{\prod_s \Gamma(d_{*,j,*,s} + \rho_s)}{\Gamma(\sum_s d_{*,j,*,s} + \rho_s)} \times \frac{\prod_s \Gamma(d_{*,m,*,s} + \rho_s)}{\Gamma(\sum_s d_{*,m,*,s} + \rho_s)}$$
$$\propto \frac{\prod_{s \neq y_{m,l}}\Gamma(d_{*,m,*,s}^{-(m,l)} + \rho_s) \times \Gamma(d_{*,m,*,y_{m,l}}^{-(m,l)} + \rho_{y_{m,l}} + 1)}{\Gamma(1 + \sum_s d_{*,m,*,s}^{-(m,l)} + \rho_s)}$$
$$= \frac{\prod_s \Gamma(d_{*,m,*,s}^{-(m,l)} + \rho_s)}{\Gamma(\sum_s d_{*,m,*,s}^{-(m,l)} + \rho_s)} \times \frac{d_{*,m,*,y_{m,l}}^{-(m,l)} + \rho_{y_{m,l}}}{d_{*,m,*,*}^{-(m,l)} + \sum_s \rho_s}$$
$$\propto d_{*,m,*,y_{m,l}}^{-(m,l)} + \rho_{y_{m,l}} \tag{25}$$

Finally, substituting Equations (20), (23) and (25) into Equation (11) gives Equation (2). Similary, substituting Equations (21), (24) and (25) into Equation (11) gives Equation (3).

# WebChild: Harvesting and Organizing Commonsense Knowledge from the Web

Niket Tandon
Max Planck Institute for Informatics
Saarbrücken, Germany
ntandon@mpi-inf.mpg.de

Gerard de Melo*
IIIS,Tsinghua University
Beijing, China
demelo@tsinghua.edu.cn

Fabian Suchanek
Télécom ParisTech
Paris, France
fabian.suchanek@telecom-paristech.fr

Gerhard Weikum
Max Planck Institute for Informatics
Saarbrücken, Germany
weikum@mpi-inf.mpg.de

## ABSTRACT

This paper presents a method for automatically constructing a large commonsense knowledge base, called WebChild[1], from Web contents. WebChild contains triples that connect nouns with adjectives via fine-grained relations like `hasShape`, `hasTaste`, `evokesEmotion`, etc. The arguments of these assertions, nouns and adjectives, are disambiguated by mapping them onto their proper WordNet senses. Our method is based on semi-supervised Label Propagation over graphs of noisy candidate assertions. We automatically derive seeds from WordNet and by pattern matching from Web text collections. The Label Propagation algorithm provides us with domain sets and range sets for 19 different relations, and with confidence-ranked assertions between WordNet senses. Large-scale experiments demonstrate the high accuracy (more than 80 percent) and coverage (more than four million fine grained disambiguated assertions) of WebChild.

## Categories and Subject Descriptors

H.4 [**Information Systems Applications**]: Miscellaneous; I.2.6 [**Artificial Intelligence**]: Learning

## Keywords

Knowledge Bases; Commonsense Knowledge; Web Mining; Label Propagation; Word Sense Disambiguation

## 1. INTRODUCTION

**Motivation.** Automatically constructed knowledge bases (KBs) have recently proven to be great assets for Web search, recommendations in social media, and text analytics. Prominent examples are the Google Knowledge Graph and the (small but effective) use of KBs in the IBM Watson project for deep question answering [29, 18]. The largest publicly available KBs are `dbpedia.org`, `freebase.com` and `yago-knowledge.org`. The strength of these KBs is in taxonomic and factual knowledge: entities in semantic classes and relationships between entities. However, they are fairly ignorant regarding commonsense knowledge: properties and statements that are easily picked up by children, but are hard to acquire by a machine.

For example, all humans know that apples are round and carrots are orange and have a longish shape. Computers completely lack this kind of commonsense knowledge, yet they would enormously benefit from such an asset for various use-cases of growing relevance: language understanding for translation or summarization, speech-based human-computer dialog, faceted search and search query suggestions, sentiment analytics on social media, and more. This paper presents a methodology for automatically extracting and cleaning commonsense properties from the Web. The resulting KB is called *WebChild.*

**State of the Art and its Limitations.** Prior work on commonsense knowledge includes the seminal projects Cyc [21] and WordNet [12], the more recent work on ConceptNet [31], and the work by [35] and [20]. Cyc has compiled complex assertions such as *every human has exactly one father and exactly one mother*, but did not aim to gather properties of things at large scale. WordNet has manually organized nouns and adjectives into lexical classes, with careful distinction between words and word senses; however, nouns and adjectives are not connected by any semantic relation, except the extremely sparse `attribute` relation (with around 1,200 links). ConceptNet is a huge collection of commonsense assertions, but the vast majority are instances of generic relations like `IsA`, `PartOf`, `ConceptuallyRelatedTo`, or `DerivedFrom`. The more specific relations like `adjectivePertainsTo` or `UsedFor` have only few instances. Tandon et al. [35] automatically compiled millions of triples of the form ⟨ *noun relation adjective* ⟩ by mining n-gram corpora, but the relations are still fairly generic such as `HasA`, `HasProperty`, or `CapableOf`. Lebani & Pianta [20] proposed encoding additional lexical relations for commonsense knowledge into WordNet, but their approach is inherently limited by relying on human input and also focuses on simple relations such as `usedFor`, `partOf`, etc.

None of these knowledge resources have refined properties like shape, size, taste, emotion, etc., and none have pro-

[1]WebChild: datasets will be publicly available at `http://mpi-inf.mpg.de/yago-naga/webchild/`

*Gerard de Melo's work was supported in part by the National Basic Research Program of China Grants 2011CBA00300, 2011CBA00301, and NSFC Grants 61033001, 61361136003.


*WSDM'14,* February 24–28, 2014, New York, New York, USA.
Copyright 2014 ACM 978-1-4503-2351-2/14/02 ...$15.00.
http://dx.doi.org/10.1145/2556195.2556245.

duced large amounts of semantically disambiguated knowledge that distinguishes the different meanings of ambiguous properties such as *hot*, which can refer to temperature, taste, or emotion. For example, the KB by [35] would merely have simple triples like ⟨*milk*, `hasProperty`, *hot*⟩, ⟨*chiliPepper*, `hasProperty`, *hot*⟩, ⟨*dress*, `hasProperty`, *hot*⟩. Thus, state-of-the-art commonsense KBs still have severe limitations: i) sparseness on aspects that go beyond generic relations, ii) focus on crude relations, without distinguishing different semantic properties, and iii) no distinction between words and their different senses.

**Our Approach.** This paper presents WebChild, a large commonsense KB automatically built from Web sources by a novel method relying on semi-supervised learning. WebChild contains more than 4 million triples for fine-grained relations such as `hasTaste`, `hasShape`, `evokesEmotion`, etc. We use a judiciously designed form of *label propagation (LP)* (see [34] for an intro) for learning the domain set, the range set, and the extension of such relations, at large scale. To this end, we first construct graphs that connect nouns, adjectives, and WordNet senses as nodes, by weighted edges. The edge-weights are derived from sense relatedness, pattern statistics, and co-occurrence statistics. We harness WordNet and Web data to obtain seeds to initialize the LP graphs, and then use LP algorithms to derive high-quality assertions for fine-grained relations between noun senses and adjective senses.

**Contributions.** Our methodology has a number of salient characteristics and results in a large commonsense KB with unique qualities:

1 **Fine-grained assertions:** WebChild is the first commonsense KB that provides refined `hasProperty` relationships between nouns and adjectives into specific and thus more informative relations. We support 19 different relations like `hasShape`, `hasSize`, `hasTaste`, `evokesEmotion`, etc.

2 **Disambiguated arguments:** The arguments of all assertions in WebChild are disambiguated by mappings to WordNet senses: noun senses for the left-hand arguments of a relation, and adjective senses for the right-hand arguments.

3 **Minimal supervision:** Our method does not require any labeled assertions for training. Instead we use bootstrapping based on Web patterns and WordNet. Our method copes well with noisy input data.

# 2. MODEL AND METHODOLOGY

## 2.1 Goal and Notation

We aim to compile a large and clean set of fine-grained commonsense properties, connecting noun senses with adjective senses by a variety of relations. In contrast to prior work that only dealt with a generic `hasProperty` relation, we use 19 different (sub-)relations like `hasShape`, `hasSize`, `hasTaste`, `hasAbility`, `evokesEmotion`, etc. The list of relation types is derived from WordNet. A noun that is the target of WordNet's `attribute` relation (e.g., *shape*, *size*) becomes a relation in our knowledge base.

Our goal is to populate these relations with *assertions* in the form of triples $\langle ns, r, as \rangle$ where $ns$ is a noun sense in WordNet, $as$ is an adjective sense in WordNet, and $r$ is one of the considered relations. Each relation $r$ has a domain $dom(r)$, the set of noun senses that appear in $r$ as left-hand arguments, and a range $rng(r)$, the set of adjective senses that appear in $r$ as right-hand arguments.

It is important to distinguish word senses from words that occur in surface text, because nouns and adjectives are often highly ambiguous. For example, the adjective *green* is associated with both plants in the botanical sense and power plants. WebChild represents assertions for the different word senses in the following form:

⟨`botanical-plant`, `hasColor`, `green-color`⟩

⟨`power-plant`, `hasQuality`, `green-environmental`⟩

where `botanical-plant`, `power-plant`, `green-color`, and `green-environmental` are specific WordNet senses[2]

Throughout this paper, we carefully distinguish words from their senses, and use different notation and fonts to make this explicit. Surface words (or composite phrases) are written in italics, whereas senses appear in typewriter font and typically suffixed with either $\texttt{-n}^i$ for noun senses or $\texttt{-a}^j$ for adjective senses. Here, $i$ and $j$ are WordNet sense numbers if a noun or adjective has multiple senses (which is usually the case). For example, *chili* is a noun and *hot* is an adjective (both are words), whereas $\texttt{chili-n}^2$ and $\texttt{hot-a}^9$ are senses.

## 2.2 Sub-Tasks

We decompose the problem of finding assertions for fine-grained commonsense relations into three sub-tasks.

1. **Range Population:** First, we compute adjective senses that occur in the range of each of the WebChild relations. For example, for the `hasColor` relation, we obtain a list of color attributes including e.g. $\texttt{green-a}^1$, the color sense of *green* from WordNet, but not the environmental sense of *green*. For the `hasShape` relation, we obtain a list of possible shapes, e.g. $\texttt{circular-a}^2$.
2. **Domain Population:** Our second task is to compute noun senses for the domain of each relation. For example, $\texttt{war-n}^1$ for the `evokesEmotion` relation, and $\texttt{pizza-n}^2$ for the `hasTaste` relation.
3. **Computing Assertions:** Finally, we aim to map generic word-level assertion candidates ⟨*noun*, `hasProperty`, *adjective*⟩, gathered from Web corpora, into fine-grained assertions about word senses. For example, ⟨*car*, `hasProperty`, *sweet*⟩ is mapped into ⟨$\texttt{car-n}^1$, `hasAppearance`, $\texttt{sweet-a}^2$⟩.

## 2.3 Candidate Gathering

For all three sub-tasks we can start with a small number of *seeds* obtained from WordNet, for example, by using the *attribute* information that connects relational noun senses (e.g., $\texttt{shape-n}^1$) with adjective senses (e.g., $\texttt{straight-a}^1$ and $\texttt{crooked-a}^1$). This is very sparse data (e.g., there are only 2 adjective senses for the attribute `shape`). Our specific choice of seeds depends on which of the three sub-tasks we are dealing with. This will be discussed later in the respective sections.

To build a knowledge base of high coverage, we gather candidates for assertions from the Web. For this purpose, we harness a

[2]WordNet shows these senses as *plant (a living organism ...)*, *power plant (an electrical generating ...)*, *green (of the color between blue and yellow ...)*, and *green (concerned with ... Green Party)*.

huge *N-gram corpus*: the Google Web 1T N-Gram Dataset Version 1 [7], which consists of 1.2 billion 5-grams (i.e., 5 consecutive words or other tokens) derived from the index of the Google search engine. Each of these 5-grams comes with its frequency of occurrences on the Web. Thus, we can use these frequencies to simulate a full Web corpus. However, we also face the restriction that N-grams are limited in length to 5.

To gather assertion candidates from this data, we employ surface patterns whose matches return N-grams that contain a noun and an adjective that are likely to be related, in a generic `hasProperty` sense. Note that the resulting candidates are still at the word level; there is no way of mapping them to senses at this stage. We define generic templates for lexical patterns of the form

"<noun> *linking_verb* [*adverb*] <adj>" or

"<adj> <noun>".

Linking verbs are different forms of "to be", "to become", "to smell", "to taste", etc.[3] Our templates capture many variations of assertions. Examples are

*apple was really <adj>*,

*apple was <adj>*,

*<adj> apple.*

Applying this family of patterns to the Google N-gram corpus results in 3.6 million noun-adjective pairs. Many of these are noise (i.e., incorrect), and none of them is disambiguated onto senses yet.

## 2.4 Semi-Supervised Inference on Graphs

The candidates obtained by the outlined procedure are usually very noisy, not yet disambiguated, and not yet assigned to our fine-grained relations – they are just word pairs for the generic `hasProperty` relation and are still ambiguous. To distill the good pairs from the noisy pool and to map words onto proper senses and noun-adjective sense pairs into specific relations, we use a semi-supervised classification method over judiciously constructed graphs. To this end, we employ the method of *Label Propagation (LP)* [37].

For each of the three sub-tasks towards building WebChild, we construct a graph with words (or word pairs) and possible word senses (or sense pairs) as nodes. A small number of nodes encodes seeds, with known relation labels. Edges reflect the relatedness of nodes, with weights derived from Web statistics and WordNet information. The specifics of the graph depend on the sub-task that we are dealing with, and will be discussed in the following sections.

LP computes scores for nodes having certain labels. In our setting, these labels are used to distinguish different relation types. For inference, we use the *MAD (modified adsorption)* algorithm [34], which has shown good performance for graphs with high numbers of incident edges per node. Our graphs have this property because adjectives usually have many possible senses.

MAD propagates labels to neighboring nodes along the graph's edges; a high edge weight implies that the incident nodes are likely to have the same label. Seed nodes are expected to retain their original labels. Additionally, regularization is employed to minimize label changes within a neighborhood, which is essential to avoid overfitting. To encode this intuition, the MAD algorithm minimizes a loss function. Assume that the graph is represented as a weighted adjacency matrix $W$ and that the label vectors of the nodes are encoded into matrices $Y$ for the initial labeling and $\hat{Y}$ for the final predicted labeling. $(Y_{*l})$ and $(\hat{Y}_{*l})$ denote the $l^{th}$ column vector of the initial matrix $Y$ and the final label matrix $\hat{Y}$, respectively. Then the loss function is:

$$L(\hat{Y}) = \sum_{l} \Big[ (Y_{*l} - \hat{Y}_{*l})^T S^l (Y_{*l} - \hat{Y}_{*l}) + \mu_2 \hat{Y}_{*l}^T L \hat{Y}_{*l} + \mu_3 \left\| \hat{Y}_{*l} - R_{*l} \right\|_2 \Big], \qquad (1)$$

The first term encodes that initial and final labels for seed nodes should mostly be the same. This is enforced by the diagonal matrix $S$ having $S_{vv} = 0$ for non-seed nodes, while for seed nodes $S_{vv}$ is set to monotonically increase with the entropy of a node's transition probabilities (such that high degree nodes are discounted). The second term encodes that neighbor nodes obtain similar labels. This effect is realized by the unnormalized graph Laplacian $L$ of the weighted adjacency matrix $W$. The third term contributes to the regularization of the estimated labels, in order to avoid over-fitting to their seed labels. This is enforced with an abandonment matrix $R$ having a zero-valued column vector corresponding to every label, except the dummy label (the dummy label is an additional label that has a large value if the node cannot be properly labeled). A pre-defined weight is computed for the dummy label, in proportion to the nodes' degrees.

The MAD algorithm is a variant of the Jacobi method (also used for PageRank, for example), an iterative process that uses the current labels of nodes to update the label scores for neighboring nodes. When this process converges or a specified number of iterations is reached, each vertex is associated with a vector indicating the estimated labels (including the dummy label). The dummy label has a large value if the node cannot be properly labeled. In our setting, we apply this procedure for each relation separately, comparing the relation labels vs. the dummy label in the resulting output. We accept the relation label only if its final score is larger than that of the dummy label.

# 3. POPULATING RELATION RANGES

We now discuss how we are able to apply this same methodology to each of the three sub-tasks introduced in Section 2.2. Our first sub-task addresses the problem of identifying possible adjective senses for the range of each of the relations supported by WebChild. For example, for `hasTaste`, we expect adjectives like *delicious*, *spicy*, *hot*, *sweet*, etc., whereas these adjectives do not make much sense for the `hasShape` relation. The main difficulty that we face with this task is to move from the word level to word senses. So actually, we aim to populate the range of `hasTaste` with senses `delicious-a`$^2$, `spicy-a`$^1$, `hot-a`$^9$, `sweet-a`$^1$, etc. Some of these surface words also appear with other relations; for example, *hot* may also denote a property for the `hasAppearance` relation, however with different senses: `hot-a`$^{10}$ and `sweet-a`$^4$. The task is to carefully discriminate the senses for the ranges of different relations (although some overlap between relations may be possible).

We solve this problem in three steps:

1. **Gathering candidates** from N-grams and other sources.
2. **Constructing a graph** that encodes association strengths between adjectives and adjective senses by weighted edges.

[3]see `http://en.wikipedia.org/wiki/List_of_English_copulae` for a full list

3. **Inferring adjective senses for a relation's range** by semi-supervised Label Propagation.

**Candidate Gathering.** We start with the raw candidates derived by extraction patterns from the Google N-gram corpus, as described in Section 2. For relation $r$, we filter the candidates by checking for the presence of the word $r$, any of its synonyms (e.g., *shape, form*, etc., or *appearance*, *look*, etc.), or any linking verb that is derivationally related to $r$ (e.g., "tastes" for `hasTaste`). We apply these patterns also to WordNet glosses (i.e., short descriptions of word senses), to collect further candidates.

In addition, we apply the Hearst pattern "<r> such as <x>" to the N-gram data, and collect the matches for $x$ as possible adjectives for relation $r$. Finally, we adopt the WebSets method [9] to HTML tables in specific articles of the English Wikipedia. The articles of choice are those whose article name corresponds to relation $r$ (or its synonyms). These were manually identified for each relation $r$.

In total we collected around 40,000 adjectives for all relations together.

**Graph Construction.** So far we have merely compiled a large set of – mostly ambiguous – words that may populate the range of a relation. We use these words as nodes in a graph, and extend this node set by *all possible adjective senses* of these words. This is a simple lookup in WordNet, without any disambiguation yet.

**Definition [Range Population Graph (RPG)]:**
The RPG of a relation $r$ is a weighted undirected graph with nodes $V_{\mathrm{RPG}}$ and edges $E_{\mathrm{RPG}}$ as follows:

- $V_{\mathrm{RPG}}$ consists of all candidate adjectives for relation $r$, and all their corresponding adjective senses.
- $E_{\mathrm{RPG}}$ consists of three kinds of edges:
  - edges between two words *w1* and *w2* if they share at least one noun in their pattern occurrences;
  - edges between two senses `w1-a`$^i$ and `w2-a`$^j$ if they are related in the WordNet structure or have WordNet glosses that suggest relatedness;
  - edges between a word *w* and all its senses `w-a`$^i$.

The left part of Figure 1 shows an example of an RPG.

**Edge Weighting.** To define meaningful edge weights, we utilize statistics from the candidate gathering (see Section 2) and from WordNet.

For weighting the *edges among words*, we harness the co-occurrences of adjectives with nouns. We derive from the large N-gram corpus two matrices $O : noun \times adjective$ and $P : noun \times adjective$ where $O_{ij}$ is the number of occurrences of the noun-adjective pair and $P_{ij}$ is the number of distinct extraction patterns that the noun-adjective pair occurs with. We normalize both matrices to have values in $[0, 1]$. For $O$, we divide all values by the maximum value. For $P$, we transform all values using the sigmoid function $f(x) = 1 - \frac{1}{e^{x-1}}$. The rationale here is to reward multiple patterns, but consider also the diminishing returns of observing many patterns. Finally, we combine $O$ and $P$ by the linear combination $\alpha O^T \times O + (1-\alpha)P^T \times P$ with hyper-parameter $\alpha$. The values of the resulting matrix are the weights for edges between two adjectives of the RPG.

For *edges between two senses* `u-a`$^i$ and `w-a`$^j$, we consider their taxonomic relatedness within WordNet. If there is a path between `u-a`$^i$ and `w-a`$^j$ using `hypernym/hyponym`, `derivationally_related`, `similar_to`, `also_see`, or `antonym` links in WordNet, then we use the Hirst measure of semantic relatedness [17].

If no such path exists, we resort to the glosses of `u-a`$^i$ and `w-a`$^j$, expanded by glosses of their respective hyponyms and hypernyms. We then compute the number of overlapping words shared by these contexts. This is essentially the concept similarity measure by [22]. All these measures are normalized to fall between 0 and 1, and we use a down-weighting coefficient for the gloss-based values, to ensure that path-related sense pairs have higher edge weights.

For *edges between words and senses*, we would ideally like to use the sense frequencies as a basis for edge weights. However, such information is hardly available.[4] We thus resort to the following statistics-based heuristics (adopted from [22, 25]). For each word *w*, we take the corresponding column from matrix $O$ (i.e., the frequencies of co-occurring nouns) as a distributional-semantics vector. For each possible sense `w-a`$^i$, we compute a context vector from its gloss and the glosses of neighboring senses, giving us another noun distribution. The normalized scalar product between the vector of *w* and the vector of `w-a`$^i$ is the weight of the edge between the adjective and its possible sense.

**Label Propagation (LP).** The final step is to run the MAD algorithm for Label Propagation on the constructed graph – one graph for each relation. We consider only two labels for each graph: the relation of interest and the dummy label (encoding *no relation* or *other relation*). We obtain seeds automatically by observing that the intersection of adjectives found in WordNet and on the Web, i.e. in more than one source, are more likely to be accurate. The sense of the WordNet adjective is considered for this. 30% of the remaining seeds were used as held-out test data to tune the parameters $\mu_2$ and $\mu_3$ of the MAD algorithm (see Section 2.4). The MAD algorithm then infers which adjective senses belong the range of the relation.

## 4. POPULATING RELATION DOMAINS

After populating the ranges of WebChild's relations, we turn to the relation domains. For each relation, such as `hasTaste`, we aim to compute the noun senses that can appear as left-hand arguments of the relation, for example, `apple-n`$^1$, `pizza-n`$^1$, `plant-n`$^2$, `beef-n`$^2$, but not `car-n`$^1$, `cow-n`$^2$, or a different sense of *plant*: `plant-n`$^1$ (the industrial plant). Analogously to the previous section, we solve this task in a three-step process: gathering candidates, constructing a graph, and LP inference for cleaning and disambiguation. We will see that we can harness the knowledge that we already acquired about adjective senses that appear in relation ranges.

**Candidate Gathering.** We use the coarse-grained generic `hasProperty` noun-adjective pairs $(n, a)$ gathered by the method of Section 2.3. Given a pair $(n, a)$, if the adjective $a$ has at least one sense that appears in the relation's range computed in Section 3, then the noun $n$ becomes a domain candidate. For example, given word pair (*beef, salty*) and having the knowledge that *salty* occurs in the range of `hasTaste`, we infer that *beef* is a noun candidate for `hasTaste`.

[4] WordNet provides senses frequencies only for a small set of words, mostly nouns, and not nearly for all of their senses.

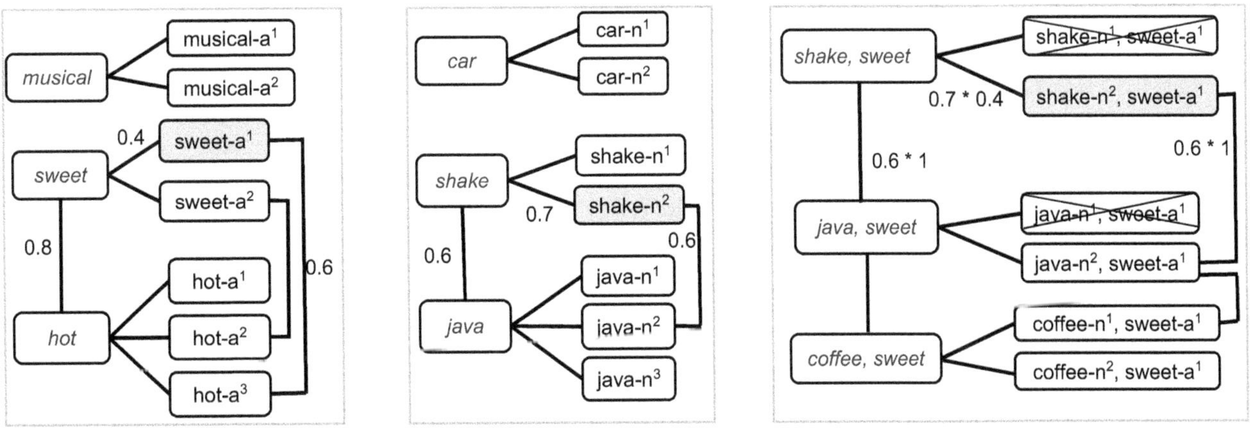


**Figure 1: Graph construction for range (left), domain (middle), and, assertions (right). Blue nodes are seeds. Crossed nodes (right) denote assertion candidates pruned based on domain and range.**

When $n$ has only one sense in WordNet, we directly use this noun sense. However, this situation is rare. A more typical candidate would be *java*, with co-occurrence pairs such as (*java,tasty*), (*java,easy*), (*java,hilly*), etc. In such situations, to move from words to senses at least in some of the cases, we harness the glosses of adjectives in WordNet to derive *semi-disambiguated* assertions where either the noun or the adjective is mapped to a WordNet sense.

Gathering *semi-disambiguated* assertions: For each adjective word in our candidate set, we find all noun-sense glosses where the adjective occurs (as a surface word). Whenever a matching noun sense gloss is found, the specific noun sense is used to replace the ambiguous surface noun in the candidate pair. We perform this analogously for nouns in adjective-sense glosses. For instance, the gloss for `sour-a`$^2$ reads "the taste experience when vinegar or lemon juice is taken ...". We generate two assertions from this: (*vinegar*, `sour-a`$^2$) and (*lemon juice*, `sour-a`$^2$). Note that although this technique goes further than the method for relation ranges, we still face a large amount of noisy candidates. An adjective such as *large* has seven word senses in WordNet, and we can obtain numerous noun-sense candidates whose glosses contain "large".

**Graph Construction.** Next, we construct a graph for subsequent Label Propagation similarly as in the method for range population (Section 3).

**Definition [Domain Population Graph (DPG)]:**
The DPG for a relation $r$ is a weighted undirected graph with nodes $V_{\text{DPG}}$ and edges $E_{\text{DPG}}$ as follows:

- $V_{\text{DPG}}$ consists of all candidate nouns for $r$ and their possible noun senses from WordNet.
- $E_{\text{DPG}}$ edges and their weights are computed exactly as described for RPGs (Section 3), with nouns taking the place of adjectives. The only difference is that we use a different sense similarity measure [19], because WordNet's nouns form a hierarchy and are thus very differently structured from the adjectives.

The middle part of Figure 1 shows a DPG example.

**Label Propagation (LP).** Again, we run the MAD algorithm for Label Propagation on the DPG for each relation. To generate seeds, we use `hasProperty` triples that have unambiguous nouns and adjectives that have been assigned to only a single relation $r$ by the Range Population method. Some of these nouns are genuinely unambiguous while others are unambiguous for us because we have previously identified the correct sense using the WordNet gloss heuristics mentioned previously in *semi-disambiguated* assertion gathering. In either case, the single noun senses of such unambiguous nouns serve as seeds. The parameters of the MAD algorithm were tuned as described previously using held-out data. The MAD output provides us with scores for the noun senses of the ambiguous nouns. For the domain of relation $r$, we accept the noun senses whose score exceeds the dummy label score.

# 5. COMPUTING ASSERTIONS

Finally, we leverage the domain and range knowledge for distilling the raw and ambiguous assertion candidates for the generic `hasProperty` relation, gathered as explained in Section 2, into word-sense pairs for fine-grained relations. Thus, we need to disambiguate the left and right arguments of the candidate assertions and determine the respective relations. Again, we build a graph representation for each relation $r$, and apply Label Propagation on these graphs.

For a candidate assertion with an ambiguous noun and adjective, we would often generate a large set of nodes when each of the two words has many different senses. To prevent the graph size from becoming intractable, we harness the already acquired knowledge about the domain and range of each $r$ and consider only those sense pairs that fall into the previously computed domain and range population, respectively. This yields an enormous pruning effect, and makes the difference between a hopelessly intractable graph and a practically viable method.

**Graph Construction.** We construct a graph for subsequent Label Propagation analogously to the method for range population (Section 3). There are two differences from the previous graphs. First, every node is a word pair instead of word. Second, there is an additional candidate node pruning step based on domain and range as described earlier. We capture these by constructing graphs of the following form for each relation.

**Definition [Assertion Graph (AG)]:**
The AG of a relation r is a weighted undirected graph with nodes $V_{\text{AG}}$ and edges $E_{\text{AG}}$ as follows:

- $V_{\text{AG}}$ consists of all word-level assertion candidates and all sense-level pairs that are not pruned by testing against the domain and range of $r$ (see above).
- $E_{\text{AG}}$ consists of three kinds of edges:
  - edges between two word-level assertions,
  - edges between a word-level assertion and a sense-level assertion, and
  - edges between two sense-level assertions.

For an example, see the right side of Figure 1.

**Edge Weighting.** For all three types of edges, we compute edge weights between two assertions $\langle n_1, r_1, a_1\rangle$ and $\langle n_2, r_2, a_2\rangle$ by considering the similarity between $n_1$ and $n_2$ and the similarity between $a_1$ and $a_2$. Here, $n_1$ and $n_2$ may be either nouns or noun senses, and similarly $a_1$ and $a_2$ may be either adjectives or adjective senses. In all cases, we use the multiplicative score

$$\text{sim}(n_1, n_2) \cdot \text{sim}(a_1, a_2)$$

as the edge weight. For example, (`car-n`$^1$, `red-a`$^1$) is similar to tuples like (`car-n`$^1$, `pink-a`$^1$), (`vehicle-n`$^1$,`red-a`$^1$), (`bus-n`$^1$, `colorful-a`$^1$).

The individual noun-noun, noun-noun sense, and noun sense-noun sense similarities (all denoted by $\text{sim}(n_1, n_2)$ here) are computed just as for the different types of edge weights earlier in Section 4. Similarly, the adjective-adjective, adjective-adjective sense, and adjective sense-adjective sense similarities (all denoted by $\text{sim}(a_1, a_2)$) are computed just as for the Range Population Graph's edge weights, described earlier in Section 3.

Since there are $O(|E_{\text{AG}}|^2)$ possible assertion edges, we use top-$k$ retrieval methods to efficiently aggregate scores from multiple ranked lists and avoid computing similarities below a threshold.

**Label Propagation (LP).** For seeds, we consider all assertions where both the noun and the adjective are unambiguous, either because they have only one sense each in WordNet or because our domain- and range-based pruning left us with only one sense pair for the two words. Again, 30 % of the remaining seeds are used for tuning the parameters of the MAD algorithm. Based on these seeds, MAD computes scores for candidate assertions. We accept all assertions for $r$ whose score exceed the dummy label score.

## 6. EXPERIMENTS

Table 1 summarizes the size of the WebChild knowledge base: the number of distinct senses and assertions, the number of instances of noun and adjectives senses (where a noun or adjective sense that occurs in $k$ different relations counts $k$ times), and the precision estimated by extensive sampling (see below). Table 2 illustrates WebChild by anecdotal examples for range, domain, and assertions. These are top-ranked results, based on a simple scoring function that rewards many occurrences as well as occurrences with multiple distinct patterns.

| | #distinct | #instances | Precision |
|---|---|---|---|
| Noun senses | 78,077 | 221,450 | 0.80 |
| Adj. senses | 5,588 | 7,783 | 0.90 |
| Assertions | 4,649,471 | 4,649,471 | 0.82 |

**Table 1: WebChild statistics**

We conducted extensive experiments to assess the viability of our approach and the quality of the resulting commonsense relations. Our experiments cover the three tasks addressed in this paper: Subsection 6.1 reports on the quality of relation ranges, Subsection 6.2 presents results on relation domains, and Subsection 6.3 discusses the quality of sense-disambiguated assertions. For each task, we compare against various baseline competitors.

### 6.1 Relation Ranges

**Baselines.** Since there is no direct competitor (see related work in Section 8), we designed several baselines as follows.

*WordNet attributes:* For some relations, WordNet provides the range directly by its `attribute` relation (e.g., `size` contains the adjective senses `small-a`$^1$ and `big-a`$^1$).

*WordNet attributes expanded:* We expanded the above data by including related word senses using synonyms, antonyms, `similar_to`, and `derivationally_related` links. We then iterated this step once more to enlarge the set, but stopped at this point to curb the inevitable topic drift.

*WordNet glosses:* WordNet provides a short gloss for each adjective. If the gloss mentions a relation, we include the adjective sense in the relation's range. For example, the gloss of `red-a`$^1$ mentions the word *color*.

*Controlled LDA MFS:* Hartung et al. [14] developed a method for creating pseudo-documents per relation $r$ (e.g. color) using nouns and adjectives that appear in the relation. An LDA model estimates the probability $P[a|d]$ for an adjective $a$ given a pseudo-document $d$, thereby approximating $P[a|r]$ to $P[a|d]$. All adjectives above a threshold for this probability form the range of the relation. We map these adjectives to their most frequent sense (MFS) according to WordNet.

*Google Sets MFS:* This service, now part of the spreadsheet processor of `docs.google.com`, expands sets of similar words given a few seeds to start with. We use it to find, for each relation, large candidate sets, using five WordNet adjectives as seeds. The resulting adjectives are mapped to the most frequent sense according to WordNet.

**Results.** We constructed a random sample of 30 adjectives for each relation from the output of WebChild (a total of 570 samples). These were manually evaluated by three people. The kappa value for inter-annotator agreement was 0.869. We likewise drew samples from the outputs of the baseline competitors (or used the entire output when less than 30), and manually assessed them, too. For statistical significance, we computed Wilson score intervals for $\alpha = 95\%$ [8].

The results of this evaluation are shown in Table 3, reporting the macro-averaged precision and the total number of results (coverage). WebChild stands out in this comparison: It discovers far more (sense-mapped) adjectives than any other method, and achieves a very good precision of 90%. WebChild's coverage is three times larger than that of the best prior method [14].

| relation | range | domain | assertions |
|---|---|---|---|
| hasTaste | sweet-a$^{1}$ | strawberry-n$^{1}$ | (chocolate-n$^{1}$,creamy-a$^{2}$) |
| | hot-a$^{9}$ | chili-n$^{1}$ | (pizza-n$^{1}$,delectable-a$^{1}$) |
| | sour-a$^{2}$ | salsa-n$^{1}$ | (salsa-n$^{1}$,spicy-a$^{2}$) |
| | salty-a$^{3}$ | sushi-n$^{1}$ | (burger-n$^{1}$,tasty-a$^{1}$) |
| | lemony-a$^{1}$ | java-n$^{2}$ | (biscuit-n$^{2}$,sweet-a$^{1}$) |
| hasShape | triangular-a$^{1}$ | leaf-n$^{1}$ | (palace-n$^{1}$,domed-a$^{1}$) |
| | meandering-a$^{1}$ | circle-n$^{1}$ | (table-n$^{2}$,flat-a$^{1}$) |
| | crescent-a$^{1}$ | ring-n$^{8}$ | (jeans-n$^{2}$,tapered-a$^{1}$) |
| | obtuse-a$^{2}$ | egg-n$^{1}$ | (tv-n$^{2}$,flat-a$^{1}$) |
| | tapered-a$^{1}$ | face-n$^{1}$ | (lens-n$^{1}$,spherical-a$^{2}$) |

**Table 2: Anecdotal example results for hasTaste, and hasShape**

| Method | Precision | Coverage |
|---|---|---|
| WordNet attributes | 1.00 | 40 |
| WordNet attributes expanded | 0.61 ± 0.03 | 5,145 |
| WordNet glosses | 0.70 ± 0.06 | 3,698 |
| Controlled LDA [14] MFS | 0.30 ± 0.06 | 2,775 |
| Google Sets MFS | 0.27 ± 0.04 | 426 |
| **WebChild** | 0.90 ± 0.03 | 7,783 |

**Table 3: Results for range population**

## 6.2 Relation Domains

**Baselines.** We compare WebChild against the following competitors.

*Extraction Unambiguous:* [2] and [13] manually defined eight patterns (e.g. "the <adj> of <noun> was") to populate the domain of a relation. We applied these patterns to the N-gram corpus and to WordNet glosses. As this technique yields nouns rather than noun senses, we consider only unambiguous nouns with a single sense in WordNet.

*Extraction MFS:* For higher coverage, we considered all nouns obtained by the previous method and mapped them to their most frequent sense according to WordNet.

*Controlled LDA MFS:* Using the method of [14] (see baselines on range population) we collect nouns $n$ with a probability $P[n|d]$ above a threshold. We map the nouns to their most frequent senses in WordNet.

*WordNet glosses:* If a relation name (e.g. *color*) appears in the WordNet gloss of a noun sense, we capture the noun sense as an instance of the relation's domain.

*WebChild adj. projections:* Our candidate gathering step extracted a large set of noun-adjective pairs from the Web. Since WebChild already has mapped adjectives to specific relations' ranges, a heuristic technique is to assign the co-occurring nouns to the domains of the same relations. Since these nouns are not yet disambiguated, we map them to the most frequent sense in WordNet.

*Google Sets:* For domain population, this technique performed very poorly due to heterogeneity of seeds; so we do not show any results below.

**Results.** Table 4 shows the results of this comparison. Again, WebChild stands out, especially by its high coverage. At the same time, its precision of 83% is still fairly high. The method based on WordNet glosses performed slightly better in terms of precision, but yields an order of magnitude lower coverage.

| Method | Precision | Coverage |
|---|---|---|
| Extraction Unambiguous | 0.76 ± 0.06 | 6,190 |
| Extraction MFS | 0.75 ± 0.05 | 30,445 |
| Controlled LDA [14] MFS | 0.71 ± 0.06 | 9,632 |
| WordNet glosses | 0.86 ± 0.03 | 14,328 |
| WebChild adj. projections | 0.71 ± 0.03 | 175,480 |
| **WebChild** | 0.83 ± 0.03 | 221,450 |

**Table 4: Results for domain population**

## 6.3 Assertions

As for the main task on commonsense knowledge acquisition, computing fine-grained assertions between noun senses and adjective senses, we can compare WebChild's performance directly with the prior method Controlled LDA (C-LDA) of [14]. C-LDA treats the task as a classification problem, with relations as the classifier's labels. We use the same data that the experiments of [14] were based on. As C-LDA works at the word rather than word-sense level, for the results of their system, a noun-adjective pair is counted as correct if there is at least one sense pair for which the relation label is meaningful. In contrast, we give WebChild the significant disadvantage of considering an assertion as correct only if the senses are correctly chosen, too. Table 5 shows the results of this experiment, demonstrating the clear superiority of WebChild over the prior state of the art.

**Baselines.** For more comprehensive studies, on our Web-scale candidates, we again designed a variety of baseline competitors.

*Controlled LDA MFS:* We use C-LDA [14] to map a hasProperty candidate pair onto fine-grained relations. Nouns and adjectives are mapped to their most frequent senses in WordNet.

*Vector Space MFS:* This is analogous to the previous baseline, except that we use the vector space model of [13] rather than LDA.

| | Precision | Recall |
|---|---|---|
| Controlled LDA [14] | 0.33 | 0.23 |
| **WebChild** | 0.93 | 0.50 |

**Table 5: Results for assertions on data of [14]**

*Web Unambiguous Adjective:* We consider only those noun-adjective pairs where the adjective has a single sense. We use WebChild's range knowledge to map the adjective to one or more relations. The noun is mapped to its most frequent sense in WordNet.

*WebChild Independence:* For a given relation, we consider all combinations of noun senses from the domain and adjective senses from the range as assertions for the relation.

**Results.** Table 6 shows the results of the comparison. WebChild yields more than 4 million assertions at a good precision of 80%. It outperforms all competitors by a large margin, with ten times higher coverage and twice better precision than the best of the prior methods [13]. Interestingly, even the relatively crude WebChild Independence technique performs better than the other baselines. However, its precision is far behind that of the full WebChild method.

| Method | Precision | Coverage |
|---|---|---|
| Controlled LDA MFS | $0.35 \pm 0.06$ | 254,576 |
| Vector Space MFS | $0.40 \pm 0.09$ | 355,018 |
| Web Unambiguous Adjective | $0.54 \pm 0.09$ | 709,337 |
| WebChild Independence | $0.62 \pm 0.06$ | 3,399,312 |
| **WebChild** | $0.82 \pm 0.03$ | 4,709,149 |

**Table 6: Results for assertions**

Table 7 shows the results of WebChild, per relation.

| relation | precision | coverage |
|---|---|---|
| ability | $0.80 \pm 0.10$ | 90,288 |
| appearance | $0.95 \pm 0.05$ | 365,201 |
| beauty | $0.70 \pm 0.15$ | 95,838 |
| color | $0.70 \pm 0.15$ | 494,380 |
| emotion | $0.90 \pm 0.09$ | 79,630 |
| feeling | $0.91 \pm 0.08$ | 141,453 |
| length | $0.70 \pm 0.15$ | 90,021 |
| motion | $0.80 \pm 0.10$ | 146,148 |
| smell | $0.82 \pm 0.10$ | 25,347 |
| quality | $0.82 \pm 0.10$ | 793,484 |
| sensitivity | $0.70 \pm 0.15$ | 5,727 |
| shape | $0.80 \pm 0.10$ | 359,789 |
| size | $0.82 \pm 0.10$ | 910,901 |
| sound | $0.71 \pm 0.15$ | 130,952 |
| state | $0.88 \pm 0.09$ | 563,022 |
| strength | $0.82 \pm 0.10$ | 165,412 |
| taste | $0.70 \pm 0.15$ | 19,892 |
| temperature | $0.80 \pm 0.13$ | 27,399 |
| weight | $0.70 \pm 0.15$ | 144,587 |
| **overall** | $0.82 \pm 0.03$ | 4,709,149 |

**Table 7: Quality of WebChild relations**

# 7. USE-CASE: POPULATING CLASSES

As a use-case that demonstrates the application benefits of WebChild, we studied the problem of populating semantic classes, such as `river`, `car`, or `singer`. This problem is often addressed as a set-expansion task [36]: Given a small number of seeds, which are instances (or hyponyms) of the same class, find as many additional instances as possible and rank them into a high-precision list. For example, for seeds like *Mississippi*, *Nile*, and *Ganges*, we would like to collect other rivers such as *Danube*, *Rhine*, *Seine*, *Mekong*, etc. A good baseline to compare with is the *Google Sets* tool, which is part of the `docs.google.com` service. Other methods like [9] may be better, but they are also much more complex and need extensive Web data not available to us.

Our method for class population is fairly simple; its main point is the way it harnesses the WebChild knowledge. For a given noun sense $\mathtt{n}$ corresponding to an instantiable semantic class, we perform the following steps:

1. We select the $m$ highest ranked adjective senses $\mathtt{a}_1, \ldots, \mathtt{a}_m$ that are connected with $\mathtt{n}$ by one or more of WebChild's fine-grained assertions. As these are senses, we can further expand them by their WordNet synonyms, thus constructing a ranked list of adjectives $a_1, \ldots, a_l$ (where usually $l \geq m$), now cast into simple words.
2. To avoid extensively used adjectives of unspecific or ambiguous nature (e.g., *great*), we compute PMI scores between the starting noun $n$ and each of the adjectives $a_i$ ($i = 1 \ldots l$):

$$\mathrm{PMI}(n, a_i) = \log_2 \frac{P[n \wedge a_i]}{P[n]\ P[a_i]}$$

   We prune all adjectives from the ranked list whose PMI score is below a specified threshold. From the remaining adjectives, we take the top $k$ words $a_1, \ldots, a_k$ (e.g., with $k = 10$).
3. Now we apply the linking-verb patterns that we introduced in Section 2 to the Google N-gram corpus and extract noun phrases from the matching N-grams. This yields frequencies for ($n$,$a_i$) co-occurrences. The noun phrases are the candidates for populating the class denoted by $n$.
4. We rank the collected noun phrases $p$ by aggregating over the co-occurrence frequencies:

$$\mathrm{score}(p) = \sum_{i=1}^{k} \mathrm{freq}(p, a_i) \times \mathrm{weight}(a_i)$$

   where $\mathrm{weight}(a_i)$ is the score of the original $\mathtt{a}_i$ for noun sense $\mathtt{n}$ in WebChild (based on pattern-matching statistics, see Section 3).

As a demonstration of the high quality that our method achieves, we evaluate its *precision@5*, in comparison to the top-5 results from Google Sets. We did this for the following 10 test cases (5 common nouns and 5 proper nouns): `river`, `ice cream`, `mountain`, `chocolate`, `keyboard`, `nile river`, `bangalore`, `tiger lily`, `parsley`, `florine`. We evaluate Google Sets with 1 seed (G-1) and 2 seeds (G-2) against WebChild, which only takes the class noun as input (W-1). G-1 runs into limitations, but G-2 performs reasonably well even in this extreme situation. For example, with seed *river* as input, G-1 gives as output *boca*, *estudiantes*, *independiente*, *racing*, *san lorenzo*; with the seed *tiger lily* as input, G-1 produces no output. G-2, with the seeds *river*, *river valley*, gives as output *canyon*, *arizona*, *valley*, *colorado*; with the seeds *tiger lily*, *panther lily* as input, G-2 gives as output *peacock iris*, *meadow saffron*, *pancratium*, *peruvian lily*, *flag*.

Table 8 shows the results. WebChild outperforms G-1 and G-2 on common nouns. On proper nouns, G-2 outperforms WebChild, but WebChild performs as well as G-1. Tables 9 and 10 show the top-10 WebChild adjectives, and the top-5 set expansions for the input `chocolate` and `keyboard` respectively.

| Approach | Genre | P@5 |
|---|---|---|
| G-1 | common noun | 0.52 |
| G-2 | common noun | 0.72 |
| W-1 | common noun | **0.92** |
| G-1 | proper noun | 0.52 |
| G-2 | proper noun | **0.68** |
| W-1 | proper noun | 0.52 |

**Table 8: Results for set expansion**

| | |
|---|---|
| top-10 adjectives | `smooth`, `assorted`, `dark`, `fine`, `delectable`, `black`, `decadent`, `white`, `yummy`, `creamy` |
| top-5 expansions | *chocolate bar, chocolate cake, milk chocolate, chocolate chip, chocolate fudge* |

**Table 9: `chocolate`: top-10 adj, top-5 expansions**

| | |
|---|---|
| top-10 adjectives | `ergonomic`, `foldable`, `sensitive`, `black`, `comfortable`, `compact`, `lightweight`, `comfy`, `pro`, `waterproof` |
| top-5 expansions | *keyboard, usb keyboard, computer keyboard, qwerty keyboard, optical mouse, touch screen* |

**Table 10: `keyboard`: top-10 adj, top-5 expansions**

# 8. RELATED WORK

Large-scale knowledge bases have received much attention in recent years, most notable endeavors being Freebase [6], DBpedia [3], and Yago [33]. These and other projects along similar lines focus on facutal knowledge, and disregard the kind of commonsense knowledge considered in this paper. Methods for open information extraction have harnessed verbal phrases and patterns derived from them [27], [10], [26]; however, their focus is still on factual knowledge and does not deliver a hierarchy of disambiguated commonsense properties.

The seminal Cyc project [21] aimed to manually compile commonsense knowledge, with emphasis on rules rather than properties. The publicly available version OpenCyc does not provide any properties of the kind addressed here. The WordNet thesaurus [12] contains a small amount of properties; we use these as seeds for WebChild and we also compare the WebChild results against using WordNet alone.

ConceptNet [23, 15, 31] is probably the largest repository of commonsense assertions about the world, covering relations such as `hasProperty`, `usedFor`, `madeOf`, `motivatedByGoal`, etc. Ongoing projects on extending ConceptNet have made use of crowdsourcing [15, 30] and pattern-based extraction from Web pages [35]. [1] and [16] present games-with-a-purpose to acquire commonsense facts. Approaches for extracting noun properties from text include pattern-based information extraction [2] and corpus co-occurrence analysis [4]. However, this line of research stayed at the level of a single generic `hasProperty` relation.

There is little prior work on methods for acquiring fine-grained commonsense relations. [2] proposed patterns like (*<object> is a/the <attribute> of <subject>*, e.g. *brown is a color of dogs*) to find more specific properties, but even on the Web this method yields only very low recall [4]. [13, 14] developed classifiers for mapping assertion candidates into a small set of 8 fine-grained relations, using vector-space features as well as LDA-based topic models. However, these methods assume that the given assertions are already correct instances of at least the generic `hasProperty` relation. So this work tackled the assertion classification problem, not the problem of computing assertions from raw data. [20] studied relations like `hasSize`, `hasShape`, etc., assigning their instances to word senses. However, it solely relied on human elicitation for 50 nouns, and is not suited for automation at large scale. Finally, [5] used WordNet and ConceptNet to infer commonsense rules, e.g., edible objects are likely to be found at a supermarket. This task is quite different from acquiring commonsense properties.

Unlike most of the above works, our method yields sense-disambiguated assertions for fine-grained relations. In contrast to all prior work, our method is able to produce large-scale output of high quality.

# 9. CONCLUSION

We presented WebChild, the first comprehensive commonsense knowledge base with fine-grained relations about sense-disambiguated nouns and adjectives. Our methodology combines pattern-based candidate gathering from Web corpora with semi-supervised Label Propagation over judiciously constructed weighted graphs. Experiments demonstrate that this methodology can achieve high precision with good coverage. WebChild is publicly available as a resource for other researchers.

As for ongoing and future work, we are considering adding value to WebChild by inferring further relationships among word senses: antonyms in addition to those known already in WordNet, and ordinal relations such as `isLargerThan` or `isDarkerThan` (cf. [11]). When applied to image annotations, this could possibly contribute to more semantic training data for computer vision. We are also exploring applications of WebChild. We believe that the rich knowledge of noun-adjective relations is a valuable asset for sentiment mining [24] in general and for analyzing feelings about images [28] in particular.

# 10. REFERENCES


[1] L. von Ahn, M. Kedia, M. Blum: Verbosity: a Game for Collecting Common-Sense Facts. CHI 2006.

[2] A. Almuhareb, M. Poesio: Attribute-Based and Value-Based Clustering: An Evaluation. EMNLP 2004.

[3] S. Auer, C. Bizer, J. Lehmann, G. Kobilarov, R. Cyganiak, Z. Ives: DBpedia: A Nucleus for a Web of Open Data. ISWC/ASWC 2007.

[4] M. Baroni, R. Zamparelli: Nouns are Vectors, Adjectives are Matrices: Representing Adjective-Noun Constructions in Semantic Space. EMNLP 2010.

[5] E. Blanco, H. C. Cankaya, and D. Moldovan: Commonsense Knowledge Extraction using Concepts Properties. FLAIRS 2011.

[6] K. Bollacker, C. Evans, P. Paritosh, T. Sturge, J. Taylor: Freebase: A Collaboratively Created Graph Database for Structuring Human Knowledge. SIGMOD 2008

[7] T. Brants, A. Franz: Web 1T 5-gram Version 1. Linguistic Data Consortium, 2006.

[8] L.D. Brown, T.T. Cai, A. Dasgupta: Interval Estimation for a Binomial Proportion. Statistical Science 16: 101–133, 2001.

[9] B. B. Dalvi, W. W. Cohen, J. Callan. Websets: Extracting Sets of Entities from the Web using Unsupervised Information Extraction. WSDM 2012.

[10] L. Del Corro, R. Gemulla. ClausIE: clause-based open information extraction. WWW 2013.

[11] G. de Melo, M. Bansal: Good, Great, Excellent: Global Inference of Semantic Intensities. Transactions of the ACL, 2013.

[12] C.D. Fellbaum, G.A. Miller (Eds.): WordNet: An Electronic Lexical Database. MIT Press, 1998.

[13] M. Hartung, A. Frank: A Structured Vector Space Model for Hidden Attribute Meaning in Adjective-Noun Phrases. COLING 2010.

[14] M. Hartung, A. Frank: Exploring Supervised LDA Models for Assigning Attributes to Adjective-Noun Phrases. EMNLP 2011.

[15] C. Havasi, R. Speer, J. Alonso: ConceptNet 3: a Flexible, Multilingual Semantic Network for Common Sense Knowledge. RANLP 2007.

[16] A. Herdagdelen, M. Baroni: Bootstrapping a Game with a Purpose for Commonsense Collection. ACM TIST 3(4): 59 (2012)

[17] G. Hirst, D. St-Onge: Lexical Chains as Representations of Context for the Detection and Correction of Malapropisms. In [12], 1998.

[18] IBM Journal of Research and Development 56(3/4), Special Issue on "This is Watson", 2012.

[19] C. Leacock and M. Chodorow: Combining local context and WordNet similarity for word sense identification. Fellbaum 1998, pp. 265âĂŞ28

[20] G.E. Lebani, E. Pianta: Encoding Commonsense Lexical Knowledge into WordNet. Global WordNet Conference 2012.

[21] Douglas B. Lenat: CYC: A Large-Scale Investment in Knowledge Infrastructure. Comm. of the ACM 38(11), pp. 32-38, 1995.

[22] M. Lesk: Automatic Sense Disambiguation using Machine Readable Dictionaries: How to Tell a Pine Cone from an Ice Cream Cone. SIGDOC 1986.

[23] H. Liu, P. Singh: ConceptNet: a Practical Commonsense Reasoning Toolkit. BT Technology Journal, 2004.

[24] B. Liu: Sentiment Analysis and Opinion Mining. Morgan & Claypool, 2012.

[25] S. Banerjee, T. Pedersen: An Adapted Lesk Algorithm for Word Sense Disambiguation using WordNet. CICLing 2002.

[26] W. Derry, P. Pratim Talukdar, T. Mitchell. PIDGIN: ontology alignment using web text as interlingua. CIKM 2013.

[27] A. Fader, S. Soderland, O. Etzioni. Identifying relations for open information extraction. EMNLP 2011.

[28] S. Siersdorfer, J. Hare: Analyzing and Predicting Sentiment of Images on the Social Web. ACM Multimedia 2010.

[29] A. Singhal: Introducing the Knowledge Graph: Things, Not Strings. `googleblog.blogspot.co.uk`, 16 May 2012.

[30] R. Speer, C. Havasi, H. Surana: Using Verbosity: Common Sense Data from Games with a Purpose. FLAIRS 2010.

[31] R. Speer, C. Havasi: Representing General Relational Knowledge in ConceptNet 5. LREC 2012.

[32] S. Staab, R. Studer (Eds.): Handbook on Ontologies, Springer, 2009.

[33] F.M. Suchanek, G. Kasneci, G. Weikum: YAGO: A Core of Semantic Knowledge. WWW 2007.

[34] P.P. Talukdar, K. Crammer: New Regularized Algorithms for Transductive Learning. ECML/PKDD 2009.

[35] N. Tandon, G. de Melo, G. Weikum: Deriving a Web-Scale Common Sense Fact Database. AAAI 2011.

[36] R.C. Wang, W.W. Cohen: Language-Independent Set Expansion of Named Entities Using the Web. ICDM 2007.

[37] X. Zhu, Z. Ghahramani, J.D. Lafferty: Semi-Supervised Learning Using Gaussian Fields and Harmonic Functions. ICML 2003.

# Using Linked Data to Mine RDF from Wikipedia's Tables

Emir Muñoz
Fujitsu (Ireland) Limited,
Swords, Co. Dublin, Ireland
emir.munoz@ie.fujitsu.com

Aidan Hogan
Dept. of Computer Science,
Universidad de Chile
ahogan@dcc.uchile.cl

Alessandra Mileo
INSIGHT at NUI Galway,
Ireland
alessandra.mileo@deri.org

## ABSTRACT

The tables embedded in Wikipedia articles contain rich, semi-structured encyclopaedic content. However, the cumulative content of these tables cannot be queried against. We thus propose methods to recover the semantics of Wikipedia tables and, in particular, to extract facts from them in the form of RDF triples. Our core method uses an existing Linked Data knowledge-base to find pre-existing relations between entities in Wikipedia tables, suggesting the same relations as holding for other entities in analogous columns on different rows. We find that such an approach extracts RDF triples from Wikipedia's tables at a raw precision of 40%. To improve the raw precision, we define a set of features for extracted triples that are tracked during the extraction phase. Using a manually labelled gold standard, we then test a variety of machine learning methods for classifying correct/incorrect triples. One such method extracts 7.9 million unique and novel RDF triples from over one million Wikipedia tables at an estimated precision of 81.5%.

## Categories and Subject Descriptors

H.2.8 [**Database Management**]: Database Applications—*Data Mining*; H.3.5 [**Information Storage & Retrieval**]: Online Information Services

## Keywords

Linked Data; Web Tables; Wikipedia; Data Mining

## 1. INTRODUCTION

Wikipedia contains a wealth of encyclopaedic knowledge collaboratively curated by millions of users. Aside from unstructured textual content, Wikipedia articles contain rich factual data encoded in millions of tables. However, although these tables are presented in a semi-structured format, they are intended for human consumption and are not directly machine readable. The individual facts that each such table encodes are not readily recoverable by automatic methods and cannot be queried by users. Though the content of these tables could be imported into a relational representation, this still does not make the task of querying the tables much easier: a user would need to know, in advance, the specific structure of each table they wish to query against, which is impractical given the native heterogeneity of relational schemata for different tables. Furthermore, performing joins across such tables would require knowledge of co-reference (when tables refer to the same entities), since suitable primary/foreign keys are often not available.

Extracting the factual content of individual Wikipedia tables into a representation that is agnostic to their native structure requires methods to interpret the *semantics* of the table [21]. Such an interpretation aims to understand which entities referenced by the table are related to which other entities, and by what relationship. Once the semantics of the tables are (partially) recovered, their factual content can be presented as semantic triples [6]: binary relations of the form $(s, p, o)$, where the subject entity $s$ is related to the object entity $o$ by the relationship $p$. The concept of semantic triples is isomorphic to that of the RDF data model [14], where URI identifiers can be used for entities and must be used for relationships. Irrespective of the structure of the originating tables, facts extracted as semantic triples could then be directly queried against using SPARQL [9]: the W3C recommended query language for the RDF data model.

Recovering the semantics of Wikipedia tables closely relates to two (mostly) orthogonal research topics.

The first area relates to works on interpreting Web tables. Cafarella et al. [4] found 14.1 billion HTML tables in a Google crawl from 2008, estimating that 154 million contain high-quality relational data. These tables are extremely diverse in terms of representation, structure and vocabulary used; they often contain polysemous (or missing or otherwise vague) attribute labels, ambiguous free-text cell content and referents, cells spanning multiple rows and/or columns, split tables, obscured contextual validity, and so forth [11]. Recovering the semantics of such tables is thus exceptionally challenging, where existing methods typically aim to rather categorise or index the schemata of such tables [4, 6, 21].

The second area relates to works that export parts of the factual content of Wikipedia as RDF, creating knowledge-bases published as Linked Data. The most prominent works in this area are DBpedia [2] and YAGO2 [10]. Both works aim to extract factual knowledge from Wikipedia, representing the results as RDF, which can be queried by SPARQL.[1]

[1] For example, see **http://dbpedia.org/sparql**


*WSDM'14*, February 24–28, 2014, New York, NY, USA.
Copyright 2014 ACM 978-1-4503-2351-2/14/02 ...$15.00.
http://dx.doi.org/10.1145/2556195.2556266.

| No. | Position | Player | No. | Position | Player |
|---|---|---|---|---|---|
| 1 | GK | Kenneth Vermeer | 21 | FW | Derk Boerrigter |
| 3 | DF | Toby Alderweireld *(vice captain)* | 22 | GK | Jasper Cillessen |
| 4 | DF | Niklas Moisander | 23 | FW | Danny Hoesen |
| 5 | MF | Christian Poulsen | 24 | DF | Ricardo van Rhijn |
| 6 | MF | Eyong Enoh | 25 | MF | Thulani Serero |
| 7 | FW | Miralem Sulejmani | 26 | DF | Dico Koppers |

Figure 1: Split table listing all current AFC Ajax squad members (abridged from the Wikipedia article **http://en.wikipedia.org/wiki/AFC_Ajax**; CC–BY–SA)

However, both works rely primarily on mining facts from Wikipedia *info-boxes*: the attribute–value tables that appear on the top, right-hand side of many Wikipedia articles. Many such info-boxes follow standard templates that serve as a hook for writing bulk manual mappings. Even in cases where templates are not available, info-boxes are relatively straightforward to semi-automatically extract semantics triples from: $s$ corresponds to the entity referred to by the article itself, $p$ corresponds to the attribute and $o$ corresponds to the value. Neither approach presents methods to extract the rich factual content present in the millions of relational tables that are embedded in the body of Wikipedia articles (which we henceforth refer to as *Wikitables*, as distinguished from info-boxes or tables-of-content).

Recently a number of works have looked to bridge these two areas—including works from Limaye et al. [12] and Mulwad et al. [17, 20, 16]—by using Linked Data knowledge-bases as references for interpreting the semantics of tables.

This paper follows on from these works with the aim of mining facts from all of Wikipedia's tables. Our methods are inspired by those from Web tables, but where we use the DBpedia Linked Data knowledge-base as a reference during the processing of tables. Though other knowledge-bases could also be used, we select DBpedia as a comprehensive dataset extracted from Wikipedia, with URIs for each subject of a Wikipedia article, and with a wide variety of relationships between those entities. We propose to first map entities in the tables to entities in the DBpedia knowledge-base. We can then query the knowledge-base for existing facts that involve those entities. By building a picture of which entities in the tables have which prior relationships, we can build an incomplete picture of the semantics of the table and attempt to extrapolate this to the rest of the table. We illustrate this idea with a motivating example.

### *Motivating Example*

Figure 1 presents a Wikitable abridged from the Wikipedia article for "AFC Ajax": a Dutch football club.[2] The table containing factual content about players: their shirt number, country and position. There are also relationships between players and the entity described by the article (their current club is AFC Ajax). However, relevant relationships do not hold across all pairs of columns: for example, there is no obvious factual relationship between positions and countries.

Aside from the **No.** columns, the cells of the table contain hyperlinks to other articles in Wikipedia, including countries, football positions, and individual players. For example, the flags link to articles for the country; MF links to the article for "Midfielder": a position in football. These links provide unambiguous referents to Wikipedia entities, which can in turn be mapped directly to DBpedia entities and descriptions. We currently focus on the extraction of relations between cells containing wiki-links and do not look at plain-string values. For example, we would not try to extract player numbers from the above table.

First we can determine the contextual entity (and in this case, the protagonist of the table [5]) by the article in which it appears. We can then query the DBpedia knowledge-base to find relations between the context entity and various entities mentioned in the table cells. For example, the following SPARQL query asks for all relationships in the DBpedia knowledge-base that hold between the entities identified by the CURIEs **dbr:Kenneth_Vermeer** and **dbr:AFC_Ajax** (this query is for the purposes of illustration only; as discussed later, for performance reasons, we do not use SPARQL):[3]

```
PREFIX dbr: <http://dbpedia.org/resource/>
SELECT ?rel WHERE { dbr:Kenneth_Vermeer ?rel dbr:AFC_Ajax }
```

This query returns the relationship **dbp:currentclub**. We find DBpedia triples with predicate **dbp:currentclub** relating $\frac{9}{12}$ entities in the **Player** to the protagonist **dbr:AFC_Ajax**. For the remaining three players in those columns, we can thus suggest the following triples as extraction candidates:

```
dbr:Niklas_Moisander dbp:currentclub dbr:AFC_Ajax .
dbr:Christian_Poulsen dbp:currentclub dbr:AFC_Ajax .
dbr:Danny_Hoesen dbp:currentclub dbr:AFC_Ajax .
```

Next we can look at relationships within the table. Taking an example for **Player** and **Position** columns:

```
SELECT ?rel WHERE { dbr:Thulani_Serero ?rel dbr:Midfielder }
```

from the reference knowledge-base, **dbp:position** is present in $\frac{11}{12}$ of the rows for entities in the **Player** column to entities in the **Position** column. We can thus suggest the missing relation as a candidate for extraction:

```
dbr:Miralem_Sulejmani dbp:position dbr:Forward .
```

Similarly, in the reference knowledge-base, the relationship **dbo:birthPlace** holds for many entities between the (unlabelled) country and **Player** columns, suggesting the analogous missing relations as candidates for extraction.

Though this method is naturally imprecise, we could suppose, for example, that the more rows for which a given relationship with a given predicate holds in the reference knowledge-base across two given columns, the higher the likelihood that that relationship exists on all such rows. Other features, such as a match between the label of the candidate relation and a column header, can strengthen confidence in the match. Such features of the extracted triple can be used to train a classifier for correct/incorrect triples.

Though a relatively "clean" example, the table depicted in Figure 1 already exhibits two potential obstacles: the table is split in two, and one cell contains multiple links ("Toby Alderweireld *(vice captain)*"). In practice, Wikitables exhibit a high-degree of diversity, which poses major challenges for extracting triples, where we rely on machine learning techniques to increase accuracy.

[2]The choice of example does not necessarily reflect the sporting allegiances of the present authors.

[3]The CURIE prefixes used in this paper are **dbr:** for **http://dbpedia.org/resource/**, dbp: for **http://dbpedia.org/property/**, and dbo: for **http://dbpedia.org/ontology/**

Our methods can ultimately be viewed from three perspectives. From the Web tables perspective, we use an existing knowledge-base as a reference to interpret the semantics of tables. From the Linked Data perspective, we enrich the reference knowledge-base with new facts mined from tables. From the Wikipedia perspective, we make the cumulative knowledge of tables available for user queries.

### *Organisation*

The rest of this paper is organised as follows:

§2. We provide an overview of related works in the areas of Web tables, mining RDF triples from Wikipedia and extracting RDF triples from tables.

§3. We survey the set of Wikitables mined from a recent Wikipedia dump, which serves as our experimental corpus.

§4. We propose our methods for extracting candidate RDF triples from Wikitables using DBPEDIA as a reference dataset (as sketched in the motivating example).

§5. We describe the features and machine learning methods that we use to classify (in)correct facts.

§6. We conclude with a summary of results and possible future directions.

This paper extends an earlier work [18] where we surveyed Wikipedia's tables and presented initial ideas for mining facts from them. In this paper, we evaluate novel features and machine learning methods to classify triples as correct or incorrect and provide extended discussion throughout.

## 2. RELATED WORK

We review recent works on three relevant topics: processing Web tables, extracting RDF from Wikipedia, and extracting RDF from Web tables.

### *Web tables:*

Hurst [11] divides the problem of processing Web tables into four sub-tasks: (1) *table location*: identifying tables in source documents, such as HTML pages; (2) *table recognition*: parsing and normalising the table into its constituent cells for further analysis; (3) *functional & structural analysis*: determining the size and nature of the table; (4) *table interpretation*: recovering the semantics of the table to allow for deep processing of its content.

In the context of HTML, sub-tasks (1) and (2) are typically carried out by looking for table-related HTML tags in the Web page (e.g. `table`, `td` and `tr`). Sub-task (2) also refers to segmenting the table into a relative spatial description, which considers issues like internal cell structure, split cells, spanning errors, and other normalisation techniques. For sub-task (2), Pivk et al. [19] proposed the TARTAR model, which normalises a table into a logical matrix.

For sub-task (3), the most common classification of tables is simply *Relational* vs. *Non-relational* (aka. *Genuine* vs. *Non-genuine*); non-relational tables include those used for formatting and navigation [22, 4]. Going further, Crestan and Pantel [6] define a taxonomy with twelve structural classes of HTML tables and Yoshida et al. [24] propose nine groups for attribute–value tables, etc.

Sub-task (4) relates to interpreting tables and attempting to recover their semantics. Cafarella et al. [4] proposed the WEBTABLES system, which adopts a distributional semantics approach, extracting co-occurrence distributions for attribute labels in tables for search and other applications. Zwicklbauer et al. [25] also use an existing knowledge-base to annotate the semantic types of individual table columns based on the most common type found in each column's cells. Venetis et al. [21] similarly look to annotate columns of tables, sourcing a set of target class and relationship labels from the Web. For interpreting attribute–value tables, Crestan et al. [6] introduce the *protagonist problem*: identifying the subject of relations for attribute–value tables in order to generate semantic triples. (We discuss works that can extract triples from tables later in this section.)

**Novelty:** We focus on the tables of Wikipedia. For subtasks (1–2), we re-use the TARTAR model [19] and parse Wikitables using HTML tags, such as `table`, `td`, etc. For sub-task (3), we simply look for tables with class `wikitable` to identify our target class of tables. Furthermore, we apply the notion of a protagonist [6] to generic relational tables (as per the AFC Ajax example). Our methods re-use and extend upon various ideas made in the Web-tables literature for extracting triples from Wikipedia tables.

### *Extracting RDF from Wikipedia*

As aforementioned, the DBPEDIA knowledge-base [2] publishes RDF extracted from Wikipedia as Linked Data. The system extracts RDF from Wikipedia articles in various languages. DBPEDIA URIs are minted for the protagonist of each Wikipedia article. RDF triples are extracted from markup including titles, abstracts, categories, images and various forms of links. The richest source of information are the attribute–value "info-boxes" presented in the top right of Wikipedia articles (where available). DBpedia supports user-contributed mappings of RDF from tables in Wikipedia, but only isolated mappings have been provided.[4]

YAGO2 [10] also extracts RDF from Wikipedia, relying on hard-coded declarative rules that specify extraction, normalisation and implication logic for mapping (primarily) infobox attributes to known terms in the ontology. Facts are enhanced and annotated through use of external knowledge-bases, such as WordNet synsets to enrich wiki-categories, and GeoNames to enrich geographical information. Estimates for the precision of YAGO2 lie at around 95% [10].

**Novelty:** Although both YAGO2 and DBpedia support manual mappings from generic tables in Wikipedia, the coverage of these mappings appears to be very limited: both works rather focus on extraction from info-boxes. To assure novelty, we thus deliberately ignore info-boxes and instead target only Wikitables embedded in the body of the article. We currently use DBPEDIA as a reference knowledge-base, but in future could also use other reference knowledge-bases that are reconcilable with Wikipedia entities, such as YAGO2 or Freebase, or perhaps even Wikidata.

### *Extracting RDF from Tables*

Various languages, such as R2RML [7], can express custom mappings from relational database tables to RDF. In terms of representing the *structure* of tables in RDF, Ding et al. [8] propose extracting each row of the table as a subject, each

[4]`http://mappings.dbpedia.org/index.php?title=Special%3APrefixIndex&prefix=Table&namespace=204`

column as a predicate and each cell as an object. Similar methods are used for the Direct Mapping standard [1].

More closely related to our own work are the methods of Limaye et al. [12] and Mulwad et al. [17, 20, 16], who take a reference knowledge-base and use it to annotate entities and columns in tables with types and relationships. As such, these approaches can be used to extract triples from tables.

**Novelty:** Our approach is automatic and does not require an input mapping (per R2RML). We export content that can be queried independently of the structure of the originating table (vs. Ding et al. [8] and the Direct Mapping).

Although Limaye et al. [12] evaluate average timings of their extraction for 250,000 Web tables, their work and the works by Mulwad et al. [17, 20, 16] evaluate the quality of relation extraction based on 25–36 hand-picked Wikitables and 150–371 hand-picked Web-tables, whereas we evaluate the quality of our extraction for over one million Wikipedia tables (all Wikitables meeting certain minimal criteria, laid out in §3.2) based on random sampling. In general, we focus specifically on the problem of relation extraction in the context of Wikipedia tables, running the extraction process over the entire corpus (post-filtering), presenting a detailed set of "row-centric" features for machine learning methods to perform classification, and evaluation based on sampling from all tables. In doing so, we exploit features specific to Wikipedia to improve results: for example, we use Wikilinks to detect entities and we extract additional relations from table cells to the protagonist of the article, etc.

## 3. SURVEY OF WIKITABLES

We begin our core contribution by formalising our notion of a table, defining the tables in Wikipedia that we consider in-scope for extraction (Wikitables), and providing some statistics on the set of Wikitables extracted from the February 13th, 2013 English Wikipedia dump.

### 3.1 Classifying Wikipedia's Tables

Wikipedia editors can choose from three classes of tables; each has a different value for the HTML attribute class in the associated table tag in the Wikipedia page, as follows:

- toc: table of contents summarising the layout of the article, typically found after its abstract;
- info-box: attribute–value tables embedded in the top-right of the article providing core information about the protagonist, typically following a standard template based on the type of protagonist (e.g., city, person, etc.);
- wikitable: tables embedded in the article's body, typically containing relational data about the protagonist.

We focus on the wikitable class since toc tables refer to article layout, not factual content, and the extraction of facts from info-box tables has already been near-exhaustively covered by works such as DBPEDIA and YAGO2. To the best of our knowledge, we are the first work to tackle a full-scale extraction of facts from the wikitable class of tables.

### 3.2 Normalising Wikipedia's Tables

The structure and content of Wikitables can be quite complex. Since these tables are intended for human consumption, their layout is guided by visual aesthetics. Tables often contain *spans* to avoid repetition: these spans cover multiple cells with one entry, and include column-spans (colspans), row-spans (rowspans) or a combination of both. To avoid tables wider than the standard display width or to avoid ugly long and narrow tables, editors will often employ split tables (as per Figure 1). Cells may also contain (i) multiple values, (ii) prose-text alongside the primary value giving justification or context for that value, (iii) superscript references to sources, (iv) images or other embedded content, (v) empty cells in "optional" columns, and so forth.

To overcome this heterogeneity, we normalise Wikitables by "squaring" them and filtering text, such that they can be represented as a logical matrix of cells prior to extraction.

Table 1: Overview of tables in the dump

| | | |
|---|---|---|
| • TOTAL ARTICLES: | 10,854,204 | 100.00% |
| ▸ ARTICLES W/TABLES: | 1,875,415 | 17.28% |
| • ALL TABLES: | 3,923,427 | 100.00% |
| ▸ ILL-FORMED: | 163,105 | 4.16% |
| ▸ WELL-FORMED: | 3,760,322 | 95.84% |
| ○ toc: | 1,648,786 | 43.85% |
| ○ info-box: | 815,350 | 21.68% |
| ○ wikitable: | 1,296,186 | 34.47% |
| ▷ $< 2 \times 2$: | 158,940 | 12.26% |
| ▷ $\geq 2 \times 2$: (*used*) | 1,137,246 | 87.74% |

#### *Table Model*

We consider as input a source of tables $\mathcal{T}$ (a set of tables). We model an individual table $T \in \mathcal{T}$ as an $m \times n$ matrix $M_T$. Table headers are very common in tables, and can be simple (one row) or hierarchical (multiple rows). We let $h$ denote the index of the bottom header row, such that $M_T(i, .)$, $i \leq h$ denotes the header rows of $M_T$.

#### *Extraction and Normalisation*

Our initial goal is to convert a Wikipedia article in HTML to a source of tables $\mathcal{T}$. Mapping HTML tables to square matrices is often challenging due to syntax-level issues (e.g., non-closed HTML tags, fewer or more columns in some rows creating jagged tables, spans, nesting, etc.).

Though we cannot *fully* normalise the tables (e.g., we do not rejoin split tables), we use TARTAR [19] to apply some standard normalisation techniques, as follows. Tables often contain their caption embedded in the first row: we discard that row when generating the matrix. Header rows are identified by the (<TH>) tag. For each table, we must also deal with colspans and rowspans: we divide such cells and copy the original content into each division. Where we find "jagged rows", we consider missing cells to contain blank strings. If the table can be parsed into a matrix $M_T$ (i.e., is syntactically valid and dense), we call the table *well-formed*. Otherwise we call it *ill-formed*. Finally, we only consider well-formed tables where the size of $M_T$ is at least $2 \times 2$; i.e., it contains at least two rows *and* at least two columns.

### 3.3 Corpus Composition

We extract our corpus of Wikitables from the February 13th, 2013 English Wikipedia dump. We first apply the Bliki engine parser[5] to convert wiki-markup to HTML articles.

[5]http://code.google.com/p/gwtwiki/

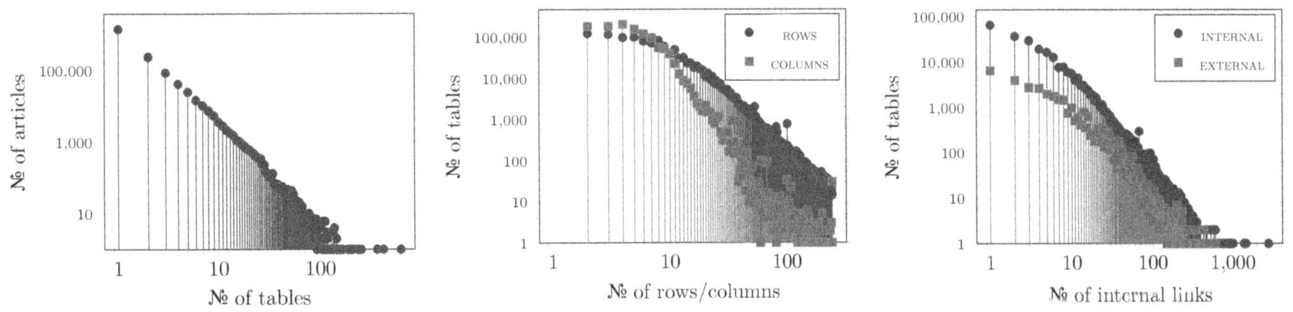


Figure 2: Various distributions for the Wikitables considered

Each HTML page is then cleaned and canonicalised (fixing syntax mistakes) using CyberNeko[6] before all HTML tables (including nested tables) are extracted.

Table 1 provides a breakdown of the high level details of the corpus. We found 10.85 million articles (more accurately "pages"), containing a total of 3.92 million HTML tables, where 17.3% of the articles contained at least one table.

In Figure 2, we plot the distributions of (a), tables per article, (b) number of tables for increasing numbers of rows/-columns, and (c) number of internal/external links per table. All distributions are plotted in log/log scale, where we see long-tailed distributions for all such dimensions. Furthermore, we make the following observations:

- The article[7] with the largest number of well-formed tables contains 623 (most of them nested inner-tables).
- Considering articles with at least one table, there are 1.66 tables per article.
- The maximum number of detected rows in a table is 250, commonly found in List_of_* articles (likely due to a Wikipedia formatting constraint). The average number of rows per table is 12.44.
- The maximum number of columns in a table[8] is 250 (due to an erroneous colspan for a caption in a table with 3 columns). The average number of columns per table is 5.55.
- The highest number of internal links in a single table is 2,774, and 594 for external links. The averages are 1.93 and 0.35 for internal and external links, respectively. Internal links are important for us since they ensure that we can map cell entries to Wikipedia articles (and thus to DBPEDIA entities).
- 19.4% of tables do not contain column headers. 79.9% contain headers only in the first row, 7.4% contain headers in the second row, and the remaining tables contain captions in further rows. 5.5% of tables contain non-empty embedded captions.

We thus view this corpus of tables as a rich source of structured data that can be exploited for information extraction and ultimately for triplification, with many tables containing a high number of internal wiki-links (as per the bottom plot in Figure 2), which can be used for entity disambiguation. After filtering toc, infobox, small and ill-formed tables, we end up considering 29.0% of all Wikipedia tables for our extraction: 1.14 million tables in total.

[6] `http://nekohtml.sourceforge.net/`

[7] `http://en.wikipedia.org/wiki/Winners_and_runners-up_in_the_legislative_ elections_of_Nepal_1994_and_1999`

[8] `http://en.wikipedia.org/wiki/2007-08_QMJHL_season`

# 4. MINING RDF FROM WIKITABLES

To extract RDF from these Wikitables, we rely on a reference knowledge-base, where we use DBPEDIA for the purposes of this paper. We extract internal links present in cells and map them directly to DBPEDIA entity URIs. We then perform lookups on DBPEDIA to find relationships that exist between entities on the same row of the table. These relationships are then proposed as candidates between entities in cells of analogous columns on other rows.

## 4.1 Reference Knowledge-base

We use English-language data from DBPEDIA v3.8, describing 9.4 million entities. The overall corpus consists of 465 million unique RDF triples, and contained 57,985 unique RDF relations (i.e., RDF predicates), 48,293 of which were in the DBPEDIA property namespace, 1,397 of which were in the curated DBPEDIA ontology namespace, and 28 of which were from external vocabularies.[9]

## 4.2 Entity/Resource Extraction

In Section 3, we described how we extract a set of tables from Wikipedia, where each table is represented as an $m \times n$ matrix $M_T$ and where each cell of the matrix $M_T(i,j)$ (for $i \leq m$, $j \leq n$) can contain a variety of content. However, we are primarily interested in internal wiki-links present in the cells since they can be directly mapped to DBPEDIA entities. We represent the set of wiki-link URLs in a cell as $W_T(i,j)$, which excludes superscript reference links, links with prefix Image: or File:, and external links. We also strip fragment identifiers from URLs (i.e., strings following a hash).[10]

For each $w \in W_T(i,j)$, we map the corresponding Wikipedia URL to a DBPEDIA entity URI by following redirects and replacing the namespace http://en.wikipedia.org/wiki/ with http://dbpedia.org/resource/; for optimisation reasons, we cache redirects. We additionally filter entities corresponding to DBPEDIA categories and list pages. We denote

[9] We also found noise where 8,267 DBPEDIA entity URIs referring to Wikipedia templates appeared as predicates.

[10] Typically these are references to sections or to footnotes, but occasionally they may refer to a sub-topic in the article. However, DBpedia does not have corresponding URIs for the entities referred to by these sub-topics.

by $E_T(i,j)$ the resulting set of DBPEDIA entity URIs extracted for wiki-links $W_T(i,j)$ for table cell $M_T(i,j)$.

## 4.3 Discovering Relations

We aim to discover two types of relations: between entities on the same row of a table and between entities in the table and the protagonist of the article.

To discover relations within tables, we query the DBPEDIA knowledge base for existing relationships between entities in different cells of the same row. We look for relations between all pairs on the same row $i$ but in different cells: $\{(e_{i,j}, e_{i,k}) \mid e_{i,j} \in E_T(i,j), e_{i,k} \in E_T(i,k), 1 \leq i \leq m, 1 \leq j < k \leq n\}$. Any relations found for $(e_{i,j}, e_{i,k})$ are suggested as candidates for relating $(e_{h,j}, e_{h,k})$ for $1 \leq h \leq m$, $h \neq i$.

To discover relations from entities in the table and $p$ the protagonist entity of the article, we query the knowledge-base for pairs $\{(e_{i,j}, p) \mid e_{i,j} \in E_T(i,j), 1 \leq i \leq m, 1 \leq j \leq n\}$. Any relations found for $(e_{i,j}, p)$ are suggested as candidates for relating $(e_{h,j}, p)$ for $1 \leq h \leq m$, $h \neq i$.

We query the DBPEDIA knowledge-base for existing relationships that hold in either direction for each such pair. We run these queries over local indexes of DBPEDIA data with in-memory caching to efficiently support repeated queries caused by colspans. Though we avoid using a SPARQL engine for performance reasons, the lookups for a pair $(e1, e2)$ would be equivalent to the following query:

```
SELECT DISTINCT ?p1 ?p2
WHERE { { <e1> ?p1 <e2> } UNION { <e2> ?p2 <e1> } }
```

The `UNION` clause in SPARQL is used to denote a disjunctive query. The terms `<e1>` and `<e2>` are instantiated with the DBPEDIA URIs of the entities in question.

**Example 4.1.** With respect to relations within tables, if we consider some example cells from row 3 of table $T$ in Figure 1, we have:

$$E_T(3,1) = \emptyset,$$
$$E_T(3,2) = \{\texttt{dbr:Belgium}\},$$
$$E_T(3,3) = \{\texttt{dbr:Defender}\},$$
$$E_T(3,4) = \{\texttt{dbr:Toby\_Alderweireld}, \texttt{dbr:Vice\_Captain}\}.$$

If we query DBPEDIA indexes looking for relationships in this row between, for example, columns 2 and 4, we could find `dbo:birthPlace` from `dbr:Toby_Alderweireld` in $E_T(3,4)$ to `dbr:Belgium` in $E_T(3,2)$. We can suggest that this relationship may hold, e.g., from entities in $E_T(2,4)$ to $E_T(2,2)$, and so forth for all other non-header rows in the table.

If we query DBPEDIA for existing relations between the entity `dbr:Toby_Alderweireld` in $E_T(3,4)$ to the article entity `dbr:AFC_Ajax`, we will find `dbp:clubs` and `dbo:team`. We consider these as candidate relations potentially holding between `dbr:AFC_Ajax` and other entities in column 4.

Of course, this process can be imprecise. We will discuss this further in Section 5. □

## 4.4 Triple Extraction

We extract all candidate relationships found for all Wikitables as RDF triples:

**Example 4.2.** Consider applying the `dbo:birthPlace` candidate relation found in Example 4.1 to row 2 (from $E_T(2,4)$ to $E_T(2,2)$). The resulting RDF triple is then:

```
dbr:Ricardo_van_Rhijn dbo:birthPlace dbr:Netherlands .
```

representing the fact that Ricardo van Rhijn was born in the Netherlands. □

Based on preliminary evaluation of the extraction process, we chose to ignore reflexive triples and triples with the predicate `dbo:wikiPageDisambiguates`, which very often pertained to incorrect facts.

Though we do not wish to focus on computational performance in this paper, we can make some high-level remarks about the general scalability of our approach. As stated previously, we use local indexes of the DBPEDIA knowledge-base for answering queries, and for each pair, we perform two atomic on-disk lookups for relations in either direction. However, given that tables can potentially contain hundreds of entities, and that the number of entity-pairs to consider is quadratic for a given row, each table may require a large amount of lookups for relations.

However, with respect to scalability of the global processing, our problem can be effectively partitioned and parallelised on a per-table basis. For example, given a cluster of shared-nothing commodity servers, if we make the full index for the reference knowledge-base available to each machine (in our scenario, a 7.7GB file), individual tables can then be assigned arbitrarily to each machine, and the extraction of triples run in an embarassingly parallel manner. We adopt this approach and using eight machines (ca. 2005) with 4GB of RAM, 160GB SATA hard-drives, 2.2GHz single-core processors, assigning an even work-load of input Wikipedia articles to each, the full process of extracting and normalising Wikitables from the articles and computing the full set of candidate triples took approximately 12 days.[11]

We extracted a total of 53.2 million candidate RDF triples, of which 37.3 million were unique, of which 34.9 million in turn were not already in DBPEDIA. These candidate triples are assigned features during extraction that serve as input to the classification process described in the next section.

# 5. LEARNING RDF TRIPLES

As alluded to before, many of the triples we extract in the previous phase are likely to be incorrect for a variety of reasons. We illustrate this with two further brief examples.

**Example 5.1.** In the table of Figure 1, we do not distinguish the entities Toby Alderweireld and *vice captain*, which appear in the same cell. Hence, when multiple entities appear in one cell, we may extract incorrect triples, such as:

```
dbr:Vice_Captain dbo:team dbr:AFC_Ajax .
```

To illustrate another common case we encountered: in our reference knowledge-base, the entity Derk Boerrigter is related to the protagonist AFC Ajax through the relation `dbp:youthclubs`. However, this relation would not hold between other players in the same column and AFC Ajax even though said candidate triples will have been produced in the previous phase: just because a relation holds for (at least) one row does not mean it *must* hold for others. □

[11] An alternative route for optimisation could be to build a compressed in-memory index over the reference knowledge-base or to use a solid-state disk, but this was not feasible for our hardware.

This section thus evaluates a variety of machine-learning methods with respect to identifying correct triples from our set of raw extracted triples. For this phase, a set of features can be associated with extracted triples to help determine if the triple is likely to be (in)correct. For example, we can consider the number of rows for which a relation holds versus the total number of rows in a table (e.g., $\frac{1}{6}$ in the case of the `dbp:youthclubs` relation mentioned in the previous example), or the presence of multiple entities in a cell (cf. Example 5.1), or string matching between a column header and a predicate label (e.g., `dbp:position` for the **Position** header in Figure 1). Along these lines, we now discuss a set of features we associate with extracted triples, which can be used by machine learning methods (described later in the section) for classification as correct/incorrect.

## 5.1 Features

In previous work, the classification problem was tackled primarily by ranking each relation according to the number of times it held in the knowledge-base between entities in those two columns. However, we feel that there are many factors—such as the structure of the table, the nature of the cell content, textual overlap with one of the column headers, etc.—that provide important signals for determining the accuracy of extracted triples. Furthermore, like Limaye et al. [12], we believe that statistics about the predicate in the reference knowledge-base serve as useful input; e.g., if a predicate is generally found to follow a one-to-one relation (e.g., `dbp:captain`), then it is unlikely to be a good relation for linking an article (e.g., `dbr:AFC_Ajax`) to multiple entities in a table column (e.g., **Players**).

The full set of features we generate is listed in Table 2, broken down by article features, table features, column features (i.e., features specific to the subject/object column from which the triple was extracted), predicate features (i.e., features specific to the predicate of the extracted triple), cell features (i.e., features specific to the subject and object cells from which the triple was extracted), predicate/column features (features that are a function of the predicate and subject/object columns) and triple features. Feature 38 tracks if the triple exists in DBPEDIA for reference only and is never used for learning. We include a wide range of features, with the goal of applying feature selection at a later stage.

Given that most of the features are self-explanatory, we give a brief explanation for non-trivial entries:

**15** The number of pairs of the form $(e_{i,s}, e_{i,o})$ for $s$ the subject column, $o$ the object column and $h < i \leq m$

**16** As per feature 15, but only unique pairs (for the given table) are counted

**17–20** All predicate features are normalised as a real value in the range $(0, 1]$ (counts are divided by the maximum such value for all predicates)

**24–25** The amount of prose text in the cells from which the subject and object of a triple is extracted, where long text is indicative of possible noise or hidden context

**26–27** A boolean value indicating the presence of, e.g., newlines, bullets or other HTML formatting tags in the source cells

**28–29** The string similarity, measured as the closer value given by the Jaro–Winkler distance and the Sørensen–Dice coefficient, between the predicate label and the header label for the subject/object column

**31** For how many rows there exists a relation in the KB with the given predicate from the subject column to the object column

**33** For how many pairs in feature 15 there exists a relation in the KB with the given predicate

**35** For how many unique pairs in feature 16 there exists a relation in the KB with the given predicate

Table 2: Full list of features

| |
|---|
| ARTICLE FEATURES |
| (1) № of tables |
| TABLE FEATURES |
| (2) table id in article |
| (3) № of rows |
| (4) № of columns |
| (5) ratio: (3)/(4) |
| (6) total relations extracted |
| COLUMN FEATURES |
| (7) subject column id |
| (8) object column id |
| (9&10) № of entities in s&o cols. |
| (11) ratio: (9)/(10) |
| (12&13) № of unique entities in s&o cols. |
| (14) ratio: (12)/(13) |
| (15) potential relations |
| (16) unique potential relations |
| PREDICATE FEATURES |
| (17) normalised triple count |
| (18) normalised unique subject count |
| (19) normalised unique object count |
| (20) ratio (18)/(19) |
| CELL FEATURES |
| (21&22) number of entities in s&o cells |
| (23) ratio (21)/(22) |
| (24&25) string length in s&o cells |
| (26&27) formatting present in s&o cells |
| PREDICATE/COLUMN FEATURES |
| (28&29) string sim. for pred and s&o header |
| (30) maximum between (28) and (29) |
| (31) № of rows where relation holds |
| (32) ratio: (31)/(3) |
| (33) № of potential relations held |
| (34) ratio: (33)/(15) |
| (35) № of unique potential relations held |
| (36) ratio: (35)/(16) |
| TRIPLE FEATURES |
| (37) from article or body relation |
| *(38) already exists in* DBPEDIA |

With respect to features 31, 33 and 35; which are similar with respect to measuring ratios of rows/relations for which a predicate exists in the KB; we include all three versions since we found that certain tables in Wikipedia can exhibit very different values for these features due to duplicate entities existing in individual cells (often due to spans).[12]

## 5.2 Machine Learning Models

We use machine learning models to classify (in)correct triples according to these features. For evaluation, we select five classifiers listed by Witten et al. [23] capturing a variety of different high-level approaches. We select one probabilistic classifier: NAÏVE BAYES; two based on trees: BAGGING DECISION TREES and RANDOM FOREST; and two based on functions: SUPPORT VECTOR MACHINES (SVM) and SIMPLE-LOGISTIC. We use all such methods to learn a classification model using 10-fold cross-validation over a gold standard of manually annotated triples (described in the next sub-section). The resulting models can then be used for the binary classification of triples (correct/incorrect) according to its supporting features. Experiments are run using the WEKA machine learning framework.[13] Full details of these machine learning techniques are out-of-scope (see, e.g., [13, 23]), here we provide a brief overview:

**Naïve Bayes** is a simple probabilistic classifier. The classification is assigned based on the probabilistic distribution of the training set. We highlight that this method (naïvely) assumes that attributes are independent, which is certainly not true in our case, but we can still apply and test the model.

**Bagging Decision Trees** consists of an ensemble of decision trees (trees of nodes that branch depending on the value of a certain feature) for each class, where the final classification decision for each instance is made based on a form of voting of the committee of classifiers.

**Random Forest** is another ensemble classifier that consists of multiple decision trees. The class is assigned according to the mode of the classes output by individual decision trees.

**Support Vector Machine** represents each feature tuple from the training data as a point in Euclidean space and searches for a good hyperplane division between the classes, which is then used for binary classification. We use SVM with a polynomial kernel.

**Simple-Logistic** uses logistic regression models, and is appropriate for classification in domains with (continuous) numeric attributes.

## 5.3 Gold Standard

We require a gold standard to train and evaluate these models. For this, we randomly selected 750 unique triples from the total set of 37.3 million triples extracted in the previous phase. Three judges (authors on this paper) then labelled the 750 triples as being *correct*, *incorrect* or *unknown*. The information available for each triple were the subject, predicate and object URIs, as well as a link to the original Wikipedia article containing the source table and a number identifying which table in the article was the source. Triples were generally validated by visiting the Wikipedia article in question to see the original table, as well as Web searches for the entities in question. We did not pre-agree on any judging strategies, where interpretation of the validity of triples was left to the discretion of individual judges.

Table 3: Inter-rater consensus for manually labelled triples

| | | |
|---|---|---|
| All *correct* | 234 | 31.2% |
| Some *correct*, Rest *unknown* | 27 | 3.6% |
| **Positive consensus** | **261** | **34.8%** |
| All *incorrect* | 195 | 26.0% |
| Some *incorrect*, Rest *unknown* | 48 | 6.4% |
| **Negative consensus** | **243** | **32.4%** |
| **Some *correct* and some *incorrect*** | **246** | **32.8%** |

In terms of inter-rater agreement for the three judges, we computed a Fleiss' $\kappa$ coefficient of 0.45 (0 indicates no agreement, 1 indicates perfect agreement), which by convention is considered as "moderate agreement". Looking through examples of disagreement, some common themes emerged. In particular, the relations of DBPEDIA are often not well defined and their meaning often has a subjective dimension (for example, `dbr:Pulp_Fiction dbo:starring dbr:Quentin_Tarantino` when he arguably only had a cameo appearance). Another recurring issue was that of temporality: for example, would stating that `dbr:Bill_Clinton` has the relation `dbp:president` to `dbr:United_States` be correct or incorrect? These questions are subjective and depend on the precise semantics for the predicate and for which DBPEDIA provides no definitive intensional answer. Table 3 summarises the consensus between raters. For the gold standard, we filter 246 examples where there were conflicting labels from different judges, leaving 504 triples.

From these results, we can also get some direct insights into the accuracy of the raw candidate triples. Based on the consensus labels, 51.8% of triples are considered correct and 48.2% considered incorrect without any further classification. However, 112 of the 504 triples appear in DBPEDIA, where the analogous results filtering these triples would be 39.6% and 60.4% respectively.[14] Next we use machine learning methods to further boost accuracy by classifying these raw extracted triples as correct/incorrect.

## 5.4 Classification Evaluation

To train and evaluate the five classifiers, we apply 10-fold cross-validation over the 504 triples with non-conflicting labels: we randomly generate 10 non-overlapping test sets with ~54 examples each, while the remaining ~450 examples are used for training purposes in each run. As a baseline, we also compare three simple rule-based models relying on features 32, 34 and 36 respectively (i.e., ratios of rows, relations and unique relations in a table for which a given predicate is found to hold), where extracted triples with a score above a threshold for the given feature are classified as positive and triples below the threshold as negative.

Given that we use many features, and that some may not be deemed relevant to the machine learning process, we

[12] See **http://en.wikipedia.org/wiki/KJEE** for such an example. The table contains 11 rows. For columns **Venue** and **City**, there exists 18 potential relations and 4 unique potential relations.

[13] **http://www.cs.waikato.ac.nz/ml/weka/**

[14] These triples are left in to provide more positive examples. Interestingly, 7 out of the 112 DBPEDIA triples were marked as incorrect (6.3%).

Table 4: Classification performance for each approach with best figures for each metric underlined

| Schema | Acc. | Pre. | Rec. | $F_1$ | Output |
|---|---|---|---|---|---|
| FEATURE 32 | 65.41 | 50.77 | 74.16 | 60.27 | 15,415,810 |
| FEATURE 34 | 70.18 | 58.08 | 78.65 | 66.81 | 3,864,653 |
| FEATURE 36 | 67.59 | 64.23 | 70.46 | 67.20 | 4,263,470 |
| NAÏVE BAYES | 75.75 | 88.85 | 71.30 | 79.11 | 3,902,861 |
| B.D. TREES | 78.13 | 81.54 | 77.37 | 79.40 | 7,871,344 |
| RAND. FOREST | 76.34 | 76.15 | 77.65 | 76.89 | 8,979,392 |
| SVM | 72.56 | 72.43 | 75.77 | 74.06 | 15,320,590 |
| SIMPLELOGISTIC | 78.53 | 79.62 | 79.01 | 79.31 | 6,376,427 |

investigated using standard "feature selection" techniques, using a greedy best-first algorithm to search for a set of features that optimises accuracy (i.e., ratio of correct true positives and true negatives) for each model. However, we found that the feature selection process had little effect on accuracy; hence we opted not to use feature selection.

Next, for the model selection, we applied a cost–benefit analysis to determine the optimal decision threshold for each classifier (aka. calibration), i.e., we maximise accuracy by varying the thresholds of each classifier below which an example is predicted for the −1 (negative) class. Considering these optimised thresholds, Table 4 compares the accuracy, recall, precision and $F_1$-measure of the eight classifiers, where the latter three metrics are given as weighted averages over the positive and negative classes. We also ran the trained models over the raw extracted triples and count the number of unique novel triples output with a positive classification (from a possible 34.9 million unique triples not appearing in DBPEDIA, of which we would expect approx. 13.8 million (39.6%) to be correct).

We first see that the single-feature baseline models are outperformed by the multi-feature models in terms of accuracy, precision and $F_1$ measures. Although FEATURE 32 classifies the most triples as correct, it does so at the cost of much lower precision. Also we see that the number of output triples can be significantly lower than would be expected based on the corresponding recall figures. We believe that this disparity is due to 40.3% of the positive examples used in the gold standard training data coming from DBPEDIA; such positive examples are removed from the 34.9 million triples classified in the output. The selected thresholds for the training data may thus be too selective for the real-world data without these examples.

Amongst the other multi-feature models, we see that there is a clear trade-off in terms of precision versus recall. Thus it is difficult to identify a "clear" winner. For example, the highest precision (88.85%) is achieved by NAÏVE BAYES, but this comes at the cost of recall and output triples captured. In terms of combined measures such as accuracy and $F_1$ measure, BAGGING DECISION TREES is close to the metrics for SIMPLELOGISTIC but outputs significantly more positive triples. On the other hand, SVM outputs nearly double the number of output triples that BAGGING DECISION TREES does, but at a lower precision. Hence it would seem that BAGGING DECISION TREES classifying 7.9 million unique novel output triples with an estimated 81.5% precision is amongst the most favourable results.

# 6. CONCLUSION

Wikipedia tables contain rich encyclopaedic knowledge but their content cannot be directly queried against. Herein we proposed methods to extract factual content from over one million Wikipedia tables. Following existing works, we use an existing Linked Data knowledge-base as a reference to guide the extraction process and to help automatically piece together the semantics of the tables.

More precisely, we look for existing relationships in the knowledge-base between entities on the same row of a table and extrapolate them as candidate relationships between entities in analogous columns on different rows of that table. We also extract relations from entities in the same column of a table to the protagonist of the article in which the table is found. Using DBPEDIA as a reference knowledge-base, we successfully mined 34.9 million unique and novel triples from 1.1 million Wikipedia tables with a precision of 40% without any further classification.

We associate each extracted triple with a rich set of features and investigate a variety of machine-learning methods to identify triples as correct or incorrect. Using a manually-labelled random-sample of extracted triples as a gold standard, we found that different classifiers produced different trade-offs with respect to precision/recall. Arguably the best result was given by the BAGGING DECISION TREES ensemble classifier, with which we mined 7.9 million unique novel triples at an estimated 78.1% accuracy, 81.5% precision, 77.4% recall and 79.4% $F_1$ measure.

Other works have also tackled relation extraction from tables using Linked Data knowledge-bases. Limaye et al. [12] report accuracy figures of 52–69% for this task over a selection of manually labelled hand-picked tables. In very recent work, Mulwad et al. [16] report $F_1$-scores of between 89–97% for this task over a similar evaluation dataset. However, the results from these papers are not directly comparable with ours since, for example, we apply extraction over all well-formed Wikitables and randomly sample our test-set (vs. using around 200 manually selected tables), we extracted relations on a per-row basis (vs. selecting the top-$k$ relations for each pair of columns), we use wiki-links to map to entities in our knowledge-base (vs. using string matching and search methods), and so forth.

To the best of our knowledge, our work is the first to look at extracting the factual content of Wikitables at full-scale and is also the first to present end-to-end results for extracting semantic triples from a large corpus of Web tables (albeit only for the easier case of Wikitables).

## *Future work*

We identify three major directions in which our work can be extended, generalised, and/or improved:

1. With respect to improving our extraction methods, we do not yet exploit the semantics of the reference knowledge-base, such as the types of entities, the domain or range of properties, the hierarchies of classes, etc. Considering such semantics could help to improve our precision and recall measures further, by, for example, splitting columns that contain multiple entities in each cell according to the type of those entities (e.g., player/position), or by rejecting relationships where the domain/range definitions do not match.

2. Our approach could be generalised to use other Linked Data knowledge-bases of encyclopaedic content—such as YAGO2 [10] or FREEBASE [3]—as an alternative to DBPEDIA. Such knowledge-bases have already been investigated by Limaye et al. [12] and Mulwad et al. [16]. Such a generalisation would require a method for mapping entities referenced in Wikipedia tables to native identifiers in the reference data-set: DBPEDIA offers links to both YAGO2 and FREEBASE that could be used for this purpose. Our approach could also take advantage of multiple knowledge-bases at once by taking the union of candidate triples produced for each such reference collection.

3. Most ambitiously, our method could potentially be generalised to Web tables in the broader sense [12, 16]. Again, a method for matching entities in the tables with the reference knowledge-base would be required, where some standard NER technique(s) could be used. For example, the DBPEDIA SPOTLIGHT tool [15] already offers entity recognition for DBPEDIA entities.

Source code, data, models and a demonstrator are available from **http://emunoz.org/wikitables/**.

**Acknowledgements:** *This work was supported in part by Fujitsu (Ireland) Ltd., by the Millennium Nucleus Center for Semantic Web Research under Grant NC120004, and by Science Foundation Ireland (SFI) under Grant Number SFI/12/RC/2289.*

## 7. REFERENCES

[1] M. Arenas, A. Bertails, E. Prud'hommeaux, and J. Sequeda. A Direct Mapping of Relational Data to RDF. W3C Recommendation, September 2012.

[2] C. Bizer, J. Lehmann, G. Kobilarov, S. Auer, C. Becker, R. Cyganiak, and S. Hellmann. DBpedia - a crystallization point for the Web of Data. *J. Web Sem.*, 7(3):154–165, 2009.

[3] K. D. Bollacker, C. Evans, P. Paritosh, T. Sturge, and J. Taylor. Freebase: a collaboratively created graph database for structuring human knowledge. In J. T.-L. Wang, editor, *SIGMOD Conference*, pages 1247–1250. ACM, 2008.

[4] M. J. Cafarella, A. Y. Halevy, D. Z. Wang, E. Wu, and Y. Zhang. WebTables: exploring the power of tables on the Web. *PVLDB*, 1(1):538–549, 2008.

[5] E. Crestan and P. Pantel. A fine-grained taxonomy of tables on the Web. In J. Huang, N. Koudas, G. J. F. Jones, X. Wu, K. Collins-Thompson, and A. An, editors, *CIKM*, pages 1405–1408. ACM, 2010.

[6] E. Crestan and P. Pantel. Web-scale table census and classification. In I. King, W. Nejdl, and H. Li, editors, *WSDM*, pages 545–554. ACM, 2011.

[7] S. Das, S. Sundara, and R. Cyganiak. R2RML: RDB to RDF Mapping Language. W3C Recommendation, September 2012.

[8] L. Ding, D. DiFranzo, A. Graves, J. Michaelis, X. Li, D. L. McGuinness, and J. Hendler. Data-gov Wiki: Towards Linking Government Data. In *AAAI Spring Symposium: Linked Data Meets Artificial Intelligence*. AAAI, 2010.

[9] S. Harris and A. Seaborne. SPARQL 1.1 Query Language. W3C Recommendation, March 2013.

[10] J. Hoffart, F. M. Suchanek, K. Berberich, and G. Weikum. YAGO2: A spatially and temporally enhanced knowledge base from Wikipedia. *Artif. Intell.*, 194:28–61, 2013.

[11] M. Hurst. Layout and language: Challenges for table understanding on the Web. In *Workshop on Web Document Analysis (WDA)*, pages 27–30, 2001.

[12] G. Limaye, S. Sarawagi, and S. Chakrabarti. Annotating and searching Web tables using entities, types and relationships. In *PVLDB*, 2010.

[13] B. Liu. *Web Data Mining: Exploring Hyperlinks, Contents, and Usage Data*. Data-Centric Systems and Applications. Springer, 2011.

[14] F. Manola and E. Miller. RDF Primer. W3C Recommendation, February 2004.

[15] P. N. Mendes, M. Jakob, A. García-Silva, and C. Bizer. DBpedia spotlight: shedding light on the web of documents. In *I-SEMANTICS*, pages 1–8, 2011.

[16] V. Mulwad, T. Finin, and A. Joshi. Semantic message passing for generating Linked Data from tables. In *ISWC*, pages 363–378, 2013.

[17] V. Mulwad, T. Finin, Z. Syed, and A. Joshi. T2LD: Interpreting and Representing Tables as Linked Data. In *ISWC Posters&Demos*, 2010.

[18] E. Muñoz, A. Hogan, and A. Mileo. Triplifying Wikipedia's Tables. In *Linked Data for Information Extraction (LD4IE) Workshop, ISWC*. CEUR, 2013.

[19] A. Pivk, P. Cimiano, Y. Sure, M. Gams, V. Rajkovic, and R. Studer. Transforming arbitrary tables into logical form with TARTAR. *Data Knowl. Eng.*, 60(3):567–595, 2007.

[20] Z. Syed, T. Finin, V. Mulwad, and A. Joshi. Exploiting a Web of Semantic Data for Interpreting Tables. In *WebSci10*, Raleigh NC, USA, April 26–27th 2010.

[21] P. Venetis, A. Halevy, J. Madhavan, M. Paşca, W. Shen, F. Wu, G. Miao, and C. Wu. Recovering semantics of tables on the Web. *PVLDB*, 4(9):528–538, June 2011.

[22] Y. Wang and J. Hu. A machine learning based approach for table detection on the web. In *WWW*, pages 242–250, New York, NY, USA, 2002. ACM.

[23] I. H. Witten, E. Frank, and M. A. Hall. *Data Mining: Practical Machine Learning Tools and Techniques, Third Edition*. Data Mining, the Morgan Kaufmann Ser. in Data Management Systems Series. Elsevier Science, 2011.

[24] M. Yoshida, K. Torisawa, and J. Tsujii. A method to integrate tables of the World Wide Web. In *Workshop on Web Document Analysis (WDA)*, pages 31–34, 2001.

[25] S. Zwicklbauer, C. Einsiedler, M. Granitzer, and C. Seifert. Towards disambiguating Web tables. In *ISWC (P&D)*, pages 205–208, 2013.

# Knowledge-based Graph Document Modeling

Michael Schuhmacher
Data and Web Science Research Group
University of Mannheim, Germany
michael@informatik.uni-mannheim.de

Simone Paolo Ponzetto
Data and Web Science Research Group
University of Mannheim, Germany
simone@informatik.uni-mannheim.de

## ABSTRACT

We propose a graph-based semantic model for representing document content. Our method relies on the use of a semantic network, namely the DBpedia knowledge base, for acquiring fine-grained information about entities and their semantic relations, thus resulting in a knowledge-rich document model. We demonstrate the benefits of these semantic representations in two tasks: entity ranking and computing document semantic similarity. To this end, we couple DBpedia's structure with an information-theoretic measure of concept association, based on its explicit semantic relations, and compute semantic similarity using a Graph Edit Distance based measure, which finds the optimal matching between the documents' entities using the Hungarian method. Experimental results show that our general model outperforms baselines built on top of traditional methods, and achieves a performance close to that of highly specialized methods that have been tuned to these specific tasks.

## Categories and Subject Descriptors

H.3.1 [**Information Storage and Retrieval**]: Content Analysis and Indexing; I.2.4 [**Artificial Intelligence**]: Semantic Networks; I.2.7 [**Artificial Intelligence**]: Natural Language Processing

## Keywords

Document modeling; Semantic network mining; DBpedia; Entity relatedness; Document semantic similarity.

## 1. INTRODUCTION

Recent years have seen a great deal of work on developing wide-coverage semantic technologies and methods embedding semantic models within a wide spectrum of applications, crucially including end-user applications like, for instance, question answering [16, 47], document search [14] and web-search results clustering [34]. Complementary to this trend, many research efforts have concentrated on the automatic acquisition of machine-readable knowledge on a large scale by mining large repositories of textual data such as the Web [2, 9] (inter alia), and exploiting collaboratively-constructed resources [40, 36, 21, 25]. As a result of this, recent years have seen a remarkable renaissance of knowledge-rich approaches for many different Natural Language Processing (NLP) and Information Retrieval (IR) tasks [27].

But while recent research trends indicate that semantic information and knowledge-rich approaches can be used effectively for high-end IR and NLP tasks, much still remains to be done in order to effectively exploit these rich models and further advance the state of the art in these fields. Most of the approaches which draw upon document representations, in fact, rely solely on morpho-syntactic information by means of 'flat' meaning representations like vector space models [44]. Although more sophisticated models have been proposed – including conceptual [17] and grounded [8] vector spaces – these still do not exploit the relational knowledge and network structure encoded within wide-coverage knowledge bases such as YAGO [25] or DBpedia [6].

In this paper, we aim at overcoming these issues by means of a knowledge-rich method to represent documents in the Web of Linked Data. Key to our approach is the combination of a fine-grained relation vocabulary with information-theoretic measures of concept associativity to produce a graph-based interpretation of texts leveraging large amounts of structured knowledge, i.e., disambiguated entities and explicit semantic relations, encoded within DBpedia. Our contributions are as follows:

- We propose a graph-based document model and present a method to produce structured representations of texts that combine disambiguated entities with fine-grained semantic relations;
- We present a variety of information-theoretic measures to weight different semantic relations within an ontology, and automatically quantify their degree of relevance with respect to the concepts they connect. Edges in the semantic graphs are thus weighted so as to capture the degree of associativity between concepts, as well as their different levels of specificity;
- We evaluate our model using two highly relevant tasks, namely entity ranking and computing document similarity. We show that our approach not only outperforms standard baselines relying on traditional, i.e., 'flat', document representations, but also produces results close to those of highly specialized methods that have been particularly tuned to the respective tasks.


*WSDM'14*, February 24–28, 2014, New York, New York, USA.
Copyright 2014 ACM 978-1-4503-2351-2/14/02 ...$15.00.
http://dx.doi.org/10.1145/2556195.2556250.

- We develop a new measure, based on graph edit distance techniques, in order to compute document similarity using our semantic graphs. Our approach views computing semantic distances within an ontology as a concept matching problem, and uses the Hungarian method for solving this combinatorial optimization problem.

As a result of this, we are able to provide a complete framework where documents are semantified by linking them to a reference knowledge base, and subgraphs of the knowledge resource are used for complex language understanding tasks like entity ranking and document semantic similarity. Results on entity ranking show that our weighting scheme helps us better estimate entity relatedness when compared with using simple, unweighted paths. Moreover, by complementing large amounts of knowledge with structured text representations we are able to achieve a robust performance on the task of computing document semantic similarity, thus competing with 'flat' approaches based on either word or conceptual vector spaces, while at the same time providing a general, *de-facto* parameter-free model.

# 2. MODELING DOCUMENT CONTENT WITH ONTOLOGY-BASED GRAPHS

We present our method to generate structured representations of textual content using DBpedia as the backend ontology. To this end, we opt for graph-based methods since: (i) they are general in nature, and can be used with *any* knowledge graph, i.e., a knowledge resource that can be viewed as a graph, regardless of its specific vocabulary; (ii) they have been shown to be effective for language understanding tasks when combined with labeled and unlabeled resources (cf., e.g., [36, 26]). In the following, we first briefly introduce DBpedia, the resource used in our methodology, in Section 2.1. Sections 2.2 through 2.3 illustrate instead the main phases of our approach.

## 2.1 DBpedia

Our approach relies on the information and structure encoded within an underlying knowledge base. In this work, we opt for DBpedia [6], since it provides a wide-coverage knowledge base with many (i.e., more than 1000) fine-grained explicit semantic relations between entities. However, our method can be also used with any other lexical or ontological resource, e.g. YAGO [25], provided it can be cast as a knowledge graph containing disambiguated entities and explicit semantic relations.

DBpedia is a community effort to extract structured information from Wikipedia and make this information available on the Web as a full-fledged ontology. The key idea behind DBpedia is to parse *infoboxes*, namely property-summarizing tables found within Wikipedia pages, in order to automatically acquire properties and relations about a large amount of entities. These are further embedded within an ontology based on Semantic Web formalisms like: i) representing data on the basis of the best practices of *linked data* [5]; ii) encoding semantic relations using the resource description framework (RDF), a generic graph-based data model for describing objects and their relationships. In the following, we refer to RDF triples in DBpedia consisting of a subject, predicate and object as a directed relation from *Subj* to *Obj*, connected by the labeled relation *Pred*.

Naturally, we can view DBpedia as a graph, whose nodes are entities and edges capture explicit semantic relations between them. For instance, an entity like "Bob Dylan" is connected in DBpedia to other entities by means of statements such as `db:Bob_Dylan rdf:type dbo:MusicalArtist` or `db:Bob_Dylan dbo:genre db:Folk_rock`, and so on[1]. We now show how we can use this structure to produce graph-based representations from an input consisting of sets of entities such as those mentioned in natural language texts.

## 2.2 Semantic graph construction

Let $C_{db}$ be the full set of DBpedia's concepts and entities[2] and $C$ an arbitrary subset of it, given as input – e.g., the set of entities mentioned within a document. In the first phase of our methodology, we create from the set of input entities a labeled, directed graph $G = (V, E)$ containing i) the entities themselves, ii) their semantic relations, as well as iii) any additional entity that is related to any of the input ones by means of some relation in the ontology. That is, $C \subseteq V \subseteq C_{db}$ and $E \subseteq V \times R \times V$, where $r \in R$ is a semantic relation found in DBpedia, e.g., `rdf:type`, `dbo:birthDate` or `dbp:genre` (we do not make any distinction between *A-box* and *T-box* statements, since we remain agnostic as to the specific vocabulary used by our underlying resource). Additionally, we want to associate a weight $w$ with each edge $(v_i, r, v_j) \in E$, in order to capture the degree of associativity between the source and target nodes – i.e., how strongly related the two corresponding entities are.

To produce our semantic graphs, we start with a set of input entities $C$ and create a labeled directed graph $G = (V, E)$ as follows: a) first, we define the set of nodes $V$ of $G$ to be made up of all input concepts, that is, we set $V := C$; b) next, we connect the nodes in $V$ based on the paths found between them in DBpedia. Nodes in $V$ are expanded into a graph by performing a depth-first search along the DBpedia graph and successively adding all outgoing relations[3] $r$, thus adding all simple directed paths $v, v_1, \ldots, v_k, v'$ of maximal length $L$ that connect them to $G$, i.e., $V := V \cup \{v_1, \ldots, v_k\}$, $E := E \cup \{(v, r_1, v_1), \ldots, (v_k, r_k, v')\}$. As a result, we obtain a sub-graph of DBpedia containing the initial concepts, together with all edges and intermediate concepts found along all paths of maximal length $L$ that connect them. In this work, we set $L = 2$ following a large body of evidence from previous related work [36, 28].

Figure 1 illustrates an example of a semantic graph generated from the set of entities { `db:Bob_Dylan`, `db:Monterey_Country_Fairgrounds`, `db:Mozambique_(Song)`, `db:Johnny_Cash` }, e.g. as found within the sentence "Dylan played Mozambique at Monterey right before Cash". Starting from these seed entities, we perform a depth-first search to add relevant intermediates concepts and relations to $G$ (e.g., `foaf:Person` or `db:Folk_music`). As a result of this, we obtain a semantically-rich graph: additional nodes and edges provide us with a rich structured context, in which the initial concepts are now connected by a variety of entities and explicit semantic relations.

[1]We abbreviate URI namespaces with common prefixes, see `http://prefix.cc` for details.

[2]Hereafter, we use *concept* and *entity* interchangeably to refer to resources of the knowledge base, i.e., DBpedia URIs.

[3]We filter out any administrative information and data using a list of stop-URIs provided by [28] and extended by us.

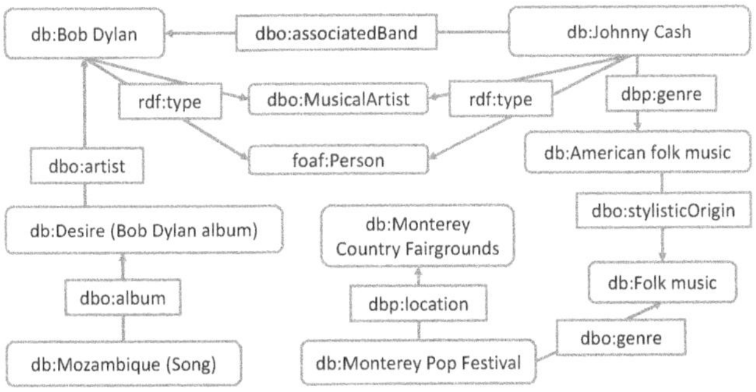


**Figure 1: Sample semantic graph.**

## 2.3 Semantic relation weighting

So far, our method simply connected a set of input entities by traversing the DBpedia graph – i.e., similar in spirit to graph-based approaches to Word Sense Disambiguation using lexical resources [36]. However, in contrast to lexical resources like WordNet, our backend ontology contains many different, fine-grained semantic relations: accordingly, not all relations are equally informative and questions arise about what kind of information to take into account when building the semantic graphs. For instance, in our example there exists multiple paths between the source nodes **db:Bob_Dylan** and **db:Johnny_Cash**, due to the typical high density of the DBpedia graph. Connecting paths, however, include highly informative relations (e.g., the two entities being linked directly via **dbo:associatedBand**), as well as generic ones (both being entities of **rdf:type foaf:Person**), which tend to apply to a very large amount of entities (i.e., all persons in DBpedia) and thus carry low discriminative power – e.g., in order to identify relations useful for computing semantic similarity (see Section 4). But while previous work [28] restricted the semantic relations used to build semantic graphs to a small, manually-selected set, we opt here instead for an automatic approach based on relation-specific edge weighting. This is because, while a manual approach ensures overall good quality, it does not scale and needs to be tuned for every knowledge base in turn. Consequently, we extend our semantic graphs by weighting their edges. Weights are meant to capture the degree of associativity between concepts in the graph – i.e., the degree of relevance of an edge (i.e., semantic relation) for the entities it connects. The key idea underlying our weighting is to reward, for a given source node, those edges and target nodes that are most specific to it. At the core of our edge weighting lies the notion of Information Content ($IC$):

$$IC_{X_{Pred}}(\omega_{Pred}) = -\log\left(P\left(\omega_{Pred}\right)\right) ,$$

where $P(\omega_{Pred})$ is the probability that the random variable $X_{Pred}$ describing the type of edge, i.e. a specific semantic relation, shows the outcome $\omega_{Pred}$. This measure makes the assumption that specificity is a good proxy for relevance – cf., for instance the **rdf:type** vs. **dbo:associatedBand** predicates. We can compute these $IC$ values for all types of predicates, as we have the full DBpedia graph available and can query for all potential realizations of the random variable $X_{Pred}$. In our example, an edge labeled with **rdf:type** will accordingly get an $IC$ which is comparably lower than, say, one labeled with **dbo:associatedBand**.

**Joint Information Content (jointIC).** While the Information Content of semantic relations provides us with a way to distinguish general vs. specific connections, it only covers the *a-priori* specificity of an edge, i.e., regardless of the entities it actually connects. However, as shown in Figure 1, the same type of edge, e.g. **rdf:type**, can lead to very general concepts with low discriminative power (**foaf:Person**), but also to very informative (because rare) ones, like **dbo:MusicalArtist**, which do, in fact, provide valuable information. We capture this by adding the conditional information content $IC(\omega_{Obj}|\omega_{Pred})$ to our weighting scheme, which accounts for the concept the predicate is pointing to, given that the edge has already been observed. Formally, given an edge $e = (Subj, Pred, Obj)$ we compute the information content of the joint probability distribution, $IC(\omega_{Pred}, \omega_{Obj})$, which we take as our weighting function:

$$w_{jointIC}(e) = IC(\omega_{Pred}) + IC(\omega_{Obj}|\omega_{Pred}) .$$

In our example, the **rdf:type** edge leading to **dbo:MusicalArtist** accordingly receives a much higher weight than that pointing to the far more generic **foaf:Person**.

**Combined Information Content (combIC).** Joint information content, although taking into account predicate and object specificity at the same time, can nevertheless penalize infrequent objects that occur with infrequent predicates – e.g., **db:American_folk_music** being overall very infrequent, but getting a high probability (and, hence, a low $IC$) when occurring conditional on **dbo:genre**. We propose to mitigate this problem by computing the joint information content while making an independence assumption between the predicated and the object. The resulting weights are then computed as the sum of the Information Content of the predicate and the object:

$$w_{combIC}(e) = IC(\omega_{Pred}) + IC(\omega_{Obj}) .$$

**Information Content and Pointwise Mutual Information (IC+PMI).** An alternative way to compute the strength of association between the predicate and the object is by means of Pointwise Mutual Information (PMI):

$$PMI(\omega_{Pred}, \omega_{Obj}) = \log \frac{P(\omega_{Pred}, \omega_{Obj})}{P(\omega_{Pred})\,P(\omega_{Obj})} .$$

PMI measures the mutual dependence between the two variable outcomes $\omega_{Pred}$ and $\omega_{Obj}$, and can thus be seen as a measure of how much deviation from independence there is between the two outcomes, i.e., the specific predicate and object found along a DBpedia graph edge. Our hunch here is to use PMI to find a middle ground between the assumption of full dependence (jointIC) or independence (combIC) between predicates and objects. We additionally combine PMI with the IC of the predicate, in order to bias our weights towards less frequent, and thus more informative, predicates:

$$w_{IC+PMI}(e) = IC(\omega_{Pred}) + PMI(\omega_{Pred}, \omega_{Obj}) .$$

# 3. GRAPH-BASED ENTITY RANKING

We present an extrinsic evaluation of the different weighting schemes we developed in order to build weighted semantic graphs from DBpedia. This is because semantic relation weighting makes a contribution of its own, and it can be

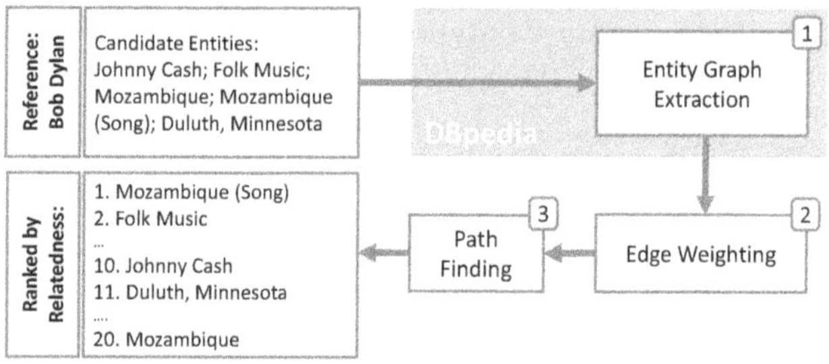


**Figure 2: Entity ranking workflow.**

used for a variety of tasks other than semantic graph construction – e.g., RDF triple ranking [23]. Consequently, we explore here a task-based evaluation on ranking related entities [24] in a knowledge base.

**Task description.** Entity ranking [12] is the task of ordering a given set of entities on the basis of their relevance with respect to a specific reference entity. In our case, since we work with DBpedia as knowledge base, we take, e.g., `db:Bob_Dylan` as reference and try to compute, how strongly `db:Johnny_Cash` is related to it, in comparison to `db:Folk_music` or `db:Mozambique_(Song)`, and so on. This ranking task has the advantage that it provides a focused, extrinsic evaluation of our different weighting methods: besides, there exists established gold standard datasets against which we can compare our approach. Entity ranking can be seen as similar in spirit to computing word relatedness [49], except that in our setting we are given as input unambiguous entity references, rather than potentially ambiguous words. Besides, entity ranking also plays a key role in Entity Linking (EL) [10, 29], since EL relies on estimating the degree of relatedness between candidate entity references of different mentions in text. That is, within a global document-level EL approach, entity mentions can be jointly disambiguated by maximizing their degree of semantic overlap as obtained, for instance, from information stored within a knowledge base – cf. AIDA [26].

**Entity ranking method.** We present an overview of our approach in Figure 2. Given a reference entity *ref* and a set of entities $E_{Cand}$ (both found in DBpedia), our method ranks these entities by performing three main steps:

1) we build a semantic graph following the procedure of Section 2.2 using all candidate entities $E_{Cand}$, as well as the reference instance as input concepts;

2) we weight graph edges by edge cost, which is defined as

$$c(e) = w_{max} - w(e) \,, \qquad (1)$$

where $w(.)$ is any of the three weighting functions defined in Section 2.3, and $w_{max}$ is the globally highest possible weight in the DBpedia graph for the selected weighting function;

3) finally, we compute (weighted) semantic distances between entity pairs – i.e., the reference entity *ref* and each of the entities *cand* in $E_{Cand}$ in turn – as the minimum path cost between them in our weighted graph:

$$distance(ref, cand) = \min_{p \in paths(ref,cand)} c_p(ref, cand) \,.$$

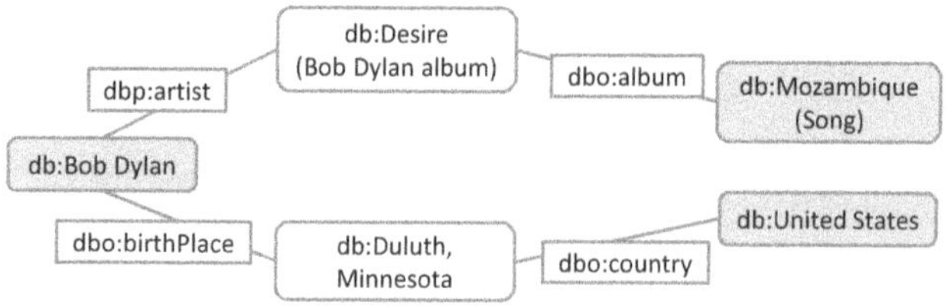


**Figure 3: Example of multiple paths between entities with different semantic specificity.**

| | Unwghtd | jointIC | combIC | IC+PMI |
|---|---|---|---|---|
| Hollywood Celebr. | 0.639 | 0.541 | **0.690** | 0.661 |
| IT Companies | 0.559 | 0.636 | **0.644** | 0.583 |
| Television Series | 0.529 | 0.595 | **0.643** | 0.602 |
| Video Games | 0.451 | **0.562** | 0.532 | 0.484 |
| Chuck Norris | 0.458 | 0.409 | **0.558** | 0.506 |
| All 21 Entities | 0.541 | 0.575 | **0.624** | 0.579 |

**Table 1: Performance on the entity ranking KORE dataset (best results are bolded).**

We then rank the entity pairs increasingly by semantic distance. Each single path cost between two entities is calculated as the sum of the edge costs along their undirected connecting path *p*:

$$c_p(ref, cand) = \sum_{e \in \{(ref,r_1,v_1),\ldots,(v_k,r_k,cand)\}} c(e) \,. \qquad (2)$$

As a result of our method, we are able to determine the degree of relatedness between two arbitrary instances within our background knowledge base as the inverse of their semantic distance. We briefly illustrate our method in Figure 3 with an example using `db:Bob_Dylan` and `db:Mozambique_(Song)` as input entity pair. When looking at the entity `db:Bob_Dylan` (the musician), we note that it is not directly connected to his song, `db:Mozambique_(Song)`. However, thanks to the fact that DBpedia encodes very specific facts – namely i) that Bob Dylan is the main artist of the album `db:Desire_(Bob_Dylan_album)`, and ii) that `db:Mozambique_(Song)` is a song contained in that very same album – we are able to estimate a high degree of semantic relatedness between the two input entities.

Note that our weighting scheme plays a crucial role in estimating the degree of semantic overlap. If we look, for instance, to another entity pair such as the one consisting of `db:Bob_Dylan` and `db:United_States`, we note that in DBpedia these entities are connected by a short, albeit rather uninformative (because unspecific), path consisting of a single intermediate entity (`db:Duluth,_Minnesota`). Our weighting captures this by assigning a low weight to edges denoting general semantic relations such as `dbo:birthPlace` and `dbo:country`. As a result of this, we are able to rank `db:Mozambique_(Song)` higher than `db:United_States`, although both are connected to the reference entity `db:Bob_Dylan` by a path of equal length.

**Experimental setting and evaluation.** We use the KORE entity ranking dataset from Hoffart et al. [24]. The dataset consists of 21 different reference entities from four different domains, namely IT companies, Hollywood celebrities, television series, video games, and Chuck Norris (a singleton dataset). For each ranking problem, Hoffart et al.

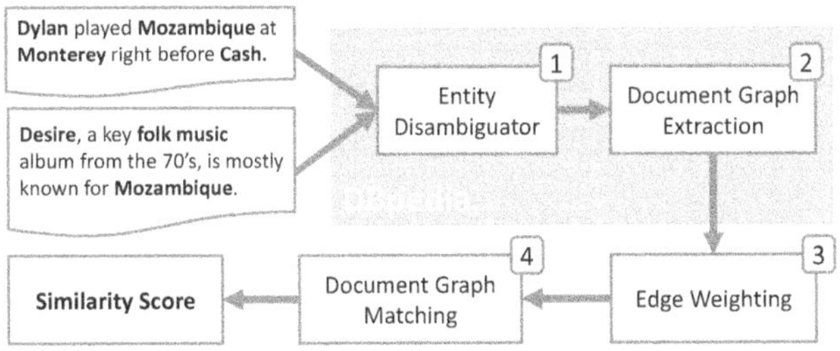


Figure 4: Document semantic similarity workflow.

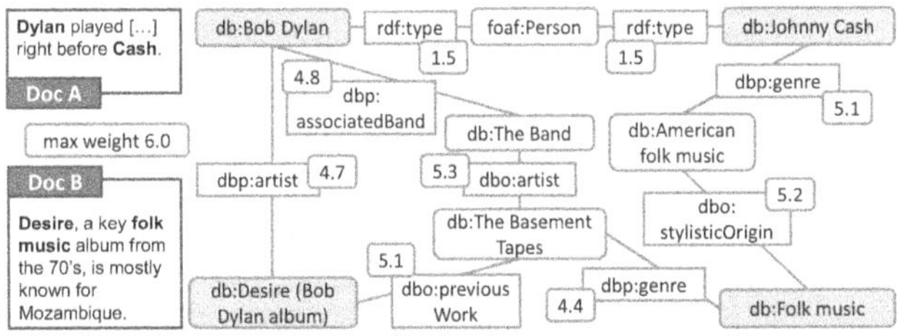


Figure 5: Graph document comparison (numbers on the graph edges indicate edge weights).

selected a set of 20 candidate entities, which were found to be related with different degrees to the reference entity. Relatedness assessments were obtained from human judges using a crowd-sourcing approach. As an example, the entity "Apple Inc." (from the 'IT Companies' category) is paired with, among others, the following other entities:

| | |
|---|---|
| **Reference entity** | Apple Inc. |
| **Related entity (rank)** | Steve Jobs (1), Steve Wozniak (2), ... Silicon Valley (9), NeXT (10) ... Ford Motor Company (20) |

Naturally, different entities have different degrees of relatedness with the concept of "Apple" as a company. "Steve Jobs", for instance, ranks highest, having been a key figure of the company. In the middle range, instead, we find related companies such as "NeXT", another company founded by Steve Jobs (rank 10). Finally, at the end of the ranking we find "Ford Motor Company", which is only marginally related to "Apple", being also an American company but from a completely different industry.

We follow the original evaluation setting of Hoffart et al. and compute Spearman's rank correlation coefficient $\rho$ for each reference entity in turn. Overall results are then obtained by averaging over all reference entities in the dataset. We report our results in Table 1, where we compare our different weighting schemes from Section 2.3. As baseline we use an unweighted version of the DBpedia graph: this amounts to computing entity relatedness simply as a function of distance in the network. Looking at the overall performance of the three alternative weighting schemes for all 21 ranking tasks, we observe that combIC consistently outperforms the baseline and both jointIC and IC+PMI on three domains out of four. When looking at specific domains, jointIC does not always improve the baseline, as results for Chuck Norris and Hollywood celebrities are actually getting worse. Nevertheless, on average all 3 weighting methods improve the baseline, with combIC, which shows an average increase of 15.5% (statistically significant for each task at $p \leq .001$ level using a paired t-test), achieving the best results. When compared with the original results from Hoffart et al. [24], our method achieves a performance slightly lower than their original proposal ($\rho = 0.673$), while at the same time outperforming all its approximations ($\rho = 0.621$ and 0.425). Overall, we take these performance figures to indicate the high quality of weighted connecting paths between entities in DBpedia. Consequently, we now take this idea one step further and use these paths to provide a structured representation of unstructured data, i.e. natural language texts. We then use these graph-based semantic representations to compute semantic similarity between documents.

# 4. COMPUTING DOCUMENT SIMILARITY

We present an application of our semantic graphs to the task of computing semantic similarity between texts. We provide an overview of our approach in Figure 4. Our method starts with the output of an entity disambiguator, which is used to identify a set of concepts from the input texts (1). Next, connecting paths between entities are collected, in order to identify the sub-graph of DBpedia covered by each document (2). Nodes in the semantic graph consist of concepts capturing the main topics of the documents: in addition, edges in the graph are weighted to identify the semantic relations that are most relevant for these concepts (3). Finally, we view computing semantic similarity as a matching problem between the concepts of different documents, and apply a Graph Edit Distance based similarity measure to identify the 'best' connecting paths between the documents' concepts (4). As a result, we are able to output the degree of similarity of the two input documents.

## 4.1 Document graph construction

Given an input text document, we first semantify it by identifying the set of concepts it contains. To this end, words and phrases are annotated with DBpedia concepts using a document entity linking system, e.g., DBpedia Spotlight [32]. Given a mention and its candidate entities, the entity linker finds its most likely meaning in context – e.g., like Spotlight, using a Vector Space Model (based on a bag-of-words approach). Accordingly, given a document, we are able to obtain a set of disambiguated entities associated with its words and phrases. In the two example documents of Figure 5, we extract, for instance, key concepts like `db:Bob_Dylan`, `db:Johnny_Cash` and `db:Desire_(Bob_Dylan_album)`. We call these extracted concepts the source nodes $V_s^d$ of a document graph $G^d = (V^d, E^d), V_s^d \subseteq V^d$ representing document $d$. $G^d$ is built by applying the procedure described in Section 2.2 while using $V_s^d$ as the set of input entities.

## 4.2 Graph-based document similarity

Since we represent documents as weighted DBpedia subgraphs (Section 2), we can naturally formulate computing document similarity as a graph matching problem. While there exist exact graph matching algorithms, e.g. based on graph isomorphism, we require our measure to be able to effectively quantify degrees of similarity. Consequently, we opt for an application of Graph Edit Distance techniques for our specific problem.

Graph Edit Distance (GED, [18]) is a general, inexact graph matching method that defines the distance between two graphs in terms of the minimum cost of edit operations needed to transform one graph into the other. In general, a GED measure needs to define edit cost functions for insertion, deletion, and modification for both nodes and edges. However, given our specific problem setting, we drop some of these requirements and define only cost functions for nodes. This is because, given a pair of semantic graphs, generated using the method from Section 2, these actually consist of two subgraphs of the same background model, namely DBpedia. As a result, no cost function over edges needs to be defined, since an edge existing or not in one graph will also be present or not in the other, given the fact that both document graphs belong in fact to the same supergraph. Thus, edit operation on edges solely cannot occur and, accordingly, we define edge cost functions to yield zero.

We define cost operations for nodes as follows. Note that, since we work with a well-defined ontology that represents concepts by unique URIs, we can rely on the fact that nodes in the DBpedia graph are unique. As a result, we do not need to account for label mismatch between concepts – e.g., the entity "Bob Dylan" being identified by `db:Robert_Allen_Zimmerman` in a graph, and referred to as `db:Bob_Dylan` in another one (or vice versa). Thus, in contrast to standard GED approaches, we define node modifications on the basis of the underlying edge structure, i.e., weighted distances in the graph, as opposed, for instance, to the application of string similarity measures like Levenshtein distance on node labels. The modification cost between two nodes is defined, analog to Section 3, as the sum of the edge costs along their connecting path (cf. Equation 2). By employing our edge cost function (Equation 1) we capture the fact that the closer (i.e., more semantically related) two nodes are, the lower the cost to modify one into the other is.

An exact solution to the GED problem can be found with a tree search over all possible edit operations, which, however, is computationally intractable for any reasonably-sized graph. In this work, we accordingly adapt an approximation method based on bipartite graph matching for finding the minimal edit cost [41]. This precomputes the cheapest node modification costs for each node pair first, and stores them into a cost matrix. Since in our case there can exist multiple paths between two nodes (and, thus, multiple such modification costs), we always select the cheapest node modification operation as the cheapest connecting path. Next, the matrix is extended with the cost for node insertion and deletion – which we define as equal to the most expensive node modification operation in the matrix (see below for details). Computing the GED is now a bipartite graph matching problem between the source nodes of the two graphs, with the objective of minimizing the edit cost and subject to the restriction of a strict one-to-one matching (as every node can only be modified exactly once). We solve this minimization problem using the Hungarian method (also known as Kuhn-Munkres or Munkres' algorithm). After computing the GED, we apply a simple normalization step to eliminate the effect of different graph, i.e., document sizes.

We summarize our approach in Algorithm 1. Given two semantic graphs $G^i$ and $G^j$, representing documents $d^i$ and $d^j$ (Section 2), we perform the following steps:

**Algorithm 1** Graph-based semantic similarity

**Input**: Document DBpedia subgraphs
$G^i = (V^i, E^i)$, $G^j = (V^j, E^j)$
**Parameter**: Maximal path length $n_{max}$

1: **function** SubgraphDistance($G^i, G^j$)
2: $P \leftarrow \emptyset$ ▷ set of cheapest paths
3: **for all** $(v^i, v^j) \in V^i_s \times V^j_s$ from $G^i, G^j$ **do**
4: **if** $v^i = v^j$ **then**
5: $c^{i,j} \leftarrow 0$
6: **else**
7: $c^{i,j} \leftarrow \mathit{DijkstraCheapestPath}(v^i, v^j)$
8: $P \leftarrow P \cup \{(p^{i,j}, c^{i,j})\}$
9: $c^{max} \leftarrow \max_{p \in P_{length \leq n_{max}}}(c_p)$
10: **for all** $(p^{i,j}, c^{i,j}) \in P$ **do**
11: **if** $p^{i,j}_{length} \leq n_{max}$ **then**
12: $c^{i,j} \leftarrow c^{i,j} / c^{max}$
13: **else**
14: $c^{i,j} \leftarrow 1$
15: $D_m \leftarrow \{d_{i,j}\}_{i=1,\ldots,m,\ j=1,\ldots,m}, m = \max(|V^i_s|, |V^j_s|)$
16: **for all** $d_{i,j}$ **do**
17: **if** $i \leq j$ **then** ▷ Be $i \geq j$
18: $d_{i,j} \leftarrow c^{i,j}$
19: **else**
20: $d_{i,j} \leftarrow c^{max}$
21: $M \leftarrow \mathit{HungarianCheapestMatching}(D_m)$
22: $\mathit{dist}(G^i, G^j) \leftarrow (\sum_{m \in M} m_{cost}) / |V^i_s \cup V^j_s|$
**return** $\mathit{dist}(G^i, G^j)$

i) **lines 1–9**: for each pair of source nodes $V^i_s \times V^j_s$ we find the cheapest undirected path $p^{i,j}$ with cost $c^{i,j}$ using Dijkstra's algorithm (edges along the path are weighted by one of our three measures from Section 2.3). In our example in Figure 5, for instance, we compute the cheapest path between `db:Bob_Dylan` and `db:Johnny_Cash` from Doc A, and each of `db:Desire_(Bob_Dylan_album)` and `db:Folk_music` from Doc B in turn. The highest weighted edge, here `dbo:artist`, is assigned a cost of 0.7 (assuming a global upper edge cost limit $w_{max} = 6.0$, Equation 1), whereas the lowest weighted edge, namely the two `rdf:type` relations, are both assigned a cost of $6.0 - 1.5 = 4.5$. Given these costs, the cheapest path between, for instance, `db:Johnny_Cash` and `db:Folk_music` is the one through `db:American_folk_music`. Note that, in order to avoid long paths between very distant (and thus semantically unrelated) concepts, we limit the search based on a maximum search depth parameter $n_{max}$.

ii) **lines 10–14**: we next compute the node modification costs for each pair of source nodes. For paths found exceeding the path limit $n_{max}$, we set their cost to that of the most expensive path $c^{max}$ found within the input graph pair. Since it might not be the case that both graphs are fully connected, we also set $c^{max}$ as the cost for unconnected source node pairs. Finally, we normalize all cost values.

iii) **lines 15–20**: we build the final edit distance matrix $D_m$ from the previously computed modification costs, as well as the costs of the node insertion and deletion operations, which we set to $c^{max}$. This is to account for the fact that, given an arbitrary document pair, the cardinality of their sets of entities does not need to be the same: in this case, additional nodes are treated the same as very distant ones.

| Tagger | Method | max depth | jointIC | combIC | IC+PMI |
|---|---|---|---|---|---|
| TagMe | Jaccard | | | | 0.51 |
| TagMe | GED | @ 2 | 0.55 | 0.59 | 0.57 |
| TagMe | GED | @ 3 | 0.52 | 0.56 | 0.54 |
| TagMe | GED | @ 4 | 0.46 | 0.49 | 0.52 |
| Spotlight | Jaccard | | | | 0.54 |
| Spotlight | GED | @ 2 | **0.60** | **0.63** | **0.63** |
| Spotlight | GED | @ 3 | 0.55 | 0.61 | 0.61 |
| Spotlight | GED | @ 4 | 0.52 | 0.55 | 0.57 |
| | DKPro [3] | | | | 0.21 |
| | TakeLab [45] | | | | 0.08 |
| | Cosine baseline | | | | 0.56 |

**Table 2: Results on the LP50 dataset (Pearson $r$ correlation coefficient, best results are bolded).**

iv) **lines 21-22**: the edit distance matrix $D_m$ represents a bipartite matching problem, which we solve with the Hungarian method. This finds the optimal, cost-minimal assignment in our node operations matrix, while ensuring that each node will only be edited once. We finally normalize the graph edit distance costs to account for the number of source entities in the two input documents.

As a result of the execution of the algorithm, the normalized graph edit distance between $G^i$ and $G^j$ is returned. In our example, we will get a mapping from `db:Bob_Dylan` to `db:Desire_(Bob_Dylan_album)` (cost 1.3) and from `db:Johnny_Cash` to `db:Folk_music` (cost 0.9 + 0.8). The final similarity score is then given by the sum of these edit costs (3.0), normalized by the number of distinct source entities in both documents (6).

## 4.3 Experiments

**Experimental setting.** We evaluate our approach with a benchmarking dataset for document semantic similarity, in order to be able to compare our method against other state-of-the-art systems. To this end, we use the **LP50** dataset [31], namely a collection of 50 news articles from the Australian Broadcasting Corporation (ABC), which were pairwise annotated with similarity rating on a Likert scale from 1 (very different) to 5 (very similar) by 8 to 12 different human annotators. To obtain the final similarity judgments, Lee et al. averaged for each pair the scores of all annotators: however, the final collection of 1,225 relatedness scores has only 67 distinct values. Consequently, Spearman's rank correlation is not appropriate to evaluate performance on this data and we opt instead, following previous work, for instance [17], for Pearson's linear correlation coefficient ($r$).

**Results and discussion.** We report our performance figures on the LP50 dataset in Table 2, where we show the Pearson product-moment correlation coefficient $r$ between the human gold standard and our graph-based approach (GED). In order to evaluate our method across different entity linking systems we test with both DBpedia Spotlight [32] and TagMe [15], two state-of-the-art systems [10]. For each tagger, we compute its performance with respect to different values for the maximum depth of the path search in the cost computation ($n_{\max}$). We compare our GED-based method with a variety of baselines:

i) a semantically-informed baseline which computes the Jaccard similarity coefficient over the set of entities identified within the input documents, namely $sim(d_1, d_2) = \frac{C^1 \cap C^2}{C^1 \cup C^2}$, where $C^1$ and $C^2$ represent the set of concepts identified by the entity tagger (i.e., TagMe or Spotlight) within documents $d_1$ and $d_2$, respectively;

ii) an unsupervised baseline computed as the cosine distance of a standard bag-of-words Vector Space Model;

iii) two strong supervised baselines based on two publicly available supervised systems, namely DKPro [3] and TakeLab [45], both trained on standard SemEval STS datasets.

In general, using our graph-based approach to document semantic similarity we are able to beat all baselines by a large margin, achieving a correlation coefficient of up to 0.63 ($n_{\max} = 2$, using Spotlight and either combIC or IC+PMI weighting). This is equal to a relative improvement of 16.0% over the semantically-informed Jaccard baseline and 11.6% over the cosine bag-of-words baseline[4]. The results indicate that our method is able to always perform above the Jaccard baseline for $n_{\max} \leq 3$, and achieves the best performance for $n_{\max} = 2$. These parameter values are indeed in-line with the optimal ones found by previous research contributions making use of graphs derived from Wikipedia or DBpedia [36, 28], which also showed the benefits of mining information from short, highly specific paths. This, in turn, makes our model virtually parameter-free, because it implies that we can simply set the only tunable parameter of our method, namely the depth of the search used for concept matching, to standard values (i.e., 2 or 3) which are known to yield good performance across many different tasks. When looking at the performance of the different weighting measures, we see that we consistently obtain the best results using either combIC or IC+PMI, which corroborates our previous findings on entity ranking (Section 3). Finally, we notice that the different baselines show large performance variations. The simple cosine baseline turns out to be a difficult competitor – e.g., outperforming the simple Jaccard baselines computed from both TagMe and Spotlight annotations – which indicates that semantifying the input texts and applying a simple entity overlap measure is not enough to yield a robust performance. The supervised baselines, DKPro and TakeLab, both show instead an extremely low performance rate, although they were reported as being among the top systems of the SemEval STS 2012 shared task. This is because both systems are supervised in nature, and thus able to yield accurate performance only when in-domain labeled data are available.

Next, in order to better understand the performance of our method, we compare it in Table 3 with an unweighted version that does not use edge weighting (i.e., all edge modifications have the same cost), as well as previous results from the literature. When computing semantic distances without weighting i.e., using the Hungarian method for mapping, but applied to unweighted paths only, we achieve up to $r = 0.61$ when using Spotlight and a maximum depth of 3 – 12.5%

[4]All differences in performance are statistically significant at $p < 0.05$ using Fisher's Z-value transformation unless otherwise noted.

| | $r$ |
|---|---|
| GED-based (weighted) | 0.63 |
| GED-based (unweighted) | 0.61 |
| Bag-of-Words [31] | 0.1-0.5 |
| LSA [31] | 0.60 |
| ESA – original [17] | 0.72 |
| ESA – reimplemented [4] | 0.46-0.59 |

**Table 3: System comparison on the LP50 data.**

above the semantically-informed Jaccard baseline and 8.3% over the cosine bag-of-words baseline. This indicates the overall robustness of our GED method, which exploits high-quality semantic paths from DBpedia. Similar to our results on entity ranking, additional performance gains can be achieved thanks to weighting semantic relations.

When comparing our approach to the state of the art on this dataset we see that, while we outperform robust methods such as LSA [11], we are nevertheless not able to achieve a performance as high as that of Explicit Semantic Analysis (ESA, [17]). Our method, however, has clear advantages over ESA in that it provides a fully unsupervised approach that practically requires no tuning, and thus can be applied to arbitrary data and domains with virtually no changes. The original performance figures for ESA [17] have been criticized in fact for being based on a cut-off value used to prune the vectors being over-fitted to the LP50 data [4] – cf. also the much lower performance obtained by re-implementations like [4] and [22], among others. Thus, we take these figures to be promising in that our approach to document semantic similarity, while being based on a general document model with many potential applications – e.g. ranking related entities (cf. Section 3) – is nevertheless able to come close in performance to a highly specialized method like ESA, which has been tuned for this specific task and dataset.

**Error analysis.** In order to gain additional insights into the performance of our method, we performed an error analysis of its output. To this end, we focused on the manual analysis of documents deemed closest or most distant from the human judgments. When looking at specific document pairs, we found that our knowledge-rich approach is able to estimate well the similarity between documents with little or partial word overlap: connecting paths between DBpedia entities, in fact, were found to implicitly cover a wide range of topical associations, ranging from near-synonymity ("U.S. intelligence" and "CIA") all the way to metonymic relations ("White House" and "Bush administration"). However, since it relies only on DBpedia entities and their document mentions, our approach will perform badly in cases where i) the input documents contain few or no entities, or ii) they share the same entities, but describe different events. For instance, our method will give a very high similarity score to the following two sentences, although they describe completely different events: (a) Obama started his second term in the White House; (b) Obama will soon leave the White House. But while our approach could be extended to include relations between entities which are automatically extracted from text, cf. recent work on building event graphs from documents [20], our results seem also to suggest that in the case of text similarity we can often get away without a deep analysis of the documents' sentences, since entity overlap is a good proxy for topical affinity. This is highlighted by the following two sentences from the LP50 data, which, albeit very different, belong to documents which were deemed highly similar by the annotators:

- Nigerian President Olusegun Obasanjo said he will weep if a single mother sentenced to death by stoning for having a child out of wedlock is killed, but added he has faith the court system will overturn her sentence. [...]
- An Islamic high court in northern Nigeria rejected an appeal today by a single mother sentenced to be stoned to death for having sex out of wedlock. [...]

## 5. RELATED WORK

The recent years have seen a great deal of work on computing semantic similarity [49]. This is arguably because semantic similarity provides a valuable model of semantic compatibility that is widely applicable to a variety of complex tasks, including both pre-processing tasks like Word Sense Disambiguation [38] and coreference resolution [39], and high-end applications such as information retrieval [14] or multi-document summarization [33], to name a few.

Most of the previous work on semantic similarity has concentrated on computing pairwise similarity of words, although recent efforts concentrated on the broader task of text similarity [4], as also shown by community efforts such as the shared tasks on Semantic Textual Similarity [1]. Overall, the best results in these evaluation campaigns have been obtained by supervised models combining large feature sets [3, 45], although questions remain on whether this approach can be easily ported to domains for which no labeled data exists. In contrast, in this work we presented an unsupervised model that requires virtually no parameter tuning and exploits the implicit supervision provided by very large amounts of structured knowledge encoded in DBpedia.

This work is, to the best of our knowledge, the first to exploit a wide-coverage ontology (i.e., other than small-scale semantic lexicons like WordNet) within a general-purpose algorithm for computing semantic similarity based on a graph-based similarity measure. Our method effectively uses large amounts of structured knowledge and can be used in principle with other such resources like, e.g., YAGO [25], provided they contain explicit semantic relations. Seminal work on representing natural language as semantic networks focused on queries [7]. Recently, graph-based representations from DBpedia have been explored by [28] for labeling topics, as obtained from a topic model, rather than providing structured representations of arbitrary texts. In addition, they limit graph construction to a small set of manually selected DBpedia relations. The work closest to ours is that of [42], who use graph-based representations of snippets for Web search results clustering. Their method also builds a document-based semantic graph from Wikipedia concepts, as obtained from the output an entity disambiguator. However, similarly to [43], they do not exploit explicit semantic relations between entities (which we show to be beneficial for both entity ranking and semantic similarity).

Previous work in computing semantic distances on linked data relied on disambiguated input [37], a requirement which is very hard to satisfy for most applications working with natural language text. In contrast, our approach relies on automatic entity linking techniques, which allow us to link entity mentions in text to well-defined entities within an ontology. From a general perspective, our work can be viewed as building upon seminal research work in IR that explored the use of controlled vocabularies [30], originally introduced for library systems. The proposed method can thus be seen as instance of an advanced Knowledge Organization System (KOS) [48, 13], since it relies at its core on a wide-coverage ontology to represent documents. However, as opposed to these approaches, we do not create a controlled vocabulary for a specific document collection, but instead reuse an existing, background ontology which contains general world knowledge. We use this knowledge source to represent the entities found documents, as opposed to using the documents' headings or metadata. The Jaccard similarity we report in Section 4.3 consists, in fact, of a baseline method that uses DBpedia as controlled vocabulary: we build upon this intuition and extend it by using the information encoded within the structure of the DBpedia network.

# 6. CONCLUSIONS

In this paper, we proposed a method for exploiting large amounts of machine-readable knowledge, i.e., entities and semantic relations, encoded within DBpedia, in order to provide a structured, i.e. graph-based, representation of natural language texts. Our results on entity ranking and document semantic similarity indicate that, thanks to an effective weighting of the semantic relations found within the semantic network, as well as a robust concept matching technique, we are able to achieve competitive performance on both these hard NLP tasks, while at the same time providing an unsupervised model which is practically parameter-free – namely, whose only tunable parameter can be fixed based on well-established findings from previous work.

This is the first proposal to exploit a Web-scale ontology to provide structured representations of document content, and computing semantic distances in a knowledge-rich fashion. We build thematically upon previous contributions which showed the beneficial effect of exploiting large amounts of knowledge for enhancing text comparison [46, 35] (*inter alia*). In our work, we take this line of research one step further by: (a) using a truly ontological resource for content modeling (as opposed, e.g., to semantic lexicons such as WordNet); (b) developing an information-theoretic measure to identify semantically specific, highly informative relations between entities in a large knowledge graph; (c) defining a new method, based on graph edit distance techniques, to quantify degrees of semantic similarity between documents: this views semantic similarity as a concept matching problem and uses the Hungarian method for solving the combinatorial optimization problem.

Our vision, ultimately, is to show how entity linking and disambiguation techniques can enable an open-domain structured representation of documents, and accordingly an even larger Web of Semantic Data, on which semantic technologies (e.g., search) can be enabled. Accordingly, we focused in this first initial step primarily on entities, since they are the bulk of wide-coverage knowledge resources like DBpedia. Clearly, extending this entity-centric model – for instance, by means of event-structured graphs [20] or RDF predicates [19] – is the next logical step. Besides, as future work we plan to develop methods to jointly perform entity disambiguation and compute semantic similarity. We are also interested in applying our techniques within domains other than newswire data, and investigating domain adaptation techniques for the graph construction phase. Our graphs naturally model fine-grained information about documents: accordingly, we will explore their application to complex, high-end task such as aspect-oriented IR, as well as fine-grained document classification and clustering for IR.

## Acknowledgments

We thank our colleagues Arnab Dutta, Christian Meilicke and Heiner Stuckenschmidt for their valuable comments on draft versions of this work.

# 7. REFERENCES

[1] E. Agirre, D. Cer, M. Diab, A. Gonzalez-Agirre, and W. Guo. *SEM 2013 shared task: Semantic textual similarity. In *Proc. of *SEM-2013*, pages 32–43, 2013.

[2] M. Banko, M. J. Cafarella, S. Soderland, M. Broadhead, and O. Etzioni. Open information extraction from the Web. In *Proc. of IJCAI-07*, pages 2670–2676, 2007.

[3] D. Bär, C. Biemann, I. Gurevych, and T. Zesch. UKP: Computing semantic textual similarity by combining multiple content similarity measures. In *Proc. of SemEval-2012*, pages 435–440, 2012.

[4] D. Bär, T. Zesch, and I. Gurevych. A reflective view on text similarity. In *Proc. of RANLP-11*, pages 515–520, 2011.

[5] C. Bizer, T. Heath, and T. Berners-Lee. Linked data – the story so far. *International Journal on Semantic Web and Information Systems*, 2012.

[6] C. Bizer, J. Lehmann, G. Kobilarov, S. Auer, C. Becker, R. Cyganiak, and S. Hellmann. DBpedia – A crystallization point for the web of data. *Journal of Web Semantics*, 7(3):154–165, 2009.

[7] J. Booth, B. D. Eugenio, I. F. Cruz, and O. Wolfson. Query sentences as semantic (sub) networks. In *Proc. of ICSC-09*, pages 89–94, 2009.

[8] E. Bruni, J. Uijlings, M. Baroni, and N. Sebe. Distributional semantics with eyes: Using image analysis to improve computational representations of word meaning. In *Proc. of MM'12*, pages 1219–1228, 2012.

[9] A. Carlson, J. Betteridge, B. Kisiel, B. Settles, E. R. H. Jr., and T. M. Mitchell. Toward an architecture for never-ending language learning. In *Proc. of AAAI-10*, pages 1306–1313, 2010.

[10] M. Cornolti, P. Ferragina, and M. Ciaramita. A framework for benchmarking entity-annotation systems. In *Proc. of WWW-13*, pages 249–260, 2013.

[11] S. Deerwester, S. T. Dumais, G. W. Furnas, T. K. Landauer, and R. Harshman. Indexing by latent semantic analysis. *Journal of the American Society for Information Science*, 41(6):391–407, 1990.

[12] G. Demartini, T. Iofciu, and A. P. de Vries. Overview of the INEX 2009 entity ranking track. In *INEX*, pages 254–264, 2009.

[13] K. Eckert. *Usage-driven Maintenance of Knowledge Organization Systems*. PhD thesis, Universität Mannheim, 2012.

[14] O. Egozi, S. Markovitch, and E. Gabrilovich. Concept-based information retrieval using Explicit Semantic Analysis. *ACM Transactions on Information Systems*, 29(2):8:1–8:34, 2011.

[15] P. Ferragina and U. Scaiella. Fast and accurate annotation of short texts with Wikipedia pages. *IEEE Software*, 29(1):70–75, 2012.

[16] D. A. Ferrucci, E. W. Brown, J. Chu-Carroll, J. Fan, D. Gondek, A. Kalyanpur, A. Lally, J. W. Murdock, E. Nyberg, J. M. Prager, N. Schlaefer, and C. A. Welty. Building Watson: An overview of the DeepQA project. *AI Magazine*, 31(3):59–79, 2010.

[17] E. Gabrilovich and S. Markovitch. Computing semantic relatedness using Wikipedia-based explicit semantic analysis. In *Proc. of IJCAI-07*, pages 1606–1611, 2007.

[18] X. Gao, B. Xiao, D. Tao, and X. Li. A survey of graph edit distance. *Pattern Analysis and Applications*, 13(1):113–129, 2010.

[19] D. Gerber and A.-C. N. Ngomo. Extracting multilingual natural-language patterns for RDF predicates. In *Proc. of EKAW-12*, pages 87–96, 2012.

[20] G. Glavaš and J. Šnajder. Recognizing identical events with graph kernels. In *Proc. of ACL-13*, pages 797–803, 2013.

[21] I. Gurevych, J. Eckle-Kohler, S. Hartmann, M. Matuschek, C. M. Meyer, and C. Wirth. UBY – a large-scale unified lexical-semantic resource based on LMF. In *Proc. of EACL-12*, pages 580–590, 2012.

[22] S. Hassan and R. Mihalcea. Semantic relatedness using salient semantic analysis. In *Proc. of AAAI-11*, pages 884–889, 2011.

[23] J. Hees, M. Khamis, R. Biedert, S. Abdennadher, and A. Dengel. Collecting links between entities ranked by human association strengths. In *Proc. of ESWC-13*, pages 517–531, 2013.

[24] J. Hoffart, S. Seufert, D. B. Nguyen, M. Theobald, and G. Weikum. KORE: Keyphrase overlap relatedness for entity disambiguation. In *Proc. of CIKM-12*, pages 545–554, 2012.

[25] J. Hoffart, F. M. Suchanek, K. Berberich, and G. Weikum. YAGO2: a spatially and temporally enhanced knowledge base from Wikipedia. *Artificial Intelligence*, 194:28–61, 2013.

[26] J. Hoffart, M. A. Yosef, I. Bordino, H. Fürstenau, M. Pinkal, M. Spaniol, B. Taneva, S. Thater, and G. Weikum. Robust disambiguation of named entities in text. In *Proc. of EMNLP-11*, pages 782–792, 2011.

[27] E. Hovy, R. Navigli, and S. P. Ponzetto. Collaboratively built semi-structured content and Artificial Intelligence: The story so far. *Artificial Intelligence*, 194:2–27, 2013.

[28] I. Hulpus, C. Hayes, M. Karnstedt, and D. Greene. Unsupervised graph-based topic labelling using DBpedia. In *Proc. of WSDM-13*, pages 465–474, 2013.

[29] H. Ji and R. Grishman. Knowledge base population: Successful approaches and challenges. In *Proc. of ACL-11*, pages 1148–1158, 2011.

[30] F. W. Lancaster. *Vocabulary Control for Information Retrieval*. Information Resources Press, 1972.

[31] M. D. Lee, B. Pincombe, and M. Welsh. An empirical evaluation of models of text document similarity. In *Proc. of CogSci 2005*, pages 1254–1259, 2005.

[32] P. N. Mendes, M. Jakob, A. García-Silva, and C. Bizer. DBpedia Spotlight : Shedding light on the web of documents. In *Proc. of I-Semantics'11*, pages 1–8, 2011.

[33] V. Nastase. Topic-driven multi-document summarization with encyclopedic knowledge and activation spreading. In *Proc. of EMNLP-08*, pages 763–772, 2008.

[34] R. Navigli and A. Di Marco. Clustering and diversifying Web search results with graph-based Word Sense Induction. *Computational Linguistics*, 39(3):709–754, 2013.

[35] R. Navigli, S. Faralli, A. Soroa, O. L. de Lacalle, and E. Agirre. Two birds with one stone: learning semantic models for Text Categorization and Word Sense Disambiguation. In *Proc. of CIKM-11*, pages 2317–2320, 2011.

[36] R. Navigli and S. P. Ponzetto. BabelNet: the automatic construction, evaluation and application of a wide-coverage multilingual semantic network. *Artificial Intelligence*, 193:217–250, 2012.

[37] A. Passant. Measuring semantic distance on linking data and using it for resources recommendations. In *Proceedings of the AAAI Spring Symposium "Linked Data Meets Artificial Intelligence"*, 2010.

[38] S. Patwardhan, S. Banerjee, and T. Pedersen. Using measures of semantic relatedness for Word Sense Disambiguation. In *Proc. of CICLing-03*, pages 241–257, 2003.

[39] S. P. Ponzetto and M. Strube. Knowledge derived from Wikipedia for computing semantic relatedness. *Journal of Artificial Intelligence Research*, 30:181–212, 2007.

[40] S. P. Ponzetto and M. Strube. Taxonomy induction based on a collaboratively built knowledge repository. *Artificial Intelligence*, 175:1737–1756, 2011.

[41] K. Riesen and H. Bunke. Approximate graph edit distance computation by means of bipartite graph matching. *Image Vision and Computing*, 27(7):950–959, 2009.

[42] U. Scaiella, P. Ferragina, A. Marino, and M. Ciaramita. Topical clustering of search results. In *Proc. of WSDM-12*, pages 223–232, 2012.

[43] W. Shen, J. Wang, P. Luo, and M. Wang. LINDEN: linking named entities with knowledge base via semantic knowledge. In *Proc. of WWW-12*, pages 449–458, 2012.

[44] P. D. Turney and P. Pantel. From frequency to meaning: Vector space models of semantics. *Journal of Artificial Intelligence Research*, 37:141–188, 2010.

[45] F. Šarić, G. Glavaš, M. Karan, J. Šnajder, and B. Dalbelo Bašić. TakeLab: Systems for measuring semantic text similarity. In *Proc. of SemEval-2012*, pages 441–448, 2012.

[46] P. Wang and C. Domeniconi. Building semantic kernels for text classification using Wikipedia. In *Proc. of KDD '08*, pages 713–721, 2008.

[47] M. Yahya, K. Berberich, S. Elbassuoni, M. Ramanath, V. Tresp, and G. Weikum. Natural language questions for the web of data. In *Proc. of EMNLP-CoNLL-12*, pages 379–390, 2012.

[48] M. L. Zeng. Knowledge Organization Systems (KOS). *Knowledge Organization*, 35(2-3):160–182, 2008.

[49] Z. Zhang, A. L. Gentile, and F. Ciravegna. Recent advances in methods of lexical semantic relatedness – a survey. *Natural Language Engineering*, 1(1):1–69, 2012.

# Trust, but Verify: Predicting Contribution Quality for Knowledge Base Construction and Curation


Chun How Tan
Google
chunhowt@google.com

Eugene Agichtein
Emory University, Google
eugene@mathcs.emory.edu

Panos Ipeirotis
New York University, Google
panos@stern.nyu.edu

Evgeniy Gabrilovich
Google
gabr@google.com



## ABSTRACT

The largest publicly available knowledge repositories, such as Wikipedia and Freebase, owe their existence and growth to volunteer contributors around the globe. While the majority of contributions are correct, errors can still creep in, due to editors' carelessness, misunderstanding of the schema, malice, or even lack of accepted ground truth. If left undetected, inaccuracies often degrade the experience of users and the performance of applications that rely on these knowledge repositories. We present a new method, CQUAL, for automatically predicting the quality of contributions submitted to a knowledge base. Significantly expanding upon previous work, our method holistically exploits a variety of signals, including the user's domains of expertise as reflected in her prior contribution history, and the historical accuracy rates of different types of facts. In a large-scale human evaluation, our method exhibits precision of 91% at 80% recall. Our model verifies whether a contribution is correct immediately after it is submitted, significantly alleviating the need for post-submission human reviewing.



## Keywords

Crowdsourcing, knowledge base construction, predicting contribution quality


## Categories and Subject Descriptors

H2.8 [Database Management]: Database Applications

## 1. INTRODUCTION

The last decade has witnessed an unprecedented growth of publicly available knowledge repositories such as the Open Directory, Wikipedia, and Freebase (and incidentally other repositories that build upon these, including YAGO, DBpedia, and Google's Knowledge Graph). These knowledge repositories thrive thanks to millions of volunteer contributors, who add new information and keep the existing knowledge up to date. All of these repositories employ the post-moderation approach, where the contributions go live immediately, but can later be edited or reverted by other users. This approach has obvious benefits, as it facilitates rapid dissemination of updated information and allows legitimate contributors to get immediate gratification from seeing their contributions online. Alas, this approach is also prone to spamming. In the largest communities, such as Wikipedia, changes on virtually any topic are often reviewed promptly [33]. However, in smaller user communities, such as Freebase, inaccurate contributions can persist for much longer periods of time until they are detected and fixed. Such errors can have significant consequences because these knowledge repositories (notably, Freebase) often serve as data sources for third-party applications, such as Google's Knowledge Graph, Bing's Satori, and Facebook's Entity Graph. Hence, it is important to maintain the knowledge repository at high accuracy level.

There are various ways to maintain high levels of accuracy. One option is to use pre-moderation, which requires all changes to be approved prior to being allowed to go live. Unfortunately, pre-moderation removes the incentive of immediate gratification and negatively affects users' propensity to contribute: in smaller communities facts can remain pending for extended periods of time until they are reviewed and approved. As an alternative to pre-moderation, new submissions can go live immediately, but be considered unverified until they stand the test of time; then, if they have not been deleted, by moderators or other users, after a number of weeks they are assumed to be correct and are released to third party applications. Both options have their shortcomings: the former allows introduction of erroneous facts, while the latter delays the inclusion of valid facts into the knowledge base.

We propose an automatic moderation technique for verifying users' contributions in real time. This approach allows a large fraction of contributions to be automatically approved instantaneously, without the need to subject them to a secondary review or let them stand the test of time. Several earlier studies have examined the quality of Wikipedia contributions based on the quality of contributor's prior work (e.g., [2, 17, 27]), however, we show that these findings do not necessarily apply in the case when contributions are *structured*, such as SPO triples[1] in Freebase. In this case,

[1]SPO stands for a triple of ⟨*subject*, *predicate*, *object*⟩, where two entities are connected by a relation predicate.



*WSDM'14,* February 24–28, 2014, New York, New York, USA.
Copyright 2014 ACM 978-1-4503-2351-2/14/02 ...$15.00.
http://dx.doi.org/10.1145/2556195.2556227.

we observed that naively using the contributors' history to compute their prior accuracy rates, yields results that are barely above the majority class baseline. Instead of using just the past rate of correctness in one's contribution history, we treat the problem of classifying user contributions holistically. We model the contributors' domain of expertise based on their past contributions, as well as the inherent "difficulty" in correctly contributing different types of information. To this end, we use a very large-scale unsupervised topic model to align the users' domains of expertise with the topics of their contributions. To infer the inherent difficulty of a contribution, we track long-term accuracy rates of contributions of different types of facts (and thus compute the prior likelihood of a contribution to be correct).

We conduct an empirical evaluation using a subset of Freebase contributions, which have been re-judged for accuracy by multiple judges to ascertain their quality. Our findings indicate that the prior correctness rate of a user (inferred from his contribution history) only has a slight predictive power with respect to the quality of his future contributions, and the prediction accuracy based on this information alone is not significantly better than that of a simple baseline that always predicts the majority class. However, we measured a significant improvement due to modeling the difficulty of facts, and a further improvement due to modeling the contributor's expertise based on her past contributions.

The contributions of this paper are fourfold. First, we propose an approach for *targeted crowdsourcing*, where we predict the quality of users' work by inferring their *domain expertise* through their past contribution history. Our approach offers a paradigm shift compared to conventional crowdsourcing techniques (e.g., the Amazon Mechanical Turk), where little prior information is available about the users, and qualification tests (even paired with their prior contribution history, if any) shed little light on the quality of their subsequent contributions. Second, our method can do well in the case of a "cold start" when the user has made no prior contributions to the knowledge base, by falling back to the prior difficulty of the type of information being contributed. Third, our empirical evaluation shows that the proposed method can instantaneously vet a very large portion (at least 80%) of the users' contributions, while offering a significant reduction in error compared to the simple test of time heuristic, as well as to the previous state of the art based on users' prior success rates. Finally, as opposed to quality control through redundancy, or via having all contributions explicitly reviewed by humans, or by letting the new contributions stand the test of time, our method offers a continuous tradeoff between the prediction accuracy and the fraction of contributions that can be approved automatically.

## 2. METHODOLOGY

In Section 2.1, we illustrate the contribution process in Freebase, a popular knowledge base, and formally define the problem of evaluating contribution quality. We then describe the signals used for estimating contribution quality in Section 2.2.

### 2.1 Life of a Freebase Contribution

Freebase[2] is one of the most popular knowledge bases (as evident by its use by major commercial search engines such

[2]http://www.freebase.com/

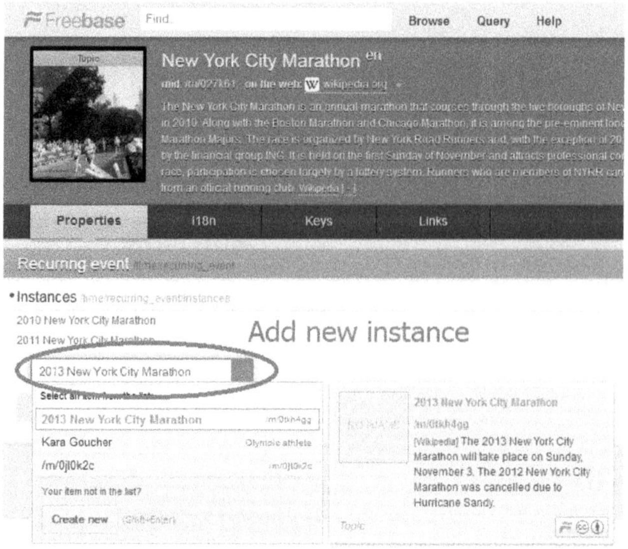


**Figure 1: An example Freebase triple contribution screen, where the user adds a new valid instance of a recurring event, namely the 2013 New York City Marathon.**

as Google and Bing) and serves as a concrete case study in the remainder of the paper. Freebase is primarily updated and expanded by volunteers and "data enthusiasts." User contributions are immediately visible, but may not be *promoted* (i.e., considered correct) until some time later. In Freebase, as in many other knowledge bases (e.g., DBpedia [7]), facts are stored as triples of the form $\langle subject, predicate, object \rangle$.

It should be emphasized, however, that this paper does not make any assumptions about the nature of the contributions that are peculiar to Freebase, beyond assuming the information is stored as triples (see the problem statement below). Consequently, the methodology proposed herein can be applied to verify the validity of contributed facts in other similarly-structured knowledge repositories. In our future work, we plan to extend our methodology to judging contributions with a more elaborate structure, such as SPOTL tuples used in YAGO [18], where each SPO triple is further annotated with Time and Location.

The example in Figure 1 illustrates the process of contributing a new triple to Freebase. A user can contribute a new triple, choosing from a rich schema of many possible predicates. For example, a user may creare a new instance of a type (as illustrated in the figure, adding the 2013 instance of the annual New York City Marathon event), or new attributes of an entity (e.g., the date of the event). While most of these contributions are valid, errors occur. Common types of errors include schema errors such as choosing a wrong type for an entity, or a wrong predicate for a relationship, entity reconciliation issues, incorrect facts, and so on. Over time, changes to the knowledge base may be reviewed, and facts can be updated or deleted (or re-added, in a case of deletion). Unfortunately, this process is time-consuming, labor-intensive, and, with existing techniques, tedious for the human reviewers. For instance, Figure 2 illustrates removing an incorrect fact for the birthplace of actor Bruce Lee, which was erroneously stated as "Chinatown," which remained unnoticed for some time, whereas the correct value

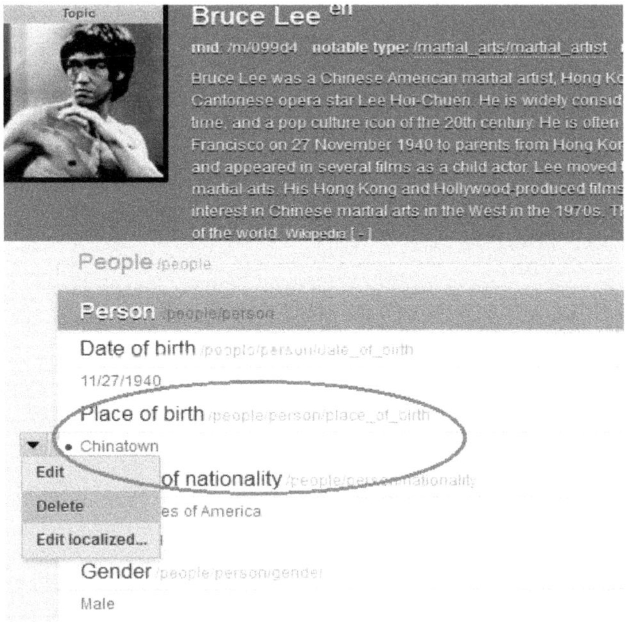


**Figure 2: An example deletion of a Freebase triple: removing incorrect birthplace value "Chinatown."**

should have been "Hong Kong." Thus, it is possible that erroneous contributions may remain unnoticed for some time, or, conversely, that good (and important) database additions may not be promoted or used by applications until they are reviewed or until they pass the test of time. For example, the contribution related to the 2013 NYC Marathon in Figure 1 is time-sensitive, since the event is scheduled to occur soon, and hence would be an ideal candidate for timely verification. Our aim is to automatically vet the contributions for correctness as soon as they are submitted. Formally, we state the problem as follows:

PROBLEM STATEMENT 1. We are given a contribution of a triple $t = \langle s,p,o \rangle$ by a user $u$. The goal is to predict whether $t$ is a correct contribution (as judged later by a human review process). The problem is thus formulated as a standard supervised binary classification. □

## 2.2 Contribution Quality Signals

Our approach is based on the idea that not all users are equally reliable, and that some predicates are inherently more difficult than others. These differences can be captured by various signals that correlate with the validity of the contribution. The signals we consider include user contribution history, user contribution expertise, and triple features (as a proxy for historical predicate difficulty).

### 2.2.1 User Contribution History

For each contribution submitted to Freebase, we use the prior contribution history of the contributing *user*, to estimate the validity of the contribution. Of all the sets of signals that we use, this one is the closest to previous work on estimating users' reputation (e.g., [2, 27, 22]), and we adapt the ideas from that line of research as a state of the art baseline. Specifically, we characterize user's prior contribution history using the features shown in Table 1. It should be noted that when modeling the user's domains of expertise

| *Feature Description* | *Scaling* |
|---|---|
| Total number of prior contributions | log |
| Total number of prior *correct* contributions | log |
| Total number of prior *incorrect* contributions | log |
| Fraction of correct contribution | – |
| Total number of deleted (*possibly* incorrect) contributions | log |
| Fraction of contributions that are deleted | – |
| Total number of prior deletion actions | log |
| Number of bad (reverted) deletions | – |
| Fraction of bad deletions | – |
| Membership lifetime of user (in days) | – |
| Number of seconds since last user action | log |

**Table 1: User contribution history features**

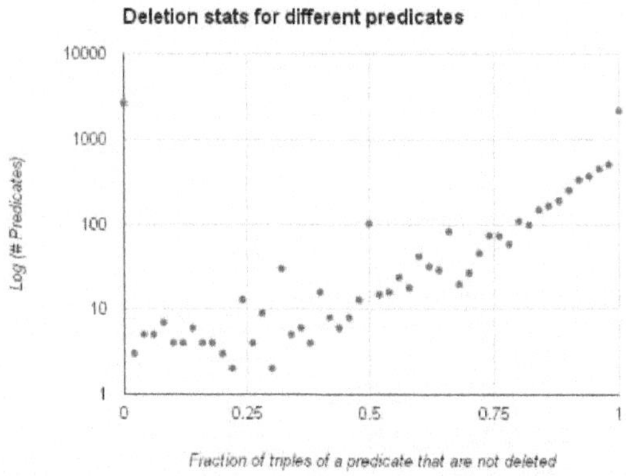


**Figure 3: Historical deletion statistics of Freebase predicates**

(cf. Section 2.2.3) we also use the set of the user's prior contributions. However, to be compatible with prior work, we only use the term "contribution history" to collectively refer to the features described in Table 1, which characterize the number and the correctness rate of the user's prior contributions.

### 2.2.2 Triple Features

Figure 3 reports the historical deletion statistics of Freebase triples, contributed by the community, for different predicates [3]. The horizontal axis is a proxy for "predicate difficulty": it is the fraction of triples, with a given predicate, that remain undeleted by the community, and are hence considered correct. A high value means that the predicate is "easy" while a low value indicates that the predicate is "difficult." The vertical axis reports the number of predicates in the Freebase schema, that have this "difficulty" value, as computed over all triple submissions with this predicate.

For example, there is a large number of predicates that historically do not contain correct values when contributed by public users (as opposed to Freebase staff, who are more knowledgeable and do not normally spam the knowledge

[3]Freebase data available at https://developers.google.com/freebase/data

| *Feature Name* | *Dimensionality* |
|---|---|
| Topics | $\sim 1,000,000$ |
| Taxonomy | $\sim 5,000$ |
| Predicates | $\sim 3,000$ |

**Table 2: Representation spaces of contributor expertise.**

base). For example, all 120 attribute instances of the predicate /martial_arts/martial_art/well_known_practitioner, which is supposed to contain references to well-known martial artists, submitted by public users, have been deleted by the community; examples of the deleted values include names such as "This is Elvis" and "Theseus", suggesting a strong prior that new values contributed for this predicate are likely to be incorrect. In contrast, values submitted for the predicate "/biology/genomic_locus/strand" are consistently preserved by the community (not deleted), providing a strong prior on accuracy. Finally, a number of predicates such as "/medicine/medical_treatment/side_effects", have roughly equal chances of being correct or incorrect.

As different predicates exhibit different historical deletion rate, the classifier can use this information as a proxy for estimating the prior likelihood of the predicate to be contributed correctly. We capture this information as a vector of features, each corresponding to a fully-specified predicate.

#### *Generalization over predicates.*

In Freebase, each predicate is of the form of "/Domain/Type/Property". Examples of top-level domains include "/biology" and "/music". For each domain, there are types associated with it such as "/music/album" and "/music/artist" for the "/music" domain. Finally, for each type, there are properties associated with it such as "/music/album/artist" and "/music/album/genre" for the "/music/album" type. In an attempt to generalize over leaf predicates, we have experimented with introducing additional features corresponding to these domains and types, but found these additional features not to be helpful. One possible explanation is that the information reflected in these features is implicitly captured through the plurality of the leaf-level features, which results in double counting. Experimenting with further refining the prior triple difficulty could be a subject of future refinements of our work.

### *2.2.3 User Contribution Expertise*

For each user, we estimate the areas of her expertise based on her previous contributions. To represent the contribution expertise of a user, we use three different concept spaces:

- *Topics*: a large topic model trained in an unsupervised manner using a large web corpus. The *Topics* space is derived from a proprietary scalable implementation of topic modeling very similar to LDA [8], with approximately one million topics.[4]
- *Taxonomy*: This space is based on an in-house taxonomy of approximately three thousand commercial topics, arranged in a four-level hierarchy, and a hierarchical text classifier [23, 13, 26] built in a supervised manner, which classifies text fragments onto the nodes of that taxonomy.
- *Predicates*: the union of all domains, types, and leaf predicates in Freebase (cf. the last paragraph in Section 2.2.2).

[4]More detailed description available at http://www.ipam.ucla.edu/abstract.aspx?tid=10734.

| *Similarity Metric* | *Space* | *Feature Sets* |
|---|---|---|
| *Dot Product* | All | All |
| *Cosine Similarity* | All | All |
| *Num. of intersecting concepts* | All | Positive, Negative |
| *Jaccard Index* | All | Positive, Negative |

**Table 3: Similarity Metrics for User Contribution Expertise Features**

To represent *user contributions*, we map from the triple contribution to the concept spaces described above. The mapping to the Freebase predicate concept space is direct, based on the predicate of the submitted triple. For the other two concept spaces, we use the text properties, and Wikipedia page of the subject and object of the triple, to construct a pseudo-document that contains the textual representation of the subject-object pair. We then process this pseudo-document using the topic model and the taxonomy classifier.

Then, to represent each *user*, we aggregate the Topic-, Taxonomy- and Predicate-representations of their prior contributions. Finally, to model the actual *expertise* of the user, we derive three feature sets based on the representations above:

- The *Positive* set, which aggregates contributions judged to be valid.
- The *Negative* set, which aggregates bad contributions.
- The *Net* set, which aggregates all contributions and is computed as the difference of the corresponding features in *Positive* and *Negative*.

That is, we explicitly model the user's expertise in each domain (represented by the different concept spaces), by tracking the aggregated valid and invalid contributions within each domain.

When a new triple is contributed, we first convert the contribution into the concept spaces described above. Then, to estimate the expertise of the user for each triple, we derive similarity features between the contribution concept distribution and the user contribution expertise distribution. Specifically, we use the similarity metrics in Table 3. Note that we compute similarity metrics involving the intersection count only for the *Positive* and *Negative* sets, but not for the *Net* set, as we just want to capture how similar is the current contribution to the previously proposed good and bad contributions.

While these results are not reported in the paper, during development we examined which of the concept space and expertise representation are most useful. Our analysis suggests that the *Taxonomy* and the *Predicates* concept spaces are more useful than the large *Topics* concept space. This is because the *Topics* concept space has of order of millions of topics, thus spreading the expertise distribution too sparse for users contributing not a lot of triples. This is especially true because the user contributions exhibit the familiar long-tail distribution, where majority of the users contribute less than hundred contributions and a small number of power users contributing more than hundred of thousands of contributions. In future works, we plan to consider smoothing/smearing the *Topics* space to reduce the number of topics and use other concept spaces. As for the various expertise representation, we observe no significant benefit of using one or the other, but the combination of all of them provide the best performance. This agrees with our intuition since each of the expertise representation intends to cover different facets of the user, i.e., the good, the bad, and the whole.

# 3. EXPERIMENTAL SETUP

We now describe our methodology for comparing the different methods for predicting the quality of the user contributions on Freebase.

## 3.1 Datasets

All experiments were performed on Freebase data, a publicly available resource. Each Freebase triple is associated with a timestamp, making it natural to split the data by time. This also allows for easy simulation of an operational environment, where we predict quality of new contributions using only historical data. We focus on contributions from *non-whitelisted users*, i.e., the majority of "regular" users in Freebase, as opposed to white-listed users who are Freebase-approved experts that "own" a particular topic and have the final say on the data therein. The non-whitelisted users have contributed almost 8 million triples to Freebase, so far. We split the data by time, into disjoint training and test sets, as described below.

**Test set, using human expert labels**: The test set is randomly sampled from the triples contributed by non-whitelisted users between June 1st, 2013 and August 15th, 2013. In total, we obtained judgments from professionally trained human experts for 3,975 triples [5].

Our human expert consists of paid contributors who are trained to do judgment on Freebase and have a deep understanding of Freebase schema. For example, our contributor can deal with intricacies of Freebase schema such as the difference between /people/person and /fictional_universe /fictional_character. All triples were judged by two experts. In case of a disagreement, a third expert adjudicated after a discussion with the original judges. As a result of this procedure, 3,414 contributions were judged as "good," and 561 as "bad."

**Training set, using heuristic, test-of-time labels**: In order to make use of the millions of historical contributions for training, we had to resort to automatic, *test-of-time heuristic labeling* (it would simply not be practical to manually label a dataset of this size). Using this approach, we assumed that all contributions that survived the "test of time" (i.e., were not deleted) for over $K$ weeks were correct. This heuristic borrows ideas from research on Wikipedia's edit history [2]. Specifically, for heuristic labeling we used the following criteria:

- All triples contributed and survive for older than $K$ weeks that are not deleted are considered good.
- All triples that have been deleted are considered bad unless the triple is reasserted and stays for more than $K$ weeks.
- The act of deleting an contribution is considered good if and only if nobody reassert the same triple that survives for more than $K$ weeks.
- Everything else is labeled as unknown and dropped from training set.

[5]Judgments can be found at http://goo.gl/0CXLYs

| *Contribution age in weeks* | *Labeling accuracy* |
|---|---|
| 2...3 | 86.5% |
| 3...4 | 87.5% |
| 4...5 | 89.3% |
| 5...6 | 88.8% |
| 6...7 | 88.4% |

**Table 4: Testing different cutoff values for the heuristic labeling of training examples.**

In order to choose a reasonable value of $K$, we experimented with different cutoff levels for how long a triple needs to "survive" in order to be considered correct. We sampled about 200 triples submitted in each one week intervals, for different $K$, (e.g., submitted less than $k+1$ but more than $k$ weeks prior) and obtained manual judgments for them using human experts similar to how we derive our test set. Note that this human-judged data set is disjoint from the test set, and was solely used for development experiments. Table 4 reports the resulting accuracy for different values of $K$. As we can see, the accuracy increases initially, as we increase $K$, and then flattens. Consequently, we chose $K = 4$ as a default value for the rest of the experiments in this paper.[6]

The generated training set consists of all triples in Freebase, contributed before June 1st, 2013. We assign labels following the the heuristic "test-of-time" criteria listed above. In total, we have 7,626,924 triples contributed by non-whitelisted Freebase users. We labeled 7,280,900 triples as "good" and 346,024 triples as "bad". The resulting training and test datasets are highly skewed towards "good" contributions (95.46% for training set and 85.9% for test set). The training set is more skewed towards "good" contributions because there might be contributions existing since the beginning of Freebase that are never corrected or that are much higher quality. This is consistent with the reputation of Freebase for being a generally high-quality source of data. Nevertheless, for many applications that rely on this data, accuracy of 86% may not be sufficient, indicating the need for validation or moderation for new contributions.

## 3.2 Methods Compared

We now summarize the different methods that we compare empirically in Section 4:

[6]We note that the heuristic labels were only used for creating the *training set* (in other words, we trained on data that could be noisy, due to the heuristic nature of the labeling). The experimental performance results are all reported on the test set, which contains only triples that have been judged for correctness by human experts.

- **CQUAL** :[7] Our method, which uses all three feature groups to estimate contribution quality, as described in Section 2.
- **Majority Class, Baseline**: Almost 86% of Freebase contributions are "good" (Section 3). Hence, we have a strong class imbalance between positive and negative examples. In this situation, it is a common practice to use a majority class predictor as a baseline, which predicts every contribution to be correct.
- **Contrib History, current state-of-the-art**: Adaptation of state-of-the-art approaches that predict quality of user contributions are using the prior contribution of the user [2, 27]. We build a supervised classifier that uses only the user contribution history features (Section 2.2.1) and we use it as a more advanced baseline to compare against.
- **Test of Time (Four Weeks)**: Unlike the first two methods, which can be used in real-time, to predict contribution quality as soon as they appear, the "test of time" method can only be used retroactively. This method considers the triples that survived four weeks of Freebase users' scrutiny, to be correct. This could be the moderation approach used in practice, say, by an application that uses data from Freebase: anything contribution submitted less than four weeks ago is not considered part of Freebase. While not truly comparable to the other methods, comparing the accuracy of our predictions to this approach provides a valuable reference point.

## 3.3 Classification Algorithms

We experimented with commonly used classifiers that could scale to the large number of examples and features.

- *Logistic Regression*
- *Gradboost*: The GradBoost algorithm by Duchi et al., [12], is a generalization of gradient-based coordinate descent methods, shown to be effective for multiclass prediction.
- *Perceptron*: Freund et al. [15].

## 3.4 Evaluation metrics

We use standard information retrieval metrics of *Precision* and *Recall*, defined respectively as fraction of predicted "good" triples that are truly correct, and the fraction of all true "good" triples identified. Precision is useful to report the rate of true positives, whereas recall measures the coverage of the "good" contributions identified by our method. We also compute the standard classification metrics, namely the ROC curves and the area under the curve (AUC), appropriate for evaluation of classification methods when the class distribution is skewed, as in our setting. We also measure *Relative Error Reduction* (RER), defined as:

$$RER = \frac{error_{baseline} - error_{\text{CQUAL}}}{error_{baseline}} \cdot 100\%.$$

The RER metric is useful to put the differences between system performance levels in perspective, by understanding how much errors we can reduce in our knowledge base using different method given the same recall level.

[7]CQUAL stands for Contribution QUALity predictor.

| *Method* | *RER@25%* | *RER@50%* | *RER@75%* |
|---|---|---|---|
| Majority | 0% | 0% | 0% |
| Contr. History | 44% | 10% | 0% |
| Test of Time | 22% | 22% | 22% |
| **CQUAL** | **65%** | **44%** | **39%** |

**Table 5: Relative Error Reduction (RER) at 25%, 50%, and 75% Recall levels.**

| *Method* | *AUC* |
|---|---|
| Majority | 0.5 |
| Contribution History | 0.543 |
| Test of Time | 0.5 |
| **CQUAL** | **0.707** |

**Table 6: The AUC values for the methods compared.**

# 4. EXPERIMENTAL RESULTS

In this section we empirically evaluate our methods for predicting the quality of the user contributions on Freebase. First, we present the main results, comparing our approach to various baselines (Section 4.1). We then analyze the results in more depth, to compare the performance of varying the underlying classification algorithms (Section 4.2) and feature sets (Section 4.3). Finally, we conduct an error analysis to provide insights into performance of our approach and possible future improvements (Section 4.4).

## 4.1 Predicting Contribution Quality

Figure 4 compares the performance of CQUAL to that of several baselines.[8] For each method, we report the interpolated precision values [34] (Y-axis) at each recall level (X-axis). We also computed, at each recall level, a paired $t$-test, to examine the statistical significance of the differences in performance between the different algorithms. We found that CQUAL outperforms all the baselines, including the retroactive "test of time" method, by a large margin. Specifically, we found CQUAL performance to be significantly superior to all other algorithms at recall levels ranging from 0.25 to 0.85, with the differences being significant at $p < 0.001$.

Table 5 reports the relative error reduction (RER) metric at key recall cut-offs, namely 25%, 50% and 75%. Table 6 lists the AUC values for the different algorithms. CQUAL provides consistent and substantial error reduction at all Recall levels considered, from 65% to 39% relative to the majority baseline, and a significantly higher AUC of 0.707 than competing methods.

## 4.2 Using different learning algorithms

We also experimented with three different learning algorithms (using all features), namely, logistic regression, gradient boosted log-linear model, and perceptron. Figures 5(a) and 5(b) show the results. Again, all three classifiers yield a substantial improvement over the existing baselines, con-

[8]In this section, we report the performance of the classifier trained using a logistic regression and using all the features described in Section 2.2. We compare performance of different classification algorithms in Section 4.2, and explore the utility of different feature classes in Section 4.3.

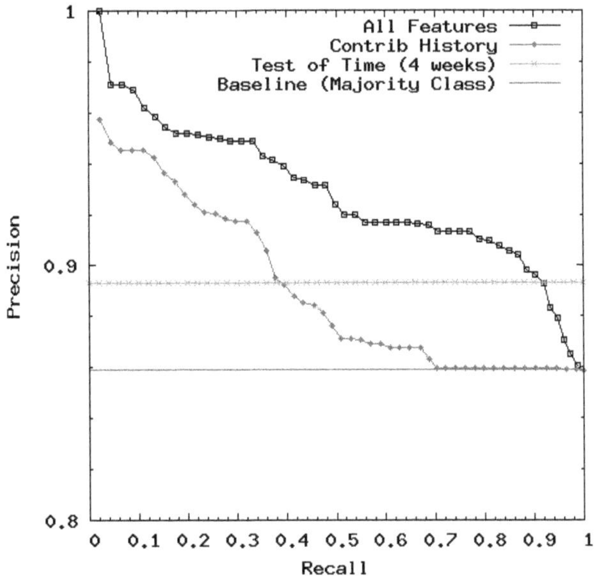


**Figure 4: Precision vs. Recall for CQUAL, User Contribution History (Contrib History), the Majority Class baseline, and the "Test of Time" approach.**

firming the informativeness of our feature sets. Logistic Regression consistently performs best, or nearly best, for all levels of recall; the performance is confirmed when considering the ROC curves. Therefore, we chose logistic regression for all our experiments and analyses.

## 4.3 Feature contribution analysis

Figure 6(a) reports the performance of classifiers using different feature groups individually. A classifier using user expertise features (Section 2.2.3) beats the baselines by a large margin. Features based on the contribution history of a user (Section 2.2.1) and those based on the prior difficulty of the different contribution types (Section 2.2.2) seem somewhat complementary, as the performance peaks and drops in different regions of the recall spectrum. Notably, the performance of the classifier that uses all three classes of features is significantly better, reaching 92.5% precision at 50% recall. Thus, for as many as half of the contributions we can make a highly accurate real-time decision whether the contribution is correct. The Precision-Recall results are complemented with analyzing the individual feature group performance through ROC curves (Figure 6(b)). Interestingly, Contribution History features only provide a lift over the majority baseline performance for low recall values (i.e., false positive ratio below 0.2), whereas Triple features (i.e., prior difficulty) accounts for a large lift for high recall levels (i.e., false positive ratio over 0.2). The ROC analysis demonstrates that these feature groups are somewhat complementary, and can be combined effectively into a single classifier (All Features). Interestingly, contribution history alone does not generate a significant improvement in performance compared to the naive "majority" baseline: The AUC value for the classifier that uses only contribution history features is at 0.543, barely above the random baseline of 0.5.

It is reasonable to anticipate that some of the feature groups are correlated, and individual feature group performance above may not contribute much to the final combined classifier. Therefore, we performed feature ablation analysis, by removing from the classifier one feature group at a time. Figure 7(a) contains the results. Interestingly, removing Triple Features (All-Triple Features in the graph) hurts performance the most, verifying that these features provide a unique signal not captured by contributor history or expertise. Somewhat puzzling is that removing Contributor History features actually *improves* performance slightly for some of the Recall levels. We conjecture that this is due to indiscriminately trusting a user who made correct contributions previously on one topic/domain to continue to make correct contributions in other domains, whereas modeling contributor *expertise* directly, as we do, does not suffer from this problem. The ROC curve results in Figure 7(b) reinforce this observation, indicating that occasionally ignoring contributor history (All-Contrib History in the graph) could improve performance. As expected, removing Triple and Contributor Expertise features consistently degrades performance. While some of the feature sets have very similar curves, based on our analysis of AUC, having all feature groups perform the best.

## 4.4 Analysis of Prediction Results

We now examine prediction results of each feature group to understand their performance in different scenarios, in order to provide more intuition about the contributions of different feature groups.

For example, the incorrect SPO triple[9] of <`/m/0kmyxvt, /film/film/initial_release_date, "2013-11-15"`>, was contributed by a user who exhibited historical accuracy of 0.88 prior to this contribution. If we had used merely the contribution history as our feature, our classifier would assign the confidence value of 0.8909 for this triple being correct, corresponding to the 55th percentile (i.e., 55% of the triples have lower classifier confidence), and would be predicted as "good". However, the other two feature groups perform better in this case, as they take into account of other signals orthogonal to the user's contribution history alone. For example, a classifier trained on triple features produced a low classifier confidence corresponding to 12th percentile (and thus would be labeled correctly as "bad"). This is likely because historically this predicate was observed to be generally challenging for "casual" Freebase users not intimately familiar with the domain. Similarly, a classifier trained using contribution expertise performs well, producing a relatively low classifier confidence of this triple, corresponding to 14th percentile (and thus would also be predicted as "bad"). This example illustrates a frequent scenario where topic- or predicate-specific features allow our classifier to outperform the contribution history-only baseline, by considering the domains and topics in which the user has previously demonstrated expertise.

Interestingly, contribution history does perform better than the other two feature groups in come cases. For example, for a correct SPO triple representing one of the Sea Otters in the Monterey Bay Acquarium, <`/m/0m55h, /zoos/zoo/`

[9]The triple is incorrect because the predicate /film/film/initial_release_date corresponds to the earliest release date of the film in any country. While the release date is 2013-11-15 in USA, this film will be released earlier in Russia on 2013-11-14.

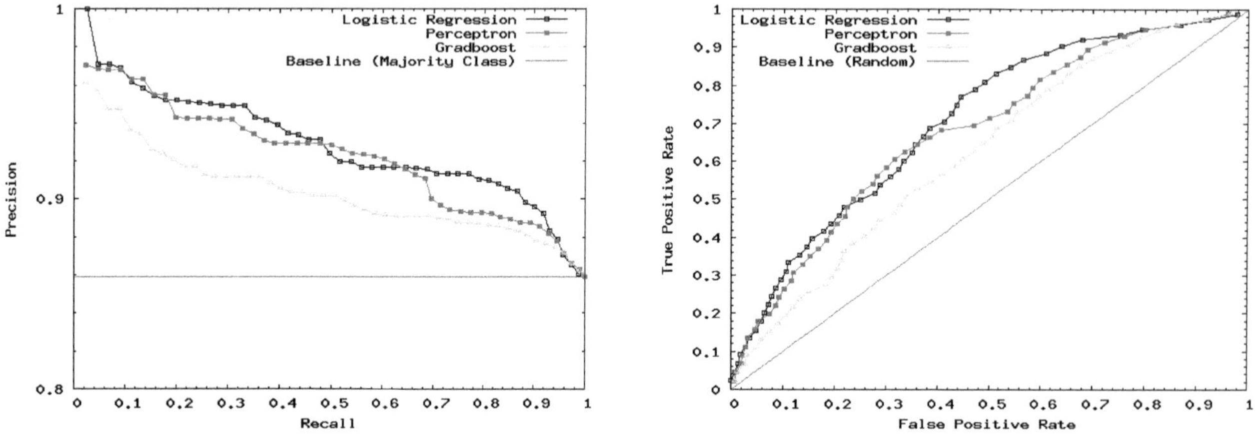


(a) Precision vs. Recall (b) ROC curves

**Figure 5: Precision-recall and ROC curves for different learning algorithms.**

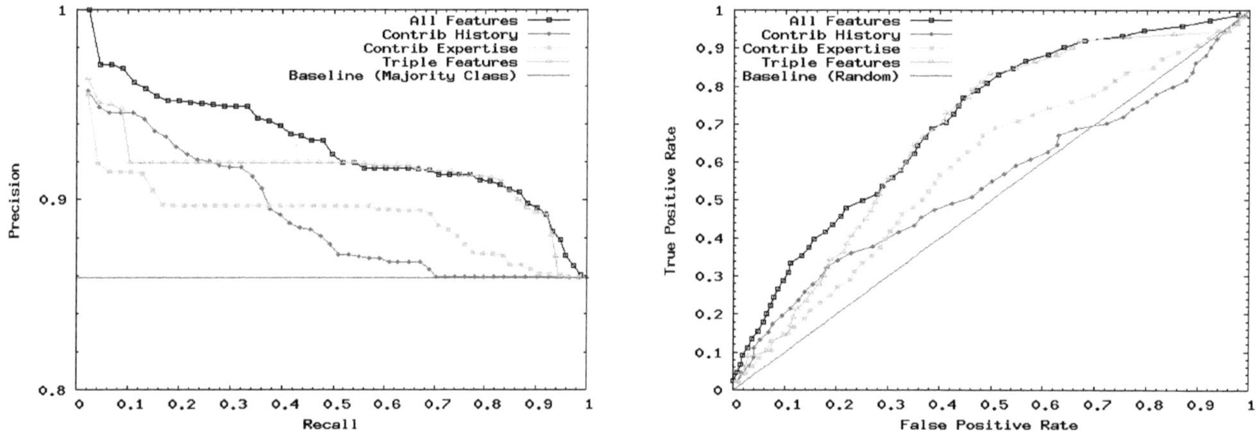


(a) Precision vs. Recall (b) ROC curves

**Figure 6: Precision-recall and ROC curves for individual feature sets.**

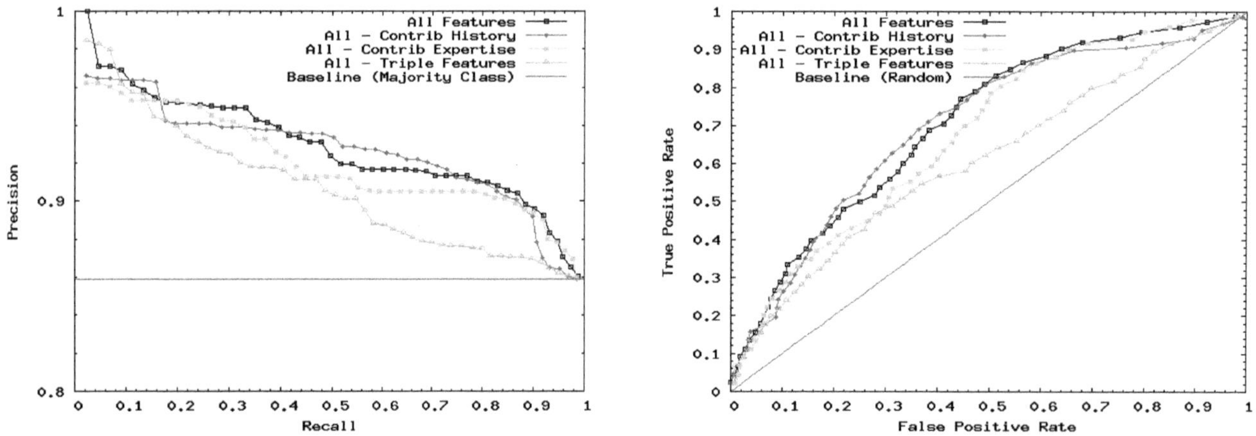


(a) Precision vs. Recall (b) ROC curves

**Figure 7: Precision-recall and ROC curves, removing one feature set at a time.**

`notable_animals, /m/0w4pq71>`, the classifier trained using contribution history predicted a much higher confidence score compared to the classifier trained using triple features or contribution expertise alone – presumably as expertise in Sea Otters is not common among Freebase contributors. As different feature groups perform well in different scenarios, it is not surprising that our classifier, trained holistically by combining the signals from all three feature groups, consistently exhibits superior performance.

# 5. RELATED WORK

**Quality Control in Crowdsourcing**: In crowdsourcing settings, the typical way of inferring the quality of the contributors is either by using questions for which we already know the answer ("gold" data) or through redundancy, or by combining the two (see, for example, [31, 30, 35, 25, 19, 5, 16]). The main disadvantage of gold data is that it requires the user to go through a phase of contributing answers for topics that we already know, effectively wasting resources and preventing contributors from making original contributions. With redundancy, this problem is avoided, but it is still not possible to infer quickly the quality of the contributions, without waiting for multiple workers to make a contribution for the same topic. Our work sidesteps these problems by using certain features derived based on prior belief on the difficulties of the fact being contributed.

An orthogonal direction that also attempts to predict the quality of the work in real-time is the work by Rzeszotarski and Kittur [28] that use micro-behavioral signals, such as mouse movements, to predict the quality of the user submission. Although we do not record such level of user behavior, it is conceivable that such approaches could be seamlessly combined with our approach to further enhance the predictive power of our system.

**Reputation systems**: Reputation mechanisms [9, 10] are also commonly used as predictors of contribution quality. The most common form of reputation is to examine the behavior of the user in similar tasks in the past and try to predict future performance (e.g., [2, 27, 22]). In our work, we use such an approach as a baseline, and show that the incorporation of a wider set of features about the user can improve significantly the predictive accuracy of our approach.

**Community question answering**: A lot of research has been conducted in the past that aims to predict the quality of online answers in "Community Question Answering" (CQA) platforms [20, 24, 3, 1, 6, 32, 29]. The general setting there is to predict the quality of a submitted answer. Our work has three major conceptual and methodological differences: First, we use as predictors a set of signals that captures domain expertise of the user based on its prior contributions; this allows us to have a much better understanding of the knowledge that a user has about a topic, and indeed the addition of these signals improve significantly the predictive performance of our system. Second, we exploit the fact that Freebase contributions happen within a schema, and we generate estimates of difficulty of filling correctly a particular triple; we are not aware of any wok that tries to estimate the inherent difficulty of providing an answer to a question in a CQA site. Third, we are predicting the quality of *short, factual, and structured* contributions: Getting quality signals from such contributions is inherently different and more difficult than extracting quality signals from longer, textual pieces of text, where a variety of other features (e.g., readability, spelling, grammar) are providing useful signals for predicting the quality of the contribution.

**Knowledge base construction**: There is also work that describes the challenges incorporating and evaluating the human contributions in a knowledge base [2, 17, 36, 11, 27, 21]. For sites like Wikipedia, a challenge is to even measure the quality of contributions; longevity of the contributions is typically a good proxy for a high-quality contribution. Freebase allows a similar model to judge correctness, (contributions that survive for longer than a certain time threshold are considered correct). However, in our case we actually procured third-party editors to verify the accuracy of the contributions and did not assume that contributions that survived for long are also de-facto correct; we are not aware of similar third-party verification of KB facts in other work. In [36], Wick et al. describe how they use human contributions as just a piece of evidence, as opposed to considering the human edit to be correct by default; our work dovetails nicely with such efforts, as we are actively providing estimates of the trust that we should place in any user contributions, therefore facilitating the adoption of such KB construction schemes.

# 6. DISCUSSION

We presented a technique for *real-time*, *automatic* evaluation of submissions in a structured knowledge repository. Past techniques either operated on a time-delay basis (facts are considered correct only after a certain time period has passed and the fact has not been changed), or auto-approved changes based on the prior history of the contributor. Our technique operates in real-time, and examines contribution history in a holistic fashion: we model both the inherent difficulty of making contributions for specific types of facts and we also model the expertise of the user in various topical parts of the space. This leads to a significant reduction in error rates, while at the same time improving the timeliness of the information that is represented in the knowledge base.

In the future, we plan on leveraging more sources of information for modeling the probability that a fact contribution is correct or not. One possible future works is to use hard constraints based on schema rules, for example, we can use the fact that a person should have a date of death after a date of birth, and that two persons born on different eras could not possibly be spouse and etc. We can also use signals from other information extraction systems to infer the likelihood that a particular contribution is correct based on the evidences from the web. Similarly, we can use Item Response Theory (IRT) [14] to jointly model in a more fine-grained mode the ability of users in different knowledge domains, potentially allowing for *actively soliciting* users to contribute facts to areas that they are contributing already and are experts on. Combining this with an appropriate design of badges [4], or other rewards, could potentially allow for a more focused and faster generation of high-quality knowledge repositories.


# Acknowledgments

We would like to thank John Giannandrea, Curt Janssen, Brian Karlak, and Kevin Murphy for helpful discussions and suggestions, and Jon Reitsma's team for providing the judgments.

## References

[1] L. A. Adamic, J. Zhang, E. Bakshy, and M. S. Ackerman. Knowledge sharing and yahoo answers: Everyone knows something. In *WWW*, 2008.

[2] B. T. Adler, L. de Alfaro, I. Pye, and V. Raman. Measuring author contributions to the wikipedia. In *4th Int'l Symposium on Wikis*. ACM, 2008.

[3] E. Agichtein, C. Castillo, D. Donato, A. Gionis, and G. Mishne. Finding high-quality content in social media. In *WSDM*, 2008.

[4] A. Anderson, D. Huttenlocher, J. Kleinberg, and J. Leskovec. Steering user behavior with badges. In *WWW*, pages 95–106, 2013.

[5] Y. Bachrach, T. Graepel, T. Minka, and J. Guiver. How to grade a test without knowing the answers—a bayesian graphical model for adaptive crowdsourcing and aptitude testing. *arXiv preprint arXiv:1206.6386*, 2012.

[6] J. Bian, Y. Liu, D. Zhou, E. Agichtein, and H. Zha. Learning to recognize reliable users and content in social media with coupled mutual reinforcement. In *WWW*, 2009.

[7] C. Bizer, J. Lehmann, G. Kobilarov, S. Auer, C. Becker, R. Cyganiak, and S. Hellmann. Dbpedia - a crystallization point for the web of data. *Web Semantics*, 7(3):154–165, Sept. 2009.

[8] D. M. Blei, A. Y. Ng, and M. I. Jordan. Latent dirichlet allocation. *JMLR*, 3:993–1022, 2003.

[9] C. Dellarocas. The digitization of word of mouth: Promise and challenges of online feedback mechanisms. *Management Science*, 2003.

[10] C. Dellarocas. Reputation mechanisms. In *Handbook on Economics and Information Systems*. Elsevier Publishing, 2006.

[11] O. Deshpande, D. S. Lamba, M. Tourn, S. Das, S. Subramaniam, A. Rajaraman, V. Harinarayan, and A. Doan. Building, maintaining, and using knowledge bases: A report from the trenches. In *SIGMOD*, 2013.

[12] J. Duchi and Y. Singer. Boosting with structural sparsity. In *ICML*, pages 297–304, 2009.

[13] S. Dumais and H. Chen. Hierarchical classification of web content. In *SIGIR'00*, pages 256–263, 2000.

[14] S. E. Embretson and S. P. Reise. *Item response theory*. Psychology Press, 2000.

[15] Y. Freund and R. E. Schapire. Large margin classification using the perceptron algorithm. *Machine learning*, 37(3):277–296, 1999.

[16] A. Galland, S. Abiteboul, A. Marian, and P. Senellart. Corroborating information from disagreeing views. In *WSDM*, 2010.

[17] A. Halfaker, A. Kittur, R. Kraut, and J. Riedl. A jury of your peers: quality, experience and ownership in wikipedia. In *5th Int'l Symposium on Wikis and Open Collaboration*, 2009.

[18] J. Hoffart, F. M. Suchanek, K. Berberich, and G. Weikum. YAGO2: A spatially and temporally enhanced knowledge base from wikipedia. *Artificial Intelligence*, 194:28–61, Jan. 2013.

[19] P. G. Ipeirotis, F. Provost, and J. Wang. Quality management on amazon mechanical turk. In *KDD Workshop on Human computation*, pages 64–67, 2010.

[20] J. Jeon, W. B. Croft, J. H. Lee, and S. Park. A framework to predict the quality of answers with non-textual features. In *SIGIR*, 2006.

[21] S. Kochhar, S. Mazzocchi, and P. Paritosh. The anatomy of a large-scale human computation engine. In *KDD Workshop on Human Computation*, pages 10–17, 2010.

[22] M. Kokkodis and P. G. Ipeirotis. Have you done anything like that?: predicting performance using inter-category reputation. In *WSDM*, pages 435–444, 2013.

[23] D. Koller and M. Sahami. Hierarchically classifying documents using very few words. In *ICML*, pages 170–178, 1997.

[24] Y. Liu, J. Bian, and E. Agichtein. Predicting information seeker satisfaction in community question answering. In *SIGIR*, 2008.

[25] V. C. Raykar, S. Yu, L. H. Zhao, G. H. Valadez, C. Florin, L. Bogoni, and L. Moy. Learning from crowds. *JMLR*, 99:1297–1322, 2010.

[26] M. E. Ruiz and P. Srinivasan. Hierarchical text categorization using neural networks. *Information Retrieval*, 5:87–118, 2002.

[27] J. Rzeszotarski and A. Kittur. Learning from history: predicting reverted work at the word level in wikipedia. In *Computer Supported Cooperative Work*, pages 437–440, 2012.

[28] J. M. Rzeszotarski and A. Kittur. Instrumenting the crowd: using implicit behavioral measures to predict task performance. In *Annual symposium on User interface software and technology*, pages 13–22. ACM, 2011.

[29] C. Shah and J. Pomerantz. Evaluating and predicting answer quality in community QA. In *SIGIR*, 2010.

[30] V. S. Sheng, F. Provost, and P. G. Ipeirotis. Get another label? improving data quality and data mining using multiple, noisy labelers. In *KDD*, pages 614–622. ACM, 2008.

[31] R. Snow, B. O'Connor, D. Jurafsky, and A. Y. Ng. Cheap and fast—but is it good?: evaluating non-expert annotations for natural language tasks. In *EMNLP*, pages 254–263. Association for Computational Linguistics, 2008.

[32] M. A. Suryanto, E.-P. Lim, and A. S. R. H. L. Chiang. Quality-aware collaborative question answering: Methods and evaluation. In *WSDM*, 2009.

[33] F. B. Viégas, M. Wattenberg, and K. Dave. Studying cooperation and conflict between authors with history flow visualizations. In *CHI*, pages 575–582, 2004.

[34] E. M. Voorhees. Overview of trec 2003. In *TREC*, pages 1–13, 2003.

[35] P. Welinder, S. Branson, S. Belongie, and P. Perona. The multidimensional wisdom of crowds. *NIPS*, 23:2424–2432, 2010.

[36] M. Wick, K. Schultz, and A. McCallum. Human-machine cooperation with epistemological dbs: supporting user corrections to knowledge bases. In *AKBC Workshop*, pages 89–94. ACL, 2012.

# Modelling Growth of Urban Crowd-Sourced Information

Giovanni Quattrone
University College London
London, UK
g.quattrone@cs.ucl.ac.uk

Afra Mashhadi
Bell Labs, Alcatel Lucent
Dublin, Ireland
afra.mashhadi@alcatel-lucent.com

Daniele Quercia
Yahoo Labs
Barcelona, Spain
dquercia@acm.org

Chris Smith-Clarke
University College London
London, UK
chris.smith@ucl.ac.uk

Licia Capra
University College London
London, UK
l.capra@cs.ucl.ac.uk

## ABSTRACT

Urban crowd-sourcing has become a popular paradigm to harvest spatial information about our evolving cities directly from citizens. OpenStreetMap is a successful example of such paradigm, with an accuracy of its user-generated content comparable to that of curated databases (e.g., Ordnance Survey). Coverage is however low and most importantly non-uniformly distributed across the city. Being able to model the spontaneous growth of digital information in these domains is required, so to be able to plan interventions aimed at gathering content about areas that would otherwise be neglected. Inspired by models of physical urban growth developed by urban planners, we build a model of digital growth of crowd-sourced spatial information that is both easy to interpret and dynamic, so to be able to determine what factors impact growth and how these change over time. We build and test the model against five years of OpenStreetMap data for the city of London, UK. We then run the model against two other cities, chosen for their different physical and digital growth's characteristics, so to stress-test the model. We conclude with a discussion of the implications of this work on both developers and users of urban crowd-sourcing applications.

## Categories and Subject Descriptors

[**Information Systems Applications**]: Spatial-temporal systems-Geographic information systems

## General Terms

Measurement

## Keywords

Crowd-sourcing, Cellular Automata, Modelling


*WSDM'14*, February 24–28, 2014, New York, New York, USA.
Copyright 2014 ACM 978-1-4503-2351-2/14/02 ...$15.00.
http://dx.doi.org/10.1145/2556195.2556244.

## 1. INTRODUCTION

Urban crowd-sourcing has become a popular mechanism to harvest knowledge about our evolving cities directly from their citizens. Equipped with powerful mobile devices, citizens have become surveyors, with council-monitoring applications like FixMyStreet;[1] reporters, with micro-blogging sites such as Twitter;[2] and cartographers, with geo-wikis like Cyclopath[3] and OpenStreetMap.[4]

OpenStreetMap (OSM) is perhaps one of the most successful examples of urban crowd-sourcing, with currently over 547,270 users, collectively building a free, openly accessible, editable map of the world. Research has shown that accuracy of the geographic information stored in OSM is very high and it sometimes supersedes the most reputable centrally-maintained geographic datasets, performing especially well in urban areas [19, 31]. As testimony of this success, businesses like Foursquare[5] are now switching from proprietary datasets to OSM.[6]

However, relying entirely on user-generated content for urban mapping raises concerns, not only in terms of accuracy of the collected information (which, for OSM, is presently high), but also in terms of its coverage. Recent studies of OSM have revealed that coverage of information is non-uniformly distributed across a city, with areas that are either further from the centre, or central but income deprived, being particularly neglected [30]. This finding raises concerns in terms of the long-term sustainability of urban crowd-sourcing: is coverage going to spontaneously grow across the city? Or are there going to be areas that will continue to be neglected? Studies so far have been limited in that they quantify coverage at one specific point in time, and in so doing they cannot disclose the factors (e.g., spatial, social, demographic) that contribute to crowd-sourcing participation over time. Being able to build a model that *explains* growth, and that accurately detects what areas are most likely to suffer from neglect, will allow location-based services that make use of crowd-sourced information to plan evidence-based targeted interventions. Such interventions may include, for example, *(i)* the use of a hybrid approach of crowd-sourced and proprietary data, whereby proprietary data is used for seeding the areas that are predicted to suffer (e.g., because far from the city center or because located in economically-deprived neighbourhoods); *(ii)* the design of incentives to call the OSM community to edit spe-

[1] `http://www.fixmystreet.com`
[2] `http://twitter.com/`
[3] `http://cyclopath.org/`
[4] `http://www.openstreetmap.org/`
[5] `https://foursquare.com`
[6] `http://blog.foursquare.com/2012/02/29/`

cific areas, for example, in the form of OSM mapping parties, that is, social events organised by OSMers to descend on an area and map it exhaustively.

We present a model inspired by Cellular Automata theory [11] that accurately captures the *digital* growth of crowd-sourced urban information. Cellular Automata are computational methods that simulate the growth of complex systems by means of a set of simple rules that afford easy interpretation. These models have been extensively used by urban planners and policy makers to understand the evolution of *physical* urban systems, to predict their natural growth, and to evaluate the impact of alternative policy interventions [22]. In this work, we consider a dynamic yet easy-to-interpret version of such models: we divide the city area into cells, we capture past crowd-sourcing activity information for each of them, then use linear regressions to model their growth. We build and test the model over five years of OSM data for the city of London, UK. We discover that the digital growth of crowd-sourced urban information depends on different factors at different times: during the bootstrapping phase of urban crowd-mapping, geodemographic factors, such as distance from the city centre and population density, play a key role (e.g., early adopters naturally start mapping central areas); physical proximity and social influence subsequently become more important; finally, for areas whose digital coverage has already become high, past activity is sufficient to correctly estimate future growth. To assess the validity of the model beyond the city of London, UK, we then stress-test it under rather different urban settings - New York City and Boston in the US. We find the model to suggest that current growth in such cities is mostly explained by geodemographic properties, indeed the same that explained growth in London in its early days of OSM mapping.

The remainder of this paper is structured as follows: after a brief overview of the state-of-the-art, we describe the urban crowd-sourcing dataset at hand and the growth metric we compute on it. The construction of our model follows, with emphasis on the properties that we have mapped onto simple cellular automata rules. We then validate the model: using OSM data for the city of London, UK, we first assess the suitability of the chosen rules individually (and thus of their underlying properties), then of the model as a whole. We then evaluate the model's accuracy and generalisability using it for two other cities in the US. Finally, we conclude the paper by stating the implications of these findings and elaborating on future directions of research.

## 2. RELATED WORK

Urban crowd-sourcing generally refers to the collective gathering of user-generated content pertaining to the urban environment. The most popular example of such content is volunteered geographic information (VGI), such as that maintained by OpenStreetMap. For years, the research community has studied the accuracy of such information [17], and compared it to traditional geographical datasets maintained by national mapping agencies, as well as proprietary datasets maintained by commercial companies such as Navteq.[7] The findings show very high positional accuracy, both in the UK [18, 19], as well as France, Germany and Switzerland [13, 29].

While accuracy is consistently high, coverage has been shown to vary considerably. Zielstra *et al.* [45] found that road coverage in Germany sharply decreases as we move away from city centres and Girres *et al.* [13] discovered a positive correlation between the number of OSM road 'objects' in an area and number of OSM contributors in that area. Shifting focus from the road network to points-of-interest (POIs), Mashhadi *et al.* [30] found that both socio-economic factors (e.g., income deprivation) and physical distance from the city centre are negatively correlated with coverage in London, UK. Another well known example of urban crowd-sourcing application is Cyclopath,[8] a geo-wiki that is being successfully used to digitally map route information for cyclists in Minneapolis. Rather than focusing on information accuracy, the researchers behind Cyclopath have investigated issues of users' motivation that lead to contributions [38], and conducted studies in terms of user's participation and behavioural analysis [37, 35, 36]. An interesting finding was that manually highlighting areas in the city which were under-covered was sufficient to trigger motivation among cyclists to go those places and map them.

A common limitation of the above studies is that they analyse coverage at one specific point in time. However, crowd-mapping is a process that takes place over time, with contributors both joining and leaving the system all the time, and with new contributions continuously being added. In order to quantify the long term success and sustainability of an urban crowd-sourcing system, we must understand how digital crowd-sourced urban information *grows* over time. Studies in this vein are limited within the area of crowd-mapping. An exception is Neis *et al.* [34], who have recently measured coverage of the OSM road network in Germany over a period of three years, and highlighted at what point the map can be considered complete with respect to commercial datasets. However, this is a retrospective study, with no attempt to model future growth.

Shifting our attention from urban crowd-sourcing to online social networks, we find several studies that have attempted to model their dynamics instead. A large stream of research has developed models of the ways in which individuals join communities. Structural properties of the users' social networks have been found to have a strong influence on subsequent tie formation [5]. Geographical properties of the social network have also been linked to tie formation [21]. For example, Kleinberg [23, 24] modelled the probability of two individuals being friends based on the intuition that friendship probability increases with geographic proximity. In 2005, Liben-Nowell et al. [28] experimentally tested this model upon a half million profiles on the blogging site LiveJournal, on which people reported their locations within the USA and lists of friends. The authors incorporated population density into the initial model and determined that 66% of LiveJournal friendships form through geographic processes. Another stream of research has looked into how information diffuses through these existing social networks. Various models have been proposed based on contagion processes (e.g., [27, 9, 15]); these models have also been expanded, to account for homophily (e.g., [2, 3]), external influences (e.g., [33]), and the language used to describe topics (e.g., [40]).

These models share our goal of modelling 'growth', interpreted in its broader sense (e.g., of ties within a social network, of nodes reached by a topic). However, none of the above models is directly applicable to the area of urban crowd-sourcing (and OpenStreetMap in particular), as such scenario lacks the existence of an explicit social network, so we cannot reason about social network structure to capture growth dynamics. We hypothesise that factors reflecting engagement, influence, and geography will still be predictors of growth in our context though. In the next section, we present a spatio-temporal model of growth that uses properties such as self-reinforcement, physical proximity, social influence and geodemographic conditioning, to model digital growth for urban crowd-sourcing scenarios.

[7] `http://www.navteq.com/`

[8] `http://cyclopath.org/`

# 3. RESEARCH METHODOLOGY

We have built and subsequently tested a growth model of urban crowd-sourced information in the context of OSM. In this section, we thus begin with a brief overview of this dataset, followed by a definition of the growth metric we used. We then delve into a detailed description of the model we built, emphasising the properties that have informed the modelling process.

## 3.1 Dataset Description

OpenStreetMap is freely available to download[9] and contains the history of all edits since 2006 on all spatial objects performed by all users. In OSM jargon, spatial objects can be one of three types: *nodes*, *ways*, and *relations*. Nodes are single geospatial points, defined using latitude/longitude coordinates, and they typically represent POIs (e.g., cafes, restaurants, hospitals, schools); ways consist of ordered sequences of nodes, and mostly represent roads (as well as streams, railway lines, and the like); finally, relations are used for grouping other objects together, based on logical (and usually local) relationships (e.g., administrative boundaries, bus routes).

To reduce the dataset to a manageable size, we restrict our analysis to the area of Greater London, United Kingdom, where OSM was originally created and launched, and for which the history of contributions is longest. Furthermore, we consider OSM nodes only, thus focusing on POIs rather than the road network. We chose to sample POIs instead of roads as the contribution processes differ greatly between the two categories: road mapping is typically done by users who have high expertise in both the geography of an area and the editing tools required to digitally represent it, while POI mapping can be performed by any city dweller, with no specific cartographic skills required. The latter category is thus more representative of the broad urban crowd-sourcing setting. Finally, to consider only genuine users' contributions, we have looked into contributions that most likely correspond to bulk imports. Two bulk imports were detected in the whole dataset, with tens of thousands of edits done in a single day by a single user, spread throughout Greater London (e.g., more than 20,000 post boxes spread across all Greater London appeared in OSM in only one day in 2009 from the same user). We chose to discard such data for two main reasons: on one hand, we intend to model genuine 'bottom-up', user-generated contributions, of which massive imports are not representative; on the other hand, these bulk 'donations' of data were not geographically concentrated in an area, but rather spread throughout the whole of Greater London. As a result, even if we kept the data (and our model failed to capture it), the result would be a constant error added almost uniformly to all areas under predictions. We should note that, apart from these two extreme cases, we have identified many other peaks of edits by single users, which may or may not be smaller imports; in these cases, we kept and modelled all the data, to avoid falsifying results.

Figure 1 illustrates the cumulative number of editors and edits for each year in the sampled dataset, with 96,357 edits done by a total of 2,240 users overall. As shown, in the very first year of OSM being launched (2006), contributors and contributions were extremely low; to avoid our modelling being skewed by this cold-start phase, during which the technology was being tested but not widely available to the public, we did not try to model 2006 activity, and in the remaining of the paper we focus on the period 2007 (year of the launch of the OSM "State of the Map" conference[10]) onwards.

[9]http://www.geofabrik.de/data/download.html
[10]http://www.stateofthemap.org

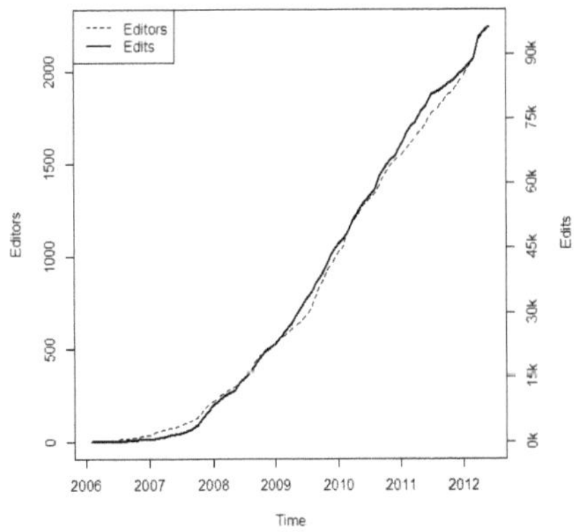


**Figure 1: Cumulative number of OSM editors and edits over time**

## 3.2 Metrics

In order to measure growth of crowd-sourced information across an urban area over time, the first step was to choose a *spatial* and *temporal* unit of analysis. In terms of spatial unit of analysis, previous studies have shown that factors such as population density and deprivation are correlated with coverage of crowd-sourced urban information [30]. We have thus chosen to operate at a level of granularity in London for which such information is available. This is the level of *wards*, of which there are about 600, as defined by London Local Authorities.[11]

In terms of temporal unit of analysis, we have tried different time units, from finer (3 months) to coarser (18 months) granularity. In the end, we chose to report the results for the smallest unit of granularity (12 months) that still afforded statistically significant results across *all areas* of Greater London. In particular, although in the very center of the city we could have chosen finer temporal granularity, doing so in the many wards falling within Greater London would not have provided us with sufficient data to have statistically significant results. This has forced us to consider 1 year as the unit of measurement for the time series.

Having defined this spatio-temporal unit of analysis, we then needed to define a metric that reflected which areas had been digitally mapped and which had been neglected instead. To this purpose, it is worth pointing out that not all areas naturally require the same amount of OSM edits to be mapped. For example, areas containing many services and attractions will require many OSM edits to be mapped (e.g., Soho in London); however, sparse areas like parks and industrial estates will require significantly less. To capture this reasoning, we chose as metric *OSM activity*, defined as the number of OSM edits *relative to* the number of physical POIs in each ward at that time:

$$\text{OSM activity} = \frac{\#\text{OSM edits}}{\#\text{POIs}} \qquad (1)$$

#OSM edits is readily available from our OSM dataset. To estimate #POIs, that is, the actual number of POIs present in each area, we use Navteq, the leading global provider of maps and location data, covering millions of POIs of varying nature, from restaurants to hospitals and gas stations. Being a commercial service, Navteq's primary objective is to ensure the highest level of accuracy of its

[11]http://data.london.gov.uk/datastore/package/ward-profiles-2011

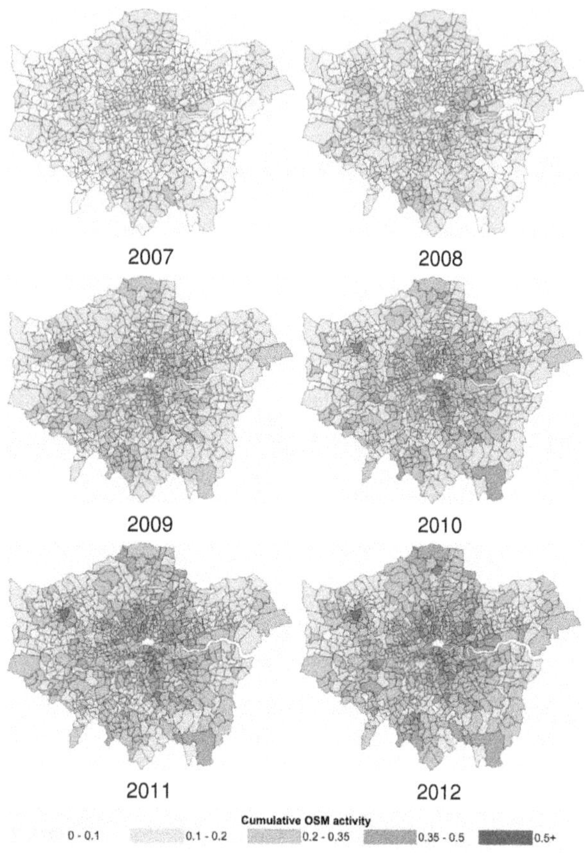


**Figure 2: Cumulative OSM activity from 2007 until 2012**

data (the information contained there is factually correct and up-to-date).

Figure 2 illustrates the cumulative temporal evolution of OSM activity (Equation 1) in London from 2007 to 2012. As shown, the vast majority of areas have low cumulative activity (with only a few wards slightly above 0.5); furthermore, complex dynamics are at play, with no clear pattern emerging (e.g., no core-to-periphery spreading). To then measure growth, in the next section we propose a model that captures how this metric changes over time.

## 3.3 Modelling Growth

Modelling the *physical* growth of urban areas has been extensively studied in the domain of urban planning [12, 1, 39]. These models offer an analysis and extrapolation of city dynamics that planners and policy makers use to forecast both natural growth and the effect of policy interventions. Cellular Automata models [11] are a well known example of such models, capable of reproducing complex spatial and temporal dynamics at a global scale, using simple local transition rules. More precisely, the urban area under investigation is first divided into a grid of cells (where each cell may correspond, for example, to a ward) and assigned an initial state $t_0$. An iterative computational process is then started, whereby the system moves from state $t$ (with $t \geq t_0$) to state $t+1$ using a set of *transition rules* that are applied at each cell in the grid. Typically, transition rules are the same for each cell and follow this general mathematical function:

$$\begin{aligned} S(c_i, t+1) = f(&S(nbh_1(c_i), t), \ldots, S(nbh_n(c_i), t), \\ &S(nbh_1(c_i), t-1), \ldots, S(nbh_n(c_i), t-1), \\ &\ldots, \\ &S(nbh_1(c_i), t_0), \ldots, S(nbh_n(c_i), t_0)) \end{aligned} \quad (2)$$

where $c_i$ is the $i$-th cell of the grid, $S(\cdot, \cdot)$ is the state of a cell at a given discretized time, $nbh_1(\cdot), \ldots, nbh_n(\cdot)$ are the neighbourhood cells relative to the input cell whose transition is being computed (usually including the cell itself), and $f$ is any mathematical function, receiving as input a list of states and returning the new state of the cell under transformation. As an example, a very simple Cellular Automata model, modelling evolution of the physical urban landscape, could comprise the following transformation rules: if a ward is non-urban and it is surrounded by three or more urban wards, then change it to urban; if the ward is urban, then keep it urban. More complex rules are used in practice, but generally all Cellular Automata models follow the basic idea that the state of urbanization of a part of the city depends on the previous state of urbanization of that part (or a sequence of its previous states), together with the previous states of urbanization of its neighbours.

In this work, we borrow from the theories of Cellular Automata to model the growth of *urban crowd-sourced information* in the *digital* domain. To this purpose, we considered each ward of London as a cell of a Cellular Automata model, and discretized time at one-year intervals. Finally, we defined the *state of a ward* $w_i$ of London at time $t$ as the OSM activity that occurred in that ward during the one year preceding $t$. In the following, we refer to such state as $act(w_i, t)$.

We built our model of crowd-sourced information growth based on processes and properties that capture factors of attractiveness, influence and geodemography.

PROPERTY 1 (SELF-REINFORCEMENT). *If a ward has been edited in the recent past, the ward will continue to be edited in the future.* □

This property paraphrases the preferential attachment process [44], and captures the intuition that, if a geographical area has attracted many contributions from OSM editors in the past (e.g., it contains 'attractions' of interest to such crowd), it will continue to do so in the future. We distinguish between recent and full history of past, so to capture a possible saturation effect that may arise when a ward has already been massively edited in the full past history, to an extent that there is not much else to edit. We then build a model where the predicted outcome $act(w_i, t+1)$ is computed as a linear function over these two quantities:

$$act(w_i, t+1) = \beta_1 \cdot act(w_i, t) + \beta_2 \cdot \hat{act}(w_i, t) + \Omega \quad (3)$$

where $act(w_i, t)$ is OSM activity measured in the last year, while $\hat{act}(w_i, t)$ is defined as $act(w_i, t) + \ldots + act(w_i, t_0)$ and condenses a whole history of activity for that ward; the parameters $\beta_1$ and $\beta_2$ are the weights we assign to $act(\cdot, \cdot)$ and $\hat{act}(\cdot, \cdot)$ respectively (in the next section, we will show how to determine them). In this and the following models, we use $\Omega$ to concisely represent linear pairwise parameter interactions.

As an OSM contributor maps an element in a ward, s/he may also do so for a neighbouring ward s/he passes through. In other words, a contagious process may take place, reminiscent of [20], leading to a spatial diffusion of OSM activity. The second property we consider is thus the following:

PROPERTY 2 (SPATIAL CORRELATION). *If the cells surrounding a ward have been heavily edited in the past, the ward is likely to be edited in the future.* □

To quantitatively capture this property, we first define two *spatial correlation scores* for each ward $w_i$ at each yearly snapshot $t$: the maximum spatial correlation score $sc_M(w_i, t)$ and the average spatial correlation score $sc_A(w_i, t)$, computed as the maximum and the average activity value of the neighbouring wards respectively:

$$\begin{aligned} sc_M(w_i,t) &= \text{Max}_{w_j \in nbh(w_i)}(act(w_j,t)) \\ sc_A(w_i,t) &= \text{Avg}_{w_j \in nbh(w_i)}(act(w_j,t)) \end{aligned}$$

where $nbh(w_i)$ indicates the list of neighbouring wards of $w_i$.

We then build a more complex model which predicts activity in a ward $w_i$ at time $t+1$, based on its own past state and that of its adjacent wards. As before, we use a linear function of the form:

$$\begin{aligned} act(w_i,t+1) &= \beta_1 \cdot act(w_i,t) + \beta_2 \cdot \hat{act}(w_i,t) + \\ &\quad +\beta_3 \cdot sc_M(w_i,t) + \\ &\quad +\beta_4 \cdot sc_A(w_i,t) + \Omega \end{aligned} \tag{4}$$

The previous property captures spatial contagion processes based on geographic adjacency between wards. A complementary definition can be given based on wards that, regardless of their spatial positioning within a city, have attracted the same OSM contributors (because they might, for example, offer related attractions/urban functions [10]). We thus formulate the third property as:

PROPERTY 3 (EDITING CORRELATION). *If a ward has been edited by contributors who have heavily edited other wards in the past year, the ward is likely to be edited in the future.* □

In other words, the activity of a ward depends on the past activity of its 'co-edited' areas, where two areas are defined as 'co-edited' if they are edited by some shared editors. To capture this property quantitatively, we define two *editing correlation scores* for each ward $w_i$ at each yearly snapshot $t$:

$$\begin{aligned} ec_M(w_i,t) &= \text{Max}_{w_j \in cdt(w_i)}(\zeta(w_i,w_j,t) \cdot act(w_j,t)) \\ ec_A(w_i,t) &= \text{Avg}_{w_j \in cdt(w_i)}(\zeta(w_i,w_j,t) \cdot act(w_j,t)) \end{aligned}$$

where $cdt(\cdot)$ returns the list of co-edited wards of the input ward (that is, the list of wards that share at least one editor with the input ward); $\zeta(\cdot,\cdot,\cdot)$ receives as input two wards $w_i$ and $w_j$, and a time window $t$, and returns a number belonging to [0,1] indicating how strongly $w_i$ and $w_j$ have been 'co-edited' in the time window $t$. Specifically, $\zeta$ returns the fraction of the edits of $w_i$ which, during year $t$, has been made by editors who edited both $w_i$ and $w_j$. Intuitively, the editing correlation score $ec_M$ of $w_i$ is high when there exists at least one ward $w_j$ that has been heavily edited in the last year, by contributors who have also edited $w_i$. For the second score $ec_A$ to be high, there must exist not just one but *several* heavily edited wards, sharing contributors with $w_i$.

The resulting model predicts the activity in a ward $w_i$ at time $t+1$, based on its past state, the past state of its physically adjacent wards, and that of its co-edited wards. Once again, we use a linear function of the form:

$$\begin{aligned} act(w_i,t+1) &= \beta_1 \cdot act(w_i,t) + \beta_2 \cdot \hat{act}(w_i,t) + \\ &\quad +\beta_3 \cdot sc_M(w_i,t) + \beta_4 \cdot sc_A(w_i,t) + \\ &\quad +\beta_5 \cdot ec_M(w_i,t) + \beta_6 \cdot ec_A(w_i,t) + \\ &\quad +\Omega \end{aligned} \tag{5}$$

All previous models rely on historical OSM activity information about a ward to be available to compute its next state. This means that, if a ward has not been edited at all in the past and neither have its adjacent ones, this ward is consistently predicted to not grow. However, Figure 2 shows this is not the case, and over time new, previously isolated areas start to be mapped. We thus consider the following factors that may determine the activation of a new ward:

*Population.* The more densely populated an area is, the more likely one of its residents will join the crowd of OSM editors and start to map the areas s/he knows (i.e., where they live). UK Census data published by the National Statistics Office[12] offers population density information at ward level; we can thus use this information within our model. On top of population density (that is, population divided by ward size), we also consider population per POIs (that is, population divided by number of physical POIs in an area), to differentiate between areas with different POI concentration.

*Deprivation.* Higher population density does not directly translate into higher number of contributors. Indeed, studies have revealed that contributors of crowd-sourced systems are a group of predominantly young, educated and wealthy males [14]. It is thus more likely that areas of low deprivation will have new OSM contributors. Furthermore, a recent study has revealed that Londoners living in well-off areas do not tend to visit areas that are deprived [26], thus increasing the probability that well-off wards will start to be mapped, as opposed to deprived ones. To quantify deprivation, we use the Index of Multiple Deprivation (IMD), a single parameter that aggregates indicators including income, employment, and education deprivation, as well as crime rates.

*Distance from the Nearest Poly-centre.* Social and economic activities tend to cluster around a small number of poly-centres in metropolitan areas [8]; a recent study [41] has found that London has 10 different polis. We expect that the further a ward is from its nearest poly-centre, the less-likely this ward will be activated, based on previous OSM studies that have shown road coverage to dramatically decrease as one moves away from the city centre [45].

Based on these considerations we formulate our final property:

PROPERTY 4 (GEODEMOGRAPHY). *The geodemographic factors of a ward (e.g., its population, deprivation, and distance from the centre) influence the probability of such ward to be mapped in the future.* □

Our final model combines all four properties above, and predicts the activity in a ward $w_i$ at time $t+1$, based on its past state, the past state of its physically adjacent wards, that of its co-edited wards, as well as its own geodemographic factors:

$$\begin{aligned} act(w_i,t+1) &= \beta_1 \cdot act(w_i,t) + \beta_2 \cdot \hat{act}(w_i,t) + \\ &\quad +\beta_3 \cdot sc_M(w_i,t) + \beta_4 \cdot sc_A(w_i,t) + \\ &\quad +\beta_5 \cdot ec_M(w_i,t) + \beta_6 \cdot ec_A(w_i,t) + \\ &\quad +\beta_7 \cdot pop\_dens(w_i) + \\ &\quad +\beta_8 \cdot pop\_poi(w_i) + \beta_9 \cdot imd(w_i) + \\ &\quad +\beta_{10} \cdot dist(w_i) + \Omega \end{aligned} \tag{6}$$

In the above formulation, $pop\_dens(\cdot)$, $pop\_poi(\cdot)$, $imd(\cdot)$, and $dist(\cdot)$ are, respectively, the population density, population per POI, IMD, and the Euclidean distance from the nearest poly-centre of a

[12] http://www.ons.gov.uk/

ward $w_i$. We have measured population density every year, and the changes are minimal in the five year span we consider. IMD is computed every three years, so for this study we have used the version released in 2010 (whose results are based on data collected mainly in 2008). The geodemographic variables are thus not time-dependent in the course of this study.

Table 1 summarises the models above, from its simplest (Equation 3, based on Property 1 only), to the most complex (Equation 6, based on all four properties):

| *Eq. Number* | *Properties* |
|---|---|
| Eq. (3) | Self-reinforcement |
| Eq. (4) | Self-reinforcement + Spatial correlation |
| Eq. (5) | Self-reinforcement + Spatial correlation + Editing correlation |
| Eq. (6) | Self-reinforcement + Spatial correlation + Editing correlation + Geodemographic |

**Table 1: Summary of Growth Models**

# 4. RESEARCH RESULTS

We structure the evaluation of the previously constructed growth model in four parts: first, we use correlation analysis to support the validity each of our properties separately; second, we use multiple linear regression to validate the models constructed from such properties, from the simplest to the more complete; third, we turn the models into a classification tool and measure their accuracy in modelling OSM activity growth; finally, we apply the models to other cities to understand their generalisability.

## 4.1 Testing the Properties

The four properties put forward in the previous section assume that the variables listed in Table 2 (e.g., OSM activity of the ward itself in the last year, OSM activity of the ward itself in all previous years, maximum and average OSM activity of the spatially correlated wards in the last year, etc.) correlate with OSM activity at time $t+1$.

As a first step in our analysis, we have thus computed the Pearson's Correlation Coefficient $r$ between the value of each such variables at year $t$ and the actual value of OSM activity registered in the following year $t+1$. As some variables exhibited a moderately skewed distribution, we first computed their square root, so to obtain a normal distribution. Correlation values computed on a yearly basis are presented in Table 3.

*Property 1 - Self-reinforcement.* According to Property 1, OSM activity in a ward at time $t+1$ depends both on its past activity at time $t$, and its cumulative past activity. Table 3 confirms this property: the correlation between future OSM activity and its past-year OSM activity goes from a minimum of $r = 0.31$ in 2007/08 to a maximum of $r = 0.37$ in 2009/10. Similarly, the correlation between future OSM activity and the cumulative past OSM activity is positive, and goes from a minimum of $r = 0.11$ in 2007/08 and a maximum of $r = 0.43$ in 2010/11. Note that there exists a positive correlation value between future OSM activity and cumulative past activity in all years analysed (i.e., the more OSM activity there has been in the aggregate past history, the more OSM activity growth will be experienced next). This suggests that OSM in London is yet far from experiencing a saturation effect.

*Property 2 - Spatial correlation.* The intuition behind Property 2 is that OSM contributors that are very active in one area are likely to spread some of their attention to adjacent areas, thus affecting their growth. Table 3 confirms this property, with OSM activity at time $t+1$ being positively correlated to both parameters we defined to capture such spatial correlation (maximum spatial correlations goes from $r = 0.27$ in 2010/11 to $r = 0.34$ in 2007/08, and average spatial correlations goes from $r = 0.28$ in 2010/11 to $r = 0.36$ in 2009/10).

| *Variable* | *Freq. Distribution* | *Max* |
|---|---|---|
| | *Self-reinforcing* | |
| Activity | | 0.56 (edit/POI) |
| Cumulative activity | | 0.92 (edit/POI) |
| | *Spatial correlation* | |
| Maximum | | 0.57 (edit/POI) |
| Average | | 0.28 (edit/POI) |
| | *Editing correlation* | |
| Maximum | | 0.34 (edit/POI) |
| Average | | 0.03 (edit/POI) |
| | *Geodemography* | |
| Population density | | 23,746.80 (ppl/ha) |
| Population per POI | | 14,310.00 (ppl/POI) |
| IMD | | 54.90 |
| Distance | | 22.90 (km) |

**Table 2: Variables used to model OSM activity growth, together with frequency distribution (starting at zero) and maximum value**

| *Variable* | 2007/08 | 2008/09 | 2009/10 | 2010/11 | 2011/12 |
|---|---|---|---|---|---|
| | | | *Self-Reinforcing* | | |
| Activity | **0.31** | **0.35** | **0.37** | **0.31** | **0.35** |
| Cumulative activity | **0.11** | **0.22** | **0.30** | **0.43** | **0.40** |
| | | | *Spatial Correlation* | | |
| Maximum | **0.34** | **0.29** | **0.29** | **0.27** | **0.28** |
| Average | **0.33** | **0.31** | **0.36** | **0.28** | **0.30** |
| | | | *Editing Correlation* | | |
| Maximum | **0.22** | **0.21** | **0.17** | **0.18** | **0.20** |
| Average | **0.21** | **0.13** | 0.00 | 0.06 | 0.04 |
| | | | *Geodemography* | | |
| Population density | **0.18** | **0.18** | **0.25** | **0.19** | **0.18** |
| Population per POI | 0.08 | 0.08 | **0.11** | 0.09 | 0.05 |
| IMD | -0.05 | -0.09 | **-0.15** | -0.06 | -0.08 |
| Distance | **-0.26** | **-0.34** | **-0.36** | **-0.32** | **-0.30** |

**Table 3: Pearson correlation $r$ between individual variables and growth (in bold are those results that are statistically significant – p-value $< 0.01$)**

*Property 3 - Editing correlation.* Next we consider Property 3, which posits that OSM activity at time $t+1$ depends on the activity occurred in the past year in co-edited wards, no matter where physically located. We considered two variables: one that expects growth to happen if *at least one* co-edited ward has seen high activity in the past ('maximum' editing correlation score), and a more stringent one, that requires *many* co-edited wards to have exhibited high activity for the ward to be affected ('average' editing correlation score). The former has weak positive correlation with OSM activity growth (from a minimum of $r = 0.17$ in 2009/10 to $r = 0.22$ in 2007/08); the latter has similar correlation in the first two years; however, in the latter two the correlation is not statistically significant (this is possibly because, in our data, the cases where the more stringent condition held true were very few).

*Property 4 - Geodemographic factors.* Finally, we turn our attention to the correlation between geodemographic factors and a ward's activity at time $t+1$. As Table 3 illustrates, distance from the closest poly-centre is the geodemographic factor with the strongest (negative) correlation (from a minimum of $r = -0.26$ in 2007/08 to $r = -0.36$ in 2009/10), supporting the intuition that, the further a cell is from the centre, the less likely it will be mapped. Weaker correlations exist for all other geodemographic factors.

## 4.2 Testing the Models

The previous analysis suggests that all four properties put forward are grounded. We now proceed to validate the growth models

| Model | Whole London | Top 75% | Top 50% | Top 25% |
|---|---|---|---|---|
| | | 2007/08 | | |
| Eq. (3): | 0.10 | 0.11 | 0.12 | 0.17 |
| Eq. (4): | 0.15 (+50%) | 0.19 (+73%) | 0.16 (+33%) | 0.20 (+18%) |
| Eq. (5): | 0.17 (+13%) | 0.23 (+21%) | 0.20 (+25%) | 0.25 (+25%) |
| Eq. (6): | 0.28 (+65%) | 0.41 (+78%) | 0.44 (+120%) | 0.54 (+116%) |
| | | 2008/09 | | |
| Eq. (3): | 0.12 | 0.10 | 0.17 | 0.17 |
| Eq. (4): | 0.15 (+25%) | 0.15 (+50%) | 0.22 (+29%) | 0.24 (+41%) |
| Eq. (5): | 0.17 (+13%) | 0.20 (+33%) | 0.31 (+41%) | 0.33 (+38%) |
| Eq. (6): | 0.23 (+35%) | 0.34 (+70%) | 0.51 (+65%) | 0.55 (+67%) |
| | | 2009/10 | | |
| Eq. (3): | 0.15 | 0.25 | 0.30 | 0.34 |
| Eq. (4): | 0.18 (+20%) | 0.30 (+20%) | 0.35 (+17%) | 0.40 (+18%) |
| Eq. (5): | 0.21 (+17%) | 0.33 (+10%) | 0.37 (+6%) | 0.42 (+5%) |
| Eq. (6): | 0.29 (+38%) | 0.45 (+36%) | 0.52 (+41%) | 0.58 (+38%) |
| | | 2010/11 | | |
| Eq. (3): | 0.20 | 0.23 | 0.31 | 0.33 |
| Eq. (4): | 0.21 (+5%) | 0.25 (+9%) | 0.34 (+10%) | 0.36 (+9%) |
| Eq. (5): | 0.24 (+14%) | 0.30 (+20%) | 0.38 (+12%) | 0.41 (+14%) |
| Eq. (6): | 0.31 (+29%) | 0.43 (+43%) | 0.53 (+39%) | 0.57 (+39%) |
| | | 2011/12 | | |
| Eq. (3): | 0.17 | 0.24 | 0.30 | 0.30 |
| Eq. (4): | 0.20 (+18%) | 0.25 (+4%) | 0.32 (+7%) | 0.32 (+7%) |
| Eq. (5): | 0.24 (+20%) | 0.28 (+12%) | 0.36 (+13%) | 0.38 (+19%) |
| Eq. (6): | 0.28 (+17%) | 0.41 (+46%) | 0.50 (+39%) | 0.54 (+42%) |

**Table 4: Adjusted multiple $R^2$ of our models, together with relative improvement w.r.t. the previous model (every model showed in this table is statistical significant – $p$-value $< 0.001$)**

we constructed based on these properties, from its simplest to its final composite one (Table 1). To this purpose, we used multiple linear regression to determine the unknown $\beta$ parameters of Equations 3–6; furthermore, we compute the adjusted $R^2$ of each such model, as a way to measure its fit with respect to modelling growth. To highlight the role that different properties play at different times in the evolution of OSM, we break down the analysis on a per-year basis. Furthermore, we decided to report results both for the whole 600 wards in London, as well as the 75%, 50% and 25% most dense wards (in terms of POIs) over the whole 600 wards in London. In so doing, we can analyse the validity of our models for areas of different growth *potential* (i.e., areas that contain only a handful of physical POIs are less amenable to growth modelling, contrary to POI-dense areas). Table 4 shows the results.

*Year-based analysis.* We observe that the complete model that combines all four properties (Equation 6) has the best fit, significantly improving over all partial models that consider only a subset of them. More interestingly, the gap between the adjusted $R^2$ of the complete model and of the partial model that leaves out the geodemographic parameters (Equation 5 – Self-reinforcing + Spatial + Editing) significantly decreases as time progresses. For example, in whole London in 2007/08, the complete model (Equation 6) improves the adjusted $R^2$ of 65% w.r.t. the second best model (Equation 5), whereas in 2010/11 the improvement is 29% only. This confirms the intuition that, in the early stages of OSM (years 2007/08 – 2008/09) all models that do not consider the geodemographic factors are not able to accurately explain OSM activity growth, possibly because of little historical OSM data available. In a second step, that is after 2009, geodemographic factors are not so important anymore, in the sense that we can have a good model of OSM activity growth even without them (possibly because the model has now plenty of historical data to be trained on).

*Density analysis.* Finally, we observe that the adjusted $R^2$ increases significantly, when considering models comprising the top 75%, top 50% and top 25% POI dense wards in London. That is, the denser the areas in terms of physical POIs, the better the models to explain their growth.

| Model | TN Rate | TP Rate | Accuracy | Senitivity |
|---|---|---|---|---|
| | | Predicted Year: 2009 | | |
| Eq. (3) | 0.59 (+18%) | 0.56 (+12%) | 0.58 (+15%) | 0.58 (+15%) |
| Eq. (4) | 0.63 (+7%) | 0.61 (+9%) | 0.62 (+8%) | 0.62 (+8%) |
| Eq. (5) | 0.67 (+6%) | 0.65 (+7%) | 0.66 (+6%) | 0.66 (+7%) |
| Eq. (6) | 0.78 (+16%) | 0.75 (+15%) | 0.77 (+16%) | 0.77 (+17%) |
| | | Predicted Year: 2010 | | |
| Eq. (3) | 0.64 (+28%) | 0.60 (+20%) | 0.62 (+24%) | 0.63 (+25%) |
| Eq. (4) | 0.66 (+3%) | 0.61 (+2%) | 0.64 (+2%) | 0.64 (+3%) |
| Eq. (5) | 0.71 (+8%) | 0.68 (+11%) | 0.70 (+9%) | 0.70 (+9%) |
| Eq. (6) | 0.81 (+14%) | 0.78 (+15%) | 0.80 (+14%) | 0.80 (+15%) |
| | | Predicted Year: 2011 | | |
| Eq. (3) | 0.66 (+32%) | 0.59 (+18%) | 0.63 (+25%) | 0.63 (+27%) |
| Eq. (4) | 0.70 (+6%) | 0.64 (+8%) | 0.67 (+7%) | 0.68 (+7%) |
| Eq. (5) | 0.75 (+7%) | 0.70 (+9%) | 0.73 (+8%) | 0.74 (+8%) |
| Eq. (6) | 0.82 (+9%) | 0.79 (+13%) | 0.81 (+11%) | 0.81 (+11%) |
| | | Predicted Year: 2012 | | |
| Eq. (3) | 0.62 (+24%) | 0.59 (+18%) | 0.61 (+21%) | 0.61 (+22%) |
| Eq. (4) | 0.68 (+10%) | 0.65 (+10%) | 0.67 (+10%) | 0.67 (+10%) |
| Eq. (5) | 0.75 (+10%) | 0.73 (+12%) | 0.74 (+11%) | 0.74 (+11%) |
| Eq. (6) | 0.79 (+5%) | 0.75 (+3%) | 0.77 (+4%) | 0.78 (+5%) |

**Table 5: True Negative Rate (slow growth), True Positive Rate (fast growth), Accuracy and Sensitivity of the classification models. Relative improvement of each model w.r.t. the preceding model is also reported in parentheses. For the baseline model of Equation 3, the improvement is computed w.r.t. a random classifier.**

## 4.3 Predicting Growth

The previous regression results afforded us the ability to understand what properties affect growth of OSM activity in different years, and to what extent. To quantify the *predictive* accuracy of our models, we have then conducted a classification experiment, whereby we first determined the unknown $\beta$ parameters of Equations 3–6 using multiple linear regression, as done before; we then used these models to classify activity for the upcoming year. For example, we used 2007/08 to estimate the parameters, then made predictions for 2009. In this case, we divided the outcome of our models in two distinct categories: 'slow future OSM activity growth' (when $act(w_i, t+1) < 0.3$) and fast future OSM activity growth' (when $act(w_i, t+1) \geq 0.3$), with 0.3 being the median value of OSM activity growth for the time windows under consideration. Finally, we considered the top 75% wards in London only, as predicting OSM activity growth of very sparse areas (e.g., parks) has little significance. Table 5 presents the results of the classification. As shown, the accuracy of our models is quite high: the simplest model based on Equation 3 already gains up to 32% for slow growth (TN rate) and up to 20% for fast growth (TP rate) over a random classifier. In all predicted years, the full model based on Equation 6 offers the highest accuracy, with up to 82% for slow growth and 79% for fast growth.

## 4.4 Beyond London

Our modelling and evaluation has so far focused on a single city, and this raises concerns in terms of the validity of our properties and models elsewhere. Indeed, London is in itself quite a peculiar city: from a geodemographic perspective, London is by far the largest city in the EU (the most densely populated within city limits), with a diverse range of people and cultures spread all over its area. In terms of OSM-related characteristics, London was the city were OSM was born, it is the one with the longest-living and largest user base, and it is considered a prime example or organic, bottom-up crowd-sourcing growth with the vast majority of OSM edits being genuine users' contributions, rather than bulk imports (i.e., data donations to the OSM foundation by third-party providers [32]).

To address this concern, we present in this section a brief study of two cities, Boston and New York City, chosen for their very different characteristics with respect to London. From a geodemographic perspective, we scale both population density and area size of a factor up (for New York City) and down (for Boston) with respect to London. From an OSM perspective, both cities are much less 'mature' than London: as shown in Table 6, they have a much smaller user base, smaller number of edits, and lower level of engagement from OSMers (edits per user), especially in New York City. This city is also fundamentally different from London in terms of growth pattern: while in London only 21% of OSM edits can be attributed to bulk imports, in New York City these represent 65% of total OSM edits. New York City thus resembles a sort of worst case scenario when it comes to predicting growth using our model, as only 35% of its contributions are actually genuine users' contributions (i.e., those that the properties in our models aim to describe). In repeating the previous analysis on Boston and New York City, we have used US census data, which is available at the level of tracts (closest US-equivalent of wards);[13] as we did not have Navteq data for the US, we have used POIs information from Yelp instead[14] (to gain confidence that Yelp was indeed a reliable source to estimate the number of physical POI in a certain area, we computed the Pearson correlation between the number of POIs in Yelp and that in Navteq for the city of London, and we found it to be above 0,9).

| *City* | *Edits* | *Users* | *Avg(edits/user)* | *Import ratio* |
|---|---|---|---|---|
| London | 96,357 | 2,240 | 43.0 | 21% |
| New York | 12,275 | 543 | 22.6 | 65% |
| Boston | 4,808 | 149 | 32.3 | 41% |

**Table 6: Comparisons between London and US Cities on OSM usage**

Table 7 shows the average adjusted $R^2$ values for the models, over the period 2007 to 2012. As observed in London, the complete model (Equation 6) is the most accurate, with an adjusted $R^2$ value as high as 0.61 for Boston, suggesting that the same properties we previously tested for London are now able to explain a large portion of this city data's variability, despite its many differences (e.g., in terms of size, population density, import ratio). The adjusted $R^2$ value for New York City is much lower (0.22); however, what is most important to observe here is that such value is in line with what observed for the whole of London in the year 2007/08 (see Table 4 - value 0.28). Furthermore, the gain in adjusted $R^2$ with respect to the model that does not account for geodemographic factors is enormous (+144% for New York City and +53% for Boston). Based on these results, we speculate that adoption of OSM in the US cities under examination is still in its infancy, and as such the geodemographic properties are those that account the most for variability in the data at this stage, as it also happened in London back in the early days of OSM adoption.

# 5. DISCUSSION AND CONCLUSION

In this paper, we have presented a model inspired by Cellular Automata theory that leverages characteristics of the urban crowd-sourcing domain to accurately describe its digital evolution over time. The model considers properties of self-reinforcement, spatial and editing correlation, and geodemographic influences. We have used correlation analysis to support each of our properties, multiple linear regression to validate the model, and classification to

[13]`http://www.census.gov/geo/reference/gtc/gtc_ct.html`

[14]`http://www.yelp.com/`

| *Model* | *New York* | *Boston* |
|---|---|---|
| Eq. (3): | 0.07 | 0.23 |
| Eq. (4): | 0.07 (+0%) | 0.24 (+4%) |
| Eq. (5): | 0.09 (+29%) | 0.40 (+67%) |
| Eq. (6): | 0.22 (+144%) | 0.61 (+53%) |

**Table 7: Adjusted multiple $R^2$ of our models, together with relative improvement w.r.t. the previous model in New York and Boston (every model showed in this table is statistical significant – $p$-value $< 0.001$)**

measure its accuracy. We now discuss the theoretical and practical implications of this work.

*Theoretical Implications.* The study reported in this paper has shown that digital mapping of spatial urban information is governed by complex dynamics, with geodemographic factors being particularly important to determine area seeding in the very early stages of technology deployment; once the bootstrapping phase is over, contagion and self-reinforcement processes explain most of the digital growth instead. This two-step process for adoption is in line with recent findings in the area of social networks, that suggest there exist two different classes of individuals who contribute to two parallel adoption processes: early participants, who start contributing and create random seeding, followed by low threshold individuals who are responsible for the subsequent contributions' spreading [4, 16, 7].

*Practical Implications.* Understanding '*what* factors are most important *when*' can be leveraged by designers of urban crowd-sourcing applications, so to better engineer them: from choosing who to target as early adopters of the technology, so to influence area seeding, to embedding gamification elements, so to drive contagion and self-reinforcement processes (e.g., via leader-boards, competitions, virtual rewards). Once the urban crowd-sourcing application is deployed, the model described in this paper can be used to monitor its growth. Being able to *predict* what areas that will not be digitally mapped gives businesses and public agencies time to plan and execute interventions. Such interventions may span a wide spectrum: from allocating financial resources to cover neglected areas, to gamification (e.g., in the form of competitions or mapping parties) to location-based social network features [43, 25] so to direct the crowd towards specific mapping goals. Having an accurate growth model at hand implies that these limited resources (human and/or financial) can be best allocated so to maximise return on investment. For example, using influence maximization schemes (e.g., [42]), one could decide how many resources to allocate to areas predicted to be severely neglected, so to maximise expected growth in the following year(s), both as an immediate result of investment *and* thanks to the contagion and self-reinforcement processes that our model estimates to follow.

## 5.1 Limitations & Future Work

Our work suffers from a number of limitations. First, we studied one specific example of urban crowd-sourcing application (OSM), on a number of cities that, even though they exhibit different characteristics, they all belong to the modern urbanised part of the world. If we were to model OSM growth in different parts of the world, different properties might have to be considered within the model. For example, our model works under the assumption that the city under examination is already urbanised and thus the physical space constraints prevents the formation of many new physical urban elements in a short period of time. This assumption does not hold for cities in developing countries, where the actual physical changes are of much higher magnitude and at a faster pace. Also, our model has been tested in a scenario where *digital* POI coverage is far from complete (indeed, there are very few areas with OSM cumulative activity above 50%, as shown in Figure 2). This means there is as yet no saturation effect to be accounted for. This is also evidenced by the fact that the positive correlation of the self-reinforcement property (for both distant and recent past) increases over the years – Table 4 (i.e., the more an area has been edited in the past, the more it will be in the future). Once saturation starts to appear, segmentation analysis should be performed, so to assess our model separately in areas under-covered and areas near-complete, as the same factors (e.g., past growth) might yield opposite effects.

Second, the 'pace' at which mapping takes place in OSM is fundamentally different to that taking place during disaster recovery efforts [46], and we do not know whether the processes of self-reinforcement and contagion that our model leverages would be able to describe growth in these settings. A direction of future work is to study the suitability of the model presented in this paper in different urban crowd-sourcing settings (both in terms of different world regions, and in terms of different applications).

We presented a model of growth that focuses on 'spatial' factors (e.g., distance to the centre) and processes (e.g., spatial contagion). In so doing, we have not investigated characteristics of the adopters of the technology themselves: their motives for taking part in digital mapping, their interests (what types of POIs they map – e.g., services vs leisure POIs), and how they respond to incentives, such as the frequently organised OSM mapping parties.[15] Modelling these factors and the processes behind adopters' dynamics is a direction of future research.

## Acknowledgment

This work was partly supported by the Knowledge and Innovation Community EIT ICT Labs, and by the Intel Collaborative Research Institute on Sustainable Connected Cities.

# 6. REFERENCES

[1] S. Alkheder and J. Shan. Cellular Automata Urban Growth Simulation and Evaluation-A Case Study of Indianapolis. In *Proceedings of the 8th International Conference on GeoComputation*, pages 1–19, 2005.

[2] A. Anagnostopoulos, R. Kumar, and M. Mahdian. Influence and correlation in social networks. In *Proceedings of the 14th ACM SIGKDD International Conference on Knowledge Discovery and Data Mining*, pages 7–15, 2008.

[3] S. Aral, L. Muchnik, and A. Sundararajan. Distinguishing influence-based contagion from homophily-driven diffusion in dynamic networks. *Proceedings of the National Academy of Sciences*, 106(51):21544–21549, December 2009.

[4] Aral, S. and Walker, D. Identifying Influential and Susceptible Members of Social Networks. *Science*, 337, 2012.

[5] L. Backstrom, D. Huttenlocher, J. Kleinberg, and X. Lan. Group formation in large social networks: membership, growth, and evolution. In *Proceedings of the 12th ACM SIGKDD International Conference on Knowledge Discovery and Data Mining*, pages 44–54. ACM, 2006.

[6] P. Bibby. Land use change in Britain. *Elsevier Journal on Land Use Policy*, 2009.

[7] A. Brodersen, S Scellato, and M. Wattenhofer. Youtube around the world: geographic popularity of videos. *WWW 2012*, 2012.

[15] `http://wiki.openstreetmap.org/wiki/Mapping_Weekend_Howto`

[8] S.D. Brunn, J.F. Williams, and D.J. Zeigler. *Cities Of The World: World Regional Urban Development*. Rowman & Littlefield Publishers, 2003.

[9] D. Cosley, D. Huttenlocher, J. Kleinberg, and S. Suri X. Lan. Sequential influence models in social networks. In *Proc. 4th International AAAI Conference on Weblogs and Social Media*, 2010.

[10] J. Cranshaw, R. Schwartz, J.I. Hong, and N. Sadeh. The livehoods project: Utilizing social media to understand the dynamics of a city. In *Proceedings of AAAI International Conference on Weblogs and Social Media (ICWSM)*, 2012.

[11] N. Ganguly, B.K. Sikdar, A. Deutsch, G. Canright, and P. Pal Chaudhuri. A Survey on Cellular Automata. Technical report, 2003.

[12] A.M. García, I. Santé, M. Boullón, and R. Crecente. A comparative analysis of cellular automata models for simulation of small urban areas in Galicia, NW Spain. *Computers, Environment and Urban Systems*, 36(4):291–301, 2012.

[13] J.F. Girres and G. Touya. Quality assessment of the french openstreetmap dataset. *Transactions in GIS*, 14(4):435–459, 2010.

[14] R. Glott, P. Schmidt, and R. Ghosh. Wikipedia Survey–overview of results. *United Nations University: Collaborative Creativity Group*, 2010.

[15] M. Gomez-Rodriguez, D. Balduzzi, and B. SchÃűlkopf. Uncovering the temporal dynamics of diffusion networks. In *Proc. of the 28th International Conference on Machine Learning*, 2011.

[16] S. González-Bailón, J. Borge-Holthoefer, A. Rivero, and Y. Moreno. The Dynamics of Protest Recruitment through an Online Network. *Scientific reports*, 1, 2011.

[17] M.F. Goodchild. Citizens as sensors: the world of volunteered geography. *GeoJournal*, 69(4):211–221, 2007.

[18] M. Haklay. How good is volunteered geographical information? A comparative study of OpenStreetMap and Ordnance Survey datasets. *Environment and Planning B: Planning and Design*, 37(4):682–703, 2010.

[19] M. Haklay, S. Basiouka, V. Antoniou, and A. Ather. How Many Volunteers Does it Take to Map an Area Well? The Validity of Linus Law to Volunteered Geographic Information. *Cartographic Journal, The*, 47(4):315–322, 2010.

[20] P. Hedström. Contagious Collectivities: On the Spatial Diffusion of Swedish Trade Unions, 1890-1940. *American Journal of Sociology*, 99(5):1157–1179, March 1994.

[21] K. Kamath, J. Caverlee, K. Lee, and Z. Cheng. Spatio-temporal dynamics of global social media. In *Proceedings of the 22nd International Conference on World Wide Web*, 2013.

[22] D. Kim and M. Batty. Calibrating Cellular Automata Models for Simulating Urban Growth. Technical Report 176, UCL Centre for Advanced Spatial Analysis, December 2011.

[23] J. Kleinberg. The small-world phenomenon: an algorithm perspective. In *Proceedings of the thirty-second annual ACM symposium on Theory of computing*, pages 163–170. ACM, 2000.

[24] J. Kleinberg. The convergence of social and technological networks. *Communications of the ACM*, 51(11):66–72, 2008.

[25] D. Laniado, R. Tasso, Y. Volkovich, and A. Kaltenbrunner. When the wikipedians talk: network and tree structure of

wikipedia discussion pages. In *Proceedings of the 5th International AAAI Conference on Weblogs and Social Media (ICWSM'11)*. AAAI, 2011.

[26] N. Lathia, D. Quercia, and J. Crowcroft. The Hidden Image of the City: Sensing Community Well-Being from Urban Mobility. In *Proc. of Pervasive*, June 2012.

[27] J. Leskovec, L. Backstrom, and J. Kleinberg. Meme-tracking and the dynamics of the news cycle. In *Proc. of the 15th ACM SIGKDD International Conference on Knowledge Discovery and Data Mining*, pages 497–506, 2009.

[28] D. Liben-Nowell, J. Novak, R. Kumar, P. Raghavan, and A. Tomkins. Geographic routing in social networks. *Proceedings of the National Academy of Sciences of the United States of America*, 102(33):11623–11628, 2005.

[29] I. Ludwig, A. Voss, and M. Krause-Traudes. A comparison of the street networks of navteq and osm in germany. *Advancing Geoinformation Science for a Changing World*, 1(2):65–84, 2011.

[30] A. Mashhadi, G. Quattrone, and L. Capra. Putting Ubiquitous Crowd-sourcing into Context. In *Proceedings of ACM CSCW*, 2013.

[31] A. Mashhadi, G. Quattrone, L. Capra, and P. Mooney. On the Accuracy of Urban Crowd-Sourcing for Maintaining Large-Scale Geospatial Databases. In *Proceedings of the 8th International Symposium on Wikis and Open Collaboration (WikiSym'12)*. ACM, 2012.

[32] P. Mooney and P. Corcoran. Who are the contributors to openstreetmap and what do they do? In *Proc. of GISRUK*, 2012.

[33] S.A. Myers, C. Zhu, and J. Leskovec. Information diffusion and external influence in networks. In *Proc. of the 18th ACM SIGKDD International Conference on Knowledge Discovery and Data Mining*, pages 33–41, 2012.

[34] P. Neis, D. Zielstra, and A. Zipf. The Street Network Evolution of Crowdsourced Maps: OpenStreetMap in Germany. *Future Internet*, 4(1):1–21, 2011.

[35] K. Panciera, R. Priedhorsky, T. Erickson, and L. Terveen. Lurking? cyclopaths?: a quantitative lifecycle analysis of user behavior in a geowiki. In *Proceedings of the 28th International Conference on Human factors in computing systems (CHI)*, pages 1917–1926. ACM, 2010.

[36] K.A. Panciera, M. Masli, and L. Terveen. "how should i go from _ to_ without getting killed?": motivation and benefits in open collaboration. In *Proceedings of the 7th International Symposium on Wikis and Open Collaboration (WikiSym'11)*, pages 183–192, 2011.

[37] R. Priedhorsky, M. Masli, and L. Terveen. Eliciting and focusing geographic volunteer work. In *Proceedings of the 13th International Conference on Computer Supported Cooperative Work (CSCW'10)*, pages 61–70. ACM, 2010.

[38] R. Priedhorsky, B. Jordan, and L. Terveen. How a personalized geowiki can help bicyclists share information more effectively. In *Proceedings of the 3rd International Symposium on Wikis and Open Collaboration (WikiSym'07)*, pages 93–98, 2007.

[39] D. Pullar and C. Pettit. Improving Urban Growth Forecasting with Cellular Automata: A Case Study for Hervey Bay. In *International Congress on Modelling and Simulation*, pages 14–17, 2003.

[40] D.M. Romero, B. Meeder, and J. Kleinberg. Differences in the mechanics of information diffusion across topics: idioms, political hashtags, and complex contagion on twitter. In *Proceedings of the 20th International Conference on World Wide Web*, pages 695–704, 2011.

[41] C. Roth, S.M. Kang, M. Batty, and M. BarthÃl'lemy. Structure of urban movements: Polycentric activity and entangled hierarchical flows. *PLoS ONE*, 6(1), 01 2011.

[42] Y. Singer. How to win friends and influence people, truthfully: influence maximization mechanisms for social networks. In *Proc.of the 5th ACM International Conference on Web Search and Data Mining*, pages 733–742, 2012.

[43] Y. Volkovich, S. Scellato, D. Laniado, C. Mascolo, and A. Kaltenbrunner. The length of bridge ties: structural and geographic properties of online social interactions. In *Proceedings of the 6th International AAAI Conference on Weblogs and Social Media (ICWSM'12)*. AAAI, 2012.

[44] G. U. Yule. A Mathematical Theory of Evolution, based on the Conclusions of Dr. J. C. Willis, F.R.S. *Philosophical Transactions of the Royal Society of London*, 213:21–87, 1925.

[45] D. Zielstra and A. Zipf. A comparative study of proprietary geodata and volunteered geographic information for germany. In *Proceedings of the 13th International Conference on Geographic Information Science*, 2010.

[46] M. Zook, M. Graham, T. Shelton, and S. Gorman. Volunteered geographic information and crowdsourcing disaster relief: A case study of the haitian earthquake. *World Medical and Health Policy*, 2(2), 2010.

# Inferring the Impacts of Social Media on Crowdfunding

Chun-Ta Lu, Sihong Xie, Xiangnan Kong, and Philip S. Yu
Department of Computer Science
University of Illinois at Chicago
Chicago, IL, USA
{clu29, sxie6, xkong4}@uic.edu, psyu@cs.uic.edu

## ABSTRACT

Crowdfunding – in which people can raise funds through collaborative contributions of general public (i.e., crowd) – has emerged as a billion dollars business for supporting more than one million ventures. However, very few research works have examined the process of crowdfunding. In particular, none has studied how social networks help crowdfunding projects to succeed. To gain insights into the effects of social networks in crowdfunding, we analyze the hidden connections between the fundraising results of projects on crowdfunding websites and the corresponding promotion campaigns in social media. Our analysis considers the dynamics of crowdfunding from two aspects: how fundraising activities and promotional activities on social media simultaneously evolve over time, and how the promotion campaigns influence the final outcomes. From our investigation, we identify a number of important principles that provide a useful guide for devising effective campaigns. For example, we observe temporal distribution of customer interest, strong correlations between a crowdfunding project's early promotional activities and the final outcomes, and the importance of concurrent promotion from multiple sources. We then show that these discoveries can help predict several important quantities, including overall popularity and the success rate of the project. Finally, we show how to use these discoveries to help design crowdfunding sites.

## Categories and Subject Descriptors

H.3.4 [**Information Systems Applications-Systems and Software**]: Information networks; J.4 [**Social and Behavioral Sciences**]: Economics

## General Terms

Experimentation

## Keywords

Crowdfunding; social media; early prediction


*WSDM'14*, February 24–28, 2014, New York, New York, USA.
Copyright 2014 ACM 978-1-4503-2351-2/14/02 ...$15.00.
http://dx.doi.org/10.1145/2556195.2556251.

## 1. INTRODUCTION

Crowdfunding, or crowd-sourced fundraising, provides a revolutionary way to support ideas and projects across a number of industries, such as technology, music, film and art. For instance, Kickstarter is one of the largest websites for crowdfunding. Three of the movie projects funded by crowd investors in Kickstarter were nominated for Oscars 2013, and one of them won the Oscar Award in the short documentary category. A recent report [1] indicates that global crowdfunding raised nearly $2.7 billion for more than 1 million campaigns in 2012, and is expected to grow into a $5.1 billion industry by 2013. Although crowdfunding has been drawing substantial attention from the business sector, many aspects of crowdfunding have not received rigorous examination [15] in research communities. In particular, social influence, the key to the success of crowdfunding projects, has not been investigated thoroughly before in data mining communities.

Unlike traditional ways of fundraising, where the enterprises used to receive a small number of major investments from venture capital firms, in crowdfunding, the enterprise receives support through a large number of small contributions from customers. As a consequence, crowdfunding presents a mixture of entrepreneurship with social network participation, in which the customers play an unexpected role: investors. Different to conventional investors in venture capital firms, customers who have invested a project may also be likely to promote the project among his/her friends through online social networks. As a fast and far reaching channel to broadcasting information, social media (e.g., Twitter, Facebook, and GooglePlus) plays an important role in promoting crowdfunding projects. Both enterprises and customers can keep track of a crowdfunding campaign on social media, and obtain useful insights in real-time. For example, enterprises can analyze social media data to forecast the prevalence of the initiatives in order to adjust strategies accordingly. While customers can also make use of social media to identify promising projects that are more likely to be successful and lead to more rewards for the investments.

Predicting the outcomes of crowdfunding projects is very important for both enterprises and customers. Previous research on social media mainly focuses on modeling how an event spreads out in social media to predict the popularity of the event. Examples include modeling patterns of popularity evolution [3, 20], analyzing social dynamics[12], and predicting speed and scale of social influence [21, 11]. However, to the best of our knowledge, none of the existing works studied how a crowdfunding campaign develops

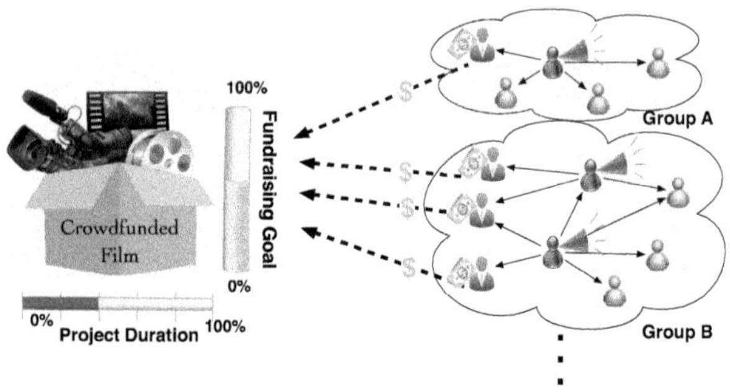


**Figure 1: Example of the process of crowdfunding, where the red persons are the promotors, the blue persons are the backers, while the green persons are just potential targets.**

in social media or what effects does social media have on the crowdfunding projects.

Crowdfunding has several unique properties that make it different from conventional information diffusion process in previous works. First, crowdfunding is usually a time-constrained process which is quite different from the everlasting process of information diffusion. For example, the fundraising process of a Kickstarter project can last from one day to 60 days[1]. Second, a project in crowdfunding should set a certain goal for fundraising, while the conventional information diffusion process doesn't have a collective objective/goal from the crowd. Third, crowdfunding involves a variety of roles, including the promoters who disseminate information about the project in social networks and the backers who pledge funds on the project. Due to these unique properties, the mechanism of crowdfunding cannot be assessed by prior works [3, 20, 12, 21, 11] effectively.

Figure 1 illustrates the process of crowdfunding. In Figure 1, the left part is a crowdfunding project, which has a pre-specified project duration and a fundraising goal to be achieved. The right part is the campaign of the project on social media, which consists of multiple groups of participants in the process of social promotion. In group A, for instance, there is a promoter who informs his/her friends of the project and one of them is influenced to invest in the project. The dashed lines in the middle of Figure 1 show the investments from backers affected by social networks. The key objective of this work is to infer the impacts of social networks on the fundraising results of a crowdfunding project, such as the number of backer of the project and the successfulness of the fundraising goal.

To infer the social impacts, we study two concrete tasks motivated by the above potential applications for both enterprises and customers. The first task is the prediction of the number of backers: given the social activities within social media during the early stage of a project, can we predict how many customers will contribute towards the project? The second task is the prediction of whether a venture will receive sufficient funding at the end of crowdfunding process. Specially, given the information of a project, the funds collected so far and the online social media activities of the project, can we predict how likely its fundraising goal will be reached?

In order to address these two tasks, we begin by investigating the dynamics of crowdfunding from the fundraising results of crowdfunding projects as well as the corresponding campaigns on social media. From our investigation, we identify some important principles that not only help infer the impacts of social media but provide a useful guide for devising effective campaigns. The first principle we identify is that the temporal distribution of customer interests regard to a project is reciprocally affected by both the freshness and the remaining duration of the project. The launch of the project sparks a burst of interests in which the majority of customers and funds arrive. The customer interests then decay significantly until the approach of the project deadline again arouses customers to achieve the fundraising goal of the project. Therefore, in order to bring in more contributions before customer interests decay, it is critical to identify potential bottlenecks so as to adjust campaign strategies by predicting the eventual outcomes at the very beginning.

Second, we observe that the results of a project are much more correlated to the early promotional activities on social media rather than its own properties (e.g. project duration and fundraising goal). More precisely, we find that the number of backers of a project has strong correlation to the volume of its promotional activities, while its success rate is more correlated to the design of its promotion campaign. In other words, a project is popularized by massive promotion, whereas the foundation of its success is established in the intensive interactions between participants. This understanding reinforces our premise that promotional activities in social media have positive impacts on the crowdfunding projects, and further hints the critical features for the two tasks we have defined.

Last but not least, we notice that the crowdfunding campaign of a project is driven by both the social promotion in social media and external stimulations outside social media. One can imagine that a campaign is composed of several groups of participants in social media. The social promotion from promoters to their friends expand the size of each group. In the mean time, the external stimulations from different channels expose the project to more groups. Thus, in order to spread a project to more contributors, the better way to process the promotion is to stimulate from social media as well as from other channels.

Overall, our goal is to contribute to a broader investigation of this perspective on crowdfunding. Our performance on the two tasks suggests that features arising from the campaign activity in social media such as Twitter can provide important information beyond simply considering the data from crowdfunding sites.

## 2. BACKGROUND

Crowdfunding originated from the concept of crowdsourcing, in which a crowd of people collaboratively contribute to the solution to a task. In crowdfunding, participants play the roles of promoters and investors in support of proposed initiatives. Therefore crowdfunding presents a mixture of entrepreneurship and social network participation.

In crowdfunding, a proposer launches a project and requests certain amount of money that needs to be raised in

[1]Statistically, projects lasting more than 30 days have lower success rates to achieve its goal, since the longer duration incites less urgency, encourages procrastination, and tends to fizzle out. `http://www.kickstarter.com/blog/shortening-the-maximum-project-length`

a specified duration [15, 16]. If they are interested in the project, investors can contribute funds to it. If the fundraising goal is reached, the funds are awarded to the proposer, and equal benefits are committed to the investors. Most of the crowdfunding sites (e.g. Kickstarter) further apply an all-or-nothing principle: if the fundraising goal is not reached by the deadline, all the funds are returned to the investors, while all commitments are cancelled. Such an all-or-nothing principle helps investors to avoid the risk of paying for nothing.

Besides fundraising activities on crowdfunding websites, typically there are also fundraising-related social activities on social networks like Twitter. Specifically, novel and creative crowdfunding projects are notably discussed on social networks where users are willing to share their interests, provide or respond to comments, promote and announce news of the projects. These activities on social networks can be seen as a complementary data source to crowdfunding websites and provide more insights into the crowdfunding process. We focus on a crowdfunding website called Kickstarter.com and related tweets on Twitter, since they exhibit the basic elements we wish to study, namely, the co-occurring fundraising and social activities on Twitter. Our observations and methodologies are applicable to other crowdfunding hosts, so long as they allow promotions on social media.

# 3. DATASET CHARACTERISTICS

We start our presentation by describing the data acquisition and processing for our analysis. We then provide the statistical characteristics of our dataset.

## 3.1 Data acquisition and processing

**Crowdfunding data:** From Kickstarter, we obtained all the projects launched after Nov. 2012 and completed before Apr. 2013. For each project we recorded its proposer, duration, webpage URL, shorten URL[2], fundraising goal and available pledging options. Within each project's duration we recorded its total pledged amount and total number of backers on a daily basis. We noticed that there were some trial projects having no backers or extremely low fundraising goals (less than $100), and we removed them from our dataset since none of them reached their fundraising goals.

**Twitter data:** We gathered all the tweets regarding Kickstarter from Nov. 2012 to Apr. 2013. The tweets are extracted by the Twitter stream API with the keywords "kickstarter" and "kck.st/"[2], ensuring they contain timestamps, authors, mentioned users, tweet texts, and URLs for our analysis. For each tweet's author, we queried Twitter API for the metadata about the author as well as the followers and followees of the author. Since a tweet is limited to 140 characters, most URLs are shortened by a URL shortening service. We expanded them to get the original URLs.

**Data preprocessing:** A crowdfunding project could be shared on different channels and referred to by various titles. An effective promotion of a project should mention its official URL to encourage others to visit it. For each project we consider only the tweets mentioning its URL within its project duration. We call the author of such a tweet a promoter. Besides, Kickstarter provides a Twitter shortcut for users to share the news of sponsoring a project in a fixed format (e.g. "I just backed project_title @kickstarter"). Hence, we further filter tweets with the keyword "backed" and the project title, and call the author of such a tweet a patron. In this paper, we distinguish the patron in Twitter from the backer in Kickstarter by assuming that a patron is not only a backer who puts a pledge on a Kickstarter project but also tweets the news of sponsoring it. Figure 2 illustrates the transition of roles in crowdfunding. In Figure 2, a potential target would become a backer of a project if he/she invests in the project, or become a promoter if he/she broadcasts the information of the project. If he/she both invests and promote the project, he/she becomes a patron.

[2] Kickstarter provides a shorten URL in the format of `http://kck.st/*` to encourage users to share the project

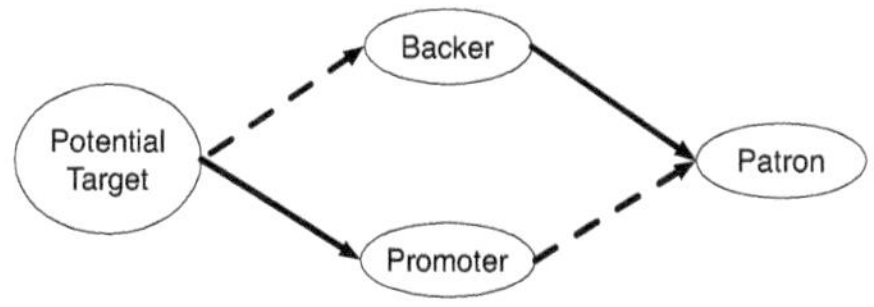


**Figure 2: Transitions of roles in crowdfunding. Solid lines show the action of broadcasting and dash lines show the action of investment.**

| | |
|---|---|
| # of projects | 1,521 |
| # of successful projects | 841 |
| # of backers | 145,032 |
| # of tweets | 62,473 |
| # of promoters | 39,051 |
| # of patrons | 16,666 |
| # of mentioned users | 14,415 |

**Table 1: Statistics of the dataset**

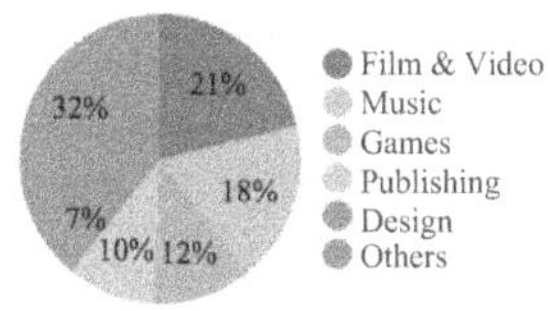


**Figure 3: Percentage of project categories.**

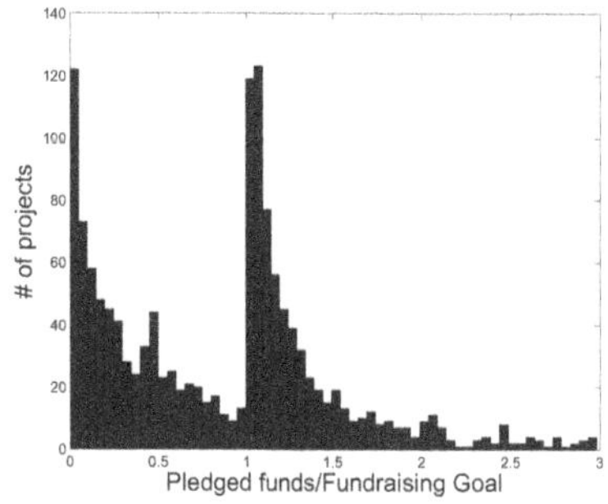


**Figure 4: Distribution of the ratio of total pledged amount to the fundraising goal. An additional 120 projects (7.8% of all projects) were funded more than 3x.**

We further filter out projects that were seldom discussed (less than 5 tweets) in the Twitter dataset, simply because there are not enough data to correctly evaluate the crowdfunding campaign through Twitter. Table 1 and Figure 3 show the basic statistics of our dataset after filtering.

## 3.2 Statistical characteristics of dataset

The distribution of the ratio of total amount of pledged funds to the fundraising goal can be found in Figure 4. It illustrates the fact that most Kickstarter projects either fail significantly or meet their goals by relatively small margins. Among all the failed projects, only twenty-five percent of

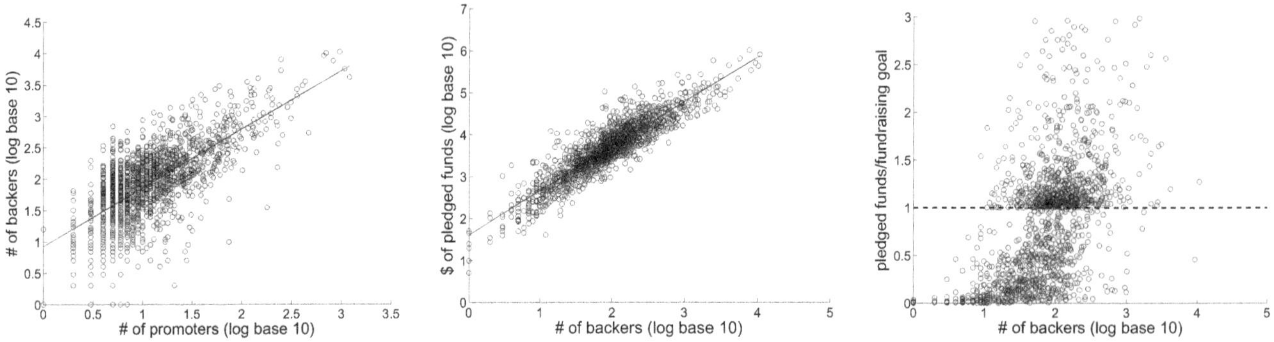


(a) Number of backers versus number of promoters (b) Amount of pledged funds versus number of backers (c) Ratio of pledged funds to fundraising goal versus number of backers

**Figure 6: Each figure shows a scatter plot of all the projects. (a) Number of backers plotted against the number of promoters, where the correlation coefficient is 0.79. (b) Amount of pledged funds plotted against the number of backers, where the correlation coefficient is 0.9. (c) Ratio of pledged funds to fundraising goal plotted against the number of backers. 44% of projects below the dash line, y=1, which means they failed to reach their fundraising goals.**

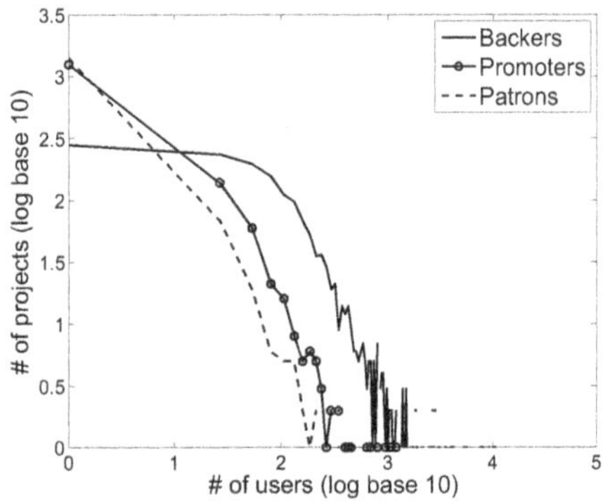


**Figure 5: Log distribution of users and projects.**

projects raise 50% of their goals. Fifty percent of projects that succeed are funded 25% or less over their goals, and only 7.8% of projects received over three times their goals. The margins of failure and success might be the result of the all-or-nothing policy. When a project shows a good chance of success, participants are more likely to invest to help the project to reach the goal.

Figure 5 displays the distribution of different types of users (i.e. backers, promoters and patrons) and the corresponding number of projects. In general, the distribution of social media users (promoters and patrons) follows the power law [3], and very few projects (1.5% of projects) are discussed by more than 100 social media users. However, the distribution of backers is unlike the distribution of social media users. It shows that there are fewer projects with few backers than one would expect from the power law, especially for the projects with less than 100 backers. The unexpected base of support seems owing to the contribution from the project proposers and their friends. Thus, simply using the number of promoters might not predict the number of backers well.

[3]Although all the projects in our dataset are referred by at least 5 tweets, some of them have less than 5 promoters because a promoter may tweet more than once.

In spite of that, there are non-negligible connections between the activities in social media and the results of crowdfunding projects. Consider the number of backers and the number of promoters in Figure 6(a) as an example. We can observe a strong correlation (0.79) between these two variables in log scale. This relationship provides a hint that social media activities are highly correlated with fundraising activities. In Section 5, we will further analyze how social activities affect the outcomes of crowdfunding projects.

# 4. PREDICTION TASKS

In this section we introduce two prediction tasks, which are based on observations of phenomena occur naturally in crowdfunding: the first is predicting the number of backers of a project and the second is predicting whether a project will receive sufficient funding. Our objective in formulating these tasks is to use them as an analytic framework, which is of practical interest to proposers and investors of crowdfunding projects.

In both prediction tasks, we focus on the early predictions that use only the data in the very early stages of crowdfunding projects to predict the outcomes of the projects. As we will see in Section 5.1, customer interests regard to a project decay significantly as the project evolves. In order to receive sufficient funds to support a project, it is important to identify potential bottlenecks as early as possible and adjust current strategies to attract more contributions before customer interests vanish. Thus, early prediction of the outcomes of projects, as well as understanding the associated properties and signals, are critical to the effectiveness of crowdfunding campaigns.

**Predicting the number of backers.** A crowdfunding project needs to raise funds and only the enrolled backers make actual monetary support. We can view the backers of a project as the buyers of a commercial product. As shown in Figure 6(b), there is an extremely high correlation (0.9) between the amount of raised funds and the number of backers (both in log scales). This high correlation suggests that the amount of raised funds strongly depends on the number of backers. Therefore, early prediction of the number of backers would help us estimate the amount of funds a project may receive.

**Predicting whether a project will reach its fundraising goal.** Although the funds of projects are highly correlated to the number of their backers, different projects may have dramatically different fundraising goals. Projects with a large amount of backers may not reach their fundraising goals. For example, Figure 6(c) shows that certain projects with more than 1,000 backers can fail to reach their fundraising goals (as shown by the points below the dash line, y=1). Our second task forms a natural complement to the first: other than predicting the number of backers of a project, we try to predict whether a project will receive sufficient funds to reach its fundraising goal or not.

Early prediction of the success rate of projects is clearly useful to investors as well as to crowdfunding services. Investors can reduce the waste of time and money by turning their attention to the projects that show more promising signs of success. The quality of crowdfunding platform can also be improved by extending current recommendation services to take into account the future success rate.

With these two prediction tasks in mind, we explore various features that affects the project results. After this exploration, we will show that the information we derive from social media helps us accurately predict both properties in Section 6.

# 5. DYNAMICS OF CROWDFUNDING

In this section we investigate the dynamics of crowdfunding from the processes of fundraising activities in crowdfunding sites as well as promotional activities in social media. We group our analysis into two parts to answer the following two questions: how participants response to a crowdfunding project over time, and how the campaigns in social media influence the eventual outcomes. In these two parts, we identify some basic principles that will be useful when we develop techniques for our prediction tasks.

## 5.1 The phases of crowdfunding activities

We start by investigating the process of crowdfunding activities along the span of a project's lifetime. Prior empirical study [7] has shown that the attention of online sharing-content peaks at the beginning and significantly decays after that. From this study one would expect that a burst followed by a power-law distribution governing the intensity of crowdfunding activities.

However, unlike conventional online content, a project has a specific deadline, after which no more action can change the results of the project. This policy arouses the potential contributors to put money into the project when the deadline is approaching. This is as if the remaining amount of activities in the long-tail of the power-law after the deadline would aggregate to the period before deadline.

Following this observation, we expect that there are threes phases in a project's lifetime: (1) starting bursty phase, when it is launched in the crowdfunding sites, (2) stationary phase, after the starting bursty follows a long period of relatively little activities and (3) final bursty phase, when its deadline is approaching.

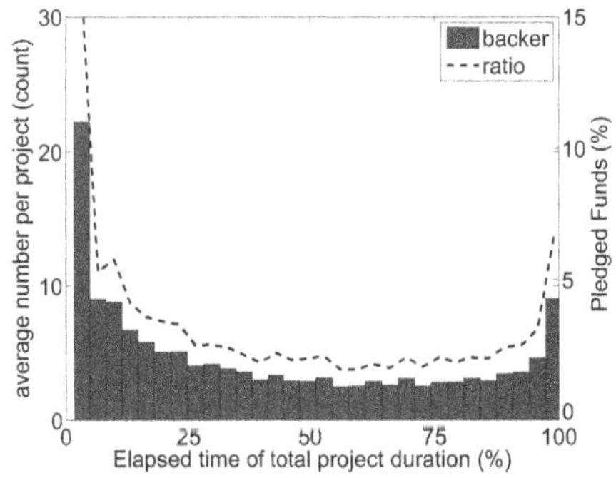


**Figure 7: Histogram of the fundraising activities in Kickstarter.**

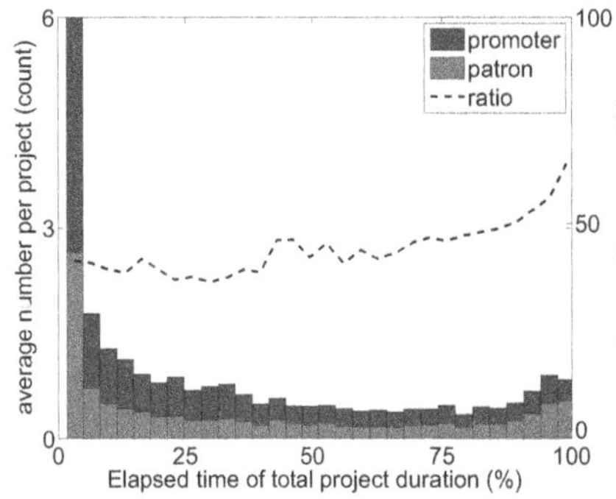


**Figure 8: Histogram of the promotional activities in Twitter.**

**Phases of fundraising activities.** In Figure 7, we examine the process of fundraising activities in Kickstarter. The blue bars represent the number of backers and the dash line shows the fraction of the raised funds in each period to the total raised funds at the target deadline. We find that the starting bursty phase happens in the first quarter of project duration, the final bursty phase appears in the last ten percent of project duration, and between these two phases is the stationary phase. A considerable portion of contribution a project receives can be attributed to the starting bursty phase, in which half of its backers invest in it and they contribute around 50% of its total raised funds. Although the majority of funding is acquired, only 14% of projects can reach their fundraising goals within the starting bursty phase. Around 60% of projects depend on the funds received in the final bursty phase to determine whether they can succeed or not (25% of projects among them succeed).

**Phases of promotional activities.** We next assess the process of promotional activities on Twitter, as shown in Figure 8. The blue bars represent the number of promoters, the red bars represent the number of patrons, and the dash line expresses the ratio of patrons to promoters in each period. We observe there also exist three similar phases in Figure 8 as in Figure 7: major amount of promotional activities in the first quarter, little attention in the middle period, and raising interests in the last ten percent of project duration.

Moreover, we notice that the patron/promoter ratio has an upward trend. It implies that the priority of crowdfund-

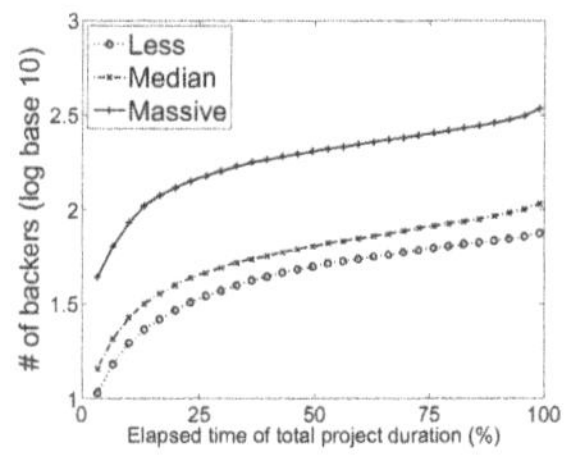


(a) Number of backers

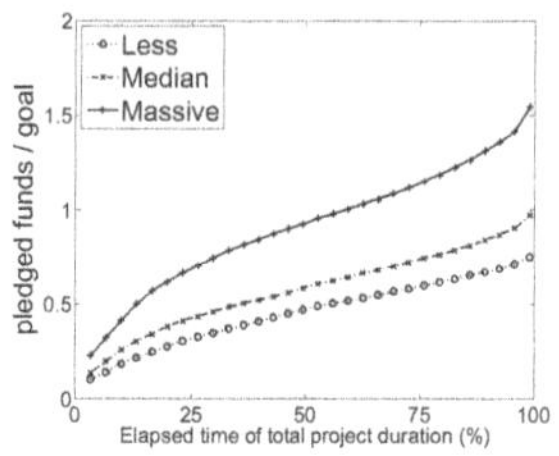


(b) Fraction of pledged funds to fundraising goal

**Figure 9: The comparison of fundraising results for different levels of promotion in starting bursty phase.**

ing activities is shifting from distributing the information to sharing the news of backing when approaching the deadline. We believe this shift is the result of the fact that it takes certain amount of time for a project to convince others to invest in, and the approaching deadline expedites the decision making in investments. Hence the longer it has been the higher percentage of the crowdfunding activities will shift from promoting to backing.

However, due to the decay of interests as time goes by, a project may not benefit much from this activity shifting. Hence, the prediction tasks we target to solve will focus on predicting the results from the data available within the starting bursty phase, as they will be more useful in practice.

**Effects of promotional activities.** The similar phases and activity shifting arise a series of interesting questions: Does this mean the fundraising activities are correlated to the promotional activities? Could we expect the projects with higher promotional activities will have better fundraising results? Could we forecast the results of crowdfunding projects from the early promotional activities?

We answer these questions by comparing with different levels of promotional activities in starting bursty phase, which is measured as the number of promoters accumulated by 25% of project duration. A project with the number of promoters between 1 and 5 is called a "less discussed project". For projects with 6-10 (11-100, respectively) promoters, we call them "median (massively, respectively) discussed projects". In Figure 9, we find that the projects with more promoters in starting bursty phase are always better in the number of backers and also in the ratio of pledged funds to fundraising goal. We stress that we are not claiming a direct causal relationship between promotional activities and the fundraising results; rather we are pointing out that there exist strong correlations between the fundraising results and early promotional activity. We will further discuss them in the following section.

## 5.2 Correlations between social promotion and fundraising results

In the previous section we observed the phases of crowdfunding activities, and demonstrated the effects of early promotional activities. Now we turn our attention to the underlying factors of crowdfunding campaigns on social media that lead to the difference in their prevalence. Specifically, we analyze correlations between the fundraising results of projects and the features extracted from corresponding campaigns on social media.

Here we treat the campaign of a crowdfunding project on a social network as the process of an information propagation on the network. A node in the campaign graph is a promoter, which is an author of a tweet regarding the project. A directed edge between a pair of nodes, e.g. $e_{u,v}$, expresses that the information of the project flows from one promoter $u$ to the other promoter $v$. There are two criteria for this information flow: 1) the earliest tweet from promoter $v$ regarding to the project is posted after that from promoter $u$, and 2) promoter $v$ follows promoter $u$ or was mentioned in promoter $u$'s tweet. If a promoter has no inward edges, there is no information flows to the promoter and the promoter must be motivated by external stimulations outside the monitored social network. Without loss of generality, the process of crowdfunding campaigns can be traced by the development of the information propagation.

After constructing the graphs of crowdfunding campaigns, we extract features from the structure of the graphs as well as from the crowdfunding activities. Overall, the features are explored from three different aspects: (1) properties of each project in crowdfunding sites, (2) activities of participants in crowdfunding campaigns, and (3) structures of the campaign graphs. The full set of features we consider is as follows:

**Project features** ($S_A$), 7 features total: project duration, elapsed days since the launch, fundraising goal, median amount of pledge options, number of backers, ratio of current raised funds to fundraising goal, and average amount of pledge per backer.

**Social activity features** ($S_B$), 6 features total: number of tweets, number of promoters, number of patrons, number of unique mentioned users, fraction of promoters from external stimulations, and fraction of patrons from external stimulations.

**Social structure features** ($S_C$), 7 features total: average number of followers of promoters, median number of followers of promoters, number of edges, diameter (largest shortest distance), number of weakly connected components, number of triads, and global clustering coefficient [9] (average local clustering coefficient [10, 23] of all nodes).

Note that the last two features in $S_B$ intend to capture the effect of external influence. The fraction of promoters (patrons) from external stimulations is measured as the fraction of the number of promoters (patrons) with no inward edges to the total number of promoters (patrons). In $S_C$, the edges represents the appearances of internal influence, and the diameter means the largest geodesic distance the cascade internal influence can reach from one node to the other one. The weakly connected components represents the groups in the crowdfunding campaigns. The number of triads and the global clustering coefficient are used to study the strength and density of the campaigns.

**Correlations between proposed features and fundraising results.** We now evaluate the correlations between the 20 features mentioned above and the final fundraising results at target deadline. The features are extracted from the information available in the starting bursty stage. Table 2 and Table 3 display the correlation values for the number of backers and the ratio of fundraising goal achievement at the target deadline, respectively. For example, in Table 2, for the row on the number of promoters, the entry on the column

| Feature | project duration (%) 5 | 10 | 25 |
|---|---|---|---|
| # of backers | 0.82 | 0.89 | 0.92 |
| # of patrons | 0.79 | 0.81 | 0.85 |
| # of promoters | 0.77 | 0.78 | 0.79 |
| # of tweets | 0.73 | 0.70 | 0.65 |
| # of weakly connected components | 0.70 | 0.69 | 0.68 |

**Table 2: Correlation of the total number of backers at target deadline and the features extracted at specified time.**

| Feature | project duration (%) 5 | 10 | 25 |
|---|---|---|---|
| raised funds/goal | 0.77 | 0.89 | 0.95 |
| # of triads | 0.47 | 0.46 | 0.45 |
| # of edges | 0.43 | 0.43 | 0.38 |
| # of patrons | 0.26 | 0.26 | 0.24 |
| # of backers | 0.18 | 0.29 | 0.30 |

**Table 3: Correlation of the ratio of raised funds to fundraising goal at target deadline and the features extracted at specified time.**

of 5% means that the correlation between the accumulated number of promoters by the end of the 5% period of the fundraising duration to the number of backers at the target deadline is 0.77. This correlation increases slightly to 0.78 and 0.79 at the end of the 10% and 25% periods, respectively.

For each table, we only report the top 5 features that have the highest correlation at each time frame. As shown in both tables, the feature that has the best correlation is the fundraising result itself. This indicates the early status of the fundraising result has good predictive power on its final value, and we should consider it as baseline for each task. Interestingly, the other top features for both objectives are extracted from social media, instead of the properties of a project on its own.

Table 2 shows that the number of backers is strongly correlated to the volume of promotional activities, i.e. the number of patrons, the number of promoters, and the number of tweets. On the other hand, Table 3 shows that the ratio of fundraising goal achievement is more correlated to the structure of campaign graphs, i.e. the number of triads and the number of edges. These observations are due to the fundamentally different properties of the volume and network structures. The number of backers is measured as the quantity of support and is primarily affected by the volume of promotion, whereas its success is determined by the quality of support, i.e. the amount of money. A popular project may receive lots of very small contributions, e.g. $1 dollar, from general public but still not be able to reach the fundraising goal. However, a successful project would target specific groups that have interests in it and acquire more money from them. The number of edges and the number of triads both suggest the strength of information flows within groups. A large number of edges and/or triads show a sign of the intensive interests among groups, and thus they are more correlated to the ratio of fundraising goal achievement.

**Concurrent processes of social promotions and external stimulations.**

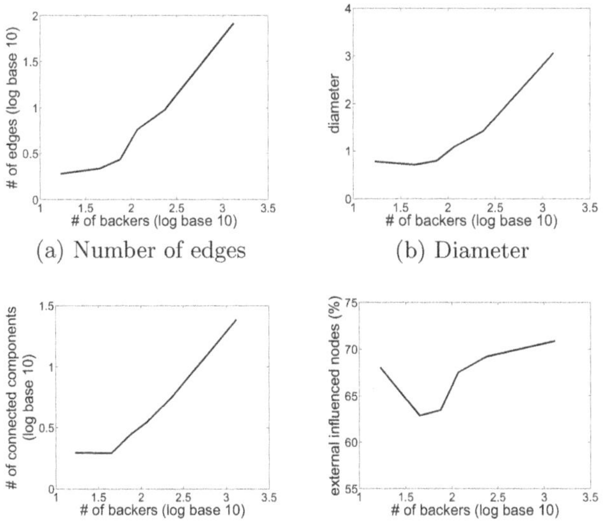


(a) Number of edges (b) Diameter

(c) Number of weakly connected components (d) fraction of nodes from external stimulations

**Figure 10: Each figure shows, given the promotional activity in the starting bursty phase, the value of a particular property as a function of the number of backers at target deadline. Top row and bottom row display the properties from the aspect of social promotions and external stimulations, respectively.**

Our above observations show that there are strong correlations between fundraising results and social features. We claim they are primarily due to the fact that if a project is more persuasive to intrigue authors in social networks to discuss it (either by social promotions or external stimulations), it is more attractive to investors. From the aspect of social promotions, we expect such a project to have a larger campaign graph. From the aspect of external stimulations, we expect there exists more groups in the campaign, each of which is represented by a weakly connected component as each component can be viewed as started by an external stimulus.

We consider the relationship between the number of backers and the social structure of its campaign in the starting bursty phase as an example to illustrate our claim. From the aspect of social promotions, as shown in Figure 10(a) and Figure 10(b), we notice that the number of backers increases with the number of edges and/or the diameter. Both features indicate the expansion of crowdfunding campaigns which is activated from the influences of social promotions. From the aspect of external stimulations, as can be seen in Figure 10(c), we observe the similar rise in the number of weakly connected components, which indicates the increase in the number of groups.

These results from both aspects suggest that social promotions and external stimulations concurrently activate the processes of crowdfunding campaigns. One may ask which one is more important? In Figure 10(d), we find that over 60% of nodes are from external stimulations. This reflects the fact that most authors access a project from external sources outside social media and motivated by personal interests to promote it. However, we also notice if there are very few social promotions, which signals the unenthusiastic response in social media, the number of backers would be very low. Hence, the effective way to promote a project is to stimulate from social media as well as stimulate from other channels. From the features extracted from social media, we could identify the bottlenecks of current campaign and devise a better campaign strategy.

# 6. EXPERIMENTS

The previous section presented a set of properties that governing the process of crowdfunding. Now we show that this understanding is directly applicable to our two prediction tasks.

The practical applications of both tasks would be to predict project results as early as possible. Accordingly, we perform the following tasks using only the information available in the starting bursty phase (within 25% of project duration after the project is posted in crowdfunding sites). We consider the features presented in the previous sections for our prediction tasks. Note that besides focusing on prediction accuracy, we also aim at obtaining explanatory insights into what features are the most relevant and useful as signals for crowdfunding processes.

## 6.1 Predicting the number of backers

Recall from Section 4 that our first task is to predict the number of backers of a project at target deadline. As suggested in [20, 18], the Relative Squared Error (RSE) is more relevant and meaningful than absolute quadratic error for online content popularity prediction. We here adopt RSE to evaluate the performance of our first task. Let $N(p)$ be the total number of backers project $p$ has received at target deadline, and $N(p|t)$ be the total number of backers predicted for project $p$ based on data from the first $t$ days. The RSE takes the form of

$$RSE = \left[\frac{N(p|t) - N(p)}{N(p)}\right]^2 = \left[\frac{N(p|t)}{N(p)} - 1\right]^2 \quad (1)$$

For the collection of projects, denoted by $C$, the mean Relative Squared Error (mRSE) is defined as the arithmetic mean of the RSE values for all projects in $C$, that is:

$$mRSE = \frac{1}{|C|} \cdot \sum_{p \in C} \left[\frac{N(p|t)}{N(p)} - 1\right]^2 \quad (2)$$

The correlation between crowdfunding activity and the future number of backers observed in previous section suggests that the number of backers can be estimated as a linear function of features. Thus, we apply a multivariate linear model [18] to predict the number of backers. We denote the feature vector of the project $p$ at time $t$ as $X(p,t)$. The future number of backers of the project can be estimated as

$$N(p|t) = \theta_t \cdot X(p,t) \quad (3)$$

where $\theta_t$ is the vector of model parameters and depends only on $t$.

Given a training set $C$, $t$, we can estimate the optimal values for the elements of $\theta_{t_i}$ as the ones that minimize the mRSE on C, i.e.:

$$\underset{\theta_t}{\operatorname{argmin}} \frac{1}{|C|} \sum_{p \in C} \left[\theta_t \cdot \frac{X(p,t)}{N(p)} - 1\right]^2 \quad (4)$$

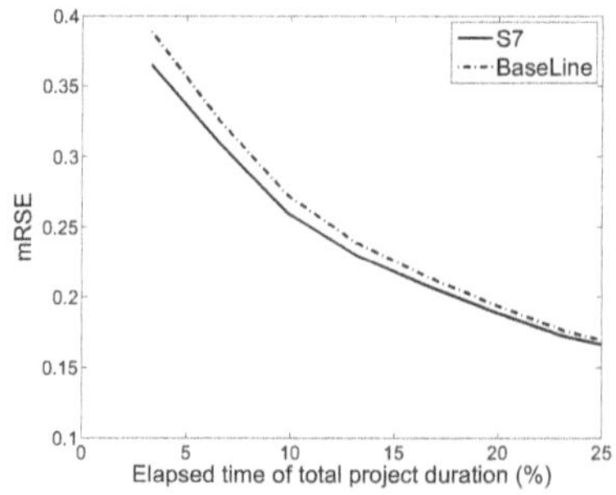


**Figure 11: The performance of the prediction of the number of backers.**

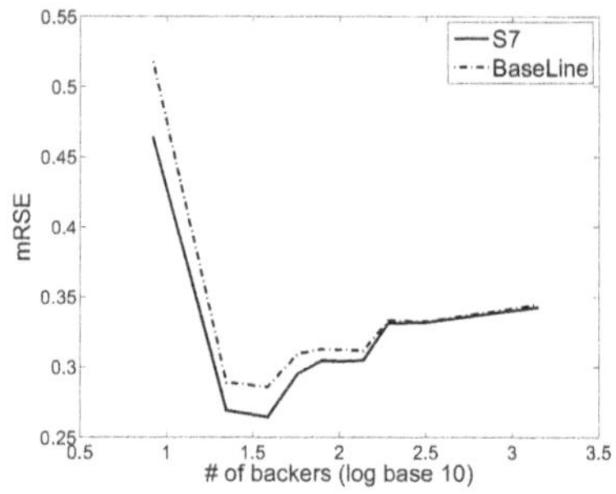


**Figure 12: The mRSE shown as a function of the number of backers at target deadline.**

which is an ordinary least squares (OLS) problem that can be solved via a singular value decomposition [5, 18].

We conduct feature selection and find a core set of 7 features that we use in this task: number of backers, number of tweets, number of promoters, number of patrons, fraction of promoters from external influence, number of edges, and number of weakly connected components. Note that except the number of backers, all the other six features are extracted from social media. The first four in the six features are from social activity features, while the last two are from social structure features. We call this set $S_7$ and compare it against the baseline that only uses the number of backers.

We perform 5-fold cross validation and report the mRSE. Figure 11 gives the results of the prediction task. We can observe that the features extracted from social media ($S_7$) inspired by our previous analyses improve the performance of prediction. For instance, when using only the data available up to 5% of project duration, the mRSE produced by the $S_7$ and by the baseline are 0.337 and 0.357, respectively, leading to an error reduction of 5.5%. If extending the time window to 25% of project duration - after which half of backers have arrived (see Section 5.1) - both mRSE values can be significantly reduced to about 0.16. The performance gains from using social media features are gradually reduced. This is reasonable, as the scale of the backers reveals more information of its final count, predictions just become easier. However, it is less meaningful to do such predictions at this stage, as it might be too late for project owners to adjust their strategies.

To further understand the performance of prediction for different popularities, in Figure 12, we analyze the mRSE values produced by comparing $S_7$ with baseline at 5% of

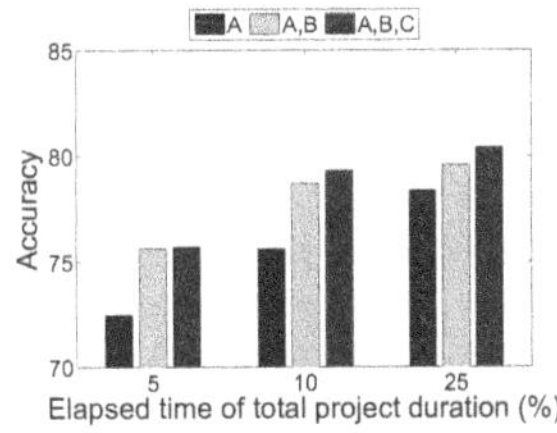


(a) Accuracy

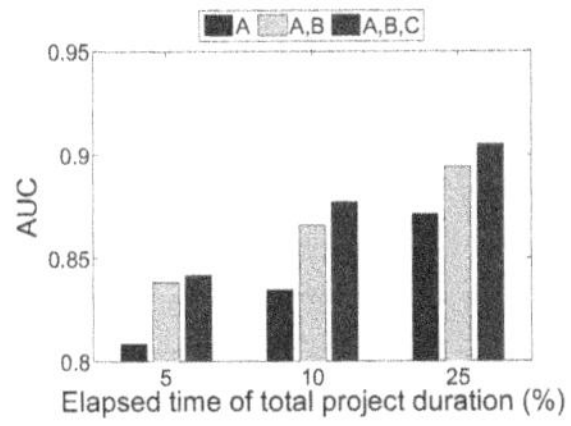


(b) AUC

**Figure 13: The performance of predicting the fundraising goal achievement.**

project duration. Note that for the most challenging case when the number of backers is small or moderate, $S_7$ performs a lot better than the baseline as it can capture other clues from the social network attributes. For example, when the number of backer is 10, the mRSE produced by the $S_7$ and by the baseline are 0.46 and 0.52, respectively, leading to an error reduction of 9.6%. More importantly, the results show that the prediction made by using $S_7$ features outperform baseline for projects with any number of backers.

## 6.2 Predicting whether a project will receive sufficient funds

We further study the performance of the four feature classes on predicting if a project will achieve its fundraising goal. Specifically, we formulate this prediction task as a binary classification task. The response variable is whether the amount of pledged funds exceeds the fundraising goal.

After performing feature selection, we reduce our features to a smaller set of 8 features: 2 from $S_A$ (number of backers, and ratio of current pledged funds to the fundraising goal), 2 from $S_B$ (number of patrons and fraction of promoters from external influence), and 4 from $S_C$ (number of edges, average number of followers, number of weakly connected component, and number of triads).

For interpretability and ease of comparison, we use a logistic regression classifier, perform 5-fold cross validation and report the classification accuracy and the area under the ROC curve (AUC). The results are reported in Figure 13. For example, in Figure 13(a), it shows that at 5% of the project duration, just using feature from the project property ($S_A$) as indicated by the label A, the prediction accuracy is around 0.725. Adding features from social activity ($S_B$) as indicated by the label (A,B) will increase the accuracy to 0.754 and further incorporating the social structure features ($S_C$) indicated by the label (A,B,C) will increase the accuracy to 0.757.

We notice that the properties of the crowdfunding projects on their own ($S_A$) have good predictive power. It gives 22% improvement in accuracy over random guessing. Although extending the time window can improve the prediction accuracy, it is less useful in practice. Moreover, extending the time window provides less improvement than adding social activity features ($S_B$), which gives a gain of 3-5% in accuracy and 3-4% in AUC in each time frame. Incorporating social structure features ($S_C$) in the prediction model further enhances the improvement. This improvement is clearer when the social structure has developed for a period of time (e.g. after 10% of project duration).

To fully appreciate the result, we emphasize that the results of 60% of projects are determined in the last ten percent of project duration, as indicated in Section 5.1. It is remarkable that we achieve 75% accuracy by using features available only up to five percent of project duration after the project was launched. From these results, we see that taking into account the rich information from social media improves performance of prediction on crowdfunding.

# 7. RELATED WORK

In this section, we will survey existing works about the determinants of the success of crowdfunding ventures. We then present some studies around the impact of social media.

**Determinants of venture success:** Crowdfunding has been drawing substantial attention from entrepreneurs, but relatively little notice from academics. Some studies focus on an important issue: the underlying factors of success and failure among crowdfunding ventures [6, 15]. To examine the determinants of venture success, Mollick et al. [15] conducted an analysis using logistic regression of the odds of successful funding from Kickstarter. Their result suggests that the size of a proposer's social network (e.g. the number of Facebook friends) help predict the success of crowdfunding efforts. However, there are only 16% of projects whose proposers have Twitter accounts in our dataset. In these 16% of projects, the number of followers of the project proposers in Twitter has very low correlations to the number of backers (-0.0117) and to the ratio of fundraising goal achievement (-0.0488). More importantly, the process of crowdfunding is not simply driven by the members in the proposer's social network; instead, it is more likely to rely on the information propagation in social media, as discussed in Section 5 and Section 6.

**Information diffusion models:** Social media platforms have recently emerged as valuable sources of realtime news, event updates, opinions, and advertising. Enormous works have been done on analyzing how an event spreads out in social media [14, 17, 22, 21, 2, 13, 4, 19]. For modeling the global influence of nodes, Yang et al. [22] proposed the Linear Influence Model that takes newly infected nodes as a function of the times when other nodes got infected in the past. However, the authors in [17] demonstrated that information reaches users not only through connections in their online social networks, but also through the influence external out-of-network sources, like the mainstream media. Thus, to solve our prediction tasks, we should consider internal influence from neighbors as well as the external influence outside the given social media.

**Prediction of future popularity:** There is a stream of research that has examined the prediction of the future popularity of online content. For example, the study in [12] presents stochastic models of user behavior on content-sharing sites (e.g. Digg[4]) for predicting popularity based on early user reactions to new content. Henrique et al. also applied historical information of early popularity measures to predict the future popularity of YouTube videos [18]. Despite that, crowdfunding campaigns has several unique properties, as discussed in the introduction, that make it different to conventional online-sharing content. Hence these approaches cannot be directly applied to our prediction tasks.

[4]http:// digg.com

**Social media as word-of-mouth wisdom:** Jansen et al. [8] used Twitter to investigate the structure of the postings, the types of expressions, and the movement in sentiments. However, the authors do not perform any analysis on the predictive aspect of Twitter. Asur et al. [4] demonstrated how Twitter can be used to predict real-world outcomes. They forecasted box-office revenues for movies by a linear regression model and further improved the result by classifying sentiments of tweets. The authors in [19] constructed time-constrained graphs from stock-market related tweets and estimated the correlation between stock-market events and micro-blogging data. These works show the possibility of using social media to predict future outcomes. Nevertheless, none of them investigate how social media create impacts to time-constrained events, such as electoral campaigns or crowdfunding campaigns.

# 8. CONCLUSION

As crowdfunding flourishes as a feasible fundraising strategy – through the collective efforts by participants who network and pool their money together – in many industries, it becomes useful to think about how to attract more contributions. In this paper, we presented the underlying connections between promotion campaigns in social media and the fundraising results of crowdfunding projects, and identified a number of important principles that guide the direction of devising an effective campaign. We also demonstrated that the features arising from social media can help improve the accuracy of predicting eventual outcomes, specifically how popular a project will be, and which projects are likely to successfully reach the fundraising goals.

In summary, our results provide a promising step towards inferring the impacts of social media on crowdfunding. We anticipate that further analysis could quantify personal interests of participants from historical behaviors, develop richer ways of assessing social influences among users, and suggest potential customers from collaborative filtering of personal interests and social influences.


## Acknowledgment

This work is supported in part by NSF through grants CNS-1115234, DBI-0960443, and OISE-1129076, US Department of Army through grant W911NF-12-1-0066, and Huawei Grant.


# 9. REFERENCES


[1] Crowdfunding industry report: Market trends, composition and crowdfunding platforms. `http://www.crowdsourcing.org/editorial/2013cf-the-crowdfunding-industry-report/25107`.

[2] C. C. Aggarwal, S. Lin, and P. S. Yu. On influential node discovery in dynamic social networks. In *SDM*, pages 636–647, 2012.

[3] M. Ahmed, S. Spagna, F. Huici, and S. Niccolini. A peek into the future: predicting the evolution of popularity in user generated content. In *WSDM*, pages 607–616, 2013.

[4] S. Asur and B. A. Huberman. Predicting the future with social media. http://arxiv.org/abs/1003.5699, 2010.

[5] S. Boyd and L. Vandenberghe. *Convex Optimization*. Cambridge University Press, New York, NY, USA, 2004.

[6] G. Burtch, A. Ghose, and S. Wattal. An Empirical Examination of the Antecedents and Consequences of Contribution Patterns in Crowd-Funded Markets. *Information Systems Research*, 2013.

[7] R. Crane and D. Sornette. Robust dynamic classes revealed by measuring the response function of a social system. *Proceedings of the National Academy of Sciences*, 105(41):15649–15653, 2008.

[8] B. J. Jansen, M. Zhang, K. Sobel, and A. Chowdury. Twitter power: Tweets as electronic word of mouth. *Journal of the American Society for Information Science and Technology*, 60(11):2169–2188, 2009.

[9] A. Kemper. *Valuation of network effects in software markets. A complex networks approach.* Contributions to Management Science., 2010.

[10] G. Kossinets and D. J. Watts. Empirical Analysis of an Evolving Social Network. *Science*, 311(5757):88–90, Jan. 2006.

[11] K. Lerman and R. Ghosh. Information contagion: An empirical study of the spread of news on digg and twitter social networks. In *ICWSM*, 2010.

[12] K. Lerman and T. Hogg. Using a model of social dynamics to predict popularity of news. In *WWW*, pages 621–630, 2010.

[13] C.-T. Li, H.-P. Hsieh, S.-D. Lin, and M.-K. Shan. Finding influential seed successors in social networks. In *WWW*, pages 557–558, 2012.

[14] Y. Matsubara, Y. Sakurai, B. A. Prakash, L. Li, and C. Faloutsos. Rise and fall patterns of information diffusion: model and implications. In *KDD*, pages 6–14, 2012.

[15] Mollick and E. R. The dynamics of crowdfunding: Determinants of success and failure. *Social Science Research Network*, 2013.

[16] M. J. Muller, W. Geyer, T. Soule, S. Daniels, and L.-T. Cheng. Crowdfunding inside the enterprise: employee-initiatives for innovation and collaboration. In *CHI*, pages 503–512, 2013.

[17] S. A. Myers, C. Zhu, and J. Leskovec. Information diffusion and external influence in networks. In *KDD*, pages 33–41, 2012.

[18] H. Pinto, J. M. Almeida, and M. A. Gonçalves. Using early view patterns to predict the popularity of youtube videos. In *WSDM*, pages 365–374, 2013.

[19] E. J. Ruiz, V. Hristidis, C. Castillo, A. Gionis, and A. Jaimes. Correlating financial time series with micro-blogging activity. In *WSDM*, pages 513–522, 2012.

[20] G. Szabo and B. A. Huberman. Predicting the popularity of online content. *Communications of the ACM*, 53(8):80–88, Aug. 2010.

[21] J. Yang and S. Counts. Predicting the speed, scale, and range of information diffusion in twitter. In *ICWSM*, 2010.

[22] J. Yang and J. Leskovec. Modeling information diffusion in implicit networks. In *ICDM*, pages 599–608, 2010.

[23] Y. Zhao, G. Wang, P. S. Yu, S. Liu, and S. Zhang. Inferring social roles and statuses in social networks. In *KDD*, 2013.

# Understanding and Promoting Micro-Finance Activities in Kiva.org

Jaegul Choo
Georgia Institute of Technology
jaegul.choo@cc.gatech.edu

Changhyun Lee
Georgia Institute of Technology
clee407@gatech.edu

Daniel Lee
Georgia Tech Research Institute
daniel.lee@gtri.gatech.edu

Hongyuan Zha
Georgia Institute of Technology
zha@cc.gatech.edu

Haesun Park
Georgia Institute of Technology
hpark@cc.gatech.edu

## ABSTRACT

Non-profit Micro-finance organizations provide loaning opportunities to eradicate poverty by financially equipping impoverished, yet skilled entrepreneurs who are in desperate need of an institution that lends to those who have little. Kiva.org, a widely-used crowd-funded micro-financial service, provides researchers with an extensive amount of publicly available data containing a rich set of heterogeneous information regarding micro-financial transactions. Our objective in this paper is to identify the key factors that encourage people to make micro-financing donations, and ultimately, to keep them actively involved. In our contribution to further promote a healthy micro-finance ecosystem, we detail our personalized loan recommendation system which we formulate as a supervised learning problem where we try to predict how likely a given lender will fund a new loan. We construct the features for each data item by utilizing the available connectivity relationships in order to integrate all the available Kiva data sources. For those lenders with no such relationships, e.g., first-time lenders, we propose a novel method of feature construction by computing joint nonnegative matrix factorizations. Utilizing gradient boosting tree methods, a state-of-the-art prediction model, we are able to achieve up to 0.92 AUC (area under the curve) value, which shows the potential of our methods for practical deployment. Finally, we point out several interesting phenomena on lenders' social behaviors in micro-finance activities.

## Categories and Subject Descriptors

H.3.3 [**Information Search and Retrieval**]: Information filtering; I.2.6 [**Artificial Intelligence**]: Learning


*WSDM'14*, February 24–28, 2014, New York, New York, USA.
Copyright 2014 ACM 978-1-4503-2351-2/14/02 ...$15.00.
http://dx.doi.org/10.1145/2556195.2556253.

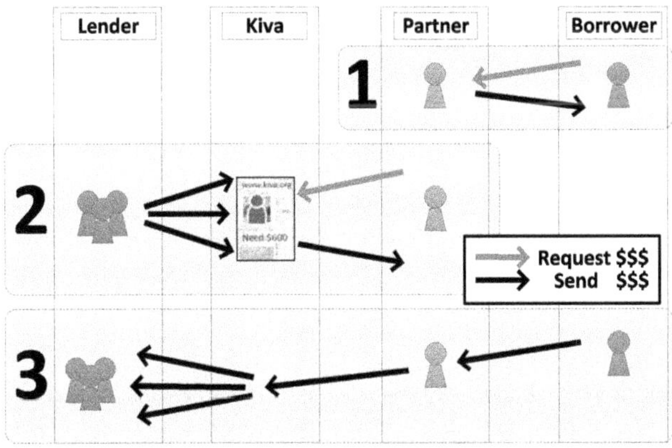


Figure 1: An overview of how Kiva works. 1. A borrower requests a loan to a (field) partner, and a loan is disbursed. 2. The partner uploads a loan request to Kiva, and lenders fund the loan. 3. The borrower makes repayments through the partner, and Kiva then repays the lenders. They can make another loan, donate to Kiva, or withdraw the money to their PayPal account.

## Keywords

Recommender systems; cold-start problem; microfinance; crowdfunding; joint matrix factorization; gradient boosting tree; heterogeneous data

## 1. INTRODUCTION

Kiva was founded by Matt Flannery and Jessica Jackley who based their concept on the inspiration of Muhammad Yunus' lecture on the Grameen Bank. The Grameen Bank, which won the Nobel Peace Prize in 2006 for its impact in helping the impoverished, was founded by Yunus in 1977 to address the lack of practical credit available to the under-utilized, yet skillful entrepreneurs in impoverished countries [32]. In Yunus' Book, he documented how he came up with the concept by noticing that the very poor could barely sustain themselves, let alone work their trade, since many times the poor were taking loans to buy the materials, only to sell their finished product back as repayment. In response, Yunus began his credit-loaning program which

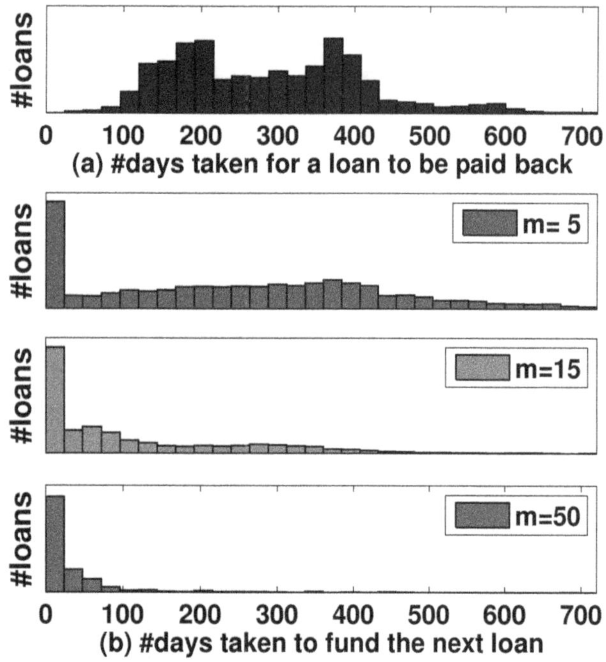


Figure 2: Temporal lending patterns for different lender groups with a specific lending count $m$

provided loans without collateral and interest, and with an easy repayment plan. There are multitudes of success stories in Yunus' book as well as on the Kiva blog[1] that portray how micro-financing has given opportunity to change the lives of the borrowers, their businesses, and their local areas.

Since its inception in 2005, Kiva and its generous lenders now impact the lives of courageous, hardworking borrowers across 72 countries. Kiva[2] is a non-profit micro-financial organization which acts as an intermediary service to provide people with the opportunity to lend money to underprivileged entrepreneurs in developing countries. Kiva's lending model is based on a crowd-funding model in which any individual can fund a particular loan by contributing to a loan individually or as a part of a lender team. The Kiva loan process is summarized in Fig. 1.[3]

Open public access to Kiva's data, provided through daily snapshots and an API, is a part of Kiva's charitable initiative to provide the working poor with an infrastructure that Kiva hopes will encourage life-changing lending. This level of transparency lies at the core of Kiva's successful growth as Matt Flannery puts it: "Transparency in this next period will be our best weapon against the challenges of growth. This model thrives on information, not marketing" [13].

Kiva data contain a wealthy set of heterogeneous information about lenders, loans, lender teams, borrowers, and field partners. As of June 2013, the publicly available Kiva data set contained over 1,100,000 lenders, 500,000 loans, and 150,000 journal entries for over 4,000,000 transactions that resulted in over 400,000,000 USD of loans issued. There are also multiple types of many-to-many relationships between each of the data entities. For example, lenders may be a part of multiple lender teams while lenders may choose any number of loans to participate in. Furthermore, borrowers may optionally update their progress to their field partner for entry into the Kiva website as a journal entry. This data set includes geospatial, temporal, and free-text data along with a variety of other numerical and categorical information, consequently forming a fascinating set of data for many data mining and social media researchers.

**Loan recommendation and diverse lender behaviors.** Kiva as a non-profit organization encourages lending by promoting the idea that those in need can create better lives for themselves and their families when given the opportunity, i.e., capital. Thus, one can naturally realize that lenders, who are also regarded as donors due to the lack of any interest or reward they receive in return for their loan, are a pivotal component to the Kiva model. Consequently, one of the keys to a healthy Kiva ecosystem relies on keeping their lenders interested in continuing in their generous donations. This is where active recommendation can play a major role by matching the lender with loans that they would be sincerely interested in.

In addition, what makes loan recommendation an interesting problem is the diversity of lenders' behaviors. How do lenders differ in their lending behaviors and what are the major factors to drive these differences? Fig. 2 displays an example showing temporal lending patterns. For a particular loan to be fully paid, it usually takes from a half to a full year (Fig. 2(a)). In case of passive lenders with a small number of lending experiences (a smaller $m$ in Fig. 2(b)), the time taken between two consecutive lending activities show a relatively high correlation with the time required for a loan to be paid, compared to the other cases. This behavior is most likely explained by the notion that some passive lenders participate in another loan when their initial loan is paid back, rather than contributing more money of their own. However, active lenders with more lending experiences continue their lending activities mainly within a short time interval, as shown in a strong peak with almost no tail in the examples with a larger $m$ in Fig. 2(b).

**Challenges in loan recommendation.** The problem of loan recommendation presents various challenges compared to other traditional recommendation problems.

The first is the *transient nature* of loans. Standard recommendation techniques based on collaborative filtering primarily utilize other similar users' ratings or preferences on the items for recommendation. The key notion is that the items being recommended such as books or movies are persistent and reusable, i.e, an item (or a copy thereof) can serve many users. Loans, on the other hand, are transient and a particular loan can only serve a single borrower. More importantly, loans are only available for a short amount of time until the loan request is fully met, often leaving little or no information available to utilize from previous lenders.

The second challenge is the *binary rating* structure. Most rating systems are composed of a multi-grade set of ratings from which a user can select, yet in Kiva, the only information available similar to a rating is whether or not s/he funded the loan.[4] Furthermore, the fact that the funding did not happen may not necessarily mean that s/he did not like it. This challenge is often found in other settings where the recommendation relies only on previous purchases, viewing of item pages, etc. Such limited information and ambigu-

[1]http://pages.kiva.org/kivablog
[2]http://www.kiva.org/
[3]http://www.kiva.org/about/how

[4]Individual loan amount could be utilized similarly to rating information, but such information is not available from Kiva API for lender privacy.

ity require more than just standard collaborative filtering approaches.

Finally, another challenge is the *heterogeneity* of data. The Kiva data set comprises a variety of intertwined entities giving rise to a rich set of heterogeneous information. Merging and fusing this diverse set of information in a unified predictive framework for loan recommendation presents a non-trivial problem.

**Overview of proposed approaches.** In order to better handle these challenges and deeply analyze various lending patterns among Kiva users, we propose a supervised learning approach to tackle this unique loan recommendation problem. That is, we formulate it as a binary classification/regression problem, where, given a lender and loan pair, the trained model computes the score that represents the likelihood of funding. In order to train our model with all the available information, we propose two main feature generation methods: (1) *graph-based feature integration* (for lenders with previous loans) (2) *feature alignment via joint nonnegative matrix factorization* (for lenders with no previous loans). The former provides us with a general framework for incorporating all the available heterogeneous information to represent a lender-loan pair. On the other hand, the latter alleviates the lack of information for newcomers, which is a well-known issue referred to as the cold-start problem in many recommendation applications.

Utilizing the proposed approaches along with a gradient boosting tree, a state-of-the-art learner model, we achieve a practically useful level of performance up to around 0.92 AUC (area under the curve) value. Furthermore, we present in-depth analysis of the resulting model and its output, revealing various interesting knowledge about lenders' social behaviors in micro-finance activities.

The rest of this paper is organized as follows. Section 2 describes our basic preprocessing steps to handle the heterogeneity of Kiva data; in addition, we have made the post-processed data readily available on the web for other researchers. Section 3 describes our main approaches for loan recommendation, and Section 4 presents the prediction performances as well as various findings from our analysis. Section 5 discusses related work. Finally, Section 6 concludes the paper and discusses future work.

## 2. BASIC DATA REPRESENTATION

The Kiva data set is composed of various entities, each of which has its own set of rich information including unstructured data (e.g., text, image, and video) as well as structured data (e.g., geo-spatial, numerical, categorical, and ordinal data). Lender entities contain basic web profile data, i.e., profile image, registration timestamp, location, loan count, and other fields, in addition to links to various types of entities. For example, a lender will have links to loans that s/he has funded and to any number of lender teams with which s/he is affiliated. Field partners manage loans within their local region, while borrowers request loans from their local field partner in respect to their lack of access to a computer with internet access.

Kiva provides a recent snapshot of its data set in JSON and XML formats,[5]. For our work, we used a 2.9 GB JSON snapshot which was collected on 5/31/2013. We preprocessed it to obtain the numerical representations of each available field. Particularly, the preprocessing of temporal, categorical, and textual fields all required a nontrivial amount of work. For temporal data, such as the loan's *posting date* and lender's *sign-up date*, we converted it to a serial date number using Matlab's *datenum* function, which represents the whole and fractional number of days from a fixed preset date of January 0 in year 0000. For categorical data, such as a lender's *gender* and a loan's *country code*, we used a dummy encoding scheme which converts a variable with $m$ categories into an $m$-dimensional binary vector where only the values in the corresponding categories are set to ones.

Finally, for textual data, we encoded each textual field separately as a bag-of-words vector where an individual dimension corresponds to a unique word. Afterwards we reduced the dimensionality using nonnegative matrix factorization[6] (NMF) [21, 19] to 100 for each textual field. We performed dimension reduction for two reasons. First, although the encoded representations may be in sparse format, the entire dimension easily amounts up to the hundreds of thousands requiring enormous computational time in learning our prediction model. Second, the reduced dimensions, which are composed of a group of words, are more semantically meaningful than individual term dimensions, and thus, they can be versatile for both good prediction performance and data/model understanding [10, 30]. The reduced dimension was set to 100 because larger values did not improve the prediction performances reported in Section 4.

As a final preprocessing step we created mappings between entities from the different tables. For example, a lender entity found in the table containing metadata for lenders may have a different identifier in another table about the lender-loan graph, and even worse, it may exist in only one table, meaning that some information about it will be completely missing. The mappings we created allow these issues to be handled with ease. We made the processed formatted data as Matlab files available at `http://fodava.gatech.edu/processed-kiva-data`.

## 3. METHODOLOGY

In this section, we describe our methodology for promoting non-profit micro-finance activities in Kiva. We formulate this task as a binary classification/regression problem. That is, we consider a pair $(u, l)$ of a lender $u$[7] and a loan $l$ as an individual data item, and given such a pair, we intend to predict how likely s/he will fund the loan, which we denote as $f(u, l)$. The associated label is set to 1 if funding occurred for the pair and 0 otherwise. Once the learner model is trained based on a set of data items along with these labels, it can then predict the likelihood of funding for any given lender-loan pair. Such a capability is broadly applicable in various loan recommendation problems. For example, it allows one to identify the best matching lender for a particular loan by solving $\arg\max_u f(u, l)$ for a fixed $l$ as well as the most appropriate loan to recommend given a particular lender by solving $\arg\max_l f(u, l)$ for a fixed $u$.

In this approach, the key procedure affecting the overall performance is feature generation, i.e., how we characterize and represent a particular lender-loan pair. This is especially challenging considering the complexity of the Kiva data set which involves heterogeneous entities, such as bor-

[5] `http://build.kiva.org/docs/data/snapshots`

[6] `http://www.cc.gatech.edu/~hpark/nmfsoftware.php`

[7] We use an acronym $u$ by viewing a lender as a kiva '$u$'ser.

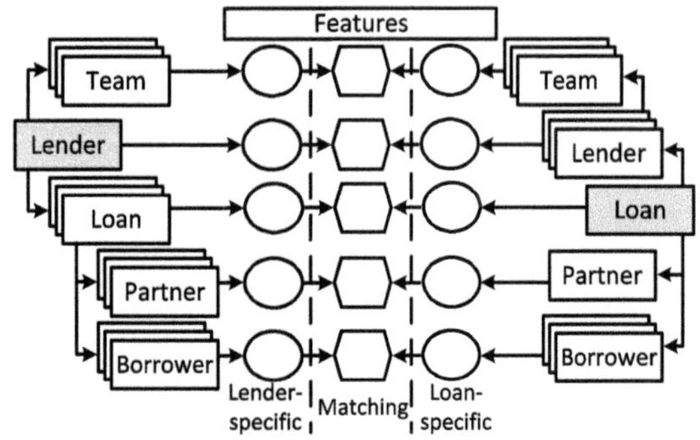

Figure 3: A graph-based feature integration for a lender-loan pair (grey-colored).

rowers, field partners, loans, lenders, and lender teams, with their own various set of information and complex relationships among them. To properly handle this issue, we act appropriately for two situations split by whether or not a lender has had previous funding experiences. In the following, we present our feature generation procedure for each case in detail.

## 3.1 Graph-based Feature Integration

When information about previous funding experiences of a particular lender is available, we utilize relationship links between different entities to take into account all the information available from the linked entities. As summarized in Fig. 3, given a lender-loan pair $(u, l)$, we first retrieve all the linked entities from both the lender and the loan. Specifically, a lender $u$ will contain links to the list of teams s/he is affiliated with, loans s/he funded previously, and partners and borrowers his/her previous loans were associated with. Similarly, a loan will contain the links to the associated partner and the lists of borrowers, lenders (excluding the lender of interest), and lender teams that lenders are affiliated with.

**Lender- and loan-specific features.** Each entity type, e.g., the $i$-th type among a borrower, a partner, a loan, a lender, and a lender team, composes the entity-type-wise feature (column) vectors, $v_i^u$ and $v_i^l$ , to represent a lender $u$ and a loan $l$, respectively, which, in turn, form a lender-specific feature vector $v^u = \begin{bmatrix} v_1^u & \cdots & v_5^u \end{bmatrix}^\mathsf{T}$and a loan-specific one $v^l = \begin{bmatrix} v_1^l & \cdots & v_5^l \end{bmatrix}^\mathsf{T}$(circles in Fig. 3).

In this process, one issue is that we may have a variable number of linked entities of the same type. For instance, one lender may have funded four loans in the past, yet another may have funded fifteen. To maintain a fixed number of dimensions for $v_i^u$ (or $v_i^l$) given a variable number of entities, we aggregate them into a single set of features by adding up all the feature vectors of individual entities. Suppose the $i$-th entity type is a loan and a lender $u$ is associated with a set of entities (loans) $\left\{(e_i^u)_j : j = 1, \cdots, n\right\}$ where an entity $(e_i^u)_j$ is represented as a feature vector $(v_i^u)_j$. The feature vector $v_i^u$ (of the $i$-th entity type) for $u$ is represented as

$$v_i^u = \sum_j (v_i^u)_j . \qquad (1)$$

For example, a loan's *requested amount* (in dollars) will correspond to the summation of the values from multiple loans, a single value indicating a total *requested amount.* For categorical variables, such as a lender's gender which is represented as a binary vector in two dimensions, after summing up the feature vectors of lenders for a particular loan, the values corresponding to the two dimensions become the number of male and females lenders, respectively. The same idea can also be applied to textual features, which are *nonnegative* representations computed by NMF.

In addition, even if there are no links to entities of a particular entity type, e.g., no associated loans for a particular lender, Eq. (1) still holds since it will produce an equal-dimensional feature vector containing all zeros.

**Lender-loan matching features.** We have described how we generate lender- and loan-specific features by including information from each of the linked entities. We note that although the resulting data include links to heterogeneous entity types, both a lender and a loan now have counterparts generated from the same entity type, which can be directly compared with each other. In other words, both lenders and loans will have all the feature sets associated with borrowers, field partners, loans, lenders, and lender teams. Intuitively, if the entities from a lender side and a loan side are similar, our predictor $f(u, l)$ should give a high score about the likelihood of funding. To leverage this in our feature representation, we generate an additional set of features $v^{ul}$ that indicate how well the entities of the same type matches in an individual feature level. To this end, we compute the product of individual features referring to them as lender-loan matching features (hexagons in Fig. 3), i.e., $v^{ul} = v^u \circ v^l$, where $\circ$ represents an element-wise product. Given the nonnegativity of $v^u$ and $v^l$, $v^{ul}$ indicates how strongly the values of a particular dimension are represented in 'both' the lender and the loan sides; this can be considered as the degree of matching at an individual feature level.

These matching features, which are originally the second-order terms of existing features, may be inherently utilized in nonlinear or kernel models, but they are potentially critical information to many other models such as linear models and other tree-based models that deal with only one variable at a time, as will be described in Section 4.1.

**Temporal features.** Inspired from the analysis discussed earlier in Section 1, we generate additional features using temporal information about a lender and a loan. Available temporal information includes a lender's *member_since* and a loan's *posted_date*, *funded_date*, and *paid_date*. By considering the relative time differences between a loan $l$ and the most recent loan, $l_r$, that a lender funded in the past, we construct six temporal features having the form of $x - y$ where $x$ is one of $l$'s *posted_date* and *funded_date* and $y$ is one of $l_r$'s *posted_date*, *funded_date*, and *paid_date*. These features basically reflect the temporal patterns of consecutive lending activities.

## 3.2 Feature Alignment via Joint Nonnegative Matrix Factorization

**Cold-start problem.** The feature generation procedure described previously is quite general and flexible when incorporating all the information from each of the heterogeneous entities, but the main limitation of this approach arises when little or no relationship link between a lender and/or a loan exists. Although details may differ, this problem, which is often referred to as a cold-start problem, is common in many recommendation applications. For instance, suppose a new Kiva user considers funding a loan for the first time and we would like to recommend the most appropriate loan they would be likely to fund. It is very likely that they may not have any connections with lender teams, previous loans, and

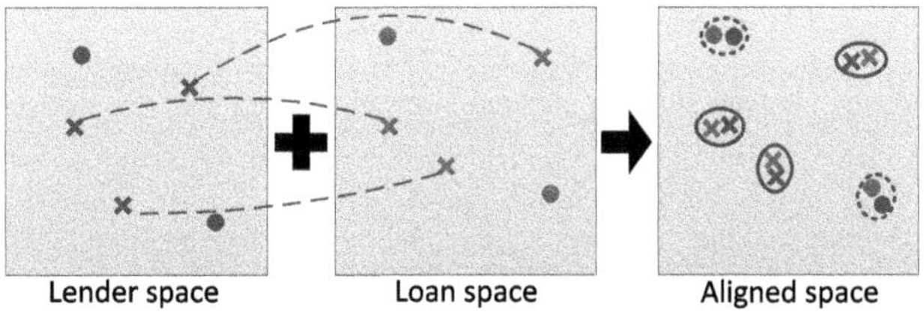


Figure 4: An overview of how joint NMF works. Given a high-dimensional space of lenders' and loans' textual data ('×'-marked) along with their linked information (dashed lines), joint NMF generates a common aligned space where linked data points are closely placed. First-time lenders and fresh loans ('•'-marked) are then mapped to the aligned space so that the resulting representations reveal their hidden linked relationships (dotted ellipses).

accordingly, any partners or borrowers. On the other hand, suppose a new loan webpage has just launched on the Kiva website and it currently has not secured a lender. In this scenario we would not have any available links to lenders and their lender teams that can be utilized in the feature generation process on the loan's side. These cold-start problems make our loan recommendation task challenging since a number of feature blocks depicted in Fig. 3 would be zero vectors, leaving little information useful for recommendation.

**How joint NMF works.** As a way to alleviate this problem, we propose a novel feature generation approach based on joint nonnegative matrix factorization (NMF) for a first-time lender and a fresh loan that have no available link information. As shown in Fig. 4, the main idea behind this approach is to transform the features generated from heterogeneous sources, one of which comes from a lender's side and the other from a loan's side, into a common space where the vectors representing a lender and a loan with which it is linked can be placed close to each other. Once we obtain the vector representations of a lender and a loan in the resulting common space, one can also easily generate the corresponding lender-loan matching features which would play a significant role in estimating the likelihood of funding.

**Input matrices for joint NMF.** To begin, we start with textual fields, e.g., a lender's *loan_because*, a lender's *occupational info*, which a lender fills out when signing up at Kiva.org, and a loan's *loan_description*. As described in Section (2), each of these textual fields is initially represented as a bag-of-words vector based on its own vocabulary. Note that the vocabulary set of a particular textual field is independent of that of any other, making each of them represented in a separate space.

Now, we form two term-document matrices $A_u$ and $A_l$ using the textual field from a lender and a loan, respectively. That is, $A_u$ encodes either a lender's *loan_because* or *occupational info* while $A_l$ encodes a loan's *loan_description*. Additionally, we assume the columns of $A_u$ and $A_l$ are aligned based on the linked relationships between lenders and loans. For example, the first column of $A_u$ and that of $A_l$ represent a lender and a loan, respectively, that have a link. Following this assumption, we exclude those lenders and loans that have no links when forming $A_u$ and $A_l$. When a particular loan, i.e., a column of $A_l$, has links to multiple lenders, we sum up the textual vectors of the corresponding lenders and put this single vector in the corresponding column of $A_u$. In this manner, we maintain a one-to-one mapping between the columns of $A_u$ and $A_l$.

**Formulation.** Given the two matrices $A_u \in \mathbb{R}_+^{m_u \times n}$ and $A_l \in \mathbb{R}_+^{m_l \times n}$, an integer $k$, and a parameter $\alpha$, joint NMF solves

$$\min_{W_u, H_u, W_l, H_l} \left\| A_u - W_u H_u^\mathsf{T} \right\|_F^2 + \left\| A_l - W_l H_l^\mathsf{T} \right\|_F^2 + +\alpha \left\| H_u - H_l \right\|_F^2, \tag{2}$$

where $W_u \in \mathbb{R}_+^{m_u \times k}$, $H_u \in \mathbb{R}_+^{n \times k}$, $W_l \in \mathbb{R}_+^{m_l \times k}$, $H_l \in \mathbb{R}_+^{n \times k}$ are nonnegative factors. In the above equation, the first and the second term correspond to standard NMF formulations, but at the same time, the third term enforces $H_u$ and $H_l$ to be close to each other. As a result, the rows of $H_u$ and $H_l$ can be considered as new vector representations in a common $k$-dimensional space where the linked lender and loan vectors are closely placed.

**Joint-NMF features for a first-time lender and a fresh loan.** Up to now, we have computed joint NMF using the textual information of lenders and loans by using their linked relationships, leading to a common space where these relationships are revealed. However, we still need to represent a first-time lender and a fresh loan to a joint-NMF space. To achieve this task, we utilize the resulting factor matrices $W_u$ and $W_l$, which provide a mapping for an arbitrary bag-of-words representation in an original space to the joint-NMF space. In detail, given $a_u \in \mathbb{R}_+^{m_u \times 1}$ and $a_l \in \mathbb{R}_+^{m_l \times 1}$ corresponding to a first-time lender and a fresh loan, respectively, we solve the following nonnegativity-constrained least squares problem,

$$\min_{h_u \geq 0} \left\| a_u - W_u h_u^\mathsf{T} \right\|_2 \text{ and } \min_{h_l \geq 0} \left\| a_l - W_l h_l^\mathsf{T} \right\|_2 \tag{3}$$

where $h_u^\mathsf{T} \in \mathbb{R}_+^{k \times 1}$ and $h_l^\mathsf{T} \in \mathbb{R}_+^{k \times 1}$ are our new representations in the joint-NMF space, i.e., joint-NMF features.

These joint-NMF features mainly have two advantages. First, even though a first-time lender and a fresh loan have no explicit links, one can expect their joint-NMF features that generated in this way to better reveal their proximity owing to the learnt factor matrices $W_u$ and $W_l$. Second, since they are considered to be in the common space, we can now generate their lender-loan matching features in a similar way presented in the previous subsection.

# 4. EXPERIMENTS AND FINDINGS

In this section, we present our experiments and analysis on two loan recommendation cases depending on whether a lender of interest has previous funding history.

## 4.1 Experimental Setup

**Learner.** Considering the heterogeneity of our data and the complexity of the problem, it is crucial to use the most suitable and powerful prediction model to date. To this end, we have chosen a gradient boosting tree (GBtree)[8] [17, 14]. A GBtree is an ensemble method where an individual learner is a decision tree [6].

The reason for choosing a GBtree for our problem is as follows: First of all, an ensemble method is known for its superior generalization capability for unseen data. More importantly, a decision tree, our base learner, uses one variable at each node when it is trained/constructed as well as when it

[8]The GBtree implementation we used is available at `https://sites.google.com/site/carlosbecker/resources/gradient-boosting-boosted-trees`

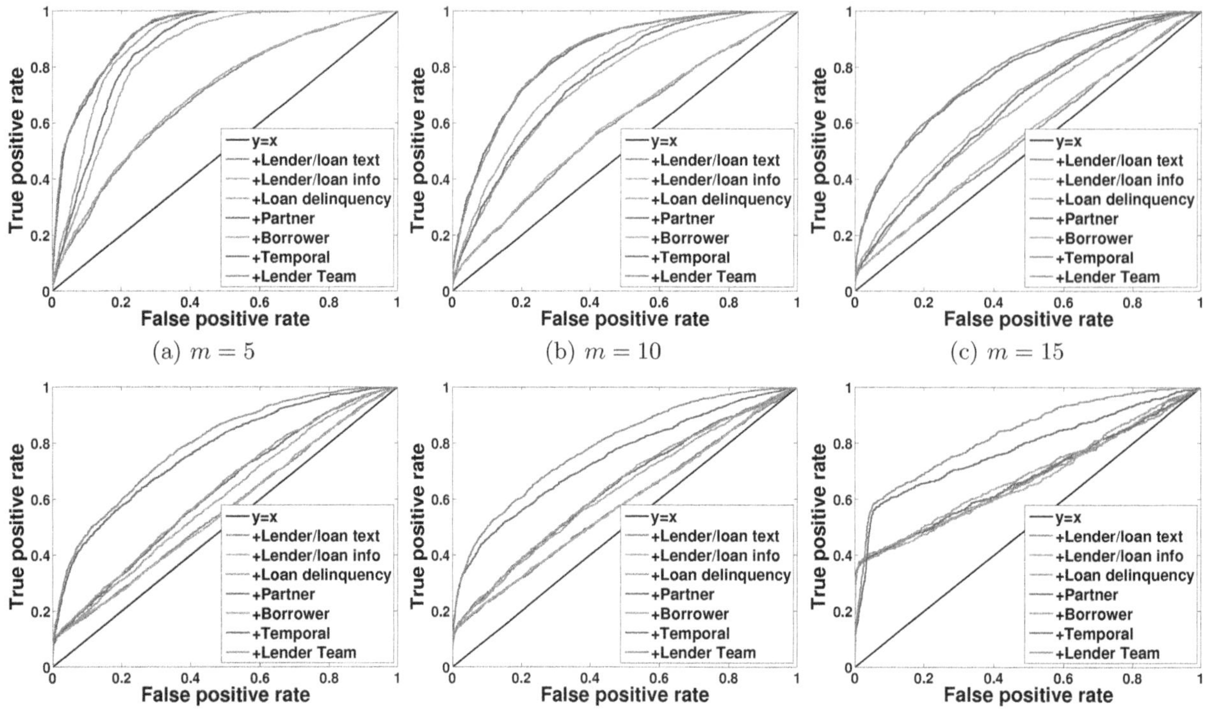


(a) $m = 5$ (b) $m = 10$ (c) $m = 15$

(d) $m = 20$ (e) $m = 25$ (f) $m = 50$

Figure 5: The ROC curve results for different lender groups with various numbers of previous loans $m$.

is applied to test data. This characteristic prevents us from worrying about heterogeneity in the features we generated. The downside to other learners, such as logistic regression and support vector machines, is that heterogeneous features have to be normalized via, say, standardization of their distributions, which transforms each feature to have zero mean and unit variance. Such normalization does not always make sense for binary and integer features, and furthermore it removes the nonnegativity of our feature representation that offers intuitive interpretation of them.

**Lender groups and data selection.** As previously highlighted, it is important to handle different user behaviors properly. Therefore, we first selected lenders that have a specific lending count $m$, where we varied $m$ from 5 to 50, indicating the degree of how actively lenders participated in loans. Then, we conducted our experiments separately on each of these lender groups. We felt that lenders within this range of $m$ contained the set of lenders not too active nor too passive, and thus we expect them to be more significantly influenced when given a recommendation for an appropriate loan.

Next, we formed a lender-by-loan adjacency matrix where only the components whose corresponding lenders funded the corresponding loans are set to 1 and 0 otherwise. From this graph, we randomly selected 5,000 positive (1-valued components) and 5,000 negative (0-valued components) samples and generated their feature vectors, as described in Section 3.[9] These samples are then used as our training and test sets under a 10-fold cross-validation setup.

[9]Note that we used balanced data sets in terms of positive vs. negative samples while original data are severely unbalanced. However, the ROC-based performance measure does not depend on the balancedness [12].

**Feature groups.** For lenders with funding history, we utilized various features presented in Section 3.1 and constructed several feature groups as follows:

**(1)** Loan/lender text (600 dimensions): Textual features from a lender's *loan_because* and a loan's *loan_description*, whose dimension is reduced by NMF (Section 2).

**(2)** Loan/lender info (183 dimensions): Features from a lender's and a loan's various fields.

**(3)** Loan delinquency (13 dimensions): Features indicating how many previous loans for a lender have been non-paid or delinquent.

**(4)** Partner (33 dimensions): Features about field partners.

**(5)** Borrower (12 dimensions): Features about borrowers, e.g., a borrower's *gender* and *pictured*.

**(6)** Temporal (6 dimensions): Time differences between a new loan and a lender's most recently funded loan (Section 3.1).

**(7)** Lender team (15 dimensions): Features about lender teams a lender is associated with.

Using this structure, a lender-loan pair, which is our data item, is represented as an 862-dimensional vector.

For lenders without funding history, many of these features are not available. Thus, the two sets of joint-NMF features described in Section 3.2 were mainly used: those generated from aligning (1-a)) a lender's *loan_because* versus a loan's *loan_description* (300-dimensional) and (1-b)) a lender's *occupational_info* versus a loan's *loan_description* (300-dimensional), respectively. Next, we included (2) loan/lender info (61-dimensional), (3) partner (11-dimensional), and (4) borrower (4-dimensional) information.

**Performance measure.** Although our experimental setting is a binary classification, the desired capability from learning the function $f(u, l)$ by a GBtree is to compute the likelihood of funding, which allows us to rank the most ap-

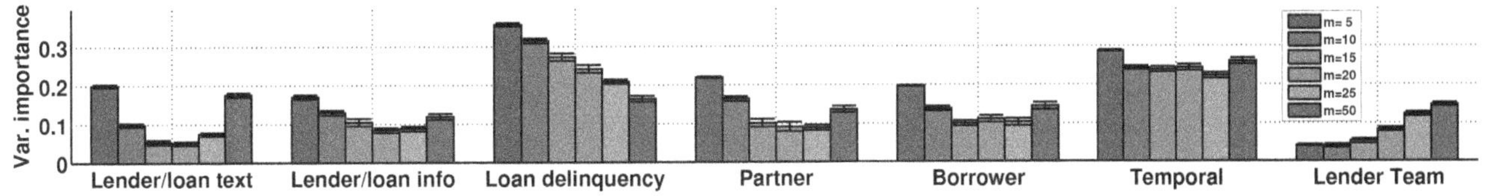


(a) The AUC value improvement over .5 when using only a particular feature group

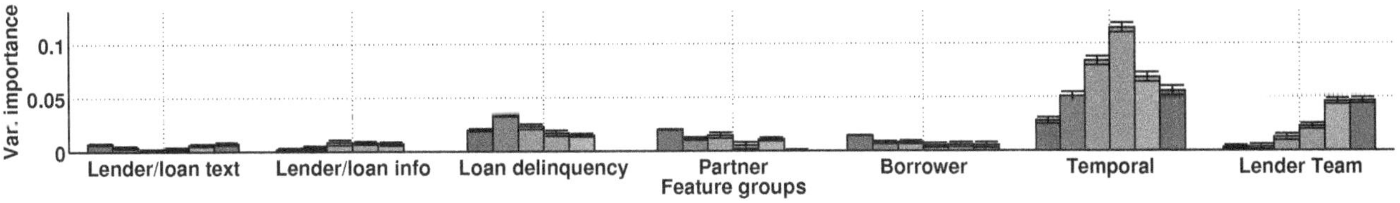


(b) The AUC value degradation due to the exclusion of a particular feature group

Figure 6: The analysis on the variable importance

Table 1: The cumulative AUC value in Fig. 5

| | The number of previous loans $m$ | | | | | |
|---|---|---|---|---|---|---|
| | 5 | 10 | 15 | 20 | 25 | 50 |
| Lender/loan text | .6938 | .5930 | .5524 | .5594 | .5788 | .6730 |
| Lender/loan info | .7010 | .5974 | .5601 | .5572 | .5793 | .6679 |
| Loan delinquency | .8416 | .7453 | .6438 | .6000 | .6265 | .6691 |
| Partner | .8646 | .7610 | .6600 | .6222 | .6301 | .6778 |
| Borrower | .8879 | .7852 | .6760 | .6275 | .6415 | .6909 |
| Temporal | .9179 | .8415 | .7736 | .7675 | .7449 | .7802 |
| Team | .9209 | .8420 | .7839 | .7923 | .7900 | .8318 |

propriate loans for a particular lender as well as the most appropriate lenders for a particular loan. Therefore, we are interested in the quality in terms of the resulting ranking of a given test set of lender-loan pairs, rather than the classification accuracy. In this respect, we report a receiver operating characteristic (ROC) curve and its area under the curve (AUC) value, which measures how much higher positive samples are ranked than negative samples.

## 4.2 Predictive Performance

### *4.2.1 Lenders with available funding history*

**Overall performance.** In cases where previous funding information of a lender is available, we gradually incorporated additional features described in Section 4.1 for different lender groups. The performance results are shown by the ROC curves in Fig. 5 along with their AUC values summarized in Table 1. The best AUC values ranged from .78 to .92, which is a significant improvement over a baseline value of .5. These results were generally achieved only when using all the features available, indicating the advantage of our feature integration framework. Among different lender groups, lenders with $15 \leq m \leq 25$ were the most difficult in predicting their likely loans to fund while lenders with a lower or higher $m$ were relatively easier.

**Analysis on feature groups.** The analysis on the variable importance of each feature group, as shown in Fig. 6, reveals various interesting knowledge about micro-finance activities, as follows:

**(1) The relative time with respect to the last funded loan plays an important role.** Temporal features, which contain elapsed time information since the most recently funded loan, e.g., when it was posted and/or when it was repaid, consistently improve the performance by a non-trivial amount for all cases.

**(2) Loan delinquencies discourage passive lenders although they do not impact active lenders as much.** The performance increase due to the loan delinquency features is substantial for lender groups with $m \leq 15$, but that increase drops significantly for lender groups with $m = 50$. Our further investigation showed these features were negatively correlated with the labels. For example, when $m = 5$, only 36% of the lenders who previously experienced loan delinquency had positive labels while 53% of the lenders without such experiences had positive labels. On the other hand, when $m = 50$, these two ratios were 49.7% and 50.1%, respectively, showing almost no correlation.

**(3) Lender teams exhibit greater influence on active lenders.** The performance due to the inclusion of lender team features improves as $m$ increases. We conjecture that it is partly because passive lenders did not join teams yet. In fact, we found that the average number of teams of each lender with $m = 50$ was .72 while that with $m = 5$ was only .25. In addition, from Figs. 5(e)(f), these features pull up the ROC curve mainly at the false positive rate value (an $x$ axis) from .4 to .7. This indicates that they are helpful in correctly classifying those somewhat ambiguous lender-loan pairs.

### *4.2.2 First-time lenders and fresh loans*

**A baseline approach.** To evaluate the effectiveness of joint-NMF features, we designed a baseline approach to compare our method against, as follows. In the baseline approach, each pair of textual fields, (a lender's *loan_because*, a loan's *loan_description*) and (a lender's *occupational_info*, a loan's *loan_description*), has been aggregated into a single document corpus, which is encoded as a list of bag-of-words vectors based on a common vocabulary set. Next, we applied standard NMF in order to obtain their reduced-dimensional vectors. Note that, similar to the joint NMF approach, the resulting vector representations of lenders' and loans' textual data exist in a common space. Nonetheless, the main difference is that joint NMF utilizes additional link information and enforces linked lenders and loans to be close to each other in the common space (Fig. 4).

**Performance comparison.** For first-time lenders and fresh loans, Fig. 7 shows the comparisons in terms of AUC measures between the joint NMF and the baseline approaches. For each case, joint NMF was computed based on a differ-

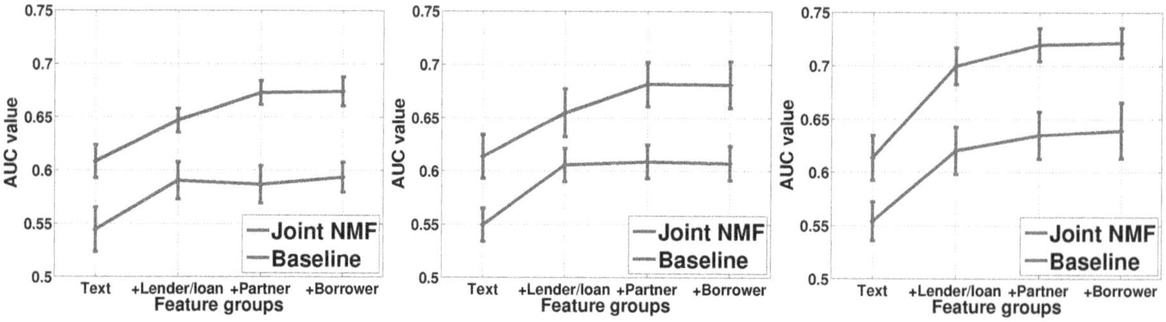


(a) $4 \le m \le 6$ (b) $15 \le m \le 20$ (c) $50 \le m \le 100$

Figure 7: The AUC values for first-time lenders and fresh loans when training joint NMF with lenders with various numbers of previous loans $m$ and their associated loans.

Table 2: The representative keywords of two topic pairs aligned by joint NMF

| Topic 1 | |
|---|---|
| a lender's *occupational_info* | a loan's *loan_description* |
| teacher, preschool, math, librarian, school | children, school, family, married, husband |
| **Topic 2** | |
| a lender's *occupational_info* | a loan's *loan_description* |
| student, mba, college, graduate, university | business, activities, entrepreneur, revenue |

ent lender group and its associated loans depending on the value range of $m$. Note that all the training/test data in the supervised learning experiments have been selected only from first-time lenders and fresh loans and that loan delinquency and temporal features were excluded since they are not available for first-time lenders.

In all the results, the joint-NMF approach shows significant improvement over the base line approach, indicating that joint-NMF features are clearly helpful in revealing hidden links between first-time lender and fresh-loans. Combined with other features available, the best AUC result, which is about .72, was found when using the active lender group with $50 \le m \le 100$. This observation is somewhat counter-intuitive since first-time lenders would be expected to have similar behaviors to those of passive lenders with a smaller value of $m$. However, it can still be explained in a sense that active lenders likely provide detailed information about themselves in a lender's textual fields, which would have provided joint NMF with vital clues in learning the mapping between lenders and loans.

**Aligned topics.** The qualitative analysis of the resulting mapping of joint NMF suggests in-depth understanding of lending behaviors. Table 2 shows the examples of aligned topics between a lender's *occupational info* and a loan's *loan_description.* These representative keywords were obtained as the most highly weighted terms in the corresponding columns of the two matrices $W_l$ and $W_u$ in Eqs. (2) and (3).

Both topics in Table 2 are related to lenders with school-oriented occupations. Lenders in Topic 1 are shown to have professional jobs in a education environment, such as teachers and librarians, while those in Topic 2 mainly consist of students. By examining the associated topic keywords in a loan' *loan_description*, one can see that the former group tends to participate in family-related loans, e.g., helping children go to school and supporting a family and/or a husband. On the contrary, the latter group (students) likes to lend to entrepreneurs with a particular business such as running a restaurant.

### 4.3 Further Discussions

Our analysis on loan recommendation and lending behaviors suggests several important directions that Kiva should take to promote micro-financial activities.

First, as seen from the significant importance of temporal features, performing loan recommendation at a right time would be crucial in keeping lenders actively involved. As shown in Fig. 2, Kiva can give recommendation (1) soon after a lender funded a loan as well as (2) when one's previous loans have been paid back. Otherwise, people tend to gradually lose interest in micro-finance activities as time goes on.

Second, Kiva should help lenders, especially passive or novice lenders, avoid potentially risky loans. From our analysis, non-paid and/or delinquent loans seem to be the major cause for passive lenders to stop their lending activities, and thus it would be important to lead them to loans with a high chance of repayment.

Finally, in order to secure active lenders as much as possible, Kiva should encourage passive lenders to join teams since lender teams seem to be one of the driving factors for active lenders.

## 5. RELATED WORK

In this section, we mainly discuss related work about (1) recommender systems (relevant to Section 3.1), (2) manifold alignment (relevant to Section 3.2), and (3) analysis on micro-financial activities.

**Recommender systems.** Basically, a recommender system, an active information filtering system [5], aims at estimating the so-called utility function for a given item and a user, which is analogous to our funding likelihood function $f(u, l)$. A recommender system typically fall within two methods: *content-based methods* which match users to products by matching a user's profile to the product's characteristics and *collaborative filtering methods* which recommend products that other users with similar preferences have chosen in the past [26, 1]. Numerous studies on recommender systems have focused on collaborative filtering approaches. These methods are generally categorized according to whether they are memory-based and model-based.

For a comprehensive summary of collaborative filtering techniques, the reader is referred to the survey articles [28, 1].

Due to the discussed challenges in Section 1, which make collaborative filtering methods inapplicable, our work partly follows the content-based approach in that the proposed lender-specific features can be viewed as a user's profile while the loan-specific features represent the product content. However, the typical content-based approach, mainly originating from information retrieval literature [4], focuses only on textual information. In order to integrate all the other information available, our approach extends it in the context of *ad-hoc* information retrieval [24], which throws various information as features and trains a learner model for predicting a relevance score of an item. These types of approaches are widely applicable in various novel applications including online dating systems [11].

**Manifold alignment.** This area has been actively studied recently in the context of image analysis [20] and cross-lingual information retrieval [29, 8, 9]. The problem setting is generally similar to that of our feature alignment where, given the different vector representations and/or relationships of the corresponding items, their new embedding in a common space is computed. Recently, from the perspective of multi-relational learning from multiple graphs or sources, several advanced methods based on joint matrix factorization have been proposed [33, 27]. In addition, a joint NMF-based approach has been proposed for multi-view clustering problems [22]. However, most of these methods focus on the best representations of existing data items while our proposed approach focuses on a generalization capability, i.e., embedding of unseen data into a common space so that their hidden correspondences are properly revealed.

**Analysis on micro-financial activities.** Previous work related to the complex micro-finance lending behavioral patterns and Kiva's now-integral role in the crowd-sourced micro-financing movement have looked at the effects of the internet on micro-financing [7] and other peer-to-peer lending transactions [3]. Studies on micro-finance decision-making have discovered that lenders favor lending opportunities not only to entities similar to themselves but also to individuals in situations that trigger an emotional reaction [2, 15].

Kiva-related findings have suggested bias in lending decisions by showing that particular borrower features generate a higher level of attraction from the wider lending audience. In particular, women and more physically attractive individuals inherit a greater chance of securing charitable loan support, at least from lenders that constitute the set of first-time and lesser-active lenders [18]. Other studies on Kiva have observed the nature of lending behavior by correlating the impact of group dynamics to lending participation [16, 23]. These studies provide a basis for our work in which we extend similar decision-making processes through automation to support our lender-loan recommendation system.

All these studies have analyzed Kiva's data in a number of ways, yet there is a lack of research that has utilized statistical numerical analysis approaches which are closer to our body of work. One such study manually defined a set of categories about the motivation of lending and applied machine learning techniques to train automatic text classifiers using a lender's *loan_because* field [23]. It also incorporated several simple features such as the loan count and team affiliations in performing regression on lending frequency and amount. This work revealed various interesting knowledge about lending behavior, but the used information and techniques are relatively limited compared to our work.

To the best of our knowledge, *our work is the first in-depth study to directly tackle the loan recommendation problem by incorporating all the heterogeneous information available from Kiva.* As seen in Section 4, *we achieve performance viable for practical application and reveal significant finding about lending behavior that has not been discussed in any previous other work.*

# 6. CONCLUSIONS AND FUTURE WORK

In this paper, we presented a novel application of loan recommendation in the non-profit micro-finance sector. Starting with an extensive data set from Kiva, a famous micro-finance service, we tackled the problem using a supervised learning approach. In order to represent any given lender-loan pair as a feature vector, which is a key procedure in this approach, we proposed two main methodologies: (1) graph-based feature integration to flexibly incorporate all the heterogeneous information available and (2) feature alignment via joint NMF to enhance the limited information of first-time lenders and fresh loans. Based on the proposed approaches combined with a gradient boosting tree, a state-of-the-art prediction model, we achieved up to .92 AUC value. Furthermore, we presented interesting phenomena about micro-financing behaviors of Kiva lenders from temporal and social aspects.

The importance of our work and the information-rich nature of the Kiva data open up various future research possibilities. We describe a few of them in the following.

**Selecting negative instances.** Although we found our experiments showed consistent results over multiple runs of different sets of random samples, it would be beneficial to choose negative samples with more care. That is, not all negative examples are truly negative. For example, a lender may not have funded a particular loan simply because he did not know about it but not because he decided not to fund it. Advanced techniques such as the one-class type approach [25] and the one leveraging the context of user-system interactions [31], which tackle these issues in other recommendation applications, could be adopted in our work.

**Fraud detection.** As seen in Section 4, non-paid and delinquent loans significantly impact further lending activities of novice lenders, and thus, it is critical to detect potentially fraudulent loans and discourage lenders from lending them. A fraud loan detection problem can be formulated and solved in a similar way to the proposed methods in this paper. Eventually, integrating the resulting potential fraud score to our feature representation will increase the loan recommendation performance even further.

# 7. ACKNOWLEDGMENTS

This work was supported in part by NSF IIS-1116886, NSF CCF-0808863, NSFC 61129001, and DARPA XDATA grant FA8750-12-2-0309. Any opinions, findings and conclusions or recommendations expressed in this material are those of the authors and do not necessarily reflect the views of funding agencies. We also thank anonymous reviewers for their insightful comments and suggestions.

## 8. REFERENCES


[1] G. Adomavicius and A. Tuzhilin. Toward the next generation of recommender systems: A survey of the state-of-the-art and possible extensions. *IEEE Transactions on Knowledge and Data Engineering (TKDE)*, 17(6):734–749, 2005.

[2] J. Andreoni. Impure altruism and donations to public goods: A theory of warm-glow giving. *The Economic Journal*, 100(401):464–477, 1990.

[3] A. Ashta and D. Assadi. Do social cause and social technology meet? impact of web 2.0 technologies on peer-to-peer lending transactions. *Cahiers du CEREN*, 29:177–192, 2009.

[4] R. Baeza-Yates and B. Ribeiro-Neto. *Modern information retrieval.* Addison-Wesley, 1999.

[5] N. J. Belkin and W. B. Croft. Information filtering and information retrieval: two sides of the same coin? *Communications of the ACM*, 35(12):29–38, 1992.

[6] L. Breiman. *Classification and regression trees.* CRC press, 1993.

[7] T. Bruett. Cows, kiva, and prosper. com: How disintermediation and the internet are changing microfinance. *Community Development Investment Review*, 3(2):44–50, 2007.

[8] P. A. Chew, B. W. Bader, T. G. Kolda, and A. Abdelali. Cross-language information retrieval using parafac2. In *Proc. the 13th ACM international conference on Knowledge discovery and data mining (SIGKDD)*, pages 143–152, 2007.

[9] J. Choo, S. Bohn, G. Nakamura, A. White, and H. Park. Heterogeneous data fusion via space alignment using nonmetric multidimensional scaling. In *Proc. the SIAM International Conference on Data Mining (SDM)*, pages 177–188, 2012.

[10] S. Deerwester, S. Dumais, G. Furnas, T. Landauer, and R. Harshman. Indexing by latent semantic analysis. *Journal of the Society for Information Science*, 41:391–407, 1990.

[11] F. Diaz, D. Metzler, and S. Amer-Yahia. Relevance and ranking in online dating systems. In *Proc. the 33rd international ACM conference on Research and development in information retrieval (SIGIR)*, pages 66–73, 2010.

[12] T. Fawcett. Roc graphs: Notes and practical considerations for researchers. *Machine Learning*, 31:1–38, 2004.

[13] M. Flannery. Kiva and the birth of person-to-person microfinance. *Innovations*, 2(1-2):31–56, 2007.

[14] J. H. Friedman. Greedy function approximation: a gradient boosting machine. *Annals of Statistics*, pages 1189–1232, 2001.

[15] J. Galak, D. Small, and A. T. Stephen. Micro-finance decision making: A field study of prosocial lending. *Journal of Marketing Research*, 48(SPL):S130–S137, 2011.

[16] S. Hartley. Kiva. org: Crowd-sourced microfinance & cooperation in group lending. 2010.

[17] T. Hastie, R. Tibshirani, and J. Friedman. *The Elements of Statistical Learning: Data Mining, Inference, and Prediction.* Springer, 2009.

[18] C. Jenq, J. Pan, and W. Theseira. What do donors discriminate on? evidence from kiva.org. 2012.

[19] H. Kim and H. Park. Sparse non-negative matrix factorizations via alternating non-negativity-constrained least squares for microarray data analysis. *Bioinformatics*, 23(12):1495–1502, 2007.

[20] S. Lafon, Y. Keller, and R. R. Coifman. Data fusion and multicue data matching by diffusion maps. *IEEE Transactions on Pattern Analysis and Machine Intelligence (TPAMI)*, 28:1784–1797, 2006.

[21] D. D. Lee and H. S. Seung. Learning the parts of objects by non-negative matrix factorization. *Nature*, 401:788–791, 1999.

[22] J. Liu, C. Wang, J. Gao, and J. Han. Multi-view clustering via joint nonnegative matrix factorization. In *Proc. the SIAM International Conference on Data Mining (SDM)*, pages 252–260, 2013.

[23] Y. Liu, R. Chen, Y. Chen, Q. Mei, and S. Salib. I loan because...: Understanding motivations for pro-social lending. In *Proc. the 5th ACM International Conference on Web Search and Data Mining (WSDM)*, pages 503–512, 2012.

[24] C. D. Manning, P. Raghavan, and H. Schütze. *Introduction to information retrieval*, volume 1. Cambridge University Press Cambridge, 2008.

[25] R. Pan and M. Scholz. Mind the gaps: weighting the unknown in large-scale one-class collaborative filtering. In *Proc. the 15th ACM international conference on Knowledge discovery and data mining (SIGKDD)*, pages 667–676, 2009.

[26] B. Sarwar, G. Karypis, J. Konstan, and J. Riedl. Analysis of recommendation algorithms for e-commerce. In *Proc. the 2nd ACM conference on Electronic commerce*, pages 158–167, 2000.

[27] A. P. Singh and G. J. Gordon. Relational learning via collective matrix factorization. In *Proc. the 14th ACM international conference on Knowledge discovery and data mining (SIGKDD)*, pages 650–658, 2008.

[28] X. Su and T. M. Khoshgoftaar. A survey of collaborative filtering techniques. *Advances in Artificial Intelligence*, 2009:4:2–4:2, 2009.

[29] C. Wang and S. Mahadevan. Manifold alignment using procrustes analysis. In *Proc. the 25th International Conference on Machine Learning (ICML)*, pages 1120–1127, 2008.

[30] W. Xu, X. Liu, and Y. Gong. Document clustering based on non-negative matrix factorization. In *Proc. the 26th international ACM conference on Research and development in informaion retrieval (SIGIR)*, pages 267–273, 2003.

[31] S.-H. Yang, B. Long, A. J. Smola, H. Zha, and Z. Zheng. Collaborative competitive filtering: learning recommender using context of user choice. In *Proc. the 34th international ACM conference on Research and development in Information Retrieval (SIGIR)*, pages 295–304, 2011.

[32] M. Yunus. *Banker to the Poor.* Penguin Books India, 1998.

[33] D. Zhou, S. Zhu, K. Yu, X. Song, B. L. Tseng, H. Zha, and C. L. Giles. Learning multiple graphs for document recommendations. In *Proc. the 17th international conference on World Wide Web (WWW)*, pages 141–150, 2008.

# Who Watches (and Shares) What on YouTube? And When? Using Twitter to Understand YouTube Viewership

Adiya Abisheva
ETH Zürich
aabisheva@ethz.ch

Venkata Rama Kiran Garimella
Qatar Computing Research Institute
gvrkirann@gmail.com

David Garcia
ETH Zürich
dgarcia@ethz.ch

Ingmar Weber
Qatar Computing Research Institute
iweber@qf.org.qa

## ABSTRACT

By combining multiple social media datasets, it is possible to gain insight into each dataset that goes beyond what could be obtained with either individually. In this paper we combine user-centric data from Twitter with video-centric data from YouTube to build a rich picture of who watches and shares what on YouTube. We study 87K Twitter users, 5.6 million YouTube videos and 15 million video sharing events from user-, video- and sharing-event-centric perspectives. We show that features of Twitter users correlate with YouTube features and sharing-related features. For example, urban users are quicker to share than rural users. We find a superlinear relationship between initial Twitter shares and the final amounts of views. We discover that Twitter activity metrics play more role in video popularity than mere amount of followers. We also reveal the existence of correlated behavior concerning the time between video creation and sharing within certain timescales, showing the time onset for a coherent response, and the time limit after which collective responses are extremely unlikely. Response times depend on the category of the video, suggesting Twitter video sharing is highly dependent on the video content. To the best of our knowledge, this is the first large-scale study combining YouTube and Twitter data, and it reveals novel, detailed insights into who watches (and shares) what on YouTube, and when.

## 1. INTRODUCTION

On July 11, 2013, @justinbieber tweeted: "so many activities it is making my head spin! haha `http://t.co/Gdg615ZZGX`", sharing a link to a short YouTube movie clip. In one day, the video received more than 100,000 views, and its owner commented: "So I checked my email today to find 500 new mail... WTF I thought.... 5 mins later I discover that Justin Bieber has tweeted this video...". The viewers of that video came from the 40 million followers that Justin Bieber has in Twitter, including large amounts of pop-loving teenagers that retweeted the video link more than 800 times in the following days.

The above example illustrates how the combination of Twitter and YouTube data provide insights on *who watches what on YouTube* *and when*. In this article we combine large datasets from both online communities, aiming at a descriptive analysis of the demographics and behavioral features of YouTube viewership through Twitter video shares. In our analysis, the *"who"* refers to the identity of Twitter users, as displayed on their public profile. We quantify this identity in three facets: a) demographic variables such as gender and location, b) social metrics that include reputation and impact metrics in the Twitter follower network, and c) personal interests and political alignment inferred from profile descriptions and followed accounts. The *"what"* refers to features of the videos, including i) the YouTube category, and ii) the popularity of videos in terms of views or likes. The *"when"* is the time lapsed between the creation of a video and its sharing in Twitter, measuring the time component of individual and collective reaction patterns to YouTube videos.

With a combined dataset of Twitter data and YouTube videos we can answer questions about the interaction between both communities. First, we explore the purpose of social sharing, distinguishing regular and promotional Twitter accounts linked to a particular YouTube channel. We then analyze to which extent the content of the videos watched by a user is similar to their interests on Twitter. Using features extracted from Twitter, we are able to quantify factors such as social sharing and influence and infer their effect on the videos consumed on YouTube. We also look at the role of political alignment in YouTube video sharing, comparing the shared topics and reaction patterns of individuals depending on their political activity on Twitter.

We analyze the times between video creation and social sharing, looking for factors that mediate the speed of video sharing. We find the demographics of users that share videos earlier than the rest, and compare how different categories elicit faster or slower reactions in Twitter. Finally, we explore the relation between the early Twitter shares of a video and its final popularity. To do so, we designed a model that includes social impact and reputation metrics of the early watchers of the video, providing early forecasts of a video's ultimate popularity.


*WSDM'14,* February 24–28, 2014, New York, New York, USA.

ACM 978-1-4503-2351-2/14/02 ...$15.00.
http://dx.doi.org/10.1145/2556195.2566588.

## 2. RELATED WORK

Since we answer "who?", "what?" and "when?", we describe related work done on Twitter profiles and online demographics, YouTube viewership and content and temporal behaviour patterns.

### 2.1 Online Demographics

Related work on "who" *does* "what" in Web search has been done in Weber and Jaimes [38] where authors analyze query logs of 2.3 million users form a web search US engine. Even though our work performs analysis on Twitter and YouTube users rather than Web search users, methodology used in previous study is of high relevance for our research. More closely related work on Twitter demographics was performed in Mislove et al. [26] where authors investigate whether Twitter users are a representative sample of society. By using (optionally) self-reported and publicly visible data of Twitter users, authors compared demographics of Twitter US users to the US population along three axes. On the geographical dimension, findings showed that Twitter users are overrepresented in highly populated US counties and underrepresented in sparsely populated regions due to different patterns of adoption of social media across regions. Across gender, the male Twitter population is greater than female especially among early Twitter adopters, but male bias decreases as Twitter evolves. On race/ethnicity authors show the distribution is highly geographically-dependent. Another study on demographics by Goel et al. [16] shows that user demographics (age, gender, race, income etc.) can be inferred from Web browsing histories. Finally, Kulshrestha et al. [22] investigate the role of offline geography in Twitter and conclude that it has a significant role in social interactions on Twitter with more tweets and links exchanged across national boundaries.

### 2.2 Research on Twitter Data

Apart from demographics, Twitter has also been studied from other perspectives: prediction of trends/hashtags [2, 34, 19]; notions of influence in Twitter [6] and using Twitter predictive data for elections and discovering political alignment of users [8, 9]. Asur et al. [2] studied trending topics/hashtags and discovered that the content of a tweet and retweeting activity rather than user attributes such as influence, number of followers and frequency of posting are the main drivers for spotting the trend and keeping it alive. In Wang and Huberman [34] a model for attention growth and persistence of trends is presented and is validated on trending topics in Twitter. In another work on trending topics, hashtags in Twitter can be clustered according to the temporal usage patterns of the hashtag: before, during and after peak of its popularity. Furthermore, the class of the hashtag correlates with social semantics of content associated with the hashtag (Lehmann et al. [24]). In a study on differences of search activity of trending topics in the Web and Twitter, Kairam et al. [19] reveal that information-seeking and information-sharing activity around trending events follows similar temporal dynamics, but social media leads Web search activity by 4.3 hours on average. More generalized study on differences between Web and Twitter search by Teevan et al. [32] found that timely and social information are primary drivers for searching on Twitter, compared to more navigational search on the Web; Twitter search is more used to monitor new content, while search on the Web is performed for developing and learning about a topic. Another perspective is the notion of influence in Twitter using followers, retweets and mentions studied by Cha et al. [6] with main finding that having a lot of followers does not necessarily mean having a high influence. Another line of work uses Twitter to monitor political opinions, increase political mobilization, and possibly predict elections' results. Conover et al. [9] present several methods to discover political alignment of Twitter users by analysing the network of political retweets and hashtags usage. In subsequent work [8], authors go beyond discovering political groups in Twitter, and analyse interaction dynamics of politically aligned subcommunities. Their findings show that right-leaning Twitter users produce more political content, spend a greater proportion of their time for political conversation and have more tightly interconnected social structure which leverages broad and fast spread of information.

### 2.3 YouTube Video Consumption

Ulges et al. [33] use YouTube concepts to predict demographic profile of viewers and also try to use demographics estimated from views statistics to predict the concepts of a video. They show that the use of demographic features improves the quality of prediction. Concerning YouTube video views, researchers have analyzed time series [11], and predicted the final views count based on properties of growth on YouTube [31]. For instance, Crane and Sornette [11] perform analysis of collective responses to YouTube videos through their time series of views. Among the classes, the most usual were videos that have a fast decaying amount of views, receiving negligible amounts of views soon after their creation. Laine et al. [23] highlighted the role of exogenous factors (such as interest groups) in the activity of YouTube viewers and Qiu et al. [29] suggested two different mechanisms that drive YouTube viewership: popularity and quality filtering. On popularity of videos in YouTube, Figueiredo et al. [12] found copyright videos gain 90% of their views early in lifetime compared to top listed YouTube or randomly chosen videos; top listed videos show *quality* popularity dynamics pattern opposed to copyright and random videos exhibiting *viral*, word-of-mouth, dynamics. And finally, related videos and internal search are most contributing towards content dissemination, but for random videos social link is also a key factor. On politics in YouTube, recent work by Garcia et al. [14] performs analysis of collective responses to the YouTube videos of US political campaigns and reveals differences in collective dynamics that suggest stronger interaction among right-leaning users. Weber et al. [36] use YouTube video tags and conclude that general YouTube videos are not polarized in terms of audience, but for subclasses of apolitical videos (e.g., tagged as "army") an audience bias can be predicted (right-leaning in this case). Finally, in Crane et al. [10] collective responses to the videos of Saddam Hussein's death show an extremely fast response and relevance of news and politics for YouTube viewers.

### 2.4 On Human Behaviour

Since our analysis involves the "when" dimension of video shares on Twitter, we review work on temporal patterns in human behaviour. Quantitative understanding of human behavior, also known as human dynamics, got a new turning point in 2005 after work by A.-L. Barabási [3], where author looked whether the timing of human activities follows any specific pattern. Results showed that there are bursts of intensive activity interchanged with long periods of inactivity (Pareto distribution) rather than events happening at regular time intervals (Poisson). Since 2005 more studies on the inhomogeneous nature of temporal processes in human dynamics have been performed [10, 20, 39]. Various proxies were used to get timing of human activity, e.g., mobile records, web server logs, SMS etc. Recent study by Wu et al. [39] suggests time patterns follow bimodal distribution with bursts of activity explained by power-law distribution in the first mode and exponentially distributed initiation of activity in the second mode.

## 3. DATA SET

We collected data from Twitter and YouTube for our analysis, and related the datasets by looking at instances where links to videos were shared on Twitter. This section describes how we obtained the 87K Twitter users, 5.6 million YouTube videos, and 15 million video sharing events we analyzed in greater detail. Data sets are available at `http://web.sg.ethz.ch/users/aabisheva/2013_YouTube_Twitter_ETH_QCRI/index.html`.

### 3.1 Twitter

The data acquisition starts with a 28 hour time slice from 6/6/2013 21:00 to 8/6/2013 1:00 (AST) of all public Tweets containing any URL provided by GNIP, a reseller of Twitter data. Of these tweets, only tweets by users with at least one follower, one friend, has non-empty profile location and English as profile language were considered. 1,271,274 tweets containing a URL from `http://www.youtube.com` or `http://youtu.be` where identified. URLs shortened by Twitter's default URL shortener `t.co` were automatically unshortened, but other services were not considered. From this set, 200K distinct tweets were sampled uniformly at random. These tweets account for 177,791 distinct users. Out of these, 100K users were sampled uniformly at random.

For each of these users we obtained (up to) their last 3,200 public tweets. In 12,922 cases this failed because the user account had been removed or made private. Along with the tweets, we obtained the user's public profile, containing the user-defined location, their followers and friends count and the set of (up to) 5,000 friends (= other Twitter users the user follows) and 5,000 followers (= other Twitter users who follow this user). 96.8% of our users had less than 5,000 followers and 98.9% had less than 5,000 friends. We also got the profile information for all these friends and followers. Finally, we had 17,013,356 unique tweets with 5,682,627 distinct YouTube video IDs, 19,004,341 friends and 22,182,881 followers for the 87,076 users. From this data we extracted a number of features related to (i) demographics, (ii) location, (iii) interests, and (iv) behavior on Twitter.

**Demographics.** We used a name dictionary to infer the self-declared gender of a Twitter user using common first names and gender from `http://www.ssa.gov/oact/babynames/limits.html`. To detect a subset of potential parents, we scanned each user's "bio" for mother/mom/wife or father/dad/husband using exact token match. Similarly, we identified a subset of potential students by scanning the bios for student/study/studying.

**Location.** Each of the users profile locations was run through Yahoo!'s Placemaker geo-coder, `http://developer.yahoo.com/yql/console/`, and for 61,250 profiles, a location could be identified. For the 23,416 users with an identified location in the US we checked if their city matched a list of the 100 biggest US cities from `http://www.city-data.com/top1.html`. This gave us an estimate of users from rural vs. urban areas.

**Interests.** To detect interests of users, we chose to analyze the users they follow. These friends were then compared against directory information from `http://wefollow.com`[1]. Concretely, we obtained information for the classes Sports, Movies, News & Politics, Finance, Comedy, Science, Non-profits, Film, Sci-Fi/Fantasy, Gaming, People, Travel, Autos, Music, Entertainment, Education, Howto, Pets, and Shows as described in Table 1. In addition to the information from wefollow.com, we labeled 32 politicians or party accounts on Twitter as either Democrats (13) or Republicans (19). The same list was also used by Weber, et al. [35, 37]. Users were then labeled as left or right according to the distribution of users they followed (if any). Following had previously been shown to be a strong signal for political orientation [7, 4, 35, 37].

**Behavior.** To quantify the activity of a user on Twitter, we extracted various features such as their number of tweets, the fraction of tweets that are retweets, or the fraction of tweets containing URLs.

[1]WeFollow is a website listing Twitter users for different topics along with a "prominence score", indicating importance of the user in the respective field. WeFollow's directory has been used in several academic studies [25, 5, 1, 27]

| Category | wefollow.com Interests |
|---|---|
| Sports | sports, baseb., basketb., soccer, footb., cricket, nfl |
| Movies | movies |
| News & Politics | economics, politics, news |
| Finance | banking, investing, finance, entrepreneur, business |
| Comedy | comedy, comedian |
| Science & Technology | tech, technology, gadgets, science, socialmedia |
| Non-profits & Activism | non-profits, non-profit, charity, philanthropy |
| Film & Animation | film, animation, cartoons |
| Sci-Fi/Fantasy | scifi, sciencefiction, fantasy |
| Gaming | games, gaming |
| People & Blogs | blogger, blogs, people, celebrity |
| Travel & Events | travel, places |
| Autos & Vehicles | automotive, autos, cars, vehicles |
| Music | music, dance, dancer |
| Entertainment | entertainment |
| Education | academic, university, education |
| Howto & Style | howto, diy, doityourself |
| Pets & Animals | animals, cats, dogs, pets |
| Shows | tv, tvshows, media |

**Table 1: Mapping of YouTube categories (left) to wefollow.com interests (right). The YouTube category "Trailers" was not mapped. The non-YouTube category "Finance" was added.**

Finally, we also aggregated features from all YouTube videos shared by a user into statistics such as the average view count or the median inter-event time ("lag") between video upload and sharing. These features are described in more detail in the next section.

### 3.2 YouTube Activity on Twitter

Given 17,013,356 unique tweets with YouTube video IDs, we retrieved 15,211,132 sharing events and identified 6,433,570 unique YouTube video IDs. We define sharing event as a tweet containing valid YouTube video ID (having category, Freebase topics and timestamp), thus a tweet with two video IDs is considered as two sharing events. A fraction of videos in initial 17 million tweets were not valid, thus such tweets and consequently derived sharing events were removed. Using the YouTube API, the following data about videos was crawled within the period 7/7/2013 – 1/8/2013: title, uploader username, number of views, number of times video has been marked as favorite, number of raters, number of likes and dislikes, number of comments, video uploaded time and categories to which videos belong. Using the Freebase API we also crawled video topics which serve as deprecated video tags and are helpful for searching content on YouTube, e.g., "hobby", "music", "book" and many others are examples of Freebase topics (`http://www.freebase.com/`).

The cleansing stage of data contained three parts: identify noise in data, introduce a filter on Twitter users with "extreme" behaviour and introduce a filter on "legacy" YouTube videos (see Section 5). In our data set, noisy data (0.53%) are those sharing events where the tweet's timestamp is earlier than the video's upload timestamp. Such negative lags spanned from 1 second up to a couple of years. We removed all such sharing events which seemed to occur 1) due to updated timestamp of streamed live videos recorded by YouTube where the time at the end of streaming is returned as published timestamp by YouTube API, and 2) due to altered timestamp of reuploaded videos by some YouTube "privileged" accounts. After removing noise, the data reduced to 15,130,439 sharing events, 5,669,907 unique video IDs and 87,069 user IDs.

Handling the data, we came across "non-human" behaviour explained by automated video sharing. We identify Twitter accounts and YouTube channels possibly owned by the same user, and label such Twitter users, as *promotional* since the primary content of such videos is advertisement. These accounts are often in top 1 percentile of Twitter users sorted by the number of YouTube videos shared. Examples of such Twitter-YouTube pairs with the number of shared videos in brackets are: *spanish_life – aspanishlife* (8,119) on real estate advertisement and *RealHollywoodTr – bootcampmc* (5,315) blogging on fitness and health, while the mean number of shares per user was found at 174 video shares. To remove *promotional* users, we applied a filtering mechanism based on a) similarity between usernames in Twitter and YouTube using longest common substring (LCS), and/or b) amount of videos in Twitter account coming from one YouTube source; for details refer to supplementary material submitted in: `http://arxiv.org/abs/1312.4511`. We follow an aggressive approach when detecting promotional users; thus, there is a possibility of some regular users being labeled as promotional but not the other way round. As a result of filtering we split Twitter accounts into 71,920 regular non-promotional and 15,149 promotional accounts.

# 4. WHO WATCHES WHAT?

In this section, we present a first analysis of who (in terms of Twitter user features) watches and shares what (in terms of YouTube video features). Though we include here user features related to the inter-event time, early video sharers are analyzed in Section 5.

## 4.1 Cluster Analysis

As a first picture of who watches and shares what we present a cluster analysis of 26,938 non-promotional, sufficiently active users who shared at least 10 YouTube videos and had at least 10 friends matched on Twitter through WeFollow (see Table 1). These users were clustered into eight groups according to the (normalized) distribution of YouTube categories of the videos they shared using an agglomerative hierarchical clustering algorithm with a cosine similarity metric [21]. Table 2 shows the results.

We were interested to see which differences for Twitter features are induced when users are grouped solely according to YouTube categories. To describe the clusters found, Table 2 first lists the *discriminative* YouTube features as output by the clustering algorithm. Below it lists the 5 most prominent terms from the Twitter bios of users in this group. These terms, which were *not* used to obtain the clustering, give fairly intuitive descriptions of the user groups. Finally, the table lists features whose average value differs statistically significantly (at 1%) between the cluster and all 27K users. These features are ranked by the absolute difference between global and within-cluster averages, divided by the standard deviation.

Inspecting the clusters, certain observations can be made. First, the discriminating YouTube categories (first block of five lines) are largely aligned with Twitter categories that are over-represented in the corresponding cluster (The "T *" in the bottom block of five lines). This alignment we will investigate more in Section 4.3. Second, there are certain correlations between the demographics and the YouTube categories. For example, Cluster 1 is focused on sports and has more male users, whereas Cluster 7 is centered around entertainment and people/blogs and has more female users. Recall that the clustering was done according to YouTube categories, whereas the demographic information comes from Twitter, indicating the possible benefits of the combination. Finally, the clustering also picks up a connection to political orientation. Concretely, Cluster 5 contains more conservative users with an increased interest in news and politics (more on this in Section 4.3).

## 4.2 Demographics

To understand the significance of the influence of variables such as gender or occupation on (i) the number of views, (ii) the polarization or controversiality[2], and (iii) the lag we applied a so-called "permutation test" [17], which unlike other tests does not make assumptions on the distribution type of the observed variables. To test, say, the impact of stating "student" in the Twitter bio on the number of views we first computed the average view count for all views by the "student" group and compared this with the average for the complement "non-student" group. Let $\delta$ be the observed difference. Then to test the significance of $\delta$ we pooled all the student and non-student labeled observations and randomly permuted the two labels to get two groups. For these two groups, obtained by a label permutation, a $\delta_p$ was then computed. This process was repeated 10,000 times to estimate the common level of variability in the $\delta_p$. We then marked the $\delta$ as significant if it was in the bottom/top 0.5% (or 2.5%) of the percentiles of the $\delta_p$. In Table 3, a ** indicates that $\delta$ was in the bottom/top 0.5% and * indicates that it was in the bottom/top 2.5%.

For Table 4 we used a similar procedure to test the statistical significance of the Spearman rank correlation coefficient. Here, to establish the common level of variability we randomly permuted both rankings to be correlated 10,000 times and observed the distribution of the Spearman rank correlation coefficients. If the original, actual coefficient fell within the bottom/top 0.5%/2.5% we marked it as significant.

Table 3 shows correlations with respect to the per-user median (i) number of views of shared videos, (ii) polarization/controversiality of shared videos and (iii) of inter-event times. One of the demographic differences that can be spotted is that men compared to women share less popular (fewer views) videos earlier (smaller lag). Some differences are hidden in this analysis though, as *both* urban *and* rural users seem to have a lower lag (share fast). The explanation for this apparent paradox is that users who have either no self-declared location or where the location is outside of the US have a comparatively larger lag, and that the comparison is with non-urban and non-rural, which mostly consist of these users, see Section 5.1 for more details.

## 4.3 Correlation Analysis

In this section we analyze the relationship between Twitter user features, such as the number of followers or the fraction of tweets that contain a hashtag, and YouTube features, such as the number of views. As a simple analysis tool we computed Spearman's rank correlation coefficient for each pair of features. To simplify the presentation, we group the Twitter features into four classes. First, to see how "social" a user is we look at (i) the number of friends, and (ii) the number of distinct users mentioned. Second, to see how common "sharing" is for a user we included the fraction of tweets that (i) are retweets, (ii) contain a hashtag, (iii) contain a YouTube URL, and (iv) contain a non-YouTube URL. Finally, we look at notions of "influence" that includes (i) the number of Twitter followers, (ii) the fraction of a user's tweets that are retweeted, (iii) the average retweet count of tweets that obtained at least one retweet, and (iv) the average number of followers of a user's followers.

For YouTube we consider the medians of (i) the number of views of videos shared by a user, (ii) the polarization of these videos, and (iii) the time lag of the video sharing events of the user. The

[2]We calculate the polarization that a YouTube video creates on its viewers through its amounts of likes $L_v$, dislikes $D_v$, and total views $V_v$, through the equation $Pol_v = \frac{L_v}{V_v^{0.849}} \cdot \frac{D_v}{V_v^{0.884}}$. The rationale behind this calculation is the rescaling of the likes and dislikes ratio based on the fact that they do not grow linearly with each other. The exponents correspond to the base rates of the logarithmically transformed amounts of views, likes and dislikes. This way we standardize the ratio over their nonlinear relation.

| | Cluster1 (2740) | Cluster2 (2327) | Cluster3 (2493) | Cluster4 (5390) | Cluster5 (2535) | Cluster6 (4052) | Cluster7 (3697) | Cluster8 (3704) |
|---|---|---|---|---|---|---|---|---|
| Discriminating features | sports | animals | non-profit | music | news/politics | film/animation | entertainment | travel |
| | music | music | music | non-profit | music | education | people/blogs | music |
| | entertainment | entertainment | sports | sports | comedy | music | howto | gaming |
| | people/blogs | people/blogs | entertainment | education | entertainment | non-profit | sports | science/tech |
| | non-profit | sports | education | animals | education | sports | music | autos |
| Top profile words | fan | music | music | music | music | music | life | music |
| | music | life | life | life | life | life | music | gamer |
| | sports | fan | fan | artist | world | fan | fan | life |
| | life | lover | world | producer | conservative | lover | live | fan |
| | football | writer | lover | live | people | time | justin | youtube |
| Top features | T sports$^+$ | Y animals$^+$ | Y non-profit$^+$ | Y music$^+$ | Y news/politics$^+$ | Y film$^+$ | Y howto$^+$ | Y gaming$^+$ |
| | Y sports$^+$ | T animals$^+$ | T non-profit$^+$ | median lag$^+$ | Y comedy$^+$ | Y education$^+$ | Y people$^+$ | Y science/tech$^+$ |
| | male$^+$ | std dev. of lag$^+$ | num. usrs rtwd$^+$ | T music$^+$ | T news/politics$^+$ | frac. Tw other URLs$^-$ | Y entertainment$^+$ | T gaming$^+$ |
| | frac. Tw other URLs$^+$ | acnt created at$^-$ | frac. of usrs Tw rtwd$^+$ | mean lag$^+$ | frac. Tw other URLs$^+$ | T movies$^+$ | female$^+$ | Y shows$^+$ |
| | avg. frnds of frnds$^-$ | T education$^+$ | frac. Tw Y videos$^-$ | Y education$^-$ | leaning republic$^+$ | Tfilm$^+$ | avg rtwt count user$^+$ | num. vids shared$^+$ |

**Table 2: Clusters obtained by clustering normalized YouTube categories distributions for each user.**

number of comments received by videos shared by a user behaved qualitatively identical to the number of views and is omitted.

Our results are presented in Table 4. Each cell in the table links a Twitter user feature group (row) with a particular YouTube video feature (columns). The three symbols in the cell indicate "+" = significant (at 1% using a permutation test as previously described) and positive, "-" = significant and negative, and "0" = not significant or below 0.05. The symbols are in the order of the features listed above in the text.

Certain general observations can be made. For example, all of our notions of "social" correlate with a drop in lag time, and out of the topics considered, News & Politics is the one that is most consistently linked with users who actively share. But other observations are more complex and, for example, only some but not other notions of influence correlate positively with a large number of views.

We also looked at relation between the Twitter user features and the fraction of video shares for various YouTube categories. Table 4 shows results for the three example categories Music, Sports and News & Politics. Again, different patterns for different definitions of "influence" can be observed. Out of the three topics, News & Politics is the one that correlates most with social and with sharing behavior.

## 4.4 Interests on Twitter vs. YouTube

Given that our analysis links Twitter behavior to YouTube sharing events it is interesting to understand if the interests on the two platforms are aligned. Though we cannot reason about YouTube views not corresponding to Twitter sharing events, we compared the topical categories of a user's shared videos with the topical categories of their Twitter friends. To infer the latter, we used the WeFollow data described in Section 3.1 where entries in WeFollow were also weighted according to their prominence score. This way, a user following @espn (prominence 99) is given a higher weight for sports than a user following @hoyarowing (prominence 23). To compare if a user's YouTube category distribution and Twitter friends WeFollow distributions are similar, we decided *not* to compare these directly due to the following expected bias. The coverage by WeFollow for the different categories is likely to differ.

| | male | female | urban | rural | student | mother | father | US |
|---|---|---|---|---|---|---|---|---|
| views | 0 | $+^{**}$ | $-^{*}$ | 0 | 0 | $-^{*}$ | $-^{*}$ | $-^{*}$ |
| polariz. | 0 | $-^{*}$ | 0 | $-^{*}$ | $-^{*}$ | $-^{*}$ | $-^{**}$ | 0 |
| lag | $-^{**}$ | $+^{*}$ | $-^{*}$ | $-^{*}$ | 0 | $+^{**}$ | $-^{*}$ | $-^{*}$ |

**Table 3: Demographics. A + indicates a positive deviation from the general population, - negative and 0 not statistically significant. $^{**}$ indicates that the significance was based on $\delta$ being in the bottom/top 0.5%, $^{*}$ for the bottom/top 2.5%.**

For a popular topic such as music, the coverage is potentially over-proportionally good compared to less popular ones. To correct for this, we first normalize as follows.

Let $c_{ij}^T$ the prominence-weighted fraction of a user $i$'s Twitter friends that are recognized in the WeFollow category $j$. Similarly, define $c_{ij}^Y$ for their shared YouTube category distribution. Now normalize both of these matrices for a fixed category $j$ such that $\hat{c}_{ij}^T = c_{ij}^T / \sum_k c_{kj}^T$. This, effectively, compares users according to their relative interest in a given topic. This is then further normalized to obtain per-user probability distributions via $\tilde{c}_{ij}^T = \hat{c}_{ij}^T / \sum_k \hat{c}_{ik}^T$, similarly for $c_{ij}^Y$.

Then, for each category $j$, we look at the distribution of the differences $\tilde{c}_{ij}^T - \tilde{c}_{ij}^Y$ across users $i$. Categories where this difference is positive indicate a relatively higher importance/preference for Twitter, cases with a negative preference indicate a relatively higher importance for YouTube. Generally, the differences were very small with the median difference not exceeding .04 in absolute value for any category and being smaller than .01 for more than half. Some categories such as Film & Animation were very slightly more prominent on YouTube (indicated by the negative mean and median), whereas Science & Tech was slightly more prominent on Twitter. This analysis was done for active users with at least 10 shared videos and at least 10 friends matched on WeFollow.

## 4.5 Politics in Twitter and YouTube

To see how *Politics* is introduced in both Twitter and YouTube, we had the following questions in mind: a) which political user groups share more politically charged content, b) what is the most frequent content of each political user group.

As mentioned in Section 3.1, to separate users into political groups we followed a US bipartite system with audience divided into left (L) and right (R) users. Users that followed more of the 13 left seed users were marked as left-leaning, users that followed more of the 19 right seed users were marked as right-leaning and users with a split preference or not following any seed user were marked as apo-

| | views | polariz. | lag | Music | Sports | News |
|---|---|---|---|---|---|---|
| Social | - - | - - | - - | + 0 | 0 + | + + |
| Sharing | 0 - - - | 0 - 0 - | - - - - | 0 - 0 - | 0 + + 0 | + + + + |
| Influence | - - + 0 | - - + 0 | 0 - - + | + 0 + 0 | 0 0 + 0 | + + - + |

**Table 4: Columns 1-3 show the relation between Twitter and per-user aggregated YouTube features. Columns 4-6 show the relation between Twitter and fractions of categories of YouTube videos shared for three example categories. Twitter features are grouped into three classes. Symbols indicate strength and direction of significance. Bold symbols indicate an absolute value of Spearman's Rank correlation coefficient > 0.1. See text for details.**

litical. Our approach resulted in three disjoint sets of left users $U_L$ ($|U_L| = 11,217$), right $U_R$ ($|U_R| = 1,046$) and apolitical users $U_A$ ($|U_A| = 57,672$).

We addressed question a) by looking at how much L, R, A users share videos in the category *News & Politics*. If left-leaning user $u_L$ shared set of videos $V_L$ with a subset of videos in the category *News & Politics*, $V_L^{News\&Politics} \in V_L$; then we looked at the distribution of ratio of number of political video shares to total amount of shares per each $u_L$, $u_R$ and $u_A$: $r_{\{u_L,u_R,u_A\}} = \frac{|V^{News\&Politics}_{\{L,R,A\}}|}{|V_{\{L,R,A\}}|}$. On average mean ratio of videos with political content for each user population is: $\mu_L = 0.06$, $\mu_R = 0.29$, $\mu_A = 0.05$, which confirms right users share more news and politics related videos compared to left users and apolitical users.

To answer question b) we calculated topic distributions of videos per each political user category and rank topics in each user group according to their frequency. In order to statistically compare the ranking of topics across groups, we applied the distance between ranks of topics method by Havlin [18]. If $R_1(\lambda)$ is the rank of topic $\lambda$ in user group 1 and $R_2(\lambda)$ is the rank of the same topic $\lambda$ in user group 2, distance $r_{12}(\lambda)$ *between the ranks of topic* $\lambda$ *in two user groups* is $r_{12}(\lambda) = |R_1(\lambda) - R_2(\lambda)|$. Thus, the distance *between two user groups* is defined as the mean square root distance between the ranks of all common topics: $r_{12} = (\frac{1}{N}\sum_\lambda r_{12}^2(\lambda))^{\frac{1}{2}}$, where $N$ is the number of common topics across user groups. We summarize the distance metric across four user groups: Left, Right, Apolitical and all population (Left, Right and Apolitical) with $N = 23,844$ and $R_{max} = 281,265$ in Table 5.

We find that the distances from right users is maximum to left, apolitical and all, and left and apolitical are close to each other in terms of distance. This suggests that right users have their own hierarchy of topics distinguished from left and apolitical users, while latter groups have more similar topics. To support our findings in distance between topic ranks, we look at the most 20 frequent Freebase topics for each user group. Right users share more politically charged content including politicians (Barack Obama, Alex Jones, Ron Paul), news channels (Russia Today, The Young Turks), military-related keywords (Gun, Police) and concepts (USA). Conversely, left-leaning users have similar interests as apolitical, giving priority to entertainment videos. For example, "Barack Obama" topic (Freebase ID */m/02mjmr*) is placed 30th popular among left users and 1st among right population.

Results of a) and b) support each other and give the following picture on political engagement of L/R/A user groups. For left users, a) says they act as apolitical users and on average do not share much political videos, with b) confirming that among top 20 video topics of left users none relate to politics. And for right users, a) states that they share more political content which is supported by b) where 9 out of top 20 topics have government, news, politics related concepts.

A possible explanation of the fact that the supposed left is much closer to the apolitical set than the right is that following *@barackobama* is not a good proxy for political orientation due to his popularity in social media. To show that following *@barackobama is* a signal for both a) being more politicized and b) being more left-leaning we perform a number of statistical tests on differences between *@barackobama* followers and non-followers. For a) we

| | Left | Right | Apolitical | All |
|---|---|---|---|---|
| Left | - | 35733.87 | 33807.2 | 25722.16 |
| Right | 35733.87 | - | 49314.69 | 37913.44 |
| Apolitical | 33807.2 | 49314.69 | - | 23879.92 |
| All | 25722.16 | 37913.44 | 23879.92 | - |

**Table 5: Distance across political, apolitical and all user groups.**

count the number of known political hashtags such as *#p2, #tcot, #obama, #ows* and others for both user groups. For b) we count the number of words *"liberal", "progressive", "democrat"* and *"conservative", "republican"* in the bios of both followers and non-followers. The idea here is that the first (abbrev. L-words) and second (abbrev. R-words) word groups are indicators of someone being left- and right- aligned respectively. Table 6 shows results with a clear message: followers of *@barackobama* are at least 4 times more likely to be left-aligned compared to non-followers (0.70% vs. 0.16%) and are twice more likely to insert political hashtags in their tweets compared to non-followers (20.5% vs. 10.3%) . Ratios were tested with a Chi-square test for equality of proportions with a 95% confidence interval with significance at $p$-value $< 10^{-15}$.

# 5. EARLY VIDEO ADOPTER

This section answers a) who shares video content faster and b) which information is shared faster. Thus, we look at another dimension linking Twitter and YouTube – the time lag between the video upload and the sharing event on Twitter, also known as inter-event time or lag and denoted as $\Delta t$. We perform inter-event time analysis on a system level and per user. For system inter-event time analysis we collected time lags, $\Delta t_v^w$, per sharing event (tweet $w$, video $v$), resulting in time lag collection $T$, i.e., $\forall w \in TWEETS, \forall v \in VIDEOS, \Delta t_v^w \in T$, where *TWEETS* is a set of all tweets in data set and *VIDEOS* is a set of all videos. Thus, a user having more than one tweet with video has more than one time lag; similarly, a video that has been shared more than once will have more than one time lag; thus, several sharing events of a video are considered as separate sharing events, and time lag of each such event becomes a member of collection $T$. For per user inter-event time analysis we calculated median time lag per each user $u$, $\langle \Delta t \rangle_u^{median}$.

One limitation of the YouTube dataset was a non-uniform distribution of video age. Thus, we removed videos before certain epochs when YouTube and Twitter underwent changes. First, Twitter was founded in 2006, nearly one year after YouTube, thus we cannot sensibly study sharing of videos uploaded in 2005-2006. The next disrupting event is the introduction of Twitter share button in YouTube on 12/8/2010, changing the ease of sharing. Additionally, our crawled dataset had another constraint: a limit of 3,200 tweets per user which mainly has effect on tweets sample of active Twitter users. Selected sample potentially contains only recent tweets and thus relatively "young" videos in those tweets. In order to get a uniform age of shared videos, we determined a cut-off time for discarding videos of certain age at which amount of shares per user is affected the least. We removed videos older than $\theta = 1/1/2012$, which automatically discards tweets containing such videos. The filtered data set contained 11, 697,550 sharing events for 2,510,653 distinct videos coming from 70,874 non-promotional users.

## 5.1 Who Shares Faster in Twitter

Question a) was addressed by comparing inter-event times per different user groups. We first looked at time differences between promotional and non-promotional Twitter accounts, see Figure 1 from a system's point of view (rather than aggregating per-user). Visually, we observe that promotional accounts are faster at shar-

| | Political # | L-words | R-words | Total |
|---|---|---|---|---|
| followers | 20.5% (3829) | 0.70% (130) | 0.28% (53) | 18664 |
| ¬followers | 10.3% (8615) | 0.16% (131) | 0.35% (281) | 83789 |

**Table 6: Percentage and counts in brackets of users having political tweet hashtags, "left"- and "right"- words in account description of @barackobama followers and non-followers.**

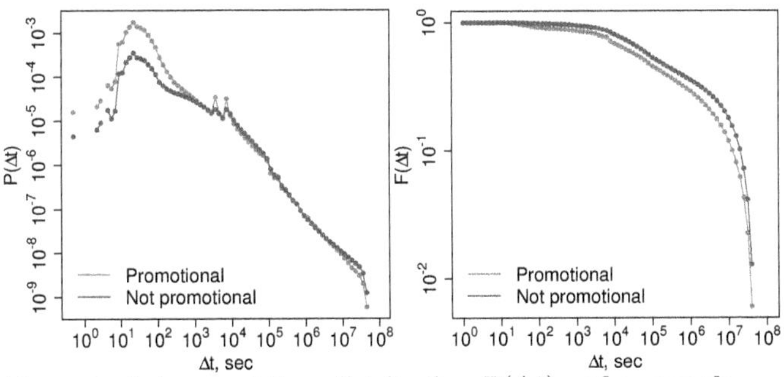


**Figure 1: Inter-event time distribution $P(\Delta t)$ and accumulative time distribution $F(\Delta t)$s of promotional (red) and non-promotional (blue) accounts.**

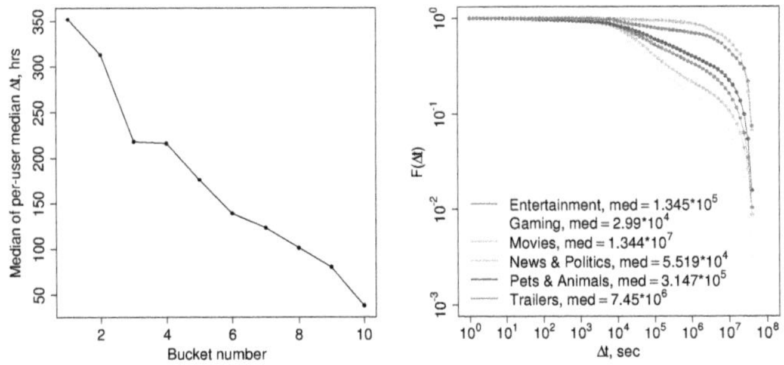


**Figure 2: Median of per-user median inter-event times for users bucketed (into deciles) by the number of YouTube videos shared (left). Accumulative time distribution $F(\Delta t)$ of videos belonging to various YouTube categories (right).**

ing content compared to regular users, see the head at $P(\Delta t)$ and tail at $F(\Delta t)$. Statistically, median(promo)= $10^{4.8}$sec (18 hours), median(non-promo) = $10^{5.1}$sec (38 hours). Within an hour promotional accounts have twice amount of shares compared to non-promotional accounts which constitutes twentieth and tenth percentile respectively.

Having confirmed that there is a difference between human and "machine" behaviour, we performed a per-user inter-event time analysis for different user groups of non-promotional accounts. For each user group $U_G$ we calculate the median lag per group (median of users' medians): $\Delta t_G = \langle\langle \Delta t\rangle_u^{median}\rangle_{u \in U_G}^{median}$.

For example, in Section 4.5 we looked at who shares what per political user groups (Left vs. Right). Here we find that on average right users share newly uploaded video content at least 3 days earlier compared to left users. Note that the set of videos being shared is different though. Our findings on the median of the median inter-event times for various user groups are presented in Table 7. Time differences in the per topic medians follow the same trend as the overall distribution (not presented here), so the observed differences cannot solely be explained by differences in category preferences for different user groups.

We highlight the following observations on who shares faster: concerning location, urban users are around 14 hours faster than rural users, and across gender women are much slower compared to men. Globally, people from Indonesia and Thailand have a reaction time in the order of a day, where as the greatest lag in the order of a half of a month is observed from people tweeting in Brazil. But as we selected only English profiles the results for other countries might be conflated with other factors.

While doing our analysis we also observed that an important dimension of the "quickness" of the users relates to how often they share videos on Twitter. Figure 2 shows the median per-user median of the inter-event times for users divided into deciles according to the number of YouTube videos they have shared. The inter-event times are given in hours and range from 352 hours for the least active to 38 hours for the most active users. As the difference is quite striking, we inspected term clouds for the Twitter bios of the least active YouTube sharers and the most active YouTube sharers. Interestingly, the two are quite similar, apart from a prominent "YouTube" for the most active users, indicating that the difference in lag time is related to the activity level, not topical interests.

## 5.2 What is Shared Faster in Twitter

To answer question b) we performed system inter-event time analysis and distributed time lags in $T$ into relevant video category. If $T_C$ is a collection of system lags of set of videos belonging to category $C$ (*VIDEOS*$^C$), then $\Delta t_v^w \in T_C, if\ v \in VIDEOS^C$. YouTube provides 19 video categories, in Figure 2 inter-event time of 6 categories which exhibit different patterns time distribution are shown, due to space limits. Remaining 13 video categories lag show similar patterns as *Entertainment* and *Pets & Animals*. Our findings show that among all videos, *Gaming* and *News & Politics* videos are the fastest shared with median time of 8 and 15 hours respectively, *Movies* and *Trailers* have the greatest lag between video uploaded and being tweeted with median of 5 and 3 months respectively.

# 6. VIDEO POPULARITY ANALYSIS

## 6.1 Forecasting Video Popularity

In this section, we present our work on early indicators of the popularity of a video, i.e., its amount of views a sufficient amount of time after its creation. Our approach is based on analyzing the Twitter attention to the video in the first moments after its creation, including the user profile information explained above. For this task, we filter our data following the cutoff date explained in Section 5, and restrict our analysis to videos that were created before June 1st 2013, a total of 4,822,675 videos created more than a month before the data retrieval date. We estimate the popularity of a video through the amount of views more than a month after its creation, following previous approaches by Szabo and Huberman [31], in line with the very fast decay of views that most videos have in YouTube as shown in Crane and Sornette [11].

| Category | Med. int. time | num. users |
|---|---|---|
| promotional | 27 | 15132 |
| non-promotional | 141 | 70874 |
| promotional urban | 40 | 2096 |
| promotional rural | 25 | 1693 |
| non-promotional urban | 143 | 5951 |
| non-promotional rural | 157 | 5928 |
| left | 163 | 11356 |
| right | 90 | 1355 |
| male | 142 | 24263 |
| female | 187 | 16293 |
| student | 156 | 877 |
| not student | 141 | 69997 |
| mother | 191 | 450 |
| not mother | 141 | 70424 |
| father | 85 | 356 |
| not father | 141 | 70518 |

**Table 7: Comparison of median of median inter-event times (in hours) for various groups of users**

For each video, we analyze its Twitter attention during the first week after its creation. We remove from our analysis all videos that, during this first week, did not have any sharing event in our data. This removes old videos that were created before Twitter grew to its actual user base, leaving us with a set of 276,488 videos. To analyze the role of user interests and promotions, we divide our analysis of Twitter data in two subsets: one only based on promotional users, and one based on non-promotional users. After such filtering, we have a total amount of 1,200,924 shares and 182,135 videos from promotional users, and 779,821 shares and 133,373 videos from non-promotional users. Note that these two datasets are disjoint in terms of Twitter data. No Twitter share is taken into account in both, but they overlap in 17,093 videos.

## 6.2 Twitter Video Metrics

We measure the early Twitter attention towards a video aggregating two types of data: i) amount of tweets or attention volume, and ii) reputation metrics calculated from the follower network and retweeting behavior of the users involved. For each video, we computed five metrics of Twitter attention that summarize different factors that potentially increase video popularity:

We measure the total attention in Twitter to a video through the *amount of shares* $S_v$ during the first week, which were produced by the set of users that shared the video in the first week, noted as $U_v \in U$. Each user $u$ created $n_v(u)$ shares of the video, which were received by the set of followers of those users. We define the *exposure* $E_v$ of a video as the sum of followers of the users that shared the video in the first week, where $F(u)$ is the set of followers of user $u$, and $f(u) = |F(u)|$. This measure approximates the size of the first order neighborhood of the accounts sharing the video, overcounting their common friends.

We aggregate the *social impact* $I_v$ of the users that shared the video estimated as their mean amount of retweets for tweets with nonzero retweets ($R_0(u)$). To improve estimation of the reputation of the users sharing the video in the first week, we approximate the size of the second-order neighborhood of the users that shared the video. For this, we calculate the *second-order exposure* $\mathcal{E}_v$, as the sum of the amount of followers of the followers of the users that shared the video.

Each user exposed to the shares of the video is subject to have its attention diluted over a set of different information sources. For this reason, we calculate the *share of voice* $A_v$ of the early users, as the ratio of their amount of followers divided by the average amount of users followed by their followers, where $f^{-1}(v)$ is the amount of users that $v$ follows. This way, we correct the case of users with many followers, who would give a lower share of voice if they follow a large amount of other users. On the other hand, a user with a low amount of followers can have a large share of voice, when its followers do not follow many other accounts.

We use these five metrics to create a video vector with a sixth dimension being its final amount of views. In the following, we present our analysis of the relations between these five metrics and the popularity of a video.

## 6.3 Factors Influencing Video Popularity

| Amount of shares | Exposure | Social impact |
|---|---|---|
| $S_v = \sum_{u \in U_v} n_v(u)$ | $E_v = \sum_{u \in U_v} f(u)$ | $I_v = \sum_{u \in U_v} R_0(u)$ |
| Second-order exposure | Share of voice | |
| $\mathcal{E}_v = \sum_{u \in U_v} \sum_{u' \in F(u)} f(u')$ | $A_v = \sum_{u \in U_v} f(u) / \langle f^{-1}(u') \rangle_{u' \in F(u)}$ | |

**Table 8: Twitter social metrics used related to video popularity.**

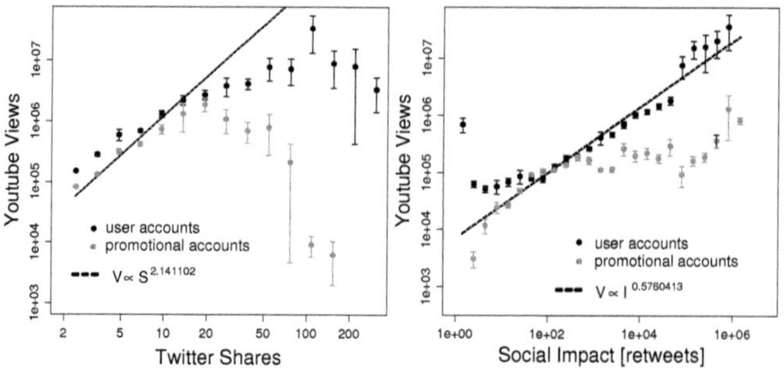


**Figure 3: Mean amount of views videos binned by amount of shares (left) and social impact of early adopters (right). Error bars show standard error, and dashed lines regression results.**

The distribution of views per video, as well as the other metrics explained above, have large variance and are skewed to the right. To avoid the uneven leverage of extreme values of these distributions, we have applied a logarithmic transformation to each one of them, reducing their variance but keeping their rank. In the first step of our analysis, we computed correlation coefficients between the logarithm of the amount of views and the other five variables. The results for promotional and non-promotional data are summarized in Table 9, revealing significant correlations for all of them. Some of this correlations are of very low magnitude or even negative sign, suggesting a more careful analysis.

Our first observation is that the amount of shares in the first week of a video is a better predictor for its popularity in the case of non-promotional users and promotional ones ($\rho = 0.184$ vs $\rho = 0.298$). The left panel of Figure 3 shows the mean amount of views of videos binned exponentially by their amount of Twitter shares.

The two types of user activities diverge after 20 shares in the first week, where for the case of non-promotional users the amount of views appears to be increasing but saturating. Regression on a power-law relation between views and shares $V \propto S^{\alpha}$ reveals a superlinear scaling with $\alpha = 2.18 \pm 0.02$, i.e., the final views of a video has a quadratic relation to the amount of regular user shares in the first week. As an example of this superlinear growth, the mean amount of views for videos with 2 shares in the first week is 151,374.5, for videos with 7 shares is 644,522.4, and for videos with 12 shares is 2,349,317. This gives an increase of almost 500K views for the five shares after the first two, but an increase of more than 1.7M for the five shares after the first seven.

The diverging pattern in both types of user activity reveals that, when promotional accounts share the same video more than 20 times in the same week, the final amount of views does not increase. In fact, there is a decreasing pattern of views, suggesting the existence of information overload or spamming behavior in promotional users.

For both types of Twitter users, the aggregated social impact in terms of mean retweet rates is the best predictor for the popularity of a video ($\rho = 0.394$ and $\rho = 0.28$). The right panel of Fig. 3 shows the mean view values for bins of the aggregated social impact, with the result of regression of the form $V \propto I^{\beta}$, where

| | $X$ | | | | | | | | | |
|---|---|---|---|---|---|---|---|---|---|---|
| Type | $S_v$ | | $E_v$ | | $I_v$ | | $\mathcal{E}_v$ | | $A_v$ | |
| Nonpr | 0.3 | 0.3 | 0.1 | 0.08 | 0.4 | 0.4 | 0.27 | 0.29 | -0.05 | -0.16 |
| Promo | 0.18 | 0.19 | 0.16 | 0.16 | 0.28 | 0.26 | 0.13 | 0.09 | 0.08 | 0.04 |

**Table 9: Pearson's (first value) and Spearman's (second value) correlation coefficients between video views and Twitter measures: $\rho(log(V_v), log(X))$, all with $p < 10^{-10}$**

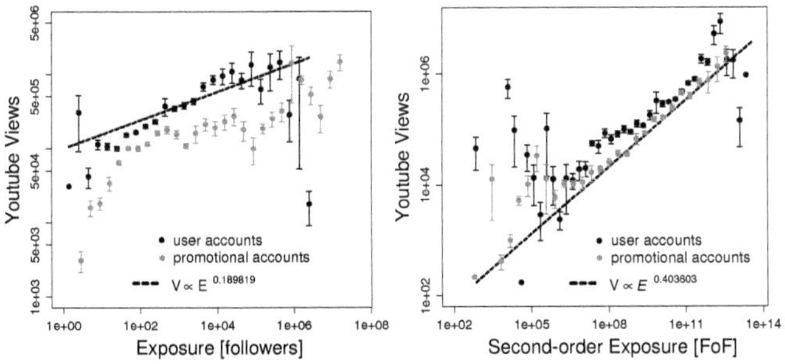


**Figure 4: Mean amount of views videos binned by first and second order exposure. Error bars show standard error, and dashed lines regression results.**

$\beta = 0.576 \pm 0.004$ for non-promotional users and $\beta = 0.358 \pm 0.003$ for promotional ones. This result reveals a sublinear relation between the amount of views and the social impact of the accounts that shared the video in the first week, close to a square root.

The amount of views of videos showed a low positive correlation coefficient with the exposure of the shares in the first week, measured through amount of followers. The left panel of Fig. 4 shows the mean amount of views versus the exposure in the first week, revealing a very soft increasing pattern in both. On the other hand, the amount of views has a more substantial correlation with the second-order exposure, with correlation coefficients of 0.268 and 0.126 for regular and promotional users respectively. The right panel of Fig. 4 shows this stronger relation, with a regression result of exponent $0.404 \pm 0.004$ for non-promotional users, and of $0.155 \pm 0.003$ for promotional ones. This comparison reveals that the second-order exposure is a much better predictor for the popularity of a video than the amount of followers of the initial sharers. This result calls for more stylized reputation metrics that take into account global information beyond amount of followers and retweet rates, for example centrality [15], or coreness [13] metrics.

Finally, the aggregated share of voice of the accounts that shared the video during the first week did not provide clear results, with a significant negative correlation of $-0.047$ for non-promotional users, and of 0.076 for promotional ones. This suggest that, if information overload and competition for attention are present in Twitter, they need to be measured with more precise approximations that the correction we presented in the previous section. Nevertheless, the share of voice of the users sharing a video still contains relevant information that we introduce in the regression model we explain below.

## 6.4 Combining Data in a Regression Model

The above results show the pairwise relation between the amount of views of a video and each one of our five Twitter metrics. This analysis ignores the possible effect of the combination of different metrics, as it can be expected that they are correlated with each other. To provide a deeper analysis on how these Twitter metrics influence the final amount of views, we propose a substitutes model in which the products of powers of each variable are proportional to the final amount of views:

$$V_v \propto \cdot S_v^{\alpha} \cdot I_v^{\beta} \cdot E_v^{\gamma} \cdot \mathcal{E}_v^{\delta} \cdot A_v^{\kappa} \quad (1)$$

This model is equivalent to a linear regression model after the logarithmic transformation of all the independent variables. Training this regressor on the promotional user data gives $R^2 = 0.107$, explaining about 10% of the variance of $log(V)$. On the non-promotional user dataset, the regressor achieves $R^2 = 0.199$, explaining almost 20% of the variance of the final amount of views of a video based exclusively on information extracted from Twitter.

| Type | $S_v$ | $E_v$ | $I_v$ | $\mathcal{E}_v$ | $A_v$ |
|---|---|---|---|---|---|
| Not promo | 1.083* | 0.096 | 0.449* | 0.118* | −0.102* |
| Promotional | 0.612* | 0.164* | 0.307* | 0.079* | 0.030 |

**Table 10: Regression coefficients for Eq. 1. Significance level * $p < 10^{-9}$, or $p > 0.01$ otherwise.**

This opens the possibility to improve previous models that used only data from YouTube [31, 28], which could also be combined with data from other online communities, as previously done in Soysa et al. [30] with a limited sample of Facebook data.

The estimated coefficients for the exponents of Eq. 1 are reported in Table 10, which allow us to compare the size of the effects of each Twitter metric. This analysis reveals the lack of relevance of the first-order exposure for the case of non-promotional users as also shown in Cha et al. [6]. The correlation between first order exposure and views shown in Fig. 4 is a confound due to the correlation of exposure with other metrics, such as impact or second-order exposure.

To assess the prediction power of our model for non-promotional users, we transformed the regression problem to a dichotomous classification, in which we tag a video as *popular* if it gathered at least 10,000 views. Using the regression model explained above, we can predict if a video will reach more than 10,000 views based on the first week of Twitter activity. If the estimator of Eq. 1 gives a value above 10,000, we classify the video as *popular*.

We performed 10-fold cross validation on the non-promotional users dataset, fitting the regressor to 90% of the data and validating it on the rest 10%. The mean base rate of popular videos for the 10 evaluations is 0.493, and our predictor achieves a mean precision of 0.715 and a mean recall of 0.534 for the *popular* class. Both values are significantly above the precision of random classifiers over the same partitions, which produced a precision of 0.492 and a recall of 0.494. This experiment shows that, using Twitter data only, a prediction can achieve a precision value much higher than expected from a random classifier.

# 7. CONCLUSIONS

We gathered a high-quality dataset based on the combination of two sources: 17 million unique public tweets for 87K users on Twitter and YouTube data for 5 million videos.

Through this combination of data sets, we could obtain novel, detailed insights into who watches (and shares) what on YouTube, and when (that is, how quickly). We applied a set of heuristics to infer demographic data including gender, location, political alignment, and interests. We designed a new method to distinguish promotional Twitter accounts, who almost exclusively share their own YouTube videos and validated our expectation that promotional users share their own videos much faster than regular ones. Our results also include a new method to characterize different user segments in terms of YouTube categories, Twitter activity, and Twitter user bios. These allowed us to analyze the relation between demographic factors and the features of YouTube videos, including their amount of views. Our detailed statistical analysis reveals correlations between Twitter behavior and YouTube video content. In addition, our clustering analysis shows that the topic preferences of the two platforms are largely aligned. Our results on politics quantitatively show that politically right users are further from the center than politically left users, and among all video categories News & Politics correlates most with social and with sharing behavior. Our detailed analysis distinguishes which user types share videos earlier/later as well as which video classes are shared earlier/later. Finally, we developed a regression model for the effect of early Twitter video shares by influential users on the final view count and we conclude by observing that second-order neighborhoods and retweet rates are much better predictors of ultimate video popularity than raw follower counts.

## 8. ACKNOWLEDGMENTS

ETH received funding from the Swiss National Science Foundation under the grant CR21I1_146499 / 1. The authors would like to thank GNIP for providing data during a free trial period of their Powertrack product.

## 9. REFERENCES

[1] F. Al Zamal, W. Liu, and D. Ruths. Homophily and latent attribute inference: Inferring latent attributes of twitter users from neighbors. In *ICWSM*, 2012.

[2] S. Asur, B. A. Huberman, G. Szabo, and C. Wang. Trends in Social Media: Persistence and Decay. In *ICWSM*, pages 434–437, 2011.

[3] A.-L. Barabasi. The origin of bursts and heavy tails in human dynamics. *Nature*, 435:207, 2005.

[4] P. Barbera. Birds of the Same Feather Tweet Together. Bayesian Ideal Point Estimation Using Twitter Data, 2012. Forthcoming.

[5] S. Bostandjiev, J. O'Donovan, and T. Höllerer. Tasteweights: A visual interactive hybrid recommender system. In *RecSys*, pages 35–42, 2012.

[6] M. Cha, H. Haddadi, F. Benevenuto, and P. K. Gummadi. Measuring user influence in twitter: The million follower fallacy. In *ICWSM*, 2010.

[7] M. Conover, J. Ratkiewicz, M. Francisco, B. Gonçalves, F. Menczer, and A. Flammini. Political polarization on twitter. In *ICWSM*, 2011.

[8] M. D. Conover, B. Gonc, A. Flammini, and F. Menczer. Partisan Asymmetries in Online Political Activity. *EPJ DataScience*, 1(6):1–17, 2012.

[9] M. D. Conover, B. Goncalves, J. Ratkiewicz, A. Flammini, and F. Menczer. Predicting the Political Alignment of Twitter Users. In *PASSAT-SocialCom*, pages 192–199, 2011.

[10] R. Crane, F. Schweitzer, and D. Sornette. Power law signature of media exposure in human response waiting time distributions. *Physical Review E*, 81(5):056101, 2010.

[11] R. Crane and D. Sornette. Robust dynamic classes revealed by measuring the response function of a social system. *PNAS*, 105(41):15649–15653, 2008.

[12] F. Figueiredo, F. Benevenuto, and J. M. Almeida. The tube over time: Characterizing popularity growth of youtube videos. In *WSDM*, pages 745–754, 2011.

[13] D. Garcia, P. Mavrodiev, and F. Schweitzer. Social resilience in online communities: The autopsy of friendster. *1st ACM Conference on Online Social Networks (Forthcoming)*, 2013.

[14] D. Garcia, F. Mendez, U. Serdült, and F. Schweitzer. Political polarization and popularity in online participatory media. In *PLEAD*, pages 3–10, Nov. 2012.

[15] D. Gayo-Avello. Nepotistic relationships in twitter and their impact on rank prestige algorithms. *Inf. Process. Manage.*, 49(6):1250–1280, 2013.

[16] S. Goel, J. M. Hofman, and M. I. Sirer. Who does what on the web: A large-scale study of browsing behavior. In *ICWSM*, 2012.

[17] P. I. Good. *Permutation, Parametric, and Bootstrap Tests of Hypotheses*. Springer, 3 edition, 2005.

[18] S. Havlin. The distance between zipf plots. *Physica A Statistical and Theoretical Physics*, 216(1-2):148–150, 1995.

[19] S. R. Kairam, M. R. Morris, J. Teevan, D. J. Liebling, and S. T. Dumais. Towards supporting search over trending events with social media. In *ICWSM*, 2013.

[20] M. Karsai, K. Kaski, A.-L. Barabási, and J. Kertész. Universal features of correlated bursty behaviour, May 2012.

[21] G. Karypis. Cluto: A clustering toolkit, 2002. `http://www.cs.umn.edu/~cluto`.

[22] J. Kulshrestha, F. Kooti, A. Nikravesh, and P. K. Gummadi. Geographic dissection of the twitter network. In *ICWSM*, 2012.

[23] M. S. S. Laine and G. Ercal. User Groups in Social Networks: An Experimental Study on YouTube. In *2011 44th Hawaii International Conference on System Sciences*, pages 1–10, Jan. 2011.

[24] J. Lehmann, B. Gonçalves, J. J. Ramasco, and C. Cattuto. Dynamical classes of collective attention in twitter. In *WWW*, page 251, New York, New York, USA, 2012.

[25] Q. V. Liao, C. Wagner, P. Pirolli, and W.-T. Fu. Understanding experts' and novices' expertise judgment of twitter users. In *CHI*, pages 2461–2464, 2012.

[26] A. Mislove, S. Lehmann, Y.-y. Ahn, J.-p. Onnela, and J. N. Rosenquist. Understanding the demographics of twitter users. In *ICWSM*, pages 554–557, 2011.

[27] M. Pennacchiotti and A.-M. Popescu. Democrats, republicans and starbucks afficionados: User classification in twitter. In *KDD*, pages 430–438, 2011.

[28] H. Pinto, J. M. Almeida, and M. A. Gonçalves. Using early view patterns to predict the popularity of youtube videos. In *WSDM*, pages 365–374, 2013.

[29] L. Qiu, Q. Tang, and A. B. Whinston. Two formulas for success in social media: Social learning and network effects, 2013. Forthcoming.

[30] D. Soysa, D. Chen, O. Au, and A. Bermak. Predicting youtube content popularity via facebook data: A network spread model for optimizing multimedia delivery. In *CIDM*, pages 214–221, 2013.

[31] G. Szabo and B. A. Huberman. Predicting the popularity of online content. *Communications of the ACM*, 53(8):80, 2010.

[32] J. Teevan, D. Ramage, and M. R. Morris. #twittersearch: A comparison of microblog search and web search. In *WSDM*, pages 35–44, 2011.

[33] A. Ulges, D. Borth, and M. Koch. Content analysis meets viewers: linking concept detection with demographics on youtube. *IJMIR*, 2(2):145–157, 2013.

[34] C. Wang and B. A. Huberman. Long trend dynamics in social media. *EPJ Data Science*, page 8, May 2012.

[35] I. Weber, V. R. K. Garimella, and E. Borra. Political search trends. In *SIGIR*, pages 1012–1012. ACM, 2012.

[36] I. Weber, V. R. K. Garimella, and E. Borra. Inferring audience partisanship for youtube videos. In *WWW*, pages 43–44, 2013.

[37] I. Weber, V. R. K. Garimella, and A. Teka. Political hashtag trends. In *ECIR*, pages 857–860, 2013.

[38] I. Weber and A. Jaimes. Who uses web search for what: and how. In *WSDM*, pages 15–24, 2011.

[39] Y. Wu, C. Zhou, J. Xiao, J. Kurths, and H. J. Schellnhuber. Evidence for a bimodal distribution in human communication. *Proceedings of the National Academy of Sciences*, 107(44):18803–18808, Oct. 2010.

# Detecting Non-Gaussian Geographical Topics in Tagged Photo Collections

Christoph Carl Kling[1], Jérôme Kunegis[2], Sergej Sizov[3], Steffen Staab[4]
[{1,2,4}] University of Koblenz-Landau, Koblenz, Germany
[3] Heinrich Heine University, Dusseldorf, Germany
{[1]ckling,[2]kunegis,[4]staab}@uni-koblenz.de, [3]sizov@hhu.de

## ABSTRACT

Nowadays, large collections of photos are tagged with GPS coordinates. The modelling of such large geo-tagged corpora is an important problem in data mining and information retrieval, and involves the use of geographical information to detect topics with a spatial component. In this paper, we propose a novel geographical topic model which captures dependencies between geographical regions to support the detection of topics with complex, non-Gaussian distributed spatial structures. The model is based on a multi-Dirichlet process (MDP), a novel generalisation of the hierarchical Dirichlet process extended to support multiple base distributions. Our method thus is called the MDP-based geographical topic model (MGTM). We show how to use a MDP to dynamically smooth topic distributions between groups of spatially adjacent documents. In systematic quantitative and qualitative evaluations using independent datasets from prior related work, we show that such a model can exploit the adjacency of regions and leads to a significant improvement in the quality of topics compared to the state of the art in geographical topic modelling.

## Categories and Subject Descriptors

H.4 [**Information Systems Applications**]: General

## General Terms

Algorithms, Theory

## Keywords

Topic models, Dirichlet process, Graphical model

## 1. INTRODUCTION

Very large amounts of geographically distributed data are available to social media websites, companies and governments. Common sources of geospatial knowledge include user-generated content with GPS coordinates (e.g. photos and messages sent from smartphones), user data with information about the place of residence, or server logs with IP-based estimations of client locations. Such geographically distributed data are a rich information source, describing the environment in which they were created. Geographical knowledge can be exploited in a broad range of applications that take into account environmental and cultural differences between locations – ranging from marketing campaigns and recommender systems to data mining applications.

Under the bag-of-words assumption, both words and geographic positions can be modelled as being generated by latent topics in a probabilistic model. Existing approaches for geographical topic modelling adopt topic models such as probabilistic latent semantic analysis (PLSA) [10] or latent Dirichlet allocation (LDA) [5] and extend the models by assigning distributions over locations to topics, or by introducing latent geographical regions. In models which extend topics for spatial distributions (such as two-dimensional normal distributions) [15], topics with a complex (i.e. non-Gaussian) spatial distribution cannot be detected. In models with latent, Gaussian distributed regions [18], documents within a complex shaped topic area do not influence the topic distribution of distant documents within the same area. Therefore, topics with a complex spatial distribution such as topics distributed along coastlines, rivers or country borders are harder to detect by such methods. More elaborate models introduce artificial assumptions about the structure of geographical distributions by introducing hierarchical structures [2] or by defining Gaussian process kernels [1] in advance. Additionally, some approaches [12, 18] do not model document-specific topic distributions.

In contrast to existing models, the multi-Dirichlet process (MDP) based geographical topic model (MGTM) presented in this paper uses a MDP mixture model that groups documents by geographical regions. A geographical network between spatially adjacent regions is used to equalise topic distributions within coherent topic areas. Consequently, it allows for constructing generative models which provide a better data fit than existing approaches.

The rest of this paper is organised as follows. Section 2 reviews previous work on geographical topic detection. In Section 3 we describe the theory and the components of MGTM. We establish the baseline reference model, introduce its extension using the MDP, and develop corresponding inference procedures. In Section 4 we evaluate our basic model against state-of-the-art models, using reference datasets that have been used in prior work. Section 5 concludes our work.


*WSDM'14,* February 24–28, 2014, New York, New York, USA.
Copyright 2014 ACM 978-1-4503-2351-2/14/02 ...$15.00.
http://dx.doi.org/10.1145/2556195.2556218.

## 2. GEOGRAPHICAL TOPIC MODELS

A geographical topic model is a statistical model of a set of spatially distributed documents that uses word co-occurrences both within texts and within geographical regions. From an application perspective, location-aware topic models should satisfy the following top-level requirements:

(1) Modelling document-specific topic distributions: Documents typically cover a small set of topics, an assumption used for prediction (e.g. tag recommendation)
(2) Recognition of topics with complex (e.g. non-Gaussian) spatial distributions
(3) Detection of coherent topic regions that form complex shaped areas of similar characteristics (e.g. countries, seas, mountain ranges, etc.)
(4) Estimation of parameters from data: Topic models should not require prior knowledge for the parameter setting

In the following, we review existing models for geographical topic modelling, focusing on these requirements.

On a high level, existing approaches to geographical topic detection can be divided in two groups: models using a discrete set of locations and models using a continuous geographical distribution associated with topics. We focus on topic models for modelling text and location only, excluding extensions for other features such as time and authors.

### 2.1 Methods Using Discrete Locations

The model of Mei et al. [12] extends probabilistic latent semantic analysis (PLSA) [10] to model spatio-temporal information by mixing the topic distribution of documents with location- and time-specific topic distributions. Locations and timestamps are modelled as discrete sets. In practice, the division of data into location and time intervals results in sparse data.

Wang et al. [17] base their model on latent Dirichlet allocation (LDA) [5]. In their model, topics are multinomial distributions both over words and a discrete set of locations. The authors are aware of the fact that some related locations, such as locations within a country, are expected to share a similar topic distribution. They suggest to introduce a hierarchy between locations such as countries or cities to share topic information by merging those locations.

Finally, Yin et al. [18] present a *location driven model* (LDM) based on PLSA, in which geographically distributed data are clustered in a preprocessing step to obtain a discrete set of locations. In the model, all documents within a spatial cluster share a common topic distribution. Clusters are independent and share a global set of topics.

### 2.2 Methods Using Continuous Locations

A first continuous approach to geographical topic modelling was proposed by Sizov [15]: GeoFolk, a model similar to the model of Wang and based on LDA [5]. Instead of using a multinomial distribution over locations, every topic in GeoFolk has a Gaussian distribution on the coordinates of a document. The drawback of this kind of topic modelling clearly is the limited geographical distribution of topics: Every topic has a normal geographical distribution and topic areas that are not normal distributed are split into independent topics.

Yin et al. [18] therefore introduce *latent geographical topic analysis* (LGTA), an extended version of GeoFolk based on PLSA. Instead of directly assigning normal distributions to topics, in the model of Yin several normal distributions are assigned to *regions* which have a distribution over the set of topics. Clearly, there now can be several Gaussian regions sharing the same topic. Regions now take the role of discrete locations as in the model of Mei. Therefore, the model inherits the problem of merging regions of one kind.

In [2], Ahmed et al. present a hierarchical topic model which models both document and region specific topic distributions and additionally models regional variations of topics. Relations between the Gaussian distributed geographical regions are modelled by assuming a strict hierarchical relation between regions that is learned during inference.

A more general approach for modelling arbitrary, complex features such as geolocations was introduced by Agovic and Banerjee [1]. Given that the similarity between topic distributions of documents directly depends on their respective position in the feature space, topic distributions of documents can be sampled from a Gaussian process (GP) prior which encodes the similarity of documents in the feature space. However, it is unclear how to choose the right GP kernel in the geographical scenario, as the similarity of document-topic distributions across the geographical space typically is hard to predict and involves complex structures such as countries or geographical zones.

### 2.3 Drawbacks of Existing Methods

The existing geographical topic models described in the previous sections have major drawbacks with respect to the four requirements discussed at the beginning of this section. The models of Yin and Hong [11, 18] do not model document-specific topic distributions; the model of Sizov [15] cannot detect topics with a complex spatial distribution; and the model of Wang [17] supports the merging of semantically related geographical regions but lacks a general merging method. Finally, only the model by Ahmed et al. is parameter-free [2].

| Model | Requirements (1) | (2) | (3) | (4) |
|---|---|---|---|---|
| Mei et al. [12] | | ✓ | | |
| Wang et al. [17] | ✓ | ✓ | (✓)[1] | |
| GeoFolk [15] | ✓ | | | |
| LDM [18] | | ✓ | | |
| LGTA [18] | | ✓ | | |
| Agovic et al. [1] | ✓ | ✓ | (✓)[1] | (✓)[1] |
| Ahmed et al. [2] | ✓ | ✓ | (✓)[1] | ✓ |
| MGTM | ✓ | ✓ | ✓ | ✓ |

**Table 1: Requirements met by existing models, and by our model (MGTM).** [1]**partial fulfilment**

Models based on a hierarchical relation between regions such as the model by Wang et al. [17] and Ahmed et al. [2] have drawbacks, not only in modelling complexity as mentioned in [17]. Particular hierarchical relations such as *city-state-country* might work for representing geographical topics such as languages or cultural behaviour. However they would be misleading e.g. for topics representing geographical features such as rivers or mountain areas. In most cases, there will be no hierarchy which fits all topics. Additionally, when introducing a hierarchy of Gaussian distributed regions as in [2], geographical topics which fit into such a hierarchy will be preferred over topics with a non-elliptic shape such as, say, coast lines, which would be poorly approximated by a hierarchy of Gaussian regions. Therefore, introducing a hierarchical relation between regions will prevent the model from properly learning topics whose complex geographical distribution does not fit such a simple hierarchical structure. Table 1 summarizes the requirements met by the models presented.

# 3. MODEL

We consider the general setting of documents consisting of words, and annotated with their geographic location. For topic modelling, words and location of documents are assumed exchangeable. Formally, we have a corpus of documents $D = \{d_1, \ldots, d_M\}$ of size $M = |D|$, and a document $d_j$ consists of a set of $N_j$ words denoted by $\mathbf{w}_j = (w_{j1}, \ldots, w_{jN_j})$ and a geographical location, a latitude and longitude pair $\text{loc}_j = (\text{lat}_j, \text{lon}_j)$. By de Finetti's theorem [5], words and location can be modelled as a mixture of independent and identically distributed random variables generated by latent factors. The document location is generated by $L$ latent factors corresponding to geographical clusters associated with continuous distributions on the geographical space. The $K$ latent factors assigned to words, written as topics $\theta_1, \ldots, \theta_K$, are multinomial distributions over the vocabulary of size $V$.

In the following section we present three novel geographical topic models: a basic model using a three-level hierarchical Dirichlet process, an extension that considers neighbour relations between regions by model selection and an improved version based on the multi-Dirichlet process introduced in this paper.

## 3.1 The Basic Model

For the basic geographical topic model, we model locations and words separately for several reasons:

*Detection of coherent topic areas.* The separation of spatial clusters and document semantics allows us to define meaningful neighbour relations between spatially adjacent clusters. In fact, as shown later, the use of these spatial adjacency relations allows us to detect coherent topic areas and to significantly improve the topic quality in the final model. Existing models that use continuous document positions do not allow a meaningful definition of spatial adjacency between geographical regions or topics as their position is influenced both by words and document locations.

*Computational complexity.* Probabilistic clustering methods in two- or three-dimensional space usually converge very fast, while samplers for probabilistic topic models usually take many iterations. Integrating both processes would result in a high computational overhead which is unacceptable for large datasets in real-world applications.

The basic topic model takes a set of geographical clusters as input. In order to get a clustering which also is a generative model of document positions, we fit a mixture of Fisher distributions to the data. The clusters are used to group documents in a three-level hierarchical Dirichlet process in order to ensure that documents within a geographical cluster share similar topics. This basic topic model is identical to the topic model for multiple corpora proposed by Teh et al. [16].

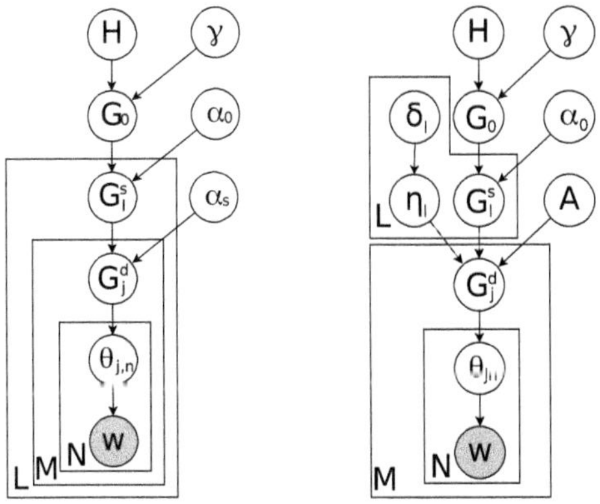

(a) Basic model (b) MGTM

**Figure 1: The graphical model for (a) the basic model and (b) MGTM.**

### 3.1.1 Geographical Clustering

Existing approaches for geographical topic modelling rely on a representation of document positions in Euclidean space of latitude and longitude. This causes problems for documents located close to the poles or to the International Date Line. Instead, we use the unit sphere as a model for the shape of the Earth. For geographical clustering, we assume that document locations follow a Fisher distribution. The Fisher distribution is a probability density function on a three-dimensional sphere comparable to an isotropic Gaussian distribution on the plane [9]. The Fisher distribution is defined as

$$f(x \mid \kappa, \mu) = \frac{\kappa}{2\pi(e^{\kappa} - e^{-\kappa})} e^{\kappa \mu^{\mathrm{T}} x}$$

where $\mu$ is the mean and $\kappa$ is the concentration parameter. Given the number of Fisher distributions $L$ and assuming a uniform prior, we use the expectation-maximisation algorithm for parameter estimation. For the concentration parameters we use the approximation given by Banerjee et al. [4]. To construct a non-parametric model where the number of regions is inferred from data, the number of clusters $L$ can be sampled using a Dirichlet process that samples from a space of Fisher distributions. The geographical distribution of topics will depend on the number of regions. In order to ensure comparability, the number of regions is kept as a fixed parameter in the algorithms evaluated in this paper.

### 3.1.2 Topic Detection

The choice of the underlying topic model is crucial for the task of geographical topic detection. Existing methods typically are based on PLSA [18] or LDA [11, 15]. We decide to base our models on the hierarchical Dirichlet process (HDP) [16] instead as it is non-parametric, yields a sound generative model and supports a grouping of documents by external factors such as geographical clusters. The hierarchical Dirichlet process is a Bayesian approach to the topic detection problem and shares many properties with LDA: There is a Dirichlet-multinomial document-topic distribution assigned to every document and every topic is represented by a Dirichlet-multinomial topic-word distribution. However, in the hierarchical Dirichlet process the number of topics is not fixed. Instead, every topic is sampled from a Dirichlet process with a base distribution over $H$, the space of possible topic-word distributions. All model parameters can be sampled using hyperparameters, resulting in a fully non-parametric model. In order to share topics between documents, the document-topic distribution is sampled from a higher-level topic-distribution, i.e. a global topic distribution which is itself a draw from a Dirichlet process [16].

It is natural to extend the hierarchical scheme by adding layers for document groups with characteristic topic distributions. We use the three-layer Dirichlet process hierarchy for modelling document corpora proposed in [16] but group the documents by geographical regions instead using the spatial clustering of documents defined before.

The three-level hierarchical topic model using geographical clusters is defined as follows: Given a set of $L$ geographical clusters, each cluster is a subset $D_l$ of the document corpus. First we draw a global probability measure $G_0$ over the topic space from a Dirichlet process with base distribution $H$ on the continuous topic space:

$$G_0 \sim DP(\gamma, H),$$

where $\gamma$ is the concentration parameter for the Dirichlet process, influencing the sparsity of the global topic distribution. A symmetric Dirichlet prior is placed over $H$. The mixture proportions $\beta$ for the global topic distribution are generated by a stick-breaking process $\beta \sim \text{Stick}(\gamma)$ [16]. For every geographical cluster, we draw a region-specific topic distribution $G_l$ from the global distribution over the topic space $G_0$:

$$G_l^s \sim DP(\alpha_0, G_0), \qquad l = 1, \dots, L$$

with mixing proportions $\beta_l^s$ and concentration parameter $\alpha_0$. The documents from each region-specific document set $D_l$ draw a document-specific topic probability measure from $G_l$:

$$G_j^d \sim DP(\alpha_s, G_l^s), \qquad d_j \in D_l$$

with mixing proportions $\pi_j$. All clusters share the common concentration parameter $\alpha_s$. The resulting model is given in Figure 1(a). A collapsed Gibbs sampler and strategies for hyperparameter inference are given in [16].

## 3.2 The Neighbour Aware Model

We modify the basic model to include adjacency relations between geographical clusters. Using geographical neighbour relations has several advantages over the basic model:

*Exploiting similarity for smoothing.* Geographical clusters adjacent in space often are similar in their topic distribution. Most geographical topics cannot be approximated by a simple spatial probability distribution such as a Gaussian or Fisher distribution and for these complex topic areas, coherent sets of multiple spatial distributions are a reasonable approximation. Therefore adjacent regions may smooth their topic distributions to increase the probability of detecting such coherent topic areas.

*Sharing emerging topics.* In the basic model, new topics emerge locally, first on the document level, then on cluster level and finally on the global level. Under the assumption that adjacent clusters are likely to be similar, new topics should be actively shared with neighbour clusters. Sharing topics through a network of adjacent clusters is a dynamic, evolutionary process which is similar to the spread of memes in social networks: Strong topics, which describe observed documents well, will survive, while poor topics will perish during the sampling process [8].

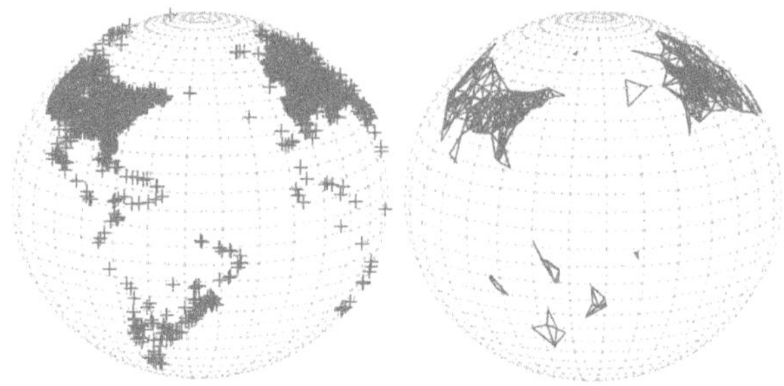

**Figure 2: Document positions (left) and geographical network (right) for the car dataset (Section 4.1)**

We call this model the *neighbour aware geographical topic model* (NAM). For defining a spatial adjacency relation, we decided to use the Delaunay triangulation, obtained as the dual of the Voronoi tesselation [3]. Triangles with side lengths greater than 1/8th of the earth radius are discarded. An example for the resulting geographical network is shown in Figure 2. Note that other definitions such as k-nearest-neighbour could have been used as well.

The idea behind the extended topic model is to include an uncertainty over the cluster membership of documents in clusters in order to more strongly connect topic distributions of adjacent geographical clusters. Each document topic distribution is assumed to be drawn either from the topic distribution of its geographical cluster or from one of the adjacent cluster distributions. $P_l$ is the union of the cluster index $l$ and the set of neighbour cluster indices, and $\lambda_j$ indicates from which cluster-specific topic distribution $\beta_r^s$ the document $d_j$ was sampled. The set of topic distributions $\beta^{\mathbf{s}}$ can be used for Bayesian model selection: Given a uniform prior over the probability for a document $d_j$ to be sampled from $G_r^s$ with $r \in P_l$, the sampling equation for $\lambda_j$ is

$$p(\lambda_j = r \mid \mathbf{z}, \mathbf{m}, \beta^{\mathbf{s}}) \propto \prod_{k=1}^{K} (\alpha_s \beta_{rk}^s)^{m_{jk}} \qquad (r \in P_l) \qquad (1)$$

which is identical to the sampling equation in [7], except that the weights of the document-specific topic distribution $\pi_j$ are integrated out. The model structure then is sampled during Gibbs sampling and the rest of the sampler remains the same as for the basic model.

## 3.3 The Multi-Dirichlet Process Based Geographical Topic Model

The neighbour aware topic model clearly leads to an interaction between adjacent cluster-topic distributions. However, in some cases this interaction does not yield the intended smoothing. Consider the example of two adjacent geographical clusters which both have a high probability for two topics, while other geographical cluster-topic distributions assign very low probabilities to both of the topics. Now, the probability of this model would clearly be maximised if one of the two clusters has a very high probability for the first topic, and the other cluster for the second topic. This (unwanted) effect occurs in cases where there are only few adjacent clusters with high probabilities for a small set of topics. In practice, this is often the case as data are sparse and the number of geographical clusters is small.

To overcome this apparent drawback, we introduce a dynamic smoothing based on the *multi-Dirichlet process* (MDP), a generalisation of the Dirichlet process that combines multiple base measures into a single mixing distribution over the space of the base measures.

### 3.3.1 The Multi-Dirichlet Process

We define the *multi-Dirichlet process* (MDP) using a notation similar to that used in [16]. Let $G_1, \dots, G_P$ be probability measures on a standard Borel space $(\Theta, \mathcal{B})$ associated with positive real parameters $\alpha_1, \dots, \alpha_P$. We define the multi-Dirichlet process $MDP(\alpha_1, \dots, \alpha_P, G_1, \dots, G_P)$ as a probability measure $G$ over $(\Theta, \mathcal{B})$, which for every finite measurable partition $(A_1, \dots, A_r)$ of $\Theta$ yields a Dirichlet distributed random vector, denoted $(G(A_1), \dots, G(A_r))$, with:

$$(G(A_1), \dots, G(A_r)) \sim Dir(\sum_{p=1}^{P} \alpha_p G_p(A_1), \dots, \sum_{p=1}^{P} \alpha_p G_p(A_r)) \quad (2)$$

In the following, we will refer to the base measures as parent distributions of the MDP. An alternative notation of the concentration parameters $\alpha_1, \dots, \alpha_P$ is given by

$$A = \sum_{p=1}^{P} \alpha_p \qquad \eta_p = \frac{\alpha_p}{A}, \quad p \in \{1, \dots, P\} \quad (3)$$

which gives a convenient parametrisation for the MDP:

$$MDP(A, \eta_1, \dots, \eta_P, G_1, \dots, G_P).$$

Using the alternative notation, the MDP can be understood as a Dirichlet process with base distribution $G_0 = \sum_{p=1}^{P} \eta_p G_p$, the weighted sum of parent distributions, and concentration parameter A. Given a set of observed samples from $G$, $\theta_1, \dots, \theta_{i-1}$, the probability of a factor $\theta_i \in \Theta$ to be sampled from $G$ can be estimated by integrating out G using the properties of the Dirichlet distributed partitions [13] and replacing the base measure with the weighted sum of parent distributions:

$$\theta_i \mid \theta_1, \dots \theta_{i-1} \sim \frac{1}{i-1+A} \sum_{j=1}^{i-1} \delta(\theta_j) + A \sum_{p=1}^{P} \frac{\eta_p}{i-1+A} G_p \quad (4)$$

with $\delta(\theta_j)$ being the Dirac delta, giving weight to a single point $\theta_j$. We immediately see that a MDP with a single parent distribution yields a standard Dirichlet process.

### 3.3.2 Inference

We sample for topic assignments by extending the inference strategies using the "Chinese restaurant franchise" representation given in [16]: For a given two-level hierarchical Dirichlet process, global "dishes" are introduced, corresponding to the Dirichlet distributed random variables on the first level from which the Dirichlet process of the second level samples factors $\theta_j$ . For factor sampling, customers corresponding to the factors $\theta_j$ form Dirichlet distributed groups sitting at tables in a restaurant and all customers at a table share the same dish. The number of customers at the $i$th table is given by $m_i$ and the tables are samples from the Dirichlet distributed base distribution of dishes. A detailed explanation of the Chinese restaurant process and its parameters is given in [16]. The Gibbs sampling equation for topic assignment $z_{ji}$ of word $w_{ji}$ in document $d_j$ is:

$$p(z_{ji}{=}k \mid \mathbf{z_{-ji}}, \mathbf{m}, \beta^{\mathbf{s}}) \propto (m_{jk} + \sum_{p \in P_l} \alpha_p \beta^s_{pk}) f_k^{-x_{ji}}(x_{ji}) \quad (5)$$

for topics already sampled, and

$$p(z_{ji}{=}k^{\text{new}} \mid \mathbf{z_{-ji}}, \mathbf{m}, \beta^{\mathbf{s}}) \propto (\sum_{p \in P_l} \alpha_p \beta^s_{pu}) f_{k^{\text{new}}}^{-x_{ji}}(x_{ji}) \quad (6)$$

for new topics where $\beta^{\mathbf{s}}_{\mathbf{p}}$ are mixing proportions of the parent distributions, $f_k^{-x_{ji}}(x_{ji})$ is a topic-specific probability function with parameters from the parent distribution and $z_{-ji}$ denotes the set of all topic assignments except for $z_{ji}$. The number of customers in document $d_j$ assigned to the $k$th factor is given by $m_{jk}$.

For sampling the number of components, the MDP can be interpreted as a multinomial extension of a Dirichlet process. This becomes apparent if we use the alternative representation from Eq. 3. Substituting $\alpha_0$ by (a sum of) $A\eta_{lp}$ in Equation 40 from [16] gives:

$$p(m_{jk}{=}\mathbf{m} \mid \mathbf{z}, \mathbf{m_{-jk}}) = \frac{\Gamma(\sum_{p \in P_l} A\eta_{lp}\beta^s_{pk})}{\Gamma((\sum_{p \in P_l} A\eta_{lp}\beta^s_{pk}) + n_{jk})} s(n_{jk}, m_{jk\cdot}) \cdot A^{m_{jk\cdot}} \binom{m_{jk\cdot}}{m_{jk1}, \dots, m_{jkP}} \prod_{p \in P_l} (\eta_{lp}\beta^s_{pk})^{m_{jkp}} \quad (7)$$

where $l$ is the index of the MDP of document $d_j$ with parent distributions $P_l$. $s(n, m)$ denotes the unsigned Stirling numbers of the first kind and $\binom{m_{jk\cdot}}{m_{jk1}, \dots, m_{jkP}}$ the multinomial coefficient. Note that we keep track of the number of tables $m_{jkp}$ for every parent distribution and sample them simultaneously. $m_{jk\cdot}$ denotes the sum of tables over all parents, $n_{jk}$ is the number of customers (topic assignments) for a given document and topic. For sampling the tables, we first drop the Gamma functions which do not depend on $\mathbf{m}$, sample for the sum of tables $m_{jk\cdot}$ and then sample the parent specific table counts $m_{jkp}$ from a multinomial with normalised parameters $\eta_{lp}\beta_{pk}$.

Sampling the weights $\beta_p$ for each $G_p$ is done using $m_{\cdot kp}$, the sum over all tables of topic $k$ and parent $p$ from documents with parent distribution $G_p$. If $G_p$ is sampled from a parent Dirichlet process with concentration parameter $\alpha_0$ and weights $\beta$, then

$$\beta_p \sim Dir(m_{\cdot 1p} + \alpha_0\beta_1, \dots, m_{\cdot Kp} + \alpha_0\beta_K, \alpha_0\beta_u) \quad (8)$$

where $\beta_k$ denotes the weight of topic $k$ in the parent Dirichlet process and $\beta_u$ is the weight of the previously unseen topics.

### 3.3.3 Estimation of Concentration Parameters

Sampling for concentration parameters $\alpha_p$ is similar to the sampling in Dirichlet processes as described in [16]. Instead of directly sampling the concentration parameters $\alpha_p$, we first sample $A$ and then sample $\eta$. We use the probability of the total table counts for all documents in the MDP:

$$p(\mathbf{m_l} \mid \mathbf{n}, \mathbf{m}, \eta, A) =$$

$$\prod_{j \in D_l} \frac{\Gamma(A)}{\Gamma(A + n_{j\cdot})} s(n_{j\cdot}, m_{j\cdot}) A^{m_{j\cdot}} \cdot \binom{m_{j\cdot}}{m_{j1}, \ldots, m_{jP}} \prod_{p \in P_l} \eta_{lp}^{m_{jp}} \tag{9}$$

where $D_l$ is the set of documents which is sampled from the MDP with index $l$. The left part of the equation is identical to Equation 44 in [16] with parameter $A$ as concentration parameter. Therefore sampling for $A$ is identical as for a normal DP. The document specific table counts $m_{j\cdot}$ are obtained by summing over the sampling results from Equation 7. Obviously, the right side of Equation 9 is a multinomial again. As $\eta$ governs the influence of parent distributions, we can set a symmetric Dirichlet prior over the sampling parameters for smoothing. For a MDP with index $l$ we then estimate $\eta_l$ using:

$$\hat{\eta}_{lp} = \frac{m_{\cdot p} + \delta}{m_{\cdot\cdot} + |P_l|\delta} \qquad \eta_l \sim Dir(\delta_l) \tag{10}$$

### 3.3.4 MDP-based Model

The extension of NAM for the multi-Dirichlet process, the multi-Dirichlet process geographical topic model (MGTM), is obtained by replacing the model selection for uncertain cluster memberships by multi-Dirichlet processes. Instead of sampling for document memberships from the set of potential parent distributions $P_l$, we use $P_l$ as indices of the parent base distributions of the MDP. Every document has several parental base distributions $G_r^s$ with $r \in P_l$, the indices of the region of the document and the adjacent regions. A schematic representation of the resulting dependencies is shown in Figure 3. The weight of region $r$ in the MDP is given by $\eta_{lr}$ and is sampled during the topic sampling process. With a concentration parameter $\delta > 1$ we smooth the cluster weights of parent distributions. The resulting model is shown in Figure 1(b). The dashed arrow connecting the cluster specific topic distributions $G_l^s$ and the document specific distributions $G_j^d$ indicates that not every cluster specific distribution is a parent base distribution of each MDP.

In MGTM, all documents of a given region share the same MDP and thus the same weights $\eta_l$ for the parent topic distributions of the region and its neighbour regions. Each region stores the influence of its adjacent regions on the topic distribution of the contained documents in the parameter $\eta_l$ which is adjusted during the Gibbs sampling process. Given $P_l$, the union of the region index $l$ and its neighbour region indices, $\eta_l$ assigns a probability to every region to be chosen as a base topic distribution by the documents $D_l$ in region $l$, and thus $\eta_{lr}$ is an indicator of similarity between the $l$th region and its $r$th neighbour.

As mentioned, it is possible to smooth the influence of adjacent regions by setting a Dirichlet prior over $\eta$. In contrast, a prior for the model selection of NAM (Eq. 1) only could re-weight but not smooth the probability for cluster memberships. Using the MDP, we obtain a more flexible and stable framework for selecting base distributions that correspond – in our case – to cluster-specific topic distributions.

The resulting model has an important advantage: For the neighbour aware model, we made the assumption that adjacent spatial clusters are similar and tried to smooth their topic distributions. The MDP ensures that the model creates homogeneous topic distributions for similar adjacent regions and at the same time prevents a smoothing of dissimilar regions by adjusting the influence parameter $\eta$ during the sampling process, leading to a *dynamic smoothing* of topic regions.

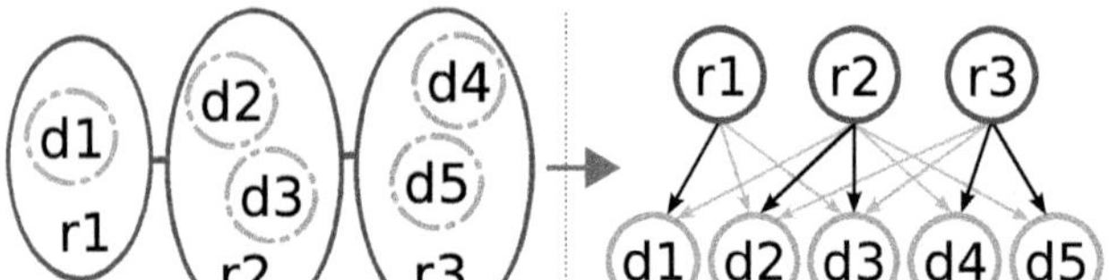


**Figure 3: The geographical adjacency of regions (left) is used in the model to derive dependencies of document-specific topic distributions from the topic distributions of regions (right). Dependencies from regions adjacent to the region of a document are shown in grey.**

## 4. EVALUATION

In this section, we demonstrate the ability of our model to improve the quality of topics by detecting more accurate, coherent topic areas. The evaluation is in four parts: First, we compare the basic model, the neighbour aware model, the multi-Dirichlet process model and a state-of-the-art model for geographical topic detection, LGTA by Yin et al., using the datasets and parameters given in [18]. Second, we analyse the influence of increased region parameters on topic quality for all four methods. We then compare the runtime of the presented methods on the largest dataset for growing region parameters. Finally, we assess the topic quality of LGTA and MGTM on the largest dataset with a user study.

## 4.1 Datasets

As the evaluation of topic models is heavily dependent on the datasets used for comparison, we use existing datasets in order to guarantee a fair comparison. We use the datasets from [18] created for the evaluation of the LGTA model. The datasets consist of photographs with geographic coordinates and text tags from the photo sharing service Flickr. The landscape dataset contains 5,791 photos, tagged by "landscape" together with the terms *mountains, mountain, beach, ocean, coast, desert* from within the US. Topic models should recognise separated topics for mountain regions, coastal regions and desert areas as they belong to different, almost mutually exclusive geographical landscapes. The activities dataset contains 1,931 images, taken within the US and tagged by "hiking" and "surfing". These two activities should be recognised as own topics of behaviour. The car dataset contains 34,707 globally distributed images annotated with *chevrolet, pontiac, cadillac, gmc, buick, audi, bmw, mercedesbenz, fiat, peugeot, citroen* or *renault*, filtered for event-like images tagged with *autoshow, show, race, racing*. Only the tags from the set of car brands were kept. Concerning the geographical topics, American, German and French car brands are expected to be detected. The manhattan dataset consists of images from New York containing the tag *manhattan*. Different parts of Manhattan should be detected. For the food dataset, Yin et al. filtered geo-tagged photos containing the tags *cuisine, food, gourmet, restaurant, restaurants, breakfast, lunch, dinner, appetizer, entree,dessert* and kept 278 co-occurring tags. Cultural food patterns such as national cuisines are latent topics hidden in the data [18]. An overview of the data is given in Table 2.

**Table 2: Collection period, document count ($M$) and vocabulary size ($V$) of the datasets used for comparison [18]**

| Dataset | Collection period | $M$ | $V$ |
|---|---|---|---|
| Landscape | 09/01/2009 – 09/01/2010 | 5.791 | 1.143 |
| Activity | 09/01/2009 – 09/01/2010 | 1.931 | 408 |
| Manhattan | 09/01/2009 – 09/01/2010 | 28.922 | 868 |
| Car | 01/01/2006 – 09/01/2010 | 34.707 | 12 |
| Food | 01/01/2006 – 09/01/2010 | 151.747 | 278 |

## 4.2 Experimental Setting

In order to test the generalisation performance of geographical topic models, we calculate the word perplexity. The word perplexity is a widely-used measure in language modelling, corresponding to the inverse of the geometric mean of the per-word likelihood of held-out documents [5] that can be understood as the ability of a topic model to predict words of new documents. Lower perplexity values indicate a better model. Yin et al. used the word perplexity in their evaluation of LGTA which they showed to be superior to GeoFolk [15] and a set of basic geographical topic models. Models that outperform LGTA in perplexity therefore also outperform GeoFolk and the basic methods evaluated by Yin [18].

The comparison between the basic Dirichlet process-based model and its extensions is needed to test the effect of including the additional information of the geographical network in the model and to compare the multi-Dirichlet process with a smoothing mechanism based on model selection.

For each perplexity calculation, a random 80% / 20% split is used to create a training set $D_{\text{train}}$ and a test set $D_{\text{test}}$. As explained in Section 3, each document $d_j$ is represented by a word set $\mathbf{w}_j$. We calculate the likelihood of words in held-out documents using the location of documents, the set of topics and other parameters sampled from the training dataset. The word perplexity is defined as [5]

$$perplexity(D_{\text{test}}) = \exp\left(\frac{-\log(\prod_{d_j \in D_{\text{test}}} p(\mathbf{w}_j))}{\sum_{d_j \in D_{\text{test}}} |\mathbf{w}_j|}\right).$$

For the hierarchical Dirichlet process-based models, the probability of a document is given by

$$p(\mathbf{w_j}) = \prod_{w_i \in \mathbf{w}_j} \sum_{k=1}^{K+1} \theta_{k,w_i} \pi_{j,k}$$

where $\theta_{k,w_i}$ is the probability of word $w_i$ under topic $k$ and $\pi_{j,k}$ is the document-topic distribution for topic $k$. $K+1$ denotes the index of a previously unseen topic and the topic-word probability $\theta_{K+1,w_i}$ is given by $\theta_{K+1,t} = 1/V,\ t \in \{1, \ldots, V\}$ as we use a symmetric Dirichlet prior over the topic space $H$ from which new topics are drawn.

For convenience, the parameters for the (multi-)Dirichlet processes are from the first model in [16]. A $Gamma(1, 0.1)$ prior is assigned to $\gamma$ and a $Gamma(1, 1)$ prior to $\alpha_0, \alpha_s$ and $A$. The concentration parameters are initialised to 1. For the multi-Dirichlet process, the weights $\eta$ of parent distributions are initialised to $1/P$ and the concentration parameter is set to $\delta = 10$. The base measure $H$ is a symmetric Dirichlet distribution with concentration parameter 0.5, except for the car dataset where the parameter is set to 5 for smooth topic-word distributions, as all car brands are expected to appear in all topic areas. We set the number of iterations of the Gibbs sampler to a low value of 200. The source code for MGTM is available from: `http://c-kling.de/mgtm`.

For the evaluation of LGTA, the parameters from the original paper [18] were used. The stopping criterion is set to a change in log-likelihood lower than 0.0001 and the background model weight is set to 0.1. LGTA sets a parameter for the number of normal distributed regions which is analogous to the number of geographical clusters (Fisher distributions) in the models presented in this paper. For comparison, we use identical numbers of regions. The setting depends on the dataset and is taken from the LGTA paper.

As the number of detected topics varies for models based on the hierarchical Dirichlet process, each of the HDP-based methods is run 100 times on each dataset and the resulting perplexity is averaged for topic counts with at least ten samples for all three models. The perplexity of LGTA is calculated for the same number of topics by averaging over ten runs.

## 4.3 Comparison with LGTA

Resulting perplexity scores for each model are given in Figure 4 (a)-(e). The experiments show that the base model, NAM and MGTM are superior to LGTA for all datasets. This finding can be explained by the ability of the models to model document-specific topic distributions that cannot be detected by LGTA. However, the performance of the HDP-based models differs. For the globally distributed datasets (car and food), MGTM performs significantly better than the base model and NAM. In contrast, for local datasets with a small number of regions, all HDP-based methods perform comparably well.

The dynamic smoothing by MGTM helps to detect coherent topic regions and can effectively improve the topic quality for large, complex structured data while for simple datasets the basic model performs similar or even better.

## 4.4 Effect of the Region Parameter

To further investigate the behaviour of MGTM for complex structured regions, we repeat the experiments for the three datasets with the smallest number of regions but increase the region parameter by a factor of ten. The results are given in Figure 4, (f)-(h). For an increased number of regions, MGTM shows an improved perplexity for all three datasets and outperforms the basic and neighbour-aware model, demonstrating its ability to effectively exploit the adjacency relation between regions for sharing topic information.

The effect of a growing number of regions for the car dataset at a fixed number of five topics is plotted in Figure 4, (i). The car dataset is adequate to demonstrate the usage of geographic information in the topic models as the documents contain only a single word, meaning that intra-document co-occurrences of words do not contribute to the

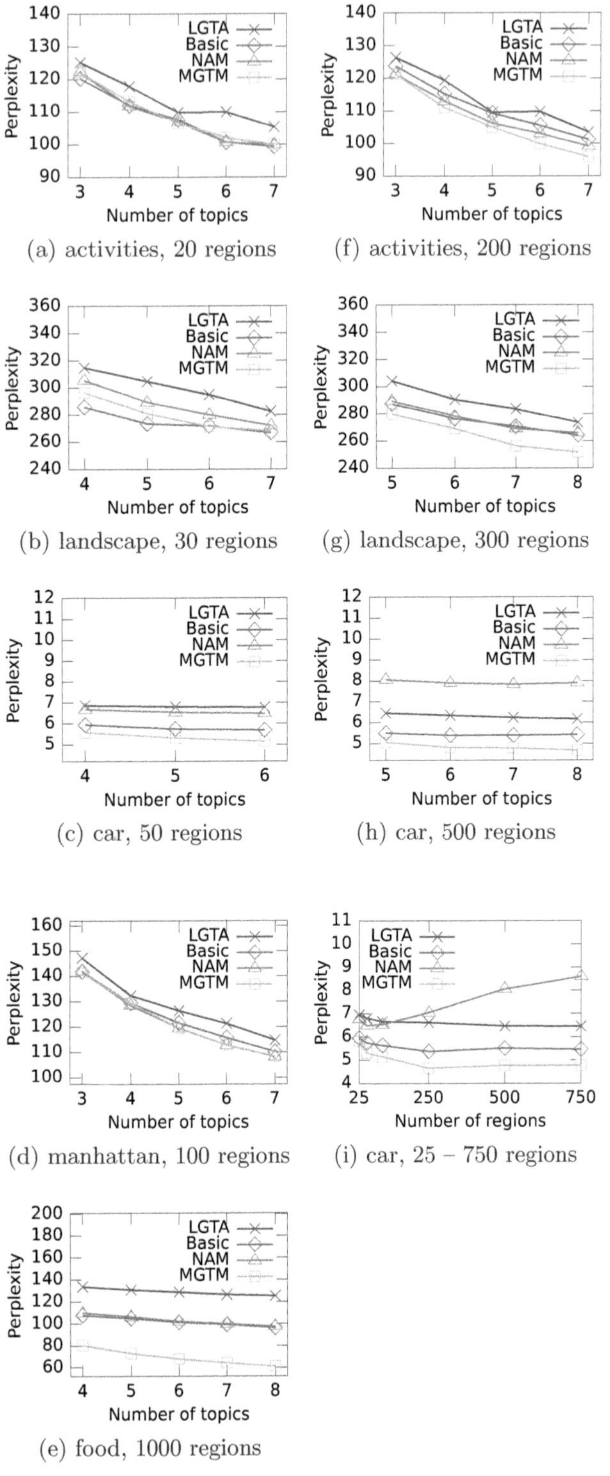


**Figure 4: Comparison of average word perplexity for LGTA, the basic model, NAM and MGTM for given topic and region counts. Lower values are better. The HDP-based models sample the number of topics, therefore the average perplexity is shown for topic counts that occur in at least 10 out of 100 runs for each method. For the car dataset, the perplexity at five topics is shown in (i) for growing numbers of regions.**

model creation. We observe that LGTA, the basic model and MGTM improve the topic quality for increased region parameters, but the improvement of MGTM is considerably larger than for LGTA and the basic model. The dynamic smoothing based on the MDP helps to improve the topic quality by exchanging topic information between similar adjacent clusters. In contrast, the perplexity of NAM dramatically gets worse for larger region counts due to the instability of the naive smoothing mechanism based on model selection.

## 4.5 User Study

A lower perplexity does not always indicate an improved topic quality [6]. Therefore we conducted a user study evaluating the semantic coherence of words within the topics detected by LGTA, the basic model, NAM and MGTM for the food dataset with 1000 regions at 4, 6 and 8 topics. Figure 3 shows the words with the highest probability for the topics detected by LGTA and MGTM at eight topics. Participants performed the "word intrusion" task introduced by Chang et al. [6]: For evaluating a topic, users are presented with a set of six words, which consists of the five words with the highest probability under the topic and a word from another topic from the same model. The user's task is to "find the word which does not fit with the other words". In case of semantically coherent topic words, the intruder can be easily found. To additionally test the interaction between topics, the intruding word was chosen from a set of words which had a low probability (not in the top 25 words) in the evaluated topic and a high probability (top 5 of the remaining words) in another topic. The study was conducted with 31 users which were presented with word sets in a random order of models and topics. Only one word set per model-topic combination was shown to the user and a total of 1,446 of word sets were rated.

In order to measure the quality of a model, we calculate an overall model precision (the percentage of intruders detected by participants) and per-topic precisions within a given model.

Table 4 shows the average precision and the median of the per-topic precisions for all four models. Clearly, MGTM performs considerably better with both an average model precision and median model precision of around 0.8 compared to about 0.6 for LGTA. Only for the case of 4 topics, the neighbour-aware model shows a comparable precision. However, for 6 topics the precision is worse compared to LGTA and for 8 topics it is only slightly better. Similarly, the basic model is worse than LGTA for 4 topics and only slightly better for 6 and 8.

To analyse the distribution of the per-topic precision, the corresponding box-and-whisker plot for the case of 8 topics is given in Figure 5. Clearly, the quality of the topics de-

| | **4 topics** | | **6 topics** | | **8 topics** | |
|---|---|---|---|---|---|---|
| | avg / | median | avg / | median | avg / | median |
| **LGTA** | 0.67 | 0.64 | 0.57 | 0.57 | 0.60 | 0.58 |
| **Basic** | 0.45 | 0.57 | 0.63 | 0.61 | 0.64 | 0.58 |
| **NAM** | **0.79** | 0.75 | 0.51 | 0.48 | 0.64 | 0.60 |
| **MGTM** | **0.79** | **0.80** | **0.82** | **0.81** | **0.78** | **0.75** |

**Table 4: Model precision and median of per-topic precisions for LGTA, the basic model, NAM and MGTM on the food dataset with 1000 regions.**

| | Topic 1 | Topic 2 | Topic 3 | Topic 4 | Topic 5 | Topic 6 | Topic 7 | Topic 8 | Map of Topic 1 |
|---|---|---|---|---|---|---|---|---|---|
| LGTA | fish<br>seafood<br>rice<br>shrimp<br>crab<br>lobster<br>chicken | chocolate<br>cheese<br>bread<br>fish<br>wine<br>tapas<br>orange | japanese<br>sushi<br>ramen<br>fish<br>noodle<br>sashimi<br>noodles | vegetarian<br>vegan<br>chocolate<br>baking<br>bread<br>cheese<br>bacon | wine<br>italian<br>coffee<br>french<br>pizza<br>chocolate<br>bakery | chinese<br>chicken<br>noodles<br>soup<br>rice<br>vietnamese<br>dimsum | mexican<br>bbq<br>chicken<br>burger<br>sandwich<br>fries<br>hamburger | sushi<br>thai<br>korean<br>japanese<br>salmon<br>rice<br>tuna | 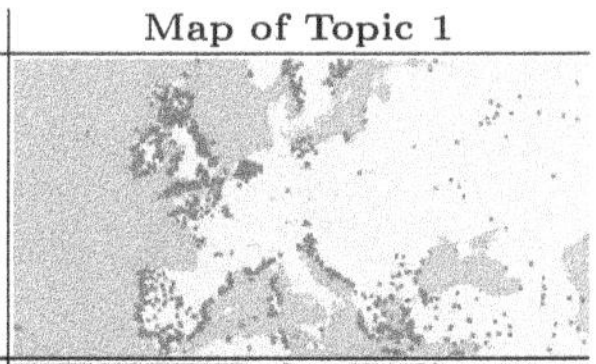 |
| MGTM | seafood<br>fish<br>lobster<br>shrimp<br>crab<br>wine<br>salmon | chocolate<br>icecream<br>strawberry<br>baking<br>cream<br>coffee<br>pie | japanese<br>sushi<br>fish<br>ramen<br>sashimi<br>rice<br>salmon | salad<br>cheese<br>tomato<br>bread<br>chicken<br>fish<br>vegetarian | wine<br>pizza<br>coffee<br>italian<br>pasta<br>cheese<br>french | chinese<br>thai<br>chicken<br>rice<br>soup<br>noodles<br>korean | mexican<br>tacos<br>taco<br>salsa<br>burrito<br>chicken<br>chips | bbq<br>burger<br>fries<br>hamburger<br>grill<br>chicken<br>sandwich |  |

**Table 3: Topic descriptions for the food dataset detected by LGTA and MGTM. The topics of MGTM were reordered to match the topics of LGTA. The maps show the positions of documents with an above average probability for Topic 1 as detected by LGTA (top) and MGTM (bottom).**

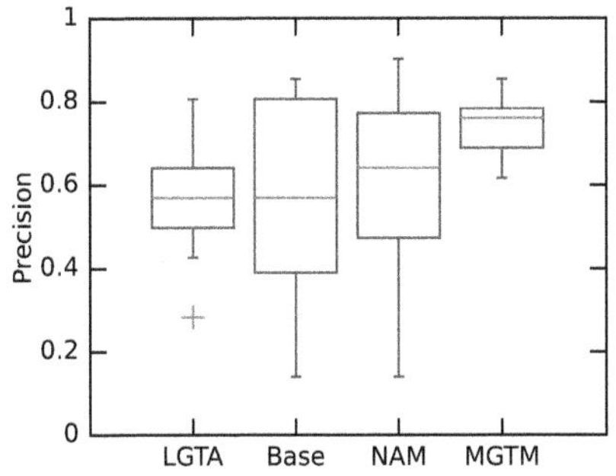


**Figure 5: Boxplots of model precision for LGTA, the basic model, NAM and MGTM on the food dataset with 1000 regions, 8 topics. Higher is better.**

tected by the basic model and NAM is mixed – the per-topic precision ranges from very low values of about 0.2 to high values greater than 0.8. The precision of LGTA is more consistent, as the topic precision is closer distributed around the median with only one outlier. Finally, the per-topic precision of MGTM is high for all topics and most homogeneous among all models.

The human evaluation supports the findings of the perplexity comparison – indeed, MGTM detects semantically more coherent topic-word distributions by exploiting the spatial structure of topics using dynamic smoothing. The differences between LGTA and MGTM can be explained by taking the topics from Table 3 as an example:

*Topic quality.* The key difference between LGTA and MGTM is the semantic coherence of the topic-word distributions. Topic 2 of LGTA assigns high probabilities to the terms *chocolate*, *cheese*, *bread* and *fish*. By contrast, the most similar topic of MGTM contains the semantically related words *chocolate*, *icecream*, *strawberry* and *baking* – all related to desserts. The incoherent word-selection of LGTA is due to the fact that these tags often occur within a small region and repetitions of similar word combinations in adjacent regions are not taken into account sufficiently.

*Globality.* The first topic from LGTA and the corresponding topic from MGTM mostly contain terms related to seafood. Clearly, the words *rice* and *chicken* from the seafood topic of LGTA do not fit – they often occur in Asia, where many photos of seafood are located. The seafood topic from MGTM is more coherent – it assigns a high probability to the word *wine*, as it is often consumed together with fish across Europe. From this example, we can see that the topics of LGTA are heavily influenced by local, region-specific patterns in tag co-occurrences whereas MGTM more is influenced by intra-document co-occurrences of tags and the global distribution of topics. The reason is that LGTA does not model document specific topic distributions, instead, all documents within a region share the same topic distribution and therefore individual deviations from the regional topics are not recognised in the model. In contrast, MGTM allows for document-specific topic distributions and permits deviations from the regional topic distribution. By detecting single documents fitting the topic of seafood in coastal regions all over the world, and by exchanging this topic information over the network of adjacent regions, a global topic of seafood is established.

*Support for non-compact topics.* Some of the topics detected in the food dataset are expected to exhibit a complex spatial distribution. As mentioned before, MGTM is able to detect such complex spatial structures. To give an example, the maps in Table 3 show the geographical distribution of documents with a higher-than-average probability for the seafood topic (Topic 1) as detected by LGTA and MGTM. We expect Topic 1 to have a distribution along coastlines. We see that this is the case for Topic 1 of both LGTA and MGTM, which covers both countries where fish is regularly eaten (such as the UK and the Netherlands) and countries where the seafood topic mainly appears at the coast (e.g. Spain, France). However, the geographical distribution of the seafood topic of LGTA has a large gap on the coast between Spain and France and is not detected in Denmark or on mainland Italy. The reason is that there are not many photos showing seafood in those areas and therefore the evidence is not sufficient for LGTA. Due to the dynamic smoothing of adjacent areas, MGTM still is able to detect such topics and thus correctly detects the seafood topic in documents along the whole coastline as seen on the map.

## 4.6 Runtime Comparison

Another advantage of the HDP-based models is the separation of geographical clustering and the topic sampling step. By excluding the distance calculation between every document and every region centre from the slowly converg-

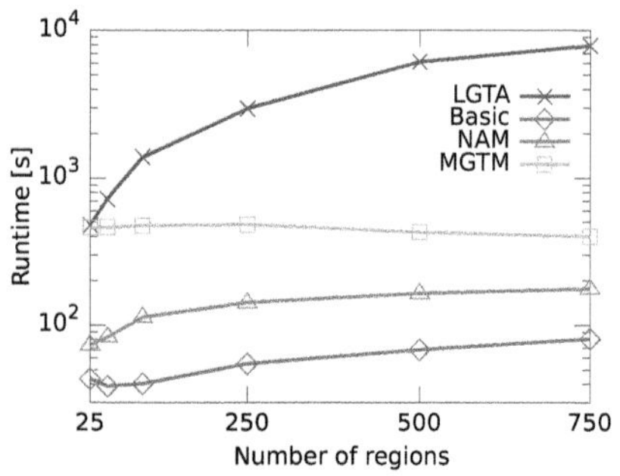


**Figure 6: Average runtimes (in seconds) of LGTA, the basic model, NAM and MGTM for the food dataset at growing numbers of regions. Note that the y-axis is a log scale.**

ing topic sampling process, we expect to dramatically decrease the runtime of our methods.

For comparing the runtime of the distinct methods, we optimised the implementation of LGTA provided by Yin and measured the runtime on the largest dataset for different settings of the region parameter on a 2.8GHz CPU with 72GB of RAM using a single core. The topic parameter of LGTA is set to 7. The runtime in seconds is given in Figure 6. We see that the runtime of LGTA linearly grows with a higher region count, as in every iteration every document has to be compared with every region for sampling its membership probability. On the other hand, the models presented in this paper use a separate geographical clustering step that can be efficiently implemented and takes only a fraction of the total runtime. The topic sampling is practically not influenced by the number of regions as it only creates additional region-specific topic distributions. MGTM shows a higher runtime compared to the basic model as the sampling of region-topic distributions in the multi-Dirichlet process is more expensive than in a normal hierarchical Dirichlet process. In return, for a larger number of regions, MGTM detects and merges topics with a coherent spatial distribution which results in a lower number of detected topics and a slightly decreased runtime. MGTM thus has a significantly reduced runtime and can be applied to much larger datasets.

Furthermore, it is straightforward to implement a distributed algorithm for MGTM as the distributed Gibbs sampling equations for hierarchical Dirichlet processes from [14] can be directly applied to multi-Dirichlet processes and region-specific topic distributions can be shared across processors with dependent document-topic distributions using the same technique as for sharing topics across processors.

# 5. CONCLUSION

The results from the user study and extensive quantitative evaluation of our model show a clear improvement in topic quality compared to state-of-the-art methods in topic modelling. MGTM detects more meaningful topics as measured by the perplexity and higher precisions in the user experiments. Additionally, the runtime analysis demonstrates that our method is highly efficient and thus suitable for large-scale applications. The model is the first to make use of adjacency relations between groups of documents for a dynamic smoothing of topic distributions. Our method is based on a multi-Dirichlet process (MDP), a generalisation of the Dirichlet process introduced in this paper. The improved performance of MGTM at higher numbers of regions shows that in real-world datasets, many geographical topics have a complex, non-Gaussian spatial distribution and that their detection can be supported. The presented topic model is just one example of how to use the MDP for dynamic smoothing. We currently are experimenting with integrating the MDP in other existing topic models to account for relations between groups of documents.

# 6. ACKNOWLEDGEMENTS

This work was supported by the EU 7th FP under grant number IST-FP7-288815 in project Live+Gov (liveandgov.eu)

# 7. REFERENCES


[1] A. Agovic and A. Banerjee. Gaussian process topic models. *CoRR*, abs/1203.3462, 2012.

[2] A. Ahmed, L. Hong, and A. Smola. Hierarchical geographical modeling of user locations from social media posts. In *WWW*, 2013.

[3] F. Aurenhammer. Voronoi diagrams – a survey of a fundamental geometric data structure. *ACM Comput. Surv.*, 23(3):345–405, 1991.

[4] A. Banerjee, I. S. Dhillon, J. Ghosh, and S. Sra. Clustering on the unit hypersphere using von Mises-Fisher distributions. *JMLR*, 6:1345–1382, 2005.

[5] D. M. Blei, A. Y. Ng, and M. I. Jordan. Latent Dirichlet allocation. *JMLR*, 3:993–1022, Mar. 2003.

[6] J. Boyd-Graber, J. Chang, S. Gerrish, C. Wang, and D. Blei. Reading tea leaves: How humans interpret topic models. In *NIPS*, 2009.

[7] K. R. Canini and T. L. Griffiths. A nonparametric Bayesian model of multi-level category learning. In *AAAI*, 2011.

[8] R. Dawkins. *The Selfish Gene*. OUP, 2006.

[9] R. Fisher. Dispersion on a sphere. *Royal Society*, 217(1130), 1953.

[10] T. Hofmann. Probabilistic latent semantic analysis. In *UAI*, pages 289–296, 1999.

[11] L. Hong, A. Ahmed, S. Gurumurthy, A. J. Smola, and K. Tsioutsiouliklis. Discovering geographical topics in the Twitter stream. In *WWW*, pages 769–778, 2012.

[12] Q. Mei, C. Liu, H. Su, and C. Zhai. A probabilistic approach to spatiotemporal theme pattern mining on weblogs. In *WWW*, pages 533–542, 2006.

[13] R. M. Neal. Markov chain sampling methods for Dirichlet process mixture models. *J. Comp. Graph. Stat.*, 9(2):249–265, 2000.

[14] D. Newman, A. U. Asuncion, P. Smyth, and M. Welling. Distributed algorithms for topic models. *JMLR*, 10:1801–1828, 2009.

[15] S. Sizov. GeoFolk: latent spatial semantics in Web 2.0 social media. In *WSDM*, pages 281–290, 2010.

[16] Y. Teh, M. Jordan, M. Beal, and D. Blei. Hierarchical Dirichlet processes. *JASA*, 2006.

[17] C. Wang, J. Wang, X. Xie, and W.-Y. Ma. Mining geographic knowledge using location aware topic model. In *GIR*, pages 65–70, 2007.

[18] Z. Yin, L. Cao, J. Han, C. Zhai, and T. S. Huang. Geographical topic discovery and comparison. In *WWW*, pages 247–256, 2011.

# Ranking in Heterogeneous Social Media

Min-Hsuan Tsai
Google
1600 Amphitheatre Pkwy
Mountain View, CA
mhtsai@google.com

Charu Aggarwal
IBM Research
1101 Kitchawan Road
Yorktown Heights, NY
charu@us.ibm.com

Thomas Huang
UIUC
2039 Beckman Institute
Urbana, Illinois
t-huang1@illinois.edu

## ABSTRACT

The problem of image search has been studied extensively in recent years because of the large and increasing repositories of images on the web, social media, and other linked networks. Most of the available techniques for keyword-based image search on the web use the text in the surrounding or linked text in order to retrieve related images.

Many image repositories on the web are built upon social media platforms such as *Flickr*. Such platforms provide a rich level of information in terms of the user linkage information to images, tags or other comments which are contributed by the users. It is reasonable to assume that the content of the images, users and other social cues such as tags and comments are often related to one another. Therefore, such cues can be useful for improving the effectiveness of search and ranking algorithms. In this paper, we propose *SocialRank*, which is a technique for using social hints in order to improve the image search and ranking process. Furthermore, we propose a holistic framework to combine social tags, social network text, linkage between actors and images, as well as the actual image features in order to create a ranking technique for image search. We design a *PageRank*-like method which can combine these different methods in order to provide an effective method for image search and ranking in social networks.

## Categories and Subject Descriptors

H.3.3 [**Information Storage and Retrieval**]: Information Search and Retrieval

## Keywords

heterogeneous network; random walk; image retrieval

## 1. INTRODUCTION

The problem of image search is an important one in the context of web and social network applications [1, 2]. The growing repository of images on the web, social networks such as *Facebook* and social media such as *Flickr* has created the need for effective methods for keyword-based search of such images. While the problem of ranking and searching large *text* collections has been studied extensively, the available solutions for keyword-based *image* search have remained relatively primitive. Typically, these methods make use of the limited knowledge of the surrounding text in order to provide query responses for a given set of keywords. These limitations are quite evident in a search engine such as *Google* in which the query results are sometimes unrelated to the keywords.

An important observation is that social networks have a rich level of information in terms of user linkages, user-to-image relationships, tags, comments, and descriptive text, which can be used in order to enhance the search process. In the context of a social network, the linkage relationships between social network actors and images may take on many different forms:

- The contribution of an image to a social network such as *Flickr* constitutes a linkage between that actor and that image.
- A comment, tag or "like" label by a user in any social network also constitutes a link between the user and the image.
- A friendship link between two users in a conventional social network such as *Facebook* may also be considered a link between the embedded images of the pages of the different users.
- The images in social networks may contain *content-based semantic links* (or *visual links*) between each other. This helps encode image similarity information into the search process.

Thus, a social network may also be considered a network of images, text, and users with heterogeneous links of different kinds between different nodes. In fact, such a network can be represented as a graph structure with nodes of different types and links representing the relationships between them. Since, the linkage information may represent user interest in images, and tags may represent image descriptions, the social network structure and content may contains rich information for improving the quality of the search process. In the traditional work on text-search in the IR-domain, such linkage information has often been leveraged in order to improve the quality of the underlying search in the context of the web. This is because similar documents are often


*WSDM'14*, February 24–28, 2014, New York, New York, USA.
Copyright 2014 ACM 978-1-4503-2351-2/14/02 ...$15.00.
http://dx.doi.org/10.1145/2556195.2556254 .

clustered together in the same network locality of most real linked entities such as the web. This class of problems is referred to as *keyword search in graphs* [10]. In the context of image data, the problem is much more complex, because of the greater heterogeneity of the problem in terms of linkage and content.

In this paper, we will use a more general approach to keyword search in graphs and allow the use of *image content information in addition to* social linkage information and the surrounding text, tags and comments for the search process. The goal of this work is to holistically use the social linkage structure with the *image and text content* of the social network.

The use of image content in the search process is still preliminary, but has seen some advances in recent years. For example, the work by [21] proposes a number of methods for using content information directly in the image retrieval process. The work in [15] uses ontological ranking, whereas the work by [4, 11] creates content-based linkages in order to provide visual cues during the search process. The content-based linkages are used in conjunction with the random surfer model of page-rank style algorithms in order to provide responses to queries. We note that since our model is general and uses a social network with heterogeneous linkages of different kinds, it is general enough to model the visual links within this framework.

Thus, the contributions of this work are as follows:

- We design an algorithm which uses the social network structure in addition to the keyword and text surrounding the image for ranking images with the use of a page-rank style algorithm. The algorithm is designed to work with and learn the importance of social links of different kinds for the ranking process. Furthermore, the surrounding or linked text of images is combined with the link structure during the ranking process using a personalized page-rank style method, so as to direct the ranking towards images which are related to the specified query-keywords.

- Since our approach is effective for ranking in networks which contain links of different kinds, it is easy to directly incorporate image content into the ranking process. Specifically, we use visual similarity between images as in [4, 11] in order to create links between images, and incorporate them into the ranking process. As in the previous case, the relative importance of different kinds of social links, keyword links and image content links is learned for the ranking process.

- One additional advantage of this approach is that it can also be used to improve the quality of retrieval in non-social scenarios by combining the effects of links of different kinds. In particular, this approach can also be used to improve the ranking quality to combining both image and keyword content effectively with the underlying network structure.

The remainder of the paper is organized as follows. In section 2, we provide a review of related work. Section 3 details a heterogeneous network model for the problem. The algorithmic design of the ranking algorithm is proposed in Section 4. The conclusions and summary are presented in section 6.

## 2. RELATED WORK

Content-based image retrieval has been a popular topic in recent years. Many of the earliest systems were developed for querying images with an image object [12, 13, 14] as the target. With the popularity of the web and related networks, keyword-based search has become increasingly relevant because of its natural semantic appeal, and the availability of surrounding text for web images. The focus of this paper is on keyword-based search, rather than image-based querying, though our ranking technique can be easily generalized to both scenarios because of its use of a heterogeneous network abstraction. Most keyword-based search methods rely purely on the use of surrounding text of the images in order to provide search results. On the other hand, for searching web-based *text* corpora, page-rank style methods are used quite often. In particular, even though *topic-sensitive* page rank methods [5, 6, 7, 9] have been used extensively in text search, their applicability has been rather limited [11] in the image domain. A natural technique for improving image ranking in the context of *network-based data* is to incorporate page-rank style random walk methods [3], which effectively combine the text, linkage structure, social cues, and image content in the search process.

Some recent work [11, 4, 15] designs methods for incorporating image features directly in the search process. The work in [15] uses content-based ontologies to improve image ranking, whereas that in [11, 4] uses *visual similarity links* between images in order to improve the ranking process. However, these techniques do not holistically use the text and image content along with network linkages in order to use all available information for ranking. The use of network linkage structure for improving the quality of retrieval has been well documented in text-based applications [10]. Nevertheless, this ability has continued to remain primitive in the context of network-based image retrieval applications. Furthermore, since many large network-based image collections are found in social media such as *Flickr*, it is also desirable to leverage this rich information in order to design an effective retrieval process. Sahbi and Audibert [23, 24] proposed to learn a network-dependent kernel or social network kernel (SNK) from the intrinsic image attributes and network linkage structure primarily for a single (image) domain, where both the target objects and the queried database correspond to images. In this paper we design a holistic framework to combine image and text content, and social and network linkage structure for effective image retrieval. We further note that our approach is not restricted to the social network scenario, but can be used for ranking in any heterogeneous network scenario containing a combination of different kinds of content and linkage information.

## 3. HETEROGENEOUS NETWORK MODEL

In this section, we define a heterogeneous network model for social media networks, which expressively utilizes multiple types of objects, linkages and their importance. We further note that the general principles of our approach can easily be extended to any kind of heterogeneous network, though the focus of this paper is on keyword-based image ranking in social networks.

Since the social network ranking process will use nodes with different kinds of data (text content, image content and users), we will first define a heterogeneous network model

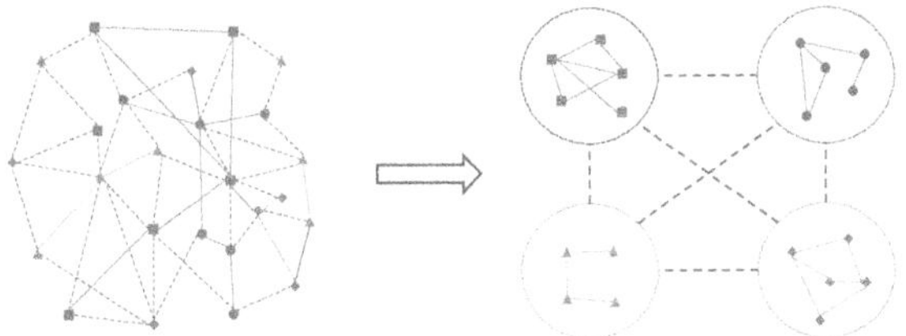

**Figure 1: Heterogeneous network can be decomposed into homogeneous sub-networks connected by heterogeneous links (dashed black lines).**

with different node *types*. We denote the set of types of nodes by $\mathcal{D}$ with the corresponding cardinality $|\mathcal{D}|$ denoted by $N$ ($N \geq 1$). We define a graph $G = \langle V, E, C \rangle$ with $N$ types of nodes in $V$, the edges (or relations) between the nodes denoted by $E$, and the content sets attached to the different nodes by $C$. We note that $C$ contains a data record for each node in $V$, which may be either text, image or a user identifier, depending upon the node type. We will see that the content plays a key role in defining the similarities and *implicit* links between nodes, which are helpful in the random walk-based ranking process. We refer to such a heterogeneous network of nodes, edges and weights as an information network. Note that a heterogeneous network has more than one type of node ($N \geq 2$), whereas a homogeneous network has only one type of node ($N = 1$).

In the case of heterogeneous networks, the graph $G$ can be decomposed into the $N$ homogeneous subgraphs $\{G^{T_i}\}_{i=1}^{N}$ whose nodes are of the same type and the inter-subgraph heterogeneous links $E^H$, as illustrated in Figure 1. Specifically, we can decompose the sets of nodes, links and the content of $G$ into the constituent homogeneous components and intra-component edges as follows:

$$V(G) = V(G^{T_1}) \cup V(G^{T_2}) \cup \ldots \cup V(G^{T_N})$$
$$E(G) = E(G^{T_1}) \cup E(G^{T_2}) \cup \ldots \cup E(G^{T_N}) \cup E^H$$
$$C(G) = C(G^{T_1}) \cup C(G^{T_2}) \cup \ldots \cup C(G^{T_N})$$

Here $E^H$ is the set of heterogeneous links between nodes from different subgraphs.

We can use the above model to decompose the heterogeneous network problem into several homogeneous network problems and solve them, as long as we are careful to propagate information between the different subgraphs. We will show that it is possible to achieve this with the use of linkage information between different domains, and an iterative ranking-based information which can effectively leverage the content and linkage information across different domains.

Next, we discuss the instantiation of this general heterogeneous information network model to the problem of of image ranking in social networks. Such social media networks can be modeled with three types of nodes, which correspond to *actor nodes*, *text nodes* and *image nodes*. These different kinds of nodes are connected by links of different kinds. We describe the different kinds of nodes and links below.

- The most basic kind of node in a social media application is an *actor* node. This could correspond to an user who may either contribute, comment on, or tag the images in the network, or to a user group whose members share the same interests toward some kinds of images. Such an actor may be linked to either text nodes corresponding to their comments, tags, wall posts, or to image nodes depending upon their image contributions, or sharing behavior. The different kinds of links may refer to the relationship between the actor and the underlying text. The actors may also be directly connected to one another with the use of friendship or membership links.
- The image nodes represent the set of images in the social network which we would like to search. Such images are linked to the nodes corresponding to their surrounding text, the tags or comments by users, and wall posts depending upon the association between the underlying text and the image. The image nodes are also linked to the actors based on contribution, or sharing behavior of likeability flags. Furthermore, in order to incorporate the effect of *content-based* similarity, images may also be linked to one another based on a measure of visual similarity.
- The text nodes represent the copious amount of text available in any social or web network. Traditionally, the text content of web networks are the key factor which are used for image search. For example, search engines such as Google use *only* the surrounding text of an image for the ranking process. In this model, the text nodes may be connected to either actor nodes or image nodes. For example, a comment by a user on an image could be considered a text node which links to both that user and the corresponding image. The traditional linkage of an image with its surrounding text or linked text is also captured by this model.

We note that different social networks can be modeled in different ways depending upon the nature of the interconnectedness between the actors, the text content and the images. Nevertheless, most social networks can be modeled with these three kinds of nodes and links of different kinds. This model is quite general and expressive in capturing social linkages, image content linkages as well as the text-to-image relationships. The key is to be able to combine them in a *directed* page-rank style algorithm which can learn the semantic importance of different kinds of linkages and leverage them for the retrieval process.

# 4. THE SOCIALRANK ALGORITHM

In this section we design an effective algorithm named *SocialRank* to incorporate social, text and image content in the ranking process. In order to achieve this goal, we design an approach, which is based on random walks on our heterogeneous network model of images, text content and users. We use both the explicit links between different domains, as well as the similarities between nodes in order to design an effective ranking method. For convenience, we will denote the set of node types by $\mathcal{D} = \{\mathsf{T}, \mathsf{I}, \mathsf{A}\}$, corresponding to to the text nodes ($v^{\mathsf{T}}$), image nodes ($v^{\mathsf{I}}$), and actor nodes ($v^{\mathsf{A}}$) respectively. While these three types suffice to expressively represent most social media networks, we note that our general heterogeneous network model can handle a wide variety of more general scenarios as well. In order to effectively rank the nodes, we introduce a measure $r_v$ for node $v$, which indicates its *relevance importance*. This is essentially the long term probability of our biased random walk to visit node $v$, and therefore provides the actual measure which is used in the ranking process. Furthermore, we use $S_{ij}^h$ to denote the similarity between node $v_i^h$ and $v_j^h$ in domain $h$, i.e., $S_{ij}^h = sim(c_i^h, c_j^h)$, with $c_i^h$ and $c_j^h$ being the content of node $v_i^h$ and $v_j^h$ respectively. This similarity is very important in regulating the random walk between nodes, because our random walk process directly encodes these similarity values. In our application, the value of $h$ is an alphanumeric superscript drawn from $\mathcal{D} = \{\mathsf{T}, \mathsf{I}, \mathsf{A}\}$, depending upon whether we are working with text, image, or actor nodes. The similarity measure $sim : \langle C, C \rangle \rightarrow [0, 1]$ may be chosen differently depending upon the domain at hand, as long as it is nonnegative and normalized in the range $[0, 1]$ such that the pair of nodes with a higher value is more similar either in a visual or semantic sense. For the particular case of our application, we defined the similarities for the different domains as follows:

- **Image Domain:** We use visual similarity as the similarity measure between image nodes. Specifically, we first quantize SIFT descriptors into visual words with the code-books built by hierarchical clustering of randomly selected descriptors from the whole image collection. The obtained image representation is typically a sparse vector and allows the use of the inverted index to accelerate the computation of the similarity scores. In particular, we use cosine similarity with three kinds of weighting for each visual word in this paper, namely (1) number of co-occurrence term (COT); (2) term frequency (TF); and (3) term frequency - inverse document frequency (TF-IDF). For two images $v_i^{\mathsf{I}}$ and $v_j^{\mathsf{I}}$ with $\mathbf{w}_i$ and $\mathbf{w}_j$ as the visual word frequency column vector, the similarity score between them is defined as follows:

  1. number of co-occurrence term (COT):
  $$S_{ij}^{\mathsf{I}} = \frac{\langle \delta(\mathbf{w}_i), \delta(\mathbf{w}_j) \rangle}{\|\delta(\mathbf{w}_i)\| \|\delta(\mathbf{w}_j)\|} \quad (1)$$
  where $\delta(\cdot)$ is an element-wise Heaviside step function and $\langle \cdot, \cdot \rangle$ being the standard Hermitian inner product.
  2. term frequency (TF):
  $$S_{ij}^{\mathsf{I}} = \frac{\langle \mathbf{w}_i, \mathbf{w}_j \rangle}{\|\mathbf{w}_i\| \|\mathbf{w}_j\|} \quad (2)$$
  3. term frequency - inverse document frequency (TF-IDF):
  $$S_{ij}^{\mathsf{I}} = \frac{\langle \mathbf{w}_i, \mathbf{w}_j \rangle_K}{\|K^{1/2}\mathbf{w}_i\| \|K^{1/2}\mathbf{w}_j\|} \quad (3)$$
  where $K$ is a diagonal matrix whose elements are the inverse document frequency weight for each visual word, given by $K_{ii} = (\log \frac{\texttt{\# documents}}{\texttt{\# doc containing word } i})^2$. And $\langle \cdot, \cdot \rangle_K$ is the Hermitian inner product characterized by the Hermitian matrix $K$.

  We will use all three of the above measures in our experimental results in order to show the effect of using different similarity measures.

- **Text Domain:** We use the normalized proportion of co-occurring words as the similarity measure in the text domain. In particular, for two text node $v_i^{\mathsf{T}}$ and $v_j^{\mathsf{T}}$ with the word frequency represented content $c_i$ and $c_j$, we have
$$S_{ij}^{\mathsf{T}} = \frac{\langle \delta(c_i), \delta(c_j) \rangle}{\|\delta(c_i)\| \|\delta(c_j)\|} \quad (4)$$
where the numerator is the number of matched words between the two texts.

- **Actor (Social) Domain:** In this case, we made the simplifying assumption that the similarity between different user groups are 0 and the self similarity is 1. That is, $S^{\mathsf{A}} = I$. This is because the actor nodes do not use any attribute-specific image content.

**Figure 2: Similarity by matching visual words.**

## 4.1 Hints from heterogeneous domains

The motivation of the proposed approach is to use the hints from other heterogeneous domains to improve the inference process during query processing. For a given query, the nodes in each of the domains can be ranked independently with a personalized-page rank style algorithm. For example, *VisualRank* [11] uses only visual content to rank the images. However, external knowledge has been shown to be very useful in recent research for a variety of mining tasks. For instance, transferring text domain knowledge from community annotated tags has demonstrated good improvement in [22], even when the tags are sometimes noisy. Besides the text domain, social linkages (which may represent user actions) are also very good knowledge sources for bridging the semantic gap by transferring the high level perception of the users into the ranking process. One example of such a phenomenon is that images favored by the same photo sharing group usually share similar visual content and perception of the underlying users.

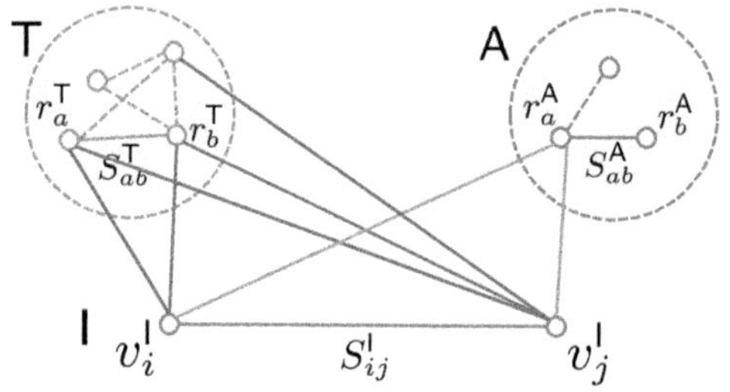


**Figure 3: Hints from heterogeneous nodes.**

While it is possible to directly use the content-based similarity value $S_{ij}^h$ in order to influence the random walk, this does not incorporate a lot of information which is available in the linkages of the images to the text and actor nodes, as well as the linkages between those nodes themselves. In order to further incorporate this information into the random walk framework, we introduce an augmented similarity value $\tilde{S}_{ij}^h$ between the different objects, which take such linkages into account. The augmented similarity is based on the idea from *SimRank* [17] that two objects are similar if they are related to similar objects. However, different from *SimRank*, the augmented similarity also considers the relevance importance of each object to the query in order to further affect the similarity function (and therefore influence the random walk). This augmented similarity value is a function of the similarity values and node relevance importance values in the other two domains. For example, Figure 3 provides an illustration in which $v_i^{\mathsf{I}}$ and $v_j^{\mathsf{I}}$ are nodes in the image domain, and their visual similarity is $S_{ij}^{\mathsf{I}}$. In such a case, the augmented similarity value $\tilde{S}_{ij}^I$ is expressed as a function $f(S_{ij}^{\mathsf{I}}, S^{\mathsf{A}}, r^{\mathsf{A}}, S^{\mathsf{T}}, r^{\mathsf{T}})$ of the original content-based similarity and the relevant parameters in the other two domains. Specifically, it is defined as follows:

$$\begin{aligned}\tilde{S}_{ij}^{\mathsf{I}} &= f(S_{ij}^{\mathsf{I}}, S^{\mathsf{A}}, r^{\mathsf{A}}, S^{\mathsf{T}}, r^{\mathsf{T}}) \\ &= S_{ij}^{\mathsf{I}} + \sum_{h\in\{\mathsf{T},\mathsf{A}\}} \beta^h \left( \sum_{a\in V_i^h, b\in V_j^h} S_{ab}^h r_a^h r_b^h \right) \end{aligned} \tag{5}$$

$V_i^h$ and $V_j^h$ are the sets of nodes in domain $h$ that have a link to nodes $v_i^{\mathsf{I}}$ and $v_j^{\mathsf{I}}$ respectively. In particular, $V_i^h = \{v | v \in V^h, (i, v) \in E^{\mathsf{I}h}\}$. $\beta^h$ are weighting parameters for each heterogeneous domain. One can generalize Eq. (5) to other (text and actor) domains as well and write the equation generally in matrix form as follows:

$$\tilde{S}^d = S^d + \sum_{h\in\mathcal{D}-\{d\}} \beta^h L^{dh} R^h S^h R^h L^{dh'} \tag{6}$$

Here $L^{dh}$ is the link map between domain $d$ and $h$ whose entry $L_{ij}^{dh}$ is 1 if node $i$ is connected to node $j$, otherwise it is 0. $R^h$ is a diagonal matrix where $R_{ii}^h = r_i^h$.

This approach provides different levels of importance to different nodes (and the incident links) in the similarity function, because they are not of equal relevance to the query. Thus, the above augmented similarity function considers not only the link structures between domains but also takes into account the relevance of the nodes such that two images, which are both linked to a more important node would have higher similarity than a pair which are linked with a less important node. Since the random walk equations will be set up with the use of this similarity matrix, this also has a direct bearing on the query results.

After the augmented similarity matrix for each domain is constructed, we use a separate random walk process for each domain in order to determine the relevance scores of the nodes. As we will see later, the separate random walk processes for the different domains will be connected to one another by re-computation of the similarity matrices with the use of inter-domain linkages in an iterative way. The re-start probability of the random walk process is denoted by $\alpha$. The probability vector $p$ is the restart vector. As we will discuss later, the value of $p$ is biased by the query. The relevance score at iteration is $t$ is denoted by $r^{(t)}$, and is determined with the use of page rank equations that are biased by the underlying similarity matrix $\tilde{S}^d$:

**Algorithm 1** SocialRank with heterogeneous random walk

**input** similarity matrices $S^d$ for each domain $d \in \mathcal{D}$, heterogeneous domain link $E^H$, parameters $\alpha, \beta$
1. Initialize bias vector $p$ by Eq. (8) or (9) and relevance score vector $r^{(0)} = [\frac{1}{N}]_{N\times 1}$
2. Set $t = 1$
**repeat**
  **for** each homogeneous sub-network $h$ **do**
3. Construct augmented similarity matrix $\tilde{S}^h$ by Eq. (6) with $\tilde{S}^{d,(t-1)}$ and $r^{d,(t-1)}$, $d \in \mathcal{D} - \{h\}$
4. Apply random walk (7) to obtain relevance score vector $r^{h,(t)}$
  **end for**
5. $t = t + 1$
**until** Convergence on $r^d$ or maximum iteration number achieves.
**output** relevance score vector $r^d$ for each domain

$$r^{(t)} = \alpha \tilde{S}^h D^{-1} r^{(t-1)} + (1 - \alpha)p \tag{7}$$

Here, $D$ is a diagonal matrix whose $i$-th diagonal entry equals to the sum of the $i$-th row of $\tilde{S}^h$. As we will see later, the bias vectors play an important role in making the random walk process query-sensitive. We note that the relevance scores are a function of the similarity in the page rank equations (Equation (7)), whereas the similarity values were determined as a function of the relevance scores (and the hints from other domains) in Equation (5). This suggests an iterative approach for computing both from each other, as discussed below.

The pseudo-code of the *SocialRank* algorithm is provided in Algorithm 1. A biased re-start vector is used in the text domain order to encode the query into the ranking process. Specifically, the random walks in the text domain use a bias vector based on the query keywords. The algorithm performs random walks separately in each homogeneous subnetwork. However, the random walks in each subnetwork are regulated by the similarity matrix as indicated in Equation (7). Since the similarity values are computed on the basis of the social cues from heterogeneous domains (based on Equation (5)), this ensures that social cues are passed from one domain to the other during the ranking process. At the same time, we re-compute the similarities between nodes in each iteration with the use of the relevance scores generated in the last iteration as indicated in Equation (5). Thus, the similarity values between nodes and the relevance importance values are inter-dependent upon one another in an iterative way. These steps are repeated until the different variables (node similarity scores and node relevance importance values) have converged. The node relevance importance values provide the ranking output for the algorithm.

## 4.2 Picking the Query-Bias Vector

The bias vector [7] is used to make the proposed *SocialRank* algorithm query-sensitive. For given query keywords

$Q$, we defined the query-bias vector $p$ in the text domain $\mathsf{T}$ with $n$ nodes $(v_1^\mathsf{T}, v_2^\mathsf{T}, \ldots, v_n^\mathsf{T})$ and their corresponding content $(c_1^\mathsf{T}, c_2^\mathsf{T}, \ldots, c_n^\mathsf{T})$ as follows:

$$p_{v_i}^\mathsf{T} = g\left(\sum_{q_j \in Q} sim(q_j, c_i^\mathsf{T})\right) \tag{8}$$

The notation $g$ represents a normalization function, which is used to ensure that the elements of the probability vector $p$ sum to 1. Here $sim(q_j, c_i^\mathsf{T})$ is the semantic similarity between the $j$-th query keyword and the text node $v_i^\mathsf{T}$ which can be WordNet similarity [19], normalized Google distance [20] or simply the 0/1 match indicator. We adopt the binary match indicator in the experiments of this paper for its simplicity.

With the bias vector, we note that the proposed *SocialRank* algorithm will not only work with the keyword type of query, but can also be used with image queries. In order to enable query by images, one needs to start the *SocialRank* algorithm with random walks in the image domain and initialize the bias vector with the visual similarities between the query images and the database images. More specifically, we set the bias vector for query by images as follows:

$$p_i^\mathsf{I} = g\left(sim(q, c_i^\mathsf{I})\right) \tag{9}$$

This general principle applies to any kind of object query in a generic heterogeneous network model. The main difference is that *one needs to define a bias vector for the appropriate node type*, just as we defined one for the case of text nodes for keyword-based search. This makes the *SocialRank* algorithm much more general in its ability to handle queries and networks of different types. For example, one can use the approach to do group recommendation or image annotation for a given query image. Thus, this approach can be used in a wide variety of heterogeneous web-based scenarios in which it is possible to query and process objects of different types.

## 4.3 Convergence of SocialRank Algorithm

Next, we will show the convergence of the *SocialRank* algorithm, which uses iterative re-computation of the parameters across different homogeneous subnetworks. For simplicity, we use the case where the heterogeneous network $G$ has only two homogeneous sub-networks, $G_1$ and $G_2$. The steps of the proof can be easily generalized to the case where there are more than two sub-networks.

Before we start the proof, it is worth noting that the augmented similarity described in section 4.1 can be employed using a biased restart vector in the random walk, rather than adjusting transition probability mentioned in section 4.1. Indeed, these two approaches to exploit the hints from heterogeneous domains are equivalent and interchangeable since by letting $\hat{p} = \frac{\alpha}{1-\alpha}\hat{S}D^{-1}r^{(t-1)}$ for given $r^{(t-1)}$ we have

$$\begin{aligned} r^{(t)} &= \alpha(S + \hat{S})D^{-1}r^{(t-1)} + (1-\alpha)p \\ &= \alpha S D^{-1} r^{(t-1)} + \alpha\hat{S}D^{-1}r^{(t-1)} + (1-\alpha)p \\ &= \alpha S D^{-1} r^{(t-1)} + (1-\alpha)(p + \hat{p}) \end{aligned}$$

Now consider the random walks on $G_1$ with a stochastic matrix $\mathbf{M}_{11}$. When we choose the damping vector to be $\mathbf{p}_1 + \frac{\alpha}{1-\alpha}\mathbf{B}_{12}\bar{\mathbf{r}}_2$, the update formula for $\mathbf{r}_1$ is as follows:

$$\mathbf{r}_1 = \alpha\mathbf{M}_{11}\mathbf{r}_1 + ((1-\alpha)\mathbf{p}_1 + \alpha\mathbf{B}_{12}\bar{\mathbf{r}}_2) \tag{10}$$

The unique solution to (10) can be obtained in the form of the following expression:

$$\hat{\mathbf{r}}_1 = (I - \alpha\mathbf{M}_{11})^{-1}((1-\alpha)\mathbf{p}_1 + \alpha\mathbf{B}_{12}\bar{\mathbf{r}}_2) \tag{11}$$

Similarly, the unique equilibrium state of the random walks on $G_2$ for a given vector $\mathbf{p}_2 + \frac{\alpha}{1-\alpha}\mathbf{B}_{21}\bar{\mathbf{r}}_1$ is as follows:

$$\hat{\mathbf{r}}_2 = (I - \alpha\mathbf{M}_{22})^{-1}((1-\alpha)\mathbf{p}_2 + \alpha\mathbf{B}_{21}\bar{\mathbf{r}}_1) \tag{12}$$

As in the *SocialRank* algorithm, we iteratively solve for the equilibrium vectors of each homogeneous subgraph. The equations (11) and (12) can be written with a superscript $t$ to indicate the iteration. Also, we denote $\bar{\mathbf{r}}$ to be the equilibrium vectors from previous iteration $\hat{\mathbf{r}}^{(t-1)}$. Therefore Equations (11) and (12) can be re-written as follows:

$$\hat{\mathbf{r}}_1^{(t)} = (I - \alpha\mathbf{M}_{11})^{-1}\left(\alpha\mathbf{B}_{12}\hat{\mathbf{r}}_2^{(t-1)} + (1-\alpha)\bar{\mathbf{p}}_1\right) \tag{13}$$

$$\hat{\mathbf{r}}_2^{(t)} = (I - \alpha\mathbf{M}_{22})^{-1}\left(\alpha\mathbf{B}_{21}\hat{\mathbf{r}}_1^{(t-1)} + (1-\alpha)\bar{\mathbf{p}}_2\right) \tag{14}$$

From (14) we can obtain $\hat{\mathbf{r}}_2^{(t-1)}$ and substitute it into (13) to get the following:

$$\begin{aligned} \hat{\mathbf{r}}_1^{(t)} &= \alpha^2(I - \alpha\mathbf{M}_{11})^{-1}\mathbf{B}_{12}(I - \alpha\mathbf{M}_{22})^{-1}\mathbf{B}_{21}\hat{\mathbf{r}}_1^{(t-2)} + \\ &(1-\alpha)(I - \alpha\mathbf{M}_{11})^{-1}\left(\mathbf{p}_1 + \alpha\mathbf{B}_{12}(I - \alpha\mathbf{M}_{22})^{-1}\mathbf{p}_2\right) \end{aligned} \tag{15}$$

From the above power iteration (15) we can see that the *SocialRank* algorithm will converge to a unique solution for $G_1$ due to the irreducibility of $\mathbf{M}_{11}$. This follows the assumption that $G_1$ is strongly connected.

To see this, we choose $\mathbf{p}_1 = \frac{1}{N}\mathbf{1} = [\frac{1}{N}]_{N\times 1}$ (for ease of illustration only, $\mathbf{p}_1$ can be any positive vector, i.e., all the elements in $\mathbf{p}_1$ are all positive) and reorganize (15) as

$$\begin{aligned} \hat{\mathbf{r}}_1^{(t)} &= (I - \alpha\mathbf{M}_{11})^{-1}\left(\alpha^2\mathbf{A}\hat{\mathbf{r}}_1^{(t-2)} + (1-\alpha)\mathbf{p}_1\right) + \alpha(1-\alpha)\mathbf{b} \\ &= (I - \alpha\mathbf{M}_{11})^{-1}\left(\alpha^2\mathbf{A} + \frac{1-\alpha}{N}\mathbf{1}\mathbf{1}^\mathsf{T}\right)\hat{\mathbf{r}}_1^{(t-2)} + \alpha(1-\alpha)\mathbf{b} \end{aligned} \tag{16}$$

where

$$\begin{aligned} \mathbf{A} &= \mathbf{B}_{12}(I - \alpha\mathbf{M}_{22})^{-1}\mathbf{B}_{21} \\ \mathbf{b} &= (I - \alpha\mathbf{M}_{11})^{-1}\mathbf{B}_{12}(I - \alpha\mathbf{M}_{22})^{-1}\mathbf{p}_2 \end{aligned}$$

Note that the matrix $(I - \alpha\mathbf{M}_{11})^{-1}\{\alpha^2\mathbf{A} + \frac{1-\alpha}{N}\mathbf{1}\mathbf{1}^\mathsf{T}\}$ is irreducible as $\mathbf{M}_{11}$ and $\mathbf{1}\mathbf{1}^\mathsf{T}$ are irreducible and $\mathbf{A}$ is nonnegative. Hence the convergence of *SocialRank* to a unique solution is guaranteed.

To obtain the equilibrium vector of (15), we rearrange it as follows:

$$\begin{aligned} (I - \alpha\mathbf{M}_{11})\hat{\mathbf{r}}_1^{(t)} &= \alpha^2\mathbf{B}_{12}(I - \alpha\mathbf{M}_{22})^{-1}\mathbf{B}_{21}\hat{\mathbf{r}}_1^{(t-2)} + \\ &(1-\alpha)\left(\mathbf{p}_1 + \alpha\mathbf{B}_{12}(I - \alpha\mathbf{M}_{22})^{-1}\mathbf{p}_2\right) \end{aligned} \tag{17}$$

When (17) reaches the equilibrium state, meaning $\hat{\mathbf{r}}_1^{(t)} = \hat{\mathbf{r}}_1^{(t-2)} = \hat{\mathbf{r}}_1^*$, we will have the following:

$$\begin{aligned} \left(I - \alpha\mathbf{M}_{11} - \alpha^2\mathbf{B}_{12}(I - \alpha\mathbf{M}_{22})^{-1}\mathbf{B}_{21}\right)\hat{\mathbf{r}}_1^* &= \\ (1-\alpha)\left(\mathbf{p}_1 + \alpha\mathbf{B}_{12}(I - \alpha\mathbf{M}_{22})^{-1}\mathbf{p}_2\right) \end{aligned} \tag{18}$$

This provides the following solution:

$$\hat{\mathbf{r}}_1^* = (1-\alpha)(I - \alpha\bar{\mathbf{M}}_{11})^{-1}\bar{\mathbf{p}}_1 \tag{19}$$

The variables on the RHS in the above equation are defined as follows:

$$\bar{\mathbf{M}}_{11} = \mathbf{M}_{11} + \alpha\mathbf{B}_{12}(I - \alpha\mathbf{M}_{22})^{-1}\mathbf{B}_{21} \quad (20)$$
$$\bar{\mathbf{p}}_1 = \mathbf{p}_1 + \alpha\mathbf{B}_{12}(I - \alpha\mathbf{M}_{22})^{-1}\mathbf{p}_2$$

# 5. EXPERIMENTAL RESULTS

We evaluated the *SocialRank* algorithm, on a number of tasks which are either directly or indirected related to the quality of the ranking process. We first describe the data sets.

## 5.1 Dataset

We evaluated the *SocialRank* algorithm with the use of images from the well known social media site known as *Flickr*. We crawled the *Flickr* site, and constructed the *Flickrgroup* dataset which includes images from 140 selected user groups in *Flickr*. The groups in *Flickr* are communities with people who have the same interests toward a target subject. The group members typically favor photos which are closely related to the target subject. A user group may favor hundreds to thousands of images favored. On the other hand, there are some groups having similar interests. Therefore, the same image may be favored by multiple user groups. The *Flickrgroup* dataset contained around 118,000 images in total, along with more than 150,000 unique tags associated with these images. We employed stop-word removal and stemming, and then selected the top 5,000 most frequent ones as the codebook tags.

For the image representation, we adopt a hierarchical vocabulary tree as the codebook to encode each image into a bag-of-words histogram. Specifically, all the images are first resized to maximum 500 × 500. Then we use David Lowe's SIFT binary[1] to extract 128-D SIFT keypoint descriptors for each image, where each descriptor is then quantized into a million of visual words with a $10^6$ hierarchical vocabulary tree (6 layers and branch factor 10, trained by 20 million randomly selected SIFT descriptors). The final image representation is a sparse $10^6$-D vector. Due to its sparsity, the storage requirement for the representation as well as the time complexity for computing similarities between images is quite modest. Moreover, the tree structured codebook made it very suitable for building inverted index files. These files were need to compute the underlying similarities between the objects.

We evaluated the proposed algorithm on three social media related tasks, corresponding to image ranking, group ranking and group recommendation.

Throughout the experiments, we set the parameters as follows:

1. the damping factor in Equation (7):
$$\alpha = 0.85 \quad (21)$$
2. the weighting parameters for each domin in Equation (6):
$$\beta^h = \gamma \cdot \max(S^d) \quad (22)$$
where $\max(S^d)$ is the maximum entry in $S^d$ and $\gamma$ is a scalar between 0 and 1, which is set to 0.5 if not mentioned.

[1]`http://www.cs.ubc.ca/~lowe/keypoints/`

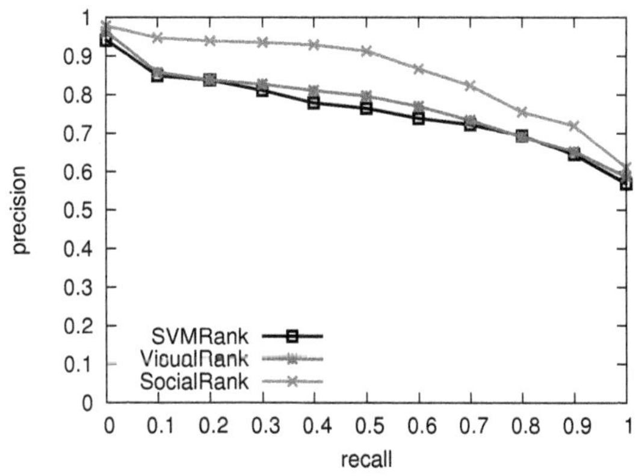


**Figure 4: Interpolated precision-recall curve on the Flickgroup dataset. The TF-IDF weighting scheme is used for similarity metric.**

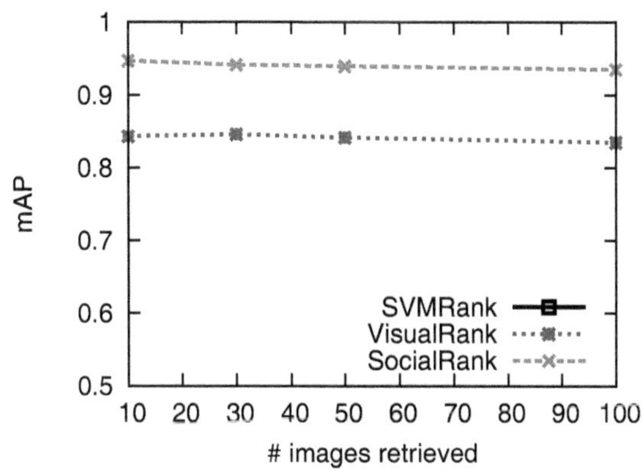


**Figure 5: Image ranking performance (mean average precision) with various number of images retrieved. TF-IDF weighting scheme is used.**

## 5.2 Image Ranking

We compare the proposed *SocialRank* algorithm with *SVMRank* [16] and *VisualRank* [11] with the standard performance metrics for information retrieval, i.e., average precision (AP). The comparison is built upon ten queries on the *Flickrgroup* dataset. We use the default linear kernel function and set the trade-off parameter for *SVMRank* as $C = 50$. The damping factor for *VisualRank* is set as $\alpha = 0.85$.

Table 1 shows the average precision of top 100 returned images (AP@100) for each query, where the proposed method demonstrates an impressive improvement over the other methods with the aid of social hints. It is interesting to note that *SVMRank* is quite sensitive to the similarity measures whereas the graph-based algorithms *VisualRank* and the proposed *SocialRank* show consistent performance with different similarity metrics. The main reason behind this would be that *SVMRank* considers only the similarities between training and testing samples while graph-based *VisualRank* and *SocialRank* additionally considers the similarities between testing samples, which provides a more robust linkage structure of samples. This reflects the advantage of semi-

**Table 1: Image ranking performance (AP@100) on the *Flickrgroup* dataset. The one with best performance for each query is indicated by an oval box.**

| Query | *SVMRank* | | | *VisualRank* | | | *SocialRank* | | |
|---|---|---|---|---|---|---|---|---|---|
| | COT | TF | TF-IDF | COT | TF | TF-IDF | COT | TF | TF-IDF |
| balloon | 0.4896 | 0.7674 | 0.8676 | 0.8694 | 0.8606 | 0.8691 | 0.9593 | 0.9607 | 0.9605 |
| bird | 0.4621 | 0.6896 | 0.9031 | 0.9032 | 0.8744 | 0.8908 | 0.9847 | 0.9922 | 0.9900 |
| box | 0.7314 | 0.8905 | 0.9313 | 0.9276 | 0.9072 | 0.9062 | 0.9945 | 0.9944 | 0.9954 |
| car | 0.4679 | 0.6113 | 0.8382 | 0.8671 | 0.8609 | 0.8673 | 0.9872 | 0.9206 | 0.9155 |
| cat | 0.4390 | 0.5157 | 0.6226 | 0.6237 | 0.6517 | 0.6437 | 0.9854 | 0.9805 | 0.9818 |
| child | 0.7037 | 0.6723 | 0.8766 | 0.8739 | 0.8849 | 0.8754 | 0.9404 | 0.9405 | 0.9384 |
| flower | 0.6123 | 0.6997 | 0.7637 | 0.8046 | 0.7301 | 0.7546 | 0.9633 | 0.8119 | 0.9909 |
| guitar | 0.6048 | 0.7380 | 0.8021 | 0.8119 | 0.8047 | 0.8197 | 0.8328 | 0.8409 | 0.8333 |
| pumpkin | 0.7269 | 0.7416 | 0.7701 | 0.8027 | 0.7816 | 0.7816 | 0.7748 | 0.7748 | 0.7748 |
| waterfall | 0.8000 | 0.8321 | 0.8405 | 0.9389 | 0.9384 | 0.9401 | 0.9720 | 0.9707 | 0.9719 |
| average | 0.6037 | 0.7158 | 0.8215 | 0.8423 | 0.8294 | 0.8348 | 0.9394 | 0.9187 | 0.9352 |

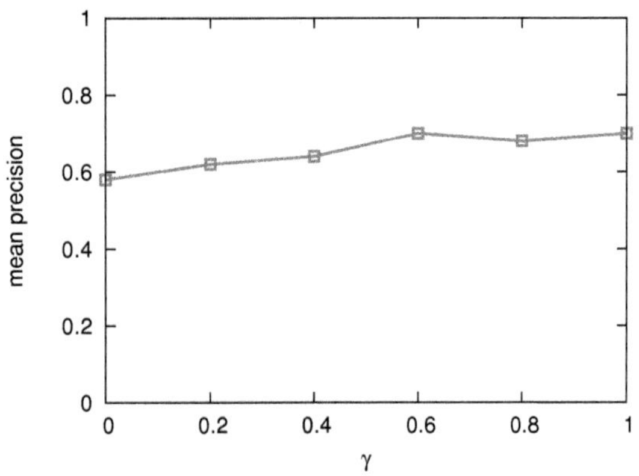


**Figure 6: Sensitivity of parameter $\gamma$ on the group ranking task.**

supervised learning over supervised learning when one has no good estimation on the distribution of samples.

Figure 4 illustrates the interpolated precision-recall curves with 500 images retrieved using the 11 cutoff recall values (i.e., the precision at a given recall level is obtained for each query, then an averaged precision over all queries is reported). This figure indicates that our proposed algorithm achieves best performance in all the recall ranges. We also varied the number of images retrieved by plotting the mean average precision (mAP) for the top 10, 30, 50, 100, 200 and 500 images in Figure 5. The mAP is calculated as an average of AP over the 10 queries obtained for each $N$. It is evident that the proposed *SocialRank* algorithm outperforms the other two methods at all level of images retrieved, with around 12% improvement.

## 5.3 Group Ranking

One of the biggest differences between traditional multimedia applications and social media applications is that the former is image-centric (or data-centric), whereas the latter is more human-centric (or actor-centric). In other words, from a social perspective, it is also relevant to search for users or groups who may be interested in particular keywords or images. One interesting aspect of the proposed *SocialRank* algorithm is that its seamless integration of different domains in the ranking process enables the search of objects of any type, including actors in social media. Indeed, the most relevant actors and images are simultaneously found by the *SocialRank* algorithm, with the use of inter-connected random walks in different domains.

Table 2 provides the top-5 results of group ranking from keyword-based queries performed for image ranking in section 5.2. The numbers in the parentheses are the relevance scores of the actor nodes in the ranking process. The groups in black color are considered the relevant groups (ground truth), based on the favored images for each group. The groups in red color are considered the irrelevant groups. The value of the precision with variation of the parameter $\gamma$ is illustrated in Figure 6. It is evident that the results are not too sensitive to the value of the parameter $\gamma$. The best overall precision over 10 queries is around 0.70 for the top 5 results, when the value of $\gamma$ was set to 0.6.

## 5.4 Group Recommendation

Recommendation is an important application in the context of a social media platform. On specific application in the context of an image sharing network such as *Flickr* is to recommend groups that may be interested in a newly shared image. Currently, such assignments are performed manually or are based on noisy tags [18]. However, none of these methods use the existing image collection of a group into account, which provide very useful hints in the commendation process. Therefore, we apply the *SocialRank* algorithm, by using a network model in which the actor nodes represent the different groups in the data. For each group, we compute a personalization vector which is proportional to the similarity between the query image and the representative images from each group. This is then used in conjunction with our ranking approach to determine the relevance scores of the group nodes. The titles of these group nodes are reported as the recommendations.

Table 3 demonstrates the group recommendation results. In each case, we have illustrated the query image, together with the titles of the group nodes which are recommended. The group names in blue are considered to be proper assignments while those in black are improper assignments.

**Table 2: Top-5 user groups ranking corresponding to queries: balloon, bird, car and flower.**

| | Balloon | Bird | Flower | Car |
|---|---|---|---|---|
| COT | Red Balloon (0.803) | Birds birds birds birds (0.502) | Flowers all kinds (0.412) | Autos (CARS) (0.668) |
| | Disney Balloons (0.032) | Birding In The Wild (0.046) | Painted Furniture (0.063) | Auto Ads (0.063) |
| | Balloons n Fireworks (0.023) | we love wildlife (0.041) | FLOWERS (0.050) | Auto Glamma (0.054) |
| | Painted Furniture (0.009) | Nature Anything Goes (0.022) | Flower Flower Flower (0.048) | Auto Shows (0.028) |
| | Party decorating ideas (0.008) | Painted Furniture (0.020) | Flowers Group (0.035) | Red Space (0.007) |
| TF | Red Balloon (0.749) | Birds birds birds birds (0.646) | Painted Furniture (0.135) | Auto Ads (0.382) |
| | Disney Balloons (0.051) | Birding In The Wild (0.025) | Flowers all kinds (0.127) | Autos (CARS) (0.334) |
| | Balloons n Fireworks (0.049) | we love wildlife (0.022) | FLOWERS (0.113) | Auto Glamma (0.109) |
| | Black 'n' Blue (0.014) | Nature Anything Goes (0.016) | Flower Flower Flower (0.109) | Auto Shows (0.017) |
| | UK night photography (0.010) | Painted Furniture (0.015) | Folk Music (0.033) | Red Space (0.005) |
| TF-IDF | Red Balloon (0.806) | Birds birds birds birds (0.635) | Flowers all kinds (0.319) | Auto Ads (0.313) |
| | Disney Balloons (0.027) | Birding In The Wild (0.026) | FLOWERS (0.222) | Autos (CARS) (0.289) |
| | Balloons n Fireworks (0.026) | we love wildlife (0.023) | Flower Flower Flower (0.156) | Auto Glamma (0.192) |
| | Black 'n' Blue (0.008) | Nature Anything Goes (0.016) | Painted Furniture (0.034) | Auto Shows (0.026) |
| | Painted Furniture (0.008) | Painted Furniture (0.014) | Flowers Group (0.017) | Red Space (0.007) |

**Table 3: Top group recommendations corresponding to image queries. The group names in blue are considered to be proper assignments while those in black are improper assignments.**

| | | | |
|---|---|---|---|
|  |  |  |  |
| Snow Leopards (0.011)<br>1st Nature n Wildlife... (0.010)<br>Natures waterfall (0.009)<br>Flower Flower Flower (0.009)<br>we love wildlife (0.009)<br>Pet Portraits (0.009) | Tennessee Parks (0.010)<br>Walls Have Paint (0.010)<br>Singin' The Blues (0.010)<br>Balloons And Fireworks (0.010)<br>Birding In The Wild (0.009)<br>Birds birds birds birds (0.009) | Street Lamps (0.026)<br>Sky Chasers (0.011)<br>The best self portraits (0.010)<br>Black 'n' Blue (0.010)<br>(Achromatic) Nature (0.009)<br>City Sunsets (0.009) | Tennessee Parks (0.012)<br>the skies above (0.010)<br>Flower Flower Flower (0.009)<br>FLOWERS (0.009)<br>Sky Chasers (0.009)<br>Flowers all kinds (0.009) |
|  |  |  |  |
| San Francisco at Night (0.013)<br>Melbourne at Night (0.012)<br>Corel Paint Shop Pro (0.012)<br>UK night photography (0.011)<br>Flickr's 1st Xmas group (0.011)<br>City Sunsets (0.010) | Electronic Music (0.011)<br>Concert Photographer (0.011)<br>San Francisco at Night (0.011)<br>Concert Photo Score Me (0.010)<br>Music Directory (0.010)<br>Concerts1 (0.010) | the skies above (0.011)<br>Black 'n' Blue (0.010)<br>Flowers all kinds (0.010)<br>FLOWERS (0.010)<br>Flower Flower Flower (0.010)<br>Family Portraiture (0.010) | Black 'n' Blue (0.010)<br>Sky Chasers (0.010)<br>Snow Riders (0.010)<br>natures composition (0.009)<br>the skies above (0.009)<br>City Sunsets (0.009) |

It is evident that the *SocialRank* algorithm makes appropriate recommendations in most cases. However, it can sometimes recommend groups, in which the specific interests are not reflected in the visual content of the query image. For instance, a query image with ground truth group as *"San Francisco at Night"* would be visually very similar to a lot of photos in the group *"Melbourne at Night"*. This is of course a challenge of the problem formulation itself (and likely to be a problem for almost any method), because it is inherently hard to make such fine grained distinctions from the subjective information in a visual object. One inherent advantage of the social rank algorithm is that it allows the simultaneous use of *query-bias vectors* from different domains. For example, we can use an *additional* query-bias vector from the text domain in order to incorporate more detailed group semantics in the ranking process. Thus, both the group semantics and the image visual content can be taken into account, which allows for more fine grained distinctions. This will be a direction of our future efforts.

## 6. CONCLUSIONS AND SUMMARY

In this paper, we proposed the *SocialRank* algorithm, which uses a heterogeneous network model to perform image ranking effectively with the use of linkages, content and social cues in the network. Our heterogeneous model is quite general, and can be used for network models which are much more complex than the social network scenario. Furthermore, while we have presented the results for the case of keyword-based queries, the method is general enough to be used for content-based queries of different types. An iterative algorithm is proposed to learn the most effective ranking based on the relationships between the different network objects. We presented experimental results which show the effectiveness of our approach over competing methods.


## Acknowledgements

Research was sponsored by the Army Research Laboratory and was accomplished under Cooperative Agreement Number W911NF-09-2-0053. The views and conclusions contained in this document are those of the authors and should not be interpreted as representing the official policies, either expressed or implied, of the Army Research Laboratory or the U.S. Government. The U.S. Government is authorized to reproduce and distribute reprints for Government purposes notwithstanding any copyright notation here on.


## 7. REFERENCES


[1] C. Aggarwal. Social network data analytics, *Springer*, 2011.

[2] C. Aggarwal and H. Wang. Managing and mining graph data, *Springer*, 2010.

[3] S. Brin and L. Page. The anatomy of a large-scale hypertextual web search engine. *WWW Conference*, 1998.

[4] L. Cao, A. D. Pozo, X. Jin, J. Luo, J. Han, and T. S. Huang. RankComplete: Simultaneous Clustering and Ranking of Web Photos, *WWW Conference*, 2010.

[5] S. Chakrabarti. Dynamic Personalized Pagerank in Entity-relation Graphs, *WWW Conference*, 2007.

[6] D. Fogaras, B. Racz, K. Csalogany, and T. Sarlos. Towards scaling fully personalized PageRank: Algorithms, lower bounds, and experiments. *Internet Mathematics*, 2(3):333-358, 2005.

[7] T. H. Haveliwala. Topic-sensitive PageRank. *WWW Conference*, pp. 517-526, 2002.

[8] X. He, W.-Y. Ma, and H. Zhang. ImageRank: Spectral Techniques for Structural Analysis of Image Database, *ICME*, vol 1, pp. 25-28, 2002.

[9] G. Jeh and J. Widom. Scaling personalized web search. *WWW Conference*, pp. 271-279, 2003.

[10] H. He, H. Wang, J. Yang, and P. Yu. BLINKS: Ranked Keyword Searches on Graphs, *SIGMOD Conference*, 2007.

[11] Y. Jing, and S. Baluja. VisualRank: Applying PageRank to Large-Scale Image Search, *IEEE Transactions on Pattern Mining and Intelligence*, Vol. 30, No. 11, 2008.

[12] R. P. A. Pentland, S. Sclaroff. Content-based Manipulation of Image Databases, *International Journal on Computer Vision*, pp. 233-254, 1996.

[13] W.-Y. Ma, and B. S. Manjunath. A Toolbox for Navigating Large Image Databases, *Multimedia Systems* 3(7), pp. 184-198, 1999.

[14] A. W. Smeulders, M. Worring, S. Santini, A. Gupta, and R. Jain. Content-based Image Retrieval in the Early Years, *IEEE Trans. on Pattern Mining and Intelligence*, 22(12), pp. 1349-1380, 2000.

[15] S.-F. Tsai, M.-H. Tsai, and T. Huang. Content-based Image Retrieval with Ontological Ranking, *SPIE*, 2010.

[16] T. Joachims. Training Linear SVMs in Linear Time, *Proceedings of the ACM Conference on Knowledge Discovery and Data Mining (KDD)*, 2006.

[17] G. Jeh and J. Widom. SimRank: a measure of structural-context similarity, *Proceedings of the ACM Conference on Knowledge Discovery and Data Mining (KDD)*, pp. 538-543, 2002.

[18] D. Liu, X.-S. Hua, L. Yang, M. Wang, H.-J. Zhang. Tag Ranking, *WWW Conference*, pp. 351-360, 2009.

[19] T. Pedersen, S. Patwardhan, J. Michelizzi. WordNet::Similarity: measuring the relatedness of concepts, *HLT-NAACL*, pp. 38-41, 2004.

[20] R. Cilibrasi and P. Vitanyi. The Google Similarity Distance, *IEEE Trans. on Knowl. and Data Eng.*, pp. 370-383, 2007.

[21] Y. Rui, T. S. Huang and S.-F. Chang. Image Retrieval: Current Techniques, Promising Directions, and Open Issues, *Journal of Visual Communication and Image Representation.*, pp. 39-62, 1999.

[22] G.-J. Qi, C. Aggarwal and T. Huang. Towards semantic knowledge propagation from text corpus to web images, *WWW Conference*, pp. 297-306, 2011.

[23] H. Sahbi and J-Y. Audibert. Network-dependent kernels for image ranking, *ICIP Conference*, pp. 2357-2360, 2010.

[24] H. Sahbi and J-Y. Audibert. Social network kernels for image ranking and retrieval, *Research Report*, TELECOM ParisTech, 2009.

# Visualizing Brand Associations from Web Community Photos

Gunhee Kim*
Carnegie Mellon University
Pittsburgh, 15213 PA
gunhee@cs.cmu.edu

Eric P. Xing
Carnegie Mellon University
Pittsburgh, 15213 PA
epxing@cs.cmu.edu

## ABSTRACT

*Brand Associations*, one of central concepts in marketing, describe customers' top-of-mind attitudes or feelings toward a brand. Thus, this consumer-driven brand equity often attains the grounds for purchasing products or services of the brand. Traditionally, brand associations are measured by analyzing the text data from consumers' responses to the survey or their online conversation logs. In this paper, we propose to go beyond text data and leverage large-scale online photo collections contributed by the general public, which have not been explored so far. As a first technical step toward the study of photo-based brand associations, we aim to jointly achieve the following two visualization tasks in a mutually-rewarding way: (i) detecting and visualizing core visual concepts associated with brands, and (ii) localizing the regions of brand in the images. With experiments on about five millions of images of 48 brands crawled from five popular online photo sharing sites, we demonstrate that our approach can discover complementary views on the brand associations that are hardly mined from the text data. We also quantitatively show that our approach outperforms other candidate methods on the both visualization tasks.

## Categories and Subject Descriptors

I.4.9 [**Image processing and computer vision**]: Applications; J.4 [**Computer Applications**]: Social and behavioral sciences—*Economics*

## Keywords

Brand associations; summarization and visualization of multimedia data; image segmentation

## 1. INTRODUCTION

*Brand equity* describes a set of values or assets linked to a brand [1, 12]. It is one of core concepts in marketing since it is a key source of bearing the competitive advantage of a company over its competitors, boosting efficiency and effectiveness of marketing programs, and attaining the price premium due to increased customer satisfaction and loyalty, to name a few. A central component of brand equity is *brand associations*, which are the set of associations that consumers perceive with the brand [12]. For example, the brand associations of *Nike* may include *Tiger Woods*, *shoes*, *basketball*, and so on. Its significance lies in that it is a *customer-driven* brand equity; that is, the brand associations are directly connected to customers' *top-of-mind* attitudes or feelings toward the brand, which provoke the reasons to preferentially purchase the products or services of the brand. For instance, if a customer strongly associates *Nike* with *golf shirts*, he may tend to first consider *Nike* products over other competitors' ones when he needs one.

Traditionally, measuring brand associations is a challenging task because it should be built from direct consumer responses to carefully designed questionnaires [2, 5, 23, 25]. With the recent emergence of online social media, it has been developed to indirectly leverage consumer-generated data on online communities such as Weblogs, boards, and Wiki. Beneficially, resources on such social media are obtainable inexpensively and almost instantaneously from a large crowd of potential customers. One typical example of such practice is the *Brand Association Map* developed by *Nielsen Online* [2, 19], in which important concepts and themes correlated with a given brand name are automatically extracted from the data of online conversations.

In this paper, in order to elicit the brand associations, we propose to go beyond textual media, and take advantage of large-scale online *photo* collections, which have not been explored so far. Admittedly, pictures can be inferior to mine users' subjective sentiments than texts (*e.g. Nike is too expensive*). However, pictures can be a complementary information modality to show customers' experiences regarding brands within a natural context. With widespread availability of digital cameras and smartphones, people can freely take pictures on any memorable moments, which include experiencing or purchasing products they like. In addition, many online tools enable people to easily share, comment, or bookmark the images of products that they wish to buy.

More specifically, as a first technical step to the study of the photo-based brand associations, we address the problem of jointly achieving the following two levels of visualization tasks for brand associations. (See Fig.1).

(1) *Detecting key pictorial concepts associated with brands*: It has been a central problem in brand association research

---

*Gunhee Kim is now at Disney Research.


*WSDM'14*, February 24–28, 2014, New York, New York, USA.

ACM 978-1-4503-2351-2/14/02 ...$15.00.
http://dx.doi.org/10.1145/2556195.2556212.

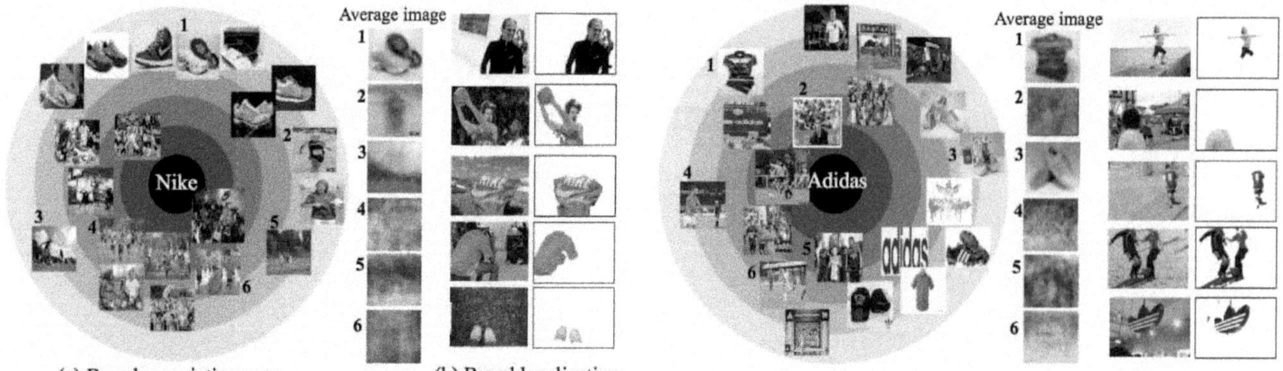


(a) Brand association map (b) Brand localization

**Figure 1: Examples of two visualization tasks for the brand association study leveraging Web community photos. We show two competing sports brands: *Nike* and *Adidas* side by side. (a) Task1: we perform exemplar detection and clustering to reconstruct brand association maps. More strongly associated clusters with the brand appear closer to the center of the map, and more similar pairs of clusters have smaller angular distances. We illustrate top 20 exemplars (*i.e.* cluster centers) in the map. On the right, we show the average images of six selected exemplars. (b) Task2: we segment the most associated regions of brand in the images.**

to identify and visualize important concepts associated with brands in the form of a network or a map [2, 6, 23, 25]. Therefore, our first task is, as shown in Fig.1.(a), to visualize core visual concepts of brands by summarizing online photos that are tagged and organized by general users. This goal involves three sub-problems: identifying a small number of image clusters and exemplars (*i.e.* cluster centers), discovering the similarity relations between clusters, and projecting them into a low-dimensional space.

(2) *Localizing the regions of brand in images*: Our second task is the *sub-image level* visualization of brand associations, while the first task addresses the *image-level* one. We aim to localize the regions that are most associated with the brand in the images in an unsupervised way (*i.e.* without any pre-defined models or human labeling), as shown in Fig.1.(b). We perform pixel-level image segmentation to delineate the regions of brand. Even though bounding boxes may be better as the final output to the general users, they can be trivially derived from segmentation results, by defining the minimum rectangle that encloses the segment while ignoring tiny unconnected dots.

We choose the above two tasks as the most fundamental building blocks for the photo-based brand associations for following reasons. The first task can provide a structural summary of large-scale and ever-growing online image data of brands, which otherwise are too overwhelming for human to grasp any underlying big picture. The second task helps reveal typical interactions between users and products in natural social scenes, which can lead a wide variety of potential benefits, ranging from content-based image retrieval to online multimedia advertisement.

Importantly, jointly solving these two tasks is *mutually rewarding*, as we will show in our experiments. The exemplar detection/clustering can generate the coherent groups of images from extremely diverse Web image set. Thus, it can promote the brand localization because we can leverage the recurring foreground signals across the images of the same group. In the reverse direction, localizing brand regions can enhance the similarity measurement between images, which subsequently contributes to better exemplar detection/clustering.

For evaluation, we collect about five millions of images for 48 brands of four categories (*i.e.* *sports*, *luxury*, *beer*, and *fastfood*) from five popular photo sharing sites, including FLICKR, PHOTOBUCKET, DEVIANTART, TWITPIC, and PINTEREST. In our experiments, we first show several examples of picture-driven brand association maps. We then demonstrate that our approach outperforms other candidate methods on the both exemplar detection/clustering and brand localization. Finally, we examine the correlations between community photos and actual sales data of the brands.

## 1.1 Relations to Previous work

We introduce two lines of research related to our work.

**Measuring brand associations**: In almost all previous research for brand associations, consumer surveys are the most popular way to collect source data. Among many methods for conducting the surveys, the *free association* procedure has been one of the simplest but often most powerful ways to profile brand associations [5, 6, 25]. In this technique, subjects are asked to freely answer their feelings and thoughts about a given brand name without any editing or censoring [18]. (*e.g.* What comes to mind when you think of *Nike*?) Our research is also based on this *free association* idea, since we view the Web photos tagged with a brand name by anonymous users as their candid pictorial impressions to the brand. Therefore, from a viewpoint of brand association research, the contribution of our work is to introduce a novel source of data for the analysis.

In this line of research, the brand association map of Nielsen Online [2, 19] is closely related to our work because both approaches explore the online data. However, our work is unique in that we explore the images, which convey complementary views on the brand associations over the texts. Furthermore, we localize the regions of brand in the images, which is another novel feature of our work.

**Analysis of product images**: Recently, with the exploding interests in electronic commerce, computer vision techniques have widely applied to analyze product images for commercial applications. Some notable examples include the product image search and ranking [10], the logo and product detection in natural images [8, 11, 16, 22], and

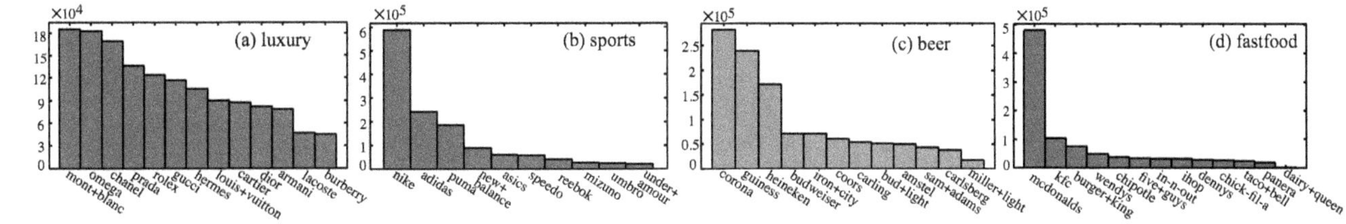


**Figure 2: The dataset of 48 brands crawled from five photo sharing sites of Table 1. The brands are classified into four categories: (a) *luxury*, (b) *sports*, (c) *beer*, and (d) *fastfood*. The total number of images is 4,720,724.**

| Web sites | Characteristics |
|---|---|
| FLICKR/ PHOTOBUCKET | Two largest and most popular photo sharing sites in terms of volumes of photos. |
| PINTEREST | Image collections bookmarked by users |
| DEVIANTART | Various forms of artwork created by users. |
| TWITPIC | Photos shared via Twitter. |

**Table 1: Five Web sites for crawling photos.**

clothing parsing in fashion photos [27]. However, the objective of our work differs in that we aim to discover and visualize the core concepts of brands from natural online images, whereas most of past work has focused on detecting a fixed number of specified product models or logos in the images. Therefore, in our work, it is important to mine the visual topics that do not explicitly contain the products but reflect the general public's experiences on the brands (*e.g.* sponsored yacht competition scenes in the *Rolex* image set).

## 1.2 Summary of Contributions

The contributions of our work are summarized as follows:

(1) We study the problem of visualizing brand associations in both image and sub-image levels by leveraging large-scale online image collections. To the best of our knowledge, our work is the first attempt so far on such photo-based brand association analysis. Consequently, our work can provide another novel and complementary way to visualize general public's opinions or experiences on the brands.

(2) We develop an algorithm to jointly achieve exemplar detection/clustering and brand localization in a mutually-rewarding way. In addition, we design an embedding algorithm to visualize the top exemplars in a circular layout.

(3) With experiments on about five million images of 48 brands, we quantitatively demonstrate that our approach outperforms other candidate methods on the both visualization tasks.

# 2. PROBLEM FORMULATION

## 2.1 Image Data Crawling

As source data, we crawl images from the five popular photo sharing sites in Table 1. The characteristics of the pictures on the five sites are different from one another as shown in Table 1. We exclude the GOOGLE IMAGE SEARCH because much of the pictures are originated from online shopping malls or news agencies. We prefer the photos that are contributed by general Web users, because we are interested in their candid views on the brands.

We query the brand names via the built-in search engines of the sites, and download all retrieved images without any filtering. We also crawl meta-data of the pictures (*e.g.* timestamps, titles, user names, texts), if available.

Fig.2 summarizes our dataset of 4,783,345 images for 48 brands, which can be classified into four categories: *luxury*, *sports*, *beer*, and *fastfood*. The number of images per brand varies much according to the popularity of the brand.

## 2.2 Overview of Our Approach

Fig.3 presents the overview of our approach. The input of our algorithm is a set of photos for a brand of interest. Let $\mathcal{I} = \{I_1, \cdots, I_N\}$ be the set of input images, where $N$ is the number of images. As shown in Fig.3.(b), our first step is to build a K-nearest neighbor (KNN) graph $\mathcal{G} = (\mathcal{I}, \mathcal{E})$ in which each image is connected with its $K$ most similar images in $\mathcal{I}$. We will present our image descriptors in section 3.1, similarity measures in section 3.2, and KNN graph construction in section 3.3.

The next step is to perform exemplar detection and clustering on the graph $\mathcal{G}$, which will be discussed in section 3.4. Its goal is to discover a small set of representative images called exemplars $\mathcal{A}(\subset \mathcal{I})$, and to partition $\mathcal{I}$ so that each image is associated with its closest exemplar, as shown in Fig.3.(c). Therefore, the clusters are the groups of contextually and visually similar images, and the exemplars are the most prototypical images of the clusters.

The clustering step is beneficial to detect brand regions in the images, because it can discover the coherent groups of images from extremely diverse Web image set. (See examples in Fig.3.(d)). In our setting, the brand localization is formulated as the problem of *cosegmentation* [13, 15], which has been actively studied in the image segmentation research. Its goal is to jointly segment out recurring objects or foregrounds across the multiple images. Obviously, the images in the same cluster are likely to share the similar themes of the brand (*e.g.* bags in Fig.3.(d)), which can be discovered by the cosegmentation approach. We summarize the procedure of cosegmentation in section 3.5.

In our closed-loop approach, the segmentation can enhance the exemplar detection/clustering by promoting a more accurate image similarity measure, which will be justified in section 3.2 with an intuitive example. Hence, after finishing the cosegmentation step, we can return to the KNN graph construction and repeat the whole algorithm again with the new segmentation-based image similarity metric.

The algorithm for the construction of brand association maps (*e.g.* Fig.1) will be presented in section 4.

# 3. APPROACH

## 3.1 Feature Extraction

For image description, we use one of standard methods in recent computer vision research: the dense feature extraction with vector quantization. We densely extract two most types of features from each image: HSV color SIFT

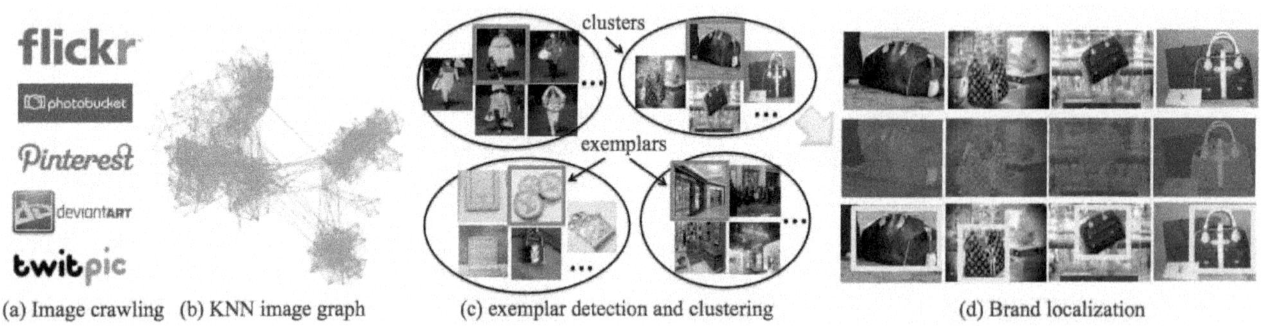


**Figure 3: The overview of the proposed approach with an example of the *Louis+Vuitton*. (a) As an input, we crawl the photos of the brand from the five photo sharing sites. (b) We build a $K$-nearest neighbor (KNN) similarity graph between images. (c) We perform the graph-based exemplar detection/clustering. (d) Finally, we cosegment the images in the same cluster in order to discover the most associated regions with the brand. As a closed-loop solution, we can return to the KNN graph construction with the new segmentation-based image similarity metric.**

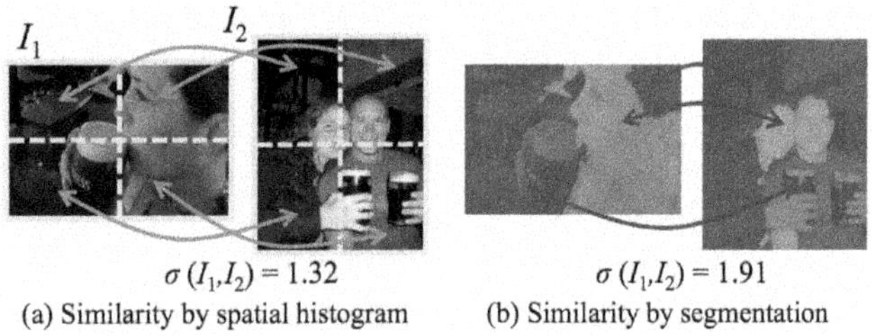


**Figure 4: The benefit of segmentation for image similarity measurement. (a) For an unsegmented image pair, the spatial pyramid histograms are constructed on the whole images, which may not be robust against the location and scale variations. (b) After segmentation, the image similarity is computed as the mean of the best assigned segment similarities.**

and histogram of oriented edge (HOG) feature on a regular grid at steps of 4 and 8 pixels, respectively. Then, we form 300 visual words for each feature type by applying K-means to randomly selected features. Finally, the nearest word is assigned to every node of the grid. We use publicly available codes[1] for the whole process of feature extraction.

## 3.2 Image Similarity Measure

One prerequisite to accurate clustering is an appropriate similarity measure between images, denoted by $\sigma : \mathcal{I} \times \mathcal{I} \rightarrow \mathbb{R}$. We assert that even imperfect segmentation helps enhance the measurement of image similarity, which can justify our closed-loop approach. Fig.4 shows a typical example, in which the two images are similar in that both include persons with glasses of *Guinness* beer. For an unsegmented image pair, the image similarity is calculated from two-level spatial pyramid histograms on the whole images [17], which are not robust against location, scale, and pose variation as shown in Fig.4.(a). On the other hand, as shown in Fig.4.(b), this issue can be largely alleviated even with an imperfect segmentation. Given the two segment sets of the images, we find the best matches between them by solving the linear assignment problem. Then, we compute the image similarity by the mean of similarities between matched segments. For the segment similarity, we use the histogram intersection kernel on the spatial pyramids of the segments.

[1]The SIFT and HOG feature extraction codes are available at http://www.vlfeat.org, and at http://www.cs.brown.edu/~pff/latent, respectively.

## 3.3 Constructing K-Nearest Neighbor Graph

Given the image descriptors and similarity measures, the construction of KNN graphs is straightforward. However, if we naively compare all pairwise similarity, it takes $\mathcal{O}(N^2)$, which can be prohibitively slow for a large $\mathcal{I}$. Fortunately, a large number of algorithms have been proposed to construct approximate KNN graphs with avoiding the quadratic complexity. We use the idea of multiple random divide-and-conquer [26], which allows to create an approximate KNN graph of high accuracy in $\mathcal{O}(N \log N)$ time. The method is simple; we randomly and recursively partition the dataset into subsets, and build an exact neighborhood graph over each subset. This random divide-and-conquer process repeats for several times, and then the aggregation of all neighborhood graphs of subsets can create an accurate approximate KNN graph with a high probability. The details of theoretic analyses can be found in [26]. In our method, meta-data of images are also exploited for the recursive random division. We repeat partitioning the image set into subsets according to each type of meta-data (*e.g.* image sources, owners, titles, or timestamps, if available). For example, in one partition, each subset includes the images taken at similar time; in another partition, each subset comprises the images owned by the same user. The basic assumption is that if images are taken at similar time or by the same user, they are likely to share similar contents. In our experiments, this heuristics is reliable to build accurate KNN graphs.

## 3.4 Exemplar detection and clustering

Given a KNN graph $\mathcal{G}$, our next step is to perform exemplar detection. As a base algorithm, we use the diversity ranking algorithm of [15], which can choose $L$ number of exemplars that are not only most central but also distinctive one another, by solving submodular optimization on the similarity graph $\mathcal{G}$. Since the $L$ exemplars are discovered in a decreasing order of ranking scores, $L$ can be set to an arbitrary large number. In this paper, we do not discuss the details of the algorithm, which can be found in [15]. Instead, we denote the exemplar detection procedure by $\mathcal{A} = \texttt{SubmDiv}(\mathbf{G}, L)$ where $\mathcal{A}$ is the set of exemplars and $\mathbf{G} \in \mathbb{R}^{N \times N}$ is the adjacency matrix of the graph $\mathcal{G}$. The pseudocode is summarized in the step **1–2** of Algorithm 1.

**Algorithm 1:** Exemplar detection and clustering.

**Input**: (1) Image graph $\mathbf{G}$. (2) Number of exemplars $L$.
**Output**: (1) Exemplar set $\mathcal{A}$ and cluster set $\mathcal{C}$.

**1**: Append a constant vector $\mathbf{z} \in \mathbb{R}^{N \times 1}$ to the end column of $\mathbf{G}$ and $\mathbf{z}^T$ to the end row of $\mathbf{G}$. ($N = |\mathbf{G}|$).
**2**: $\mathcal{A} =$ `SubmDiv`$(\mathbf{G}, L)$.
**3**: $\{\mathcal{C}_l\}_{l=1}^{L} =$ `ClustSrc`$(\mathbf{G}, \mathcal{A})$.

/* Select $L$ number of central and diverse exemplars $\mathcal{A}$.
**Function** $[\mathcal{A}] =$ `SubmDiv`$(\mathbf{G}, L)$
  **1**: $\mathcal{A} \leftarrow \emptyset$. $\mathbf{u} = \mathbf{0} \in \mathbb{R}^{(N+1)\times 1}$.
  **while** $|\mathcal{A}| \leq L$ **do**
    **2**: **for** $i = 1 : N$ **do** $\mathbf{u}(i) =$ `TempSrc`$(\mathbf{G}, \{\mathcal{A} \cup i\})$.
    **3**: $\mathcal{A} \leftarrow \mathcal{A} \cup \operatorname{argmax}_i \mathbf{u}$.

/* Get marginal gain $u$ from the $\mathbf{G}$ and the node set $\mathcal{P}$.
**Function** $[u] =$ `TempSrc`$(\mathbf{G}, \mathcal{P})$
  **1**: Solve $\mathbf{u} = \mathbf{L}\mathbf{u}$ where $\mathbf{L}$ is the Laplacian of $\mathbf{G}$ under constraints of $\mathbf{u}(\mathcal{P}) = 1$ and $\mathbf{u}(N+1) = 0$.
  **2**: Compute the marginal gain $u = |\mathbf{u}|_1$.

/* Get cluster set $\mathcal{C}$ from the graph $\mathbf{G}$ and exemplars $\mathcal{A}$.
**Function** $\mathcal{C} =$ `ClustSrc`$(\mathbf{G}, \mathcal{A})$
  **1**: Let $L = |\mathcal{A}|$ and $M = |\mathbf{G}|$. $\mathcal{V}$ is vertext set of $\mathbf{G}$.
  **2**: Compute the matrix $\mathbf{X} \in \mathbb{R}^{(M-L)\times L}$ by solving $\mathbf{L}_u\mathbf{X} = -\mathbf{B}^T\mathbf{I}_s$ where if we let $\mathcal{X} = \mathcal{V}\backslash\mathcal{A}$, $\mathbf{L}_u = \mathbf{L}(\mathcal{X}, \mathcal{X})$, $\mathbf{B} = \mathbf{L}(\mathcal{A}, \mathcal{X})$, and $\mathbf{I}_s$ is an $L \times L$ identity matrix.
  **3**: Each vertex $v \in \mathcal{V}$ is clustered $c_v = \operatorname{argmax}_k \mathbf{X}(v, k)$.

Next, the clustering is performed using the random walk model [9]; each image $i$ is associated with the exemplar that a random walker starting at $i$ is most likely to reach first. Then, we cluster the images that share the same exemplar as the most probable destination. This procedure is implemented as a function `ClustSrc` of Algorithm 1.

Our exemplar detection/clustering runs in $\mathcal{O}(L|\mathcal{E}|)$ where $|\mathcal{E}|$ is the number of edges. Since we use sparse KNN graphs where each vertex links to a constant number of neighbors, its overall computation runs in a linear time $\mathcal{O}(LN)$.

### 3.5 Brand Localization via Cosegmentation

As the clustering output, we obtain the groups of coherent images $\mathcal{C} = \{\mathcal{C}_l\}_{l=1}^{L}$. The brand localization is achieved by separately applying the cosegmentation algorithm to each cluster. This separate cosegmentation scheme is advantageous not only for parallelization but also for performance. Especially, for performance, it prevents cosegmenting the images of no commonality, which contradicts the basic assumption of cosegmentation algorithms. For instance, given the *Prada* brand, cosegmenting bag and jewelry images could be worsen than individually segmenting each image.

The cosegmentation partitions each of multiple images into foreground (*i.e.* the regions recurring across the images like *bags* in Fig.3.(d)) and background (*i.e.* the other regions). We select the MFC method [13] as our base cosegmentation algorithm, since it is scalable and has been successfully tested with Flickr user images. The MFC algorithm consists of two procedures, which are *foreground modeling* and *region assignment*. The foreground modeling step learns the appearance models for foreground and background. It is implemented by the Gaussian mixture model (GMM) on the RGB color space. The foreground models compute the values of any given regions with respect to the foregrounds and background, based on which the region assignment allocates the regions of an image via a combinatorial-auction style optimization to maximize the overall allocation values. More details of the algorithm can be referred to [13].

**Algorithm 2:** Brand localization via cosegmentation.

**Input**: (1) Cluster set $\mathcal{C} = \{\mathcal{C}_l\}_{l=1}^{L}$. (2) Image graph $\mathbf{G}$.
**Output**: (1) Segmentation of each image $i \in \mathcal{I}$ into foreground $\mathcal{F}_i$ and background $\mathcal{B}_i$.

**foreach** $\mathcal{C}_l \in \mathcal{C}$ **do**
  **1**: Find central image $c =$ `SubmDiv`$(\mathbf{G}_l, 1)$ where $\mathbf{G}_l = \mathbf{G}(\mathcal{C}_l)$ is the subgraph of $\mathcal{C}_l$.
  **2**: Apply the unsupervised MFC algorithm [13] to $\{c \cup \mathcal{N}_c\}$ where $\mathcal{N}_c$ is the neighbor of $c$ in the graph $\mathbf{G}_l$. As a result, we obtain segmentation for $\{c \cup \mathcal{N}_c\}$.
  **3**: Let $\mathcal{S}_l \leftarrow \{c \cup \mathcal{N}_c\}$ and $\mathcal{U}_l \leftarrow \mathcal{C}_l \backslash \mathcal{S}_l$.
  **while** $\mathcal{U}_l \neq \emptyset$ **do**
    **4**: Sample an image $i$ from $\{\mathcal{U}_l \cap \mathcal{N}_{\mathcal{S}_l}\}$.
    **5**: Get foreground model $\{v_i\} =$ `FM` $(\{\mathcal{N}_i \cap \mathcal{S}_l\})$.
    **6**: Segment the image $i$: $(\mathcal{F}_i, \mathcal{B}_i) =$ `RA` $(i, \{v_i\})$.
    **7**: Let $\mathcal{S}_l \leftarrow \mathcal{S}_l \cup i$ and $\mathcal{U}_l \leftarrow \mathcal{U}_l \backslash i$.

/* $\{v_i\} =$ `FM` $(\mathcal{S}_i)$ is the function to learn foreground model $\{v_i\}$ of MFC [13] from the segmented images $\mathcal{S}_i$.
/* $(\mathcal{F}_i, \mathcal{B}_i) =$ `RA` $(i, \{v_i\})$ is the function to run region assign- ment of MFC [13] on image $i$ using $\{v_i\}$.

For each cluster $\mathcal{C}_l$, we perform the cosegmentation by iteratively applying the foreground modeling and region assignment steps under the guidance of the subgraph $\mathcal{G}(\mathcal{C}_l)$ whose vertex set is $\mathcal{C}_l$ [14]. Its basic idea is that the neighboring images in $\mathcal{G}(\mathcal{C}_l)$ are visually similar, and thus they are likely to share enough commonality to be segmented together. Therefore, we iteratively segment each image $i$ by using the learned foreground models from its neighbors in the graph. Then, the segmented image $i$ is subsequently used to learn the foreground models for its neighbors' segmentation. That is, we iteratively run foreground modeling and region assignment by following the edges of $\mathcal{G}(\mathcal{C}_l)$. The overall algorithm, which runs in a linear time $\mathcal{O}(|\mathcal{C}_l|)$, is summarized in Algorithm 2. For initialization, as shown in step **1**–**2** of Algorithm 2, we run the unsupervised version of the MFC algorithm to the exemplar of $C_l$ and its neighbors, from which the iterative cosegmentation starts.

## 4. BRAND ASSOCIATION MAPS

We visualize the clusters (or exemplars) in a circular layout, in order to concisely represent both short-range and long-range interactions between them. We place the visual clusters by using two different metrics, the *radial distance* and *angular distance*, inspired by the Nielsen's method [2]:

1. The *radial distance* of a cluster reflects how strongly it associates with the brand. A larger cluster appears closer to the center of the map.

2. The *angular distance* between a pair of clusters shows their closeness. The smaller the angular distance between the two is, the higher the correlation is.

Since Nielsen's algorithm is unknown and no photo-based brand association mapping has been developed yet, we design a new embedding algorithm that satisfies the above requirements. Our objective is to calculate $(\mathbf{r}, \boldsymbol{\theta}) \in \mathbb{R}^{L\times 2}$,

**Algorithm 3:** Computing polar coordinates of clusters.

**Input:** (a) Cluster set $\mathcal{C} = \{\mathcal{C}_l\}_{l=1}^{L}$. (b) Image graph $\mathbf{G}$. (c) Image sizes to be drawn $\mathbf{t} \in \mathbb{R}^{L\times 1}$.
**Output:** Polar coordinates $(\mathbf{r}, \boldsymbol{\theta}) \in \mathbb{R}^{L\times 2}$ of $\mathcal{C}$.

/* *Radial coordinates.* */
**1:** Compute transition matrix $\mathbf{P}$ by row-normalizing $\mathbf{G}$.
**2:** Solve Eq.(1) to get stationary distribution $\boldsymbol{\pi} \in \mathbb{R}^{N\times 1}$.
**3:** **foreach** $\mathcal{C}_a \in \mathcal{C}$ **do** compute $\pi_a = \sum_{i\in\mathcal{C}_a} \boldsymbol{\pi}(i)$.
**4:** Let $\pi_{min} = \min_{a\in\mathcal{C}} \boldsymbol{\pi}_a$ and $\pi_{max} = \max_{a\in\mathcal{C}} \boldsymbol{\pi}_a$.
**5:** **foreach** $\mathcal{C}_a \in \mathcal{C}$ **do** obtain $\mathbf{r}(a)$ by solving Eq.(2).
/* *Angular coordinates.* */
**6:** Obtain the cluster similarity $\mathbf{S} \in \mathbb{R}^{L\times L}$ from Eq.(4).
**7:** Initialize $\boldsymbol{\theta}$ by polar dendrogram of hierarchical clustering on $\mathbf{S}$, $J = 0$, $J_{old}$ = a large number.
**while** $|J - J_{old}| > \epsilon$ **do**
  **8:** Calculate $\frac{\partial}{\partial\boldsymbol{\theta}} J \in \mathbb{R}^{L\times 1}$. For each $a \in \mathcal{C}$, $\frac{\partial}{\partial\theta_a} J = \sum_{b\in\mathcal{C}} (\mathbf{S}(a,b) - \gamma|\theta_a - \theta_b|^{\gamma-1}) G$ where $G = -2(1-\cos(\theta_a-\theta_b))^{-1/2}(-\sin\theta_a\cos\theta_b + \cos\theta_a\sin\theta_b)$.
  **9:** $\boldsymbol{\theta}_{new} = \boldsymbol{\theta} + \mu\frac{\partial}{\partial\boldsymbol{\theta}} J$.
  **10:** $J_{new} = \sum_a \sum_b \mathbf{S}(a,b)|\theta_a - \theta_b| - \sum\sum|\theta_a - \theta_b|^{\gamma}$.
  **11:** Update $J_{old} = J, J = J_{new}, \boldsymbol{\theta} = \boldsymbol{\theta}_{new}$.
/* *Force-directed refinement.* */
**12:** Obtain Cartesian coordinates $\mathbf{x} \in \mathbb{R}^{L\times 2}$ from $(\mathbf{r}, \boldsymbol{\theta})$ and a pariwse distance matrix $\mathbf{D}$. Store the original $\mathbf{x}_0$.
**while** $\mathbf{x}$ *is updated* **do**
  **13:** Set the displacement vector $\mathbf{d} = \mathbf{0}$. Set attractive and repulsive forces: $f_{at}(x) = x^2/k$ and $f_{re}(x) = k^2/x$.
  **foreach** *pair* $(a,b)$ *if* $\mathbf{D}(a,b) < \gamma(\mathbf{t}(a) + \mathbf{t}(b))$ **do**
    **14:** $\mathbf{d}(b) += f_{re}(|\mathbf{x}(b) - \mathbf{x}(a)|)$.
  **15:** **foreach** $a \in \mathcal{C}$ **do** $\mathbf{d}(a) -= f_{at}(|\mathbf{x}(a) - \mathbf{x}_0(a)|)$.
  **16:** **foreach** $a \in \mathcal{C}$ **do** $\mathbf{x}(a) += \mathbf{d}(a)$.
**17:** Obtain the final $(\mathbf{r}, \boldsymbol{\theta})$ from $\mathbf{x}$.

which are the polar coordinates of all clusters of $\mathcal{C}$. Algorithm 3 summarizes the whole mapping procedure.

**Radial distances of clusters**: According to the requirement 1, a larger cluster has a smaller radial distance (*i.e.* closer to the center). In order to estimate the cluster sizes, we first compute the stationary distribution $\boldsymbol{\pi} \in \mathbb{R}^{N\times 1}$ of the graph $\mathcal{G}$, where $\boldsymbol{\pi}(i)$ indicates a random walker's visiting probability of node $i$. We assume that the size of cluster $\mathcal{C}_a$ is proportional to the sum of stationary distribution of the nodes in $\mathcal{C}_a$, which means the portion of time that a random walker traversing the graph stays in the cluster $\mathcal{C}_a$. That is, in a larger cluster, a random walker stays longer.

Given the transition matrix $\mathbf{P}$ obtained by normalizing the rows of $\mathbf{G}$, the stationary probability vector $\boldsymbol{\pi}$ can be computed by solving $\boldsymbol{\pi} = \mathbf{P}^T\boldsymbol{\pi}$ with $\|\boldsymbol{\pi}\|_1 = 1$. However, it is well known from the success of PageRank that a regularized stationary distribution is more robust and can incorporate a prior knowledge; it can be obtained by solving

$$\boldsymbol{\pi} = \widetilde{\mathbf{P}}^T\boldsymbol{\pi} \quad \text{where } \widetilde{\mathbf{P}} = \lambda\mathbf{P} + (1-\lambda)\mathbf{1}\mathbf{v}^T \tag{1}$$

where $\mathbf{v} \in \mathbb{R}^{N\times 1}$ is the teleporting probability such that $\mathbf{v}(i) \geq 0$, $\|\mathbf{v}\|_1 = 1$. It can supply a prior ranking to each node; without it, one can let $\mathbf{v} = [1/N, \cdots, 1/N]^T$ be uniform. $\mathbf{1}$ is an all-one vector, and $\lambda$ is a regularization parameter to weight the random walker's behavior between edge following and random transporting. We set $\lambda = 0.9$ in all experiments.

Once we have $\boldsymbol{\pi}$, then we compute the stationary probability $\pi_a$ of each cluster $\mathcal{C}_a$ by summing over the values of vertices in the cluster: $\pi_a = \sum_{i\in\mathcal{C}_a} \boldsymbol{\pi}(i)$. Let $r_{max}$ and $r_{min}$ be max and min radius of the circular layout, and $\pi_{max}$ and $\pi_{min}$ be max and min cluster stationary probability, respectively. Finally, the radial coordinate $\mathbf{r}(a)$ of cluster $\mathcal{C}_a$ is

$$\mathbf{r}(a) = \frac{r_{max} - r_{min}}{\pi_{max} - \pi_{min}}(\pi_{max} - \pi_a) + r_{min}. \tag{2}$$

**Angular coordinates of clusters**: In order to obtain the angular coordinates $\boldsymbol{\theta}$ of clusters $\mathcal{C}$, we first compute all pairwise similarities $\mathbf{S} \in \mathbb{R}^{L\times L}$ between the clusters, and then apply the modified spherical *Laplacian Eigenmap* technique [3, 4] to project the clusters on a circular manifold.

We use the *random walk with restart* (RWR) algorithm [24] to define the cluster similarity on a graph. The similarity values of all nodes $\mathbf{s}_a$ with respect to cluster $\mathcal{C}_a$ is defined as

$$\mathbf{s}_a = \lambda\mathbf{P}\mathbf{s}_a + (1-\lambda)\mathbf{v}_a^T \text{with } \mathbf{v}_a(i) = \begin{cases} 1/|\mathcal{C}_a| & \text{if } i \in \mathcal{C}_a \\ 0 & \text{otherwise} \end{cases} \tag{3}$$

The score $\mathbf{s}_a(i)$ means the probability that a random walker stays at node $i$ when the walker follows the edge of graph with probability $\lambda$ and return to uniformly random nodes of cluster $\mathcal{C}_a$ with $1-\lambda$. It is straightforward to compute the similarity score from $\mathcal{C}_a$ to $\mathcal{C}_b$, denoted by $\mathbf{S}(a,b)$, as follows:

$$\mathbf{S}(a,b) = \sum_{i\in\mathcal{C}_b} \mathbf{s}_a(i)/S_a \quad \text{where } S_a = 1 - \sum_{i\in\mathcal{C}_a} \mathbf{s}_a(i). \tag{4}$$

Next, we project the clusters on a unit circle. Our circular embedding is based on the *Spherical Laplacian Information Maps* (SLIM) [4], which extends the Laplacian eigenmap (LEM) optimization [3] with an additional constraint of embedding data on the surface of sphere.

Conceptually, if a pair of clusters is similar to each other, then their angular difference in embedding should be small. Hence, the objective is formulated as finding $\boldsymbol{\theta}$ to minimize

$$\boldsymbol{\theta} = \text{argmin} \sum_{a\in\mathcal{C}}\sum_{b\in\mathcal{C}} \mathbf{S}(a,b)|\theta_a - \theta_b| - \sum_{a\in\mathcal{C}}\sum_{b\in\mathcal{C}} |\theta_a - \theta_b|^{\gamma}. \tag{5}$$

The LEM objective (*i.e.* the first term of Eq.(5)) enforces nearby points in the graph to be as close together as possible in the angular representation. However, the optimization using only the LEM objective attains a trivial solution to collapse all data to the same point. Therefore, the regularizer (*i.e.* the second term) is included in order to spread the embedded clusters on a circle. It leads the optimization to prefer large angular distances between all pairs of clusters. We set the constant $\gamma = 0.5$ in our experiments.

Since the optimization problem in Eq.(5) has no closed-form solution, we employ a gradient descent procedure, as summarized in step **7–11** of Algorithm 3. By nature, the final embedding highly depends on the initialization, for which we first perform hierarchical clustering on $\mathbf{S}$, and then use its polar dendrogram. This initialization enables similar nodes to have small geodesic distances.

**Layout refinement**: We slightly update the coordinates of clusters $(\mathbf{r}, \boldsymbol{\theta})$ so that the final layout is more visually pleasant. We separate any pair of exemplars that are too much overlapped, by using a force-directed drawing algorithm called Fruchterman and Reingold's method. The cluster positions are updated to reach equilibrium states by the attractive and repulsive forces. The attractive forces encourage the updated positions to be as similar to the original $(\mathbf{r}, \boldsymbol{\theta})$ as possible, while the repulsive forces take part severely overlapped exemplars. This refinement is summarized in step **12–17** of Algorithm 3.

# 5. EXPERIMENTS

In our experiments, we first present the examples of brand association maps in section 5.1. Then, we quantitatively evaluate the proposed approach from two technical perspectives: exemplar detection/clustering in section 5.2, and brand localization via image cosegmentation in section 5.3. Since the main goal of this paper is to achieve the two technical visualization tasks, we focus on validating the algorithmic performance over other candidate methods instead of user study. Finally, we examine the correlation between our findings from community photos and the actual sales data of brands in section 5.4.

## 5.1 Visualization of Brand Association Maps

We present the brand association maps of six competing brands of the *luxury* category in Fig.5. We show top 20 exemplars (*i.e.* cluster centers) in the map. We make several interesting observations as follows. First of all, our algorithm successfully discovers brands' characteristic visual themes (*e.g.* the watch clusters in the *Rolex* and the iconic check patterns of the *Burberry*). Second, much of highly ranked clusters attribute to some specific scenes where phototaking is preferred. For example, in the *Rolex*, the clusters of horse-riding and auto-racing events that are sponsored by the *Rolex* are as dominant as those of its main product watches. Such event topics are more favorable to be recorded as pictures rather than texts. In the *Louis+Vuitton*, there are lots of *wedding* related clusters; it makes sense because the wedding is not only an event where the products of luxury brands are purchased much, but also a memorable moment where the photos are taken a lot.

Although our photo-based brand association map is novel and promising, there are several issues to be explored further. First, we may need to correctly handle highly redundant or noisy clusters, which are mainly caused by the imperfection of image processing and clustering. Second, we also need to deal with polysemous brand names; for example, the *Mont+Blanc* is also the name of the mountain. If we use additional keywords during image crawling to filter them out, the volume of retrieved images decreases severely.

## 5.2 Results on Clustering

**Task**: We evaluate the performance of our algorithm and the baselines for the exemplar detection/clustering task as follows. We choose 20 brands (*i.e.* five brands per category), and generate 100 sets of groundtruth per brand as follows. We randomly sample three images $(i, j, k)$ from the image set of each brand, and manually label which of $j$ and $k$ is more similar to $i$. We denote $j \succ k|i$ if $j$ is more similar to $i$ than $k$. After applying each algorithm, suppose that $C_i$, $C_j$, and $C_k$ denote the clusters that include image $i$, $j$, and $k$, respectively. Then, we compute the similarity between clusters $\sigma(C_j, C_i)$ and $\sigma(C_k, C_i)$ by using the RWR algorithm in section 4. Finally, we compute the accuracy of the algorithm using the Wilcoxon–Mann–Whitney statistics:

$$ACC := \frac{\sum_{(i,j,k)} \mathbb{I}(j \succ k|i \ \wedge \ \sigma(C_j, C_i) > \sigma(C_k, C_i))}{\sum_{(i,j,k)} \mathbb{I}(j \succ k|i)} \quad (6)$$

where $\mathbb{I}$ is an indicator function. The accuracy increases only if the algorithm can partition the image set into coherent clusters, and the similarities between clusters coincide well with human's judgment of groundtruth.

**Baselines**: We compare our algorithm with four baselines. The (`KMean`) and the (`Spect`) are the two popular clustering methods, K-means and spectral clustering, respectively. The (`LP`) is a label propagation algorithm for community detection [20], and the (`AP`) is the *affinity propagation* [7], which is a message-passing based clustering algorithm. Our method is tested in two different ways, according to whether image segmentation is in a loop or not. The (`Sub`) does not exploit the image cosegmentation output, whereas the (`Sub-M`) is our fully geared approach. That is, this comparison can justify the usefulness of our alternating approach between clustering and cosegmentation. For all algorithms, we set the number of clusters as $L = 300$, and use the same image features and KNN similarity graphs of section 3.

**Quantitative results**: Fig.6 reports the results of our algorithm and four baselines across 20 brand classes. The leftmost bar set is the average accuracies of 20 classes. In most brand classes, the accuracies of our method (`Sub-M`) are better than those of all the baselines. The average accuracy of our (`Sub-M`) is 62.0%, which is much higher than 51.7% of the best baseline (`AP`). In addition, the average accuracies of the (`Sub-M`) are notably better than (`Sub`), which implicates that the cosegmentation for brand localization can improve the clustering performance as expected.

## 5.3 Results on Brand Localization

**Task**: The brand localization task is evaluated as follows. As groundtruths, we manually annotate 50 randomly sampled images per brand, for the same 20 brands in the previous experiments. We do not label too obvious images depicting products on white background, since they are too trivial to correctly evaluate the performances of algorithms. The accuracy is measured by the intersection-over-union metric $(GT_i \cap R_i)/(GT_i \cup R_i)$, where $GT_i$ is the groundtruth of image $i$ and $R_i$ is the regions segmented by the algorithm. It is a standard metric in segmentation literature [13, 15]. We compute the average accuracy from all annotated images.

**Baselines**: We select two baselines that can segment object regions from a large number of images in an unsupervised manner (*i.e.* with no labeled seed images). The (`LDA`) [21] is an LDA-based unsupervised localization method, and the (`COS`) [15] is a state-of-art submodular optimization based cosegmentation algorithm. Our algorithm is tested in three different versions, according to whether exemplar detection/clustering is in a loop or not. The (`MFC`) runs our cosegmentation without involving our clustering output (but using a random partitioning instead), in order to show the importance of the clustering step when segmenting highly diverse Web images. The (`MFC-S`) is a single loop of our exemplar detection/clustering and cosegmentation, and (`MFC-M`) iterates this process more than twice. In almost all cases, it converges in two iterations. Hence, this comparison can quantify the accuracy increase by the iterations. We run all algorithms in an unsupervised way for a fair comparison. Since it is hard to know the best number of foregrounds $K$

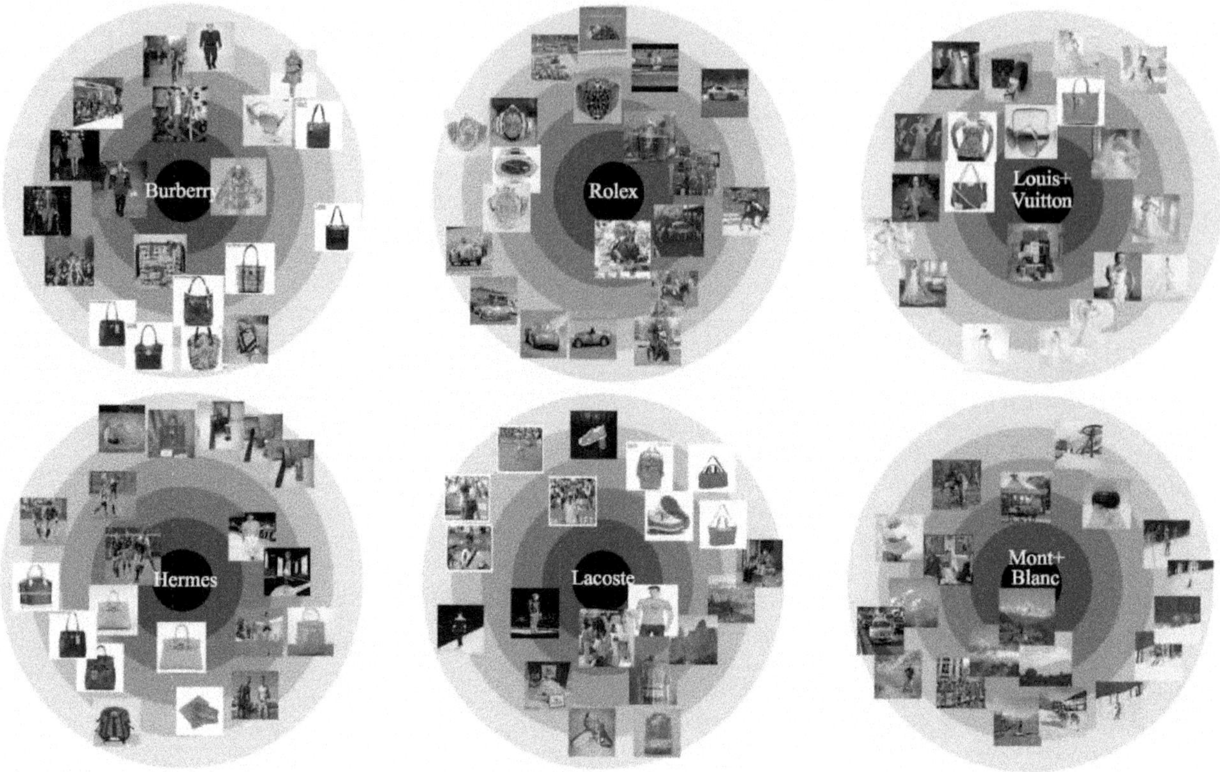


**Figure 5: Examples of brand association maps for six brands of the *luxury* category.**

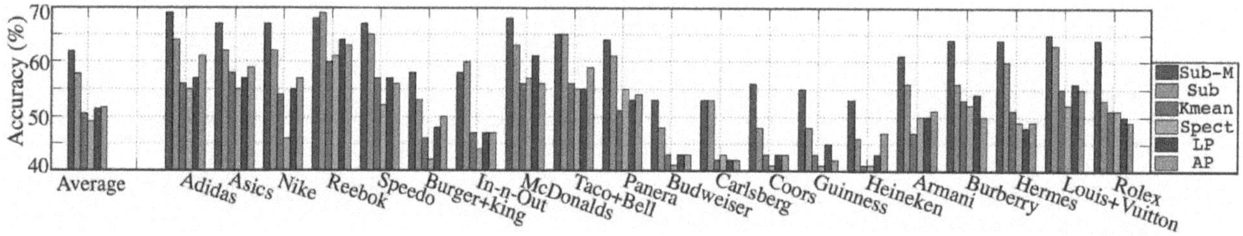


**Figure 6: Clustering accuracies of two variants of our approach (`Sub-*`) and four baselines for the 20 selected brands. The average accuracies over the 20 brands, shown in the leftmost bar set, are (`Sub-M`): 62.0%, (`Sub`): 57.8%, (`Kmean`): 50.5%, (`Spect`): 49.2%, (`LP`): 51.4%, and (`AP`): 51.7%.**

in advance (*e.g.* multiple foregrounds may exist in each image), we repeat each method by changing $K$ from one to five, and report the best results.

**Quantitative results**: Fig.7 shows that our method outperforms other candidate methods in almost all classes. Especially, our average accuracy is 49.5%, which is notably higher than 36.7% of the best baseline (`COS`). In addition, the average accuracy of the (`MFC-M`) is also higher than those of (`MFC-S`) and (`MFC`), which demonstrates that the clustering and cosegmentation are mutually-rewarding.

**Qualitative analysis**: Fig.8 shows six sets of brand localization examples. The images of each set belong to the same cluster, and thus are cosegmented. We observe that the subjects and their appearances severely vary across the pictures even though they are associated with the same brands. However, our approach can quickly cluster a large-scale image set and segment out common regions in an unsupervised and bottom-up way, which can be an useful function for various Web applications, including detecting regions of brand for online multimedia advertisement.

## 5.4 Correlation with Sales Data

Since our work is the first attempt on exploring online photo collections for brand associations, we additionally report the statistics of correlations between image data and sales data of the brands. We conduct two different comparisons. First, we observe how the photo volumes of brands are correlated with their market shares. For example, the average annual revenue of the *Nike* is higher than that of the *Adidas* by about 40% from 2006 to 2011. We examine whether the *Nike* is also dominant over the *Adidas* in the volumes of Web photos. Second, we study in-depth correlation between the product groups of each brand. For example, the annual reports of the *Louis+Vuitton* classify their business into several product groups such as leather goods, perfume, jewelry, and wine. We compare between the proportions of product groups in image data and sales data of the brand.

We obtain the sales data from the annual reports that are publicly available on the companies' webpages. We ignore the brands held by private companies (*e.g. Chanel*), because it is often hard to know accurate financial information. In this analysis, we use image and sales data from 2006 to 2011.

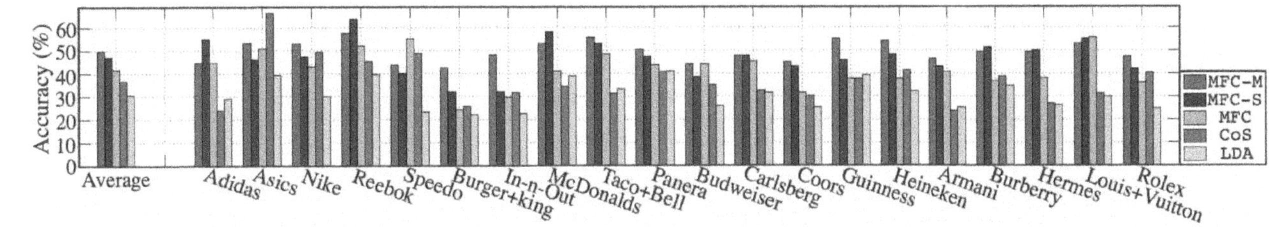


**Figure 7: Brand localization accuracies of three variants of our approach (MFC-*) and two baselines. The average accuracies of the leftmost bar set are (MFC-M): 49.5%, (MFC-S): 46.8%, (MFC): 41.7%, (COS): 36.7%, and (LDA): 30.6%.**

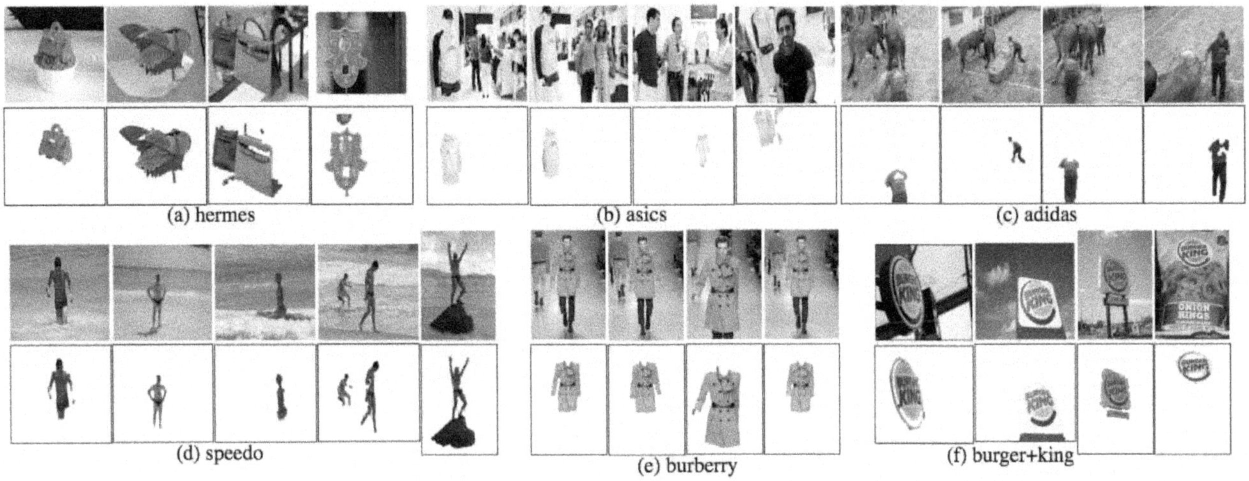


**Figure 8: Six groups of brand localization examples. We show input images (top) and their segmentation output (bottom). In each group, we sample four or five images that belong to the same cluster, and thus are jointly segmented.**

**Correlation between photo volumes and market shares**: Fig.9 shows the proportions of photo volumes and market shares for the brands per category. The ranking of the brands in the two data types are roughly similar, but the percentages do not agree each other because the preferred scenes or situations of photo taking are different from those of product purchase. For example, the *Guinness* has a larger percentage value in the photo volume than in the sales thanks to its positioning as premium beer. On the contrary, *Taco+Bell* occupies a small portion of photo volumes. It may be because the *Taco+Bell* is a cheap fastfood brand, which hardly attracts people to take pictures for the brand.

**Correlation between product groups**: Now we turn to the comparison between product groups in each brand. The main challenge here is that it is difficult for both human and computers to correctly classify millions of images into the predefined product groups. For human, the data size is too large to manually classify them. For computers, there is no classifier applicable to noisy Web images with high accuracies. Thus, we take advantage of our exemplar detection/clustering results. We manually classify each exemplar into one of predefined groups, and all the images in the same cluster are labeled as the same. The classification of product groups is based on the brand's annual reports.

Fig.10 shows the results of product group analysis for four luxury brands. We first label exemplar images by one of three groups: *product*, *company*, and *personal*. The *product* group comprises the photos whose main contents are the products of the brand. The *company* group includes the images that are directly relevant to the brand but not to any particular products. It consists of four subgroups: *advertisement*, *logo*, *shop*, and *event*. The final one is the *personal* group for the private pictures whose contents are not explicitly associated with brands.

We summarize several observations as follows. First, in most brands, the *personal* group is the first or second largest one, which may result from that people usually take pictures on personal matters. Second, the *company* group is also very popular; for examples, people are interested in luxurious *Louis+Vuitton*'s stores or advertisement as much as its products. Moreover, the events hosted by brands are also popularly taken such as fashion shows, music concerts, and sports activities. Third, in the *product* group, one or two leading product types take the majority of photo volumes while some product segments like *wines*, *perfume*, and *jewelry* rarely appear.

# 6. CONCLUSION

In this paper, we addressed the problem of visualizing the brand associations by leveraging large-scale online photo collections. We developed a novel approach to jointly performing exemplar detection/clustering and brand localization in a mutually-rewarding way. With the experiments of about five millions of images for 48 brands, we have shown the superiority of our approach for the two visualization tasks over other candidate methods. The empirical results assured that our method can be a fundamental component to achieve our ultimate goal: developing an interactive system for both marketers and general users to automatically elicit and visualize brand associations from online images, which is a next direction of our future work.

**Acknowledgement**: This work is supported in part by NSF IIS-1115313, AFOSR FA9550010247, Google, and Alfred P. Sloan Foundation.

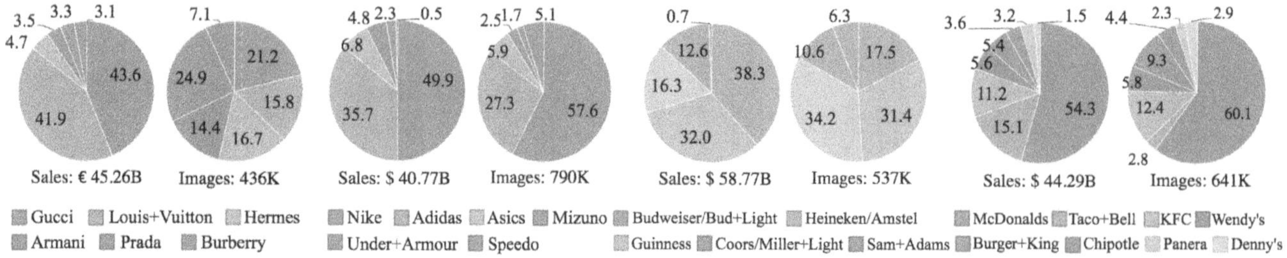


(a) luxury (b) sports (c) beer (d) fastfood

**Figure 9: Comparison between the market shares (left) and the portions of photo volumes (right) for the brands of four categories: (a) *luxury*, (b) *sports*, (c) *beer*, and (d) *fastfood*. The numbers indicate percentage values.**

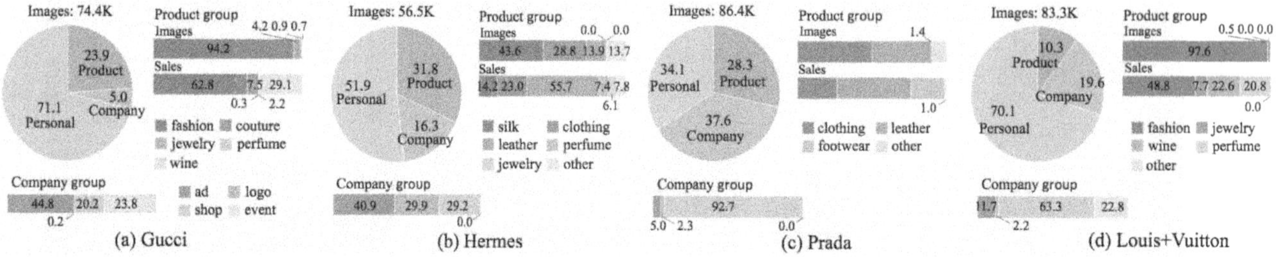


(a) Gucci (b) Hermes (c) Prada (d) Louis+Vuitton

**Figure 10: Results of the product group analysis for four luxury brands. Each pie chart shows the proportions of three groups in the image volume: *product*, *company*, and *personal*. In the bottom, the images of the *company* group are further classified into one of *advertisement*, *logo*, *shop*, and *event*. In the right, bar charts show the proportions of the images (top) and the actual revenues (bottom) for the *product* group. The numbers indicate percentage values.**

# 7. REFERENCES


[1] D. A. Aaker. Measuring Brand Equity Across Products and Markets. *Cal. Manag. Rev.*, 38(3):102–120, 1996.

[2] N. Akiva, E. Greitzer, Y. Krichman, and J. Schler. Mining and Visualizing Online Web Content Using BAM: Brand Association Map. In *ICWSM*, 2008.

[3] M. Belkin and P. Niyogi. Laplacian Eigenmaps for Dimensionality Reduction and Data Representation. *neural computation*, 15(6):1373–1396, 2003.

[4] K. M. Carter, R. Raich, and A. O. Hero. Spherical Laplacian Information Maps (SLIM) for dimensionality reduction. In *SSP*, 2009.

[5] A. C. H. Chen. Using Free Association to Examine the Relationship between the Characteristics of Brand Associations and Brand Equity. *J. Product Brand Management*, 10(7):439–451, 2001.

[6] J. E. Danes, J. S. Hess, J. W. Story, and J. L. York. Brand Image Associations for Large Virtual Groups. *Qualitative Market Research*, 13(3):309–323, 2010.

[7] B. J. Frey and D. Dueck. Clustering by Passing Messages Between Data Points. *Science*, 315:972–976, 2007.

[8] K. Gao, S. Lin, Y. Zhang, S. Tang, and D. Zhang. Logo Detection Based on Spatial-Spectral Saliency and Partial Spatial Context. In *ICME*, 2009.

[9] L. Grady. Random Walks for Image Segmentation. *IEEE PAMI*, 28:1768–1783, 2006.

[10] Y. Jing and S. Baluja. PageRank for Product Image Search. In *WWW*, 2008.

[11] H. Kang, M. Hebert, A. A. Efros, and T. Kanade. Connecting Missing Links: Object Discovery from Sparse Observations Using 5 Million Product Images. In *ECCV*, 2012.

[12] K. L. Keller. Conceptualizing, Measuring, and Managing Customer-Based Brand Equity. *J. Marketing*, 57(1):1–22, 1993.

[13] G. Kim and E. P. Xing. On Multiple Foreground Cosegmentation. In *CVPR*, 2012.

[14] G. Kim and E. P. Xing. Jointly Aligning and Segmenting Multiple Web Photo Streams for the Inference of Collective Photo Storylines. In *CVPR*, 2013.

[15] G. Kim, E. P. Xing, L. Fei-Fei, and T. Kanade. Distributed Cosegmentation via Submodular Optimization on Anisotropic Diffusion. In *ICCV*, 2011.

[16] J. Kleban, X. Xie, and W.-Y. Ma. Spatial Pyramid Mining for Logo Detection in Natural Scenes. In *ICME*, 2008.

[17] S. Lazebnik, C. Schmid, and J. Ponce. Beyond Bags of Features: Spatial Pyramid Matching for Recognizing Natural Scene Categories. In *CVPR*, 2006.

[18] D. L. Nelson, C. L. McEvoy, and T. A. Schreiber. The University of South Florida Free Association, Rhyme, and Word Fragment Norms. *Behavior Research Methods, Instruments, Computers*, 36(3):402–407, 2004.

[19] Nielsen Online. Brand Association Map, 2010.

[20] U. N. Raghavan, R. Albert, and S. Kumara. Near Linear Time Algorithm to Detect Community Structures in Large-Scale Networks. *Phys Rev E*, 76(036106), 2007.

[21] B. C. Russell, A. Efros, J. Sivic, W. T. Freeman, and A. Zisserman. Using Multiple Segmentations to Discover Objects and their Extent in Image Collections. In *CVPR*, 2006.

[22] S. Sanyal and S. H. Srinivasan. LogoSeeker: A System for Detecting and Matching Logos in Natural Images. In *ACM MM*, 2007.

[23] O. Schnittka, H. Sattler, and S. Zenker. Advanced Brand Concept Maps: A New Approach for Evaluating the Favorability of Brand Association Networks. *I. J. Research in Marketing*, 2012.

[24] J. Sun, H. Qu, D. Chakrabarti, and C. Faloutsos. Neighborhood Formation and Anomaly Detection in Bipartite Graphs. In *ICDM*, 2005.

[25] B. D. Till, D. Baack, and B. Waterman. Strategic Brand Association Maps: Developing Brand Insight. *J. Product Brand Management*, 20(2):92–100, 2011.

[26] J. Wang, J. Wang, G. Zeng, Z. Tu, R. Gan, and S. Li. Scalable k-NN Graph Construction for Visual Descriptors. In *CVPR*, 2012.

[27] K. Yamaguchi, M. H. Kiapour, L. E. Ortiz, and T. L. Berg. Parsing Clothing in Fashion Photographs. In *CVPR*, 2012.

# Is a Picture Really Worth a Thousand Words? - On the Role of Images in E-commerce

Wei Di, Neel Sundaresan, Robinson Piramuthu, Anurag Bhardwaj
eBay Research Labs, eBay Inc.
2145 Hamilton Ave., San Jose, CA, USA
wedi, nsundaresan, rpiramuthu, anbhardwaj@ebay.com

## ABSTRACT

In online peer-to-peer commerce places where physical examination of the goods is infeasible, textual descriptions, images of the products, reputation of the participants, play key roles. Visual image is a powerful channel to convey crucial information towards e-shoppers and influence their choice. In this paper, we investigate a well-known online marketplace where over millions of products change hands and most are described with the help of one or more images. We present a systematic data mining and knowledge discovery approach that aims to quantitatively dissect the role of images in e-commerce in great detail. Our goal is two-fold. First, we aim to get a thorough understanding of impact of images across various dimensions: product categories, user segments, conversion rate. We present quantitative evaluation of the influence of images and show how to leverage different image aspects, such as quantity and quality, to effectively raise sale. Second, we study interaction of image data with other selling dimensions by jointly modeling them with user behavior data. Results suggest that "watch" behavior encodes complex signals combining both attention and hesitation from buyer, in which image still holds an important role when compared to other selling variables, especially for products for which appearance is important. We conclude on how these findings can benefit sellers in a high competitive online e-commerce market.

## Categories and Subject Descriptors

G.3 [**PROBABILITY AND STATISTICS**]: Correlation and regression analysis, Experimental design; H.2.8 [**Database Applications**]: [data mining, image databases]

## Keywords

E-commerce, Online shopping, Multimodal data mining, Image, Image Quality, Buyer Behavior, User Engagement

## 1. INTRODUCTION

Consumers enjoy the convenience and low price offered by online shopping. However, since there is no physical interaction between buyers and sellers, these benefits may be diminished by increased risk due to product uncertainty and seller uncertainty. In online transaction, trust is an essential dimension of success [16]. Online reputation systems can reflect seller credits based on past transaction and crowd wisdom [8, 24]. Yet, each individual product purchase involves understanding the product better. Information and communication with sellers are mostly limited through text, creating a sense of anxiety among online shoppers [28]. Fortunately, product images (or other multimedia format) provide a unique yet profound channel to convey visual information to buyer. It provides buyer, who must put considerable dollars at risk, a way to view and inspect the item before making the decision.

Pictures from online personal albums and social sites are typically used to record events or share visual elements of creativity and beauty. On the other hand, product images are used to provide a clear and attractive picture in a trust-worthy way in order to convey information to consumers about the product and its quality.

With the advent of digital cameras and phone-based cameras, capturing and sharing of images and videos have become prevalent. For instance, according to one source, over 200K images are uploaded to Facebook per minute; 16 billion images have been shared on Instagram; eBay sellers upload above 20 million product images everyday. While most images are for human consumption, on platforms like Amazon, Craigslist and eBay, images form an important component for commerce to happen. While Amazon curates and standardizes the images given its catalog-based commerce, on eBay, given the diversity of the products, product conditions, and the sellers, there are huge variations among images in terms of quantity and quality. In fact, a large portion of inventory images are taken by individual sellers who do not possess professional photography skills, which leads to significant variations in image quality [11].

Studies on selling strategies and trust issues for online shopping are widespread in the literature [6, 28, 16], without focus on role of product images. Previous research on importance of images in an e-commerce scenario can be found in [3, 4, 10, 26, 17, 20, 14, 27]. However, studies related to image quality and quantity are only drawn from small user groups, which may not be extensible to realistic vast online markets. Large scale studies only look at inclusion of images in the success of auctions, without importance to image quality or quantity. Also, we still know little about the effects of image in marketplace where majority of images are taken by individual customers rather being well designed by merchandising standard, and little of to what extent, images influence user's online shopping choice and behavior.

The goal of this research is to get a thorough understanding of impact of images across various key dimensions. While a successful online transaction is dependent on many factors, such as *prod-*


*WSDM'14,* February 24–28, 2014, New York, New York, USA.

ACM 978-1-4503-2351-2/14/02 ...$15.00.
http://dx.doi.org/10.1145/2556195.2556226.

*uct* (price & quality), *advertisement* (listing title, description, and image), *service* (shipping & return & communication & security), *buyer's intention* and *seller's qualification*, we particularly focus on answering the following questions in relation to product images in e-commerce:

- How images of listings differ across categories, sellers, or specific attributes of the item, such as condition?
- Does visual information always help to improve the conversion rate for online shopping by increasing trust and reducing perceived risk, and if it does, in what respect and to what extent?
- How to leverage various image properties (display format, quality or quantity) to raise sale cost-effectively?
- How images impact buyer behavior/experience? For instance, how sensitive are experienced buyers to different quality and quantity of product images?
- How important are images as compared to other selling variables?

Specifically, we choose three important aspects of images: 1) the display format, 2) number of images per product, and 3) image quality. We do a cross study of their relationship with multiple key dimensions in e-commerce, such as conversion rate, seller and buyer, buyer experience and engagement.

We believe that given the significant growth in online shopping, investigation of these issues allows better selling strategies to be designed and better understanding of consumer's behavior and their preference.

The rest of the paper is organized as follows. In section 2, we review research background, formulate our problem and discuss previous related work in literature. Two major data sets are introduced in section 3. Section 4 presents an overview of the role of images in e-commerce in terms of category, seller and buyer segments, buyer activity and experience, and conversion rate. Also, using product resale (where buyers resell products purchased from other sellers in the same marketplace) as an exemplar, we show improved sell-through and profit by improving image factors. Section 5 studies factors that affect buyer's behavior of adding items to watch list. We show that the "watch" action is double-faced with complex signals that can be attributed to various factors, including those related to image. Moreover, we propose a binomial action model, and describe the use of logistic regression as a means of combining individual variables and determining significant factors. Section 6 lists some concluding remarks and possible future work.

## 2. BACKGROUND AND RELATED WORK

Online marketplaces have significantly grown in the past decade affording both local and global online trade. Many of these markets are peer-to-peer in nature and have encouraged useful research on topics like consumer behavior, trust, selling strategy, cross-border languages [6].

Online shopping process consists of five steps similar to those associated with traditional shopping behavior [19], including a) a need for some product or service, b) search online marketplace for need-related information, c) attracted by information about products or services, d) evaluate/compare alternatives, e) make the final decision for purchasing and being provided with post-sale services.

Studies have shown that shopping behavior is significantly influenced by trust and perceived risk, consumer's attitude, social influence, etc. [21]. Trust and the perceived risk are the very essential issues for online market [28, 16]. This is mainly due to the information asymmetry of online market [2], which causes difficulty for sellers to credibly disclose product information and for buyers to obtain relevant information to evaluate product quality. Risk in each transaction is essentially created by the threats to obtain misleading/incorrect information from the item, thus facing adverse consequences of engaging in e-commerce. With no buildings or staff to evaluate, and no physical items to inspect, consumer decisions rest purely on the the descriptions and pictures provided [13]. Therefore, effective communication between buyer and seller is very important to break up this asymmetry hurdle. Effective product presentation must be visible, clear, and credible [22]. However, text information such as title and listing description can only provide information within the scope of language, while the valuable visual information is lost.

Previous research has shown the use of pictures to be important to buyers when buying on one of the largest e-commerce market - eBay [3, 10, 4, 20, 26]. Study in [5] indicated that product picture is one of the most influential risk-reducing factors. The author found in their particular case that either a real picture of the product actually being sold or a stock picture is a risk-reducing factor that will improve the outcomes of the auction for the seller. The inclusion of the real picture is proved to be effective in increasing auction success, effectiveness, and the value of the final bid. While a stock picture also significantly increases the final bid, the probability of auction success is not enhanced. Study in [18] looks at number of images embedded in item descriptions in eBay motors and draws the conclusion that more images help to boost the selling, especially for old cars. The author also found strong correlation of photo and price for non-dealers, which is possibly because buyers cannot rely on reputation as an alternate source of information about quality.

Moreover, evidence has been presented that clear and detailed pictures of the products also help to reduce perceived risk associated with online purchasing [14, 17, 27]. Based on the study of a smaller user group, the Keynote study in 2005 ([15]) reveals the importance of better quality images as a number of shoppers expressed their preference to see both higher quality photographs and more images in item descriptions.

Recent study showed that certain image features can also help to improve click through rate in product search engine [11, 7]. The authors conducted experiments to show that including image features in a machine learned click based ranking model improves the NDCG (normalized discounted cumulative gain) of the search results. The work in [4] studies the ability to attract customers and likelihood of transaction by including a binary variable indicating whether an image is associated with the listing. They found positive evidence for inexpensive products that providing image can increase number of bidding.

The above mentioned research work address the observed benefit of using images for listing descriptions. However, none of the above work has done a systematic and thorough study on the impact of images on online shopping, either from both the quantity and quality sides of image, or cross various dimensions of online shopping - from seller to buyer, or from user experience to user behavior. Also, these work do not provide the answers to the question that, given known importance of image presence for online transaction, to what extend image affect user's attention and decision for a product, how does it compare to other key factors such as price or seller reputation, etc.

## 3. DATA PREPARATION

To avoid bias from studying a smaller user group, in this study, we collect data from real online listing at a large scale. We construct two major data sets from the universe of product listings from a popular online peer-to-peer marketplace. We want to understand, at the highest level, the impact on user engagement and purchase of the number of images; the quality of images; and the way they are laid out (display type). We would also like to know what kind of sellers benefit from these aspects of images. Particularly, the data focuses on three different aspects of a listing image: a) the display type, b) the number of images per listing, and c) the image quality for the dominant image (the one shown up on the product search page).

The first dataset includes randomly chosen product listings from the year 2011-2012. Since displaying type or using multiple images are optional for seller (and costs the sellers), the data may be sparse. It is used to learn the first two aspects of images in relation to conversion rate and seller type. Detailed results are presented in section 4.1 and 4.2. The second data set is mainly used for studying image quality factors. The data covers randomly sampled listings created on several random selected months in the year of 2012. In this dataset, there are in total 4658711 listings. Among them, 889541 are fixed price listings, and others are auctions. This data is used to perform analysis in section 4.3 and 5.2. We further expand this data set with great details to study buyer's "watch" behavior in section 5.3. Detailed information include title, seller information, item condition, shipping information, gallery type, displaying type, auction type, stock photo indicator, listing duration, image quality and counts, etc..

One additional resale data is also collected as special exemplar case to gain deeper understandings on our major findings. Detailed information can be found in section 4.4.

# 4. AN OVERVIEW OF IMAGES IN E-COMMERCE

In this section, we study the impact of image display type, the number of images, and the quality of images.

## 4.1 Photo Display Type

**Question 1**: *What is the effect of custom photos versus original catalog photos on users?*

Stock photos are catalog images with high quality. Seller can choose "use stock photo" option without taking and uploading their own photos, but a note stating that the item picture is a stock photo will appear below the photo. We investigate the conversion rate of items using and not using stock photo. Result shows that the conversion rate for items in our dataset using stock photo is only about about half of what it is for items not using stock photo. This result is consistent with previous finding that an actual digital picture of the item being sold will likely increase the probability of success, and the benefit to using a stock source of photos is rather limited [5].

**Question 2**: *Does Size Matter?*

The default format for displaying photo is the *Standard Show*. The platform also provides seller with few other enhanced features with small amount of additional fees. There are features like *EPS Picture Show* that enables buyers to browse the item pictures or run them in a slide show at the top of the item listing; *Picture Pack* that offers special pricing for multiple pictures (up to 12). *Super Size Picture* will display images in an enlarged manner. Table 1 shows the conversion rate of few major options. Results indicate that larger photos, which provide more information for buyer to inspect details of the product, increase the chance of success for an online selling.

| Display Type | Sold | Listing | Conversion rate |
|---|---|---|---|
| Standard Show | 420.7M | 2958.5M | 14.2% |
| Large Photo Show | 4.5M | 19.9M | 22.9% |
| Picture Pack | 316.3M | 1411.5M | 22.4% |
| EPS Picture Show | 3.4M | 9.0M | 37.9% |
| Super Size Picture | 7.7M | 26.0M | 29.5% |

Table 1: Conversion Rate vs. Photo Display Type, which shows larger picture and pleasing browsing experience increase chance of success in sale. Numbers of sold and listed items are rounded to millions (M).

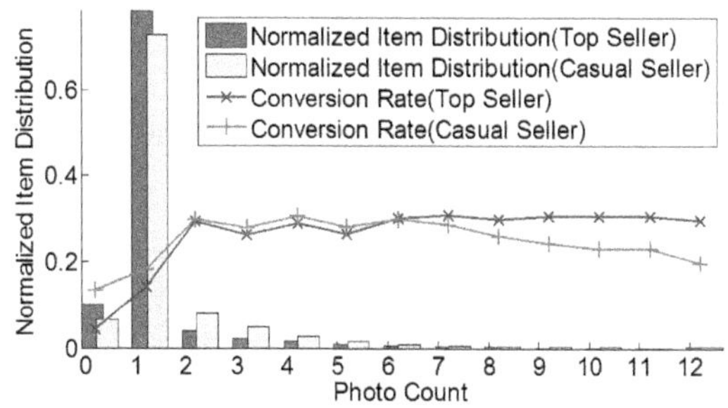


Figure 3: Photo Count distribution vs. Conversion Rate for top sellers and casual sellers. Observed from the curve plots, conversion rate doubled twice when using two images as compared to using one picture. Observed from the bar plots, casual sellers tend to upload more pictures than top sellers as they have low volume to sell and can afford more effort on each item to add more pictures.

## 4.2 Photo Count

**Question 3**: *More pictures, more information? Better conversion?*

Figure 3 shows the normalized distribution of items sold by experienced sellers (green bar) and casual sellers (yellow bar), and the conversion rate (red and blue curves) in terms of number of images per item (photo count). Common to both experienced seller and casual seller, most of the items only have one image. Also, both the conversion rate shows a log-like growth pattern at the beginning. Clearly, by giving buyers more complete information from different views of object, the probability of success is increased, as we can see that conversion rate is almost doubled twice by using two images as compared to using a single one. In our data, more than 3 pictures seem to have a small impact. Further, comparing the normalized distribution of experienced and casual sellers (bar plot), we can see that casual sellers tend to use more images than experienced sellers. One possible explanation is that casual sellers have lower volume of items to be sold, thus can afford more effort for each single item to take or upload more images.

## 4.3 Image Quality

Quality of product images is important in helping the customer make decisions [14, 27, 17, 15]. Not only they are important to convey the visual information to buyers, also they are viewed as a visual proof of the quality of the real product and even the seller. Buyers expect clear, clean and even visually enjoyable images. A high quality or professionally photographed image may help to draw attentions from buyer or boost buyer's confidence for the product that they are interested in. On the contrary, poor images may countermand this benefit.

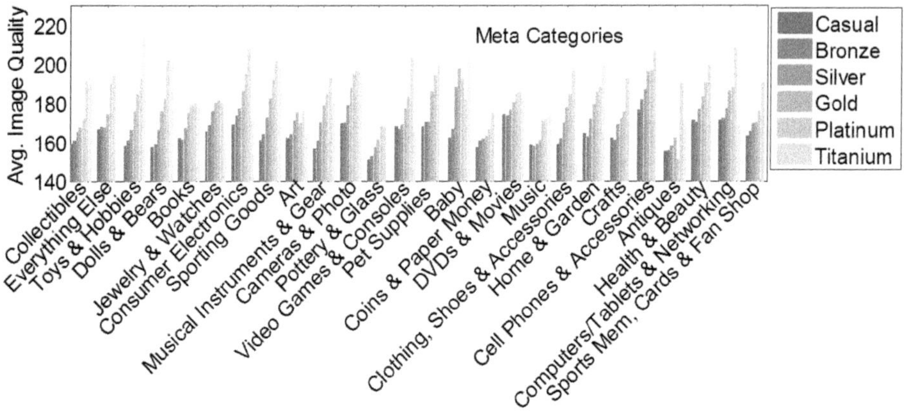


Figure 1: Image quality vs. Seller type for each meta category. Casual sellers are low volume seller, where titanium seller are of highest selling volume. Top sellers tend to use better quality images and casual sellers generally have lower quality images.

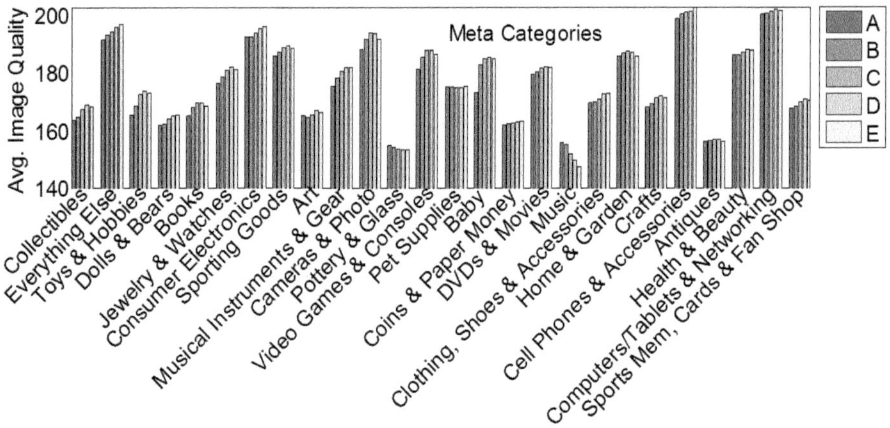


Figure 2: Image quality vs. Buyer type for each meta category for complete transactions. A-type buyer are the most frequent buyer, and E-type buyer are least active buyer. Experienced buyers show less sensitivity as compared to inexperienced buyers who show more concern about the quality of image.

While image quality is a highly content dependent and subjective concept, a proper measurement for this fundamental property is to evaluate whether a listing image is able to convey accurate information about the product effectively. In a peer-to-peer marketplace, where there is huge diversity of content providers, image quality can vary quite a bit even for similar products. Common image quality problems include: bad lighting, cluttered background, blur, specular reflection, and bad composition. Thus, focusing on the preference of product image from e-commerce perspective, we employ quality score that emphasizes on the clarity of the foreground object, high brightness, strong contrast between foreground and background, clean and uniform background, etc.. For each image, scores that represent each of these visual aspects, e.g. brightness or contrast, are computed and used as features to describe the image. A linear regression model is trained based on human rated data, where each annotator rates the image quality to be good, fair or bad. The learned model is then used to aggregate all the features to predict the overall quality of the image. Because some of the these features are computed from RGB values (0-255), as a convention, the range of quality score is also kept in $[0, 255]$, whereas a score of 255 means the best quality. Potential readers are referred to [7, 11] for details.

We study image qualities in relation to seller, buyer and their experience. Sellers are divided into different levels (casual, bronze, silver, gold, platinum, titanium) based on increasing amount of sales made and revenue generated. Buyers are also grouped into several levels (A,B,C,D,E) based on their spend over the last 12 months. A-type buyer spends the most, while E-type buyer spends the least. What we focus here on is the relative grades between sellers and between buyers.

Figures 1 and 2 show the evidences that:

**Question 4**: *How do quality of pictures vary with seller levels?*

**Question 5**: *How do different classes of buyers respond to image quality?*

We found that more successful the sellers are, the better quality images they use for their listings. However, limited to professional photograph tools and skills, qualities by casual seller are generally worse than top seller. This also corresponds to our finding that quality of images for *used* items are generally lower than that for *new* items (as casual sellers typically sell *used* products).

On the other hand, Figure 2 shows that, in general, new buyers prefer listings with high quality images which can provide more assurance on the product, whereas frequent buyers show less concern on possible risk for listings with low quality images, with few exceptions for categories such as Music and Antiques. This confirms the previous findings that perceived risk can be reduced by knowledge, skill, and experience on the Internet ([23, 25, 12]).

## 4.4 Resale: Profiting from better pictures

To understand how changes in image (quantity & quality) can make a difference, we collect a set of pairs of resale data. The initial sale are listings ended at several randomly selected time windows across 3 months of 2012. Each window covers 15 days. A valid resale is identified if the same buyer re-lists the item within 3 months after he/she bought from the initial sale. We restrict that both listings have the same title and are listed under the same leaf category. We are aware that there are professional sellers who conduct resale at the site by buying lots and then selling individually after modifying titles and other descriptions. However,we found that relaxing the condition to include pairs with similar titles introduces noise and the data become unreliable. We also filter out any items that use stock photos. The final data set consists of 55396 pairs of listings in total.

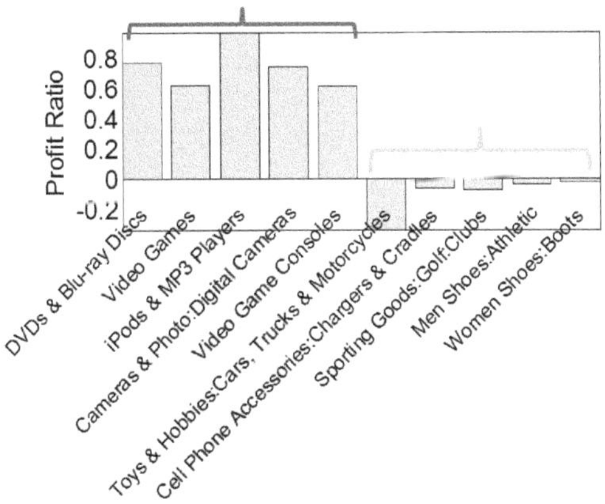


Figure 4: The most and least profitable leaf categories in resale, and their profit ratio. Electronic categories shows to be more profitable.

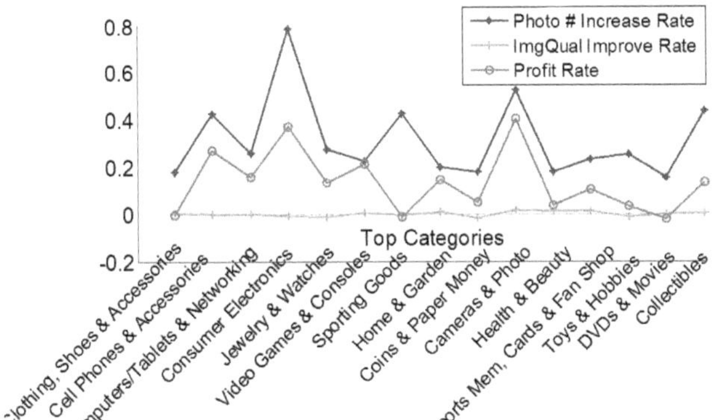


Figure 5: Resale profit rate vs. photo count increment rate for top 15 meta-categories. Strong correlation between increment in photo count and profit rate.

To analyze the changes of image factors and profit made from the resale, we compute relative changes in photo count $C$, image quality $Q$ and price $P$ (item price plus shipping & handling fees) by comparing resale (denoted by $b$) with initial sale (denoted by $a$):

$$
\begin{aligned}
R_P &= \frac{P_b - P_a}{P_a} \\
R_Q &= \frac{Q_b - Q_a}{Q_a} \\
R_C &= \frac{\alpha + C_b - C_a}{\alpha + C_a}
\end{aligned}
\tag{1}
$$

where $R_P$ is the profit rate and $R_Q$ is the quality improvement rate. $\alpha$ is a smoothing parameter as some of the initial sale items may not have any image. We choose $\alpha = 0.1$ in the experiments. As shown in Figure 3, increment of conversion rate follows a logarithmic-like growth pattern at the beginning. Hence, we formulate $R_C$ as the incremental rate of photo count, rather than using the absolute photo number.

Figure 4 shows the most profit and least profit leaf categories, along with their average profit rate. One can see that resale of Electronic items tends to be easier to make profit. Figure 5 shows the relationship between average $R_C$, $R_Q$ and $R_P$ for top meta-categories. We found a clear trend that as photo count increases, the probability of making profit also increases. However, image quality shows very small changes between the initial listing and the resale item. We also compute the correlation between $R_C$ and $R_P$ for top 20 leaf categories, resulting in 0.788, while correlation between $R_Q$ and $R_P$ is only about 0.032. Note that correlation is computed using scores from each item, not from the average profit rate that is shown in Figure 5.

By browsing image pairs in this resale dataset, we notice that reseller may change product images, but in general is able to maintain the quality of picture since the initial sale serves as an example of selling. Some resellers even copy photos from the previous seller, and only make slight modification, such as cropping the image. An example is shown in Figure 6.

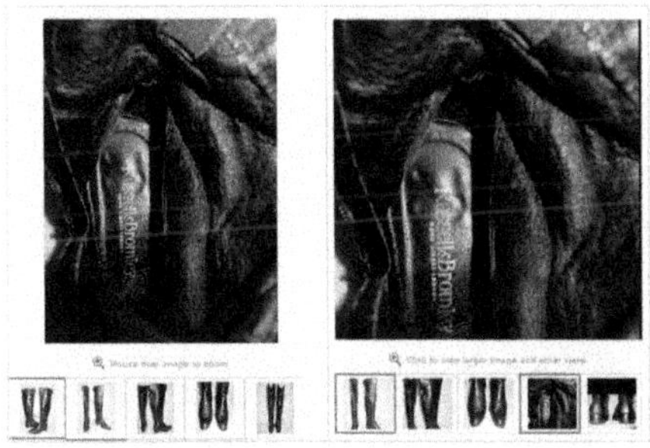

Figure 6: An example of resale, where reseller simply copied of the images from the initial sale, and modified some of them by cropping and scaling. Item title *"Black Leather Russell Bromley Knee Overknee Boots Sz 37 5 4 5 5 GC "*. **Left figure**: pictures in initial listing in Aug., 2012, **Right figure**: pictures for re-listing in Sept., 2012.

# 5. WATCHING THE WHEELS

Shopping processes can involve various states and stages like "viewing a product","sharing with friends", "adding to wish list", "adding to watch list", "adding to shopping cart", and finally, "buying". We would like to understand the role of images in these steps in the pipeline of a shopping process.

Among all kinds of buyer behaviors, in this paper, we investigate the buyer's "add-to-watch-list" behavior. We believe that although "add-to-watch-list" may not necessarily lead to a check out action, it embeds a more *serious* shopping attitude and intention than others behaviors, such as click-through, or visiting a page.

Unlike actions such as "add-to-cart", whereas users have to either confirm their decision for purchase or replace/remove the item from the cart later on, "watch" action comes with lower cost and pressure since no further action is required. It can also be used to reserve an item for a long term purpose. Moreover, "watch" encodes more individual preference, and is less influenced by other buyers in the market. Unlike other actions, the number of watch is always hidden from buyer. For example, at the search result page, the current bidding price and number of bids are often shown to buyers. Study has shown that in competitive situations, online auctions are likely to intensify, as bidders are emotionally involved [1]. Similarly, at the listing page, numbers of actions for "like", "want", and "own" are also shown. Buyers may be biased towards items with a higher number of bids or being liked by many people.

However, it would be naive to assume that "watch" only encodes user's interest and attention for the product. It's essentially a coin with two sides. As consumers are in the middle stage of a shopping process (browse, compare, decide, checkout), the "watch" behavior should therefore involve buyer's a) interest/intention for the item which causes them to seriously put the item under check, and b) hesitation as they are putting the item on hold to compare with other similar items, weigh the risk and take time to make the decision.

To understand this behavior, in the following section, we first analyze the relationship between watch and conversion rate. The goal is to see if our assumption that watch action encodes user's interest in the item is true. Second, we decompose this action by analyzing influential/related selling variables, particularly incorporate image related factors.

## 5.1 Buying Myself a Chance

The action of watching an item can be attributed to many things. Although we can not directly quantify how much interest the user has for the item through this action, we can assume that higher interest may transfer to higher probability of purchase. To prove this, Figure 7 (a) shows the changes in conversion rate given the watch popularity (in terms of the frequency of watch). It clearly shows that more "watch" indicates the product draws more interest from user, and resulting in higher conversion rate. This phenomenon peaks at about 20 watches, with a slightly down trend afterwards, which is possibly due to the lack of data samples to obtain a stable prediction (items with higher watch numbers are very sparse). It is also possible that a higher watch number indicates more competitive market. To get a sense of how watched item is compared to the overall inventory, Figure 7 (b) shows the averaged conversion rate per meta-category. In general, having more than 10 watches indicates higher market demand, and an above average conversion rate.

Figure 8 shows the percentage of the transactions that is made from watchers (buyers that made the watch action), for the items being watched and successfully sold. It can be seen that nearly one-third of the transactions come from watchers. Especially, percentage is higher for "unique" items, such as categories: music, crafts, and books. This is possibly due to that buyers often have clearer intentions for items in these categories or because items are "unique", buyers have fewer alternative options and end up going back to purchase the one they bookmarked through watching.

## 5.2 Better Image = More Watch?

As many variables may affect "watch" behavior, we particularly want to understand the influence of image factors. Does a better image lead to more attention from buyer and how does it compare

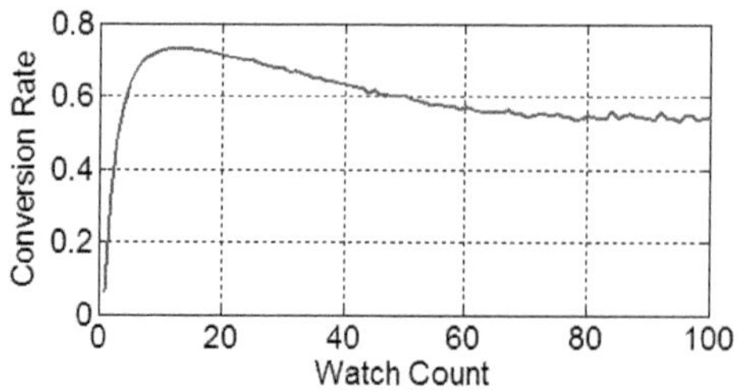


(a) Conversion rate vs. watch popularity

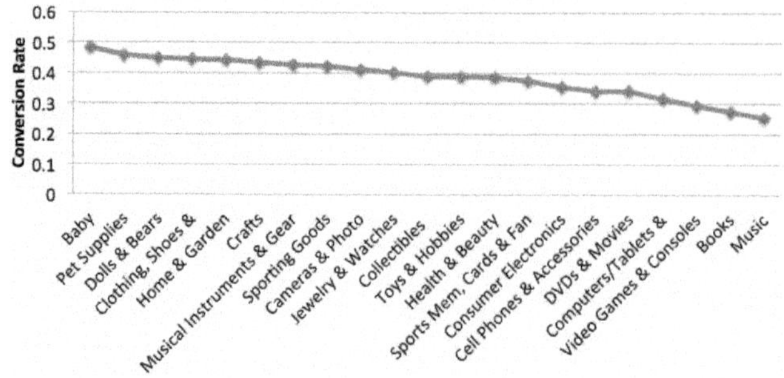


(b) Overview of conversion rate for various meta-categories

Figure 7: Conversion Rate w.r.t watch popularity and overall rate for each meta-category.

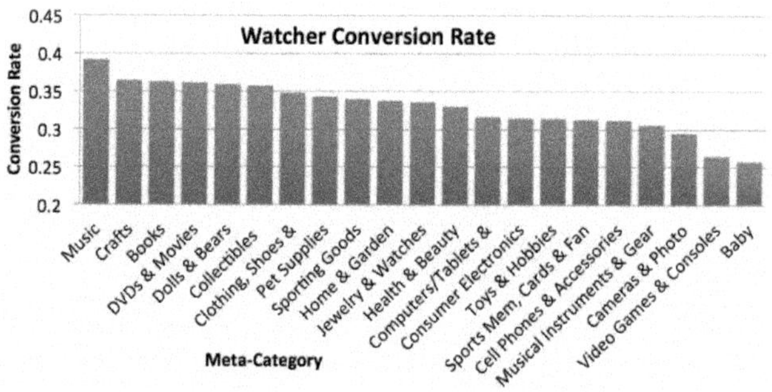


Figure 8: Conversion rate vs. watch popularity.

to other key factors that also influence this action? Also, some products rely more on their visual, e.g. clothing. Other products, e.g. electronics, rely more on their specifications and functionality, since only limited design models are available. Given such intrinsic difference, will it affect the importance of image in presenting the product?

To answer these questions, we collect listing data during the Fall season of 2012. Detailed information of this dataset is given in section 3. We first compare image quality with the number of "watch" per item. As shown in Figure 9, irrespective of the category of the products, data exhibits a strong correlation between image quality and watch count.

In order to understand buyer's behavior from the product category level, we also look at the performance of four top meta-categories. We divide these four categories into two groups. Type-A-categ, including Clothing, Shoes and Accessories, Consumer Electronics, is more apparel based and popular. On the other hand, type-B-categ is of more unique product, which includes Coins & Paper Money, Books. It can be seen from Figure 11 that type-A-categ shows much stronger response to image quality than type-B-categ. Type-A-categ also has higher average watch action as com-

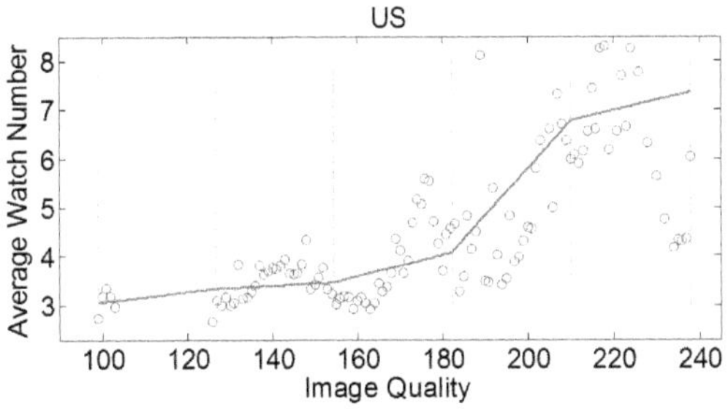


Figure 9: Overall trend of "watch" per item versus image quality score.

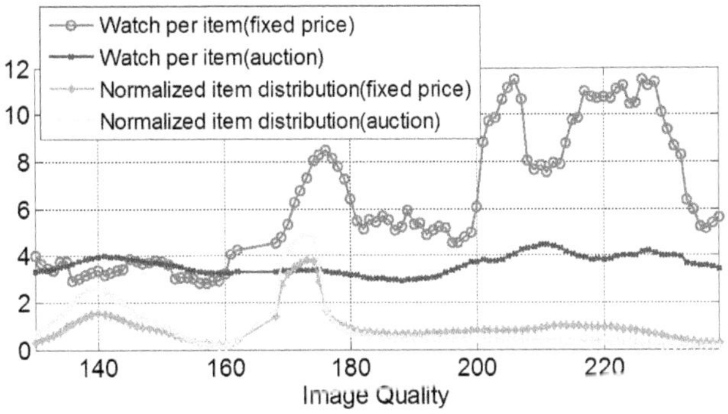


Figure 10: Different "watch" behavior for fixed-price and auction listings (red & blue curves). Yellow and green curves show the distributions of items in relation to image quality for auction and fixed-price items, respectively.

pared to type-B-categ. Differences between categories indicate the different roles of images cross various products. It is reasonable to assume that for products that more depend on their looking, image is likely to be a more important channel for communication. Trendy categories also imply that high competition may cause buyer to hold the item and look around for other candidates. This is less likely to happen for type-B-categ. Because items are unique, there are less competition from peers and fewer available alternatives in the market.

Figure 10 also plots the normalized item distribution in terms of image quality for fixed-price (green) and auctions (yellow), respectively. The peak around 170-180 shows that many images have moderate qualities. We also found a similar peak around the same position in the red curve, which is the watch number per item for fixed-price listings. We think this co-occurrence is not random. It's possibly because intensive competition between similar items holds back buyers from immediate purchase and increases the possibility that buyer adds the item into watch list for further comparison.

## 5.3 Action Model: A Regression Explanation

As shown in above section, "watch" action as one of the user engagement factor reveals complex signals combining both attention and hesitation from buyer. In order to model this action, we need to consider factors from both sides of the coin.

Assume each action "watch"(or not) from the buyer is a binary outcome $W$ from a set of selling variables. It can be modeled by *Bernoulli trial* as "watch"($W_i = 1$) and "not-watch"($W_i = 0$) for the $i$th trial with probability:

$$Pr(W_i = 1) = \pi_i \tag{2}$$

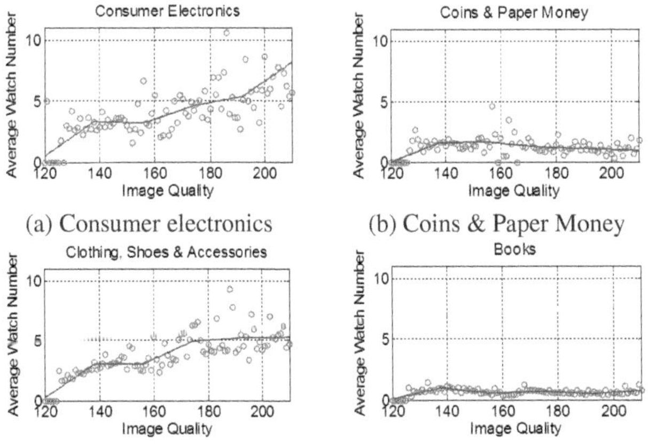


(a) Consumer electronics (b) Coins & Paper Money (c) Clothing, Shoes & Accessories (d) Books

Figure 11: Examples of several top meta-categories: correlation of "watch" per item versus image quality score.

Then the amount of "watch" $Y$ (watch count) that a listing item received can be viewed as a result of a sequence of each these trials. The distribution of this count in the $N$th trial is a binomial distribution $Y \sim Binomial(N, \pi)$.

Logistic regression models are often used to understand the role of input variables in explaining the outcome [9], where the response variable follows a binomial distribution. It can be formulated as:

$$\begin{aligned} log(\frac{\pi}{1-\pi}) &= \beta_0 + \beta_1 x_1 + \ldots + \beta_n x_n \\ &+ \delta_1 d_1 + \ldots + \delta_m d_m + \epsilon \end{aligned} \tag{3}$$

where the log value of the odds $\frac{\pi}{1-\pi}$ of taking action can be approximated by a linear combination of continuous input variables $x_1 \ldots x_n$, and dichotomous variables $d_1 \ldots d_m$ with values 0 or 1.

Based on the observations and discussions we had in previous sections, we select several selling dimensions and image related factors as input variables, including item price, shipping price, number of photos per item (photo count), number of word tokens in title (title length), seller type (0 as casual seller, 1 as top seller), item condition (new or used), seller's feedback positive ratio (percentage of positive feedback over all feedback), log of total feedback score, auction duration days (auct-durn-days), bold-title (0 as standard title, 1 as bold title), three gallery types, two display types, and keyword popularity ($Pop_{kw}$).

The three gallery types are: Standard, Gallery and Gallery Plus. *Gallery* as gallery view which is using a bigger size of images. *Gallery Plus* enhances the image displaying in the search results by displaying a larger picture and provide a magnifying glass and enlarge link. Photo display type include: Standard and Picture Pack which offers special pricing for multiple pictures. We have also discussed these features in section 4.1.

Keyword Popularity is used to encode the competition especially between popular items. We only use the title information as the product search engine highly depends on title. To compute this score, we first group listings based on their leaf category. Then, we parse each title to get tokens of words and corresponding count. We choose top tokens as the most popular keywords for each leaf category. In the experiment, for each leaf category we choose average token count as the threshold to select the popular keyword set $S_{kw}(c)$, where $S_{kw}$ is the popular keyword set for leaf category $c$. For a listing $l(c)$ from leaf category $c$ with title $t$, the keyword popularity score is computed by:

$$Pop_{kw}(t(l),c) = \frac{\mid f(S_w(t)) \bigcap S_{kw}(c) \mid}{\mid f(S_w(t)) \mid} \quad (4)$$

where $\mid S \mid$ is the cardinality of the set $S$. $S_w(t)$ is the set of word tokens for title $t$. $f$ is the function to filter out some stop words and punctuation, such as "the", "of", "!", etc. We kept some common words such as "new", "free", "size". Although they are commonly seen in titles and do not provide discriminative information to differentiate listings, our goal is instead to highlight the competition. These words are usually top queries and play important role in product search as many buyers try to search product with certain condition or with free shipping and handling. Taking the leaf category "*iPad/Tablet/eBook Accessories*" as an example, the popular keyword set $S_{kw}$ includes: " *crystal, protective, touchpad, apple, ereader, portable, magnetic, compatible, dual, camera, bluetooth, slim, amazon, 3gs, 4s* ", and many others. While for "*Women's Clothing:Athletic Apparel*" category, the popular keyword list instead consists of "*yoga, v-neck, seamless, nike, gym, fit, golf, hoodie, cotton, compression, zip, workout, cycling, combat, adidas, shot, stretch*", and so on.

## 5.4 Regression Results & Discussion

Since market and consumer's intention change dramatically cross different categories, we therefore apply regression model to each meta-category. Category variables include item condition (new or used), seller type (casual, top), gallery types, bold title, and display types. Regression is computed using the first level of each category variable as reference. Others are treated as continuous variables. We also filter out items with watch count over 50, which rarely occur. Then we normalize the count to be within the range of [0, 1]. Tables 2 and 3 show the regression results for *Clothing, Shoes & Accessories* (CSA), and *Consumer Electronics*.

For both categories, common significant factors include photo count, item condition, keyword popularity score and auction duration days. *Photo count* shows significant positive impact as we expected. Using *condition-new* as reference, *condition(used)* shows negative impact on attracting the buyer. With longer listing time, item has more chances to be exposed to consumers, therefore *auction duration days* is one of the major factors. Keywords help the item to have higher exposure, thus be search-able and accessible to the buyers. A higher keyword popularity score means larger overlap between title and the popular keyword set from the leaf-category that the item belongs to. This also indicates more intensive competition from peers.

Besides *photo count*, other image related variables, such as image quality and display types show more significant impact on CSA as compared to Electronics. We also found similar results for other electronic related categories. This corresponds to our assumption that apparel related category may gain more benefits from providing visual content for consumers. Also, we notice that Electronic category has overall better quality images since it's easier to obtain standard product image. Sellers also tend to employ good quality images from other sellers. Therefore, the competition between sellers and the focuses from buyers in regards to the product more likely rely on other factors instead of image.

# 6. CONCLUSIONS AND FUTURE WORK

Given only scattered evidence in literature that inclusion of image or other multimedia information may help improve transaction rate, in this paper, we dive into three major aspects of image: display format, number of views presented per item, and their quality. We focus on understanding not only yes or no question but to what extent images affect online transactions, and how they compare with other selling variables. We analyze conversion rate, seller & buyer segments, consumer experience and interaction behavior in responding to each of the image aspects.

| **Coefficients** | **Estimate** | **Std. Err.** | **z Value** | **Pr(>\|z\|)** |
|---|---|---|---|---|
| (Intercept) | -1.99487 | 3.30301 | -0.604 | 0.54587 |
| Photo count | 0.05396 | 0.00899 | 6.000 | 1.97e-09 *** |
| Title length | -0.00360 | 0.00825 | -0.436 | 0.66285 |
| Condition(used) | -0.47499 | 0.05602 | -8.479 | < 2e-16 *** |
| Item price | 0.00071 | 0.00013 | 5.426 | 5.76e-08 *** |
| Shipping price | 0.00835 | 0.00395 | 2.109 | 0.03498 * |
| Seller(top) | -0.08114 | 0.06183 | -1.312 | 0.18944 |
| Image quality | 0.69101 | 0.21363 | 3.235 | 0.00122 ** |
| Keyword-popul | 0.79942 | 0.12590 | 6.350 | 2.16e-10 *** |
| Positive ratio | -1.75245 | 0.59897 | -2.926 | 0.00344 ** |
| Log-feedback | -0.46535 | 0.23888 | -1.948 | 0.05141 . |
| Auct-durtn-days | 1.33312 | 0.08567 | 15.561 | < 2e-16 *** |
| Bold title | 0.32979 | 0.39621 | 0.832 | 0.40521 |
| Gallery | 0.60296 | 3.24548 | 0.186 | 0.85261 |
| Gallery plus | 0.62745 | 3.24748 | 0.193 | 0.84679 |
| Picture Pack | -0.60578 | 0.09780 | -6.182 | 6.34e-10 *** |

Signif. codes: 0 "***" 0.001 "**" 0.01 "*" 0.05 "." 0.1 " " 1

Table 2: Logistic Regression Results for "Clothing, Shoes & Accessories". Result shows that image quality and display types exhibit significant impact on products that rely more on visual.

| **Coefficients** | **Estimate** | **Std. Err.** | **z Value** | **Pr(>\|z\|)** |
|---|---|---|---|---|
| (Intercept) | -1.50325 | 2.28782 | -0.657 | 0.511148 |
| Photo count | 0.06847 | 0.02025 | 3.381 | 0.000723 *** |
| Title length | 0.04172 | 0.01499 | 2.782 | 0.005405 ** |
| Condition(used) | -0.22298 | 0.11860 | -1.880 | 0.060097 . |
| Item price | 0.00086 | 0.00017 | 5.210 | 1.89e-07 *** |
| Shipping price | 0.00979 | 0.00443 | 2.212 | 0.027001 * |
| Seller(top) | -0.02553 | 0.10188 | -0.251 | 0.802130 |
| Image Quality | -0.69671 | 0.38630 | -1.804 | 0.071302 . |
| Keyword-popul | 1.31181 | 0.19120 | 6.861 | 6.84e-12 *** |
| Positive ratio | -1.69386 | 2.29103 | -0.739 | 0.459697 |
| Log-feedback | -0.85510 | 0.45418 | -1.883 | 0.059734 . |
| Auct-durtn-days | 1.49221 | 0.15275 | 9.769 | < 2e-16 *** |
| Bold title | 0.59359 | 0.38452 | 1.544 | 0.122657 |
| Gallery plus | 0.37636 | 0.21863 | 1.721 | 0.085170 . |
| Picture Pack | -0.20458 | 0.22484 | -0.910 | 0.362883 |

Signif. codes: 0 "***" 0.001 "**" 0.01 "*" 0.05 "." 0.1 " " 1

Table 3: Logistic Regression Results for "Consumer Electronics". Image quality appears to be less significant for Electronics as compared to CSA category. This is due to high similarity among product photos used by sellers, which drives shopper's attention to other selling factors.

Our results show positive evidence that images help increase buyer's attention, trust and conversion rate. Among the three properties of images, our study shows that increasing number of images of the product, which is equivalent to providing more complete visual representation of the product, is an effective way to improve sell-through. For marketplaces that cater to used, refurbished, and resale products where most sellers are casual sellers, the impact of image quality is limited to certain extent, since users, especially experienced users, may have developed certain level of tolerance towards poor quality images. However, image quality still serves as an important factor especially for goods where appearance plays a key role. Additionally, one should be aware that the norm of market can dramatically change when comparing this type of market to other markets where only high-quality images are used. In that case, quality of product may become a symbol of the quality of the marketplace, and will affect user's choice on which market to shop online. In other words, cross-market seller should be aware of differences between markets, and adapt their strategy accordingly.

We believe this is the first systematic analysis on this subject that jointly considers key e-commerce dimensions. Our studies provide a deeper understanding of the role of images in the e-commerce flow.

Future studies include developing content based image quality to understand the impact of image aesthetics on attracting buyer's attention. We will also pursue modeling "watch" action using Graphical model for causal relationship analysis, to discover the transition relationship between "watch" and other behaviors, such as click-through, purchasing and adding-to-cart.

## 7. REFERENCES


[1] D. Ariely and I. Simonson. Buying, bidding, playing, or competing? value assessment and decision dynamics in online auctions. *Journal of Consumer Psychology*, 13(1):113–123, 2003.

[2] S. Ba, A. B. Whinston, and H. Zhang. Building trust in the electronic market through an economic incentive mechanism. In *Proceedings of the 20th international conference on Information Systems*, pages 208–213. Association for Information Systems, 1999.

[3] P. Bajari and A. Hortacsu. Winner's curse, reserve prices and endogenous entry: Empirical insights from ebay auctions. *Reserve Prices and Endogenous Entry: Empirical Insights from eBay Auctions*, 2000.

[4] E. M. Bland, G. S. Black, and K. Lawrimore. Determinants of effectiveness and success for ebay auctions. *The Coastal Business Journal*, 4(1):5–15, 2005.

[5] E. M. Bland, G. S. Black, and K. Lawrimore. Risk-reducing and risk-enhancing factors impacting online auction outcomes: empirical evidence from ebay auctions. *Journal of Electronic Commerce Research*, 8(4):236–243, 2007.

[6] L. Chen. *Online consumer behavior: An empirical study based on theory of planned behavior.* The university of Nebraska-lincoln, 2009.

[7] S. H. Chung, A. Goswami, H. Lee, and J. Hu. The impact of images on user clicks in product search. In *Proceedings of the Twelfth International Workshop on Multimedia Data Mining*, pages 25–33. ACM, 2012.

[8] C. Dellarocas. Analyzing the economic efficiency of ebay-like online reputation reporting mechanisms. In *Proceedings of the 3rd ACM Conference on Electronic Commerce*, pages 171–179. ACM, 2001.

[9] J. Friedman, T. Hastie, and R. Tibshirani. *The elements of statistical learning*, volume 1. Springer Series in Statistics, 2001.

[10] J. H. Gilkeson and K. Reynolds. Determinants of internet auction success and closing price: An exploratory study. *Psychology & Marketing*, 20(6):537–566, 2003.

[11] A. Goswami, N. Chittar, and C. H. Sung. A study on the impact of product images on user clicks for online shopping. In *Proceedings of the 20th international conference companion on World wide web*, pages 45–46. ACM, 2011.

[12] H.-J. Han, R. Ocker, and J. Fjermestad. An investigation of university students' on-line shopping behavior. In *Proceedings of the 7th Americas Conference on Information Systems*, pages 930–933, 2001.

[13] A. Haywood. Online auctions: User experience insights from ebay. *Chimera Working Paper*, 10:2006, 2006.

[14] M. G. Helander. Theories and models of electronic commerce. In *Proceedings of the Human Factors and Ergonomics Society Annual Meeting*, volume 44, pages 2–770. SAGE Publications, 2000.

[15] Keynote. ebay. keynote case study[oneline, accessed 18/02/2013]. "http://www.keynote.com/docs/success_stories/cs_eBay.pdf".

[16] D. J. Kim, D. L. Ferrin, and H. R. Rao. A trust-based consumer decision-making model in electronic commerce: The role of trust, perceived risk, and their antecedents. *Decision support systems*, 44(2):544–564, 2008.

[17] D. Koehn. The nature of and conditions for online trust. *Journal of Business Ethics*, 43(1):3–19, 2003.

[18] G. Lewis. Asymmetric information, adverse selection and online disclosure: The case of ebay motors. *The American Economic Review*, 2009.

[19] T.-P. Liang and H.-J. Lai. Electronic store design and consumer choice: an empirical study. In *Proceedings of the 33rd Annual Hawaii International Conference on System Sciences*, pages 10–pp. IEEE, 2000.

[20] G. L. Lohse and P. Spiller. Electronic shopping. *Communications of the ACM*, 41(7):81–87, 1998.

[21] M. H. Moshrefjavadi, H. R. Dolatabadi, M. Nourbakhsh, A. Poursaeedi, and A. Asadollahi. An analysis of factors affecting on online shopping behavior of consumers. *International Journal of Marketing Studies*, 4(5):p81, 2012.

[22] P. Pavlou and A. Dimoka. Understanding and mitigating product uncertainty in online auction marketplaces. In *Industry Studies Conference Paper*, 2008.

[23] B. T. Ratchford, D. Talukdar, and M.-S. Lee. A model of consumer choice of the internet as an information source. *International Journal of Electronic Commerce*, 5:7–22, 2001.

[24] P. Resnick, K. Kuwabara, R. Zeckhauser, and E. Friedman. Reputation systems. *Communications of the ACM*, 43(12):45–48, 2000.

[25] N. Sukpanich and L. Chen. Antecedents of desirable consumer behaviors in electronic commerce. In *Proceedings of the 5th Americas Conference on Information Systems*, pages 550–552, 1999.

[26] P. J. Trocchia and S. Janda. A phenomenological investigation of internet usage among older individuals. *Journal of consumer marketing*, 17(7):605–616, 2000.

[27] M. Wolfinbarger and M. C. Gilly. Shopping online for freedom, control, and fun. *California Management Review*, 43(2):34–55, 2001.

[28] T. P. y Monsuwé, B. G. Dellaert, and K. De Ruyter. What drives consumers to shop online? a literature review. *International Journal of Service Industry Management*, 15(1):102–121, 2004.

# Integration of Large Scale Knowledge Bases using Probabilistic Graphical Models

Arnab Kumar Dutta
Data and Web Science
Universität Mannheim
68159 Mannheim, Germany
arnab@informatik.uni-mannheim.de

## ABSTRACT

Over the recent past, information extraction (IE) systems such as NELL and REVERB have attained much success in creating large knowledge resources with minimal supervision. But, these resources in general, lack schema information and contain facts with high degree of ambiguity which are often difficult to interpret. Whereas, Wikipedia-based IE projects like DBPEDIA and YAGO are structured, have disambiguated facts with unique identifiers and maintain a well-defined schema. In this work, we propose a probabilistic method to integrate these two types of IE projects where the structured knowledge bases benefit from the wide coverage of the semi-supervised IE projects and the latter benefits from the schema information of the former.

## Categories and Subject Descriptors

I.2.4 [ **Knowledge Representation Formalisms and Methods**]: [Representations (procedural and rule-based)]; I.2.3 [**Deduction and Theorem Proving**]: [Uncertainty, fuzzy, and probabilistic reasoning]

## Keywords

Data Integration, Probabilistic Inference, Knowledge Bases

## 1. INTRODUCTION

### 1.1 Motivation

Research in information extraction (IE) systems has experienced a strong momentum in recent years. While Wikipedia based information extraction projects such as DBPEDIA [1, 16] and YAGO [23] have been in development for several years, systems such as NELL [5] and REVERB [9] that work on very large and unstructured text corpora have more recently achieved impressive results. The developers of the latter systems have coined the term *open* information extraction (OIE) [2] to describe information extraction systems that are not constrained by the boundaries of encyclopedic knowledge and the corresponding fixed schemata that are, for instance, used by YAGO and DBPEDIA. The data maintained by OIE systems is important for analyzing, reasoning about, and discovering novel facts on the web and has the potential to result in a new generation of web search engines [8]. In this context, there are latent advantages in integrating these two IE systems in producing better knowledge repositories which can be harvested to further enable state-of-the-art performance on a wide range of NLP applications. This is especially promising, since NELL and REVERB typically achieve a very large coverage, but still lack a full-fledged, clean ontological structure which, on the other hand, could be provided by large-scale ontologies like DBPEDIA or YAGO.


*WSDM'14*, February 24–28, 2014, New York, New York, USA.

http://dx.doi.org/10.1145/2556195.2556202.

### 1.2 Problem Statement

In order to integrate existing IE projects, we have to solve the problem of entity resolution. The fact that makes this task challenging is that triples from OIE systems are often underspecified and ambiguous. For instance, consider a NELL triple, where two terms (subject and object) are linked with some relationship (predicate):

`agentcollaborateswithagent(times, bob herbert)`

Here, `times` and `bob herbert` are two terms which are linked by a predicate called `agentcollaborateswithagent`. The problem of interpreting the terms is difficult since the term `times` by itself can have several meanings. Interpreting this sentence's meaning poses a challenging task even to humans. Here, `times` refers to the newspaper company *The New York Times* and `bob herbert` refers to the journalist *Bob Herbert*.

Furthermore, the task of integration gets more complicated as the triples extracted from the web are often not certain. OIE systems attach a *degree of truth* to the facts. Even, if the disambiguated terms refer to the correct entities in the given context, it is difficult to determine the correctness of the triple itself. This becomes evident with the following example,

`0.86: agentcollaborateswithagent(fox, obama)`

In this given context, the triple is of significantly low confidence and even if `fox` refers to the *news corporation* and `obama` to *Barack Obama*, the certainty of the fact is questionable. Thus, the free text terms within OIE facts can have multiple meanings and varying confidences across different contexts. In this work, we take some steps towards overcoming this problem by providing a probabilistic approach for the integration of different large-scale knowledge bases.

| Anchor | Article | Link Counts |
|---|---|---|
| carbon | Carbon | 2256 |
| carbon | Carbon County, Pennsylvania | 120 |
| ... | ... | ... |
| lincoln | Lincoln, England | 1844 |
| lincoln | Lincoln (2012 film) | 496 |
| ... | ... | ... |

**Table 1: Snippet of articles linked to using the anchors *carbon* and *lincoln*.**

## 2. PROPOSED SOLUTION

We propose a three step approach towards a solution of the problem. In Section 2.1 we discuss a way to create probabilistic set of `sameAs` hypotheses between instances from NELL and DBPEDIA. In Section 2.2 we formulate the problem using Markov Logic Networks [19], which is an efficient way of combining logic with uncertainty. Finally, in Section 2.3 we filter out incorrect `sameAs` hypotheses, if any, by solving an inference task on a Markov network created from our markov logic formulation. In the process, we want to find an answer to the question if it is possible with probabilistic reasoning to exploit the inconsistencies in linking entities occurring in web-extracted facts to improve the integration task. Note that, although NELL has a schema of its own, we do not exploit it keeping in mind a generalized approach towards the problem, since other OIE projects, like REVERB lack such a schema.

### 2.1 Linking terms

In this work we use Wikipedia as an entity-tagged corpus [4] in order to bridge knowledge encoded in NELL with DBPEDIA. It contains information about each article, anchors present, outgoing links etc. Note that, there are alternative data sets such as the CROSSWIKI data [21], but we opted instead for exploiting only Wikipedia internal-link anchors, which are expected to be a cleaner source of data. Since there is a corresponding DBPEDIA instance for each Wikipedia article [3], we can safely assume an article to be an exact counterpart of the DBPEDIA instance. However, the problem is that, due to polysemy, often a term from NELL can refer to several different articles in Wikipedia or, analogously, instances in DBPEDIA.

Table 1 shows two examples, where a particular anchor can refer to multiple Wikipedia articles with varying number of link counts[1]. This fosters the idea to adopt a probabilistic approach in selecting the best possible DBPEDIA resource. For any given anchor in Wikipedia, the fraction of articles the links points to, is proportional to the probability that the anchor term refers to the particular article [21]. Formally, if some anchor $e$ refers to $N$ articles $A_1, \ldots, A_N$ with $n_1, \ldots, n_N$ respective links counts, then the conditional probability $P$ of $e$ referring to $A_j$ is given by, $P(A_j|e) = n_j/\sum_{i=1}^{N} n_i$. We compute the probabilities for each terms we are interested in and from a ranked list of $P(A_j|e)$, top-$k$ candidates are selected.

We apply this procedure on every term occurring as subject and object in a NELL triple. These terms are analogous to the anchors in Wikipedia. We generate a set of `sameAs` hypotheses between the NELL terms and the most probable DBPEDIA instance with confidences given by $P$. For further details and empirical results, refer to the paper [7].

[1]We used WikiPrep [13, 12] for parsing the Wikipedia dumps and finding the link counts for anchor-article pairs.

| Axiom Type | Atom | Example of a Ground Atom |
|---|---|---|
| $\mathtt{A} \sqsubseteq \mathtt{B}$ | csub(A, B) | *csub(Student,Person)* |
| $\mathtt{A} \sqsubseteq \neg\mathtt{B}$ | cdis(A, B) | *cdis(Vehicle,Actor)* |
| $\mathtt{P} \sqsubseteq \mathtt{Q}$ | psub(P, Q) | *psub(husbandof, hasspouse)* |
| $\mathtt{a} : \mathtt{C}$ | isType(C, a) | *isType(President, Obama)* |
| $\mathtt{a} \neq \mathtt{b}$ | diffFrom(a, b) | *diffFrom(Obama, Bush)* |
| $\exists\mathtt{R}.\top \sqsubseteq \mathtt{A}$ | dom(R, A) | *dom(lakeinstate, BodyOfWater)* |
| $\top \sqsubseteq \forall\mathtt{R}.\mathtt{A}$ | ran(R, A) | *ran(lakeinstate, Place)* |

**Table 2: *unweighted atomic formulae* used for the modeling.**

### 2.2 Modeling with Markov Logic Networks

For the integration task, we create a knowledge base $\mathcal{K}$, consisting of two types of information. An *uncertain* type consisting of `sameAs` hypotheses described in the previous section. The other being the *certain* type which encodes the information from the *closed* domain IE, DBPEDIA in particular. In our case, we employ Markov Logic Network (MLN) which provides the perfect template to model scenarios consisting of certain and uncertain aspects, as present in our knowledge base.

#### Unweighted Atoms

We translate the axioms of the DBPEDIA ontology[2] to *atomic formulae* or *atoms*[3] as indicated by Table 2. These atoms are defined for both the terminological axioms ($\mathcal{T}$-box) and the assertions involving instances ($\mathcal{A}$-box) in $\mathcal{K}$. Since these atoms model the information from DBPEDIA, we want them to hold under all circumstances, hence they are unweighted. All possible instantiations of the atoms lead to *ground atoms* or specifically *hard evidences*. Examples of such hard evidences are shown in Table 2. The atoms are formulated using the ontology provided by DBPEDIA with the exception of class disjointness. Particularly, atoms of the form cdis(A, B) were taken from the works of [11], where disjointness axioms were learnt automatically.

#### Weighted Atoms

Weighted atomic formulae represent the *uncertain* information in $\mathcal{K}$. In our linking task, we create a set of `sameAs` hypotheses having confidence values attached. Using MLN, we define weighted `sameAs` atoms as

$$w : \mathtt{sameAs}(\mathtt{a}, \mathtt{b})$$

where, $w$ are the confidences as computed in Section 2.1. Instantiating the atoms with a set of constants leads to grounding them and creates *soft evidences*, for instance `0.498 : sameAs(Special Air Service, sas)`.

[2]http://downloads.dbpedia.org/3.8/dbpedia_3.8.owl.bz2
[3]Classes are denoted with $A, B, C, D$, properties with $R, S$ and instances with $a, b, c$.

The property assertions from OIE can also be modeled in a similar fashion as

$$w : \texttt{pAss(P, a, b)}$$

where, $w$ are the confidence values obtained from the web extracts of the OIE projects. Grounding these type of atoms leads to the set of soft evidences like
0.967 : pAss(bookwriter, pickwick papers, dickens). Note that every ground atom, is binary valued.

**Unweighted Rules**

The atoms, in disjunction with each other, enable us to formulate a set of first order logic *rules*. Generally, a knowledge base is a conjunction of all such rules. Hence, $\mathcal{K}$ can have an exponential number of states with every possible combination of a boolean value assignment to the ground atoms. Every such state is a *world*. A possible world is necessarily a truth assignment to the ground atoms.

Unweighted rules are the *hard* constraints which should hold in every world. If they are violated, the world is improbable. By translating the DBPEDIA axioms into atoms, we loose the semantics associated with the Description Logic (DL) axioms in DBPEDIA. Hence, there is a need to add explicitly deduction rules to exploit the inference mechanisms implicit in the DL semantics.

$$\Rightarrow \texttt{csub(C, D)} \quad (1a)$$
$$\Rightarrow \texttt{!cdis(C, C)} \quad (1b)$$
$$\texttt{csub(B, C)} \wedge \texttt{csub(C, D)} \Rightarrow \texttt{csub(B, D)} \quad (1c)$$
$$\texttt{csub(A, B)} \wedge \texttt{cdis(B, C)} \Rightarrow \texttt{cdis(A, C)} \quad (1d)$$
$$\texttt{dom(R, C)} \wedge \texttt{csub(C, B)} \Rightarrow \texttt{dom(R, B)} \quad (1e)$$
$$\texttt{ran(R, C)} \wedge \texttt{csub(C, B)} \Rightarrow \texttt{ran(R, B)} \quad (1f)$$

These rules are a subset of the rules used in [10]. We further extend our rule set with support for inference with the $\mathcal{A}$-box.

$$\texttt{csub(C, B)} \wedge \texttt{isType(C, a)} \Rightarrow \texttt{isType(B, a)} \quad (2a)$$
$$\texttt{pAss(R, a, b)} \wedge \texttt{psub(R, S)} \Rightarrow \texttt{pAss(S, a, b)} \quad (2b)$$
$$\texttt{pAss(R, a, b)} \wedge \texttt{dom(R, C)} \Rightarrow \texttt{isType(C, a)} \quad (2c)$$
$$\texttt{pAss(R, a, b)} \wedge \texttt{ran(R, C)} \Rightarrow \texttt{isType(C, b)} \quad (2d)$$

So far we have defined rules required to capture the general behavior of the $\mathcal{A}$-box and the $\mathcal{T}$-box. But there needs to be a restriction which ensures that an incorrect hypothesis introduces an inconsistency into our knowledge base.

$$\Rightarrow \texttt{sameAs(a, a)} \quad (3a)$$
$$\texttt{sameAs(a, b)} \Rightarrow \texttt{sameAs(b, a)} \quad (3b)$$
$$\texttt{sameAs(a, b)} \wedge \texttt{sameAs(b, c)} \Rightarrow \texttt{sameAs(a, c)} \quad (3c)$$
$$\texttt{isType(C, a)} \wedge \texttt{sameAs(a, b)} \Rightarrow \texttt{isType(C, b)} \quad (3d)$$
$$\texttt{cdis(C, B)} \wedge \texttt{isType(C, a)} \Rightarrow \texttt{!isType(B, a)} \quad (3e)$$
$$\texttt{diffFrom(a, b)} \Rightarrow \texttt{!sameAs(a, b)} \quad (3f)$$

(3e) enforces a conflict into the modeling by stating that if two classes are disjoint with each other they cannot be the type of the same instance. (3f) limits the possibility for an entity representing two different real world instances.

**Weighted Rules**

These are *soft* rules, which can be violated but if they are, that world becomes less probable compared to the world where they hold true. In our modeling, we have not used any soft rules. This remains as an open issue which is discussed further in Section 4.

## 2.3 Inference

Here, we discuss the idea behind solving the problem as an inference task in MLN. In particular, we are interested in the maximum a-posteriori (MAP) state. The aim is to find the most probable world. Usually, we observe the state of some variables and try to infer the state of the hidden variables. Let, $E$ be the observed variables and $Q$ be the set of hidden variables, then a MAP state tries to find an assignment for $Q$ so that $\underset{Q}{\operatorname{argmax}}\, P(Q|E)$ , i.e. the assignment which makes $P$ maximum. Such an assignment is the most probable world.

In our problem scenario, only the evidences containing pAss and sameAs are hidden. The rule set in Section 2.2 provides a template for creating a Markov Network where each node represents a ground atom or an evidence. Intuitively, a possible world is a truth value assignment to every evidence without any hard rules being violated. Whenever an evidence involving a sameAs is in a conflict with others, it makes that world less likely and it gets penalized by the weight $w$ associated with it. There can be multiple such possible worlds, but we are interested in the world with maximal sum of the weights of the weighted evidences. This world is called the *most probable* world which contains a subset of the initial sameAs hypotheses.

# 3. EMPIRICAL RESULTS

In the following we report about the experiments we conducted so far, focusing primarily on the sameAs hypotheses. In Section 3.1 we analyze our approach described in Section 2.1 in generating good mapping hypotheses among the $top-k$ proposals. These proposals will finally be the input to our Markov Logic based method and serve as a baseline for comparison as well. It is thus important to understand the characteristics of our method for generating linking proposals in details. In Section 3.2 we report on first results for applying the ML based approach in a simple setting. The results of these experiments give a first impression of the benefits of our approach.

## 3.1 Linking Entities

For the task of linking, we sample a set of NELL properties having atleast 100 instances each. We annotated them to come up with a gold standard for which the data set is publicly available[4]. We ran our baseline algorithm against the gold standard. In Figure 1, we show the *precision*@1 and *recall*@1 values obtained on this set of NELL predicates. Using micro-average method, for the $top-1$ matches we achieved a precision of 82.78% and an average recall of 81.31% across all the predicates. In the case of macro-averaging, instead, we achieved precision of 82.61% and recall of 81.42%.

These results indicate that there is significant room for improvement. Our extended experiments showed a steady

[4]http://web.informatik.uni-mannheim.de/data/nell-dbpedia/NellGoldStandard.tar

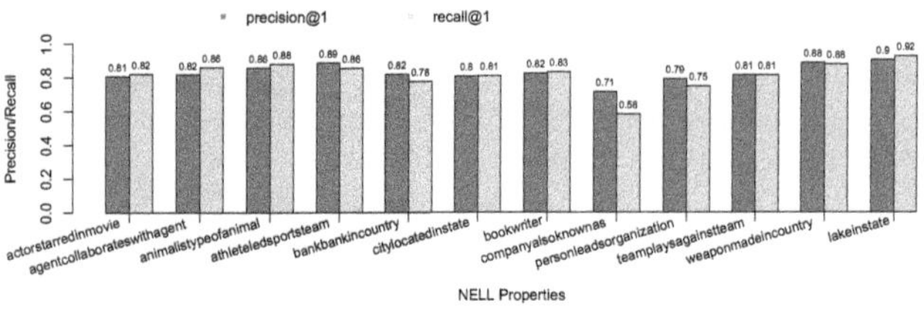


**Figure 1: *precision*@1 and *recall*@1 of the baseline method.**

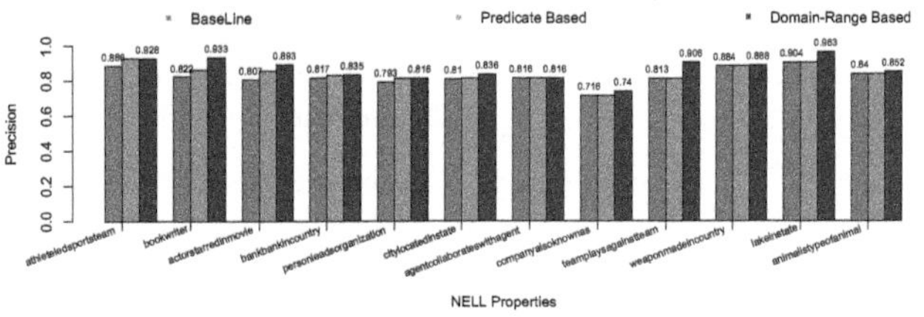


**Figure 2: precision values comparison of baseline method and MLN based approach.**

rise in recall for $top-2$ and beyond with a saturation after $top-5$ ([7]). This denotes that there are good candidate matches within $top-5$ and with probabilistic reasoning we can influence the precision and recall in such cases where the $top-1$ is not the best candidate choice. Intuitively, in other cases, there is nothing to improve.

## 3.2 MLN Based Approach

Initially, we adopt a naive way of manually mapping the NELL properties to a DBPEDIA property. The rationale is to link properties with a subsumption axiom. We add hard evidences of the form `psub(bookwriter, author)`. For some properties, like `actorstarredinmovie`, we had to extend our rule set with the addition of `invpsub` to capture their behavior (similar to rule 2b). We observed, there are few properties for which a DBPEDIA counterpart was not found.

Hence, we extended our experiments with a different approach. We manually specified the *domain* and *range* restrictions for the NELL properties in terms of DBPEDIA classes. Table 3 gives the collective details of the manual mappings for the set of NELL properties; analogous DBPEDIA properties it is in subsumption with and the domain/range values used. Figure 2 reports our first results using MLN. It shows a comparison of the two above mentioned approaches with the baseline. Note that properties which were not possible to be mapped initially, had considerable improvements with the domain and range based mapping. We used Rockit [18] for computing the MAP state for our inference task.

In particular, even though manual methods showed some improvements, we need to develop automated techniques to generate such property mappings and domain/range restrictions in order to make our approach applicable to the complete data set from NELL and REVERB as well.

# 4. RESEARCH ISSUES

**Distant Supervision**: However, we intend to incorporate semi-supervised techniques to automatically learn such restrictions between NELL and DBPEDIA. For a given NELL

| Nell Property | DBpedia Property | Domain | Range |
|---|---|---|---|
| bookwriter | author | WrittenWork | Person |
| athleteledsportsteam | formerTeam | Athlete | SportsTeam |
| bankbankincountry | regionServed | Organisation | Country |
| citylocatedinstate | location | City | Place |
| personleads organization | employer | Person | Organisation |
| actorstarredinmovie | starring* | Person | Film |
| agentcollaborates withagent | - | Agent | Agent |
| animalistypeof animal | - | Animal | Animal |
| teamplaysagainst team | - | SportsTeam | SportsTeam |
| companyalso knownas | - | Organisation | Organisation |
| weaponmade incountry | - | Device | Country |
| lakeinstate | - | BodyOfWater | Place |

**Table 3: Property Mappings of Nell to DBpedia.(* : inverse property subsumption)**

property, we can sample a certain number of triples and for each one of them we can find an analogous DBPEDIA triple with the similar subject-object combination. This can give a probability distribution of *domain* and *range* of the NELL property over a set of possible DBPEDIA triples. For instance, NELL property *bookwriter* has domain as DBPEDIA concept *Book* with 56% probability and *Work* with 78% probability. Similar values can also be computed for range.

**Weight Learning**: It is important to weigh the evidences we create between NELL and DBPEDIA. For instance, `psub` discussed in Section 3.2. In an ideal setting, we cannot claim a strict property subsumption restriction between properties across different domains. The choice of the weight is critical otherwise, it can lead to a degraded model. Our initial experiments, lead to deteriorated results while trying to set weights manually to such rules. This motivates us, to adopt an efficient weight learning strategy. There have been works on efficient weight learning strategies [15], which are expected to work better than pseudo likelihood, as was proposed in [19].

**Similar Type but Incorrect Mapping**: There are two broad types of the problem we aim to address. Firstly, a scenario where a particular assignment of the `sameAs` statement is wrong and it has incorrect type information. For instance, the term *jaguar* in some NELL triple refers to the animal but it should have been the car company. And, secondly there can be a scenario where an assignment is wrong but the type is correct. For instance, a term like *steve* in some triple refers to *SteveNash*, the basketball player and not *SteveJobs*, the ex-CEO of Apple. Both are of type persons in this case and we need a way to deal with such scenarios. Essentially, every entity involved in some relation, has some inherent characteristics. For e.g. entities involved in a *hasSpouse* relationship cannot have age-difference more than 100 years, *bookwriter* cannot have author's birth year later than the publication date of the book, and so on. We had exploited this characteristics for a small set of OIE properties and efficiently employed non-parametric ways of estimating the probability density function of the variables. We used Kernel Density Estimation (KDE) to rank entities based on their estimation function values. However, the biggest challenge still is to discover such features we intend to use in an automated setting.

## 5. RELATED WORK

OIE further focused on approaches that do not need any manually-labeled data [9], however, the output of these systems still needs to be disambiguated by linking it to entities and relations from a knowledge base. Recent work has extensively explored the usage of distant supervision for IE, namely by harvesting sentences containing concepts whose relation is known and leveraging these sentences as training data for supervised extractors [24, 14]. There has been closely related work in entity linking in the past. Machine learning based approach try to indicate equivalent instances that refer to the same real-world object [20]. Our approach closely relates to the work using linking features such as string matching. Extraction frameworks like NELL, TextRunner [2], are of prime importance in providing massive data sets of web-extracted statements. PARIS [22] takes a probabilistic approach to align ontologies. This work is aimed towards ontology alignment and utilizes the interdependence of instances and schema to compute probabilities for the instance matches. Please note the important distinction between entity resolution in text and integrating triples from information extraction projects. The latter can explicitly take into account the semantics of the relations that links subject and object in each of the triples.

Reasoning in general, on large scale data was applied in enriching Yago [17]. But this used MaxSat-based constraint reasoning and did not compute MAP state. There have been works in disambiguating entities using MLN [6] but they use much of the background knowledge of entities in coming up with their disambiguation formulae.

## 6. REFERENCES

[1] S. Auer, C. Bizer, G. Kobilarov, J. Lehmann, R. Cyganiak, and Z. Ive. Dbpedia: A nucleus for a web of open data. In *Proceedings of ISWC+ASWC 2007*, pages 722–735, 2007.

[2] M. Banko, M. J. Cafarella, S. Soderland, M. Broadhead, and O. Etzioni. Open information extraction from the web. In *IJCAI*, pages 2670–2676, 2007.

[3] C. Bizer, J. Lehmann, G. Kobilarov, S. Auer, C. Becker, R. Cyganiak, and S. Hellmann. DBpedia – A crystallization point for the web of data. *Journal of Web Semantics*, 7(3):154–165, 2009.

[4] R. Bunescu and M. Paşca. Using encyclopedic knowledge for named entity disambiguation. In *Proc. of EACL-06*, pages 9–16, 2006.

[5] A. Carlson, J. Betteridge, B. Kisiel, B. Settles, E. R. Hruschka, and T. M. Mitchell. Toward an architecture for never-ending language learning. In *Proc. of AAAI-10*, pages 1306–1313, 2010.

[6] H.-J. Dai, R. T.-H. Tsai, and W.-L. Hsu. Entity disambiguation using a markov-logic network. In *Proceedings of 5th IJCNLP*, pages 846–855, 2011.

[7] A. Dutta, M. Niepert, C. Meilicke, and S. P. Ponzetto. Integrating Open and Closed Information Extraction : Challenges and First Steps. *Proceedings of the NLP and DBpedia workshop ISWC*, 1064, 2013.

[8] O. Etzioni. Search needs a shake-up. *Nature*, 476(7358):25–26, 2011.

[9] A. Fader, S. Soderland, and O. Etzioni. Identifying relations for open information extraction. In *Proc. of EMNLP-11*, pages 1535–1545, 2011.

[10] D. Fleischhacker, C. Meilicke, J. Völker, and M. Niepert. Computing incoherence explanations for learned ontologies. In *RR*, pages 80–94. Springer, 2013.

[11] D. Fleischhacker and J. Völker. Inductive learning of disjointness axioms. In *On the Move to Meaningful Internet Systems: OTM 2011*, volume 7045, pages 680–697. Springer, 2011.

[12] E. Gabrilovich and S. Markovitch. Overcoming the brittleness bottleneck using wikipedia: Enhancing text categorization with encyclopedic knowledge. In *Proc. of AAAI-06*, pages 1301–1306, 2006.

[13] E. Gabrilovich and S. Markovitch. Computing semantic relatedness using wikipedia-based explicit semantic analysis. In *Proc. of IJCAI-07*, pages 1606–1611, 2007.

[14] R. Hoffmann, C. Zhang, and D. S. Weld. Learning 5000 relational extractors. In *Proc. of ACL-10*, pages 286–295, 2010.

[15] D. Lowd and P. Domingos. Efficient weight learning for markov logic networks. In *Proceedings of the Eleventh European Conference on Principles and Practice of Knowledge Discovery in Databases*, pages 200–211, 2007.

[16] P. Mendes, M. Jakob, and C. Bizer. Dbpedia: A multilingual cross-domain knowledge base. In *Proc. of LREC-12*, 2012.

[17] N. Nakashole, M. Theobald, and G. Weikum. Scalable knowledge harvesting with high precision and high recall. In *Proceedings of the Fourth ACM WSDM*, WSDM '11, pages 227–236. ACM, 2011.

[18] J. Noessner, M. Niepert, and H. Stuckenschmidt. Rockit: Exploiting parallelism and symmetry for map inference in statistical relational models. In *AAAI*, 2013.

[19] M. Richardson and P. Domingos. Markov logic networks. *Mach. Learn.*, 62(1-2):107–136, 2006.

[20] S. Rong, X. Niu, E. Xiang, H. Wang, Q. Yang, and Y. Yu. A machine learning approach for instance matching based on similarity metrics. In *The Semantic Web – ISWC 2012*, volume 7649, pages 460–475. Springer-Verlag, 2012.

[21] V. I. Spitkovsky and A. X. Chang. A cross-lingual dictionary for english wikipedia concepts. In *Proc of LREC-12*, pages 3168–3175, 2012.

[22] F. M. Suchanek, S. Abiteboul, and P. Senellart. Paris: probabilistic alignment of relations, instances, and schema. *Proc. VLDB Endow.*, 5(3):157–168, 2011.

[23] F. M. Suchanek, G. Kasneci, and G. Weikum. Yago: A Core of Semantic Knowledge. In *WWW 2007*, New York, NY, USA, 2007. ACM Press.

[24] F. Wu and D. S. Weld. Open information extraction using wikipedia. In *Proc. of ACL-10*, pages 118–127, 2010.

# Strategy in Action: Analyzing Online Search Behavior by Mining Search Strategies

Chathra Hendahewa
Department of Computer Science
Rutgers, The State University of New Jersey
110 Frelinghuysen Road
Piscataway, NJ 08854-8019, USA
chathrah@cs.rutgers.edu

## ABSTRACT

Analyzing people's Web search behavior has been a significant topic of interest in the Information Retrieval domain and search engine industry over the past decade. Research in this area has focused on improving search and retrieval capabilities leading to high demands and expectations of Web search users. Understanding and analyzing the Web search process when users are performing Web search tasks is a challenging problem due to many reasons such as subjectivity, dynamic nature, difficulty in measurement of success and difficulty in evaluation. I propose to analyze the users' Web search behavior in order to identify the strategies and tactics they use in fulfilling their task. In order to achieve this, I intend to use data mining and machine learning methods with an emphasis on time series analysis given that the user search process can be considered as a sequence of time related events.

## Categories and Subject Descriptors

H.3.3 [**Information Storage and Retrieval**]: Information Search and Retrieval; H.3.3.h [**Information Search and Retrieval**]: Search Process; H.4.m [**Information Systems Applications**]: Miscellaneous

## General Terms

Measurement, Experimentation, Human Factors

## Keywords

Web search, Information Retrieval, User Behavior, Time series analysis, Data Mining

## 1. INTRODUCTION

In the context of Web search, when a user issues a query or search for information on the Web, the *Information Retrieval* (IR) methodologies implemented in the search engines retrieve a set of documents/Web pages from the vast online information sources based on the indexes. *Information Seeking* (IS) on the other hand is the activity of attempting to obtain information in both human and technological contexts. Since different users have different information needs they require different information seeking strategies. The new digital environment not only forces people to apply more than one type of information-seeking strategy, but also requires people to change from one information seeking strategy to another in the information-seeking process. However, current IR systems in the domain of Web search such as Google, Yahoo!, Ask, Bing are designed mainly to support query formulation and limited browsing. Therefore, we can see that although IR systems and methodologies are essential for IS, the latter is a more complex task that is not only dependent on the information retrieved from a search query but, how that information would be made useful for fulfilling the information need of a user. This research will focus on IR with IS as the context for search activities and tasks.

### 1.1 Problem Definition

In an online search task, an information seeker undergoes various cognitive activities in order to formulate the strategies and tactics required to achieve his/her goal. Once a user comes up with a mental model and the required cognitive processes, generally a strategy is formulated as an overall plan to be executed to perform a task in order to achieve a desired goal.

*Strategies* can be broken down into sequences of actions or individual actions known as *tactics*[5]. Based on these tactics a user would access Web pages and other Web documents to find information he/she needs to complete the task and in most cases, some of those documents would be relevant or useful. Based on the tactics performed, one could assess how the user is performing and whether the tactics are eventually useful or not in achieving his/her goal. For this reason, the analysis of search performance becomes imperative on this aspect.

Understanding and analyzing all the different aspects of the search process when users are performing online search tasks is a challenging problem for many reasons including, but not limited to the points mentioned below.

- Dynamic nature
- Uniqueness for each user based on internal and external factors
- Inherent subjectivity in the process


*WSDM'14*, February 24–28, 2014, New York, New York, USA.
ACM 978-1-4503-2351-2/14/02.
http://dx.doi.org/10.1145/2556195.2556203.

- Difficulty in capturing the cognitive process
- Difficulty in asking or interviewing a user about inner cognitive processes

As explained above, it is a difficult task to identify strategies/tactics undertaken by a user when performing an online search task, which if could be identified would assist in providing useful recommendation and search performance prediction to provide a much richer search experience to the user.

## 1.2 Research Hypothesis

In the process of searching for information online, based on the *Search Engine Result Page* (SERP) a user retrieves from queries he/she issues on the search engine, he/she navigates thorough the information he/she deems as relevant to his/her information need. There has been previous work done on building user satisfaction models to determine whether a user has satisfied his/her search goals or not [11] based on the information they were able to find with actions such as querying, visiting Web pages resulted from querying, etc. Based on the results that a user obtains from the sequence of actions he/she performs relating to the retrieved Web documents, he/she often abandons his/her searches [6]. In some cases, the participants abandoned the SERPs because they decided on a better query before they examined the search results [6]. Further, O'Day and Jeffries [14] defined a number of triggers that motivate a user to switch from one search strategy to another, such as encountering a change or violation of previous expectations or encountering inconsistencies with or gaps in previous understanding. These findings indicate that users could be dissatisfied with the information obtained based on the actions they pursued due to an inability to find relevant information to complete their information related task, which ultimately induces them to change or abandon the current path/tactics and move on to formulating new strategies leading to a different set of tactics.

We can hypothesize that by identifying the tactics used at the early stage of the search process and inferring the underlying strategy/strategies, one could find ways to minimize user search abandonments relating to dissatisfaction. This would pave a way to evaluate user search performance based on the tactics and strategies they undertake and provide useful recommendations and personalization to improve overall search performance and thereby improve the user satisfaction and ability to achieve the final search goal.

It can be argued that the actions performed during a search process are the artifacts generated as a result of the thought process and strategy formulation that occur in a user's mind. Some theoretical frameworks such as Norman's execution-evaluation model [13], explains that formulating a search problem and expressing the information need via queries or navigation in a search system corresponds to executing actions. Therefore, we can assume that the inner cognitive senses that pave way to making expressing the information needs are modeled and executed via the actions an information seeker uses in the information seeking process. Although there is no direct way to capture these inner cognitive senses (other than monitoring EEG signals of the brain and then classifying them into the cognitive processes), how a user handles a search process should provide us with a good understanding of the strategies and tactics used in a task. This process will be different for each user due to many factors such as expertise in the task area, prior knowledge, experience in online searching, cognitive factors, environment he/she is operating in, whether he/she is working individually or collaboratively, etc. Therefore, it is important to typify these search strategies by analyzing their related search process in order to provide useful recommendations, which would yield more effective search results in a personalized manner.

# 2. BACKGROUND

Previous work on understanding user search behavior and search strategies have spanned various domains such as Information Retrieval, Data mining, Machine Learning and Personalized Search. The following section summarizes the previous work from major sub areas related to the proposed research.

## 2.1 Information Retrieval

In the domain of Information Retrieval (IR), the main focus is on retrieving relevant information in response to user queries[8]. A pre-collected set of documents containing information is pre-indexed and stored in a storage such as a database. When a user issues a query, based on the similarity of the indexed documents to the query, a set of relevant documents are returned to the user. One of the main research areas in IR is how to make the a effective ranking of the documents that are retrieved for a specific user query. Another research area is how to make sure that the required information is returned to the user in as fast as possible making the retrieval system efficient. Therefore, the terms *effectiveness* and *efficiency* are key terms that appear in the IR domain. Both of these characteristics are important parts of a good IR system since a rational user would prefer to find relevant information in a timely manner to meet his/her information needs. In order to measure the goodness of the information retrieved, the measures such as Precision, Recall, F-score have been widely used in the IR domain.

Various retrieval methods have been proposed over the years to find the similarity between a user issued query and the documents[8]. Most retrieval methods are based on the heuristic that if one can find the highest commonality in the terms appearing in a query and a document, then that document is highly relevant to the user. Some of such methods in the IR domain are vector space model, probabilistic retrieval model and latent semantic indexing. All of these methods and measures merely focus on the product: such as Web pages (documents), queries but, not on the user. If we select one specific method and ask two users to execute the same query, the retrieved set of documents would be the same, given that all other resources used are identical. Thus, these methods do not take in to account about the characteristics of the user such as his/her search pattern, what he/she mostly clicks on, what is the ultimate goal of his/her search, etc. This leads to other areas of research widely known as recommender systems and search personalization.

## 2.2 Personalized Search

Personalized search tries to go beyond the generic framework of queries and documents and try to incorporate what we know about the user in providing the search results. It is tailored to each individual's profile so that it goes beyond the specific query he/she executes. Two general approaches in personalizing search results have been defined by [15], one that involves modifying the user's query and another that re-ranks the search results originally returned by the search engine. Almost all the search engines nowadays provide some sort of personalization based on the general information about the user, based on location where the query is originated from (based on IP address) and also analyzing past search behavior of users.

## 2.3 Machine Learning and Data Mining

The problem of discovering episodes or patterns in the data can be closely related to the idea of identifying stages or underlying strategies in an information seeking process. Time series clustering is a important topic in Machine Learning and Data mining domain, which has been widely researched by many scientists due to its vast applicability to many fields such as finance, business, meteorology, medical analysis, motion capture, etc. Distance based measures to find similarity between time series signals has been the main focal point in this area of research. Most commonly used distance measures have been Euclidean distance and Dynamic Time warping and despite their wide use and applicability to most cases, their inherent issues such as non-resilience to noise and missing data causing issues had led researchers to go beyond these conventional distance measures to perform time series based clustering. Some recent methods have been proposed [17] , where they used unsupervised-shapelet based methods to cluster sequences bypassing results obtained by all the state of the art methods before. There had been work on exploiting temporal information embedded in documents for presentation, clustering, and exploration of search results[3]. In such work the temporal aspect is used on the documents or the information objects level, but not at the search process level.

Another focus on data mining related to IR is the problem of search trend prediction. By analyzing the query logs of search engines, researchers seek to accurately predict what are the most trending items on the Web. This feature has been actively implemented in almost all of the current popular search engines such as Google trends, Yahoo! trending now and Bing trends. Various attempts have been made to make such search trend prediction more accurate with low latency relative to the actual event that sparked the trend [7].

Analysis to evaluate the effectiveness of task trails in three different search applications relating to user satisfaction, user search interest prediction and query suggestion was also conducted by researchers [12]. In order to evaluate success of search goals, Hassan et al. [10] have proposed modeling user search behavior using a Markovian model with transition times based on user search process based features. Such model of predicting user search goal success has shown empirically that it is significantly accurate than the traditional relevance based models.

Recently, it was shown that analysis of Web search behavior over time leads to discovering and predicting important patterns about how people search information online [16]. They look at seasonal patterns, trends and surprises of the current and past behavioral data to construct models for user search behavior. This kind of modeling provides users with a much richer searching experience by providing more personalized search results and more relevant information.

## 2.4 Predictive Models

With relation to behavioral studies research has been conducted to explore user models that help anticipating specific aspects of the search process. Agichtein et al. [2] investigated different patterns that can be identified in tasks that require multiple sessions. As a result, they [2] have devised an algorithm capable of predicting whether users will continue or abandon the task. Similar work is described in Diriye et al. [6], which focuses on predicting and understanding of why and when users abandon Web searches. There have been also attempts to understand past users' behaviors in order to predict future ones in similar conditions [1].

From an IR perspective, Radinski et al. [16] explored models to predict users' behaviors in a population in order to improve results from IR systems. The authors also developed a learning algorithm capable of selecting an appropriate predictive model depending on the situation and time. Several works have been conducted on query performance prediction, focusing on developing techniques that help IR system to anticipate whether a query will be effective or not to provide results that satisfy users' needs. For example, Guo et al. [9] found that features derived from search results and interactions features offer better prediction results than a prediction baseline defined in terms of query features.

# 3. RESEARCH QUESTIONS

Identifying and recommending search strategies to users who are searching information online is of importance in order to improve the overall search process and ultimately lead to successful completion of the task at hand. As previously mentioned, the analysis of the search process that deals with many aspects such as mental model, cognitive processes, strategies and tactics is a challenging problem. Even if one could successfully identify the tactics and strategies that a user is adopting while performing a search task, merely informing about that to the user would not be that helpful from the point of view of the user. A user would be more interested in knowing whether the underlying thought process that affects his/her strategies will eventually lead to the successful task completion to meet the required goals and if not what he/she should do to ensure that as early as possible in the search process.

One such attempt in addressing this problem is to assume that once a user strategizes how to tackle the task at hand in his/her brain and those ideas, thoughts and path is reflected in the actions he/she chooses along the search process. These actions such as the queries executed, the way they form queries (simple, descriptive, refined), the Web pages they visit, what they bookmark or consider as useful information, when and how they revisit pages, re-execute queries etc., all are considered not as part of a random thought process but, part of a search strategy that they form in their inner consciousness. Some early work has been done in the area of identifying strategies like the use of bookmarks, multiple browser windows and tabs, the way they capture and store relevant information (such as emailing or bookmarking useful Web pages, going through the history of the browser) [4]. Although such search strategies have been analyzed, these strategies are analyzed only with relation to the information seeking search process artifacts, but not in relation to the actual search process in identifying whether the user is adopting a specific strategy or not. It is also important to see whether a user changes the strategy based on the task they are approaching or the environment they are operating (individual/collaborative setting) in.

The above discussion leads to the following set of research questions.

- **RQ 1**: How can we identify different search strategies that people use during different search tasks by analyzing the actions they perform?
  - ***RQ 1.1***: What are the specific search process based features or characteristics of different search strategies of users?
  - ***RQ 1.2***: Do users use the same strategy repeatedly and/or does strategy vary by task?
- **RQ 2**: How well can we predict whether a specific user strategy is going to yield a good search performance or not?
  - ***RQ 2.1***: Which performance measures to quantify the strategies should we consider when evaluating the user search performance?
  - ***RQ 2.2***: How effectively can we recommend a search strategy to a user if we identify he/she is not performing well in a given search task?

## 4. PROPOSED APPROACH

In this research, I propose to analyze the search process which can be considered as a collection of user actions that a typical user would do when performing a Web search task, including but not limited to the following.

- Issue a query
- Scan the search result pages
- Visit a particular Web page
- Bookmarking or saving the page for future use
- Reformulating a query
- Revisiting a Web page
- Collecting a passage from a Web page
- Recommend a Web page/part of it to someone

The proposed approach would focus on the process rather than the information objects in contrast to traditional approaches as depicted in table 1. It will use time series analysis to evaluate the user search process since the actions have a temporal aspect over the search process and the information retrieved at different points in time will have different meanings when examined from the perspective of strategy formulation and execution. Instead of considering information as a collection of discrete documents, here the search is considered as a continuous process. In order to provide prediction of user search performance, the proposed approach would be considered as two-fold; one that uses the users's past search behavior (which has been widely used in the literature) and the second that combines the former with the current identified strategies/tactics. Thus, the proposed approach is a hybrid way of capturing the dependency of the future performance on *what* a user did in the past, in addition to discovering *how* the user came in to deciding on those past actions based on the strategies he/she possessed that would help in the future performance.

**Table 1: Comparison of Proposed approach and Traditional IR based approach.**

| *Factor* | **Traditional IR Based Approach** | **Proposed Approach** |
|---|---|---|
| *Unit of consideration* | Information Objects (E.g: Web pages, queries, etc.) | Process (E.g: Search process, strategies, tactics) |
| *Product/Process type* | Discrete | Continuous (Time Series) |
| *Prediction Based on* | User's Past Search Behavior | User's Past Search Behavior + Current Strategies/Tactics |

This would pave a way to evaluate user search performance based on the tactics and strategies they undertake and provide useful recommendations and personalization to improve overall search performance and thereby improve the user satisfaction and ability to achieve the final search goal.

## 5. PRELIMINARY ANALYSIS

This section provides brief overview of a preliminary analysis conducted using log data collected from user studies conducted in-house involving Web search to perform a certain task.

One dataset contains search session logs of 49 single users performing an exploratory search task. I have also conducted another user study to collect data from users for a different exploratory search task comprising of 12 individual users. Logs for each user correspond to approximately 20 to 30 minutes of active search. The log data consists of the time stamped records of all the user actions (such as page visits, queries, snippets, bookmarks) from task initiation to task completion.

Each action sequence which were separated in to sub sequences were then grouped in to different clusters, were positioned along the search process. After the cluster analysis, each of the sub-sequences that were clustered were mapped to their original position in the user search process and visualized in figure 1. It can be observed that each user has a different transition among different clusters along the search process and the clusters also alternate between these stages. It can also be noted that most users are in stage 2/Cluster 2 towards the end of the search process. This shows that users go through different steps during the search process over time, which by using further analysis could be linked to search strategies/tactics.

## 6. ISSUES FOR DISCUSSION

Although I have come up with some measures to be used in quantifying and evaluating the search strategies among users, which is crucial to this approach, I would like to discuss whether such measures are worthy of being considered.

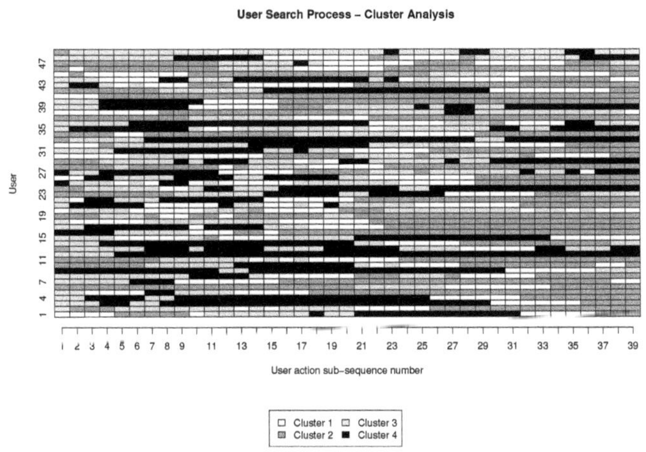


**Figure 1: Cluster Analysis of User Search Process**

I would also like to discuss about other possible evaluation measures and features that could be relevant to this approach.

While I have access to a couple of data sets based on the user studies we have conducted in-house and potential use of TREC Session track data, I would like to find whether there are any other datasets that I am unaware of that could be used in this analysis. This would allow me to evaluate whether the methods I come up with are generalizable across different data sets, which is a key aspect in such methods being considered useful to a wider research audience.

# 7. CONCLUSION

Understanding user online search process with respect to its inherent latent strategies and tactics used to find information is considered a complex task. In this research, I propose to develop methods and techniques to make such analysis and evaluation of log search data to undermine search strategies and tactics of the users, possible. I believe my proposed research would be able to contribute towards enhancing user experience in Web search, by exploiting the analysis of user search strategies and tactics.

# 8. ACKNOWLEDGEMENT

The work reported here is supported by Institute of Museum and Library Services (IMLS) Early Career Development grant #RE-04-12-0105-12 to Dr. Chirag Shah.

# 9. REFERENCES

[1] E. Adar, D. Weld, B. Bershad, and S. Gribble. Why we search: Visualizing and predicting user behavior. *In Proceedings of World Wide Web (WWW) Conference*, 2007.

[2] E. Agichtein, R. White, S. Dumais, and P. Bennett. Search interrupted: Understanding and predicting search task continuation. *In Proceedings of the Annual ACM Conference on Research and Development in Information Retrieval*, 2012.

[3] O. Alonso, M. Gertz, and R. A. Baeza-Yates. On the value of temporal information in information retrieval. *SIGIR Forum*, 41(2):35–41, 2007.

[4] A. Aula, N. Jhaveri, and M. Käki. Information search and re-access strategies of experienced web users. In *Proceedings of the 14th international conference on World Wide Web*, WWW '05, pages 583–592, 2005.

[5] M. Bates. Information search tactics. *Journal of the American Society for Information Science*, 30(4):205–214, 1979.

[6] A. Diriye, R. White, G. Buscher, and S. Dumais. Leaving so soon?: Understanding and predicting web search abandonment rationales. In *Proceedings of the 21st ACM international conference on Information and knowledge management*, CIKM '12, pages 1025–1034, 2012.

[7] N. G. Golbandi, L. K. Katzir, Y. K. Koren, and R. L. Lempel. Expediting search trend detection via prediction of query counts. In *Proceedings of the sixth ACM international conference on Web search and data mining*, WSDM '13, pages 295–304, 2013.

[8] D. A. Grossman and O. Frieder. *Information Retrieval, Algorithms and Heuristics*, volume 15 of *The Information Retrieval Series*. Springer, 2004.

[9] Q. Guo, R. W. White, S. T. Dumais, J. Wang, and B. Anderson. Predicting query performance using query, result, and user interaction features. In *Adaptivity, Personalization and Fusion of Heterogeneous Information*, RIAO '10, pages 198–201, 2010.

[10] A. Hassan, R. Jones, and K. L. Klinkner. Beyond DCG: User behavior as a predictor of a successful search. In *Proceedings of the third ACM international conference on Web search and data mining*, WSDM '10, pages 221–230, 2010.

[11] A. Hassan, Y. Song, and L.-w. He. A task level metric for measuring web search satisfaction and its application on improving relevance estimation. In *Proceedings of the 20th ACM international conference on Information and knowledge management*, CIKM '11, pages 125–134, 2011.

[12] Z. Liao, Y. Song, L.-w. He, and Y. Huang. Evaluating the effectiveness of search task trails. In *Proceedings of the 21st international conference on World Wide Web*, WWW '12, pages 489–498, 2012.

[13] D. A. Norman. *The Psychology of Everyday Things*. Basic Books, New York, 1998.

[14] V. L. O'Day and R. Jeffries. Orienteering in an information landscape: How information seekers get from here to there. In *Proceedings of the INTERACT '93 and CHI '93 Conference on Human Factors in Computing Systems*, CHI '93, pages 438–445, 1993.

[15] J. Pitkow, H. Schütze, T. Cass, R. Cooley, D. Turnbull, A. Edmonds, E. Adar, and T. Breuel. Personalized search. *Commun. ACM*, 45(9):50–55, Sept. 2002.

[16] K. Radinsky, K. Svore, S. Dumais, J. Teevan, A. Bocharov, and E. Horvitz. Modeling and predicting behavioral dynamics on the web. In *Proceedings of the 21st international conference on World Wide Web*, WWW '12, pages 599–608, 2012.

[17] J. Zakaria, A. Mueen, and E. Keogh. Clustering time series using unsupervised-shapelets. *IEEE International Conference on Data Mining*, 2012.

# On Discovering non-Obvious Recommendations: Using Unexpectedness and Neighborhood Selection Methods in Collaborative Filtering Systems

Panagiotis Adamopoulos
Department of Information, Operations and Management Sciences
Leonard N. Stern School of Business, New York University
padamopo@stern.nyu.edu

## ABSTRACT

This paper proposes a number of studies in order to move the field of recommender systems beyond the traditional paradigm and the classical perspective of rating prediction accuracy. We contribute to existing helpful but less explored recommendation strategies and propose new approaches targeting to more useful recommendations for both users and businesses. Working toward this direction, we discuss the studies we have conducted so far and present our future research plans. The overall goal of this research program is to expand our focus from even more accurate rating predictions toward a more holistic experience for the users, by providing them with non-obvious but high quality recommendations and avoiding the *over-specialization* and *concentration bias* problems. In particular, we propose a new *probabilistic neighborhood-based method* as an improvement of the standard $k$-nearest neighbors approach, alleviating some of the most common problems of collaborative filtering recommender systems, based on classical metrics of dispersion and diversity as well as some newly proposed metrics. Furthermore, we propose a concept of *unexpectedness* in recommender systems and operationalize it by suggesting various mechanisms for specifying the *expectations of the users* and proposing a recommendation method for providing the users with unexpected but high quality personalized recommendations that fairly match their interests. Besides, in order to generate utility-based recommendations for Massive Open Online Courses (MOOCs) that better serve the educational needs of students, we study the satisfaction of users with online courses vis-à-vis student retention. Finally, we summarize the conclusions of the conducted studies, discuss the limitations of our work and also outline the managerial implications of the proposed stream of research.

## Categories and Subject Descriptors

H.1.2 [**Models and Principles**]: User/Machine Systems - Human Factors; H.3.3 [**Information Storage and Retrieval**]: Information Search and Retrieval - Information filtering, Selection process, Retrieval models; I.2.6 [**Learning**]: Parameter learning

## Keywords

Algorithm Design; Unexpectedness; Recommender Systems


*WSDM'14,* February 24–28, 2014, New York, New York, USA.
Copyright 2014 ACM 978-1-4503-2351-2/14/02.
http://dx.doi.org/10.1145/2556195.2556204.

## 1. INTRODUCTION

Over the last two decades, a wide variety of different types of recommender systems (RSes) has been developed and successfully used across several domains [9]. During this time, many researchers have focused mainly on the development and improvement of efficient algorithms for more accurate rating predictions. Although the recommendations of the latest class of systems are significantly more accurate than they used to be a decade ago [13] and the broad social and business acceptance of RSes has already been achieved, there is still a long way to go in terms of satisfaction of the actual needs of the users [23, 7]. This is primarily due to the fact that many existing RSes focus on providing even more accurate rather than more useful recommendations. Besides, common recommenders, such as collaborative filtering (CF) algorithms, recommend products based on prior sales and ratings. Hence, they tend not to recommend products with limited historical data, even if these items would be rated favorably. These recommenders can create a rich-get-richer effect for popular items while this *concentration bias* can prevent what may otherwise be better consumer-product matches [17]. At the same time, common RSes usually recommend items very similar to what the users have already purchased or liked in the past [1]. This *over-specialization* of recommendations, however, is often inconsistent with sales goals and consumers' preferences. Some of the main problems pertaining to this narrow rating prediction focus of many existing recommender systems [16, 2] and the ways to broaden the current approaches have been discussed in [26].

Even though the aforementioned rating prediction perspective is the prevailing paradigm in recommender systems, there are other approaches that try to alleviate the problems pertaining to this narrow focus and have been gaining significant attention in the field of RSes [20]. In particular, some of the most recent perspectives maintain that recommender systems should make the users familiar with the various product categories and the whole product catalog. In addition, RSes should provide personalized recommendations from a wide range of items and enable the users to find relevant items that are hard to discover. Also, they should increase user satisfaction and engagement while offering a superior user experience. Recommender systems should also be able to reduce user search costs, improve the quality of decisions that consumers make, and increase their welfare. Besides, from a business perspective, RSes should increase the overall sales volume and conversion rates as well as promote items from the long tail that usually exhibit significantly lower marginal cost and, at the same time, higher marginal profit.

Moving beyond the classical perspective of the rating prediction accuracy, the main objective of this stream of research is to extend existing but less explored paradigms of RSes as well as propose new approaches that will result in more useful recommendations for both users and businesses. Working toward this direction, we discuss the studies we have conducted so far and present our future research plans. In particular, we shift our focus from even more accurate rating predictions and aim at offering a better experience to the users by avoiding the over-specialization and concentration bias of recommendations and providing the users with non-obvious (unexpected) but high quality recommendations that fairly match their interests.

## 2. RELATED WORK

Two of the most important problems of many recommender systems that have been identified in the literature and hinder user satisfaction are the *over-specialization* and *concentration* bias of recommendations. The problem of over-specialization is often practically addressed by introducing randomness in the recommendation procedure [11], filtering out items which are too similar to items the user has rated in the past [14], or increasing the diversity of recommendations [32]. Regarding the concentration bias of recommendations, [19] compared different RS algorithms with respect to aggregate diversity and their tendency to focus on certain parts of the product spectrum and showed that popular algorithms may lead to an undesired popularity boost of already popular items. Finally, [17] showed that this concentration bias can create a rich-get-richer effect for popular products leading to a subsequent reduction in profits and sales diversity.

Other streams of research that improve recommender systems going beyond rating prediction accuracy include work on *human-computer interaction* (HCI) [30], which involves the study and design of the interaction between users and RSes, as well as *explanations* for recommendations [28] that provide transparency into the recommendation process exposing the reasoning and data behind each recommendation. Besides, other approaches pertain to *diversification* [8, 31], which maximizes the variety of items in a recommendation list, *group recommenders* [27], which recommend items for groups of people, rather than individuals, and recommendation *sequences* [25], where sequences of ordered items are recommended instead of single items.

## 3. RESEARCH STUDIES

In this stream of research, working toward providing even more useful recommendations for both users and businesses and effectively moving beyond the narrow focus of the rating prediction accuracy, we designed a number of research studies to explore issues related to several new approaches.

In particular, Section 3.1.1, focusing on neighborhood selection, proposes a new *probabilistic neighborhood-based approach* ($k$-PN) as an improvement of the standard $k$-nearest neighbors ($k$-NN) algorithm, alleviating some of the most common problems of collaborative filtering recommender systems, based on classical metrics of dispersion and diversity as well as some newly proposed metrics. Then, Section 3.1.2 proposes a concept of *unexpectedness* in recommender systems and fully operationalizes it by suggesting various mechanisms for specifying the expectations of the users and proposing a recommendation method for providing the users with non-obvious but high quality personalized recommendations that fairly match their interests based on specific metrics of unexpectedness. Finally, Section 3.2 studies the satisfaction of students with massive open online courses (MOOCs) vis-à-vis student retention, in order to generate utility-based recommendations using the aforementioned methods and then experimentally evaluate the corresponding approaches in a real-world application. All these research studies go beyond the classical perspective of RSes and aim at providing the users with non-obvious but high quality recommendation sets that fairly match their interests and they will remarkably like. Thorough discussions of these concepts, implementation details, and experimental results are provided in [3, 4, 5, 6].

### 3.1 Beyond over-specialization

Sections 3.1.1 and 3.1.2 address the over-specialization and concentration bias problems in recommender systems focusing on *unexpectedness* and the related concepts of coverage, novelty, serendipity, and diversity of recommendation lists [4, 5].

#### *3.1.1 Probabilistic Neighborhoods*

In [6], we propose a new probabilistic method for neighborhood selection in collaborative filtering models. In particular, we illustrate the practical implementation of the proposed approach presenting a specific variation of the classical $k$-nearest neighbors ($k$-NN) CF method in which the neighborhood selection is based on an underlying probability distribution instead of just the $k$ neighbors with the highest similarity level to the target user. For the probabilistic neighborhood selection ($k$-PN), we use an efficient method for weighted sampling [29] of $k$ neighbors without replacement that also takes into consideration the similarity levels between the target user and the $n$ candidate neighbors. The key intuition for this *probabilistic nearest neighbors* collaborative filtering method is two-fold. First, using the neighborhood with the most similar users in order to estimate unknown ratings and recommend candidate items, the generated recommendation lists usually consist of known items with which the users are already familiar. Second, because of the multi-dimensionality of users' tastes, there are many items that the target user may like and are unknown to the $k$ most similar users to her/him. The theoretical motivation for this approach is based on ensemble learning theory according to which the generalization error of an ensemble, in addition to the bias and variance of the individual estimators (and the noise variance), also depends on the covariance between the individuals. Thus, we propose the use of probabilistic neighborhood selection in order to alleviate the aforementioned problems and move beyond the limited focus of rating prediction accuracy.

To investigate this claim, we conducted an empirical study and tested the proposed method in a very large number of experimental settings. In detail, we used a number of probability distributions from different families with various location and shape parameters in order to compare the proposed probabilistic method for neighborhood selection against the standard collaborative filtering approach in terms of popular evaluation metrics for item prediction accuracy, utility-based ranking, diversity, and dispersion as well as a newly proposed metric of mobility of recommendations.

The experimental results illustrate that the proposed method generates recommendation lists that are very different from those generated based on the classical collaborative filtering approach and alleviates the over-specialization and concentration bias problems. We also demonstrate that using probability distributions which sample mainly from the nearest neighbors and also some further neighbors, the proposed method outperforms, by a wide margin in most cases, the standard user-based $k$-NN method in terms of both item prediction accuracy and utility-based ranking measures, such as the F-measure and the normalized discounted cumulative gain (nDCG), across various experimental settings. This performance improvement is due to the reduction of covariance among the selected neighbors and is in accordance with the ensemble learning theory. Additionally, we showed that the performance improvement is not achieved at the expense of other popular performance measures that go beyond the rating prediction accuracy, such as catalog coverage, aggregate diversity, recommendation dispersion, and mobility. Finally, we identified a particular implementation of the $k$-PN method that consistently performs well across various experimental settings.

### 3.1.2 Expecting the Unexpected

In [4, 5], we propose a concept of unexpected recommendations as recommending those items that significantly depart from the expectations of the users. We also suggest a method for generating such recommendations, based on the utility theory of economics, as well as specific metrics to measure the unexpectedness of recommendation lists.

In particular, we formally define the concept of *unexpectedness* in recommender systems taking into account the actual *expectations* of the users and discuss how the concept of unexpectedness is differentiated from various related notions, such as novelty, serendipity, and diversity. Following the Greek philosopher Heraclitus, we approach this problem of finding and recommending unexpected items by first capturing the items expected by the users. Toward this direction, we suggest several mechanisms for specifying users' expectations that can be applied across various domains. Such mechanisms include the past transactions performed by the users, knowledge discovery and data mining techniques, and experts' domain knowledge. Besides, we formulate and fully operationalize the notion of unexpectedness and present an algorithm for providing unexpected recommendations of high quality that are hard to discover but fairly match the users' interests, based on the *utility theory* of economics. Moreover, we propose specific performance metrics to measure the unexpectedness of the generated recommendation lists taking into account also the usefulness of individual items.

Using "real-world" data sets, various examples of sets of expected recommendations, and different utility functions and distance metrics, we were able to test the proposed method in a large number of experimental settings including various levels of sparsity, different mechanisms for specifying users' expectations, and different cardinalities of these sets of expectations. The empirical study showed that all the examined variations of the proposed method significantly outperformed in terms of unexpectedness the standard baseline algorithms, including item-based and user-based $k$-Nearest Neighbors [22], Slope One, and Matrix Factorization [24]. This demonstrates that the proposed method indeed effectively captures the concept of unexpectedness since, in principle, it should do better than unexpectedness-agnostic methods. Furthermore, the proposed method for unexpected recommendations performed at least as well as, and in some cases even better than, the baseline algorithms in terms of the classical accuracy-based measures, such as root-mean-square error (RMSE) and the F-measure, as well as other popular performance measures, such as catalog coverage, aggregate diversity, serendipity, and the Gini coefficient. In addition, we presented a number of actual recommendation examples, generated by the proposed method and the employed baseline approaches, and provided insightful qualitative comments and recommendation explanations.

One of the main premises of the proposed method is that the users' expectations should be explicitly considered in order to provide them with unexpected recommendations of high quality that are hard to discover but fairly match their interests. Hence, the greatest improvements in terms of both unexpectedness and accuracy were observed in the experiments using the more accurate sets of user expectations. Moreover, the use of utility functions of standard form illustrates that the proposed method can be easily implemented in existing recommender systems as a new component that enhances unexpectedness of recommendations, without the need to further modify the current rating prediction procedures.

## 3.2 Massive Open Online Learning

In [3], we study the satisfaction of students with *Massive Open Online Courses* (MOOCs) vis-à-vis student retention in order to use the aforementioned approaches and generate utility-based recommendations for online courses that better serve the educational needs of students.

In particular, MOOCs are a recent development in the area of e-learning and distant education that has remarkably expanded during the last years. MOOCs are larger in scale than traditional courses, have no restrictions on individual participation, are globally distributed across a variety of networks, and aim at revolutionizing the way education happens. Such massive online courses are offered in a wide range of topics by dozens of top universities with the vision to provide free high-level education all over the world. Even though MOOCs have been broadly accepted, the very high drop-out rates indicate that much more should be done in order to satisfy the actual educational needs of the students. Tackling this important problem, we employ interdisciplinary research methods that complement each other. More specifically, we employ the *Grounded Theory Method* (GTM) on quantitative data, a less frequently applied paradigm which prioritizes exploration of the given phenomenon in a inductive *theory development* paradigm. In addition, we integrate state-of-the-art *econometric, text mining, opinion mining, and machine learning techniques* with the iterative approach of GTM, building both explanatory and predictive models, toward a more complete and in-depth analysis of the information captured by user-generated content. Overall, we present a novel mixed-methods analysis using a real-world data set with user-generated online reviews, where we both identify the emergent concepts related to different *student*, *course*, *platform*, and *university* characteristics that affect student retention and study their relative effect in a hedonic-like framework. Applying the methodological ideas of GTM to explanatory quantitative analysis and predictive models and going beyond descriptive statistics of coded verbal data, we contribute to the related literature by discovering new rich findings and provide actionable insights with significant implications for both MOOCs and traditional education.

The proposed approach and the corresponding findings have several implications for the universities and platforms offering online courses. They can be utilized for real-time detection of dissatisfied students as well as the design of better and more engaging courses that will increase retention rates. In detail, the results suggest that the course characteristics (e.g. estimated difficulty, workload, duration, whether there is automated grading, etc.) are important determinants of students' satisfaction and suggest useful guidelines for course design. For instance, MOOCs in general should have a specific instructor-based timetable, but for the most difficult courses students should be allowed to follow their own pace. Also, the findings suggest that there is room for improvement in the current form of certifications, which should be redesigned in order to become more useful for the students and further motivate them to successfully complete the corresponding course by ensuring knowledge verification and student identification. Additionally, while better technical solutions are needed for automatically providing feedback and evaluating the assignments of the students, peer assessment remains an important component of the learning process in MOOCs. Besides, professors and course instructors are the most important factor in online course retention and have the largest positive effect on the probability of a student to successfully complete a course. Our results also illustrate that, in addition to discussion forums, improved mechanisms or complementary technologies, such as wikis, are still needed in order to successfully advise, assist, connect, and motivate the students. Furthermore, our results show that open textbooks, in contrast to paid textbooks, have a positive effect. Finally, apart from the implications in education and the methodological ideas of GTM, we also discuss the managerial implications of the proposed analytical approach in other domains, such as social media and online commerce.

# 4. DISCUSSION AND FUTURE WORK

Successfully completing the aforementioned work will help the recommender systems field move further beyond the perspective of rating prediction accuracy. Following the proposed stream of research and adhering to our main objective of improving the usefulness of recommendations for both users and businesses, we both contribute to existing helpful but less explored recommender systems approaches and propose new valuable perspectives. Working toward this direction, we discussed the studies we have conducted so far and presented in detail some of our future research plans. In particular, the studies discussed in Section 3 move our focus from further improving the rating prediction accuracy and aim at offering a holistic experience to the users by avoiding the over-specialization and concentration bias of classical recommender systems and providing the users with non-obvious but high quality personalized recommendations that fairly match their interests.

In detail, Section 3.1.1, focusing on neighborhood selection, proposes a novel probabilistic neighborhood-based method ($k$-PN) as an improvement of the standard $k$-nearest neighbors recommendation algorithm, alleviating some of the most common problems of collaborative filtering recommender systems, based on classical metrics of dispersion and diversity as well as some newly proposed metrics. Then, Section 3.1.2 proposes a concept of *unexpectedness* in recommender systems and fully operationalizes it by suggesting various mechanisms for specifying the expectations of the users and proposing a recommendation method for providing the users with non-obvious but high quality personalized recommendations that fairly match their interests based on specific metrics of unexpectedness. Finally, Section 3.2 examines the satisfaction of students with massive open online courses (MOOCs) vis-à-vis student retention in order to generate utility-based recommendations using the aforementioned methods and then experimentally evaluate the corresponding approaches in a real-world application.

The aforementioned research studies have important managerial implications. Adhering to our main research objective, we work toward the direction of providing more useful recommendations for both users and businesses. Avoiding obvious and expected recommendations while maintaining high predictive accuracy levels, we can alleviate the common problems of over-specialization and concentration bias and, therefore, we have the potential to further increase user satisfaction and engagement and offer a superior experience to the users [12, 21]. In addition, unexpectedness and its related notions can improve the welfare of consumers by allowing them to locate and buy products that otherwise they would not have purchased. Introducing unexpectedness in RSes can vastly reduce customers' search costs by recommending items that the users would rate highly but it would be quite unlikely to discover on their own. As a result, the inefficiencies caused by buyer search costs are reduced, while the ability of markets to optimally allocate productive resources is increased [10]. Furthermore, the generated recommendations should be useful not only for the users but for the businesses, too. The proposed approach exhibits a potential positive economic impact based on the direct effect of increased sales and willingness-to-pay as well as the enhanced customer loyalty leading to lasting and valuable relationships [18] through offering more useful recommendations from a wider range of items and making the users familiar with the whole product catalog. Apart from the significant gains in producer welfare from the additional sales [15], businesses might also leverage revenues from market niches [17]. Thus, there is a potential positive economic impact based on the effect of recommending items from the long tail and not focusing mostly on bestsellers that usually exhibit higher marginal costs and lower profit margins because of acquisition costs, licenses, and increased competition.

As part of our future work, we would like to further optimize and streamline the proposed methods as well as to integrate them with related existing approaches in the fields of web search and data mining. Moreover, we would like to implement and evaluate the proposed approaches in both MOOCs and a traditional on-line retail setting. Besides, we would like to conduct a series of live controlled experiments with human subjects in order to study the on-line user behavior, examine and actively adjust the trade-off between exploration (e.g. unexpectedness, serendipity, diversity, etc.) and exploitation (e.g. accuracy) of recommender systems, and better evaluate the proposed perspectives in a user-centric framework for top-$N$ recommendations. In addition, we plan to investigate how the proposed recommendation approaches and perspectives can be effectively combined with traditional approaches in hybrid recommender systems aiming at accurate and non-obvious recommendation lists that the users will remarkably like.

## 5. ACKNOWLEDGMENTS

I would like to thank my advisor and co-author, Prof. Alexander Tuzhilin, for his support, guidance, and valuable feedback.

## 6. REFERENCES

[1] Z. Abbassi, S. Amer-Yahia, L. V. Lakshmanan, S. Vassilvitskii, and C. Yu. Getting recommender systems to think outside the box. In *RecSys '09*, pages 285–288. ACM, 2009.

[2] P. Adamopoulos. Beyond Rating Prediction Accuracy: On New Perspectives in Recommender Systems. In *RecSys '13*, pages 459–462. ACM, 2013.

[3] P. Adamopoulos. What Makes a Great MOOC? An Interdisciplinary Analysis of Student Retention in Online Courses. In *ICIS '13*. AIS, 2013.

[4] P. Adamopoulos and A. Tuzhilin. On Unexpectedness in Recommender Systems: Or How to Expect the Unexpected. In *DiveRS 2011 - ACM RecSys 2011 Workshop on Novelty and Diversity in Recommender Systems*, RecSys '11. ACM, 2011.

[5] P. Adamopoulos and A. Tuzhilin. On Unexpectedness in Recommender Systems: Or How to Better Expect the Unexpected. *Working Paper: CBA-13-03, New York University*, 2013. http://hdl.handle.net/2451/31832.

[6] P. Adamopoulos and A. Tuzhilin. Probabilistic Neighborhood Selection in Collaborative Filtering Systems. *Working Paper: CBA-13-04, New York University*, 2013. http://hdl.handle.net/2451/31988.

[7] P. Adamopoulos and A. Tuzhilin. Recommendation Opportunities: Improving Item Prediction Using Weighted Percentile Methods in Collaborative Filtering Systems. In *RecSys '13*, pages 351–354. ACM, 2013.

[8] G. Adomavicius and Y. Kwon. Improving aggregate recommendation diversity using ranking-based techniques. *Knowledge and Data Engineering, IEEE Transactions on*, 24(5):896 –911, 2012.

[9] G. Adomavicius and A. Tuzhilin. Toward the next generation of recommender systems: A survey of the state-of-the-art and possible extensions. *IEEE Trans. on Knowl. and Data Eng.*, 17(6):734–749, 2005.

[10] J. Y. Bakos. Reducing buyer search costs: implications for electronic marketplaces. *Manage. Sci.*, 43(12):1676–1692, 1997.

[11] M. Balabanović and Y. Shoham. Fab: content-based, collaborative recommendation. *Communications of the ACM*, 40(3):66–72, 1997.

[12] W. J. Baumol and E. A. Ide. Variety in retailing. *Management Science*, 3(1):pp. 93–101, 1956.

[13] R. M. Bell, J. Bennett, Y. Koren, and C. Volinsky. The million dollar programming prize. *IEEE Spectr.*, 46(5):28–33, 2009.

[14] D. Billsus and M. J. Pazzani. User modeling for adaptive news access. *User Modeling and User-Adapted Interaction*, 10(2-3):147–180, 2000.

[15] E. Brynjolfsson, Y. J. Hu, and M. D. Smith. Consumer surplus in the digital economy: Estimating the value of increased product variety at online booksellers. *Manage. Sci.*, 49(11):1580–1596, 2003.

[16] P. Cremonesi, F. Garzotto, S. Negro, A. V. Papadopoulos, and R. Turrin. Looking for "good" recommendations: a comparative evaluation of recommender systems. In *INTERACT '11*, 2011.

[17] D. Fleder and K. Hosanagar. Blockbuster culture's next rise or fall: The impact of recommender systems on sales diversity. *Manage. Sci.*, 55(5):697–712, 2009.

[18] M. Gorgoglione, U. Panniello, and A. Tuzhilin. The effect of context-aware recommendations on customer purchasing behavior and trust. In *RecSys '11*, pages 85–92. ACM, 2011.

[19] D. Jannach, L. Lerche, F. Gedikli, and G. Bonnin. What recommenders recommend–an analysis of accuracy, popularity, and sales diversity effects. In *UMAP '13*, pages 25–37. Springer, 2013.

[20] D. Jannach, M. Zanker, A. Felfernig, and G. Friedrich. *Recommender systems: an introduction.* Cambridge University Press, 2010.

[21] B. Kahn, D. Lehmann, and W. S. M. Dept. *Modeling choice among assortments.* Working paper (Wharton School. Marketing Dept.). Wharton School, University of Pennsylvania, Marketing Department, 1991.

[22] J. A. Konstan, B. N. Miller, D. Maltz, J. L. Herlocker, L. R. Gordon, and J. Riedl. Grouplens: applying collaborative filtering to usenet news. *Comm. of the ACM*, 40(3), 1997.

[23] J. A. Konstan and J. T. Riedl. Recommender systems: from algorithms to user experience. *User Modeling and User-Adapted Interaction*, 22:101–123, 2012.

[24] Y. Koren, R. Bell, and C. Volinsky. Matrix factorization techniques for recommender systems. *Computer*, 42(8), 2009.

[25] J. Masthoff. Group recommender systems: Combining individual models. In *Recommender Systems Handbook*, pages 677–702. Springer, 2011.

[26] S. M. McNee, J. Riedl, and J. A. Konstan. Being accurate is not enough: how accuracy metrics have hurt recommender systems. In *CHI '06*, pages 1097–1101. ACM, 2006.

[27] M. O'Connor, D. Cosley, J. A. Konstan, and J. Riedl. Polylens: a recommender system for groups of users. In *ECSCW '01*. Kluwer Academic Publishers, 2001.

[28] N. Tintarev and J. Masthoff. Designing and evaluating explanations for recommender systems. In *Recommender Systems Handbook*, pages 479–510. Springer, 2011.

[29] C.-K. Wong and M. C. Easton. An efficient method for weighted sampling without replacement. *SIAM Journal on Computing*, 9(1):111–113, 1980.

[30] K.-H. Yoo, U. Gretzel, and M. Zanker. *Persuasive Recommender Systems: Conceptual Background and Implications.* Springer, 2013.

[31] T. Zhou, Z. Kuscsik, J.-G. Liu, M. Medo, J. R. Wakeling, and Y.-C. Zhang. Solving the apparent diversity-accuracy dilemma of recommender systems. *Proceedings of the National Academy of Sciences*, 107(10):4511–4515, 2010.

[32] C.-N. Ziegler, S. M. McNee, J. A. Konstan, and G. Lausen. Improving recommendation lists through topic diversification. In *WWW '05*, pages 22–32. ACM, 2005.

# Exploratory Search with Semantic Transformations using Collaborative Knowledge Bases

Yegin Genc
Howe School of Technology Management
Stevens Institute of Technology
Hoboken, NJ
ygenc@stevens.edu

## ABSTRACT

Sometimes we search for simple facts. Other times we search for relationships between concepts. While existing information retrieval systems work well for simple searches, they are less satisfying for complex inquiries because of the ill-structured nature of many searches and the cognitive load involved in the search process. Search can be improved by leveraging the network of concepts that are maintained by collaborative knowledge bases such as Wikipedia. By treating exploratory search inquires as networks of concepts – and then mapping documents to these concepts, exploratory search performance can be improved. This method is applied to an exploratory search task: given a journal abstract, abstracts are ranked based their relevancy to the seed abstract. The results show comparable relevancy scores to state of the art techniques while at the same time providing better diversity.

## Categories and Subject Descriptors

H.3.3 [**Information Storage and Retrieval**]: Information Search and Retrieval—*Search process, Selection process*

## General Terms

Exploratory search, Collaborative Knowledge Bases, wikipedia, concept networks

## 1. INTRODUCTION

Learning new topics, or investigating unfamiliar subjects are complex search activities because we need to interpret and often critically assess the new information. Such search activities, commonly known as exploratory searches, are mixed with other information or cognitive behaviors such as sense making, organizing & analyzing data, and decision making [20].

For exploratory search tasks, information needs are not initially well recognized because (a) such tasks are motivated by ill-structured problems and (b) searchers lack the necessary prior background knowledge [32]. Ill-structuredness can be defined as not having a specific problem definition or a single right approach to execute the search. Consequently, searchers find it difficult to develop a proper solution path or even recognize a valid solution [28]. Similarly, if searchers lacks prior background knowledge, they struggle with determining the information needs and integrating new knowledge. Heit [15] suggests, human perception and learning new categories are affected by a person's knowledge and theories about the world [29] in at least three respects: integration, selective weighting, and facilitation effects.

To recognize the information needs, exploratory search starts with formulating a 'focus'. During this process, searchers look for background information to improve their mental models about the search task [28]. As their mental model gets more structured, information requirements clarifies and a solution space is formulated. In parallel, the notion of relevancy also shifts. What is considered as relevant in the early stages of the search, i.e. pre-focus, can be dropped later once the focus is established. In short, until the information needs clarify, it is hard for the searchers to represent their information needs or recognize relevant documents.

Existing IR systems are problematic in exploratory search because they rely on the searchers' ability to represent the information need properly. That is, the searcher needs to formulate proper queries, make sense of the retrieved results, and, based on these results, adjust queries and reiterate the search if necessary. These system are less efficient when users lack the knowledge or contextual awareness to formulate queries or navigate complex information spaces [31] – two key characteristics of exploratory search. Another potential issue with these systems is that search results can fail to cover all aspects of the search topics. On an analysis of the IR systems based on TREC results, Buckely [4] suggests that one major reason for failure common across different systems is that top retrieved documents do not reflect some aspects of the search topics.

In this work, I propose a methodology to improve search by leveraging the network of concepts that are maintained by collaborative knowledge bases such as Wikipedia. Drawing from the cognitive view of the information retrieval [16], I consider documents and exploratory search inquires, that are in the form of unstructured text, as networks of concepts. Ranking documents based on their concept coverage returns highly relevant and diverse set of documents.

The rest of the paper is structured as follows. Section 2 discusses related work on exploratory search and using


*WSDM'14*, February 24–28, 2014, New York, New York, USA.
ACM 978-1-4503-2351-2/14/02.
http://dx.doi.org/10.1145/2556195.2556205.

Wikipedia in information retrieval. Section 3 describes the model and Section 4 presents the experiment before Section 5 concludes with results and discussions.

## 2. RELATED WORK

### 2.1 Exploratory Search

Information Retrieval studies have long been working on various aspects information seeking behaviors in complex search tasks [2, 27, 19]. However, after 2005, we started seeing dedicated workshops and special issues on exploratory search [31, 30]. In one of these special issues, Marchionini [20] described exploratory search activities and how it is different from simpler search activities – i.e., lookups. Kang et. al[17] investigated how domain expertise effects exploratory search tasks when using traditional search engines – such as google.com, and social tagging systems – such as delicious.com. This study is a variation of Duggan and his colleges' work [8] that investigated effects of background knowledge in web searches. Fu et. al [11] proposed a learning model that characterizes learning activities and exploratory search processes by studying how users interacted with social tagging systems.

One of the challenges in studying exploratory search tasks is performance evaluation due to their ill-structured nature. In [28], Vakkari analyzes characteristics exploratory search activities in order to provide insight on how to evaluate exploratory search systems. This study also provides a good reference list for Vakkari's previous work on exploratory search. Wildemuth et. al [32] also provides an extensive review of the exploratory studies and the experimental exploratory search tasks that are used in some of these previous studies.

### 2.2 Wikipedia in Information Retrieval

In recent years Wikipedia has gained popularity for extracting meaning from text. It has potential to serve as encyclopedia, corpus, thesaurus, database, ontology, and network structure. All these features combined make Wikipedia an attractive resource in natural language processing, information retrieval, information extraction and ontology building [21]. The benefits of extracting a set of concepts from text go far beyond boosting content. It is an important step in detecting semantic relationships among textual data and automated classification of text.

When every concept in a text corpus is matched to an entity in Wikipedia, text can be represented as a set of these concepts or annotations. Cross-referencing concepts in text with Wikipedia articles using this technique is called wikification. 'Wikify!' [24] and MilneâĂŹs system [25] are two examples that annotate text with slightly different disambiguation techniques. Cucerzan [6] employed a space vector model by creating vector representation of Wikipedia entities and comparing them with vector representations of processed documents in the process. Meij et al. [23] classifies tweets into concepts in Wikipedia by applying machine learning. Dredze et al. [7] applied a more generalized approach that can be extended to other knowledge bases and their method 'learns' to predict entities that will not appear in the Knowledge Base. Like [23], this method also requires a supervised learning process.

One of the most prominent work that use Wikipedia as an *interpreter* for understanding online text is called Explicit Semantic Analysis (ESA) [9, 10, 12, 13]. In ESA concepts are defined as Wikipedia pages and meaning is defined as the "strength of its association with concepts that we know" [12]. This way words can be expressed as weighted vectors of concepts - wikipedia pages. ESA requires a preprocessing step that takes several hours but once done, it can be used to improve the relevancy of search results [10].

## 3. METHODOLOGY

Our method essentially ranks the documents of a corpus based on their relevancy to a seed document that represents the exploratory search inquiry. This method has three stages: (1) Extract the concept network from the seed document using Wikipedia, (2) Map the explored documents onto the concepts in the network, and (3) Rank the documents based on their concept coverage. These stages are described in turn.

### 3.1 Extracting concept network

To extract concepts from a document, the text is segmented into phrases – single words, bi–grams, and tri–grams – that overlap in a sliding window fashion. The resulting candidate phrases are then submitted as search criteria for the page titles of Wikipedia articles using the Wikipedia API. The process captures important concepts of the document, but there are usually a number of matches that are not appropriate if context is considered. As an example, in an abstract on computer language representation, the term '*the observer*' lands on the Wikipedia page for the British newspaper 'The Observer' [1]. To filter out such concepts, the ontology of the concepts based on their Wikipedia categories are extracted, and ontology extended by traversing both up and down the hierarchy of categories.

The process usually results in one large connected component and a few disconnected components (Figure 1). The disconnected components, in general, contain concepts that are irrelevant or unnecessary. Thus, by taking only the largest component into account, we filter out extraneous concepts.

### 3.2 Mapping documents to concepts

In order that a document set is analyzed in the context of a seed document, each document of the set is seen as a distribution over the concepts (the Wikipedia page titles) extracted from the seed document. Each concept is seen as a word frequency distribution that sum up to its explicit definitions in its content page. This wiki method is similar in structure to topic models, such as Latent Dirichlet Allocation [3]. However, concepts are observable Wikipedia page word frequencies, rather than inferred latent word distributions. This way, we can drop the computationally expensive step of inferring topic distributions and simply observe word frequencies of Wikipedia pages. By observing just the word frequencies in Wikipedia pages and documents, we can calculate topic distributions of documents. Topic distributions are considered as $\Theta = (\theta_{j,k})$ such that the element (j,k) represents relevancy of the document j, to the topic represented by Wikipedia page j.

By observing the word frequencies in Wikipedia pages (W) and documents (D), the concept frequencies of documents

[1] `http://en.wikipedia.org/wiki/The_Observer`

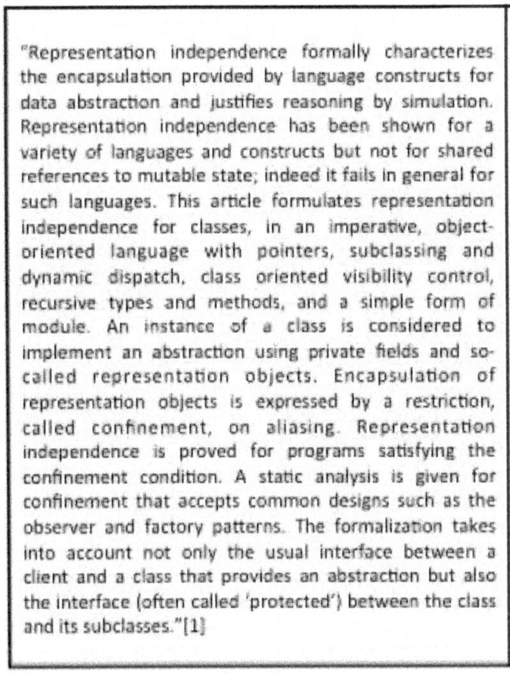

"Representation independence formally characterizes the encapsulation provided by language constructs for data abstraction and justifies reasoning by simulation. Representation independence has been shown for a variety of languages and constructs but not for shared references to mutable state; indeed it fails in general for such languages. This article formulates representation independence for classes, in an imperative, object-oriented language with pointers, subclassing and dynamic dispatch, class oriented visibility control, recursive types and methods, and a simple form of module. An instance of a class is considered to implement an abstraction using private fields and so-called representation objects. Encapsulation of representation objects is expressed by a restriction, called confinement, on aliasing. Representation independence is proved for programs satisfying the confinement condition. A static analysis is given for confinement that accepts common designs such as the observer and factory patterns. The formalization takes into account not only the usual interface between a client and a class that provides an abstraction but also the interface (often called 'protected') between the class and its subclasses."[1]

**Figure 1: An example abstract [1] and its concept network based extracted from Wikipedia. Concepts are connected through their categories. In further analysis, the smaller components of the graph are usually out of context or do not provide value about understanding the topic of the document.**

can be calculate as:

$$\Theta = D^T W$$

Let $V = \{v_1, v_2, ..., v_n\}$ be the vocabulary of documents in the corpus. $D = (d_{i,j})$ is the document word frequency matrix where element (i,j) represents the frequency of term $i (i \in V)$ in document j. $W = (w_{i,k})$ is the Wikipedia word frequency matrix where element (i,k) represents the frequency of term $i (i \in V)$ in Wikipedia page k.

To address the noise from commonly used words across all documents and Wikipedia pages, a Term Frequency-Inverse Document Frequency (tfidf) transformation is applied to both D and W, making the concept frequencies:

$$\Theta = tfidf(D)^T tfidf(W)$$

## 3.3 Ranking

Concept frequencies of a document indicate how relevant the document is to each concept. As a result, the most intuitive way to rank a set of documents based on their relevancy to a seed document is to sort them by the sum of extracted concept frequencies: the higher the total, the more relevant the document to the concepts:

$$Ranking\Theta_j = argsort_j \left( \sum_{i=0}^{k} \theta_i \right)$$

Observing only concept frequency sums allows frequency distributions to vary. That is, two documents that are seemingly equally related to the seed document (equal frequency sums) can easily be related to different concepts in it (different concept frequency distributions). By allowing variance in the concept frequency distributions, I expect a topical diversity in results.

# 4. EXPERIMENT

The model is applied to an exploratory search task: given a journal abstract, abstracts are ranked based their relevancy to the seed abstract. Our goal is to find highly relevant and diverse results.

The experiment included 619 abstracts of the Journal of the ACM (JACM) and their references. For each abstract, the top-k (5,10,15, and 20) relevant abstracts were selected from the set using the method above. The selections were evaluated based on the average relevancy to the seed documents, as well as the diversity of the top-k documents. Relevancy was measured using latent semantic analysis vector cosine similarity between the documents:

$$Sim(D_i, D_j) = cosine\left(\overrightarrow{LSA(D_i)}, \overrightarrow{LSA(D_j)}\right) \quad (1)$$

Diversity was measured through the coverage of the references, a common diversity measure for experiments using journal articles data sets [22], [18]. The coverage measure for a subset of articles is the inverse of the density of the references sub-graph. To evaluate density, a directed network graph of document references was generated. For each document, on average, half of all the references had unique identifiers since they were also stored in the digital library (DL) of the ACM. For references without unique identifiers, the titles from the reference entries were extracted and hashed. Digital Library notifies that article references were entered using Optical Character Recognition (OCR) software. To

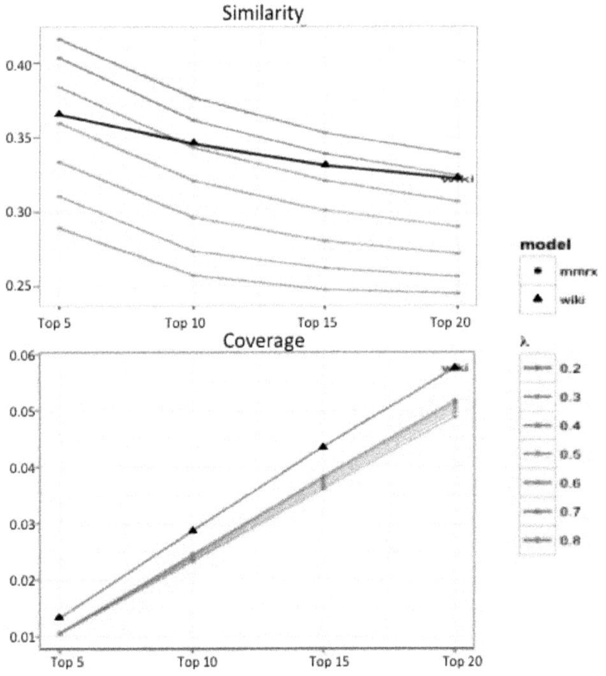


**Figure 2: Comparison of the proposed model (wiki) with Maximal Marginal Relevance method (mmrx) at different relevance to diversity ratios (λ) .**

account for OCR issues, we consider pairs of titles with Levensthein String Edit distances higher than 0.9 as the same.

# 5. RESULTS AND DISCUSSIONS

The wiki method was compared to a probabilistic information retrieval algorithm, Okapi BM25 [26]. In order to produce diversity, the Maximal Marginal Relevance (MMR) algorithm was used at varying relevance to diversity ratios (λ) [5]. The details of BM225 and MMR are in Appendix A.

Figure 2 (bottom) shows that the wiki method provides considerably better diversity results than the highest diversity MMR can provide. Moreover, when diversity is closest to the Wikipedia results, MMR's average relevance to the seed documents is considerably lower than the wiki method.

Information in collaborative data can help us explore complex information spaces more efficiently and effectively. If we can automate the understanding of text, we can reduce the cognitive load involved in the process. In this and previous work (i.e., [14] ) I have shown the layers of information in Wikipedia, such as linkages, categorizations and the content can help people navigate unstructured text even when they lack the knowledge or contextual awareness.

My focus, so far, was to find machine algorithms that can support exploratory search. I think Wikipedia has more to offer to support exploratory search. To give an example, visual interfaces similar to Figure 1 can help searchers understand either the problem space –the queries– or the solution space – query results. Although experiments so far are promising, this remains to be an ambitious goal. Concept maps generated from Wikipedia can be quite complicated at times and rather than helping users, they can potentially increase the cognitive load.

Another challenge in studying exploratory search is evaluating task performance. While information retrieval tasks are commonly evaluated by precision and recall on pre-labelled datasets, such measures are insufficient in gauging how well users articulate the topics they are searching [28]. A potential solution is to design experiments with outcomes that can be judged by humans – i.e. asking users to write reports on a topic they need to investigate and have such reports evaluated by subject matter experts. For authenticity – and external validity, the tasks need to be kept as ill-defined as possible. Then the evaluation becomes more complicated. When there is multiple solution paths, and multiple right answers, the inter-rater reliability measures tend to decrease.

# 6. REFERENCES

[1] A. Banerjee and D. A. Naumann. Ownership confinement ensures representation independence for object-oriented programs. *Journal of the ACM*, 52(6):894–960, Nov. 2005.

[2] N. J. Belkin, R. N. Oddy, and H. M. Brooks. ASK for Information Retrieval: Part I. Background and Theory. *Journal of Documentation*, 38(2):61–71, 1982.

[3] D. M. Blei, A. Y. Ng, and M. I. Jordan. Latent dirichlet allocation. *The Journal of Machine Learning Research*, 3:993–1022, Mar. 2003.

[4] C. Buckley. Why current IR engines fail. *Proceedings of the 27th annual international ACM SIGIR conference on Research and development in information retrieval*, pages 584–585, 2004.

[5] J. Carbonell and J. Goldstein. The use of MMR, diversity-based reranking for reordering documents and producing summaries. *Proceedings of the 21st annual international ACM SIGIR conference on Research and development in information retrieval*, pages 335–336, 1998.

[6] S. Cucerzan. Large-scale named entity disambiguation based on Wikipedia data. In *Proceedings of EMNLP-CoNLL*, 2007.

[7] M. Dredze, P. McNamee, D. Rao, A. Gerber, and T. Finin. Entity disambiguation for knowledge base population. *Proceedings of the 23rd International Conference on Computational Linguistics*, pages 277–285, 2010.

[8] G. B. Duggan and S. J. Payne. Knowledge in the head and on the web. In *Proceeding of the twenty-sixth annual CHI conference*, pages 39–48, New York, New York, USA, 2008. ACM Press.

[9] O. Egozi, E. Gabrilovich, and S. Markovitch. Concept-based feature generation and selection for information retrieval. *AAAI'08*, 2008.

[10] O. Egozi, S. Markovitch, and E. Gabrilovich. Concept-Based Information Retrieval Using Explicit Semantic Analysis. *ACM Transactions on Information Systems*, 29(2):1–34, Apr. 2011.

[11] W.-T. Fu, T. G. Kannampallil, and R. Kang. A semantic imitation model of social tag choices. 4:66–73, 2009.

[12] E. Gabrilovich and S. Markovitch. Computing semantic relatedness using wikipedia-based explicit semantic analysis. *IJCAI*, 7, 2007.

[13] E. Gabrilovich and S. Markovitch. Wikipedia-based semantic interpretation for natural language processing. *Journal of Artificial Intelligence Research*, 34(1):443–498, 2009.
[14] Y. Genc, Y. Sakamoto, and J. Nickerson. Discovering context: Classifying tweets through a semantic transform based on wikipedia. *Foundations of Augmented Cognition. Directing the Future of Adaptive Systems*, pages 484–492, 2011.
[15] E. Heit. Knowledge and concept learning. *Knowledge, concepts, and categories*, pages 7–41, 1997.
[16] P. Ingwersen and K. Järvelin. The Turn: Integration of Information Seeking and Retrieval in Context. 2005.
[17] R. Kang, W.-T. Fu, and T. G. Kannampallil. Exploiting knowledge-in-the-head and knowledge-in-the-social-web. In *the 28th international conference*, pages 393–402, New York, New York, USA, 2010. ACM Press.
[18] O. Küçüktunç, E. Saule, K. Kaya, and Ü. V. Çatalyürek. Diversified recommendation on graphs: pitfalls, measures, and algorithms. *Proceedings of the 22nd international conference on World Wide Web*, pages 715–726, 2013.
[19] C. C. Kuhlthau. Inside the search process: Information seeking from the user's perspective. *JASIS*, 1991.
[20] G. Marchionini. Exploratory search: from finding to understanding. *Communications of the ACM*, 49(4):41–46, 2006.
[21] O. Medelyan, D. Milne, C. Legg, and I. H. Witten. Mining meaning from Wikipedia. *International Journal of Human-Computer Studies*, 67(9):716–754, Sept. 2009.
[22] Q. Mei, J. Guo, and D. Radev. Divrank: the interplay of prestige and diversity in information networks. *Proceedings of the 16th ACM SIGKDD international conference on Knowledge discovery and data mining*, pages 1009–1018, 2010.
[23] E. Meij, W. Weerkamp, and M. de Rijke. Adding semantics to microblog posts. In *WSDM '12: Proceedings of the fifth ACM international conference on Web search and data mining*. ACM Request Permissions, Feb. 2012.
[24] R. Mihalcea and A. Csomai. Wikify!: linking documents to encyclopedic knowledge. *Proceedings of the sixteenth ACM conference on Conference on information and knowledge management*, pages 233–242, 2007.
[25] D. Milne and I. Witten. Learning to link with wikipedia. *Proceedings of the 17th ACM conference on Information and knowledge management*, pages 509–518, 2008.
[26] S. E. Robertson and S. Walker. Okapi/Keenbow at TREC-8. *The Eighth Text REtrieval Conference (TREC 8). NIST Special Publication*, 8:151–162, 1999.
[27] P. Vakkari. A theory of the task-based information retrieval process: a summary and generalisation of a longitudinal study. *Journal of Documentation*, 57(1):44–60, 2001.
[28] P. Vakkari. Exploratory searching as conceptual exploration. *Proceedings of HCIR*, pages 24–27, 2010.
[29] K. E. Weick. *Sensemaking in Organizations*. Sage Publications, Incorporated, May 1995.
[30] R. W. White, S. M. Drucker, G. Marchionini, M. Hearst, and m. c. schraefel. Exploratory search and HCI. In *CHI '07 extended abstracts*, pages 2877–2880, New York, New York, USA, 2007. ACM Press.
[31] R. W. White, B. Kules, and S. M. Drucker. Supporting exploratory search, introduction, special issue, communications of the ACM. *Communications of the ACM*, 49(4):36–39, 2006.
[32] B. M. Wildemuth and L. Freund. Assigning search tasks designed to elicit exploratory search behaviors. *Proceedings of the Symposium on Human-Computer Interaction and Information Retrieval*, page 4, 2012.

## 7. ACKNOWLEDGMENTS

This material is based upon work supported by the National Science Foundation under Grant Number 0968561.

# APPENDIX

## A. RELEVANCE AND DIVERSITY

### A.1 Best Match 25 (BM25)

BM25 is a probabilistic retrieval function stems from TREC-8 [26]. It scores, and ranks, documents based on their similarities to a given query Q containing keywords $(q_i, ..., q_n)$ is:

$$sim(Q, d) = \sum_{i=1}^{n} \frac{k \times tf(q_i)}{K + tf(q_i)} idf(q_i)$$

The principle is similar to TF-IDF where query terms are weighted based on frequency in a document (tf) and across the corpus (idf). In addition, ratio of the document length to the average document length is taken into account in K and BM25 is parameterized for further optimization. We used xapianâĂŹs implementation of BM25 with default parameters.

### A.2 Maximal Marginal Relevance (MMR)

One approach to diversify search result is optimizing the search results based on two criteria: similarity to the query – relevance, and dissimilarity to the other relevant documents – novelty. Maximal Marginal Relevance (MMR) [5], for example, work on this principle: similarity of a document to a query is adjusted based on its similarity to the other documents that are more similar to the query.

$$MMR = \underset{D_i \in R \setminus S}{argmax} \left[ \lambda Sim_1(D_i, Q) - (1 - \lambda) \max_{D_j \in S} (Sim_2(D_i, D_j)) \right]$$

Given a query Q, R is a ranked list of document and S is a subset that is already retrieved. Sim1 is the similarity metric between the query and the documents, and Sim2 is the similarity metric between among, $Sim_2$ can be a different metric than $Sim_1$. $\lambda$ is the importance of relevance over diversity: with lower $\lambda$ values, the diversity is expected to improve while relevancy deteriorates.

# Search by Multiple Examples

Mingzhu Zhu
Information Systems Department, New Jersey Institute of Technology
University Heights, Newark, NJ 07102, USA
mz59@njit.edu

Yi-Fang Brook Wu
Information Systems Department, New Jersey Institute of Technology
University Heights, Newark, NJ 07102, USA
wu@njit.edu

## ABSTRACT
It is often difficult for users to adopt keywords to express their information needs. Search-By-*Multiple*-Examples (SBME), a promising method for overcoming this problem, allows users to specify their information needs as a set of *relevant documents* rather than as a set of keywords. Most of the studies on SBME adopt the Positive Unlabeled learning (PU learning) techniques by treating the users' provided examples (denote as query examples) as positive set and the entire data collection as unlabeled set. However, it is inefficient to treat the entire data collection as unlabeled set, as its size can be huge. In addition, the query examples are treated as being relevant to a single topic, but it is often the case that they can be relevant to multiple topics. As the query examples are much fewer than the unlabeled data, the system performance may downgrade dramatically because of the class imbalance problem. What's more, the experiments conducted in these studies have not taken into account the settings in online search, which are very different from the controlled experiments scenario.

This proposed research seeks to explore how to improve SBME by exploring: (1) how to predict user' information needs by modeling the content of the documents using probabilistic topic models; (2) how to deal with the class imbalance problem by reducing the size of the unlabeled data and adopting machine learning techniques. We will also conduct extensive experiments to better evaluate SBME using different sizes of query examples to simulate users' information needs.

## Categories and Subject Descriptors
H.3.3 [**Information Storage and Retrieval**]: Information Search and Retrieval

## General Terms
Algorithms, Experimentation

## Keywords
Information Retrieval, Positive Unlabeled Learning, Transductive Inference, Search by Multiple Examples

## 1. INTRODUCTION
Information overload is a common problem with the volume of digital information being created increasing exponentially. This is especially true for those researchers who need to keep up with the relevant literature in their research domain. Traditionally, most researchers keep themselves up to date with the literature by using keyword-based Information Retrieval (IR) systems such as Google Scholar, ACM digital libraries and PubMed. Although these tools play an indispensable role in assisting users to combat the overload of information, there are many cases where the keyword-based search is unsatisfactory, as most of the knowledge in the modern era is a combination of concepts, topics, methods, and ideas.


*WSDM'14,* February 24–28, 2014, New York, New York, USA.
ACM 978-1-4503-2351-2/14/02.
http://dx.doi.org/10.1145/2556195.2556206

The main reason for the shortcomings of the keyword-based search is that it is often hard for users to express their information needs as a simple string of keywords. For instance, with the growing popularity of interdisciplinary studies, researchers often need to search articles related to multiple domains, it would be difficult for them to express the information needs using keywords, especially when they are not familiar with the domain of the articles of interest. To overcome this problem, a new search paradigm named Search-By-Multiple-Examples (SBME) [1][2][3][4] has been proposed to enable users to express their information needs using multiple relevant examples (denoted as query examples). For instances, in the article search scenario, having already read some papers on a specific topic, the researchers can use these examples as queries to get more relevant articles.

Most of the previous studies on SBME adopt the Positive Unlabeled learning (PU learning) techniques by treating the query examples as positive training data P and the documents in the entire data collection as unlabeled data U. Not only do such methods suffer efficiency issues as the size of the entire data collection in an online database is often huge, but also that the system performance may downgrade dramatically because of the class imbalance problem: the size of the positive examples P (denoted as |P|) is much smaller than the size of U (denoted as |U|).

Another issue of the previous methods is that the query examples are treated as being relevant to a single topic to build a query vector [2][3][4], but it is often the case that they can be relevant to multiple topics. The ignorance of the topic diversity issue makes these methods perform not well when a large number of documents are chosen as query examples, which are high likely belonging to multiple topics.

In addition, the experiments conducted in these studies have not taken into account the settings in online search, which are very different from the controlled experiments scenario. For instance, in online search, different users may provide different numbers of query examples for the same information need. Even for the same user, the query examples can be different from case to case.

To evaluate the performance of an SBME system, most of the previous studies simply use a large number of relevant examples to simulate user's query. This is biased, as the performance of certain models, which perform well when they are built on a large size of training data, may perform poorly when they are built on a small size of training data. In order to adopt PU learning for SBME, it is important to identify which PU learning algorithms perform well in online settings, where it is often the case that only a few query examples are available.

In this proposed research, we investigate how to improve SBME by (1) exploring how to use topic analysis techniques to predict users' true information needs from the query examples; and (2) examining how to deal with the class imbalance problem by reducing the size of the unlabeled data and adopting machine learning techniques. We will also conduct extensive experiments to better evaluate SBME using different sizes of query examples to simulate users' information needs. Our previous studies show that it's promising to adopt ensemble learning and under-sampling to solve the class-imbalance problem in the PU learning based SBME system [4]. We will further explore how to improve SBME using other machine learning techniques such as topic modeling and ensemble learning.

After reviewing related work in Section 2, Section 3 describes the proposed framework and research questions. Evaluation methods are described in Section 4, followed by a conclusion in Section 5.

# 2. RELATED WORK

In this section, we give a brief overview about the related work to this proposed research, which includes: 1) Search by Multiple Examples, 2) Positive Unlabeled Learning, 3) Transductive Inference and 4) Relevance Feedback.

## 2.1 Search by Multiple Examples

Our research follows the paradigm of SBME. Different from the traditional keyword-based search, SBME allows users to express their information needs using a set of relevant examples rather than a set of simple string keywords. Although it is a valuable research topic, there are only a few studies in the literature [1][2][3]. In [1], the entire list of references of a group of papers is adopted to find related publications. The query is defined as a small set of papers that are relevant to the research task at hand. More relevant articles are selected by "optimizing an object function based on a fine-grained notion of influence between documents." The authors define a directed, acyclic graph for each concept in the document collection to capture how ideas travel between documents. In the graph, nodes represent articles that contain the concept and the edges represent citations and common authorship. The degree of influence is captured by calculating a weight for each edge between two nodes. The weight of the edge represents the probability of direct influence from the head to the tail of the edge with respect to the concept that is contained by the articles (nodes) in the graph. Given these edge weights, they define a probabilistic, concept-specific notion of influence between any two articles in the document collection. One concern of this method is that not all documents are cited because some articles may be newly published or their importance has not been recognized by the community. The proposed method is based on Vector Space Model which doesn't depend on the citation information. Thus it is applicable in broader areas.

Another direction for SBME is based on PU learning. Employing the same idea of using multiple examples to express users' information needs, Zhang and Lee [2] consider the problem of SBME from the perspective of PU learning in two scenarios: online queries and offline queries. For the online queries, they propose a one-class SVM learning from the query set; for offline queries, they propose to learn a SVM model from the query set as well as the entire corpus. Zhu et al. [4] also adopts PU learning and propose an under-sampling based method to solve the class imbalanced problem that |P| is much smaller than |U|.

The main issue of these studies is that considering the entire data collection as unlabeled data is inefficient. Besides, the one-class SVM performs extremely poor [8], especially when |P| is small, as it does not consider useful information in the unlabeled examples. Thus the one-class SVM is actually not a good approach for online search. We will propose a new approach by first reducing the scope of the unlabeled data from the entire data collection to a subset of the data collection, then training a more effective PU learning model on the smaller subset.

Duh and Kirchhoff [3] present a transductive learning framework exploring how to improve ranking performance using partially labeled data. They adopt KernelPCA to generate better features from the unlabeled data and use the features via Boosting for learning different ranking functions adapted to the individual test queries. As the method in [3] needs both positive and negative training data, it is not applicable in the setting where users only have positive examples.

In addition, most of the precious studies of SBME take no consideration of the change of |P| for evaluation. The PU learning algorithms perform well with a large positive set may perform poorly when |P| is small. Thus it is still unknown which PU learning algorithms should be chosen for SBME, where the query examples from users can be very small. In this proposed research, we will compare different PU learning algorithm for SBME with different sizes of query examples.

## 2.2 Positive Unlabeled Learning

Many approaches of using unlabeled data to improve the performance of the supervised learning algorithms have been proposed. The specific approach of using a small size of labeled set and a large size of unlabeled set is called semi-supervised learning, where positive instances, negative instances and unlabeled data are needed. As a special case of semi-supervised learning, the PU learning works on only a positive set P and an unlabeled set U [5]. It aims to identify the hidden positive documents or negative documents from the unlabeled data (denoted as NU).

Nigam et al. [9] use a small set of labeled instances and a large set of unlabeled instances to build a classifier. When both positive and unlabeled data are available, the positive training data can be used to estimate the positive class' conditional probability $p(x|+)$, and the unlabeled data can be used to estimate $p(x)$. With the prior $p(+)$, which is known or can be estimated using data from other sources, the negative class' conditional probability can be obtained as follows:

$$p(x \mid -)=(p(x)-p(+)p(x \mid +))/(1-p(+))$$

Denis et al. adopt the conditional probability $p(x|-)$ to perform text classification with Naive Bayes methods [10].

Yu et al. propose a mapping-convergence algorithm for PU learning. There are two stages in their algorithm: mapping stage and convergence stage. In the mapping stage, they perform initial approximation of reliable negative examples (denoted as RN). In the convergence stage, they iteratively run an internal classifier that maximizes margins to progressively achieve the true boundary of the positive class in the feature space [11].

Most PU learning algorithms belong to such a two-stage strategy category. For instance, Li et al [7] propose to identify RN using Rocchio classifier in the first step. In the second step, a set of SVM classifiers run iteratively to identify the best classifier. They show that this method (denoted as RcSVM) outperforms the precious PU learning algorithms significantly.

Another direction of using PU learning is identifying positive examples from unlabeled data directly. Noto et al. [12] adopt the Transforming Prediction Model (TPM) [6], which is the state-of-the-art PU learning method, to learn a traditional classifier for biomedical documents identification. They show that their algorithm works well in identifying documents related to proteins.

## 2.3 Transductive Inference

Our research also follows the transductive learning paradigm. Transductive learning is an extension of standard supervised learning in the setting of semi-supervised learning. It adopts the test data to train a model, which is in turn applied on the test data.

Different from the inductive inference, in which the learner tries to induce a model from the training data aiming to have a low error rate on the test data that is unseen when the model is built, transductive learning focuses on a given set of instances (i.e. a test set) and tries to classify them with least errors [13].

Let $D_{train}=\{(x_1,y_1),\ldots.(x_n,y_n)\}$denote an i.i.d (Independent and Identically Distributed) sample of $n$ training instances, an inductive learner L seeks a function $h$:X($D_{train}$)→Y, where X($D_{train}$) is the input space and Y is the output space, by minimizing the structure risk using a penalty function to control the bias/variance tradeoff. The function is used for making predictions on a test data $D_{test}$ which is also an i.i.d sample from the population, from which the training data $D_{train}$ is sampled. In inductive learning, the test dataset is different from the training data set, which means the testing data set is not used to build the function or classifier. In transductive learning setting, the learner is built using both the training data $D_{train}$ and the test set $D_{test}$ $=\{(x_1,?,),\ldots.(x_m,?)\}$, where the question mark denotes that the class or label for the instance $x_i$ is unknown in the training process, such that the erroneous predictions on the test instances is minimized.

Since both the training and test set is available in the training process, the function can be learned to adapt to the test data, thus transductive inference has the potential to outperform inductive learning. In recent years, transducitve learning has attracted booming interests from researchers in machine learning and text mining fields [3][14].

Transductive Support Vector Machines (TSVM) [14] is one of the most widely used tranductive learning method. Different from Support Vector Machines (SVM) [15], which tries to induce a general decision boundary for a learning task, TSVM incorporates the test set into the training process and aims to minimize prediction errors of just those particular instances in the test set.

We will adopt the same idea of transductive inference that the test data is included in the training process, but we don't need negative training data.

## 2.4 Relevance Feedback

The proposed work can also be put into the relevance feedback category [16], in that the query examples can be regarded as the feedback documents from a user. However, the system performance of a relevance feedback system is highly dependent on the quality of the original query that is constructed manually. The feedback documents are usually the top ranked documents in the returned search result list. If the original query is poorly constructed, the top ranked documents may not represent user's true information needs. Besides, screening the returned search result list to specify relevant documents is often tedious and time consuming, especially when the user is not familiar with the content of the top ranked documents. The proposed method makes it easier for users to adopt multiple examples to express their information needs. As there is no need to construct short queries manually, the only thing they need to do is to use the relevant documents at hand to get more similar documents. Thus the proposed method is easier to use than the traditional relevance feedback method.

Of course, the traditional relevance feedback system can be integrated into the SBME system. For instance, the users can add more relevant documents into the query examples to run the SBME system iteratively until they are satisfied with the results.

# 3. THE PROPOSED FRAMEWORK

In this research, we propose a framework of applying PU learning for SBME using latent topics identified by a topic model for predicting users' information needs. The framework, illustrated in Figure 1, consists of three main components: 1) Query Processing, 2) PU learning based Re-ranking, and 3) Feature Selection.

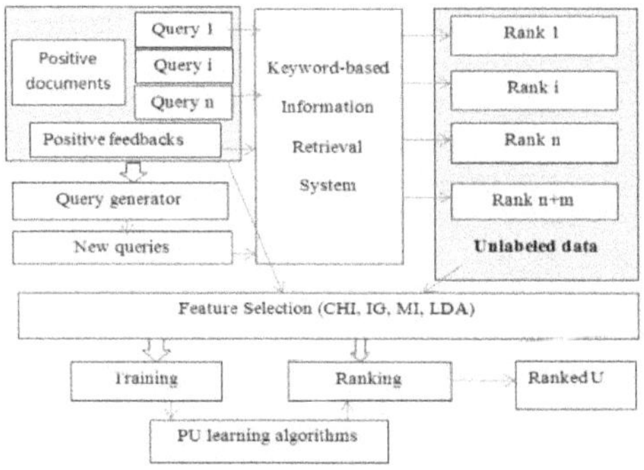


**Figure 1. The Proposed Framework.**

## 3.1 Query Processing

The query processing module enables users to input their queries to the search system. Theoretically, when the query is a set of documents, the entire corpus in the database can be considered as the searching space, but the size of the entire corpus is often so large that this method is inefficient. The query processing module serves to reduce the searching space by enabling users to initialize the scope of the text collection. This is also helpful for those users who are only interested in the articles contained some specific keywords, or published in some specific journals.

When a set of keywords are used for expressing an information need, the searching space can be formed by using these keywords for conducting a standard keyword-based search. However, when the information need is expressed as a set of relevant documents, forming the searching space becomes difficult. A simple method is using the centroid of the query examples as the query to conduct a keyword-based search, but this method treats the query examples belonging to a single topic. As the query examples often belong to multiple topics, it may be beneficial to conduct topic analysis to predict the user's true information needs more accurately. We will adopt a topic model to infer the topic distributions of the query examples for predicting the most likely topics that the user is interested in. Only those topics, of which the probability values exceed a threshold, are considered for selecting the terms associated with them as the queries that represent users' information needs. The words associated with each of the selected topics will be used as queries for conducting a set of standard keyword-based searches. Several lists of documents will be returned to form the unlabeled data U. The user can specify the relevant documents as the positive feedback, which will also be used to construct more queries using the above mentioned procedure.

## 3.2 PU learning based Re-ranking

The final output to a user is a list of documents that are ranked by the likelihood that they are relevant to the query examples and the positive feedback documents. We use PU learning algorithms to re-rank the documents returned from the search engine. Considering these documents as unlabeled data, and the positive examples and the positive feedback documents from the user as the positive training data, a PU learning algorithm is used to rank the unlabeled data based on the likelihood that they are predicted as being positive.

### *3.2.1 Studying How the Change of |P| Affects the Performance of the Proposed System*

In the online search environment, the size of query examples is often varying, which may affect the performance of the system. For instance, the size of the query examples provided by a specific user can vary from case to case. Even for the same search task, the query examples from different users can be different. It is important to examine how the change of |P| affects the system performance, as it can provide insights to other researchers as well as online users the relationship between |P| and the system performance. We will explore how the change of |P| affects the performance of the system by randomly generating different datasets with different size of query examples for simulating the real online search environment.

### *3.2.2 Studying How to Overcome the Class Imbalance Problem in the Proposed Framework*

In traditional supervised learning, when a dataset is imbalanced, the performance of the learning model can decrease dramatically. In the proposed framework, when |P| is much smaller than |U|, the dataset for learning becomes seriously imbalanced, which may degrade the performance of the classifier seriously. In an online search environment, it's often the case that the training data for PU learning is imbalanced, so it is necessary to investigate how to overcome the class imbalance problem in the proposed framework. An efficient strategy for dealing with class imbalance is under-sampling [20]. We will propose a novel method that combines under-sampling with PU learning for the SBME system.

## 3.3 Feature Selection

There are two stages involved in the PU learning based ranking methods: 1) document preprocessing, 2) using PU Learning algorithms to rank the unlabeled data. In the first stage, documents are usually transformed into term vectors after feature selection and feature weight determination. In the second stage, PU Learning algorithms are applied on the prepared data (i.e. term vectors) for learning classifiers and making predictions on the unlabeled data. Thus, the key for a given PU learning algorithm to achieve good performance is to select a set of good features and use appropriate feature weighting methods.

Most PU learning algorithms are based on the Vector Space Model, where a document is treated as a vector, of which the features are terms in the collections. Such a term-vector based document representation brings high dimensionality problems; or even worse, some noisy features seriously degrade the performance of the learning algorithms. So it's important to conduct feature selection to improve the efficiency as well as the effectiveness of PU learning algorithms. We will examine how feature selection methods such as Information Gain and Chi square test can be used to improve the system performance.

# 4. EVALUATIONS

## 4.1 Data Collections

Three benchmark datasets will be used for the empirical evaluation. The first one is the Reuters-21578 dataset, which is a commonly used benchmark news article collection in text classification. The second dataset is the WebKB collection [17], which contains web pages gathered from university computer science departments. The pages are grouped into seven categories. The third dataset is the 20 Newsgroup (20NG) dataset [21], which is a collection of 20,000 messages collected from twenty different Usenet groups. The dataset is categories by newsgroup names. We will also employ a scientific literature dataset to evaluate how the proposed methods perform in scientific literature search.

## 4.2 Evaluation Methods

Two standard IR evaluation measures, Mean Average Precision (MAP) [18] and *p@k*, will be adopted to evaluate the system performance.. In ranking the results of a query, MAP represents the mean of the Average Precision (AP) scores. Let L be a ranked list of documents, and R be the relevant documents being retrieved. The AP score is calculated using the following formula:

$$\mathrm{AP(L)} = \frac{1}{|R|}\sum_{k=1}^{n}\left(p(k) \times rel(k)\right)$$

where $|R|$ is the number of retrieved relevant documents; $k$ is the rank in the sequence of the retrieved documents; $n$ is the number of retrieved documents; $p(k)$ is the precision at cut-off k in the list; $rel(k)$ is an indicator function equaling 1 if the item at rank $k$ is a relevant document, and zero otherwise The MAP score is the mean arithmetical value of the AP scores.

In IR, users are often interested in the precision on the top returned documents [19], which is denoted as *p@k*. Compared with MAP, *p@k* is a more user-oriented measure, as users hope to find relevant documents by only scanning the top few (e.g. 30) documents in the returned search result list.

## 4.3 Experimental Design

Each run of an experiment will be conducted using the procedure proposed in [4]. For each topic of interest in a data collection, the documents belonging to it are considered as positive examples to form the positive pool, and other documents in the same data collection form the negative pool. From a positive pool, a subset of |P| examples will be randomly sampled to simulate user' query examples. In default, the documents in the negative pool and the remaining documents in the positive pool form the searching space. In the proposed framework, we reduce the searching space through conducting a keyword-based search from the default searching space using the terms extracted from the query examples as the query. The top N documents, which are potentially relevant, in the search result list form the new searching space. N should be chosen for making a trade-off between the efficiency and effectiveness of the system. When N is too small, only a small fraction of the positive documents are included in the unlabeled data, when N is large, the efficiency of the system sacrifices.

A transductive learning model is trained using the query examples and the unlabeled data, which will be ranked by the model. An AP, and $p@k$ ($k$=10, 20, 30) will be calculated for the rank. The MAP and average $p@k$ scores for each run of the experiments are calculated using the mean AP, and mean $p@k$ for all the selected topics. For each data collection, we will carry out 10 runs for an experiment, and the final MAP and average $p@k$ scores are calculated by averaging over the MAP and average $p@k$ scores from the 10 runs.

## 5. CONCLUSIONS

In document search, it is often difficult for users to express their information needs using simple keywords. The proposed work tries to solve this issue by exploring how to improve SBME. The resulted SBME system can be deployed in online digital libraries. This will bring significant convenience for researchers to keep up to date their knowledge of their research interests. For instance, it will be helpful for researchers to collect articles on a specific topic for a literature review. The proposed work also offers novel methodologies that are helpful for conducting text analysis in other domains such as government, health and academia. For instance, it provides insights to domain experts on constructing text datasets for a special purpose. In supervised learning, in order to make sure the learned model has a good performance, domain experts often need to build a large set of training data, which is often time consuming and tedious. The proposed system will be helpful for them to get more relevant documents using the documents at hand. The utilization of under-sampling for solving the class imbalance problem and the investigation of how to use topic modeling for users' information needs prediction will also provide inspirations to the researchers in the community.

## 6. ACKNOWLEDGMENTS

The work is supported in part by the Natural Science Foundation of China (No. 71373192, Title: Study on mobile reading recommendation system based on context). We thank the peer reviewers for their helpful comments and constructive criticism.

## 7. REFERENCES

[1] K. El-Arini and C Guestrin. Beyond keyword search: discovering relevant scientific literature. *Proceedings of the 17th ACM SIGKDD international conference on knowledge discovery and data mining*, 439-447, 2011.

[2] D. Zhang and W.S. Lee. Query-By-Multiple-Examples using Support Vector Machines. Journal of Digital Information Management. 7(4): 202-210, 2009.

[3] K. Duh and K. Kirchhoff. Learning to rank with partially-labeled data. *Proceedings of the 31st annual international ACM SIGIR conference on Research and development in information retrieval*, 251-258, 2008.

[4] M. Zhu, C. Xu, and Y. B. Wu. IFME: information filtering by multiple examples with under-sampling in a digital library environment. *Proceedings of the 13th ACM/IEEE-CS joint conference on Digital libraries*. 2013.

[5] B. Liu. Web data mining: exploring hyperlinks, contents, and usage data: Springer Verlag, 2007.

[6] C. Elkan and K. Noto. Learning classifiers from only positive and unlabeled data. *Proceedings of the 14th ACM SIGKDD international conference on Knowledge discovery and data mining*, 213-220, 2008.

[7] B. Liu, Y. Dai, X. Li, W. S. Lee, and P. S. Yu. Building text classifiers using positive and unlabeled examples. *Third IEEE International Conference on Data Mining*, 179-186, 2003.

[8] X. Li, and B. Liu. Learning to classify texts using positive and unlabeled data. *Proceedings of the Eighteenth International Joint Conference on Artificial Intelligence*, 587-592, 2003.

[9] K. Nigam, A. McCallum, S. Thrun, and T. Mitchell. Learning to classify text from labeled and unlabeled documents. *Proceedings of the Fifteenth National Conference on Artificial Intelligence*, 792-799, 1998.

[10] F. Denis, R. Gilleron, and M. Tommasi. Text classification from positive and unlabeled examples. *Proceedings of the 9th International Conference on Information Processing and Management of Uncertainty in Knowledge-Based Systems*, 1927-1934, 2002.

[11] H. Yu, J. Han, and K. C. Chang. PEBL: Web page classification without negative examples. *IEEE-Transactions on Knowledge and Data Engineering*. 16(1): 70-81, 2004.

[12] K. Noto, M. Saier, and C. Elkan. Learning to find relevant biological articles without negative training examples. *Proceedings of 21st Australasian Joint Conference on Artificial Intelligence*, 202-213, 2008.

[13] V. Vapnik. Statistical Learning Theory. Wiley, 1998.

[14] T. Joachims, Transductive inference for text classification using support vector machines. *Proceedings of the Sixteenth International Conference on Machine Learning*, vol. 99, 200-209.1999.

[15] M. A. Hearst , S. T. Dumais, E. Osman, J. Platt, and B. Scholkopf . Support vector machines. *Intelligent Systems and their Applications*, IEEE, 13(4), 18-28, 1998.

[16] G. Salton, and C. Buckley. Improving retrieval performance by relevance feedback. Readings in information retrieval 24 (1997): 5.

[17] M. Craven, D. DiPasquo, D. Freitag, A. McCallum, T. Mitchell, K. Nigam, and S. Slattery. Learning to extract symbolic knowledge from the World Wide Web. *AAAI-98*, 1998.

[18] E. Agichtein, E. Brill, and S. Dumais. Improving web search ranking by incorporating user behavior information. In *Proceedings of the 29th annual international ACM SIGIR conference on Research and development in information retrieval*, pages 19-26, 2006.

[19] C. D. Manning, C.D. P. Raghavan, and H. Sch¨utze. Introduction to Information Retrieval. Cambridge University Press, 2008.

[20] C. Drummond and R. C. Holte. C4. 5, class imbalance, and cost sensitivity: Why under-sampling beats over-sampling. *Workshop on Learning from Imbalanced Datasets II*, 2003.

[21] T. Joachims. A probabilistic analysis of the Rocchio algorithm with TFIDF for text categorization. *Proceedings of the Fourteenth International Conference on Machine Learning*, 1997.

# Behavioral Data Mining and Network Analysis in Massive Online Games

Muhammad Aurangzeb Ahmad
Department of Computer Science
University of Minnesota
Minneapolis, MN 55455
mahmad@cs.umn.edu

Jaideep Srivastava
Department of Computer Science
University of Minnesota
Minneapolis, MN 55455
srivastav@cs.umn.edu

## ABSTRACT

The last decade has been characterized by an explosion of social media in a variety of forms. Since the data is captured in digital form it has become possible for the first time study human behavior at a massive scale. Not only is it possible to address traditional questions in the social sciences regarding collective dynamics of human behaviors but it is also possible to study new types of human behaviors which have arisen as a result of usage of new mediums like twitter, YouTube, Facebook, one games etc. Each of these mediums has its respective limitations and affordances. Out of all these mediums the most complex and data rich medium is that of Massive Online Games (MOGs).

MOGs refer to massive online persistent environments (World of Warcraft, EVE Online, EverQuest etc) shared by millions of people . In general these environments are characterized by a rich array of activities and social interactions with a wide array of behaviors e.g., cooperation, trade, quest, deceit, mentoring etc. Such environments allow one to study human behavior at a level of granularity where it was not possible to do so previously. Given the challenges associated with analyzing this type of data traditional techniques in data mining and social network analysis have to be extended with insights from the social sciences. The tutorial will cover predictive and generative models in the study of MOGs. Additionally we will cover some SNA techniques which are more appropriate for MOGs given the multi-dimensionality of the data (P*/ERGM Models, IR Based Network Analysis, Hypergrah based Techniques, Coextensive Social Networks etc). We also describe the various ways in which MOGs exhibit similarities to the real world e.g., economic behaviors, clandestine behaviors, mentoring etc).

Massive Online Games collect behavioral and social data of their players in the form of operational logs. These datasets provide an unbiased view of social relationships between individuals. This gives us an unprecedented opportunity to study large social networks, and there is a need to develop new scalable computational models for finding interesting patterns from these data. The nature of MOGs also imply that traditional social network analysis methods which were developed with a different setting in mind can only take one so far. Thus data from MOGs tends to be very high dimensional, since a large number of variables are being collected. Second, the data is of multiple types, including text, spatial, clicks, trade, grouping etc.; and usually a much larger fraction compared to numeric measures. Third, the data has very strong temporal characteristics, with the set of variables collected often changing as time progresses. Finally, the data tends to be extremely large, and also very sparse. Based on these characteristics, there is a clear need to develop scalable techniques for the exploratory analysis of high-dimensional, sparse, and very large datasets.

This tutorial will provide an up-to-date introduction to the emerging field of analysis of massive online games. The main emphasis will be on data mining, social network analysis and machine learning techniques which are informed by social science theories. An overview of current and future research directions in this field will also be given. In this tutorial, we first provide an introduction to massive online game and methodological issues in associated research. We will then survey the research in this area from the perspective of social sciences as well as computer science. Next, an overview of emerging research in data mining for social network analysis in the context of massive online games is presented. This tutorial will help researchers by providing a survey on the research till date, enable the understanding of how specific techniques in data mining, machine learning in this area can foment new research. It will also be useful for practitioners from industrial organizations to understand where the state of the art stands since it has direct commercial applications as well given the size of the gaming industry. The promise of gaining valuable insights and answering traditional questions in sociology is limited by limitations in data collection, data availability and ethical concerns. These limitations will also be discussed. Lastly the tutorial will also reference our extensive research in this area in the form of the Virtual World Observatory (http://vwobservatory.com/) project which is the leading research collaborative in this area.


*WSDM'14*, February 24–28, 2014, New York, New York, USA.
ACM 978-1-4503-2351-2/14/02.
http://dx.doi.org/10.1145/2556195.2556196 .

# Exploration and Mining of Web Repositories

Nan Zhang
The George Washington University
Washington, District of Columbia, USA
nzhang10@gwu.edu

Gautam Das
The University of Texas at Arlington
Arlington, Texas, USA
gdas@uta.edu

## ABSTRACT
With the proliferation of very large data repositories hidden behind web interfaces, e.g., keyword search, form-like search and hierarchical/graph-based browsing interfaces for Amazon.com, eBay.com, etc., efficient ways of searching, exploring and/or mining such web data are of increasing importance.

There are two key challenges facing these tasks: how to properly understand web interfaces, and how to bypass the interface restrictions. In this tutorial, we start with a general overview of web search and data mining, including various exciting applications enabled by the effective search, exploration, and mining of web repositories. Then, we focus on the fundamental developments in the field, including web interface understanding, crawling, sampling, and data analytics over web repositories with various types of interfaces. We also discuss the potential changes required for query processing, data mining and machine learning algorithms to be applied to web data. Our goal is two-fold: one is to promote the awareness of existing web data search/exploration/mining techniques among all web researchers who are interested in leveraging web data, and the other is to encourage researchers, especially those who have not previously worked in web search and mining before, to initiate their own research in these exciting areas.

## Categories and Subject Descriptors
H.3.5 [**Information Storage and Retrieval**]: Online Information Services – *Web-based services.*

H.2.8 [**Database Management**]: Database Applications – *Data Mining.*

## General Terms
Algorithms, Management, Measurement.

## Keywords
Web Repositories, Web Databases, Deep Web, Data Analytics.

## 1. INTRODUCTION
Given the recent development of crawling, sampling and analytical processing techniques over deep web repositories, we believe that now is the time for researchers to be aware of these deep-web exploration and mining techniques, so as to effectively leverage the vast amounts of valuable data in the deep web. It is also the time for Web researchers to initiate their own research and enable exciting application over the gold mine of data provided by deep web repositories. This is our main goal for presenting the tutorial at WSDM 2014.


*WSDM'14*, February 24–28, 2014, New York, New York, USA.
ACM 978-1-4503-2351-2/14/02.
http://dx.doi.org/10.1145/2556195.2556197

## 2. TARGET AUDIENCE
The anticipated audience will consist of search and data mining researchers, researchers in the related communities of database, IR, WWW, and machine learning, as well as engineers, web developers, and information systems designers from industrial companies. No specific prerequisite other than general knowledge of data mining is required.

## 3. OUTLINE OF TUTORIAL
Part I (Introduction): The tutorial shall begin with general overview of web search and data mining, including a series of real-world examples of web repositories that enable various exciting applications related to search, exploration, and mining. We shall then use these examples to motivate the importance of efficient exploration and mining over hidden web repositories. We shall describe three important tasks commonly desired for the exploration and mining of web repositories: crawling, sampling, and data analytics/mining.

Part II (Challenges): Our tutorial shall next discuss why the three tasks are difficult to accomplish over very large web repositories. We summarize two key challenges, one on understanding the interface - e.g., how to model web query interfaces and perform schema matching - and the other on the efficient exploration of data - e.g., how to determine which queries/browsing requests to issue, especially given the extremely restrictive input and output interfaces of a hidden web repository. We shall summarize the fundamental developments for interface understanding here, and devote the rest of the tutorial to addressing exploration challenge.

Part III (Crawling, Sampling and Data Analytics): In this part of the tutorial, our focus is on discussing the crawling, sampling and mining of a web repository *after* its interface is properly understood. We shall start with using real-world examples to motivate each of the three tasks, and then discuss exciting recent developments for addressing each task over web repositories with various types of input/output web interfaces. Throughout this part, we shall illustrate the potential changes required for query processing, data mining and machine learning algorithms to be applied to web data.

Part IV (Conclusions and Future Directions): To encourage researchers to initiate their own research in the future, we first discuss how the challenging problems of crawling, sampling and analytics/mining over web repositories require expertise in many related areas, e.g., traditional query processing, IR, social networks, data mining as well as algorithms. Then, we shall conclude by identifying open challenges. In particular, we discuss the privacy implications of the above-described exploration and mining techniques, especially when the data owners are unwilling to share certain sensitive knowledge about the underlying data.

# Big Graph Mining for the Web and Social Media: Algorithms, Anomaly Detection, and Applications

U Kang
Korea Advanced Institute of Science and Technology
ukang@cs.kaist.ac.kr

Leman Akoglu
Stony Brook University
Dept. of Computer Science
leman@cs.stonybrook.edu

Duen Horng Chau
College of Computing
Georgia Tech
polo@gatech.edu

## 1. AIMS & LEARNING OBJECTIVES

Graphs are everywhere: social networks, computer networks, mobile call networks, the World Wide Web, protein interaction networks, and many more. The lower cost of disk storage, the success of social networking websites and Web 2.0 applications, and the high availability of data sources lead to graphs being generated at unprecedented size. They are now measured in terabytes or even petabytes, with more than billions of nodes and edges.

Finding patterns on large graphs have a lot of applications including cyber security on the Web, social media mining (Facebook, Twitter), and fraud detection, among others. This tutorial will cover topics related to *finding patterns and anomalies and sensemaking in large-scale graphs with applications to real-world problems in social media and the Web.* Specifically, we aim to answer the following questions: How can we scale up graph mining algorithms for massive graphs with billions of edges? How can we find anomalies in such large-scale graphs? How can we make sense of disk-resident large graphs, what and how can we do visual analytics? How can we use the algorithms and anomaly detection techniques to solve challenging real-world problems that play key role in social media and the Web?

Our tutorial consists of three main parts. We start with scalable graph mining algorithms for billion-scale graphs, including structure analysis, eigensolvers, storage and indexing, and graph layout and graph compression. Next we describe anomaly detection techniques for large scale graphs with applications on social media. Finally, we discuss visual analytics techniques which leverage these algorithms and anomaly detection techniques in the previous parts.

## 2. RELATION TO WSDM AREAS

Our tutorial is broadly relevant to all major WSDM areas: *Web Search*, *Web Mining* and *Social Search and Mining*; as we will cover foundational and scalable algorithms and techniques that support WSDM-related research. Our focus on discussing applications for the web and social media further strengthens our tutorial's relevance.

## 3. LENGTH

We plan to deliver a *half-day* tutorial, and will be happy to adjust its length according to the conference's schedule. We will spend 1/3 of the time on algorithms; 1/3 on anomaly detection, and 1/3 on applications and visualization.

## 4. TARGET AUDIENCE

The target audience consists of social network, data bases, and data mining professionals who wish to have a comprehensive understandings on large-scale graph mining and management algorithms, applications, and anomaly detection tools. The audience will learn recent developments on big graph mining and how they could utilize these tools for real-world problems that they are facing with in the wild.

## 5. ABOUT THE INSTRUCTORS

**U Kang** is an assistant professor in Computer Science Department at KAIST. He received the 2013 KDD Dissertation Award, Honorable Mention. He won two best paper awards, and he has published many refereed articles in major data mining and database venues. He holds four U.S. patents. His research interests include data mining in big graphs. He leads the research on the award-winning PEGASUS system.

**Leman Akoglu** is an assistant professor at Stony Brook University. She received her Ph.D. from Carnegie Mellon University in 2012. Her research has won 2 "Best Paper" awards, and led to several peer-reviewed publications in major data mining venues, and 3 U.S. patents, filed by IBM T. J. Watson Research. Her research interests are in data mining, machine learning, and applied statistics with a focus on pattern mining, and anomaly and event detection in large dynamic data using graph mining and compression.

**Duen Horng (Polo) Chau** is an Assistant Professor at Georgia Tech's College of Computing. His Ph.D. thesis received Carnegie Mellon's Computer Science Dissertation Award, runner up for bridging Data Mining and Human-Computer Interaction (HCI) for making sense of large graphs. His Polonium malware detection technology (with Symantec, patented) helps protect 120 million people worldwide. Polo is the only two-time Symantec fellow. His NetProbe auction fraud detection system appeared on The Wall Street Journal, CNN, TV and radio.


*WSDM'14*, February 24-28, 2014, New York, NY, USA.
ACM 978-1-4503-2351-2/14/02.

# Diversity and Novelty in Web Search, Recommender Systems and Data Streams

Rodrygo L. T. Santos
Univ. Federal de Minas Gerais
Belo Horizonte, MG, Brazil
rodrygo@dcc.ufmg.br

Pablo Castells
Univ. Autónoma de Madrid
Madrid, Spain
pablo.castells@uam.es

Ismail Sengor Altingovde
Middle East Technical University
Ankara, Turkey
altingovde@ceng.metu.edu.tr

Fazli Can
Bilkent University
Ankara, Turkey
canf@cs.bilkent.edu.tr

## ABSTRACT

This tutorial aims to provide a unifying account of current research on diversity and novelty in the domains of web search, recommender systems, and data stream processing.

## Categories and Subject Descriptors

H.3.3 [**Information Storage and Retrieval**]: Information Search and Retrieval—*search process*

## Keywords

Relevance, Diversity, Novelty, Ambiguity, Redundancy

## 1. OVERVIEW

Information retrieval (IR) is traditionally approached as a pursuit of relevant information, under the assumption that the users' information needs are unambiguously conveyed by their information requests. Arguably, such an assumption does not hold for the multitude of users' needs in modern IR systems, such as web search engines, recommender systems, and stream processing engines. In order to identify relevant information under the uncertainty posed by the users' requests, an effective approach is to diversify the retrieved results. By doing so, an IR system can minimize the chance of wrongly guessing the users' needs, which may cause the users to abandon their retrieval task.

Through a stream of active research and experiences, diversity and novelty can be said to have by now consolidated into a significant body of techniques, methodologies, theories, and knowledge in the field of information retrieval. This tutorial aims to provide a unifying account of current research on diversity and novelty in different IR domains. In particular, we will cover the motivations, as well as the most established approaches for producing and evaluating diverse results in the context of search engines, recommender systems, and data streams. By contrasting the state-of-the-art in these multiple domains, this tutorial aims to derive a common understanding of the diversification problem and the existing solutions, their commonalities and differences, as a means to foster new research directions.

In particular, the tutorial attendees will:

- understand the importance and complexities of achieving diversity/novelty for various IR domains;
- learn the state-of-the-art approaches for promoting diversity and novelty in web search, recommender systems, and data streams;
- learn the fundamental evaluation metrics and have an overview of past and current evaluation campaigns;
- get an overview of other related application areas that include query suggestions, query ambiguity detection, and aggregated search;
- obtain a unifying view of the topic by exploring the similarities and differences between the methods employed in different domains.

## 2. TUTORIAL OUTLINE

1. Practical and Theoretical Background
2. Diversity in Web Search
    - *Implicit and Explicit Diversification*
    - *Advanced Topics in Web Search Diversification*
    - *Diversity Evaluation*
3. Diversity in Recommender Systems
    - *Motivation and Notions*
    - *Novelty and Diversity Enhancement*
    - *Novelty and Diversity Evaluation*
4. Diversity in Data Streams
    - *Document-level Novelty*
    - *Novelty and Diversification of Document Streams*
    - *Evaluation*
5. Other Application Areas


*WSDM'14*, February 24–28, 2014, New York, New York, USA.
ACM 978-1-4503-2351-2/14/02.
http://dx.doi.org/10.1145/2556195.2556199.

# Multilingual Probabilistic Topic Modeling and its Applications in Web Mining and Search

Marie-Francine Moens and Ivan Vulić
Department of Computer Science
KU Leuven, Belgium
marie-francine.moens@cs.kuleuven.be, ivan.vulic@cs.kuleuven.be

## ABSTRACT

Multilingual topic models are a fairly novel group of unsupervised, language-independent and generative machine learning models. This tutorial covers all key aspects of their probabilistic framework and demonstrates how to easily integrate these models into frameworks for cross-lingual and multilingual Web mining and search.

## 1. TUTORIAL GOALS AND MOTIVATION

In the current international data-driven society, it becomes increasingly important to quickly and correctly find answers to a user's information need, so as not to lose the desired data in a vast ocean of information. Companies are increasingly interested in mining multilingual and multi-jargon Web data, and in linking Web data. In such a multilingual, multi-idiomatic and multi-domain (or simply *multi**) setting there is a need to access and mine information across multiple different languages and jargons, that is, we desire effective and cheap tools for cross-lingual information retrieval and search, semantic similarity, and for cross-language clustering, classification and linking of content.

Multilingual topic models can be effectively trained on large-volume of non-parallel, comparable multi* data and capture the properties of multi* data directly (e.g., multilingual Wikipedia, news, user-generated content, e-commerce data). They offer an elegant way to represent content across different languages, domains and jargons. State-of-the-art multilingual topic models follow the modeling paradigm established for monolingual settings by probabilistic Latent Semantic Analysis (pLSA) and Latent Dirichlet Allocation (LDA) [1]. A multilingual topic model learns topic distributions over documents (the so-called *per-document topic distributions*) and word distributions over topics (the so-called *per-topic word distributions*). The set of language-independent topics serves as a bridge between languages, jargons and other multi* content. Each document, regardless of its actual language, can be presented as a mixture of the language-independent cross-lingual concepts, that is cross-lingual topics (modeled by per-document word distributions), while each topic has its own language-specific representation in each language involved in training (modeled by per-topic word distributions). Due to its generic language-independent nature and the power of inference on unseen documents, these models have been used in a variety of cross-lingual (or -domain and -jargon, or simply *cross-**) tasks that are of large interest for both academia and industry.


*WSDM'14*, February 24–28, 2014, New York, New York, USA.
ACM 978-1-4503-2351-2/14/02.
http://dx.doi.org/10.1145/2556195.2556200.

## 2. TUTORIAL OVERVIEW

The tutorial covers recent advances in multilingual topic modeling, with an emphasis on its applications in Web mining and search, and e-commerce. It includes: (1) A high-level overview of the key intuitions and assumptions behind topic modeling in general (starting from monolingual settings) and multi* topic modeling in specific; (2) The methodology and mathematical foundations including training and inference (e.g., variational Dirichlet, Gibbs sampling); and (3) The application of these models in various cross-lingual and even cross-modal tasks, with a special focus on cross-lingual information retrieval, cross-lingual and cross-jargon Web mining and search, and the evaluation of these tasks.

The tutorial is illustrated with practical cases (e.g., [2, 3]) of using multilingual probabilistic topic models among which are cross-lingual event clustering, cross-lingual document classification, cross-lingual semantic word similarity, and translation and transliteration mining. The tutorial explains cross-lingual information retrieval starting from simpler query likelihood models [3] and leading to more elaborate retrieval models which combine cross-lingual topical knowledge with the relevance modeling retrieval framework [4] and use the topical knowledge for query expansion [3]. It goes deeper into linking user interests to the Web e-commerce data such as linking pins to webshops, processing user generated content such as summarizing tweets, and utilizing the topical knowledge in recommendation systems [5]. In a broader framework the tutorial is relevant for searching social media content, user profiling, computational advertising and multimodal data mining.

## 3. PARTIAL BIBLIOGRAPHY

[1] D. M. Blei, A. Y. Ng, and M. I. Jordan. Latent Dirichlet Allocation. *Journal of Machine Learning Research*, 3:993–1022, 2003.

[2] X. Ni, J.-T. Sun, J. Hu, and Z. Chen. Cross lingual text classification by mining multilingual topics from Wikipedia. In *WSDM*, pages 375–384, 2011.

[3] I. Vulić, W. De Smet, and M.-F. Moens. Cross-language information retrieval models based on latent topic models trained with document-aligned comparable corpora. *Information Retrieval*, 16(3):331–368, 2013.

[4] I. Vulić and M.-F. Moens. A unified framework for monolingual and cross-lingual relevance modeling based on probabilistic topic models. In *ECIR*, pages 98–109, 2013.

[5] S. Zoghbi, I. Vulić, and M.-F. Moens. I pinned it. Where can i buy one like it? Automatically linking Pinterest pins to online Webshops. In *DUBMOD*, pages 9–12, 2013.

# Entity Linking and Retrieval for Semantic Search

Edgar Meij
Yahoo! Research
Barcelona, Spain
emeij@yahoo-inc.com

Krisztian Balog
University of Stavanger
Stavanger, Norway
krisztian.balog@uis.no

Daan Odijk
ISLA, University of Amsterdam
Amsterdam, The Netherlands
d.odijk@uva.nl

## ABSTRACT

More and more search engine users are expecting direct answers to their information needs, rather than links to documents. Semantic search and its recent applications enabled search engines to organize their wealth of information around entities. Entity linking and retrieval provide the building stones for organizing the web of entities. This tutorial aims to cover all facets of semantic search from a unified point of view and connect real-world applications with results from scientific publications. We provide a comprehensive overview of entity linking and retrieval in the context of semantic search and thoroughly explore techniques for query understanding, entity-based retrieval and ranking on unstructured text, structured knowledge repositories, and a mixture of these. We point out the connections between published approaches and applications, and provide hands-on examples on real-world use cases and datasets.

## Categories and Subject Descriptors

H.3 [**Information Storage and Retrieval**]: H.3.1 Content Analysis and Indexing; H.3.3 Information Search and Retrieval; H.3.4 Systems and Software

## Keywords

Entity linking, entity retrieval, semantic search

## 1. OVERVIEW

The explosive increase in the amount of unstructured textual data being produced calls for advanced methodologies for making sense of this data. Recent advances have enabled a precise manner of analysis, where phrases—consisting of a single term or sequence of terms—are automatically linked to entries in a knowledge base. This process is commonly known as *entity linking*. Entity linking facilitates advanced forms of searching and browsing in various domains and contexts. For example, it can be used to anchor textual resources in background knowledge. In search engines, linking queries to entities to improve the user experience is becoming increasingly prevalent. More and more, users want to find the actual entities that satisfy their information need, rather than merely the documents that mention them; a process known as *entity retrieval*.

Entities are a key enabling component for semantic search, as many information needs can be answered by returning a list of entities, their properties, and/or their relations. They can be used to enrich the search result page to enable direct answers or serendipitous results, and are able to bridge the gap between unstructured and structured data.

The goal of this tutorial is to cover all facets of semantic search from a unified point of view and connect real-world applications with results from scientific publications. Its main highlights are that we: (i) provide a comprehensive overview of entity linking and retrieval in the context of semantic search, (ii) thoroughly explore techniques for query understanding, entity-based retrieval and ranking on unstructured text, structured knowledge repositories, and a mixture of these, and (iii) point out the connections between published approaches and applications, and provide hands-on examples on real-world use cases and datasets.

The half-day tutorial is structured into five parts. Part I sets the scene by introducing the data landscape. We make a case for entity retrieval that is built on the observation that web search engine users prefer to express information needs using short keyword queries and that many of these revolve around entities. Part II zooms in on the congruent relationship between textual and structural evidence for entities. These come in two main flavors: (i) entity linking and (ii) knowledge base population/acceleration, i.e., given a massive text corpus, populate a knowledge base with new entities, relations, and attributes. Part III starts with an overview of traditional methods for keyword-based search in the IR, DB, and semantic web communities. Then, we discuss methods that combine these aspects and where query understanding may involve some inferencing. Part IV continues with settings where the aim is to provide the user with an improved overall search experience, e.g. by providing an enriched SERP which lists recent match results when searching for a football team or displaying restaurants on a map. Alternatively, the standard document-based result list can be augmented with entity-oriented components for serendipitous discovery. Finally, Part V concludes the tutorial with an overview and an outlook of future challenges. Each block discusses a particular topic and is be followed by hands-on exercises, illustrating the theory presented before.

The slides, bibliography, and resources of the current and previous editions can be found at `http://bit.ly/ELR-slides`.


*WSDM'14*, February 24–28, 2014, New York, New York, USA.
ACM 978-1-4503-2351-2/14/02.
http://dx.doi.org/10.1145/2556195.2556201.

# WSDM'14 Workshop Summary
# Log-based Personalization: the 4th Web Search Click Data (WSCD) workshop

Pavel Serdyukov
Yandex
Leo Tolstoy 16
Moscow, Russia
pavser@yandex-team.ru

Georges Dupret
Yahoo! Labs
701 First Avenue
Sunnyvale, USA
gdupret@yahoo-inc.com

Nick Craswell
Microsoft Corporation
One Microsoft Way
Redmond, WA USA
nickcr@microsoft.com

## ABSTRACT

WSCD 2014[1] is the fourth workshop on Web Search Click Data, following WSCD 2009, WSCD 2011, WSCD 2012 and WSCD 2013. It is a forum for new research relating to Web search usage logs and for discussing desirable properties of publicly released search log datasets. Research relating to search logs has been hampered by the limited availability of click datasets. This series of workshops comes with new datasets based on logged user search behaviour and accompanying data mining challenges. This year the challenge and the workshop are focused on the tasks of personalization using logs.

## 1. INTRODUCTION

Web search click data has caught the interest of a growing community of professionals during the last decade. It provides a snapshot of the typical information access patterns of the user population, unlike a group of relevance judges or the tags provided on collaborative sites. Issued queries and clicked document records have the potential to give an accurate view of millions of people's daily interests, how these interests evolve, how they are related, etc.

Of particular interest is the relation between log data and the user decision process that generated it. A user interacting with a search engine might at any point decide to click on a new link, request a new page of results, reformulate his query, switch search engine or end the session. Understanding how a sequence of actions relates to the user satisfaction is key to improve the experience and the popularity of the search engine. This applies to web search in general but also to most verticals like "local search" and to newer research areas like "diversity" where the question is how to introduce diversity in document ranking or "personalization" where the goal is to adapt the search results to take into account what is known from the user who issued the query.

[1]http://research.microsoft.com/en-us/um/people/nickcr/wscd2014/


*WSDM'14*, February 24–28, 2014, New York, New York, USA.
ACM 978-1-4503-2351-2/14/02.
http://dx.doi.org/10.1145/2556195.2556207.

## 2. WORKSHOP FOCUS

This year's workshop focuses on log-based methods, for application in search systems and recommender systems, that tailor results for the current user. The logs can be used to uncover characteristics, patterns and preferences in users and cohorts of users. Logs can also be used to train the personalized search/recommender system. The goal is to improve results by showing different results to different users.

In one application, a search system might detect a user's current interest in rock music, so reorder the results for the query 'chicago' to promote the band above the city. In another application, a news recommender system might use a contextual bandit approach to learn from click logs and personalize news article recommendation.

The workshop is a forum for discussion of current work and problems in the area. For this reason we invited position papers on the following topics and attemping to answer the following questions:

- Specific models for log-based personalization.
- Data mining methods for identifying and characterizing interests of users in logged data.
- Insights into personalization evidence and features derived from logs. For example via demographics, topical interests or memorizing specific past actions.
- Specific application(s) of log-based personalization. How useful is it? What works? What doesn't?
- Does log-based personalization narrow options into a filter bubble? Or, does log-based personalization broaden people's options like on Amazon.
- What machine learning problems arise in training log-based personalized models.
- What IR evaluation problems arise in testing log-based models.
- What datasets are available, or should be available, for studying log-based personalization.

## 3. CHALLENGE

This year's challenge is the Personalized Web Search Challenge, which uses anonymized data from Yandex (about 35mln search sessions) and is hosted by Kaggle[2]. The goal of this competition is to re-rank top-10 URLs returned by the search engine in response to a user query using the history of clicks on URLs for all users and the user issuing the current query in particular. This may involve using long-term (user history based) and short-term (session based) user context. The dataset includes anonymized user ids, queries, query terms, urls, url domains and clicks.

The evaluation rewards a reranking if the promoted URL had a long-dwell click by the current user. The training period shared with participants corresponds to 27 days of search activity. The next 3 days correspond to the test period.

Challenge winners are encouraged to write a report on their participation and present their results at the workshop. The Challenge is intended as a logical follow-up to the previous two challenges on predicting relevance of documents using search logs[3] and detection of search engine switchings in search sessions[4].

## 4. ADDITIONAL ORGANIZERS

The Challenge is also co-organized by Eugene Kharitonov from Yandex, who has done the most work on data preprocessing and configuting the submission system. We also gratefully acknowledge the support of Will Cukierski and Ben Hamner from Kaggle who kindly invited us to host the Challenge at Kaggle and continuosly helped us with its setup before and during the competition.

[2]https://www.kaggle.com/c/yandex-personalized-web-search-challenge

[3]http://imat-relpred.yandex.ru/en

[4]http://switchdetect.yandex.ru/en

# Web-Scale Classification: Web Classification in the Big Data Era

[Workshop Overview]

Ioannis Partalas
Université Joseph Fourier
Grenoble, France
ioannis.partalas@imag.fr

Massih-Reza Amini
Université Joseph Fourier
Grenoble, France
massih-reza.amini@imag.fr

Ion Androutsopoulos
Athens University of Economics and Business
Athens, Greece
ion@aueb.gr

Thierry Artieres, Patrick Gallinari
LIP6, UPMC
Sorbonne Université
Paris, France
firstname.lastname@lip6.fr

Eric Gaussier
Université Joseph Fourier
Grenoble, France
eric.gaussier@imag.fr

Georgios Paliouras
NCSR "Demokritos"
Athens, Greece
paliourg@iit.demokritos.gr

## ABSTRACT

This paper provides an overview of the workshop *Web-Scale Classification: Web Classification in the Big Data Era* which was held in New York City, on February $28^{th}$ as a workshop of the seventh International Conference on Web Search and Data Mining. The goal of the workshop was to discuss and assess recent research focusing on classification and mining in Web-scale category systems. The workshop brought together members of several communities such web mining, machine learning, text classification and social media mining.

## Categories and Subject Descriptors

H.3 [**Information Storage and Retrieval**]: Miscellaneous; H.2.8 [**Database Applications**]: Data Mining

## General Terms

Algorithms

## Keywords

web-scale classification; large-scale text classification; social media prediction

## 1. OVERVIEW

The huge amount of data available in the Web in various forms (text, images, videos etc.) pose challenging and difficult problems towards the extraction and assessment of useful information. Intelligent systems for knowledge extraction are nowadays of utmost importance due to the scale of the data in the Web. A key module for any intelligent system is the capability of identifying and classifying correctly data items in a pre-defined set of classes. For example, in the e-commerce setting the goal is to classify product items in a set of categories (contained in the inventory). In order to ease the classification and organization of the data many real world systems use taxonomies over the set of categories which are typically organized in a hierarchical structure with parent-child relations. Typical examples of such taxonomies are DMOZ[1], the International Patent Classification[2] or Wikipedia.

In this setting a number of interesting problems arise for Web classification systems as the both the size of the hierarchies and the data grow. In particular it is one of the rare situations where data sparsity remains an issue despite the vastness of available data. The reasons for this are the simultaneous increase in the number of classes and their hierarchical organization. The latter leads to a very high imbalance between the classes at different levels of the hierarchy. Additionally, the statistical dependence of the classes poses challenges and opportunities for learning approaches.

The goal of this workshop was to discuss and assess recent research focusing on classification and mining in Web-scale category systems. In particular, we wanted to attract researchers developing new ways to exploit such Web-scale systems, e.g. by exploring how different category systems can be combined (though multi- task or transfer learning for example) to improve classification accuracy or by exploring how hierarchies can be refined or simplified for classification and mining purposes. We also wanted to attract studies that reveal new properties of large scale category systems, as the type of data distributions underlying large scale systems. The following topics were of interest to the workshop (this list is not exhaustive):


*WSDM'14*, February 24–28, 2014, New York, New York, USA.
ACM 978-1-4503-2351-2/14/02.
http://dx.doi.org/10.1145/2556195.2556208

[1]http://www.dmoz.org/
[2]http://www.wipo.int/classifications/ipc/en/

- (semi-)Supervised, transfer or multi-task learning for Web-Scale Classification (WSC)
- Deep learning approaches to WSC
- Clustering and hierarchy refinement
- Mining large scale (hierarchical) category systems
- Large scale classification for e-commerce
- Image and video classification and annotation
- Classification and prediction in social networks

The workshop brought together members of several communities such web mining, machine learning, text classification and social media mining. It was held in New York City, on February $28^{th}$ as a workshop of the seventh International Conference on Web Search and Data Mining. Paper submissions went through an exhaustive peer-review process. All papers received at last two independent reviews and some papers even three. The review process was handled by 11 members of the program committee:

- Sihem Amer-Yahia, Laboratoire d'Informatique de Grenoble, France
- Rohit Babbar, Laboratoire d'Informatique de Grenoble, France
- Anurag Bhardwaj, ebay Research Labs, USA
- Cyril Goutte, National Research Council Canada, Canada
- Vignesh Jagadeesh , ebay Research Labs, USA
- Ioannis Katakis, National and Kapodistrian University of Athens, Greece
- Alessandro Moschitti, University of Trento, Italy
- Ingo Frommholz, University of Bredfordshire, UK
- Benjamin Piwowarski, University Pierre et Marie Curie, France
- Jean-Michel Renders, Xerox Research Centre Europe, France
- Grigorios Tsoumakas, Aristotle University of Thessaloniki, Greece

## 2. RELATED WORKSHOPS AND EVENTS

This workshop builds upon a series of successful challenges and workshops on large-scale hierarchical text classification [1].[3] More specifically, we have recently organized three editions of the Large Scale Hierarchical Text Classification (LSHTC) challenge, which were successfully completed in December 2009, June 2011 and June 2012 respectively. These challenges attracted more than 50 teams from around the world (USA, Europe and Asia). The results of the challenges were presented at subsequent workshops (Workshops on Large Scale Hierarchical Classification) at the conferences ECIR 2010, ECML/PKDD 2011 and ECML/PKDD 2012, our challenge being the discovery challenge of ECML/PKDD 2012.

The current workshop has an enlarged scope, including various media (images, video, social networks), various applications (e-commerce, mining and clustering) and new technologies that have to be deployed on these types of data. These new aspects were not covered in the above mentioned workshops.

## 3. ACKNOWLEDGEMENTS

We would like to thank all the authors who submitted papers to the workshop as well as all the participants. We are also grateful to the program committee members for their indispensable help during the review period for providing with high quality reviews in a very short period of time. The organization of the workshop was partially supported by the ANR project Class-Y and the European FP7/2007-2013 project BioASQ (grant agreement n$^o$ 318652).

## 4. REFERENCES

[1] A. Kosmopoulos, É. Gaussier, G. Paliouras, and S. Aseervatham. The ecir 2010 large scale hierarchical classification workshop. *SIGIR Forum*, 44(1):23–32, 2010.

[3] http://lshtc.iit.demikritos.gr

# 1st Workshop on Diffusion Networks and Cascade Analytics


Peng Cui
Tsinghua University
Beijing, China
cuip@tsinghua.edu.cn

Fei Wang
IBM Watson Research Center
Yorktown Heights. NY, U.S.
fwang@us.ibm.com

Hanghang Tong
City University of New York
New York, USA
tong@cs.ccny.cuny.edu

Manuel Gomez Rodriguez
MPI for Intelligent Systems
Munich, Germany
manuelgr@tue.mpg.de



## ABSTRACT

Diffusion and cascades have been studied for many years in sociology, and different theoretical models have been developed. However, experimental validation has been always carried out in relatively small datasets. In recent years, with the availability of large-scale network and cascade data, research on cascading and diffusion phenomena has aroused considerable interests from various fields in computer science. One of the main goals is to discover different propagation patterns from historical cascade data. In this context, understanding the mechanisms underlying diffusion in both micro- and macro-scale levels and further develop predictive model of diffusion are fundamental problems of crucial importance.



## Categories and Subject Descriptors

H.1.2 [Information Systems]: Models and Principles—Human factors; I.2.6 [Computing Methodologies]: Artificial Intelligence—Knowledge acquisition

## General Terms

Algorithms, Experimentation

## Keywords

Diffusion Networks, Cascade Modeling


## 1. CONTENTS AND MAIN GOALS

Diffusion of various types of behavior, information, rumors, ideas and infectious diseases are all instances of stochastic processes that occur over the edges of an underlying network. A contagion appears at some node of a network and then spreads like an epidemic from node to node over the edges of the network, creating a cascade. For example, in case of information propagation, the contagion represents a piece of information and infection events correspond to times when nodes mention or copy the information from one of their neighbors in the network. Developing computational methods to analyze different cascade patterns, understand the mechanism underlying diffusion, and eventually predict the cascading outbreaks, is of paramount importance since it would allow to stop disease spread, avoid rumor and misinformation spread, or mitigate traffic congestion and, on the other side, design optimal marketing strategies, maximize sales of a product, or detect viral ideas and content in an early stage [1][2].

Diffusion and cascades have been studied for many years in sociology, and different theoretical models have been developed. However, experimental validation has been always carried out in relatively small datasets. In recent years, with the availability of large-scale network and cascade data, research on cascading and diffusion phenomena has aroused considerable interests from various fields in computer science. One of the main goals has been to discover different propagation patterns from historical cascade data. In this context, understanding the mechanisms underlying diffusion in both micro- and macro-scale levels and further develop predictive model of diffusion are fundamental problems of crucial importance. Due to its complexity, modeling diffusion entails some challenges:

1. Diffusion and cascades are node-dependent. For example, information cascades in social networks are microscopically caused by users' forwarding behavior. How do diffusion and cascades depend on the nodes' characteristics? How should nodes' characteristics be included in the analysis and prediction of diffusion networks and cascades?

2. The diffusion and cascades are network-dependent. Diffusion and cascades take places over underlying networks. For example, diseases spread over physical social networks, traffic-jams occur over road networks, and information propagates over online social networks. How do diffusion and cascades depend on the underlying network structure? How should the underlying network structure be included in the analysis and prediction of diffusion networks and cascades?

3. The diffusion and cascades are information-dependent. It is perhaps conventional wisdom that information content is one of the driving factors for information diffusion processes. How do diffusion and cascades depend on the content? How should information content be included in the analysis and prediction of diffusion networks and cascades?



*WSDM'14*, February 24–28, 2014, New York, New York, USA.
ACM 978-1-4503-2351-2/14/02.
http://dx.doi.org/10.1145/2556195.2556209

In addition to these challenges and since diffusion and cascades take places over increasingly larger networks, diffusion models and methods for analysis, inference and prediction need to be highly scalable and efficiently to handle streaming data.

## 2. TOPICS

Topics of interest for the workshop include (but are not limited to) the following:

- Cascading behavior analysis and prediction
- Cascades pattern mining and analysis
- Cascading outbreak detection and prediction
- Network inference from cascades
- Information diffusion in social networks
- Social influence analysis and prediction
- Homophily, social contagion and causality
- Rumor, misinformation, and anti-spam detection
- Mobility patterns mining and analysis
- Disease dynamics and vaccination strategies in social networks
- Games in networks
- Link prediction in graphs

## 3. WORKSHOP ORGANIZERS

Dr. Peng Cui is an Assistant Professor in Department of Computer Science and Technology, Tsinghua University. He received his PhD in Computer Science from Tsinghua University in 2010. His research interests include social network analysis and social multimedia computing. His recent research work has been published in leading conferences and journals, such as SIGKDD, SIGIR, AAAI, ACM MM, ICDM, IEEE TMM, IEEE TIP, DMKD, etc. He has been the recipient of several awards, include Best Paper Award in MMM'2013, and Grand Challenge Award in ACM MM 2012. He organized workshops, special sessions, tutorials and special issues in ACM MM 2011&2012, ICME 2011, and Information Retrieval Journal.

Dr. Fei Wang is a Research Staff Member in healthcare analytics research group, IBM T. J. Watson Research Center. His research interest is mainly data mining algorithms and their application in healthcare and social informatics. Dr. Wang has published over 100 scientific articles in the relevant venues including KDD, ICML, AAAI, IJCAI, ICDM, SDM, CIKM. He received the Best Research Paper Honorable Mention Award from ICDM 2010. He regularly serves as the program committee members of the top conferences such as KDD, ICDM and SDM. He presented tutorials in CIKM 2008, SDM 2009, SDM 2012 and SDM 2013.

Dr. Hanghang Tong is currently an assistant professor at Computer Science Department, City College, City University of New York. Before that, he was a research staff member at IBM T.J. Watson Research Center and a Post-doctoral fellow in Carnegie Mellon University. He received his M.Sc and Ph.D. degree from Carnegie Mellon University in 2008 and 2009, both majored in Machine Learning. His research interest is in large scale data mining for graphs and multimedia. His research has been funded by NSF, DARPA and ARL. He has received several awards, including best paper award in CIKM 2012, best paper award in SDM 2008 and best research paper award in ICDM 2006. He has published over 60 referred articles and more than 20 patents. He has served as a program committee member in top data mining, databases and artificial intelligence venues (e.g., SIGKDD, SIGMOD, AAAI, WWW, CIKM, etc).

Dr. Manuel Gomez Rodriguez is a Research Scientist at Max Planck Institute for Intelligent Systems. His research interests include diffusion processes in the context of information and social networks. Dr. Gomez Rodriguez has published his research in top data mining and machine learning conferences such as KDD, WSDM, ICML, or NIPS. He has received a Best Research Paper Honorable Mention at KDD'10 for his research on network inference. Manuel has been a Barrie de la Maza Graduate Fellow and a Caja Madrid Graduate Fellow. He has served as program committee member of top conferences such as WSDM, ICML and NIPS and as reviewer for leading journals such as JMLR, TKDD and PLOS One. He holds a M.S. and Ph.D. in Electrical Engineering from Stanford University.

## 4. PROGRAM COMMITTEE MEMBERS

- Lada Adamic, U Michigan
- Leman Akoglu, Stony Brook University
- Alex Beutel, CMU
- Petko Bogdanov, UCSB
- Francesco Bonchi, Yahoo Research
- Wei Chen, Microsoft Research
- Chong-Tat Chua, Singapore Management University
- Peng Cui, Tsinghua University
- Aram Galstyan, USC
- Manuel Gomez Rodriguez, MPI for Intelligent Systems
- Krishna Gummadi, MPI for Software Systems
- David Kempe, USC
- Irwin King, The Chinese University of Hong Kong
- David Liben-Nowell, Carleton College
- Yaron Singer, Harvard University
- Chaoming Song, Northeastern University
- Le Song, Georgia Tech
- Hanghang Tong, CUNY
- Johan Ugander, Cornell University
- William Wallace, RPI
- Chi Wang, University of Illinois
- Fei Wang, IBM T.J. Watson Research Center
- Hui Xiong, Rutgers University
- Jiayu Zhou, IBM T.J. Watson Research Center


## 5. ACKNOWLEDGMENTS

The organizers would like to thank all the authors for contributing to the 1st workshop on Diffusion Networks and Cascade Analytics and all the members of the program committee for ascertaining the scientific quality of the workshop.


## 6. REFERENCES


[1] Peng Cui, Shifei Jin, Linyun Yu, Fei Wang, Wenwu Zhu, Shiqiang Yang. Cascading Outbreak Prediction in Networks: A Data-Driven Approach. ACM SIGKDD, 2013.

[2] Manuel Gomez Rodriguez, Jure Leskovec, Bernhard Schoelkopf, Modeling Information Propagation with Survival Theory, ICML, 2013.

# Workshop on Large-Scale and Distributed Systems for Information Retrieval (LSDS-IR 2014)

Ismail Sengor Altingovde
Middle East Technical University
Ankara, Turkey
altingovde@ceng.metu.edu.tr

B. Barla Cambazoglu
Yahoo Labs
Barcelona, Spain
barla@yahoo-inc.com

Craig Macdonald
University of Glasgow
Glasgow, UK
craigm@dcs.gla.ac.uk

Nicola Tonellotto
National Research Council
Pisa, Italy
nicola.tonellotto@isti.cnr.it

## ABSTRACT

The LSDS-IR'14 workshop aims to bring together information retrieval practitioners from industry and academic researchers concerned with efficient and distributed IR systems. The workshop also welcomes contributions that propose different ways of leveraging diversity and multiplicity of resources available in distributed systems. The main goal of the workshop is to attract people from industry and academia to present and discuss ideas, problems, and results related to the efficiency of large scale and distributed information retrieval systems.

## Categories and Subject Descriptors

H.3.3 [**Information Storage Systems**]: Information Retrieval Systems

## Keywords

Distributed search; large-scale systems; scalability; efficiency

## 1. OVERVIEW

The growth of the Web and other Big Data sources lead to important performance problems for large-scale distributed information retrieval (IR) systems. Scalability and efficiency of these systems also have an impact on their effectiveness. Consequently, scalability and efficiency in the context of retrieval systems continue to be an important topic in IR research. Even within research laboratory settings, the size of the standard datasets have become exceedingly large, requiring efficient and often distributed architectures to facilitate large-scale experimentation. Traditionally, web-scale search engines employ large and highly replicated systems, operating on computer clusters in one or few data centers. Coping with the increasing number of user requests and indexable pages requires adding more resources. However, data centers cannot grow indefinitely. Scalability problems in information retrieval have to be addressed and new distributed applications are likely to drive the way in which people search the Web. Distributed IR is the point in which these two directions converge. This workshop provides space for researchers to discuss these problems and to define new directions for the work on distributed information retrieval.


*WSDM'14*, February 24–28, 2014, New York, New York, USA.
ACM 978-1-4503-2351-2/14/02.
http://dx.doi.org/10.1145/2556195.2556210.

## 2. TOPICS OF INTEREST

We solicited technical and position paper submissions in the following research areas:

- Novel distributed IR applications
- Web search in the cloud: applications of cloud computing to IR
- Big Data techniques for IR applications
- Energy-aware processing techniques for web search
- IR algorithms on novel computing architectures
- Efficiency for feature-based models
- Efficiency and scalability in distributed query processing
- Multi-site web search engines
- Inverted index partitioning and replication models
- Lossy and lossless inverted index compression
- Collection selection and result merging in federated IR
- Distributed web crawling
- Distributed indexing and retrieval of dynamic information sources
- Caching for search engines
- Retrieval models for distributed IR
- Standards and benchmarks for distributed IR
- Evaluation of the impact of search efficiency on user satisfaction
- IR on large-scale web archives
- IR algorithms for exotic high-performance computer architectures

## 3. WORKSHOP ORGANIZERS

**Ismail Sengor Altingovde.** Ismail Sengor Altingovde recently served as a PC member in SIGIR 2011, ECIR 2012, CIKM 2013, ECIR 2013 as well as the previous editions of LSDS-IR in 2010 and 2011, and he co-chaired LSDS-IR'12. He published papers in prestigious journals, including ACM TODS, TOIS, TWEB, JASIST, IEEE Intelligent Systems, Inf. Syst. and IP&M, as well as top-tier conferences including SIGIR, WWW, and CIKM, mostly on efficiency related topics such as crawling, caching, index pruning and query processing for Web search engines.

**B. Barla Cambazoglu.** B. Barla Cambazoglu was a co-organizer of the LSDS-IR'10 and LSDS-IR'11 workshops. He was also the proceedings chair for WSDM'09 and the poster and proceedings chairs for ECIR'12. He served as a PC member in WSDM'09, WWW'11, CIKM'11, WSDM'12, SIGIR'12, WSDM'13, SIGIR'13, and KDD'13. He has papers published in prestigious journals including IEEE TPDS, JPDC, ACM TWEB, Inf. Syst., IP&M as well as top-tier conferences including SIGIR, CIKM, WSDM, WWW, and KDD, mainly in the areas of information retrieval and distributed computing.

**Craig Macdonald.** Craig Macdonald was a co-chair of CIKM 2011 with workshop remit. Craig was also a past local organiser and Industry Day Chair of ECIR, and also co-presented a tutorial on the Terrier IR platform at ECIR 2008. Craig co-chaired LSDS-IR 2013, and has also co-chaired the 2011 and 2012 editions of the Diversity in Document Retrieval (DDR) workshops, co-located with ECIR 2011 in Dublin, Ireland, and with WSDM 2012 in Seattle, USA, respectively. Craig is the lead maintainer of the Terrier information retrieval platform, and has developed many of the efficient yet effective retrieval functionalities within the platform. In conjunction with Nicola Tonellotto, Craig has several publications on efficient information retrieval, at venues including TOIS, SIGIR, ECIR, ICTIR, and WSDM as well as past editions of LSDS-IR.

**Nicola Tonellotto.** Nicola Tonellotto served as a PC member in CIKM 2011 and previous editions of LSDS-IR in 2010 and 2011. Previously, he served as a PC member and reviewer in several HPC conferences. Nicola has published papers on efficiency topics in information retrieval in prestigious journals and conferences such as ACM TOIS, SIGIR, ECIR, ICTIR, WSDM. Nicola has contributed to the development of several open source software packages, such as the Terrier information retrieval platform.

## 4. PROGRAM COMMITTEE

- Fabrizio Silvestri (Yahoo Labs)
- Eitan Frachtenberg (Facebook)
- Torsten Suel (Polytechnic Institute of NYU)
- Marcus Fontoura (Microsoft)
- Ruey-Cheng Chen (National Taiwan University)
- Shuai Ding (Google)
- Xiao Bai (Yahoo Labs)
- Vassilis Plachouras (IMIS/ATHENA R.C.)
- Sebastiano Vigna (University of Milan)
- Alexandros Ntoulas (Zynga)
- Simon Jonassen (cXense)
- Veronica Gil Costa (National University of San Luis)
- Avishek Anand (Max Planck Institute)
- Mauricio Marin (Yahoo Labs)
- Rifat Ozcan (Turgut Ozal University)

# Data Design for Personalization: Current Challenges and Emerging Opportunities

Elizabeth F. Churchill
eBay Research Labs, eBay Inc., San Jose, USA
churchill@acm.org

Atish Das Sarma
eBay Research Labs, eBay Inc., San Jose, USA
atish.dassarma@gmail.com

## ABSTRACT

There are several definitions of personalization but one that relates specifically to internet technologies is the following: *Personalization technology enables the dynamic insertion, customization or suggestion of content in any format that is relevant to the individual user, based on the user's implicit behavior and preferences, and explicitly given details*[1].

Personalization is central to most Internet experiences. Personalization is a data-driven process, whether the data are explicitly gathered (e.g., by asking people to fill out forms) or implicitly (e.g. through analysis of behavioral data).

It is clear that designing for effective personalization poses interesting engineering and computer science challenges. However, personalization is also a user experience issue. We believe that encouraging dialogue and collaboration between data mining experts, content providers, and user-focused researchers will offer gains in the area of personalization for search and for other domains. This is increasingly the case as devices enable more forms of data to be gathered, are always on/connected and are always with users. This workshop brings researchers interested in the area of personalization to share their research, explore possibilities for collaboration, and work on defining an agenda for Data Design for Personalization.

## 1. WORKSHOP DESCRIPTION

### Challenges and Opportunities

In recent years as Internet enabled devices are increasingly mobile and data services increasingly affordable, there has been a significant focus on understanding users in and across varied contexts and in very different personal and social circumstances. There is much competition to offer the best services; service providers, application developers, and device manufacturers are all scrambling for user attention and engagement. Novel designs, tailored towards personalized needs are becoming the norm. Further, with users being flooded with numerous apps and experiences across multiple platforms on various devices and gadgets (mobile, sensors, accelerometers), from various sources (social, local, advertisements), the expectations on experience and quality of recommendations has risen dramatically and businesses are seeing setting-appropriate personalization as being a major competitive advantage.

Arguably, effective personalization could have a positive impact on many daily activities. However, there are tensions: although users may value more personalized services that are more efficient, many also desire serendipity, data transparency, and potential for curation, if not total control of their data. The challenge is on: how can we design more effective, situationally sensitive services that offer users the most efficient, enjoyable and setting-appropriate experiences, without being invasive, intrusive, and privacy insensitive. This is the Holy Grail of content and presentation personalization.

This workshop brings together researchers to elaborate emerging challenges in the area of Personalization, share ideas and ongoing research, and investigate novel design paradigms in conjunction with new forms of data, user demands, and recommendation algorithms.

### Who Cares?

There are many interesting research and business questions to be posed. These address search, ranking, social interactions, content consumption and beyond. Typical perspectives on personalization are (1) the needs/desires and perspectives of content providers, (2) the needs and desires of users, and (3) the views of the technology researchers and developers. Common goals of these different perspectives include efficiency and elegance, impact (technology uptake, business impact, needs/wants satisfied), and reduced effort in achieving these.

At the *content provider's* end, this challenge brings new opportunity in the form of the potential to leverage varying types of data, and sources of user preferences. There is also the possibility of designing radically new experiences, by explicitly *asking* for user preferences (such as questions on profile pages in social networks, surveys or choices on mobile apps), as well as implicitly *inferring* interests based on mining data from previous interactions. There is a shift from classic personalization to novel methods and experiences that: engage across multiple devices; leverage contextual information; strive for privacy-preserving and socially

[1]from Wikipedia


*WSDM'14*, February 24–28, 2014, New York, New York, USA.
ACM 978-1-4503-2351-2/14/02.
http://–enter the whole DOI string from rightsreview form confirmation.

acceptable, yet heavily tailored transparent recommendations; and potentially bring the user as part of the process through self-curation.

*Users* are now taking an increasingly central role in all forms of web and online interactions. As they engage with several different kinds of devices and through varying locations, users now provide implicit and explicit signals for their needs. However, as new modes of interaction and several kinds of applications become ubiquitous, the awareness and expectations of individuals are rising dramatically on all dimensions, including the quality of service provided, ease of interaction, greater control on privacy, and highly personalized content.

For *researchers*, the emerging sources and formats of data, computational challenges and the clear needs expressed by both businesses and users needs are tantalizing. Several instances arise in everyday search: local recommendation search, informational search, and search for products on a commerce site.

Consider searching for a restaurant recommendation. Naturally in this example, we are already accustomed to search results being filtered based on user's query-time, geographic location and sometimes even potentially distance/driving-time in current traffic. However, in addition, several factors may be helpful for more effective personalization and the provision of a good experience: knowledge of the user's dietary constraints (vegetarian, vegan, food allergies etc.); propensity and current need for novelty or familiar comfort (some users like going back to the same places over and over, while others like new experiences); previous reviews and likelihood of taking advice from others such as from Yelp/Zagat, friends' recommendations or preferences; budgetary constraints; time constraints; clothing constraints (casual versus formal); time of planned meal (as that determines which places are open, and dinner menu vs. lunch menu), availability of discount coupons (either offered by the restaurants or by external providers, or could be modulated by user specific factors such as member of AAA); ambiance preferences; number of people in party (table availability for the user's family-size) and so on.....

Consider the search experience on a commerce site like eBay. The end users include buyers and sellers, and the browse experience is designed for multiple devices such as mobile phones, tablets, and desktops, and the search methods span different modalities like eBay presentation of potentially interesting items in feeds (where interests are asked for explicitly and also learned implicitly), and conventional search where user's query terms, and the back-end algorithms leverage transaction histories, learned user similarities, inferred economic status or budget constraints, reputation scores, and perhaps even social and local signals.

While we can imagine some of the rich data that could be available and what may be needed, we are only at the beginning of setting a research agenda for what data is available, what the best data sources, formats, and granularity are for describing and understanding any particular situation, and how to involve users in more effective and comfortable data sharing and collaborative data curation. We therefore believe these emerging challenges are best faced by multi-disciplinary collaborations. To date, there has been a lack of exchange of ideas across disciplinary borders. This workshop proposal focuses on cross disciplinary collaboration to develop the new face of personalization.

### Cross Disciplinary Perspectives

This workshop provides a forum to discuss recent innovations, brainstorm ideas, and showcase works that take into consideration this broader view of Personalization, and to address the issues of data design as new forms of user data are beginning to become available. The focus of this workshop is on methods for and effects of personalization on search experiences, but we believe insights from the workshop will have broad implications. For example, how will new forms of data collection (such as social and local) change our models? How will new forms of interaction with devices (such as gesture, voice, eye gaze and other sensor based interactions) change the data that are available for personalization algorithms? What kinds of expectation will users develop for control and curation (including deletion) of their data and what will that mean for personalization? These emerging challenges are best faced by multi-disciplinary collaborations, across computer science, human-computer intereaction, and design.

## 2. WORKSHOP ORGANIZERS

### Elizabeth F. Churchill:

Elizabeth Churchill is a Director at eBay leading HCI (Human Computer Interaction) research. A psychologist by training, Elizabeth has a PhD in Cognitive Science from the University of Cambridge in UK. Earlier, Elizabeth led HCI research at Yahoo labs, PARC (the Palo Alto Research Center) and FX Palo Laboratory, Fuji Xerox's lab in Palo Alto. She is the current Executive Vice President of the ACM's Special Interest Group on Computer Human Interaction (SigCHI). She is a Distinguished Scientist of the Association for Computing Machinery (ACM) and Distinguished Visiting Scholar at Stanford University's Media X.

### Atish Das Sarma:

Atish Das Sarma is a Research Scientist at eBay Research Labs. Atish was previously at Google Research and earlier received a Ph.D. in Computer Science from Georgia Tech. He received the Best Paper Award at PODS-2008, a Facebook award in 2009 for work done that was named a top-50 fbFund Finalist for most promising upcoming start-up ideas, and Google awards for "excellent paper in structured data" and "best paper of 2012 in Information Retrieval". His works have been featured in New Scientist, MIT Technology Review, and invited to interview at NPR. Atish has published over 40 research papers and serves on numerous international program committees.

### Program committee members:

- **Gordon Baxter:** University of St. Andrews
- **Smriti Bhagat:** Technicolor Labs.
- **Andy Brooks:** UC Berkeley.
- **Sreenivas Gollapudi:** Microsoft Research.
- **Silvio Lattanzi:** Google Research.
- **Ashwin Machanavajjhala:** Duke University.
- **Lester D. Nelson:** PARC.
- **Ben Y. Zhao:** UC Santa Barbara.

# Author Index

www.ingramcontent.com/pod-product-compliance
Ingram Content Group UK Ltd.
Pitfield, Milton Keynes, MK11 3LW, UK
UKHW051419290926
15471UKWH00009B/1690

9 781450 330978